Merriam-Webster's
Spanish-English
Dictionary

Merriam-Webster's Spanish-English Dictionary

MERRIAM-WEBSTER, INCORPORATED
Springfield, Massachusetts, U.S.A.

A GENUINE MERRIAM-WEBSTER

The name *Webster* alone is no guarantee of excellence. It is used by a number of publishers and may serve mainly to mislead an unwary buyer.

Merriam-Webster™ is the name you should look for when you consider the purchase of dictionaries or other fine reference books. It carries the reputation of a company that has been publishing since 1831 and is your assurance of quality and authority.

Library of Congress Cataloging-in-Publication Data

Names: Merriam-Webster, Inc., editor.
Title: Merriam-Webster's Spanish-English dictionary.
Other titles: Spanish-English dictionary
Description: Springfield, Massachusetts : Merriam-Webster, Incorporated, [2021] | Summary: "Merriam-Webster's Spanish-English Dictionary is a bilingual, bidirectional dictionary designed to help users communicate effectively in American Spanish and English, which includes up-to-date coverage of essential, current vocabulary"—Provided by publisher.
Identifiers: LCCN 2021022099 | ISBN 9780877793724 (hardcover)
Subjects: LCSH: Spanish language—Dictionaries—English. | English language—Dictionaries—Spanish.
Classification: LCC PC4640 .M47 2021 | DDC 463/.21—dc23
LC record available at https://lccn.loc.gov/2021022099

Merriam-Webster's Spanish-English Dictionary, principal copyright 1998

PRINTED IN INDIA

1st printing Thomson Press India Ltd. Faridabad 9/2021

Contents   Índice

Preface

MERRIAM-WEBSTER'S SPANISH-ENGLISH DICTIONARY is a completely new dictionary designed to meet the needs of English and Spanish speakers in a time of ever-expanding communication among the countries of the Western Hemisphere. It is intended for language learners, teachers, office workers, tourists, business travelers—anyone who needs to communicate effectively in the Spanish and English languages as they are spoken and written in the Americas. This new dictionary provides accurate and up-to-date coverage of current vocabulary in both languages, as well as abundant examples of words used in context to illustrate idiomatic usage. The selection of Spanish words and idioms was based on evidence drawn from a wide variety of modern Latin-American sources and interpreted by trained Merriam-Webster bilingual lexicographers. The English entries were chosen by Merriam-Webster editors from the most recent Merriam-Webster dictionaries, and they represent the current basic vocabulary of American English.

All of this material is presented in a format which is based firmly upon and, in many important ways, is similar to the traditional styling found in the Merriam-Webster monolingual dictionaries. The reader who is familiar with Merriam-Webster dictionaries will immediately recognize this style, with its emphasis on convenience and ease of use, clarity and conciseness of the information presented, precise discrimination of senses, and frequent inclusion of example phrases showing words in actual use. Other features include pronunciations (in the International Phonetic Alphabet) for all English words, full coverage of irregular verbs in both languages, a section on basic Spanish grammar, tables of the most common Spanish and English abbreviations, and a detailed Explanatory Notes section which answers any questions the reader might have concerning the use of this book.

Merriam-Webster's Spanish-English Dictionary represents the combined efforts of many members of the Merriam-Webster Editorial Department, along with advice and assistance from consultants outside the company. The primary defining work was done by Charlene M. Chateauneuf, Seán O'Mannion-Espejo, Karen L. Wilkinson, and Jocelyn Woods; early contributions to the text were also submitted by Cèsar Alegre, Hilton Alers, Marién Díaz, Anne Gatschet, and María D. Guijarro, with Victoria E. Neufeldt, Ph.D., and James L. Rader providing helpful suggestions regarding style. Proofreading was done by Susan L. Brady, Daniel B. Brandon, Charlene M. Chateauneuf, Deanna Stathis Chiasson, Seán O'Mannion-Espejo, James L. Rader, Donna L. Rickerby, Adrienne M. Scholz, Amy West, Karen L. Wilkinson, and Linda Picard Wood. Brian M. Sietsema, Ph.D., provided the pronunciations. Cross-reference services were provided by Donna L. Rickerby.

Karen L. Levister assisted in inputting revisions. Carol Fugiel contributed many hours of clerical assistance and other valuable support. The editorial work relating to typesetting and production was begun by Jennifer Goss Duby and continued by Susan L. Brady, who also offered helpful suggestions regarding format. Madeline L. Novak provided guidance on typographic matters. John M. Morse was responsible for the conception of this book as well as for numerous ideas and continued support along the way.

Eileen M. Haraty
Editor
2003

This new revision of *Merriam-Webster's Spanish-English Dictionary* adds more than 350 new words and meanings from areas such as science, medicine, technology, and popular culture, and provides updates to nearly 130 existing vocabulary entries. It builds on the substantial work already completed in previous updates, which added more than 4,600 new vocabulary terms, updated more than 6,000 existing entries, and incorporated significantly expanded coverage of more than 700 of the entries for the most essential English and Spanish vocabulary. Included in this expanded coverage were many additional meanings, thousands of new examples showing how the words are typically used in context, and more than 2,000 common idioms and phrasal verbs in which these essential words often appear.

Many members of the Merriam-Webster editorial staff contributed to this update. Defining and cross-reference work were done by Sarah S. Carragher. Proofreading was done by Paul S. Wood and editor Carragher, with outside assistance from Mark A. Stevens and Tasha Martino Bigelow. Joshua S. Guenter, Ph.D., provided the pronunciations. Data file management was performed by Anne E. McDonald, who also entered the revisions. Editor Wood oversaw the book's typesetting and final production. Madeline L. Novak and Emily A. Vezina assisted in planning the update, and also provided guidance and support throughout the course of the project.

Karen L. Wilkinson
Editor
2021

Prefacio

El DICCIONARIO ESPAÑOL-INGLÉS MERRIAM-WEBSTER es un diccionario completamente nuevo, diseñado con el fin de satisfacer las necesidades de lenguaje de angloparlantes e hispanoparlantes en una era de continuo crecimiento en la comunicación entre los países del hemisferio occidental. El diccionario está destinado a los estudiantes de estos idiomas, así como a los maestros, oficinistas, turistas, viajeros de negocios, o a cualquier persona que necesite expresarse claramente y eficazmente en los idiomas inglés o español tal como se hablan y se escriben en las Américas. Este diccionario provee una cobertura exacta y actualizada del vocabulario corriente en ambos idiomas, así como abundantes ejemplos de palabras empleadas en contexto para ilustrar su uso idiomático. La selección de vocablos y modismos en español se efectuó a base de una vasta gama de fuentes latinoamericanas modernas y fue interpretada por especialistas en lexicografía bilingüe de Merriam-Webster. Las voces inglesas fueron extraídas de los más recientes diccionarios Merriam-Webster por editores de Merriam-Webster, y representan el vocabulario básico actual del inglés americano.

El material se ha organizado en un formato basado en el estilo tradicional característico de los diccionarios monolingües Merriam-Webster. El lector ya familiarizado con los diccionarios Merriam-Webster reconocerá de inmediato este estilo, con su énfasis en la conveniencia y la facilidad de uso, en la claridad y la concisión de la información presentada, en el preciso discernimiento de los sentidos de cada vocablo, y en la frecuente inclusión de frases ejemplares que ilustran el uso de una palabra. Aparecen también pronunciaciones (compuestas en el Alfabeto Fonético Internacional) para todas las voces inglesas, así como una cobertura plena de verbos irregulares en ambos idiomas, una sección de gramática inglesa básica, tablas de abreviaturas comunes, y una sección de Notas explicativas que contesta en detalle cualquier pregunta que pueda tener el lector tocante al uso de este libro.

El *Diccionario Español-Inglés Merriam-Webster* es el fruto del esfuerzo combinado de muchos miembros del departamento editorial de Merriam-Webster, junto con el asesoramiento y la asistencia de consultores exteriores. La obra de definición primaria fue llevada a cabo por Charlene M. Chateauneuf, Seán O'Mannion-Espejo, Karen L. Wilkinson, y Jocelyn Woods; contribuciones textuales preliminares fueron aportadas por Cèsar Alegre, Hilton Alers, Marién Díaz, Anne Gatschet, y María D. Guijarro, y valiosas sugerencias con respecto al estilo del diccionario fueron hechas por Victoria E. Neufeldt, Ph.D., y James L. Rader. La corrección de pruebas fue realizada por Susan L. Brady, Daniel B. Brandon, Charlene M. Chateauneuf, Deanna Stathis Chiasson, Seán O'Mannion-Espejo, James L. Rader, Donna L. Rickerby, Adrienne M. Scholz, Amy West, Karen L. Wilkinson, y Linda Picard Wood.

Las pronunciaciones fueron proporcionadas por Brian M. Sietsema, Ph.D. Los servicios de remisión textual fueron provistos por Donna L. Rickerby. Karen L. Levister ayudó con la entrada de revisiones. Carol Fugiel contribuyó muchas horas de labor de oficina y otros valiosos apoyos. La labor editorial de composición y producción fue comenzada por Jennifer Goss Duby y fue continuada por Susan L. Brady, la cual también ofreció sugerencias importantes con respecto al formato. Madeline L. Novak proveyó orientación en asuntos tipográficos. John M. Morse fue responsable de la concepción de este libro, y contribuyó numerosas ideas y apoyo continuo durante su elaboración.

Eileen M. Haraty
Editor
2003

Esta nueva versión corregida del *Diccionario Español-Inglés Merriam-Webster* añade más de 350 vocablos y significados nuevos de áreas tales como la ciencia, la medicina, la tecnología, y la cultura popular, y proporciona actualizaciones de casi 130 entradas ya existentes. Continúa el considerable trabajo ya realizado en versiones anteriores, en las cuales se añadieron más de 4600 vocablos, se actualizaron más de 6000 entradas, y se incorporaron cobertura considerablemente ampliada en más de 700 de las entradas que corresponden al vocabulario más esencial del inglés y el español. Esta ampliación abarcaba muchos significados adicionales, miles de ejemplos que muestran el uso típico de las palabras en contexto, y más de dos mil de los modismos y verbos preposicionales en los cuales estas palabras tan esenciales suelen aparecer.

Muchos miembros del departamento editorial de Merriam-Webster contribuyeron a la actualización de este libro. La obra de definición primaria y de verificación de remisiones fue realizada por Sarah S. Carragher. La corrección de pruebas fue hecha por Paul S. Wood y la redactora Carragher, con la ayuda externa de Mark A. Stevens y Tasha Martino Bigelow. Las pronunciaciones fueron provistas por Joshua S. Guenter, Ph.D. La administración de archivos de datos fue ejecutada por Anne E. McDonald, quien también tecleó las revisiones. El redactor Wood supervisó la composición del libro. Madeline L. Novak y Emily A. Vezina ayudaron con la planificación del proyecto de actualización, y también proporcionaron orientación y apoyo general en el curso del proyecto.

Karen L. Wilkinson
Editora
2021

Explanatory Notes

Entries

1. Headwords

A boldface letter, word, or phrase appearing at the left edge of a column of type is a headword or main entry word. The headword may consist of letters set solid, of letters joined by a hyphen, or of letters separated by a space:

>   **cafetalero**[1]**, -ra** *adj* . . .
>   **lip–read** . . . *vi* . . .
>   **computer science** *n* . . .

The headword, together with the material that follows it on the same line and succeeding indented lines, constitutes a dictionary entry.

2. Order of Entries

Alphabetical order throughout the dictionary follows the order of the English alphabet, with one exception: the Spanish letter *ñ* follows the letter *n* and comes before the letter *o*. The headwords are ordered alphabetically letter by letter without regard to intervening spaces or hyphens; for example, *shake-up* follows *shaker*.

Homographs (words with the same spelling) having different parts of speech are usually given separate dictionary entries. These entries have superscript numerals after the headword:

>   **hail**[1] . . . *vt* . . .
>   **hail**[2] *n* . . .
>   **hail**[3] *interj* . . .
>   **madrileño**[1]**, -ña** *adj* . . .
>   **madrileño**[2]**, -ña** *n* . . .

Headwords in a numbered sequence are listed in this order: verb, adverb, adjective, noun, conjunction, preposition, pronoun, interjection, article.

Homographs having the same part of speech are normally included at the same dictionary entry even if they have different origins. On the English-to-Spanish side, however, separate entries are made if the homographs have different inflected forms or if they have different pronunciations. On the Spanish-to-English side, separate entries are made if the homographs differ in gender.

3. Guide Words

A pair of guide words is printed at the top of each page, indicating the first and last main entries that appear on that page:

balanca · bañar

4. Variants

When a headword is followed by the word *or* and another spelling, the two spellings are variants. Both are standard, and you may choose to use either one:

> **jailer** *or* **jailor** . . . *n* . . .
>
> **quizá** *or* **quizás** *adv* . . .

Occasionally, a variant spelling is used only for a particular sense of a word. In these cases, the variant spelling is listed after the sense number of the sense to which it pertains:

> **electric** . . . *adj* **1** *or* **electrical** . . .

Sometimes the headword is used interchangeably with a longer phrase containing the headword. For the purposes of this dictionary, such phrases are considered variants of the headword:

> **bunk²** *n* **1** *or* **bunk bed** . . .
>
> **angina** *nf* **1** *or* **angina de pecho** . . .

Variant wordings of boldface phrases may also be shown:

> **madera** *nf* . . . **3 madera dura** *or* **madera noble** . . .
>
> **atención¹** *nf* . . . **2 poner atención** *or* **prestar atención** . . .
>
> **gasto** *nm* . . . **3 gastos fijos/generales/indirectos** . . .

5. Run-On Entries

A main entry may be followed by one or more derivatives or by a homograph with a different functional label. These are run-on entries. Each is introduced by a boldface dash and each has a functional label. They are not defined, however, since their equivalents can be readily derived by adding the corresponding foreign-language suffix to the terms used to define the main entry word or, in the case of homographs, simply substituting the appropriate part of speech:

> **illegal** . . . *adj* : ilegal — **illegally** *adv*
> [the Spanish adverb is *ilegalmente*]
>
> **transferir** . . . *vt* TRASLADAR : to transfer — **transferible** *adj*
> [the English adjective is *transferable*]
>
> **Bosnian** . . . *n* : bosnio *m*, -nia *f* — **Bosnian** *adj*
> [the Spanish adjective is *bosnio, -nia*]

On the Spanish-to-English side of the dictionary, reflexive verbs are sometimes run on undefined:

> **enrollar** *vt* : to roll up, to coil — **enrollarse** *vr*

The absence of a definition means that *enrollarse* has the simple reflexive meaning "to become rolled up or coiled," "to roll itself up."

6. Boldface phrases

A main entry may be followed by one or more phrases in dark, boldface type that contain the main entry word or an inflected form of it. Each boldface phrase is defined at its own numbered sense:

> **álamo** *nm* **1** : poplar **2 álamo tem-blón** : aspen
>
> **hold**[1] . . . *v* . . . — *vi* . . . **3 to hold forth** : . . . **4 to hold off** WAIT : . . .

If the boldface phrase consists only of the entry word and a single preposition, the entry word is represented by a boldface swung dash ∼ :

> **pegar** . . . *vt* . . . — *vi* . . . **3** ∼ **con** : . . .

The same boldface phrase may appear at two or more senses if it has more than one distinct meaning:

> **wear**[1] . . . *v* . . . *vt* . . . **8 to wear out** : gastar . . . **9 to wear out** EXHAUST : agotar, fatigar . . .
>
> **estar** . . . *v aux* . . . *vi* . . . **16** ∼ **por** : to be in favor of **17** ∼ **por** : to be about to . . .

A slash / is used between words in a boldface phrase when either of the words separated by the slash can be used in that part of the phrase:

> **casa** *nf* . . . **11 echar/tirar/botar la casa por la ventana** . . .
>
> **same**[2] *pron* . . . **4 all/just the same** . . .

Words separated by slashes in boldface phrases do not always have the same meaning.

When a boldface phrase contains a slash, a corresponding slash may or may not be included in the definition that follows the phrase:

> **agua** *nf* . . . **4 agua dulce/salada** : fresh/salt water . . .
>
> **go**[1] . . . *v* . . . *vi* . . . **59 to go down well/badly** : caer bien/mal, tener una buena/mala acogida . . .
>
> **pedir** . . . *vt* . . . **3 pedir disculpas/perdón** : to apologize . . .
>
> **break**[1] . . . *v* . . . *vt* . . . — *vi* . . . **17 to break free/loose** : soltarse . . .

When no corresponding slash is included in the definition, all wordings shown for the boldface phrase have the same meaning.

If a word in a boldface phrase is followed by "(etc.)", other words similar to the one that precedes the "(etc.)" may be used in that place in the phrase:

> **part**[2] *n* . . . **6 for my/his (etc.) part** : por mi/su (etc.) parte . . .

> **hablar** . . . — **hablarse** *vr* . . . **2 se**
> **habla inglés (etc.)** : English (etc.)
> spoken

A corresponding "(etc.)" is included in the definition unless a verbal illustration is shown instead of a definition, or the definition is worded in a way that makes the inclusion of "(etc.)" unnecessary:

> **ser¹** . . . *vi* . . . **17 sea cual/quien**
> **(etc.) sea** <sean cuales sean las cir-
> cunstancias : whatever the circum-
> stances might be> . . .
>
> **hell** . . . *n* . . . **8 like hell I did/will**
> **(etc.)!** *fam* : ¡y un cuerno! . . .

If the use of the entry word is commonly restricted to one particular phrase, then only the phrase will be defined:

> **ward¹** . . . *vt* **to ward off** : desviar,
> protegerse contra

Pronunciation

1. Pronunciation of English Entry Words

The text between a pair of brackets [ ] following the entry word of an English-to-Spanish entry indicates the pronunciation. The symbols used are explained in the Pronunciation Symbols chart on page 85a.

When more than one pronunciation is shown for a word, different educated speakers of English pronounce that word in different ways. The pronunciation shown second may be just as common as the one shown first. All pronunciations shown are common and acceptable:

> **tomato** [tə'meɪt̬o, -'mɑ-] . . .

When less than a full pronunciation is shown for a compound word, the rest of the pronunciation can be found at the separate entry for that individual part of the compound:

> **gamma ray** ['gæmə] . . .
> **ray** ['reɪ] . . .
> **smoke¹** ['smoːk] . . .
> **smoke detector** [dɪ'tɛktər] . . .

In general, no pronunciation is given for open compounds consisting of two or more English words that are main entries at their own alphabetical place:

> **water lily** *n* : nenúfar *m*

Only the first headword in a series of numbered homographs is given a pronunciation if their pronunciations are the same:

> **dab¹** ['dæb] *vt* . . .
> **dab²** *n* . . .

No pronunciation is shown for principal parts of verbs that are formed regularly by adding a suffix or for other derivative words formed by common suffixes.

2. Pronunciation of Spanish Entry Words

Spanish pronunciation is highly regular, so no pronunciations are given in most Spanish-to-English entries. Exceptions have been made for certain words (such as foreign borrowings) whose Spanish pronunciations are not evident from their spellings:

> **pizza** [ˈpitsa, ˈpisa] . . .
> **footing** [ˈfuˌtɪŋ] . . .

Functional Labels

An italic label indicating a part of speech or some other functional classification follows the pronunciation or, if no pronunciation is given, the headword. The eight traditional parts of speech—adjective, adverb, conjunction, interjection, noun, preposition, pronoun, and verb—are indicated as follows:

> **daily²** *adj* . . .
> **vagamente** *adv* . . .
> **and** . . . *conj* . . .
> **huy** *interj* . . .
> **jackal** . . . *n* . . .
> **para** *prep* . . .
> **neither³** *pron* . . .
> **leer** . . . *v* . . .

Verbs that are intransitive are labeled *vi*, and verbs that are transitive are labeled *vt*:

> **deliberar** *vi* : to deliberate . . .
> **necessitate** . . . *vt* **-tated; -tating**
>   : necesitar, requerir

Verbs that are both transitive and intransitive are labeled *v* if all listed senses are both transitive and intransitive. If some senses are only transitive or only intransitive, the entry is subdivided into transitive and intransitive sections, each with its own *vt* or *vi* label, respectively:

> **scrawl¹** . . . *v* : garabatear
> **crack¹** . . . *vt* . . . — *vi* . . .
> **esperar** *vt* . . . — *vi* . . .

If a subdivided verb entry includes irregular verb inflections, it is labeled *v* immediately before the inflections, with the labels *vt* and *vi* serving to introduce the transitive and intransitive subdivisions:

> **satisfy** . . . *v* **-fied; -fying** *vt* . . . —
>   *vi* . . .

Spanish reflexive verbs are labeled *vr*:

> **jactarse** *vr* . . .
>
> **abandonar** *vt* . . . — **abando-**
> **narse** . . . *vr* . . .

Two other labels are used to indicate functional classifications of verbs: *v aux* (auxiliary verb) and *v impers* (impersonal verb).

> **may** . . . *v aux, past* **might** . . .
>
> **hacer** . . . *vt* . . . — *vi* . . . — *v impers*
> **1** *(referring to weather)* <hace frío
> : it's cold> . . .

Entries for prefixes are labeled *pref*:

> **ciber-** *pref* . . .
>
> **e-** *pref* . . .

Entries for suffixes are labeled *suf*:

> **-less** . . . *suf* . . .
>
> **-ísimo, -ma** *suf* . . .

Entries for English-language and Spanish-language trademarks are labeled *trademark* and *marca registrada*, respectively:

> **Q–tips** . . . *trademark* — se usa para
> hisopos
>
> **Kleenex** . . . *marca registrada, m* —
> used for a paper tissue

Entries for English-language service marks (words or names that organizations use to identify their services) are labeled *service mark*:

> **Realtor** . . . *service mark* . . .

Gender Labels

In Spanish-to-English noun entries and trademark entries, the gender of the headword is indicated by an italic *m* (masculine), *f* (feminine), or *mf* (masculine or feminine). In noun entries, the gender label immediately follows the functional label:

> **magnesio** *nm* . . .
>
> **galaxia** *nf* . . .
>
> **turista** *nmf* . . .

In trademark entries, the gender label follows the functional label and is preceded by a comma and a space:

> **Ping–Pong** *marca registrada, m* . . .

If both the masculine and feminine forms are shown for a noun referring to a person, the label is simply *n:*

> **director, -tora** *n* . . .

Spanish noun equivalents of English headwords are also labeled for gender:

> **amnesia** ... *n* : amnesia *f*
> **earache** ... *n* : dolor *m* de oído(s)
> **gamekeeper** ... *n* : guardabosque *mf*

Inflected Forms

1. Nouns

The plurals of nouns are shown in this dictionary when they are irregular, if the root word changes in spelling or accentuation when a plural suffix is added, when an English noun ends in a consonant plus *-o* or in *-ey,* when an English noun ends in *-oo,* when an English noun is a compound that pluralizes the first element instead of the last, when a noun has variant plurals, or whenever the dictionary user might have reasonable doubts regarding the spelling of a plural:

> **tooth** ... *n, pl* **teeth** ...
> **garrafón** *nm, pl* **-fones** ...
> **potato** ... *n, pl* **-toes** ...
> **abbey** ... *n, pl* **-beys** ...
> **cuckoo**[2] *n, pl* **-oos** ...
> **brother–in–law** ... *n, pl* **brothers–in–law** ...
> **fish**[2] *n, pl* **fish** *or* **fishes** ...
> **hábitat** *nm, pl* **-tats** ...
> **tahúr** *nm, pl* **tahúres** ...

Cutback (partial) inflected forms are shown for most nouns on the English-to-Spanish side, regardless of the number of syllables in the word. On the Spanish-to-English side, cutback inflections are given for nouns that have three or more syllables; plurals for shorter words are written out in full:

> **shampoo**[2] *n, pl* **-poos** ...
> **calamity** ... *n, pl* **-ties** ...
> **mouse** ... *n, pl* **mice** ...
> **sartén** *nmf, pl* **sartenes** ...
> **hámster** ... *nm, pl* **hámsters** ...
> **federación** *nf, pl* **-ciones** ...

If only one gender form has a plural which is irregular, that plural form will be given with the appropriate label:

> **campeón, -peona** *n, mpl* **-peones**
> : champion

The plurals of nouns are usually not shown when the base word is unchanged by the addition of the regular plural suffix or when the noun is unlikely to occur in the plural:

> **apple** ... *n* : manzana *f*
> **inglés**[3] *nm* : English (language)

Nouns that are always plural in form and occur in plural constructions are labeled *npl* for English nouns, *nmpl* for Spanish masculine nouns, *nfpl* for Spanish feminine nouns, or *nmfpl* for Spanish nouns that can be masculine or feminine:

> **knickers** ... *npl* ...
> **enseres** *nmpl* ...
> **mancuernas** *nfpl* ...
> **panties** ... *nmfpl* ...

Entry words that are unchanged in the plural are labeled *ns & pl* for English nouns, *nms & pl* for Spanish masculine nouns, *nfs & pl* for Spanish feminine nouns, or *nmfs & pl* for Spanish nouns that can be masculine or feminine:

> **deer** ... *ns & pl* ...
> **lavaplatos** *nms & pl* ...
> **tesis** *nfs & pl* ...
> **rompehuelgas** *nmfs & pl* ...

2. Verbs

ENGLISH VERBS

The principal parts of verbs are shown in English-to-Spanish entries when they are irregular, if the spelling of the root word changes when the verb suffix is added, when the verb ends in *-ey,* when there are variant inflected forms, or whenever the dictionary user might have reasonable doubts about the spelling of an inflected form:

> **break¹** ... *v* **broke** ... ; **broken** ... ;
>   **breaking** ...
> **drag¹** ... *v* **dragged; dragging** ...
> **monkey¹** ... *vi* **-keyed; -keying** ...
> **label¹** ... *vt* **-beled** *or* **-belled; -beling**
>   *or* **-belling** ...
> **imagine** ... *vt* **-ined; -ining** ...

Cutback inflected forms are usually shown when the verb has two or more syllables:

> **multiply** ... *v* **-plied; -plying** ...
> **bevel¹** ... *v* **-eled** *or* **-elled; -eling** *or*
>   **-elling** ...
> **forgo** *or* **forego** ... *vt* **-went; -gone;**
>   **-going** ...
> **commit** ... *vt* **-mitted; -mitting** ...

The principal parts of an English verb are not shown if the base word does not change when *-s, -ed,* and *-ing* are added:

> **delay¹** ... *vt*
> **pitch¹** ... *vt*

SPANISH VERBS

Entries for irregular Spanish verbs are cross-referenced by number to the model conjugations appearing in the Conjugation of Spanish Verbs section on pages 72a–78a:

> **abnegarse** {49} *vr* . . .
> **volver** {89} *vi* . . .

Entries for Spanish verbs with regular conjugations are not cross-referenced; however, model conjugations for regular Spanish verbs are included on pages 68a–69a in the Conjugation of Spanish Verbs section.

3. Adverbs and Adjectives

The comparative and superlative forms of English adjective and adverb main entries are shown if the spelling of the root word changes when the suffix is added, if the inflection is irregular, or if there are variant inflected forms:

> **wet**[2] *adj* **wetter; wettest** . . .
> **good**[2] *adj* **better** . . . ; **best** . . .
> **evil**[1] . . . *adj* **eviler** *or* **eviller; evilest**
> *or* **evillest** . . .

For adjectives and adverbs that have more than one syllable, only the shortened form *-est* is usually shown for the superlative:

> **early**[1] . . . *adv* **earlier; -est** . . .
> **gaudy** . . . *adj* **gaudier; -est** . . .
> **secure**[2] *adj* **securer; -est** . . .

At a few entries only the superlative form is shown because there is no evidence that the comparative form is used:

> **mere** . . . *adj, superlative* **merest** . . .

The comparative and superlative forms of adjectives and adverbs are usually not shown if the base word does not change when the suffix is added:

> **quiet**[3] *adj* **1** . . .

Usage

1. Usage Labels

Two types of usage labels are used in this dictionary—regional and stylistic. Spanish words that are limited in use to a specific area or areas of Latin America, or to Spain, are given labels indicating the countries in which they are most commonly used:

> **guarachear** *vi Cuba, PRi fam* . . .
> **bucket** . . . *n* : . . . cubeta *f Mex*

The following regional labels are used in this dictionary: *Arg* (Argentina), *Bol* (Bolivia), *CA* (Central America), *Car* (Caribbean), *Chile* (Chile), *Col* (Colombia), *CoRi* (Costa Rica), *Cuba* (Cuba), *DomRep* (Dominican Republic), *Ecua* (Ecuador), *Sal* (El Salvador), *Guat* (Guatemala), *Hond* (Honduras), *Mex* (Mexico), *Nic* (Nicaragua), *Pan* (Panama), *Par* (Paraguay), *Peru* (Peru), *PRi* (Puerto Rico), *Spain* (Spain), *Uru* (Uruguay), *Ven* (Venezuela).

Since this dictionary focuses on the Spanish spoken in Latin America, only the most common regionalisms from Spain have been included.

A number of words are given a *fam* (familiar) label, indicating that these words are suitable for informal contexts but would not normally be used in formal writing or speaking. The labels *disparaging*, *vulgar*, and *offensive* are used for words or senses that are intended to hurt or shock or that are likely to give offense; such words are entered and defined in this dictionary only if they are very commonly used. The labels are intended to warn the reader that the word or sense in question may be inappropriate in polite conversation.

2. Usage Notes

Usage notes that give information about meaning or grammar may appear in parentheses before the definition:

> **not** ... *adv* **1** (*used to form a negative*) : no ...
>
> **within**[2] *prep* ... **2** (*in expressions of distance*) : ... **3** (*in expressions of time*) : ...
>
> **e**[2] *conj* (*used instead of* **y** *before words beginning with i- or hi-*) : ...
>
> **poder**[1] ... *v aux* ... **2** (*expressing possibility*) : ... **3** (*expressing permission*) : ...

Orientation about meaning is also sometimes given in parentheses within the definition:

> **calibrate** ... *vt* ... : calibrar (armas), graduar (termómetros)
>
> **palco** *nm* : box (in a theater or stadium)

Occasionally a usage note is used in place of a definition. This is usually done when the entry word has no simple equivalent in the other language. This type of usage note is accompanied by examples of common use:

> **shall** ... *v aux* ... **1** (*used formally to express a command*) <you shall do as I say : harás lo que te digo> ...

3. Illustrations of Usage

Definitions are sometimes followed by verbal illustrations that show a typical use of the word in context or a common idiomatic usage. These verbal illustrations include a translation and are enclosed in angle brackets:

> **lejos** *adv* **1 :** far away, distant <a lo lejos : in the distance, far off> ...
>
> **make¹** ... *v* ... *vt* ... **15** ... : hacer (dinero, amigos) <to make a living : ganarse la vida> ...

A slash / is used between words in a verbal illustration when either of the words separated by the slash can occur in that position in the phrase:

> **tener** ... *vt* ... **2 :** to have (available) <tener dinero/tiempo para : to have money/time for> ...
>
> **money** ... *n* ... **1 :** dinero *m*, plata *f* <to make/lose money : ganar/perder dinero> ...

Words separated by slashes in verbal illustrations do not always have the same meaning.

When a word in a verbal illustration is followed by "(etc.)," other words similar to the one before the "(etc.)" can occur in that position in the phrase:

> **dar** ... *vt* ... **16** CAUSAR **:** to cause <darle miedo/sed (etc.) a alguien : to make someone frightened/thirsty (etc.)> ...
>
> **turn²** *n* ... **3** INTERSECTION **:** bocacalle *f* <we took a wrong turn : nos equivocamos de calle/salida (etc.), ...> ...

Occasionally verbal illustrations are used in place of a definition. This is usually done when a boldface phrase has no single-phrase equivalent in the other language, or when its use is more easily understood in context:

> **saber¹** ... *vt* ... **6 qué sé yo** <diamantes, perlas, y qué sé yo : diamonds, pearls, and whatnot> <y qué sé yo dónde : and who knows where (else)> ...
>
> **all¹** ... *adv* ... **8 ~ over** *fam* <to be all over someone for something : criticar duramente a alguien por algo> ...

Definitions

A definition in this dictionary consists of one or more translations for a single sense of a main entry word, a run-on entry word, or a boldface phrase. A boldface colon is used to introduce a definition:

> **fable** ... *n* **:** fábula *f*
>
> **sonrojar** ... — **sonrojarse** *vr* **:** to blush

> **aback** . . . *adv* . . . **2 to be taken**
> **aback :** quedarse desconcertado

If more than one translation word or phrase is included in the same definition, the translations are usually separated by commas:

> **as of** *prep* : desde, a partir de

When commas are used within a definition for other reasons, the translations are separated by semicolons instead of commas:

> **love²** *n* . . . **3** BELOVED : amor *m;*
> amado *m*, -da *f;* enamorado *m*, -da
> *f* . . .

A slash / is used between words in a translation phrase when either of the words separated by the slash can be used in that position in the phrase:

> **bajar** *vt* . . . **2 :** to bring/take/carry
> down, to get/lift down . . .

Words separated by slashes in translations do not always have the same meaning.

Sense Division

When a word has more than one sense, each sense begins with a boldface numeral:

> **laguna** *nf* **1 :** lagoon **2 :** gap

Whenever some information (such as a synonym, a boldface word or phrase, a usage note, a cross-reference, or a label) follows a sense number, it applies only to that specific sense:

> **abanico** *nm* . . . **2** GAMA : . . .
> **tonic²** *n* . . . **2** *or* **tonic water :** . . .
> **grillo** *nm* . . . **2 grillos** *nmpl* : . . .
> **fairy** . . . *n, pl* **fairies** . . . **2 fairy tale**
> **:** . . .
> **myself** . . . *pron* **1** (*used reflexively*)
> **:** . . .
> **pike** . . . *n* . . . **3** → **turnpike**
> **atado²** *nm* . . . **2** *Arg* : . . .

Cross-References

An arrow in an entry means that information about the word you have looked up is available at the separate entry for the word that appears after the arrow. If the word you have looked up is an inflected form, the cross-reference after the arrow will point you to the base form of the word:

> **fue, etc.** → **ir, ser**
> **mice** → **mouse**

In other cases, the cross-reference will point you to the entry for a word that has the same meaning as the word you have looked up:

> scapula ... → **shoulder blade**
> amuck ... → **amok**

Synonyms

A synonym in small capital letters is often provided before the boldface colon that precedes a definition:

> **seleccionar** *vt* ELEGIR : ...
> **turn**[1] *vt* ... — *vi* ... **1** ROTATE, SPIN
> : ...
> **carta** *nf* ... **2** NAIPE : ...

These synonyms are all main entries or boldface phrases elsewhere in the dictionary. They serve as a helpful guide to the meaning of the entry or sense and also give you an additional term that might be substituted in a similar context.

Notas explicativas

Entradas

1. Lemas

Toda letra, palabra o frase en negrita que aparece al margen izquierdo de una columna de texto de la que forma parte es un lema, o entrada principal. La composición del lema puede constar de letras continuas, de letras unidas por un guión, o bien de letras separadas por un espacio:

> **cafetalero[1], -ra** *adj* . . .
> **lip–read** . . . *vi* . . .
> **computer science** *n* . . .

El lema, junto con el texto que lo sigue tanto en la misma línea como en las líneas sangradas subsiguientes, constituye una entrada del diccionario.

2. Orden de los lemas

El orden alfabético del diccionario concuerda con el orden alfabético latino universal, en el que la letra *ñ* aparece después de la *n* y antes de la *o*, y la *ch* y la *ll* no se consideran letras independientes. Los lemas se suceden alfabéticamente, letra por letra, sin tener en cuenta guiones o espacios intermediarios; por ejemplo, *shake-up* aparece después de *shaker*.

Los homógrafos (palabras que se escriben igual) que pertenecen a distintas categorías gramaticales por lo general aparecen en entradas individuales. Estas entradas tienen un número volado:

> **hail[1]** . . . *vt* . . .
> **hail[2]** *n* . . .
> **hail[3]** *interj* . . .
> **madrileño[1], -ña** *adj* . . .
> **madrileño[2], -ña** *n* . . .

Las entradas que siguen una secuencia numerada se listan en el siguiente orden: verbo, adverbio, adjetivo, sustantivo, conjunción, preposición, pronombre, interjección, y por último, artículo.

Los homógrafos que se clasifican bajo una misma categoría gramatical son normalmente incluidos dentro de la misma entrada del diccionario, sin tener en cuenta diferencias de origen semántico. Sin embargo, en la sección Inglés-Español se les asigna a cada uno de estos homógrafos una entrada individual si entre ellos existe alguna diferencia ya sea en la inflexión o en la pronunciación. En la sección Español-Inglés, se les asigna una entrada individual si existe una diferencia de género.

3. Palabras guía

En el margen superior de cada página aparecen dos palabras guía, que indican la primera y última entrada de la página correspondiente:

balanca · bañar

4. Variantes

Cuando un lema aparece seguido de la palabra *or* y otra ortografía, las dos ortografías se consideran como variantes. Ambas ortografías son estándares, y cualquiera de las dos puede usarse:

> **jailer** *or* **jailor** . . . *n* . . .
> **quizá** *or* **quizás** *adv* . . .

Hay ocasiones en las que una variante ortográfica se emplea únicamente para una de las acepciones de una palabra. En tales casos, la variante ortográfica aparece después del número de la acepción a la cual corresponde:

> **electric** . . . *adj* 1 *or* **electrical** . . .

En otros casos, el lema puede usarse intercambiablemente con una frase de la que forma parte. Para los fines de este diccionario, tales frases se consideran como variantes del lema:

> **bunk²** *n* 1 *or* **bunk bed** . . .
> **angina** *nf* 1 *or* **angina de pecho** . . .

Las frases en negrita también pueden, a su vez, presentar variantes:

> **madera** *nf* . . . 3 **madera dura** *or*
>   **madera noble** . . .
> **atención¹** *nf* . . . 2 **poner atención** *or*
>   **prestar atención** . . .
> **gasto** *nm* . . . 3 **gastos fijos/genera-**
>   **les/indirectos** . . .

5. Entradas secundarias

Una entrada principal puede ser seguida de uno o más derivados del lema, o de un homógrafo de distinta categoría gramatical. Éstas son entradas secundarias. Cada una de estas entradas aparece después de un guión en negrita, y cada una posee su propio calificativo. Tales entradas aparecen sin definición, ya que sus equivalentes en el idioma extranjero pueden derivarse fácilmente al combinar la definición del lema con el sufijo correspondiente, o como sucede con los homógrafos, al sustituir la categoría gramatical por otra. Véase por ejemplo:

> **illegal** . . . *adj* : ilegal — **illegally** *adv*
> [el adverbio español es *ilegalmente*]
> **transferir** . . . *vt* TRASLADAR : to
> transfer — **transferible** *adj*
> [el adjetivo inglés es *transferable*]
> **Bosnian** . . . *n* : bosnio *m*, -nia *f* —
> **Bosnian** *adj*
> [el adjetivo español es *bosnio, -nia*]

En la sección Español-Inglés, los verbos pronominales aparecen en ocasiones como entradas secundarias, sin definición:

> **enrollar** *vt* : to roll up, to coil —
>   **enrollarse** *vr*

La ausencia de la definición en este caso comunica al lector que el verbo *enrollarse* tiene una función expresamente reflexiva. Esto elimina la necesidad de agregar una definición que resultaría superflua como "to become rolled up or coiled," o "to roll itself up."

6. Frases en negrita

Un lema puede aparecer acompañado de una o varias frases en negrita que contienen ya sea el lema, o una inflexión de éste. Cada una de estas frases se presenta como una de las acepciones numeradas del lema:

> **álamo** *nm* **1** : poplar **2 álamo temblón** : aspen
>
> **hold**[1] . . . *v* . . . — *vi* . . . **3 to hold forth** : . . . **4 to hold off** WAIT : . . .

Cuando la frase en negrita consta únicamente de una combinación del lema con una preposición, el lema se representa entonces por medio de una tilde en negrita ~ :

> **pegar** . . . *vt* . . . — *vi* . . . **3 ~ con** : . . .

Si la frase en cuestión tiene más de un sentido, entonces puede aparecer en dos o más acepciones del mismo lema:

> **wear**[1] . . . *v* . . . *vt* . . . **8 to wear out** : gastar . . . **9 to wear out** EXHAUST : agotar, fatigar . . .
>
> **estar** . . . *v aux* . . . *vi* . . . **16 ~ por** : to be in favor of **17 ~ por** : to be about to . . .

Se utiliza una barra inclinada / entre las palabras de una frase en negrita para indicar que cualquiera de las palabras así separadas puede usarse en esa posición dentro de la frase:

> **casa** *nf* . . . **11 echar/tirar/botar la casa por la ventana** . . .
>
> **same**[2] *pron* . . . **4 all/just the same** . . .

Las palabras separadas por barras no siempre tienen el mismo significado.

Cuando una frase en negrita contiene una barra, la definición que sigue puede o no contener una barra correspondiente:

> **agua** *nf* . . . **4 agua dulce/salada** : fresh/salt water . . .
>
> **go**[1] . . . *v* . . . *vi* . . . **59 to go down well/badly** : caer bien/mal, tener una buena/mala acogida . . .
>
> **pedir** . . . *vt* . . . **3 pedir disculpas/perdón** : to apologize . . .
>
> **break**[1] . . . *v* . . . *vt* . . . — *vi* . . . **17 to break free/loose** : soltarse . . .

Si la definición no incluye una barra correspondiente, esto indica que todas las versiones de la frase en negrita tienen el mismo significado.

Cuando una de las palabras de una frase en negrita aparece seguida de "(etc.)", esto indica que hay otras palabras parecidas a la que precede al "(etc.)" que pueden usarse en esa posición dentro de la frase:

> **part**[2] *n* . . . **6 for my/his (etc.) part**
> : por mi/su (etc.) parte . . .
>
> **hablar** . . . — **hablarse** *vr* . . . **2 se**
> **habla inglés (etc.)** : English (etc.)
> spoken

Un "(etc.)" correspondiente se incluye en la definición que sigue a no ser que ésta o se sustituya por un ejemplo de uso o esté construída de tal manera que el "(etc.)" no haga falta:

> **ser**[1] . . . *vi* . . . **17 sea cual/quien**
> **(etc.) sea** <sean cuales sean las cir-
> cunstancias : whatever the circum-
> stances might be> . . .
>
> **hell** . . . *n* . . . **8 like hell I did/will**
> **(etc.)!** *fam* : ¡y un cuerno! . . .

Si el uso común de una palabra es generalmente limitado a una frase determinada, la frase es presentada como la única acepción del lema:

> **ward**[1] . . . *vt* **to ward off** : desviar,
> protegerse contra

Pronunciación

1. Pronunciación de los lemas ingleses

El texto que aparece entre corchetes [ ] inmediatamente después de un lema en la sección Inglés-Español indica la pronunciación del lema. Para una explicación de los símbolos empleados, véase la tabla titulada Símbolos de pronunciación que aparece en la página 85a.

Cuando se incluyen dos o más pronunciaciones que corresponden a la misma palabra, esto indica que diferentes hablantes educados del idioma pronuncian esta palabra de distintas maneras. La segunda variante puede ser tan común como la primera. Todas las pronunciaciones incluidas son comunes y aceptables:

> **tomato** [təˈmeɪt̬o, -ˈmɑ-] . . .

Cuando un término compuesto aparece con sólo una pronunciación parcial, el resto de la pronunciación puede obtenerse bajo la entrada que corresponde a la parte del término cuya pronunciación se ha omitido:

> **gamma ray** [ˈgæmə] . . .
> **ray** [ˈreɪ] . . .
> **smoke**[1] [ˈsmoːk] . . .
> **smoke detector** [dɪˈtɛktər] . . .

En general, no se indica la pronunciación de términos compuestos cuando éstos están formados de dos o más palabras inglesas que aparecen en el diccionario como lemas:

> **water lily** *n* : nenúfar *m*

Solamente la primera entrada en una serie de homógrafos numerados incluye la pronunciación si ésta es la misma para todos los otros homógrafos:

> **dab¹** ['dæb] *vt* . . .
> **dab²** *n* . . .

No se indica la pronunciación de las partes principales de los verbos formados regularmente por añadir un sufijo, ni por otros derivados formados por sufijos comunes.

2. Pronunciación de los lemas españoles

Dada la alta regularidad de la pronunciación del español, no se indica la pronunciación de la mayor parte de las entradas que aparecen en la sección Español-Inglés. Sin embargo, se han hecho excepciones para ciertas palabras (tales como aquéllas que se han adaptado de otras lenguas) cuya pronunciación en español no puede derivarse naturalmente de su ortografía:

> **pizza** ['pitsa, 'pisa] . . .
> **footing** ['fu‚tɪŋ] . . .

Calificativos funcionales

Un calificativo en itálicas que indica la categoría gramatical u otra clasificación funcional del lema aparece inmediatamente después de la pronunciación, o si la pronunciación se ha omitido, después del lema. Las ocho categorías gramaticales tradicionales—el adjetivo, el adverbio, la conjunción, la interjección, el sustantivo, la preposición, el pronombre, y el verbo—se indican como sigue:

> **daily²** *adj* . . .
> **vagamente** *adv* . . .
> **and** . . . *conj* . . .
> **huy** *interj* . . .
> **jackal** . . . *n* . . .
> **para** *prep* . . .
> **neither³** *pron* . . .
> **leer** . . . *v* . . .

Los verbos intransitivos se identifican con el calificativo *vi,* y los transitivos, *vt*:

> **deliberar** *vi* : to deliberate . . .
> **necessitate** . . . *vt* -tated; -tating
>   : necesitar, requerir

Los verbos que son a la vez transitivos e intransitivos llevan el calificativo *v* si todas las acepciones que aparecen en la entrada son tanto transitivas como intransitivas; si algunas son o únicamente transitivas o únicamente intransitivas, la entrada se subdivide en

dos secciones, y cada una de éstas es introducida con el calificativo
vt o *vi*, respectivamente:

> **scrawl**[1] ... *v* : garabatear
> **crack**[1] ... *vt* ... — *vi* ...
> **esperar** *vt* ... — *vi* ...

Si una entrada así subdividida incluye inflexiones irregulares, el
calificativo *v* aparece inmediatamente delante de las inflexiones, y
las acepciones transitivas e intransitivas son introducidas con los
calificativos *vt* y *vi*, respectivamente:

> **satisfy** ... *v* -fied; -fying *vt* ... —
> *vi* ...

Los verbos pronominales españoles se identifican con el calificativo *vr*:

> **jactarse** *vr* ...
> **abandonar** *vt* ... — **abando-**
> **narse** ... *vr* ...

Por último, dos otros calificativos se emplean para indicar la
clasificación funcional de los verbos: *v aux* (auxiliary verb) y *v
impers* (impersonal verb).

> **may** ... *v aux, past* **might** ...
> **hacer** ... *vt* ... — *vi* ... — *v impers*
> **1** *(referring to weather)* <hace frío
> : it's cold> ...

Los prefijos se identifican con el calificativo *pref*:

> **ciber-** *pref* ...
> **e-** *pref* ...

Los sufijos se identifican con el calificativo *suf*:

> **-less** ... *suf* ...
> **-ísimo, -ma** *suf* ...

Los lemas ingleses y españoles que son marcas registradas se
indican con los calificativos *trademark* y *marca registrada*, respectivamente:

> **Q–tips** ... *trademark* — se usa para
> hisopos
> **Kleenex** ... *marca registrada, m* —
> used for a paper tissue

Los lemas ingleses que son marcas de servicio (palabras o nombres utilizados por una organización para identificar sus servicios)
se indican con el calificativo *service mark*:

> **Realtor** ... *service mark* ...

Calificativos de género

En toda entrada de la sección Español-Inglés cuyo lema es un
sustantivo o una marca registrada, el género del lema se indica con
los calificativos *m* (masculino), *f* (femenino), o *mf* (masculino o

femenino). Si el lema es un sustantivo, el calificativo de género aparece inmediatamente después del calificativo funcional:

> **magnesio** *nm* . . .
> **galaxia** *nf* . . .
> **turista** *nmf* . . .

Si el lema es una marca registrada, el calificativo de género aparece después del calificativo funcional y va precedido por una coma y un espacio:

> **Ping–Pong** *marca registrada, m* . . .

Si se dan las formas tanto masculina como femenina de un sustantivo que denota a una persona, se aplica el calificativo *n*:

> **director, -tora** *n* . . .

Todo sustantivo español que aparece como definición de un lema inglés es acompañado de un calificativo de género:

> **amnesia** . . . *n* : amnesia *f*
> **earache** . . . *n* : dolor *m* de oído(s)
> **gamekeeper** . . . *n* : guardabosque
>   *mf*

Inflexiones

1. Sustantivos

En este diccionario se indica el plural de un sustantivo en los siguientes casos: cuando el plural es irregular, cuando la acentuación o la ortografía del vocablo raíz cambia al añadir el sufijo del plural, cuando un sustantivo inglés termina en una consonante seguida de *-o* o de *-ey,* cuando un sustantivo inglés termina en *-oo,* cuando un sustantivo inglés es un término compuesto del cual el elemento a pluralizar es el primero y no el último, cuando un sustantivo tiene variantes en el plural, o cuando podría suscitarse una duda razonable en cuanto a la ortografía del plural:

> **tooth** . . . *n, pl* **teeth** . . .
> **garrafón** *nm, pl* **-fones** . . .
> **potato** . . . *n, pl* **-toes** . . .
> **abbey** . . . *n, pl* **-beys** . . .
> **cuckoo**[2] *n, pl* **-oos** . . .
> **brother–in–law** . . . *n, pl* **brothers–** **in–law** . . .
> **fish**[2] *n, pl* **fish** *or* **fishes** . . .
> **hábitat** *nm, pl* **-tats** . . .
> **tahúr** *nm, pl* **tahúres** . . .

En la sección Inglés-Español, la forma plural de la mayor parte de los sustantivos se indica por medio de una inflexión reducida, sin tener en cuenta el número de sílabas que el lema contenga. En la sección Español-Inglés, se dan inflexiones reducidas sólo para aquellos sustantivos que contengan tres o más sílabas, mientras que las formas plurales de sustantivos más breves se presentan enteras:

> **shampoo²** *n, pl* **-poos** ...
> **calamity** ... *n, pl* **-ties** ...
> **mouse** ... *n, pl* **mice** ...
> **sartén** *nmf, pl* **sartenes** ...
> **hámster** ... *nm, pl* **hámsters** ...
> **federación** *nf, pl* **-ciones** ...

Si se produce un plural irregular en sólo uno de los géneros, la forma plural se da con el calificativo correspondiente:

> **campeón, -peona** *n, mpl* **-peones**
> : champion

La forma plural de un sustantivo generalmente no aparece si el vocablo raíz permanece inalterado por la adición del sufijo plural regular, o cuando no es probable que el sustantivo se use en el plural:

> **apple** ... *n* : manzana *f*
> **inglés³** *nm* : English (language)

Aquellos sustantivos que siempre son plurales en forma y que ocurren en construcciones plurales son clasificados *npl* si son sustantivos ingleses, *nmpl* si son sustantivos masculinos españoles, *nfpl* si son sustantivos femeninos españoles, o *nmfpl* si son sustantivos españoles que pueden ser o masculino o femenino:

> **knickers** ... *npl* ...
> **enseres** *nmpl* ...
> **mancuernas** *nfpl* ...
> **panties** ... *nmfpl* ...

Toda entrada que permanece inalterada en el plural es clasificada *ns & pl* si es un sustantivo inglés, *nms & pl* si es un sustantivo masculino español, *nfs & pl* si es un sustantivo femenino español, y *nmfs & pl* si es un sustantivo español que puede ser o masculino o femenino:

> **deer** ... *ns & pl* ...
> **lavaplatos** *nms & pl* ...
> **tesis** *nfs & pl* ...
> **rompehuelgas** *nmfs & pl* ...

2. Verbos

VERBOS INGLESES

En la sección Inglés-Español, las partes principales de los verbos se indican en los siguientes casos: cuando el verbo es irregular, cuando la ortografía del vocablo raíz cambia al añadir un sufijo verbal, cuando el verbo termina en *-ey*, cuando una inflexión tiene variantes, o cuando puede suscitarse una duda razonable en cuanto a la ortografía de una inflexión:

> **break**[1] . . . *v* **broke** . . . ; **broken** . . . ; **breaking** . . .
>
> **drag**[1] . . . *v* **dragged; dragging** . . .
>
> **monkey**[1] . . . *vi* **-keyed; -keying** . . .
>
> **label**[1] . . . *vt* **-beled** *or* **-belled; -beling** *or* **-belling** . . .
>
> **imagine** . . . *vt* **-ined; -ining** . . .

Si el verbo consta de dos o más sílabas, se da generalmente una forma reducida de la inflexión:

> **multiply** . . . *v* **-plied; -plying** . . .
>
> **bevel**[1] . . . *v* **-eled** *or* **-elled; -eling** *or* **-elling** . . .
>
> **forgo** *or* **forego** . . . *vt* **-went; -gone; -going** . . .
>
> **commit** . . . *vt* **-mitted; -mitting** . . .

Las partes principales de un verbo inglés no aparecen cuando el vocablo raíz no cambia al añadir *-s, -ed,* y *-ing*:

> **delay**[1] . . . *vt*
>
> **pitch**[1] . . . *vt*

VERBOS ESPAÑOLES

En cada entrada correspondiente a un verbo irregular español aparece un número entre llaves que remite al lector a los modelos de conjugación que aparecen en las páginas 72a a 78a de la sección titulada Conjugation of Spanish Verbs:

> **abnegarse** {49} *vr* . . .
>
> **volver** {89} *vi* . . .

Aunque estas remisiones no aparecen en las entradas que corresponden a los verbos regulares españoles, los modelos de conjugación de estas formas pueden consultarse en la susodicha sección, que comienza en la página 68a.

3. Adverbios y adjetivos

ADVERBIOS Y ADJETIVOS INGLESES

Los lemas de adjetivos y adverbios ingleses incluyen las formas comparativas y superlativas cuando la ortografía del vocablo raíz cambia al añadir un sufijo, cuando la inflexión es de forma irregular, o cuando existen variantes de la inflexión:

> **wet**[2] *adj* **wetter; wettest** . . .
>
> **good**[2] *adj* **better** . . . ; **best** . . .
>
> **evil**[1] . . . *adj* **eviler** *or* **eviller; evilest** *or* **evillest** . . .

Las formas superlativas de adjetivos y adverbios ingleses de más de una sola sílaba son representadas generalmente por la forma reducida -*est*:

> **early**[1] ... *adv* **earlier; -est** ...
> **gaudy** ... *adj* **gaudier; -est** ...
> **secure**[2] *adj* **securer; -est** ...

En algunas entradas aparece únicamente la forma superlativa porque no existe evidencia del uso de la forma comparativa:

> **mere** ... *adj, superlative* **merest** ...

Las formas comparativas y superlativas de los adjetivos y adverbios generalmente no se muestran si el vocablo raíz no cambia al añadir el sufijo:

> **quiet**[3] *adj* **1** ...

Uso

1. Calificativos de uso

En este diccionario se emplean dos tipos de calificativo de uso: regional y estilístico. Las palabras españolas cuyo uso se limita a ciertas regiones de Latinoamérica o a España reciben calificativos que indican los países en que suelen usarse con más frecuencia:

> **guarachear** *vi Cuba, PRi fam* ...
> **bucket** ... *n* : ... cubeta *f Mex*

Los siguientes calificativos regionales se han empleado en la redacción de este libro: *Arg* (Argentina), *Bol* (Bolivia), *CA* (Centroamérica), *Car* (el Caribe), *Chile* (Chile), *Col* (Colombia), *CoRi* (Costa Rica), *Cuba* (Cuba), *DomRep* (República Dominicana), *Ecua* (Ecuador), *Sal* (El Salvador), *Guat* (Guatemala), *Hond* (Honduras), *Mex* (México), *Nic* (Nicaragua), *Pan* (Panamá), *Par* (Paraguay), *Peru* (Perú), *PRi* (Puerto Rico), *Spain* (España), *Uru* (Uruguay), *Ven* (Venezuela).

Dado el foco primordialmente latinoamericano de este diccionario, la mayoría de los regionalismos que contiene provienen de América Latina. Sin embargo, se han incluido también algunos regionalismos comunes de España.

Varios vocablos reciben un calificativo de *fam* (familiar), lo cual indica que el uso de tales palabras es apropiado solamente en contextos informales. Los calificativos *disparaging* (despreciativo), *vulgar* (vulgar o soez), y *offensive* (ofensivo) se emplean para palabras o acepciones que se usan con la intención de lastimar o escandalizar, o que tienen una alta probabilidad de ofender. Tales voces aparecen definidas en este diccionario solamente si su uso es muy común. El propósito de estos calificativos es, pues, de servir de advertencia al lector.

2. Notas de uso

En algunos casos, una acepción puede venir precedida de una nota entre paréntesis que proporciona al lector información semántica o gramatical:

> **not** . . . *adv* **1** (*used to form a negative*)
> : no . . .
>
> **within²** *prep* . . . **2** (*in expressions of distance*) : . . . **3** (*in expressions of time*) : . . .
>
> **e²** *conj* (*used instead of* **y** *before words beginning with* i- *or* hi-) : . . .
>
> **poder¹** . . . *v aux* . . . **2** (*expressing possibility*) : . . . **3** (*expressing permission*) : . . .

Este tipo de orientación semántica puede aparecer también entre paréntesis como parte de la definición:

> **calibrate** . . . *vt* . . . : calibrar (armas), graduar (termómetros)
>
> **palco** *nm* : box (in a theater or stadium)

En algunas ocasiones, una nota de uso aparece en lugar de una definición. Esto ocurre generalmente cuando el lema carece de un equivalente sencillo en el otro idioma. Estas notas de uso aparecen acompañadas de ejemplos que ilustran el uso común del lema:

> **shall** . . . *v aux* . . . **1** (*used formally to express a command*) <you shall do as I say : harás lo que te digo> . . .

3. Ejemplos de uso

Varias definiciones vienen acompañadas de ejemplos de uso. Estos ejemplos sirven para ilustrar un empleo típico del lema en un contexto dado, o un uso idiomático común de la palabra. Los ejemplos de uso incluyen una traducción, y aparecen entre paréntesis angulares:

> **lejos** *adv* **1** : far away, distant <a lo lejos : in the distance, far off> . . .
>
> **make¹** . . . *v* . . . *vt* . . . **15** . . . : hacer (dinero, amigos) <to make a living : ganarse la vida> . . .

Se utiliza una barra inclinada / entre las palabras de un ejemplo de uso para indicar que cualquiera de las palabras así separadas puede usarse en esa posición dentro de la frase:

> **tener** . . . *vt* . . . **2** : to have (available) <tener dinero/tiempo para : to have money/time for> . . .
>
> **money** . . . *n* . . . **1** : dinero *m*, plata *f* <to make/lose money : ganar/perder dinero> . . .

Las palabras separadas por barras no siempre tienen el mismo significado.

Cuando una de las palabras de un ejemplo de uso aparece seguida de "(etc.)", esto indica que hay otras palabras parecidas a la que precede al "(etc.)" que pueden usarse en esa posición dentro de la frase:

> **dar** . . . *vt* . . . **16** CAUSAR : to cause
> \<darle miedo/sed (etc.) a alguien : to
> make someone frightened/thirsty
> (etc.)> . . .
>
> **turn²** *n* . . . **3** INTERSECTION : boca-
> calle *f* \<we took a wrong turn : nos
> equivocamos de calle/salida (etc.),
> . . .> . . .

En algunas ocasiones, un ejemplo de uso aparece en lugar de una definición. Esto ocurre generalmente cuando una frase en negrita carece de un equivalente en el otro idioma de una sola frase, o cuando su uso se entiende mejor en contexto:

> **saber¹** . . . *vt* . . . **6 qué sé yo** \<dia-
> mantes, perlas, y qué sé yo : dia-
> monds, pearls, and whatnot> \<y qué
> sé yo dónde : and who knows where
> (else)> . . .
>
> **all¹** . . . *adv* . . . **8 ~ over** *fam* \<to be
> all over someone for something : criti-
> car duramente a alguien por
> algo> . . .

Definiciones

En este diccionario, una definición consta de una o más traducciones que corresponden a una sola acepción de un lema, una entrada secundaria, o una frase en negrita. Se introduce una acepción o definición por medio de dos puntos en negrita:

> **fable** . . . *n* : fábula *f*
>
> **sonrojar** . . . — **sonrojarse** *vr* : to
> blush
>
> **aback** . . . *adv* . . . **2 to be taken
> aback** : quedarse desconcertado

Si se incluye más de una traducción dentro de la misma definición, las traducciones generalmente se separan por comas:

> **as of** *prep* : desde, a partir de

Cuando las comas aparecen en una definición por otras razones, las traducciones se separan por un punto y coma en lugar de una coma:

> **love²** *n* . . . **3** BELOVED : amor *m;*
> amado *m,* -da *f;* enamorado *m,* -da
> *f* . . .

Se utiliza una barra inclinada / entre las palabras de una traducción para indicar que cualquiera de las palabras así separadas puede usarse en esa posición dentro de la frase:

> **bajar** *vt* . . . **2** : to bring/take/carry
> down, to get/lift down . . .

Las palabras separadas por barras no siempre tienen el mismo significado.

División de las acepciones

Cuando una entrada principal tiene varias acepciones, éstas se indican con un número arábigo, compuesto también en negrita:

> **laguna** *nf* **1** : lagoon **2** : gap

Cuando alguna información (como un sinónimo, una palabra o frase en negrita, una nota de uso, una remisión, o un calificativo) aparece después de un número de acepción, ésta se aplica específicamente a dicha acepción:

> **abanico** *nm* . . . 2 GAMA : . . .
> **tonic²** *n* . . . 2 *or* **tonic water** : . . .
> **grillo** *nm* . . . 2 **grillos** *nmpl* : . . .
> **fairy** . . . *n, pl* **fairies** . . . 2 **fairy tale**
> : . . .
> **myself** . . . *pron* 1 (*used reflexively*)
> : . . .
> **pike** . . . *n* . . . 3 → **turnpike**
> **atado²** *nm* . . . 2 *Arg* : . . .

Remisiones

Una flecha indica que información correspondiente al lema que precede a la flecha puede encontrarse en la entrada que corresponde a la palabra que la sigue. Si el lema es una inflexión, la remisión que viene después de la flecha dirige al lector a la forma raíz de la palabra:

> **fue, etc.** → **ir, ser**
> **mice** → **mouse**

En otros casos, la remisión señala otro lema que tiene el mismo significado que la palabra buscada:

> **scapula** . . . → **shoulder blade**
> **amuck** . . . → **amok**

Sinónimos

Frecuentemente se provee un sinónimo compuesto en mayúsculas pequeñas antes de los dos puntos en negrita que preceden a una definición:

> **seleccionar** *vt* ELEGIR : . . .
> **turn¹** *vt* . . . — *vi* . . . 1 ROTATE, SPIN
> : . . .
> **carta** *nf* . . . 2 NAIPE : . . .

Toda palabra empleada como sinónimo tiene su propia entrada en el diccionario, ya sea como lema o como frase en negrita. El propósito de estos sinónimos es de orientar al lector y ayudarlo a elegir la acepción correcta, así como de proveer un término que podría usarse alternativamente en el mismo contexto.

Spanish Grammar

Accentuation

Spanish word stress is generally determined according to the following rules:

- Words ending in a vowel, or in -*n* or -*s,* are stressed on the next-to-last syllable (*za<u>pa</u>to, <u>lla</u>man*).

- Words ending in a consonant other than -*n* or -*s* are stressed on the last syllable (*per<u>diz</u>, curiosi<u>dad</u>*).

Exceptions to these rules have a written accent mark over the stressed vowel (*<u>fá</u>cil, habla<u>rá</u>, <u>úl</u>timo*).

There are also a few words which take accent marks in order to distinguish them from homonyms (*si, sí; que, qué; el, él;* etc.)*.

Adverbs ending in -*mente* have two stressed syllables since they retain both the stress of the root word and of the -*mente* suffix (*<u>len</u>ta<u>men</u>te, difí<u>cilmen</u>te*). Many compounds also have two stressed syllables (*<u>lim</u>piaparab<u>ri</u>sas*).

Punctuation and Capitalization

Questions and exclamations in Spanish are preceded by an inverted question mark ¿ and an inverted exclamation mark ¡, respectively:

¿Cuándo llamó Ana?
Y tú, ¿qué piensas?

¡No hagas eso!
Pero, ¡qué lástima!

In Spanish, unlike English, the following words are not capitalized:

- Names of days, months, and languages (*jueves, octubre, español*).

- Spanish adjectives or nouns derived from proper nouns (*los nicaragüenses, una teoría marxista*).

---

*The Real Academia Española (Royal Spanish Academy) now recommends always omitting the accent marks from the adverb *solo,* which was previously written as *sólo* to distinguish it from the adjective *solo;* and from all demonstrative pronouns (see Demonstrative Pronouns on page 51a for more information about the latter). Nevertheless, the accented variants of these words are still commonly encountered as of this writing.

Articles

1. Definite Article

Spanish has five forms of the definite article: *el* (masculine singular), *la* (feminine singular), *los* (masculine plural), *las* (feminine plural), and *lo* (neuter). The first four agree in gender and number with the nouns they limit (*el carro*, the car; *las tijeras*, the scissors), although the form *el* is used with feminine singular nouns beginning with a stressed *a-* or *ha-* (*el águila, el hambre*).

The neuter article *lo* is used with the masculine singular form of an adjective to express an abstract concept (*lo mejor de este método*, the best thing about this method; *lo meticuloso de su trabajo*, the meticulousness of her work; *lo mismo para mí*, the same for me).

Whenever the masculine article *el* immediately follows the words *de* or *a*, it combines with them to form the contractions *del* and *al*, respectively (*viene del campo, vi al hermano de Roberto*).

The use of *el, la, los,* and *las* in Spanish corresponds largely to the use of *the* in English; some exceptions are noted below.

The definite article is used:

- When referring to something as a class (*los gatos son ágiles*, cats are agile; *me gusta el café*, I like coffee).

- In references to meals and in most expressions of time (*¿comiste el almuerzo?*, did you eat lunch?; *vino el año pasado*, he came last year; *son las dos*, it's two o'clock; *prefiero el verano*, I prefer summer; *la reunión es el lunes*, the meeting is on Monday; but: *hoy es lunes*, today is Monday).

- Before titles (except *don, doña, san, santo, santa, fray,* and *sor*) in third-person references to people (*la señora Rivera llamó*, Mrs. Rivera called; but: *hola, señora Rivera*, hello, Mrs. Rivera).

- In references to body parts and personal possessions (*me duele la cabeza*, my head hurts; *dejó el sombrero*, he left his hat).

- To mean "the one" or "the ones" when the subject is already understood (*la de plástico*, the plastic one; *los que vi ayer*, the ones I saw yesterday).

The definite article is omitted:

- Before a noun in apposition, if the noun is not modified (*Caracas, capital de Venezuela;* but: *Pico Bolívar, la montaña más alta de Venezuela*).

- Before a number in a royal title (*Carlos Quinto*, Charles the Fifth).

2. Indefinite Article

The forms of the indefinite article in Spanish are *un* (masculine singular), *una* (feminine singular), *unos* (masculine plural), and *unas* (feminine plural). They agree in number and gender with the nouns they limit (*una mesa*, a table; *unos platos*, some plates), although the form *un* is used with feminine singular nouns beginning with a stressed *a-* or *ha-* (*un ala*, *un hacha*).

The use of *un, una, unos,* and *unas* in Spanish corresponds largely to the use of *a, an,* and *some* in English, with some exceptions:

* Indefinite articles are generally omitted before nouns identifying someone or something as a member of a class or category (*Paco es profesor/católico*, Paco is a professor/Catholic; *se llama páncreas*, it's called a pancreas).

* They are also often omitted in instances where quantity is understood from context (*vine sin chaqueta*, I came without a jacket; *no tengo carro*, I don't have a car).

Nouns

1. Gender

Nouns in Spanish are either masculine or feminine. A noun's gender can often be determined according to the following guidelines:

* Nouns ending in *-aje, -o,* or *-or* are usually masculine (*el traje, el libro, el sabor*), with some exceptions (*la mano, la foto, la labor,* etc.).

* Nouns ending in *-a, -dad, -ión, -tud,* or *-umbre* are usually feminine (*la alfombra, la capacidad, la excepción, la juventud, la certidumbre*). Exceptions include: *el día, el mapa,* and many learned borrowings ending in *-ma* (*el idioma, el tema*).

Most nouns referring to people or animals agree in gender with the subject (*el hombre, la mujer; el hermano, la hermana; el perro, la perra*). However, some nouns referring to people, including those ending in *-ista,* use the same form for both sexes (*el artista, la artista; el modelo, la modelo;* etc.).

A few names of animals exist in only one gender form (*la jirafa, el sapo,* etc.). In these instances, the adjectives *macho* and *hembra* are sometimes used to distinguish males and females (*una jirafa macho*, a male giraffe).

2. Pluralization

Plurals of Spanish nouns are formed as follows:

* Nouns ending in an unstressed vowel or an accented *-é* are pluralized by adding *-s* (*la vaca, las vacas; el café, los cafés*).

- Nouns ending in a consonant other than *-s,* or in a stressed vowel other than *-é,* are generally pluralized by adding *-es* (*el papel, los papeles; el rubí, los rubíes*). Exceptions include *papá* (*papás*) and *mamá* (*mamás*).

- Nouns with an unstressed final syllable ending in *-s* usually have a zero plural (*la crisis, las crisis; el jueves, los jueves*). Other nouns ending in *-s* add *-es* to form the plural (*el mes, los meses; el país, los países*).

- Nouns ending in *-z* are pluralized by changing the *-z* to *-c* and adding *-es* (*el lápiz, los lápices; la vez, las veces*).

- Many compound nouns have a zero plural (*el paraguas, los paraguas; el aguafiestas, los aguafiestas*).

- The plurals of *cualquiera* and *quienquiera* are *cualesquiera* and *quienesquiera,* respectively.

Adjectives

1. Gender and Number

Most adjectives agree in gender and number with the nouns they modify (*un chico alto, una chica alta, unos chicos altos, unas chicas altas*). Some adjectives, including those ending in *-e* and *-ista* (*fuerte, altruista*) and comparative adjectives ending in *-or* (*mayor, mejor*), vary only for number.

Adjectives whose masculine singular forms end in *-o* generally change the *-o* to *-a* to form the feminine (*pequeño → pequeña*). Masculine adjectives ending in *-án, -ón,* or *-dor,* and masculine adjectives of nationality which end in a consonant, usually add *-a* to form the feminine (*holgazán → holgazana; llorón → llorona; trabajador → trabajadora; irlandés → irlandesa*).

Adjectives are pluralized in much the same manner as nouns:

- The plurals of adjectives ending in an unstressed vowel or an accented *-é* are formed by adding an *-s* (*un postre rico,* unos postres *ricos;* una camisa *café,* unas camisas *cafés*).

- Adjectives ending in a consonant, or in a stressed vowel other than *-é,* are generally pluralized by adding *-es* (*un niño cortés,* unos niños *corteses;* una persona *iraní,* unas personas *iraníes*).

- Adjectives ending in *-z* are pluralized by changing the *-z* to *-c* and adding *-es* (*una respuesta sagaz,* unas respuestas *sagaces*).

2. Shortening

- The following masculine singular adjectives drop their final *-o* when they occur before a masculine singular noun: *bueno* (*buen*), *malo* (*mal*), *uno* (*un*), *alguno* (*algún*), *ninguno* (*ningún*), *primero* (*primer*), *tercero* (*tercer*).

- *Grande* shortens to *gran* before any singular noun.
- *Ciento* shortens to *cien* before any noun.
- *Cualquiera* shortens to *cualquier* before any noun.
- The title *Santo* shortens to *San* before all masculine names except those beginning with *To-* or *Do-* (*San Juan, Santo Tomás*).

3. Position

Descriptive adjectives generally follow the nouns they modify (*una cosa útil, un actor famoso*). However, adjectives that express an inherent quality often precede the noun (*la blanca nieve*).

Some adjectives change meaning depending on whether they occur before or after the noun: *un pobre niño,* a poor (pitiable) child; *un niño pobre,* a poor (not rich) child; *un gran hombre,* a great man; *un hombre grande,* a big man; *el único libro,* the only book; *el libro único,* the unique book; etc.

4. Comparative and Superlative Forms

The comparative of Spanish adjectives is generally rendered as *más . . . que* (more . . . than) or *menos . . . que* (less . . . than): *soy más alta que él,* I'm taller than he (is), I'm taller than him *fam; son menos inteligentes que tú,* they're less intelligent than you.

The superlative of Spanish adjectives usually follows the formula *definite article + (noun +) más/menos + adjective: ella es la estudiante más trabajadora,* she is the hardest-working student; *él es el menos conocido,* he's the least known.

A few Spanish adjectives have irregular comparative and superlative forms:

Adjective	Comparative/Superlative
bueno (good)	**mejor** (better, best)
malo (bad)	**peor** (worse, worst)
grande[1] (big, great), **viejo** (old)	**mayor** (greater, older; greatest, oldest)
pequeño[1] (little), **joven** (young)	**menor** (lesser, younger; least, youngest)
mucho (much), **muchos** (many)	**más** (more, most)
poco (little), **pocos** (few)	**menos** (less, least)

[1] These words have regular comparative and superlative forms when used in reference to physical size: *él es más grande que yo; nuestra casa es la más pequeña.*

ABSOLUTE SUPERLATIVE

The absolute superlative is formed by placing *muy* before the adjective, or by adding the suffix *-ísimo* (*ella es muy simpática* or *ella es simpatiquísima,* she is very nice). The absolute superlative using *-ísimo* is formed according to the following rules:

- Adjectives ending in a consonant other than *-z* simply add the *-ísimo* ending (*fácil* → *facilísimo*).

- Adjectives ending in *-z* change this consonant to *-c* and add *-ísimo* (*feliz* → *felicísimo*).

- Adjectives ending in a vowel or diphthong drop the vowel or diphthong and add *-ísimo* (*claro* → *clarísimo; amplio* → *amplísimo*).

- Adjectives ending in *-co* or *-go* change these endings to *-qu* and *-gu,* respectively, and add *-ísimo* (*rico* → *riquísimo; largo* → *larguísimo*).

- Adjectives ending in *-ble* change this ending to *-bil* and add *-ísimo* (*notable* → *notabilísimo*).

- Adjectives containing the stressed diphthong *ie* or *ue* will sometimes change these to *e* and *o,* respectively (*ferviente* → *fervientísimo* or *ferventísimo; bueno* → *buenísimo* or *bonísimo*).

Adverbs

Adverbs can be formed by adding the adverbial suffix *-mente* to virtually any adjective (*fácil* → *fácilmente*). If the adjective varies for gender, the feminine form is used as the basis for forming the adverb (*rápido* → *rápidamente*).

Pronouns

1. Personal Pronouns

The personal pronouns in Spanish are:

Person	Singular		Plural	
FIRST	yo	I	nosotros, -tras	we
SECOND	tú	you (familiar)	vosotros[2], -tras[2]	you, all of you
	vos[1]	you		
	usted	you (formal)	ustedes[3]	you, all of you
THIRD	él	he	ellos, ellas	they
	ella	she		
	ello	it (neuter)		

[1] Familiar form used in addition to *tú* in South and Central America.
[2] Familiar form used in Spain.
[3] Formal form used in Spain; familiar and formal form used in Latin America.

FAMILIAR VS. FORMAL

The second-person personal pronouns exist in both familiar and formal forms. The familiar forms are generally used when addressing relatives, friends, and children, although usage varies considerably from region to region; the formal forms are used in other contexts to show courtesy, respect, or emotional distance.

In Spain and in the Caribbean, *tú* is used exclusively as the familiar singular "you." In South and Central America, however, *vos* either competes with *tú* to varying degrees or replaces it entirely. (For a more detailed explanation of *vos* and its corresponding verb forms, refer to the Conjugation of Spanish Verbs section.)

The plural familiar form *vosotros, -tras* is used only in Spain, where *ustedes* is reserved for formal contexts. In Latin America, *vosotros, -tras* is not used, and *ustedes* serves as the all-purpose plural "you."

It should be noted that while *usted* and *ustedes* are regarded as second-person pronouns, they take the third-person form of the verb.

USAGE

In Spanish, personal pronouns are generally omitted (*voy al cine,* I'm going to the movies; *¿llamaron?,* did they call?), although they are sometimes used for purposes of emphasis or clarity (*se lo diré yo,* I will tell them; *vino ella, pero él se quedó,* she came, but he stayed behind). The forms *usted* and *ustedes* are usually included out of courtesy (*¿cómo está usted?,* how are you?).

Personal pronouns are not generally used in reference to inanimate objects or living creatures other than humans; in these instances, the pronoun is most often omitted (*¿es nuevo? no, es viejo,* is it new? no, it's old).

The neuter third-person pronoun *ello* is reserved for indefinite subjects (such as abstract concepts): *todo ello implica* . . . , all of this implies . . . ; *por si ello fuera poco* . . . , as if that weren't enough . . . . It most commonly appears in formal writing and speech. In less formal contexts, *ello* is often either omitted or replaced with *esto, eso,* or *aquello.*

2. Prepositional Pronouns

Prepositional pronouns are used as the objects of prepositions (*¿es para mí?*, is it for me?; *se lo dio a ellos*, he gave it to them).

The prepositional pronouns in Spanish are:

Singular		Plural	
mí	me	**nosotros, -tras**	us
ti	you	**vosotros¹, -tras¹**	you
usted	you (formal)	**ustedes**	you
él	him	**ellos, ellas**	them
ella	her		
ello	it (neuter)		
sí	yourself, himself, herself, itself, oneself	**sí**	yourselves, themselves

¹Used primarily in Spain.

When the preposition *con* is followed by *mí, ti,* or *sí,* both words are replaced by *conmigo, contigo,* and *consigo,* respectively (*¿vienes conmigo?*, are you coming with me?; *habló contigo,* he spoke with you; *no lo trajo consigo,* she didn't bring it with her).

3. Object Pronouns

DIRECT OBJECT PRONOUNS

Direct object pronouns indicate the person or thing that receives the action of a verb. The direct object pronouns in Spanish are:

Singular		Plural	
me	me	**nos**	us
te	you	**os¹**	you
le²	you, him	**les²**	you³, them
lo	you (formal), him, it	**los**	you³, them
la	you (formal), her, it	**las**	you³, them

¹ Used only in Spain.
² Used mainly in Spain.
³ See explanation below.

Agreement

The third-person forms agree in both gender and number with the nouns they replace or the people they refer to (*pintó las paredes,* she painted the walls → *las pintó,* she painted them; *visitaron al señor Juárez,* they visited Mr. Juárez → *lo visitaron,* they visited him). The remaining forms vary only for number.

Position

Direct object pronouns are normally affixed to the end of an affirmative command, a simple infinitive, or a present participle (*¡hazlo!,* do it!; *es difícil hacerlo,* it's difficult to do it; *haciéndolo, aprenderás,* you'll learn by doing it). With constructions involving an auxiliary verb and an infinitive or present participle, the pronoun may occur either immediately before the construction or suffixed to it (*lo voy a hacer* or *voy a hacerlo,* I'm going to do it; *estoy haciéndolo* or *lo estoy haciendo,* I'm doing it). In all other cases, the pronoun immediately precedes the conjugated verb (*no lo haré,* I won't do it).

Regional Variation

The second-person ("you") familiar plural form *os* is restricted to Spain. In most parts of Latin America, *los* and *las* are used as both the familiar and formal second-person plural forms.

In Spain and in a few areas of Latin America, *le* and *les* are used in place of *lo* and *los,* respectively, when referring to or addressing people (*le vieron,* they saw him; *les vistió,* she dressed them; *encantado de conocerle,* pleased to meet you).

INDIRECT OBJECT PRONOUNS

Indirect object pronouns represent the secondary goal of the action of a verb (*me dio el regalo,* he gave me the gift; *les dije que no,* I told them no). The indirect object pronouns in Spanish are:

Singular		Plural	
me	(to, for, from) me	nos	(to, for, from) us
te	(to, for, from) you	os[1]	(to, for, from) you
le	(to, for, from) you, him, her, it	les	(to, for, from) you, them
se[2]		se[2]	

[1] Used only in Spain.
[2] See explanation below.

Position

Indirect object pronouns follow the same rules as direct object pronouns with regard to their position in relation to verbs. When they occur with direct object pronouns, the indirect object pronoun always precedes (*nos lo dio,* she gave it to us; *estoy trayéndotela,* I'm bringing it to you).

Use of *Se*

When the indirect object pronouns *le* or *les* occur before any direct object pronoun beginning with an *l-,* the indirect object pronouns *le* and *les* convert to *se* (*les mandé la carta,* I sent them the letter → *se la mandé,* I sent it to them; *vamos a comprarle los aretes,* let's buy her the earrings → *vamos a comprárselos,* let's buy them for her).

4. Reflexive Pronouns

Reflexive pronouns are used to refer back to the subject of the verb (*me hice daño,* I hurt myself; *se vistieron,* they got dressed, they dressed themselves; *nos lo compramos,* we bought it for ourselves).

The reflexive pronouns in Spanish are:

Singular		Plural	
me	myself	**nos**	ourselves
te	yourself	**os**[1]	yourselves
se	yourself, himself, herself, itself	**se**	yourselves, themselves

[1] Used only in Spain.

Reflexive pronouns are also used:

- When the verb describes an action performed to one's own body, clothing, etc. (*me quité los zapatos,* I took off my shoes; *se arregló el pelo,* he fixed his hair).

- In the plural, to indicate reciprocal action (*se hablan con frecuencia,* they speak with each other frequently).

- In the third-person singular and plural, as an indefinite subject reference (*se dice que es verdad,* they say it's true; *nunca se sabe,* one never knows; *se escribieron miles de páginas,* thousands of pages were written).

It should be noted that many verbs which take reflexive pronouns in Spanish have intransitive equivalents in English (*ducharse,* to shower; *quejarse,* to complain; etc.).

5. Relative Pronouns

Relative pronouns introduce subordinate clauses acting as nouns or modifiers (*el libro que escribió* . . . , the book that he wrote . . . ; *las chicas a quienes conociste* . . . , the girls whom you met . . .). In Spanish, the relative pronouns are:

que (that, which, who, whom)

quien, quienes (who, whom, that, whoever, whomever)

el cual, la cual, los cuales, las cuales (which, who)

el que, la que, los que, las que (which, who, whoever)

lo cual (which)

lo que (what, which, whatever)

cuanto, cuanta, cuantos, cuantas (all those that, all that, whatever, whoever, as much as, as many as)

Relative pronouns are not omitted in Spanish as they often are in English: *el carro que vi ayer,* the car (that) I saw yesterday. When relative pronouns are used with prepositions, the preposition precedes the clause (*la película sobre la cual le hablé,* the film I spoke to you about).

The relative pronoun *que* can be used in reference to both people and things. Unlike other relative pronouns, *que* does not take the personal *a** when used as a direct object referring to a person (*el hombre que llamé,* the man that I called; but: *el hombre a quien llamé,* the man whom I called).

Quien is used only in reference to people. It varies in number with the explicit or implied antecedent (*las mujeres con quienes charlamos* . . . , the women we chatted with; *quien lo hizo pagará,* whoever did it will pay).

El cual and *el que* vary for both number and gender, and are therefore often used in situations where *que* or *quien(es)* might create ambiguity: *nos contó algunas cosas sobre los libros, las cuales eran interesantes,* he told us some things about the books which (the things) were interesting.

Lo cual and *lo que* are used to refer back to a whole clause, or to something indefinite (*dijo que iría, lo cual me alegró,* he said he would go, which made me happy; *pide lo que quieras,* ask for whatever you want).

Cuanto varies for both number and gender with the implied antecedent: *conté a cuantas* (*personas*) *pude,* I counted as many (people) as I could. If an indefinite mass quantity is referred to, the masculine singular form is used (*anoté cuanto decía,* I jotted down whatever he said).

*The personal *a* is generally used: 1) before direct objects (except direct object pronouns or reflexive pronouns) that refer to people or to something that is personified: *cuida a los niños,* he takes care of the children; *amar a la patria,* to love one's country; and 2) before indirect objects (except indirect object pronouns or reflexive pronouns): *permiten a los pasajeros usar sus teléfonos,* they allow passengers to use their phones; *a mí no me importa,* it doesn't matter to me.

Possessives

1. Possessive Adjectives

UNSTRESSED FORMS

Singular		Plural	
mi(s)	my	**nuestro(s), nuestra(s)**	our
tu(s)	your	**vuestro(s)[1], vuestra(s)[1]**	your
su(s)	your, his, her, its	**su(s)**	your, their

[1] Used only in Spain.

STRESSED FORMS

Singular		Plural	
mío(s), **mía(s)**	my, mine, of mine	**nuestro(s),** **nuestra(s)**	our, ours, of ours
tuyo(s), **tuya(s)**	your, yours, of yours	**vuestro(s)[1],** **vuestra(s)[1]**	your, yours, of yours
suyo(s), **suya(s)**	your, yours, of yours; his, of his; her, hers, of hers; its, of its	**suyo(s),** **suya(s)**	your, yours, of yours; their, theirs, of theirs

[1] Used only in Spain.

The unstressed forms of possessive adjectives precede the nouns they modify (*mis zapatos,* my shoes; *nuestra escuela,* our school).

The stressed forms occur after the noun and are often used for purposes of emphasis (*el carro tuyo,* your car; *la pluma es mía,* the pen is mine; *unos amigos nuestros,* some friends of ours).

All possessive adjectives agree with the noun in number. The stressed forms, as well as the unstressed forms *nuestro* and *vuestro,* also vary for gender.

2. Possessive Pronouns

The possessive pronouns have the same forms as the stressed possessive adjectives (see table above). They are always preceded by the definite article, and they agree in number and gender with the nouns they replace (*las llaves mías,* my keys → *las mías,* mine; *los guantes nuestros,* our gloves → *los nuestros,* ours).

Demonstratives

1. Demonstrative Adjectives

The demonstrative adjectives in Spanish are:

Singular		Plural	
este, esta	this	**estos, estas**	these
ese, esa	that	**esos, esas**	those
aquel, aquella	that	**aquellos, aquellas**	those

Demonstrative adjectives agree in gender and number with the nouns they modify (*esta chica, aquellos árboles*). They normally precede the noun, but may occasionally occur after for purposes of emphasis or to express contempt: *en la época aquella de cambio,* in that era of change; *el perro ese ha ladrado toda la noche,* that (awful, annoying, etc.) dog barked all night long.

The forms *aquel, aquella, aquellos,* and *aquellas* are generally used in reference to people and things that are relatively distant from the speaker in space or time: *ese libro,* that book (a few feet away); *aquel libro,* that book (way over there).

2. Demonstrative Pronouns

The demonstrative pronouns in Spanish are orthographically identical to the demonstrative adjectives. Formerly, Spanish rules of orthography required that the demonstrative pronouns include an accent mark over the stressed vowel (*éste, ése, aquél,* etc.) to distinguish them from the corresponding demonstrative adjectives. However, the Real Academia Española (Royal Spanish Academy) now recommends the omission of the accent mark from these pronouns. This supersedes a previous recommendation calling for the inclusion of the accent mark only when needed to resolve cases of ambiguity. Nevertheless, both the accented and unaccented variants are in common use as of this writing, and are reflected in this dictionary.

In addition, there are three neuter forms—*esto, eso,* and *aquello*—which are used when referring to abstract ideas or unidentified things (*¿te dijo eso?,* he said that to you?; *¿qué es esto?,* what is this?; *tráeme todo aquello,* bring me all that stuff).

Except for the neuter forms, demonstrative pronouns agree in gender and number with the nouns they replace (*esta silla,* this chair → *esta/ésta,* this one; *aquellos vasos,* those glasses → *aquellos/aquéllos,* those ones).

Gramática inglesa

El adjetivo

El adjetivo inglés es invariable en cuanto a número o género, y suele preceder al sustantivo que modifica:

the *tall* woman
(la mujer *alta*)

the *tall* women
(las mujeres *altas*)

a *happy* child
(un niño *contento*)

happy children
(niños *contentos*)

1. Adjetivos positivos, comparativos, y superlativos

Las formas comparativas y superlativas del adjetivo inglés se pueden construir de tres maneras. Cuando el adjetivo positivo consta de una sola sílaba, la construcción más común es de añadir los sufijos *-er* o *-est* al vocablo raíz; si el adjetivo positivo consta de más de dos sílabas, suele entonces combinarse con los adverbios *more, most, less* o *least;* al adjetivo positivo de dos sílabas puede aplicarse cualquiera de las dos fórmulas; y por último, existen los adjetivos irregulares cuyas formas comparativas y superlativas son únicas:

Positivo	Comparativo	Superlativo
clean (limpio)	**cleaner** (más limpio)	**cleanest** (el más limpio)
narrow (angosto)	**narrower** (más angosto)	**narrowest** (el más angosto)
meaningful (significativo)	**more meaningful** (más significativo)	**most meaningful** (el más significativo)
less meaningful (menos significativo)	**least meaningful** (el menos significativo)	
good (bueno)	**better** (mejor)	**best** (el mejor)
bad (malo)	**worse** (peor)	**worst** (el peor)

2. Adjetivos demostrativos

Los adjetivos demostrativos *this* y *that* corresponden a los adjetivos españoles *este* y *ese*, respectivamente, y sirven esencialmente la misma función. Debe notarse que este tipo de adjetivo es el único que tiene forma plural:

Singular		Plural	
this	este, esta	**these**	estos, estas
that	ese, esa	**those**	esos, esas

3. Adjetivos descriptivos

Un adjetivo descriptivo describe o indica una cualidad, clase o condición (*a fascinating conversation,* una conversación fascinante; *a positive attitude,* una actitud positiva; *a fast computer,* una computadora rápida).

4. Adjetivos indefinidos

Un adjetivo indefinido se usa para designar personas o cosas no identificadas (*some children,* unos niños o algunos niños; *other hotels,* otros hoteles).

5. Adjetivos interrogativos

El adjetivo interrogativo se usa para formular preguntas:

Whose office is this?
(*¿De quién* es esta oficina?)

Which book do you want?
(*¿Cuál* libro quieres?)

6. El sustantivo empleado como adjetivo

Un sustantivo puede usarse para modificar otro sustantivo. De esta manera el sustantivo funciona igual que un adjetivo (*the Vietnam War,* la Guerra de Vietnam; *word processing,* procesamiento de textos).

7. Adjetivos posesivos

Llámase adjetivo posesivo a la forma posesiva del pronombre personal. A continuación se listan los adjetivos posesivos ingleses y algunos ejemplos de su uso:

Singular	Plural
my	our
your	your
his/her/its	their

Where's *my* watch?
(¿Dónde está *mi* reloj?)

Your cab's here.
(Ha llegado *su/tu* taxi.)

It was *her* idea.
(Fue *su* idea.)

They read *his* book.
(Leyeron *su* libro.)

the box and *its* contents
(la caja y *su* contenido)

We paid for *their* ticket.
(Pagamos por *su* boleto.)

Your tables are ready.
(*Sus* mesas están listas.)

8. Adjetivos predicativos

Un adjetivo predicativo modifica el sujeto de un verbo copula-
tivo (como *be, become, feel, taste, smell,* o *seem*):

She is *happy* with the outcome.
(Está *contenta* con el resultado.)

The milk tastes *sour*.
(La leche sabe *agria*.)

The student seems *puzzled*.
(El estudiante parece estar *desconcertado*.)

9. Adjetivos propios

Un adjetivo propio es derivado de un nombre propio y suele
escribirse con mayúscula:

Victorian furniture
(muebles *victorianos*)

a *Puerto Rican* product
(un producto *puertorriqueño*)

10. Adjetivos relativos

Un adjetivo relativo (tal como *which, that, who, whom, whose,
where*) se emplea para introducir una cláusula adjetival o sustantiva:

toward late April, by *which* time the report should be finished
(para fines de abril, fecha para *la cual* deberá estar listo el reporte)

a person *whose* identity is unknown
(una persona *cuya* identidad se desconoce)

El adverbio

La mayor parte de los adverbios ingleses se forman a partir de un adjetivo al que se le agrega el sufijo *-ly*:

mad*ly*
(loca*mente*)

wonderful*ly*
(maravillosa*mente*)

Para formar un adverbio de un adjetivo que termina en *-y*, suele cambiarse primero esta terminación a una *-i*, y luego se añade el sufijo *-ly*:

happ*ily*
(feliz*mente*)

daint*ily*
(delicada*mente*)

La forma adverbial que corresponde a varios adjetivos que terminan en *-ic* recibe el sufijo *-ally*:

basic*ally*
(básica*mente*)

numeric*ally*
(numérica*mente*)

Si un adjetivo termina en *-ly*, el adverbio que le corresponde suele escribirse de la misma manera:

she called her mother *daily*
(llamaba a su madre *todos los días*)

the show started *early*
(la función empezó *temprano*)

Por último, hay adverbios que no terminan en *-ly*, por ejemplo:

again (otra vez)
now (ahora)

too (demasiado)
too (también)

1. Adverbios positivos, comparativos, y superlativos

Al igual que el adjetivo, la mayoría de los adverbios ingleses poseen tres grados de comparación: positivo, comparativo, y superlativo. Como regla general, a un adverbio monosilábico se le añade el sufijo *-er* cuando es comparativo, y *-est* cuando es superlativo. Si el adverbio consta de tres o más sílabas, las formas comparativas y superlativas se forman al combinarlo con los adverbios *more/most* o *less/least*. Las formas comparativas y superlativas de un adverbio de dos sílabas pueden obtenerse empleando uno u otro de los dos métodos:

Positivo	Comparativo	Superlativo
fast	faster	fastest
easy	easier	easiest
madly	more madly	most madly
happily	more happily	most happily

Finalmente, hay algunos adverbios, tales como *quite* y *very*, que no poseen comparativo.

2. Adverbios de énfasis

Adverbios tales como *just* y *only* suelen usarse para poner el énfasis en otras palabras. El énfasis producido puede cambiar según la posición del adverbio en la oración:

He *just* nodded to me as he passed.
(*Sólo* me saludó con la cabeza al pasar.)

He nodded to me *just* as he passed.
(Me saludó con la cabeza *justamente* cuando me pasó.)

3. Adverbios relativos

Los adverbios relativos (tales como *when*, *where*, y *why*) se utilizan principalmente para introducir preguntas:

When will he return?
(*¿Cuándo* volverá?)

Where have the children gone?
(*¿A dónde* fueron los niños?)

Why did you do it?
(*¿Por qué* lo hiciste?)

El artículo

1. El artículo definido

En inglés existe solamente una forma del artículo definido, *the*. Este artículo es invariable en cuanto a género o número:

The boys were expelled.
(*Los* chicos fueron expulsados.)

The First Lady dined with *the* ambassador.
(*La* Primera Dama cenó con *el* embajador.)

2. El artículo indefinido

El artículo indefinido *a* se usa con cualquier sustantivo o abreviatura que comience ya sea con una consonante, o con un *sonido* consonántico:

a door	*a* hat
a B.A. degree	*a* one-way street
a union	*a* U.S. Senator

El artículo *a* se emplea también antes de un sustantivo cuya primera sílaba comienza con *h-*, y esta sílaba o no es acentuada, o tiene solamente una acentuación moderada (*a historian, a heroic attempt, a hilarious performance*). Sin embargo, en el inglés hablado, suele más usarse el artículo *an* en estos casos (*an historian, an heroic attempt, an hilarious performance*). Ambas formas son perfectamente aceptables.

El artículo indefinido *an* se usa con cualquier sustantivo o abreviatura que comience con un *sonido* vocal, sin tener en cuenta si la primera letra del sustantivo es vocal o consonante (*an icicle, an nth degree, an honor, an FBI investigation*).

La conjunción

Existen tres tipos principales de conjunciones: la conjunción coordinante, la correlativa, y la subordinante.

1. Conjunciones coordinantes

Las conjunciones coordinantes, tales como *and, because, but, or, nor, since, so,* y *yet,* se emplean para unir elementos gramaticales de igual valor. Estos elementos pueden ser palabras, frases, cláusulas subordinadas, cláusulas principales, u oraciones completas. Las conjunciones coordinantes se emplean para unir elementos similares, para excluir o contrastar, para indicar una alternativa, para indicar una razón, o para precisar un resultado:

unión de elementos similares:
She ordered pencils, pens, *and* erasers.

exclusión o contraste:
He is a brilliant *but* arrogant man.
They offered a promising plan, *but* it had not yet been tested.

alternativa:
She can wait here *or* go on ahead.

razón:
The report is useless, *since* its information is no longer current.

resultado:

His diction is excellent, *so* every word is clear.

2. Conjunciones correlativas

Las conjunciones correlativas se usan en pares, y sirven para unir alternativas y elementos de igual valor gramatical:

Either you go *or* you stay.
(*O* te vas *o* te quedas.)

He had *neither* looks *nor* wit.
(No tenía *ni* atractivo físico *ni* inteligencia.)

3. Conjunciones subordinantes

Las conjunciones subordinantes se usan para unir una cláusula subordinada a una cláusula principal. Estas conjunciones pueden emplearse para expresar la causa, la condición o concesión, el modo, el propósito o resultado, el tiempo, el lugar o la circunstancia, así como las condiciones o posibilidades alternativas:

causa:
Because she learns quickly, she is doing well in her new job.

condición o concesión:
Don't call *unless* you are coming.

modo:
We'll do it *however* you tell us to.

propósito o resultado:
He distributes the mail early *so that* they can read it.

tiempo:
She kept meetings to a minimum *when* she was president.

El sustantivo

A diferencia del sustantivo español, el sustantivo inglés generalmente carece de género. En algunos sustantivos, el género femenino se identifica por la presencia del sufijo *-ess* (*empress, hostess*); existen también aquellos sustantivos que sólo se aplican a miembros de uno u otro sexo, por ejemplo: *husband, wife; father, mother; brother, sister;* así como nombres de ciertos animales: *bull, cow; buck, doe;* etc. Sin embargo, la mayoría de los sustantivos ingleses son neutros. Cuando es preciso atribuirle un género a un sustantivo neutro, suele combinarse éste con palabras como *male, female, man, woman,* etc., por ejemplo:

a *male* parrot
(un loro *macho*)

women writers
(escritoras)

1. Usos básicos

Los sustantivos ingleses suelen usarse como sujetos, objetos directos, objetos de una preposición, objetos indirectos, objetos retenidos, nominativos predicativos, complementos objetivos, construcciones apositivas, y en trato directo:

sujeto:
The *office* was quiet.

objeto directo:
He locked the *office*.

objeto de una preposición:
The file is in the *office*.

objeto indirecto:
He gave his *client* the papers.

objeto retenido:
His client was given the *papers*.

nominativo predicativo:
Mrs. Adams is the managing *partner*.

complemento objetivo:
They made Mrs. Adams managing *partner*.

construcción apositiva:
Mrs. Adams, the managing *partner*, wrote that memo.

trato directo:
Mrs. Adams, may I present Mr. Bonkowski.

2. El sustantivo empleado como adjetivo

Los sustantivos desempeñan una función adjetival cuando preceden a otros sustantivos:

olive oil
(aceite *de oliva*)

business management
(administración *de empresas*)

emergency room
(sala *de emergencias*)

3. La formación del plural

La mayoría de los sustantivos ingleses se pluralizan añadiendo *-s* al final del singular (*book, books; cat, cats; dog, dogs; tree, trees*).

Cuando el sustantivo singular termina en *-s, -x, -z, -ch,* o *-sh,* su forma plural se obtiene añadiendo *-es* al final (*cross, crosses; fox, foxes; witch, witches; wish, wishes; fez, fezes*).

Si el sustantivo singular termina en -*y* precedida de una consonante, la -*y* es convertida en -*i* y se le añade la terminación -*es* (*fairy, fairies; pony, ponies; guppy, guppies*).

No todos los sustantivos ingleses obedecen estas normas. Hay algunos sustantivos (generalmente nombres de animales) que no siempre cambian en el plural (*fish, fish* o *fishes; caribou, caribou* o *caribous*). Por último, hay algunos sustantivos que poseen una forma plural única (*foot, feet; mouse, mice; knife, knives*).

4. El posesivo

La forma posesiva del sustantivo singular generalmente se obtiene al añadir un apóstrofe seguido de una -*s* al final:

Jackie's passport
(el pasaporte *de Jackie*)

this hat is *Billy's*
(este sombrero es *de Billy*)

Cuando el sustantivo termina en -*s,* suele añadirse únicamente el apóstrofe, como sigue:

the *neighbors'* dog
(el perro *de los vecinos*)

Mr. Collins' briefcase
(el portafolios *del Sr. Collins*)

La preposición

La preposición inglesa se combina generalmente con un sustantivo, un pronombre, o el equivalente de un sustantivo (como una frase o cláusula) para formar una frase con función adjetival, adverbial, o sustantiva. Suele distinguirse dos tipos de preposiciones: la preposición simple, es decir, aquélla que consta de una sola palabra (p. ej., *against, from, near, of, on, out,* o *without*), y la compuesta, que consta de más de un elemento (como *according to, by means of,* o *in spite of*).

1. Usos básicos

La preposición se emplea generalmente para unir un sustantivo, un pronombre, o el equivalente de un sustantivo al resto de la oración. Una frase preposicional suele emplearse como adverbio o adjetivo:

She expected resistance *on his part.*
He sat down *beside her.*

2. La conjunción vs. la preposición

Las palabras inglesas *after, before, but, for*,* y *since* pueden funcionar como preposiciones así como conjunciones. El papel que

---

*La conjunción *for* se emplea principalmente en el lenguaje formal y literario.

desempeñan estas palabras suele determinarse según su posición
dentro de la oración. Las conjunciones generalmente sirven para
unir dos elementos de igual valor gramatical, mientras que las preposiciones suelen preceder a un sustantivo, un pronombre, o una
frase sustantiva:

conjunción:
I was a bit concerned *but* not panicky. (*but* vincula dos adjetivos)

preposición:
I was left with nothing *but* hope. (*but* precede a un sustantivo)

conjunción:
The device conserves fuel, *for* it is battery-powered. (*for* vincula
dos cláusulas)

preposición:
The device conserves fuel *for* residual heating. (*for* precede a una
frase sustantiva)

3. Posición

Una preposición puede aparecer antes de un sustantivo o un pronombre (*below the desk, beside them*), después de un adjetivo (*antagonistic to, insufficient in, symbolic of*), o después de un elemento
verbal con el cual combina para formar una frase con función
verbal (*take for, take over, come across*).

A diferencia de la preposición española, la preposición inglesa
puede aparecer al final de una oración, lo cual sucede frecuentemente en el uso común, especialmente si la preposición forma
parte de una frase con función verbal:

After Rourke left, Joyce took *over*.
What does this all add up *to*?

El pronombre

Los pronombres pueden poseer las características siguientes: caso (nominativo, posesivo, u objetivo); número (singular o
plural); persona (primera, segunda, o tercera), y género (masculino, femenino, o neutro). Los pronombres ingleses se clasifican en
siete categorías principales, de las cuales cada una juega un papel
específico.

1. Pronombres demostrativos

Las palabras *this, that, these* y *those* se consideran como pronombres cuando funcionan como sustantivos. (Se les clasifica como
adjetivos demostrativos cuando modifican un sustantivo.) El

pronombre demostrativo indica a una persona o cosa para distinguirla de otras:

These are the best designs we've seen to date.
Those are strong words.

El pronombre demostrativo también se usa para distinguir a una persona o cosa cercana de otra que se encuentre a mayor distancia (*this is my desk; that is yours*).

2. Pronombres indefinidos

El pronombre indefinido se emplea para designar a una persona o cosa cuya identidad se desconoce o no se puede establecer de inmediato. Estos pronombres se usan generalmente como referencias en la tercera persona, y no se distinguen en cuanto a género. A continuación se listan ejemplos de pronombres indefinidos:

all	either	none
another	everybody	no one
any	everyone	one
anybody	everything	other
anyone	few	several
anything	many	some
both	much	somebody
each	neither	someone
each one	nobody	something

Los pronombres indefinidos deben concordar en cuanto a número con los verbos que les corresponden. Los siguientes pronombres son singulares y deben usarse con un verbo conjugado en singular: *another, anything, each, each one, everything, much, nobody, no one, one, other, someone, something.*

Much is being done.
No one wants to go.

Los pronombres indefinidos *both, few, many, several* entre otros son plurales, y por lo tanto deben emplearse con verbos conjugados en plural:

Many were called; *few were* chosen.

Algunos pronombres, tales como *all, any, none,* y *some,* pueden presentar un problema ya que pueden usarse tanto con verbos singulares como plurales. Como regla general, los pronombres que se usan con sustantivos no numerables emplean verbos singulares, mientras que aquéllos que se usan con sustantivos numerables suelen tomar un verbo plural:

con sustantivo no numerable:
All of the property *is* affected.
None of the soup *was* spilled.
Some of the money *was* spent.

con sustantivo numerable:

All of my shoes *are* black.
None of the clerks *were* available.
Some of your friends *were* there.

3. Pronombres interrogativos

Los pronombres interrogativos *what, which, who, whom,* y *whose,* así como las combinaciones de estos con el sufijo *-ever* (*whatever, whichever,* etc.) se usan para introducir una pregunta:

Who is she?
He asked me *who* she was.

Whoever can that be?
We wondered *whoever* that could be.

4. Pronombres personales

El pronombre personal refleja la persona, el número, y el género del ser u objeto que representa. La mayoría de los pronombres personales toman una forma distinta para cada uno de estos tres casos:

Persona	Nominativo	Posesivo	Objetivo
PRIMERA			
SINGULAR:	I	my, mine	me
PLURAL:	we	our, ours	us
SEGUNDA			
SINGULAR:	you	your, yours	you
PLURAL:	you	your, yours	you
TERCERA			
SINGULAR:	he	his, his	him
	she	her, hers	her
	it	its, its	it
PLURAL:	they	their, theirs	them

Nótese que los pronombres personales en el caso posesivo no llevan apóstrofe, y no deben confundirse con los homófonos *you're, they're, there's, it's.*

5. Pronombres recíprocos

Los pronombres recíprocos *each other* y *one another* se emplean para indicar una acción o relación mutua:

They do not quarrel with *one another*.
(No se pelean (el uno con el otro).)

Lou and Andy saw *each other* at the party.
(Lou y Andy se vieron en la fiesta.)

Un pronombre recíproco puede usarse también en el caso posesivo:

They always borrowed *one another's* money.
(Siempre se prestaban dinero.)

The two companies depend on *each other's* success.
(Cada una de las dos compañías depende del éxito de la otra.)

6. Pronombres reflexivos

Los pronombres reflexivos se forman al combinar los pronombres personales *him, her, it, my, our, them* y *your* con *-self* o *-selves*. El pronombre reflexivo se usa generalmente para expresar una acción reflexiva, o bien para recalcar el sujeto de una oración, cláusula, o frase:

She dressed *herself.*
He asked *himself* if it was worth it.
I *myself* am not concerned.

7. Pronombres relativos

Los pronombres relativos son *that, what, which, who, whom,* y *whose,* así como las combinaciones de éstos con la terminación *-ever*. Estos pronombres se emplean para introducir oraciones subordinadas con función sustantiva o adjetival.

El pronombre relativo *who* se usa para referirse a personas y, en ciertas ocasiones, algunos animales. *Which* suele usarse para referirse a animales o cosas, y *that* puede usarse para personas, animales, o cosas:

a man *who* sought success
a woman *whom* we trust
Kentucky Firebolt, *who* won yesterday's horse race
a movie *which* was a big hit
a dog *which* kept barking
a boy *that* behaves well
a movie *that* was a big hit
a dog *that* kept barking

En ciertas ocasiones el pronombre relativo puede omitirse:

The man (*whom*) I was talking to is the senator.

El verbo

El verbo inglés posee típicamente las siguientes características: inflexión (p. ej., *help, helps, helping, helped*), persona (primera, segunda, o tercera), número (singular o plural), tiempo (presente, pasado, futuro), aspecto (categorías temporales distintas a los tiempos simples de presente, pasado y futuro), voz (activa o pasiva), y modo (indicativo, subjuntivo e imperativo).

1. La inflexión

Los verbos regulares ingleses tienen cuatro inflexiones diferentes, las cuales se producen al añadir los sufijos -*s* o -*es*, -*ed*, e -*ing*. La mayoría de los verbos irregulares poseen cuatro o cinco inflexiones (p. ej., *see, sees, seeing, saw, seen*); y el verbo *be* tiene ocho (*be, is, am, are, being, was, were, been*).

Los verbos que terminan en una -*e* muda conservan por lo general la -*e* al añadírsele un sufijo que comienza con una consonante (como -*s*), pero esta -*e* desaparece si el sufijo comienza con una vocal (como sucede con -*ed* o -*ing*):

arrange; arranges; arranged; arranging
hope; hopes; hoped; hoping

Sin embargo, algunos de estos verbos conservan la -*e* final para no ser confundidos con otras palabras de ortografía igual, por ejemplo:

dye; dyes; dyed; dyeing
(vs. *dying*, del verbo *die*)
singe; singes; singed; singeing
(vs. *singing*, del verbo *sing*)

Si un verbo consta de una sílaba y termina en una sola consonante a la cual precede una sola vocal, la consonante final se repite al añadir el sufijo -*ed* o -*ing*:

brag; brags; bra**gg**ed; bra**gg**ing
grip; grips; gri**pp**ed; gri**pp**ing

Cuando un verbo posee esta misma terminación, pero consta de dos o más sílabas, y la última de éstas es acentuada, se repite también al añadir el sufijo -*ed* o -*ing*:

commit; commits; commi**tt**ed; commi**tt**ing
occur; occurs; occu**rr**ed; occu**rr**ing

Los verbos que terminan en -*y*, precedida de una consonante, suelen cambiar esta -*y* en -*i* en toda inflexión excepto cuando el sufijo correspondiente es -*ing*:

carry; carr**i**es; carr**i**ed; carrying
study; stud**i**es; stud**i**ed; studying

Cuando un verbo termina en -*c*, se le añade una -*k* en inflexiones cuyos sufijos comienzan con -*e* o -*i*:

mimic; mimics; mimi**ck**ed; mimi**ck**ing
traffic; traffics; traffi**ck**ed; traffi**ck**ing

2. El tiempo y el aspecto

Los verbos ingleses exhiben generalmente su presente simple o pasado simple en una sola palabra, por ejemplo:

I *do*, I *did*
we *write*, we *wrote*

El tiempo futuro suele expresarse al combinar el verbo auxiliar *shall* o *will* con la forma presente simple o presente progresiva del verbo:

I *shall do* it.
(Lo *haré*.)

We *will come* tomorrow.
(*Vendremos* mañana.)

He *will be arriving* later.
(*Llegará* más tarde.)

Llámase aspecto de un verbo a aquellos tiempos que difieren del presente simple, pasado simple, o futuro simple. A continuación se presentan cuatro de estos tiempos o aspectos: el progresivo, el presente perfecto, el pasado perfecto, y el futuro perfecto.

El tiempo progresivo expresa una acción en progreso:

He *is reading* the paper.
(*Está leyendo* el periódico.)

I *was working* when she called.
(*Estaba trabajando* cuando llamó.)

El presente perfecto se emplea para expresar una acción que ha comenzado en el pasado y que continúa en el presente, o también para expresar una acción que haya tenido lugar en un momento indefinido del pasado:

She *has written* a book.
(*Ha escrito* un libro.)

El pasado perfecto expresa una acción que fue llevada a cabo antes de otra acción o evento en el pasado:

She *had written* many books previously.
(*Había escrito* muchos libros anteriormente.)

El futuro perfecto indica una acción que será llevada a cabo antes de una acción o evento en el futuro:

We *will have finished* the project by then.
(A esas alturas *habremos terminado* el proyecto.)

3. La voz

La voz (activa o pasiva) indica si el sujeto de la oración es el que desempeña la acción del verbo o si es el objeto de esta acción:

Voz activa:
He *respected* his colleagues.
(*Respetaba* a sus colegas.)

Voz pasiva:
He *was respected* by his colleagues.
(*Era respetado* por sus colegas.)

4. El modo

En inglés existen tres modos: indicativo, imperativo, y subjuntivo.

El modo indicativo se emplea ya sea para indicar un hecho, o para hacer una pregunta:

He *is* here.
(*Está* aquí.)

Is he here?
(¿*Está* aquí?)

El modo imperativo se usa para expresar una orden o una petición:

Come here.
(*Ven* aquí.)

Please *come* here.
(*Ven* aquí, por favor.)

El modo subjuntivo expresa una condición contraria a los hechos. El modo subjuntivo en inglés ha caído en desuso, pero suele aparecer en cláusulas introducidas por *if*, y después del verbo *wish*:

I wish he *were* here.
(Quisiera que *estuviera* él aquí.)

If she *were* there, she could have answered that.
(Si *estuviera* ella allá, podría haberlo contestado.)

5. Verbos transitivos e intransitivos

Como en español, el verbo inglés puede ser transitivo o intransitivo. El verbo transitivo es el que puede llevar un complemento directo:

She *sold* her car.
(*Vendió* su coche.)

El verbo intransitivo no lleva un complemento directo:

He *talked* all day.
(*Habló* todo el día.)

Conjugation of Spanish Verbs

Simple Tenses

Tense	Regular Verbs Ending in -AR hablar	
PRESENT INDICATIVE	hablo	hablamos
	hablas	habláis
	habla	hablan
PRESENT SUBJUNCTIVE	hable	hablemos
	hables	habléis
	hable	hablen
PRETERIT INDICATIVE	hablé	hablamos
	hablaste	hablasteis
	habló	hablaron
IMPERFECT INDICATIVE	hablaba	hablábamos
	hablabas	hablabais
	hablaba	hablaban
IMPERFECT SUBJUNCTIVE	hablara	habláramos
	hablaras	hablarais
	hablara	hablaran
	or	
	hablase	hablásemos
	hablases	hablaseis
	hablase	hablasen
FUTURE INDICATIVE	hablaré	hablaremos
	hablarás	hablaréis
	hablará	hablarán
FUTURE SUBJUNCTIVE	hablare	habláremos
	hablares	hablareis
	hablare	hablaren
CONDITIONAL	hablaría	hablaríamos
	hablarías	hablaríais
	hablaría	hablarían
IMPERATIVE		hablemos
	habla	hablad
	hable	hablen
PRESENT PARTICIPLE (GERUND)	hablando	
PAST PARTICIPLE	hablado	

Regular Verbs Ending in -ER		Regular Verbs Ending in -IR	
	comer		vivir
como	comemos	vivo	vivimos
comes	coméis	vives	vivís
come	comen	vive	viven
coma	comamos	viva	vivamos
comas	comáis	vivas	viváis
coma	coman	viva	vivan
comí	comimos	viví	vivimos
comiste	comisteis	viviste	vivisteis
comió	comieron	vivió	vivieron
comía	comíamos	vivía	vivíamos
comías	comíais	vivías	vivíais
comía	comían	vivía	vivían
comiera	comiéramos	viviera	viviéramos
comieras	comierais	vivieras	vivierais
comiera	comieran	viviera	vivieran
or		*or*	
comiese	comiésemos	viviese	viviésemos
comieses	comieseis	vivieses	vivieseis
comiese	comiesen	viviese	viviesen
comeré	comeremos	viviré	viviremos
comerás	comeréis	vivirás	viviréis
comerá	comerán	vivirá	vivirán
comiere	comiéremos	viviere	viviéremos
comieres	comiereis	vivieres	viviereis
comiere	comieren	viviere	vivieren
comería	comeríamos	viviría	viviríamos
comerías	comeríais	vivirías	viviríais
comería	comerían	viviría	vivirían
	comamos		vivamos
come	comed	vive	vivid
coma	coman	viva	vivan
comiendo		viviendo	
comido		vivido	

Compound Tenses

1. Perfect Tenses

The perfect tenses are formed with *haber* and the past participle:

PRESENT PERFECT

he hablado, etc. (*indicative*)
haya hablado, etc. (*subjunctive*)

PAST PERFECT

había hablado, etc. (*indicative*)
hubiera hablado, etc. (*subjunctive*)
or
hubiese hablado, etc. (*subjunctive*)

PRETERIT PERFECT

hube hablado, etc. (*indicative*)

FUTURE PERFECT

habré hablado, etc. (*indicative*)

CONDITIONAL PERFECT

habría hablado, etc. (*indicative*)

2. Progressive Tenses

The progressive tenses are formed with *estar* and the present participle:

PRESENT PROGRESSIVE

estoy llamando, etc. (*indicative*)
esté llamando, etc. (*subjunctive*)

IMPERFECT PROGRESSIVE

estaba llamando, etc. (*indicative*)
estuviera llamando, etc. (*subjunctive*)
or
estuviese llamando, etc. (*subjunctive*)

PRETERIT PROGRESSIVE

estuve llamando, etc. (*indicative*)

FUTURE PROGRESSIVE

estaré llamando, etc. (*indicative*)

CONDITIONAL PROGRESSIVE

estaría llamando, etc. (*indicative*)

PRESENT PERFECT PROGRESSIVE

he estado llamando, etc. (*indicative*)
haya estado llamando, etc. (*subjunctive*)

PAST PERFECT PROGRESSIVE

había estado llamando, etc. (*indicative*)
hubiera estado llamando, etc. (*subjunctive*)
or
hubiese estado llamando, etc. (*subjunctive*)

Use of *Vos*

In parts of South and Central America, *vos* often replaces or competes with *tú* as the second-person familiar personal pronoun. It is particularly well established in the Río de la Plata region and much of Central America.

The pronoun *vos* often takes a distinct set of verb forms, usually in the present tense and the imperative. These vary widely from region to region; examples of the most common forms are shown below:

INFINITIVE FORM	hablar	comer	vivir
PRESENT INDICATIVE	vos hablás	vos comés	vos vivís
PRESENT SUBJUNCTIVE	vos hablés	vos comás	vos vivás
IMPERATIVE	hablá	comé	viví

In some areas, *vos* may take the *tú* or *vosotros* forms of the verb, while in others (such as Uruguay), *tú* is combined with the *vos* verb forms.

Irregular Verbs

The *imperfect subjunctive,* the *future subjunctive,* the *conditional*, and most forms of the *imperative* are not included in the model conjugations list, but can be derived as follows:

The *imperfect subjunctive* and the *future subjunctive* are formed from the third-person plural form of the preterit tense by removing the last syllable (*-ron*) and adding the appropriate suffix:

PRETERIT INDICATIVE, THIRD-PERSON PLURAL (querer)	quisieron
IMPERFECT SUBJUNCTIVE (querer)	quisiera, quisieras, etc.
	or
	quisiese, quisieses, etc.
FUTURE SUBJUNCTIVE (querer)	quisiere, quisieres, etc.

The conditional uses the same stem as the future indicative:

FUTURE INDICATIVE (poner)   pondré, pondrás, etc.
CONDITIONAL (poner)   pondría, pondrías, etc.

The third-person singular, first-person plural, and third-person plural forms of the *imperative* are the same as the corresponding forms of the present subjunctive.

The second-person plural (*vosotros*) form of the *imperative* is formed by removing the final -*r* of the infinitive form and adding a -*d* (ex.: *oír* → *oíd*).

Model Conjugations of Irregular Verbs

The model conjugations below include the following simple tenses: the *present indicative* (IND), the *present subjunctive* (SUBJ), the *preterit indicative* (PRET), the *imperfect indicative* (IMPF), the *future indicative* (FUT), the second-person singular form of the *imperative* (IMPER), the *present participle* or *gerund* (PRP), and the *past participle* (PP). Each set of conjugations is preceded by the corresponding infinitive form of the verb, shown in bold type. Only tenses containing irregularities are listed, and the irregular verb forms within each tense are displayed in bold type.

Each irregular verb entry in the Spanish-English section of this dictionary is cross-referred by number to one of the following model conjugations. These cross-reference numbers are shown in curly braces { } immediately following the entry's functional label.

1 **abolir** *(defective verb)* : *IND* abolimos, abolís *(other forms not used); SUBJ (not used); IMPER (only second-person plural is used)*

2 **abrir** : *PP* abierto

3 **actuar** : *IND* **actúo, actúas, actúa,** actuamos, actuáis, **actúan;** *SUBJ* **actúe, actúes, actúe,** actuemos, actuéis, **actúen;** *IMPER* **actúa**

4 **adquirir** : *IND* **adquiero, adquieres, adquiere,** adquirimos, adquirís, **adquieren;** *SUBJ* **adquiera, adquieras, adquiera,** adquiramos, adquiráis, **adquieran;** *IMPER* **adquiere**

5 **airar** : *IND* **aíro, aíras, aíra,** airamos, airáis, **aíran;** *SUBJ* **aíre, aíres, aíre,** airemos, airéis, **aíren;** *IMPER* **aíra**

6 **andar** : *PRET* **anduve, anduviste, anduvo, anduvimos, anduvisteis, anduvieron**

7 **asir** : *IND* **asgo,** ases, ase, asimos, asís, asen; *SUBJ* **asga, asgas, asga, asgamos, asgáis, asgan**

8 **aunar** : *IND* **aúno, aúnas, aúna,** aunamos, aunáis, **aúnan;** *SUBJ* **aúne, aúnes, aúne,** aunemos, aunéis, **aúnen;** *IMPER* **aúna**

9 **avergonzar** : *IND* **avergüenzo, avergüenzas, avergüenza,** avergonzamos, avergonzáis, **avergüenzan;** *SUBJ* **avergüence, avergüences, avergüence, avergoncemos, avergoncéis, avergüencen;** *PRET* **avergoncé;** *IMPER* **avergüenza**

10 **averiguar** : *SUBJ* **averigüe, averigües, averigüe, averigüemos, averigüéis, averigüen;** *PRET* **averigüé,** averiguaste, averiguó, averiguamos, averiguasteis, averiguaron

11 **bendecir** : *IND* **bendigo, bendices, bendice,** bendecimos, bendecís, **bendicen;** *SUBJ* **bendiga, bendigas, bendiga, bendigamos, bendigáis, bendigan;** *PRET* **bendije, bendijiste, bendijo, bendijimos, bendijisteis, bendijeron;** *IMPER* **bendice**

12 **caber** : *IND* **quepo,** cabes, cabe, cabemos, cabéis, caben; *SUBJ* **quepa, quepas, quepa, quepamos, quepáis, quepan;** *PRET* **cupe, cupiste, cupo, cupimos, cupisteis, cupieron;** *FUT* **cabré, cabrás, cabrá, cabremos, cabréis, cabrán**

13 **caer** : *IND* **caigo,** caes, cae, caemos, caéis, caen; *SUBJ* **caiga, caigas, caiga, caigamos, caigáis, caigan;** *PRET* **caí, caíste, cayó, caímos, caísteis, cayeron;** *PRP* **cayendo;** *PP* **caído**

14 **cocer** : *IND* **cuezo, cueces, cuece,** cocemos, cocéis, **cuecen;** *SUBJ* **cueza, cuezas, cueza, cozamos, cozáis, cuezan;** *IMPER* **cuece**

15 **coger** : *IND* **cojo,** coges, coge, cogemos, cogéis, cogen; *SUBJ* **coja, cojas, coja, cojamos, cojáis, cojan**

16 **colgar** : *IND* **cuelgo, cuelgas, cuelga,** colgamos, colgáis, **cuelgan;** *SUBJ* **cuelgue, cuelgues, cuelgue, colguemos, colguéis, cuelguen;** *PRET* **colgué,** colgaste, colgó, colgamos, colgasteis, colgaron; *IMPER* **cuelga**

17 **concernir** *(defective verb; used only in the third-person singular and plural of the present indicative, present subjunctive, and imperfect subjunctive)* see **25 discernir**

18 **conocer** : *IND* **conozco,** conoces, conoce, conocemos, conocéis, conocen; *SUBJ* **conozca, conozcas, conozca, conozcamos, conozcáis, conozcan**

19 **contar** : *IND* **cuento, cuentas, cuenta,** contamos, contáis, **cuentan;** *SUBJ* **cuente, cuentes, cuente,** contemos, contéis, **cuenten;** *IMPER* **cuenta**

20 **creer** : *PRET* creí, **creíste, creyó, creímos, creísteis, creyeron;** *PRP* **creyendo;** *PP* **creído**

21 **cruzar** : *SUBJ* **cruce, cruces, cruce, crucemos, crucéis, crucen;** *PRET* **crucé,** cruzaste, cruzó, cruzamos, cruzasteis, cruzaron

22 **dar** : *IND* **doy,** das, da, damos, **dais,** dan; *SUBJ* **dé,** des, **dé,** demos, **deis,** den; *PRET* **di, diste, dio, dimos, disteis, dieron**

23 **decir** : *IND* **digo, dices, dice,** decimos, decís, **dicen;** *SUBJ* **diga, digas, diga, digamos, digáis, digan;** *PRET* **dije, dijiste, dijo, dijimos, dijisteis, dijeron;** *FUT* **diré, dirás, dirá, diremos, diréis, dirán;** *IMPER* **di;** *PRP* **diciendo;** *PP* **dicho**

24 **delinquir** : *IND* **delinco,** delinques, delinque, delinquimos, delinquís, delinquen; *SUBJ* **delinca, delincas, delinca, delincamos, delincáis, delincan**

25 **discernir** : *IND* **discierno, disciernes, discierne,** discernimos, discernís, **disciernen;** *SUBJ* **discierna, disciernas, discierna,** discernamos, discernáis, **disciernan;** *IMPER* **discierne**

26 **distinguir** : *IND* **distingo,** distingues, distingue, distinguimos, distinguís, distinguen; *SUBJ* **distinga, distingas, distinga, distingamos, distingáis, distingan**

27 **dormir** : *IND* **duermo, duermes, duerme,** dormimos, dormís, **duermen;** *SUBJ* **duerma, duermas, duerma, durmamos, durmáis, duerman;** *PRET* dormí, dormiste, **durmió,** dormimos, dormisteis, **durmieron;** *IMPER* **duerme;** *PRP* **durmiendo**

28 **elegir** : *IND* **elijo, eliges, elige,** elegimos, elegís, **eligen;** *SUBJ* **elija, elijas, elija, elijamos, elijáis, elijan;** *PRET* elegí, elegiste, **eligió,** elegimos, elegisteis, **eligieron;** *IMPER* **elige;** *PRP* **eligiendo**

29 **empezar** : *IND* **empiezo, empiezas, empieza,** empezamos, empezáis, **empiezan;** *SUBJ* **empiece, empieces, empiece, empecemos, empecéis, empiecen;** *PRET* **empecé,** empezaste, empezó, empezamos, empezasteis, empezaron; *IMPER* **empieza**

30 **enraizar** : *IND* **enraízo, enraízas, enraíza,** enraizamos, enraizáis, **enraízan;** *SUBJ* **enraíce, enraíces, enraíce, enraicemos, enraicéis, enraícen;** *PRET* **enraicé,** enraizaste, enraizó, enraizamos, enraizasteis, enraizaron; *IMPER* **enraíza**

31 **erguir** : *IND* **irgo** *or* **yergo, irgues** *or* **yergues, irgue** *or* **yergue,** erguimos, erguís, **irguen** *or* **yerguen;** *SUBJ* **irga** *or* **yerga, irgas** *or* **yergas, irga** *or* **yerga, irgamos, irgáis, irgan** *or* **yergan;** *PRET* erguí, erguiste, **irguió,** erguimos, erguisteis, **irguieron;** *IMPER* **irgue** *or* **yergue;** *PRP* **irguiendo**

32 **errar** : *IND* **yerro, yerras, yerra,** erramos, erráis, **yerran;** *SUBJ* **yerre, yerres, yerre,** erremos, erréis, **yerren;** *IMPER* **yerra**

33 **escribir** : *PP* **escrito**

34 **estar** : *IND* **estoy, estás, está,** estamos, estáis, **están;** *SUBJ* **esté, estés, esté,** estemos, estéis, **estén;** *PRET* **estuve, estuviste, estuvo, estuvimos, estuvisteis, estuvieron;** *IMPER* **está**

35 **exigir** : *IND* **exijo,** exiges, exige, exigimos, exigís, exigen; *SUBJ* **exija, exijas, exija, exijamos, exijáis, exijan**

36 **forzar** : *IND* **fuerzo, fuerzas, fuerza,** forzamos, forzáis, **fuerzan;** *SUBJ* **fuerce, fuerces, fuerce, forcemos, forcéis, fuercen;** *PRET* **forcé,** forzaste, forzó, forzamos, forzasteis, forzaron; *IMPER* **fuerza**

37 **freír** : *IND* **frío, fríes, fríe, freímos,** freís, **fríen;** *SUBJ* **fría, frías, fría, friamos, friáis, frían;** *PRET* freí, **freíste, frió, freímos, freísteis, frieron;** *IMPER* **fríe;** *PRP* **friendo;** *PP* **frito**

38 **gruñir** : *PRET* gruñí, gruñiste, **gruñó,** gruñimos, gruñisteis, **gruñeron;** *PRP* **gruñendo**

39 haber : *IND* **he, has, ha, hemos,** habéis, **han;** *SUBJ* **haya, hayas, haya, hayamos,** hayáis, **hayan;** *PRET* **hube, hubiste, hubo, hubimos,** hubisteis, **hubieron;** *FUT* **habré, habrás, habrá, habremos,** habréis, **habrán;** *IMPER* **he**

40 hacer : *IND* **hago,** haces, hace, hacemos, hacéis, hacen; *SUBJ* **haga, hagas, haga, hagamos, hagáis, hagan;** *PRET* **hice, hiciste, hizo, hicimos,** hicisteis, **hicieron;** *FUT* **haré, harás, hará, haremos, haréis, harán;** *IMPER* **haz;** *PP* **hecho**

41 huir : *IND* **huyo, huyes, huye,** huimos, huís, **huyen;** *SUBJ* **huya, huyas, huya, huyamos,** huyáis, **huyan;** *PRET* **huí,** huiste, **huyó,** huimos, huisteis, **huyeron;** *IMPER* **huye;** *PRP* **huyendo**

42 imprimir : *PP* **impreso**

43 ir : *IND* **voy, vas, va, vamos, vais, van;** *SUBJ* **vaya, vayas, vaya, vayamos,** vayáis, **vayan;** *PRET* **fui, fuiste, fue, fuimos, fuisteis, fueron;** *IMPF* **iba, ibas, iba, íbamos, ibais, iban;** *IMPER* **ve;** *PRP* **yendo;** *PP* **ido**

44 jugar : *IND* **juego, juegas, juega,** jugamos, jugáis, **juegan;** *SUBJ* **juegue, juegues, juegue, juguemos, juguéis, jueguen;** *PRET* **jugué,** jugaste, jugó, jugamos, jugasteis, jugaron; *IMPER* **juega**

45 lucir : *IND* **luzco,** luces, luce, lucimos, lucís, lucen; *SUBJ* **luzca, luzcas, luzca, luzcamos, luzcáis, luzcan**

46 morir : *IND* **muero, mueres, muere,** morimos, morís, **mueren;** *SUBJ* **muera, mueras, muera, muramos, muráis, mueran;** *PRET* morí, moriste, **murió,** morimos, moristeis, **murieron;** *IMPER* **muere;** *PRP* **muriendo;** *PP* **muerto**

47 mover : *IND* **muevo, mueves, mueve,** movemos, movéis, **mueven;** *SUBJ* **mueva, muevas, mueva,** movamos, mováis, **muevan;** *IMPER* **mueve**

48 nacer : *IND* **nazco,** naces, nace, nacemos, nacéis, nacen; *SUBJ* **nazca, nazcas, nazca, nazcamos, nazcáis, nazcan**

49 negar : *IND* **niego, niegas, niega,** negamos, negáis, **niegan;** *SUBJ* **niegue, niegues, niegue, neguemos, neguéis, nieguen;** *PRET* **negué,** negaste, negó, negamos, negasteis, negaron; *IMPER* **niega**

50 oír : *IND* **oigo, oyes, oye, oímos,** oís, **oyen;** *SUBJ* **oiga, oigas, oiga, oigamos, oigáis, oigan;** *PRET* **oí, oíste, oyó, oímos, oísteis, oyeron;** *IMPER* **oye;** *PRP* **oyendo;** *PP* **oído**

51 oler : *IND* **huelo, hueles, huele,** olemos, oléis, **huelen;** *SUBJ* **huela, huelas, huela,** olamos, oláis, **huelan;** *IMPER* **huele**

52 pagar : *SUBJ* **pague, pagues, pague, paguemos, paguéis, paguen;** *PRET* **pagué,** pagaste, pagó, pagamos, pagasteis, pagaron

53 parecer : *IND* **parezco,** pareces, parece, parecemos, parecéis, parecen; *SUBJ* **parezca, parezcas, parezca, parezcamos, parezcáis, parezcan**

54 pedir : *IND* **pido, pides, pide,** pedimos, pedís, **piden;** *SUBJ* **pida, pidas, pida, pidamos, pidáis, pidan;** *PRET* pedí, pediste, **pidió,** pedimos, pedisteis, **pidieron;** *IMPER* **pide;** *PRP* **pidiendo**

55 **pensar** : *IND* **pienso, piensas, piensa,** pensamos, penséis, **piensan;** *SUBJ* **piense, pienses, piense,** pensemos, penséis, **piensen;** *IMPER* **piensa**

56 **perder** : *IND* **pierdo, pierdes, pierde,** perdemos, perdéis, **pierden;** *SUBJ* **pierda, pierdas, pierda,** perdamos, perdáis, **pierdan;** *IMPER* **pierde**

57 **placer** : *IND* **plazco,** places, place, placemos, placéis, placen; *SUBJ* **plazca, plazcas, plazca, plazcamos, plazcáis, plazcan;** *PRET* plací, placiste, plació *or* **plugo,** placimos, placisteis, placieron *or* **pluguieron**

58 **poder** : *IND* **puedo, puedes, puede,** podemos, podéis, **pueden;** *SUBJ* **pueda, puedas, pueda,** podamos, podáis, **puedan;** *PRET* **pude, pudiste, pudo, pudimos, pudisteis, pudieron;** *FUT* **podré, podrás, podrá, podremos, podréis, podrán;** *IMPER* **puede;** *PRP* **pudiendo**

59 **podrir** *or* **pudrir** : *PP* **podrido** *(all other forms based on* pudrir*)*

60 **poner** : *IND* **pongo,** pones, pone, ponemos, ponéis, ponen; *SUBJ* **ponga, pongas, ponga, pongamos, pongáis, pongan;** *PRET* **puse, pusiste, puso, pusimos, pusisteis, pusieron;** *FUT* **pondré, pondrás, pondrá, pondremos, pondréis, pondrán;** *IMPER* **pon;** *PP* **puesto**

61 **producir** : *IND* **produzco,** produces, produce, producimos, producís, producen; *SUBJ* **produzca, produzcas, produzca, produzcamos, produzcáis, produzcan;** *PRET* **produje, produjiste, produjo, produjimos, produjisteis, produjeron**

62 **prohibir** : *IND* **prohíbo, prohíbes, prohíbe,** prohibimos, prohibís, **prohíben;** *SUBJ* **prohíba, prohíbas, prohíba,** prohibamos, prohibáis, **prohíban;** *IMPER* **prohíbe**

63 **proveer** : *PRET* **proveí, proveíste, proveyó, proveímos, proveísteis, proveyeron;** *PRP* **proveyendo;** *PP* **provisto**

64 **querer** : *IND* **quiero, quieres, quiere,** queremos, queréis, **quieren;** *SUBJ* **quiera, quieras, quiera,** queramos, queráis, **quieran;** *PRET* **quise, quisiste, quiso, quisimos, quisisteis, quisieron;** *FUT* **querré, querrás, querrá, querremos, querréis, querrán;** *IMPER* **quiere**

65 **raer** : *IND* **rao** *or* **raigo** *or* **rayo,** raes, rae, raemos, raéis, raen; *SUBJ* **raiga** *or* **raya, raigas** *or* **rayas, raiga** *or* **raya, raigamos** *or* **rayamos, raigáis** *or* **rayáis, raigan** *or* **rayan;** *PRET* **raí, raíste, rayó, raímos, raísteis, rayeron;** *PRP* **rayendo;** *PP* **raído**

66 **reír** : *IND* **río, ríes, ríe, reímos,** reís, **ríen;** *SUBJ* **ría, rías, ría, riamos, riáis, rían;** *PRET* reí, **reíste, rió, reímos, reísteis, rieron;** *IMPER* **ríe;** *PRP* **riendo;** *PP* **reído**

67 **reñir** : *IND* **riño, riñes, riñe,** reñimos, reñís, **riñen;** *SUBJ* **riña, riñas, riña, riñamos, riñáis, riñan;** *PRET* reñí, reñiste, **riñó,** reñimos, reñisteis, **riñeron;** *IMPER* **riñe;** *PRP* **riñendo**

68 reunir : *IND* **reúno, reúnes, reúne,** reunimos, reunís, **reúnen;** *SUBJ* **reúna, reúnas, reúna,** reunamos, reunáis, **reúnan;** *IMPER* **reúne**

69 roer : *IND* roo *or* **roigo** *or* **royo,** roes, roe, roemos, roéis, roen; *SUBJ* roa *or* **roiga** *or* **roya,** roas *or* **roigas** *or* **royas,** roa *or* **roiga** *or* **roya,** roamos *or* **roigamos** *or* **royamos,** roáis *or* **roigáis** *or* royáis, roan *or* **roigan** *or* **royan;** *PRET* roí, **roíste, royó, roímos, roísteis, royeron;** *PRP* **royendo;** *PP* **roído**

70 romper : *PP* **roto**

71 saber : *IND* **sé,** sabes, sabe, sabemos, sabéis, saben; *SUBJ* **sepa, sepas, sepa, sepamos, sepáis, sepan;** *PRET* **supe, supiste, supo, supimos, supisteis, supieron;** *FUT* **sabré, sabrás, sabrá, sabremos, sabréis, sabrán**

72 sacar : *SUBJ* **saque, saques, saque, saquemos, saquéis, saquen;** *PRET* **saqué,** sacaste, sacó, sacamos, sacasteis, sacaron

73 salir : *IND* **salgo,** sales, sale, salimos, salís, salen; *SUBJ* **salga, salgas, salga, salgamos, salgáis, salgan;** *FUT* **saldré, saldrás, saldrá, saldremos, saldréis, saldrán;** *IMPER* **sal**

74 satisfacer : *IND* **satisfago,** satisfaces, satisface, satisfacemos, satisfacéis, satisfacen; *SUBJ* **satisfaga, satisfagas, satisfaga, satisfagamos, satisfagáis, satisfagan;** *PRET* **satisfice, satisficiste, satisfizo, satisficimos, satisficisteis, satisficieron;** *FUT* **satisfaré, satisfarás, satisfará, satisfaremos, satisfaréis, satisfarán;** *IMPER* **satisfaz** *or* satisface; *PP* **satisfecho**

75 seguir : *IND* **sigo, sigues, sigue,** seguimos, seguís, **siguen;** *SUBJ* **siga, sigas, siga, sigamos, sigáis, sigan;** *PRET* seguí, seguiste, **siguió,** seguimos, seguisteis, **siguieron;** *IMPER* **sigue;** *PRP* **siguiendo**

76 sentir : *IND* **siento, sientes, siente,** sentimos, sentís, **sienten;** *SUBJ* **sienta, sientas, sienta, sintamos, sintáis, sientan;** *PRET* sentí, sentiste, **sintió,** sentimos, sentisteis, **sintieron;** *IMPER* **siente;** *PRP* **sintiendo**

77 ser : *IND* **soy, eres, es, somos, sois, son;** *SUBJ* **sea, seas, sea, seamos, seáis, sean;** *PRET* **fui, fuiste, fue, fuimos, fuisteis, fueron;** *IMPF* **era, eras, era, éramos, erais, eran;** *IMPER* **sé;** *PRP* **siendo;** *PP* **sido**

78 soler *(defective verb; used only in the present, preterit, and imperfect indicative, and the present and imperfect subjunctive) see* **47 mover**

79 tañer : *PRET* tañí, tañiste, **tañó,** tañimos, tañisteis, **tañeron;** *PRP* **tañendo**

80 tener : *IND* **tengo, tienes, tiene,** tenemos, tenéis, **tienen;** *SUBJ* **tenga, tengas, tenga, tengamos, tengáis, tengan;** *PRET* **tuve, tuviste, tuvo, tuvimos, tuvisteis, tuvieron;** *FUT* **tendré, tendrás, tendrá, tendremos, tendréis, tendrán;** *IMPER* **ten**

81 **traer** : *IND* **traigo**, traes, trae, traemos, traéis, traen; *SUBJ* **traiga, traigas, traiga, traigamos, traigáis, traigan;** *PRET* **traje, trajiste, trajo, trajimos, trajisteis, trajeron;** *PRP* **trayendo;** *PP* **traído**

82 **trocar** : *IND* **trueco, truecas, trueca,** trocamos, trocáis, **truecan;** *SUBJ* **trueque, trueques, trueque, troquemos, troquéis, truequen;** *PRET* **troqué,** trocaste, trocó, trocamos, trocasteis, trocaron; *IMPER* **trueca**

83 **uncir** : *IND* **unzo**, unces, unce, uncimos, uncís, uncen; *SUBJ* **unza, unzas, unza, unzamos, unzáis, unzan**

84 **valer** : *IND* **valgo**, vales, vale, valemos, valéis, valen; *SUBJ* **valga, valgas, valga, valgamos, valgáis, valgan;** *FUT* **valdré, valdrás, valdrá, valdremos, valdréis, valdrán**

85 **variar** : *IND* **varío, varías, varía**, variamos, variáis, **varían;** *SUBJ* **varíe, varíes, varíe**, variemos, variéis, **varíen;** *IMPER* **varía**

86 **vencer** : *IND* **venzo**, vences, vence, vencemos, vencéis, vencen; *SUBJ* **venza, venzas, venza, venzamos, venzáis, venzan**

87 **venir** : *IND* **vengo, vienes, viene**, venimos, venís, **vienen;** *SUBJ* **venga, vengas, venga, vengamos, vengáis, vengan;** *PRET* **vine, viniste, vino, vinimos, vinisteis, vinieron;** *FUT* **vendré, vendrás, vendrá, vendremos, vendréis, vendrán;** *IMPER* **ven;** *PRP* **viniendo**

88 **ver** : *IND* **veo, ves, ve, vemos, veis, ven;** *PRET* **vi, viste, vio, vimos, visteis, vieron;** *IMPER* **ve;** *PRP* **viendo;** *PP* **visto**

89 **volver** : *IND* **vuelvo, vuelves, vuelve**, volvemos, volvéis, **vuelven;** *SUBJ* **vuelva, vuelvas, vuelva**, volvamos, volváis, **vuelvan;** *IMPER* **vuelve;** *PP* **vuelto**

90 **yacer** : *IND* **yazco** or **yazgo** or **yago**, yaces, yace, yacemos, yacéis, yacen; *SUBJ* **yazca** or **yazga** or **yaga, yazcas** or **yazgas** or **yagas, yazca** or **yazga** or **yaga, yazcamos** or **yazgamos** or **yagamos, yazcáis** or **yazgáis** or **yagáis, yazcan** or **yazgan** or **yagan;** *IMPER* **yace** or **yaz**

Verbos irregulares en inglés

INFINITIVO	PRETÉRITO	PARTICIPIO PASADO
arise	arose	arisen
awake	awoke	awoken o awaked
be	was, were	been
bear	bore	borne
beat	beat	beaten o beat
become	became	become
befall	befell	befallen
begin	began	begun
behold	beheld	beheld
bend	bent	bent
beseech	beseeched o besought	beseeched o besought
beset	beset	beset
bet	bet	bet
bid	bade o bid	bidden o bid
bind	bound	bound
bite	bit	bitten
bleed	bled	bled
blow	blew	blown
break	broke	broken
breed	bred	bred
bring	brought	brought
build	built	built
burn	burned o burnt	burned o burnt
burst	burst	burst
buy	bought	bought
can	could	—
cast	cast	cast
catch	caught	caught
choose	chose	chosen
cling	clung	clung
come	came	come
cost	cost	cost
creep	crept	crept
cut	cut	cut
deal	dealt	dealt
dig	dug	dug
dive	dived o dove	dived
do	did	done
draw	drew	drawn
dream	dreamed o dreamt	dreamed o dreamt
drink	drank	drunk o drank
drive	drove	driven
dwell	dwelled o dwelt	dwelled o dwelt
eat	ate	eaten
fall	fell	fallen
feed	fed	fed
feel	felt	felt
fight	fought	fought
find	found	found
flee	fled	fled
fling	flung	flung
fly	flew	flown
forbid	forbade	forbidden

INFINITIVO	PRETÉRITO	PARTICIPIO PASADO
forecast	forecast	forecast
forego	forewent	foregone
foresee	foresaw	foreseen
foretell	foretold	foretold
forget	forgot	forgotten o forgot
forgive	forgave	forgiven
forsake	forsook	forsaken
freeze	froze	frozen
get	got	got o gotten
give	gave	given
go	went	gone
grind	ground	ground
grow	grew	grown
hang	hung	hung
have	had	had
hear	heard	heard
hide	hid	hidden o hid
hit	hit	hit
hold	held	held
hurt	hurt	hurt
keep	kept	kept
kneel	knelt o kneeled	knelt o kneeled
know	knew	known
lay	laid	laid
lead	led	led
leap	leaped o leapt	leaped o leapt
leave	left	left
lend	lent	lent
let	let	let
lie	lay	lain
light	lit o lighted	lit o lighted
lose	lost	lost
make	made	made
may	might	—
mean	meant	meant
meet	met	met
mow	mowed	mowed o mown
overcome	overcame	overcome
pay	paid	paid
put	put	put
quit	quit	quit
read	read	read
rend	rent	rent
rid	rid	rid
ride	rode	ridden
ring	rang	rung
rise	rose	risen
run	ran	run
saw	sawed	sawed o sawn
say	said	said
see	saw	seen
seek	sought	sought

INFINITIVO	PRETÉRITO	PARTICIPIO PASADO
sell	sold	sold
send	sent	sent
set	set	set
sew	sewed	sewn *o* sewed
shake	shook	shaken
shall	should	—
shear	sheared	sheared *o* shorn
shed	shed	shed
shine	shone *o* shined	shone *o* shined
shoot	shot	shot
show	showed	shown *o* showed
shrink	shrank *o* shrunk	shrunk *o* shrunken
shut	shut	shut
sing	sang *o* sung	sung
sink	sank *o* sunk	sunk
sit	sat	sat
slay	slew	slain
sleep	slept	slept
slide	slid	slid
sling	slung	slung
smell	smelled *o* smelt	smelled *o* smelt
sow	sowed	sown *o* sowed
speak	spoke	spoken
speed	sped *o* speeded	sped *o* speeded
spend	spent	spent
spin	spun	spun
spit	spit *o* spat	spit *o* spat
split	split	split
spread	spread	spread
spring	sprang *o* sprung	sprung
stand	stood	stood
steal	stole	stolen
stick	stuck	stuck
sting	stung	stung
stink	stank *o* stunk	stunk
stride	strode	stridden
strike	struck	struck
swear	swore	sworn
sweep	swept	swept
swell	swelled	swelled *o* swollen
swim	swam	swum
swing	swung	swung
take	took	taken
teach	taught	taught
tear	tore	torn
tell	told	told
think	thought	thought
throw	threw	thrown
thrust	thrust	thrust
tread	trod	trodden *o* trod
undergo	underwent	undergone
understand	understood	understood

Verbos irregulares en inglés

INFINITIVO	PRETÉRITO	PARTICIPIO PASADO
undo	undid	undone
wake	woke	woken *o* waked
waylay	waylaid	waylaid
wear	wore	worn
weave	wove *o* weaved	woven *o* weaved
weep	wept	wept
will	would	—
win	won	won
wind	wound	wound
withdraw	withdrew	withdrawn
withhold	withheld	withheld
withstand	withstood	withstood
wring	wrung	wrung
write	wrote	written

Abbreviations in This Work (Abreviaturas empleadas en este libro)

Abbreviation (Abreviatura)	English Expansion (Expansión en inglés)	Spanish Meaning (Significado en español)
adj	adjective	adjetivo
adv	adverb	adverbio
Arg	Argentina	Argentina
Bol	Bolivia	Bolivia
Brit	British	británico
CA	Central America	Centroamérica
Car	Caribbean region	Región del Caribe
Col	Colombia	Colombia
conj	conjunction	conjunción
CoRi	Costa Rica	Costa Rica
DomRep	Dominican Republic	República Dominicana
Ecua	Ecuador	Ecuador
esp	especially	especialmente
f	feminine	femenino
fam	familiar or colloquial	familiar o coloquial
fpl	feminine plural	femenino plural
Guat	Guatemala	Guatemala
Hond	Honduras	Honduras
interj	interjection	interjección
m	masculine	masculino
Mex	Mexico	México
mf	masculine or feminine	masculino o femenino
mfpl	masculine or feminine plural	plural masculino o femenino
mpl	masculine plural	plural masculino
n	noun	sustantivo
nf	feminine noun	sustantivo femenino
nfpl	feminine plural noun	sustantivo plural femenino
nfs & pl	invariable singular or plural feminine noun	sustantivo femenino, invariable en cuanto a número
Nic	Nicaragua	Nicaragua
nm	masculine noun	sustantivo masculino
nmf	masculine or feminine noun	sustantivo masculino o femenino
nmfpl	plural noun invariable for gender	sustantivo plural, invariable en cuanto a género
nmfs & pl	noun invariable for both gender and number	sustantivo invariable en cuanto a género y número
nmpl	masculine plural noun	sustantivo plural masculino

Abbreviation (Abreviatura)	English Expansion (Expansión en inglés)	Spanish Meaning (Significado en español)
nms & pl	invariable singular or plural masculine noun	sustantivo masculino, invariable en cuanto a número
npl	plural noun	sustantivo plural
ns & pl	noun invariable for plural	sustantivo invariable en cuanto a número
Pan	Panama	Panamá
Par	Paraguay	Paraguay
pl	plural	plural
pp	past participle	participio pasado
pref	prefix	prefijo
prep	preposition	preposición
PRi	Puerto Rico	Puerto Rico
pron	pronoun	pronombre
s	singular	singular
Sal	El Salvador	El Salvador
suf	suffix	sufijo
Uru	Uruguay	Uruguay
usu	usually	generalmente
v	verb	verbo
v aux	auxiliary verb	verbo auxiliar
Ven	Venezuela	Venezuela
vi	intransitive verb	verbo intransitivo
v impers	impersonal verb	verbo impersonal
vr	reflexive verb	verbo pronominal
vt	transitive verb	verbo transitivo

Pronunciation Symbols
(Símbolos de pronunciación)

VOWELS (VOCALES)

æ	ask, bat, glad	ask, bat, glad
ɑ	cot, bomb	cot, bomb
a	*New England* aunt, *British* ask, glass, *Spanish* casa	*Nueva Inglaterra* aunt, *inglés británico* ask, glass, *español* casa
e	*Spanish* peso, jefe	*español* peso, jefe
ɛ	egg, bet, fed	egg, bet, fed
ə	about, javelin, Alabama	about, javelin, Alabama
ə	indicates a syllabic pronunciation of the consonant as in bottle, prism	denota una pronunciación silábica del consonante, como en bottle, prism
i	very, any, thirty, *Spanish* piña	very, any, thirty, *español* piña
i:	eat, bead, bee	eat, bead, bee
ɪ	id, bid, pit	id, bid, pit
o	Ohio, yellower, potato, *Spanish* óvalo	Ohio, yellower, potato, *español* óvalo
o:	oats, own, zone, blow	oats, own, zone, blow
ɔ	awl, maul, caught, paw	awl, maul, caught, paw
ʊ	should, could	should, could
u	*Spanish* uva, culpa	*español* uva, culpa
u:	boot, few, coo	boot, few, coo
ʌ	under, putt, bud	under, putt, bud
eɪ	eight, wade, bay	eight, wade, bay
aɪ	ice, bite, tie	ice, bite, tie
aʊ	out, gown, plow	out, gown, plow
ɔɪ	oyster, coil, boy	oyster, coil, boy
ər	further, stir	further, stir
ø	*French* deux, *German* Höhle	*francés* deux, *alemán* Höhle
~	(tilde as in ɔ̃) *French* bon	(tilde como en ɔ̃) *francés* bon
:	indicates that the preceding vowel is long	indica que la vocal precedente es larga

CONSONANTS (CONSONANTES)

b	baby, labor, cab	baby, labor, cab
d	day, ready, kid	day, ready, kid
ʤ	just, badger, fudge	just, badger, fudge
ð	then, either, bathe	then, either, bathe
f	foe, tough, buff	foe, tough, buff
g	go, bigger, bag	go, bigger, bag
h	hot, aha	hot, aha
j	yes, vineyard	yes, vineyard
k	cat, keep, lacquer, flock	cat, keep, lacquer, flock
l	law, hollow, boil	law, hollow, boil
m	mat, hemp, hammer, rim	mat, hemp, hammer, rim
n	new, tent, tenor, run	new, tent, tenor, run
ŋ	rung, hang, swinger	rung, hang, swinger
p	pay, lapse, top	pay, lapse, top
r	rope, burn, tar	rope, burn, tar
s	sad, mist, kiss	sad, mist, kiss
ʃ	shoe, mission, slush	shoe, mission, slush

t	toe, button, mat	toe, button, mat
t̪	indicates a voiced alveolar flap [ɾ], as in later, catty, battle	indica un flap alveolar sonoro [ɾ], como en later, catty, battle
t͡ʃ	choose, batch	choose, batch
θ	thin, ether, bath	thin, ether, bath
v	vat, never, cave	vat, never, cave
w	wet, software	wet, software
x	*German* Ba**ch**, *Scots* lo**ch**, *Spanish* **g**ente, **j**efe	*alemán* Ba**ch**, *escocés* lo**ch**, *español* **g**ente, **j**efe
z	zoo, easy, buzz	zoo, easy, buzz
ʒ	**j**aborandi, a**z**ure, bei**g**e	**j**aborandi, a**z**ure, bei**g**e
h, k,	indicate sounds which are	denotan sonidos presentes en la
p, t	present in the pronunciation of some speakers of English but absent in that of others	forma de pronunciar de algunos angloparlantes pero ausentes en el habla de otros angloparlantes

STRESS MARKS (MARCAS DE ACENTUACIÓN)

ˈ	[high stress] **pen**manship	[acento alto] **pen**manship
ˌ	[low stress] penman**ship**	[acento bajo] penman**ship**

Spelling-to-Sound Correspondences in Spanish

For example words for the phonetic symbols below, see Pronunciation Symbols on page 85a.

VOWELS

a   [a]

e   [e] in open syllables (syllables ending with a vowel); [ɛ] in closed syllables (syllables ending with a consonant)

i   [i]; before another vowel in the same syllable pronounced as [j] ([ʒ] or [ʃ] in Argentina and Uruguay; [ʤ] when at the beginning of a word in the Caribbean)

o   [o] in open syllables (syllables ending with a vowel); [ɔ] in closed syllables (syllables ending with a consonant)

u   [u]; before another vowel in the same syllable pronounced as [w]

y   [i]; before another vowel in the same syllable pronounced as [j] ([ʒ] or [ʃ] in Argentina and Uruguay; [ʤ] when at the beginning of a word in the Caribbean)

CONSONANTS

b   [b] at the beginning of a word or after *m* or *n*; [β] elsewhere

c   [s] before *i* or *e* in Latin America and parts of southern Spain, [θ] in northern Spain; [k] elsewhere

ch   [ʧ]; frequently [ʃ] in Chile and Panama; sometimes [ts] in Chile

d   [d] at the beginning of a word or after *n* or *l*; [ð] elsewhere, frequently silent between vowels

f   [f]; [Φ] in Honduras (no English equivalent for this sound; like [f] but made with both lips)

g   [x] before *i* or *e* ([h] in the Caribbean and Central America); [g] at the beginning of a word or after *n* and not before *i* or *e*; [ɣ] elsewhere, frequently silent between vowels

gu   [gw] at the beginning of a word before *a, o*; [ɣw] elsewhere before *a, o*; frequently just [w] between vowels; [g] at the beginning of a word before *i, e*; [ɣ] elsewhere before *i, e*; frequently silent between vowels

gü   [gw] at the beginning of a word, [ɣw] elsewhere; frequently just [w] between vowels

h   silent

j   [x] ([h] in the Caribbean and Central America)

k   [k]

l   [l]

ll   [j]; [ʒ] or [ʃ] in Argentina and Uruguay; [ʤ] when at the beginning of a word in the Caribbean; [lʲ] in Bolivia, Paraguay, Peru, and parts of northern Spain (no English equivalent; like "lli" in *million*)

m   [m]

n   [n]; frequently [ŋ] at the end of a word when next word begins with a vowel

ñ   [ɲ]

p   [p]

qu   [k]

r [r] (no English equivalent; a trilled sound) at the beginning of words; [t]/[ɾ] elsewhere

rr [r] (no English equivalent; a trilled sound)

s [s]; frequently [z] before *b, d, g, m, n, l, r*; at the end of a word [h] or silent in many parts of Latin America and some parts of Spain

t [t]

v [b] at the beginning of a word or after *m* or *n*; [β] elsewhere

x [ks] or [gz] between vowels; [s] before consonants

z [s] in Latin America and parts of southern Spain, [θ] in northern Spain; at the end of a word [h] or silent in many parts of Latin America and some parts of Spain

Diccionario
Español-Inglés

Spanish-English
Dictionary

A

a¹ *nf* : first letter of the Spanish alphabet

a² *prep* **1** (*indicating direction*) : to ⟨vamos a México : we're going to Mexico⟩ ⟨fui a casa : I went home⟩ ⟨gira a la derecha : turn right⟩ **2** (*indicating location*) : at ⟨llegué al hotel : I arrived at the hotel⟩ ⟨al fondo del pasillo : at the end of the hall⟩ ⟨a mi lado : beside me⟩ ⟨vivo a cinco minutos de aquí : I live five minutes from here⟩ **3** (*used before direct objects referring to persons*) ⟨¿llamaste a tu papá? : did you call your dad?⟩ **4** (*used before indirect objects*) ⟨como a usted le guste : as you wish⟩ ⟨le echó un vistazo a la página : she glanced over the page⟩ **5** : in the manner of ⟨papas a la francesa : french fries⟩ ⟨una boda a lo Hollywood : a Hollywood-style wedding⟩ **6** : on, by means of ⟨a pie : on foot⟩ ⟨a mano : by hand⟩ **7** : per, each ⟨tres pastillas al día : three pills per day⟩ **8** (*indicating rate or measure*) ⟨lo venden a 50 pesos el kilo : they sell it for 50 pesos a kilo⟩ ⟨a una velocidad de . . . : at a speed of . . .⟩ **9** (*indicating comparison*) : to ⟨prefiero el vino a la cerveza : I prefer wine to beer⟩ ⟨un margen de dos a uno : a two-to-one margin⟩ **10** (*indicating time*) : at, on ⟨a las dos : at two o'clock⟩ ⟨al principio : at first⟩ ⟨al salir : on/upon leaving⟩ ⟨al día siguiente : on the following day⟩ **11** (*with infinitive*) ⟨enséñales a leer : teach them to read⟩ ⟨problemas a resolver : problems to be solved⟩

a- *pref* : a-

ábaco *nm* : abacus

abad *nm* : abbot

abadesa *nf* : abbess

abadía *nf* : abbey

abajo *adv* **1** : down ⟨póngalo más abajo : put it lower (down)⟩ ⟨arriba y abajo : up and down⟩ ⟨cuesta/río abajo : downhill/downstream⟩ **2** : downstairs ⟨los vecinos de abajo : the downstairs neighbors⟩ **3** : under, beneath ⟨el abajo firmante : the undersigned⟩ **4** : down with ⟨¡abajo la violencia! : down with violence!⟩ **5 ~ de** : under, beneath **6 de ~** : bottom ⟨el cajón de abajo : the bottom drawer⟩ **7 hacia ~** *or* **para ~** : downwards

abalanzarse {21} *vr* : to hurl oneself, to rush

abalorio *nm* : glass bead

abanderado, -da *n* : standard-bearer

abandonado, -da *adj* **1** : abandoned, deserted **2** : neglected **3** : slovenly, unkempt

abandonar *vt* **1** DEJAR : to abandon, to leave **2** : to give up, to quit ⟨abandonaron la búsqueda : they gave up the search⟩ — **abandonarse** *vr* **1** : to neglect oneself **2 ~ a** : to succumb to, to give oneself over to

abandono *nm* **1** : abandonment **2** : neglect **3** : withdrawal ⟨ganar por abandono : to win by default⟩

abanicar {72} *vt* : to fan — **abanicarse** *vr*

abanico *nm* **1** : fan **2** GAMA : range, gamut

abaratamiento *nm* : price reduction

abaratar *vt* : to lower the price of — **abaratarse** *vr* : to go down in price

abarcar {72} *vt* **1** : to cover, to include, to embrace **2** : to undertake **3** : to monopolize

abaritonado, -da *adj* : baritone

abarrotado, -da *adj* : packed, crammed

abarrotar *vt* : to fill up, to pack

abarrotería *nf CA, Mex* : grocery store

abarrotero, -ra *n Col, Mex* : grocer

abarrotes *nmpl* **1** : groceries, supplies **2 tienda de abarrotes** : general store, grocery store

abastecedor, -dora *n* : supplier

abastecer {53} *vt* : to supply, to stock — **abastecerse** *vr* : to stock up

abastecimiento → **abasto**

abasto *nm* : supply, supplying ⟨no da abasto : there isn't enough for all⟩

abatible *adj* **1** : reclining (of a chair) **2** : folding

abatido, -da *adj* : dejected, depressed

abatimiento *nm* **1** : drop, reduction **2** : dejection, depression

abatir *vt* **1** DERRIBAR : to demolish, to knock down **2** : to shoot down **3** DEPRIMIR : to depress, to bring low — **abatirse** *vr* **1** DEPRIMIRSE : to get depressed **2 ~ sobre** : to swoop down on

abdicación *nf, pl* **-ciones** : abdication

abdicar {72} *vt* : to relinquish, to abdicate

abdomen *nm, pl* **-dómenes** : abdomen

abdominal *adj* : abdominal

abecé *nm* : ABC's *pl*

abecedario *nm* ALFABETO : alphabet

abedul *nm* : birch (tree)

abeja *nf* : bee

abejorro *nm* : bumblebee

aberración *nf, pl* **-ciones** : aberration

aberrante *adj* : aberrant, perverse

abertura *nf* **1** : aperture, opening **2** AGUJERO : hole **3** : slit (in a skirt, etc.) **4** GRIETA : crack

abeto *nm* : fir (tree)

abierto¹ *pp* → **abrir**

abierto², -ta *adj* **1** : open ⟨una puerta/boca/caja abierta : an open door/mouth/box⟩ ⟨heridas abiertas : open wounds⟩ ⟨con los brazos abiertos : with open arms⟩ **2** : open (for business, traffic, etc.) **3** DESABROCHADO : open, undone **4** : unlocked, open **5** : on, running (of a faucet) **6** : open, overt ⟨guerra abierta : open warfare⟩ **7** FRANCO : open, frank **8** RECEPTIVO : open, receptive — **abiertamente** *adv*

abigarrado, -da *adj* : multicolored, variegated

abigeato *nm* : rustling (of livestock)

abismal *adj* : abysmal, vast
abismo *nm* : abyss, chasm ⟨al borde del abismo : on the brink of ruin⟩
abjurar *vi* ∼ de : to abjure — abjuración *nf*
ablandamiento *nm* : softening, moderation
ablandar *vt* 1 SUAVIZAR : to soften 2 CALMAR : to soothe, to appease — *vi* : to moderate, to get milder — ablandarse *vr* 1 : to become soft, to soften 2 CEDER : to yield, to relent
-able *suf* : -able
ablución *nf, pl* -ciones : ablution
abnegación *nf, pl* -ciones : self-denial
abnegado, -da *adj* : self-sacrificing, selfless
abnegarse {49} *vr* : to deny oneself
abobado, -da *adj* 1 : silly, stupid 2 : bewildered
abocado, -da *adj* ∼ a 1 : headed for 2 : committed to
abocarse {72} *vr* 1 DIRIGIRSE : to head, to direct oneself 2 DEDICARSE : to dedicate oneself
abochornar *vt* AVERGONZAR : to embarrass, to shame — abochornarse *vr*
abofetear *vt* : to slap
abogacía *nf* : law, legal profession
abogado, -da *n* : lawyer, attorney
abogar {52} *vi* ∼ por : to plead for, to defend, to advocate
abolengo *nm* LINAJE : lineage, ancestry
abolición *nf, pl* -ciones : abolition
abolir {1} *vt* DEROGAR : to abolish, to repeal
abolladura *nf* : dent
abollar *vt* : to dent
abombar *vt* : to warp, to cause to bulge — abombarse *vr* : to decompose, to go bad
abominable *adj* ABORRECIBLE : abominable
abominación *nf, pl* -ciones : abomination
abominar *vt* ABORRECER : to abominate, to abhor
abonado, -da *n* : subscriber
abonar *vt* 1 : to pay 2 FERTILIZAR : to fertilize — abonarse *vr* : to subscribe
abono *nm* 1 : payment, installment 2 FERTILIZANTE : fertilizer 3 : season ticket
abordaje *nm* : boarding
abordar *vt* 1 : to address, to broach 2 : to accost, to waylay 3 : to come on board
aborigen[1] *adj, pl* -rígenes : aboriginal, native
aborigen[2] *nmf, pl* -rígenes : aborigine, indigenous inhabitant
aborrecer {53} *vt* ABOMINAR, ODIAR : to abhor, to detest, to hate
aborrecible *adj* ABOMINABLE, ODIOSO : abominable, detestable
aborrecimiento *nm* : abhorrence, loathing
abortar *vi* : to have an abortion — *vt* 1 : to abort 2 : to quash, to suppress
abortivo, -va *adj* : abortive
aborto *nm* 1 : abortion 2 : miscarriage

abotonar *vt* : to button — abotonarse *vr* : to button up
abovedado, -da *adj* : vaulted
abrasador, -dora *adj* : burning, scorching
abrasar *vt* QUEMAR : to burn, to sear, to scorch
abrasivo[1], -va *adj* : abrasive
abrasivo[2] *nm* : abrasive
abrazadera *nf* : clamp, brace
abrazar {21} *vt* : to hug, to embrace — abrazarse *vr*
abrazo *nm* : hug, embrace
abrebotellas *nms & pl* : bottle opener
abrecartas *nms & pl* : letter opener
abrelatas *nms & pl* : can opener
abrevadero *nm* BEBEDERO : watering trough
abreviación *nf, pl* -ciones : abbreviation
abreviar *vt* 1 : to abbreviate 2 : to shorten, to cut short
abreviatura → abreviación
abridor *nm* : bottle opener, can opener
abrigadero *nm* : shelter, windbreak
abrigado, -da *adj* 1 : sheltered 2 : warm, wrapped up (with clothing)
abrigar {52} *vt* 1 : to shelter, to protect 2 : to keep warm, to dress warmly 3 : to cherish, to harbor ⟨abrigar esperanzas : to cherish hopes⟩ — abrigarse *vr* : to dress warmly
abrigo *nm* 1 : coat, overcoat 2 : shelter, refuge
abril *nm* : April ⟨el dos de abril : (on) April second⟩
abrillantador *nm* : polish
abrillantar *vt* : to polish, to shine
abrir {2} *vt* 1 : to open (a door, an umbrella, etc.) 2 : to open, to clear ⟨abrir paso a : to make way for⟩ 3 : to open (a business, an account) 4 : to unlock (a lock, a house), to undo (clothing) 5 : to turn on (a tap or faucet) 6 INICIAR : to open, to start — *vi* : to open, to open up ⟨abren a las nueve : they open at nine⟩ — abrirse *vr* 1 : to open, to open up 2 : to clear (of the skies)
abrochar *vt* : to button, to fasten — abrocharse *vr* : to fasten, to hook up
abrogación *nf, pl* -ciones : annulment, repeal
abrogar {52} *vt* : to abrogate, to annul, to repeal
abrojo *nm* : bur (of a plant)
abrumador, -dora *adj* : crushing, overwhelming
abrumar *vt* 1 AGOBIAR : to overwhelm 2 OPRIMIR : to oppress, to burden
abrupto, -ta *adj* 1 : abrupt 2 ESCARPADO : steep — abruptamente *adv*
absceso *nm* : abscess
absolución *nf, pl* -ciones 1 : absolution 2 : acquittal
absolutismo *nm* : absolutism
absoluto, -ta *adj* 1 : absolute, unconditional 2 en ∼ : (not) at all ⟨no me gustó en absoluto : I did not like it at all⟩ — absolutamente *adv*
absolver {89} *vt* 1 : to absolve 2 : to acquit
absorbencia *nf* : absorbency

absorbente *adj* **1** : absorbent **2** : absorbing, engrossing
absorber *vt* **1** : to absorb, to soak up **2** : to occupy, to take up, to engross
absorción *nf, pl* **-ciones** : absorption
absorto, -ta *adj* : absorbed, engrossed
abstemio[1], -mia *adj* : abstemious, teetotal
abstemio[2], -mia *n* : teetotaler
abstención *nf, pl* **-ciones** : abstention — **abstencionismo** *nm*
abstenerse {80} *vr* : to abstain, to refrain
abstinencia *nf* : abstinence
abstracción *nf, pl* **-ciones** : abstraction
abstracto, -ta *adj* : abstract
abstraer {81} *vt* : to abstract — **abstraerse** *vr* : to lose oneself in thought
abstraído, -da *adj* : preoccupied, withdrawn
abstruso, -sa *adj* : abstruse
abstuvo, etc. → **abstenerse**
absuelto *pp* → **absolver**
absurdo[1], -da *adj* DISPARATADO, RIDÍCULO : absurd, ridiculous — **absurdamente** *adv*
absurdo[2] *nm* : absurdity
abuchear *vt* : to boo, to jeer
abucheo *nm* : booing, jeering
abuela *nf* **1** : grandmother **2** : old woman **3** **¡tu abuela!** *fam* : no way!, forget about it!
abuelita *nf fam* : grandma *fam*
abuelito *nm fam* : grandpa *fam*
abuelo *nm* **1** : grandfather **2** : old man **3** **abuelos** *nmpl* : grandparents, ancestors
abulia *nf* : apathy, lethargy
abúlico, -ca *adj* : lethargic, apathetic
abultado, -da *adj* : bulging, bulky
abultar *vi* : to bulge — *vt* : to enlarge, to expand
abundancia *nf* : abundance
abundante *adj* : abundant, plentiful — **abundantemente** *adv*
abundar *vi* **1** : to abound, to be plentiful **2** ~ **en** : to be in agreement with
aburrido, -da *adj* **1** : bored, tired, fed up **2** TEDIOSO : boring, tedious
aburrimiento *nm* : boredom, weariness
aburrir *vt* : to bore, to tire — **aburrirse** *vr* : to get bored
abusado, -da *adj Mex fam* : sharp, on the ball
abusador, -dora *n* : abuser
abusar *vi* **1** : to go too far, to do something to excess **2** ~ **de** : to abuse (as drugs) **3** ~ **de** : to take unfair advantage of
abusivo, -va *adj* **1** : abusive **2** : outrageous, excessive
abuso *nm* **1** : abuse **2** : injustice, outrage
abyecto, -ta *adj* : despicable, contemptible
acá *adv* **1** AQUÍ : here, over here ⟨¡ven acá! : come here!⟩ ⟨de acá para allá : back and forth⟩ **2** (*in expressions of time*) ⟨de 2010 (para) acá : from 2010 to now, since 2010⟩
acabado[1], -da *adj* **1** : finished, done, completed **2** : old, worn-out

acabado[2] *nm* : finish ⟨un acabado brillante : a glossy finish⟩
acabar *vi* **1** TERMINAR : to finish, to end ⟨ya acabo : I'm almost done⟩ **2** ~ **de** : to have just ⟨acabo de ver a tu hermano : I just saw your brother⟩ **3** ~ **con** : to put an end to, to stamp out **4** **acabar por hacer algo** *or* **acabar haciendo algo** : to end up doing something — *vt* TERMINAR : to finish — **acabarse** *vr* TERMINARSE : to come to an end, to run out ⟨se me acabó el dinero : I ran out of money⟩ ⟨¡se acabó! : that's it!⟩
acabose *or* **acabóse** *nm fam* COLMO : extreme, limit ⟨¡esto es el acabóse! : this is the limit!⟩
acacia *nf* : acacia
academia *nf* : academy
académico[1], -ca *adj* : academic, scholastic — **académicamente** *adv*
académico[2], -ca *n* : academic, academician
acaecer {53} *vt* (*3rd person only*) : to happen, to take place
acalambrarse *vr* : to cramp up, to get a cramp
acallar *vt* : to quiet, to silence
acalorado, -da *adj* : emotional, heated
acaloramiento *nm* **1** : heat **2** : ardor, passion
acalorar *vt* : to heat up, to inflame — **acalorarse** *vr* : to get upset, to get worked up
acampada *nf* : camp, camping ⟨ir de acampada : to go camping⟩
acampar *vi* : to camp
acanalar *vt* **1** : to groove, to furrow **2** : to corrugate
acantilado *nm* : cliff
acanto *nm* : acanthus
acantonar *vt* : to station, to quarter
acaparador, -dora *adj* : greedy, selfish
acaparar *vt* **1** : to stockpile, to hoard **2** : to monopolize
acápite *nm* : paragraph
acaramelado, -da *adj* **1** : caramel-coated **2** : caramel-colored **3** : sugary **4** : very affectionate (of a couple)
acariciar *vt* : to caress, to stroke, to pet
ácaro *nm* : mite
acarrear *vt* **1** : to haul, to carry **2** : to bring, to give rise to ⟨los problemas que acarrea : the problems that come along with it⟩
acarreo *nm* : transport, haulage
acartonarse *vr* **1** : to stiffen **2** : to become wizened
acaso *adv* **1** : perhaps, by any chance **2** **por si acaso** : just in case
acatamiento *nm* : compliance, observance
acatar *vt* : to comply with, to respect
acatarrarse *vr* : to catch a cold
acaudalado, -da *adj* RICO : wealthy, rich
acaudillar *vt* : to lead, to command
acceder *vi* ~ **a** **1** : to accede to, to agree to **2** : to assume (a position) **3** : to gain access to
accesar *vt* : to access (on a computer)
accesibilidad *nf* : accessibility

accesible *adj* ASEQUIBLE : accessible, attainable

acceso *nm* **1** : access **2** : admittance, entrance

accesorio[1], **-ria** *adj* **1** : accessory **2** : incidental

accesorio[2] *nm* **1** : accessory **2** : prop (in the theater)

accidentado[1], **-da** *adj* **1** : eventful, turbulent **2** : rough, uneven **3** : injured

accidentado[2], **-da** *n* : accident victim

accidental *adj* : accidental, unintentional — **accidentalmente** *adv*

accidentarse *vr* : to have an accident

accidente *nm* **1** : accident **2** : unevenness **3 accidente geográfico** : geographical feature

acción *nf, pl* **acciones** **1** : action **2** ACTO : act, deed **3** : share, stock

accionamiento *nm* : activation

accionar *vt* : to put into motion, to activate — *vi* : to gesticulate

accionario, -ria *adj* : stock ⟨mercado accionario : stock market⟩

accionista *nmf* : stockholder, shareholder

acebo *nm* : holly

acechar *vt* **1** : to watch, to spy on **2** : to stalk, to lie in wait for

acecho *nm* **al acecho** : lying in wait

acedera *nf* : sorrel (herb)

aceitar *vt* : to oil

aceite *nm* **1** : oil **2 aceite de ricino** : castor oil **3 aceite de oliva** : olive oil

aceitera *nf* **1** : cruet (for oil) **2** : oilcan **3** *Mex* : oil refinery

aceitoso, -sa *adj* : oily

aceituna *nf* OLIVA : olive

aceituno *nm* OLIVO : olive tree

aceleración *nf, pl* **-ciones** : acceleration, speeding up

acelerado, -da *adj* : accelerated, speedy

acelerador *nm* : accelerator

aceleramiento *nm* → **aceleración**

acelerar *vt* **1** : to accelerate, to speed up **2** AGILIZAR : to expedite — *vi* : to accelerate (of an automobile) — **acelerarse** *vr* : to hasten, to hurry up

acelga *nf* : chard, Swiss chard

acendrar *vt* : to purify, to refine

acento *nm* **1** : accent **2** : stress, emphasis

acentuado, -da *adj* : marked, pronounced

acentuar {3} *vt* **1** : to accent **2** : to emphasize, to stress — **acentuarse** *vr* : to become more pronounced

acepción *nf, pl* **-ciones** SIGNIFICADO : sense, meaning

aceptabilidad *nf* : acceptability

aceptable *adj* : acceptable

aceptación *nf, pl* **-ciones** **1** : acceptance **2** APROBACIÓN : approval

aceptar *vt* **1** : to accept **2** : to approve

acequia *nf* **1** : irrigation ditch **2** *Mex* : sewer

acera *nf* : sidewalk

acerado, -da *adj* **1** : made of steel **2** : steely, tough

acerbo, -ba *adj* **1** : harsh, cutting ⟨comentarios acerbos : cutting remarks⟩ **2** : bitter — **acerbamente** *adv*

acerca *prep* ~ **de** : about, concerning

acercamiento *nm* : rapprochement, reconciliation

acercar {72} *vt* APROXIMAR, ARRIMAR : to bring near, to bring closer — **acercarse** *vr* APROXIMARSE, ARRIMARSE : to approach, to draw near

acería *nf* : steel mill

acerico *nm* : pincushion

acero *nm* : steel ⟨acero inoxidable : stainless steel⟩

acérrimo, -ma *adj* **1** : staunch, steadfast **2** : bitter ⟨un acérrimo enemigo : a bitter enemy⟩

acertado, -da *adj* CORRECTO : accurate, correct, on target — **acertadamente** *adv*

acertante[1] *adj* : winning

acertante[2] *nmf* : winner

acertar {55} *vt* : to guess correctly — *vi* **1** ATINAR : to be correct, to be on target **2** ~ **a** : to manage to

acertijo *nm* ADIVINANZA : riddle

acervo *nm* **1** : pile, heap **2** : wealth, heritage ⟨el acervo artístico del instituto : the artistic treasures of the institute⟩

acetato *nm* : acetate

acetileno *nm* : acetylene

acetona *nf* **1** : acetone **2** : nail-polish remover

achacar {72} *vt* : to attribute, to impute ⟨te achaca todos sus problemas : he blames all his problems on you⟩

achacoso, -sa *adj* : frail, sickly

achaparrado, -da *adj* : stunted, scrubby ⟨árboles achaparrados : scrubby trees⟩

achaque *nm* : ailment

achaques *nmpl* : aches and pains

achatar *vt* : to flatten

achicar {72} *vt* **1** REDUCIR : to make smaller, to reduce **2** : to intimidate **3** : to bail out (water) — **achicarse** *vr* : to become intimidated

achicharrar *vt* : to scorch, to burn to a crisp

achicoria *nf* : chicory

achiote *or* **achote** *nm* : annatto

achispado, -da *adj fam* : tipsy

achuchón *nm, pl* **-chones** **1** : push, shove **2** *fam* : squeeze, hug **3** *fam* : mild illness

aciago, -ga *adj* : fateful, unlucky

acicalar *vt* **1** PULIR : to polish **2** : to dress up, to adorn — **acicalarse** *vr* : to get dressed up

acicate *nm* **1** : spur **2** INCENTIVO : incentive, stimulus

acidez *nf, pl* **-deces** **1** : acidity **2** : sourness **3 acidez estomacal** : heartburn

ácido[1], **-da** *adj* AGRIO : acid, sour

ácido[2] *nm* **1** : acid **2 ácido clorhídrico** : hydrochloric acid **3 ácido nítrico** : nitric acid **4 ácido sulfúrico** : sulfuric acid

acierto *nm* **1** : correct answer, right choice **2** : accuracy, skill

acimut *nm* : azimuth

acitronar *vt Mex* : to fry until crisp

aclamación *nf, pl* **-ciones** : acclaim, acclamation

aclamar *vt* : to acclaim, to cheer, to applaud

aclaración *nf, pl* **-ciones** CLARIFICACIÓN : clarification, explanation

aclarar *vt* **1** CLARIFICAR : to clarify, to explain, to resolve **2** : to lighten **3** **aclarar la voz** : to clear one's throat — *vi* **1** : to get light, to dawn **2** : to clear up — **aclararse** *vr* : to become clear

aclaratorio, -ria *adj* : explanatory

aclimatar *vt* : to acclimatize — **aclimatarse** *vr* ~ **a** : to get used to — **aclimatación** *nf*

acné *nm* : acne

acobardar *vt* INTIMIDAR : to frighten, to intimidate — **acobardarse** *vr* **1** : to get frightened, to chicken out **2** : to cower

acodarse *vr* ~ **en** : to lean (one's elbows) on

acogedor, -dora *adj* : cozy, warm, friendly

acoger {15} *vt* **1** REFUGIAR : to take in, to shelter **2** : to receive, to welcome — **acogerse** *vr* **1** REFUGIARSE : to take refuge **2** ~ **a** : to resort to, to avail oneself of

acogida *nf* **1** AMPARO, REFUGIO : refuge, protection **2** RECIBIMIENTO : reception, welcome

acolchar *vt* **1** : to pad (a wall, etc.) **2** : to quilt

acólito *nm* **1** MONAGUILLO : altar boy **2** : follower, helper, acolyte

acomedido, -da *adj* : helpful, obliging

acometer *vt* **1** ATACAR : to attack, to assail **2** EMPRENDER : to undertake, to begin — *vi* ~ **contra** : to rush against

acometida *nf* ATAQUE : attack, assault

acomodado, -da *adj* **1** : suitable, appropriate **2** : well-to-do, prosperous

acomodador, -dora *n* : usher, usherette *f*

acomodar *vt* **1** : to accommodate, to make room for **2** : to adjust, to adapt — **acomodarse** *vr* **1** : to settle in **2** ~ **a** : to adjust to

acomodaticio, -cia *adj* : accommodating, obliging

acomodo *nm* **1** : job, position **2** : arrangement, placement **3** : accommodation, lodging

acompañamiento *nm* : accompaniment

acompañante *nmf* **1** COMPAÑERO : companion **2** : accompanist

acompañar *vt* : to accompany, to go with

acompasado, -da *adj* : rhythmic, regular, measured

acompasar *vt* : to synchronize

acomplejado, -da *adj* : full of complexes, neurotic

acomplejar *vt* : to give a complex, to make neurotic

acondicionado, -da *adj* **1** : equipped **2** **bien acondicionado** : in good shape, in a fit state

acondicionador *nm* **1** : conditioner **2** **acondicionador de aire** : air conditioner

acondicionar *vt* **1** : to condition **2** : to fit out, to furnish

acongojado, -da *adj* : distressed, upset

acongojarse *vr* : to grieve, to become distressed

aconsejable *adj* : advisable

aconsejar *vt* : to advise, to counsel

acontecer {53} *vt* (*3rd person only*) : to occur, to happen

acontecimiento *nm* SUCESO : event

acopiar *vt* : to gather, to collect, to stockpile

acopio *nm* : collection, stock

acoplamiento *nm* : connection, coupling

acoplar *vt* : to couple, to connect — **acoplarse** *vr* : to fit together

acoquinar *vt* : to intimidate

acorazado[1], -da *adj* BLINDADO : armored

acorazado[2] *nm* : battleship

acordado, -da *adj* : agreed upon

acordar {19} *vt* **1** : to agree on **2** OTORGAR : to award, to bestow — **acordarse** *vr* RECORDAR : to remember, to recall

acorde[1] *adj* **1** : in agreement, in accordance **2** ~ **con** : in keeping with

acorde[2] *nm* : chord

acordeón *nm, pl* **-deones** : accordion — **acordeonista** *nmf*

acordonar *vt* **1** : to cordon off **2** : to lace up **3** : to mill (coins)

acorralar *vt* ARRINCONAR : to corner, to hem in, to corral

acortar *vt* : to shorten, to cut short — **acortarse** *vr* **1** : to become shorter **2** : to end early

acosar *vt* PERSEGUIR : to pursue, to hound, to harass

acoso *nm* ASEDIO : harassment ⟨acoso sexual : sexual harassment⟩

acostar {19} *vt* **1** : to lay (something) down **2** : to put to bed — **acostarse** *vr* **1** : to lie down **2** : to go to bed

acostumbrado, -da *adj* **1** HABITUADO : accustomed **2** HABITUAL : usual, customary

acostumbrar *vt* : to accustom — *vi* : to be accustomed, to be in the habit — **acostumbrarse** *vr*

acotación *nf, pl* **-ciones** **1** : marginal note **2** : stage direction

acotado, -da *adj* : enclosed

acotamiento *nm Mex* : shoulder (of a road)

acotar *vt* **1** ANOTAR : to note, to annotate **2** DELIMITAR : to mark off (land), to demarcate

acre[1] *adj* **1** : acrid, pungent **2** MORDAZ : caustic, biting

acre[2] *nm* : acre

acrecentamiento *nm* : growth, increase

acrecentar {55} *vt* AUMENTAR : to increase, to augment

acreditación *nf, pl* **-ciones** : accreditation

acreditado, -da *adj* **1** : accredited, authorized **2** : reputable

acreditar *vt* **1** : to accredit, to authorize **2** : to credit **3** : to prove, to verify — **acreditarse** *vr* : to gain a reputation

acreedor[1], -dora *adj* : deserving, worthy

acreedor[2], -dora *n* : creditor

acribillar *vt* **1** : to riddle, to pepper (with bullets, etc.) **2** : to hound, to harass

acrílico *nm* : acrylic

acrimonia *nf* **1** : pungency **2** : acrimony

acrimonioso, -sa *adj* : acrimonious

acriollarse *vr* : to adopt local customs, to go native

acristalamiento *nm Spain* : glazing, windows *pl*

acritud *nf* **1** : pungency, bitterness **2** : intensity, sharpness **3** : harshness, asperity

acrobacia *nf* : acrobatics

acróbata *nmf* : acrobat

acrobático, -ca *adj* : acrobatic

acrónimo *nm* : acronym

acta *nf* **1** : document, certificate ⟨acta de nacimiento/defunción : birth/death certificate⟩ **2 actas** *nfpl* : minutes (of a meeting)

actitud *nf* **1** : attitude **2** : posture, position

activación *nf, pl* **-ciones 1** : activation, stimulation **2** ACELERACIÓN : acceleration, speeding up

activar *vt* **1** : to activate **2** : to stimulate, to energize **3** : to speed up

actividad *nf* : activity

activista *nmf* : activist — **activismo** *nm*

activo¹, -va *adj* : active — **activamente** *adv*

activo² *nm* : assets *pl* ⟨activo y pasivo : assets and liabilities⟩

acto *nm* **1** ACCIÓN : act, deed **2** : act (in a play) **3 el acto sexual** : sexual intercourse **4 en el acto** : right away, on the spot **5 acto seguido** : immediately after

actor *nm* ARTISTA : actor

actriz *nf, pl* **actrices** ARTISTA : actress

actuación *nf, pl* **-ciones 1** : performance **2 actuaciones** *nfpl* DILIGENCIAS : proceedings

actual *adj* PRESENTE : present, current

actualidad *nf* **1** : present time ⟨en la actualidad : at present⟩ **2 actualidades** *nfpl* : current affairs

actualización *nf, pl* **-ciones** : updating, modernization

actualizar {21} *vt* : to modernize, to bring up to date

actualmente *adv* : at present, nowadays

actuar {3} *vi* : to act, to perform

actuarial *adj* : actuarial

actuario, -ria *n* : actuary

acuarela *nf* : watercolor

acuario *nm* : aquarium

Acuario¹ *nm* : Aquarius (sign or constellation)

Acuario² *nmf* : Aquarius (person)

acuartelar *vt* : to quarter (troops)

acuático, -ca *adj* : aquatic, water

acuchillar *vt* APUÑALAR : to knife, to stab

acuciante *adj* : pressing, urgent

acucioso, -sa → **acuciante**

acudir *vi* **1** : to go, to come (someplace for a specific purpose) ⟨acudió a la puerta : he went to the door⟩ ⟨acudimos en su ayuda : we came to her aid⟩ **2** : to be present, to show up ⟨acudí a la cita : I showed up for the appointment⟩ **3 ∼ a** : to turn to, to have recourse to ⟨hay que acudir al médico : you must consult the doctor⟩

acueducto *nm* : aqueduct

acuerdo *nm* **1** : agreement **2 estar de acuerdo** : to agree **3 de acuerdo con** : in accordance with **4 de ∼** : OK, all right

acullá *adv* : yonder, over there

acumulación *nf, pl* **-ciones** : accumulation

acumulador *nm* : storage battery

acumular *vt* : to accumulate, to amass — **acumularse** *vr* : to build up, to pile up

acumulativo, -va *adj* : cumulative — **acumulativamente** *adv*

acunar *vt* : to rock, to cradle

acuñar *vt* : to coin, to mint

acuoso, -sa *adj* : aqueous, watery

acupuntura *nf* : acupuncture

acurrucarse {72} *vr* : to cuddle, to nestle, to curl up

acusación *nf, pl* **-ciones 1** : accusation, charge **2 la acusación** : the prosecution

acusado¹, -da *adj* : prominent, marked

acusado², -da *n* : defendant ⟨el acusado : the defendant, the accused⟩

acusador, -dora *n* **1** : accuser **2** FISCAL : prosecutor

acusar *vt* **1** : to accuse, to charge **2** : to reveal, to betray ⟨sus ojos acusaban la desconfianza : his eyes revealed distrust⟩ — **acusarse** *vr* : to confess

acusativo *nm* : objective (in grammar)

acusatorio, -ria *adj* : accusatory

acuse *nm* **acuse de recibo** : acknowledgment of receipt

acústica *nf* : acoustics

acústico, -ca *adj* : acoustic

adagio *nm* REFRÁN : adage, proverb

adalid *nm* : leader, champion

adaptable *adj* : adaptable — **adaptabilidad** *nf*

adaptación *nf, pl* **-ciones** : adaptation, adjustment

adaptado, -da *adj* : suited, adapted

adaptador *nm* : adapter (in electricity)

adaptar *vt* **1** MODIFICAR : to adapt **2** : to adjust, to fit — **adaptarse** *vr* : to adapt oneself, to conform

adecentar *vt* : to tidy up

adecuación *nf, pl* **-ciones** ADAPTACIÓN : adaptation

adecuadamente *adv* : adequately

adecuado, -da *adj* **1** IDÓNEO : suitable, appropriate **2** : adequate

adecuar {8} *vt* : to adapt, to make suitable — **adecuarse** *vr* **∼ a** : to be appropriate for, to fit in with

adefesio *nm* : eyesore, monstrosity

adelantado, -da *adj* **1** : advanced, ahead **2** : fast (of a clock or watch) **3 por ∼** : in advance

adelantamiento *nm* **1** : advancement **2** : speeding up

adelantar *vt* **1** : to advance, to move forward ⟨adelantar el reloj : to set one's watch/clock ahead⟩ ⟨adelantar una fecha : to move up a date⟩ **2** : to pass, to overtake **3** : to reveal (information) in advance **4** : to advance, to lend (money) — **adelantarse** *vr* **1** : to go ahead ⟨se adelantó para recibirlos : she went ahead to meet them⟩ **2** : to run fast (of a watch or clock) **3** : to get ahead ⟨alguien se me adelantó : someone beat me to it⟩ ⟨no nos adelantemos : let's not get ahead of ourselves⟩ **4 adelantarse a su tiempo** : to be ahead of one's time

adelante *adv* **1** : forward, ahead, in front ⟨dar un paso adelante : to take a step forward⟩ ⟨seguimos adelante con el proyecto : we went ahead with the project⟩ **2 de ahora/ahí en adelante** : from now/then on **3 hacia/para** ~ : forward, toward the front **4 más adelante** : further on, later on **5 ¡adelante!** : come in!

adelanto *nm* **1** : advance, progress **2** : advance payment **3** : earliness ⟨llevamos una hora de adelanto : we're running an hour ahead of time⟩

adelfa *nf* : oleander

adelgazar {21} *vt* : to thin, to reduce — *vi* : to lose weight

ademán *nm, pl* **-manes** **1** GESTO : gesture **2 ademanes** *nmpl* : manners

además *adv* **1** : besides, furthermore **2** ~ **de** : in addition to, as well as

adenoides *nfpl* : adenoids

adentrarse *vr* ~ **en** : to go into, to penetrate

adentro *adv* **1** : in, inside ⟨fuimos adentro : we went inside⟩ ⟨estoy aquí adentro : I'm in here⟩ **2 mar adentro** : out to sea **3 tierra adentro** : inland

adentros *nmpl* **decirse para sus adentros** : to say to oneself ⟨me dije para mis adentros que nunca regresaría : I told myself that I'd never go back⟩

adepto¹, -ta *adj* : supportive ⟨ser adepto a : to be a follower of⟩

adepto², -ta *n* PARTIDARIO : follower, supporter

aderezar {21} *vt* **1** SAZONAR : to season, to dress (salad) **2** : to embellish, to adorn

aderezo *nm* **1** : dressing, seasoning **2** : adornment, embellishment

adeudar *vt* **1** : to debit **2** DEBER : to owe

adeudo *nm* **1** DÉBITO : debit **2** *Mex* : debt, indebtedness

adherencia *nf* **1** : adherence (to a rule, etc.) **2** : adhesion

adherente *adj* : adhesive, sticky

adherir {76} *vt* : to stick to — **adherirse** *vr* : to adhere, to stick

adhesión *nf, pl* **-siones** **1** : adhesion **2** : attachment, commitment (to a cause, etc.)

adhesivo¹, -va *adj* : adhesive

adhesivo² *nm* : adhesive

adicción *nf, pl* **-ciones** : addiction

adición *nf, pl* **-ciones** : addition

adicional *adj* : additional — **adicionalmente** *adv*

adicionar *vt* : to add

adictivo, -va *adj* : addictive

adicto¹, -ta *adj* **1** : addicted **2** : devoted, dedicated

adicto², -ta *n* **1** : addict **2** PARTIDARIO : supporter, advocate

adiestrador, -dora *n* : trainer

adiestramiento *nm* : training

adiestrar *vt* : to train

adinerado, -da *adj* : moneyed, wealthy

adiós *nm, pl* **adioses** **1** DESPEDIDA : farewell, good-bye **2 ¡adiós!** : good-bye!

aditamento *nm* : attachment, accessory

aditivo *nm* : additive

adivinación *nf, pl* **-ciones** **1** : guess **2** : divination, prediction

adivinanza *nf* ACERTIJO : riddle

adivinar *vt* **1** : to guess **2** : to foretell, to predict

adivino, -na *n* : fortune-teller

adjetivo¹, -va *adj* : adjectival

adjetivo² *nm* : adjective

adjudicación *nf, pl* **-ciones** **1** : adjudication **2** : allocation, awarding, granting

adjudicar {72} *vt* **1** : to judge, to adjudicate **2** : to assign, to allocate ⟨adjudicar la culpa : to assign the blame⟩ **3** : to award, to grant

adjuntar *vt* : to enclose, to attach

adjunto¹, -ta *adj* : enclosed, attached

adjunto², -ta *n* : deputy, assistant

adjunto³ *nm* **1** : adjunct **2** : attachment (in an e-mail)

administración *nf, pl* **-ciones** **1** : administration, management **2 administración de empresas** : business administration

administrador, -dora *n* : administrator, manager

administrar *vt* : to administer, to manage, to run

administrativo, -va *adj* : administrative — **administrativamente** *adv*

admirable *adj* : admirable, impressive — **admirablemente** *adv*

admiración *nf, pl* **-ciones** : admiration

admirador, -dora *n* : admirer

admirar *vt* **1** : to admire **2** : to amaze, to astonish — **admirarse** *vr* : to be amazed

admirativo, -va *adj* : admiring

admisible *adj* : admissible, allowable

admisión *nf, pl* **-siones** : admission, admittance

admitir *vt* **1** : to admit, to let in **2** : to acknowledge, to concede **3** : to allow, to make room for ⟨la ley no admite cambios : the law doesn't allow for changes⟩

admonición *nf, pl* **-ciones** : admonition, warning

admonitorio, -ria *adj* : admonishing

ADN *nm* (*á*cido *d*esoxirribo*n*ucleico) : DNA

adobar *vt* : to marinate

adobe *nm* : adobe

adobo *nm* **1** : marinade, seasoning **2** *Mex* : spicy marinade used for cooking pork

adoctrinamiento *nm* : indoctrination

adoctrinar *vt* : to indoctrinate

adolecer {53} *vi* PADECER : to suffer ⟨adolece de timidez : he suffers from shyness⟩

adolescencia *nf* : adolescence

adolescente¹ *adj* : adolescent, teenage

adolescente² *nmf* : adolescent, teenager

adonde *conj* : where ⟨el lugar adonde vamos es bello : the place where we're going is beautiful⟩

adónde *adv* : where ⟨¿adónde vamos? : where are we going?⟩

adondequiera *adv* : wherever, anywhere ⟨adondequiera que vayas : anywhere you go⟩

adopción *nf, pl* **-ciones** : adoption

adoptar *vt* **1** : to adopt (a measure), to take (a decision) **2** : to adopt (children)

adoptivo, -va *adj* **1** : adopted (children, country) **2** : adoptive (parents)

adoquín *nm, pl* **-quines** : paving stone, cobblestone

-ador, -adora *suf* : -er ⟨trabajador, trabajadora : worker⟩

adorable *adj* : adorable, lovable

adoración *nf, pl* **-ciones** : adoration, worship

adorador[1], **-dora** *adj* : adoring, worshipping

adorador[2], **-dora** *n* : worshipper

adorar *vt* : to adore, to worship

adormecer {53} *vt* **1** : to make sleepy, to lull to sleep **2** : to numb — **adormecerse** *vr* **1** : to doze off **2** : to go numb

adormecimiento *nm* **1** SUEÑO : drowsiness, sleepiness **2** INSENSIBILIDAD : numbness

adormilarse *vr* : to doze, to drowse

adornar *vt* DECORAR : to decorate, to adorn

adorno *nm* : ornament, decoration

adosado, -da *adj* : attached (of a structure) ⟨casa adosada : duplex, row house⟩

adosar *vt* **1** : to place against, to affix **2** : to enclose, to attach (to a letter)

adquirido, -da *adj* **1** : acquired **2 mal adquirido** : ill-gotten

adquirir {4} *vt* **1** : to acquire, to gain **2** COMPRAR : to purchase

adquisición *nf, pl* **-ciones** **1** : acquisition **2** COMPRA : purchase

adquisitivo, -va *adj* **poder adquisitivo** : purchasing power

adrede *adv* : intentionally, on purpose

adrenalina *nf* : adrenaline

adscribir {33} *vt* : to assign, to appoint — **adscribirse** *vr* ∼ **a** : to become a member of

adscripción *nf, pl* **-ciones** : assignment, appointment

adscrito *pp* → **adscribir**

aduana *nf* : customs, customs office

aduanero[1], **-ra** *adj* : customs

aduanero[2], **-ra** *n* : customs officer

aducir {61} *vt* : to adduce, to offer as proof

adueñarse *vr* ∼ **de** : to take possession of, to take over

adulación *nf, pl* **-ciones** : adulation, flattery

adulador[1], **-dora** *adj* : flattering

adulador[2], **-dora** *n* : flatterer, toady

adular *vt* LISONJEAR : to flatter

adulteración *nf, pl* **-ciones** : adulteration

adulterar *vt* : to adulterate

adulterio *nm* : adultery

adúltero[1], **-ra** *adj* : adulterous

adúltero[2], **-ra** *n* : adulterer

adultez *nf* : adulthood

adulto, -ta *adj & n* : adult

adusto, -ta *adj* : harsh, severe

advenedizo, -za *n* **1** : upstart, parvenu **2** : newcomer

advenimiento *nm* : advent

adverbio *nm* : adverb — **adverbial** *adj*

adversario[1], **-ria** *adj* : opposing, contrary

adversario[2], **-ria** *n* OPOSITOR : adversary, opponent

adversidad *nf* : adversity

adverso, -sa *adj* DESFAVORABLE : adverse, unfavorable — **adversamente** *adv*

advertencia *nf* AVISO : warning

advertir {76} *vt* **1** AVISAR : to warn **2** : to notice, to tell ⟨no advertí que estuviera enojada : I couldn't tell she was angry⟩

Adviento *nm* : Advent

adyacente *adj* : adjacent

aéreo, -rea *adj* **1** : aerial, air **2 correo aéreo** : airmail

aeróbic *nm* : aerobics

aeróbico, -ca *adj* : aerobic

aerobio, -bia *adj* : aerobic

aerodeslizador *nm* : hovercraft

aerodinámica *nf* : aerodynamics

aerodinámico, -ca *adj* : aerodynamic, streamlined

aeródromo *nm* : airfield

aeroespacial *adj* : aerospace

aerogenerador *nm* : wind-powered generator

aerolínea *nf* : airline

aeromozo, -za *n* : flight attendant, steward *m*, stewardess *f*

aeronáutica *nf* : aeronautics

aeronáutico, -ca *adj* : aeronautical

aeronave *nf* : aircraft

aeropostal *adj* : airmail

aeropuerto *nm* : airport

aerosol *nm* : aerosol, aerosol spray

aeróstata *nmf* : balloonist

aerotransportado, -da *adj* : airborne

aerotransportar *vt* : to airlift

afabilidad *nf* : affability

afable *adj* : affable — **afablemente** *adv*

afamado, -da *adj* : well-known, famous

afán *nm, pl* **afanes** **1** ANHELO : eagerness, desire **2** EMPEÑO : effort, determination

afanador, -dora *n Mex* : cleaning person, cleaner

afanarse *vr* : to toil, to strive

afanosamente *adv* : zealously, industriously, busily

afanoso, -sa *adj* **1** : eager, industrious **2** : arduous, hard

afear *vt* : to make ugly, to disfigure

afección *nf, pl* **-ciones** **1** : fondness, affection **2** : illness, complaint

afectación *nf, pl* **-ciones** : affectation

afectado, -da *adj* **1** : affected, mannered **2** : influenced **3** : afflicted **4** : feigned

afectar *vt* **1** : to affect **2** : to upset **3** : to feign, to pretend

afectísimo, -ma *adj* **suyo afectísimo** : yours truly

afectivo, -va *adj* : emotional

afecto[1], **-ta** *adj* **1** : affected, afflicted **2** : fond, affectionate

afecto[2] *nm* CARIÑO : affection

afectuoso, -sa *adj* CARIÑOSO : affectionate — **afectuosamente** *adv*

afeitadora *nf* : shaver, electric razor

afeitar *vt* RASURAR : to shave — **afeitarse** *vr*

afelpado, -da *adj* : plush

afeminado, -da *adj* : effeminate

aferrado, -da *adj* : obstinate, stubborn

aferrarse {55} *vr* : to cling, to hold on

affidávit *nm, pl* **-dávits** : affidavit

afgano, -na *adj & n* : Afghan

AFI *nm* (Alfabeto Fonético Internacional) : IPA

afianzar {21} *vt* **1** : to secure, to strengthen **2** : to guarantee, to vouch for — **afianzarse** *vr* ESTABLECERSE : to establish oneself — **afianzamiento** *nm*

afiche *nm* : poster

afición *nf, pl* **-ciones** **1** : enthusiasm, penchant, fondness ⟨afición al deporte : love of sports⟩ **2** PASATIEMPO : hobby

aficionado[1], **-da** *adj* ENTUSIASTA : enthusiastic, keen

aficionado[2], **-da** *n* **1** ENTUSIASTA : enthusiast, fan **2** : amateur

aficionar *vt* : to interest ⟨aficionar a alguien a algo : to get someone interested in something⟩ — **aficionarse** *vr*

áfido *nm* : aphid

afiebrado, -da *adj* : feverish

afilado, -da *adj* **1** : sharp **2** : long, pointed ⟨una nariz afilada : a sharp nose⟩

afilador *nm* : sharpener

afilalápices *nms & pl* : pencil sharpener

afilar *vt* : to sharpen

afiliación *nf, pl* **-ciones** : affiliation

afiliado[1], **-da** *adj* : affiliated

afiliado[2], **-da** *n* : member

afiliarse *vr* ∼ **a** : to become a member of, to join

afín *adj, pl* **afines** **1** PARECIDO : related, similar ⟨la biología y disciplinas afines : biology and related disciplines⟩ **2** PRÓXIMO : adjacent, nearby

afinación *nf, pl* **-ciones** **1** : tune-up **2** : tuning (of an instrument)

afinador, -dora *n* : tuner (of musical instruments)

afinar *vt* **1** : to perfect, to refine **2** : to tune (an instrument) — *vi* : to sing or play in tune

afincarse {72} *vr* : to establish oneself, to settle in

afinidad *nf* : affinity, similarity

afirmación *nf, pl* **-ciones** **1** : statement **2** : affirmation

afirmar *vt* **1** : to state, to affirm **2** REFORZAR : to make firm, to strengthen

afirmativo, -va *adj* : affirmative — **afirmativamente** *adv*

aflicción *nf, pl* **-ciones** DESCONSUELO, PESAR : grief, sorrow

afligido, -da *adj* : grief-stricken, sorrowful

afligir {35} *vt* **1** : to distress, to upset **2** : to afflict — **afligirse** *vr* : to grieve

aflojar *vt* **1** : to loosen, to slacken **2** *fam* : to pay up, to fork over — *vi* : to slacken, to ease up — **aflojarse** *vr* : to become loose, to slacken

aflorar *vi* : to come to the surface, to emerge

afluencia *nf* **1** : flow, influx **2** : abundance, plenty

afluente *nm* : tributary

afluir {41} *vi* **1** : to flock ⟨la gente afluía a la frontera : people were flocking to the border⟩ **2** : to flow

afónico, -ca *adj* **quedarse afónico** : to lose one's voice, to get laryngitis

aforismo *nm* : aphorism

aforo *nm* **1** : appraisal, assessment **2** : maximum capacity (of a theater, highway, etc.)

afortunado, -da *adj* : fortunate, lucky — **afortunadamente** *adv*

afrecho *nm* : bran, mash

afrenta *nf* : affront, insult

afrentar *vt* : to affront, to dishonor, to insult

africano, -na *adj & n* : African

afroamericano, -na *adj & n* : Afro-American

afrodisíaco *or* **afrodisíaco** *nm* : aphrodisiac

afrontamiento *nm* : confrontation

afrontar *vt* : to confront, to face up to

afrutado, -da *adj* : fruity

aftershave ['afterʃeif] *nm* : aftershave

afuera *adv* **1** (*indicating direction*) : out, outside ⟨¡afuera! : get out!⟩ **2** (*indicating location*) FUERA : out, outside ⟨estoy aquí afuera : I'm out here, I'm outside⟩ **3 afuera de** : out of, outside

afueras *nfpl* ALEDAÑOS : outskirts

agachadiza *nf* : snipe (bird)

agachar *vt* : to lower (a part of the body) ⟨agachar la cabeza : to bow one's head⟩ — **agacharse** *vr* : to crouch, to stoop, to bend down

agalla *nf* **1** BRANQUIA : gill **2 tener agallas** *fam* : to have guts, to have courage

agarradera *nf* ASA, ASIDERO : handle, grip

agarrado, -da *adj fam* : cheap, stingy

agarrar *vt* **1** : to grab, to grasp **2** : to catch, to take — *vi* **agarrar y** *fam* : to do (something) abruptly ⟨el día siguiente agarró y se fue : the next day he up and left⟩ — **agarrarse** *vr* **1** : to hold on, to cling **2** *fam* : to get into a fight ⟨se agarraron a golpes : they came to blows⟩

agarre *nm* : grip, grasp

agarrotarse *vr* **1** : to stiffen up **2** : to seize up

agasajar *vt* : to fête, to wine and dine

agasajo *nm* : lavish attention

ágata *nf* : agate

agazaparse *vr* **1** AGACHARSE : to crouch **2** : to hide

agencia *nf* : agency, office

agenciar *vt* : to obtain, to procure — **agenciarse** *vr* : to manage, to get by

agenda *nf* **1** : agenda **2** : appointment book

agénero *adj* : agender ⟨las personas agénero : agender people⟩

agente *nmf* **1** : agent **2 agente de viajes** : travel agent **3 agente de bolsa** : stockbroker **4 agente de tráfico** : traffic officer

agigantado, -da *adj* GIGANTESCO : gigantic

agigantar *vt* **1** : to increase greatly, to enlarge **2** : to exaggerate

ágil *adj* **1** : agile, nimble **2** : sharp, lively (of a response, etc.) — **ágilmente** *adv*

agilidad *nf* : agility, nimbleness

agilizar {21} *vt* ACELERAR : to expedite, to speed up

agitación *nf, pl* **-ciones 1** : agitation **2** NERVIOSISMO : nervousness

agitado, -da *adj* **1** : agitated, excited **2** : choppy, rough, turbulent

agitador, -dora *n* PROVOCADOR : agitator

agitar *vt* **1** : to agitate, to shake **2** : to wave, to flap **3** : to stir up — **agitarse** *vr* **1** : to toss about, to flap around **2** : to get upset

aglomeración *nf, pl* **-ciones 1** : conglomeration, mass **2** GENTÍO : crowd

aglomerar *vt* : to cluster, to amass — **aglomerarse** *vr* : to crowd together

aglutinar *vt* : to bring together, to bind

agnóstico, -ca *adj & n* : agnostic

agobiado, -da *adj* : weary, worn-out, weighted down

agobiante *adj* **1** : exhausting, overwhelming **2** : stifling, oppressive

agobiar *vt* **1** OPRIMIR : to oppress, to burden **2** ABRUMAR : to overwhelm **3** : to wear out, to exhaust

agobio *nm Spain fam* : burden, pressure

agolparse *vr* : to crowd together

agonía *nf* : agony, death throes

agonizante *adj* : dying

agonizar {21} *vi* **1** : to be dying **2** : to be in agony **3** : to dim, to fade

agorero, -ra *adj* : ominous

agostar *vt* **1** : to parch **2** : to wither — **agostarse** *vr*

agosto *nm* **1** : August ⟨el cinco de agosto : (on) August fifth⟩ **2 hacer uno su agosto** : to make a fortune, to make a killing

agotado, -da *adj* **1** : exhausted, used up **2** : sold out **3** FATIGADO : worn-out, tired

agotador, -dora *adj* : exhausting

agotamiento *nm* FATIGA : exhaustion

agotar *vt* **1** : to exhaust, to use up **2** : to weary, to wear out — **agotarse** *vr*

agraciado¹, -da *adj* **1** : attractive **2** : fortunate

agraciado², -da *n* : winner

agradable *adj* **1** GRATO, PLACENTERO : pleasant, agreeable **2 ser agradable a la vista** : to be easy on the eye(s) — **agradablemente** *adv*

agradar *vi* : to be pleasing ⟨nos agradó mucho el resultado : we were very pleased with the result⟩

agradecer {53} *vt* **1** : to be grateful for **2** : to thank

agradecido, -da *adj* : grateful, thankful

agradecimiento *nm* : gratitude, thankfulness

agrado *nm* **1** GUSTO : taste, liking ⟨no es de su agrado : it's not to his liking⟩ **2** : graciousness, helpfulness **3 con** ～ : with pleasure, willingly ⟨lo haré con agrado : I will be happy to do it⟩

agrandar *vt* **1** : to exaggerate **2** : to enlarge — **agrandarse** *vr*

agrario, -ria *adj* : agrarian, agricultural

agravación *nf, pl* **-ciones** : aggravation, worsening

agravante *adj* : aggravating

agravar *vt* **1** : to increase (weight), to make heavier **2** EMPEORAR : to aggravate, to worsen — **agravarse** *vr*

agraviar *vt* INJURIAR, OFENDER : to offend, to insult

agravio *nm* INJURIA : affront, offense, insult

agredir {1} *vt* : to assail, to attack

agregado¹, -da *n* **1** : attaché **2** : assistant professor

agregado² *nm* **1** : aggregate **2** AÑADIDURA : addition, something added

agregar {52} *vt* **1** AÑADIR : to add, to attach **2** : to appoint — **agregarse** *vr* : to join

agresión *nf, pl* **-siones 1** : aggression **2** ATAQUE : attack

agresividad *nf* : aggressiveness, aggression

agresivo, -va *adj* : aggressive — **agresivamente** *adv*

agresor¹, -sora *adj* : hostile, attacking

agresor², -sora *n* **1** : aggressor **2** : assailant, attacker

agreste *adj* **1** CAMPESTRE : rural **2** : wild, untamed

agriar *vt* **1** : to sour, to make sour **2** : to embitter — **agriarse** *vr* : to turn sour

agrícola *adj* : agricultural

agricultor, -tora *n* : farmer, grower

agricultura *nf* : agriculture, farming

agridulce *adj* **1** : bittersweet **2** : sweet-and-sour

agrietar *vt* : to crack — **agrietarse** *vr* **1** : to crack **2** : to become chapped

agrimensor, -sora *n* : surveyor

agrimensura *nf* : surveying

agrio, agria *adj* **1** ÁCIDO : sour **2** : caustic, acrimonious

agriparse *vr* : to catch the flu

agroindustria *nf* : agribusiness

agropecuario, -ria *adj* : pertaining to livestock and agriculture

agrupación *nf, pl* **-ciones** GRUPO : group, association

agrupamiento *nm* : grouping, concentration

agrupar *vt* : to group together

agua *nf* **1** : water **2 agua bendita** : holy water **3 agua corriente** : running water **4 agua dulce/salada** : fresh/salt water **5 agua mineral** : mineral water **6 agua oxigenada** : hydrogen peroxide **7 agua potable** : drinking water **8 aguas** *nfpl* : waters ⟨en aguas internacionales : in international waters⟩ **9 aguas negras/residuales** : sewage **10 como agua para chocolate** *Mex fam* : furious **11 echar aguas** *Mex fam* : to keep an eye

out, to be on the lookout **12 ¡aguas!**
Mex fam : look out!

aguacate *nm* : avocado

aguacero *nm* : shower, downpour

aguado, -da *adj* **1** DILUIDO : diluted **2**
CA, Col, Mex fam : soft, flabby **3** *Mex,*
Peru fam : dull, boring

aguafiestas *nmfs & pl* : killjoy, stick-in-
the-mud, spoilsport

aguafuerte *nf* : etching

aguamarina *nf* **1** : aquamarine **2 color**
aguamarina : aqua

aguanieve *nf* : sleet ⟨caer aguanieve : to
be sleeting⟩

aguantar *vt* **1** SOPORTAR : to bear, to tolerate **2** : to hold ⟨aguántame la puerta
: hold the door for me⟩ **3** : to take, to
withstand (weight, etc.) **4** DURAR : to
last **5 aguantar las ganas (de hacer**
algo) : to resist the urge (to do something) — *vi* **1** : to tolerate ⟨no aguanto
más : I can't take it anymore⟩ **2** : to
hold out, to last **3** : to hold (under pressure, etc.) — **aguantarse** *vr* **1** : to resign oneself **2** : to restrain oneself

aguante *nm* **1** TOLERANCIA : tolerance,
patience **2** RESISTENCIA : endurance,
strength

aguar {10} *vt* **1** : to water down, to dilute
2 aguar la fiesta *fam* : to spoil the party

aguardar *vt* ESPERAR : to wait for, to
await — *vi* : to be in store

aguardiente *nm* : clear brandy

aguarrás *nm* : turpentine

agudeza *nf* **1** : keenness, sharpness **2**
: sharpness (of a sound) **3** : witticism

agudizar {21} *vt* : to intensify, to heighten

agudo, -da *adj* **1** : sharp (of a point, etc.)
2 : acute (of an angle), sharp (of an increase) **3** : acute (of an illness), severe
(of a crisis) ⟨un dolor agudo : a sharp
pain⟩ **4** ESTRIDENTE : shrill **5** : sharp
(of eyes or ears) **6** PERSPICAZ : clever,
shrewd **7** : acute (of an accent) — **agu-**
damente *adv*

agüero *nm* AUGURIO, PRESAGIO : augury,
omen

aguijón *nm, pl* **-jones 1** : stinger (of a
bee, etc.) **2** : goad

aguijonear *vt* : to goad

águila *nf* **1** : eagle **2 águila o sol** *Mex*
: heads or tails

aguileño, -ña *adj* : aquiline

aguilera *nf* : aerie, eagle's nest

aguilón *nm, pl* **-lones** : gable

aguinaldo *nm* **1** : Christmas bonus, year-
end bonus **2** *PRi, Ven* : Christmas carol

agüitarse *vr Mex fam* : to have the blues,
to feel discouraged

aguja *nf* **1** : needle **2** : steeple, spire

agujerear *vt* : to make a hole in, to pierce

agujero *nm* **1** : hole **2 agujero negro**
: black hole (in astronomy)

agujeta *nf* **1** *Mex* : shoelace **2 agujetas**
nfpl : muscular soreness or stiffness

agusanado, -da *adj* : wormy

aguzar {21} *vt* **1** : to sharpen ⟨aguzar el
ingenio : to sharpen one's wits⟩ **2 agu-**
zar el oído : to prick up one's ears

ah *interj* : oh!

ahí *adv* **1** : there ⟨ahí está : there it is⟩
⟨pasé por ahí : I went by/through there⟩
⟨ahí está el problema : therein lies the
problem⟩ **2** : then ⟨desde ahí : since
then⟩ **3 por** ~ : (around) there ⟨lo he
visto por ahí : I've seen him around
there⟩ ⟨debe estar por ahí : it must be
there somewhere⟩ ⟨en 1950 o por ahí
: in 1950 or thereabouts⟩ **4 de ahí**
: hence **5 de ahí que** : with the result
that, so that

ahijado, -da *n* : godchild, godson *m*, goddaughter *f*

ahijar {5} *vt* : to adopt (a child)

ahínco *nm* : eagerness, zeal

ahogar {52} *vt* **1** : to drown **2** : to
smother **3** : to choke back, to stifle —
ahogarse *vr*

ahogo *nm* : breathlessness, suffocation

ahondar *vt* : to deepen — *vi* : to elaborate,
to go into detail

ahora *adv* **1** : now ⟨ahora voy : I'm coming now⟩ **2** : just (now) ⟨como te decía
ahora . . . : as I was just telling you
(now) . . .⟩ **3 ahora bien** : however **4**
ahora mismo : right now **5 hasta** ~
: so far **6 por** ~ : for the time being

ahorcar {72} *vt* : to hang, to kill by hanging — **ahorcarse** *vr*

ahorita *adv fam* : right now, right away

ahorquillado, -da *adj* : forked

ahorrador, -dora *adj* : thrifty

ahorrante *nmf Chile, CoRi, DomRep, Hon*
AHORRISTA : investor (in savings)

ahorrar *vt* **1** : to save (money) **2** : to
spare, to conserve — *vi* : to save up —
ahorrarse *vr* : to spare oneself

ahorrativo, -va *adj* : thrifty, frugal

ahorrista *nmf Arg, Uru, Ven* AHORRANTE
: investor (in savings)

ahorro *nm* : saving ⟨cuenta de ahorro(s)
: savings account⟩

ahuecar {72} *vt* **1** : to hollow out **2** : to
cup (one's hands) **3** : to plump up, to
fluff up

ahuizote *nm Mex fam* : annoying person,
pain in the neck

ahumado, -da *adj* : smoked

ahumar {8} *vt* : to smoke, to cure

ahuyentar *vt* **1** : to scare away, to chase
away **2** : to banish, to dispel ⟨ahuyentar
las dudas : to dispel doubts⟩

airado, -da *adj* FURIOSO : angry, irate

airar {5} *vt* : to make angry, to anger

airbag ['erbag] *nm, pl* **airbags** *or* **airbag**
: airbag

aire *nm* **1** : air ⟨aire frío : cold air⟩ ⟨un
aire caliente : a hot breeze⟩ **2** : air ⟨un
aire de autoridad : an air of authority⟩
3 aire acondicionado : air-conditioning
4 al aire libre : in the open air **5 darse**
aires : to give oneself airs **6 en el aire**
: on the air, broadcasting **7 en el aire**
: up in the air, unresolved

airear *vt* : to air, to air out — **airearse** *vr*
: to get some fresh air

airoso, -sa *adj* **1** : elegant, graceful **2**
salir airoso : to come out winning

aislado, -da *adj* : isolated, alone

aislador *nm* : insulator (part)

aislamiento *nm* 1 : isolation 2 : insulation

aislante *nm* : insulator, nonconductor

aislar {5} *vt* 1 : to isolate 2 : to insulate

ajado, -da *adj* 1 : worn, shabby 2 : wrinkled, crumpled

ajar *vt* : to wear out, to spoil

ajardinar *vt* : to landscape

ajedrecista *nmf* : chess player

ajedrez *nm, pl* **-dreces** 1 : chess 2 : chess set

ajeno, -na *adj* 1 : alien 2 : of another, of others ⟨propiedad ajena : somebody else's property⟩ 3 ~ **a** : foreign to 4 ~ **de** : devoid of, free from

ajetreado, -da *adj* : hectic, busy

ajetrearse *vr* : to bustle about, to rush around

ajetreo *nm* : hustle and bustle, fuss

ají *nm, pl* **ajíes** : chili pepper

ajillo *nm* **al ajillo** : in a garlic sauce

ajo *nm* : garlic

ajonjolí *nm, pl* **-líes** : sesame

ajuar *nm* : trousseau

ajustable *adj* : adjustable

ajustado, -da *adj* 1 CEÑIDO : tight, tight-fitting 2 : close, tight ⟨una ajustada victoria : a close victory⟩

ajustar *vt* 1 : to adjust (wages, settings, etc.) 2 ADECUAR : to adapt 3 : to tighten (a bolt, etc.) 4 : to fit (a part) 5 : to take in (clothing) 6 : to fix, to set (a price) 7 SALDAR : to settle — *vi* : to fit — **ajustarse** *vr* : to fit, to conform

ajuste *nm* 1 : adjustment 2 : tightening

ajusticiar *vt* EJECUTAR : to execute, to put to death

al *prep contraction of* A *and* EL → **a²**

ala *nf* 1 : wing 2 : brim (of a hat) 3 : end (in football) ⟨ala cerrada : tight end⟩

Alá *nm* : Allah

alabanza *nf* ELOGIO : praise

alabar *vt* : to praise — **alabarse** *vr* : to boast

alabastro *nm* : alabaster

alabear *vt* : to warp — **alabearse** *vr*

alabeo *nm* : warp, warping

alacena *nf* : cupboard, larder

alacrán *nm, pl* **-cranes** ESCORPIÓN : scorpion

ala delta *nf* 1 : hang glider 2 → **aladeltismo**

aladeltismo *nm* : hang gliding

alado, -da *adj* : winged

alambique *nm* : still (to distill alcohol)

alambrada *nf* : wire fence

alambre *nm* 1 : wire 2 **alambre de púas** : barbed wire

alameda *nf* 1 : poplar grove 2 : tree-lined avenue

álamo *nm* 1 : poplar 2 **álamo temblón** : aspen

alar *nm* : eaves *pl*

alarde *nm* 1 : show, display 2 **hacer alarde de** : to make show of, to boast about

alardear *vi* PRESUMIR : to boast, to brag

alargado, -da *adj* : elongated, slender

alargador *nm* : extension cord

alargamiento *nm* : lengthening, extension, elongation

alargar {52} *vt* 1 : to extend, to lengthen 2 PROLONGAR : to prolong — **alargarse** *vr*

alargue *nm* 1 *Arg* → **alargador** 2 *Arg, Chile, Uru* : overtime (in sports)

alarido *nm* : howl, shriek

alarma *nf* : alarm

alarmante *adj* : alarming — **alarmantemente** *adv*

alarmar *vt* : to alarm

alazán *nm, pl* **-zanes** : sorrel (color or animal)

alba *nf* AMANECER : dawn, daybreak

albacea *nmf* TESTAMENTARIO : executor, executrix *f*

albahaca *nf* : basil

albanés, -nesa *adj & n, mpl* **-neses** : Albanian

albañil *nmf* : bricklayer, mason

albañilería *nf* : bricklaying, masonry

albaricoque *nm* : apricot

albatros *nm* : albatross

albedrío *nm* : will ⟨libre albedrío : free will⟩

alberca *nf* 1 : reservoir, tank 2 *Mex* : swimming pool

albergar {52} *vt* ALOJAR : to house, to lodge, to shelter

albergue *nm* 1 : shelter, refuge 2 : hostel

albino, -na *adj & n* : albino — **albinismo** *nm*

albóndiga *nf* : meatball

albor *nm* 1 : dawning, beginning 2 BLANCURA : whiteness

alborada *nf* : dawn

alborear *v impers* : to dawn

alborotado, -da *adj* 1 : excited, agitated 2 : rowdy, unruly

alborotador¹, -dora *adj* 1 : noisy, boisterous 2 : rowdy, unruly

alborotador², -dora *n* : agitator, troublemaker, rioter

alborotar *vt* 1 : to excite, to agitate 2 : to incite, to stir up — **alborotarse** *vr* 1 : to get excited 2 : to riot

alboroto *nm* 1 : disturbance, ruckus 2 MOTÍN : riot

alborozado, -da *adj* : jubilant

alborozar {21} *vt* : to gladden, to cheer

alborozo *nm* : joy, elation

álbum *nm* : album ⟨álbum de fotos : photo album⟩ ⟨álbum de recortes : scrapbook⟩

albúmina *nf* : albumin

albur *nm* 1 : chance, risk 2 *Mex* : pun

alca *nf* : auk

alcachofa *nf* : artichoke

alcahuete, -ta *n* CHISMOSO : gossip

alcaide *nm* : warden (in a prison)

alcalde, -desa *n* : mayor

alcaldía *nf* 1 : mayor's office (job) 2 AYUNTAMIENTO : city hall

álcali *nm* : alkali

alcalino, -na *adj* : alkaline — **alcalinidad** *nf*

alcance *nm* 1 : reach 2 : range, scope

alcancía *nf* 1 : piggy bank, money box 2 : collection box (for alms, etc.)

alcanfor *nm* : camphor
alcantarilla *nf* CLOACA : sewer, drain
alcantarillado *nm* : sewer system
alcanzar {21} *vt* **1** : to reach **2** : to catch up with **3** LOGRAR : to achieve, to attain — *vi* **1** DAR : to suffice, to be enough **2** ~ **a** : to manage to
alcaparra *nf* : caper
alcapurria *nf PRi* : stuffed fritter made with taro and green banana
alcaravea *nf* : caraway
alcayata *nf* : hook
alcázar *nm* : fortress, castle
alce[1], etc. → **alzar**
alce[2] *nm* : moose, European elk
alcista *adj* : upward (of a trend), bullish (of markets)
alcoba *nf* : bedroom
alcohol *nm* : alcohol
alcoholemia *nf* **prueba de alcoholemia** : sobriety test
alcohólico, -ca *adj & n* : alcoholic
alcoholismo *nm* : alcoholism
alcoholizarse {21} *vr* : to become an alcoholic
alcornoque *nm* **1** : cork oak **2** *fam* : idiot, fool
alcurnia *nf* : ancestry, lineage
aldaba *nf* : door knocker
aldea *nf* : village
aldeano[1], **-na** *adj* : village, rustic
aldeano[2], **-na** *n* : villager
aleación *nf, pl* **-ciones** : alloy
alear *vt* : to alloy
aleatorio, -ria *adj* : random, fortuitous — **aleatoriamente** *adv*
alebrestar *vt* : to excite, to make nervous — **alebrestarse** *vr*
aleccionar *vt* : to lecture, to teach
aledaño, -ña *adj* : bordering, neighboring
aledaños *nmpl* AFUERAS : outskirts, surrounding area
alegación *nf, pl* **-ciones** **1** *CA, Car* : allegation **2** : statement (in law)
alegar {52} *vt* : to assert, to allege — *vi* DISCUTIR : to argue
alegato *nm* **1** : allegation, claim **2** *Mex* : argument, summation (in law) **3** : argument, dispute
alegoría *nf* : allegory
alegórico, -ca *adj* : allegorical
alegrar *vt* : to make happy, to cheer up ⟨me alegra mucho que . . . : I'm very happy that . . .⟩ — **alegrarse** *vr* : to be glad, to be happy ⟨me alegro de (ver) que . . . : I'm glad (to see) that . . .⟩ ⟨me alegro por ti : I'm happy for you⟩
alegre *adj* **1** : glad, cheerful **2** : colorful, bright **3** *fam* : tipsy
alegremente *adv* : happily, cheerfully
alegría *nf* : joy, cheer, happiness
alejado, -da *adj* : remote
alejamiento *nm* **1** : removal, separation **2** : estrangement
alejar *vt* **1** : to remove, to move away **2** : to estrange, to alienate — **alejarse** *vr* **1** : to move away, to stray **2** : to drift apart
alelado, -da *adj* **1** : bewildered, stupefied **2** : foolish, stupid

aleluya *interj* : hallelujah!, alleluia!
alemán[1], **-mana** *adj & n, mpl* **-manes** : German
alemán[2] *nm* : German (language)
alentador, -dora *adj* : encouraging
alentar {55} *vt* : to encourage, to inspire — *vi* : to breathe
alerce *nm* : larch
alérgeno *nm* : allergen
alergia *nf* : allergy
alérgico, -ca *adj* : allergic
alero *nm* **1** : eaves *pl* **2** : forward (in basketball)
alerón *nm, pl* **-rones** : aileron
alerta[1] *adv* : on the alert
alerta[2] *adj & nf* : alert
alertar *vt* : to alert
aleta *nf* **1** : fin **2** : flipper **3** : small wing
aletargado, -da *adj* : lethargic, sluggish, torpid
aletargarse {52} *vr* : to feel drowsy, to become lethargic
aletear *vi* : to flutter, to flap one's wings
aleteo *nm* : flapping, flutter
alevín *nm, pl* **-vines** **1** : fry, young fish **2** PRINCIPIANTE : beginner
alevosía *nf* **1** : treachery **2** : premeditation
alevoso, -sa *adj* : treacherous
alfabético, -ca *adj* : alphabetical — **alfabéticamente** *adv*
alfabetismo *nm* : literacy
alfabetizado, -da *adj* : literate
alfabetizar {21} *vt* : to alphabetize — **alfabetización** *nf*
alfabeto *nm* : alphabet
alfalfa *nf* : alfalfa
alfanje *nm* : cutlass
alfarería *nf* : pottery
alfarero, -ra *n* : potter
alféizar *nm* : sill, windowsill
alfeñique *nm fam* : wimp, weakling
alférez *nmf, pl* **-reces** **1** : second lieutenant **2** : ensign
alfil *nm* : bishop (in chess)
alfiler *nm* **1** : pin **2** BROCHE : brooch
alfiletero *nm* : pincushion
alfombra *nf* : carpet, rug
alfombrado *nm* : carpeting
alfombrar *vt* : to carpet
alfombrilla *nf* **1** : small rug, mat **2** **alfombrilla de/para ratón** : mouse pad
alforfón *nm, pl* **-fones** : buckwheat
alforja *nf* : saddlebag
alforza *nf* : pleat, tuck
alga *nf* **1** : aquatic plant, alga **2** : seaweed
algarabía *nf* **1** : gibberish, babble **2** : hubbub, uproar
álgebra *nf* : algebra
algebraico, -ca *adj* : algebraic
álgido, -da *adj* **1** : critical, decisive **2** : icy cold
algo[1] *adv* : somewhat, rather ⟨estaba algo nervioso : he was a little nervous⟩
algo[2] *pron* **1** : something, anything ⟨¿pasa algo? : is something wrong?⟩ ⟨¿dijo algo más? : did he say anything else?⟩ ⟨por algo lo escogió : she chose him for a reason⟩ ⟨algo para/de comer

: something to eat⟩ **2** ~ **de** : some, a little ⟨tengo algo de dinero : I've got some money⟩ **3 (o) algo así** : (or) something like that
algodón *nm, pl* **-dones** : cotton
algodoncillo *nm* : milkweed
algodón de azúcar *nm* : cotton candy
algodonero¹, -ra *adj* : cotton
algodonero², -ra *n* : cotton farmer
algoritmo *nm* : algorithm
alguacil *nm* : constable
alguien *pron* **1** : somebody, someone ⟨alguien gritó : someone shouted⟩ ⟨hablaba con alguien : he was talking to somebody⟩ **2** : anybody, anyone ⟨¿hay alguien en casa? : is there anybody home?⟩
alguno¹, -na *adj* (**algún** before masculine singular nouns) **1** : some, any ⟨en algunos casos : in some cases⟩ ⟨algún día : someday, one day⟩ ⟨algunas semanas después : a few weeks later⟩ ⟨¿alguna pregunta? : any questions?⟩ **2** (*in negative constructions*) : not any, not at all ⟨no tengo noticia alguna : I have no news at all⟩ **3 algún que otro, alguna que otra** : the odd, the occasional
alguno², -na *pron* **1** : one, any ⟨alguno de los libros/niños : one of the books/children⟩ ⟨alguno se ofendió : someone got offended⟩ ⟨¿falta alguno? : are there any missing?⟩ **2 algunos, -nas** *pl* : some, a few, any ⟨algunos de los libros/niños : some of the books/children⟩ ⟨algunos dicen que . . . : some (people) say that . . .⟩ ⟨¿hay algunos que te gusten? : are there any that you like?⟩
alhaja *nf* : jewel, gem
alhajar *vt* : to adorn with jewels
alhajero *nm* : jewelry box
alharaca *nf* : fuss
alhelí *nm, pl* **alhelíes** : wallflower
aliado¹, -da *adj* : allied
aliado², -da *n* : ally
alianza *nf* : alliance
aliar {85} *vt* : to ally — **aliarse** *vr* : to form an alliance, to ally oneself
alias *adv & nm* : alias
alicaído, -da *adj* : depressed, discouraged
alicates *nmpl* PINZAS : pliers
aliciente *nm* **1** INCENTIVO : incentive **2** ATRACCIÓN : attraction
alienación *nf, pl* **-ciones** : alienation, derangement
alienar *vt* ENAJENAR : to alienate
aliento *nm* **1** : breath **2** : courage, strength **3 dar aliento a** : to encourage
aligerar *vt* **1** : to lighten **2** ACELERAR : to hasten, to quicken
alijo *nm* : cache, consignment (of contraband)
alimaña *nf* : pest, vermin
alimentación *nf, pl* **-ciones** **1** NUTRICIÓN : nutrition, nourishment **2** : feed ⟨mecanismo de alimentación : feed (mechanism)⟩
alimentar *vt* **1** NUTRIR : to feed, to nourish **2** MANTENER : to support (a family) **3** FOMENTAR : to nurture, to foster — **alimentarse** *vr* ~ **con** : to live on

alimentario, -ria → **alimenticio**
alimenticio, -cia *adj* **1** : nutritional, food, dietary **2** : nutritious, nourishing
alimento *nm* : food, nourishment
alineación *nf, pl* **-ciones** **1** : alignment **2** : lineup (in sports)
alineamiento *nm* : alignment
alinear *vt* **1** : to align **2** : to line up — **alinearse** *vr* **1** : to fall in, to line up **2** ~ **con** : to align oneself with
aliñar *vt* **1** : to dress (salad) **2** CONDIMENTAR : to season
aliño *nm* : seasoning, dressing
alipús *nm, pl* **-puses** *Mex fam* : booze, drink
alisar *vt* : to smooth
aliscafo *or* **alíscafo** *nm* : hydrofoil
alistamiento *nm* : enlistment, recruitment
alistar *vt* **1** : to recruit **2** : to make ready — **alistarse** *vr* : to join up, to enlist
aliteración *nf, pl* **-ciones** : alliteration
aliviar *vt* MITIGAR : to relieve, to alleviate, to soothe — **aliviarse** *vr* : to recover, to get better
alivio *nm* : relief
aljaba *nf* : quiver (for arrows)
aljibe *nm* : cistern, well
allá *adv* **1** : there, over there ⟨allá arriba : up there⟩ ⟨allá en Cuba : over (there) in Cuba⟩ **2** ~ **por** : back in ⟨allá por los años 80 : back in the 80's⟩ **3 allá tú** : that's up to you **4 ¡allá voy!** : here I come!, here I go! **5 más allá** : farther away **6 más allá de** : beyond
allanamiento *nm* **1** : (police) raid **2 allanamiento de morada** : breaking and entering
allanar *vt* **1** : to raid, to search **2** : to resolve, to solve **3** : to smooth, to level off/out — **allanarse** *vr* : to even out, to level off/out
allegado¹, -da *adj* : close, intimate
allegado², -da *n* : close friend, relation ⟨parientes y allegados : friends and relations⟩
allegar {52} *vt* : to gather, to collect
allende¹ *adv* : beyond, on the other side
allende² *prep* : beyond ⟨allende las montañas : beyond the mountains⟩
allí *adv* : there, over there ⟨todos están allí : everyone's there⟩ ⟨allí mismo : right there⟩ ⟨hasta allí : up to that point⟩
alma *nf* **1** : soul **2** : person, human being **3 no tener alma** : to be pitiless **4 tener el alma en un hilo** : to have one's heart in one's mouth
almacén *nm, pl* **-cenes** **1** BODEGA : warehouse, storehouse **2** TIENDA : shop, store **3 gran almacén** *Spain* : department store
almacenaje → **almacenamiento**
almacenamiento *nm* : storage ⟨almacenamiento de datos : data storage⟩
almacenar *vt* : to store, to put in storage
almacenero, -ra *n* : shopkeeper
almacenista *nm* MAYORISTA : wholesaler
almádena *nf* : sledgehammer
almanaque *nm* : almanac
almeja *nf* : clam

almendra *nf* **1** : almond **2** : kernel
almendro *nm* : almond tree
almiar *nm* : haystack
almíbar *nm* : syrup
almidón *nm, pl* **-dones** : starch
almidonar *vt* : to starch
alminar *nm* MINARETE : minaret
almirantazgo *nm* : admiralty
almirante *nm* : admiral
almizcle *nm* : musk
almohada *nf* : pillow
almohadilla *nf* **1** : small pillow, cushion **2** : bag, base (in baseball) **3 almohadilla de/para ratón** : mouse pad
almohadón *nm, pl* **-dones** : bolster, cushion
almohazar {21} *vt* : to curry (a horse)
almoneda *nf* SUBASTA : auction
almorranas *nfpl* HEMORROIDES : hemorrhoids, piles
almorzar {36} *vi* : to have lunch — *vt* : to have for lunch
almuerzo *nm* : lunch
alocado, -da *adj* **1** : crazy **2** : wild, reckless **3** : silly, scatterbrained
alocución *nf, pl* **-ciones** : speech, address
áloe *or* **aloe** *nm* : aloe
alojamiento *nm* : lodging, accommodations *pl*
alojar *vt* ALBERGAR : to house, to lodge — **alojarse** *vr* : to lodge, to room
alondra *nf* : lark, skylark
alpaca *nf* : alpaca
alpargata *nf Arg, Spain, Uru, Ven* : espadrille
alpinismo *nm* : mountain climbing, mountaineering
alpinista *nmf* : mountain climber
alpino, -na *adj* : Alpine, alpine
alpiste *nm* : birdseed
alquilar *vt* ARRENDAR : to rent, to lease
alquiler *nm* ARRENDAMIENTO : rent, rental
alquimia *nf* : alchemy
alquimista *nmf* : alchemist
alquitrán *nm, pl* **-tranes** BREA : tar
alquitranar *vt* : to tar, to cover with tar
alrededor *adv* **1** : around ⟨lo que sucede alrededor : the things happening around us/you (etc.)⟩ **2** ~ **de** : around ⟨la Tierra gira alrededor del sol : the Earth revolves around the sun⟩ **3** ~ **de** : about, around ⟨alrededor de quince personas : about fifteen people⟩ ⟨alrededor de diciembre : around December⟩ **4 a mi/tu (etc.) alrededor** : around me/you (etc.)
alrededores *nmpl* ALEDAÑOS : surroundings, outskirts
alta *nf* **1** : admission, entry, enrollment **2 dar de alta** : to release, to discharge (a patient)
altanería *nf* ALTIVEZ, ARROGANCIA : arrogance, haughtiness
altanero, -ra *adj* ALTIVO, ARROGANTE : arrogant, haughty — **altaneramente** *adv*
altar *nm* : altar
altavoz *nm, pl* **-voces** ALTOPARLANTE : loudspeaker

alteración *nf, pl* **-ciones** **1** MODIFICACIÓN : alteration, modification **2** PERTURBACIÓN : disturbance, disruption
alterado, -da *adj* : upset
alterar *vt* **1** MODIFICAR : to alter, to modify **2** PERTURBAR : to disturb, to disrupt — **alterarse** *vr* : to get upset, to get worked up
altercado *nm* DISCUSIÓN, DISPUTA : altercation, argument, dispute
altercar {72} *vi* : to argue
alternador *nm* : alternator
alternancia *nf* : alternation, rotation
alternar *vi* **1** : to alternate **2** : to mix, to socialize — *vt* : to alternate — **alternarse** *vr* : to take turns
alternativa *nf* OPCIÓN : alternative, option
alternativo, -va *adj* **1** : alternating **2** : alternative — **alternativamente** *adv*
alterno, -na *adj* : alternate ⟨corriente alterna : alternating current⟩
alteza *nf* **1** : loftiness, lofty height **2 Alteza** : Highness
altibajos *nmpl* **1** : unevenness (of terrain) **2** : ups and downs
altiplanicie *nf* → **altiplano**
altiplano *nm* : high plateau, upland
altisonante *adj* **1** : pompous, affected (of language) **2** *Mex* : rude, obscene (of language)
altitud *nf* : altitude
altivez *nf, pl* **-veces** ALTANERÍA, ARROGANCIA : arrogance, haughtiness
altivo, -va *adj* ALTANERO, ARROGANTE : arrogant, haughty
alto[1] *adv* **1** : high **2** : loud, loudly — **altamente** *adv*
alto[2]**, -ta** *adj* **1** : tall, high ⟨un hombre/edificio alto : a tall man/building⟩ ⟨altas montañas : high mountains⟩ **2** : high ⟨altas temperaturas : high temperatures⟩ ⟨de alta calidad : of high quality⟩ **3** : high ⟨la alta sociedad : high society⟩ ⟨un alto funcionario : a high-ranking official⟩ **4** : upper ⟨el Alto Nilo : the Upper Nile⟩ **5** : loud ⟨en voz alta : aloud, out loud⟩ **6 en alta mar** : on the high seas **7 en alto** : in the air ⟨con la cabeza en alto : with her head held high⟩ **8 en lo alto de** : high up on/in **9 por todo lo alto** : in high style
alto[3] *nm* **1** ALTURA : height, elevation ⟨tiene un metro de alto : it's one meter tall/high⟩ **2** : stop, halt **3 altos** *nmpl* : upper floors
alto[4] *interj* : halt!, stop!
alto el fuego *nm, pl* **altos el fuego** : ceasefire
altoparlante *nm* ALTAVOZ : loudspeaker
altozano *nm* : hillock
altruismo *nm* : altruism
altruista *adj* : altruistic
altura *nf* **1** : height ⟨una altura de dos metros : a height of two meters⟩ ⟨a la altura del pecho : at chest height⟩ ⟨no estuvo a la altura de las expectativas : it didn't meet our expectations⟩ **2** : altitude **3** : loftiness, nobleness **4 a la altura de** : (up) by, (up) near ⟨en la avenida San Antonio a la

altura de la calle Tres : on San Antonio Avenue up by Third Street⟩ **5 a estas alturas** : at this point, at this stage

alubia *nf* : kidney bean

alucinación *nf, pl* **-ciones** : hallucination

alucinante *adj* : hallucinatory

alucinar *vi* : to hallucinate

alucinógeno¹, -na *adj* : hallucinogenic

alucinógeno² *nm* : hallucinogen

alud *nm* AVALANCHA : avalanche, landslide

aludido, -da *n* **1** : person in question ⟨el aludido : the aforesaid⟩ **2 darse por aludido** : to take it personally

aludir *vi* : to allude, to refer

alumbrado *nm* ILUMINACIÓN : lighting

alumbramiento *nm* **1** : lighting **2** : childbirth

alumbrar *vt* **1** ILUMINAR : to light, to illuminate **2** : to give birth to

alumbre *nm* : alum

aluminio *nm* : aluminum

alumnado *nm* : student body

alumno, -na *n* : pupil, student ⟨ex-alumno, ex-alumna : alumnus, alumna⟩ ⟨ex-alumnos, ex-alumnas : alumni, alumnae⟩

alusión *nf, pl* **-siones** : allusion, reference

alusivo, -va *adj* ∼ **a** : in reference to, regarding

aluvión *nm, pl* **-viones** : flood, barrage

alza *nf* SUBIDA : rise ⟨precios en alza : rising prices⟩

alzacuello *nm* : clerical collar

alzamiento *nm* LEVANTAMIENTO : uprising, insurrection

alzar {21} *vt* **1** ELEVAR, LEVANTAR : to lift, to raise **2** : to erect — **alzarse** *vr* LEVANTARSE : to rise up ⟨alzarse en armas : to rise up in arms⟩

Alzheimer [al'seimer] *nm* : Alzheimer's, Alzheimer's disease

ama *nf* → amo

amabilidad *nf* : kindness

amable *adj* : kind, nice — **amablemente** *adv*

amado¹, -da *adj* : beloved, darling

amado², -da *n* : sweetheart, loved one

amaestrar *vt* : to train (animals)

amafiarse *vr Mex fam* : to conspire, to be in cahoots *fam*

amagar {52} *vt* **1** : to show signs of (an illness, etc.) **2** : to threaten — *vi* **1** : to be imminent, to threaten **2** : to feint, to dissemble

amago *nm* **1** AMENAZA : threat **2** : sign, hint

amainar *vi* : to abate, to ease up, to die down

amalgama *nf* : amalgam

amalgamar *vt* : to amalgamate, to unite

amamantar *v* : to breast-feed, to nurse, to suckle

amanecer¹ {53} *v impers* **1** : to dawn **2** : to begin to show, to appear **3** : to wake up (in the morning)

amanecer² *nm* ALBA : dawn, daybreak

amanerado, -da *adj* : affected, mannered

amansar *vt* **1** : to tame **2** : to soothe, to calm down — **amansarse** *vr*

amante¹ *adj* : loving, fond

amante² *nmf* : lover

amañar *vt* : to rig, to fix, to tamper with — **amañarse** *vr* **amañárselas** : to manage

amaño *nm* **1** : skill, dexterity **2** : trick, ruse

amapola *nf* : poppy

amar *vt* : to love — **amarse** *vr*

amargado, -da *adj* : embittered, bitter

amargar {52} *vt* : to make bitter, to embitter — *vi* : to taste bitter

amargo¹, -ga *adj* : bitter — **amargamente** *adv*

amargo² *nm* : bitterness, tartness

amargura *nf* **1** : bitterness **2** : grief, sorrow

amarilis *nf* : amaryllis

amarillear *vi* : to yellow, to turn yellow

amarillento, -ta *adj* : yellowish

amarillismo *nm* : sensationalism

amarillo¹, -lla *adj* : yellow

amarillo² *nm* : yellow

amarra *nf* **1** : mooring, mooring line **2 soltar las amarras de** : to loosen one's grip on

amarrar *vt* **1** : to moor (a boat) **2** ATAR : to fasten, to tie up, to tie down

amartillar *vt* : to cock (a gun)

amasar *vt* **1** : to amass **2** : to knead **3** : to mix, to prepare

amasijo *nm* : jumble, hodgepodge

amasio, -sia *n* : lover

amateur *adj & nmf* : amateur — **amateurismo** *nm*

amatista *nf* : amethyst

amazona *nf* **1** : Amazon (in mythology) **2** : horsewoman

amazónico, -ca *adj* : amazonian

ambages *nmpl* **sin** ∼ : without hesitation, straight to the point

ámbar *nm* **1** : amber **2 ámbar gris** : ambergris

ambición *nf, pl* **-ciones** : ambition

ambicionar *vt* : to aspire to, to seek

ambicioso, -sa *adj* : ambitious — **ambiciosamente** *adv*

ambidextro, -tra *adj* : ambidextrous

ambientación *nf, pl* **-ciones** : setting, atmosphere

ambiental *adj* : environmental — **ambientalmente** *adv*

ambientalista *nmf* : environmentalist

ambientar *vt* : to give atmosphere to, to set (in literature and drama) — **ambientarse** *vr* : to adjust, to get one's bearings

ambiente *nm* **1** : atmosphere **2** : environment **3** : surroundings *pl*

ambigüedad *nf* : ambiguity

ambiguo, -gua *adj* : ambiguous

ámbito *nm* : domain, field, area

ambivalencia *nf* : ambivalence

ambivalente *adj* : ambivalent

ambos, -bas *adj & pron* : both

ambulancia *nf* : ambulance

ambulante *adj* **1** : traveling, itinerant **2 vendedor ambulante** : street vendor

ambulatorio¹, -ria *adj* : outpatient

ambulatorio² *nm Spain, Ven* : clinic

ameba *nf* : amoeba — **amébico** *adj*

amedrentar *vt* : to frighten, to intimidate — **amedrentarse** *vr*

amén *nm, pl* **amenes 1** : amen **2** ~ **de** : in addition to, besides **3 en un decir amén** : in an instant

amenaza *nf* : threat ⟨amenazas de muerte/ bomba : death/bomb threats⟩

amenazador, -dora *adj* : threatening, menacing

amenazante → **amenazador**

amenazar {21} *vt* **1** : to threaten ⟨me amenazó con demandarme : she threatened to sue me⟩ ⟨fue amenazado de muerte : he received death threats⟩ — *vi* **1** : to threaten ⟨amenazan con sanciones : they're threatening sanctions⟩

amenguar {10} *vt* **1** : to diminish **2** : to belittle, to dishonor

amenidad *nf* : pleasantness, amenity

amenizar {21} *vt* **1** : to make pleasant **2** : to brighten up, to add life to

ameno, -na *adj* : agreeable, pleasant

americano, -na *adj & n* : American

amerindio, -dia *adj & n* → **nativo americano**

ameritar *vt* MERECER : to deserve

ametralladora *nf* : machine gun

amianto *nm* : asbestos

amiba → **ameba**

amienemigo, -ga *n fam* : frenemy

amigable *adj* : friendly, amicable — **amigablemente** *adv*

amígdala *nf* : tonsil

amigdalitis *nf* : tonsillitis

amigo[1], -ga *adj* **1** : friendly, close ⟨es muy amigo mío : he's a very good friend of mine⟩ **2 hacerse (muy) amigo (de)** : to become (good) friends (with) **3 ser (muy) amigo de algo** : to be (very) fond of something

amigo[2], -ga *n* **1** : friend ⟨un buen/íntimo amigo : a good/close friend⟩ ⟨es una amiga suya : she's a friend of his⟩ **2 hacer amigos** : to make friends

amigote *nm* : crony, pal

amilanar *vt* **1** : to frighten **2** : to daunt, to discourage — **amilanarse** *vr* : to lose heart

aminoácido *nm* : amino acid

aminorar *vt* : to reduce, to lessen — *vi* : to diminish

amistad *nf* : friendship

amistoso, -sa *adj* : friendly — **amistosamente** *adv*

amnesia *nf* : amnesia

amnésico, -ca *adj & n* : amnesiac

amnistía *nf* : amnesty

amnistiar {85} *vt* : to grant amnesty to

amo, ama *n* **1** : master *m*, mistress *f* **2** : owner, keeper (of an animal) **3 ama de casa** : housewife **4 ama de llaves** : housekeeper

amodorrado, -da *adj* : drowsy

amolar {19} *vt* **1** : to grind, to sharpen **2** : to pester, to annoy

amoldable *adj* : adaptable

amoldar *vt* **1** : to mold **2** : to adapt, to adjust — **amoldarse** *vr*

amonestación *nf, pl* **-ciones 1** APERCIBIMIENTO : admonition, warning **2 amonestaciones** *nfpl* : banns

amonestar *vt* APERCIBIR : to admonish, to warn

amoníaco *or* **amoniaco** *nm* : ammonia

amontonamiento *nm* : accumulation, piling up

amontonar *vt* **1** APILAR : to pile up, to heap up **2** : to collect, to gather **3** : to hoard — **amontonarse** *vr*

amor *nm* **1** : love ⟨un poema de amor : a love poem⟩ ⟨su amor por/a la música : his love of music⟩ **2** : loved one, beloved ⟨sí, mi amor : yes, my love⟩ **3 amor propio** : self-esteem **4 hacer el amor** : to make love **5 por amor al arte** : for the love of it **6 ¡por el amor de Dios!** : for God's sake!

amoral *adj* : amoral

amoratado, -da *adj* : black-and-blue, bruised, livid

amordazar {21} *vt* **1** : to gag, to muzzle **2** : to silence

amorfo, -fa *adj* : shapeless, amorphous

amorío *nm* : love affair, fling

amoroso, -sa *adj* **1** : loving, affectionate **2** : amorous ⟨una mirada amorosa : an amorous glance⟩ **3** : charming, cute — **amorosamente** *adv*

amortiguación *nf* : cushioning, absorption

amortiguador *nm* : shock absorber

amortiguar {10} *vt* : to soften (an impact)

amortizar {21} *vt* : to amortize, to pay off — **amortización** *nf*

amotinado[1], -da *adj* : rebellious, insurgent, mutinous

amotinado[2], -da *n* : rebel, insurgent, mutineer

amotinamiento *nm* : uprising, rebellion

amotinar *vt* : to incite (to riot), to agitate — **amotinarse** *vr* **1** : to riot, to rebel **2** : to mutiny

amparar *vt* : to safeguard, to protect — **ampararse** *vr* **1** ~ **de** : to take shelter from **2** ~ **en** : to have recourse to

amparo *nm* ACOGIDA, REFUGIO : protection, refuge

amperímetro *nm* : ammeter

amperio *nm* : ampere

ampliación *nf, pl* **-ciones** : expansion, extension

ampliar {85} *vt* **1** : to expand, to extend **2** : to widen **3** : to enlarge (photographs) **4** : to elaborate on, to develop (ideas)

amplificador *nm* : amplifier

amplificar {72} *vt* : to amplify — **amplificación** *nf*

amplio, -plia *adj* **1** : broad, wide (of a street, etc.), spacious (of a room, etc.) ⟨una amplia gama de : a broad range of⟩ ⟨en el sentido más amplio : in the broadest sense⟩ **2** : full, comprehensive **3** : loose, full (of clothes) — **ampliamente** *adv*

amplitud *nf* **1** : breadth, extent **2** : space, spacious quality

ampolla *nf* **1** : blister **2** : vial

ampollar *vt* : to blister — **ampollarse** *vr*

ampolleta *nf* **1** : small vial **2** : hourglass **3** *Chile* : light bulb

ampulosidad *nf* : pomposity, bombast

ampuloso, -sa *adj* GRANDILOCUENTE : pompous, bombastic — **ampulosamente** *adv* amputar *vt* : to amputate — **amputación** *nf*

amueblar *vt* : to furnish

amuleto *nm* TALISMÁN : amulet, charm

amurallar *vt* : to wall in, to fortify

anacardo *nm* : cashew nut

anaconda *nf* : anaconda

anacrónico, -ca *adj* : anachronistic

anacronismo *nm* : anachronism

ánade *nmf* 1 : duck 2 **ánade real** : mallard

anagrama *nm* : anagram

anal *adj* : anal

anales *nmpl* : annals

analfabetismo *nm* : illiteracy

analfabeto, -ta *adj & n* : illiterate

analgésico[1], -ca *adj* : analgesic

analgésico[2] *nm* : painkiller, analgesic

análisis *nm* : analysis

analista *nmf* : analyst

analítico, -ca *adj* : analytical, analytic — **analíticamente** *adv*

analizar {21} *vt* : to analyze

analogía *nf* : analogy

analógico, -ca *adj* 1 : analogical 2 : analog ⟨computadora analógica : analog computer⟩

análogo, -ga *adj* : analogous, similar

ananá *or* ananás *nm, pl* -nás : pineapple

anaquel *nm* REPISA : shelf

anaranjado[1], -da *adj* NARANJA : orange-colored

anaranjado[2] *nm* NARANJA : orange (color)

anarquía *nf* : anarchy

anárquico, -ca *adj* : anarchic

anarquismo *nm* : anarchism

anarquista *adj & nmf* : anarchist

anatema *nm* : anathema

anatomía *nf* : anatomy — **anatomista** *nmf*

anatómico, -ca *adj* : anatomical — **anatómicamente** *adv*

ancas *nfpl* 1 : haunches, hindquarters 2 **ancas de rana** : frogs' legs

ancestral *adj* 1 : ancient, traditional 2 : ancestral

ancestro *nm* ASCENDIENTE : ancestor, forefather *m*

ancho[1], -cha *adj* 1 : wide, broad ⟨calles anchas : wide streets⟩ 2 : full, loose-fitting 3 **a lo ancho** : across (the width of) 4 **a sus anchas** : at home, comfortable

ancho[2] *nm* 1 : width, breadth ⟨tiene dos metros de ancho : it's two meters wide⟩ 2 **ancho de banda** : bandwidth

anchoa *nf* : anchovy

anchura *nf* : width, breadth

ancianidad *nf* SENECTUD : old age

anciano[1], -na *adj* : aged, old, elderly

anciano[2], -na *n* : elderly person

ancla *nf* : anchor

ancladero → **anclaje**

anclaje *nm* : anchorage

anclar *v* FONDEAR : to anchor

andadas *nfpl* 1 : tracks 2 **volver a las andadas** : to go back to one's old ways, to backslide

andador[1] *nm* 1 : walker, baby walker 2 *Mex* : walkway

andador[2], -dora *n* : walker, one who walks

andadura *nf* : course, journey ⟨su agotadora andadura al campeonato : his exhausting journey to the championship⟩

ándale → **andar**

andaluz, -luza *adj & n, mpl* -luces : Andalusian

andamiaje *nm* 1 : scaffolding 2 ESTRUCTURA : structure, framework

andamio *nm* : scaffold

andanada *nf* 1 : volley, broadside 2 **soltarle una andanada a alguien** : to reprimand someone

andanzas *nfpl* : adventures

andar[1] {6} *vi* 1 CAMINAR : to walk 2 IR : to go, to travel 3 FUNCIONAR : to run, to function ⟨el auto anda bien : the car runs well⟩ 4 : to ride ⟨andar en bicicleta : to ride a bike⟩ ⟨andar a caballo : to ride on horseback⟩ 5 : to be ⟨su madre no anda bien : his mother isn't well⟩ ⟨lo andaban buscando : they were looking for him⟩ 6 **¡anda!** *or Mex* **¡ándale!** : come on!, go on! 7 ~ **con** SALIR CON : to go out with, to date 8 ~ **con** : to associate with 9 ~ **con/sin** ⟨andaba sin camisa : he had no shirt on⟩ ⟨siempre anda con su guitarra : she always has her guitar with her⟩ 10 **andar detrás de** : to be after 11 ~ **en** : to be involved with 12 ~ **en** REVOLVER : to rummage through 13 ~ **por** : to be about ⟨anda por los 25 años : she's about 25 years old⟩ — *vt* : to walk, to travel — **andarse** *vr* : to leave, to go

andar[2] *nm* : walk, gait

andas *nfpl* : stand (for a coffin), bier

andén *nm, pl* andenes 1 : (train) platform 2 *CA, Col* : sidewalk

andino, -na *adj* : Andean

andorrano, -na *adj & n* : Andorran

andrajos *nmpl* : rags, tatters

andrajoso, -sa *adj* : ragged, tattered

andrógino, -na *adj* : androgynous

andurriales *nmpl* : remote place

anea *nf* : cattail

anduvo, etc. → **andar**

anécdota *nf* : anecdote

anecdótico, -ca *adj* : anecdotal

anegar {52} *vt* 1 INUNDAR : to flood 2 AHOGAR : to drown 3 : to overwhelm — **anegarse** *vr* : to be flooded

anejo *nm* → **anexo**[2]

anemia *nf* : anemia

anémico, -ca *adj* : anemic

anémona *nf* : anemone

anestesia *nf* : anesthesia

anestesiar *vt* : to anesthetize

anestésico[1], -ca *adj* : anesthetic

anestésico[2] *nm* : anesthetic

anestesista *nmf* : anesthetist

aneurisma *nmf* : aneurysm

anexar *vt* : to annex, to attach

anexión *nf, pl* -xiones : annexation

anexo[1], -xa *adj* : attached, joined, annexed

anexo[2] *nm* 1 : annex 2 : supplement (to a book), appendix

anfetamina *nf* : amphetamine

anfibio[1], -bia *adj* : amphibious

anfibio[2] *nm* : amphibian
anfiteatro *nm* **1** : amphitheater **2** : lecture hall
anfitrión, -triona *n, mpl* **-triones** : host, hostess *f*
ánfora *nf* **1** : urn, jar (with two handles) **2** *Mex, Peru* : ballot box
ángel *nm* **1** : angel **2 ángel de la guarda** : guardian angel **3 ángel exterminador** : Angel of Death
angelical *adj* : angelic, angelical
angélico, -ca *adj* → angelical
angina *nf* **1** *or* **angina de pecho** : angina **2** *Mex* : tonsil
anglicano, -na *adj & n* : Anglican
angloparlante[1] *adj* : English-speaking
angloparlante[2] *nmf* : English speaker
anglosajón, -jona *adj & n, mpl* **-jones** : Anglo-Saxon
angoleño, -ña *adj & n* : Angolan
angora *nf* : angora
angostar *vt* : to narrow — **angostarse** *vr*
angosto, -ta *adj* : narrow
angostura *nf* : narrowness
anguila *nf* : eel
angular *adj* : angular — **angularidad** *nf*
ángulo *nm* **1** : angle **2** : corner **3 ángulo muerto** : blind spot
anguloso, -sa *adj* : angular, sharp ⟨una cara angulosa : an angular face⟩ — **angulosidad** *nf*
angustia *nf* **1** CONGOJA : anguish, distress **2** : anxiety, worry
angustiar *vt* **1** : to anguish, to distress **2** : to worry — **angustiarse** *vr*
angustioso, -sa *adj* **1** : anguished, distressed **2** : distressing, worrisome
anhelante *adj* : yearning, longing
anhelar *vt* : to yearn for, to crave
anhelo *nm* : longing, yearning
anidar *vi* **1** : to nest **2** : to make one's home, to dwell — *vt* : to shelter
anilla *nf* : ring
anillo *nm* SORTIJA : ring
ánima *n* ALMA : soul
animación *nf, pl* **-ciones** **1** : animation **2** VIVEZA : liveliness
animado, -da *adj* **1** : animated, lively **2** : cheerful — **animadamente** *adv*
animador, -dora *n* **1** : (television) host **2** : cheerleader
animadversión *nf, pl* **-siones** ANIMOSIDAD : animosity, antagonism
animal[1] *adj* **1** : animal **2** ESTÚPIDO : stupid, idiotic **3** : rough, brutish
animal[2] *nm* : animal
animal[3] *nmf* **1** IDIOTA : idiot, fool **2** : brute, beastly person
animar *vt* **1** ALENTAR : to encourage, to inspire **2** : to animate, to enliven **3** : to brighten up, to cheer up — **animarse** *vr*
anímico, -ca *adj* : mental ⟨estado anímico : state of mind⟩
ánimo *nm* **1** ALMA : spirit, soul **2** : mood, spirits *pl* **3** : encouragement **4** PROPÓSITO : intention, purpose ⟨sociedad sin ánimo de lucro : nonprofit organization⟩ **5** : energy, vitality
animosidad *nf* ANIMADVERSIÓN : animosity, ill will

animoso, -sa *adj* : brave, spirited — **animosamente** *adv*
aniñado, -da *adj* : childlike
aniquilación *nf* → aniquilamiento
aniquilamiento *nm* : annihilation, extermination
aniquilar *vt* **1** : to annihilate, to wipe out **2** : to overwhelm, to bring to one's knees — **aniquilarse** *vr*
anís *nm* **1** : anise **2 semilla de anís** : aniseed
aniversario *nm* : anniversary
ano *nm* : anus
anoche *adv* : last night
anochecer[1] {53} *v impers* : to get dark
anochecer[2] *nm* : dusk, nightfall
anodino, -na *adj* : insipid, dull
ánodo *nm* : anode
anomalía *nf* : anomaly
anómalo, -la *adj* : anomalous
anonadado, -da *adj* : dumbfounded, speechless
anonadar *vt* : to dumbfound, to stun
anonimato *nm* : anonymity
anónimo, -ma *adj* : anonymous — **anónimamente** *adv*
anorak [ano'rak] *nm, pl* **-raks** : anorak
anorexia *nf* : anorexia
anoréxico, -ca *adj* : anorexic
anormal *adj* : abnormal — **anormalmente** *adv*
anormalidad *nf* : abnormality
anotación *nf, pl* **-ciones** **1** : annotation, note **2** : scoring (in sports) ⟨lograron una anotación : they managed to score a goal⟩
anotador, -dora *n* : scorer (in sports) ⟨el máximo anotador : the top scorer, the top-scoring player⟩
anotar *vt* **1** : to annotate **2** APUNTAR, ESCRIBIR : to write down, to jot down **3** : to score (in sports) — *vi* : to score
anquilosado, -da *adj* **1** : stiff (of a joint) **2** : stagnated, stale
anquilosamiento *nm* **1** : stiffness (of joints) **2** : stagnation, paralysis
anquilosarse *vr* **1** : to stagnate **2** : to become stiff or paralyzed
anquilostoma *nm* : hookworm
ánsar *nm* : goose
ansarino *nm* : gosling
ansia *nf* **1** INQUIETUD : anxiety, uneasiness **2** ANGUSTIA : anguish, distress **3** ANHELO : longing, yearning
ansiar {85} *vt* : to long for, to yearn for
ansiedad *nf* : anxiety
ansioso, -sa *adj* **1** : anxious, worried **2** : eager — **ansiosamente** *adv*
antagónico, -ca *adj* : conflicting, opposing
antagonismo *nm* : antagonism
antagonista[1] *adj* : antagonistic
antagonista[2] *nmf* : antagonist, opponent
antagonizar {21} *vt* : to antagonize
antaño *adv* : yesteryear, long ago
antártico, -ca *adj* **1** : antarctic **2 círculo antártico** : antarctic circle
ante[1] *nm* **1** : elk, moose **2** : suede
ante[2] *prep* **1** : before, in front of **2** : considering, in view of **3 ante todo** : first and foremost, above all

anteanoche *adv* : the night before last
anteayer *adv* : the day before yesterday
antebrazo *nm* : forearm
antecedente[1] *adj* : previous, prior
antecedente[2] *nm* **1** : precedent **2 antecedentes** *nmpl* : record, background
anteceder *v* : to precede
antecesor, -sora *n* **1** ANTEPASADO : ancestor **2** PREDECESOR : predecessor
antedicho, -cha *adj* : aforesaid, above
antelación *nf, pl* **-ciones 1** : advance notice **2 con ~** : in advance, beforehand
antemano *adv* **de ~** : in advance ⟨se lo agradezco de antemano : I thank you in advance⟩
antena *nf* : antenna ⟨antena parabólica : satellite dish⟩
antenoche → anteanoche
anteojera *nf* **1** : glasses case **2 anteojeras** *nfpl* : blinders
anteojos *nmpl* GAFAS : glasses, eyeglasses
antepasado[1], **-da** *adj* : before last ⟨el domingo antepasado : the Sunday before last⟩
antepasado[2], **-da** *n* ANTECESOR : ancestor
antepecho *nm* **1** : guardrail **2** : ledge, sill
antepenúltimo, -ma *adj* : third from last
anteponer {60} *vt* **1** : to place before ⟨anteponer al interés de la nación el interés de la comunidad : to place the interests of the community before national interest⟩ **2** : to prefer
anteproyecto *nm* **1** : draft, proposal **2 anteproyecto de ley** : bill
antera *nf* : anther
anterior *adj* **1** : previous **2** : earlier ⟨tiempos anteriores : earlier times⟩ **3** : anterior, forward, front
anterioridad *nf* **1** : priority **2 con ~** : beforehand, in advance
anteriormente *adv* : previously, beforehand
antes *adv* **1** : before ⟨no se me ocurrió antes : it didn't occur to me before⟩ ⟨es igual que antes : it's the same as before⟩ ⟨una hora antes : an hour earlier⟩ ⟨antes eran más baratos : they used to be cheaper⟩ **2** : rather, sooner ⟨antes prefiero morir : I'd rather die⟩ **3 ~ de** : before, previous to ⟨antes de hoy : before today⟩ ⟨antes de salir : before leaving⟩ ⟨antes de un mes : within a month⟩ **4 antes que** : before ⟨antes que llegue Luis : before Luis arrives⟩ **5 cuanto antes** *or* **lo antes posible** : as soon as possible **6 antes bien** : on the contrary
antesala *nf* **1** : lobby, waiting room **2** : prelude, prologue
anti- *pref* : anti-, against, opposing
antiaborto, -ta *adj* : antiabortion
antiácido *nm* : antacid
antiadherente *adj* : nonstick
antiaéreo, -rea *adj* : antiaircraft
antiamericano, -na *adj* : anti-American
antibalas *adj* : bulletproof
antibiótico[1], **-ca** *adj* : antibiotic
antibiótico[2] *nm* : antibiotic
anticipación *nf, pl* **-ciones 1** : expectation, anticipation **2 con ~** : in advance

anticipado, -da *adj* **1** : advance, early **2 por ~** : in advance
anticipar *vt* **1** : to anticipate, to forestall, to deal with in advance **2** : to pay in advance — **anticiparse** *vr* **1** : to be early **2** ADELANTARSE : to get ahead
anticipo *nm* **1** : advance (payment) **2** : foretaste, preview
anticlimático, -ca *adj* : anticlimactic
anticlímax *nm* : anticlimax
anticomunismo *nm* : anticommunism
anticomunista *adj & nmf* : anticommunist
anticoncepción *nf, pl* **-ciones** : birth control, contraception
anticonceptivo *nm* : contraceptive — **anticonceptivo, -va** *adj*
anticongelante *nm* : antifreeze
anticonstitucional *adj* : not constitutional
anticuado, -da *adj* : antiquated, outdated
anticuario[1], **-ria** *adj* : antique, antiquarian
anticuario[2], **-ria** *n* : antiquarian, antiquary
anticuario[3] *nm* : antique shop
anticuerpo *nm* : antibody
antidemocrático, -ca *adj* : antidemocratic
antidepresivo *nm* : antidepressant
antidisturbios[1] *adj* : riot ⟨policía antidisturbios : riot police⟩
antidisturbios[2] *nmpl* : riot police
antídoto *nm* : antidote
antidrogas *adj* : antidrug
antier → anteayer
antiestético, -ca *adj* : unsightly, unattractive
antifascista *adj & nmf* : antifascist
antifaz *nm, pl* **-faces** : mask
antifeminista *adj & nmf* : antifeminist
antífona *nf* : anthem
antígeno *nm* : antigen
antigualla *nf* **1** : antique **2** : relic, old thing
antiguamente *adv* **1** : formerly, once **2** : long ago
antigüedad *nf* **1** : antiquity **2** : seniority **3** : age ⟨con siglos de antigüedad : centuries-old⟩ **4 antigüedades** *nfpl* : antiques
antiguo, -gua *adj* **1** : ancient, old **2** : former **3** : old-fashioned ⟨a la antigua : in the old-fashioned way⟩ **4 Antiguo Testamento** : Old Testament
antihigiénico, -ca *adj* INSALUBRE : unhygienic, unsanitary
antihistamínico *nm* : antihistamine
antiimperialismo *nm* : anti-imperialism
antiimperialista *adj & nmf* : anti-imperialist
antiinflacionario, -ria *adj* : anti-inflationary
antiinflamatorio, -ria *adj* : anti-inflammatory
antillano[1], **-na** *adj* CARIBEÑO : Caribbean, West Indian
antillano[2], **-na** *n* : West Indian
antílope *nm* : antelope
antimonio *nm* : antimony
antimonopolista *adj* : antitrust

antinatural *adj* : unnatural, perverse
antipatía *nf* : aversion, dislike
antipático, -ca *adj* : obnoxious, unpleasant
antipatriótico, -ca *adj* : unpatriotic
antirrábico, -ca *adj* : rabies ⟨vacuna antirrábica : rabies vaccine⟩
antirreglamentario, -ria *adj* 1 : unlawful, illegal 2 : foul (in sports)
antirrevolucionario, -ria *adj & n* : anti-revolutionary
antirrobo, -ba *adj* : antitheft
antisemita *adj* : anti-Semitic
antisemitismo *nm* : anti-Semitism
antiséptico¹, -ca *adj* : antiseptic
antiséptico² *nm* : antiseptic
antisocial *adj* : antisocial
antitabaco *adj* : antismoking
antiterrorista *adj* : antiterrorist
antítesis *nf* : antithesis
antitoxina *nf* : antitoxin
antitranspirante *nm* : antiperspirant
antiviral *adj* : antiviral
antivirus *nm, pl* **antivirus** : antivirus software
antojadizo, -za *adj* CAPRICHOSO : capricious
antojarse *vr* 1 APETECER : to be appealing, to be desirable ⟨se me antoja un helado : I feel like having ice cream⟩ 2 : to seem, to appear ⟨los árboles se antojaban fantasmas : the trees seemed like ghosts⟩
antojitos *nmpl Mex* : traditional Mexican snack foods
antojo *nm* 1 CAPRICHO : whim 2 : craving
antología *nf* 1 : anthology 2 **de** ∼ *fam* : fantastic, incredible
antónimo *nm* : antonym
antonomasia *nf* **por** ∼ : par excellence
antorcha *nf* : torch
antracita *nf* : anthracite
antro *nm* 1 : cave, den 2 : dive, seedy nightclub
antropofagia *nf* CANIBALISMO : cannibalism
antropófago¹, -ga *adj* : cannibalistic
antropófago², -ga *n* CANÍBAL : cannibal
antropoide *adj & nmf* : anthropoid
antropología *nf* : anthropology
antropológico, -ca *adj* : anthropological
antropólogo, -ga *n* : anthropologist
anual *adj* : annual, yearly — **anualmente** *adv*
anualidad *nf* : annuity
anuario *nm* : yearbook, annual
anudar *vt* : to knot, to tie in a knot — **anudarse** *vr*
anuencia *nf* : consent
anulación *nf, pl* **-ciones** : annulment, cancellation
anular *vt* : to annul, to cancel
anunciador, -dora *n* → **anunciante**
anunciante *nmf* : advertiser
anunciar *vt* 1 : to announce 2 : to advertise
anuncio *nm* 1 : announcement 2 : advertisement, commercial
anzuelo *nm* 1 : fishhook 2 **morder el anzuelo** : to take the bait

añadido *nm* : addition
añadidura *nf* 1 : additive, addition 2 **por** ∼ : in addition, furthermore
añadir *vt* 1 AGREGAR : to add 2 AUMENTAR : to increase
añejar *vt* : to age, to ripen
añejo, -ja *adj* 1 : aged, vintage 2 : ancient, musty, stale
añicos *nmpl* : smithereens, bits ⟨hacer(se) añicos : to shatter⟩
añil *nm* 1 : indigo 2 : bluing
año *nm* 1 : year ⟨el año pasado : last year⟩ ⟨en el año 1990 : in (the year) 1990⟩ ⟨en los años '70 : in the '70's⟩ ⟨tiene diez años : she is ten years old⟩ ⟨cumple hoy 80 años : he turns 80 today⟩ ⟨los menores de 18 años : those under the age of 18⟩ 2 : grade ⟨cuarto año : fourth grade⟩ 3 **año bisiesto** : leap year 4 **año luz** : light-year 5 **Año Nuevo** : New Year
añoranza *nf* : longing, yearning
añorar *vt* 1 DESEAR : to long for 2 : to grieve for, to miss — *vi* : to mourn, to grieve
añoso, -sa *adj* : aged, old
añublo *nm* : blight
aorta *nf* : aorta
apa *interj Mex fam* : wow!
apabullante *adj* : overwhelming, crushing
apabullar *vt* : to overwhelm
apacentar {55} *vt* : to pasture, to put to pasture
apache *adj & nmf* : Apache
apachurrado, -da *adj fam* : depressed, down
apachurrar *vt* : to crush, to squash
apacible *adj* : gentle, mild, calm — **apaciblemente** *adv*
apaciguador, -dora *adj* : calming
apaciguamiento *nm* : appeasement
apaciguar {10} *vt* APLACAR : to appease, to pacify — **apaciguarse** *vr* : to calm down
apadrinar *vt* 1 : to be a godparent to 2 : to sponsor, to support
apagado, -da *adj* 1 : off, out ⟨la luz está apagada : the light is off⟩ 2 : dull, subdued
apagador *nm Mex* : switch
apagar {52} *vt* 1 : to turn off, to shut off 2 : to put out, to extinguish — **apagarse** *vr* 1 : to go out (of a light, flame, etc.) 2 DISMINUIR : to wane, to die down
apagón *nm, pl* **-gones** : blackout (of power), power failure
apalabrar *vt* : to arrange with (someone), to arrange for (something)
apalancamiento *nm* : leverage
apalancar {72} *vt* 1 : to jack up 2 : to pry open
apalear *vt* : to beat up, to thrash
apanar *Col, Ecua, Peru* → **empanar**
apantallar *vt Mex* : to dazzle, to impress
apañar *vt* 1 : to seize, to grasp 2 : to repair, to mend — **apañarse** *vr* : to manage, to get along
apaño *nm fam* 1 : patch 2 HABILIDAD : skill, knack
apapachar *vt Mex fam* : to cuddle, to caress — **apapacharse** *vr*

apapacho *nm Mex fam* : cuddle, caress
aparador *nm* **1** : sideboard, cupboard **2** ESCAPARATE, VITRINA : shop window
aparato *nm* **1** : machine, appliance, apparatus ⟨aparato auditivo : hearing aid⟩ ⟨aparato de televisión : television set⟩ **2** : system ⟨aparato digestivo : digestive system⟩ **3** : display, ostentation ⟨sin aparato : without ceremony⟩ **4 aparatos** *nmpl* : braces (for the teeth) **5** : ride (in an amusement park)
aparatoso, -sa *adj* **1** : ostentatious **2** : spectacular
aparcamiento *nm Spain* **1** : parking **2** : parking lot
aparcar {72} *v Spain* : to park
aparcero, -ra *n* : sharecropper
aparear *vt* **1** : to mate (animals) **2** : to match up — **aparearse** *vr* : to mate
aparecer {53} *vi* **1** : to appear **2** PRESENTARSE : to show up **3** : to turn up, to be found — **aparecerse** *vr* : to appear
aparejado, -da *adj* **1 ir aparejado con** : to go hand in hand with **2 llevar aparejado** : to entail
aparejar *vt* **1** PREPARAR : to prepare, to make ready **2** : to harness (a horse) **3** : to fit out (a ship)
aparejo *nm* **1** : equipment, gear **2** : harness, saddle **3** : rig, rigging (of a ship)
aparentar *vt* **1** : to seem, to appear ⟨no aparentas tu edad : you don't look your age⟩ **2** FINGIR : to feign, to pretend
aparente *adj* **1** : apparent **2** : showy, striking — **aparentemente** *adv*
aparición *nf, pl* **-ciones 1** : appearance **2** PUBLICACIÓN : publication, release **3** FANTASMA : apparition, vision
apariencia *nf* **1** ASPECTO : appearance, look **2 en ～** : seemingly, apparently
apartado *nm* **1** : section, paragraph **2 apartado postal** : P.O. Box
apartamento *nm* DEPARTAMENTO : apartment
apartar *vt* **1** ALEJAR : to move away, to put at a distance **2** : to put aside, to set aside, to separate — **apartarse** *vr* **1** : to step aside, to move away **2** DESVIARSE : to stray
aparte¹ *adv* **1** : apart, aside ⟨modestia aparte : if I say so myself⟩ **2** : separately **3 ～ de** : apart from, besides
aparte² *adj* : separate, special
aparte³ *nm* : aside (in theater)
apartheid *nm* : apartheid
apasionado, -da *adj* : passionate, enthusiastic — **apasionadamente** *adv*
apasionante *adj* : fascinating, exciting
apasionar *vt* : to enthuse, to excite — **apasionarse** *vr*
apatía *nf* : apathy
apático, -ca *adj* : apathetic
apátrida *adj* **1** : without nationality **2** *Ven* : unpatriotic
apearse *vr* **1** DESMONTAR : to dismount **2** : to get out of or off (a vehicle)
apechugar {52} *vi fam* : to put up with the situation ⟨apechugar con : to put up with, to deal with⟩
apedrear *vt* : to stone, to throw stones at

apegado, -da *adj* : attached, close, devoted ⟨es muy apegado a su familia : he is very devoted to his family⟩
apegarse {52} *vr* **～ a** : to become attached to, to grow fond of
apego *nm* AFICIÓN : attachment, fondness, inclination
apelación *nf, pl* **-ciones** : appeal (in court)
apelar *vi* **1** : to appeal **2 ～ a** : to resort to
apelativo *nm* APELLIDO : last name, surname
apellidarse *vr* : to have for a last name ⟨¿cómo se apellida? : what is your last name?⟩
apellido *nm* : last name, surname
apelotonar *vt* : to roll into a ball, to bundle up
apenar *vt* : to sadden — **apenarse** *vr* **1** : to be saddened **2** : to become embarrassed
apenas¹ *adv* : hardly, scarcely
apenas² *conj* : as soon as
apéndice *nm* **1** : appendix **2** : appendage
apendicectomía *nf* : appendectomy
apendicitis *nf* : appendicitis
apercibimiento *nm* **1** : preparation **2** AMONESTACIÓN : warning
apercibir *vt* **1** DISPONER : to prepare, to make ready **2** AMONESTAR : to warn **3** OBSERVAR : to observe, to perceive — **apercibirse** *vr* **1** : to get ready **2 ～ de** : to notice
aperitivo *nm* **1** : appetizer **2** : aperitif
apero *nm* : tool, implement
apersonarse *vr* **1** : to appear, to show up **2 ～ de** *Col* : to take charge of, to oversee
apertura *nf* **1** : opening, aperture **2** : commencement, beginning **3** : openness
apesadumbrar *vt* : to distress, to sadden — **apesadumbrarse** *vr* : to be weighed down
apestar *vt* **1** : to infect with the plague **2** : to corrupt — *vi* : to stink
apestoso, -sa *adj* : stinking, foul
apetecer {53} *vt* **1** : to crave, to long for ⟨apeteció la fama : he longed for fame⟩ **2** : to appeal to ⟨me apetece un bistec : I feel like having a steak⟩ ⟨¿cuándo te apetece ir? : when do you want to go?⟩ — *vi* : to be appealing
apetecible *adj* : appetizing, appealing
apetito *nm* : appetite
apetitoso, -sa *adj* : appetizing
apiadarse *vr* **～ de** : to take pity on
apiario *nm* : apiary
ápice *nm* **1** : apex, summit **2** PIZCA : bit, smidgen
apicultor, -tora *n* : beekeeper
apicultura *nf* : beekeeping
apilar *vt* AMONTONAR : to heap up, to pile up — **apilarse** *vr*
apiñado, -da *adj* : jammed, crowded
apiñar *vt* : to pack, to cram — **apiñarse** *vr* : to crowd together, to huddle
apio *nm* : celery

apisonadora *nf* : steamroller
apisonar *vt* : to pack down, to tamp
aplacamiento *nm* : appeasement
aplacar {72} *vt* APACIGUAR : to appease, to placate — **aplacarse** *vr* : to calm down
aplanadora *nf* : steamroller
aplanar *vt* : to flatten, to level
aplastante *adj* : crushing, overwhelming
aplastar *vt* : to crush, to squash
aplaudir *v* : to applaud
aplauso *nm* 1 : applause, clapping 2 : praise, acclaim
aplazamiento *nm* : postponement
aplazar {21} *vt* : to postpone, to defer
aplicable *adj* : applicable — **aplicabilidad** *nf*
aplicación *nf, pl* **-ciones** 1 : application 2 : diligence, dedication
aplicado, -da *adj* : diligent, industrious
aplicador *nm* : applicator
aplicar {72} *vt* : to apply — **aplicarse** *vr* : to apply oneself
aplique *or* **apliqué** *nm* : appliqué
aplomar *vt* : to plumb, to make vertical
aplomo *nm* : aplomb, composure
apocado, -da *adj* : timid
apocalipsis *nms & pl* : apocalypse ⟨el Libro del Apocalipsis : the Book of Revelation⟩
apocalíptico, -ca *adj* : apocalyptic
apocamiento *nm* : timidity
apocarse {72} *vr* 1 : to shy away, to be intimidated 2 : to humble oneself, to sell oneself short
apócrifo, -fa *adj* : apocryphal
apodar *vt* : to nickname, to call — **apodarse** *vr*
apoderado, -da *n* : proxy, agent
apoderar *vt* : to authorize, to empower — **apoderarse** *vr* ~ **de** : to seize, to take over
apodo *nm* SOBRENOMBRE : nickname
apogeo *nm* : acme, peak, zenith
apolillado, -da *adj* 1 : moth-eaten, worm-eaten 2 : old-fashioned
apolítico, -ca *adj* : apolitical
apología *nf* : defense, apology
apoplejía *nf* : apoplexy, stroke
apoplético, -ca *adj* : apoplectic
aporrear *vt* : to bang on, to beat, to bludgeon
aportación *nf, pl* **-ciones** : contribution
aportar *vt* CONTRIBUIR : to contribute, to provide
aporte *nm* → **aportación**
aposento *nm* : chamber, room ⟨los aposentos reales : the royal chambers⟩
apósito *nm* : dressing (for a wound)
apostador, -dora *n* : bettor, better
apostar {19} *v* : to bet, to wager ⟨apuesto que no viene : I bet he's not coming⟩
apostasía *nf* : apostasy
apóstata *nmf* : apostate
apostilla *nf* : note
apostillar *vt* : to annotate
apóstol *nm* : apostle
apostólico, -ca *adj* : apostolic
apóstrofe *nmf* → **apóstrofo**
apóstrofo *nm* : apostrophe

apostura *nf* : elegance, gracefulness
apoteósico, -ca *adj* : tremendous
apoyabrazos *nms & pl* : armrest
apoyacabezas *nms & pl* : headrest
apoyapiés *nms & pl* : footrest
apoyar *vt* 1 : to support, to back 2 : to lean, to rest — **apoyarse** *vr* 1 ~ **en** : to lean on 2 ~ **en** : to be based on, to rest on
apoyo *nm* : support, backing
app ['ap] *nf, pl* **apps** : app, application
apreciable *adj* : appreciable, substantial, considerable
apreciación *nf, pl* **-ciones** 1 : appreciation 2 : appraisal, evaluation
apreciar *vt* 1 ESTIMAR : to appreciate, to value 2 EVALUAR : to appraise, to assess — **apreciarse** *vr* : to appreciate, to increase in value
apreciativo, -va *adj* : appreciative
aprecio *nm* 1 ESTIMO : esteem, appreciation 2 EVALUACIÓN : appraisal, assessment
aprehender *vt* 1 : to apprehend, to capture 2 : to conceive of, to grasp
aprehensión *nf, pl* **-siones** : apprehension, capture, arrest
apremiante *adj* : pressing, urgent
apremiar *vt* INSTAR : to pressure, to urge — *vi* URGIR : to be urgent ⟨el tiempo apremia : time is of the essence⟩
apremio *nm* : pressure, urgency
aprender *v* : to learn — **aprenderse** *vr*
aprendiz, -diza *n, mpl* **-dices** : apprentice, trainee
aprendizaje *nm* 1 : apprenticeship 2 : learning
aprensión *nf, pl* **-siones** : apprehension, dread
aprensivo, -va *adj* : apprehensive, worried
apresamiento *nm* : seizure, capture
apresar *vt* : to capture, to seize
aprestar *vt* : to make ready, to prepare — **aprestarse** *vr* : to get ready
apresuradamente *adv* 1 : hurriedly 2 : hastily, too fast
apresurado, -da *adj* : hurried, in a rush
apresuramiento *nm* : hurry, haste
apresurar *vt* : to quicken, to speed up — **apresurarse** *vr* : to hurry up, to make haste
apretado, -da *adj* 1 : tight 2 *fam* : cheap — **apretadamente** *adv*
apretar {55} *vt* 1 : to press, to push (a button) 2 : to tighten 3 : to squeeze, to clasp ⟨apretar el gatillo : to pull the trigger⟩ 4 : to press together ⟨apretar los dientes : to grit one's teeth⟩ — *vi* 1 : to press, to push 2 : to fit tightly, to be too tight ⟨los zapatos me aprietan : my shoes are too tight⟩ — **apretarse** *vr*
apretón *nm, pl* **-tones** 1 : squeeze 2 **apretón de manos** : handshake
apretujado, -da *adj* : cramped, squeezed together
apretujar *vt* : to squash, to squeeze — **apretujarse** *vr*
aprieto *nm* APURO : predicament, difficulty ⟨estar en un aprieto : to be in a fix⟩

aprisa *adv* : quickly, hurriedly
aprisionar *vt* 1 : to imprison 2 : to trap, to box in
aprobación *nf, pl* -ciones : approval, endorsement
aprobar {19} *vt* 1 : to approve of 2 : to pass (a law) 3 : to pass (an exam) 4 : to pass (a student) — *vi* : to pass (in school)
aprobatorio, -ria *adj* : approving
aprontar *vt Chile, Uru* : to prepare, to ready — aprontarse *vr* : to get ready
apropiación *nf, pl* -ciones : appropriation
apropiado, -da *adj* : appropriate, proper, suitable — apropiadamente *adv*
apropiarse *vr* ~ de : to take possession of, to appropriate
aprovechable *adj* : usable
aprovechado[1], -da *adj* 1 : diligent, hardworking 2 : pushy, opportunistic
aprovechado[2], -da *n* : pushy person, opportunist
aprovechamiento *nm* : use, exploitation
aprovechar *vt* : to take advantage of (an opportunity, etc.), to make good use of (time, etc.) — *vi* : to make the most of it — aprovecharse *vr* ~ de : to take advantage of, to exploit
aprovisionamiento *nm* : provisions *pl*, supplies *pl*
aprovisionar *vt* : to provide, to supply (with provisions)
aproximación *nf, pl* -ciones 1 : approximation, estimate 2 : rapprochement
aproximado, -da *adj* : approximate, estimated — aproximadamente *adv*
aproximar *vt* ACERCAR, ARRIMAR : to approximate, to bring closer — aproximarse *vr* ACERCARSE, ARRIMARSE : to approach, to move closer
aptitud *nf* : aptitude, capability
apto, -ta *adj* 1 : suitable, suited, fit 2 HÁBIL : capable, competent
apuesta *nf* : bet, wager
apuesto, -ta *adj* : elegant, good-looking
apuntador, -dora *n* : prompter
apuntalar *vt* : to prop up, to shore up
apuntar *vt* 1 : to point (a finger, etc.) 2 : to point at 3 ANOTAR : to write down 4 INSCRIBIR : to sign up 5 : to point out (a fact, etc.) 6 : to prompt (in the theater) — *vi* 1 : to aim ⟨apuntó al blanco con el revólver : she aimed the gun at the target⟩ 2 ~ a/hacia : to point to/toward — apuntarse *vr* 1 : to sign up, to enroll 2 : to score
apunte *nm* : note
apuñalar *vt* : to stab
apuradamente *adv* 1 : with difficulty 2 : hurriedly, hastily
apurado, -da *adj* 1 APRESURADO : rushed, pressured 2 : poor, needy 3 : difficult, awkward 4 : embarrassed
apurar *vt* 1 APRESURAR : to hurry, to rush 2 : to use up, to exhaust 3 : to trouble — apurarse *vr* 1 APRESURARSE : to hurry up 2 PREOCUPARSE : to worry
apuro *nm* 1 : predicament, jam ⟨en apuros : in a bind⟩ ⟨me sacó del apuro : he

got me out of a jam⟩ 2 : rush, hurry ⟨tengo apuro : I'm in a hurry⟩ ⟨con/sin apuro : in a hurried/leisurely way⟩ 3 : embarrassment
aquejado, -da *adj* ~ de : suffering from
aquejar *vt* : to afflict
aquel[1], aquella *adj, mpl* aquellos : that, those
aquel[2], aquella *or* aquél, aquélla *pron, mpl* aquellos *or* aquéllos 1 : that (one), those (ones) ⟨aquel/aquél fue un año récord : that was a record year⟩ ⟨aquellos/aquéllos que la conocieron : those who knew her⟩ 2 : the former (of two) 3 todo aquel/aquél que : anyone who
aquello *pron* (*neuter*) : that, that matter, that business ⟨aquello fue algo serio : that was something serious⟩
aquí *adv* 1 : here ⟨aquí está : here it is⟩ ⟨ven aquí : come here⟩ ⟨aquí adentro : in here⟩ ⟨aquí mismo : right here⟩ ⟨como dicen (por) aquí . . . : as they say (around) here . . .⟩ ⟨de aquí para allá : back and forth⟩ 2 : now ⟨de aquí en adelante : from now on⟩
aquiescente *adj* : acquiescent
aquiescencia *nf* : acquiescence, approval
aquietar *vt* : to allay, to calm — aquietarse *vr* : to calm down
aquilatar *vt* 1 : to assay 2 : to assess, to size up
ara *nf* 1 : altar 2 en aras de : in the interests of, for the sake of
árabe[1] *adj & nmf* : Arab, Arabian
árabe[2] *nm* : Arabic (language)
arabesco *nm* : arabesque — arabesco, -ca *adj*
arábigo, -ga *adj* 1 : Arabic, Arabian 2 número arábigo : Arabic numeral
arable *adj* : arable
arado *nm* : plow
aragonés[1], -nesa *adj, mpl* -neses : of or from Aragón
aragonés[2], -nesa *n, mpl* -neses : person from Aragón
arancel *nm* : tariff, duty
arancelario, -ria *adj* : tariff, duty ⟨barreras arancelarias : tariff barriers⟩
arándano *nm* : blueberry
arandela *nf* : washer (for a faucet, etc.)
araña *nf* 1 : spider 2 : chandelier
arañar *v* : to scratch, to claw
arañazo *nm* : scratch
arar *v* : to plow
arbitraje *nm* 1 : arbitration 2 : refereeing (in sports)
arbitrar *v* 1 : to arbitrate 2 : to referee, to umpire
arbitrariedad *nf* 1 : arbitrariness 2 INJUSTICIA : injustice, wrong
arbitrario, -ria *adj* 1 : arbitrary 2 : unfair, unjust — arbitrariamente *adv*
arbitrio *nm* 1 ALBEDRÍO : will 2 JUICIO : judgment
árbitro, -tra *n* 1 : arbitrator, arbiter 2 : referee, umpire
árbol *nm* 1 : tree 2 árbol genealógico : family tree
arbolado[1], -da *adj* : wooded
arbolado[2] *nm* : woodland

arboleda *nf* : grove, wood
arbóreo, -rea *adj* : arboreal
arbusto *nm* : shrub, bush, hedge
arca *nf* **1** : ark **2** : coffer, chest
arcada *nf* **1** : arcade, series of arches **2**
  arcadas *nfpl* : retching ⟨hacer arcadas
  : to retch⟩
arcaico, -ca *adj* : archaic
arcángel *nm* : archangel
arcano, -na *adj* : arcane
arce *nm* : maple tree
arcén *nm, pl* **arcenes** : hard shoulder,
  berm
archiconocido, -da *adj* : well-known, famous
archidiócesis *nfs & pl* → **arquidiócesis**
archipiélago *nm* : archipelago
archivador *nm* : filing cabinet
archivar *vt* **1** : to file **2** : to archive
archivero, -ra *n* : archivist
archivista *nmf* : archivist
archivo *nm* **1** : file **2** : archive, archives
  pl
arcilla *nf* : clay
arco *nm* **1** : arch, archway **2** : bow (in
  archery) **3** : arc **4** : wicket (in croquet)
  5 PORTERÍA : goal, goalposts *pl* **6 arco**
  iris : rainbow
arcón *nm, pl* **-cones** : large chest
arder *vi* **1** : to burn ⟨el bosque está ardiendo : the forest is in flames⟩ ⟨arder de
  ira : to burn with anger, to be seething⟩
  2 : to smart, to sting, to burn ⟨le ardía el
  estómago : he had heartburn⟩
ardid *nm* : scheme, ruse
ardiente *adj* **1** : burning **2** : ardent, passionate — **ardientemente** *adv*
ardilla *nf* **1** : squirrel **2** *or* **ardilla listada**
  : chipmunk
ardor *nm* **1** : heat **2** : passion, ardor
ardoroso, -sa *adj* : heated, impassioned
arduo, -dua *adj* : arduous, grueling — **arduamente** *adv*
área *nf* : area
arena *nf* **1** : sand ⟨arena movediza
  : quicksand⟩ **2** : arena
arenal *nm* : sandy area
arenga *nf* : harangue, lecture
arengar {52} *vt* : to harangue, to lecture
arenilla *nf* **1** : fine sand **2 arenillas** *nfpl*
  : kidney stones
arenisca *nf* : sandstone
arenoso, -sa *adj* : sandy, gritty
arenque *nm* : herring
arepa *nf* : cornmeal bread
arete *nm* : earring
argamasa *nf* : mortar (cement)
argelino, -na *adj & n* : Algerian
argentino, -na *adj & n* : Argentinian, Argentine
argolla *nf* : hoop, ring
argón *nm* : argon
argot *nm* : slang
argucia *nf* : sophistry, subtlety
argüir {41} *vi* : to argue — *vt* **1** ARGU-
  MENTAR : to contend, to argue **2** INFE-
  RIR : to deduce **3** PROBAR : to prove
argumentación *nf, pl* **-ciones** : line of
  reasoning, argument
argumentar *vt* : to argue, to contend

argumento *nm* **1** : argument, reasoning
  2 : plot, story line
aria *nf* : aria
aridez *nf, pl* **-deces** : aridity, dryness
árido, -da *adj* : arid, dry
Aries[1] *nm* : Aries (sign or constellation)
Aries[2] *nmf* : Aries (person)
ariete *nm* : battering ram
arisco, -ca *adj* : surly, sullen, unsociable
arista *nf* **1** : ridge, edge **2** : beard (of a
  plant) **3 aristas** *nfpl* : rough edges,
  complications, problems
aristocracia *nf* : aristocracy
aristócrata *nmf* : aristocrat
aristocrático, -ca *adj* : aristocratic
aritmética *nf* : arithmetic
aritmético, -ca *adj* : arithmetic, arithmetical — **aritméticamente** *adv*
arlequín *nm, pl* **-quines** : harlequin
arma *nf* **1** : weapon ⟨arma nuclear : nuclear weapon⟩ ⟨arma química/biológica
  : chemical/biological weapon⟩ ⟨arma de
  destrucción masiva : weapon of mass de-
  struction⟩ **2 armas** *nfpl* : armed forces
  3 arma blanca : sharp object (used as a
  weapon) **4 arma de fuego** : firearm
armada *nf* : navy, fleet
armadillo *nm* : armadillo
armado, -da *adj* **1** : armed **2** : assem-
  bled, put together **3** *PRi* : obstinate,
  stubborn
armador, -dora *n* : owner of a ship
armadura *nf* **1** : armor **2** ARMAZÓN
  : skeleton, framework
armamento *nm* : armament, arms *pl*,
  weaponry
armar *vt* **1** : to assemble, to put together
  2 : to create, to cause ⟨armar un
  escándalo : to cause a scene⟩ **3** : to arm
  (soldiers, etc.) — **armarse** *vr* ~ **de** : to
  arm oneself with ⟨armarse de valor : to
  steel oneself⟩
armario *nm* **1** CLÓSET, ROPERO : closet
  2 ALACENA : cupboard
armatoste *nm fam* : monstrosity, contraption
armazón *nmf, pl* **-zones** **1** ESQUELETO
  : framework, skeleton ⟨armazón de
  acero : steel framework⟩ **2** : frames *pl*
  (of eyeglasses)
armenio, -nia *adj & n* : Armenian
armería *nf* **1** : armory **2** : arms museum
  3 : gunsmith's shop **4** : gunsmith's craft
armero, -ra *n* : gunsmith
armiño *nm* : ermine
armisticio *nm* : armistice
armonía *nf* : harmony
armónica *nf* : harmonica
armónico, -ca *adj* **1** : harmonic **2** : harmonious — **armónicamente** *adv*
armonioso, -sa *adj* : harmonious — **ar-
  moniosamente** *adv*
armonizar {21} *vt* **1** : to harmonize **2**
  : to reconcile — *vi* : to harmonize, to
  blend together
arnés *nm, pl* **arneses** : harness
aro *nm* **1** : hoop **2** : napkin ring **3** *Arg,
  Chile, Uru* : earring
aroma *nm* : aroma, scent
aromático, -ca *adj* : aromatic

arpa *nf* : harp
arpillera *nf* : burlap
arpista *nmf* : harpist
arpón *nm, pl* **arpones** : harpoon — **arponear** *vt*
arquear *vt* : to arch, to bend ⟨arquear las cejas : to raise one's eyebrows⟩ — **arquearse** *vr* : to bend, to bow
arqueología *nf* : archaeology
arqueológico, -ca *adj* : archaeological
arqueólogo, -ga *n* : archaeologist
arquero, -ra *n* **1** : archer **2** PORTERO : goalkeeper, goalie
arquetípico, -ca *adj* : archetypal
arquetipo *nm* : archetype
arquidiócesis *nfs & pl* : archdiocese
arquitecto, -ta *n* : architect
arquitectónico, -ca *adj* : architectural — **aquitectónicamente** *adv*
arquitectura *nf* : architecture
arrabal *nm* **1** : slum **2 arrabales** *nmpl* : outskirts, outlying area
arracada *nf* : hoop earring
arracimarse *vr* : to cluster together
arraigado, -da *adj* : deep-seated, ingrained
arraigar {52} *vi* : to take root, to become established — **arraigarse** *vr*
arraigo *nm* : roots *pl* ⟨con mucho arraigo : deep-rooted⟩
arrancar {72} *vt* **1** : to pull out (hair), to tear out (a page), to pull up (a weed), to pull off (a piece) **2** : to pick (a flower) **3** : to draw (applause, tears) **4** : to start (a car, etc.), to boot (a computer) **5** ARREBATAR : to snatch — *vi* **1** : to start, to boot (of a computer) **2** : to get going — **arrancarse** *vr* : to pull out, to pull off
arrancón *nm, pl* **-cones** *Mex* **1** : sudden loud start (of a car) **2 carrera de arrancones** : drag race
arranque *nm* **1** : starter (of a car) **2** ARREBATO : outburst, fit **3 punto de arranque** : beginning, starting point
arrasar *vt* **1** : to level, to smooth **2** : to devastate, to destroy **3** : to fill to the brim
arrastrar *vt* **1** : to drag, to tow **2** : to draw, to attract — *vi* : to hang down, to trail — **arrastrarse** *vr* **1** : to crawl **2** : to grovel
arrastre *nm* **1** : dragging **2** : pull, attraction **3 red de arrastre** : dragnet, trawling net
arrayán *nm, pl* **-yanes** MIRTO : myrtle
arrear *vt* : to urge on, to drive — *vi* : to hurry along
arrebatado, -da *adj* **1** PRECIPITADO : impetuous, hotheaded, rash **2** : flushed, blushing
arrebatador, -dora *adj* : breathtaking, impressive
arrebatar *vt* **1** : to snatch, to seize **2** CAUTIVAR : to captivate — **arrebatarse** *vr* : to get carried away (with anger, etc.)
arrebato *nm* ARRANQUE : fit, outburst
arreciar *vi* : to intensify, to worsen
arrecife *nm* : reef
arreglado, -da *adj* **1** : fixed, repaired **2** : settled, sorted out **3** : neat, tidy **4** : smart, dressed-up

arreglar *vt* **1** COMPONER : to repair, to fix **2** : to tidy, to straighten ⟨arregla tu cuarto : pick up your room⟩ ⟨deja que te arregle : let me fix your clothes/hair⟩ **3** : to arrange (flowers, etc.) **4** : to solve (a problem), to work out (plans) ⟨quiero arreglar este asunto : I want to settle this matter⟩ — **arreglarse** *vr* **1** : to get ready, to get dressed (up) **2** : to fix, to do ⟨arreglarse el pelo : to fix/do one's hair⟩ **3** : to have/get done ⟨arreglarse el pelo : to have/get one's hair done⟩ **4 arreglárselas** *fam* : to get by, to manage
arreglo *nm* **1** : repair **2** : arrangement **3** : agreement, understanding
arrellanarse *vr* : to settle (in a chair)
arremangarse {52} *vr* : to roll up one's sleeves
arremeter *vi* EMBESTIR : to attack, to charge
arremetida *nf* EMBESTIDA : attack, onslaught
arremolinarse *vr* **1** : to crowd around, to mill about **2** : to swirl (about)
arrendador, -dora *n* **1** : landlord, landlady *f* **2** : tenant, lessee
arrendajo *nm* : jay
arrendamiento *nm* **1** ALQUILER : rental, leasing **2 contrato de arrendamiento** : lease
arrendar {55} *vt* ALQUILAR : to rent, to lease
arrendatario, -ria *n* : tenant, lessee, renter
arreos *nmpl* GUARNICIONES : tack, harness, trappings
arrepentido, -da *adj* : repentant, remorseful
arrepentimiento *nm* : regret, remorse, repentance
arrepentirse {76} *vr* **1** : to regret, to be sorry **2** : to repent
arrestar *vt* DETENER : to arrest, to detain
arresto *nm* **1** DETENCIÓN : arrest **2 arrestos** *nmpl* : boldness, daring
arriar {85} *vt* **1** : to lower (a flag, etc.) **2** : to slacken (a rope, etc.)
arriate *nm* *Mex, Spain* : bed (for plants), border
arriba *adv* **1** : up, upwards ⟨póngalo más arriba : put it higher (up)⟩ ⟨arriba y abajo : up and down⟩ ⟨¡manos arriba! : (put your) hands up!⟩ ⟨cuesta/río arriba : uphill/upstream⟩ **2** : above, overhead ⟨desde arriba : from above⟩ ⟨el arriba mencionado : the above-mentioned⟩ **3** : upstairs ⟨los vecinos de arriba : the upstairs neighbors⟩ **4** : up with ⟨¡arriba la democracia! : up with democracy!⟩ **5 ~ de** : above, on top of **6 ~ de** : more than ⟨arriba de cien : more than a hundred⟩ **7 de ~** : top, upper ⟨el cajón de arriba : the top drawer⟩ **8 de arriba abajo** : from top to bottom, from head to foot **9 hacia/para ~** : upwards
arribar *vi* **1** : to arrive **2** : to dock, to put into port
arribista *nmf* : parvenu, upstart
arribo *nm* : arrival
arriendo *nm* ARRENDAMIENTO : rent, rental

arriero, -ra *n* : mule driver

arriesgado, -da *adj* **1** : risky **2** : bold, daring

arriesgar {52} *vt* : to risk, to venture — **arriesgarse** *vr* : to take a chance

arrimado, -da *n Mex fam* : sponger, freeloader

arrimar *vt* ACERCAR, APROXIMAR : to bring closer, to draw near — **arrimarse** *vr* ACERCARSE, APROXIMARSE : to approach, to get close

arrinconar *vt* **1** ACORRALAR : to corner, to box in **2** : to push aside, to abandon

arroba *nf* **1** (*used for the symbol @*) : at sign ⟨arroba merriam-webster punto com : at merriam-webster dot com⟩ **2** : former unit of measurement

arrobamiento *nm* : rapture, ecstasy

arrobar *vt* : to enrapture, to enchant — **arrobarse** *vr*

arrocero¹, -ra *adj* : rice

arrocero², -ra *n* : rice grower

arrodillarse *vr* : to kneel (down)

arrogancia *nf* ALTANERÍA, ALTIVEZ : arrogance, haughtiness

arrogante *adj* ALTANERO, ALTIVO : arrogant, haughty

arrogarse {52} *vr* : to usurp, to arrogate

arrojado, -da *adj* : daring, fearless

arrojar *vt* **1** : to hurl, to cast, to throw **2** : to give off, to spew out **3** : to yield, to produce **4** *fam* : to vomit — **arrojarse** *vr* PRECIPITARSE : to throw oneself, to leap

arrojo *nm* : boldness, fearlessness

arrollador, -dora *adj* : sweeping, overwhelming

arrollar *vt* **1** : to sweep away, to carry away **2** : to crush, to overwhelm **3** : to run over (with a vehicle)

arropar *vt* : to clothe, to cover (up) — **arroparse** *vr*

arrostrar *vt* : to confront, to face (up to)

arroyo *nm* **1** RIACHUELO : brook, creek, stream **2** : gutter

arroz *nm, pl* **arroces** : rice

arrozal *nm* : rice field, rice paddy

arruga *nf* : wrinkle, fold, crease

arrugado, -da *adj* : wrinkled, creased, lined

arrugar {52} *vt* : to wrinkle, to crease, to pucker — **arrugarse** *vr*

arruinar *vt* : to ruin, to wreck — **arruinarse** *vr* **1** : to be ruined **2** : to fall into ruin, to go bankrupt

arrullar *vt* : to lull to sleep — *vi* : to coo

arrullo *nm* **1** : lullaby **2** : coo (of a dove)

arrumaco *nm fam* : kissing, cuddling

arrumbar *vt* **1** : to lay aside, to put away **2** : to floor, to leave speechless

arsenal *nm* : arsenal

arsénico *nm* : arsenic

arte *nmf* (*usually m in singular, f in plural*) **1** : art ⟨artes y oficios : arts and crafts⟩ ⟨bellas artes : fine arts⟩ ⟨obra de arte : work of art⟩ **2** HABILIDAD : art, skill ⟨el arte de hacer amigos : the art of making friends⟩ ⟨tener arte para : to be skilled at⟩ **3** *artes* *nfpl* : cunning, guile

artefacto *nm* **1** : artifact **2** DISPOSITIVO : device

artemisa *nf* : sagebrush

arteria *nf* : artery — **arterial** *adj*

arteriosclerosis *nf* : arteriosclerosis, hardening of the arteries

artero, -ra *adj* : wily, crafty

artesanal *adj* : pertaining to crafts or craftsmanship, handmade

artesanía *nf* **1** : craftsmanship **2** : handicrafts *pl*

artesano, -na *n* : artisan, craftsman

ártico, -ca *adj* : arctic

articulación *nf, pl* **-ciones 1** : articulation, pronunciation **2** COYUNTURA : joint

articular *vt* **1** : to articulate, to utter **2** : to connect with a joint **3** : to coordinate, to orchestrate

articulista *nmf* : columnist

artículo *nm* **1** : article, thing **2** : item, feature, report **3 artículo de comercio** : commodity **4 artículos de primera necesidad** : essentials **5 artículos de tocador** : toiletries

artífice *nmf* **1** ARTESANO : artisan **2** : mastermind, architect

artificial *adj* **1** : artificial, man-made **2** : feigned, false — **artificialmente** *adv*

artificio *nm* **1** HABILIDAD : skill **2** APARATO : device, appliance **3** ARDID : artifice, ruse

artificioso, -sa *adj* **1** : skillful **2** : cunning, deceptive

artillería *nf* : artillery

artillero, -ra *n* : gunner

artilugio *nm* : gadget, contraption

artimaña *nf* : ruse, trick

artista *nmf* **1** : artist **2** ACTOR, ACTRIZ : actor, actress *f*

artístico, -ca *adj* : artistic — **artísticamente** *adv*

artrítico, -ca *adj* : arthritic

artritis *nfs & pl* : arthritis

artrópodo *nm* : arthropod

arveja *nf* GUISANTE : pea

arzobispado *nm* : archbishopric

arzobispo *nm* : archbishop

as *nm* : ace

asa *nf* AGARRADERA, ASIDERO : handle, grip

asado¹, -da *adj* : roasted, grilled, broiled

asado² ** *nm* **1 : roast **2** : barbecued meat **3** : barbecue, cookout

asador *nm* : spit, rotisserie

asaduras *nfpl* : entrails, offal

asalariado¹, -da *adj* : wage-earning, salaried

asalariado², -da *n* : wage earner

asaltante *nmf* **1** : mugger, robber **2** : assailant

asaltar *vt* **1** : to assault **2** : to mug, to rob **3 asaltar al poder** : to seize power

asalto *nm* **1** : assault **2** : mugging, robbery **3** : round (in boxing) **4 asalto al poder** : coup d'état

asamblea *nf* : assembly, meeting

asambleísta *nmf* : assemblyman *m*, assemblywoman *f*

asar *vt* : to roast, to grill — **asarse** *vr fam* : to roast, to be dying from heat

asbesto *nm* : asbestos

ascendencia *nf* **1** : ancestry, descent **2** ~ **sobre** : influence over
ascendente *adj* : ascending, upward ⟨un curso ascendente : an upward trend⟩
ascender {56} *vt* **1** : to ascend, to rise up **2** : to be promoted ⟨ascendió a gerente : she was promoted to manager⟩ **3** ~ **a** : to amount to, to reach ⟨las deudas ascienden a 20 millones de pesos : the debt amounts to 20 million pesos⟩ — *vt* : to promote
ascendiente¹ *nmf* ANCESTRO : ancestor
ascendiente² *nm* INFLUENCIA : influence, ascendancy
ascensión *nf, pl* **-siones 1** : ascent, rise **2 Fiesta de la Ascensión** : Ascension Day
ascenso *nm* **1** : ascent, rise **2** : promotion
ascensor *nm* ELEVADOR : elevator
asceta *nmf* : ascetic
ascético, -ca *adj* : ascetic
ascetismo *nm* : asceticism
asco *nm* **1** : disgust ⟨¡qué asco! : that's disgusting!, how revolting!⟩ **2 darle asco a alguien** : to disgust someone **3 estar hecho un asco** : to be filthy **4 hacerle ascos a algo** : to turn up one's nose at something
ascua *nf* **1** BRASA : ember **2 estar en ascuas** *fam* : to be on edge
aseado, -da *adj* : clean, neat
asear *vt* **1** : to wash, to clean **2** : to tidy up — **asearse** *vr*
asechanza *nf* : snare, trap
asechar *vt* : to set a trap for
asediar *vt* **1** SITIAR : to besiege **2** ACOSAR : to harass
asedio *nm* **1** : siege **2** ACOSO : harassment
asegurador¹, -dora *adj* **1** : insuring, assuring **2** : pertaining to insurance
asegurador², -dora *n* : insurer, underwriter
aseguradora *nf* : insurance company
asegurar *vt* **1** : to assure **2** : to secure **3** : to insure — **asegurarse** *vr* **1** CERCIORARSE : to make sure **2** : to take out insurance, to insure oneself
asemejar *vt* **1** : to make similar ⟨ese bigote te asemeja a tu abuelo : that mustache makes you look like your grandfather⟩ **2** *Mex* : to be similar to, to resemble — **asemejarse** *vr* ~ **a** : to look like, to resemble
asentaderas *nfpl fam* : bottom, buttocks *pl*
asentado, -da *adj* : settled, established
asentamiento *nm* : settlement
asentar {55} *vt* **1** : to lay down, to set down, to place **2** : to settle, to establish **3** *Mex* : to state, to affirm — **asentarse** *vr* **1** : to settle **2** ESTABLECERSE : to settle down, to establish oneself
asentimiento *nm* : assent, consent
asentir {76} *vi* : to consent, to agree
aseo *nm* : cleanliness
aséptico, -ca *adj* : aseptic
asequible *adj* ACCESIBLE : accessible, attainable

aserción *nf, pl* **-ciones** → **aserto**
aserradero *nm* : sawmill
aserrar {55} *vt* : to saw
aserrín *nm, pl* **-rrines** : sawdust
aserto *nm* : assertion, affirmation
asesinar *vt* **1** : to murder **2** : to assassinate
asesinato *nm* **1** : murder **2** : assassination
asesino¹, -na *adj* : murderous, homicidal
asesino², -na *n* **1** : murderer, killer **2** : assassin
asesor, -sora *n* : advisor, consultant
asesoramiento *nm* : advice, counsel
asesorar *vt* : to advise, to counsel — **asesorarse** *vr* ~ **de** : to consult
asesoría *nf* **1** : consulting, advising **2** : consultant's office
asestar {55} *vt* **1** : to aim, to point (a weapon) **2** : to deliver, to deal (a blow)
aseveración *nf, pl* **-ciones** : assertion, statement
aseverar *vt* : to assert, to state
asexual *adj* : asexual — **asexualmente** *adv*
asfaltado¹, -da *adj* : paved (with asphalt)
asfaltado² *nm* PAVIMENTO : pavement, asphalt
asfaltar *vt* : to pave, to blacktop
asfalto *nm* : asphalt
asfixia *nf* : asphyxia, asphyxiation, suffocation
asfixiante *adj* **1** : asphyxiating **2** AGOBIANTE : oppressive
asfixiar *vt* : to asphyxiate, to suffocate, to smother — **asfixiarse** *vr*
asga, etc. → **asir**
así¹ *adv* **1** : like this, like that, so ⟨así se hace : that's how it's done⟩ ⟨no puede seguir así : it can't go on like this⟩ ⟨así sea : so be it⟩ ⟨y así sucesivamente : and so on⟩ **2 así así** : so-so, fair **3** ~ **como** : as well as **4 así como así** *or* **así nomás** : just like that **5** ~ **de** : so, about so ⟨una caja así de grande : a box about so big⟩ **6 así mismo** → **asimismo 7 así que** : so, therefore **8 así y todo** : even so
así² *adj* : such, such a, like that ⟨un talento así : a talent like that⟩ ⟨algo así : something like that⟩ ⟨así es la vida : that's life⟩ ⟨si es así . . . : if that's the case . . .⟩
así³ *conj* AUNQUE : even if, even though ⟨no irá, así le paguen : he won't go, even if they pay him⟩
asiático¹, -ca *adj* : Asian
asiático², -ca *n* : Asian
asidero *nm* **1** AGARRADERA, ASA : grip, handle **2** AGARRE : grip, hold
asiduamente *adv* : regularly, frequently
asiduidad *nf* **con** ~ : regularly, frequently
asiduo, -dua *adj* **1** : assiduous **2** : frequent, regular
asiento *nm* **1** : seat, chair ⟨asiento trasero : back seat⟩ **2** : location, site
asignación *nf, pl* **-ciones 1** : allocation **2** : appointment, designation **3** : allowance, pay **4** *PRi* : homework, assignment

asignar *vt* **1** : to assign, to allocate **2** : to appoint
asignatura *nf* MATERIA : subject, course
asilado, -da *n* : exile, refugee
asilo *nm* : asylum, refuge, shelter
asimetría *nf* : asymmetry
asimétrico, -ca *adj* : asymmetrical, asymmetric
asimilación *nf, pl* **-ciones** : assimilation
asimilar *vt* : to assimilate — **asimilarse** *vr* ～ **a** : to be similar to, to resemble
asimismo *adv* **1** IGUALMENTE : similarly, likewise **2** TAMBIÉN : as well, also
asir {7} *vt* : to seize, to grasp — **asirse** *vr* ～ **a** : to cling to
asistencia *nf* **1** : attendance **2** : assistance **3** : assist (in sports) **4 asistencia médica** *or Spain* **asistencia sanitaria** : health care, medical care
asistente[1] *adj* : attending, in attendance
asistente[2] *nmf* **1** : assistant **2 los asistentes** : those present, those in attendance
asistido, -da *adj* : assisted
asistir *vi* : to attend, to be present ⟨asistir a clase : to attend class⟩ — *vt* : to aid, to assist
asma *nf* : asthma
asmático, -ca *adj* : asthmatic
asno *nm* BURRO : ass, donkey
asociación *nf, pl* **-ciones** **1** : association, relationship **2** : society, group, association
asociado[1], **-da** *adj* : associate, associated
asociado[2], **-da** *n* : associate, partner
asociar *vt* **1** : to associate, to connect **2** : to pool (resources) **3** : to take into partnership — **asociarse** *vr* **1** : to become partners **2** ～ **a** : to join, to become a member of
asolar {19} *vt* : to devastate, to destroy
asoleado, -da *adj* : sunny
asolear *vt* : to put in the sun — **asolearse** *vr* : to sunbathe
asomar *vt* : to show, to stick out — *vi* : to appear, to become visible — **asomarse** *vr* **1** : to show, to appear **2** : to lean out, to look out ⟨se asomó por la ventana : he leaned out the window⟩
asombrar *vt* MARAVILLAR : to amaze, to astonish — **asombrarse** *vr* : to marvel, to be amazed
asombro *nm* : amazement, astonishment
asombroso, -sa *adj* : amazing, astonishing — **asombrosamente** *adv*
asomo *nm* **1** : hint, trace **2 ni por asomo** : by no means
aspa *nf* : blade (of a fan or propeller)
aspaviento *nm* : exaggerated movement, fuss, flounce
aspecto *nm* **1** : aspect **2** APARIENCIA : appearance, look
aspereza *nf* RUDEZA : roughness, coarseness
áspero, -ra *adj* : rough, coarse, abrasive — **ásperamente** *adv*
aspersión *nf, pl* **-siones** : sprinkling
aspersor *nm* : sprinkler
aspiración *nf, pl* **-ciones** **1** : inhalation, breathing in **2** ANHELO : aspiration, desire

aspiradora *nf* : vacuum cleaner
aspirante *nmf* : applicant, candidate
aspirar *vi* ～ **a** : to aspire to — *vt* : to inhale, to breathe in
aspirina *nf* : aspirin
asqueante *adj* : sickening, disgusting
asquear *vt* : to sicken, to disgust
asquerosidad *nf* : filth, foulness
asqueroso, -sa *adj* : disgusting, sickening, repulsive — **asquerosamente** *adv*
asta *nf* **1** : flagpole ⟨a media asta : at half-mast⟩ **2** : horn, antler **3** : shaft (of a weapon)
ástaco *nm* : crayfish
astado, -da *adj* : horned
aster *nm* : aster
asterisco *nm* : asterisk
asteroide *nm* : asteroid
astigmatismo *nm* : astigmatism
astil *nm* : shaft (of an arrow or feather)
astilla *nf* **1** : splinter, chip **2 de tal palo, tal astilla** : like father, like son
astillar *vt* : to splinter — **astillarse** *vr*
astillero *nm* : dry dock, shipyard
astral *adj* : astral
astringente *adj & nm* : astringent — **astringencia** *nf*
astro *nm* **1** : heavenly body **2** : star
astrología *nf* : astrology
astrológico, -ca *adj* : astrological
astrólogo, -ga *n* : astrologer
astronauta *nmf* : astronaut
astronáutica *nf* : astronautics
astronáutico, -ca *adj* : astronautic, astronautical
astronave *nf* : spaceship
astronomía *nf* : astronomy
astronómico, -ca *adj* : astronomical — **astronómicamente** *adv*
astrónomo, -ma *n* : astronomer
astroso, -sa *adj* DESALIÑADO : slovenly, untidy
astucia *nf* **1** : astuteness, shrewdness **2** : cunning, guile
astuto, -ta *adj* **1** : astute, shrewd **2** : crafty, tricky — **astutamente** *adv*
asueto *nm* : time off, break
asumir *vt* **1** : to assume, to take on ⟨asumir el cargo : to take office⟩ **2** SUPONER : to assume, to suppose
asunción *nf, pl* **-ciones** : assumption
asunto *nm* **1** CUESTIÓN, TEMA : affair, matter, subject **2 asuntos** *nmpl* : affairs, business
asustadizo, -za *adj* : nervous, jumpy, skittish
asustado, -da *adj* : frightened, afraid
asustar *vt* ESPANTAR : to scare, to frighten — **asustarse** *vr*
atacante *nmf* : assailant, attacker
atacar {72} *v* : to attack
atado[1], **-da** *adj* : shy, inhibited
atado[2] *nm* **1** : bundle, bunch **2** *Arg* : pack (of cigarettes)
atadura *nf* LIGADURA : tie, bond
atajada *nf* : save (in sports)
atajar *vt* **1** IMPEDIR : to block, to stop **2** INTERRUMPIR : to interrupt, to cut off **3** CONTENER : to hold back, to restrain — *vi* ～ **por** : to take a shortcut through

atajo *nm* : shortcut
atalaya *nf* **1** : watchtower **2** : vantage point
atañer {79} *vt* ~ **a** (*3rd person only*) : to concern, to have to do with ⟨eso no me atañe : that does not concern me⟩
ataque *nm* **1** : attack, assault **2** : fit ⟨ataque de risa : fit of laughter⟩ **3 ataque de nervios** : nervous breakdown **4 ataque de pánico/ansiedad** : panic/ anxiety attack **5 ataque cardíaco** *or* **ataque al corazón** : heart attack
atar *vt* AMARRAR : to tie, to tie up, to tie down — **atarse** *vr*
atarantado, -da *adj fam* **1** : restless : dazed, stunned
atarantar *vt fam* : to daze, to stun
atarazana *nf* : shipyard
atardecer[1] *v impers* : to get dark
atardecer[2] *nm* : late afternoon, dusk
atareado, -da *adj* : busy, overworked
atascar {72} *vt* **1** ATORAR : to block, to clog, to stop up **2** : to hinder — **atascarse** *vr* **1** : to become obstructed **2** : to get bogged down **3** PARARSE : to stall
atasco *nm* **1** : blockage **2** EMBOTELLA-MIENTO : traffic jam
ataúd *nm* : coffin, casket
ataviar {85} *vt* **1** : to dress, to clothe — **ataviarse** *vr* : to dress up
atavío *nm* ATUENDO : dress, attire
ateísmo *nm* : atheism
atemorizar {21} *vt* : to frighten, to intimidate — **atemorizarse** *vr*
atemperar *vt* : to temper, to moderate
atención[1] *nf, pl* **-ciones** **1** : attention **2 poner atención** *or* **prestar atención** : to pay attention **3 llamar la atención** : to attract attention **4 en atención a** : in view of
atención[2] *interj* **1** : attention! **2** : watch out!
atender {56} *vt* **1** : to help, to wait on **2** : to look after, to take care of **3** : to heed, to listen to — *vi* : to pay attention
atenerse {80} *vr* : to abide ⟨tendrás que atenerte a las reglas : you will have to abide by the rules⟩
atentado *nm* : attack, assault
atentamente *adv* **1** : attentively, carefully **2** (*used in correspondence*) : sincerely, sincerely yours
atentar {55} *vi* ~ **contra** : to make an attempt on, to threaten ⟨atentaron contra su vida : they made an attempt on his life⟩
atento, -ta *adj* **1** : attentive, mindful **2** CORTÉS : courteous
atenuación *nf, pl* **-ciones** **1** : lessening **2** : understatement
atenuante[1] *adj* : extenuating, mitigating
atenuante[2] *nmf* : extenuating circumstance, excuse
atenuar {3} *vt* **1** MITIGAR : to extenuate, to mitigate **2** : to dim (light), to tone down (colors) **3** : to minimize, to lessen
ateo[1], **atea** *adj* : atheistic
ateo[2], **atea** *n* : atheist
aterciopelado, -da *adj* : velvety, downy
aterido, -da *adj* : freezing, frozen

aterrador, -dora *adj* : terrifying
aterrar {55} *vt* : to terrify, to frighten
aterrizaje *nm* : landing (of a plane)
aterrizar {21} *vt* : to land, to touch down
aterrorizar {21} *vt* **1** : to terrify **2** : to terrorize — **aterrorizarse** *vr* : to be terrified
atesorar *vt* : to hoard, to amass
atestado, -da *adj* : crowded, packed
atestar {55} *vt* **1** ATIBORRAR : to crowd, to pack **2** : to witness, to testify to — *vi* : to testify
atestiguar {10} *vt* : to testify to, to bear witness to — *vi* DECLARAR : to testify
atiborrar *vt* : to pack, to crowd — **atiborrarse** *vr* : to stuff oneself
ático *nm* **1** : penthouse **2** BUHARDILLA, DESVÁN : attic
atigrado, -da *adj* : tabby (of cats), striped (of fur)
atildado, -da *adj* : smart, neat, dapper
atildar *vt* **1** : to put a tilde over **2** : to clean up, to smarten up — **atildarse** *vr* : to get spruced up
atinar *vi* ACERTAR : to be accurate, to be on target
atingencia *nf* : bearing, relevance
atípico, -ca *adj* : atypical
atiplado, -da *adj* : shrill, high-pitched
atirantar *vt* : to make taut, to tighten
atisbar *vt* **1** : to spy on, to watch **2** : to catch a glimpse of, to make out
atisbo *nm* : glimpse, sign, hint
atizador *nm* : poker (for a fire)
atizar {21} *vt* **1** : to poke, to stir, to stoke (a fire) **2** : to stir up, to rouse **3** *fam* : to give, to land (a blow)
atlántico, -ca *adj* : Atlantic
atlas *nm* : atlas
atleta *nmf* : athlete
atlético, -ca *adj* : athletic
atletismo *nm* : athletics
atmósfera *nf* : atmosphere
atmosférico, -ca *adj* : atmospheric
atole *nm Mex* **1** : thick hot beverage prepared with cornmeal **2 darle atole con el dedo a alguien** : to string someone along
atolladero *nm* : predicament, fix
atollarse *vr* : to get stuck, to get bogged down
atolón *nm, pl* **-lones** : atoll
atolondrado, -da *adj* **1** ATURDIDO : bewildered, dazed **2** DESPISTADO : scatterbrained, absentminded
atómico, -ca *adj* : atomic
atomizador *nm* : atomizer
atomizar {21} *vt* FRAGMENTAR : to fragment, to break into bits
átomo *nm* : atom
atónito, -ta *adj* : astonished, amazed
atontar *vt* **1** : to stupefy **2** : to bewilder, to confuse
atorar *vt* ATASCAR : to block, to clog — **atorarse** *vr* **1** ATASCARSE : to get stuck **2** ATRAGANTARSE : to choke
atormentador, -dora *n* : tormentor
atormentar *vt* : to torment, to torture — **atormentarse** *vr* : to torment oneself, to agonize
atornillar *vt* : to screw (in, on, down)

atorrante *nmf Arg* : bum, loafer
atosigar {52} *vt* : to harass, to annoy
atracadero *nm* : dock, pier
atracador, -dora *n* : robber, mugger
atracar {72} *vt* : to dock, to land — *vt* : to hold up, to rob, to mug — **atracarse** *vr fam* ~ **de** : to gorge oneself with
atracción *nf, pl* **-ciones** : attraction
atraco *nm* : holdup, robbery
atracón *nm, pl* **-cones** *fam* **darse un atracón (de)** : to pig out (on)
atractivo¹, -va *adj* : attractive — **atractivamente** *adv*
atractivo² *nm* : attraction, appeal, charm
atraer {81} *vt* : to attract — **atraerse** *vr* 1 : to attract (each other) 2 GANARSE : to gain, to win
atragantarse *vr* : to choke (on food)
atrancar {72} *vt* : to block, to bar — **atrancarse** *vr*
atrapada *nf* : catch
atrapar *vt* : to trap, to capture
atrás *adv* 1 DETRÁS : back, behind ⟨la parte de atrás : the back/rear part⟩ ⟨dar un paso atrás : to take a step back⟩ 2 ANTES : ago ⟨mucho tiempo atrás : long ago⟩ 3 ~ **de** : in back of, behind 4 **desde** ~ : from behind, from the rear 5 **hacia/para** ~ : backwards, toward the rear 6 **dejar atrás** : to leave (the past, etc.) behind 7 **quedarse atrás** : to fall behind, to get left behind
atrasado, -da *adj* 1 : late, overdue 2 : backward 3 : old-fashioned 4 : slow (of a clock or watch)
atrasar *vt* : to delay, to put off — *vi* : to lose time — **atrasarse** *vr* : to fall behind
atraso *nm* 1 RETRASO : lateness, delay ⟨llegó con 20 minutos de atraso : he was 20 minutes late⟩ 2 : backwardness 3 **atrasos** *nmpl* : arrears
atravesar {55} *vt* 1 CRUZAR : to cross, to go across 2 : to pierce 3 : to lay across 4 : to go through (a situation or crisis) — **atravesarse** *vr* 1 : to be in the way ⟨se me atravesó : it blocked my path⟩ 2 : to interfere, to meddle
atrayente *adj* : attractive
atreverse *vr* 1 : to dare 2 : to be insolent
atrevido, -da *adj* 1 : bold, daring 2 : insolent
atrevimiento *nm* 1 : daring, boldness 2 : insolence
atribución *nf, pl* **-ciones** : attribution
atribuible *adj* IMPUTABLE : attributable, ascribable
atribuir {41} *vt* 1 : to attribute, to ascribe 2 : to grant, to confer — **atribuirse** *vr* : to take credit for
atribular *vt* : to afflict, to trouble — **atribularse** *vr*
atributo *nm* : attribute
atril *nm* : lectern, stand
atrincherar *vt* : to entrench — **atrincherarse** *vr* 1 : to dig in, to entrench oneself 2 ~ **en** : to hide behind
atrio *nm* 1 : atrium 2 : portico
atrocidad *nf* : atrocity
atrofia *nf* : atrophy

atrofiar *v* : to atrophy
atronador, -dora *adj* : thunderous, deafening
atropellado, -da *adj* 1 : rash, hasty 2 : brusque, abrupt — **atropelladamente** *adv*
atropellamiento → **atropello**
atropellar *vt* 1 : to knock down, to run over 2 : to violate, to abuse — **atropellarse** *vr* : to rush through (a task), to trip over one's words
atropello *nm* : abuse, violation, outrage
atroz *adj, pl* **atroces** : atrocious, appalling — **atrozmente** *adv*
atuendo *nm* ATAVÍO : attire, costume
atufar *vt* : to vex, to irritate — **atufarse** *vr* 1 : to get angry 2 : to smell bad, to stink
atún *nm, pl* **atunes** : tuna fish, tuna
aturdimiento *nm* : bewilderment, confusion
aturdir *vt* 1 : to stun, to shock 2 : to bewilder, to confuse, to stupefy — **aturdido, -da** *adj*
atuvo, etc. → **atenerse**
audacia *nf* OSADÍA : boldness, audacity
audaz *adj, pl* **audaces** : bold, audacious, daring — **audazmente** *adv*
audible *adj* : audible
audición *nf, pl* **-ciones** 1 : hearing 2 : audition
audiencia *nf* : audience
audífono *nm* 1 : hearing aid 2 **audífonos** *nmpl* : headphones, earphones
audio *nm* : audio
audiolibro *nm* : audiobook
audiovisual *adj* : audiovisual
auditar *vt* : to audit
auditivo, -va *adj* : auditory, hearing, aural ⟨aparato auditivo : hearing aid⟩
auditor, -tora *n* : auditor
auditoría *nf* : audit
auditorio *nm* 1 : auditorium 2 : audience
auge *nm* 1 : peak, height 2 : boom, upturn
augur *nm* : augur
augurar *vt* : to predict, to foretell
augurio *nm* AGÜERO, PRESAGIO : augury, omen
augusto, -ta *adj* : august
aula *nf* : classroom
aullar {8} *vt* : to howl, to wail
aullido *nm* : howl, wail
aumentar *vt* ACRECENTAR : to increase, to raise — *vi* : to rise, to increase, to grow
aumento *nm* INCREMENTO : increase, rise
aun *adv* 1 : even ⟨ni aun en coche llegaría a tiempo : I wouldn't arrive on time even if I drove⟩ 2 **aun así** : even so 3 **aun más** : even more
aún *adv* TODAVÍA : still, yet ⟨aún falta mucho por hacer : there's still a lot left to do⟩ ⟨aún no lo sabe : she doesn't know yet⟩
aunar {8} *vt* : to join, to combine — **aunarse** *vr* : to unite
aunque *conj* 1 : though, although, even if, even though 2 **aunque sea** : at least
aura *nf* 1 : aura 2 : turkey buzzard

áureo, -rea *adj* : golden
aureola *nf* 1 : halo 2 : aura (of power, fame, etc.)
aurícula *nf* : auricle
auricular *nm* 1 : telephone receiver 2 auriculares *nmpl* : headphones, earphones 3 auriculares de tapón : earbuds
aurora *nf* 1 : dawn 2 aurora boreal : aurora borealis
ausencia *nf* : absence
ausentarse *vr* 1 : to leave, to go away 2 ~ de : to stay away from
ausente[1] *adj* : absent, missing
ausente[2] *nmf* 1 : absentee 2 : missing person
auspiciar *vt* 1 PATROCINAR : to sponsor 2 FOMENTAR : to foster, to promote
auspicios *nmpl* : sponsorship, auspices
austeridad *nf* : austerity
austero, -ra *adj* : austere
austral[1] *adj* : southern
austral[2] *nm* : former monetary unit of Argentina
australiano, -na *adj & n* : Australian
austriaco *or* austríaco, -ca *adj & n* : Austrian
autenticar {72} *vt* : to authenticate — autenticación *nf*
autenticidad *nf* : authenticity
auténtico, -ca *adj* : authentic — auténticamente *adv*
autentificar {72} *vt* : to authenticate — autentificación *nf*
autismo *nm* : autism
autista *adj* : autistic
auto *nm* : auto, car
auto- *pref* : self-
autoabastecerse {18} *vr* : to be self-sufficient
autoayuda *nf* : self-help
autobiografía *nf* : autobiography
autobiográfico, -ca *adj* : autobiographical
autobomba *nf Arg, Spain, Uru* : fire truck
auto bomba *nf Chile* : car bomb
autobús *nm, pl* -buses : bus
autocar *Spain* → autobús
autocine *nm* : drive-in
autocompasión *nf* : self-pity
autocontrol *nm* : self-control
autocorrector *nm* : autocorrect
autocracia *nf* : autocracy
autócrata *nmf* : autocrat
autocrático, -ca *adj* : autocratic
autóctono, -na *adj* : indigenous, native
⟨arte autóctono : indigenous art⟩
autodefensa *nf* : self-defense
autodenominarse *vr* : to call oneself
autodestrucción *nf* : self-destruction — autodestructivo, -va *adj*
autodeterminación *nf* : self-determination
autodidacta[1] *adj* : self-taught
autodidacta[2] *nmf* : self-taught person
autodidacto[1], -ta *adj* → autodidacta[1]
autodidacto[2], -ta *n* → autodidacta[2]
autodisciplina *nf* : self-discipline
autoedición *nf* : desktop publishing
autoescuela *nf Spain* : driving school
autoestima *nf* : self-esteem

autofoto *nf* : selfie
autogobierno *nm* : self-government
autografiar *vt* : to autograph
autógrafo *nm* : autograph
autoinfligido, -da *adj* : self-inflicted
automación → automatización
autómata *nm* : automaton
automático, -ca *adj* : automatic — automáticamente *adv*
automatización *nf* : automation
automatizar {21} *vt* : to automate
automercado *nm Ven* : supermarket
automotor, -tora *adj* 1 : self-propelled 2 : automotive, car
automotriz[1] *adj, pl* -trices : automotive, car
automotriz[2] *nf, pl* -trices : automaker
automóvil *nm* : automobile
automovilista *nmf* : motorist
automovilístico, -ca *adj* : automobile, car
⟨accidente automovilístico : automobile accident⟩
autonombrado, -da *adj* : self-appointed
autonomía *nf* : autonomy
autonómico, -ca *adj* : autonomous
autónomo, -ma *adj* : autonomous — autónomamente *adv*
autopista *nf* : expressway, highway
autoproclamado, -da *adj* : self-proclaimed, self-appointed
autopropulsado, -da *adj* : self-propelled
autopsia *nf* : autopsy
autor, -tora *n* 1 : author 2 : perpetrator
autoría *nf* : authorship
autoridad *nf* : authority
autoritario, -ria *adj* : authoritarian
autorización *nf, pl* -ciones : authorization
autorizado, -da *adj* 1 : authorized 2 : authoritative
autorizar {21} *vt* : to authorize, to approve
autorretrato *nm* : self-portrait
autoservicio *nm* 1 : self-service restaurant 2 SUPERMERCADO : supermarket
autostop *nm* 1 : hitchhiking 2 hacer autostop : to hitchhike
autostopista *nmf* : hitchhiker
autosuficiencia *nf* : self-sufficiency — autosuficiente *adj*
autovía *nf* : divided highway
auxiliar[1] *vt* : to aid, to assist
auxiliar[2] *adj* : assistant, auxiliary
auxiliar[3] *nmf* 1 : assistant, helper 2 auxiliar de vuelo : flight attendant
auxilio *nm* 1 : aid, assistance 2 primeros auxilios : first aid
aval *nm* : guarantee, endorsement
avalancha *nf* ALUD : avalanche
avalar *vt* : to guarantee, to endorse
avaluar {3} *vt* : to evaluate, to appraise
avalúo *nm* : appraisal, evaluation
avance *nm* ADELANTO : advance
avanzado, -da *adj* 1 : advanced 2 : progressive
avanzar {21} *vi* 1 : to advance, to move forward, to make progress — *vt* 1 : to advance, to move forward 2 : to advance, to put forward
avaricia *nf* CODICIA : greed, avarice
avaricioso, -sa *adj* : avaricious, greedy

avaro¹, -ra *adj* : miserly, greedy
avaro², -ra *n* : miser
avasallador, -dora *adj* : overwhelming
avasallamiento *nm* : domination
avasallar *vt* : to overpower, to subjugate
avatar *nm* **1** : avatar **2 avatares** *nmpl*
: vagaries, vicissitudes
ave *nf* **1** : bird **2 aves de corral** : poultry
3 ave rapaz *or* **ave de presa** : bird of prey
avecinarse *vr* : to approach, to come near
avecindarse *vr* : to settle, to take up residence
avellana *nf* : hazelnut, filbert
avellano *nm* : hazel
avena *nf* **1** : oat, oats *pl* **2** : oatmeal
avenencia *nf* : agreement, pact
avenida *nf* : avenue
avenir {87} *vt* : to reconcile, to harmonize
— **avenirse** *vr* **1** : to agree, to come to terms **2** : to get along
aventajado, -da *adj* : outstanding
aventajar *vt* **1** : to be ahead of, to lead **2**
: to surpass, to outdo
aventar {55} *vt* **1** : to fan **2** : to winnow
3 *Col, Mex* : to throw, to toss — **aventarse** *vr* **1** *Col, Mex* : to hurl oneself **2**
Mex fam : to dare, to take a chance
aventón *nm, pl* **-tones** *Col, Mex fam*
: ride, lift
aventura *nf* **1** : adventure **2** RIESGO
: venture, risk **3** : love affair
aventurado, -da *adj* : hazardous, risky
aventurar *vt* : to venture, to risk — **aventurarse** *vr* : to take a risk
aventurero¹, -ra *adj* : adventurous
aventurero², -ra *n* : adventurer
avergonzado, -da *adj* **1** : ashamed **2**
: embarrassed
avergonzar {9} *vt* APENAR : to shame, to embarrass — **avergonzarse** *vr* APENARSE
: to be ashamed, to be embarrassed
avería *nf* **1** : damage **2** : breakdown, malfunction
averiado, -da *adj* **1** : damaged, faulty **2**
: broken down
averiar {85} *vt* : to damage — **averiarse** *vr*
: to break down
averiguación *nf, pl* **-ciones** : investigation, inquiry
averiguar {10} *vt* **1** : to find out, to ascertain **2** : to investigate
aversión *nf, pl* **-siones** : aversion, dislike
avestruz *nm, pl* **-truces** : ostrich
avezado, -da *adj* : seasoned, experienced
aviación *nf, pl* **-ciones** : aviation
aviador, -dora *n* : aviator, flyer
aviar {85} *vt* **1** : to prepare, to make ready
2 : to tidy up **3** : to equip, to supply
avícola *adj* : poultry
avicultor, -tora *n* : poultry farmer
avicultura *nf* : poultry farming
avidez *nf, pl* **-deces** : eagerness
ávido, -da *adj* : eager, avid — **ávidamente** *adv*
avieso, -sa *adj* **1** : twisted, distorted **2**
: wicked, depraved
avinagrado, -da *adj* : vinegary, sour
avío *nm* **1** : preparation, provision **2**
: loan (for agriculture or mining) **3**
avíos *nmpl* : gear, equipment

avión *nm, pl* **aviones** : airplane
avionazo *nm Mex* : plane crash
avioneta *nf* : light airplane
avisar *vt* **1** : to notify, to inform **2** : to advise, to warn
aviso *nm* **1** : notice **2** : advertisement, ad **3** ADVERTENCIA : warning **4 estar sobre aviso** : to be on the alert
avispa *nf* : wasp
avispado, -da *adj fam* : clever, sharp
avispero *nm* : wasps' nest
avispón *nm, pl* **-pones** : hornet
avistamiento *nm* : sighting
avistar *vt* : to sight, to catch sight of
avituallar *vt* : to supply with food, to provision
avivar *vt* **1** : to enliven, to brighten **2**
: to strengthen, to intensify
avizorar *vt* **1** ACECHAR : to spy on, to watch **2** : to observe, to perceive ⟨se avizoran dificultades : difficulties are expected⟩
axila *nf* : armpit
axioma *nm* : axiom
axiomático, -ca *adj* : axiomatic
ay *interj* **1** : oh! **2** : ouch!, ow!
ayer¹ *adv* : yesterday ⟨ayer por/en la mañana : yesterday morning⟩ ⟨antes de ayer : the day before yesterday⟩
ayer² *nm* ANTAÑO : yesteryear, days gone by
ayote *nm CA, Mex* : squash, pumpkin
ayuda *nf* **1** : help, assistance **2 ayuda de cámara** : valet
ayudante *nmf* : helper, assistant
ayudar *vt* : to help, to assist ⟨ayúdame a levantar esta caja : help me lift this box⟩ ⟨¿en qué puedo ayudarle? : how can I help you?⟩ ⟨¿te ayudo con tus cosas? : can I help you with your things?⟩ —
ayudarse *vr* ~ **de** : to make use of
ayunar *vi* : to fast
ayunas *nfpl* **en** ~ : fasting ⟨este medicamento ha de tomarse en ayunas : this medication should be taken on an empty stomach⟩
ayuno *nm* : fast
ayuntamiento *nm* **1** : town hall, city hall **2** : town or city council
azabache *nm* : jet ⟨negro azabache : jet black⟩
azada *nf* : hoe
azafata *nf* **1** : stewardess *f* **2** : hostess *f* (on a TV show)
azafrán *nm, pl* **-franes** **1** : saffron **2**
: crocus
azahar *nm* : orange blossom
azalea *nf* : azalea
azar *nm* **1** : chance ⟨juegos de azar : games of chance⟩ **2** : accident, misfortune **3 al azar** : at random, randomly
azaroso, -sa *adj* **1** : perilous, hazardous **2** : turbulent, eventful
azimut *nm* : azimuth
azogue *nm* : mercury
azorado, -da *adj* **1** : embarrassed, flustered **2** : amazed, stunned
azorar *vt* **1** : to alarm, to startle **2** : to fluster, to embarrass — **azorarse** *vr* : to get embarrassed

azotar *vt* **1** : to whip, to flog **2** : to lash, to batter **3** : to devastate, to afflict

azote *nm* **1** LÁTIGO : whip, lash **2** *fam* : spanking, licking **3** : calamity, scourge

azotea *nf* : flat roof, terraced roof

azteca *adj & nmf* : Aztec

azúcar *nmf* : sugar — **azucarar** *vt*

azucarado, -da *adj* : sweetened, sugary

azucarera *nf* : sugar bowl

azucarero, -ra *adj* : sugar ⟨industria azucarera : sugar industry⟩

azucena *nf* : white lily

azuela *nf* : adze

azufre *nm* : sulfur — **azufroso, -sa** *adj*

azul *adj & nm* : blue

azulado, -da *adj* : bluish

azulejo *nm* : ceramic tile, floor tile

azuloso, -sa *adj* : bluish

azulete *nm* : bluing

azur[1] *adj* CELESTE : azure

azur[2] *n* CELESTE : azure, sky blue

azuzar {21} *vt* : to incite, to egg on

B

b *nf* : second letter of the Spanish alphabet

baba *nf* **1** : spittle, saliva **2** : dribble, drool (of a baby) **3** : slime, ooze

babear *vi* **1** : to drool, to slobber **2** : to ooze

babero *nm* : bib

babor *nm* : port, port side ⟨a babor : to port⟩

babosa *nf* : slug (mollusk)

babosada *nf CA, Mex* : silly act or remark

baboso, -sa *adj* **1** : drooling, slobbering **2** : slimy **3** *CA, Mex fam* : silly, dumb

babucha *nf* : slipper

babuino *nm* : baboon

baca *nf* : luggage/roof rack

bacalao *nm* : cod (fish)

bacán[1] *adj, pl* **bacanes** *fam* **1** *Arg, Uru* : posh, classy, rich **2** *Chile, Ecua, Peru* : cool, neat, great

bacán[2] *n, pl* **bacanes** *Arg, Col, Uru* : rich person

bacano, -na *adj Col fam* : cool, great

bache *nm* **1** : pothole **2** : air pocket **3** : bad period, rough time, slump

bachiller *nmf* : high school graduate

bachillerato *nm* : high school diploma

bacinica *nf* : chamber pot, potty (for children)

bacon *nm Spain* : bacon

bacteria *nf* : bacterium

bacteriano, -na *adj* : bacterial

báculo *nm* : staff, stick

badajo *nm* : clapper (of a bell)

badén *nm, pl* **badenes** **1** VADO : ford **2** : dip, ditch (in a road) **3** : speed bump

bádminton *nm* : badminton

bafle *or* **baffle** *nm* : speaker, loudspeaker

bagaje *nm* **1** → **equipaje** **2** : background, knowledge ⟨bagaje cultural : cultural heritage⟩

bagre *nm* : catfish

baguette *nf* : baguette

bah *interj* (*expressing disapproval*) : huh!

bahía *nf* : bay

bailar *vt* : to dance — *vi* **1** : to dance **2** : to spin **3** : to be loose, to be too big

bailarín[1], **-rina** *adj, mpl* **-rines** **1** : dancing **2** : fond of dancing

bailarín[2], **-rina** *n, mpl* **-rines** **1** : dancer **2** : ballet dancer, ballerina *f* ⟨prima bailarina : prima ballerina⟩

baile *nm* **1** : dance **2** : dance party, ball **3 llevarse al baile a** *Mex fam* : to take advantage of

baja *nf* **1** DESCENSO : fall, drop **2** : slump, recession **3** : loss, casualty **4 dar de baja** : to discharge, to dismiss **5 darse de baja** : to withdraw, to drop out, to resign

bajada *nf* **1** : descent **2** : dip, slope **3** : decrease, drop **4 bajada de bandera** *Arg, Spain* : minimum fare

bajar *vt* **1** : to lower (a blind, zipper, etc.), to let down (a hem) **2** : to bring/take/carry down, to get/lift down **3** REDUCIR : to lower (prices, a fever, one's voice, etc.) **4** INCLINAR : to lower (the eyes, etc.), to bow (the head) **5** : to go/come down (stairs) **6** DESCARGAR : to download **7 bajar de categoría** : to downgrade — *vi* **1** DISMINUIR : to drop, to fall, to go down **2** : to come/go down ⟨bajar por la escalera : to come/go down the stairs⟩ **3** : to ebb (of tides) — **bajarse** *vr* ~ **de** : to get off (a train, etc.), to get out of (a car)

bajeza *nf* **1** : low or despicable act **2** : baseness

bajío *nm* **1** : lowland **2** : shoal, sandbank, shallows

bajista *nmf* : bass player, bassist

bajo[1] *adv* **1** : low **2** : softly, quietly

bajo[2], **-ja** *adj* **1** : low **2** : short (of stature) **3** : soft, faint, low ⟨en voz baja : in a low voice⟩ **4** : low, deep (in tone) **5** : lower ⟨el bajo Amazonas : the lower Amazon⟩ ⟨la planta baja : the ground/first floor⟩ **6** : lowered ⟨con la mirada baja : with lowered eyes⟩ **7** : base, vile **8 los bajos fondos** : the underworld

bajo[3] *nm* **1** : bass, double bass **2** : bass, bass guitar **3** : first floor, ground floor **4** : hemline

bajo[4] *prep* : under, beneath, below

bajón *nm, pl* **bajones** : sharp drop, slump

bajorrelieve *nm* : bas-relief

bala *nf* **1** : bullet ⟨a prueba de balas : bulletproof⟩ **2** : bale **3 lanzamiento de bala** : shot put

balacear → **balear**

balacera *nf* → **baleo**

balada *nf* : ballad

balance *nm* 1 : balance 2 : balance sheet 3 : outcome, result 4 **hacer balance de** : to take stock of
balancear *vt* 1 : to balance 2 : to swing (one's arms, etc.) 3 : to rock (a boat) — **balancearse** *vr* OSCILAR : to swing, to sway, to rock
balanceo *nm* : swaying, rocking, swinging
balancín *nm, pl* **-cines** 1 : rocking chair 2 SUBIBAJA : seesaw
balandra *nf* : sloop
balanza *nf* : scales *pl*, balance ⟨balanza comercial : balance of trade⟩ ⟨balanza de pagos : balance of payments⟩
balar *vi* : to bleat
balaustrada *nf* : balustrade
balazo *nm* 1 TIRO : shot, gunshot 2 : bullet wound
balboa *nf* : balboa (monetary unit of Panama)
balbucear *vi* 1 : to mutter, to stammer 2 : to babble
balbuceo *nm* 1 : mumbling, stammering 2 : babbling
balbucir → **balbucear**
balcánico, -ca *adj* : Balkan
balcón *nm, pl* **balcones** : balcony
balde *nm* 1 CUBO : bucket, pail 2 **en ~** : in vain, to no avail
baldío¹, -día *adj* 1 : fallow 2 : useless, vain
baldío² *nm* 1 : wasteland 2 *Mex* : vacant lot
baldosa *nf* LOSETA : floor tile, paving tile/stone, paving block
balear *vt* : to shoot, to shoot at
baleo *nm* : shooting, shoot-out
balero *nm* 1 *Mex* : ball bearing 2 *Mex, PRi* : cup-and-ball toy
balido *nm* : bleat
balín *nm, pl* **balines** : pellet
balística *nf* : ballistics
balístico, -ca *adj* : ballistic
baliza *nf* 1 : buoy 2 : beacon (for aircraft)
ballena *nf* : whale
ballenero¹, -ra *adj* : whaling
ballenero², -ra *n* : whaler
ballenero³ *nm* : whaleboat, whaler
ballesta *nf* 1 : crossbow 2 : spring (of an automobile)
ballet [ba'le] *nm* : ballet
balneario *nm* : spa, bathing resort
balompié *nm* FUTBOL : soccer
balón *nm, pl* **balones** 1 : ball 2 TANQUE : tank
baloncelista *PRi* → **basquetbolista**
baloncesto *nm* BASQUETBOL : basketball
balonmano *nm* : handball
balsa *nf* 1 : raft 2 : balsa 3 : pond, pool
balsámico, -ca *adj* : soothing
bálsamo *nm* : balsam, balm
balsero, -ra *n* : boat person, refugee
báltico, -ca *adj* : Baltic
baluarte *nm* : bulwark, bastion
bambalina *nf* **tras/entre bambalinas** : behind the scenes
bambolear *vi* 1 : to sway, to swing 2 : to wobble — **bambolearse** *vr*
bamboleo *nm* 1 : swaying, swinging 2 : wobbling

bambú *nm, pl* **bambúes** *or* **bambús** : bamboo
banal *adj* : banal — **banalidad** *nf*
banana *nf* : banana
bananero¹, -ra *adj* : banana
bananero² *nm* : banana tree
banano *nm* 1 : banana tree 2 *CA, Col* : banana
banca *nf* 1 : banking, banks 2 : bank (in games) 3 BANCO : bench 4 BANQUILLO : bench (in sports)
bancada *nf* 1 : group, faction 2 : workbench
bancal *nm* 1 : terrace (in agriculture) 2 : plot (of land)
bancario, -ria *adj* : bank, banking
bancarrota *nf* QUIEBRA : bankruptcy ⟨en bancarrota : bankrupt⟩
banco *nm* 1 : bank ⟨banco central : central bank⟩ ⟨banco de datos : data bank⟩ ⟨banco de sangre : blood bank⟩ 2 BARRA : bank, bar ⟨banco de arena : sandbank⟩ 3 BANCA : stool, bench 4 : pew 5 : school (of fish)
banda *nf* 1 : band, strip 2 : band (on arm), sash 3 *Mex* : belt ⟨banda transportadora : conveyor belt⟩ 4 : (frequency) band 5 : band (of musicians) 6 : gang (of persons), flock (of birds) 7 : side (of a ship) 8 : touchline (in soccer) 9 **banda ancha** : broadband 10 **banda de rodadura** : tread (of a tire) 11 **banda sonora** *or* **banda de sonido** : sound track
bandada *nf* : flock (of birds), school (of fish)
bandazo *nm* **dar bandazos** : to move from side to side
bandearse *vr* : to look after oneself, to cope
bandeja *nf* 1 : tray, platter 2 **bandeja de entrada** : in-box 3 **bandeja de salida** : out-box
bandera *nf* : flag, banner
banderazo *nm* : starting signal (in sports)
banderilla *nf* : dart (in bullfighting)
banderín *nm, pl* **-rines** : pennant, small flag
bandido, -da *n* BANDOLERO : bandit, outlaw
bando *nm* 1 FACCIÓN : faction, side 2 EDICTO : proclamation
bandolero, -ra *n* BANDIDO : bandit, outlaw
banjo *nm* : banjo
banquero, -ra *n* : banker
banqueta *nf* 1 : footstool, stool, bench 2 *Mex* : sidewalk
banquete *nm* : banquet ⟨banquete de bodas : wedding reception⟩
banquetear *v* : to feast
banquillo *nm* 1 BANCA : bench (in sports) 2 : dock, defendant's seat
banquina *nf* *Arg, Uru* : shoulder (of a road)
bañadera *Arg, Uru* → **bañera**
bañador *nm* *Spain* : swimsuit, bathing suit
bañar *vt* 1 : to bathe, to wash 2 : to immerse, to dip 3 : to coat, to cover

⟨bañado en lágrimas : bathed in tears⟩ — **bañarse** *vr* **1** : to take a bath, to bathe **2** : to swim, to go swimming

bañera *nf* **1** TINA : bathtub **2 bañera de hidromasaje** : hot tub, whirlpool, Jacuzzi *trademark*

bañero, -ra *n Arg, Uru* : lifeguard

bañista *nmf* : bather

baño *nm* **1** : bath ⟨darse un baño : to take a bath⟩ ⟨baño de espuma/burbujas : bubble bath⟩ **2** : swim, dip **3** : bathroom ⟨baños públicos : public restrooms⟩ **4** BAÑERA : bathtub **5** GLASEADO : icing, frosting **6 baño de sangre** : bloodbath

baptista → **bautista**

baqueta *nf* **1** : ramrod **2 baquetas** *nfpl* : drumsticks

bar *nm* : bar

baraja *nf* : deck of cards

barajar *vt* **1** : to shuffle (cards) **2** : to consider

baranda *nf* → **barandal 1**

barandal *nm* **1** : rail, railing **2** : banister, handrail

barandilla *nf Spain* → **barandal**

barata *nf* **1** *Mex* : sale, bargain **2** *Chile* : cockroach

baratija *nf* : bauble, trinket

baratillo *nm* : rummage sale, flea market

barato[1] *adv* : cheap, cheaply ⟨te lo vendo barato : I'll sell it to you cheap⟩

barato[2], **-ta** *adj* : cheap, inexpensive

barba *nf* **1** : beard, stubble **2** : chin

barbacoa *nf* **1** PARRILLA : barbecue **2** : barbecued meat

bárbaramente *adv* : barbarously

barbaridad *nf* **1** : barbarity, atrocity **2** BURRADA : stupid act or remark **3** MONTÓN : ton, load **4 ¡qué barbaridad!** : that's outrageous!

barbarie *nf* : savagery

bárbaro[1] **pasarlo bárbaro** *fam* : to have a great time

bárbaro[2], **-ra** *adj* **1** : barbarian (in history) **2** CRUEL : cruel **3** GROSERO : rude, crass **4** *fam* : great, fantastic

bárbaro[3], **-ra** *n* : barbarian

barbecho *nm* : fallow land ⟨dejar en barbecho : to leave fallow⟩

barbería *nf* : barbershop

barbero *nm* : barber

barbilla *nf* MENTÓN : chin

barbitúrico *nm* : barbiturate

barbudo[1], **-da** *adj* : bearded

barbudo[2] *nm* : bearded man

barca *nf* : boat

barcaza *nf* : barge

barcia *nf* : chaff

barco *nm* **1** BARCA : boat ⟨viajar en barco : to travel by boat/ship⟩ ⟨barco de guerra/vapor/vela : warship/steamship/sailboat⟩ ⟨barco pesquero : fishing boat⟩ **2** BUQUE, NAVE : ship

barda *nf Mex* **1** MURO : wall **2** CERCO : fence

bardo *nm* : bard

baremo *nm* : scale

barítono *nm* : baritone

barman *nm* : bartender

barniz *nm, pl* **barnices** : varnish

barnizar {21} *vt* : to varnish

barómetro *nm* : barometer — **barométrico, -ca** *adj*

barón *nm, pl* **barones** : baron

baronesa *nf* : baroness

barquero, -ra *n* : boatman *m*, boatwoman *f*

barquillo *nm* **1** : wafer **2** CONO : ice-cream cone

barra *nf* **1** : bar (of metal), rod (for curtains) **2** : bar (of soap, etc.), block (of ice) **3** MOSTRADOR : bar, counter **4** : gang (of friends) **5** : slash (in punctuation) ⟨barra oblicua : forward slash⟩ ⟨barra invertida/inversa : backslash⟩ **6** BANCO : bar, bank ⟨barra de arena : sandbar⟩ **7 barra de herramientas** : toolbar **8 barra de labios** : lipstick **9 barra de pan** *Mex, Spain* : baguette

barraca *nf* **1** CHOZA : shack **2** PUESTO, CASETA : booth, stall

barracuda *nf* : barracuda

barranca *nf* **1** : hillside, slope **2** → **barranco**

barranco *nm* : ravine, gorge

barredora *nf* : street sweeper (machine)

barrena *nf* **1** TALADRO : drill, auger, gimlet **2** : tailspin

barrenar *vt* : to drill

barrendero, -ra *n* : sweeper, street cleaner

barrer *vt* **1** : to sweep **2** : to sweep away **3** : to crush, to defeat — *vi* **1** : to sweep **2** : to make a clean sweep **3** ~ **con** : to sweep away **4** ~ **con** : to wipe out (an enemy), to crush (a sports opponent) — **barrerse** *vr* : to slide (in sports)

barrera *nf* OBSTÁCULO : barrier, obstacle ⟨barrera de sonido : sound barrier⟩ ⟨barrera comercial : trade barrier⟩

barreta *nf Arg, Mex* : crowbar

barriada *nf* **1** : district, quarter **2** : shantytown, slums *pl*

barrica *nf* BARRIL, TONEL : barrel, cask, keg

barricada *nf* : barricade

barrida *nf* **1** : sweep **2** : slide (in sports) **3** : clean sweep (in a competition)

barrido *nm* : sweeping

barriga *nf* : belly

barrigón, -gona *adj, mpl* **-gones** *fam* : potbellied

barril *nm* **1** BARRICA : barrel, keg **2 cerveza de barril** : draft beer

barrio *nm* **1** : neighborhood, district **2 barrios bajos** : slums *pl* **3 barrio de invasión** *Col* → **invasión 4 barrio de chabolas** *Spain* : shantytown, slums *pl*

barrizal *nm* : quagmire

barro *nm* **1** LODO : mud **2** ARCILLA : clay ⟨vajilla de barro : earthenware dishes⟩ **3** ESPINILLA, GRANO : pimple, blackhead

barroco, -ca *adj* : baroque — **barroco** *nm*

barroso, -sa *adj* ENLODADO : muddy

barrote *nm* : bar (on a window)

bártulos *nmpl* : things, belongings ⟨liar los bártulos : to pack one's things⟩

barullo *nm* **1** BULLA : racket, ruckus **2** CONFUSIÓN : mess, confusion

basa *nf* : base, pedestal

basalto *nm* : basalt
basar *vt* FUNDAR : to base — **basarse** *vr* FUNDARSE **1** ~ **en** : to be based on **2** ~ **en** : to base one's position on
báscula *nf* BALANZA : balance, scales *pl*
base *nf* **1** : base, bottom **2** : base (in baseball) **3** FUNDAMENTO : basis, foundation ⟨sentar las bases de : to lay the foundation for⟩ **4** : base ⟨base naval/ aérea : naval/air base⟩ **5** REGLAS : rules *pl* **6** *or* **base de maquillaje** : foundation (makeup) **7** **a base de** : based on, by means of **8** **base de datos** : database **9** **en base a** : based on, on the basis of
básico, -ca *adj* FUNDAMENTAL : basic — **básicamente** *adv*
basílica *nf* : basilica
basket *or* **básquet** → **basquetbol**
basquetbol *or* **básquetbol** *nm* BALONCESTO : basketball
basquetbolista *nmf* : basketball player
basset *nm* : basset hound
bastante¹ *adv* **1** : enough, sufficiently ⟨he trabajado bastante : I have worked enough⟩ ⟨lo bastante alto (como) para alcanzar : tall enough to reach⟩ **2** : fairly, rather, quite ⟨llegaron bastante temprano : they arrived quite early⟩ ⟨me gustó bastante : I liked it a lot⟩
bastante² *adj* **1** : enough, sufficient ⟨¿hay bastantes sillas? : are there enough chairs?⟩ **2** : plenty of, a lot of ⟨había bastante gente : there were a lot of people⟩
bastante³ *pron* : enough ⟨hemos visto bastante : we have seen enough⟩ ⟨no hay bastantes : there aren't enough⟩
bastar *vi* : to be enough, to suffice ⟨con uno basta (y sobra) : one is (more than) enough⟩ ⟨¡basta (ya)! : that's enough!⟩ — **bastarse** *vr* : to be able to manage on one's own
bastardilla *nf* CURSIVA : italic type, italics *pl*
bastardo¹, -da *adj* **1** ILEGÍTIMO : bastard **2** VIL : base
bastardo², -da *n* : bastard *usu offensive*
bastidor *nm* **1** : framework, frame **2** : wing (in theater) ⟨entre bastidores : backstage, behind the scenes⟩
bastión *nf, pl* **bastiones** BALUARTE : bastion, bulwark
basto¹, -ta *adj* : coarse, rough
basto² *nm* : club (in the Spanish deck of cards)
bastón *nm, pl* **bastones** **1** : cane, walking stick **2** : baton **3** *or* **bastón de esquí** : ski pole **4** **bastón de mando** : staff (of authority)
basura *nf* : garbage, trash ⟨tirar/echar/ botar algo a la basura : to throw something in the garbage⟩ ⟨sacar la basura : to take out the garbage⟩
basural → **basurero 2**
basurero¹, -ra *n* : garbage collector
basurero² *nm* **1** *Mex* : garbage can **2** VERTEDERO, BASURAL : garbage dump
bata *nf* **1** : bathrobe, housecoat **2** : smock, coveralls, lab coat
batacazo *nm* **1** : wallop **2** **dar el/un batacazo** *Arg, Uru* : to pull off an unexpected win

batalla *nf* **1** : battle ⟨batalla campal : pitched battle⟩ **2** : fight, struggle **3 de** ~ : ordinary, everyday
batallar *vi* LIDIAR, LUCHAR : to battle, to fight
batallón *nm, pl* **-llones** : battalion
batata *nf* : yam, sweet potato
batazo *nm* HIT : hit (in baseball)
bate *nm* : baseball bat
batea *nf* **1** : tray, pan **2** : punt (boat)
bateador, -dora *n* : batter, hitter
batear *vi* : to bat — *vt* : to hit
bateo *nm* : batting (in baseball)
batería *nf* **1** PILA : battery **2** : drum kit, drums *pl* **3** **batería de cocina** : kitchen utensils *pl*
baterista *nmf* : drummer
batida *nf* REDADA, ALLANAMIENTO : raid
batido *nm* LICUADO : milk shake
batidor *nm* : eggbeater, whisk, mixer
batidora *nf* : (electric) mixer
batir *vt* **1** GOLPEAR : to beat, to hit **2** VENCER : to defeat **3** : to whisk, to beat (eggs), to whip (cream), to cream (butter and sugar) **4** : to flap, to beat (wings) **5** RASTREAR : to comb, to search **6** : to break (a record) **7** **batir palmas** : to clap — **batirse** *vr* : to fight
batuta *nf* **1** : baton **2** **llevar la batuta** : to be in charge
baúl *nm* **1** : trunk, chest **2** (*in various countries*) : trunk (of a car)
bautismal *adj* : baptismal
bautismo *nm* : baptism, christening
bautista *adj & nmf* : Baptist
bautizar {21} *vt* : to baptize, to christen
bautizo → **bautismo**
bávaro, -ra *adj & n* : Bavarian
baya *nf* : berry
bayeta *nf* : cleaning cloth
bayoneta *nf* : bayonet
baza *nf* : trick (in card games)
bazar *nm* : bazaar
bazo *nm* : spleen
bazofia *nf* **1** : table scraps *pl* **2** : slop, swill **3** : rubbish
bazuca *nf* : bazooka
be *or* **be larga** *or* **be grande** *nf* : (letter) b
beagle *nm* : beagle
beatífico, -ca *adj* : beatific
beato, -ta *adj* **1** : blessed **2** : devout **3** : overly devout
bebe, -ba *n Arg, Uru* : baby
bebé *nm* : baby
bebedero *nm* **1** ABREVADERO : watering trough **2** *Mex* : drinking fountain
bebedor, -dora *n* : (heavy) drinker
beber *v* TOMAR : to drink
bebida *nf* : drink, beverage
bebido, -da *adj* BORRACHO : drunk
beca *nf* : grant, scholarship
becado, -da *n* : grant recipient, scholarship holder
becar {72} *vt* : to award a grant or scholarship to
becario, -ria → **becado**
becerro, -rra *n* : calf
bedel *nmf* : janitor
begonia *nf* : begonia
beige *adj & nm* : beige

beisbol or **béisbol** nm : baseball
beisbolista nmf : baseball player
beldad nf BELLEZA, HERMOSURA : beauty
belén nf, pl **belenes** NACIMIENTO : Nativity scene
belga adj & nmf : Belgian
belicista[1] adj : militaristic
belicista[2] nmf : warmonger
bélico, -ca adj GUERRERO : war, fighting, military ⟨conflicto bélico : armed conflict⟩
belicoso, -sa adj 1 : warlike, martial 2 : aggressive, belligerent
beligerancia nf : belligerence
beligerante adj & nmf : belligerent
bellaco[1], **-ca** adj : sly, cunning
bellaco[2], **-ca** n : rogue, scoundrel
belleza nf BELDAD, HERMOSURA : beauty
bello, -lla adj 1 HERMOSO : beautiful 2 **bellas artes** : fine arts — **bellamente** adv
bellota nf : acorn
bemol nm : flat (in music) — **bemol** adj
bencina nf Chile GASOLINA : gas, gasoline
bencinera nf Chile : gas station
bendecir {11} vt 1 : to bless 2 **bendecir la mesa** : to say grace
bendición nf, pl **-ciones** : benediction, blessing
bendiga, bendijo etc. → **bendecir**
bendito[1], **-ta** adj 1 : blessed, holy 2 : fortunate
bendito[2], **-ta** n : simple person
benefactor[1], **-tora** adj : charitable
benefactor[2], **-tora** n : benefactor, benefactress f
beneficencia nf : charity
beneficiar vt : to benefit — **beneficiarse** vr : to benefit ⟨beneficiarse con/de : to benefit from⟩
beneficiario, -ria n 1 : beneficiary 2 : payee (of a check)
beneficio nm 1 GANANCIA : profit 2 : benefit 3 **en/a beneficio de** : in aid of, to benefit 4 **en beneficio de alguien** : in someone's interest
beneficioso, -sa adj : beneficial
benéfico, -ca adj : charitable
benemérito, -ta adj : meritorious, worthy
beneplácito nm : approval, consent
benevolencia nf BONDAD : benevolence, kindness
benevolente → **benévolo**
benévolo, -la adj BONDADOSO : benevolent, kind, good
bengala nf **luz de bengala** 1 : flare (signal) 2 : sparkler
benigno, -na adj : benign, mild
benjamín, -mina n, mpl **-mines** : youngest child
beodo, -da adj & n : drunk
berberecho nm : cockle
berenjena nf : eggplant
bergantín nm, pl **-tines** : brig (ship)
berlinés[1], **-nesa** adj : of or from Berlin
berlinés[2], **-nesa** n : person from Berlin
berma nf Chile, Col, Ecua, Peru : shoulder (of a road)
bermudas nfpl : Bermuda shorts
berrear vi 1 : to bellow, to low 2 : to bawl, to howl

berrido nm 1 : bellowing 2 : howl, scream
berrinche nm fam : tantrum ⟨hacer (un) berrinche : to throw a tantrum⟩
berro nm : watercress
besar vt : to kiss — **besarse** vr : to kiss (each other)
beso nm : kiss ⟨tirarle un beso a alguien : to blow someone a kiss⟩
bestia[1] adj 1 : ignorant, stupid 2 : boorish, rude
bestia[2] nf 1 : beast — 2 BRUTO : brute
bestia[3] nmf 1 IGNORANTE : ignoramus 2 : brute
bestial adj 1 : bestial, beastly 2 fam : huge, enormous ⟨hace un frío bestial : it's freezing cold⟩ 3 fam : great, fantastic
bestialidad nf 1 BRUTALIDAD : brutality 2 DISPARATE : stupid act or remark 3 MONTÓN : load, ton
best–seller [bes'seler] nm, pl **-sellers** : best seller
beta nf : beta (software)
besuquear vt fam : to cover with kisses — **besuquearse** vr fam : to neck, to smooch
betabel nm Mex : beet
betún nm, pl **betunes** 1 : shoe polish 2 Mex : icing
bi- pref : bi-
bianual adj : biannual
biberón nm, pl **-rones** : baby's bottle ⟨le dio el biberón al bebé : she gave the baby his bottle⟩
biblia nf 1 : bible 2 **la Biblia** : the Bible
bíblico, -ca adj : biblical
bibliografía nf : bibliography — **bibliográfico, -ca** adj
bibliógrafo, -fa n : bibliographer
biblioteca nf 1 : library 2 ESTANTERÍA : bookcase, bookshelves
bibliotecario, -ria n : librarian
bicameral adj : bicameral
bicarbonato nm 1 : bicarbonate 2 **bicarbonato de soda** : sodium bicarbonate, baking soda
bicentenario nm : bicentennial
bíceps nms & pl : biceps
bicho nm 1 : small animal 2 INSECTO : bug 3 **bicho raro** : weirdo
bici nf fam : bike
bicicleta nf 1 : bicycle ⟨ir en bicicleta : to cycle, to bicycle⟩ ⟨andar/montar en bicicleta : to ride a bicycle⟩ 2 **bicicleta de montaña** mountain bike
bicolor adj : two-tone
bidé or **bidet** nm : bidet
bidireccional adj : two-way
bidón nm, pl **bidones** : large can, (oil) drum
bien[1] adv 1 : well ⟨¿dormiste bien? : did you sleep well?⟩ ⟨todo va bien : everything's going well⟩ 2 : well, right, properly ⟨nos trata bien : she treats us well⟩ ⟨funcionar bien : to work right⟩ 3 : well, skillfully ⟨canta bien : she sings well⟩ ⟨¡bien dicho! : well said!⟩ 4 : well, thoroughly ⟨piénsalo bien : think it over carefully⟩ ⟨bien documentado : well-

documented⟩ **5** : very, quite ⟨era bien divertido : it was very enjoyable⟩ **6** : easily ⟨bien podría decirse que . . . : it could very well be said that . . .⟩ **7 bien que** : willingly, readily ⟨no ayuda pero bien que critica : he doesn't help but he's quick to criticize⟩ **8 más bien** : rather **9 no bien** : as soon as **10 si bien** : although

bien² *adj* **1** : well, OK, all right ⟨¿te sientes bien? : are you feeling all right?⟩ ⟨estoy bien, gracias : I'm fine, thanks⟩ **2** : good, nice, pleasant ⟨las flores huelen bien : the flowers smell very nice⟩ ⟨se está bien aquí : it's very pleasant here⟩ **3** : fine, OK, all right ⟨me parece bien : it seems fine to me⟩ ⟨está bien, no te preocupes : it's OK—don't worry about it⟩ **4** : right, correct, proper ⟨esta frase no está bien : this sentence isn't right⟩ ⟨no está bien que te hable así : it's not right for him to speak to you like that⟩

bien³ *nm* **1** : good ⟨el bien y el mal : good and evil⟩ **2** : good, sake ⟨por tu (propio) bien : for your (own) good⟩ **3 bienes** *nmpl* : property, goods, possessions ⟨bienes de consumo : consumer goods⟩ ⟨bienes muebles : personal property⟩ ⟨bienes raíces/inmuebles : real estate⟩

bien⁴ *conj* **(o) bien . . . (o) bien . . .** : either . . . or . . .

bien⁵ *interj* **1** BUENO : well, so ⟨bien, empecemos : well, let's get started⟩ ⟨bien, como iba diciendo . . . : so as I was saying . . .⟩ **2 ¡(muy) bien!** : (very) good!, well done! **3 ¡qué bien!** : great!

bienal *adj & nf* : biennial — **bienalmente** *adv*

bienaventurado, -da *adj* **1** : blessed **2** : fortunate, happy

bienestar *nm* **1** : welfare, well-being **2** CONFORT : comfort

bienintencionado, -da *adj* : well-meaning

bienvenida *nf* **1** : welcome **2 dar la bienvenida a** : to welcome

bienvenido, -da *adj* : welcome

bies *nm* : bias (in sewing)

bife *nm Arg, Chile, Uru* : steak

bífido, -da *adj* : forked

bifocales *nmpl* : bifocals — **bifocal** *adj*

bifurcación *nf, pl* **-ciones** : fork (in a river or road)

bifurcarse {72} *vr* : to fork

bigamia *nf* : bigamy

bígamo, -ma *n* : bigamist

bigote *nm* **1** : mustache **2** : whisker (of an animal)

bigotón, -tona *adj, mpl* **-tones** *CA, Mex* : having a big mustache

bikini *nm* : bikini

bilateral *adj* : bilateral — **bilateralmente** *adv*

biliar *adj* : bile ⟨cálculo biliar : gallstone⟩

bilingüe *adj* : bilingual

bilis *nf* : bile

billar *nm* : pool, billiards

billete *nm* **1** : bill ⟨un billete de cinco dólares : a five-dollar bill⟩ ⟨billete de banco : banknote⟩ **2** *Spain* → **boleto**

billetera *nf* : billfold, wallet

billetero, -ra *n CA, Car* : lottery ticket vendor

billón *nm, pl* **billones 1** : billion (Great Britain) **2** : trillion (U.S.A.)

bimensual *adj* : bimonthly, semimonthly

bimestral *adj* : bimonthly ⟨una revista bimestral : a bimonthly magazine, a magazine that's published every two months⟩ — **bimestralmente** *adv*

bimestre *nm* : two-month period

bimotor *adj* : twin-engine

binacional *adj* : binational

binario, -ria *adj* : binary

bingo *nm* : bingo

binocular *adj* : binocular

binoculares *nmpl* : binoculars

bio- *pref* : bio-

biodegradable *adj* : biodegradable

biodiversidad *nf* : biodiversity

biografía *nf* : biography

biográfico, -ca *adj* : biographical

biógrafo, -fa *n* : biographer

biología *nf* : biology

biológico, -ca *adj* : biological, biologic — **biológicamente** *adv*

biólogo, -ga *n* : biologist

biombo *nm* MAMPARA : folding screen, room divider

biopsia *nf* : biopsy

bioquímica *nf* : biochemistry

bioquímico¹, -ca *adj* : biochemical

bioquímico², -ca *n* : biochemist

biosfera *or* **biósfera** *nf* : biosphere

biotecnología *nf* : biotechnology — **biotecnológico, -ca** *adj*

bip *nm* PITIDO : beep

bipartidismo *nm* : two-party system

bipartidista *adj* : bipartisan

bípedo *nm* : biped

biquini → **bikini**

birlar *vt fam* : to swipe, to pinch

birmano, -na *adj & n* : Burmese

birrete *nm* **1** : mortarboard **2** : biretta

bis¹ *adv* **1** : twice, again (in music) **2** : a, A ⟨artículo 47 bis : Article 47A⟩ ⟨calle 15, número 70 bis : 15th Street, number 70A⟩

bis² *nm* : encore

bis- *pref* : great ⟨bisnieto : great-grandson⟩

bisabuelo, -la *n* : great-grandfather *m*, great-grandmother *f*, great-grandparent

bisagra *nf* : hinge

bisecar {72} *vt* : bisect

bisel *nm* : bevel

biselar *vt* : to bevel

bisexual *adj* : bisexual — **bisexualidad** *nf*

bisiesto *adj* **año bisiesto** : leap year

bisnieto, -ta *n* : great-grandson *m*, great-granddaughter *f*, great-grandchild

bisonte *nm* : bison, buffalo

bisoñé *nm* : hairpiece, toupee

bisoño¹, -ña *adj* : inexperienced

bisoño², -ña *n* : rookie

bistec *nm* : steak, beefsteak

bisturí *nm, pl* **-ríes** ESCALPELO : scalpel

bisutería *nf* : costume jewelry

bit *nm* : bit (unit of information)

bitácora *nf* 1 : ship's log 2 BLOG : blog
bitcoin [bit'koin] *nm, pl* **bitcoins** : Bitcoin
bizco, -ca *adj* : cross-eyed
bizcocho *nm* 1 : sponge cake 2 : biscuit
blanca *nf* : half note (in music)
blanco¹, -ca *adj* 1 : white 2 **en blanco** : blank (of a paper, etc.) 3 **pasar la noche en blanco** : to have a sleepless night
blanco², -ca *n* : white person
blanco³ *nm* 1 : white (color) 2 : white (of the eye) 3 : target, bull's-eye ⟨dar en el blanco : to hit the target, to hit the nail on the head⟩
blancura *nf* : whiteness
blancuzco, -ca *adj* 1 : whitish, off-white 2 PÁLIDO : pale
blandir {1} *vt* : to wave, to brandish
blando, -da *adj* 1 SUAVE : soft (of a bed, etc.), tender (of meat) 2 : weak (in character) 3 : lenient
blandura *nf* 1 : softness, tenderness 2 : leniency
blanqueador *nm* : bleach, whitener
blanquear *vt* 1 : to bleach (clothes), to whitewash (a wall) 2 : to shut out (in sports) 3 : to launder (money) — *vi* : to turn white
blanqueo *nm* 1 : bleaching, whitewashing 2 : money laundering
blanquillo *nm CA, Mex* : egg
blasfemar *vi* : to blaspheme
blasfemia *nf* : blasphemy
blasfemo, -ma *adj* : blasphemous
blazer *nm* : blazer
bledo *nm* **(no) me importa un bledo** *fam* : I don't give a damn
blindado, -da *adj* ACORAZADO : armored
blindaje *nm* 1 : armor, armor plating 2 : shield (for cables, machinery, etc.)
bloc *nm, pl* **blocs** : notepad, pad (of paper)
blof *nm Col, Mex* : bluff
blofear *vi Col, Mex* : to bluff
blog ['blox] *nm, pl* **blogs** BITÁCORA : blog
blondo, -da *adj* : blond, flaxen
bloque *nm* 1 : block (of wood, etc.) 2 GRUPO : bloc ⟨el bloque comunista : the Communist bloc⟩ 3 **en bloque** : en masse
bloquear *vt* 1 OBSTRUIR : to block (a road, etc.) 2 : to blockade (a port) 3 : to jam (a mechanism) 4 : to freeze (an account) — **bloquearse** *vr* : to jam, to stick, to lock
bloqueo *nm* 1 : blocking 2 : blockade (of a port, etc.)
blues ['blus] *nm* : blues (music)
blusa *nf* : blouse
blusón *nm, pl* **blusones** : loose shirt, smock
boa *nf* : boa
boato *nm* : ostentation, show
bobada *nf* 1 : stupid remark or action 2 **decir bobadas** : to talk nonsense
bobalicón, -cona *adj, mpl* **-cones** *fam* : silly, stupid
bobina *nf* 1 : roll, spool (of thread), bobbin (in sewing machine) 2 : (electrical) coil

bobo¹, -ba *adj* : silly, stupid
bobo², -ba *n* : fool
bobsleigh ['bobsle] *nm* : bobsled
boca *nf* 1 : mouth 2 : entrance 3 : mouth (of a jar, etc.), muzzle (of a gun) 4 **boca arriba** : face up 5 **boca abajo** : face down 6 **boca del estómago** : pit of the stomach 7 **boca de riego/incendios** : hydrant 8 **correr de boca en boca** : to spread by word of mouth 9 **el boca a boca** : mouth-to-mouth (resuscitation) ⟨hacerle el boca a boca a alguien : to give someone mouth-to-mouth⟩ 10 **en boca de todos** : on everyone's lips 11 **por boca de** : according to
bocacalle *nf* : entrance to a street ⟨gire a la última bocacalle : turn onto the last side street⟩
bocadillo *nm Spain* : sandwich
bocado *nm* 1 : bite, mouthful ⟨no probó bocado : he didn't have a bite to eat⟩ 2 FRENO : bit (of a bridle)
bocajarro *nm* **a ~** : point-blank
bocallave *nf* : keyhole
bocanada *nf* 1 : mouthful (of smoke, etc.) 2 : gust (of air)
boceto *nm* : sketch, outline
bochinche *nm fam* : ruckus, uproar
bochorno *nm* 1 VERGÜENZA : embarrassment 2 : hot and humid weather 3 : hot flash
bochornoso, -sa *adj* 1 EMBARAZOSO : embarrassing 2 : hot and muggy
bocina *nf* 1 : horn, trumpet 2 : automobile horn 3 : mouthpiece (of a telephone) 4 *Mex* : loudspeaker
bocinazo *nm* : honk (of a horn)
bocio *nm* : goiter
bocón, -cona *n, mpl* **bocones** *fam* : blabbermouth, loudmouth
boda *nf* : wedding ⟨bodas de oro/plata : golden/silver anniversary⟩
bodega *nf* 1 : wine cellar 2 : wine shop 3 : wine bar 4 : winery, wine producer 5 SÓTANO : cellar 6 : (ship's) hold 7 *Chile, Col, Mex* : storeroom, warehouse 8 (*in various countries*) : grocery store
bodegón *nm, pl* **-gones** : still life
bofetada *nf* CACHETADA : slap on the face
bofetear *vt* CACHETEAR : to slap
bofetón *nm, pl* **-tones** → **bofetada**
boga *nf* : fashion, vogue ⟨estar en boga : to be in style⟩
bogey ['bogi] *nm* : bogey (in golf)
bogotano¹, -na *adj* : of or from Bogotá
bogotano², -na *n* : person from Bogotá
bohemio, -mia *adj & n* : bohemian, Bohemian
bohío *nm* (*in various countries*) : hut
boicot *nm, pl* **boicots** : boycott
boicotear *vt* : to boycott
bóiler *nm Mex* : water heater
boina *nf* : beret
bol *nm* : bowl
bola *nf* 1 : ball ⟨bola de nieve : snowball⟩ ⟨bola de billar : billiard ball⟩ 2 CANICA : marble 3 : scoop (of ice cream) 4 *fam* : lie, fib *fam* 5 *Mex fam* : bunch ⟨una bola de rateros/mentiras : a bunch of thieves/lies⟩ 6 *Mex* : up-

roar, tumult **7 hacerse bolas con** *Mex* : to muddle up (facts), to make a mess of

bolchevique *adj & nmf* : Bolshevik

bolear *vt Mex* : to polish (shoes)

bolera *nf* : bowling alley

bolero[1] *nm* : bolero

bolero[2], **-ra** *n Mex* : shoeshine boy/man *m*, shoeshine girl/woman *f*

boleta *nf* **1** : receipt, ticket, slip **2** : (traffic/parking) ticket **3** *Arg, Mex* FACTURA : bill **4** *or* **boleta electoral** : ballot **5 boleta de calificaciones** *Mex* : report card

boletaje *nm Mex* : tickets *pl*

boletería *nf* TAQUILLA : box office, ticket office

boletín *nm, pl* **-tines 1** : bulletin **2** : journal, review **3 boletín informativo** : news bulletin **4 boletín de prensa** : press release

boleto *nm* **1** : ticket, fare ⟨boleto de ida/ de ida y vuelta : one-way/round-trip ticket⟩ **2** : ticket (for a lottery, etc.)

boli *nm Spain* → **bolígrafo**

boliche *nm* **1** BOLOS : bowling **2** BO-LERA : bowling alley **3** *Arg, Uru* : bar, nightclub **4** *Arg, Chile, Uru* : small store

bólido *nm* **1** : race car **2** METEORO : meteor

bolígrafo *nm* : ballpoint pen

bolillo *nm* **1** : bobbin **2** *Mex* : roll, bun

bolita *nf* CANICA : marble

bolívar *nm* : bolivar (monetary unit of Venezuela)

boliviano[1], **-na** *adj & n* : Bolivian

boliviano[2] *nm* : boliviano (monetary unit of Bolivia)

bollo *nm* **1** : bun, sweet roll **2** *Arg, Uru* : ball

bolo *nm* : bowling pin

bolos *nmpl* BOLICHE : bowling

bolsa *nf* **1** : bag, sack ⟨bolsa de basura/ plástico : garbage/plastic bag⟩ **2** *Mex* : pocketbook, purse **3** *Mex* : pocket **4** : pouch (of a marsupial) **5** : pocket (of minerals, etc.) **6** *or* **Bolsa** *or* **bolsa de valores** : stock market, stock exchange **7 bolsa de agua caliente** : hot-water bottle **8 bolsa de aire** : airbag **9 bolsa de trabajo** : job bank

bolsear *vt Mex* : to pick (someone's) pocket

bolsillo *nm* **1** : pocket **2 dinero de bolsillo** : pocket change

bolsita *nf* : small bag ⟨bolsita de té : tea bag⟩

bolso *nm* : pocketbook, handbag

bomba *nf* **1** : bomb ⟨bomba atómica : atomic/atom bomb⟩ ⟨bomba de tiempo, bomba de relojería *Spain* : time bomb⟩ **2** : bubble **3** : pump ⟨bomba de agua : water pump⟩ **4** *or* **bomba desta-pacaños** : plunger (for toilets, etc.) **5** (*in various countries*) : gas station **6** BOMBAZO : bombshell, shocker **7 pa-sarlo bomba** : to have a great time

bombacha *nf Arg, Uru* **1** : panties **2** → **bombachos**

bombachos *nmpl* : baggy pants, bloomers

bombardear *vt* **1** : to bomb **2** : to bombard

bombardeo *nm* **1** : bombing, shelling **2** : bombardment

bombardero *nm* : bomber (airplane)

bombástico, -ca *adj* : bombastic

bombazo *nm* **1** : bombshell, shocker **2** *Mex* : (bomb) explosion

bombear *vt* : to pump

bombero, -ra *n* : firefighter, fireman *m*

bombilla *nf* **1** : lightbulb **2** : tube, straw (for maté)

bombillo *nm CA, Col, Ven* : lightbulb

bombín *nm, pl* **-bines** : derby (hat)

bombita *Arg, Uru* → **bombilla**

bombo *nm* **1** : bass drum **2** *fam* : fanfare, hype ⟨con bombos y platillos : with great fanfare⟩

bombón *nm, pl* **bombones 1** : bonbon, chocolate **2** *Mex* : marshmallow

bombona *nf Ecua, Spain, Ven* : tank (container)

bonachón[1], **-chona** *adj, mpl* **-chones** *fam* : good-natured, kindhearted

bonachón[2], **-chona** *n, mpl* **-chones** *fam* BUENAZO : kindhearted person

bonaerense[1] *adj* : of or from Buenos Aires

bonaerense[2] *nmf* : person from Buenos Aires

bonanza *nf* **1** PROSPERIDAD : prosperity **2** : calm weather **3** : rich ore deposit, bonanza

bondad *nf* BENEVOLENCIA : goodness, kindness ⟨tener la bondad de hacer algo : to be kind enough to do something⟩

bondadoso, -sa *adj* BENÉVOLO : kind, kindly, good — **bondadosamente** *adv*

bonete *nm* : cap, mortarboard

bongo *or* **bongó** *nm, pl* **bongos** *or* **bon-góes** : bongo

boniato *nm* : sweet potato

bonificación *nf, pl* **-ciones 1** : discount **2** : bonus, extra

bonito[1] *adv* : nicely, well

bonito[2], **-ta** *adj* LINDO : pretty, lovely

bonito[3] *nm* : bonito (tuna)

bono *nm* **1** : bond ⟨bono bancario : bank bond⟩ **2** : voucher

boqueada *nf* : gasp ⟨dar la última bo-queada : to give one's last gasp⟩

boquear *vi* **1** : to gasp **2** : to be dying

boquerón *nm, pl* **-rones** : anchovy

boquete *nm* : hole, opening

boquiabierto, -ta *adj* : open-mouthed, speechless, agape

boquilla *nf* **1** : mouthpiece (of a musical instrument), stem (of a pipe) **2** : cigarette holder **3** : nozzle

borbotar *or* **borbotear** *vi* : to bubble

borboteo *nm* : bubbling

borbotón *nm, pl* **-tones 1 hervir a bor-botones** : to boil rapidly **2 salir a bor-botones** : to gush out

borda *nf* : gunwale ⟨echar/tirar algo por la borda : to throw something overboard⟩

bordado *nm* : embroidery

bordar *v* : to embroider

borde *nm* **1** : edge (of a table, etc.), rim (of a glass, etc.) **2** : side (of a road, etc.) **3 al borde de** : on the verge of

bordear *vt* **1** : to border (a city, etc.), to line (a street) **2** : to skirt, to follow (a coastline, etc.) **3** : to border on ⟨bordea la genialidad : it borders on genius⟩
bordillo *nm* : curb
bordo *nm* a ~ : aboard, on board
bordón *nm, pl* **-dones** **1** : bass string (of a guitar, etc.), snare (of a drum) **2** BASTÓN : staff
boreal *adj* : northern
borgoña *nf* : burgundy
boricua *adj & nmf fam* : Puerto Rican
borinqueño, -ña → **boricua**
borla *nf* **1** : pom-pom, tassel **2** : powder puff
borrachera *nf* : drunkenness ⟨(se) agarró una borrachera : he got drunk⟩
borrachín, -china *n, mpl* **-chines** *fam* : lush, drunk
borracho¹, -cha *adj* EBRIO : drunk
borracho², -cha *n* : drunk, drunkard
borrador *nm* **1** : rough copy, first draft ⟨en borrador : in the rough⟩ **2** BOSQUEJO : sketch **3** : (blackboard) eraser
borrar *vt* **1** : to erase (on paper), to delete (on a computer) **2** : to wipe, to erase (a disk, etc.) **3** : to erase, to wipe off (a blackboard) **4** : to erase, to blot out (a memory) — **borrarse** *vr* **1** : to fade, to fade away **2** : to resign, to drop out **3** *Mex fam* : to split, to leave ⟨me borro : I'm out of here⟩
borrasca *nf* **1** : area of low pressure **2** TORMENTA : squall, storm
borrascoso, -sa *adj* : blustery, stormy
borrego, -ga *n* : lamb, sheep
borrico → **burro**
borrón *nm, pl* **borrones** : smudge, blot ⟨hacer borrón y cuenta nueva : to start with a clean slate⟩
borronear *vt* : to smudge, to blot
borroso, -sa *adj* : blurry, fuzzy
boscoso, -sa *adj* : wooded
bosnio, -nia *adj & n* : Bosnian
bosque *nm* : woods, forest ⟨bosque tropical : rain forest⟩
bosquecillo *nm* : grove, copse, thicket
bosquejar *vt* ESBOZAR : to outline, to sketch
bosquejo *nm* **1** TRAZADO : outline, sketch **2** : draft
bostezar {21} *vi* : to yawn
bostezo *nm* : yawn
bot ['bot] *nm, pl* **bots** : bot
bota *nf* **1** : boot **2** : wineskin (small) **3** **botas vaqueras** *Mex* : cowboy boots
botadero *nm* : garbage dump
botana *nf Mex* : snack, appetizer
botánica *nf* : botany
botánico¹, -ca *adj* : botanical
botánico², -ca *n* : botanist
botar *vt* **1** ARROJAR : to throw, to fling, to hurl **2** TIRAR : to throw out, to throw away **3** ECHAR : to throw (someone) out **4** : to bounce **5** : to launch (a ship) — *vi* **1** SALTAR : to jump **2** *Spain* REBOTAR : to bounce
bote *nm* **1** : small boat ⟨bote de remos : rowboat⟩ ⟨bote salvavidas : lifeboat⟩ **2** : can, jar **3** : jump, bounce ⟨dar botes : to bounce⟩ **4** *Mex fam* : jail **5** **bote de basura** *CA, Mex* : garbage can, trash can
botella *nf* : bottle
botica *nf* FARMACIA : drugstore, pharmacy
boticario, -ria *n* FARMACÉUTICO : pharmacist, druggist
botín *nm, pl* **botines** **1** : baby's bootee **2** : ankle boot **3** : booty, plunder
botiquín *nm, pl* **-quines** **1** : medicine cabinet **2** : first aid kit
botón *nm, pl* **botones** **1** : button **2** : bud **3** INSIGNIA : badge
botones *nmfs & pl* : bellhop
botulismo *nm* : botulism
boulevard [,bule'var] → **bulevar**
bouquet [bu'ke] *nm, pl* **-quets** **1** RAMO : bouquet **2** : bouquet, aroma
bourbon *nm* : bourbon
boutique [bu'tik] *nf* : boutique
bóveda *nf* **1** : vault, dome **2** CRIPTA : crypt
bovino, -na *adj* : bovine
box *nm, pl* **boxes** **1** : pit (in auto racing) **2** *CA, Mex* : boxing
boxeador, -dora *n* : boxer
boxear *vi* : to box
boxeo *nm* : boxing
boxers *nmpl* : boxer shorts
boya *nf* : buoy
boyante *adj* : buoyant
bozal *nm* **1** : muzzle **2** : halter (for a horse)
bracear *vi* **1** : to wave one's arms **2** : to make strokes (in swimming)
bracero, -ra *n* : migrant worker, day laborer
bragas *nfpl Spain* : panties
braguero *nm* : truss (in medicine)
bragueta *nf* : fly, pants zipper
braille *adj & nm* : braille
bramante *nm* : twine, string
bramar *vi* **1** RUGIR : to roar, to bellow **2** : to howl (of the wind)
bramido *nm* : bellowing, roar
brandy *nm* : brandy
branquia *nf* AGALLA : gill
brasa *nf* ASCUA : ember ⟨a la brasa : grilled⟩
brasero *nm* : brazier
brasier *or* **brassiere** *nm Col, Mex* : brassiere, bra
brasileño, -ña *adj & n* : Brazilian
brasilero, -ra → **brasileño**
bravata *nf* **1** JACTANCIA : boast **2** AMENAZA : threat
bravío, -vía *adj* : wild, fierce
bravo, -va *adj* **1** FEROZ : ferocious, fierce **2** : angry **3** : rough (of the sea) **4** ¡bravo! : bravo!, well done!
bravucón, -cona *n, mpl* **-cones** : bully
bravuconadas *nfpl* : bravado
bravura *nf* **1** FEROCIDAD : fierceness, ferocity **2** VALENTÍA : bravery
braza *nf* **1** *or* **estilo braza** *Spain* : breaststroke ⟨nadar a braza : to swim the breaststroke⟩ **2** : fathom (unit of length)
brazada *nf* : stroke (in swimming)
brazalete *nm* **1** PULSERA : bracelet, bangle **2** BANDA : armband

brazo *nm* **1** : arm ⟨tomar del brazo : to take by the arm⟩ ⟨con los brazos cruzados : with one's arms crossed⟩ ⟨llevar en brazos : to carry in one's arms⟩ **2** : arm (of an object), limb (of a tree) **3** : branch (of a river), inlet (of the sea) **4 brazo derecho** : right-hand man **5 brazos** *nmpl* : hands, laborers

brea *nf* ALQUITRÁN : tar, pitch

brebaje *nm* : potion, brew

brecha *nf* **1** : gap, breach, opening **2** : breach (of defenses) **3** DIFERENCIA : gap, difference **4** TAJO : gash

brega *nf* **1** LUCHA : struggle **2** : hard work

bregar {52} *vi* **1** LUCHAR : to struggle **2** : to toil **3** ~ **con** : to deal with

breve *adj* **1** CORTO : brief, short **2 en** ~ : shortly, in short — **brevemente** *adv*

brevedad *nf* **1** : brevity, shortness **2 con la mayor brevedad** *or* **a la brevedad posible** : as soon as possible

brezo *nm* : heather

bribón, -bona *n*, *mpl* **bribones** : rascal, scamp

bricolaje *or* **bricolage** *nm* : do-it-yourself, DIY

brida *nf* : bridle

bridge ['brɪʤ, 'brɪʒ, 'brɪtʃ] *nm* : bridge (game)

brigada *nf* **1** : brigade **2** : team, squad

brigadier *nm* : brigadier

brillante[1] *adj* **1** : bright (of color, light, etc.) **2** LUSTROSO : shiny, glossy **3** RELUCIENTE : sparkling **4** GENIAL : brilliant — **brillantemente** *adv*

brillante[2] *nm* DIAMANTE : diamond

brillantez *nf* : brilliance, brightness

brillar *vi* : to shine, to sparkle

brillo *nm* **1** : brilliance **2** : luster, shine, gloss ⟨sacarle/darle brillo a : to polish⟩ **3** ESPLENDOR : splendor

brilloso, -sa *adj* LUSTROSO : lustrous, shiny

brincar {72} *vi* **1** SALTAR : to jump (up and down) ⟨brincar de alegría : to jump for joy⟩ **2** : to hop (of a rabbit, etc.), to gambol

brinco *nm* **1** SALTO : jump, leap, skip **2 dar un brinco** : to jump

brindar *vi* : to drink a toast ⟨brindar por : to toast, to drink to⟩ — *vt* : to offer, to provide — **brindarse** *vr* **brindarse a hacer algo** : to volunteer to do something

brindis *nm* : toast, drink ⟨hacer un brindis : to drink a toast⟩

brinque, etc. → **brincar**

brío *nm* **1** : force, determination **2** : spirit, verve

brioso, -sa *adj* : spirited

brisa *nf* : breeze

británico[1], **-ca** *adj* : British

británico[2], **-ca** *n* **1** : British person **2 los británicos** : the British

brizna *nf* **1** : strand **2** : blade (of grass)

broca *nf* : drill bit

brocado *nm* : brocade

brocha *nf* : paintbrush

broche *nm* **1** ALFILER : brooch **2** : fastener, clasp, clip **3** *Mex* : barrette, hair clip **4** *Arg* GRAPA : staple **5 broche de oro** : finishing touch

brocheta *nf* : skewer

brócoli *nm* : broccoli

broma *nf* **1** : joke, prank ⟨le hizo una broma : she played a joke on him⟩ **2 en** ~ : in jest, jokingly

bromear *vi* : to joke

bromista[1] *adj* : joking, playful

bromista[2] *nmf* : joker, prankster

bromo *nm* : bromine

bronca *nf* **1** *fam* : fight, quarrel, fuss ⟨armar una bronca : to kick up a fuss⟩ **2** *fam* : anger ⟨dar bronca : to piss off⟩ ⟨estar con bronca : to be pissed off⟩ ⟨tener bronca con : to have a beef with⟩ **3** *fam* : scolding ⟨echarle (la) bronca a alguien : to tell someone off⟩

bronce *nm* : bronze

bronceado[1], **-da** *adj* **1** : tanned, suntanned **2** : bronze

bronceado[2] *nm* **1** : suntan, tan **2** : bronzing

bronceador *nm* : suntan lotion

broncear *vt* : to tan — **broncearse** *vr* : to get a suntan

bronco, -ca *adj* **1** : harsh, rough **2** : untamed, wild

bronquial *adj* : bronchial

bronquio *nm* : bronchial tube

bronquitis *nf* : bronchitis

broqueta *nf* : skewer

brotar *vi* **1** : to bud, to sprout **2** : to spring up, to stream, to gush forth **3** : to appear (of a rash, etc.)

brote *nm* **1** : outbreak **2** : sprout, bud, shoot

broza *nf* **1** : brushwood **2** MALEZA : scrub, undergrowth

bruces → **de bruces**

brujería *nf* HECHICERÍA : witchcraft, sorcery

brujo[1], **-ja** *adj* : bewitching

brujo[2], **-ja** *n* : witch *f*, sorcerer

brújula *nf* : compass

bruma *nf* : haze, mist

brumoso, -sa *adj* : hazy, misty

bruñir {38} *vt* : to burnish, to polish (metals)

brusco, -ca *adj* **1** SÚBITO : sudden, abrupt **2** : curt, brusque — **bruscamente** *adv*

brusquedad *nf* **1** : abruptness, suddenness **2** : brusqueness

brutal *adj* **1** : brutal **2** *fam* : incredible, terrific — **brutalmente** *adv*

brutalidad *nf* : brutality

brutalizar {21} *vt* : to brutalize, to maltreat

bruto[1], **-ta** *adj* **1** : gross ⟨peso bruto : gross weight⟩ ⟨ingresos brutos : gross income⟩ **2** : raw, unrefined ⟨petróleo (en) bruto : crude oil⟩ ⟨diamantes en bruto : uncut diamonds⟩ **3** ESTÚPIDO : brutish, stupid

bruto[2], **-ta** *n* **1** : brute **2** : dunce, blockhead

bubónico, -ca *adj* : bubonic ⟨peste bubónica : bubonic plague⟩

bucal *adj* : oral

bucanero *nm* : buccaneer
buceador, -dora *n* : diver, scuba diver
bucear *vi* **1** : to dive, to swim underwater **2** : to explore, to delve
buceo *nm* : diving, scuba diving
buche *nm* **1** : crop (of a bird) **2** *fam* : belly **3 hacer buches** : to rinse one's mouth
bucle *nm* **1** : curl, ringlet **2** : loop
bucólico, -ca *adj* : bucolic
budín *nm, pl* **budines** : pudding
budismo *nm* : Buddhism
budista *adj & nmf* : Buddhist
buen *adj* → **bueno**[1]
buenamente *adv* **1** : easily **2** : willingly
buenaventura *nf* **1** : good luck **2** : fortune, future ⟨le dijo la buenaventura : she told his fortune⟩
buenazo, -za *n fam* BONACHÓN : kind-hearted person
bueno[1]**, -na** *adj* (**buen** *before masculine singular nouns*) **1** : good ⟨una buena idea : a good idea⟩ ⟨en buenas condiciones : in good condition⟩ **2** : good, kind ⟨un buen hombre : a good man⟩ ⟨ser bueno con alguien : to be good to someone⟩ **3** : good, proper ⟨buenos modales : good manners⟩ ⟨es bueno ayudar a la gente : it's good to help people⟩ **4** : good, pleasant ⟨buen tiempo : good weather⟩ **5** : good, tasty ⟨esta sopa está buena : this soup is good⟩ **6** FRESCO : fresh **7** : good, healthy ⟨una buena alimentación : a good diet⟩ ⟨es bueno para el corazón : it's good for your heart⟩ **8** *fam* : sexy, hot *fam* ⟨está bueno : he's a hunk⟩ **9** : good, competent ⟨un buen abogado : a good lawyer⟩ ⟨hiciste un buen trabajo : you did a good job⟩ ⟨ser bueno para/en algo : to be good at something⟩ **10** : considerable, goodly ⟨una buena cantidad : a goodly amount, a lot⟩ **11 buenos días** : hello, good day **12 buenas tardes** : good afternoon **13 buenas noches** : good evening, good night **14 de buenas a primeras** : suddenly **15 ¡qué bueno!** : great! **16 un buen día** : one day
bueno[2] *interj* **1** : OK!, all right! **2** *Mex* : hello! (on the telephone)
bueno[3]**, -na** *n* **1** : good guy (in a story, etc.) **2 el bueno de, la buena de** : good old ⟨el bueno de Carlos : good old Carlos⟩
buey *nm* : ox, steer
búfalo *nm* **1** : buffalo **2 búfalo de agua** : water buffalo
bufanda *nf* : scarf
bufar *vi* : to snort
bufet *or* **bufé** *nm* : buffet (meal)
bufete *nm* : law firm, law office
bufido *nm* : snort
bufo, -fa *adj* : comic
bufón, -fona *n, mpl* **bufones 1** : jester **2** : clown, buffoon
bufonada *nf* : antic ⟨hacer bufonadas : to clown around⟩
buhardilla *nf* **1** ÁTICO, DESVÁN : attic **2** : dormer window
búho *nm* **1** : owl **2** *fam* : hermit, recluse
buhonero, -ra *n* MERCACHIFLE : peddler

buitre *nm* : vulture
bujía *nf* : spark plug
bula *nf* : papal bull
bulbo *nm* : bulb
bulboso, -sa *adj* : bulbous
bulevar *nm* : boulevard
búlgaro, -ra *adj & n* : Bulgarian
bulla *nf* BARULLO : racket, rowdiness
bulldog [bul'dog] *nm, pl* **bulldogs** : bulldog
bulldozer [bul'doser] *nm, pl* **-zers** : bulldozer
bullicio *nm* **1** : ruckus, uproar **2** : hustle and bustle
bullicioso, -sa *adj* : noisy, busy, turbulent
bullir {38} *vi* **1** HERVIR : to boil **2** MOVERSE : to stir, to bustle about
bullying ['bulin] *nm* : bullying
bulto *nm* **1** : package, bundle **2** : piece of luggage, bag **3** : size, bulk, volume **4** : form, shape ⟨pude distinguir unos bultos : I could make out some shapes⟩ **5** : lump (on the body), swelling, bulge
bumerán *nm, pl* **-ranes** : boomerang
búnker *nm, pl* **búnkers** : bunker
búnquer → **búnker**
buñuelo *nm* : doughnut, fried pastry
buque *nm* BARCO : ship, vessel ⟨buque de guerra : warship⟩
burbuja *nf* : bubble
burbujeante *adj* : bubbly
burbujear *vi* **1** : to bubble **2** : to fizz
burdel *nm* : brothel
burdo, -da *adj* **1** : coarse, rough **2** : crude, clumsy ⟨una burda mentira : an obvious lie⟩ — **burdamente** *adj*
burgués, -guesa *adj & n, mpl* **burgueses** : bourgeois
burguesía *nf* : bourgeoisie, middle class
burla *nf* **1** : mockery, ridicule **2** : joke, trick **3 hacer burla de** : to make fun of, to mock
burlar *vt* **1** ENGAÑAR : to trick, to deceive **2** ELUDIR : to evade — **burlarse** *vr* ~ **de** : to make fun of
burlesco, -ca *adj* : burlesque, comic
burlón[1]**, -lona** *adj, mpl* **burlones** : joking, mocking
burlón[2]**, -lona** *n, mpl* **burlones** : joker
burocracia *nf* : bureaucracy
burócrata *nmf* : bureaucrat
burocrático, -ca *adj* : bureaucratic
burrada *nf fam* : stupid act or remark, nonsense
burrito *nm* : burrito
burro[1]**, -rra** *adj fam* : dumb, stupid
burro[2]**, -rra** *n* **1** ASNO : donkey, ass **2** *fam* : idiot, dunce
burro[3] *nm* **1** : sawhorse **2** *Mex* : ironing board **3** *Mex* : stepladder
bursátil *adj* : stock-market
bus *nm* : bus
busca[1] *nf* : search ⟨en busca de : in search of⟩
busca[2] *nm Spain* → **buscapersonas**
buscador[1] *nm* : search engine
buscador[2]**, -dora** *n* : hunter (for treasure, etc.), prospector
buscapersonas *nms & pl* : beeper, pager
buscapleitos *nmfs & pl* : troublemaker

buscar {72} *vt* **1** : to look for (a person, an object, etc.), to seek (revenge, etc.) **2** : to fetch, to get ⟨ve a buscar ayuda : go (and) get help⟩ **3** : to look for (trouble, etc.) **4** : to look up (in a book, etc.), to search (on the Web) **5 ir a buscar** RE-COGER : to pick up (at a place) — *vi* : to look, to search ⟨buscó en los bolsillos : he searched through his pockets⟩ — **buscarse** *vr* : to ask for, to look for ⟨te la estás buscando : you're asking for it/ trouble⟩

buscavidas *nmfs & pl* : go-getter
busero, -ra *n* CA : bus driver
buseta *nf* Col, CoRi, Ecua, Ven : minibus
busque, etc. → buscar

búsqueda *nf* : search ⟨en búsqueda de : in search of⟩ ⟨la búsqueda de la verdad : the search for the truth⟩
busto *nm* : bust
butaca *nf* **1** SILLÓN : armchair, easy chair **2** : seat (in a theatre) **3** *Mex* : pupil's desk
buzo¹, -za *adj* Mex fam : smart, astute ⟨¡ponte buzo! : get with it!, get on the ball!⟩
buzo² *nm* **1** : diver **2** *Arg, Col* : sweatshirt, hoodie **3** *Uru* : sweater **4** *Chile, Peru* : tracksuit
buzón *nm, pl* **buzones** : mailbox ⟨buzón de voz : voice mail⟩
byte *nm* : byte

C

c *nf* : third letter of the Spanish alphabet
cabal *adj* **1** : exact, correct **2** : complete **3** : upright, honest
cabales *nmpl* **no estar en sus cabales** : not to be in one's right mind
cabalgar {52} *vi* : to ride (on horseback)
cabalgata *nf* : cavalcade, procession
cabalidad *nf* **a** ~ : thoroughly, conscientiously
caballa *nf* : mackerel
caballar *adj* EQUINO : horse, equine
caballeresco, -ca *adj* : gallant, chivalrous
caballería *nf* **1** : cavalry **2** : horse, mount **3** : knighthood, chivalry
caballeriza *nf* : stable
caballero¹ → caballeroso
caballero² *nm* **1** : gentleman **2** : knight ⟨caballero andante : knight errant⟩
caballerosidad *nf* : chivalry, gallantry
caballeroso, -sa *adj* : gentlemanly, chivalrous
caballete *nm* **1** : ridge **2** : easel **3** : trestle (for a table, etc.) **4** : bridge (of the nose) **5** : sawhorse
caballista *nmf* : horseman *m*, horsewoman *f*
caballito *nm* **1** : rocking horse **2 caballito de mar** : sea horse **3 caballitos** *nmpl* : merry-go-round
caballo *nm* **1** : horse **2** : knight (in chess) **3 caballo de fuerza** *or* **caballo de vapor** : horsepower
cabalmente *adv* : fully, exactly
cabaña *nf* : cabin, hut
cabaret [kaba'reʳ] *nm, pl* **-rets** : nightclub, cabaret
cabecear *vt* : to head (in soccer) — *vi* **1** : to nod one's head **2** : to lurch, to pitch
cabeceo *nm* : pitch (of a boat, etc.)
cabecera *nf* **1** : headboard **2** : head ⟨cabecera de la mesa : head of the table⟩ **3** : heading, headline **4** : headwaters *pl* **5 médico de cabecera** : family doctor **6 cabecera municipal** CA, Mex : downtown area
cabecilla *nmf* : ringleader
cabellera *nf* : head of hair, mane

cabello *nm* : hair
cabelludo, -da *adj* **1** : hairy **2 cuero cabelludo** : scalp
caber {12} *vi* **1** : to fit, to go ⟨¿cabremos todos? : will we all fit?⟩ **2** : to be possible ⟨no cabe duda alguna : there's no doubt about it⟩ ⟨cabe la posibilidad que llegue mañana : it's possible he'll come tomorrow⟩
cabestrillo *nm* : sling ⟨llevo el brazo en cabestrillo : my arm is in a sling⟩
cabestro *nm* : halter (for an animal)
cabeza *nf* **1** : head ⟨de pies a cabeza : from head to toe⟩ ⟨negar/asentir con la cabeza : to shake/nod one's head⟩ ⟨levantar/bajar/volver la cabeza : to raise/lower/turn one's head⟩ **2** : head, mind ⟨pasar por la cabeza : to cross one's mind⟩ **3** PELO : hair **4** : head, leader **5** : head, front, top **6** : head ⟨por cabeza : each, a head⟩ ⟨500 cabezas de ganado : 500 head of cattle⟩ **7** : head (of cabbage, etc.) **8** : head (measurement) **9 de** ~ : headfirst **10 dolor de cabeza** : headache
cabezada *nf* **1** : head butt **2** : nod ⟨echar una cabezada : to take a nap, to doze off⟩ **3** → cabeceo
cabezal *nm* : bolster
cabeza rapada *nmf* : skinhead
cabezazo *nm* : head butt
cabezón, -zona *adj, mpl* **-zones** *fam* **1** : having a big head **2** : pigheaded, stubborn
cabida *nf* **1** : room, space, capacity **2 dar cabida a** : to accommodate, to hold
cabildear *vi* : to lobby
cabildeo *nm* : lobbying
cabildero, -ra *n* : lobbyist
cabildo *nm* AYUNTAMIENTO **1** : town or city hall **2** : town or city council
cabina *nf* **1** : cabin **2** : booth **3** : cab (of a truck), cockpit (of an airplane)
cabizbajo, -ja *adj* : dejected, downcast
cable *nm* **1** : cable ⟨cables de arranque, cables pasacorriente Mex⟩ : jumper cables⟩ **2** : cable, cable television **3 cable tensor** : guy, guy line

cableado *nm* : wiring
cabo *nm* **1** : end ⟨al cabo de dos semanas : at the end of two weeks⟩ **2** : stub, end piece **3** : corporal **4** : cape, headland ⟨el Cabo Cañaveral : Cape Canaveral⟩ **5 al fin y al cabo** : after all, in the end **6 llevar a cabo** : to carry out, to do
cabrá, etc. → **caber**
cabra *nf* : goat
cabrío, -ría *adj* : goat
cabriola *nf* **1** : skip, jump **2 hacer cabriolas** : to prance
cabriolar *vi* : to prance
cabrito *nm* : kid, baby goat
cabro, cabra *n* : kid, youth
cabrón, cabrona *n, mpl* **cabrones** *Spain, Mex offensive* : bastard *m offensive*, bitch *f fam + offensive*
cabús *nm, pl* **cabuses** *Mex* : caboose
caca *nf fam* : poop ⟨hacer caca : to poop⟩ ⟨hacerse caca : to poop one's pants/diaper (etc.)⟩
cacahuate *nm Mex* : peanut
cacahuete *nm Spain* : peanut
cacalote *nm Mex* : crow
cacao *nm* **1** : cacao, cocoa bean **2** : hot chocolate, cocoa (drink)
cacarear *vi* : to crow, to cackle, to cluck — *vt fam* : to boast about, to crow about
cacareo *nm* **1** : clucking (of a hen), crowing (of a rooster) **2** : boasting
cacatúa *nf* : cockatoo
cace, etc. → **cazar**
cacería *nf* CAZA : hunt, hunting **2** : hunting party
cacerola *nf* : pan, saucepan
cacha *nf* : butt (of a gun)
cachalote *nm* : sperm whale
cachar *vt fam* : to catch
cacharro *nm* **1** *fam* : thing, piece of junk **2** *fam* : jalopy **3 cacharros** *nmpl* : pots and pans
cache *nm* : cache, cache memory
caché *nm* : cachet
cachear *vt* : to search, to frisk
cachemir *nm* : cashmere
cachemira *nf* → **cachemir**
cacheo *nm* : frisking, body search
cachetada *nf* BOFETADA : slap on the face
cachete *nm* : cheek
cachetear *vt* BOFETEAR : to slap
cachiporra *nf* : bludgeon, club, blackjack
cachirul *nm Mex fam* : cheating ⟨hacer cachirul : to cheat⟩
cachivache *nm fam* : thing, piece of junk ⟨cachivaches : stuff, junk⟩
cacho *nm fam* : piece, bit
cachondo, -da *adj Mex & Spain fam* : horny, lustful
cachorro, -rra *n* **1** : cub **2** PERRITO : puppy
cachucha *nf Mex* : cap, baseball cap
cacique *nm* **1** : chief (of a tribe) **2** : boss (in politics)
caco *nm fam* : thief
cacofonía *nf* : cacophony
cacto *nm* : cactus
cactus → **cacto**
cada *adj* **1** : each, every ⟨cuestan diez pesos cada una : they cost ten pesos each⟩ ⟨cada vez : each/every time⟩ **2** : every ⟨cada dos semanas : every two weeks, every other week⟩ ⟨cada cinco metros : every five meters⟩ **3** : every ⟨cuatro de cada cinco : four out of (every) five⟩ **4** : such, some ⟨sales con cada historia : you come up with such crazy stories⟩ **5 cada vez más** : more and more, increasingly **6 cada vez menos** : less and less
cadalso *nm* : scaffold, gallows
cadáver *nm* : corpse, cadaver
cadavérico, -ca *adj* **1** : cadaverous **2** : cadaveric (in medicine)
caddie *or* **caddy** *nmf, pl* **caddies** : caddy
cadena *nf* **1** : chain **2** : network, channel **3 cadena de montaje** : assembly line **4 cadena perpetua** : life sentence
cadencia *nf* : cadence, rhythm
cadencioso, -sa *adj* : rhythmic, rhythmical
cadera *nf* : hip
cadete *nmf* : cadet
cadmio *nm* : cadmium
caducar {72} *vi* : to expire
caducidad *nf* : expiration
caduco, -ca *adj* **1** : outdated, obsolete **2** : deciduous
caer {13} *vi* **1** : to fall ⟨cayó al suelo : he fell on the floor/ground⟩ ⟨lo dejó caer : she dropped it⟩ **2** : to drop away, to slope **3** : to fall (of night) **4** : to collapse, to fall **5** : to hang (down) **6** : to realize, to understand ⟨caer (en) que . . . : to realize that . . .⟩ **7 ∼ en** : to fall into (a trap, etc.) ⟨caer en el error de : to make the mistake of⟩ ⟨caer en manos de : to fall into the hands of⟩ ⟨caer en la tentación : to give in to temptation⟩ **8 caer en desgracia** : to fall out of favor **9 caer enfermo** : to fall ill **10 caerle bien/mal a alguien** *fam* : to sit well/poorly with someone ⟨me caes bien : I like you⟩ — **caerse** *vr* : to fall (down) ⟨se cayó de rodillas : she fell to her knees⟩
café¹ *adj* : brown ⟨ojos cafés : brown eyes⟩
café² *nm* **1** : coffee **2** : café
cafeína *nf* : caffeine
cafetal *nm* : coffee plantation
cafetalero¹, -ra *adj* : coffee ⟨cosecha cafetalera : coffee harvest⟩
cafetalero², -ra *n* : coffee grower
cafetera *nf* : coffeepot, coffeemaker
cafetería *nf* **1** : coffee shop, café **2** : lunchroom, cafeteria
cafetero¹, -ra *adj* : coffee-producing
cafetero², -ra *n* : coffee grower
caficultura *Mex* → **caficultura**
caficultor, -tora *n* : coffee grower
caficultura *nf* : coffee industry
caguama *nf* **1** : large Caribbean turtle **2** *Mex* : large bottle of beer
caída *nf* **1** BAJA, DESCENSO : fall, drop **2** : collapse, downfall
caído, -da *adj* **1** : fallen **2** : drooping, sagging
caiga, etc. → **caer**
caimán *nm, pl* **caimanes** : alligator

caimito *nm* : star apple
caja *nf* 1 : box, case 2 *or* caja registradora : cash register, checkout 3 : bed
(of a truck) 4 *fam* : coffin 5 caja de
cambios : gearbox 6 caja fuerte *or*
caja de caudales : safe 7 caja de seguridad : safe-deposit box 8 caja negra
: black box 9 caja torácica : rib cage
cajero, -ra *n* 1 : cashier 2 : teller 3 cajero automático : automated teller machine, ATM
cajeta *nf Mex* : sweet caramel-flavored
spread
cajetilla *nf* : pack (of cigarettes)
cajón *nm, pl* cajones 1 : drawer, till 2
: crate, case 3 ATAÚD : coffin, casket 4
cajón de arena : sandbox 5 cajón de
estacionamiento *Mex* : parking space
cajuela *nf Mex* : trunk (of a car)
cal *nf* : lime
cala *nf* : cove, inlet
calabacín *nm, pl* -cines : zucchini
calabacita *nf Mex* : zucchini
calabaza *nf* 1 : pumpkin, squash 2
: gourd 3 dar calabazas a : to give the
brush-off to, to jilt
calabozo *nm* 1 : prison 2 : jail cell
calado[1], -da *adj* : drenched
calado[2] *nm* : draft (of a ship)
calamar *nm* 1 : squid 2 calamares
nmpl : calamari
calambre *nm* 1 ESPASMO : cramp 2
: electric shock, jolt
calamidad *nf* DESASTRE : calamity, disaster
calamina *nf* : calamine
calamitoso, -sa *adj* : calamitous, disastrous
calaña *nf* : ilk, kind, sort ⟨una persona de
mala calaña : a bad sort⟩
calar *vt* 1 : to soak through 2 : to pierce,
to penetrate — *vi* : to catch on — ca-
larse *vr* : to get drenched
calavera[1] *nf* 1 : skull 2 *Mex* : taillight
calavera[2] *nm* : rake, rogue
calcar {72} *vt* 1 : to trace 2 : to copy, to
imitate
calce, etc. → calzar
calceta *nf* : knee-high stocking
calcetería *nf* : hosiery
calcetín *nm, pl* -tines : sock
calcinar *vt* : to char, to burn
calcio *nm* : calcium
calco *nm* 1 : transfer, tracing 2 : copy,
image
calcomanía *nf* : decal, transfer
calculador, -dora *adj* : calculating
calculadora *nf* : calculator
calcular *vt* 1 : to calculate, to estimate 2
: to plan, to scheme
cálculo *nm* 1 : calculation, estimation
: calculus 3 : plan, scheme 4 cálculo
biliar : gallstone 5 hoja de cálculo
: spreadsheet
caldear *vt* : to heat, to warm — caldearse
vr 1 : to heat up 2 : to become heated,
to get tense
caldera *nf* 1 : cauldron 2 : boiler
caldero *nm* : cauldron
caldo *nm* 1 : broth, stock 2 caldo de cultivo : culture medium, breeding ground

caldoso, -sa *adj* : watery
calefacción *nf, pl* -ciones : heating, heat
calefactor *nm* : heater
caleidoscopio → calidoscopio
calendario *nm* 1 : calendar 2 : timetable, schedule
caléndula *nf* : marigold
calentador *nm* : heater
calentamiento *nm* 1 : heating, warming
⟨calentamiento global : global warming⟩
2 : warm-up (in sports)
calentar {55} *vt* 1 : to heat, to warm 2
fam : to annoy, to anger 3 *fam* : to excite, to turn on — calentarse *vr* 1 : to
get warm, to heat up 2 : to warm up (in
sports) 3 *fam* : to become sexually
aroused 4 *fam* : to get mad
calentura *nf* 1 FIEBRE : temperature, fever 2 : cold sore
calesa *nf* : buggy
calibrador *nm* : gauge, calipers *pl*
calibrar *vt* : to calibrate — calibración *nf*
calibre *nm* 1 : caliber, gauge 2 : importance, excellence 3 : kind, sort ⟨un
problema de grueso calibre : a serious
problem⟩
calicó *nm* : calico (cloth)
calidad *nf* 1 : quality, grade 2 : position, status 3 en calidad de : as, in the
capacity of
cálido, -da *adj* 1 : hot ⟨un clima cálido
: a hot climate⟩ 2 : warm ⟨una cálida
bienvenida : a warm welcome⟩
calidoscopio *nm* : kaleidoscope
caliente *adj* 1 : hot, warm ⟨mantenerse
caliente : to stay warm⟩ 2 : heated, fiery
⟨una disputa caliente : a heated argu-
ment⟩ 3 *fam* : sexually excited, horny
calificación *nf, pl* -ciones 1 NOTA
: grade (for a course) 2 : rating, score
3 CLASIFICACIÓN : qualification, qualifying ⟨ronda de calificación : qualifying
round⟩
calificar {72} *vt* 1 : to grade 2 : to describe, to rate ⟨la calificaron de buena
alumna : they described her as a good
student⟩ 3 : to qualify, to modify (in
grammar)
calificativo[1], -va *adj* : qualifying
calificativo[2] *nm* : qualifier, epithet
caligrafía *nf* 1 LETRA : handwriting 2
: calligraphy
calipso *nm* : calypso
calistenia *nf* : calisthenics
cáliz *nm, pl* cálices 1 : chalice, goblet 2
: calyx
caliza *nf* : limestone
calizo, -za *adj* : chalky, limy
callado, -da *adj* : quiet, silent — calladamente *adv*
callampa *nf Chile* 1 : mushroom 2 ca-
llampas *pl* : slums, shantytown
callar *vi* : to keep quiet, to be silent — *vt*
1 : to silence, to hush ⟨¡calla a los niños!
: keep the children quiet!⟩ 2 : to keep
secret — callarse *vr* : to remain silent
⟨¡cállate! : be quiet!, shut up!⟩
calle *nf* : street, road ⟨calle de sentido
único : one-way street⟩ ⟨calle sin salida

: dead-end street⟩ ⟨salir a la calle : to go out/outside⟩ ⟨salir a la(s) calle(s) : to take to the streets⟩ ⟨la echó a la calle : he kicked her out⟩
callejear vi : to wander about the streets, to hang out
callejero, -ra adj : street ⟨perro callejero : stray dog⟩
callejón nm, pl **-jones** 1 : alley 2 **callejón sin salida** : dead-end street
callejuela nf 1 : alley 2 : narrow street, side street
callo nm 1 : callus, corn 2 **callos** nmpl : tripe
calloso, -sa adj : callous
calma nf : calm, quiet
calmante¹ adj : calming, soothing
calmante² nm : tranquilizer, sedative
calmar vt : to calm, to soothe — **calmarse** vr 1 : to calm down 2 : to ease (of pain, etc.)
calmo, -ma adj : calm, tranquil
calmoso, -sa adj 1 : calm, quiet 2 LENTO : slow
caló nm : Gypsy slang
calor nm 1 : heat ⟨hace calor : it's hot outside⟩ ⟨tener calor : to feel hot⟩ ⟨entrar en calor : to warm up, to get warm⟩ 2 : warmth, affection 3 : ardor, passion
caloria nf : calorie
calórico, -ca adj : caloric
calorífico, -ca adj : caloric
calque, etc. → calcar
calumnia nf : slander, libel — **calumnioso, -sa** adj
calumniar vt : to slander, to libel
caluroso, -sa adj 1 : hot 2 : warm, enthusiastic — **calurosamente** adv
calva nf : bald spot, bald head
calvario nm : ordeal, misery ⟨vivir un calvario : to go through hell⟩
calvicie nf : baldness
calvo¹, -va adj : bald
calvo², -va n : bald person
calza nf : block, wedge
calzada nf : roadway, avenue
calzado nm : footwear
calzador nm : shoehorn
calzar {21} vt 1 : to wear (shoes) ⟨¿de cuál calza? : what is your shoe size?⟩ ⟨calzar tenis : to wear sneakers⟩ 2 : to provide with shoes
calzoncillos nmpl : underpants, briefs
calzones nmpl : underpants, panties
cama nf 1 : bed 2 **cama elástica** : trampoline
camada nf : litter, brood
camafeo nm : cameo
camaleón nm, pl **-leones** : chameleon
cámara nf 1 : camera 2 : chamber, room 3 : house (in government) 4 : inner tube
camarada nmf 1 : comrade, companion 2 : colleague
camaradería nf : camaraderie
camarero, -ra n 1 MESERO : waiter, waitress f 2 BARMAN : bartender 3 : bellhop m, chambermaid f (in a hotel) 4 : steward m, stewardess f (on a ship, etc.)
camarilla nf : political clique

camarín nm, pl **-rines** 1 Chile, Peru, Uru : locker room 2 Arg, Uru : dressing room
camarógrafo, -fa n : cameraman m, camerawoman f
camarón nm, pl **-rones** 1 : shrimp 2 : prawn
camarote nm : cabin, stateroom
camastro nm : small hard bed, pallet
cambalache nm fam : swap
cambiable adj : changeable
cambiante adj 1 : changing 2 VARIABLE : changeable, variable
cambiar vt 1 : to change ⟨le cambió la vida : it changed her life⟩ ⟨cambiaron el menú : they changed the menu⟩ ⟨cambiar algo de lugar : to move something⟩ 2 : to exchange, to trade ⟨lo cambió por otro : she exchanged it for another⟩ 3 : to change (money) ⟨cambiar pesos a euros : to change pesos into euros⟩ 4 : to change, to replace ⟨cambió la llanta/contraseña : he changed the tire/password⟩ ⟨le cambié el pañal : I changed her diaper⟩ — vi 1 : to change ⟨el tiempo cambió : the weather changed⟩ ⟨cambiar de color : to change color⟩ ⟨cambiar de tema : to change the subject⟩ ⟨cambiar de opinión/idea : to change one's mind⟩ 2 **cambiar de velocidad** : to shift gears — **cambiarse** vr 1 : to change ⟨se ha cambiado mucho : she's changed a lot⟩ 2 or **cambiarse de ropa** : to change (clothes) 3 MUDARSE : to move (to a new address)
cambio nm 1 : change, alteration ⟨cambio climático : climate change⟩ ⟨cambio de horario : schedule change⟩ ⟨cambio de domicilio : change of address⟩ 2 : exchange (of goods, etc.) 3 : change (money) 4 : currency exchange 5 : gear ⟨palanca de cambio : gearshift⟩ ⟨caja de cambios : gearbox⟩ 6 a **cambio (de)** : in exchange (for) 7 **en ~** : instead 8 **en ~** : however, on the other hand
cambista nmf : exchange broker, money changer
camboyano, -na adj & n : Cambodian
cambur nm Ven : banana
camello nm 1 : camel 2 fam TRAFICANTE : drug dealer, pusher
camellón nm, pl **-llones** Mex : traffic island
camerino nm : dressing room
camilla nf : stretcher
camillero, -ra n : orderly (in a hospital)
caminante nmf : wayfarer, walker
caminar vi 1 ANDAR : to walk ⟨prefiero ir caminando : I prefer to walk⟩ 2 : to move, to progress 3 FUNCIONAR : to work, to run — vt : to walk, to cover (a distance)
caminata nf : hike, long walk
camino nm 1 : path, road 2 : journey ⟨ponerse en camino : to set off⟩ 3 : way ⟨a medio camino : halfway there⟩
camión nm, pl **camiones** 1 : truck 2 Mex : bus
camionero, -ra n 1 : truck driver 2 Mex : bus driver

camioneta *nf* : light truck, van
camisa *nf* **1** : shirt **2 camisa de fuerza** : straitjacket
camiseta *nf* **1** : T-shirt **2** : undershirt
camisón *nm, pl* **-sones** : nightshirt, nightgown
camomila *nf* MANZANILLA : chamomile
camorra *nf fam* : fight, trouble ⟨buscar camorra : to pick a fight⟩
camote *nm* **1** : root vegetable similar to the sweet potato **2 hacerse camote** *Mex fam* : to get mixed up
campal *adj* : pitched, fierce (of a battle)
campamento *nm* : camp
campana *nf* : bell
campanada *nf* : stroke (of a clock), peal (of bells)
campanario *nm* : bell tower, belfry
campanazo *nm* **1** → **campanada 2 campanazo inicial** : starting bell
campanilla *nf* **1** : bluebell **2** : uvula **3 campanilla blanca** : snowdrop
campante *adj* : nonchalant, smug ⟨seguir tan campante : to go on as if nothing had happened⟩
campaña *nf* **1** CAMPO : countryside, country **2** : campaign **3 tienda de campaña** : tent
campañol *nm* : vole
campechana *nf Mex* : puff pastry
campechano, -na *adj* : friendly and down-to-earth
campeón, -peona *n, mpl* **-peones** : champion
campeonato *nm* : championship
cámper *nm* : camper (vehicle)
campera *nf* CHAQUETA : jacket
campero, -ra *adj* : country, rural
campesino, -na *n* : peasant, farm laborer
campestre *adj* : rural, rustic
camping *nm* **1** : camping **2** : campsite
campiña *nf* CAMPO : countryside, country
campista *nmf* : camper
campo *nm* **1** CAMPAÑA : countryside, country **2** : field (of crops, ice, etc.) **3** : field (in sports), course (in golf) **4** : field, area ⟨su campo de responsabilidad : her area of responsibility⟩ ⟨el campo tecnológico : the field of technology⟩ **5** : camp ⟨campo de refugiados : refugee camp⟩ ⟨campo de concentración : concentration camp⟩ **6 campo de aviación** : airfield **7 campo de batalla** : battlefield **8 campo magnético** : magnetic field **9 estudio de campo** : field study
camposanto *nm* : graveyard, cemetery
campus *nms & pl* : campus
camuflaje *nm* : camouflage
camuflajear *vt* : to camouflage
camuflar → **camuflajear**
can *nm* : hound, dog
cana *nf* **1** : gray hair ⟨le salen canas : he's going gray⟩ **2 echar una cana al aire** : to let one's hair down
canadiense *adj & nmf* : Canadian
canal[1] *nm* **1** : canal **2** : channel **3** : feed (on social media)
canal[2] *nmf* : gutter, groove
canalé *nm* : rib, ribbing (in fabric)

canaleta *nf* : gutter
canalete *nm* : paddle
canalizar {21} *vt* : to channel
canalla[1] *adj fam* : low, rotten
canalla[2] *nmf fam* : bastard, swine
canapé *nm* **1** : canapé **2** SOFÁ : couch, sofa
canario[1]**, -ria** *adj* : of or from the Canary Islands
canario[2]**, -ria** *n* : Canary Islander
canario[3] *nm* : canary
canasta *nf* : basket
canasto *nm* : (large) basket
cancel *nm* **1** : sliding door **2** : partition
cancelación *nf, pl* **-ciones 1** : cancellation **2** : payment in full
cancelar *vt* **1** : to cancel **2** : to pay off, to settle
cáncer *nm* : cancer
Cáncer[1] *nm* : Cancer (sign or constellation)
Cáncer[2] *nmf* : Cancer (person)
cancerígeno[1]**, -na** *adj* : carcinogenic
cancerígeno[2] *nm* : carcinogen
canceroso, -sa *adj* : cancerous
cancha *nf* : court, field (for sports) ⟨cancha de golf : golf course⟩
canciller *nm* : chancellor
cancillería *nf* : ministry of foreign affairs
canción *nf, pl* **canciones 1** : song **2 canción de cuna** : lullaby
cancionero[1] *nm* : songbook
cancionero[2]**, -ra** *n Mex* : singer
candado *nm* : padlock
candela *nf* **1** : flame, fire **2** : candle
candelabro *nm* : candelabra
candelero *nm* **1** : candlestick **2 estar en el candelero** : to be in the spotlight
candente *adj* : red-hot, white-hot
candidato, -ta *n* : candidate, applicant
candidatura *nf* : candidacy
candidez *nf* **1** : simplicity **2** INGENUIDAD : naïveté, ingenuousness
cándido, -da *adj* **1** : simple, unassuming **2** INGENUO : naive, ingenuous
candil *nm* : oil lamp
candilejas *nfpl* : footlights
candor *nm* : naïveté, innocence
caneca *nf Col* **1** : garbage can **2** PAPELERA : wastebasket **3** BIDÓN : drum
canela *nf* : cinnamon
canelones *nmpl* : cannelloni
cangrejo *nm* JAIBA : crab
canguro[1] *nm* : kangaroo
canguro[2] *nmf Spain fam* : baby-sitter
caníbal[1] *adj* : cannibalistic
caníbal[2] *nmf* ANTROPÓFAGO : cannibal
canibalismo *nm* ANTROPOFAGIA : cannibalism
canica *nf* : marble ⟨jugar a las canicas : to play marbles⟩
caniche *nm* : poodle
canijo, -ja *adj* **1** *fam* : puny, weak **2** *Mex fam* DIFÍCIL : tough, hard
canilla *nf* **1** : shin **2** *Arg, Uru* : faucet
canillita *nmf Arg* : newspaper vendor
canino[1]**, -na** *adj* : canine
canino[2] *nm* **1** COLMILLO : canine (tooth) **2** : dog, canine
canje *nm* : exchange, trade

canjeable *adj* : exchangeable
canjear *vt* : to exchange, to trade
cannabis *nm* : cannabis
cano, -na *adj* : gray ⟨un hombre de pelo cano : a gray-haired man⟩
canoa *nf* : canoe
canon *nm, pl* **cánones** : canon
canónico, -ca *adj* : canonical
canónigo *nm* : canon (of a church)
canonizar {21} *vt* : to canonize — **canonización** *nf*
canoso, -sa → **cano**
cansado, -da *adj* 1 : tired ⟨estar cansado : to be tired⟩ 2 : tiresome ⟨ser cansado : to be tiring⟩
cansancio *nm* : tiredness
cansar *vt* : to tire — *vi* : to be tiresome — **cansarse** *vr* 1 : to tire oneself out 2 : to get bored
cansino, -na *adj* : slow, weary, lethargic
cantaleta *nf fam* : nagging ⟨la misma cantaleta : the same old story⟩
cantalupo *nm* : cantaloupe
cantante[1] *adj* : singing
cantante[2] *nmf* : singer
cantar[1] *vi* 1 : to sing 2 CACAREAR : to crow 3 CHIRRIAR : to chirp (of insects) — *vt* 1 : to sing 2 : to call out, to recite ⟨cantar victoria : to claim victory⟩
cantar[2] *nm* : song, ballad
cántaro *nm* 1 : pitcher, jug 2 **llover a cántaros** *fam* : to rain cats and dogs
cantata *nf* : cantata
cantautor, -tora *n* : singer-songwriter
cantera *nf* : quarry
cantero *nm* 1 MAMPOSTERO : mason, stonemason 2 ARRIATE : bed (for plants)
cántico *nm* : chant
cantidad[1] *adv fam* : a lot ⟨me gustó cantidad : I liked it a lot⟩ ⟨ese carro me costó cantidad : that car cost me plenty⟩
cantidad[2] *nf* 1 : quantity 2 : sum, amount (of money) 3 *fam* : a lot, a great many ⟨había cantidad de gente : there were tons of people⟩
cantillos *nmpl* : jacks *pl*
cantimplora *nf* : canteen, water bottle
cantina *nf* 1 : tavern, bar 2 : canteen, mess, dining quarters *pl*
cantinero, -ra *n* : bartender
canto *nm* 1 : singing 2 : chant ⟨canto gregoriano : Gregorian chant⟩ 3 : song (of a bird) 4 : edge, end ⟨de canto : on end, sideways⟩ 5 **canto rodado** : boulder
cantón *nm, pl* **cantones** 1 : canton 2 *Mex fam* : place, home
cantonés[1], **-nesa** *adj & n, mpl* **-neses** : Cantonese
cantonés[2] *nm, pl* **-neses** : Cantonese (language)
cantor[1], **-tora** *adj* 1 : singing 2 **pájaro cantor** : songbird
cantor[2], **-tora** *n* 1 : singer 2 : cantor
canturrear *v* : to sing softly
caña *nf* 1 : cane ⟨caña de azúcar : sugarcane⟩ 2 : reed 3 **caña de pescar** : fishing rod 4 **caña del timón** : tiller (of a boat)

cañada *nf* : ravine, gully
cáñamo *nm* : hemp
cañaveral *nm* : sugarcane field
cañería *nf* TUBERÍA : pipes *pl*, piping
cañero[1], **-ra** *adj* : sugar cane
cañero[2], **-ra** *n* 1 : sugar cane grower 2 : sugar cane worker
caño *nm* 1 : pipe 2 : spout 3 : channel (for navigation)
cañón *nm, pl* **cañones** 1 : cannon 2 : barrel (of a gun) 3 : canyon
cañonazo *nm* : firing (of a cannon) ⟨saludo de 21 cañonazos : 21-gun salute⟩
cañonear *vt* : to shell, to bombard
cañonero *nm* : gunboat
caoba *nf* : mahogany
caos *nm* : chaos
caótico, -ca *adj* : chaotic
capa *nf* 1 : cape, cloak 2 : coating 3 : layer, stratum 4 : (social) class, stratum
capacidad *nf* 1 : capacity 2 : capability, ability
capacitación *nf, pl* **-ciones** : training
capacitar *vt* : to train, to qualify
capar *vt* : to castrate
caparazón *nm, pl* **-zones** : shell
capataz[1] *nmf, pl* **-taces** : foreman *m*, forewoman *f*
capataz[2], **taza** *n* → **capataz**[1]
capaz *adj, pl* **capaces** 1 : capable, able ⟨capaz de trabajar : able to work⟩ ⟨es capaz de cualquier cosa : he's capable of anything⟩ 2 COMPETENTE : competent, capable 3 : spacious ⟨capaz para : with room for⟩
capcioso, -sa *adj* : cunning, deceptive ⟨pregunta capciosa : trick question⟩
capea *nf* : amateur bullfight
capear *vt* 1 : to make a pass with the cape (in bullfighting) 2 : to weather (a storm, crisis, etc.)
capellán *nm, pl* **-llanes** : chaplain
capilar[1] *adj* 1 : capillary 2 : hair
capilar[2] *nm* : capillary
capilla *nf* : chapel
capirotada *nf Mex* : traditional bread pudding
capirotazo *nm* : flip, flick
capital[1] *adj* 1 : capital 2 : chief, principal
capital[2] *nm* : capital ⟨capital de riesgo : venture capital⟩
capital[3] *nf* : capital, capital city
capitalino[1], **-na** *adj* : of or from a capital city
capitalino[2], **-na** *n* : inhabitant of a capital city
capitalismo *nm* : capitalism
capitalista *adj & nmf* : capitalist
capitalizar {21} *vt* : to capitalize — **capitalización** *nf*
capitán, -tana *n, mpl* **-tanes** 1 : captain 2 **capitán de corbeta** : lieutenant commander
capitanear *vt* : to captain, to command
capitel *nm* : capital (of a column)
capitolio *nm* : capitol
capitulación *nf, pl* **-ciones** : capitulation
capitular *vi* : to capitulate, to surrender

capítulo *nm* **1** : chapter, section **2** : matter, subject

capo, capa *n* : boss

capó *nm* : hood (of a car)

capón *nm, pl* **capones** : capon

caporal *nm* **1** : chief, leader **2** : foreman (on a ranch)

capot → **capó**

capota *nf* : top (of a convertible)

capote *nm* **1** : cloak, overcoat **2** : bullfighter's cape **3** *Mex* : hood (of a car)

capricho *nm* : whim, caprice

caprichoso, -sa *adj* : capricious, fickle

Capricornio[1] *nm* : Capricorn (sign or constellation)

Capricornio[2] *nmf* : Capricorn (person)

cápsula *nf* : capsule

captar *vt* **1** : to catch, to grasp **2** : to gain, to attract **3** : to harness, to collect (waters)

captor, -tora *n* : captor

captura *nf* : capture, seizure

capturar *vt* : to capture, to seize

capucha *nf* : hood, cowl

capuchino *nm* : cappuccino

capullo *nm* **1** : cocoon **2** : bud (of a flower)

caqui *adj & nm* : khaki

cara *nf* **1** : face **2** : look, appearance ⟨¡qué buena cara tiene ese pastel! : that cake looks delicious!⟩ **3** *fam* : nerve, gall **4 (de) cara a** : facing **5 de cara a** : in view of, in the light of

carabina *nf* : carbine

carabinero, -ra *n* : police officer

caracol *nm* **1** : snail **2** CONCHA : conch, seashell **3** : ringlet

caracola *nf* : conch

carácter *nm, pl* **caracteres** **1** ÍNDOLE : character, kind, nature **2** TEMPERAMENTO : character, temperament **3** : character (in writing)

característica *nf* RASGO : trait, feature, characteristic

característico, -ca *adj* : characteristic — **característicamente** *adv*

caracterizar {21} *vt* : to characterize — **caracterización** *nf*

caradura *adj* DESCARADO : cheeky, impudent

caramba *interj* **1** (*expressing annoyance or anger*) : darn!, heck! **2** (*expressing surprise*) : wow!, good Lord!

carámbano *nm* : icicle

carambola *nf* **1** : carom **2** : ruse, trick ⟨por carambola : by a lucky chance⟩

caramelo *nm* **1** : caramel **2** DULCE : candy

caramillo *nm* **1** : pipe, small flute **2** : heap, pile

caraqueño[1], **-ña** *adj* : of or from Caracas

caraqueño[2], **-ña** *n* : person from Caracas

carátula *nf* **1** : title page **2** : cover, dust jacket **3** CARETA : mask **4** *Mex* : face, dial (of a clock or watch)

caravana *nf* **1** : caravan **2** : convoy **3** REMOLQUE : trailer

caray → **caramba**

carbohidrato *nm* : carbohydrate

carbón *nm, pl* **carbones** **1** : coal **2** : charcoal

carbonatado, -da *adj* : carbonated

carboncillo *nm* : charcoal

carbonera *nf* : coal cellar, coal bunker (on a ship)

carbonero, -ra *adj* : coal

carbonizar {21} *vt* : to char — **carbonizarse** *vr*

carbono *nm* : carbon

carburador *nm* : carburetor

carburante *nm* : fuel

carca *nmf fam* : old fogy

carcacha *nf fam* : jalopy, wreck

carcaj *nm* : quiver (for arrows)

carcajada *nf* : loud laugh, guffaw ⟨reírse a carcajadas : to roar with laughter⟩

carcajearse *vr* : to roar with laughter, to be in stitches

cárcel *nf* PRISIÓN : jail, prison

carcelario, -ria *adj* : prison

carcelero, -ra *n* : jailer

carcinogénico, -ca *adj* → **cancerígeno**

carcinógeno *nm* → **cancerígeno**

carcinoma *nm* : carcinoma

carcomer *vt* : to eat away at, to consume

carcomido, -da *adj* **1** : worm-eaten **2** : decayed, rotten

cardar *vt* : to card, to comb

cardenal *nm* **1** : cardinal (in religion) **2** : bruise

cardíaco *or* **cardiaco, -ca** *adj* : cardiac, heart

cárdigan *nm, pl* **-gans** : cardigan

cardinal *adj* : cardinal

cardiología *nf* : cardiology

cardiólogo, -ga *n* : cardiologist

cardiovascular *adj* : cardiovascular

cardo *nm* : thistle

cardumen *nm* : school of fish

carecer {53} *vi* ∼ **de** : to lack ⟨el cheque carecía de fondos : the check had insufficient funds⟩

carencia *nf* **1** FALTA : lack **2** ESCASEZ : shortage **3** DEFICIENCIA : deficiency

carente *adj* ∼ **de** : lacking (in)

careo *nm* : confrontation, face-off

carero, -ra *adj fam* : pricey

carestía *nf* **1** : rise in cost ⟨la carestía de la vida : the high cost of living⟩ **2** : dearth, scarcity

careta *nf* MÁSCARA : mask

carey *nm* **1** : sea turtle **2** : tortoiseshell

carga *nf* **1** : loading **2** : freight, load, cargo **3** : burden, responsibility **4** : charge ⟨carga eléctrica : electrical charge⟩ **5** : attack, charge

cargada *nf Arg, Uru* : joke

cargado, -da *adj* **1** : loaded **2** : bogged down, weighted down **3** : close, stuffy **4** : full, fraught ⟨cargado de tensión/errores : fraught with tension/errors⟩ **5** FUERTE : strong ⟨café cargado : strong coffee⟩ **6 cargado de hombros** : round-shouldered

cargador[1], **-dora** *n* : longshoreman *m*, longshorewoman *f*

cargador[2] *nm* **1** : magazine (for a firearm) **2** : charger (for batteries)

cargamento *nm* : cargo, load

cargar {52} *vt* **1** : to carry **2** : to load, to fill **3** : to charge **4** : to burden ⟨car-

gado de deudas : burdened with debts⟩
5 SUBIR : to upload — *vi* **1** : to load **2**
: to rest (in architecture) **3** ~ **con** : to
shoulder, to take on (a responsibility,
etc.) **4** ~ **sobre** : to fall upon
cargo *nm* **1** : burden, load **2** : charge ⟨es-
tar a cargo de : to be in charge of⟩ ⟨correr
a cargo de : to be paid by⟩ ⟨hacerse cargo
de : to take charge of, to take care of⟩
⟨tener a su cargo : to be in charge of⟩ **3**
: charge, cost **4** : position, office
cargue[1], etc. → **cargar**
cargue[2] *nm Col* : loading
carguero[1], **-ra** *adj* : freight, cargo ⟨tren
carguero : freight train⟩
carguero[2] *nm* : freighter, cargo ship
cariarse *vr* : to decay (of teeth)
caribe *adj* : Caribbean ⟨el mar Caribe
: the Caribbean Sea⟩
caribeño, -ña *adj* : Caribbean
caribú *nm, pl* **caribúes** : caribou
caricatura *nf* **1** : caricature **2** : cartoon
caricaturista *nmf* : caricaturist, cartoonist
caricaturizar {21} *vt* : to caricature
caricia *nf* **1** : caress **2 hacer caricias**
: to pet, to stroke
caridad *nf* : charity
caries *nfs & pl* : cavity (in a tooth)
cariño[1] *nm* AFECTO : affection, love
cariño[2], **-ña** *n* : darling, sweetheart
cariñoso, -sa *adj* AFECTUOSO : affectionate, loving — **cariñosamente** *adv*
carioca[1] *adj* : of or from Rio de Janeiro
carioca[2] *nmf* : person from Rio de Janeiro
carisma *nf* : charisma
carismático, -ca *adj* : charismatic
carita *adj Mex fam* : cute (said of a man)
⟨se cree muy carita : he thinks he's gor-
geous⟩
carita sonriente *nf* : smiley face (emoticon or drawing)
caritativo, -va *adj* : charitable
cariz *nm, pl* **carices** : appearance, aspect
carmesí *adj & nm* : crimson
carmín *nm, pl* **carmines** **1** : carmine **2**
: lipstick
carnada *nf* CEBO : bait
carnal *adj* **1** : carnal **2 primo carnal**
: first cousin
carnaval *nm* : carnival
carne *nf* **1** : meat ⟨carne molida : ground
beef⟩ **2** : flesh ⟨carne de gallina : goose
bumps⟩
carné → **carnet**
carnero *nm* **1** : ram, sheep **2** : mutton
carnet *nm* **1** : identification card, ID **2**
: membership card **3 carnet de condu-
cir** *Spain* : driver's license
carnicería *nf* **1** : butcher shop **2** MA-
TANZA : slaughter, carnage
carnicero, -ra *n* : butcher
carnitas *nfpl Mex* : small chunks of
cooked pork
carnívoro[1], **-ra** *adj* : carnivorous
carnívoro[2] *nm* : carnivore
carnoso, -sa *adj* : fleshy, meaty
caro[1] *adv* : a lot ⟨costar/pagar caro : to
cost/pay a lot⟩ ⟨vender caro : to sell

high, to sell at a high price⟩ ⟨un error
que me costó caro : a mistake that cost
me dearly⟩
caro[2], **-ra** *adj* **1** : expensive, dear ⟨es
muy/demasiado caro : it's very/too ex-
pensive⟩ **2** QUERIDO : dear, beloved
carpa *nf* **1** : carp **2** : big top (of a circus)
3 : tent
carpeta *nf* : folder, binder, portfolio (of
drawings, etc.)
carpetazo *nm* **dar carpetazo a** : to shelve,
to defer
carpintería *nf* **1** : carpentry **2** : carpenter's workshop
carpintero, -ra *n* : carpenter
carraspear *vi* : to clear one's throat
carraspera *nf* : hoarseness ⟨tener carraspera : to have a frog in one's throat⟩
carrera *nf* **1** : run, running ⟨a la carrera
: at full speed⟩ ⟨de carrera : hastily⟩ **2**
: race ⟨carrera de caballos : horse race⟩
3 : course of study ⟨estudiar la carrera
de medicina : to study medicine⟩ **4** : career, profession **5** : run (in baseball)
carreta *nf* : cart, wagon
carrete *nm* **1** : spool (for thread), bobbin
(in sewing machine), reel (for film, etc.)
⟨carrete de pesca : fishing reel⟩ **2** : roll
of film **3** : (electrical) coil
carretear *vi* : to taxi
carretel → **carrete**
carretera *nf* : highway, road ⟨carretera de
peaje : turnpike⟩
carretero, -ra *adj* : highway ⟨el sistema
carretero : the highway system⟩
carretilla *nf* **1** : wheelbarrow **2 carretilla elevadora** : forklift
carril *nm* **1** : lane ⟨carretera de doble
carril : two-lane highway⟩ **2** : rail (on a
railroad track)
carrillo *nm* : cheek, jowl
carrito *nm* : cart ⟨carrito de compras, carrito de la compra *Mexico, Spain* : shopping cart⟩
carrizo *nm* JUNCO : reed
carro *nm* **1** COCHE : car **2** : cart **3**
Chile, Mex : coach (of a train) **4 carro
alegórico** : float (in a parade) **5 carro
bomba** : car bomb **6 carro de compras**
or **carro de la compra** *Spain* : shopping
cart
carrocería *nf* : bodywork, body (of a vehicle)
carroña *nf* : carrion
carroñero, -ra *n* : scavenger (animal)
carroza *nf* **1** : carriage **2** : float (in a
parade)
carruaje *nm* : carriage
carrusel *nm* **1** : merry-go-round **2** : carousel ⟨carrusel de equipaje : luggage
carousel⟩
carta *nf* **1** : letter ⟨carta de amor : love
letter⟩ ⟨carta de renuncia : letter of res-
ignation⟩ **2** NAIPE : playing card **3**
: charter, constitution **4** MENÚ : menu
5 : map, chart **6 tomar cartas en** : to
intervene in
carta blanca *nf* : carte blanche
carta bomba *nf* : letter bomb

cartearse *vr* : to write to one another, to correspond

cartel *nm* : sign, poster

cártel *or* **cartel** *nm* : cartel

cartelera *nf* **1** : billboard **2** : marquee

cartera *nf* **1** BILLETERA : wallet, billfold **2** BOLSO : pocketbook, purse **3** : portfolio ⟨cartera de acciones : stock portfolio⟩

carterista *nmf* : pickpocket

cartero, -ra *n* : letter carrier, mailman *m*

cartílago *nm* : cartilage

cartilla *nf* **1** : primer, reader **2** : booklet ⟨cartilla de ahorros : bankbook⟩

cartografía *nf* : cartography

cartógrafo, -fa *n* : cartographer

cartón *nm, pl* **cartones** **1** : cardboard ⟨cartón madera : fiberboard⟩ **2** : carton

cartucho *nm* : cartridge

cartulina *nf* : poster board, cardboard

casa *nf* **1** : house ⟨una casa de dos pisos : a two-story house⟩ ⟨la casa blanca : the White House⟩ **2** HOGAR : home ⟨en casa : at home⟩ ⟨ir a casa : to go home⟩ **3** : home (in sports) ⟨equipo de casa : home team⟩ ⟨partido en casa : home game⟩ ⟨partido fuera de casa : away game⟩ **4** : household, family **5** : company, firm **6 casa de cambio** : currency exchange **7 casa de empeños** : pawnshop **8 casa de (altos) estudios** : institute of (higher) learning, college, university **9 casa de salud** : clinic **10 casa matriz** : headquarters **11 echar/tirar/botar la casa por la ventana** : to spare no expense

casaca *nf* : jacket

casado¹, -da *adj* : married

casado², -da *n* : married person

casamentero, -ra *n* : matchmaker

casamiento *nm* **1** : marriage **2** BODA : wedding

casar *vt* : to marry ⟨el cura que nos casó : the priest who married us⟩ — *vi* : to go together, to match up — **casarse** *vr* **1** : to get married **2** ~ **con** : to marry

casateniente *nmf Mex* : landlord, landlady *f*

cascabel¹ *nm* : small bell

cascabel² *nf* : rattlesnake

cascada *nf* CATARATA, SALTO : waterfall, cascade

cascajo *nm* **1** : pebble, rock fragment **2** *fam* : piece of junk

cascanueces *nms & pl* : nutcracker

cascar {72} *vt* : to crack (a shell) — **cascarse** *vr* : to crack, to chip

cáscara *nf* **1** : skin, peel, rind, husk **2** : shell (of a nut or egg)

cascarón *nm, pl* **-rones** **1** : eggshell **2** *Mex* : shell filled with confetti

cascarrabias *nmfs & pl fam* : grouch, crab

casco *nm* **1** : helmet **2** : hull **3** : hoof **4** : fragment, shard **5** : center (of a town) **6** *Mex* : empty bottle **7 cascos** *nmpl* : headphones

caserío *nm* **1** : country house **2** : hamlet

casero¹, -ra *adj* **1** : domestic, household **2** : homemade

casero², -ra *n* DUEÑO : landlord *m*, landlady *f*

caseta *nf* **1** : booth, stand, stall ⟨caseta de peaje, caseta de cobro *CA, Mex* : tollbooth⟩ **2** : doghouse **3** : dugout (in sports)

casete → **cassette**

casi *adv* **1** : almost, nearly ⟨casi un año : almost a year⟩ ⟨casi me desmayo : I almost fainted⟩ **2** (*in negative phrases*) : hardly ⟨casi nunca : hardly ever⟩ ⟨no hace casi nada : he hardly does anything⟩

casilla *nf* **1** : booth **2** : pigeonhole **3** : box (on a form) **4 casilla de correos** *Arg* : P.O. box

casillero *nm* **1** : pigeonhole **2** : set of pigeonholes

casino *nm* **1** : casino **2** : (social) club

caso *nm* **1** : case ⟨en caso de : in case of⟩ ⟨en este/ese caso : in this/that case⟩ ⟨en todo/cualquier caso : in any case⟩ ⟨en el mejor/peor de los casos : at best/worst⟩ ⟨el caso es que . . . . : the fact/thing is (that) . . .⟩ **2** : case (in law or medicine) **3 hacer caso** : to pay attention ⟨hacer caso de algo : to pay attention to something, to notice something⟩ ⟨hacerle caso a alguien : to pay attention to someone, to listen to someone⟩ **4 hacer caso omiso de** : to ignore, to take no notice of **5 no hay caso** : it's useless, there's no point **6 no venir al caso** : to be beside the point

caspa *nf* : dandruff

casque, etc. → **cascar**

casquete *nm* **1** : skullcap **2 casquete glaciar** : ice cap **3 casquete polar** : polar ice cap **4 casquete corto** *Mex* : crew cut

casquillo *nm* : case, casing (of a bullet)

cassette *nmf* : cassette

casta *nf* **1** : caste **2** : lineage, stock ⟨de casta : thoroughbred, purebred⟩ **3 sacar la casta** *Mex* : to come out ahead

castaña *nf* : chestnut

castañetear *vi* : to chatter (of teeth)

castañeteo *nm* : chatter, chattering (of teeth)

castaño¹, -ña *adj* : chestnut, brown

castaño² *nm* **1** : chestnut tree **2** : chestnut, brown

castañuela *nf* : castanet

castellano¹, -na *adj & n* : Castilian

castellano² *nm* ESPAÑOL : Spanish, Castilian (language)

castidad *nf* : chastity

castigar {52} *vt* : to punish

castigo *nm* : punishment

castillo *nm* **1** : castle **2 castillo de proa** : forecastle **3 castillo de arena** : sand castle

castizo, -za *adj* **1** AUTÉNTICO : authentic, genuine, pure **2** TRADICIONAL : traditional

casto, -ta *adj* : chaste, pure — **castamente** *adv*

castor *nm* : beaver

castración *nf, pl* **-ciones** : castration
castrar *vt* **1** : to castrate, to spay, to neuter **2** DEBILITAR : to weaken, to debilitate
castrense *adj* : military
casual *adj* **1** : chance ⟨no es casual : it's no accident⟩ **2** *Mex* : casual (of clothing)
casualidad *nf* **1** : chance **2 por** ∼ *or* **de** ∼ : by chance, by any chance
casualmente *adv* : accidentally, by chance
casucha *or* **casuca** *nf* : shanty, hovel
cataclismo *nm* : cataclysm
catacumbas *nfpl* : catacombs
catador, -dora *n* : wine taster
catalán¹, -lana *adj & n, mpl* **-lanes** : Catalan
catalán² *nm* : Catalan (language)
catalizador *nm* **1** : catalyst **2** : catalytic converter
catalogar {52} *vt* : to catalog, to classify
catálogo *nm* : catalog
catamarán *nm, pl* **-ranes** : catamaran
cataplasma *nf* : poultice
catapulta *nf* : catapult
catapultar *vt* : to catapult
catar *vt* **1** : to taste, to sample **2** : to look at, to examine
catarata *nf* **1** CASCADA, SALTO : waterfall **2** : cataract
catarro *nm* RESFRIADO : cold, catarrh
catarsis *nf* : catharsis — **catártico, -ca** *adj*
catastro *nm* : property registry
catástrofe *nf* DESASTRE : catastrophe, disaster
catastrófico, -ca *adj* DESASTROSO : catastrophic, disastrous
catcher *nmf* : catcher (in baseball)
catecismo *nm* : catechism
cátedra *nf* **1** : (tenured) professorship **2** : department chair (at a university) **3** : subject, class **4 libertad de cátedra** : academic freedom
catedral *nf* : cathedral
catedrático, -ca *n* **1** PROFESOR : (tenured) professor **2** : department chair (at a university)
categoría *nf* **1** CLASE : category **2** RANGO : rank, standing **3 categoría gramatical** : part of speech **4 de** ∼ : first-rate, outstanding
categórico, -ca *adj* : categorical, unequivocal — **categóricamente** *adv*
categorizar {21} *vt* : categorize
cateo *CA, Mex* → **cacheo**
catering *or* **cátering** *nm* : catering, food service
catéter *nm* : catheter
cátodo *nm* : cathode
catolicismo *nm* : Catholicism
católico, -ca *adj & n* : Catholic
catorce *adj & nm* : fourteen — **catorce** *pron*
catorceavo¹, -va *adj* : fourteenth
catorceavo² *nm* : fourteenth
catre *nm* : cot
catsup *nm* : ketchup
caucásico, -ca *adj & n* : Caucasian

cauce *nm* **1** LECHO : riverbed **2** : means *pl*, channel
caucho *nm* **1** GOMA : rubber **2** : rubber tree **3** *Ven* : tire
caución *nf, pl* **cauciones** FIANZA : bail, security
caudal *nm* **1** : volume of water **2** RIQUEZA : capital, wealth **3** ABUNDANCIA : abundance
caudaloso, -sa *adj* **1** : large, mighty (of a river) **2** RICO : rich, wealthy
caudillo *nm* : leader, commander
causa *nf* **1** MOTIVO : cause, reason, motive ⟨a causa de : because of⟩ **2** IDEAL : cause ⟨morir por una causa : to die for a cause⟩ **3** : lawsuit
causal¹ *adj* : causal — **causalidad** *nf*
causal² *nm* : cause, grounds *pl*
causante¹ *adj* ∼ **de** : causing, responsible for
causante² *nmf Mex* : taxpayer
causar *vt* **1** : to cause **2** : to provoke, to arouse ⟨eso me causa gracia : I find that funny⟩
cáustico, -ca *adj* : caustic
cautela *nf* : caution, prudence
cautelar *adj* : precautionary, preventive
cauteloso, -sa *adj* : cautious, prudent — **cautelosamente** *adv*
cauterizar {21} *vt* : to cauterize
cautivador, -dora *adj* : captivating
cautivar *vt* : to captivate, to charm
cautiverio *nm* : captivity
cautivo, -va *adj & n* : captive
cauto, -ta *adj* : cautious, careful
cava *nm* : a Spanish sparkling wine
cavar *vt* : to dig — *vi* ∼ **en** : to delve into, to probe
caverna *nf* : cavern, cave
cavernícola *nmf* : caveman *m*, cavewoman *f*
cavernoso, -sa *adj* **1** : cavernous **2** : deep, resounding
caviar *nm* : caviar
cavidad *nf* : cavity
cavilar *vi* : to ponder, to deliberate
cayado *nm* : crook, staff
cayena *nf* : cayenne pepper
cayo *nm* ISLOTE : key, islet
cayó, etc. → **caer**
caza¹ *nf* **1** CACERÍA : hunt, hunting **2** : game
caza² *nm* : fighter plane
cazador, -dora *n* **1** : hunter **2 cazador furtivo** : poacher
cazadora *nf* : jacket, bomber jacket
cazar {21} *vt* **1** : to hunt **2** : to catch, to bag **3** *fam* : to land (a job, a spouse) — *vi* : to go hunting
cazatalentos *nmfs & pl* : talent scout
cazo *nm* **1** : saucepan, pot **2** CUCHARÓN : ladle
cazuela *nf* **1** : pan, saucepan **2** : casserole
cazurro, -ra *adj* : sullen, surly
CD *nm* : CD, compact disk
CD–ROM [sedeʳrom] *nm* : CD-ROM
ce *nf* : (letter) c
cebada *nf* : barley

cebar *vt* **1** : to bait **2** : to feed, to fatten **3** : to prime (a pump, etc.) — **cebarse** *vr* ～ **en** : to take it out on

cebo *nm* CARNADA : bait **2** : feed **3** : primer (for firearms)

cebolla *nf* : onion

cebolleta *nf* : scallion, green onion

cebollino *nm* **1** : chive **2** : scallion

cebra *nf* : zebra

cebú *nm, pl* **cebús** *or* **cebúes** : zebu (cattle)

cecear [θeθe'ar] *vi* **1** : to lisp **2** : to pronounce the Spanish letter *s* as /θ/

ceceo [θe'θeo] *nm* **1** : lisp **2** : pronunciation of the Spanish letter *s* as /θ/

cecina *nf* : dried beef, beef jerky

cedazo *nm* : sieve

ceder *vi* **1** : to yield, to give way **2** : to diminish, to abate **3** : to give in, to relent — *vt* : to cede, to hand over

cedro *nm* : cedar

cédula *nf* : document, certificate

cegador, -dora *adj* : blinding

cegar {49} *vt* **1** : to blind **2** : to block, to stop up — *vi* : to be blinded, to go blind

ceguera *nf* : blindness

ceiba *nf* : silk-cotton tree

ceja *nf* **1** : eyebrow ⟨fruncir las cejas : to knit one's brows⟩ **2** : flange, rim

cejar *vi* : to give in, to back down

celada *nf* : trap, ambush

celador, -dora *n* GUARDIA : guard, warden

celda *nf* : cell (of a jail)

celebración *nf, pl* **-ciones** : celebration

celebrado, -da *adj* → **célebre**

celebrante *nmf* OFICIANTE : celebrant

celebrar *vt* **1** : to celebrate **2** : to hold (a meeting) **3** : to say (Mass) **4** : to welcome, to be happy about — *vi* : to be glad — **celebrarse** *vr* **1** : to be celebrated, to fall **2** : to be held, to take place

célebre *adj* : celebrated, famous

celebridad *nf* **1** : celebrity **2** FAMA : fame, celebrity

celeridad *nf* : swiftness

celeste[1] *adj* **1** : celestial **2** : sky blue, azure

celeste[2] *nm* : sky blue

celestial *adj* : heavenly, celestial

celibato *nm* : celibacy

célibe *adj & nmf* : celibate

cello ['tʃelo] → **chelo**

celo *nm* **1** : zeal, fervor **2** : heat (of females), rut (of males) **3** **celos** *nmpl* : jealousy ⟨tenerle celos a alguien : to be jealous of someone⟩

celofán *nm, pl* **-fanes** : cellophane

celosía *nf* **1** : lattice window **2** : lattice, trellis

celoso, -sa *adj* **1** : jealous **2** : zealous — **celosamente** *adv*

celta[1] *adj* : Celtic

celta[2] *nmf* : Celt

célula *nf* : cell ⟨célula madre : stem cell⟩

celular[1] *adj* : cellular

celular[2] *nm* : cell phone

celulitis *nf* : cellulite

celuloide *nm* **1** : celluloid **2** : film, cinema

celulosa *nf* : cellulose

cementar *vt* : to cement

cementerio *nm* : cemetery

cemento *nm* : cement

cena *nf* : supper, dinner

cenador *nm* : arbor, gazebo

cenagal *nm* : bog, quagmire

cenagoso, -sa *adj* : swampy

cenar *vi* : to have dinner, to have supper — *vt* : to have for dinner or supper ⟨cenamos tamales : we had tamales for supper⟩

cencerro *nm* : cowbell

cenicero *nm* : ashtray

ceniciento, -ta *adj* : ashen

cenit *nm* : zenith, peak

ceniza *nf* **1** : ash **2 cenizas** *nfpl* : ashes (of a deceased person)

cenizo *nm* : jinx

cenote *nm Mex* : natural deposit of spring water

censar *vt* : to take a census of

censo *nm* : census

censor, -sora *n* : censor, critic

censura *nf* **1** : censorship **2** : censure, criticism

censurable *adj* : reprehensible, blameworthy

censurar *vt* **1** : to censor **2** : to censure, to criticize

centauro *nm* : centaur

centavo *nm* **1** : cent (in English-speaking countries) **2** : centavo (unit of currency in various Latin-American countries)

centella *nf* **1** : lightning flash **2** : spark

centellear *vi* **1** : to twinkle **2** : to gleam, to sparkle

centelleo *nm* : twinkling, sparkle

centena *nf* : hundred ⟨una centena de personas : a hundred people⟩

centenar *nm* **1** : hundred **2 a centenares** : by the hundreds

centenario[1]**, -ria** *adj & n* : hundred-year-old

centenario[2] *nm* : centennial

centeno *nm* : rye

centésima *nf* : hundredth

centésimo[1]**, -ma** *adj* : hundredth

centésimo[2] *nm* **1** : hundredth **2** : centesimo (Panamanian and Uruguayan unit of currency)

centi- *pref* : centi-

centígrado *adj* : centigrade, Celsius

centigramo *nm* : centigram

centímetro *nm* : centimeter

céntimo *nm* **1** : centimo (unit of currency in various Spanish- and Portuguese-speaking countries) **2** : cent (subdivision of the euro) **3** : centime (unit of currency in various French- and Portuguese-speaking countries)

centinela *nmf* : sentinel, sentry

centrado, -da *adj* **1** EQUILIBRADO : stable **2** : centered **3** ～ **en** : focused on

central[1] *adj* **1** : central **2** PRINCIPAL : main, principal

central[2] *nf* **1** : main office, headquarters **2** : power plant, power station **3 central camionera** *Mex* : bus terminal

centralista *adj & nmf* : centralist

centralita *nf* : switchboard
centralizar {21} *vt* : to centralize — **centralización** *nf*
centrar *vt* **1** : to center **2** : to focus — **centrarse** *vr* ~ **en** : to focus on, to concentrate on
céntrico, -ca *adj* : central
centrifugar {52} *vt* : to spin (clothing)
centrista *adj & nmf* : centrist
centro[1] *nmf* : center (in sports)
centro[2] *nm* **1** MEDIO : center ⟨centro de atención/gravedad : center of attention/gravity⟩ **2** : downtown **3 centro comercial** : shopping plaza **4 centro de mesa** : centerpiece **5 centro de votación** : polling place
centroamericano, -na *adj & n* : Central American
centrocampista *nmf* : midfielder
ceñido, -da *adj* AJUSTADO : tight, tight-fitting
ceñir {67} *vt* **1** : to encircle, to surround **2** : to hug, to cling to ⟨me ciñe demasiado : it's too tight on me⟩ — **ceñirse** *vr* ~ **a** : to restrict oneself to, to stick to
ceño *nm* **1** : frown, scowl **2 fruncir el ceño** : to frown, to knit one's brows
cepa *nf* **1** : stump (of a tree) **2** : stock (of a vine) **3** LINAJE : ancestry, stock
cepillar *vt* **1** : to brush **2** : to plane (wood) — **cepillarse** *vr*
cepillo *nm* **1** : brush ⟨cepillo de dientes : toothbrush⟩ **2** : plane (for woodworking)
cepo *nm* : trap (for animals)
cera *nf* **1** : wax ⟨cera de abejas : beeswax⟩ **2** : polish
cerámica *nf* **1** : ceramics *pl* **2** : pottery
cerámico, -ca *adj* : ceramic
ceramista *nmf* ALFARERO : potter
cerca[1] *adv* **1** : nearby, close by ⟨vive cerca : he lives nearby⟩ **2** : close, near ⟨cerca de aquí : near here⟩ ⟨su cumpleaños está cerca : her birthday is almost here⟩ **3** ~ **de** : nearly, almost, close to ⟨cerca de 100 personas : nearly 100 people⟩ **4 de** ~ : close up ⟨seguir de cerca : to follow closely⟩
cerca[2] *nf* **1** : fence **2** : (stone) wall
cercado *nm* : enclosure
cercanía *nf* **1** PROXIMIDAD : proximity, closeness **2 cercanías** *nfpl* : outskirts, suburbs
cercano, -na *adj* : near, close
cercar {72} *vt* **1** : to fence in, to enclose **2** : to surround
cercenar *vt* **1** : to cut off, to amputate, to sever **2** : to diminish, to curtail
cerceta *nf* : teal (duck)
cerciorarse *vr* ASEGURARSE ~ **de** : to make sure of, to verify
cerco *nm* **1** : siege **2** : cordon, circle **3** : fence
cerda *nf* **1** : bristle **2** : sow
cerdo *nm* **1** : pig, hog **2 carne de cerdo** : pork
cereal *nm* : cereal — **cereal** *adj*
cerebelo *nm* : cerebellum
cerebral *adj* : cerebral
cerebro *nm* : brain

ceremonia *nf* : ceremony ⟨sin ceremonias : informal/informally, without ceremony⟩ — **ceremonial** *adj*
ceremonioso, -sa *adj* : ceremonious
cereza *nf* : cherry
cerezo *nm* : cherry tree
cerilla *nf* **1** : match **2** : earwax
cerillo *nm* (*in various countries*) : match
cerner {56} *vt* : to sift — **cernerse** *vr* **1** : to hover **2** ~ **sobre** : to loom over, to threaten
cernidor *nm* : sieve
cernir → **cerner**
cero *nm* : zero
ceroso, -sa *adj* : waxy
cerque, etc. → **cercar**
cerquillo *nm* : bangs *pl*
cerquita *adv fam* : very close, very near
cerrado, -da *adj* **1** : closed, shut **2** : thick, broad (of an accent) **3** : cloudy, overcast **4** : quiet, reserved **5** : dense, stupid
cerradura *nf* : lock
cerrajería *nf* : locksmith's shop
cerrajero, -ra *n* : locksmith
cerrar {55} *vt* **1** : to close, to shut (a door, a book, etc.) ⟨cerrar los ojos : to close one's eyes⟩ ⟨cerrar algo (con llave) : to lock something⟩ **2** : to turn off (a faucet, etc.) **3** : to close, to put the top on (a jar, etc.) **4** : to fasten, to button up (buttons), to zip up (a zipper) **5** CONCLUIR : to bring to an end, to close ⟨cerrar (la) sesión : to log off/out⟩ **6** : to close (a business, an account) **7** : to close, to close off (a street, etc.) — *vi* **1** : to close up, to lock up **2** : to close down — **cerrarse** *vr* **1** : to close **2** : to fasten, button up, to zip up **3** : to conclude, to end
cerrazón *nf, pl* **-zones** : obstinacy, stubbornness
cerro *nm* COLINA, LOMA : hill
cerrojo *nm* PESTILLO : bolt, latch
certamen *nm, pl* **-támenes** : competition, contest
certero, -ra *adj* : accurate, precise — **certeramente** *adv*
certeza *nf* : certainty
certidumbre *nf* : certainty
certificable *adj* : certifiable
certificación *nf, pl* **-ciones** : certification
certificado[1]**, -da** *adj* **1** : certified **2** : registered (of mail)
certificado[2] *nm* **1** : certificate ⟨certificado de matrimonio/difunción/nacimiento : marriage/death/birth certificate⟩ ⟨certificado de regalo : gift certificate⟩ **2** : registered letter
certificar {72} *vt* **1** : to certify **2** : to register (mail)
cerumen *nm* : earwax
cervato *nm* : fawn
cervecera *nf* : brewery
cervecero, -ra *n* : brewer
cervecería *nf* **1** : brewery **2** : beer hall, bar
cerveza *nf* : beer ⟨cerveza de barril : draft beer⟩
cervical *adj* : cervical

cerviz *nf, pl* **cervices** : nape of the neck
cesación *nf, pl* **-ciones** : cessation, suspension
cesante *adj* : laid off, unemployed
cesantía *nf* : unemployment
cesar *vi* : to cease, to stop — *vt* : to dismiss, to lay off
cesárea *nf* : cesarean
cesáreo, -rea *adj* : cesarean
cese *nm* **1** : cessation, stop ⟨cese del fuego : cease-fire⟩ **2** : dismissal
cesio *nm* : cesium
cesión *nf, pl* **cesiones** : transfer, assignment (of property, etc.)
césped *nm* : lawn, grass
cesta *nf* **1** : basket **2** : jai alai racket
cesto *nm* **1** : hamper **2** : basket (in basketball) **3 cesto de (la) basura** : wastebasket
cetro *nm* : scepter
ch *nf* : fourth letter of the Spanish alphabet — not usually considered a separate letter in alphabetization
chabacano¹, -na *adj* : tacky, tasteless
chabacano² *nm Mex* : apricot
chabola *nf Spain* : shack, shanty **2 barrio de chabolas** → **barrio**
chacal *nm* : jackal
cháchara *nf fam* **1** : small talk, chatter **2 chácharas** *nfpl* : trinkets, junk
chacharear *vi fam* : to chatter, to gab
chacra *nf Arg, Chile, Peru* : small farm
chal *nm* MANTÓN : shawl
chalado¹, -da *adj fam* : crazy, nuts
chalado², -da *n* : nut, crazy person
chalán *nm, pl* **chalanes** *Mex* : barge
chalé → **chalet**
chaleco *nm* : vest
chalet *nm Spain* : house
chalupa *nf* **1** : small boat **2** *Mex* : small stuffed tortilla
chamaco, -ca *n Mex fam* : kid, boy *m*, girl *f*
chamarra *nf* **1** : sheepskin jacket **2** : poncho, blanket
chamba *nf Mex, Peru fam* : job, work
chambear *vi Mex, Peru fam* : to work
chamo, -ma *n Ven fam* **1** : kid, boy *m*, girl *f* **2** : buddy, pal
champaña *or* **champán** *nm* : champagne
champiñón *nm, pl* **-ñones** : mushroom
champú *nm, pl* **-pus** *or* **-púes** : shampoo
champurrado *nm Mex* : hot chocolate thickened with cornstarch
chamuco *nm Mex fam* : devil
chamuscar {72} *vt* : to singe, to scorch — **chamuscarse** *vr*
chamusquina *nf* : scorch
chance *nm* OPORTUNIDAD : chance, opportunity
chancho¹, -cha *adj fam* : dirty, filthy, gross
chancho², -cha *n* **1** : pig, hog **2** *fam* : slob
chanchullero, -ra *adj fam* : shady, crooked
chanchullo *nm fam* : shady deal, scam
chancla *nf* **1** : thong sandal, slipper **2** : old shoe
chancleta → **chancla**

chanclo *nm* **1** : clog **2 chanclos** *nmpl* : overshoes, galoshes, rubbers
chándal *nm, pl* **chándals** *Spain* : sweatsuit, tracksuit
changarro *nm Mex* : small shop, stall
chango, -ga *n Mex* : monkey
chantaje *nm* : blackmail
chantajear *vt* : to blackmail
chantajista *nmf* : blackmailer
chanza *nf* **1** : joke, jest **2** *Mex fam* : chance, opportunity
chao *interj fam* : bye!
chapa *nf* **1** *Arg, Uru* : license plate **2** : sheet, panel, veneer **3** : lock **4** : badge **5** TAPÓN : cap, bottle cap
chapado, -da *adj* **1** : plated **2 chapado a la antigua** : old-fashioned
chapar *vt* **1** : to add a veneer to **2** : to plate (metals)
chaparro¹, -rra *adj* : short and squat, stocky
chaparro², -rra *n* : short, stocky person
chaparrón *nm, pl* **-rrones** **1** : downpour **2** : great quantity, torrent
chapeado, -da *adj Col, Mex* : flushed
chaperón, -rona *n, mpl* **-rones** : chaperon, chaperone
chapín, chapina *adj & n CA* : Guatemalan
chapopote *nm Mex* : tar, blacktop
chapotear *vi* : to splash about
chapucero¹, -ra *adj* **1** : crude, shoddy **2** *Mex fam* : dishonest
chapucero², -ra *n* **1** : sloppy worker, bungler **2** *Mex fam* : cheat, swindler
chapulín *nm, pl* **-lines** *CA, Mex* : grasshopper, locust
chapurrear *or* **chapurrar** *vt* **chapurrear el inglés/español** (etc.) : to speak broken English/Spanish (etc.)
chapuza *nf* **1** : botched job **2** *Mex fam* : fraud, trick ⟨hacer chapuzas : to cheat⟩
chapuzón *nm, pl* **-zones** : dip, swim ⟨darse un chapuzón : to go for a quick dip⟩
chaqueta *nf* : jacket
chara *nf* : jay
charada *nf* : charades (game)
charango *nm* : traditional Andean stringed instrument
charca *nf* : pond, pool
charco *nm* : puddle, pool
charcutería *nf* : delicatessen
charla *nf* : chat, talk
charlar *vi* : to chat, to talk
charlatán¹, -tana *adj* : talkative, chatty
charlatán², -tana *n, mpl* **-tanes** **1** : chatterbox **2** FARSANTE : charlatan, phony
charol *nm* **1** : lacquer, varnish **2** : patent leather **3** : tray
charola *nf Bol, Mex, Peru* : tray
charqui *nm Chile, Peru* : dried beef, beef jerky
charreada *nf Mex* : rodeo
charretera *nf* : epaulet
charro¹, -rra *adj* **1** : gaudy, tacky **2** *Mex* : pertaining to charros
charro², -rra *n Mex* : charro (Mexican cowboy or cowgirl)
charrúa *adj & nmf* : Uruguayan

chárter *adj* : charter
chascarrillo *nm fam* : joke, funny story
chasco *nm* 1 BROMA : trick, joke 2 DE-CEPCIÓN : disappointment
chasis *or* chasís *nm* : chassis
chasquear *vt* 1 : to snap (the fingers), to click (the tongue) 2 : to snap (a whip)
chasquido *nm* 1 : snap (of fingers), click (of the tongue) 2 : snap, crack
chat *nm, pl* chats : chat room
chatarra *nf* : scrap metal
chato, -ta *adj* 1 : pug-nosed 2 : flat
chauvinismo *nm* : chauvinism
chauvinista[1] *adj* : chauvinistic
chauvinista[2] *nmf* : chauvinist
chaval, -vala *n fam* : kid, boy *m*, girl *f*
chavalo, -vala *Mex, Nic* → chaval
chavo[1], -va *adj Mex fam* : young
chavo[2], -va *n Mex fam* : kid, boy *m*, girl *f*
chavo[3] *nm fam* : cent, buck ⟨no tengo un chavo : I'm broke⟩
che[1] *nf* : (letter) ch
che[2] *interj Arg, Uru* ⟨che, ¡mirá! : hey, look!⟩ ⟨che, ¡qué mal! : wow, how awful!⟩ ⟨en serio, che : hey, I'm being serious⟩
checar {72} *vt Mex* : to check, to verify
checo[1], -ca *adj & n* : Czech
checo[2] *nm* : Czech (language)
checoslovaco, -ca *adj & n* : Czechoslovakian
cheddar *nm* : cheddar
chef *nm* : chef
chelín *nm, pl* chelines : shilling
chelo *nm* : cello, violoncello
cheque[1], etc. → checar
cheque[2] *nm* 1 : check 2 cheque de viajero : traveler's check
chequear *vt* 1 : to check, to verify 2 : to check in (baggage)
chequeo *nm* 1 INSPECCIÓN : check, inspection 2 : checkup, examination
chequera *nf* : checkbook
chévere *adj fam* : great, fantastic
chic *adj & nm* : chic
chica → chico
chicano, -na *adj & n* : Chicano *m*, Chicana *f*
chicha *nf* : fermented alcoholic beverage made from corn
chícharo *nm* : pea
chicharra *nf* 1 CIGARRA : cicada 2 : buzzer
chicharrón *nm, pl* -rrones 1 : pork rind 2 darle chicharrón a algo/alguien *Mex fam* : to get rid of something/someone
chiche *nm Arg, Uru* JUGUETE : toy
chichón *nm, pl* chichones : bump, swelling
chicle *nm* : chewing gum
chicloso *nm Mex* : taffy
chico[1], -ca *adj* 1 : little, small 2 : young
chico[2], -ca *n* 1 : child, boy *m*, girl *f* 2 : young man *m*, young woman *f*
chicote *nm* LÁTIGO : whip, lash
chido, -da *adj Mex fam* : cool, great
chiffon → chifón
chiflado[1], -da *adj fam* : nuts, crazy
chiflado[2], -da *n fam* : crazy person, lunatic

chiflar *vi* : to whistle — *vt* : to whistle at, to boo — chiflarse *vr fam* ~ por : to be crazy about
chiflido *nm* : whistle, whistling
chiflón *nm, pl* chiflones : draft (of air)
chifón *nm, pl* chifones : chiffon
chii[1] *adj* CHIITA : Shiite
chii[2] *nmf* CHIITA : Shia, Shiite
chiismo *or* chiísmo *nm* : Shia
chiita[1] *or* chiíta *adj & n* → chii[1]
chiita[2] *or* chiíta *nmf* → chii[2]
chilango[1], -ga *adj Mex fam* : of or from Mexico City
chilango[2], -ga *n Mex fam* : person from Mexico City
chilaquiles *nmpl Mex* : shredded tortillas in sauce
chile *nm* : chili pepper
chileno, -na *adj & n* : Chilean
chillar *vi* 1 : to squeal, to screech 2 : to scream, to yell 3 : to be gaudy, to clash
chillido *nm* 1 : scream, shout 2 : squeal, screech, cry (of an animal)
chillo *nm PRi* : red snapper
chillón, -llona *adj, mpl* chillones 1 : piercing, shrill 2 : loud, gaudy
chilpayate *nmf Mex fam* : child, little kid
chimbo[1], -ba *adj* 1 : fake, false ⟨un cheque chimbo : a bad check⟩ 2 *Ven* : crummy, lousy
chimbo[2] *nm Hond* : tank (container)
chimenea *nf* 1 : chimney 2 : fireplace
chimichurri *nm Arg* : traditional hot sauce
chimpancé *nm* : chimpanzee
china *nf* 1 : pebble, small stone 2 *PRi* : orange
chinchar *vt Spain fam* : to annoy, to pester — chincharse *vr Spain fam* : to put up with something
chinche[1] *nf* 1 : bedbug 2 *Ven* : ladybug 3 : thumbtack
chinche[2] *nmf fam* : nuisance, pain in the neck
chinchilla *nf* : chinchilla
chino[1], -na *adj* 1 : Chinese 2 *Mex* : curly, kinky
chino[2], -na *n* : Chinese person
chino[3] *nm* : Chinese (language)
chintz ['tʃ ints] *or* chinz *nm* : chintz
chip *nm, pl* chips : chip ⟨chip de memoria : memory chip⟩
chipote *nm Mex fam* : bump (on the head)
chipotle *nm Mex* : chipotle
chiquear *vt Mex* : to spoil, to indulge
chiquero *nm* POCILGA : pigpen, pigsty
chiquillada *nf* : childish prank
chiquillo[1], -lla *adj* : very young, little
chiquillo[2], -lla *n* : kid, youngster
chiquito[1], -ta *adj* : tiny
chiquito[2], -ta *n* : little one, baby
chiribita *nf* 1 : spark 2 chiribitas *nfpl* : spots before the eyes
chiribitil *nm* 1 DESVÁN : attic, garret 2 : cubbyhole
chirigota *nf fam* : joke
chirimía *nf* : traditional reed pipe
chiripa *nf* 1 : fluke 2 de ~ : by sheer luck

chirivía *nf* : parsnip
chirona *nf fam* : jail
chirriar {85} *vi* **1** : to squeak, to creak **2** : to screech — **chirriante** *adj*
chirrido *nm* **1** : squeak, squeaking **2** : screech, screeching
chirrión *nm, pl* **chirriones** *Mex* : whip, lash
chis *or* **chist** *interj* **1** : sh! **2** : hey!
chisme *nm* **1** : gossip, tale **2** *Spain fam* : gadget, thingamajig
chismear *vi* : to gossip
chismorrear → **chismear**
chismoso[1], **-sa** *adj* : gossipy, gossiping
chismoso[2], **-sa** *n* **1** : gossiper, gossip **2** *Mex fam* : tattletale
chispa[1] *adj* **1** *Mex fam* : lively, vivacious ⟨un perrito chispa : a frisky puppy⟩ **2** *Spain fam* : tipsy
chispa[2] *nf* **1** : spark **2 echar chispas** : to be furious
chispeante *adj* : sparkling, scintillating
chispear *vi* **1** : to give off sparks **2** : to sparkle
chisporrotear *vi* : to crackle, to sizzle
chistar *vi* **sin chistar** : without a word (of complaint)
chiste *nm* **1** : joke, funny story **2 tener chiste** : to be funny **3 tener su chiste** *Mex* : to be tricky
chistera *nf Spain* : top hat
chistoso[1], **-sa** *adj* **1** : funny, humorous **2** : witty
chistoso[2], **-sa** *n* : wit, joker
chiva *nf* **1** *Col, Ecua, Pan* : rural bus **2 chivas** *nfpl Mex fam* : stuff, odds and ends
chivato, -ta *n Cuba, Spain* **1** : informant, snitch **2** : tattletale
chivo[1], **-va** *n* **1** : kid, young goat **2 chivo expiatorio** : scapegoat
chivo[2] *nm* **1** : billy goat **2** : fit of anger
chocante *adj* **1** : shocking **2** : unpleasant, rude
chocar {72} *vi* **1** : to crash, to collide **2** : to clash, to conflict **3** : to be shocking ⟨le chocó : he was shocked⟩ **4** *Mex, Ven fam* : to be unpleasant or obnoxious ⟨me choca tu jefe : I can't stand your boss⟩ — *vt* **1** : to shake (hands) **2** : to clink glasses
chochear *vi* **1** : to be senile **2** ~ **por** : to dote on, to be soft on
chochín *nm, pl* **-chines** : wren
chocho, -cha *adj* **1** : senile **2** : doting
choclo *nm* **1** : ear of corn, corncob **2** : corn **3 meter el choclo** *Mex fam* : to make a mistake
chocolate *nm* **1** : chocolate ⟨chocolate con leche : milk chocolate⟩ ⟨chocolate oscuro/amargo/negro : dark chocolate⟩ ⟨chocolate blanco : white chocolate⟩ **2** : hot chocolate, cocoa
chocolatín *nm, pl* **-tines** → **chocolatina**
chocolatina *nf* : chocolate bar
chofer *or* **chófer** *nm* **1** : chauffeur **2** : driver
choke *nm* : choke (of an automobile)
chole *interj Mex fam* **¡ya chole!** : enough!, cut it out!
cholo, -la *adj & n* : mestizo

cholla *nf fam* : head
chollo *nm Spain fam* : bargain
chongo *nm* **1** *Mex* : bun (chignon) **2 chongos** *nmpl Mex* : dessert made with fried bread
choque[1], etc. → **chocar**
choque[2] *nm* **1** : crash, collision **2** : clash, conflict **3** : shock
chorizo *nm* : chorizo, pork sausage
choro *nm* **1** MEJILLÓN : mussel **2** : crook, criminal
chorrear *vi* **1** : to drip **2** : to pour out, to gush out
chorrito *nm* : squirt, splash
chorro *nm* **1** : flow, stream, jet **2** *Mex fam* : heap, ton
choteado, -da *adj Mex fam* : worn-out, stale ⟨esa canción está bien choteada : that song's been played to death⟩
chotear *vt* : to make fun of
choteo *nm* : joking around, kidding
chovinismo, chovinista → **chauvinismo, chauvinista**
chow–chow [ˈtʃautʃau] *nmf* : chow
choza *nf* : hut, shack
christmas *or* **crismas** *nm Spain* : Christmas card
chubasco *nm* : downpour, storm
chuchería *nf* : knickknack, trinket
chucho, -cha *n fam* **1** *CA, Mex, Spain* : mongrel, mutt **2 chuchos de frío** *Arg, Uru* : shivers
chueco, -ca *adj* **1** : crooked, bent **2** *Chile, Mex fam* : dishonest, shady
chulada *nf Mex, Spain fam* : cute or pretty thing ⟨¡qué chulada de vestido! : what a lovely dress!⟩
chulear *vt Mex fam* : to compliment
chuleta *nf* : cutlet, chop
chulla *nmf* : person from Quito, Ecuador
chulo[1], **-la** *adj* **1** *fam* : cute, pretty **2** *Spain fam* : cocky, arrogant
chulo[2] *nm Spain* : pimp
chupada *nf* **1** : suck, sucking **2** : puff, drag (on a cigarette)
chupado, -da *adj fam* **1** : gaunt, skinny **2** : plastered, drunk
chupaflor *nm* COLIBRÍ : hummingbird
chupamirto *nm Mex* : hummingbird
chupar *vt* **1** : to suck **2** : to absorb **3** : to puff on **4** *fam* : to drink, to guzzle — *vi* : to suckle — **chuparse** *vr* **1** : to waste away **2** *fam* : to put up with **3 ¡chúpate esa!** *fam* : take that!
chupete *nm* **1** : pacifier **2** *Chile, Peru* : lollipop
chupetear *vt* : to suck (at)
chupón *nm, pl* **chupones** **1** : sucker (of a plant) **2** : baby bottle, pacifier
churrasco *nm* **1** : steak **2** : barbecued meat
churro *nm* **1** : fried dough **2** *fam* : attractive person
chusco, -ca *adj* : funny, amusing
chusma *nf* GENTUZA : riffraff, rabble
chutar *vi* : to shoot (in soccer)
chute *nm* : shot (in soccer)
chutney [ˈʃatni] *nm* : chutney
CI *or* **coeficiente intelectual** *nm* : IQ, intelligence quotient

cianotipo *nm* : blueprint
cianuro *nm* : cyanide
ciber- *pref* : cyber-
ciberacoso *nm* : cyberbullying
cibercafé *nm* : Internet café
cibernético, -ca *adj* : cybernetic, cyber-
cicatriz *nf, pl* **-trices** : scar
cicatrizar {21} *vi* : to form a scar, to heal
cicatrizarse *vr* → **cicatrizar**
cíclico, -ca *adj* : cyclical
ciclismo *nm* : bicycling
ciclista *nmf* : bicyclist
ciclo *nm* : cycle
ciclomotor *nm* : moped
ciclón *nm, pl* **ciclones** : cyclone
cicuta *nf* : hemlock
ciega, ciegue etc. → **cegar**
ciego¹, -ga *adj* **1** INVIDENTE : blind **2 a ciegas** : blindly **3 quedarse ciego** : to go blind — **ciegamente** *adv*
ciego², -ga *n* INVIDENTE : blind person
cielo *nm* **1** : sky **2** : heaven **3** : ceiling
ciempiés *nms & pl* : centipede
cien¹ *adj* **1** : a hundred, hundred ⟨las primeras cien páginas : the first hundred pages⟩ **2 cien por cien** *or* **cien por ciento** : a hundred percent, through and through, wholeheartedly — **cien** *pron*
cien² *nm* : one hundred
ciénaga *nf* : swamp, bog
ciencia *nf* **1** : science **2** : learning, knowledge **3 a ciencia cierta** : for a fact, for certain
cieno *nm* : mire, mud, silt
científico¹, -ca *adj* : scientific — **científicamente** *adv*
científico², -ca *n* : scientist
ciento¹ *adj* (*used in compound numbers*) : one hundred ⟨ciento uno : one hundred and one⟩
ciento² *nm* **1** : hundred ⟨cientos de personas/años : hundreds of people/years⟩ **2 por ~** : percent
cierne, etc. → **cerner**
cierra, etc. → **cerrar**
cierre *nm* **1** : closing, closure **2** : fastener, clasp, zipper
cierto, -ta *adj* **1** : true, certain, definite ⟨lo cierto es que . . . : the fact is that . . .⟩ **2** : certain, one ⟨cierto día de verano : one summer day⟩ ⟨bajo ciertas circunstancias : under certain circumstances⟩ **3 por ~** : in fact, as a matter of fact — **ciertamente** *adv*
ciervo, -va *n* : deer, stag *m*, hind *f*
cifra *nf* **1** : figure, number **2** : quantity, amount **3** CLAVE : code, cipher
cifrar *vt* **1** : to write in code **2** : to place, to pin ⟨cifró su esperanza en la lotería : he pinned his hopes on the lottery⟩ **3** : to encrypt (a file, etc.) — **cifrarse** *vr* : to amount ⟨cifrarse en : to amount to⟩
cigarra *nf* CHICHARRA : cicada
cigarrera *nf* : cigarette case
cigarrillo *nm* **1** : cigarette **2 cigarrillo electrónico** : electronic cigarette, e-cigarette
cigarro *nm* **1** : cigarette **2** PURO : cigar
cigoto *nm* : zygote
cigüeña *nf* : stork

cilantro *nm* : cilantro, coriander
cilindrada *nf* : cubic capacity (of an engine)
cilíndrico, -ca *adj* : cylindrical
cilindro *nm* : cylinder
cima *nf* CUMBRE : peak, summit, top
cimarrón, -rrona *adj, mpl* **-rrones** : untamed, wild
címbalo *nm* : cymbal
cimbrar *vt* : to shake, to rock — **cimbrarse** *vr* : to sway, to swing
cimentar {55} *vt* **1** : to lay the foundation of, to establish **2** : to strengthen, to cement
cimientos *nmpl* : base, foundation(s)
cinc *nm* : zinc
cincel *nm* : chisel
cincelar *vt* **1** : to chisel **2** : to engrave
cincha *nf* : cinch, girth
cinchar *vt* : to cinch (a horse)
cinco¹ *adj & nm* : five ⟨mi hija tiene cinco años : my daughter is five (years old)⟩ ⟨el cinco de junio : (on) the fifth of June, (on) June fifth⟩
cinco² *pron* : five ⟨seremos cinco : there will be five of us⟩ ⟨son las cinco y media : it's five-thirty⟩
cincuenta *adj & nm* : fifty — **cincuenta** *pron*
cincuentavo¹, -va *adj* : fiftieth
cincuentavo² *nm* : fiftieth (fraction)
cine *nm* **1** : cinema, movies *pl* **2** : movie theater
cineasta *nmf* : filmmaker
cinéfilo, -la *n* : cinephile, movie buff
cinematografía *nf* : cinematography
cinematográfico, -ca *adj* : movie, film, cinematic ⟨la industria cinematográfica : the film industry⟩
cínico¹, -ca *adj* **1** : cynical **2** : shameless, brazen — **cínicamente** *adv*
cínico², -ca *n* : cynic
cinismo *nm* : cynicism
cinta *nf* **1** : ribbon **2** : tape ⟨cinta métrica : tape measure⟩ **3** : strap, belt ⟨cinta transportadora : conveyor belt⟩
cinto *nm* : strap, belt
cintura *nf* **1** : waist, waistline **2 meter en cintura** *fam* : to bring into line, to discipline
cinturilla *nf* : waistband
cinturón *nm, pl* **-rones** **1** : belt **2 cinturón de seguridad** : seat belt **3 cinturón de miseria** : shantytown, slums *pl*
ciñe, etc. → **ceñir**
ciprés *nm, pl* **cipreses** : cypress
circo *nm* : circus
circuitería *nf* : circuitry
circuito *nm* : circuit
circulación *nf, pl* **-ciones** **1** : circulation **2** : movement **3** : traffic
circular¹ *vi* **1** : to circulate **2** : to move along **3** : to drive
circular² *adj* : circular
circular³ *nf* : circular, flier
circulatorio, -ria *adj* : circulatory
círculo *nm* **1** : circle **2** : club, group
circuncidar *vt* : to circumcise
circuncisión *nf, pl* **-siones** : circumcision
circundar *vt* : to surround — **circundante** *adj*

circunferencia *nf* : circumference

circunflejo, -ja *adj* **acento circunflejo** : circumflex

circunlocución *nf, pl* **-ciones** : circumlocution

circunloquio *nm* → **circunlocución**

circunnavegar {52} *vt* : to circumnavigate — **circunnavegación** *nf*

circunscribir {33} *vt* : to circumscribe, to constrict, to limit — **circunscribirse** *vr*

circunscripción *nf, pl* **-ciones 1** : limitation, restriction **2** : constituency

circunscrito *pp* → **circunscribir**

circunspecto, -ta *adj* : circumspect, prudent

circunstancia *nf* : circumstance

circunstancial *adj* : circumstantial, incidental

circunstante *nmf* **1** : onlooker, bystander **2 los circunstantes** : those present

circunvalación *nf, pl* **-ciones** : surrounding, encircling ⟨carretera de circunvalación : bypass, beltway⟩

circunvecino, -na *adj* : surrounding, neighboring

cirio *nm* : large candle

cirrosis *nf* : cirrhosis

ciruela *nf* **1** : plum **2 ciruela pasa** : prune

cirugía *nf* : surgery ⟨cirugía cardíaca : heart surgery⟩ ⟨cirugía plástica/estética : plastic/cosmetic surgery⟩

cirujano, -na *n* : surgeon

cisgénero *adj* : cisgender, cis ⟨las personas cisgénero : cisgender people⟩

cisma *nm* : schism, rift

cisne *nm* : swan

cisterna *nf* : cistern, tank

cita *nf* **1** : quote, quotation **2** : appointment, date

citable *adj* : quotable

citación *nf, pl* **-ciones** EMPLAZAMIENTO : summons, subpoena

citadino¹, -na *adj* : of the city, urban

citadino², -na *n* : city dweller

citado, -da *adj* : said, aforementioned

citar *vt* **1** : to quote, to cite **2** : to make an appointment with **3** : to summon (to court), to subpoena — **citarse** *vr* ∼ **con** : to arrange to meet (someone)

citatorio *nm* : subpoena

-cito *suf* → **-ito**

cítrico *nm* : citrus

ciudad *nf* **1** : city, town **2 ciudad deportiva** : sports complex **3 ciudad natal** : native city/town **4 ciudad perdida** *Mex* : shantytown **5 ciudad universitaria** : college or university campus

ciudadanía *nf* **1** : citizenship **2** : citizenry, citizens *pl*

ciudadano¹, -na *adj* : civic, city

ciudadano², -na *n* **1** NACIONAL : citizen **2** HABITANTE : resident, city dweller

ciudadela *nf* : citadel, fortress

cívico, -ca *adj* **1** : civic **2** : civic-minded

civil¹ *adj* **1** : civil **2** : civilian **3 de** ∼ : in plain/civilian clothes ⟨un policía de civil : a plainclothes policeman⟩

civil² *nmf* : civilian

civilidad *nf* : civility, courtesy

civilización *nf, pl* **-ciones** : civilization

civilizado, -da *adj* : civilized

civilizar {21} *vt* : to civilize

civismo *nm* : community spirit, civics

cizaña *nf* **sembrar cizaña** : to sow discord

clamar *vi* : to clamor, to raise a protest — *vt* : to cry out for

clamor *nm* : clamor, outcry

clamoroso, -sa *adj* : clamorous, resounding, thunderous

clan *nm* : clan

clandestinidad *nf* : secrecy ⟨en la clandestinidad : underground⟩

clandestino, -na *adj* : clandestine, secret — **clandestinamente** *adv*

clara *nf* : egg white

claraboya *nf* : skylight

claramente *adv* : clearly

clarear *v impers* **1** : to clear, to clear up **2** : to get light, to dawn — *vi* : to go gray, to turn white

claridad *nf* **1** NITIDEZ : clarity **2** : brightness, light

clarificación *nf, pl* **-ciones** ACLARACIÓN : clarification, explanation

clarificar {72} *vt* ACLARAR : to clarify, to explain

clarín *nm, pl* **clarines** : bugle

clarinete *nm* : clarinet

clarividencia *nf* **1** : clairvoyance **2** : perspicacity, discernment

clarividente¹ *adj* **1** : clairvoyant **2** : perspicacious, discerning

clarividente² *nmf* : clairvoyant

claro¹ *adv* **1** : clearly ⟨habla más claro : speak more clearly⟩ **2** : of course, surely ⟨¡claro!, ¡claro que sí! : absolutely!, of course!⟩ ⟨claro que entendió : of course she understood⟩

claro², -ra *adj* **1** : bright, clear **2** : pale, fair, light **3** : clear, evident

claro³ *nm* **1** : clearing **2 claro de luna** : moonlight

clase *nf* **1** : class **2** ÍNDOLE, TIPO : sort, kind, type **3 clase alta/baja** : upper/lower class

clasicismo *nm* : classicism

clásico¹, -ca *adj* **1** : classic **2** : classical

clásico² *nm* : classic

clasificación *nf, pl* **-ciones 1** : classification, sorting out **2** : rating **3** CALIFICACIÓN : qualification (in competitions)

clasificado, -da *adj* : classified ⟨aviso clasificado : classified ad⟩

clasificar {72} *vt* **1** : to classify, to sort out **2** : to rate, to rank — *vi* CALIFICAR : to qualify (in competitions) — **clasificarse** *vr*

clasificatorio, -ria *adj* : qualifying

claudicación *nf, pl* **-ciones** : surrender, abandonment of one's principles

claudicar {72} *vi* : to back down, to abandon one's principles

claustro *nm* : cloister

claustrofobia *nf* : claustrophobia

claustrofóbico, -ca *adj* : claustrophobic

cláusula *nf* : clause

clausura *nf* **1** : closure, closing **2** : closing ceremony **3** : cloister

clausurar *vt* **1** : to close, to bring to a close **2** : to close down

clavada *nf* : slam dunk (in basketball)

clavadista *nmf* : diver

clavado¹, -da *adj* **1** : nailed, fixed, stuck **2** *fam* : punctual, on the dot **3** *fam* : identical ⟨es clavado a su padre : he's the image of his father⟩

clavado² *nm* : dive

clavar *vt* **1** : to nail, to hammer **2** HIN-CAR : to plunge, to stick **3** : to fix (one's eyes) on — **clavarse** *vr* : to stick oneself (with a sharp object)

clave¹ *adj* : key, essential

clave² *nf* **1** CIFRA : code **2** : key ⟨la clave del misterio : the key to the mystery⟩ **3** : clef ⟨clave de sol/fa : treble/bass clef⟩

clavel *nm* : carnation

clavelito *nm* : pink (flower)

clavicémbalo *nm* : harpsichord

clavícula *nf* : collarbone

clavija *nf* **1** : plug **2** : peg, pin

clavo *nm* **1** : nail ⟨clavo grande : spike⟩ **2** : clove **3 dar en el clavo** : to hit the nail on the head

claxon *nm, pl* **cláxones** : horn (of an automobile)

clemencia *nf* : clemency, mercy

clemente *adj* : merciful

cleptomanía *nf* : kleptomania

cleptómano, -na *n* : kleptomaniac

clerecía *nf* : ministry, ministers *pl*

clerical *adj* : clerical

clérigo, -ga *n* : cleric, member of the clergy

clero *nm* : clergy

clic *or* **click** *nm, pl* **clics** *or* **clicks** : click ⟨haz clic aquí : click here⟩ ⟨doble clic : double click⟩ ⟨hacer clic derecho/izquierdo : to right-click/left-click⟩

cliché *nm* **1** : cliché **2** : stencil **3** : negative (of a photograph)

cliente, -ta *n* : customer, client

clientela *nf* : clientele, customers *pl*

clima *nm* **1** : climate **2** AMBIENTE : atmosphere, ambience

climático, -ca *adj* : climatic

climatización *nf, pl* **-ciones** : air-conditioning

climatizar {21} *vt* : to air-condition — **climatizado, -da** *adj*

clímax *nm* : climax

clinch *nm* : clinch (in boxing)

clínica *nf* : clinic

clínico, -ca *adj* : clinical — **clínicamente** *adv*

clip *nm, pl* **clips** **1** : clip **2** : paper clip

clíper *nm* : clipper

clítoris *nms & pl* : clitoris

cloaca *nf* ALCANTARILLA : sewer

clocar {82} *vi* : to cluck

cloche *nm* CA, Car, Col, Ven : clutch (of an automobile)

clon *nm* : clone

clonar *vt* : to clone

cloqué, etc. → **clocar**

cloquear *vi* : to cluck

cloqueo *nm* : cluck, clucking

clorar *vt* : to chlorinate — **cloración** *nf*

clorhídrico, -ca *adj* **ácido clorhídrico** → **ácido²**

cloro *nm* : chlorine

clorofila *nf* : chlorophyll

cloroformo *nm* : chloroform

cloruro *nm* : chloride

clóset *nm, pl* **clósets** **1** : closet **2** : cupboard

club *nm* : club

clueca, clueque etc. → **clocar**

clutch [ˈklatʃ] *nm* : clutch

coa *nf Mex* : hoe

coacción *nf, pl* **-ciones** : coercion, duress

coaccionar *vt* : to coerce

coactivo, -va *adj* : coercive

coagular *v* : to clot, to coagulate — **coagulación** *nf*

coágulo *nm* : clot

coalición *nf, pl* **-ciones** : coalition

coartada *nf* : alibi

coartar *vt* : to restrict, to limit

coba *nf fam* **1** : flattery ⟨darle coba a alguien : to suck up to someone⟩ **2** *Ven* MENTIRA : lie

cobalto *nm* : cobalt

cobarde¹ *adj* : cowardly

cobarde² *nmf* : coward

cobardía *nf* : cowardice

cobaya *nf* : guinea pig

cobertizo *nm* : shed, shelter

cobertor *nm* COLCHA : bedspread, quilt

cobertura *nf* **1** : coverage **2** : cover, collateral

cobija *nf* FRAZADA, MANTA : blanket

cobijar *vt* : to shelter — **cobijarse** *vr* : to take shelter

cobijo *nm* : shelter

cobra *nf* : cobra

cobrador, -dora *n* **1** : collector **2** : conductor (of a bus or train)

cobrar *vt* **1** : to charge **2** : to collect, to draw, to earn **3** : to acquire, to gain **4** : to recover, to retrieve **5** : to cash (a check) **6** : to claim, to take (a life) **7** : to shoot (game), to bag — *vi* **1** : to be paid **2 llamar por cobrar** *Mex* : to call collect

cobre *nm* : copper

cobrizo, -za *adj* : coppery

cobro *nm* : collection (of money), cashing (of a check)

coca *nf* **1** : coca **2** *fam* : coke, cocaine

Coca *nf* (*Coca-Cola*, marca registrada) : Coke™, Coca-Cola™

cocaína *nf* : cocaine

cocal *nm* : coca plantation

cocción *nf, pl* **cocciones** : cooking

cocear *vi* : to kick (of an animal)

cocer {14} *vt* **1** COCINAR : to cook **2** HERVIR : to boil

cochambre *nmf fam* : filth, grime

cochambroso, -sa *adj* : filthy, grimy

coche *nm* **1** : car, automobile **2** : coach, carriage **3 coche bomba** : car bomb **4 coche cama** : sleeping car **5 coche fúnebre** : hearse

cochecito *nm* : baby carriage, stroller

cochera *nf* GARAJE : garage, carport

cochinada *nf fam* **1** : filthy language **2** : disgusting behavior **3** : dirty trick

cochinillo *nm* : suckling pig, piglet
cochino¹, -na *adj* **1** : dirty, filthy, disgusting **2** *fam* : rotten, lousy
cochino², -na *n* : pig, hog
cocido¹, -da *adj* **1** : boiled, cooked **2 bien cocido** : well-done
cocido² *nm* ESTOFADO, GUISADO : stew
cociente *nm* : quotient
cocimiento *nm* : cooking, baking
cocina *nf* **1** : kitchen **2** : stove **3** : cuisine, cooking
cocinar *v* : to cook
cocinero, -ra *n* : cook, chef
cocineta *nf Mex* : kitchenette
coco *nm* **1** : coconut **2** *fam* : head **3** *fam* : bogeyman
cocoa *nf* : cocoa, hot chocolate
cocodrilo *nm* : crocodile
cocotero *nm* : coconut palm
coctel *or* **cóctel** *nm* **1** : cocktail **2** : cocktail party
coctelera *nf* : cocktail shaker
codazo *nm* **1 darle un codazo a alguien** : to elbow someone, to nudge someone **2 abrirse paso a codazos** : to elbow one's way through
codear *vt* : to elbow, to jog, to nudge — **codearse** *vr* : to rub elbows, to hobnob
codeína *nf* : codeine
códice *nm* : codex, manuscript
codicia *nf* AVARICIA : avarice
codiciar *vt* : to covet
codicioso, -sa *adj* : avaricious, covetous
codificar {72} *vt* **1** : to codify **2** : to code, to encode
código *nm* **1** : code **2 código de barras** : bar code **3 código postal** : zip code **4 código morse** : Morse code
codo¹, -da *adj Mex* : cheap, stingy
codo², -da *n Mex* : tightwad, cheapskate
codo³ *nm* : elbow
codorniz *nf, pl* **-nices** : quail
coeficiente *nm* **1** : coefficient **2 coeficiente intelectual** : IQ, intelligence quotient
coexistir *vi* : to coexist — **coexistencia** *nf*
cofradía *nf* **1** : (religious) brotherhood **2** GREMIO : guild
cofre *nm* **1** BAÚL : trunk, chest **2** *Mex* CAPOTE : hood (of a car)
coger {15} *vt* **1** : to seize, to take hold of **2** : to catch **3** : to pick up **4** : to gather, to pick **5** : to gore — **cogerse** *vr* AGARRARSE : to hold on
cogida *nf* **1** : gathering, harvest **2** : goring
cognición *nf, pl* **-ciones** : cognition
cognitivo, -va *adj* : cognitive
cogollo *nm* **1** : heart (of a vegetable) **2** : bud, bulb **3** : core, crux ⟨el cogollo de la cuestión : the heart of the matter⟩
cogote *nm* : scruff, nape
cohabitar *vi* : to cohabit — **cohabitación** *nf*
cohechar *vt* SOBORNAR : to bribe
cohecho *nm* SOBORNO : bribe, bribery
coherencia *nf* : coherence — **coherente** *adj*
cohesión *nf, pl* **-siones** : cohesion

cohesivo, -va *adj* : cohesive
cohete *nm* : rocket
cohibición *nf, pl* **-ciones** **1** : (legal) restraint **2** INHIBICIÓN : inhibition
cohibido, -da *adj* : inhibited, shy
cohibir {62} *vt* : to inhibit, to make self-conscious — **cohibirse** *vr* : to feel shy or embarrassed
cohorte *nf* : cohort
coima *nf Arg, Chile, Peru* : bribe
coimear *vt Arg, Chile, Peru* : to bribe
coincidencia *nf* **1** CASUALIDAD : coincidence **2** ACUERDO : agreement
coincidente *adj* **1** : coincident **2** ACORDE : coinciding
coincidir *vi* **1** : to coincide **2** : to agree
coito *nm* : sexual intercourse, coitus
coja, etc. → **coger**
cojear *vi* **1** : to limp **2** : to wobble, to rock **3 cojear del mismo pie** : to be two of a kind
cojera *nf* : limp
cojín *nm, pl* **cojines** : cushion, throw pillow
cojinete *nm* **1** : bearing, bushing **2 cojinete de bola** : ball bearing
cojo¹, -ja *adj* **1** : limping, lame **2** : wobbly **3** : weak, ineffectual
cojo², -ja *n* : lame person
cojones *nmpl usu vulgar* **1** : balls *pl, usu vulgar*; testicles *pl* **2** : balls *pl, usu vulgar*; guts *pl*; courage
col *nf* **1** REPOLLO : cabbage **2 col de Bruselas** : Brussels sprout **3 col rizada** : kale
cola *nf* **1** RABO : tail ⟨cola de caballo : ponytail⟩ **2** FILA : line (of people) ⟨hacer cola : to wait in line⟩ **3** : cola, drink **4** : train (of a dress) **5** : tails *pl* (of a tuxedo) **6** PEGAMENTO : glue **7** *fam* : buttocks *pl*, rear end
colaboracionista *nmf* : collaborator, traitor
colaborador, -dora *n* **1** : contributor (to a periodical) **2** : collaborator
colaborar *vi* : to collaborate — **colaboración** *nf*
colación *nf, pl* **-ciones** **1** : light meal **2** : conferring (of a degree) **3 traer a colación** : to bring up, to broach
colada *nf Spain* : laundry, wash, washing
coladera *nf Mex* : drain
colador *nm* **1** : colander, strainer **2** *PRi* : small coffeepot
colapsar *vt* **1** : to collapse **2** : to paralyze, to bring to a standstill — *vi* : to collapse
colapso *nm* **1** : collapse **2** : standstill
colar {19} *vt* : to strain, to filter — **colarse** *vr* **1** : to sneak in **2** : to cut in line **3** : to slip up, to make a mistake
colateral¹ *adj* : collateral — **colateralmente** *adv*
colateral² *nm* : collateral
colcha *nf* COBERTOR : bedspread, quilt
colchón *nm, pl* **colchones** **1** : mattress **2** : cushion, padding, buffer
colchoneta *nf* : mat (for gymnastic sports)
colear *vi* **1** : to wag its tail **2 vivito y coleando** *fam* : alive and kicking

colección *nf, pl* -ciones : collection
coleccionable *adj* : collectible
coleccionar *vt* : to collect, to keep a collection of
coleccionista *nmf* : collector
colecta *nf* : collection (of donations)
colectar *vt* : to collect
colectivero, -ra *n* 1 *Arg* : bus driver 2 *Chile* : taxi driver
colectividad *nf* : community, group
colectivo¹, -va *adj* : collective — colectivamente *adv*
colectivo² *nm* 1 : collective 2 (*in various countries*) : city bus 3 *Chile* : fixed-route taxi
colector¹, -tora *n* : collector ⟨colector de impuestos : tax collector⟩
colector² *nm* 1 : sewer 2 : manifold (of an engine)
colega *nmf* 1 : colleague 2 HOMÓLOGO : counterpart 3 *fam* : buddy
colegiado, -da *n* 1 ÁRBITRO : referee 2 : member (of a professional association)
colegial¹, -giala *adj* 1 : school 2 *Mex fam* : green, inexperienced
colegial², -giala *n* : schoolboy *m,* schoolgirl *f*
colegiatura *nf Mex* : tuition
colegio *nm* 1 : school 2 : college ⟨colegio electoral : electoral college⟩ 3 : professional association
colegir {28} *vt* 1 JUNTAR : to collect, to gather 2 INFERIR : to infer, to deduce
cólera¹ *nm* : cholera
cólera² *nf* FURIA, IRA : anger, rage
colérico, -ca *adj* 1 FURIOSO : angry 2 IRRITABLE : irritable
colesterol *nm* : cholesterol
coleta *nf* 1 : ponytail 2 : pigtail
coletazo *nm* : lash, flick (of a tail)
colgado, -da *adj* 1 : hanging, hanged 2 : pending 3 dejar colgado a : to disappoint, to let down
colgante¹ *adj* : hanging, dangling
colgante² *nm* : pendant, charm (on a bracelet)
colgar {16} *vt* 1 : to hang (up), to put up 2 AHORCAR : to hang (someone) 3 : to hang up (a telephone) 4 *fam* : to fail (an exam) — colgarse *vr* 1 : to hang, to be suspended 2 AHORCARSE : to hang oneself 3 : to hang up a telephone
colibrí *nm* CHUPAFLOR : hummingbird
cólico *nm* : colic
coliflor *nf* : cauliflower
colilla *nf* : butt (of a cigarette)
colín *nm, pl* colines *Spain* : breadstick
colina *nf* CERRO, LOMA : hill
colindante *adj* CONTIGUO : adjacent, neighboring
colindar *vi* : to adjoin, to be adjacent
colirio *nm* : eyedrops *pl*
coliseo *nm* : coliseum
colisión *nf, pl* -siones : collision
colisionar *vi* : to collide
collage *nm* : collage
collar *nm* 1 : collar (for an animal) 2 : necklace
collie [ˈkoli] *nmf* : collie
colmado, -da *adj* : heaping

colmar *vt* 1 : to fill to the brim 2 : to fulfill, to satisfy 3 : to heap, to shower ⟨me colmaron de regalos : they showered me with gifts⟩
colmena *nf* : beehive
colmenar *nm* APIARIO : apiary
colmillo *nm* 1 CANINO : canine (tooth), fang 2 : tusk
colmilludo, -da *adj Mex, PRi* : astute, shrewd, crafty
colmo *nm* : height, extreme, limit ⟨el colmo de la locura : the height of folly⟩ ⟨¡eso es el colmo! : that's the last straw!⟩ ⟨para colmo : to top it all off⟩
colocación *nf, pl* -ciones 1 : placement, placing 2 : position, job 3 : investment
colocar {72} *vt* 1 PONER : to place, to put 2 : to find a job for 3 : to invest — colocarse *vr* 1 SITUARSE : to position oneself 2 : to get a job
colofonia *nf* : rosin
colombiano, -na *adj & n* : Colombian
colon *nm* : (intestinal) colon
colón *nm, pl* colones : colón (Costa Rican and Salvadoran unit of currency)
colonia *nf* 1 : colony 2 : cologne 3 *Mex* : residential area, neighborhood
colonial *adj* : colonial
colonización *nf, pl* -ciones : colonization
colonizador¹, -dora *adj* : colonizing
colonizador², -dora *n* : colonist
colonizar {21} *vt* : to colonize, to settle
colono, -na *n* 1 : settler, colonist 2 : tenant farmer
coloquial *adj* : colloquial
coloquio *nm* 1 : discussion, talk 2 : conference, symposium
color *nm* 1 : color 2 : paint, dye 3 colores *nmpl* : colored pencils
coloración *nf, pl* -ciones : coloring, coloration
colorado¹, -da *adj* 1 ROJO : red 2 ponerse colorado : to blush 3 chiste colorado *Mex* : off-color joke
colorado² *nm* ROJO : red
colorante *nm* : coloring ⟨colorante de alimentos : food coloring⟩
colorear *vt* : to color — *vi* 1 : to redden 2 : to ripen
colorete *nm* : blush, rouge
colorido *nm* : color, coloring
colorín *nm, pl* -rines 1 : bright color 2 : goldfinch
colosal *adj* : colossal
coloso *nm* : colossus
coludir *vi* : to conspire
columna *nf* 1 : column 2 columna vertebral : spine, backbone
columnata *nf* : colonnade
columnista *nmf* : columnist
columpiar *vt* : to push (on a swing) — columpiarse *vr* : to swing
columpio *nm* : swing
colusión *nf, pl* -siones : collusion
colza *nf* : rape (plant)
coma¹ *nm* : coma ⟨entrar en coma : to go into a coma⟩
coma² *nf* 1 : comma 2 coma decimal : decimal point

comadre *nf* **1** : godmother of one's child **2** : mother of one's godchild **3** *fam* : neighbor, female friend **4** *fam* : gossip

comadrear *vi fam* : to gossip

comadreja *nf* : weasel

comadrona *nf* : midwife

comal *nm CA, Mex* : tortilla griddle

comanche *nmf* : Comanche

comandancia *nf* **1** : command headquarters **2** : command

comandante *nmf* **1** : commander, commanding officer **2** : major

comandar *vt* : to command, to lead

comando *nm* **1** : commando **2** : command (for computers)

comarca *nf* REGIÓN : region

comarcal *adj* REGIONAL : regional, local

comatoso, -sa *adj* : comatose

comba *nf* **1** : bend, sag **2** *Spain* : jump rope

combar *vt* : to bend, to curve — **combarse** *vr* **1** : to bend, to buckle **2** : to warp, to bulge, to sag

combate *nm* **1** : combat **2** : fight, boxing match

combatiente *nmf* : combatant, fighter

combatir *vt* : to combat, to fight against — *vi* : to fight

combatividad *nf* : fighting spirit

combativo, -va *adj* : combative, spirited

combi *nf Arg, Mex, Peru* : minibus

combinación *nf, pl* **-ciones** **1** : combination **2** : connection (in travel)

combinado *nm* **1** COCTEL : cocktail **2** EQUIPO : team

combinar *vt* **1** UNIR : to combine, to mix together **2** : to match, to put together — **combinarse** *vr* : to get together, to conspire

combo *nm* **1** : (musical) band **2** *Chile, Peru* : sledgehammer **3** *Chile, Peru* : punch

combustible¹ *adj* : combustible

combustible² *nm* : fuel

combustión *nf, pl* **-tiones** : combustion

comedero *nm* : trough, feeder

comedia *nf* : comedy

comediante *nmf* **1** : actor, actress *f* **2** FARSANTE : fraud

comedido, -da *adj* MESURADO : moderate, restrained

comediógrafo, -fa *n* : playwright

comedor *nm* : dining room

comején *nm, pl* **-jenes** : termite

comelón¹, -lona *adj, mpl* **-lones** *fam* : gluttonous

comelón², -lona *n, pl* **-lones** *fam* : big eater, glutton

comensal *nmf* : dinner guest

comentador, -dora *n* → **comentarista**

comentar *vt* **1** : to comment on, to discuss **2** : to mention, to remark

comentario *nm* **1** : comment, remark ⟨sin comentarios : no comment⟩ **2** : commentary

comentarista *nmf* : commentator

comenzar {29} *v* EMPEZAR : to begin, to start ⟨comenzó a trabajar : he started to work⟩ ⟨comenzó diciendo que . . . , comenzó por decir que . . . : she started by saying that . . .⟩

comer¹ *vt* **1** : to eat **2** : to consume, to eat up, to eat into — *vi* **1** : to eat **2** CENAR : to have a meal **3** **dar de comer** : to feed — **comerse** *vr* : to eat up

comer² *nm* : eating, dining

comercial *adj & nm* : commercial — **comercialmente** *adv*

comercializar {21} *vt* **1** : to commercialize **2** : to market — **comercialización** *nf*

comerciante *nmf* : merchant, dealer

comerciar *vi* : to do business, to trade

comercio *nm* **1** : commerce, trade **2** NEGOCIO : business, place of business **3** **comercio electrónico** : e-commerce

comestible¹ *adj* : edible

comestible² *nm* **1** : foodstuff, food **2** **comestibles** *nmpl* VÍVERES : groceries, food

cometa¹ *nm* : comet

cometa² *nf* : kite

cometer *vt* **1** : to commit **2** **cometer un error** : to make a mistake

cometido *nm* : assignment, task

comezón *nf, pl* **-zones** PICAZÓN : itchiness, itching

comible *adj fam* : eatable, edible

comic *or* **cómic** *nm* : comic strip, comic book

comicidad *nf* HUMOR : humor, wit

comicios *nmpl* : elections, voting

cómico¹, -ca *adj* : comic, comical

cómico², -ca *n* HUMORISTA : comic, comedian, comedienne *f*

comida *nf* **1** : food **2** : meal **3** CENA : dinner **3** *Mex, Spain* ALMUERZO : lunch **5** **comida basura** *or* **comida chatarra** : junk food **6** **comida rápida** : fast food

comidilla *nf* : talk, gossip

comienzo *nm* **1** : start, beginning **2** **al comienzo** : at first **3** **dar comienzo** : to begin

comillas *nfpl* : quotation marks ⟨entre comillas : in quotes⟩

comilón, -lona → **comelón, -lona**

comilona *nf fam* : feast

comino *nm* **1** : cumin **2** **me vale un comino** *fam* : not to matter to someone ⟨no me importa un comino : I couldn't care less⟩

comisaría *nf* : police station

comisario, -ria *n* : commissioner

comisión *nf, pl* **-siones** **1** : commission, committing **2** : committee, commission **3** : percentage, commission ⟨comisión sobre las ventas : sales commission⟩ ⟨trabajar a comisión : to work on commission⟩

comisionado¹, -da *adj* : commissioned, entrusted

comisionado², -da *n* → **comisario**

comisionar *vt* : to commission

comisura *nf* **comisura de los labios** : corner of the mouth

comité *nm* : committee

comitiva *nf* : retinue, entourage

como¹ *adv* **1** : around, about ⟨cuesta como 500 pesos : it costs around 500 pesos⟩ **2** : kind of, like ⟨tengo como mareos : I'm kind of dizzy⟩

como[2] *conj* **1** : how, as ⟨hazlo como dijiste que lo harías : do it the way you said you would⟩ **2** : since, given that ⟨como estaba lloviendo, no salí : since it was raining, I didn't go out⟩ **3** : if ⟨como lo vuelva a hacer lo arrestarán : if he does that again he'll be arrested⟩ **4 como quiera** : in any way

como[3] *prep* **1** : like, as ⟨ligero como una pluma : light as a feather⟩ **2 así como** : as well as

cómo *adv* : how ⟨¿cómo estás? : how are you?⟩ ⟨¿a cómo están las peras? : how much are the pears?⟩ ⟨¿cómo? : excuse me?, what was that?⟩ ⟨no sé cómo lo hace : I don't know how she does it⟩ ⟨¿cómo es eso? : how come?⟩ ⟨¿cómo que no hay dinero? : what do you mean there's no money?⟩ ⟨¿se puede? ¡cómo no! : may I? of course!⟩ ⟨¡cómo cambian los tiempos! : how times change!⟩

cómoda *nf* : bureau, chest of drawers

comodidad *nf* **1** : comfort **2** : convenience

comodín *nm, pl* **-dines** **1** : joker, wild card **2** : wildcard (symbol) **3** : all-purpose word or thing **4** : pretext, excuse

cómodo, -da *adj* **1** COMFORTABLE ; comfortable **2** : convenient — **cómodamente** *adv*

comodoro *nm* : commodore

comoquiera *adv* **1** : in any way **2 comoquiera que** : in whatever way, however ⟨comoquiera que sea eso : however that may be⟩

compa *nm fam* : buddy, pal

compactar *vt* : to compact, to compress

compact disc ['kompak'dis, -'disk] *nm, pl* **compact discs** ['kompak'dis, -'disks] : compact disc, CD

compacto, -ta *adj* : compact

compadecer {53} *vt* : to sympathize with, to feel sorry for — **compadecerse** *vr* **1** ∼ **de** : to take pity on **2** ∼ **con** : to fit, to accord (with)

compadre *nm* **1** : godfather of one's child **2** : father of one's godchild **3** *fam* : buddy, pal

compaginar *vt* **1** COORDINAR : to combine, to coordinate **2** : to collate

compañerismo *nm* : camaraderie

compañero, -ra *n* : companion, mate, partner ⟨compañero de clase : classmate⟩ ⟨compañero de trabajo : coworker⟩

compañía *nf* **1** : company ⟨en compañía de su madre : accompanied by his mother⟩ ⟨me hacía compañía : she was keeping me company⟩ ⟨andar en/con malas compañías : to keep bad company⟩ **2** EMPRESA, FIRMA : company, firm **3** : company (in theater) **4** : company (in the military)

comparable *adj* : comparable

comparación *nf, pl* **-ciones** : comparison

comparado, -da *adj* : comparative ⟨literatura comparada : comparative literature⟩

comparar *vt* : to compare

comparativo[1]**, -va** *adj* : comparative, relative — **comparativamente** *adv*

comparativo[2] *nm* : comparative degree or form

comparecencia *nf* **1** : appearance (in court) **2 orden de comparecencia** : subpoena, summons

comparecer {53} *vi* : to appear (in court)

comparsa *nmf* : extra (in a film, etc.)

compartimiento *or* **compartimento** *nm* : compartment

compartir *vt* : to share

compás *nm, pl* **-pases** **1** : beat, rhythm, time **2** : compass

compasión *nf, pl* **-siones** : compassion, pity

compasivo, -va *adj* : compassionate

compatibilidad *nf* : compatibility

compatible *adj* : compatible

compatriota *nmf* PAISANO : compatriot, fellow countryman

compeler *vt* : to compel

compendiar *vt* : to summarize, to condense

compendio *nm* : summary

compenetración *nf, pl* **-ciones** : rapport, mutual understanding

compenetrarse *vr* **1** : to understand each other **2** ∼ **con** : to identify oneself with

compensación *nf, pl* **-ciones** : compensation

compensar *vt* : to compensate for, to make up for — *vi* : to be worth one's while

compensatorio, -ria *adj* : compensatory

competencia *nf* **1** : competition, rivalry **2** : competence

competente *adj* : competent, able — **competentemente** *adv*

competición *nf, pl* **-ciones** : competition

competidor[1]**, -dora** *adj* RIVAL : competing, rival

competidor[2]**, -dora** *n* RIVAL : competitor, rival

competir {54} *vi* : to compete

competitividad *nf* : competitiveness

competitivo, -va *adj* : competitive — **competitivamente** *adv*

compilar *vt* : to compile — **compilación** *nf*

compinche *nmf fam* **1** : buddy, pal **2** : partner in crime, accomplice

complacencia *nf* : pleasure, satisfaction

complacer {57} *vt* : to please — **complacerse** *vr* ∼ **en** : to take pleasure in

complaciente *adj* : obliging, eager to please

complejidad *nf* : complexity

complejo[1]**, -ja** *adj* : complex

complejo[2] *nm* : complex

complementar *vt* : to complement, to supplement — **complementarse** *vr*

complementario, -ria *adj* : complementary

complemento *nm* **1** : complement, supplement **2** : supplementary pay, allowance

completamente *adv* : completely, totally

completar *vt* TERMINAR : to complete, to finish

completo, -ta *adj* **1** : complete, full, whole ⟨las obras completas : the complete works⟩ ⟨su nombre completo : his full name⟩ **2** : complete, absolute ⟨por completo : completely⟩ **3** DETALLADO : full, detailed **4** VERSÁTIL : well-rounded, versatile

complexión *nf, pl* **-xiones** : (physical) constitution

complicación *nf, pl* **-ciones** : complication

complicado, -da *adj* : complicated

complicar {72} *vt* **1** : to complicate **2** : to involve — **complicarse** *vr*

cómplice *nmf* : accomplice

complicidad *nf* : complicity

complot *nm, pl* **complots** CONFABULA-CIÓN, CONSPIRACIÓN : conspiracy, plot

componenda *nf* : shady deal, scam

componente *adj & nm* : component, constituent

componer {60} *vt* **1** ARREGLAR : to fix, to repair **2** CONSTITUIR : to make up, to compose **3** : to compose, to write **4** : to set (a bone) — **componerse** *vr* **1** : to improve, to get better **2** ~ **de** : to consist of

comportamiento *nm* CONDUCTA : behavior, conduct

comportarse *vr* : to behave, to conduct oneself

composición *nf, pl* **-ciones** **1** OBRA : composition, work **2** : makeup, arrangement

compositor, -tora *n* : composer, songwriter

compostura *nf* **1** : composure **2** : mending, repair

compota *nf* : compote

compra *nf* **1** : purchase **2 ir de compras** : to go shopping **3 orden de compra** : purchase order

comprador, -dora *n* : buyer, shopper

comprar *vt* : to buy, to purchase

compraventa *nf* : buying and selling

comprender *vt* **1** ENTENDER : to comprehend, to understand **2** ABARCAR : to cover, to include — *vi* : to understand ⟨¡ya comprendo! : now I understand!⟩

comprensible *adj* : understandable — **comprensiblemente** *adv*

comprensión *nf, pl* **-siones** **1** : comprehension, understanding **2** : understanding, sympathy

comprensivo, -va *adj* : understanding

compresa *nf* **1** : compress **2** *or* **compresa higiénica** : sanitary napkin

compresión *nf, pl* **-siones** : compression

compresor *nm* : compressor

comprimido *nm* PÍLDORA, TABLETA : pill, tablet

comprimir *vt* : to compress

comprobable *adj* : provable

comprobación *nf, pl* **-ciones** : verification, confirmation

comprobante *nm* **1** : proof ⟨comprobante de identidad : proof of identity⟩ **2** : voucher, receipt ⟨comprobante de ventas : sales slip⟩

comprobar {19} *vt* **1** : to verify, to check **2** : to prove

comprometedor, -dora *adj* : compromising

comprometer *vt* **1** : to compromise **2** : to jeopardize **3** : to commit, to put under obligation — **comprometerse** *vr* **1** : to commit oneself **2** ~ **con** : to get engaged to

comprometido, -da *adj* **1** : compromising, awkward **2** : committed, obliged **3** : engaged (to be married)

compromiso *nm* **1** : obligation, commitment **2** : engagement ⟨anillo de compromiso : engagement ring⟩ **3** : agreement **4** : awkward situation, fix

compuerta *nf* : floodgate

compuesto¹ *pp* → **componer**

compuesto², -ta *adj* **1** : fixed, repaired **2** : compound, composite **3** : decked out, spruced up **4** ~ **de** : made up of, consisting of

compuesto³ *nm* : compound

compulsión *nf, pl* **-siones** : compulsion

compulsivo, -va *adj* **1** : compelling, urgent **2** : compulsive — **compulsivamente** *adv*

compungido, -da *adj* : contrite, remorseful

compungirse {35} *vr* : to feel remorse

compuso, etc. → **componer**

computable *adj* : countable ⟨años computables : years accrued⟩ ⟨ingresos computables : qualifying income⟩

computación *nf, pl* **-ciones** : computing, computers *pl*

computador *nm* → **computadora**

computadora *nf* **1** : computer **2 computadora portátil** : laptop computer

computar *vt* : to compute, to calculate

computarizar {21} *vt* : to computerize

cómputo *nm* : computation, calculation

comulgar {52} *vi* : to receive Communion

común *adj, pl* **comunes** **1** : common **2 común y corriente** : ordinary, regular **3 por lo común** : generally, as a rule

comuna *nf* : commune

comunal *adj* : communal

comunicación *nf, pl* **-ciones** **1** : communication **2** : access, link **3** : message, report

comunicado *nm* **1** : communiqué **2 comunicado de prensa** : press release

comunicador, -dora *n* : commentator, analyst

comunicar {72} *vt* **1** : to communicate, to convey **2** : to notify — **comunicarse** *vr* ~ **con** **1** : to contact, to get in touch with **2** : to be connected to

comunicativo, -va *adj* : communicative, talkative

comunidad *nf* : community

comunión *nf, pl* **-niones** **1** : communion, sharing **2** : Communion

comunismo *nm* : communism, Communism

comunista *adj & nmf* : communist

comunitario, -ria *adj* : community, communal

comúnmente *adv* : commonly

con *prep* **1** : with ⟨vengo con mi padre : I'm going with my father⟩ ⟨¿con quién hablas? : who are you speaking to?⟩ **2** : in spite of ⟨con todo : in spite of it all⟩

3 : to, towards ⟨ser amable con : to be kind to⟩ **4** : by ⟨con llegar temprano : by arriving early⟩ **5 con (tal) que** : as/ so long as

conato *nm* : attempt, effort ⟨conato de robo : attempted robbery⟩

cóncavo, -va *adj* : concave

concebible *adj* : conceivable

concebir {54} *vt* **1** : to conceive **2** : to conceive of, to imagine — *vi* : to conceive, to become pregnant

conceder *vt* **1** : to grant, to bestow **2** : to concede, to admit

concejal, -jala *n* : councilman *m*, councilwoman *f*; alderman *mf*

concejo *nm* : council ⟨concejo municipal : town council⟩

concentración *nf, pl* **-ciones** : concentration

concentrado *nm* : concentrate

concentrar *vt* : to concentrate — **concentrarse** *vr*

concéntrico, -ca *adj* : concentric

concepción *nf, pl* **-ciones** : conception

concepto *nm* NOCIÓN : concept, idea, opinion

conceptual *adj* : conceptual — **conceptualmente** *adv*

conceptualizar {21} *vt* : conceptualize — **conceptualización** *nf*

conceptuar {3} *vt* : to regard, to judge

concernir {17} *vi* : to be of concern

concertar {55} *vt* **1** : to arrange, to set up **2** : to agree on, to settle **3** : to harmonize — *vi* : to be in harmony

concesión *nf, pl* **-siones** **1** : concession **2** : awarding, granting

concesionario, -ria *n* : franchisee

concha *nf* : conch, seashell

concho *nm DomRep* : fixed-route taxi

conciencia *nf* **1** : conscience **2** : consciousness, awareness

concienciar → **concientizar**

concientización *nf, pl* **-ciones** : awareness, awareness-raising

concientizar {21} *vt* : to make aware — **concientizarse** *vr* ∼ **de** : to realize, to become aware of

concienzudo, -da *adj* : conscientious

concierto *nm* **1** : concert **2** : agreement **3** : concerto

conciliador[1], -dora *adj* : conciliatory

conciliador[2], -dora *n* : arbitrator, peacemaker

conciliar *vt* : to reconcile — **conciliación** *nf*

conciliatorio, -ria *adj* → **conciliador[1]**

concilio *nm* : (church) council

conciso, -sa *adj* : concise — **concisamente** *adv* — **concisión** *nf*

concitar *vt* : to arouse

conciudadano, -na *n* : fellow citizen

cónclave *nm* : conclave, private meeting

concluir {41} *vt* **1** TERMINAR : to conclude, to finish **2** DEDUCIR : to deduce, to conclude — *vi* : to end, to conclude

conclusión *nf, pl* **-siones** : conclusion

concluyente *adj* : conclusive

concomitante *adj* : accompanying, attendant

concordancia *nf* : agreement, accordance

concordar {19} *vi* : to agree, to coincide — *vt* : to reconcile

concordia *nf* : concord, harmony

concretar *vt* **1** : to pinpoint, to specify **2** : to fulfill, to realize — **concretarse** *vr* : to become real, to take shape

concretizar → **concretar**

concreto[1], -ta *adj* **1** : concrete, actual **2** : definite, specific ⟨en concreto : specifically⟩ — **concretamente** *adv*

concreto[2] *nm* HORMIGÓN : concrete

concurrencia *nf* **1** : audience, turnout **2** : concurrence

concurrente *adj* : concurrent — **concurrentemente** *adv*

concurrido, -da *adj* : busy, crowded

concurrir *vi* **1** : to converge, to come together **2** : to concur, to agree **3** : to take part, to participate **4** : to attend, to be present ⟨concurrir a una reunión : to attend a meeting⟩ **5** ∼ **a** : to contribute to

concursante *nmf* : contestant, competitor

concursar *vt* : to compete in — *vi* : to compete, to participate

concurso *nm* **1** : contest, competition **2** : concurrence, coincidence **3** : crowd, gathering **4** : cooperation, assistance

condado *nm* **1** : county **2** : earldom

conde, -desa *n* : count *m*, earl *m*, countess *f*

condecoración *nf, pl* **-ciones** : decoration, medal

condecorar *vt* : to decorate, to award (a medal)

condena *nf* **1** : condemnation **2** SENTENCIA : sentence

condenable *adj* : reprehensible

condenación *nf, pl* **-ciones** **1** : condemnation **2** : damnation

condenado[1], -da *adj* **1** : fated, doomed **2** : convicted, sentenced **3** *fam* : darn, damned

condenado[2], -da *n* : convict

condenar *vt* **1** : to condemn **2** : to sentence **3** : to board up, to wall up — **condenarse** *vr* : to be damned

condenatorio, -ria *adj* : condemning ⟨sentencia condenatoria : conviction⟩

condensación *nf, pl* **-ciones** : condensation

condensar *vt* : to condense

condesa *nf* → **conde**

condescendencia *nf* : condescension

condescender {56} *vi* **1** : to condescend **2** : to agree, to acquiesce

condescendiente *adj* **1** : condescending **2** : accommodating, obliging

condición *nf, pl* **-ciones** **1** : condition, state ⟨en buenas/malas condiciones : in good/bad condition⟩ ⟨no está en condiciones de trabajar : she's in no shape to work⟩ **2** : capacity, position ⟨estar en condiciones de : to be in a position to⟩ **3** : condition, stipulation ⟨a condición de que, con la condición de que : on the condition that⟩ **4 condiciones** *nfpl* : conditions, circumstances ⟨condicio-

nes de vida : living conditions⟩ ⟨en igualdad de condiciones : on equal footing⟩
condicional *adj* : conditional — **condicionalmente** *adv*
condicionamiento *nm* : conditioning
condicionar *vt* **1** : to condition, to determine **2** ~ **a** : to be contingent on, to depend on
condimentar *vt* SAZONAR : to season, to spice
condimento *nm* : condiment, seasoning, spice
condolencia *nf* : condolence, sympathy
condolerse {47} *vr* : to sympathize
condominio *nm* : condominium, condo
condón *nm*, *pl* **condones** : condom
cóndor *nm* : condor
conducción *nf*, *pl* **-ciones 1** : conduction (of electricity, etc.) **2** DIRECCIÓN : management, direction
conducir {61} *vt* **1** DIRIGIR, GUIAR : to direct, to lead **2** MANEJAR : to drive (a vehicle) — *vi* **1** : to drive a vehicle **2** ~ **a** : to lead to — **conducirse** *vr* PORTARSE : to behave, to conduct oneself
conducta *nf* COMPORTAMIENTO : conduct, behavior
conductividad *nf* : conductivity
conducto *nm* : conduit, channel, duct
conductor¹, -tora *adj* : conducting, leading
conductor², -tora *n* : driver
conductor³ *nm* : conductor (of electricity, etc.)
conectar *vt* : to connect — *vi* ~ **con** : to link up with, to communicate with
conectivo, -va *adj* : connective — **conectividad** *nf*
conector *nm* : connector
conejera *nf* : rabbit hutch
conejillo *nm* **conejillo de Indias** : guinea pig
conejo, -ja *n* : rabbit
conexión *nf*, *pl* **-xiones** : connection
confabulación *nf*, *pl* **-ciones** COMPLOT, CONSPIRACIÓN : plot, conspiracy
confabularse *vr* : to plot, to conspire
confección *nf*, *pl* **-ciones 1** : preparation **2** : tailoring, dressmaking
confeccionar *vt* : to make, to produce, to prepare
confederación *nf*, *pl* **-ciones** : confederation
confederarse *vr* : to confederate, to form a confederation
conferencia *nf* **1** REUNIÓN : conference, meeting **2** : lecture
conferenciante *nmf* : lecturer
conferencista → **conferenciante**
conferir {76} *vt* : to confer, to bestow
confesar {55} *v* : to confess — **confesarse** *vr* : to go to confession
confesión *nf*, *pl* **-siones 1** : confession **2** : creed, denomination
confesionario *nm* : confessional
confesor *nm* : confessor
confeti *nm* : confetti
confiable *adj* : trustworthy, reliable
confiado, -da *adj* **1** : confident, self-confident **2** : trusting — **confiadamente** *adv*

confianza *nf* **1** : trust ⟨de poca confianza : untrustworthy⟩ **2** : confidence, self-confidence
confianzudo, -da *adj* : forward, presumptuous
confiar {85} *vt* **1** : to confide **2** : to entrust — *vi* ~ **en** : to trust, to have faith/confidence in — **confiarse** *vr* **1** : to be overconfident **2** ~ **a** : to confide in
confidencia *nf* : confidence, secret
confidencial *adj* : confidential — **confidencialmente** *adv*
confidencialidad *nf* : confidentiality
confidente *nmf* **1** : confidant, confidante *f* **2** : informer
configuración *nf*, *pl* **-ciones** : configuration, shape
configurar *vt* **1** : to shape, to form **2** : to configure (a computer, etc.)
confín *nm*, *pl* **confines** : boundary, limit
confinamiento *nm* : confinement
confinar *vt* **1** : to confine, to limit **2** : to exile — *vi* ~ **con** : to border on
confirmación *nf*, *pl* **-ciones** : confirmation
confirmar *vt* : to confirm, to substantiate
confiscación *nf*, *pl* **-ciones** : confiscation
confiscar {72} *vt* DECOMISAR : to confiscate, to seize
confitado, -da *adj* : candied
confite *nm* : sugar-coated candy
confitería *nf* **1** DULCERÍA : candy store, confectionery **2** : tearoom, café
confitero, -ra *n* : confectioner
confitura *nf* : preserves, jam
conflagración *nf*, *pl* **-ciones 1** : conflagration, fire **2** : war
conflictivo, -va *adj* **1** : troubled **2** : controversial
conflicto *nm* : conflict
confluencia *nf* : junction, confluence
confluir {41} *vi* **1** : to converge, to join **2** : to gather, to assemble
conformación *nf*, *pl* **-ciones** : makeup, composition
conformar *vt* **1** : to form, to create **2** : to constitute, to make up — **conformarse** *vr* **1** RESIGNARSE : to resign oneself **2** : to comply, to conform **3** ~ **con** : to be content with
conforme¹ *adj* **1** : content, satisfied **2** ~ **a** : in accordance with
conforme² *conj* : as ⟨irá mejorando conforme avance el día : it will improve as the day goes on⟩
conformidad *nf* **1** : agreement, consent **2** : resignation
confort *nm* : comfort
confortable *adj* CÓMODO : comfortable
confortar *vt* CONSOLAR : to comfort, to console
confraternidad *nf* : brotherhood, fraternity
confraternizar {21} *vi* : to fraternize — **confraternización** *nf*
confrontación *nf*, *pl* **-ciones** : confrontation
confrontar *vt* **1** ENCARAR : to confront **2** : to compare **3** : to bring face-to-face — *vi* : to border — **confrontarse** *vr* ~ **con** : to face up to

confundir *vt* : to confuse, to mix up — **confundirse** *vr* : to make a mistake, to be confused ⟨confundirse de número : to get the wrong number⟩

confusión *nf, pl* **-siones** : confusion

confuso, -sa *adj* **1** DESORDENADO : confused, confusing ⟨ideas confusas : confused ideas⟩ ⟨una situación confusa : a confused/confusing situation⟩ ⟨unas voces confusas : a confusion of voices⟩ **2** ATURDIDO, TURBADO : confused, flustered, embarrassed **3** VAGO : hazy, indistinct

congelación *nf, pl* **-ciones** **1** : freezing **2** : frostbite (on skin), exposure

congelado, -da *adj* HELADO : frozen

congelador *nm* HELADORA : freezer

congelamiento *nm* → **congelación**

congelar *vt* : to freeze — **congelarse** *vr*

congeniar *vi* : to get along (with someone)

congénito, -ta *adj* : congenital

congestión *nf, pl* **-tiones** : congestion

congestionado, -da *adj* : congested

congestionamiento *nm* → **congestión**

congestionarse *vr* **1** : to become flushed **2** : to become congested

conglomerado¹, -da *adj* : conglomerate, mixed

**conglomerado² ** *nm* : conglomerate, conglomeration

congoja *nf* ANGUSTIA : anguish, grief

congoleño, -ña *adj & n* : Congolese

congraciarse *vr* : to ingratiate oneself

congratular *vt* FELICITAR : to congratulate

congregación *nf, pl* **-ciones** : congregation, gathering

congregar {52} *vt* : to bring together — **congregarse** *vr* : to congregate, to assemble

congresista *nmf* : congressman *m*, congresswoman *f*

congreso *nm* : congress, conference

congruencia *nf* **1** : congruence **2** COHERENCIA : coherence — **congruente** *adj*

cónico, -ca *adj* : conical, conic

conífera *nf* : conifer

conífero, -ra *adj* : coniferous

conjetura *nf* : conjecture, guess

conjeturar *vt* : to guess, to conjecture

conjugación *nf, pl* **-ciones** : conjugation

conjugar {52} *vt* **1** : to conjugate **2** : to combine

conjunción *nf, pl* **-ciones** : conjunction

conjuntivitis *nf* : conjunctivitis

conjuntivo, -va *adj* : connective ⟨tejido conjuntivo : connective tissue⟩

conjunto¹, -ta *adj* : joint — **conjuntamente** *adv*

conjunto² ** *nm* **1 : collection, group **2** : ensemble, outfit **3** : ensemble, musical group **4** : whole, entirety ⟨en conjunto : as a whole, altogether⟩

conjurar *vt* **1** : to exorcise **2** : to avert, to ward off — *vi* CONSPIRAR : to conspire, to plot

conjuro *nm* **1** : exorcism **2** : spell

conllevar *vt* **1** : to bear, to suffer **2** IMPLICAR : to entail, to involve

conmemorar *vt* : to commemorate — **conmemoración** *nf*

conmemorativo, -va *adj* : commemorative, memorial

conmigo *pron* : with me ⟨habló conmigo : he talked with me⟩

conminar *vt* AMENAZAR : to threaten, to warn

conmiseración *nf, pl* **-ciones** : pity, commiseration

conmoción *nf, pl* **-ciones** **1** : shock, upheaval **2** *or* **conmoción cerebral** : concussion

conmocionar *vt* : to shake, to shock

conmovedor, -dora *adj* EMOCIONANTE : moving, touching

conmover {47} *vt* **1** EMOCIONAR : to move, to touch **2** : to shake up — **conmoverse** *vr*

conmutador *nm* **1** : switch **2** : switchboard

conmutar *vt* **1** : to commute (a sentence) **2** : to switch, to exchange

connivencia *nf* : connivance

connotación *nf, pl* **-ciones** : connotation

connotar *vt* : to connote, to imply

cono *nm* : cone

conocedor¹, -dora *adj* : knowledgeable

conocedor², -dora *n* : connoisseur, expert

conocer {18} *vt* **1** : to know, to be acquainted with ⟨¿lo conoces? : do you know him?⟩ **2** : to meet ⟨ya la conocí : I've already met her⟩ **3** : to know, to be familiar with (a topic, etc.) **4** : to get to know, to experience ⟨me gustaría conocer otros países : I'd like to visit other countries⟩ ⟨conocer de primera mano : to experience firsthand⟩ **5** RECONOCER : to recognize ⟨no te conocí : I didn't recognize you⟩ **6 dar a conocer** : to disclose, to announce **7 darse a conocer** : to make oneself known — **conocerse** *vr* **1** : to know each other **2** : to meet **3** : to know oneself

conocible *adj* : knowable

conocido¹, -da *adj* **1** : familiar **2** : well-known, famous

conocido², -da *n* : acquaintance

conocimiento *nm* **1** : knowledge **2** SENTIDO : consciousness

conque *conj* : so, so then, and so ⟨¡ah, conque esas tenemos! : oh, so that's what's going on!⟩

conquista *nf* : conquest

conquistador¹, -dora *adj* : conquering

conquistador², -dora *n* : conqueror

conquistar *vt* : to conquer

consabido, -da *adj* : usual, typical

consagración *nf, pl* **-ciones** : consecration

consagrar *vt* **1** : to consecrate **2** DEDICAR : to dedicate, to devote

consciencia → **conciencia**

consciente *adj* : conscious, aware — **conscientemente** *adv*

conscripción *nf, pl* **-ciones** : conscription, draft

conscripto, -ta *n* : conscript, inductee

consecución *nf, pl* **-ciones** : attainment

consecuencia *nf* **1** : consequence, result ⟨a consecuencia de : as a result of⟩ **2 en ~** : accordingly

consecuente *adj* : consistent — **consecuentemente** *adv*

consecutivo, -va *adj* : consecutive, successive — **consecutivamente** *adv*

conseguir {75} *vt* **1** : to get, to obtain **2** : to achieve, to attain (a goal, etc.) **3** : to manage to ⟨consiguió acabar : she managed to finish⟩ ⟨conseguí que lo aceptara : I got him to accept it⟩

consejero, -ra *n* : adviser, counselor

consejo *nm* **1** : piece of advice ⟨me dio algunos consejos : she gave me some advice⟩ ⟨por consejo de : on the advice of⟩ **2** : council ⟨consejo de guerra : court-martial⟩

consenso *nm* : consensus

consensuar *vt* : to reach a consensus on

consentido, -da *adj* : spoiled, pampered

consentimiento *nm* : consent, permission

consentir {76} *vt* **1** PERMITIR : to consent to, to allow **2** MIMAR : to pamper, to spoil — *vi* **~ en** : to agree to, to approve of

conserje *nmf* : custodian, janitor, caretaker

conserva *nf* **1** : preserve(s), jam **2 conservas** *nfpl* : canned goods

conservación *nf, pl* **-ciones** : conservation, preservation

conservacionista *nmf* : conservationist

conservador¹, -dora *adj & n* : conservative

conservador² *nm* : preservative

conservadurismo *nf* : conservatism

conservante *nm* : preservative

conservar *vt* **1** : to preserve **2** GUARDAR : to keep, to conserve

conservatorio *nm* : conservatory

considerable *adj* : considerable — **considerablemente** *adv*

consideración *nf, pl* **-ciones** **1** : consideration **2** : respect **3 de ~** : considerable, important

considerado, -da *adj* **1** : considerate, thoughtful **2** : respected

considerar *vt* **1** : to consider, to think about ⟨considerar la posibilidad : to consider the possibility⟩ ⟨considerando su edad : considering his age⟩ **2** : to consider, to regard as ⟨lo considera necesario : she considers it necessary⟩ **3** : to treat with consideration — **considerarse** *vr* : to consider oneself

consigna *nf* **1** ESLOGAN : slogan **2** : assignment, orders *pl* **3** : luggage storage

consignación *nf, pl* **-ciones** **1** : consignment **2** ASIGNACIÓN : allocation

consignar *vt* **1** : to consign **2** : to record, to write down **3** : to assign, to allocate

consigo *pron* : with her, with him, with you, with oneself ⟨se llevó las llaves consigo : she took the keys with her⟩

consiguiente *adj* **1** : resulting, consequent **2 por ~** : consequently, as a result

consistencia *nf* : consistency

consistente *adj* **1** : firm, strong, sound **2** : consistent — **consistentemente** *adv*

consistir *vi* **1 ~ en** : to consist of **2 ~ en** : to lie in, to consist in

consola *nf* : console

consolación *nf, pl* **-ciones** : consolation ⟨premio de consolación : consolation prize⟩

consolar {19} *vt* CONFORTAR : to console, to comfort

consolidar *vt* : to consolidate — **consolidación** *nf*

consomé *nm* CALDO : consommé, clear soup

consonancia *nf* **1** : harmony **2 en consonancia con** : in accordance with

consonante¹ *adj* : consonant, harmonious

consonante² *nf* : consonant

consorcio *nm* : consortium

consorte *nmf* : consort, spouse

conspicuo, -cua *adj* : eminent, famous

conspiración *nf, pl* **-ciones** COMPLOT, CONFABULACIÓN : conspiracy, plot

conspirador, -dora *n* : conspirator

conspirar *vi* CONJURAR : to conspire, to plot

constancia *nf* **1** PRUEBA : proof, certainty **2** : record, evidence ⟨que quede constancia : for the record⟩ **3** : perseverance, constancy

constante¹ *adj* : constant — **constantemente** *adv*

constante² *nf* : constant

constar *vi* **1** : to be evident, to be on record ⟨que conste : believe me, have no doubt⟩ **2 ~ de** : to consist of

constatación *nf, pl* **-ciones** : confirmation, proof

constatar *vt* **1** : to verify **2** : to state

constelación *nf, pl* **-ciones** : constellation

consternación *nf, pl* **-ciones** : consternation, dismay

consternar *vt* : to dismay, to appall

constipación *nf, pl* **-ciones** : constipation

constipado¹, -da *adj* **estar constipado** : to have a cold

constipado² *nm* RESFRIADO : cold

constiparse *vr* : to catch a cold

constitución *nf, pl* **-ciones** : constitution — **constitucional** *adj* — **constitucionalmente** *adv*

constitucionalidad *nf* : constitutionality

constituir {41} *vt* **1** FORMAR : to constitute, to make up, to form **2** FUNDAR : to establish, to set up — **constituirse** *vr* **~ en** : to set oneself up as, to become

constitutivo, -va *adj* : constituent, component

constituyente *adj & nmf* : constituent

constreñir {67} *vt* **1** FORZAR, OBLIGAR : to constrain, to oblige **2** LIMITAR : to restrict, to limit

construcción *nf, pl* **-ciones** : construction, building

constructivo, -va *adj* : constructive — **constructivamente** *adv*

constructor, -tora *n* : builder

constructora *nf* : construction company

construir {41} *vt* : to build, to construct
consuelo *nm* : consolation, comfort
consuetudinario, -ria *adj* **1** : customary, habitual **2 derecho consuetudinario** : common law
cónsul *nmf* : consul — **consular** *adj*
consulado *nm* : consulate
consulta *nf* **1** : consultation **2** : inquiry
consultar *vt* : to consult
consultivo, -va *adj* : advisory
consultor¹, -tora *adj* : consulting ⟨firma consultora : consulting firm⟩
consultor², -tora *n* : consultant
consultoría *nf* : consultancy
consultorio *nm* **1** : office (of a doctor or dentist) **2** → **consultoría**
consumación *nf, pl* **-ciones** : consummation
consumado, -da *adj* : consummate, perfect
consumar *vt* **1** : to consummate, to complete **2** : to commit, to carry out
consumible *adj* : consumable
consumición *nf, pl* **-ciones** **1** : consumption **2** : drink (in a restaurant)
consumido, -da *adj* : thin, emaciated
consumidor, -dora *n* : consumer
consumir *vt* : to consume — **consumirse** *vr* : to waste away
consumismo *nm* : consumerism
consumo *nm* : consumption (of food, fuel, etc.)
contabilidad *nf* **1** : accounting, bookkeeping **2** : accountancy
contabilizar {21} *vt* : to enter, to record (in accounting)
contable¹ *adj* : countable
contable² *nmf Spain* : accountant, bookkeeper
contactar *vt* : to contact — *vi* ~ **con** : to get in touch with, to contact
contacto *nm* : contact
contado¹, -da *adj* **1** : counted ⟨tenía los días contados : his days were numbered⟩ **2** : rare, scarce ⟨en contadas ocasiones : on rare occasions⟩
contado² *nm* **al contado** : cash ⟨pagar al contado : to pay in cash⟩
contador¹, -dora *n* : accountant
contador² *nm* : meter ⟨contador de agua : water meter⟩ ⟨contador Geiger : Geiger counter⟩
contaduría *nf* **1** : accounting office **2** CONTABILIDAD : accountancy
contagiar *vt* **1** : to infect **2** : to transmit (a disease) — **contagiarse** *vr* **1** : to be contagious **2** : to become infected
contagio *nm* : contagion, infection
contagioso, -sa *adj* : contagious, catching
contaminación *nf, pl* **-ciones** : contamination, pollution
contaminante *nm* : pollutant, contaminant
contaminar *vt* : to contaminate, to pollute
contante *adj* **dinero contante y sonante** → **dinero**
contar {19} *vt* **1** : to count ⟨contar el dinero : to count the money⟩ **2** : to tell ⟨cuéntame un cuento : tell me a story⟩

⟨me lo contó todo : she told me everything⟩ **3** : to include, to count — *vi* **1** : to count (up) ⟨contar de diez en diez : to count by tens⟩ **2** : to count, to matter ⟨eso no cuenta : that doesn't count⟩ **3** ~ **con** : to count on, to rely on **4** ~ **con** : to expect, to count on ⟨no contaba con que . . . : I didn't count on the fact that . . .⟩ **5** ~ **con** : to have (support, resources, etc.) — **contarse** *vr* ~ **entre** : to be numbered among
contemplación *nf, pl* **-ciones** : contemplation — **contemplativo, -va** *adj*
contemplar *vt* **1** : to contemplate, to ponder **2** : to gaze at, to look at
contemporáneo, -nea *adj & n* : contemporary
contención *nf, pl* **-ciones** : containment, holding
contencioso, -sa *adj* : contentious
contender {56} *vi* **1** : to contend, to compete **2** : to fight
contendiente *nmf* : contender
contenedor *nm* **1** : container, receptacle **2** : Dumpster™
contener {80} *vt* **1** : to contain, to hold **2** ATAJAR : to restrain, to hold back — **contenerse** *vr* : to restrain oneself
contenido¹, -da *adj* : restrained, reserved
contenido² *nm* : contents *pl*, content
contentar *vt* : to please, to make happy — **contentarse** *vr* : to be satisfied, to be pleased
contento¹, -ta *adj* : contented, glad, happy
contento² *nm* : joy, happiness
conteo *nm* : count
contestación *nf, pl* **-ciones** **1** : answer, reply **2** : protest
contestador *nm or* **contestador automático** : answering machine
contestadora *nf* → **contestador**
contestar *vt* RESPONDER : to answer — *vi* **1** RESPONDER : to answer, to reply **2** : to talk back, to be disrespectful
contexto *nm* : context
contienda *nf* **1** : dispute, conflict **2** : contest, competition
contigo *pron* : with you ⟨voy contigo : I'm going with you⟩
contiguo, -gua *adj* COLINDANTE : contiguous, adjacent
continente *nm* : continent — **continental** *adj*
contingencia *nf* : contingency, eventuality
contingente *adj & nm* : contingent
continuación *nf, pl* **-ciones** **1** : continuation **2 a** ~ : next ⟨más detalles a continuación : more details below⟩ **3 a continuación de** : after, following
continuar {3} *v* : to continue ⟨continuó trabajando : she continued working, she continued to work⟩ ⟨continuar (con) algo : to continue (with) something⟩
continuidad *nf* : continuity
continuo, -nua *adj* : continuous, steady, constant — **continuamente** *adv*
contonearse *vr* : to sway one's hips
contoneo *nm* : swaying, wiggling (of the hips)

contorno *nm* **1** : outline **2 contornos** *nmpl* : outskirts

contorsión *nf, pl* **-siones** : contortion

contra[1] *nf* **1** *fam* : difficulty, snag **2 llevar la contra a** : to oppose, to contradict

contra[2] *nm* : con ⟨los pros y los contras : the pros and cons⟩

contra[3] *prep* **1** : against ⟨se apoyó contra la pared : he leaned against the wall⟩ ⟨luchar contra : to fight against⟩ **2 en contra** : against ⟨las razones en contra : the reasons against it⟩ ⟨protestas en contra del gobierno : anti-government protests⟩

contra- *pref* : counter- ⟨contraataque : counterattack⟩

contraalmirante *nm* : rear admiral

contraatacar {72} *v* : to counterattack — **contraataque** *nm*

contrabajo *nm* : double bass

contrabalancear *vt* : to counterbalance — **contrabalanza** *nf*

contrabandear *v* : to smuggle

contrabandista *nmf* : smuggler, black market dealer

contrabando *nm* **1** : smuggling **2** : contraband

contracción *nf, pl* **-ciones** : contraction

contracepción *nf, pl* **-ciones** : contraception

contraceptivo *nm* ANTICONCEPTIVO : contraceptive

contrachapado *nm* : plywood

contracorriente *nf* **1** : crosscurrent **2 ir a contracorriente** : to go against the tide

contractual *adj* : contractual

contradecir {11} *vt* DESMENTIR : to contradict — **contradecirse** *vr* DESDECIRSE : to contradict oneself

contradicción *nf, pl* **-ciones** : contradiction

contradictorio, -ria *adj* : contradictory

contraer {81} *vt* **1** : to contract (a disease) **2** : to establish by contract ⟨contraer matrimonio : to get married⟩ **3** : to tighten, to contract — **contraerse** *vr* : to contract, to tighten up

contrafuerte *nm* : buttress

contragolpe *nm* **1** : counterattack **2** : backlash

contrahuella *nf* : riser (of a stair)

contralor, -lora *n* : comptroller

contraloría *nf* : office of the comptroller

contralto *nmf* : contralto

contraluz *nm, pl* **-luces a contraluz** : against the light

contramandar *vt* : to countermand

contramano *nm* a ∼ : the wrong way (on a street)

contramedida *nf* : countermeasure

contraparte *nf* **1** : counterpart **2 en** ∼ : on the other hand

contrapartida *nf* : compensation

contrapelo *nm* a ∼ : in the wrong direction, against the grain

contrapesar *vt* : to counterbalance

contrapeso *nm* : counterbalance

contraponer {60} *vt* **1** : to counter, to oppose **2** : to contrast, to compare

contraportada *nf* : back cover, back page

contraposición *nf, pl* **-ciones** : comparison

contraproducente *adj* : counterproductive

contrapunto *nm* : counterpoint

contrariar {85} *vt* **1** : to contradict, to oppose **2** : to vex, to annoy

contrariedad *nf* **1** : setback, obstacle **2** : vexation, annoyance

contrario, -ria *adj* **1** : contrary, opposite ⟨al contrario : on the contrary⟩ **2** : conflicting, opposed

contrarreloj *adj* **1** : timed **2 a** ∼ : against the clock

contrarrestar *vt* : to counteract

contrarrevolución *nf, pl* **-ciones** : counterrevolution — **contrarrevolucionario, -ria** *adj & n*

contrasentido *nm* : contradiction

contraseña *nf* : password

contrastante *adj* : contrasting

contrastar *vt* **1** : to resist **2** : to check, to confirm — *vi* : to contrast

contraste *nm* : contrast

contratar *vt* **1** : to contract for **2** : to hire, to engage

contratiempo *nm* **1** PERCANCE : mishap, accident **2** DIFICULTAD : setback, difficulty

contratista *nmf* : contractor

contrato *nm* : contract

contravenir {87} *vt* : to contravene, to infringe

contraventana *nf* : shutter

contravía *nf Col* **ir en contravía** : to drive the wrong way (down a street)

contribución *nf, pl* **-ciones** : contribution

contribuidor, -dora *n* : contributor

contribuir {41} *vt* **1** APORTAR : to contribute **2** : to pay (in taxes) — *vi* **1** : contribute, to help out **2** : to pay taxes

contribuyente[1] *adj* : contributing

contribuyente[2] *nmf* : taxpayer

contrición *nf, pl* **-ciones** : contrition

contrincante *nmf* : rival, opponent

contrito, -ta *adj* : contrite, repentant

control *nm* **1** : control ⟨control remoto : remote control⟩ ⟨control de natalidad : birth control⟩ **2** : inspection, check **3** : checkpoint, roadblock

controlable *adj* : controllable

controlador, -dora *n* : controller ⟨controlador aéreo : air traffic controller⟩

controlar *vt* **1** : to control **2** : to monitor, to check

controversia *nf* : controversy

controversial → **controvertido**

controvertido, -da *adj* : controversial

controvertir {76} *vt* : to dispute, to argue about — *vi* : to argue, to debate

contubernio *nm* : conspiracy

contundencia *nf* **1** : forcefulness, weight **2** : severity

contundente *adj* **1** : blunt ⟨un objeto contundente : a blunt instrument⟩ **2** : forceful, convincing — **contundentemente** *adv*

contusión *nf, pl* **-siones** : bruise, contusion

contusionar *vt* MAGULLAR : to bruise

contuvo, etc. → **contener**
conurbano *nm Arg* : suburbs *pl*
convalecencia *nf* : convalescence
convalecer {53} *vi* : to convalesce, to recover
convaleciente *adj & nmf* : convalescent
convalidar *vt* : to recognize, to validate
convección *nf, pl* **-ciones** : convection
convencer {86} *vt* : to convince, to persuade — **convencerse** *vr*
convencimiento *nm* : belief, conviction
convención *nf, pl* **-ciones** **1** : convention, conference **2** : pact, agreement **3** : convention, custom
convencional *adj* : conventional — **convencionalmente** *adv*
conveniencia *nf* **1** : convenience **2** : fitness, suitability, advisability
conveniente *adj* **1** : convenient **2** : suitable, advisable
convenio *nm* PACTO : agreement, pact
convenir {87} *vi* **1** : to be suitable, to be advisable **2** : to agree
conventillo *nm Arg, Uru* : tenement
convento *nm* **1** : convent **2** : monastery
convergencia *nf* : convergence
convergente *adj* : convergent, converging
converger {15} *or* **convergir** {35} *vi* **1** : to converge **2** ~ **en** : to concur on
conversación *nf, pl* **-ciones** : conversation
conversador, -dora *n* : conversationalist, talker
conversar *vi* : to converse, to talk
conversatorio *nm CA, Carib, Mex* : talk, discussion
conversión *nf, pl* **-siones** : conversion
converso, -sa *n* : convert
convertible *adj & nm* : convertible
convertidor *nm* : converter ⟨convertidor catalítico : catalytic converter⟩
convertir {76} *vt* **1** : to convert (someone) **2** : to convert (money, etc.) **3** ~ **en** : to turn (someone or something) into (something) — **convertirse** *vr* **1** : to convert **2** ~ **en** : to turn into, to become
convexo, -xa *adj* : convex
convicción *nf, pl* **-ciones** : conviction
convicto¹, -ta *adj* : convicted
convicto², -ta *n* : convict, prisoner
convidado, -da *n* : guest
convidar *vt* **1** INVITAR : to invite **2** : to offer
convincente *adj* : convincing — **convincentemente** *adv*
convivir *vi* **1** : to coexist **2** : to live together
convocar {72} *vt* : to convoke, to call together
convocatoria *nf* : summons, call
convoy *nm* : convoy
convulsión *nf, pl* **-siones** **1** : convulsion **2** : agitation, upheaval
convulsionar *vt* : to shake, to convulse — **convulsionarse** *vr*
convulsivo, -va *adj* : convulsive
conyugal *adj* : conjugal
cónyuge *nmf* : spouse, partner

coñac *nm* : cognac, brandy
cooperación *nf, pl* **-ciones** : cooperation
cooperador, -dora *adj* : cooperative
cooperar *vi* : to cooperate
cooperativa *nf* : cooperative, co-op
cooperativo, -va *adj* : cooperative
cooptar *vt* : to co-opt
coordenada *nf* : coordinate
coordinación *nf, pl* **-ciones** : coordination
coordinador, -dora *n* : coordinator
coordinar *vt* COMPAGINAR : to coordinate, to combine
copa *nf* **1** : wineglass, goblet **2** : drink ⟨irse de copas : to go out drinking⟩ **3** : cup, trophy **4** : top, crown (of a tree) **5 copas** *nfpl* : cups (suit in the Spanish deck of cards)
copar *vt* **1** : to take ⟨ya está copado el puesto : the job is already taken⟩ **2** : to fill, to crowd
copartícipe *nmf* : joint partner
copero, -ra *adj* : cup ⟨partido copero : cup game⟩
copete *nm* **1** : tuft (of hair) **2 estar hasta el copete** : to be completely fed up
copia *nf* **1** : copy **2** : imitation, replica **3 copia oculta** : blind carbon copy
copiadora *nf* : photocopier
copiar *vt* : to copy
copiloto *nmf* : copilot
copión, -piona *n, pl* **copiones** : copycat
copioso, -sa *adj* : copious, abundant
copla *nf* **1** : popular song or ballad **2** : stanza
copo *nm* **1** : snowflake **2 copos de avena** : rolled oats **3 copos de maíz** : cornflakes
coprotagonista *nmf* : co-star
cópula *nf* : copulation
copular *vi* : to copulate
coque *nm* : coke (fuel)
coqueta *nf* : dressing table
coquetear *vi* : to flirt
coqueteo *nm* : flirting
coqueto¹, -ta *adj* : flirtatious
coqueto², -ta *n* : flirt
coraje *nm* **1** VALOR : valor, courage **2** IRA : anger ⟨darle coraje a alguien : to make someone angry⟩
corajudo, -da *adj* : brave
coral¹ *adj* : choral
coral² *nm* **1** : coral **2** : chorale
coral³ *nf* : choir
Corán *nm* **el Corán** : the Koran
coraza *nf* **1** : armor, armor plating **2** : shell (of an animal)
corazón *nm, pl* **-zones** **1** : heart ⟨de todo corazón : wholeheartedly⟩ ⟨de buen corazón : kindhearted⟩ **2** : core **3** : darling, sweetheart
corazonada *nf* : hunch, impulse
corbata *nf* : tie, necktie
corcel *nm* : steed, charger
corchete *nm* **1** : hook and eye, clasp **2** : square bracket
corcho *nm* : cork
corcholata *nf Mex* : cap, bottle top
corcovear *vi* : to buck

cordel *nm* : cord, string
cordero *nm* : lamb
cordial[1] *adj* : cordial, affable — **cordialmente** *adv*
cordial[2] *nm* : cordial (liqueur)
cordialidad *nf* : cordiality, warmth
cordillera *nf* : mountain range
córdoba *nf* : córdoba (Nicaraguan unit of currency)
cordón *nm, pl* **cordones** 1 : cord ⟨cordón umbilical : umbilical cord⟩ 2 : cordon
cordoncillo *nm* : piping (of clothing, etc.)
cordura *nf* 1 : sanity 2 : prudence, good judgment
coreano[1], **-na** *adj & n* : Korean
coreano[2] *nm* : Korean (language)
corear *vt* : to chant, to chorus
coreografía *nf* : choreography
coreografiar {85} *vt* : to choreograph
coreográfico, -ca *adj* : choreographic
coreógrafo, -fa *n* : choreographer
corista *nmf* 1 : chorister 2 : chorus girl *f*
cormorán *nm, pl* **-ranes** : cormorant
cornada *nf* : goring, butt (with the horns)
córnea *nf* : cornea
cornear *vt* : to gore
cornejo *nm* : dogwood (tree)
córner *nm* : corner kick
corneta *nf* : bugle, horn, cornet
cornisa *nf* : cornice
cornucopia *nf* : cornucopia
cornudo, -da *adj* : horned
coro *nm* 1 : choir 2 : chorus
corola *nf* : corolla
corolario *nm* : corollary
corona *nf* 1 : crown 2 : wreath, garland 3 : corona (in astronomy)
coronación *nf, pl* **-ciones** : coronation
coronar *vt* 1 : to crown 2 : to reach the top of, to culminate
coronario, -ria *adj* : coronary
coronel, -nela *n* : colonel
coronilla *nf* 1 : crown (of the head) 2 **estar hasta la coronilla** : to be completely fed up
corpiño *nm* 1 : bodice 2 *Arg* : brassiere, bra
corporación *nf, pl* **-ciones** : corporation
corporal *adj* : corporal, bodily
corporativo, -va *adj* : corporate
corpóreo, -rea *adj* : corporeal, physical
corpulencia *nf* : stoutness, sturdiness
corpulento, -ta *adj* : robust, stout, sturdy
corpúsculo *nm* : corpuscle
corral *nm* 1 : farmyard 2 : corral, pen, stockyard 3 *or* **corralito** : playpen
correa *nf* 1 : strap, belt 2 TRAÍLLA : leash
correcaminos *nms & pl* : roadrunner
corrección *nf, pl* **-ciones** 1 : correction 2 : correctness, propriety 3 : rebuke, reprimand 4 **corrección de pruebas** : proofreading 5 **corrección ortográfica** : spell-check
correccional *nm* REFORMATORIO : reform school
correctivo, -va *adj* : corrective ⟨lentes correctivos : corrective lenses⟩

correcto, -ta *adj* 1 : correct, right 2 : courteous, polite — **correctamente** *adv*
corrector, -tora *n* : proofreader
corrector automático *nm* : autocorrect
corrector ortográfico *nm* : spellchecker
corredizo, -za *adj* : sliding ⟨puerta corrediza : sliding door⟩ ⟨nudo corredizo : slipknot⟩
corredor[1], **-dora** *n* 1 : runner, racer 2 : agent, broker ⟨corredor de bolsa : stockbroker⟩
corredor[2] *nm* PASILLO : corridor, hallway
correduría *nf* → **corretaje**
corregir {28} *vt* 1 : to correct, to edit (text), to grade (exams) 2 : to reprimand 3 **corregir pruebas** : to proofread — **corregirse** *vr* : to reform, to mend one's ways
correlación *nf, pl* **-ciones** : correlation
correo *nm* 1 : mail 2 : post office 3 **correo aéreo** : airmail 4 **correo electrónico** : e-mail, email
correoso, -sa *adj* : leathery, rough
correr *vi* 1 : to run ⟨corrió a/hacia la puerta : he ran to/towards the door⟩ ⟨salí corriendo : I took off running⟩ 2 : to race (in sports) 3 : to rush ⟨¡corre, que se acaban! : hurry, they're almost gone/done!⟩ 4 : to flow, to run 5 **a todo correr** : at top speed, in a hurry — *vt* 1 : to run, to race in 2 : to move, to slide, to roll, to draw (curtains) 3 ~ **con** : to be responsible for ⟨correr con los gastos : to foot the bill⟩ 4 **correr peligro** : to be in danger 5 **correr un riesgo** : to run a risk — **correrse** *vr* 1 : to move along 2 : to run, to spill over
correspondencia *nf* 1 : correspondence, mail 2 : equivalence 3 : connection, interchange
corresponder *vi* 1 : to correspond ⟨corresponder a/con : to correspond to/with, to match, to fit⟩ 2 : to belong ⟨el título que le corresponde : the title that is rightfully hers⟩ 3 : to be the responsibility of ⟨no le corresponde intervenir : it's not his place to intervene⟩ 4 : to be appropriate, to be fitting ⟨como corresponde : as is appropriate⟩ 5 : to reciprocate — **corresponderse** *vr* : to write to each other
correspondiente *adj* : corresponding, respective
corresponsal *nmf* : correspondent
corretaje *nm* : brokerage
corretear *vi* 1 VAGAR : to loiter, to wander about 2 : to run around, to scamper about — *vt* : to pursue, to chase
correteo *nm* : running around
corrida *nf* 1 : run, dash 2 : bullfight
corrido[1], **-da** *adj* 1 : straight, continuous 2 : worldly, experienced
corrido[2] *nm* : Mexican narrative folk song
corriente[1] *adj* 1 : common, everyday 2 : current, present 3 *Mex* : cheap, trashy 4 **perro corriente** *Mex* : mutt
corriente[2] *nf* 1 : current ⟨corriente alterna : alternating current⟩ ⟨corriente

continua : direct current⟩ **2** : draft **3** TENDENCIA : tendency, trend
corrillo *nm* : small group, clique
corro *nm* **1** : ring, circle (of people)
corroboración *nf, pl* **-ciones** : corroboration
corroborar *vt* : to corroborate
corroer {69} *vt* **1** : to corrode **2** : to erode, to wear away
corromper *vt* **1** : to corrupt **2** : to rot — **corromperse** *vr*
corrompido, -da *adj* CORRUPTO : corrupt, rotten
corrosión *nf, pl* **-siones** : corrosion
corrosivo, -va *adj* : corrosive
corrugar {52} *vt* : to corrugate — **corrugación** *nf*
corrupción *nf, pl* **-ciones 1** : decay **2** : corruption
corruptela *nf* : corruption, abuse of power
corruptible *adj* : corruptible
corrupto, -ta *adj* CORROMPIDO : corrupt
corsé *nm* : corset
cortacésped *nm Spain* : lawn mower
cortada *nf* : cut, gash
cortador, -dora *n* : cutter
cortadora *nf* : cutter, slicer
cortadura *nf* : cut, slash
oortafuegos *nms & pl* **1** : firebreak **2** : firewall (program)
cortante *adj* : cutting, sharp
cortar *vt* **1** : to cut ⟨lo cortó en dos : he cut it in half⟩ ⟨cortar en pedazos : to cut into pieces⟩ ⟨cortar en rebanadas/trozos (etc.) : to slice⟩ ⟨cortar leña : to chop wood⟩ ⟨cortar el pasto : to mow the lawn, to cut the grass⟩ **2** CERCENAR : to cut off, to sever **3** TALAR : to cut down, to chop down **4** RECORTAR : to cut out, to clip (coupons, etc.) **5** EDITAR : to cut, to edit **6** INTERRUMPIR : to cut off, to interrupt **7** BLOQUEAR, CERRAR : to block (off), to close (off) **8** : to curdle (milk) — *vi* **1** : to cut **2** : to break up ⟨cortar con alguien : to break up with someone⟩ **3** : to hang up (the telephone) — **cortarse** *vr* **1** : to cut oneself ⟨cortarse el pelo : to cut one's hair⟩ **2** : to be cut off **3** : to sour, to separate (of milk)
cortaúñas *nms & pl* : nail clippers
corte[1] *nm* **1** : cut, cutting ⟨corte de pelo : haircut⟩ **2** : cut (of clothes) **3** : cutoff, interruption ⟨corte comercial/publicitario : commercial break⟩ ⟨corte de luz, corte de energía eléctrica : power failure⟩
corte[2] *nf* **1** : court ⟨corte suprema : supreme court⟩ **2 hacer la corte a** : to court, to woo
cortejar *vt* GALANTEAR : to court, to woo
cortejo *nm* **1** GALANTEO : courtship **2** : retinue, entourage
cortés *adj* : courteous, polite — **cortésmente** *adv*
cortesano[1]**, -na** *adj* : courtly
cortesano[2]**, -na** *n* : courtier
cortesía *nf* **1** : courtesy, politeness **2 de ∼** : complimentary, free

corteza *nf* **1** : bark **2** : crust **3** : peel, rind **4** : cortex ⟨corteza cerebral : cerebral cortex⟩
cortijo *nm* : farmhouse
cortina *nf* : curtain
cortisona *nf* : cortisone
corto[1]**, -ta** *adj* **1** : short (in length or duration) **2** : scarce **3** : timid, shy **4 corto de vista** : nearsighted
corto[2] *nm* → **cortometraje**
cortocircuito *nm* : short circuit
cortometraje *nm* : short (film)
corvejón *nm, pl* **-jones** JARRETE : hock
corvo, -va *adj* : curved, bent
cosa *nf* **1** : thing, object **2** : matter, affair **3 otra cosa** : anything else, something else
cosecha *nf* : harvest, crop
cosechador, -dora *n* : harvester, reaper
cosechadora *nf* : harvester (machine)
cosechar *vt* **1** : to harvest, to reap **2** : to win, to earn, to garner — *vi* : to harvest
coser *vt* **1** : to sew **2** : to stitch up — *vi* : to sew
cosmético[1]**, -ca** *adj* : cosmetic
cosmético[2] *nm* : cosmetic
cósmico, -ca *adj* : cosmic
cosmonauta *nmf* : cosmonaut
cosmopolita *adj & nmf* : cosmopolitan
cosmos *nm* : cosmos
cosquillas *nfpl* **1** : tickling **2 hacer cosquillas** : to tickle
cosquilleo *nm* : tickling sensation, tingle
cosquilloso, -sa *adj* : ticklish
costa *nf* **1** : coast, shore **2** : cost ⟨a toda costa : at all costs⟩ ⟨a costa de : at the expense of⟩
costado *nm* **1** : side **2 al costado** : alongside
costal *nm* **1** : sack **2 ser harina de otro costal** → **harina**
costanera *nf* : boardwalk, waterfront path
costar {19} *v* : to cost ⟨¿cuánto cuesta? : how much does it cost?⟩
costarricense *adj & nmf* : Costa Rican
costarriqueño, -ña → **costarricense**
coste → **costo**
costear *vt* : to pay for, to finance
costero, -ra *adj* : coastal, coast
costilla *nf* **1** : rib **2** : chop, cutlet **3** *fam* : better half, wife
costo *nm* **1** : cost, price **2 costo de vida** : cost of living
costoso, -sa *adj* : costly, expensive
costra *nf* **1** : crust **2** POSTILLA : scab
costumbre *nf* **1** : custom **2** HÁBITO : habit
costura *nf* **1** : seam **2** : sewing, dressmaking **3 alta costura** : haute couture
costurera *nf* : seamstress *f*
costurero *nm* : sewing box
cota *nf* **1** : altitude **2** : level ⟨su máxima cota : its maximum level⟩
cotejar *vt* : to compare, to collate
cotejo *nm* **1** : comparison **2** : match, game
cotidiano, -na *adj* : daily, everyday ⟨la vida cotidiana : daily life⟩
cotilla *nmf Spain fam* : gossip, gossiper

cotización *nf, pl* **-ciones** **1** : market price **2** : quote, estimate

cotizado, -da *adj* : in demand, sought after

cotizar {21} *vt* : to quote, to value — **cotizarse** *vr* : to be worth

coto *nm* **1** : enclosure, reserve **2 poner coto a** : to put a stop to

cotonete *nf Mex* : (cotton) swab

cotorra *nf* **1** : small parrot **2** *fam* : chatterbox

cotorrear *vi fam* : to chatter, to gab, to blab

cotorreo *nm fam* : chatter, prattle

cowboy [kao'boi] *nm, pl* **-boys** [kao'bois] : cowboy

coyote *nm* **1** : coyote **2** *Mex fam* : smuggler (of illegal immigrants)

coyuntura *nf* **1** ARTICULACIÓN : joint **2** : occasion, moment

coz *nf, pl* **coces** : kick (of an animal)

CPU [sepe'u] *nmf* : CPU

crac *nm, pl* **cracs** : crash (of the stock market)

crack *nm* : crack (cocaine)

cozamos, etc. → **cocer**

craneal *adj* : cranial

craneano, -na *adj* : cranial

cráneo *nf* : cranium, skull — **craneano, -na** *adj*

cráter *nm* : crater

crayón *nm, pl* **-yones** : crayon

creación *nf, pl* **-ciones** : creation

creador[1], -dora *adj* : creative, creating

creador[2], -dora *n* : creator

crear *vt* **1** : to create, to cause **2** : to originate

creatividad *nf* : creativity

creativo, -va *adj* : creative — **creativamente** *adv*

creces *nfpl* **con creces** ⟨cumple con creces las expectativas : it more than meets expectations⟩ ⟨superar con creces : to greatly exceed⟩ ⟨pagar con creces : to pay dearly (for)⟩

crecer {53} *vi* **1** : to grow **2** : to increase, to grow (in number, etc.)

crecida *nf* : flooding, floodwater

crecido, -da *adj* **1** : grown, grown-up **2** : large (of numbers)

creciente *adj* **1** : growing, increasing **2 luna creciente** : waxing moon

crecimiento *nm* **1** : growth **2** : increase

credencial *adj* **cartas credenciales** : credentials

credenciales *nfpl* : documents, documentation, credentials ⟨credenciales de acceso/usuario : login/user credentials⟩

credibilidad *nf* : credibility

crediticio, -cia *adj* : credit

crédito *nm* : credit

credo *nm* : creed, credo

credulidad *nf* : credulity

crédulo, -la *adj* : credulous, gullible

creencia *nf* : belief

creer {20} *v* **1** : to believe ⟨creer en : to believe in⟩ **2** : to think, to suppose ⟨creo que sí : I think so⟩ ⟨creo que no : I don't think so⟩ ⟨no creo que sea necesario : I don't think it's necessary⟩ **3 ¡ya lo creo!** : of course!, indeed! — **creerse** *vr* **1** : to believe, to think **2** : to regard oneself as ⟨se cree muy guapo : he thinks he's so handsome⟩

creíble *adj* : believable, credible

creído, -da *adj* **1** *fam* : conceited **2** : confident, sure

crema *nf* **1** : cream ⟨crema batida : whipped cream⟩ **2 la crema y nata** : the pick of the crop

cremación *nf, pl* **-ciones** : cremation

cremallera *nf* : zipper

cremar *vt* : to cremate

crematorio *nm* : crematorium

cremoso, -sa *adj* : creamy

crepa *nf Mex* : crepe (pancake)

crepe *or* **crep** *nmf* : crepe (pancake)

crepé *nm* **1** → **crespón** **2 papel crepé** : crepe paper

crepúsculo *nm* : twilight

crescendo *nm* : crescendo

crespo, -pa *adj* : curly, frizzy

crespón *nm, pl* **crespones** : crepe (fabric)

cresta *nf* **1** : crest **2** : comb (of a rooster)

creta *nf* : chalk (mineral)

cretino, -na *n* **1** : cretin *often offensive* **2** : idiot, moron, cretin

creyente[1] *adj* : faithful ⟨personas creyentes : believers⟩

creyente[2] *nmf* : believer

creyó, etc. → **creer**

crezca, etc. → **crecer**

cría *nf* **1** : breeding, rearing **2** : young **3** : litter

criadero *nm* : hatchery

criado[1], -da *adj* **1** : raised, brought up **2 bien criado** : well-bred

criado[2], -da *n* : servant, maid *f*

criador, -dora *n* : breeder

crianza *nf* : upbringing, rearing

criar {85} *vt* **1** : to breed **2** : to bring up, to raise — **criarse** *vr* : to grow up

criatura *nf* **1** : baby, child **2** : creature

criba *nf* : sieve, screen

cribar *vt* : to sift

cric *nm, pl* **crics** : jack

cricket *nm* : cricket (sport)

crimen *nm, pl* **crímenes** : crime

criminal *adj & nmf* : criminal

criminalidad *nf* : crime ⟨alta criminalidad : high crime rates⟩

crin *nf* **1** : mane **2** : horsehair

crío, cría *n Spain* : kid

criollo[1], -lla *adj* **1** : Creole **2** : native, national ⟨comida criolla : native cuisine⟩

criollo[2], -lla *n* : Creole

criollo[3] *nm* : Creole (language)

cripta *nf* : crypt

críptico, -ca *adj* **1** : cryptic, coded **2** : enigmatic, cryptic

criptodivisa → **criptomoneda**

criptomoneda *nf* : cryptocurrency

criptón *nm* : krypton

críquet *nm* : cricket (game)

crisálida *nf* : chrysalis, pupa

crisantemo *nm* : chrysanthemum

crisis *nf* **1** : crisis **2 crisis nerviosa** : nervous breakdown

crisma *nf fam* : head ⟨romperle la crisma a alguien : to knock someone's block off⟩

crismas → **christmas**

crisol *nm* **1** : crucible **2** : melting pot

crispar *vt* **1** : to cause to contract **2** : to irritate, to set on edge ⟨eso me crispa : that gets on my nerves⟩ — **crisparse** *vr* : to tense up

cristal *nm* **1** VIDRIO : glass, piece of glass **2** : crystal

cristalería *nf* **1** : glassware shop **2** : glassware, crystal

cristalino¹, -na *adj* : crystalline, clear

cristalino² *nm* : lens (of the eye)

cristalizar {21} *vi* : to crystallize — **cristalización** *nf*

cristiandad *nf* : Christendom

cristianismo *nm* : Christianity

cristiano, -na *adj & n* : Christian

Cristo *nm* : Christ

criterio *nm* **1** : criterion **2** : judgment, sense

crítica *nf* **1** : criticism **2** : review, critique

criticar {72} *vt* : to criticize

crítico¹, -ca *adj* : critical — **críticamente** *adv*

crítico², -ca *n* : critic

criticón¹, -cona *adj, mpl* **-cones** *fam* : hypercritical

criticón², -cona *n, mpl* **-cones** *fam* : faultfinder, critic

croar *vi* : to croak

croata *adj & nmf* : Croatian

crocante *adj* : crunchy

croché *or* **crochet** *nm* : crochet

croissant [krwa'san, -'zan] *nm, pl* **croissants** [krwa'sans, -'zans] : croissant

crol *nm* : crawl (in swimming)

cromático, -ca *adj* : chromatic

cromo *nm* **1** : chromium, chrome **2** : picture card, sports card

cromosoma *nm* : chromosome

crónica *nf* **1** : news report **2** : chronicle, history

crónico, -ca *adj* : chronic

cronista *nmf* **1** : reporter, newscaster **2** HISTORIADOR : chronicler, historian

cronograma *nm* : schedule, timetable

cronología *nf* : chronology

cronológico, -ca *adj* : chronological — **cronológicamente** *adv*

cronometrador, -dora *n* : timekeeper

cronometrar *vt* : to time, to clock

cronómetro *nm* : chronometer

croquet *nm* : croquet

croqueta *nf* : croquette

croquis *nm* : rough sketch

cruasán *nm, pl* **cruasanes** → **croissant**

cruce¹, etc. → **cruzar**

cruce² *nm* **1** : crossing, cross **2** : crossroads, intersection ⟨cruce peatonal : crosswalk⟩

crucero *nm* **1** : cruise **2** : cruiser, warship **3** *Mex* : intersection

crucial *adj* : crucial — **crucialmente** *adv*

crucificar {72} *vt* : to crucify

crucifijo *nm* : crucifix

crucifixión *nf, pl* **-fixiones** : crucifixion

crucigrama *nm* : crossword puzzle

cruda *nf Mex fam* : hangover

crudeza *nf* : harshness

crudo¹, -da *adj* **1** : raw **2** : crude, harsh

crudo² *nm* : crude oil

cruel *adj* : cruel — **cruelmente** *adv*

crueldad *nf* : cruelty ⟨la crueldad del tirano : the tyrant's cruelty⟩ ⟨las crueldades de la guerra : the cruelties of war⟩

cruento, -ta *adj* : bloody

crujido *nm* **1** : rustling **2** : creaking **3** : crackling (of a fire) **4** : crunching

crujiente *adj* : crunchy, crisp

crujir *vi* **1** : to rustle **2** : to creak, to crack **3** : to crunch

crup *nm* : croup

crustáceo *nm* : crustacean

crutón *nm, pl* **crutones** : crouton

cruz *nf, pl* **cruces** : cross

cruza *nf* : cross (hybrid)

cruzada *nf* : crusade

cruzado¹, -da *adj* : crossed

cruzado² *nm* **1** : crusader **2** : Brazilian unit of currency

cruzar {21} *vt* **1** : to cross ⟨cruzar la calle : to cross the street⟩ ⟨cruzar las piernas : to cross one's legs⟩ **2** : to exchange (words, greetings) **3** : to cross, to interbreed — *vi* : to cross — **cruzarse** *vr* **1** : to intersect **2** : to meet, to pass each other **3 cruzarse de brazos** : to cross one's arms

cuaderno *nm* LIBRETA : notebook

cuadra *nf* **1** : city block **2** : stable

cuadrado¹, -da *adj* : square

cuadrado² *nm* : square ⟨elevar al cuadrado : to square (a number)⟩

cuadragésimo¹, -ma *adj* : fortieth, forty-

cuadragésimo², -ma *n* : fortieth, forty- (in a series)

cuadrante *nm* **1** : quadrant **2** : dial

cuadrar *vi* : to conform, to agree — *vt* : to square — **cuadrarse** *vr* : to stand at attention

cuadriculado *nm* : grid (on a map, etc.)

cuadrilátero *nm* **1** : quadrilateral **2** : ring (in sports)

cuadrilla *nf* : gang, team, group

cuadro *nm* **1** : square ⟨una blusa a cuadros : a checkered blouse⟩ **2** : painting, picture **3** : baseball diamond, infield **4** : panel, board, cadre

cuádruple *adj* : quadruple

cuadruplicar {72} *vt* : to quadruple — **cuadruplicarse** *vr*

cuajada *nf* : curd

cuajar *vi* **1** : to curdle **2** COAGULAR : to clot, to coagulate **3** : to set, to jell **4** : to be accepted ⟨su idea no cuajó : his idea didn't catch on⟩ — *vt* **1** : to curdle **2** ∼ **de** : to fill with

cual¹ *prep* : like, as

cual² *pron* **1 el cual, la cual, los cuales, las cuales** : who, whom, which ⟨la razón por la cual lo dije : the reason I said it⟩ **2 lo cual** : which ⟨se rió, lo cual me dio rabia : he laughed, which made me mad⟩ **3 cada cual** : everyone, everybody

cuál¹ *adj* : which, what ⟨¿cuáles libros? : which books?⟩

cuál² *pron* **1** (*in questions*) : which (one), what (one) ⟨¿cuál es el mejor? : which one is the best?⟩ ⟨¿cuál es tu apellido? : what is your last name?⟩ **2 cuál más, cuál menos** : some more, some less

cualidad *nf* : quality, trait

cualificado, -da *adj Spain* : qualified, trained

cualitativo, -va *adj* : qualitative — **cualitativamente** *adv*

cualquier *adj* → **cualquiera¹**

cualquiera¹ *cualquier* before nouns *adj, pl* **cualesquiera 1** : any, whichever ⟨cualquier persona : any person⟩ **2** : everyday, ordinary ⟨un hombre cualquiera : an ordinary man⟩

cualquiera² *pron, pl* **cualesquiera 1** : anyone, anybody, whoever **2** : whatever, whichever

cuán *adv* : how ⟨¡cuán feliz era! : how happy I was!⟩

cuando¹ *conj* **1** : when ⟨cuando llegó : when he arrived⟩ **2** : since, if ⟨cuando lo dices : if you say so⟩ **3 cuando más/menos** : at the most/least **4 de vez en cuando** : from time to time

cuando² *prep* : during, at the time of ⟨cuando la guerra : during the war⟩

cuándo *adv & conj* **1** : when ⟨¿cuándo llegará? : when will she arrive?⟩ ⟨no sabemos cuándo será : we don't know when it will be⟩ **2 ¿de cuándo acá?** : since when?, how come?

cuantía *nf* **1** : quantity, extent **2** : significance, import

cuántico, -ca *adj* : quantum ⟨teoría cuántica : quantum theory⟩

cuantificar {72} *vt* : to quantify

cuantioso, -sa *adj* **1** : abundant, considerable **2** : heavy, grave ⟨cuantiosos daños : heavy damage⟩

cuantitativo, -va *adj* : quantitative — **cuantitativamente** *adv*

cuanto¹ *adv* **1** : as much as ⟨come cuanto puedas : eat as much as you can⟩ **2 cuanto antes** : as soon as possible **3 en ~** : as soon as **4 en cuanto a** : as for, as regards

cuanto², -ta *adj* : as many, whatever ⟨llévate cuantas flores quieras : take as many flowers as you wish⟩

cuanto³, -ta *pron* **1** : as much as, all that, everything ⟨tengo cuanto deseo : I have all that I want⟩ **2 unos cuantos, unas cuantas** : a few

cuánto¹ *adv* : how much, how many ⟨¿a cuánto están las peras? : how much are the pears?⟩ ⟨no sé cuánto desean : I don't know how much they want⟩

cuánto², -ta *adj* : how much, how many ⟨¿cuántos niños tiene? : how many children do you have?⟩

cuánto³, -ta *pron* : how much, how many ⟨¿cuántos quieren participar? : how many want to take part?⟩ ⟨¿cuánto cuesta? : how much does it cost?⟩

cuáquero, -ra *adj & n* : Quaker

cuarenta *adj & nm* : forty — **cuarenta** *pron*

cuarentavo¹, -va *adj* : fortieth

cuarentavo² *adj & nm* : fortieth (fraction)

cuarentena *nf* **1** : group of forty **2** : quarantine

Cuaresma *nf* : Lent

cuarta *nf* : fourth (gear)

cuartear *vt* **1** : to quarter **2** : to divide up — **cuartearse** *vr* AGRIETARSE : to crack, to split

cuartel *nm* **1** : barracks, headquarters **2** : mercy ⟨una guerra sin cuartel : a merciless war⟩

cuartelazo *nm* : coup d'état

cuarteto *nm* : quartet

cuartilla *nf* : sheet (of paper)

cuarto¹, -ta *adj & n* : fourth ⟨la cuarta (persona) : the fourth (person)⟩ ⟨llegó la cuarta : she came in fourth (place)⟩ ⟨una/la cuarta parte de : a quarter of, a fourth of⟩

cuarto² *nm* **1** : quarter, fourth ⟨un cuarto de : a quarter of, a fourth of⟩ ⟨cuarto de galón : quart⟩ **2** HABITACIÓN : room

cuarto oscuro *nm* : darkroom

cuarzo *nm* : quartz

cuasi- *pref* : quasi-

cuate, -ta *n Mex* **1** : twin **2** *fam* : buddy, pal

cuatrero, -ra *n* : rustler

cuatrillizo, -za *n* : quadruplet

cuatro¹ *adj & nm* : four ⟨tiene cuatro años : she's four years old⟩ ⟨el cuatro de agosto : (on) the fourth of August, (on) August fourth⟩

cuatro² *pron* : four ⟨son cuatro : there are four of them⟩ ⟨son las cuatro y cuarto : it's four fifteen, it's (a) quarter after four⟩

cuatrocientos, -tas *adj & nm* : four hundred — **cuatrocientos** *pron*

cuba *nf* BARRIL : cask, barrel

cubano, -na *adj & n* : Cuban

cubertería *nf* : flatware, silverware

cubeta *nf* **1** : keg, cask **2** : bulb (of a thermometer) **3** *Mex* : bucket, pail

cúbico, -ca *adj* : cubic, cubed

cubículo *nm* : cubicle

cubierta *nf* **1** : covering **2** FORRO : cover, jacket (of a book) **3** : deck

cubierto¹ *pp* → **cubrir**

cubierto² *nm* **1** : cover, shelter ⟨bajo cubierto : under cover⟩ **2** : table setting **3** : utensil, piece of silverware

cubil *nm* : den, lair

cúbito *nm* : ulna

cubo *nm* **1** : cube **2** *Spain* BALDE : pail, bucket, can ⟨cubo de basura : garbage can⟩ **3** : hub (of a wheel)

cubrecama *nm* COLCHA : bedspread

cubrir {2} *vt* **1** : to cover ⟨cubierto de algo : covered in/with something⟩ **2** : to cover (costs, etc.) — **cubrirse** *vr*

cucaracha *nf* : cockroach, roach

cuchara *nf* : spoon

cucharada *nf* : spoonful

cucharadita *nf* : teaspoon, teaspoonful

cucharilla *or* **cucharita** *nf* : teaspoon

cucharón *nm, pl* **-rones** : ladle

cuchichear *vi* : to whisper

cuchicheo *nm* : whisper

cuchilla *nf* **1** : kitchen knife, cleaver **2** : blade ⟨cuchilla de afeitar : razor blade, (safety) razor⟩ **3** : crest, ridge

cuchillada *nf* : stab, knife wound

cuchillo *nm* : knife

cuclillas *nfpl* en ∼ : squatting, crouching

cuclillo *nm* : cuckoo

cuco[1], **-ca** *adj fam* : pretty, cute

cuco[2] *nm* **1** : cuckoo **2** *Arg, Chile, Peru, Uru fam* COCO : bogeyman

cucurucho *nm* : ice-cream cone

cuece, cueza etc. → cocer

cuela, cueza etc. → colar

cuelga, cuelgue etc. → colgar

cuello *nm* **1** : neck **2** : collar, neck (of a shirt) ⟨cuello en V : V-neck⟩ **3 cuello del útero** : cervix

cuenca *nf* **1** : river basin **2** : eye socket

cuenco *nm* : bowl, basin

cuenta[1], etc. → contar

cuenta[2] *nf* **1** : calculation, count **2** : account ⟨cuenta corriente : checking account⟩ ⟨cuenta de ahorro(s) : savings account⟩ ⟨cuenta de correo(s) electrónico(s), cuenta de email : e-mail account⟩ **3** : responsibility, liability ⟨corre por cuenta del gobierno : the government is footing the bill⟩ ⟨trabajar por cuenta propia : to be self-employed⟩ **4** : check, bill **5 a fin de cuentas** : in the end **6 darse cuenta** : to realize **7 en buenas cuentas** *Chile* : in short **8 por cuenta de** : on account of, because of **9 rendir cuentas** : to be held accountable **10 tener en cuenta** : to bear in mind **11 tomar en cuenta** : to take into account

cuentagotas *nfs & pl* **1** : dropper **2 con** ∼ : little by little

cuentakilómetros *nm* **1** : odometer **2** VELOCÍMETRO : speedometer

cuentista *nmf* **1** : short story writer **2** *fam* : liar, fibber

cuento *nm* **1** : story, tale **2 cuento chino** : tall tale **3 cuento de hadas** : fairy tale **4 sin** ∼ : countless

cuerda *nf* **1** : cord, rope, string **2 cuerdas vocales** : vocal cords **3 darle cuerda a algo** : to wind something up

cuerdo, -da *adj* : sane, sensible

cuerno *nm* **1** : horn, antler **2** : cusp (of the moon) **3** : horn (musical instrument)

cuero *nm* **1** : leather, hide **2 cuero cabelludo** : scalp

cuerpo *nm* **1** : body **2** : corps ⟨cuerpo policial : police force⟩

cuervo *nm* : crow, raven

cuesta[1], etc. → costar

cuesta[2] *nf* **1** : slope ⟨cuesta arriba : uphill⟩ **2 a cuestas** : on one's back

cuestión *nf, pl* **-tiones** ASUNTO, TEMA : matter, affair

cuestionable *adj* : questionable, dubious

cuestionamiento *nm* **1** : question, doubt ⟨hacer cuestionamientos a/sobre : to raise questions about⟩ **2** : questioning

cuestionar *vt* : to question

cuestionario *nm* **1** : questionnaire **2** : quiz

cueva *nf* : cave

cuidado *nm* **1** : care ⟨cuidado personal : self-care⟩ **2** : worry, concern **3 tener cuidado** : to be careful **4 ¡cuidado!** : watch out!, be careful!

cuidador, -dora *n* : caretaker

cuidadoso, -sa *adj* : careful, attentive — **cuidadosamente** *adv*

cuidar *vt* **1** : to take care of, to look after **2** : to pay attention to — *vi* **1** ∼ **de** : to look after **2 cuidar de que** : to make sure that — **cuidarse** *vr* : to take care of oneself

culata *nf* : butt (of a gun)

culatazo *nf* : kick, recoil

culebra *nf* SERPIENTE : snake

culebrón *nm, pl* **-brones** : soap, soap opera

culinario, -ria *adj* : culinary

culminante *adj* **punto culminante** : peak, high point, climax

culminar *vi* : to culminate — **culminación** *nf*

culo *nm* **1** *fam* : backside, behind **2** : bottom (of a glass)

culpa *nf* **1** : fault, blame ⟨echarle la culpa a alguien : to blame someone⟩ **2** : sin

culpabilidad *nf* : guilt

culpable[1] *adj* : guilty

culpable[2] *nmf* : culprit, guilty party

culpar *vt* : to blame

culposo, -sa *adj* : culpable, negligent

cultivable *adj* : arable

cultivado, -da *adj* **1** : cultivated, farmed **2** : cultured

cultivador, -dora *n* : grower

cultivar *vt* **1** : to cultivate **2** : to foster

cultivo *nm* **1** : cultivation, farming **2** : crop

culto[1], **-ta** *adj* : cultured, educated

culto[2] *nm* **1** : worship **2** : cult

cultura *nf* : culture

cultural *adj* : cultural — **culturalmente** *adv*

culturismo *nm* : bodybuilding

cumbre *nf* CIMA : top, peak, summit

cumpleañero, -ra *n* : birthday boy *m*, birthday girl *f*

cumpleaños *nms & pl* : birthday

cumplido[1], **-da** *adj* **1** : complete, full **2** : courteous, correct

cumplido[2] *nm* : compliment, courtesy ⟨por cumplido : out of courtesy⟩ ⟨andarse con cumplidos : to stand on ceremony⟩

cumplidor, -dora *adj* : reliable

cumplimentar *vt* **1** : to congratulate **2** : to carry out, to perform

cumplimiento *nm* **1** : completion, fulfillment **2** : performance

cumplir *vt* **1** : to accomplish, to carry out **2** : to comply with, to fulfill **3** : to attain, to reach ⟨su hermana cumple (los) 20 (años) el viernes : her sister will be 20 on Friday⟩ — *vi* **1** : to expire, to fall due **2** : to fulfill one's obligations ⟨cumplir con su deber : to do one's duty⟩ ⟨cumplir con su palabra : to keep one's word⟩ — **cumplirse** *vr* **1** : to come true, to be fulfilled ⟨se cumplieron

sus sueños : her dreams came true〉 **2**
: to run out, to expire
cúmulo *nm* **1** MONTÓN : heap, pile **2**
: cumulus
cuna *nf* **1** : cradle **2** : birthplace, origin
cundir *vi* **1** : to spread, to propagate (of
panic, etc.) **2** : to progress, to make
headway
cuneta *nf* : ditch (in a road), gutter
cuña *nf* : wedge
cuñado, -da *n* : brother-in-law *m,* sister-
in-law *f*
cuño *nm* : die (for stamping)
cuota *nf* **1** : fee, dues **2** : quota, share **3**
: installment, payment
cupé *nm* : coupe
cupo[1]**, etc.** → **caber**
cupo[2] *nm* **1** : quota, share **2** : capacity,
room
cupón *nm, pl* **cupones 1** : coupon,
voucher **2 cupón federal** : food stamp
cúpula *nf* : dome, cupola
cura[1] *nm* : priest
cura[2] *nf* **1** CURACIÓN, TRATAMIENTO
: cure, treatment **2** : dressing, bandage
curación *nf, pl* **-ciones** CURA, TRATA-
MIENTO : cure, treatment
curador, -dora *n* **1** : healer **2** CONSER-
VADOR : curator
curandero, -ra *nm* **1** : witch doctor **2**
: quack, charlatan
curar *vt* **1** : to cure, to heal **2** : to treat,
to dress **3** CURTIR : to tan **4** : to cure
(meat) — *vi* : to get well, to recover —
curarse *vr*
curativo, -va *adj* : healing
curiosear *vi* **1** : to snoop, to pry **2** : to
browse — *vt* : to look over, to check
curiosidad *nf* **1** : curiosity **2** : curio
curioso, -sa *adj* **1** : curious, inquisitive
2 : strange, unusual, odd — **curiosamente** *adv*
curita *nf* (*Curitas,* marca registrada)
: bandage, Band-Aid™

currículo → **currículum**
currículum *nm, pl* **-lums 1** : résumé, curriculum vitae **2** : curriculum, course of
study
curruca *nf* : warbler
curry [ˈkurri] *nm, pl* **-rries 1** : curry powder **2** : curry (dish)
cursar *vt* **1** : to attend (school), to take (a
course) **2** : to dispatch, to pass on
cursi *adj fam* : affected, pretentious
cursilería *nf* **1** : vulgarity, poor taste **2**
: pretentiousness
cursillo *nm* : short course
cursiva *nf* BASTARDILLA : italic type, italics *pl*
cursivo, -va *adj* : italic
curso *nm* **1** : course, direction **2**
: school year **3** : course, subject (in
school)
cursor *nm* : cursor
curtido, -da *adj* : weather-beaten, leathery (of skin)
curtidor, -dora *n* : tanner
curtiduría *nf* : tannery
curtir *vt* **1** : to tan **2** : to harden, to
weather — **curtirse** *vr*
curul *nf* ESCAÑO : seat (in a legislative
body)
curva *nf* : curve, bend
curvar *vt* : to bend
curvatura *nf* : curvature
curvilíneo, -nea *adj* : shapely
curvo, -va *adj* : curved, bent
cúspide *nf* : zenith, apex, peak
custodia *nf* : custody
custodiar *vt* : to guard, to look after
custodio, -dia *n* : keeper, guardian
cutáneo, -nea *adj* : skin, cutaneous
cúter *nm* : cutter (boat)
cutícula *nf* : cuticle
cutis *nms & pl* : skin, complexion
cuyo, -ya *adj* **1** : whose, of whom, of
which **2 en cuyo caso** : in which case

D

d *nf* : fifth letter of the Spanish alphabet
dactilar *adj* **huellas dactilares** : finger-
prints
dádiva *nf* : gift, handout
dadivoso, -sa *adj* : generous
dado, -da *adj* **1** : given **2 dado que**
: given that, since
dados *nmpl* : dice
daga *nf* : dagger
dalia *nf* : dahlia
dálmata *nm* : dalmatian
daltónico, -ca *adj* : color-blind
daltonismo *nm* : color blindness
dama *nf* **1** : lady **2 damas** *nfpl* : checkers
damasco *nm* : damask
damisela *nf* : damsel
damnificado, -da *n* : victim (of a disaster)
dance, etc. → **danzar**
dandi *nm* : dandy

danés[1]**, -nesa** *adj* : Danish
danés[2]**, -nesa** *n, mpl* **daneses** : Dane,
Danish person
danza *nf* : dance, dancing 〈danza
folklórica : folk dance〉
danzante, -ta *n* BAILARÍN : dancer
danzar {21} *v* BAILAR : to dance
dañar *vt* **1** : to damage, to spoil **2** : to
harm, to hurt — **dañarse** *vr*
dañino, -na *adj* : harmful
daño *nm* **1** : damage **2** : harm, injury
〈daños colaterales : collateral damages〉
3 hacer daño a : to harm, to damage **4
hacerse daño** : to hurt oneself 〈me he
hecho daño en la mano : I've hurt my
hand〉 **5 daños y perjuicios** : damages
dar {22} *vt* **1** : to give (a gift, a donation,
etc.) **2** ENTREGAR : to give, to hand
(over) **3** PROPORCIONAR : to give (sup-

plies, support, etc.) ⟨dale una oportunidad : give him a chance⟩ **4** CONCEDER : to give (time, permission, etc.) **5** ADMINISTRAR : to give (medicine, etc.) **6** EXPRESAR : to give, to express ⟨dales recuerdos de mi parte : give them my regards⟩ ⟨darle las gracias a : to thank⟩ ⟨dar su palabra : to give one's word⟩ **7** MOSTRAR : to give (an indication, etc.) **8** OFRECER : to give (a reason, etc.) **9** : to give (an impression, etc.) **10** GOLPEAR : to hit ⟨me dio en la cara : it hit me in the face⟩ **11** : to strike ⟨el reloj dio las doce : the clock struck twelve⟩ **12** PRODUCIR : to yield, to produce **13** : to give (a performance, a party, etc.), to show (a film, etc.) **14** : to do (an action) ⟨dar un grito : to give a shout⟩ ⟨dar un paseo : to go for a walk⟩ ⟨me dio un beso : she gave me a kiss⟩ **15** VENDER : to give, to sell **16** CAUSAR : to cause ⟨darle miedo/sed (etc.) a alguien : to make someone frightened/thirsty (etc.)⟩ ⟨me da risa : it makes me laugh, it's funny⟩ ⟨le da problemas/esperanza : it gives her trouble/hope⟩ **17** APLICAR : to apply ⟨dale una mano de pintura : give it a coat of paint⟩ ⟨dar un impulso a : to give a boost to⟩ **18** CONFERIR : to give, to impart (a quality) **19 dar como/por** : to regard as, to consider ⟨dar por hecho : to take for granted⟩ ⟨dar a alguien por muerto : to give someone up for dead⟩ — *vi* **1** : to provide (enough) ⟨no me da para dos pasajes : I don't have enough for two fares⟩ ⟨no me da tiempo : I don't have time⟩ ⟨esto no da para más : this can't go on⟩ ⟨a todo lo que da : at full speed/power (etc.)⟩ **2** : to hand something over ⟨dame : give it to me⟩ **3** : to deal (in cards) **4** : to hit ⟨dar en el blanco : to hit the target⟩ **5** : to give a result ⟨dio positivo al virus : he tested positive for the virus⟩ **6 dale que dale** *or Spain* **dale que te pego** ⟨están dale que dale con el teléfono : they're constantly on the phone⟩ ⟨y ella dale que te pego con sus problemas : and she was going on and on about her problems⟩ **7 darle a** : to press (a button, etc.), to turn (a dial, etc.) **8 ~ a/sobre** : to overlook, to look out on **9 ~ con** : to run into **10 ~ con** : to hit upon (an idea) **11 dar de sí** : to give, to stretch (of clothing, etc.) — **darse** *vr* **1** : to consider oneself ⟨se dio por vencido : he gave in⟩ **2** : to occur, to arise **3** : to grow, to come up **4 ~ con/contra** : to hit oneself against, to bump into **5 dárselas de** : to boast about ⟨se las da de muy listo : he thinks he's very smart⟩ **6 dársele bien algo a uno** : to be good at something ⟨se le dan muy bien las matemáticas : she's very good at math⟩

dardo *nm* : dart

dársena *nf* : dock

data *nf* **1** : byline **2 de larga data** : long-standing

datar *vt* : to date — *vi* **~ de** : to date from, to date back to

dátil *nm* : date (fruit)

dato *nm* **1** : fact, piece of information **2 datos** *nmpl* : data, information

dé → **dar**

de¹ *nf* : (letter) d

de² *prep* **1** (*indicating connection or belonging*) : of ⟨la casa de Pepe : Pepe's house⟩ ⟨el cuatro de abril : the fourth of April, April fourth⟩ ⟨la reina de Inglaterra : the Queen of England⟩ ⟨el mejor de todos : the best of all⟩ **2** (*indicating a quality or condition*) : of ⟨un asunto de gran importancia : a matter of great importance⟩ ⟨un niño de tres años : a three-year-old boy⟩ ⟨estoy de vacaciones : I'm on vacation⟩ **3** (*indicating content, material, or quantity*) : of ⟨un vaso de agua : a glass of water⟩ ⟨una casa de ladrillo : a brick house, a house made of brick⟩ ⟨una gran cantidad de lluvia : a large amount of rain⟩ **4** (*indicating a source or starting point*) : from ⟨es de Managua : she's from Managua⟩ ⟨salió del edificio : he left the building⟩ **5** (*with time*) : in, at ⟨a las tres de la mañana : at three in the morning⟩ ⟨salen de noche : they go out at night⟩ **6** (*with numbers*) : than ⟨más de tres : more than three⟩ **7** (*indicating a particular example*) : of ⟨el mes de junio : the month of June⟩ **8** (*indicating a cause*) ⟨morirse de hambre : to be dying of/from starvation⟩ ⟨gritar de alegría : to shout with/for joy⟩ **9** : about ⟨libros de historia : history books, books about history⟩ **10** (*indicating purpose*) : for ⟨ropa de deporte : sportswear, athletic clothes⟩ ⟨máquina de coser : sewing machine⟩ **11** : as ⟨ella trabaja de camionera : she works as a truck driver⟩ **12** : if ⟨de haberlo sabido : if I had known⟩ ⟨de continuar esta situación : if this situation continues⟩

deambular *vi* : to wander, to roam

deán *nm, pl* **deanes** : dean (of clergy)

debacle *nf* : debacle

debajo *adv* **1** : underneath, below, on the bottom **2 ~ de** : under, underneath **3 por ~** : below, beneath

debate *nm* : debate

debatir *vt* : to debate, to discuss — **debatirse** *vr* : to struggle

debe *nm* : debit column, debit

deber¹ *vt* : to owe — *v aux* **1** : must, have to ⟨debo ir : I must go⟩ ⟨no debes hacerlo : you mustn't do it⟩ **2** : should, ought to ⟨deberías buscar trabajo : you should look for work⟩ ⟨debería darte vergüenza : you ought to be ashamed of yourself⟩ **3** (*expressing probability*) : must ⟨debe ser muy tarde : it must be very late⟩ — **deberse** *vr* **1 ~ a** : to be due to **2 ~ a** : to have a responsibility towards

deber² *nm* **1** OBLIGACIÓN : duty, obligation **2 deberes** *nmpl Spain* : homework

debidamente *adv* : properly, duly

debido, -da *adj* **1** : right, proper, due **2 ~ a** : due to, owing to

débil *adj* : weak, feeble — **débilmente** *adv*

debilidad *nf* : weakness, debility, feebleness

debilitamiento *nm* : weakening

debilitar *vt* : to debilitate, to weaken — **debilitarse** *vr*

debilucho¹, -cha *adj* : weak, frail

debilucho², -cha *n* : weakling

debitar *vt* : to debit

débito *nm* **1** DEUDA : debt **2** : debit

de bruces *adv* : facedown, face-first ⟨caer de bruces : to fall flat on one's face⟩

debut [de'but] *nm, pl* **debuts** : debut

debutante¹ *nmf* : beginner, newcomer

debutante² *nf* : debutante *f*

debutar *vi* : to debut, to make a debut

década *nf* DECENIO : decade

decadencia *nf* **1** : decadence **2** : decline

decadente *adj* **1** : decadent **2** : declining

decaer {13} *vi* **1** : to decline, to decay, to deteriorate **2** FLAQUEAR : to weaken, to flag

decaído, -da *adj fam* : depressed, sad

decaiga, etc. → **decaer**

decano, -na *n* **1** : dean **2** : senior member

decapitar *vt* : to decapitate, to behead

decayó, etc. → **decaer**

decena *nf* : group of ten

decencia *nf* : decency

decenio *nm* DÉCADA : decade

decente *adj* : decent — **decentemente** *adv*

decepción *nf, pl* **-ciones** : disappointment, letdown

decepcionante *adj* : disappointing

decepcionar *vt* : to disappoint, to let down — **decepcionarse** *vr*

deceso *nm* DEFUNCIÓN : death, passing

dechado *nm* **1** : sampler (of embroidery) **2** : model, paragon

decibelio *or* **decibel** *nm* : decibel

decidido, -da *adj* : decisive, determined, resolute — **decididamente** *adv*

decidir *vt* **1** : to decide ⟨decidí ir : I decided to go⟩ ⟨no he decidido nada : I haven't made a decision⟩ **2** : to make (someone) decide, to persuade (someone) — *vi* : to decide ⟨decidir sobre : to make a decision about⟩ — **decidirse** *vr* : to make up one's mind ⟨decidirse por : to decide on, to choose⟩

décima *nf* : tenth (fraction)

decimal *adj* : decimal

décimo¹, -ma *adj & n* : tenth ⟨la décima (persona) : the tenth (person)⟩ ⟨una/la décima parte de : a tenth of, one tenth of⟩ ⟨en décimo lugar : in tenth place⟩

décimo² *nm Spain* → **décima**

decimoctavo¹, -va *adj* : eighteenth

decimoctavo², -va *n* : eighteenth (in a series)

decimocuarto¹, -ta *adj* : fourteenth

decimocuarto², -ta *n* : fourteenth (in a series)

decimonoveno¹, -na *or* **decimonono, -na** *adj* : nineteenth

decimonoveno², -na *or* **decimonono, -na** *n* : nineteenth (in a series)

decimoquinto¹, -ta *adj* : fifteenth

decimoquinto², -ta *n* : fifteenth (in a series)

decimoséptimo¹, -ma *adj* : seventeenth

decimoséptimo², -ma *n* : seventeenth (in a series)

decimosexto¹, -ta *adj* : sixteenth

decimosexto², -ta *n* : sixteenth (in a series)

decimotercero¹, -ra *adj* : thirteenth

decimotercero², -ra *n* : thirteenth (in a series)

decir¹ {23} *vt* **1** : to say ⟨dice que no irá : she says she won't go⟩ **2** : to tell ⟨dime lo que estás pensando : tell me what you're thinking⟩ ⟨ya te lo decía yo : I told you so⟩ **3** : to tell, to say ⟨haz lo que te digo : do as I say, do what I tell you⟩ ⟨te dije que callaras : I told you to be quiet⟩ **4** : to speak, to talk ⟨no digas tonterías : don't talk nonsense⟩ **5** : to call ⟨me dicen Rosy : they call me Rosy⟩ **6 como quien dice** : so to speak **7 es decir** : that is to say **8 dicho y hecho** : no sooner said than done **9 (o) mejor dicho** : (or) rather **10 ¡no me digas!** : you're kidding!, you don't say! **11 por así decirlo** : so to speak **12 querer decir** : to mean ⟨¿qué quiere decir? : what do you mean?⟩ — **decirse** *vr* **1** : to say to oneself **2** : to be said ⟨¿cómo se dice "lápiz" en francés? : how do you say "pencil" in French?⟩

decir² *nm* DICHO : saying, expression

decisión *nf, pl* **-siones** **1** : decision, choice ⟨tomar una decisión : to make a decision⟩ **2** : decisiveness

decisivo, -va *adj* : decisive, conclusive — **decisivamente** *adv*

declamar *vi* : to declaim — *vt* : to recite

declaración *nf, pl* **-ciones** **1** : declaration, statement ⟨hacer una declaración : to issue a statement⟩ **2** TESTIMONIO : deposition, testimony ⟨prestar declaración : to give evidence, to testify⟩ **3 declaración de derechos** : bill of rights **4 declaración jurada** : affidavit **5 declaración de la renta** : income tax return

declarado, -da *adj* : professed, open — **declaradamente** *adv*

declarar *vt* : to declare, to state ⟨declarar culpable : to find guilty⟩ ⟨declarar inocente : to find not guilty⟩ — *vi* ATESTIGUAR : to testify — **declararse** *vr* **1** : to declare oneself (to be) ⟨declararse en huelga : to go on strike⟩ ⟨declararse en bancarrota : to declare bankruptcy⟩ **2** : to confess one's love **3** : to plead (in court) ⟨declararse culpable : to plead guilty⟩ ⟨declararse inocente : to plead not guilty⟩ **4** : to testify **5** : to break out (of a fire, etc.)

declinar *vt* : to decline, to turn down — *vi* **1** : to draw to a close **2** : to diminish, to decline

declive *nm* **1** DECADENCIA : decline **2** : slope, incline

decodificador *nm* : decoder

decolar *vi Chile, Col, Ecua* : to take off (of an airplane)

decolorar *vt* : to bleach — **decolorarse** *vr* : to fade

decomisar *vt* CONFISCAR : to seize, to confiscate

decomiso *nm* : seizure, confiscation

decoración *nf, pl* **-ciones** **1** : decoration **2** : decor **3** : stage set, scenery

decorado *nm* : stage set, scenery

decorador, -dora *n* : decorator

decorar *vt* ADORNAR : to decorate, to adorn

decorativo, -va *adj* : decorative, ornamental

decoro *nm* : decorum, propriety

decoroso, -sa *adj* : decent, proper, respectable

decrecer {53} *vi* : to decrease, to wane, to diminish — **decreciente** *adj*

decrecimiento *nm* : decrease, decline

decrépito, -ta *adj* : decrepit

decretar *vt* : to decree, to order

decreto *nm* : decree

decúbito *nm* : horizontal position ⟨en decúbito prono/supino : prone/supine⟩

dedal *nm* : thimble

dedalera *nf* DIGITAL : foxglove

dedicación *nf, pl* **-ciones** : dedication, devotion

dedicar {72} *vt* : to dedicate, to devote — **dedicarse** *vr* ~ **a** : to devote oneself to, to engage in

dedicatoria *nf* : dedication (of a book, song, etc.)

dedillo *nm* **conocer algo al dedillo** : to know something backward and forward

dedo *nm* **1** : finger ⟨dedo meñique : little finger⟩ ⟨no mover un dedo : not to lift a finger⟩ ⟨hacer dedo, ir a dedo : to hitchhike⟩ ⟨poner el dedo en la llaga : to hit a nerve⟩ **2 dedo del pie** : toe

deducción *nf, pl* **-ciones** : deduction

deducible *adj* : deductible

deducir {61} *vt* **1** INFERIR : to deduce **2** DESCONTAR : to deduct

defecar {72} *vi* : to defecate — **defecación** *nf*

defecto *nm* **1** : defect, flaw, shortcoming **2 en su defecto** : lacking that, in the absence of that

defectuoso, -sa *adj* : defective, faulty

defender {56} *vt* : to defend, to protect — **defenderse** *vr* **1** : to defend oneself **2** : to get by, to know the basics ⟨su inglés no es perfecto pero se defiende : his English isn't perfect but he gets by⟩

defendible *adj* : tenable

defensa[1] *nf* **1** : defense ⟨salió en nuestra defensa : he came to our defense⟩ ⟨actuar en defensa propia : to act in self-defense⟩ ⟨clase de defensa personal : self-defense class⟩ **2** : defense (in sports)

defensa[2] *nmf* : defender, back (in sports)

defensiva *nf* : defensive, defense

defensivo, -va *adj* : defensive — **defensivamente** *adv*

defensor[1], **-sora** *adj* : defending, defense

defensor[2], **-sora** *n* **1** : defender, advocate **2** : defense counsel

defeño, -ña *n* : person from the Federal District (Mexico City)

deferencia *nf* : deference

deferir {76} *vi* **deferir a** : to defer to

deficiencia *nf* : deficiency, flaw

deficiente *adj* : deficient

déficit *nm, pl* **-cits** **1** : deficit **2** : shortage, lack

deficitario, -ria *adj* : with a deficit (of a country, etc.), negative (of a balance) ⟨una empresa deficitaria : a business that is losing money⟩

definición *nf, pl* **-ciones** : definition

definido, -da *adj* : definite, well-defined

definir *vt* **1** : to define **2** : to determine

definitivamente *adv* **1** : finally **2** : permanently, for good **3** : definitely, absolutely

definitivo, -va *adj* **1** : definitive, conclusive **2 en definitiva** : all in all, on the whole **3 en definitiva** *Mex* : permanently, for good

deflación *nf, pl* **-ciones** : deflation

deforestación *nf, pl* **-ciones** : deforestation

deformación *nf, pl* **-ciones** **1** : deformation **2** : distortion

deformar *vt* **1** : to deform, to disfigure **2** : to distort — **deformarse** *vr*

deforme *adj* : deformed, misshapen

deformidad *nf* : deformity

defraudación *nf, pl* **-ciones** : fraud

defraudar *vt* **1** ESTAFAR : to defraud, to cheat **2** : to disappoint

defunción *nf, pl* **-ciones** DECESO : death, passing

degeneración *nf, pl* **-ciones** **1** : degeneration **2** DEPRAVACIÓN : depravity

degenerado, -da *adj* DEPRAVADO : degenerate

degenerar *vi* : to degenerate

degenerativo, -va *adj* : degenerative

degollar {19} *vt* **1** : to slit the throat of, to slaughter **2** DECAPITAR : to behead **3** : to ruin, to destroy

degradación *nf, pl* **-ciones** **1** : degradation **2** : demotion

degradante *adj* : degrading

degradar *vt* **1** : to degrade, to debase **2** : to demote

degustación *nf, pl* **-ciones** : tasting, sampling

degustador, -dora *n* : taster

degustar *vt* : to taste

dehesa *nf* : meadow

deidad *nf* : deity

deificar {72} *vt* : to idolize, to deify

dejadez *nf* : neglect, slovenliness

dejado, -da *adj* **1** : slovenly **2** : careless, lazy

dejar *vt* **1** : to leave ⟨dejé la cartera en casa : I left my purse at home⟩ ⟨déjalo allí : leave it there⟩ ⟨déjalo conmigo : leave it with me⟩ **2** : to drop (someone) off **3** : to leave (a tip, a package, etc.) **4** LEGAR : to leave, to bequeath **5** ABANDONAR : to leave (a spouse, a job, etc.), to give up (an activity) **6** : to leave alone, to let be **7** : to drop (a subject) ⟨déjalo, no importa : forget it—it's not important⟩ **8** POSPONER : to leave, to put off **9** : to leave ⟨dejé las luces encendidas : I left the lights on⟩ ⟨no me dejes esperando : don't leave me waiting⟩ **10** GUARDAR : to leave, to set aside **11** : to leave (a mark, etc.) **12** PERMITIR : to let, to allow ⟨déjalo hablar : let him speak⟩ ⟨deja que se enfríe : let it cool⟩ — *vi* **1** ~ **de** : to stop, to quit ⟨dejar de fumar : to quit smoking⟩ **2 no dejar de** : to be sure to ⟨no dejes de llamar : be sure to call⟩ — **dejarse** *vr* **1** : to let oneself be ⟨se deja insultar : he lets himself be insulted⟩ **2** : to forget, to leave ⟨me dejé las llaves en el carro : I left the keys in the car⟩ **3** : to neglect oneself, to let oneself go **4** : to grow ⟨me estoy dejando el pelo largo : I'm growing my hair long⟩

dejo *nm* **1** : aftertaste **2** : touch, hint **3** : (regional) accent

del *contraction of* DE *and* EL → **de**

delación *nf, pl* **-ciones** : denunciation, betrayal

delantal *nm* **1** : apron **2** : pinafore

delante *adv* **1** ENFRENTE : ahead, in front **2** ~ **de** : before, in front of

delantera *nf* **1** : front, front part, front row ⟨tomar la delantera : to take the lead⟩ **2** : forward line (in sports)

delantero¹, -ra *adj* **1** : front, forward **2 tracción delantera** : front-wheel drive

delantero², -ra *n* : forward (in sports)

delatar *vt* **1** : to betray, to reveal **2** : to denounce, to inform against

delator, -tora *adj* : incriminating

delegación *nf, pl* **-ciones** : delegation

delegado, -da *n* : delegate, representative

delegar {52} *vt* : to delegate

deleitar *vt* : to delight, to please — **deleitarse** *vr*

deleite *nm* : delight, pleasure

deletrear *vi* : to spell ⟨¿como se deletrea? : how do you spell it?⟩

deleznable *adj* **1** : brittle, crumbly **2** : slippery **3** : weak, fragile ⟨una excusa deleznable : a weak excuse⟩

delfín *nm, pl* **delfines** : dolphin

delgadez *nf* : thinness

delgado, -da *adj* **1** FLACO : thin, skinny **2** ESBELTO : slender, slim **3** DELICADO : delicate, fine **4** AGUDO : sharp, clever

deliberado, -da *adj* : deliberate, intentional — **deliberadamente** *adv*

deliberar *vi* : to deliberate — **deliberación** *nf*

delicadamente *adv* : delicately

delicadeza *nf* **1** : delicacy, fineness **2** : gentleness, softness **3** : tact, discretion, consideration

delicado, -da *adj* **1** : delicate, fine **2** : sensitive, frail **3** : delicate, tricky **4** : fussy **5** : tactful, considerate

delicia *nf* : delight

delicioso, -sa *adj* **1** RICO : delicious **2** : delightful

delictivo, -va *adj* : criminal

delictuoso, -sa → **delictivo**

delimitación *nf, pl* **-ciones** **1** : demarcation **2** : defining, specifying

delimitar *vt* **1** : to demarcate **2** : to define, to specify

delincuencia *nf* : delinquency, crime

delincuente¹ *adj* : delinquent

delincuente² *nmf* CRIMINAL : delinquent, criminal

delineador *nm* : eyeliner

delinear *vt* **1** : to delineate, to outline **2** : to draft, to draw up

delinquir {24} *vi* : to break the law

delirante *adj* : delirious

delirar *vi* **1** DESVARIAR : to be delirious **2** : to rave, to talk nonsense

delirio *nm* **1** : delirium **2** FRENESÍ : mania, frenzy ⟨¡fue el delirio! : it was wild!⟩ **3 delirios** *pl* DISPARATES : nonsense, ravings *pl* ⟨delirios de grandeza : delusions of grandeur⟩

delito *nm* : crime, offense

delta *nm* : delta

demacrado, -da *adj* : emaciated, gaunt

demagogo, -ga *n* : demagogue

demanda *nf* **1** : demand ⟨la oferta y la demanda : supply and demand⟩ ⟨tener mucha demanda : to be in great demand⟩ **2** : petition, request **3** : lawsuit

demandado, -da *n* : defendant

demandante *nmf* : plaintiff

demandar *vt* **1** : to demand **2** REQUERIR : to call for, to require **3** : to sue, to file a lawsuit against

demarcar {72} *vt* : to demarcate — **demarcación** *nf*

demás¹ *adj* : remaining ⟨las demás tareas : the rest of the chores⟩

demás² *pron* **1 lo (la, los, las) demás** : the rest, everyone else, everything else ⟨Pepe, Rosa, y los demás : Pepe, Rosa, and everybody else⟩ **2 estar por demás** : to be of no use, to be pointless ⟨no estaría por demás : it couldn't hurt, it's worth a try⟩ **3 por demás** : extremely **4 por lo demás** : otherwise **5 y demás** : and so on, et cetera

demasía *nf en* ~ : excessively, in excess

demasiado¹ *adv* **1** : too ⟨vas demasiado aprisa : you're going too fast⟩ **2** : too much ⟨comí demasiado : I ate too much⟩

demasiado², -da *adj* : too much, too many, excessive

demencia *nf* **1** : dementia **2** LOCURA : madness, insanity

demencial *adj fam* : crazy, insane

demente¹ *adj* : insane, mad

demente² *nmf* : insane person

demeritar *vt* **1** : to detract from **2** : to discredit

demérito *nm* **1** : fault **2** : discredit, disrepute

demo *nf* **1** : demo, demo product/version (etc.) **2** : demo, demo tape

democracia *nf* : democracy

demócrata¹ *adj* : democratic

demócrata² *nmf* : democrat

democrático, -ca *adj* : democratic — **democráticamente** *adv*

democratizar {21} *vt* : to democratize, to make democratic — **democratización** *nf*

demografía *nf* 1 : demography 2 : demographics *pl*

demográfico, -ca *adj* : demographic

demoledor, -dora *adj* : devastating

demoler {47} *vt* DERRIBAR, DERRUMBAR : to demolish, to destroy

demolición *nf, pl* **-ciones** : demolition

demoníaco, -ca *adj* : demonic, demoniac

demonio *nm* 1 DIABLO : devil, demon 2 ¿qué demonios . . . ? : what on earth . . . ?, what the hell . . . ?

demora *nf* : delay

demorar *vt* 1 RETRASAR : to delay 2 TARDAR : to take, to last ⟨la reparación demorará varios días : the repair will take several days⟩ — *vi* : to delay, to linger ⟨no demores : don't delay, don't take too long⟩ — **demorarse** *vr* 1 : to be slow, to take a long time 2 : to take too long

demostración *nf, pl* **-ciones** : demonstration

demostrar {19} *vt* 1 PROBAR : to demonstrate, to prove 2 MANIFESTAR : to show 3 : to demonstrate (a procedure, etc.)

demostrativo, -va *adj* : demonstrative

demudar *vt* : to change, to alter — **demudarse** *vr* : to change one's expression

denegación *nf, pl* **-ciones** : denial, refusal

denegar {49} *vt* : to deny, to turn down

dengue *nm* : dengue

denigrante *adj* : degrading, humiliating

denigrar *vt* 1 DIFAMAR : to denigrate, to disparage 2 : to degrade, to humiliate

denominación *nf, pl* **-ciones** 1 : name, designation 2 : denomination (of money)

denominador *nm* : denominator

denominar *vt* : to designate, to name, to call

denostar {19} *vt* : to revile

denotar *vt* : to denote, to show

densidad *nf* : density, thickness

denso, -sa *adj* : dense, thick — **densamente** *adv*

dentado, -da *adj* SERRADO : serrated, jagged

dentadura *nf* 1 : teeth *pl* 2 **dentadura postiza** : dentures *pl*

dental *adj* : dental

dentellada *nf* 1 : bite 2 : tooth mark

dentera *nf* 1 : envy, jealousy 2 **dar dentera** : to set one's teeth on edge

dentífrico *nm* : toothpaste

dentista *nmf* : dentist

dentro *adv* 1 ADENTRO : in, inside ⟨por dentro : on the inside⟩ ⟨estoy aquí dentro : I'm in here⟩ 2 ~ **de** : within, inside, in ⟨dentro de la tienda : inside the store⟩ ⟨dentro de los límites de : within the limits of⟩ 3 ~ **de** : in, within (a time period) ⟨dentro de poco : soon, shortly⟩ 4 **dentro de todo** : all in all, all things considered 5 **por** ~ : inwardly, inside

denuncia *nf* 1 : denunciation, condemnation 2 : police report

denunciante *nmf* : accuser (of a crime)

denunciar *vt* 1 : to denounce, to condemn 2 : to report (to the authorities)

deparar *vt* : to have in store for, to provide with ⟨no sabemos lo que nos depara el destino : we don't know what fate has in store for us⟩

departamental *adj* 1 : departmental 2 **tienda departamental** *Mex* : department store

departamento *nm* 1 : department 2 APARTAMENTO : apartment

departir *vi* : to converse

dependencia *nf* 1 : dependence, dependency ⟨dependencia del alcohol : dependence on alcohol⟩ 2 : agency, branch office

depender *vi* 1 : to depend 2 ~ **de** : to depend on 3 ~ **de** : to be subordinate to

dependiente¹ *adj* : dependent

dependiente², -ta *n* : clerk, salesperson

depilar *vt* : to wax, to shave

deplorable *adj* : deplorable

deplorar *vt* 1 : to deplore 2 LAMENTAR : to regret

deponer {60} *vt* 1 : to depose, to overthrow 2 : to abandon (an attitude or stance) 3 **deponer las armas** : to lay down one's arms — *vi* 1 TESTIFICAR : to testify, to make a statement 2 EVACUAR : to defecate

deportación *nf, pl* **-ciones** : deportation

deportar *vt* : to deport

deporte *nm* 1 : sport, sports *pl* ⟨hacer deporte : to engage in sports⟩ ⟨practicar un deporte : to do a sport⟩ ⟨por deporte : for the fun of it, for sport⟩ 2 **deporte extremo** : extreme sport 3 **deporte de invierno/equipo** : winter/team sport

deportista¹ *adj* 1 : fond of sports 2 : sporty

deportista² *nmf* 1 : sports fan 2 : athlete, sportsman *m*, sportswoman *f*

deportividad *nf Spain* : sportsmanship

deportivo, -va *adj* 1 : sports, sporting ⟨artículos deportivos : sporting goods⟩ 2 : sporty

deposición *nf, pl* **-ciones** 1 : statement, testimony 2 : removal from office

depositar *vt* 1 : to deposit, to place 2 : to store — **depositarse** *vr* : to settle

depósito *nm* 1 : deposit ⟨hacer un depósito : to make a deposit⟩ 2 : warehouse, storehouse ⟨depósito de armas : arms depot⟩ 3 : tank ⟨depósito de gasolina : gas tank⟩

depravación *nf, pl* **-ciones** : depravity

depravado, -da *adj* DEGENERADO : depraved, degenerate

depravar *vt* : to deprave, to corrupt

depreciación *nf, pl* **-ciones** : depreciation

depreciar *vt* : to depreciate, to reduce the value of — **depreciarse** *vr* : to lose value

depredador¹, -dora *adj* : predatory

depredador² *nm* 1 : predator 2 SAQUEADOR : plunderer

depresión *nf, pl* **-siones** 1 : depression 2 : hollow, recess 3 : drop, fall 4 : slump, recession

depresivo *nm* : depressant
deprimente *adj* : depressing
deprimir *vt* **1** : to depress **2** : to lower —
— **deprimirse** *vr* ABATIRSE : to get depressed
deprisa *adv* : fast
depuesto *pp* → deponer
depuración *nf, pl* **-ciones 1** PURIFICACIÓN : purification **2** PURGA : purge **3** : refinement, polish
depurar *vt* **1** PURIFICAR : to purify **2** PURGAR : to purge
depuso, *etc.* → deponer
derby *nm, pl* **derbies** *or* **derbys 1** : derby (in horse racing) **2** : derby (hat) **3** *Spain* : local game
derecha *nf* **1** : right **2** : right hand, right side **3** : right wing, right (in politics)
derechazo *nm* **1** : pass with the cape on the right hand (in bullfighting) **2** : right (in boxing) **3** : forehand (in tennis)
derechista[1] *adj* : rightist, right-wing
derechista[2] *nmf* : right-winger, rightist
derecho[1] *adv* **1** : straight ⟨todo derecho : straight ahead⟩ **2** : upright **3** : directly ⟨ir derecho al tema : to get straight to the point⟩
derecho[2], **-cha** *adj* **1** : right **2** : right-hand ⟨el margen derecho : the right-hand margin⟩ **3** RECTO : straight, upright, erect ⟨siéntate derecho : sit up straight⟩
derecho[3] *nm* **1** : right ⟨derechos humanos : human rights⟩ ⟨el derecho al voto : the right to vote⟩ ⟨derecho de nacimiento : birthright⟩ ⟨tener derecho a : to have a right to⟩ ⟨hacer valer sus derechos : to exercise one's rights⟩ ⟨estás en tu derecho : you're within your rights⟩ ⟨no hay derecho : it's not fair⟩ **2** : law ⟨derecho civil : civil law⟩ ⟨derecho de familia : family law⟩ ⟨un estudiante de derecho : a law student⟩ **3** : right side (of cloth or clothing) ⟨ponlo del derecho : turn it right side up/out⟩
de refilón *adv* **1** : sidelong, obliquely **2** : briefly
deriva *nf* **1** : drift **2 a la deriva** : adrift
derivación *nf, pl* **-ciones 1** : derivation **2** RAMIFICACIÓN : ramification, consequence
derivar *vi* **1** : to drift **2** ∼ **de** : to come from, to derive from **3** ∼ **en** : to result in — *vt* : to steer, to direct ⟨derivó la discusión hacia la política : he steered the discussion over to politics⟩ — **derivarse** *vr* : to be derived from, to arise from
dermatología *nf* : dermatology
dermatólogo, -ga *n* : dermatologist
derogación *nf, pl* **-ciones** : abolition, repeal
derogar {52} *vt* ABOLIR : to abolish, to repeal
derramamiento *nm* **1** : spilling, overflowing **2 derramamiento de sangre** : bloodshed
derramar *vt* **1** : to spill **2** : to shed (tears, blood) — **derramarse** *vr* **1** : to spill over **2** : to scatter

derrame *nm* **1** : spilling, shedding **2** : leakage, overflow **3** : discharge, hemorrhage ⟨derrame cerebral : stroke⟩
derrapar *vi* : to skid
derrape *nm* : skid
derredor *nm* **al derredor** *or* **en derredor** : around, round about
derrengado, -da *adj* **1** : bent, twisted **2** : exhausted
derretir {54} *vt* : to melt, to thaw — **derretirse** *vr* **1** : to melt, to thaw **2** ∼ **por** *fam* : to be crazy about
derribar *vt* **1** DEMOLER, DERRUMBAR : to demolish, to knock down **2** : to shoot down, to bring down (an airplane) **3** DERROCAR : to overthrow
derribo *nm* **1** : demolition, razing **2** : shooting down **3** : overthrow
derrocamiento *nm* : overthrow
derrocar {72} *vt* DERRIBAR : to overthrow, to topple
derrochador[1], **-dora** *adj* : extravagant, wasteful
derrochador[2], **-dora** *n* : spendthrift
derrochar *vt* : to waste, to squander
derroche *nm* : extravagance, waste
derrota *nf* **1** : defeat, rout **2** : course (at sea)
derrotar *vt* : to defeat
derrotero *nm* RUTA : course
derrotista *adj & nmf* : defeatist
derruir {41} *vt* : to demolish, to tear down
derrumbamiento *nm* : collapse
derrumbar *vt* **1** DEMOLER, DERRIBAR : to demolish, to knock down **2** DESPEÑAR : to cast down, to topple — **derrumbarse** *vr* DESPLOMARSE : to collapse, to break down
derrumbe *nm* **1** DESPLOME : collapse, fall ⟨el derrumbe del comunismo : the fall of Communism⟩ **2** : landslide
des- *pref* : de-, dis-, un-
desabastecimiento *nm* : shortage, scarcity
desabasto *nm Mex* : shortage, scarcity
desabotonar *vt* : to unbutton, to undo — **desabotonarse** *vr* : to come undone
desabrido, -da *adj* : tasteless, bland
desabrigar {52} *vt* **1** : to undress **2** : to uncover **3** : to deprive of shelter
desabrochar *vt* : to unbutton, to undo — **desabrocharse** *vr* : to come undone
desacato *nm* **1** : disrespect **2** : contempt (of court)
desacelerar *vi* : to decelerate, to slow down
desacertado, -da *adj* **1** : mistaken **2** : unwise
desacertar {55} *vi* ERRAR : to err, to be mistaken
desacierto *nm* ERROR : error, mistake
desaconsejable *adj* : inadvisable
desaconsejado, -da *adj* : ill-advised, unwise
desaconsejar *vt* : to advise against
desacostumbrado, -da *adj* : unaccustomed, unusual
desacreditar *vt* DESPRESTIGIAR : to discredit, to disgrace
desactivar *vt* : to deactivate, to defuse

desacuerdo *nm* : disagreement

desafiante *adj* : defiant

desafiar {85} *vt* RETAR : to defy, to challenge

desafilado, -da *adj* : blunt

desafilar *vt* : to dull, to blunt

desafinado, -da *adj* : out-of-tune, off-key

desafinarse *vr* : to go out of tune

desafío *nm* 1 RETO : challenge 2 RESISTENCIA : defiance

desaforado, -da *adj* : wild, unrestrained

desafortunado, -da *adj* : unfortunate, unlucky — **desafortunadamente** *adv*

desafuero *nm* ABUSO : injustice, outrage

desagradable *adj* : unpleasant, disagreeable — **desagradablemente** *adv*

desagradar *vi* : to be unpleasant, to be disagreeable

desagradecido, -da *adj* : ungrateful

desagrado *nm* 1 : displeasure 2 con ~ : reluctantly

desagravio *nm* 1 : apology 2 : amends, reparation

desagregarse {52} *vr* : to break up, to disintegrate

desaguar {10} *vi* : to drain, to empty

desagüe *nm* 1 : drain 2 : drainage

desaguisado *nm* : mess

desahogado, -da *adj* 1 : well-off, comfortable 2 : spacious, roomy

desahogar {52} *vt* 1 : to relieve, to ease 2 : to give vent to — **desahogarse** *vr* 1 : to recover, to feel better 2 : to unburden oneself, to let off steam

desahogo *nm* 1 : relief, outlet 2 con ~ : comfortably

desahuciar *vt* 1 : to deprive of hope 2 : to evict — **desahuciarse** *vr* : to lose all hope

desahucio *nm* : eviction

desairar {5} *vt* : to snub, to rebuff

desaire *nm* : rebuff, snub, slight

desajustar *vt* 1 : to disarrange, to put out of order 2 : to upset (plans)

desajuste *nm* 1 : maladjustment 2 : imbalance 3 : upset, disruption

desalentador, -dora *adj* : discouraging, disheartening

desalentar {55} *vt* DESANIMAR : to discourage, to dishearten — **desalentarse** *vr*

desaliento *nm* : discouragement

desaliñado, -da *adj* : sloppy, untidy (of a person's appearance) — **desaliñadamente** *adv*

desaliño *nm* : sloppiness, untidiness (of a person's appearance)

desalmado, -da *adj* : heartless, callous

desalojar *vt* 1 : to remove, to clear 2 EVACUAR : to evacuate, to vacate 3 : to evict

desalojo *nm* 1 : removal, expulsion 2 : evacuation 3 : eviction

desamarrar *vt* 1 : to cast off 2 : to untie

desamor *nm* 1 FRIALDAD : indifference 2 ENEMISTAD : dislike, enmity

desamparado, -da *adj* DESVALIDO : helpless, destitute

desamparar *vt* : to abandon, to forsake

desamparo *nm* 1 : abandonment, neglect 2 : helplessness

desamueblado, -da *adj* : unfurnished

desandar {6} *vt* : to go back, to return to the starting point

desangelado, -da *adj* : dull, lifeless

desangrar *vt* : to bleed, to bleed dry — **desangrarse** *vr* 1 : to be bleeding 2 : to bleed to death

desanimar *vt* DESALENTAR : to discourage, to dishearten — **desanimarse** *vr*

desánimo *nm* DESALIENTO : discouragement, dejection

desapacible *adj* : unpleasant, disagreeable

desaparecer {53} *vt* : to cause to disappear — *vi* : to disappear, to vanish

desaparecido¹, -da *adj* 1 : late, deceased 2 : missing

desaparecido², -da *n* : missing person

desaparición *nf, pl* **-ciones** : disappearance

desapasionado, -da *adj* : dispassionate, impartial — **desapasionadamente** *adv*

desapego *nm* : coolness, indifference

desapercibido, -da *adj* 1 : unnoticed 2 DESPREVENIDO : unprepared, off guard

desaprobación *nf, pl* **-ciones** : disapproval

desaprobar {19} *vt* REPROBAR : to disapprove of

desaprovechar *vt* MALGASTAR : to waste, to misuse — *vi* : to lose ground, to slip back

desarmador *nm Mex* : screwdriver

desarmar *vt* 1 : to disarm 2 DESMONTAR : to disassemble, to take apart

desarme *nm* : disarmament

desarraigado, -da *adj* : rootless

desarraigar {52} *vt* : to uproot, to root out

desarregladamente *adv* : untidily, messily

desarreglado, -da *adj* : untidy, disorganized

desarreglar *vt* 1 : to mess up 2 : to upset, to disrupt

desarreglo *nm* 1 : untidiness 2 : disorder, confusion

desarrollar *vt* 1 : to develop 2 : to carry out (an action, etc.) 3 : to explain (a theory, etc.) — **desarrollarse** *vr* 1 : to develop 2 : to take place, to unfold

desarrollo *nm* : development ⟨países en vías de desarrollo : developing countries⟩

desarticulación *nf, pl* **-ciones** 1 : dislocation 2 : breaking up, dismantling

desarticular *vt* 1 DISLOCAR : to dislocate 2 : to break up, to dismantle

desasosiego *nm* : sense of unease

desastre *nm* CATÁSTROFE : disaster

desastroso, -sa *adj* : disastrous, catastrophic — **desastrosamente** *adv*

desatar *vt* 1 : to undo, to untie 2 : to unleash 3 : to trigger, to precipitate — **desatarse** *vr* 1 : to come undone 2 : to break out, to erupt

desatascador *nm* : plunger (for toilets, etc.)

desatascar {72} *vt* : to unblock, to clear

desatención *nf, pl* **-ciones** 1 : absentmindedness, distraction 2 : discourtesy

desatender {56} *vt* **1** : to disregard **2** : to neglect **3** : to leave unattended

desatento, -ta *adj* **1** DISTRAÍDO : absent-minded **2** GROSERO : discourteous, rude

desatinado, -da *adj* : foolish, silly

desatino *nm* : folly, mistake

desatorador *nm* **1** : plunger (for toilets, etc.) **2** : drain cleaner (liquid)

desatornillar → **destornillar**

desautorizar {21} *vt* : to deprive of authority, to discredit

desavenencia *nf* DISCORDANCIA : disagreement, dispute

desayunar *vi* : to have breakfast — *vt* : to have for breakfast

desayuno *nm* : breakfast

desazón *nf, pl* **-zones** INQUIETUD : uneasiness, anxiety

desbalance *nm* : imbalance

desbancar {72} *vt* : to displace, to oust

desbandada *nf* : scattering, dispersal

desbarajuste *nm* DESORDEN : disarray, disorder, mess

desbaratar *vt* **1** ARRUINAR : to destroy, to ruin **2** DESCOMPONER : to break, to break down — **desbaratarse** *vr* : to fall apart

desbloquear *vt* **1** : to open up, to clear, to break through **2** : to free, to release

desbocado, -da *adj* : unbridled, rampant

desbocarse {72} *vr* : to run away, to bolt

desbordamiento *nm* : overflowing

desbordante *adj* : overflowing, bursting ⟨desbordante de energía : bursting with energy⟩

desbordar *vt* **1** : to overflow, to spill over **2** : to surpass, to exceed — **desbordarse** *vr*

descabellado, -da *adj* : outlandish, ridiculous

descafeinado, -da *adj* : decaffeinated

descalabrar *vt* : to hit on the head — **descalabrarse** *vr*

descalabro *nm* : setback, misfortune, loss

descalificación *nf, pl* **-ciones** **1** : disqualification **2** : disparaging remark

descalificar {72} *vt* **1** : to disqualify **2** DESACREDITAR : to discredit — **descalificarse** *vr*

descalzarse {21} *vr* : take off one's shoes

descalzo, -za *adj* : barefoot

descampado *nm* : open area

descansado, -da *adj* **1** : rested, refreshed **2** : restful, peaceful

descansar *vi* : to rest, to relax ⟨¡descansen! : at ease!⟩ — *vt* : to rest ⟨descansar la vista : to rest one's eyes⟩

descansillo *nm Spain* DESCANSO : landing (of a staircase)

descanso *nm* **1** : rest, relaxation **2** : break **3** : landing (of a staircase) **4** : intermission (in a show), halftime (in sports)

descapotable *adj & nm* : convertible

descarado, -da *adj* : brazen, impudent — **descaradamente** *adv*

descarga *nf* **1** : discharge **2** : unloading

descargable *adj* : downloadable

descargar {52} *vt* **1** : to discharge **2** : to unload **3** : to release, to free **4** : to take out, to vent (anger, etc.) **5** : to download (a file, etc.) — **descargarse** *vr* **1** : to unburden oneself **2** : to quit **3** : to lose power

descargo *nm* **1** : unloading **2** : defense ⟨testigo de descargo : witness for the defense⟩

descarnado, -da *adj* : scrawny, gaunt

descaro *nm* : audacity, nerve

descarriado, -da *adj* : lost, gone astray

descarriarse *vr* : to go astray

descarrilar *vi* : to derail — **descarrilarse** *vr* — **descarrilamiento** *n*

descartar *vt* : to rule out, to reject — **descartarse** *vr* : to discard

descascarar *vt* : to peel, to shell, to husk — **descascararse** *vr* : to peel off, to chip

descendencia *nf* **1** : descendants *pl* **2** LINAJE : descent, lineage

descendente *adj* : downward, descending

descender {56} *vt* **1** : to descend, to go down **2** BAJAR : to lower, to take down, to let down — *vi* **1** : to descend, to come down **2** : to drop, to fall **3** ~ **de** : to be a descendant of

descendiente *adj & nm* : descendant

descenso *nm* **1** : descent **2** BAJA, CAÍDA : drop, fall

descentralizar {21} *vt* : to decentralize — **descentralizarse** *vr* — **descentralización** *nf*

descifrar *vt* : to decipher, to decode — **descifrable** *adj*

desclasificar {72} *vt* : to declassify

descodificador → **decodificador**

descodificar {72} *vt* : to decode

descolgar {16} *vt* **1** : to take down, to let down **2** : to pick up, to answer (the telephone)

descollar {19} *vi* SOBRESALIR : to stand out, to be outstanding, to excel

descolorido, -da *adj* : discolored, faded

descomponer {60} *vt* **1** : to rot, to decompose **2** DESBARATAR : to break, to break down **3** : to damage **4** : to mess up — **descomponerse** *vr* **1** : to break down **2** : to decompose

descomposición *nf, pl* **-ciones** **1** : breakdown, decomposition **2** : decay

descompuesto¹ *pp* → **descomponer**

descompuesto², -ta *adj* **1** : broken down, out of order **2** : rotten, decomposed

descomunal *adj* **1** ENORME : enormous, huge **2** EXTRAORDINARIO : extraordinary

desconcentrar *vt* DISTRAER : to distract

desconcertante *adj* : disconcerting

desconcertar {55} *vt* : to disconcert — **desconcertarse** *vr*

desconchar *vt* : to chip — **desconcharse** *vr* : to chip off, to peel

desconcierto *nm* : uncertainty, confusion

desconectar *vt* **1** : to disconnect, to switch off **2** : to unplug

desconfiado, -da *adj* : distrustful, suspicious

desconfianza *nf* RECELO : distrust, suspicion

desconfiar {85} *vi* ∼ **de** : to distrust, to be suspicious of

descongelar *vt* **1** : to thaw **2** : to defrost (a refrigerator, etc.) **3** : to unfreeze (assets) — **descongelarse** *vr*

descongestionante *adj & nm* : decongestant

descongestionar *vt* : to clear, to unclog ⟨descongestionar el tráfico : to reduce traffic congestion⟩

desconocer {18} *vt* **1** IGNORAR : to be unaware of **2** : to fail to recognize

desconocido¹, -da *adj* : unknown, unfamiliar

desconocido², -da *n* EXTRAÑO : stranger

desconocimiento *nm* : ignorance

desconsiderado, -da *adj* : inconsiderate, thoughtless — **desconsideradamente** *adj*

desconsolado, -da *adj* : disconsolate, heartbroken, despondent

desconsuelo *nm* AFLICCIÓN : grief, distress, despair

descontaminar *vt* : to decontaminate — **descontaminación** *nf*

descontar {19} *vt* **1** : to discount, to deduct **2** EXCEPTUAR : to except, to exclude

descontento¹, -ta *adj* : discontented, dissatisfied

descontento² *nm* : discontent, dissatisfaction

descontinuar {3} *vt* : to discontinue (a product, etc.)

descontrol *nm* : lack of control, disorder, chaos

descontrolarse *vr* : to get out of control, to be out of hand

desconvocar {72} *vt* : to cancel

descorazonado, -da *adj* : disheartened, discouraged

descorchar *vt* : to uncork

descorrer *vt* : to draw back

descortés *adj, pl* **-teses** : discourteous, rude

descortesía *nf* : discourtesy, rudeness

descrédito *nm* DESPRESTIGIO : discredit

descremado, -da *adj* : nonfat, skim

describir {33} *vt* : to describe

descripción *nf, pl* **-ciones** : description

descriptivo, -va *adj* : descriptive

descrito *pp* → **describir**

descuartizar {21} *vt* **1** : to cut up, to quarter **2** : to tear to pieces

descubierto¹ *pp* → **descubrir**

descubierto², -ta *adj* **1** : exposed, revealed **2 al descubierto** : out in the open

descubridor, -dora *n* : discoverer, explorer

descubrimiento *nm* : discovery

descubrir {2} *vt* **1** HALLAR : to discover, to find out **2** REVELAR : to uncover, to reveal **3** DEVELAR : to unveil **4** DELATAR : to give away — **descubrirse** *vr*

descuento *nm* REBAJA : discount

descuidado, -da *adj* **1** : neglectful, careless **2** : neglected, unkempt

descuidar *vt* : to neglect, to overlook — *vi* : to be careless — **descuidarse** *vr* **1** : to be careless, to drop one's guard **2** : to let oneself go

descuido *nm* **1** : carelessness, negligence **2** : slip, oversight

desde *prep* **1** : from ⟨desde arriba : from above⟩ ⟨desde la cabeza hasta los pies : from head to foot/toe⟩ **2** : since, from ⟨desde el lunes : since Monday⟩ ⟨desde el principio : right from the start⟩ ⟨desde la mañana hasta la noche : from morning to/until night⟩ **3 desde ahora** : from now on **4 desde entonces** : since then **5 desde hace** : for, since (a time) ⟨ha estado nevando desde hace dos días : it's been snowing for two days⟩ **6 desde luego** : of course **7 desde que** : since, ever since **8 desde ya** : right now, immediately

desdecir {11} *vi* **1** ∼ **de** : to be unworthy of **2** ∼ **de** : to clash with — **desdecirse** *vr* **1** CONTRADECIRSE : to contradict oneself **2** RETRACTARSE : to go back on one's word

desdén *nm, pl* **desdenes** DESPRECIO : disdain, scorn

desdentado, -da *adj* : toothless

desdeñar *vt* DESPRECIAR : to disdain, to scorn, to despise

desdeñoso, -sa *adj* : disdainful, scornful — **desdeñosamente** *adv*

desdibujar *vt* : to blur — **desdibujarse** *vr*

desdicha *nf* **1** : misery **2** : misfortune

desdichado¹, -da *adj* **1** : unfortunate **2** : miserable, unhappy

desdichado², -da *n* : wretch

desdicho *pp* → **desdecir**

desdiga, desdijo etc. → **desdecir**

desdoblar *vt* DESPLEGAR : to unfold

deseable *adj* : desirable

desear *vt* **1** : to wish ⟨te deseo buena suerte : I wish you good luck⟩ **2** QUERER : to want, to desire ⟨dejar mucho que desear : to leave much to be desired⟩

desecar {72} *vt* : to dry (flowers, etc.)

desechable *adj* : disposable

desechar *vt* **1** : to discard, to throw away **2** RECHAZAR : to reject

desecho *nm* **1** : reject **2 desechos** *nmpl* RESIDUOS : rubbish, waste

desembarazarse {21} *vr* ∼ **de** : to get rid of

desembarcar {72} *vi* : to disembark — *vt* : to unload

desembarco *nm* **1** : landing, arrival **2** : unloading

desembarque → **desembarco**

desembocadura *nf* **1** : mouth (of a river) **2** : opening, end (of a street)

desembocar {72} *vi* ∼ **en** *or* ∼ **a** **1** : to flow into, to join **2** : to lead to, to result in

desembolsar *vt* PAGAR : to disburse, to pay out

desembolso *nm* PAGO : disbursement, payment

desempacar {72} *v* : to unpack
desempatar *vi* : to break a tie
desempate *nm* : tiebreaker, play-off
desempeñar *vt* **1** : to play (a role) **2** : to fulfill, to carry out **3** : to redeem (from a pawnshop) — **desempeñarse** *vr* : to function, to act
desempeño *nm* **1** : fulfillment, carrying out **2** : performance
desempleado¹, -da *adj* : unemployed
desempleado², -da *n* : unemployed person
desempleo *nm* : unemployment
desempolvar *vt* **1** : to dust off **2** : to resurrect, to revive
desencadenar *vt* **1** : to unchain **2** : to trigger, to unleash — **desencadenarse** *vr*
desencajar *vt* **1** : to dislocate (a bone) **2** : to pop out of place, to disengage — **desencajarse** *vr*
desencantar *vt* : to disenchant, to disillusion — **desencantarse** *vr*
desencanto *nm* : disenchantment, disillusionment
desenchufar *vt* : to disconnect, to unplug
desenfadado, -da *adj* **1** : uninhibited, carefree **2** : confident, self-assured
desenfado *nm* **1** DESENVOLTURA : self-assurance, confidence **2** : naturalness, ease
desenfocado, -da *adj* : unfocused, blurry
desenfrenadamente *adv* : wildly, with abandon
desenfrenado, -da *adj* : unbridled, unrestrained
desenfreno *nm* : abandon, lack of restraint
desenfundar *vt* : to draw (a gun)
desenganchar *vt* : to unhitch, to uncouple
desengañar *vt* : to disillusion, to disenchant — **desengañarse** *vr*
desengaño *nm* : disenchantment, disillusionment
desenlace *nm* : ending, outcome
desenmarañar *vt* : to disentangle, to unravel
desenmascarar *vt* : to unmask, to expose
desenredar *vt* **1** : to untangle, to disentangle **2** : to straighten out, to sort out
desenrollar *vt* : to unroll, to unwind
desenroscar *vt* **1** : to unscrew **2** : to unroll — **desenroscarse** *vr*
desentenderse {56} *vr* **1** ~ **de** : to want nothing to do with, to be uninterested in **2** ~ **de** : to pretend ignorance of
desenterrar {55} *vt* **1** EXHUMAR : to exhume **2** : to unearth, to dig up
desentonar *vi* **1** : to clash, to conflict **2** : to be out of tune, to sing off-key
desentrañar *vt* : to get to the bottom of, to unravel
desenvainar *vt* : to draw, to unsheathe (a sword)
desenvoltura *nf* **1** DESENFADO : confidence, self-assurance **2** ELOCUENCIA : eloquence, fluency
desenvolver {89} *vt* : to unwrap, to open — **desenvolverse** *vr* **1** : to unfold, to develop **2** : to manage, to cope
desenvuelto¹ *pp* → **desenvolver**

desenvuelto², -ta *adj* : confident, relaxed, self-assured
deseo *nm* : wish, desire
deseoso, -sa *adj* : eager, anxious
desequilibrado, -da *adj* **1** : off-balance **2** : insane
desequilibrar *vt* : to unbalance, to throw off balance — **desequilibrarse** *vr*
desequilibrio *nm* : imbalance
deserción *nf, pl* **-ciones** : desertion, defection
desertar *vi* **1** : to desert, to defect **2** ~ **de** : to abandon, to neglect
desértico, -ca *adj* **1** : desert **2** : uninhabited
desertor, -tora *n* : deserter, defector
desesperación *nf, pl* **-ciones** : desperation, despair
desesperado, -da *adj* : desperate, despairing, hopeless — **desesperadamente** *adv*
desesperante *adj* **1** : exasperating **2** : agonizing, excruciating
desesperanza *nf* : despair, hopelessness
desesperar *vt* : to exasperate — *vi* : to despair, to lose hope — **desesperarse** *vr* : to become exasperated
desestabilizar {21} *vt* : to make unstable
desestimar *vt* **1** : to reject, to disallow **2** : to have a low opinion of
desfachatez *nf, pl* **-teces** : audacity, nerve, cheek
desfalcador, -dora *n* : embezzler
desfalcar {72} *vt* : to embezzle
desfalco *nm* : embezzlement
desfallecer {53} *vi* **1** : to weaken **2** : to faint
desfallecimiento *nm* **1** : weakness **2** : fainting
desfasado, -da *adj* **1** : out of sync **2** : out of step, behind the times
desfase *nm* : gap, lag ⟨desfase (de) horario : jet lag⟩
desfavorable *adj* : unfavorable, adverse — **desfavorablemente** *adv*
desfavorecido, -da *adj* : underprivileged
desfigurar *vt* **1** : to disfigure, to mar **2** : to distort, to misrepresent
desfiladero *nm* : narrow gorge, defile
desfilar *vi* : to parade, to march
desfile *nm* : parade, procession
desfogar {52} *vt* **1** : to vent **2** *Mex* : to unclog, to unblock — **desfogarse** *vr* : to vent one's feelings, to let off steam
desgajar *vt* **1** : to tear off **2** : to break apart — **desgajarse** *vr* : to come apart
desgana *nf* **1** INAPETENCIA : lack of appetite **2** APATÍA : apathy, unwillingness, reluctance
desgano *nm* → **desgana**
desgarbado, -da *adj* : ungainly
desgarrador, -dora *adj* : heartbreaking
desgarradura *nf* : tear, rip
desgarrar *vt* **1** : to tear, to rip **2** : to break (one's heart) — **desgarrarse** *vr*
desgarre → **desgarro**
desgarro *nm* : tear
desgarrón *nm, pl* **-rrones** : rip, tear
desgastar *vt* **1** : to use up **2** : to wear away, to wear down

desgaste *nm* : deterioration, wear and tear

desglosar *vt* : to break down, to itemize

desglose *nm* : breakdown, itemization

desgobierno *nm* : anarchy, disorder

desgracia *nf* 1 : misfortune 2 : disgrace 3 por ～ : unfortunately

desgraciadamente *adv* : unfortunately

desgraciado¹, -da *adj* 1 : unfortunate, unlucky 2 : vile, wretched

desgraciado², -da *n* : unfortunate person, wretch

desgranar *vt* : to shuck, to shell

desgravar *vt* : to deduct (from taxes), to exempt — **desgravación** *n*

desguazar {21} *vt Spain* : to scrap

deshabitado, -da *adj* : unoccupied, uninhabited

deshacer {40} *vt* 1 : to destroy, to ruin 2 DESATAR : to undo, to untie 3 : to break apart, to crumble 4 : to dissolve, to melt 5 : to break, to cancel — **deshacerse** *vr* 1 : to fall apart, to come undone 2 ～ de : to get rid of

deshecho¹ *pp* → **deshacer**

deshecho², -cha *adj* 1 : destroyed, ruined 2 : devastated, shattered 3 : undone, untied

deshelar {55} *vt* 1 : to thaw 2 : to deice (a plane), to defrost — **deshelarse** *vr* 1 : to thaw 2 : to defrost

desherbar *vt* : to weed

desheredado, -da *adj* MARGINADO : dispossessed, destitute

desheredar *vt* : to disinherit

deshicieron, etc. → **deshacer**

deshidratar *vt* : to dehydrate — **deshidratación** *nf*

deshielo *nm* : thaw, thawing

deshierbar → **desherbar**

deshilachar *vt* : to fray — **deshilacharse** *vr*

deshizo → **deshacer**

deshojar *vt* 1 : to remove petals from 2 : to remove pages from

deshollinador, -dora *n* : chimney sweep

deshonestidad *nf* : dishonesty

deshonesto, -ta *adj* : dishonest

deshonor *nm* : dishonor, disgrace

deshonra *nf* : dishonor, disgrace

deshonrar *vt* : to dishonor, to disgrace

deshonroso, -sa *adj* : dishonorable, disgraceful

deshora *nf* a deshoras : at odd times

deshuesadero *nm Mex* : dump

deshuesar *vt* 1 : to pit (a fruit, etc.) 2 : to bone

desidia *nf* 1 APATÍA : apathy, indolence 2 NEGLIGENCIA : negligence, sloppiness

desierto¹, -ta *adj* : deserted, uninhabited

desierto² *nm* : desert

designación *nf, pl* -ciones NOMBRAMIENTO : appointment, naming (to an office, etc.)

designar *vt* NOMBRAR : to designate, to appoint, to name

designio *nm* : plan

desigual *adj* 1 : unequal 2 DISPAREJO : uneven 3 : variable, changeable — **desigualmente** *adv*

desigualdad *nf* 1 : inequality 2 : unevenness

desilusión *nf, pl* -siones DESENCANTO, DESENGAÑO : disillusionment, disenchantment

desilusionar *vt* DESENCANTAR, DESENGAÑAR : to disillusion, to disenchant — **desilusionarse** *vr*

desinfectante *adj & nm* : disinfectant

desinfectar *vt* : to disinfect — **desinfección** *nf*

desinflar *vt* : to deflate — **desinflarse** *vr*

desinformar *vt* : to misinform

desinhibido, -da *adj* : uninhibited, unrestrained

desintegración *nf, pl* -ciones : disintegration

desintegrar *vt* : to disintegrate, to break up — **desintegrarse** *vr*

desinterés *nm* 1 : lack of interest, indifference 2 : unselfishness

desinteresado, -da *adj* GENEROSO : unselfish

desintoxicación *nf, pl* -ciones : detoxification, detox *fam*

desintoxicar {72} *vt* : to detoxify, to detox *fam* — **desintoxicarse** *vr*

desistir *vi* 1 : to desist, to stop 2 ～ de : to give up, to relinquish

deslave *nm Mex* : landslide

desleal *adj* INFIEL : disloyal — **deslealmente** *adv*

deslealtad *nf* : disloyalty

desligar {52} *vt* 1 : to separate, to undo 2 : to free (from an obligation) — **desligarse** *vr* ～ de : to extricate oneself from

deslindar *vt* 1 : to mark the limits of, to demarcate 2 : to define, to clarify

deslinde *nm* : demarcation

desliz *nm, pl* **deslices** : error, mistake, slip ⟨desliz de la lengua : slip of the tongue⟩

deslizador *nm* 1 : speedboat 2 *Mex* : hang glider

deslizamiento *nm* : slip, slide ⟨deslizamiento de tierras : landslide⟩

deslizar {21} *vt* 1 : to slide, to slip 2 : to slip in — **deslizarse** *vr* 1 : to slide, to glide 2 : to slip away

deslomarse *vr* : to wear oneself out, to work oneself to death

deslucido, -da *adj* 1 : lackluster, dull 2 : faded, dingy, tarnished

deslucir {45} *vt* 1 : to spoil 2 : to fade, to dull, to tarnish 3 : to discredit

deslumbrar *vt* : to dazzle — **deslumbrante** *adj*

deslustrado, -da *adj* : dull, lusterless

deslustrar *vt* : to tarnish, to dull

deslustre *nm* : tarnish

desmadrarse *vr* : to get out of hand

desmadre *nm fam* : chaos

desmán *nm, pl* **desmanes** 1 : outrage, abuse 2 : misfortune

desmandarse *vr* : to behave badly, to get out of hand

desmantelar *vt* DESMONTAR : to dismantle

desmañado, -da *adj* : clumsy, awkward

desmarcarse {72} *vr* : to distance oneself

desmayado, -da *adj* **1** : fainting, weak **2** : dull, pale

desmayar *vi* : to lose heart, to falter — **desmayarse** *vr* DESVANECERSE : to faint, to swoon

desmayo *nm* **1** : faint, fainting **2 sufrir un desmayo** : to faint

desmedido, -da *adj* DESMESURADO : excessive, undue

desmejorar *vt* : to weaken, to make worse — *vi* : to decline (in health), to get worse

desmembrar {55} *vt* **1** : to dismember **2** : to break up

desmemoriado, -da *adj* : absentminded, forgetful

desmentido *nm* : denial

desmentir {76} *vt* **1** NEGAR : to deny, to refute **2** CONTRADECIR : to contradict

desmenuzar {21} *vt* **1** : to break down, to scrutinize **2** : to crumble, to shred — **desmenuzarse** *vr*

desmerecer {53} *vt* : to be unworthy of — *vi* **1** : to decline in value **2** ~ **de** : to compare unfavorably with

desmesurado, -da *adj* DESMEDIDO : excessive, inordinate — **desmesuradamente** *adv*

desmigajar *vt* : to crumble — **desmigajarse** *vr*

desmilitarizar {21} *vt* : to demilitarize

desmitificar {72} *vt* : to demystify, to dispel the myths surrounding

desmontable *adj* : removable

desmontar *vt* **1** : to clear, to level off **2** DESMANTELAR : to dismantle, to take apart — *vi* : to dismount

desmonte *nm* : clearing, leveling

desmoralizador, -dora *adj* : demoralizing

desmoralizante → **desmoralizador**

desmoralizar {21} *vt* DESALENTAR : to demoralize, to discourage

desmoronamiento *nm* : crumbling, falling apart

desmoronar *vt* : to wear away, to erode — **desmoronarse** *vr* : to crumble, to deteriorate, to fall apart

desmovilizar {21} *vt* : to demobilize — **desmovilización** *nf*

desnatado, -da *Spain* → **descremado**

desnaturalizar {21} *vt* **1** : to denature **2** : to distort, to alter

desnivel *nm* **1** : disparity, difference **2** : unevenness (of a surface)

desnivelado, -da *adj* **1** : uneven **2** : unbalanced

desnivelar *vt* **1** : to make uneven **2** : to tip (the balance)

desnucar {72} *vt* : to break the neck of — **desnucarse** *vr* : to break one's neck

desnudar *vt* **1** : to undress **2** : to strip, to lay bare — **desnudarse** *vr* : to undress, to strip off one's clothing

desnudez *nf, pl* **-deces** : nudity, nakedness

desnudo[1], **-da** *adj* : nude, naked, bare

desnudo[2] *nm* : nude

desnutrición *nf, pl* **-ciones** MALNUTRICIÓN : malnutrition

desnutrido, -da *adj* MALNUTRIDO : malnourished, undernourished

desobedecer {53} *v* : to disobey

desobediencia *nf* : disobedience — **desobediente** *adj*

desocupación *nf, pl* **-ciones** : unemployment

desocupado, -da *adj* **1** : vacant, empty **2** : free, unoccupied **3** : unemployed

desocupar *vt* **1** : to empty **2** : to vacate, to move out of — **desocuparse** *vr* : to leave, to quit (a job)

desodorante *adj & nm* : deodorant

desolación *nf, pl* **-ciones** : desolation

desolado, -da *adj* **1** : desolate **2** : devastated, distressed

desolador, -dora *adj* **1** : devastating **2** : bleak, desolate

desolar {19} *vt* : to devastate

desollar *vt* : to skin, to flay

desorbitado, -da *adj* **1** : excessive, exorbitant **2 con los ojos desorbitados** : with eyes popping out of one's head

desorden *nm, pl* **desórdenes** **1** DESBARAJUSTE : disorder, mess **2** : disorder, disturbance, upset

desordenadamente *adv* : messily, in a disorderly way

desordenado, -da *adj* **1** : untidy, messy **2** : disorderly, unruly

desordenar *vt* : to mess up — **desordenarse** *vr* : to get messed up

desorganización *nf, pl* **-ciones** : disorganization

desorganizar {21} *vt* : to disrupt, to disorganize

desorientar *vt* : to disorient, to mislead, to confuse — **desorientarse** *vr* : to become disoriented, to lose one's way

desovar *vi* : to spawn

despachar *vt* **1** : to complete, to conclude **2** : to deal with, to take care of, to handle **3** : to dispatch, to send off **4** *fam* : to finish off, to kill **5** : to serve — *vi* : to serve — **despacharse** *vr fam* : to gulp down, to polish off

despacho *nm* **1** : dispatch, shipment **2** OFICINA : office, study

despacio *adv* LENTAMENTE, LENTO : slowly, slow ⟨¡despacio! : take it easy!, easy does it!⟩

despampanante *adj fam* : breathtaking, stunning

desparasitar *vt* : to worm (an animal), to rid of fleas/ticks/lice (etc.)

desparpajo *nm fam* **1** : self-confidence, nerve **2** *CA* : confusion, muddle

desparramar *vt* **1** : to spill, to splatter **2** : to spread, to scatter

despatarrarse *vr* : to sprawl (out)

despavorido, -da *adj* : terrified, horrified

despecho *nm* **1** : spite **2 a despecho de** : despite, in spite of

despectivo, -va *adj* **1** : contemptuous, disparaging **2** : derogatory, pejorative — **despectivamente** *adv*

despedazar {21} *vt* : to cut to pieces, to tear apart

despedida *nf* **1** : farewell, good-bye **2 despedida de soltera** : bridal shower

despedir {54} *vt* **1** : to see off, to show out **2** : to dismiss, to fire **3** EMITIR : to give off, to emit ⟨despedir un olor : to give off an odor⟩ — **despedirse** *vr* : to take one's leave, to say good-bye

despegado, -da *adj* **1** : separated, detached **2** : cold, distant

despegar {52} *vt* : to remove, to detach — *vi* : to take off, to lift off, to blast off

despegue *nm* : takeoff, liftoff

despeinar *vt* **despeinar a alguien** : to mess up someone's hair — **despeinarse** *vr* ⟨me despeiné : I messed up my hair, my hair got messed up⟩

despejado, -da *adj* **1** : clear, fair **2** : alert **3** : uncluttered, unobstructed

despejar *vt* **1** : to clear, to free **2** : to clarify — *vi* **1** : to clear up **2** : to punt (in sports)

despeje *nm* **1** : clearing **2** : punt (in sports)

despellejar *vt* : to skin (an animal)

despelote *nm* : mess, disaster

despenalizar {21} *vt* : to legalize — **despenalización** *nf*

despensa *nf* **1** : pantry, larder **2** PROVISIONES : provisions *pl*, supplies *pl*

despeñadero *nm* : cliff, precipice

despeñar *vt* : to hurl down

desperdiciar *vt* **1** DESAPROVECHAR, MALGASTAR : to waste **2** : to miss, to miss out on

desperdicio *nm* **1** : waste **2 desperdicios** *nmpl* RESIDUOS : refuse, scraps, rubbish

desperdigar {52} *vt* DISPERSAR : to disperse, to scatter

desperezarse {21} *vr* : to stretch

desperfecto *nm* **1** DEFECTO : flaw, defect **2** : damage

despertador *nm* : alarm clock

despertar {55} *vi* : to awaken, to wake up — *vt* **1** : to arouse, to wake **2** EVOCAR : to elicit, to evoke — **despertarse** *vr* : to wake (oneself) up

despiadado, -da *adj* CRUEL : cruel, merciless, pitiless — **despiadadamente** *adv*

despido *nm* : dismissal, layoff

despierto, -ta *adj* **1** : awake, alert **2** LISTO : clever, sharp ⟨con la mente despierta : with a sharp mind⟩

despilfarrador¹, -dora *adj* : extravagant, wasteful

despilfarrador², -dora *n* : spendthrift, prodigal

despilfarrar *vt* MALGASTAR : to squander, to waste

despilfarro *nm* : extravagance, wastefulness

despintar *vt* : to strip the paint from — **despintarse** *vr* : to fade, to wash off, to peel off

despistado¹, -da *adj* **1** DISTRAÍDO : absentminded, forgetful, scatterbrained **2** CONFUSO : confused, bewildered

despistado², -da *n* : absentminded person

despistar *vt* : to throw off the track, to confuse — **despistarse** *vr*

despiste *nm* **1** : absentmindedness **2** : mistake, slip

desplantador *nm* : garden trowel

desplante *nm* : insolence, rudeness

desplazamiento *nm* **1** : movement, displacement **2** : journey

desplazar {21} *vt* **1** : to replace, to displace **2** TRASLADAR : to move, to shift **3** : to scroll (in computing) — **desplazarse** *vr*

desplegar {49} *vt* **1** : to display, to show, to manifest **2** DESDOBLAR : to unfold, to unfurl **3** : to spread (out) **4** : to deploy

despliegue *nm* **1** : display **2** : deployment

desplomarse *vr* **1** : to plummet, to fall **2** DERRUMBARSE : to collapse, to break down

desplome *nm* **1** : fall, drop **2** : collapse

desplumar *vt* : to pluck (a chicken, etc.)

despoblación *nf, pl* **-ciones** : large population decrease

despoblado¹, -da *adj* : uninhabited, deserted

despoblado² *nm* : open country, deserted area

despoblar {19} *vt* : to reduce the population of ⟨un lugar despoblado : a deserted place⟩

despojar *vt* **1** : to strip, to clear **2** : to divest, to deprive — **despojarse** *vr* **1** ∼ **de** : to remove (clothing) **2** ∼ **de** : to relinquish, to renounce

despojos *nmpl* **1** : remains, scraps **2** : plunder, spoils

desportillar *vt* : to chip — **desportillarse** *vr*

desposar *vt* : to marry — **desposarse** *vr*

desposeer {20} *vt* : to dispossess

déspota *nmf* : despot, tyrant

despotismo *nm* : despotism — **despótico, -ca** *adj*

despotricar {72} *vi* : to rant and rave, to complain excessively

despreciable *adj* **1** : despicable, contemptible **2** : negligible ⟨nada despreciable : not inconsiderable, significant⟩

despreciar *vt* DESDEÑAR, MENOSPRECIAR : to despise, to scorn, to disdain

despreciativo, -va *adj* : scornful, disdainful

desprecio *nm* DESDÉN, MENOSPRECIO : disdain, contempt, scorn

desprender *vt* **1** SOLTAR : to detach, to loosen, to unfasten **2** EMITIR : to emit, to give off — **desprenderse** *vr* **1** : to come off, to come undone **2** : to be inferred, to follow **3** ∼ **de** : to part with, to get rid of

desprendido, -da *adj* : generous, unselfish, disinterested

desprendimiento *nm* **1** : detachment **2** GENEROSIDAD : generosity **3 desprendimiento de tierras** : landslide

despreocupación *nf, pl* **-ciones** : indifference, lack of concern

despreocupadamente *adv* : in a carefree, easygoing, or unconcerned way

despreocupado, -da *adj* : carefree, easygoing, unconcerned

desprestigiar *vt* DESACREDITAR : to discredit, to disgrace — **desprestigiarse** *vr* : to lose prestige

desprestigio nm DESCRÉDITO : discredit, disrepute

desprevenido, -da adj DESAPERCIBIDO : unprepared, off guard, unsuspecting

desprolijo, -ja adj : untidy, messy

desproporción nf, pl **-ciones** : disproportion, disparity

desproporcionado, -da adj : out of proportion

despropósito nm : piece of nonsense, absurdity

desprotegido, -da adj : unprotected, vulnerable

desprovisto, -ta adj ~ **de** : devoid of, lacking in

después adv **1** : afterward, later ⟨mucho después : much later⟩ ⟨me lo dijo después : she told me about it afterward⟩ **2** : then, next ⟨primero uno y después el otro : first one and then the other⟩ ⟨¿que hago después? : what do I do next?⟩ **3** ~ **de** : after, next after ⟨después de comer : after eating⟩ ⟨después del semáforo : after the stoplight⟩ **4 después (de) que** : after ⟨después que lo acabé : after I finished it⟩ **5 después de todo** : after all **6 poco después** : shortly after, soon thereafter

despuntado, -da adj : blunt, dull

despuntar vt : to blunt — vi **1** : to dawn **2** : to sprout **3** : to excel, to stand out

desquiciado, -da adj : crazy

desquiciar vt **1** : to unhinge (a door) **2** : to drive crazy — **desquiciarse** vr : to go crazy

desquitarse vr **1** : to get even, to retaliate **2** ~ **con** : to take it out on

desquite nm : revenge

desregulación nf, pl **-ciones** : deregulation

desregular vt : to deregulate

desregularización nf, pl **-ciones** → **desregulación**

destacadamente adv : outstandingly, prominently

destacado, -da adj **1** : outstanding, prominent **2** : stationed, posted

destacamento nm : detachment (of troops)

destacar {72} vt **1** ENFATIZAR, SUBRAYAR : to emphasize, to highlight, to stress ⟨cabe destacar . . . : it's worth mentioning . . .⟩ **2** REALZAR : to highlight, to bring out **3** : to station, to post — vi : to stand out — **destacarse** vr : to stand out

destajo nm **1** : piecework **2 a** ~ : by the item, by the job

destapacaños nm Mex : plunger (for toilets, etc.)

destapador nm : bottle opener

destapar vt **1** : to open, to take the top off **2** DESCUBRIR : to reveal, to uncover **3** : to unblock, to unclog

destape nm : uncovering, revealing

destartalado, -da adj : dilapidated, tumbledown

destellar vi **1** : to sparkle, to flash, to glint **2** : to twinkle

destello nm **1** : flash, sparkle, twinkle **2** : glimmer, hint

destemplado, -da adj **1** : out of tune **2** : irritable, out of sorts **3** : unpleasant (of weather)

desteñir {67} vi : to run, to fade — **desteñirse** vr : to fade

desterrado[1], -da adj : banished, exiled

desterrado[2], -da n : exile

desterrar {55} vt **1** EXILIAR : to banish, to exile **2** ERRADICAR : to eradicate, to do away with

destetar vt : to wean

destiempo adv **a** ~ : at the wrong time

destierro nm EXILIO : exile

destilación nf, pl **-ciones** : distillation

destilador, -dora n : distiller

destilar vt **1** : to exude **2** : to distill

destilería nf : distillery

destinación nf, pl **-ciones** DESTINO : destination

destinado, -da adj : destined, bound

destinar vt **1** : to appoint, to assign **2** ASIGNAR : to earmark, to allot

destinatario, -ria n **1** : addressee **2** : payee

destino nm **1** : destiny, fate **2** DESTINACIÓN : destination **3** : use **4** : assignment, post

destitución nf, pl **-ciones** : dismissal, removal from office

destituir {41} vt : to dismiss, to remove from office

destornillador nm : screwdriver

destornillar vt : to unscrew

destrabar vt **1** : to untie, to undo, to ease up **2** : to separate

destreza nf HABILIDAD : dexterity, skill

destronar vt : to depose, to dethrone

destrozado, -da adj **1** : ruined, destroyed **2** : devastated, brokenhearted

destrozar {21} vt **1** : to smash, to shatter **2** : to destroy, to wreck — **destrozarse** vr

destrozo nm **1** DAÑO : damage **2** : havoc, destruction

destrucción nf, pl **-ciones** : destruction

destructivo, -va adj : destructive

destructor[1], -tora adj : destructive

destructor[2] nm : destroyer (ship)

destruir {41} vt : to destroy — **destruirse** vr

desubicado, -da adj **1** : out of place **2** : confused, disoriented

desunión nf, pl **-niones** : lack of unity

desunir vt : to split, to divide

desusado, -da adj **1** INSÓLITO : unusual **2** OBSOLETO : obsolete, disused, antiquated

desuso nm : disuse, obsolescence ⟨caer en desuso : to fall into disuse⟩

desvaído, -da adj **1** : pale, washed-out **2** : vague, blurred

desvalido, -da adj DESAMPARADO : destitute, helpless

desvalijar vt **1** : to ransack **2** : to rob

desvalorización nf, pl **-ciones 1** DEVALUACIÓN : devaluation **2** : depreciation

desvalorizar {21} vt : to devalue

desván nm, pl **desvanes** ÁTICO, BUHARDILLA : attic

desvanecer {53} vt **1** DISIPAR : to make disappear, to dispel **2** : to fade, to blur

— **desvanecerse** *vr* **1** : to vanish, to disappear **2** : to fade **3** DESMAYARSE : to faint, to swoon

desvanecimiento *nm* **1** : disappearance **2** DESMAYO : faint **3** : fading

desvariar {85} *vi* **1** DELIRAR : to be delirious **2** : to rave, to talk nonsense

desvarío *nm* **1** DELIRIO : delirium **2 desvaríos** *nmpl* : ravings *pl*

desvelado, -da *adj* : sleepless

desvelar *vt* **1** : to keep awake **2** REVELAR : to reveal, to disclose — **desvelarse** *vr* **1** : to stay awake **2** : to do one's utmost

desvelo *nm* **1** : insomnia **2 desvelos** *nmpl* : efforts, pains

desvencijado, -da *adj* : dilapidated, rickety

desventaja *nf* : disadvantage, drawback

desventajoso, -sa *adj* : disadvantageous, unfavorable

desventura *nf* INFORTUNIO : misfortune

desventurado, -da *adj* : unfortunate, illfated

desvergonzado, -da *adj* : shameless, impudent

desvergüenza *nf* : audacity, impudence

desvestir {54} *vt* : to undress — **desvestirse** *vr* : to get undressed

desviación *nf, pl* -**ciones 1** : deviation, departure **2** : detour, diversion

desviar {85} *vt* **1** : to change the course of, to divert **2** : to turn away, to deflect — **desviarse** *vr* **1** : to branch off **2** APARTARSE : to stray

desvinculación *nf, pl* -**ciones** : dissociation

desvincular *vt* ~ **de** : to separate from, to dissociate from — **desvincularse** *vr*

desvío *nm* **1** : diversion, detour **2** : deviation

desvirtuar {3} *vt* **1** : to impair, to spoil **2** : to detract from **3** : to distort, to misrepresent

desvivirse *vr* : to be devoted to

detalladamente *adv* : in detail, at great length

detallar *vt* : to detail

detalle *nm* **1** : detail ⟨entrar en detalles : to go into detail⟩ **2 al detalle** : retail **3** : thoughtful gesture ⟨tener un detalle con alguien : to do something nice for someone⟩

detallista[1] *adj* **1** : meticulous **2** : retail

detallista[2] *nmf* **1** : perfectionist **2** : retailer

detección *nf, pl* -**ciones** : detection

detectar *vt* : to detect — **detectable** *adj*

detective *nmf* : detective ⟨detective privado/privada : private detective⟩

detector *nm* : detector ⟨detector de mentiras : lie detector⟩

detención *nf, pl* -**ciones 1** ARRESTO : detention, arrest **2** : stop, halt **3** : delay, holdup

detener {80} *vt* **1** ARRESTAR : to arrest, to detain **2** PARAR : to stop, to halt **3** : to keep, to hold back — **detenerse** *vr* **1** : to stop **2** : to delay, to linger

detenidamente *adv* : thoroughly, at length

detenimiento *nm* **con** ~ : carefully, in detail

detentar *vt* : to hold, to retain

detergente *nm* : detergent

deteriorado, -da *adj* : damaged, worn

deteriorar *vt* ESTROPEAR : to damage, to spoil — **deteriorarse** *vr* **1** : to get damaged, to wear out **2** : to deteriorate, to worsen

deterioro *nm* **1** : deterioration, wear **2** : worsening, decline

determinación *nf, pl* -**ciones 1** : determination, resolve **2 tomar una determinación** : to make a decision

determinado, -da *adj* **1** : certain, particular **2** : determined, resolute

determinante[1] *adj* : determining, deciding

determinante[2] *nm* : determinant

determinar *vt* **1** : to determine **2** : to cause, to bring about — **determinarse** *vr* : to make up one's mind, to decide

detestar *vt* : to detest — **detestable** *adj*

detonación *nf, pl* -**ciones** : detonation

detonador *nm* : detonator

detonante[1] *adj* : detonating, explosive

detonante[2] *nm* **1** → **detonador 2** : catalyst, cause

detonar *vi* : to detonate, to explode

detractor, -tora *n* : detractor, critic

detrás *adv* **1** : behind ⟨caminábamos detrás : we walked along behind⟩ **2** ~ **de** : in back of, behind **3 por** ~ : from behind, in/at the back

detrimento *nm* : detriment ⟨en detrimento de : to the detriment of⟩

detuvo, etc. → **detener**

deuda *nf* **1** DÉBITO : debt **2 en deuda con** : indebted to

deudo, -da *n* : relative

deudor[1], **-dora** *adj* : indebted

deudor[2], **-dora** *n* : debtor

devaluación *nf, pl* -**ciones** DESVALORIZACIÓN : devaluation

devaluar {3} *vt* : to devalue — **devaluarse** *vr* : to depreciate

devanarse *vr* **devanarse los sesos** : to rack one's brains

devaneo *nm* **1** : flirtation, fling **2** : idle pursuit

devastador, -dora *adj* : devastating

devastar *vt* : to devastate — **devastación** *nf*

develar *vt* **1** REVELAR : to reveal, to uncover **2** : to unveil

devenir {87} *vi* **1** : to come about **2** ~ **en** : to become, to turn into

devoción *nf, pl* -**ciones** : devotion

devolución *nf, pl* -**ciones** REEMBOLSO : return, refund

devolver {89} *vt* **1** : to return, to give back **2** REEMBOLSAR : to refund, to pay back **3** : to vomit, to bring up — *vi* : to vomit, to throw up — **devolverse** *vr* : to return, to come back, to go back

devorar *vt* **1** : to devour **2** : to consume

devoto[1], **-ta** *adj* : devout — **devotamente** *adv*

devoto[2], **-ta** *n* : devotee, admirer

di → **dar, decir**

día *nm* **1** : day ⟨buenos días : hello, good morning⟩ ⟨todos los días : every day⟩ ⟨todo el día : all day⟩ ⟨un día sí y otro no : every other day⟩ ⟨ocho horas al día : eight hours a day⟩ ⟨día hábil : workday, business day⟩ ⟨día festivo/feriado : public holiday⟩ ⟨día de pago : payday⟩ ⟨¿qué día es hoy? : what day is today?⟩ ⟨el día 21 de abril : the 21st of April, April 21st⟩ ⟨el día anterior : the previous day, the day before⟩ **2** : daytime, daylight ⟨de día : by day, in the daytime⟩ ⟨en pleno día : in broad daylight⟩ ⟨día y noche : day and night⟩ **3 al día** : up-to-date ⟨ponerse al día con : to get up to date with, to catch up on⟩ ⟨poner al día : to bring up to date, to update⟩ **4 en su día** : in due time **5 hoy (en) día** : nowadays, these days

diabetes *nf* : diabetes
diabético, -ca *adj & n* : diabetic
diablillo *nm* : little devil, imp
diablo *nm* **1** DEMONIO : devil **2 ¿qué diablos . . . ?** : what on earth . . . ?, what the hell . . . ?
diablura *nf* **1** : prank **2 diabluras** *nfpl* : mischief
diabólico, -ca *adj* : diabolical, diabolic, devilish
diaconisa *nf* : deaconess
diácono *nm* : deacon
diacrítico, -ca *adj* : diacritic, diacritical
diadema *nf* : diadem, crown
diáfano, -na *adj* **1** CLARO : clear **2** TRASLÚCIDO : sheer (of fabric), translucent **3** : bright (of a light, room, etc.)
diafragma *nm* : diaphragm
diagnosticar {72} *vt* : to diagnose
diagnóstico¹, -ca *adj* : diagnostic
diagnóstico² *nm* : diagnosis
diagonal¹ *adj* : diagonal — **diagonalmente** *adv*
diagonal² *nf* **1** : diagonal **2** : slash (punctuation mark)
diagrama *nm* **1** : diagram **2 diagrama de flujo** ORGANIGRAMA : flow chart
dial *nm* : dial (on a radio, etc.)
dialecto *nm* : dialect
dialogar {52} *vi* : to have a talk, to converse
diálogo *nm* : dialogue
diamante *nm* : diamond
diámetro *nm* : diameter
diana *nf* **1** : target, bull's-eye **2 or toque de diana** : reveille
diapasón *nm, pl* -**sones** : tuning fork
diapositiva *nf* : slide, transparency
diariamente *adv* : daily, every day
diario¹ *adv Mex* : every day, daily
diario², -ria *adj* **1** : daily, everyday ⟨la vida diaria : everyday life⟩ ⟨ocho horas diarias : eight hours a day⟩ **2 a diario** : every day, daily
diario³ *nm* **1** : diary **2** PERIÓDICO : newspaper **3 de ~** : everyday
diarrea *nf* : diarrhea
diatriba *nf* : diatribe, tirade
dibujante *nmf* **1** : draftsman *m*, draftswoman *f* **2** CARICATURISTA : cartoonist

dibujar *vt* **1** : to draw, to sketch **2** : to portray, to depict
dibujo *nm* **1** : drawing ⟨dibujo lineal : line drawing⟩ ⟨dibujo a lápiz : pencil drawing⟩ ⟨dibujo a pulso, dibujo a mano alzada : freehand sketch⟩ **2** : design, pattern **3 dibujos animados** : (animated) cartoons
dicción *nf, pl* -**ciones** : diction
diccionario *nm* : dictionary
dícese → **decir**
dicha *nf* **1** SUERTE : good luck **2** FELICIDAD : happiness, joy
dicho¹ *pp* → **decir**
dicho², -cha *adj* : said, aforementioned ⟨las personas dichas : the aforementioned people⟩
dicho³ *nm* DECIR : saying, proverb
dichoso, -sa *adj* **1** : blessed **2** FELIZ : happy **3** AFORTUNADO : fortunate, lucky
diciembre *nm* : December ⟨el primero de diciembre : (on) December first⟩
diciendo → **decir**
dictado *nm* : dictation
dictador, -dora *n* : dictator
dictadura *nf* : dictatorship
dictamen *nm, pl* **dictámenes** **1** : report **2** : judgment, opinion
dictaminar *vt* : to report — *vi* : to give an opinion, to pass judgment
dictar *vt* **1** : to dictate **2** : to pronounce (a judgment) **3** : to give, to deliver (a lecture, etc.)
dictatorial *adj* : dictatorial
didáctico, -ca *adj* : didactic
diecinueve *adj & nm* : nineteen — **diecinueve** *pron*
diecinueveavo¹, -va *adj* : nineteenth
diecinueveavo² *nm* : nineteenth (fraction)
dieciocho *adj & nm* : eighteen — **dieciocho** *pron*
dieciochoavo¹, -va *or* **dieciochavo, -va** *adj* : eighteenth
dieciochoavo² *or* **dieciochavo** *nm* : eighteenth (fraction)
dieciséis *adj & nm* : sixteen — **dieciséis** *pron*
dieciseisavo¹, -va *adj* : sixteenth
dieciseisavo² *nm* : sixteenth (fraction)
diecisiete *adj & nm* : seventeen — **diecisiete** *pron*
diecisieteavo¹, -va *adj* : seventeenth
diecisieteavo² *nm* : seventeenth (in a series)
diente *nm* **1** : tooth ⟨diente canino : eyetooth, canine tooth⟩ ⟨cepillarse los dientes : to brush one's teeth⟩ ⟨le están saliendo los dientes : he's teething⟩ **2** : tusk, fang **3** : prong, tine **4** : clove (of garlic) **5 diente de león** : dandelion **6 entre dientes** : under one's breath, quietly ⟨hablar entre dientes : to mutter, to mumble⟩
dieron, etc. → **dar**
diesel [ˈdisɛl] *nm* : diesel
diestra *nf* : right hand
diestro¹, -tra *adj* **1** : right **2** : skillful, accomplished

diestro[2] *nm* : bullfighter, matador

dieta *nf* : diet

dietético, -ca *adj* : dietary, diet

dietista *nmf* : dietitian

diez[1] *nm, pl* **dieces** : ten ⟨el diez de julio : (on) the tenth of July, (on) July tenth⟩ ⟨un as y dos dieces : an ace and two tens⟩

diez[2] *adj* : ten ⟨tiene diez años : he's ten (years old)⟩

diez[3] *pron* : ten ⟨somos diez : there are ten of us⟩ ⟨son las diez : it's ten o'clock⟩

difamación *nf, pl* **-ciones** : defamation, slander

difamar *vt* : to defame, to slander

difamatorio, -ria *adj* : slanderous, defamatory, libelous

diferencia *nf* **1** : difference ⟨partir la diferencia : to split the difference⟩ **2 a diferencia de** : unlike, in contrast to **3 con ∼** : by far

diferenciación *nf, pl* **-ciones** : differentiation

diferencial *adj & nm* : differential

diferenciar *vt* : to differentiate between, to distinguish — **diferenciarse** *vr* : to differ

diferendo *nm* : dispute, conflict

diferente *adj* DISTINTO : different ⟨diferente a/de : different from⟩ — **diferentemente** *adv*

diferido *adj* **en ∼** ⟨un programa en diferido : a prerecorded program⟩ ⟨transmitir en diferido : to broadcast later⟩

diferir {76} *vt* DILATAR, POSPONER : to postpone, to put off — *vi* : to differ

difícil *adj* : difficult, hard ⟨difícil de describir : hard to describe⟩ ⟨una persona difícil : a difficult person⟩ ⟨lo veo difícil : I think it's unlikely⟩

difícilmente *adv* **1** : with difficulty **2** : hardly

dificultad *nf* : difficulty

dificultar *vt* : to make difficult, to obstruct

dificultoso, -sa *adj* : difficult, hard

difteria *nf* : diphtheria

difuminar *vt* : to blur

difundir *vt* **1** : to diffuse, to spread out **2** : to broadcast, to spread

difunto, -ta *adj & n* FALLECIDO : deceased

difusión *nf, pl* **-siones 1** : spreading **2** : diffusion (of heat, etc.) **3** : broadcast, broadcasting ⟨los medios de difusión : the media⟩

difuso, -sa *adj* : diffuse, widespread

diga, etc. → **decir**

digerir {76} *vt* : to digest — **digerible** *adj*

digestión *nf, pl* **-tiones** : digestion

digestivo, -va *adj* : digestive

digital[1] *adj* : digital — **digitalmente** *adv*

digital[2] *nf* DEDALERA : foxglove

digitalizar {21} *vt* : to digitalize

digitaria *nf* : crabgrass

dígito *nm* : digit

dignarse *vr* : to deign, to condescend ⟨no se dignó contestar : he didn't deign to answer⟩

dignatario, -ria *n* : dignitary

dignidad *nf* **1** : dignity **2** : dignitary

dignificar {72} *vt* : to dignify

digno, -na *adj* **1** HONORABLE : honorable **2** : worthy ⟨digno de : worthy of⟩ **3** : decent (of a salary, etc.) — **dignamente** *adv*

digresión *nf, pl* **-ciones** : digression

dije *nm* : charm (on a bracelet)

dijo, etc. → **decir**

dilación *nf, pl* **-ciones** : delay

dilapidar *vt* : to waste, to squander

dilatar *vt* **1** : to dilate, to widen, to expand **2** DIFERIR, POSPONER : to put off, to postpone — **dilatarse** *vr* **1** : to expand (of gases, metals, etc.) **2** *Mex* : to take long, to be long

dilatorio, -ria *adj* : delaying

dilema *nm* : dilemma

diletante *nmf* : dilettante

diligencia *nf* **1** : diligence, care **2** : promptness, speed **3** : action, step **4** : task, errand **5** : stagecoach **6 diligencias** *nfpl* : judicial procedures, formalities

diligente *adj* : diligent — **diligentemente** *adv*

dilucidar *vt* : to elucidate, to clarify

dilución *nf, pl* **-ciones** : dilution

diluir {41} *vt* : to dilute

diluviar *v impers* : to pour (with rain), to pour down

diluvio *nm* **1** : flood **2** : downpour

dimensión *nf, pl* **-siones** : dimension — **dimensional** *adj*

dimensionar *vt* : to measure, to gauge

diminutivo[1], **-va** *adj* : diminutive

diminutivo[2] *nm* : diminutive

diminuto, -ta *adj* : minute, tiny

dimisión *nf, pl* **-siones** : resignation

dimitir *vi* : to resign, to step down

dimos → **dar**

dinámica *nf* : dynamics

dinámico, -ca *adj* : dynamic — **dinámicamente** *adv*

dinamismo *nm* : energy, vigor

dinamita *nf* : dynamite

dinamitar *vt* : to dynamite

dínamo *or* **dinamo** *nm* : dynamo

dinastía *nf* : dynasty

dineral *nm* : fortune, large sum of money

dinero *nm* **1** : money ⟨hacer/ganar/recaudar dinero : to make/earn/raise money⟩ **2 dinero de bolsillo** : pocket money **3 dinero contante y sonante** : cold cash, hard cash **4 dinero en efectivo** : cash

dinosaurio *nm* : dinosaur

dintel *nm* : lintel

dio, etc. → **dar**

diócesis *nfs & pl* : diocese

dios, diosa *n* : god, goddess *f*

Dios *nm* : God ⟨gracias a Dios : thank God⟩ ⟨si Dios quiere : God willing⟩ ⟨¡por Dios! : for God's sake!⟩ ⟨¡Dios mío! : good God!⟩ ⟨¡vaya por Dios! : for heaven's sake!⟩ ⟨¡Dios me libre! : God/heaven forbid!⟩ ⟨que Dios te bendiga : God bless you⟩ ⟨como Dios manda : proper, properly⟩

dióxido de carbono *nm* : carbon dioxide

diploma *nm* : diploma

diplomacia *nf* : diplomacy

diplomado[1], **-da** *adj* : qualified, trained
diplomado[2] *nm Mex* : seminar
diplomático[1], **-ca** *adj* : diplomatic — **diplomáticamente** *adv*
diplomático[2], **-ca** *n* : diplomat
diptongo *nm* : diphthong
diputación *nf, pl* **-ciones** : deputation, delegation
diputado, -da *n* : delegate, representative
dique *nm* : dike
dirá, etc. → **decir**
dirección *nf, pl* **-ciones** 1 : address ⟨dirección particular/electrónica : home/e-mail address⟩ 2 : direction ⟨en dirección a : towards⟩ ⟨en dirección contraria : the opposite direction, the other way⟩ 3 : management, leadership 4 : steering (of an automobile) ⟨dirección asistida : power steering⟩
direccional[1] *adj* : directional
direccional[2] *nf* : directional, turn signal
directa *nf* : high gear
directamente *adv* : straight, directly
directiva *nf* 1 ORDEN : directive 2 DIRECTORIO, JUNTA : board of directors
directivo[1], **-va** *adj* : executive, managerial
directivo[2], **-va** *n* : executive, director
directo, -ta *adj* 1 : direct, straight, immediate 2 **en** ~ : live (in broadcasting)
director, -tora *n* 1 : director, manager, head 2 : conductor (of an orchestra)
directorial → **directivo**[1]
directorio *nm* 1 : directory 2 DIRECTIVA, JUNTA : board of directors
directriz *nf, pl* **-trices** : guideline
dirigencia *nf* : leaders *pl*, leadership
dirigente[1] *adj* : directing, leading
dirigente[2] *nmf* : director, leader
dirigible *nm* : dirigible, blimp
dirigir {35} *vt* 1 : to run, to manage (a business, etc.), to lead (a group, etc.) 2 : to conduct (music), to direct (a film) 3 : to address (a letter, comment, etc.) 4 : to aim, to point ⟨dirigir la mirada a/hacia : to look at/towards⟩ ⟨dirigir la atención hacia : to turn one's attention to⟩ — **dirigirse** *vr* ~ **a** 1 : to go towards 2 : to speak to, to address
dirimir *vt* 1 : to resolve, to settle 2 : to annul, to dissolve (a marriage)
discapacidad *nf* MINUSVALÍA : disability, handicap *sometimes offensive*
discapacitado[1], **-da** *adj* : disabled, handicapped *sometimes offensive*
discapacitado[2], **-da** *n* : disabled person, handicapped person *sometimes offensive*
discar {72} *v* : to dial
discernimiento *nm* : discernment
discernir {25} *v* : to discern, to distinguish
disciplina *nf* : discipline
disciplinar *vt* : to discipline — **disciplinario, -ria** *adj*
discípulo, -la *n* : disciple, follower
disc jockey [ˌdiskˈjoke, -ˈdʒo-] *nmf* : disc jockey
disco *nm* 1 : record ⟨parecer un disco rayado : to sound like a broken record⟩ 2 : disc, disk ⟨disco compacto : compact disc⟩ ⟨disco volador : Frisbee *trademark*⟩ 3 : discus

disco duro *nm* 1 : hard disk 2 *or* **unidad de disco duro** : hard drive
discografía *nf* : list of records (by a musician)
díscolo, -la *adj* : unruly, disobedient
disconforme *adj* : in disagreement
discontinuidad *nf* : discontinuity
discontinuo, -nua *adj* : discontinuous
discordancia *nf* DESAVENENCIA : conflict, disagreement
discordante *adj* 1 : discordant 2 : conflicting
discordia *nf* : discord
discoteca *nf* 1 : disco, discotheque 2 *CA, Mex* : record store
discreción *nf, pl* **-ciones** : discretion
discrecional *adj* : discretionary
discrepancia *nf* : discrepancy
discrepar *vi* 1 : to disagree 2 : to differ
discreto, -ta *adj* : discreet — **discretamente** *adv*
discriminación *nf, pl* **-ciones** : discrimination
discriminar *vt* 1 : to discriminate against 2 : to distinguish, to differentiate
discriminatorio, -ria *adj* : discriminatory
disculpa *nf* 1 : apology 2 : excuse
disculpable *adj* : excusable
disculpar *vt* : to excuse, to pardon — **disculparse** *vr* : to apologize
discurrir *vi* 1 : to flow 2 : to pass, to go by 3 : to ponder, to reflect
discurso *nm* 1 ORACIÓN : speech, address 2 : discourse, treatise
discusión *nf, pl* **-siones** 1 : discussion 2 ALTERCADO, DISPUTA : argument
discutible *adj* : arguable, debatable
discutidor, -dora *adj* : argumentative
discutir *vt* 1 : to discuss 2 : to dispute — *vi* ALTERCAR : to argue, to quarrel
disecar {72} *vt* 1 : to dissect 2 : to stuff (for preservation)
disección *nf, pl* **-ciones** : dissection
diseminación *nf, pl* **-ciones** : dissemination, spreading
diseminar *vt* : to disseminate, to spread
disensión *nf, pl* **-siones** : dissension, disagreement
disenso *nm* : dissent, disagreement
disentería *nf* : dysentery
disentimiento → **disenso**
disentir {76} *vi* : to dissent, to disagree
diseñador, -dora *n* : designer
diseñar *vt* 1 : to design, to plan 2 : to lay out, to outline
diseño *nm* : design
disertación *nf, pl* **-ciones** 1 : lecture, talk 2 : dissertation
disertar *vi* : to lecture, to give a talk
disfraz *nm, pl* **disfraces** 1 : disguise 2 : costume 3 : front, pretense
disfrazar {21} *vt* 1 : to disguise 2 : to mask, to conceal — **disfrazarse** *vr* : to wear a costume, to be in disguise
disfrutar *vt* : to enjoy — *vi* : to enjoy oneself, to have a good time
disfrute *nm* : enjoyment
disfunción *nf, pl* **-ciones** : dysfunction — **disfuncional** *adj*

disgregar {52} *vt* : to break up, to disintegrate — **disgregarse** *vr*

disgustar *vt* : to upset, to displease, to make angry ⟨darle un disgusto a alguien : to upset someone⟩ ⟨llevarse un disgusto : to be upset⟩ — **disgustarse** *vr*

disgusto *nm* **1** : annoyance, displeasure **2** : argument, quarrel **3** : trouble, misfortune

disidencia *nf* : dissent

disidente *adj & nmf* : dissident

disímbolo, -la *adj Mex* : dissimilar

disímil *adj* : dissimilar

disimuladamente *adv* : furtively, slyly

disimulado, -da *adj* **1** : concealed, disguised **2** : furtive, sly

disimular *vi* : to dissemble, to pretend — *vt* : to conceal, to hide

disimulo *nm* **1** : dissembling, pretense **2** : slyness, furtiveness **3** : tolerance

disipar *vt* **1** : to dissipate, to dispel **2** : to squander — **disiparse** *vr*

diskette [di'skɛt] *nm* : floppy disk, diskette

dislexia *nf* : dyslexia — **disléxico, -ca** *adj*

dislocar {72} *vt* : to dislocate — **dislocación** *nf*

disminución *nf, pl* **-ciones** : decrease, drop, fall

disminuir {41} *vt* REDUCIR : to reduce, to decrease, to lower — *vi* **1** : to lower **2** : to drop, to fall

disociar *vt* : to dissociate, to separate — **disociación** *nf*

disolución *nf, pl* **-ciones** **1** : dissolution, dissolving **2** : breaking up **3** : dissipation

disoluto, -ta *adj* : dissolute, dissipated

disolvente *nm* : solvent

disolver {89} *vt* **1** : to dissolve **2** : to break up — **disolverse** *vr*

disonancia *nf* : dissonance — **disonante** *adj*

dispar *adj* **1** : different, disparate **2** DIVERSO : diverse **3** DESIGUAL : inconsistent

disparado, -da *adj* **salir disparado** *fam* : to take off in a hurry, to rush away

disparar *vi* **1** : to shoot, to fire **2** *Mex fam* : to pay — *vt* **1** : to shoot **2** *Mex fam* : to treat to, to buy — **dispararse** *vr* : to shoot up, to skyrocket

disparatado, -da *adj* ABSURDO, RIDÍCULO : absurd, ridiculous, crazy

disparate *nm* : silliness, stupidity ⟨decir disparates : to talk nonsense⟩

disparejo, -ja *adj* DESIGUAL : uneven

disparidad *nf* : disparity

disparo *nm* TIRO : shot

dispendio *nm* : wastefulness, extravagance

dispendioso, -sa *adj* : wasteful, extravagant

dispensa *nf* : dispensation

dispensador *nm* : dispenser

dispensar *vt* **1** : to dispense, to give, to grant **2** EXCUSAR : to excuse, to forgive **3** EXIMIR : to exempt

dispensario *nm* **1** : dispensary, clinic **2** *Mex* : dispenser

dispersar *vt* DESPERDIGAR : to disperse, to scatter

dispersión *nf, pl* **-siones** : dispersion

disperso, -sa *adj* : dispersed, scattered

displicencia *nf* : indifference, coldness, disdain

displicente *adj* : indifferent, cold, disdainful

disponer {60} *vt* **1** : to arrange, to lay out **2** : to stipulate, to order **3** : to prepare — *vi* ~ **de** : to have at one's disposal — **disponerse** *vr* ~ **a** : to prepare to, to be about to

disponibilidad *nf* : availability

disponible *adj* : available

disposición *nf, pl* **-ciones** **1** : disposition **2** : aptitude, talent **3** : order, arrangement **4** : willingness, readiness **5** **última disposición** : last will and testament

dispositivo *nm* **1** APARATO, MECANISMO : device, mechanism **2** : force, detachment

dispositivo intrauterino *nm* : intrauterine device, IUD

dispuesto[1] *pp* → **disponer**

dispuesto[2]**, -ta** *adj* PREPARADO : ready, prepared, disposed

dispuso, etc. → **disponer**

disputa *nf* ALTERCADO, DISCUSIÓN : dispute, argument

disputar *vi* : to argue, to contend, to vie — *vt* : to dispute, to question — **disputarse** *vr* : to compete for

disquera *nf* : record label, recording company

disquete → **diskette**

disquisición *nf, pl* **-ciones** **1** : formal discourse **2 disquisiciones** *nfpl* : digressions

distancia *nf* **1** : distance ⟨la distancia entre la Tierra y el Sol : the distance between the Earth and the Sun⟩ ⟨está a dos cuadras de distancia : it's two blocks away⟩ **2** : (emotional) distance ⟨guardar/mantener las distancias : to keep one's distance⟩ **3 a** ~ : from/at a distance ⟨mando a distancia : remote control⟩

distanciamiento *nm* **1** : distancing **2** : rift, estrangement

distanciar *vt* **1** : to space out **2** : to draw apart — **distanciarse** *vr* : to grow apart, to become estranged

distante *adj* **1** : distant, far-off **2** : aloof

distar *vi* ~ **de** : to be far from ⟨dista de ser perfecto : he is far from perfect⟩

diste → **dar**

distender {56} *vt* : to distend, to stretch

distendido, -da *adj* : relaxed

distensión *nf, pl* **-siones** : easing of relations

distinción *nf, pl* **-ciones** : distinction

distinguible *adj* : distinguishable

distinguido, -da *adj* : distinguished, refined

distinguir {26} *vt* **1** : to distinguish **2** : to honor **3** : to characterize — **distinguirse** *vr*

distintivo, -va *adj* : distinctive — **distintivamente** *adv*

distinto, -ta *adj* **1** DIFERENTE : different
⟨distinto de/a : different from/than⟩ **2**
CLARO : distinct, clear, evident **3 distin-**
tos, -tas *pl* : various
distorsión *nf, pl* **-siones** : distortion
distorsionar *vt* : to distort
distracción *nf, pl* **-ciones** **1** : distraction,
amusement **2** : forgetfulness **3** : oversight
distraer {81} *vt* **1** : to distract **2** ENTRE-
TENER : to entertain, to amuse — **dis-**
traerse *vr* **1** : to get distracted **2** : to
amuse oneself
distraídamente *adv* : absentmindedly
distraído[1] *pp* → **distraer**
distraído[2], **-da** *adj* **1** : distracted, preoccupied **2** DESPISTADO : absentminded
distribución *nf, pl* **-ciones** : distribution
distribuidor, -dora *n* : distributor
distribuir {41} *vt* : to distribute
distributivo, -va *adj* : distributive
distrital *adj* : district, of the district
distrito *nm* : district
distrofia *nf* : dystrophy ⟨distrofia muscular : muscular dystrophy⟩
disturbio *nm* : disturbance
disuadir *vt* : to dissuade, to discourage
disuasión *nf, pl* **-siones** : deterrence
disuasivo, -va *adj* : deterrent, discouraging
disuasorio, -ria *adj* : discouraging
disuelto *pp* → **disolver**
disyuntiva *nf* : dilemma
DIU ['diu] *nm* (*dispositivo intrauterino*)
: IUD, intrauterine device
diurno, -na *adj* : day, daytime
diva *nf* → **divo**
divagar {52} *vi* : to digress
diván *nm, pl* **divanes** : divan
divergencia *nf* : divergence, difference
divergente *adj* : divergent, differing
divergir {35} *vi* **1** : to diverge **2** : to differ, to disagree
diversidad *nf* : diversity, variety
diversificación *nf, pl* **-ciones** : diversification
diversificar {72} *vt* : to diversify
diversión *nf, pl* **-siones** ENTRETENI-
MIENTO : fun, amusement, diversion
diverso, -sa *adj* : diverse, various ⟨opin-
iones diversas : diverse opinions⟩ ⟨de
diverso(s) tipo(s) : of various kinds⟩
divertido, -da *adj* **1** : amusing, funny **2**
: entertaining, enjoyable
divertir {76} *vt* ENTRETENER : to amuse,
to entertain — **divertirse** *vr* : to have
fun, to have a good time
dividendo *nm* : dividend
dividir *vt* **1** : to divide, to split **2** : to distribute, to share out — **dividirse** *vr*
divinidad *nf* : divinity
divino, -na *adj* : divine
divisa *nf* **1** : currency **2** LEMA : motto
3 : emblem, insignia
divisar *vt* : to discern, to make out
divisible *adj* : divisible
división *nf, pl* **-siones** : division
divisivo, -va *adj* : divisive
divisor *nm* : denominator
divisorio, -ria *adj* : dividing

divo, -va *n* **1** : prima donna **2** : celebrity, star
divorciado[1], **-da** *adj* **1** : divorced **2**
: split, divided
divorciado[2], **-da** *n* : divorcé *m*, divorcée *f*
divorciar *vt* : to divorce — **divorciarse** *vr*
: to get a divorce
divorcio *nm* : divorce
divulgación *nf, pl* **-ciones** **1** : spreading,
dissemination **2** : popularizing
divulgar {52} *vt* **1** : to spread, to circulate
2 REVELAR : to divulge, to reveal **3** : to
popularize — **divulgarse** *vr*
dizque *adv* : supposedly, apparently
do *nm* **1** : C ⟨do sostenido/bemol : C
sharp/flat⟩ **2** : do (in singing)
dobladillo *nm* : hem
doblado, -da *adj* **1** : folded **2** : dubbed
doblaje *nm* : dubbing
doblar *vt* **1** : to double **2** PLEGAR : to
fold, to bend **3** : to turn ⟨doblar la esquina : to turn the corner⟩ **4** : to dub —
vi **1** : to turn **2** : to toll, to ring —
doblarse *vr* **1** : to fold up, to double
over **2** : to give in, to yield
doble[1] *adj* : double ⟨doble el número de
: double the number of⟩ ⟨doble sentido
: double meaning⟩ — **doblemente** *adv*
doble[2] *nm* **1** : double **2** : toll (of a bell),
knell
doble[3] *nmf* : stand-in, double
doblegar {52} *vt* **1** : to fold, to crease **2**
: to force to yield — **doblegarse** *vr* : to
yield, to bow
doble uve *nf Spain* → **ve doble**
doble ve → **ve doble**
doblez[1] *nm, pl* **dobleces** : fold, crease
doblez[2] *nmf* : duplicity, deceitfulness
doce *adj* & *nm* : twelve — **doce** *pron*
doceavo[1], **-va** *adj* : twelfth
doceavo[2] *nm* : twelfth (fraction)
docena *nf* **1** : dozen **2 docena de fraile**
: baker's dozen
docencia *nf* : teaching
docente[1] *adj* : educational, teaching
docente[2] *n* : teacher, lecturer
dócil *adj* : docile — **dócilmente** *adv*
docilidad *nf* : meekness
docto, -ta *adj* : learned, erudite
doctor, -tora *n* : doctor ⟨doctor en pedagogía : doctor of education⟩
doctorado *nm* : doctorate
doctorarse *vr* : to earn one's doctorate
doctrina *nf* : doctrine — **doctrinal** *adj*
documentación *nf, pl* **-ciones** : documentation
documental *adj* & *nm* : documentary
documentar *vt* : to document
documento *nm* : document
dogma *nm* : dogma
dogmático, -ca *adj* : dogmatic
dogmatismo *nm* : dogmatism
doguillo *nm* : pug (dog)
dólar *nm* : dollar
dolencia *nf* : ailment, malaise
doler {47} *vi* **1** : to hurt, to ache ⟨me duele la cabeza : my head hurts⟩ ⟨no duele
nada : it doesn't hurt at all⟩ **2** : to grieve
— **dolerse** *vr* **1** : to be distressed **2** : to
complain

doliente *nmf* : mourner, bereaved
dolor *nm* **1** : pain, ache ⟨dolor de cabeza/muelas/espalda : headache/toothache/backache⟩ **2** PENA, TRISTEZA : grief, sorrow
dolorido, -da *adj* **1** : sore, aching **2** : hurt, upset
doloroso, -sa *adj* **1** : painful **2** : distressing — **dolorosamente** *adv*
doloso, -sa *adj* : fraudulent — **dolosamente** *adv*
domador, -dora *n* : tamer
domar *vt* : to tame, to break in
domesticado, -da *adj* : domesticated, tame
domésticamente *adv* : domestically
domesticar {72} *vt* : to domesticate, to tame
doméstico, -ca *adj* : domestic, household
domiciliado, -da *adj* : residing
domiciliario, -ria *adj* **1** : home **2 arresto domiciliario** : house arrest
domiciliarse *vr* RESIDIR : to reside
domicilio *nm* : home, residence ⟨cambio de domicilio : change of address⟩
dominación *nf, pl* **-ciones** : domination
dominante *adj* **1** : dominant **2** : domineering
dominar *vt* **1** : to dominate **2** : to master, to be proficient at **3** : to overlook, to offer a view of — *vi* **1** : to predominate, to prevail — **dominarse** *vr* : to control oneself
domingo *nm* **1** : Sunday ⟨el domingo : on Sunday⟩ ⟨Domingo de Pascua/Resurrección : Easter Sunday⟩
dominical *adj* : Sunday ⟨periódico dominical : Sunday newspaper⟩
dominicano, -na *adj & n* : Dominican
dominico, -ca *adj & n* : Dominican (in religion)
dominio *nm* **1** : dominion, power ⟨dominio de/sobre sí mismo : self-control⟩ **2** : mastery **3** : domain, field
dominó *nm, pl* **-nós 1** : domino (tile) **2** : dominoes *pl* (game)
domo *nm* : dome
don[1] *nm* **1** : gift, present **2** : talent, gift ⟨don de gente(s)/mando : people/leadership skills⟩ ⟨tener el don de la palabra : to have a way with words⟩
don[2] *nm* **1** : title of courtesy preceding a man's first name **2 don nadie** : nobody, insignificant person
dona *nf Mex* : doughnut, donut
donación *nf, pl* **-ciones** : donation
donador, -dora *n* : donor
donaire *nm* **1** GARBO : grace, poise **2** : witticism
donante *nf* → **donador**
donar *vt* : to donate
donativo *nm* : donation
doncella *nf* : maiden, damsel
donde[1] *conj* : where ⟨el pueblo donde vivo : the town where I live⟩ ⟨el lugar de donde viene : the place that/where he comes from⟩ ⟨regresamos por donde venimos : we went back the way we came⟩
donde[2] *prep* : over by ⟨lo encontré donde la silla : I found it over by the chair⟩

dónde *adv* : where ⟨¿dónde está su casa? : where is your house?⟩ ⟨¿de dónde eres? : where are you from?⟩ ⟨no sé por dónde empezar : I don't know where to begin⟩
dondequiera *adv* **1** : anywhere, no matter where **2 dondequiera que** : wherever, everywhere
donqueo *nm* : slam dunk
doña *nf* : title of courtesy preceding a woman's first name
dopado, -da *adj* : drugged
dopar *vt* : to drug, to dope — **doparse** *vr*
doping *nm* : doping (in sports)
doquier *adv* **por ~** : everywhere, all over
dorado[1], **-da** *adj* : gold, golden
dorado[2], **-da** *nm* : gilt
dorar *vt* **1** : to gild **2** : to brown (food)
dormido, -da *adj* **1** : asleep **2** : numb ⟨tiene el pie dormido : her foot's numb, her foot's gone to sleep⟩
dormilón, -lona *n, mpl* **-lones** : late riser
dormir {27} *vi* : to sleep — *vt* **1** : to put to sleep/bed **2** : to put to sleep (from boredom, etc.) **3** ANESTESIAR : to put to sleep, to anesthetize **4 dormir la siesta** : to have a nap — **dormirse** *vr* : to fall asleep
dormitar *vi* : to snooze, to doze
dormitorio *nm* **1** : bedroom **2** : dormitory
dorsal[1] *adj* : dorsal
dorsal[2] *nm* : number (worn in sports)
dorso *nm* **1** : back ⟨el dorso de la mano : the back of the hand⟩ **2** *or* **estilo dorso** *Mex* : backstroke
dos[1] *adj & nm* : two ⟨ella tiene dos años : she's two (years old)⟩ ⟨el dos de junio : (on) the second of June, (on) June second⟩
dos[2] *pron* : two ⟨somos dos : there are two of us⟩ ⟨ya somos dos : that makes two of us⟩ ⟨son las dos de la tarde : it's two o'clock in the afternoon⟩
doscientos[1], **-tas** *adj & pron* : two hundred
doscientos[2] *nms & pl* : two hundred (in a series)
dosel *nm* : canopy
dosificación *nf, pl* **-ciones** : dosage
dosificar {72} *vt* **1** : to dose **2** : to use sparingly
dosis *nfs & pl* **1** : dose **2** : amount, quantity
dossier *nm* : dossier
dotación *nf, pl* **-ciones 1** : endowment, funding **2** : staff, personnel
dotado, -da *adj* **1** : gifted **2 ~ de** : endowed with, equipped with
dotar *vt* **1** : to provide, to equip **2** : to endow
dote *nf* **1** : dowry **2 dotes** *nfpl* : talent, gift
doy → **dar**
draga *nf* : dredge
dragado *nm* : dredging
dragar {52} *vt* : to dredge
dragón *nm, pl* **dragones 1** : dragon **2** : snapdragon
drague, etc. → **dragar**

drama *nm* : drama
dramático, -ca *adj* : dramatic — **dramáticamente** *adv*
dramatizar {21} *vt* : to dramatize — **dramatización** *nf*
dramaturgo, -ga *n* : dramatist, playwright
drástico, -ca *adj* : drastic — **drásticamente** *adv*
drenaje *nm* : drainage
drenar *vt* : to drain
drene *nm Mex* : drain
driblar *vi* : to dribble (in basketball)
drible *nm* : dribble (in basketball)
droga *nf* : drug
drogadicción *nf, pl* **-ciones** : drug addiction
drogadicto, -ta *n* : drug addict
drogar {52} *vt* : to drug — **drogarse** *vr* : to take drugs
drogodependiente *nmf* : drug addict
drogue, etc. → **drogar**
droguería *nf* FARMACIA : drugstore
dromedario *nm* : dromedary
dual *adj* : dual
dualidad *nf* : duality
dualismo *nm* : dualism
ducha *nf* : shower ⟨darse una ducha : to take a shower⟩
ducharse *vr* : to take a shower
ducho, -cha *adj* : experienced, skilled, expert
ducto *nm* **1** : duct, shaft **2** : pipeline
duda *nf* **1** : doubt ⟨no cabe duda : there's no doubt about it⟩ ⟨no tengo ninguna duda que . . . : I have no doubt that . . .⟩ ⟨si tienes alguna duda . . . : if you have any questions . . .⟩ ⟨poner algo en duda : to call something into question⟩ ⟨salir de dudas : to set one's mind at ease⟩ ⟨sin sombra de duda : beyond the shadow of a doubt⟩ **2 sin ∼** : undoubtedly, without a doubt, no doubt
dudar *vt* : to doubt ⟨lo dudo mucho : I doubt that very much⟩ — *vi* ∼ **en** : to hesitate to ⟨no dudes en pedirme ayuda : don't hesitate to ask me for help⟩
dudoso, -sa *adj* **1** : doubtful **2** : dubious, questionable — **dudosamente** *adv*
duela *nf Mex* : floorboard
duele, etc. → **doler**
duelo *nm* **1** : duel **2** LUTO : mourning

duende *nm* **1** : elf, goblin **2** ENCANTO : magic, charm ⟨una bailarina que tiene duende : a dancer with a certain magic⟩
dueño, -ña *n* **1** : owner, proprietor **2** : landlord, landlady *f*
duerme, etc. → **dormir**
dueto *nm* : duet
dulce¹ *adv* : sweetly, softly
dulce² *adj* **1** : sweet **2** : mild, gentle, mellow — **dulcemente** *adv*
dulce³ *nm* : candy, sweet
dulcería *nf* : candy store
dulcificar {72} *vt* : to sweeten
dulzura *nf* **1** : sweetness **2** : gentleness, mellowness
duna *nf* : dune
dúo *nm* : duo, duet
duodécimo¹, -ma *adj* : twelfth
duodécimo², -ma *nm* : twelfth (in a series)
dúplex *nms & pl* : duplex apartment
duplicación *nf, pl* **-ciones** : duplication, copying
duplicado *nm* : duplicate, copy
duplicar {72} *vt* **1** : to double **2** : to duplicate, to copy
duplicidad *nf* : duplicity
duque *nm* : duke
duquesa *nf* : duchess
durabilidad *nf* : durability
durable → **duradero**
duración *nf, pl* **-ciones** : duration, length
duradero, -ra *adj* : durable, lasting
duramente *adv* **1** : harshly, severely **2** : hard
durante *prep* : during ⟨durante todo el día : all day long⟩ ⟨trabajó durante tres horas : he worked for three hours⟩
durar *v* : to last
durazno *nm* **1** : peach **2** : peach tree
dureza *nf* **1** : hardness, toughness **2** : severity, harshness
durmiente¹ *adj* : sleeping
durmiente² *nmf* : sleeper
durmió, etc. → **dormir**
duro¹ *adv* : hard ⟨trabajé tan duro : I worked so hard⟩
duro², -ra *adj* **1** FIRME : hard (of a surface, etc.), tough (of meat) **2** DIFÍCIL : hard, tough **3** : harsh, severe ⟨no seas tan duro con él : don't be so hard on him⟩
DVD *nm* : DVD

E

e¹ *nf* : sixth letter of the Spanish alphabet
e² *conj* (*used instead of* **y** *before words beginning with* i- *or* hi-) : and
ebanista *nmf* : cabinetmaker
ébano *nm* : ebony
e-book [ˈibuk] *nm, pl* **e-books** : e-book, electronic book
ebriedad *nf* EMBRIAGUEZ : inebriation, drunkenness
ebrio, -bria *adj* EMBRIAGADO : inebriated, drunk
ebullición *nf, pl* **-ciones** : boiling

eccema → **eczema**
eccéntrico → **excéntrico**
echar *vt* **1** LANZAR : to throw, to toss (a coin), to cast (an anchor, a net) ⟨lo echó a la basura : she threw it away⟩ ⟨echar la cabeza hacia atrás : to throw one's head back⟩ **2** : to throw out (of a place), to expel (from school) ⟨me echaron de la casa : they threw me out of the house⟩ **3** DESPEDIR : to fire, to dismiss **4** EMITIR : to emit, to give off **5** BROTAR : to sprout **6** : to put in, to add **7** : to take,

to have (a look) **8** : to mail **9** : to pour **10** : to give (a blessing, etc.), to put (a curse) on **11** : to turn (a key), to slide (a bolt) ⟨echarle (la) llave (a la puerta) : to lock the door⟩ **12 echar abajo** : to demolish **13 echar a perder** : to spoil, to ruin **14 echar de menos** : to miss ⟨echan de menos a su madre : they miss their mother⟩ — *vi* **1** : to start off **2 ~ a** : to begin to ⟨se echó a llorar : he began to cry⟩ — **echarse** *vr* **1** : to throw oneself ⟨se echó en sus brazos : she threw herself into his arms⟩ **2** : to lie down **3** : to put on **4 ~ a** : to begin to **5 echarse a perder** : to go bad, to spoil **6 echárselas de** : to pose as

ecléctico, -ca *adj* : eclectic

eclesiástico¹, -ca *adj* : ecclesiastical, ecclesiastic

eclesiástico² *nm* CLÉRIGO : cleric, clergyman

eclipsar *vt* **1** : to eclipse **2** : to outshine, to surpass

eclipse *nm* : eclipse

eco *nm* **1** : echo **2 hacerse eco de** : to echo, to repeat

eco- *pref* : eco-

ecografía *nf* : ultrasound scanning

ecología *nf* : ecology

ecológico, -ca *adj* : ecological — **ecológicamente** *adv*

ecologismo *nm* : environmentalism

ecologista *nmf* : ecologist, environmentalist

ecólogo, -ga *n* : ecologist

economía *nf* **1** : economy **2** : economics

económicamente *adv* : financially

económico, -ca *adj* : economic, economical

economista *nmf* : economist

economizar {21} *vt* : to save, to economize on — *vi* : to save money, to be frugal

ecosistema *nm* : ecosystem

ecoturismo *nm* : ecotourism — **ecoturístico, -ca** *adj*

ecuación *nf, pl* **-ciones** : equation

ecuador *nm* : equator

ecuánime *adj* **1** : even-tempered **2** : impartial

ecuanimidad *nf* **1** : equanimity **2** : impartiality

ecuatorial *adj* : equatorial

ecuatoriano, -na *adj & n* : Ecuadorian

ecuestre *adj* : equestrian

ecuménico, -ca *adj* : ecumenical

eczema *nm* : eczema

edad *nf* **1** : age ⟨¿qué edad tiene? : how old is she?⟩ ⟨tiene 20 años de edad : she is 20 years old⟩ ⟨ser mayor de edad : to be of age⟩ ⟨ser menor de edad : to be a minor, to be underage⟩ ⟨una persona de edad : an elderly person⟩ ⟨desde temprana edad : from an early age⟩ **2** : age, epoch, era ⟨la edad media : the Middle Ages⟩ ⟨la edad de oro/bronce : the Golden/Bronze Age⟩

edamame *nm* : edamame

edecán *nm, pl* **-canes** : aide, assistant

edema *nm* : edema

Edén *nm, pl* **Edenes** : Eden, paradise

edición *nf, pl* **-ciones** **1** : edition **2** : publication, publishing

edicto *nm* : edict, proclamation

edificación *nf, pl* **-ciones** **1** : edification **2** : construction, building

edificar {72} *vt* **1** : to edify **2** CONSTRUIR : to build, to construct

edificio *nm* : building, edifice

edil, edila *n* : councillor, councilman *m*, councilwoman *f*

editar *vt* **1** : to edit **2** PUBLICAR : to publish

editor¹, -tora *adj* : publishing ⟨casa editora : publishing house⟩

editor², -tora *n* **1** : editor **2** : publisher

editor³ *nm* : editor (software)

editora *nf* : publisher, publishing company

editorial¹ *adj* **1** : publishing **2** : editorial

editorial² *nm* : editorial

editorial³ *nf* : publishing house

edredón *nm, pl* **-dones** COBERTOR, COLCHA : comforter, eiderdown, quilt

educación *nf, pl* **-ciones** **1** ENSEÑANZA : education ⟨educación primaria/secundaria/superior : primary/secondary/higher education⟩ **2** : manners *pl* ⟨es de mala educación : it's bad manners⟩ — **educacional** *adj*

educado, -da *adj* : polite, well-mannered

educador, -dora *n* : educator

educando, -da *n* ALUMNO, PUPILO : pupil, student

educar {72} *vt* **1** : to educate **2** CRIAR : to bring up, to raise **3** : to train — **educarse** *vr* : to be educated

educativo, -va *adj* : educational

efe *nf* : (letter) f

efectista *adj* : dramatic, sensational

efectivamente *adv* : really, actually

efectividad *nf* : effectiveness

efectivo¹, -va *adj* **1** : effective **2** : real, actual **3** : permanent, regular (of employment)

efectivo² *nm* : cash

efecto *nm* **1** : effect ⟨tener efecto : to take effect⟩ ⟨surtir efecto, producir un efecto : to have an effect⟩ ⟨bajo los efectos del alcohol : under the influence of alcohol⟩ **2 en ~** : actually, in fact **3 efecto dominó** : domino effect **4 efecto secundario** : side effect **5 efectos** *nmpl* : goods, property ⟨efectos personales : personal effects⟩ **6 efectos** *nmpl* : effects ⟨efectos especiales : special effects⟩ ⟨efectos de sonido : sound effects⟩

efeméride *nf* : major event

efectuar {3} *vt* : to carry out, to bring about

efervescencia *nf* : effervescence — **efervescente** *adj*

eficacia *nf* **1** : effectiveness, efficacy **2** : efficiency

eficaz *adj, pl* **-caces** **1** : effective **2** EFICIENTE : efficient — **eficazmente** *adv*

eficiencia *nf* : efficiency

eficiente *adj* EFICAZ : efficient — **eficientemente** *adv*

eficientizar {21} *vt Mex* : to streamline, to make more efficient
efigie *nf* : effigy
efímera *nf* : mayfly
efímero, -ra *adj* : ephemeral
efluentes *nmpl* : effluent(s), (liquid) waste
efusión *nf, pl* **-siones** 1 : warmth, effusiveness 2 **con** ~ : effusively
efusivo, -va *adj* : effusive — **efusivamente** *adv*
egipcio, -cia *adj & n* : Egyptian
eglefino *nm* : haddock
ego *nm* : ego
egocéntrico, -ca *adj* : egocentric, self-centered
egoísmo *nm* : selfishness, egoism
egoísta[1] *adj* : selfish, egoistic
egoísta[2] *nmf* : egoist, selfish person
egotismo *nm* : egotism, conceit
egotista[1] *adj* : egotistic, egotistical, conceited
egotista[2] *nmf* : egotist, conceited person
egresado, -da *n* : graduate
egresar *vi* : to graduate
egreso *nm* 1 : graduation 2 **ingresos y egresos** : income and expenditure
eh *interj* 1 : hey! 2 : eh?, huh?
eje *nm* 1 : axle 2 : axis
ejecución *nf, pl* **-ciones** : execution
ejecutante *nmf* : performer
ejecutar *vt* 1 : to execute, to put to death 2 : to carry out, to perform
ejecutivo, -va *adj & n* : executive
ejecutor, -tora *n* : executor
ejem *interj* : ahem!
ejemplar[1] *adj* : exemplary, model
ejemplar[2] *nm* 1 : copy (of a book, magazine, etc.) 2 : specimen, example
ejemplificar {72} *vt* : to exemplify, to illustrate
ejemplo *nm* 1 : example 2 **por** ~ : for example 3 **dar ejemplo** : to set an example
ejercer {86} *vi* ~ **de** : to practice as, to work as — *vt* 1 : to practice 2 : exercise (a right) 3 : to exert
ejercicio *nm* 1 : exercise 2 : practice
ejercitar *vt* 1 : to exercise 2 ADIESTRAR : to drill, to train
ejército *nm* : army
ejidal *adj Mex* : cooperative
ejidatario, -ria *n Mex* : member of a cooperative
ejido *nm* 1 : common land 2 *Mex* : cooperative
ejote *nm Mex* : green bean
el[1] *pron* (*referring to masculine nouns*) 1 : the one ⟨me gusta el verde : I like the green one⟩ ⟨el de la camisa roja : the one with the red shirt⟩ ⟨mi papá y el tuyo : my dad and yours⟩ ⟨el partido de ayer y el de hoy : yesterday's game and today's⟩ 2 **el que** : the one that/who, whoever, he who ⟨el que vino ayer : the one who came yesterday⟩ ⟨el que compré : the one (that) I bought⟩ ⟨el que gane : whoever wins⟩ ⟨el que trabaja duro estará contento : he who works hard will be happy⟩

el[2], **la** *art, pl* **los, las** : the ⟨los niños están en la casa : the boys/children are in the house⟩ ⟨me duele el pie : my foot hurts⟩ ⟨¿te gusta el té? : do you like tea?⟩ ⟨los gatos son inteligentes : cats are intelligent⟩ ⟨el lago Titicaca : Lake Titicaca⟩ ⟨llamó el señor Núñez : Mr. Núñez called⟩ ⟨viene el lunes : he's coming on Monday⟩ ⟨son las dos : it's two o'clock⟩ ⟨el cinco por ciento : five percent⟩ ⟨un dólar la docena : a dollar a dozen⟩
él *pron* : he, him ⟨él es mi amigo : he's my friend⟩ ⟨un amigo de él : a friend of his⟩ ⟨a él no le interesa : it doesn't interest him⟩ ⟨hablaremos con él : we will speak with him⟩
elaboración *nf, pl* **-ciones** 1 PRODUCCIÓN : production, making 2 : preparation, devising
elaborado, -da *adj* : elaborate
elaborar *vt* 1 : to make, to produce 2 : to devise, to draw up
elasticidad *nf* : elasticity
elástico[1], **-ca** *adj* 1 FLEXIBLE : flexible 2 : elastic
elástico[2] *nm* 1 : elastic (material) 2 : rubber band
elastizado, -da *adj* : elastic
ele *nf* : (letter) l
elección *nf, pl* **-ciones** 1 SELECCIÓN : choice, selection 2 : election
electivo, -va *adj* : elective
electo, -ta *adj* : elect ⟨el presidente electo : the president-elect⟩
elector, -tora *n* : voter
electorado *nm* : electorate
electoral *adj* : electoral, election
electricidad *nf* : electricity
electricista *nmf* : electrician
eléctrico, -ca *adj* : electric, electrical
electrificar {72} *vt* : to electrify — **electrificación** *nf*
electrizar {21} *vt* : to electrify, to thrill — **electrizante** *adj*
electrocardiógrafo *nm* : electrocardiograph
electrocardiograma *nm* : electrocardiogram
electrocutar *vt* : to electrocute — **electrocución** *nf*
electrodo *nm* : electrode
electrodoméstico *nm* : electric appliance
electroimán *nm, pl* **-manes** : electromagnet
electrólisis *nfs & pl* : electrolysis
electrolito *nm* : electrolyte
electromagnético, -ca *adj* : electromagnetic
electromagnetismo *nm* : electromagnetism
electrón *nm, pl* **-trones** : electron
electrónica *nf* : electronics
electrónico, -ca *adj* : electronic, electronics — **electrónicamente** *adv*
elefante, -ta *n* : elephant
elegancia *nf* : elegance
elegante *adj* : elegant, smart — **elegantemente** *adv*
elegía *nf* : elegy
elegíaco, -ca *adj* : elegiac

elegible *adj* : eligible — **elegibilidad** *nf*

elegido, -da *adj* 1 : chosen, selected 2 : elected

elegir {28} *vt* 1 ESCOGER, SELECCIONAR : to choose, to select 2 : to elect

elemental *adj* 1 : elementary, basic 2 : fundamental, essential

elemento *nm* : element

elenco *nm* : cast (of actors)

elevación *nf, pl* **-ciones** : elevation, height

elevado, -da *adj* 1 : elevated, lofty 2 : high

elevador *nm* ASCENSOR : elevator

elevar *vt* 1 ALZAR : to raise, to lift 2 AUMENTAR : to raise, to increase 3 : to elevate (in a hierarchy), to promote 4 : to present, to submit — **elevarse** *vr* : to rise

elfo *nm* : elf

eliminación *nf, pl* **-ciones** : elimination, removal

eliminar *vt* 1 : to eliminate, to remove 2 : to do in, to kill

eliminatoria *nf* : qualifying round (in a competition)

eliminatorio, -ria *adj* : qualifying

elipse *nf* : ellipse

elipsis *nf* : ellipsis

elíptico, -ca *adj* : elliptical, elliptic

elite *or* **élite** *nf* : elite

elitista *adj & nmf* : elitist

elixir *or* **elíxir** *nm* : elixir

ella *pron* : she, her ⟨ella es mi amiga : she is my friend⟩ ⟨un amigo de ella : a friend of hers⟩ ⟨a ella no le interesa : it doesn't interest her⟩ ⟨nos fuimos con ella : we left with her⟩

ello *pron* : it ⟨es por ello que me voy : that's why I'm going⟩

ellos, ellas *pron pl* 1 : they, them ⟨ellas son mis hermanas : they're my sisters⟩ ⟨un amigo de ellos : a friend of theirs⟩ ⟨a ellos no les interesa : it doesn't interest them⟩ ⟨fuimos con ellos : we went with them⟩ 2 **de ellos, de ellas** : theirs

elocución *nf, pl* **-ciones** : elocution

elocuencia *nf* : eloquence

elocuente *adj* : eloquent — **elocuentemente** *adv*

elogiar *vt* ENCOMIAR : to praise

elogio *nm* : praise

elote *nm* 1 *Mex* : corn, maize 2 *CA, Mex* : corncob

elucidación *nf, pl* **-ciones** ESCLARECIMIENTO : elucidation

elucidar *vt* ESCLARECER : to elucidate

eludir *vt* EVADIR : to evade, to avoid, to elude

em- → **en-**

email [ˈimeil] *nm, pl* **emails** : e-mail ⟨enviar algo por email : to e-mail something⟩

emanación *nf, pl* **-ciones** : emanation

emanar *vi* ~ **de** : to emanate from — *vt* : to exude

emancipar *vt* : to emancipate — **emancipación** *nf*

embadurnar *vt* EMBARRAR : to smear, to daub

embajada *nf* : embassy

embajador, -dora *n* : ambassador

embalaje *nm* : packing, packaging

embalar *vt* EMPAQUETAR : to pack

embaldosar *vt* : to tile, to pave with tiles

embalsamar *vt* : to embalm

embalse *nm* : dam, reservoir

embarazada¹ *adj* ENCINTA, PREÑADA : pregnant, expecting

embarazada² *nf* : pregnant woman

embarazar {21} *vt* 1 : to obstruct, to hamper 2 PREÑAR : to make pregnant

embarazo *nm* 1 : pregnancy 2 IMPEDIMENTO : obstacle, obstruction 3 VERGÜENZA : embarrassment

embarazoso, -sa *adj* : embarrassing, awkward

embarcación *nf, pl* **-ciones** : boat, craft

embarcadero *nm* : wharf, pier, jetty

embarcar {72} *vi* : to embark, to board — *vt* : to load

embarco *nm* : embarkation

embargar {52} *vt* 1 : to seize, to impound 2 : to overwhelm

embargo *nm* 1 : seizure 2 : embargo 3 **sin ~** : however, nevertheless

embarque *nm* 1 : embarkation 2 : shipment

embarrancar {72} *vi* 1 : to run aground 2 : to get bogged down

embarrar *vt* 1 : to cover with mud 2 EMBADURNAR : to smear

embate *nm* 1 : onslaught 2 : battering (of waves or wind)

embaucador, -dora *n* : swindler, deceiver

embaucar {72} *vt* : to trick, to swindle

embeber *vt* : to absorb, to soak up — *vi* : to shrink

embelesado, -da *adj* : spellbound

embelesar *vt* : to enchant, to captivate

embellecer {53} *vt* : to embellish, to beautify

embellecimiento *nm* : beautification, embellishment

embestida *nf* 1 : charge (of a bull) 2 ARREMETIDA : attack, onslaught

embestir {54} *vt* : to hit, to run into, to charge at — *vi* ARREMETER : to charge, to attack

emblanquecer {53} *vt* BLANQUEAR : to bleach, to whiten — **emblanquecerse** *vr* : to turn white

emblema *nm* : emblem

emblemático, -ca *adj* : emblematic

embobado, -da *adj* 1 : captivated, spellbound 2 : dazed

embolar *vt Col* : to polish (shoes)

embolia *nf* : embolism

émbolo *nm* : piston

embolsarse *vr* 1 : to pocket (money) 2 : to collect (payment)

embonar *vi Mex* ENCAJAR : to fit

emborracharse *vr* EMBRIAGARSE : to get drunk

emborronar *vt* 1 : to blot, to smudge 2 GARABATEAR : to scribble

emboscada *nf* : ambush

emboscar {72} *vt* : to ambush — **emboscarse** *vr* : to lie in ambush

embotar *vt* 1 : to dull, to blunt 2 : to weaken, to enervate

embotellamiento *nm* ATASCO : traffic jam

embotellar *vt* ENVASAR : to bottle — **embotellado, -da** *adj*
embragar {52} *vi* : to engage the clutch
embrague *nm* : clutch
embriagado, -da *adj* : inebriated, drunk
embriagador, -dora *adj* : intoxicating
embriagar {52} *vt* : to intoxicate, to make drunk — **embriagarse** *vr* EMBORRACHARSE : to get drunk
embriaguez *nf* EBRIEDAD : drunkenness, inebriation
embridar *vt* : to bridle (a horse)
embrión *nm, pl* **embriones** : embryo
embrionario, -ria *adj* : embryonic
embrollo *nm* ENREDO : confusion, mess, tangle
embrujado *adj* **1** : bewitched **2** : haunted (of a house, etc.)
embrujar *vt* HECHIZAR : to bewitch
embrujo *nm* : spell, curse
embrutecer {18} *vt* **1** : to make dull **2** ATONTAR : to stupefy
embudo *nm* : funnel
embuste *nm* **1** MENTIRA : lie, fib *fam* **2** ENGAÑO : trick, hoax
embustero¹, -ra *adj* : lying, deceitful
embustero², -ra *n* : liar, cheat
embutido *nm* **1** : sausage **2** : inlaid work
embutir *vt* **1** : to cram, to stuff, to jam **2** : to inlay
eme *nf* : (letter) m
emergencia *nf* **1** : emergency **2** : emergence
emergente *adj* **1** : emergent **2** : consequent, resultant
emerger {15} *vi* : to emerge, to surface
emigración *nf, pl* **-ciones** **1** : emigration **2** : migration
emigrante *adj & nmf* : emigrant
emigrar *vi* **1** : to emigrate **2** : to migrate
eminencia *nf* : eminence
eminente *adj* : eminent, distinguished
eminentemente *adv* : basically, essentially
emisario¹, -ria *n* : emissary
emisario² *nm* : outlet (of a body of water)
emisión *nf, pl* **-siones** **1** : emission **2** : broadcast **3** : issue ⟨emisión de acciones : stock issue⟩
emisor *nm* TRANSMISOR : television or radio transmitter
emisora *nf* : radio station
emitir *vt* **1** : to emit, to give off **2** : to broadcast **3** : to issue **4** : to cast (a vote)
emoción *nf, pl* **-ciones** : emotion — **emocional** *adj* — **emocionalmente** *adv*
emocionado, -da *adj* **1** : moved, affected by emotion **2** ENTUSIASMADO : excited
emocionante *adj* **1** CONMOVEDOR : moving, touching **2** EXCITANTE : exciting, thrilling
emocionar *vt* **1** CONMOVER : to move, to touch **2** : to excite, to thrill — **emocionarse** *vr*
emoji [e'moji] *nm, pl* **emojis** *or* **emoji** : emoji
emoticón *or* **emoticono** *nm, pl* **-cones** *or* **-conos** : emoticon

emotivo, -va *adj* : emotional, moving
empacador, -dora *n* : packer
empacar {72} *vt* **1** EMPAQUETAR : to pack **2** : to bale — *vi* : to pack — **empacarse** *vr* **1** : to balk, to refuse to budge **2** *Col, Mex fam* : to eat ravenously, to devour
empachar *vt* **1** ESTORBAR : to obstruct **2** : to give indigestion to **3** DISFRAZAR : to disguise, to mask — **empacharse** *vr* **1** INDIGESTARSE : to get indigestion **2** AVERGONZARSE : to be embarrassed
empacho *nm* **1** INDIGESTIÓN : indigestion **2** VERGÜENZA : embarrassment **3** **no tener empacho en** : to have no qualms about
empadronarse *vr* : to register to vote
empalagar {52} *vt* **1** : to seem cloying to ⟨me empalaga : I find it cloying⟩ **2** FASTIDIAR : to annoy, to bother
empalagoso, -sa *adj* MELOSO : cloying
empalar *vt* : to impale
empalizada *nf* : palisade (fence)
empalmar *vt* **1** : to splice, to link **2** : to combine — *vi* : to meet, to converge
empalme *nm* **1** CONEXIÓN : connection, link **2** : junction
empanada *nf* : pie, turnover
empanadilla *nf* : meat or seafood pie
empanar *vt* : to bread
empantanar *vt* **1** INUNDAR : to swamp, to bog down **2** ESTANCAR : to bog down, to delay — **empantanarse** *vr*
empañar *vt* **1** : to steam up **2** : to tarnish, to sully
empapado, -da *adj* : soggy, sodden
empapar *vt* MOJAR : to soak, to drench — **empaparse** *vr* **1** : to get soaking wet **2** ~ **de** : to absorb, to be imbued with
empapelar *vt* : to wallpaper
empaque *nm fam* **1** : presence, bearing **2** : pomposity **3** DESCARO : impudence, nerve
empaquetar *vt* EMBALAR : to pack, to package — **empaquetarse** *vr fam* : to dress up
emparedado *nm* : sandwich
emparedar *vt* : to wall in, to confine
emparejar *vt* **1** : to pair, to match up **2** : to make even, to even out — *vi* : to catch up — **emparejarse** *vr* **1** : to pair up **2** : to become even, to even out
emparentado, -da *adj* : related
emparentar {55} *vi* : to become related by marriage
emparrillado *nm Mex* : gridiron (in football)
empastar *vt* **1** : to fill (a tooth) **2** : to bind (a book)
empaste *nm* : filling (of a tooth)
empatar *vt* : to tie, to connect — *vi* : to result in a draw, to be tied — **empatarse** *vr Ven* : to hook up, to link together
empate *nm* : draw, tie
empatía *nf* : empathy
empecinado, -da *adj* TERCO : stubborn
empecinarse *vr* OBSTINARSE : to be stubborn, to persist
empedernido, -da *adj* INCORREGIBLE : hardened, inveterate

empedrado *nm* : paving, pavement
empedrar {55} *vt* : to pave (with stones)
empeine *nm* : instep
empellón *nm, pl* **-llones** : shove, push
empelotado, -da *adj* **1** *Mex fam* : madly in love **2** *fam* : stark naked
empeñado, -da *adj* : determined, committed
empeñar *vt* **1** : to pawn **2** : to pledge, to give (one's word) — **empeñarse** *vr* **1** : to insist stubbornly **2** : to make an effort
empeño *nm* **1** : pledge, commitment **2** : insistence **3** ESFUERZO : effort, determination ⟨poner mucho empeño : to put in a lot of effort⟩ ⟨trabajar con empeño : to work hard⟩ **4** : pawning ⟨casa de empeños : pawnshop⟩
empeoramiento *nm* : worsening, deterioration
empeorar *vi* : to deteriorate, to get worse — *vt* : to make worse
empequeñecer {53} *vi* : to diminish, to become smaller — *vt* : to minimize, to make smaller
emperador *nm* : emperor
emperatriz *nf, pl* **-trices** : empress
empero *conj* : however, nevertheless
empezar {29} *v* COMENZAR : to start, to begin ⟨empezar a hacer algo : to start to do something, to start doing something⟩ ⟨empezar por algo/alguien : to start with something/someone⟩ ⟨empezar por hacer algo : to start by doing something⟩ ⟨empezó diciendo que . . . : she started out by saying that . . .⟩ ⟨para empezar : to begin with⟩
empinado, -da *adj* : steep
empinar *vt* ELEVAR : to lift, to raise — **empinarse** *vr* : to stand on tiptoe
empírico, -ca *adj* : empirical — **empíricamente** *adv*
emplasto *nm* : poultice, dressing
emplazamiento *nm* **1** : location, site **2** CITACIÓN : summons, subpoena
emplazar {21} *vt* **1** CONVOCAR : to convene, to summon **2** : to subpoena **3** UBICAR : to place, to position
empleado, -da *n* : employee
empleador, -dora *n* PATRÓN : employer
emplear *vt* **1** : to employ **2** USAR : to use — **emplearse** *vr* **1** : to get a job **2** : to occupy oneself
empleo *nm* **1** OCUPACIÓN : employment, occupation, job **2** : use, usage
emplomadura *nm* *Arg, Uru* : filling (in a tooth)
emplumar *vt* : to feather
empobrecer {53} *vt* : to impoverish — *vi* : to become poor — **empobrecerse** *vr*
empobrecimiento *nm* : impoverishment
empollar *vi* : to brood eggs — *vt* : to incubate
empolvar *vt* **1** : to cover with dust **2** : to powder — **empolvarse** *vr* **1** : to gather dust **2** : to powder one's face
emporio *nm* **1** : center, capital, empire ⟨un emporio cultural : a cultural center⟩ ⟨un emporio financiero : a financial empire⟩ **2** : department store

empotrado, -da *adj* : built-in ⟨armarios empotrados : built-in cabinets⟩
empotrar *vt* : to build into, to embed
emprendedor, -dora *adj* : enterprising
emprender *vt* : to undertake, to begin
empresa *nf* **1** COMPAÑÍA, FIRMA : company, corporation, firm **2** : undertaking, venture
empresariado *nm* **1** : business world **2** : management, managers *pl*
empresarial *adj* : business, managerial, corporate
empresario, -ria *n* **1** : manager **2** : businessman *m*, businesswoman *f* **3** : impresario
empréstito *nm* : loan
empujar *vi* : to push, to shove — *vt* **1** : to push **2** PRESIONAR : to spur on, to press
empuje *nm* : impetus, drive
empujón *nm, pl* **-jones** : push, shove
empuñadura *nf* MANGO : hilt, handle
empuñar *vt* **1** ASIR : to grasp **2** empuñar las armas : to take up arms
emú *nm, pl* **emú** *or* **emús** *or* **emúes** : emu
emular *vt* IMITAR : to emulate — **emulación** *nf*
emulsión *nf, pl* **-siones** : emulsion
emulsionante *nm* : emulsifier
emulsionar *vt* : to emulsify
en *prep* **1** : in (a box, building, city, etc.) ⟨en el aire : in the air⟩ ⟨en el bolsillo : in one's pocket⟩ **2** : on (a surface, etc.) ⟨está en la mesa : it's on the table⟩ ⟨en la costa : on the coast⟩ ⟨en la planta baja : on the ground floor⟩ ⟨en la calle Sur : on South Street⟩ **3** : at (a place or event) ⟨en casa : at home⟩ ⟨en el trabajo : at work⟩ ⟨en la reunión : at the meeting⟩ ⟨todos en la mesa : everyone at the table⟩ ⟨en el 30 de la calle Sur : at 30 South Street⟩ **4** : in, on, as part of ⟨en la película : in the movie⟩ ⟨en el equipo : on the team⟩ **5** : on (television, etc.) **6** : by (plane, train, etc.) **7** : in, within (a day, week, etc.) **8** : in, during (a period) **9** : on, at ⟨en esa ocasión : on that occasion⟩ ⟨en ese momento : at that moment⟩ **10** : in (a form) ⟨en francés/metros/pedazos : in French/meters/pieces⟩ **11** (*with numbers*) ⟨se ubica en el 26% : it's at 26%⟩ ⟨aumentó en un 90% : it increased by 90%⟩ ⟨se cifran en millones : they amount to millions⟩ **12** : in, made of (a material) **13** : in (a state, manner, circumstance) ⟨en peligro : in danger⟩ ⟨en broma : in jest⟩ ⟨en ese caso : in that case⟩ **14** : on (a subject) ⟨un experto en animales : an animal expert⟩ **15** : in (a field or profession) **16** (*with an infinitive verb*) ⟨el primero en ganar el título : the first to win the title⟩
en- *or* **em-** *pref* : en-, em- ⟨enredar : entangle⟩ ⟨empatía : empathy⟩
enagua *nf* : petticoat, slip
enajenación *nf, pl* **-ciones** **1** : transfer (of property) **2** : alienation **3** : absentmindedness
enajenado, -da *adj* : out of one's mind
enajenar *vt* **1** : to transfer (property) **2** : to alienate **3** : to enrapture — **enaje-**

narse *vr* **1** : to become estranged **2** : to go mad
enaltecer {53} *vt* : to praise, to extol
enamorado[1], **-da** *adj* : in love
enamorado[2], **-da** *n* : lover, sweetheart
enamoramiento *nm* : infatuation, crush
enamorar *vt* : to enamor, to win the love of — **enamorarse** *vr* : to fall in love
enamorizado, -da *adj* : amorous, passionate
enano[1], **-na** *adj* : tiny, minute
enano[2], **-na** *n* **1** *sometimes offensive* : little person, dwarf *sometimes offensive*, midget *sometimes offensive* **2** : dwarf (in stories) **3** *often disparaging* : shorty, shrimp *usu disparaging*
enarbolar *vt* **1** : to hoist, to raise **2** : to brandish
enardecer {53} *vt* **1** : to arouse (anger, passions) **2** : to stir up, to excite — **enardecerse** *vr*
encabezado *nm Mex* : headline
encabezamiento *nm* **1** : heading **2** : salutation, opening
encabezar {21} *vt* **1** : to head, to lead **2** : to put a heading on
encabritarse *vr* **1** : to rear up **2** *fam* : to get angry
encadenar *vt* **1** : to chain **2** : to connect, to link **3** INMOVILIZAR : to immobilize
encajar *vi* : to fit, to fit together, to fit in — *vt* **1** : to insert, to stick **2** : to take, to cope with ⟨encajó el golpe : he withstood the blow⟩
encaje *nm* **1** : lace **2** : financial reserve
encajonar *vt* **1** : to box, to crate **2** : to cram in
encalar *vt* : to whitewash
encallar *vi* **1** : to run aground **2** : to get stuck
encallecido, -da *adj* : callused
encamar *vt* : to confine to a bed
encaminado, -da *adj* **1** : on the right track **2** ~ **a** : aimed at, designed to
encaminar *vt* **1** : to direct, to channel **2** : to head in the right direction — **encaminarse** *vr* ~ **a** : to head for, to aim at
encandilar *vt* : to dazzle
encanecer {53} *vi* : to gray, to go gray
encantado, -da *adj* **1** : charmed, bewitched **2** : delighted **3** : haunted
encantador[1], **-dora** *adj* : charming, delightful
encantador[2], **-dora** *n* : magician
encantamiento *nm* : enchantment, spell
encantar *vt* **1** : to enchant, to bewitch **2** : to charm, to delight ⟨me encanta esta canción : I love this song⟩
encanto *nm* **1** : charm, fascination **2** HECHIZO : spell **3** : delightful person or thing
encañonar *vt* : to point (a gun) at, to hold up
encapotado, -da *adj* : cloudy, overcast
encaprichado, -da *adj* : infatuated
encaprichamiento *nm* : infatuation
encapuchado, -da *adj* : hooded
encarado, -da *adj* **estar mal encarado** *fam* : to be ugly-looking, to look mean

encaramar *vt* : to raise, to lift up — **encaramarse** *vr* : to perch
encarar *vt* CONFRONTAR : to face, to confront
encarcelación *nf, pl* **-ciones** → **encarcelamiento**
encarcelamiento *nm* : incarceration, imprisonment
encarcelar *vt* : to incarcerate, to imprison
encarecer {53} *vt* **1** : to increase, to raise (price, value) **2** : to beseech, to entreat — **encarecerse** *vr* : to become more expensive
encarecidamente *adv* : insistently, urgently
encarecimiento *nm* : increase, rise (in price)
encargado[1], **-da** *adj* : in charge
encargado[2], **-da** *n* : manager, person in charge
encargar {52} *vt* **1** : to put in charge of **2** : to recommend, to advise **3** : to order, to request — **encargarse** *vr* ~ **de** : to take charge of
encargo *nm* **1** : errand **2** : job assignment **3** : order ⟨hecho de encargo : custom-made, made to order⟩
encariñarse *vr* ~ **con** : to become fond of, to grow attached to
encarnación *nf, pl* **-ciones** : incarnation, embodiment
encarnado[1], **-da** *adj* **1** : incarnate **2** : flesh-colored **3** : red **4** : ingrown
encarnado[2] *nm* : red
encarnar *vt* : to incarnate, to embody — **encarnarse** *vr* **encarnarse una uña** : to have an ingrown nail
encarnizado, -da *adj* **1** : bloodshot, inflamed **2** : fierce, bloody
encarnizar {21} *vt* : to enrage, to infuriate — **encarnizarse** *vr* : to be brutal, to attack viciously
encarrilar *vt* : to guide, to put on the right track
encasillar *vt* CLASIFICAR : to classify, to pigeonhole, to categorize
encausar *vt* : to prosecute, to charge
encauzar {21} *vt* : to channel, to guide — **encauzarse** *vr*
encebollado, -da *adj* : cooked with onions
encefalitis *nms & pl* : encephalitis
enceguecedor, -dora *n* : blinding
encendedor *nm* : lighter
encender {56} *vi* : to light — *vt* **1** : to light, to set fire to **2** PRENDER : to switch on **3** : to start (a motor) **4** : to arouse, to kindle — **encenderse** *vr* **1** : to get excited **2** : to blush
encendido[1], **-da** *adj* **1** : burning **2** : flushed **3** : fiery, passionate
encendido[2] *nm* : ignition
encerado *nm* **1** : waxing, polishing **2** : blackboard
encerar *vt* : to wax, to polish
encerrar {55} *vt* **1** : to lock (up), to shut away/up ⟨la encerraron en una celda : they locked her in a cell⟩ ⟨está encerrado en su cuarto : he's shut up in his room⟩ **2** : to contain, to include **3** : to involve, to entail

encerrona *nf* **1** TRAMPA : trap, setup **2 prepararle una encerrona a alguien** : to set a trap for someone, to set someone up

encestar *vi* : to make a basket (in basketball)

enchapado *nm* : plating, coating (of metal)

encharcamiento *nm* : flood, flooding

encharcar {72} *vt* : to flood — **encharcarse** *vr* **1** : to flood, to get flooded **2** : to pool

enchilada *nf* : enchilada

enchilar *vt Mex* : to season with chili

enchuecar {72} *vt Chile, Mex fam* : to make crooked, to twist

enchufar *vt* **1** : to plug in **2** : to connect, to fit together

enchufe *nm* **1** : connection **2** : plug, socket

encía *nf* : gum (tissue)

-encia *suf* : -ence ⟨independencia : independence⟩

enciclopedia *nf* : encyclopedia — **enciclopédico, -ca** *adj*

encierro *nm* **1** : confinement **2** : enclosure

encima *adv* **1** : on, on top (of) ⟨se me cayó encima : it fell on (top of) me⟩ ⟨con queso (por) encima : with cheese on top⟩ ⟨no llevo dinero encima : I don't have any money on me⟩ **2** ADEMÁS : as well, besides ⟨y encima : and on top of that⟩ **3 ~ de** : on, on top of, over, above ⟨encima de la mesa : on (top of) the table⟩ ⟨encima de las nubes : above the clouds⟩ ⟨viven encima de la librería : they live above the bookstore⟩ ⟨miró por encima del hombro : he looked over his shoulder⟩ **4 por ~** : superficially **5 por encima de** : above, beyond ⟨por encima de la ley : above the law⟩ ⟨por encima de la media : above average⟩ ⟨por encima de todo : above all⟩ ⟨vive por encima de sus posibilidades : she lives above her means⟩ **6 echarse encima** : to take upon oneself **7 estar encima de** *fam* : to nag, to criticize **8 quitarse de encima** : to get rid of

encina *nf* : evergreen oak

encinta *adj* EMBARAZADA, PREÑADA : pregnant, expecting

enclaustrado, -da *adj* : cloistered, shut away

enclavado, -da *adj* : buried

enclenque *adj* : weak, sickly

encoger {15} *vt* **1** : to shrink, to make smaller **2** : to intimidate — *vi* : to shrink, to contract — **encogerse** *vr* **1** : to shrink **2** : to be intimidated, to cower, to cringe **3 encogerse de hombros** : to shrug (one's shoulders)

encogido, -da *adj* **1** : shriveled, shrunken **2** TÍMIDO : shy, inhibited

encogimiento *nm* **1** : shrinking, shrinkage **2** : shrug **3** TIMIDEZ : shyness

encolerizar {21} *vt* ENFURECER : to enrage, to infuriate — **encolerizarse** *vr*

encomendar {55} *vt* CONFIAR : to entrust, to commend — **encomendarse** *vr*

encomiable *adj* : commendable, praiseworthy

encomiar *vt* ELOGIAR : to praise, to pay tribute to

encomienda *nf* **1** : charge, mission **2** : royal land grant **3** : parcel

encomio *nm* : praise, eulogy

enconar *vt* **1** : to irritate, to anger **2** : to inflame — **enconarse** *vr* **1** : to become heated **2** : to fester

encono *nm* **1** RENCOR : animosity, rancor **2** : inflammation, infection

encontrado, -da *adj* : contrary, opposing

encontrar {19} *vt* **1** HALLAR : to find ⟨encontré el libro : I found the book⟩ ⟨encontraron al culpable : they found the culprit⟩ **2** : to encounter, to meet **3** : to find ⟨lo encuentro muy interesante : I find it very interesting⟩ — **encontrarse** *vr* **1** : to clash, to conflict **2** : to be, to feel ⟨su padre se encuentra mejor : her father is (feeling/doing) better⟩ **3 ~ con** : to meet, to bump into

encorvar *vt* : to bend, to curve — **encorvarse** *vr* : to hunch over, to stoop

encrespar *vt* **1** : to curl, to ruffle, to ripple **2** : to annoy, to irritate — **encresparse** *vr* **1** : to curl one's hair **2** : to become choppy **3** : to get annoyed

encriptar *vt* : to encrypt

encrucijada *nf* : crossroads

encuadernación *nf*, *pl* **-ciones** : binding (of books)

encuadernar *vt* EMPASTAR : to bind (a book) — **encuadernador, -dora** *n*

encuadrar *vt* **1** ENMARCAR : to frame **2** ENCAJAR : to fit, to insert **3** COMPRENDER : to contain, to include

encubierto *pp* → **encubrir**

encubrimiento *nm* : cover-up

encubrir {2} *vt* : to cover up, to conceal

encuentro *nm* **1** : meeting, encounter **2** : conference, congress

encuerado, -da *adj fam* : naked

encuerar *vt fam* : to undress

encuesta *nf* **1** INVESTIGACIÓN, PESQUISA : inquiry, investigation **2** SONDEO : survey

encuestador, -dora *n* : pollster

encuestar *vt* : to poll, to take a survey of

encumbrado, -da *adj* **1** : lofty, high **2** : eminent, distinguished

encumbrar *vt* **1** : to exalt, to elevate **2** : to extol — **encumbrarse** *vr* : to reach the top

encurtir *vt* ESCABECHAR : to pickle

ende *adv* **por ~** : therefore, consequently

endeble *adj* : feeble, weak

endemoniado, -da *adj* : fiendish, diabolical

enderezar {21} *vt* **1** : to straighten (out) **2** : to stand on end, to put upright — **enderezarse** *vr* **1** : to straighten up, to sit/stand (up) straight **2** ARREGLARSE : to straighten out, to improve

endeudado, -da *adj* : in debt, indebted

endeudamiento *nm* : indebtedness, debt

endeudarse *vr* **1** : to go into debt **2** : to feel obliged

endiablado, -da *adj* **1** : devilish, diabolical **2** : complicated, difficult

endibia or **endivia** nf : endive
endilgar {52} vt fam : to spring, to foist ⟨me endilgó la responsabilidad : he saddled me with the responsibility⟩
endocrino, -na adj : endocrine
endogamia nf : inbreeding
endosar vt : to endorse
endoso nm : endorsement
endulzante nm : sweetener
endulzar {21} vt 1 : to sweeten 2 : to soften, to mellow — **endulzarse** vr
endurecer {53} vt : to harden, to toughen — **endurecerse** vr
ene nf : (letter) n
enebro nm : juniper
eneldo nm : dill
enema nm : enema
enemigo, -ga adj & n : enemy
enemistad nf : enmity, hostility
enemistar vt : to make enemies of — **enemistarse** vr ~ **con** : to fall out with
energético, -ca adj 1 : energy ⟨consumo energético : energy consumption⟩ 2 : lively, spirited
energía nf : energy
enérgico, -ca adj 1 : energetic, vigorous 2 : forceful, emphatic — **enérgicamente** adv
energúmeno, -na n fam : lunatic, crazy person
enero nm : January ⟨el primero de enero : (on) January first⟩
enervar vt 1 : to enervate 2 fam : to annoy, to get on one's nerves — **enervante** adj
enésimo, -ma adj : umpteenth, nth
enfadado, -da adj : angry, annoyed
enfadar vt : to annoy, to make angry — **enfadarse** vr : to get angry, to get annoyed
enfado nm : anger, annoyance
enfardar vt : to bale
énfasis nms & pl : emphasis
enfático, -ca adj : emphatic — **enfáticamente** adv
enfatizar {21} vt DESTACAR, SUBRAYAR : to emphasize
enfermar vt : to make sick — vi : to fall ill, to get sick — **enfermarse** vr
enfermedad nf 1 INDISPOSICIÓN : illness, sickness ⟨por enfermedad : due to illness⟩ 2 : illness, disease ⟨contraer una enfermedad : to catch/contract an illness⟩ ⟨enfermedad infecciosa : infectious disease⟩ ⟨enfermedad mental : mental illness⟩ ⟨enfermedad de Alzheimer : Alzheimer's disease⟩
enfermería nf : infirmary
enfermero, -ra n : nurse
enfermizo, -za adj : sickly
enfermo¹, -ma adj : sick, ill
enfermo², -ma n 1 : sick person, invalid 2 PACIENTE : patient
enfilar vt 1 : to take, to go along ⟨enfiló la carretera de Montevideo : she went up the road to Montevideo⟩ 2 : to line up, to put in a row 3 : to string, to thread 4 : to aim, to direct — vi : to make one's way
enflaquecer {53} vi : to lose weight, to become thin — vt : to emaciate

enfocar {72} vt 1 : to focus (on) 2 : to consider, to look at
enfoque nm : focus
enfrascarse {72} vr ~ **en** : to immerse oneself in, to get caught up in
enfrentamiento nm : clash, confrontation
enfrentar vt : to confront, to face — **enfrentarse** vr 1 ~ **con** : to clash with 2 ~ **a** : to face up to
enfrente adv 1 DELANTE : in front 2 : opposite
enfriamiento nm 1 CATARRO : chill, cold 2 : cooling off, damper
enfriar {85} vt 1 : to chill, to cool 2 : to cool down, to dampen — vi : to get cold — **enfriarse** vr : to get chilled, to catch a cold
enfundar vt : to sheathe, to encase
enfurecer {53} vt ENCOLERIZAR : to infuriate — **enfurecerse** vr : to fly into a rage
enfurecido, -da adj : furious, raging
enfurruñarse vr fam : to sulk
engalanar vt : to decorate, to deck out — **engalanarse** vr : to dress up
enganchar vt 1 : to hook, to snag 2 : to attach, to hitch up — **engancharse** vr 1 : to get snagged, to get hooked 2 : to enlist
enganche nm 1 : hook 2 : coupling, hitch 3 Mex : down payment
engañar vt 1 EMBAUCAR : to trick, to deceive, to mislead 2 : to cheat on, to be unfaithful to — **engañarse** vr 1 : to be mistaken 2 : to deceive oneself
engaño nm 1 : deception, trick 2 : fake, feint (in sports)
engañoso, -sa adj 1 : deceitful 2 : misleading, deceptive
engarzar {21} vt 1 : to set (a gem) 2 ENSARTAR : to string 3 HILAR : to string together — **engarzarse** vr ~ **en** : to get involved in, to get caught up in
engatusar vt : to coax, to cajole
engendrar vt 1 : to beget, to father 2 : to give rise to, to engender
engendro nm 1 : fetus 2 MONSTRUO : monstrosity, freak
engentarse vr Mex : to become confused and overwhelmed
englobar vt : to include, to embrace
engomado nm Mex : sticker
engomar vt : to glue, to coat with glue
engordar vt : to fatten, to fatten up — vi : to gain weight
engorroso, -sa adj : bothersome
engranaje nm : gears pl, cogs pl
engranar vt : to mesh, to engage — vi : to mesh gears
engrandecer {53} vt 1 : to enlarge 2 : to exaggerate 3 : to exalt
engrandecimiento nm 1 : enlargement 2 : exaggeration 3 : exaltation
engrane nm Mex : cogwheel
engrapadora nf : stapler
engrapar vt : to staple
engrasar vt : to grease, to lubricate
engrase nm : greasing, lubrication
engreído, -da adj PRESUMIDO, VANIDOSO : vain, conceited, stuck-up

engreimiento *nm* ARROGANCIA : arrogance, conceit

engreír {66} *vt* ENVANECER : to make vain — **engreírse** *vr* : to become conceited

engrosar {19} *vt* : to enlarge, to increase, to swell — *vi* ENGORDAR : to gain weight

engrudo *nm* : paste

engullir {38} *vt* : to gulp down, to gobble up — **engullirse** *vr*

enharinar *vt* : to flour

enhebrar *vt* ENSARTAR : to string, to thread

enhilar *vt* : to thread (a needle, etc.)

enhorabuena *nf* FELICIDADES : congratulations *pl*

enigma *nm* : enigma, mystery

enigmático, -ca *adj* : enigmatic — **enigmáticamente** *adv*

enjabonar *vt* : to soap up, to lather — **enjabonarse** *vr*

enjaezar {21} *vt* : to harness

enjalbegar {52} *vt* : to whitewash

enjambrar *vi* : to swarm

enjambre *nm* 1 : swarm 2 MUCHEDUMBRE : crowd, mob

enjaular *vt* 1 : to cage 2 *fam* : to jail, to lock up

enjuagar {52} *vt* : to rinse — **enjuagarse** *vr* : to rinse out

enjuague *nm* 1 : rinse 2 **enjuague bucal** : mouthwash

enjugar {52} *vt* : to wipe away (tears)

enjuiciar *vt* 1 : to indict, to prosecute 2 JUZGAR : to try

enlace *nm* 1 : bond, link, connection 2 : liaison 3 HIPERENLACE : link

enlatar *vt* ENVASAR : to can — **enlatado, -da** *adj*

enlazar {21} *v* : to join, to link, to fit together

enlistar *vt* : to list — **enlistarse** *vr* : to enlist

enlodado, -da *adj* LODOSO : muddy

enlodar *vt* 1 : to cover with mud 2 : to stain, to sully — **enlodarse** *vr*

enlodazar → **enlodar**

enloquecedor, -dora *adj* : maddening

enloquecer {53} *vt* : to drive crazy — **enloquecerse** *vr* : to go crazy

enlutarse *vr* : to go into mourning

enmarañar *vt* 1 : to tangle 2 : to complicate 3 : to confuse, to mix up — **enmarañarse** *vr*

enmarcar {72} *vt* 1 ENCUADRAR : to frame 2 : to provide the setting for

enmascarar *vt* : to mask, to disguise — **enmascarado, -da** *adj*

enmasillar *vt* : to putty, to caulk

enmendar {55} *vt* 1 : to amend 2 CORREGIR : to emend, to correct 3 COMPENSAR : to compensate for — **enmendarse** *vr* : to mend one's ways

enmienda *nf* 1 : amendment 2 : correction, emendation

enmohecerse {53} *vr* 1 : to become moldy 2 OXIDARSE : to rust, to become rusty

enmudecer {53} *vt* : to mute, to silence — *vi* : to fall silent

ennegrecer {53} *vt* : to blacken, to darken — **ennegrecerse** *vr*

ennoblecer {53} *vt* 1 : to ennoble 2 : to embellish

enojadizo, -za *adj* IRRITABLE : irritable, cranky

enojado, -da *adj* 1 : annoyed 2 : angry, mad

enojar *vt* 1 : to anger 2 : to annoy, to upset — **enojarse** *vr*

enojo *nm* 1 CÓLERA : anger 2 : annoyance

enojón, -jona *adj*, *pl* -**jones** *Chile, Mex fam* : irritable, cranky

enojoso, -sa *adj* FASTIDIOSO, MOLESTOSO : annoying, irritating

enorgullecer {53} *vt* : to make proud — **enorgullecerse** *vr* : to pride oneself

enorme *adj* INMENSO : enormous, huge — **enormemente** *adv*

enormidad *nf* 1 : enormity, seriousness 2 : immensity, hugeness

enraizado, -da *adj* : deep-seated, deeply rooted

enraizar {30} *vi* : to take root

enramada *nf* : arbor, bower

enramar *vt* : to cover with branches

enrarecer {53} *vt* : to rarefy — **enrarecerse** *vr*

enredadera *nf* : climbing plant, vine

enredar *vt* 1 : to tangle up, to entangle 2 : to confuse, to complicate 3 : to involve, to implicate — **enredarse** *vr*

enredo *nm* 1 EMBROLLO : muddle, confusion 2 MARAÑA : tangle

enrejado *nm* 1 : railing 2 : grating, grille 3 : trellis, lattice

enrevesado, -da *adj* : complicated, involved

enriquecer {53} *vt* : to enrich — **enriquecerse** *vr* : to get rich

enriquecido, -da *adj* : enriched

enriquecimiento *nm* : enrichment

enrojecer {53} *vt* : to make red, to redden — **enrojecerse** *vr* : to blush

enrolar *vt* RECLUTAR : to recruit — **enrolarse** *vr* INSCRIBIRSE : to enlist, to sign up

enrollado, -da *adj* 1 : rolled up, coiled 2 **estar enrollado con** *Spain* : to be involved with (romantically)

enrollar *vt* : to roll up, to coil — **enrollarse** *vr*

enronquecerse {53} *vr* : to become hoarse

enroscar {72} *vt* TORCER : to twist — **enroscarse** *vr* : to coil, to twine

ensacar {72} *vt* : to bag (up)

ensalada *nf* : salad

ensaladera *nf* : salad bowl

ensalmo *nm* : incantation, spell

ensalzar {21} *vt* 1 : to praise, to extol 2 EXALTAR : to exalt

ensamblaje *nm* : assembly

ensamblar *vt* 1 : to assemble 2 : to join, to fit together

ensanchar *vt* 1 : to widen 2 : to expand, to extend — **ensancharse** *vr*

ensanche *nm* 1 : widening 2 : expansion, development

ensangrentado, -da *adj* : bloody, blood-stained

ensangrentar {55} *vt* : to cover or stain with blood

ensañarse *vr* : to act cruelly, to be merciless

ensartar *vt* **1** ENHEBRAR : to string, to thread **2** : to skewer, to pierce

ensayar *vi* : to rehearse — *vt* **1** : to try out, to test **2** : to assay

ensayista *nmf* : essayist

ensayo *nm* **1** : essay **2** : trial, test **3** : rehearsal **4** : assay (of metals)

enseguida *adv* INMEDIATAMENTE : right away, immediately, at once

ensenada *nf* : cove, inlet

enseña *nf* **1** INSIGNIA : emblem, insignia **2** : standard, banner

enseñanza *nf* **1** EDUCACIÓN : education **2** : teaching

enseñar *vt* **1** : to teach **2** MOSTRAR : to show, to display — **enseñarse** *vr* ~ **a** : to learn to, to get used to

enseres *nmpl* : equipment, furnishings *pl* ⟨enseres domésticos : household goods⟩

ensillar *vt* : to saddle (up)

ensimismado, -da *adj* : absorbed, engrossed

ensimismarse *vr* : to lose oneself in thought

ensombrecer {53} *vt* : to cast a shadow over, to darken — **ensombrecerse** *vr*

ensoñación *nf, pl* **-ciones** : fantasy

ensopar *vt* **1** : to drench **2** : to dunk, to dip

ensordecedor, -dora *adj* : deafening, thunderous

ensordecer {53} *vt* : to deafen — *vi* : to go deaf

ensuciar *vt* : to soil, to dirty — **ensuciarse** *vr*

ensueño *nm* **1** : daydream, reverie **2** FANTASÍA : illusion, fantasy

entablar *vt* **1** : to cover with boards **2** : to initiate, to enter into, to start

entallar *vt* AJUSTAR : to tailor, to fit, to take in — *vi* QUEDAR : to fit

entarimado *nm* : flooring, floorboards *pl*

ente *nm* **1** : being, entity **2** : body, organization ⟨ente rector : ruling body⟩ **3** *fam* : eccentric, crackpot

entenado, -da *n Mex* : stepchild, stepson *m*, stepdaughter *f*

entender[1] {56} *vt* **1** COMPRENDER : to understand ⟨no entiendo por qué : I don't understand why⟩ ⟨me has entendido mal : you've misunderstood me⟩ ⟨mis padres no me entienden : my parents don't understand me⟩ ⟨dar a entender : to imply⟩ **2** : to think, to believe ⟨él no lo entiende así : he doesn't see it that way⟩ **3** : to know, to get ⟨si me entiendes : if you know what I mean⟩ **4** : to infer ⟨dar algo a entender : to imply something⟩ — *vi* **1** : to understand ⟨¡ya entiendo! : now I understand!⟩ **2** ~ **de** : to know about **3** ~ **en** : to be in charge of — **entenderse** *vr* **1** : to be understood **2** : to get along well **3** ~ **con** : to deal with

entender[2] *nm* **a mi entender** : in my opinion

entendible *adj* : understandable

entendido[1], -da *adj* **1** : skilled, expert, knowledgeable **2 tener entendido** : to understand, to be under the impression ⟨teníamos entendido que vendrías : we were under the impression you would come⟩ **3 darse por entendido** : to go without saying

entendido[2] *nm* : expert, authority, connoisseur

entendimiento *nm* **1** : intellect, mind **2** : understanding, agreement

enterado, -da *adj* : aware, well-informed ⟨estar enterado de : to be privy to⟩ ⟨darse por enterado : to get the message⟩

enteramente *adv* : entirely, completely

enterar *vt* INFORMAR : to inform — **enterarse** *vr* INFORMARSE : to find out, to learn

entereza *nf* **1** INTEGRIDAD : integrity **2** FORTALEZA : fortitude **3** FIRMEZA : resolve

enternecedor, -dora *adj* CONMOVEDOR : touching, moving

enternecer {53} *vt* CONMOVER : to move, to touch

entero[1], -ra *adj* **1** : entire, whole **2** : complete, absolute **3** : intact — **enteramente** *adv*

entero[2] *nm* **1** : integer, whole number **2** : point (in finance)

enterramiento *nm* : burial

enterrar {55} *vt* : to bury

entibiar *vt* : to cool (down) — **entibiarse** *vr* : to become lukewarm

entidad *nf* **1** ENTE : entity **2** : body, organization **3** : firm, company **4** : importance, significance

entierro *nm* **1** : burial **2** : funeral

entintar *vt* : to ink

entoldado *nm* : awning

entomología *nf* : entomology

entomólogo, -ga *n* : entomologist

entonación *nf, pl* **-ciones** : intonation

entonar *vi* : to be in tune — *vt* **1** : to intone **2** : to tone up

entonces *adv* **1** : then **2 desde** ~ : since then **3 en aquel entonces** : in those days

entornado, -da *adj* ENTREABIERTO : half-closed, ajar

entornar *vt* ENTREABRIR : to leave ajar

entorno *nm* : surroundings *pl*, environment

entorpecer {53} *vt* **1** : to hinder, to obstruct **2** : to dull — **entorpecerse** *vr* : to dull the senses

entrada *nf* **1** : entrance, entry ⟨prohibida la entrada : do not enter⟩ **2** : entrance ⟨entrada principal : main entrance⟩ **3** : ticket, admission ⟨entrada gratuita/libre : free admission⟩ **4** : beginning, onset ⟨de entrada : from the start⟩ **5** : entrée **6** : cue (in music) **7 entradas** *nfpl* : income ⟨entradas y salidas : income and expenditures⟩ **8 tener entradas** : to have a receding hairline

entrado, -da *adj* **entrado en años** : elderly

entramado *nm* : framework

entrampar *vt* **1** ATRAPAR : to entrap, to ensnare **2** ENGAÑAR : to deceive, to trick

entrante *adj* **1** : next, upcoming ⟨el año entrante : next year⟩ **2** : incoming, new ⟨el presidente entrante : the president elect⟩

entraña *nf* **1** MEOLLO : core, heart, crux **2 entrañas** *nfpl* VÍSCERAS : entrails

entrañable *adj* : close, intimate

entrañar *vt* : to entail, to involve

entrar *vi* **1** : to enter, to go in, to come in ⟨entré a la casa : I went in the house⟩ ⟨entrar por : to come/go in (through)⟩ ⟨¿puedo entrar? : can I come in?⟩ ⟨la llave no entra : the key won't go in⟩ **2** : to fit ⟨este vestido no me entra : this dress doesn't fit me⟩ **3** : to begin ⟨entro a trabajar a las ocho : I start work at eight⟩ **4** : to affect ⟨me entra el hambre : I'm getting hungry⟩ **5** ~ **en** : to enter (a phase, etc.) **6** ~ **en** : to be included/considered in **7** ~ **en** : to go into, to discuss (details, etc.) **8** ~ **en** : to enter into (negotiations, battle, etc.), to come into (contact, conflict, etc.), to go into (effect) **9** ~ **en** : to enter (college), to join (an organization), to go into (a profession) — *vt* **1** : to bring in, to introduce **2** : to access

entre *prep* **1** : between ⟨entre las dos ciudades/fechas : between the two cities/dates⟩ ⟨lo dividimos entre los dos : we divided it between the two of us⟩ ⟨la diferencia entre los dos : the difference between the two⟩ ⟨entre todos lo logramos : between all of us we managed it⟩ ⟨entre tú y yo : between you and me⟩ **2** : among ⟨entre las hojas : among the leaves⟩ ⟨entre amigos : among friends⟩ ⟨lo dividimos entre los cuatro : we divided it among the four of us⟩ ⟨conversaban entre sí : they talked among themselves⟩

entreabierto[1] *pp* → **entreabrir**

entreabierto[2], **-ta** *adj* ENTORNADO : half-open, ajar

entreabrir {2} *vt* ENTORNAR : to leave ajar

entreacto *nm* : intermission, interval

entrecano, -na *adj* : grayish, graying

entrecejo *nm* **fruncir el entrecejo** : to knit one's brows

entrecomillar *vt* : to place in quotation marks

entrecortadamente *adv* **1** : breathlessly **2** : falteringly

entrecortado, -da *adj* **1** : labored, difficult ⟨respiración entrecortada : shortness of breath⟩ **2** : faltering, hesitant ⟨con la voz entrecortada : with a catch in his voice⟩

entrecortarse *vr* : to falter (of the voice or breath)

entrecruzar {21} *vt* ENTRELAZAR : to interweave, to intertwine — **entrecruzarse** *vr*

entredicho *nm* **1** DUDA : doubt, question **2** : prohibition

entrega *nf* **1** : delivery **2** : handing over, surrender **3** : installment ⟨entrega inicial : down payment⟩

entregar {52} *vt* **1** : to deliver **2** DAR : to give, to present **3** : to hand in, to hand over — **entregarse** *vr* **1** : to surrender, to give in **2** : to devote oneself

entrelazar {21} *vt* ENTRECRUZAR : to interweave, to intertwine

entremedias *adv* **1** : in between, halfway **2** : in the meantime

entremés *nm*, *pl* **-meses 1** APERITIVO : appetizer, hors d'oeuvre **2** : interlude, short play

entremeterse → **entrometerse**

entremetido → **entrometido**

entremezclar *vt* : to intermingle

entrenador, -dora *n* : trainer, coach

entrenamiento *nm* : training, drill, practice

entrenar *vt* : to train, to drill, to practice — **entrenarse** *vr* : to train, to spar (in boxing)

entrepierna *nf* **1** : inner thigh **2** : crotch **3** : inseam

entrepiso *nm* : mezzanine

entretanto[1] *adv* : meanwhile

entretanto[2] *nm* **en el entretanto** : in the meantime

entretejer *vt* : to interweave

entretela *nf* : facing (of a garment)

entretelones *nmpl* : inside details

entretención *nf*, *pl* **-ciones** ENTRETENIMIENTO : entertainment

entretener {80} *vt* **1** DIVERTIR : to entertain, to amuse **2** DISTRAER : to distract **3** DEMORAR : to delay, to hold up — **entretenerse** *vr* **1** : to amuse oneself **2** : to dally

entretenido, -da *adj* DIVERTIDO : entertaining, amusing

entretenimiento *nm* **1** : entertainment, pastime **2** DIVERSIÓN : fun, amusement

entretiempo *nm* **1** → **medio tiempo 2** : period between seasons

entrever {88} *vt* **1** : to catch a glimpse of **2** : to make out, to see indistinctly

entreverar *vt* : to mix, to intermingle

entrevero *nm* : confusion, disorder

entrevista *nf* : interview

entrevistador, -dora *n* : interviewer

entrevistar *vt* : to interview — **entrevistarse** ~ **con** : to meet with

entristecer {53} *vt* : to sadden

entrometerse *vr* : to interfere, to meddle

entrometido, -da *n* : meddler, busybody

entroncar {72} *vt* RELACIONAR : to establish a relationship between, to connect — *vi* **1** : to be related **2** : to link up, to be connected

entronque *nm* **1** : kinship **2** VÍNCULO : link, connection

entuerto *nm* : wrong, injustice

entumecer {53} *vt* : to make numb, to be numb — **entumecerse** *vr* : to go numb, to fall asleep

entumecido, -da *adj* **1** : numb **2** : stiff (of muscles, joints, etc.)

entumecimiento *nm* : numbness

enturbiar *vt* **1** : to cloud **2** : to confuse — **enturbiarse** *vr*

entusiasmar *vt* : to excite, to fill with enthusiasm — **entusiasmarse** *vr* : to get excited

entusiasmo *nm* : enthusiasm

entusiasta[1] *adj* : enthusiastic

entusiasta[2] *nmf* AFICIONADO : enthusiast

enumerar *vt* : to enumerate — **enumeración** *nf*

enunciación *nf, pl* **-ciones** : enunciation, statement

enunciado *nm* : statement

enunciar *vt* : to enunciate, to state

envainar *vt* : to sheathe

envalentonar *vt* : to make bold, to encourage — **envalentonarse** *vr*

envanecer {53} *vt* ENGREÍR : to make vain — **envanecerse** *vr*

envasar *vt* **1** EMBOTELLAR : to bottle **2** ENLATAR : to can **3** : to pack in a container

envase *nm* **1** : packaging, packing **2** : container **3** LATA : can **4** : empty bottle

envejecer {53} *vt* : to age, to make look old — *vi* : to age, to grow old

envejecido, -da *adj* : aged, old-looking

envejecimiento *nm* : aging

envenenamiento *nm* : poisoning

envenenar *vt* **1** : to poison **2** : to embitter

envergadura *nf* **1** : span, breadth, spread **2** : importance, scope

envés *nm, pl* **enveses** : reverse, opposite side

enviado, -da *n* : envoy, correspondent

enviar {85} *vt* **1** : to send **2** : to ship

envidia *nf* : envy, jealousy

envidiar *vt* : to envy — **envidiable** *adj*

envidioso, -sa *adj* : envious, jealous

envilecer {53} *vt* : to degrade, to debase

envío *nm* **1** : shipment **2** : remittance

enviudar *vi* : to be widowed, to become a widower

envoltorio *nm* **1** : bundle, package **2** : wrapping, wrapper

envoltura *nf* : wrapper, wrapping

envolver {89} *vt* **1** : to wrap **2** : to envelop, to surround **3** : to entangle, to involve — **envolverse** *vr* **1** : to become involved **2** : to wrap oneself (up)

envuelto *pp* → **envolver**

enyerbar *vt Mex* : to bewitch

enyesar *vt* **1** : to plaster **2** ESCAYOLAR : to put (a broken limb) in a cast

enzima *nf* : enzyme

eón *nm, pl* **eones** : aeon

eperlano *nm* : smelt (fish)

epicentro *nm* : epicenter

épico, -ca *adj* : epic

epicúreo[1]**, -rea** *adj* : epicurean

epicúreo[2]**, -rea** *n* : epicure

epidemia *nf* : epidemic

epidémico, -ca *adj* : epidemic

epidemiología *nf* : epidemiology — **epidemiológico, -ca** *adj*

epifanía *nf* : feast of the Epiphany (January 6th)

epigrama *nm* : epigram

epilepsia *nf* : epilepsy

epiléptico, -ca *adj & n* : epileptic

epílogo *nm* : epilogue

episcopal *adj* : episcopal

episcopaliano, -na *adj & n* : Episcopalian

episódico, -ca *adj* : episodic

episodio *nm* : episode

epístola *nf* : epistle

epitafio *nm* : epitaph

epíteto *nm* : epithet, name

epítome *nm* : summary, abstract

época *nf* **1** EDAD, ERA, PERÍODO : epoch, age, period **2** : time of year, season **3** de ～ : vintage, antique

epopeya *nf* : epic poem

equidad *nf* JUSTICIA : equity, justice, fairness

equilátero, -ra *adj* : equilateral

equilibrado, -da *adj* : well-balanced

equilibrar *vt* : to balance — **equilibrarse** *vr*

equilibrio *nm* **1** : balance, equilibrium ⟨perder el equilibrio : to lose one's balance⟩ ⟨equilibrio político : balance of power⟩ **2** : poise, aplomb

equilibrista *nmf* ACRÓBATA : acrobat, tightrope walker

equino, -na *adj* : equine

equinoccio *nm* : equinox

equipaje *nm* BAGAJE : baggage, luggage

equipamiento *nm* : equipping, equipment

equipar *vt* : to equip — **equiparse** *vr*

equiparable *adj* : comparable

equiparar *vt* **1** ～ **a/con** : to put on the same level as/with **2** COMPARAR : to compare

equipo *nm* **1** : team, crew **2** : gear, equipment

equis *nf* : (letter) x

equitación *nf, pl* **-ciones** : horseback riding, horsemanship

equitativo, -va *adj* JUSTO : equitable, fair, just — **equitativamente** *adv*

equivalencia *nf* : equivalence

equivalente *adj & nm* : equivalent

equivaler {84} *vi* : to be equivalent

equivocación *nf, pl* **-ciones** ERROR : error, mistake

equivocado, -da *adj* : mistaken, wrong — **equivocadamente** *adv*

equivocar {72} *vt* **1** : to confuse (someone), to make (someone) mess up **2** : to choose badly — **equivocarse** *vr* : to make a mistake, to be wrong ⟨se equivocó de casa : he got the wrong house⟩

equívoco[1]**, -ca** *adj* AMBIGUO : ambiguous, equivocal

equívoco[2] *nm* : misunderstanding

era[1]**, etc.** → **ser**

era[2] *nf* EDAD, ÉPOCA : era, age

erario *nm* : public treasury

ere *nf* : (letter) r

erección *nf, pl* **-ciones** : erection, raising

erecto, -ta *adj* : erect

eremita *nmf* ERMITAÑO : hermit

ergonomía *nf* : ergonomics

erguido, -da *adj* : erect, upright

erguir {31} *vt* : to raise, to lift up — **erguirse** *vr* : to straighten up

erigir {35} *vt* : to build, to erect — **erigirse** *vr* ～ **en** : to set oneself up as

erizado, -da *adj* : bristly

erizar {21} *vt* **1** : to make (hair, etc.) stand on end ⟨me eriza la piel : it gives me goose bumps⟩ **2** : to irritate, to grate on (someone) — **erizarse** *vr* : to stand on end

erizo *nm* **1** : hedgehog **2 erizo de mar** : sea urchin

ermitaño[1], **-ña** *n* EREMITA : hermit, recluse

ermitaño[2] *nm* : hermit crab

erogación *nf, pl* **-ciones** : expenditure

erogar {52} *vt* **1** : to pay out **2** : to distribute

erosión *nf, pl* **-siones** : erosion

erosionar *vt* : to erode

erótico, -ca *adj* : erotic

erotismo *nm* : eroticism

erradicar {72} *vt* : to eradicate — **erradicación** *nf*

errado, -da *adj* : wrong, mistaken

errante *adj* VAGABUNDO : errant, wandering

errar {32} *vt* FALLAR : to miss — *vi* **1** DESACERTAR : to be wrong, to be mistaken **2** VAGAR : to wander

errata *nf* : misprint, error

errático, -ca *adj* : erratic — **erráticamente** *adv*

erre *nf* : (letter) r (especially when trilled)

erróneo, -nea *adj* EQUIVOCADO : erroneous, wrong — **erróneamente** *adv*

error *nm* EQUIVOCACIÓN : error, mistake ⟨cometer un error : to make a mistake⟩ ⟨estar en un error : to be mistaken⟩ ⟨por error : by mistake⟩ ⟨error de cálculo : miscalculation⟩ ⟨error de imprenta : misprint⟩ ⟨error de hecho : factual error⟩

eructar *vi* : to belch, to burp

eructo *nm* : belch, burp

erudición *nf, pl* **-ciones** : erudition, learning

erudito[1], **-ta** *adj* LETRADO : erudite, learned

erudito[2], **-ta** *n* : scholar

erupción *nf, pl* **-ciones** **1** : eruption **2** SARPULLIDO : rash

eruptivo, -va *adj* : eruptive

es → ser

esbelto, -ta *adj* DELGADO : slender, slim

esbirro *nm* : henchman

esbozar {21} *vt* BOSQUEJAR : to sketch, to outline

esbozo *nm* **1** : sketch **2** : rough draft

escabechar *vt* **1** ENCURTIR : to pickle **2** *fam* : to kill, to rub out

escabeche *nm* : brine (for pickling)

escabel *nm* : footstool

escabroso, -sa *adj* **1** : rugged, rough **2** : difficult, tough **3** : risqué

escabullirse {38} *vr* : to slip away, to escape

escafandra *nf* : (protective) suit

escala *nf* **1** : scale ⟨en escala de 1 a 10 : on a scale of 1 to 10⟩ ⟨a escala : to scale⟩ ⟨a escala mundial : on a worldwide scale⟩ ⟨producción a gran escala : large-scale production⟩ **2** : scale (in music) **3** ESCALERA : ladder **4** : stopover, layover ⟨hacer escala : to lay over⟩

escalada *nf* : ascent, climb

escalador, -dora *n* ALPINISTA : mountain climber

escalafón *nm, pl* **-fones** **1** : list of personnel **2** : salary scale, rank

escalar *vt* : to climb, to scale — *vi* **1** : to go climbing **2** : to escalate

escaldar *vt* : to scald

escalera *nf* **1** : ladder ⟨escalera de tijera : stepladder⟩ **2** : stairs *pl*, staircase **3 escalera mecánica** : escalator

escalfar *vt* : to poach (eggs)

escalinata *nf* : flight of stairs

escalofriante *adj* : horrifying, bloodcurdling

escalofrío *nm* : shiver, chill, shudder

escalón *nm, pl* **-lones** **1** : echelon **2** : step, rung

escalonado, -da *adj* GRADUAL : gradual, staggered

escalonar *vt* **1** : to terrace **2** : to stagger, to alternate

escalpelo *nm* BISTURÍ : scalpel

escama *nf* **1** : scale (of fish or reptiles) **2** : flake (of skin)

escamar *vt* **1** : to scale (fish) **2** : to make suspicious

escamocha *nf Mex* : fruit salad

escamoso, -sa *adj* : scaly

escamotear *vt* **1** : to palm, to conceal **2** *fam* : to lift, to swipe **3** : to hide, to cover up

escampar *v impers* : to stop raining

escandalizar {21} *vt* : to shock, to scandalize — *vi* : to make a fuss — **escandalizarse** *vr* : to be shocked

escándalo *nm* **1** : scandal **2** : scene, commotion

escandaloso, -sa *adj* **1** : shocking, scandalous **2** RUIDOSO : noisy, rowdy **3** : flagrant, outrageous — **escandalosamente** *adv*

escandinavo, -va *adj & n* : Scandinavian

escandir *vt* : to scan (poetry)

escanear *vt* : to scan (documents)

escáner *nm* **1** : scan **2** : scanner

escaño *nm* **1** : seat (in a legislative body) **2** BANCO : bench

escapada *nf* HUIDA : flight, escape

escapar *vi* HUIR : to escape, to flee, to run away — **escaparse** *vr* : to escape notice, to leak out

escaparate *nm* **1** : shop window **2** : showcase

escapatoria *nf* **1** : loophole, excuse, pretext ⟨no tener escapatoria : to have no way out⟩ **2** ESCAPADA : escape, flight

escape *nm* **1** FUGA : escape **2** : exhaust (from a vehicle)

escapismo *nm* : escapism — **escapista** *adj*

escápula *nf* OMÓPLATO : scapula, shoulder blade

escarabajo *nm* : beetle

escaramuza *nf* **1** : skirmish **2** : scrimmage

escaramuzar {21} *vi* : to skirmish

escarapela *nf* : rosette (ornament)

escarbar *vt* **1** : to dig, to scratch up **2** : to poke, to pick **3** ~ **en** : to investigate, to pry into

escarcha nf **1** : frost **2** Mex, PRi : glitter
escarchar vt **1** : to frost, to sugar **2** : to candy (fruit)
escardar vt **1** : to weed, to hoe **2** : to weed out
escarlata adj & nf : scarlet
escarlatina nf : scarlet fever
escarmentar {55} vt : to punish, to teach a lesson to — vi : to learn one's lesson
escarmiento nm **1** : lesson, warning **2** CASTIGO : punishment
escarnio nm : ridicule, mockery
escarola nf : escarole
escarpa nf : escarpment, steep slope
escarpado, -da adj : steep, sheer
escasamente adv : scarcely, barely
escasear vi : to be scarce, to run short
escasez nf, pl **-seces** : shortage, scarcity
escaso, -sa adj **1** : scarce, scant **2** ~ **de** : short of
escatimar vt : to skimp on, to be sparing with ⟨no escatimar esfuerzos : to spare no effort⟩
escayola nf Spain **1** : plaster (for casts) **2** : cast (in medicine)
escayolar vt Spain : to put (a broken limb) in a cast
escena nf **1** : scene **2** : stage
escenario nm **1** ESCENA : stage **2** : setting, scene ⟨el escenario del crimen : the scene of the crime⟩
escénico, -ca adj **1** : scenic **2** : stage
escenificar {72} vt : to stage, to dramatize
escenografía nf : set design
escepticismo nm : skepticism
escéptico[1], -ca adj : skeptical
escéptico[2], -ca n : skeptic
escindirse vr **1** : to split **2** : to break away
escisión nf, pl **-siones** : split, division
esclarecer {53} vt **1** ELUCIDAR : to elucidate, to clarify **2** ILUMINAR : to illuminate, to light up
esclarecimiento nm ELUCIDACIÓN : elucidation, clarification
esclavitud nf : slavery
esclavización nf, pl **-ciones** : enslavement
esclavizar {21} vt : to enslave
esclavo, -va n : slave
esclerosis nf **esclerosis múltiple** : multiple sclerosis
esclusa nf : floodgate, lock (of a canal)
escoba nf : broom
escobilla nf : small broom, brush, whisk broom
escocer {14} vi ARDER : to smart, to sting — **escocerse** vr : to be sore
escocés[1], -cesa adj, mpl **-ceses** **1** : Scottish **2** : tartan, plaid
escocés[2], -cesa n, mpl **-ceses** : Scottish person, Scot
escocés[3] nm **1** : Scottish, Scots (language) **2** pl **-ceses** : Scotch (whiskey)
escofina nf : file, rasp
escoger {15} vt ELEGIR, SELECCIONAR : to choose, to select
escogido, -da adj : choice, select
escolar[1] adj : school
escolar[2] nmf : student, pupil

escolaridad nf : schooling ⟨escolaridad obligatoria : compulsory education⟩
escolarización nf, pl **-ciones** : education, schooling
escolarizar {21} vt : to educate
escollo nm **1** : reef **2** OBSTÁCULO : obstacle
escolta nmf : escort
escoltar vt : to escort, to accompany
escombro nm **1** : debris, rubbish **2** **escombros** nmpl : ruins, rubble
esconder vt OCULTAR : to hide, to conceal
escondidas nfpl **1** : hide-and-seek **2** a ~ : secretly, in secret
escondite nm **1** ESCONDRIJO : hiding place **2** ESCONDIDAS : hide-and-seek
escondrijo nm ESCONDITE : hiding place
escopeta nf : shotgun
escoplo nm : chisel
escorar vi : to list, to heel (of a boat)
escorbuto nm : scurvy
escoria nf **1** : slag, dross **2** HEZ : dregs pl, scum ⟨la escoria de la sociedad : the dregs of society⟩
Escorpio[1] or **Escorpión** nm : Scorpio (sign or constellation)
Escorpio[2] or **Escorpión** nmf : Scorpio (person)
escorpión nm, pl **-piones** ALACRÁN : scorpion
escotado, -da adj : low-cut (of clothing)
escote nm **1** : (low) neckline ⟨escote en V : V-neck⟩ **2** pagar a escote : to go dutch
escotilla nf : hatch, hatchway
escozor nm : smarting, stinging
escriba nm : scribe
escribanía nf CoRi, Arg, Uru : office of a notary public
escribano, -na n **1** : court clerk **2** NOTARIO : notary public
escribir {33} v **1** : to write ⟨escribir una novela/palabra : to write a novel/word⟩ ⟨escribir a lápiz : to write in pencil⟩ ⟨escribir a mano : to write by hand⟩ ⟨escribir a máquina : to type⟩ **2** : to spell ⟨¿cómo se escribe? : how do you spell it?⟩ — **escribirse** vr CARTEARSE : to write to one another, to correspond
escrito[1] pp → **escribir**
escrito[2], -ta adj : written
escrito[3] nm **1** : written document **2** **escritos** nmpl : writings, works
escritor, -tora n : writer
escritorio nm : desk
escritorzuelo, -la n : hack (writer)
escritura nf **1** : writing, handwriting **2** : deed **3** las Escrituras : the Scriptures
escroto nm : scrotum
escrúpulo nm : scruple
escrupuloso, -sa adj **1** : scrupulous **2** METICULOSO : exact, meticulous — **escrupulosamente** adv
escrutador, -dora adj : penetrating, searching
escrutar vt ESCUDRIÑAR : to scrutinize, to examine closely
escrutinio nm : scrutiny

escuadra *nf* **1** : square (instrument) **2** : fleet, squadron

escuadrilla *nf* : squadron, formation, flight

escuadrón *nm, pl* **-drones** : squadron

escuálido, -da *adj* **1** : skinny, scrawny **2** INMUNDO : filthy, squalid

escuchar *vt* **1** : to listen to **2** : to hear — *vi* : to listen — **escucharse** *vr*

escudar *vt* : to shield — **escudarse** *vr* ~ **en** : to hide behind

escudería *nf* : team (in car racing)

escudero *nm* : squire

escudo *nm* **1** : shield **2 escudo de armas** : coat of arms

escudriñar *vt* **1** ESCRUTAR : to scrutinize **2** : to inquire into, to investigate

escuela *nf* **1** : school ⟨escuela privada/pública : private/public school⟩ ⟨escuela nocturna : night school⟩ ⟨escuela de verano : summer school⟩ **2** DEPARTAMENTO : school, department

escueto, -ta *adj* **1** : plain, simple **2** : succinct, concise — **escuetamente** *adv*

escuincle, -cla *n Mex fam* : child, kid

escular {72} *vt* : to search

esculpir *vt* **1** : to sculpt **2** : to carve, to engrave — *vi* : to sculpt

escultor, -tora *n* : sculptor

escultórico, -ca *adj* : sculptural

escultura *nf* : sculpture

escultural *adj* : statuesque

escupir *v* : to spit

escupitajo *nm* : spit, gob of spit

escurridizo, -za *adj* : slippery, elusive

escurridor *nm* **1** : dish rack **2** : colander

escurrir *vt* **1** : to wring out **2** : to drain — *vi* : to drain **2** : to drip, to drip-dry — **escurrirse** *vr* : to slip away

ese¹, esa *adj, mpl* **esos** : that, those ⟨ese mismo día : that very day⟩ ⟨esos niños : those children⟩ ⟨sale con la chica esa : he's dating that girl⟩

ese² *nf* : (letter) s

ese³, esa *or* **ése, ésa** *pron, mpl* **esos** *or* **ésos** : that (one), those (ones) *pl* ⟨ese/ése es el mío : that one is mine⟩ ⟨esa/ésa no fue la primera vez : that wasn't the first time⟩ ⟨ese/ése no es el hombre : that's not the man⟩

esencia *nf* : essence

esencial *adj* : essential — **esencialmente** *adv*

esfera *nf* **1** : sphere (object or shape) **2** : sphere ⟨esfera de influencia : sphere of influence⟩ ⟨en las altas esferas : in the highest circles⟩ **3** : face, dial (of a clock)

esférico¹, -ca *adj* : spherical

esférico² *nm* : ball (in sports)

esfinge *nf* : sphinx

esforzado, -da *adj* **1** : energetic, vigorous **2** VALIENTE : courageous, brave

esforzar {36} *vt* : to strain — **esforzarse** *vr* : to make an effort

esfuerzo *nm* **1** : effort **2** ÁNIMO, VIGOR : spirit, vigor **3 sin ~** : effortlessly

esfumar *vt* : to tone down, to soften — **esfumarse** *vr* **1** : to fade away, to vanish **2** *fam* : to take off, to leave

esgrima *nf* : fencing (sport)

esgrimir *vt* **1** : to brandish, to wield **2** : to use, to resort to — *vi* : to fence

esgrimista *nmf* : fencer

esguince *nm* : sprain, strain (of a muscle)

eslabón *nm, pl* **-bones** : link

eslavo¹, -va *adj* : Slavic

eslavo², -va *n* : Slav

eslogan *nm, pl* **-lóganes** : slogan

eslora *nf* : length

eslovaco, -ca *adj & n* : Slovakian, Slovak

esloveno, -na *adj & nm* : Slovene, Slovenian

esmaltar *vt* : to enamel

esmalte *nm* **1** : enamel **2 esmalte de uñas** : nail polish

esmerado, -da *adj* : careful, painstaking

esmeralda *nf* : emerald

esmerarse *vr* : to take great pains, to do one's utmost

esmeril *nm* : emery

esmero *nm* : meticulousness, great care

esmoquin *nm, pl* **-quins** **1** : tuxedo (suit) **2** : tuxedo jacket, dinner jacket

esnob¹ *adj, pl* **esnobs** : snobbish

esnob² *nmf, pl* **esnobs** : snob

esnobismo *nm* : snobbery, snobbishness

esnórquel *nm* : snorkel

eso *pron* (*neuter*) **1** : that ⟨eso no me gusta : I don't like that⟩ **2 ¡eso es!** : that's it!, that's right! **3 a eso de** : around ⟨a eso de las tres : around three o'clock⟩ **4 en ~** : at that point, just then **5 por ~** : for that reason ⟨por eso me voy : that's why I'm leaving⟩

esófago *nm* : esophagus

esos → ese

ésos → ése

esotérico, -ca *adj* : esoteric — **esotéricamente** *adv*

espabilado, -da *adj* : bright, smart

espabilarse *vr* **1** : to awaken **2** : to get a move on **3** : to get smart, to wise up

espacial *adj* **1** : space **2** : spatial

espaciar *vt* DISTANCIAR : to space out, to spread out

espacio *nm* **1** : space, room ⟨hay mucho espacio : there is plenty of space⟩ ⟨ocupa demasiado espacio : it takes up too much space⟩ ⟨espacios abiertos : open spaces⟩ **2** : space (in printing) ⟨a doble espacio : double-spaced⟩ **3** : period, length (of time) ⟨por espacio de : over a period of⟩ **4** : time slot (in television, etc.) **5** : program ⟨espacio televisivo : television program⟩ **6 espacio exterior** : outer space

espacioso, -sa *adj* : spacious, roomy

espada¹ *nf* **1** : sword **2 espadas** *nfpl* : swords (in the Spanish deck of cards)

espada² *nm* MATADOR, TORERO : bullfighter, matador

espadaña *nf* **1** : belfry **2** : cattail

espagueti *nm or* **espaguetis** *nmpl* : spaghetti

espalda *nf* **1** : back **2 espaldas** *nfpl* : shoulders, back **3** *or* **estilo espalda** : backstroke **4 por la espalda** : from behind

espaldarazo *nm* **1** : recognition, support **2** : slap on the back
espantajo *nm* : scarecrow
espantapájaros *nms & pl* : scarecrow
espantar *vt* ASUSTAR : to scare, to frighten — **espantarse** *vr*
espanto *nm* : fright, fear, horror
espantoso, -sa *adj* **1** : frightening, terrifying **2** : frightful, dreadful — **espantosamente** *adv*
español¹, -ñola *adj* : Spanish
español², -ñola *n* : Spaniard
español³ *nm* CASTELLANO : Spanish (language)
esparadrapo *nm* : adhesive bandage, Band-Aid™
esparcimiento *nm* **1** DIVERSIÓN, RECREO : entertainment, recreation **2** DESCANSO : relaxation **3** DISEMINACIÓN : dissemination, spreading
esparcir {83} *vt* DISPERSAR : to scatter, to spread — **esparcirse** *vr* **1** : to spread out **2** DESCANSARSE : to take it easy **3** DIVERTIRSE : to amuse oneself
espárrago *nm* : asparagus
espartano, -na *adj* : severe, austere
espasmo *nm* : spasm
espasmódico, -ca *adj* : spasmodic — **espasmódicamente** *adv*
espástico, -ca *adj* : spastic
espátula *nf* : spatula
especia *nf* : spice
especial *adj & nm* : special
especialidad *nf* : specialty
especialista *nmf* : specialist, expert
especialización *nf, pl* **-ciones** : specialization
especializarse {21} *vr* : to specialize
especialmente *adv* : especially, particularly
especie *nf* **1** : species **2** CLASE, TIPO : type, kind, sort
especificación *nf, pl* **-ciones** : specification
especificar {72} *vt* : to specify
específico, -ca *adj* : specific — **específicamente** *adv*
espécimen *nm, pl* **especímenes** : specimen
espectacular *adj* : spectacular — **espectacularmente** *adv*
espectáculo *nm* **1** : spectacle, sight **2** : show, performance
espectador, -dora *n* : spectator, onlooker
espectro *nm* **1** : ghost, specter **2** : spectrum
especulación *nf, pl* **-ciones** : speculation
especulador, -dora *n* : speculator
especular *vi* : to speculate
especulativo, -va *adj* : speculative
espejismo *nm* **1** : mirage **2** : illusion
espejo *nm* : mirror
espejuelos *nmpl* ANTEOJOS : spectacles, glasses
espeluznante *adj* : hair-raising, terrifying
espera *nf* : wait
esperado, -da *adj* : anticipated
esperanza *nf* : hope, expectation ⟨dar esperanzas : to give hope⟩ ⟨perder la esperanza : to lose hope⟩ ⟨esperanza de vida : life expectancy⟩
esperanzado, -da *adj* : hopeful
esperanzador, -dora *adj* : encouraging, promising
esperanzar {21} *vt* : to give hope to
esperar *vt* **1** AGUARDAR : to wait for ⟨espero a un amigo : I'm waiting for a friend⟩ ⟨esperé una hora : I waited for an hour⟩ **2** : to expect ⟨no esperaba visitas : I wasn't expecting visitors⟩ ⟨como era de esperar : as was to be expected⟩ ⟨cuando uno menos lo espera : when you least expect it⟩ **3** : to hope ⟨espero poder trabajar : I hope to be able to work⟩ ⟨espero que sí/no : I hope so/not⟩ ⟨espero que llame : I hope he calls⟩ — *vi* : to wait ⟨espere un momento, por favor : just a moment, please⟩ ⟨hay que esperar a que llueva : we have to wait for it to rain⟩ — **esperarse** *vr* **1** : to expect, to be hoped ⟨como podría esperarse : as would be expected⟩ **2** : to hold on, to hang on ⟨espérate un momento : hold on a minute⟩
esperma *nmf* : sperm
esperpéntico, -ca *adj* GROTESCO : grotesque
esperpento *nm fam* MAMARRACHO : sight, fright ⟨voy hecha un esperpento : I really look a sight⟩
espesante *nm* : thickener
espesar *vt* : to thicken — **espesarse** *vr*
espeso, -sa *adj* : thick, heavy, dense
espesor *nm* : thickness, density
espesura *nf* **1** : thickness **2** : thicket
espetar *vt* **1** : to blurt out **2** : to skewer
espía *nmf* : spy
espiar {85} *vt* : to spy on, to observe — *vi* : to spy
espiga *nf* **1** : ear (of wheat) **2** : spike (of flowers)
espigado, -da *adj* : willowy, slender
espigar {52} *vt* : to glean, to gather — **espigarse** *vr* : to grow quickly, to shoot up
espigón *nm, pl* **-gones** : breakwater
espina *nf* **1** : thorn **2** : spine ⟨espina dorsal : spinal column⟩ **3** : fish bone **4 darle mala espina a alguien** : to make someone uneasy
espinaca *nf* **1** : spinach (plant) **2 espinacas** *nfpl* : spinach (food)
espinal *adj* : spinal
espinazo *nm* : backbone
espinilla *nf* **1** BARRO, GRANO : pimple **2** : shin
espino *nm* : hawthorn
espinoso, -sa *adj* **1** : thorny, prickly **2** : bony (of fish) **3** : knotty, difficult
espionaje *nm* : espionage
espiración *nf, pl* **-ciones** : exhalation
espiral *adj & nf* : spiral
espirar *vt* EXHALAR : to breathe out, to give off — *vi* : to exhale
espiritismo *nm* : spiritualism
espiritista *nmf* : spiritualist
espíritu *nm* **1** : spirit **2** ÁNIMO : state of mind, spirits *pl* **3 el Espíritu Santo** : the Holy Ghost

espiritual adj : spiritual — espiritual-
mente adv
espiritualidad nf : spirituality
espita nf : spigot, tap
esplendidez nf, pl -deces ESPLENDOR
: magnificence, splendor
espléndido, -da adj 1 : splendid, magnificent 2 : generous, lavish — espléndidamente adv
esplendor nm ESPLENDIDEZ : splendor
esplendoroso, -sa adj MAGNÍFICO : magnificent, grand
espliego nm LAVANDA : lavender
espolear vt : to spur on
espoleta nf 1 DETONADOR : detonator,
fuse 2 : wishbone
espolón nm, pl -lones : spur (of poultry),
fetlock (of a horse)
espolvorear vt : to sprinkle, to dust
esponja nf 1 : sponge 2 tirar la esponja
: to throw in the towel
esponjado, -da adj : spongy
esponjoso, -sa adj 1 : spongy 2 : soft,
fluffy
esponsales nmpl : betrothal, engagement
espontaneidad nf : spontaneity
espontáneo, -nea adj : spontaneous —
espontáneamente adv
espora nf : spore
esporádico, -ca adj : sporadic —
esporádicamente adv
esposar vt : to handcuff
esposas nfpl : handcuffs
esposo, -sa n : spouse, wife f, husband m
espray nm, pl esprays : spray
esprint nm : sprint
esprintar vi : to sprint
esprínter nmf : sprinter
espuela nf : spur
espuma nf 1 : foam ⟨espuma de afeitar
: shaving cream⟩ ⟨espuma de baño
: bubble bath (soap)⟩ ⟨baño de espuma
: bubble bath⟩ ⟨crecer/subir como la
espuma : to mushroom, to skyrocket⟩ 2
: lather 3 : froth, head (on beer)
espumadera nf : slotted spoon
espumar vi : to foam, to froth — vt : to
skim off
espumoso, -sa adj : foamy, frothy
espurio, -ria adj : spurious
esqueje nm : cutting (from a plant)
esquela nf 1 : note 2 : notice, announcement
esquelético, -ca adj : emaciated, skeletal
esqueleto nm 1 : skeleton 2 ARMAZÓN
: framework
esquema nm BOSQUEJO : outline, sketch,
plan
esquemático, -ca adj : schematic
esquí nm, pl esquíes 1 : ski 2 esquí
acuático : water ski, waterskiing
esquiador, -dora n : skier
esquiar {85} vi : to ski
esquilar vt TRASQUILAR : to shear
esquimal adj & nmf : Eskimo now sometimes offensive
esquina nf : corner
esquinazo nm 1 : corner 2 dar esquinazo a fam : to stand up, to give the slip
to

esquirla nf : splinter (of bone, glass, etc.)
esquirol nm ROMPEHUELGAS : strikebreaker, scab
esquisto nm : shale
esquivar vt 1 EVADIR : to dodge, to
evade 2 EVITAR : to avoid
esquivo, -va adj 1 HURAÑO : aloof, unsociable 2 : shy 3 : elusive, evasive
esquizofrenia nf : schizophrenia
esquizofrénico, -ca adj & n : schizophrenic
esta adj → este[1]
ésta → éste[1]
estabilidad nf : stability
estabilizar {21} vt : to stabilize — estabilizarse vr — estabilización nf — estabi-
lizador nm
estable adj : stable, steady
establecer {53} vt 1 FUNDAR, INSTITUIR
: to establish, to found (a city, etc.), to
set up (a system, etc.) 2 : to establish (a
law, etc.), to set (a standard, etc.) 3 : to
establish (relations, etc.) 4 DEMOSTRAR
: to establish, to show, to prove — establecerse vr 1 INSTALARSE : to settle, to
establish oneself 2 : to establish, to
show, to prove
establecimiento nm 1 : establishing 2
: establishment, institution, office
establo nm : stable
estaca nf : stake, picket, post
estacada nf 1 : picket fence 2 : stockade
estacar {72} vt 1 : to stake out 2 : to
fasten down with stakes — estacarse vr
: to remain rigid
estación nf, pl -ciones 1 : station ⟨es-
tación de servicio : service station, gas
station⟩ 2 : season
estacional adj : seasonal
estacionamiento nm 1 : parking 2
: parking lot
estacionar vt 1 : to place, to station 2
: to park — estacionarse vr 1 : to park
2 : to remain stationary
estacionario, -ria adj 1 : stationary 2
: stable
estada nf → estadía
estadía nf ESTANCIA : stay, sojourn
estadio nm 1 : stadium 2 : phase, stage
estadista nmf : statesman
estadística nf 1 : statistic, figure 2 : statistics
estadístico[1], -ca adj : statistical — es-
tadísticamente adv
estadístico[2], -ca n : statistician
estado nm 1 : state, condition ⟨estar en
buen/mal estado : to be in good/bad
condition⟩ 2 : state (nation or region)
⟨los Estados Unidos : the United States⟩
3 : state, government 4 : status ⟨estado
civil : marital status⟩ 5 estado de
ánimo : state of mind 6 estado de
cuenta : account statement 7 estado
de emergencia : state of emergency 8
estado de la nación : state of the nation
9 estado de salud : (state of) health,
condition 10 estar en estado : to be
expecting, to be pregnant

estadounidense *adj* & *nmf* AMERICANO, NORTEAMERICANO : American
estafa *nf* : swindle, fraud
estafador, -dora *n* : cheat, swindler
estafar *vt* DEFRAUDAR : to swindle, to defraud
estafeta *nf* **1** : baton (in a relay race) **2** : post office
estalactita *nf* : stalactite
estalagmita *nf* : stalagmite
estallar *vi* **1** REVENTAR : to burst, to explode, to erupt **2** : to break out
estallido *nm* **1** EXPLOSIÓN : explosion **2** : report (of a gun) **3** : outbreak, outburst
estambre *nm* **1** : worsted (fabric) **2** : stamen
estamento *nm* : stratum, class
estampa *nf* **1** ILUSTRACIÓN, IMAGEN : printed image, illustration **2** ASPECTO : appearance, demeanor
estampado¹, -da *adj* : patterned, printed
estampado² *nm* : print, pattern
estampar *vt* : to stamp, to print, to engrave
estampida *nf* : stampede
estampido *nm* ESTALLIDO : bang
estampilla *nf* **1** : rubber stamp **2** SELLO, TIMBRE : postage stamp
estancado, -da *adj* : stagnant
estancamiento *nm* : stagnation
estancar {72} *vt* **1** : to dam up, to hold back **2** : to bring to a halt, to deadlock — **estancarse** *vr* **1** : to stagnate **2** : to be brought to a standstill, to be deadlocked
estancia *nf* **1** ESTADÍA : stay, sojourn **2** : ranch, farm
estanciero, -ra *n* : rancher, farmer
estanco, -ca *adj* : watertight
estándar *adj* & *nm* : standard
estandarización *nf, pl* **-ciones** : standardization
estandarizar {21} *vt* : to standardize
estandarte *nm* : standard, banner
estanque *nm* **1** : pool, pond **2** : tank, reservoir
estanquillo *nm Mex* : general store
estante *nm* REPISA : shelf
estantería *nf* : shelves *pl*, bookcase
estaño *nm* : tin
estaquilla *nf* **1** : peg **2** ESPIGA : spike
estar {34} *v aux* : to be ⟨estoy aprendiendo inglés : I'm learning English⟩ ⟨está terminado : it's finished⟩ — *vi* **1** (*indicating a state or condition*) : to be ⟨está lleno : it's full⟩ ⟨está claro que . . . : it's clear that . . .⟩ ⟨¿ya estás mejor? : are you feeling better now?⟩ ⟨estoy casado : I'm married⟩ ⟨está sin trabajo : she's out of work, she has no job⟩ ⟨está muy alto : he's so tall, he's gotten very tall⟩ **2** (*indicating location*) : to be ⟨están en la mesa : they're on the table⟩ ⟨estamos en la página 2 : we're on page 2⟩ ⟨ahí está el problema : therein lies the problem⟩ **3** : to be at home ⟨¿está Julia? : is Julia in?⟩ **4** : to be, to remain ⟨estaré aquí 5 días : I'll be here for 5 days⟩ **5** : to be ready, to be done ⟨estará para las diez

: it will be ready by ten o'clock⟩ **6** : to agree ⟨¿estamos? : are we in agreement?⟩ ⟨estoy contigo : I'm with you⟩ **7** ¿**cómo estás?** : how are you? **8** ¡**está bien!** : all right!, that's fine! **9** ⁓ **a** : to cost **10** ⁓ **a** : to be ⟨¿a qué día estamos? : what day is today?, what's today's date?⟩ ⟨está a 15 kilómetros del centro : it's 15 kilometers from the downtown⟩ **11** ⁓ **con** : to have ⟨está con fiebre : she has a fever⟩ **12** ⁓ **de** : to be ⟨estoy de vacaciones : I'm on vacation⟩ ⟨está de director hoy : he's acting as director today⟩ **13 estar bien/mal** : to be well/sick **14** ⁓ **para** : to be in the mood for **15** ⁓ **para** : to be for (a purpose) ⟨para eso está : that's what it's here for⟩ **16** ⁓ **por** : to be in favor of **17** ⁓ **por** : to be about to ⟨está por cerrar : it's on the verge of closing⟩ **18 estar de más** : to be unnecessary **19 estar que** (*indicating a state or condition*) ⟨está que echa chispas : he's hopping mad⟩ — **estarse** *vr* QUEDARSE : to stay, to remain ⟨¡estáte quieto! : be still!⟩
estarcir {83} *vt* : to stencil
estárter *nm* : choke (of a motor)
estatal *adj* : state, national
estática *nf* : static
estático, -ca *adj* : static
estatizar {21} *vt* : to nationalize — **estatización** *nf*
estatua *nf* : statue
estatuilla *nf* : statuette, figurine
estatura *nf* : height, stature ⟨de mediana estatura : of medium height⟩
estatus *nm* : status, prestige
estatutario, -ria *adj* : statutory
estatuto *nm* : statute
este¹, esta *adj, mpl* **estos** : this, these ⟨este año : this year⟩ ⟨estas señoras : these ladies⟩ ⟨es un sinvergüenza el tipo este : this guy is a crook⟩
este² *adj* : eastern, east
este³ *nm* **1** ORIENTE : east **2** : east wind **3 el Este** : the East, the Orient
este⁴, esta *or* **éste, ésta** *pron, mpl* **estos** *or* **éstos** **1** : this (one), these (ones) *pl* ⟨este/éste es el mío : this one is mine⟩ ⟨esta/ésta no es la primera vez : this isn't the first time⟩ ⟨un día de estos/éstos : one of these days⟩ **2** : the latter ⟨se lo dijo a su hijo, y este/éste me llamó : he told his son, who called me⟩
estela *nf* **1** : wake (of a ship) **2** RASTRO : trail (of dust, smoke, etc.)
estelar *adj* : stellar
estelarizar {21} *vt Mex* : to star in, to be the star of
esténcil *nm* : stencil
estepa *nf* : steppe
estera *nf* : mat
estéreo *adj* & *nm* : stereo
estereofónico, -ca *adj* : stereophonic
estereotipado, -da *adj* : stereotyped
estereotipar *vt* : to stereotype
estereotipo *nm* : stereotype
estéril *adj* **1** : sterile **2** : infertile, sterile, barren **3** : futile, vain
esterilidad *nf* **1** : sterility **2** : infertility

esterilizar {21} vt 1 : to sterilize, to disinfect 2 : to sterilize (a person), to spay (an animal) — esterilización nf
esterlina adj : sterling
esternón nm, pl -nones : sternum
estero nm : estuary
esteroide nm : steroid
estertor nm : death rattle
estética nf : aesthetics
esteticista nmf : beautician
estético, -ca adj : aesthetic — estéticamente adv
estetoscopio nm : stethoscope
estibador, -dora n : longshoreman, stevedore
estiércol nm : dung, manure
estigma nm : stigma
estigmatizar {21} vt : to stigmatize, to brand
estilarse vr : to be in fashion
estilete nm : stiletto
estilista nmf : stylist
estilizar {21} vt : to stylize
estilo nm 1 : style ⟨estilo de vida : lifestyle⟩ 2 : fashion, manner 3 : stylus
estilográfica nf : fountain pen
estima nf ESTIMACIÓN : esteem, regard
estimable adj 1 : considerable 2 : estimable, esteemed
estimación nf, pl -ciones 1 ESTIMA : esteem, regard 2 : estimate
estimado, -da adj : esteemed, dear ⟨Estimado señor Ortiz : Dear Mr. Ortiz⟩
estimar vt 1 APRECIAR : to esteem, to respect 2 EVALUAR : to estimate, to appraise 3 OPINAR : to consider, to deem
estimulación nf, pl -ciones 1 : stimulation 2 estimulación hidráulica Arg, Col : fracking
estimulante¹ adj : stimulating
estimulante² nm : stimulant
estimular vt 1 : to stimulate 2 : to encourage
estímulo nm 1 : stimulus 2 INCENTIVO : incentive, encouragement
estío nm : summertime
estipendio nm 1 : salary 2 : stipend, remuneration
estipular vt : to stipulate — estipulación nf
estirado, -da adj 1 : stretched, extended 2 PRESUMIDO : stuck-up, conceited
estiramiento nm 1 : stretching 2 estiramiento facial : face-lift
estirar vt : to stretch (out), to extend — estirarse vr
estirón nm, pl -rones 1 : pull, tug 2 dar un estirón : to grow quickly, to shoot up
estirpe nf LINAJE : lineage, stock
estival adj VERANIEGO : summer
esto pron (neuter) 1 : this ⟨¿qué es esto? : what is this?⟩ 2 en ~ : at this point 3 por ~ : for this reason
estocada nf 1 : final thrust (in bullfighting) 2 : thrust, lunge (in fencing)
estofa nf CLASE : class, quality ⟨de baja estofa : low-class, poor-quality⟩
estofado nm COCIDO, GUISADO : stew
estofar vt GUISAR : to stew
estoicismo nm : stoicism

estoico¹, -ca adj : stoic, stoical
estoico², -ca n : stoic
estola nf : stole
estolón nm, pl -lones : runner (of a plant)
estomacal adj GÁSTRICO : stomach, gastric
estómago nm : stomach
estoniano, -na adj & n : Estonian
estonio, -nia adj & n : Estonian
estopa nf 1 : tow (yarn or cloth) 2 : burlap
estopilla nf : cheesecloth
estoque nm : rapier, sword
estorbar vt OBSTRUIR : to obstruct, to hinder — vi : to get in the way
estorbo nm 1 : obstacle, hindrance 2 : nuisance
estornino nm : starling
estornudar vi : to sneeze
estornudo nm : sneeze
estos adj → este¹
éstos → éste
estoy → estar
estrabismo nm : squint
estrado nm 1 : dais, platform 2 : bench (of a judge) 3 : witness stand 4 estrados nmpl : courts of law
estrafalario, -ria adj ESTRAMBÓTICO, EXCÉNTRICO : eccentric, bizarre
estragar {52} vt DEVASTAR : to ruin, to devastate
estragón nm : tarragon
estragos nmpl 1 : ravages, destruction, devastation ⟨los estragos de la guerra : the ravages of war⟩ 2 hacer estragos en or causar estragos entre : to play havoc with
estrambótico, -ca adj ESTRAFALARIO, EXCÉNTRICO : eccentric, bizarre
estrangulador, -dora n : strangler
estrangulamiento nm : strangling, strangulation
estrangular vt AHOGAR : to strangle — estrangulación nf
estratagema nf ARTIMAÑA : stratagem, ruse
estratega nmf : strategist
estrategia nf : strategy
estratégico, -ca adj : strategic, tactical — estratégicamente adv
estratificado, -da adj : stratified
estrato nm : stratum, layer
estratosfera nf : stratosphere
estratosférico, -ca adj 1 : stratospheric 2 : astronomical, exorbitant
estrechamiento nm 1 : narrowing 2 : narrow point 3 : tightening, strengthening (of relations)
estrechar vt 1 : to narrow 2 : to tighten, to strengthen (a bond) 3 : to hug, to embrace 4 estrechar la mano de : to shake hands with — estrecharse vr
estrechez nf, pl -checes 1 : tightness, narrowness 2 estrecheces nfpl : financial problems
estrecho¹, -cha adj 1 : tight, narrow 2 ÍNTIMO : close — estrechamente adv
estrecho² nm : strait, narrows
estrella nf 1 ASTRO : star ⟨estrella fugaz : shooting star⟩ 2 : destiny ⟨tener buena

estrella : to be born lucky⟩ **3** : movie star **4 estrella de mar** : starfish

estrellado, -da *adj* **1** : starry **2** : star-shaped **3 huevos estrellados** : fried eggs

estrellamiento *nm* : crash, collision

estrellar *vt* : to smash, to crash — **estrellarse** *vr* : to crash, to collide

estrellato *nm* : stardom

estremecedor, -dora *adj* : horrifying

estremecer {53} *vt* : to cause to shake — *vi* : to tremble, to shake — **estremecerse** *vr* : to shudder, to shiver (with emotion)

estremecimiento *nm* : trembling, shaking, shivering

estrenar *vt* **1** : to use for the first time **2** : to premiere, to open — **estrenarse** *vr* : to make one's debut

estreno *nm* DEBUT : debut, premiere

estreñido, -da *adj* : constipated

estreñimiento *nm* : constipation

estreñir {67} *vt* : to constipate, to make constipated — *vi* : to cause constipation — **estreñirse** *vr* to get constipated

estrépito *nm* ESTRUENDO : clamor, din

estrepitoso, -sa *adj* : clamorous, noisy — **estrepitosamente** *adv*

estrés *nm, pl* **estreses** : stress

estresante *adj* : stressful

estresar *vt* : to stress, to stress out — **estresado, -da** *adj*

estría *nf* : fluting, groove

estribación *nf, pl* **-ciones** **1** : spur, ridge **2 estribaciones** *nfpl* : foothills

estribar *vi* FUNDARSE ∼ **en** : to be due to, to stem from

estribillo *nm* : refrain, chorus

estribo *nm* **1** : stirrup **2** : abutment, buttress **3 perder los estribos** : to lose one's temper

estribor *nm* : starboard

estricto, -ta *adj* SEVERO : strict, severe — **estrictamente** *adv*

estridente *adj* : strident, shrill, loud — **estridentemente** *adv*

estrofa *nf* : stanza, verse

estrógeno *nm* : estrogen

estropajo *nm* : scouring pad

estropear *vt* **1** ARRUINAR : to ruin, to spoil **2** : to break, to damage — **estropearse** *vr* **1** : to spoil, to go bad **2** : to break down — **estropeado, -da** *adj*

estropicio *nm* DAÑO : damage, breakage

estructura *nf* : structure, framework

estructuración *nf, pl* **-ciones** : structuring, structure

estructural *adj* : structural — **estructuralmente** *adv*

estructurar *vt* : to structure, to organize

estruendo *nm* ESTRÉPITO : racket, din, roar

estruendoso, -sa *adj* : resounding, thunderous

estrujar *vt* APRETAR : to press, to squeeze

estuario *nm* : estuary

estuche *nm* : kit, case

estuco *nm* : stucco

estudiado, -da *adj* : affected, mannered

estudiantado *nm* : student body, students *pl*

estudiante *nmf* : student

estudiantil *adj* : student ⟨la vida estudiantil : student life⟩

estudiar *v* : to study

estudio *nm* **1** : study ⟨estar en estudio : to be under consideration⟩ ⟨un estudio sobre la salud nacional : a study of the nation's health⟩ **2** : studio (room or office) **3** : studio (for filming, etc.) **4** : studio (apartment) **5 estudios** *nmpl* : studies, education ⟨estudios primarios/secundarios/superiores : primary/secondary/higher education⟩ ⟨tener estudios en/de algo : to have studied something⟩

estudioso, -sa *adj* : studious

estufa *nf* **1** : stove, heater **2** *Col, Mex* : cooking stove, range

estupefacción *nf, pl* **-ciones** : astonishment

estupefaciente[1] *adj* : narcotic

estupefaciente[2] *nm* DROGA, NARCÓTICO : drug, narcotic

estupefacto, -ta *adj* : astonished, stunned

estupendo, -da *adj* MARAVILLOSO : stupendous, marvelous — **estupendamente** *adv*

estupidez *nf, pl* **-deces** **1** : stupidity **2** : nonsense

estúpido[1], **-da** *adj* : stupid — **estúpidamente** *adj*

estúpido[2], **-da** *n* IDIOTA : idiot, fool

estupor *nm* **1** : stupor **2** : amazement

esturión *nm, pl* **-riones** : sturgeon

estuvo, etc. → **estar**

esvástica *nf* : swastika

etanol *nm* : ethanol

etapa *nf* FASE : stage, phase

etcétera[1] : et cetera, and so on

etcétera[2] *nmf* : et cetera

éter *nm* : ether

etéreo, -rea *adj* : ethereal, heavenly

eternidad *nf* : eternity

eternizar {21} *vt* PERPETUAR : to make eternal, to perpetuate — **eternizarse** *vr fam* : to take forever

eterno, -na *adj* : eternal, endless — **eternamente** *adv*

ética *nf* : ethics

ético, -ca *adj* : ethical — **éticamente** *adv*

etílico, -ca *adj* **1** : alcohol, alcoholic ⟨intoxicación etílica : alcohol poisoning⟩ **2** : inebriated, drunken

etimología *nf* : etymology

etimológico, -ca *adj* : etymological

etíope *adj & nmf* : Ethiopian

etiqueta *nf* **1** : etiquette **2** : tag, label **3** : hashtag (on social media) **4 de** ∼ : formal, dressy

etiquetar *vt* : to label

etnia *nf* : ethnic group

étnico, -ca *adj* : ethnic

eucalipto *nm* : eucalyptus

Eucaristía *nf* : Eucharist, communion

eufemismo *nm* : euphemism

eufemístico, -ca *adj* : euphemistic

euforia *nf* : euphoria, joyousness

eufórico, -ca *adj* : euphoric, exuberant, joyous — **eufóricamente** *adv*

eunuco *nm* : eunuch

euro *nm* : euro
europeo, -pea *adj & n* : European
euskera *nm* : Basque (language)
eutanasia *nf* : euthanasia
evacuación *nf, pl* **-ciones** : evacuation
evacuar *vt* **1** : to evacuate, to vacate **2** : to carry out — *vi* : to have a bowel movement, to move one's bowels
evadir *vt* ELUDIR : to evade, to avoid — **evadirse** *vr* : to escape, to slip away
evaluación *nf, pl* **-ciones** : assessment, evaluation
evaluador, -dora *n* : assessor
evaluar {3} *vt* : to evaluate, to assess, to appraise
evangélico, -ca *adj* : evangelical — **evangélicamente** *adv*
evangelio *nm* : gospel
evangelismo *nm* : evangelism
evangelista *nm* : evangelist
evangelizador, -dora *n* : evangelist, missionary
evaporación *nf, pl* **-ciones** : evaporation
evaporar *vt* : to evaporate — **evaporarse** *vr* ESFUMARSE : to disappear, to vanish
evasión *nf, pl* **-siones** **1** : escape, flight **2** : evasion, dodge
evasiva *nf* : excuse, pretext
evasivo, -va *adj* : evasive
evento *nm* : cvcnt
eventual *adj* **1** : possible **2** : temporary ⟨trabajadores eventuales : temporary workers⟩ — **eventualmente** *adv*
eventualidad *nf* : possibility, eventuality
evidencia *nf* **1** : evidence, proof **2 poner en evidencia** : to demonstrate, to make clear
evidenciar *vt* : to demonstrate, to show — **evidenciarse** *vr* : to be evident
evidente *adj* : evident, obvious, clear — **evidentemente** *adv*
eviscerar *vt* : to eviscerate
evitable *adj* : avoidable, preventable
evitar *vt* **1** : to avoid **2** PREVENIR : to prevent **3** ELUDIR : to escape, to elude
evocación *nf, pl* **-ciones** : evocation
evocador, -dora *adj* : evocative
evocar {72} *vt* **1** : to evoke **2** RECORDAR : to recall
evolución *nf, pl* **-ciones** **1** : evolution **2** : development, progress
evolucionar *vi* **1** : to evolve **2** : to change, to develop
evolutivo, -va *adj* : evolutionary
ex *nmf* : ex
ex- or ex *pref* : ex-, former ⟨exmarido, ex marido : ex-husband⟩
exabrupto *nm* : pointed remark
exacerbar *vt* **1** : to exacerbate, to aggravate **2** : to irritate, to exasperate
exactamente *adv* : exactly
exactitud *nf* PRECISIÓN : accuracy, precision, exactitude
exacto, -ta *adj* PRECISO : accurate, precise, exact
exageración *nf, pl* **-ciones** : exaggeration
exagerado, -da *adj* **1** : exaggerated **2** : excessive — **exageradamente** *adv*
exagerar *v* : to exaggerate

exaltación *nf, pl* **-ciones** **1** : exaltation **2** : excitement, agitation
exaltado¹, -da *adj* : excitable, hotheaded
exaltado², -da *n* : hothead
exaltar *vt* **1** ENSALZAR : to exalt, to extol **2** : to excite, to agitate — **exaltarse** *vr* ACALORARSE : to get overexcited
ex–alumno → **alumno**
examen *nm, pl* **exámenes** **1** : examination, test ⟨examen final/oral : final/written exam⟩ ⟨examen de manejo/conducir : driving test⟩ ⟨hacer/dar un examen : to take a test⟩ **2** : consideration, investigation ⟨someter algo a examen : to examine something⟩
examinar *vt* **1** : to examine **2** INSPECCIONAR : to inspect — **examinarse** *vr* : to take an exam
exánime *adj* **1** : lifeless **2** : exhausted
exasperante *adj* : exasperating
exasperar *vt* IRRITAR : to exasperate, to irritate — **exasperación** *nf*
excavación *nf, pl* **-ciones** : excavation
excavadora *nf* : excavator
excavar *v* : to excavate, to dig
excedente¹ *adj* **1** : excessive **2** : excess, surplus
excedente² *nm* : surplus, excess
exceder *vt* : to exceed, to surpass — **excederse** *vr* : to go too far
excelencia *nf* **1** : excellence **2** : excellency ⟨Su Excelencia : His Excellency⟩
excelente *adj* : excellent — **excelentemente** *adv*
excelso, -sa *adj* : lofty, sublime
excentricidad *nf* : eccentricity
excéntrico, -ca *adj & n* : eccentric
excepción *nf, pl* **-ciones** : exception ⟨a/con excepción de : with the exception of⟩
excepcional *adj* EXTRAORDINARIO : exceptional, extraordinary, rare — **excepcionalmente** *adv*
excepto *prep* SALVO : except
exceptuar {3} *vt* EXCLUIR : to except, to exclude
excesivo, -va *adj* : excessive — **excesivamente** *adv*
exceso *nm* **1** : excess **2 excesos** *nmpl* : excesses, abuses **3 exceso de velocidad** : speeding
excitabilidad *nf* : excitability
excitación *nf, pl* **-ciones** : excitement
excitante *adj* : exciting
excitar *vt* : to excite, to arouse — **excitarse** *vr*
exclamación *nf, pl* **-ciones** : exclamation
exclamar *v* : to exclaim
excluir {41} *vt* EXCEPTUAR : to exclude, to leave out
exclusión *nf, pl* **-siones** : exclusion
exclusividad *nf* **1** : exclusiveness **2** : exclusive rights *pl*
exclusivo, -va *adj* : exclusive — **exclusivamente** *adv*
excombatiente *nmf* : war veteran
excomulgar {52} *vt* : to excommunicate
excomunión *nf, pl* **-niones** : excommunication
excreción *nf, pl* **-ciones** : excretion

excremento *nm* : excrement

excretar *vt* : to excrete

exculpar *vt* : to exonerate, to exculpate — **exculpación** *nf*

excursión *nf, pl* **-siones** : excursion, outing

excursionista *nmf* **1** : sightseer, tourist **2** : hiker

excusa *nf* **1** PRETEXTO : excuse ⟨poner excusas : to make excuses⟩ **2** DISCULPA : apology

excusado *nm Mex* : toilet

excusar *vt* **1** : to excuse **2** : to exempt — **excusarse** *vr* : to apologize, to send one's regrets

execrable *adj* : detestable, abominable

exención *nf, pl* **-ciones** : exemption

exento, -ta *adj* **1** : exempt, free **2** **exento de impuestos** : tax-exempt

exequias *nfpl* FUNERALES : funeral rites

exesposa *or* **ex esposa** *nf* : ex-wife

exhalación *nf, pl* **-ciones** **1** : exhalation **2** : shooting star ⟨salió como una exhalación : he took off like a shot⟩

exhalar *vt* ESPIRAR : to exhale, to give off

exhaustivo, -va *adj* : exhaustive — **exhaustivamente** *adv*

exhausto, -ta *adj* AGOTADO : exhausted, worn-out

exhibición *nf, pl* **-ciones** **1** : exhibition, show **2** : showing

exhibir *vt* : to exhibit, to show, to display — **exhibirse** *vr*

exhortación *nf, pl* **-ciones** : exhortation

exhortar *vt* : to exhort

exhumar *vt* DESENTERRAR : to exhume — **exhumación** *nf*

exigencia *nf* : demand, requirement

exigente *adj* : demanding, exacting

exigir {35} *vt* **1** : to demand, to require **2** : to exact, to levy

exiguo, -gua *adj* : meager

exiliado¹, -da *adj* : exiled, in exile

exiliado², -da *n* : exile

exiliar *vt* DESTERRAR : to exile, to banish — **exiliarse** *vr* : to go into exile

exilio *nm* DESTIERRO : exile

eximio, -mia *adj* : distinguished, eminent

eximir *vt* EXONERAR : to exempt

existencia *nf* **1** : existence **2** **existencias** *nfpl* MERCANCÍA : goods, stock

existente *adj* **1** : existing, in existence **2** : in stock

existir *vi* : to exist

exitazo *nm* : big/huge success, big/huge hit, smash

éxito *nm* **1** TRIUNFO : success, hit **2** **tener éxito** : to be successful

exitoso, -sa *adj* : successful — **exitosamente** *adv*

exmarido *or* **ex marido** *nm* : ex-husband

éxodo *nm* : exodus

exoneración *nf, pl* **-ciones** EXENCIÓN : exoneration, exemption

exonerar *vt* **1** EXIMIR : to exempt, to exonerate **2** DESPEDIR : to dismiss

exorbitante *adj* : exorbitant

exorcismo *nm* : exorcism — **exorcista** *nmf*

exorcizar {21} *vt* : to exorcise

exótico, -ca *adj* : exotic

expandir *vt* EXPANSIONAR : to expand — **expandirse** *vr* : to spread

expansión *nf, pl* **-siones** **1** : expansion, spread **2** DIVERSIÓN : recreation, relaxation

expansionar *vt* EXPANDIR : to expand — **expansionarse** *vr* **1** : to expand **2** DIVERTIRSE : to amuse oneself, to relax

expansivo, -va *adj* : expansive

expatriado, -da *adj & n* : expatriate

expatriar {85} *vt* : to expatriate, to exile — **expatriarse** *vr* **1** EMIGRAR : to emigrate **2** : to go into exile

expectación *nf, pl* **-ciones** : expectation, anticipation

expectante *adj* : expectant

expectativa *nf* **1** : expectation, hope ⟨estar a la expectativa de : to await, to wait for⟩ ⟨expectativa(s) de la vida : life expectancy⟩ **2 expectativas** *nfpl* : prospects

expedición *nf, pl* **-ciones** : expedition

expediente *nm* **1** : expedient, means **2** ARCHIVO : file, dossier, record

expedir {54} *vt* **1** EMITIR : to issue **2** DESPACHAR : to dispatch, to send

expedito, -ta *adj* **1** : free, clear **2** : quick, easy

expeler *vt* : to expel, to eject

expendedor, -dora *n* : dealer, seller

expendio *nm* TIENDA : store, shop

expensas *nfpl* **1** : expenses, costs **2 a expensas de** : at the expense of

experiencia *nf* **1** : experience **2** EXPERIMENTO : experiment

experimentación *nf, pl* **-ciones** : experimentation

experimentado, -da *adj* : experienced

experimental *adj* : experimental

experimentar *vi* : to experiment — *vt* **1** : to experiment with, to test out **2** : to experience

experimento *nm* EXPERIENCIA : experiment

experto, -ta *adj & n* : expert

expiación *nf, pl* **-ciones** : expiation, atonement

expiar {85} *vt* : to expiate, to atone for

expiración *nf, pl* **-ciones** VENCIMIENTO : expiration

expirar *vi* **1** FALLECER, MORIR : to pass away, to die **2** : to expire

explanada *nf* **1** TERRAZA : terrace **2** PATIO : courtyard, patio **3** : seaside walk, boardwalk

explayar *vt* : to extend — **explayarse** *vr* : to expound, to speak at length

explicable *adj* : explicable, explainable

explicación *nf, pl* **-ciones** : explanation

explicar {72} *vt* **1** : to explain — **explicarse** *vr* **1** : to understand **2** : to explain oneself

explicativo, -va *adj* : explanatory

explicitar *vt* : to state explicitly, to specify

explícito, -ta *adj* : explicit — **explícitamente** *adv*

exploración *nf, pl* **-ciones** : exploration

explorador, -dora *n* : explorer, scout

explorar *vt* : to explore — **exploratorio, -ria** *adj*

explosión *nf, pl* **-siones 1** ESTALLIDO : explosion **2** : outburst ⟨una explosión de ira — *vi* : an outburst of anger⟩
explosionar *vi* : to explode
explosivo, -va *adj* : explosive
explotación *nf, pl* **-ciones 1** : exploitation **2** : operation, running
explotar *vt* **1** : to exploit **2** : to operate, to run — *vi* ESTALLAR, REVENTAR : to explode — **explotable** *adj*
exponencial *adj* : exponential — **exponencialmente** *adv*
exponente *nm* : exponent
exponer {60} *vt* **1** : to exhibit, to show, to display **2** : to explain, to present, to set forth **3** : to expose, to risk — *vi* : to exhibit
exportación *nf, pl* **-ciones 1** : exportation **2 exportaciones** *nfpl* : exports
exportador, -dora *n* : exporter
exportar *vt* : to export — **exportable** *adj*
exposición *nf, pl* **-ciones 1** EXHIBICIÓN : exposition, exhibition **2** : exposure **3** : presentation, statement
expósito, -ta *n* : foundling
expositor, -tora *n* **1** : exhibitor **2** : exponent
exprés[1] *adj* : express
exprés[2] *nms & pl* **1** : express, express train **2** : espresso
expresamente *adv* : expressly, on purpose
expresar *vt* : to express — **expresarse** *vr*
expresión *nf, pl* **-siones** : expression
expresivo, -va *adj* **1** : expressive **2** CARIÑOSO : affectionate — **expresivamente** *adv*
expreso[1], **-sa** *adj* **1** : express, specific **2** : express ⟨correo expreso : express mail⟩
expreso[2] *nm* **1** : express train, express **2** : express mail
express → **exprés**
exprimidor *nm* : juicer
exprimir *vt* **1** : to squeeze **2** : to exploit
expropiar *vt* : to expropriate, to commandeer — **expropiación** *nf*
expuesto[1] *pp* → **exponer**
expuesto[2], **-ta** *adj* **1** : exposed **2** : hazardous, risky
expulsar *vt* : to expel, to eject — **expulsarse** *vr*
expulsión *nf, pl* **-siones** : expulsion
expurgar {52} *vt* : to expurgate
expuso, etc. → **exponer**
exquisitez *nf, pl* **-teces 1** : exquisiteness, refinement **2** : delicacy, special dish
exquisito, -ta *adj* **1** : exquisite **2** : delicious
extasiarse {85} *vr* : to be in ecstasy, to be enraptured
éxtasis *nms & pl* **1** : ecstasy, rapture **2** : Ecstasy (drug)
extático, -ca *adj* : ecstatic
extemporáneo, -nea *adj* **1** : unseasonable **2** : untimely
extender {56} *vt* **1** : to spread out, to stretch out **2** : to broaden, to expand ⟨extender la influencia : to broaden one's influence⟩ **3** : to draw up (a document), to write out (a check) — **extenderse** *vr* **1** : to spread **2** : to last

extendido, -da *adj* **1** : outstretched **2** : widespread **3** : extended ⟨garantía extendida : extended warranty⟩
extensamente *adv* : extensively, at length
extensible *adj* : extendable
extensión *nf, pl* **-siones 1** : extension, stretching **2** : expanse, spread **3** : extent, range **4** : length, duration **5** : extension cord
extensivamente *adv* : widely, broadly
extensivo, -va *adj* **1** : extensive **2 hacer extensivo** : to extend
extenso, -sa *adj* **1** : extensive, detailed **2** : spacious, vast
extenuar {3} *vt* : to exhaust, to tire out — **extenuarse** *vr* — **extenuante** *adj*
exterior[1] *adj* **1** : exterior, external **2** : foreign ⟨asuntos exteriores : foreign affairs⟩
exterior[2] *nm* **1** : outside **2** : abroad
exteriorizar {21} *vt* : to express, to reveal
exteriormente *adv* : outwardly
exterminador[1], **-dora** *adj* → **ángel**
exterminador[2], **-dora** *n* **exterminador -dora de plagas** : exterminator
exterminar *vt* : to exterminate — **exterminación** *nf*
exterminio *nm* : extermination
externalización *nf, pl* **-ciones** : outsourcing
externalizar {21} *vt* : to outsource
externar *vt Mex* : to express, to display
externo, -na *adj* : external, outward
extinción *nf, pl* **-ciones** : extinction
extinguidor *nm* : fire extinguisher
extinguir {26} *vt* **1** APAGAR : to extinguish, to put out **2** : to wipe out — **extinguirse** *vr* **1** APAGARSE : to go out, to fade out **2** : to die out, to become extinct
extinto, -ta *adj* : extinct
extintor *nm* : extinguisher
extirpación *n, pl* **-ciones** : removal (of a tumor, etc.)
extirpar *vt* : to eradicate, to remove, to excise — **extirparse** *vr*
extorsión *nf, pl* **-siones 1** : extortion **2** : harm, trouble
extorsionar *vt* : to extort
extra[1] *adv* : extra
extra[2] *adj* **1** : additional, extra **2** : superior, top-quality
extra[3] *nmf* : extra (in movies)
extra[4] *nm* : extra expense ⟨paga extra : bonus⟩
extra- *pref* : extra-
extracción *nf, pl* **-ciones** : extraction
extracto *nm* **1** : extract ⟨extracto de vainilla : vanilla extract⟩ **2** : abstract, summary
extractor *nm* : extractor
extracurricular *adj* : extracurricular
extradición *nf, pl* **-ciones** : extradition
extraditar *vt* : to extradite
extraer {81} *vt* : to extract
extraído *pp* → **extraer**
extrajudicial *adj* : out-of-court
extrajudicialmente *adv* : out of court
extralimitarse *vr* : to go too far, to overstep one's bounds

extramatrimonial *adj* : extramarital
extranjero[1], **-ra** *adj* : foreign
extranjero[2], **-ra** *n* : foreigner
extranjero[3] *nm* : foreign countries *pl* ⟨viajó al extranjero : he traveled abroad⟩ ⟨trabajan en el extranjero : they work overseas⟩
extrañamente *adv* : strangely, oddly
extrañamiento *nm* ASOMBRO : amazement, surprise, wonder
extrañar *vt* : to miss (someone) — **extrañarse** *vr* : to be surprised
extrañeza *nf* **1** : strangeness, oddness **2** : surprise
extraño[1], **-ña** *adj* **1** RARO : strange, odd **2** EXTRANJERO : foreign
extraño[2], **-ña** *n* DESCONOCIDO : stranger
extraoficial *adj* OFICIOSO : unofficial — **extraoficialmente** *adv*
extraordinario, -ria *adj* EXCEPCIONAL : extraordinary — **extraordinariamente** *adv*
extrapolar *vt* : to extrapolate — **extrapolación** *nf*
extrarradio *nm* : outskirts *pl*
extrasensorial *adj* : extrasensory ⟨percepción extrasensorial : extrasensory perception⟩
extraterrestre *adj* & *nmf* : extraterrestrial, alien
extravagancia *nf* **1** : extravagance, flamboyance **2** : outrageous or outlandish thing
extravagante *adj* **1** : extravagant, flamboyant **2** : outrageous, outlandish
extraviado, -da *adj* : lost, stray
extraviar {85} *vt* **1** : to mislead, to lead astray **2** : to misplace, to lose — **extraviarse** *vr* : to get lost, to go astray
extravío *nm* **1** PÉRDIDA : loss **2** : misconduct

extremado, -da *adj* : extreme — **extremadamente** *adv*
extremar *vt* : to carry to extremes — **extremarse** *vr* : to do one's utmost
extremidad *nf* **1** : extremity, tip, edge **2 extremidades** *nfpl* : extremities
extremista *adj* & *nmf* : extremist
extremo[1], **-ma** *adj* **1** : extreme, great ⟨frío extremo : extreme cold⟩ ⟨extrema pobreza : extreme poverty⟩ **2** : extreme, severe ⟨condiciones extremas : extreme conditions⟩ **3** EXTREMISTA : extreme ⟨opiniones extremas : extreme views⟩ **4** : extreme ⟨deportes extremos : extreme sports⟩ **5 en caso extremo** : as a last resort
extremo[2] *nm* **1** : extreme ⟨de un extremo a otro : from one extreme to the other⟩ **2** : end ⟨el otro extremo de la calle : the other end of the street⟩ ⟨el extremo sur : the southern end/tip⟩ **3 al extremo de** : to the point of **4 en ∼** : in the extreme
extrovertido[1], **-da** *adj* : extroverted, outgoing
extrovertido[2], **-da** *n* : extrovert
extrudir *vt* : to extrude
exuberancia *nf* **1** : exuberance **2** : luxuriance, lushness
exuberante *adj* : exuberant, luxuriant — **exuberantemente** *adv*
exudar *vt* : to exude
exultación *nf, pl* **-ciones** : exultation, elation
exultante *adj* : exultant, elated — **exultantemente** *adv*
exultar *vi* : to exult, to rejoice
eyacular *vi* : to ejaculate — **eyaculación** *nf*
eyección *nf, pl* **-ciones** : ejection, expulsion
eyectar *vt* : to eject, to expel — **eyectarse** *vr*

F

f *nf* : seventh letter of the Spanish alphabet
fa *nm* **1** : F ⟨fa sostenido/bemol : F sharp/flat⟩ **2** : fa (in singing)
fábrica *nf* FACTORÍA : factory
fabricación *nf, pl* **-ciones** : manufacture
fabricante *nmf* : manufacturer
fabricar {72} *vt* MANUFACTURAR : to manufacture, to make
fabril *adj* INDUSTRIAL : industrial, manufacturing
fábula *nf* **1** : fable **2** : fabrication, fib *fam*
fabuloso, -sa *adj* **1** : fabulous, fantastic **2** : mythical, fabled
facción *nf, pl* **facciones 1** : faction **2 facciones** *nfpl* RASGOS : features
faceta *nf* : facet
facha *nf* : appearance, look ⟨estar hecho una facha : to look a sight⟩
fachada *nf* : facade
facial *adj* : facial

fácil *adj* **1** : easy **2** : likely, probable ⟨es fácil que no pase : it probably won't happen⟩
facilidad *nf* **1** : facility, ease ⟨con facilidad : with ease, easily⟩ ⟨tener facilidad para : to have a gift for⟩ **2 facilidades** *nfpl* : facilities, services ⟨facilidades de pago : payment plans⟩ **3 facilidades** *nfpl* : opportunities ⟨tenían todas las facilidades : they had every opportunity⟩
facilitar *vt* **1** : to make easier, to facilitate **2** : to provide, to supply — **facilitador, -dora** *n*
fácilmente *adv* : easily, readily
facsímil *nm* **1** : facsimile, copy **2** : fax
factibilidad *nf* : feasibility
factible *adj* : feasible, practicable
factor[1], **-tora** *n* **1** : agent, factor **2** : baggage clerk
factor[2] *nm* ELEMENTO : factor, element
factoría *nf* FÁBRICA : factory
factura *nf* **1** : making, manufacturing **2** : bill, invoice

facturación *nf, pl* **-ciones 1** : invoicing, billing **2** : check-in

facturar *vt* **1** : to bill, to invoice **2** : to register, to check in

facultad *nf* **1** : faculty, ability ⟨facultades mentales : mental faculties⟩ **2** : authority, power **3** : school (of a university) ⟨facultad de derecho : law school⟩

facultar *vt* : to authorize, to empower

facultativo, -va *adj* **1** OPTATIVO : voluntary, optional **2** : medical ⟨informe facultativo : medical report⟩

faena *nf* : task, job, work ⟨faenas domésticas : housework⟩

faenar *vi* **1** : to work, to labor **2** PESCAR : to fish

fagot *nm* : bassoon

Fahrenheit *adj* : Fahrenheit

faisán *nm, pl* **faisanes** : pheasant

faja *nf* **1** : sash, belt **2** : girdle **3** : strip (of land)

fajar *vt* **1** : to wrap (a sash or girdle) around **2** : to hit, to thrash — **fajarse** *vr* **1** : to put on a sash or girdle **2** : to come to blows

fajín *nm, pl* **-jines** : sash, belt

fajo *nm* : bundle, sheaf ⟨un fajo de billetes : a wad of cash⟩

falacia *nf* : fallacy

falaz, -laza *adj, mpl* **falaces** FALSO : fallacious, false

falda *nf* **1** : skirt ⟨falda escocesa : kilt⟩ ⟨falda de tubo : pencil skirt⟩ **2** REGAZO : lap (of the body) **3** VERTIENTE : side, slope

faldón *nm, pl* **-dones 1** : tail (of a shirt, etc.) **2** : full skirt **3** : christening gown

falible *adj* : fallible

fálico, -ca *adj* : phallic

falla *nf* **1** : flaw, defect **2** : (geological) fault **3** : fault, failing

fallar *vi* **1** FRACASAR : to fail, to go wrong **2** : to rule (in a court of law) — *vt* **1** ERRAR : to miss (a target) **2** : to pronounce judgment on

fallecer {53} *vi* MORIR : to pass away, to die

fallecido, -da *adj & n* DIFUNTO : deceased

fallecimiento *nm* : demise, death

fallido, -da *adj* : failed, unsuccessful

fallo *nm* **1** SENTENCIA : sentence, judgment, verdict **2** : error, fault

falo *nm* : phallus, penis

falsamente *adv* : falsely

falsear *vt* **1** : to falsify, to fake **2** : to distort — *vi* **1** CEDER : to give way **2** : to be out of tune

falsedad *nf* **1** : falseness, hypocrisy **2** MENTIRA : falsehood, lie

falsete *nm* : falsetto

falsificación *nf, pl* **-ciones 1** : counterfeit, forgery **2** : falsification

falsificador, -dora *n* : counterfeiter, forger

falsificar {72} *vt* **1** : to counterfeit, to forge **2** : to falsify

falso, -sa *adj* **1** FALAZ : false, untrue **2** : counterfeit, forged

falta *nf* **1** CARENCIA : lack ⟨falta de dinero/interés : lack of money/interest⟩ **2** DEFECTO : defect, fault, error ⟨falta de ortografía : spelling mistake⟩ ⟨falta de educación : bad manners⟩ **3** AUSENCIA : absence **4** : offense, misdemeanor **5** : foul (in basketball), fault (in tennis) **6 a falta de** : in the absence of **7 hacer falta** : to be lacking, to be needed ⟨nos hace falta un líder : we need a leader⟩ ⟨no hace falta : it's not necessary⟩ ⟨me hace mucha falta mi familia : I really miss my family⟩ **8 por falta de** : for lack of **9 sin ～** : without fail

faltar *vi* **1** : to be lacking, to be needed ⟨me falta tiempo : I don't have time⟩ ⟨le falta imaginación : he lacks imagination⟩ ⟨le falta sal : it needs salt⟩ ⟨falta algo : something's missing⟩ ⟨al libro le falta una página : the book is missing a page⟩ ⟨nos faltan sillas : we need more chairs⟩ **2** : to be absent, to be missing ⟨faltan Juan y María : Juan and María aren't here⟩ ⟨faltar al trabajo/colegio : to miss work/school⟩ **3** QUEDAR : to remain, to be left ⟨falta un mes para la boda : there's a month to go until the wedding, the wedding is a month away⟩ ⟨falta mucho por hacer : there is still a lot to be done⟩ ⟨¿te falta mucho? : are you almost ready/done?⟩ **4 faltar a su promesa/palabra** : not to keep one's promise/word **5 ¡no faltaba más!** : don't mention it!, you're welcome!

faltante *nm* : shortage

falto, -ta *adj* **～ de** : lacking (in), short of

fama *nf* **1** : fame **2** REPUTACIÓN : reputation **3 de mala fama** : disreputable

famélico, -ca *adj* HAMBRIENTO : starving, famished

familia *nf* **1** : family ⟨ser como de la familia : to be like one of the family⟩ ⟨sentir como en familia : to feel at home⟩ ⟨le viene de familia : he inherited it, it runs in the family⟩ **2 en ～** : in private **3 familia nuclear** : nuclear family **4 familia política** : in-laws

familiar¹ *adj* **1** CONOCIDO : familiar **2** : familial, family **3** INFORMAL : informal

familiar² *nmf* PARIENTE : relation, relative

familiaridad *nf* **1** : familiarity **2** : informality

familiarizar {21} *vt* : to familiarize — **familiarizarse** *vr*

famoso¹, -sa *adj* CÉLEBRE : famous

famoso², -sa *n* : celebrity

fan *nmf, pl* **fans** AFICIONADO : fan

fanal *nm* **1** : beacon, signal light **2** *Mex* : headlight

fanático, -ca *adj & n* : fanatic

fanatismo *nm* : fanaticism

fandango *nm* : fandango

fanfarria *nf* **1** : (musical) fanfare **2** : pomp, ceremony

fanfarrón¹, -rrona *adj, mpl* **-rrones** *fam* : bragging, boastful

fanfarrón², -rrona *n, mpl* **-rrones** *fam* : braggart

fanfarronada *nf* : boast, bluster

fanfarronear *vi* : to brag, to boast

fango *nm* LODO : mud, mire
fangoso, -sa *adj* LODOSO : muddy
fantasear *vi* : to fantasize, to daydream
fantasía *nf* 1 : fantasy 2 : imagination
fantasioso, -sa *adj* : fanciful
fantasma *nm* : ghost, phantom
fantasmagórico, -ca *adj* : ghostly, eerie
fantasmal *adj* : ghostly
fantástico, -ca *adj* 1 : fantastic, imaginary, unreal 2 *fam* : great, fantastic
FAQ ['fak] *nm, pl* **FAQs** : FAQ
farándula *nf* : show business, theater
faraón *nm, pl* **faraones** : pharaoh
fardo *nm* 1 : bale 2 : bundle
farfullar *v* : to jabber
faringe *nf* : pharynx
fariña *nf* : coarse manioc flour
farmacéutico¹, -ca *adj* : pharmaceutical
farmacéutico², -ca *n* : pharmacist
farmacia *nf* : drugstore, pharmacy
fármaco *nm* : medicine, drug
farmacología *nf* : pharmacology
faro *nm* 1 : lighthouse 2 : headlight
farol *nm* 1 : streetlight 2 : lantern, lamp 3 *fam* : bluff 4 *Mex* : headlight
farola *nf* 1 : lamppost 2 : streetlight
farra *nf* : spree, revelry
fárrago *nm* REVOLTIJO : hodgepodge, jumble
farsa *nf* 1 : farce 2 : fake, sham
farsante *nmf* CHARLATÁN : charlatan, fraud, phony
fascículo *nm* : part (of a publication)
fascinación *nf, pl* **-ciones** : fascination
fascinante *adj* : fascinating
fascinar *vt* 1 : to fascinate 2 : to charm, to captivate
fascismo *nm* : fascism
fascista *adj & nmf* : fascist
fase *nf* : phase, stage
fastidiar *vt* 1 MOLESTAR : to annoy, to bother, to hassle 2 ABURRIR : to bore — *vi* : to be annoying or bothersome — **fastidiarse** *vr* : to put up with something
fastidio *nm* 1 MOLESTIA : annoyance, nuisance, hassle 2 ABURRIMIENTO : boredom
fastidioso, -sa *adj* 1 MOLESTO : annoying, bothersome 2 ABURRIDO : boring — **fastidiosamente** *adv*
fastuoso, -sa *adj* : lavish, luxurious
fatal *adj* 1 MORTAL : fatal 2 *fam* : awful, terrible 3 : fateful, unavoidable
fatalidad *nf* 1 : fatality 2 DESGRACIA : misfortune, bad luck
fatalismo *nm* : fatalism
fatalista¹ *adj* : fatalistic
fatalista² *nmf* : fatalist
fatalmente *adv* 1 : unavoidably 2 : unfortunately
fatídico, -ca *adj* : fateful, momentous
fatiga *nf* CANSANCIO : fatigue
fatigado, -da *adj* AGOTADO : weary, tired
fatigar {52} *vt* CANSAR : to fatigue, to tire — **fatigarse** *vr* : to wear oneself out
fatigoso, -sa *adj* : fatiguing, tiring
fatuo, -tua *adj* 1 : fatuous 2 PRESUMIDO : vain
fauces *nfpl* : jaws *pl*, maw
faul *nm, pl* **fauls** : foul, foul ball

fauna *nf* : fauna
fausto *nm* : splendor, magnificence
favor *nm* 1 : favor ⟨¿me haces un favor? : will you do me a favor?⟩ ⟨quiero pedirte un favor : I want to ask you (for) a favor⟩ 2 **a/en favor de** : in favor of 3 **en favor de** : in support of, in the interests of ⟨trabajar en favor de una causa : to work for a cause⟩ 4 **por ~** : please
favorable *adj* : favorable — **favorablemente** *adv*
favorecedor, -dora *adj* : becoming, flattering
favorecer {53} *vt* 1 : to favor 2 : to look well on, to suit
favorecido, -da *adj* 1 : flattering 2 : fortunate
favoritismo *nm* : favoritism
favorito, -ta *adj & n* : favorite
fax *nm* : fax, facsimile
fayuca *nf Mex* 1 : contraband 2 : black market
faz *nf* 1 : face, countenance ⟨la faz de la tierra : the face of the earth⟩ 2 : side (of coins, fabric, etc.)
fe *nf* 1 : faith 2 : assurance, testimony ⟨dar fe de : to bear witness to⟩ 3 : intention, will ⟨de buena fe : bona fide, in good faith⟩
fealdad *nf* : ugliness
febrero *nm* : February ⟨el primero de febrero : (on) February first⟩
febril *adj* : feverish — **febrilmente** *adv*
fecal *adj* : fecal
fecha *nf* 1 : date ⟨hasta la fecha : to date⟩ ⟨a partir de esta fecha : from today⟩ ⟨adelantar/atrasar la fecha : to move up/back the date⟩ 2 **fecha de caducidad/vencimiento** : expiration date 3 **fecha límite** : deadline
fechar *vt* : to date, to put a date on
fechoría *nf* : misdeed
fécula *nf* : starch (food)
fecundar *vt* : to fertilize (an egg) — **fecundación** *nf*
fecundidad *nf* 1 : fecundity, fertility 2 : productivity
fecundo, -da *adj* FÉRTIL : fertile, fecund
federación *nf, pl* **-ciones** : federation
federal *adj* : federal
federalismo *nm* : federalism — **federalista** *adj & nmf*
federar *vt* : to federate
fehaciente *adj* : reliable, irrefutable — **fehacientemente** *adv*
felicidad *nf* 1 : happiness 2 ¡**felicidades!** : best wishes!, congratulations!, happy birthday!
felicitación *nf, pl* **-ciones** 1 : congratulation ⟨¡felicitaciones! : congratulations!⟩ 2 : greeting card
felicitar *vt* CONGRATULAR : to congratulate — **felicitarse** *vr* **~ de** : to be glad about
feligrés, -gresa *n, mpl* **-greses** : parishioner
feligresía *nf* : parish
felino, -na *adj & n* : feline
feliz *adj, pl* **felices** 1 : happy 2 **Feliz Navidad** : Merry Christmas

felizmente *adv* **1** : happily **2** : fortunately, luckily

felonía *nf* : felony

felpa *nf* **1** : terry cloth **2** : plush

felpudo *nm* : doormat

femenil *adj* : women's, girls' ⟨futbol femenil : women's soccer⟩

femenino, -na *adj* **1** : feminine **2** : women's ⟨derechos femeninos : women's rights⟩ **3** : female

fémina *nf* : woman

femineidad *or* **feminidad** *nf* : femininity

feminismo *nm* : feminism

feminista *adj* & *nmf* : feminist

femoral *adj* : femoral

fémur *nm* : femur, thighbone

fenecer {53} *vi* **1** : to die, to pass away **2** : to come to an end, to cease

fénix *nm* : phoenix

fenomenal *adj* **1** : phenomenal **2** *fam* : fantastic, terrific — **fenomenalmente** *adv*

fenómeno *nm* **1** : phenomenon **2** : prodigy, genius

feo[1] *adv* : badly, bad

feo[2]**, fea** *adj* **1** : ugly **2** : unpleasant, nasty ⟨un olor feo : a nasty smell⟩ ⟨me dijo cosas feas : he said awful things to me⟩ ⟨la cosa se pone fea : things are getting ugly⟩

féretro *nm* ATAÚD : coffin, casket

feria *nf* **1** : fair, market **2** : festival, holiday **3** *Mex* : change (money)

feriado, -da *adj* **día feriado** : public holiday

ferial *nm* : fairground

fermentar *v* : to ferment — **fermentación** *nf*

fermento *nm* : ferment

ferocidad *nf* : ferocity, fierceness

feroz *adj*, *pl* **feroces** FIERO : ferocious, fierce — **ferozmente** *adv*

férreo, -rrea *adj* **1** : iron **2** : strong, steely ⟨una voluntad férrea : an iron will⟩ **3** : strict, severe **4 vía férrea** : railroad track

ferretería *nf* **1** : hardware store **2** : hardware **3** : foundry, ironworks

ferrocarril *nm* : railroad, railway

ferrocarrilero → **ferroviario**

ferroviario, -ria *adj* : rail, railroad

ferry *nm*, *pl* **ferrys** : ferry

fértil *adj* FECUNDO : fertile, fruitful

fertilidad *nf* : fertility

fertilizante[1] *adj* : fertilizing ⟨droga fertilizante : fertility drug⟩

fertilizante[2] *nm* ABONO : fertilizer

fertilizar *vt* ABONAR : to fertilize — **fertilización** *nf*

ferviente *adj* FERVOROSO : fervent — **fervientemente** *adv*

fervor *nm* : fervor, zeal

fervoroso, -sa *adj* FERVIENTE : fervent, zealous

festejar *vt* **1** CELEBRAR : to celebrate **2** AGASAJAR : to entertain, to wine and dine **3** *Mex fam* : to thrash, to beat

festejo *nm* : celebration, festivity

festín *nm*, *pl* **festines** : banquet, feast

festinar *vt* : to hasten, to hurry up

festival *nm* : festival

festividad *nf* **1** : festivity **2** : (religious) feast, holiday

festivo, -va *adj* **1** : festive **2 día festivo** : holiday — **festivamente** *adv*

festón *nm*, *pl* **-tones** : scallop (decoration)

fetal *adj* : fetal

fetiche *nm* : fetish

fétido, -da *adj* : fetid, foul

feto *nm* : fetus

feudal *adj* : feudal — **feudalismo** *nm*

fiabilidad *nf* : reliability, trustworthiness

fiable *adj* : trustworthy, reliable

fiado, -da *adj* : on credit

fiador, -dora *n* : bondsman, guarantor

fiambrería *nf* : delicatessen

fiambres *nmpl* : cold cuts

fianza *nf* **1** CAUCIÓN : bail, bond **2** : surety, deposit

fiar {85} *vt* **1** : to sell on credit **2** : to guarantee — **fiarse** *vr* ~ **de** : to place trust in

fiasco *nm* FRACASO : fiasco, failure

fibra *nf* **1** : fiber **2 fibra de vidrio** : fiberglass

fibroso, -sa *adj* : fibrous

ficción *nf*, *pl* **ficciones** **1** : fiction **2** : fabrication, lie

ficha *nf* **1** : index card **2** : file, record **3** : token **4** : domino, checker, counter, poker chip

fichaje *nm* : signing (in sports)

fichar *vt* **1** : to open a file on **2** : to sign up — *vi* : to punch in, to punch out

fichero *nm* **1** : card file **2** : filing cabinet

ficticio, -cia *adj* : fictitious

fidedigno, -na *adj* FIABLE : reliable, trustworthy

fideicomisario, -ria *n* : trustee

fideicomiso *nm* : trust ⟨guardar en fideicomiso : to hold in trust⟩

fidelidad *nf* : fidelity, faithfulness

fideo *nm* : noodle

fiduciario[1]**, -ria** *adj* : fiduciary

fiduciario[2]**, -ria** *n* : trustee

fiebre *nf* **1** CALENTURA : fever, temperature ⟨fiebre amarilla : yellow fever⟩ **2** : fever, excitement

fiel[1] *adj* **1** : faithful, loyal **2** : accurate — **fielmente** *adv*

fiel[2] *nm* **1** : pointer (of a scale) **2 los fieles** : the faithful

fieltro *nm* : felt

fiera *nf* **1** : wild animal, beast **2** : fiend, demon ⟨una fiera para el trabajo : a demon for work⟩

fiereza *nf* : fierceness, ferocity

fiero, -ra *adj* FEROZ : fierce, ferocious

fierro *nm* HIERRO : iron

fiesta *nf* **1** : party, fiesta ⟨fiesta de cumpleaños : birthday party⟩ ⟨no estoy para fiestas : I am in no mood to celebrate⟩ ⟨aguarle la fiesta a alguien : to rain on someone's parade⟩ **2** : holiday, feast day (in religion) ⟨hoy es (día de) fiesta : today is a holiday⟩

figura *nf* **1** : figure ⟨figura retórica : figure of speech⟩ ⟨figuras políticas : political figures⟩ **2** : shape, form **3** : figure, body shape

figuración *nf, pl* **-ciones** : imagining
figurado, -da *adj* : figurative — **figuradamente** *adv*
figurar *vi* **1** : to figure, to be included ⟨Rivera figura entre los más grandes pintores de México : Rivera is among Mexico's greatest painters⟩ **2** : to be prominent, to stand out — *vt* : to represent ⟨esta línea figura el horizonte : this line represents the horizon⟩ — **figurarse** *vr* : to imagine, to think ⟨¡figúrate el lío en que se metió! : imagine the mess she got into!⟩
fijación *nf, pl* **-ciones** **1** : fixation, obsession **2** : fixing, establishing **3** : fastening, securing
fijador *nm* : hair spray
fijamente *adv* : fixedly
fijar *vt* **1** : to fasten, to affix **2** ESTABLECER : to establish, to set up ⟨fijar su residencia : to take up residence⟩ **3** CONCRETAR : to set, to fix ⟨fijar la fecha : to set the date⟩ ⟨fijar la atención en : to focus one's attention on⟩ ⟨fijar la mirada en : to fix one's gaze on⟩ — **fijarse** *vr* **1** : to settle, to become fixed **2** : to notice ⟨fijarse en algo : to notice something, to pay attention to something⟩ ⟨me he fijado que . . . : I noticed that . . .⟩
fijeza *nf* **1** : firmness (of convictions) **2** : persistence, constancy ⟨mirar con fijeza a : to stare at⟩
fijo, -ja *adj* **1** : fixed, firm, steady **2** PERMANENTE : permanent
fila *nf* **1** HILERA : line, file ⟨ponerse en fila : to get in line⟩ ⟨en fila india : (in) single file⟩ **2** : rank, row **3 filas** *nfpl* : ranks ⟨cerrar filas : to close ranks⟩
filamento *nm* : filament
filantropía *nf* : philanthropy
filantrópico, -ca *adj* : philanthropic
filántropo, -pa *n* : philanthropist
filarmónica *nf* : philharmonic
filatelia *nf* : philately, stamp collecting
fildeador, -dora *n* : fielder
filete *nm* **1** : fillet **2** SOLOMILLO : sirloin **3** : thread (of a screw)
filiación *nf, pl* **-ciones** **1** : affiliation, connection **2** : particulars *pl*, (police) description
filial[1] *adj* : filial
filial[2] *nf* : affiliate, subsidiary
filigrana *nf* **1** : filigree **2** : watermark (on paper)
filipino, -na *adj & n* : Filipino
filmación *nf, pl* **-ciones** : filming, shooting
filmar *vt* : to film, to shoot
filme *or* **film** *nm* PELÍCULA : film, movie
filmoteca *nf* : film library
filo *nm* **1** : cutting edge, blade **2** : edge ⟨al filo del escritorio : at the edge of the desk⟩ ⟨al filo de la medianoche : at the stroke of midnight⟩
filón *nm, pl* **filones** **1** : seam, vein (of minerals) **2** *fam* : successful business, gold mine
filoso, -sa *adj* : sharp
filosofar *vi* : to philosophize
filosofía *nf* : philosophy

filosófico, -ca *adj* : philosophic, philosophical — **filosóficamente** *adv*
filósofo, -fa *n* : philosopher
filtración *nf, pl* **-ciones** : seeping, leaking
filtrar *v* : to filter — **filtrarse** *vr* : to seep through, to leak
filtro *nm* : filter
fin *nm* **1** : end ⟨dar/poner fin a : to end, to put an end to⟩ ⟨llegar a su fin : to come to an end⟩ **2** : purpose, aim, objective **3 a fin de cuentas** : in the end **4 a fin de que** : in order to **5 a fines de mes/año (etc.)** : at the end of the month/year (etc.) **6 al fin y al cabo** : after all **7 con el fin de** *or* **a fin de** : with the purpose of **8 con este fin** : to this end, with this purpose **9 en** ∼ : in short **10 fin de semana** : weekend **11 por** ∼ : finally, at last
finado, -da *adj & n* DIFUNTO : deceased
final[1] *adj* : final, ultimate — **finalmente** *adv*
final[2] *nm* **1** CONCLUSIÓN : end ⟨al final : at the end⟩ **2 a finales de mes/año (etc.)** : at the end of the month/year (etc.)
final[3] *nf* : final, play-off
finalidad *nf* **1** : purpose, aim **2** : finality
finalista *nmf* : finalist
finalización *nf, pl* **-ciones** : completion, end
finalizar {21} *v* : to finish, to end
financiación *nf, pl* **-ciones** : financing, funding
financiamiento *nm* → **financiación**
financiar *vt* : to finance, to fund
financiero[1], **-ra** *adj* : financial
financiero[2], **-ra** *n* : financier
financista *nmf* : financier
finanzas *nfpl* : finances, finance ⟨altas finanzas : high finance⟩
finca *nf* **1** : farm, ranch **2** : country house
fineza *nf* FINURA, REFINAMIENTO : refinement
fingido, -da *adj* : false, feigned
fingimiento *nm* : pretense
fingir {35} *v* : to feign, to pretend
finiquitar *vt* **1** : to settle (an account) **2** : to conclude, to bring to an end
finiquito *nm* : settlement (of an account)
finito, -ta *adj* : finite
finja, etc. → **fingir**
finlandés, -desa *adj & n* : Finnish
fino[1], **-na** *adj* **1** : fine, excellent **2** : delicate, slender **3** REFINADO : refined **4** : sharp, acute ⟨olfato fino : keen sense of smell⟩ **5** : subtle
fino[2] *nm* : dry sherry
finta *nf* : feint
fintar *or* **fintear** *vi* : to feint
finura *nf* **1** : fineness, high quality **2** FINEZA, REFINAMIENTO : refinement
fiordo *nm* : fjord
firma *nf* **1** : signature **2** : signing **3** EMPRESA : firm, company
firmamento *nm* : firmament, sky
firmante *nmf* : signer, signatory
firmar *v* : to sign
firme *adj* **1** : firm, resolute **2** : steady, stable

firmemente *adv* : firmly

firmeza *nf* 1 : firmness, stability 2 : strength, resolve

fiscal[1] *adj* : fiscal — fiscalmente *adv*

fiscal[2] *nmf* : district attorney, prosecutor

fiscalizar {21} *vt* 1 : to audit, to inspect 2 : to oversee 3 : to criticize

fisco *nm* : Treasury (en EEUU), Exchequer (en Gran Bretaña)

fisgar {52} *vt* HUSMEAR : to pry into, to snoop on

fisgón, -gona *n, mpl* fisgones : snoop, busybody

fisgonear *vi* : to snoop, to pry

fisgue, etc. → fisgar

física *nf* : physics

físico[1], -ca *adj* : physical — físicamente *adv*

físico[2], -ca *n* : physicist

físico[3] *nm* : physique, figure

fisiología *nf* : physiology

fisiológico, -ca *adj* : physiological, physiologic

fisiólogo, -ga *n* : physiologist

fisión *nf, pl* fisiones : fission — fisionable *adj*

fisionomía → fisonomía

fisioterapeuta *nmf* : physical therapist

fisioterapia *nf* : physical therapy

fisonomía *nf* : physiognomy, features *pl*

fistol *nm Mex* : tie clip

fisura *nf* : fissure, crevasse

flaccidez *nf* : limpness

fláccido, -da *or* flácido, -da *adj* : flaccid, flabby

flaco, -ca *adj* 1 DELGADO : thin, skinny 2 : feeble, weak ⟨una flaca excusa : a feeble excuse⟩

flagelo *nm* 1 : scourge, whip 2 : calamity

flagrante *adj* : flagrant, glaring, blatant — flagrantemente *adv*

flama *nf* LLAMA : flame

flamable *adj Mex* : flammable

flamante *adj* 1 : bright, brilliant 2 : brand-new

flamear *vi* 1 LLAMEAR : to flame, to blaze 2 ONDEAR : to flap, to flutter

flamenco[1], -ca *adj* 1 : flamenco 2 : Flemish

flamenco[2], -ca *n* : Fleming, Flemish person

flamenco[3] *nm* 1 : Flemish (language) 2 : flamingo 3 : flamenco (music or dance)

flan *nm* : flan

flanco *nm* : flank, side

flanquear *vt* : to flank

flaquear *vi* DECAER : to flag, to weaken

flaqueza *nf* 1 DEBILIDAD : frailty, feebleness 2 : thinness 3 : weakness, failing

flash *nm* : flash (in photography)

flashback *nm, pl* flashbacks : flashback

flatulento, -ta *adj* : flatulent — flatulencia *nf*

flauta *nf* 1 : flute 2 flauta dulce : recorder

flautín *nm, pl* flautines : piccolo

flautista *nmf* : flute player, flutist

flecha *nf* : arrow

flechazo *nm* : love at first sight

fleco *nm* 1 : bangs *pl* 2 : fringe

flema *nf* : phlegm

flemático, -ca *adj* : phlegmatic, stolid, impassive

flequillo *nm* : bangs *pl*

fletar *vt* 1 : to charter, to hire 2 : to load (freight)

flete *nm* 1 : charter fee 2 : shipping cost 3 : freight, cargo

fletero *nm* : shipper, carrier

flexibilidad *nf* : flexibility

flexibilizar {21} *vt* : to make more flexible

flexible[1] *adj* : flexible

flexible[2] *nm* 1 : flexible electrical cord 2 : soft hat

flexión *nf, pl* flexiones 1 : push-up 2 : squat

flexionar *vt* : to bend (a limb, etc.)

flirtear *vi* : to flirt

flojear *vi* 1 DEBILITARSE : to weaken, to flag 2 : to idle, to loaf around

flojedad *nf* : weakness

flojera *nf fam* 1 : lethargy, feeling of weakness 2 : laziness

flojo, -ja *adj* 1 SUELTO : loose, slack 2 : weak, poor ⟨está flojo en las ciencias : he's weak in science⟩ 3 PEREZOSO : lazy

flor *nf* 1 : flower 2 a flor de piel : easily noticed or affected ⟨con los nervios a flor de piel : with one's nerves on edge⟩ ⟨canta con las emociones a flor de piel : her singing is full of emotion⟩ 3 en ∼ : in bloom 4 flor de Pascua : poinsettia

flora *nf* : flora

floración *nf, pl* -ciones : flowering ⟨en plena floración : in full bloom⟩

floral *adj* : floral

floreado, -da *adj* : flowered, flowery

florear *vi* FLORECER : to flower, to bloom — *vt* 1 : to adorn with flowers 2 *Mex* : to flatter, to compliment

florecer {53} *vi* 1 : to bloom, to blossom 2 : to flourish, to thrive

floreciente *adj* 1 : flowering 2 PRÓSPERO : flourishing, thriving

florecimiento *nm* : flowering

floreo *nm* : flourish

florería *nf* : flower shop, florist's

florero[1], -ra *n* : florist

florero[2] *nm* JARRÓN : vase

florete *nm* : foil (in fencing)

florido, -da *adj* 1 : full of flowers 2 : florid, flowery ⟨escritos floridos : flowery prose⟩

florista *nmf* : florist

floristería → florería

floritura *nf* : frill, embellishment

flota *nf* : fleet

flotabilidad *nf* : buoyancy

flotación *nf, pl* -ciones : flotation

flotador *nm* 1 : float 2 : life preserver

flotante *adj* : floating, buoyant

flotar *vi* : to float

flote *nm* a ∼ : afloat

flotilla *nf* : flotilla, fleet

fluctuar {3} *vi* 1 : to fluctuate 2 VACILAR : to vacillate — fluctuación *nf* — fluctuante *adj*

fluidez *nf* **1** : fluency **2** : fluidity
fluido¹, -da *adj* **1** : flowing **2** : fluent **3** : fluid
fluido² *nm* : fluid
fluir {41} *vi* : to flow
flujo *nm* **1** : flow ⟨el flujo y reflujo : the ebb and flow⟩ **2** : discharge
flúor *nm* : fluorine
fluorescencia *nf* : fluorescence — **fluorescente** *adj*
fluorescente *nm* : fluorescent light — **fluorescente** *adj*
fluoruro *nm* : fluoride
fluye, etc. → **fluir**
fobia *nf* : phobia
foca *nf* : seal (animal)
focal *adj* : focal
foco *nm* **1** : focus **2** : center, pocket **3** : lightbulb **4** : spotlight **5** : headlight
fofo, -fa *adj* **1** ESPONJOSO : soft, spongy **2** : flabby
fogata *nf* : campfire, bonfire
fogón *nm, pl* **fogones** **1** : bonfire, campfire **2** : burner, stove **3** : fireplace
fogonazo *nm* : flash, explosion
fogoso, -sa *adj* ARDIENTE : ardent
foguear *vt* : to inure, to accustom
fogueo *nm* **de** ~ ⟨un cartucho de fogueo : a blank, a dummy round⟩
foja *nf* : sheet (of paper)
folículo *nm* : follicle
folio *nm* : folio, leaf
folk ['fok, 'folk] *nm* : folk (music) — **folk** *adj*
folklore *nm* : folklore
folklórico, -ca *adj* : folk, traditional
follaje *nm* : foliage
folleto *nm* : pamphlet, leaflet, circular
follón *nm, pl* **follones** *Spain* **1** : commotion, fuss **2** : mess
fomentar *vt* **1** : to foment, to stir up **2** PROMOVER : to promote, to foster
fomento *nm* : promotion, encouragement
fonda *nf* **1** POSADA : inn **2** : small restaurant
fondeado, -da *adj fam* : rich, in the money
fondear *vt* **1** : to sound **2** : to sound out, to examine **3** *Mex* : to fund, to finance — *vi* ANCLAR : to anchor — **fondearse** *vr fam* : to get rich
fondeo *nm* **1** : anchoring **2** *Mex* : funding, financing
fondillos *mpl* : seat, bottom (of clothing)
fondista *nmf* : long-distance runner
fondo *nm* **1** : bottom ⟨el fondo del océano/barril : the bottom of the ocean/barrel⟩ ⟨llegar al fondo de algo : to get to the bottom of something⟩ **2** : rear, back, end ⟨al fondo de la casa : at the back of the house⟩ **3** PROFUNDIDAD : depth **4** : background ⟨al fondo : in the background⟩ ⟨música de fondo : background music⟩ **5** CONTENIDO : content **6** *Mex* : slip, petticoat **7** : fund ⟨fondo de inversiones/pensiones : investment/pension fund⟩ ⟨fondo común : joint fund⟩ **8 fondos** *nmpl* : funds, resources ⟨cheque sin fondos : bounced check⟩ ⟨recaudar fondos : to raise funds⟩ ⟨fondos públicos : public funds⟩ ⟨fondos de campaña : campaign funds⟩ **9 a** ~ : thoroughly, in depth **10 de** ~ : fundamental **11 de** ~ : long-distance (in sports) **12 en** ~ : abreast **13 en el fondo** : deep down, at heart **14 tocar fondo** : to touch bottom (in the sea, etc.), to hit rock bottom
fondue *nf* : fondue
fonema *nm* : phoneme
fonética *nf* : phonetics
fonético, -ca *adj* : phonetic
fontanería *nf* PLOMERÍA : plumbing
fontanero, -ra *n* PLOMERO : plumber
footing ['fu,tɪŋ] *nm* : jogging ⟨hacer footing : to jog⟩
forajido, -da *n* : bandit, fugitive, outlaw
foráneo, -nea *adj* : foreign, strange
forastero, -ra *n* : stranger, outsider
forcejear *vi* : to struggle
forcejeo *nm* : struggle
fórceps *nms & pl* : forceps *pl*
forense¹ *adj* : forensic, legal
forense² *nmf* : forensic scientist
forestal *adj* : forest
forja *nf* FRAGUA : forge
forjar *vt* **1** : to forge **2** : to shape, to create ⟨forjar un compromiso : to hammer out a compromise⟩ **3** : to invent, to concoct
forma *nf* **1** : form, shape ⟨tomar forma : to take shape⟩ ⟨dar forma a : to form, to give shape to⟩ ⟨en forma de corazón : in the shape of a heart⟩ **2** MANERA, MODO : manner, way ⟨su forma de vida : their way of life⟩ ⟨formas de pago : payment methods⟩ **3** : fitness ⟨estar en forma : to be fit, to be in shape⟩ ⟨estar en baja forma : to be out of shape⟩ **4 formas** *nfpl* : appearances, conventions ⟨guardar las formas : to keep up appearances⟩ **5 de cualquier forma** *or* **de todas formas** : anyway, in any case **6 de forma que** : so that
formación *nf, pl* **-ciones** **1** : formation **2** : training ⟨formación profesional : vocational training⟩
formal *adj* **1** : formal **2** : serious, dignified **3** : dependable, reliable
formaldehído *nm* : formaldehyde
formalidad *nf* **1** : formality **2** : seriousness, dignity **3** : reliability
formalizar {21} *vt* : to formalize, to make official
formalmente *adv* : formally
formar *vt* **1** : to form, to make **2** CONSTITUIR : to make up, to constitute **3** : to train, to educate — **formarse** *vr* **1** DESARROLLARSE : to develop, to take shape **2** EDUCARSE : to be educated
formatear *vt* : to format
formativo, -va *adj* : formative
formato *nm* : format
formidable *adj* **1** : formidable, tremendous **2** *fam* : fantastic, terrific
formón *nm, pl* **formones** : chisel
fórmula *nf* : formula
formulación *nf, pl* **-ciones** : formulation
formular *vt* **1** : to formulate, to draw up **2** : to make, to lodge (a protest or complaint)

formulario *nm* : form ⟨rellenar un formulario : to fill out a form⟩
fornicar {72} *vi* : to fornicate — **fornicación** *nf*
fornido, -da *adj* : well-built, burly, hefty
foro *nm* 1 : forum 2 : public assembly, open discussion
forraje *nm* 1 : fodder 2 : foraging 3 *fam* : hodgepodge
forrajear *vi* : to forage
forrar *vt* 1 : to line (a garment) 2 : to cover (a book)
forro *nm* 1 : lining 2 CUBIERTA : book cover
forsitia *nf* : forsythia
fortalecer {53} *vt* : to strengthen, to fortify — **fortalecerse** *vr*
fortalecimiento *nm* 1 : strengthening, fortifying 2 : fortifications
fortaleza *nf* 1 : fortress 2 FUERZA : strength 3 : resolution, fortitude
fortificación *nf, pl* **-ciones** : fortification
fortificar {72} *vt* 1 : to fortify 2 : to strengthen
fortín *nm, pl* **fortines** : small fort
fortuito, -ta *adj* : fortuitous
fortuna *nf* 1 SUERTE : fortune, luck 2 RIQUEZA : wealth, fortune
forúnculo *nm* : boil
forzado, -da *adj* : forced (of a smile, etc.)
forzar {36} *vt* 1 OBLIGAR : to force, to compel 2 : to force open 3 : to strain ⟨forzar los ojos : to strain one's eyes⟩
forzosamente *adv* 1 : forcibly, by force 2 : necessarily, inevitably ⟨forzosamente tendrán que pagar : they'll have no choice but to pay⟩
forzoso, -sa *adj* 1 : forced, compulsory 2 : necessary, inevitable
fosa *nf* 1 : ditch, pit ⟨fosa séptica : septic tank⟩ 2 TUMBA : grave 3 : cavity ⟨fosas nasales : nasal cavities, nostrils⟩
fosfato *nm* : phosphate
fosforescencia *nf* : phosphorescence — **fosforescente** *adj*
fósforo *nm* 1 CERILLA : match 2 : phosphorus
fósil¹ *adj* : fossilized, fossil
fósil² *nm* : fossil
fosilizar {21} *vt* : to fossilize — **fosilizarse** *vr*
foso *nm* 1 FOSA, ZANJA : ditch 2 : pit (of a theater) 3 : moat
foto *nf* : photo, picture
fotocopia *nf* : photocopy — **fotocopiar** *vt*
fotocopiadora *nf* COPIADORA : photocopier
fotoeléctrico, -ca *adj* : photoelectric
fotogénico, -ca *adj* : photogenic
fotografía *nf* 1 : photograph 2 : photography
fotografiar {85} *vt* : to photograph
fotográfico, -ca *adj* : photographic — **fotográficamente** *adv*
fotógrafo, -fa *n* : photographer
fotosíntesis *nf* : photosynthesis
foul *nm, pl* **fouls** : foul (in sports)
frac *nm, pl* **fracs** : tailcoat, tails *pl*
fracasado¹, -da *adj* : unsuccessful, failed
fracasado², -da *n* : failure

fracasar *vi* 1 FALLAR : to fail 2 : to fall through
fracaso *nm* FIASCO : failure
fracción *nf, pl* **fracciones** 1 : fraction 2 : part, fragment 3 : faction, splinter group
fraccionamiento *nm* 1 : division, breaking up 2 *Mex* : residential area, housing development
fraccionar *vt* : to divide, to break up
fraccionario, -ria *adj* : fractional
fracking ['frakiŋ] *nm* : fracking
fractura *nf* 1 : fracture 2 **fractura hidráulica** : fracking
fracturación hidráulica *nf* : fracking
fracturar *vt* : to fracture — **fracturarse** *vr*
fragancia *nf* : fragrance, scent
fragante *adj* : fragrant
fragata *nf* : frigate
frágil *adj* 1 : fragile 2 : frail, delicate
fragilidad *nf* 1 : fragility 2 : frailty, delicacy
fragmentar *vt* : to fragment — **fragmentación** *nf*
fragmentario, -ria *adj* : fragmentary, sketchy
fragmento *nm* 1 : fragment, shard 2 : bit, snippet 3 : excerpt, passage
fragor *nm* : clamor, din, roar
fragua *nf* FORJA : forge
fraguar {10} *vt* 1 : to forge 2 : to conceive, to concoct, to hatch — *vi* : to set, to solidify
fraile *nm* : friar, monk
frambuesa *nf* : raspberry
francamente *adv* 1 : frankly, candidly 2 REALMENTE : really ⟨es francamente admirable : it's really impressive⟩
francés¹, -cesa *adj, mpl* **franceses** : French
francés², -cesa *n, mpl* **franceses** : French person, Frenchman *m*, Frenchwoman *f*
francés³ *nm* : French (language)
franciscano, -na *adj & n* : Franciscan
francmasón, -sona *n, mpl* **-sones** : Freemason — **francmasonería** *nf*
franco¹, -ca *adj* 1 CÁNDIDO : frank, candid 2 PATENTE : clear, obvious 3 : free ⟨franco a bordo : free on board⟩
franco² *nm* : franc
francotirador, -dora *n* : sniper
franela *nf* : flannel
franja *nf* 1 : stripe, band 2 : border, fringe
franquear *vt* 1 : to clear 2 ATRAVESAR : to cross, to go through 3 : to pay the postage on
franqueo *nm* : postage
franqueza *nf* : frankness
franquicia *nf* 1 EXENCIÓN : exemption 2 : franchise
frasco *nm* : small bottle, flask, vial
frase *nf* 1 : phrase 2 ORACIÓN : sentence
frasear *vt* : to phrase
fraternal *adj* : fraternal, brotherly
fraternidad *nf* 1 : brotherhood 2 : fraternity
fraternizar {21} *vi* : to fraternize — **fraternización** *nf*

fraterno, -na *adj* : fraternal, brotherly

fraude *nm* : fraud

fraudulento, -ta *adj* : fraudulent — **fraudulentamente** *adv*

fray *nm* : brother (title of a friar) ⟨Fray Bartolomé : Brother Bartholomew⟩

frazada *nf* COBIJA, MANTA : blanket

frecuencia *nf* : frequency

frecuentar *vt* : to frequent, to haunt

frecuente *adj* : frequent — **frecuentemente** *adv*

freelance[1] [fri'lans] *adj, pl* **freelance** : freelance

freelance[2] *nmf* : freelancer

fregadero *nm* : kitchen sink

fregado[1]**, -da** *adj fam* : annoying, bothersome

fregado[2] *nm* **1** : scrubbing, scouring **2** *fam* : mess, muddle

fregar {49} *vt* **1** : to scrub, to scour, to wash ⟨fregar los trastes : to do the dishes⟩ ⟨fregar el suelo : to scrub the floor⟩ **2** *fam* : to annoy — *vi* **1** : to wash the dishes **2** : to clean, to scrub **3** *fam* : to be annoying

fregona *nf Spain* : mop

freidera *nf Mex* : frying pan

freír {37} *vt* : to fry — **freírse** *vr*

fréjol *Ecua* → **frijol**

frenado *nm* : braking (of a vehicle)

frenar *vt* **1** : to brake **2** DETENER : to curb, to check — *vi* **1** : to apply the brakes — **frenarse** *vr* : to restrain oneself

frenazo *nm* : sudden stop (in a vehicle) ⟨dar un frenazo : to brake hard⟩

frenesí *nm, pl* **-síes** : frenzy

frenético, -ca *adj* : frantic, frenzied — **frenéticamente** *adv*

freno *nm* **1** : brake ⟨freno de mano : handbrake, emergency brake⟩ **2** : bit (of a bridle) **3** : check, restraint **4 frenos** *nmpl Mex* : braces (for teeth)

frente[1] *nm* **1** : front ⟨en frente : in front, opposite⟩ **2** : facade **3** : front line, front **4** : front (in politics) **5** : front (in meteorology) ⟨frente frío : cold front⟩ **6 de ~** : head-on ⟨chocar de frente a/con : to run head-on into⟩ **7 de frente a** : facing **8 ~ a** : opposite, in front of **9 ~ a** : in the face of (a crisis, etc.), against (an opponent, etc.) **10 estar al ~ de** : to be at the head of, to lead **11 hacer frente a** : to face up to

frente[2] *nf* **1** : forehead, brow **2 frente a frente** : face to face

fresa *nf* **1** : strawberry **2** : drill (in dentistry)

fresco[1]**, -ca** *adj* **1** : fresh **2** : cool **3** *fam* : insolent, nervy

fresco[2] *nm* **1** : coolness **2** : fresh air ⟨al fresco : in the open air, outdoors⟩ **3** : fresco **4** → **refresco**

frescor *nm* : cool air ⟨el frescor de la noche : the cool of the evening⟩

frescura *nf* **1** : freshness **2** : coolness **3** : calmness **4** DESCARO : nerve, audacity

fresno *nm* : ash (tree)

frialdad *nf* **1** : coldness **2** INDIFERENCIA : coldness, indifference

fríamente *adv* : coldly, indifferently

fricción *nf, pl* **fricciones 1** : friction **2** : rubbing, massage **3** : discord, disagreement ⟨fricción entre los hermanos : friction between the brothers⟩

friccionar *vt* **1** FROTAR : to rub **2** : to massage

friega[1]**, friegue, etc.** → **fregar**

friega[2] *nf* **1** FRICCIÓN : massage **2** : annoyance, bother

frigidez *nf* : (sexual) frigidity

frigorífico *nm Spain* : refrigerator

frijol *nm* : bean ⟨frijoles refritos : refried beans⟩

frío[1]**, fría** *adj* **1** : cold **2** INDIFERENTE : cool, indifferent ⟨me deja frío : it leaves me cold⟩ **3** ESTUPEFACTO, PASMADO : shocked, stunned

frío[2] *nm* **1** : cold ⟨hace mucho frío esta noche : it's very cold tonight⟩ **2** INDIFERENCIA : coldness, indifference **3 tener frío** : to feel cold ⟨tengo frío : I'm cold⟩ **4 tomar frío** RESFRIARSE : to catch a cold

friolento, -ta *adj* : sensitive to cold

friolera *nf* (*used ironically or humorously*) : trifling amount ⟨una friolera de mil dólares : a mere thousand dollars⟩

friolero, -ra → **friolento**

friso *nm* : frieze

fritar *vt* : to fry

frito[1] *pp* → **freír**

frito[2]**, -ta** *adj* **1** : fried **2** *fam* : worn-out, fed up ⟨tener frito a alguien : to get on someone's nerves⟩ **3** *fam* : fast asleep ⟨se quedó frito en el sofá : she fell asleep on the couch⟩ **4** *Arg, Chile, Peru, Uru fam* : done for, in trouble

fritura *nf* **1** : frying **2** : fried food

frivolidad *nf* : frivolity

frívolo, -la *adj* : frivolous — **frívolamente** *adv*

fronda *nf* **1** : frond **2 frondas** *nfpl* : foliage

frondoso, -sa *adj* : leafy, luxuriant

frontal *adj* : frontal, head-on ⟨un choque frontal : a head-on collision⟩

frontalmente *adv* : head-on

frontera *nf* : border, frontier

fronterizo, -za *adj* : border, on the border ⟨estados fronterizos : neighboring states⟩

frontón *nm, pl* **frontones 1** : jai alai **2** : jai alai court

frotar *vt* **1** : to rub **2** : to strike (a match) — **frotarse** *vr* : to rub (together)

frote *nm* : rubbing, rub

fructífero, -ra *adj* : fruitful, productive

fructificar {72} *vi* **1** : to bear or produce fruit **2** : to be productive

fructuoso, -sa *adj* : fruitful

frugal *adj* : frugal, thrifty — **frugalmente** *adv*

frugalidad *adj* : frugality

fruncido *nm* : gathering (of fabric)

fruncir {83} *vt* **1** : to gather (fabric) **2 fruncir el ceño** : to knit one's brow, to frown **3 fruncir la boca** : to pucker up, to purse one's lips

frunza, etc. → **fruncir**

frustración *nf, pl* **-ciones** : frustration

frustrado, -da *adj* **1** : frustrated **2** : failed, unsuccessful

frustrante *adj* : frustrating

frustrar *vt* : to frustrate, to thwart — **frustrarse** *vr* FRACASAR : to fail, to come to nothing ⟨se frustraron sus esperanzas : his hopes were dashed⟩

fruta *nf* : fruit

frutal[1] *adj* : fruit, fruit-bearing

frutal[2] *nm* : fruit tree

frutería *nf* : fruit store

frutero[1], **-ra** *n* : fruit seller

frutero[2] *nm* : fruit bowl

frutilla *nf* : South American strawberry

fruto *nm* **1** : fruit ⟨los frutos de la tierra : the fruits of the earth⟩ **2** : fruit, result ⟨los frutos de su trabajo : the fruits of his labor⟩

fucsia *adj & nm* : fuchsia

fue, etc. → ir, ser

fuego *nm* **1** : fire ⟨prender fuego a algo : to set something on fire⟩ ⟨jugar con fuego : to play with fire⟩ ⟨abrir fuego contra : to open fire on⟩ **2** : light ⟨¿tienes fuego? : have you got a light?⟩ **3** : flame, burner (on a stove) ⟨a fuego lento : on low heat⟩ **4** : ardor, passion **5** : skin eruption, cold sore **6 fuegos artificiales** : fireworks

fuelle *nm* : bellows

fuente *nf* **1** MANANTIAL : spring **2** : fountain **3** ORIGEN : source ⟨fuentes informativas : sources of information⟩ ⟨fuente de alimentación/energía : food/energy source⟩ **4** : platter, serving dish **5 fuente de noticias** : news feed **6 fuente de soda** : soda fountain

fuera *adv* **1** AFUERA : outside, out ⟨por fuera : on the outside⟩ ⟨hacia fuera : out, outside, outwards⟩ **2** : abroad, away **3 ~ de** : out of, outside of, beyond ⟨fuera del alcance : out of reach⟩ ⟨fuera de peligro : out of danger⟩ **4 ~ de** : besides, in addition to ⟨fuera de eso : aside from that⟩ **5 fuera de lugar** : out of place, amiss

fuerce, fuerza etc. → forzar

fuero *nm* **1** JURISDICCIÓN : jurisdiction **2** : privilege, exemption **3 fuero interno** : conscience, heart of hearts

fuerte[1] *adv* **1** : strongly, tightly, hard **2** : loudly **3** : abundantly

fuerte[2] *adj* **1** : strong ⟨brazos fuertes : strong arms⟩ **2** RESISTENTE : strong, sturdy **3** : intense (of pain, etc.), strong (of a drug, odor, etc.) **4** : powerful, strong (of wind), heavy (of rain) ⟨un fuerte golpe : a hard blow⟩ **5** : sharp, marked ⟨un fuerte incremento : a sharp increase⟩ **6** : loud ⟨hablar más fuerte : to speak up⟩ **7** : extreme, excessive **8 hacerse fuerte** : to pull oneself together — **fuertemente** *adv*

fuerte[3] *nm* **1** : fort, stronghold **2** : forte, strong point

fuerza *nf* **1** : strength ⟨tener fuerzas para : to have the strength to⟩ ⟨cobrar fuerza : to gather strength⟩ ⟨recuperar fuerzas : to get one's strength back⟩ ⟨con todas sus fuerzas : with all your might⟩ **2** VIO-LENCIA : force ⟨fuerza bruta : brute force⟩ **3** : force, strength, power ⟨la fuerza del impacto : the force of the impact⟩ **4** : force, power ⟨fuerza de costumbre : force of habit⟩ ⟨fuerza de voluntad : willpower⟩ ⟨la fuerza de la razón : the power of reason⟩ **5** : (natural) force ⟨la fuerza de la gravedad : the force of gravity⟩ **6** : force ⟨fuerzas armadas/militares : armed/military forces⟩ ⟨fuerzas de seguridad : security forces⟩ ⟨fuerza pública, fuerzas del orden : police⟩ ⟨fuerza de trabajo : workforce⟩ **7 a fuerza de** : by, by dint of **8 a/por la fuerza** : by force, forcibly **9 con ~** : hard, firmly, tightly **10 por ~** : necessarily, unavoidably

fuerza centrífuga *nf* : centrifugal force

fuete *nm* : riding crop

fuga *nf* **1** HUIDA : flight, escape **2** : fugue **3** : leak ⟨fuga de gas : gas leak⟩

fugarse {52} *vr* **1** : to escape **2** HUIR : to flee, to run away **3** : to elope

fugaz *adj, pl* **fugaces** : brief, fleeting

fugitivo, -va *adj & n* : fugitive

fulana *nf disparaging* : hooker, slut *disparaging + offensive*

fulano, -na *n* : so-and-so, what's-his-name, what's-her-name ⟨fulano, mengano, y zutano : Tom, Dick, and Harry⟩ ⟨señora fulana de tal : Mrs. so-and-so⟩

fulcro *nm* : fulcrum

fulgor *nm* : brilliance, splendor

fulminante *adj* : devastating, terrible ⟨una mirada fulminante : a withering look⟩

fulminar *vt* : to strike down ⟨fulminar a alguien con la mirada : to look daggers at someone⟩

fumador, -dora *n* : smoker

fumar *v* : to smoke

fumble *nm* : fumble (in football)

fumblear *vt* : to fumble (in football)

fumigar {52} *vt* : to fumigate — **fumigación** *nf* — **fumigador, -dora** *n*

función *nf, pl* **funciones** **1** : function **2** : duty ⟨el presidente en funciones : the acting president⟩ **3** : performance, show **4 en función de** : according to

funcional *adj* : functional — **funcionalmente** *adv*

funcionamiento *nm* **1** : functioning **2 en ~** : in operation

funcionar *vi* **1** : to function **2** : to run, to work

funcionario, -ria *n* : civil servant, official

funda *nf* **1** : case, cover, sheath **2** : pillowcase

fundación *nf, pl* **-ciones** : foundation, establishment

fundado, -da *adj* : well-founded, justified

fundador, -dora *n* : founder

fundamental *adj* BÁSICO : fundamental, basic — **fundamentalmente** *adv*

fundamentalismo *nm* : fundamentalism — **fundamentalista** *nmf*

fundamentar *vt* **1** : to lay the foundations for **2** : to support, to back up **3** : to base, to found

fundamento *nm* : basis, foundation, groundwork

fundar *vt* **1** ESTABLECER, INSTITUIR : to found, to establish **2** BASAR : to base — **fundarse** *vr* ~ **en** : to be based on, to stem from

fundición *nf, pl* **-ciones** **1** : founding, smelting **2** : foundry

fundir *vt* **1** : to melt down, to smelt **2** : to fuse, to merge **3** : to burn out (a lightbulb) — **fundirse** *vr* **1** : to fuse together, to blend, to merge **2** : to melt, to thaw **3** : to fade (in television or movies)

fúnebre *adj* **1** : funeral, funereal **2** LÚGUBRE : gloomy, mournful

funeral[1] *adj* : funeral

funeral[2] *nm* **1** : funeral **2 funerales** *nmpl* EXEQUIAS : funeral rites

funeraria *nf* **1** : funeral home, funeral parlor **2 director de funeraria** : funeral director, undertaker

funerario, -ria *adj* : funeral

funesto, -ta *adj* : terrible, disastrous ⟨consecuencias funestas : disastrous consequences⟩

fungicida *nm* : fungicide

fungir {35} *vi* : to act, to function ⟨fungir de asesor : to act as a consultant⟩

funicular *nm* : cable car (on a mountain)

funja, etc. → **fungir**

furgón *nm, pl* **furgones** **1** : van, truck **2** : freight car, boxcar **3 furgón de cola** : caboose

furgoneta *nf* : van

furia *nf* **1** CÓLERA, IRA : fury, rage **2** : violence, fury ⟨la furia de la tormenta : the fury of the storm⟩

furibundo, -da *adj* : furious

furiosamente *adv* : furiously, frantically

furioso, -sa *adj* **1** AIRADO : furious, irate **2** : intense, violent

furor *nm* **1** : fury, rage **2** : violence (of the elements) **3** : passion, frenzy **4** : enthusiasm ⟨hacer furor : to be all the rage⟩

furtivo, -va *adj* : furtive — **furtivamente** *adv*

fuselaje *nm* : fuselage

fusible *nm* : (electrical) fuse

fusil *nm* : rifle

fusilar *vt* **1** : to shoot, to execute (by firing squad) **2** *fam* : to plagiarize, to pirate

fusilería *nf* **1** : rifles *pl*, rifle fire **2 descarga de fusilería** : fusillade

fusión *nf, pl* **fusiones** **1** : fusion **2** : union, merger

fusionar *vt* **1** : to fuse **2** : to merge, to amalgamate — **fusionarse** *vr*

fusta *nf* : riding crop

fuste *nm* **1** : shaft **2 de fuste** : important, significant

fustigar {52} *vt* **1** AZOTAR : to whip, to lash **2** : to upbraid, to berate

futbol *or* **fútbol** *nm* **1** : soccer **2 futbol americano** : football

futbolista *nmf* : soccer player

fútbol sala *nm* : indoor soccer

futesa *nf* **1** : small thing, trifle **2 futesas** *nfpl* : small talk

fútil *adj* : trifling, trivial

futón *nm, pl* **-tones** : futon

futurista *adj* : futuristic

futuro[1], **-ra** *adj* : future

futuro[2] *nm* PORVENIR : future

G

g *nf* : eighth letter of the Spanish alphabet

gabán *nm, pl* **gabanes** : topcoat, overcoat

gabardina *nf* **1** : gabardine **2** : trench coat, raincoat

gabarra *nf* : barge

gabinete *nm* **1** : cabinet (in government) **2** : study, office (in the home) **3** : (professional) office

gablete *nm* : gable

gabonés, -nesa *adj & n, mpl* **-neses** : Gabonese

gacela *nf* : gazelle

gaceta *nf* : gazette, newspaper

gachas *nfpl* : porridge

gacho, -cha *adj* **1** : drooping, turned downward **2** *Mex fam* : nasty, awful **3 ir a gachas** *fam* : to go on all fours

gaélico[1], **-ca** *adj* : Gaelic

gaélico[2] *nm* : Gaelic (language)

gafas *nfpl* ANTEOJOS : eyeglasses, glasses

gafe *nm* *Spain fam* : jinx, bad luck

gaita *nf* : bagpipes *pl*

gajes *nmpl* **gajes del oficio** : occupational hazards

gajo *nm* **1** : broken branch (of a tree) **2** : cluster, bunch (of fruit) **3** : segment (of citrus fruit)

gala *nf* **1** : gala ⟨vestido de gala : formal dress⟩ ⟨tener algo a gala : to be proud of something⟩ **2 galas** *nfpl* : finery, attire

galáctico, -ca *adj* : galactic

galán *nm, pl* **galanes** **1** : ladies' man, gallant **2** : leading man, hero **3** : boyfriend, suitor

galano, -na *adj* **1** : elegant **2** *Mex* : mottled

galante *adj* : gallant, attentive — **galantemente** *adv*

galantear *vt* **1** CORTEJAR : to court, to woo **2** : to flirt with

galanteo *nm* **1** CORTEJO : courtship **2** : flirtation, flirting

galantería *nf* **1** : gallantry, attentiveness **2** : compliment

galápago *nm* : aquatic turtle

galardón *nm, pl* **-dones** : award, prize

galardonado, -da *adj* : prizewinning

galardonar *vt* : to give an award to

galaxia *nf* : galaxy

galeno *nm* *fam* : physician, doctor

galeón *nm, pl* **galeones** : galleon

galera *nf* : galley

galería *nf* **1** : gallery, balcony (in a theater) ⟨galería comercial : shopping mall⟩ **2** : corridor, passage

galerón *nm, pl* **-rones** *Mex* : large hall
galés¹, -lesa *adj* : Welsh
galés², -lesa *n, mpl* **galeses** **1** : Welshman *m*, Welshwoman *f* **2 los galeses** : the Welsh
galés³ *nm* : Welsh (language)
galgo *nm* : greyhound
galimatías *nms & pl* : gibberish, nonsense
galio *nm* : gallium
gallardete *nm* : pennant, streamer
gallardía *nf* **1** VALENTÍA : bravery **2** APOSTURA : elegance, gracefulness
gallardo, -da *adj* **1** VALIENTE : brave **2** APUESTO : elegant, graceful
gallear *vi* : to show off, to strut around
gallego¹, -ga *adj* **1** : Galician **2** *fam* : Spanish
gallego², -ga *n* **1** : Galician **2** *fam* : Spaniard
galleta *nf* **1** : cookie **2** : cracker
gallina *nf* **1** : hen **2 gallina de Guinea** : guinea fowl
gallinazo *nm* : vulture, buzzard
gallinero *nm* : chicken coop
gallito, -ta *adj fam* : cocky, belligerent
gallo *nm* **1** : rooster, cock **2** *fam* : squeak or crack in the voice **3** *Mex* : serenade **4 gallo de pelea** : gamecock
galochas *nfpl* : galoshes
galón *nm, pl* **galones** **1** : gallon **2** : stripe (military insignia)
galopada *nf* : gallop
galopante *adj* : galloping ⟨inflación galopante : galloping inflation⟩
galopar *vi* : to gallop
galope *nm* : gallop
galpón *nm, pl* **galpones** : shed, storehouse
galvanizar {21} *vt* : to galvanize — **galvanización** *nf*
gama *nf* **1** : range, spectrum, gamut **2** → **gamo**
gamba *nf Arg, Spain, Uru* : large shrimp, prawn
gamberrada *nf Spain* **1** : act of vandalism **2** : crude thing (to say or do)
gamberro, -rra *n Spain* : hooligan, troublemaker
gambiano, -na *adj & n* : Gambian
gambito *nm* : gambit (in chess)
gamo, -ma *n* : fallow deer
gamuza *nf* **1** : suede **2** : chamois
gana *nf* **1** : desire, inclination **2 con ∼s** : enthusiastically, heartily ⟨trabajar con ganas : to work enthusiastically⟩ ⟨llover con ganas : to be pouring rain⟩ **3 darle ganas a alguien de hacer algo** : to make someone feel like doing something **4 de buena gana** : willingly, readily, gladly **5 de mala gana** : reluctantly, halfheartedly **6 tener ganas de hacer algo** : to feel like doing something ⟨tengo ganas de bailar : I feel like dancing⟩ **7 morirse de ganas de hacer algo** : to be dying to do something **8 ponerle ganas a algo** : to put effort into something **9 quedarse con las ganas (de hacer algo)** : to end up not doing something

ganadería *nf* **1** : cattle raising **2** : cattle ranch **3** GANADO : cattle *pl*, livestock
ganadero¹, -ra *adj* : cattle, ranching
ganadero², -ra *n* : rancher
ganado *nm* **1** : cattle *pl*, livestock **2 ganado ovino** : sheep *pl* **3 ganado porcino** : swine *pl*
ganador¹, -dora *adj* : winning
ganador², -dora *n* : winner
ganancia *nf* **1** : profit **2 ganancias** *nfpl* : winnings, gains
ganancioso, -sa *adj* : profitable
ganar *vt* **1** : to win **2** : to gain ⟨ganar tiempo : to buy time⟩ **3** : to earn ⟨ganar dinero : to make money⟩ **4** : to acquire, to obtain — *vi* **1** : to win **2** : to profit ⟨salir ganando : to come out ahead⟩ — **ganarse** *vr* **1** : to gain, to win ⟨ganarse a alguien : to win someone over⟩ **2** : to earn ⟨ganarse la vida : to make a living⟩ **3** : to deserve
ganchillo *nm* : crochet hook
gancho *nm* **1** : hook **2** : clothes hanger **3** : hairpin, bobby pin **4** *Col* : safety pin
gandul¹ *nm CA, Car, Col* : pigeon pea
gandul², -dula *n fam* : idler, lazybones
gandulear *vi* : to idle, to loaf, to lounge about
ganga *nf* : bargain
ganglio *nm* **1** : ganglion **2** : gland
gangrena *nf* : gangrene — **gangrenoso, -sa** *adj*
gángster *nmf, pl* **gángsters** : gangster
gansada *nf* : silly thing, nonsense
ganso, -sa *n* **1** : goose, gander *m* **2** : idiot, fool
gañido *nm* : yelp (of a dog)
gañir {38} *vi* : to yelp
garabatear *v* : to scribble, to scrawl, to doodle
garabato *nm* **1** : doodle **2 garabatos** *nmpl* : scribble, scrawl
garaje *nm* : garage
garante *nmf* : guarantor
garantía *nf* **1** : guarantee, warranty **2** : security ⟨garantía de trabajo : job security⟩
garantizar {21} *vt* : to guarantee
garapiña *nf* : pineapple drink
garapiñar *vt* : to candy
garbanzo *nm* : chickpea
garbo *nm* **1** DONAIRE : grace, poise **2** : jauntiness
garboso, -sa *adj* **1** : graceful **2** : elegant, stylish
garceta *nf* : egret
gardenia *nf* : gardenia
garfio *nm* : hook, gaff
gargajo *nm fam* : phlegm
garganta *nf* **1** : throat **2** : neck (of a person or a bottle) **3** : ravine, narrow pass
gargantilla *nf* : choker, necklace
gárgara *nf* **1** : gargle, gargling **2 hacer gárgaras** : to gargle
gargarizar *vi* : to gargle
gárgola *nf* : gargoyle
garita *nf* **1** : cabin, hut **2** : sentry box, lookout post
garito *nm* : gambling hall

garoso, -sa *adj Col, Ven* : gluttonous, greedy
garra *nf* 1 : claw 2 : hand, paw 3 **garras** *nfpl* : claws, clutches ⟨caer en las garras de alguien : to fall into someone's clutches⟩
garrafa *nf* : decanter, carafe
garrafal *adj* : terrible, monstrous
garrafón *nm, pl* **-fones** : large decanter, large bottle
garrapata *nf* : tick
garrobo *nm CA* : large lizard, iguana
garrocha *nf* 1 : lance, pike 2 : pole ⟨salto con/de garrocha : pole vault⟩
garrotazo *nm* : blow (with a club)
garrote *nm* 1 : club, stick 2 *Mex* : brake
garúa *nf* : drizzle
garuar {3} *v impers* LLOVIZNAR : to drizzle
garza *nf* : heron
garzón, -zona *n, mpl* **-zones** *Chile* : waiter *m*, waitress *f*
gas *nm* : gas, vapor, fumes *pl* ⟨gas lacrimógeno : tear gas⟩
gasa *nf* : gauze
gasear *vt* 1 : to gas 2 : to aerate (a liquid)
gaseosa *nf* REFRESCO : soda, soft drink
gaseoso, -sa *adj* 1 : gaseous 2 : carbonated, fizzy
gasfitería *nf Chile, Peru* : plumbing
gasfitero, -ra *n Chile, Peru* : plumber
gasoducto *nm* : gas pipeline
gasoil *nm* : diesel oil, fuel oil
gasóleo → **gasoil**
gasolina *nf* : gasoline, gas
gasolinera *nf* : gas station, service station
gastado, -da *adj* 1 : spent 2 : worn, worn-out
gastador[1], -dora *adj* : extravagant, spendthrift
gastador[2], -dora *n* : spendthrift
gastar *vt* 1 : to spend 2 CONSUMIR : to consume, to use up 3 : to squander, to waste 4 : to wear ⟨gasta un bigote : he sports a mustache⟩ — **gastarse** *vr* 1 : to spend, to expend 2 : to run down, to wear out
gasto *nm* 1 : expense, expenditure 2 DETERIORO : wear 3 **gastos fijos/generales/indirectos** : overhead 4 **cubrir gastos** : to cover costs, to break even 5 **gastos de seguro** : insurance costs 6 **gastos de la casa** : household expenses 7 **gastos de viaje** : travel expenses 8 **gastos de envío** : shipping and handling 9 **gasto público** : public spending
gástrico, -ca *adj* : gastric
gastronomía *nf* : gastronomy
gastronómico, -ca *adj* : gastronomic
gastrónomo, -ma *n* : gourmet
gatas *adv* **andar a gatas** : to crawl, to go on all fours
gatear *vi* 1 : to crawl 2 : to climb, to clamber (up)
gatillero *nm Mex* : gunman
gatillo *nm* : trigger
gatito, -ta *n* : kitten
gato[1], -ta *n* 1 : cat ⟨gato manchado : calico cat⟩ ⟨gato montés : wildcat⟩ 2

(aquí) **hay gato encerrado** : there's something fishy going on (here) 3 **dar gato por liebre a alguien** : to swindle someone 4 **llevarse el gato al agua** : to pull it off, to manage it
gato[2] *nm* : jack (for an automobile)
gauchada *nf Arg, Uru* : favor, kindness
gaucho *nm* : gaucho
gaveta *nf* 1 CAJÓN : drawer 2 : till
gavilán *nm, pl* **-lanes** : sparrow hawk
gavilla *nf* 1 : gang, band 2 : sheaf
gaviota *nf* : gull, seagull
gay ['ge, 'gai] *adj* : gay (homosexual)
gaza *nf* : loop
gazapo *nm* 1 : young rabbit 2 : misprint, error
gazmoñería *nf* MOJIGATERÍA : prudery, primness
gazmoño[1], -ña *adj* : prudish, prim
gazmoño[2], -ña *n* MOJIGATO : prude, prig
gaznate *nm* : throat, gullet
gazpacho *nm* : gazpacho
ge *nf* : (letter) g
géiser *or* **géyser** *nm* : geyser
gel *nm* : gel
gelatina *nf* : gelatin
gélido, -da *adj* : icy, freezing cold
gelificarse *vr* : to jell
gema *nf* : gem
gemelo[1], -la *adj & n* MELLIZO : twin
gemelo[2] *nm* 1 : cuff link 2 **gemelos** *nmpl* BINOCULARES : binoculars
gemido *nm* : moan, groan, wail
Géminis[1] *nm* : Gemini (sign or constellation)
Géminis[2] *nmf* : Gemini (person)
gemir {54} *vi* : to moan, to groan, to wail
gen *or* **gene** *nm* : gene
gendarme *nmf* POLICÍA : police officer, policeman *m*, policewoman *f*
gendarmería *nf* : police
genealogía *nf* : genealogy
genealógico, -ca *adj* : genealogical
generación *nf, pl* **-ciones** 1 : generation ⟨tercera generación : third generation⟩ 2 : generating, creating 3 : class ⟨la generación del '97 : the class of '97⟩
generacional *adj* : generation, generational
generador *nm* : generator
general[1] *adj* 1 : general 2 **en ∼** *or* **por lo general** : in general, generally
general[2] *nmf* 1 : general 2 **general de división** : major general
generalidad *nf* 1 : generality, generalization 2 : majority
generalización *nf, pl* **-ciones** 1 : generalization 2 : escalation, spread
generalizado, -da *adj* : generalized, widespread
generalizar {21} *vi* : to generalize — *vt* : to spread, to spread out — **generalizarse** *vr* : to become widespread
generalmente *adv* : usually, generally
generar *vt* : to generate — **generarse** *vr*
genérico, -ca *adj* : generic
género *nm* 1 : genre, class, kind ⟨el género humano : the human race, mankind⟩ 2 : gender (in grammar) 3 : gender (of a person) ⟨identidad de género

: gender identity⟩ **4 géneros** *nmpl*
: goods, commodities **5 de género neutro** : gender-neutral
generosidad *nf* : generosity
generoso, -sa *adj* **1** : generous, unselfish **2** : ample — **generosamente** *adv*
genética *nf* : genetics
genético, -ca *adj* : genetic — **genéticamente** *adv*
genetista *nmf* : geneticist
genial *adj* **1** AGRADABLE : genial, pleasant **2** : brilliant ⟨una obra genial : a work of genius⟩ **3** *fam* FORMIDABLE : fantastic, terrific
genialidad *nf* **1** : genius **2** : stroke of genius **3** : eccentricity
genio *nm* **1** : genius **2** : temper, disposition ⟨de mal genio : bad-tempered⟩ **3** : genie
genital *adj* : genital
genitales *nmpl* : genitals
genocidio *nm* : genocide
gente *nf* **1** : people **2** : relatives *pl*, folks *pl* **3 gente menuda** *fam* : children, kids *pl* **4 ser buena gente** : to be nice, to be kind
gentil[1] *adj* **1** AMABLE : kind **2** : gentile
gentil[2] *nmf* : gentile
gentileza *nf* **1** AMABILIDAD : kindness **2** CORTESÍA : courtesy
gentilicio, -cia *adj* **1** : national, tribal **2** : family
gentilmente *adv* : kindly
gentío *nm* MUCHEDUMBRE, MULTITUD : crowd, mob
gentuza *nf* CHUSMA : riffraff, rabble
genuflexión *nf, pl* **-xiones** **1** : genuflection **2 hacer una genuflexión** : to genuflect
genuino, -na *adj* : genuine — **genuinamente** *adv*
geografía *nf* : geography
geográfico, -ca *adj* : geographic, geographical — **geográficamente** *adv*
geógrafo, -fa *n* : geographer
geología *nf* : geology
geológico, -ca *adj* : geologic, geological — **geológicamente** *adv*
geólogo, -ga *n* : geologist
geometría *nf* : geometry
geométrico, -ca *adj* : geometric, geometrical — **geométricamente** *adv*
geopolítico, -ca *adj* : geopolitical
georgiano, -na *adj & n* : Georgian
geranio *nm* : geranium
gerbo *nm* : gerbil
gerencia *nf* : management, administration
gerencial *adj* : managerial
gerente *nmf* : manager, director
geriatría *nf* : geriatrics
geriátrico, -ca *adj* : geriatric
germanio *nm* : germanium
germano, -na *adj* : Germanic, German
germen *nm, pl* **gérmenes** : germ
germicida *nf* : germicide
germinación *nf, pl* **-ciones** : germination
germinar *vi* : to germinate, to sprout
gerundio *nm* : gerund
gesta *nf* : deed, exploit

gestación *nf, pl* **-ciones** : gestation
gesticular *vi* : to gesticulate — **gesticulación** *nf*
gestión *nf, pl* **gestiones** **1** TRÁMITE : procedure, step **2** ADMINISTRACIÓN : management **3 gestiones** *nfpl* : negotiations **4 gestión de datos** : data management
gestionar *vt* **1** : to negotiate, to work towards **2** ADMINISTRAR : to manage, to handle
gesto *nm* **1** ADEMÁN : gesture **2** : facial expression **3** MUECA : grimace
gestor[1]**, -tora** *adj* : facilitating, negotiating, managing
gestor[2]**, -tora** *n* : facilitator, manager
géyser → **géiser**
ghanés, -nesa *adj & n, mpl* **ghaneses** : Ghanaian
ghetto → **gueto**
giba *nf* **1** : hump (of an animal) **2** : person with a hump, hunchback *offensive*, humpback *offensive*
gibón *nm, pl* **gibones** : gibbon
giboso[1]**, -sa** *adj* : hunchbacked, humpbacked
giboso[2]**, -sa** *n* : person with a hump, hunchback *offensive*, humpback *offensive*
giga[1] *nf* : jig
giga[2] *nmf fam* : gig, gigabyte
gigabyte *nm* : gigabyte
gigante[1] *adj* : giant, gigantic
gigante[2]**, -ta** *n* : giant
gigantesco, -ca *adj* : gigantic, huge
gime, etc. → **gemir**
gimnasia *nf* : gymnastics
gimnasio *nm* : gymnasium, gym
gimnasta *nmf* : gymnast
gimnástico, -ca *adj* : gymnastic
gimotear *vi* LLORIQUEAR : to whine, to whimper
gimoteo *nm* : whimpering
ginebra *nf* : gin
ginecología *nf* : gynecology
ginecológico, -ca *adj* : gynecologic, gynecological
ginecólogo, -ga *n* : gynecologist
ginseng *nm* : ginseng
gira *nf* : tour
giralda *nf* : weather vane
girar *vi* **1** : to turn around, to revolve **2** : to swing around, to swivel — *vt* **1** : to turn, to twist, to rotate **2** : to draft (checks) **3** : to transfer (funds)
girasol *nm* MIRASOL : sunflower
giratorio, -ria *adj* : revolving
giro *nm* **1** VUELTA : turn, rotation **2** : change of direction ⟨giro de 180 grados, giro en U : U-turn, about-face⟩ **3 giro bancario** : bank draft **4 giro postal** : money order
giroscopio *or* **giróscopo** *nm* : gyroscope
gis *nm Mex* : chalk
gitano, -na *adj & n* : Gypsy *sometimes offensive*
glacial *adj* : glacial, icy — **glacialmente** *adv*
glaciar *nm* : glacier
gladiador *nm* : gladiator

gladiolo *or* **gladíolo** *nm* : gladiolus
glamping ['glampin] *nm fam* : glamping
glándula *nf* : gland — **glandular** *adj*
glaseado *nm* : glaze, icing
glasear *vt* : to glaze
glaucoma *nm* : glaucoma
glena *nf* : socket
glicerina *nf* : glycerin
glicinia *nf* : wisteria
global *adj* 1 : global, worldwide 2 : full, comprehensive 3 : total, overall
globalizar {21} *vt* 1 ABARCAR : to include, to encompass 2 : to extend worldwide — **globalización** *nf*
globalmente *adv* : globally, as a whole
globo *nm* 1 : globe, sphere 2 : balloon 3 **globo ocular** : eyeball
glóbulo *nm* 1 : globule 2 : blood cell, corpuscle
gloria *nf* 1 : glory 2 : fame, renown 3 : delight, enjoyment 4 : star, legend ⟨las glorias del cine : the great names in motion pictures⟩
glorieta *nf* 1 : rotary, traffic circle 2 : bower, arbor 3 : gazebo
glorificar {72} *vt* ALABAR : to glorify — **glorificación** *nf*
glorioso, -sa *adj* : glorious — **gloriosamente** *adv*
glosa *nf* 1 : gloss 2 : annotation, commentary
glosar *vt* 1 : to gloss 2 : to annotate, to comment on (a text)
glosario *nm* : glossary
glotón¹, -tona *adj, mpl* **glotones** : gluttonous
glotón², -tona *n, mpl* **glotones** : glutton
glotón³ *nm, pl* **glotones** : wolverine
glotonería *nf* GULA : gluttony
glucosa *nf* : glucose
glutinoso, -sa *adj* : glutinous
gnomo ['nomo] *nm* : gnome
gobernación *nf, pl* **-ciones** : governing, government
gobernador, -dora *n* : governor
gobernante¹ *adj* : ruling, governing
gobernante² *nmf* : ruler, leader, governor
gobernar {55} *vt* 1 : to govern, to rule 2 : to steer, to sail (a ship) — *vi* 1 : to govern 2 : to steer
gobierno *nm* : government
goce¹, etc. → **gozar**
goce² *nm* 1 PLACER : enjoyment, pleasure 2 : use, possession
gol *nm* : goal (in soccer)
goleada *nf* : rout, defeat (in sports)
goleador, -dora *n* : scorer (of goals) ⟨el máximo goleador del equipo : the team's top scorer⟩
golear *vt* 1 : to rout, to score many goals against (in soccer)
goleta *nf* : schooner
golf *nm* : golf
golfista *nmf* : golfer
golfo *nm* : gulf, bay
golondrina *nf* 1 : swallow (bird) 2 **golondrina de mar** : tern
golosina *nf* : sweet, snack
goloso, -sa *adj* : fond of sweets ⟨ser goloso : to have a sweet tooth⟩

golpazo *nm* : heavy blow, bang, thump
golpe *nm* 1 : blow ⟨caerle/cogerle a golpes a alguien : to give someone a beating⟩ ⟨darse un golpe en la cabeza : to hit one's head⟩ 2 : knock 3 : job, heist ⟨dar el golpe : to do the job⟩ 4 **de ~** : suddenly 5 **de un golpe** : all at once, in one fell swoop 6 **golpe de estado** : coup, coup d'etat 7 **golpe de gracia** : coup de grâce 8 **golpe de suerte** : stroke of luck 9 **golpe de viento** : gust of wind 10 **no dar/pegar (ni) golpe** : not to lift a finger, not to do a bit of work
golpeado, -da *adj* 1 : beaten, hit 2 : bruised (of fruit) 3 : dented
golpear *vt* 1 : to beat (up), to hit 2 : to slam, to bang, to strike — *vi* 1 : to knock (at a door) 2 : to beat ⟨la lluvia golpeaba contra el tejado : the rain beat against the roof⟩ — **golpearse** *vr*
golpetear *v* : to knock, to rattle, to tap
golpeteo *nm* : banging, knocking, tapping
golpista¹ *adj* 1 : coup, coup-related ⟨intentona golpista : attempted coup, coup attempt⟩ 2 : pro-coup
golpista² *mf* 1 : coup supporter 2 : military insurgent
golpiza *nf* : beating, pummeling
goma *nf* 1 : gum ⟨goma de mascar : chewing gum⟩ ⟨goma de pegar : glue⟩ 2 CAUCHO : rubber ⟨goma espuma : foam rubber⟩ **goma** : glue 4 : rubber band 5 *Arg* : tire 6 *or* **goma de borrar** : eraser 6 *CA fam* : hangover
gomina *nf* : hair gel
gomita *nf* : rubber band
gomoso, -sa *adj* : gummy, sticky
góndola *nf* : gondola
gong *nm* : gong
gonorrea *nf* : gonorrhea
googlear [gugle'ar] *vt* (*Google*, marca registrada) : to google
gorda *nf Mex* : thick corn tortilla
gordinflón¹, -flona *adj, mpl* **-flones** *fam* : chubby, pudgy
gordinflón², -flona *n, mpl* **-flones** *fam* : chubby person
gordo¹, -da *adj* 1 : fat 2 : thick 3 : fatty, greasy, oily 4 : unpleasant ⟨me cae gorda tu tía : I can't stand your aunt⟩
gordo², -da *n* : fat person
gordo³ *nm* 1 GRASA : fat 2 : jackpot
gordura *nf* : fatness, flab
gorgojo *nm* : weevil
gorgorito *nm* : trill
gorgotear *vi* : to gurgle, to bubble
gorgoteo *nm* : gurgle
gorila *nm* 1 : gorilla 2 *Spain fam* : bouncer
gorjear *vi* 1 : to chirp, to tweet, to warble 2 : to gurgle
gorjeo *nm* 1 : chirping, warbling 2 : gurgling
gorra *nf* 1 : bonnet 2 : cap 3 **de ~** *fam* : for free, at someone else's expense ⟨vivir de gorra : to sponge, to freeload⟩
gorrear *vt fam* : to bum, to scrounge — *vi fam* : to freeload

gorrero, -ra *n fam* : freeloader, sponger
gorrión *nm, pl* **gorriones** : sparrow
gorro *nm* **1** : cap ⟨gorro de ducha : shower cap⟩ **2 estar hasta el gorro** : to be fed up
gorrón, -rrona *n, mpl* **gorrones** *fam* : freeloader, scrounger
gorronear *vt fam* : to bum, to scrounge — *vi fam* : to freeload
gota *nf* **1** : drop ⟨una gota de sudor : a bead of sweat⟩ ⟨como dos gotas de agua : like two peas in a pod⟩ ⟨sudar la gota gorda : to sweat buckets, to work very hard⟩ **2** : gout
gotear *v* **1** : to drip **2** : to leak — *v impers* LLOVIZNAR : to drizzle
goteo *nm* : drip, dripping
gotera *nf* **1** : leak **2** : stain (from dripping water)
gotero *nm* : (medicine) dropper
gótico, -ca *adj* : Gothic
gourmet *nmf* : gourmet
gozar {21} *vi* **1** : to enjoy oneself, to have a good time **2** ~ **de** : to enjoy, to have, to possess ⟨gozar de buena salud : to enjoy good health⟩ **3** ~ **con** : to take delight in
gozne *nm* BISAGRA : hinge
gozo *nm* **1** : joy **2** PLACER : enjoyment, pleasure
gozoso, -sa *adj* : joyful
GPS [hepeˈese] *nm, pl* **GPS** : GPS
grabación *nf, pl* **-ciones** : recording
grabado *nm* **1** : engraving **2 grabado al aguafuerte** : etching
grabador, -dora *n* **1** : engraver **2** → **grabadora**
grabadora *nf* : recorder, tape recorder ⟨grabadora de DVD : DVD recorder⟩
grabar *vt* **1** : to engrave **2** : to record, to tape — *vi* **grabar al aguafuerte** : to etch — **grabarse** *vr* **grabársele a alguien en la memoria** : to become engraved on someone's mind
gracia *nf* **1** : grace ⟨lo hizo con gracia : she did it gracefully⟩ ⟨una casa con mucha gracia : a very stylish/elegant house⟩ **2** : favor, kindness ⟨por la gracia de Dios : by the grace of God⟩ **3** : humor, wit ⟨su comentario no me hizo gracia : I wasn't amused by his remark⟩ ⟨tener gracia : to be funny⟩ **4** : grace, respite ⟨una semana de gracia : a week's grace⟩ ⟨período de gracia : grace period⟩ **5 gracias** *nfpl* : thanks ⟨¡gracias! : thank you!⟩ ⟨dar gracias : to give thanks⟩
grácil *adj* **1** : graceful **2** : delicate, slender, fine
gracilidad *nm* : gracefulness
gracioso, -sa *adj* **1** CHISTOSO : funny, amusing **2** : cute, attractive
grada *nf* **1** : harrow **2** PELDAÑO : step, stair **3 gradas** *nfpl* : bleachers, grandstand
gradación *nf, pl* **-ciones** : gradation, scale
gradar *vt* : to harrow, to hoe
gradería *nf* : tiers *pl*, stands *pl*, rows *pl* (in a theater)
gradiente *nf* : gradient, slope

grado *nm* **1** : degree (in meteorology and mathematics) ⟨grado centígrado : degree centigrade⟩ **2** : extent, level, degree ⟨en grado sumo : greatly, to the highest degree⟩ **3** RANGO : rank **4** : year, class (in education) **5 de buen grado** : willingly, readily
graduable *adj* : adjustable
graduación *nf, pl* **-ciones** **1** : graduation (from a school) **2** GRADO : rank **3** : alcohol content, proof
graduado¹, -da *adj* **1** : graduated **2 lentes graduados** : prescription lenses
graduado², -da *n* : graduate
gradual *adj* : gradual — **gradualmente** *adv*
graduar {3} *v* **1** : to regulate, to adjust **2** CALIBRAR : to calibrate, to gauge — **graduarse** *vr* : to graduate (from a school)
graffiti *or* **grafiti** *nmpl* : graffiti *pl*
gráfica *nf* → **gráfico²**
gráfico¹, -ca *adj* : graphic — **gráficamente** *adv*
gráfico² *nm* **1** : graph, chart **2** : graphic (for a computer, etc.) **3 gráfico de barras** : bar graph
grafismo *nm* : graphics *pl*
grafito *nm* : graphite
gragea *nf* **1** : coated pill or tablet **2 grageas** *nfpl* : sprinkles, jimmies
grajo *nm* : rook (bird)
grama *nf* : grass
gramática *nf* : grammar
gramatical *adj* : grammatical — **gramaticalmente** *adv*
gramilla *f* : crabgrass
gramo *nm* : gram
gran → **grande**
grana *nf* : scarlet, deep red
granada *nf* **1** : pomegranate **2** : grenade ⟨granada de mano : hand grenade⟩
granaderos *nmpl Mex* : riot squad
granadino, -na *adj* & *n* : Grenadian
granado, -da *adj* **1** DISTINGUIDO : distinguished **2** : choice, select
granate *nm* **1** : garnet **2** : deep red, maroon
grande *adj* (**gran** *before singular nouns*) **1** : large, big ⟨un libro grande : a big book⟩ ⟨un grupo grande : a large group⟩ ⟨grandes cantidades : large quantities⟩ ⟨grandes corporaciones : big corporations⟩ ⟨esta camisa me queda grande : this shirt's (too) big on me⟩ **2** ALTO : tall ⟨¡qué grande estás! : look how much you've grown!⟩ **3** NOTABLE : great ⟨un gran autor : a great writer⟩ **4** (*indicating significance*) : big ⟨un gran error : a big mistake⟩ ⟨su gran oportunidad : his big chance⟩ **5** (*indicating degree*) : great, big ⟨con gran placer : with great pleasure⟩ ⟨un gran éxito : a big/great success⟩ ⟨a gran velocidad : at great speed⟩ ⟨grandes amigos : great friends⟩ ⟨un gran admirador : a great/big admirer, a big fan⟩ **6** : old, grown-up, big ⟨hijos grandes : grown children⟩ ⟨ya eres (una niña/un niño) grande

: you're a big girl/boy now⟩ **7 a lo grande** : in style
grandeza *nf* **1** MAGNITUD : greatness, size **2** : nobility **3** : generosity, graciousness **4** : grandeur, magnificence
grandilocuencia *nf* : bombast
grandilocuente *adj* : bombastic
grandiosidad *nf* : grandeur
grandioso, -sa *adj* **1** MAGNÍFICO : grand, magnificent **2** : grandiose
granel *adv* **1 a** ~ : galore, in great quantities **2 a** ~ : in bulk ⟨vender a granel : to sell in bulk⟩
granero *nm* : barn, granary
granito *nm* : granite
granizada *nf* : hailstorm
granizado *nm* : drink made with crushed ice
granizar {21} *v impers* : to hail
granizo *nm* : hail
granja *nf* : farm
granjear *vt* : to earn, to win — **granjearse** *vr* : to gain, to earn
granjero, -ra *n* : farmer
grano *nm* **1** PARTÍCULA : grain, particle ⟨un grano de arena : a grain of sand⟩ **2** : grain (of rice, etc.), bean (of coffee), seed **3** : grain (of wood or rock) **4** BARRO, ESPINILLA : pimple **5 apartar el grano de la paja** *fam* : to separate the wheat from the chaff **6 ir al grano** : to get to the point
granoso, -sa *adj* : grainy
granuja *nmf* PILLUELO : rascal, urchin
granular *adj* : granular, grainy
granularse *vr* : to break out in spots
granuloso, -sa → **granular**
granza *nf* : chaff
grapa *nf* **1** : staple **2** : clamp
grapadora *nf* ENGRAPADORA : stapler
grapar *vt* ENGRAPAR : to staple
grasa *nf* **1** : grease **2** : fat **3** *Mex* : shoe polish
grasiento, -ta *adj* : greasy, oily
graso, -sa *adj* **1** : fatty **2** : greasy, oily
grasoso, -sa *adj* GRASIENTO : greasy, oily
gratificación *nf, pl* **-ciones** **1** SATISFACCIÓN : gratification **2** : bonus **3** RECOMPENSA : recompense, reward
gratificante *adj* : satisfying, gratifying
gratificar {72} *vt* **1** SATISFACER : to satisfy, to gratify **2** RECOMPENSAR : to reward **3** : to give a bonus to
gratinado, -da *adj* : au gratin
gratis[1] *adv* GRATUITAMENTE : free, for free, gratis
gratis[2] *adj* GRATUITO : free, gratis
gratitud *nf* : gratitude
grato, -ta *adj* AGRADABLE, PLACENTERO : pleasant, agreeable — **gratamente** *adv*
gratuitamente *adv* **1** : gratuitously **2** GRATIS : free, for free, gratis
gratuito, -ta *adj* **1** : gratuitous, unwarranted **2** GRATIS : free, gratis
grava *nf* : gravel
gravamen *nm, pl* **-vámenes** **1** : burden, obligation **2** : (property) tax
gravar *vt* **1** : to burden, to encumber **2** : to levy (a tax)

grave *adj* **1** : grave, important **2** : serious, somber **3** : serious (of an illness)
gravedad *nf* **1** : gravity ⟨centro de gravedad : center of gravity⟩ **2** : seriousness, severity, gravity
gravemente *adv* : gravely, seriously
gravilla *nf* : (fine) gravel
gravitación *nf, pl* **-ciones** : gravitation
gravitacional *adj* : gravitational
gravitar *vi* **1** : to gravitate **2** ~ **sobre** : to rest on **3** ~ **sobre** : to loom over
gravoso, -sa *adj* **1** ONEROSO : burdensome, onerous **2** : costly
graznar *vi* : to caw, to honk, to quack, to squawk
graznido *nm* : cawing, honking, quacking, squawking
gregario, -ria *adj* : gregarious
gremial *adj* SINDICAL : union, labor
gremialista *nmf* : union supporter
gremio *nm* SINDICATO : union, guild
greña *nf* **1** : mat, tangle **2 greñas** *nfpl* MELENAS : shaggy hair, mop
greñudo, -da *n* HIPPIE, MELENUDO : hippie
gresca *nf fam* : fight, ruckus
grey *nf* : congregation, flock
griego[1]**, -ga** *adj & n* : Greek
griego[2] *nm* : Greek (language)
grieta *nf* : crack, crevice
grifo *nm* **1** : faucet ⟨agua del grifo : tap water⟩ **2** *Peru* : gas station
grillete *nm* : shackle
grillo *nm* **1** : cricket **2 grillos** *nmpl* : fetters, shackles
grima *nf* **1** : disgust, uneasiness **2 darle grima a alguien** : to get on someone's nerves
gringo, -ga *adj & n often disparaging* YANQUI : Yankee, gringo *often disparaging*
gripa *nf Col, Mex* : flu
gripe *nf* : flu
gris *adj* **1** : gray **2** : overcast, cloudy
grisáceo, -cea *adj* : grayish
grisín *nm, pl* **grisines** *Arg, Uru* : breadstick
gritar *v* : to shout, to scream, to cry
gritería *nf* : shouting, clamor
grito *nm* **1** : shout, scream, cry ⟨a grito pelado : at the top of one's voice⟩ **2 ser el último grito** : to be the latest fashion
groenlandés, -desa *adj & n* : Greenlander
grogui *adj fam* : dazed, groggy
grosella *nf* **1** : currant **2 grosella espinosa** : gooseberry
grosería *nf* **1** : insult, coarse language **2** : rudeness, discourtesy
grosero[1]**, -ra** *adj* **1** : rude, fresh **2** : coarse, vulgar — **groseramente** *adv*
grosero[2]**, -ra** *n* : rude person
grosor *nm* : thickness
grosso *adj* **a grosso modo** : roughly, broadly, approximately
grotesco, -ca *adj* : grotesque, hideous
grúa *nf* **1** : crane (machine) **2** : tow truck
gruesa *nf* : gross
grueso[1]**, -sa** *adj* **1** : thick, bulky **2** : heavy, big **3** : stout
grueso[2] *nm* **1** : thickness **2** : main body, mass **3 en** ~ : in bulk

grulla *nf* : crane (bird)
grumo *nm* : lump, glob
gruñido *nm* : growl, grunt
gruñir {38} *vi* **1** : to growl, to grunt **2** : to grumble
gruñón[1], **-ñona** *adj, mpl* **gruñones** *fam* : grumpy, crabby
gruñón[2], **-ñona** *n, mpl* **gruñones** *fam* : grumpy person, nag
grupa *nf* : rump, hindquarters *pl*
grupo *nm* : group
gruta *nf* : grotto, cave
guacal *nm Col, Mex, Ven* : crate
guacamayo *nm* : macaw
guacamole *or* **guacamol** *nm* : guacamole
guacamote *nm Mex* : manioc, cassava
guachimán *nm, pl* **-manes** *fam* : watchman
guachinango → **huachinango**
guacho, -cha *adj* **1** *Arg, Col, Chile, Peru* : orphaned **2** *Chile, Peru* : odd (of a shoe, glove, etc.)
guadaña *nf* : scythe
guagua *nf* **1** *Arg, Col, Chile, Peru* : baby **2** *Cuba, PRi* : bus
guaira *nf* **1** *CA* : traditional flute **2** *Peru* : smelting furnace
guajiro, -ra *n Cuba* : peasant
guajolote *nm Mex* : turkey
guanábana *nf* : soursop (fruit)
guanaco *nm* : guanaco (South American mammal)
guandú *nm, pl* **guandú** *or* **guandúes** *CA, Car, Col* : pigeon pea
guango, -ga *adj Mex* **1** : loose-fitting, baggy **2** : slack, loose
guano *nm* : guano
guante *nm* **1** : glove ⟨guante de boxeo : boxing glove⟩ **2 arrojarle el guante (a alguien)** : to throw down the gauntlet (to someone)
guantelete *nm* : gauntlet
guantera *nf* : glove compartment
guapo, -pa *adj* **1** : handsome, good-looking, attractive **2** : elegant, smart **3** *fam* : bold, dashing
guarache → **huarache**
guarachear *vi Cuba, PRi fam* : to go on a spree, to go out on the town
guarangada *nf Arg, Uru fam* : rude or insulting remark
guaraní[1] *nmf, pl* **-níes** : Guarani (person) — **guaraní** *adj*
guaraní[2] *nm* **1** : Guarani (language of Paraguay) **2** : guarani (Paraguayan unit of currency)
guarda *nmf* **1** GUARDIÁN : security guard **2** : keeper, custodian
guardabarros *nms & pl* : fender, mudguard
guardabosque *nmf* : forest ranger, gamekeeper
guardacostas[1] *nmfs & pl* : member of the coast guard
guardacostas[2] *nms & pl* : coast guard vessel
guardaespaldas *nmfs & pl* : bodyguard
guardafangos *nms & pl* : fender
guardameta *nmf* ARQUERO, PORTERO : goalkeeper, goalie
guardapelo *nm* : locket

guardapolvo *nm* **1** : dustcover **2** : duster, housecoat
guardar *vt* **1** : to guard **2** : to maintain, to preserve **3** CONSERVAR : to put away **4** RESERVAR : to save **5** : to keep (a secret or promise) — **guardarse** *vr* **1 ~ de** : to refrain from **2 ~ de** : to guard against, to be careful not to
guardarropa *nm* **1** : coat check **2** ARMARIO : closet, wardrobe
guardavallas *nmf* : goalkeeper
guardería *nf* : nursery, day-care center
guardia[1] *nf* **1** : guard, defense **2** : guard duty, watch **3 en ~** : on guard
guardia[2] *nmf* **1** : sentry, guard **2** : police officer, policeman *m*, policewoman *f*
guardiamarina *nmf* : midshipman
guardián, -diana *n, mpl* **guardianes 1** GUARDA : security guard, watchman **2** : guardian, keeper **3 perro guardián** : watchdog
guarecer {53} *vt* : to shelter, to protect — **guarecerse** *vr* : to take shelter
guarida *nf* **1** : den, lair **2** : hideout
guarismo *nm* : figure, numeral
guarnecer {53} *vt* **1** : to adorn **2** : to garnish **3** : to garrison
guarnición *nf, pl* **-ciones 1** : garnish **2** : garrison **3** : decoration, trimming, setting (of a jewel)
guaro *nm CA* : liquor distilled from sugarcane
guarrada *nf Spain fam* **1** : filthy mess **2** : dirty trick **3 decir guarradas** : to say filthy/disgusting things, to be vulgar
guarro[1], **-rra** *adj Spain fam* : dirty, filthy
guarro[2], **-rra** *n Spain fam* : filthy, disgusting, or vulgar person
guarura *nm Mex fam* : bodyguard
guasa *nf fam* **1** : joking, fooling around **2 de ~** : in jest, as a joke
guasón[1], **-sona** *adj, mpl* **guasones** *fam* : funny, witty
guasón[2], **-sona** *n, mpl* **guasones** *fam* : joker, clown
guatemalteco, -ca *adj & n* : Guatemalan
guau *interj* : wow!
guay *adj Spain fam* : cool, neat, great
guayaba *nf* : guava (fruit)
guayín *nm, pl* **guayines** *Mex* : station wagon
gubernamental *adj* : governmental
gubernativo, -va → **gubernamental**
gubernatura *nf Mex* : governing body
guepardo *nm* : cheetah
güero, -ra *adj Mex* : blond, fair
guerra *nf* **1** : war ⟨declarar la guerra : to declare war⟩ ⟨estar en guerra : to be at war⟩ ⟨guerra sin cuartel : all-out war⟩ ⟨guerra civil/nuclear : civil/nuclear war⟩ ⟨hacer la guerra : to wage war⟩ **2** : warfare ⟨guerra de guerrillas : guerrilla warfare⟩ ⟨guerra biológica : biological warfare⟩ **3** LUCHA : conflict, struggle ⟨guerra a muerte : fight to the death⟩ **4 dar guerra** *fam* : to be annoying, to cause trouble
guerrear *vi* : to wage war
guerrero[1], **-ra** *adj* **1** : war, fighting **2** : warlike
guerrero[2], **-ra** *n* : warrior

guerrilla *nf* : guerrilla warfare
guerrillero, -ra *adj & n* : guerrilla
gueto *nm* : ghetto
guía[1] *nf* **1** : directory, guidebook **2** ORIENTACIÓN : guidance, direction ⟨la conciencia me sirve como guía : conscience is my guide⟩
guía[2] *nmf* : guide, leader ⟨guía de turismo : tour guide⟩
guiar {85} *vt* **1** : to guide, to lead **2** CONDUCIR : to manage — **guiarse** *vr* : to be guided by, to go by
guija *nf* : pebble
guijarro *nm* : pebble
guillotina *nf* : guillotine — **guillotinar** *vt*
guinda[1] *adj & nm Mex* : maroon (color)
guinda[2] *nf* : morello (cherry)
guindilla *nf* : chili
guineo *nm Car* : banana
guinga *nf* : gingham
guiñada → **guiño**
guiñar *vi* : to wink
guiño *nm* : wink
guiñol *nm* : puppet theater
guión *nm, pl* **guiones** **1** : script, screenplay **2** : hyphen, dash **3** ESTANDARTE : standard, banner
guionista *nmf* : scriptwriter
guirnalda *nf* : garland
guisa *nf* **1** : manner, fashion **2 a guisa de** : like, by way of **3 de tal guisa** : in such a way
guisado ESTOFADO *nm* : stew
guisante *nm* : pea
guisar *vt* **1** ESTOFAR : to stew **2** *Spain* : to cook
guiso *nm* **1** : stew **2** : casserole
güisqui → **whisky**
guita *nf* : string, twine

guitarra *nf* : guitar
guitarrista *nmf* : guitarist
gula *nf* GLOTONERÍA : gluttony, greed
guppy *nm* : guppy
gusano *nm* **1** LOMBRIZ : worm, earthworm ⟨gusano de seda : silkworm⟩ **2** : caterpillar, maggot, grub
gustar *vt* **1** : to taste **2** : to like ⟨¿gustan pasar? : would you like to come in?⟩ — *vi* **1** : to be pleasing ⟨me gustan los dulces : I like sweets⟩ ⟨a María le gusta Carlos : Maria is attracted to Carlos⟩ ⟨no me gusta que me griten : I don't like to be yelled at⟩ **2 ~ de** : to like, to enjoy ⟨no gusta de chismes : she doesn't like gossip⟩ **3 como guste** : as you wish, as you like
gustativo, -va *adj* : taste ⟨papilas gustativas : taste buds⟩
gusto *nm* **1** : flavor, taste ⟨tiene gusto a chocolate : it tastes like chocolate⟩ **2** : taste, style ⟨de buen/mal gusto : in good/bad taste⟩ ⟨no es de mi gusto : it's not to my taste⟩ **3** : pleasure, liking ⟨tener el gusto de : to have the pleasure of⟩ ⟨con mucho gusto : gladly, with pleasure⟩ ⟨dar gusto : to be a pleasure⟩ ⟨darse el gusto de : to treat oneself to⟩ **4** : whim, fancy ⟨a gusto : at will⟩ **5 a ~** : comfortable, at ease **6 al gusto** : to taste, as one likes **7 mucho gusto** : pleased to meet you **8 por ~** : for pleasure
gustosamente *adv* : gladly
gustoso, -sa *adj* **1** : willing, glad ⟨nuestra empresa participará gustosa : our company will be pleased to participate⟩ **2** : zesty, tasty
gutural *adj* : guttural

H

h *nf* : ninth letter of the Spanish alphabet
ha → **haber**
haba *nf* : broad bean
habanero[1] **, -ra** *adj* : of or from Havana
habanero[2] **, -ra** *n* : native or resident of Havana
habano, -na *n* **1** → **habanero** **2** : cigar from Havana
haber[1] {39} *v aux* **1** : have, has ⟨no ha llegado el envío : the shipment hasn't arrived⟩ ⟨de haberlo sabido : if I had known⟩ ⟨debería haberlo pensado : I should have thought of it⟩ **2 ~ de** : must ⟨ha de ser tarde : it must be late⟩ — *v impers* (**hay** *in the present indicative*) **1** : there is, there are ⟨hay dos mensajes : there are two messages⟩ ⟨¿hay postre? : do you have any dessert?⟩ ⟨hubo muchos errores : there were a lot of errors⟩ ⟨ha habido varios casos : there have been various cases⟩ **2 hay que** : it is necessary ⟨hay que trabajar más rápido : you/we (etc.) have to work faster⟩ ⟨habrá que hacerlo : it will have

to be done⟩ ⟨hubo que esperar : we had to wait⟩ **3 no hay de qué** : you're welcome, don't mention it **4 ¿qué hay?** *fam* : what's up?, how are things? **5 ¿qué hay de nuevo?** *fam* : what's new?
haber[2] *nm* **1** : assets *pl* **2** : credit, credit side **3 haberes** *nmpl* : salary, income, remuneration
habichuela *nf* **1** : bean, kidney bean **2** : green bean
hábil *adj* **1** : able, skillful **2** : work, working ⟨días hábiles : workdays, business days⟩
habilidad *nf* CAPACIDAD : ability, skill
habilidoso, -sa *adj* : skillful, clever
habilitación *nf, pl* **-ciones** **1** : authorization **2** : furnishing, equipping
habilitar *vt* **1** : to enable, to authorize, to empower (someone) **2** : to equip, to furnish
hábilmente *adv* : skillfully, expertly
habiloso, -sa *adj Chile fam* : bright, smart, clever
habitable *adj* : habitable, inhabitable

habitación *nf, pl* **-ciones 1** CUARTO : room **2** DORMITORIO : bedroom **3** : habitation, occupancy

habitante *nmf* : inhabitant, resident

habitar *vt* : to inhabit — *vi* : to reside, to dwell

hábitat *nm, pl* **-tats** : habitat

hábito *nm* **1** : habit, custom **2** : habit (of a monk or nun)

habitual *adj* : habitual, customary — **habitualmente** *adv*

habituar {3} *vt* : to accustom, to habituate — **habituarse** *vr* ~ **a** : to get used to, to grow accustomed to

habla *nf* **1** : speech ⟨dejar a alguien sin habla : to leave someone speechless⟩ ⟨quedarse sin habla : to be left speechless⟩ **2** : language, dialect **3 de** ~ : speaking ⟨de habla inglesa : English-speaking⟩

hablado, -da *adj* **1** : spoken **2 mal hablado** : foulmouthed

hablador[1]**, -dora** *adj* : talkative

hablador[2]**, -dora** *n* : chatterbox

habladuría *nf* **1** : rumor **2 habladurías** *nfpl* : gossip, scandal

hablante *nmf* : speaker

hablar *vi* **1** : to speak, to talk ⟨hablar en broma : to be joking⟩ ⟨hablar más alto : to speak up, to speak/talk louder⟩ ⟨hablar más bajo : to lower one's voice, to speak/talk more quietly⟩ **2** ~ **con** : to talk to, to speak to/with **3** ~ **de** : to mention, to talk about ⟨hablar bien/mal de : to speak well/ill of⟩ **4 dar que hablar** : to make people talk ⟨va a dar que hablar : people will start talking/gossiping about him⟩ **5 ¡ni hablar!** : no way! — *vt* **1** : to speak (a language) **2** : to talk about, to discuss ⟨háblalo con tu jefe : discuss it with your boss⟩ — **hablarse** *vr* **1** : to speak to each other, to be on speaking terms **2 se habla inglés (etc.)** : English (etc.) spoken

habrá, etc. → **haber**

hacedor, -dora *n* : creator, maker, doer

hacendado, -da *n* : landowner

hacendoso, -sa *adj* : hardworking, industrious

hacer {40} *vt* **1** CREAR, CONSTRUIR : to make (a cake, a list, a law, etc.), to build (a building), to write (a book, a check) ⟨hacer planes : to make plans⟩ ⟨hacer una película : to make a movie⟩ ⟨hacer un fuego : to make/build a fire⟩ ⟨lo hizo de madera : he made it out of wood⟩ **2** : to do (a task, an activity, etc.), to make (a gesture, an agreement, etc.), to pay (a visit) ⟨hacer mandados : to do/run errands⟩ ⟨hacer los deberes : to do one's homework⟩ ⟨¿me haces un favor? : will you do me a favor?⟩ **3** : to make, to cause, to produce ⟨hacer ruido : to make noise⟩ **4** EXPRESAR : to voice (an objection, etc.), to ask (a question) **5** : to make, to force, to oblige ⟨los hice esperar : I made them wait⟩ ⟨hizo que todos se callaran : he made everyone be quiet⟩ **6** : to make, to cause, to provoke ⟨me hizo reír/llorar : it made me laugh/

cry⟩ ⟨¿te hice daño? : did I hurt you?⟩ **7** : to make, to cause to (be) ⟨la hizo famosa : it made her famous⟩ ⟨te hará (un) hombre : it will make a man out of you⟩ ⟨lo hizo funcionar : she made it work⟩ ⟨hace que el color parezca más oscuro : it makes the color seem darker⟩ **8** : to make (a bed), to pack (a suitcase) **9** PREPARAR : to make, to fix (a meal, etc.) **10** ADQUIRIR : to make (money, friends, etc.) — *vi* **1** : to act ⟨haces bien : you're doing the right thing⟩ **2** : to serve as, to function as **3** ~ **de** : to play, to perform as ⟨hizo de Ofelia en "Hamlet" : she played Ophelia in "Hamlet"⟩ **4 hacer como que/si** : to act as if **5 hacer por** : to try to ⟨hicieron por entendernos : they tried to understand us⟩ **6 hacer y deshacer** : to do as one pleases — *v impers* **1** (*referring to weather*) ⟨hace frío : it's cold⟩ ⟨hacía mucho viento : it was very windy⟩ **2** (*referring to time*) ⟨eso pasó hace mucho tiempo : that happened a long time ago⟩ ⟨vivo aquí desde hace dos años, hace dos años que vivo aquí : I've lived here for two years⟩ ⟨hacía años que no sabía nada de él : I hadn't heard from him in years⟩ **3 hacer falta** : to be necessary, to be needed **4 no le hace** : it doesn't matter, it makes no difference — **hacerse** *vr* **1** : to become **2** : to pretend, to act, to play ⟨hacerse el tonto : to play dumb⟩ **3** : to seem ⟨el examen se me hizo difícil : the exam seemed difficult to me⟩ **4** : to get, to grow ⟨se hace tarde : it's getting/growing late⟩

hacha *nf* : hatchet, ax

hachazo *nm* : blow, chop (with an ax)

hache *nf* : (letter) h

hachís *nm* : hashish

hacia *prep* **1** : toward, towards ⟨hacia abajo : downward⟩ ⟨hacia adelante : forward⟩ **2** : near, around, about ⟨hacia las seis : about six o'clock⟩

hacienda *nf* **1** : estate, ranch, farm **2** : property **3** : livestock **4 la Hacienda** : department of revenue, tax office

hacinamiento *nm* : overcrowding

hacinar *vt* **1** : to pile up, to stack **2** : to crowd, to cram — **hacinarse** *vr* : to crowd together

hackear *vt fam* : to hack, to hack into (a system, etc.)

hacker *nmf, pl* **hackers** *fam* : hacker

hada *nf* : fairy

hado *nm* : destiny, fate

haga, etc. → **hacer**

haitiano, -na *adj & n* : Haitian

hala *interj Spain* **1** (*expressing encouragement or disbelief*) : come on! **2** (*expressing surprise*) : wow! **3** (*expressing protest*) : hey!

halagador[1]**, -dora** *adj* : flattering

halagador[2]**, -dora** *n* : flatterer

halagar {52} *vt* : to flatter, to compliment

halago *nm* : flattery, praise

halagüeño, -ña *adj* **1** : flattering **2** : encouraging, promising

halar *vt CA, Car* → **jalar**

halcón *nm, pl* **halcones** : hawk, falcon
halibut *nm, pl* **-buts** : halibut
hálito *nm* **1** : breath **2** : gentle breeze
hallar *vt* **1** ENCONTRAR : to find **2** DES-
CUBRIR : to discover, to find out — **hal-**
larse *vr* **1** : to be situated, to find oneself **2** : to feel ⟨no se halla bien : he
doesn't feel comfortable, he feels out of
place⟩
hallazgo *nm* **1** : discovery **2** : find ⟨¡es
un verdadero hallazgo! : it's a real find!⟩
halo *nm* **1** : halo **2** : aura
halterofilia *nf* : weight lifting
hamaca *nf* : hammock
hambre *nf* **1** : hunger **2** : starvation **3**
tener hambre : to be hungry **4** dar
hambre : to make hungry
hambriento, -ta *adj* : hungry, starving
hambruna *nf* : famine
hamburguesa *nf* **1** : hamburger, burger
2 : patty, burger ⟨una hamburguesa de
pavo : a turkey patty/burger⟩
hampa *nf* : criminal underworld
hampón, -pona *n, mpl* **hampones** : criminal, thug
hámster [ˈxamster] *nm, pl* **hámsters**
: hamster
han → haber
handicap *or* hándicap [ˈhandiˌkap] *nm, pl*
-caps : handicap (in sports)
hangar *nm* : hangar
Hanukkah → Janucá
hará, etc. → hacer
haragán[1], -gana *adj, mpl* **-ganes** : lazy,
idle
haragán[2], -gana *n, mpl* **-ganes**
HOLGAZÁN : slacker, good-for-nothing
haraganear *vi* : to be lazy, to waste one's
time
haraganería *nf* : laziness
harapiento, -ta *adj* : ragged, tattered
harapos *nmpl* ANDRAJOS : rags, tatters
hardware [ˈhardˌwɛr] *nm* : computer
hardware
harén *nm, pl* **harenes** : harem
harina *nf* **1** : flour **2** harina de maíz
: cornmeal **3** ser harina de otro costal
: to be a horse of a different color
hartar *vt* **1** : to glut, to satiate **2** FASTI-
DIAR : to tire, to irritate, to annoy —
hartarse *vr* **1** : to be weary, to get fed
up **2** ~ de : to gorge oneself on
harto[1] *adv* : most, extremely, very
harto[2], -ta *adj* **1** : full, satiated **2** : fed
up **3** MUCHO : a lot of, much ⟨tiene
harto dinero : he has lots of money⟩
hartura *nf* **1** : surfeit **2** : abundance,
plenty
has → haber
hashtag [ˈhaʃtag] *nm, pl* **hashtags**
: hashtag
hasta[1] *adv* : even
hasta[2] *prep* **1** : until, up until ⟨hasta
ahora/entonces : until now/then⟩ ⟨until
Friday : hasta el viernes⟩ ⟨¡hasta luego!
: see you later!⟩ **2** : as far as ⟨nos fuimos hasta Managua : we went all the
way to Managua⟩ **3** : to, up/down to
⟨hasta cierto punto : up to a certain
point⟩ ⟨tengo el pelo hasta la cintura

: my hair is down to my waist⟩ **4 hasta**
que : until ⟨hasta que lleguen : until
they arrive⟩
hastiar {85} *vt* **1** : to make weary, to bore
2 : to disgust, to sicken — **hastiarse** *vr*
~ de : to get tired of
hastío *nm* **1** TEDIO : tedium **2** REPUG-
NANCIA : disgust
hatchback *nm* : hatchback (car)
hatillo *nm* : bundle (of clothes)
hato *nm* **1** : flock, herd **2** : bundle (of
possessions)
hawaiano, -na *adj & n* : Hawaiian
hay → haber[1]
haya[1], etc. → haber
haya[2] *nf* : beech (tree and wood)
hayuco *nm* : beechnut
haz[1] → hacer
haz[2] *nm, pl* **haces 1** FARDO : bundle **2**
: beam (of light)
haz[3] *nf, pl* **haces 1** : face **2 haz de la**
tierra : surface of the earth
hazaña *nf* PROEZA : feat, exploit
hazmerreír *nm fam* : laughingstock
he[1] {39} → haber
he[2] *v impers* he aquí : here is, here are,
behold
hebilla *nf* : buckle, clasp
hebra *nf* : strand, thread
hebreo[1], -brea *adj & n* : Hebrew
hebreo[2] *nm* : Hebrew (language)
hecatombe *nf* **1** MATANZA : massacre **2**
: disaster
heces → hez
hechicería *nf* **1** BRUJERÍA : sorcery,
witchcraft **2** : curse, spell
hechicero[1], -ra *adj* : bewitching, enchanting
hechicero[2], -ra *n* : sorcerer, sorceress *f*
hechizar {21} *vt* **1** EMBRUJAR : to bewitch **2** CAUTIVAR : to charm
hechizo *nm* **1** SORTILEGIO : spell, enchantment **2** ENCANTO : charm, fascination
hecho[1] *pp* → hacer
hecho[2], -cha *adj* **1** : made, done ⟨hecho
a mano : handmade⟩ **2** : complete, finished ⟨hecho y derecho : full-fledged⟩
hecho[3] *nm* **1** : fact **2** : event ⟨hechos
históricos : historic events⟩ **3** : act, action **4** de ~ : in fact, in reality
hechura *nf* **1** : style **2** : craftsmanship,
workmanship **3** : product, creation
hectárea *nf* : hectare
heder {56} *vi* : to stink, to reek
hediondez *nf, pl* **-deces** : stink, stench
hediondo, -da *adj* MALOLIENTE : foul-
smelling, stinking
hedor *nm* : stench, stink
hegemonía *nf* **1** : dominance **2** : hegemony (in politics)
helada *nf* : frost (in meteorology)
heladería *nf* : ice-cream parlor, ice-cream
stand
helado[1], -da *adj* **1** GÉLIDO : icy, freezing
cold **2** CONGELADO : frozen
helado[2] *nm* : ice cream
heladora *nf* CONGELADOR : freezer
helar {55} *v* CONGELAR : to freeze — *v*
impers : to produce frost ⟨anoche heló
: there was frost last night⟩ — **helarse** *vr*

helecho *nm* : fern, bracken
hélice *nf* 1 : spiral, helix 2 : propeller
helicóptero *nm* : helicopter
helio *nm* : helium
helipuerto *nm* : heliport
hematoma *nm* 1 : hematoma 2 MORE-TÓN : bruise
hembra *adj & nf* : female
hemisférico, -ca *adj* : hemispheric, hemispherical
hemisferio *nm* : hemisphere
hemofilia *nf* : hemophilia
hemofílico, -ca *adj & n* : hemophiliac
hemoglobina *nf* : hemoglobin
hemorragia *nf* 1 : hemorrhage 2 hemorragia nasal : nosebleed
hemorroides *nfpl* ALMORRANAS : hemorrhoids, piles
hemos → haber
henchido, -da *adj* : swollen, bloated
henchir {54} *vt* 1 : to stuff, to fill 2 : to swell, to swell up — henchirse *vr* 1 : to stuff oneself 2 LLENARSE : to fill up, to be full
hender {56} *vt* : to cleave, to split
hendidura *nf* : crack, crevice, fissure
heno *nm* : hay
hepatitis *nf* : hepatitis
heráldica *nf* : heraldry
heráldico, -ca *adj* : heraldic
heraldo *nm* : herald
herbario, -ria *adj* : herbal
herbicida *nm* : herbicide, weed killer
herbívoro[1], -ra *adj* : herbivorous
herbívoro[2] *nm* : herbivore
hercio *nm* : hertz
hercúleo, -lea *adj* : herculean
heredar *vt* : to inherit
heredero, -ra *n* : heir, heiress *f*
hereditario, -ria *adj* : hereditary
hereje *nmf* : heretic
herejía *nf* : heresy
herencia *nf* 1 : inheritance 2 : heritage 3 : heredity
herético, -ca *adj* : heretical
herida *nf* : injury, wound
herido[1], -da *adj* 1 : injured, wounded 2 : hurt, offended
herido[2], -da *n* : injured person, casualty
herir {76} *vt* 1 : to injure, to wound 2 : to hurt, to offend
hermafrodita *nmf* : hermaphrodite
hermanar *vt* 1 : to unite, to bring together 2 : to match up, to twin (cities)
hermanastro, -tra *n* 1 : half brother *m*, half sister *f* 2 : stepbrother *m*, stepsister *f*
hermandad *nf* 1 FRATERNIDAD : brotherhood ⟨hermandad de mujeres : sisterhood, sorority⟩ 2 : association
hermano, -na *n* : sibling, brother *m*, sister *f* ⟨hermano mayor/menor : big/little brother⟩ ⟨hermana gemela : twin sister⟩
hermético, -ca *adj* : hermetic, watertight — herméticamente *adv*
hermoso, -sa *adj* BELLO : beautiful, lovely — hermosamente *adv*
hermosura *nf* BELLEZA : beauty, loveliness
hernia *nf* : hernia

herniarse *vr* : to get a hernia, to rupture oneself
héroe *nm* : hero
heroicidad *nf* : heroism, heroic deed
heroico, -ca *adj* : heroic — heroicamente *adv*
heroína *nf* 1 : heroine 2 : heroin
heroinómano, -na *n* : heroin addict
heroísmo *nm* : heroism
herpes *nms & pl* 1 : herpes 2 : shingles
herradura *nf* : horseshoe
herraje *nm* : ironwork
herramienta *nf* : tool
herrar {55} *vt* : to shoe (a horse)
herrería *nf* : blacksmith's shop
herrero, -ra *n* : blacksmith
herrumbre *nf* ORÍN : rust
herrumbroso, -sa *adj* OXIDADO : rusty
hertzio → hercio
hervidero *nm* 1 : mass, swarm 2 : hotbed (of crime, etc.)
hervidor *nm* : kettle
hervir {76} *vi* 1 BULLIR : to boil, to bubble 2 ~ de : to teem with, to be swarming with — *vt* : to boil
hervor *nm* 1 : boiling 2 : fervor, ardor
heterogéneo, -nea *adj* : heterogeneous
heterosexual *adj & nmf* : heterosexual
heterosexualidad *nf* : heterosexuality
hexágono *nm* : hexagon — hexagonal *adj*
hez *nf, pl* heces 1 ESCORIA : scum, dregs *pl* 2 : sediment, lees *pl* 3 heces *nfpl* : feces, excrement
hiato *nm* : hiatus
hibernar *vi* : to hibernate — hibernación *nf*
híbrido[1], -da *adj* : hybrid
híbrido[2] *nm* : hybrid
hicieron, etc. → hacer
hidalgo, -ga *n* : nobleman *m*, noblewoman *f*
hidrante *nm* CA, Col : hydrant
hidratar *vt* : to moisturize — hidratante *adj*
hidrato de carbono *nm* : carbohydrate
hidráulico, -ca *adj* : hydraulic
hidroala *nm* : hydrofoil
hidroavión *nm, pl* -viones : seaplane
hidrocarburo *nm* : hydrocarbon
hidroeléctrico, -ca *adj* : hydroelectric
hidrofobia *nf* RABIA : hydrophobia, rabies
hidrófugo, -ga *adj* : water-repellent
hidrógeno *nm* : hydrogen
hidromasaje *nm* bañera de hidromasaje → bañera
hidroplano *nm* : hydroplane
hiede, etc. → heder
hiedra *nf* 1 : ivy 2 hiedra venenosa : poison ivy
hiel *nf* 1 BILIS : bile 2 : bitterness
hiela, etc. → helar
hielo *nm* 1 : ice 2 : coldness, reserve ⟨romper el hielo : to break the ice⟩
hiena *nf* : hyena
hiende, etc. → hender
hierba *nf* 1 : herb 2 : grass 3 mala hierba : weed
hierbabuena *nf* : mint, spearmint
hiere, etc. → herir

hierra, etc. → **herrar**
hierro nm **1** : iron ⟨hierro fundido : cast iron⟩ **2** : branding iron
hierve, etc. → **hervir**
hígado nm : liver
higiene nf : hygiene
higiénico, -ca adj : hygienic — **higiénicamente** adv
higienista nmf : hygienist
higo nm **1** : fig **2 higo chumbo** : prickly pear (fruit)
higrómetro nm : hygrometer
higuera nf : fig tree
hijab → **hiyab**
hijastro, -tra n : stepson m, stepdaughter f
hijo, -ja n : son m, daughter f ⟨hijo adoptivo : adopted son⟩ ⟨soy hija única : I'm an only child⟩ ⟨tiene dos hijos/hijas : she has two sons/daughters⟩ ⟨nuestros hijos : our children⟩
hijo de puta nm sometimes offensive : son of a bitch sometimes offensive, bastard offensive
híjole interj Mex : wow!, good grief!
hilacha nf **1** : ravel, loose thread **2 mostrar la hilacha** : to show one's true colors
hilado nm **1** : spinning **2** HILO : yarn, thread
hilar vt **1** : to spin (thread) **2** : to consider, to string together (ideas) — vi **1** : to spin **2 hilar delgado** : to split hairs
hilarante adj **1** : humorous, hilarious **2 gas hilarante** : laughing gas
hilaridad nf : hilarity
hilera nf FILA : file, row, line
hilo nm **1** : thread ⟨colgar de un hilo : to hang by a thread⟩ ⟨hilo dental : dental floss⟩ **2** LINO : linen **3** : (electric) wire ⟨conexión sin hilos : wireless connection⟩ **4** : theme, thread (of a discourse) **5** : trickle (of water, etc.)
hilvanar vt **1** : to baste, to tack **2** : to piece together
himnario nm : hymnal
himno nm **1** : hymn **2 himno nacional** : national anthem
hincapié nm **hacer hincapié en** : to emphasize, to stress
hincar {72} vt CLAVAR : to stick, to plunge — **hincarse** vr **hincarse de rodillas** : to kneel down, to fall to one's knees
hincha nmf fam : fan, supporter
hinchado, -da adj **1** : swollen, inflated **2** : pompous, overblown
hinchar vt **1** INFLAR : to inflate **2** : to exaggerate — **hincharse** vr **1** : to swell up **2** : to become conceited, to swell with pride
hinchazón nf, pl **-zones** : swelling
hinche, etc. → **henchir**
hindi nm : Hindi
hindú adj & nmf : Hindu
hinduismo nm : Hinduism
hiniesta nf : broom (plant)
hinojo nm **1** : fennel **2 de hinojos** : on bended knee
hinque, etc. → **hincar**
hipar vi : to hiccup
hiperactividad nf : hyperactivity

hiperactivo, -va adj : hyperactive, overactive
hipérbole nf : hyperbole
hiperbólico, -ca adj : hyperbolic, exaggerated
hipercrítico, -ca adj : hypercritical
hiperenlace nm : hyperlink
hipermercado nm : large supermarket, hypermarket
hipermétrope adj : farsighted
hipermetropía nf : farsightedness
hipersensibilidad nf : hypersensitivity
hipertensión nf, pl **-siones** : hypertension, high blood pressure
hip–hop [ˌxipˈxop] nm : hip-hop (music)
hípico, -ca adj : equestrian ⟨concurso hípico : horse show⟩
hipil → **huipil**
hipnosis nfs & pl : hypnosis
hipnótico, -ca adj : hypnotic
hipnotismo nm : hypnotism
hipnotizador¹, -dora adj **1** : hypnotic **2** : spellbinding, mesmerizing
hipnotizador², -dora n : hypnotist
hipnotizar {21} vt : to hypnotize
hipo nm : hiccup, hiccups pl
hipocampo nm : sea horse
hipocondría nf : hypochondria
hipocondríaco, -ca adj & n : hypochondriac
hipocresía nf : hypocrisy
hipócrita¹ adj : hypocritical — **hipócritamente** adv
hipócrita² nmf : hypocrite
hipodérmico, -ca adj **aguja hipodérmica** : hypodermic needle
hipódromo nm : racetrack
hipopótamo nm : hippopotamus
hipoteca nf : mortgage
hipotecar {72} vt **1** : to mortgage **2** : to compromise, to jeopardize
hipotecario, -ria adj : mortgage
hipotensión nf, pl **-siones** : low blood pressure
hipotenusa nf : hypotenuse
hipotermia nf : hypothermia
hipótesis nfs & pl : hypothesis
hipotético, -ca adj : hypothetical — **hipotéticamente** adv
hippie or **hippy** [ˈhipi] nmf, pl **hippies** [-pis] : hippie
hiriente adj : hurtful, offensive
hirió, etc. → **herir**
hirsuto, -ta adj **1** : hairy **2** : bristly, wiry
hirviente adj : boiling
hirvió, etc. → **hervir**
hisopo nm : cotton swab
hispánico, -ca adj & n : Hispanic
hispano¹, -na adj : Hispanic ⟨de habla hispana : Spanish-speaking⟩
hispano², -na n : Hispanic (person)
hispanoamericano¹, -na adj LATINOAMERICANO : Latin-American
hispanoamericano², -na n LATINOAMERICANO : Latin American
hispanohablante¹ adj : Spanish-speaking
hispanohablante² nmf : Spanish speaker
histerectomía nf : hysterectomy
histeria nf **1** : hysteria **2** : hysterics

histérico, -ca *adj* : hysterical — **histéri-camente** *adv*
histerismo *nm* 1 : hysteria 2 : hysterics
historia *nf* 1 : history ⟨historia universal : world history⟩ ⟨pasará a la historia como un gran jugador de béisbol : he'll go down in history as a great baseball player⟩ 2 NARRACIÓN, RELATO : story 3 **dejarse de** ∼**s** : to say something directly, to stop beating around the bush 4 **hacer** ∼ : to make history
historiador, -dora *n* : historian
historial *nm* 1 : record, document 2 CU-RRÍCULUM : résumé, curriculum vitae
histórico, -ca *adj* 1 : historical 2 : historic, important — **históricamente** *adv*
historieta *nf* : comic strip
histrionismo *nm* : histrionics, acting
hit ['hit] *nm, pl* **hits** 1 ÉXITO : hit, popular song 2 : hit (in baseball)
hito *nm* : milestone, landmark
hiyab *nm, pl* **hiyabs** : hijab
hizo → **hacer**
hobby ['hɔbi] *nm, pl* **hobbies** [-bis] : hobby
hocico *nm* : snout, muzzle
hockey ['hɔke, -ki] *nm* : hockey ⟨hockey sobre césped : field hockey⟩
hogar *nm* 1 : home ⟨labores del hogar : housework⟩ ⟨hogar, dulce hogar : home sweet home⟩ 2 : hearth, fireplace
hogareño, -ña *adj* 1 : domestic, homey 2 **ser muy hogareño** : to be a homebody
hogaza *nf* : large loaf (of bread)
hoguera *nf* 1 FOGATA : bonfire, campfire 2 **morir en la hoguera** : to burn at the stake
hoja *nf* 1 : leaf, petal, blade (of grass) 2 : sheet (of paper), page (of a book) ⟨hoja de cálculo : spreadsheet⟩ 3 FORMULA-RIO : form ⟨hoja de pedido : order form⟩ 4 : blade (of a knife) ⟨hoja de afeitar : razor blade⟩
hojalata *nf* : tinplate
hojaldre *nm* : puff pastry
hojarasca *nf* : fallen leaves *pl*
hojear *vt* : to leaf through (a book or magazine)
hojuela *nf* 1 : leaflet, young leaf 2 : flake
hola *interj* : hello!, hi!
holandés¹, -desa *adj, mpl* **-deses** : Dutch
holandés², -desa *n, mpl* **-deses** : Dutch person ⟨los holandeses : the Dutch⟩
holandés³ *nm* : Dutch (language)
holgadamente *adv* : comfortably, easily ⟨vivir holgadamente : to be well-off⟩
holgado, -da *adj* 1 : loose, baggy 2 : at ease, comfortable
holganza *nf* : leisure, idleness
holgar {16} *vi* : to be unnecessary ⟨huelga decir que . . . : it goes without saying that . . .⟩
holgazán¹, -zana *adj, mpl* **-zanes** : lazy
holgazán², -zana *n, mpl* **-zanes** HARAGÁN : slacker, idler
holgazanear *vi* HARAGANEAR : to laze around, to loaf

holgazanería *nf* PEREZA : idleness, laziness
holgura *nf* 1 : looseness 2 COMODIDAD : comfort, ease
holístico, -ca *adj* : holistic
hollar {19} *vt* : to tread on, to trample
hollín *nm, pl* **hollines** TIZNE : soot
holocausto *nm* : holocaust
holograma *nm* : hologram
hombre¹ *nm* 1 : man ⟨el hombre : man, mankind⟩ ⟨la escuela hizo de él un hombre : the school made a man out of him⟩ 2 **hombre de confianza** : right-hand man 3 **hombre de estado** : statesman 4 **hombre de negocios** : businessman 5 **hombre lobo** : werewolf 6 **el hombre de la calle** : the man in/on the street, the average person
hombre² *interj fam* 1 : well, hey 2 : of course!, you bet! 3 : come on!
hombrera *nf* 1 : shoulder pad 2 : epaulet
hombría *nf* : manliness
hombro *nm* 1 : shoulder ⟨encogerse de hombros : to shrug one's shoulders⟩ ⟨hombro con hombro : shoulder to shoulder⟩ ⟨llevé mi hija en hombros : I carried my daughter on my shoulders⟩ 2 **arrimar el hombro** : to lend a hand, to pull one's weight
hombruno, -na *adj* : mannish
homenaje *nm* : homage, tribute ⟨rendir homenaje a : to pay tribute to⟩
homenajeado, -da *n* : guest of honor
homenajear *vt* : to pay homage to, to honor
homeopatía *nf* : homeopathy — **homeopático, -ca** *adj*
homicida¹ *adj* : homicidal, murderous
homicida² *nmf* ASESINO : murderer
homicidio *nm* ASESINATO : homicide, murder
homilía *nf* : homily, sermon
homófono *nm* : homophone
homogeneidad *nf* : homogeneity
homogeneizar {21} *vt* : to homogenize
homogéneo, -nea *adj* : homogeneous — **homogéneamente** *adv*
homógrafo *nm* : homograph
homologación *nf, pl* **-clones** 1 : sanctioning, approval 2 : parity
homologar {52} *vt* 1 : to sanction 2 : to bring into line
homólogo¹, -ga *adj* : homologous, equivalent
homólogo², -ga *n* : counterpart
homónimo¹, -ma *n* TOCAYO : namesake
homónimo² *nm* : homonym
homosexual *adj & nmf* : homosexual
homosexualidad *nf* : homosexuality
honda *nf* : sling
hondo¹ *adv* : deeply
hondo², -da *adj* PROFUNDO : deep ⟨en lo más hondo de : in the depths of⟩ — **hondamente** *adv*
hondonada *nf* 1 : hollow, depression 2 : ravine, gorge
hondura *nf* : depth
hondureño, -ña *adj & n* : Honduran

honestidad *nf* 1 : decency, modesty 2 : honesty

honesto, -ta *adj* 1 : decent, virtuous 2 : honest, honorable — **honestamente** *adv*

hongo *nm* 1 : fungus 2 : mushroom

honor *nm* 1 : honor ⟨en honor a la verdad : to be quite honest⟩ 2 **honores** *nmpl* : honors ⟨hacer los honores : to do the honors⟩

honorable *adj* HONROSO : honorable — **honorablemente** *adv*

honorario, -ria *adj* : honorary

honorarios *nmpl* : payment, fees (for professional services)

honorífico, -ca *adj* : honorary ⟨mención honorífica : honorable mention⟩

honra *nf* 1 : dignity, self-respect ⟨tener a mucha honra : to take great pride in⟩ 2 : good name, reputation

honradamente *adv* : honestly, decently

honradez *nf, pl* **-deces** : honesty, integrity, probity

honrado, -da *adj* 1 HONESTO : honest, upright 2 : honored

honrar *vt* 1 : to honor 2 : to be a credit to ⟨su generosidad lo honra : his generosity does him credit⟩

honroso, -sa *adj* HONORABLE : honorable — **honrosamente** *adv*

hora *nf* 1 : hour ⟨media hora : half an hour⟩ ⟨se pasa horas viendo televisión : he spends hours watching television⟩ 2 : time ⟨¿qué hora es? : what time is it?⟩ ⟨llegar a la hora : to arrive on time⟩ ⟨a la hora en punto : on the dot⟩ ⟨a la hora de comer : at mealtime⟩ ⟨a la última hora : at the last minute⟩ ⟨a primera hora : first thing⟩ ⟨antes de la hora : early, ahead of time⟩ ⟨es hora de irnos a casa : it's time to go home⟩ ⟨ya es hora de tomarlo en serio : it's about time we took it seriously⟩ 3 CITA : appointment ⟨pedir/dar/tener hora : to make/give/have an appointment⟩ 4 **hora de cierre** : closing time 5 **hora local** : local time 6 **horas de oficina/trabajo** : office/work hours 7 **hora pico** : rush hour 8 **horas extras** : overtime 9 **las altas horas** : the wee hours 10 **trabajar por horas** : to work by the hour

horadar *vt* : to drill a hole in

horario *nm* : schedule, timetable, hours *pl* ⟨horario de visita : visiting hours⟩

horca *nf* 1 : gallows *pl* 2 : pitchfork

horcajadas *nfpl* **a ~** : astride, astraddle

horchata *nf* : cold sweet drink usually made with a kind of tuber

horcón *nm, pl* **horcones** : wooden post, prop

horda *nf* : horde

horizontal *adj* : horizontal — **horizontalmente** *adv*

horizonte *nm* : horizon, skyline

horma *nf* 1 : shoe tree 2 : shoemaker's last

hormiga *nf* : ant

hormigón *nm, pl* **-gones** CONCRETO : concrete

hormigonera *nf* : cement mixer

hormigueo *nm* 1 : tingling, pins and needles *pl* 2 : uneasiness

hormiguero *nm* 1 : anthill 2 : swarm (of people)

hormona *nf* : hormone — **hormonal** *adj*

hornacina *nf* : niche, recess

hornada *nf* : batch

hornear *vt* : to bake

hornilla *nf* : burner (of a stove)

hornillo *nm* : portable stove

horno *nm* 1 : oven ⟨horno de microondas : microwave oven⟩ 2 : kiln

horóscopo *nm* : horoscope

horqueta *nf* 1 : fork (in a river or road) 2 : crotch (in a tree) 3 : small pitchfork

horquilla *nf* 1 : hairpin, bobby pin 2 : pitchfork

horrendo, -da *adj* : horrendous, horrible

horrible *adj* : horrible, dreadful — **horriblemente** *adv*

horripilante *adj* : horrifying, hair-raising

horripilar *vt* : to horrify, to terrify

horror *nm* : horror, dread

horrorizado, -da *adj* : terrified

horrorizar {21} *vt* : to horrify, to terrify — **horrorizarse** *vr*

horroroso, -sa *adj* 1 : horrifying, terrifying 2 : dreadful, bad

hortaliza *nf* 1 : vegetable 2 **hortalizas** *nfpl* : garden produce

hortera *adj Spain fam* : tacky, gaudy

hortícola *adj* : horticultural

horticultura *nf* : horticulture

hosco, -ca *adj* : sullen, gloomy — **hoscamente** *adv*

hospedaje *nm* : lodging, accommodations *pl*

hospedar *vt* : to provide with lodging, to put up — **hospedarse** *vr* : to stay, to lodge

hospicio *nm* : orphanage

hospital *nm* : hospital

hospitalario, -ria *adj* : hospitable

hospitalidad *nf* : hospitality

hospitalización *nf, pl* **-ciones** : hospitalization

hospitalizar {21} *vt* : to hospitalize — **hospitalizarse** *vr*

hostal *nm* : cheap hotel

hostelería *nf* : the hotel industry

hostería *nf* POSADA : inn

hostia *nf* : host, Eucharist

hostigamiento *nm* : harassment

hostigar {52} *vt* ACOSAR, ASEDIAR : to harass, to pester

hostil *adj* : hostile

hostilidad *nf* 1 : hostility, antagonism 2 **hostilidades** *nfpl* : (military) hostilities

hostilizar {21} *vt* : to harass

hotel *nm* : hotel

hotelero¹, -ra *adj* : hotel ⟨la industria hotelera : the hotel business⟩

hotelero², -ra *n* : hotel manager, hotelier

hoy *adv* 1 : today ⟨hoy mismo : right now, this very day⟩ 2 : now, nowadays ⟨de hoy en adelante : from now on⟩

hoyo *nm* AGUJERO : hole

hoyuelo *nm* : dimple

hoz *nf, pl* **hoces** : sickle

hozar {21} *vi* : to root (of a pig)

huachinango *nm Mex* : red snapper
huarache *nm* : sandal
hubo, etc. → haber
hueco¹, -ca *adj* 1 : hollow, empty 2 : soft, spongy 3 : hollow, resonant 4 : proud, conceited 5 : superficial
hueco² *nm* 1 : hole, hollow, cavity 2 : gap, space 3 : recess, alcove
huele, etc. → oler
huelga *nf* 1 PARO : strike 2 hacer huelga : to strike, to go on strike
huelguista *nmf* : striker
huella¹, etc. → hollar
huella² *nf* 1 : footprint ⟨seguir las huellas de alguien : to follow in someone's footsteps⟩ 2 : mark, impact ⟨dejar huella : to leave one's mark⟩ ⟨sin dejar huella : without a trace⟩ 3 huella digital *or* huella dactilar : fingerprint
huérfano¹, -na *adj* 1 : orphan, orphaned 2 : defenseless 3 ~ de : lacking, devoid of
huérfano², -na *n* : orphan
huerta *nf* 1 : large vegetable garden, truck farm 2 : orchard 3 : irrigated land
huerto *nm* 1 : vegetable garden 2 : orchard
hueso *nm* 1 : bone 2 : pit, stone (of a fruit)
huésped¹, -peda *n* INVITADO : guest
huésped² *nm* : host ⟨organismo huésped : host organism⟩
huestes *nfpl* 1 : followers 2 : troops, army
huesudo, -da *adj* : bony
hueva *nf* : roe, spawn
huevo *nm* 1 : egg ⟨huevos revueltos : scrambled eggs⟩ ⟨huevo de Pascua : Easter egg⟩ 2 huevos *nmpl usu vulgar* : balls *pl*, *usu vulgar*; testicles *pl*
huida *nf* : flight, escape
huidizo, -za *adj* 1 ESCURRIDIZO : elusive, slippery 2 : shy, evasive
huipil *nm CA, Mex* : traditional sleeveless blouse or dress
huir {41} *vi* 1 ESCAPAR : to escape, to flee 2 ~ de : to avoid
huiro *nm Chile, Peru* : seaweed
huizache *nm* : acacia
hule *nm* 1 : oilcloth, oilskin 2 *Mex* : rubber 3 hule espuma *Mex* : foam rubber
hulera *nf Mex* : slingshot
humanidad *nf* 1 : humanity, mankind 2 : humanity, compassion 3 humanidades *nfpl* : humanities *pl*
humanismo *nm* : humanism
humanista *nmf* : humanist
humanístico, -ca *adj* : humanistic
humanitario, -ria *adj & n* : humanitarian
humanizar {21} *vt* : to humanize
humano¹, -na *adj* 1 : human 2 BENÉVOLO : humane, benevolent — humanamente *adv*
humano² *nm* : human being, human
humareda *nf* : cloud of smoke
humeante *adj* 1 : smoky 2 : smoking, steaming

humear *vi* 1 : to smoke 2 : to steam
humectante¹ *adj* : moisturizing
humectante² *nm* : moisturizer
humedad *nf* 1 : humidity 2 : dampness, moistness
humedecer {53} *vt* 1 : to humidify 2 : to moisten, to dampen
húmedo, -da *adj* 1 : humid 2 : moist, damp
humidificador *nm* : humidifier
humidificar {72} *vt* : to humidify
humildad *nf* 1 : humility 2 : lowliness
humilde *adj* 1 : humble 2 : lowly ⟨gente humilde : poor people⟩
humildemente *adv* : meekly, humbly
humillación *nf, pl* -ciones : humiliation
humillante *adj* : humiliating
humillar *vt* : to humiliate — humillarse *vr* : to humble oneself ⟨humillarse a hacer algo : to stoop to doing something⟩
humo *nm* 1 : smoke, steam, fumes 2 humos *nmpl* : airs *pl*, conceit
humor *nm* 1 : humor 2 : mood, temper ⟨está de buen humor : she's in a good mood⟩
humorada *nf* 1 BROMA : joke, witticism 2 : whim, caprice
humorismo *nm* : humor, wit
humorista *nmf* : humorist, comedian, comedienne *f*
humorístico, -ca *adj* : humorous — humorísticamente *adv*
humoso, -sa *adj* : smoky, steamy
humus *nm* : humus
hundido, -da *adj* 1 : sunken 2 : depressed
hundimiento *nm* 1 : sinking 2 : collapse, ruin
hundir *vt* 1 : to sink 2 : to destroy, to ruin — hundirse *vr* 1 : to sink down 2 : to cave in 3 : to break down, to go to pieces
húngaro¹, -ra *adj & n* : Hungarian
húngaro² *nm* : Hungarian (language)
huracán *nm, pl* -canes : hurricane
huraño, -ña *adj* 1 : unsociable, aloof 2 : timid, skittish (of an animal)
hurgar {52} *vt* : to poke, to jab, to rake (a fire) — *vi* ~ en : to rummage in, to poke through
hurgue, etc. → hurgar
hurón *nm, pl* hurones : ferret
huronear *vi* : to pry, to snoop
hurra *interj* : hurrah!, hooray!
hurtadillas *nfpl* a ~ : stealthily, on the sly
hurtar *vt* ROBAR : to steal
hurto *nm* 1 : theft, robbery 2 : stolen property, loot
husmear *vt* 1 : to follow the scent of, to track 2 : to sniff out, to pry into — *vi* 1 : to pry, to snoop 2 : to sniff around (of an animal)
huso *nm* 1 : spindle 2 huso horario : time zone
huy *interj* : ow!, ouch!
huye, etc. → huir

I

i *nf* : tenth letter of the Spanish alphabet
i- → **in-**
iba, etc. → **ir**
ibérico, -ca *adj* : Iberian
ibero, -ra *or* **íbero, -ra** *adj & n* : Iberian
iberoamericano, -na *adj* HISPANOAMERICANO, LATINOAMERICANO : Latin-American
-ible *suf* : -ible
ice, etc. → **izar**
iceberg *nm, pl* **icebergs** : iceberg
icono *nm* : icon
iconoclasia *nf* : iconoclasm
iconoclasta *nmf* : iconoclast
ictericia *nf* : jaundice
ictérico, -ca *adj* : jaundiced
id *nm* : id
ida *nf* **1** : going, departure **2 ida y vuelta** : round trip **3 idas y venidas** : comings and goings
idea *nf* **1** : idea, notion ⟨una buena/mala idea : a good/bad idea⟩ ⟨tengo una idea : I have an idea⟩ ⟨no tengo (ni) idea : I have no idea⟩ ⟨me hago una idea de cómo es : I'm getting an/some idea of what he's like⟩ **2** : opinion, belief ⟨siempre puedes cambiar de idea : you can always change your mind⟩ ⟨¿de dónde sacaste esa idea? : where did you get that idea?⟩ **3** PROPÓSITO : intention, idea ⟨la idea era llegar temprano : the idea was to arrive early⟩
ideal *adj & nm* : ideal — **idealmente** *adv*
idealismo *nm* : idealism
idealista[1] *adj* : idealistic
idealista[2] *nmf* : idealist
idealizar {21} *vt* : to idealize — **idealización** *nf*
idear *vt* : to devise, to think up
ideario *nm* : ideology
ídem *nm* : the same, ditto
idéntico, -ca *adj* : identical, alike — **idénticamente** *adv*
identidad *nf* : identity
identificable *adj* : identifiable
identificación *nf, pl* **-ciones 1** : identification, identifying **2** : identification document, ID
identificar {72} *vt* : to identify — **identificarse** *vr* **1** : to identify oneself **2** ~ **con** : to identify with
ideología *nf* : ideology — **ideológicamente** *adv*
ideológico, -ca *adj* : ideological
ideólogo, -ga *n* : ideologue
idílico, -ca *adj* : idyllic
idilio *nm* **1** : idyll **2** AMORÍO : love affair, romance
idioma *nm* : language ⟨el idioma inglés : the English language⟩
idiomático, -ca *adj* : idiomatic — **idiomáticamente** *adv*
idiosincrasia *nf* : idiosyncrasy
idiosincrásico, -ca *adj* : idiosyncratic
idiota[1] *adj* : idiotic, stupid, foolish
idiota[2] *nmf* **1** : idiot, foolish person **2** *dated, now offensive* : idiot (in medicine) *dated, now offensive*

idiotez *nf, pl* **-teces 1** : idiocy (in medicine) *dated, now offensive* **2** : idiotic act or remark ⟨¡no digas idioteces! : don't talk nonsense!⟩
ido[1], **ida** *adj* : crazy, nutty
ido[2] *pp* → **ir**
idólatra[1] *adj* : idolatrous
idólatra[2] *nmf* : idolater
idolatrar *vt* : to idolize
idolatría *nf* : idolatry
ídolo *nm* : idol
idoneidad *nf* : suitability
idóneo, -nea *adj* ADECUADO : suitable, fitting
iglesia *nf* : church
iglú *nm, pl* **iglús** *or* **iglúes** : igloo
ignición *nf, pl* **-ciones** : ignition
ignífugo, -ga *adj* : fireproof
ignominia *nf* : ignominy, disgrace
ignominioso, -sa *adj* : ignominious, shameful
ignorancia *nf* : ignorance
ignorante[1] *adj* : ignorant — **ignorantemente** *adv*
ignorante[2] *nmf* : ignorant person, ignoramus
ignorar *vt* **1** : to ignore **2** DESCONOCER : to be unaware of ⟨lo ignoramos por absoluto : we have no idea⟩
ignoto, -ta *adj* : unknown
i griega *nf* : (letter) i
igual[1] *adv* **1** : in the same way ⟨las cosas siguen igual : things are the same as ever⟩ **2** : perhaps ⟨igual llueve : it might rain, it may rain⟩ **3** : anyway ⟨iba a venir igual : I was going to come anyway⟩ **4 al igual que** : as well as **5 igual que** : (just) like, the same as ⟨juega básquetbol, igual que su prima : she plays basketball, just like her cousin⟩ ⟨pienso igual que tú : I agree with you, I think the same thing⟩ **6 por ~** : equally
igual[2] *adj* **1** : equal ⟨ser igual a : to be equal to⟩ **2** IDÉNTICO : the same, alike ⟨son iguales : they're the same⟩ ⟨ser igual a : to be the same as⟩ ⟨me es/da igual : it makes no difference to me⟩ **3** : even, smooth **4** SEMEJANTE : similar **5** CONSTANTE : constant
igual[3] *nmf* : equal, peer ⟨sin igual : without equal, unequaled⟩
igualado, -da *adj* **1** : even (of a score) **2** : level **3** *Mex* : disrespectful
igualar *vt* **1** : to equalize **2** NIVELAR : to level, to flatten, to straighten **3** : to tie ⟨igualar el marcador : to even the score⟩ — **igualarse** *vr* ~ **a/con** : to equal, to be equal to, to be a match for
igualdad *nf* **1** : equality **2** UNIFORMIDAD : evenness, uniformity
igualitario, -ria *adj* : egalitarian
igualmente *adv* **1** : equally **2** ASIMISMO : likewise
iguana *nf* : iguana
ijada *nf* : flank, loin, side
ijar *nm* → **ijada**

ilegal[1] *adj* : illegal, unlawful — **ilegalmente** *adv*
ilegal[2] *nmf CA, Mex* : illegal alien
ilegalidad *nf* : illegality
ilegibilidad *nf* : illegibility
ilegible *adj* : illegible — **ilegiblemente** *adv*
ilegitimidad *nf* : illegitimacy
ilegítimo, -ma *adj* : illegitimate, unlawful
ileso, -sa *adj* : uninjured, unharmed
ilícito, -ta *adj* : illicit — **ilícitamente** *adv*
ilimitado, -da *adj* : unlimited
ilógico, -ca *adj* : illogical — **ilógicamente** *adv*
iluminación *nf, pl* **-ciones** **1** : illumination **2** ALUMBRADO : lighting
iluminado, -da *adj* : illuminated, lighted
iluminar *vt* **1** : to illuminate, to light (up) **2** : to enlighten
ilusión *nf, pl* **-siones** **1** : illusion, delusion **2** ESPERANZA : hope ⟨hacerse ilusiones : to get one's hopes up⟩ **3** *Spain* : happiness, excitement, enthusiasm ⟨¡me hace mucha ilusión que te haya gustado! : I'm so glad you liked it!⟩ ⟨no me hace ilusión ir : I'm not looking forward to going⟩ **4 ilusión óptica** : optical illusion
ilusionado, -da *adj* ESPERANZADO : hopeful, eager
ilusionar *vt* : to build up hope, to excite — **ilusionarse** *vr* : to get one's hopes up
iluso[1]**, -sa** *adj* : naive, gullible
iluso[2]**, -sa** *n* SOÑADOR : dreamer, visionary
ilusorio, -ria *adj* ENGAÑOSO : illusory, misleading
ilustración *nf, pl* **-ciones** **1** : illustration **2** : erudition, learning ⟨la Ilustración : the Enlightenment⟩
ilustrado, -da *adj* **1** : illustrated **2** DOCTO : learned, erudite
ilustrador, -dora *n* : illustrator
ilustrar *vt* **1** : to illustrate **2** ACLARAR, CLARIFICAR : to explain
ilustrativo, -va *adj* : illustrative
ilustre *adj* : illustrious, eminent
im- → in-
imagen *nf, pl* **imágenes** : image, picture
imaginable *adj* : imaginable, conceivable
imaginación *nf, pl* **-ciones** : imagination
imaginar *vt* : to imagine — **imaginarse** *vr* **1** : to suppose, to imagine **2** : to picture
imaginario, -ria *adj* : imaginary
imaginativo, -va *adj* : imaginative — **imaginativamente** *adv*
imaginería *nf* **1** : imagery **2** : image making (in religion)
imán *nm, pl* **imanes** : magnet
imantar *vt* : to magnetize
imbatible *adj* : unbeatable
imbécil[1] *adj* : stupid, idiotic
imbécil[2] *nmf* **1** *dated, now offensive* : imbecile (in medicine) *dated, now offensive* **2** *fam* : idiot, dope
imbecilidad *nf* **1** : imbecility (in medicine) *dated, now offensive* **2** IDIOTEZ : stupid thing to say or do
imborrable *adj* : indelible
imbuir {41} *vt* : to imbue — **imbuirse** *vr*

imitación *nf, pl* **-ciones** **1** : imitation **2** : mimicry, impersonation
imitador[1]**, -dora** *adj* : imitative
imitador[2]**, -dora** *n* **1** : imitator **2** : mimic
imitar *vt* **1** : to imitate, to copy **2** : to mimic, to impersonate
imitativo, -va *adj* → **imitador**[1]
impaciencia *nf* : impatience
impacientar *vt* : to make impatient, to exasperate — **impacientarse** *vr*
impaciente *adj* : impatient — **impacientemente** *adv*
impactado, -da *adj* : shocked, stunned
impactante *adj* **1** : shocking **2** : impressive, powerful
impactar *vt* **1** GOLPEAR : to hit **2** IMPRESIONAR : to impact, to affect — **impactarse** *vr*
impacto *nm* **1** : impact, effect **2** : shock, collision
impagable *adj* **1** : unpayable **2** : priceless
impago[1] *adj* : outstanding, unpaid
impago[2] *nm* : nonpayment
impala *nm* : impala
impalpable *adj* INTANGIBLE : impalpable, intangible
impar[1] *adj* : odd ⟨números impares : odd numbers⟩
impar[2] *nm* : odd number
imparable *adj* : unstoppable
imparcial *adj* : impartial — **imparcialmente** *adv*
imparcialidad *nf* : impartiality
impartir *vt* : to impart, to give
impasible *adj* : impassive, unmoved — **impasiblemente** *adv*
impasse *nm* : impasse
impavidez *nf* : fearlessness
impávido, -da *adj* : undaunted
impecable *adj* INTACHABLE : impeccable, faultless — **impecablemente** *adv*
impedido[1]**, -da** *adj* : disabled, crippled
impedido[2]**, -da** *n* : disabled person, handicapped person *sometimes offensive*
impedimento *nm* **1** : impediment, obstacle **2** : disability
impedir {54} *vt* **1** : to prevent, to block **2** : to impede, to hinder
impeler *vt* **1** : to drive, to propel **2** : to impel
impenetrable *adj* : impenetrable — **impenetrabilidad** *nf*
impenitente *adj* : unrepentant
impensable *adj* : unthinkable
impensado, -da *adj* : unforeseen, unexpected
imperante *adj* : prevailing
imperar *vi* **1** : to reign, to rule **2** PREDOMINAR : to prevail
imperativo[1]**, -va** *adj* **1** : imperative **2** : authoritative, commanding
imperativo[2] *nm* : imperative
imperceptible *adj* : imperceptible — **imperceptiblemente** *adv*
imperdible *nm Spain* : safety pin
imperdonable *adj* : unforgivable
imperecedero, -ra *adj* **1** : imperishable **2** INMORTAL : immortal, everlasting

imperfección *nf, pl* **-ciones** 1 : imperfection 2 DEFECTO : defect, flaw
imperfecto¹, -ta *adj* : imperfect, flawed
imperfecto² *nm* : imperfect tense
imperial *adj* : imperial
imperialismo *nm* : imperialism
imperialista *adj & nmf* : imperialist
impericia *nf* : lack of skill, incompetence
imperio *nm* 1 : empire 2 : authority, rule ⟨el imperio de la ley : the rule of law⟩
imperioso, -sa *adj* 1 : imperious 2 : pressing, urgent — **imperiosamente** *adv*
impermeabilizante *nm* : water repellent, waterproofing
impermeabilizar {21} *vt* : to waterproof
impermeable¹ *adj* 1 : impervious 2 : impermeable, waterproof
impermeable² *nm* : raincoat
impersonal *adj* : impersonal — **impersonalmente** *adv*
impersonar *vt Mex* : to impersonate
impertinencia *nf* INSOLENCIA : impertinence, insolence
impertinente *adj* 1 INSOLENTE : impertinent, insolent 2 INOPORTUNO : inappropriate, uncalled-for 3 IRRELEVANTE : irrelevant
impertinentemente *adv* : impertinently
imperturbable *adj* : imperturbable, impassive, stolid
ímpetu *nm* 1 : impetus, momentum 2 : vigor, energy 3 : force, violence
impetuoso, -sa *adj* : impetuous, impulsive — **impetuosamente** *adv*
impiedad *nf* : impiety
impío, -pía *adj* : impious, ungodly
implacable *adj* : implacable, relentless — **implacablemente** *adv*
implantación *nf, pl* **-ciones** 1 : implantation 2 ESTABLECIMIENTO : establishment, introduction
implantado, -da *adj* : well-established
implantar *vt* 1 : to implant 2 ESTABLECER : to establish, to introduce — **implantarse** *vr*
implante *nm* : implant
implementar *vt* : to implement — **implementarse** *vr* — **implementación** *nf*
implemento *nm* : implement, tool
implicación *nf, pl* **-ciones** : implication
implicancia *nf* : implication
implicar {72} *vt* 1 ENREDAR, ENVOLVER : to involve, to implicate 2 : to imply
implícito, -ta *adj* : implied, implicit — **implícitamente** *adv*
implorar *vt* : to implore
implosión *nf, pl* **-siones** : implosion — **implosivo, -va** *adj*
implosionar *vi* : to implode
imponderable *adj & nm* : imponderable
imponente *adj* : imposing, impressive
imponer {60} *vt* 1 : to impose 2 : to confer 3 : to introduce, to establish, to set (a fashion) — *vi* : to be impressive, to command respect — **imponerse** *vr* 1 : to take on (a duty) 2 : to assert oneself 3 : to prevail
imponible *adj* : taxable

impopular *adj* : unpopular — **impopularidad** *nf*
importación *nf, pl* **-ciones** 1 : importation 2 **importaciones** *nfpl* : imports
importado, -da *adj* : imported
importador¹, -dora *adj* : importing
importador², -dora *n* : importer
importancia *nf* : importance
importante *adj* : important, significant — **importantemente** *adv*
importar *vi* 1 : to matter, to be important ⟨no importa : it doesn't matter, it's not important⟩ ⟨lo que importa es el resultado : what matters is the result⟩ ⟨no le importa lo que piensen : she doesn't care what they think⟩ ⟨¿qué importa que no les guste? : who cares if they don't like it?⟩ ⟨(no) me importa un bledo/comino : I don't give a damn, I couldn't care less⟩ ⟨no te importo : you don't care about me⟩ 2 : to bother ⟨no le importa hacerlo : he doesn't mind doing it⟩ ⟨si no te importa : if you don't mind, if it's OK with you⟩ — *vt* 1 : to import (goods, etc.) 2 : to import (in computing)
importe *nm* 1 : price, cost 2 : sum, amount
importunar *vt* : to bother, to inconvenience — *vi* : to be inconvenient
importuno, -na *adj* 1 : inopportune, inconvenient 2 : bothersome, annoying
imposibilidad *nf* : impossibility
imposibilitado, -da *adj* 1 : disabled, crippled 2 **verse imposibilitado** : to be unable (to do something)
imposibilitar *vt* 1 : to make impossible 2 : to disable, to incapacitate — **imposibilitarse** *vr* : to become disabled
imposible *adj* : impossible — **imposiblemente** *adv*
imposición *nf, pl* **-ciones** 1 : imposition 2 EXIGENCIA : demand, requirement 3 : tax 4 : deposit
impositivo, -va *adj* : tax ⟨tasa impositiva : tax rate⟩
impostor, -tora *n* : impostor
impostura *nf* 1 : fraud 2 CALUMNIA : slander
impotencia *nf* 1 : impotence, helplessness, powerlessness 2 : impotence (in medicine)
impotente *adj* 1 : helpless, powerless 2 : impotent
impracticable *adj* : impracticable
imprecisión *nf, pl* **-siones** 1 : imprecision, vagueness 2 : inaccuracy
impreciso, -sa *adj* 1 : imprecise, vague 2 : inaccurate
impredecible *adj* : unpredictable
impregnar *vt* : to impregnate
imprenta *nf* 1 : printing 2 : printing shop, press 3 **letra(s) de imprenta** → letra
imprescindible *adj* : essential, indispensable
impresión *nf, pl* **-siones** 1 : print, printing 2 : impression, feeling ⟨causar una buena/mala impresión : to make a good/bad impression⟩
impresionable *adj* : impressionable

impresionante *adj* : impressive, incredible, amazing, shocking (of video, etc.), horrific (of an accident, etc.) — **impresionantemente** *adv*
impresionar *vt* **1** : to impress, to strike **2** : to affect, to move **3** : to shock **4** : to expose (film) to light — *vi* : to make an impression — **impresionarse** *vr* : to be affected, to be moved
impresionismo *nm* : impressionism
impresionista[1] *adj* : impressionist
impresionista[2] *nmf* : impressionist
impreso[1] *pp* → **imprimir**
impreso[2], **-sa** *adj* : printed
impreso[3] *nm* **1** PUBLICACIÓN : printed matter, publication **2** FORMULARIO : form
impresor, -sora *n* : printer
impresora *nf* **1** : (computer) printer **2** **impresora de inyección de tinta** : inkjet printer **3 impresora láser** : laser printer
imprevisible *adj* : unforeseeable, unpredictable
imprevisión *nf, pl* **-siones** : lack of foresight, thoughtlessness
imprevisto[1], **-ta** *adj* : unexpected, unforeseen
imprevisto[2] *nm* : unexpected occurrence, contingency
imprimir {42} *vt* **1** : to print **2** : to imprint, to stamp, to impress
improbabilidad *nf* : improbability
improbable *adj* : improbable, unlikely
improcedente *adj* **1** : inadmissible **2** : inappropriate, improper
improductivo, -va *adj* : unproductive
impronta *nf* : mark, stamp ⟨dejar su impronta : to leave one's mark⟩
improperio *nm* : affront, insult
impropiedad *nf* : impropriety
impropio, -pia *adj* **1** : improper, incorrect **2** INADECUADO : unsuitable, inappropriate
improvisación *nf, pl* **-ciones** : improvisation, ad-lib
improvisado, -da *adj* : improvised, ad-lib
improvisar *v* : to improvise, to ad-lib
improviso *adj* **de ~** : all of a sudden, unexpectedly
imprudencia *nf* **1** : mistake, indiscretion **2** : carelessness, recklessness
imprudente *adj* **1** : imprudent, unwise, indiscreet **2** : careless, reckless — **imprudentemente** *adv*
impúdico, -ca *adj* : shameless, indecent
impuesto[1] *pp* → **imponer**
impuesto[2] *nm* : tax
impugnar *vt* : to challenge, to contest
impulsar *vt* **1** : to propel, to drive **2** : to boost, to promote
impulsividad *nf* : impulsiveness
impulsivo, -va *adj* : impulsive — **impulsivamente** *adv*
impulso *nm* **1** : drive, thrust **2** : impulse, urge
impulsor, -sora *n* : force, impetus ⟨el principal impulsor de la iniciativa : the main/driving force behind the initiative⟩
impune *adj* : unpunished
impunemente *adv* : with impunity

impunidad *nf* : impunity
impuntualidad *nf* : lack of punctuality
impureza *nf* : impurity
impuro, -ra *adj* : impure
impuso, etc. → **imponer**
imputable *adj* ATRIBUIBLE : attributable
imputación *nf, pl* **-ciones** **1** : attribution **2** : accusation
imputar *vt* ATRIBUIR : to impute, to attribute
in- *or* **im-** *or* **i-** *or* **ir-** *pref* : in-, im-, il-, un- ⟨inexacto : inexact⟩ ⟨imperfecto : imperfect⟩ ⟨ilegal : illegal⟩ ⟨inaceptable : unacceptable⟩
inacabable *adj* : endless
inacabado, -da *adj* INCONCLUSO : unfinished
inaccesibilidad *nf* : inaccessibility
inaccesible *adj* **1** : inaccessible **2** : unattainable
inacción *nf, pl* **-ciones** : inactivity, inaction
inaceptable *adj* : unacceptable
inactividad *nf* : inactivity, idleness
inactivo, -va *adj* : inactive, idle
inadaptado[1], **-da** *adj* : maladjusted
inadaptado[2], **-da** *n* : misfit
inadecuación *nf, pl* **-ciones** : inadequacy
inadecuado, -da *adj* **1** : inadequate **2** IMPROPIO : inappropriate **inadecuadamente** *adv*
inadmisible *adj* **1** : inadmissible **2** : unacceptable
inadvertencia *nf* : oversight
inadvertidamente *adv* : inadvertently
inadvertido, -da *adj* **1** : unnoticed ⟨pasar inadvertido : to go unnoticed⟩ **2** DESPISTADO, DISTRAÍDO : inattentive, distracted
inagotable *adj* : inexhaustible
inaguantable *adj* INSOPORTABLE : insufferable, unbearable
inalámbrico, -ca *adj* : wireless, cordless ⟨acceso inalámbrico a Internet : wireless Internet access⟩ ⟨un teléfono inalámbrico : a cordless phone⟩
inalcanzable *adj* : unreachable, unattainable
inalienable *adj* : inalienable
inalterable *adj* **1** : unalterable, unchangeable **2** : impassive **3** : colorfast
inamovible *adj* : immovable, fixed
inanición *nf, pl* **-ciones** : starvation
inanimado, -da *adj* : inanimate
inapelable *adj* : indisputable
inapetencia *nf* : lack of appetite
inaplicable *adj* : inapplicable
inapreciable *adj* **1** : imperceptible, negligible **2** : invaluable
inapropiado, -da *adj* : inappropriate, unsuitable — **inapropiadamente** *adv*
inarticulado, -da *adj* : inarticulate, unintelligible — **inarticuladamente** *adv*
inasequible *adj* : unattainable, inaccessible
inasistencia *nf* AUSENCIA : absence
inatacable *adj* : unassailable, indisputable
inaudible *adj* : inaudible
inaudito, -ta *adj* : unheard-of, unprecedented

inauguración *nf, pl* **-ciones 1** : inauguration, opening **2** : inauguration, beginning

inaugural *adj* : inaugural, opening

inaugurar *vt* **1** : to inaugurate **2** : to open

inauténtico, -ca *adj* : counterfeit, inauthentic

inca *adj & nmf* : Inca

incaico, -ca *adj* : Inca, Incan

incalculable *adj* : incalculable

incalificable *adj* : indescribable

incandescencia *nf* : incandescence — **incandescente** *adj*

incansable *adj* INFATIGABLE : tireless — **incansablemente** *adv*

incapacidad *nf* **1** : inability, incapacity **2** : disability, handicap *sometimes offensive* **3** : incompetence **4** *Col, CoRi* : sick leave

incapacitado, -da *adj* **1** : disqualified **2** : disabled, handicapped

incapacitar *vt* **1** : to incapacitate, to disable **2** : to disqualify

incapaz *adj, pl* **-paces 1** : incapable, unable **2** : incompetent, inept

incautación *nf, pl* **-ciones** : seizure, confiscation

incautar *vt* CONFISCAR : to confiscate, to seize — **incautarse** *vr*

incauto, -ta *adj* : unwary, unsuspecting

incendiar *vt* : to set fire to, to burn (down) — **incendiarse** *vr* : to catch fire, to burn down

incendiario[1], -ria *adj* : incendiary, inflammatory

incendiario[2], -ria *n* : arsonist

incendio *nm* **1** : fire **2 incendio provocado** : arson

incensario *nm* : censer

incentivar *vt* : to encourage, to stimulate

incentivo *nm* : incentive

incertidumbre *nf* : uncertainty, suspense

incesante *adj* : incessant — **incesantemente** *adv*

incesto *nm* : incest

incestuoso, -sa *adj* : incestuous

incidencia *nf* **1** : incident **2** : effect, impact **3 por ~** : by chance, accidentally

incidental *adj* : incidental

incidentalmente *adv* : by chance

incidente *nm* : incident, occurrence

incidir *vi* **1 ~ en** : to fall into, to enter into ⟨incidimos en el mismo error : we fell into the same mistake⟩ **2 ~ en** : to affect, to influence, to have a bearing on

incienso *nm* : incense

incierto, -ta *adj* **1** : uncertain **2** : untrue **3** : unsteady, insecure

incinerador *nm* : incinerator

incinerar *vt* **1** : to incinerate **2** : to cremate

incipiente *adj* : incipient

incisión *nf, pl* **-siones** : incision

incisivo[1], -va *adj* : incisive

incisivo[2] *nm* : incisor

inciso *nm* **1** : digression, aside **2** : paragraph, subsection

incitación *nf, pl* **-ciones** : incitement

incitador[1], -dora *n* : instigator, agitator

incitador[2], -dora *adj* : provocative

incitante *adj* : provocative

incitar *vt* : to incite, to rouse

incivilizado, -da *adj* : uncivilized

inclemencia *nf* : inclemency, severity

inclemente *adj* : inclement

inclinación *nf, pl* **-ciones 1** PROPENSIÓN : inclination, tendency **2** : incline, slope **3** : bow ⟨inclinación de cabeza : nod⟩

inclinado, -da *adj* **1** : sloping, tilted **2** : inclined, apt

inclinar *vt* : to tilt, to lean, to incline ⟨inclinar la cabeza : to bow one's head⟩ — **inclinarse** *vr* **1** : to lean, to lean over **2** : to bow **3 ~ a** : to be inclined to

incluir {41} *vt* : to include

inclusión *nf, pl* **-siones** : inclusion

inclusive *adv* : inclusive ⟨niños de entre dos y cinco años inclusive : children ages two through five inclusive⟩ ⟨hasta el sábado inclusive : up to and including Saturday, through Saturday⟩

inclusivo, -va *adj* : inclusive, open

incluso *adv* AUN : even, in fact ⟨es importante e incluso crucial : it is important and even crucial⟩

incógnita *nf* **1** : unknown quantity (in mathematics) **2** : mystery

incógnito, -ta *adj* **1** : unknown **2 de incógnito** : incognito

incoherencia *nf* : incoherence

incoherente *adj* : incoherent — **incoherentemente** *adv*

incoloro, -ra *adj* : colorless

incombustible *adj* : fireproof

incomible *adj* : inedible

incomodar *vt* **1** : to make uncomfortable **2** : to inconvenience — **incomodarse** *vr* : to put oneself out, to take the trouble

incomodidad *nf* **1** : discomfort, awkwardness **2** MOLESTIA : inconvenience, bother

incómodo, -da *adj* **1** : uncomfortable, awkward **2** INCONVENIENTE : inconvenient — **incómodamente** *adv*

incomparable *adj* : incomparable

incompatibilidad *nf* : incompatibility

incompatible *adj* : incompatible

incompetencia *nf* : incompetence

incompetente *adj & nmf* : incompetent

incompleto, -ta *adj* : incomplete

incomprendido, -da *adj* : misunderstood

incomprensible *adj* : incomprehensible

incomprensión *nf, pl* **-siones** : lack of understanding, incomprehension

incomunicación *nf, pl* **-ciones** : lack of communication

incomunicado, -da *adj* **1** : cut off, isolated **2** : in solitary confinement

inconcebible *adj* : inconceivable, unthinkable — **inconcebiblemente** *adv*

inconcluso, -sa *adj* INACABADO : unfinished

incondicional *adj* : unconditional — **incondicionalmente** *adv*

inconexo, -xa *adj* **1** : unrelated, unconnected **2** : disjointed

inconfesable *adj* : unspeakable, shameful

inconforme *adj & nmf* : nonconformist

inconformidad *nf* : nonconformity

inconformista *adj & nmf* : nonconformist
inconfundible *adj* : unmistakable, obvious — **inconfundiblemente** *adv*
incongruencia *nf* : incongruity
incongruente *adj* : incongruous
inconmensurable *adj* : vast, immeasurable
inconquistable *adj* : unyielding
inconsciencia *nf* **1** : unconsciousness, lack of awareness **2** : irresponsibility
inconsciente[1] *adj* **1** : unconscious, unaware **2** : reckless, needless — **inconscientemente** *adv*
inconsciente[2] *nm* **el inconsciente** : the unconscious
inconsecuente *adj* : inconsistent — **inconsecuencia** *nf*
inconsiderado, -da *adj* : inconsiderate, thoughtless
inconsistencia *nf* : inconsistency
inconsistente *adj* **1** : weak, flimsy **2** : inconsistent, weak (of an argument)
inconsolable *adj* : inconsolable — **inconsolablemente** *adv*
inconstancia *nf* : fickleness
inconstante *adj* : fickle, changeable
inconstitucional *adj* : unconstitutional — **inconstitucionalidad** *nf*
incontable *adj* INNUMERABLE : countless, innumerable
incontenible *adj* : uncontrollable, unstoppable
incontestable *adj* INCUESTIONABLE, INDISCUTIBLE : irrefutable, indisputable
incontinencia *nf* : incontinence — **incontinente** *adj*
incontrolable *adj* : uncontrollable
incontrolado, -da *adj* : uncontrolled, out of control
incontrovertible *adj* : indisputable
inconveniencia *nf* **1** : inconvenience, trouble **2** : inappropriateness **3** : tactless remark
inconveniente[1] *adj* **1** INCÓMODO : inconvenient **2** INAPROPIADO : improper, unsuitable
inconveniente[2] *nm* **1** : obstacle, problem, snag **2** : objection ⟨no tengo inconveniente en hacerlo : I don't mind doing it⟩ **3** : disadvantage, drawback ⟨las ventajas e inconvenientes : the advantages and disadvantages⟩
incordiar *vt Spain* : to annoy, to pester
incorporación *nf, pl* **-ciones** : incorporation
incorporado *adj* : built-in
incorporar *vt* **1** : to incorporate **2** : to add, to include — **incorporarse** *vr* **1** : to sit up **2** ~ **a** : to join
incorpóreo, -rea *adj* : incorporeal, bodiless
incorrección *n, pl* **-ciones** : impropriety, improper word or action
incorrecto, -ta *adj* **1** : incorrect **2** : impolite, rude — **incorrectamente** *adv*
incorregible *adj* : incorrigible — **incorregibilidad** *nf*
incorruptible *adj* : incorruptible
incredulidad *nf* : incredulity, skepticism
incrédulo[1], **-la** *adj* : incredulous, skeptical

incrédulo[2], **-la** *n* : skeptic
increíble *adj* : incredible, unbelievable — **increíblemente** *adv*
incrementar *vt* : to increase — **incrementarse** *vr*
incremento *nm* AUMENTO : increase
increpar *vt* : to tell off *fam*, to yell at, to rebuke
incriminar *vt* : to incriminate — **incriminación** *nf*
incriminatorio, -ria *adj* : incriminating, incriminatory
incruento, -ta *adj* : bloodless
incrustación *nf, pl* **-ciones** : inlay
incrustar *vt* **1** : to embed **2** : to inlay — **incrustarse** *vr* : to become embedded
incubación *nf, pl* **-ciones** : incubation
incubadora *nf* : incubator
incubar *v* : to incubate
incuestionable *adj* INCONTESTABLE, INDISCUTIBLE : unquestionable, indisputable — **incuestionablemente** *adv*
inculcar {72} *vt* : to inculcate, to instill
inculpado, -da *n* : defendant ⟨el inculpado : the defendant, the accused⟩
inculpar *vt* ACUSAR : to accuse, to charge
inculto, -ta *adj* **1** : uncultured, ignorant **2** : uncultivated, fallow
incultura *adj* : ignorance, lack of culture
incumbencia *nf* : obligation, responsibility
incumbir *vi* (*3rd person only*) ~ **a** : to be incumbent upon, to be of concern to ⟨a mí no me incumbe : it's not my concern⟩
incumplido, -da *adj* : irresponsible, unreliable
incumplimiento *nm* **1** : failure to fulfill (conditions, obligations, etc.) ⟨incumplimiento de la ley : failure to comply with the law⟩ ⟨incumplimiento de pago : failure to make payment, default⟩ **2 incumplimiento de contrato** : breach of contract **3 incumplimiento de deberes** : neglect of duty
incumplir *vt* : to fail to carry out, to break (a promise, a contract)
incurable *adj* : incurable
incurrir *vi* **1** ~ **en** : to incur ⟨incurrir en gastos : to incur expenses⟩ **2** ~ **en** : to fall into, to commit ⟨incurrió en un error : he made a mistake⟩
incursión *nf, pl* **-siones** : incursion, raid
incursionar *vi* **1** : to raid **2** ~ **en** : to go into, to enter ⟨el actor incursionó en el baile : the actor worked in dance for a while⟩
indagación *nf, pl* **-ciones** : investigation, inquiry
indagar {52} *vt* : to inquire into, to investigate
indagatoria *nf* **1** : statement, deposition **2** : investigation, inquiry, inquest
indebido, -da *adj* : improper, undue — **indebidamente** *adv*
indecencia *nf* : indecency, obscenity
indecente *adj* : indecent, obscene
indecible *adj* : indescribable, inexpressible
indecisión *nf, pl* **-siones** : indecision
indeciso, -sa *adj* **1** IRRESOLUTO : indecisive **2** : undecided

indeclinable *adj* : unavoidable
indecoro *nm* : impropriety, indecorousness
indecoroso, -sa *adj* : indecorous, unseemly
indefectible *adj* : unfailing, sure
indefendible *adj* : indefensible
indefensión *nf* : defenselessness
indefenso, -sa *adj* : defenseless, helpless
indefinible *adj* : indefinable
indefinido, -da *adj* 1 : undefined, vague 2 INDETERMINADO : indefinite — **indefinidamente** *adv*
indeleble *adj* : indelible — **indeleblemente** *adv*
indelicado, -da *adj* : indelicate, tactless
indemne *adj* : unharmed, unhurt
indemnidad *nf* : indemnity
indemnización *nf, pl* -ciones 1 : indemnity 2 **indemnización por despido** : severance pay
indemnizar {21} *vt* : to indemnify, to compensate
independencia *nf* : independence
independiente *adj* : independent — **independientemente** *adv*
independista[1] *adj* : pro-independence
independista[2] *nmf* : independence supporter
independizar {21} *vt* : to make independent — **independizarse** *vr*
indescifrable *adj* : indecipherable
indescriptible *adj* : indescribable — **indescriptiblemente** *adv*
indeseable *adj & nmf* : undesirable
indestructible *adj* : indestructible
indeterminado, -da *adj* 1 INDEFINIDO : indefinite 2 : indeterminate
indexar *vt* INDICIAR : to index (wages, prices, etc.)
indicación *nf, pl* -ciones 1 : sign, signal 2 : direction, instruction 3 : suggestion, hint
indicado, -da *adj* 1 APROPIADO : appropriate, suitable 2 : specified, indicated ⟨al día indicado : on the specified day⟩
indicador *nm* 1 : gauge, dial, meter 2 : indicator ⟨indicadores económicos : economic indicators⟩
indicar {72} *vt* 1 SEÑALAR : to indicate 2 ENSEÑAR, MOSTRAR : to show
indicativo[1]**, -va** *adj* : indicative
indicativo[2] *nm* : indicative (mood)
índice *nm* 1 : index 2 : contents *pl*, table of contents 3 : index finger, forefinger 4 INDICIO : indication
indiciar *vt* : to index (prices, wages, etc.)
indicio *nm* 1 : indication, sign 2 **indicios** *nmpl* : evidence
indiferencia *nf* : indifference
indiferente *adj* 1 : indifferent, unconcerned 2 **ser indiferente** : to be of no concern ⟨me es indiferente : it doesn't matter to me⟩
indiferentemente *adv* : indifferently
indígena[1] *adj* : indigenous, native
indígena[2] *nmf* : native
indigencia *nf* MISERIA : poverty, destitution
indigente *adj & nmf* : indigent

indigestarse *vr* 1 EMPACHARSE : to have indigestion 2 *fam* : to nauseate, to disgust ⟨ese tipo se me indigesta : that guy makes me sick⟩
indigestión *nf, pl* -tiones EMPACHO : indigestion
indigesto, -ta *adj* : indigestible, difficult to digest
indignación *nf, pl* -ciones : indignation
indignado, -da *adj* : indignant
indignante *adj* : outrageous, infuriating
indignar *vt* : to outrage, to infuriate — **indignarse** *vr*
indignidad *nf* : indignity
indigno, -na *adj* 1 : unworthy 2 : contemptible, despicable
índigo *nm* : indigo
indio, -dia *adj & n* 1 *sometimes offensive* : Indian *often offensive*, Native American 2 : Indian (from India)
indio–americano, india–americana → **nativo americano**
indirecta *nf* 1 : hint, innuendo 2 **echar indirectas** *or* **lanzar indirectas** : to drop a hint, to insinuate
indirecto, -ta *adj* : indirect — **indirectamente** *adv*
indisciplina *nf* : lack of discipline, unruliness
indisciplinado, -da *adj* : undisciplined, unruly
indiscreción *nf, pl* -ciones 1 IMPRUDENCIA : indiscretion 2 : tactless remark
indiscreto, -ta *adj* IMPRUDENTE : indiscreet, imprudent — **indiscretamente** *adv*
indiscriminado, -da *adj* : indiscriminate — **indiscriminadamente** *adv*
indiscutible *adj* 1 INCONTESTABLE, INCUESTIONABLE : indisputable, unquestionable 2 : undisputed ⟨el campeón indiscutible : the undisputed champion⟩ — **indiscutiblemente** *adv*
indiscutido, -da *adj* : undisputed
indispensable *adj* : indispensable — **indispensablemente** *adv*
indisponer {60} *vt* 1 : to spoil, to upset 2 : to make ill — **indisponerse** *vr* 1 : to become ill 2 ∼ **con** : to fall out with
indisposición *nf, pl* -ciones : illness
indispuesto, -ta *adj* : unwell, indisposed
indistinguible *adj* : indistinguishable
indistintamente *adv* 1 : indistinctly 2 : indiscriminately
indistinto, -ta *adj* : indistinct, vague, faint
individual[1] *adj* : individual — **individualmente** *adv*
individual[2] *nm* 1 : place mat 2 **individuales** *nmpl* : singles (in sports)
individualidad *nf* : individuality
individualismo *nm* : individualism
individualista[1] *adj* : individualistic
individualista[2] *nmf* : individualist
individualizar {21} *vt* : to individualize
individuo *nm* : individual, person
indivisible *adj* : indivisible — **indivisibilidad** *nf*
indocumentado, -da *n* : illegal immigrant
índole *nf* 1 : nature, character 2 CLASE, TIPO : sort, kind

indolencia *nf* : indolence, laziness
indolente *adj* : indolent, lazy
indoloro, -ra *adj* : painless
indomable *adj* **1** : indomitable **2** : unruly, unmanageable
indómito, -ta *adj* **1** : indomitable **2** : untamed
indonesio, -sia *adj & n* : Indonesian
inducción *nf, pl* **-ciones** : induction
inducir {61} *vt* **1** : to induce, to cause **2** : to infer, to deduce
inductivo, -va *adj* : inductive
indubable *adj* : unquestionable, beyond doubt
indudablemente *adv* : undoubtedly, unquestionably
indulgencia *nf* **1** : indulgence, leniency **2** : indulgence (in religion)
indulgente *adj* : indulgent, lenient
indultar *vt* : to pardon, to reprieve
indulto *nm* : pardon, reprieve
indumentaria *nf* : clothing, attire
industria *nf* : industry
industrial[1] *adj* : industrial
industrial[2] *nmf* : industrialist, manufacturer
industrialización *nf, pl* **-ciones** : industrialization
industrializar {21} *vt* : to industrialize
industrioso, -sa *adj* : industrious
inédito, -ta *adj* **1** : unpublished **2** : unprecedented
inefable *adj* : ineffable
ineficacia *nf* **1** : inefficiency **2** : lack of effectiveness
ineficaz *adj, pl* **-caces** **1** : inefficient **2** : ineffective — **ineficazmente** *adv*
ineficiencia *nf* : inefficiency
ineficiente *adj* : inefficient — **ineficientemente** *adv*
inelegancia *nf* : inelegance — **inelegante** *adj*
inelegible *adj* : ineligible — **inelegibilidad** *nf*
ineludible *adj* : inescapable, unavoidable — **ineludiblemente** *adv*
ineptitud *nf* : ineptitude, incompetence
inepto[1]**, -ta** *adj* : inept, incompetent
inepto[2]**, -ta** *n* : incompetent
inequidad *nf* : inequity
inequitativo, -va *adj* : inequitable
inequívoco, -ca *adj* : unequivocal, unmistakable — **inequívocamente** *adv*
inercia *nf* **1** : inertia **2** : apathy **3 por ∼** : out of habit
inerme *adj* : unarmed, defenseless
inerte *adj* : inert
inescrupuloso, -sa *adj* : unscrupulous
inescrutable *adj* : inscrutable
inesperado, -da *adj* : unexpected — **inesperadamente** *adv*
inestabilidad *nf* : instability, unsteadiness
inestable *adj* **1** : unstable, unsteady **2** : changeable (of weather)
inestimable *adj* : inestimable, invaluable
inevitabilidad *nf* : inevitability
inevitable *adj* : inevitable, unavoidable — **inevitablemente** *adv*
inexactitud *nf* : inaccuracy
inexacto, -ta *adj* : inexact, inaccurate

inexcusable *adj* **1** : inexcusable, unforgivable **2** : unavoidable
inexistencia *nf* : lack, nonexistence
inexistente *adj* : nonexistent
inexorable *adj* : inexorable — **inexorablemente** *adv*
inexperiencia *nf* : inexperience
inexperto, -ta *adj* : inexperienced, unskilled
inexplicable *adj* : inexplicable — **inexplicablemente** *adv*
inexplorado, -da *adj* : unexplored
inexpresable *adj* : inexpressible
inexpresivo, -va *adj* : expressionless
inexpugnable *adj* : impregnable
inextricable *adj* : inextricable — **inextricablemente** *adv*
infalibilidad *nf* : infallibility
infalible *adj* : infallible — **infaliblemente** *adv*
infame *adj* **1** : infamous **2** : loathsome, vile ⟨tiempo infame : terrible weather⟩
infamia *nf* : infamy, disgrace
infancia *nf* **1** NIÑEZ : infancy, childhood **2** : children *pl* **3** : beginnings *pl*
infante[1]**, -ta** *n* : prince *m*, princess *f*
infante[2] *nm* : infantry soldier
infantería *nf* **1** : infantry **2 infantería de marina** : marines *pl*
infantil *adj* **1** : childish, infantile **2** : child's, children's
infarto *nm* **1** : heart attack **2 infarto cerebral** : stroke
infatigable *adj* : indefatigable, tireless — **infatigablemente** *adv*
infección *nf, pl* **-ciones** : infection
infeccioso, -sa *adj* : infectious
infectar *vt* : to infect — **infectarse** *vr*
infecto, -ta *adj* **1** : infected **2** : repulsive, sickening
infecundidad *nf* : infertility
infecundo, -da *adj* : infertile, barren
infelicidad *nf* : unhappiness
infeliz[1] *adj, pl* **-lices** **1** : unhappy **2** : hapless, unfortunate, wretched
infeliz[2] *nmf, pl* **-lices** : wretch
inferencia *nf* : inference
inferior[1] *adj* : inferior, lower
inferior[2] *nmf* : inferior, underling
inferioridad *nf* : inferiority
inferir {76} *vt* **1** DEDUCIR : to infer, to deduce **2** : to cause (harm or injury), to inflict
infernal *adj* : infernal, hellish
infertilidad *nf* : infertility
infestación *n, pl* **-ciones** : infestation
infestar *vt* **1** : to infest ⟨infestar de : to infest with⟩ **2** : to overrun, to invade
inficción *nf, pl* **-ciones** *Mex* : pollution
infidelidad *nf* : unfaithfulness, infidelity
infiel[1] *adj* : unfaithful, disloyal
infiel[2] *nmf* : infidel, heathen *often offensive*
infierno *nm* **1** : hell **2** : bedlam, madness **3** : hellhole, hellish place **4 el quinto infierno** : the middle of nowhere
infiltrado, -da *n* : infiltrator
infiltrar *vt* : to infiltrate — **infiltrarse** *vr* — **infiltración** *nf*
ínfimo, -ma *adj* **1** : minuscule, negligible **2** : lousy, very poor

infinidad *nf* **1** : infinity **2** SINFÍN : great number, huge quantity ⟨una infinidad de veces : countless times⟩
infinitesimal *adj* : infinitesimal
infinitivo *nm* : infinitive
infinito[1] *adv* : infinitely, vastly
infinito[2], **-ta** *adj* **1** : infinite **2** : limitless, endless — **infinitamente** *adv*
infinito[3] *nm* : infinity
inflable *adj* : inflatable
inflación *nf*, *pl* **-ciones** : inflation
inflacionario, -ria *adj* : inflationary
inflacionista → **inflacionario**
inflamable *adj* : flammable
inflamación *nf*, *pl* **-ciones** **1** : inflammation **2** : ignition, combustion
inflamar *vt* **1** : to inflame **2** : to ignite
inflamatorio, -ria *adj* : inflammatory
inflar *vt* **1** HINCHAR : to inflate **2** EXAGERAR : to exaggerate — **inflarse** *vr* **1** : to swell **2** : to become conceited
inflexibilidad *nf* : inflexibility
inflexible *adj* : inflexible, unyielding
inflexión *nf*, *pl* **-xiones** : inflection
infligir {35} *vt* : to inflict
influencia *nf* **1** INFLUJO : influence **2** **influencias** *nfpl* : contacts *pl*, influence ⟨tráfico de influencias : influence peddling⟩
influenciable *adj* : easily influenced, suggestible
influenciar *vt* : to influence
influenza *nf* : influenza
influir {41} *vt* : to influence — *vi* ∼ **en** *or* ∼ **sobre** : to have an influence on, to affect
influjo *nm* INFLUENCIA : influence
influyente *adj* : influential
infografía *nf* : computer graphics *pl*
información *nf*, *pl* **-ciones** **1** : information ⟨centro/oficina de información : information center/office⟩ **2** : information, directory assistance **3** INFORME : report, inquiry **4** NOTICIAS : news
informado, -da *adj* : informed ⟨bien informado : well-informed⟩
informador, -dora *n* : informer, informant
informal *adj* **1** : unreliable (of persons) **2** : informal, casual **3** : informal, unofficial (in economics) — **informalmente** *adv*
informalidad *nf* : informality
informante *nmf* : informant
informar *vt* ENTERAR : to inform — *vi* : to report — **informarse** *vr* ENTERARSE : to get information, to find out
informática *nf* : computer science, computing
informático[1], **-ca** *adj* : computer ⟨sistema informático : computer system⟩
informático[2], **-ca** *n* : computer specialist
informativo[1], **-va** *adj* : informative, informational
informativo[2] *nm* : news program, news
informatización *nf*, *pl* **-ciones** : computerization
informatizar {21} *vt* : to computerize
informe[1] *adj* AMORFO : shapeless, formless

informe[2] *nm* **1** : report **2** : reference (for employment) **3 informes** *nmpl* : information, data
infortunado, -da *adj* : unfortunate, unlucky
infortunio *nm* **1** DESGRACIA : misfortune **2** CONTRATIEMPO : mishap
infracción *nf*, *pl* **-ciones** : violation, offense, infraction
infractor, -tora *n* : offender
infraestructura *nf* : infrastructure
in fraganti *adv* : red-handed
infrahumano, -na *adj* : subhuman
infranqueable *adj* **1** : impassable **2** : insurmountable
infrarrojo, -ja *adj* : infrared
infrecuente *adj* : infrequent
infringir {35} *vt* : to infringe, to breach
infructuoso, -sa *adj* : fruitless — **infructuosamente** *adv*
ínfulas *nfpl* **1** : conceit **2 darse ínfulas** : to put on airs
infundado, -da *adj* : unfounded, baseless
infundio *nm* : false story, lie, tall tale ⟨todo eso son infundios : that's a pack of lies⟩
infundir *vt* **1** : to instill (fear, confidence), to arouse (enthusiasm) **2 infundir ánimo a** : to encourage
infusión *nf*, *pl* **-siones** : infusion, tea
ingeniar *vt* : to devise, to think up — **ingeniarse** *vr* : to manage, to find a way
ingeniería *nf* : engineering
ingeniero, -ra *n* : engineer
ingenio *nm* **1** : ingenuity **2** CHISPA : wit, wits **3** : device, apparatus **4 ingenio azucarero** : sugar refinery
ingenioso, -sa *adj* **1** : ingenious **2** : clever, witty — **ingeniosamente** *adv*
ingente *adj* : huge, enormous
ingenuidad *nf* : naïveté, ingenuousness
ingenuo[1], **-nua** *adj* CÁNDIDO : naive — **ingenuamente** *adv*
ingenuo[2], **-nua** *n* : naive person
ingerencia → **injerencia**
ingerir {76} *vt* : to ingest, to consume
ingesta *nf* : consumption, ingestion
ingestión *nf*, *pl* **-tiones** : ingestion
ingle *nf* : groin
inglés[1], **-glesa** *adj, mpl* **ingleses** : English
inglés[2], **-glesa** *n, mpl* **ingleses** : Englishman *m*, Englishwoman *f*
inglés[3] *nm* : English (language)
inglete *nm* : miter joint
ingobernable *adj* : ungovernable, lawless
ingratitud *nf* : ingratitude
ingrato[1], **-ta** *adj* **1** : ungrateful **2** : thankless, difficult
ingrato[2], **-ta** *n* : ingrate
ingrávido, -da *adj* : weightless
ingrediente *nm* : ingredient
ingresar *vt* **1** : to admit ⟨ingresaron a Luis al hospital : Luis was admitted into the hospital⟩ **2** : to deposit — *vi* **1** : to enter, to go in **2** ∼ **en** : to join, to enroll in
ingreso *nm* **1** : entrance, entry **2** : admission **3** : deposit **4 ingresos** *nmpl* : income, earnings *pl*
íngrimo, -ma *adj* : all alone, all by oneself

inhábil *adj* : clumsy
inhabilidad *nf* 1 : lack of skill 2 : lack of suitability
inhabilitar *vt* 1 : to disqualify, to bar 2 : to disable
inhabitable *adj* : uninhabitable
inhabitado, -da → deshabitado
inhabituado, -da *adj* ~ a : unaccustomed to
inhalador *nm* : inhaler
inhalante *nm* : inhalant
inhalar *vt* : to inhale — inhalación *nf*
inherente *adj* : inherent
inhibición *nf, pl* -ciones COHIBICIÓN : inhibition
inhibir *vt* : to inhibit — inhibirse *vr*
inhóspito, -ta *adj* : inhospitable
inhumación *nf, pl* -ciones : interment, burial
inhumanidad *nf* : inhumanity
inhumano, -na *adj* : inhuman, cruel, inhumane
inhumar *vt* : to inter, to bury
iniciación *nf, pl* -ciones 1 : initiation 2 : introduction
iniciado, -da *n* : initiate
iniciador¹, -dora *adj* : initiatory
iniciador², -dora *n* : originator
inicial¹ *adj* : initial, original — inicialmente *adv*
inicial² *nf* : initial (letter)
iniciar *vt* 1 COMENZAR : to initiate, to begin ⟨iniciar (la) sesión : to log in/on⟩ 2 : to initiate (someone) — iniciarse *vr*
iniciativa *nf* : initiative
inicio *nm* COMIENZO : beginning
inicuo, -cua *adj* : iniquitous, wicked
inigualable *adj* : incomparable (of a person, view, etc.), unrivaled (of popularity, etc.), unbeatable (of prices, etc.)
inigualado, -da *adj* : unequaled
inimaginable *adj* : unimaginable
inimitable *adj* : inimitable
ininteligible *adj* : unintelligible
ininterrumpido, -da *adj* : uninterrupted, continuous — ininterrumpidamente *adv*
iniquidad *nf* : iniquity, wickedness
injerencia *nf* : interference
injerirse {76} *vr* ENTROMETERSE, INMISCUIRSE : to meddle, to interfere
injertar *vt* : to graft
injerto *nm* : graft ⟨injerto de piel : skin graft⟩
injuria *nf* AGRAVIO : affront, insult
injuriar *vt* INSULTAR : to insult, to revile
injurioso, -sa *adj* : insulting, abusive
injusticia *nf* : injustice, unfairness
injustificable *adj* : unjustifiable
injustificadamente *adv* : unjustifiably, unfairly
injustificado, -da *adj* : unjustified, unwarranted
injusto, -ta *adj* : unfair, unjust — injustamente *adv*
inmaculado, -da *adj* : immaculate, spotless
inmadurez *nf, pl* -reces : immaturity
inmaduro, -ra *adj* 1 : immature 2 : unripe

inmediaciones *nfpl* : environs, surrounding area
inmediatamente *adv* ENSEGUIDA : immediately
inmediatez *nf, pl* -teces : immediacy
inmediato, -ta *adj* 1 : immediate 2 CONTIGUO : adjoining 3 de ~ : immediately, right away 4 ~ a : next to, close to
inmejorable *adj* : excellent, unbeatable
inmemorial *adj* : immemorial ⟨tiempos inmemoriales : time immemorial⟩
inmensidad *nf* : immensity, vastness
inmenso, -sa *adj* ENORME : immense, huge, vast — inmensamente *adv*
inmensurable *adj* : boundless, immeasurable
inmerecido, -da *adj* : undeserved — inmerecidamente *adv*
inmersión *nf, pl* -siones : immersion
inmerso, -sa *adj* 1 : immersed 2 : involved, absorbed
inmigración *nf, pl* -ciones : immigration
inmigrado, -da *adj & n* : immigrant
inmigrante *adj & nmf* : immigrant
inmigrar *vi* : to immigrate
inminencia *nf* : imminence
inminente *adj* : imminent — inminentemente *adv*
inmiscuirse {41} *vr* ENTROMETERSE, INJERIRSE : to meddle, to interfere
inmobiliaria *nf* 1 : real estate agency 2 : developer
inmobiliario, -ria *adj* : real estate, property
inmoderación *n, pl* -ciones : intemperance, lack of moderation
inmoderado, -da *adj* : immoderate, excessive — inmoderadamente *adv*
inmodestia *nf* : immodesty — inmodesto, -ta *adj*
inmoral *adj* : immoral
inmoralidad *nf* : immorality
inmortal *adj & nmf* : immortal
inmortalidad *nf* : immortality
inmortalizar {21} *vt* : to immortalize
inmotivado, -da *adj* 1 : unmotivated 2 : groundless
inmovible *adj* : immovable, fixed
inmóvil *adj* 1 : still, motionless 2 : steadfast
inmovilidad *nf* : immobility
inmovilizar {21} *vt* : to immobilize — inmovilización *nf*
inmueble *nm* : building, property
inmundicia *nf* : dirt, filth, trash
inmundo, -da *adj* : dirty, filthy, nasty
inmune *adj* : immune
inmunidad *nf* : immunity
inmunizar {21} *vt* : to immunize — inmunización *nf*
inmunología *nf* : immunology
inmunológico, -ca *adj* : immune ⟨sistema inmunológico : immune system⟩
inmutable *adj* : immutable, unchangeable
inmutar *vt* : to upset — inmutarse *vr* : to get upset, to look upset ⟨ni se inmutó : he didn't even bat an eyelash⟩
innato, -ta *adj* : innate, inborn
innecesario, -ria *adj* : unnecessary — innecesariamente *adv*

innegable *adj* : undeniable
innoble *adj* : ignoble — **innoblemente** *adv*
innovación *nf, pl* **-ciones** : innovation
innovador¹, -dora *adj* : innovative
innovador², -dora *n* : innovator
innovar *vt* : to introduce — *vi* : to innovate
innumerable *adj* INCONTABLE : innumerable, countless
inobjetable *adj* : indisputable, unobjectionable
inocencia *nf* : innocence
inocentada *nf* : practical joke
inocente¹ *adj* **1** : innocent **2** INGENUO : naive — **inocentemente** *adv*
inocente² *nmf* : innocent person
inocentón¹, -tona *adj, mpl* **-tones -tones** : naive, gullible
inocentón², -tona *n, mpl* **-tones** : simpleton, dupe
inocuidad *nf* : harmlessness
inocular *vt* : to inoculate, to vaccinate — **inoculación** *nf*
inocuo, -cua *adj* : innocuous, harmless
inodoro¹, -ra *adj* : odorless
inodoro² *nm* : toilet
inofensivo, -va *adj* : inoffensive, harmless
inolvidable *adj* : unforgettable
inoperable *adj* : inoperable
inoperante *adj* : ineffective, inoperative
inopinado, -da *adj* : unexpected — **inopinadamente** *adv*
inoportuno, -na *adj* : untimely, inopportune, inappropriate
inorgánico, -ca *adj* : inorganic
inoxidable *adj* **1** : rustproof **2 acero inoxidable** : stainless steel
inquebrantable *adj* : unshakable, unwavering
inquietamente *adv* **1** : anxiously, uneasily **2** : restlessly
inquietante *adj* : disturbing, worrisome
inquietar *vt* PREOCUPAR : to disturb, to upset, to worry — **inquietarse** *vr*
inquieto, -ta *adj* **1** : anxious, uneasy, worried **2** : restless
inquietud *nf* **1** : anxiety, uneasiness, worry **2** AGITACIÓN : restlessness
inquilinato *nm* : tenancy
inquilino, -na *n* : tenant, occupant
inquina *nf* **1** : aversion, dislike **2** : ill will ⟨tener inquina a alguien : to have a grudge against someone⟩
inquirir {4} *vi* : to make inquiries — *vt* : to investigate
inquisición *nf, pl* **-ciones** : investigation, inquiry
inquisidor¹, -dora *adj* : inquisitive
inquisidor² *nm* : inquisitor
inquisitivo, -va *adj* : inquisitive, curious — **inquisitivamente** *adv*
insaciable *adj* : insatiable
insalubre *adj* **1** : unhealthy **2** ANTIHIGIÉNICO : unsanitary
insalvable *adj* : insurmountable
insano, -na *adj* **1** LOCO : insane, mad **2** INSALUBRE : unhealthy
insatisfacción *nf, pl* **-ciones** : dissatisfaction

insatisfactorio *nm* : unsatisfactory
insatisfecho, -cha *adj* **1** : dissatisfied **2** : unsatisfied
inscribir {33} *vt* **1** MATRICULAR : to enroll, to register **2** GRABAR : to engrave — **inscribirse** *vr* : to register, to sign up
inscripción *nf, pl* **-ciones** **1** MATRÍCULA : enrollment, registration **2** : inscription
inscrito *pp* → **inscribir**
insecticida¹ *adj* : insecticidal
insecticida² *nm* : insecticide
insecto *nm* : insect
inseguridad *nf* **1** : insecurity **2** : lack of safety **3** : uncertainty
inseguro, -ra *adj* **1** : insecure **2** : unsafe **3** : uncertain — **inseguramente** *adv*
inseminar *vt* : to inseminate — **inseminación** *nf*
insensatez *nf, pl* **-teces** : foolishness, stupidity
insensato¹, -ta *adj* : foolish, senseless — **insensatamente** *adv*
insensato², -ta *n* : fool
insensibilidad *nf* : insensitivity
insensible *adj* : insensitive, unfeeling — **insensiblemente** *adv*
inseparable *adj* : inseparable — **inseparablemente** *adv*
inserción *nf, pl* **-ciones** : insertion
insertar *vt* : to insert
inservible *adj* INÚTIL : useless, unusable
insidia *nf* **1** : snare, trap **2** : malice
insidioso, -sa *adj* : insidious
insigne *adj* : noted, famous
insignia *nf* ENSEÑA : insignia, emblem, badge
insignificancia *nf* **1** : insignificance **2** NIMIEDAD : trifle, triviality
insignificante *adj* : insignificant
insincero, -ra *adj* : insincere — **insinceramente** *adv* — **insinceridad** *nf*
insinuación *nf, pl* **-ciones** : insinuation, hint
insinuante *adj* : suggestive
insinuar {3} *vt* : to insinuate, to hint at — **insinuarse** *vr* **1** ∼ **a** : to make advances to **2** ∼ **en** : to worm one's way into
insípido, -da *adj* : insipid, bland
insistencia *nf* : insistence
insistente *adj* : insistent — **insistentemente** *adv*
insistir *v* : to insist
insociable *adj* : unsociable
insolación *nf, pl* **-ciones** : sunstroke
insolencia *nf* IMPERTINENCIA : insolence
insolente *adj* IMPERTINENTE : insolent — **insolentemente** *adv*
insólito, -ta *adj* : rare, unusual
insoluble *adj* : insoluble — **insolubilidad** *nf*
insolvencia *nf* : insolvency, bankruptcy
insolvente *adj* : insolvent, bankrupt
insomne *adj & nmf* : insomniac
insomnio *nm* : insomnia
insonorizado, -da *adj* : soundproof
insoportable *adj* INAGUANTABLE : unbearable, intolerable
insoslayable *adj* : unavoidable, inescapable

insospechado, -da *adj* : unexpected, unforeseen
insostenible *adj* 1 : not sustainable (of a rate, etc.) 2 : untenable
inspección *nf, pl* -ciones : inspection
inspeccionar *vt* : to inspect
inspector, -tora *n* : inspector
inspiración *nf, pl* -ciones 1 : inspiration 2 INHALACIÓN : inhalation
inspirador, -dora *adj* : inspiring
inspirar *vt* : to inspire — *vi* INHALAR : to inhale — **inspirarse** *vr*
instalación *nf, pl* -ciones : installation
instalar *vt* 1 : to install (a device, etc.) 2 : to install, to induct — **instalarse** *vr* ESTABLECERSE : to settle, to establish oneself
instancia *nf* 1 : petition, request 2 **en última instancia** : as a last resort
instantánea *nf* : snapshot
instantáneo, -nea *adj* 1 : instantaneous 2 : instant ⟨café instantáneo : instant coffee⟩ — **instantáneamente** *adv*
instante *nm* 1 : instant, moment 2 **al instante** : immediately 3 **a cada instante** : frequently, all the time 4 **por instantes** : constantly, incessantly
instar *vt* APREMIAR : to urge, to press — *vi* URGIR : to be urgent or pressing ⟨insta que vayamos pronto : it is imperative that we leave soon⟩
instauración *nf, pl* -ciones : establishment
instaurar *vt* : to establish
instigador, -dora *n* : instigator
instigar {52} *vt* : to instigate, to incite
instintivo, -va *adj* : instinctive — **instintivamente** *adv*
instinto *nm* : instinct
institución *nf, pl* -ciones : institution
institucional *adj* : institutional — **institucionalmente** *adv*
institucionalizar {21} *vt* : to institutionalize
instituir {41} *vt* ESTABLECER, FUNDAR : to institute, to establish, to found
instituto *nm* : institute
institutriz *nf, pl* -trices : governess *f*
instrucción *nf, pl* -ciones 1 EDUCACIÓN : education, training 2 **instrucciones** *nfpl* : instructions, directions
instructivo, -va *adj* : instructive, educational
instructor, -tora *n* : instructor
instruir {41} *vt* 1 ADIESTRAR : to instruct, to train 2 ENSEÑAR : to educate, to teach
instrumentación *nf, pl* -ciones : orchestration
instrumental[1] *adj* : instrumental
instrumental[2] *nm* : instruments *pl*
instrumentar *vt* : to orchestrate
instrumentista *nmf* : instrumentalist
instrumento *nm* 1 : (musical) instrument 2 : instrument (tool or device) 3 : instrument, means *pl*
insubordinado, -da *adj* : insubordinate — **insubordinación** *nf*
insubordinarse *vr* : to rebel

insuficiencia *nf* 1 : insufficiency, inadequacy 2 **insuficiencia cardíaca** : heart failure
insuficiente[1] *adj* 1 : insufficient, inadequate 2 : poor, unsatisfactory — **insuficientemente** *adv*
insuficiente[2] *nm* : F, failing grade
insufrible *adj* : insufferable
insular *adj* : insular
insularidad *nf* : insularity
insulina *nf* : insulin
insulso, -sa *adj* 1 INSÍPIDO : insipid, bland 2 : dull
insultante *adj* : insulting
insultar *vt* : to insult
insulto *nm* : insult
insumos *nmpl* : supplies ⟨insumos agrícolas : agricultural supplies⟩
insuperable *adj* 1 : insurmountable 2 : unbeatable
insurgente *adj* & *nmf* : insurgent — **insurgencia** *nf*
insurrección *nf, pl* -ciones : insurrection, uprising
insustancial *adj* : insubstantial, flimsy
insustituible *adj* : irreplaceable
intachable *adj* : irreproachable, faultless
intacto, -ta *adj* : intact
intangible *adj* IMPALPABLE : intangible, impalpable
integración *nf, pl* -ciones : integration
integral *adj* 1 : integral, essential 2 **pan integral** : whole grain bread
integrante[1] *adj* : integrating, integral
integrante[2] *nmf* : member
integrar *vt* : to make up, to compose — **integrarse** *vr* : to integrate, to fit in
integridad *nf* 1 RECTITUD : integrity, honesty 2 : integrity, soundness ⟨integridad física : personal safety⟩
integrismo *nm* : fundamentalism
integrista *adj* & *nmf* : fundamentalist
íntegro, -gra *adj* 1 : honest, upright 2 ENTERO : whole, complete 3 : unabridged
intelecto *nm* : intellect
intelectual *adj* & *nmf* : intellectual — **intelectualmente** *adv*
intelectualidad *nf* : intelligentsia
inteligencia *nf* : intelligence
inteligente *adj* : intelligent — **inteligentemente** *adv*
inteligible *adj* : intelligible — **inteligibilidad** *nf*
intemperancia *adj* : intemperance, excess
intemperie *nf* 1 : bad weather, elements *pl* 2 **a la intemperie** : in the open air, outside
intempestivo, -va *adj* : inopportune, untimely — **intempestivamente** *adv*
intención *nf, pl* -ciones 1 : intention, plan ⟨tenías buenas intenciones : you had good intentions, your intentions were good⟩ ⟨tener la intención de hacer algo : to intend to do something⟩ ⟨con/sin intención : intentionally/unintentionally⟩ ⟨con la mejor intención : with the best (of) intentions⟩ 2 **segunda intención** : ulterior motive
intencionadamente → intencionalmente

intencionado, -da → **intencional**

intencional *adj* : intentional

intencionalmente *adv* : intentionally

intendencia *nf* **1** : management, administration **2** *Arg, Par, Uru* : city council, town council **3** *Chile* : governorship

intendente *nmf* **1** : quartermaster **2** *Arg, Par, Uru* : mayor **3** *Chile* : governor

intensidad *nf* : intensity

intensificación *nf, pl* **-ciones** : intensification

intensificador *nm* : intensifier (in linguistics)

intensificar {72} *vt* : to intensify — **intensificarse** *vr*

intensivo, -va *adj* : intensive — **intensivamente** *adv*

intenso, -sa *adj* : intense — **intensamente** *adv*

intentar *vt* : to attempt, to try

intento *nm* **1** PROPÓSITO : intent, intention **2** TENTATIVA : attempt, try

intentona *nf* : attempt ⟨intentona golpista : attempted coup⟩

inter- *pref* : inter-

interacción *nf, pl* **-ciones** : interaction

interactivo, -va *adj* : interactive

interactuar {3} *vi* : to interact

intercalar *vt* : to intersperse, to insert

intercambiable *adj* : interchangeable

intercambiar *vt* CANJEAR : to exchange, to trade

intercambio *nm* CANJE : exchange, trade

interceder *vi* : to intercede

intercepción → **interceptación**

interceptación *nf, pl* **-ciones** : interception

interceptar *vt* **1** : to intercept, to block **2 interceptar las líneas** : to wiretap

intercesión *nf, pl* **-siones** : intercession

interconectar *vt* : to connect, to interconnect

interconfesional *adj* : interdenominational

intercontinental *adj* : intercontinental

interdepartamental *adj* : interdepartmental

interdependencia *nf* : interdependence — **interdependiente** *adj*

interdicción *nf, pl* **-ciones** : prohibition

interdisciplinario, -ria *adj* : interdisciplinary

interés *nm, pl* **-reses** **1** : interest ⟨su interés por la ciencia : her interest in science⟩ ⟨tiene interés en aprender español : he is interested in learning Spanish⟩ ⟨perder interés : to lose interest⟩ **2** BENEFICIO : interest ⟨por su propio interés : for one's own benefit⟩ ⟨por puro interés : purely out of self-interest⟩ ⟨el interés público : the public interest⟩ ⟨conflicto de intereses : conflict of interest⟩ **3** : interest, interest rate **4 intereses** *nmpl* : interest, stake ⟨tener intereses en : to have an interest in⟩

interesado[1], -da *adj* **1** : interested **2** : selfish, self-seeking

interesado[2], -da *n* **1** : interested party ⟨los interesados deberán rellenar una solicitud : anyone who is interested should fill out an application⟩ **2** : self-centered person

interesante *adj* : interesting

interesar *vt* : to interest — *vi* : to be of interest, to be interesting — **interesarse** *vr*

interestatal *adj* : interstate ⟨autopista interestatal : interstate highway⟩

interestelar *adj* : interstellar

interfase → **interfaz**

interfaz *nf, pl* **-faces** : interface

interferencia *nf* : interference, static

interferir {76} *vi* : to interfere, to meddle — *vt* : to interfere with, to obstruct

interfón *nm, pl* **-fones** *Mex* : intercom

interfono *nm Spain* : intercom

intergaláctico, -ca *adj* : intergalactic

intergubernamental *adj* : intergovernmental

interín[1] *or* **ínterin** *adv* : meanwhile

interín[2] *or* **ínterin** *nm, pl* **-rines** : meantime, interim ⟨en el interín : in the meantime⟩

interinamente *adv* : temporarily

interinato *nm* : temporary position

interino[1], -na *adj* : acting, temporary, interim

interino[2], -na *n* : substitute, temp

interior[1] *adj* **1** : interior, inside, inner ⟨parte interior : inside⟩ ⟨bolsillo interior : inside pocket⟩ ⟨patio interior : inner courtyard⟩ **2** : inner ⟨voz interior : inner voice⟩ **3** : domestic, internal

interior[2] *nm* **1** : interior, inside **2** : inland region

interiormente *adv* : inwardly

interjección *nf, pl* **-ciones** : interjection

interlocutor, -tora *n* : speaker

interludio *nm* : interlude

intermediario, -ria *adj & n* : intermediary, go-between

intermedio[1], -dia *adj* : intermediate

intermedio[2] *nm* **1** : intermission **2 por intermedio de** : by means of

interminable *adj* : interminable, endless — **interminablemente** *adv*

intermisión *nf, pl* **-siones** : intermission, pause

intermitente[1] *adj* **1** : intermittent **2** : flashing, blinking (of a light) — **intermitentemente** *adv*

intermitente[2] *nm* : blinker, turn signal

internacional *adj* : international — **internacionalmente** *adv*

internacionalizar {21} *vt* : to internationalize — **internacionalización** *nf*

internado *nm* : boarding school

internamiento *nm* **1** : internment, confinement **2** : admission

internar *vt* : to admit (to a hospital, etc.), to commit (to an institution) — **internarse** *vr* **1** : to penetrate, to advance into **2 ~ en** : to go into, to enter **3 ~ en** : to be admitted to

internauta *nmf* : Internet user

Internet *or* **internet** *nmf* : Internet

internista *nmf* : internist

interno[1], -na *adj* : internal ⟨la política interna : domestic policy⟩ — **internamente** *adv*

interno², **-na** *n* **1** : intern **2** : inmate
interpelación *nf, pl* **-ciones** : appeal, plea
interpelar *vt* : to question (formally)
interpersonal *adj* : interpersonal
interpolar *vt* : to insert, to interpolate
interponer {60} *vt* : to interpose — **interponerse** *vr* : to intervene
interpretación *nf, pl* **-ciones** : interpretation
interpretar *vt* **1** : to interpret **2** : to play, to perform
interpretativo, **-va** *adj* : interpretive
intérprete *nmf* **1** TRADUCTOR : interpreter **2** : performer
interpuesto *pp* → **interponer**
interracial *adj* : interracial
interrelación *nf, pl* **-ciones** : interrelationship
interrelacionar *vi* : to interrelate
interrogación *nf, pl* **-ciones** **1** : interrogation, questioning **2** *or* **signo de interrogación** : question mark
interrogador, **-dora** *n* : interrogator, questioner
interrogante¹ *adj* : questioning
interrogante² *nm* : question mark
interrogante³ *nmf* : question
interrogar {52} *vt* : to interrogate, to question
interrogativo, **-va** *adj* : interrogative
interrogatorio *nm* : interrogation, questioning
interrumpir *v* : to interrupt
interrupción *nf, pl* **-ciones** : interruption
interruptor *nm* **1** : (electrical) switch **2** : circuit breaker
intersecarse {72} *vr Spain* → **intersectarse**
intersección *nf, pl* **-ciones** : intersection
intersectarse *vr* : to intersect
intersticio *nm* : interstice — **intersticial** *adj*
interuniversitario, **-ria** *adj* : intercollegiate
interurbano, **-na** *adj* **1** : intercity **2** : long-distance ⟨llamadas interurbanas : long-distance calls⟩
intervalo *nm* : interval
intervención *nf, pl* **-ciones** **1** : intervention **2** : audit **3** : intercepting (of mail, etc.), tapping (of phones) **4** **intervención quirúrgica** : operation
intervenir {87} *vi* **1** : to take part **2** INTERCEDER : to intervene, to intercede — *vt* **1** : to control, to supervise **2** : to audit **3** : to operate on **4** : to tap, to wiretap (a phone)
interventor, **-tora** *n* **1** : inspector **2** : auditor, comptroller
intestado, **-da** *adj* : intestate
intestinal *adj* : intestinal
intestino¹, **-na** *adj* : internal, internecine
intestino² *nm* : intestine
intimar *vi* ~ **con** : to become friendly with — *vt* : to require, to call on
intimidación *nf, pl* **-ciones** : intimidation
intimidad *nf* **1** : intimacy **2** : privacy, private life
intimidante *adj* : intimidating
intimidar *vt* ACOBARDAR : to intimidate

intimidatorio, **-ria** *adj* : intimidating
íntimo, **-ma** *adj* **1** : intimate, close **2** PRIVADO : private — **íntimamente** *adv*
intitular *vt* : to entitle, to title
intocable *adj* : untouchable
intolerable *adj* : intolerable, unbearable
intolerancia *nf* : intolerance
intolerante¹ *adj* : intolerant
intolerante² *nmf* : intolerant person, bigot
intoxicación *nf, pl* **-ciones** : poisoning
intoxicante *nm* : poison
intoxicar {72} *vt* : to poison
intranquilidad *nf* PREOCUPACIÓN : worry, anxiety
intranquilizar {21} *vt* : to upset, to make uneasy — **intranquilizarse** *vr* : to get worried, to be anxious
intranquilo, **-la** *adj* PREOCUPADO : uneasy, worried
intransferible *adj* : nontransferable
intransigencia *nf* : intransigence
intransigente *adj* : intransigent, unyielding
intransitable *adj* : impassable
intransitivo, **-va** *adj* : intransitive
intrascendente *adj* : unimportant, insignificant
intratable *adj* **1** : intractable **2** : awkward **3** : unsociable
intravenoso, **-sa** *adj* : intravenous
intrepidez *nf* : fearlessness
intrépido, **-da** *adj* : intrepid, fearless
intriga *nf* : intrigue
intrigante *nmf* : schemer
intrigar {52} *v* : to intrigue — **intrigante** *adj*
intrincado, **-da** *adj* : intricate, involved
intrínseco, **-ca** *adj* : intrinsic — **intrínsecamente** *adv*
introducción *nf, pl* **-ciones** : introduction
introducir {61} *vt* **1** : to introduce **2** : to bring in **3** : to insert **4** : to input, to enter — **introducirse** *vr* : to penetrate, to get into
introductorio, **-ria** *adj* : introductory
intromisión *nf, pl* **-siones** : interference, meddling
introspección *nf, pl* **-ciones** : introspection
introspectivo, **-va** *adj* : introspective
introvertido¹, **-da** *adj* : introverted
introvertido², **-da** *n* : introvert
intrusión *nf, pl* **-siones** : intrusion
intruso¹, **-sa** *adj* : intrusive
intruso², **-sa** *n* : intruder
intuición *nf, pl* **-ciones** : intuition
intuir {41} *vt* : to intuit, to sense
intuitivo, **-va** *adj* : intuitive — **intuitivamente** *adv*
inundación *nf, pl* **-ciones** : flood, inundation
inundar *vt* : to flood, to inundate — **inundarse** *vr*
inusitado, **-da** *adj* : unusual, uncommon — **inusitadamente** *adv*
inusual *adj* : unusual, uncommon — **inusualmente** *adv*
inútil¹ *adj* INSERVIBLE : useless — **inútilmente** *adv*
inútil² *nmf* : good-for-nothing

inutilidad *nf* : uselessness
inutilizar {21} *vt* **1** : to make useless **2** INCAPACITAR : to disable, to put out of commission
invadir *vt* : to invade
invalidar *vt* : to nullify, to invalidate
invalidez *nf, pl* **-deces 1** : invalidity **2** : disability
inválido, -da *adj & n* : invalid
invalorable *adj* : invaluable
invaluable *adj* : invaluable
invariable *adj* : invariable — **invariablemente** *adv*
invasión *nf, pl* **-siones 1** : invasion **2** *or* **barrio de invasión** *Col* : shantytown, slums *pl*
invasivo, -va *adj* : invasive
invasor[1], -sora *adj* : invading
invasor[2], -sora *n* : invader
invectiva *nf* : invective, abuse
invencibilidad *nf* : invincibility
invencible *adj* **1** : invincible **2** : insurmountable
invención *nf, pl* **-ciones 1** INVENTO : invention **2** MENTIRA : fabrication, lie
inventar *vt* **1** : to invent **2** : to fabricate, to make up — **inventarse** *vr* : to fabricate, to make up
inventariar {85} *vt* : to inventory
inventario *nm* : inventory
inventiva *nf* : ingenuity, inventiveness
inventivo, -va *adj* : inventive
invento *nm* INVENCIÓN : invention
inventor, -tora *n* : inventor
invernadero *nm* : greenhouse, hothouse
invernal *adj* : winter, wintry
invernar {55} *vi* **1** : to spend the winter **2** HIBERNAR : to hibernate
inverosímil *adj* : unlikely, far-fetched
inverosimilitud *nf* : implausibility, improbability
inversión *nf, pl* **-siones 1** : inversion **2** : investment
inversionista *nmf* : investor
inverso[1], -sa *adj* **1** : inverse, inverted **2** CONTRARIO : opposite **3 a la inversa** : the other way around, vice versa **4 en orden inverso** : in reverse order — **inversamente** *adv*
inverso[2] *n* : inverse
inversor, -sora *n* : investor
invertebrado[1], -da *adj* : invertebrate
invertebrado[2] *nm* : invertebrate
invertir {76} *vt* **1** : to invert, to reverse **2** : to invest — *vi* : to make an investment — **invertirse** *vr* : to be reversed
investidura *nf* : investiture, inauguration
investigación *nf, pl* **-ciones 1** ENCUESTA, INDAGACIÓN : investigation, inquiry **2** : research ⟨investigación y desarrollo : research and development⟩
investigador[1], -dora *adj* : investigative
investigador[2], -dora *n* **1** : investigator ⟨investigador privado, investigadora privada : private investigator⟩ **2** : researcher
investigar {52} *vt* **1** INDAGAR : to investigate **2** : to research — *vi* ~ **sobre** : to do research into
investigativo, -va *adj* : investigative

investir {54} *vt* **1** : to empower **2** : to swear in, to inaugurate
inveterado, -da *adj* : inveterate, deep-seated
inviable *adj* : not viable, not feasible
invicto, -ta *adj* : undefeated
invidente[1] *adj* CIEGO : blind, sightless
invidente[2] *nmf* CIEGO : blind person
invierno *nm* : winter, wintertime
inviolable *adj* : inviolable — **inviolabilidad** *nf*
inviolado, -da *adj* : inviolate, pure
invisibilidad *nf* : invisibility
invisible *adj* : invisible — **invisiblemente** *adv*
invitación *nf, pl* **-ciones** : invitation
invitado, -da *n* : guest
invitar *vt* : to invite — *vi* : to pay for ⟨invita la casa : it's on the house⟩ ⟨invito yo : it's on me, it's my treat⟩
invocación *nf, pl* **-ciones** : invocation
invocar {72} *vt* : to invoke, to call on
involucramiento *nm* : involvement
involucrar *vt* : to implicate, to involve — **involucrarse** *vr* : to get involved
involuntario, -ria *adj* : involuntary — **involuntariamente** *adv*
invulnerable *adj* : invulnerable
inyección *nf, pl* **-ciones** : injection, shot
inyectado, -da *adj* **ojos inyectados** : bloodshot eyes
inyectar *vt* : to inject — **inyectarse** *vr*
ion *nm* : ion
iónico, -ca *adj* : ionic
ionizar {21} *vt* : to ionize — **ionización** *nf*
ionosfera *nf* : ionosphere
ir {43} *vi* **1** : to go ⟨ir a pie : to go on foot, to walk⟩ ⟨ir a caballo : to ride horseback⟩ ⟨ir a casa : to go home⟩ ⟨ir por mar : to go by sea⟩ ⟨iba para el aeropuerto : he was headed for the airport⟩ ⟨fui a ver una película : I went to see a movie⟩ ⟨el ir y venir de la gente : the comings and goings (of the people)⟩ ⟨vamos : let's go⟩ ⟨¡voy! : I'm coming!⟩ **2** : to lead, to extend, to stretch ⟨el camino va de Cali a Bogotá : the road goes from Cali to Bogotá⟩ **3** FUNCIONAR : to work, to function ⟨esta computadora ya no va : this computer doesn't work anymore⟩ **4** : to get on, to get along ⟨¿cómo te va? : how are you?, how's it going?⟩ ⟨el negocio no va bien : the business isn't doing well⟩ ⟨ir a mejor/peor : to get better/worse⟩ ⟨ir de mal en peor : to go from bad to worse⟩ **5** : to suit ⟨ese vestido te va bien : that dress really suits you⟩ ⟨el cambio te irá bien : the change will do you good⟩ **6** ~ **a** ASISTIR : to go to, to attend **7** ~ **con/en/de** : to wear ⟨voy a ir con/en falda : I'm going to wear a skirt⟩ ⟨iba de azul : she was wearing blue⟩ **8** ~ **con** (*with a noun*) : to be ⟨ir con prisa : to be in a hurry⟩ ⟨ir con cuidado : to be cautious⟩ **9** ~ **con** : to go with, to complement **10** ~ **para** : to be studying to be ⟨va para médico : she's studying to be a doctor⟩ **11** ~ **para** : to be going on, to be close to (an age) **12** ~ **por** : to be aimed at ⟨también va por

ti : that goes for you, too⟩ **13** ~ **por**
: to follow, to go along ⟨fueron por la
costa : they followed the shoreline⟩ **14**
~ **por** : to be up to (a point or stage)
⟨voy por la última página : I'm on the
last page⟩ **15** ~ **por** : to go (and) get, to
fetch **16 dejarse ir** : to let oneself go
17 ir a parar : to end up **18 ¡qué va!**
fam : hardly! **19 ¡vamos!** : come on!
20 vamos a ver : let's see — *v aux* **1**
(*indicating manner*) ⟨ir caminando : to
walk, to go on foot⟩ ⟨¡voy corriendo!
: I'll be right there!⟩ **2** (*indicating a process*) ⟨va mejorando : he's getting better⟩
⟨lo iremos haciendo poco a poco : we'll
do it little by little⟩ **3** ~ **a** : to be going
to ⟨voy a hacerlo : I'm going to do it⟩ ⟨el
avión va a despegar : the plane is about
to take off⟩ — **irse** *vr* **1** : to leave, to go
⟨¡vámonos! : let's go!⟩ ⟨todo el mundo se
fue : everyone left⟩ **2** ESCAPARSE : to
leak **3** GASTARSE : to be used up, to be
gone
ira *nf* CÓLERA, FURIA : wrath, anger
iracundo, -da *adj* **1** : irate, angry ⟨estar
iracundo : to be angry⟩ **2** : irascible
⟨ser iracundo : to be irascible⟩
iraní *adj & nmf* : Iranian
iraquí *adj & nmf* : Iraqi
irascible *adj* : irascible, irritable — **irascibilidad** *nf*
irga, irgue etc. → **erguir**
iridio *nm* : iridium
iridiscencia *nf* : iridescence — **iridiscente** *adj*
iris *nms & pl* **1** : iris **2 arco iris** : rainbow
irlandés¹, -desa *adj, mpl* **-deses -deses**
: Irish
irlandés², -desa *n, pl* **-deses** : Irish person, Irishman *m*, Irishwoman *f*
irlandés³ *nm* : Irish (language)
ironía *nf* : irony
irónico, -ca *adj* : ironic, ironical — **iróni-
camente** *adv*
ironizar {21} *vi* : to speak ironically — *vt*
: to say ironically
irracional *adj* : irrational — **irracionalmente** *adv*
irracionalidad *nf* : irrationality
irradiación *nf, pl* **-ciones** : irradiation
irradiar *vt* : to radiate, to irradiate
irrazonable *adj* : unreasonable
irreal *adj* : unreal
irrebatible *adj* : unanswerable, irrefutable
irreconciliable *adj* : irreconcilable
irreconocible *adj* : unrecognizable
irrecuperable *adj* : irrecoverable, irretrievable
irredimible *adj* : irredeemable
irreductible *adj* : unyielding
irreemplazable *adj* : irreplaceable
irreflexión *nf, pl* **-xiones** : thoughtlessness
irreflexivo, -va *adj* : rash, unthinking —
irreflexivamente *adv*
irrefrenable *adj* : uncontrollable, unstoppable ⟨un impulso irrefrenable : an irresistible urge⟩
irrefutable *adj* : irrefutable

irregular *adj* : irregular — **irregular-
mente** *adv*
irregularidad *nf* : irregularity
irrelevante *adj* : irrelevant — **irrelevancia** *nf*
irreligioso, -sa *adj* : irreligious
irremediable *adj* : incurable — **irreme-
diablemente** *adv*
irreparable *adj* : irreparable
irrepetible *adj* : unrepeatable, unique
irreprimible *adj* : irrepressible
irreprochable *adj* : irreproachable
irresistible *adj* : irresistible — **irresisti-
blemente** *adv*
irresolución *nf, pl* **-ciones** : indecision,
hesitation
irresoluto, -ta *adj* INDECISO : undecided
irrespetar *vt CA, Carib* : to disrespect, to
be disrespectful to
irrespeto *nm* : disrespect
irrespetuoso, -sa *adj* : disrespectful —
irrespetuosamente *adv*
irrespirable *adj* : unbreathable
irresponsabilidad *nf* : irresponsibility
irresponsable *adj* : irresponsible —
irresponsablemente *adv*
irrestricto, -ta *adj* : unrestricted, unconditional
irreverencia *nf* : disrespect
irreverente *adj* : irreverent, disrespectful
irreversible *adj* : irreversible
irrevocable *adj* : irrevocable — **irrevoca-
blemente** *adv*
irrigar {52} *vt* : to irrigate — **irrigación** *nf*
irrisible *adj* : laughable
irrisión *nf, pl* **-siones** : derision, ridicule
irrisorio, -ria *adj* RISIBLE : ridiculous, ludicrous
irritabilidad *nf* : irritability
irritable *adj* : irritable
irritación *nf, pl* **-ciones** : irritation
irritante *adj* : irritating
irritar *vt* : to irritate
irrompible *adj* : unbreakable
irrumpir *vi* ~ **en** : to burst into
irrupción *nf, pl* **-ciones** **1** : emergence **2**
: invasion
-ísimo, -ma *suf* : very, extremely
isla *nf* : island
Islam *nm* : Islam
islámico, -ca *adj* : Islamic, Muslim
islamismo *nm* **1** : Islam **2** : Islamism —
islamista *adj & nmf*
islandés¹, -desa *adj, mpl* **-deses** : Icelandic
islandés², -desa *n, mpl* **-deses** : Icelander
islandés³ *nm* : Icelandic (language)
isleño¹, -ña *adj* : island
isleño², -ña *n* : islander
islote *nm* : islet
isometría *nfs & pl* : isometrics
isométrico, -ca *adj* : isometric
isósceles *adj* : isosceles ⟨triángulo isósceles : isosceles triangle⟩
isótopo *nm* : isotope
israelí *adj & nmf* : Israeli
istmo *nm* : isthmus
itacate *nm Mex* : pack, provisions *pl*
italiano¹, -na *adj & n* : Italian
italiano² *nm* : Italian (language)

ítem *nm* : item
itinerante *adj* AMBULANTE : traveling, itinerant
itinerario *nm* : itinerary, route
-ito *or* **-cito** *suf* **1** : little ⟨un pedacito : a little piece⟩ ⟨su hermanita : his little/baby sister⟩ ⟨sólo un ratito : just a little while⟩ **2** (*used to show affection*) ⟨mi abuelito : my grandpa⟩ ⟨¡pobrecita! : poor thing!⟩ ⟨dame un besito : give me

a kiss⟩ ⟨¿quieres un cafecito? : do you want a nice cup of coffee?⟩ **3** (*used for emphasis*) ⟨bien calentito : nice and hot⟩ ⟨al verlo se quedó calladita : when she saw him she went quiet⟩
izar {21} *vt* : to hoist, to raise ⟨izar la bandera : to raise the flag⟩
izquierda *nf* : left
izquierdista *adj & nmf* : leftist
izquierdo, -da *adj* : left

J

j *nf* : tenth letter of the Spanish alphabet
ja *interj* **1** : ha! **2 ja, ja** : ha-ha!
jaba *nf* **1** *Car* : bag, sack **2** *Mex, CA* : crate, box
jabalí *nm, pl* **-líes** : wild boar
jabalina *nf* : javelin
jabón *nm, pl* **jabones** : soap
jabonar *vt* ENJABONAR : to soap up, to lather — **jabonarse** *vr*
jabonera *nf* : soap dish
jabonoso, -sa *adj* : soapy
jaca *nf* **1** : pony **2** YEGUA : mare
jacal *nm Mex* : shack, hut
jacinto *nm* : hyacinth
jactancia *nf* **1** : boastfulness **2** : boasting, bragging
jactancioso¹, -sa *adj* : boastful
jactancioso², -sa *n* : boaster, braggart
jactarse *vr* : to boast, to brag ⟨jactarse de algo : to brag about something⟩
Jacuzzi [ja'kuzi, -'kusi] *marca registrada, m* — used for a whirlpool bath
jade *nm* : jade
jadear *vi* : to pant, to gasp, to puff — **jadeante** *adj*
jadeo *nm* : panting, gasping, puffing
jaez *nm, pl* **jaeces** **1** : harness **2** : kind, sort, ilk **3 jaeces** *nmpl* : trappings
jaguar *nm* : jaguar
jai alai *nm* : jai alai
jaiba *nf* CANGREJO : crab
jalapeño *nm Mex* : jalapeño pepper
jalar *vt* **1** : to pull, to tug **2** *fam* : to attract, to draw in ⟨las ideas nuevas lo jalan : new ideas appeal to him⟩ — *vi* **1** : to pull, to pull together ⟨jalar de algo : to pull on something⟩ **2** *fam* : to hurry up, to get going **3** *Mex fam* : to be in working order ⟨esta máquina no jala : this machine doesn't work⟩
jalbegue *nm* : whitewash
jalea *nf* : jelly
jalear *vt* : to encourage, to urge on
jaleo *nm* **1** *fam* : uproar, ruckus, racket **2** *fam* : confusion, mess, hassle **3** : cheering and clapping (for a dance)
jalón *nm, pl* **jalones** **1** : milestone, landmark **2** TIRÓN : pull, tug
jalonar *vt* : to mark, to stake out
jalonear *vt Mex, Peru fam* : to tug at — *vi* **1** *fam* : to pull, to tug **2** *CA fam* : to haggle
jamaicano, -na → jamaiquino

jamaiquino, -na *adj & n* : Jamaican
jamás *adv* **1** NUNCA : never ⟨jamás vi tal cosa : I've never seen such a thing⟩ ⟨no lo olvidaré jamás : I'll never forget it⟩ **2 nunca jamás** *or* **jamás de los jamases** : never ever **3 para siempre jamás** : for ever and ever
jamba *nf* : jamb
jamelgo *nm* : nag (horse)
jamón *nm, pl* **jamones** **1** : ham **2 jamón serrano** : cured Spanish ham
Janucá *or* **Januká** *nmf* : Hanukkah
japonés¹, -nesa *adj & n, mpl* **-neses** : Japanese ⟨los japoneses : the Japanese (people)⟩
japonés² *nm, pl* **-neses** : Japanese (language)
jaque *nm* **1** : check (in chess) ⟨jaque mate : checkmate⟩ ⟨dar jaque mate a : to checkmate⟩ **2 tener en jaque** : to intimidate, to bully
jaquear *vi* : to check (in chess)
jaqueca *nf* : headache, migraine
jarabe *nm* **1** : syrup ⟨jarabe para la tos : cough syrup⟩ **2** : Mexican folk dance
jarana *nf* **1** *fam* : revelry, partying, spree **2** *fam* : joking, fooling around **3** : small guitar
jaranear *vi fam* : to go on a spree, to party
jarcia *nf* **1** : rigging **2** : fishing tackle
jardín *nm, pl* **jardines** **1** : garden **2** : yard (of a house) **3 jardín de niños** *CA, Mex or* **jardín infantil** *Chile or* **jardín de infancia** *Spain* : kindergarten **4 jardín izquierdo/central/derecho** : left/center/right field **5 los jardines** : the outfield
jardinera *nf* **1** : planter **2** : plant stand
jardinería *nf* : gardening
jardinero, -ra *n* **1** : gardener **2** : outfielder (in baseball)
jarra *nf* **1** : pitcher, jug **2** : stein, mug **3 de jarras** *or* **en jarras** : akimbo
jarrete *nm* **1** : back of the knee **2** CORVEJÓN : hock
jarro *nm* **1** : pitcher, jug **2** : mug
jarrón *nm, pl* **jarrones** FLORERO : vase
jaspe *nm* : jasper
jaspeado, -da *adj* **1** VETEADO : streaked, veined **2** : speckled, mottled
jaula *nf* : cage
jauría *nf* : pack of hounds
javanés, -nesa *adj & n* : Javanese

jazmín *nm, pl* **jazmines** : jasmine
jazz ['jas, 'ʤas] *nm* : jazz
je *interj* → **ja**
jeans ['jins, 'ʤins] *nmpl* : jeans
jeep ['jip, 'ʤip] *nm, pl* **jeeps** : jeep (military vehicle)
Jeep *marca registrada, m* — used for a small truck
jefatura *nf* **1** : leadership **2** : headquarters ⟨jefatura de policía : police headquarters⟩
jefe, -fa *n* **1** : chief, head, leader ⟨jefe de bomberos/policía : fire/police chief⟩ ⟨jefe del departamento : department head⟩ ⟨jefe de oficina : office manager⟩ ⟨jefe de Estado/gobierno : head of state/government⟩ ⟨jefe de redacción : editor in chief⟩ **2** : boss
Jehová *nm* : Jehovah
jején *nm, pl* **jejenes** : gnat, small mosquito
jengibre *nm* : ginger
jeque *nm* : sheikh, sheik
jerarca *nmf* : leader, chief
jerarquía *nf* **1** : hierarchy **2** RANGO : rank
jerárquico, -ca *adj* : hierarchical
jerbo *nm* : gerbil
jerez *nm, pl* **jereces** : sherry
jerga *nf* **1** : jargon, slang **2** : coarse cloth
jerigonza *nf* GALIMATÍAS : mumbo jumbo, gibberish
jeringa *nf* : syringe
jeringar {52} *vt* **1** : to inject **2** *fam* JOROBAR : to annoy, to pester — *vi fam* JOROBAR : to be annoying, to be a nuisance
jeringuear → **jeringar**
jeringuilla → **jeringa**
jeroglífico *nm* : hieroglyphic
jersey *nm, pl* **jerseys** **1** : jersey (fabric) **2** *Spain* : sweater
Jesucristo *nm* : Jesus Christ
jesuita *adj & nm* : Jesuit
Jesús *nm* **1** : Jesus **2** ¡Jesús! : goodness!, good heavens! **3** ¡Jesús! : bless you! (said to someone who has sneezed)
jet *nm* : jet (airplane)
jeta *nf* **1** : snout **2** *fam* : face, mug
jíbaro, -ra *adj* **1** : Jivaro **2** : rustic, rural
jibia *nf* : cuttlefish
jícama *nf* : jicama
jícara *nf Mex* : calabash
jicotea *nf CA, Car, Mex* : turtle
jihad *nmf* → **yihad**
jilguero *nm* : European goldfinch
jinete *nmf* : horseman, horsewoman *f*, rider
jinetear *vt* **1** : to ride, to perform (on horseback) **2** DOMAR : to break in (a horse) — *vi* CABALGAR : to ride horseback
jingoísmo [ˌjɪŋgoˈizmo, ˌʤɪŋ-] *nm* : jingoism
jingoísta *adj* : jingoist, jingoistic
jiote *nm Mex* : rash
jira *nf* : outing, picnic
jirafa *nf* **1** : giraffe **2** : boom microphone
jirón *nm, pl* **jirones** **1** : shred, rag ⟨hecho jirones : in tatters⟩ **2** *Peru* : street

jitomate *nm Mex* : tomato
jockey ['jɔki, 'ʤɔ-] *nmf, pl* **jockeys** [-kis] : jockey
jocosidad *nf* : humor, jocularity
jocoso, -sa *adj* : playful, jocular — **jocosamente** *adv*
jofaina *nf* : washbowl
jogging ['jɔgɪŋ, 'ʤɔ-,] *nm* **1** : jogging **2** *Arg* : sweatpants **3** *Arg* : sweatsuit, tracksuit
jolgorio *nm* : merrymaking, fun
jonrón *nm, pl* **jonrones** : home run
jordano, -na *adj & n* : Jordanian
jornada *nf* **1** : expedition, day's journey **2** jornada laboral *or* jornada de trabajo : workday **3** jornadas *nfpl* : conference, congress
jornal *nm* **1** : day's pay **2 a** ∼ : by the day
jornalero, -ra *n* : day laborer
joroba *nf* **1** GIBA : hump **2** *fam* : nuisance, pain in the neck
jorobado¹, -da *adj* GIBOSO : hunchbacked, humpbacked
jorobado², -da *n* GIBOSO : person with a hump, hunchback *offensive*, humpback *offensive*
jorobar *vt fam* JERINGAR : to bother, to annoy — *vi fam* JERINGAR : to be annoying, to be a nuisance
jorongo *nm Mex* : full-length poncho
jota *nf* **1** : jot, bit ⟨no entiendo ni jota : I don't understand a word of it⟩ ⟨no se ve ni jota : you can't see a thing⟩ **2** : jack (in playing cards) **3** : (letter) j
joven¹ *adj, pl* **jóvenes** **1** : young **2** : youthful
joven² *nmf, pl* **jóvenes** : young man *m*, young woman *f*, young person
jovial *adj* : jovial, cheerful — **jovialmente** *adv*
jovialidad *nf* : joviality, cheerfulness
joya *nf* **1** : jewel, piece of jewelry **2** : treasure, gem ⟨la nueva empleada es una joya : the new employee is a real gem⟩
joyería *nf* **1** : jewelry store **2** : jewelry **3** joyería de fantasía : costume jewelry
joyero, -ra *n* **1** : jeweler **2** : jewelry box
joystick ['jɔistik] *nm, pl* **joysticks** : joystick
juanete *nm* : bunion
jubilación *nf, pl* **-ciones** **1** : retirement ⟨jubilación anticipada : early retirement⟩ **2** PENSIÓN : pension
jubilado¹, -da *adj* : retired, in retirement
jubilado², -da *nmf* : retired person, retiree
jubilar *vt* **1** : to retire, to pension off **2** *fam* : to get rid of, to discard — **jubilarse** *vr* : to retire
jubileo *nm* : jubilee
júbilo *nm* : jubilation, joy
jubiloso, -sa *adj* : jubilant, joyous
judaico, -ca *adj* : Judaic, Jewish
judaísmo *nm* : Judaism
judía *nf* **1** : bean **2** *or* judía verde : green bean, string bean
judicatura *nf* **1** : judiciary, judges *pl* **2** : office of judge

judicial *adj* : judicial — **judicialmente**
adv
judío¹, -día *adj* : Jewish
judío², -día *n* : Jewish person, Jew
judo [ˈjuðo, ˈdʒu-] *nm* : judo
juega, juegue etc. → **jugar**
juego *nm* **1** : play, playing ⟨poner/entrar
en juego : to bring/come into play⟩
⟨juego limpio/sucio : fair/foul play⟩ **2**
: game, sport ⟨juego de cartas : card
game⟩ ⟨juego de mesa : board game⟩
⟨juego de azar : game of chance⟩
⟨Juegos Olímpicos : Olympic Games⟩ **3**
: gaming, gambling ⟨el juego ilegal : illegal gambling⟩ ⟨estar en juego : to be at
stake⟩ **4** : ride (at an amusement park)
5 : set ⟨un juego de herramientas/platos
: a set of tools/dishes⟩ **6** SOLTURA
: play, slack **7 fuera de juego** : offside
8 hacer juego : to go together, to match
9 hacerle el juego a : to play along with
10 juego de manos : trick, sleight of
hand **11 juego de palabras** : play on
words, pun
juerga *nf* : partying, binge ⟨irse de juerga
: to go on a spree⟩
juerguista *nmf* : reveler, carouser
jueves *nms & pl* : Thursday ⟨el jueves
: (on) Thursday⟩ ⟨los jueves : (on)
Thursdays⟩ ⟨cada (dos) jueves : every
(other) Thursday⟩ ⟨el jueves pasado
: last Thursday⟩ ⟨el próximo jueves
: next Thursday⟩
juez¹ *nmf, pl* **jueces 1** : judge **2** ÁRBI-
TRO : umpire, referee **3 juez de paz**
: justice of the peace
juez², jueza *n* → **juez¹**
jugada *nf* **1** : play, move **2** : trick ⟨hacer
una mala jugada : to play a dirty trick⟩
jugador, -dora *n* **1** : player **2** : gambler
jugar {44} *vi* **1** : to play ⟨jugar al fútbol
: to play soccer⟩ ⟨jugar a la lotería : to
play the lottery⟩ ⟨jugar a las muñecas
: to play with dolls⟩ ⟨jugar limpio/sucio
: to play fair/dirty⟩ **2** APOSTAR : to
gamble, to bet ⟨jugar a la Bolsa : to play
the stock market⟩ **3** : to joke, to kid **4**
jugar con alguien : to toy with someone
— *vt* **1** : to play ⟨jugar un papel : to
play a role⟩ ⟨jugar una carta : to play a
card⟩ **2** : to bet ⟨jugarlo todo a : to bet
everything on⟩ — **jugarse** *vr* **1** : to risk,
to gamble away ⟨jugarse la vida : to risk
one's life⟩ **2 jugarse el todo por el todo**
: to risk everything
jugarreta *nf fam* : prank, dirty trick
juglar *nm* : minstrel
jugo *nm* **1** : juice ⟨jugo de naranja : orange juice⟩ **2** : substance, essence
⟨sacarle el jugo a algo : to get the most
out of something⟩
jugosidad *nf* : juiciness
jugoso, -sa *adj* **1** : juicy **2** : lucrative,
profitable
juguete *nm* **1** : toy **2 de ∼** : toy ⟨un
camión de juguete : a toy truck⟩
juguetear *vi* **1** : to play, to cavort, to
frolic **2** : to toy, to fiddle
juguetería *nf* : toy store

juguetón, -tona *adj, mpl* **-tones** : playful
— **juguetonamente** *adv*
juicio *nm* **1** : good judgment, reason,
sense ⟨perder el juicio : to lose one's
mind⟩ ⟨en su sano juicio : in one's right
mind⟩ **2** : opinion ⟨a mi juicio : in my
opinion⟩ **3** : trial ⟨llevar/ir a juicio : to
take/go to court⟩ ⟨un juicio civil/crimi-
nal : a civil/criminal trial⟩
juicioso, -sa *adj* : judicious, wise — **jui-
ciosamente** *adv*
julio *nm* : July ⟨el primero de julio : (on)
July first⟩
jumper [ˈdʒumper] *nm, pl* **jumpers**
[ˈdʒumpers] : jumper, pinafore
juncia *nf* : sedge
junco *nm* **1** : reed, rush **2** : junk (boat)
jungla *nf* : jungle
junio *nm* : June ⟨el primero de junio
: (on) June first⟩
junquillo *nm* : jonquil
junta *nf* **1** : board, committee ⟨junta directiva : board of directors⟩ **2** REUNIÓN
: meeting, session **3** : junta **4** : regional
government (in Spain) **5** : joint, gasket
juntamente *adv* **1** : jointly, together
⟨juntamente con : together with⟩ **2** : at
the same time
juntar *vt* **1** UNIR : to unite, to combine,
to put together **2** REUNIR : to collect, to
gather together, to assemble **3** : to close
partially ⟨juntar la puerta : to leave the
door ajar⟩ — **juntarse** *vr* **1** : to join together **2** : to move closer together **3**
: to get together ⟨nos juntamos a conversar : we got together to chat⟩ ⟨volvió a
juntarse con el grupo : he got back together with the group⟩
junto, -ta *adj* **1** UNIDO : joined, united **2**
: close, adjacent ⟨colgaron los dos retra-
tos juntos : they hung the two paintings
side by side⟩ **3** (*used adverbially*) : together ⟨llegamos juntos : we arrived to-
gether⟩ ⟨sabe más que todos juntos : she
knows more than all of us put together⟩
4 ∼ a : next to, alongside of **5 ∼ con**
: together with, along with
juntura *nf* : joint, coupling
Júpiter *nm* : Jupiter
jura *nf* : oath, pledge ⟨jura de bandera
: pledge of allegiance⟩
jurado¹ *nm* : jury (in a trial), panel of
judges (in a contest)
jurado², -da *nmf* **1** : juror **2** : judge (in a
contest)
juramentación *nf, pl* **-ciones** : swearing
in
juramentar *vt* : to swear in
juramento *nm* **1** : oath ⟨prestar juramento : to swear, to take an oath⟩ ⟨to-
marle juramento a : to swear in (an official), to place (a witness) under oath⟩ **2**
: swearword, oath
jurar *vt* **1** : to swear ⟨jurar lealtad : to
swear loyalty⟩ ⟨jurar bandera : to pledge
allegiance to the flag⟩ ⟨no lo sabía, ¡te lo
juro! : I swear I didn't know!⟩ **2** : to
take an oath ⟨el alcalde juró su cargo
: the mayor took the oath of office⟩ **3**

tenérsela jurada a alguien : to have it in for someone — *vi* : to curse, to swear
jurídico, -ca *adj* : legal
jurisdicción *nf, pl* **-ciones** : jurisdiction — **jurisdiccional** *adj*
jurisprudencia *nf* : jurisprudence, law
jurista *nmf* : jurist
justa *nf* **1** : joust **2** TORNEO : tournament, competition
justamente *adv* **1** PRECISAMENTE : precisely, exactly **2** : justly, fairly
justar *vi* : to joust
justicia *nf* **1** : justice, fairness ⟨hacerle justicia a : to do justice to⟩ ⟨ser de justicia : to be only fair⟩ ⟨en justicia : in all fairness⟩ ⟨pedir justicia : to demand justice⟩ **2 la justicia** : the law ⟨tomarse la justicia por su mano : to take the law into one's own hands⟩
justiciero, -ra *adj* : righteous, avenging
justificable *adj* : justifiable
justificación *nf, pl* **-ciones** : justification
justificante *nm* **1** : justification **2** : proof, voucher
justificar {72} *vt* **1** : to justify **2** : to excuse, to vindicate — **justificarse** *vr*

justo¹ *adv* **1** : justly **2** : right, exactly ⟨justo en ese momento : right at that moment⟩ ⟨justo en el centro : right in the center/middle⟩ ⟨justo a tiempo : just in time⟩ **3** : tightly
justo², -ta *adj* **1** : just, fair **2** : right, exact ⟨la cantidad justa : the exact amount⟩ ⟨lo justo para vivir : just enough to live on⟩ **3** : tight ⟨estos zapatos me quedan muy justos : these shoes are too tight⟩
justo³, -ta *n* : just person ⟨los justos : the just⟩
juvenil *adj* **1** : juvenile (of crimes, etc.), youth ⟨una organización juvenil : a youth organization⟩ **2** : young, youthful (in appearance, etc.) **3** ADOLESCENTE : teenage **4** : junior (in sports)
juventud *nf* **1** : youth **2** : young people
juzgado *nm* TRIBUNAL : court, tribunal
juzgar {52} *vt* **1** : to try, to judge (a case in court) **2** : to pass judgment on **3** CONSIDERAR : to consider, to deem ⟨a juzgar por los resultados : judging by the results⟩
juzgue, etc. → **juzgar**

K

k *nf* : twelfth letter of the Spanish alphabet
ka *nf* : (letter) k
káiser *nm* : kaiser
kaki → **caqui**
kaleidoscopio → **caleidoscopio**
kamikaze *adj & nm* : kamikaze
kan *nm* : khan
karaoke *nm* : karaoke
karate *or* **kárate** *nm* : karate
kayac *or* **kayak** *nm, pl* **kayacs** *or* **kayaks** : kayak
kebab [ke'bab] *nm, pl* **kebabs** [ke'babs] : kebab
keniano, -na *adj & n* : Kenyan
kermesse *or* **kermés** [kɛr'mɛs] *nf, pl* **kermesses** *or* **kermeses** [-'mɛsɛs] : charity fair, bazaar
kerosene *or* **kerosén** *or* **keroseno** *nm* : kerosene, paraffin
ketchup ['ketʃap, -tʃup] *nm* : ketchup, catsup
kibutz *or* **kibbutz** *nms & pl* : kibbutz
kilo *nm* **1** : kilo, kilogram **2** *fam* : large amount
kilobyte [ˌkilo'bait] *nm* : kilobyte
kilociclo *nm* : kilocycle
kilogramo *nm* : kilogram

kilohertzio *nm* : kilohertz
kilometraje *nm* : distance in kilometers, mileage
kilométrico, -ca *adj fam* : endless, very long
kilómetro *nm* : kilometer
kilovatio *nm* : kilowatt
kimono *nm* : kimono
kinder ['kɪndɛr,] → **kindergarten**
kindergarten [ˌkɪndɛr'gartɛn] *nm, pl* **kindergartens** [-tɛns] **1** : kindergarten **2** : nursery school
kinesiología *nf* : physical therapy
kinesiólogo, -ga *n* : physical therapist
kiosco, kiosko → **quiosco**
kiosquero, -ra → **quiosquero**
kit *nm, pl* **kits** : kit
kiwi ['kiwi] *nm* **1** : kiwi (bird) **2** : kiwifruit
klaxon → **claxon**
Kleenex ['klines, -neks] *marca registrada, m* — used for a paper tissue
knockout [nɔ'kaut] → **nocaut**
koala *nm* : koala bear
kriptón *nm* : krypton
kurdo¹, -da *adj* : Kurdish
kurdo², -da *n* : Kurd
kuwaití [kuˌwai'ti] *adj & nmf* : Kuwaiti

L

l *nf* : thirteenth letter of the Spanish alphabet

la¹ *nm* **1** : A ⟨la sostenido/bemol : A sharp/flat⟩ **2** : la (in singing)

la² *pron* (*referring to feminine nouns*) **1** : her, it ⟨llámala hoy : call her today⟩ ⟨sacó la botella y la abrió : he took out the bottle and opened it⟩ **2** (*formal*) : you ⟨no la vi a usted, Señora Díaz : I didn't see you, Mrs. Díaz⟩ **3** : the one ⟨me gusta la roja : I like the red one⟩ ⟨la de la camisa azul : the one with the blue shirt⟩ ⟨mi mamá y la tuya : my mom and yours⟩ ⟨la clase de ayer y la de hoy : yesterday's class and today's⟩ **4 la que** : the one that/who, whoever ⟨la que vino ayer : the one who came yesterday⟩ ⟨la que compré : the one (that) I bought⟩ ⟨la que gane : whoever wins⟩

la³ *art* → **el²**

laberíntico, -ca *adj* : labyrinthine

laberinto *nm* : labyrinth, maze

labia *nf fam* : gift of gab ⟨tu amigo tiene labia : your friend has a way with words⟩

labial *adj* : labial, lip ⟨lápiz labial : lipstick⟩

labio *nm* : lip

labor *nf* : work, labor

laborable *adj* **1** : arable **2** : work, working ⟨día laborable : workday, business day⟩

laboral *adj* : work, labor ⟨costos laborales : labor costs⟩

laborar *vi* : to work

laboratorio *nm* : laboratory, lab

laboriosamente *adv* **1** : laboriously **2** : industriously, diligently

laboriosidad *nf* : industriousness, diligence

laborioso, -sa *adj* **1** : laborious, hard **2** : industrious, hardworking

labrado¹, -da *adj* **1** : cultivated, tilled **2** : carved, wrought

labrado² *nm* : cultivated field

labrador, -dora *n* : farmer

labranza *nf* : farming

labrar *vt* **1** : to carve, to work (metal) **2** : to cultivate, to till **3** : to cause, to bring about

labriego, -ga *n* : farm worker

laburar *vi Arg, Uru* TRABAJAR : to work

laburo *nm Arg, Uru* TRABAJO : work, job

laca *nf* **1** : lacquer, shellac **2** : hair spray **3 laca de uñas** : nail polish

lacayo *nm* : lackey

lace, etc. → **lazar**

lacear *vt* : to lasso

laceración *nf, pl* **-ciones** : laceration

lacerante *adj* : hurtful, wounding

lacerar *vt* **1** : to lacerate, to cut **2** : to hurt, to wound (one's feelings)

lacio, -cia *adj* **1** : limp, lank **2 pelo lacio** : straight hair

lacónico, -ca *adj* : laconic — **lacónicamente** *adv*

lacra *nf* **1** : scar, mark (on the skin) **2** : stigma, blemish

lacrar *vt* : to seal (with wax)

lacrimógeno, -na *adj* **gas lacrimógeno** : tear gas

lacrimoso, -sa *adj* : tearful, moving

lacrosse *nm* : lacrosse

lactancia *nf* : breast-feeding

lactante *nmf* : nursing infant, suckling

lactar *v* : to breast-feed

lácteo¹, -tea *adj* **1** : dairy **2 Vía Láctea** : Milky Way

lácteo² *nm* : dairy product ⟨evito los lácteos : I avoid dairy⟩

ladeado, -da *adj* : crooked, tilted, lopsided

ladear *vt* : to tilt, to tip — **ladearse** *vr* : to bend (over)

ladera *nf* : slope, hillside

ladino¹, -na *adj* **1** : cunning, shrewd **2** *CA, Mex* : mestizo

ladino², -na *n* **1** : trickster **2** *CA, Mex* : Spanish-speaking person of indigenous descent **3** *CA, Mex* : mestizo

lado *nm* **1** : side ⟨el lado izquierdo/derecho : the left/right side⟩ ⟨el otro lado : the other side⟩ ⟨el lado de arriba/abajo : the top/bottom⟩ **2** PARTE : place ⟨miró por todos lados : he looked everywhere⟩ **3** : side (in an argument, etc.) ⟨se puso de mi lado : she took my side⟩ **4 al ~** ⟨los que viven al lado : the people who live next door⟩ ⟨tenemos una tienda al lado : there's a store beside/near us⟩ **5 al lado de** : next to, beside ⟨al lado de la calle : on/at the side of the road⟩ ⟨a mi lado : beside me⟩ **6 de al lado** ⟨los de al lado : the next-door neighbors⟩ ⟨el asiento de al lado : the seat next to mine/yours (etc.)⟩ **7 de ~** : tilted, sideways ⟨está de lado : it's lying on its side⟩ **8 de un lado a otro** : to and fro, back and forth **9 dejar a un lado** : to set aside **10 hacerse a un lado** : to step aside **11 lado a lado** : side by side **12 por un lado ..., por otro lado ...** : on the one hand ..., on the other hand ...

ladrar *vi* : to bark

ladrido *nm* : bark (of a dog), barking

ladrillo *nm* **1** : brick **2** AZULEJO : tile

ladrón, -drona *n, mpl* **ladrones** : robber, thief, burglar

lagartija *nf* : small lizard

lagarto *nm* **1** : lizard **2 lagarto de Indias** : alligator

lago *nm* : lake

lágrima *nf* : tear, teardrop

lagrimal *nm* : corner of the eye

lagrimear *vi* **1** : to water (of eyes) **2** : to weep easily

laguna *nf* **1** : lagoon **2** : gap

laicado *nm* : laity

laico¹, -ca *adj* : lay, secular

laico², -ca *n* : layman *m*, laywoman *f*

laja *nf* : slab

lama¹ *nf* : slime, ooze

lama² *nm* : lama

lamber *vt* : to lick

lamentable *adj* 1 : unfortunate, lamentable 2 : pitiful, sad

lamentablemente *adv* : unfortunately, regrettably

lamentación *nf, pl* **-ciones** : lamentation, groaning, moaning

lamentar *vt* 1 : to lament 2 : to regret ⟨lo lamento : I'm sorry⟩ — **lamentarse** *vr* : to grumble, to complain

lamento *nm* : lament, groan, cry

lamer *vt* 1 : to lick 2 : to lap against

lamida *nf* : lick

lámina *nf* 1 PLANCHA : sheet, plate 2 : plate, illustration

laminado¹, -da *adj* : laminated

laminado² *nm* : laminate

laminar *vt* : to laminate — **laminación** *nf*

lámpara *nf* : lamp

lampiño, -ña *adj* : hairless

lamprea *nf* : lamprey

lana *nf* 1 : wool ⟨lana de acero : steel wool⟩ 2 *Mex fam* : money, dough

lance¹, etc. → **lanzar**

lance² *nm* 1 INCIDENTE : event, incident 2 RIÑA : quarrel 3 : throw, cast (of a net, etc.) 4 : move, play (in a game), throw (of dice)

lancear *vt* : to spear

lancha *nf* 1 : small boat, launch 2 **lancha motora** : motorboat, speedboat

langosta *nf* 1 : lobster 2 : locust

langostino *nm* : prawn, crayfish

languidecer {53} *vi* : to languish

languidez *nf, pl* **-deces** : languor, listlessness

lánguido, -da *adj* : languid, listless — **lánguidamente** *adv*

lanolina *nf* : lanolin

lanudo, -da *adj* : woolly

lanza *nf* : spear, lance

lanzadera *nf* 1 : shuttle (for weaving) 2 **lanzadera espacial** : space shuttle

lanzado, -da *adj* 1 : impulsive, brazen 2 : forward, determined ⟨ir lanzado : to hurtle along⟩

lanzador, -dora *n* : thrower, pitcher

lanzallamas *nms & pl* : flamethrower

lanzamiento *nm* 1 : throw 2 : pitch (in baseball) 3 : launching, launch

lanzar {21} *vt* 1 : to throw, to hurl 2 : to pitch 3 : to launch — **lanzarse** *vr* 1 : to throw oneself (at, into) 2 ∼ **a** : to embark upon, to undertake

laosiano, -na *adj & n* : Laotian

lapa *nf* : limpet

lapicera *nf Arg, Uru* : pen

lapicero *nm* 1 : mechanical pencil 2 *CA, Peru* : ballpoint pen

lápida *nf* : marker, tombstone

lapidar *vt* APEDREAR : to stone

lápiz *nm, pl* **lápices** 1 : pencil 2 **lápiz labial** *or* **lápiz de labios** : lipstick

lapón, -pona *adj & n, mpl* **lapones** : Lapp

lapso *nm* : lapse, space (of time)

lapsus *nms & pl* : error, slip

laptop *nm, pl* **laptops** : laptop

laquear *vt* : to lacquer, to varnish, to shellac

larga *nf* 1 **a la larga** : in the long run 2 **darle largas a** : to put off, to stall

largamente *adv* 1 : at length, extensively 2 : easily, comfortably 3 : generously

largar {52} *vt* 1 SOLTAR : to let loose, to release 2 AFLOJAR : to loosen, to slacken 3 *fam* : to give, to hand over 4 *fam* : to hurl, to let fly (insults, etc.) — **largarse** *vr fam* : to scram, to beat it

largo¹, -ga *adj* 1 : long 2 **a lo largo** : lengthwise 3 **a lo largo de** : along 4 **a lo largo y ancho de** : the length and breadth of, all over

largo² *nm* : length ⟨tres metros de largo : three meters long⟩

largometraje *nm* : feature film

largue, etc. → **largar**

largueza *nf* : generosity, largesse

larguirucho, -cha *adj fam* : lanky

largura *nf* : length

laringe *nf* : larynx

laringitis *nfs & pl* : laryngitis

larva *nf* : larva — **larval** *adj*

las → **el²**, **los¹**

lasaña *nf* : lasagna

lasca *nf* : chip, chipping

lascivia *nf* : lasciviousness, lewdness

lascivo, -va *adj* : lascivious, lewd — **lascivamente** *adv*

láser *nm* : laser

lasitud *nf* : weariness

laso, -sa *adj* : languid, weary

lástima *nf* 1 : compassion, pity 2 PENA : shame, pity ⟨¡qué lástima! : what a shame!⟩ ⟨es una lástima que . . . : it's a shame that . . .⟩ ⟨tener/sentir lástima de : to feel sorry for⟩

lastimadura *nf* : injury, wound

lastimar *vt* 1 DAÑAR, HERIR : to hurt, to injure 2 AGRAVIAR : to offend — **lastimarse** *vr* : to hurt oneself

lastimero, -ra *adj* : pitiful, wretched

lastimoso, -sa *adj* 1 : shameful 2 : pitiful, terrible

lastrar *vt* 1 : to ballast 2 : to burden, to encumber

lastre *nm* 1 : burden 2 : ballast

lata *nf* 1 : tin 2 : tin can 3 *fam* : pest, bother, nuisance 4 **dar lata** *fam* : to bother, to annoy

latente *adj* : latent

lateral¹ *adj* 1 : lateral, side 2 : indirect — **lateralmente** *adv*

lateral² *nm* : end piece, side

látex *nms & pl* : latex

latido *nm* : beat, throb ⟨latido del corazón : heartbeat⟩

latifundio *nm* : large estate

latigazo *nm* : lash (with a whip)

látigo *nm* AZOTE : whip

latín *nm* : Latin (language)

latino¹, -na *adj* 1 : Latin 2 *fam* : Latin-American

latino², -na *n fam* : Latin American

latinoamericano¹, -na *adj* HISPANOAMERICANO : Latin American

latinoamericano², -na *n* : Latin American

latir *vi* 1 : to beat, to throb 2 **latirle a uno** *Mex fam* : to have a hunch ⟨me late que no va a venir : I have a feeling he's not going to come⟩

latitud *nf* 1 : latitude 2 : breadth

lato, -ta *adj* **1** : extended, lengthy **2** : broad (in meaning)

latón *nm, pl* **latones** : brass

latoso¹, -sa *adj fam* : annoying, bothersome

latoso², -sa *n fam* : pest, nuisance

latrocinio *nm* : larceny

laúd *nm* : lute

laudable *adj* : laudable, praiseworthy

laudo *nm* : findings, decision

laureado, -da *adj & n* : laureate

laurear *vt* : to award, to honor

laurel *nm* **1** : laurel, bay (in cooking) ⟨hoja de laurel : bay leaf⟩ **2 dormirse en sus laureles** : to rest on one's laurels

lava *nf* : lava

lavable *adj* : washable

lavabo *nm* **1** LAVAMANOS : sink, washbowl **2** : lavatory, toilet

lavadero *nm* : laundry room

lavado *nm* **1** : laundry, wash **2** : laundering ⟨lavado de dinero : money laundering⟩

lavadora *nf* : washing machine

lavamanos *nms & pl* LAVABO : sink, washbowl

lavanda *nf* ESPLIEGO : lavender

lavandería *nf* : laundry (service)

lavandero, -ra *n* : launderer, laundress *f*

lavaplatos *nms & pl* **1** : dishwasher **2** *Chile, Col, Mex* : kitchen sink

lavar *vt* **1** : to wash, to clean **2** : to launder (money) **3 lavar en seco** : to dry-clean — **lavarse** *vr* **1** : to wash oneself **2 lavarse las manos de** : to wash one's hands of

lavarropas *nms & pl Arg, Uru* : washing machine

lavativa *nf* : enema

lavatorio *nm* : lavatory, washroom

lavavajillas *nms & pl* : dishwasher

laxante *adj & nm* : laxative

laxitud *nf* : laxity, slackness

laxo, -xa *adj* : lax, slack

lazada *nf* : bow, loop

lazar {21} *vt* : to rope, to lasso

lazo *nm* **1** VÍNCULO : link, bond **2** : bow, ribbon **3** : lasso, lariat

LCD *nm* : LCD, liquid crystal display

le *pron* **1** : to her, to him, to it ⟨¿qué le dijiste? : what did you tell him?⟩ **2** : from her, from him, from it ⟨el ladrón le robó la cartera : the thief stole his wallet⟩ **3** : for her, for him, for it ⟨cómprale flores a tu mamá : buy your mom some flowers⟩ **4** *(formal)* : to you, for you ⟨le traje un regalo : I brought you a gift⟩

leal *adj* : loyal, faithful — **lealmente** *adv*

lealtad *nf* : loyalty, allegiance

lebrel *nm* : hound

lección *nf, pl* **lecciones** : lesson

lechada *nf* **1** : whitewash **2** : grout

lechal *adj* : suckling ⟨cordero lechal : suckling lamb⟩

leche *nf* **1** : milk ⟨leche en polvo : powdered milk⟩ **2** : milk (of a plant) **3 leche de magnesia** : milk of magnesia

lechera *nf* **1** : milk jug **2** : dairymaid *f*

lechería *nf* : dairy store

lechero¹, -ra *adj* : dairy

lechero², -ra *n* : milkman *m*, milk dealer

lecho *nm* **1** : bed ⟨un lecho de rosas : a bed of roses⟩ ⟨lecho de muerte : deathbed⟩ **2** : riverbed **3** : layer, stratum (in geology)

lechón, -chona *n, mpl* **lechones** : suckling pig

lechoso, -sa *adj* : milky

lechuga *nf* : lettuce

lechuza *nf* BÚHO : owl, barn owl

lectivo, -va *adj* : school ⟨año lectivo : school year⟩

lector¹, -tora *adj* : reading ⟨nivel lector : reading level⟩

lector², -tora *n* : reader

lector³ *nm* **1** : scanner, reader **2 lector electrónico** *or* **lector de libros electrónicos** : e-reader

lectura *nf* **1** : reading **2** : reading matter

LED *or* **led** *nm* : LED

leer {20} *v* : to read ⟨leer los labios : to lip-read, to read lips⟩ ⟨leer entre las líneas : to read between the lines⟩

legación *nf, pl* **-ciones** : legation

legado *nm* **1** : legacy, bequest **2** : legate, emissary

legajo *nm* : dossier, file

legal *adj* : legal, lawful — **legalmente** *adv*

legalidad *nf* : legality

legalista *adj* : legalistic

legalizar {21} *vt* : to legalize — **legalización** *nf*

legañas *nfpl* : sleep (in the eyes)

legar {52} *vt* **1** : to bequeath, to hand down **2** DELEGAR : to delegate

legendario, -ria *adj* : legendary

legible *adj* : legible — **legibilidad** *nf*

legión *nf, pl* **legiones** : legion

legionario, -ria *n* : legionnaire

legislación *nf, pl* **-ciones** **1** : legislation (act) **2** : laws *pl*, legislation

legislador¹, -dora *adj* : legislative

legislador², -dora *n* : legislator

legislar *vi* : to legislate

legislativo, -va *adj* : legislative

legislatura *nf* **1** : legislature **2** : term of office

legitimar *vt* **1** : to legitimize **2** : to authenticate — **legitimación** *nf*

legitimidad *nf* : legitimacy

legítimo, -ma *adj* **1** : legitimate **2** : genuine, authentic — **legítimamente** *adv*

lego¹, -ga *adj* **1** : secular, lay **2** : uninformed, ignorant

lego², -ga *n* : layperson, layman *m*, laywoman *f*

legua *nf* **1** : league **2 notarse a leguas** : to be very obvious ⟨se notaba a leguas : you could tell from a mile away⟩

legue, etc. → **legar**

legumbre *nf* **1** HORTALIZA : vegetable **2** : legume

leíble *adj* : readable

leída *nf* : reading, read ⟨de una leída : in one reading, at one go⟩

leído¹ *pp* → **leer**

leído², -da *adj* : well-read

lejanía *nf* : remoteness, distance

lejano, -na *adj* : remote, distant, far away

lejía *nf* **1** : lye **2** : bleach
lejos *adv* **1** : far away, distant ⟨a lo lejos : in the distance, far off⟩ ⟨desde lejos : from a distance⟩ **2** : long ago, a long way off ⟨está lejos de los 50 años : he's a long way from 50 years old⟩ **3 de** ~ : by far ⟨esta decisión fue de lejos la más fácil : this decision was by far the easiest⟩ **4** ~ **de** : far from ⟨lejos de ser reprobado, recibió una nota de B : far from failing, he got a B⟩ **5 ir demasiado lejos** : to go too far
lelo, -la *adj* : silly, stupid
lema *nm* : motto, slogan
lemming *nm* : lemming
lempira *nf* : lempira (Honduran unit of currency)
lencería *nf* : lingerie
lengua *nf* **1** : tongue ⟨se me traba la lengua : I have trouble speaking, I get tongue-tied⟩ **2** IDIOMA : language ⟨lengua materna : mother tongue⟩ ⟨lengua nativa : native language⟩ ⟨lengua muerta : dead language⟩ **3** : tongue (of flame) **4** : spit (of land) **5 irse de la lengua** : to let something slip, to blab **6 morderse la lengua** : to bite one's tongue **7 sacarle la lengua a alguien** : to stick one's tongue out at someone
lenguado *nm* : sole, flounder
lenguaje *nm* **1** : language, speech **2 lenguaje gestual** *or* **lenguaje de gestos** : sign language **3 lenguaje de programación** : programming language
lengüeta *nf* **1** : tongue (of a shoe), tab, flap **2** : reed (of a musical instrument) **3** : barb, point
lengüetada *nf* **beber a lengüetadas** : to lap (up)
lenidad *nf* : leniency
lenitivo, -va *adj* : soothing
lente *nmf* **1** : lens ⟨lentes de contacto : contact lenses⟩ **2 lentes** *nmpl* ANTEOJOS : eyeglasses ⟨lentes de sol : sunglasses⟩
lenteja *nf* : lentil
lentejuela *nf* : sequin, spangle
lentilla *nf Spain* : contact lens
lentitud *nf* : slowness
lento¹ *adv* DESPACIO : slowly
lento², -ta *adj* **1** : slow **2** : slow-witted, dull — **lentamente** *adv*
leña *nf* : wood, firewood
leñador, -dora *n* : lumberjack, woodcutter
leñera *nf* : woodshed
leño *nm* : log
leñoso, -sa *adj* : woody
Leo¹ *nm* : Leo (sign or constellation)
Leo² *nmf* : Leo (person)
león, -ona *n, mpl* **leones 1** : lion, lioness *f* **2** (*in various countries*) : puma, cougar
leonado, -da *adj* : tawny
leonino, -na *adj* **1** : lion-like **2** : one-sided, unfair
leopardo *nm* : leopard
leotardo *nm* MALLA : leotard, tights *pl*
leperada *nf Mex* : obscenity
lépero, -ra *adj Mex* : vulgar, coarse
lepra *nf* : leprosy

leproso¹, -sa *adj* : leprous
leproso², -sa *n* : leper
lerdo, -da *adj* **1** : clumsy **2** : dull, oafish, slow-witted
les *pron* **1** : to them ⟨dales una propina : give them a tip⟩ **2** : from them ⟨se les privó de su herencia : they were deprived of their inheritance⟩ **3** : for them ⟨les hice sus tareas : I did their homework for them⟩ **4** : to you *pl*, for you *pl* ⟨les compré un regalo : I bought you all a present⟩
lesbiana *nf* : lesbian — **lesbiano, -na** *adj*
lesbianismo *nm* : lesbianism
lesera *nf Chile fam* : stupid thing
lesión *nf, pl* **lesiones** HERIDA : lesion, wound, injury ⟨una lesión grave : a serious injury⟩
lesionado, -da *adj* HERIDO : injured, wounded
lesionar *vt* : to injure, to wound — **lesionarse** *vr* : to hurt oneself
lesivo, -va *adj* : harmful, damaging
letal *adj* MORTÍFERO : deadly, lethal — **letalmente** *adv*
letanía *nf* **1** : litany **2** *fam* : spiel, song and dance
letárgico, -ca *adj* : lethargic
letargo *nm* : lethargy, torpor
letón¹, -tona *adj & n, mpl* **letones** : Latvian
letón² *nm* : Latvian (language)
letra *nf* **1** : letter ⟨letra mayúscula/minúscula : capital/lowercase letter⟩ ⟨letra en negrilla/negrita : boldface, bold type⟩ ⟨letra cursiva : italics, italic type⟩ ⟨leer la letra pequeña/chica : to read the small print⟩ ⟨aprender las primeras letras : to learn how to read and write⟩ **2** CALIGRAFÍA : handwriting, lettering **3** : lyrics *pl* **4 al pie de la letra** : word for word, by the book **5 letra(s) de molde** *or* **letra(s) de imprenta** : print ⟨escribió su nombre en/con letra(s) de molde/imprenta : she printed her name⟩ **6 letras** *nfpl* : arts (in education)
letrado¹, -da *adj* ERUDITO : learned, erudite
letrado², -da *n* : attorney, lawyer
letrero *nm* RÓTULO : sign, notice
letrina *nf* : latrine
letrista *nmf* : lyricist, songwriter
leucemia *nf* : leukemia
leva *nf* : cam
levadura *nf* **1** : yeast, leavening **2 levadura en polvo** : baking powder
levantado, -da *adj* : awake, up
levantamiento *nm* **1** ALZAMIENTO : uprising **2** : raising, lifting ⟨levantamiento de pesas : weight lifting⟩
levantar *vt* **1** ALZAR : to lift, to raise ⟨levanté la tapa : I lifted the lid⟩ ⟨levantar pesas : to lift weights⟩ ⟨levantar la mano : to raise one's hand⟩ ⟨levantar la mirada/vista : to look up⟩ ⟨levantar la voz : to raise one's voice⟩ **2** : to put up, to erect (a building, etc.) **3** : to give a boost to ⟨me levantó el ánimo : it lifted my spirits⟩ ⟨un plan para levantar al país : a plan to get the country back on its

feet⟩ **4** : to lift (an embargo, etc.), to call off (a strike, etc.), to adjourn (a meeting, etc.) **5** : to give rise to, to arouse ⟨levantar sospechas : to arouse suspicion⟩ ⟨levantar una polémica : to spark controversy⟩ **6 levantar cabeza** : to get back on one's feet, to recover — **levantarse** *vr* **1** : to rise, to stand up **2** : to get out of bed, to get up ⟨se levanta a las seis : he gets up at six⟩

levante *nm* **1** : east (direction) **2** : east wind

levar *vt* **levar anclas** : to weigh anchor

leve *adj* **1** : light, slight **2** : trivial, unimportant — **levemente** *adv*

levedad *nf* : lightness

levemente *adv* LIGERAMENTE : lightly, softly

leviatán *nm, pl* **-tanes** : leviathan

levitar *vi* : to levitate

léxico[1], **-ca** *adj* : lexical

léxico[2] *nm* : lexicon, glossary

lexicografía *nf* : lexicography

lexicográfico, -ca *adj* : lexicographical, lexicographic

lexicógrafo, -fa *n* : lexicographer

ley *nf* **1** : law ⟨aprobar/derogar una ley : to pass/repeal a law⟩ ⟨violar la ley : to break the law⟩ ⟨fuera de la ley : outside the law⟩ ⟨proyecto de ley : bill (of law)⟩ ⟨la ley de gravedad : the law of gravity⟩ ⟨es ley de vida : it's a fact of life⟩ ⟨con todas las de la ley : proper, properly⟩ **2** : purity (of metals) ⟨oro de ley : pure gold⟩

leyenda *nf* **1** : legend **2** : caption, inscription

leyó, etc. → **leer**

liar {85} *vt* **1** ATAR : to bind, to tie (up) **2** : to roll (a cigarette) **3** : to confuse — **liarse** *vr* : to get mixed up

libanés, -nesa *adj & n, mpl* **-neses** : Lebanese

libar *vt* **1** : to suck (nectar) **2** : to sip, to swig (liquor, etc.)

libelo *nm* **1** : libel, lampoon **2** : petition (in court)

libélula *nf* : dragonfly

liberación *nf, pl* **-ciones** : liberation, deliverance ⟨liberación de la mujer : women's liberation⟩

liberado, -da *adj* **1** : liberated ⟨una mujer liberada : a liberated woman⟩ **2** : freed, delivered

liberal *adj & nmf* : liberal

liberalidad *nf* : generosity, liberality

liberalismo *nm* : liberalism

liberalizar {21} *vt* : to liberalize — **liberalización** *nf*

liberar *vt* : to liberate, to free — **liberarse** *vr* : to get free of

liberiano, -na *adj & n* : Liberian

libertad *nf* **1** : freedom, liberty ⟨tomarse la libertad de : to take the liberty of⟩ ⟨poner a alguien en libertad : to set someone free⟩ ⟨libertad de expresión : freedom of speech⟩ **2 libertad bajo fianza** : bail **3 libertad condicional** : parole, probation

libertador[1], **-dora** *adj* : liberating

libertador[2], **-dora** *n* : liberator

libertar *vt* LIBRAR : to set free

libertario, -ria *adj & n* : libertarian

libertinaje *nm* : licentiousness, dissipation

libertino[1], **-na** *adj* : licentious, dissolute

libertino[2], **-na** *n* : libertine

libidinoso, -sa *adj* : lustful, lewd

libido *nf* : libido

libio, -bia *adj & n* : Libyan

libra *nf* **1** : pound **2 libra esterlina** : pound sterling

Libra[1] *nm* : Libra (sign or constellation)

Libra[2] *nmf* : Libra (person)

libramiento *nm* **1** : liberating, freeing **2** LIBRANZA : order of payment **3** *Mex* : beltway

libranza *nf* : order of payment

librar *vt* **1** LIBERTAR : to free (from punishment, etc.), to save (from death, etc.) ⟨líbranos del mal : deliver us from evil⟩ ⟨librar de culpas : to absolve of guilt⟩ **2** : to wage ⟨librar batalla : to do battle⟩ **3** : to issue ⟨librar una orden : to issue an order⟩ — **librarse** *vr* ~ **de** : to free oneself from, to get out of ⟨se libró de pagar una multa : he got out of paying a fine⟩ ⟨librarse de morir : to escape death⟩

libre[1] *adj* **1** : free ⟨un país libre : a free country⟩ ⟨libre de : free from, exempt from⟩ ⟨libre albedrío : free will⟩ ⟨ratos libres : free/spare time⟩ **2** DESOCUPADO : vacant **3 día libre** : day off

libre[2] *nm Mex* : taxi

librea *nf* : livery

librecambio *nm* : free trade

libremente *adv* : freely

librería *nf* : bookstore

librero[1], **-ra** *n* : bookseller

librero[2] *nm Mex* : bookcase

libresco, -ca *adj* : bookish

libreta *nf* CUADERNO : notebook

libretista *nmf* **1** : librettist **2** : scriptwriter

libreto *nm* : libretto, script

libro *nm* **1** : book ⟨libro de texto/cocina : textbook/cookbook⟩ ⟨libro de consulta : reference book⟩ ⟨libro en rústica, libro de tapa/pasta blanda : paperback⟩ ⟨libro de tapa/pasta dura : hardcover⟩ ⟨libro de instrucciones : instruction manual⟩ **2 libros** *nmpl* : books (in bookkeeping), accounts ⟨llevar los libros : to keep the books⟩

liceal *nmf Uru* : high school student

liceano, -na *n Chile* → **liceal**

liceísta *nmf CoRi, Ven* → **liceal**

licencia *nf* **1** : permission **2** : leave, leave of absence **3** : permit, license ⟨licencia de conducir : driver's license⟩

licenciado, -da *n* **1** : university graduate **2** ABOGADO : lawyer

licenciar *vt* **1** : to license, to permit, to allow **2** : to discharge **3** : to grant a university degree to — **licenciarse** *vr* : to graduate

licenciatura *nf* **1** : college degree **2** : course of study (at a college or university)

licencioso, -sa *adj* : licentious, lewd

liceo *nm* (*in various countries*) : secondary school, high school

licitación *nf, pl* -ciones : bid, bidding
licitar *vt* : to bid on
lícito, -ta *adj* 1 : lawful, licit 2 JUSTO : just, fair
licor *nm* 1 : liquor 2 : liqueur
licorera *nf* : decanter
licuado *nm* BATIDO : milk shake
licuadora *nf* : blender
licuar {3} *vt* : to liquefy — licuarse *vr*
lid *nf* 1 : fight, combat 2 : argument, dispute 3 lides *nfpl* : matters, affairs 4 en buena lid : fair and square
líder¹ *adj* : leading, foremost
líder² *nmf* : leader
liderar *vt* DIRIGIR : to lead, to head
liderato *nm* : leadership, leading
liderazgo → liderato
lidia *nf* 1 : bullfighting 2 : bullfight
lidiar *vt* : to fight — *vi* BATALLAR, LUCHAR : to struggle, to battle, to wrestle
liebre *nf* : hare
liendre *nf* : nit
lienzo *nm* 1 : linen 2 : canvas, painting 3 : stretch of wall or fencing
liga *nf* 1 ASOCIACIÓN : league 2 GOMITA : rubber band 3 : garter
ligado, -da *adj* : linked, connected
ligadura *nf* 1 ATADURA : tie, bond 2 : ligature
ligamento *nm* : ligament
ligar {52} *vt* : to bind, to tie (up)
ligeramente *adv* 1 : slightly 2 LEVEMENTE : lightly, gently 3 : casually, lightly
ligereza *nf* 1 : lightness 2 : flippancy 3 : agility
ligero, -ra *adj* 1 : light, lightweight 2 : slight, minor 3 : agile, quick 4 : lighthearted, superficial
light [ˈlait] *adj* : light, low-calorie
ligue, etc. → ligar
liguero, -ra *adj* : league
lija *nf or* papel de lija : sandpaper
lijar *vt* : to sand
lila¹ *adj* : lilac, light purple
lila² *nf* : lilac
lima *nf* 1 : lime (fruit) 2 : file ⟨lima de uñas : nail file⟩
limar *vt* 1 : to file 2 : to polish, to put the final touch on 3 : to smooth over ⟨limar asperezas : to iron out differences⟩
limbo *nm* 1 : limbo 2 : limb (in botany and astronomy)
limeño¹, -ña *adj* : of or from Lima, Peru
limeño², -ña *n* : person from Lima, Peru
limero *nm* : lime tree
limitación *nf, pl* -ciones 1 : limitation 2 : limit, restriction ⟨sin limitación : unlimited⟩
limitado, -da *adj* 1 RESTRINGIDO : limited 2 : dull, slow-witted
limitar *vt* RESTRINGIR : to limit, to restrict — *vi* ~ con : to border on — limitarse *vr* ~ a : to limit oneself to
límite *nm* 1 : boundary, border 2 : limit ⟨el límite de mi paciencia : the limit of my patience⟩ ⟨límite de velocidad : speed limit⟩ 3 fecha límite : deadline
limítrofe *adj* LINDANTE, LINDERO : bordering, adjoining

limo *nm* : slime, mud
limón *nm, pl* limones 1 : lemon 2 : lemon tree 3 limón verde *Mex* : lime
limonada *nf* : lemonade
limonero *nm* : lemon tree
limosna *nf* : alms, charity
limosnear *vi* : to beg (for alms)
limosnero, -ra *n* MENDIGO : beggar
limoso, -sa *adj* : slimy
limpiabotas *nmfs & pl* : shoeshine boy/man *m*, shoeshine girl/woman *f*
limpiacristales *nms & pl Spain* 1 : glass cleaner (fluid) 2 : window washer (person)
limpiador¹, -dora *adj* : cleaning
limpiador², -dora *n* : cleaning person, cleaner
limpiamente *adv* : cleanly, honestly, fairly
limpiaparabrisas *nms & pl* : windshield wiper
limpiar *vt* 1 : to clean, to cleanse 2 : to clean up, to remove defects 3 *fam* : to clean out (in a game) 4 *fam* : to swipe, to pinch — *vi* : to clean — limpiarse *vr*
limpiavidrios *nmfs & pl* 1 *Mex* : windshield wiper 2 : glass cleaner (fluid) 3 : window washer (person)
límpido, -da *adj* : limpid
limpieza *nf* 1 : cleanliness, tidiness 2 : cleaning 3 HONRADEZ : integrity, honesty 4 DESTREZA : skill, dexterity
limpio¹ *adv* : fairly
limpio², -pia *adj* 1 : clean, neat 2 : honest ⟨un juego limpio : a fair game⟩ 3 : free ⟨limpio de impurezas : pure, free from impurities⟩ 4 : clear, net ⟨ganancia limpia : clear profit⟩
limusina *nf* : limousine
linaje *nm* ABOLENGO : lineage, ancestry
lince *nm* : lynx
linchamiento *nm* : lynching
linchar *vt* : to lynch
lindante *adj* LIMÍTROFE, LINDERO : bordering, adjoining
lindar *vi* 1 ~ con : to border, to skirt 2 ~ con BORDEAR : to border on, to verge on
linde *nmf* : boundary, limit
lindero¹, -ra *adj* LIMÍTROFE, LINDANTE : bordering, adjoining
lindero² *nm* : boundary, limit
lindeza *nf* 1 : prettiness 2 : clever remark 3 lindezas *nfpl* (*used ironically*) : insults
lindo¹ *adv* 1 : beautifully, wonderfully ⟨canta lindo tu mujer : your wife sings beautifully⟩ 2 de lo lindo : a lot, a great deal ⟨los zancudos nos picaban de lo lindo : the mosquitoes were biting away at us⟩
lindo², -da *adj* 1 BONITO : pretty, lovely 2 MONO : cute
línea *nf* 1 : line ⟨línea divisoria : dividing line⟩ ⟨línea de banda : sideline⟩ ⟨línea de meta : finish line⟩ ⟨línea de puntos : dotted line⟩ ⟨líneas enemigas : enemy lines⟩ ⟨línea de producción : production line⟩ ⟨leer entre líneas : to read between the lines⟩ 2 : line, course, position ⟨en

líneas generales : in general terms, along general lines) ⟨línea de conducta : course of action⟩ ⟨línea de investigación : line of inquiry⟩ ⟨la línea del partido : the party line⟩ **3** : line, range ⟨línea de productos : product line⟩ **4** : line, side ⟨línea de sucesión : line of succession⟩ ⟨un primo suyo por línea materna : a cousin on his mother's side⟩ **5** : line, service ⟨línea aérea : airline⟩ ⟨línea telefónica : telephone line⟩ ⟨en línea : online⟩ ⟨fuera de línea : off-line⟩ **6** : figure ⟨guardar la línea : to watch one's figure⟩

línea de crédito *nf* : line of credit

lineal *adj* : linear

lineamientos *nmpl* : guidelines

linfa *nf* : lymph

linfático, -ca *adj* : lymphatic

lingote *nm* : ingot

lingüista *nmf* : linguist

lingüística *nf* : linguistics

lingüístico, -ca *adj* : linguistic

linimento *nm* : liniment

lino *nm* **1** : linen **2** : flax

linóleo *nm* : linoleum

linterna *nf* **1** : lantern **2** : flashlight

lío *nm fam* **1** : confusion, mess **2** : hassle, trouble, jam ⟨meterse en un lío : to get into a jam⟩ **3** : affair, liaison

liofilizar {21} *vt* : to freeze-dry

lioso, -sa *adj fam* : confusing, muddled

liquen *nm* : lichen

liquidación *nf, pl* **-ciones 1** : liquidation **2** : clearance sale **3** : settlement, payment

liquidar *vt* **1** : to liquefy **2** : to liquidate **3** : to settle, to pay off **4** *fam* : to rub out, to kill

liquidez *nf, pl* **-deces** : liquidity

líquido¹, -da *adj* **1** : liquid, fluid **2** : net ⟨ingresos líquidos : net income⟩

líquido² *nm* **1** : liquid, fluid ⟨líquido de frenos : brake fluid⟩ **2** : ready cash, liquid assets

lira *nf* : lyre

lírica *nf* : lyric poetry

lírico, -ca *adj* : lyric, lyrical

lirio *nm* **1** : iris **2 lirio de los valles** MUGUETE : lily of the valley

lirón *nm, pl* **lirones** : dormouse

lisiado¹, -da *adj* : disabled, crippled

lisiado², -da *n offensive* : disabled person, cripple *offensive*

lisiar *vt* : to cripple, to disable — **lisiarse** *vr*

liso, -sa *adj* **1** : smooth **2** : flat **3** : straight ⟨pelo liso : straight hair⟩ **4** : plain, unadorned ⟨liso y llano : plain and simple⟩

lisonja *nf* : flattery

lisonjear *vt* ADULAR : to flatter

lista *nf* **1** : list ⟨es la primera/última de la lista : she's first/last on the list⟩ **2** : roster, roll ⟨pasar lista : to take attendance⟩ **3** : stripe, strip **4** : menu

listado¹, -da *adj* : striped

listado² *nm* : listing

listar *vt* : to list

listeza *nf* : smartness, alertness

listo, -ta *adj* **1** DISPUESTO, PREPARADO : ready ⟨¿estás listo? : are you ready?⟩ **2** : clever, smart ⟨pasarse de listo : to be too clever⟩

listón *nm, pl* **listones 1** : ribbon **2** : strip (of wood), lath **3** : high bar (in sports)

lisura *nf* : smoothness

litera *nf* : bunk bed, berth

literal *adj* : literal — **literalmente** *adv*

literario, -ria *adj* : literary

literato, -ta *n* : writer, author

literatura *nf* : literature

litigante *adj & nmf* : litigant

litigar {52} *vi* : to litigate, to be in litigation

litigio *nm* **1** : litigation, lawsuit **2 en ~** : in dispute

litio *nm* : lithium

litografía *nf* **1** : lithography **2** : lithograph

litógrafo, -fa *n* : lithographer

litoral¹ *adj* : coastal

litoral² *nm* : shore, seaboard

litosfera *nf* : lithosphere

litro *nm* : liter

lituano¹, -na *adj & n* : Lithuanian

lituano² *nm* : Lithuanian (language)

liturgia *nf* : liturgy

litúrgico, -ca *adj* : liturgical — **litúrgicamente** *adv*

liviandad *nf* LIGEREZA : lightness

liviano, -na *adj* **1** : light, slight **2** INCONSTANTE : fickle

lividez *nf* PALIDEZ : pallor

lívido, -da *adj* **1** AMORATADO : livid **2** PÁLIDO : pallid, extremely pale

living *nm* : living room

ll *nf* : fourteenth letter of the Spanish alphabet not usually considered a separate letter in alphabetization

llaga *nf* : sore, wound

llama *nf* **1** : flame **2** : llama

llamada *nf* : call ⟨llamada a larga distancia : long-distance call⟩ ⟨llamada al orden : call to order⟩

llamado¹, -da *adj* : named, called ⟨una mujer llamada Rosa : a woman called Rosa⟩

llamado² → **llamamiento**

llamador *nm* : door knocker

llamamiento *nm* : call, appeal

llamar *vt* **1** : to call, to name ⟨la llamamos Paulita : we call her Paulita⟩ ⟨lo llamaban loco : they called him crazy⟩ ⟨así lo llamamos en Cuba : that's what we call it in Cuba⟩ **2** : to call, to summon ⟨llamar un taxi : to call a taxi⟩ ⟨me llamó desde abajo : she called up to me (from downstairs)⟩ ⟨fue llamado a declarar : he was called to testify⟩ **3** : to call (up), to phone ⟨me llama todos los días : she calls me every day⟩ — *vi* : to knock (on a door), to ring a doorbell ⟨llaman a la puerta : there's someone at the door⟩ — **llamarse** *vr* : to be called, to be named ⟨¿cómo te llamas? : what's your name?⟩ ⟨me llamo Ana : my name is Ana⟩

llamarada *nf* **1** : flare-up, sudden blaze **2** : flushing (of the face)

llamativo, -va *adj* : flashy, showy, striking
llameante *adj* : flaming, blazing
llamear *vi* : to flame, to blaze
llana *nf* **1** : trowel **2** → **llano²**
llanamente *adv* : simply, plainly ⟨es, simple y llanamente, un desastre : it's a disaster, plain and simple⟩
llaneza *nf* : simplicity, naturalness
llano¹, -na *adj* **1** : even, flat **2** : frank, open **3** LISO : plain, simple
llano² *nm* : plain
llanta *nf* **1** NEUMÁTICO : tire **2** : rim
llantén *nm, pl* **llantenes** : plantain (weed)
llanto *nm* : crying, weeping
llanura *nf* : plain, prairie
llave *nf* **1** : key ⟨bajo llave : under lock and key⟩ ⟨llave maestra : master key⟩ ⟨cerrar (algo) con llave : to lock (something)⟩ **2** : faucet **3** : valve (in plumbing) **4** INTERRUPTOR : switch **5** : (curly) brace, curly bracket (punctuation mark) **6** : wrench ⟨llave inglesa : monkey wrench⟩
llavero *nm* : key chain, key ring
llegada *nf* : arrival
llegar {52} *vi* **1** : to arrive ⟨llegar temprano/tarde : to arrive early/late⟩ ⟨llegué a Lisboa : I arrived in Lisbon⟩ ⟨llegué al hotel : I arrived at the hotel⟩ ⟨llegó hasta la frontera : he got as far as the border⟩ ⟨cuando llegue el momento : when the time comes⟩ ⟨va a llegar lejos : she's going to go far⟩ **2** : to be enough ⟨no nos llega el sueldo para todo : we can't afford it all on our salary⟩ **3** ~ a/hasta : to reach ⟨llega hasta el techo : it goes (all the way) up to the ceiling⟩ ⟨llegué hasta la página 85 : I got up to page 85, I got as far as page 85⟩ ⟨podría llegar a los 35 grados : it could get up to 35 degrees⟩ **4** ~ a : to reach (an agreement, etc.) **5** ~ a : to manage to ⟨llegó a terminar la novela : she managed to finish the novel⟩ **6 llegar a ser** : to become ⟨llegó a ser presidente : he became President⟩
llegue, etc. → **llegar**
llenar *vt* **1** : to fill, to fill up, to fill in **2** : to meet, to fulfill ⟨los regalos no llenaron sus expectativas : the gifts did not meet her expectations⟩ — **llenarse** *vr* : to fill up, to become full
llenito, -ta *adj fam* REGORDETE : chubby, plump
lleno¹, -na *adj* **1** : full, filled **2 de ~** : completely, fully **3 estar lleno de sí mismo** : to be full of oneself
lleno² *nm* **1** *fam* : plenty, abundance **2** : full house
llevadero, -ra *adj* : bearable
llevar *vt* **1** : to carry, to take (away) ⟨le llevé las maletas : I carried her bags⟩ ⟨siempre lo lleva consigo : he always has it with him⟩ ⟨me gusta, me lo llevo : I like it—I'll take it⟩ **2** : to wear ⟨llevaba un vestido azul : she wore a blue dress⟩ ⟨llevar el pelo corto/largo : to wear one's hair short/long⟩ **3** : to take ⟨llevamos a Pedro al cine : we took Pedro to the movies⟩ ⟨la llevaron al hospital : they

took her to the hospital⟩ **4** : to lead ⟨nos llevó por un pasillo : he led us down a hallway⟩ ⟨me lleva a pensar que . . . : it leads me to believe that . . .⟩ **5** : to lead ⟨llevar una vida sana : to lead a healthy life⟩ **6** : to run, to be in charge of ⟨lleva la biblioteca : she runs the library⟩ **7** : to keep ⟨llevar el ritmo : to keep time⟩ ⟨llevar un diario : to keep a diary⟩ **8** : to take, to require ⟨le llevó horas hacerlo : it took him hours to do it⟩ **9** : to have . . . more than ⟨nos llevan cinco puntos : they're five points ahead of us⟩ ⟨te llevo tres años : I'm three years older than you⟩ **10 llevar a cabo** : to carry out **11 llevar adelante** : to carry on with, to keep going with — *vi* : to lead ⟨un problema lleva al otro : one problem leads to another⟩ — *v aux* : to have ⟨llevo mucho tiempo buscándolo : I've been looking for it for a long time⟩ ⟨lleva leído medio libro : he's halfway through the book⟩ — **llevarse** *vr* **1** : to take away, to carry off/away ⟨una ola se lo llevó : a wave carried him away⟩ ⟨se llevó el primer premio : she took/won first prize⟩ **2** : to get along ⟨siempre nos llevábamos bien : we always got along well⟩
llorar *vi* : to cry, to weep — *vt* : to mourn, to bewail
lloriquear *vi* : to whimper, to whine
lloriqueo *nm* : whimpering, whining
lloro *nm* : crying
llorón, -rona *n, mpl* **llorones** : crybaby, whiner
lloroso, -sa *adj* : tearful, sad
llovedizo, -za *adj* : rain ⟨agua llovediza : rainwater⟩
llover {47} *v impers* : to rain ⟨está lloviendo : it's raining⟩ ⟨llover a cántaros : to rain cats and dogs⟩ — *vi* : to rain down, to shower ⟨le llovieron regalos : he was showered with gifts⟩
llovizna *nf* : drizzle, sprinkle
lloviznar *v impers* : to drizzle, to sprinkle
llueve, etc. → **llover**
lluvia *nf* **1** : rain, rainfall **2** : barrage, shower **3 lluvia ácida** : acid rain
lluvioso, -sa *adj* : rainy
lo¹ *pron (referring to masculine nouns)* **1** : him, it ⟨lo vi ayer : I saw him yesterday⟩ ⟨lo entiendo : I understand it⟩ ⟨no lo creo : I don't believe so⟩ **2** *(formal)* : you ⟨disculpe, señor, no lo oí : excuse me, sir, I didn't hear you⟩ **3 lo que** : what, that which ⟨eso es lo que más le gusta : that's what he likes the most⟩
lo² *art* **1** : the ⟨lo mejor : the best, the best thing⟩ **2** : how ⟨sé lo bueno que eres : I know how good you are⟩ ⟨lo más rápido posible : as quickly as possible⟩
loa *nf* : praise
loable *adj* : laudable, praiseworthy — **loablemente** *adv*
loar *vt* : to praise, to laud
lobato, -ta *n* : wolf cub
lobby *nm* : lobby, pressure group
lobo, -ba *n* : wolf
lobotomía *nf* : lobotomy

lóbrego, -ga *adj* SOMBRÍO : gloomy, dark
lobulado, -da *adj* : lobed
lóbulo *nm* : lobe ⟨lóbulo de la oreja : earlobe⟩
locación *nf, pl* **-ciones** **1** : location (for filming) **2** *Mex* : place
local[1] *adj* : local — **localmente** *adv*
local[2] *nm* : premises *pl*
localidad *nf* : town, locality
localización *nf, pl* **-ciones** **1** : locating, localization **2** : location
localizar {21} *vt* **1** UBICAR : to locate, to find **2** : to localize — **localizarse** *vr* UBICARSE : to be located ⟨se localiza en el séptimo piso : it is located on the seventh floor⟩
locamente *adv* **1** : madly **2** : wildly, recklessly
locatario, -ria *n* : tenant
loción *nf, pl* **lociones** : lotion
lócker *nm, pl* **lóckers** : locker
loco[1], **-ca** *adj* **1** DEMENTE : crazy, insane, mad **2 a lo loco** : wildly, recklessly **3 volverse loco** : to go mad
loco[2], **-ca** *n* **1** : crazy person, lunatic **2 hacerse el loco** : to act the fool
locomoción *nf, pl* **-ciones** : locomotion
locomotor, -tora *adj* : locomotive
locomotora *nf* **1** : locomotive **2** : driving force
locuaz *adj, pl* **locuaces** : loquacious, talkative
locución *nf, pl* **-ciones** : locution, phrase ⟨locución adverbial : adverbial phrase⟩
locura *nf* **1** : insanity, madness **2** : crazy thing, folly
locutor, -tora *n* : announcer
lodazal *nm* : bog, quagmire
lodo *nm* BARRO : mud, mire
lodoso, -sa *adj* : muddy
logaritmo *nm* : logarithm
logia *nf* : lodge ⟨logia masónica : Masonic lodge⟩
lógica *nf* : logic
lógico, -ca *adj* : logical — **lógicamente** *adv*
login [¹login] *nm* **1** : login, logon (act of logging in) **2** : login (user credentials)
logística *nf* : logistics *pl*
logístico, -ca *adj* : logistic
logo → **logotipo**
logotipo *nm* : logo
logrado, -da *adj* : successful, skillfully done ⟨un efecto muy logrado : a very convincing effect⟩
lograr *vt* **1** : to get, to obtain **2** : to achieve, to attain — **lograrse** *vr* : to be successful
logro *nm* : achievement, attainment
loma *nf* : hill, hillock
lombriz *nf, pl* **lombrices** : worm ⟨lombriz de tierra : earthworm, night crawler⟩ ⟨lombriz solitaria : tapeworm⟩ ⟨tener lombrices : to have worms⟩
lomo *nm* **1** : back (of an animal) **2** : loin ⟨lomo de cerdo : pork loin⟩ **3** : spine (of a book) **4** : blunt edge (of a knife)
lona *nf* : canvas
loncha *nf* LONJA, REBANADA : slice

lonche *nm* **1** *Mex* ALMUERZO : lunch **2** *Mex* : submarine sandwich **3** *Peru* MERIENDA : afternoon snack, tea
lonchería *nf Mex* : snack bar
londinense[1] *adj* : of or from London
londinense[2] *nmf* : Londoner
longaniza *nf* : spicy pork sausage
longevidad *nf* : longevity
longevo, -va *adj* : long-lived
longitud *nf* **1** LARGO : length ⟨longitud de onda : wavelength⟩ **2** : longitude
longitudinal *adj* : longitudinal — **longitudinalmente** *adv*
lonja *nf* LONCHA, REBANADA : slice
lontananza *nf* : background ⟨en lontananza : in the distance, far away⟩
lord *nm, pl* **lores** (*title in England*) : lord
loro *nm* : parrot
los[1], **las** *pron* **1** : them ⟨no los conozco muy bien : I don't know them very well⟩ ⟨hice galletas y se las di a los nuevos vecinos : I made cookies and gave them to the new neighbors⟩ **2** : you ⟨voy a llevarlos a los dos : I am going to take both of you⟩ **3** : the ones ⟨me gustan las rojas : I like the red ones⟩ ⟨los de las camisas azules : the ones in the blue shirts⟩ ⟨mis padres y los tuyos : my parents and yours⟩ ⟨las reuniones de ayer y las de hoy : yesterday's meetings and today's⟩ **4 los que, las que** : those, who, the ones ⟨los que van a cantar deben venir temprano : those who are singing must come early⟩ **5** (*used with* **haber**) ⟨los hay en varios colores : they come in various colors⟩
los[2] *art* → **el**[2]
losa *nf* : flagstone, paving stone
loseta *nf* BALDOSA : floor tile
lote *nm* **1** : part, share **2** : batch, lot **3** : plot of land, lot
lotería *nf* : lottery
loto *nm* : lotus
loza *nf* **1** : crockery, earthenware **2** : china
lozanía *nf* **1** : healthiness, robustness **2** : luxuriance, lushness
lozano, -na *adj* **1** : robust, healthy-looking ⟨un rostro lozano : a smooth, fresh face⟩ **2** : lush, luxuriant
LSD *nm* : LSD
lubina *nf* : sea bass
lubricante[1] *adj* : lubricating
lubricante[2] *nm* : lubricant
lubricar {72} *vt* : to lubricate, to oil — **lubricación** *nf*
lucero *nm* : bright star ⟨lucero del alba : morning star⟩
lucha *nf* **1** : struggle, fight **2** : wrestling
luchador, -dora *n* **1** : fighter **2** : wrestler
luchar *vi* **1** : to fight, to struggle **2** : to wrestle
luchón, -chona *adj, mpl* **luchones** *Mex* : industrious, hardworking
lucidez *nf, pl* **-deces** : lucidity, clarity
lucido, -da *adj* MAGNÍFICO : magnificent, splendid
lúcido, -da *adj* : lucid
luciente *adj* : bright, shining

luciérnaga *nf* : firefly, glowworm

lucimiento *nm* **1** : brilliance, splendor, sparkle **2** : triumph, success ⟨salir con lucimiento : to succeed with flying colors⟩

lucio *nm* : pike (fish)

lucir {45} *vi* **1** : to shine **2** : to look good, to stand out **3** : to seem, to appear ⟨ahora luce contento : he looks happy now⟩ — *vt* **1** : to wear, to sport **2** : to flaunt, to show off — **lucirse** *vr* **1** : to distinguish oneself, to excel **2** : to show off

lucrarse *vr* : to make a profit

lucrativo, -va *adj* : lucrative, profitable — **lucrativamente** *adv*

lucro *nm* GANANCIA : profit, gain

luctuoso, -sa *adj* : mournful, tragic

lúdico, -ca *adj* : play, playful

luego¹ *adv* **1** DESPUÉS : then, afterwards **2** : later (on) **3 desde ~** : of course **4 ¡hasta luego!** : see you later! **5 luego que** : as soon as **6 luego luego** *Mex fam* : right away, immediately

luego² *conj* : therefore ⟨pienso, luego existo : I think, therefore I am⟩

lugar *nm* **1** : place, position ⟨lugar de nacimiento/trabajo : birthplace/workplace⟩ ⟨en algún lugar : somewhere⟩ ⟨en otro lugar : somewhere else⟩ ⟨cambiar algo de lugar : to move something⟩ ⟨poner las cosas en su lugar : to put things away, to straighten up⟩ ⟨te guardo el lugar : I'll save your spot⟩ ⟨yo en tu lugar : if I were in your place, if I were you⟩ ⟨se llevó el primer lugar : she took first place⟩ **2** ESPACIO : space, room ⟨no hay lugar para todos : there isn't room for everyone⟩ **3 dar lugar a** : to give rise to, to lead to ⟨puede dar lugar a complicaciones : it can lead to complications⟩ **4 en lugar de** : instead of, on behalf of **5 en primer lugar** : in the first place, firstly **6 en último lugar** : last, lastly **7 lugar común** : cliché, platitude **8 sin lugar a dudas** : without a doubt, undoubtedly **9 tener lugar** : to take place

lugareño¹, -ña *adj* : village, rural

lugareño², -ña *n* : villager

lugarteniente *nmf* : lieutenant, deputy

lúgubre *adj* : gloomy, lugubrious

lujo *nm* **1** : luxury **2 de ~** : deluxe

lujoso, -sa *adj* : luxurious

lujuria *nf* : lust, lechery

lujurioso, -sa *adj* : lustful, lecherous

lumbago *nm* : lumbago

lumbar *adj* : lumbar

lumbre *nf* **1** FUEGO : fire **2** : brilliance, splendor **3 poner en la lumbre** : to put on the stove, to warm up

lumbrera *nf* **1** : skylight **2** : vent, port **3** : brilliant person, luminary

luminaria *nf* **1** : altar lamp **2** LUMBRERA : luminary, celebrity

luminiscencia *nf* : luminescence — **luminiscente** *adj*

luminosidad *nf* : luminosity, brightness

luminoso, -sa *adj* : shining, luminous

luna *nf* **1** : moon **2 luna de miel** : honeymoon

lunar¹ *adj* : lunar

lunar² *nm* **1** : mole, beauty spot **2** : defect, blemish **3** : polka dot

lunático, -ca *adj & n* : lunatic

lunes *nms & pl* : Monday ⟨el lunes : (on) Monday⟩ ⟨los lunes : (on) Mondays⟩ ⟨cada (dos) lunes : every (other) Monday⟩ ⟨el lunes pasado : last Monday⟩ ⟨el lunes por la noche : on Monday night⟩ ⟨el próximo lunes : next Monday⟩

luneta *nf* **1** : lens (of eyeglasses) **2** : windshield (of an automobile) **3** : crescent

lupa *nf* : magnifying glass

lúpulo *nm* : hops (plant)

lustrabotas → **limpiabotas**

lustrar *vt* : to shine, to polish

lustre *nm* **1** BRILLO : luster, shine **2** : glory, distinction

lustro *nm* : five-year period

lustroso, -sa *adj* BRILLOSO : lustrous, shiny

luto *nm* : mourning ⟨estar de luto : to be in mourning⟩

luxación *nf, pl* **-ciones** : dislocation

luz *nf, pl* **luces** **1** : light ⟨luz del sol : sunlight⟩ ⟨luz eléctrica/artificial : electric/artificial light⟩ ⟨iluminado con una luz tenue : dimly lit⟩ ⟨a plena luz del día : in full/broad daylight⟩ **2** *fam* : power, electricity ⟨se fue la luz : the power/electricity went out⟩ ⟨cortar la luz : to cut off the power⟩ ⟨pagar la luz : to pay the electricity bill⟩ **3** : light, lamp ⟨apagar la luz : to turn off the light⟩ ⟨encender/prender la luz : to turn on the light⟩ ⟨luz de bengala : flare⟩ ⟨luz neón/LED : neon/LED light⟩ **4** : span, spread (between supports) **5 a la luz de** : in light of **6 a todas luces** : by any measure **7 dar a luz** : to give birth **8 sacar a la luz** : to make known, to bring to light **9 salir a la luz** : to become known, to come to light **10 traje de luces** : matador's costume

luzca, etc. → **lucir**

M

m *nf* : fifteenth letter of the Spanish alphabet

macabro, -bra *adj* : macabre

macadán *nm, pl* **-danes** : macadam

macana *nf* **1** : club, cudgel **2** *fam* : nonsense, silliness **3** *fam* : lie, fib *fam*

macanear *vi Arg, Chile, Uru fam* : to talk nonsense — *vt Mex, PRi fam* : to beat

macanudo, -da *adj fam* : great, fantastic

macarrón *nm, pl* **-rrones 1** : macaroon **2 macarrones** *nmpl* : macaroni

macerar *vt* : to soak (food)

maceta *nf* **1** : flowerpot **2** : mallet **3** *Mex fam* : head

macetero *nm* **1** : plant stand **2** TIESTO : flowerpot, planter

machacar {72} *vt* **1** : to crush, to grind **2** : to beat, to pound — *vi* : to insist, to go on (about)

machacón, -cona *adj, mpl* **-cones** : insistent, tiresome

machete *nm* : machete

machetear *vt* : to hack with a machete — *vi Mex fam* : to plod, to work tirelessly

machismo *nm* **1** : machismo **2** : male chauvinism

machista *nm* : male chauvinist

macho¹ *adj* **1** : male **2** : macho, virile, tough

macho² *nm* **1** : male **2** : he-man

machote *nm* **1** *fam* : tough guy, he-man **2** *CA, Mex* : rough draft, model **3** *Mex* : blank form

machucar {72} *vt* **1** : to pound, to beat, to crush **2** : to bruise

machucón *nm, pl* **-cones 1** MORETÓN : bruise **2** : smashing, pounding

macilento, -ta *adj* : gaunt, wan

macis *nm* : mace (spice)

macizo, -za *adj* **1** : solid ⟨oro macizo : solid gold⟩ **2** : strong, strapping **3** : massive

mácula *nf* : blemish, stain

macuto *nm Spain* : backpack

madeja *nf* **1** : skein, hank **2** : tangle (of hair)

madera *nf* **1** : wood ⟨de madera : made of wood, wooden⟩ ⟨tener madera de algo : to have the makings of something⟩ **2** : lumber, timber **3 madera dura** *or* **madera noble** : hardwood

maderero, -ra *adj* : timber, lumber

madero *nm* : piece of lumber, plank

madrastra *nf* : stepmother

madrazo *nm Mex fam* : punch, blow ⟨se agarraron a madrazos : they beat each other up⟩

madre *nf* **1** : mother ⟨madre biológica/adoptiva : biological/adoptive mother⟩ ⟨madre de alquiler : surrogate mother⟩ ⟨madre soltera : single/unwed mother⟩ **2 madre política** : mother-in-law **3 la Madre Patria** : the mother country (said of Spain)

madrear *vt Mex fam* : to beat up

madreperla *nf* NÁCAR : mother-of-pearl

madreselva *nf* : honeysuckle

madriguera *nf* : burrow, den, lair

madrileño¹, -ña *adj* : of or from Madrid

madrileño², -ña *n* : person from Madrid

madrina *nf* **1** : godmother **2** : mother of the groom, matron of honor **3** : sponsor

madrugada *nf* **1** : early morning, wee hours **2** ALBA : dawn, daybreak

madrugador, -dora *n* : early riser

madrugar {52} *vi* **1** : to get up early **2** : to get a head start

madurar *v* **1** : to ripen **2** : to mature

madurez *nf, pl* **-reces 1** : maturity **2** : ripeness

maduro, -ra *adj* **1** : mature **2** : ripe

maestría *nf* **1** : mastery, skill **2** : master's degree

maestro¹, -tra *adj* **1** : masterly, skilled **2** : chief, main **3** : trained ⟨un elefante maestro : a trained elephant⟩

maestro², -tra *n* **1** : teacher (in elementary and middle school) ⟨no hay mejor maestro que la necesidad : necessity is the mother of invention⟩ **2** : expert, master ⟨maestro de cocina : chef⟩ ⟨maestro de ceremonias : master of ceremonies⟩ **3** : maestro

Mafia *nf* : Mafia

mafioso, -sa *n* : mafioso, gangster

magdalena *nf* : bun, muffin

magenta *adj & n* : magenta

magia *nf* : magic

mágico, -ca *adj* : magic, magical — **mágicamente** *adv*

magisterio *nm* **1** : teaching **2** : teachers *pl*, teaching profession

magistrado, -da *n* : magistrate, judge

magistral *adj* : masterful, skillful

magistralmente *adv* : masterfully, brilliantly

magistratura *nf* : office of judge/magistrate

magma *nm* : magma

magnanimidad *nf* : magnanimity

magnánimo, -ma *adj* GENEROSO : magnanimous — **magnánimamente** *adv*

magnate *nmf* : magnate, tycoon

magnesio *nm* : magnesium

magnético, -ca *adj* : magnetic

magnetismo *nm* : magnetism

magnetizar {21} *vt* : to magnetize

magnetofónico, -ca *adj* **cinta magnetofónica** : magnetic tape

magnificar {72} *vt* **1** : to magnify **2** EXAGERAR : to exaggerate **3** ENSALZAR : to exalt, to extol, to praise highly

magnificencia *nf* : magnificence, splendor

magnífico, -ca *adj* ESPLENDOROSO : magnificent, splendid — **magníficamente** *adv*

magnitud *nf* : magnitude

magnolia *nf* : magnolia (flower)

magnolio *nm* : magnolia (tree)

mago, -ga *n* **1** : magician **2** : wizard (in folk tales, etc.) **3 los Reyes Magos** : the Magi

magro, -gra *adj* **1** : lean (of meat) **2** : meager

maguey *nm* : maguey

magulladura *nf* MORETÓN : bruise

magullar *vt* : to bruise — **magullarse** *vr*

mahometano¹, -na *adj* ISLÁMICO : Islamic, Muslim

mahometano², -na *n* : Muslim

mahonesa → **mayonesa**

maicena *nf* : cornstarch

mainframe ['mein,freim] *nm* : mainframe

maíz *nm* : corn, maize

maizal *nm* : cornfield

maja *nf* : pestle

majadería *nf* **1** TONTERÍA : stupidity, foolishness **2** *Mex* LEPERADA : insult, obscenity

majadero¹, -ra *adj* **1** : foolish, silly **2** *Mex* LÉPERO : crude, vulgar

majadero², -ra *n* **1** TONTO : fool **2** *Mex* : rude person, boor

majar *vt* : to crush, to mash

majestad *nf* : majesty ⟨Su Majestad : Your Majesty⟩

majestuosamente *adv* : majestically

majestuosidad *nf* : majesty, grandeur

majestuoso, -sa *adj* : majestic, stately

majo, -ja *adj Spain* **1** : nice, likeable **2** GUAPO : attractive, good-looking

mal¹ *adv* **1** : badly, poorly ⟨baila muy mal : he dances very badly⟩ ⟨hablar mal de alguien : to speak ill of someone⟩ ⟨hice mal en decirlo : I was wrong to say it⟩ ⟨comió algo que le hizo mal : he ate something that didn't agree with him⟩ ⟨algo anda mal : something's wrong⟩ ⟨todo le salió mal : everything went wrong for her⟩ ⟨el primer día no me fue mal : my first day wasn't bad⟩ **2** : wrong, incorrectly ⟨me entendió mal : she misunderstood me⟩ ⟨no lo tomes a mal : don't take it the wrong way⟩ ⟨esta palabra está mal escrita : this word is spelled wrong⟩ ⟨si mal no recuerdo : if I remember correctly⟩ **3** : hardly, with difficulty ⟨te oigo mal : I can hardly hear you⟩ ⟨mal se pueden comparar : you can hardly compare them⟩ ⟨mal puedo esperar : I can hardly wait⟩ **4 de mal en peor** : from bad to worse **5 menos mal** : it's a good thing, it's just as well ⟨menos mal que reaccioné a tiempo : it's a good thing I reacted in time⟩ ⟨menos mal que no viniste : it's just as well you didn't come⟩

mal² *adj* → **malo**

mal³ *nm* **1** : evil, wrong ⟨un mal necesario : a necessary evil⟩ **2** DAÑO : harm, damage ⟨las acusaciones le hicieron mucho mal : the accusations did him a lot of harm⟩ **3** DESGRACIA : misfortune **4** ENFERMEDAD : illness, sickness **5 mal de ojo** : evil eye

malabar *adj* **juegos malabares** : juggling

malabares *nmpl* : juggling ⟨hacer malabares : to juggle⟩

malabarismos → **malabares**

malabarista *nmf* : juggler

malaconsejado, -da *adj* : ill-advised

malacostumbrado, -da *adj* CONSENTIDO : spoiled, pampered

malacostumbrar *vt* : to spoil

malagradecido, -da *adj* INGRATO : ungrateful

malaisio → **malasio**

malanga *nf* TARO : taro

malaria *nf* PALUDISMO : malaria

malasio, -sia *adj & n* : Malaysian

malauiano, -na *adj & n* : Malawian

malaventura *nf* : misadventure, misfortune

malaventurado, -da *adj* MALHADADO : ill-fated, unfortunate

malayo, -ya *adj & n* : Malay, Malayan

malbaratar *vt* **1** MALGASTAR : to squander **2** : to undersell

malcriado¹, -da *adj* **1** : ill-bred, ill-mannered **2** : spoiled, pampered

malcriado², -da *n* : spoiled brat

malcriar *vt* : to spoil, to raise badly

maldad *nf* **1** : evil, wickedness **2** : evil deed

maldecir {11} *vt* : to curse, to damn — *vi* **1** : to curse, to swear **2 ~ de** : to speak ill of, to slander, to defame

maldición *nf, pl* **-ciones** : curse

maldiga, maldijo etc. → **maldecir**

maldito, -ta *adj* **1** : cursed, damned ⟨¡maldita sea! : damn it all!⟩ **2** : wicked

maldoso, -sa *adj Mex* : mischievous

maleable *adj* : malleable

maleante *nmf* : crook, thug

malecón *nm, pl* **-cones** : jetty, breakwater

maleducado, -da *adj* : ill-mannered, rude

maleficio *nm* : curse, hex

maléfico, -ca *adj* : evil, harmful

malentender {56} *vt* : to misunderstand

malentendido *nm* : misunderstanding

malestar *nm* **1** : discomfort **2** IRRITACIÓN : annoyance **3** INQUIETUD : uneasiness, unrest

maleta *nf* : suitcase, bag ⟨haz tus maletas : pack your bags⟩

maletera *nf Peru* → **maletero²**

maletero¹, -ra *n* : porter

maletero² *nm* : trunk (of an automobile)

maletín *nm, pl* **-tines** **1** PORTAFOLIO : briefcase **2** : overnight bag, satchel

malevolencia *nf* : malevolence, wickedness

malévolo, -la *adj* : malevolent, wicked

maleza *nf* **1** : thicket, underbrush **2** : weeds *pl*

malformación *nf, pl* **-ciones** : malformation

malgache *adj & nmf* : Madagascan

malgastar *vt* : to squander (resources), to waste (time, effort)

mal habido, -da *adj* : ill-gotten, dirty

malhablado, -da *adj* : foulmouthed

malhadado, -da *adj* MALAVENTURADO : ill-fated

malhechor, -chora *n* : criminal, delinquent, wrongdoer

malherir {76} *vt* : to injure seriously

malhumor *nm* : bad mood

malhumorado, -da *adj* : bad-tempered, cross

malicia *nf* **1** : wickedness, malice **2** : mischief, naughtiness **3** : cunning, craftiness

malicioso, -sa *adj* **1** : malicious **2** PÍCARO : mischievous

malignidad *nf* **1** : malignancy **2** MALDAD : evil

maligno, -na *adj* **1** : malignant ⟨un tumor maligno : a malignant tumor⟩ **2** : evil, harmful, malign

malinchismo *nm Mex* : preference for foreign goods or people — **malinchista** *adj*

malintencionado, -da *adj* : malicious, spiteful

malinterpretar *vt* : to misinterpret

mall ['mol] *nm, pl* **malls** : (shopping) mall

malla *nf* **1** : mesh **2** LEOTARDO : leotard, tights *pl* **3** **malla de baño** *Arg, Uru* : swimsuit, bathing suit

mallorquín, -quina *adj & n* : Majorcan

malnutrición *nf, pl* **-ciones** DESNUTRICIÓN : malnutrition

malnutrido, -da *adj* DESNUTRIDO : malnourished, undernourished

malo[1], -la *adj* (**mal** *before masculine singular nouns*) **1** : bad ⟨mala suerte : bad luck⟩ ⟨malas noticias : bad news⟩ ⟨es mala idea : it's a bad idea⟩ ⟨mal aliento : bad breath⟩ ⟨un mal sabor : a bad taste⟩ ⟨un mal actor : a bad actor⟩ ⟨tener un mal día : to have a bad day⟩ ⟨una situación muy mala : a very bad situation⟩ ⟨recibió muy malas críticas : it got very bad reviews⟩ ⟨ese sombrero te queda mal : that hat doesn't look good on you⟩ ⟨llegaste en mal momento : you arrived at a bad time⟩ **2** : bad, poor ⟨en malas condiciones : in bad condition⟩ ⟨es de mala calidad : it's poor quality⟩ **3** : bad, wicked, naughty ⟨una mala persona : a bad person⟩ ⟨malas intenciones : bad intentions⟩ ⟨fuiste muy malo : you were very bad⟩ **4** : bad, improper ⟨ser de mala educación : to be bad manners⟩ ⟨malas palabras : bad words⟩ **5** : bad, harmful ⟨malo para la salud : bad for one's health⟩ **6** (*using the form* **mal**) : sick, ill, unwell ⟨estar/ponerse mal : to be/fall ill⟩ ⟨me siento/encuentro mal : I feel sick⟩ ⟨ando mal del estómago : my stomach is upset⟩ ⟨estar mal del corazón : to have heart trouble⟩ **7** : bad, spoiled (of food) **8** **estar de malas** : to be in a bad mood

malo[2], -la *n* : villain, bad guy (in novels, movies, etc.)

malogrado, -da *adj* : failed, unsuccessful

malograr *vt* **1** : to spoil, to ruin **2** : to waste (an opportunity, time) — **malograrse** *vr* **1** FRACASAR : to fail **2** : to die young

malogro *nm* **1** : untimely death **2** FRACASO : failure

maloliente *adj* HEDIONDO : foul-smelling, smelly

malparado, -da *adj* **salir malparado** or **quedar malparado** : to come out of (something) badly, to end up in a bad state

malpensado, -da *adj* : distrustful, suspicious

malquerencia *nf* AVERSIÓN : ill will, dislike

malquerer {64} *vt* : to dislike

malquiso, etc. → **malquerer**

malsano, -na *adj* : unhealthy

malsonante *adj* : rude, offensive ⟨palabras malsonantes : foul language⟩

malta *nf* : malt

malteada *nf* : malted milk ⟨malteada de chocolate : chocolate malt⟩

maltratar *vt* **1** : to mistreat, to abuse **2** : to damage, to spoil

maltrato *nm* : mistreatment, abuse

maltrecho, -cha *adj* : battered, damaged

malucho, -cha *adj fam* : sick, under the weather

malva *adj & nm* : mauve

malvado[1], -da *adj* : evil, wicked

malvado[2], -da *n* : evildoer, wicked person

malvavisco *nm* : marshmallow

malvender *vt* : to sell at a loss

malversación *nf, pl* **-ciones** : misappropriation (of funds), embezzlement

malversador, -dora *n* : embezzler

malversar *vt* : to embezzle

malvivir *vi* : to live badly, to just scrape by

malware ['malwer] *nm* : malware

mamá *nf fam* : mom, mama

mamadera *nf* : baby bottle

mamar *vi* **1** : to suckle **2** **darle de mamar a** : to breast-feed — *vt* **1** : to suckle, to nurse **2** : to learn from childhood, to grow up with — **mamarse** *vr fam* : to get drunk

mamario, -ria *adj* : mammary

mamarracho *nm fam* **1** ESPERPENTO : mess, sight **2** : laughingstock, fool **3** : rubbish, junk

mambo *nm* : mambo

mameluco *nm* : overalls *pl*

mami *nf fam* : mommy

mamífero[1], -ra *adj* : mammalian

mamífero[2] *nm* : mammal

mamila *nf* **1** : nipple **2** *Mex* : baby bottle, pacifier

mamografía *nf* : mammogram

mamola *nf* : pat, chuck under the chin

mamotreto *nm fam* **1** : huge book, tome **2** ARMATOSTE : hulk, monstrosity

mampara *nf* BIOMBO : screen, room divider

mamparo *nm* : bulkhead

mampostería *nf* : masonry, stonemasonry

mampostero *nm* : mason, stonemason

mamut *nm, pl* **mamuts** : mammoth

maná *nm* : manna

manada *nf* **1** : flock, herd, pack **2** *fam* : horde, mob ⟨llegaron en manada : they came in droves⟩

manager or **mánager** *nmf, pl* **-gers** : manager

manantial *nm* **1** FUENTE : spring **2** : source

manar *vi* **1** : to flow **2** : to abound

manaza *nf* MANO : hand, mitt

manazas *nmfs & pl* : clumsy person, klutz, oaf

manatí *nm, pl* **-tíes** : manatee

mancha *nf* **1** : stain, spot, mark ⟨mancha de sangre : bloodstain⟩ **2** : blemish, blot ⟨una mancha en su reputación : a blemish on his reputation⟩ **3** : patch
manchado, -da *adj* : stained
manchar *vt* **1** ENSUCIAR : to stain, to soil **2** DESHONRAR : to sully, to tarnish — **mancharse** *vr* : to get dirty
mancillar *vt* : to sully, to besmirch
manco, -ca *adj* : one-armed, with one arm/hand
mancomunar *vt* : to combine, to pool — **mancomunarse** *vr* : to unite, to join together
mancomunidad *nf* **1** : commonwealth **2** : association, confederation
mancuernas *nfpl* : cuff links
mancuernillas *nf Mex* : cuff links
mandadero, -ra *n* : errand boy *m*, errand girl *f*, messenger
mandado *nm* **1** : order, command **2** : errand ⟨hacer los mandados : to run errands, to go shopping⟩
mandamás *nmf, pl* **-mases** *fam* : boss, bigwig, honcho
mandamiento *nm* **1** : commandment **2** : command, order, warrant ⟨mandamiento judicial : warrant, court order⟩
mandar *vt* **1** ORDENAR : to command, to order ⟨los mandó (a) callar, los mandó (a) que callaran : she ordered them to be quiet⟩ ⟨mandó (a) construir un monumento : he had a monument built⟩ **2** ENVIAR : to send ⟨te manda saludos : he sends you his regards⟩ ⟨la mandaron a Buenos Aires : they sent her to Buenos Aires⟩ **3** ECHAR : to hurl, to throw **4** ¿mande? *Mex* : yes?, pardon? **5** mandar algo a arreglar : to have something fixed **6** mandar (a) decir : to send word, to send a message **7** mandar (a) llamar : to send for, to summon — *vi* : to be the boss, to be in charge — **mandarse** *vr Mex* : to take liberties, to take advantage
mandarín *nm* : Mandarin
mandarina *nf* : mandarin orange, tangerine
mandatario, -ria *n* **1** : leader (in politics) ⟨primer mandatario : head of state⟩ **2** : agent (in law)
mandato *nm* **1** : term of office **2** : mandate
mandíbula *nf* **1** : jaw **2** : mandible
mandil *nm* **1** DELANTAL : apron **2** : horse blanket
mandilón *nm, pl* **-lones** *fam* : wimp, coward
mandioca *nf* **1** : manioc, cassava **2** : tapioca
mando *nm* **1** : command, leadership **2** : control (for a device) ⟨mando a distancia : remote control⟩ **3** al mando de : in charge of **4** al mando de : under the command of
mandolina *nf* : mandolin
mandón, -dona *adj, mpl* **mandones** : bossy, domineering
mandonear *vt fam* MANGONEAR : to boss around

manecilla *nf* : hand (of a clock), pointer
manejable *adj* **1** : manageable **2** : docile, easily led
manejar *vt* **1** CONDUCIR : to drive (a car) **2** OPERAR : to handle, to operate **3** : to manage **4** : to manipulate (a person) — *vi* : to drive — **manejarse** *vr* **1** COMPORTARSE : to behave **2** : to get along, to manage
manejo *nm* **1** : handling, operation **2** : management
manera *nf* **1** MODO : way, manner, fashion ⟨cada uno lo hace a su manera : everyone does it their own way⟩ ⟨a mi manera de ver : the way I see it⟩ ⟨de esta/esa manera : in this/that way⟩ ⟨de una manera u otra : one way or another⟩ ⟨de manera inmediata : immediately⟩ ⟨de mala manera : badly, rudely⟩ **2** a manera de : by way of **3** de alguna manera : somehow, in some way **4** de cualquier manera *or* de todas maneras : anyway, anyhow ⟨de todas maneras tenía que hacerlo : I had to do it anyway⟩ **5** de manera que : so, in order that **6** de ninguna manera : by no means, absolutely not **7** de otra manera : differently, in another way ⟨para decirlo de otra manera : in other words⟩ ⟨de otra manera no hubiera sobrevivido : otherwise he wouldn't have survived⟩ **8** manera de ser : personality, demeanor **9** no hay manera : there's no way, it's not possible ⟨no hay manera de saberlo : there's no way to know⟩ **10** maneras *nfpl* : manners
manga *nf* **1** : sleeve ⟨en mangas de camisa : in shirt sleeves⟩ ⟨sin mangas : without sleeves, sleeveless⟩ **2** MANGUERA : hose
manganeso *nm* : manganese
manglar *nm* : mangrove swamp
mangle *nm* : mangrove
mango *nm* **1** : hilt, handle **2** : mango
mangonear *vt fam* : to boss around, to bully — *vi* **1** : to be bossy **2** : to loaf, to fool around
mangosta *nf* : mongoose
manguera *nf* : hose
manguito *nm* **1** : muff **2** : sleeve (of a pipe, etc.), hose (of a car)
maní *nm, pl* **maníes** : peanut
manía *nf* **1** OBSESIÓN : mania, obsession **2** : craze, fad **3** : odd habit, peculiarity **4** : dislike, aversion
maníaco[1], -ca *or* **maniaco, -ca** *adj* **1** : manic **2** *fam* CRAZED : maniacal
maníaco[2], -ca *or* **maniaco, -ca** *n* : maniac
maniatar *vt* : to tie the hands of
maniático[1], -ca *adj* **1** MANÍACO : maniacal **2** : obsessive **3** : fussy, finicky
maniático[2], -ca *n* **1** MANÍACO : maniac, lunatic **2** : obsessive person, fanatic **3** : eccentric, crank
manicomio *nm fam* **1** : insane asylum, madhouse *now often offensive* **2** (*used figuratively*) : madhouse
manicura *nf* : manicure
manicuro, -ra *n* : manicurist
manido, -da *adj* : hackneyed, stale, trite

manifestación *nf, pl* **-ciones 1** : manifestation, sign **2** : demonstration, rally
manifestante *nmf* : demonstrator
manifestar {55} *vt* **1** : to demonstrate, to show **2** : to declare — **manifestarse** *vr* **1** : to be or become evident **2** : to state one's position ⟨se han manifestado a favor del acuerdo : they have declared their support for the agreement⟩ **3** : to demonstrate, to rally
manifiesto¹, -ta *adj* : manifest, evident, clear — **manifiestamente** *adv*
manifiesto² *nm* : manifesto
manija *nf* MANGO : handle
manilla → **manecilla**
manillar *nm* : handlebars *pl*
maniobra *nf* : maneuver, stratagem
maniobrar *v* : to maneuver
manipulación *nf, pl* **-ciones** : manipulation
manipulador¹, -dora *adj* : manipulating, manipulative
manipulador², -dora *n* : manipulator
manipular *vt* **1** : to manipulate **2** MANEJAR : to handle
maniquí¹ *nmf, pl* **-quíes** : mannequin, model
maniquí² *nm, pl* **-quíes** : mannequin, dummy
manirroto¹, -ta *adj* : extravagant
manirroto², -ta *n* : spendthrift
manitas *nmfs & pl Spain* : handyman *m*, handywoman *f*
manito, -ta → **mano²**
manivela *nf* : crank
manjar *nm* : delicacy, special dish
mano¹ *nf* **1** : hand ⟨lávate las manos : wash your hands⟩ ⟨agárralo con las dos manos : hold it with both hands⟩ ⟨tenía algo en la mano : she had something in her hand⟩ ⟨con mis propias manos : with my own two hands⟩ **2** : coat (of paint or varnish) **3** : hand (in games) **4** a ∼ : by hand **5** a ∼ *or* a la mano : handy, at hand, nearby ⟨tenía los libros a (la) mano : I kept the books handy⟩ **6** bajo ∼ : secretly, on the sly **7** caer en manos de : to fall into the hands of **8** con las manos en la masa : red-handed **9** darle la mano a alguien : to shake someone's hand **10** darse la mano : to shake hands **11** de la mano : by the hand, hand in hand ⟨me tomó de la mano : he took me by the hand⟩ ⟨la política y la economía van de la mano : politics and economics go hand in hand⟩ **12** de mano en mano : from one person to the next ⟨pasar de mano en mano : to be passed along/around⟩ **13** de primera mano : firsthand, at first-hand ⟨conocer de primera mano : to experience firsthand⟩ **14** de segunda mano : secondhand, used ⟨ropa de segunda mano : secondhand clothing⟩ **15** echar una mano : to lend a hand **16** mano a mano : one-on-one **17** mano de obra : labor, manpower **18** mano de mortero : pestle **19** mano negra *Mex fam* : shady dealings *pl* **20** ¡manos arriba! *or* ¡arriba las manos! : stick 'em

up!, (put your) hands up! **21** tener (buena) mano para : to be good at
mano², -na *n fam* : buddy, pal ⟨¡oye, mano! : hey man!⟩
manojo *nm* PUÑADO : handful, bunch ⟨ser un manojo de nervios : to be a bag/bundle of nerves⟩
manómetro *nm* : pressure gauge
manopla *nf* **1** : mitten, mitt **2** : brass knuckles *pl*
manosear *vt* **1** : to handle or touch excessively **2** ACARICIAR : to fondle, to caress
manoseo *nm* **1** : touching, handling **2** : groping, fondling
manotazo *nm* : slap, smack, swipe
manotear *vi* : to wave one's hands, to gesticulate
mansalva *adv* a ∼ : at close range
mansarda *nf* BUHARDILLA : attic
mansedumbre *nf* : gentleness, meekness
mansión *nf, pl* **-siones** : mansion
manso, -sa *adj* **1** : gentle, meek **2** : tame — **mansamente** *adv*
manta *nf* **1** COBIJA, FRAZADA : blanket **2** : poncho **3** *Mex* : coarse cotton fabric
manteca *nf* **1** GRASA : lard, fat **2** : butter
mantecado *nm* **1** PRi HELADO : ice cream **2** (*in various countries*) : unflavored ice cream **3** *Spain* : shortbread (made with lard)
mantecoso, -sa *adj* : buttery
mantel *nm* **1** : tablecloth **2** : altar cloth
mantelería *nf* : table linen
mantener {80} *vt* **1** SUSTENTAR : to support, to feed ⟨mantener uno su familia : to support one's family⟩ **2** CONSERVAR : to keep, to preserve ⟨mantener la calma : to keep one's calm⟩ ⟨mantener la paz : to keep the peace⟩ **3** CONTINUAR : to keep up, to sustain ⟨mantener una correspondencia : to keep up a correspondence⟩ **4** AFIRMAR : to maintain, to affirm — **mantenerse** *vr* **1** : to support oneself, to subsist **2** mantenerse firme : to hold one's ground
mantenimiento *nm* **1** : maintenance, upkeep **2** : sustenance, food **3** : preservation
mantequera *nf* **1** : churn **2** : butter dish
mantequería *nf* **1** : creamery, dairy **2** : grocery store
mantequilla *nf* : butter
mantilla *nf* : scarf (worn over the head and shoulders)
mantis *nf* **mantis religiosa** : praying mantis
manto *nm* **1** : cloak **2** : mantle (in geology)
mantón *nm, pl* **-tones** CHAL : shawl
mantuvo, etc. → **mantener**
manual¹ *adj* **1** : manual ⟨trabajo manual : manual labor⟩ **2** : handy, manageable — **manualmente** *adv*
manual² *nm* : manual, handbook
manualidades *nfpl* : handicrafts (in schools)
manubrio *nm* **1** : handle, crank **2** : handlebars *pl*

manufactura *nf* **1** FABRICACIÓN : manufacture **2** : manufactured item, product **3** FÁBRICA : factory

manufacturar *vt* FABRICAR : to manufacture

manufacturero¹, -ra *adj* : manufacturing

manufacturero², -ra *n* FABRICANTE : manufacturer

manuscrito¹, -ta *adj* : handwritten

manuscrito² *nm* : manuscript

manutención *nf, pl* **-ciones** : maintenance, support

manzana *nf* **1** : apple **2** CUADRA : block (enclosed by streets or buildings) **3** *or* **manzana de Adán** : Adam's apple

manzanal *nm* **1** : apple orchard **2** MANZANO : apple tree

manzanar *nm* : apple orchard

manzanilla *nf* **1** : chamomile **2** : chamomile tea

manzano *nm* : apple tree

maña *nf* **1** : dexterity, skill **2** : cunning, guile **3 mañas** *or* **malas mañas** *nfpl* : bad habits, vices

mañana *nf* **1** : morning ⟨a las cuatro de la mañana : at four in the morning⟩ ⟨por la mañana : in the morning⟩ **2** : tomorrow

mañanero, -ra *adj* MATUTINO : morning ⟨rocío mañanero : morning dew⟩

mañanitas *nfpl Mex* : birthday serenade

mañoso, -sa *adj* **1** HÁBIL : skillful **2** ASTUTO : cunning, crafty **3** : fussy, finicky

mapa *nm* CARTA : map

mapache *nm* : raccoon

mapamundi *nm* : map of the world

maqueta *nf* : model

maquila *nf* **1** : production, manufacture (for export) **2** → **maquiladora**

maquiladora *nf* : foreign-owned factory

maquillador, -dora *n* : makeup artist

maquillaje *nm* : makeup

maquillarse *vr* : to put on makeup, to make oneself up

máquina *nf* **1** : machine ⟨máquina de afeitar : electric razor⟩ ⟨máquina de coser : sewing machine⟩ ⟨máquina de escribir : typewriter⟩ ⟨máquina tragamonedas : slot machine⟩ ⟨máquina del tiempo : time machine⟩ ⟨máquina de votación : voting machine⟩ ⟨máquina expendedora : vending machine⟩ ⟨hecho a máquina : machine-made⟩ ⟨escribir a máquina : to type⟩ **2** LOCOMOTORA : engine, locomotive **3** : machine (in politics) **4** *or* **máquina de fotos** CÁMARA : camera **5 a toda máquina** : at full speed

maquinación *nf, pl* **-ciones** : machination, scheme, plot

maquinal *adj* : mechanical, automatic — **maquinalmente** *adv*

maquinar *vt* : to plot, to scheme

maquinaria *nf* **1** : machinery **2** : mechanism, works *pl*

maquinilla *nf* **1** : small machine or device **2** *CA, Car* : typewriter

maquinista *nmf* **1** : machinist **2** : railroad engineer

mar *nmf* **1** : sea ⟨un mar agitado : a rough sea⟩ ⟨hacerse a la mar : to set sail⟩ **2 alta mar** : high seas

maraca *nf* : maraca

maraña *nf* **1** : thicket **2** ENREDO : tangle, mess

marasmo *nm* : paralysis, stagnation

maratón *nm, pl* **-tones** : marathon

maravilla *nf* **1** : wonder, marvel ⟨a las mil maravillas : wonderfully, marvelously⟩ ⟨hacer maravillas : to work wonders⟩ **2** : marigold

maravillar *vt* ASOMBRAR : to astonish, to amaze — **maravillarse** *vr* : to be amazed, to marvel

maravilloso, -sa *adj* ESTUPENDO : wonderful, marvelous — **maravillosamente** *adv*

marbete *nm* **1** ETIQUETA : label, tag **2** *PRi* : registration sticker (of a car)

marca *nf* **1** : mark ⟨marca de nacimiento : birthmark⟩ **2** : brand, make ⟨artículos de marca : brand-name items⟩ **3** : trademark ⟨marca registrada : registered trademark⟩ **4** : record (in sports) ⟨batir la marca : to beat the record⟩

marcado, -da *adj* : marked ⟨un marcado contraste : a marked contrast⟩ — **marcadamente** *adv*

marcador *nm* **1** TANTEADOR : scoreboard **2** : marker, felt-tip pen **3 marcador de libros** : bookmark

marcaje *nm* **1** : scoring (in sports) **2** : guarding (in sports)

marcapasos *nms & pl* : pacemaker

marcar {72} *vt* **1** : to mark **2** : to brand (livestock) **3** : to indicate, to show **4** RESALTAR : to emphasize **5** : to dial (a telephone) **6** : to guard (an opponent) **7** ANOTAR : to score (a goal, a point) — *vi* **1** ANOTAR : to score **2** : to dial

marcha *nf* **1** : march ⟨cerrar la marcha : to bring up the rear⟩ **2** : hike, walk ⟨ir de marcha : to go hiking⟩ **3** : pace, speed ⟨a toda marcha : at top speed⟩ **4** : gear (of an automobile) ⟨marcha atrás : reverse, reverse gear⟩ ⟨dar marcha atrás : to go into reverse⟩ **5** : departure **6** : march (in music) ⟨marcha fúnebre/nupcial : funeral/wedding march⟩ **7** : course ⟨la marcha de los acontecimientos : the course of events⟩ **8 dar marcha atrás (en algo)** : to backtrack (on something) **9 en ～** : in motion, in gear, under way ⟨poner en marcha : to activate, to start, to set in motion⟩ ⟨ponerse en marcha : to set off⟩

marchar *vi* **1** IR : to go, to travel **2** ANDAR : to walk **3** FUNCIONAR : to work, to go **4** : to march — **marcharse** *vr* : to leave

marchitar *vi* : to make wither, to wilt — **marchitarse** *vr* **1** : to wither, to shrivel up, to wilt **2** : to languish, to fade away

marchito, -ta *adj* : withered, faded

marcial *adj* : martial, military

marciano, -na *adj & n* : Martian

marco *nm* **1** : frame, framework **2** : goalposts *pl* **3** AMBIENTE : setting, atmosphere **4** : mark (unit of currency)

marea *nf* **1** : tide **2 marea negra** : oil slick

mareado, -da *adj* **1** : dizzy, light-headed **2** : queasy, nauseous **3** : seasick, airsick, carsick

marear *vt* **1** : to make sick ⟨los gases me marearon : the fumes made me sick⟩ **2** : to bother, to annoy — **marearse** *vr* **1** : to get sick, to become nauseated **2** : to feel dizzy **3** : to get tipsy

marejada *nf* **1** : surge, swell (of the sea) **2** : undercurrent, ferment, unrest

maremoto *nm* : tidal wave

mareo *nm* **1** : dizzy spell **2** : nausea **3** : seasickness, motion sickness **4** : annoyance, vexation

marfil *nm* : ivory

margarina *nf* : margarine

margarita *nf* **1** : daisy **2** : margarita (cocktail)

margen[1] *nf, pl* **márgenes** : bank (of a river), side (of a street)

margen[2] *nm, pl* **márgenes** **1** : edge, border ⟨dejar al margen : to exclude⟩ **2** : margin ⟨margen de ganancia : profit margin⟩ ⟨margen de error : margin of error⟩

marginación *nf, pl* **-ciones** : marginalization, exclusion

marginado[1], **-da** *adj* **1** DESHEREDADO : outcast, alienated, dispossessed **2 clases marginadas** : underclass

marginado[2], **-da** *n* : outcast, misfit

marginal *adj* : marginal, fringe

marginar *vt* : to ostracize, to exclude

mariachi *nm* **1** : mariachi band **2** : mariachi musician **3** : mariachi music

maridaje *nm* : marriage, union

maridar *vt* UNIR : to marry, to unite

marido *nm* ESPOSO : husband

marihuana *or* **mariguana** *or* **marijuana** *nf* : marihuana

marimacho *nmf fam* **1** : mannish woman **2** : tomboy

marimba *nf* : marimba

marina *nf* **1** : coast, coastal area **2** : navy, fleet ⟨marina mercante : merchant marine⟩

marinada *nf* : marinade

marinar *vt* : to marinate

marinero[1], **-ra** *adj* **1** : seaworthy **2** : sea, marine

marinero[2] *nm* : sailor

marino[1], **-na** *adj* : marine, sea

marino[2] *nm* : sailor, seaman

marioneta *nf* TÍTERE : puppet, marionette

mariposa *nf* **1** : butterfly **2 mariposa nocturna** : moth

mariquita[1] *nf* : ladybug

mariquita[2] *nm fam + disparaging* : sissy *fam + disparaging*, wimp

mariscal *nm* **1** : marshal **2 mariscal de campo** : field marshal (in the military), quarterback (in football)

marisco *nm* **1** : shellfish **2 mariscos** *nmpl* : seafood

marisma *nf* : marsh, salt marsh

marital *adj* : marital, married ⟨la vida marital : married life⟩

marítimo, -ma *adj* : maritime, shipping ⟨la industria marítima : the shipping industry⟩

marketing [ˈmarketin] *nm* : marketing

marmita *nf* : (cooking) pot

mármol *nm* : marble

marmóreo, -rea *adj* : marble

marmota *nf* **1** : marmot **2 marmota de América** : woodchuck, groundhog

maroma *nf* **1** : rope **2** : acrobatic stunt **3** *Mex* : somersault

marque, etc. → **marcar**

marqués, -quesa *n, pl* **marqueses** : marquis *m*, marquess *m*, marquise *f*, marchioness *f*

marquesina *nf* **1** : marquee, canopy **2** : shelter (at a bus stop, etc.)

marqueta *nf Mex* : block (of chocolate), lump (of sugar or salt)

marranada *nf* **1** : disgusting thing **2** : dirty trick

marrano[1], **-na** *adj* : filthy, disgusting

marrano[2], **-na** *n* **1** CERDO : pig, hog **2** *fam* : dirty pig, slob

marrar *vt* : to miss (a target) — *vi* : to fail, to go wrong

marras *adj* **1** : long ago **2 de ~** : said, aforementioned ⟨el individuo de marras : the individual in question⟩

marrasquino *nm* : maraschino

marrón *adj & nm, pl* **marrones** CASTAÑO : brown

marroquí *adj & nmf, pl* **-quíes** : Moroccan

marsopa *nf* : porpoise

marsupial *nm* : marsupial

marta *nf* **1** : marten **2 marta cebellina** : sable (animal)

Marte *nm* : Mars

martes *nms & pl* **1** : Tuesday ⟨el martes : (on) Tuesday⟩ ⟨los martes : (on) Tuesdays⟩ ⟨cada (dos) martes : every (other) Tuesday⟩ ⟨el martes pasado : last Tuesday⟩ ⟨el próximo martes : next Tuesday⟩ **2 martes de Carnaval** : Mardi Gras

martillar *or* **martillear** *v* : to hammer

martillazo *nm* : blow with a hammer

martillo *nm* **1** : hammer **2 martillo neumático** : jackhammer

martín pescador *nm, pl* **martines pescadores** : kingfisher

martinete *nm* **1** : heron **2** : pile driver

mártir *nmf* : martyr

martirio *nm* **1** : martyrdom **2** : ordeal, torment

martirizar {21} *vt* **1** : to martyr **2** ATORMENTAR : to torment

marxismo *nm* : Marxism

marxista *adj & nmf* : Marxist

marzo *nm* : March ⟨el nueve de marzo : (on) the ninth of March, (on) March ninth⟩

mas *conj* PERO : but

más[1] *adv* **1** : more ⟨¿hay algo más grande? : is there anything bigger?⟩ ⟨unos días más tarde : a few days later⟩ ⟨es más complicado de lo que parece : it's more complicated than it seems⟩ ⟨no puedo esperar más : I can't wait any longer⟩ ⟨éste me gusta más que ése : I like this one better than that one⟩ ⟨ahora más que nunca : now more than ever⟩ **2** : most ⟨Luis es el más alto (del grupo) : Luis is the tallest (in the group)⟩ ⟨el que más me gusta : the one I like the most/best⟩ ⟨estudia lo más posible : he studies as much as possible⟩ **3** : rather ⟨más querría andar : I would rather walk⟩ **4 a** ∼ : besides, in addition **5 más allá** : further, farther ⟨la tienda está más allá : the shop is farther down⟩ **6 más allá de** : beyond, past ⟨está más allá de la iglesia : it's beyond/past the church⟩ ⟨ir más allá de los límites : to go beyond the limits⟩ **7** ∼ **de** : more than (a number or amount) ⟨más de cien personas : more than a hundred people⟩ ⟨más de una hora : more than an hour⟩ **8 qué . . . más . . .** : what . . . , what a . . . ⟨¡qué día más bonito! : what a beautiful day!⟩

más² *adj* **1** : more ⟨dáme dos kilos más : give me two more kilos⟩ **2** : most ⟨la que ganó más dinero : the one who earned the most money⟩ **3** : else ⟨¿quién más quiere vino? : who else wants wine?⟩ ⟨nadie más : nobody else⟩

más³ *n* : plus sign

más⁴ *prep* : plus ⟨tres más dos es igual a cinco : three plus two equals five⟩

más⁵ *pron* **1** : more ⟨¿tienes más? : do you have more?⟩ **2 a lo más** : at most **3 de** ∼ : extra, excess **4** ∼ **bien** : rather **5 más o menos** : more or less, approximately **6 por más que** : no matter how much ⟨por más que corras no llegarás a tiempo : no matter how fast you run you won't arrive on time⟩

masa *nf* **1** : mass, volume ⟨masa atómica : atomic mass⟩ ⟨producción en masa : mass production⟩ **2** : dough, batter **3 masas** *nfpl* : people, masses ⟨las masas populares : the common people⟩ **4 masa harina** *Mex* : corn flour (for tortillas, etc.) **5 en masa** : en masse

masacrar *vt* : to massacre

masacre *nf* : massacre

masaje *nm* : massage

masajear *vt* : to massage

masajista *nmf* : masseur *m*, masseuse *f*

mascar {72} *v* MASTICAR : to chew

máscara *nf* **1** CARETA : mask **2** : appearance, pretense **3 máscara antigás** : gas mask

mascarada *nf* : masquerade

mascarilla *nf* **1** : mask (in medicine) ⟨mascarilla de oxígeno : oxygen mask⟩ **2** : facial mask (treatment)

mascota *nf* **1** : mascot **2** : pet

masculinidad *nf* : masculinity

masculino, -na *adj* **1** : masculine, male **2** : manly **3** : masculine (in grammar)

mascullar *v* : to mumble, to mutter

masificación *nf, pl* **-ciones 1** : mass adoption, propagation **2** *Spain* : overcrowding

masificado, -da *adj* : overcrowded

masilla *nf* : putty

masivamente *adv* : en masse

masivo, -va *adj* : mass ⟨comunicación masiva : mass communication⟩

masón *nm, pl* **masones** FRANCMASÓN : Mason, Freemason

masonería *nf* FRANCMASONERÍA : Masonry, Freemasonry

masónico, -ca *adj* : Masonic

masoquismo *nm* : masochism

masoquista¹ *adj* : masochistic

masoquista² *nmf* : masochist

masque, etc. → **mascar**

Máster *nm* : Master's degree

masticar {72} *v* MASCAR : to chew, to masticate

mástil *nm* **1** : mast **2** ASTA : flagpole **3** : neck (of a stringed instrument)

mastín *nm, pl* **mastines** : mastiff

mástique *nm* : putty, filler

mastodonte *nm* : mastodon

masturbación *nf, pl* **-ciones** : masturbation

masturbarse *vr* : to masturbate

mata *nf* **1** ARBUSTO : bush, shrub **2** : plant ⟨mata de tomate : tomato plant⟩ **3** : sprig, tuft **4 mata de pelo** : mop of hair

matadero *nm* : slaughterhouse, abattoir

matado, -da *adj Mex* : strenuous, exhausting

matador *nm* TORERO : matador, bullfighter

matamoscas *nms & pl* : flyswatter

matanza *nf* MASACRE : slaughter, butchering

matar *vt* **1** : to kill **2** : to slaughter, to butcher **3** APAGAR : to extinguish, to put out (fire, light) **4** : to tone down (colors) **5** : to pass, to waste (time) **6** : to trump (in card games) — *vi* : to kill — **matarse** *vr* **1** : to be killed **2** SUICIDARSE : to commit suicide **3** *fam* : to exhaust oneself ⟨se mató tratando de terminarlo : he knocked himself out trying to finish it⟩

matasanos *nms & pl fam* : quack

matasellar *vt* : to cancel (a stamp), to postmark

matasellos *nms & pl* : postmark

matatena *nf Mex* : jacks

mate¹ *adj* : matte, dull

mate² *nm* **1** : maté **2** : slam dunk (in basketball) **3 jaque mate** : checkmate ⟨darle mate a *or* darle jaque mate a : to checkmate⟩

matemática → **matemáticas**

matemáticas *nfpl* : mathematics, math

matemático¹, -ca *adj* : mathematical — **matemáticamente** *adv*

matemático², -ca *n* : mathematician

materia *nf* **1** : matter ⟨materia gris : gray matter⟩ **2** : material ⟨materia prima : raw material⟩ **3** : (academic) subject **4 en materia de** : on the subject of, concerning

material¹ *adj* **1** : material, physical, real **2 daños materiales** : property damage

material² *nm* **1** : material ⟨material de construcción : building material⟩ **2** EQUIPO : equipment, gear **3 material gráfico** : illustrations *pl*, artwork

materialismo *nm* : materialism

materialista¹ *adj* : materialistic

materialista² *nmf* **1** : materialist **2** *Mex* : truck driver

materializar {21} *vt* : to bring to fruition, to realize — **materializarse** *vr* : to materialize, to come into being

materialmente *adv* **1** : physically ⟨materialmente imposible : physically impossible⟩ **2** : really, absolutely

maternal *adj* : maternal, motherly

maternidad *nf* **1** : maternity, motherhood **2** : maternity hospital, maternity ward

materno, -na *adj* : maternal

matinal *adj* MATUTINO : morning ⟨la pálida luz matinal : the pale morning light⟩

matinée *or* **matiné** *nf* : matinee

matiz *nm, pl* **matices** **1** : hue, shade **2** : nuance

matización *nf, pl* **-ciones** **1** : tinting, toning, shading **2** : clarification (of a statement)

matizar {21} *vt* **1** : to tinge, to tint (colors) **2** : to vary, to modulate (sounds) **3** : to qualify (statements)

matón *nm, pl* **matones** : thug, bully

matorral *nm* **1** : thicket **2** : scrub

matraca *nf* **1** : rattle, noisemaker **2 dar la matraca a** : to pester, to nag

matriarca *nf* : matriarch

matriarcado *nm* : matriarchy

matrícula *nf* **1** : list, roll, register **2** INSCRIPCIÓN : registration, enrollment **3** : registration number : (of a vehicle) **4** *or* **placa de matrícula** : license plate, tag

matriculación *nf, pl* **-ciones** : matriculation, registration

matricular *vt* **1** INSCRIBIR : to enroll, to register (a person) **2** : to register (a vehicle) — **matricularse** *vr* : to matriculate

matrimonial *adj* : marital, matrimonial ⟨la vida matrimonial : married life⟩

matrimonio *nm* **1** : marriage, matrimony ⟨matrimonio civil/religioso : civil/religious wedding⟩ ⟨nació fuera del matrimonio : he was born out(side) of wedlock⟩ **2** : married couple

matriz *nf, pl* **matrices** **1** : uterus, womb **2** : original, master copy **3** : main office, headquarters **4** : stub (of a check) **5** : matrix ⟨matriz de puntos : dot matrix⟩

matrona *nf* : matron

matronal *adj* : matronly

matutino¹, -na *adj* : morning ⟨la edición matutina : the morning edition⟩

matutino² *nm* : morning paper

maullar {8} *vi* : to meow

maullido *nm* : meow

mauritano, -na *adj & n* : Mauritanian

mausoleo *nm* : mausoleum

maxilar *nm* : jaw, jawbone

máxima *nf* : maxim

máxime *adv* ESPECIALMENTE : especially, principally

maximizar {21} *vt* : to maximize

máximo¹, -ma *adj* : maximum, greatest, highest

máximo² *nm* **1** : maximum **2 al máximo** : to the utmost **3 como ~** : at the most, at the latest

maya¹ *adj & nmf* : Mayan

maya² *nmf* : Maya, Mayan

mayo *nm* : May ⟨el primero de mayo : (on) the first of May, (on) May first⟩

mayonesa *nf* : mayonnaise

mayor¹ *adj* **1** *comparative of* GRANDE : bigger, larger, greater, elder, older **2** *superlative of* GRANDE : biggest, largest, greatest, eldest, oldest **3** : grown-up, mature ⟨hacerse mayor : to grow up⟩ **4** : main, major **5** : elderly **6** : major ⟨una sonata en re mayor : a sonata in D major⟩ **7 mayor de edad** : of (legal) age **8 al por mayor** *or* **por ~** : wholesale

mayor² *nmf* **1** : major (in the military) **2** : adult, grown-up ⟨tus mayores : your elders⟩ ⟨las personas mayores : the elderly⟩

mayoral *nm* CAPATAZ : foreman, overseer

mayordomo *nm* : butler

mayoreo *nm* : wholesale

mayoría *nf* **1** : majority ⟨la mayoría de : most of, the majority of⟩ ⟨estar en mayoría : to be in the majority⟩ ⟨mayoría de edad : adulthood, age of majority⟩ **2 en su mayoría** : on the whole

mayorista¹ *adj* ALMACENISTA : wholesale

mayorista² *nmf* : wholesaler

mayoritariamente *adv* : primarily, chiefly

mayoritario, -ria *adj & n* : majority ⟨un consenso mayoritario : a majority consensus⟩

mayormente *adv* : primarily, chiefly

mayúscula *nf* : capital letter

mayúsculo, -la *adj* **1** : capital, uppercase **2** : huge, terrible ⟨un problema mayúsculo : a huge problem⟩

maza *nf* **1** : mace (weapon) **2** : drumstick **3** *fam* : bore, pest

mazacote *nm* **1** : concrete **2** : lumpy mess (of food) **3** : eyesore, crude work of art

mazapán *nm, pl* **-panes** : marzipan

mazmorra *nf* CALABOZO : dungeon

mazo *nm* **1** : mallet **2** : pestle **3** MANOJO : handful, bunch

mazorca *nf* **1** CHOCLO : cob, ear of corn **2 pelar la mazorca** *Mex fam* : to smile from ear to ear

me *pron* **1** : me ⟨me vieron : they saw me⟩ **2** : to me, for me, from me ⟨dame el libro : give me the book⟩ ⟨me lo compró : he bought it for me⟩ ⟨me robaron la cartera : they stole my pocketbook⟩ **3** : myself, to myself, for myself, from myself ⟨me preparé una buena comida : I cooked myself a good dinner⟩ ⟨me equivoqué : I made a mistake⟩

meada *nf usu vulgar* : piss *usu vulgar* ⟨echar una meada : to take a piss⟩

meados *nmpl usu vulgar* ORINA : piss *usu vulgar*

mear *vi usu vulgar* : to piss *usu vulgar*, to take a piss *usu vulgar*

mecánica *nf* : mechanics

mecánico¹, -ca *adj* : mechanical — **mecánicamente** *adv*

mecánico², -ca *n* **1** : mechanic **2** : technician ⟨mecánico dental : dental technician⟩

mecanismo *nm* : mechanism
mecanización *nf, pl* **-ciones** : mechanization
mecanizar {21} *vt* : to mechanize
mecanografía *nf* : typing
mecanografiar {85} *vt* : to type
mecanógrafo, -fa *n* : typist
mecate *nm CA, Mex, Ven* : rope, twine, cord
mecedor *nm* : glider (seat)
mecedora *nf* : rocking chair
mecenas *nmfs & pl* : patron (of the arts), sponsor
mecenazgo *nm* PATROCINIO : sponsorship, patronage
mecer {86} *vt* **1** : to rock **2** COLUMPIAR : to push (on a swing) — **mecerse** *vr* : to rock, to swing, to sway
mecha *nf* **1** : fuse **2** : wick **3 mechas** *nfpl* : highlights (in hair)
mechero *nm* **1** : burner **2** *Spain* : lighter
mechón *nm, pl* **mechones** : lock (of hair)
medalla *nf* : medal, medallion
medallista *nmf* : medalist
medallón *nm, pl* **-llones** **1** : medallion **2** : locket
media *nf* **1** CALCETÍN : sock **2** : average, mean **3 medias** *nfpl* : stockings, hose, tights **4 a medias** : by halves, half and half, halfway ⟨ir a medias : to go halves⟩ ⟨verdad a medias : half-truth⟩
mediación *nf, pl* **-ciones** : mediation
mediado, -da *adj* **1** : half full, half empty, half over **2** : halfway through ⟨mediada la tarea : halfway through the job⟩
mediador, -dora *n* : mediator
mediados *nmpl* **a mediados de** : halfway through, in the middle of ⟨a mediados del mes : towards the middle of the month, mid-month⟩
medialuna *nf* **1** : crescent **2** : croissant, crescent roll
medianamente *adv* : fairly, moderately
medianero, -ra *adj* **1** : dividing **2** : mediating
medianía *nf* **1** : middle position **2** : mediocre person, mediocrity
mediano, -na *adj* **1** : medium, average ⟨la mediana edad : middle age⟩ **2** : mediocre
medianoche *nf* : midnight
mediante *prep* : through, by means of ⟨Dios mediante : God willing⟩
mediar *vi* **1** : to mediate ⟨mediar en algo : to mediate something⟩ ⟨mediar por : to intercede on behalf of⟩ ⟨mediar con/ante : to intercede with⟩ **2** : to be in the middle, to be halfway through **3** : to elapse, to pass ⟨mediaron cinco años entre el inicio de la guerra y el armisticio : five years passed between the start of the war and the armistice⟩ **4** : to be a consideration ⟨media el hecho de que cuesta mucho : one must take into account that it is costly⟩ **5** : to come up, to happen ⟨medió algo urgente : something pressing came up⟩
mediatizar {21} *vt* : to influence, to interfere with

medicación *nf, pl* **-ciones** : medication, treatment
medicamento *nm* : medication, medicine, drug
medicar {72} *vt* : to medicate — **medicarse** *vr* : to take medicine
medicatura *nf Ven* : first aid clinic
medicina *nf* : medicine
medicinal *adj* **1** : medicinal **2** : medicated
medicinar *vt* : to give medication to, to dose
medición *nf, pl* **-ciones** : measuring, measurement
médico¹, -ca *adj* : medical ⟨una receta médica : a doctor's prescription⟩
médico², -ca *n* DOCTOR : doctor, physician
medida *nf* **1** : measurement, measure ⟨hecho a medida : custom-made⟩ ⟨tomar las medidas de algo : to measure something⟩ ⟨tomarle las medidas a alguien : to measure someone⟩ **2** : measure, step ⟨tomar medidas : to take steps⟩ ⟨medidas cautelares : precautionary measures⟩ ⟨medidas de seguridad : security measures⟩ **3** : moderation, prudence ⟨sin medida : immoderately⟩ **4** : extent, degree ⟨en cierta/gran medida : to a certain/great extent⟩ ⟨en la medida de lo posible : as far as possible, to the extent possible⟩ **5 a medida que** : as ⟨a medida que aumenta : as it increases⟩
medidor *nm* : meter, gauge
medieval *adj* : medieval — **medievalista** *nmf*
medievo → **medioevo**
medio¹ *adv* **1** : half ⟨está medio dormida : she's half asleep⟩ **2** : rather, kind of ⟨está medio aburrida esta fiesta : this party is rather boring⟩
medio², -dia *adj* **1** : half ⟨una media hora : half an hour⟩ ⟨medio hermano : half brother⟩ ⟨estar a media luz : to be dimly lit⟩ ⟨son las tres y media : it's half past three, it's three-thirty⟩ **2** : midway, halfway ⟨a medio camino : halfway there⟩ ⟨a media tarde : (in the) mid-afternoon⟩ **3** : middle ⟨la clase media : the middle class⟩ **4** : average ⟨la temperatura media : the average temperature⟩
medio³ *nm* **1** CENTRO : middle, center ⟨en medio de : in the middle of, amid⟩ ⟨estar en medio : to be in the way⟩ ⟨ponerse en medio : to get in the way⟩ **2** AMBIENTE : milieu, environment **3** : medium, spiritualist **4** : means *pl*, way ⟨por medio de : by means of⟩ ⟨los medios de comunicación : the media⟩ ⟨medios sociales : social media⟩ **5 medios** *nmpl* : means, resources
medioambiental *adj* : environmental
medio ambiente *nm* : environment
mediocampista *nmf* : midfielder
mediocre *adj* : mediocre, average
mediocridad *nf* : mediocrity
mediodía *nm* : noon, midday
medioevo *nm* : Middle Ages

medio tiempo *nm* : halftime
medir {54} *vt* **1** : to measure **2** : to weigh, to consider ⟨medir los riesgos : to weigh the risks⟩ — *vi* : to measure — **medirse** *vr* : to be moderate, to exercise restraint
meditabundo, -da *adj* PENSATIVO : pensive, thoughtful
meditación *nf, pl* **-ciones** : meditation, thought
meditar *vi* : to meditate, to think ⟨meditar sobre la vida : to contemplate life⟩ — *vt* **1** : to think over, to consider **2** : to plan, to work out
meditativo, -va *adj* : pensive
mediterráneo, -nea *adj* : Mediterranean
médium *nmf, pl* **médiums** : medium (person)
medrar *vi* **1** PROSPERAR : to prosper, to thrive **2** AUMENTAR : to increase, to grow
medro *nm* PROSPERIDAD : prosperity, growth
medroso, -sa *adj* : fainthearted, fearful
médula *nf* **1** : marrow, pith **2 médula espinal** : spinal cord
medular *adj* : fundamental, core ⟨el punto medular : the crux of the matter⟩
medusa *nf* : jellyfish
megabyte *nm* : megabyte
megáfono *nm* : megaphone
megahercio *nm* : megahertz
megahertzio *nm* : megahertz
megatón *nm, pl* **-tones** : megaton
megavatio *nm* : megawatt
mejicano → **mexicano**
mejilla *nf* : cheek
mejillón *nm, pl* **-llones** : mussel
mejor[1] *adv* **1** : better ⟨Carla cocina mejor que Ana : Carla cooks better than Ann⟩ **2** : best ⟨ella es la que lo hace mejor : she's the one who does it best⟩ **3** : rather ⟨mejor morir que rendirme : I'd rather die than give up⟩ **4** : it's better that . . . ⟨mejor te vas : you'd better go⟩ **5 a lo mejor** : maybe, perhaps
mejor[2] *adj* **1** *comparative of* BUENO : better ⟨a falta de algo mejor : for lack of something better⟩ **2** *comparative of* BIEN : better ⟨está mucho mejor : he's much better⟩ **3** *superlative of* BUENO : best, the better ⟨mi mejor amigo : my best friend⟩ **4** *superlative of* BIEN : best, the better ⟨duermo mejor en un clima seco : I sleep best in a dry climate⟩ **5** PREFERIBLE : preferable, better **6 lo mejor** : the best thing, the best part
mejor[3] *nmf* (*with definite article*) : the better (one), the best (one)
mejora *nf* : improvement
mejoramiento *nm* : improvement
mejorana *nf* : marjoram
mejorar *vt* : to improve, to make better — *vi* : to improve, to get better — **mejorarse** *vr*
mejoría *nf* : improvement, betterment
mejunje *nm* : concoction, brew
melancolía *nf* : melancholy, sadness
melancólico, -ca *adj* : melancholy, sad
melanoma *nm* : melanoma

melaza *nf* : molasses
melena *nf* **1** : mane **2** : long hair **3 melenas** *nfpl* GREÑAS : shaggy hair, mop
melenudo, -da *adj fam* : long-haired
melindroso[1]**, -sa** *adj* **1** : affected **2** : fussy, finicky
melindroso[2]**, -sa** *n* : finicky person, fussbudget
melisa *nf* : lemon balm
mella *nf* **1** : dent, nick **2 hacer mella en** : to have an effect on, to make an impression on
mellado, -da *adj* **1** : chipped, dented **2** : gap-toothed
mellar *vt* : to dent, to nick
mellizo, -za *adj & n* GEMELO : twin
melocotón *nm, pl* **-tones** : peach
melodía *nf* : melody, tune
melódico, -ca *adj* : melodic
melodioso, -sa *adj* : melodious
melodrama *nm* : melodrama
melodramático, -ca *adj* : melodramatic
melón *nm, pl* **melones** : melon, cantaloupe
meloso, -sa *adj* **1** : sweet **2** EMPALAGOSO : cloying, saccharine
membrana *nf* **1** : membrane **2 membrana interdigital** : web, webbing (of a bird's foot) — **membranoso, -sa** *adj*
membresía *nf* : membership, members *pl*
membrete *nm* : letterhead, heading ⟨papel con membrete : official stationery, letterhead⟩
membrillo *nm* : quince
membrudo, -da *adj* FORNIDO : muscular, well-built
memez *nf, pl* **memeces** : stupid thing
memo, -ma *adj* : silly, stupid
memorabilia *nf* : memorabilia
memorable *adj* : memorable
memorándum *or* **memorando** *nm, pl* **-dums** *or* **-dos** **1** : memorandum, memo **2** : memo book, appointment book
memoria *nf* **1** : memory ⟨de memoria : by heart⟩ ⟨hacer memoria : to try to remember⟩ ⟨traer a la memoria : to call to mind⟩ **2** RECUERDO : remembrance, memory ⟨su memoria perdurará para siempre : his memory will live forever⟩ **3** : report ⟨memoria anual : annual report⟩ **4** : memory (in computing) **5 memorias** *nfpl* : memoirs *pl* **6 memoria de acceso aleatorio** : random-access memory, RAM **7 memoria flash** : flash memory
memorizar {21} *vt* : to memorize — **memorización** *nf*
mena *nf* : ore
menaje *nm* : household goods *pl*, furnishings *pl*
mención *nf, pl* **-ciones** : mention
mencionar *vt* : to mention, to refer to
mendaz *adj, pl* **mendaces** : false, untruthful, dishonest
mendicidad *nf* : begging
mendigar {52} *vi* : to beg — *vt* : to beg for
mendigo, -ga *n* LIMOSNERO : beggar
mendrugo *nm* : crust (of bread)
menear *vt* **1** : to shake (one's head) **2** : to sway, to wiggle (one's hips) **3** : to

wag (a tail) **4** : to stir (a liquid) —
menearse *vr* **1** : to wiggle one's hips **2**
: to fidget
meneo *nm* **1** : movement **2** : shake, toss
3 : swaying, wagging, wiggling **4** : stir,
stirring
menester *nm* **1** : activity, occupation,
duties *pl* **2 ser menester** : to be necessary ⟨es menester que vengas : you must
come⟩
menestra *nf* **1** *Ecua* : legume stew **2**
Peru : legume **3** *Spain* : mixed cooked
vegetables
mengano, -na → fulano
mengua *nf* **1** : decrease, decline **2**
: lack, want **3** : discredit, dishonor
menguar *vt* : to diminish, to lessen — *vi*
1 : to decline, to decrease **2** : to wane —
menguante *adj*
meningitis *nf* : meningitis
menisco *nm* : cartilage
menjurje → **mejunje**
menopausia *nf* : menopause
menopáusico, -ca *nf* : menopausal
menor[1] *adj* **1** *comparative of* PEQUEÑO
: smaller, lesser, younger ⟨es menor que
su hermana : he's younger than his sis-
ter⟩ ⟨en menor medida : to a lesser ex-
tent/degree⟩ **2** *superlative of* PEQUEÑO
: smallest, least, youngest **3** : minor ⟨un
problema menor : a minor problem⟩ **4**
: minor (in music) ⟨en tono de mi menor
: in the key of E minor⟩ **5 al por menor**
: retail **6 ser menor de edad** : to be a
minor, to be underage
menor[2] *nmf* : minor, juvenile
menos[1] *adv* **1** : less ⟨llueve menos en
agosto : it rains less in August⟩ ⟨éste me
gusta menos que ése : I like this one less
than that one⟩ ⟨soy menos alta que mis
hermanas : I'm not as tall as my sisters⟩
⟨es menos difícil de lo que parece : it's
less difficult than it looks⟩ **2** : least ⟨el
coche menos caro : the least expensive
car⟩ ⟨en el momento menos pensado
: when you least expect it⟩ ⟨es lo menos
que puedo hacer : it's the least I can do⟩
⟨trabaja lo menos posible : he works as
little as possible⟩ ⟨los que menos ganan
: those who earn the least⟩ ⟨lo que menos necesitamos es otra crisis : the last
thing we need is another crisis⟩ **3** ∼ **de**
: less than, fewer than ⟨tienen menos de
50 empleados : they have fewer than 50
employees⟩ ⟨en menos de un minuto : in
less than a minute⟩
menos[2] *adj* **1** : less, fewer ⟨tengo más
trabajo y menos tiempo : I have more
work and less time⟩ ⟨hay menos sillas
que personas : there are fewer chairs
than people⟩ **2** : least, fewest ⟨la clase
que tiene menos estudiantes : the class
that has the fewest students⟩
menos[3] *prep* **1** SALVO, EXCEPTO : except
2 : minus ⟨quince menos cuatro son
once : fifteen minus four is eleven⟩
menos[4] *pron* **1** : less, fewer ⟨no deberías
aceptar menos : you shouldn't accept
less⟩ **2 al menos** *or* **por lo menos** : at

least **3 a menos que** : unless **4 lo de
menos** : the least important thing
menoscabar *vt* **1** : to lessen, to diminish
2 : to disgrace, to discredit **3** PERJUDI-
CAR : to harm, to damage
menoscabo *nm* **1** : lessening, diminish-
ing **2** : disgrace, discredit **3** : harm,
damage
menospreciar *vt* **1** DESPRECIAR : to
scorn, to look down on **2** : to underestimate, to undervalue
menosprecio *nm* DESPRECIO : contempt,
scorn
mensaje *nm* **1** : message **2 mensaje
instantáneo** : instant message
mensajear *v fam* : to message, to text
mensajería *nf* **1** : messaging **2 mensajería instantánea** : instant messaging
mensajero, -ra *n* : messenger
menso, -sa *adj Mex fam* : foolish, stupid
menstrual *adj* : menstrual
menstruar {3} *vi* : to menstruate —
menstruación *nf*
mensual *adj* : monthly
mensualidad *nf* **1** : monthly payment,
installment **2** : monthly salary
mensualmente *adv* : every month,
monthly
mensurable *adj* : measurable
menta *nf* **1** : mint, peppermint **2 menta
verde** : spearmint
mentado, -da *adj* **1** : aforementioned **2**
FAMOSO : renowned, famous
mental *adj* : mental, intellectual — **mentalmente** *adv*
mentalidad *nf* : mentality
mentalizar {21} *vt* : to prepare mentally
— **mentalizarse** *vr*
mentar {55} *vt* **1** : to mention, to name **2
mentar la madre a** *fam* : to insult, to
swear at
mente *nf* : mind ⟨tener en mente : to have
in mind⟩
-mente *suf* : -ly ⟨frecuentemente : fre-
quently⟩
mentecato[1], **-ta** *adj* : foolish, simple
mentecato[2], **-ta** *n* : fool, idiot
mentir {76} *vi* : to lie
mentira *nf* : lie
mentirijillas *nfpl fam* **de** ∼ : as a joke, in
fun
mentiroso[1], **-sa** *adj* EMBUSTERO : lying,
untruthful
mentiroso[2], **-sa** *n* EMBUSTERO : liar
mentís *nm, pl* **mentises** : denial, repudiation ⟨dar el mentís a : to deny, to refute⟩
mentol *nm* : menthol — **mentolado, -da**
adj
mentón *nm, pl* **mentones** BARBILLA
: chin
mentor *nm* : mentor, counselor
menú *nm, pl* **menús** : menu
menudear *vi* : to occur frequently — *vt*
: to do repeatedly
menudencia *nf* **1** : trifle **2 menudencias** *nfpl* : giblets
menudeo *nm* : retail, retailing
menudillos *nmpl* : giblets
menudo[1], **-da** *adj* **1** : minute, small **2 a**
∼ FRECUENTEMENTE : often, frequently

menudo² *nm* **1** *Mex* : tripe stew **2 menudos** *nmpl* : giblets
meñique *nm or* **dedo meñique** : little finger, pinkie
meollo *nm* **1** MÉDULA : marrow **2** SESO : brains *pl* **3** ENTRAÑA : essence, core ⟨el meollo del asunto : the heart of the matter⟩
mequetrefe *nm fam* : good-for-nothing
meramente *adv* : merely, purely
mercachifle *nm* : peddler, hawker
mercadeo *nm* : marketing
mercader *nmf* : merchant
mercadería *nf* : merchandise, goods *pl*
mercadillo *nm Spain* : flea market
mercado *nm* **1** : market **2 mercado de pulgas** (*in various countries*) : flea market **3 mercado de trabajo/valores** : labor market **4 mercado de valores** *or* **mercado bursátil** : stock market
mercadotecnia *nf* : marketing
mercancía *nf* : merchandise, goods *pl*
mercante *nmf* : merchant, dealer
mercantil *adj* COMERCIAL : commercial, mercantile
merced *nf* **1** : favor **2** ∼ **a** : thanks to, due to **3 a merced de** : at the mercy of
mercenario, -ria *adj & n* : mercenary
mercería *nf* : notions store
Mercosur *nm* : economic community consisting of Argentina, Brazil, Paraguay, and Uruguay
mercurio *nm* : mercury
Mercurio *nm* : Mercury (planet)
merecedor, -dora *adj* : deserving, worthy
merecer {53} *vt* : to deserve, to merit — *vi* : to be worthy
merecidamente *adv* : rightfully, deservedly
merecido *nm* : something merited, due ⟨recibieron su merecido : they got their just deserts⟩
merecimiento *nm* : merit, worth
merendar {55} *vi* : to have an afternoon snack — *vt* : to have as an afternoon snack
merendero *nm* **1** : lunchroom, snack bar **2** : picnic area
merengue *nm* **1** : meringue **2** : merengue (music or dance)
meridiano¹, -na *adj* **1** : midday **2** : crystal clear
meridiano² *nm* : meridian
meridional *adj* SUREÑO : southern
merienda *nf* : afternoon snack, tea
mérito *nm* : merit
meritorio¹, -ria *adj* : deserving, meritorious
meritorio², -ria *n* : intern, trainee
merluza *nf* : hake
merma *nf* **1** : decrease, cut **2** : waste, loss
mermar *vi* : to decrease, to diminish — *vt* : to reduce, to cut down
mermelada *nf* : marmalade, jam
mero¹, -ra *adv Mex fam* **1** : nearly, almost ⟨ya mero me caí : I almost fell⟩ **2** : just, exactly ⟨aquí mero : right here⟩
mero², -ra *adj* **1** : mere, simple **2** *Mex fam* (*used as an intensifier*) : very ⟨en el

mero centro : in the very center of town⟩
mero³ *nm* : grouper
merodeador, -dora *n* **1** : marauder **2** : prowler
merodear *vi* **1** : to maraud, to pillage **2** : to prowl around, to skulk
mes *nm* : month
mesa *nf* **1** : table ⟨mesa de cocina : kitchen table⟩ ⟨mesa de noche : nightstand, night table⟩ **2** : committee, board ⟨mesa directiva : executive board⟩
mesada *nf* : allowance, pocket money
mesarse *vr* : to pull at ⟨mesarse los cabellos : to tear one's hair⟩
mesero, -ra *n* CAMARERO : waiter, waitress *f*
meseta *nf* : plateau
Mesías *nm* : Messiah
mesita *or Spain* **mesilla** *nf* **1** : small table **2** *or* **mesita/mesilla de noche** : nightstand, night table
mesón *nm, pl* **mesones** : inn
mesonero, -ra *nm* : innkeeper
mesteño, -ña *adj* **caballo mesteño** : wild horse, mustang
mestizo¹, -za *adj* **1** : of mixed ancestry, mestizo **2** HÍBRIDO : hybrid
mestizo², -za *n* : person of mixed ancestry, mestizo
mesura *nf* **1** MODERACIÓN : moderation, discretion **2** CORTESÍA : courtesy **3** GRAVEDAD : seriousness, dignity
mesurado, -da *adj* COMEDIDO : moderate, restrained
mesurar *vt* : to moderate, to restrain, to temper — **mesurarse** *vr* : to restrain oneself
meta *nf* : goal, objective
metabólico, -ca *adj* : metabolic
metabolismo *nm* : metabolism
metabolizar {21} *vt* : to metabolize
metafísica *nf* : metaphysics
metafísico, -ca *adj* : metaphysical
metáfora *nf* : metaphor
metafórico, -ca *adj* : metaphoric, metaphorical
metal *nm* **1** : metal **2** *or* **metales** *nmpl* : brass, brass section (in an orchestra)
metálico, -ca *adj* : metallic, metal
metalistería *nf* : metalworking
metalizado, -da *adj* : metallic
metalurgia *nf* : metallurgy
metalúrgico¹, -ca *adj* : metallurgical
metalúrgico², -ca *n* : metalworker
metamorfosis *nfs & pl* : metamorphosis
metano *nm* : methane
metedura *nf* **metedura de pata** : blunder, faux pas
meteórico, -ca *adj* : meteoric
meteorito *nm* : meteorite
meteoro *nm* : meteor
meteorología *nf* : meteorology
meteorológico, -ca *adj* : meteorologic, meteorological
meteorólogo, -ga *n* : meteorologist
meter *vt* **1** : to put ⟨lo metió en un cajón : he put it in a drawer⟩ ⟨metieron su dinero en el banco : they put their money in the bank⟩ ⟨se le metió en la

cabeza que . . . : he got it in his head that . . .⟩ **2** : to shut (in a place) ⟨la metieron en la cárcel : they put her in jail⟩ ⟨estuve todo el día metida en la casa : I was stuck in the house all day⟩ **3** : to fit, to squeeze ⟨puedes meter dos líneas más en esa página : you can fit two more lines on that page⟩ **4** : to place (in a job) ⟨lo metieron de dependiente : they got him a job as a store clerk⟩ **5** : to involve ⟨lo metió en un buen lío : she got him in an awful mess⟩ **6** : to make, to cause ⟨meten demasiado ruido : they make too much noise⟩ ⟨un cuento que mete miedo : a scary story⟩ **7** : to spread (a rumor) **8** : to strike (a blow) **9** : to score (a goal or point) **10** : to take up, to take in (clothing) **11 a todo meter** : at top speed — **meterse** vr **1** : to get (in), to enter ⟨se metió en la cama : she got in bed⟩ ⟨el ladrón se metió por la ventana : the thief got in through the window⟩ ⟨¿dónde te has metido? : where are you hiding?, where have you gotten to?⟩ **2** : to put, to stick ⟨no te lo metas en la boca : don't put it in your mouth⟩ ⟨se metió la mano en el bolsillo : he stuck his hand in his pocket⟩ **3** fam : to meddle ⟨no te metas en lo que no te importa : mind your own business⟩ **4** ~ **con** fam : to pick a fight with, to provoke ⟨no te metas conmigo : don't mess with me⟩ **5** ~ **a/de** : to become ⟨se metió a monja : she became a nun⟩

metiche[1] adj Mex fam : nosy

metiche[2] nmf Mex fam : busybody

meticulosidad nf : thoroughness, meticulousness

meticuloso, -sa adj : meticulous, thorough — **meticulosamente** adv

metida nf **metida de pata** fam : blunder, gaffe, blooper

metódico, -ca adj : methodical — **metódicamente** adv

metodista adj & nmf : Methodist

método nm : method

metodología nf : methodology

metomentodo nmf fam : busybody

metraje nm : length (of a film) ⟨de largo metraje : feature-length⟩

metralla nf : shrapnel

metralleta nf : submachine gun

métrico, -ca adj **1** : metric **2 cinta métrica** : tape measure

metro nm **1** : meter **2** : subway

metrónomo nm : metronome

metrópoli nf or **metrópolis** nfs & pl : metropolis

metropolitano, -na adj : metropolitan

mexicanismo nm : Mexican word or expression

mexicano, -na adj & n : Mexican

mexicoamericano, -na adj & n : Mexican-American

mexiquense[1] adj Mex : of or from Mexico City

mexiquense[2] nmf Mex : person from Mexico City

meza, etc. → **mecer**

mezcla nf **1** : mixing **2** : mixture, blend **3** : mortar (masonry material)

mezclar vt **1** : to mix, to blend **2** : to mix up, to muddle **3** INVOLUCRAR : to involve — **mezclarse** vr **1** : to get mixed up (in) **2** : to mix, to mingle (socially)

mezclilla nf Chile, Mex : denim ⟨pantalones de mezclilla : jeans⟩

mezcolanza nf : jumble, hodgepodge

mezquindad nf **1** : meanness, stinginess **2** : petty deed, mean action

mezquino[1], -na adj **1** : mean, petty **2** : stingy **3** : paltry

mezquino[2] nm Mex : wart

mezquita nf : mosque

mi[1] adj : my

mi[2] nm **1** : E ⟨mi sostenido/bemol : E sharp/flat⟩ **2** : mi (in singing)

mí pron **1** : me ⟨es para mí : it's for me⟩ ⟨a mí no me importa : it doesn't matter to me⟩ **2 mí mismo, mí misma** : myself

miasma nm : miasma

miau nm : meow

mica nf : mica

mico nm : monkey, long-tailed monkey

micro nm **1** Chile, Arg : minibus **2** : microphone

micro- pref : micro-

microbio nm : microbe, germ

microbiología nf : microbiology

microbús nm, pl **-buses** : minibus

microchip nm, pl **microchips** : microchip

microcomputadora nf : microcomputer

microcosmos nms & pl : microcosm

microfilm nm, pl **-films** : microfilm

micrófono nm : microphone

micrómetro nm : micrometer

microonda nf : microwave

microondas nms & pl : microwave, microwave oven

microordenador nm Spain : microcomputer

microorganismo nm : microorganism

microprocesador nm : microprocessor

microscópico, -ca adj : microscopic

microscopio nm : microscope

mide, etc. → **medir**

miedo nm **1** TEMOR : fear ⟨le tiene miedo al perro : he's scared of the dog⟩ ⟨tenían miedo de hablar : they were afraid to speak⟩ ⟨morirse de miedo : to be scared to death⟩ ⟨temblar de miedo : to tremble with fear⟩ ⟨miedo escénico : stage fright⟩ **2 dar miedo** : to frighten

miedoso, -sa adj TEMEROSO : fearful

miel nf : honey

miembro nm **1** : member **2** EXTREMIDAD : limb, extremity

mienta, etc. → **mentar**

miente, etc. → **mentir**

-miento suf : -ment ⟨entretenimiento : entertainment⟩

mientras[1] adv **1** or **mientras tanto** : meanwhile, in the meantime **2 mientras más** : the more ⟨mientras más como, más quiero : the more I eat, the more I want⟩

mientras[2] conj **1** : while, as ⟨roncaba mientras dormía : he snored while he was sleeping⟩ **2** : as long as ⟨luchará mientras pueda : he will fight as long as he is able⟩ **3 mientras que** : while, whereas ⟨él es alto mientras que ella es muy baja : he is tall, whereas she is very short⟩

miércoles *nms & pl* **1** : Wednesday ⟨el miércoles : (on) Wednesday⟩ ⟨los miércoles : (on) Wednesdays⟩ ⟨cada (dos) miércoles : every (other) Wednesday⟩ ⟨el miércoles pasado : last Wednesday⟩ ⟨el próximo miércoles : next Wednesday⟩ ⟨el miércoles por la noche : Wednesday night⟩ **2 Miércoles de Ceniza** : Ash Wednesday

miga *nf* **1** : crumb **2 hacer buenas (malas) migas con** : to get along well (poorly) with

migaja *nf* **1** : crumb **2 migajas** *nfpl* SOBRAS : leftovers, scraps

migra *nf Mex fam* **la migra** : the immigration police

migración *nf, pl* **-ciones** : migration

migrante *nmf* : migrant

migraña *nf* : migraine

migrar *vi* : to migrate

migratorio, -ria *adj* : migratory

mijo *nm* : millet

mil[1] *adj & pron* : thousand

mil[2] *nm* : one thousand, a thousand

milagro *nm* : miracle ⟨de milagro : miraculously⟩

milagroso, -sa *adj* : miraculous, marvelous — **milagrosamente** *adv*

milenario[1], **-ria** *adj* : millennial

milenario[2], **-ria** *n* : millennial (person born in the 1980s or 1990s)

milenial → milenario[2]

milenio *nm* : millennium

milésima *nf* → **milésimo**[2]

milésimo[1], **-ma** *adj* : thousandth

milésimo[2] *nm* : thousandth

mili *nf Spain fam* : military service

milicia *nf* **1** : militia **2** : military service

miligramo *nm* : milligram

mililitro *nm* : milliliter

milímetro *nm* : millimeter

militancia *nf* : militancy

militante[1] *adj* : militant

militante[2] *nmf* : militant, activist

militar[1] *vi* **1** : to serve (in the military) **2** : to be active (in politics)

militar[2] *adj* : military

militar[3] *nmf* SOLDADO : soldier

militarismo *nm* : militarism

militarista *adj* : militaristic

militarizar {21} *vt* : to militarize

milla *nf* : mile

millar *nm* : thousand

millón *nm, pl* **millones** : million

millonario, -ria *n* : millionaire

millonésima *nf* → **millonésimo**[2]

millonésimo[1], **-ma** *adj* : millionth

millonésimo[2] *nm* **1** : millionth (in a series) **2** : millionth (fraction)

mil millones *nms & pl* : billion

milmillonésimo[1], **-ma** *adj* : billionth

milmillonésimo[2] *nm* **1** : billionth (in a series) **2** : billionth (fraction)

milpa *nf CA, Mex* : cornfield

milpiés *nms & pl* : millipede

mimar *vt* CONSENTIR : to pamper, to spoil

mimbre *nm* : wicker

mimeógrafo *nm* : mimeograph

mímica *nf* **1** : mime, sign language **2** IMITACIÓN : mimicry

mimo *nm* **1** : pampering, indulgence ⟨hacerle mimos a alguien : to pamper someone⟩ **2** : mime

mimoso, -sa *adj* **1** : fussy, finicky **2** : affectionate, clinging

mina *nf* **1** : mine **2** : lead (for pencils)

minar *vt* **1** : to mine **2** DEBILITAR : to undermine

minarete *nm* ALMINAR : minaret

mineral *adj & nm* : mineral

mineralogía *nf* : mineralogy

minería *nf* : mining

minero[1], **-ra** *adj* : mining

minero[2], **-ra** *n* : miner, mine worker

mini- *pref* : mini-

miniatura *nf* : miniature

minicomputadora *nf* : minicomputer

minifalda *nf* : miniskirt

minifundio *nm* : small farm

minimizar {21} *vt* : to minimize

mínimo[1], **-ma** *adj* **1** : minimum ⟨salario mínimo : minimum wage⟩ **2** : least, smallest ⟨es lo mínimo que puede hacer : it's the least he can do⟩ **3** : very small, minute ⟨no tengo la más mínima idea : I haven't the slightest idea⟩

mínimo[2] *nm* **1** : minimum, least amount **2** : modicum, small amount **3 como ~** : at least

minino, -na *n fam* : kitty, pussy

miniserie *nf* : miniseries

ministerial *adj* : ministerial

ministerio *nm* : ministry, department

ministro, -tra *n* : minister, secretary ⟨primer ministro, primera ministra : prime minister⟩ ⟨Ministro de Defensa : Secretary of Defense⟩

minivan [ˌminiˈban, -ˈvan] *nf, pl* **-vanes** : minivan

minoría *nf* : minority

minorista[1] *adj* : retail

minorista[2] *nmf* : retailer

minoritario, -ria *adj* : minority

mintió, etc. → mentir

minucia *nf* **1** : (minor) detail **2** INSIGNIFICANCIA : trifle, triviality **3 con minucia** : in detail

minuciosamente *adv* **1** : minutely **2** : in great detail **3** : thoroughly, meticulously

minucioso, -sa *adj* **1** : minute **2** DETALLADO : detailed **3** : thorough, meticulous

minué *nm* : minuet

minúsculo, -la *adj* DIMINUTO : tiny, minuscule

minusvalía *nf* : disability, handicap *sometimes offensive*

minusválido[1], **-da** *adj* : handicapped, disabled

minusválido[2], **-da** *n* : handicapped person

minuta *nf* **1** BORRADOR : rough draft **2** : bill, fee

minutero *nm* : minute hand

minuto *nm* : minute

mío¹, mía *adj* **1** : my, of mine ⟨¡Dios mío! : my God!, good heavens!⟩ ⟨una amiga mía : a friend of mine⟩ **2** : mine ⟨es mío : it's mine⟩

mío², mía *pron* (*with definite article*) : mine, my own ⟨tus zapatos son iguales a los míos : your shoes are just like mine⟩

miope *adj* : nearsighted, myopic

miopía *nf* : myopia, nearsightedness

mira *nf* **1** : sight (of a firearm or instrument) **2** : aim, objective ⟨con miras a : with the intention of, with a view to⟩ ⟨de amplias miras : broad-minded⟩ ⟨poner la mira en : to aim at, to aspire to⟩

mirada *nf* **1** : look, glance, gaze ⟨apartar la mirada : to look away⟩ ⟨dirigir/lanzar la mirada a : to glance at⟩ ⟨hay miradas que matan : if looks could kill⟩ **2** EXPRESIÓN : look, expression ⟨una mirada de sorpresa : a look of surprise⟩

mirado, -da *adj* **1** : cautious, careful **2** : considerate **3 bien mirado** : well thought of **4 mal mirado** : disliked, disapproved of

mirador *nm* : balcony, lookout, vantage point

miramiento *nm* **1** CONSIDERACIÓN : consideration, respect **2 sin miramientos** : without due consideration, carelessly

mirar *vt* **1** : to look at ⟨miró el reloj : she looked at her watch⟩ ⟨mirar fijamente : to stare at⟩ ⟨mirar algo (muy) por encima : to glance something over⟩ ⟨la miré en los ojos : I looked her straight in the eye⟩ **2** OBSERVAR : to watch ⟨mirar televisión : to watch television⟩ **3** REFLEXIONAR : to consider, to think over ⟨míralo desde su punto de vista : look at it from her point of view⟩ **4** (*used for emphasis*) ⟨¡mira que eres lista! : you're so clever!⟩ ⟨mire que no soy experto, pero . . . : I'm no expert, but . . .⟩ ⟨¡mira qué gracia! : how funny!⟩ — *vi* **1** : to look ⟨miraba por la ventana : I was looking out the window⟩ ⟨mira bien y lo verás : look carefully and you'll see it⟩ ⟨¡mira! ahí está : look! there he is⟩ ⟨mira, a mí no me importa : look, it doesn't matter to me⟩ **2** : to face, to overlook **3 ~ por** : to look after, to look out for — **mirarse** *vr* **1** : to look at oneself **2** : to look at each other

mirasol *nm* GIRASOL : sunflower

miríada *nf* : myriad

mirlo *nm* : blackbird

mirón, rona *n, mpl* **-rones 1** : gawker, onlooker **2** : voyeur

mirra *nf* : myrrh

mirto *nm* ARRAYÁN : myrtle

misa *nf* : Mass

misantropía *nf* : misanthropy

misantrópico, -ca *adj* : misanthropic

misántropo, -pa *n* : misanthrope

miscelánea *nf* : miscellany

misceláneo, -nea *adj* : miscellaneous

miserable *adj* **1** LASTIMOSO : miserable, wretched **2** : paltry, meager **3** MEZ-QUINO : stingy, miserly **4** : despicable, vile

miserablemente *adv* **1** : miserably, wretchedly **2** : shamefully, disgracefully

miseria *nf* **1** POBREZA : poverty **2** : misery, suffering **3** : pittance, meager amount

misericordia *nf* COMPASIÓN : mercy, compassion

misericordioso, -sa *adj* : merciful

mísero, -ra *adj* **1** : wretched, miserable **2** : stingy **3** : paltry, meager

misil *nm* : missile

misión *nf, pl* **misiones** : mission

misionero, -ra *adj & n* : missionary

misiva *nf* : missive, letter

mismísimo, -ma *adj* (*used as an intensifier*) : very, selfsame ⟨el mismísimo día : that very same day⟩

mismo¹ *adv* (*used as an intensifier*) : right, exactly ⟨hazlo ahora mismo : do it right now⟩ ⟨te llamará hoy mismo : he'll definitely call you today⟩

mismo², -ma *adj* **1** : same ⟨la misma historia de siempre : the same old story⟩ ⟨ya no es el mismo de antes : he's not the same as he was before⟩ **2** (*used as an intensifier*) : very ⟨en ese mismo momento : at that very moment⟩ **3** : oneself ⟨lo hizo ella misma : she made it herself⟩ **4 por lo mismo** : for that reason

misoginia *nf* : misogyny

misógino *nm* : misogynist

miss *nf* : miss ⟨Miss Universo : Miss Universe⟩

misterio *nm* : mystery

misterioso, -sa *adj* : mysterious — **misteriosamente** *adv*

misticismo *nm* : mysticism

místico¹, -ca *adj* : mystic, mystical

místico², -ca *n* : mystic

mitad *nf* **1** : half ⟨mitad y mitad : half and half⟩ **2** MEDIO : middle ⟨a mitad de : halfway through⟩ ⟨por la mitad : in half⟩

mítico, -ca *adj* : mythical, mythic

mitigar {52} *vt* ALIVIAR : to mitigate, to alleviate — **mitigación** *nf*

mitin *nm, pl* **mítines** : (political) meeting, rally

mito *nm* LEYENDA : myth, legend

mitología *nf* : mythology

mitológico, -ca *adj* : mythological

mitosis *nfs & pl* : mitosis

mitra *nf* : miter (bishop's hat)

mixto, -ta *adj* **1** : mixed, joint **2** : coeducational

mixtura *nf* : mixture, blend

mnemónico, -ca *adj* : mnemonic

mobbing ['mobiŋ] *nm Spain* : workplace bullying

mobiliario *nm* : furniture

mocasín *nm, pl* **-sines** : moccasin

mocedad *nf* **1** JUVENTUD : youth **2** : youthful prank

mochila *nf* MORRAL : backpack, knapsack

moción *nf, pl* **-ciones 1** MOVIMIENTO : motion, movement **2** : motion (to a court or assembly)

moco *nm* **1** : mucus **2** *fam* : snot ⟨limpiarse los mocos : to wipe one's (runny) nose⟩

mocoso, -sa *n disparaging* : kid, brat *disparaging*

moda *nf* **1** : fashion, style **2 a la moda** *or* **de** ~ : in style, fashionable **3 moda pasajera** : fad

modales *nmpl* : manners

modalidad *nf* **1** CLASE : kind, type **2** MANERA : way, manner

modelaje *nm* (*in various countries*) : modeling

modelar *vt* : to model, to mold — **modelarse** *vr* : to model oneself after, to emulate

modelo¹ *adj* : model ⟨una casa modelo : a model home⟩

modelo² *nm* : model, example, pattern

modelo³ *nmf* : model, mannequin

módem *or* **modem** [¹moðɛm] *nm* : modem

moderación *nf, pl* **-ciones** MESURA : moderation

moderado, -da *adj & n* : moderate — **moderadamente** *adv*

moderador, -dora *n* : moderator, chair

moderar *vt* **1** TEMPERAR : to temper, to moderate **2** : to curb, to reduce ⟨moderar gastos : to curb spending⟩ **3** PRESIDIR : to chair (a meeting) — **moderarse** *vr* **1** : to restrain oneself **2** : to diminish, to calm down

modernidad *nf* **1** : modernity **2** : modern age

modernismo *nm* : modernism

modernista¹ *adj* : modernist

modernista² *nmf* : modernist

modernizar {21} *vt* : to modernize — **modernización** *nf*

moderno, -na *adj* : modern, up-to-date

modestia *nf* : modesty

modesto, -ta *adj* : modest — **modestamente** *adv*

módico, -ca *adj* : modest, reasonable

modificación *nf, pl* **-ciones** : alteration

modificador¹, -dora *adj* : modifying, moderating

modificador² → **modificante**

modificante *nm* : modifier

modificar {72} *vt* ALTERAR : to modify, to alter, to adapt

modismo *nm* : idiom

modista *nmf* **1** : dressmaker **2** : fashion designer

modisto *nm* : fashion designer

modo *nm* **1** MANERA : way, manner, mode ⟨de un modo u otro : one way or another⟩ ⟨a mi modo de ver : to my way of thinking⟩ ⟨modo de vida : way of life⟩ **2** : mood (in grammar) **3** : mode (in music) **4 a modo de** : by way of, in the manner of, like ⟨a modo de ejemplo : by way of example⟩ **5 de este/ese modo** : in this/that way **6 de cualquier modo** : in any case, anyway **7 de modo que** : so, in such a way that **8 de ningún modo** : (in) no way **9 de todos modos** : in any case, anyway **10 en cierto modo** : in a way, to a certain extent

modorra *nf* : drowsiness, lethargy

modular¹ *v* : to modulate — **modulación** *nf*

modular² *adj* : modular

módulo *nm* : module, unit

mofa *nf* **1** : mockery, ridicule **2 hacer mofa de** : to make fun of, to ridicule

mofarse *vr* ~ **de** : to scoff at, to make fun of

mofeta *nf* ZORRILLO : skunk

mofle *nm* *CA, Mex* : muffler (of a car)

moflete *nm fam* : fat cheek

mofletudo, -da *adj fam* : chubby-cheeked, chubby

mohín *nm, pl* **mohines** : grimace, face

mohino, -na *adj* : gloomy, melancholy

moho *nm* **1** : mold, mildew **2** : rust

mohoso, -sa *adj* **1** : moldy **2** : rusty

moisés *nm, pl* **moiseses** : bassinet, cradle

mojado¹, -da *adj* : wet

mojado², -da *n Mex fam* : illegal immigrant

mojar *vt* **1** : to wet, to moisten **2** : to dunk — **mojarse** *vr* : to get wet

mojigatería *nf* **1** : hypocrisy **2** GAZMOÑERÍA : primness, prudery

mojigato¹, -ta *adj* : prudish, prim — **mojigatamente** *adv*

mojigato², -ta *n* : prude, prig

mojón *nm, pl* **mojones** : boundary stone, marker

molar *nm* MUELA : molar

molcajete *nm Mex* : mortar

molde *nm* **1** : mold, form **2 letra(s) de molde** → **letra**

moldear *vt* **1** FORMAR : to mold, to shape **2** : to cast

moldura *nf* : molding

mole¹ *nm Mex* **1** : spicy sauce made with chilies and usually chocolate **2** : meat served with mole sauce

mole² *nf* : mass, bulk

molécula *nf* : molecule — **molecular** *adj*

moler {47} *vt* **1** : to grind, to crush **2** CANSAR : to exhaust, to wear out

molestar *vt* **1** FASTIDIAR : to annoy, to bother ⟨no me molesta : it doesn't bother me, I don't mind⟩ **2** : to disturb, to disrupt — *vi* : to be a nuisance — **molestarse** *vr* **1** : to get annoyed, to be offended **2** ~ **en** : to take the trouble to

molestia *nf* **1** FASTIDIO : annoyance, bother, nuisance **2** : trouble ⟨se tomó la molestia de investigar : she took the trouble to investigate⟩ **3** MALESTAR : discomfort

molesto, -ta *adj* **1** ENOJADO : bothered, annoyed **2** FASTIDIOSO : bothersome, annoying

molestoso, -sa *adj* : bothersome, annoying

molido, -da *adj* **1** MACHACADO : ground, crushed **2 estar molido** : to be exhausted

molienda *nf* : milling, grinding

molinero, -ra *n* : miller

molinillo *nm* : grinder, mill ⟨molinillo de café : coffee grinder⟩

molino *nm* 1 : mill 2 **molino de viento** : windmill

molla *nf* : soft fleshy part, flesh (of fruit), lean part (of meat)

molleja *nf* : gizzard

molusco *nm* : mollusk

momentáneamente *adv* : momentarily

momentáneo, -nea *adj* 1 : momentary 2 TEMPORARIO : temporary

momento *nm* 1 : moment, instant ⟨espera un momentito : wait just a moment⟩ 2 : time, period of time ⟨momentos difíciles : hard times⟩ 3 : time, moment (in time) ⟨en este momento : right now, at the moment⟩ ⟨llegar en mal momento : to come at a bad time⟩ ⟨momento decisivo : turning point, critical time⟩ 4 : present, moment ⟨los atletas del momento : the athletes of the moment, today's popular athletes⟩ 5 : momentum 6 **a cada momento** : constantly 7 **al momento** : right away, at once 8 **de ~** : at the moment, for the moment 9 **de un momento a otro** : any time now 10 **en algún momento** : at some point, sometime 11 **en cualquier momento** : at any time 12 **en ningún momento** : never, at no time 13 **en todo momento** : at all times 14 **en un primer momento** : at first, initially 15 **por el momento** : for the time being 16 **por ~s** : at times

momia *nf* : mummy

monada *nf* 1 : attractive person 2 : cute or pretty thing

monaguillo *nm* ACÓLITO : altar boy

monarca *nmf* : monarch

monarquía *nf* : monarchy

monárquico, -ca *n* : monarchist

monasterio *nm* : monastery

monástico, -ca *adj* : monastic

monda *nf* 1 : peel 2 **ser la monda** *Spain fam* : to be hilarious

mondadientes *nms & pl* PALILLO : toothpick

mondar *vt* : to peel

mondongo *nm* ENTRAÑAS : innards *pl*, insides *pl*, guts *pl*

moneda *nf* 1 : coin 2 : money, currency

monedero *nm* : change purse

monetario, -ria *adj* : monetary, financial

mongol, -gola *adj & n* : Mongol, Mongolian

monigote *nm* 1 : rag doll 2 : paper doll

monitor¹, -tora *n* : instructor (in sports)

monitor² *nm* : monitor ⟨monitor de televisión : television monitor⟩

monitorear *vt* : to monitor

monja *nf* : nun

monje *nm* : monk

mono¹, -na *adj fam* : lovely, pretty, cute, darling

mono², -na *n* : monkey

monóculo *nm* : monocle

monogamia *nf* : monogamy

monógamo, -ma *adj* : monogamous

monografía *nf* : monograph

monograma *nm* : monogram

monolingüe *adj* : monolingual

monolítico, -ca *adj* : monolithic

monolito *nm* : monolith

monólogo *nm* : monologue

monomanía *nf* : obsession

monopatín *nm, pl* **-tines** 1 : scooter 2 : skateboard

monopatinaje *nm* : skateboarding

monopolio *nm* : monopoly

monopolizar {21} *vt* : to monopolize — **monopolización** *nf*

monosilábico, -ca *adj* : monosyllabic

monosílabo *nm* : monosyllable

monoteísmo *nm* : monotheism

monoteísta¹ *adj* : monotheistic

monoteísta² *nmf* : monotheist

monotonía *nf* 1 : monotony 2 : monotone

monótono, -na *adj* : monotonous — **monótonamente** *adv*

monóxido *nm* **monóxido de carbono** : carbon monoxide

monovolumen *nm, pl* **-lúmenes** *Spain* : minivan

monseñor *nm* : monsignor

monserga *nf* : gibberish, drivel

monstruo *nm* : monster

monstruosidad *nf* : monstrosity

monstruoso, -sa *adj* : monstrous — **monstruosamente** *adv*

monta *nf* 1 : sum, total 2 : importance, value ⟨de poca monta : unimportant, insignificant⟩

montacargas *nms & pl* : freight elevator

montaje *nm* 1 : assembling, assembly 2 : montage

montante *nm* : transom, fanlight

montaña *nf* 1 MONTE : mountain 2 **montaña rusa** : roller coaster

montañero, -ra *n* : mountaineer, mountain climber

montañismo *nm* : mountaineering, (mountain) climbing

montañoso, -sa *adj* : mountainous

montar *vt* 1 : to mount, to get on 2 : to ride (a horse, a bicycle, etc.) 3 ESTABLECER : to set up, to establish 4 ARMAR : to assemble, to put together, to set up 5 : to set, to mount (gems, etc.) 6 : to edit (a film) 7 : to stage, to put on (a show) 8 : to cock (a gun) 9 : to mount (of a male animal) — *vi* 1 : to get on (a bus, etc), to get in (a car, a truck), to mount (a horse) 2 **montar en bicicleta** : to ride a bicycle 3 **montar a caballo** CABALGAR : to ride horseback — **montarse** *vr* 1 : to get in, to get on, to mount ⟨se montó en el avión : she got on the plane⟩ ⟨volvió a montarse : he got back on again⟩

monte *nm* 1 MONTAÑA : mountain, mount 2 : woodland ⟨monte bajo : underbrush⟩ 3 : outskirts (of a town), surrounding country 4 **monte de piedad** : pawnshop

montés *adj, pl* **monteses** : wild (of animals or plants)

montículo *nm* 1 : mound, heap 2 : hillock, knoll

monto *nm* : amount, total

montón *nm, pl* **-tones** 1 : heap, pile 2 *fam* : ton, load ⟨un montón de preguntas

: a ton of questions⟩ ⟨montones de gente
: loads of people⟩
montonero, -ra *n* : guerrilla
montura *nf* **1** : mount (horse) **2** : saddle, tack **3** : setting, mounting (of jewelry) **4** : frame (of glasses)
monumental *adj fam* **1** : tremendous,
terrific **2** : massive, huge
monumento *nm* : monument
monzón *nm, pl* **monzones** : monsoon
moño *nm* **1** : bun (chignon) **2** LAZO
: bow, knot ⟨corbata de moño : bow tie⟩
moquear *vi* : to snivel
moqueta *nf Spain* : wall-to-wall carpet
moquette *nf Arg, Uru* : wall-to-wall carpet
moquillo *nm* : distemper
mora *nf* **1** : blackberry **2** : mulberry
morada *nf* RESIDENCIA : dwelling, abode
morado¹, -da *adj* : purple
morado² *nm* : purple
morador, -dora *n* : dweller, inhabitant
moral¹ *adj* : moral — **moralmente** *adv*
moral² *nf* **1** MORALIDAD : ethics, morality, morals *pl* **2** ÁNIMO : morale, spirits
pl
moraleja *nf* : moral (of a story)
moralidad *nf* : morality
moralista¹ *adj* : moralistic
moralista² *nmf* : moralist
morar *vi* : to dwell, to reside
moratón *nm, pl* **-tones** : bruise
moratoria *nf* : moratorium
mórbido, -da *adj* : morbid
morbo *nm* : morbid fascination
morboso, -sa *adj* : morbid — **morbosidad** *nf*
morcilla *nf* : blood sausage, blood pudding
mordacidad *nf* : bite, sharpness
mordaz *adj* : caustic, scathing
mordaza *nf* **1** : gag **2** : clamp
mordedura *nf* : bite (of an animal)
morder {47} *v* : to bite — **morderse** *vr* : to
bite ⟨morderse la lengua/las uñas : to
bite one's tongue/nails⟩
mordida *nf* **1** : bite **2** *CA, Mex* : bribe,
payoff
mordisco *nm* : bite, nibble
mordisquear *vt* : to nibble (on), to bite
morena *nf* **1** : moraine **2** : moray (eel)
moreno¹, -na *adj* **1** : brunette **2** : dark,
dark-skinned
moreno², -na *n* **1** : brunette **2** : dark-
skinned person
morera *nf* : mulberry
moretón *nm, pl* **-tones** : bruise
morfina *nf* : morphine
morfología *nf* : morphology
morgue *nf* : morgue
moribundo¹, -da *adj* : dying, moribund
moribundo², -da *n* : dying person
morillo *nm* : andiron
morir {46} *vi* **1** FALLECER : to die ⟨murió
de cáncer : he died of cancer⟩ **2** APA-
GARSE : to die out, to go out — **morirse**
vr **1** : to die **2** ~ **de** (*expressing an extreme state*) ⟨¡me muero de frío/hambre!
: I'm freezing/starving!⟩ ⟨cuando lo vi
casi me muero de vergüenza : when I
saw it I nearly died of embarrassment⟩

⟨morirse de risa : to die laughing⟩ **3** ~
por : to be dying for (something), to be
dying to (do something) ⟨se muere por
jugar : she's dying to play⟩ ⟨se muere
por ti : he's crazy about you⟩
mormón, -mona *adj & n, pl* **mormones**
: Mormon
moro¹, -ra *adj* : Moorish
moro², -ra *n* **1** : Moor **2** : Muslim
morocho¹, -cha *adj* : dark-haired
morocho², -cha *n* : dark-haired person
morosidad *nf* **1** : delinquency (in payment) **2** : slowness
moroso, -sa *adj* **1** : delinquent, in arrears ⟨cuentas morosas : delinquent ac-
counts⟩ **2** : slow, sluggish
morral *nm* MOCHILA : backpack, knapsack
morralla *nf* **1** : small fish **2** : trash, riffraff **3** *Mex* : small change
morriña *nf* : homesickness
morro *nm* HOCICO : snout
morsa *nf* : walrus
morse *nm* : Morse code
mortadela *nf* : mortadella
mortaja *nf* SUDARIO : shroud
mortal¹ *adj* **1** : mortal **2** FATAL : fatal,
deadly — **mortalmente** *adv*
mortal² *nmf* : mortal
mortalidad *nf* : mortality
mortandad *nf* **1** : loss of life, death toll
2 : carnage, slaughter
mortero *nm* : mortar (bowl, cannon, or
building material)
mortífero, -ra *adj* LETAL : deadly, fatal
mortificación *nf, pl* **-ciones** **1** : mortification **2** TORMENTO : anguish, torment
mortificar {72} *vt* **1** : to mortify **2** TOR-
TURAR : to trouble, to torment — **morti-
ficarse** *vr* : to be mortified, to feel embarrassed
mosaico *nm* : mosaic
mosca *nf* **1** : fly **2** **mosca común**
: housefly
moscada *adj* **nuez moscada** : nutmeg
mosquearse *vr* **1** : to become suspicious
2 : to take offense
mosquete *nm* : musket
mosquetero *nm* : musketeer
mosquitero *nm* : mosquito net
mosquito *nm* ZANCUDO : mosquito
mostachón *nm, pl* **-chones** : macaroon
mostaza *nf* : mustard
mosto *nm* : must (from a grape)
mostrador *nm* : counter (in a store)
mostrar {19} *vt* **1** : to show **2** EXHIBIR
: to exhibit, to display — **mostrarse** *vr*
: to show oneself, to appear
mota *nf* **1** : fleck, speck **2** : defect,
blemish
mote *nm* SOBRENOMBRE : nickname
moteado, -da *adj* : dotted, spotted, dappled
motel *nm* : motel
motín *nm, pl* **motines** **1** : riot **2** : rebellion, mutiny
motivación *nf, pl* **-ciones** : motivation —
motivacional *adj*
motivar *vt* **1** CAUSAR : to cause **2** IM-
PULSAR : to motivate

motivo *nm* **1** MÓVIL : motive ⟨el motivo del crimen : the motive for the crime⟩ **2** CAUSA : cause, reason ⟨da motivos para el optimismo : it's cause for optimism⟩ **3** TEMA : theme, motif

moto *nf* : motorcycle, motorbike

motocicleta *nf* : motorcycle

motociclismo *nm* : motorcycling

motociclista *nmf* : motorcyclist

motoneta *nf* : scooter

motor¹, -ra *adj* MOTRIZ : motor

motor² *nm* **1** : motor, engine **2** : driving force, cause

motora *nf* : motorboat

motorismo *nm* : motorcycle riding, motorcycling

motorista *nmf* : motorist

motorizado, -da *adj* : motorized

motriz *adj*, *pl* **motrices** : driving

motu proprio *adv* **de motu proprio** [de'-motu'proprio] : voluntarily, of one's own accord

mousse ['mus] *nmf* : mousse

movedizo, -za *adj* **1** : movable **2** : moving **3** : restless

mover {47} *vt* **1** TRASLADAR : to move, to shift **2** AGITAR : to shake, to move ⟨mover la cabeza (diciendo que sí) : to nod⟩ ⟨mover la cabeza (diciendo que no) : to shake one's head⟩ **3** ACCIONAR : to power, to drive **4** ~ **a** : to cause to (do something) ⟨me movió a pensar : it made me think⟩ ⟨lo movió a escribir : it inspired him to write⟩ — **moverse** *vr* **1** : to move **2** : to hurry, to get a move on **3** : to get moving, to make an effort

movible *adj* : movable

movida *nf* : move (in a game)

móvil¹ *adj* : mobile

móvil² *nm* **1** MOTIVO : motive **2** : mobile

movilidad *nf* : mobility

movilizar {21} *vt* : to mobilize — **movilización** *nf*

movimiento *nm* : movement, motion ⟨movimiento del cuerpo : bodily movement⟩ ⟨movimiento sindicalista : labor movement⟩

mozo¹, -za *adj* : young, youthful

mozo², -za *n* **1** JOVEN : young man *m*, young woman *f*, youth **2** : helper, servant **3** *Arg, Chile, Col, Peru* : waiter *m*, waitress *f*

MP3 *nm*, *pl* **MP3** : MP3

mucamo, -ma *n* : servant, maid *f*

muchacha *nf* : maid

muchacho, -cha *n* **1** : kid, boy *m*, girl *f* **2** JOVEN : young man *m*, young woman *f*

muchedumbre *nf* MULTITUD : crowd, multitude

mucho¹ *adv* : (very) much, a lot ⟨mucho más fácil/rápido/grande : much easier/faster/bigger⟩ ⟨mucho más tarde : much later⟩ ⟨te quiero mucho : I love you very much⟩ ⟨lo siento mucho : I'm very sorry⟩ ⟨le gusta mucho : he likes it a lot⟩ ⟨¿viajas mucho? : do you travel a lot?⟩ ⟨no habla mucho : she doesn't talk (very) much⟩

mucho², -cha *adj* **1** : a lot of, many, much ⟨mucha gente : a lot of people,

many people⟩ ⟨mucho dinero : a lot of money⟩ ⟨¡muchas gracias! : thank you very much!⟩ ⟨no tengo mucha hambre : I'm not very hungry⟩ ⟨hace mucho tiempo que no lo veo : I haven't seen him in ages⟩ **2 muchas veces** : often

mucho³, -cha *pron* **1** : a lot, many, much ⟨hay mucho que hacer : there is a lot to do⟩ ⟨muchos no vinieron : many didn't come⟩ **2 mucho** : long, a long time ⟨tardó mucho en venir : he was a long time getting here⟩ ⟨¿te falta mucho? : will you be much longer?⟩ ⟨hace mucho que no te veo : it's been a long time since I've seen you⟩ **3 cuando/como** ~ : at most **4 con** ~ : by far **5 ni mucho menos** : not at all, far from it **6 por mucho que** : no matter how much, (as) much as ⟨por mucho que quiera no puedo : as much as I would like to, I can't⟩

mucílago *nm* : mucilage

mucosidad *nf* : mucus

mucoso, -sa *adj* : mucous, slimy

muda *nf* **1** : change ⟨muda de ropa : change of clothes⟩ **2** : molt, molting

mudanza *nf* **1** CAMBIO : change **2** TRASLADO : move, moving

mudar *v* **1** CAMBIAR : to change **2** : to molt, to shed — **mudarse** *vr* **1** TRASLADARSE : to move (one's residence) **2** : to change (clothes)

mudo¹, -da *adj* **1** SILENCIOSO : silent ⟨el cine mudo : silent films⟩ **2** : mute, dumb *now often offensive*

mudo², -da *n* : mute *sometimes offensive*

mueble *nm* **1** : piece of furniture **2 muebles** *nmpl* : furniture, furnishings

mueblería *nf* : furniture store

mueca *nf* : grimace, face

muela *nf* **1** : tooth, molar ⟨dolor de muelas : toothache⟩ ⟨muela del juicio : wisdom tooth⟩ **2** : millstone **3** : whetstone

muele, etc. → **moler**

muelle¹ *adj* : soft, comfortable, easy

muelle² *nm* **1** : wharf, dock **2** RESORTE : spring

muérdago *nm* : mistletoe

muerde, etc. → **morder**

muere, etc. → **morir**

muerte *nf* : death ⟨amenaza de muerte : death threat⟩ ⟨dar un susto de muerte : to scare half to death⟩ ⟨morir de muerte natural : to die of natural causes⟩

muerto¹ *pp* → **morir**

muerto², -ta *adj* **1** : dead ⟨caer muerto : to die, to drop dead⟩ **2** : lifeless, flat, dull **3** ~ **de** : dying of ⟨estoy muerto de hambre : I'm dying of hunger⟩ ⟨muerto de miedo : scared to death⟩

muerto³, -ta *nm* DIFUNTO : dead person, deceased

muesca *nf* : nick, notch

muestra¹, etc. → **mostrar**

muestra² *nf* **1** : sample **2** SEÑAL : sign, show ⟨una muestra de respeto : a show of respect⟩ **3** EXPOSICIÓN : exhibition, exposition **4** : pattern, model

muestreo *nm* : sample

mueve, etc. → **mover**
mugido *nm* : moo, lowing, bellow
mugir {35} *vi* : to moo, to low, to bellow
mugre *nf* SUCIEDAD : grime, filth
mugriento, -ta *adj* : filthy
muguete *nm* : lily of the valley
muja, etc. → **mugir**
mujer *nf* **1** : woman **2** ESPOSA : wife
mújol *nm* : mullet (fish)
mulato, -ta *adj & n* : mulatto *now sometimes offensive*
muleta *nf* : crutch
muletilla *nf* : favorite word or phrase
mullido, -da *adj* **1** : soft, fluffy **2** : spongy, springy
mulo, -la *n* : mule
multa *nf* : fine
multar *vt* : to fine
multi- *pref* : multi-
multicine *nm* : multiplex
multicolor *adj* : multicolored
multicultural *adj* : multicultural
multidisciplinario, -ria *adj* : multidisciplinary
multifacético, -ca *adj* : multifaceted
multifamiliar *adj* : multifamily
multilateral *adj* : multilateral
multimedia *nf* : multimedia
multimillonario, -ria *n* : multimillionaire
multinacional *adj* : multinational
múltiple *adj* : multiple
multiplicación *nf, pl* **-ciones** : multiplication
multiplicar {72} *v* **1** : to multiply **2** : to increase — **multiplicarse** *vr* **1** : to multiply, to reproduce **2** : to increase, to multiply ⟨multiplicarse por cinco : to increase fivefold⟩
multiplicidad *nf* : multiplicity
múltiplo *nm* : multiple
multipropiedad *nf* : time share
multitarea *nf* : multitasking
multitud *nf* MUCHEDUMBRE : crowd, multitude
multitudinario, -ria *adj* : well-attended ⟨manifestaciones multitudinarias : mass protests⟩ ⟨un concierto multitudinario : a concert with a huge turnout⟩
multiuso, -sa *adj* : multipurpose
multivitamínico, -ca *adj* : multivitamin
mundano, -na *adj* : worldly, earthly
mundial *adj* : world, worldwide
mundialmente *adv* : worldwide, all over the world
mundo *nm* **1** : world ⟨alrededor del mundo : around the world⟩ ⟨el mundo entero : the whole world⟩ ⟨el mundo actual : today's world⟩ ⟨el Tercer Mundo : the Third World⟩ ⟨el mundo de la moda : the world of fashion⟩ **2** VIDA : world, life ⟨su mundo se derrumbó : his world fell apart⟩ **3** PLANETA : world, planet **4 del mundo** : in the world ⟨el mejor del mundo : the best in the world⟩ ⟨por nada del mundo : not for anything in the world⟩ ⟨tener todo el tiempo del mundo : to have all the time

in the world⟩ **5 el otro mundo** : the afterlife, the hereafter ⟨no es nada del otro mundo : it's nothing special⟩ **6 en su mundo** *fam* : in one's own world, in a world of one's own **7 por/en/de todo el mundo** : the (whole) world over **8 todo el mundo** : everyone, everybody
municiones *nfpl* : ammunition, munitions
municipal *adj* : municipal
municipio *nm* **1** : municipality **2** AYUNTAMIENTO : town council
muñeca *nf* **1** : doll ⟨muñeca de trapo : rag doll⟩ **2** MANIQUÍ : mannequin **3** : wrist
muñeco *nm* **1** : doll, boy doll **2** MARIONETA : puppet
muñequera *nf* : wristband
muñón *nm, pl* **muñones** : stump (of an arm or leg)
mural *adj & nm* : mural
muralla *nf* : rampart, wall
murciélago *nm* : bat (animal)
murga *nf* : band of street musicians
murió, etc. → **morir**
murmullo *nm* **1** : murmur, murmuring **2** : rustling, rustle ⟨el murmullo de las hojas : the rustling of the leaves⟩
murmuraciones *nfpl* : gossip
murmurar *vt* **1** : to murmur, to mutter **2** : to whisper (gossip) — *vi* **1** : to murmur **2** CHISMEAR : to gossip
muro *nm* : wall
musa *nf* : muse
musaraña *nf* : shrew
muscular *adj* : muscular
musculatura *nf* : muscles *pl*, musculature
músculo *nm* : muscle
musculoso, -sa *adj* : muscular, brawny
muselina *nf* : muslin
museo *nm* : museum
musgo *nm* : moss
musgoso, -sa *adj* : mossy
música *nf* : music
musical *adj* : musical — **musicalmente** *adv*
músico[1]**, -ca** *adj* : musical
músico[2]**, -ca** *n* : musician
musitar *vt* : to mumble, to murmur
muslo *nm* : thigh
mustio, -tia *adj* : withered (of a plant)
musulmán, -mana *adj & n, mpl* **-manes** : Muslim
mutación *nf, pl* **-ciones** : mutation
mutante *adj & nm* : mutant
mutar *v* : to mutate
mutilar *vt* : to mutilate — **mutilación** *nf*
mutis *nm* **1** : exit (in theater) **2** : silence
mutismo *nm* : silence
mutual *adj* : mutual
mutuo, -tua *adj* : mutual, reciprocal — **mutuamente** *adv*
muy *adv* **1** : very, quite ⟨es muy inteligente : she's very intelligent⟩ ⟨muy bien : very well, fine⟩ ⟨eso es muy americano : that's typically American⟩ ⟨muy poca comida : very little food⟩ **2** : too ⟨es muy grande para él : it's too big for him⟩

N

n *nf* : sixteenth letter of the Spanish alphabet

nabo *nm* : turnip

nácar *nm* MADREPERLA : mother-of-pearl

nacarado, -da *adj* : pearly

nacer {48} *vi* **1** : to be born ⟨nací en Guatemala : I was born in Guatemala⟩ ⟨no nació ayer : he wasn't born yesterday⟩ **2** : to hatch **3** : to bud, to sprout **4** : to rise, to originate **5 nacer para algo** : to be born to be something **6 volver a nacer** : to have a lucky escape

nacido¹, -da *adj* **1** : born **2 recién nacido** : newborn

nacido², -da *n* **1 los nacidos** : those born (at a particular time) **2 recién nacido** : newborn baby

naciente *adj* **1** : newfound, growing **2** : rising ⟨el sol naciente : the rising sun⟩

nacimiento *nm* **1** : birth **2** : source (of a river) **3** : beginning, origin **4** BELÉN : Nativity scene, crèche

nación *nf, pl* **naciones** : nation, country, people (of a country)

nacional¹ *adj* : national

nacional² *nmf* CIUDADANO : national, citizen

nacionalidad *nf* : nationality

nacionalismo *nm* : nationalism

nacionalista¹ *adj* : nationalist, nationalistic

nacionalista² *nmf* : nationalist

nacionalización *nf, pl* **-ciones 1** : nationalization **2** : naturalization

nacionalizar {21} *vt* **1** : to nationalize **2** : to naturalize (as a citizen) — **nacionalizarse** *vr*

naco, -ca *adj Mex* : trashy, vulgar, common

nada¹ *adv* : not at all, not in the least ⟨no estamos nada cansados : we are not at all tired⟩ ⟨no me importa nada : it doesn't matter at all to me⟩

nada² *nf* **1** : nothingness **2** : smidgen, bit ⟨una nada le disgusta : the slightest thing upsets him⟩

nada³ *pron* **1** : nothing ⟨no estoy haciendo nada : I'm not doing anything⟩ ⟨es mejor que nada : it's better than nothing⟩ ⟨empecé sin nada : I started out with nothing⟩ ⟨no tengo nada que decir : I have nothing to say⟩ ⟨no tiene nada de extraño : there's nothing strange about it⟩ ⟨esta pluma no sirve para nada : this pen is useless⟩ ⟨no me interesa para nada : it doesn't interest me at all⟩ ⟨no es nada comparado con . . . : it's nothing compared to . . .⟩ ⟨no hay nada como la comida casera : there's nothing like home cooking⟩ **2 antes que nada** : first of all (in order), above all (in importance) **3 casi nada** : next to nothing **4 de ~** : you're welcome **5 dentro de nada** : very soon, in no time **6 nada de eso** : nothing of the kind, nothing like that **7 nada más** : nothing else, nothing

more **8 nada más** : as soon as, no sooner . . . than ⟨nada más comenzar el partido, marcó : as soon as the game started, he scored; no sooner did the game start than he scored⟩ **9 pues nada** *fam* : anyway

nadador, -dora *n* : swimmer

nadar *vi* **1** : to swim **2 ~ en** : to be swimming in, to be rolling in — *vt* : to swim

nadería *nf* : small thing, trifle

nadie *pron* : nobody, no one ⟨no vi a nadie : I didn't see anyone⟩

nadir *nm* : nadir

nado *nm* **1** *Mex* : swimming **2 a ~** : swimming ⟨cruzó el río a nado : he swam across the river⟩

nafta *nf* **1** : naphtha **2** (*in various countries*) : gasoline

naftalina *nf* : mothballs *pl*

náhuatl¹ *adj & nmf, pl* **nahuas** : Nahuatl

náhuatl² *nm* : Nahuatl (language)

nailon → nilón

naipe *nm* : playing card

nalga *nf* **1** : buttock **2 nalgas** *nfpl* : buttocks, bottom

nalgada *nf* : smack on the bottom, spanking

namibio, -bia *adj & n* : Namibian

nana *nf* **1** : lullaby **2** *fam* : grandma **3** *CA, Col, Mex, Ven* : nanny

nanay *interj fam* : no way!, not likely!

nanotecnología *nf* : nanotechnology

naranja¹ *adj & nm* : orange (color)

naranja² *nf* : orange (fruit)

naranjada *nf* : orangeade

naranjal *nm* : orange grove

naranjo *nm* : orange tree

narcisismo *nm* : narcissism

narcisista¹ *adj* : narcissistic

narcisista² *nmf* : narcissist

narciso *nm* : narcissus, daffodil

narco *nmf fam* → **narcotraficante**

narcótico¹, -ca *adj* : narcotic

narcótico² *nm* : narcotic

narcotizar {21} *vt* : to drug, to dope

narcotraficante *nmf* : drug trafficker

narcotráfico *nm* : drug trafficking

narigón, -gona *adj, mpl* **-gones** : big-nosed

narigudo → narigón

nariz *nf, pl* **narices 1** : nose ⟨sonar(se) la nariz : to blow one's nose⟩ **2** : sense of smell

narración *nf, pl* **-ciones** : narration, account

narrador, -dora *n* : narrator

narrar *vt* : to narrate, to tell

narrativa *nf* : narrative, story

narrativo, -va *adj* : narrative

nasa *nf* : creel

nasal *adj* : nasal

nata *nf* **1** *Spain* : cream ⟨nata montada : whipped cream⟩ **2** : skin (on boiled milk)

natación *nf, pl* **-ciones** : swimming

natal *adj* : native, natal

natalicio *nm* : birthday ⟨el natalicio de George Washington : George Washington's birthday⟩
natalidad *nf* : birthrate
natillas *nfpl* : custard
natividad *nf* : birth, nativity
nativo, -va *adj & n* : native
nativo americano, nativa americana *adj & n* : Native American
nato, -ta *adj* : born, natural
natural[1] *adj* **1** : natural **2** : normal ⟨como es natural : naturally, as expected⟩ **3** ~ **de** : native of, from **4 de tamaño natural** : life-size
natural[2] *nm* **1** CARÁCTER : disposition, temperament **2** : native ⟨un natural de Venezuela : a native of Venezuela⟩
naturaleza *nf* **1** : nature ⟨la madre naturaleza : mother nature⟩ **2** ÍNDOLE : nature, disposition, constitution ⟨la naturaleza humana : human nature⟩ **3 naturaleza muerta** : still life
naturalidad *nf* : simplicity, naturalness
naturalismo *nm* : naturalism
naturalista[1] *adj* : naturalistic
naturalista[2] *nmf* : naturalist
naturalización *nf, pl* **-ciones** : naturalization
naturalizar {21} *vt* : to naturalize — **naturalizarse** *vr* NACIONALIZARSE : to become naturalized
naturalmente *adv* **1** : naturally, inherently **2** : of course
naufragar {52} *vi* **1** : to be shipwrecked **2** FRACASAR : to fail, to collapse
naufragio *nm* **1** : shipwreck **2** FRACASO : failure, collapse
náufrago[1], **-ga** *adj* : shipwrecked, castaway
náufrago[2], **-ga** *n* : shipwrecked person, castaway
náusea *nf* **1** : nausea **2 dar náuseas** : to nauseate, to disgust **3 náuseas matutinas** : morning sickness
nauseabundo, -da *adj* : nauseating, sickening
náutica *nf* : navigation
náutico, -ca *adj* : nautical
nautilo *nm* : nautilus
navaja *nf* **1** : pocketknife, penknife ⟨navaja de muelle : switchblade⟩ **2 navaja de afeitar** : straight razor
navajazo *nm* : knife wound
navajo, -ja *adj & n* : Navajo
naval *adj* : naval
nave *nf* **1** : ship ⟨nave capitana : flagship⟩ ⟨nave espacial : spaceship⟩ **2** : nave ⟨nave lateral : aisle⟩ **3 quemar uno sus naves** : to burn one's bridges
navegabilidad *nf* : navigability
navegable *adj* : navigable
navegación *nf, pl* **-ciones** : navigation
navegador *nm* : browser ⟨navegador web : web browser⟩
navegante[1] *adj* : sailing, seafaring
navegante[2] *nmf* : navigator
navegar {52} *v* : to navigate, to sail
Navidad *nf* : Christmas ⟨Feliz Navidad : Merry Christmas⟩
navideño, -ña *adj* : Christmas

naviero, -ra *adj* : shipping
navío *nm* : (large) ship
nazca, etc. → **nacer**
nazi *adj & nmf* : Nazi
nazismo *nm* : Nazism
neandertal *or* **neanderthal** *nm* **1 Neandertal** *or* **Neanderthal** *or* **hombre de Neandertal/Neanderthal** : Neanderthal (man) **2** *fam* : Neanderthal
nébeda *nf* : catnip
neblina *nf* : light fog, mist
neblinoso, -sa *adj* : misty, foggy
nebulosa *nf* : nebula
nebulosidad *nf* : mistiness, haziness
nebuloso, -sa *adj* **1** : hazy, misty **2** : nebulous, vague
necedad *nf* : stupidity, foolishness ⟨decir necedades : to talk nonsense⟩
necesariamente *adv* : necessarily
necesario, -ria *adj* **1** : necessary **2 si es necesario** : if need be **3 hacerse necesario** : to be required
neceser *nm* : toilet kit, vanity case
necesidad *nf* **1** : need, necessity ⟨por necesidad : out of necessity⟩ ⟨en caso de necesidad : if necessary, if need be⟩ **2** : poverty, want **3 necesidades** *nfpl* : hardships **4 hacer sus necesidades** : to relieve oneself
necesitado, -da *adj* : needy
necesitar *vt* **1** : to need **2** : to necessitate, to require — *vi* ~ **de** : to have need of
necio[1], **-cia** *adj* **1** : foolish, silly, dumb **2** *fam* : naughty **3** *Mex* : stubborn
necio[2], **-cia** *n* **1** ESTÚPIDO : fool, idiot **2** *Mex* : stubborn person
necrología *nf* : obituary
necrópolis *nfs & pl* : cemetery
néctar *nm* : nectar
nectarina *nf* : nectarine
neerlandés[1], **-desa** *adj, mpl* **-deses** HOLANDÉS : Dutch
neerlandés[2], **-desa** *n, mpl* **-deses** HOLANDÉS : Dutch person
nefando, -da *adj* : unspeakable, heinous
nefario, -ria *adj* : nefarious
nefasto, -ta *adj* **1** : ill-fated, unlucky **2** : disastrous, terrible
negación *nf, pl* **-ciones** **1** : negation, denial **2** : negative (in grammar)
negado, -da *adj* : useless
negar {49} *vt* **1** : to deny **2** REHUSAR : to refuse **3** : to disown — **negarse** *vr* **1** : to refuse **2** : to deny oneself
negativa *nf* **1** : denial **2** : refusal
negativo[1], **-va** *adj* : negative — **negativamente** *adv*
negativo[2] *nm* : negative (of a photograph)
negligé *nm* : negligee
negligencia *nf* : negligence
negligente *adj* : neglectful, negligent — **negligentemente** *adv*
negociable *adj* : negotiable
negociación *nf, pl* **-ciones** **1** : negotiation **2 negociación colectiva** : collective bargaining
negociador, -dora *n* : negotiator
negociante *nmf* : businessman *m*, businesswoman *f*

negociar *vt* : to negotiate — *vi* : to deal, to do business
negocio *nm* **1** : business, place of business ⟨el mundo de los negocios : the business world⟩ **2** : deal, transaction **3 negocios** *nmpl* : commerce, trade, business
negra *nf* : quarter note
negrero, -ra *n* **1** : slave trader **2** *fam* : slave driver, brutal boss
negrita *or* **negrilla** *nf* : boldface (type)
negro¹, -gra *adj* **1** : black, dark **2** BRONCEADO : suntanned **3** : gloomy, awful, desperate ⟨la cosa se está poniendo negra : things are looking bad⟩ **4 mercado negro** : black market
negro², -gra *n* **1** : dark-skinned person, black person **2** *fam* : darling, dear
negro³ *nm* : black (color)
negrura *nf* : blackness
negruzco, -ca *adj* : blackish
nene, -na *n* : baby, small child
nenúfar *nm* : water lily
neocelandés → **neozelandés**
neófito, -ta *n* : neophyte, novice
neologismo *nm* : neologism
neón *nm, pl* **neones** : neon
neoyorquino¹, -na *adj* : of or from New York
neoyorquino², -na *n* : New Yorker
neozelandés¹, -desa *adj, mpl* **-deses** : of or from New Zealand
neozelandés², -desa *n, mpl* **-deses** : New Zealander
nepalés, -lesa *adj & n, mpl* **-leses** : Nepali
nepotismo *nm* : nepotism
Neptuno *nm* : Neptune
nervio *nm* **1** : nerve **2** : tendon, sinew, gristle (in meat) **3** : energy, drive **4** : rib (of a vault) **5 nervios** *nmpl* : nerves ⟨estar mal de los nervios : to be a bag/bundle of nerves⟩ ⟨tener los nervios de punta : to be on edge, to have one's nerves on edge⟩ ⟨crisparle los nervios a alguien : to get on someone's nerves⟩ ⟨ataque de nervios : nervous breakdown⟩ ⟨una guerra de nervios : a war of nerves⟩ ⟨nervios de acero : nerves of steel⟩
nerviosamente *adv* : nervously
nerviosidad → **nerviosismo**
nerviosismo *nf* : nervousness, anxiety
nervioso, -sa *adj* **1** : nervous, nerve ⟨sistema nervioso : nervous system⟩ **2** : high-strung, restless, anxious ⟨ponerse nervioso : to get nervous⟩ **3** : vigorous, energetic
nervudo, -da *adj* : sinewy, wiry
neta *nf Mex fam* : truth ⟨la neta es que me cae mal : the truth is, I don't like her⟩
netamente *adv* : clearly, obviously
neto, -ta *adj* **1** : net ⟨peso neto : net weight⟩ **2** : clear, distinct
neumático¹, -ca *adj* : pneumatic
neumático² *nm* LLANTA : tire
neumonía *nf* PULMONÍA : pneumonia
neural *adj* : neural
neuralgia *nf* : neuralgia
neuritis *nf* : neuritis

neurología *nf* : neurology
neurológico, -ca *adj* : neurological, neurologic
neurólogo, -ga *n* : neurologist
neurosis *nfs & pl* : neurosis
neurótico, -ca *adj & n* : neurotic
neutral *adj* : neutral
neutralidad *nf* : neutrality
neutralizar {21} *vt* : to neutralize — **neutralización** *nf*
neutro, -tra *adj* **1** : neutral **2** : neuter
neutrón *nm, pl* **neutrones** : neutron
nevada *nf* : snowfall
nevado, -da *adj* **1** : snowcapped **2** : snow-white
nevar {55} *v impers* : to snow
nevasca *nf* : snowstorm, blizzard
nevera *nf* REFRIGERADOR : refrigerator
nevería *nf Mex* : ice cream parlor
nevisca *nf* : light snowfall, flurry
nevoso, -sa *adj* : snowy
nexo *nm* VÍNCULO : link, connection, nexus
ni *conj* **1** : neither, nor ⟨no es (ni) bueno ni malo : it's neither good nor bad⟩ ⟨ni hoy ni mañana : neither today nor tomorrow⟩ ⟨ni confirma ni niega las acusaciones : he neither confirms nor denies the allegations⟩ ⟨zonas sin agua ni electricidad : areas without water or power, areas with no water or power⟩ ⟨no pagó ni un centavo : he didn't pay a single cent⟩ ⟨él no lo cree, ni yo tampoco : he doesn't believe it, and neither do I⟩ ⟨no le beneficia a ella ni a nadie : it doesn't benefit her or anyone else⟩ **2 ni que** : not even if, not as if ⟨ni que me pagaran : not even if they paid me⟩ ⟨ni que fuera (yo) su madre : it's not as if I were his mother⟩ **3 ni siquiera** : not even ⟨ni siquiera nos llamaron : they didn't even call us⟩
nicaragüense *adj & nmf* : Nicaraguan
nicho *nm* : niche
nicotina *nf* : nicotine
nidada *nf* : brood (of chicks)
nido *nm* **1** : nest **2** : hiding place, den
niebla *nf* : fog, mist
niega, niegue *etc.* → **negar**
nieto, -ta *n* **1** : grandson *m*, granddaughter *f* **2 nietos** *nmpl* : grandchildren
nieva, *etc.* → **nevar**
nieve *nf* **1** : snow **2** *Cuba, Mex, PRi* : sherbet
nigeriano, -na *adj & n* : Nigerian
nigua *nf* : sand flea, chigger
nihilismo *nm* : nihilism
nilón *or* **nilon** *nm, pl* **nilones** : nylon
nimbo *nm* : halo
nimiedad *nf* INSIGNIFICANCIA : trifle, triviality
nimio, -mia *adj* INSIGNIFICANTE : insignificant, trivial
ninfa *nf* : nymph
ningunear *vt Mex fam* : to disrespect
ninguno¹, -na (**ningún** *before masculine singular nouns*) *adj, mpl* **ningunos** : no, none ⟨no es ninguna tonta : she's no fool⟩ ⟨no dieron ninguna razón : they gave no reason, they didn't give a reason⟩ ⟨no debe hacerse en ningún mo-

mento : that should never be done⟩ ⟨no tenemos ninguna idea : we have no idea⟩

ninguno², -na *pron* **1** : neither, none ⟨ninguno de los dos ha vuelto aún : neither one has returned yet⟩ ⟨ninguno de ellos : none of them⟩ **2** : no one, no other ⟨te quiero más que a ninguna : I love you more than any other⟩ ⟨ninguno me dice nada : nobody tells me anything⟩

niña *nf* **1** PUPILA : pupil (of the eye) **2 la niña de los ojos** : the apple of one's eye

niñada *nf* **1** : childishness **2** : trifle, silly thing

niñería → niñada

niñero, -ra *n* : baby-sitter, nanny

niñez *nf, pl* **niñeces** INFANCIA : childhood

niño, -ña *n* : child, boy *m*, girl *f* ⟨los niños : the children⟩ ⟨esperar un niño : to be pregnant, to be expecting a baby⟩

nipón, -pona *adj & n, mpl* **nipones** JAPONÉS : Japanese

níquel *nm* : nickel

nitidez *nf, pl* **-deces** CLARIDAD : clarity, vividness, sharpness

nítido, -da *adj* CLARO : clear, vivid, sharp

nitrato *nm* : nitrate

nítrico, -ca *adj* ácido nítrico → ácido²

nitrógeno *nm* : nitrogen

nitroglicerina *nf* : nitroglycerin

nivel *nm* **1** : level, height ⟨nivel del mar : sea level⟩ ⟨al nivel de : level with⟩ ⟨al nivel del suelo : at floor level⟩ **2** : level, standard ⟨nivel de vida : standard of living⟩ ⟨al mismo nivel que : on a level/par with⟩ ⟨de alto nivel : high-level⟩

nivelador, -dora *n* : leveler

nivelar *vt* : to level (off/out), to even (out) — **nivelarse** *vr*

nixtamal *nm Mex* : corn cooked with lime (used for tortillas)

no¹ *adv* **1** (*indicating a negative response*) : no ¿quieres más? no, gracias : do you want more? no, thanks⟩ ⟨¿la conoces? no : do you know her? no⟩ **2** : no, not ⟨no sé : I don't know⟩ ⟨no tengo ni idea : I have no idea⟩ ⟨¡no hagas eso! : don't do that!⟩ ⟨no le gusta : she doesn't like it⟩ ⟨no es fácil : it's not easy⟩ ⟨creo que no : I don't think so⟩ ⟨no puedo ver nada : I can't see a thing, I can't see anything⟩ ⟨no hay nadie : there's no one there⟩ ⟨es interesante, ¿no? : it's interesting, isn't it?⟩ ⟨¡se casó! ¡no! : he got married! no way!⟩ **3** : non- ⟨no fumador : non-smoker⟩ **4** ¡cómo no! : of course! **5 no bien** : as soon as, no sooner

no² *nm, pl* **noes** : no

noble¹ *adj* : noble — **noblemente** *adv*

noble² *nmf* : nobleman *m*, noblewoman *f*

nobleza *nf* **1** : nobility **2** HONRADEZ : honesty, integrity

nocaut *nm* : knockout, KO

noche *nf* **1** : night, nighttime, evening ⟨esta noche : tonight⟩ ⟨la noche anterior : the night before⟩ ⟨la noche del lunes : (on) Monday night⟩ ⟨todas las noches : every night⟩ ⟨a altas horas de la noche

: late at night⟩ ⟨en medio/mitad de la noche : in the middle of the night⟩ ⟨las diez de la noche : ten (o'clock) at night⟩ ⟨al caer la noche : at nightfall⟩ ⟨pasar la noche : to spend the night⟩ **2 buenas noches** : good evening, good night **3 de noche** *or* **en/por/a la noche** : at night ⟨salir de noche : to go out at night⟩ ⟨era de noche : it was nighttime⟩ ⟨mañana en/por/a la noche : tomorrow night⟩ **4 de la noche a la mañana** : overnight, suddenly **5 hacerse de noche** : to get dark

Nochebuena *nf* : Christmas Eve

nochecita *nf* : dusk

Nochevieja *nf* : New Year's Eve

noción *nf, pl* **nociones** **1** CONCEPTO : notion, concept **2 nociones** *nfpl* : smattering, rudiments *pl*

nocivo, -va *adj* DAÑINO : harmful, noxious

noctámbulo, -la *n* **1** : sleepwalker **2** : night owl

nocturno¹, -na *adj* : night, nocturnal

nocturno² *nm* : nocturne

nodriza *nf* : wet nurse

nódulo *nm* : nodule

nogal *nm* **1** : walnut tree **2** *Mex* : pecan tree **3 nogal americano** : hickory

nómada¹ *adj* : nomadic

nómada² *nmf* : nomad

nomás *adv* : only, just ⟨lo hice nomás porque sí : I did it just because⟩ ⟨nomás de recordarlo me enojo : I get angry just remembering it⟩ ⟨nomás faltan dos semanas para Navidad : there are only two weeks left till Christmas⟩

nombradía *nf* RENOMBRE : fame, renown

nombrado, -da *adj* : famous, well-known

nombramiento *nm* : appointment, nomination

nombrar *vt* **1** : to appoint **2** : to mention, to name

nombre *nm* **1** : name ⟨nombre y apellido : first and last name, full name⟩ ⟨nombre de pila : first name⟩ ⟨nombre de soltera : maiden name⟩ ⟨nombre de usuario : user name⟩ ⟨nombre artístico : stage name⟩ ⟨nombre de pluma : pen name⟩ ⟨nombre comercial : trade name⟩ ⟨en nombre de : on behalf of⟩ ⟨sin nombre : nameless⟩ ⟨sólo de nombre : in name only⟩ ⟨lo cambiaron de nombre : they changed its name⟩ ⟨no lo conozco de nombre : I don't know him by name⟩ ⟨lo que están haciendo no tiene nombre : what they're doing is an outrage⟩ **2** : noun ⟨nombre propio : proper noun⟩ **3** : fame, renown ⟨hacerse un nombre : to make a name for oneself⟩

nomenclatura *nf* : nomenclature

nomeolvides *nmfs & pl* : forget-me-not

nómina *nf* : payroll

nominación *nf, pl* **-ciones** : nomination

nominal *adj* : nominal — **nominalmente** *adv*

nominar *vt* : to nominate

nominativo¹, -va *adj* : nominative

nominativo² *nm* : nominative (case)

nomo *nm* : gnome

non[1] *adj* IMPAR : odd, not even
non[2] *nm* : odd number
nonagésimo[1], **-ma** *adj* : ninetieth, ninety-
nonagésimo[2], **-ma** *n* : ninetieth, ninety-
(in a series)
nono, -na *adj* : ninth — **nono** *nm*
nopal *nm* : prickly pear
nopalitos *nmpl Mex* : pickled prickly
pear leaves
noquear *vt* : to knock out, to KO
norcoreano, -na *adj & n* : North Korean
nordeste[1] *or* **noreste** *adj* 1 : northeastern 2 : northeasterly
nordeste[2] *or* **noreste** *nm* : northeast
nórdico, -ca *adj & n* 1 ESCANDINAVO
: Scandinavian 2 : Norse
noreste → **nordeste**
noria *nf* 1 : waterwheel 2 : Ferris wheel
norirlandés[1], **-desa** *adj, mpl* **-deses**
: Northern Irish
norirlandés[2], **-desa** *n, mpl* **-deses** : person from Northern Ireland
norma *nf* 1 : rule, regulation 2 : norm,
standard
normal *adj* 1 : normal, usual 2 : standard 3 **escuela normal** : teacher-train-
ing college
normalidad *nf* : normality, normalcy
normalización *nf, pl* **-ciones** *nf* 1 REGU-
LARIZACIÓN : normalization 2 ESTAN-
DARIZACIÓN : standardization
normalizar {21} *vt* 1 REGULARIZAR : to
normalize 2 ESTANDARIZAR : to standardize — **normalizarse** *vr* : to return to
normal
normalmente *adv* GENERALMENTE : ordinarily, generally
noroeste[1] *adj* 1 : northwestern 2
: northwesterly
noroeste[2] *nm* : northwest
norte[1] *adj* : north, northern
norte[2] *nm* 1 : north 2 : north wind 3
META : aim, objective
norteamericano, -na *adj & n* 1 : North
American 2 AMERICANO, ESTADOUNI-
DENSE : American, native or inhabitant
of the United States
norteño[1], **-ña** *adj* : northern
norteño[2], **-ña** *n* : Northerner
noruego[1], **-ga** *adj & n* : Norwegian
noruego[2] *nm* : Norwegian (language)
nos *pron pl* 1 : us ⟨nos enviaron a la
frontera : they sent us to the border⟩ 2
: ourselves ⟨nos divertimos muchísimo
: we enjoyed ourselves a great deal⟩ 3
: each other, one another ⟨nos vimos
desde lejos : we saw each other from far
away⟩ 4 : to us, for us, from us ⟨nos lo
dio : he gave it to us⟩ ⟨nos lo compraron
: they bought it from us⟩
nosotros, -tras *pron pl* 1 : we ⟨nosotros
llegamos ayer : we arrived yesterday⟩ 2
: us ⟨ven con nosotros : come with us⟩
⟨a nosotros no nos afecta : it doesn't affect us⟩ ⟨ninguna de nosotras : neither
of us⟩ ⟨el de nosotros es mejor : ours is
better⟩ 3 **nosotros mismos** : ourselves
⟨lo arreglamos nosotros mismos : we
fixed it ourselves⟩

nostalgia *nf* 1 : nostalgia, longing 2
: homesickness
nostálgico, -ca *adj* 1 : nostalgic 2
: homesick
nota *nf* 1 : note, message ⟨tomar notas
: to take notes⟩ 2 : announcement
⟨nota de prensa : press release⟩ 3
: grade, mark (in school) 4 : characteristic, feature, touch 5 : note (in music)
6 : bill, check (in a restaurant)
notable *adj* 1 : notable, noteworthy 2
: outstanding
notablemente *adv* 1 : notably, markedly
2 : outstandingly
notación *nf, pl* **-ciones** : notation
notar *vt* 1 : to notice ⟨hacer notar algo
: to point out something⟩ 2 : to tell ⟨la
diferencia se nota inmediatamente : you
can tell the difference right away⟩ —
notarse *vr* 1 : to be evident, to show 2
: to feel, to seem
notaría *nf* : notary's office
notario, -ria *n* : notary, notary public
notebook *nf* : notebook (computer)
noticia *nf* 1 : news item, piece of news
⟨noticia bomba : shocking news, bomb-
shell⟩ 2 **noticias** *nfpl* : news
noticiero *or* **noticiario** *nm* : news, news
program, newscast
noticioso, -sa *adj* : news ⟨agencia noti-
ciosa : news agency⟩
notificación *nf, pl* **-ciones** : notification
notificar {72} *vt* : to notify, to inform
notoriedad *nf* 1 : knowledge 2 : fame,
notoriety
notorio, -ria *adj* 1 OBVIO : obvious, evident 2 CONOCIDO : well-known
novato[1], **-ta** *adj* : inexperienced, new
novato[2], **-ta** *n* : beginner, novice
novecientos[1], **-tas** *adj & pron* : nine hundred
novecientos[2] *nms & pl* : nine hundred
novedad *nf* 1 : newness, novelty 2 : innovation 3 : news, development 4 **sin
∼** : the same as before 5 **sin ∼** : without incident, safely
novedoso, -sa *adj* : original, novel
novel *adj* NOVATO : inexperienced, new
novela *nf* 1 : novel 2 : soap opera
novelar *vt* : to make a novel out of
novelesco, -ca *adj* 1 : fictional 2 : fantastic, fabulous
novelista *nmf* : novelist
novena *nf* : novena
noveno, -na *adj & n* : ninth ⟨el noveno
piso : the ninth floor⟩ ⟨la novena (persona) : the ninth (person)⟩ ⟨un noveno
de . . . : one ninth of . . .⟩
noventa *adj & nm* : ninety — **noventa**
pron
noventavo[1], **-va** *adj* : ninetieth
noventavo[2] *nm* : ninetieth (fraction)
noviar *vi* : to date, to go out ⟨noviar con
: to go out with⟩
noviazgo *nm* 1 : courtship, relationship
2 : engagement, betrothal
novicio, -cia *n* 1 : novice (in religion) 2
PRINCIPIANTE : novice, beginner
noviembre *nm* : November ⟨el primero
de noviembre : (on) November first⟩

novilla *nf* : heifer
novillada *nf* : bullfight featuring young bulls
novillero, -ra *n* : apprentice bullfighter
novillo *nm* : young bull
novio, -via *n* 1 : boyfriend *m*, girlfriend *f* 2 PROMETIDO : fiancé *m*, fiancée *f* 3 : bridegroom *m*, bride *f*
novocaína *nf* : novocaine
nubarrón *nm, pl* -rrones : storm cloud
nube *nf* 1 : cloud ⟨andar en las nubes : to have one's head in the clouds⟩ ⟨por las nubes : sky-high⟩ 2 : cloud (of dust), swarm (of insects, etc.) 3 : cloud ⟨computación en la nube : cloud computing⟩
nublado¹, -da *adj* 1 NUBOSO : cloudy, overcast 2 : clouded, dim
nublado² *nm* 1 : storm cloud 2 AMENAZA : menace, threat
nublar *vt* 1 : to cloud 2 OSCURECER : to obscure — nublarse *vr* : to get cloudy
nubosidad *nf* : cloudiness
nuboso, -sa *adj* NUBLADO : cloudy
nuca *nf* : nape, back of the neck
nuclear *adj* : nuclear
núcleo *nm* 1 : nucleus 2 : center, heart, core
nudillo *nm* : knuckle
nudismo *nm* : nudism
nudista *adj & nmf* : nudist
nudo *nm* 1 : knot ⟨nudo de rizo : square knot⟩ ⟨nudo corredizo : slipknot⟩ ⟨un nudo en la garganta : a lump in one's throat⟩ 2 : node 3 : junction, hub ⟨nudo de comunicaciones : communication center⟩ 4 : crux, heart (of a problem, etc.)
nudoso, -sa *adj* : knotty, gnarled
nuera *nf* : daughter-in-law
nuestro¹, -tra *adj* : our
nuestro², -tra *pron* (*with definite article*) : ours, our own ⟨el nuestro es más grande : ours is bigger⟩ ⟨es de los nuestros : it's one of ours⟩
nuevamente *adv* : again, anew
nuevas *nfpl* : tidings *pl*
nueve¹ *adj & nm* : nine ⟨tengo nueve años : I am nine years old⟩ ⟨el nueve de noviembre : (on) the ninth of November, (on) November ninth⟩
nueve² *pron* : nine ⟨somos nueve : there are nine of us⟩ ⟨son las nueve : it's nine o'clock⟩
nuevecito, -ta *adj* : brand-new
nuevo, -va *adj* 1 : new ⟨una casa nueva : a new house⟩ ⟨¿qué hay de nuevo? : what's new?⟩ 2 de ~ : again, once more 3 Nuevo Testamento : New Testament
nuez *nf, pl* nueces 1 : nut 2 : walnut 3 *Mex* : pecan 4 nuez de Adán : Adam's apple 5 nuez de Brasil : Brazil nut 6 nuez moscada : nutmeg

nulidad *nf* 1 : nullity 2 : incompetent person ⟨¡es una nulidad! : he's hopeless!⟩
nulo, -la *adj* 1 : null, null and void 2 INEPTO : useless, inept ⟨es nula para la cocina : she's hopeless at cooking⟩
numen *nm* : poetic muse, inspiration
numerable *adj* : countable
numeración *nf, pl* -ciones 1 : numbering 2 : numbers *pl*, numerals ⟨numeración romana : Roman numerals⟩
numerador *nm* : numerator
numeral *adj* : numeral
numerar *vt* : to number
numerario, -ria *adj* : long-standing, permanent ⟨profesor numerario : tenured professor⟩
numérico, -ca *adj* : numerical — numéricamente *adv*
número *nm* 1 : number ⟨número impar : odd number⟩ ⟨número primo : prime number⟩ ⟨número ordinal : ordinal number⟩ ⟨número arábigo : Arabic numeral⟩ ⟨número quebrado : fraction⟩ 2 : issue (of a publication) 3 : size ⟨¿qué número calza? : what's his shoe size?⟩ 4 : lottery ticket 5 : act, routine, number 6 sin ~ : countless
numeroso, -sa *adj* : numerous
numismática *nf* : numismatics
nunca *adv* 1 : never, ever ⟨nunca es tarde : it's never too late⟩ ⟨no trabaja casi nunca : he hardly ever works⟩ 2 nunca más : never again 3 nunca jamás : never ever
nuncio *nm* : harbinger, herald
nupcial *adj* : nuptial, wedding
nupcias *nfpl* : nuptials *pl*, wedding
nutria *nf* 1 : otter 2 : nutria
nutrición *nf, pl* -ciones : nutrition, nourishment
nutricionista *nmf* : nutritionist
nutrido, -da *adj* 1 : nourished ⟨mal nutrido : undernourished, malnourished⟩ 2 : considerable, abundant ⟨de nutrido : full of, abounding in⟩
nutriente *nm* : nutrient
nutrimento *nm* : nutriment
nutrir *vt* 1 ALIMENTAR : to feed, to nourish 2 : to foster, to provide
nutritivo, -va *adj* : nourishing, nutritious
nylon → nilón
ñ *nf* : seventeenth letter of the Spanish alphabet
ñame *nm* : yam
ñandú *nm, pl* ñandú *or* ñandúes : rhea
ñapa *nf* : extra amount ⟨de ñapa : for good measure⟩
ñato, -ta *adj* : snub-nosed
ñoñear *vi fam* : to whine
ñoñería *nf* : inanity
ñoño, -ña *adj fam* : whiny, fussy ⟨no seas tan ñoño : don't be such a wimp⟩
ñu *nm* : gnu

O

o¹ *nf* : eighteenth letter of the Spanish alphabet

o² *conj* (**u** *before words beginning with* o- *or* ho-) **1** : or ⟨¿vienes con nosotros o te quedas? : are you coming with us or staying?⟩ **2** : either ⟨o vienes con nosotros o te quedas : either you come with us or you stay⟩ **3 o sea** : that is to say, in other words

oasis *nms & pl* : oasis

obcecado, -da *adj* **1** : blinded ⟨obcecado por la ira : blinded by rage⟩ **2** : stubborn, obstinate

obcecar {72} *vt* : to blind (by emotions) — **obcecarse** *vr* : to become stubborn

obedecer {53} *vt* : to obey ⟨obedecer órdenes : to obey orders⟩ ⟨obedece a tus padres : obey your parents⟩ — *vi* **1** : to obey **2** ∼ **a** : to respond to **3** ∼ **a** : to be due to, to result from

obediencia *nf* : obedience

obediente *adj* : obedient — **obedientemente** *adv*

obelisco *nm* : obelisk

obertura *nf* : overture

obesidad *nf* : obesity

obeso, -sa *adj* : obese

óbice *nm* : obstacle, impediment

obispado *nm* DIÓCESIS : bishopric, diocese

obispo *nm* : bishop

obituario *nm* : obituary

objeción *nf, pl* **-ciones** : objection ⟨ponerle objeciones a algo : to object to something⟩

objetar *v* : to object ⟨no tengo nada que objetar : I have no objections⟩

objetividad *nf* : objectivity

objetivo¹, -va *adj* : objective — **objetivamente** *adv*

objetivo² *nm* **1** META : objective, goal, target **2** : lens

objeto *nm* **1** COSA : object, thing ⟨objetos de valor : valuables⟩ **2** OBJETIVO : objective, purpose ⟨con objeto de : in order to, with the aim of⟩ **3 objeto volador no identificado** : unidentified flying object

objetor, -tora *n* : objector ⟨objetor de conciencia : conscientious objector⟩

oblea *nf* **1** : wafer **2 hecho una oblea** *fam* : skinny as a rail

oblicuo, -cua *adj* : oblique — **oblicuamente** *adv*

obligación *nf, pl* **-ciones** **1** DEBER : obligation, duty **2** : bond

obligado, -da *adj* **1** : obliged **2** : obligatory, compulsory **3** : customary

obligar {52} *vt* : to force, to require, to oblige — **obligarse** *vr* : to commit oneself, to undertake (to do something)

obligatorio, -ria *adj* : mandatory, required, compulsory

obliterar *vt* : to obliterate, to destroy — **obliteración** *nf*

oblongo, -ga *adj* : oblong

obnubilación *nf, pl* **-ciones** : bewilderment, confusion

obnubilar *vt* : to daze, to bewilder

oboe¹ *nm* : oboe

oboe² *nmf* : oboist

obra *nf* **1** : work ⟨obra de arte : work of art⟩ ⟨obra de teatro : play⟩ ⟨obra de consulta : reference work⟩ **2** : deed ⟨una buena obra : a good deed⟩ **3** : construction work ⟨en obra(s) : under construction⟩ ⟨obras viales : roadwork⟩ **4** : construction site, building site **5 obra maestra** : masterpiece **6 obras públicas** : public works **7 poner en obra** : to put into effect **8 por obra de** : thanks to, because of

obrar *vt* : to work, to produce ⟨obrar milagros : to work miracles⟩ — *vi* **1** : to act, to behave ⟨obrar con cautela : to act with caution⟩ **2 obrar en poder de** : to be in possession of

obrero¹, -ra *adj* : working ⟨la clase obrera : the working class⟩

obrero², -ra *n* : worker, laborer

obscenidad *nf* : obscenity

obsceno, -na *adj* : obscene

obscurecer, obscuridad, obscuro → **oscurecer, oscuridad, oscuro**

obsequiar *vt* REGALAR : to give, to present ⟨lo obsequiaron con una placa : they presented him with a plaque⟩

obsequio *nm* REGALO : gift, present

obsequiosidad *nf* : attentiveness, deference

obsequioso, -sa *adj* : obliging, attentive

observable *adj* : observable

observación *nf, pl* **-ciones** **1** : observation, watching ⟨bajo/en observación : under observation⟩ **2** : remark, comment

observador¹, -dora *adj* : observant

observador², -dora *n* : observer, watcher

observancia *nf* : observance

observante *adj* : observant ⟨los judíos observantes : observant Jews⟩

observar *vt* **1** : to observe, to watch ⟨estábamos observando a los niños : we were watching the children⟩ **2** NOTAR : to notice **3** ACATAR : to obey, to abide by **4** COMENTAR : to remark, to comment

observatorio *nm* : observatory

obsesión *nf, pl* **-siones** : obsession

obsesionar *vt* : to obsess, to preoccupy excessively — **obsesionarse** *vr*

obsesivo, -va *adj* : obsessive

obseso, -sa *adj* : obsessed

obsolescencia *nf* DESUSO : obsolescence — **obsolescente** *adj*

obsoleto, -ta *adj* DESUSADO : obsolete

obstaculizar {21} *vt* IMPEDIR : to obstruct, to hinder

obstáculo *nm* IMPEDIMENTO : obstacle

obstante¹ *conj* **no obstante** : nevertheless, however

obstante² *prep* **no obstante** : in spite of, despite ⟨mantuvo su inocencia no obstante la evidencia : he maintained his innocence in spite of the evidence⟩

obstar *v impers* ~ **a** *or* ~ **para** : to hinder, to prevent ⟨eso no obsta para que me vaya : that doesn't prevent me from leaving⟩

obstetra *nmf* TOCÓLOGO : obstetrician

obstetricia *nf* : obstetrics

obstétrico, -ca *adj* : obstetric, obstetrical

obstinación *nf, pl* **-ciones** **1** TERQUEDAD : obstinacy, stubbornness **2** : perseverance, tenacity

obstinado, -da *adj* **1** TERCO : obstinate, stubborn **2** : persistent — **obstinadamente** *adv*

obstinarse *vr* EMPECINARSE : to be obstinate, to be stubborn

obstrucción *nf, pl* **-ciones** : obstruction, blockage

obstruccionismo *nm* : filibustering (en política)

obstruccionista *adj* : filibustering (en política)

obstructor, -tora *adj* : obstructive

obstruir {41} *vt* BLOQUEAR : to obstruct, to block, to clog — **obstruirse** *vr*

obtención *nf, pl* **-ciones** : obtaining, procurement

obtener {80} *vt* : to obtain, to secure, to get — **obtenible** *adj*

obturador *nm* : shutter (of a camera)

obturar *vt* : to block

obtuso, -sa *adj* : obtuse

obtuvo, etc. → **obtener**

obús *nm, pl* **obuses** **1** : mortar (weapon) **2** : mortar shell

obviar *vt* : to get around (a difficulty), to avoid

obvio, -via *adj* : obvious — **obviamente** *adv*

oca *nf* : goose

ocasión *nf, pl* **-siones** **1** : occasion, time ⟨en alguna ocasión : occasionally, sometimes⟩ **2** : opportunity, chance **3** : bargain **4 de** ~ : secondhand **5 aviso de ocasión** *Mex* : classified ad

ocasional *adj* **1** : occasional **2** : chance, fortuitous

ocasionalmente *adv* **1** : occasionally **2** : by chance

ocasionar *vt* CAUSAR : to cause, to occasion

ocaso *nm* **1** ANOCHECER : sunset, sundown **2** DECADENCIA : decline, fall

occidental *adj* : western

occidente *nm* **1** OESTE, PONIENTE : west **2 el Occidente** : the West

oceánico, -ca *adj* : oceanic

océano *nm* : ocean

oceanografía *nf* : oceanography — **oceanográfico, -ca** *adj*

ocelote *nm* : ocelot

ochenta *adj & nm* : eighty — **ochenta** *pron*

ochentavo¹, -va *adj* : eightieth

ochentavo² *nm* : eightieth (fraction)

ocho¹ *adj & nm* : eight ⟨tiene ocho años : he's eight (years old)⟩ ⟨el ocho de mayo : (on) the eighth of May, (on) May eighth⟩

ocho² *pron* : eight ⟨somos ocho : there are eight of us⟩ ⟨son las ocho : it's eight o'clock⟩

ochocientos¹, -tas *adj & pron* : eight hundred

ochocientos² *nms & pl* : eight hundred

ocio *nm* **1** : free time, leisure **2** : idleness

ociosamente *adv* : idly

ociosidad *nf* : idleness, inactivity

ocioso, -sa *adj* **1** INACTIVO : idle, inactive **2** INÚTIL : pointless, useless

ocre *nm* : ocher

octágono *nm* : octagon — **octagonal** *adj*

octava *nf* : octave

octavilla *nf* : pamphlet

octavo, -va *adj & n* : eighth ⟨el octavo grado : the eighth grade⟩ ⟨la octava (persona) : the eighth (person)⟩ ⟨un octavo de . . . : one eighth of . . .⟩

octeto *nm* : byte

octogésimo¹, -ma *adj* : eightieth, eighty- (in a series)

octogésimo², -ma *n* : eightieth, eighty- (in a series)

octubre *nm* : October ⟨el primero de octubre : (on) October first⟩

ocular *adj* **1** : ocular, eye ⟨músculos oculares : eye muscles⟩ **2 testigo ocular** : eyewitness

oculista *nmf* : oculist, ophthalmologist

ocultación *nf, pl* **-ciones** : concealment

ocultar *vt* ESCONDER : to conceal, to hide — **ocultarse** *vr*

oculto, -ta *adj* **1** ESCONDIDO : hidden, concealed **2** : occult

ocupación *nf, pl* **-ciones** **1** : occupation, activity **2** : occupancy **3** EMPLEO : employment, job

ocupacional *adj* : occupational, job-related

ocupado, -da *adj* **1** : busy **2** : taken ⟨este asiento está ocupado : this seat is taken⟩ **3** : occupied ⟨territorios ocupados : occupied territories⟩ **4 señal de ocupado** : busy signal

ocupante *nmf* : occupant

ocupar *vt* **1** : to occupy, to take possession of **2** : to hold (a position) **3** : to employ, to keep busy **4** : to fill (space, time) **5** : to inhabit (a dwelling) **6** : to bother, to concern — **ocuparse** *vr* ~ **de** **1** : to be concerned with **2** : to take care of

ocurrencia *nf* **1** : occurrence, event **2** : witticism **3** : bright idea

ocurrente *adj* **1** : witty **2** : clever, sharp

ocurrir *vi* : to occur, to happen — **ocurrirse** *vr* ~ **a** : to occur to, to strike ⟨se me ocurrió una mejor idea : a better idea occurred to me⟩

oda *nf* : ode

odiar *vt* ABOMINAR, ABORRECER : to hate

odio *nm* : hate, hatred

odioso, -sa *adj* ABOMINABLE, ABORRECIBLE : hateful, detestable

odisea *nf* : odyssey

odómetro *nm* : odometer

odontología *nf* : dentistry, dental surgery

odontólogo, -ga *n* : dentist, dental surgeon

odre *nm* : wineskin

oeste[1] *adj* **1** : west, western ⟨la región oeste : the western region⟩ **2** : westerly

oeste[2] *nm* **1** : west, West **2** : west wind

ofender *vt* AGRAVIAR : to offend, to insult — *vi* : to offend, to be insulting — **ofenderse** *vr* : to take offense

ofensa *nf* : offense, insult

ofensiva *nf* : offensive ⟨pasar a la ofensiva : to go on the offensive⟩

ofensivo, -va *adj* : offensive, insulting — **ofensivamente** *adv*

ofensor, -sora *n* : offender

oferente *nmf* **1** : supplier **2** FUENTE : source ⟨un oferente no identificado : an unidentified source⟩

oferta *nf* **1** : offer **2** : sale, bargain ⟨las camisas están en oferta : the shirts are on sale⟩ **3 oferta y demanda** : supply and demand

ofertar *vt* OFRECER : to offer

oficial[1] *adj* : official — **oficialmente** *adv*

oficial[2] *nmf* **1** : officer, police officer, commissioned officer (in the military) **2** : skilled worker

oficializar {21} *vt* : to make official

oficiante *nmf* : celebrant

oficiar *vt* **1** : to inform officially **2** : to officiate at, to celebrate (Mass) — *vi* ~ **de** : to act as

oficina *nf* : office

oficinista *nmf* : office worker

oficio *nm* **1** : trade, profession ⟨es electricista de oficio : he's an electrician by trade⟩ **2** : function, role **3** : official communication **4** : experience ⟨tener oficio : to be experienced⟩ **5** : religious ceremony

oficioso, -sa *adj* **1** EXTRAOFICIAL : unofficial **2** : officious — **oficiosamente** *adv*

ofimática *nf* : office automation, office computing

ofrecer {53} *vt* **1** : to offer **2** : to provide, to give **3** : to present (an appearance, etc.) — **ofrecerse** *vr* **1** : to offer oneself, to volunteer **2** : to open up, to present itself

ofrecimiento *nm* : offer, offering

ofrenda *nf* : offering

oftalmología *nf* : ophthalmology

oftalmólogo, -ga *n* : ophthalmologist

ofuscación *nf, pl* **-ciones** : blindness, confusion

ofuscar {72} *vt* **1** : to blind, to dazzle **2** CONFUNDIR : to bewilder, to confuse — **ofuscarse** *vr* ~ **con** : to be blinded by

ogro *nm* : ogre

oh *interj* : oh ⟨¡oh, no! : oh no!⟩ ⟨oh, ¡qué raro! : oh, how odd!⟩

ohm *nm, pl* **ohms** : ohm

ohmio → **ohm**

oídas *nfpl* **de** ~ : by hearsay

oído *nm* **1** : ear ⟨oído interno : inner ear⟩ **2** : hearing ⟨duro de oído : hard of hearing⟩ **3 tocar de oído** : to play by ear

oiga, etc. → **oír**

oír {50} *vi* : to hear — *vt* **1** : to hear **2** ESCUCHAR : to listen to **3** : to pay atten-

tion to, to heed **4 ¡oye!** *or* **¡oiga!** : listen!, excuse me!, look here!

ojal *nm* : buttonhole

ojalá *interj* **1** : I hope so!, if only!, God willing! **2** : I hope, I wish, hopefully ⟨¡ojalá que le vaya bien! : I hope things go well for her!⟩ ⟨¡ojalá no llueva! : hopefully it won't rain!⟩

ojeada *nf* : glimpse, glance ⟨echar una ojeada : to have a quick look⟩

ojear *vt* : to eye, to have a look at

ojeras *nfpl* : bags/circles under one's eyes

ojeriza *nf fam* : grudge

ojeroso, -sa *adj* : with bags/circles under one's eyes

ojete *nm* : eyelet

ojiva *nf* : warhead

ojo *nm* **1** : eye ⟨un hombre con/de ojos verdes : a man with green eyes⟩ ⟨ojos negros : dark eyes⟩ ⟨la miré a los ojos : I looked her in the eye⟩ ⟨lo vi con mis propios ojos : I saw it with my own two eyes⟩ ⟨apareció ante nuestros ojos : it appeared before our very eyes⟩ ⟨con los ojos abiertos : with one's eyes open⟩ **2** : judgment, sharpness ⟨tener buen ojo para : to be a good judge of, to have a good eye for⟩ **3** : hole (in cheese), eye (in a needle), center (of a storm) ⟨ojo de cerradura : keyhole⟩ **4** : span (of a bridge) **5 a ojos vistas** : obviously, visibly **6 andar con ojo** : to be careful **7 costar un ojo de la cara** : to cost an arm and a leg **8 en un abrir y cerrar de ojos** : in the blink of an eye **9 ojo de agua** *Mex* : spring, source **10 ¡ojo!** : look out!, pay attention! **11 tener ojos de águila** : to have eyes like a hawk

okupa *nf fam* : squatter

ola *nf* **1** : wave **2 ola de calor** : heat wave

oleada *nf* : swell, wave ⟨una oleada de protestas : a wave of protests⟩

oleaje *nm* : waves *pl*, surf

óleo *nm* **1** : oil **2** : oil painting

oleoducto *nm* : oil pipeline

oleoso, -sa *adj* : oily

oler {51} *vt* **1** : to smell **2** INQUIRIR : to pry into, to investigate **3** AVERIGUAR : to smell out, to uncover — *vi* **1** : to smell ⟨huele mal : it smells bad⟩ ⟨todo esto huele mal : there's something fishy about all of this⟩ **2** ~ **a** : to smell like, to smell of ⟨huele a pino : it smells like pine⟩ — **olerse** *vr* : to have a hunch, to suspect

olfatear *vt* **1** : to sniff **2** : to sense, to sniff out

olfativo, -va *adj* : olfactory

olfato *nm* **1** : sense of smell **2** : nose, instinct

oligarquía *nf* : oligarchy

olimpiada *or* **olimpíada** *nf* **1** : Olympiad **2** *or* **olympiadas** *nfpl* : Olympics *pl*

olímpico, -ca *adj* : Olympic

olisquear *vt* : to sniff at

oliva *nf* ACEITUNA : olive ⟨aceite de oliva : olive oil⟩

olivar *nm* : olive grove

olivo *nm* : olive tree

olla *nf* **1** : pot ⟨olla de presión : pressure cooker⟩ ⟨olla de cocción lenta, olla de cocimiento lento : slow cooker⟩ **2 olla podrida** : Spanish stew **3 olla vaporera** → **vaporera**

olmeca *adj & nmf* : Olmec

olmo *nm* : elm

olor *nm* : smell, odor

oloroso, -sa *adj* : scented, fragrant

olote *nm Mex* : cob, corncob

olvidadizo, -za *adj* : forgetful, absent-minded

olvidar *vt* **1** : to forget, to forget about ⟨olvida lo que pasó : forget about what happened⟩ **2** : to leave behind ⟨olvidé mi chequera en la casa : I left my checkbook at home⟩ — **olvidarse** *vr* : to forget ⟨se me olvidó mi cuaderno : I forgot my notebook⟩ ⟨se le olvidó llamarme : he forgot to call me⟩

olvido *nm* **1** : forgetfulness **2** : oblivion **3** DESCUIDO : oversight

omaní *adj & nmf* : Omani

ombligo *nm* : navel, belly button

ombudsman *nmfs & pl* : ombudsman

omelette *nmf* : omelet

ominoso, -sa *adj* : ominous — **ominosamente** *adv*

omisión *nf, pl* **-siones** : omission, neglect

omiso, -sa *adj* **1** NEGLIGENTE : neglectful **2 hacer caso omiso de** → **caso**

omitir *vt* **1** : to omit, to leave out **2** : to fail to ⟨omitió dar su nombre : he failed to give his name⟩

ómnibus *n, pl* **-bus** *or* **-buses** : bus, coach

omnipotencia *nf* : omnipotence

omnipotente *adj* TODOPODEROSO : omnipotent, almighty

omnipresencia *nf* : omnipresence

omnipresente *adj* : ubiquitous, omnipresent

omnisciente *adj* : omniscient — **omnisciencia** *nf*

omnívoro, -ra *adj* : omnivorous

omóplato *or* **omoplato** *nm* : shoulder blade

once¹ *adj & nm* : eleven ⟨tiene once años : she's eleven (years old)⟩ ⟨el once de noviembre : (on) the eleventh of November, (on) November eleventh⟩

once² *pron* : eleven ⟨son las once : it's eleven o'clock⟩ ⟨somos once : there are eleven of us⟩

onceavo¹, -va *adj* : eleventh

onceavo² *nm* : eleventh (fraction)

onda *nf* **1** : wave, ripple, undulation ⟨onda sonora : sound wave⟩ **2** : wave (in hair) **3** : scallop (on clothing) **4** *fam* : wavelength, understanding ⟨agarrar la onda : to get the point⟩ ⟨en la onda : on the ball, with it⟩ **5 ¿qué onda?** *fam* : what's happening?, what's up?

ondear *vi* : to ripple, to undulate, to flutter

ondulación *nf, pl* **-ciones** : undulation

ondulado, -da *adj* **1** : wavy ⟨pelo ondulado : wavy hair⟩ **2** : undulating

ondulante *adj* : undulating

ondular *vt* : to wave (hair) — *vi* : to undulate, to ripple

oneroso, -sa *adj* GRAVOSO : onerous, burdensome

ónix *nm* : onyx

online [on'lain] *adj & adv* : online

onza *nf* : ounce

opacar {72} *vt* **1** : to make opaque or dull **2** : to outshine, to overshadow

opacidad *nf* **1** : opacity **2** : dullness

opaco, -ca *adj* **1** : opaque **2** : dull

ópalo *nm* : opal

opción *nf, pl* **opciones** **1** ALTERNATIVA : option, choice **2** : right, chance ⟨tener opción a : to be eligible for⟩

opcional *adj* : optional — **opcionalmente** *adv*

ópera *nf* : opera

operación *nf, pl* **-ciones** **1** : operation **2** : transaction, deal

operacional *adj* : operational

operador, -dora *n* **1** : operator **2** : projectionist, camera operator

operante *adj* : operating, working

operar *vt* **1** : to produce, to bring about **2** INTERVENIR : to operate on ⟨me operaron : I had an operation, I had surgery⟩ ⟨me operaron de la rodilla : I had surgery on my knee, I had knee surgery⟩ ⟨la operaron de cáncer : she had cancer surgery⟩ ⟨fue operado de un tumor : he had surgery to remove a tumor⟩ **3** *Mex* : to operate, to run (a machine) — *vi* **1** : to operate, to function **2** : to deal, to do business — **operarse** *vr* **1** : to come about, to take place **2** : to have an operation, to have surgery

operario, -ria *n* : laborer, worker

operático, -ca → **operístico**

operativo¹, -va *adj* **1** : operating ⟨capacidad operativa : operating capacity⟩ **2** : operative

operativo² *nm* : operation ⟨operativo militar : military operation⟩

opereta *nf* : operetta

operístico, -ca *adj* : operatic

opiato *nm* : opiate

opinable *adj* : arguable

opinar *vi* **1** : to think, to have an opinion **2** : to express an opinion **3 opinar bien de** : to think highly of — *vt* : to think ⟨opinamos lo mismo : we're of the same opinion, we're in agreement⟩

opinión *nf, pl* **-niones** : opinion, belief

opio *nm* : opium

oponente *nmf* : opponent

oponer {60} *vt* **1** CONTRAPONER : to oppose, to place against **2 oponer resistencia** : to resist, to put up a fight — **oponerse** *vr* ~ **a** : to object to, to be against

oporto *nm* : port (wine)

oportunamente *adv* **1** : at the right time, opportunely **2** : appropriately

oportunidad *nf* : opportunity, chance

oportunismo *nm* : opportunism

oportunista¹ *adj* : opportunistic

oportunista² *nmf* : opportunist

oportuno, -na *adj* **1** : opportune, timely **2** : suitable, appropriate

oposición *nf, pl* **-ciones** : opposition

opositor, -tora *n* ADVERSARIO : opponent

oposum *nm* ZARIGÜEYA : opossum
opresión *nf, pl* **-siones** **1** : oppression **2**
  opresión de pecho : tightness in the
  chest
opresivo, -va *adj* : oppressive
opresor¹, -sora *adj* : oppressive
opresor², -sora *n* : oppressor
oprimir *vt* **1** : to oppress **2** : to press, to
  squeeze ⟨oprima el botón : push the but-
  ton⟩
oprobio *nm* : opprobrium, shame
optar *vi* **1** ~ **por** : to opt for, to choose
  2 ~ **a** : to aspire to, to apply for ⟨dos
  candidatos optan a la presidencia : two
  candidates are running for president⟩
optativo, -va *adj* FACULTATIVO : optional
óptica *nf* **1** : optics **2** : optician's shop
  3 : viewpoint
óptico¹, -ca *adj* : optical, optic
óptico², -ca *n* : optician
optimismo *nm* : optimism
optimista¹ *adj* : optimistic
optimista² *nmf* : optimist
óptimo, -ma *adj* : optimum, optimal
optometría *nf* : optometry — **optometrista** *nmf*
opuesto¹ *pp* → **oponer**
opuesto² *adj* **1** : opposite, contrary **2**
  : opposed
opulencia *nf* : opulence — **opulento, -ta**
  adj
opus *nm* : opus
opuso, etc. → **oponer**
ora *conj* : now ⟨los matices eran variados,
  ora verdes, ora ocres : the hues were varied, now green, now ocher⟩
oración *nf, pl* **-ciones** **1** DISCURSO : oration, speech **2** PLEGARIA : prayer **3**
  FRASE : sentence, clause
oráculo *nm* : oracle
orador, -dora *n* : speaker, orator
oral *adj* : oral — **oralmente** *adv*
órale *interj Mex fam* **1** : sure!, OK! ⟨¿los
  dos por cinco pesos? ¡órale! : both for
  five pesos? you've got a deal!⟩ **2** : come
  on! ⟨¡órale, vámonos! : come on, let's
  go!⟩
orangután *nm, pl* **-tanes** : orangutan
orar *vi* REZAR : to pray
oratoria *nf* : oratory
oratorio *nm* **1** CAPILLA : oratory, chapel
  2 : oratorio
orbe *nm* **1** : orb, sphere **2** GLOBO
  : globe, world
órbita *nf* **1** : orbit **2** : eye socket **3**
  ÁMBITO : sphere, field
orbital *adj* : orbital
orbitar *v* : to orbit
orca *nf* : orca, killer whale
orden¹ *nm, pl* **órdenes** **1** : order ⟨todo
  está en orden : everything's in order⟩ ⟨por
  orden cronológico : in chronological or-
  der⟩ **2 orden del día** : agenda (at a meeting) **3 orden público** : law and order
orden² *nf, pl* **órdenes** **1** : order ⟨una orden religiosa : a religious order⟩ ⟨una
  orden de tacos : an order of tacos⟩ **2
  orden de compra** : purchase order **3
  estar a la orden del día** : to be the order
  of the day, to be prevalent

ordenación *nf, pl* **-ciones** **1** : ordination
  2 : ordering, organizing
ordenadamente *adv* : in an orderly fashion, neatly
ordenado, -da *adj* : orderly, neat
ordenador *nm Spain* : computer
ordenamiento *nm* **1** : ordering, organizing **2** : code (of laws)
ordenanza¹ *nf* REGLAMENTO : ordinance,
  regulation
ordenanza² *nm* : orderly (in the armed
  forces)
ordenar *vt* **1** MANDAR : to order, to command **2** ARREGLAR : to put in order, to
  arrange **3** : to ordain (a priest) — **orde-
  narse** *vr* : to be ordained
ordeñar *vt* : to milk
ordeño *nm* : milking
ordinal *nm* : ordinal (number)
ordinariamente *adv* **1** : usually **2**
  : coarsely
ordinariez *nf* : coarseness, vulgarity
ordinario, -ria *adj* **1** : ordinary **2** : coarse,
  common, vulgar **3 de** ~ : usually
orear *vt* : to air
orégano *nm* : oregano
oreja *nf* : ear
orfanato *nm* : orphanage
orfanatorio *nm Mex* : orphanage
orfandad *nf* : state of being an orphan
orfebre *nmf* : goldsmith, silversmith
orfebrería *nf* : articles of gold or silver
orfelinato *nm* : orphanage
orgánico, -ca *adj* : organic —
  orgánicamente *adv*
organigrama *nm* : organization chart,
  flow chart
organismo *nm* **1** : organism **2** : agency,
  organization
organista *nmf* : organist
organización *nf, pl* **-ciones** : organization
organizador¹, -dora *adj* : organizing
organizador², -dora *n* : organizer ⟨orga-
  nizador de bodas : wedding planner⟩
organizar {21} *vt* : to organize, to arrange
  — **organizarse** *vr* : to get organized
organizativo, -va *adj* : organizational
órgano *nm* : organ
orgasmo *nm* : orgasm
orgía *nf* : orgy
orgullo *nm* : pride
orgulloso, -sa *adj* : proud — **orgullosa-
  mente** *adv*
orientación *nf, pl* **-ciones** **1** : orientation
  2 DIRECCIÓN : direction, course **3** GUÍA
  : guidance, direction
oriental¹ *adj* **1** : eastern **2** *now sometimes offensive when used of people* : oriental *now usu offensive when used of
  people* **3** *Arg, Uru* : Uruguayan
oriental² *nmf* **1** : Easterner **2** *dated now
  sometimes offensive* : Oriental *dated, now
  usu offensive* **3** *Arg, Uru* : Uruguayan
orientar *vt* **1** : to orient, to position **2** : to
  guide, to direct — **orientarse** *vr* **1** : to
  orient oneself, to get one's bearings **2** ~
  hacia : to turn towards, to lean towards
oriente *nm* **1** : east, East **2 el Oriente**
  : the Orient

orífice *nmf* : goldsmith
orificio *nm* : orifice, opening
origen *nm, pl* **orígenes 1** : origin **2** : lineage, birth **3 dar origen a** : to give rise to **4 en su origen** : originally
original *adj & nm* : original — **originalmente** *adv*
originalidad *nf* : originality
originar *vt* : to originate, to give rise to — **originarse** *vr* : to originate, to begin
originario, -ria *adj* ~ **de** : native of
originariamente *adv* : originally
orilla *nf* **1** BORDE : border, edge **2** : bank (of a river) **3** : shore
orillar *vt* **1** : to skirt, to go around **2** : to trim, to edge (cloth) **3** : to settle, to wind up **4** *Mex* : to pull over (a vehicle)
orín *nm* **1** HERRUMBRE : rust **2 orines** *nmpl* : urine
orina *nf* : urine
orinación *nf* : urination
orinal *nm* : urinal (vessel)
orinar *vi* : to urinate — **orinarse** *vr* : to wet oneself
oriol *nm* OROPÉNDOLA : oriole
oriundo, -da *adj* ~ **de** : native of
orla *nf* : border, edging
orlar *vt* : to edge, to trim
ornamentación *nf, pl* **-ciones** : ornamentation
ornamental *adj* : ornamental
ornamentar *vt* ADORNAR : to ornament, to adorn
ornamento *nm* : ornament, adornment
ornar *vt* : to adorn, to decorate
ornitología *nf* : ornithology
ornitólogo, -ga *n* : ornithologist
ornitorrinco *nm* : platypus
oro *nm* **1** : gold **2 oros** *nmpl* : gold coins (in the Spanish deck of cards)
orondo, -da *adj* **1** : rounded, potbellied (of a container) **2** *fam* : smug, self-satisfied
oropel *nm* : glitz, glitter, tinsel
oropéndola *nf* : oriole
orquesta *nf* : orchestra ⟨orquesta sinfónica : symphony (orchestra)⟩ — **orquestal** *adj*
orquestar *vt* : to orchestrate — **orquestación** *nf*
orquídea *nf* : orchid
ortiga *nf* : nettle
ortodoncia *nf* : orthodontics
ortodoncista *nmf* : orthodontist
ortodoxia *nf* : orthodoxy
ortodoxo, -xa *adj* : orthodox
ortografía *nf* : orthography, spelling
ortográfico, -ca *adj* : orthographic, spelling
ortopedia *nf* : orthopedics
ortopédico, -ca *adj* : orthopedic
ortopedista *nmf* : orthopedist
oruga *nf* **1** : caterpillar **2** : track (of a tank, etc.)
orzuelo *nm* : sty, stye (in the eye)
os *pron pl objective form of* VOSOTROS **1** *Spain* : you, to you ⟨os veo pronto : I'll see you soon⟩ **2** : yourselves, to yourselves **3** : each other, to each other
osa *nf* → **oso**

osadía *nf* **1** VALOR : boldness, daring **2** AUDACIA : audacity, nerve
osado, -da *adj* **1** : bold, daring **2** : audacious, impudent — **osadamente** *adv*
osamenta *nf* : skeletal remains *pl*, bones *pl*
osar *vi* : to dare
oscilación *nf, pl* **-ciones 1** : oscillation **2** : fluctuation **3** : vacillation, wavering
oscilar *vi* **1** BALANCEARSE : to swing, to sway, to oscillate **2** FLUCTUAR : to fluctuate **3** : to vacillate, to waver
oscuramente *adv* : obscurely
oscurecer {53} *vt* **1** : to darken **2** : to obscure, to confuse, to cloud **3 al oscurecer** : at dusk, at nightfall — *v impers* : to grow dark, to get dark — **oscurecerse** *vr* : to darken, to dim
oscuridad *nf* **1** : darkness **2** : obscurity
oscuro, -ra *adj* **1** : dark **2** : obscure **3 a oscuras** : in the dark, in darkness
óseo, ósea *adj* : skeletal, bony
ósmosis *or* **osmosis** *nf* : osmosis
oso, osa *n* **1** : bear **2 Osa Mayor** : Big Dipper **3 Osa Menor** : Little Dipper **4 oso blanco** : polar bear **5 oso hormiguero** : anteater **6 oso de peluche** : teddy bear
ostensible *adj* : ostensible, apparent — **ostensiblemente** *adv*
ostentación *nf, pl* **-ciones** : ostentation, display
ostentar *vt* **1** : to display, to flaunt **2** POSEER : to have, to hold ⟨ostenta el récord mundial : he holds the world record⟩
ostentoso, -sa *adj* : ostentatious, showy — **ostentosamente** *adv*
osteópata *nmf* : osteopath
osteopatía *n* : osteopathy
osteoporosis *nf* : osteoporosis
ostión *nm, pl* **ostiones 1** *Mex* : oyster **2** *Chile* : scallop
ostra *nf* : oyster
ostracismo *nm* : ostracism
otear *vt* : to scan, to survey, to look over
otero *nm* : knoll, hillock
otitis *nf* : otitis, inflammation of the ear
otomana *nf* : ottoman (furniture)
otomano, -na *adj & n* : Ottoman
otoñal *adj* : autumn, autumnal
otoño *nm* : autumn, fall
otorgamiento *nm* : granting, awarding
otorgar {52} *vt* **1** : to grant, to award **2** : to draw up, to frame (a legal document)
otorrino, -na *n* : ear, nose, and throat doctor
otro¹, otra *adj* **1** : other **2** : another ⟨en otro juego, ellos ganaron : in another game, they won⟩ **3 otra vez** : again **4 de otra manera** : otherwise **5 otra parte** : elsewhere **6 en otro tiempo** : once, formerly
otro², otra *pron* **1** : another one ⟨dame otro : give me another⟩ ⟨¡otra! : encore!⟩ **2** : other one ⟨el uno o el otro : one or the other⟩ **3 los otros, las otras** : the others, the rest ⟨me dio una y se quedó con las otras : he gave me one and kept the rest⟩

ovación *nf, pl* **-ciones** : ovation
ovacionar *vt* : to cheer, to applaud
oval → ovalado
ovalado, -da *adj* : oval
óvalo *nm* : oval
ovárico, -ca *adj* : ovarian
ovario *nm* : ovary
oveja *nf* 1 : sheep, ewe 2 **oveja negra** : black sheep
overol *nm* : overalls *pl*
ovillar *vt* : to roll into a ball
ovillo *nm* 1 : ball (of yarn) 2 : tangle
ovni *or* OVNI *nm* (objeto volador no identificado) : UFO
ovoide *adj* : ovoid, ovoidal
ovulación *nf, pl* **-ciones** : ovulation
ovular *vi* : to ovulate

óvulo *nm* : ovum
oxidación *nf, pl* **-ciones** 1 : oxidation 2 : rusting
oxidado, -da *adj* : rusty
oxidar *vt* 1 : to cause to rust 2 : to oxidize — **oxidarse** *vr* : to rust, to become rusty
óxido *nm* 1 HERRUMBRE, ORÍN : rust 2 : oxide
oxigenar *vt* 1 : to oxygenate 2 : to bleach (hair)
oxígeno *nm* : oxygen
oxiuro *nm* : pinworm
oye, etc. → oír
oyente *nmf* 1 : listener 2 : auditor, auditing student
ozono *nm* : ozone

P

p *nf* : nineteenth letter of the Spanish alphabet
pabellón *nm, pl* **-llones** 1 : pavilion (at a fair, etc.) 2 GLORIETA : gazebo, pavilion 3 : building (of a hospital, etc.) 4 : flag (of a vessel)
pabilo *nm* MECHA : wick
paca *nf* FARDO : bale
pacana *nf* : pecan
pacer {48} *v* : to graze, to pasture
paces → paz
pachanga *nf fam* : party, bash
paciencia *nf* : patience ⟨tener paciencia : to be patient⟩ ⟨perder la paciencia : to lose (one's) patience⟩
paciente *adj & nmf* : patient — **pacientemente** *adv*
pacíficamente *adv* : peacefully, peaceably
pacificar {72} *vt* : to pacify, to calm — **pacificarse** *vr* : to calm down, to abate — **pacificación** *nf*
pacífico, -ca *adj* : peaceful, pacific
pacifismo *nm* : pacifism
pacifista *adj & nmf* : pacifist
pacotilla *nf* de ∼ : shoddy, trashy
pactar *vt* : to agree on (terms, etc.) — *vi* : to come to an agreement
pacto *nm* CONVENIO : pact, agreement
paddock ['padok] *nm* : paddock
padecer {53} *vt* : to suffer (hardship, etc.), to suffer from (an illness) — *vi* 1 ADOLECER : to suffer 2 ∼ **de** : to suffer from
padecimiento *nm* 1 : suffering 2 : ailment, condition
padrastro *nm* 1 : stepfather 2 : hangnail
padre¹ *adj Mex fam* : fantastic, great
padre² *nm* 1 : father 2 : Father (title of a priest) 3 **padres** *nmpl* : parents
padrenuestro *nm* : Lord's Prayer
padrino *nm* 1 : godfather 2 : father of the bride 3 : sponsor, patron 4 **padrinos** *nmpl* : godparents

padrón *nm, pl* **padrones** : register, roll ⟨padrón municipal : city register⟩ ⟨padrón electoral : electoral/voter roll⟩
paella *nf* : paella
paga *nf* 1 : payment 2 : pay, wages *pl* 3 : allowance (given to a child)
pagadero, -ra *adj* : payable
pagado, -da *adj* 1 : paid 2 **pagado de sí mismo** : self-satisfied, smug
pagador, -dora *n* : payer
paganismo *nm* : paganism
pagano, -na *adj & n* : pagan
pagar {52} *vt* 1 : to pay (a bill), to pay for (a purchase), to pay off (a debt) 2 : to pay for (a crime, etc.) 3 : to repay (a favor) — *vi* : to pay
pagaré *nm* VALE : promissory note, IOU
página *nf* 1 : page ⟨la página seis : page six⟩ 2 **página de inicio** : home page 3 **página web** : web page
pago *nm* 1 : payment 2 **en pago de** : in return for 3 **pago al contado** : cash payment 4 **pago anticipado** : advance payment 5 **pago inicial** : down payment
pagoda *nf* : pagoda
pague, etc. → pagar
paila *nf* 1 : large shallow dish or pan 2 *Hond* : cargo area (of a vehicle)
país *nm* 1 NACIÓN : country, nation 2 REGIÓN : region, territory
paisaje *nm* : scenery, landscape
paisajismo *nm* : landscaping
paisajista *nmf* : landscaper
paisano, -na *n* 1 COMPATRIOTA : compatriot, fellow countryman 2 **de** ∼ : in plain/civilian clothes ⟨un policía de paisano : a plainclothes policeman⟩
paja *nf* 1 : straw 2 *fam* : trash, tripe
pajar *nm* : hayloft, haystack
pajarera *nf* : aviary
pajarita *nf Spain* : bow tie
pájaro *nm* : bird ⟨pájaro cantor : songbird⟩ ⟨pájaro bobo : penguin⟩ ⟨pájaro carpintero : woodpecker⟩

paje *nm* : page (person)
pajita *or* **pajilla** *nf* : (drinking) straw
pajote *nm* : straw, mulch
pakistaní *adj & nmf, pl* **-níes** : Pakistani
pala *nf* **1** : shovel, spade **2** : blade (of an oar or a rotor) **3** : paddle, racket **4** : spatula (for serving food)
palabra *nf* **1** VOCABLO : word ⟨en otras palabras : in other words⟩ ⟨no dijo ni una palabra : she didn't say a word⟩ **2** PROMESA : word, promise ⟨un hombre de palabra : a man of his word⟩ ⟨cumplió (con) su palabra : she kept her word⟩ ⟨le di mi palabra : I gave him my word⟩ **3** HABLA : speech ⟨acuerdo de palabra : verbal agreement⟩ **4** : right to speak ⟨tener/tomar la palabra : to have/take the floor⟩ ⟨pidió la palabra : he asked to speak⟩
palabrería *nf* : empty talk
palabrota *nf* : swearword ⟨decir palabrotas : to swear⟩
palacio *nm* **1** : palace, mansion **2 palacio de justicia** : courthouse **3 palacio municipal** : city hall
paladar *nm* **1** : palate **2** GUSTO : taste
paladear *vt* SABOREAR : to savor
paladín *nm, pl* **-dines** : champion, defender
palanca *nf* **1** : lever, crowbar **2** *fam* : leverage, influence **3 palanca de cambios/velocidad** : gearshift **4 palanca de mando** JOYSTICK : joystick
palangana *nf* : washbowl
palanqueta *nf* : jimmy, small crowbar
palapa *nf Mex* : shelter (thatched with palms)
palco *nm* : box (in a theater or stadium)
palear *vt* **1** : to shovel **2** : to paddle
palenque *nm* **1** ESTACADA : stockade, palisade **2** : arena, ring
paleontología *nf* : paleontology
paleontólogo, -ga *n* : paleontologist
palestino, -na *adj & n* : Palestinian
palestra *nf* : arena ⟨salir a la palestra : to join the fray⟩
paleta *nf* **1** : palette **2** : trowel **3** : spatula **4** : blade, vane **5** : paddle **6** *CA, Mex* : lollipop, Popsicle
paletilla *nf* : shoulder blade
paliacate *nm Mex* : bandanna, scarf
paliar *vt* MITIGAR : to alleviate
paliativo¹, -va *adj* : palliative ⟨cuidados paliativos : palliative care⟩ ⟨centro de cuidados paliativos : hospice⟩
paliativo² *nm* : palliative
palidecer {53} *vi* : to turn pale
palidez *nf, pl* **-deces** : paleness, pallor
pálido, -da *adj* : pale ⟨se puso pálida : she turned pale⟩
palillo *nm* **1** *or* **palillo de dientes** MONDADIENTES : toothpick **2** *or* **palillo de tambor** : drumstick **3 palillos** *nmpl* : chopsticks
paliza *nf* **1** : beating, pummeling ⟨darle una paliza a : to beat, to thrash⟩ **2** DERROTA : rout, defeat
palma *nf* **1** : palm (of the hand) **2** : palm (tree or leaf) **3 batir/dar palmas** : to clap, to applaud **4 llevarse la palma** *fam* : to take the cake

palmada *nf* **1** : pat ⟨le dio unas palmadas en el hombro : she patted him on the shoulder⟩ **2** BOFETADA, CACHETADA : slap **3** : clap ⟨dar palmadas : to clap⟩
palmarés *nm* : record (of achievements)
palmario, -ria *adj* MANIFIESTO : clear, manifest
palmeado, -da *adj* : webbed
palmear *vt* : to slap on the back — *vi* : to clap, to applaud
palmera *nf* : palm tree
palmito *nm* : heart of palm
palmo *nm* **1** : span, small amount **2 palmo a palmo** : bit by bit, inch by inch **3 palmo a palmo** : thoroughly **4 dejar con un palmo de narices** : to disappoint
palmotear *vi* : to applaud
palmoteo *nm* : clapping, applause
palo *nm* **1** : stick, pole, post **2** : shaft, handle ⟨palo de escoba : broomstick⟩ **3** : mast, spar **4** *or* **palo de golf** : golf club **5** : wood **6** : blow (with a stick) **7** : suit (of cards) **8 de tal palo, tal astilla** : he/she (etc.) is a chip off the old block
paloma *nf* **1** : pigeon, dove **2 paloma de la paz** : dove of peace **3 paloma mensajera** : carrier pigeon
palomilla *nf* : moth
palomitas *nfpl* : popcorn
palpable *adj* : palpable, tangible
palpar *vt* : to feel, to touch — **palparse** *vr* ⟨se palpó la cabeza : he felt/touched his head⟩
palpitación *nf, pl* **-ciones** : palpitation
palpitar *vi* : to palpitate, to throb — **palpitante** *adj*
pálpito *nm* : feeling, hunch
palta *nf Arg, Chile, Peru, Uru* : avocado
paludismo *nm* MALARIA : malaria
palurdo, -da *n* : boor, yokel, bumpkin
pampa *nf* : pampas *pl*
pampeano, -na *adj* : pampas
pampero → **pampeano**
pan *nm* **1** : bread ⟨una rebanada de pan : a slice of bread⟩ ⟨pan rallado : (grated) bread crumbs⟩ **2** : loaf of bread **3** : cake, bar ⟨pan de jabón : bar of soap⟩ **4 pan árabe** *Arg, Ven, Uru* : pita, pita bread **5 pan blanco** : white bread **6 pan de molde** : sandwich bread (baked in a loaf pan) **7 pan dulce** *CA, Mex* : traditional pastry **8 pan integral** : whole wheat bread **9 pan tostado** : toast **10 ser pan comido** *fam* : to be a piece of cake, to be a cinch
pan- *pref* : pan- ⟨panacea : panacea⟩
pana¹ *nf* : corduroy
pana² *nmf PRi, Ven* : buddy, friend
panacea *nf* : panacea
panadería *nf* : bakery, bread shop
panadero, -ra *n* : baker
panal *nm* : honeycomb
panameño, -ña *adj & n* : Panamanian
pancarta *nf* : placard, sign, banner
panceta *nf* : bacon
pancho *nm Arg, Uru* : hot dog
pancita *nf Mex* : tripe
páncreas *nms & pl* : pancreas
panda *nmf* : panda
pandeado, -da *adj* : warped

pandearse *vr* 1 : to warp 2 : to bulge, to sag
pandemonio *or* **pandemónium** *nm* : pandemonium
pandereta *nf* : tambourine
pandero *nm* : tambourine
pandilla *nf* 1 : group, clique 2 : gang
panecillo *Spain* → **panecito**
panecito *nm* : roll, bun
panegírico *nm* : eulogy
panel *nm* 1 : panel ⟨paneles de madera : wood panels⟩ ⟨panel solar : solar panel⟩ 2 TABLERO : board — **panelista** *nmf*
panela *nf Col, Ecua* : unrefined sugar
panera *nf* : bread box (for storage), bread basket (for serving)
panfleto *nm* : pamphlet
pánico *nm* : panic ⟨tener(le) pánico a algo : to be terrified of something⟩ ⟨pánico escénico : stage fright⟩
panificadora *nf* : bakery
panini *nm, pl* **panini** *or* **paninis** : panini
panorama *nm* 1 VISTA : panorama, view 2 : scene, situation ⟨el panorama nacional : the national scene⟩ 3 PERSPECTIVA : outlook
panorámico, -ca *adj* : panoramic
panqueque *nm* : pancake
pansexual *adj* : pansexual ⟨las personas pansexuales : pansexual people⟩
pantaletas *nfpl* : panties
pantalla *nf* 1 : screen, monitor 2 : lampshade 3 : fan 4 **pantalla táctil** : touchscreen
pantalón *nm, pl* **-lones** 1 : pants *pl*, trousers *pl* 2 **pantalones cortos** : shorts 3 **pantalones vaqueros/tejanos** : jeans 4 **pantalones de mezclilla** *Chile, Mex* : jeans 5 **pantalones de montar** : jodhpurs
pantano *nm* 1 : swamp, marsh, bayou 2 : reservoir 3 : obstacle, difficulty
pantanoso, -sa *adj* 1 : marshy, swampy 2 : difficult, thorny
panteón *nm, pl* **-teones** 1 CEMENTERIO : cemetery 2 : pantheon, mausoleum
pantera *nf* : panther
panties *or* **pantys** *or* **pantis** *nmfpl* 1 *CA, Car* : panties *pl* 2 *Spain* : panty hose
pantimedias *nfpl Mex* : panty hose
pantomima *nf* : pantomime
pantorrilla *nf* : calf (of the leg)
pants *nms & pl Mex* 1 : sweatpants 2 : sweatsuit, tracksuit
pantufla *nf* ZAPATILLA : slipper
panty *or* **panti** *nmf, pl* **-tys** *or* **-ties** *or* **-tis** → **panties**
panza *nf* BARRIGA : belly, paunch
panzón, -zona *adj, mpl* **panzones** : potbellied
pañal *nm* 1 : diaper ⟨pañal desechable : disposable diaper⟩ 2 **estar en pañales** : to be in its infancy (of things), to be a beginner (of people)
pañería *nf* 1 : cloth, material 2 : fabric store
pañito *nm* : doily
paño *nm* 1 : cloth ⟨en paños menores : in one's underwear⟩ 2 : rag, dust cloth

3 *or* **paño de cocina** : dishcloth 4 **paño higiénico** : sanitary napkin
pañoleta *nf* 1 : head scarf 2 : kerchief, scarf (for the neck) 3 CHAL : shawl
pañuelo *nm* 1 : handkerchief 2 : head scarf 3 : scarf (for the neck)
papa[1] *nm* : pope ⟨el Papa : the Pope⟩
papa[2] *nf* 1 : potato 2 **papa dulce** : sweet potato 3 **papas fritas** : potato chips, french fries 4 **papas a la francesa** *Mex* : french fries
papá *nm fam* 1 : dad *fam*, pop *fam* 2 **papás** *nmpl* : parents, folks *fam*
papada *nf* 1 : double chin, jowl 2 : dewlap
papagayo *nm* LORO : parrot
papal *adj* : papal
papalote *nm CA, Car, Mex* : kite
Papanicolau *nm* : Pap smear
Papá Noel *nm* : Santa Claus
papaya *nf* : papaya
papel *nm* 1 : paper, piece of paper 2 : role, part ⟨hizo el papel de Romeo : he played the part of Romeo⟩ ⟨jugar un papel importante en algo : to play an important role in something⟩ 3 **papel (de) aluminio** : tinfoil, aluminum foil 4 **papel de carta** : writing paper 5 **papel de empapelar** *or* **papel pintado** : wallpaper 6 **papel de envolver** : wrapping paper 7 **papel de fumar** : cigarette paper 8 **papel de lija** : sandpaper 9 **papel de periódico** : newspaper, newsprint 10 **papel de seda** : tissue paper 11 **papel film** : plastic wrap 12 **papel higiénico** : toilet paper, bathroom tissue 13 **papel maché** : papier-mâché 14 **papel moneda** : paper money
papeleo *nm* : paperwork, red tape
papelera *nf* 1 : wastebasket (indoors), trash can (on street) 2 : paper mill
papelería *nf* : stationery store
papelero, -ra *adj* : paper
papeleta *nf* 1 : ballot 2 : ticket, slip
paperas *nfpl* : mumps
papi *nm fam* : daddy, papa
papila gustativa *nf* : taste bud
papilla *nf* 1 : pap (for sick people), baby food 2 **hacer papilla** : to beat to a pulp
papiro *nm* : papyrus
paprika *nf* : paprika
paquete *nm* 1 BULTO : package, parcel ⟨paquete bomba : mail bomb⟩ 2 : package (of cookies, etc.), pack (of cigarettes) 3 : package, bundle ⟨paquete turístico : tour package⟩ ⟨paquete de software : software bundle⟩
paquistaní *adj & nmf* : Pakistani
par[1] *adj* : even (in number)
par[2] *nm* 1 : pair, couple ⟨un par de zapatos : a pair of shoes⟩ 2 : equal, peer ⟨sin par : matchless, peerless⟩ 3 : par (in golf) 4 : rafter 5 **de par en par** : wide open
par[3] *nf* 1 : par ⟨por encima de la par : above par⟩ 2 **a la par que** : at the same time as, as well as ⟨interesante a la par que instructivo : both interesting and informative⟩
para *prep* 1 (*indicating a recipient*) : for ⟨un regalo para ti : a present for you⟩ 2

(*indicating a purpose or goal*) : for ⟨la comida es para la fiesta : the food is for the party⟩ ⟨¿para qué? : what for?⟩ **3** (*indicating comparison*) : for ⟨alta para su edad : tall for her age⟩ ⟨es bueno para lo que cuesta : it's good for what it costs⟩ **4** : for (a time) ⟨una cita para el lunes : an appointment for Monday⟩ **5** : to (a time) ⟨faltan cinco para las ocho : it's five (minutes) to eight⟩ **6** : around, by (a time) ⟨para mañana estarán listos : they'll be ready by tomorrow⟩ **7** : to, towards ⟨para adelante/atrás : forwards/ backwards⟩ ⟨para la derecha/izquierda : to the right/left⟩ ⟨van para el río : they're heading towards the river⟩ **8** (*used before an infinitive*) : to, in order to ⟨lo hace para molestarte : he does it to annoy you⟩ ⟨para no ser visto : in order not to be seen⟩ **9** (*used before an infinitive*) : to ⟨estoy listo para salir : I'm ready to leave⟩ ⟨demasiado joven para entender : too young to understand⟩ ⟨lo compré para devolverlo el mismo día : I bought it only to return it the same day⟩ **10 para que** : so, so that, in order that ⟨te lo digo para que sepas : I'm telling you so you'll know⟩

parabién *nm, pl* **-bienes** : congratulations *pl*

parábola *nf* **1** : parable **2** : parabola

parabrisas *nms & pl* : windshield

paracaídas *nms & pl* : parachute ⟨saltar/ lanzarse en paracaídas : to parachute⟩

paracaidista *nmf* **1** : parachutist **2** : paratrooper

parachoques *nms & pl* : bumper

parada *nf* **1** : stop ⟨parada de autobús : bus stop⟩ **2** : stop (action) **3** : catch, save, parry (in sports) **4** DESFILE : parade

paradero *nm* **1** : whereabouts **2** : bus stop

paradigma *nm* : paradigm

paradisíaco, -ca *or* **paradisiaco, -ca** *adj* : heavenly

parado¹, -da *adj* **1** : motionless, idle, stopped **2** : standing (up) ⟨estar parado : to stand, to be standing⟩ **3** : confused, bewildered **4 bien/mal parado** : in good/bad shape ⟨salió bien parado : it turned out well for him⟩

parado², -da *n Spain* : unemployed person

paradoja *nf* : paradox

paradójico, -ca *adj* : paradoxical

parador *nm* **1** : roadside inn **2** : state-run hotel (in Spain) **3 parador en corto** *Car, Mex, Ven* : shortstop

parafernalia *nf* : paraphernalia

parafina *nf* **1** : paraffin **2** *Chile* : kerosene

parafrasear *vt* : to paraphrase

paráfrasis *nfs & pl* : paraphrase

paragolpes *nms & pl Arg, Par, Uru* : bumper

paraguas *nms & pl* : umbrella

paraguayo, -ya *adj & n* : Paraguayan

paraíso *nm* **1** : paradise, heaven **2 paraíso fiscal** : tax shelter

paraje *nm* : spot, place

paralelismo *nm* : parallel, similarity

paralelo¹, -la *adj* : parallel

paralelo² *nm* : parallel

paralelogramo *nm* : parallelogram

parálisis *nfs & pl* **1** : paralysis **2** : standstill **3 parálisis cerebral** : cerebral palsy

paralizar {21} *vt* **1** : to paralyze **2** : to paralyze, to bring to a standstill — **paralizarse** *vr*

paramédico, -ca *n* : paramedic

parámetro *nm* : parameter

páramo *nm* : barren plateau, moor

parangón {21} *nm, pl* **-gones 1** : comparison **2 sin ~** : incomparable

paraninfo *nm* : auditorium, assembly hall

paranoia *nf* : paranoia

paranoico, -ca *adj & n* : paranoid

paranormal *adj* : paranormal

parapente *nm* : paragliding

parapetarse *vr* : to take cover

parapeto *nm* : parapet, rampart

parapléjico, -ca *adj & n* : paraplegic

parar *vt* **1** DETENER : to stop **2** : to stand, to prop ⟨parar la oreja : to perk up one's ears⟩ **3** : to stop, to block (a blow, etc.) — *vi* **1** CESAR : to stop ⟨habla sin parar : she talks nonstop⟩ ⟨no paraba de llorar : he wouldn't stop crying⟩ **2** : to stay, to put up **3** : to go on strike **4 ir a parar** : to end up, to wind up ⟨ir a parar a manos de alguien : to fall into someone's hands⟩ ⟨va a parar al hospital : he's going to end up in the hospital⟩ — **pararse** *vr* **1** : to stop ⟨pararse en seco : to stop dead⟩ **2** ATASCARSE : to stall (out) **3** : to stand up, to get up

pararrayos *nms & pl* : lightning rod

parasitario, -ria *adj* : parasitic

parásito *nm* : parasite

parasol *nm* SOMBRILLA : parasol

parcela *nf* : parcel, tract of land

parcelar *vt* : to parcel (land)

parchar *vt* : to patch, to patch up

parche *nm* : patch

parcial¹ *adj* **1** : partial ⟨un éxito parcial : a partial success⟩ **2** TENDENCIOSO : partial, biased — **parcialmente** *adv*

parcial² *nm* : exam (covering a portion of a semester's or trimester's material)

parcialidad *nf* : partiality, bias

parco, -ca *adj* **1** : sparing, frugal **2** : moderate, temperate **3** LACÓNICO : laconic, concise

pardo, -da *adj* : brownish grey

pardusco → pardo

parecer¹ {53} *vi* **1** : to seem, to look, to appear to be ⟨parece fácil : it looks easy⟩ ⟨parece que van a ganar : it looks like they're going to win⟩ ⟨así parece : so it seems⟩ ⟨pareces una princesa : you look like a princess⟩ **2** (*expressing an opinion*) ⟨¿qué te parece? : what do you think?⟩ ⟨me parece que sí : I think so⟩ ⟨me parece bien : that seems fine to me⟩ **3** : to like, to be in agreement ⟨si te parece : if you like, if it's all right with you⟩ — **parecerse** *vr* **~ a** : to resemble

parecer² *nm* **1** OPINIÓN : opinion ⟨en mi parecer : in my opinion⟩ ⟨es del parecer

que . . . : he's of the opinion that . . .⟩ 2
ASPECTO : appearance ⟨al parecer : apparently⟩
parecido¹, -da *adj* 1 : similar, alike 2
bien parecido : good-looking
parecido² *nm* : resemblance, similarity
⟨tener un parecido con : to bear a resemblance to⟩
pared *nf* 1 : wall ⟨las paredes oyen : the
walls have ears⟩ 2 : face (of a mountain)
paredón *nm, pl* **-dones** 1 : rock face 2
: wall (for executions by firing squad)
pareja *nf* 1 : couple, pair ⟨por parejas
: in pairs⟩ ⟨vivir en pareja : to live together⟩ ⟨pareja de hecho : unmarried
couple living together⟩ 2 : partner,
mate ⟨tu pareja ideal : your ideal mate⟩
3 : mate (to a glove, etc.)
parejo, -ja *adj* 1 : even, smooth, level 2
: equal, similar 3 **al parejo de** : on a par
with
parentela *nf* : relations *pl*, kinfolk
parentesco *nm* : relationship, kinship
paréntesis *nms & pl* 1 : parenthesis ⟨entre paréntesis : in parentheses⟩ 2 : digression 3 **entre ∼** : by the way
parentético, -ca *adj* : parenthetic, parenthetical
pargo *nm* : red snapper
paria *nmf* : pariah, outcast
paridad *nf* : parity, equality
pariente *nmf* : relative, relation
parir *vi* : to give birth — *vt* : to give birth
to, to bear
paritario, -ria *adj* : equal, of peers/equals
parka *nf* : parka
parking *nm* : parking lot
parkour [par'kor] *nm* : parkour
parlamentar *vi* : to talk, to parley
parlamentario¹, -ria *adj* : parliamentary
parlamentario², -ria *n* : member of parliament
parlamento *nm* 1 : parliament 2 : negotiations *pl*, talks *pl*
parlanchín¹, -china *adj, mpl* **-chines**
: chatty, talkative
parlanchín², -china *n, mpl* **-chines** : chatterbox
parlante *nm* ALTOPARLANTE : loudspeaker
parlotear *vi fam* : to gab, to chat, to prattle
parloteo *nm fam* : prattle, chatter
paro *nm* 1 HUELGA : strike 2 : stoppage, stopping 3 *Spain* : unemployment
4 *Spain* : unemployment benefits 5
paro cardíaco/cardiaco : cardiac arrest
6 **paro forzoso** : layoff
parodia *nf* : parody
parodiar *vt* : to parody
paroxismo *nm* 1 : fit, paroxysm 2
: peak, height ⟨llevar al paroxismo : to
carry to the extreme⟩
parpadear *vi* 1 : to blink 2 : to flicker
parpadeo *nm* 1 : blink, blinking 2
: flickering
párpado *nm* : eyelid
parque *nm* 1 : park 2 CORRAL : playpen
(for children) 3 **parque de diversio-**

nes/atracciones : amusement park 4
parque infantil : playground 5 **parque
natural** : nature preserve 6 **parque nacional** : national park 7 **parque
temático** : theme park
parqueadero *nm Col* : parking lot
parquear *vt* : to park — **parquearse** *vr*
parqueo *nm* : parking
parquet *or* **parqué** *nm* : parquet
parquímetro *nm* : parking meter
parra *nf* : vine, grapevine
párrafo *nm* : paragraph
parranda *nf fam* : party, spree ⟨irse de
parranda : to party, to go partying⟩
parrilla *nf* 1 : broiler, grill ⟨a la parrilla
: broiled, grilled⟩ 3 : grill (restaurant)
4 : grate 5 BACA : luggage rack, roof
rack
parrillada *nf* 1 BARBACOA : barbecue 2
: grill (restaurant)
párroco *nm* : parish priest
parroquia *nf* 1 : parish 2 : parish church
3 : customers *pl*, clientele
parroquial *adj* : parochial
parroquiano, -na *nm* 1 : parishioner 2
: customer, patron
parsimonia *nf* 1 : calm 2 : thrift
parsimonioso, -sa *adj* 1 : calm, unhurried 2 : parsimonious, thrifty
parte¹ *nm* : report, dispatch ⟨parte meteorológico : weather report⟩
parte² *nf* 1 : part (of a whole) ⟨la mayor
parte de : the majority of⟩ ⟨una quinta
parte de : one fifth of⟩ 2 : place, part
⟨en alguna/cualquier parte : somewhere/anywhere⟩ ⟨en ninguna parte
: nowhere, not anywhere⟩ ⟨por todas
partes : everywhere⟩ ⟨ir a otra parte : to
go somewhere else⟩ 3 : party (in negotiations, etc.) 4 **de parte de** : on behalf
of ⟨de mi parte : on my behalf, for me⟩
5 **¿de parte de quién?** : may I ask who's
calling? 6 **en gran parte** : largely, in
large part 7 **en ∼** : partly, in part 8 **la
mayor parte de** : most of, the majority
of 9 **por otra parte** : on the other hand
10 **por parte de** : on the part of ⟨por mi
parte : on my part, as far as I'm concerned⟩ 11 **tomar parte** : to take part
partero, -ra *n* : midwife
partición *nf, pl* **-ciones** : division, sharing
participación *nf, pl* **-ciones** 1 : participation 2 : share, interest 3 : announcement, notice
participante *nmf* 1 : participant 2
: competitor, entrant
participar *vi* 1 : to participate, to take
part ⟨participar en algo : to participate
in something⟩ 2 **∼ en** : to have a share
in — *vt* : to announce, to notify
partícipe *nmf* : participant
participio *nm* : participle
partícula *nf* : particle
particular¹ *adj* 1 : particular, specific ⟨en
particular : in particular⟩ 2 : private
⟨clases particulares : private lessons⟩
⟨una casa particular : a private home⟩
3 : special, unique ⟨¿qué tiene de particular? : what's so special about it?⟩ 4
de ∼ *Arg, Uru* : in plain/civilian clothes

⟨un policía de particular : a plainclothes policeman⟩

particular² *nm* **1** : matter, detail **2** : individual

particularidad *nf* : characteristic, peculiarity

particularizar {21} *vt* **1** : to distinguish, to characterize **2** : to specify

particularmente *adv* **1** : particularly, especially **2** : personally

partida *nf* **1** : departure **2** : item, entry **3** : certificate ⟨partida de nacimiento : birth certificate⟩ **4** : game, match, hand **5** : party, group

partidario, -ria *n* : follower, supporter ⟨soy partidario de . . . : I'm in favor of . . . , I support . . .⟩

partido *nm* **1** : (political) party **2** : game, match ⟨partido de futbol : soccer game⟩ ⟨partido amistoso : non-league game, non-championship game⟩ **3** APOYO : support, following **4** PROVECHO : profit, advantage ⟨sacar partido de : to profit from⟩ **5 un buen partido** : a good catch (for marriage)

partir *vt* **1** : to cut, to split **2** : to break, to crack **3** : to share (out), to divide — *vi* **1** : to leave, to depart **2** ~ **de** : to start from **3 a partir de** : as of, from ⟨a partir de hoy : as of today⟩ — **partirse** *vr* **1** : to smash, to split open **2** : to become chapped

partisano, -na *adj & n* : partisan

partitura *nf* : (musical) score

parto *nm* **1** : childbirth, delivery, labor ⟨estar de parto : to be in labor⟩ **2** : product, creation, brainchild

parvulario *nm* **1** : nursery school **2** : kindergarten

párvulo, -la *n* : toddler, preschooler

pasa *nf* **1** : raisin **2 pasa de Corinto** : currant

pasable *adj* : passable, tolerable — **pasablemente** *adv*

pasada *nf* **1** : passage, passing **2** : pass, wipe, coat (of paint) **3 de** ~ : in passing **4 mala pasada** : dirty trick

pasadizo *nm* : passageway, corridor

pasado¹, -da *adj* **1** : past ⟨el año pasado : last year⟩ ⟨pasado mañana : the day after tomorrow⟩ ⟨pasadas las siete : after seven o'clock⟩ **2** : overripe (of fruit), slightly spoiled **3** : well done (of meat), overcooked **4** : past tense (in grammar) **5** *or* **pasado de moda** : old-fashioned, out-of-date

pasado² *nm* : past

pasador *nm* **1** : bolt, latch **2** : barrette **3** *Mex* : bobby pin **4** : quarterback (in American football)

pasaje *nm* **1** : ticket (for travel) **2** TARIFA : fare **3** : passageway **4** : passengers *pl* **5** : passage (from a book, etc.)

pasajero¹, -ra *adj* : passing, fleeting

pasajero², -ra *n* : passenger

pasamanos *nms & pl* : banister (of a staircase), handrail

pasamontañas *nms & pl* : balaclava, ski mask

pasante *nmf* : assistant

pasapalos *nmpl Ven* : snacks, hors d'oeuvres

pasaporte *nm* : passport

pasar *vi* **1** : to pass, to go ⟨la gente que pasa : the people who are passing (by), the people who pass by⟩ ⟨nos dejaron pasar : they let us (go) through⟩ ⟨pasamos por el centro : we went through the downtown⟩ ⟨nunca paso por esa calle : I never go down that street⟩ ⟨pasé por delante de la escuela : I went by/past the school⟩ **2** : to pass (of time) **3** : to pass, to pass down ⟨el trono pasó a su hijo : the throne passed to his son⟩ **4** : to go (on), to move (on) ⟨pasaron a la final : they moved on to the finals⟩ ⟨pasar a ser : to go on to become⟩ ⟨pasar de . . . a . . . : to go from . . . to . . .⟩ **5** : to drop by/in, to stop by ⟨pasamos por su casa : we dropped by his house⟩ **6** : to come in, to enter ⟨¿se puede pasar? : may we come in?⟩ **7** CABER : to go through, to fit **8** : to happen ⟨¿qué pasa? : what's happening?, what's going on?⟩ ⟨lo que pasa es que . . . : what's happening is that . . . , the thing is that . . .⟩ ⟨¿qué le pasa? : what's the matter with him?⟩ ⟨pase lo que pase : come what may⟩ **9** : to manage, to get by ⟨pasar sin algo : to manage without something⟩ **10** : to be acceptable, to pass ⟨puede pasar : it will do⟩ **11** : to pass (in an exam, etc.) **12** TERMINAR : to be over, to end **13** ~ **de** : to exceed, to go beyond **14** ~ **por** : to pass as/for ⟨podría pasar por tu hermana : she could pass as/for your sister⟩ **15** ~ **por** : to go through, to experience (difficulties, etc.) — *vt* **1** : to pass, to give ⟨¿me pasas la sal? : would you pass me the salt?⟩ **2** PEGAR : to give (an illness) **3** : to pass (a test) **4** : to cross (a bridge, river, etc.), to go through (a barrier) **5** : to spend (time) ⟨pasamos una semana en Acapulco : we spent a week in Acapulco⟩ **6** TOLERAR : to tolerate **7** SUFRIR : to go through, to suffer **8** : to show (a movie, etc.) **9** ADELANTAR, SUPERAR : to overtake, to pass, to surpass **10** : to pass (something over something) ⟨le pasó un trapo : he wiped it with a cloth⟩ ⟨pasar la aspiradora (por algo) : to vacuum (something)⟩ **11** ~ **con** : to put (a caller) through to ⟨pásame con el jefe : put me through to the boss⟩ **12 pasar de largo** : to go right past (without stopping) **13 pasarlo/pasarla bien** : to have a good time **14 pasarlo/pasarla mal** : to have a bad time, to have a hard time **15** ~ **por** : to put through ⟨pasa la sopa por un colador : put the soup through a strainer⟩ **16 pasar por alto** : to overlook, to omit — **pasarse** *vr* **1** : to pass, to go away ⟨se me pasó el mareo : the/my nausea has passed⟩ **2** : to stop by **3** : to slip one's mind, to slip by ⟨la fecha se me pasó : the date slipped by me⟩ **4** : to go too far ⟨se pasa de listo : he's too clever for his own good⟩ ⟨no te pases con la sal

: go easy with/on the salt⟩ **5** : to go bad, to spoil

pasarela *nf* **1** : gangplank **2** : footbridge **3** : runway, catwalk

pasatiempo *nm* : pastime, hobby

Pascua *nf* **1** : Easter ⟨Domingo de Pascua : Easter Sunday⟩ **2** : Passover **3** : Christmas **4 Pascuas** *nfpl* : Christmas season

pase *nm* **1** PERMISO : pass, permit **2** : pass (in sports) **3 pase de abordar** *Mex* : boarding pass

paseante *nmf* : walker (person)

pasear *vi* : to take a walk, to go for a ride — *vt* **1** : to take for a walk **2** : to parade around, to show off — **pasearse** *vr* : to walk around, to go for a ride

paseo *nm* **1** : walk, stroll ⟨dar un paseo : to go for a walk⟩ **2** : ride **3** EXCURSIÓN : outing, trip **4** : avenue, walk **5** *or* **paseo marítimo** : boardwalk

pasiflora *nf* PASIONARIA : passionflower

pasillo *nm* CORREDOR : hallway, corridor, aisle

pasión *nf, pl* **pasiones** : passion

pasional *adj* : passionate ⟨crimen pasional : crime of passion⟩

pasionaria → pasiflora

pasivo¹, -va *adj* : passive — **pasivamente** *adv*

pasivo² *nm* **1** : liability ⟨activos y pasivos : assets and liabilities⟩ **2** : debit side (of an account)

pasmado, -da *adj* : stunned, flabbergasted

pasmar *vt* : to amaze, to stun — **pasmarse** *vr*

pasmo *nm* **1** : shock, astonishment **2** : wonder, marvel

pasmoso, -sa *adj* : incredible, amazing — **pasmosamente** *adv*

paso¹, -sa *adj* : dried ⟨ciruela pasa : prune⟩

paso² *nm* **1** : passage, passing ⟨de paso : in passing, on the way⟩ ⟨estar de paso : to be passing through⟩ ⟨el paso del tiempo : the passage of time⟩ **2** : way, path ⟨abrir/dejar paso a : to make way for⟩ ⟨ceda el paso : yield⟩ ⟨prohibido el paso : do not enter, no entry⟩ **3** : crossing ⟨paso de peatones : crosswalk⟩ ⟨paso elevado : overpass⟩ ⟨paso subterráneo : underpass, tunnel⟩ ⟨paso a desnivel : underpass, overpass⟩ ⟨paso a nivel : railroad crossing⟩ **4** : pass (through mountains) ⟨salir del paso : to get out of a jam⟩ **5** : step ⟨dar un paso para adelante/atrás : to take a step forward/back⟩ ⟨estar a un paso de : to be within spitting distance of⟩ ⟨oír pasos : to hear footsteps⟩ **6** : step (in a process) ⟨paso a paso : step by step⟩ ⟨un paso positivo : a step in the right direction⟩ **7** : pace, gait ⟨a buen paso : quickly, at a good rate⟩ ⟨a este paso : at this rate⟩

pasta *nf* **1** : paste ⟨pasta de dientes *or* pasta dental : toothpaste⟩ **2** : pasta **3** : pastry dough **4 libro en pasta dura** : hardcover book **5 tener pasta de** : to have the makings of

pastar *vi* : to graze — *vt* : to put to pasture

pastel¹ *adj* : pastel

pastel² *nm* **1** : cake ⟨pastel de cumpleaños : birthday cake⟩ **2** : pie, turnover **3** : pastel

pastelería *nf* **1** : bakery, pastry shop **2** : baking, pastry making

pasteurización *nf, pl* **-ciones** : pasteurization

pasteurizar {21} *vt* : to pasteurize

pastilla *nf* **1** COMPRIMIDO, PÍLDORA : pill, tablet **2** : lozenge ⟨pastilla para la tos : cough drop⟩ **3** : cake (of soap), bar (of chocolate)

pastizal *nm* : pasture, grazing land

pasto *nm* **1** : pasture **2** HIERBA : grass, lawn

pastor, -tora *n* **1** : shepherd, shepherdess *f* **2** : minister, pastor **3 pastor alemán** : German shepherd

pastoral *adj & nf* : pastoral

pastorear *vt* : to shepherd, to tend

pastorela *nf Mex* : traditional Christmas play

pastoso, -sa *adj* **1** : pasty, doughy **2** : smooth, mellow (of sounds)

pata¹ *nf* **1** : paw, leg (of an animal) **2** *fam* : foot, leg (of a person) **3** : foot, leg (of furniture) **4 mala pata** *fam* : bad luck **5 meter la pata** *fam* : to put one's foot in it, to make a faux pas **6 patas de gallo** : crow's-feet **7 patas (para) arriba** : upside-down

pata² *nm Peru* : pal, buddy

patada *nf* **1** PUNTAPIÉ : kick ⟨le dio una patada : she kicked him⟩ **2** : stamp (of the foot)

patalear *vi* **1** : to kick **2** : to stamp one's feet

pataleta *nf fam* : tantrum

patán¹ *adj, pl* **patanes** : boorish, crude

patán² *nm, pl* **patanes** : boor, lout

patata *nf Spain* **1** : potato **2 patatas fritas** : potato chips, french fries

paté *nm* : pâté

pateador, -dora *n* : kicker (in sports)

patear *vt* : to kick — *vi* : to stamp one's foot

patentar *vt* : to patent

patente¹ *adj* EVIDENTE : obvious, patent — **patentemente** *adv*

patente² *nf* **1** : patent **2** *Arg, Chile, Uru* : license plate

paternal *adj* : fatherly, paternal

paternidad *nf* **1** : fatherhood, paternity **2** : parenthood **3** : authorship

paterno, -na *adj* : paternal ⟨abuela paterna : paternal grandmother⟩

patético, -ca *adj* : pathetic, moving

patetismo *nm* : pathos

patíbulo *nm* : gallows, scaffold

patilla *nf* **1** : arm (of glasses) **2** *Col* : watermelon **3 patillas** *nfpl* : sideburns

patín *nm, pl* **patines** : skate ⟨patín de ruedas : roller skate⟩ ⟨patín en línea : in-line skate⟩

pátina *nf* : patina

patinador, -dora *n* : skater

patinaje *nm* : skating ⟨patinaje artístico : figure skating⟩
patinar *vi* **1** : to skate **2** : to skid, to slip **3** *fam* : to slip up, to blunder
patinazo *nm* **1** : skid **2** *fam* : blunder, slipup
patineta *nf* **1** : scooter **2** : skateboard
patinete *nm* : scooter
patio *nm* **1** : courtyard, patio **2 patio de recreo** : playground
patito, -ta *n* : duckling
patizambo, -ba *adj* : knock-kneed
pato, -ta *n* **1** : duck **2 pato real** : mallard **3 pagar el pato** *fam* : to take the blame
patología *nf* : pathology
patológico, -ca *adj* : pathological
patólogo, -ga *n* : pathologist
patoso, -sa *adj Spain* : clumsy
patovica *nm Arg, Uru fam* : bouncer
patraña *nf* : tall tale, humbug, nonsense
patria *nf* : native land
patriarca *nm* : patriarch — **patriarcal** *adj*
patriarcado *nm* : patriarchy
patrimonio *nm* : patrimony, legacy
patrio, -tria *adj* **1** : native, home ⟨suelo patrio : native soil⟩ **2** : paternal
patriota[1] *adj* : patriotic
patriota[2] *nmf* : patriot
patriotería *nf* : jingoism, chauvinism
patriotero[1], **-ra** *adj* : jingoistic, chauvinistic
patriotero[2], **-ra** *n* : jingoist, chauvinist
patriótico, -ca *adj* : patriotic
patriotismo *nm* : patriotism
patrocinador, -dora *n* : sponsor, patron
patrocinar *vt* : to sponsor
patrocinio *nm* : sponsorship, patronage
patrón[1], **-trona** *n, mpl* **patrones 1** JEFE : boss **2** CAPITÁN : skipper **3** *Spain* CASERO : landlord *m*, landlady *f* **4** : patron saint
patrón[2] *nm, pl* **patrones 1** : standard **2** : pattern (in sewing)
patronal *adj* **1** : management, employers' ⟨sindicato patronal : employers' association⟩ **2** : pertaining to a patron saint ⟨fiesta patronal : patron saint's day⟩
patronato *nm* **1** : board, council **2** : foundation, trust
patrono, -na *n* **1** : employer **2** : patron saint
patrulla *nf* **1** : patrol **2** : police car, cruiser
patrullar *v* : to patrol
patrullero *nm* **1** : police car **2** : patrol boat **3** : patrol plane
paulatino, -na *adj* : gradual
paupérrimo, -ma *adj* : destitute, poverty-stricken
pausa *nf* : pause, break ⟨hacer una pausa : to pause, to break⟩ ⟨pausa comercial/ publicitaria : commercial break⟩
pausado[1] *adv* : slowly, deliberately ⟨habla más pausado : speak more slowly⟩
pausado[2], **-da** *adj* : slow, deliberate — **pausadamente** *adv*
pauta *nf* **1** : rule, guideline **2** : lines *pl* (on paper)

pava *nf Arg, Bol, Chile* : kettle
pavimentar *vt* : pave
pavimento *nm* : pavement
pavo, -va *n* **1** : turkey **2 pavo real** : peacock **3 comer pavo** : to be a wallflower
pavón *nm, pl* **pavones** : peacock
pavonearse *vr* **1** : to strut, to swagger **2 pavonearse de** : to brag about
pavoneo *nm* : strut, swagger
pavor *nm* TERROR : dread, terror
pavoroso, -sa *adj* ATERRADOR : dreadful, terrifying
paya *nf Chile* → **payada**
payada *nf Arg, Uru* : song with improvised lyrics
payasada *nf* **1** : antic ⟨hacer payasadas : to clown around⟩ **2** TONTERÍA : foolish thing **3** FARSA : joke, farce
payasear *vi* : to clown around
payaso, -sa *n* **1** : clown **2** : clown, funny person
paz *nf, pl* **paces 1** : peace **2 descanse en paz** : rest in peace **3 dejar en paz** : to leave alone **4 hacer las paces** : to make up, to reconcile
pazca, etc. → **pacer**
PC [pe'se, pi'si] *nmf* : PC, personal computer
PDA [pede'a, pidi'e] *nm* : PDA
pe *nf* : (letter) p
peaje *nm* : toll
peatón *nm, pl* **-tones** : pedestrian
peatonal *adj* : pedestrian
peca *nf* : freckle
pecado *nm* : sin
pecador[1], **-dora** *adj* : sinful, sinning
pecador[2], **-dora** *n* : sinner
pecaminoso, -sa *adj* : sinful
pecar {72} *vi* **1** : to sin **2** ~ **de** ⟨pecan de optimistas/optimismo : they're too optimistic⟩
pécari *or* **pecarí** *nm* : peccary
pececillo *nm* : small fish
pecera *nf* : fishbowl, fish tank
pecho *nm* **1** : chest **2** SENO : breast, bosom **3** : heart, courage **4 dar el pecho** : to breast-feed **5** *or* **estilo (de) pecho** : breaststroke **6 tomarse algo a pecho** : to take something to heart
pechuga *nf* : breast (of fowl)
pecoso, -sa *adj* : freckled
pectoral *adj* : pectoral
peculado *nm* : embezzlement
peculiar *adj* **1** CARACTERÍSTICO : particular, characteristic **2** RARO : peculiar, uncommon
peculiaridad *nf* : peculiarity
pecuniario, -ria *adj* : pecuniary
pedagogía *nf* : pedagogy
pedagógico, -ca *adj* : pedagogic, pedagogical
pedagogo, -ga *n* : educator
pedal *nm* : pedal ⟨pedal del acelerador : accelerator pedal⟩
pedalear *vi* : to pedal
pedante[1] *adj* : pedantic
pedante[2] *nmf* : pedant
pedantería *nf* : pedantry
pedazo *nm* TROZO : piece, bit, chunk ⟨caerse a pedazos : to fall to pieces⟩

⟨hacer pedazos : to tear into shreds, to smash to pieces⟩
pedernal *nm* : flint
pedestal *nm* : pedestal
pedestre *adj* : commonplace, pedestrian
pediatra *nmf* : pediatrician
pediatría *nf* : pediatrics
pediátrico, -ca *adj* : pediatric
pedido *nm* 1 : order (of merchandise) ⟨hacer un pedido : to place an order⟩ 2 : request
pedigrí *nm, pl* **-gríes** : pedigree
pedir {54} *vt* 1 : to ask for, to request ⟨le pedí un préstamo a Claudia : I asked Claudia for a loan⟩ ⟨le pedí que nos llamara : I asked her to call us⟩ ⟨me pidieron ayuda/permiso : they asked me for help/permission⟩ ⟨pide 200 dólares por la bici : he's asking 200 dollars for the bike⟩ 2 : to order (food, merchandise) 3 **pedir disculpas/perdón** : to apologize — *vi* 1 : to order 2 : to beg
pedo *nm fam* : fart *often vulgar*
pedrada *nf* 1 : blow (with a rock or stone) ⟨la ventana se quebró de una pedrada : the window was broken by a rock⟩ 2 *fam* : cutting remark, dig
pedregal *nm* : rocky ground
pedregoso, -sa *adj* : rocky, stony
pedrera *nf* CANTERA : quarry
pedrería *nf* : precious stones *pl*, gems *pl*
pega *nf Chile* : work
pegadizo, -za *adj* : catchy
pegado, -da *adj* 1 : glued, stuck, stuck together 2 ~ **a** : right next to
pegajoso, -sa *adj* 1 : sticky, gluey 2 : catchy ⟨una tonada pegajosa : a catchy tune⟩ 3 : clingy (of a person)
pegamento *nm* : adhesive, glue
pegar {52} *vt* 1 : to stick, to glue, to paste 2 : to attach, to sew on 3 : to infect with, to give ⟨me pegó el resfriado : he gave me his cold⟩ 4 : to give (a slap, a kick, etc.), to deal (a blow) ⟨le pegó un tiro/puñetazo : she shot/punched him⟩ ⟨me pegó un susto : he startled me⟩ 5 : to give (a shout, a jump, etc.) ⟨pegó un alarido : she let out a scream⟩ 6 : to put against, to put near 7 : to paste (into a computer document) — *vi* 1 ADHERIRSE : to stick, to adhere 2 : to hit ⟨pegar en algo : to hit (against) something⟩ ⟨pegarle a alguien : to hit someone⟩ 3 ~ **con** : to match, to go with — **pegarse** *vr* 1 : to hit oneself ⟨me pegué en el codo : I hit my elbow⟩ 2 : to hit each other 3 : to stick, to take hold 4 : to be contagious
pegote *nm* 1 : sticky mess 2 *Mex* : sticker, adhesive label
pegue, etc. → **pegar**
peinado *nm* : hairstyle, hairdo
peinador, -dora *n* : hairdresser
peinar *vt* 1 : to comb (hair) 2 : to style, to do (hair) 3 RASTREAR : to comb, to search — **peinarse** *vr* 1 : to comb one's hair 2 : to get one's hair done
peine *nm* : comb
peineta *nf* : ornamental comb
peladez *nf, pl* **-deces** *Mex fam* : obscenity, bad language

pelado, -da *adj* 1 : bald, hairless 2 : peeled 3 : bare, barren 4 : broke, penniless 5 *Mex fam* : coarse, crude
pelador *nm* : peeler
pelagra *nf* : pellagra
pelaje *nm* : coat (of an animal), fur
pelapapas *nm* : (potato) peeler
pelar *vt* 1 : to peel, to shell 2 : to skin 3 : to pluck 4 : to remove hair from 5 *fam* : to clean out (of money) — **pelarse** *vr* 1 : to peel 2 *fam* : to get a haircut 3 *Mex fam* : to split, to leave
peldaño *nm* 1 : step, stair 2 : rung
pelea *nf* 1 LUCHA : fight 2 : quarrel
pelear *vi* 1 LUCHAR : to fight 2 DISPUTAR : to quarrel — **pelearse** *vr*
pelele *nm* : puppet
peleón, -ona *adj, mpl* **-ones** *Spain* : quarrelsome, argumentative
peleonero, -ra *adj Mex* : quarrelsome
peletería *nf* 1 : fur shop 2 : fur trade
peletero, -ra *n* : furrier
peliagudo, -da *adj* : tricky, difficult, ticklish
pelícano *nm* : pelican
película *nf* 1 : movie, film ⟨dar/poner una película : to show a movie⟩ ⟨película de acción/suspenso/terror : action/suspense/horror movie⟩ ⟨película de vaqueros : Western⟩ 2 : (photographic) film 3 : thin covering, layer
peligrar *vi* : to be in danger
peligro *nm* 1 : danger, peril ⟨estar en peligro : to be in danger⟩ ⟨estar fuera de peligro : to be out of danger⟩ ⟨poner en peligro : to put in danger, to endanger⟩ ⟨peligro de incendio : fire hazard⟩ 2 : risk ⟨correr (el) peligro de : to run the risk of⟩
peligroso, -sa *adj* : dangerous, hazardous
pelirrojo¹, -ja *adj* : red-haired, redheaded
pelirrojo², -ja *n* : redhead
pellejo *nm* 1 : hide, skin 2 **salvar el pellejo** : to save one's neck
pellizcar {72} *vt* 1 : to pinch 2 : to nibble on
pellizco *nm* : pinch ⟨me dio un pellizco : she gave me a pinch⟩ ⟨un pellizco de : a pinch of⟩
pelmazo¹, -za *adj fam* : boring
pelmazo², -za *n fam* : bore
pelo *nm* 1 : hair 2 : fur 3 : pile, nap 4 **a pelo** : bareback 5 **con pelos y señales** : in great detail 6 **no tener pelos en la lengua** : not to mince words, to be blunt 7 **ponerle los pelos de punta a alguien** : to make someone's hair stand on end 8 **por un pelo** : just barely 9 **tomarle el pelo a alguien** : to tease someone, to pull someone's leg
pelón¹, -lona *adj, mpl* **pelones** 1 : bald 2 *fam* : broke 3 *Mex fam* : tough, difficult
pelón², -lona *n, mpl* **pelones** : bald person
pelota *nf* 1 : ball 2 *fam* : head 3 **en pelotas** *fam* : naked 4 **jugar a la pelota** : to play ball 5 **pasar la pelota** *fam* : to pass the buck 6 **pelota vasca** : jai alai
pelotera *nf* 1 : fight 2 : ruckus, row

pelotón *nm, pl* **-tones** : squad, detachment

peltre *nm* : pewter

peluca *nf* : wig

peluche *nm* : plush (fabric) ⟨oso de peluche : teddy bear⟩

peludo, -da *adj* : hairy, shaggy, bushy

peluquería *nf* **1** : hairdresser's, barbershop **2** : hairdressing

peluquero, -ra *n* : barber, hairdresser

peluquín *nm, pl* **-quines** TUPÉ : hairpiece, toupee

pelusa *nf* **1** : down **2** : lint (on clothes)

pélvico, -ca *adj* : pelvic

pelvis *nfs & pl* : pelvis

pena *nf* **1** SENTENCIA : sentence, penalty ⟨pena de muerte, pena capital : death penalty⟩ **2** AFLICCIÓN : sorrow, grief ⟨me da pena : it makes me sad⟩ ⟨morir de pena : to die of a broken heart⟩ ⟨¡qué pena! : what a shame!, how sad!⟩ **3** VERGÜENZA : shame, embarrassment **4** **penas** *nfpl* : problems, troubles ⟨olvidar tus penas : to forget your troubles⟩ **5** **penas** *nfpl* : difficulty, trouble ⟨a duras penas : with great difficulty⟩ **6 valer la pena** : to be worthwhile

penacho *nm* **1** : crest, tuft **2** : plume (of feathers)

penal¹ *adj* : criminal, penal

penal² *nm* CÁRCEL : prison, penitentiary

penalidad *nf* **1** : hardship **2** : penalty, punishment

penalizar {21} *vt* : to penalize

penalty *nm* : penalty (in sports)

penar *vt* : to punish, to penalize — *vi* : to suffer, to grieve

pendenciero, -ra *adj* : argumentative, quarrelsome

pender *vi* **1** : to hang **2** : to be pending

pendiente¹ *adj* **1** : pending ⟨asuntos pendientes : unfinished business⟩ ⟨cuentas pendientes : outstanding bills⟩ **2 estar pendiente de** : to pay a lot of attention to **3 estar pendiente de** : to be awaiting

pendiente² *nm Spain* : earring

pendiente³ *nf* : slope, incline

pendón *nm, pl* **pendones** : banner

péndulo *nm* : pendulum

pene *nm* : penis

penetración *nf, pl* **-ciones** **1** : penetration **2** : insight

penetrante *adj* **1** : penetrating ⟨una mirada/mente penetrante : a penetrating look/mind⟩ **2** : bitter (of cold or wind), pungent (of smells) **3** ESTRIDENTE : piercing, shrill

penetrar *vi* **1** : to penetrate, to sink in **2** ~ **por** *or* ~ **en** : to pierce, to go in, to enter into ⟨el frío penetra por la ventana : the cold comes right in through the window⟩ — *vt* **1** : to penetrate, to permeate **2** : to pierce ⟨el dolor penetró su corazón : sorrow pierced her heart⟩ **3** : to fathom, to understand

penicilina *nf* : penicillin

península *nf* : peninsula — **peninsular** *adj*

penique *nm* : penny

penitencia *nf* : penance, penitence

penitenciaría *nf* : penitentiary

penitente *adj & nmf* : penitent

penol *nm* : yardarm

penosamente *adv* : with difficulty

penoso, -sa *adj* **1** : painful, distressing **2** : difficult, arduous **3** : shy, bashful

pensado, -da *adj* **1 bien pensado** : well thought-out **2 en el momento menos pensado** : when least expected **3 poco pensado** : badly thought-out **4 mal pensado** : evil-minded

pensador, -dora *n* : thinker

pensamiento *nm* **1** : thought **2** : thinking **3** : pansy

pensar {55} *vi* **1** : to think ⟨pensar bien/mal de alguien : to think well/poorly of someone⟩ **2** ~ **en** : to think about ⟨pensaba en otra cosa : I was thinking about something else⟩ **3 dar que pensar** : to provide food for thought — *vt* **1** : to think ⟨pienso que es necesario : I think it's necessary⟩ ⟨¿qué piensas de su nueva canción? : what do you think about her new song?⟩ **2** : to think about ⟨está pensando comprar una casa : she's thinking about buying a house⟩ **3** : to intend, to plan on ⟨¿qué piensas hacer? : what do you plan to do?⟩ ⟨no pienso casarme : I don't intend to get married⟩ — **pensarse** *vr* : to think over

pensativo, -va *adj* : pensive, thoughtful

pensión *nf, pl* **pensiones** **1** JUBILACIÓN : pension **2** : boarding house **3 pensión alimenticia** : alimony

pensionado, -da *n* → **pensionista**

pensionista *nmf* **1** JUBILADO : pensioner, retiree **2** : boarder, lodger

pentágono *nm* : pentagon — **pentagonal** *adj*

pentagrama *nm* : staff (in music)

penthouse ['pent,haus] *nm* : penthouse

penúltimo, -ma *adj* : next to last, penultimate

penumbra *nf* : partial darkness, shadow

penuria *nf* **1** ESCASEZ : shortage, scarcity **2** : poverty

peña *nf* : rock, crag

peñasco *nm* : crag, large rock

peñascoso, -sa *adj* : craggy

peñón → **peñasco**

peón *nm, pl* **peones** **1** : laborer, peon **2** : pawn (in chess)

peonía *nf* : peony

peor¹ *adv* **1** *comparative of* MAL : worse ⟨se llevan peor que antes : they get along worse than before⟩ **2** *superlative of* MAL : worst ⟨me fue peor que a nadie : I did the worst of all⟩ ⟨el secreto peor guardado : the worst-kept secret⟩ **3 cada vez peor** : worse and worse **4 de mal en peor** : from bad to worse

peor² *adj* **1** *comparative of* MALO : worse ⟨es peor que el original : it's worse than the original⟩ **2** *superlative of* MALO : worst ⟨la peor parte : the worst part⟩ ⟨el peor de todos : the worst of all⟩

pepa *nf* : seed, pit (of a fruit)

pepenador, -dora *n CA, Mex* : scavenger

pepenar *vt CA, Mex* : to scavenge, to scrounge

pepinillo *nm* : pickle, gherkin
pepino *nf* : cucumber
pepita *nf* **1** : seed, pip **2** : nugget **3** *Mex* : dried pumpkin seed
peque, etc. → pecar
pequeñez *nf, pl* **-ñeces 1** : smallness **2** : trifle, triviality **3 pequeñez de espíritu** : pettiness
pequeño¹, -ña *adj* **1** : small, little ⟨un libro pequeño : a small book⟩ **2** : young, little ⟨su hermana pequeña : his little sister⟩ **3** CORTO : short **4** LIGERO : slight
pequeño², -ña *n* : child, little one
pera *nf* **1** : pear **2** *Arg, Chile, Uru* BARBILLA, MENTÓN : chin **3** *Arg, Chile, Uru* : goatee **4** : rubber bulb (for suction, etc.) **5 pedirle peras al olmo** : to ask the impossible
peral *nm* : pear tree
peraltar *vt* : to bank (a road)
peralte *nm* : bank (of a road)
perca *nf* : perch (fish)
percal *nm* : percale
percance *nm* : mishap, misfortune
per cápita *adv & adj* : per capita
percatarse *vr* ~ **de** : to notice, to become aware of
percebe *nm* : barnacle
percepción *nf, pl* **-ciones 1** : perception **2** : idea, notion **3** COBRO : receipt (of payment), collection
perceptible *adj* : perceptible, noticeable — **perceptiblemente** *adv*
percha *nf* **1** : perch **2** : coat hanger **3** : coatrack, coat hook
perchero *nm* : coatrack
percibir *vt* **1** : to perceive, to notice, to sense **2** : to earn, to draw (a salary)
percudido, -da *adj* : grimy
percudir *vt* : to make grimy — **percudirse** *vr*
percusión *nf, pl* **-siones** : percussion
percusor *or* **percutor** *nm* : hammer (of a firearm)
perdedor¹, -dora *adj* : losing
perdedor², -dora *n* : loser
perder {56} *vt* **1** : to lose ⟨perdió las llaves : he lost his keys⟩ ⟨perder dinero/peso : to lose money/weight⟩ ⟨perder la paciencia/confianza : to lose patience/confidence⟩ ⟨perder la vida : to lose one's life⟩ **2** : to lose (a game, contest, etc.) **3** : to miss (a train, an event, etc.) ⟨perdimos la oportunidad : we missed the opportunity⟩ **4** : to waste (time) — *vi* : to lose — **perderse** *vr* **1** EXTRAVIARSE : to get lost **2** : to miss **3** DESAPARECER : to disappear
perdición *nf, pl* **-ciones** : ruin
pérdida *nf* **1** : loss ⟨pérdidas económicas : economic losses⟩ **2** : waste (of time, money, etc.) **3** : leak (of liquid, gas, etc.)
perdidamente *adv* : hopelessly
perdido, -da *adj* **1** : lost ⟨objetos perdidos : lost and found⟩ ⟨una bala perdida : a stray bullet⟩ **2** : inveterate, incorrigible ⟨es un caso perdido : he's a hopeless case⟩ ⟨dar algo por perdido : to give

something up as a lost cause⟩ **3 de** ~ *Mex fam* : at least **4 estar perdido** : to be in trouble, to be done for
perdigón *nm, pl* **-gones** : shot, pellet
perdiz *nf, pl* **perdices** : partridge
perdón¹ *nm, pl* **perdones** : forgiveness, pardon ⟨me pidió perdón : she apologized to me⟩
perdón² *interj* : excuse me!, sorry!
perdonable *adj* : forgivable
perdonar *vt* **1** DISCULPAR : to forgive, to pardon ⟨¿me perdonas? : do you forgive me?⟩ ⟨perdona que te interrumpa : pardon me for interrupting⟩ **2** : to excuse from (a task, etc.), to write off (a debt) ⟨perdonarle la vida a alguien : to spare someone's life⟩ — *vi* : to excuse, to pardon ⟨perdona, pero . . . : excuse/pardon me, but . . .⟩
perdurable *adj* : lasting
perdurar *vi* : to last, to endure, to survive
perecedero, -ra *adj* : perishable
perecer {53} *vi* : to perish, to die
peregrinación *nf, pl* **-ciones** : pilgrimage
peregrinaje *nm* → peregrinación
peregrino¹, -na *adj* **1** : unusual, odd **2** MIGRATORIO : migratory
peregrino², -na *n* : pilgrim
perejil *nm* : parsley
perenne *adj* : perennial ⟨árbol de hoja perenne : evergreen tree⟩
perentorio, -ria *adj* **1** : peremptory **2** URGENTE : urgent **3** FIJO : fixed, set
pereza *nf* FLOJERA, HOLGAZANERÍA : laziness, idleness
perezoso¹, -sa *adj* FLOJO, HOLGAZÁN : lazy
perezoso² *nm* : sloth (animal)
perfección *nf, pl* **-ciones** : perfection ⟨a la perfección : perfectly⟩
perfeccionamiento *nm* : perfecting, refinement
perfeccionar *vt* **1** : to perfect **2** : to improve, to refine
perfeccionismo *nm* : perfectionism
perfeccionista *nmf* : perfectionist
perfecto, -ta *adj* : perfect — **perfectamente** *adv*
perfidia *nf* : treachery
pérfido, -da *adj* : perfidious
perfil *nm* **1** : profile ⟨de perfil : from the side, in profile⟩ **2** CONTORNO : profile, outline **3 perfiles** *nmpl* RASGOS : features, characteristics
perfilar *vt* : to outline, to define — **perfilarse** *vr* **1** : to be outlined, to be silhouetted **2** : to take shape
perforación *nf, pl* **-ciones 1** : perforation **2** : drilling
perforadora *nf* **1** : hole punch (for paper) **2** : drill (in mining, etc.)
perforar *vt* **1** : to perforate, to pierce **2** : to drill, to bore
perfumar *vt* : to perfume, to scent — **perfumarse** *vr* : to put on perfume
perfume *nm* : perfume, scent
perfumería *nf* **1** : perfume shop **2** : perfumes *pl* **3** : perfume industry
pergamino *nm* : parchment
pérgola *nf* : arbor

pericia *nf* : skill, expertise
pericial *adj* : expert ⟨testigo pericial : expert witness⟩
perico *nm* COTORRA : small parrot
periferia *nf* : periphery, outskirts
periférico¹, -ca *adj* : outlying, peripheral
periférico² *nm* **1** *CA, Mex* : beltway **2** : peripheral
perilla *nf* **1** : goatee **2** : pommel (on a saddle) **3** *Col, Mex* : knob, handle **4** **perilla de la oreja** : earlobe **5 de perillas** *fam* : handy, just right
perímetro *nm* : perimeter
periódico¹, -ca *adj* : periodic — **periódicamente** *adv*
periódico² *nm* DIARIO : newspaper
periodismo *nm* : journalism
periodista *nmf* : journalist
periodístico, -ca *adj* : journalistic, news
período *or* **periodo** *nm* : period
peripecia *nf* VICISITUD : vicissitude, reversal ⟨las peripecias de su carrera : the ups and downs of her career⟩ ⟨contar las peripecias de : to tell the adventures of⟩
periquera *nf Mex* : high chair (for a baby)
periquito *nm* : parakeet
periscopio *nm* : periscope
perito, -ta *adj & n* : expert
perjudicar {72} *vt* : to harm, to be detrimental to ⟨perjudicar la salud : to be bad for your health⟩
perjudicial *adj* : harmful, detrimental ⟨ser perjudicial para : to be harmful to⟩
perjuicio *nm* **1** : harm, damage ⟨causar perjuicio a : to cause damage to⟩ **2 en perjuicio de** : to the detriment of **3 sin perjuicio de** : without detriment to, without affecting
perjurar *vi* : to perjure oneself
perjurio *nm* : perjury
perla *nf* **1** : pearl **2 de perlas** *fam* : wonderfully ⟨me viene de perlas : it suits me just fine⟩
permanecer {53} *vi* **1** QUEDARSE : to remain, to stay **2** SEGUIR : to remain, to continue to be
permanencia *nf* **1** : permanence, continuance **2** ESTANCIA : stay
permanente¹ *adj* **1** : permanent **2** : constant — **permanentemente** *adv*
permanente² *nf* : perm, permanent (wave) ⟨hacerse la permanente : to get a perm⟩
permeabilidad *nf* : permeability
permeable *adj* : permeable
permisible *adj* : permissible, allowable
permisividad *nf* : permissiveness
permisivo, -va *adj* : permissive
permiso *nm* **1** : permission ⟨dar permiso : to give permission⟩ **2** : permit, license ⟨permiso de conducir : driver's license⟩ ⟨permiso de residencia : green card⟩ ⟨permiso de trabajo : work permit⟩ **3** : leave, furlough **4 con ∼** : excuse me, pardon me **5 de ∼** : on leave
permitir *vt* **1** : to permit, to allow ⟨no me permitió pasar : he wouldn't let me through⟩ ⟨¿me permite? : may I?⟩ **2** POSIBILITAR : to enable, to allow — **permitirse** *vr* : to allow oneself ⟨permitirse

el lujo de : to allow oneself the luxury of⟩
permuta *nf* : exchange
permutación *nf, pl* **-ciones** : permutation
permutar *vt* INTERCAMBIAR : to exchange
pernera *nf* : leg (of pants, etc.)
pernicioso, -sa *adj* : pernicious, destructive
pernil *nm* **1** : haunch (of an animal) **2** : leg (of meat), ham **3** : trouser leg
perno *nm* : bolt, pin
pernoctar *vi* : to stay overnight, to spend the night
pero¹ *nm* **1** : fault, defect ⟨ponerle peros a : to find fault with⟩ **2** : objection
pero² *conj* **1** : but ⟨lo siento, pero no puedo : I'm sorry, but I can't⟩ **2** (*used for emphasis*) ⟨¿pero que le ve? : what on earth does she see in him?⟩ ⟨es muy, pero muy caro : it's extremely expensive⟩
perogrullada *nf* : truism, platitude, cliché
peroné *nm* : fibula
perorar *vi* : to deliver a speech
perorata *nf* : oration, long-winded speech
peróxido *nm* : peroxide
perpendicular *adj & nf* : perpendicular
perpetrar *vt* : to perpetrate
perpetuar {3} *vt* ETERNIZAR : to perpetuate
perpetuidad *nf* : perpetuity
perpetuo, -tua *adj* : perpetual — **perpetuamente** *adv*
perplejidad *nf* : perplexity
perplejo, -ja *adj* : perplexed, puzzled
perrada *nf fam* : dirty trick
perrera *nf* : kennel, dog pound
perrero, -ra *n* : dogcatcher
perrito, -ta *n* CACHORRO : puppy, small dog
perro, -rra *n* **1** : dog, bitch *f* **2 perro callejero** : stray dog **3 perro caliente** : hot dog **4 perro cobrador** : retriever **5 perro faldero** : lapdog **6 perro guardián** : guard dog **7 perro guía/lazarillo** : guide dog **8 perro pastor** : sheepdog **9 perro policía** : police dog **10 perro rastreador** : tracking dog **11 perro salchicha** : dachshund
persa¹ *adj & nmf* : Persian
persa² *nm* : Persian (language)
per se *adv* : per se
persecución *nf, pl* **-ciones** **1** : pursuit, chase **2** : persecution
perseguible *adj* : chargeable
perseguidor, -dora *n* **1** : pursuer **2** : persecutor
perseguir {75} *vt* **1** : to pursue, to chase **2** : to persecute **3** : to pester, to annoy
perseverancia *nf* : perseverance
perseverante *adj* : persistent
perseverar *vi* : to persevere
persiana *nf* : blind, venetian blind
persignarse *vr* SANTIGUARSE : to cross oneself, to make the sign of the cross
persistir *vi* **1** : to persist **2 ∼ en** : to persist in — **persistencia** *nf* — **persistente** *adj*
persona *nf* **1** : person ⟨miles de personas : thousands of people⟩ **2 en ∼** : in person **3 por ∼** : per person

personaje *nm* **1** : character (in drama or literature) **2** : personage, celebrity

personal[1] *adj* : personal — **personalmente** *adv*

personal[2] *nm* : personnel, staff

personalidad *nf* **1** : personality **2** PERSONAJE : personage, celebrity

personalizar {21} *vt* : to personalize — *vi* : to name names

personero, -ra *n* **1** : representative **2** : spokesperson, spokesman *m*, spokeswoman *f*

personificar {72} *vi* : to personify — **personificación** *nf*

perspectiva *nf* **1** : perspective **2** VISTA : view **3** : prospect, outlook ⟨tener buenas perspectivas : to have good prospects⟩ ⟨en perspectiva : in the offing, in prospect⟩ **4** : perspective, point of view ⟨mirándolo en perspectiva : looking back (at it), (looking at it) in retrospect/hindsight⟩

perspicacia *nf* : shrewdness, perspicacity, insight

perspicaz *adj, pl* **-caces** : shrewd, perspicacious

persuadir *vt* : to persuade ⟨lo persuadí de/para que viniera : I persuaded him to come⟩ — **persuadirse** *vr* : to become convinced

persuasión *nf, pl* **-siones** : persuasion

persuasivo, -va *adj* : persuasive

pertenecer {53} *vi* : to belong ⟨pertenecer a : to belong to⟩

perteneciente *adj* ∼ **a** : belonging to

pertenencia *nf* **1** : membership **2** : ownership **3 pertenencias** *nfpl* : belongings, possessions

pértiga *nf* GARROCHA : pole ⟨salto con/de pértiga : pole vault⟩

pertinaz *adj, pl* **-naces 1** OBSTINADO : obstinate **2** PERSISTENTE : persistent

pertinencia *nf* : pertinence, relevance

pertinente *adj* **1** : pertinent, relevant **2** : appropriate

pertrechos *nmpl* : equipment, gear

perturbación *nf, pl* **-ciones** : disturbance, disruption

perturbador, -dora *adj* **1** INQUIETANTE : disturbing, troubling **2** : disruptive

perturbar *vt* **1** : to disturb, to trouble **2** : to disrupt

peruano, -na *adj & n* : Peruvian

perversidad *nf* : perversity, depravity

perversión *nf, pl* **-siones** : perversion

perverso, -sa *adj* : wicked, depraved

pervertido[1], **-da** *adj* DEPRAVADO : perverted, depraved

pervertido[2], **-da** *n* : pervert

pervertir {76} *vt* : to pervert, to corrupt

pesa *nf* **1** : weight **2 levantamiento de pesas** : weight lifting

pesadamente *adv* **1** : heavily **2** : slowly, clumsily

pesadez *nf, pl* **-deces 1** : heaviness **2** ABURRIMIENTO : tediousness **3** PLOMO : drag, bore

pesadilla *nf* : nightmare

pesado[1], **-da** *adj* **1** : heavy **2** LENTO : slow **3** MOLESTO : irritating, annoying

4 ABURRIDO : tedious, boring **5** DIFÍCIL : tough, difficult

pesado[2], **-da** *n fam* : bore, pest

pesadumbre *nf* AFLICCIÓN : grief, sorrow, sadness

pésame *nm* : condolences *pl* ⟨darle el pésame a alguien : to give someone one's condolences⟩ ⟨mi más sentido pésame : my heartfelt condolences⟩

pesar[1] *vt* **1** : to weigh ⟨pesa dos kilos : it weighs two kilos⟩ **2** EXAMINAR : to consider, to think over — *vi* **1** : to weigh ⟨¿cuánto pesa? : how much does it weigh?⟩ **2** : to be heavy **3** : to weigh heavily, to be a burden ⟨la responsabilidad le pesa : the responsibility is a burden on him⟩ **4** INFLUIR : to carry weight, to have bearing **5** (*with personal pronouns*) : to grieve, to sadden ⟨me pesa mucho no haber ido : I really regret not having gone⟩ **6 pese a** : in spite of, despite **7 pese a que** : in spite of the fact that

pesar[2] *nm* **1** AFLICCIÓN, PENA : sorrow, grief **2** REMORDIMIENTO : remorse **3 a pesar de** : in spite of, despite ⟨a pesar de todo : in spite of it all⟩ **4 a pesar de que** : in spite of the fact that

pesaroso, -sa *adj* **1** : sad, mournful **2** ARREPENTIDO : sorry, regretful

pesca *nf* **1** : fishing ⟨ir de pesca : to go fishing⟩ **2** : catch

pescadería *nf* : fish market

pescado *nm* : fish (as food)

pescador, -dora *n* : fisherman *m*, fisherwoman *f*

pescar {72} *vt* **1** : to fish for **2** : to catch **3** *fam* : to get a hold of, to land — *vi* : to fish, to go fishing

pescuezo *nm* : neck

pesebre *nm* **1** : manger **2** : Nativity scene

pesebrera *nf Col* : stable

pesera *nf* → **pesero**

pesero *nm Mex* : minibus

peseta *nf* : peseta (Spanish unit of currency)

pesimismo *nm* : pessimism

pesimista[1] *adj* : pessimistic

pesimista[2] *nmf* : pessimist

pésimo, -ma *adj* : dreadful, abominable

peso *nm* **1** : weight, heaviness ⟨perder/ganar peso : to lose/gain weight⟩ ⟨peso bruto/neto : gross/net weight⟩ **2** : burden, responsibility **3** : weight (in sports) ⟨peso pesado : heavyweight⟩ **4** BÁSCULA : scale **5** : peso (currency)

pesque, etc. → **pescar**

pesquería *nf* : fishery

pesquero[1], **-ra** *adj* : fishing ⟨pueblo pesquero : fishing village⟩

pesquero[2] *nm* : fishing boat

pesquisa *nf* INVESTIGACIÓN : inquiry, investigation

pestaña *nf* **1** : eyelash **2** : flange, rim **3** : tab (in a browser, etc.)

pestañear *vi* : to blink

pestañeo *nm* : blink

peste *nf* **1** : plague, pestilence **2** : stench, stink **3** : nuisance, pest

pesticida *nm* : pesticide
pestilencia *nf* **1** : stench, foul odor **2** : pestilence
pestillo *nm* CERROJO : bolt, latch
petaca *nf* **1** *Mex* : suitcase **2 petacas** *nfpl Mex fam* : bottom, behind
pétalo *nm* : petal
petardear *vi* : to backfire
petardeo *nm* : backfiring
petardo *nm* : firecracker
petate *nm Hond, Mex* : mat
petición *nf, pl* **-ciones** : petition, request ⟨a petición de : at the request of⟩
peticionar *vt* : to petition
peticionario, -ria *n* : petitioner
petirrojo *nm* : robin
petiso, -sa *or* **petizo, -za** *n* : shorty
peto *nm* : bib (of clothing)
pétreo, -trea *adj* : stone, stony
petrificar {72} *vt* : to petrify
petróleo *nm* : oil, petroleum
petrolero[1], -ra *adj* : oil ⟨industria petrolera : oil industry⟩
petrolero[2] *nm* : oil tanker
petrolífero, -ra *adj* → **petrolero[1]**
petulancia *nf* INSOLENCIA : insolence, petulance
petulante *adj* INSOLENTE : insolent, petulant — **petulantemente** *adv*
petunia *nf* : petunia
peyorativo, -va *adj* : pejorative
pez[1] *nm, pl* **peces 1** : fish **2 pez de colores** : goldfish **3 pez espada** : swordfish **4 pez gordo** : big shot
pez[2] *nf, pl* **peces** : pitch, tar
pezón *nm, pl* **pezones** : nipple
pezuña *nf* : hoof ⟨pezuña hendida : cloven hoof⟩
pH ['pe¹atʃe, ¹pi¹etʃ] *nm* : pH
phishing ['fiʃiŋ] *nm* : phishing
phylum ['filum] *nm* : phylum
pi *nf* : pi
piadoso, -sa *adj* **1** : compassionate, merciful **2** DEVOTO : pious, devout — **piadosamente** *adv*
pianista *nmf* : pianist, piano player
piano *nm* : piano ⟨piano de cola : grand piano⟩
piar {85} *vi* : to chirp, to cheep, to tweet
pibe, -ba *n Arg, Uru fam* : kid, child
pica *nf* **1** : pike, lance **2** : goad (in bullfighting) **3** : spade (in playing cards)
picada *nf* **1** : bite, sting (of an insect) **2** : sharp descent
picadero *nm* **1** : exercise ring (for horses) **2** : riding school
picadillo *nm* **1** : minced meat, hash **2 hacer picadillo a** : to beat to a pulp
picado, -da *adj* **1** : perforated **2** : ground (of meat), chopped **3** : decayed (of teeth) **4** : choppy, rough **5** *fam* : annoyed, miffed
picador *nm* : picador
picadura *nf* **1** : sting, bite **2** : prick, puncture **3** : decay, cavity
picaflor *nm* **1** COLIBRÍ : hummingbird **2** : womanizer
picana *nf* : goad, prod
picante[1] *adj* **1** : hot, spicy **2** : sharp, cutting **3** : racy, risqué

picante[2] *nm* **1** : spiciness **2** : hot spices *pl*, hot sauce
picaporte *nm* **1** : latch **2** : door handle **3** ALDABA : door knocker
picar {72} *vt* **1** : to sting (of bees, etc.), to bite (of fleas, etc.) **2** : to peck at (of birds) **3** COMER : to nibble on **4** : to prick (of a needle, etc.), to punch (a ticket) **5** : to break, to chip (stone, etc.) **6** : to grind, to chop **7** : to goad, to incite **8** : to pique, to provoke — *vi* **1** : to itch ⟨esta camisa me pica : this shirt is itchy⟩ **2** : to sting **3** : to be spicy, to be hot **4** : to nibble **5** : to take the bait **6** ~ **en** : to dabble in **7 picar muy alto** : to aim too high — **picarse** *vr* **1** : to get a cavity, to decay **2** : to go bad (of food) **3** : to get annoyed, to take offense **4** : to become choppy (of the sea)
picardía *nf* **1** : cunning, craftiness **2** : prank, dirty trick
picaresco, -ca *adj* **1** : picaresque **2** : mischievous, naughty
pícaro[1], -ra *adj* **1** : mischievous **2** : cunning, sly **3** : off-color, risqué
pícaro[2], -ra *n* **1** : rogue, scoundrel **2** : rascal
picazón *nf, pl* **-zones** COMEZÓN : itch
picea *nf* : spruce (tree)
pichel *nm* : pitcher, jug
pichón, -chona *n, mpl* **pichones 1** : young pigeon, squab **2** *Mex fam* : novice, greenhorn
picnic *nm* : picnic
pico *nm* **1** : peak **2** : point **3** : corner **4** : beak, bill **5** *fam* : mouth **6** : pick, pickax **7 y pico** : and a little, and a bit ⟨las siete y pico : a little after seven⟩ ⟨dos metros y pico : a bit over two meters⟩
picor *nm* : itch, irritation
picoso, -sa *adj Mex* : very hot, spicy
picota *nf* **1** : pillory, stock **2 poner a alguien en la picota** : to put someone on the spot
picotada *nf* → **picotazo**
picotazo *nm* : peck (of a bird)
picotear *vt* : to peck — *vi* : to nibble, to pick
pictórico, -ca *adj* : pictorial
picudo, -da *adj* **1** : pointy, sharp **2** ~ **para** *Mex fam* : clever at, good at
pide, etc. → **pedir**
pie *nm* **1** : foot **2** : base, bottom, stem, foot ⟨pie de la cama : foot of the bed⟩ ⟨pie de una lámpara : base of a lamp⟩ ⟨pie de la escalera : bottom of the stairs⟩ ⟨pie de una copa : stem of a glass⟩ ⟨pie de la página : foot of the page⟩ ⟨pie de foto : caption⟩ **3** : foot (in measurement) ⟨pie cuadrado : square foot⟩ **4** : cue (in theater) **5 a** ~ : on foot **6 de** ~ : on one's feet, standing ⟨estar de pie : to be standing⟩ ⟨ponerse de pie : to stand up⟩ **7 en** ~ : standing ⟨mantenerse en pie : to remain standing⟩ ⟨seguir en pie : to remain valid, to stand⟩ **8 al pie de la letra** : word for word **9 con buen pie** : well ⟨comenzar con buen pie : to start on the right foot, to get off to a

good start⟩ **10 con pies de plomo** : very cautiously **11 dar pie a** : to give cause for, to give rise to **12 de a pie** : average, ordinary **13 de pies a cabeza** : from head to toe **14 en pie de guerra** : ready for war **15 en pie de igualdad** : on equal footing **16 hacer pie** : to touch bottom (in water) **17 no tener ni pies ni cabeza** : to make no sense

piedad *nf* **1** COMPASIÓN : mercy, pity **2** DEVOCIÓN : piety, devotion

piedra *nf* **1** : stone **2** : flint (of a lighter) **3** : hailstone **4 piedra angular** : cornerstone **5 piedra arenisca** : sandstone **6 piedra caliza** : limestone **7 piedra de afilar** : whetstone, grindstone **8 piedra de molino** : millstone **9 piedra de pómez** : pumice stone **10 piedra de toque** : touchstone **11 piedra imán** : lodestone **12 piedra preciosa** : precious stone

piel *nf* **1** : skin **2** CUERO : leather, hide ⟨piel de venado : deerskin⟩ **3** : fur, pelt **4** CÁSCARA : peel, skin **5 piel de gallina** : goose bumps *pl* ⟨me pone la piel de gallina : it gives me goose bumps⟩

piélago *nm* **el piélago** : the deep, the ocean

piensa, etc. → **pensar**

pienso *nm* : feed, fodder

pierde, etc. → **perder**

pierna *nf* : leg ⟨cruzar las piernas : to cross one's legs⟩

pieza *nf* **1** ELEMENTO : piece, part, component ⟨vestido de dos piezas : two-piece dress⟩ ⟨pieza de recambio/repuesto : spare part⟩ ⟨pieza clave : key element⟩ **2** : piece (in chess) **3** OBRA : piece, work ⟨pieza de teatro : play⟩ **4** : room, bedroom

pífano *nm* : fife

pifia *nf fam* : goof, blunder

pifiar *vt fam* : to mess up, to bungle

pigargo *nm* : osprey

pigmentación *nf, pl* **-ciones** : pigmentation

pigmento *nm* : pigment

pigmeo, -mea *adj & n* : pygmy, Pygmy

pijama *nm* : pajamas *pl*

pila *nf* **1** BATERÍA : battery ⟨pila de linterna : flashlight battery⟩ **2** MONTÓN : pile, heap **3** : sink, basin, font ⟨pila bautismal : baptismal font⟩ ⟨pila para pájaros : birdbath⟩

pilar *nm* **1** : pillar, column **2** : support, mainstay

píldora *nf* PASTILLA : pill ⟨tomar la píldora (anticonceptiva) : to be on the pill⟩

pileta *nf Arg, Uru* **1** FREGADERO, LAVABO : sink **2** PISCINA : swimming pool

pillaje *nm* : pillage, plunder

pillar *vt* **1** *fam* : to catch ⟨¡cuidado! ¡nos pillarán! : watch out! they'll catch us!⟩ **2** *fam* : to grasp, to catch on ⟨¿no lo pillas? : don't you get it?⟩ — **pillarse** *vr* : to catch (one's finger, etc.)

pillo[1], **-lla** *adj* : cunning, crafty

pillo[2], **-lla** *n* **1** : rascal, brat **2** : rogue, scoundrel

pilluelo, -la *n* : urchin

pilón *nm, pl* **pilones 1** PILA : basin **2** : pillar, tower (for cables), pylon (of a bridge) **3** *Mex* : extra, free gift

pilotar *vt* : to pilot (a plane), to steer (a ship), to drive (an automobile)

pilote *nm* : pile (stake)

pilotear → **pilotar**

piloto[1] *nm* **1** : pilot light **2** *Arg* : raincoat **3 piloto automático** : autopilot, automatic pilot

piloto[2] *nmf* : pilot (of a plane or ship), driver (of an automobile)

piltrafa *nf* **1** : poor quality meat **2** : wretch **3 piltrafas** *nfpl* : food scraps

pimentero *nm* : pepper shaker

pimentón *nm, pl* **-tones 1** : paprika **2** : cayenne pepper

pimienta *nf* **1** : pepper (condiment) ⟨pimienta blanca/negra : white/black pepper⟩ **2 pimienta de Jamaica** : allspice

pimiento *nm* : pepper (fruit) ⟨pimiento verde : green pepper⟩ ⟨pimiento morrón : pimiento, pimento⟩

pináculo *nm* **1** : pinnacle (of a building) **2** : peak, acme

pinar *nm* : pine forest

pinball [pin**'**bol] *nm* : pinball

pincel *nm* **1** : paintbrush **2** : makeup brush

pincelada *nf* **1** : brushstroke **2 últimas pinceladas** : final touches

pinchar *vt* **1** : to puncture (a tire, balloon, etc.) **2** : to prick, to stick, to jab **3** PROVOCAR : to goad, to tease, to needle **4** : to give an injection **5** : to click on (a link, etc.) ⟨pinche aquí : click here⟩ **6** *fam* : to tap, to wiretap (a phone) — *vi* **1** : to be prickly **2** : to get a flat tire **3** *fam* : to get beaten, to lose out — **pincharse** *vr* **1** INYECTARSE : to shoot up **2** : to go flat (of a tire)

pinchazo *nm* **1** : prick, jab **2** : puncture, flat tire

pinche[1] *adj Mex* MALDITO : damned

pinche[2] *nmf* : kitchen assistant

pincho *nm* **1** : thorn, spine (of a plant) **2** *Spain* : bar snack

Ping–Pong *marca registrada, m* — used for table tennis

pingüe *adj* **1** : rich, huge (of profits) **2** : lucrative

pingüino *nm* : penguin

pininos *or* **pinitos** *nmpl* : first steps ⟨hacer pininos : to take one's first steps, to toddle⟩

pino *nm* : pine, pine tree

pinta *nf* **1** : dot, spot **2** : pint **3** *fam* : aspect, appearance ⟨las peras tienen buena pinta : the pears look good⟩ ⟨tener pinta de : to look like⟩ **4 pintas** *nfpl Mex* : graffiti

pintadas *nfpl* : graffiti

pintado, -da *adj* : spotted

pintalabios *nms & pl* : lipstick

pintar *vt* **1** : to paint **2** : to draw, to mark **3** : to describe, to depict — *vi* **1** : to paint, to draw **2** : to look ⟨no pinta bien : it doesn't look good⟩ **3** *fam* : to count ⟨aquí no pinta nada : he has no say here⟩ — **pintarse** *vr* **1** MAQUI-

LLARSE : to put on makeup **2**
pintárselas solo *fam* : to manage by
oneself, to know it all
pintarrajear *vt* : to daub (with paint)
pinto, -ta *adj* : speckled, spotted
pintor, -tora *n* **1** : painter (artist) **2** *or*
pintor de brocha gorda : painter (of
buildings, etc.)
pintoresco, -ca *adj* : picturesque, quaint
pintura *nf* **1** : paint **2** : painting ⟨pintura
al óleo : oil painting⟩ ⟨pintura a la acuarela : watercolor painting⟩
pinza *nf* **1** : clothespin **2** HORQUILLA
: bobby pin **3** : claw, pincer (of a crab,
etc.) **4** : pleat, dart (in clothing) **5 pinzas** *nfpl* : tweezers **6 pinzas** *nfpl* ALICA-
TES : pliers, pincers **7 pinzas** *nfpl*
: tongs (for food)
pinzón *nm, pl* **pinzones** : finch
piña *nf* **1** : pineapple **2** : pine cone
piñata *nf* : piñata
piñón *nm, pl* **piñones 1** : pine nut **2**
: pinion (of a machine), sprocket (of a
bicycle)
pío[1]**, pía** *adj* **1** DEVOTO : pious, devout **2**
: pied, dappled
pío[2] *nm* **1** : peep, tweet, cheep **2 no decir ni pío** : not to say a word
piocha *nf* **1** : pickax **2** *Mex* : goatee
piojo *nm* : louse
piojoso, -sa *adj* **1** : lousy **2** : filthy
piola[1] *adj fam* **1** *Arg* : cool *fam*, good **2
pasar piola** *Chile, Peru* : to go unnoticed
piola[2] *nf* : cord
pionero[1]**, -ra** *adj* : pioneering
pionero[2]**, -ra** *n* : pioneer
pipa *nf* **1** : pipe (for smoking) **2** *Cuba,
Mex* : tanker truck **3** *Spain* : seed
pipí *nm fam* : pee *fam* ⟨hacer pipí : to
take a pee⟩
pipián *nm, pl* **pipianes** *Mex* : a spicy
sauce or stew
pipiolo, -la *n fam* **1** : greenhorn, novice
2 : kid, youngster
pique[1]**, etc.** → **picar**
pique[2] *nm* **1** : pique, resentment **2** : rivalry, competition **3 a pique de** : about
to, on the verge of **4 irse a pique** : to
sink, to founder
piqueta *nf* : pickax
piquete *nm* **1** : picketers *pl*, picket line
2 : squad, detachment **3** *Mex* : prick,
jab **4** *Mex* : insect bite
piquetear *vt* **1** : to picket **2** *Mex* : to
prick, to jab
pira *nf* : pyre
piragua *nf* : canoe
piragüismo *nm* : canoeing
piragüista *nmf* : canoeist, canoer
pirámide *nf* : pyramid
piraña *nf* : piranha
pirata[1] *adj* **1** : bootleg, pirated **2** : pirate
⟨un barco pirata : a pirate ship⟩
pirata[2] *nmf* **1** : pirate **2** : pirate, bootlegger **3 pirata aéreo** : hijacker **4 pirata
informático** : hacker
piratear *vt* **1** : to hijack, to commandeer
2 : to bootleg, to pirate
piratería *nf* : piracy, bootlegging
piromanía *nf* : pyromania

pirómano, -na *n* : pyromaniac
piropo *nm* : flirtatious compliment
pirotecnia *nf* : fireworks *pl*, pyrotechnics
pl
pirotécnico, -ca *adj* : fireworks, pyrotechnic
pírrico, -ca *adj* : Pyrrhic
pirueta *nf* : pirouette
pirulí *nm* : cone-shaped lollipop
pis → **pipí**
pisada *nf* **1** : footstep **2** HUELLA : footprint
pisapapeles *nms & pl* : paperweight
pisar *vt* **1** : to step on/in ⟨no pises las
flores : don't step on the flowers⟩ **2** : to
set foot in (a place) **3** : to walk all over,
to mistreat — *vi* : to step, to walk, to
tread
piscina *nf* **1** : swimming pool **2** : fish
pond
Piscis[1] *nm* : Pisces (sign or constellation)
Piscis[2] *nmf* : Pisces (person)
piso *nm* **1** PLANTA : floor, story **2** SUELO
: floor **3** PAVIMENTO : surface (of a road)
4 CAPA : layer **5** *Spain* : apartment
pisotear *vt* **1** : to stamp on, to trample **2**
PISAR : to walk all over **3** : to flout, to
disregard
pisotón *nm, pl* **-tones** : stamp, step ⟨su-
frieron empujones y pisotones : they
were pushed and stepped on⟩
pista *nf* **1** RASTRO : trail, track ⟨siguen la
pista de los sospechosos : they're on the
trail of the suspects⟩ **2** : clue **3** CA-
MINO : road, trail **4** : track, racetrack
5 *Chile* : lane (of a road) **6** : ring, arena,
rink ⟨pista de patinaje/hielo : skating/ice
rink⟩ **7** : track (of a recording) **8 pista
de aterrizaje** : runway, airstrip **9 pista
de baile** : dance floor **10 pista de tenis**
Spain : tennis court
pistacho *nm* : pistachio
pistilo *nm* : pistil
pistola *nf* **1** : pistol, handgun **2** : spray
gun
pistolera *nf* : holster
pistolero *nm* : gunman
pistón *nm, pl* **pistones 1** : piston **2**
: key, valve (of an instrument)
pita *nf* **1** : twine **2** : pita (bread)
pitar *vi* **1** : to blow a whistle **2** : to whistle, to boo **3** : to beep, to honk, to toot
— *vt* **1** : to whistle at, to boo **2** : to call,
to signal (a foul)
pitido *nm* **1** : whistle, whistling **2** : beep,
honk, toot
pitillo *nm* : cigarette
pito *nm* **1** SILBATO : whistle **2** CLAXON,
BOCINA : horn **3 no me importa un pito**
fam : I don't give a damn
pitón *nm, pl* **pitones 1** : python **2**
: point of a bull's horn
pitonisa *nf* : fortune-teller
pituitario, -ria *adj* : pituitary
pívot *nmf, pl* **pívots** : center (in basketball)
pivote *nm* : pivot
piyama *nmf* : pajamas *pl*
pizarra *nf* **1** : slate **2** : blackboard **3**
: scoreboard

pizarrón *nm, pl* -rrones : blackboard, chalkboard
pizca *nf* 1 : pinch ⟨una pizca de canela : a pinch of cinnamon⟩ 2 : speck, trace ⟨ni pizca : not a bit⟩ 3 *Mex* : harvest
pizcar {72} *vt Mex* : to harvest
pizque, etc. → pizcar
pizza ['pitsa, 'pisa] *nf* : pizza
pizzería *nf* : pizzeria, pizza parlor
placa *nf* 1 : sheet, plate 2 : plaque 3 : plate (in photography) 4 : badge, insignia 5 **placa de circuito(s)** : circuit board 6 **placa de matrícula** : license plate, tag 7 **placa dental** : plaque, tartar
placard [pla'kar] *nm, pl* -cards *Arg, Uru* : built-in closet
placebo *nm* : placebo
placenta *nf* : placenta
placentero, -ra *adj* AGRADABLE, GRATO : pleasant, agreeable — **placenteramente** *adv*
placer[1] {57} *vi* GUSTAR : to be pleasing ⟨hazlo como te plazca : do it however you please⟩
placer[2] *nm* 1 : pleasure, enjoyment ⟨ha sido un placer : it has been a pleasure⟩ 2 a ~ : as much as one wants
plácido, -da *adj* TRANQUILO : placid, calm
plaga *nf* 1 : plague, infestation (of insects, etc.), blight (of crops, etc.) 2 CALAMIDAD : disaster, scourge
plagado, -da *adj* ~ de : filled with, covered with
plagar {52} *vt* : to plague
plagiar *vt* 1 : to plagiarize 2 SECUESTRAR : to kidnap, to abduct
plagiario, -ria *n* 1 : plagiarist 2 SECUESTRADOR : kidnapper, abductor
plagio *nm* 1 : plagiarism 2 SECUESTRO : kidnapping, abduction
plague, etc. → plagar
plan *nm* 1 : plan, strategy, program ⟨plan de inversiones : investment plan⟩ ⟨plan de estudios : curriculum⟩ 2 PLANO : plan, diagram 3 : attitude, intent, purpose ⟨ponte en plan serio : be serious⟩ ⟨estamos en plan de divertirnos : we're looking to have some fun⟩
plana *nf* 1 : page ⟨noticias en primera plana : front-page news⟩ 2 **plana mayor** : staff (in the military)
plancha *nf* 1 : iron, ironing 2 : grill, griddle ⟨a la plancha : grilled⟩ 3 : sheet, plate ⟨plancha para hornear : baking sheet⟩ 4 *fam* : blunder, blooper
planchada *nf* : ironing, pressing
planchado *nm* → planchada
planchar *v* : to iron
planchazo *nm fam* : goof, blunder
plancton *nm* : plankton
planeación *nf, pl* -ciones *Col, Hon, Mex* → planeamiento
planeador *nm* : glider (aircraft)
planeamiento *nm* : plan, planning
planear *vt* : to plan — *vi* : to glide (in the air)
planeo *nm* : gliding, soaring
planeta *nm* : planet
planetario[1], -ria *adj* 1 : planetary 2 : global, worldwide

planetario[2] *nm* : planetarium
planicie *nf* : plain
planificación *nf, pl* -ciones : planning ⟨planificación familiar : family planning⟩
planificador, -dora *n* : planner
planificar {72} *vt* : to plan
planilla *nf* 1 LISTA : list 2 NÓMINA : payroll 3 TABLA : chart, table 4 *Mex* : slate, ticket (of candidates) 5 **planilla de cálculo** *Arg, Chile* : spreadsheet
plano[1], -na *adj* : flat, level, plane
plano[2] *nm* 1 PLAN : map, plan 2 : plane (surface) 3 NIVEL : level ⟨en un plano personal : on a personal level⟩ 4 : shot (in photography) ⟨primer plano : close-up⟩ 5 de ~ : flatly, outright, directly ⟨se negó de plano : he flatly refused⟩
planta *nf* 1 : plant ⟨planta de interior : houseplant⟩ 2 FÁBRICA : plant, factory 3 PISO : floor, story ⟨planta baja : ground floor, first floor⟩ 4 : staff, employees *pl* 5 : sole (of the foot)
plantación *nf, pl* -ciones 1 : plantation 2 : planting
plantado, -da *adj* 1 : planted 2 **dejar plantado** *fam* : to stand up (a date), to dump (a lover)
plantar *vt* 1 : to plant, to sow ⟨plantar de flores : to plant with flowers⟩ 2 : to put in, to place 3 *fam* : to plant, to land ⟨plantar un beso : to plant a kiss⟩ 4 *fam* : to leave, to jilt — **plantarse** *vr* 1 : to stand firm 2 *fam* : to arrive, to show up 3 *fam* : to balk
planteamiento *nm* 1 : approach, position ⟨el planteamiento feminista : the feminist viewpoint⟩ 2 : explanation, exposition 3 : proposal, suggestion, plan
plantear *vt* 1 : to set forth (an argument, etc.), to bring up (a topic, possibility, etc.), to suggest (an idea, etc.) ⟨no lo plantearía así : I wouldn't describe/explain it like that⟩ 2 : to establish, to set up 3 : to create, to pose (a problem) — **plantearse** *vr* 1 : to think about 2 : to arise
plantel *nm* 1 : educational institution 2 : staff, team
planteo → planteamiento
plantilla *nf* 1 : insole 2 : pattern, template, stencil 3 *Mex, Spain* : staff, roster of employees
plantío *nm* : field (planted with a crop)
plantón *nm, pl* plantones 1 : seedling 2 : long wait ⟨darle (un) plantón a alguien : to stand someone up⟩
plañidero[1], -ra *adj* : mournful
plañidero[2], -ra *nf* : hired mourner
plañir {38} *v* : to mourn, to lament
plasma *nm* : plasma
plasmar *vt* : to express, to give form to — **plasmarse** *vr*
plasta *nf* : soft mass, lump
plástica *nf* : modeling, sculpture
plasticidad *nf* : plasticity
plástico[1], -ca *adj* : plastic
plástico[2] *nm* : plastic
plastificar {72} *vt* : to laminate
plata *nf* 1 : silver (metal) 2 : silver, silverware 3 : money

plataforma *nf* **1** ESTRADO, TARIMA : platform, dais **2** : platform (in politics) **3** : springboard, stepping stone **4 plataforma continental** : continental shelf **5 plataforma de lanzamiento** : launchpad **6 plataforma petrolífera** : oil rig (at sea)

platal *nm* : large sum of money, fortune

platanal *or* **platanar** *nm* : banana plantation

platanero[1], -ra *adj* : banana, banana-producing

platanero[2], -ra *n* : banana grower

plátano *nm* **1** : banana (plant, fruit) **2** : plantain (plant, fruit) **3** : plane tree **plátano macho** *Mex* : plantain

platea *nf* : orchestra seats *pl* (in a theater)

plateado, -da *adj* **1** : silver, silvery **2** : silver-plated

platería *nf* **1** : silver, silverware **2** : silver shop

plática *nf* **1** : talk, lecture **2** : chat, conversation

platicar {72} *vi* : to talk, to chat — *vt Mex* : to tell, to say

platija *nf* : flatfish, flounder

platillo *nm* **1** : saucer ⟨platillo volador : flying saucer⟩ **2** : cymbal **3** : pan (of a scale) **4** *Mex* : dish ⟨platillos típicos : local dishes⟩

platino *nm* : platinum

plato *nm* **1** : plate, dish ⟨lavar los platos : to do the dishes⟩ **2** : serving, helping **3** : course (of a meal) ⟨primer/segundo plato : first/second course⟩ ⟨plato fuerte/principal : main course⟩ **4** : dish ⟨plato típico : typical dish⟩ ⟨plato dulce/salado : sweet/savory dish⟩ **5** : home plate (in baseball) **6 plato hondo** : soup bowl **7 plato llano** : dinner plate

plató *nm* : set (in the movies)

platónico, -ca *adj* : platonic

playa *nf* **1** : beach, seashore **2 playa de estacionamiento** : parking lot

playera *nf* **1** : canvas sneaker **2** *CA, Mex* : T-shirt

playboy [plei'boi] *nm, pl* **playboys** : playboy

plaza *nf* **1** : square, plaza **2** : marketplace **3** : space, seat (in a vehicle) **4** EMPLEO, PUESTO : post, position **5** : place, spot (on a team, etc.) **6 plaza fuerte** : stronghold, fortified city **7 plaza de toros** : bullring

plazca, etc. → placer

plazo *nm* **1** : period, term ⟨un plazo de cinco días : a period of five days⟩ ⟨préstamos a corto/largo plazo : short-term/long-term loans⟩ ⟨el plazo se cumplió : the deadline has passed⟩ **2** ABONO : installment ⟨pagar a plazos : to pay in installments⟩

plazoleta *nf* : small square

plazuela → plazoleta

pleamar *nf* : high tide

plebe *nf* : common people, masses *pl*

plebeyo[1], -ya *adj* : plebeian

plebeyo[2], -ya *n* : plebeian, commoner

plegable *adj* : folding, collapsible

plegadizo → plegable

plegar {49} *vt* DOBLAR : to fold, to bend — **plegarse** *vr* : to give in, to yield

plegaria *nf* ORACIÓN : prayer

pleito *nm* **1** : lawsuit **2** : fight, argument, dispute

plenamente *adv* COMPLETAMENTE : fully, completely

plenario, -ria *adj* : full

plenilunio *nm* : full moon

plenitud *nf* : fullness, abundance

pleno, -na *adj* (*often used as an intensifier*) COMPLETO : full, complete ⟨en pleno uso de sus facultades : in full command of his faculties⟩ ⟨en plena noche : in the middle of the night⟩ ⟨a plena luz (del día) : in broad daylight⟩ ⟨en pleno corazón de la ciudad : right in the heart of the city⟩ ⟨en plena cara : right in the face⟩

plétora *nf* : plethora

pleuresía *nf* : pleurisy

plexiglás *nm* (*Plexiglas*, trademark) *Spain* : plexiglass

pliega, pliegue etc. → plegar

pliego *nm* **1** HOJA : sheet of paper **2** : sealed document

pliegue *nm* **1** DOBLEZ : crease, fold **2** : pleat

plisar *vt* : to pleat

plomada *nf* **1** : plumb line **2** : weight, sinker

plomería *nf* FONTANERÍA : plumbing

plomero, -ra *n* FONTANERO : plumber

plomizo, -za *adj* : leaden

plomo *nm* **1** : lead ⟨sin plomo : unleaded⟩ **2** : plumb line **3** : weight, sinker **4** *Spain* FUSIBLE : fuse **5** *fam* : bore, drag **6 a** ~ : plumb, straight

plugo, etc. → placer

pluma *nf* **1** : feather, quill (for writing) **2** : pen **3** LLAVE : faucet **4 pluma fuente** : fountain pen

plumaje *nm* : plumage

plumero *nm* : feather duster

plumilla *nf* : nib

plumón *nm, pl* **plumones** **1** : down **2** : marker, felt-tip pen

plumoso, -sa *adj* : feathery, downy

plural *adj & nm* : plural

pluralidad *nf* : plurality

pluralizar {21} *vt* **1** : to pluralize **2** : to expand, to multiply

pluriempleado, -da *adj* : holding more than one job

pluriempleo *nm* : moonlighting

plus *nm* : bonus

pluscuamperfecto *nm* : pluperfect — **pluscuamperfecto, -ta** *adj*

plusvalía *nf* : appreciation, capital gain

Plutón *nm* : Pluto

plutocracia *nf* : plutocracy

plutonio *nm* : plutonium

población *nf, pl* **-ciones** **1** : population ⟨población activa : working population⟩ **2** : city, town, village **3 población callampa** *Chile* : shantytown, slums *pl*

poblado[1], -da *adj* **1** : inhabited, populated **2** : full, thick ⟨cejas pobladas : bushy eyebrows⟩

poblado[2] *nm* : village, settlement

poblador, -dora *n* : settler

poblar {19} *vt* **1** : to populate, to inhabit **2** : to settle, to colonize **3** ~ **de** : to

stock with, to plant with — **poblarse** *vr*
: to fill up, to become crowded
pobre[1] *adj* **1** : poor, impoverished **2**
: poor, unfortunate ⟨¡pobre de mí!
: poor me!⟩ **3** : poor, bad (in quality)
⟨pobres resultados : poor results⟩ **4**
: poor, deficient ⟨una dieta pobre : a
poor diet⟩
pobre[2] *nmf* : poor person ⟨los pobres
: the poor⟩ ⟨¡pobre! : poor thing!⟩
pobremente *adv* : poorly
pobreza *nf* : poverty
pocilga *nf* CHIQUERO : pigsty, pigpen
pocillo *nm* : small coffee cup, demitasse
poción *or* **pócima** *nf, pl* **pociones** *or* **pó-
cimas** : potion
poco[1] *adv* **1** : little, not much ⟨poco
probable : not very likely⟩ ⟨come poco
: he doesn't eat much⟩ **2** : a short time,
a while ⟨tardaremos poco : we won't be
very long⟩ **3 poco antes** : shortly before **4 poco después** : shortly after
poco[2], **-ca** *adj* **1** : little, not much, (a)
few ⟨tengo poco dinero : I don't have
much money⟩ ⟨en no pocas ocasiones
: on more than a few occasions⟩ ⟨unos
pocos meses : a few months⟩ ⟨muy poca
gente : very few people⟩ **2 pocas veces**
: rarely
poco[3], **-ca** *pron* **1** : little, few ⟨le falta
poco para terminar : he's almost fin-
ished⟩ ⟨uno de los pocos que quedan
: one of the remaining few⟩ **2 un poco**
: a little, a bit ⟨un poco de vino : a little
wine⟩ ⟨un poco extraño : a bit strange⟩
3 a ~ *Mex* (*used to express disbelief*) ⟨¿a
poco no se te hizo difícil? : you mean
you didn't find it difficult?⟩ **4 de a
poco** : little by little **5 dentro de poco**
: shortly, in a little while **6 hace poco**
: not long ago **7 poco a poco** : little by
little **8 por ~** : nearly, almost
podar *vt* : to prune, to trim
podcast [pod'kast] *nm, pl* **podcasts**
: podcast
poder[1] {58} *v aux* **1** : to be able to, can
⟨no puede hablar : he can't speak⟩ ⟨no
pude acabarlo : I couldn't finish it⟩ **2**
(*expressing possibility*) : might, may
⟨puede llover : it may rain at any mo-
ment⟩ ⟨¿cómo puede ser? : how can that
be?⟩ ⟨se podría/podía haber evitado : it
could have been avoided⟩ **3** (*expressing
permission*) : can, may ⟨¿puedo ir a la
fiesta? : can I go to the party?⟩ ⟨¿se
puede? : may I come in?⟩ **4** (*expressing
a request*) : can ⟨¿me puedes ayudar?
: can you help me?⟩ ⟨¿me lo podrías explicar? : could/would you explain it to
me?⟩ **5** (*expressing annoyance*) : can
⟨¿no puedes estarte quieto? : can't you
sit still?⟩ ⟨¡podrías/podías haberme llamado! : you could have called me!⟩ **6**
(*expressing moral obligation*) : can ⟨no
puedo juzgarlo : I can't judge him⟩ — *vi*
1 : to beat, to defeat ⟨cree que le puede a
cualquiera : he thinks he can beat any-
one⟩ **2** : to be possible ⟨¿crees que
vendrán? — puede (que sí) : do you think
they'll come? — maybe⟩ **3 ~ con** : to

cope with, to manage ⟨¡no puedo con estos niños! : I can't handle these children!⟩
4 a/hasta más no poder ⟨es competitivo
a más no poder : he's as competitive as
they come⟩ ⟨comimos hasta más no
poder : we ate until we couldn't eat another bite⟩ **5 no poder más** : to have
had enough ⟨no puede más : she can't
take anymore⟩ **6 no poder menos que**
: not to be able to help (doing something)
⟨no pudo menos que asombrarse : she
couldn't help but be amazed⟩
poder[2] *nm* **1** : power, control ⟨tener
poder sobre alguien : to have power over
someone⟩ **2** : power, influence ⟨el
poder del amor : the power of love⟩ **3**
: power, ability ⟨poderes mágicos : magical powers⟩ ⟨poder adquisitivo : purchasing power⟩ **4** : power, control (of a
country, etc.) ⟨llegar al poder : to come
to power⟩ ⟨estar en el poder : to be in
power⟩ **5** : power, authority ⟨el poder
de veto : veto power⟩ ⟨tener el poder
para : to have the authority to⟩ **6**
: branch (of government) ⟨el poder legislativo : the legislature⟩ ⟨los poderes
públicos : the authorities⟩ **7** : power,
force ⟨poder militar : military might⟩ **8**
: possession ⟨estar en el poder de : to be
in the hands of⟩ **9** : power of attorney
poderío *nm* **1** : power **2** : wealth, influence
poderosamente *adv* : powerfully
poderoso, -sa *adj* **1** : powerful **2**
: wealthy, influential **3** : effective
podiatría *nf* : podiatry
podio *nm* : podium
pódium → **podio**
podología *nf* : podiatry, chiropody
podólogo, -ga *n* : podiatrist, chiropodist
podrá, etc. → **poder**
podredumbre *nf* **1** : decay, rottenness **2**
: corruption
podrido, -da *adj* **1** : rotten, decayed **2**
: corrupt **3** *Arg, Chile, Uru* HARTO : fed
up
podrir → **pudrir**
poema *nm* : poem
poesía *nf* **1** : poetry **2** POEMA : poem
poeta *nmf* : poet
poético, -ca *adj* : poetic, poetical
poetisa *nf* : poetess *f*, poet
pogrom *nm* : pogrom
póker *or* **poker** *nm* : poker (card game)
polaco[1], **-ca** *adj* : Polish
polaco[2], **-ca** *n* : Pole, Polish person
polaco[3] *nm* : Polish (language)
polar *adj* : polar
polarizar {21} *vt* : to polarize — **polari-
zarse** *vr* — **polarización** *nf*
Polaroid *marca registrada, f* — used for a
camera that produces developed photos
or for the photos produced in this way
polea *nf* : pulley
polémica *nf* CONTROVERSIA : controversy, polemics
polémico, -ca *adj* CONTROVERTIDO
: controversial, polemical
polemizar {21} *vi* : to argue, to debate
polemonio *nm* : phlox

polen *nm, pl* **pólenes** : pollen
polera *nf Chile* : T-shirt
polerón *nm, pl* **-rones** *Chile* : sweatshirt
policía¹ *nf* : police
policía² *nmf* : police officer, policeman *m*, policewoman *f*
policíaco, -ca *or* **policiaco, -ca** *adj* : police ⟨novela policíaca : detective story⟩
policial *adj* : police
polideportivo *nm* : sports center
poliéster *nm* : polyester
polifacético, -ca *adj* : versatile, multifaceted
poligamia *nf* : polygamy
polígamo¹, -ma *adj* : polygamous
polígamo², -ma *n* : polygamist
poligonal *adj* : polygonal
polígono *nm* **1** : polygon **2** *Spain* : zone
poliinsaturado, -da *adj* : polyunsaturated
polilla *nf* : moth
polímero *nm* : polymer
polinesio, -sia *adj & n* : Polynesian
polinizar {21} *vt* : to pollinate — **polinización** *nf*
polio *nf* : polio
poliomielitis *nf* : poliomyelitis, polio
polisón *nm, pl* **-sones** : bustle (on clothing)
politeísmo *nm* : polytheism — **politeísta** *adj & nmf*
política *nf* **1** : politics **2** : policy ⟨política interior/exterior : domestic/foreign policy⟩
políticamente *adv* : politically
político¹, -ca *adj* **1** : political **2** : tactful, politic **3** : by marriage ⟨padre político : father-in-law⟩
político², -ca *n* : politician
póliza *nf* : policy ⟨póliza de seguros : insurance policy⟩
polizón *nm, pl* **-zones** : stowaway ⟨viajar de polizón : to stow away⟩
polka *nf* : polka
polla *nf* **1** APUESTA : bet **2** *Chile* LOTERÍA : lottery
pollera *nf* **1** : chicken coop **2** : skirt
pollero, -ra *n* **1** : poultry farmer **2** : poultry farm **3** *Mex fam* COYOTE : smuggler of illegal immigrants
pollito, -ta *n* : chick, young bird, fledgling
pollo, -lla *n* **1** : chicken **2** POLLITO : chick **3** JOVEN : young man *m*, young lady *f*
polluelo *nm* → **pollito**
polo *nm* **1** : pole ⟨el Polo Norte : the North Pole⟩ ⟨polo negativo : negative pole⟩ **2** : polo (sport) **3** : polo shirt **4** : focal point, center **5 polo opuesto** : exact opposite
pololo, -la *n Chile fam* : boyfriend *m*, girlfriend *f*
poltrona *nf* : armchair, easy chair
polución *nf, pl* **-ciones** CONTAMINACIÓN : pollution
polvareda *nf* **1** : cloud of dust **2** : uproar, fuss
polvera *nf* : compact (for face powder)
polvo *nm* **1** : dust ⟨quitar/limpiar el polvo : to dust⟩ **2** : powder ⟨polvo(s) de hornear : baking powder⟩ **3 polvos**

nmpl : face powder **4 en** ~ : powdered, ground **5 estar hecho polvo** *fam* : to be worn out **6 hacer polvo** *fam* : to crush, to shatter
pólvora *nf* **1** : gunpowder **2** : fireworks *pl*
polvoriento, -ta *adj* : dusty, powdery
polvorín *nm, pl* **-rines** : magazine, ammunition dump
pomada *nf* : ointment, cream
pomelo *nm* : grapefruit
pómez *nf or* **piedra pómez** : pumice
pomo *nm* **1** : pommel (on a sword) **2** : knob, handle **3** : perfume bottle
pompa *nf* **1** : bubble **2** : pomp, splendor **3 pompas fúnebres** : funeral
pompón *nm, pl* **pompones** BORLA : pompom
pomposidad *nf* **1** : pomp, splendor **2** : pomposity, ostentation
pomposo, -sa *adj* : pompous — **pomposamente** *adv*
pómulo *nm* : cheekbone
pon → **poner**
ponchadura *nf Mex* : puncture, flat (tire)
ponchar *vt* **1** *Car, CA, Col, Ven* : to strike out (in baseball) **2** *Mex* : to puncture — **poncharse** *vr* **1** *Car, CA, Col, Ven* : to strike out (in baseball) **2** *Mex* : to blow out (of a tire)
ponche *nm* **1** : punch (drink) **2 ponche de huevo** : eggnog
poncho *nm* : poncho
ponderación *nf, pl* **-ciones** **1** : consideration, deliberation **2** : high praise
ponderar *vt* **1** : to weigh, to consider **2** : to speak highly of
pondrá, etc. → **poner**
ponedora *nf* : layer (bird)
ponencia *nf* **1** DISCURSO : paper, presentation, address **2** INFORME : report
ponente *nmf* : speaker, presenter
poner {60} *vt* **1** COLOCAR : to put, to place ⟨pon el libro en la mesa : put the book on the table⟩ **2** AGREGAR, AÑADIR : to put in, to add (an ingredient, etc.) **3** : to put on (clothes) ⟨le puse el suéter : I put her sweater on (her)⟩ **4** CONTRIBUIR : to contribute **5** ESCRIBIR : to put in writing ⟨no le puso su nombre : he didn't put his name on it⟩ **6** : to give (a task, etc.), to impose (a fine) **7** : to prepare, to arrange ⟨poner la mesa : to set the table⟩ **8** : to name ⟨le pusimos Ana : we called her Ana⟩ **9** ESTABLECER : to set up, to establish ⟨puso un restaurante : he opened up a restaurant⟩ **10** INSTALAR : to install, to put in **11** (*with an adjective or adverb*) : to make ⟨me pone nervioso : it makes me nervous⟩ ⟨siempre lo pones de mal humor : you always put him in a bad mood⟩ **12** : to turn on, to switch on **13** : to set (an alarm, etc.) ⟨pon la música más alta/fuerte : turn up the music⟩ **14** SUPONER : to suppose ⟨pongamos que no viene : supposing he doesn't come⟩ **15** : to give (an example) **16** : to raise (objections), to create (problems, etc.) **17** : to lay (eggs) **18** ~ **a** : to start (some-

one doing something) ⟨lo puse a trabajar : I put him to work⟩ **19** ~ **de** : to place as ⟨la pusieron de directora : they made her director⟩ **20** ~ **en** : to put in (a state or condition) ⟨poner en duda : to call into question⟩ ⟨lo puso en peligro : she put him in danger⟩ — *vi* **1** : to contribute **2** : to lay eggs — **ponerse** *vr* **1** : to move (into a position) ⟨ponerse de pie : to stand up⟩ **2** : to put on, to wear **3** : to become, to turn ⟨se puso colorado : he turned red⟩ **4** : to start ⟨me puse a llorar : I started to cry⟩ **5** : to set (of the sun or moon)

poni *or* **poney** *nm* : pony

ponga, etc. → **poner**

poniente *nm* **1** OCCIDENTE : west **2** : west wind

ponqué *nm Col, Ven* : cake

pontificar {72} *vi* : to pontificate

pontífice *nm* : pontiff, pope

pontón *nm, pl* **pontones** : pontoon

ponzoña *nf* VENENO : poison — **ponzoñoso, -sa** *adj*

pop [ˈpop] *adj & nm* : pop (music)

popa *nf* **1** : stern **2 a** ~ : astern, abaft, aft

popelín *nm, pl* **-lines** : poplin

popelina *nf* : poplin

popó *nm fam* **1** : poop **2 hacer popó** : to poop, to go poop

popote *nm Mex* : straw, drinking straw

populachero, -ra *adj* : common, popular, vulgar

populacho *nm* : rabble, masses *pl*

popular *adj* **1** : popular **2** : traditional **3** : colloquial — **popularmente** *adv*

popularidad *nf* : popularity

popularizar {21} *vt* : to popularize — **popularizarse** *vr*

populista *adj & nmf* : populist — **populismo** *nm*

populoso, -sa *adj* : populous

popurrí *nm* : potpourri

por *prep* **1** : for, during ⟨se quedaron allí por la semana : they stayed there for the week⟩ ⟨por el momento : for now, at the moment⟩ **2** : around, during ⟨por noviembre empieza a nevar : around November it starts to snow⟩ ⟨por la mañana : in the morning⟩ ⟨por la noche : at night⟩ **3** : around (a place) ⟨debe estar por allí : it must be over there⟩ ⟨por todas partes : everywhere⟩ **4** : by, through, along ⟨por la puerta : through the door⟩ ⟨pasamos por el centro : we went through the downtown⟩ ⟨pasé por tu casa : I stopped by your house⟩ ⟨por la costa : along the coast⟩ ⟨caminando por la calle : walking down the street⟩ **5** : for, for the sake of ⟨lo hizo por su madre : he did it for his mother⟩ ⟨¡por Dios! : for heaven's sake!⟩ **6** : because of, on account of ⟨llegué tarde por el tráfico : I arrived late because of the traffic⟩ ⟨dejar por imposible : to give up as impossible⟩ ⟨perdón por la demora : sorry for the delay⟩ **7** : per ⟨60 millas por hora : 60 miles per hour⟩ ⟨por docena : by the dozen⟩ **8** : for, in ex-

change for, instead of ⟨su hermana habló por él : his sister spoke on his behalf⟩ ⟨lo vendió por cien dólares : he sold it for a hundred dollars⟩ **9** : by means of ⟨hablar por teléfono : to talk on the phone⟩ ⟨por escrito : in writing⟩ ⟨por avión : by plane⟩ **10** : as for ⟨por mí : as far as I'm concerned⟩ **11** : times ⟨tres por dos son seis : three times two is six⟩ **12** SEGÚN : from, according to ⟨por lo que dices : judging from what you're telling me⟩ **13** : as, for ⟨por ejemplo : for example⟩ **14** : by ⟨hecho por mi abuela : made by my grandmother⟩ ⟨por correo : by mail⟩ **15** : for, in order to ⟨lucha por ganar su respeto : he struggles to win her respect⟩ **16 estar por** : to be about to **17 por ciento** : percent **18 por favor** : please **19 por lo tanto** : therefore, consequently **20 ¿por qué?** : why? **21 por que** → **porque 22 por ... que** : no matter how ⟨por mucho que intente : no matter how hard I try⟩ **23 por si** *or* **por si acaso** : just in case

porcelana *nf* : china, porcelain

porcentaje *nm* : percentage

porche *nm* : porch

porción *nf, pl* **porciones** **1** : portion **2** PARTE : part, share **3** RACIÓN : serving, helping

pordiosear *vi* MENDIGAR : beg

pordiosero, -ra *n* MENDIGO : beggar

porfiado, -da *adj* OBSTINADO, TERCO : obstinate, stubborn — **porfiadamente** *adv*

porfiar {85} *vi* : to insist, to persist

pormenor *nm* DETALLE : detail

pormenorizar {21} *vi* : to go into detail — *vt* : to tell in detail

pornografía *nf* : pornography

pornográfico, -ca *adj* : pornographic

poro *nm* : pore

poroso, -sa *adj* : porous — **porosidad** *nf*

poroto *nm Arg, Chile, Uru* : bean

porque *conj* **1** : because **2** *or* **por que** : in order that

porqué *nm* : reason, cause ⟨no explicó el porqué : he didn't explain the reason⟩

porquería *nf* **1** SUCIEDAD : dirt, filth **2** : nastiness, vulgarity **3** : worthless thing, trifle **4** : junk food

porra *nf* **1** : nightstick, club **2** *Mex* : fans *pl* **3** *Mex* : cheer, yell ⟨los aficionados le echaban porras : the fans cheered him on⟩ **4 mandar a alguien a la porra** : to tell someone to go to hell

porrazo *nm* **1** : blow, whack **2 de golpe y porrazo** : suddenly

porrista *nmf* **1** : cheerleader **2** : fan, supporter

porro *nm fam* : joint *fam*, marijuana cigarette

portaaviones *nms & pl* : aircraft carrier

portada *nf* **1** : title page **2** : cover **3** : facade, front

portador, -dora *n* : carrier, bearer ⟨cheque al portador : check payable to bearer⟩

portaequipajes *nms & pl* **1** : luggage rack, roof rack **2** : trunk (of a car)

portafolio or **portafolios** nm, pl **-lios** 1 MALETÍN : briefcase 2 : portfolio (of investments)
portal nm 1 : portal, doorway 2 VESTÍBULO : vestibule, hall 3 : portal (on the web)
portar vt 1 : to carry, to bear 2 : to wear — **portarse** vr CONDUCIRSE : to behave ⟨pórtate bien : behave yourself⟩ ⟨se portó mal con ella : he treated her badly⟩
portátil[1] adj : portable
portátil[2] nmf : laptop computer
portaviandas nms & pl : lunch box
portaviones nm → **portaaviones**
portavoz nmf, pl **-voces** : spokesperson, spokesman m, spokeswoman f
portazo nm : slam ⟨dar un portazo : to slam the door⟩
porte nm 1 ASPECTO : bearing, demeanor 2 TRANSPORTE : transport, carrying ⟨porte pagado : postage paid⟩ 3 : size ⟨de gran porte : large-sized⟩
portento nm MARAVILLA : marvel, wonder
portentoso, -sa adj MARAVILLOSO : marvelous, wonderful
porteño, -ña adj : of or from Buenos Aires
portería nf 1 ARCO : goal, goalposts pl 2 : superintendent's office
portero, -ra n 1 ARQUERO : goalkeeper, goalie 2 : doorman m (at a hotel, etc.), bouncer (at a nightclub, etc.) 3 : janitor, superintendent
pórtico nm : portico
portilla nf : porthole
portón nm, pl **portones** 1 : main door 2 : gate
portorriqueño, -ña → **puertorriqueño**
portugués[1], **-guesa** adj & n, mpl **-gueses** : Portuguese
portugués[2] nm : Portuguese (language)
porvenir nm FUTURO : future
pos adv **en pos de** : in pursuit of
pos- or **post-** pref : post-
posada nf 1 : inn 2 Mex : Advent celebration
posaderas nfpl : bottom, backside
posadero, -ra n : innkeeper
posar vi : to pose — vt : to place, to lay — **posarse** vr 1 : to land, to light, to perch 2 : to settle, to rest
posavasos nms & pl : coaster (for drinks)
posdata → **postdata**
pose nf : pose
poseedor, -dora n : possessor, holder
poseer {20} vt : to possess, to hold, to have
poseído, -da adj : possessed
posesión nf, pl **-siones** : possession
posesionarse vr ~ **de** : to take possession of, to take over
posesivo[1], **-va** adj : possessive
posesivo[2] nm : possessive case
posfechar vt : to postdate
posguerra nf : postwar period
posibilidad nf 1 : possibility ⟨existe la posibilidad de que . . . : the possibility exists that . . .⟩ 2 **posibilidades** nfpl : means, income

posibilitar vt : to make possible, to permit
posible adj 1 : possible ⟨es posible que . . . : it's possible that . . .⟩ 2 **a/de ser posible** : if possible 3 **dentro de lo posible** or **en lo posible** : as far as possible 4 **hacer todo lo posible** : to do everything possible 5 **lo mejor/antes (etc.) posible** : as well/soon (etc.) as possible 6 **si es posible** : if possible — **posiblemente** adv
posición nf, pl **-ciones** 1 : position, place ⟨en posición vertical : in an upright position⟩ 2 : status, standing 3 : attitude, stance
posicionar vt 1 : to position, to place 2 : to establish — **posicionarse** vr
positivo[1], **-va** adj : positive — **positivamente** adv
positivo[2] nm : print (in photography)
posmoderno, -na adj : postmodern
poso nm 1 : sediment, dregs pl 2 : grounds pl (of coffee)
posoperatorio, -ria adj : postoperative
posparto adj : postnatal ⟨depresión posparto : postpartum depression⟩
posponer {60} vt 1 : to postpone 2 : to put behind, to subordinate
pospuso, etc. → **posponer**
post nm, pl **post** or **posts** : post (on social media)
posta nf 1 : relay race 2 : post, station 3 Chile : emergency medical center
postal[1] adj : postal
postal[2] nf : postcard
postdata nf : postscript
poste nm 1 : post, pole ⟨poste de teléfonos : telephone pole⟩ 2 : goalpost (in sports)
postear vt fam : to post (on social media)
posteo nm → **post**
póster or **poster** nm, pl **pósters** or **posters** : poster, placard
postergación nf, pl **-ciones** : postponement, deferring
postergar {52} vt 1 : to delay, to postpone 2 : to pass over (an employee)
posteridad nf : posterity
posterior adj 1 ULTERIOR : later, subsequent 2 TRASERO : back, rear
posterioridad nf **con** ~ : subsequently, later
posteriormente adv : subsequently
postgrado nm : graduate course
postgraduado, -da n : graduate student, postgraduate
postguerra → **posguerra**
postigo nm 1 CONTRAVENTANA : shutter 2 : small door, wicket gate
postilla nf : scab
Post-it marca registrada, m — used for a slip of paper with a sticky edge
postizo, -za adj : artificial, false ⟨dentadura postiza : dentures⟩
postnatal adj : postnatal
postor, -tora n : bidder ⟨mejor postor : highest bidder⟩
postración nf, pl **-ciones** 1 : prostration 2 ABATIMIENTO : depression
postrado, -da adj 1 : prostrate 2 **postrado en cama** : bedridden

potranco, -ca *n* → **potro**[1]

postrar *vt* DEBILITAR : to debilitate, to weaken — **postrarse** *vr* : to prostrate oneself

postre[1] *nm* : dessert ⟨de postre comimos helado : we had ice cream for dessert⟩

postre[2] *nf* **a la postre** : in the end

postrero, -ra *adj* (*postrer* before masculine singular nouns) ÚLTIMO : last

postulación *nf, pl* **-ciones** 1 : collection 2 : nomination (of a candidate)

postulado *nm* : postulate, assumption

postulante, -ta *n* : candidate, applicant

postular *vt* 1 : to postulate 2 : to nominate 3 : to propose — **postularse** *vr* : to run, to be a candidate

póstumo, -ma *adj* : posthumous — **póstumamente** *adv*

postura *nf* 1 : posture, position (of the body) 2 ACTITUD, POSICIÓN : position, stance

potable *adj* : drinkable, potable ⟨agua potable : (safe) drinking water⟩

potaje *nm* : thick vegetable soup

potasa *nf* : potash

potasio *nm* : potassium

pote *nm* 1 OLLA : pot 2 : jar, container

potencia *nf* 1 : power ⟨potencias extranjeras : foreign powers⟩ ⟨elevado a la tercera potencia : raised to the third power⟩ 2 : capacity, potency 3 **en ~** : in the making ⟨un líder en potencia : a leader in the making⟩

potencial *adj & nm* : potential

potenciar *vt* : to promote, to foster

potenciómetro *nm* : dimmer, dimmer switch

potentado, -da *n* 1 SOBERANO : sovereign, ruler 2 MAGNATE : tycoon, magnate

potente *adj* 1 : powerful, strong 2 : potent, virile

potestad *nf* 1 AUTORIDAD : authority, jurisdiction 2 **patria potestad** : custody, guardianship

potrero *nm* 1 : field, pasture 2 : cattle ranch

potro[1], **-tra** *n* : colt *m*, filly *f*

potro[2] *nm* 1 : rack (for torture) 2 : horse (in gymnastics)

pozo *nm* 1 : well ⟨pozo de petróleo, pozo petrolero : oil well⟩ 2 : deep pool (in a river) 3 : mine shaft 4 *Arg, Par, Uru* : pothole 5 **pozo séptico** : cesspool

pozole *nm Mex* : spicy stew made with pork and hominy

práctica *nf* 1 : practice, experience 2 : practice ⟨la práctica de la medicina : the practice of medicine⟩ 3 : practice ⟨en la práctica : in practice⟩ ⟨poner en práctica : to put into practice⟩ 4 **prácticas** *nfpl* : practice, training

practicable *adj* : practicable, feasible

prácticamente *adv* : practically

practicante[1] *adj* : practicing ⟨católicos practicantes : practicing Catholics⟩

practicante[2] *nmf* : practitioner

practicar {72} *vt* 1 : to practice 2 : to perform, to carry out 3 : to exercise (a profession), to play (a sport) — *vi* : to practice

práctico, -ca *adj* : practical ⟨a efectos prácticos : for all practical purposes⟩

pradera *nf* : grassland, prairie

prado *nm* 1 CAMPO : field, meadow 2 : park

pragmático, -ca *adj* : pragmatic — **pragmáticamente** *adv*

pragmatismo *nm* : pragmatism

pre- *pref* : pre-

preadolescente *nmf* : preteen

preámbulo *nm* 1 INTRODUCCIÓN : preamble, introduction 2 RODEO : evasion ⟨gastar preámbulos : to beat around the bush⟩

prebélico, -ca *adj* : antebellum

prebenda *nf* : privilege

precalentar {55} *vt* : to preheat

precariedad *nf* : precariousness

precario, -ria *adj* : precarious — **precariamente** *adv*

precaución *nf, pl* **-ciones** 1 : precaution ⟨medidas de precaución : precautionary measures⟩ 2 PRUDENCIA : caution, care ⟨con precaución : cautiously⟩

precautorio, -ria *adj* : precautionary

precaver *vt* PREVENIR : to prevent, to guard against — **precaverse** *vr* PREVENIRSE : to take precautions, to be on guard

precavido, -da *adj* CAUTELOSO : cautious, prudent

precedencia *nf* : precedence, priority

precedente[1] *adj* : preceding, previous

precedente[2] *nm* : precedent

preceder *v* : to precede

precepto *nm* : rule, precept

preciado, -da *adj* : esteemed, prized, valuable

preciarse *vr* 1 JACTARSE : to boast, to brag 2 **~ de** : to pride oneself on

precintar *vt* 1 : to seal 2 : to shut down (a business), to seal off (an area)

precinto *nm* : seal

precio *nm* 1 : price ⟨¿qué precio tiene? : how much is it?⟩ ⟨no tener precio : to be priceless⟩ 2 : cost, sacrifice ⟨a cualquier precio : at any cost⟩ 3 **precio de salida** : starting price 4 **precio de venta** : retail price

preciosidad *nf* : beautiful thing ⟨este vestido es una preciosidad : this dress is lovely⟩

precioso, -sa *adj* 1 HERMOSO : beautiful, exquisite 2 VALIOSO : precious, valuable

precipicio *nm* 1 : precipice 2 RUINA : ruin

precipitación *nf, pl* **-ciones** 1 PRISA : haste, hurry, rush 2 : precipitation, rain, snow

precipitado, -da *adj* 1 : hasty, sudden 2 : rash — **precipitadamente** *adv*

precipitar *vt* 1 APRESURAR : to hasten, to speed up 2 ARROJAR : to hurl, to throw — **precipitarse** *vr* 1 APRESURARSE : to rush 2 : to act rashly ⟨tal vez me precipito : perhaps I'm being too hasty⟩ 3 ARROJARSE : to throw oneself

precisamente *adv* JUSTAMENTE : precisely, exactly

precisar *vt* **1** : to specify, to determine exactly **2** NECESITAR : to need, to require — *vi* : to be necessary

precisión *nf, pl* **-siones 1** EXACTITUD : precision, accuracy **2** CLARIDAD : clarity (of style, etc.) **3** NECESIDAD : necessity ⟨tener precisión de : to have need of⟩

preciso, -sa *adj* **1** EXACTO : precise **2** : very, exact ⟨en ese preciso instante : at that very instant⟩ **3** NECESARIO : necessary ⟨es preciso que . . . : it is necessary that . . .⟩

precocidad *nf* : precocity

precocinar *vt* : to precook

preconcebido, -da *adj* : preconceived

precondición *nf, pl* **-ciones** : precondition

preconizar {21} *vt* **1** : to recommend, to advocate **2** : to extol

precoz *adj, pl* **precoces 1** : precocious **2** : early, premature — **precozmente** *adv*

precursor, -sora *n* : forerunner, precursor

predecesor, -sora *n* ANTECESOR : predecessor

predecir {11} *vt* : to foretell, to predict

predestinado, -da *adj* : predestined, fated

predestinar *vt* : to predestine — **predestinación** *nf*

predeterminar *vt* : to predetermine

prédica *nf* SERMÓN : sermon

predicado *nm* : predicate

predicador, -dora *n* : preacher

predicar {72} *v* : to preach

predicción *nf, pl* **-ciones 1** : prediction **2** PRONÓSTICO : forecast ⟨predicción del tiempo : weather forecast⟩

prediga, predijo etc. → **predecir**

predilección *nf, pl* **-ciones** : predilection, preference

predilecto, -ta *adj* : favorite

predio *nm* : property, piece of land

predisponer {60} *vt* **1** : to predispose, to incline **2** : to prejudice, to bias

predisposición *nf, pl* **-ciones 1** : predisposition, tendency **2** : prejudice, bias

predispuesto, -ta *adj* ∼ **a** : prone to

predominante *adj* : predominant — **predominantemente** *adv*

predominar *vi* PREVALECER : to predominate, to prevail

predominio *nm* : predominance, prevalence

preeminente *adj* : preeminent — **preeminencia** *nf*

preescolar *adj & nm* : preschool

preestreno *nm* : preview

prefabricado, -da *adj* : prefabricated

prefacio *nm* : preface

prefecto *nm* : prefect

preferencia *nf* **1** : preference **2** PRIORIDAD : priority **3** : right-of-way (of traffic) **4 de** ∼ : preferably

preferencial *adj* : preferential

preferente *adj* : preferential, special ⟨trato preferente : special treatment⟩

preferentemente *adv* : preferably

preferible *adj* : preferable ⟨es preferible que . . . : it's better that . . .⟩ ⟨ser preferible a : to be preferable to⟩

preferido, -da *adj & n* : favorite

preferir {76} *vt* : to prefer ⟨prefiero ir : I'd rather go⟩ ⟨prefiero que no vayas : I'd rather (that) you didn't go⟩ ⟨prefiero éste a ése : I prefer this one to/over that one⟩

prefigurar *vt* : to foreshadow, prefigure

prefijo *nm* **1** : prefix (in linguistics) **2** *Spain* : area code

pregonar *vt* **1** : to proclaim, to announce **2** : to hawk (merchandise) **3** : to extol **4** : to reveal, to disclose

pregrabado, -da *adj* : prerecorded

pregunta *nf* **1** : question **2 hacer una pregunta** : to ask a question

preguntar *vt* : to ask, to question — *vi* : to ask, to inquire ⟨preguntar por : to ask about⟩ — **preguntarse** *vr* : to wonder

preguntón, -tona *adj, mpl* **-tones** : inquisitive

prehistórico, -ca *adj* : prehistoric

prejuiciado, -da *adj* : prejudiced

prejuicio *nm* : prejudice ⟨tener prejuicios contra : to be prejudiced against⟩

prejuzgar {52} *vt* : to prejudge

prelado *nm* : prelate

preliminar *adj & nm* : preliminary

preludio *nm* : prelude

prematrimonial *adj* : premarital

prematuro, -ra *adj* : premature

premeditación *nf, pl* **-ciones** : premeditation

premeditar *vt* : to premeditate, to plan

premenstrual *adj* : premenstrual

premiado[1], -da *adj* : winning, prizewinning

premiado[2], -da *n* : prizewinner

premiar *vt* **1** : to award a prize to **2** : to reward

premier *nmf* : premier, prime minister

premio *nm* **1** : prize ⟨premio gordo : grand prize, jackpot⟩ ⟨dar/ganar un premio : to give/win a prize⟩ **2** : reward **3** : premium

premisa *nf* : premise, basis

premolar *nm* : bicuspid (tooth)

premonición *nf, pl* **-ciones** : premonition

premura *nf* : haste, urgency

prenatal *adj* : prenatal

prenda *nf* **1** : piece of clothing **2** : security, pledge **3** : forfeit (in a game)

prendar *vt* **1** : to charm, to captivate **2** : to pawn, to pledge — **prendarse** *vr* ∼ **de** : to fall in love with

prendedor *nm* : brooch, pin

prender *vt* **1** SUJETAR : to pin, to fasten **2** APRESAR : to catch, to apprehend **3** : to light (a cigarette, a match) **4** : to turn on ⟨prende la luz : turn on the light⟩ **5 prender fuego a** : to set fire to — *vi* **1** : to take root **2** : to catch fire **3** : to catch on — **prenderse** *vr* : to catch fire

prensa *nf* **1** : printing press **2** : press ⟨conferencia de prensa : press conference⟩ ⟨la prensa : the press, the newspapers⟩

prensar *vt* : to press
prensil *adj* : prehensile
preñado, -da *adj* **1** : pregnant **2** ～ **de** : filled with
preñar *vt* EMBARAZAR : to make pregnant
preñez *nf, pl* **preñeces** : pregnancy
preocupación *nf, pl* **-ciones** INQUIETUD : worry, concern
preocupado, -da *adj* : worried ⟨preocupado por : worried about⟩
preocupante *adj* : worrisome
preocupar *vt* INQUIETAR : to worry, to concern ⟨eso me preocupa : that worries me⟩ — **preocuparse** *vr* **1** APURARSE : to worry, to be concerned ⟨preocuparse por : to worry about⟩ **2** ～ **de** : to take care of (something) ⟨preocuparse de que . . . : to make sure that . . .⟩
preparación *nf, pl* **-ciones** **1** : preparation, readiness **2** : education, training **3** : (medicinal) preparation
preparado[1], -da *adj* **1** : ready, prepared **2** : trained
preparado[2] *nm* : preparation, mixture
preparar *vt* **1** : to prepare ⟨preparé el almuerzo : I made lunch, I got lunch ready⟩ ⟨preparar un examen : to prepare for an exam⟩ **2** : to teach, to train, to coach — **prepararse** *vr* : to get ready, to prepare ⟨prepararse para algo : to get ready for something⟩ ⟨se prepara para salir : she's getting ready to leave⟩
preparativos *nmpl* : preparations
preparatoria *nf Mex* : high school
preparatorio, -ria *adj* : preparatory
preponderante *adj* : preponderant, predominant — **preponderancia** *nf* — **preponderantemente** *adv*
preposición *nf, pl* **-ciones** : preposition — **preposicional** *adj*
prepotente *adj* : arrogant, domineering, overbearing — **prepotencia** *nf*
prerrogativa *nf* : prerogative, privilege
presa *nf* **1** : capture, seizure ⟨hacer presa de : to seize⟩ **2** : catch, prey ⟨presa de : prey to, seized with⟩ **3** : claw, fang **4** DIQUE : dam **5** : morsel, piece (of food)
presagiar *vt* : to presage, to portend
presagio *nm* : omen, portent
presbiterio *nm* : sanctuary (of a church)
prescindible *adj* : expendable, dispensable
prescindir *vi* ～ **de** **1** : to do without, to dispense with **2** DESATENDER : to ignore, to disregard **3** OMITIR : to omit, to skip
prescribir {33} *vt* : to prescribe
prescripción *nf, pl* **-ciones** : prescription
prescrito *pp* → **prescribir**
presencia *nf* **1** : presence ⟨en presencia de : in the presence of⟩ **2** ASPECTO : appearance
presenciar *vt* **1** : to witness **2** : to be present at, to attend
presentable *adj* : presentable
presentación *nf, pl* **-ciones** **1** : presentation **2** : introduction **3** : appearance
presentador, -dora *n* : host (of a show), anchor (of a newscast)

presentar *vt* **1** MOSTRAR : to present, to show **2** : to have, to show (a symptom) **3** : to offer, to give (an excuse, etc.) **4** : to submit (a document), to file (a complaint) **5** : to launch (a product) **6** : to introduce (a person) **7** : to host (a show), to anchor (a newscast) — **presentarse** *vr* **1** : to show up, to appear ⟨preséntese en la oficina central : report to the central office⟩ **2** SURGIR : to arise, to come up **3** : to introduce oneself **4** ～ **a** : to enter (a competition), to run in (an election)
presente[1] *adj* **1** : present, in attendance **2** : present, current ⟨del presente mes/año : of the current month/year⟩ **3 tener presente** : to keep in mind
presente[2] *nf* **por la presente** : hereby (in a letter)
presente[3] *nm* : present (time, tense)
presente[4] *nmf* : one present ⟨entre los presentes se encontraban . . . : those present included . . .⟩
presentimiento *nm* : premonition, hunch, feeling
presentir {76} *vt* : to sense, to intuit ⟨presentía lo que iba a pasar : he sensed what was going to happen⟩
preservación *nf, pl* **-ciones** : preservation
preservar *vt* **1** : to preserve **2** : to protect
preservativo *nm* CONDÓN : condom
presidencia *nf* **1** : presidency **2** : chairmanship
presidencial *adj* : presidential
presidente[1] *nmf* → **presidente[2]**
presidente[2], -ta *n* **1** : president **2** : chair, chairperson (of a group or event) **3** : presiding judge
presidiario, -ria *n* : convict, prisoner
presidio *nm* : prison, penitentiary
presidir *vt* **1** MODERAR : to preside over, to chair **2** : to dominate, to rule over
presilla *nf* : eye, loop, fastener
presión *nf, pl* **presiones** **1** : pressure **2 presión arterial** : blood pressure
presionar *vt* **1** : to pressure **2** : to press, to push — *vi* : to put on the pressure
preso[1], -sa *adj* **1** : imprisoned ⟨estar preso : to be imprisoned⟩ **2 llevarse/tomar preso a** : to imprison, to take prisoner
preso[2], -sa *n* : prisoner
prestación *nf, pl* **-ciones** **1** : providing, provision **2** : benefit ⟨prestaciones sociales : welfare, government assistance⟩ **3** : feature
prestado, -da *adj* **1** : borrowed, on loan **2 pedir prestado** : to borrow, to ask to borrow **3 tomar prestado** : to borrow
prestamista *nmf* : moneylender, pawnbroker
préstamo *nm* **1** : loan **2** : lending, borrowing **3** BARBARISMO : loanword, borrowing
prestar *vt* **1** : to lend, to loan ⟨¿me prestas el paraguas? : can I borrow your umbrella?⟩ **2** : to render (a service), to give (aid) **3 prestar atención** : to pay atten-

tion **4 prestar declaración** : to testify **5 prestar juramento** : to take an oath — **prestarse** *vr* ~ **a/para 1** : to lend oneself to ⟨se presta a confusiones : it lends itself to confusion⟩ **2** : to agree to **3** : to participate in

prestatario, -ria *n* : borrower

presteza *nf* : promptness, speed

prestidigitación *nf, pl* **-ciones** : sleight of hand

prestidigitador, -dora *n* : conjurer, magician

prestigio *nm* : prestige — **prestigioso, -sa** *adj*

presto¹ *adv* : promptly, at once

presto², -ta *adj* **1** : quick, prompt **2** DISPUESTO, PREPARADO : ready

presumido, -da *adj* VANIDOSO : conceited, vain

presumir *vt* SUPONER : to presume, to suppose — *vi* **1** ALARDEAR : to boast, to show off **2** ~ **de** : to consider oneself ⟨presume de inteligente : he thinks he's intelligent⟩

presunción *nf, pl* **-ciones 1** SUPOSICIÓN : presumption, supposition **2** VANIDAD : conceit, vanity

presunto, -ta *adj* : presumed, supposed, alleged — **presuntamente** *adv*

presuntuoso, -sa *adj* : conceited

presuponer {60} *vt* : to presuppose

presupuestal *adj* : budget, budgetary

presupuestar *vi* : to budget — *vt* : to budget for

presupuestario, -ria *adj* : budget, budgetary

presupuesto *nm* **1** : budget, estimate **2** : assumption, supposition

presurizar {21} *vt* : to pressurize

presuroso, -sa *adj* : hasty, quick

pretencioso, -sa *adj* : pretentious — **pretenciosamente** *adv*

pretender *vt* **1** INTENTAR : to attempt, to try ⟨pretendo estudiar : I'm trying to study⟩ **2** AFIRMAR : to claim ⟨pretende ser pobre : he claims he's poor⟩ **3** : to seek, to aspire to ⟨¿qué pretendes tú? : what are you after?⟩ **4** CORTEJAR : to court **5 pretender que** : to expect ⟨¿pretendes que lo crea? : do you expect me to believe you?⟩

pretendido, -da *adj* **1** SUPUESTO : supposed, so-called **2** FALSO : feigned, false

pretendiente¹ *nmf* **1** : candidate, applicant **2** : pretender, claimant (to a throne, etc.)

pretendiente² *nm* : suitor

pretensión *nf, pl* **-siones 1** : intention, hope, plan **2** : claim (to a throne, etc.) **3** : pretension ⟨sin pretensiones : unpretentious⟩

pretérito *nm* : preterit, past (tense)

pretextar *vt* : to claim, to feign

pretexto *nm* EXCUSA : pretext, excuse

pretil *nm* : parapet, railing

prevalecer {53} *vi* : to prevail, to triumph

prevaleciente *adj* : prevailing, prevalent

prevalerse {84} *vr* ~ **de** : to avail oneself of, to take advantage of

prevención *nf, pl* **-ciones 1** : prevention **2** : preparation, readiness **3** : precautionary measure **4** : prejudice, bias

prevenido, -da *adj* **1** PREPARADO : prepared, ready **2** ADVERTIDO : forewarned **3** CAUTELOSO : cautious

prevenir {87} *vt* **1** : to prevent **2** : to warn — **prevenirse** *vr* ~ **contra** *or* ~ **de** : to take precautions against

preventivo, -va *adj* : preventive, precautionary

prever {88} *vt* **1** ANTICIPAR : to foresee, to anticipate **2** PLANEAR : to plan

previo¹, -via *adj* **1** : previous, prior **2** PRELIMINAR : preliminary

previo², -via *prep* : after, upon ⟨previo pago : after paying, upon payment⟩

previsible *adj* : foreseeable

previsión *nf, pl* **-siones 1** : foresight **2** : prediction, forecast **3** : precaution **4 previsión social** : welfare

previsor, -sora *adj* : farsighted, prudent

prieto, -ta *adj* **1** : dark **2** *Car, Mex* : dark-skinned **3** : tight, compressed

prima *nf* **1** : premium **2** : bonus **3** → **primo**

primacía *nf* **1** : precedence, priority **2** : superiority, supremacy

primado *nm* : primate (bishop)

primario, -ria *adj* : primary

primate *nm* : primate

primavera *nf* **1** : spring (season) **2** PRÍMULA : primrose

primaveral *adj* : spring

primera *nf* **1** : first (gear) **2** : first class

primeramente *adv* : firstly, first of all

primero¹ *adv* **1** : first **2** : rather, sooner

primero², -ra *adj* (*primer before masculine singular nouns*) **1** : first ⟨el primer paso : the first step⟩ **2** : top, leading ⟨de primera clase : first-class⟩ **3** : main, basic ⟨nuestro primer objetivo : our main objective⟩ ⟨lo primero es no alarmarse : the most important thing is not to panic⟩ **4 de primera** : first-rate

primero³, -ra *n* : first ⟨el primero de enero : (on) the first of January, (on) January first⟩ ⟨el primero en llegar : the first to arrive⟩ ⟨la primera de tres fases : the first of three stages⟩

primicia *nf* **1** : first fruits **2** : scoop, exclusive

primigenio, -nia *adj* : original, primary

primitivo, -va *adj* **1** : primitive **2** ORIGINAL : original

primo¹ *adj* **1** : prime (of a number) **2** : raw ⟨materia prima : raw material⟩

primo², -ma *n* **1** : cousin ⟨primo hermano : first cousin⟩ **2** *Spain* : sucker

primogénito, -ta *adj & n* : firstborn

primor *nm* **1** : skill, care **2** : beauty, elegance

primordial *adj* **1** : primordial **2** : basic, fundamental

primoroso, -sa *adj* **1** : exquisite, fine, delicate **2** : skillful

prímula *nf* : primrose

princesa *nf* : princess

principado *nm* : principality

principal¹ *adj* **1** : main, principal **2** : foremost, leading

principal² *nm* : capital, principal

principalmente *adv* : mainly, chiefly

príncipe *nm* : prince
principesco, -ca *adj* : princely
principiante[1] *adj* : beginning
principiante[2] *nmf* : beginner, novice
principiar *vt* EMPEZAR : to begin
principio *nm* 1 COMIENZO : beginning
⟨empieza por el principio : start at the
beginning⟩ 2 : principle (theory, law)
3 : principle (moral belief) 4 **al principio** : at first 5 **a principios de** : at the
beginning of ⟨a principios de agosto : at
the beginning of August⟩ 6 **en ~** : in
principle 7 **en un principio** : at first 8
por ~ : on principle
pringar {52} *vt* 1 : to dip (in grease) 2
: to soil, to spatter (with grease) — **prin-
garse** *vr*
pringoso, -sa *adj* : greasy
pringue[1], etc. → pringar
pringue[2] *nm* : grease, drippings *pl*
prior, priora *n* : prior *m*, prioress *f*
priorato *nm* : priory
prioridad *nf* : priority, precedence
prisa *nf* 1 : hurry, rush 2 **a ~ or de ~**
: quickly, fast 3 **a toda prisa** : as fast as
possible 4 **correr prisa** : to be urgent 5
darse prisa : to hurry 6 **tener prisa** : to
be in a hurry
prisión *nf, pl* **prisiones** 1 CÁRCEL
: prison, jail 2 ENCARCELAMIENTO
: imprisonment
prisionero, -ra *n* : prisoner
prisma *nm* : prism
prismáticos *nmpl* : binoculars
prístino, -na *adj* : pristine
privacidad *nf* : privacy
privación *nf, pl* **-ciones** 1 : deprivation
⟨privación de libertad : deprivation of
liberty⟩ 2 : privation, want
privado, -da *adj* : private ⟨en privado : in
private⟩ — **privadamente** *adv*
privar *vt* 1 DESPOJAR : to deprive ⟨privar
a alguien de algo : to deprive someone of
something⟩ 2 : to stun, to knock out —
privarse *vr* : to deprive oneself
privativo, -va *adj* : exclusive, particular
privatizar {21} *vt* : to privatize
privilegiado, -da *adj* 1 : privileged 2
EXCEPCIONAL : exceptional
privilegiar *vt* : to grant a privilege to, to
favor
privilegio *nm* : privilege
pro[1] *nm* 1 : pro, advantage ⟨los pros y
contras : the pros and cons⟩ 2 **en pro
de** : for, in favor of
pro[2] *prep* : for, in favor of ⟨grupos pro
derechos humanos : groups supporting
human rights⟩
pro- *pref* : pro-
proa *nf* : bow, prow
probabilidad *nf* : probability ⟨con toda
probabilidad : in all likelihood⟩
probable *adj* : probable, likely ⟨es probable que pierdan : it's likely that they'll
lose⟩
probablemente *adv* : probably
probador[1] *nm* : fitting room, dressing room
probador[2], **-dora** *n* : tester
probar {19} *vt* 1 : to demonstrate, to
prove 2 : to test, to try out 3 : to try on

(clothing) 4 : to taste, to sample — *vi*
: to try ⟨probar a hacer algo : to try doing something⟩ — **probarse** *vr* : to try
on (clothing)
probeta *nf* : test tube
probidad *nf* : probity
problema *nm* : problem ⟨resolver un
problema : to solve a problem⟩
problemática *nf* : set of problems ⟨la
problemática que debemos enfrentar
: the problems we must face⟩
proboscide *nf* : proboscis
problemático, -ca *adj* : problematic
procaz *adj, pl* **procaces** 1 : insolent, impudent 2 : indecent
procedencia *nf* : origin, source
procedente *adj* 1 : proper, fitting 2 ~
de : coming from
proceder *vi* 1 AVANZAR : to proceed 2
: to act, to behave 3 : to be appropriate,
to be fitting 4 ~ **a** : to proceed to 5 ~
de : to originate from, to come from
procedimiento *nm* 1 : procedure, process 2 : proceedings *pl* (in law)
prócer *nmf* : eminent person, leader
procesado, -da *n* : accused, defendant
procesador *nm* : processor ⟨procesador
de textos : word processor⟩
procesamiento *nm* : processing ⟨pro-
cesamiento de datos : data processing⟩
procesar *vt* 1 : to prosecute, to try 2
: to process
procesión *nf, pl* **-siones** : procession
proceso *nm* 1 : process 2 : trial, proceedings *pl* 3 → **procesamiento**
proclama *nf* : proclamation
proclamación *nf, pl* **-ciones** : proclamation
proclamar *vt* : to proclaim — **procla-
marse** *vr*
proclive *adj* ~ **a** : inclined to, prone to
proclividad *nf* : proclivity, inclination
procrear *vi* : to procreate — **procreación**
nf
procurador, -dora *n* ABOGADO : attorney
procurar *vt* 1 INTENTAR : to try, to endeavor ⟨procura llegar temprano : try to
arrive early⟩ ⟨procura que no se enteren
: make sure they don't find out⟩ 2 CON-
SEGUIR : to obtain, to procure
prodigar {52} *vt* : to lavish, to be generous
with
prodigio *nm* : wonder, marvel
prodigioso, -sa *adj* : prodigious, marvelous
pródigo[1], **-ga** *adj* 1 : generous, lavish 2
: wasteful, prodigal
pródigo[2], **-ga** *n* : spendthrift, prodigal
producción *nf, pl* **-ciones** 1 : production
(action or quantity) 2 : production (in
cinema, etc.) 3 **producción en serie**
: mass production
producir {61} *vt* 1 : to produce, to make,
to manufacture 2 : to cause, to bring
about 3 : to bear (interest) — **producirse** *vr* : to take place, to occur
productividad *nf* : productivity
productivo, -va *adj* 1 : productive 2 LU-
CRATIVO : profitable
producto *nm* : product ⟨producto alimenticio : foodstuff⟩ ⟨producto interno

bruto : gross domestic product⟩ **2** : proceeds *pl*, yield

productor[1], **-tora** *adj* : producing

productor[2], **-tora** *n* : producer

productora *nf* : production company

proeza *nf* HAZAÑA : feat, exploit

profanar *vt* : to profane, to desecrate — **profanación** *nf*

profano[1], **-na** *adj* **1** : profane **2** : worldly, secular, lay

profano[2], **-na** *n* **1** : layman *mf*, layperson *mf* **2** LAICO : layman *m*, laywoman *f*, layperson *mf* (in religion)

profecía *nf* : prophecy

proferir {76} *vt* **1** : to utter **2** : to hurl (insults)

profesar *vt* **1** : to profess, to declare **2** : to practice, to exercise

profesión *nf, pl* **-siones** : profession, occupation

profesional *adj & nmf* : professional — **profesionalmente** *adv*

profesionalismo *nm* : professionalism

profesionalizar {21} *vt* : to make (more) professional

profesionista *nmf Mex* : professional

profesor, **-sora** *n* **1** : teacher (of older children) **2** : professor (in a university) **3** : instructor, tutor

profesorado *nm* **1** : faculty **2** : teaching profession

profeta *nm* : prophet

profético, **-ca** *adj* : prophetic

profetizar {21} *vt* : to prophesy

prófugo, **-ga** *adj & n* : fugitive

profundidad *nf* **1** : depth, profundity **2** en ~ : in depth, thoroughly

profundizar {21} *vt* **1** : to deepen **2** : to study in depth — *vi* ~ **en** : to go deeply into, to study in depth

profundo, **-da** *adj* **1** HONDO : deep ⟨poco profundo : shallow⟩ **2** : profound — **profundamente** *adv*

profusión *nf, pl* **-siones** : abundance, profusion

profuso, **-sa** *adj* : profuse, abundant, extensive

progenie *nf* : progeny, offspring

progenitor, **-tora** *n* **1** : father *m*, mother *f* ⟨sus progenitores : his parents⟩ **2** ANTEPASADO : ancestor, progenitor

progesterona *nf* : progesterone

prognóstico *nm* : prognosis

programa *nm* **1** : program (on television, etc.) **2** : program (pamphlet) **3** : plan, schedule **4** : program (on a computer) **5** *or* **programa de estudios** : curriculum, syllabus

programable *adj* : programmable

programación *nf, pl* **-ciones 1** : programming (on television) **2** : programming (of computers) **3** : planning (of an event)

programador, **-dora** *n* : programmer

programar *vt* **1** : to schedule (times, shows, etc.), to plan (an event) **2** : to program (a computer, etc.)

progresar *vi* : to progress, to make progress

progresista *adj & nmf* : progressive

progresivo, **-va** *adj* : progressive, gradual — **progresivamente** *adv*

progreso *nm* : progress ⟨hacer progresos : to make progress⟩

prohibición *nf, pl* **-ciones** : ban, prohibition

prohibir {62} *vt* : to prohibit, to ban, to forbid ⟨prohibido fumar : no smoking⟩ ⟨prohibido el paso : do not enter⟩ ⟨me prohibió ir : she forbade me to go⟩ ⟨se prohibe el uso de pesticidas : the use of pesticides is banned/prohibited⟩

prohibitivo, **-va** *adj* : prohibitive

prohijar {5} *vt* ADOPTAR : to adopt

prójimo *nm* : neighbor, fellow man

prole *nf* : offspring, progeny

proletariado *nm* : proletariat, working class

proletario, **-ria** *adj & n* : proletarian

proliferar *vi* : to proliferate — **proliferación** *nf*

prolífico, **-ca** *adj* : prolific

prolijo, **-ja** *adj* : wordy, long-winded

prólogo *nm* : prologue, preface, foreword

prolongación *nf, pl* **-ciones** : extension, lengthening

prolongar {52} *vt* **1** : to prolong (a life, a war, etc.), to extend (a visit, etc.) **2** : to extend, to lengthen (in size) — **prolongarse** *vr* CONTINUAR : to last, to continue

promediar *vt* **1** : to average **2** : to divide in half — *vi* : to be half over

promedio *nm* **1** : average ⟨como promedio : on average⟩ **2** : middle, midpoint

promesa *nf* : promise ⟨cumplir (con) una promesa : to keep a promise⟩

prometedor, **-dora** *adj* : promising, hopeful

prometer *vt* : to promise ⟨¿me lo prometes? : (do you) promise?⟩ — *vi* : to show promise — **prometerse** *vr* COMPROMETERSE : to get engaged

prometido[1], **-da** *adj* : engaged

prometido[2], **-da** *n* NOVIO : fiancé *m*, fiancée *f*

prominente *adj* : prominent — **prominencia** *nf* — **prominentemente** *adv*

promiscuo, **-cua** *adj* : promiscuous — **promiscuidad** *nf*

promisorio, **-ria** *adj* **1** : promising **2** : promissory

promoción *nf, pl* **-ciones 1** : promotion **2** : class, year **3** : play-off (in soccer)

promocionar *vt* : to promote — **promocional** *adj*

promontorio *nm* : promontory, headland

promotor, **-tora** *n* **1** : promoter **2** INSTIGADOR : instigator **3** : developer (of real estate)

promover {47} *vt* **1** FOMENTAR : to promote, to encourage **2** : to promote (in rank, etc.) **3** PROVOCAR : to provoke, to cause

promulgación *nf, pl* **-ciones 1** : enactment **2** : proclamation, enactment

promulgar {52} *vt* **1** : to promulgate, to proclaim **2** : to enact (a law or decree)

prono, **-na** *adj* : prone

pronombre *nm* : pronoun

pronosticar {72} *vt* : to predict, to forecast

pronóstico *nm* **1** PREDICCIÓN : forecast, prediction ⟨pronóstico del tiempo : weather forecast⟩ **2** : prognosis

prontitud *nf* **1** PRESTEZA : promptness, speed **2 con** ∼ : promptly, quickly

pronto[1] *adv* **1** : quickly, promptly **2** : soon **3 de** ∼ : suddenly **4 ¡hasta pronto!** : see you soon! **5 lo más pronto posible** : as soon as possible **6 por de pronto** : for now **7 tan pronto como** : as soon as

pronto[2], **-ta** *adj* **1** RÁPIDO : quick, speedy, prompt **2** PREPARADO : ready

pronunciación *nf, pl* **-ciones** : pronunciation

pronunciado, -da *adj* **1** : pronounced, sharp, steep **2** : marked, noticeable

pronunciamiento *nm* **1** : pronouncement **2** : military uprising

pronunciar *vt* **1** : to pronounce, to say **2** : to give, to deliver (a speech) **3 pronunciar un fallo** : to pronounce sentence — **pronunciarse** *vr* : to declare oneself (for or against), to make a statement

propagación *nf, pl* **-ciones** : propagation, spreading

propaganda *nf* **1** : propaganda **2** PUBLICIDAD : advertising (activity or materials)

propagar {52} *vt* **1** : to propagate **2** : to spread, to disseminate — **propagarse** *vr*

propalar *vt* **1** : to divulge **2** : to spread

propano *nm* : propane

propasarse *vr* **1** : to go too far, to overstep one's bounds **2** ∼ **con** : to make sexual advances towards

propensión *nf, pl* **-siones** INCLINACIÓN : inclination, propensity

propenso, -sa *adj* ∼ **a** : prone to, susceptible to

propiamente *adv* **1** : properly, correctly **2** : exactly, precisely ⟨propiamente dicho : strictly speaking⟩

propiciar *vt* **1** : to propitiate **2** : to favor, to foster

propicio, -cia *adj* : favorable, propitious

propiedad *nf* **1** : property ⟨propiedad privada : private property⟩ ⟨ser propiedad de : to be the property of⟩ **2** : ownership **3** CUALIDAD : property, quality **4** : suitability, appropriateness ⟨con propiedad : appropriately, properly⟩

propietario[1], **-ria** *adj* : proprietary

propietario[2], **-ria** *n* DUEÑO : proprietor (of a business), owner

propina *nf* : tip, gratuity ⟨le di una buena propina : I tipped him well⟩

propinar *vt* : to give, to strike ⟨propinar una paliza : to give a beating⟩

propio, -pia *adj* **1** : own ⟨su propia casa : his own house⟩ ⟨tienen recursos propios : they have their own resources⟩ **2** APROPIADO : appropriate, suitable **3** CARACTERÍSTICO : characteristic, typical ⟨es propio de la región : it's typical of the region⟩ **4** MISMO : oneself ⟨el propio director : the director himself⟩

proponer {60} *vt* **1** : to propose, to suggest **2** : to nominate — **proponerse** *vr* : to intend, to plan, to set out ⟨lo que se propone lo cumple : he does what he sets out to do⟩

proporción *nf, pl* **-ciones** **1** : proportion ⟨en proporción a : in proportion to⟩ **2** : ratio (in mathematics) **3 proporciones** *nfpl* : proportions, size ⟨de grandes proporciones : very large⟩

proporcionado, -da *adj* **1** : proportionate **2** : proportioned ⟨bien proporcionado : well-proportioned⟩ — **proporcionadamente** *adv*

proporcional *adj* : proportional — **proporcionalmente** *adv*

proporcionar *vt* **1** : to provide, to give ⟨les proporcionó la información : she provided them with the information⟩ **2** : to proportion, to adapt

proposición *nf, pl* **-ciones** : proposal, proposition

propósito *nm* **1** INTENCIÓN : purpose, intention **2 a** ∼ : by the way **3 a** ∼ : on purpose, intentionally **4 a propósito de** : on the subject of

propuesta *nf* PROPOSICIÓN : proposal

propulsar *vt* **1** IMPULSAR : to propel, to drive **2** PROMOVER : to promote, to encourage

propulsión *nf, pl* **-siones** : propulsion ⟨propulsión a chorro : jet propulsion⟩

propulsor[1] *nm* : propellant

propulsor[2], **-sora** *n* : promoter, proponent

propulsor[3], **-sora** *adj* : propellant

propuso, etc. → **proponer**

prórroga *nf* **1** : extension, deferment **2** : overtime (in sports)

prorrogar {52} *vt* **1** : to extend (a deadline) **2** : to postpone

prorrumpir *vi* : to burst forth, to break out ⟨prorrumpí en lágrimas : I burst into tears⟩

prosa *nf* : prose

prosaico, -ca *adj* : prosaic, mundane

proscribir {33} *v* **1** PROHIBIR : to prohibit, to ban, to proscribe **2** DESTERRAR : to banish, to exile

proscripción *nf, pl* **-ciones** **1** PROHIBICIÓN : ban **2** DESTIERRO : banishment

proscrito[1] *pp* → **proscribir**

proscrito[2], **-ta** *n* **1** DESTERRADO : exile **2** : outlaw

prosecución *nf, pl* **-ciones** **1** : continuation **2** : pursuit

proseguir {75} *vt* **1** CONTINUAR : to continue **2** : to pursue (studies, goals) — *vi* : to continue, to go on

prospección *nf, pl* **-ciones** : prospecting, exploration

prospectar *vi* : to prospect

prospecto *nm* **1** : leaflet, brochure **2** : prospectus (for investors, etc.)

prospector, -tora *n* : prospector

prosperar *vi* : to prosper, to thrive

prosperidad *nf* : prosperity

próspero, -ra *adj* : prosperous, flourishing

próstata *nf* : prostate

prostíbulo *nm* : brothel
prostitución *nf, pl* -ciones : prostitution
prostituir {41} *vt* : to prostitute — **prostituirse** *vr* : to prostitute oneself
prostituto, -ta *n* : prostitute
protagonista *nmf* 1 : protagonist, main character 2 : star (in a film, etc.) 3 : leader, central figure
protagonizar {21} *vt* 1 : to star in 2 : to cause (an accident, etc.), to carry out (an attack, a campaign, etc.)
protección *nf, pl* -ciones : protection
protector[1], -tora *adj* : protective ⟨chaleco protector : chest protector⟩
protector[2], -tora *n* 1 : protector, guardian 2 : patron
protector[3] *nm* : protector, guard ⟨protector de pantallas : screen saver⟩
protectorado *nm* : protectorate
proteger {15} *vt* : to protect, to defend ⟨proteger de/contra algo : to protect against something⟩ — **protegerse** *vr*
protegido, -da *n* : protégé
proteína *nf* : protein
prótesis *nfs & pl* : prosthesis
protesta *nf* 1 : protest 2 *Mex* : promise, oath
protestante *adj & nmf* : Protestant
protestantismo *nm* : Protestantism
protestar *vi* 1 : to protest, to object 2 ~ **por** : to complain about — *vt* : to protest, to object to
protocolo *nm* : protocol
protón *nm, pl* protones : proton
protoplasma *nm* : protoplasm
prototipo *nm* : prototype
protuberancia *nf* : protuberance — **protuberante** *adj*
provecho *nm* 1 : benefit, advantage ⟨sacar provecho de : to benefit from⟩ 2 ¡buen provecho! : bon appétit!
provechoso, -sa *adj* BENEFICIOSO : beneficial, profitable, useful — **provechosamente** *adv*
proveedor, -dora *n* : provider, supplier
proveedor de servicios de Internet *or* PSI *nm* : Internet service provider, ISP
proveer {63} *vt* : to provide, to supply ⟨proveer a alguien de algo : to provide someone with something⟩ — **proveerse** *vr* ~ **de** : to obtain, to supply oneself with
provenir {87} *vi* ~ **de** : to come from
provenzal[1] *adj* : Provençal
provenzal[2] *nmf* : Provençal
provenzal[3] *nm* : Provençal (language)
proverbio *nm* REFRÁN : proverb — **proverbial** *adj*
providencia *nf* 1 : providence, foresight 2 : Providence, God 3 providencias *nfpl* : steps, measures
providencial *adj* : providential
provincia *nf* : province — **provincial** *adj*
provinciano, -na *adj* : provincial, unsophisticated
provisión *nf, pl* -siones 1 : provision, providing 2 provisiones *nfpl* : provisions, supplies
provisional *adj* : provisional, temporary

provisionalmente *adv* : provisionally, tentatively
provisorio, -ria *adj* : provisional, temporary
provisto *pp* → proveer
provocación *nf, pl* -ciones : provocation
provocador[1], -dora *adj* : provocative, provoking
provocador[2], -dora *n* AGITADOR : agitator
provocar {72} *vt* 1 CAUSAR : to provoke, to cause 2 IRRITAR : to provoke, to pique 3 : to arouse (sexually) 4 *Col, Peru, Ven fam* APETECER : to appeal to ⟨¿qué te provoca comer? : what would you like to eat?⟩
provocativo, -va *adj* : provocative
proxeneta *nmf* : pimp *m*
próximamente *adv* : shortly, soon
proximidad *nf* 1 : nearness, proximity 2 proximidades *nfpl* : vicinity
próximo, -ma *adj* 1 : near, close ⟨la Navidad está próxima : Christmas is almost here⟩ ⟨las próximas elecciones : the coming election⟩ ⟨en un futuro próximo : in the near future⟩ ⟨próximo a la ciudad : near the city⟩ 2 SIGUIENTE : next, following ⟨la próxima semana : the following week, next week⟩ — **próximo, -ma** *pron*
proyección *nf, pl* -ciones 1 : projection 2 : showing, screening (of a film) 3 : range, influence, diffusion
proyeccionista *nmf* : projectionist
proyectar *vt* 1 : to plan 2 LANZAR : to throw, to hurl 3 : to project, to cast (light or shadow) 4 : to show, to screen (a film)
proyectil *nm* : projectile, missile
proyecto *nm* 1 : plan, project 2 proyecto de ley : bill
proyector *nm* 1 : projector 2 : spotlight
prudencia *nf* : prudence, care, discretion
prudencial *adj* : prudent, sensible, cautious ⟨a una distancia prudencial : at a safe distance⟩
prudente *adj* : prudent, sensible, cautious
prueba[1], etc. → probar
prueba[2] *nf* 1 : proof, (piece of) evidence ⟨como prueba de : as proof of⟩ ⟨pruebas científicas : scientific evidence⟩ 2 : trial, test ⟨prueba del embarazo : pregnancy test⟩ ⟨vamos a hacer la prueba : let's try it⟩ 3 : proof (in printing or photography) 4 : event, qualifying round (in sports) 5 a ~ : on a trial basis 6 a prueba de agua : waterproof 7 prueba de fuego : acid test 8 poner a prueba : to put to the test
prurito *nm* 1 : itching 2 : desire, urge
PSI → proveedor de servicios de Internet
psicoanálisis *nm* : psychoanalysis — **psicoanalista** *nmf*
psicoanalítico, -ca *adj* : psychoanalytic
psicoanalizar {21} *vt* : to psychoanalyze
psicodélico, -ca *adj* : psychedelic
psicología *nf* : psychology
psicológico, -ca *adj* : psychological — **psicológicamente** *adv*

psicólogo, -ga *n* : psychologist
psicópata *nmf* : psychopath
psicopático, -ca *adj* : psychopathic
psicosis *nfs & pl* : psychosis
psicosomático, -ca *adj* : psychosomatic
psicoterapeuta *nmf* : psychotherapist
psicoterapia *nf* : psychotherapy
psicótico, -ca *adj & n* : psychotic
psique *nf* : psyche
psiquiatra *nmf* : psychiatrist
psiquiatría *nf* : psychiatry
psiquiátrico[1], -ca *adj* : psychiatric
psiquiátrico[2] *nm* : mental hospital
psíquico, -ca *adj* : psychic
psiquis *nfs & pl* : psyche
psoriasis *nf* : psoriasis
púa *nf* 1 : barb ⟨alambre de púas : barbed wire⟩ 2 : tooth (of a comb) 3 : quill, spine (of an animal) 4 : thorn, spine (of a plant) 5 : pick (for a guitar, etc.)
pub ['pub, 'pab] *nm, pl* pubs : bar, night-club
pubertad *nf* : puberty
pubiano → púbico
púbico, -ca *adj* : pubic
publicación *nf, pl* -ciones : publication
publicar {72} *vt* 1 : to publish 2 DIVULGAR : to divulge, to disclose
publicidad *nf* 1 : publicity 2 : advertising
publicista *nmf* : publicist
publicitar *vt* 1 : to publicize 2 : to advertise
publicitario, -ria *adj* : advertising, publicity ⟨agencia publicitaria : advertising agency⟩
público[1], -ca *adj* : public ⟨hacer público : to make public⟩ — **públicamente** *adv*
público[2] *nm* 1 : public ⟨en público : in public⟩ 2 : audience, spectators *pl*
puchero *nm* 1 : pot 2 : stew 3 : pout ⟨hacer pucheros : to pout⟩
pucho *nm* 1 : waste, residue 2 : cigarette 3 : cigarette butt 4 a puchos : little by little, bit by bit
púdico, -ca *adj* : chaste, modest
pudiente *adj* 1 : powerful 2 : rich, wealthy
pudín *nm, pl* pudines BUDÍN : pudding
pudo, etc. → poder
pudor *nm* : modesty, reserve
pudoroso, -sa *adj* : modest, reserved, shy
pudrir {59} *vt* 1 : to rot 2 *fam* : to annoy, to upset — **pudrirse** *vr* 1 : to rot 2 : to languish
puebla, etc. → poblar
pueblerino, -na *adj* : provincial
pueblo *nm* 1 NACIÓN : people 2 : common people 3 ALDEA, POBLADO : town, village 4 pueblo joven *Peru* : shantytown, slums *pl*
puede, etc. → poder
puente *nm* 1 : bridge 2 : bridge (in dentistry) 3 puente aéreo : airlift (military), air shuttle (commercial) 4 puente levadizo : drawbridge
puerco[1], -ca *adj* : dirty, filthy
puerco[2], -ca *n* 1 CERDO, MARRANO : pig, hog 2 : pig, dirty or greedy person 3 puerco espín : porcupine

puericultura *nf* : infant care, childcare
pueril *adj* : childish, puerile
puerro *nm* : leek
puerta *nf* 1 : door (of a house, etc.), entrance (of a hotel, etc.), gate (in a fence, etc.) ⟨llamar a la puerta : to knock at/on the door⟩ ⟨puerta principal : front door, main entrance⟩ ⟨puerta trasera : back door⟩ 2 a las puertas de : on the verge of 3 a puerta cerrada : behind closed doors 4 puerta de embarque : gate (in an airport)
puerto *nm* 1 : port, harbor ⟨puerto pesquero : fishing port⟩ ⟨puerto marítimo : seaport⟩ 2 : mountain pass 3 : port (in a computer)
puertorriqueño, -ña *adj & n* : Puerto Rican
pues *conj* 1 : since, because, for ⟨lo hicieron, pues consideraron que era necesario : they did it because they considered it necessary⟩ 2 (*used interjectionally*) : well, then ⟨pues claro que sí! : well, of course!⟩ ⟨pues no voy! : well then, I'm not going!⟩
puesta *nf* 1 : setting ⟨puesta de/del sol : sunset⟩ 2 : laying (of eggs) 3 puesta al día : updating 4 puesta a punto : tune-up 5 puesta en escena : production (in theater) 6 puesta en marcha : start, starting up
puestero, -ra *n* : seller, vendor
puesto[1] *pp* → poner
puesto[2], -ta *adj* 1 : dressed ⟨bien puesto : well-dressed⟩ 2 : set (of a table)
puesto[3] *nm* 1 LUGAR, SITIO : place, position 2 : place (in a ranking) 3 : kiosk, stand, stall 4 : post, station ⟨puesto de policía : police station⟩ ⟨puesto de socorro : first-aid post⟩ 5 *or* puesto de trabajo : position, job 6 puesto que : since, given that
púgil → pugilista
pugilato *nm* BOXEO : boxing
pugilista *nmf* BOXEADOR : boxer (athlete)
pugna *nf* 1 CONFLICTO, LUCHA : conflict, struggle 2 en ∼ : at odds, in conflict
pugnar *vi* ∼ por : to strive to (do something), to strive for (something)
pugnaz *adj* : pugnacious
pujante *adj* : mighty, powerful
pujanza *nf* : strength, vigor ⟨pujanza económica : economic strength⟩
pujar *vi* 1 : to push, to strain 2 ∼ por : to struggle to (do something), to struggle for (something)
pulcritud *nf* 1 : neatness, tidiness 2 ESMERO : meticulousness
pulcro, -cra *adj* 1 : clean, neat 2 : exquisite, delicate, refined
pulga *nf* 1 : flea 2 tener malas pulgas : to be bad-tempered
pulgada *nf* : inch
pulgar *nm* 1 : thumb 2 : big toe
pulir *vt* 1 : to polish, to shine 2 REFINAR : to refine, to perfect
pulla *nf* 1 : cutting remark, dig, gibe 2 : obscenity
pulmón *nm, pl* pulmones : lung

pulmonar *adj* : pulmonary
pulmonía *nf* NEUMONÍA : pneumonia
pulóver *nm, pl* **-veres** : pullover, sweater
pulpa *nf* : pulp, flesh
pulpería *nf* : small grocery store
púlpito *nm* : pulpit
pulpo *nm* : octopus
pulque *nm* : Mexican alcoholic drink made from maguey sap
pulsación *nf, pl* **-ciones** 1 : beat, pulsation, throb 2 : keystroke
pulsar *vt* 1 APRETAR : to press, to push 2 : to strike (a key), to pluck (a string) 3 : to assess — *vi* : to beat, to throb
pulsera *nf* : bracelet
pulso *nm* 1 : pulse ⟨tomarle el pulso a alguien : to take someone's pulse⟩ ⟨tomarle el pulso a la opinión : to sound out opinion⟩ 2 : steady hand ⟨dibujo a pulso : freehand sketch⟩ ⟨a pulso : through effort, through hard work⟩
pulular *vi* ABUNDAR : to abound, to swarm ⟨en el río pululan los peces : the river is teeming with fish⟩
pulverizador *nm* 1 : atomizer, spray 2 : spray gun
pulverizar {21} *vt* 1 : to pulverize, to crush 2 : to spray
pum *interj* : bang!
puma *nf* : cougar, puma
puna *nf* 1 : Andean plateau 2 : altitude sickness
punción *nf, pl* **punciones** : puncture
punible *adj* : punishable
punitivo, -va *adj* : punitive
punce, etc. → **punzar**
punk[1] *adj* : punk
punk[2] *nm* : punk, punk rock
punk[3] *nmf* : punk, punk rocker
punta *nf* 1 : tip, end ⟨punta del dedo : fingertip⟩ ⟨en la punta de la lengua : at the tip of one's tongue⟩ ⟨en la otra punta del país : on the other side of the country⟩ ⟨cortar las puntas : to trim (hair)⟩ 2 : point (of a weapon, pencil, etc.) ⟨punta de lanza : spearhead⟩ ⟨acabar en punta : to be pointed⟩ ⟨sacar punta a : to sharpen⟩ 3 : point, headland 4 : bunch, lot ⟨una punta de ladrones : a bunch of thieves⟩ 5 **a punta de** : by, by dint of 6 **de ~** : on end
puntada *nf* 1 : stitch (in sewing) 2 PUNZADA : sharp pain, stitch, twinge 3 *Mex* : witticism, quip
puntal *nm* : prop, support
puntapié *nm* PATADA : kick ⟨darle un puntapié a alguien : to kick someone⟩
puntazo *nm* CORNADA : wound (from a goring)
puntear *vt* 1 : to pluck (a guitar) 2 : to lead (in sports)
puntería *nf* : aim, marksmanship
puntero *nm* 1 : pointer 2 : leader
puntiagudo, -da *adj* : sharp, pointed
puntilla *nf* 1 : lace edging 2 : dagger (in bullfighting) 3 **de puntillas** : on tiptoe
puntilloso, -sa *adj* : punctilious
punto *nm* 1 : dot, point 2 : period (in punctuation) 3 : point, item, question 4 : spot, place 5 : point, moment, stage

6 : point, extent 7 : point (in a score) 8 : stitch 9 **en ~** : on the dot, sharp ⟨a las dos en punto : at two o'clock sharp⟩ 10 **al punto** : at once 11 **a punto de** : about to, on the verge of ⟨estaba a punto de salir : I was about to leave⟩ ⟨a punto del colapso : on the verge of collapse⟩ 12 **a punto fijo** : exactly, certainly 13 **dos puntos** : colon 14 **en su punto** : just right 15 **hasta cierto punto** : up to a point 16 **punto decimal** : decimal point 17 **punto de partida** : starting point 18 **punto de vista** : point of view 19 **punto final** : period (in punctuation) ⟨poner punto final a algo : to end something⟩ 20 **punto fuerte/débil** : strong/weak point 21 **punto muerto** : neutral (in an automobile), deadlock (in talks, etc.) 22 **puntos cardinales** : points of the compass 23 **puntos suspensivos** : ellipsis (in punctuation) 24 **punto y aparte** : (period and) new paragraph 25 **punto y coma** : semicolon 26 **y punto** : period ⟨es el mejor que hay y punto : it's the best there is, period⟩
puntocom *nm, pl* **puntocom** : dot-com
puntuación *nf, pl* **-ciones** 1 : punctuation 2 : scoring (action), score, grade
puntual *adj* 1 : prompt, punctual 2 : exact, accurate — **puntualmente** *adv*
puntualidad *nf* : promptness, punctuality
puntualizar {21} *vt* 1 : to specify, to state 2 : to point out
puntuar {3} *vt* : to punctuate — *vi* : to score points
punzada *nf* : sharp pain, twinge, stitch
punzante *adj* 1 : sharp 2 CÁUSTICO : biting, caustic
punzar {21} *vt* : to pierce, to puncture
punzón *nm, pl* **punzones** 1 : awl 2 : hole punch
puñado *nm* 1 : handful 2 **a puñados** : lots of, by the handful
puñal *nm* DAGA : dagger
puñalada *nf* : stab, stab wound
puñetazo *nm* : punch (with the fist) ⟨le dio un puñetazo en la cara : she punched him in the face⟩
puño *nm* 1 : fist 2 : handful, fistful 3 : cuff (of a shirt) 4 : handle, hilt 5 **de su puño y letra** : in one's own handwriting
pupa *nf* CRISÁLIDA : pupa, chrysalis
pupila *nf* : pupil (of the eye)
pupilente *nm Mex* : contact lens
pupilo, -la *n* 1 : pupil, student 2 : ward, charge
pupitre *nm* : writing desk
puramente *adv* : purely
puré *nm* : puree ⟨puré de papas : mashed potatoes⟩
pureza *nf* : purity
purga *nf* 1 : laxative 2 : purge
purgante *adj & nm* : laxative, purgative
purgar {52} *vt* 1 : to purge, to cleanse 2 : to liquidate (in politics) 3 : to give a laxative to — **purgarse** *vr* 1 : to take a laxative 2 **~ de** : to purge oneself of
purgatorio *nm* : purgatory
purgue, etc. → **purgar**
purificador *nm* : purifier

purificar {72} *vt* : to purify — **purificación** *nf*
puritano[1], **-na** *adj* : puritanical, puritan
puritano[2], **-na** *n* **1** : Puritan **2** : puritan
puro[1] *adv* : sheer, much ⟨de puro terco : out of sheer stubbornness⟩
puro[2], **-ra** *adj* **1** : pure ⟨aire puro : fresh air⟩ **2** : plain, simple, sheer ⟨por pura curiosidad : from sheer curiosity⟩ **3** : only, just ⟨emplean puras mujeres : they only employ women⟩ **4 pura sangre** : Thoroughbred horse
puro[3] *nm* : cigar
púrpura *nf* : purple

purpúreo, -rea *adj* : purple
purpurina *nf* : glitter (for decoration)
pus *nm* : pus
pusilánime *adj* COBARDE : cowardly
puso, etc. → **poner**
pústula *nf* : pustule, pimple
puta *nf offensive* : whore, prostitute
putrefacción *nf, pl* **-ciones** : putrefying, rotting
putrefacto, -ta *adj* **1** PODRIDO : putrid, rotten **2** : decayed
pútrido, -da *adj* : putrid, rotten
puya *nf* **1** : point (of a lance) **2 lanzar una puya** : to gibe, to taunt

Q

q *nf* : twentieth letter of the Spanish alphabet
que[1] *conj* **1** : that ⟨dice que está listo : he says (that) he's ready⟩ ⟨espero que lo haga : I hope (that) she does it⟩ ⟨es posible que vuelva a pasar : it's possible (that) it will happen again⟩ ⟨estaba tan cansado que casi se durmió : he was so tired (that) he almost fell asleep⟩ ⟨me di cuenta de que era ella : I realized (that) it was her⟩ **2** : than ⟨ella es más alta que él : she is taller than he is⟩ ⟨más que nada : more than anything⟩ **3** (*expressing permission or desire*) ⟨¡que entre! : send him in!⟩ ⟨¡que te vaya bien! : I wish you well!⟩ **4** (*used in repeating a statement or question*) ⟨¡que no lo toques! : I told you not to touch it!⟩ ⟨que si quieres más : I asked if you wanted more⟩ ⟨¿cómo que no lo sabes? : what do you mean you don't know?⟩ **5** (*indicating a reason or cause*) ⟨¡cuidado, que te caes! : be careful, you're about to fall!⟩ ⟨no provoques al perro, que te va a morder : don't provoke the dog or (else) he'll bite⟩ **6** (*indicating a continuing or repeated action*) ⟨estaba todo el día corre que (te) corre : I was running around nonstop all day⟩ **7 es que** : the thing is that, I'm afraid that ⟨es que no tengo ganas de ir : the thing is that I don't want to go⟩ **8 yo que tú** : if I were you
que[2] *pron* **1** : who, that ⟨la niña que viene : the girl who is coming⟩ ⟨todos los chicos que están aquí : all (of) the boys who are here⟩ ⟨es el hombre que llamó ayer : he's the man who called yesterday⟩ ⟨no conozco a nadie que lo crea : I don't know anyone who believes it⟩ **2** : whom, that ⟨los alumnos que enseñé : the students that I taught⟩ ⟨la persona con que habló : the person with whom he spoke⟩ ⟨el hombre al que pertenece : the man to whom it belongs⟩ **3** : that, which ⟨el carro que me gusta : the car that I like⟩ ⟨el asunto al que hizo referencia : the matter to which he referred⟩ ⟨el delito del que fue acusado

: the crime of which he was accused⟩ **4 el (la, lo, las, los) que** → **el**[1], **la**[1], **lo**[1], **los**[1]
qué[1] *adv* : how, what ⟨¡qué bonito! : how pretty!⟩
qué[2] *adj* : what, which ⟨¿qué hora es? : what time is it?⟩
qué[3] *pron* : what ⟨¿qué quieres? : what do you want?⟩ ⟨¿y qué? : so what?⟩ ⟨¿qué es eso? : what is that?⟩ ⟨¿sabes qué? : you know what?⟩ ⟨qué de . . . : what a lot of . . .⟩
quebracho *nm* : quebracho (tree)
quebrada *nf* DESFILADERO : ravine, gorge
quebradero *nm* **quebradero de cabeza** : headache, problem
quebradizo, -za *adj* FRÁGIL : breakable, delicate, fragile
quebrado[1], **-da** *adj* **1** : bankrupt **2** : rough, uneven **3** ROTO : broken
quebrado[2] *nm* : fraction
quebrantamiento *nm* **1** : breaking **2** : deterioration, weakening
quebrantar *vt* **1** : to break, to split, to crack **2** : to weaken **3** : to violate (a law or contract)
quebranto *nm* **1** : break, breaking **2** AFLICCIÓN : affliction, grief **3** PÉRDIDA : loss
quebrar {55} *vt* **1** ROMPER : to break **2** DOBLAR : to bend, to twist — *vi* **1** : to go bankrupt **2** : to fall out, to break up — **quebrarse** *vr*
queda *nf* : curfew
quedar *vi* **1** PERMANECER : to remain, to stay ⟨queda abierto hasta el 31 : it will remain open until the 31st⟩ **2** : to be, to end up being ⟨quedamos contentos con las mejoras : we were pleased with the improvements⟩ ⟨el partido quedó empatado : the game ended in a tie⟩ ⟨el pastel quedó muy rico : the cake came out really well, the cake was delicious⟩ ⟨queda claro que . . . : it's clear that . . .⟩ **3** : to be situated ⟨queda muy lejos : it's very far, it's too far away⟩ **4** : to be left ⟨quedan sólo dos alternativas : there are only two options left⟩ ⟨no me queda mucho

dinero : I don't have much money left⟩ ⟨queda mucho por hacer : there's still a lot left to do⟩ **5** : to fit, to suit ⟨estos zapatos no me quedan : these shoes don't fit⟩ ⟨me queda grande : it's big on me⟩ ⟨ese color te queda bien : that color looks good on you⟩ **6** : to agree to meet ⟨¿a qué hora quedamos? : what time are we meeting?⟩ ⟨quedé con un amigo para cenar : I arranged to have dinner with a friend⟩ **7 quedar bien/mal con alguien** : to make a good/bad impression on someone **8 ~ en** : to agree, to arrange ⟨¿en qué quedamos? : what's the plan?, what are we doing?⟩ — **quedarse** *vr* **1** : to stay ⟨se quedó en casa : she stayed at home⟩ **2** : to keep on ⟨se quedó esperando : he kept on waiting⟩ **3 quedarse atrás** : to stay behind, to get left behind ⟨no quedarse atrás : to be no slouch⟩ **4 ~ con** : to remain ⟨me quedé con hambre después de comer : I was still hungry after I ate⟩

quedo[1] *adv* : softly, quietly

quedo[2], **-da** *adj* : quiet, still

queer [ˈker] *adj & nmf, pl* **queer** *or* **queers** : queer *sometimes disparaging + offensive*

quehacer *nm* **1** : work **2 quehaceres** *nmpl* : chores

queja *nf* : complaint

quejarse *vr* **1** : to complain **2** : to groan, to moan

quejica[1] *adj fam* : whiny

quejica[2] *nmf fam* : whiny person

quejido *nm* **1** : groan, moan **2** : whine, whimper

quejoso, -sa *adj* : complaining, whining

quema *nf* **1** FUEGO : fire **2** : burning

quemado, -da *adj* **1** : burned, burnt **2** : annoyed **3** : burned out **4** : sunburned

quemador *nm* : burner

quemadura *nf* : burn

quemar *vt* **1** : to burn (wood, letters, etc.), to burn down (a building) **2** : to burn (calories, etc.) **3** : to burn, to overcook **4** : to burn (skin, clothes, etc.) ⟨te ha quemado el sol : you have a sunburn⟩ **5** DERROCHAR : to squander **6** : to burn (a DVD, etc.) **7** : to burn out (an engine), to blow (a fuse) — *vi* **1** : to burn ⟨en el trópico el sol quema mucho : the sun is very strong in the tropics⟩ **2** : to be burning hot — **quemarse** *vr* **1** : to burn, to burn down **2** : to burn oneself ⟨me quemé la mano : I burned my hand⟩ **3** : to get sunburned **4** : to burn out, to blow

quemarropa *nf* **a ~** : point-blank

quemazón *nf, pl* **-zones** **1** : burning **2** : intense heat **3** : itch **4** : cutting remark

quena *nf* : Peruvian reed flute

quepa, etc. → caber

querella *nf* **1** : complaint **2** : lawsuit

querellante *nmf* : plaintiff

querellarse *vr* **~ contra** : to bring suit against, to sue

querer[1] {64} *vt* **1** DESEAR : to want, to desire ⟨quiere ser profesor : he wants to be a teacher⟩ ⟨¿cuánto quieres por esta computadora? : how much do you want for this computer?⟩ ⟨¿qué quieres que haga? : what do you want me to do?⟩ ⟨quiero que ella me ayude : I want her to help me⟩ ⟨quisiera cancelar la cuenta : I'd like to cancel the account⟩ ⟨quisiera que no fuera así : I wish it weren't so⟩ ⟨léelo cuando quieras : read it whenever you like⟩ ⟨no quería decírselo : he didn't want to tell her⟩ ⟨no quiso dar detalles : she wouldn't give any details⟩ **2** : to love, to like, to be fond of ⟨te quiero : I love you⟩ ⟨te quiere bien : he's very fond of you⟩ **3** (*indicating a request*) ⟨¿quieres pasarme la leche? : please pass the milk⟩ ⟨¿quieres decirme qué pasa? : do you mind telling me what's going on?⟩ **4 querer decir** : to mean ⟨¿qué quieres decir con eso? : what do you mean by that?⟩ ⟨eso no es lo que quiero decir : that's not what I meant to say⟩ **5 sin ~** : unintentionally — *vi* : like, want ⟨si quieres : if you like⟩ ⟨¡no quiero! : I don't want to!⟩

querer[2] *nm* : love, affection

querido[1], **-da** *adj* : dear, beloved

querido[2], **-da** *n* : dear, sweetheart

queroseno *nm* : kerosene

querrá, etc. → querer

querúbico, -ca *adj* : cherubic

querubín *nm, pl* **-bines** : cherub

quesadilla *nf* : quesadilla

quesería *nf* : cheese shop

queso *nm* : cheese

quetzal *nm* **1** : quetzal (bird) **2** : quetzal (monetary unit of Guatemala)

quiche *nf* : quiche

quicio *nm* **1 estar fuera de quicio** : to be beside oneself **2 sacar de quicio** : to exasperate, to drive crazy

quid *nm* : crux, gist ⟨el quid de la cuestión : the crux of the matter⟩

quiebra[1], **etc. → quebrar**

quiebra[2] *nf* **1** : break, crack **2** BANCARROTA : failure, bankruptcy

quien *pron, pl* **quienes** **1** : who, whom ⟨no sé quien ganará : I don't know who will win⟩ ⟨las personas con quienes trabajo : the people with whom I work⟩ ⟨su amigo, a quien conoció en México : his friend, whom he met in Mexico⟩ **2** : whoever, whomever ⟨quien quiere salir que salga : whoever wants to can leave⟩ **3** : anyone, some people ⟨hay quienes no están de acuerdo : some people don't agree⟩ ⟨no hay quien lo aguante : there's no one who would tolerate it⟩

quién *pron, pl* **quiénes** **1** : who, whom ⟨¿quién sabe? : who knows?⟩ ⟨¿con quién hablo? : with whom am I speaking?⟩ **2 de ~** : whose ⟨¿de quién es este libro? : whose book is this?⟩

quienquiera *pron, pl* **quienesquiera** : whoever, whomever

quiere, etc. → querer

quieto, -ta *adj* **1** : calm, quiet **2** INMÓVIL : still

quietud *nf* **1** : calm, tranquility **2** INMOVILIDAD : stillness

quijada *nf* : jaw, jawbone
quijotesco, -ca *adj* : quixotic
quilate *nm* : karat
quilla *nf* : keel
quimera *nf* : chimera, illusion
quimérico, -ca *adj* : fanciful
química *nf* : chemistry
químico¹, -ca *adj* : chemical
químico², -ca *n* : chemist
quimioterapia *nf* : chemotherapy
quimono *nm* : kimono
quincalla *nf* : trinkets *pl*
quince *adj & nm* : fifteen — quince *pron*
quinceañero, -ra *n* : fifteen-year-old, teenager
quinceavo¹, -va *adj* : fifteenth
quinceavo² *nm* : fifteenth (fraction)
quincena *nf* : two week period, fortnight
quincenal *adj* : bimonthly, semimonthly
quincuagésimo¹, -ma *adj* : fiftieth, fifty-
quincuagésimo², -ma *n* : fiftieth, fifty-
(in a series)
quingombó *nm* : okra
quiniela *nf* : sports lottery
quinientos¹, -tas *adj & pron* : five hundred
quinientos² *nms & pl* : five hundred
quinina *nf* : quinine
quino *nm* : cinchona
quinqué *nm* : oil lamp
quinquenal *adj* : five-year ⟨un plan quin-quenal : a five-year plan⟩
quinta *nf* : country house, villa
quintaesencia *nf* : quintessence — quin-taesencial *adj*
quintal *nm* : hundredweight
quinteto *nm* : quintet
quintillizo, -za *n* : quintuplet
quinto, -ta *adj & n* : fifth ⟨el quinto grado : the fifth grade⟩ ⟨la quinta (persona) : the fifth (person)⟩ ⟨llegó el quinto : he came in fifth (place)⟩ ⟨un quinto de : a fifth of⟩
quíntuplo, -la *adj* : quintuple, five-fold
quiosco *nm* 1 : kiosk 2 : newsstand 3 quiosco de música : bandstand
quiosquero, -ra *n* : kiosk vendor

quirófano *nm* : operating room
quiromancia *nf* : palmistry
quiropráctica *nf* : chiropractic
quiropráctico, -ca *n* : chiropractor
quirúrgico, -ca *adj* : surgical — quirúrgicamente *adv*
quiso, etc. → querer
quisquilloso¹, -sa *adj* : fastidious, fussy
quisquilloso², -sa *n* : fussy person, fuss-budget
quiste *nm* : cyst
quitaesmalte *nm* : nail polish remover
quitamanchas *nms & pl* : stain remover
quitanieves *nms & pl* : snowplow
quitar *vt* 1 : to remove, to take away/off/out ⟨quita la olla del fuego : take the pot off the heat/burner⟩ ⟨quitarle el polvo a algo : to dust something⟩ ⟨quítalo de en medio : get it out of the way⟩ ⟨¡quítame las manos (de encima)! : get your hands off me!⟩ 2 : to take, to take away ⟨le quitó las llaves : she took away his keys⟩ ⟨trataron de quitarle el dinero : they tried to take her money⟩ ⟨le quitaron la vida : they took his life, they killed him⟩ ⟨no me quita el sueño : I'm not losing any sleep over it⟩ 3 : to take off (clothes) ⟨le quitó los zapatos al paciente : she took the patient's shoes off⟩ 4 : to get rid of, to relieve ⟨quitar el dolor : to relieve the pain⟩ ⟨nadie le va a quitar esa idea de la cabeza : nobody's going to change his mind⟩ 5 : to take up (time) — quitarse *vr* 1 : to withdraw, to leave, to go away ⟨se me quitaron las ganas de salir : I don't feel like going out any-more⟩ 2 : to take off (one's clothes) 3 ~ de : to give up (a habit) 4 quitarse de encima : to get rid of ⟨me he quitado un peso de encima : that's a load off my mind⟩
quitasol *nm* : parasol
quiteño¹, -ña *adj* : of or from Quito
quiteño², -ña *n* : person from Quito
quizá *or* quizás *adv* : maybe, perhaps
quórum *nm, pl* quórums : quorum

R

r *nf* : twenty-first letter of the Spanish al-phabet
rábano *nm* 1 : radish 2 rábano picante : horseradish
rabí *nmf, pl* rabíes : rabbi
rabia *nf* 1 HIDROFOBIA : rabies, hydro-phobia 2 : rage, anger
rabiar *vi* 1 : to rage, to be furious 2 : to be in great pain 3 a ~ *fam* : like crazy, like mad
rabieta *nf* BERRINCHE : tantrum
rabillo *nm* : corner (of the eye)
rabino, -na *n* : rabbi
rabioso, -sa *adj* 1 : enraged, furious 2 : rabid
rabo *nm* 1 COLA : tail 2 el rabo del ojo : the corner of one's eye

rácano, -na *adj fam* : stingy
racha *nf* 1 : gust of wind 2 : run, series, string ⟨racha perdedora : losing streak⟩
racheado, -da *adj* : gusty, windy
racial *adj* : racial
racimo *nm* : bunch, cluster ⟨un racimo de uvas : a bunch of grapes⟩
raciocinio *nm* : reason, reasoning
ración *nf, pl* raciones 1 : share, ration 2 PORCIÓN : portion, helping
racional *adj* : rational, reasonable — ra-cionalmente *adv*
racionalidad *nf* : rationality
racionalización *nf, pl* -ciones : rational-ization
racionalizar {21} *vt* 1 : to rationalize 2 : to streamline

racionamiento *nm* : rationing
racionar *vt* : to ration
racismo *nm* : racism
racista *adj & nmf* : racist
radar *nm* : radar
radiación *nf, pl* **-ciones** : radiation, irradiation
radiactividad *nf* : radioactivity
radiactivo, -va *adj* : radioactive
radiador *nm* : radiator
radial *adj* 1 : radial 2 : radio, broadcasting ⟨emisora radial : radio transmitter⟩
radiante *adj* : radiant — **radiantemente** *adv*
radiar *vt* 1 : to radiate 2 : to irradiate 3 : to broadcast (on the radio)
radical[1] *adj* : radical, extreme — **radicalmente** *adv*
radical[2] *nmf* : radical
radicalismo *nm* : radicalism
radicar {72} *vi* 1 : to be found, to lie 2 ARRAIGAR : to take root — **radicarse** *vr* : to settle, to establish oneself
radio[1] *nm* 1 : radius 2 : radium
radio[2] *nmf* : radio
radioactividad *nf* : radioactivity
radioactivo, -va *adj* : radioactive
radioaficionado, -da *n* : ham radio operator
radiodifusión *nf, pl* **-siones** : radio broadcasting
radiodifusora *nf* : radio station
radioemisora *nf* : radio station
radiofaro *nm* : radio beacon
radiofónico, -ca *adj* : radio ⟨estación radiofónica pública : public radio station⟩
radiofrecuencia *nf* : radio frequency
radiografía *nf* : X ray (photograph)
radiografiar {85} *vt* : to x-ray
radiología *nf* : radiology
radiólogo, -ga *n* : radiologist
radionovela *nf* : radio soap opera
radioterapia *nf* : radiation therapy
radioyente *nmf* : radio listener
radón *nm* : radon
raer {65} *vt* RASPAR : to scrape, to scrape off
ráfaga *nf* 1 : gust (of wind) 2 : flash, burst ⟨una ráfaga de luz : a flash of light⟩
rafting *nm* : rafting
ragtime *nm* : ragtime
raid *nm* CA, Mex fam : lift, ride
raído, -da *adj* : worn, shabby
raiga, etc. → raer
raíz *nf, pl* **raíces** 1 : root 2 : origin, source 3 **a raíz de** : following, as a result of 4 **echar raíces** : to take root
raja *nf* 1 : crack, slit 2 : slice, wedge
rajá *nm* : raja
rajadura *nf* : crack, split
rajar *vt* HENDER : to crack, to split — *vi* 1 fam : to chatter 2 fam : to boast, to brag — **rajarse** *vr* 1 : to crack, to split open 2 fam : to back out
rajatabla *adv* **a ~** : strictly, to the letter
ralea *nf* : kind, sort, ilk ⟨son de la misma ralea : they're two of a kind⟩
ralentí *nm* **dejar al ralentí** : to leave (a motor) idling

rallado, -da *adj* 1 : grated 2 **pan rallado** : bread crumbs *pl*
rallador *nm* : grater
rallar *vt* : to grate
ralo, -la *adj* : sparse, thin
RAM *nf* : RAM, random-access memory
rama *nf* : branch
Ramadán *nm, pl* **-danes** : Ramadan
ramaje *nm* : branches *pl*
ramal *nm* 1 : spur (of a railroad line) 2 : halter, strap
rambla *nf* 1 : avenue, boulevard 2 Arg, Uru : seaside walk, boardwalk
ramera *nf* : harlot, prostitute
ramificación *nf, pl* **-ciones** : ramification
ramificarse {72} *vr* : to branch out, to divide into branches
ramillete *nm* 1 RAMO : bouquet 2 : select group, cluster
ramo *nm* 1 : branch 2 RAMILLETE : bouquet 3 : division (of science or industry) 4 **Domingo de Ramos** : Palm Sunday
rampa *nf* : ramp, incline
rana *nf* 1 : frog 2 **rana toro** : bullfrog
ranchera *nf* Mex : traditional folk song
ranchería *nf* : settlement
ranchero, -ra *n* : rancher, farmer
rancho *nm* 1 : ranch, farm 2 : hut 3 : settlement, camp 4 : food, mess (for soldiers, etc.)
rancio, -cia *adj* 1 : aged, mellow (of wine) 2 : ancient, old 3 : rancid
rango *nm* 1 : rank, status 2 : high social standing 3 : pomp, splendor
ransomware [ˈransomwer] *nm* : ransomware
ranúnculo *nm* : buttercup
ranura *nf* : groove, slot
rap *nm* : rap (music)
rapar *vt* 1 : to crop 2 : to shave
rapaz[1] *adj, pl* **rapaces** : rapacious, predatory
rapaz[2], **-paza** *n, mpl* **rapaces** : youngster, child
rape *nm* : close haircut
rapé *nm* : snuff
rapero, -ra *n* : rapper, rap artist
rapidez *nf* : rapidity, speed
rápido[1] *adv* : quickly, fast ⟨¡manejas tan rápido! : you drive so fast!⟩
rápido[2], **-da** *adj* : rapid, quick — **rápidamente** *adv*
rápido[3] *nm* 1 : express train 2 **rápidos** *nmpl* : rapids
rapiña *nf* 1 : plunder, pillage 2 **ave de rapiña** : bird of prey
raposa *nf* : vixen (fox)
rapsodia *nf* : rhapsody
raptar *vt* SECUESTRAR : to abduct, to kidnap
rapto *nm* 1 SECUESTRO : kidnapping, abduction 2 ARREBATO : fit, outburst
raptor, -tora *n* SECUESTRADOR : kidnapper
raquero, -ra *n* : beachcomber
raqueta *nf* 1 : racket (in sports) 2 : snowshoe
raquítico, -ca *adj* 1 : scrawny, weak 2 : measly, skimpy

raquitismo *nm* : rickets
raramente *adv* : seldom, rarely
rareza *nf* 1 : rarity 2 : peculiarity, oddity
raro, -ra *adj* 1 EXTRAÑO : odd, strange, peculiar 2 : unusual, rare 3 : exceptional 4 **rara vez** : seldom, rarely
ras *nm* **a ras de** : level with
rasar *vt* 1 : to skim, to graze 2 : to level
rascacielos *nms & pl* : skyscraper
rascar {72} *vt* 1 : to scratch 2 : to scrape — **rascarse** *vr* : to scratch an itch
rasgadura *nf* : tear, rip
rasgar {52} *vt* : to rip, to tear — **rasgarse** *vr*
rasgo *nm* 1 : stroke (of a pen) ⟨a grandes rasgos : in broad outlines⟩ 2 CARACTERÍSTICA : trait, characteristic 3 : gesture, deed 4 **rasgos** *nmpl* FACCIONES : features
rasgón *nm, pl* **rasgones** : rip, tear
rasgue, etc. → rasgar
rasguear *vt* : to strum
rasguñar *vt* 1 : to scratch 2 : to sketch, to outline
rasguño *nm* 1 : scratch 2 : sketch
raso[1], -sa *adj* 1 : level, flat 2 **soldado raso** : private (in the army) ⟨los soldados rasos : the ranks⟩
raso[2] *nm* : satin
raspadura *nf* 1 : scratching, scraping 2 **raspaduras** *nfpl* : scrapings
raspar *vt* 1 : to scrape 2 : to file down, to smooth — *vi* : to be rough
rasposo, -sa *adj* : rough, scratchy
rasque, etc. → rascar
rastra *nf* 1 : harrow 2 **a rastras** : by dragging, unwillingly
rastrear *vt* 1 : to track, to trace 2 : to comb, to search 3 : to trawl
rastrero, -ra *adj* 1 : creeping, crawling 2 : vile, despicable
rastrillar *vt* : to rake, to harrow
rastrillo *nm* 1 : rake 2 *Mex* : razor
rastro *nm* 1 PISTA : trail, track 2 VESTIGIO : trace, sign
rastrojo *nm* : stubble (of plants)
rasuradora *nf Mex, CA* : electric razor, shaver
rasurar *vt* AFEITAR : to shave — **rasurarse** *vr*
rata[1] *nm fam* : pickpocket, thief
rata[2] *nf* 1 : rat 2 *Col, Pan, Peru* : rate, percentage
rata almizclera *nf* : muskrat
ratear *vt* : to pilfer, to steal
ratero, -ra *n* : petty thief
ratificación *nf, pl* **-ciones** : ratification
ratificar {72} *vt* 1 : to ratify 2 : to confirm
rato *nm* 1 : while 2 **pasar el rato** : to pass the time 3 **a cada rato** : all the time, constantly ⟨les sacaba dinero a cada rato : he was always taking money from them⟩ 4 **al poco rato** : later, shortly after 5 **pasar un mal rato** : to have a bad/hard/tough time
ratón[1], -tona *n, mpl* **ratones** 1 : mouse 2 **ratón de biblioteca** *fam* : bookworm
ratón[2] *nm, pl* **ratones** 1 : (computer) mouse 2 *CoRi* : biceps

ratonera *nf* : mousetrap
raudal *nm* 1 : torrent 2 **a raudales** : in abundance
raviolis *or* **ravioles** *nmpl* : ravioli
raya[1], etc. → raer
raya[2] *nf* 1 : line ⟨pasarse de la raya : to go over the line, to go too far⟩ 2 : stripe 3 : skate, ray 4 : part (in the hair) ⟨hacerse la raya : to part one's hair⟩ 5 : crease (in clothing)
rayado, -da *adj* : striped, lined
rayar *vt* 1 ARAÑAR : to scratch 2 : to scrawl on, to mark up ⟨rayaron las paredes : they covered the walls with graffiti⟩ — *vi* 1 : to scratch 2 AMANECER : to dawn, to break ⟨al rayar el alba : at break of day⟩ 3 ~ **con** : to be adjacent to, to be next to 4 ~ **en** : to border on, to verge on ⟨su respuesta raya en lo ridículo : his answer borders on the ridiculous⟩ — **rayarse** *vr*
rayo *nm* 1 : ray, beam ⟨rayo láser : laser beam⟩ ⟨rayo gamma : gamma ray⟩ ⟨rayo de sol : sunbeam⟩ 2 RELÁMPAGO : lightning bolt 3 **rayo X** : X-ray
rayón *nm, pl* **rayones** : rayon
rayuela *nf* : hopscotch
raza *nf* 1 : race ⟨raza humana : human race⟩ 2 : breed, strain 3 **de** ~ : thoroughbred (of a horse), purebred, pedigreed
razón *nf, pl* **razones** 1 MOTIVO : reason, motive ⟨en razón de : by reason of, because of⟩ ⟨tuvo sus razones : she had her reasons⟩ ⟨razón de más para hacerlo : all the more reason to do it⟩ 2 : reasoning, sense ⟨perder la razón : to lose one's mind⟩ 3 **con** ~ : with good reason ⟨se quejaron, y con razón : they complained, and with good reason⟩ ⟨con razón no tiene novia : no wonder he doesn't have a girlfriend⟩ 4 **con razón o sin ella** : rightly or wrongly 5 **tener razón** : to be right ⟨en algo tiene razón : he's right about one thing⟩ 6 **darle la razón a alguien** : to say/admit that someone is right
razonable *adj* : reasonable — **razonablemente** *adv*
razonado, -da *adj* : itemized, detailed
razonamiento *nm* : reasoning
razonar *v* : to reason, to think
re *nm* 1 : D ⟨re sostenido/bemol : D sharp/flat⟩ 2 : re (in singing)
re- *pref* : re-
reabastecimiento *nm* : replenishment
reabierto *pp* → reabrir
reabrir {2} *vt* : to reopen — **reabrirse** *vr*
reacción *nf, pl* **-ciones** 1 : reaction 2 **motor a reacción** : jet engine
reaccionar *vi* : to react, to respond
reaccionario, -ria *adj & n* : reactionary
reacio, -cia *adj* : resistant, opposed
reacondicionar *vt* : to recondition
reactivación *nf, pl* **-ciones** : reactivation, revival
reactivar *vt* : reactivate, revive
reactor *nm* 1 : reactor ⟨reactor nuclear : nuclear reactor⟩ 2 : jet engine 3 : jet airplane, jet

reafirmar *vt* : to reaffirm, to assert, to strengthen

reagruparse *vr* : to regroup

reajustar *vt* : to readjust, to adjust

reajuste *nm* : readjustment ⟨reajuste de precios : price increase⟩

real[1] *adj* **1** : real, true **2** : royal

real[2] *nm* : real (monetary unit of Brazil)

realce *nm* **1** : embossing, relief **2 dar realce** : to highlight, to bring out

realeza *nf* : royalty

realidad *nf* **1** : reality **2 en ～** : in truth, actually **3 realidad aumentada** : augmented reality

realinear *vt* : to realign — **realineamiento** *nm*

realismo *nm* **1** : realism **2** : royalism

realista[1] *adj* **1** : realistic **2** : realist : royalist

realista[2] *nmf* **1** : realist **2** : royalist

realizable *adj* : feasible, attainable, workable

realización *nf, pl* **-ciones** : execution, realization

realizador, -dora *n* : (television or movie) producer

realizar {21} *vt* **1** : to carry out, to execute **2** : to produce, to direct (a film or play) **3** : to fulfill, to achieve **4** : to realize (a profit) — **realizarse** *vr* **1** : to come true **2** : to fulfill oneself

realmente *adv* : really, in reality

realzar {21} *vt* **1** : to heighten, to raise **2** : to highlight, to enhance

reanimación *nf, pl* **-ciones** : revival, resuscitation

reanimar *vt* **1** : to revive, to restore **2** : to resuscitate — **reanimarse** *vr* **1** : to come around, to recover

reanudación *nf, pl* **-ciones** : resumption, renewal

reanudar *vt* : to resume, to renew — **reanudarse** *vr* : to resume, to continue

reaparecer {53} *vi* **1** : to reappear **2** : to make a comeback

reaparición *nf, pl* **-ciones** : reappearance

reapertura *nf* : reopening

reata *nf* **1** : rope **2** *Mex* : lasso, lariat **3 de ～** : single file

reavivar *vt* : to revive, to reawaken

rebaja *nf* **1** : reduction **2** DESCUENTO : discount **3 rebajas** *nfpl* : sale

rebajar *vt* **1** : to reduce, to lower ⟨a precios rebajados : at reduced prices, on sale⟩ **2** : to lessen, to diminish **3** : to humiliate — **rebajarse** *vr* **1** : to humble oneself **2 rebajarse a** : to stoop to

rebanada *nf* : slice

rebanadora *nf* : slicer

rebañar *vt* : to mop up, to sop up

rebaño *nm* **1** : flock **2** : herd

rebasar *vt* **1** : to surpass, to exceed **2** *Mex* : to pass, to overtake

rebatiña *nf* : scramble, fight (over something)

rebatir *vt* REFUTAR : to refute

rebato *nm* **1** : surprise attack **2 tocar a rebato** : to sound the alarm

rebeca *nf Spain* : cardigan

rebelarse *vr* : to rebel

rebelde[1] *adj* : rebellious, unruly

rebelde[2] *nmf* **1** : rebel **2** : defaulter

rebeldía *nf* **1** : rebelliousness **2 en ～** : in default

rebelión *nf, pl* **-liones** : rebellion

reblandecer {18} *vt* : to soften

rebobinar *vt* : to rewind

reborde *nm* : border, flange, rim

rebosante *adj* : brimming, overflowing ⟨rebosante de salud : brimming with health⟩

rebosar *vi* **1** : to overflow **2 ～ de** : to abound in, to be bursting with — *vt* : to radiate

rebotar *vi* **1** : to bounce **2** : to ricochet, to rebound

rebote *nm* **1** : bounce **2** : rebound, ricochet

rebozar {21} *vt* : to coat in batter

rebozo *nm* **1** : shawl, wrap **2 sin ～** : frankly, openly

rebullir {38} *v* : to move, to stir — **rebullirse** *vr*

rebuscado, -da *adj* : affected, pretentious

rebuscar {72} *vi* : to search thoroughly

rebuznar *vi* : to bray

rebuzno *nm* : bray, braying

recabar *vt* **1** : to gather, to obtain, to collect **2 recabar fondos** : to raise money

recado *nm* **1** : message ⟨mandar recado : to send word⟩ **2** *Spain* : errand

recaer {13} *vi* **1** : to relapse **2 ～ en** *or* **～ sobre** : to fall on, to fall to

recaída *nf* : relapse

recaiga, etc. → recaer

recalar *vi* : to arrive

recalcar {72} *vt* : to emphasize, to stress

recalcitrante *adj* : recalcitrant

recalentar {55} *vt* **1** : to reheat, to warm up **2** : to overheat

recámara *nf* **1** *Col, Mex, Pan* : bedroom **2** : chamber (of a firearm)

recamarera *nf Mex* : chambermaid

recambio *nm* **1** : spare part **2** : refill (for a pen, etc.)

recapacitar *vi* **1** : to reconsider **2 ～ en** : to reflect on, to weigh

recapitular *v* : to recapitulate — **recapitulación** *nf*

recargable *adj* : rechargeable

recargado, -da *adj* : overly elaborate or ornate

recargar {52} *vt* **1** : to recharge (a battery), to reload (a gun) **2** : to reload (a web page, etc.) **3** : to overload — **recargarse** *vr Mex* **～ contra** : to lean against

recargo *nm* : surcharge

recatado, -da *adj* MODESTO : modest, demure

recato *nm* PUDOR : modesty

recaudación *nf, pl* **-ciones** **1** : collection **2** : earnings *pl*, takings *pl*

recaudador, -dora *n* **recaudador de impuestos** : tax collector

recaudar *vt* : to collect

recaudo *nm* : safe place ⟨a (buen) recaudo : in safe keeping⟩

recayó, etc. → recaer

rece, etc. → rezar

recelar *vi* **～ de** : to distrust, to be suspicious of ⟨recelábamos de ella : we didn't trust her, we were suspicious of her⟩

recelo *nm* : distrust, suspicion
receloso, -sa *adj* : distrustful, suspicious
recepción *nf, pl* **-ciones** : reception
recepcionista *nmf* : receptionist
receptáculo *nm* : receptacle
receptividad *nf* : receptiveness
receptivo, -va *adj* : receptive
receptor¹, -tora *adj* : receiving
receptor², **-tora** *n* **1** : recipient **2** : catcher (in baseball), receiver (in football)
receptor³ *nm* : receiver ⟨receptor de televisión : television set⟩
recesión *nf, pl* **-siones** : recession
recesivo, -va *adj* : recessive
receso *nm* : recess, adjournment
receta *nf* **1** : recipe **2** : prescription
recetar *vt* : to prescribe (medications)
rechazar {21} *vt* **1** : to reject **2** : to turn down, to refuse
rechazo *nm* : rejection, refusal
rechifla *nf* : booing, jeering
rechinar *vi* **1** : to squeak **2** : to grind, to gnash ⟨hacer rechinar los dientes : to grind one's teeth⟩
rechistar *vi* : to complain, to answer back ⟨trabajó sin rechistar : he worked without complaint⟩
rechoncho, -cha *adj fam* : chubby, squat
rechupete *adj fam* **de ∼** : delicious, scrumptious
recibidor *nm* : vestibule, entrance hall
recibimiento *nm* : reception, welcome
recibir *vt* **1** : to receive, to get **2** : to receive, to greet (visitors) — *vi* : to receive visitors — **recibirse** *vr* **1** : to graduate **2 ∼ de** : to qualify as
recibo *nm* : receipt
reciclable *adj* : recyclable
reciclado → **reciclaje**
reciclaje *nm* **1** : recycling **2** : retraining
reciclar *vt* **1** : to recycle **2** : to retrain
recién *adv* **1** : newly, recently ⟨recién nacido : newborn⟩ ⟨recién casados : newlyweds⟩ ⟨recién llegado : newcomer⟩ **2** : just, only just ⟨recién ahora me acordé : I just now remembered⟩
reciente *adj* : recent — **recientemente** *adv*
recinto *nm* **1** : enclosure **2** : site, premises *pl*
recio¹ *adv* **1** : strongly, hard **2** : loudly, loud
recio², -cia *adj* **1** : severe, harsh **2** : tough, strong
recipiente¹ *nm* : container, receptacle
recipiente² *nmf* : recipient
reciprocar {72} *vi* : to reciprocate
reciprocidad *nf* : reciprocity
recíproco, -ca *adj* : reciprocal, mutual — **recíprocamente** *adv*
recitación *nf, pl* **-ciones** : recitation, recital
recital *nm* : recital
recitar *vt* : to recite
reclamación *nf, pl* **-ciones** **1** : claim, demand **2** QUEJA : complaint
reclamar *vt* **1** EXIGIR : to demand, to require **2** : to claim — *vi* : to complain

reclamo *nm* **1** : bird call, lure **2** : lure, decoy **3** : inducement, attraction **4** : advertisement **5** : complaint
reclinable *adj* : reclining
reclinar *vt* : to rest, to lean — **reclinarse** *vr* : to recline, to lean back
recluir {41} *vt* : to confine, to lock up — **recluirse** *vr* : to shut oneself up, to withdraw
reclusión *nf, pl* **-siones** : imprisonment
recluso, -sa *n* **1** : inmate, prisoner **2** SOLITARIO : recluse
recluta *nmf* : recruit, draftee
reclutamiento *nm* : recruitment, recruiting
reclutar *vt* ENROLAR : to recruit, to enlist
recobrar *vt* : to recover, to regain — **recobrarse** *vr* : to recover, to recuperate
recocer {14} *vt* : to overcook, to cook again
recodo *nm* : bend
recogedor *nm* : dustpan
recogepelotas *nmfs & pl* : ball boy *m*, ball girl *f*
recoger {15} *vt* **1** : to collect, to gather **2** : to get, to pick up, to retrieve **3** : to clean up, to tidy (up)
recogido, -da *adj* : quiet, secluded
recogimiento *nm* **1** : collecting, gathering **2** : withdrawal **3** : absorption, concentration
recolección *nf, pl* **-ciones** **1** : collection ⟨recolección de basura : trash pickup⟩ **2** : harvest
recolectar *vt* **1** : to gather, to collect **2** : to harvest, to pick
recomendable *adj* : advisable, recommended
recomendación *nf, pl* **-ciones** : recommendation
recomendar {55} *vt* **1** : to recommend **2** ACONSEJAR : to advise
recompensa *nf* : reward, recompense
recompensar *vt* **1** PREMIAR : to reward **2** : to compensate
reconciliación *nf, pl* **-ciones** : reconciliation
reconciliar *vt* : to reconcile — **reconciliarse** *vr*
recóndito, -ta *adj* **1** : remote, isolated **2** : hidden **3 en lo más recóndito de** : in the depths of
reconfortar *vt* : to comfort — **reconfortante** *adj*
reconocer {18} *vt* **1** : to recognize **2** : to admit **3** : to examine
reconocible *adj* : recognizable
reconocido, -da *adj* **1** : recognized, accepted **2** : grateful
reconocimiento *nm* **1** : acknowledgment, recognition, avowal **2** : (medical) examination **3** : reconnaissance
reconquista *nf* : reconquest
reconquistar *vt* **1** : to reconquer, to recapture **2** RECUPERAR : to regain, to recover
reconsiderar *vt* : to reconsider — **reconsideración** *nf*
reconstrucción *nf, pl* **-ciones** : reconstruction

reconstructivo, -va *adj* : reconstructive
reconstruir {41} *vt* : to rebuild, to reconstruct
reconversión *nf, pl* **-siones** : restructuring
reconvertir {76} *vt* **1** : to restructure **2** : to retrain
recopilación *nf, pl* **-ciones 1** : summary **2** : collection, compilation
recopilar *vt* : to compile, to collect
récord *or* **record** ['rɛkɔr] *nm, pl* **récords** *or* **records** [-kɔrs] : record ⟨record mundial : world record⟩ — **récord** *or* **record** *adj*
recordar {19} *vt* **1** : to recall, to remember **2** : to remind — *vi* **1** ACORDARSE : to remember ⟨si mal no recuerdo : if I recall/remember correctly⟩ **2** DESPERTAR : to wake up
recordatorio¹, -ria *adj* : commemorative
recordatorio² *nm* : reminder
recorrer *vt* **1** : to travel through, to tour **2** : to cover (a distance) **3** : to go over, to look over
recorrido *nm* **1** : journey, trip **2** : path, route, course **3** : round (in golf)
recortar *vt* **1** : to cut, to reduce **2** : to cut out **3** : to trim, to cut off **4** : to outline — **recortarse** *vr* : to stand out ⟨los árboles se recortaban en el horizonte : the trees were silhouetted against the horizon⟩
recorte *nm* **1** : cut, reduction **2** : clipping ⟨recortes de periódicos : newspaper clippings⟩
recostar {19} *vt* : to lean, to rest — **recostarse** *vr* : to lie down, recline
recoveco *nm* **1** VUELTA : bend, turn **2** : nook, corner **3 recovecos** *nmpl* : intricacies, ins and outs
recreación *nf, pl* **-ciones 1** : re-creation **2** DIVERSIÓN : recreation, entertainment
recrear *vt* **1** : to re-create **2** : to entertain, to amuse — **recrearse** *vr* : to enjoy oneself
recreativo, -va *adj* : recreational
recreo *nm* **1** DIVERSIÓN : entertainment, amusement **2** : recess, break
recriminación *nf, pl* **-ciones** : reproach, recrimination
recriminar *vt* : to reproach — **recriminarse** *vr*
recrudecer {53} *v* : to intensify, to worsen — **recrudecerse** *vr*
recta *nf* : straight line
rectal *adj* : rectal
rectangular *adj* : rectangular
rectángulo *nm* : rectangle
rectificación *nf, pl* **-ciones** : rectification, correction
rectificar {72} *vt* **1** : to rectify, to correct **2** : to straighten (out)
rectitud *nf* : honesty, rectitude
recto¹ *adv* : straight
recto², -ta *adj* **1** : straight **2** : upright, honorable **3** : sound
recto³ *nm* : rectum
rector¹, -tora *adj* : governing, managing
rector², -tora *n* : rector
rectoría *nf* : rectory

recuadro *nm* : box (containing text, etc.)
recubierto *pp* → **recubrir**
recubrir {2} *vt* : to cover, to coat
recuento *nm* : recount, count ⟨un recuento de los votos : a recount of the votes⟩
recuerdo *nm* **1** : memory **2** : souvenir, memento **3 recuerdos** *nmpl* : regards
recular *vi* **1** : to back up **2** REPLEGARSE : to retreat, to fall back **3** RETRACTARSE : to back down
recuperación *nf, pl* **-ciones 1** : recovery, recuperation **2 recuperación de datos** : data retrieval
recuperar *vt* **1** : to recover, to get back, to retrieve **2** : to recuperate **3** : to make up for ⟨recuperar el tiempo perdido : to make up for lost time⟩ — **recuperarse** *vr* ~ **de** : to recover from, to get over
recurrente *adj* : recurrent, recurring
recurrir *vi* **1** ~ **a** : to turn to, to appeal to **2** ~ **a** : to resort to **3** : to appeal (in law)
recurso *nm* **1** : recourse ⟨el último recurso : the last resort⟩ **2** : appeal (in law) **3 recursos** *nmpl* : resources, means ⟨recursos naturales : natural resources⟩
red *nf* **1** : net, mesh **2** : network, system, chain ⟨redes sociales : social media⟩ **3** : trap, snare **4 la red/Red** : the Internet, the Web **5 red barredera** : dragnet
redacción *nf, pl* **-ciones 1** : writing, composition **2** : editing
redactar *vt* **1** : to write, to draft **2** : to edit
redactor, -tora *n* : editor
redada *nf* **1** : raid **2** : catch, haul
redecorar *v* : to redecorate
redefinir *vt* : to redefine — **redefinición** *nf*
redención *nf, pl* **-ciones** : redemption
redentor¹, -tora *adj* : redeeming
redentor², -tora *n* : redeemer
redescubierto *pp* → **redescubrir**
redescubrir {2} *vt* : to rediscover
redicho, -cha *adj fam* : affected, pretentious
redil *nm* **1** : sheepfold **2 volver al redil** : to return to the fold
redimir *vt* : to redeem, to deliver (from sin)
rediseñar *vt* : to redesign
redistribuir {41} *vt* : to redistribute — **redistribución** *nf*
rédito *nm* : return, yield
redituar {3} *vt* : to produce, to yield
redoblar *vt* : to redouble, to strengthen — **redoblado, -da** *adj*
redoble *nm* : drum roll
redomado, -da *adj* **1** : sly, crafty **2** : utter, out-and-out
redonda *nf* **1** : region, surrounding area **2 a la redonda** ALREDEDOR : around ⟨de diez millas a la redonda : for ten miles around⟩ **3** : whole note
redondear *vt* : to round off, to round out
redondel *nm* **1** : ring, circle **2** : bullring, arena

redondez *nf* : roundness

redondo, -da *adj* **1** : round ⟨mesa redonda : round table⟩ **2** : great, perfect ⟨un negocio redondo : an excellent deal⟩ **3** : straightforward, flat ⟨un rechazo redondo : a flat refusal⟩ **4** *Mex* : round-trip **5 en ～** : around

reducción *nf, pl* **-ciones** : reduction, decrease

reducido, -da *adj* **1** : reduced, limited **2** : small

reducir {61} *vt* **1** DISMINUIR : to reduce, to decrease, to cut **2** : to subdue **3** : to boil down — **reducirse** *vr* ～ **a** : to come down to, to be nothing more than

redundancia *nf* : redundancy

redundante *adj* : redundant

reedición *nf, pl* **-ciones** : reprint

reeditar *vt* : to reprint

reelegir {28} *vt* : to reelect — **reelección** *nf*

reembolsable *adj* : refundable

reembolsar *vt* **1** : to refund, to reimburse **2** : to repay

reembolso *nm* : refund, reimbursement

reemplazable *adj* : replaceable

reemplazar {21} *vt* : to replace, to substitute

reemplazo *nm* : replacement, substitution

reencarnación *nf, pl* **-ciones** : reincarnation

reencuentro *nm* : reunion

reestablecer {53} *vt* : to reestablish

reestructurar *vt* : to restructure

reexaminar *vt* : to reexamine

refacción *nf, pl* **-ciones 1** *Mex* : spare part, replacement part **2** : repair, renovation

refaccionar *vt* : to repair, to renovate

refaccionaria *nf Mex* : repair shop

referencia *nf* **1** : reference **2 hacer referencia a** : to refer to

referendo → **referéndum**

referéndum *nm, pl* **-dums** : referendum

referente *adj* ～ **a** : concerning

réferi *or* **referi** [ˈrɛfɛri] *nmf* : referee

referir {76} *vt* **1** : to relate, to tell **2** : to refer ⟨nos refirió al diccionario : she referred us to the dictionary⟩ — **referirse** *vr* ～ **a 1** : to refer to **2** : to be concerned, to be in reference to ⟨en lo que se refiere a la educación : as far as education is concerned⟩

refilón → **de refilón**

refinado¹, -da *adj* : refined

refinado² *nm* : refining

refinamiento *nm* **1** : refining **2** FINURA : refinement

refinanciar *vt* : to refinance

refinar *vt* : to refine

refinería *nf* : refinery

reflectante *adj* : reflective, reflecting

reflector¹, -tora *adj* : reflecting

reflector² *nm* **1** : spotlight, searchlight **2** : reflector

reflejar *vt* : to reflect — **reflejarse** *vr* : to be reflected ⟨la decepción se refleja en su rostro : the disappointment shows on her face⟩

reflejo *nm* **1** : reflection **2** : reflex **3 reflejos** *nmpl* : highlights, streaks (in hair)

reflexión *nf, pl* **-xiones** : reflection, thought

reflexionar *vi* : to reflect, to think

reflexivo, -va *adj* **1** : reflective, thoughtful **2** : reflexive

reflujo *nm* **1** : ebb, ebb tide **2 el flujo y reflujo** : the ebb and flow

reforma *nf* **1** : reform **2** : alteration, renovation

reformador, -dora *n* : reformer

reformar *vt* **1** : to reform **2** : to change, to alter **3** : to renovate, to repair — **reformarse** *vr* : to mend one's ways

reformatorio *nm* : reform school

reforzar {36} *vt* **1** : to reinforce, to strengthen **2** : to encourage, to support

refracción *nf, pl* **-ciones** : refraction

refractar *vt* : to refract — **refractarse** *vr*

refrán *nm, pl* **refranes** ADAGIO : proverb, saying

refregar {49} *vt* : to scrub

refrenar *vt* **1** : to rein in (a horse) **2** : to restrain, to check — **refrenarse** *vr* : to restrain oneself

refrendar *vt* **1** : to countersign, to endorse **2** : to stamp (a passport)

refrescante *adj* : refreshing

refrescar {72} *vt* **1** : to refresh, to cool **2** : to brush up (on) **3 refrescar la memoria** : to refresh one's memory — *vi* : to turn cooler

refresco *nm* : refreshment, soft drink ⟨refresco de cola : cola⟩

refriega *nf* : skirmish, scuffle

refrigeración *nf, pl* **-ciones 1** : refrigeration **2** : air-conditioning

refrigerador *nmf* NEVERA : refrigerator

refrigeradora *nf Col, Peru* : refrigerator

refrigerante *nm* : coolant

refrigerar *vt* **1** : to refrigerate **2** : to air-condition

refrigerio *nm* : snack, refreshments *pl*

refrito¹, -ta *adj* : refried

refrito² *nm* : fried dish

refuerzo *nm* : reinforcement, support

refugiado, -da *n* : refugee

refugiar *vt* : to shelter — **refugiarse** *vr* ACOGERSE : to take refuge

refugio *nm* : refuge, shelter

refulgencia *nf* : brilliance, splendor

refulgir {35} *vi* : to shine brightly

refundir *vt* **1** : to recast (metals) **2** : to revise, to rewrite

refunfuñar *vi* : to grumble, to groan

refutar *vt* : to refute — **refutación** *nf*

regadera *nf* **1** : watering can **2** : shower head, shower **3** : sprinkler

regaderazo *nm Mex* : shower

regadío *nm* **tierra de ～** : irrigated land

regalado, -da *adj* **1** : dirt cheap **2** : comfortable, easy

regalar *vt* **1** OBSEQUIAR : to present (as a gift), to give away **2** : to regale, to entertain **3** : to flatter, to make a fuss over — **regalarse** *vr* : to pamper oneself

regalía *nf* : royalty, payment

regaliz *nm, pl* **-lices** : licorice

regalo *nm* **1** OBSEQUIO : gift, present **2** : pleasure, comfort **3** : treat

regalón, -lona *adj, mpl* **-lones** *Chile fam* : spoiled (of a person)

regañadientes *mpl* **a** ~ : reluctantly, unwillingly

regañar *vt* : to scold, to give a talking to — *vi* **1** QUEJARSE : to grumble, to complain **2** REÑIR : to quarrel, to argue

regañina *nf fam* : scolding

regaño *nm fam* : scolding

regañón, -ñona *adj, mpl* **-ñones** *fam* : grumpy, irritable

regar {49} *vt* **1** : to irrigate **2** : to water **3** : to wash, to hose down **4** : to spill, to scatter

regata *nf* : regatta, yacht race

regate *nm* : dodge, feint

regatear *vt* **1** : to haggle over **2** ESCATIMAR : to skimp on, to be sparing with — *vi* : to bargain, to haggle

regateo *nm* : bargaining, haggling

regatón *nm, pl* **-tones** : cap, tip

regazo *nm* : lap (of a person)

regencia *nf* : regency

regenerar *vt* : to regenerate — **regenerarse** *vr* — **regeneración** *nf*

regentar *vt* : to run, to manage

regente *nmf* : regent

reggae ['rege, 'rigi] *nm* : reggae

regidor, -dora *n* : town councillor

régimen *nm, pl* **regímenes 1** : regime **2** : diet **3** : regimen, rules *pl* ⟨régimen de vida : lifestyle⟩

regimiento *nm* : regiment

regio, -gia *adj* **1** : great, magnificent **2** : regal, royal

región *nf, pl* **regiones** : region, area

regional *adj* : regional — **regionalmente** *adv*

regir {28} *vt* **1** : to rule **2** : to manage, to run **3** : to control, to govern ⟨las costumbres que rigen la conducta : the customs which govern behavior⟩ — *vi* : to apply, to be in force ⟨las leyes rigen en los tres países : the laws apply in all three countries⟩ — **regirse** *vr* ~ **por** : to go by, to be guided by

registrador¹, -dora *adj* **caja registradora** : cash register

registrador², -dora *n* : registrar, recorder

registrar *vt* **1** : to register, to record **2** GRABAR : to record, to tape **3** : to search, to examine — **registrarse** *vr* **1** INSCRIBIRSE : to register **2** OCURRIR : to happen, to occur

registro *nm* **1** : register **2** : registration **3** : registry, record office **4** : range (of a voice or musical instrument) **5** : search

regla *nf* **1** NORMA : rule, regulation **2** : ruler ⟨regla de cálculo : slide rule⟩ **3** MENSTRUACIÓN : period, menstruation

reglamentación *nf, pl* **-ciones 1** : regulation **2** : rules *pl*

reglamentar *vt* : to regulate, to set rules for

reglamentario, -ria *adj* : regulation, official ⟨equipo reglamentario : standard equipment⟩

reglamento *nm* : regulations *pl*, rules *pl* ⟨reglamento de tráfico : traffic regulations⟩

regocijar *vt* : to gladden, to delight — **regocijarse** *vr* : to rejoice

regocijo *nm* : delight, rejoicing

regodearse *vr* : to delight, to gloat ⟨regodearse en/con : to delight in, to gloat about/over⟩

regordete, -ta *adj fam* LLENITO : chubby

regresar *vt* DEVOLVER : to give back — *vi* : to return, to come back, to go back

regresión *nf, pl* **-siones** : regression, return

regresivo, -va *adj* : regressive

regreso *nm* **1** : return **2 estar de regreso** : to be back, to be home

reguero *nm* **1** : irrigation ditch **2** : trail, trace **3 propagarse como reguero de pólvora** : to spread like wildfire

regulable *adj* : adjustable

regulación *nf, pl* **-ciones** : regulation, control

regulador¹, -dora *adj* : regulating, regulatory

regulador² *nm* **1** : regulator, governor **2 regulador de tiro** : damper (in a chimney)

regular¹ *vt* : to regulate, to control

regular² *adj* **1** : regular **2** : fair, OK, soso **3** : medium, average **4 por lo regular** : in general, generally

regularidad *nf* : regularity

regularización *nf, pl* **-ciones** NORMALIZACIÓN : normalization

regularizar {21} *vt* NORMALIZAR : to normalize, to make regular

regularmente *adv* : regularly

regurgitar *vi* : to regurgitate

regusto *nm* : aftertaste

rehabilitar *vt* **1** : to rehabilitate **2** : to reinstate **3** : renovate, to restore — **rehabilitación** *nf*

rehacer {40} *vt* **1** : to redo **2** : to remake, to repair; to renew — **rehacerse** *vr* **1** : to recover **2** ~ **de** : to get over

rehecho *pp* → rehacer

rehén *nm, pl* **rehenes** : hostage

rehicieron, etc. → rehacer

rehizo → rehacer

rehuir {41} *vt* : to avoid, to shun

rehusar {8} *v* : to refuse

reimprimir *vt* : to reprint

reina *nf* : queen

reinado *nm* : reign

reinante *adj* **1** : reigning **2** : prevailing, current

reinar *vi* **1** : to reign **2** : to prevail

reincidencia *nf* : recidivism

reincidente *adj & nmf* : recidivist

reincidir *vi* : to backslide, to relapse

reincorporar *vt* : to reinstate — **reincorporarse** *vr* ~ **a** : to return to, to rejoin

reiniciar *vt* **1** : to resume, to restart **2** : to reboot (a computer)

reino *nm* : kingdom, realm ⟨reino animal : animal kingdom⟩

reinstalar *vt* **1** : to reinstall **2** : to reinstate

reintegración *nf, pl* **-ciones 1** : reinstatement, reintegration **2** : refund, reimbursement

reintegrar *vt* **1** : to reintegrate, reinstate **2** : to refund, to reimburse — **reintegrarse** *vr* ~ **a** : to return to, to rejoin

reintegro *nm* : refund, reimbursement

reintroducir {61} *vt* : to reintroduce

reír {66} *vi* : to laugh — *vt* : to laugh at — **reírse** *vr*

reiteración *nf, pl* **-ciones** : reiteration, repetition

reiterado, -da *adj* : repeated ⟨lo explicó en reiteradas ocasiones : he explained it repeatedly⟩ — **reiteradamente** *adv*

reiterar *vt* : to reiterate, to repeat

reiterativo, -va *adj* : repetitive, repetitious

reivindicación *nf, pl* **-ciones** **1** : demand, claim **2** : vindication

reivindicar {72} *vt* **1** : to vindicate **2** : to demand, to claim **3** : to restore

reja *nf* **1** : grille, grating ⟨entre rejas : behind bars⟩ **2** : plowshare

rejego, -ga *adj Mex fam* : stubborn

rejilla *nf* : grille, grate, screen

rejuvenecer {53} *vt* : to rejuvenate — *vi* : to be rejuvenated — **rejuvenecerse** *vr*

rejuvenecimiento *nm* : rejuvenation

relación *nf, pl* **-ciones** **1** : relation, connection, relevance **2** : relationship **3** RELATO : account **4** LISTA : list **5** : ratio (in mathematics) **6 con relación a** *or* **en relación con** : in relation to, concerning **7 relaciones públicas** : public relations, PR

relacionar *vt* : to relate, to connect — **relacionarse** *vr* ~ **con** : to be connected to, to be linked with

relajación *nf, pl* **-ciones** : relaxation

relajado, -da *adj* **1** : relaxed, loose **2** : dissolute, depraved

relajante *adj* : relaxing

relajar *vt* : to relax, to slacken — *vi* : to be relaxing — **relajarse** *vr*

relajo *nm* **1** : commotion, ruckus **2** : joke, laugh ⟨lo hizo de relajo : he did it for a laugh⟩

relamerse *vr* : to smack one's lips, to lick one's chops

relámpago *nm* : flash of lightning

relampaguear *vi* : to flash

relanzar {21} *vt* : to relaunch

relatar *vt* : to relate, to tell

relatividad *nf* : relativity

relativismo *nm* : relativism

relativo, -va *adj* **1** : relative **2 en lo relativo a** : with regard to, concerning — **relativamente** *adv*

relato *nm* **1** : story, tale **2** : account

relax [re'las] *nm* : relaxation

releer {20} *vt* : to reread

relegar {52} *vt* **1** : to relegate **2 relegar al olvido** : to consign to oblivion

relevante *adj* : outstanding, important

relevar *vt* **1** : to relieve, to take over from **2** ~ **de** : to exempt from — **relevarse** *vr* : to take turns

relevo *nm* **1** : relief, replacement **2** : relay ⟨carrera de relevos : relay race⟩

relicario *nm* **1** : shrine, container (for relics) **2** : locket

relieve *nm* **1** : relief, projection ⟨mapa en relieve : relief map⟩ ⟨letras en relieve : embossed letters⟩ **2** : prominence, importance **3 poner en relieve** : to highlight, to emphasize

religión *nf, pl* **-giones** : religion

religiosamente *adv* : religiously, faithfully

religioso[1], -sa *adj* : religious

religioso[2], -sa *n* : monk *m*, nun *f*

relinchar *vi* : to neigh, to whinny

relincho *nm* : neigh, whinny

reliquia *nf* **1** : relic **2 reliquia de familia** : family heirloom

rellano *nm* : landing (of a stairway)

rellenar *vt* **1** : to refill **2** : to stuff, to fill **3** : to fill out

relleno[1], -na *adj* : stuffed, filled

relleno[2] *nm* : stuffing, filling

reloj *nm* **1** : clock **2** : watch **3 reloj de arena** : hourglass **4 reloj de pulsera** : wristwatch **5 como un reloj** : like clockwork

relojería *nf* **1** : watchmaker's shop **2** : watchmaking, clockmaking

relojero, -ra *n* : watchmaker, clockmaker

reluciente *adj* : brilliant, shining

relucir {45} *vi* **1** : to glitter, to shine **2 salir a relucir** : to come to the surface **3 sacar a relucir** : to bring up, to mention

relumbrante *adj* : dazzling

relumbrar *vi* : to shine brightly

relumbrón *nm, pl* **-brones** **1** : flash, glare **2 de** ~ : flashy, showy

remachar *vt* **1** : to rivet **2** : to clinch (a nail) **3** : to stress, to drive home — *vi* : to smash, to spike (a ball)

remache *nm* **1** : rivet **2** : smash, spike (in sports)

remanente *nm* **1** : remainder, balance **2** : surplus

remangar {52} *vt* : to roll up — **remangarse** *vr* : to roll up one's sleeves

remanso *nm* : pool

remar *vi* **1** : to row, to paddle **2** : to struggle, to toil

remarcar {72} *vt* : to emphasize, to stress

rematado, -da *adj* : utter, complete

rematador, -dora *n* : auctioneer

rematar *vt* **1** : to finish off **2** : to auction — *vi* **1** : to shoot **2** : to end

remate *nm* **1** : shot (in sports) ⟨sacar un remate : to take a shot⟩ **2** : auction **3** : end, conclusion **4 como** ~ : to top it off **5 de** ~ : completely, utterly

remecer {86} *vt* : to sway, to swing

remedar *vt* **1** IMITAR : to imitate, to copy **2** : to mimic, to ape

remediar *vt* **1** : to remedy, to repair **2** : to help out, to assist **3** EVITAR : to prevent, to avoid

remedio *nm* **1** : remedy, cure **2** : solution **3** : option ⟨no me quedó más remedio : I had no other choice⟩ ⟨no hay remedio : it can't be helped⟩ **4 poner remedio a** : to put a stop to **5 sin** ~ : unavoidable, inevitable

remedo *nm* : imitation

rememorar *vi* : to recall ⟨rememorar los viejos tiempos : to reminisce⟩

remendar {55} *vt* **1** : to mend, to patch, to darn **2** : to correct

remera *nf Arg, Uru* : T-shirt
remero, -ra *n* : rower
remesa *nf* 1 : remittance 2 : shipment
remezón *nm, pl* **-zones** : mild earthquake, tremor
remiendo *nm* 1 : patch 2 : correction
remilgado, -da *adj* 1 : prim, prudish 2 : affected
remilgo *nm* : primness, affectation
reminiscencia *nf* : reminiscence
remisión *nf, pl* **-siones** 1 ENVÍO : sending, delivery 2 : remission 3 : reference, cross-reference
remiso, -sa *adj* 1 : lax, remiss 2 : reluctant
remite *nm* : return address
remitente¹ *nm* : return address
remitente² *nmf* : sender (of a letter, etc.)
remitir *vt* 1 : to send, to remit 2 ~ **a** : to refer to, to direct to ⟨nos remitió al diccionario : he referred us to the dictionary⟩ — *vi* : to subside, to let up — **remitirse** *vr* ~ **a** : to refer to
remo *nm* 1 : paddle, oar 2 : rowing (sport)
remoción *nf, pl* **-ciones** 1 : removal 2 : dismissal
remodelación *nf, pl* **-ciones** 1 : remodeling 2 : reorganization, restructuring
remodelar *vt* 1 : to remodel 2 : to restructure
remojar *vt* 1 : to soak, to steep 2 : to dip, to dunk 3 : to celebrate with a drink
remojo *nm* 1 : soaking, steeping 2 **poner en remojo** : to soak, to leave soaking
remolacha *nf* : beet
remolcador *nm* : tugboat
remolcar {72} *vt* : to tow, to haul
remolino *nm* 1 : whirlwind 2 : eddy, whirlpool 3 : crowd, throng 4 : cowlick
remolón, -lona *adj, mpl* **-lones** : lazy
remolque *nm* 1 : towing, tow 2 : trailer 3 **a** ~ : in tow
remontar *vt* 1 : to overcome 2 SUBIR : to go up — **remontarse** *vr* 1 : to soar 2 ~ **a** : to date from, to go back to
rémora *nf* : obstacle, hindrance
remorder {47} *vt* INQUIETAR : to trouble, to distress
remordimiento *nm* : remorse
remotamente *adv* : remotely, vaguely
remoto, -ta *adj* 1 : remote, unlikely ⟨hay una posibilidad remota : there is a slim possibility⟩ 2 : distant, far-off
remover {47} *vt* 1 : to stir 2 : to move around, to turn over 3 : to stir up 4 : to remove 5 : to dismiss
removible *adj* : removable
remozamiento *nm* : renovation
remozar {21} *vt* 1 : to renew, to brighten up 2 : to redo, to renovate
remuneración *nf, pl* **-ciones** : remuneration, pay
remunerar *vt* : to pay, to remunerate
renacer {48} *vi* : to be reborn, to revive
renacimiento *nm* 1 : rebirth, revival 2 **el Renacimiento** : the Renaissance
renacuajo *nm* : tadpole, pollywog

renal *adj* : renal, kidney
rencilla *nf* : quarrel
renco, -ca *adj* : lame
rencor *nm* 1 : rancor, enmity, hostility 2 **guardar rencor** : to hold a grudge ⟨guardarle rencor a alguien por algo : to resent someone for something, to hold a grudge against someone for something⟩
rencoroso, -sa *adj* : resentful, bitter, rancorous
rendición *nf, pl* **-ciones** 1 : surrender, submission 2 : yield, return
rendido, -da *adj* 1 : submissive 2 : worn-out, exhausted 3 : devoted
rendija *nf* GRIETA : crack, split
rendimiento *nm* 1 : performance 2 : yield, efficiency
rendir {54} *vt* 1 : to render, to give ⟨rendir las gracias : to give thanks⟩ ⟨rendir homenaje a : to pay homage to⟩ 2 : to yield 3 CANSAR : to exhaust — *vi* 1 CUNDIR : to progress, to make headway 2 : to last, to go a long way — **rendirse** *vr* : to surrender, to give up
renegado, -da *n* : renegade
renegar {49} *vi* 1 ~ **de** : to renounce, to disown, to give up 2 ~ **de** : to complain about — *vt* 1 : to deny vigorously 2 : to abhor, to hate
renglón *nm, pl* **renglones** 1 : line (of writing) 2 : merchandise, line (of products)
rengo, -ga *adj* : lame
renguear *vi* : to limp
reno *nm* : reindeer
renombrado, -da *adj* : renowned, famous
renombre *nm* NOMBRADÍA : renown, fame
renovable *adj* : renewable
renovación *nf, pl* **-ciones** 1 : renewal ⟨renovación de un contrato : renewal of a contract⟩ 2 : change, renovation
renovar {19} *vt* 1 : to renew, to restore 2 : to renovate
renquear *vi* : to limp, to hobble
renquera *nf* COJERA : limp, lameness
renta *nf* 1 : income 2 : rent 3 **impuesto sobre la renta** : income tax
rentable *adj* : profitable — **rentabilidad** *nf*
rentar *vt* 1 : to produce, to yield 2 ALQUILAR : to rent
renuencia *nf* : reluctance, unwillingness
renuente *adj* : reluctant, unwilling
renuncia *nf* 1 : resignation 2 : renunciation 3 : waiver
renunciar *vi* 1 : to resign 2 ~ **a** : to renounce, to relinquish ⟨renunció al título : he relinquished the title⟩
reñido, -da *adj* 1 : tough, hard-fought 2 : at odds, on bad terms
reñir {67} *vi* 1 : to argue 2 ~ **con** : to fall out with, to go up against — *vt* : to scold, to reprimand
reo, rea *n* 1 : accused, defendant 2 : offender, culprit
reojo *nm* **de** ~ : out of the corner of one's eye ⟨una mirada de reojo : a sidelong glance⟩
reorganizar {21} *vt* : to reorganize — **reorganización** *nf*

repantigarse {52} *vr* : to slouch, to loll about

reparación *nf, pl* **-ciones** 1 : reparation, amends 2 : repair

reparador, -dora *adj* : refreshing

reparar *vt* 1 : to repair, to fix, to mend 2 : to make amends for 3 : to correct 4 : to restore, to refresh — *vi* 1 ~ **en** : to observe, to take notice of 2 ~ **en** : to consider, to think about ⟨sin reparar en las consecuencias : without thinking about the consequences⟩ ⟨no repararon en gastos : they spared no expense, money was no object⟩

reparo *nm* 1 : repair, restoration 2 : reservation, qualm ⟨no tuvieron reparos en decírmelo : they didn't hesitate to tell me⟩ 3 **poner reparos a** : to find fault with, to object to

repartición *nf, pl* **-ciones** 1 : distribution 2 : department, division

repartidor[1], -dora *adj* : delivery ⟨camión repartidor : delivery truck⟩

repartidor[2], -dora *n* : delivery person, distributor

repartimiento *nm* → **repartición**

repartir *vt* 1 : to allocate 2 DISTRIBUIR : to distribute, to hand out 3 : to spread

reparto *nm* 1 : allocation 2 : distribution 3 : cast (of characters)

repasador *nm Arg, Uru* : dish towel

repasar *vt* 1 : to pass by again 2 : to review, to go over 3 : to mend

repaso *nm* 1 : review 2 : mending 3 : checkup, overhaul

repatriar {85} *vt* : to repatriate — **repatriación** *nf*

repavimentar *vt* : to resurface

repelente[1] *adj* : repellent, repulsive

repelente[2] *nm* : repellent ⟨repelente de insectos : insect repellent⟩

repeler *vt* 1 : to repel, to resist, to repulse 2 : to reject 3 : to disgust ⟨el sabor me repele : I find the taste repulsive⟩

repensar {55} *v* : to rethink, to reconsider

repente *nm* 1 : sudden movement, start ⟨de repente : suddenly⟩ 2 : fit, outburst ⟨un repente de ira : a fit of anger⟩

repentino, -na *adj* : sudden — **repentinamente** *adv*

repercusión *nf, pl* **-siones** : repercussion

repercutir *vi* 1 : to reverberate, to echo 2 ~ **en** : to have effects on, to have repercussions on

repertorio *nm* : repertoire

repetición *nf, pl* **-ciones** 1 : repetition 2 : rerun, repeat

repetidamente *adv* : repeatedly

repetido, -da *adj* 1 : repeated, numerous 2 **repetidas veces** : repeatedly, time and again

repetir {54} *vt* 1 : to repeat 2 : to have a second helping of — *vi* 1 : to repeat a year (in school) 2 : to have a second helping 3 : to give indigestion — **repetirse** *vr* 1 : to repeat oneself 2 : to recur

repetitivo, -va *adj* : repetitive, repetitious

repicar {72} *vt* : to ring — *vi* : to ring out, to peal

repique *nm* : ringing, pealing

repiqueteo *nm* 1 : ringing, pealing 2 : drumming

repisa *nf* : shelf, ledge ⟨repisa de chimenea : mantelpiece⟩ ⟨repisa de ventana : windowsill⟩

replantear *vt* : to redefine, to restate — **replantearse** *vr* : to reconsider

replegar {49} *vt* : to fold — **replegarse** *vr* RETIRARSE : to retreat, to withdraw

repleto, -ta *adj* 1 : replete, full 2 ~ **de** : packed with, crammed with

réplica *nf* 1 : reply 2 : replica, reproduction 3 : aftershock

replicación *nf, pl* **-ciones** : replication

replicar {72} *vi* 1 : to reply, to retort 2 : to argue, to answer back

repliegue *nm* 1 : fold 2 : retreat, withdrawal

repollo *nm* COL : cabbage

reponer {60} *vt* 1 : to replace, to put back 2 : to reinstate 3 : to reply — **reponerse** *vr* : to recover

reportaje *nm* : article, story, report

reportar *vt* 1 : to check, to restrain 2 : to bring, to carry, to yield ⟨me reportó numerosos beneficios : it brought me many benefits⟩ 3 : to report — **reportarse** *vr* 1 CONTENERSE : to control oneself 2 PRESENTARSE : to report, to show up

reporte *nm* : report

reportear *vt* : to report on, to cover

reportero, -ra *n* 1 : reporter 2 **reportero gráfico** : photojournalist

reposado, -da *adj* : calm

reposapiés *nm, pl* **reposapiés** : footrest

reposar *vi* 1 : to rest, to repose 2 : to stand, to settle ⟨deje reposar la masa media hora : let the dough stand for half an hour⟩ 3 : to lie, to be buried — **reposarse** *vr* : to settle

reposición *nf, pl* **-ciones** 1 : replacement 2 : reinstatement 3 : revival

repositorio *nm* : repository

reposo *nm* : repose, rest

repostar *vi* 1 : to stock up 2 : to refuel

repostear *vt* : to repost (on social media)

repostería *nf* 1 : confectioner's shop 2 : pastry-making

repostero, -ra *n* : confectioner

repreguntar *vt* : to cross-examine

repreguntas *nfpl* : cross-examination

reprender *vt* : to reprimand, to scold

reprensible *adj* : reprehensible

represa *nf* : dam

represalia *nf* 1 : reprisal, retaliation 2 **tomar represalias** : to retaliate

represar *vt* : to dam

representación *nf, pl* **-ciones** 1 : representation 2 : performance 3 **en representación de** : on behalf of

representante *nmf* 1 : representative 2 : performer

representar *vt* 1 : to represent, to act for 2 : to perform 3 : to look, to appear as 4 : to symbolize, to stand for 5 : to signify, to mean — **representarse** *vr* : to imagine, to picture

representativo, -va *adj* : representative

represión *nf, pl* **-siones** : repression
represivo, -va *adj* : repressive
reprimenda *nf* : reprimand
reprimir *vt* **1** : to repress **2** : to suppress, to stifle
reprobable *adj* : reprehensible, culpable
reprobación *nf, pl* **-ciones** : disapproval
reprobar {19} *vt* **1** DESAPROBAR : to condemn, to disapprove of **2** : to fail (a course)
reprobatorio, -ria *adj* : disapproving, admonishing
reprochable *adj* : reprehensible
reprochar *vt* : to reproach — **reprocharse** *vr*
reproche *nm* : reproach
reproducción *nf, pl* **-ciones** : reproduction
reproducir {61} *vt* : to reproduce — **reproducirse** *vr* **1** : to breed, to reproduce **2** : to recur
reproductor[1], **-tora** *adj* : reproductive
reproductor[2] *nm* : player ⟨reproductor de DVD : DVD player⟩
reptar *vi* : to crawl, to slither
reptil[1] *adj* : reptilian
reptil[2] *nm* : reptile
república *nf* : republic
republicano, -na *adj & n* : republican — **republicanismo** *nm*
repudiar *vt* : to repudiate — **repudiación** *nf*
repudio *nm* : repudiation
repuesto[1] *pp* → **reponer**
repuesto[2] *nm* **1** : spare part **2 de ~** : spare ⟨rueda de repuesto : spare wheel⟩
repugnancia *nf* : repugnance
repugnante *adj* : repulsive, repugnant, revolting
repugnar *vt* : to cause repugnance, to disgust — **repugnarse** *vr*
repujar *vt* : to emboss
repulsa *nf* **1** : rejection **2** : condemnation
repulsivo, -va *adj* : repulsive
repuntar *vt Arg, Chile* : to round up (cattle) — *vi* : to begin to appear — **repuntarse** *vr* : to fall out, to quarrel
repuso, etc. → **reponer**
reputación *nf, pl* **-ciones** : reputation
reputar *vt* : to consider, to deem
requerir {76} *vt* **1** : to require, to call for **2** : to summon, to send for
requesón *nm, pl* **-sones** : curd cheese, cottage cheese
réquiem *nm* : requiem
requisa *nf* **1** : requisition **2** : seizure **3** : inspection
requisar *vt* **1** : to requisition **2** : to seize **3** INSPECCIONAR : to inspect
requisito *nm* **1** : requirement **2 requisito previo** : prerequisite
res *nf* **1** : beast, animal **2** *CA, Mex* : beef **3 reses** *nfpl* : cattle ⟨60 reses : 60 head of cattle⟩
resabio *nm* **1** VICIO : bad habit, vice **2** DEJO : aftertaste
resaca *nf* **1** : undertow **2** : hangover
resaltar *vi* **1** SOBRESALIR : to stand out **2 hacer resaltar** : to bring out, to highlight — *vt* : to stress, to emphasize

resarcimiento *nm* **1** : compensation **2** : reimbursement
resarcir {83} *vt* : to compensate, to indemnify — **resarcirse** *vr* **~ de** : to make up for
resbalada *nf* : slip
resbaladizo, -za *adj* **1** RESBALOSO : slippery **2** : tricky, ticklish, delicate
resbalar *vi* **1** : to slip, to slide **2** : to slip up, to make a mistake **3** : to skid — **resbalarse** *vr*
resbalón *nm, pl* **-lones** : slip
resbaloso, -sa *adj* : slippery
rescatar *vt* **1** : to rescue, to save **2** : to recover, to get back
rescate *nm* **1** : rescue **2** : recovery **3** : ransom
rescindir *vt* : to rescind, to annul, to cancel
rescisión *nf, pl* **-siones** : annulment, cancellation
rescoldo *nm* : embers *pl*
resecar {72} *vt* : to make dry, to dry up — **resecarse** *vr* : to dry up
reseco, -ca *adj* : dry
resentido, -da *adj* : resentful
resentimiento *nm* : resentment
resentirse {76} *vr* **1** : to suffer, to be weakened **2** OFENDERSE : to be/get upset ⟨se resintió porque la insultaron : she got upset when they insulted her, she resented being insulted⟩ **3 ~ de** : to feel the effects of — **resentir** *vt* **1** : to feel (effects, etc.) **2** : to resent
reseña *nf* **1** : report, summary, review **2** : description
reseñar *vt* **1** : to review **2** DESCRIBIR : to describe
reserva *nf* **1** : reservation **2** : reserve **3** : confidence, privacy ⟨con la mayor reserva : in strictest confidence⟩ **4 de ~** : spare, in reserve **5 reservas** *nfpl* : reservations, doubts
reservación *nf, pl* **-ciones** : reservation
reservado, -da *adj* **1** : reserved, reticent **2** : confidential
reservar *vt* : to reserve — **reservarse** *vr* **1** : to save oneself **2** : to conceal, to keep to oneself
reservorio *nm* : reservoir, reserve
resfriado *nm* CATARRO : cold
resfriar {85} *vt* : to cool — **resfriarse** *vr* **1** : to cool off **2** : to catch a cold
resfrío *nm* : cold
resguardar *vt* : to safeguard, to protect — **resguardarse** *vr*
resguardo *nm* **1** : safeguard, protection **2** : receipt, voucher **3** : border guard, coast guard
residencia *nf* **1** : residence **2** : boarding house
residencial *adj* : residential
residente *adj & nmf* : resident
residir *vi* **1** VIVIR : to reside, to dwell **2 ~ en** : to lie in, to consist of
residual *adj* : residual
residuo *nm* **1** : residue **2** : remainder **3 residuos** *nmpl* : waste ⟨residuos nucleares : nuclear waste⟩
resignación *nf, pl* **-ciones** : resignation

resignar *vt* : to resign — **resignarse** *vr* ~ **a** : to resign oneself to

resina *nf* **1** : resin **2 resina epoxídica** : epoxy

resistencia *nf* **1** : resistance **2** AGUANTE : endurance, strength, stamina **3** : heating element

resistente *adj* **1** : resistant **2** : strong, tough

resistir *vt* **1** TOLERAR : to stand, to bear, to tolerate **2** : to withstand, to resist **3** : to resist (temptation, etc.) — *vi* : to resist ⟨resistió hasta el último minuto : he held out until the last minute⟩ — **resistirse** *vr* ~ **a** : to be resistant to, to be reluctant ⟨se resiste a aceptarlo : she's reluctant to accept it⟩

resma *nf* : ream

resollar {19} *vi* : to breathe heavily, to wheeze

resolución *nf, pl* **-ciones** **1** : resolution, settlement **2** : decision **3** : determination, resolve

resolver {89} *vt* **1** : to resolve, to settle **2** : to decide — **resolverse** *vr* : to make up one's mind

resonancia *nf* **1** : resonance **2** : impact, repercussions *pl*

resonante *adj* **1** : resonant **2** : tremendous, resounding ⟨un éxito resonante : a resounding success⟩

resonar {19} *vi* : to resound, to ring

resoplar *vi* **1** : to puff, to pant **2** : to snort

resoplo *nm* **1** : puffing, panting **2** : snort

resorte *nm* **1** MUELLE : spring **2** : elasticity **3** : influence, means *pl* ⟨tocar resortes : to pull strings⟩

resortera *nf Mex* : slingshot

respaldar *vt* : to back, to support, to endorse — **respaldarse** *vr* : to lean back

respaldo *nm* **1** : back (of an object) **2** : support, backing

respectar *vt* : to concern, to relate to ⟨por lo que a mí respecta : as far as I'm concerned⟩

respectivo, -va *adj* : respective — **respectivamente** *adv*

respecto *nm* **1** ~ **a** : in regard to, concerning **2 al respecto** : on this matter, in this respect

respetable *adj* : respectable — **respetabilidad** *nf*

respetar *vt* : to respect

respeto *nm* **1** : respect, consideration **2 respetos** *nmpl* : respects ⟨presentar sus respetos : to pay one's respects⟩

respetuosidad *nf* : respectfulness

respetuoso, -sa *adj* : respectful — **respetuosamente** *adv*

respingado, -da *adj* : snub-nosed

respingo *nm* : start, jump

respiración *nf, pl* **-ciones** **1** : respiration, breathing **2 respiración boca a boca** : mouth-to-mouth resuscitation

respiradero *nm* : vent, ventilation shaft

respirador *nm* : respirator

respirar *v* : to breathe

respiratorio, -ria *adj* : respiratory

respiro *nm* **1** : breath **2** : respite, break

resplandecer {53} *vi* **1** : to shine **2** : to stand out

resplandeciente *adj* **1** : resplendent, shining **2** : radiant

resplandor *nm* **1** : brightness, brilliance, radiance **2** : flash

responder *vt* : to answer — *vi* **1** : to answer, to reply, to respond **2** ~ **a** : to respond to ⟨responder al tratamiento : to respond to treatment⟩ **3** ~ **de** : to answer for, to vouch for (something) **4** ~ **por** : to vouch for (someone)

respondón, -dona *adj, mpl* **-dones** *fam* : sassy, fresh, impertinent

responsabilidad *nf* : responsibility ⟨tener la responsabilidad de : to be responsible for⟩ ⟨exigen responsabilidades a la compañía : the company is being held responsible/accountable⟩

responsabilizarse {21} *vr* : to accept responsibility ⟨responsabilizarse de : to accept responsibility for⟩

responsable[1] *adj* : responsible — **responsablemente** *adv*

responsable[2] *nmf* : person responsible ⟨los responsables del proyecto : those in charge of the project⟩ ⟨los responsables del desastre : those responsible for the disaster⟩

respuesta *nf* : answer, response

resquebrajar *vt* : to split, to crack — **resquebrajarse** *vr*

resquemor *nm* : resentment, bitterness

resquicio *nm* **1** : crack **2** : opportunity, chance **3** : trace ⟨sin un resquicio de remordimiento : without a trace of remorse⟩ **4 resquicio legal** : loophole

resta *nf* SUSTRACCIÓN : subtraction

restablecer {53} *vt* : to reestablish, to restore — **restablecerse** *vr* : to recover

restablecimiento *nm* **1** : reestablishment, restoration **2** : recovery

restallar *vi* : to crack, to crackle, to click

restallido *nm* : crack, crackle

restante *adj* **1** : remaining **2 lo restante, los restantes** : the rest

restañar *vt* : to stanch

restar *vt* **1** : to deduct, to subtract ⟨restar un punto : to deduct a point⟩ **2** : to minimize, to play down — *vi* : to remain, to be left

restauración *nf, pl* **-ciones** **1** : restoration **2** : catering, food service

restaurante *nm* : restaurant

restaurar *vt* : to restore

restitución *nf, pl* **-ciones** : restitution, return

restituir {41} *vt* : to return, to restore, to reinstate

resto *nm* **1** : rest, remainder **2 restos** *nmpl* : remains ⟨restos de comida : leftovers⟩ ⟨restos arqueológicos : archeological ruins⟩ **3 restos mortales** : mortal remains

restorán *nm, pl* **-ranes** : restaurant

restregadura *nf* : scrub, scrubbing

restregar {49} *vt* **1** : to rub **2** : to scrub — **restregarse** *vr*

restricción *nf, pl* **-ciones** : restriction, limitation

restrictivo, -va *adj* : restrictive

restringido, -da *adj* LIMITADO : limited, restricted

restringir {35} *vt* LIMITAR : to restrict, to limit

restructuración *nf, pl* **-ciones** : restructuring

restructurar *vt* : to restructure

resucitación *nf, pl* **-ciones** : resuscitation ⟨resucitación cardiopulmonar : CPR, cardiopulmonary resuscitation⟩

resucitar *vt* **1** : to resuscitate, to revive, to resurrect **2** : to revitalize

resuello *nm* **1** : puffing, heavy breathing, wheezing **2** : break, breather

resueltamente *adv* : resolutely

resuelto[1] *pp* → **resolver**

resuelto[2], **-ta** *adj* : determined, resolved, resolute

resulta *nf* **1** : consequence, result **2 a resultas de** *or* **de resultas de** : as a result of

resultado *nm* : result, outcome

resultante *adj & nf* : resultant

resultar *vi* **1** : to work, to work out ⟨mi idea no resultó : my idea didn't work out⟩ **2** : to be, to turn out to be, to end up being ⟨resultó bien simpático : he turned out to be very nice⟩ ⟨resultó cancelado : it was canceled, it ended up being canceled⟩ ⟨resulta más sencillo/barato : it's simpler/cheaper, it ends up being simpler/cheaper⟩ ⟨me resulta muy interesante : I find it very interesting⟩ ⟨resultó (ser) una falsa alarma : it turned out to be a false alarm⟩ ⟨resulta que ya lo había hecho : it turns out she'd already done it⟩ ⟨resultó con heridas graves : he sustained serious injuries⟩ **3** ~ **en** : to lead to, to result in **4** ~ **de** : to be the result of

resumen *nm, pl* **-súmenes** **1** : summary, summation **2 en** ~ : in summary, in short

resumidero *nm* : drain

resumir *v* : to summarize, to sum up

resurgimiento *nm* : resurgence

resurgir {35} *vi* : to reappear, to revive

resurrección *nf, pl* **-ciones** : resurrection **2** *or* **Domingo de Resurrección** : Easter, Easter Sunday

retablo *nm* : tableau

retador, -dora *n* : challenger (in sports)

retaguardia *nf* : rear guard

retahíla *nf* : string, series ⟨una retahíla de insultos : a volley of insults⟩

retaliación *nf, pl* **-ciones** : retaliation

retama *nf* : broom (plant)

retar *vt* DESAFIAR : to challenge, to defy

retardar *vt* **1** RETRASAR : to delay, to retard **2** : to postpone

retazo *nm* **1** : remnant, scrap **2** : fragment, piece ⟨retazos de su obra : bits and pieces from his writings⟩

retén *nm, pl* **retenes** **1** : squad, patrol ⟨de retén : on call, on duty⟩ **2** CONTROL : checkpoint, roadblock **3** *Ven* : reform school

retención *nf, pl* **-ciones** **1** : retention **2** : deduction, withholding

retener {80} *vt* **1** : to retain, to keep **2** : to withhold **3** : to detain

retentivo, -va *adj* : retentive

reticencia *nf* **1** : reluctance, reticence **2** : insinuation

reticente *adj* **1** : reluctant, reticent **2** : insinuating, misleading

retina *nf* : retina

retintín *nm, pl* **-tines** **1** : jingle, jangle **2** **con** ~ : sarcastically

retirada *nf* **1** : retreat ⟨batirse en retirada : to withdraw, to beat a retreat⟩ **2** : withdrawal (of funds) **3** : retirement **4** : refuge, haven

retirado, -da *adj* **1** : remote, distant, far off **2** : secluded, quiet

retirar *vt* **1** : to remove, to take away, to recall **2** : to withdraw, to take out — **retirarse** *vr* **1** REPLEGARSE : to retreat, to withdraw **2** JUBILARSE : to retire

retiro *nm* **1** JUBILACIÓN : retirement **2** : withdrawal, retreat **3** : seclusion

reto *nm* DESAFÍO : challenge, dare

retocar {72} *vt* : to touch up

retomar *vt* : to pick up, to resume

retoñar *vi* : to sprout

retoño *nm* : sprout, shoot

retoque *nm* : touch-up, finishing touch

retorcer {14} *vt* **1** : to twist **2** : to wring — **retorcerse** *vr* **1** : to get twisted, to get tangled up **2** : to squirm, to writhe, to wiggle about

retorcido, -da *adj* **1** : twisted **2** : complicated

retorcijón *nm, pl* **-jones** : cramp, sharp pain

retórica *nf* : rhetoric

retórico, -ca *adj* : rhetorical — **retóricamente** *adv*

retornar *v* : to return

retorno *nm* : return

retozar {21} *vi* : to frolic, to romp

retozo *nm* : frolicking

retozón, -zona *adj, mpl* **-zones** : playful

retracción *nf, pl* **-ciones** : retraction, withdrawal

retractable *adj* : retractable

retractación *nf, pl* **-ciones** : retraction (of a statement, etc.)

retractarse *vr* **1** : to withdraw, to back down **2** ~ **de** : to take back, to retract

retraer {81} *vt* **1** : to bring back **2** : to dissuade — **retraerse** *vr* **1** RETIRARSE : to withdraw, to retire **2** REFUGIARSE : to take refuge

retraído, -da *adj* : withdrawn, retiring, shy

retraimiento *nm* **1** : shyness, timidity **2** : withdrawal

retransmisión *nf, pl* **-siones** *Spain* : broadcast

retransmitir *vt* *Spain* : to broadcast

retrasado[1], **-da** *adj* **1** *dated, now usu offensive* : retarded *dated, now usu offensive*, mentally slow **2** : behind, in arrears **3** : backward (of a country) **4** : slow (of a watch)

retrasado[2], **-da** *n* *or* **retrasado mental** *dated, now offensive* : retarded person *dated, now usu offensive*; moron *dated, now offensive*

retrasar *vt* **1** DEMORAR, RETARDAR : to delay, to hold up **2** : to put off, to postpone **3** : to turn back (a clock) — **retrasarse** *vr* **1** : to be late **2** : to fall behind **3** : to lose time (of a clock)

retraso *nm* **1** ATRASO : delay, lateness **2 retraso mental** *dated, now sometimes offensive* : mental retardation *dated, now sometimes offensive*

retratar *vt* **1** : to portray, to depict **2** : to photograph **3** : to paint a portrait of

retrato *nm* **1** : depiction, portrayal **2** : portrait, photograph

retrete *nm* : restroom, toilet

retribución *nf, pl* **-ciones** **1** : pay, payment **2** : reward

retribuir {41} *vt* **1** : to pay **2** : to reward

retroactivo, -va *adj* : retroactive — **retroactivamente** *adv*

retroalimentación *nf, pl* **-ciones** : feedback

retroceder *vi* **1** : to move back, to turn back **2** : to back off, to back down **3** : to recoil (of a firearm)

retroceso *nm* **1** : backward movement **2** : backing down **3** : setback, relapse **4** : recoil

retrógrado, -da *adj* **1** : reactionary **2** : rctrograde

retropropulsión *nf* : jet propulsion

retroproyector *nm* : overhead projector

retrospectiva *nf* : retrospective, hindsight

retrospectivamente *adv* : in retrospect

retrospectivo, -va *adj* **1** : retrospective **2 mirada retrospectiva** : backward glance

retrovisor *nm* : rearview mirror

retruécano *nm* : pun, play on words

retuitear *vt* : to retweet

retumbar *vi* **1** : to boom, to thunder **2** : to resound, to reverberate

retumbo *nm* : booming, thundering, roll

retuvo, etc. → **retener**

reubicar {72} *vt* : to relocate — **reubicación** *nf*

reuma *or* **reúma** *nmf* → **reumatismo**

reumático, -ca *adj* : rheumatic

reumatismo *nm* : rheumatism

reunión *nf, pl* **-niones** **1** : meeting **2** : gathering, reunion

reunir {68} *vt* **1** : to unite, to join, to bring together **2** : to have, to possess ⟨reunieron los requisitos necesarios : they fulfilled the necessary requirements⟩ **3** : to gather, to collect, to raise (funds) — **reunirse** *vr* : to meet

reutilizable *adj* : reusable

reutilizar {21} *vt* : to recycle, to reuse

revalidar *vt* **1** : to confirm, to ratify **2** : to defend (a title)

revalorizar {21} *vt* : to reevaluate, to reassess

revaluar {3} *vt* : to reevaluate — **revaluación** *n*

revancha *nf* **1** DESQUITE : revenge **2** : rematch

revelación *nf, pl* **-ciones** : revelation

revelado *nm* : developing (of film)

revelador¹, -dora *adj* : revealing

revelador² *nm* : developer

revelar *vt* **1** : to reveal, to disclose **2** : to develop (film)

revendedor, -dora *n* **1** : scalper **2** DETALLISTA : retailer

revender *vt* **1** : to resell **2** : to scalp

reventa *nf* **1** : resale **2** : scalping

reventar {55} *vi* **1** ESTALLAR, EXPLOTAR : to burst, to blow up **2** ~ **de** : to be bursting with — *vt* **1** : to burst **2** *fam* : to annoy, to rile — **reventarse** *vr* : to burst

reventón *nm, pl* **-tones** **1** : burst, bursting **2** : blowout, flat tire **3** *Mex fam* : bash, party

reverberar *vi* : to reverberate — **reverberación** *nf*

reverdecer {53} *vi* **1** : to grow green again **2** : to revive

reverencia *nf* **1** : reverence **2** : bow, curtsy

reverenciar *vt* : to revere, to venerate

reverendo¹, -da *adj* **1** : reverend **2** *fam* : total, absolute ⟨es un reverendo imbécil : he is a complete idiot⟩

reverendo², -da *n* : reverend

reverente *adj* : reverent

reversa *nf Col, Mex* : reverse (gear)

reversible *adj* : reversible

reversión *nf, pl* **-siones** : reversion

reverso *nm* **1** : back, other side **2 el reverso de la medalla** : the complete opposite

revertir {76} *vi* **1** : to revert, to go back **2** ~ **en** : to result in, to end up as — *vt* : to reverse (a decision, etc.)

revés *nm, pl* **reveses** **1** : back, wrong side **2** : setback, reversal **3** : backhand (in sports) **4 al revés** : the other way around, upside down, inside out **5 al revés de** : contrary to

revestimiento *nm* : covering, facing (of a building)

revestir {54} *vt* **1** : to coat, to cover, to surface **2** : to conceal, to disguise **3** : to take on, to assume ⟨la reunión revistió gravedad : the meeting took on a serious note⟩

revisar *vt* **1** : to examine, to inspect, to check **2** : to check over, to overhaul (machinery) **3** : to revise

revisión *nf, pl* **-siones** **1** : revision **2** : inspection, check ⟨revisión de cuentas : (financial) audit⟩ ⟨revisión médica : checkup⟩

revisor, -sora *n* **1** : inspector **2** : conductor (on a train)

revista *nf* **1** : magazine, journal **2** : revue **3 pasar revista** : to review, to inspect

revistar *vt* : to review, to inspect

revistero *nm* : magazine rack

revitalizar {21} *vt* : to revitalize — **revitalización** *nf*

revivir *vi* : to revive, to come alive again — *vt* : to relive

revocación *nf, pl* **-ciones** **1** : revocation, repeal **2** : reversal

revocar {72} *vt* **1** : to revoke, to repeal **2** : to plaster (a wall)

revolcar {82} *vt* : to knock over, to knock down — **revolcarse** *vr* : to roll around, to wallow
revolcón *nm, pl* **-cones** *fam* : tumble, fall
revolotear *vi* : to flutter around, to flit
revoloteo *nm* : fluttering, flitting
revoltijo *or* **revoltillo** *nm* **1** FÁRRAGO : mess, jumble **2** *Mex* : traditional seafood dish
revoltoso, -sa *adj* : unruly, rebellious
revolución *nf, pl* **-ciones** : revolution
revolucionar *vt* : to revolutionize
revolucionario, -ria *adj & n* : revolutionary
revolver {89} *vt* **1** : to move about, to mix, to shake, to stir **2** : to upset (one's stomach) **3** : to mess up, to rummage through ⟨revolver la casa : to turn the house upside down⟩ — **revolverse** *vr* **1** : to toss and turn **2** VOLVERSE : to turn around
revólver *nm* : revolver
revoque *nm* : plaster
revuelo *nm* **1** : fluttering **2** : commotion, stir
revuelta *nf* : uprising, revolt
revuelto¹ *pp* → **revolver**
revuelto², -ta *adj* **1** : choppy, rough ⟨mar revuelto : rough sea⟩ **2** : untidy **3 huevos revueltos** : scrambled eggs
rey *nm* : king
reyerta *nf* : brawl, fight
rezagado, -da *n* : straggler, latecomer
rezagar {52} *vt* **1** : to leave behind **2** : to postpone — **rezagarse** *vr* : to fall behind, to lag
rezar {21} *vi* **1** : to pray **2** : to say ⟨como reza el refrán : as the saying goes⟩ **3 ~ con** : to concern, to have to do with — *vt* : to say, to recite ⟨rezar un Ave María : to say a Hail Mary⟩
rezo *nm* : prayer, praying
rezongar {52} *vi* : to gripe, to grumble
rezumar *v* : to ooze, to leak
ría, etc. → **reír**
riachuelo *nm* ARROYO : brook, stream
riada *nf* : flood
ribera *nf* : bank, shore
ribete *nm* **1** : border, trim **2** : frill, adornment **3 ribetes** *nmpl* : hint, touch ⟨tiene sus ribetes de genio : there's a touch of genius in him⟩
ribetear *vt* : to border, to edge, to trim
ricachón¹, -chona *adj, mpl* **-chones** *fam* : rich, wealthy
ricachón², -chona *n, mpl* **-chones** *fam* : rich person
ricamente *adv* : richly, splendidly
rice, etc. → **rizar**
rickshaw ['rikʃo] *nm* : rickshaw
rico¹, -ca *adj* **1** : rich, wealthy **2** : fertile **3** : luxurious, valuable **4** : delicious **5** : adorable, lovely **6** : great, wonderful
rico², -ca *n* : rich person
ridiculez *nf, pl* **-leces** : absurdity
ridiculizar {21} *vt* : to ridicule
ridículo¹, -la *adj* ABSURDO, DISPARATADO : ridiculous, ludicrous — **ridículamente** *adv*
ridículo², -la *n* **1 hacer el ridículo** : to make a fool of oneself **2 poner en ridículo** : to ridicule

ríe, etc. → **reír**
riega, riegue etc. → **regar**
riego *nm* : irrigation
riel *nm* : rail, track
rienda *nf* **1** : rein **2 dar rienda suelta a** : to give free rein to **3 llevar las riendas** : to be in charge **4 tomar las riendas** : to take control
riesgo *nm* : risk
riesgoso, -sa *adj* : risky
rifa *nf* : raffle
rifar *vt* : to raffle — *vi* : to quarrel, to fight
rifle *nm* : rifle
rige, rija etc. → **regir**
rigidez *nf, pl* **-deces 1** : rigidity, stiffness ⟨rigidez cadavérica : rigor mortis⟩ **2** : inflexibility
rígido, -da *adj* **1** : rigid, stiff **2** : strict — **rígidamente** *adv*
rigor *nm* **1** : rigor, harshness **2** : precision, meticulousness **3 de ~** : usual ⟨la respuesta de rigor : the standard reply⟩ **4 de ~** : essential, obligatory **5 en ~** : strictly speaking, in reality
riguroso, -sa *adj* : rigorous — **rigurosamente** *adv*
rima *nf* **1** : rhyme **2 rimas** *nfpl* : verse, poetry
rimar *vi* : to rhyme
rimbombante *adj* **1** : grandiose, showy **2** : bombastic, pompous
rímel *or* **rimel** *or* **rimmel** *nm* : mascara
rin *nm Col, Mex* : wheel, rim (of a tire)
rincón *nm, pl* **rincones** : corner, nook
rinde, etc. → **rendir**
ring ['rin] *nm, pl* **rings** : (boxing) ring
ringtone ['rinton] *nm* : ringtone
rinoceronte *nm* : rhinoceros
riña *nf* **1** : fight, brawl **2** : dispute, quarrel
riñe, etc. → **reñir**
riñón *nm, pl* **riñones** : kidney
río¹ → **reír**
río² *nm* **1** : river **2** : torrent, stream ⟨un río de lágrimas : a flood of tears⟩
ripio *nm* **1** : debris, rubble **2** : gravel
riqueza *nf* **1** : wealth, riches *pl* **2** : richness **3 riquezas naturales** : natural resources
risa *nf* **1** : laughter, laugh **2 dar risa** : to make laugh ⟨me dio mucha risa : I found it very funny⟩ **3** *fam* **morirse de la risa** : to die laughing, to crack up
risco *nm* : crag, cliff
risible *adj* IRRISORIO : ludicrous, laughable
risita *nf* : giggle, titter, snicker
risotada *nf* : guffaw
ristra *nf* : string, series *pl*
risueño, -ña *adj* **1** : cheerful, pleasant **2** : promising
rítmico, -ca *adj* : rhythmical, rhythmic — **rítmicamente** *adv*
ritmo *nm* **1** : rhythm **2** : pace, tempo ⟨trabajó a ritmo lento : she worked at a slow pace⟩
rito *nm* : rite, ritual
ritual *adj & nm* : ritual — **ritualmente** *adv*
rival *adj & nmf* COMPETIDOR : rival
rivalidad *nf* : rivalry, competition

rivalizar {21} *vi* ~ **con** : to rival, to compete with

rizado, -da *adj* **1** : curly **2** : ridged **3** : rippled, undulating

rizar {21} *vt* **1** : to curl **2** : to ripple, to ruffle (a surface) **3** : to crumple, to fold — **rizarse** *vr* **1** : to frizz **2** : to ripple

rizo *nm* **1** : curl **2** : loop (in aviation)

robalo *or* **róbalo** *nm* : sea bass

robar *vt* **1** : to steal **2** : to rob, to burglarize **3** SECUESTRAR : to abduct, to kidnap **4** : to captivate — *vi* ~ **en** : to break into

roble *nm* : oak

robo *nm* : robbery, theft ⟨robo de identidad : identity theft⟩

robot *nm, pl* **robots** : robot — **robótico, -ca** *adj*

robótica *nf* : robotics

robustecer {53} *vt* : to grow stronger, to strengthen

robustez *nf* : sturdiness, robustness

robusto, -ta *adj* : robust, sturdy

roca *nf* : rock, boulder

roce[1], etc. → **rozar**

roce[2] *nm* **1** : rubbing, chafing **2** : brush, graze, touch **3** : close contact, familiarity **4** : friction, disagreement

rociador *nm* : sprinkler

rociar {85} *vt* : to spray, to sprinkle

rocío *nm* **1** : dew **2** : shower, light rain

rock *or* **rock and roll** *nm* : rock, rock and roll

rocola *nf* : jukebox

rocoso, -sa *adj* : rocky

rodada *nf* : track (of a tire), rut

rodado, -da *adj* **1** : wheeled **2** : dappled (of a horse)

rodadura *nf* : rolling, taxiing

rodaja *nf* : round, slice

rodaje *nm* **1** : filming, shooting **2** : breaking in (of a vehicle)

rodamiento *nm* **1** : bearing ⟨rodamiento de bolas : ball bearings⟩ **2** : rolling

rodante *adj* : rolling

rodar {19} *vi* **1** : to roll, to roll down, to roll along ⟨rodé por la escalera : I tumbled down the stairs⟩ ⟨todo rodaba bien : everything was going along well⟩ **2** GIRAR : to turn, to go around **3** : to move about, to travel ⟨andábamos rodando por todas partes : we drifted along from place to place⟩ — *vt* **1** : to film, to shoot **2** : to break in (a new vehicle)

rodear *vt* **1** : to surround ⟨rodeado de montañas : surrounded by mountains⟩ **2** : to round up (cattle) — *vi* ~ : to go around **2** : to beat around the bush — **rodearse** *vr* ~ **de** : to surround oneself with

rodeo *nm* **1** : rodeo, roundup **2** DESVÍO : detour **3** : evasion ⟨andar con rodeos : to beat around the bush⟩ ⟨sin rodeos : without reservations⟩

rodilla *nf* : knee

rodillera *nf* : knee pad

rodillo *nm* **1** : roller **2** : rolling pin

rododendro *nm* : rhododendron

roedor[1], **-dora** *adj* : gnawing

roedor[2] *nm* : rodent

roer {69} *vt* **1** : to gnaw **2** : to eat away at, to torment

rogar {16} *vt* : to beg, to request — *vi* **1** : to beg, to plead **2** : to pray

roiga, etc. → **roer**

rojez *nf* : redness

rojizo, -za *adj* : reddish

rojo[1], **-ja** *adj* **1** : red **2 ponerse rojo** : to blush

rojo[2] *nm* : red

rol *nm* **1** : role **2** : list, roll

rollizo, -za *adj* : chubby, plump

rollo *nm* **1** : roll, coil ⟨un rollo de cinta : a roll of tape⟩ ⟨en rollo : rolled up⟩ **2** *fam* : roll of fat **3** *fam* : boring speech, lecture

ROM *nf, pl* **ROM** *or* **ROMs** : ROM

romance *nm* **1** : Romance language **2** : ballad **3** : romance **4 en buen romance** : simply stated, simply put

romano, -na *adj & n* : Roman

romanticismo *nm* : romanticism

romántico, -ca *adj* : romantic — **romántico, -ca** *n* — **románticamente** *adv*

rombo *nm* : rhombus

romería *nf* **1** : pilgrimage, procession **2** : crowd, gathering

romero[1], **-ra** *n* PEREGRINO : pilgrim

romero[2] *nm* : rosemary

romo, -ma *adj* : blunt, dull

rompecabezas *nms & pl* : puzzle, riddle

rompecorazones *nmfs & pl* : heartbreaker

rompehielos *nms & pl* : icebreaker (ship)

rompehuelgas *nmfs & pl* ESQUIROL : strikebreaker, scab

rompenueces *nms & pl* : nutcracker

rompeolas *ns & pl* : breakwater, jetty

romper {70} *vt* **1** : to break (a glass, a bone, etc.) **2** : to rip, to tear (cloth, paper) **3** : to break off (relations), to break (a contract) **4** : to break through/down (a door, etc.) **5** GASTAR : to wear out **6** : to break ⟨romper el hielo/silencio : to break the ice/silence⟩ — *vi* **1** : to break ⟨al romper del día : at the break of day⟩ **2** ~ **a** : to begin to, to burst out with ⟨romper a llorar : to burst into tears⟩ **3** ~ **con** : to break with (tradition, etc.), to break away from **4** ~ **con alguien** : to break up with someone — **romperse** *vr*

rompope *nm CA, Mex* : drink similar to eggnog

ron *nm* : rum

roncar {72} *vi* **1** : to snore **2** : to roar

roncha *nf* : rash

ronco, -ca *adj* **1** : hoarse **2** : husky (of the voice) — **roncamente** *adv*

ronda *nf* **1** : beat, patrol **2** : round (of drinks, of negotiations, of a game)

rondar *vt* **1** : to patrol **2** : to hang around ⟨siempre está rondando la calle : he's always hanging around the street⟩ **3** : to be approximately ⟨debe rondar los cincuenta : he must be about 50⟩ — *vi* **1** : to be on patrol **2** : to prowl around, to roam about

ronque, etc. → **roncar**

ronquera *nf* : hoarseness
ronquido *nm* **1** : snore **2** : roar
ronronear *vi* : to purr
ronroneo *nm* : purr, purring
ronzal *nm* : halter (for an animal)
ronzar {21} *v* : to munch, to crunch
roña *nf* **1** : mange **2** : dirt, filth **3** *fam* : stinginess
roñoso, -sa *adj* **1** : mangy **2** : dirty **3** *fam* : stingy
ropa *nf* **1** : clothes *pl*, clothing ⟨ropa sucia : dirty clothes, (dirty) laundry⟩ ⟨ropa de abrigo : warm clothes⟩ ⟨cambiarse de ropa : to change one's clothes, to get changed⟩ **2 ropa interior** : underwear
ropaje *nm* : apparel, garments *pl*, regalia
ropero *nm* ARMARIO, CLÓSET : wardrobe, closet
rosa¹ *adj* : rose-colored, pink
rosa² *nm* : rose, pink (color)
rosa³ *nf* : rose (flower)
rosáceo, -cea *adj* : pinkish
rosado¹, -da *adj* **1** : pink **2 vino rosado** : rosé
rosado² *nm* : pink (color)
rosal *nm* : rosebush
rosario *nm* **1** : rosary **2** : series ⟨un rosario de islas : a string of islands⟩
rosbif *nm* : roast beef
rosca *nf* **1** : thread (of a screw) ⟨una tapa a rosca : a screw top⟩ **2** : ring, coil
roscón *nm, pl* **roscones** : ring-shaped cake
roseta *nf* : rosette
rosetón *nm, pl* **-tones** : rose window
rosquilla *nf* : ring-shaped pastry, doughnut
rostro *nm* : face, countenance
rotación *nf, pl* **-ciones** : rotation
rotar *vt* : to rotate, to turn — *vi* : to turn, to spin
rotativo¹, -va *adj* : rotary
rotativo² *nm* : newspaper
rotatorio, -ria *adj* → rotativo¹
roto¹ *pp* → romper
roto², -ta *adj* **1** : broken **2** : ripped, torn
rotonda *nf* **1** : traffic circle, rotary **2** : rotunda
rotor *nm* : rotor
rotoso, -sa *adj Arg, Uru, Peru* : ragged, scruffy
rótula *nf* : kneecap
rotulador *nm Spain* **1** : felt-tip pen **2** : highlighter
rotular *vt* **1** : to head, to entitle **2** : to label
rótulo *nm* **1** : heading, title **2** : label, sign
rotundo, -da *adj* **1** REDONDO : round **2** : categorical, absolute ⟨un éxito rotundo : a resounding success⟩ — **rotundamente** *adv*
rotura *nf* : break, tear, fracture
rough [ˈruf, ˈraf] *nm* **el rough** : the rough (in golf)
router *nm, pl* **routers** : router (in computing)
roya¹ *nf* : plant rust
roya², etc. → roer
rozado, -da *adj* GASTADO : worn

rozadura *nf* **1** : scratch, abrasion **2** : rubbed spot, sore
rozamiento *nf* : rubbing, friction
rozar {21} *vt* **1** : to chafe, to rub against **2** : to border on, to touch on **3** : to graze, to touch lightly — **rozarse** *vr* ∼ **con** *fam* : to rub shoulders with
ruandés, -desa *adj & n* : Rwandan
rubéola *nf* : German measles, rubella
rubí *nm, pl* **rubíes** : ruby
rubicundo, -da *adj* : ruddy ⟨una cara rubicunda : a ruddy face⟩
rubio, -bia *adj & n* : blond
rublo *nm* : ruble
rubor *nm* **1** : flush, blush **2** : blush, rouge
ruborizarse {21} *vr* : to blush
rúbrica *nf* : title, heading
rubricar {72} *vt* **1** : sign with a flourish ⟨firmado y rubricado : signed and sealed⟩ **2** : to endorse, to sanction
rubro *nm* **1** : heading, title **2** : line, area (in business)
rucio, rucia *adj* : gray
rudeza *nf* ASPEREZA : roughness, coarseness
rudimentario, -ria *adj* : rudimentary — **rudimentariamente** *adv*
rudimento *nm* : rudiment, basics *pl*
rudo, -da *adj* **1** : rough, harsh **2** : coarse, unpolished — **rudamente** *adv*
rueda¹, etc. → rodar
rueda² *nf* **1** : wheel **2** RODAJA : round slice **3** : circle, ring **4 rueda de andar** : treadmill **5 rueda de prensa** : press conference **6 ir sobre ruedas** : to go smoothly
ruedita *nf* : caster (on furniture)
ruedo *nm* **1** : bullring, arena **2** : rotation, turn **3** : hem
ruega, ruegue etc. → rogar
ruego *nm* : request, appeal, plea
rufián *nf, pl* **rufianes** : villain, scoundrel, ruffian
rugby *nm* : rugby
rugido *nm* : roar
rugir {35} *vi* : to roar
rugoso, -sa *adj* **1** : rough, bumpy **2** : wrinkled
ruibarbo *nm* : rhubarb
ruido *nm* : noise, sound
ruidoso, -sa *adj* : loud, noisy — **ruidosamente** *adv*
ruin *adj* **1** : base, despicable **2** : mean, stingy
ruina *nf* **1** : ruin, destruction ⟨llevar a alguien a la ruina : to ruin someone, to bring someone to ruin⟩ ⟨estar en la ruina : to be ruined⟩ **2** : ruin, downfall ⟨la avaricia será su ruina : greed will be his ruin⟩ **3** : collapse (of a building, etc.) ⟨amenazar ruina : to threaten to collapse⟩ **4 ruinas** *nfpl* : ruins, remains ⟨ruinas romanas : Roman ruins⟩ ⟨estar/quedar en ruinas : to be/lie in ruins⟩
ruinoso, -sa *adj* **1** : run-down, dilapidated **2** : ruinous, disastrous
ruiseñor *nm* : nightingale
ruja, etc. → rugir
rulero *nm Arg, Peru, Uru* : curler, roller

ruleta *nf* : roulette
ruletero, -ra *n Mex fam* : taxi driver
rulo *nm* : curler, roller
ruma *nf Chile, Peru, Ven* : pile, heap
rumano, -na *n* : Romanian, Rumanian
rumba *nf* : rumba
rumbo *nm* **1** : direction, course ⟨con rumbo a : bound for, heading for⟩ ⟨perder el rumbo : to go off course, to lose one's bearings⟩ ⟨sin rumbo : aimless, aimlessly⟩ **2** : ostentation, pomp **3** : lavishness, generosity
rumiante *adj & nm* : ruminant
rumiar *vt* : to ponder, to mull over — *vi* **1** : to chew the cud **2** : to ruminate, to ponder
rummy *nm* : rummy (card game)
rumor *nm* **1** : rumor **2** : murmur
rumorearse *or* **rumorarse** *vr* : to be rumored ⟨se rumorea que se va : rumor

has it that she's leaving⟩ — **rumoreado, -da** *adj*
rumoroso, -sa *adj* : murmuring, babbling ⟨un arroyo rumoroso : a babbling brook⟩
rupestre *adj* : cave ⟨pinturas rupestres : cave paintings⟩
rupia *nf* : rupee
ruptura *nf* **1** : break **2** : breaking, breach (of a contract) **3** : breaking off, breakup
rural *adj* : rural
ruso¹, -sa *adj & n* : Russian
ruso² *nm* : Russian (language)
rústico¹, -ca *adj* : rural, rustic
rústico², -ca *n* : rustic, country dweller
ruta *nf* : route
rutina *nf* : routine, habit
rutinario, -ria *adj* : routine, ordinary ⟨visita rutinaria : routine visit⟩ — **rutinariamente** *adv*

S

s *nf* : twenty-second letter of the Spanish alphabet
sábado *nm* **1** : Saturday ⟨el sábado : (on) Saturday⟩ ⟨los sábados : (on) Saturdays⟩ ⟨cada (dos) sábados : every (other) Saturday⟩ ⟨el sábado pasado : last Saturday⟩ ⟨el próximo sábado : next Saturday⟩ **2** : Sabbath
sábalo *nm* : shad
sabana *nf* : savanna
sábana *nf* : sheet, bedsheet
sabandija *nf* BICHO : bug, small reptile, pesky creature
sabático, -ca *adj* : sabbatical
sabedor, -dora *adj* : aware, informed
sabelotodo *nmf fam* : know-it-all
saber¹ {71} *vt* **1** : to know ⟨no lo sé : I don't know⟩ ⟨no sé qué decirte : I don't know what to tell you⟩ ⟨no sabes lo que te espera : you don't know what you're in for⟩ ⟨saber la respuesta : to know the answer⟩ ⟨sabe mucho de política : he knows a lot about politics⟩ ⟨¿sabes dónde está? : do you know where it is?⟩ ⟨creo que no, pero ¿qué sé yo? : I don't think so, but what do I know?⟩ ⟨quién sabe qué va a pasar : who knows what will happen⟩ **2** : to know how to, to be able to ⟨sabe tocar el violín : she can play the violin⟩ **3** : to learn, to find out ⟨lo supe ayer : I found out yesterday⟩ ⟨no sé nada de ellos : I haven't heard from them⟩ **4 a ~** : to wit, namely **5 que yo sepa** : as far as I know **6 qué sé yo** ⟨diamantes, perlas, y qué sé yo : diamonds, pearls, and whatnot⟩ ⟨y qué sé yo dónde : and who knows where (else)⟩ — *vi* **1** : to know, to suppose ⟨¿quién sabe? : who knows?⟩ ⟨nunca se sabe : you never know, one never knows⟩ **2** : to be informed ⟨supimos del desastre : we heard about the disaster⟩ **3** : to taste ⟨esto no sabe bien : this doesn't

taste right⟩ **4 ~ a** : to taste like ⟨sabe a naranja : it tastes like orange⟩ — **saberse** *vr* : to know ⟨ese chiste no me lo sé : I don't know that joke⟩
saber² *nm* : knowledge, learning
sabiamente *adv* : wisely
sabido, -da *adj* : well-known
sabiduría *nf* **1** : wisdom **2** : learning, knowledge
sabiendas *adv* **1 a ~** : knowingly **2 a sabiendas de que** : knowing full well that
sabihondo, -da *n fam* : know-it-all
sabio¹, -bia *adj* **1** PRUDENTE : wise, sensible **2** DOCTO : learned
sabio², -bia *n* **1** : wise person **2** : learned person
sable *nm* : saber, cutlass
sablear *vt* **1** : to bum, to scrounge, to sponge **2** : to scrounge off, to sponge off
sabor *nm* **1** : flavor, taste **2 sin ~** : flavorless
saborear *vt* **1** : to taste, to savor **2** : to enjoy, to relish
saborizante *nm* : flavor, flavoring
sabotaje *nm* : sabotage
saboteador, -dora *n* : saboteur
sabotear *vt* : to sabotage
sabrá, etc. → **saber**
sabroso, -sa *adj* **1** RICO : delicious, tasty **2** AGRADABLE : pleasant, nice, lovely
sabueso *nm* **1** : bloodhound **2** *fam* : detective, sleuth
sacacorchos *nms & pl* : corkscrew
sacapuntas *nms & pl* : pencil sharpener
sacar {72} *vt* **1** : to pull out, to take out ⟨saca el pollo del congelador : take the chicken out of the freezer⟩ ⟨me sacaron de la cama : they dragged me out of bed⟩ ⟨sacó un as : he drew an ace⟩ ⟨sacar la basura : to take out the garbage⟩ ⟨¡sácalo de la casa! : get it out of the

house!⟩ **2** : to get, to obtain ⟨saqué un 100 en el examen : I got 100 on the exam⟩ ⟨sacó cuatro puntos de ventaja : she got a four-point lead⟩ **3** : to get out, to extract ⟨le saqué la información : I got the information from him⟩ ⟨sacar sangre : to draw blood⟩ ⟨me sacó de un apuro : she got me out of a jam⟩ ⟨sacar provecho de : to benefit from⟩ **4** : to take (someone) out ⟨lo saqué a comer : I took him out to eat⟩ ⟨la sacó a bailar : he asked her to dance⟩ **5** : to stick out ⟨sacar la lengua : to stick out one's tongue⟩ **6** : to bring out, to introduce ⟨sacar un libro : to publish a book⟩ ⟨sacaron una moda nueva : they introduced a new style⟩ ⟨sacar algo a la venta : to release something for sale⟩ ⟨sacar a relucir un tema : to bring up a topic⟩ **7** : to take (a photo, a shot) **8** : to make (copies) **9** RETIRAR : to withdraw (money) **10** : to draw, to reach (a conclusion) **11** CALCULAR : to work out, to tally up **12 sacar adelante** AVANZAR : to get started, to move forward **13 sacar adelante** MANTENER : to support, to keep afloat **14 sacar de encima** : to get rid of — *vi* **1** : to kick off (in soccer or football) **2** : to serve (in sports)

sacarina *nf* : saccharin

sacarosa *nf* : sucrose

sacerdocio *nm* : priesthood

sacerdotal *adj* : priestly

sacerdote, -tisa *n* : priest *m*, priestess *f*

saciar *vt* **1** HARTAR : to sate, to satiate **2** SATISFACER : to satisfy

saciedad *nf* **1** : fullness ⟨comer hasta la saciedad : to eat one's fill⟩ **2 hacer algo hasta la saciedad** : to do something ad nauseam

saco *nm* **1** : bag, sack **2** : sac **3** : jacket, sport coat

sacramento *nm* : sacrament — **sacramental** *adj*

sacrificar {72} *vt* **1** : to sacrifice **2** : to euthanize, to put down — **sacrificarse** *vr* : to sacrifice oneself, to make sacrifices

sacrificio *nm* : sacrifice

sacrilegio *nm* : sacrilege

sacrílego, -ga *adj* : sacrilegious

sacristán *nm, pl* **-tanes** : sexton

sacristía *nf* : vestry

sacro, -cra *adj* SAGRADO : sacred ⟨arte sacro : sacred art⟩

sacrosanto, -ta *adj* : sacrosanct

sacudida *nf* **1** : shaking **2** : jerk, jolt, shock **3** : shake-up, upheaval

sacudir *vt* **1** : to shake, to beat **2** : to jerk, to jolt **3** : to dust off **4** CONMOVER : to shake up, to shock — **sacudirse** *vr* : to shake off

sacudón *nm, pl* **-dones** : intense jolt or shake-up

sádico[1], -ca *adj* : sadistic

sádico[2], -ca *n* : sadist

sadismo *nm* : sadism

safari *nm* : safari

saga *nf* : saga

sagacidad *nf* : shrewdness

sagaz *adj, pl* **sagaces** PERSPICAZ : shrewd, discerning, sagacious

sagazmente *adv* : shrewdly

Sagitario[1] *nm* : Sagittarius (sign or constellation)

Sagitario[2] *nmf* : Sagittarius (person)

sagrado, -da *adj* : sacred, holy

sainete *nm* : comedy sketch, one-act farce ⟨este proceso es un sainete : these proceedings are a farce⟩

sajar *vt* : to lance, to cut open

sal[1] → **salir**

sal[2] *nf* **1** : salt **2** *CA, Mex* : misfortune, bad luck

sala *nf* **1** : living room **2** : room, hall ⟨sala de conferencias : lecture hall⟩ ⟨sala de urgencias : emergency room⟩ ⟨sala de baile : ballroom⟩

salado, -da *adj* **1** : salty **2 agua salada** : salt water

salamandra *nf* : salamander

salami *nm* : salami

salar *vt* **1** : to salt **2** : to spoil, to ruin **3** *CoRi, Mex* : to jinx, to bring bad luck

salarial *adj* : salary, salary-related

salario *nm* **1** : salary **2 salario mínimo** : minimum wage

salaz *adj, pl* **salaces** : salacious, lecherous

salchicha *nf* **1** : sausage **2** : frankfurter, wiener

salchichón *nf, pl* **-chones** : a type of deli meat

salchichonería *nf Mex* **1** : delicatessen **2** : cold cuts *pl*

saldar *vt* : to settle, to pay off ⟨saldar una cuenta : to settle an account⟩

saldo *nm* **1** : settlement, payment **2** : balance ⟨saldo de cuenta : account balance⟩ **3** : remainder, leftover merchandise

saldrá, etc. → **salir**

salero *nm* **1** : salt shaker **2** : wit, charm

salga, etc. → **salir**

salida *nf* **1** : exit ⟨salida de emergencia/incendios : emergency/fire exit⟩ ⟨una calle sin salida : a dead-end street⟩ **2** : leaving, departure **3** SOLUCIÓN : way out, solution **4** : start (of a race) **5** OCURRENCIA : wisecrack, joke **6 salida del sol** : sunrise

salido *adj* : protuding

saliente[1] *adj* **1** : departing, outgoing **2** : projecting **3** DESTACADO : salient, prominent

saliente[2] *nm* **1** : projection, protrusion **2 ventana en saliente** : bay window

salinidad *nf* : salinity, saltiness

salino, -na *adj* : saline ⟨solución salina : saline solution⟩

salir {73} *vi* **1** : to go out, to come out, to get out ⟨salió del edificio : she came/went out of the building⟩ ⟨salí a la calle : I went outside⟩ ⟨salimos todas las noches : we go out every night⟩ ⟨salimos a desayunar : we went out for breakfast⟩ ⟨me ayudó a salir del apuro : he helped me out of a jam⟩ ⟨salieron ilesos : they escaped unharmed⟩ ⟨por la tarde salió el sol : in the afternoon the sun came out⟩

2 PARTIR : to leave, to depart ⟨salí de casa a las seis : I left home at six (o'clock)⟩ ⟨salió del hospital : she's out of the hospital⟩ ⟨salieron para Bogotá : they left for Bogotá⟩ ⟨salió a buscarla : he went to go pick her up⟩ ⟨¿a qué hora sale el vuelo? : what time does the flight leave?⟩ ⟨salió corriendo : she took off running⟩ **3** APARECER : to appear ⟨salió en todos los diarios : it came out in all the papers⟩ ⟨le están saliendo los dientes : she's teething⟩ ⟨me salen canas : I'm going gray, I'm getting gray hairs⟩ ⟨le salen granos : she breaks out, she gets pimples⟩ ⟨le salió un sarpullido : he broke out in a rash⟩ **4** : to come out, to become available ⟨su libro acaba de salir : her book just came out⟩ ⟨salir a la venta : to be released (for sale)⟩ **5** : to rise (of the sun) **6** : to come up (of a topic), to come out (of news) ⟨salir a relucir : to come out, to come to light⟩ **7** : to project, to stick out **8** : to cost, to come to ⟨sale muy caro : it's very expensive⟩ **9** RESULTAR : to turn out, to prove ⟨salir bien/mal : to turn out well/badly⟩ **10** : to come up, to occur ⟨salga lo que salga : whatever happens⟩ ⟨salió una oportunidad : an opportunity came up⟩ **11 ~ a** : to take after, to look like, to resemble **12 salir adelante** : to overcome difficulties, to advance ⟨salir adelante en la vida : to get ahead in life⟩ ⟨es difícil, pero saldremos adelante : it's difficult, but we'll get through it⟩ ⟨sin ello el país/proyecto no saldrá adelante : without it the country/project won't move forward⟩ **13 ~ con** : to go out with, to date — **salirse** vr **1** : to escape, to get out, to leak out **2** : to come loose, to come off **3 salirse con la suya** : to get one's own way

saliva nf : saliva

salival adj : salivary ⟨glándula salival : salivary gland⟩

salivar vi : to salivate

salmo nm : psalm

salmodia nf : chant

salmodiar v : to chant

salmón[1] adj : salmon-colored

salmón[2] nm, pl **salmones** : salmon

salmuera nf : brine

salobre adj : brackish, briny

salón nm, pl **salones** **1** : hall, large room ⟨salón de clase : classroom⟩ ⟨salón de baile : ballroom⟩ **2** : salon ⟨salón de belleza : beauty salon⟩ **3** : parlor, sitting room

salpicadera nf Mex : fender

salpicadero nm Spain : dashboard

salpicadura nf : spatter, splash

salpicar {72} vt **1** : to spatter, to splash **2** : to sprinkle, to scatter about

salpimentar {55} vt **1** : to season (with salt and pepper) **2** : to spice up

salpullido → sarpullido

salsa nf **1** : sauce ⟨salsa picante : hot sauce⟩ ⟨salsa inglesa : Worcestershire sauce⟩ ⟨salsa tártara : tartar sauce⟩ **2** : gravy **3** : salsa (music) **4 salsa mexicana** : salsa (sauce)

salsero, -ra n : salsa musician

saltador, -dora n : jumper

saltamontes nms & pl : grasshopper

saltar vi **1** BRINCAR : to jump, to leap ⟨saltó de la silla : he jumped out of his chair⟩ ⟨el gato saltó sobre el ratón : the cat pounced on the mouse⟩ ⟨saltó a la fama : she rose to fame⟩ **2** REBOTAR : to bounce **3** : to come off, to pop out ⟨el corcho saltó de la botella : the cork popped out of the bottle⟩ **4** : to shatter, to break **5** : to explode, to blow up **6** : to jump, to increase ⟨saltó de 500.000 a un millón : it jumped from 500,000 to a million⟩ **7 saltar a la vista** : to be glaringly obvious **8 saltar de alegría** : to jump for joy — vt **1** : to jump, to jump over ⟨saltó la reja : he jumped over the railing⟩ **2** : to skip, to miss — **saltarse** vr **1** OMITIR : to skip, to omit ⟨me salté ese capítulo : I skipped that chapter⟩ **2** : to come off, to fall off

saltarín, -rina adj, mpl **-rines** : leaping, hopping ⟨frijol saltarín : jumping bean⟩

salteado, -da adj **1** : sautéed **2** : jumbled up ⟨los episodios se transmitieron salteados : the episodes were broadcast in random order⟩

salteador nm : highwayman

saltear vt **1** SOFREÍR : to sauté **2** : to skip around, to skip over

saltimbanqui nmf : acrobat

salto nm **1** BRINCO : jump, leap, skip **2** : jump, dive (in sports) ⟨salto de longitud, salto (en) largo : long jump⟩ **3** : gap, omission **4 dar saltos** : to jump up and down **5** or **salto de agua** CATARATA : waterfall

saltón, -tona adj, mpl **saltones** : bulging, protruding

salubre adj : healthful, salubrious

salubridad nf : healthiness, health

salud nf **1** : health ⟨buena salud : good health⟩ **2 ¡salud!** : bless you! (when someone sneezes) **3 ¡salud!** : cheers!, to your health!

saludable adj **1** SALUBRE : healthful **2** SANO : healthy, well

saludar vt **1** : to greet, to say hello to **2** : to salute — **saludarse** vr

saludo nm **1** : greeting, regards pl **2** : salute

salutación nf, pl **-ciones** : salutation

salva nf **1** : salvo, volley **2 salva de aplausos** : round of applause

salvación nf, pl **-ciones** **1** : salvation **2** RESCATE : rescue

salvado nm : bran

salvador, -dora n **1** : savior, rescuer **2 el Salvador** : the Savior

salvadoreño, -ña adj & n : Salvadoran, El Salvadoran

salvaguardar vt : to safeguard

salvaguardia or **salvaguarda** nf : safeguard, defense

salvajada nf ATROCIDAD : atrocity, act of savagery

salvaje[1] adj **1** : wild ⟨animales salvajes : wild animals⟩ **2** : savage, cruel **3** : primitive, uncivilized

salvaje[2] *nmf* : savage

salvajismo *nm* : savagery

salvamanteles *nms & pl* : trivet

salvamento *nm* **1** : rescuing, lifesaving **2** : salvation **3** : refuge

salvapantallas *nms & pl* : screen saver

salvar *vt* **1** : to save, to rescue **2** : to cover (a distance) **3** : to get around (an obstacle), to overcome (a difficulty) **4** : to cross, to jump across **5 salvando** : except for, excluding — **salvarse** *vr* **1** : to survive, to escape **2** : to save one's soul

salvavidas[1] *nms & pl* **1** : life preserver **2 bote salvavidas** : lifeboat

salvavidas[2] *nmf* : lifeguard

salvedad *nf* **1** EXCEPCIÓN : exception **2** : proviso, stipulation

salvia *nf* : sage (plant)

salvo[1], **-va** *adj* **1** : unharmed, sound ⟨sano y salvo : safe and sound⟩ **2 a ∼** : safe from danger

salvo[2] *prep* **1** EXCEPTO : except (for), save ⟨todos asistirán salvo Jaime : all will attend except for Jaime⟩ **2 salvo que** : unless ⟨salvo que llueva : unless it rains⟩

salvoconducto *nm* : safe-conduct

samba *nf* : samba

San *adj* → **santo**[1]

sanar *vt* : to heal, to cure — *vi* : to get well, to recover

sanatorio *nm* **1** : sanatorium **2** : clinic, private hospital

sanción *nf, pl* **sanciones** : sanction

sancionar *vt* **1** : to penalize, to impose a sanction on **2** : to sanction, to approve

sancochar *vt* : to parboil

sandalia *nf* : sandal

sándalo *nm* : sandalwood

sandez *nf, pl* **sandeces** ESTUPIDEZ : nonsense, silly thing to say

sandía *nf* : watermelon

sandwich [ˈsandwitʃ, ˈsaŋgwitʃ] *nm, pl* **sandwiches** [-dwitʃɛs, -gwi-] EMPAREDADO : sandwich

saneamiento *nm* **1** : cleaning up, sanitation **2** : reorganizing, streamlining

sanear *vt* **1** : to clean up, to sanitize **2** : to reorganize, to streamline

sangrante *adj* **1** : bleeding **2** : flagrant, blatant

sangrar *vi* : to bleed — *vt* : to indent (a paragraph, etc.)

sangre *nf* **1** : blood **2 a sangre fría** : in cold blood **3 a sangre y fuego** : by violent force **4 pura sangre** : thoroughbred

sangría *nf* **1** : bleeding (in medicine) **2** : sangria (wine punch) **3** : drain, draining ⟨una sangría fiscal : a financial drain⟩ **4** : indentation, indenting

sangriento, -ta *adj* **1** : bloody **2** : cruel

sanguijuela *nf* **1** : leech, bloodsucker **2** : sponger, leech

sanguinario, -ria *adj* : bloodthirsty

sanguíneo, -nea *adj* **1** : blood ⟨vaso sanguíneo : blood vessel⟩ **2** : sanguine, ruddy

sanidad *nf* **1** : health **2** : public health, sanitation

sanitario[1], **-ria** *adj* **1** : sanitary **2** : health ⟨centro sanitario : health center⟩

sanitario[2], **-ria** *n* : sanitation worker

sanitario[3] *nm Col, Mex, Ven* : toilet ⟨los sanitarios : the toilets, the restroom⟩

sano, -na *adj* **1** SALUDABLE : healthy **2** : wholesome **3** : whole, intact

santiaguino, -na *adj* : of or from Santiago, Chile

santiamén *nm* **en un santiamén** : in no time at all

santidad *nf* : holiness, sanctity

santificar {72} *vt* : to sanctify, to consecrate, to hallow

santiguarse {10} *vr* PERSIGNARSE : to cross oneself

santo[1], **-ta** *adj* **1** : holy, saintly ⟨el Santo Padre : the Holy Father⟩ ⟨una vida santa : a saintly life⟩ **2 Santo, Santa** (*San before names of masculine saints except those beginning with D or T*) : Saint ⟨Santa Clara : Saint Claire⟩ ⟨Santo Tomás : Saint Thomas⟩ ⟨San Francisco : Saint Francis⟩

santo[2], **-ta** *n* : saint

santo[3] *nm* **1** : saint's day **2** CUMPLEAÑOS : birthday

santuario *nm* : sanctuary

santurrón, -rrona *adj, mpl* **-rrones** : overly pious, sanctimonious — **santurronamente** *adv*

saña *nf* **1** : fury, rage **2** : viciousness ⟨con saña : viciously⟩

sapo *nm* : toad

saque[1], etc. → **sacar**

saque[2] *nm* **1** : kickoff (in soccer or football) **2** : serve, service (in sports)

saqueador, -dora *n* DEPREDADOR : plunderer, looter

saquear *vt* : to sack, to plunder, to loot

saqueo *nm* : sacking, plunder, looting

sarampión *nm* : measles *pl*

sarape *nm CA, Mex* : blanket (worn as a poncho)

sarcasmo *nm* : sarcasm

sarcástico, -ca *adj* : sarcastic

sarcófago *nm* : sarcophagus

sardina *nf* : sardine

sardónico, -ca *adj* : sardonic

sarga *nf* : serge

sargento *nmf* : sergeant

sari *nm* : sari

sarna *nf* : mange

sarnoso, -sa *adj* : mangy

sarpullido *nm* ERUPCIÓN : rash

sarro *nm* **1** : deposit, coating **2** : tartar, plaque

sarta *nf* **1** : string, series (of insults, etc.) **2** : string (of pearls, etc.)

sartén *nmf, pl* **sartenes** **1** : frying pan **2 tener la sartén por el mango** : to call the shots, to be in control

sasafrás *nm* : sassafras

sastre, -tra *n* : tailor

sastrería *nf* **1** : tailoring **2** : tailor's shop

Satanás *or* **Satán** *nm* : Satan, the devil

satánico, -ca *adj* : satanic

satélite *nm* : satellite

satín *or* **satén** *nm, pl* **satines** *or* **satenes** : satin

satinado, -da *adj* : satin, glossy
sátira *nf* : satire
satírico, -ca *adj* : satirical, satiric
satirizar {21} *vt* : to satirize
sátiro *nm* : satyr
satisfacción *nf, pl* -ciones : satisfaction
satisfacer {74} *vt* 1 : to satisfy 2 : to fulfill, to meet 3 : to pay, to settle — sa-
tisfacerse *vr* 1 : to be satisfied 2 : to
take revenge
satisfactorio, -ria *adj* : satisfactory — sa-
tisfactoriamente *adv*
satisfecho, -cha *adj* : satisfied, content,
pleased
saturación *nf, pl* -ciones : saturation
saturar *vt* 1 : to saturate, to fill up 2 : to
satiate, to surfeit
saturnismo *nm* : lead poisoning
Saturno *nm* : Saturn
sauce *nm* : willow
saúco *nm* : elder (tree)
saudí *or* saudita *adj & nmf* : Saudi, Saudi
Arabian
sauna *nmf* : sauna
savia *nf* : sap
saxo¹ *nm fam* : sax *fam*, saxophone
saxo² *nmf fam* : sax player *fam*, saxophone player
saxofón *nm, pl* -fones : saxophone — sa-
xofonista *nmf*
sazón¹ *nf, pl* sazones 1 : flavor, seasoning 2 : ripeness, maturity ⟨en sazón : in
season, ripe⟩ 3 a la sazón : at that time,
then
sazón² *nmf, pl* sazones *Mex* : flavor, seasoning
sazonar *vt* CONDIMENTAR : to season, to
spice
scanner [es'kaner] → escáner
scout [es'kaut] *nmf, pl* scouts : scout
se *pron* 1 : to him, to her, to you, to
them ⟨se los daré a ella : I'll give them to
her⟩ 2 : each other, one another ⟨se
abrazaron : they hugged each other⟩ 3
: himself, herself, itself, yourself, yourselves, themselves ⟨se afeitó antes de
salir : he shaved before leaving⟩ 4 (*used
in passive constructions*) ⟨se dice que es
hermosa : they say she's beautiful⟩ ⟨se
habla inglés : English spoken⟩
sé → saber, ser
sea, etc. → ser
sebo *nm* 1 : grease, fat 2 : tallow 3
: suet
secado *nm* : drying
secador *nm* : hair dryer
secadora *nf* 1 : dryer, clothes dryer 2
Mex : hair dryer
secamente *adv* : curtly, brusquely
secante *nm* : blotting paper, blotter
secar {72} *v* : to dry — secarse *vr* 1 : to
get dry 2 : to dry up
sección *nf, pl* secciones 1 : section
⟨sección transversal : cross section⟩ 2
: department, division
seccionar *vt* : to section, to divide
seco, -ca *adj* 1 : dry 2 DISECADO : dried
⟨fruta seca : dried fruit⟩ 3 : thin, lean
4 : curt, brusque 5 : sharp ⟨un golpe
seco : a sharp blow⟩ 6 : dry, alcohol-

free 7 a secas : simply, just ⟨se llama
Chico, a secas : he's just called Chico⟩ 8
en ~ : abruptly, suddenly ⟨frenar en
seco : to make a sudden stop⟩
secoya *nf* : sequoia, redwood
secreción *nf, pl* -ciones : secretion
secretar *vt* : to secrete
secretaría *nf* 1 : secretariat, administrative department 2 *Mex* : ministry, cabinet office
secretariado *nm* 1 : secretariat 2 : secretarial profession
secretario, -ria *n* : secretary — secretarial *adj*
secreto¹, -ta *adj* : secret — secretamente
adv
secreto² *nm* 1 : secret 2 : secrecy
secta *nf* : sect
sectario, -ria *adj & n* : sectarian
sector *nm* : sector
secuaz *nmf, pl* secuaces : follower,
henchman, underling
secuela *nf* : consequence, sequel ⟨las secuelas de la guerra : the aftermath of the
war⟩
secuencia *nf* : sequence
secuestrador, -dora *n* 1 : kidnapper, abductor 2 : hijacker
secuestrar *vt* 1 RAPTAR : to kidnap, to
abduct 2 : to hijack, to commandeer 3
CONFISCAR : to confiscate, to seize
secuestro *nm* 1 RAPTO : kidnapping, abduction 2 : hijacking 3 : seizure, confiscation
secular *adj* : secular — secularismo *nm*
— secularización *nf*
secundar *vt* : to support, to second
secundaria *nf* 1 : secondary education,
high school 2 *Mex* : junior high school,
middle school
secundario, -ria *adj* : secondary
secuoya *nf* : sequoia
sed *nf* 1 : thirst ⟨tener sed : to be thirsty⟩
2 tener sed de : to hunger for, to thirst
for
seda *nf* : silk
sedación *nf, pl* -ciones : sedation
sedal *nm* : fishing line
sedán *nm, pl* sedanes : sedan
sedante *adj & nm* CALMANTE : sedative
sedar *vt* : to sedate
sede *nf* 1 : seat, headquarters 2 : venue,
site 3 la Santa Sede : the Holy See
sedentario, -ria *adj* : sedentary
sedición *nf, pl* -ciones : sedition — sedicioso, -sa *adj*
sediento, -ta *adj* : thirsty, thirsting
sedimento *nm* : sediment — sedimenta-
rio, -ria *adj* — sedimentación *nf*
sedoso, -sa *adj* : silky, silken
seducción *nf, pl* -ciones : seduction
seducir {61} *vt* 1 : to seduce 2 : to captivate, to charm
seductivo, -va *adj* : seductive
seductor¹, -tora *adj* 1 SEDUCTIVO : seductive 2 ENCANTADOR : charming, al-
luring
seductor², -tora *n* : seducer
segador¹, *nm* : daddy longlegs
segador², -dora *n* : harvester

segar {49} *vt* **1** : to reap, to harvest, to cut **2** : to sever abruptly ⟨una vida segada por la enfermedad : a life cut short by illness⟩

seglar[1] *adj* LAICO : lay, secular

seglar[2] *nm* LAICO : layperson, layman *m*, laywoman *f*

segmentado, -da *adj* : segmented

segmento *nm* : segment

segregación *nf, pl* **-ciones** : segregation

segregar {52} *vt* **1** : to segregate **2** SE-CRETAR : to secrete

seguida *nf* **en** ~ : right away, immediately ⟨vuelvo en seguida : I'll be right back⟩

seguidamente *adv* **1** : next, immediately after **2** : without a break, continuously

seguido[1] *adv* **1** RECTO : straight, straight ahead **2** : often, frequently

seguido[2], **-da** *adj* **1** CONSECUTIVO : consecutive, successive ⟨tres días seguidos : three days in a row⟩ **2** : straight, unbroken **3** ~ **por** *or* ~ **de** : followed by

seguidor, -dora *n* : follower, supporter

seguimiento *nm* **1** : following, pursuit **2** : continuation ⟨darle seguimiento a : to follow up (on)⟩ **3** : tracking, monitoring

seguir {75} *vt* **1** : to follow ⟨el policía los siguió : the policeman followed them⟩ ⟨me siguieron con la mirada : they followed me with their eyes⟩ ⟨seguiré tu consejo : I'll follow your advice⟩ ⟨seguir el ejemplo de : to follow the example of⟩ ⟨me cuesta seguirle el ritmo : I have trouble keeping up with her⟩ ⟨seguir el procedimiento : to follow procedure⟩ ⟨en los meses que siguieron a la tragedia : in the months that followed the tragedy⟩ **2** : to go along, to keep on ⟨seguimos toda la carretera panamericana : we continued along the PanAmerican Highway⟩ ⟨siguió hablando : he kept on talking⟩ ⟨sigue aumentando : it continues to increase⟩ ⟨lo sigue creyendo : he still believes it⟩ ⟨seguir el curso : to stay on course⟩ **3** : to take (a course, a treatment) — *vi* **1** : to go on, to keep going ⟨sigue adelante : keep going, carry on⟩ ⟨sigue derecho : keep going straight⟩ **2** : to remain, to continue to be ⟨¿todavía sigues aquí? : you're still here?⟩ ⟨sigue con vida : she's still alive⟩ ⟨todo sigue igual : everything's still the same⟩ ⟨seguimos a la espera de noticias : we're still awaiting news⟩ **3** : to follow, to come after ⟨la frase que sigue : the following sentence⟩ ⟨¿qué sigue después? : what comes next?⟩

según[1] *adv* : it depends ⟨según y como : it all depends on⟩

según[2] *conj* **1** COMO, CONFORME : as, just as ⟨según lo dejé : just as I left it⟩ ⟨hace anotaciones según va leyendo : she makes notes as she reads⟩ **2** : depending on how ⟨según se vea : depending on how one sees it⟩

según[3] *prep* **1** : according to ⟨según los rumores : according to the rumors⟩ **2** : depending on ⟨según los resultados : depending on the results⟩

segundero *nm* : second hand (on a clock)

segundo[1], **-da** *adj* : second ⟨el segundo lugar : second place⟩ ⟨el segundo piso : the second floor⟩ ⟨llegó la segunda : she came in second⟩

segundo[2], **-da** *n* **1** : second (in a series) **2** : second (person), second in command

segundo[3] *nm* : second ⟨sesenta segundos : sixty seconds⟩

seguramente *adv* **1** : for sure, surely **2** : probably

seguridad *nf* **1** : safety (against accidents, etc.), security (against attacks, etc.) ⟨seguridad ciudadana : public safety⟩ ⟨seguridad nacional : national security⟩ ⟨de alta/máxima seguridad : high/maximum security⟩ ⟨medidas de seguridad : safety/security measures⟩ **2** : (financial) security ⟨seguridad social : Social Security⟩ **3** CERTEZA : certainty, assurance ⟨con toda seguridad : with complete certainty⟩ **4** : confidence, self-confidence

seguro[1] *adv* : certainly, definitely ⟨va a llover, seguro : it's going to rain for sure⟩ ⟨¡seguro que sí! : of course!⟩

seguro[2], **-ra** *adj* **1** : safe, secure **2** : sure, certain ⟨estoy segura que es él : I'm sure that's him⟩ **3** : reliable, trustworthy **4** : self-assured

seguro[3] *nm* **1** : insurance ⟨seguro de vida : life insurance⟩ **2** : fastener, clasp **3** *Mex* : safety pin

seis[1] *adj & nm* : six ⟨tiene seis años : she's six (years old)⟩ ⟨el seis de agosto : (on) the sixth of August, (on) August sixth⟩

seis[2] *pron* : six ⟨somos seis : there are six of us⟩ ⟨son las seis : it's six o'clock⟩

seiscientos[1], **-tas** *adj & pron* : six hundred

seiscientos[2] *nms & pl* : six hundred

seísmo *nm Spain* : earthquake

selección *nf, pl* **-ciones** **1** ELECCIÓN : selection, choice **2** **selección natural** : natural selection

seleccionador, -dora *n* : manager (in sports)

seleccionar *vt* ELEGIR : to select, to choose

selectividad *nf Spain* : entrance examination

selectivo, -va *adj* : selective — **selectivamente** *adv*

selecto, -ta *adj* **1** : choice, select **2** EXCLUSIVO : exclusive

selenio *nm* : selenium

selfie *or* **selfi** [ˈselfi] *nm* : selfie

self–service [selfˈserbis] *nm* : self-service restaurant

sellar *vt* **1** : to seal **2** : to stamp

sello *nm* **1** : seal **2** ESTAMPILLA, TIMBRE : postage stamp **3** : hallmark, characteristic

selva *nf* **1** BOSQUE : woods *pl*, forest ⟨selva húmeda : rain forest⟩ **2** JUNGLA : jungle

selvático, -ca *adj* **1** : forest, jungle ⟨sendero selvático : jungle path⟩ **2** : wild

semáforo *nm* **1** : traffic light **2** : stop signal

semana *nf* : week

semanal *adj* : weekly — **semanalmente** *adv*

semanario *nm* : weekly (publication)

semántica *nf* : semantics

semántico, -ca *adj* : semantic

semblante *nm* 1 : countenance, face 2 : appearance, look

semblanza *nf* : biographical sketch, profile

sembrado *nm* : cultivated field

sembrar {55} *vt* 1 : to plant, to sow 2 : to scatter, to strew ⟨sembrar el pánico : to spread panic⟩

semejante[1] *adj* 1 PARECIDO : similar, alike 2 TAL : such ⟨nunca he visto cosa semejante : I have never seen such a thing⟩

semejante[2] *nm* PRÓJIMO : fellowman

semejanza *nf* PARECIDO : similarity, resemblance

semejar *vi* : to resemble, to look like — **semejarse** *vr* : to be similar, to look alike

semen *nm* : semen

semental *nm* : stud (animal) ⟨caballo semental : stallion⟩

semestral *adj* : biannual, semiannual

semestre *nm* : semester

semi- *pref* : semi-

semibreve *nf* : whole note

semicírculo *nm* : semicircle, half circle

semiconductor *nm* : semiconductor

semidiós *nm, pl* **-dioses** : demigod *m*

semifinal *nf* : semifinal

semilla *nf* : seed

semillero *nm* 1 : bed (for plants), seed tray 2 : hotbed, breeding ground

seminario *nm* 1 : seminary 2 : seminar, graduate course

semiprecioso, -sa *adj* : semiprecious

semita *nmf* : Semite — **semítico, -ca** *adj*

sémola *nf* : semolina

sempiterno, -na *adj* ETERNO : eternal, everlasting

senado *nm* : senate

senador, -dora *n* : senator

sencillamente *adv* : simply, plainly

sencillez *nf* : simplicity

sencillo[1], **-lla** *adj* 1 : simple, easy 2 : plain, unaffected 3 : single

sencillo[2] *nm* 1 : single (recording) 2 : small change (coins) 3 : one-way ticket

senda *nf* CAMINO, SENDERO : path, way

senderismo *nm* : hiking

sendero *nm* CAMINO, SENDA : path, way

sendos, -das *adj pl* : each, both ⟨llevaban sendos vestidos nuevos : they were each wearing a new dress⟩

senectud *nf* ANCIANIDAD : old age

senegalés, -lesa *adj & n, mpl* **-leses** : Senegalese

senil *adj* : senile — **senilidad** *nf*

seno *nm* 1 : breast, bosom ⟨los senos : the breasts⟩ ⟨el seno de la familia : the bosom of the family⟩ 2 : sinus 3 **seno materno** : womb

sensación *nf, pl* **-ciones** 1 IMPRESIÓN : feeling ⟨tener la sensación : to have a feeling⟩ 2 : sensation ⟨causar sensación : to cause a sensation⟩

sensacional *adj* : sensational

sensacionalismo *nm* : sensationalism — **sensacionalista** *adj*

sensatez *nf* 1 : good sense 2 **con ~** : sensibly

sensato, -ta *adj* : sensible, sound — **sensatamente** *adv*

sensibilidad *nf* 1 : sensitivity, sensibility 2 SENSACIÓN : feeling

sensibilizar {21} *vt* : to sensitize

sensible *adj* 1 : sensitive 2 APRECIABLE : considerable, significant 3 : sentient, capable of feeling

sensiblemente *adv* : considerably, significantly

sensiblería *nf* : sentimentality, mush

sensiblero, -ra *adj* : mawkish, sentimental, mushy

sensitivo, -va *adj* 1 : sense ⟨órganos sensitivos : sense organs⟩ 2 : sentient, capable of feeling

sensor *nm* : sensor

sensorial *adj* : sensory

sensual *adj* : sensual, sensuous — **sensualmente** *adv*

sensualidad *nf* : sensuality

sentado, -da *adj* 1 : sitting, seated 2 : established, settled ⟨dar por sentado : to take for granted⟩ ⟨dejar sentado : to make clear⟩ 3 : sensible, steady, judicious

sentar {55} *vt* 1 : to seat, to sit 2 : to establish, to set — *vi* 1 : to suit ⟨ese color te sienta : that color suits you⟩ 2 : to agree with (of food or drink) ⟨las cebollas no me sientan : onions don't agree with me⟩ 3 : to please ⟨le sentó mal el paseo : she didn't enjoy the trip⟩ — **sentarse** *vr* : to sit, to sit down ⟨siéntese, por favor : please have a seat⟩

sentencia *nf* 1 : sentence, judgment 2 : maxim, saying

sentenciar *vt* : to sentence

sentido[1], **-da** *adj* 1 : heartfelt, sincere ⟨mi más sentido pésame : my sincerest condolences⟩ 2 : touchy, sensitive 3 : offended, hurt

sentido[2] *nm* 1 : sense ⟨sentido común : common sense⟩ ⟨los cinco sentidos : the five senses⟩ ⟨sin sentido : senseless⟩ 2 CONOCIMIENTO : consciousness 3 SIGNIFICADO : meaning, sense ⟨doble sentido : double entendre⟩ 4 : direction ⟨calle de sentido único : one-way street⟩

sentimental *adj* 1 : sentimental 2 : love, romantic ⟨vida sentimental : love life⟩

sentimentalismo *nm* : sentimentality

sentimiento *nm* 1 : feeling, emotion 2 PESAR : regret, sorrow

sentir {76} *vt* 1 : to feel, to experience ⟨no siento nada de dolor : I don't feel any pain⟩ ⟨sentía sed : he was feeling thirsty⟩ ⟨sentir amor : to feel love⟩ 2 PERCIBIR : to perceive, to sense ⟨sentir un ruido : to hear a noise⟩ 3 LAMENTAR : to regret, to feel sorry for ⟨lo siento mucho : I'm very sorry⟩ — *vi* 1 : to have feeling, to feel 2 **sin ~** : without noticing, inadvertently — **sentirse** *vr* 1 : to feel ⟨¿te sientes mejor? : are you feeling better?⟩ **2** *Chile, Mex* : to take offense

seña *nf* **1** : sign, signal ⟨hablar por señas : to talk in sign language⟩ **2 dar señas de** : to show signs of

señal *nf* **1** : signal ⟨señales de radio/televisión : radio/television signals⟩ **2** : sign ⟨señal de tráfico/tránsito : traffic sign⟩ **3** : signal (with the hand, etc.) ⟨señales de humo : smoke signals⟩ **4** INDICIO : sign, indication ⟨señales de vida : signs of life⟩ ⟨señal de alarma/alerta : warning sign⟩ ⟨no hay señales de violencia : there are no signs of violence⟩ ⟨como señal de protesta : as a sign of protest⟩ ⟨en señal de : as a token of⟩ ⟨sin dejar señal : without leaving a trace⟩ ⟨una buena señal : a good sign⟩ **5** MARCA : mark

señalado, -da *adj* : distinguished, notable

señalador *nm* : marker ⟨señalador de libros : bookmark⟩

señalar *vt* **1** INDICAR : to indicate, to show **2** : to mark **3** : to point out, to stress **4** : to fix, to set — **señalarse** *vr* : to distinguish oneself

señalización *nf, pl* **-ciones 1** : signs *pl*, signage **2** : installing of signs

señalizar {21} *vt* **1** : to mark (with signs or guides) ⟨la ruta está claramente señalizada : the route is clearly marked⟩ **2** : to put up signs on/in

señor, -ñora *n* **1** : gentleman *m*, man *m*, lady *f*, woman *f*, wife *f* ⟨señoras y señores : ladies and gentlemen⟩ ⟨un señor de setenta años : a 70-year-old man⟩ ⟨la señora de la casa : the lady of the house⟩ ⟨mi señora : my wife⟩ **2** : Mr. *m*, Mrs. *f* ⟨buenos días, señor López : good morning, Mr. López⟩ ⟨¿conoces a la señora Ortega? : do you know Mrs. Ortega?⟩ **3** : Sir *m*, Madam *f* ⟨Estimados señores : Dear Sirs⟩ **4** : Mr. *m*, Madam *f* ⟨Señora presidenta: . . . : Madam President: . . .⟩ ⟨Señor presidente: . . . : Mr. President: . . .⟩ ⟨habló con el señor embajador : she spoke with the ambassador⟩ **5** : lord *m*, lady *f* ⟨el Señor : the Lord⟩

señoría *nf* **1** : lordship **2 Su Señoría** : Your Honor

señorial *adj* : stately, regal

señorío *nm* **1** : manor, estate **2** : dominion, power **3** : elegance, class

señorita *nf* **1** : young lady, young woman **2** : Miss

señuelo *nm* **1** : decoy **2** : bait

sepa, etc. → *saber*

separación *nf, pl* **-ciones 1** : separation, division **2** : gap, space

separadamente *adv* : separately, apart

separado¹, -da *adj* **1** : separated **2** : separate ⟨vidas separadas : separate lives⟩ **3 por ~** : separately

separado², -da *n* : person who is separated ⟨separados y divorciados : separated and divorced people⟩

separador *nm* : divider

separar *vt* **1** : to separate, to divide **2** : to split up, to pull apart **3** : to put aside, to set aside — **separarse** *vr* **1** : to

separate, to split up ⟨sus padres se separaron : his parents separated⟩ ⟨separarse de alguien : to separate from someone⟩ **2** : to split up (of a group, etc.)

separo *nm Mex* : cell (in a jail or prison)

sepelio *nm* : interment, burial

sepia¹ *adj & nm* : sepia

sepia² *nf* : cuttlefish

septentrional *adj* : northern

séptico, -ca *adj* : septic

septiembre *nm* : September ⟨el cinco de septiembre : (on) the fifth of September⟩

séptimo, -ma *adj & n* : seventh ⟨el séptimo piso : the seventh floor⟩ ⟨llegó la séptima : she came in seventh (place)⟩ ⟨un séptimo de : a seventh of⟩

septuagésimo¹, -ma *adj* : seventieth

septuagésimo² *nm* : seventieth

sepulcral *adj* **1** : deathly **2** : dismal, gloomy

sepulcro *nm* TUMBA : tomb, sepulchre

sepultar *vt* ENTERRAR : to bury

sepultura *nf* **1** : burial **2** TUMBA : grave, tomb

seque, etc. → *secar*

sequedad *nf* **1** : dryness **2** : brusqueness, curtness

sequía *nf* : drought

séquito *nm* : retinue, entourage

ser¹ {77} *vi* **1** (*expressing identity*) : to be ⟨él es mi hermano : he is my brother⟩ ⟨¿quién es? : who is it?⟩ ⟨soy yo : it's me⟩ **2** (*expressing a quality*) : to be ⟨Camila es linda : Camila is pretty⟩ ⟨no seas tonto : don't be silly⟩ ⟨éste es el mejor : this one is the best⟩ ⟨es mío : it's mine⟩ ⟨es para ti : it's for you⟩ ⟨es para abrir latas : it's for opening cans⟩ ⟨son de Juan : they're Juan's⟩ ⟨somos de Managua : we're from Managua⟩ ⟨no creo que sea necesario : I don't think it's necessary⟩ ⟨quiero que seas feliz : I want you to be happy⟩ **3** (*indicating group, category, etc.*) : to be ⟨soy abogada : I'm a lawyer⟩ ⟨es un mamífero : it's a mammal⟩ **4** : to be, to exist, to live ⟨ser, o no ser : to be or not to be⟩ **5** : to be, to take place, to occur ⟨el concierto es el domingo : the concert is on Sunday⟩ ⟨la reunión fue en la escuela : the meeting was at the school⟩ **6** (*expressing time, date, season*) ⟨son las diez : it's ten o'clock⟩ ⟨hoy es el 9 : today's the 9th⟩ **7** : to be (a price), to cost, to come to ⟨¿cuánto es? : how much is it?⟩ **8** : to be, to equal ⟨dos más dos son cuatro : two plus two is four⟩ **9** (*with the future tense*) ⟨¿será posible? : can it be possible?⟩ ⟨serán las ocho : it must be eight o'clock⟩ **10 a no ser que** : unless **11 como sea** *or* **sea como sea** : one way or another, somehow ⟨hay que terminarlo como sea; hay que terminarlo, sea como sea : one way or another, we have to finish it⟩ **12 cuando sea** : anytime, whenever **13 donde sea** : anywhere, wherever **14 es que** : the thing is that ⟨es que no lo conozco : it's just that I don't know him⟩ **15 o sea** : in other words **16 ¡sea!** : agreed!, all right! **17 sea**

cual/quien (etc.) sea ⟨sean cuales sean las circunstancias : whatever the circumstances might be⟩ ⟨sea quien sea, no lo van a permitir : no matter who he is, they're not going to allow it⟩ **18 sea** ... **sea** : either ... or — *v aux* (*used in passive constructions*) : to be ⟨la cuenta ha sido pagada : the bill has been paid⟩ ⟨él fue asesinado : he was murdered⟩

ser[2] *nm* : being ⟨ser humano : human being⟩

seráfico, -ca *adj* : angelic

serbio[1]**, -bia** *adj & n* : Serb, Serbian

serbio[2] *nm* : Serbian (language)

serbocroata[1] *adj* : Serbo-Croatian

serbocroata[2] *nm* : Serbo-Croatian (language)

serenar *vt* : to calm, to soothe — **serenarse** *vr* CALMARSE : to calm down

serenata *nf* : serenade

serenidad *nf* : serenity, calmness

sereno[1]**, -na** *adj* **1** SOSEGADO : serene, calm, composed **2** : fair, clear (of weather) **3** : calm, still (of the sea) — **serenamente** *adv*

sereno[2] *nm* : night watchman

seriado, -da *adj* : serial

serial *nm* : serial (on radio or television)

seriamente *adv* : seriously

serie *nf* **1** : series **2** SERIAL : serial **3 fabricación en serie** : mass production **4 fuera de serie** : extraordinary, amazing

seriedad *nf* **1** : seriousness, earnestness **2** : gravity, importance

serio, -ria *adj* **1** : serious, earnest **2** : reliable, responsible **3** : important **4 en ~** : seriously, in earnest — **seriamente** *adv*

sermón *nm, pl* **sermones 1** : sermon **2** *fam* : harangue, lecture

sermonear *vt fam* : to harangue, to lecture

seropositivo *adj* **1** : positive (in blood testing) ⟨es seropositivo : he's positive, he tested positive⟩ **2** : HIV positive

serpentear *vi* : to twist, to wind — **serpenteante** *adj*

serpentina *nf* : paper streamer

serpiente *nf* : serpent, snake

serrado, -da *adj* DENTADO : serrated

serranía *nf* : mountainous area

serrano, -na *adj* : from the mountains

serrar {55} *vt* : to saw

serrín *nm, pl* **serrines** : sawdust

serruchar *vt* : to saw up

serrucho *nm* : saw, handsaw

servicentro *nm Peru* : gas station

servicial *adj* : obliging, helpful

servicio *nm* **1** : service ⟨servicio postal : postal service⟩ ⟨servicios sociales : social services⟩ ⟨servicio público : public service⟩ **2** SAQUE : serve (in sports) **3** : help, servants *pl* **4 servicios** *nmpl* : restrooms **5 fuera de servicio** : out of service

servidor, -dora *n* **1** : servant **2 su seguro servidor** : yours truly (in correspondence)

servidumbre *nf* **1** : servitude **2** : help, servants *pl*

servil *adj* **1** : servile, subservient **2** : menial

servilismo *nm* : servility

servilleta *nf* : napkin

servir {54} *vi* **1** : to work, to be useful ⟨esta máquina no sirve para nada : this machine is completely useless⟩ ⟨esa excusa no sirve : that excuse doesn't work⟩ ⟨su talento no le sirvió de mucho : his talent didn't do him much good⟩ ⟨deshazte de lo que no te sirve : get rid of what you don't need⟩ ⟨¿para qué sirve? : what's it for?⟩ **2** : to serve ⟨¿en qué puedo servirle? : how may I help you?⟩ **3** : to serve (in sports) **4** : to serve (in the military, etc.) **5 ~ de** : to serve as ⟨servir de ejemplo : to serve as an example⟩ — *vt* **1** : to serve ⟨¿en qué puedo servirlo? : how may I help you?⟩ ⟨¿te sirvo más café? : would you like more coffee?⟩ **2** SURTIR : to fill (an order) — **servirse** *vr* **1** : to help oneself to **2** : to be kind enough ⟨sírvase enviarnos un catálogo : please send us a catalog⟩

sésamo *nm* AJONJOLÍ : sesame, sesame seeds *pl*

sesear *vi* : to pronounce the Spanish letter *c* before *i* or *e* or the Spanish letter *z* as /s/

sesenta *adj & nm* : sixty — **sesenta** *pron*

sesentavo[1]**, -va** *adj* : sixtieth

sesentavo[2] *n* : sixtieth (fraction)

seseo *nm* : pronunciation of the Spanish letter *c* before *i* or *e* or the Spanish letter *z* as /s/

sesgado, -da *adj* **1** : inclined, tilted **2** : slanted, biased

sesgar {52} *vt* **1** : to cut on the bias **2** : to tilt **3** : to bias, to slant

sesgo *nm* : bias

sesgue, etc. → **sesgar**

sesión *nf, pl* **sesiones 1** : session (of a legislature, etc.), meeting **2** : showing, performance ⟨sesión de tarde : afternoon showing⟩

sesionar *vi* REUNIRSE : to meet, to be in session

seso *nm* **1** : brains, intelligence **2 sesos** *nmpl* : brains (as food)

sesudo, -da *adj* **1** : prudent, sensible **2** : brainy

set *nm, pl* **sets** : set (in tennis)

seta *nf* : mushroom

setecientos[1]**, -tas** *adj & pron* : seven hundred

setecientos[2] *nms & pl* : seven hundred

setenta *adj & nm* : seventy — **setenta** *pron*

setentavo[1]**, -va** *adj* : seventieth

setentavo[2] *nm* : seventieth

setiembre → **septiembre**

seto *nm* **1** : fence, enclosure **2 seto vivo** : hedge

setter *nm, pl* **setter** *or* **setters** : setter (dog)

seudónimo *nm* : pseudonym

severidad *nf* **1** : harshness, severity **2** : strictness

severo, -ra *adj* **1** : harsh, severe **2** ESTRICTO : strict — **severamente** *adv*

sexagésimo¹, -ma *adj* : sixtieth, sixty-
sexagésimo², -ma *n* : sixtieth, sixty- (in a series)
sexismo *nm* : sexism — **sexista** *adj & nmf*
sexo *nm* : sex
sextante *nm* : sextant
sexteto *nm* : sextet
sexto, -ta *adj & n* : sixth ⟨el sexto lugar : sixth place⟩ ⟨llegó la sexta : she came in sixth (place)⟩ ⟨un sexto de : a sixth of⟩
sexual *adj* : sexual, sex ⟨educación sexual : sex education⟩ — **sexualmente** *adv*
sexualidad *nf* : sexuality
sexy *adj, pl* **sexy** *or* **sexys** : sexy
sheriff *nmf, pl* **sheriffs** : sheriff
shock [ˈʃɔk, ˈtʃɔk] *nm* : shock ⟨estado de shock : state of shock⟩
short *nm, pl* **shorts** : shorts *pl*
show *nm, pl* **shows** : show
si¹ *nm* **1** : B ⟨si sostenido/bemol : B sharp/flat⟩ **2** : ti (in singing)
si² *conj* **1** : if ⟨lo haré si me pagan : I'll do it if they pay me⟩ ⟨si lo supiera te lo diría : if I knew it I would tell you⟩ **2** : whether, if ⟨no importa si funciona o no : it doesn't matter whether it works (or not)⟩ **3** (*expressing desire, protest, or surprise*) ⟨si supiera la verdad : if only I knew the truth⟩ ⟨¡si no quiero! : but I don't want to!⟩ **4 si bien** : although ⟨si bien se ha progresado : although progress has been made⟩ **5 si no** : otherwise, or else ⟨si no, no voy : otherwise I won't go⟩
sí¹ *adv* **1** : yes ⟨sí, gracias : yes, please⟩ ⟨creo que sí : I think so⟩ **2 sí que** : indeed, absolutely ⟨esta vez sí que ganaré : this time I'm sure to win⟩ **3 porque sí** *fam* : because, just because ⟨lo hizo porque sí : she did it just because⟩
sí² *nm, pl* **síes** : yes ⟨dar el sí : to say yes, to express consent⟩
sí³ *pron* **1** : oneself, yourself, yourselves *pl*, itself, himself, herself, themselves *pl* ⟨puede decidir por sí mismo : he can decide for himself⟩ ⟨los hechos hablan por sí solos : the facts speak for themselves⟩ ⟨se culpa a sí misma : she blames herself⟩ ⟨dio lo mejor de sí : he gave it his all⟩ **2 de por sí** *or* **en sí** : by itself, in itself, per se **3 fuera de sí** : beside oneself/yourself (etc.) **4 para sí (mismo)** : to oneself/yourself (etc.), for oneself/yourself (etc.) ⟨¿qué quiere decir?—dijo para sí : "what does it mean?" she said to herself⟩ ⟨lo hicieron para sí mismos : they did it for themselves⟩ **5 entre ～** : among themselves
siamés, -mesa *adj & n, mpl* **siameses** : Siamese
sicario, -ria *n* : hired killer, hit man
siciliano, -na *adj & n* : Sicilian
sico- → **psico-**
sicomoro *or* **sicómoro** *nm* : sycamore
SIDA *or* **sida** *nm* (síndrome de *i*nmun*o*deficiencia *a*dquirida) : AIDS
siderurgia *nf* : iron and steel industry
siderúrgico, -ca *adj* : steel, iron ⟨la industria siderúrgica : the steel industry⟩

sidra *nf* : hard cider
siega¹, siegue, etc. → **segar**
siega² *nf* **1** : harvesting **2** : harvest time **3** : harvested crop
siembra¹, etc. → **sembrar**
siembra² *nf* **1** : sowing **2** : sowing season **3** SEMBRADO : cultivated field
siempre *adv* **1** : always ⟨siempre tienes hambre : you're always hungry⟩ **2** : still ⟨¿siempre te vas? : are you still going?⟩ **3** *Mex* : after all ⟨siempre no fui : I didn't go after all⟩ **4 siempre que** : whenever, every time ⟨siempre que pasa : every time he walks by⟩ **5 para ～** : forever, for good **6 siempre y cuando** : provided that
sien *nf* : temple (on the forehead)
sienta, etc. → **sentar**
siente, etc. → **sentir**
sierpe *nf* : serpent, snake
sierra¹, etc. → **serrar**
sierra² *nf* **1** : saw ⟨sierra de vaivén : jigsaw⟩ **2** CORDILLERA : mountain range **3** : mountains *pl* ⟨viven en la sierra : they live in the mountains⟩
siervo, -va *n* **1** : slave **2** : serf
siesta *nf* : nap, siesta
siete¹ *adj & nm* : seven ⟨tiene siete años : she's seven (years old)⟩ ⟨la página siete : page seven⟩ ⟨el siete de junio : (on) the seventh of June, (on) June seventh⟩
siete² *pron* : seven ⟨somos siete : there are seven of us⟩ ⟨son las siete : it's seven o'clock⟩
sífilis *nf* : syphilis
sifón *nm, pl* **sifones** : siphon
siga, sigue etc. → **seguir**
sigilo *nm* : secrecy, stealth
sigiloso, -sa *adj* FURTIVO : furtive, stealthy — **sigilosamente** *adv*
sigla *nf* : acronym, abbreviation
siglo *nm* **1** : century **2** : age ⟨el Siglo de Oro : the Golden Age⟩ ⟨hace siglos que no te veo : I haven't seen you in ages⟩ **3** : world, secular life
signar *vt* : to sign (a treaty or agreement)
signatario, -ria *n* : signatory
significación *nf, pl* **-ciones** **1** : significance, importance **2** : meaning
significado *nm* **1** : sense, meaning **2** : significance
significante *adj* : significant
significar {72} *vt* **1** : to mean, to signify **2** : to express, to make known — **significarse** *vr* **1** : to draw attention, to become known **2** : to take a stance
significativo, -va *adj* **1** : significant, important **2** : meaningful — **significativamente** *adv*
signo *nm* **1** : sign ⟨signo de igual : equal sign⟩ ⟨un signo de alegría : a sign of happiness⟩ **2** : (punctuation) mark ⟨signo de interrogación : question mark⟩ ⟨signo de admiración : exclamation point⟩ ⟨signo de intercalación : caret⟩
siguiente *adj* : next, following
sílaba *nf* : syllable
silábico, -ca *adj* : syllabic
silbar *v* : to whistle
silbato *nm* PITO : whistle

silbido *nm* : whistle, whistling
silenciador *nm* **1** : muffler (of an automobile) **2** : silencer
silenciar *vt* **1** : to silence **2** : to muffle
silencio *nm* **1** : silence, quiet ⟨¡silencio! : be quiet!⟩ **2** : rest (in music)
silencioso, -sa *adj* : silent, quiet — **silenciosamente** *adv*
sílice *nf* : silica
silicio *nm* : silicon
silla *nf* **1** : chair **2 silla alta** : high chair (for a baby) **3 silla de ruedas** : wheelchair
sillín *nm, pl* **sillines** : saddle
sillón *nm, pl* **sillones** : armchair, easy chair
silo *nm* : silo
silueta *nf* **1** : silhouette **2** : figure, shape
silvestre *adj* : wild ⟨flor silvestre : wildflower⟩
silvicultor, -tora *n* : forester
silvicultura *nf* : forestry
sima *nf* ABISMO : chasm, abyss
simbólico, -ca *adj* : symbolic — **simbólicamente** *adj*
simbolismo *nm* : symbolism
simbolizar {21} *vt* : to symbolize
símbolo *nm* : symbol
simetría *nf* : symmetry
simétrico, -ca *adj* : symmetrical, symmetric
simiente *nf* : seed
símil *nm* **1** : simile **2** : analogy, comparison
similar *adj* SEMEJANTE : similar, alike
similitud *nf* : similarity, resemblance
simio *nm* : ape
simpatía *nf* **1** : liking, affection ⟨tomarle simpatía a : to take a liking to⟩ **2** : warmth, friendliness **3** : support, solidarity
simpático, -ca *adj* : nice, friendly, likeable
simpatizante *nf* : sympathizer, supporter
simpatizar {21} *vi* **1** : to get along, to hit it off ⟨simpaticé mucho con él : I really liked him⟩ **2** ~ **con** : to sympathize with, to support
simple¹ *adj* **1** SENCILLO : plain, simple, easy **2** : pure, mere ⟨por simple vanidad : out of pure vanity⟩ **3** : simpleminded, foolish
simple² *n* : fool, simpleton
simplemente *adv* : simply, merely, just
simpleza *nf* **1** : foolishness **2** NECEDAD : nonsense
simplicidad *nf* : simplicity
simplificar {72} *vt* : to simplify — **simplificación** *nf*
simplista *adj* : simplistic
simposio *or* **simposium** *nm* : symposium
simulación *nf, pl* **-ciones** : simulation
simulacro *nm* : imitation, sham ⟨simulacro de juicio : mock trial⟩
simular *vt* **1** : to simulate **2** : to feign, to pretend
simultáneo, -nea *adj* : simultaneous — **simultáneamente** *adv*
sin *prep* **1** : without ⟨sin querer : unintentionally⟩ ⟨sin refinar : unrefined⟩ ⟨café sin leche : coffee without milk⟩ ⟨un vuelo sin escalas : a nonstop flight⟩ **2 sin que** : without ⟨lo hicimos sin que él se diera cuenta : we did it without him noticing⟩

sinagoga *nf* : synagogue
sinceridad *nf* : sincerity
sincero, -ra *adj* : sincere, honest, true — **sinceramente** *adv*
síncopa *nf* : syncopation
sincopar *vt* : to syncopate
sincronizar {21} *vt* : to synchronize — **sincronización** *nf*
sindical *adj* GREMIAL : union, labor ⟨representante sindical : union representative⟩
sindicalismo *nm* : unionism — **sindicalista** *nmf*
sindicalizar {21} *vt* : to unionize — **sindicalizarse** *vr* **1** : to form a union **2** : to join a union
sindicar → **sindicalizar**
sindicato *nm* GREMIO : union, guild
síndrome *nm* : syndrome ⟨síndrome de Down : Down's syndrome⟩ ⟨síndrome tóxico : poisoning⟩
síndrome premenstrual *nm* : premenstrual syndrome, PMS
sinfín *nm* : endless number ⟨un sinfín de problemas : no end of problems⟩
sinfonía *nf* : symphony
sinfónica *nf* : symphony orchestra
sinfónico, -ca *adj* : symphonic, symphony
singular¹ *adj* **1** : singular, unique **2** PARTICULAR : peculiar, odd **3** : singular (in grammar) — **singularmente** *adv*
singular² *nm* : singular
singularidad *nf* **1** : uniqueness **2** : strangeness, peculiarity
singularizar {21} *vt* : to make unique or distinct — **singularizarse** *vr* : to stand out, to distinguish oneself
siniestrado, -da *adj* : damaged, wrecked ⟨zona siniestrada : disaster zone⟩
siniestro¹, -tra *adj* **1** IZQUIERDO : left, left-hand **2** MALVADO : sinister, evil
siniestro² *nm* : accident, disaster
sinnúmero → **sinfín**
sino *conj* **1** : but, rather ⟨no será hoy, sino mañana : it won't be today, but tomorrow⟩ **2** EXCEPTO : but, except ⟨no hace sino despertar suspicacias : it does nothing but arouse suspicion⟩
sinónimo¹, -ma *adj* : synonymous
sinónimo² *nm* : synonym
sinopsis *nfs & pl* RESUMEN : synopsis, summary
sinrazón *nf, pl* **-zones** : wrong, injustice
sinsabores *nmpl* : woes, troubles
sinsonte *nm* : mockingbird
sintáctico, -ca *adj* : syntactic
sintaxis *nfs & pl* : syntax
síntesis *nfs & pl* **1** : synthesis, fusion **2** SINOPSIS : synopsis, summary
sintético, -ca *adj* : synthetic — **sintéticamente** *adv*
sintetizador *nm* : synthesizer
sintetizar {21} *vt* **1** : to synthesize **2** RESUMIR : to summarize
sintió, etc. → **sentir**

síntoma *nm* : symptom
sintomático, -ca *adj* : symptomatic
sintonía *nf* **1** : tuning in (of a radio) **2 en sintonía con** : in tune with, attuned to
sintonizador *nm* : tuner, knob for tuning (of a radio, etc.)
sintonizar {21} *vt* : to tune (in) to — *vi* **1** : to tune in **2** ∼ **con** : to be in tune with, to empathize with
sinuoso, -sa *adj* **1** : winding, sinuous **2** : devious
sinvergüenza[1] *adj* **1** DESCARADO : shameless, brazen, impudent **2** TRAVIESO : naughty
sinvergüenza[2] *nmf* **1** : rogue, scoundrel **2** : brat, rascal
sionista *adj & nmf* : Zionist — **sionismo** *nm*
siqui- → **psiqui-**
siquiera *adv* **1** : at least ⟨dame siquiera un poquito : at least give me a little bit⟩ **2** (*in negative constructions*) : not even ⟨ni siquiera nos saludaron : they didn't even say hello to us⟩
sir *nm* : sir (in titles)
sirena *nf* **1** : mermaid **2** : siren ⟨sirena de niebla : foghorn⟩
sirio, -ria *adj & n* : Syrian
sirope *nm* : syrup
sirve, etc. → **servir**
sirviente, -ta *n* : servant, maid *f*
sisear *vi* : to hiss
siseo *nm* : hiss
sísmico, -ca *adj* : seismic
sismo *nm* **1** TERREMOTO : earthquake **2** TEMBLOR : tremor
sismógrafo *nm* : seismograph
sistema *nm* **1** : system ⟨sistema nervioso : nervous system⟩ ⟨el sistema métrico : the metric system⟩ ⟨sistema solar : solar system⟩ ⟨entrar al sistema : to log in⟩ ⟨salir del sistema : to log out⟩ **2** : method ⟨trabajar con sistema : to work methodically⟩
sistemático, -ca *adj* : systematic — **sistemáticamente** *adv*
sistematizar {21} *vt* : to systematize
sistémico, -ca *adj* : systemic
sitiar *vt* ASEDIAR : to besiege
sitio *nm* **1** LUGAR : place, site ⟨vámonos a otro sitio : let's go somewhere else⟩ **2** ESPACIO : room, space ⟨hacer sitio a : to make room for⟩ **3** : siege ⟨estado de sitio : state of siege⟩ **4** *Mex* : taxi stand **5** *or* **sitio web** : site, web site
situación *nf, pl* **-ciones** : situation
situado, -da *adj* : situated, placed
situar {3} *vt* UBICAR : to place, to locate — **situarse** *vr* **1** : to be placed, to be located **2** : to make a place for oneself, to do well
skateboard [es'keitbor] *nm, pl* **skateboards** : skateboard
skateboarding [es'keitbordin] *nm* : skateboarding
sketch *nm* : sketch, skit
slider [esli'der] *nm, pl* **sliders** : slider (in baseball)
slip *nm* : briefs *pl*, underpants *pl*

smartphone ['smartfon] *nm* : smartphone
smog *nm* : smog
smoking → **esmoquin**
SMS ['ese'eme'ese, 'es'em'es] *nm, pl* **SMS** : text message
snob → **esnob**
snorkel → **esnórquel**
snowboard *nm, pl* **snowboards 1** : snowboard **2** : snowboarding
so *prep* : under ⟨so pena de : under penalty of⟩
sobaco *nm* : armpit
sobado, -da *adj* **1** : worn, shabby **2** : well-worn, hackneyed
sobar *vt* **1** : to finger, to handle **2** : to knead **3** : to rub, to massage **4** *fam* : to beat, to pummel
soberanía *nf* : sovereignty
soberano, -na *adj & n* : sovereign
soberbia *nf* **1** ORGULLO : pride, arrogance **2** MAGNIFICENCIA : magnificence
soberbio, -bia *adj* **1** : proud, arrogant **2** : grand, magnificent
sobornar *vt* : to bribe
soborno *nm* **1** : bribery **2** : bribe
sobra *nf* **1** : excess, surplus **2 de** ∼ : extra, to spare **3 sobras** *nfpl* : leftovers, scraps
sobrado, -da *adj* : abundant, excessive, more than enough
sobrante[1] *adj* : remaining, superfluous
sobrante[2] *nm* : remainder, surplus
sobrar *vi* : to be in excess, to be superfluous ⟨más vale que sobre a que falte : it's better to have too much than not enough⟩
sobre[1] *nm* **1** : envelope **2** : packet ⟨un sobre de sazón : a packet of seasoning⟩
sobre[2] *prep* **1** : on, on top of ⟨sobre la mesa : on the table⟩ ⟨apilados uno sobre otro : piled one on top of another⟩ **2** : over, above ⟨hay montañas sobre la ciudad : there are mountains above the city⟩ ⟨se inclinó sobre mí : she leaned over me⟩ ⟨temperaturas sobre los 30 grados : temperatures above 30 degrees⟩ **3** : about ⟨¿tiene libros sobre Bolivia? : do you have books on Bolivia?⟩ **4 sobre todo** : especially, above all
sobrealimentar *vt* : to overfeed
sobrecalentar {55} *vt* : to overheat — **sobrecalentarse** *vr*
sobrecama *nmf* : bedspread
sobrecarga *nf* **1** : excess weight **2** : overload
sobrecargar {52} *vt* : to overload, to overburden, to weigh down
sobrecargo *nm* : purser
sobrecogedor, -dora *adj* : shocking
sobrecoger {15} *vt* **1** : to surprise, to startle **2** : to scare — **sobrecogerse** *vr*
sobrecubierta *nf* : dust jacket
sobredosis *nfs & pl* : overdose
sobreentender {56} *vt* : to infer, to understand
sobreestimar *vt* : to overestimate, to overrate
sobreexcitado, -da *adj* : overexcited
sobreexponer {60} *vt* : to overexpose

sobregirar *vt* : to overdraw
sobregiro *nm* : overdraft
sobrehumano, -na *adj* : superhuman
sobrellevar *vt* : to endure, to bear
sobremanera *adv* : exceedingly
sobremesa *nf* : after-dinner conversation
sobrenatural *adj* : supernatural
sobrenombre *nm* APODO : nickname
sobrentender → **sobreentender**
sobrepasar *vt* : to exceed, to surpass —
sobrepasarse *vr* PASARSE : to go too far
sobrepeso *nm* 1 : excess weight 2 : overweight, obesity
sobrepoblación, sobrepoblado → **superpoblación, superpoblado**
sobreponer {60} *vt* 1 SUPERPONER : to superimpose 2 ANTEPONER : to put first, to give priority to — **sobreponerse** *vr* 1 : to pull oneself together 2 ~ **a** : to overcome
sobreprecio *nm* : surcharge
sobreprotector, -tora *adj* : overprotective
sobresaliente[1] *adj* 1 : protruding, projecting 2 : outstanding, noteworthy 3 : significant, salient
sobresaliente[2] *nmf* : understudy
sobresalir {73} *vi* 1 : to protrude, to jut out, to project 2 : to stand out, to excel
sobresaltar *vt* : to startle, to frighten — **sobresaltarse** *vr*
sobresalto *nm* : start, fright
sobresueldo *nm* : bonus, additional pay
sobretasa *nf* : surcharge ⟨sobretasa a la gasolina : gas tax⟩
sobretodo *nm* : overcoat
sobrevalorar *or* **sobrevaluar** {3} *vt* : to overrate
sobrevender *vt* : to oversell
sobrevenir {87} *vi* ACAECER : to take place, to come about ⟨podrían sobrevenir complicaciones : complications could occur⟩
sobrevivencia → **supervivencia**
sobreviviente → **superviviente**
sobrevivir *vi* : to survive — *vt* : to outlive, to outlast
sobrevolar {19} *vt* : to fly over, to overfly
sobriedad *nf* : sobriety, moderation
sobrino, -na *n* : nephew *m*, niece *f*
sobrio, -bria *adj* : sober — **sobriamente** *adv*
socarrón, -rrona *adj, mpl* **-rrones** 1 : sly, cunning 2 : sarcastic
socavar *vt* : to undermine
socavón *nm, pl* **-vones** : pothole
sociabilidad *nf* : sociability
sociable *adj* : sociable
social *adj* : social — **socialmente** *adv*
socialista *adj & nmf* : socialist — **socialismo** *nm*
socializar {21} *vt* 1 : to nationalize 2 : to socialize — *vi* : to socialize
sociedad *nf* 1 : society ⟨sociedad democrática : democratic society⟩ ⟨una sociedad secreta : a secret society⟩ 2 : company, enterprise 3 **sociedad anónima** : incorporated company
socio, -cia *n* 1 : member 2 : partner
socioeconómico, -ca *adj* : socioeconomic

sociología *nf* : sociology
sociológico, -ca *adj* : sociological — **sociológicamente** *adv*
sociólogo, -ga *n* : sociologist
socorrer *vt* : to assist, to come to the aid of
socorrido, -da *adj* ÚTIL : handy, practical
socorrismo *nm* : lifesaving
socorrista *nmf* 1 : rescue worker 2 : lifeguard
socorro *nm* AUXILIO 1 : aid, help ⟨equipo de socorro : rescue team⟩ 2 **¡socorro!** : help!
soda *nf* 1 : soda, soda water 2 *CA, Car* REFRESCO : soda, soda pop
sodio *nf* : sodium
soez *adj, pl* **soeces** GROSERO : rude, vulgar — **soezmente** *adv*
sofá *nm* : couch, sofa
sofistería *nf* : sophistry — **sofista** *nmf*
sofisticación *nf, pl* **-ciones** : sophistication
sofisticado, -da *adj* : sophisticated
sofocante *adj* : suffocating, stifling
sofocar {72} *vt* 1 AHOGAR : to suffocate, to smother 2 EXTINGUIR : to extinguish, to put out (a fire) 3 APLASTAR : to crush, to put down ⟨sofocar una rebelión : to crush a rebellion⟩ — **sofocarse** *vr* 1 : to suffocate 2 *fam* : to get upset, to get mad
sofoco *nm* : hot flash
sofreír {66} *vt* : to sauté
sofrito[1], **-ta** *adj* : sautéed
sofrito[2] *nm* : seasoning sauce
softbol *nm* : softball
software *nm* : software
soga *nf* : rope
soja → **soya**
sojuzgar *vt* : to subdue, to conquer, to subjugate
sol[1] *nm* 1 : G ⟨sol sostenido/bemol : G sharp/flat⟩ 2 : so, sol (in singing)
sol[2] *nm* 1 : sun ⟨a pleno sol : in the sun⟩ ⟨tomar el sol : to sunbathe⟩ 2 : sol (Peruvian unit of currency)
solamente *adv* SÓLO : only, just
solapa *nf* 1 : lapel (of a jacket) 2 : flap (of an envelope)
solapado, -da *adj* : secret, underhanded
solapar *vt* : to cover up, to keep secret — **solaparse** *vr* : to overlap
solar[1] {19} *vt* : to floor, to tile
solar[2] *adj* : solar, sun
solar[3] *nm* 1 TERRENO : lot, piece of land, site 2 *Cuba, Peru* : tenement building
solariego, -ga *adj* : ancestral
solaz *nm, pl* **solaces** 1 CONSUELO : solace, comfort 2 DESCANSO : relaxation, recreation
solazarse {21} *vr* : to relax, to enjoy oneself
soldado *nm* 1 : soldier 2 **soldado raso** : private, enlisted man
soldador[1], **-dora** *n* : welder
soldador[2] *nm* : soldering iron
soldadura *nf* 1 : welding 2 : soldering, solder
soldar {19} *vt* 1 : to weld 2 : to solder
soleado, -da *adj* : sunny
soledad *nf* : loneliness, solitude

solemne *adj* : solemn — **solemnemente** *adv*

solemnidad *nf* : solemnity

soler {78} *vi* : to be in the habit of, to tend to ⟨solía tomar café por la tarde : she usually drank coffee in the afternoon⟩ ⟨eso suele ocurrir : that frequently happens⟩

solera *nf* **1** : prop, support **2** : tradition

solfeo *nm* : sol-fa

solicitante *nmf* : applicant

solicitar *vt* **1** : to request, to solicit **2** : to apply for ⟨solicitar empleo : to apply for employment⟩

solícito, -ta *adj* : solicitous, attentive, obliging

solicitud *nf* **1** : solicitude, concern **2** : request **3** : application

solidaridad *nf* : solidarity

solidario, -ria *adj* : supportive, united in support ⟨se declararon solidarios con la nueva ley : they declared their support for the new law⟩ ⟨espíritu solidario : spirit of solidarity⟩

solidarizar {21} *vi* : to be in solidarity ⟨solidarizamos con la huelga : we support the strike⟩

solidez *nf* **1** : solidity, firmness **2** : soundness (of an argument, etc.)

solidificar {72} *vt* : to solidify, to make solid — **solidificarse** *vr* — **solidificación** *nf*

sólido¹, -da *adj* **1** : solid, firm **2** : sturdy, well-made **3** : sound, well-founded — **sólidamente** *adv*

sólido² *nm* : solid

soliloquio *nm* : soliloquy

solista *nmf* : soloist

solitaria *nf* TENIA : tapeworm

solitario¹, -ria *adj* **1** : lonely **2** : lone, solitary **3** DESIERTO : deserted, lonely ⟨una calle solitaria : a deserted street⟩

solitario², -ria *n* : recluse, loner

solitario³ *nm* : solitaire

sollozar {21} *vi* : to sob

sollozo *nm* : sob

solo¹, -la *adj* **1** : alone, by oneself ⟨me dejaron solo : they left me on my own⟩ ⟨lo hizo ella sola : she did it all by herself⟩ **2** : lonely **3** ÚNICO : only, sole, unique ⟨hay un solo problema : there's only one problem⟩ **4 a solas** : alone

solo² *nm* : solo

solo³ *or* **sólo** *adv* SOLAMENTE : just, only

solomillo *nm* : sirloin, loin

solsticio *nm* : solstice

soltar {19} *vt* **1** : to let go of, to drop ⟨¡suéltame el brazo! : let go of my arm!⟩ ⟨soltó las riendas : he dropped the reins⟩ **2** : to release, to set free **3** : to pay out (a rope, etc.) **4** AFLOJAR : to loosen, to slacken **5** : to undo, to untie (a knot, etc.) **6** : to give, to let out (a shout, etc.) **7** : to come out with (a swearword, etc.) — **soltarse** *vr* **1** : to get loose, to break free **2** : to come undone

soltería *nf* : state of being single

soltero¹, -ra *adj* : single, unmarried

soltero², -ra *n* **1** : bachelor *m*, single man *m*, single woman *f* **2 apellido de soltera** : maiden name

soltura *nf* **1** : looseness, slackness **2** : fluency (of language) **3** : agility, ease of movement

soluble *adj* : soluble — **solubilidad** *nf*

solución *nf, pl* **-ciones 1** : solution (in a liquid) **2** : answer, solution

solucionar *vt* RESOLVER : to solve, to resolve — **solucionarse** *vr*

solvencia *nf* **1** : solvency **2** : settling, payment (of debts) **3** : reliability ⟨solvencia moral : trustworthiness⟩

solvente¹ *adj* **1** : solvent **2** : reliable, trustworthy

solvente² *nm* : solvent

sombra *nf* **1** : shadow **2** : shade **3 sombras** *nfpl* : darkness, shadows *pl* **4 sin sombra de duda** : without a shadow of a doubt **5 sombra de ojos** : eye shadow

sombreado, -da *adj* **1** : shady **2** : shaded, darkened

sombrear *vt* : to shade

sombrerero, -ra *n* : milliner, hatter

sombrero *nm* **1** : hat **2 sin ~** : bareheaded **3 sombrero hongo** : derby

sombrilla *nf* : parasol, umbrella

sombrío, -bría *adj* LÓBREGO : dark, somber, gloomy — **sombríamente** *adv*

somero, -ra *adj* : superficial, cursory, shallow

someter *vt* **1** : to subjugate, to conquer **2** : to subordinate **3** : to subject (to treatment or testing) **4** : to submit, to present ⟨lo someterán a votación : they will put it to a vote⟩ ⟨someter a la justicia : to bring to justice⟩ — **someterse** *vr* **1** : to submit, to yield **2** : to undergo

sometimiento *nm* **1** : submission, subjection **2** : presentation

somier *nm, pl* **somieres** *or* **somiers** : box spring

somnífero¹, -ra *adj* : soporific

somnífero² *nm* : sleeping pill

somnolencia *nf* : drowsiness, sleepiness

somnoliento, -ta *adj* : drowsy, sleepy

somorgujo *or* **somormujo** *nm* : loon, grebe

somos → **ser**

son¹ → **ser**

son² *nm* **1** : sound ⟨al son de la trompeta : at the sound of the trumpet⟩ **2** : news, rumor **3 en son de** : as, in the manner of, by way of ⟨en son de broma : as a joke⟩ ⟨en son de paz : in peace⟩

sonado, -da *adj* : celebrated, famous, much-discussed

sonaja *nf* : rattle

sonajero *nm* : rattle (toy)

sonambulismo *nm* : sleepwalking

sonámbulo, -la *n* : sleepwalker

sonante *adj* **dinero contante y sonante** → **dinero**

sonar¹ {19} *vi* **1** : to sound ⟨suena bien : it sounds good⟩ ⟨sonaba contenta : she sounded happy⟩ **2** : to sound, to ring (of bells, a phone, etc.), to go off (of an alarm), to ring out (of shots), to play (of music) **3** : to be pronounced (of a letter) **4** : to look or sound familiar ⟨me suena ese nombre : that name rings a bell⟩ **5** : to fly (of rumors), to be talked about ⟨suena para reemplazar a Díaz : there is talk that he might replace Díaz⟩ **6 ~ a** : to sound like — *vt* **1** : to ring **2** : to blow (a trumpet, a nose) — **sonarse** *vr* : to blow one's nose

sonar² *nm* : sonar

sonata *nf* : sonata

sonda *nf* **1** : sounding line **2** : probe **3** CATÉTER : catheter

sondar *vt* **1** : to sound, to probe (in medicine, drilling, etc.) **2** : to probe, to explore (outer space)

sondear *vt* **1** : to sound **2** : to probe **3** : to sound out, to test (opinions, markets)

sondeo *nm* **1** : sounding, probing **2** : drilling **3** ENCUESTA : survey, poll

soneto *nm* : sonnet

sónico, -ca *adj* : sonic

sonido *nm* : sound

sonoridad *nf* : resonance

sonoro, -ra *adj* **1** : resonant, sonorous, voiced (in linguistics) **2** : resounding, loud **3 banda sonora** : soundtrack

sonreír {66} *vi* : to smile

sonriente *adj* : smiling

sonrisa *nf* : smile

sonrojar *vt* : to cause to blush — **sonrojarse** *vr* : to blush

sonrojo *nm* RUBOR : blush

sonrosado, -da *adj* : rosy, pink

sonsacar {72} *vt* : to wheedle, to extract

sonsonete *nm* **1** : tapping **2** : drone **3** : mocking tone

soñador¹, -dora *adj* : dreamy

soñador², -dora *n* : dreamer

soñar {19} *v* **1** : to dream **2 ~ con** : to dream about **3 soñar despierto** : to daydream

soñoliento, -ta *adj* : sleepy, drowsy

sopa *nf* **1** : soup **2 estar hecho una sopa** : to be soaked to the bone

sopapa *nm Arg* : plunger (for toilets, etc.)

sopapo *nm fam* : slap

sopera *nf* : soup tureen

sopesar *vt* : to weigh, to evaluate

soplar *vi* : to blow — *vt* : to blow on, to blow out, to blow off

soplete *nm* : blowtorch

soplido *nm* : puff

soplo *nm* : puff, gust

soplón, -plona *n, mpl* **soplones** *fam* : tattletale, sneak

soponcio *nm fam* **1** : fainting spell ⟨sufrió un soponcio : he fainted⟩ **2** : shock, fit ⟨cuando se enteró le dio un/el soponcio : when he found out, he was horrified⟩

sopor *nm* SOMNOLENCIA : drowsiness, sleepiness

soporífero, -ra *adj* : soporific

soportable *adj* : bearable, tolerable

soportar *vt* **1** SOSTENER : to support, to hold up **2** RESISTIR : to withstand, to resist **3** AGUANTAR : to bear, to tolerate

soporte *nm* : base, stand, support

soprano *nmf* : soprano

sor *nf* : Sister (religious title)

sorber *vt* **1** : to sip, to suck in **2** : to absorb, to soak up

sorbete *nm* : sherbet

sorbo *nm* **1** : sip, gulp, swallow **2 beber a sorbos** : to sip

sordera *nf* : deafness

sórdido, -da *adj* : sordid, dirty, squalid

sordina *nf* : mute (for a musical instrument)

sordo, -da *adj* **1** : deaf **2** : muted, muffled

sordomudo, -da *n offensive* : deaf-mute *often offensive*

sorgo *nm* : sorghum

soriasis *nfs & pl* : psoriasis

sorna *nf* : sarcasm, mocking tone

soroche *nm Peru* : altitude sickness

sorprendente *adj* : surprising — **sorprendentemente** *adv*

sorprender *vt* : to surprise — **sorprenderse** *vr*

sorpresa *nf* : surprise

sorpresivo, -va *adj* **1** : surprising, surprise **2** IMPREVISTO : sudden, unexpected

sortear *vt* **1** RIFAR : to raffle, to draw lots for **2** : to dodge, to avoid

sorteo *nm* : drawing, raffle

sortija *nf* **1** ANILLO : ring **2** : curl, ringlet

sortilegio *nm* **1** HECHIZO : spell, charm **2** HECHICERÍA : sorcery

SOS *nm* : SOS

sosegado, -da *adj* SERENO : calm, tranquil, serene

sosegar {49} *vt* : to calm, to pacify — **sosegarse** *vr*

sosiego *nm* : tranquillity, serenity, calm

soslayar *vt* ESQUIVAR : to dodge, to evade

soslayo *nm* **de ~** : obliquely, sideways ⟨mirar de soslayo⟩ : to look askance⟩

soso, -sa *adj* **1** INSÍPIDO : bland, flavorless **2** ABURRIDO : dull, boring

sospecha *nf* : suspicion

sospechar *vt* : to suspect — *vi* : to be suspicious

sospechosamente *adv* : suspiciously

sospechoso¹, -sa *adj* : suspicious, suspect

sospechoso², -sa *n* : suspect

sostén *nm, pl* **sostenes** **1** APOYO : support **2** : sustenance **3** : brassiere, bra

sostener {80} *vt* **1** : to support, to hold up **2** : to hold ⟨sostenme la puerta : hold the door for me⟩ ⟨sostener una conversación : to hold a conversation⟩ **3** : to sustain, to maintain — **sostenerse** *vr* **1** : to stand, to hold oneself up **2** : to continue, to remain

sostenible *adj* : sustainable, tenable — **sostenibilidad** *nf*

sostenido¹, -da *adj* **1** : sustained, prolonged **2** : sharp (in music)

sostenido² *nm* : sharp (in music)

sostuvo, etc. → **sostener**

sota *nf* : jack (in the Spanish deck of cards)

sotana *nf* : cassock

sótano *nm* : basement

sotavento *nm* : lee ⟨a sotavento : leeward⟩

soterrar {55} *vt* **1** : to bury **2** : to conceal, to hide away

soto *nm* : grove, copse
souvenir *nm, pl* **-nirs** RECUERDO : souvenir, memento
soviético, -ca *adj* : Soviet
soy → **ser**
soya *nf* : soy, soybean
spaghetti → **espagueti**
spam *nm, pl* **spams** : spam (e-mail)
spaniel *nm, pl* **spaniels** : spaniel
SPM → **síndrome premenstrual**
sport [ɛ'spor] *adj* : sport, casual
sprint [ɛ'sprin, -'sprint] *nm* : sprint —
sprinter *nmf*
squash [ɛ'skwaʃ, -'skwatʃ] *nm* : squash
(sport)
Sr. *nm* : Mr.
Sra. *nf* : Mrs., Ms.
Srta. *or* **Srita.** *nf* : Miss, Ms.
staccato *adj* : staccato
stand *nm, pl* **stands** : stand, kiosk
standard → **estándar**
statu quo *nm* : status quo
stop [es'top] *nm* : stop sign
streaming ['strimin] *nm* : streaming (of
audio, video, etc.) ⟨un streaming en vivo
: a livestream⟩
stress → **estrés**
su *adj* **1** : his, her, its, their, one's ⟨su libro : her book⟩ ⟨sus consecuencias : its
consequences⟩ **2** (*formal*) : your
⟨tómese su medicina, señor : take your
medicine, sir⟩
suave *adj* **1** BLANDO : soft **2** LISO
: smooth **3** : gentle, mild **4** *Mex fam*
: great, fantastic
suavemente *adj* : smoothly, gently, softly
suavidad *nf* : softness, smoothness, mellowness
suavizante *nm* : softener, fabric softener
suavizar {21} *vt* **1** : to soften, to smooth
out **2** : to tone down — **suavizarse** *vr*
sub- *pref* : sub-
subacuático, -ca *adj* : underwater
subalterno[1], -na *adj* **1** SUBORDINADO
: subordinate **2** SECUNDARIO : secondary
subalterno[2], -na *n* SUBORDINADO : subordinate
subarrendar {55} *vt* : to sublet
subasta *nf* : auction
subastador, -dora *n* : auctioneer
subastar *vt* : to auction, to auction off
subcampeón, -peona *n, mpl* **-peones**
: runner-up
subcomisión *nf, pl* **-siones** : subcommittee
subcomité *nm* : subcommittee
subconsciente *adj & nm* : subconscious
— **subconscientemente** *adv*
subcontratar *vt* : to subcontract
subcontratista *nmf* : subcontractor
subcultura *nf* : subculture
subdesarrollado, -da *adj* : underdeveloped
subdesarrollo *nm* : underdevelopment
subdirector, -tora *n* : assistant manager
súbdito, -ta *n* : subject (of a monarch)
subdividir *vt* : to subdivide
subdivisión *nf, pl* **-siones** : subdivision
subestimar *vt* : to underestimate, to undervalue

subexponer {60} *vt* : to underexpose
subexposición *nf, pl* **-ciones** : underexposure
subgrupo *nm* : subgroup
subibaja *nm* : seesaw
subida *nf* **1** : ascent, climb **2** : rise, increase **3** : slope, hill ⟨ir de subida : to go
uphill⟩
subido, -da *adj* **1** : intense, strong ⟨amarillo subido : bright yellow⟩ **2** **subido
de tono** : risqué
subir *vt* **1** : to bring/take/carry up, to lift
up **2** : to climb, to go/come up (stairs,
etc.) **3** : to raise (a blind, etc.), to pull
up (a zipper, etc.), to take up (a hem) **4**
AUMENTAR : to raise (prices, etc.) ⟨subir
el volumen : to turn up the volume⟩ **5**
CARGAR : to upload — *vi* **1** : to go/
come up **2** AUMENTAR : to rise, to increase **3** : to be promoted **4** ∼ **a** : to
get on, to mount ⟨subir a un tren : to get
on a train⟩ — **subirse** *vr* **1** : to climb
(up) **2** : to pull up (clothing) **3** **subirse
a la cabeza** : to go to one's head
súbito, -ta *adj* **1** REPENTINO : sudden **2**
de ∼ : all of a sudden, suddenly —
súbitamente *adv*
subjetivo, -va *adj* : subjective — **subjetivamente** *adv* — **subjetividad** *nf*
subjuntivo[1], -va *adj* : subjunctive
subjuntivo[2] *nm* : subjunctive
sublevación *nf, pl* **-ciones** ALZAMIENTO
: uprising, rebellion
sublevar *vt* : to incite to rebellion — **sublevarse** *vr* : to rebel, to rise up
sublimar *vt* : to sublimate — **sublimación** *nf*
sublime *adj* : sublime
submarinismo *nm* : scuba diving
submarinista *nmf* : scuba diver
submarino[1], -na *adj* : submarine, undersea
submarino[2] *nm* : submarine
subnormal[1] *adj* **1** *usu offensive* : mentally handicapped *sometimes offensive* **2**
: idiotic
subnormal[2] *nmf* **1** *usu offensive* : mentally handicapped person **2** : moron,
idiot
suboficial *nmf* : noncommissioned officer, petty officer
subordinado, -da *adj & n* : subordinate
subordinar *vt* : to subordinate — **subordinarse** *vr* — **subordinación** *nf*
subproducto *nm* : by-product
subrayar *vt* **1** : to underline, to underscore **2** ENFATIZAR : to highlight, to
emphasize
subrepticio, -cia *adj* : surreptitious —
subrepticiamente *adv*
subsanar *vt* **1** RECTIFICAR : to rectify, to
correct **2** : to overlook, to excuse **3**
: to make up for
subscribir → **suscribir**
subsecretario, -ria *n* : undersecretary
subsecuente *adj* : subsequent — **subsecuentemente** *adv*
subsidiar *vt* : to subsidize
subsidiaria *nf* : subsidiary
subsidio *nm* : subsidy

subsiguiente *adj* : subsequent
subsistencia *nf* **1** : subsistence **2** : sustenance
subsistir *vi* **1** : to subsist, to live **2** : to endure, to survive
substancia → **sustancia**
subte *nm Arg, Uru* : subway
subteniente *nmf* : second lieutenant
subterfugio *nm* : subterfuge
subterráneo¹, -nea *adj* : underground, subterranean
subterráneo² *nm* **1** : underground passage, tunnel **2** *Arg, Uru* : subway
subtitular *vt* : to subtitle
subtítulo *nm* : subtitle, subheading
subtotal *nm* : subtotal
suburbano, -na *adj* : suburban
suburbio *nm* **1** : suburb **2** : slum (outside a city)
subvención *nf, pl* **-ciones** : subsidy, grant
subvencionar *vt* : to subsidize
subversivo, -va *adj & n* : subversive — **subversión** *nf*
subvertir {76} *vt* : to subvert
subyacente *adj* : underlying
subyacer *vi* ∼ **en/a** : to underlie
subyugar {52} *vt* : to subjugate — **subyugación** *nf*
succión *nf, pl* **succiones** : suction
succionar *vt* : to suck up, to draw in
sucedáneo *nm* : substitute ⟨sucedáneo de azúcar : sugar substitute⟩
suceder *vi* **1** OCURRIR : to happen, to occur ⟨¿qué sucede? : what's going on?⟩ ⟨suceda lo que suceda : come what may⟩ **2** ∼ **a** : to follow, to succeed ⟨a la primavera sucede el verano : summer follows spring⟩ — *vt* : to succeed ⟨suceder a alguien : to succeed someone⟩
sucesión *nf, pl* **-siones** **1** : succession **2** : sequence, series **3** : issue, heirs *pl* **4** : estate, inheritance
sucesivamente *adv* : successively, consecutively ⟨y así sucesivamente : and so on⟩
sucesivo, -va *adj* : successive ⟨en los días sucesivos : in the days that followed⟩
suceso *nm* **1** : event, happening, occurrence **2** : incident, crime
sucesor, -sora *n* : successor
suciedad *nf* **1** : dirtiness, filthiness **2** MUGRE : dirt, filth
sucinto, -ta *adj* CONCISO : succinct, concise — **sucintamente** *adv*
sucio, -cia *adj* : dirty, filthy
sucre *nm* : Ecuadoran unit of currency
suculento, -ta *adj* : succulent
sucumbir *vi* : to succumb
sucursal *nf* : branch (of a business)
sudadera *nf* **1** : sweatshirt **2** : sweatsuit, tracksuit
sudado, -da → **sudoroso**
sudafricano, -na *adj & n* : South African
sudamericano, -na *adj & n* : South American
sudanés, -nesa *adj & n, mpl* **-neses** : Sudanese
sudar *vi* TRANSPIRAR : to sweat, to perspire
sudario *nm* : shroud

sudeste → **sureste**
sudoeste → **suroeste**
sudor *nm* TRANSPIRACIÓN : sweat, perspiration
sudoroso, -sa *adj* : sweaty
sueco¹, -ca *adj* : Swedish
sueco², -ca *n* : Swede
sueco³ *nm* : Swedish (language)
suegro, -gra *n* **1** : father-in-law *m*, mother-in-law *f* **2 suegros** *nmpl* : in-laws
suela *nf* : sole (of a shoe)
suelda, etc. → **soldar**
sueldo *nm* : salary, wage
suele, etc. → **soler**
suelo *nm* **1** : ground ⟨caerse al suelo : to fall down, to hit the ground⟩ **2** : floor, flooring **3** TIERRA : soil, land
suelta, etc. → **soltar**
suelto¹, -ta *adj* **1** : loose, free, unattached ⟨dinero suelto : loose change⟩ ⟨una camisa suelta : a loose shirt⟩ ⟨cabos sueltos : loose ends⟩ ⟨el perro estaba suelto : the dog was loose⟩ ⟨un papelito suelto : a scrap of paper⟩ ⟨con el pelo suelto : with one's hair down⟩ **2** : individual, separate, odd ⟨¿las venden sueltas? : do they sell them individually?⟩ **3** : fluent, fluid
suelto² *nm* : loose change
suena, etc. → **sonar**
sueña, etc. → **soñar**
sueño *nm* **1** : dream **2** : sleep ⟨perder el sueño : to lose sleep⟩ **3** : sleepiness ⟨tener sueño : to be sleepy⟩
suero *nm* **1** : serum **2** : whey **3 suero de mantequilla/manteca** : buttermilk
suerte *nf* **1** FORTUNA : luck, fortune ⟨tener suerte : to be lucky⟩ ⟨estar de suerte : to be in luck⟩ ⟨le deseo suerte : I wish him luck⟩ ⟨¡buena suerte! : good luck!⟩ ⟨por suerte : luckily⟩ ⟨con suerte : with any luck⟩ ⟨traer mala suerte : to be/bring bad luck⟩ ⟨fue una suerte que . . . : it's a lucky thing that . . .⟩ **2** DESTINO : fate, destiny, lot ⟨tentar a la suerte : to tempt fate⟩ ⟨la dejaron a su suerte : they left her to her fate⟩ ⟨correr la misma suerte : to meet the same fate⟩ **3** CLASE, GÉNERO : sort, kind ⟨toda suerte de cosas : all kinds of things⟩
suertudo¹, -da *adj fam* : lucky
suertudo², -da *n fam* : lucky person
suéter *nm* : sweater
suficiencia *nf* **1** : adequacy **2** : competence, fitness **3** : self-satisfaction
suficiente *adj* **1** BASTANTE : enough, sufficient ⟨tener suficiente : to have enough⟩ **2** : suitable, fit **3** : smug, complacent
suficientemente *adv* : sufficiently, enough
sufijo *nm* : suffix
suflé *nm* : soufflé
sufragar {52} *vt* **1** AYUDAR : to help out, to support **2** : to defray (costs) — *vi* : to vote
sufragio *nm* : suffrage, vote
sufrido, -da *adj* **1** : long-suffering, patient **2** : sturdy, serviceable (of clothing)

sufrimiento *nm* : suffering
sufrir *vt* **1** : to suffer ⟨sufrir una pérdida : to suffer a loss⟩ **2** : to tolerate, to put up with ⟨ella no lo puede sufrir : she can't stand him⟩ — *vi* : to suffer
sugerencia *nf* : suggestion
sugerente *adj* **1** : suggestive (of words, etc.), revealing (of clothes) **2** : intriguing, provocative
sugerir {76} *vt* **1** PROPONER, RECOMENDAR : to suggest, to recommend, to propose **2** : to suggest, to bring to mind
sugestión *nf, pl* **-tiones** : suggestion, prompting ⟨poder de sugestión : power of suggestion⟩
sugestionable *adj* : suggestible, impressionable
sugestionar *vt* : to influence, to sway — **sugestionarse** *vr* ~ **con** : to talk oneself into, to become convinced of
sugestivo, -va *adj* **1** : suggestive **2** : interesting, stimulating
suicida¹ *adj* : suicidal
suicida² *nmf* : suicide victim, suicide
suicidarse *vr* : to commit suicide
suicidio *nm* : suicide
suite *nf* : suite
suizo, -za *adj & n* : Swiss
sujeción *nf, pl* **-ciones 1** : holding, fastening **2** : subjection
sujetador *nm* **1** : fastener **2** : holder ⟨sujetador de tazas : cup holder⟩
sujetalibros *nms & pl* : bookend
sujetapapeles *nms & pl* CLIP : paper clip
sujetar *vt* **1** : to hold on to, to steady, to hold down **2** FIJAR : to fasten, to attach **3** DOMINAR : to subdue, to conquer — **sujetarse** *vr* **1** : to hold on, to hang on **2** ~ **a** : to abide by
sujeto¹, -ta *adj* **1** : secure, fastened **2** ~ **a** : subject to
sujeto² *nm* **1** INDIVIDUO : individual, character **2** : subject (in grammar)
sulfúrico, -ca *adj* **ácido sulfúrico** → **ácido²**
sulfuro *nm* : sulfur
sultán *nm, pl* **sultanes** : sultan
suma *nf* **1** CANTIDAD : sum, quantity **2** : addition
sumamente *adv* : extremely, exceedingly
sumar *vt* **1** : to add, to add up **2** : to add up to, to total — *vi* : to add up — **sumarse** *vr* ~ **a** : to join
sumariamente *adv* : summarily
sumario¹, -ria *adj* SUCINTO : succinct, summary
sumario² *nm* : summary
sumergible *adj* : waterproof
sumergir {35} *vt* : to submerge, to immerse, to plunge — **sumergirse** *vr*
sumersión *nf, pl* **-siones** : submerging, immersion
sumidero *nm* : drain, sewer
suministrar *vt* : to supply, to provide
suministro *nm* : supply, provision
sumir *vt* SUMERGIR : to plunge, to immerse, to sink — **sumirse** *vr*
sumisión *nf, pl* **-siones 1** : submission **2** : submissiveness

sumiso, -sa *adj* : submissive, acquiescent, docile
sumo, -ma *adj* **1** : extreme, great, high ⟨la suma autoridad : the highest authority⟩ **2 a lo sumo** : at the most
sunita *nmf* : Sunni
suntuoso, -sa *adj* : sumptuous, lavish — **suntuosamente** *adv*
supeditar *vt* SUBORDINAR : to subordinate — **supeditación** *nf*
super¹ *or* **súper** *adj fam* : super, great
super² *nm* SUPERMERCADO : market, supermarket
super- *pref* : super-
superabundancia *nf* : overabundance — **superabundante** *adj*
superación *nf, pl* **-ciones** : surpassing, overcoming
superar *vt* **1** : to surpass, to exceed **2** : to overcome, to surmount — **superarse** *vr* : to improve oneself
superávit *nm, pl* **-vit** *or* **-vits** : surplus
superchería *nf* : trickery, fraud
supercomputadora *nf* : supercomputer
superdotado, -da *n* : a very talented person
superestrella *nf* : superstar
superestructura *nf* : superstructure
superficial *adj* : superficial — **superficialmente** *adv*
superficialidad *nf* : superficiality
superficie *nf* **1** : surface **2** : area ⟨la superficie de un triángulo : the area of a triangle⟩
superfluo, -flua *adj* : superfluous — **superfluidad** *nf*
superintendente *nmf* : supervisor, superintendent
superior¹ *adj* **1** : superior **2** : upper ⟨nivel superior : upper level⟩ **3** : higher ⟨educación superior : higher education⟩ **4** ~ **a** : above, higher than, in excess of
superior² *nm* : superior
superioridad *nf* : superiority
superlativo¹, -va *adj* : superlative
superlativo² *nm* : superlative
supermercado *nm* : supermarket
superpoblación *nf, pl* **-ciones** : overpopulation
superpoblado, -da *adj* : overpopulated
superponer {60} *vt* : to superimpose
superpotencia *nf* : superpower
superproducción → **sobreproducción**
supersónico, -ca *adj* : supersonic
superstición *nf, pl* **-ciones** : superstition
supersticioso, -sa *adj* : superstitious
supervisar *vt* : to supervise, to oversee
supervisión *nf, pl* **-siones** : supervision
supervisor, -sora *n* : supervisor, overseer
supervivencia *nf* : survival
superviviente *nmf* : survivor
supino, -na *adj* : supine
suplantación *nf, pl* **-ciones** : supplanting, replacement ⟨suplantación de identidad : identity theft⟩
suplantar *vt* : to supplant, to replace
suplemental → **suplementario**
suplementario, -ria *adj* : supplementary, additional, extra

suplemento *nm* : supplement

suplencia *nf* : substitution, replacement

suplente *adj & nmf* : substitute ⟨equipo suplente : replacement team⟩

supletorio, -ria *adj* : extra, additional ⟨teléfono supletorio : extension phone⟩ ⟨cama supletoria : spare bed⟩

súplica *nf* : plea, entreaty

suplicar {72} *vt* IMPLORAR, ROGAR : to entreat, to implore, to supplicate

suplicio *nm* TORMENTO : ordeal, torture

suplir *vt* **1** COMPENSAR : to make up for, to compensate for **2** REEMPLAZAR : to replace, to substitute

supo, etc. → **saber**

suponer {60} *vt* **1** PRESUMIR : to suppose, to assume ⟨supongo que sí : I guess so, I suppose so⟩ ⟨se supone que van a llegar mañana : they're supposed to arrive tomorrow⟩ **2** : to imply, to suggest **3** : to involve, to entail ⟨el éxito supone mucho trabajo : success involves a lot of work⟩

suposición *nf, pl* **-ciones** PRESUNCIÓN : supposition, assumption

supositorio *nm* : suppository

supremacía *nf* : supremacy

supremo, -ma *adj* : supreme

supresión *nf, pl* **-siones** **1** : suppression, elimination **2** : deletion

suprimir *vt* **1** : to suppress, to eliminate **2** : to delete

supuestamente *adv* : supposedly, allegedly

supuesto, -ta *adj* **1** : supposed, alleged ⟨los supuestos expertos : the supposed experts⟩ ⟨un nombre supuesto : an assumed name⟩ **2 por ~** : of course, absolutely

supurar *vi* : to ooze, to discharge

supuso, etc. → **suponer**

sur[1] *adj* : southern, southerly, south

sur[2] *nm* **1** : south, South **2** : south wind

surafricano, -na → **sudafricano**

suramericano, -na → **sudamericano**

surcar {72} *vt* **1** : to plow (through) **2** : to groove, to score, to furrow

surco *nm* : groove, furrow, rut

sureño[1]**, -ña** *adj* : southern, Southern

sureño[2]**, -ña** *n* : Southerner

sureste[1] *adj* **1** : southeast, southeastern **2** : southeasterly

sureste[2] *nm* : southeast, Southeast

surf *nm* : surfing

surfear *vi* : to surf

surfing → **surf**

surfista *nmf* : surfer

surgimiento *nm* : rise, emergence

surgir {35} *vi* : to rise, to arise, to emerge

suroeste[1] *adj* **1** : southwest, southwestern **2** : southwesterly

suroeste[2] *nm* : southwest, Southwest

surrealismo *nm* : surrealism

surrealista[1] *adj* : surreal, surrealistic

surrealista[2] *nmf* : surrealist

surtido[1]**, -da** *adj* **1** : assorted, varied **2** : stocked, provisioned

surtido[2] *nm* : assortment, selection

surtidor *nm* **1** : jet, spout **2** *Arg, Chile, Spain* : gas pump

surtir *vt* **1** : to supply, to provide ⟨surtir un pedido : to fill an order⟩ **2 surtir efecto** : to have an effect — *vi* : to spout, to spurt up — **surtirse** *vr* : to stock up

susceptible *adj* : susceptible, sensitive — **susceptibilidad** *nf*

suscitar *vt* : to provoke, to give rise to

suscribir {33} *vt* **1** : to sign (a formal document) **2** : to endorse, to sanction — **suscribirse** *vr* ~ **a** : to subscribe to

suscripción *nf, pl* **-ciones** **1** : subscription **2** : endorsement, sanction **3** : signing

suscriptor, -tora *n* : subscriber

susodicho, -cha *adj* : aforementioned, aforesaid

suspender *vt* **1** COLGAR : to suspend, to hang **2** : to suspend, to discontinue **3** : to suspend, to dismiss

suspense *nm Spain* → **suspenso**

suspensión *nf, pl* **-siones** : suspension

suspenso *nm* : suspense

suspensores *nmpl Chile* : suspenders

suspicacia *nf* : suspicion, mistrust

suspicaz *adj, pl* **-caces** DESCONFIADO : suspicious, wary

suspirar *vi* : to sigh

suspiro *nm* : sigh

surque, etc. → **surcar**

suscrito *pp* → **suscribir**

sustancia *nf* **1** : substance **2 sin ~** : shallow, lacking substance

sustancial *adj* **1** : substantial **2** ESENCIAL, FUNDAMENTAL : essential, fundamental — **sustancialmente** *adv*

sustancioso, -sa *adj* **1** NUTRITIVO : hearty, nutritious **2** : substantial, solid

sustantivo *nm* : noun

sustentación *nf, pl* **-ciones** SOSTÉN : support

sustentar *vt* **1** : to support, to hold up **2** : to sustain, to nourish **3** : to maintain, to hold (an opinion) — **sustentarse** *vr* : to support oneself

sustento *nm* **1** : means of support, livelihood **2** : sustenance, food

sustitución *nf, pl* **-ciones** : replacement, substitution

sustituir {41} *vt* **1** : to replace, to substitute for **2** : to stand in for

sustituto, -ta *n* : substitute, stand-in

susto *nm* : fright, scare

sustracción *nf, pl* **-ciones** **1** RESTA : subtraction **2** : theft

sustraer {81} *vt* **1** : to remove, to take away **2** RESTAR : to subtract **3** : to steal — **sustraerse** *vr* ~ **a** : to avoid, to evade

susurrar *vi* **1** : to whisper **2** : to murmur **3** : to rustle (leaves, etc.) — *vt* : to whisper

susurro *nm* **1** : whisper **2** : murmur **3** : rustle, rustling

sutil *adj* **1** : delicate, thin, fine **2** : subtle — **sutilmente** *adv*

sutileza *nf* **1** : delicacy **2** : subtlety

sutura *nf* : suture, stitch

SUV [esuˈbi, esjuˈ-] *nm, pl* **SUV** *or* **SUVs** [esuˈbis, esjuˈ-] : SUV

suyo¹, -ya *adj* **1** : his, her, its, theirs ⟨los libros suyos : his books⟩ ⟨un amigo suyo : a friend of hers⟩ ⟨esta casa es suya : this house is theirs⟩ **2** (*formal*) : yours ⟨¿este abrigo es suyo, señor? : is this your coat, sir?⟩

suyo², -ya *pron* **1** : his, hers, theirs ⟨mi guitarra y la suya : my guitar and hers⟩ ⟨ellos trajeron las suyas : they brought theirs, they brought their own⟩ **2** (*formal*) : yours ⟨usted olvidó la suya : you forgot yours⟩

switch *nm* : switch

T

t *nf* : twenty-third letter of the Spanish alphabet

taba *nf* : anklebone

tabacalero¹, -ra *adj* : tobacco ⟨industria tabacalera : tobacco industry⟩

tabacalero², -ra *n* : tobacco grower

tabaco *nm* : tobacco

tábano *nm* : horsefly

tabaquería *nf* : tobacco shop

tabaquismo *nm* **tabaquismo pasivo** : passive smoking

taberna *nf* : tavern, bar

tabernáculo *nm* : tabernacle

tabernero, -ra *n* **1** : bar owner **2** : bartender

tabicar {72} *vt* : to wall up

tabique *nm* : thin wall, partition

tabla *nf* **1** : table, list ⟨tabla de multiplicar : multiplication table⟩ **2** : board, plank, slab ⟨tabla de planchar : ironing board⟩ **3** : plot, strip (of land) **4** : box pleat **5 tablas** *nfpl* : stage, boards *pl*

tablado *nm* **1** : floor **2** : platform, scaffold **3** : stage

tablao *nm* : flamenco bar

tablero *nm* **1** : bulletin board **2** : board (in games) ⟨tablero de ajedrez : chessboard⟩ ⟨tablero de damas : checkerboard⟩ ⟨tablero de circuitos : circuit board⟩ **3** PIZARRA : blackboard **4** : switchboard **5 tablero de instrumentos** : dashboard, instrument panel

tablet → **tableta**

tableta *nf* **1** COMPRIMIDO, PÍLDORA : tablet, pill **2** : bar (of chocolate) **3** : tablet (computer)

tabletear *vi* : to rattle, to clack

tableteo *nm* : clack, rattling

tablilla *nf* **1** : small board or tablet **2** : bulletin board **3** : splint

tabloide *nm* : tabloid

tablón *nm, pl* **tablones 1** : plank, beam **2 tablón de anuncios** : bulletin board

tabú¹ *adj* : taboo

tabú² *nm, pl* **tabúes** *or* **tabús** : taboo

tabulador *nm* **1** : tabulator **2** : tab, tab key

tabular¹ *vt* : to tabulate

tabular² *adj* : tabular

taburete *nm* : footstool, stool

tacañería *nf* : stinginess

tacaño¹, -ña *adj* MEZQUINO : stingy, miserly

tacaño², -ña *n* : miser, tightwad

tacha *nf* **1** : flaw, blemish, defect **2 poner tacha a** : to find fault with **3 sin ∼** : flawless

tachadura *nf* : erasure, correction

tachar *vt* **1** : to cross out, to delete **2 ∼ de** : to accuse of, to label as ⟨lo tacharon de mentiroso : they accused him of being a liar⟩

tacho *nm* *Arg, Chile, Ecua, Peru, Uru* **1** : wastebasket **2 ∼ de (la) basura** : garbage can

tachón *nm, pl* **tachones** : stud, hobnail

tachonar *vt* : to stud

tachuela *nf* : tack, hobnail, stud

tácito, -ta *adj* : tacit, implicit — **tácitamente** *adv*

taciturno, -na *adj* **1** : taciturn **2** : sullen, gloomy

tacle *nm* : tackle

tacleada *nf* : tackle (in football)

taclear *vt* : to tackle (in football)

taco *nm* **1** : wad, stopper, plug **2** : pad (of paper) **3** : cleat **4** : heel (of a shoe) **5** : cue (in billiards) **6** : light snack, bite **7** : taco

tacón *nm, pl* **tacones** : heel (of a shoe) ⟨de tacón alto : high-heeled⟩

taconazo *nm* **1** PATADA : (heel) kick **2** : stamp, heel tap ⟨dar un taconazo : to click one's heels⟩

táctica *nf* : tactic, tactics *pl*

táctico, -ca *adj* : tactical

táctil *adj* : tactile

tacto *nm* **1** : touch, touching, feel **2** DELICADEZA : tact

tafeta *nf* *Arg, Mex, Uru* : taffeta

tafetán *nm, pl* **-tanes** : taffeta

tahúr *nm, pl* **tahúres** : gambler

tailandés¹, -desa *adj & n, pl* **-deses** : Thai

tailandés² *nm* : Thai (language)

taimado, -da *adj* **1** : crafty, sly **2** *Chile* : sullen, sulky

tajada *nf* **1** : slice **2 sacar tajada** *fam* : to get one's share

tajante *adj* **1** : cutting, sharp **2** : decisive, categorical

tajantemente *adj* : emphatically, categorically

tajar *vt* : to cut, to slice

tajear *vt* **1** : to cut **2** : to hack, to slash

tajo *nm* **1** : cut, slash, gash **2** ESCARPA : steep cliff

tal¹ *adv* **1** : so, in such a way **2 tal como** : just as ⟨tal como lo hice : just the way I did it⟩ **3 con tal que** : provided that, as long as **4 ¿qué tal?** : how are you?, how's it going?

tal² *adj* **1** : such, such a ⟨a tal grado : to such a degree⟩ ⟨de tal manera que : such that, in such a way that⟩ ⟨¡yo no dije tal cosa! : I said no such thing!⟩ **2** (*indicating an unspecified person or thing*) ⟨en tal día, a tal hora : on such and such a day at such and such a time⟩ ⟨un tal Pérez : a Mr. Pérez, some guy named Pérez⟩ **3 tal vez** : maybe, perhaps

tal³ *pron* **1** : such a one, someone **2** : such a thing, something **3 tal para cual** : two of a kind

tala *nf* : felling (of trees)

taladradora *nf* : jackhammer

taladrar *vt* : to drill

taladro *nm* : drill, auger ⟨taladro eléctrico : power drill⟩

talante *nm* **1** HUMOR : mood, disposition **2** VOLUNTAD : will, willingness

talar *vt* **1** : to cut down, to fell **2** DEVASTAR : to devastate, to destroy

talco *nm* **1** : talc **2** : talcum powder

talego *nm* : sack

talento *nm* : talent, ability

talentoso, -sa *adj* : talented, gifted

talismán *nm, pl* **-manes** AMULETO : talisman, charm

talla *nf* **1** ESTATURA : height **2** : size (in clothing) **3** : stature, status **4** : sculpture, carving

tallar *vt* **1** : to sculpt, to carve **2** : to measure (someone's height) **3** : to deal (cards)

tallarín *nf, pl* **-rines** : noodle

talle *nm* **1** : size **2** : waist, waistline **3** : figure, shape

taller *nm* **1** : shop, workshop **2** : studio (of an artist)

tallo *nm* : stalk, stem ⟨tallo de maíz : cornstalk⟩

talón *nm, pl* **talones 1** : heel (of the foot) **2** : stub (of a check) **3 talón de Aquiles** : Achilles' heel

talonario *nm* : checkbook

taltuza *nf* : gopher

talud *nm* : slope, incline

tamal *nm* : tamale

tamaño¹, -ña *adj* : such a big ⟨¿crees tamaña mentira? : do you believe such a lie?⟩

tamaño² ** *nm* **1 : size **2 de tamaño natural** : life-size

tamarindo *nm* : tamarind

tambaleante *adj* **1** : wobbly, unsteady, teetering **2** : staggering, swaying, tottering

tambalear *vi* → **tambalearse**

tambalearse *vr* **1** : to teeter **2** : to stagger, to sway, to totter

tambaleo *nm* : staggering, lurching, swaying

también *adv* : too, as well, also

tambor *nm* : drum

tamborilear *vi* : to drum, to tap

tamborileo *nm* : tapping, drumming

tamiz *nm* : sieve

tamizar {21} *vt* : to sift

tampoco *adv* : neither, not either ⟨ni yo tampoco : me neither⟩

tampón *nm, pl* **tampones 1** : ink pad **2** : tampon

tam–tam *nm* : tom-tom

tan¹ *adv* **1** : so, so very ⟨no es tan difícil : it is not that difficult⟩ **2** : as ⟨tan pronto como : as soon as⟩ **3 tan siquiera** : at least, at the least **4 tan sólo** : only, merely

tan² *pron* **tan es así** : so much so

tanda *nf* **1** : turn, shift **2** : batch, lot, series

tándem *nm* **1** : tandem (bicycle) **2** : duo, pair

tangente *adj & nf* : tangent — **tangencial** *adj*

tangerina *nf* : tangerine

tangible *adj* : tangible

tango *nm* : tango

tanino *nm* : tannin

tanque *nm* **1** : tank ⟨buque tanque : tanker (ship)⟩ **2** : tank (vehicle)

tanteador *nm* MARCADOR : scoreboard

tantear *vt* **1** : to feel, to grope **2** : to size up, to weigh — *vi* **1** : to keep score **2** : to feel one's way

tanteo *nm* **1** : estimate, rough calculation **2** : testing, sizing up **3** : scoring

tanto¹ *adv* **1** : so much ⟨te quiero tanto : I love you so much⟩ ⟨ha cambiado tanto que no lo reconocí : he has changed so much that I didn't recognize him⟩ ⟨tanto mejor : so much the better⟩ **2** : so long ⟨¿por qué te tardaste tanto? : why did you take so long?⟩ **3 tanto como** : as much as ⟨trabajo tanto como ella : I work as much as she does⟩ ⟨¿te gustó tanto como a mí? : did you like it as much as I did?⟩

tanto², -ta *adj* **1** : so much, so many, such ⟨no hagas tantas preguntas : don't ask so many questions⟩ ⟨tiene tanto encanto : he has such charm, he's so charming⟩ **2** : as much, as many ⟨come tantos dulces como yo : she eats as many sweets as I do⟩ **3** : odd, however many ⟨cuarenta y tantos años : forty-odd years⟩

tanto³ *nm* **1** : certain amount **2** : goal, point (in sports) **3 al tanto** : abreast, in the picture **4 un tanto** : somewhat, rather ⟨un tanto cansado : rather tired⟩

tanto⁴, -ta *pron* **1** : so much, so many ⟨tiene tanto que hacer : she has so much to do⟩ ⟨no me des tantos! : don't give me so many!⟩ **2 en ~** : while **3 entre ~** : meanwhile **4 otro tanto** : again as much, again as many ⟨tiene un metro de ancho y otro tanto de altura : it's a meter wide and a meter high⟩ ⟨otro tanto podría decirse de . . . : the same can be said of . . .⟩ **5 por lo tanto** : therefore **6 tanto es así** : so much so

tañer {79} *vt* **1** : to ring (a bell) **2** : to play (a musical instrument)

tañido *nm* **1** CAMPANADA : ring, peal, toll **2** : sound (of an instrument)

tapa *nf* **1** : cover, top, lid **2** *Spain* : bar snack

tapacubos *nms & pl* : hubcap

tapadera *nf* **1** : cover, lid **2** : front, cover (for an organization or person)

tapar *vt* **1** CUBRIR : to cover, to cover up **2** OBSTRUIR : to block, to obstruct — **taparse** *vr*

taparrabos *nms & pl* : loincloth

tapete *nm* **1** : small rug, mat **2** : table cover **3 poner sobre el tapete** : to bring up for discussion

tapia *nf* : (adobe) wall, garden wall

tapiar *vt* **1** : to wall in **2** : to enclose, to block off

tapicería *nf* **1** : upholstery **2** TAPIZ : tapestry

tapicero, -ra *n* : upholsterer

tapioca *nf* : tapioca

tapir *nm* : tapir

tapiz *nm, pl* **tapices** : tapestry

tapizado *nm* : upholstery

tapizar {21} *vt* **1** : to upholster **2** : to cover, to carpet

tapón *nm, pl* **tapones** **1** : cork **2** : bottle cap **3** : plug, stopper **4** *fam* : traffic jam **5** *Arg* : fuse

taponar *vt* : to block, to stop up

tapujo *nm* **1** : deceit, pretension **2 sin tapujos** : openly, frankly

taquigrafía *nf* : stenography, shorthand

taquigráfico, -ca *adj* : stenographic

taquígrafo, -fa *n* : stenographer

taquilla *nf* **1** : box office, ticket office **2** : earnings *pl*, take

taquillero, -ra *adj* : box-office, popular ⟨un éxito taquillero : a box-office success⟩

tara *nf* : defect

tarántula *nf* : tarantula

tararear *vt* : to hum

tardanza *nf* : lateness, delay

tardar *vi* **1** : to take time, to delay ⟨tardaron en responder : they took a while to respond⟩ **2 a más tardar** : at the latest — *vt* DEMORAR : to take (time) ⟨tarda una hora : it takes an hour⟩ ⟨tardar mucho : to take a long time⟩ ⟨tardar el doble : to take twice as long⟩ — **tardarse** *vr*

tarde¹ *adv* **1** : late **2 tarde o temprano** : sooner or later

tarde² *nf* **1** : afternoon, evening **2 ¡buenas tardes!** : good afternoon!, good evening! **3 en la tarde** *or* **por la tarde** : in the afternoon, in the evening

tardío, -día *adj* : late, tardy

tardo, -da *adj* : slow

tarea *nf* **1** : task, job **2** : homework

tarifa *nf* **1** : rate ⟨tarifas postales : postal rates⟩ **2** : fare (for transportation) **3** : price list **4** ARANCEL : duty

tarima *nf* PLATAFORMA : dais, platform, stage

tarjeta *nf* : card ⟨tarjeta de crédito/débito : credit/debit card⟩ ⟨tarjeta postal : postcard⟩ ⟨tarjeta (de) regalo : gift card⟩ ⟨tarjeta de felicitación : greeting card⟩ ⟨tarjeta navideña, tarjeta de Navidad : Christmas card⟩ ⟨tarjeta de video/memoria : video/memory card⟩ ⟨tarjeta de visita : business card, calling card⟩

taro *nm* : taro

tarrina *nf* : tub

tarro *nm* **1** : jar, pot **2** *Arg, Chile, CoRi, Uru* : can, tin

tarta *nf* **1** : tart **2** *Spain* : cake

tartaleta *nf* : tart

tartamudear *vi* : to stammer, to stutter

tartamudeo *nm* : stutter, stammer

tartamudo¹, -da *adj* : stuttering, stammering

tartamudo², -da *n* : person who stutters or stammers

tartán *nm, pl* **tartanes** : tartan, plaid

tártaro *nm* : tartar

tartera *nf* *Spain* : lunch box

tasa *nf* **1** : rate ⟨tasa de desempleo : unemployment rate⟩ **2** : tax, fee **3** : appraisal, valuation

tasación *nf, pl* **-ciones** : appraisal, assessment

tasador, -dora *n* : assessor, appraiser

tasajo *nm* : dried beef, beef jerky

tasar *vt* **1** VALORAR : to appraise, to value **2** : to set the price of **3** : to ration, to limit

tasca *nf* : cheap bar, dive

tatarabuela *nf* : great-great-grandmother

tatarabuelo *nm* : great-great-grandfather

tatuaje *nm* : tattoo, tattooing

tatuar {3} *vt* : to tattoo

taurino, -na *adj* : bull, bullfighting

Tauro¹ *nm* : Taurus (sign or constellation)

Tauro² *nmf* : Taurus (person)

tauromaquia *nf* : (art of) bullfighting

taxi *nm, pl* **taxis** : taxi, taxicab

taxidermia *nf* : taxidermy

taxidermista *nmf* : taxidermist

taxista *nmf* : taxi driver

taza *nf* **1** : cup **2** : cupful **3** : (toilet) bowl **4** : basin (of a fountain)

tazón *nm, pl* **tazones** **1** : bowl **2** : large cup, mug

te¹ *nf* : (letter) t

te² *pron* **1** : you ⟨te quiero : I love you⟩ **2** : for you, to you, from you ⟨me gustaría dártelo : I would like to give it to you⟩ **3** : yourself, for yourself, to yourself, from yourself ⟨¡cálmate! : calm yourself!⟩ ⟨¿te guardaste uno? : did you keep one for yourself?⟩ **4** : thee

té *nm* **1** : tea **2** : tea party

tea *nf* : torch

teatral *adj* : theatrical — **teatralmente** *adv*

teatro *nm* **1** : theater **2 hacer teatro** : to put on an act, to exaggerate

teca *nf* : teak

techado *nm* **1** : roof **2 bajo techado** : under cover, indoors

techar *vt* : to roof, to shingle

techo *nm* **1** TEJADO : roof **2** : ceiling **3** : upper limit, ceiling

techumbre *nf* : roofing

tecla *nf* **1** : key (of a musical instrument or a machine) ⟨la tecla Tab : the tab key⟩ **2 dar en la tecla** : to hit the nail on the head

teclado *nm* **1** : keyboard — **2 teclado numérico** : (number) keypad

teclear *vt* : to type in, to enter

técnica *nf* **1** : technique, skill **2** : technology

técnico¹, -ca *adj* : technical — **técnicamente** *adv*

técnico², -ca *n* : technician, expert, engineer

tecnología *nf* : technology

tecnológico, -ca *adj* : technological — **tecnológicamente** *adv*

tecolote *nm Mex* : owl

tedio *nm* : tedium, boredom

tedioso, -sa *adj* : tedious, boring — **tediosamente** *adv*

tee ['ti] *nm* : tee (in golf)

teja *nf* : tile

tejado *nm* TECHO : roof

tejanos *nmpl* : jeans

tejar *vt* : to tile

tejedor, -dora *n* : weaver

tejemaneje *nm* **1** : intrigue, machination **2** : fuss, commotion

tejer *vt* **1** : to knit, to crochet **2** : to weave **3** FABRICAR : to concoct, to make up, to fabricate

tejido *nm* **1** TELA : fabric, cloth **2** : weave, texture **3** : tissue ⟨tejido muscular : muscle tissue⟩

tejo *nm* **1** : yew **2** : hopscotch (children's game)

tejón *nm, pl* **tejones** : badger

tela *nf* **1** : fabric, cloth, material **2 tela de araña** : spiderweb **3 poner en tela de juicio** : to call into question, to doubt

telar *nm* : loom

telaraña *nf* : spiderweb, cobweb

tele *nf fam* : TV, television

telecomunicación *nf, pl* **-ciones** : telecommunication

teleconferencia *nf* : teleconference

telediario *nm Spain* : news, news program

teledifusión *nf, pl* **-siones** : television broadcasting

teledirigido, -da *adj* : remote-controlled

teleférico *nm* : cable car

telefonazo *nm fam* : (telephone) call

telefonear *v* : to telephone, to call

telefónico, -ca *adj* : phone, telephone ⟨llamada telefónica : phone call⟩

telefonista *nmf* : telephone operator

teléfono *nm* **1** : telephone ⟨contestar el teléfono : to answer the phone⟩ ⟨número de teléfono : phone number⟩ ⟨teléfono celular : cell phone, mobile phone⟩ **2 llamar por teléfono** : to telephone, to make a phone call **3 teléfono inteligente** : smartphone

telegrafiar {85} *v* : to telegraph

telégrafo *nm* : telegraph

telegrama *nm* : telegram

telemárketing *nm* : telemarketing

telenovela *nf* : soap opera

telepatía *nf* : telepathy

telepático, -ca *adj* : telepathic — **telepáticamente** *adv*

telerrealidad *nf* : reality TV, reality television

telescópico, -ca *adj* : telescopic

telescopio *nm* : telescope

telesilla *nmf* : ski lift

telespectador, -dora *n* : (television) viewer

telesquí *nm, pl* **-squís** : ski lift

televidente *nmf* : (television) viewer

televisar *vt* : to televise

televisión *nf, pl* **-siones** : television, TV ⟨televisión de alta definición : high definition television⟩ ⟨hay un programa de ciencia en la televisión : there's a science program on TV⟩

televisivo, -va *adj* : television ⟨serie televisiva : television series⟩

televisor *nm* : television set

telón *nm, pl* **telones** **1** : curtain (in theater) **2 telón de fondo** : backdrop, background

tema *nm* **1** ASUNTO : theme, topic, subject **2** MOTIVO : motif, central theme

temario *nm* **1** : set of topics (for study) **2** : agenda

temática *nf* : subject matter

temático, -ca *adj* : thematic

temblar {55} *vi* **1** : to tremble, to shake, to shiver ⟨le temblaban las rodillas : his knees were shaking⟩ **2** : to shudder, to be afraid ⟨tiemblo con sólo pensarlo : I shudder to think of it⟩

temblor *nm* **1** : shaking, trembling **2** : tremor, earthquake

temblorosamente *adv* : shakily

tembloroso, -sa *adj* : tremulous, trembling, shaking ⟨con la voz temblorosa : with a shaky voice⟩

temer *vt* : to fear, to dread ⟨temíamos lo peor : we feared the worst⟩ — *vi* : to be afraid ⟨temer por alguien/algo : to fear for someone/something⟩ — **temerse** *vr*

temerario, -ria *adj* : reckless, rash — **temerariamente** *adv*

temeridad *nf* **1** : temerity, recklessness, rashness **2** : rash act

temeroso, -sa *adj* MIEDOSO : fearful, frightened

temible *adj* : fearsome, dreadful

temor *nm* MIEDO : fear, dread

témpano *nm* : ice floe

temperamento *nm* : temperament — **temperamental** *adj*

temperancia *nf* : temperance

temperar *vt* MODERAR : to temper, to moderate — *vi* : to have a change of air

temperatura *nf* : temperature

tempestad *nf* **1** : storm, tempest **2 tempestad de arena** : sandstorm

tempestuoso, -sa *adj* : tempestuous, stormy

templado, -da *adj* **1** : temperate, mild **2** : moderate, restrained **3** : warm, lukewarm **4** VALIENTE : courageous, bold

templanza *nf* **1** : temperance, moderation **2** : mildness (of weather)

templar *vt* **1** : to temper (steel) **2** : to restrain, to moderate **3** : to tune (a musical instrument) **4** : to warm up, to cool down — **templarse** *vr* **1** : to be moderate **2** : to warm up, to cool down

temple *nm* **1** : temper (of steel, etc.) **2** HUMOR : mood ⟨de buen temple : in a good mood⟩ **3** : tuning **4** VALOR : courage

templo *nm* **1** : temple **2** : church, chapel

tempo *nm* : tempo (in music)

temporada *nf* **1** : season, time ⟨temporada de béisbol : baseball season⟩ **2** : period, spell ⟨por temporadas : on and off⟩

temporal[1] *adj* **1** : temporal **2** : temporary

temporal[2] *nm* **1** : storm **2 capear el temporal** : to weather the storm
temporalmente *adv* : temporarily
temporario, -ria *adj* : temporary — **temporariamente** *adv*
temporero[1], **-ra** *adj* : temporary, seasonal
temporero[2], **-ra** *n* : temporary or seasonal worker
temporizador *nm* : timer
tempranero, -ra *adj* : early
temprano[1] *adv* : early ⟨lo más temprano posible : as soon as possible⟩ ⟨por la mañana temprano : early in the morning⟩
temprano[2], **-na** *adj* : early ⟨la parte temprana del siglo : the early part of the century⟩
ten → **tener**
tenacidad *nf* : tenacity, perseverance
tenacillas *nfpl* **1** : tongs **2** : curling iron (for hair)
tenaz *adj*, *pl* **tenaces** **1** : tenacious, persistent **2** : strong, tough
tenaza *nf*, *or* **tenazas** *nfpl* **1** : pliers, pincers **2** : tongs **3** : claw (of a crustacean)
tenazmente *adv* : tenaciously
tendedero *nm* : clothesline
tendencia *nf* **1** PROPENSIÓN : tendency, inclination **2** : trend
tendencioso, -sa *adj* : biased
tendente → **tendiente**
tender {56} *vt* **1** EXTENDER : to spread out, to lay out **2** EXTENDER : to extend, to hold out (one's hand) **3** : to hang out (clothes) **4** : to run (cables, etc.) **5** : to set (a trap) **6** : to set (a table), to make (a bed) — *vi* ~ **a** : to tend, to have a tendency towards — **tenderse** *vr* : to stretch out, to lie down
tenderete *nm* : (market) stall
tendero, -ra *n* : shopkeeper, storekeeper
tendido *nm* **1** : laying (of cables, etc.) **2** : seats *pl*, section (at a bullfight)
tendiente *adj* ~ **a** : aimed at, designed to
tendón *nm*, *pl* **tendones** : tendon
tenebrosidad *nf* : darkness, gloom
tendrá, etc. → **tener**
tenebroso, -sa *adj* **1** OSCURO : gloomy, dark **2** SINIESTRO : sinister
tenedor[1], **-dora** *n* **1** : holder **2 tenedor de libros, tenedora de libros** : bookkeeper
tenedor[2] *nm* : table fork
teneduría *nf* **teneduría de libros** : bookkeeping
tenencia *nf* **1** : possession, holding **2** : tenancy **3** : tenure
tener {80} *vt* **1** : to have ⟨tiene un coche azul : he has a blue car⟩ ⟨¿lo tienes contigo? : do you have it with you?⟩ ⟨tienen tres hijos : they have three children⟩ ⟨tiene ojos verdes : she has green eyes⟩ ⟨tiene mucha experiencia : she has a lot of experience⟩ ⟨¿tiene hora? : do you have the time?, can you tell me what time it is?⟩ **2** : to have (available) ⟨tener dinero/tiempo para : to have money/time for⟩ ⟨no tuve más remedio : I had no choice⟩ **3** : to have (plans, etc.) ⟨tengo mucho que hacer : I have a lot to do⟩ ⟨hoy tiene clase : he has class today⟩ **4** : to have, to cause (consequences, etc.)

5 (*indicating age*) ⟨tiene veinte años : he's twenty years old⟩ **6** (*indicating dimensions*) ⟨tiene un metro de largo : it's one meter long⟩ **7** (*expressing thoughts, feelings, or sensations*) ⟨tengo frío/hambre/miedo : I'm cold/hungry/scared⟩ ⟨no tengo ni idea : I have no idea⟩ ⟨tengo confianza en ti : I have confidence in you⟩ ⟨eso nos tiene contentos : that makes us happy⟩ **8** : to have (an illness or injury) **9** : to have, to experience (problems, etc.) ⟨tuve un buen día : I had a good day⟩ **10** : to have, to receive (news, etc.) **11** : to have, to show (a quality) ⟨tienes razón : you're right⟩ ⟨eso no tiene sentido : that doesn't make sense⟩ ⟨no tiene nada de malo/raro : there's nothing bad/strange about it⟩ **12** : to have, to include ⟨el libro tiene 500 páginas : the book has 500 pages⟩ **13** : to use, to exercise ⟨tener cuidado : to be careful⟩ **14** (*indicating condition*) ⟨tenía la camisa manchada : his shirt was stained⟩ **15** (*indicating position*) ⟨tenía las manos en los bolsillos : she had her hands in her pockets⟩ **16** : to hold ⟨ten esto : hold this⟩ **17** : to have, to give birth to **18** ~ **por** : to think, to consider ⟨me tienes por loco : you think I'm crazy⟩ — *v aux* **1 tener que** : to have to ⟨tengo que salir : I have to leave⟩ ⟨tiene que estar aquí : it has to be here, it must be here⟩ **2** (*with past participle*) ⟨tenía pensado escribirte : I've been thinking of writing to you⟩ **3** (*in expressions of time*) ⟨tengo diez años haciendo esto : I have been doing this for ten years⟩ ⟨tiene años de estar aquí : it's been here for tenwork⟩ — **tenerse** *vr* **1** : to stand up **2** ~ **por** : to consider oneself ⟨me tengo por afortunado : I consider myself lucky⟩
tenería *nf* CURTIDURÍA : tannery
tenga, etc. → **tener**
tenia *nf* SOLITARIA : tapeworm
teniente *nmf* **1** : lieutenant **2 teniente coronel** : lieutenant colonel
tenis *nms & pl* **1** : tennis **2 tenis** *nmpl* : sneakers *pl*
tenista *nmf* : tennis player
tenor *nm* **1** : tenor **2** : tone, sense
tensar *vt* **1** : to tense, to make taut **2** : to draw (a bow) — **tensarse** *vr* : to become tense
tensión *nf*, *pl* **tensiones** **1** : tension, tautness **2** : stress, strain **3 tensión arterial** : blood pressure **4** : voltage, tension ⟨de alta tensión : high-tension⟩
tenso, -sa *adj* : tense — **tensamente** *adv*
tentación *nf*, *pl* **-ciones** : temptation ⟨caer en la tentación : to give in to temptation⟩ ⟨caer en la tentación de : to be tempted into⟩ ⟨resistir la tentación de : to resist the temptation to⟩
tentáculo *nm* : tentacle, feeler
tentador[1], **-dora** *adj* : tempting
tentador[2], **-dora** *n* : tempter, temptress *f*
tentar {55} *vt* **1** TOCAR : to feel, to touch **2** PROBAR : to test, to try **3** ATRAER : to tempt, to entice

tentativa *nf* : attempt, try
tentempié *nm fam* : snack, bite
tenue *adj* **1** : tenuous **2** : faint, weak, dim **3** : light, fine **4** : thin, slender
teñir {67} *vt* **1** : to dye **2** : to stain
teología *nf* : theology
teológico, -ca *adj* : theological
teólogo, -ga *n* : theologian
teorema *nm* : theorem
teoría *nf* : theory
teórico¹, -ca *adj* : theoretical — **teóricamente** *adv*
teórico², -ca *n* : theorist
teorizar {21} *vi* : to theorize
tepe *nm* : sod, turf
teponaztle *nm Mex* : traditional drum
tequila *nm* : tequila
terapeuta *nmf* : therapist
terapéutica *nf* : therapeutics
terapéutico, -ca *adj* : therapeutic
terapia *nf* **1** : therapy **2 terapia intensiva** : intensive care
tercer → **tercero**
tercermundista *adj* : third-world
tercero¹, -ra *adj* (**tercer** *before masculine singular nouns*) **1** : third ⟨el tercer piso/grado : the third floor/grade⟩ ⟨una/la tercera parte de : a third of, one third of⟩ **2 el Tercer Mundo** : the Third World
tercero², -ra *n* : third (in a series)
terceto *nm* **1** : triplet (in literature) **2** : trio (in music)
terciar *vt* **1** : to place diagonally **2** : to divide into three parts — *vi* **1** : to mediate **2** ~ **en** : to take part in
terciario, -ria *adj* : tertiary
tercio¹, -cia → **tercero**
tercio² *nm* : third ⟨dos tercios : two thirds⟩
terciopelo *nm* : velvet
terco, -ca *adj* OBSTINADO : obstinate, stubborn
tergiversación *nf, pl* **-ciones** : distortion
tergiversar *vt* : to distort, to twist
termal *adj* : thermal, hot
termas *nfpl* : hot springs
térmico, -ca *adj* : thermal, heat ⟨energía térmica : thermal energy⟩
terminación *nf, pl* **-ciones** : termination, conclusion
terminal¹ *adj* : terminal — **terminalmente** *adv*
terminal² *nm* (*in some regions f*) : (electric or electronic) terminal
terminal³ *nf* (*in some regions m*) : terminal, station
terminante *adj* : final, definitive, categorical — **terminantemente** *adv*
terminar *vt* **1** CONCLUIR : to end, to conclude **2** ACABAR : to complete, to finish off — *vi* **1** : to finish **2** : to stop, to end — **terminarse** *vr* **1** : to run out **2** : to come to an end
término *nm* **1** CONCLUSIÓN : end, conclusion **2** : term, expression **3** : period, term of office **4** : place, position ⟨en primer término : first of all⟩ **5 término medio** : happy medium **6 por término medio** : on average **7 términos** *nmpl*

: terms, specifications ⟨los términos del acuerdo : the terms of the agreement⟩
terminología *nf* : terminology
termita *nf* : termite
termo *nm* : thermos
termodinámica *nf* : thermodynamics
termómetro *nm* : thermometer
termostato *nm* : thermostat
ternera *nf* : veal
ternero, -ra *n* : calf
terno *nm* **1** : set of three **2** : three-piece suit
ternura *nf* : tenderness
terquedad *nf* OBSTINACIÓN : obstinacy, stubbornness
terracota *nf* : terra-cotta
terraplén *nm, pl* **-plenes** : terrace, embankment
terráqueo, -quea *adj* **1** : earth **2 globo terráqueo** : the earth, globe (of the earth)
terrateniente *nmf* : landowner
terraza *nf* **1** : terrace, veranda **2** : balcony (in a theater) **3** : terrace (in agriculture)
terremoto *nm* : earthquake
terrenal *adj* : worldly, earthly
terreno *nm* **1** : terrain **2** SUELO : earth, ground **3** : plot, tract of land **4 perder terreno** : to lose ground **5 preparar el terreno** : to pave the way
terrestre *adj* : terrestrial
terrible *adj* : terrible, horrible — **terriblemente** *adv*
terrier *nmf* : terrier
territorial *adj* : territorial
territorio *nm* : territory
terrón *nm, pl* **terrones** **1** : clod (of earth) **2 terrón de azúcar** : lump of sugar
terror *nm* : terror
terrorífico, -ca *adj* : horrific, terrifying
terrorismo *nm* : terrorism
terrorista *adj & nmf* : terrorist
terroso, -sa *adj* : earthy ⟨colores terrosos : earthy colors⟩
terruño *nm* : native land, homeland
terso, -sa *adj* **1** : smooth **2** : glossy, shiny **3** : polished, flowing (of a style)
tersura *nf* **1** : smoothness **2** : shine
tertulia *nf* : gathering, group ⟨tertulia literaria : literary circle⟩
tesauro *nm* : thesaurus
tesis *nfs & pl* : thesis
tesón *nm* : persistence, tenacity
tesonero, -ra *adj* : persistent, tenacious
tesorería *nf* : treasurer's office
tesorero, -ra *n* : treasurer
tesoro *nm* **1** : treasure **2** : thesaurus **3** : treasury
test *nm* : test
testaferro *nm* : figurehead
testamentario, -ria *n* ALBACEA : executor
testamento *nm* : testament, will
testar *vi* : to draw up a will
testarudo, -da *adj* : stubborn, pigheaded
testículo *nm* : testicle
testificar {72} *v* : to testify
testigo *nmf* **1** : witness **2 testigo presencial** : eyewitness
testimonial *adj* **1** : testimonial **2** : token
testimoniar *vi* : to testify

testimonio *nm* : testimony, statement
teta *nf* : teat
tétano *or* **tétanos** *nm* : tetanus, lockjaw
tetera *nf* 1 : teapot 2 : teakettle
tetilla *nf* 1 : teat 2 : nipple
tetina *nf* : nipple (on a bottle)
tétrico, -ca *adj* : somber, gloomy
textear *v fam* : to text
textil *adj & nm* : textile
texto *nm* : text
textual *adj* : literal, exact — **textualmente** *adv*
textura *nf* : texture
tez *nf, pl* **teces** : complexion, coloring
thumbnail ['tomneil] *nm, pl* **thumbnails** : thumbnail (in computing)
ti *pron* 1 : you ⟨es para ti : it's for you⟩ 2 **ti mismo, ti misma** : yourself 3 : thee
tía → **tío**
tiamina *nf* : thiamine
tianguis *nm Mex* : open-air market
tibetano¹, -na *adj & n* : Tibetan
tibetano² *nm* : Tibetan (language)
tibia *nf* : tibia
tibieza *nf* 1 : warmth, mildness 2 : lack of enthusiasm, coolness, indifference
tibio, -bia *adj* 1 : lukewarm, tepid 2 : cool, unenthusiastic
tiburón *nm, pl* **-rones** 1 : shark 2 : raider (in finance)
tic *nm* 1 : click, tick 2 **tic nervioso** : tic
tico, -ca *adj & n fam* : Costa Rican
tictac *nm* 1 : ticking, tick-tock 2 **hacer tictac** : to tick
tiembla, etc. → **temblar**
tiempo *nm* 1 : time ⟨justo a tiempo : just in time⟩ ⟨ahorrar/matar/perder tiempo : to save/kill/waste time⟩ ⟨ganar tiempo : to buy time⟩ ⟨tiempo libre : spare time⟩ ⟨al poco tiempo : soon after⟩ ⟨al tiempo que : (while) at the same time⟩ ⟨con tiempo : in good time, in advance⟩ ⟨con el tiempo : in/with/over time⟩ ⟨no tengo tiempo, no me da tiempo : I don't have time⟩ ⟨hace tiempo que vive aquí : she has lived here for a while⟩ ⟨desde hace mucho tiempo : for quite a while⟩ 2 : period of time ⟨un tiempo de : a period of⟩ ⟨esperamos un tiempo : we waited a while⟩ ⟨cada cierto tiempo : every so often⟩ ⟨en los tiempos que corren : nowadays⟩ 3 : season, moment ⟨antes de tiempo : prematurely⟩ ⟨fuera de tiempo : at the wrong time⟩ 4 : weather ⟨hace buen tiempo : the weather is fine, it's nice outside⟩ 5 : tempo (in music) 6 : half (in sports) 7 : tense (in grammar) 8 : half (in sports) ⟨medio tiempo : halftime⟩ 9 **medio tiempo** *or* **tiempo parcial** ⟨un empleo de medio tiempo, un empleo a tiempo parcial : a part-time job⟩ ⟨trabajar medio tiempo, trabajar a tiempo parcial : to work part-time⟩ 10 **tiempo compartido** : timeshare 11 **tiempo completo** : full-time ⟨un empleo de tiempo completo : a full-time job⟩ ⟨trabajar a/de tiempo completo : to work full-time⟩
tienda *nf* 1 : store, shop 2 *or* **tienda de campaña** : tent

tiende, etc. → **tender**
tiene, etc. → **tener**
tienta¹, etc. → **tentar**
tienta² *nf* **andar a tientas** : to feel one's way, to grope around
tiernamente *adv* : tenderly
tierno, -na *adj* 1 : affectionate, tender 2 : tender, young
tierra *nf* 1 : land ⟨vender tierra : to sell land⟩ 2 SUELO : ground, earth ⟨camino de tierra : dirt road⟩ ⟨tomar tierra : to land⟩ ⟨caer a tierra : to fall to earth⟩ 3 : country, homeland, soil 4 **tierra adentro** : inland 5 **tierra firme** : dry/solid ground 6 **tierra natal** : native land 7 **tierras altas** : highlands 8 **tierras bajas** : lowlands 9 **la Tierra** : the Earth
tieso, -sa *adj* 1 : stiff, rigid 2 : upright, erect
tiesto *nm* MACETA : flowerpot
tiesura *nf* : stiffness, rigidity
tifoidea *nf* : typhoid
tifoideo, -dea *adj* : typhoid ⟨fiebre tifoidea : typhoid fever⟩
tifón *nm, pl* **tifones** : typhoon
tifus *nm* : typhus
tigre, -gresa *n* 1 : tiger, tigress *f* 2 : jaguar
tijera *nf* 1 *or* **tijeras** *nfpl* : scissors 2 **de ~** : folding ⟨escalera de tijera : stepladder⟩
tijereta *nf* : earwig
tijeretada *nf or* **tijeretazo** *nm* : cut, snip
tila *nf* : lime blossom tea
tildar *vt* **~ de** : to brand as, to call ⟨lo tildaron de traidor : they branded him as a traitor⟩
tilde *nf* 1 : accent mark 2 : tilde (accent over ñ)
tilín *nm, pl* **tilines** : tinkle
tilo *nm* : linden (tree)
timador, -dora *n* : swindler
timar *vt* : to swindle, to cheat
timbal *nm* 1 : kettledrum 2 **timbales** *nmpl* : timpani
timbre *nm* 1 : bell ⟨tocar el timbre : to ring the doorbell⟩ 2 : tone, timbre 3 SELLO : seal, stamp 4 *CA, Mex* : postage stamp
timidez *nf* : timidity, shyness
tímido, -da *adj* : timid, shy — **tímidamente** *adv*
timo *nm fam* : swindle, trick, hoax
timón *nm, pl* **timones** : rudder ⟨estar al timón : to beat the helm⟩
timonel *nm* : coxswain
timorato, -ta *adj* 1 : timorous 2 : sanctimonious
tímpano *nm* 1 : eardrum 2 **tímpanos** *nmpl* : timpani, kettledrums
tina *nf* 1 BAÑERA : tub, bathtub 2 : vat
tinaco *nm Mex* : water tank
tinaja *nf* : large clay pot/jar
tinieblas *nfpl* 1 OSCURIDAD : darkness 2 : ignorance
tino *nm* 1 : good judgment, sense 2 : tact, sensitivity, insight
tinta *nf* : ink
tinte *nm* 1 : dye, coloring 2 : overtone ⟨tintes raciales : racial overtones⟩

tintero *nm* **1** : inkwell **2 quedarse en el tintero** : to remain unsaid
tintinear *vt* : to jingle, to clink, to tinkle
tintineo *nm* : clink, jingle, tinkle
tinto, -ta *adj* **1** : dyed, stained ⟨tinto en sangre : bloodstained⟩ **2** : red (of wine)
tintorería *nf* : dry cleaner (service)
tintura *nf* **1** : dye, tint **2** : tincture ⟨tintura de yodo : tincture of iodine⟩
tiña *nf* : ringworm
tiñe, etc. → **teñir**
tío, tía *n* : uncle *m,* aunt *f*
tiovivo *nm* : merry-go-round
tipear *vt* (*in various countries*) : to type
tipi *nm* : tepee
típico, -ca *adj* : typical — **típicamente** *adv*
tipificar {72} *vt* **1** : to classify, to categorize **2** : to typify
tiple *nm* : soprano
tipo[1] *nm* **1** CLASE : type, kind, sort **2** : figure, build, appearance **3** : rate ⟨tipo de interés : interest rate⟩ **4** : (printing) type, typeface **5** : style, model ⟨un vestido tipo 60's : a 60's-style dress⟩
tipo[2]**, -pa** *n fam* : guy *m,* gal *f,* character
tipografía *nf* : typography, printing
tipográfico, -ca *adj* : typographic, typographical
tipógrafo, -fa *n* : printer, typographer
tique *or* **tiquet** *nm* **1** : ticket **2** : receipt
tira *nf* **1** : strip, strap **2 tira cómica** : comic, comic strip
tirabuzón *nf, pl* **-zones** : corkscrew
tirachinas *nms & pl* : slingshot
tirada *nf* **1** : throw **2** : distance, stretch **3** IMPRESIÓN : printing, issue
tiradero *nm Mex* **1** : dump **2** : mess, clutter
tirado, -da *adj Spain fam* **1** : dirt cheap **2** : very easy
tirador[1] *nm* : handle, knob
tirador[2]**, -dora** *n* : marksman *m,* markswoman *f*
tiragomas *nms & pl* : slingshot
tiranía *nf* : tyranny
tiránico, -ca *adj* : tyrannical
tiranizar {21} *vt* : to tyrannize
tirano[1]**, -na** *adj* : tyrannical, despotic
tirano[2]**, -na** *n* : tyrant
tirante[1] *adj* **1** : tense, strained **2** : taut
tirante[2] *nm* **1** : shoulder strap **2 tirantes** *nmpl* : suspenders
tirantez *nf* **1** : tautness **2** : tension, friction, strain
tirar *vt* **1** : to throw, to hurl, to toss ⟨tírame la pelota : throw/toss me the ball⟩ **2** BOTAR : to throw away/out (garbage), to waste (money, etc.) **3** DERRIBAR : to knock down **4** : to shoot, to fire, to launch (a rocket), to drop (a bomb) **5** : to shoot (in sports) **6** *Car, Spain* : to take (a photo) **7** : to print, to run off **8** *Arg, Chile, Uru* : to pull — *vi* **1** : to pull, to draw **2** : to shoot ⟨tirar a matar : to shoot to kill⟩ **3** : to shoot (in sports) **4** : to attract **5** : to get by, to manage ⟨va tirando : he's getting along, he's managing⟩ **6 ~ a** : to tend towards, to be rather ⟨tira a picante : it's a

bit spicy⟩ — **tirarse** *vr* **1** : to throw oneself **2** *fam* : to spend (time)
tiritar *vi* : to shiver, to tremble
tiro *nm* **1** BALAZO, DISPARO : shot, gunshot ⟨pegarle un tiro a alguien : to shoot someone⟩ ⟨matar a alguien a tiros : to shoot someone dead⟩ ⟨errar el tiro : to miss the mark⟩ **2** : shot, kick (in sports) ⟨tiro libre : free shot/throw/kick⟩ ⟨tiro penal : penalty shot/kick⟩ **3** : flue **4** : team (of horses, etc.) **5 a ~** : within range ⟨ponerse a tiro : to come within range⟩ ⟨estar a tiro : to be within range, to be within reach⟩ **6 al tiro** : right away **7 tiro de gracia** : coup de grâce, death blow
tiroideo, -dea *adj* : thyroid
tiroides *nmf* : thyroid, thyroid gland — **tiroides** *adj*
tirolés, -lesa *adj* : Tyrolean
tirón *nm, pl* **tirones** **1** : pull, tug, yank **2 de un tirón** : all at once, in one go **3 tirón de orejas** : slap on the wrist, minor punishment
tiroteo *nm* **1** : shooting **2** : gunfight, shoot-out
tirria *nf* **tener tirria a** *fam* : to have a grudge against
titánico, -ca *adj* : titanic, huge
titanio *nm* : titanium
títere *nm* : puppet
tití *nm, pl* **tití** *or* **titíes** *or* **titís** : marmoset
titilar *vi* : to twinkle, to flicker
titileo *nm* : twinkle, flickering
titiritero, -ra *n* **1** : puppeteer **2** : acrobat
tito, tita *n fam* : uncle *m,* auntie *f*
titubear *vi* **1** : to hesitate **2** : to stutter, to stammer — **titubeante** *adj*
titubeo *nm* **1** : hesitation **2** : stammering
titulado, -da *adj* **1** : titled, entitled **2** : qualified
titular[1] *vt* : to title, to entitle — **titularse** *vr* **1** : to be called, to be entitled **2** : to receive a degree
titular[2] *adj* : titular, official
titular[3] *nm* : headline
titular[4] *nmf* **1** : owner, holder **2** : officeholder, incumbent
titularidad *nf* **1** : ownership, title **2** : position, office (with a title) **3** : starting position (in sports)
título *nm* **1** : title **2** : degree, qualification **3** : security, bond **4 a título de** : by way of, in the capacity of
tiza *nf* : chalk
tiznar *vt* : to blacken (with soot, etc.)
tizne *nm* HOLLÍN : soot
tiznón *nm, pl* **tiznones** : stain, smudge
tlapalería *nf Mex* : hardware store
TNT *nm* (trinitrotolueno) : TNT
toalla *nf* **1** : towel **2 tirar la toalla** : to throw in the towel
toallita *nf* : washcloth
tobillo *nm* : ankle
tobogán *nm, pl* **-ganes** **1** : toboggan, sled **2** : slide, chute
tocadiscos *nms & pl* : record player
tocado[1]**, -da** *adj* **1** : bad, bruised (of fruit) **2** *fam* : touched, not all there

tocado[2] *nm* : headdress
tocador[1] *nm* **1** : dressing table, vanity table **2 artículos de tocador** : toiletries
tocador[2], **-dora** *n* : player (of music)
tocante *adj* ~ **a** : with regard to, regarding
tocar {72} *vt* **1** : to touch, to feel, to handle **2** : to touch on, to refer to **3** : to concern, to affect **4** : to play (a musical instrument) **5** : to ring (a bell), to sound **6 tocar fondo** : to hit/reach rock bottom — *vi* **1** : to knock ⟨tocar a la puerta : to knock on the door⟩ **2** : to sound, to ring ⟨tocó el timbre : the doorbell rang⟩ **3** : to fall to, to be up to, to be one's turn ⟨¿a quién le toca manejar? : whose turn is it to drive?⟩ ⟨a él le toca decidir : it's up to him to decide⟩ ⟨nos toca el 50 por ciento : we get 50 percent⟩ **4** : to come by chance ⟨les tocó la lotería : they won the lottery⟩ ⟨nos toca vivir en tiempos difíciles : it's our fate to live in difficult times⟩ **5** ~ **en** : to touch on, to border on ⟨eso toca en lo ridículo : that's almost ludicrous⟩ — **tocarse** *vr* **1** : to touch ⟨se tocó la frente : he touched his forehead⟩ **2** : to touch (each other)
tocayo, -ya *n* : namesake
tocineta *nf Col, Ven* : bacon
tocino *nm* **1** : bacon **2** : salt pork
tocología *nf* OBSTETRICIA : obstetrics
tocólogo, -ga *n* OBSTETRA : obstetrician
tocón *nm, pl* **tocones** CEPA : stump (of a tree)
todavía *adv* **1** AÚN : still, yet ⟨todavía puedes verlo : you can still see it⟩ **2** : even ⟨todavía más rápido : even faster⟩ **3 todavía no** : not yet
todo[1], **-da** *adj* **1** : all, whole, entire ⟨toda la comunidad : the whole community⟩ ⟨toda la noche : all night, the whole night⟩ ⟨todo tipo de : all kinds of⟩ ⟨con toda sinceridad : with all sincerity⟩ **2** : every, each, any ⟨a todo nivel : at every level⟩ ⟨todos los días : every day⟩ ⟨toda persona menor de 18 años : anyone under the age of 18⟩ **3** : maximum ⟨a toda velocidad : at top speed⟩ **4 todo el mundo** : everyone, everybody
todo[2] *nm* : whole
todo[3], **-da** *pron* **1** : everything, all, every bit ⟨lo sabe todo : he knows it all⟩ ⟨tienen de todo : they have some of everything⟩ ⟨hizo todo lo que pudo : she did everything she could⟩ ⟨no los encontré todos : I didn't find all of them⟩ ⟨es todo un soldado : he's a soldier through and through⟩ ⟨fue todo un éxito : it was quite a success⟩ **2 todos, -das** *pl* : everybody, everyone, all ⟨todos estamos de acuerdo : everybody agrees, we all agree⟩ ⟨¿estamos todos? : are we all here?⟩ ⟨es mejor para todos : it's better for everyone⟩ ⟨agradeció a todos : he thanked everyone⟩ ⟨es la más famosa de todos : she's the most famous of them all⟩ **3 ante** ~ : above all, first and foremost **4 con todo (y eso)** : even so, nevertheless **5 del todo** : completely **6 sobre** ~ : above all

todopoderoso, -sa *adj* OMNIPOTENTE : almighty
todoterreno *nm* : all-terrain vehicle
toga *nf* **1** : toga **2** : gown, robe (for magistrates, etc.)
toldo *nm* : awning, canopy
tolerable *adj* : tolerable — **tolerablemente** *adv*
tolerancia *nf* : tolerance, toleration
tolerante *adj* : tolerant — **tolerantemente** *adv*
tolerar *vt* : to tolerate
tolete *nm* : oarlock
tolva *nf* : hopper (container)
toma *nf* **1** : taking, seizure, capture **2** DOSIS : dose **3** : take, shot **4 toma de corriente** : wall socket, outlet **5 toma y daca** : give-and-take
tomado *adj* : drunk
tomar *vt* **1** : to take ⟨tomé el libro : I took the book⟩ ⟨tomar un taxi : to take a taxi⟩ ⟨tomar una foto : to take a photo⟩ ⟨toma dos años : it takes two years⟩ ⟨tomaron medidas drásticas : they took drastic measures⟩ **2** : to make (a decision) **3** BEBER : to drink **4** CONSUMIR : to have (food), to take (medicine) **5** CAPTURAR : to capture, to seize **6** : to take, to interpret ⟨no lo tomes a mal : don't take it the wrong way⟩ **7** ~ **por** : to take for, to mistake for **8 tomar el sol** : to sunbathe **9 tomar prestado** : to borrow **10 tomar tierra** : to land — *vi* **1** : to take something ⟨toma, te lo presto : here, I'll lend it to you⟩ **2** : to drink (alcohol) — **tomarse** *vr* **1** : to take ⟨tomarse la molestia de : to take the trouble to⟩ **2** : to drink, to eat, to have
tomate *nm* : tomato
tomillo *nm* : thyme
tomo *nm* : volume, tome
ton *nm* **sin ton ni son** : without rhyme or reason
tonada *nf* **1** : tune, song **2** : accent
tonalidad *nf* : tones *pl*, color scheme
tonel *nm* BARRICA : barrel, cask
tonelada *nf* : ton
tonelaje *nm* : tonnage
tónica *nf* **1** : tonic (water) **2** : tonic (in music) **3** : trend, tone ⟨dar la tónica : to set the tone⟩
tónico[1], **-ca** *adj* : tonic
tónico[2] *nm* : tonic ⟨tónico capilar : hair tonic⟩
tonificar {72} *vt* : to tone, to tone up
tono *nm* **1** : tone ⟨tono muscular : muscle tone⟩ **2** : shade (of colors) **3** : key (in music) **4 tono de llamada** : ringtone
tontamente *adv* : foolishly, stupidly
tontear *vi* **1** : to fool around, to play the fool **2** : to flirt
tontería *nf* **1** : foolishness **2** : stupid remark or action **3 decir tonterías** : to talk nonsense
tonto[1], **-ta** *adj* **1** : dumb, stupid **2** : silly **3 a tontas y a locas** : without thinking, haphazardly
tonto[2], **-ta** *n* : fool, idiot
topacio *nm* : topaz

toparse *vr* ~ **con** : to bump into, to run into, to come across ⟨me topé con algunas dificultades : I ran into some problems⟩
tope *nm* **1** : limit, end ⟨hasta el tope : to the limit, to the brim⟩ **2** : stop, check, buffer ⟨tope de puerta : doorstop⟩ **3** : bump, collision **4** *Mex* : speed bump
tópico¹, -ca *adj* **1** : topical, external **2** : trite, commonplace
tópico² *nm* **1** : topic, subject **2** : cliché, trite expression
topo *nm* **1** : mole (animal) **2** *fam* : clumsy person
topografía *nf* : topography
topográfico, -ca *adj* : topographic, topographical
toque¹, etc. → **tocar**
toque² *nm* **1** : touch ⟨el último toque : the finishing touch⟩ ⟨un toque de color : a touch of color⟩ **2** : ringing, peal, chime **3** *Mex* : shock, jolt **4 toque de queda** : curfew **5 toque de diana** : reveille
toquetear *vt* : to touch, to handle, to finger
toquilla *nf* : shawl
tórax *nm* : thorax
torbellino *nm* : whirlwind
torcedura *nf* **1** : twisting, buckling **2** : sprain
torcer {14} *vt* **1** : to bend, to twist **2** : to sprain **3** : to turn (a corner) **4** : to wring, to wring out **5** : to distort — *vi* : to turn — **torcerse** *vr*
torcido, -da *adj* **1** : twisted, crooked **2** : devious
tordo *nm* ZORZAL : thrush
torear *vt* **1** : to fight (bulls) **2** : to dodge, to sidestep
toreo *nm* : bullfighting
torero, -ra *n* MATADOR : bullfighter, matador
tormenta *nf* **1** : storm ⟨tormenta de nieve : snowstorm⟩ **2** : turmoil, frenzy
tormento *nm* **1** : torment, anguish **2** : torture
tormentoso, -sa *adj* : stormy, turbulent — **tormentosamente** *adv*
tornado *nm* : tornado
tornamesa *nmf* : turntable
tornar *vt* **1** : to return, to give back **2** : to make, to render — *vi* : to go back — **tornarse** *vr* : to become, to turn into
tornasol *nm* **1** : reflected light **2** : sunflower **3** : litmus
tornear *vt* : to turn (in carpentry)
torneo *nm* : tournament
tornillo *nm* **1** : screw **2 tornillo de banco** : vise
torniquete *nm* **1** : tourniquet **2** : turnstile
torno *nm* **1** : lathe **2** : winch **3 torno de banco** : vise **4 en torno a** : around, about ⟨en torno a este asunto : about this issue⟩ ⟨en torno suyo : around him⟩
toro *nm* : bull
toronja *nf* : grapefruit
toronjil *nm* : balm, lemon balm
torpe *adj* **1** DESMAÑADO : clumsy, awkward **2** : stupid, dull — **torpemente** *adv*

torpedear *vt* : to torpedo
torpedero, -ra *n* : shortstop
torpedo *nm* : torpedo
torpeza *nf* **1** : clumsiness, awkwardness **2** : stupidity **3** : blunder
torre *nf* **1** : tower ⟨torre de perforación : oil rig⟩ **2** : turret **3** : rook, castle (in chess)
torreja *nf* : French toast
torrencial *adj* : torrential — **torrencialmente** *adv*
torrente *nm* **1** : torrent **2 torrente sanguíneo** : bloodstream
torreón *nm, pl* **-rreones** : tower (of a castle)
torreta *nf* : turret (of a tank, ship, etc.)
tórrido, -da *adj* : torrid
torrija *nf Spain* → **torreja**
torso *nm* : torso, trunk
torta *nf* **1** (*in various countries*) : cake **2** : pie, tart **3** *Mex* : sandwich
tortazo *nm fam* : blow, wallop
tortícolis *nf* : stiff neck
tortilla *nf* **1** : tortilla **2** *or* **tortilla de huevo** : omelet
tórtola *nf* : turtledove
tortuga *nf* **1** : turtle, tortoise **2 tortuga de agua dulce** : terrapin **3 tortuga boba** : loggerhead
tortuoso, -sa *adj* : tortuous, winding
tortura *nf* : torture
torturador, -dora *n* : torturer
torturar *vt* : to torture, to torment
torvo, -va *adj* : grim, stern, baleful
torzamos, etc. → **torcer**
tos *nf* **1** : cough **2 tos ferina** : whooping cough
tosco, -ca *adj* : rough, coarse
toser *vi* : to cough
tosquedad *nf* : coarseness, roughness
tostada *nf* **1** : piece of toast **2** *Mex* : fried tortilla
tostador *nm* **1** : toaster **2** : roaster (for coffee)
tostadora *nf* **1** : toaster **2** : roaster (for coffee)
tostar {19} *vt* **1** : to toast **2** : to roast (coffee) **3** : to tan — **tostarse** *vr* : to get a tan
tostón *nm, pl* **tostones** *Car* : fried plantain chip
total¹ *adv* : in the end, so ⟨total, que no fui : in short, I didn't go⟩
total² *adj & nm* : total — **totalmente** *adv*
totalidad *nf* : totality, whole
totalitario, -ria *adj & n* : totalitarian
totalitarismo *nm* : totalitarianism
totalizar {21} *vt* : to total, to add up to
tótem *nm, pl* **tótems** : totem
totopo *nm CA, Mex* : tortilla chip
totuma *nf* : calabash
touchdown *nm* : touchdown (in football)
tour [ˈtur] *nm, pl* **tours** : tour, excursion
toxicidad *nf* : toxicity
tóxico¹, -ca *adj* : toxic, poisonous
tóxico² *nm* : poison
toxicomanía *nf* : drug addiction
toxicómano, -na *n* : drug addict
toxina *nf* : toxin
tozudez *nf* : stubbornness, obstinacy

tozudo, -da *adj* : stubborn, obstinate — **tozudamente** *adv*

traba *nf* **1** : tie, bond **2** : obstacle, hindrance

trabajador¹, -dora *adj* : hardworking

trabajador², -dora *n* : worker

trabajar *vi* **1** : to work ⟨trabaja mucho : he works hard⟩ ⟨trabajo de secretaria : I work as a secretary⟩ **2** : to strive ⟨trabajan por mejores oportunidades : they're striving for better opportunities⟩ **3** : to act, to perform ⟨trabajar en una película : to be in a movie⟩ — *vt* **1** : to work (metal) **2** : to knead **3** : to till **4** : to work on ⟨tienes que trabajar el español : you need to work on your Spanish⟩

trabajo *nm* **1** : work, job **2** LABOR : labor, work ⟨tengo mucho trabajo : I have a lot of work to do⟩ ⟨¡buen trabajo! : good job!, good work!⟩ **3** TAREA : task **4** ESFUERZO : effort **5** : piece of writing, essay, paper **6 costar trabajo** : to be difficult **7 tomarse el trabajo** : to take the trouble **8 trabajo en equipo** : teamwork **9 trabajos** *nmpl* : hardships, difficulties

trabajoso, -sa *adj* LABORIOSO : laborious — **trabajosamente** *adv*

trabalenguas *nms & pl* : tongue twister

trabar *vt* **1** : to join, to connect **2** : to impede, to hold back **3** : to strike up (a conversation), to form (a friendship) **4** : to thicken (sauces) — **trabarse** *vr* **1** : to jam **2** : to become entangled **3** : to be tongue-tied, to stammer

trabucar {72} *vt* : to confuse, to mix up

trabuco *nm* : blunderbuss

tracalero, -ra *adj Mex* : dishonest, tricky

tracción *nf* : traction

trace, etc. → **trazar**

tracto *nm* : tract

tractor *nm* : tractor

tradición *nf, pl* **-ciones** : tradition

tradicional *adj* : traditional — **tradicionalmente** *adv*

traducción *nf, pl* **-ciones** : translation

traducible *adj* : translatable

traducir {61} *vt* **1** : to translate **2** : to convey, to express — **traducirse** *vr* ∼ **en** : to result in

traductor, -tora *n* : translator

traer {81} *vt* **1** : to bring ⟨trae una ensalada : bring a salad⟩ **2** CAUSAR : to cause, to bring about ⟨el problema puede traer graves consecuencias : the problem could have serious consequences⟩ **3** : to carry, to have ⟨todos los periódicos traían las mismas noticias : all of the newspapers carried the same news⟩ **4** LLEVAR : to wear — **traerse** *vr* **1** : to bring along **2 traérselas** : to be difficult

traficante *nmf* : dealer, trafficker

traficar {72} *vi* **1** : to trade, to deal **2** ∼ **con** : to traffic in

tráfico *nm* **1** : trade **2** : traffic

tragaluz *nf, pl* **-luces** : skylight, fanlight

tragamonedas *nmfs & pl* : slot machine

tragaperras *nmfs & pl Spain* → **tragamonedas**

tragar {52} *v* : to swallow — **tragarse** *vr*

tragedia *nf* : tragedy

trágico, -ca *adj* : tragic — **trágicamente** *adv*

trago *nm* **1** : swallow, swig **2** : drink, liquor **3 trago amargo** : hard time

trague, etc. → **tragar**

traición *nf, pl* **traiciones** **1** : treason **2** : betrayal, treachery

traicionar *vt* : to betray

traicionero, -ra → **traidor**

traidor¹, -dora *adj* : traitorous, treacherous

traidor², -dora *n* : traitor

traiga, etc. → **traer**

tráiler [ˈtrailer] *or* **trailer** [ˈtrailer, ˈtreiler] *nm* : trailer

trailla *nf* **1** : leash **2** : harrow

traje *nm* **1** : suit **2** : dress **3** : costume **4 traje de baño** : swimsuit, bathing suit **5 traje de luces** : matador's outfit **6 traje de neopreno/buzo** : wet suit

trajín *nm, pl* **trajines** **1** : transport **2** *fam* : hustle and bustle

trajinar *vt* : to transport, to carry — *vi* : to rush around

trajo, etc. → **traer**

trama *nf* **1** : plot **2** : weave, weft (fabric)

tramar *vt* **1** : to plot, to plan **2** : to weave

tramitación *nf, pl* **-ciones** : processing

tramitar *vt* : to transact, to negotiate, to handle

trámite *nm* : procedure, step

tramo *nm* **1** : stretch, section **2** : flight (of stairs)

trampa *nf* **1** : trap ⟨trampa mortal : death trap⟩ **2 hacer trampas** : to cheat

trampear *vt* : to cheat

trampero, -ra *n* : trapper

trampilla *nf* : trapdoor

trampolín *nm, pl* **-lines** **1** : diving board **2** : trampoline **3** : springboard ⟨un trampolín al éxito : a springboard to success⟩ **4** : ski jump

tramposo¹, -sa *adj* : crooked, cheating

tramposo², -sa *n* : cheat, swindler

tranca *nf* **1** : stick, club **2** : bar, crossbar

trancar {72} *vt* : to bar (a door or window)

trancazo *nm* GOLPE : blow, hit

trance *nm* **1** : critical juncture, tough time **2** : trance **3 en trance de** : in the process of ⟨en trance de extinción : on the verge of extinction⟩

tranco *nm* **1** : stride **2** UMBRAL : threshold

tranque, etc. → **trancar**

tranquilidad *nf* : tranquility, peace

tranquilizador, -dora *adj* **1** : soothing **2** : reassuring

tranquilizante¹ *adj* **1** : reassuring **2** : tranquilizing

tranquilizante² *nm* : tranquilizer

tranquilizar {21} *vt* CALMAR : to calm down, to soothe ⟨tranquilizar la conciencia : to ease the conscience⟩ — **tranquilizarse** *vr*

tranquilo, -la *adj* CALMO : calm, tranquil ⟨una vida tranquila : a quiet life⟩ — **tranquilamente** *adv*

trans ['trans] *adj* 1 TRANSGÉNERO
: trans, transgender 2 TRANSEXUAL
: trans, transsexual
transacción *nf, pl* -ciones : transaction
transar *vi* TRANSIGIR : to give way, to
compromise — *vt* : to buy and sell
transatlántico[1], -ca *adj* : transatlantic
transatlántico[2] *nm* : ocean liner
transbordador *nm* 1 : ferry 2 transbordador espacial : space shuttle
transbordar *v* : to transfer
transbordo *nm* : transfer
transcendencia → trascendencia
transcender → trascender
transcribir {33} *vt* : to transcribe
transcrito *pp* → transcribir
transcripción *nf, pl* -ciones : transcription
transcurrir *vi* : to elapse, to pass
transcurso *nm* : course, progression ⟨en
el transcurso de cien años : over the
course of a hundred years⟩
transeúnte *nmf* 1 : passerby 2 : transient
transexual *adj & nmf* : transsexual
transferencia *nf* : transfer, transference
transferir {76} *vt* TRASLADAR : to transfer
— transferible *adj*
transfigurar *vt* : to transfigure, to transform — transfiguración *nf*
transformación *nf, pl* -ciones : transformation, conversion
transformador *nm* : transformer
transformar *vt* 1 CONVERTIR : to convert
2 : to transform, to change, to alter —
transformarse *vr*
tránsfuga *nmf* : defector, turncoat
transfusión *nf, pl* -siones : transfusion
transgénero *adj* : transgender ⟨las personas transgénero : transgender people⟩
transgénico[1], -ca *adj* : genetically modified
transgénico[2] *nm* : genetically modified
plant or animal
transgredir {1} *vt* : to transgress — transgresión *nf* — transgresor, -sora *n*
transición *nf, pl* -ciones : transition
⟨período de transición : transition pe-
riod⟩
transido, -da *adj* : overcome, beset ⟨tran-
sido de dolor : racked with pain⟩
transigir {35} *vi* 1 : to give in, to compromise 2 ∼ con : to tolerate, to put up
with
transistor *nm* : transistor
transitable *adj* : passable
transitar *vi* : to go, to pass, to travel ⟨tran-
sitar por la ciudad : to travel through the
city⟩
transitivo, -va *adj* : transitive
tránsito *nm* 1 TRÁFICO : traffic ⟨hora de
máximo tránsito : rush hour⟩ 2 : transit, passage, movement 3 : death, passing
transitorio, -ria *adj* 1 : transitory 2
: provisional, temporary — transitoria-
mente *adv*
translúcido, -da *adj* : translucent
translucir → traslucir
transmisible *adj* : transmissible

transmisión *nf, pl* -siones 1 : transmission, broadcast 2 : transfer 3 : transmission (of an automobile)
transmisor *nm* : transmitter
transmitir *vt* 1 : to transmit, to broadcast
2 : to pass on, to transfer — *vi* : to transmit, to broadcast
transparencia *nf* : transparency
transparentar *vt* : to reveal, to betray —
transparentarse *vr* 1 : to be transparent 2 : to show through
transparente[1] *adj* : transparent — trans-
parentemente *adv*
transparente[2] *nm* : shade, blind
transpiración *nf, pl* -ciones SUDOR : perspiration, sweat
transpirado, -da *adj* : sweaty
transpirar *vi* 1 SUDAR : to perspire, to
sweat 2 : to transpire
transplantar, transplante → trasplantar,
trasplante
transponer {60} *vt* 1 : to transpose, to
move about 2 TRASPLANTAR : to transplant — transponerse *vr* 1 OCULTARSE
: to hide 2 PONERSE : to set, to go down
(of the sun or moon) 3 DORMITAR : to
doze off
transportación *nf, pl* -ciones : transportation
transportador *nm* 1 : protractor 2
: conveyor
transportar *vt* 1 : to transport, to carry
2 : to transmit 3 : to transpose (music)
— transportarse *vr* : to get carried away
transporte *nm* : transport, transportation
⟨transporte público : public transit,
mass transit⟩
transportista *nmf* : hauler, carrier, trucker
transpuso, etc. → transponer
transversal *adj* : transverse, cross ⟨corte
transversal : cross section⟩
transversalmente *adv* : obliquely
transverso, -sa *adj* : transverse
tranvía *nm* : streetcar, trolley
trapeador *nm* : mop
trapear *vt* : to mop
trapecio *nm* 1 : trapezoid 2 : trapeze
trapecista *nmf* : trapeze artist
trapezoide *nm* : trapezoid
trapo *nm* 1 : cloth, rag ⟨trapo de polvo
: dust cloth⟩ 2 soltar el trapo : to burst
into tears 3 trapos *nmpl fam* : clothes
tráquea *nf* : trachea, windpipe
traquetear *vi* : to clatter, to jolt
traqueteo *nm* 1 : jolting 2 : clattering,
clatter
tras *prep* 1 : after ⟨día tras día : day after
day⟩ ⟨uno tras otro : one after another⟩
2 : behind ⟨tras la puerta : behind the
door⟩
trasbordar, trasbordo → transbordar,
transbordo
trascendencia *nf* 1 : importance, significance 2 : transcendence
trascendental *adj* 1 : transcendental 2
: important, momentous
trascendente *adj* 1 : important, significant 2 : transcendent
trascender {56} *vi* 1 : to leak out, to become known 2 : to spread, to have a

wide effect **3** ~ **a** : to smell of ⟨la casa trascendía a flores : the house smelled of flowers⟩ **4** ~ **de** : to transcend, to go beyond — *vt* : to transcend
trasero[1], **-ra** *adj* POSTERIOR : rear, back
trasero[2] *nm* : buttocks
trasfondo *nm* **1** : background, backdrop **2** : undertone, undercurrent
trasformación → **transformación**
trasgo *nm* : goblin, imp
trasgredir → **transgredir**
trashumante *adj* : seasonally migratory
trasiego *nm* **1** : coming and going **2** : transfer
trasladar *vt* **1** TRANSFERIR : to transfer, to move **2** POSPONER : to postpone **3** TRADUCIR : to translate **4** COPIAR : to copy, to transcribe — **trasladarse** *vr* MUDARSE : to move, to relocate
traslado *nm* **1** : transfer, move **2** : copy
traslapar *vt* : to overlap — **traslaparse** *vr*
traslapo *nm* : overlap
traslúcido, -da → **translúcido**
traslucir {45} *vi* : to reveal, to show — **traslucirse** *vr* : to show through
trasluz *nm, pl* **-luces al trasluz** : against the light
trasmano *nm* **a** ~ : out of the way, out of reach
trasmisión, trasmitir → **transmisión, transmitir**
trasnochar *vi* : to stay up all night
traspapelar *vt* : to misplace, to mislay (papers, etc.)
trasparencia, trasparente → **transparencia, transparente**
traspasar *vt* **1** PERFORAR : to pierce, to go through **2** : to go beyond ⟨traspasar los límites : to overstep the limits⟩ **3** ATRAVESAR : to cross, to go across **4** : to sell, to transfer
traspaso *nm* : transfer, sale
traspié *nm* **1** : stumble **2** : blunder
traspiración → **transpiración**
trasplantar *vt* : to transplant
trasplante *nm* : transplant
trasponer → **transponer**
trasportar, trasporte → **transportar**
trasquilar *vt* ESQUILAR : to shear
trastada *nf fam* : dirty trick
traste *nm* **1** : fret (on a guitar) **2** *CA, Mex, PRi* : kitchen utensil ⟨lavar los trastes : to do the dishes⟩ **3 dar al traste con** : to ruin, to destroy **4 irse al traste** : to fall through
trastero *nm* : junk room
trastienda *nf* : back room
trastornar *vt* : to disturb, to upset, to disrupt — **trastornarse** *vr*
trastorno *nm* **1** : disorder ⟨trastorno mental : mental disorder⟩ **2** : disturbance, upset
trastos *nmpl* **1** : implements, utensils **2** *fam* : pieces of junk, stuff
trasunto *nm* : image, likeness
tratable *adj* **1** : friendly, sociable **2** : treatable
tratado *nm* **1** : treatise **2** : treaty
tratamiento *nm* : treatment
tratante *nmf* : dealer, trader

tratar *vi* **1** ~ **con** : to deal with, to have contact with ⟨no trato mucho con los clientes : I don't have much contact with customers⟩ **2** ~ **de** : to try to ⟨estoy tratando de comer : I am trying to eat⟩ **3** ~ **de/sobre** : to be about, to concern ⟨el libro trata de las plantas : the book is about plants⟩ **4** ~ **en** : to deal in ⟨trata en herramientas : he deals in tools⟩ — *vt* **1** : to treat ⟨tratan bien a sus empleados : they treat their employees well⟩ **2** : to treat (a patient, a condition) **3** : to handle ⟨trató el tema con delicadeza : he handled the subject tactfully⟩ **4** : to treat (wood, etc.) — **tratarse** *vr* **1** : to socialize with **2** ~ **de** : to be about, to concern
trato *nm* **1** : deal, agreement **2** : relationship, dealings *pl* **3** : treatment ⟨malos tratos : ill-treatment⟩
trauma *nm* : trauma
traumático, -ca *adj* : traumatic — **traumáticamente** *adv*
traumatismo *nm* : injury ⟨traumatismo cervical : whiplash⟩
través *nm* **1 a través de** : across, through **2 al través** : crosswise, across **3 de través** : sideways
travesaño *nm* **1** : crossbar **2** : transom (of a window), crosspiece
travesía *nf* : voyage, crossing (of the sea)
travesti *or* **travestí** *adj & nmf, pl* **-tis** *or* **-ties** : transvestite
travesura *nf* **1** : prank, mischievous act **2 travesuras** *nfpl* : mischief
travieso, -sa *adj* : mischievous, naughty — **traviesamente** *adv*
trayecto *nm* **1** : journey **2** : route **3** : trajectory, path
trayectoria *nf* **1** : course, path, trajectory **2** : history (of a company, etc.), career (of a person)
trayendo → **traer**
traza *nf* **1** DISEÑO : design, plan **2** : appearance
trazado *nm* **1** BOSQUEJO : outline, sketch **2** PLAN : plan, layout
trazar {21} *vt* **1** : to trace **2** : to draw up, to devise **3** : to outline, to sketch
trazo *nm* **1** : stroke, line **2** : sketch, outline
trébol *nm* **1** : clover, shamrock **2** : club (playing card)
trece *adj & nm* : thirteen — **trece** *pron*
treceavo[1], **-va** *adj* : thirteenth
treceavo[2] *nm* : thirteenth (fraction)
trecho *nm* **1** : stretch, period ⟨de trecho en trecho : at intervals⟩ **2** : distance, space
tregua *nf* **1** : truce **2** : lull, respite **3 sin** ~ : relentless, unrelenting
treinta *adj & nm* : thirty — **treinta** *pron*
treintavo[1], **-va** *adj* : thirtieth
treintavo[2] *nm* : thirtieth (fraction)
tremendamente *adv* : tremendously
tremendo, -da *adj* **1** : tremendous, enormous **2** : terrible, dreadful **3** *fam* : great, super
trementina *nf* AGUARRÁS : turpentine
trémulo, -la *adj* **1** : trembling, shaky **2** : flickering

tren *nm* **1** : train **2** : set, assembly ⟨tren de aterrizaje : landing gear⟩ ⟨tren motriz : drive train⟩ **3** : speed, pace ⟨a todo tren : at top speed⟩

trenca *nf Spain* : duffle coat

trence, etc. → **trenzar**

trenza *nf* : braid, pigtail

trenzar {21} *vt* : to braid — **trenzarse** *vr* : to get involved

trepador, -dora *adj* : climbing ⟨rosal trepador : rambling rose⟩

trepadora *nf* **1** : climbing plant, climber **2** : nuthatch

trepar *vi* **1** : to climb ⟨trepar a un árbol : to climb up a tree⟩ **2** : to creep, to spread (of a plant)

trepidación *nf, pl* **-ciones** : vibration

trepidante *adj* **1** : vibrating **2** : fast, frantic

trepidar *vi* **1** : to shake, to vibrate **2** : to hesitate, to waver

tres[1] *adj & nm* : three ⟨tiene tres años : she's three years old⟩ ⟨el tres de mayo : (on) the third of May, (on) May third⟩ ⟨el siglo tres : the third century⟩

tres[2] *pron* : three ⟨somos tres : there are three of us⟩ ⟨son las tres : it's three (o'clock)⟩

trescientos[1], **-tas** *adj & pron* : three hundred

trescientos[2] *nms & pl* : three hundred

tresillo *nm* **1** : three-piece suit **2** *Spain* : three-piece furniture set **3** *Spain* : three-seat sofa

treta *nf* : trick, ruse

tri- *pref* : tri-

tríada *nf* : triad

triángulo *nm* : triangle — **triangular** *adj*

tribal *adj* : tribal

tribu *nf* : tribe

tribulación *nf, pl* **-ciones** : tribulation

tribuna *nf* **1** : dais, platform **2** : stands *pl*, bleachers *pl*, grandstand

tribunal *nm* : court, tribunal

tributar *vt* : to pay, to render — *vi* : to pay taxes

tributario[1], **-ria** *adj* : tax ⟨evasión tributaria : tax evasion⟩

tributario[2] *nm* : tributary

tributo *nm* **1** : tax **2** : tribute

triciclo *nm* : tricycle

tricolor *adj* : tricolor

tricotar *vt Spain* : to knit

tridente *nm* : trident

tridimensional *adj* : three-dimensional, 3-D

trienal *adj* : triennial

trifulca *nf fam* : row, ruckus

trigal *nm* : wheat field

trigésimo[1], **-ma** *adj* : thirtieth, thirty-

trigésimo[2], **-ma** *n* : thirtieth, thirty- (in a series)

trigo *nm* **1** : wheat **2 trigo sarraceno** : buckwheat

trigonometría *nf* : trigonometry

trigueño, -ña *adj* **1** : light brown (of hair) **2** MORENO : dark, olive-skinned

trillado, -da *adj* : trite, hackneyed

trilladora *nf* : thresher, threshing machine

trillar *vt* : to thresh

trillizo, -za *n* : triplet

trilogía *nf* : trilogy

trimestral *adj* : quarterly — **trimestralmente** *adv*

trimestre *nm* : trimester

trinar *vi* **1** : to thrill **2** : to warble

trinchar *vt* : to carve, to cut up

trinchera *nf* **1** : trench, ditch **2** : trench coat

trineo *nm* : sled, sleigh

trinidad *nf* **la Trinidad** : the Trinity

trino *nm* : trill, warble

trinquete *nm* : ratchet

trío *nm* : trio

tripa *nf* **1** INTESTINO : gut, intestine **2 tripas** *nfpl fam* : belly, tummy, insides *pl* ⟨dolerle a uno las tripas : to have a stomach ache⟩

tripartito, -ta *adj* : tripartite

triple *adj & nm* : triple

triplicado *nm* : triplicate

triplicar {72} *vt* : to triple, to treble

trípode *nm* : tripod

tripulación *nf, pl* **-ciones** : crew

tripulante *nmf* : crew member

tripular *vt* : to man

triquiñuela *nf* : trick

tris *nm* **estar en un tris de** : to be within an inch of, to be very close to

triste *adj* **1** : sad, gloomy ⟨ponerse triste : to become sad⟩ **2** : desolate, dismal ⟨una perspectiva triste : a dismal outlook⟩ **3** : sorry, sorry-looking ⟨la triste verdad : the sorry truth⟩

tristemente *adv* : sadly

tristeza *nf* DOLOR : sadness, grief

tristón, -tona *adj, mpl* **-tones** : melancholy, downhearted

tritón *nm, pl* **tritones** : newt

triturador *nm* → **trituradora**

trituradora *nf* **1** : grinder **2 trituradora de papel** : paper shredder **3 trituradora de basura** : garbage disposal

triturar *vt* : to crush, to grind

triunfador[1], **-dora** *adj* : triumphal, triumphant

triunfador[2], **-dora** *n* : winner

triunfal *adj* : triumphal, triumphant — **triunfalmente** *adv*

triunfante *adj* : triumphant, victorious

triunfar *vi* : to triumph, to win

triunfo *nm* **1** : triumph, victory **2** ÉXITO : success **3** : trump (in card games)

triunvirato *nm* : triumvirate

trivial *adj* **1** : trivial **2** : trite, commonplace

trivialidad *nf* : triviality

triza *nf* **1** : shred, bit **2 hacer trizas** : to tear into shreds, to smash to pieces

trocar {82} *vt* **1** CAMBIAR : to exchange, to trade **2** CAMBIAR : to change, to alter, to transform **3** CONFUNDIR : to confuse, to mix up

trocear *vt* : to carve, to cut up

trocha *nf* : path, trail

troce, etc. → **trozar**

trofeo *nm* : trophy

tromba *nf* **1** : whirlwind **2 tromba de agua** : downpour, cloudburst

trombón *nm, pl* **trombones** **1** : trombone **2** : trombonist — **trombonista** *nmf*

trombosis *nf* : thrombosis
trompa *nf* **1** : trunk (of an elephant), proboscis (of an insect) **2** : horn ⟨trompa de caza : hunting horn⟩ **3** : tube, duct (in the body)
trompada *nf fam* **1** : punch, blow **2** : bump, collision (of persons)
trompazo *nm fam* : bang, bump, smack
trompear *vt fam* : to punch
trompeta *nf* : trumpet
trompetista *nmf* : trumpet player, trumpeter
trompicón *nm*, *pl* **-cones 1** : stumble, lurch **2 a trompicones** : in fits and starts
trompo *nm* : spinning top
trona *nf Spain* : high chair (for a baby)
tronada *nf* : thunderstorm
tronado, -da *adj fam* : nuts, crazy
tronar {19} *vi* **1** : to thunder, to roar **2** : to be furious, to rage **3** *CA, Mex fam* : to shoot — *v impers* : to thunder ⟨está tronando : it's thundering⟩
tronchar *vt* **1** : to snap, to break off **2** : to cut off (relations)
tronco *nm* **1** : trunk (of a tree) **2** : log **3** : torso
trono *nm* **1** : throne **2** *fam* : toilet
tropa *nf* **1** : troop, soldiers *pl* **2** : crowd, mob **3** : herd (of livestock)
tropel *nm* : mob, swarm
tropezar {29} *vi* **1** : to trip, to stumble **2** : to slip up, to blunder **3** ~ **con** : to run into, to bump into **4** ~ **con** : to come up against (a problem) — **tropezarse** *vr* ~ **con** : to run into, to bump into
tropezón *nm*, *pl* **-zones 1** : stumble **2** : mistake, slip
tropical *adj* : tropical
trópico *nm* **1** : tropic ⟨trópico de Cáncer : tropic of Cancer⟩ **2 el trópico** : the tropics
tropiezo *nm* **1** CONTRATIEMPO : snag, setback **2** EQUIVOCACIÓN : mistake, slip
troqué, etc. → **trocar**
troquel *nm* : die (for stamping)
trotamundos *nmf* : globe-trotter
trotar *vi* **1** : to trot **2** : to jog **3** *fam* : to rush about
trote *nm* **1** : trot **2** *fam* : rush, bustle **3 de** ~ : durable, for everyday use
troupe *nf* : troupe
trovador, -dora *n* : troubadour
trozar {21} *vt* : to cut up, to dice
trozo *nm* **1** PEDAZO : piece, bit, chunk **2** : passage, extract
trucha *nf* : trout
truco *nm* **1** : trick **2** : knack
truculento, -ta *adj* : horrifying, gruesome
trueca, trueque etc. → **trocar**
truena, etc. → **tronar**
trueno *nm* : thunder
trueque *nm* : barter, exchange
trufa *nf* : truffle
truhán, truhana *n*, *pl* **truhanes** : rogue, scoundrel
truncar {72} *vt* **1** : to truncate, to cut short **2** : to thwart, to frustrate ⟨truncó sus esperanzas : she shattered their hopes⟩

trunco, -ca *adj* **1** : truncated **2** : unfinished, incomplete
trunque, etc. → **truncar**
trust *nm* : trust (business group)
tu *adj* **1** : your ⟨tu vestido : your dress⟩ ⟨toma tus vitaminas : take your vitamins⟩ **2** : thy
tú *pron* **1** : you ⟨tú eres mi hijo : you are my son⟩ **2** : thou
tuba *nf* : tuba
tubérculo *nm* : tuber
tuberculosis *nf* : tuberculosis
tuberculoso, -sa *adj* : tuberculous, tubercular
tubería *nf* : pipes *pl*, tubing
tuberoso, -sa *adj* : tuberous
tubo *nm* **1** : tube ⟨tubo de ensayo : test tube⟩ **2** : pipe ⟨tubo de desagüe : drainpipe⟩ **3 tubo digestivo** : alimentary canal
tubular *adj* : tubular
tuerca *nf* : nut ⟨tuercas y tornillos : nuts and bolts⟩
tuerce, etc. → **torcer**
tuerto, -ta *adj* : one-eyed, blind in one eye
tuerza, etc. → **torcer**
tuesta, etc. → **tostar**
tuétano *nm* : marrow
tufo *nm* **1** : fume, vapor **2** *fam* : stench, stink
tugurio *nm* : hovel
tuit *nm*, *pl* **tuits** : tweet (on the social network Twitter)
tuitear *v* : to tweet (on the social network Twitter)
tul *nm* : tulle
tulipán *nm*, *pl* **-panes** : tulip
tullido[1], -da *adj* : disabled, crippled
tullido[2], -da *n* : disabled person
tumba *nf* **1** SEPULCRO : tomb **2** FOSA : grave **3** : felling of trees
tumbar *vt* **1** : to knock down **2** : to fell, to cut down — *vi* : to fall down — **tumbarse** *vr* ACOSTARSE : to lie down
tumbo *nm* **1** : tumble, fall **2 dar tumbos** : to jolt, to bump around
tumbona *nf Spain* : deck chair
tumor *nm* : tumor
túmulo *nm* : burial mound
tumulto *nm* **1** ALBOROTO : commotion, tumult **2** MOTÍN : riot **3** MULTITUD : crowd
tumultuoso, -sa *adj* : tumultuous
tuna *nf* : prickly pear (fruit)
tunante, -ta *n* : crook, scoundrel
tundra *nf* : tundra
tunecino, -na *adj & n* : Tunisian
túnel *nm* : tunnel
tungsteno *nm* : tungsten
túnica *nf* : tunic
tupé *nm* PELUQUÍN : toupee
tupido, -da *adj* **1** DENSO : dense, thick **2** OBSTRUIDO : obstructed, blocked up
turba *nf* **1** : peat **2** : mob, throng
turbación *nf*, *pl* **-ciones 1** : disturbance **2** : alarm, concern **3** : confusion
turbante *nm* : turban
turbar *vt* **1** : to disturb, to disrupt **2** : to worry, to upset **3** : to confuse
turbina *nf* : turbine

turbio, -bia *adj* **1** : cloudy, murky, turbid **2** : dim, blurred **3** : shady, crooked
turbulencia *nf* : turbulence
turbulento, -ta *adj* : turbulent
turco¹, -ca *adj* : Turkish
turco², -ca *n* : Turk
turco³ *nm* : Turkish (language)
turgente *adj* : turgid, swollen
turismo *nm* : tourism, tourist industry
turista *nmf* : tourist, vacationer
turístico, -ca *adj* : tourist, travel
turnar *vi* : to take turns, to alternate
turno *nm* **1** : turn ⟨ya te tocará tu turno : you'll get your turn⟩ **2** : shift, duty ⟨turno de noche : night shift⟩ **3 por turno** : alternately
turón *nm, pl* **turones** : polecat
turquesa *nf* : turquoise
turrón *nm, pl* **turrones** : nougat

tusa *nf* : corn husk
tutear *vt* : to address as *tú*
tutela *nf* **1** : guardianship **2** : tutelage, protection
tuteo *nm* : addressing as *tú*
tutor, -tora *n* **1** : tutor **2** : guardian
tutoría *nf* : guardianship
tutorial *nm* : tutorial
tuvo, etc. → **tener**
tuyo¹, -ya *adj* : yours, of yours ⟨un amigo tuyo : a friend of yours⟩ ⟨¿es tuya esta casa? : is this house yours?⟩
tuyo², -ya *pron* **1** : yours ⟨ése es el tuyo : that one is yours⟩ ⟨trae la tuya : bring your own⟩ **2 los tuyos** : your relations, your friends ⟨¿vendrán los tuyos? : are your folks coming?⟩
tweed ['twið] *nm* : tweed
tweet ['twit] → **tuit**
twittear → **tuitear**

U

u¹ *nf* : twenty-fourth letter of the Spanish alphabet
u² *conj* (used instead of **o** before words beginning with o- or ho-) : or
uapití *nm, pl* **-tíes** or **-tís** or **-tí** : American elk, wapiti
ubicación *nf, pl* **-ciones** : location, position
ubicar {72} *vt* **1** SITUAR : to place, to put, to position **2** LOCALIZAR : to locate, to find — **ubicarse** *vr* **1** LOCALIZARSE : to be placed, to be located **2** SITUARSE : to position oneself
ubicuo, -cua *adj* : ubiquitous
ubre *nf* : udder
UCP [use'pe] (unidad central de procesamiento) → **CPU**
ucraniano¹, -na *adj* & *n* : Ukrainian
ucraniano² *nm* : Ukrainian (language)
Ud., Uds. → **usted**
uf *interj* : phew!
ufanarse *vr* ~ **de** : to boast about
ufano, -na *adj* **1** ORGULLOSO : proud **2** : self-satisfied, smug
ugandés, -desa *adj* & *n, mpl* **-deses** : Ugandan
ukelele *nm* : ukulele
úlcera *nf* : ulcer — **ulceroso, -sa** *adj*
ulcerar *vt* : to ulcerate — **ulcerarse** *vr*
ulterior *adj* : later, subsequent — **ulteriormente** *adv*
últimamente *adv* : lately, recently
ultimar *vt* **1** : to complete, to finish, to finalize **2** MATAR : to kill
ultimátum *nm, pl* **-tums** : ultimatum
último¹, -ma *adj* **1** : last, final ⟨la última galleta : the last cookie⟩ ⟨en último caso : as a last resort⟩ ⟨estar en último lugar : to be in last place⟩ **2** : last, latest, most recent ⟨su último viaje a España : her last trip to Spain⟩ ⟨en los últimos años : in recent years⟩ ⟨las últimas noticias : the latest news⟩ ⟨a última hora : at the

last moment⟩ **3** : last, farthest ⟨el último piso : the top floor⟩ **4 por** ~ : finally
último², -ma *n* : last one
ultra- *pref* : ultra-
ultrajar *vt* : to offend, to outrage, to insult
ultraje *nm* : outrage, insult
ultramar *nm* **de** ~ or **en** ~ : overseas, abroad
ultranza *nf* **1 a** ~ : to the extreme ⟨defender a ultranza : to defend fiercely⟩ **2 a** ~ : extreme, out-and-out ⟨perfeccionismo a ultranza : rabid perfectionism⟩
ultrarrojo, -ja *adj* : infrared
ultrasecreto, -ta *adj* : top secret
ultrasónico, -ca *adj* : ultrasonic
ultrasonido *nm* : ultrasound
ultravioleta *adj* : ultraviolet
ulular *vi* **1** : to hoot **2** : to howl, to wail
ululato *nm* : hoot (of an owl), wail (of a person)
umbilical *adj* : umbilical ⟨cordón umbilical : umbilical cord⟩
umbral *nm* : threshold, doorstep
un¹ *adj* → **uno¹**
un², una *art, mpl* **unos** **1** : a, an ⟨un año : a year⟩ ⟨una persona : a person⟩ **2 unos** or **unas** *pl* : some, a few ⟨hace unas semanas : a few weeks ago⟩ **3 unos** or **unas** *pl* : about, approximately ⟨unos veinte años antes : about twenty years before⟩
unánime *adj* : unanimous — **unánimemente** *adv*
unanimidad *nf* **1** : unanimity **2 por** ~ : unanimously
uncir {83} *vt* : to yoke
undécimo¹, -ma *adj* : eleventh
undécimo², -ma *n* : eleventh (in a series)
ungir {35} *vt* : to anoint
ungüento *nm* : ointment, salve
ungulado, -da *adj* : hoofed
únicamente *adv* : only, solely

único¹, -ca *adj* **1** : only, sole ⟨lo único que necesito : the only thing I need⟩ ⟨es hijo único : he's an only child⟩ **2** : unique, extraordinary

único², -ca *n* : only one ⟨los únicos que vinieron : the only ones who showed up⟩

unicornio *nm* : unicorn

unidad *nf* **1** : unity **2** : unit (of army, currency, etc.) **3** : drive, unit ⟨unidad (de memoria) flash : flash drive⟩

unido, -da *adj* **1** : joined, united **2** : close (of friends, etc.)

unificar {72} *vt* : to unify — **unificación** *nf*

uniformado, -da *adj* : uniformed

uniformar *vt* : to standardize, to make uniform

uniforme¹ *adj* : uniform — **uniforme-mente** *adv*

uniforme² *nm* : uniform

uniformidad *nf* : uniformity

unilateral *adj* : unilateral — **unilateral-mente** *adv*

unión *nf, pl* **uniones 1** : union (partnership) ⟨Unión Europea : European Union⟩ **2** : union, joining **3** JUNTURA : joint, coupling

unir *vt* **1** JUNTAR : to unite, to join **2** CONECTAR : to link, to connect **3** COMBINAR : to combine, to blend — **unirse** *vr* **1** : to join together **2** : to combine, to mix together **3** ∼ **a** : to join (a group, etc.)

unísono *nm* : unison ⟨al unísono : in unison⟩

unitario, -ria *adj* : unitary, unit ⟨precio unitario : unit price⟩

universal *adj* : universal — **universalidad** *nf* — **universalmente** *adv*

universidad *nf* : university

universitario¹, -ria *adj* : university, college

universitario², -ria *n* : university student, college student

universo *nm* : universe

unja, etc. → **ungir**

uno¹, una *adj* (*un before masculine singular nouns*) : one ⟨una cosa más : one more thing⟩ ⟨tiene treinta y un años : he's thirty-one years old⟩ ⟨el tomo uno : volume one⟩

uno² *nm* : one, number one

uno³, una *pron* **1** : one (number) ⟨uno por uno : one by one⟩ ⟨es la una : it's one o'clock⟩ **2** : one (person or thing) ⟨una es mejor que las otras : one (of them) is better than the others⟩ ⟨hacerlo uno mismo : to do it oneself⟩ ⟨uno no puede vivir así : you/one can't live like that⟩ **3** **unos, unas** *pl* : some (ones), some people **4** **uno y otro** : both **5** **unos y otros** : all of them **6** **el uno al otro** : one another, each other ⟨se enseñaron los unos a los otros : they taught each other⟩

untar *vt* **1** : to anoint **2** : to smear, to grease **3** : to bribe

unza, etc. → **uncir**

uña *nf* **1** : fingernail, toenail **2** : claw, hoof, stinger

UPC [upeˈse] (*unidad de procesamiento central*) → **CPU**

uranio *nm* : uranium

Urano *nm* : Uranus

urbanismo *nm* : city planning

urbanización *nf, pl* **-ciones** : housing development, residential area

urbanizar {21} *vt* : to develop (an area) — **urbanizado, -da** *adj* — **urbanizadora** *nf*

urbano, -na *adj* **1** : urban **2** CORTÉS : urbane, polite

urbe *nf* : large city, metropolis

urdimbre *nf* : warp (in a loom)

urdir *vt* : to engineer, to devise

uretra *nf* : urethra

urgencia *nf* **1** : urgency ⟨con urgencia : urgently⟩ **2** EMERGENCIA : emergency ⟨sala de urgencias : emergency room⟩ ⟨fue intervenido de urgencia : he had emergency surgery⟩

urgente *adj* **1** : urgent **2** : express (mail) — **urgentemente** *adv*

urgido, -da *adj* **estar urgido de** : to be in urgent need of

urgir {35} *v impers* : to be urgent, to be pressing ⟨me urge localizarlo : I urgently need to find him⟩ ⟨el tiempo urge : time is running out⟩

urinario, -ria *adj* : urinary

urja, etc. → **urgir**

urna *nf* **1** : urn **2** : ballot box ⟨acudir a las urnas : to go to the polls⟩

urogallo *nm* : grouse (bird)

urraca *nf* **1** : magpie **2** **urraca de América** : blue jay

urticaria *nf* : hives

uruguayo, -ya *adj & n* : Uruguayan

usado, -da *adj* **1** : used, secondhand **2** : worn, worn-out

usanza *nf* : custom, usage

usar *vt* **1** : to use, to make use of ⟨lo usó de martillo : he used it as a hammer⟩ **2** CONSUMIR : to consume, to use (up) **3** LLEVAR : to wear **4** **de usar y tirar** : disposable — **usarse** *vr* **1** : to be used **2** : to be in fashion

usina *nf* : power plant

uso *nm* **1** : use ⟨hacer uso de : to make use of⟩ ⟨objetos de uso personal : personal items⟩ **2** : wear ⟨uso y desgaste : wear and tear⟩ **3** COSTUMBRE : custom **4** **al uso** : typical, standard ⟨una casa al uso : a typical house⟩

usted *pron* **1** (*formal form of address in most countries; often written as Ud. or Vd.*) : you ⟨usted la conoce : you know her⟩ ⟨¿a usted le gusta el café? : do you like coffee?⟩ ⟨con/para usted : with/for you⟩ **2** **ustedes** *pl* (*often written as Uds. or Vds.*) : you, all of you ⟨muchos de ustedes : many of you⟩

usual *adj* : usual, common, normal ⟨poco usual : not very common⟩ — **usualmente** *adv*

usuario, -ria *n* : user

usura *nf* : usury

usurpador, -dora *n* : usurper

usurpar *vt* : to usurp — **usurpación** *nf*

utensilio *nm* : utensil, tool

uterino, -na *adj* : uterine

útero *nm* : uterus, womb
útil *adj* : useful, handy, helpful
utilería *nf* : props *pl*
útiles *nmpl* : implements, tools
utilidad *nf* **1** : utility, usefulness **2 utilidades** *nfpl* : profits
utilitario, -ria *adj* : utilitarian
utilizable *adj* : usable, fit for use
utilización *nf, pl* **-ciones** : utilization, use

utilizar {21} *vt* : to use, to utilize
útilmente *adv* : usefully
utopía *nf* : utopia
utópico, -ca *adj* : utopian
uva *nf* : grape
uve *nf Spain* → **ve²**
uve doble *nf Spain* → **ve doble**
úvula *nf* : uvula
uy *interj* **1** : oh! **2** : ow!

V

v *nf* : twenty-fifth letter of the Spanish alphabet
va → **ir**
vaca *nf* : cow
vacación *nf, pl* **-ciones 1** : vacation ⟨dos semanas de vacaciones : two weeks of vacation⟩ **2 estar de vacaciones** : to be on vacation **3 irse de vacaciones** : to go on vacation
vacacionar *vi Mex* : to vacation
vacacionista *nmf CA, Mex* : vacationer
vacante¹ *adj* : vacant, empty
vacante² *nf* : vacancy (for a job)
vaciar {85} *vt* **1** : to empty, to empty out, to drain **2** AHUECAR : to hollow out **3** : to cast (in a mold) — *vi* ∼ **en** : to flow into, to empty into
vacilación *nf, pl* **-ciones** : hesitation, vacillation
vacilante *adj* **1** : hesitant, unsure **2** : shaky, unsteady **3** : flickering
vacilar *vi* **1** : to hesitate, to vacillate, to waver **2** : to be unsteady, to wobble **3** : to flicker **4** *fam* : to joke, to fool around
vacío¹, -cía *adj* **1** : vacant **2** : empty **3** : meaningless
vacío² *nm* **1** : emptiness, void **2** : space, gap **3** : vacuum **4 hacerle el vacío a alguien** : to ostracize someone, to give someone the cold shoulder
vacuidad *nf* : vacuousness
vacuna *nf* : vaccine
vacunación *nf, pl* **-ciones** INOCULACIÓN : vaccination, inoculation
vacunar *vt* INOCULAR : to vaccinate, to inoculate
vacuno¹, -na *adj* : bovine ⟨ganado vacuno : cattle⟩
vacuno² *nm* : bovine
vacuo, -cua *adj* : empty, shallow, inane
vadear *vt* : to ford, to wade across
vado *nm* : ford
vagabundear *vi* : to wander, to roam about
vagabundo¹, -da *adj* **1** ERRANTE : wandering **2** : stray
vagabundo², -da *n* : vagrant, bum, vagabond
vagamente *adv* : vaguely
vagancia *nf* **1** : vagrancy **2** PEREZA : laziness, idleness
vagar {52} *vi* ERRAR : to roam, to wander
vagina *nf* : vagina — **vaginal** *adj*

vago¹, -ga *adj* **1** : vague **2** PEREZOSO : lazy, idle
vago², -ga *n* **1** : idler, loafer **2** VAGABUNDO : vagrant, bum
vagón *nm, pl* **vagones** : car (of a train)
vagoneta *nf* : station wagon
vague, etc. → **vagar**
vaguedad *nf* : vagueness
vahído *nm* : dizzy spell
vaho *nm* **1** : breath **2** : vapor, steam (on glass, etc.)
vaina *nf* **1** : sheath, scabbard **2** : pod (of a pea or bean) **3** *fam* MOLESTIA : nuisance, bother **4** *fam* COSA : thing
vainilla *nf* : vanilla
vaivén *nm, pl* **vaivenes 1** : swinging, swaying, rocking **2** : change, fluctuation ⟨los vaivenes de la vida : life's ups and downs⟩
vajilla *nf* : dishes *pl*, set of dishes
valdrá, etc. → **valer**
vale *nm* **1** : voucher **2** PAGARÉ : promissory note, IOU
valedero, -ra *adj* : valid
valentía *nf* : courage, valor
valer {84} *vt* **1** : to be worth ⟨valen una fortuna : they're worth a fortune⟩ ⟨no vale protestar : there's no point in protesting⟩ ⟨valer la pena : to be worth the trouble⟩ **2** : to cost ⟨¿cuánto vale? : how much does it cost?⟩ **3** : to earn, to gain ⟨le valió una reprimenda : it earned him a reprimand⟩ **4** : to protect, to aid ⟨¡válgame Dios! : God help me!⟩ **5** : to be equal to — *vi* **1** : to have value ⟨sus consejos no valen para nada : his advice is worthless⟩ **2** : to be valid, to count ⟨¡eso no vale! : that doesn't count!⟩ **3 hacerse valer** : to assert oneself **4 más vale** : it's better ⟨más vale que te vayas : you'd better go⟩ — **valerse** *vr* **1** ∼ **de** : to take advantage of **2 valerse solo** *or* **valerse por sí mismo** : to look after oneself **3** *Mex* : to be fair ⟨no se vale : it's not fair⟩
valeroso, -sa *adj* : brave, valiant
valet [ˈbalɛt, -ˈle] *nm* : jack (in playing cards)
valga, etc. → **valer**
valía *nf* : value, worth
validar *vt* : to validate — **validación** *nf*
validez *nf* : validity
válido, -da *adj* : valid
valiente *adj* **1** : brave, valiant **2** (*used ironically*) : fine, great ⟨¡valiente amiga!

: what a fine friend!⟩ — **valientemente**
adv
valija *nf* : suitcase, valise
valioso, -sa *adj* PRECIOSO : valuable, precious
Valium *marca registrada, m* — used for a drug that reduces anxiety and stress
valla *nf* **1** : fence, barricade **2** : hurdle (in sports) **3** : obstacle, hindrance
vallar *vt* : to fence, to put a fence around
valle *nm* : valley, vale
valor *nm* **1** : value, worth, importance **2** CORAJE : courage, valor **3 valores** *nmpl* : values, principles **4 valores** *nmpl* : securities, bonds **5 sin ~** : worthless
valoración *nf, pl* **-ciones 1** EVALUACIÓN : valuation, appraisal, assessment **2** APRECIACIÓN : appreciation
valorar *vt* **1** EVALUAR : to evaluate, to appraise, to assess **2** APRECIAR : to value, to appreciate
valorizarse {21} *vr* : to appreciate, to increase in value — **valorización** *nf*
vals *nm* : waltz
valuación *nf, pl* **-ciones** : valuation, appraisal
valuar {3} *vt* : to value, to appraise, to assess
válvula *nf* **1** : valve **2 válvula reguladora** : throttle
vamos → **ir**
vampiro *nm* : vampire
van → **ir**
vanagloriarse *vr* : to boast, to brag
vandalismo : vandalism
vándalo *nm* : vandal — **vandalismo** *nm*
vanguardia *nf* **1** : vanguard **2** : avant-garde **3 a la vanguardia** : at the forefront
vanguardista[1] *adj* : avant-garde
vanguardista[2] *nmf* : avant-gardist
vanidad *nf* : vanity
vanidoso, -sa *adj* PRESUMIDO : vain, conceited
vano, -na *adj* **1** INÚTIL : vain, useless **2** : vain, worthless ⟨vanas promesas : empty promises⟩ **3 en ~** : in vain, of no avail — **vanamente** *adv*
vapear *v* : to vape
vapor *nm* **1** : vapor, steam **2** : steamer, steamship **3 al vapor** : steamed
vaporeador *nm* : e-cigarette
vaporera *nf* : steamer (for cooking)
vaporizador *nm* **1** : vaporizer **2** : e-cigarette
vaporizar {21} *vt* : to vaporize — **vaporizarse** *vr* — **vaporización** *nf*
vaporoso, -sa *adj* : sheer, airy
vapulear *vt* : to beat, to thrash
vaquero[1]**, -ra** *adj* : cowboy ⟨pantalón vaquero : jeans⟩
vaquero[2]**, -ra** *n* : cowboy *m*, cowgirl *f*
vaqueros *nmpl* JEANS : jeans
vaquilla *nf* : heifer
vara *nf* **1** : pole, stick, rod **2** : staff (of office) **3** : lance, pike (in bullfighting) **4** : yardstick **5 vara de oro** : goldenrod
varado, -da *adj* **1** : beached, aground **2** : stranded
varar *vt* : to beach (a ship), to strand — *vi* : to run aground

variable *adj & nf* : variable — **variabilidad** *nf*
variación *nf, pl* **-ciones** : variation
variado, -da *adj* : varied, diverse
variante *adj & nf* : variant
varianza *nf* : variance
variar {85} *vt* **1** : to change, to alter **2** : to diversify — *vi* **1** : to vary, to change **2 variar de opinión** : to change one's mind
varicela *nf* : chicken pox
várices *or* **varices** *nfpl* : varicose veins
varicoso, -sa *adj* : varicose
variedad *nf* DIVERSIDAD : variety, diversity
varilla *nf* **1** : rod, bar **2** : spoke (of a wheel) **3** : rib (of an umbrella)
vario, -ria *adj* **1** : varied, diverse **2** : variegated, motley **3** : changeable **4 varios, varias** *pl* : various, several
variopinto, -ta *adj* : diverse, assorted, motley
varita *nf* : wand ⟨varita mágica : magic wand⟩
varón *nm, pl* **varones 1** HOMBRE : man, male **2** NIÑO : boy
varonil *adj* **1** : masculine, manly **2** : mannish
vas → **ir**
vasallo, -lla *n* : vassal — **vasallaje** *nm*
vasco[1]**, -ca** *adj & n* : Basque
vasco[2] *nm* : Basque (language)
vascular *adj* : vascular
vaselina *nf* : petroleum jelly
vasija *nf* : container, vessel
vaso *nm* **1** : glass, tumbler **2** : glassful **3** : vessel ⟨vaso sanguíneo : blood vessel⟩ **4 ahogarse en un vaso de agua** : to make a mountain out of a molehill **5 una tormenta en un vaso de agua** : a tempest in a teapot
vástago *nm* **1** : offspring, descendant **2** : shoot (of a plant)
vastedad *nf* : vastness, immensity
vasto, -ta *adj* : vast, immense
vataje *nm* : wattage
váter *nm* **1** : toilet **2** : bathroom
vaticinar *vt* : to predict, to foretell
vaticinio *nm* : prediction, prophecy
vatio *nm* : watt
vaya, etc. → **ir**
Vd., Vds. → **usted**
ve[1]**, etc.** → **ir, ver**
ve[2] *or* **ve corta** *or* **ve pequuña** *or* **ve chica** *nf* : (letter) v
vea, etc. → **ver**
vecinal *adj* : local
vecindad *nf* **1** : neighborhood, vicinity **2 casa de vecindad** : tenement
vecindario *nm* **1** : neighborhood, area **2** : residents *pl*
vecino[1]**, -na** *adj* : neighboring
vecino[2]**, -na** *n* **1** : neighbor **2** : resident, inhabitant
veda *nf* **1** PROHIBICIÓN : prohibition **2** : closed season (for hunting or fishing)
vedar *vt* **1** : to prohibit, to ban **2** IMPEDIR : to impede, to prevent
ve doble *or* **doble ve** *nf* : (letter) w
vegetación *nf, pl* **-ciones 1** : vegetation **2 vegetaciones** *nfpl* : adenoids

vegetal *adj & nm* : vegetable, plant
vegetar *vi* : to vegetate
vegetariano, -na *adj & n* : vegetarian — **vegetarianismo** *nm*
vegetativo, -va *adj* : vegetative
vehemente *adj* : vehement — **vehemencia** *nf* — **vehementemente** *adv*
vehículo *nm* : vehicle ⟨vehículo deportivo utilitario : sport-utility vehicle⟩ — **vehicular** *adj*
veía, etc. → **ver**
veinte *adj & nm* : twenty — **veinte** *pron*
veinteavo[1], -va *adj* : twentieth
veinteavo[2] *nm* : twentieth (fraction)
veintena *nf* : group of twenty, score ⟨una veintena de participantes : about twenty participants⟩
vejación *nf, pl* **-ciones** : ill-treatment, humiliation
vejete *nm* : old fellow, codger
vejez *nf* : old age
vejiga *nf* **1** : bladder **2** AMPOLLA : blister
vela *nf* **1** : watch, vigil, wake **2** : candle **3** : sail **4** : sailing **5 pasar la noche en vela** : to be up all night
velada *nf* : evening party
velado, -da *adj* **1** : veiled, hidden **2** : blurred **3** : muffled
velador[1], -dora *n* : guard, night watchman
velador[2] *nm* **1** : candlestick **2** : night table
velar *vt* **1** : to hold a wake over **2** : to watch over, to sit up with **3** : to blur, to expose (a photo) **4** : to veil, to conceal — *vi* **1** : to stay awake **2** ~ **por** : to watch over, to look after
velatorio *nm* VELORIO : wake (for the dead)
velcro *marca registrada, m* — used for a type of nylon fastener
veleidad *nf* **1** : fickleness **2** : whim, caprice
veleidoso, -sa *adj* : fickle, capricious
velero *nm* **1** : sailing ship **2** : sailboat
veleta *nf* : weather vane
vello *nm* **1** : body hair **2** : down, fuzz
vellón *nm, pl* **vellones 1** : fleece, sheepskin **2** *PRi* : nickel (coin)
vellosidad *nf* : fuzziness, hairiness
velloso, -sa *adj* : downy, fuzzy, hairy
velludo, -da *adj* : hairy
velo *nm* : veil
velocidad *nf* **1** : speed, velocity ⟨límite de velocidad : speed limit⟩ ⟨exceso de velocidad : speeding⟩ ⟨a gran velocidad : at high speed⟩ ⟨de alta velocidad : high-speed⟩ **2** MARCHA : gear (of an automobile)
velocímetro *nm* : speedometer
velocista *nmf* : sprinter
velorio *nm* VELATORIO : wake (for the dead)
velour *nm* : velour, velours
veloz *adj, pl* **veloces** : fast, quick, swift — **velozmente** *adv*
ven → **venir**
vena *nf* **1** : vein ⟨vena yugular : jugular vein⟩ **2** : vein, seam, lode **3** : grain (of wood) **4** : style ⟨en vena lírica : in a

lyrical vein⟩ **5** : strain, touch ⟨una vena de humor : a touch of humor⟩ **6** : mood
venado *nm* **1** : deer **2** : venison
venal *adj* : venal
vencedor, -dora *n* : winner, victor
vencejo *nm* : swift (bird)
vencer {86} *vt* **1** DERROTAR : to vanquish, to defeat **2** SUPERAR : to overcome, to surmount — *vi* **1** GANAR : to win, to triumph **2** CADUCAR : to expire ⟨el plazo vence el jueves : the deadline is Thursday⟩ **3** : to be due, to mature
vencerse *vr* **1** DOMINARSE : to control oneself **2** : to break, to collapse
vencido, -da *adj* **1** : defeated **2** : expired **3** : due, payable **4 darse por vencido** : to give up
vencimiento *nm* **1** : defeat **2** : expiration **3** : maturity (of a loan)
venda *nf* : bandage
vendaje *nm* : bandage, dressing
vendar *vt* **1** : to bandage **2 vendar los ojos** : to blindfold
vendaval *nm* : gale, strong wind
vendedor, -dora *n* : salesperson, salesman *m*, saleswoman *f*
vender *vt* **1** : to sell **2** : to sell out, to betray — **venderse** *vr* **1** : to be sold ⟨se vende : for sale⟩ **2** : to sell out
vendetta *nf* : vendetta
vendible *adj* : salable, marketable
vendimia *nf* : grape harvest
vendrá, etc. → **venir**
veneno *nm* **1** : poison **2** : venom
venenoso, -sa *adj* : poisonous, venomous
venerable *adj* : venerable
veneración *nf, pl* **-ciones** : veneration, reverence
venerar *vt* : to venerate, to revere
venéreo, -rea *adj* : venereal ⟨enfermedad venérea : venereal disease⟩
venero *nm* **1** VENA : seam, lode, vein **2** MANANTIAL : spring **3** FUENTE : origin, source
venezolano, -na *adj & n* : Venezuelan
venga, etc. → **venir**
venganza *nf* : vengeance, revenge
vengar {52} *vt* : to avenge — **vengarse** *vr* : to get even, to revenge oneself
vengativo, -va *adj* : vindictive, vengeful
vengue, etc. → **vengar**
venia *nf* **1** PERMISO : permission, leave **2** PERDÓN : pardon **3** : bow (of the head)
venial *adj* : venial
venida *nf* **1** LLEGADA : arrival, coming **2** REGRESO : return **3 idas y venidas** : comings and goings
venidero, -ra *adj* : coming, future
venir {87} *vi* **1** : to come ⟨lo vi venir : I saw him coming⟩ ⟨vino a verte : she came to see you⟩ ⟨vino a/de la oficina : he came to/from the office⟩ ⟨¡no me vengas con cuentos! : I don't want to hear your excuses!⟩ ⟨¡venga! : come on!⟩ **2** : to arrive ⟨vinieron en coche : they came by car⟩ **3** : to come, to originate ⟨sus zapatos vienen de Italia : her shoes are from Italy⟩ **4** : to come, to be available ⟨viene envuelto en plástico : it

comes wrapped in plastic⟩ **5** : to come back, to return ⟨no vengas tarde : don't come back late⟩ **6** : to affect, to overcome ⟨me vino un vahído : a dizzy spell came over me⟩ **7** : to fit ⟨te viene un poco grande : it's a little big for you⟩ **8** *(with the present participle)* : to have been ⟨viene entrenando diariamente : he's been training daily⟩ **9** ~ **a** *(with the infinitive)* : to end up, to turn out ⟨viene a ser lo mismo : it comes out the same⟩ **10 que viene** : coming, next ⟨el año que viene : next year⟩ **11 venir bien** : to be suitable, to be just right — **venirse** *vr* **1** : to come, to arrive ⟨¿te vienes conmigo? : are you coming with me?⟩ **2** : to come back **3 venirse abajo** : to fall apart, to collapse

venta *nf* **1** : sale **2 venta al por menor** *or* **venta al detalle** : retail **3 venta al por mayor** : wholesale **4 venta por correo** : mail order

ventaja *nf* **1** : advantage **2** : lead, head start ⟨llevar (la) ventaja : to be in the lead⟩ **3 ventajas** *nfpl* : perks, extras

ventajoso, -sa *adj* **1** : advantageous **2** : profitable — **ventajosamente** *adv*

ventana *nf* **1** : window (of a building) **2** : window (on a computer) **3 ventana de la nariz** : nostril

ventanal *nm* : large window

ventanilla *nf* **1** : window (of a vehicle or airplane) **2** : ticket window, box office

ventero, -ra *n* : innkeeper

ventilación *nf, pl* **-ciones** : ventilation

ventilador *nm* **1** : ventilator **2** : fan

ventilar *vt* **1** : to ventilate, to air out **2** : to air, to discuss **3** : to make public, to reveal — **ventilarse** *vr* : to get some air

ventisca *nf* : snowstorm, blizzard

ventisquero *nm* : snowdrift

ventolera *nf* : gust of wind

ventosa *nf* : sucker

ventosear *vi* : to break wind

ventosidad *nf* : wind, flatulence

ventoso, -sa *adj* : windy

ventrículo *nm* : ventricle

ventrílocuo, -cua *n* : ventriloquist

ventriloquia *nf* : ventriloquism

ventura *nf* **1** : fortune, luck, chance **2** : happiness **3 a la ventura** : at random, as it comes

venturoso, -sa *adj* **1** AFORTUNADO : fortunate, lucky **2** : successful

Venus *nm* : Venus

venza, etc. → **vencer**

ver¹ {88} *vt* **1** : to see ⟨no veo nada : I can't see anything⟩ ⟨lo vi con mis propios ojos : I saw it with my own eyes⟩ ⟨vimos una película : we saw a movie⟩ **2** ENTENDER : to understand, to see ⟨ya lo veo : (so) I get it⟩ ⟨no veo por qué : I don't see why⟩ ⟨¿ves lo que quiero decir? : do you see what I mean?⟩ **3** EXAMINAR : to examine, to look into ⟨lo veré : I'll take a look at it⟩ **4** JUZGAR : to see, to judge ⟨otra forma de verlo : another way of looking at it⟩ ⟨lo veo bien : I think it's good/fine⟩ **5** VISITAR : to see, to meet, to visit ⟨vino a verte

: she came to see you⟩ **6** AVERIGUAR : to see, to find out ⟨vino a ver cómo estabas : she came to see how you were⟩ — *vi* **1** : to see **2** ENTERARSE : to learn, to find out **3** ENTENDER : to understand ⟨ya veo : (so) I see⟩ ⟨a mi modo de ver : to my way of thinking, the way I see it⟩ **4 (vamos) a ver** : let's see — **verse** *vr* **1** HALLARSE : to find oneself **2** PARECER : to look, to appear **3** ENCONTRARSE : to see each other, to meet

ver² *nm* **1** : looks *pl*, appearance **2** : opinion ⟨a mi ver : in my view⟩

vera *nf* : side ⟨a la vera del camino : alongside the road⟩

veracidad *nf* : truthfulness, veracity

veranda *nf* : veranda

veraneante *nmf* : summer vacationer

veranear *vi* : to spend the summer

veraneo *nm* : summer vacation

veraniego, -ga *adj* **1** ESTIVAL : summer ⟨el sol veraniego : the summer sun⟩ **2** : summery

verano *nm* : summer

veras *nfpl* **de** ~ : really, truly

veraz *adj, pl* **veraces** : truthful

verbal *adj* : verbal — **verbalmente** *adv*

verbalizar {21} *vt* : to verbalize, to express

verbena *nf* FIESTA : festival, fair

verbigracia *adv* : for example

verbo *nm* : verb

verbosidad *nf* : wordiness

verboso, -sa *adj* : verbose, wordy

verdad *nf* **1** : truth ⟨es verdad : it's true⟩ ⟨a decir verdad : to tell the truth⟩ **2 de** ~ : really, truly **3 de** ~ : real ⟨un amigo de verdad : a true friend⟩ **4 ¿verdad?** : right?, isn't that so?

verdaderamente *adv* : really, truly

verdadero, -dera *adj* **1** REAL, VERÍDICO : true, real **2** AUTÉNTICO : genuine

verde¹ *adj* **1** : green (in color) **2** : green, unripe **3** : inexperienced, green **4** : dirty, risqué

verde² *nm* : green

verdeante *adj* : verdant

verdín *nm, pl* **verdines** : slime, scum

verdor *nm* : greenness

verdoso, -sa *adj* : greenish

verdugo *nm* **1** : executioner, hangman **2** : tyrant

verdugón *nm, pl* **-gones** : welt (on the body)

verdulería *nf* : greengrocer's store

verdulero, -ra *n* : greengrocer

verdura *nf* : vegetable(s), green(s)

vereda *nf* **1** SENDA : path, trail **2** : sidewalk, pavement

veredicto *nm* : verdict

verga *nf* : spar, yard (of a ship)

vergonzoso, -sa *adj* **1** : disgraceful, shameful **2** : bashful, shy — **vergonzosamente** *adv*

vergüenza *nf* **1** : embarrassment ⟨me hiciste pasar vergüenza : you embarrassed me⟩ ⟨me da vergüenza : I'm embarrassed (about it)⟩ ⟨¡qué vergüenza! : how embarrassing!⟩ **2** : disgrace, shame ⟨ser una vergüenza para : to be a disgrace to⟩ **3** : bashfulness, shyness

vericueto *nm* : rough terrain

verídico, -ca *adj* **1** REAL, VERDADERO : true, real **2** VERAZ : truthful

verificación *nf, pl* **-ciones 1** : verification **2** : testing, checking

verificador, -dora *n* : inspector, tester

verificar {72} *vt* **1** : to verify, to confirm **2** : to test, to check **3** : to carry out, to conduct — **verificarse** *vr* **1** : to take place, to occur **2** : to come true

verja *nf* **1** : rails *pl* (of a fence) **2** : grating, grille **3** : gate

vermut *nm, pl* **vermuts** : vermouth

vernáculo, -la *adj* : vernacular

vernal *adj* : vernal, spring

verosímil *adj* **1** : probable, likely **2** : credible, realistic

verosimilitud *nf* **1** : probability, plausibility **2** : realism

verraco *nm* : boar

verruga *nf* : wart

versado, -da *adj* ~ **en** : versed in, knowledgeable about

versar *vi* ~ **sobre** : to deal with, to be about

versátil *adj* **1** : versatile **2** : fickle

versatilidad *nf* **1** : versatility **2** : fickleness

versículo *nm* : verse (in the Bible)

versión *nf, pl* **versiones 1** : version **2** : translation

verso *nm* : verse

versus *prep* : versus, against

vértebra *nf* : vertebra — **vertebral** *adj*

vertebrado[1], -da *adj* : vertebrate

vertebrado[2] *nm* : vertebrate

vertedero *nm* **1** : garbage dump **2** DESAGÜE : drain, outlet

verter {56} *vt* **1** : to pour (liquid), to dump (waste) **2** DERRAMAR : to spill, to shed **3** VACIAR : to empty out **4** EXPRESAR : to express, to voice **5** TRADUCIR : to translate, to render — *vi* : to flow

vertical *adj & nf* : vertical — **verticalmente** *adv*

vértice *nm* : vertex, apex

vertido *nm* : spilling, spill

vertiente *nf* **1** : slope **2** : aspect, side, element

vertiginoso, -sa *adj* : dizzying — **vertiginosamente** *adv*

vértigo *nm* : vertigo, dizziness

vesícula *nf* **1** : vesicle **2 vesícula biliar** : gallbladder

vespertino, -na *adj* : evening

vestíbulo *nm* : vestibule, hall, lobby, foyer

vestido *nm* **1** : dress, costume, clothes *pl* **2** : dress (garment)

vestidor *nm* : dressing room

vestiduras *nfpl* **1** : clothing, raiment, regalia **2** : vestments (of a priest)

vestigio *nm* : vestige, sign, trace

vestimenta *nf* ROPA : clothing, clothes *pl*

vestir {54} *vt* **1** : to dress, to clothe **2** LLEVAR : to wear ⟨vestir de blanco : to wear white⟩ **3** ADORNAR : to decorate, to dress up — *vi* **1** : to dress ⟨vestir bien : to dress well⟩ **2** : to look good, to suit

the occasion — **vestirse** *vr* **1** : to get dressed **2** ~ **con** : to wear, to dress in **3** ~ **de** : to dress up as ⟨se vistieron de soldados : they dressed up as soldiers⟩ **4** ~ **de** : to wear, to dress in

vestuario *nm* **1** : wardrobe **2** : dressing room, locker room

veta *nf* **1** : grain (in wood) **2** : vein, seam, lode **3** : trace, streak ⟨una veta de terco : a stubborn streak⟩

vetar *vt* : to veto

veteado, -da *adj* : streaked, veined

veteranía *nf* **1** EXPERIENCIA : experience **2** ANTIGÜEDAD : seniority

veterano, -na *adj & n* : veteran

veterinaria *nf* : veterinary medicine

veterinario[1], -ria *adj* : veterinary

veterinario[2], -ria *n* : veterinarian

veto *nm* : veto

vetusto, -ta *adj* ANTIGUO : ancient, very old

vez *nf, pl* **veces 1** : time, occasion ⟨a la vez : at the same time⟩ ⟨a veces : at times, occasionally⟩ ⟨algunas veces : sometimes⟩ ⟨cada vez : each/every time⟩ ⟨cada vez más : more and more⟩ ⟨cada vez menos : less and less⟩ ⟨de vez en cuando : from time to time⟩ **2** (*with numbers*) : time ⟨una vez : once⟩ ⟨dos veces : twice⟩ ⟨de una vez : all at once⟩ ⟨dc una vcz para sicmpre : once and for all⟩ ⟨una y otra vez : time after time, again and again⟩ **3** : turn ⟨a su vez : in turn⟩ ⟨en vez de : instead of⟩ ⟨hacer las veces de : to act as, to stand in for⟩ **4 alguna vez** : sometime (in the future), on occasion (in the past) ⟨¿has viajado alguna vez? : have you ever traveled?⟩

vía[1] *nf* **1** RUTA, CAMINO : road, route, way ⟨vía pública : public thoroughfare⟩ ⟨Vía Láctea : Milky Way⟩ **2** MEDIO : means, way ⟨por la vía diplomática : through diplomatic channels⟩ ⟨por vía aérea : by air, airmail⟩ ⟨por vía oral : orally⟩ **3** : track, line (of a railroad) **4** : tract ⟨vía urinaria : urinary tract⟩ **5 en vías de** : in the process of ⟨en vías de solución : on the road to a solution⟩ ⟨países en vías de desarrollo : developing countries⟩ ⟨animales en vías de extinción : endangered animals⟩

vía[2] *prep* : via

viable *adj* : viable, feasible — **viabilidad** *nf*

viaducto *nm* : viaduct

viajante *mf* : traveling salesman, traveling saleswoman

viajar *vi* : to travel, to journey

viaje *nm* : trip, journey ⟨ir de viaje : to go on a trip⟩ ⟨estar de viaje : to be away⟩ ⟨¡buen viaje! : have a good trip!⟩ ⟨viaje de ida : one-way trip⟩ ⟨viaje de ida y vuelta/regreso : round trip⟩ ⟨viaje de regreso/vuelta : return trip⟩ ⟨viaje de negocios : business trip⟩ ⟨viaje en tren : train trip⟩

viajero[1], -ra *adj* : traveling

viajero[2], -ra *n* **1** : traveler **2** PASAJERO : passenger

vial *adj* : road, traffic

viático *nm* : travel allowance, travel expenses *pl*
víbora *nf* : viper
vibración *nf, pl* **-ciones** : vibration
vibrador *nm* : vibrator
vibrante *adj* 1 : vibrant 2 : vibrating
vibrar *vi* : to vibrate
vicario, -ria *n* : vicar
vice- *pref* : vice-
vicealmirante *nmf* : vice admiral
vicepresidente, -ta *n* : vice president — **vicepresidencia** *nf*
viceversa *adv* : vice versa, conversely
viciado, -da *adj* : stuffy, close
viciar *vt* 1 : to corrupt 2 : to invalidate 3 FALSEAR : to distort 4 : to pollute, to adulterate
vicio *nm* 1 : vice, depravity 2 : bad habit 3 : defect, blemish
vicioso, -sa *adj* : depraved, corrupt
vicisitud *nf* : vicissitude
víctima *nf* : victim
victimario, -ria *n* ASESINO : killer, murderer
victimizar {21} *vt Arg, Mex* : to victimize
victoria *nf* : victory — **victorioso, -sa** *adj* — **victoriosamente** *adv*
victoriano, -na *adj* : Victorian
vid *nf* : vine, grapevine
vida *nf* 1 : life ⟨con vida : alive⟩ ⟨sin vida : lifeless, dead⟩ ⟨perder/quitarse la vida : to lose/take one's life⟩ 2 : life ⟨la vida cotidiana : everyday life⟩ ⟨vida nocturna : nightlife⟩ ⟨estilo de vida : lifestyle, way of life⟩ ⟨así es la vida : that's life⟩ 3 : life, lifetime ⟨nunca en mi/la vida : never in my life⟩ ⟨de por vida : for life⟩ 4 : life ⟨vida animal/vegetal : animal/plant life⟩ 5 BIOGRAFÍA : life, biography 6 : living, livelihood ⟨ganarse la vida : to earn one's living⟩ 7 VIVEZA : life, liveliness 8 **media vida** : half-life
vidente *nmf* 1 : psychic, clairvoyant 2 : sighted person
video *or* **vídeo** *nm* : video
videocinta *nf* : videotape
videocasete *or* **videocassette** *nm* : videocassette
videocasetera *or* **videocassettera** *nf* : videocassette recorder, video recorder, VCR
videocámara *nf* : video camera
videoclip *nm, pl* **-clips** : video
videoclub *nm* : video store
videoconferencia *nf* : videoconference
videograbar *vt Mex* : to videotape
videojuego *nm* : video game
videojugador, -dora *n* : gamer
videollamada *nf* : video call
vidriado *nm* : glaze
vidriar *vt* : to glaze (pottery, tile, etc.)
vidriera *nf* 1 : stained-glass window 2 : glass door or window 3 : store window
vidriero, -ra *n* : glazier
vidrio *nm* 1 : glass, piece of glass 2 : windowpane
vidrioso, -sa *adj* 1 : brittle, fragile 2 : slippery 3 : glassy, glazed (of eyes) 4 : touchy, delicate
vieira *nf* 1 : scallop 2 : scallop shell

viejo¹, -ja *adj* 1 ANCIANO : old, elderly 2 ANTIGUO : former, long-standing ⟨viejas tradiciones : old traditions⟩ ⟨viejos amigos : old friends⟩ 3 GASTADO : old, worn, worn-out 4 **hacerse viejo** : to get old
viejo², -ja *n* ANCIANO : old man *m*, old woman *f*
viene, etc. → **venir**
viento *nm* 1 : wind 2 **hacer viento** : to be windy 3 **contra viento y marea** : against all odds 4 **viento en popa** : splendidly, successfully
vientre *nm* 1 : abdomen, belly 2 : womb 3 : bowels *pl*
viernes *nms & pl* : Friday ⟨el viernes : (on) Friday⟩ ⟨los viernes : (on) Fridays⟩ ⟨cada (dos) viernes : every (other) Friday⟩ ⟨el viernes pasado : last Friday⟩ ⟨el próximo viernes : next Friday⟩
vierte, etc. → **verter**
vietnamita¹ *adj & nmf* : Vietnamese
vietnamita² *nf* : Vietnamese (language)
viga *nf* 1 : beam, rafter, girder 2 **viga voladiza** : cantilever
vigencia *nf* 1 : validity 2 : force, effect ⟨entrar en vigencia : to go into effect⟩
vigente *adj* : valid, in force
vigésimo¹, -ma *adj* 1 : twentieth, twenty- ⟨la vigésima segunda edición : the twenty-second edition⟩
vigésimo², -ma *n* : twentieth, twenty- (in a series)
vigía *nmf* : lookout
vigilancia *nf* : vigilance, watchfulness ⟨bajo vigilancia : under surveillance⟩
vigilante¹ *adj* : vigilant, watchful
vigilante² *nmf* : watchman, guard
vigilar *vt* 1 CUIDAR : to look after, to keep an eye on 2 GUARDAR : to watch over, to guard — *vi* 1 : to be watchful 2 : to keep watch
vigilia *nf* 1 VELA : wakefulness 2 : night work 3 : vigil (in religion)
vigor *nm* 1 : vigor, energy, strength 2 VIGENCIA : force, effect ⟨entrar en vigor : to take effect⟩
vigorizante *adj* : invigorating
vigorizar {21} *vt* : to strengthen, to invigorate
vigoroso, -sa *adj* : vigorous — **vigorosamente** *adv*
VIH *nm* (virus de inmunodeficiencia humana) : HIV
vikingo, -ga *adj & n* : Viking
vil *adj* : vile, despicable, base
vileza *nf* 1 : vileness 2 : despicable action, villainy
vilipendiar *vt* : to vilify, to revile
villa *nf* 1 : town, village 2 : villa 3 **villa miseria** *or* **villa de emergencia** *Arg* : shantytown, slums *pl*
villancico *nm* : carol, Christmas carol
villano, -na *n* 1 : villain 2 : peasant
vilmente *adv* : basely
vilo *nm* 1 **en ~** : in the air 2 **en ~** : uncertain, in suspense
vinagre *nm* : vinegar
vinagrera *nf* : cruet (for vinegar)
vinagreta *nf* : vinaigrette

vinatería *nf* : wine shop
vinculación *nf, pl* -ciones 1 : linking 2 RELACIÓN : bond, link, connection
vincular *vt* CONECTAR, RELACIONAR : to tie, to link, to connect
vínculo *nm* 1 LAZO : tie, link, bond 2 HIPERENLACE : link
vindicación *nf, pl* -ciones : vindication
vindicar *vt* 1 : to vindicate 2 : to avenge
vinilo *nm* : vinyl
vino¹, etc. → venir
vino² *nm* : wine
viña *nf* : vineyard
viñedo *nm* : vineyard
viñeta *nf* : cartoon
vio, etc. → ver
viola *nf* : viola
violación *nf, pl* -ciones 1 : violation, offense 2 : rape
violador¹, -dora *n* : violator, offender
violador² *nm* : rapist
violar *vt* 1 : to rape 2 : to violate (a law or right) 3 PROFANAR : to desecrate
violencia *nf* : violence
violentamente *adv* : by force, violently
violentar *vt* 1 FORZAR : to break open, to force 2 : to distort (words or ideas) — violentarse *vr* : to force oneself
violento, -ta *adj* 1 : violent 2 EMBARAZOSO, INCÓMODO : awkward, embarrassing
violeta¹ *adj & n* : violet (color)
violeta² *nf* : violet (flower)
violín *nm, pl* -lines : violin
violinista *nmf* : violinist
violonchelista *nmf* : cellist
violonchelo *nm* : cello, violoncello
VIP *nmf, pl* VIPs : VIP
viraje *nm* 1 : turn, swerve 2 : change
viral *adj* : viral
virar *vi* : to tack, to turn, to veer
virgen¹ *adj* : virgin ⟨lana virgen : virgin wool⟩
virgen² *nmf, pl* vírgenes : virgin ⟨la Santísima Virgen : the Blessed Virgin⟩
virginal *adj* : virginal, chaste
virginidad *nf* : virginity
Virgo¹ *nm* : Virgo (sign or constellation)
Virgo² *nmf* : Virgo (person)
vírico, -ca *adj Spain* : viral
viril *adj* : virile — virilidad *nf*
virrey, -rreina *n* : viceroy *m*
virtual *adj* : virtual — virtualmente *adv*
virtud *nf* 1 : virtue 2 en virtud de : by virtue of
virtuosismo *nm* : virtuosity
virtuoso¹, -sa *adj* : virtuous
virtuoso², -sa *n* : virtuoso
viruela *nf* 1 : smallpox 2 : pockmark
virulencia *nf* : virulence
virulento, -ta *adj* : virulent
virus *nm* : virus
viruta *nf* : shaving
visa *nf* : visa
visado *nm Spain* : visa
visceral *adj* : visceral
vísceras *nfpl* : viscera, entrails
viscosidad *nf* : viscosity
viscoso, -sa *adj* : viscous
visera *nf* : visor

visibilidad *nf* : visibility
visible *adj* : visible — visiblemente *adv*
visillo *nm* : sheer curtain, lace curtain
visión *nf, pl* visiones 1 : vision, eyesight 2 : view, perspective 3 : vision, illusion ⟨ver visiones : to be seeing things⟩
visionario, -ria *adj & n* : visionary
visita *nf* 1 : visit, call ⟨hacer una visita : to pay a visit⟩ ⟨ir de visita : to go visiting⟩ 2 : visitor ⟨tener visita(s) : to have company⟩
visitador, -dora *n* : visitor, frequent caller
visitante¹ *adj* : visiting
visitante² *nmf* : visitor
visitar *vt* : to visit
vislumbrar *vt* 1 : to discern, to make out 2 : to begin to see, to have an inkling of
vislumbre *nf* : glimmer, gleam
viso *nm* 1 APARIENCIA : appearance ⟨tener visos de : to seem, to show signs of⟩ 2 DESTELLO : glint, gleam 3 : sheen, iridescence
visón *nm, pl* visones : mink
visor *nm* 1 : viewfinder (of a camera), sight (of a gun) 2 : scout (in sports)
víspera *nf* 1 : eve, day before 2 vísperas *nfpl* : vespers
vista *nf* 1 VISIÓN : vision, eyesight ⟨perder la vista : to lose one's eyesight⟩ 2 MIRADA : look, gaze, glance ⟨bajó la vista : he looked down⟩ ⟨fijar la vista en : to fix one's gaze on⟩ 3 PANORAMA : view, vista, panorama 4 : hearing (in court) 5 a la vista : in sight, in view 6 a primera vista : at first sight 7 con vistas a : with a view to 8 en vistas de : in view of 9 hacer la vista gorda : to turn a blind eye 10 ¡hasta la vista! : so long!, see you! 11 perder de vista : to lose sight of 12 punto de vista : point of view 13 saltar a la vista : to be obvious, to stand out
vistazo *nm* : glance, look
viste, etc. → ver¹, vestir
visto¹ *pp* → ver
visto², -ta *adj* 1 : obvious, clear 2 : in view of, considering 3 estar bien visto : to be approved of 4 estar mal visto : to be frowned upon 5 por lo visto : apparently 6 nunca visto : unheard-of 7 visto que : since, given that
visto³ *nm* visto bueno : approval
vistoso, -sa *adj* : colorful, bright
visual *adj* : visual — visualmente *adv*
visualizador *nm* : display (of a device)
visualizar {21} *vt* 1 : to visualize 2 : to display (on a screen)
vital *adj* 1 : vital 2 : lively, dynamic
vitalicio, -cia *adj* : life, lifetime
vitalidad *nf* : vitality
vitamina *nf* : vitamin
vitamínico, -ca *adj* : vitamin ⟨complejos vitamínicos : vitamin compounds⟩
viticultor, -ra *n* : wine producer
viticultura *nf* : wine producing
vítor *nm* : cheer
vitorear *vt* : to cheer
vitral *nm* : stained-glass window
vítreo, -rea *adj* : glass, glassy

vitrina *nf* **1** : showcase, display case **2** : store window
vitriolo *nm* : vitriol
vituperar *vt* : to condemn, to lambaste
viudez *nf* : state of being widowed ⟨su primer año de viudez : his first year as a widower⟩
viudo, -da *n* : widower *m*, widow *f*
viva *nm* : cheer
vivacidad *nf* VIVEZA : vivacity, liveliness
vivamente *adv* **1** : in a lively manner **2** : vividly **3** : strongly, acutely ⟨lo recomendamos vivamente : we strongly recommend it⟩
vivar *vi* : to cheer
vivaracho, -cha *adj* **1** : lively, vivacious **2** : bright, sparkling
vivaz *adj, pl* **vivaces** **1** : lively, vivacious **2** : clever, sharp **3** : perennial
vivencia *nf* : experience
víveres *nmpl* : provisions, supplies, food
vivero *nm* **1** : nursery (for plants) **2** : hatchery, fish farm
viveza *nf* **1** VIVACIDAD : liveliness **2** BRILLO : vividness, brightness **3** ASTUCIA : cleverness, sharpness
vívidamente *adv* : vividly
vívido, -da *adj* : vivid, lively
vividor, -dora *n* : sponger, parasite
vivienda *nf* **1** : housing **2** MORADA : dwelling, home
viviente *adj* : living
vivificar {72} *vt* : to revitalize, to give life to
vivir[1] *vi* **1** : to live, to be alive ⟨¡viva la democracia! : long live democracy!⟩ **2** SUBSISTIR : to subsist, to make a living **3** RESIDIR : to reside **4** : to spend one's life ⟨vive para trabajar : she lives to work⟩ **5** ∼ **de** : to live on — *vt* **1** : to live ⟨vivir su vida : to live one's life⟩ **2** EXPERIMENTAR : to go through, to experience
vivir[2] *nm* **1** : life, lifestyle **2 de mal vivir** : disreputable
vivisección *nf, pl* **-ciones** : vivisection
vivo, -va *adj* **1** : alive **2** INTENSO : vivid, bright, intense **3** ANIMADO : lively, vivacious **4** ASTUTO : sharp, clever **5 en** ∼ : live ⟨transmisión en vivo : live broadcast⟩ **6 al rojo vivo** : red-hot
vocablo *nm* PALABRA : word
vocabulario *nm* : vocabulary
vocación *nf, pl* **-ciones** : vocation
vocacional *adj* : vocational
vocal[1] *adj* : vocal
vocal[2] *nmf* : member (of a committee, board, etc.)
vocal[3] *nf* : vowel
vocalista *nmf* CANTANTE : singer, vocalist
vocalizar {21} *vi* : to vocalize
vocear *v* : to shout
vocerío *nm* : clamor, shouting
vocero, -ra *n* PORTAVOZ : spokesperson, spokesman *m*, spokeswoman *f*
vociferante *adj* : vociferous
vociferar *vi* GRITAR : to shout, to yell
vodevil *nm* : vaudeville
vodka *nm* : vodka
voladizo[1], **-za** *adj* : projecting

voladizo[2] *nm* : projection
volador, -dora *adj* : flying
volando *adv* : quickly, in a hurry
volante[1] *adj* : flying
volante[2] *nm* **1** : steering wheel **2** FOLLETO : flier, circular **3** : shuttlecock **4** : flywheel **5** : balance wheel (of a watch) **6** : ruffle, flounce
volantín *nm, pl* **-tines** : kite
volar {19} *vi* **1** : to fly **2** CORRER : to go quickly, to rush ⟨el tiempo vuela : time flies⟩ ⟨pasar volando : to fly past⟩ **3** DESAPARECER : to disappear ⟨el dinero ya voló : the money's already gone⟩ — *vt* **1** : to blow up, to demolish **2** : to irritate
volátil *adj* : volatile — **volatilidad** *nf*
volcán *nm, pl* **volcanes** : volcano
volcánico, -ca *adj* : volcanic
volcar {82} *vt* **1** : to upset, to knock over, to turn over **2** : to empty out **3** : to make dizzy **4** : to cause a change of mind in **5** : to irritate — *vi* **1** : to overturn, to tip over **2** : to capsize — **volcarse** *vr* **1** : to overturn **2** : to do one's utmost
volea *nf* : volley (in sports)
volear *vi* : to volley (in sports)
voleibol *nm* : volleyball
voleo *nm* **al voleo** : haphazardly, at random
volframio *nm* : wolfram, tungsten
volibol *Car, Hond, Mex* → **voleibol**
volición *nf, pl* **-ciones** : volition
volqué, etc. → **volcar**
voltaje *nm* : voltage ⟨de alto voltaje : high-voltage⟩
voltear *vt* **1** : to turn over, to turn upside down **2** : to reverse, to turn inside out **3** : to turn ⟨voltear la cara : to turn one's head⟩ **4** : to knock down — *vi* **1** : to roll over, to do somersaults **2** : to turn ⟨volteó a la izquierda : he turned left⟩ — **voltearse** *vr* **1** : to turn around **2** : to change one's allegiance
voltereta *nf* : somersault, tumble
voltio *nm* : volt
volubilidad *nf* : fickleness
voluble *adj* : fickle, changeable
volumen *nm, pl* **-lúmenes** **1** TOMO : volume, book **2** : capacity, size, bulk **3** CANTIDAD : amount ⟨el volumen de ventas : the volume of sales⟩ **4** : volume, loudness
voluminoso, -sa *adj* : voluminous, massive, bulky
voluntad *nf* **1** : will, volition ⟨por propia voluntad : of one's own free will⟩ **2** DESEO : desire, wish **3** INTENCIÓN : intention **4 a voluntad** : at will **5 buena voluntad** : good will **6 mala voluntad** : ill will **7 fuerza de voluntad** : willpower
voluntariado *nm* : volunteer service ⟨programa de voluntariado : volunteer program⟩
voluntario[1], **-ria** *adj* : voluntary — **voluntariamente** *adv*
voluntario[2], **-ria** *n* : volunteer
voluntarioso, -sa *adj* **1** : stubborn **2** : willing, eager
voluptuosidad *nf* : voluptuousness

voluptuoso, -sa *adj* : voluptuous — **vo-luptuosamente** *adv*
voluta *nf* : spiral, column (of smoke)
volver {89} *vi* **1** : to return, to come/go back ⟨volver a casa : to return home⟩ ⟨volver de vacaciones : to get back from vacation⟩ ⟨no vuelvas por aquí : don't come back here⟩ ⟨volver atrás : to turn back⟩ **2** ∼ **a** : to return to ⟨volver al tema : to get back to the subject⟩ ⟨volver a la normalidad : to get back to normal⟩ **3** ∼ **a** : to do again ⟨volvieron a llamar : they called again⟩ ⟨volver a pasar/ocurrir/suceder : to happen again⟩ **4 volver en sí** : to come to, to regain consciousness — *vt* **1** : to turn, to turn over, to turn inside out **2** : to return, to repay, to restore **3** : to cause, to make ⟨la volvía loca : it was driving her crazy⟩ — **volverse** *vr* **1** : to become ⟨se volvió deprimido : he became depressed⟩ **2** : to turn around
vomitar *vi* : to vomit — *vt* **1** : to vomit **2** : to spew out (lava, etc.)
vómito *nm* **1** : vomiting **2** : vomit
voracidad *nf* : voracity
vorágine *nf* : whirlpool, maelstrom
voraz *adj, pl* **voraces** : voracious — **vo-razmente** *adv*
vórtice *nm* **1** : whirlpool, vortex **2** TOR-BELLINO : whirlwind
vos *pron* (*in some regions of Latin America*) : you ⟨para vos : for you⟩ ⟨¿vos sos José? : are you José?⟩
vosear *vt* : to address as *vos*
vosotros, -tras *pron pl Spain* **1** : you, yourselves **2** : ye
votación *nf, pl* **-ciones** : vote, voting ⟨someter a votación : to put to a vote, to vote on⟩
votante *nmf* : voter
votar *vi* : to vote ⟨votar por : to vote for⟩ ⟨votar a favor de : to vote in favor of⟩ ⟨votar en contra de : to vote against⟩ — *vt* : to vote for
voto *nm* **1** : vote **2** : vow (in religion) **3 votos** *nmpl* : good wishes
voy → **ir**
voz *nf, pl* **voces** **1** : voice ⟨alzar la voz : to raise one's voice⟩ **2** : opinion, say **3** GRITO : shout, yell **4** : sound **5** VOCA-BLO : word, term **6** : rumor **7 a voces** : loudly, in a loud voice **8 a voz en cue-llo** : at the top of one's lungs **9 dar vo-ces** : to shout **10 en voz alta** : aloud, in a loud voice **11 en voz baja** : softly, in a low voice

vudú *nm* : voodoo
vuelco *nm* **1** : upset, overturning ⟨dar un vuelco : to overturn⟩ ⟨me dio un vuelco el corazón : my heart skipped a beat⟩ **2** : drastic change, reversal ⟨dar un vuelco inesperado : to take an unexpected turn⟩
vuela, etc. → **volar**
vuelca, vuelque etc. → **volcar**
vuelo *nm* **1** : flight, flying ⟨alzar el vuelo : to take flight⟩ ⟨remontar el vuelo : to climb, to fly up⟩ **2** : flight (of an aircraft) ⟨un vuelo directo : a direct flight⟩ **3** : flare, fullness (of clothing) **4 al vuelo** : on the wing
vuelta *nf* **1** GIRO : turn ⟨se dio la vuelta : he turned around⟩ ⟨vuelta en U : U-turn, about-face⟩ **2** REVOLUCIÓN : circle, revolution ⟨dio la vuelta al mundo : she went around the world⟩ ⟨las ruedas daban vueltas : the wheels were spinning⟩ **3** : flip, turn ⟨le dio la vuelta : she flipped it over⟩ **4** : bend, curve ⟨a la vuelta de la esquina : around the corner⟩ **5** REGRESO : return ⟨de ida y vuelta : round-trip⟩ ⟨a vuelta de correo : by return mail⟩ **6** : round, lap (in sports or games) **7** PASEO : walk, drive, ride ⟨dio una vuelta : he went for a walk⟩ **8** DORSO, REVÉS : back, other side ⟨a la vuelta : on the back⟩ **9** : cuff (of pants) **10 darle vueltas a algo** : to think something over **11 darle vuelta a la página** : to move on, to begin a new phase **12 dar una vuelta de campana** : to roll over (completely) **13 estar de vuelta** : to be back
vuelto *pp* → **volver**
vuelve, etc. → **volver**
vuestro[1], -stra *adj Spain* : your, of yours ⟨vuestros coches : your cars⟩ ⟨una amiga vuestra : a friend of yours⟩
vuestro[2], -stra *pron Spain* (*with definite article*) : yours ⟨la vuestra es más grande : yours is bigger⟩ ⟨esos son los vuestros : those are yours⟩
vulgar *adj* **1** : common **2** : vulgar
vulgaridad *nf* : vulgarity
vulgarmente *adv* : vulgarly, popularly
vulgo *nm* **el vulgo** : the masses, common people
vulnerable *adj* : vulnerable — **vulnerabi-lidad** *nf*
vulnerar *vt* **1** : to injure, to damage (one's reputation or honor) **2** : to violate, to break (a law or contract)

W

w *nf* : twenty-sixth letter of the Spanish alphabet
wafle *nm* : waffle
waflera *nf* : waffle iron
wapití *nm, pl* **-tíes** *or* **-tís** *or* **-tí** : wapiti, elk
wáter → **váter**
web *nmf* : web, World Wide Web
webcam *nf, pl* **webcams** : webcam

webmaster *nmf, pl* **-ters** : Webmaster
western *nm, pl* **westerns** : western
whisky *nm, pl* **whiskys** *or* **whiskies** : whiskey
wicca *nf* : Wicca
wiccano, -na *adj & n* : Wiccan
wigwam *nm* : wigwam
windsurf ['winsurf] *nm* : windsurfing

X

x *nf* : twenty-seventh letter of the Spanish alphabet
xenofobia *nf* : xenophobia
xenófobo[1], -ba *adj* : xenophobic
xenófobo[2], -ba *n* : xenophobe

xenón *nm* : xenon
xerografiar *vt* : to photocopy, to xerox
Xerox *marca registrada, f* — used for a photocopier
xilófono *nm* : xylophone

Y

y[1] *nf* : twenty-eighth letter of the Spanish alphabet
y[2] *conj* (**e** *before words beginning with* i- *or* hi-) **1** : and ⟨mi hermano y yo : my brother and I⟩ ⟨más y más : more and more⟩ ⟨¿y los demás? : and (what about) the others?⟩ **2** (*used in numbers*) ⟨cincuenta y cinco : fifty-five⟩ **3** *fam* : well ⟨y por supuesto : well, of course⟩ **4** ¿y qué? : so what?
ya[1] *adv* **1** : already ⟨ya terminó : she's finished already⟩ ⟨ya en los años sesenta : as early as the 1960's⟩ **2** : now, right now ⟨¡hazlo ya! : do it now!⟩ ⟨ya mismo : right away⟩ ⟨desde ya : as of now, immediately⟩ **3** : later, soon ⟨ya iremos : we'll go later on⟩ **4** : no longer, anymore ⟨ya no fuma : he no longer smokes⟩ **5** : yes, right ⟨ya, pero . . . : yes, I know, but . . .⟩ **6** (*used for emphasis*) ⟨¡ya lo sé! : I know!⟩ ⟨ya lo creo : of course⟩ **7** no ya : not only ⟨no ya lloran sino gritan : they're not only crying but screaming⟩ **8** ya que : now that, since ⟨ya que sabe la verdad : now that she knows the truth⟩
ya[2] *conj* ya . . . ya : whether . . . or, first . . . then ⟨ya le gusta, ya no : first he likes it, then he doesn't⟩
yac *nm* : yak
yacer {90} *vi* : to lie ⟨en esta tumba yacen sus abuelos : his grandparents lie in this grave⟩
yacimiento *nm* : bed, deposit ⟨yacimiento petrolífero : oil field⟩
yaga, etc. → **yacer**
yang *nm* : yang ⟨el yin y el yang : (the) yin and yang⟩
yanqui *adj & nmf* : Yankee
yarda *nf* : yard

yate *nm* : yacht
yayo, yaya *n fam* : grandpa *m*, grandma *f*
yaz, yazca yazga etc. → **yacer**
yedra *nf* : ivy
yegua *nf* : mare
yelmo *nm* : helmet
yema *nf* **1** : bud, shoot **2** : yolk (of an egg) **3** yema del dedo : fingertip
yen *nm* : yen (currency)
yendo → **ir**
yerba *nf* **1** *or* **yerba mate** : maté **2** → **hierba**
yerga, yergue etc. → **erguir**
yermo[1], -ma *adj* : barren, deserted
yermo[2] *nm* : wasteland
yerno *nm* : son-in-law
yerra, etc. → **errar**
yerro *nm* : blunder, mistake
yesca *nf* : tinder
yeso *nm* **1** : plaster (material) **2** : cast (for a limb) **3** : gypsum
yiddish ['jidiʃ] *or* **yidis** ['jidis] *adj & nm* : Yiddish
yihad [ji'ad] *nmf, pl* **yihads** : jihad — **yihadista** *nmf*
yin *nm* : yin ⟨el yin y el yang : (the) yin and yang⟩
yo[1] *nm* : ego, self
yo[2] *pron* **1** : I ⟨yo la vi : I saw her⟩ ⟨¿quién lo hizo? yo : who did it? I did⟩ **2** : me ⟨todos menos yo : everyone except me⟩ ⟨tan bajo como yo : as short as me⟩ **3** soy yo : it's me
yodo *nm* : iodine
yoga *nm* : yoga
yogurt *or* **yogur** *nm* : yogurt
Yom Kippur *n* : Yom Kippur
yoyo *or* **yoyó** *nm* : yo-yo
yuca *nf* **1** : yucca (plant) **2** : cassava, manioc

yucateco[1], **-ca** *adj* : of or from the Yucatán

yucateco[2], **-ca** *n* : person from the Yucatán

yudo → **judo**

yugo *nm* : yoke

yugoslavo, -va *adj & n* : Yugoslavian

yugular *adj* : jugular ⟨vena yugular : jugular vein⟩

yungas *nfpl Bol, Chile, Peru* : warm tropical valleys

yunque *nm* : anvil

yunta *nf* : yoke, team (of oxen)

yuppy *nmf, pl* **yuppies** : yuppie

yute *nm* : jute

yuxtaponer {60} *vt* : to juxtapose — **yuxtaposición** *nf*

yuyo *nm* (*in various countries*) **1** : weed **2** : herb

Z

z *nf* : twenty-ninth letter of the Spanish alphabet

zacate *nm CA, Mex* **1** : grass, fodder **2** : hay

zafacón *nm, pl* **-cones** *Car* : wastebasket

zafar *vt* : to loosen, to untie — **zafarse** *vr* **1** : to loosen up, to come undone **2** : to get free of

zafio, -fia *adj* : coarse, crude

zafiro *nm* : sapphire

zaga *nf* **1** : defense (in sports) **2 a la zaga** *or* **en ~** : behind, in the rear

zagual *nm* : paddle (of a canoe)

zaguán *nm, pl* **zaguanes** : front hall, vestibule

zaherir {76} *vt* **1** : to criticize sharply **2** : to wound, to mortify

zahones *nmpl* : chaps

zaino, -na *adj* : chestnut (color)

zalamería *nf* : flattery, sweet talk

zalamero[1], **-ra** *adj* : flattering, fawning

zalamero[2], **-ra** *n* : flatterer

zambullida *nf* : dive, plunge

zambullir {38} *vt* : to dip, to submerge — **zambullirse** *vr* : to dive, to plunge

zamparse *vr* : to gobble, to wolf down (food)

zanahoria *nf* : carrot

zancada *nf* : stride, step

zancadilla *nf* **1** : trip, stumble **2** *fam* : trick, ruse

zanco *nm* : stilt

zancuda *nf* : wading bird

zancudo *nm* MOSQUITO : mosquito

zángano *nm* : drone, male bee

zanja *nf* : ditch, trench

zanjar *vt* ACLARAR : to settle, to clear up, to resolve

zapallo *nm Arg, Chile, Peru, Uru* : pumpkin

zapapico *nm* : pickax

zapata *nf* : brake shoe

zapatear *vi* : to stamp one's feet

zapatería *nf* **1** : shoemaker's, shoe factory **2** : shoe store

zapatero[1], **-ra** *adj* : dry, tough, poorly cooked

zapatero[2], **-ra** *n* : shoemaker, cobbler

zapatilla *nf* **1** PANTUFLA : slipper **2** *Mex* : women's shoe **3** *or* **zapatilla de deporte** : sneaker

zapato *nm* : shoe

zapping ['sapin, 'θapin] *nm* : channel surfing

zar, zarina *n* : czar *m*, czarina *f*

zarandear *vt* **1** : to sift, to sieve **2** : to shake, to jostle, to jiggle

zarapito *nm* : curlew

zarcillo *nm* **1** : earring **2** : tendril (of a plant)

zarigüeya *nf* : opossum

zarpa *nf* : paw

zarpar *vi* : to set sail, to raise anchor

zarpazo *nm* : swipe (with a paw)

zarza *nf* : bramble, blackberry bush

zarzamora *nf* **1** : blackberry **2** : bramble, blackberry bush

zarzaparrilla *nf* : sarsaparilla

zarzuela *nf* : Spanish operetta

zas *interj* : bam!, wham!

zepelín *nm, pl* **-lines** : zeppelin

zeta *nf* : (letter) z

zigoto *nm* : zygote

zigzag *nm, pl* **zigzags** *or* **zigzagues** : zigzag

zigzaguear *vi* : to zigzag

zimbabuense *adj & nmf* : Zimbabwean

zinc *nm* : zinc

zinnia *nf* : zinnia

zíper *nm CA, Mex* : zipper

zócalo *nm Mex* : main square

zodíaco *or* **zodiaco** *nm* : zodiac — **zodíacal** *adj*

zombi *or* **zombie** *nmf* : zombie

zona *nf* : zone, district, area ⟨zona comercial : business district⟩ ⟨zonas rurales/urbanas : rural/urban areas⟩ ⟨zona de conflicto : conflict zone⟩

zonzo[1], **-za** *adj* : stupid, silly

zonzo[2], **-za** *n* : idiot, nitwit

zoo *nm* : zoo

zoología *nf* : zoology

zoológico[1], **-ca** *adj* : zoological

zoológico[2] *nm* : zoo

zoólogo, -ga *n* : zoologist

zoom *nm* : zoom lens

zopilote *nm CA, Mex* : buzzard

zoquete *nmf fam* : oaf, blockhead

zorrillo *nm* MOFETA : skunk

zorro[1], **-rra** *adj* : sly, crafty

zorro[2], **-rra** *n* **1** : fox, vixen **2** : sly crafty person

zorzal *nm* : thrush

zozobra *nf* : anxiety, worry

zozobrar *vi* : to capsize

zueco *nm* : clog (shoe)

zulú[1] *adj & nmf, pl* **zulúes** *or* **zulús** *or* **zulú** : Zulu

zulú[2] *nm* : Zulu (language)
zumaque *nm* : sumac
zumbar *vi* : to buzz, to hum ⟨le zumba-
ban los oídos : her ears were ringing⟩ —
vt fam **1** : to hit, to thrash **2** : to make
fun of
zumbido *nm* : buzzing, humming

zumo *nf* JUGO : juice
zurcir {83} *vt* : to darn, to mend
zurdo[1], **-da** *adj* : left-handed
zurdo[2], **-da** *n* : left-handed person
zurrón *nm, pl* **zurrones** : leather bag
zurza, etc. → zurcir
zutano, -na → fulano

English-Spanish Dictionary

Diccionario Inglés-Español

A

a¹ ['eɪ] *n, pl* **a's** *or* **as** ['eɪz] **1** : primera letra del alfabeto inglés **2 A** : la *m* ⟨A sharp/flat : la sostenido/bemol⟩

a² [ə, 'eɪ] (**an** [ən, 'æn] *before vowel or silent h*) *art* **1** : un *m*, una *f* ⟨a house : una casa⟩ ⟨a little more : un poco más⟩ ⟨half an hour : media hora⟩ ⟨what a surprise! : ¡qué sorpresa!⟩ ⟨she's a lawyer : es abogada⟩ ⟨it's a Rembrandt : es un Rembrandt⟩ ⟨a Mr. Jones called : llamó un tal señor Jones⟩ **2** PER : por, a la, al ⟨30 kilometers an hour : 30 kilómetros por hora⟩ ⟨twice a month : dos veces al mes⟩

a- [ə] *pref* : a-

aardvark ['ɑrd,vɑrk] *n* : oso *m* hormiguero

aback [ə'bæk] *adv* **1** : por sorpresa **2 to be taken aback** : quedarse desconcertado

abacus ['æbəkəs] *n, pl* **abaci** ['æbə,saɪ, -,ki:] *or* **abacuses** : ábaco *m*

abaft [ə'bæft] *adv* : a popa

abandon¹ [ə'bændən] *vt* **1** DESERT, FORSAKE : abandonar, desamparar (a alguien), desertar de (algo) **2** GIVE UP, SUSPEND : renunciar a, suspender ⟨he abandoned the search : suspendió la búsqueda⟩ **3** EVACUATE, LEAVE : abandonar, evacuar, dejar ⟨to abandon ship : abandonar el buque⟩ **4 to abandon oneself** : entregarse, abandonarse

abandon² *n* : desenfreno *m* ⟨with wild abandon : desenfrenadamente⟩

abandoned [ə'bændənd] *adj* **1** DESERTED : abandonado **2** UNRESTRAINED : desenfrenado, desinhibido

abandonment [ə'bændənmənt] *n* : abandono *m*, desamparo *m*

abase [ə'beɪs] *vt* **abased; abasing** : degradar, humillar, rebajar

abash [ə'bæʃ] *vt* : avergonzar, abochornar

abashed [ə'bæʃt] *adj* : avergonzado

abate [ə'beɪt] *vi* **abated; abating** : amainar, menguar, disminuir

abattoir ['æbə,twɑr] *n* : matadero *m*

abbess ['æbɪs, -,bɛs, -bəs] *n* : abadesa *f*

abbey ['æbi] *n, pl* **-beys** : abadía *f*

abbot ['æbət] *n* : abad *m*

abbreviate [ə'bri:vi,eɪt] *vt* **-ated; -ating** : abreviar

abbreviation [ə,bri:vi'eɪʃən] *n* : abreviación *f*, abreviatura *f*

ABC's [,eɪ,bi:'si:z] *npl* : abecé *m*

abdicate ['æbdɪ,keɪt] *v* **-cated; -cating** : abdicar

abdication [,æbdɪ'keɪʃən] *n* : abdicación *f*

abdomen ['æbdəmən, æb'do:mən] *n* : abdomen *m*, vientre *m*

abdominal [æb'dɑmənəl] *adj* : abdominal — **abdominally** *adv*

abduct [æb'dʌkt] *vt* : raptar, secuestrar

abduction [æb'dʌkʃən] *n* : rapto *m*, secuestro *m*

abductor [æb'dʌktər] *n* : raptor *m*, -tora *f*; secuestrador *m*, -dora *f*

abed [ə'bɛd] *adv & adj* : en cama

aberrant [æ'bɛrənt, 'æbərənt] *adj* **1** ABNORMAL : anormal, aberrante **2** ATYPICAL : anómalo, atípico

aberration [,æbə'reɪʃən] *n* **1** : aberración *f* **2** DERANGEMENT : perturbación *f* mental

abet [ə'bɛt] *vt* **abetted; abetting** ASSIST : ayudar ⟨to aid and abet : ser cómplice de⟩

abeyance [ə'beɪənts] *n* : desuso *m*, suspensión *f*

abhor [əb'hɔr, æb-] *vt* **-horred; -horring** : abominar, aborrecer

abhorrence [əb'hɔrənts, æb-] *n* : aborrecimiento *m*, odio *m*

abhorrent [əb'hɔrənt, æb-] *adj* : abominable, aborrecible, odioso

abide [ə'baɪd] *v* **abode** [ə'boːd] *or* **abided; abiding** *vt* STAND : soportar, tolerar ⟨I can't abide them : no los puedo ver⟩ — *vi* **1** ENDURE : quedar, permanecer **2** DWELL : morar, residir **3 to abide by** : atenerse a

ability [ə'bɪləti] *n, pl* **-ties 1** CAPABILITY : aptitud *f*, capacidad *f*, facultad *f* **2** COMPETENCE : competencia *f* **3** TALENT : talento *m*, don *m*, habilidad *f*

abject ['æb,dʒɛkt, æb'-] *adj* **1** WRETCHED : miserable, desdichado **2** HOPELESS : abatido, desesperado **3** SERVILE : servil ⟨abject flattery : halagos serviles⟩ — **abjectly** *adv*

abjure [æb'dʒʊr] *vt* **-jured; -juring** : abjurar de

ablaze [ə'bleɪz] *adj* **1** BURNING : ardiendo, en llamas **2** RADIANT : resplandeciente, radiante

able ['eɪbəl] *adj* **abler; ablest 1** CAPABLE : capaz, hábil **2** COMPETENT : competente

-able *suf* : -able

ablution [ə'bluːʃən] *n* : ablución *f* ⟨to perform one's ablutions : lavarse⟩

ably ['eɪbəli] *adv* : hábilmente, eficientemente

abnormal [æb'nɔrməl] *adj* : anormal — **abnormally** *adv*

abnormality [,æbnər'mæləti, -nɔr-] *n, pl* **-ties** : anormalidad *f*

aboard¹ [ə'bord] *adv* : a bordo

aboard² *prep* : a bordo de

abode¹ → **abide**

abode² [ə'boːd] *n* : morada *f*, residencia *f*, vivienda *f*

abolish [ə'bɑlɪʃ] *vt* : abolir, suprimir

abolition [,æbə'lɪʃən] *n* : abolición *f*, supresión *f*

abominable [ə'bɑmənəbəl] *adj* DETESTABLE : abominable, aborrecible, espantoso

abominate [ə'bɑmə,neɪt] *vt* **-nated; -nating** : abominar, aborrecer

abomination [ə,bɑmə'neɪʃən] *n* : abominación *f*

aboriginal [,æbə'rɪdʒənəl] *adj* : aborigen, indígena

aborigine [ˌæbəˈrɪʤəni] *n* NATIVE : aborigen *mf*, indígena *mf*

abort [əˈbɔrt] *vt* **1** : abortar (en medicina) **2** CALL OFF : suspender, abandonar — *vi* : abortar, hacerse un aborto

abortion [əˈbɔrʃən] *n* : aborto *m*

abortive [əˈbɔrtɪv] *adj* UNSUCCESSFUL : fracasado, frustrado, malogrado

abound [əˈbaʊnd] *vi* **to abound in** : abundar en, estar lleno de

about¹ [əˈbaʊt] *adv* **1** APPROXIMATELY : aproximadamente, casi, más o menos ⟨about a hundred dollars : unos cien dólares⟩ **2** AROUND : por todas partes, alrededor ⟨the children are running about : los niños están corriendo por todas partes⟩ **3 to be about to** : estar a punto de **4 to be out and about** → out³ **5 to be up and about** → up³

about² *prep* **1** AROUND : alrededor de (un lugar, una persona, etc.) **2** CONCERNING : de, acerca de, sobre ⟨he always talks about politics : siempre habla de política⟩ ⟨she's worried about him : está preocupada por él⟩ ⟨you need to do something about it : tienes que hacer algo⟩ **3** (*indicating a quality*) ⟨there's something weird about it : hay algo raro (en el asunto)⟩ ⟨there's something about her : tiene algo, tiene un no sé qué⟩ **4** (*indicating manner*) ⟨be quick about it : date prisa, apúrate⟩ **5 to be (all) about** : tratarse de (dícese de un asunto), ser muy partidario de (dícese de una persona)

about–face [əˈbaʊtˈfeɪs] *n* **1** : media vuelta *f* **2** : cambio *m* total (de opinión, etc.), giro *m* de 180 grados

above¹ [əˈbʌv] *adv* **1** OVERHEAD : por encima, arriba ⟨the floor above : el piso de arriba⟩ ⟨I looked at the sky above : alcé la vista hacia el cielo⟩ **2** : más arriba ⟨as stated above : como se indica más arriba⟩ **3** OVER, MORE : más ⟨groups of six and above : grupos de seis o más⟩ ⟨children age 10 and above : niños a partir de los 10 años⟩ **4** : sobre cero (dícese de temperaturas) **5 from above** : de arriba, desde arriba ⟨looking down from above : mirando desde arriba⟩ ⟨orders from above : órdenes de arriba⟩

above² *adj* **1** : anterior, antedicho ⟨for the above reasons : por las razones antedichas⟩ **2 the above** : lo anterior

above³ *prep* **1** OVER : encima de, arriba de, sobre **2** : superior a, por encima de ⟨he's above those things : él está por encima de esas cosas⟩ **3** : más de, superior a ⟨he earns above $50,000 : gana más de $50,000⟩ ⟨a number above 10 : un número superior a 10⟩ **4 above all** : sobre todo

aboveboard¹ [əˈbʌvˌbord, -ˌbord] *adv or* **open and aboveboard** : sin tapujos

aboveboard² *adj* : legítimo, sincero

aboveground *adj* : sobre el nivel del suelo

abrade [əˈbreɪd] *vt* **abraded; abrading 1** ERODE : erosionar, corroer **2** SCRAPE : raspar

abrasion [əˈbreɪʒən] *n* **1** SCRAPE, SCRATCH : raspadura *f*, rasguño *m* **2** EROSION : erosión *f*

abrasive¹ [əˈbreɪsɪv] *adj* **1** ROUGH : abrasivo, áspero **2** BRUSQUE, IRRITATING : brusco, irritante

abrasive² *n* : abrasivo *m*

abreast [əˈbrɛst] *adv* **1** : en fondo, al lado ⟨to march three abreast : marchar de tres en fondo⟩ **2 to keep abreast** : mantenerse al día

abridge [əˈbrɪʤ] *vt* **abridged; abridging** : compendiar, resumir

abridgment *or* **abridgement** [əˈbrɪʤ-mənt] *n* : compendio *m*, resumen *m*

abroad [əˈbrɔd] *adv* **1** ABOUT, WIDELY : por todas partes, en todas direcciones ⟨the news spread abroad : la noticia corrió por todas partes⟩ **2** OVERSEAS : en el extranjero, en el exterior

abrogate [ˈæbrəˌgeɪt] *vt* **-gated; -gating** : abrogar

abrupt [əˈbrʌpt] *adj* **1** SUDDEN : abrupto, repentino, súbito **2** BRUSQUE, CURT : brusco, cortante — **abruptly** *adv*

abruptness [əˈbrʌptnəs] *n* **1** SUDDENNESS : lo repentino **2** BRUSQUENESS : brusquedad *f*

abscess [ˈæbˌsɛs] *n* : absceso *m*

abscond [æbˈskɑnd] *vi* : huir, fugarse

absence [ˈæbsənts] *n* **1** : ausencia *f* (de una persona) **2** LACK : falta *f*, carencia *f*

absent¹ [æbˈsɛnt] *vt* **to absent oneself** : ausentarse

absent² [ˈæbsənt] *adj* : ausente

absentee [ˌæbsənˈtiː] *n* : ausente *mf*

absentminded [ˌæbsəntˈmaɪndəd] *adj* : distraído, despistado

absentmindedly [ˌæbsəntˈmaɪndədli] *adv* : distraídamente

absentmindedness [ˌæbsəntˈmaɪndəd-nəs] *n* : distracción *f*, despiste *m*

absolute [ˈæbsəˌluːt, ˌæbsəˈluːt] *adj* **1** COMPLETE, PERFECT : completo, pleno, perfecto **2** UNCONDITIONAL : absoluto, incondicional **3** DEFINITE : categórico, definitivo

absolutely [ˈæbsəˌluːtli, ˌæbsəˈluːtli] *adv* **1** COMPLETELY : completamente, absolutamente **2** CERTAINLY : desde luego ⟨do you agree? absolutely! : ¿estás de acuerdo? ¡desde luego!⟩

absolution [ˌæbsəˈluːʃən] *n* : absolución *f*

absolutism [ˈæbsəˌluːˌtɪzəm] *n* : absolutismo *m*

absolve [əbˈzɑlv, æb-, -ˈsɑlv] *vt* **-solved; -solving** : absolver, perdonar

absorb [əbˈzɔrb, æb-, -ˈsɔrb] *vt* **1** : absorber, embeber (un líquido), amortiguar (un golpe, la luz) **2** ENGROSS : absorber **3** ASSIMILATE : asimilar

absorbed [əbˈzɔrbd, æb-, -ˈsɔrbd] *adj* ENGROSSED : absorto, ensimismado

absorbency [əbˈzɔrbəntsi, æb-, -ˈsɔr-] *n* : absorbencia *f*

absorbent [əbˈzɔrbənt, æb-, -ˈsɔr-] *adj* : absorbente

absorbing [əbˈzɔrbɪŋ, æb-, -ˈsɔr-] *adj* : absorbente, fascinante

absorption [əbˈzɔrpʃən, æb-, -ˈsɔrp-] *n* **1**
: absorción *f* **2** CONCENTRATION : concentración *f*
abstain [əbˈsteɪn, æb-] *vi* : abstenerse
abstainer [əbˈsteɪnər, æb-] *n* : abstemio
m, -mia *f*
abstemious [æbˈstiːmiəs] *adj* : abstemio,
sobrio — **abstemiously** *adv*
abstention [əbˈstɛntʃən, æb-] *n* : abstención *f*
abstinence [ˈæbstənənts] *n* : abstinencia *f*
abstract[1] [æbˈstrækt, ˈæb-] *vt* **1** EXTRACT
: abstraer, extraer **2** SUMMARIZE : compendiar, resumir
abstract[2] *adj* : abstracto — **abstractly**
[æbˈstræktli, ˈæb-] *adv*
abstract[3] [ˈæbˌstrækt] *n* : resumen *m*,
compendio *m*, sumario *m*
abstraction [æbˈstrækʃən] *n* **1** : abstracción *f*, idea *f* abstracta **2** ABSENTMIND-
EDNESS : distracción *f*
abstruse [əbˈstruːs, æb-] *adj* : abstruso,
recóndito — **abstrusely** *adv*
absurd [əbˈsərd, -ˈzərd] *adj* : absurdo,
ridículo, disparatado — **absurdly** *adv*
absurdity [əbˈsərdəti, -ˈzər-] *n, pl* **-ties**
1 : absurdo *m* **2** NONSENSE : disparate *m*,
despropósito *m*
abundance [əˈbʌndənts] *n* : abundancia *f*
abundant [əˈbʌndənt] *adj* : abundante,
cuantioso, copioso
abundantly [əˈbʌndəntli] *adv* : abundantemente, en abundancia
abuse[1] [əˈbjuːz] *vt* **abused; abusing 1**
MISUSE : abusar de **2** MISTREAT
: maltratar **3** REVILE : insultar, injuriar,
denostar
abuse[2] [əˈbjuːs] *n* **1** MISUSE : abuso *m* **2**
MISTREATMENT : abuso *m*, maltrato
m **3** INSULTS : insultos *mpl*, impro-
perios *mpl* ⟨a string of abuse : una serie
de improperios⟩
abuser [əˈbjuːzər] *n* : abusador *m*, -dora *f*
abusive [əˈbjuːsɪv] *adj* **1** ABUSING : abusivo **2** INSULTING : ofensivo, injurioso,
insultante — **abusively** *adv*
abut [əˈbʌt] *v* **abutted; abutting** *vt* : bordear — *vi* **to abut on** : colindar con
abutment [əˈbʌtmənt] *n* BUTTRESS : contrafuerte *m*, estribo *m*
abysmal [əˈbɪzməl] *adj* TERRIBLE : atroz,
desastroso
abysmally [əˈbɪzməli] *adv* : desastrosamente, terriblemente
abyss [əˈbɪs, ˈæbɪs] *n* : abismo *m*, sima *f*
acacia [əˈkeɪʃə] *n* : acacia *f*
academic[1]   [ˌækəˈdɛmɪk]   *adj*   **1**
: académico **2** THEORETICAL : teórico
— **academically** [-mɪkli] *adv*
academic[2] *n* : académico *m*, -ca *f*
academician [ˌækədəˈmɪʃən] *n* → **academic**
academy [əˈkædəmi] *n, pl* **-mies** : academia *f*
acanthus [əˈkænθəs] *n* : acanto *m*
accede [ækˈsiːd] *vi* **-ceded; -ceding 1**
AGREE : acceder, consentir **2** ASCEND
: subir, acceder ⟨he acceded to the
throne : subió al trono⟩

accelerate [ɪkˈsɛləˌreɪt, æk-] *v* **-ated;
-ating** *vt* : acelerar, apresurar — *vi*
: acelerar (dícese de un carro)
acceleration [ɪkˌsɛləˈreɪʃən, æk-] *n* : aceleración *f*
accelerator [ɪkˈsɛləˌreɪtər, æk-] *n* : acelerador *m*
accent[1] [ˈækˌsɛnt, ækˈsɛnt] *vt* : acentuar
accent[2] [ˈækˌsɛnt, -sənt] *n* **1** : acento
m **2** EMPHASIS, STRESS : énfasis *m*, acento *m*
accentuate [ɪkˈsɛntʃuˌeɪt, æk-] *vt* **-ated;
-ating** : acentuar, poner énfasis en
accept [ɪkˈsɛpt, æk-] *vt* **1** : aceptar **2** AC-
KNOWLEDGE : admitir, reconocer
acceptability [ɪkˌsɛptəˈbɪləti, æk-] *n*
: aceptabilidad *f*
acceptable [ɪkˈsɛptəbəl, æk-] *adj* : aceptable, admisible — **acceptably** [-bli] *adv*
acceptance [ɪkˈsɛptənts, æk-] *n* : aceptación *f*, aprobación *f*
access[1] [ˈækˌsɛs] *vt* : obtener acceso a, entrar a
access[2] *n* : acceso *m*
accessibility [ɪkˌsɛsəˈbɪləti, æk-] *n, pl* **-ties**
: accesibilidad *f*
accessible [ɪkˈsɛsəbəl, æk-] *adj* : accesible, asequible
accession [ɪkˈsɛʃən, æk-] *n* **1** : ascenso *f*,
subida *f* (al trono, etc.) **2** ACQUISITION
: adquisición *f*
accessory[1] [ɪkˈsɛsəri, æk-] *adj* : auxiliar
accessory[2] *n, pl* **-ries 1** : accesorio *m*,
complemento *m* **2** ACCOMPLICE : cómplice *mf*
accident [ˈæksədənt] *n* **1** MISHAP : accidente *m* **2** CHANCE : casualidad *f*
accidental [ˌæksəˈdɛntəl] *adj* : accidental,
casual, imprevisto, fortuito
accidentally [ˌæksəˈdɛntəli, -ˈdɛntli] *adv* **1**
BY CHANCE : por casualidad **2** UNIN-
TENTIONALLY : sin querer, involuntariamente
acclaim[1] [əˈkleɪm] *vt* : aclamar, elogiar
acclaim[2] *n* : aclamación *f*, elogio *m*
acclamation [ˌækləˈmeɪʃən] *n* : aclamación
f
acclimate [ˈækləˌmeɪt, əˈklaɪmət] → **acclimatize**
acclimatize [əˈklaɪməˌtaɪz] *v* **-tized; -tiz-
ing** *vt* **1** : aclimatar **2 to acclimatize
oneself** : aclimatarse
accolade [ˈækəˌleɪd, -ˌlɑd] *n* **1** PRAISE
: elogio *m* **2** AWARD : galardón *m*
accommodate [əˈkɑməˌdeɪt] *vt* **-dated;
-dating 1** ADAPT : acomodar, adaptar **2**
SATISFY : tener en cuenta, satisfacer **3**
HOLD : dar cabida a, tener cabida para
accommodating   [əˈkɑməˌdeɪtɪŋ]   *adj*
: complaciente, acomodaticio
accommodation   [əˌkɑməˈdeɪʃən]   *n*   **1**
: adaptación *f*, adecuación *f* **2 accommodations** *npl* LODGING : alojamiento
m, hospedaje *m*
accompaniment [əˈkʌmpənəmənt, -ˈkɑm-]
n : acompañamiento *m*
accompanist [əˈkʌmpənɪst, -ˈkɑm-] *n*
: acompañante *mf*
accompany [əˈkʌmpəni, -ˈkɑm-] *vt* **-nied;
-nying** : acompañar

accomplice [ə'kɑmpləs, -'kʌm-] *n* : cómplice *mf*

accomplish [ə'kɑmplɪʃ, -'kʌm-] *vt* : efectuar, realizar, lograr, llevar a cabo

accomplished [ə'kɑmplɪʃt, -'kʌm-] *adj* : consumado, logrado

accomplishment [ə'kɑmplɪʃmənt, -'kʌm-] *n* **1** ACHIEVEMENT : logro *m*, éxito *m* **2** SKILL : destreza *f*, habilidad *f*

accord¹ [ə'kɔrd] *vt* GRANT : conceder, otorgar — *vi* **to accord with** : concordar con, conformarse con

accord² *n* **1** AGREEMENT : acuerdo *m*, convenio *m* **2** VOLITION : voluntad *f* ⟨of one's own accord : voluntariamente, de motu proprio⟩

accordance [ə'kɔrdənts] *n* **1** ACCORD : acuerdo *m*, conformidad *f* **2 in accordance with** : conforme a, según, de acuerdo con

accordingly [ə'kɔrdɪŋli] *adv* **1** CORRESPONDINGLY : en consecuencia **2** CONSEQUENTLY : por consiguiente, por lo tanto

according to [ə'kɔrdɪŋ] *prep* : según, de acuerdo con, conforme a

accordion [ə'kɔrdiən] *n* : acordeón *m*

accordionist [ə'kɔrdiənɪst] *n* : acordeonista *mf*

accost [ə'kɔst] *vt* : abordar, dirigirse a

account¹ [ə'kaʊnt] *vt* : considerar, estimar ⟨he accounts himself lucky : se considera afortunado⟩ — *vi* **to account for** : dar cuenta de, explicar

account² *n* **1** : cuenta *f* ⟨bank/checking account : cuenta bancaria/corriente⟩ ⟨savings account : cuenta de ahorro(s)⟩ ⟨e-mail account : cuenta de email, cuenta de correo(s) electrónico(s)⟩ **2** EXPLANATION : versión *f*, explicación *f* **3** REPORT : relato *m*, informe *m* **4** IMPORTANCE : importancia *f* ⟨to be of no account : no tener importancia⟩ **5** **accounts** *npl* : contabilidad *f* **6 by all accounts** : a decir de todos **7 by one's own account** ⟨by her own account : según ella misma⟩ **8 on account of** BECAUSE OF : a causa de, debido a, por **9 on no account** : de ninguna manera **10 on someone's account** : por alguien **11 to take into account** : tener en cuenta

accountability [ə,kaʊntə'bɪləʧi] *n* : responsabilidad *f*

accountable [ə'kaʊntəbəl] *adj* : responsable

accountancy [ə'kaʊntəntsi] *n* : contabilidad *f*

accountant [ə'kaʊntənt] *n* : contador *m*, -dora *f*; contable *mf Spain*

accounting [ə'kaʊntɪŋ] *n* : contabilidad *f*

accoutrements *or* **accouterments** [ə'ku:trəmənts, -'ku:tər-] *npl* **1** EQUIPMENT : equipo *m*, avíos *mpl* **2** ACCESSORIES : accesorios *mpl* **3** TRAPPINGS : símbolos *mpl* ⟨the accoutrements of power : los símbolos del poder⟩

accredit [ə'krɛdət] *vt* : acreditar, autorizar

accreditation [ə,krɛdə'teɪʃən] *n* : acreditación *f*, homologación *f*

accrual [ə'kru:əl] *n* : incremento *m*, acumulación *f*

accrue [ə'kru:] *vi* **-crued; -cruing** : acumularse, aumentarse

accumulate [ə'kju:mjə,leɪt] *v* **-lated; -lating** *vt* : acumular, amontonar — *vi* : acumularse, amontonarse

accumulation [ə,kju:mjə'leɪʃən] *n* : acumulación *f*, amontonamiento *m*

accuracy ['ækjərəsi] *n* : exactitud *f*, precisión *f*

accurate ['ækjərət] *adj* : exacto, correcto, fiel, preciso — **accurately** *adv*

accusation [,ækjə'zeɪʃən] *n* : acusación *f*

accusatory [ə'kju:zə,tori] *adj* : acusatorio

accuse [ə'kju:z] *vt* **-cused; -cusing** : acusar, delatar, denunciar

accused [ə'kju:zd] *ns & pl* DEFENDANT : acusado *m*, -da *f*

accuser [ə'kju:zər] *n* : acusador *m*, -dora *f*

accustom [ə'kʌstəm] *vt* : acostumbrar, habituar

ace ['eɪs] *n* : as *m*

acerbic [ə'sərbɪk, æ-] *adj* : acerbo, mordaz

acetate ['æsə,teɪt] *n* : acetato *m*

acetone ['æsə,to:n] *n* : acetona *f*

acetylene [ə'sɛt̬ələn, -t̬ə,li:n] *n* : acetileno *m*

ache¹ ['eɪk] *vi* **ached; aching 1** : doler **2 to ache for** : anhelar, ansiar

ache² *n* : dolor *m*

achieve [ə'tʃi:v] *vt* **achieved; achieving** : lograr, alcanzar, conseguir, realizar

achievement [ə'tʃi:vmənt] *n* : logro *m*, éxito *m*, realización *f*

Achilles' heel [ə'kɪliz-] *n* : talón *m* de Aquiles

acid¹ ['æsəd] *adj* **1** SOUR : ácido, agrio **2** CAUSTIC, SHARP : acerbo, mordaz — **acidly** *adv*

acid² *n* : ácido *m*

acidic [ə'sɪdɪk, æ-] *adj* : ácido

acidity [ə'sɪdət̬i, æ-] *n*, *pl* **-ties** : acidez *f*

acid rain *n* : lluvia *f* ácida

acid test *n* : prueba *f* de fuego

acknowledge [ɪk'nɑlɪʤ, æk-] *vt* **-edged; -edging 1** ADMIT : reconocer, admitir **2** RECOGNIZE : reconocer **3 to acknowledge receipt of** : acusar recibo de

acknowledgment [ɪk'nɑlɪʤmənt, æk-] *n* **1** RECOGNITION : reconocimiento *m* **2** THANKS : agradecimiento *m*

acme ['ækmi] *n* : colmo *m*, apogeo *m*, cúspide *f*

acne ['ækni] *n* : acné *m*

acolyte ['ækə,laɪt] *n* : acólito *m*

acorn ['eɪ,kɔrn, -kərn] *n* : bellota *f*

acoustic [ə'ku:stɪk] *or* **acoustical** [-stɪkəl] *adj* : acústico — **acoustically** *adv*

acoustics [ə'ku:stɪks] *ns & pl* : acústica *f*

acquaint [ə'kweɪnt] *vt* **1** INFORM : enterar, informar **2** FAMILIARIZE : familiarizar **3 to be acquainted with** : conocer a (una persona), estar al tanto de (un hecho)

acquaintance [ə'kweɪntənts] *n* **1** KNOWLEDGE : conocimiento *m* **2** : conocido *m*, -da *f* ⟨friends and acquaintances : amigos y conocidos⟩

acquiesce [ˌækwiˈɛs] *vi* -**esced; -escing** : consentir, conformarse

acquiescence [ˌækwiˈɛsənts] *n* : consentimiento *m*, aquiescencia *f*

acquiescent [ˌækwiˈɛsənt] *adj* : acquiescente

acquire [əˈkwaɪr] *vt* -**quired; -quiring** : adquirir, obtener

acquisition [ˌækwəˈzɪʃən] *n* : adquisición *f*

acquisitive [əˈkwɪzətɪv] *adj* : adquisitivo, codicioso

acquit [əˈkwɪt] *vt* -**quitted; -quitting** 1 : absolver, exculpar 2 **to acquit oneself** : comportarse, defenderse

acquittal [əˈkwɪtəl] *n* : absolución *f*, exculpación *f*

acre [ˈeɪkər] *n* : acre *m*

acreage [ˈeɪkərɪdʒ] *n* : superficie *f* en acres

acrid [ˈækrəd] *adj* 1 BITTER : acre 2 CAUSTIC : acre, mordaz — **acridly** *adv*

acrimonious [ˌækrəˈmoːniəs] *adj* : áspero, cáustico, sarcástico

acrimony [ˈækrəˌmoːni] *n, pl* -**nies** : acrimonia *f*

acrobat [ˈækrəˌbæt] *n* : acróbata *mf*, saltimbanqui *mf*

acrobatic [ˌækrəˈbæṭɪk] *adj* : acrobático

acrobatics [ˌækrəˈbæṭɪks] *ns & pl* : acrobacia *f*

acronym [ˈækrəˌnɪm] *n* : acrónimo *m*

across[1] [əˈkrɔs] *adv* 1 CROSSWISE : al través 2 : a través, del otro lado ⟨he's already across : ya está del otro lado⟩ 3 : de ancho ⟨40 feet across : 40 pies de ancho⟩

across[2] *prep* 1 : al otro lado de ⟨across the street : al otro lado de la calle⟩ 2 : a través de ⟨a log across the road : un tronco a través del camino⟩

across–the–board *adj* : general, para todos

acrylic [əˈkrɪlɪk] *n* : acrílico *m*

act[1] [ˈækt] *vi* 1 : actuar ⟨he acted alone : actuó solo⟩ ⟨she acted courageously : actuó con coraje⟩ ⟨to act in one's own interests : actuar uno en su propio interés⟩ 2 : tomar medidas ⟨he acted to save the business : tomó medidas para salvar el negocio⟩ 3 BEHAVE : comportarse ⟨to act like children : actuar como niños⟩ 4 PERFORM : actuar, interpretar 5 : fingir, simular ⟨to act dumb : hacerse el tonto⟩ ⟨he acted as if nothing had happened : actuó como si no hubiera pasado nada⟩ 6 FUNCTION : actuar, servir, funcionar 7 **to act as** : servir de, hacer de 8 **to act on** : seguir (un consejo, etc.), actuar respecto a 9 **to act on** AFFECT : actuar sobre 10 **to act out** MISBEHAVE : portarse mal (para hacerse notar) 11 **to act out** PERFORM : representar 12 **to act up** MISBEHAVE : portarse mal 13 **to act up** MALFUNCTION : funcionar mal 14 **to act up** WORSEN : agravarse

act[2] *n* 1 DEED : acto *m*, hecho *m*, acción *f* 2 DECREE : ley *f*, decreto *m* 3 : acto *m*

(en una obra de teatro), número *m* (en un espectáculo) 4 PRETENSE : fingimiento *m*

acting[1] [ˈæktɪŋ] *adj* INTERIM : interino, en funciones

acting[2] *n* : interpretación *f*, actuación *f*

action [ˈækʃən] *n* 1 DEED : acción *f*, acto *m*, hecho *m* ⟨to take action : tomar medidas⟩ 2 BEHAVIOR : actuación *f*, comportamiento *m* 3 LAWSUIT : demanda *f* 4 MOVEMENT : movimiento *m* 5 COMBAT : combate *m* 6 PLOT : acción *f*, trama *f* 7 MECHANISM : mecanismo *m* 8 **in** ～ : en acción 9 **to go into action** : entrar en acción

activate [ˈæktəˌveɪt] *vt* -**vated; -vating** : activar

activation [ˌæktəˈveɪʃən] *n* : activación *f*

active [ˈæktɪv] *adj* 1 MOVING : activo, en movimiento 2 LIVELY : vigoroso, enérgico 3 : en actividad ⟨an active volcano : un volcán en actividad⟩ 4 OPERATIVE : vigente

actively [ˈæktɪvli] *adv* : activamente, enérgicamente

activist [ˈæktɪvɪst] *n* : activista *mf* — **activism** [-ˌvɪzəm] *n* — **activist** *adj*

activity [ækˈtɪvəṭi] *n, pl* -**ties** 1 MOVEMENT : actividad *f*, movimiento *m* 2 VIGOR : vigor *m*, energía *f* 3 OCCUPATION : actividad *f*, ocupación *f*

actor [ˈæktər] *n* : actor *m*, artista *mf*

actress [ˈæktrəs] *n* : actriz *f*

actual [ˈæktʃuəl] *adj* : real, verdadero

actuality [ˌæktʃuˈæləṭi] *n, pl* -**ties** : realidad *f*

actually [ˈæktʃuəli, -ʃəli] *adv* : realmente, en realidad

actuary [ˈæktʃuˌɛri] *n, pl* -**aries** : actuario *m*, -ria *f* de seguros — **actuarial** [ˌæktʃuˈɛriəl] *adj*

acumen [əˈkjuːmən] *n* : perspicacia *f*

acupuncture [ˈækjuˌpʌŋktʃər] *n* : acupuntura *f*

acute [əˈkjuːt] *adj* **acuter; acutest** 1 SHARP : agudo 2 PERCEPTIVE : perspicaz, sagaz 3 KEEN : fino, muy desarrollado, agudo ⟨an acute sense of smell : un fino olfato⟩ 4 SEVERE : grave 5

acute angle : ángulo *m* agudo

acutely [əˈkjuːtli] *adv* : intensamente ⟨to be acutely aware : estar perfectamente consciente⟩

acuteness [əˈkjuːtnəs] *n* : agudeza *f*

ad [ˈæd] → **advertisement**

adage [ˈædɪdʒ] *n* : adagio *m*, refrán *m*, dicho *m*

adamant [ˈædəmənt, -ˌmænt] *adj* : firme, categórico, inflexible — **adamantly** *adv*

Adam's apple [ˈædəmz] *n* : nuez *f* de Adán

adapt [əˈdæpt] *vt* : adaptar, ajustar — *vi* : adaptarse

adaptability [əˌdæptəˈbɪləṭi] *n* : adaptabilidad *f*, flexibilidad *f*

adaptable [əˈdæptəbəl] *adj* : adaptable, amoldable

adaptation [ˌæˌdæpˈteɪʃən, -dəp-] *n* 1 : adaptación *f*, modificación *f* 2 VERSION : versión *f*

adapter [ə'dæptər] *n* : adaptador *m*
add ['æd] *vt* **1** : añadir, agregar ⟨add the flour : añadir la harina⟩ **2** : agregar, añadir ⟨to add a comment : añadir una observación⟩ **3** : sumar (números) **4** INCLUDE : incluir **5 to add up** : sumar ⟨add up the costs : suma los gastos⟩ — *vi* **1** : sumar **2 to add to** INCREASE : aumentar ⟨to add to the confusion : para aumentar la confusión⟩ **3 to add up** SQUARE : cuadrar **4 to add up to** : sumar en total
adder ['ædər] *n* : víbora *f*
addict¹ [ə'dɪkt] *vt* : causar adicción en
addict² ['ædɪkt] *n* **1** : adicto *m*, -ta *f* **2 drug addict** : drogadicto *m*, -ta *f*; toxicómano *m*, -na *f*
addicted [ə'dɪktəd] *adj* : adicto
addiction [ə'dɪkʃən] *n* **1** : adicción *f*, dependencia *f* **2 drug addiction** : drogadicción *f*
addictive [ə'dɪktɪv] *adj* : adictivo
addition [ə'dɪʃən] *n* **1** : adición *f*, añadidura *f* **2 in ~** : además, también
additional [ə'dɪʃənəl] *adj* : extra, adicional, de más
additionally [ə'dɪʃənəli] *adv* : además, adicionalmente
additive ['ædətɪv] *n* : aditivo *m*
addle ['ædəl] *vt* **-dled; -dling** : confundir, enturbiar
address¹ [ə'drɛs] *vt* **1** : dirigirse a, pronunciar un discurso ante ⟨to address a jury : dirigirse a un jurado⟩ **2** : dirigir, ponerle la dirección a ⟨to address a letter : dirigir una carta⟩
address² [ə'drɛs, 'æˌdrɛs] *n* **1** SPEECH : discurso *m*, alocución *f* **2** : dirección *f* (de una residencia, etc.)
addressee [ˌæˌdrɛ'siː, ə-] *n* : destinatario *m*, -ria *f*
adduce [ə-'duːs, 'djuːs] *vt* **-duced; -ducing** : aducir
adenoids ['ædəˌnɔɪd, -dənˌɔɪd] *npl* : adenoides *fpl*
adept [ə'dɛpt] *adj* : experto, hábil — **adeptly** *adv*
adequacy ['ædɪkwəsi] *n, pl* **-cies** : lo adecuado, lo suficiente
adequate ['ædɪkwət] *adj* **1** SUFFICIENT : adecuado, suficiente **2** ACCEPTABLE, PASSABLE : adecuado, aceptable
adequately ['ædɪkwətli] *adv* : suficientemente, apropiadamente
adhere [æd'hɪr, əd-] *vi* **-hered; -hering 1** STICK : pegarse, adherirse **2 to adhere to** : adherirse a (una política, etc.), cumplir con (una promesa)
adherence [æd'hɪrənts, əd-] *n* : adhesión *f*, adherencia *f*, observancia *f* (de una ley, etc.)
adherent¹ [æd'hɪrənt, əd-] *adj* : adherente, adhesivo, pegajoso
adherent² *n* : adepto *m*, -ta *f*; partidario *m*, -ria *f*
adhesion [æd'hiːʒən, əd-] *n* : adhesión *f*, adherencia *f*
adhesive¹ [æd'hiːsɪv, əd-, -zɪv] *adj* : adhesivo
adhesive² *n* : adhesivo *m*, pegamento *m*

adjacent [ə'ʤeɪsənt] *adj* : adyacente, colindante, contiguo
adjective ['æʤɪktɪv] *n* : adjetivo *m* — **adjectival** [ˌæʤɪk'taɪvəl] *adj*
adjoin [ə'ʤɔɪn] *vt* : lindar con, colindar con
adjoining [ə'ʤɔɪnɪŋ] *adj* : contiguo, colindante
adjourn [ə'ʤərn] *vt* : levantar, suspender ⟨the meeting is adjourned : se levanta la sesión⟩ — *vi* : aplazarse
adjournment [ə'ʤərnmənt] *n* : suspensión *f*, aplazamiento *m*
adjudicate [ə'ʤuːdɪˌkeɪt] *vt* **-cated; -cating** : juzgar, arbitrar
adjudication [əˌʤuːdɪ'keɪʃən] *n* **1** JUDGING : arbitrio *m* (judicial) **2** JUDGMENT : fallo *m*
adjunct ['æˌʤʌŋkt] *n* : adjunto *m*, complemento *m*
adjust [ə'ʤʌst] *vt* : ajustar, arreglar, regular — *vi* **to adjust to** : adaptarse a
adjustable [ə'ʤʌstəbəl] *adj* : ajustable, regulable, graduable
adjustment [ə'ʤʌstmənt] *n* : ajuste *m*, modificación *f*
ad-lib¹ ['æd'lɪb] *v* **-libbed; -libbing** : improvisar
ad-lib² *adj* : improvisado
administer [æd'mɪnəstər, əd-] *vt* : administrar
administration [ædˌmɪnə'streɪʃən, əd-] *n* **1** MANAGING : administración *f*, dirección *f* **2** GOVERNMENT, MANAGEMENT : administración *f*, gobierno *m*
administrative [æd'mɪnəˌstreɪtɪv, əd-] *adj* : administrativo — **administratively** *adv*
administrator [æd'mɪnəˌstreɪtər, əd-] *n* : administrador *m*, -dora *f*
admirable ['ædmərəbəl] *adj* : admirable, loable — **admirably** *adv*
admiral ['ædmərəl] *n* : almirante *mf*
admiralty ['ædmərəlti] *n* : almirantazgo *m*
admiration [ˌædmə'reɪʃən] *n* : admiración *f*
admire [æd'maɪr] *vt* **-mired; -miring** : admirar
admirer [æd'maɪrər] *n* : admirador *m*, -dora *f*
admiring [æd'maɪrɪŋ] *adj* : admirativo, de admiración
admiringly [æd'maɪrɪŋli] *adv* : con admiración
admissible [æd'mɪsəbəl] *adj* : admisible, aceptable
admission [æd'mɪʃən] *n* **1** ADMITTANCE : entrada *f*, admisión *f* **2** ACKNOWLEDGMENT : reconocimiento *m*, admisión *f*
admit [æd'mɪt, əd-] *vt* **-mitted; -mitting 1** : admitir, dejar entrar ⟨the museum admits children : el museo deja entrar a los niños⟩ **2** ACKNOWLEDGE : reconocer, admitir
admittance [æd'mɪtənts, əd-] *n* : admisión *f*, entrada *f*, acceso *m*
admittedly [æd'mɪtədli, əd-] *adv* : la verdad es que, lo cierto es que ⟨admittedly we went too fast : la verdad es que fuimos demasiado de prisa⟩
admonish [æd'mɑnɪʃ, əd-] *vt* : amonestar, reprender

admonition [ˌædmə'nɪʃən] n : admonición f

ad nauseam [æd'nɔziəm] adv : hasta la saciedad

ado [ə'du:] n 1 FUSS : ruido m, alboroto m 2 TROUBLE : dificultad f, lío m 3 **without further ado** : sin más preámbulos

adobe [ə'do:bi] n : adobe m

adolescence [ˌædəl'ɛsənts] n : adolescencia f

adolescent¹ [ˌædəl'ɛsənt] adj : adolescente, de adolescencia

adolescent² n : adolescente mf

adopt [ə'dɑpt] vt : adoptar

adopted [ə'dɑptəd] adj : adoptivo

adoption [ə'dɑpʃən] n : adopción f

adoptive [ə'dɑptɪv] adj : adoptivo

adorable [ə'dorəbəl] adj : adorable, encantador

adorably [ə'dorəbli] adv : de manera adorable

adoration [ˌædə'reɪʃən] n : adoración f

adore [ə'dor] vt **adored; adoring** 1 WORSHIP : adorar 2 LOVE : querer, adorar 3 LIKE : encantarle (algo a uno), gustarle mucho (algo a uno) ⟨I adore your new dress : me encanta tu vestido nuevo⟩

adorn [ə'dorn] vt : adornar, ornar, engalanar

adornment [ə'dornmənt] n : adorno m, decoración f

adrenaline [ə'drɛnələn] n : adrenalina f

adrift [ə'drɪft] adj & adv : a la deriva

adroit [ə'drɔɪt] adj : diestro, hábil — **adroitly** adv

adroitness [ə'drɔɪtnəs] n : destreza f, habilidad f

adulation [ˌædʒəleɪʃən] n : adulación f

adult¹ [ə'dʌlt, 'æˌdʌlt] adj : adulto

adult² n : adulto m, -ta f

adulterate [ə'dʌltəˌreɪt] vt **-ated; -ating** : adulterar — **adulteration** [əˌdʌltə'reɪʃən] n

adulterer [ə'dʌltərər] n : adúltero m, -ra f

adulterous [ə'dʌltərəs] adj : adúltero

adultery [ə'dʌltəri] n, pl **-teries** : adulterio m

adulthood [ə'dʌltˌhʊd] n : adultez f, edad f adulta

advance¹ [æd'vænts, əd-] v **-vanced; -vancing** vt 1 : avanzar, adelantar ⟨to advance troops : avanzar las tropas⟩ 2 PROMOTE : ascender, promover 3 PROPOSE : proponer, presentar 4 : adelantar, anticipar ⟨they advanced me next month's salary : me adelantaron el sueldo del próximo mes⟩ — vi 1 PROCEED : avanzar, adelantarse 2 PROGRESS : progresar

advance² adj : anticipado ⟨advance notice : previo aviso⟩

advance³ n 1 PROGRESSION : avance m 2 PROGRESS : adelanto m, mejora f, progreso m 3 RISE : aumento m, alza f 4 LOAN : anticipo m, préstamo m 5 **in** ~ : por adelantado

advanced [æd'vænst, əd-] adj 1 DEVELOPED : avanzado, desarrollado 2 PRECOCIOUS : adelantado, precoz 3 HIGHER : superior

advancement [æd'væntsmənt, əd-] n 1 FURTHERANCE : fomento m, adelantamiento m, progreso m 2 PROMOTION : ascenso m

advantage [əd'væntɪʤ, æd-] n 1 SUPERIORITY : ventaja f, superioridad f ⟨to have the/an advantage : tener ventaja⟩ 2 GAIN : provecho m, partido m 3 **to take advantage of** : aprovecharse de

advantageous [ˌædˌvæn'teɪʤəs, -vən-] adj : ventajoso, provechoso — **advantageously** adv

advent ['ædˌvɛnt] n 1 **Advent** : Adviento m 2 ARRIVAL : advenimiento m, venida f

adventure [æd'vɛntʃər, əd-] n : aventura f

adventurer [æd'vɛntʃərər, əd-] n : aventurero m, -ra f

adventurous [æd'vɛntʃərəs, əd-] adj 1 : intrépido, aventurero ⟨an adventurous traveler : un viajero intrépido⟩ 2 RISKY : arriesgado, aventurado

adverb ['ædˌvərb] n : adverbio m — **adverbial** [æd'vərbiəl] adj

adversary ['ædvərˌseri] n, pl **-saries** : adversario m, -ria f

adverse [æd'vərs, 'ædˌ] adj 1 OPPOSING : opuesto, contrario 2 UNFAVORABLE : adverso, desfavorable — **adversely** adv

adversity [æd'vərsəti, əd-] n, pl **-ties** : adversidad f

advertise ['ædvərˌtaɪz] v **-tised; -tising** vt : anunciar, hacerle publicidad a — vi : hacer publicidad, hacer propaganda

advertisement ['ædvərˌtaɪzmənt;, ædˈvərtəzmənt] n : anuncio m, aviso m

advertiser ['ædvərˌtaɪzər] n : anunciante mf

advertising ['ædvərˌtaɪzɪŋ] n : publicidad f, propaganda f

advice [æd'vaɪs] n : consejo m, recomendación f ⟨take my advice : sigue mis consejos⟩

advisability [ædˌvaɪzə'bɪləti, əd-] n : conveniencia f

advisable [æd'vaɪzəbəl, əd-] adj : aconsejable, recomendable, conveniente

advise [æd'vaɪz, əd-] v **-vised; -vising** vt 1 COUNSEL : aconsejar, asesorar ⟨I advise that you wait : le aconsejo que espere⟩ ⟨I advise you to wait : le aconsejo esperar⟩ ⟨she advised us against buying it : nos aconsejó que no lo compráramos⟩ 2 RECOMMEND : recomendar ⟨I advise that you wait, I advise waiting : les aconsejo que esperen⟩ ⟨he advised caution : aconsejó actuar con cautela⟩ 3 INFORM : informar, notificar ⟨they advised him of his rights : le informaron de sus derechos⟩ — vi : dar consejo ⟨to advise against : desaconsejar⟩

adviser or **advisor** [æd'vaɪzər, əd-] n : consejero m, -ra f; asesor m, -sora f

advisory [æd'vaɪzəri, əd-] adj 1 : consultivo 2 **in an advisory capacity** : como asesor

advocacy ['ædvəkəsi] n : promoción f, apoyo m

advocate¹ ['ædvəˌkeɪt] vt **-cated; -cating** : recomendar, abogar por, ser partidario de advocate² ['ædvəkət] *n* : defensor *m*, -sora *f*; partidario *m*, -ria *f*

adze ['ædz] *n* : azuela *f*

aeon ['i:ən, 'i:,ɑn] *n* : eón *m*, siglo *m*, eternidad *f*

aerate ['ær,eɪt] *vt* -ated; -ating : gasear (un líquido), oxigenar (la sangre)

aerial¹ ['æriəl] *adj* : aéreo

aerial² *n* : antena *f*

aerie ['æri, 'ɪri, 'eɪəri] *n* : aguilera *f*

aerobic [,ær'o:bɪk] *adj* : aerobio, aeróbico ⟨aerobic exercises : ejercicios aeróbicos⟩

aerobics [,ær'o:bɪks] *ns & pl* : aeróbic *m*

aerodynamic [,æro:daɪ'næmɪk] *adj* : aerodinámico — aerodynamically [-mɪkli] *adv*

aerodynamics [,æro:daɪ'næmɪks] *n* : aerodinámica *f*

aeronautical [,ærə'nɔtɪkəl] *adj* : aeronáutico

aeronautics [,ærə'nɔtɪks] *n* : aeronáutica *f*

aerosol ['ærə,sɔl] *n* : aerosol *m*

aerospace¹ ['æro,speɪs] *adj* : aeroespacial

aerospace² *n* : espacio *m*

aesthetic [es'θɛtɪk] *adj* : estético — aesthetically [-tɪkli] *adv*

aesthetics [ɛs'θɛtɪks] *n* : estética *f*

afar [ə'fɑr] *adv* : lejos, a lo lejos

affability [,æfə'bɪləti] *n* : afabilidad *f*

affable ['æfəbəl] *adj* : afable — affably *adv*

affair [ə'fær] *n* 1 MATTER : asunto *m*, cuestión *f*, caso *m* 2 EVENT : ocasión *f*, acontecimiento *m* 3 LIAISON : amorío *m*, aventura *f* 4 business affairs : negocios *mpl* 5 current affairs : actualidades *fpl*

affect [ə'fɛkt, æ-] *vt* 1 INFLUENCE, TOUCH : afectar, tocar 2 FEIGN : fingir

affectation [,æ,fɛk'teɪʃən] *n* : afectación *f*

affected [ə'fɛktəd, æ-] *adj* 1 FEIGNED : afectado, fingido 2 MOVED : conmovido

affecting [ə'fɛktɪŋ, æ-] *adj* : conmovedor

affection [ə'fɛkʃən] *n* : afecto *m*, cariño *m*

affectionate [ə'fɛkʃənət] *adj* : afectuoso, cariñoso — affectionately *adv*

affidavit [,æfə'deɪvət, 'æfə-] *n* : declaración *f* jurada, affidávit *m*

affiliate¹ [ə'fɪli,eɪt] *v* -ated; -ating *vt* to be affiliated with : estar afiliado a

affiliate² [ə'fɪliət] *n* : afiliado *m*, -da *f* (persona), filial *f* (organización)

affiliation [ə,fɪli'eɪʃən] *n* : afiliación *f*, filiación *f*

affinity [ə'fɪnəti] *n, pl* -ties : afinidad *f*

affirm [ə'fərm] *vt* : afirmar, aseverar, declarar

affirmation [,æfər'meɪʃən] *n* : afirmación *f*, aserto *m*, declaración *f*

affirmative¹ [ə'fərmətɪv] *adj* : afirmativo ⟨affirmative action : acción afirmativa⟩

affirmative² *n* 1 : afirmativa *f* 2 to answer in the affirmative : responder afirmativamente, dar una respuesta afirmativa

affix [ə'fɪks] *vt* : fijar, poner, pegar

afflict [ə'flɪkt] *vt* 1 : afligir, aquejar 2 to be afflicted with : padecer de, sufrir de

affliction [ə'flɪkʃən] *n* 1 TRIBULATION : tribulación *f* 2 AILMENT : enfermedad *f*, padecimiento *m*

affluence ['æ,flu:ənts;, æ'flu:-, ə-] *n* : afluencia *f*, abundancia *f*, prosperidad *f*

affluent ['æ,flu:ənt; æ'flu:-, ə-] *adj* : próspero, adinerado

afford [ə'ford] *vt* 1 : tener los recursos para, permitirse el lujo de ⟨I can afford it : puedo permitírmelo, tengo con que comprarlo⟩ 2 PROVIDE : ofrecer, proporcionar, dar

affordable [ə'fordəbəl] *adj* : asequible (dícese de precios)

affront¹ [ə'frʌnt] *vt* : afrentar, insultar, ofender

affront² *n* : afrenta *f*, insulto *m*, ofensa *f*

Afghan ['æf,gæn, -gən] *n* : afgano *m*, -na *f* — Afghan *adj*

afield [ə'fi:ld] *adv* farther afield : más lejos

afire [ə'faɪr] *adj* : ardiendo, en llamas

aflame [ə'fleɪm] *adj* : llameante, en llamas

afloat [ə'flo:t] *adv & adj* : a flote

afoot [ə'fut] *adj* 1 WALKING : a pie, andando 2 UNDER WAY : en marcha ⟨something suspicious is afoot : algo sospechoso se está tramando⟩

aforementioned [ə'for'mentʃənd] : antedicho, susodicho

aforesaid [ə'for,sɛd] *adj* : antes mencionado, antedicho

afraid [ə'freɪd] *adj* 1 to be afraid : tener miedo ⟨she's afraid of the dark : le tiene miedo a la oscuridad⟩ ⟨I was afraid to look down : me daba miedo mirar para abajo⟩ 2 to be afraid that : temerse que ⟨I'm afraid not : me temo que no⟩

afresh [ə'frɛʃ] *adv* 1 : de nuevo, otra vez 2 to start afresh : volver a empezar

African ['æfrɪkən] *n* : africano *m*, -na *f* — African *adj*

African–American¹ [,æfrɪkənə'mɛrɪkən] *adj* : afroamericano

African–American² *n* : afroamericano *m*, -na *f*

Afro–American¹ [,æfroə'mɛrɪkən] *adj* → African-American¹

Afro–American² *n* → African-American²

aft ['æft] *adv* : a popa

after¹ ['æftər] *adv* 1 AFTERWARD : después 2 BEHIND : detrás, atrás

after² *adj* : posterior, siguiente ⟨in after years : en los años posteriores⟩

after³ *conj* : después de, después de que ⟨after we ate : después, de que comimos, después de comer⟩

after⁴ *prep* 1 FOLLOWING : después de, tras ⟨after Saturday/lunch : después del sábado/almuerzo⟩ ⟨after a year : después de un año⟩ ⟨day after day : día tras día⟩ ⟨the day after tomorrow : pasado mañana⟩ ⟨it's ten (minutes) after six : son las seis y diez⟩ ⟨I shouted after him : le grité (mientras se alejaba)⟩ ⟨I'm not cleaning up after you : no voy a limpiar lo que tú ensucias⟩ 2 BEHIND : tras, detrás de ⟨she ran after the dog : corrió tras el perro⟩ 3 CONCERNING : por ⟨they asked after you : preguntaron por ti⟩ 4 CONSIDERING : después de 5 PURSUING : tras ⟨to be after someone : andar tras alguien⟩ 6 : al estilo de ⟨to be named after : llevar el nombre de⟩ ⟨to take after : parecerse a⟩ 7 **after all** : después de todo

aftereffect [ˈæftəriˌfɛkt] n : efecto m secundario

afterlife [ˈæftərˌlaɪf] n : vida f venidera, vida f después de la muerte

aftermath [ˈæftərˌmæθ] n : consecuencias fpl, resultados mpl

afternoon [ˌæftərˈnuːn] n : tarde f

aftershave [ˈæftərˌʃeɪv] n : aftershave m, loción f para después de afeitarse

aftershock [ˈæftərˌʃɑk] n : réplica f (de un terremoto)

aftertaste [ˈæftərˌteɪst] n : resabio m, regusto m

afterthought [ˈæftərˌθɔt] n : ocurrencia f tardía, idea f tardía

afterward [ˈæftərwərd] or **afterwards** [-wərdz] adv : después, luego ⟨soon afterward : poco después⟩

again [əˈgɛn, -ˈgɪn] adv 1 ANEW, OVER : de nuevo, otra vez ⟨all over again : otra vez desde el principio⟩ ⟨never again : nunca más⟩ ⟨again and again : una y otra vez⟩ 2 BESIDES : además 3 **then again** : por otra parte ⟨I may stay, then again I may not : puede ser que me quede, por otra parte, puede que no⟩

against [əˈgɛnst, -ˈgɪnst] prep 1 TOUCHING : contra ⟨against the wall : contra la pared⟩ 2 OPPOSING : contra, en contra de ⟨I voted against the proposal : voté en contra de la propuesta⟩ ⟨he acted against my advice : no siguió mi consejo⟩ ⟨against her wishes/will : en contra de su voluntad⟩

agape [əˈgeɪp] adj : boquiabierto

agate [ˈægət] n : ágata f

age¹ [ˈeɪdʒ] vi **aged; aging** : envejecer, madurar

age² n 1 : edad f ⟨ten years of age : diez años de edad⟩ ⟨at the age of 35 : a los 35 años, a la edad de 35⟩ ⟨at your age : a tu edad⟩ ⟨people of all ages : personas de todas las edades⟩ ⟨those under age 18 : los menores de 18 años⟩ ⟨from an early age : desde pequeño⟩ ⟨to be of age : ser mayor de edad⟩ ⟨to come of age : cumplir la mayoría de edad⟩ ⟨he came of age as a writer : alcanzó su madurez como escritor⟩ ⟨to act one's age : actuar con madurez⟩ 2 PERIOD : era f, siglo m, época f 3 **old age** : vejez f 4 **ages** npl : siglos mpl, eternidad f ⟨it's been ages since I've seen her : hace mucho tiempo que no la veo⟩

aged n 1 [ˈeɪdʒəd, ˈeɪdʒd] OLD : anciano, viejo, vetusto 2 [ˈeɪdʒd] (indicating a specified age) ⟨a girl aged 10 : una niña de 10 años de edad⟩

ageless [ˈeɪdʒləs] adj 1 YOUTHFUL : eternamente joven 2 TIMELESS : eterno, perenne

agency [ˈeɪdʒəntsi] n, pl **-cies** 1 : agencia f, oficina f ⟨travel agency : agencia de viajes⟩ 2 **through the agency of** : a través de, por medio de

agenda [əˈdʒɛndə] n : agenda f, orden m del día

agender [eɪˈdʒɛndər] adj : agénero ⟨agender people : las personas agénero⟩

agent [ˈeɪdʒənt] n 1 MEANS : agente m, medio m, instrumento m 2 REPRESENTATIVE : agente mf, representante mf

aggravate [ˈægrəˌveɪt] vt **-vated; -vating** 1 WORSEN : agravar, empeorar 2 ANNOY : irritar, exasperar

aggravation [ˌægrəˈveɪʃən] n 1 WORSENING : empeoramiento m 2 ANNOYANCE : molestia f, irritación f, exasperación f

aggregate¹ [ˈægrɪˌgeɪt] vt **-gated; -gating** : juntar, sumar

aggregate² [ˈægrɪgət] adj : total, global, conjunto

aggregate³ [ˈægrɪgət] n 1 CONGLOMERATE : agregado m, conglomerado m 2 WHOLE : total m, conjunto m

aggression [əˈgrɛʃən] n 1 ATTACK : agresión f 2 AGGRESSIVENESS : agresividad f

aggressive [əˈgrɛsɪv] adj : agresivo — **aggressively** adv

aggressiveness [əˈgrɛsɪvnəs] n : agresividad f

aggressor [əˈgrɛsər] n : agresor m, -sora f

aggrieved [əˈgriːvd] adj : ofendido, herido

aghast [əˈgæst] adj : espantado, aterrado, horrorizado

agile [ˈædʒəl] adj : ágil

agility [əˈdʒɪləti] n, pl **-ties** : agilidad f

aging¹ [ˈeɪdʒɪŋ] adj 1 : envejecido 2 : anticuado

aging² [ˈeɪdʒɪŋ] n : envejecimiento

agitate [ˈædʒəˌteɪt] v **-tated; -tating** vt 1 SHAKE : agitar 2 UPSET : inquietar, perturbar — vi **to agitate against** : hacer campaña en contra de

agitated [ˈædʒəˌteɪtəd] adj : agitado, inquieto

agitation [ˌædʒəˈteɪʃən] n : agitación f, inquietud f

agitator [ˈædʒəˌteɪtər] n : agitador m, -dora f

agnostic [ægˈnɑstɪk] n : agnóstico m, -ca f

ago [əˈgoː] adv : hace ⟨two years ago : hace dos años⟩ ⟨long ago : hace tiempo, hace mucho tiempo⟩

agog [əˈgɑg] adj : ansioso, curioso

agonize [ˈægəˌnaɪz] vi **-nized; -nizing** 1 : atormentarse, angustiarse 2 **to agonize over** : preocuparse mucho por

agonizing [ˈægəˌnaɪzɪŋ] adj : angustioso, terrible — **agonizingly** [-zɪŋli] adv

agony [ˈægəni] n, pl **-nies** 1 PAIN : dolor m 2 ANGUISH : angustia f

agrarian [əˈgrɛriən] adj : agrario

agree [əˈgriː] v **agreed; agreeing** vt 1 : estar de acuerdo ⟨we all agree that . . . : todos estamos de acuerdo que . . .⟩ 2 ADMIT, CONCEDE : reconocer, admitir 3 : acceder a, consentir en ⟨she agreed to come : accedió a venir⟩ ⟨he agreed that she could come : consintió en que viniera⟩ ⟨she agreed to be interviewed : concedió una entrevista⟩ — vi 1 CON-

CUR : estar de acuerdo ⟨to agree with someone/something : estar de acuerdo con alguien/algo⟩ ⟨we agree on/about . . . : estamos de acuerdo en . . .⟩ ⟨we can't agree on a date : no nos ponemos de acuerdo en la fecha⟩ **2** TALLY, SQUARE : concordar **3** : concordar (en gramática) **4 to agree on** : ponerse de acuerdo en **5 to agree to** : acceder a ⟨he agreed to the plan : accedió al plan⟩ **6 to agree with** SUIT : sentarle bien (a alguien)

agreeable [ə'griːəbəl] *adj* **1** PLEASANT : agradable, simpático **2** WILLING : dispuesto **3** ACCEPTABLE : aceptable ⟨is it agreeable to you? : ¿te parece bien?⟩

agreeableness [ə'griːəbəlnəs] *n* **1** PLEASANTNESS : simpatía *f* **2** WILLINGNESS : disposición *f*, buena voluntad *f* **3** ACCEPTABILITY : aceptabilidad *f*

agreeably [ə'griːəbli] *adv* : agradablemente

agreement [ə'griːmənt] *n* **1** : acuerdo *m*, conformidad *f* ⟨in agreement with : de acuerdo con⟩ **2** CONTRACT, PACT : acuerdo *m*, pacto *m*, convenio *m* **3** CONCORD, HARMONY : concordia *f*

agribusiness ['ægrɪˌbɪznəs, -nəz] *n* : agroindustria *f*

agricultural [ˌægrɪ'kʌltʃərəl] *n* : agrícola *f*

agriculture ['ægrɪˌkʌltʃər] *n* : agricultura *f*

aground [ə'graʊnd] *adj* : encallado, varado

ahead [ə'hɛd] *adv* **1** : al frente, delante, adelante ⟨he walked ahead : caminó delante⟩ ⟨to go straight ahead : ir todo recto⟩ **2** BEFOREHAND : por adelantado, con antelación **3** LEADING : a la delantera **4 to get ahead** : adelantar, progresar **5 to look/think ahead** : mirar hacia el futuro

ahead of *prep* **1** : al frente de, delante de, antes de **2 to get ahead of** : adelantarse a

ahem [ə'hɛm] *interj* : ¡ejem!

ahoy [ə'hɔɪ] *interj* **ship ahoy!** : ¡barco a la vista!

aid¹ ['eɪd] *vt* : ayudar, auxiliar

aid² *n* **1** HELP : ayuda *f*, asistencia *f* **2** ASSISTANT : asistente *mf*

aide ['eɪd] *n* : ayudante *mf*

AIDS ['eɪdz] *n* : SIDA *m*, sida *m*

ail ['eɪl] *vt* : molestar, afligir — *vi* : sufrir, estar enfermo

aileron ['eɪləˌrɑn] *n* : alerón *m*

ailment ['eɪlmənt] *n* : enfermedad *f*, dolencia *f*, achaque *m*

aim¹ ['eɪm] *vt* **1** POINT : apuntar (un arma, una cámara, etc.) **2** DIRECT : dirigir ⟨he aimed the stone at the window : arrojó la piedra hacia la ventana⟩ ⟨a well-aimed blow : un golpe certero⟩ **3** INTEND : proponerse, querer ⟨he aims to do it tonight : se propone hacerlo esta noche⟩ ⟨we aim to please : nuestro objetivo es complacer⟩ **4 to be aimed at** ⟨his criticism wasn't aimed at her : sus críticas no iban dirigidas a ella⟩ ⟨it's aimed at reducing costs : tiene como objetivo la reducción de gastos⟩ — *vi* **1**

POINT : apuntar ⟨she aimed at the target : le apuntó al blanco⟩ **2** ASPIRE : aspirar ⟨to aim high/low : aspirar a mucho/poco⟩ **3 to aim at/for** ⟨it aims at reducing costs : tiene como objetivo la reducción de gastos⟩ ⟨to aim for a goal : proponerse como meta⟩

aim² *n* **1** MARKSMANSHIP : puntería *f* **2** GOAL : propósito *m*, objetivo *m*, fin *m*

aimless ['eɪmləs] *adj* : sin rumbo, sin objeto

aimlessly ['eɪmləsli] *adv* : sin rumbo, sin objeto

ain't ['eɪnt] *fam contraction of* AM NOT *or* ARE NOT *or* IS NOT *or* HAVE NOT *or* HAD NOT → **be, have**

air¹ ['ær] *vt* **1** *or* **to air out** : airear, ventilar ⟨to air out a mattress : airear un colchón⟩ **2** EXPRESS : airear, manifestar, comunicar **3** BROADCAST : transmitir, emitir

air² *n* **1** : aire *m* ⟨in the open air : al aire libre⟩ ⟨to vanish into thin air : desaparecerse⟩ **2** MELODY : aire *m* **3** APPEARANCE : aire *m*, aspecto *m* **4** → **air-conditioning** **5 airs** *npl* : aires *mpl*, afectación *f* **6 by ~** : por avión (dícese de una carta), en avión (dícese de una persona) **7 to be on the air** : estar en el aire, estar emitiendo **8 to be up in the air** : estar en el aire, no estar resuelto

airbag ['ærˌbæg] *n* : bolsa *f* de aire, airbag *m*

airbase ['ærˌbeɪs] *n* : base *f* aérea

airborne ['ærˌborn] *adj* **1** : aerotransportado ⟨airborne troops : tropas aerotransportadas⟩ **2** FLYING : volando, en el aire

air–condition [ˌærkən'dɪʃən] *vt* : climatizar, condicionar con el aire

air–conditioned [-ʃənd] *adj* : climatizado, con aire acondicionado

air conditioner [ˌærkən'dɪʃənər] *n* : acondicionador *m* de aire

air–conditioning [ˌærkən'dɪʃənɪŋ] *n* : aire *m* acondicionado

aircraft ['ærˌkræft] *ns & pl* **1** : avión *m*, aeronave *f* **2 aircraft carrier** : portaaviones *m*

airfield ['ærˌfiːld] *n* : aeródromo *m*, campo *m* de aviación

air force *n* : fuerza *f* aérea

airlift ['ærˌlɪft] *n* : puente *m* aéreo, transporte *m* aéreo

airline ['ærˌlaɪn] *n* : aerolínea *f*, línea *f* aérea

airliner ['ærˌlaɪnər] *n* : avión *m* de pasajeros

airmail¹ ['ærˌmeɪl] *vt* : enviar por vía aérea

airmail² *n* : correo *m* aéreo

airman ['ærmən] *n, pl* **-men** [-mən, -ˌmɛn] **1** AVIATOR : aviador *m*, -dora *f* **2** : soldado *m* de la fuerza aérea

airplane ['ærˌpleɪn] *n* : avión *m*

airport ['ærˌport] *n* : aeropuerto *m*

airship ['ærˌʃɪp] *n* : dirigible *m*, zepelín *m*

airsick ['ærˌsɪk] *adj* : mareado (al viajar en avión)

airstrip ['ærˌstrɪp] *n* : pista *f* de aterrizaje

airtight ['ær₁taɪt] *adj* : hermético, herméticamente cerrado

air vent → **vent**²

airwaves ['ær₁weɪvz] *npl* : radio *m*, televisión *f*

airy ['æri] *adj* **airier** [-iər]; **-est** 1 DELICATE, LIGHT : delicado, ligero 2 BREEZY : aireado, bien ventilado

aisle ['aɪl] *n* : pasillo *m*, nave *f* lateral (de una iglesia)

ajar [ə'dʒɑr] *adj* : entreabierto, entornado

akimbo [ə'kɪmbo] *adj & adv* : en jarras

akin [ə'kɪn] *adj* 1 RELATED : emparentado 2 SIMILAR : semejante, parecido

alabaster ['ælə₁bæstər] *n* : alabastro *m*

alacrity [ə'lækrəti] *n* : presteza *f*, prontitud *f*

alarm¹ [ə'lɑrm] *vt* 1 WARN : alarmar, alertar 2 FRIGHTEN : asustar

alarm² *n* 1 WARNING : alarma *f*, alerta *f* 2 APPREHENSION, FEAR : aprensión *f*, inquietud *f*, temor *m* 3 **alarm clock** : despertador *m*

alarming [ə'lɑrmɪŋ] *adj* : alarmante

alas [ə'læs] *interj* : ¡ay!

Albanian [æl'beɪniən] *n* : albanés *m*, -nesa *f* — **Albanian** *adj*

albatross ['ælbə₁trɔs] *n, pl* **-tross** *or* **-trosses** : albatros *m*

albeit [ɔl'bi:ət, æl-] *conj* : aunque

albino [æl'baɪno] *n, pl* **-nos** : albino *m*, -na *f*

album ['ælbəm] *n* : álbum *m* ⟨photo album : álbum de fotos⟩

albumen [æl'bju:mən] *n* 1 : clara *f* de huevo 2 → **albumin**

albumin [æl'bju:mən] *n* : albúmina *f*

alchemist ['ælkəmɪst] *n* : alquimista *mf*

alchemy ['ælkəmi] *n, pl* **-mies** : alquimia *f*

alcohol ['ælkə₁hɔl] *n* 1 ETHANOL : alcohol *m*, etanol *m* 2 LIQUOR : alcohol *m*, bebidas *fpl* alcohólicas

alcohol–free *adj* : sin alcohol

alcoholic¹ [₁ælkə'hɔlɪk] *adj* : alcohólico

alcoholic² *n* : alcohólico *m*, -ca *f*

alcoholism ['ælkəhɔ₁lɪzəm] *n* : alcoholismo *m*

alcove ['æl₁ko:v] *n* : nicho *m*, hueco *m*

alderman ['ɔldərmən] *n, pl* **-men** [-mən, -₁mɛn] : concejal *mf*

ale ['eɪl] *n* : cerveza *f*

alert¹ [ə'lərt] *vt* : alertar, poner sobre aviso

alert² *adj* 1 WATCHFUL : alerta, vigilante 2 QUICK : listo, vivo

alert³ *n* : alerta *f*, alarma *f*

alertly [ə'lərtli] *adv* : con listeza

alertness [ə'lərtnəs] *n* 1 WATCHFULNESS : vigilancia *f* 2 ASTUTENESS : listeza *f*, viveza *f*

alfalfa [æl'fælfə] *n* : alfalfa *f*

alga ['ælgə] *n, pl* **-gae** ['æl₁dʒi:] : alga *f*

algebra ['ældʒəbrə] *n* : álgebra *m*

algebraic [₁ældʒə'breɪk] *adj* : algebraico — **algebraically** [-ɪkli] *adv*

Algerian [æl'dʒɪriən] *n* : argelino *m*, -na *f* — **Algerian** *adj*

algorithm ['ælgə₁rɪðəm] *n* : algoritmo *m*

alias¹ ['eɪliəs] *adv* : alias

alias² *n* : alias *m*

alibi¹ ['ælə₁baɪ] *vi* : ofrecer una coartada

alibi² *n* 1 : coartada *f* 2 EXCUSE : pretexto *m*, excusa *f*

alien¹ ['eɪliən] *adj* 1 STRANGE : ajeno, extraño 2 FOREIGN : extranjero, foráneo 3 EXTRATERRESTRIAL : extraterrestre

alien² *n* 1 FOREIGNER : extranjero *m*, -ra *f*; forastero *m*, -ra *f* 2 EXTRATERRESTRIAL : extraterrestre *mf*

alienate ['eɪliə₁neɪt] *vt* **-ated**; **-ating** 1 ESTRANGE : alienar, enajenar 2 **to alienate oneself** : alejarse, distanciarse

alienation [₁eɪliə'neɪʃən] *n* : alienación *f*, enajenación *f*

alight [ə'laɪt] *vi* 1 DISMOUNT : bajarse, apearse 2 LAND : posarse, aterrizar

align [ə'laɪn] *vt* : alinear

alignment [ə'laɪnmənt] *n* : alineación *f*, alineamiento *m*

alike¹ [ə'laɪk] *adv* : igual, del mismo modo

alike² *adj* : igual, semejante, parecido

alimentary [₁ælə'mɛntəri] *adj* 1 : alimenticio 2 **alimentary canal** : tubo *m* digestivo

alimony ['ælə₁mo:ni] *n, pl* **-nies** : pensión *f* alimenticia

alive [ə'laɪv] *adj* 1 LIVING : vivo, viviente ⟨alive and kicking : vivito y coleando⟩ 2 LIVELY : animado, activo 3 ACTIVE : vigente, en uso 4 AWARE : consciente ⟨alive to the danger : consciente del peligro⟩

alkali ['ælkə₁laɪ] *n, pl* **-lies** [-₁laɪz] *or* **-lis** [-₁laɪz] : álcali *m*

alkaline ['ælkələn, -₁laɪn] *adj* : alcalino

all¹ ['ɔl] *adv* 1 COMPLETELY : todo, completamente ⟨all wet : todo mojado⟩ ⟨all alone : completamente solo⟩ ⟨all too often : con demasiada frecuencia⟩ ⟨it's all yours : es todo para ti⟩ ⟨I'm all for it : estoy totalmente a su favor⟩ ⟨she forgot all about it : lo olvidó por completo⟩ 2 : igual ⟨the score is 14 all : es 14 iguales, están empatados a 14⟩ 3 **all around** : para todos 4 **all but** ALMOST : casi 5 **~ of** ONLY : sólo, solamente 6 **~ of** AT LEAST : por lo menos 7 **~ over** EVERYWHERE : por todas partes 8 **~ over** *fam* ⟨to be all over someone for something : criticar duramente a alguien por algo⟩ 9 **~ over** : aglomerados alrededor de ⟨to be all over each other : estar muy acaramelados⟩ 10 **all that** : tan ⟨it hasn't changed all that much : no ha cambiado tanto/demasiado⟩ ⟨it's not all that bad : no es para tanto⟩ 11 **all the better** : tanto mejor 12 **all the more** : aún más, todavía más

all² *adj* : todo ⟨all the children : todos los niños⟩ ⟨in all likelihood : con toda probabilidad, con la mayor probabilidad⟩ ⟨all night : toda la noche⟩ ⟨people of all kinds : gente de todo tipo⟩

all³ *pron* 1 : todo ⟨they ate it all : lo comieron todo⟩ ⟨that's all : eso es todo⟩ ⟨enough for all : suficiente para todos⟩ ⟨the best of all : el mejor de todos⟩ ⟨some of the girls, but not all : algunas de las muchachas, pero no todas⟩ ⟨all I know is that . . . : lo único que sé es que . . . , todo lo que sé es que . . .⟩ ⟨for all I know : que yo sepa⟩ **2 all in all** : en general **3 all told** *or* **in all** : en total **4 and all** : y todo eso **5 at all** (*in questions*) ⟨did you find out anything at all? : ¿supiste algo?⟩ **6 (not) at all** (*in negative constructions*) : en absoluto, para nada ⟨he did nothing at all, he didn't do anything at all : no hizo nada en absoluto⟩ ⟨I don't like it at all : no me gusta para nada⟩ **7 to give it one's all** : dar todo de sí **8 when all is said and done** : a fin de cuentas

Allah [ˈɑlɑ, ɑˈlɑ] *n* : Alá *m*

all–around [ˌɔləˈraʊnd] *adj* : completo, amplio

allay [əˈleɪ] *vt* **1** ALLEVIATE : aliviar, mitigar **2** CALM : aquietar, calmar

allegation [ˌælɪˈɡeɪʃən] *n* : alegato *m*, acusación *f*

allege [əˈlɛdʒ] *vt* **-leged; -leging 1** : alegar, afirmar **2 to be alleged** : decirse, pretenderse ⟨she is alleged to be wealthy : se dice que es adinerada⟩

alleged [əˈlɛdʒd, əˈlɛdʒəd] *adj* : presunto, supuesto

allegedly [əˈlɛdʒədli] *adv* : supuestamente, según se alega

allegiance [əˈliːdʒənts] *n* : lealtad *f*, fidelidad *f* ⟨to pledge allegiance to : jurar lealtad a⟩

allegorical [ˌæləˈɡɔrɪkəl] *adj* : alegórico

allegory [ˈæləˌɡori] *n, pl* **-ries** : alegoría *f*

alleluia [ˌɑləˈluːjə, ˌæ-] → **hallelujah**

allergen [ˈælərdʒən] *n* : alérgeno *m*

allergic [əˈlərdʒɪk] *adj* : alérgico

allergy [ˈælərdʒi] *n, pl* **-gies** : alergia *f*

alleviate [əˈliːviˌeɪt] *vt* **-ated; -ating** : aliviar, mitigar, paliar

alleviation [əˌliːviˈeɪʃən] *n* : alivio *m*

alley [ˈæli] *n, pl* **-leys 1** : callejón *m* **2 bowling alley** : bolera *f*

alliance [əˈlaɪənts] *n* : alianza *f*, coalición *f*

alligator [ˈæləˌɡeɪtər] *n* : caimán *m*

all–important [ˌɔlɪmˈpɔrtənt] *adj* : crucial, de fundamental importancia

alliteration [əˌlɪtəˈreɪʃən] *n* : aliteración *f*

all–night [ˈɔlˈnaɪt] *adj* **1** : que dura toda la noche (dícese de una fiesta, etc.) **2** : que está abierto toda la noche (dícese de un restaurante, etc.)

all–nighter [ˈɔlˈnaɪtər] *n fam* **to pull an all–nighter** : trasnochar (estudiando, etc.)

allocate [ˈæləˌkeɪt] *vt* **-cated; -cating** : asignar, adjudicar

allocation [ˌæləˈkeɪʃən] *n* : asignación *f*, reparto *m*, distribución *f*

allot [əˈlɑt] *vt* **-lotted; -lotting** : repartir, distribuir, asignar

allotment [əˈlɑtmənt] *n* : reparto *m*, asignación *f*, distribución *f*

all–out [ˈɔlˈaʊt] *adj* : total, con todo ⟨all-out war : guerra sin cuartel⟩

allow [əˈlaʊ] *vt* **1** PERMIT : permitir, dejar ⟨she allowed him to leave : le permitió irse, le permitió que se fuera⟩ ⟨we won't allow that to happen : no permitiremos que eso pase⟩ ⟨it allows you to create web pages : permite crear páginas web⟩ ⟨no dogs allowed : no se admiten pe-

rros⟩ **2** ALLOT : conceder, dar (tiempo, etc.) **3** ADMIT, CONCEDE : admitir, conceder **4** : admitir (pruebas) — *vi* **to allow for** : tener en cuenta

allowable [əˈlaʊəbəl] *adj* **1** PERMISSIBLE : permisible, lícito **2** : deducible ⟨allowable expenditure : gasto deducible⟩

allowance [əˈlaʊənts] *n* **1** : complemento *m* (para gastos, etc.), mesada *f* (para niños) **2 to make allowance(s)** : tener en cuenta, disculpar

alloy [ˈæˌlɔɪ] *n* : aleación *f*

all–purpose [ˈɔlˈpərpəs] *adj* : multiuso ⟨all-purpose flour : harina común⟩

all right[1] *adv* **1** YES : sí, por supuesto **2** WELL : bien ⟨I did all right : me fue bien⟩ **3** DEFINITELY : bien, ciertamente, sin duda ⟨he's sick all right : está bien enfermo⟩

all right[2] *adj* **1** OK : bien ⟨are you all right? : ¿estás bien?⟩ **2** SATISFACTORY : bien, bueno ⟨your work is all right : tu trabajo es bueno⟩

all–round [ˌɔlˈraʊnd] → **all-around**

allspice [ˈɔlspaɪs] *n* : pimienta *f* de Jamaica

all–terrain vehicle [ˈɔltəˈreɪn-] *n* : todoterreno *m*, vehículo *m* todoterreno

all–time [ˈɔlˌtaɪm] *adj* : de todos los tiempos, histórico ⟨my all-time favorite : mi favorito de todos los tiempos⟩ ⟨an all-time record/high/low : un récord/máximo/mínimo histórico⟩

allude [əˈluːd] *vi* **-luded; -luding** : aludir, referirse

allure [əˈlʊr] *vt* **-lured; -luring** : cautivar, atraer

allure[2] *n* : atractivo *m*, encanto *m*

allusion [əˈluːʒən] *n* : alusión *f*

ally[1] [əˈlaɪ, ˈæˌlaɪ] *vi* **-lied; -lying** : aliarse

ally[2] [ˈæˌlaɪ, əˈlaɪ] *n* : aliado *m*, -da *f*

almanac [ˈɔlməˌnæk, ˈæl-] *n* : almanaque *m*

almighty [ɔlˈmaɪti] *adj* : omnipotente, todopoderoso

almond [ˈɑmənd, ˈɑl-, ˈæ-, ˈæl-] *n* : almendra *f*

almost [ˈɔlˌmoːst, ɔlˈmoːst] *adv* : casi, prácticamente

alms [ˈɑmz, ˈɑlmz, ˈælmz] *ns & pl* : limosna *f*, caridad *f*

aloe [ˈæloː] *n* : áloe *m*

aloft [əˈlɔft] *adv* : en alto, en el aire

alone[1] [əˈloːn] *adv* : sólo, solamente, únicamente

alone[2] *adj* : solo ⟨they're alone in the house : están solos en la casa⟩

along[1] [əˈlɔŋ] *adv* **1** FORWARD : adelante ⟨farther along : más adelante⟩ ⟨move along! : ¡circulen, por favor!⟩ **2 to bring along** : traer **3 ~ with** : con, junto con **4 all along** : desde el principio

along[2] *prep* **1** : por, a lo largo de ⟨along the coast : a lo largo de la costa⟩ **2** : en, en el curso de, por ⟨along the way : en el curso del viaje⟩

alongside[1] [əˌlɔŋˈsaɪd] *adv* : al costado, al lado

alongside[2] *or* **alongside of** *prep* : junto a, al lado de

aloof [ə'lu:f] *adj* : distante, reservado
aloofness [ə'lu:fnəs] *n* : reserva *f*, actitud *f* distante
aloud [ə'laʊd] *adv* : en voz alta
alpaca [æl'pækə] *n* : alpaca *f*
alphabet ['ælfə,bɛt] *n* : alfabeto *m*
alphabetical [,ælfə'bɛtɪkəl] *or* **alphabetic** [-'bɛtɪk] *adj* : alfabético — **alphabetically** [-tɪkli] *adv*
alphabetize ['ælfəbə,taɪz] *vt* **-ized; -izing** : alfabetizar, poner en orden alfabético
alpine ['æl,paɪn] *adj* : alpino
already [ɔl'rɛdi] *adv* : ya
also ['ɔl,so:] *adv* : también, además
altar ['ɔltər] *n* : altar *m*
alter ['ɔltər] *vt* : alterar, cambiar, modificar
alteration [,ɔltə'reɪʃən] *n* : alteración *f*, cambio *m*, modificación *f*
altercation [,ɔltər'keɪʃən] *n* : altercado *m*, disputa *f*
alternate¹ ['ɔltər,neɪt] *v* **-nated; -nating** : alternar
alternate² ['ɔltərnət] *adj* **1** : alterno ⟨alternate cycles of inflation and depression : ciclos alternos de inflación y depresión⟩ **2** : uno sí y otro no ⟨he cooks on alternate days : cocina un día sí y otro no⟩
alternate³ ['ɔltərnət] *n* : suplente *mf*; sustituto *m*, -ta *f*
alternately ['ɔltərnətli] *adv* : alternativamente, por turno
alternating current ['ɔltər,neɪtɪŋ] *n* : corriente *f* alterna
alternation [,ɔltər'neɪʃən] *n* : alternancia *f*, rotación *f*
alternative¹ [ɔl'tərnətɪv] *adj* : alternativo
alternative² *n* : alternativa *f*
alternatively [ɔl'tərnətɪvli] *adv* (*indicating another option*) ⟨(or,) alternatively, you could come here : (o,) si prefieres, podrías venir aquí⟩
alternator ['ɔltər,neɪtər] *n* : alternador *m*
although [ɔl'ðo:] *conj* : aunque, a pesar de que
altitude ['æltə,tu:d, -,tju:d] *n* : altitud *f*, altura *f*
alto ['æl,to:] *n*, *pl* **-tos** : alto *mf*, contralto *mf*
altogether [,ɔltə'gɛðər] *adv* **1** COMPLETELY : completamente, totalmente, del todo **2** ON THE WHOLE : en suma, en general
altruism ['æltru,ɪzəm] *n* : altruismo *m*
altruistic [,æltru'ɪstɪk] *adj* : altruista — **altruistically** [-tɪkli] *adv*
alum ['æləm] *n* : alumbre *m*
aluminum [ə'lu:mənəm] *n* : aluminio *m*
alumna [ə'lʌmnə] *n*, *pl* **-nae** [-,ni:] : exalumna *f*
alumnus [ə'lʌmnəs] *n*, *pl* **-ni** [-,naɪ] : exalumno *m*
always ['ɔlwiz, -,weɪz] *adv* **1** INVARIABLY : siempre, invariablemente **2** FOREVER : para siempre
Alzheimer's ['ɑlts,haɪmərz] *or* **Alzheimer's disease** *n* : (enfermedad *f* de) Alzheimer *m*
am → **be**

amalgam [ə'mælgəm] *n* : amalgama *f*
amalgamate [ə'mælgə,meɪt] *vt* **-ated; -ating** : amalgamar, unir, fusionar
amalgamation [ə,mælgə'meɪʃən] *n* : fusión *f*, unión *f*
amaryllis [,æmə'rɪləs] *n* : amarilis *f*
amass [ə'mæs] *vt* : amasar, acumular
amateur ['æmət̬ər, -tər, -,tʊr, -,tjʊr] *n* **1** : amateur *mf* **2** BEGINNER : principiante *mf*; aficionado *m*, -da *f*
amateurish ['æmə,tʃərɪʃ, -,tər-, -,tʊr-, -,tjʊr-] *adj* : amateur, inexperto
amaze [ə'meɪz] *vt* **amazed; amazing** : asombrar, maravillar, pasmar
amazement [ə'meɪzmənt] *n* : asombro *m*, sorpresa *f*
amazing [ə'meɪzɪŋ] *adj* : asombroso, sorprendente — **amazingly** [-zɪŋli] *adv*
Amazon ['æmə,zɑn] *n* : amazona *f* (en mitología)
Amazonian [,æmə'zo:niən] *adj* : amazónico
ambassador [æm'bæsədər] *n* : embajador *m*, -dora *f*
amber ['æmbər] *n* : ámbar *m*
ambergris ['æmbər,grɪs, -,gri:s] *n* : ámbar *m* gris
ambidextrous [,æmbi'dɛkstrəs] *adj* : ambidextro — **ambidextrously** *adv*
ambience *or* **ambiance** ['æmbiənts, 'ɑmbi,ɑnts] *n* : ambiente *m*, atmósfera *f*
ambiguity [,æmbə'gju:əṭi] *n*, *pl* **-ties** : ambigüedad *f*
ambiguous [æm'bɪgjuəs] *adj* : ambiguo
ambition [æm'bɪʃən] *n* : ambición *f*
ambitious [æm'bɪʃəs] *adj* : ambicioso — **ambitiously** *adv*
ambivalence [æm'bɪvələnts] *n* : ambivalencia *f*
ambivalent [æm'bɪvələnt] *adj* : ambivalente
amble¹ ['æmbəl] *vi* **-bled; -bling** : ir tranquilamente, pasearse despreocupadamente
amble² *n* : paseo *m* tranquilo
ambulance ['æmbjələnts] *n* : ambulancia *f*
ambush¹ ['æm,bʊʃ] *vt* : emboscar
ambush² *n* : emboscada *f*, celada *f*
ameliorate [ə'mi:ljə,reɪt] *v* **-rated; -rating** IMPROVE : mejorar
amelioration [ə,mi:ljə'reɪʃən] *n* : mejora *f*
amen ['eɪ'mɛn, 'ɑ-] *interj* : amén
amenable [ə'mi:nəbəl, -'mɛ-] *adj* RESPONSIVE : susceptible, receptivo, sensible
amend [ə'mɛnd] *vt* **1** IMPROVE : mejorar, enmendar **2** CORRECT : enmendar, corregir
amendment [ə'mɛndmənt] *n* : enmienda *f*
amends [ə'mɛndz] *ns & pl* : compensación *f*, reparación *f*, desagravio *m*
amenity [ə'mɛnəṭi, -'mi:-] *n*, *pl* **-ties 1** PLEASANTNESS : lo agradable, amenidad *f* **2 amenities** *npl* : servicios *mpl*, comodidades *fpl*
American [ə'mɛrɪkən] *n* : americano *m*, -na *f* — **American** *adj*
American Indian *n sometimes offensive* → **Native American**
amethyst ['æməθəst] *n* : amatista *f*
amiability [,eɪmi:ə'bɪləṭi] *n* : amabilidad *f*, afabilidad *f*

amiable ['eɪmi:əbəl] *adj* : amable, afable — **amiably** [-bli] *adv*

amicable ['æmɪkəbəl] *adj* : amigable, amistoso, cordial — **amicably** [-bli] *adv*

amid [ə'mɪd] *or* **amidst** [ə'mɪdst] *prep* : en medio de, entre

amino acid [ə'mi:no] *n* : aminoácido *m*

amiss[1] [ə'mɪs] *adv* : mal, fuera de lugar ⟨to take amiss : tomar a mal, llevar a mal⟩

amiss[2] *adj* **1** WRONG : malo, inoportuno **2** there's something amiss : pasa algo, algo anda mal

ammeter ['æˌmi:t̬ər] *n* : amperímetro *m*

ammonia [ə'mo:njə] *n* : amoníaco *m*

ammunition [ˌæmjə'nɪʃən] *n* **1** : municiones *fpl* **2** ARGUMENTS : argumentos *mpl*

amnesia [æm'ni:ʒə] *n* : amnesia *f*

amnesiac [æm'ni:ʒiˌæk] *n* : amnésico *m*, -ca *f* — **amnesiac** *adj*

amnesty ['æmnəsti] *n, pl* **-ties** : amnistía *f*

amoeba [ə'mi:bə] *n, pl* **-bas** *or* **-bae** [-ˌbi:] : ameba *f* — **amoebic** [ə'mi:bɪk] *adj*

amok [ə'mʌk, -'mɑk] *adv* **to run amok** : correr a ciegas, enloquecerse, desbocarse (dícese de la economía, etc.)

among [ə'mʌŋ] *or* **amongst** [ə'mʌŋkst] *prep* : entre

amoral [eɪ'mɔrəl] *adj* : amoral

amorous ['æmərəs] *adj* **1** PASSIONATE : apasionado **2** ENAMORED : enamorado **3** LOVING : amoroso, cariñoso

amorously ['æmərəsli] *adv* : con cariño

amorphous [ə'mɔrfəs] *adj* : amorfo, informe

amortize ['æmərˌtaɪz, ə'mɔr-] *vt* **-tized; -tizing** : amortizar

amount[1] [ə'maʊnt] *vi* **to amount to 1** : equivaler a, significar ⟨that amounts to treason : eso equivale a la traición⟩ **2** : ascender (a) ⟨my debts amount to $2000 : mis deudas ascienden a $2000⟩

amount[2] *n* : cantidad *f*, suma *f*

ampere ['æmˌpɪr] *n* : amperio *m*

ampersand ['æmpərˌsænd] *n* : el signo &

amphetamine [æm'fɛt̬əˌmi:n] *n* : anfetamina *f*

amphibian [æm'fɪbiən] *n* : anfibio *m*

amphibious [æm'fɪbiəs] *adj* : anfibio

amphitheater ['æmfəˌθi:ət̬ər] *n* : anfiteatro *m*

ample ['æmpəl] *adj* **ampler; amplest 1** LARGE, SPACIOUS : amplio, extenso, grande **2** ABUNDANT : abundante, generoso

amplifier ['æmpləˌfaɪər] *n* : amplificador *m*

amplify ['æmpləˌfaɪ] *vt* **-fied; -fying** : amplificar

amply ['æmpli] *adv* : ampliamente, abundantemente, suficientemente

amputate ['æmpjəˌteɪt] *vt* **-tated; -tating** : amputar

amputation [ˌæmpjə'teɪʃən] *n* : amputación *f*

amuck [ə'mʌk] → **amok**

amulet ['æmjələt] *n* : amuleto *m*, talismán *m*

amuse [ə'mju:z] *vt* **amused; amusing 1** ENTERTAIN : entretener, distraer **2**

: hacer reír, divertir ⟨the joke amused us : la broma nos hizo reír⟩

amusement [ə'mju:zmənt] *n* **1** ENTERTAINMENT : diversión *f*, entretenimiento *m*, pasatiempo *m* **2** LAUGHTER : risa *f*

amusement park *n* : parque *m* de diversiones

an *art* → **a**[2]

anachronism [ə'nækrəˌnɪzəm] *n* : anacronismo *m*

anachronistic [əˌnækrə'nɪstɪk] *adj* : anacrónico

anaconda [ˌænə'kɑndə] *n* : anaconda *f*

anagram ['ænəˌgræm] *n* : anagrama *m*

anal ['eɪnəl] *adj* : anal

analgesic [ˌænəl'dʒi:zɪk, -sɪk] *n* : analgésico *m*

analog ['ænəˌlɔg] *adj* : analógico

analogical [ˌænə'lɑdʒɪkəl] *adj* : analógico — **analogically** [-kli] *adv*

analogous [ə'næləgəs] *adj* : análogo

analogy [ə'nælədʒi] *n, pl* **-gies** : analogía *f*

analysis [ə'næləsəs] *n, pl* **-yses** [-ˌsi:z] **1** : análisis *m* **2** PSYCHOANALYSIS : psicoanálisis *m*

analyst ['ænəlɪst] *n* **1** : analista *mf* **2** PSYCHOANALYST : psicoanalista *mf*

analytic [ˌænə'lɪt̬ɪk] *or* **analytical** [-t̬ɪkəl] *adj* : analítico — **analytically** [-t̬ɪkli] *adv*

analyze ['ænəˌlaɪz] *vt* **-lyzed; -lyzing** : analizar

anarchic [æ'nɑrkɪk] *adj* : anárquico — **anarchically** [-kɪkli] *adv*

anarchism ['ænərˌkɪzəm, -nɑr-] *n* : anarquismo *m*

anarchist ['ænərkɪst, -nɑr-] *n* : anarquista *mf*

anarchy ['ænərki, -nɑr-] *n* : anarquía *f*

anathema [ə'næθəmə] *n* : anatema *m*

anatomic [ˌænə'tɑmɪk] *or* **anatomical** [-mɪkəl] *adj* : anatómico — **anatomically** [-mɪkli] *adv*

anatomy [ə'næt̬əmi] *n, pl* **-mies** : anatomía *f*

ancestor ['ænˌsɛstər] *n* : antepasado *m*, -da *f*; antecesor *m*, -sora *f*

ancestral [æn'sɛstrəl] *adj* : ancestral, de los antepasados

ancestry ['ænˌsɛstri] *n* **1** DESCENT : ascendencia *f*, linaje *m*, abolengo *m* **2** ANCESTORS : antepasados *mpl*, -das *fpl*

anchor[1] ['æŋkər] *vt* **1** MOOR : anclar, fondear **2** FASTEN : sujetar, asegurar, fijar

anchor[2] *n* **1** : ancla *f* **2** → **anchorman 3** → **anchorwoman**

anchorage ['æŋkərɪdʒ] *n* : anclaje *m*

anchorman ['æŋkərˌmæn] *n, pl* **-men** [-mən, -ˌmɛn] : presentador *m* (de televisión)

anchorwoman ['æŋkərˌwʊmən] *n, pl* **-women** [-ˌwɪmən] : presentadora *f* (de televisión)

anchovy ['ænˌtʃo:vi, æn'tʃo:-] *n, pl* **-vies** *or* **-vy** : anchoa *f*, boquerón *m*

ancient ['eɪntʃənt] *adj* **1** : antiguo ⟨ancient history : historia antigua⟩ **2** OLD : viejo

ancients ['eɪntʃənts] *npl* : los antiguos *mpl*

and ['ænd] *conj* **1** : y (**e** *before words beginning with* i- *or* hi-) ⟨books and papers

: libros y papeles⟩ ⟨six and a half : seis y medio⟩ ⟨a hundred and ten : ciento diez⟩ ⟨2 and 2 equals 4 : 2 más 2 es igual a 4⟩ ⟨at (the corner of) First and Main : en la esquina de First y Main⟩ **2** : con ⟨ham and eggs : huevos con jamón⟩ **3** IN ORDER TO : a, de ⟨go and see : ve a ver⟩ ⟨try and finish it : trata de terminarlo⟩ **4** (*indicating continuation*) ⟨she cried and cried : no dejaba de llorar⟩ **5** (*used for emphasis*) ⟨hundreds and hundreds of people : cientos de personas⟩ ⟨more and more difficult : cada vez más difícil⟩

Andalusian [ˌændəˈluːʒən] *n* : andaluz *m*, -luza *f* — **Andalusian** *adj*

Andean [ˈændiən] *adj* : andino

andiron [ˈænˌdaɪərn] *n* : morillo *m*

Andorran [ænˈdɔrən] *n* : andorrano *m*, -na *f* — **Andorran** *adj*

androgynous [ænˈdrɑʤənəs] *adj* : andrógino

anecdotal [ˌænɪkˈdoːʈəl] *adj* : anecdótico

anecdote [ˈænɪkˌdoːt] *n* : anécdota *f*

anemia [əˈniːmiə] *n* : anemia *f*

anemic [əˈniːmɪk] *adj* : anémico

anemone [əˈnɛməni] *n* : anémona *f*

anesthesia [ˌænəsˈθiːʒə] *n* : anestesia *f*

anesthetic[1] [ˌænəsˈθɪk] *adj* : anestésico

anesthetic[2] *n* : anestésico *m*

anesthetist [əˈnɛsθətɪst] *n* : anestesista *mf*

anesthetize [əˈnɛsθəˌtaɪz] *vt* **-tize; -tized** : anestesiar

aneurysm [ˈænjəˌrɪzəm] *n* : aneurisma *mf*

anew [əˈnuː, -ˈnjuː] *adv* : de nuevo, otra vez, nuevamente

angel [ˈeɪnʤəl] *n* : ángel *m* ⟨the Angel of Death : el ángel exterminador⟩

angelic [ænˈʤɛlɪk] *or* **angelical** [-lɪkəl] *adj* : angélico, angelical — **angelically** [-lɪkli] *adv*

anger[1] [ˈæŋgər] *vt* : enojar, enfadar

anger[2] *n* : enojo *m*, enfado *m*, ira *f*, cólera *f*, rabia *f*

angina [ænˈʤaɪnə] *n* : angina *f*

angle[1] [ˈæŋgəl] *v* **angled; angling** *vt* DIRECT, SLANT : orientar, dirigir — *vi* FISH : pescar (con caña)

angle[2] *n* **1** : ángulo *m* **2** POINT OF VIEW : perspectiva *f*, punto *m* de vista

angler [ˈæŋglər] *n* : pescador *m*, -dora *f*

Anglican [ˈæŋglɪkən] *n* : anglicano *m*, -na *f* — **Anglican** *adj*

angling [ˈæŋglɪŋ] *n* : pesca *f* con caña

Anglo–Saxon[1] [ˌæŋgloˈsæksən] *adj* : anglosajón

Anglo–Saxon[2] *n* : anglosajón *m*, -jona *f*

Angolan [æŋˈgoːlən, æn-] *n* : angoleño *m*, -ña *f* — **Angolan** *adj*

angora [æŋˈgorə, æn-] *n* : angora *f*

angrily [ˈæŋgrəli] *adv* : furiosamente, con ira

angry [ˈæŋgri] *adj* **angrier; -est** : enojado, enfadado, furioso

anguish [ˈæŋgwɪʃ] *n* : angustia *f*, congoja *f*

anguished [ˈæŋgwɪʃt] *adj* : angustiado, acongojado

angular [ˈæŋgjələr] *adj* : angular (dícese de las formas), anguloso (dícese de las caras)

animal [ˈænəməl] *n* **1** : animal *m* **2** BRUTE : bruto *m*, -ta *f*

animate[1] [ˈænəˌmeɪt] *vt* **-mated; -mating** : animar

animate[2] [ˈænəmət] *adj* : animado

animated [ˈænəˌmeɪʈəd] *adj* **1** LIVELY : animado, vivo, vivaz **2 animated cartoon** : dibujos *mpl* animados

animation [ˌænəˈmeɪʃən] *n* : animación *f*

animosity [ˌænəˈmɑsəʈi] *n*, *pl* **-ties** : animosidad *f*, animadversión *f*

anise [ˈænəs] *n* : anís *m*

aniseed [ˈænəsˌsiːd] *n* : anís *m*, semilla *f* de anís

ankle [ˈæŋkəl] *n* : tobillo *m*

anklebone [ˈæŋkəlˌboːn] *n* : taba *f*

annals [ˈænəlz] *npl* : anales *mpl*, crónica *f*

annatto [əˈnɑto] *n* : achiote *m*

anneal [əˈniːl] *vt* **1** TEMPER : templar **2** STRENGTHEN : fortalecer

annex[1] [əˈnɛks, ˈæˌnɛks] *vt* : anexar

annex[2] [ˈæˌnɛks, -nɪks] *n* : anexo *m*, anejo *m*

annexation [ˌæˌnɛkˈseɪʃən] *n* : anexión *f*

annihilate [əˈnaɪəˌleɪt] *vt* **-lated; -lating** : aniquilar

annihilation [əˌnaɪəˈleɪʃən] *n* : aniquilación *f*, aniquilamiento *m*

anniversary [ˌænəˈvɔrsəri] *n*, *pl* **-ries** : aniversario *m*

annotate [ˈænəˌteɪt] *vt* **-tated; -tating** : anotar

annotation [ˌænəˈteɪʃən] *n* : anotación *f*

announce [əˈnaʊnts] *vt* **-nounced; -nouncing** : anunciar

announcement [əˈnaʊntsmənt] *n* : anuncio *m*

announcer [əˈnaʊntsər] *n* : anunciador *m*, -dora *f*; comentarista *mf*; locutor *m*, -tora *f*

annoy [əˈnɔɪ] *vt* : molestar, fastidiar, irritar

annoyance [əˈnɔɪənts] *n* **1** IRRITATION : irritación *f*, fastidio *m* **2** NUISANCE : molestia *f*, fastidio *m*

annoying [əˈnɔɪɪŋ] *adj* : molesto, fastidioso, engorroso — **annoyingly** [-ɪŋli] *adv*

annual[1] [ˈænjʊəl] *adj* : anual — **annually** *adv*

annual[2] *n* **1** : planta *f* anual **2** YEARBOOK : anuario *m*

annuity [əˈnuːəʈi] *n*, *pl* **-ties** : anualidad *f*

annul [əˈnʌl] *vt* **anulled; anulling** : anular, invalidar

annulment [əˈnʌlmənt] *n* : anulación *f*

anode [ˈæˌnoːd] *n* : ánodo *m*

anoint [əˈnɔɪnt] *vt* : ungir

anomalous [əˈnɑmələs] *adj* : anómalo

anomaly [əˈnɑməli] *n*, *pl* **-lies** : anomalía *f*

anonymity [ˌænəˈnɪməʈi] *n* : anonimato *m*

anonymous [əˈnɑnəməs] *adj* : anónimo — **anonymously** *adv*

anorak [ˈænəˌræk] *n* : anorak *m*

anorexia [ˌænəˈrɛksiə] *n* : anorexia *f*

anorexic [ˌænəˈrɛksɪk] *adj* : anoréxico

another[1] [əˈnʌðər] *adj* **1** : otro ⟨another drink : otra copa⟩ ⟨another two days : dos días más, otros dos días⟩ ⟨yet another example : otro ejemplo más⟩ ⟨it was just another day : fue un día como cualquier otro〉 **2** : otro 〈at another time : en otro momento, en otra ocasión〉 〈that's another matter : eso es otra cuestión〉 **3** (*indicating similarity*) : otro 〈another Great Depression : otra Gran Depresión〉

another² *pron* : otro 〈one after another : uno tras otro, una tras otra〉 〈at one time or another : en algún momento〉 〈for one reason or another : por alguna razón〉 〈one way or another : de una u otra forma/manera〉

answer¹ ['æn*t*sər] *vt* **1** : contestar (a) 〈to answer the telephone : contestar el teléfono〉 〈to answer a question : contestar (a) una pregunta〉 〈he didn't answer me : no me contestó〉 **2** FULFILL : satisfacer **3** : responder a (acusaciones, etc.) — *vi* **1** : contestar, responder **2 to answer back** TALK BACK : contestar (con impertinencia) **3 to answer for someone** : contestar por alguien **4 to answer for something** : responder de algo, pagar por algo 〈she'll answer for that mistake : pagará por ese error〉 **5 to answer to** : responder a

answer² *n* **1** REPLY : respuesta *f*, contestación *f* 〈a straight answer : una respuesta clara〉 〈there's no answer : no contestan (el teléfono)〉 〈I never got an answer : nunca me dieron respuesta〉 〈in answer to your question : en respuesta a su pregunta〉 **2** : respuesta *f*, solución *f* (en un examen, etc.) **3** SOLUTION : solución *f* 〈there's no easy answer : no tiene una solución fácil〉

answerable ['æn*t*sərəbəl] *adj* : responsable

answering machine *n* : contestador *m* (automático)

ant ['ænt] *n* : hormiga *f*

antacid [ænt'æsəd, 'æn,tæ-] *n* : antiácido *m*

antagonism [æn'tægə,nɪzəm] *n* : antagonismo *m*, hostilidad *f*

antagonist [æn'tægənɪst] *n* : antagonista *mf*

antagonistic [æn,tægə'nɪstɪk] *adj* : antagonista, hostil

antagonize [æn'tægə,naɪz] *vt* **-nized; -nizing** : antagonizar

antarctic [ænt'arktɪk, -'artɪk] *adj* : antártico

antarctic circle *n* : círculo *m* antártico

anteater ['ænt,i:tər] *n* : oso *m* hormiguero

antebellum [,æntə'beləm] *adj* : prebélico

antecedent¹ [,æntə'si:dənt] *adj* : antecedente, precedente

antecedent² *n* : antecedente *mf*; precursor *m*, -sora *f*

antelope ['æntəl,o:p] *n, pl* **-lope** *or* **-lopes** : antílope *m*

antenatal [,ænti'neitəl] → **prenatal**

antenna [æn'tɛnə] *n, pl* **-nae** [-,ni:, -,nai] *or* **-nas** : antena *f*

anterior [æn'tɪriər] *adj* : anterior

anthem ['ænθəm] *n* : himno *m* 〈national anthem : himno nacional〉

anther ['ænθər] *n* : antera *f*

anthill ['ænt,hɪl] *n* : hormiguero *m*

anthology [æn'θɑlədʒi] *n, pl* **-gies** : antología *f*

anthracite ['ænθrə,saɪt] *n* : antracita *f*

anthropoid¹ ['ænθrə,pɔɪd] *adj* : antropoide

anthropoid² *n* : antropoide *mf*

anthropological [,ænθrəpə'lɑdʒɪkəl] *adj* : antropológico

anthropologist [,ænθrə'pɑlədʒɪst] *n* : antropólogo *m*, -ga *f*

anthropology [,ænθrə'pɑlədʒi] *n* : antropología *f*

anti- [,ænti, ,æntai] *pref* : anti-

antiabortion [,ænti ə'bɔrʃən, ,æntai-] *adj* : antiaborto

antiaircraft [,ænti'ær,kræft, ,æntai-] *adj* : antiaéreo

anti–American [,æntiə'mɛrɪkən, ,æntai-] *adj* : antiamericano

antibiotic¹ [,æntibai'ɑtɪk, ,æntai-, -bi-] *adj* : antibiótico

antibiotic² *n* : antibiótico *m*

antibody ['ænti,bɑdi] *n, pl* **-bodies** : anticuerpo *m*

antic¹ ['æntɪk] *adj* : extravagante, juguetón

antic² *n* : payasada *f*, travesura *f*

anticipate [æn'tɪsə,peɪt] *vt* **-pated; -pating** **1** FORESEE : anticipar, prever **2** EXPECT : esperar, contar con

anticipation [æn,tɪsə'peɪʃən] *n* **1** FORESIGHT : previsión *f* **2** EXPECTATION : anticipación *f*, expectación *f*, esperanza *f*

anticipatory [æn'tɪsəpə,tori] *adj* : en anticipación, en previsión

anticlimactic [,æntiklai'mæktɪk] *adj* : anticlimático, decepcionante

anticlimax [,ænti'klai,mæks] *n* : anticlímax *m*

anticommunism [,ænti'kɑmjə,nɪzəm, ,æntai-] *n* : anticomunismo *m*

anticommunist¹ [,ænti'kɑmjənɪst, ,æntai-] *adj* : anticomunista

anticommunist² *n* : anticomunista *mf*

antidemocratic [,ænti,demə'krætɪk, ,æntai-] *adj* : antidemocrático

antidepressant [,æntidi'prɛsənt] *n* : antidepresivo *m* — **antidepressant** *adj*

antidote ['ænti,do:t] *n* : antídoto *m*

antidrug [,ænti'drʌg, ,æntai-;, 'ænti,drʌg, 'æntai-] *adj* : antidrogas

antifascist [,ænti'fæʃɪst, ,æntai-] *adj* : antifascista

antifeminist [,ænti'fɛmənɪst, ,æntai-] *adj* : antifeminista

antifreeze ['ænti,fri:z] *n* : anticongelante *m*

antigen ['æntɪdʒən, -,dʒɛn] *n* : antígeno *m*

antihistamine [,ænti'hɪstə,mi:n, -mən] *n* : antihistamínico *m*

anti–imperialism [,æntiɪm'pɪriə,lɪzəm, ,æntai-] *n* : antiimperialismo *m*

anti–imperialist [,æntiɪm'pɪriəlɪst, ,æntai-] *adj* : antiimperialista

anti–inflammatory [,ætiɪn'flæmətori] *adj* : antiinflamatorio

anti–inflationary [,æntiɪn'fleɪʃə,nɛri, ,æntai-] *adj* : antiinflacionario

antimony ['æntə,mo:ni] *n* : antimonio *m*

antipathy [æn'tɪpəθi] *n, pl* **-thies** : antipatía *f*, aversión *f*

antiperspirant [ˌænti'pərspərənt, ˌæntaɪ-] n : antitranspirante m

antiquarian¹ [ˌæntə'kwɛriən] adj : antiguo, anticuario ⟨an antiquarian book : un libro antiguo⟩

antiquarian² n : anticuario m, -ria f

antiquary ['æntəˌkwɛri] n → **antiquarian²**

antiquated ['æntəˌkweɪtəd] adj : anticuado, pasado de moda

antique¹ [æn'tiːk] adj 1 OLD : antiguo, de época ⟨an antique mirror : un espejo antiguo⟩ 2 OLD-FASHIONED : anticuado, pasado de moda

antique² n : antigüedad f

antiquity [æn'tɪkwəti] n, pl -ties : antigüedad

antirevolutionary [ˌæntiˌrɛvə'luːʃəˌnɛri, ˌæntaɪ-] adj : antirrevolucionario

anti-Semitic [ˌæntisə'mɪtɪk, ˌæntaɪ-] adj : antisemita

anti-Semitism [ˌænti'sɛməˌtɪzəm, ˌæntaɪ-] n : antisemitismo m

antiseptic¹ [ˌæntə'sɛptɪk] adj : antiséptico — **antiseptically** [-tɪkli] adv

antiseptic² n : antiséptico m

antismoking [ˌænti'smoːkɪŋ, ˌæntaɪ-] adj : antitabaco

antisocial [ˌænti'soːʃəl, ˌæntaɪ-] adj 1 : antisocial 2 UNSOCIABLE : poco sociable

antiterrorist [ˌænti'tɛrərɪst, ˌæntaɪ-] adj : antiterrorista

antitheft [ˌænti'θɛft, ˌæntaɪ-] adj : antirrobo

antithesis [æn'tɪθəsɪs] n, pl -eses [-ˌsiːz] : antítesis f

antitoxin [ˌænti'tɑksən, ˌæntaɪ-] n : antitoxina f

antitrust [ˌænti'trʌst, ˌæntaɪ-] adj : antimonopolista

antiviral [ˌænti'vaɪrəl, ˌæntaɪ-] adj : antiviral

antivirus [ˌænti'vaɪrəs, ˌæntaɪ-] adj → **antiviral**

antivirus software n : antivirus m

antler ['æntlər] n : asta f, cuerno m

antonym ['æntəˌnɪm] n : antónimo m

anus ['eɪnəs] n : ano m

anvil ['ænvəl, -vɪl] n : yunque m

anxiety [æŋk'zaɪəti] n, pl -eties 1 UNEASINESS : inquietud f, preocupación f, ansiedad f 2 APPREHENSION : ansiedad f, angustia f

anxious ['æŋkʃəs] adj 1 WORRIED : inquieto, preocupado, ansioso 2 WORRISOME : preocupante, inquietante 3 EAGER : ansioso, deseoso

anxiously ['æŋkʃəsli] adv : con inquietud, con ansiedad

any¹ ['ɛni] adv 1 : algo ⟨is it any better? : ¿está (algo) mejor?⟩ ⟨I can't stand it any more : no lo soporto más⟩ ⟨do you want any more? : ¿quiere más?⟩ 2 : para nada ⟨it is not any good : no sirve para nada⟩

any² adj 1 : alguno ⟨is there any doubt? : ¿hay alguna duda?⟩ ⟨call me if you have any questions : llámeme si tiene alguna pregunta⟩ 2 : cualquier ⟨I can

answer any question : puedo responder a cualquier pregunta⟩ 3 : todo ⟨in any case : en todo caso⟩ 4 : ningún ⟨he would not accept it under any circumstances : no lo aceptaría bajo ninguna circunstancia⟩

any³ pron 1 : alguno ⟨are there any left? : ¿queda alguno?⟩ ⟨did you see any of the girls? : ¿viste a alguna de las chicas?⟩ 2 : ninguno ⟨I don't want any : no quiero ninguno⟩ ⟨I couldn't attend any of the meetings : no pude asistir a ninguna de las reuniones⟩

anybody ['ɛniˌbʌdi, -ˌbɑ-] → **anyone**

anyhow ['ɛniˌhaʊ] adv 1 HAPHAZARDLY : de cualquier manera 2 IN ANY CASE : de todos modos, en todo caso

anymore [ˌɛni'mor] adv 1 : ya, ya más ⟨he doesn't dance anymore : ya no baila más⟩ 2 : todavía ⟨do they sing anymore? : ¿cantan todavía?⟩

anyone ['ɛniˌwʌn] pron 1 : alguien ⟨is anyone here? : ¿hay alguien aquí?⟩ ⟨if anyone wants to come : si alguno quiere venir⟩ 2 : cualquiera ⟨anyone can play : cualquiera puede jugar⟩ 3 : nadie ⟨I don't want anyone here : no quiero a nadie aquí⟩

anyplace ['ɛniˌpleɪs] → **anywhere**

anything ['ɛniˌθɪŋ] pron 1 : algo, alguna cosa ⟨do you want anything (else)? : ¿quieres algo (más)?, ¿quieres alguna cosa (más)?⟩ 2 : nada ⟨hardly anything : casi nada⟩ 3 : cualquier cosa ⟨I eat anything : como de todo⟩ 4 ~ but : no . . . ni mucho menos ⟨he was anything but pleased : no estaba contento, ni mucho menos⟩ 5 anything goes : todo vale 6 ~ like ⟨it wasn't anything like what I expected : no fue en absoluto lo que esperaba⟩ ⟨we don't have anything like enough : no tenemos suficiente, ni mucho menos⟩

anytime ['ɛniˌtaɪm] adv : en cualquier momento, a cualquier hora, cuando sea

anyway ['ɛniˌweɪ] or **anyways** [-ˌweɪz] → **anyhow**

anywhere ['ɛniˌʍɛr] adv 1 : en algún sitio, en alguna parte ⟨do you see it anywhere? : ¿lo ves en alguna parte?⟩ 2 : en ningún sitio, por ninguna parte ⟨I can't find it anywhere : no puedo encontrarlo por ninguna parte⟩ 3 : en cualquier parte, dondequiera, donde sea ⟨put it anywhere : ponlo dondequiera⟩

aorta [eɪ'ɔrtə] n, pl -tas or -tae [-ˌti, -ˌtaɪ] : aorta f

Apache [ə'pætʃi] n, pl **Apache** or **Apaches** : apache mf

apart [ə'pɑrt] adv 1 SEPARATELY : aparte, separadamente 2 ASIDE : aparte, a un lado 3 to fall apart : deshacerse, hacerse pedazos 4 to take apart : desmontar, desmantelar

apartheid [ə'pɑrˌteɪt, -ˌtaɪt] n : apartheid m

apartment [ə'pɑrtmənt] n : apartamento m, departamento m, piso m Spain

apartment building n : bloque m de apartamentos/departamentos, bloque m de pisos Spain

apathetic [ˌæpə'θɛtɪk] *adj* : apático, indiferente — **apathetically** [-tɪkli] *adv*

apathy ['æpəθi] *n* : apatía *f*, indiferencia *f*

ape[1] ['eɪp] *vt* **aped; aping** : imitar, remedar

ape[2] *n* : simio *m*; mono *m*, -na *f*

aperitif [əˌpɛrə'ti:f] *n* : aperitivo *m*

aperture ['æpərtʃər, -ˌtʃʊr] *n* : abertura *f*, rendija *f*, apertura *f* (en fotografía)

apex ['eɪˌpɛks] *n, pl* **apexes** *or* **apices** ['eɪpəˌsi:z, 'æ-] : ápice *m*, cúspide *f*, cima *f*

aphid ['eɪfɪd, 'æ-] *n* : áfido *m*

aphorism ['æfəˌrɪzəm] *n* : aforismo *m*

aphrodisiac [ˌæfrə'di:ziˌæk, -'dɪ-] *n* : afrodisíaco *m*

apiary ['eɪpiˌɛri] *n, pl* **-aries** : apiario *m*, colmenar *m*

apiece [ə'pi:s] *adv* : cada uno

aplenty [ə'plɛnti] *adj* : en abundancia

aplomb [ə'plɑm, -'plʌm] *n* : aplomo *m*

apocalypse [ə'pɑkəˌlɪps] *n* : apocalipsis *m*

apocalyptic [əˌpɑkə'lɪptɪk] *adj* : apocalíptico

apocrypha [ə'pɑkrəfə] *n* : textos *mpl* apócrifos

apocryphal [ə'pɑkrəfəl] *adj* : apócrifo

apolitical [ˌeɪpə'lɪtɪkəl] *adj* : apolítico

apologetic [əˌpɑlə'dʒɛtɪk] *adj* : lleno de disculpas

apologetically [əˌpɑlə'dʒɛtɪkli] *adv* : disculpándose, con aire de disculpas

apologize [ə'pɑləˌdʒaɪz] *vi* **-gized; -gizing** : disculparse, pedir perdón

apology [ə'pɑlədʒi] *n, pl* **-gies** : disculpa *f*, excusa *f*

apoplectic [ˌæpə'plɛktɪk] *adj* : apoplético

apoplexy ['æpəˌplɛksi] *n* : apoplejía *f*

apostasy [ə'pɑstəsi] *n, pl* **-sies** : apostasía *f*

apostate [ə'pɑsˌteɪt] *n* : apóstata *mf*

apostle [ə'pɑsəl] *n* : apóstol *m*

apostolic [ˌæpə'stɑlɪk] *adj* : apostólico

apostrophe [ə'pɑstrəˌfi:] *n* : apóstrofo *m* (ortográfico)

apothecary [ə'pɑθəˌkɛri] *n, pl* **-caries** : boticario *m*, -ria *f*

app ['æp] *n* : app *f*, aplicación *f*

appall [ə'pɔl] *vt* : consternar, horrorizar

appalling [ə'pɔlɪŋ] *adj* : atroz, horroroso

apparatus [ˌæpə'ræt̬əs, -'reɪ-] *n, pl* **-tuses** *or* **-tus** : aparato *m*, equipo *m*

apparel [ə'pærəl] *n* : atavío *m*, ropa *f*

apparent [ə'pærənt] *adj* **1** VISIBLE : visible **2** OBVIOUS : claro, evidente, manifiesto **3** SEEMING : aparente, ostensible

apparently [ə'pærəntli] *adv* : aparentemente, al parecer

apparition [ˌæpə'rɪʃən] *n* : aparición *f*, visión *f*

appeal[1] [ə'pi:l] *vt* : apelar ⟨to appeal a decision : apelar contra una decisión⟩ — *vi* **1 to appeal for** : pedir, solicitar **2 to appeal to** : atraer a ⟨that doesn't appeal to me : eso no me atrae⟩

appeal[2] *n* **1** : apelación *f* (en derecho) **2** PLEA : ruego *m*, súplica *f* **3** ATTRACTION : atracción *f*, atractivo *m*, interés *m*

appear [ə'pɪr] *vi* **1** : aparecer, aparecerse, presentarse ⟨he suddenly appeared

: apareció de repente⟩ **2** COME OUT : aparecer, salir, publicarse **3** : comparecer (ante el tribunal), actuar (en el teatro) **4** SEEM : parecer

appearance [ə'pɪrənts] *n* **1** APPEARING : aparición *f*, presentación *f*, comparecencia *f* (ante un tribunal), publicación *f* (de un libro) **2** LOOK : apariencia *f*, aspecto *m* **3 by all appearances** : según parece **4 to keep up appearances** : guardar las apariencias **5 to make an appearance** : hacer acto de presencia

appease [ə'pi:z] *vt* **-peased; -peasing 1** CALM, PACIFY : aplacar, apaciguar, sosegar **2** SATISFY : satisfacer, mitigar

appeasement [ə'pi:zmənt] *n* : aplacamiento *m*, apaciguamiento *m*

append [ə'pɛnd] *vt* : agregar, añadir, adjuntar

appendage [ə'pɛndɪdʒ] *n* **1** ADDITION : apéndice *m*, añadidura *f* **2** LIMB : miembro *m*, extremidad *f*

appendectomy [ˌæpən'dɛktəmi] *n, pl* **-mies** : apendicectomía *f*

appendicitis [əˌpɛndə'saɪt̬əs] *n* : apendicitis *f*

appendix [ə'pɛndɪks] *n, pl* **-dixes** *or* **-dices** [-dəˌsi:z] : apéndice *m*

appetite ['æpəˌtaɪt] *n* **1** CRAVING : apetito *m*, deseo *m*, ganas *fpl* **2** PREFERENCE : gusto *m*, preferencia *f* ⟨the cultural appetites of today : los gustos culturales de hoy⟩

appetizer ['æpəˌtaɪzər] *n* : aperitivo *m*, entremés *m*, botana *f Mex*, tapa *f Spain*

appetizing ['æpəˌtaɪzɪŋ] *adj* : apetecible, apetitoso — **appetizingly** [-zɪŋli] *adv*

applaud [ə'plɔd] *v* : aplaudir

applause [ə'plɔz] *n* : aplauso *m*

apple ['æpəl] *n* : manzana *f*

apple tree *n* : manzano *m*

appliance [ə'plaɪənts] *n* **1** : aparato *m* **2 household appliance** : electrodoméstico *m*, aparato *m* electrodoméstico

applicability [ˌæplɪkə'bɪlət̬i, əˌplɪkə-] *n* : aplicabilidad *f*

applicable ['æplɪkəbəl, ə'plɪkə-] *adj* : aplicable, pertinente

applicant ['æplɪkənt] *n* : solicitante *mf*, aspirante *mf*, postulante *mf*; candidato *m*, -ta *f*

application [ˌæplə'keɪʃən] *n* **1** USE : aplicación *f*, empleo *m*, uso *m* **2** DILIGENCE : aplicación *f*, diligencia *f*, dedicación *f* **3** REQUEST : solicitud *f*, petición *f*, demanda *f* **4** PROGRAM : aplicación *f*, app *f*

applicator ['æpləˌkeɪt̬ər] *n* : aplicador *m*

appliqué[1] [ˌæplə'keɪ] *vt* : decorar con apliques

appliqué[2] *n* : aplique *m*

apply [ə'plaɪ] *v* **-plied; -plying** *vt* **1** : aplicar (una sustancia, los frenos, el conocimiento) **2 to apply oneself** : dedicarse, aplicarse — *vi* **1** : aplicarse, referirse ⟨the rules apply to everyone : las reglas se aplican a todos⟩ **2 to apply for** : solicitar, pedir

appoint [ə'pɔɪnt] *vt* **1** NAME : nombrar, designar **2** FIX, SET : fijar, señalar, desig-

nar ⟨to appoint a date : fijar una fecha⟩
3 EQUIP : equipar ⟨a well-appointed office
: una oficina bien equipada⟩
appointee [ə,pɔɪn'tiː, ,æ-] *n* : persona *f*
designada
appointment [ə'pɔɪntmənt] *n* **1** APPOIN-
TING : nombramiento *m*, designación
f **2** ENGAGEMENT : cita *f*, hora *f* ⟨to
have/make an appointment : tener/con-
certar una cita⟩ **3** POST : puesto *m*
apportion [ə'porʃən] *vt* : distribuir, repartir
apportionment [ə'porʃənmənt] *n* : distribución *f*, repartición *f*, reparto *m*
apposite ['æpəzət] *adj* : apropiado, oportuno, pertinente — **appositely** *adv*
appraisal [ə'preɪzəl] *n* : evaluación *f*, valoración *f*, tasación *f*, apreciación *f*
appraise [ə'preɪz] *vt* **-praised; -praising**
: evaluar, valorar, tasar, apreciar
appraiser [ə'preɪzər] *n* : tasador *m*, -dora
f
appreciable [ə'priːʃəbəl, -'priʃiə-] *adj*
: apreciable, sensible, considerable —
appreciably [-bli] *adv*
appreciate [ə'priːʃi,eɪt, -'prɪ-] *v* **-ated;
-ating** *vt* **1** VALUE : apreciar, valorar **2**
: agradecer ⟨we appreciate his frankness
: agradecemos su franqueza⟩ **3** UN-
DERSTAND : darse cuenta de, entender
— *vi* : apreciarse, valorizarse
appreciation [ə,priːʃi'eɪʃən, -,prɪ-] *n* **1**
GRATITUDE : agradecimiento *m*, reconocimiento *m* **2** VALUING : apreciación *f*,
valoración *f*, estimación *f* ⟨art appreciation : apreciación artística⟩ **3** UNDERS-
TANDING : comprensión *f*, entendimiento *m*
appreciative [ə'priːʃətɪv, -'prɪ-;, ə'priːʃi,eɪ-]
adj **1** : apreciativo ⟨an appreciative audience : un público apreciativo⟩ **2** GRA-
TEFUL : agradecido **3** ADMIRING : de
admiración
apprehend [,æprɪ'hɛnd] *vt* **1** ARREST
: aprehender, detener, arrestar **2**
DREAD : temer **3** COMPREHEND : comprender, entender
apprehension [,æprɪ'hɛntʃən] *n* **1**
ARREST : arresto *m*, detención *f*, aprehensión *f* **2** ANXIETY : aprensión *f*, ansiedad
f, temor *m* **3** UNDERSTANDING : comprensión *f*, percepción *f*
apprehensive [,æprɪ'hɛntsɪv] *adj* : aprensivo, inquieto — **apprehensively** *adv*
apprentice¹ [ə'prɛntɪs] *vt* **-ticed; -ticing**
: colocar de aprendiz
apprentice² *n* : aprendiz *m*, -diza *f*
apprenticeship [ə'prɛntɪs,ʃɪp] *n* : aprendizaje *f*
apprise [ə'praɪz] *vt* **-prised; -prising** : informar, avisar
approach¹ [ə'proːtʃ] *vt* **1** NEAR : acercarse a **2** APPROXIMATE : aproximarse a
3 : abordar, dirigirse a ⟨I approached my
boss with the proposal : me dirigí a mi
jefe con la propuesta⟩ **4** TACKLE : abordar, enfocar, considerar — *vi* : acercarse,
aproximarse
approach² *n* **1** NEARING : acercamiento
m, aproximación *f* **2** POSITION : en-

foque *m*, planteamiento *m* **3** OFFER
: propuesta *f*, oferta *f* **4** ACCESS : acceso
m, vía *f* de acceso
approachable [ə'proːtʃəbəl] *adj* : accesible, asequible
approbation [,æprə'beɪʃən] *n* : aprobación *f*
appropriate¹ [ə'proːpri,eɪt] *vt* **-ated; -ating**
1 SEIZE : apropiarse de **2** ALLOCATE
: destinar, asignar
appropriate² [ə'proːpriət] *adj* : apropiado,
adecuado, idóneo — **appropriately** *adv*
appropriateness [ə'proːpriətnəs] *n* : idoneidad *f*, propiedad *f*
appropriation [ə,proːpri'eɪʃən] *n* **1** SEI-
ZURE : apropiación *f* **2** ALLOCATION
: asignación *f*
approval [ə'pruːvəl] *n* **1** : aprobación *f*,
visto *m* bueno **2 on approval** : a prueba
approve [ə'pruːv] *vt* **-proved; -proving 1**
: aprobar, sancionar, darle el visto bueno
a **2 to approve of** : consentir en, aprobar ⟨he doesn't approve of smoking
: está en contra del tabaco⟩
approximate¹ [ə'praksə,meɪt] *vt* **-mated;
-mating** : aproximarse a, acercarse a
approximate² [ə'praksəmət] *adj* : aproximado
approximately [ə'praksəmətli] *adv* : aproximadamente, más o menos
approximation [ə,praksə'meɪʃən] *n*
: aproximación *f*
appurtenance [ə'pərtənənts] *n* : accesorio
m
apricot ['æprə,kɑt, 'eɪ-] *n* : albaricoque *m*,
chabacano *m* Mex
April ['eɪprəl] *n* : abril *m* ⟨they arrived on
the 23rd of April, they arrived on April
23rd : llegaron el 23 de abril⟩
apron ['eɪprən] *n* : delantal *m*, mandil *m*
apropos¹ [,æprə'poː, 'æprə,poː] *adv* : a
propósito
apropos² *adj* : pertinente, oportuno,
acertado
apropos of *prep* : a propósito de
apt ['æpt] *adj* **1** FITTING : apto, apropiado, acertado, oportuno **2** LIABLE
: propenso, inclinado **3** CLEVER, QUICK
: listo, despierto
aptitude ['æptə,tuːd, -,tjuːd] *n* **1** : aptitud
f, capacidad *f* ⟨aptitude test : prueba de
aptitud⟩ **2** TALENT : talento *m*, facilidad *f*
aptly ['æptli] *adv* : acertadamente
aqua ['ækwə, 'ɑ-] *n* : color *m* aguamarina
aquamarine [,ɑkwəmə'riːn, ,æ-] *n* **1** : aguamarina *f* **2** → **aqua**
aquarium [ə'kwæriəm] *n, pl* **-iums** *or* **-ia**
[-iə] : acuario *m*
Aquarius [ə'kwæriəs] *n* **1** : Acuario *m*
(signo o constelación) **2** : Acuario *mf*
(persona)
aquatic [ə'kwɑtɪk, -'kwæ-] *adj* : acuático
aqueduct ['ækwə,dʌkt] *n* : acueducto *m*
aqueous ['eɪkwiəs, 'æ-] *adj* : acuoso
aquiline ['ækwə,laɪn, -lən] *adj* : aguileño
Arab¹ ['ærəb] *adj* : árabe
Arab² *n* : árabe *mf*
arabesque [,ærə'bɛsk] *n* : arabesco *m*
Arabian¹ [ə'reɪbiən] *adj* : árabe

Arabian² *n* → **Arab²**

Arabic¹ ['ærəbɪk] *adj* : árabe

Arabic² *n* : árabe *m* (idioma)

arable ['ærəbəl] *adj* : arable, cultivable

arbiter ['ɑrbəṭər] *n* : árbitro *m*, -tra *f*

arbitrariness ['ɑrbə,trɛrinəs] *n* : arbitrariedad *f*

arbitrary ['ɑrbə,trɛri] *adj* : arbitrario — **arbitrarily** [,ɑrbə'trɛrəli] *adv*

arbitrate ['ɑrbə,treɪt] *v* **-trated; -trating** : arbitrar

arbitration [,ɑrbə'treɪʃən] *n* : arbitraje *m*

arbitrator ['ɑrbə,treɪṭər] *n* : árbitro *m*, -tra *f*

arbor ['ɑrbər] *n* : cenador *m*, pérgola *f*

arboreal [ɑr'boriəl] *adj* : arbóreo

arc¹ ['ɑrk] *vi* **arced; arcing** : formar un arco

arc² *n* : arco *m*

arcade [ɑr'keɪd] *n* **1** ARCHES : arcada *f* **2** MALL : galería *f* comercial

arcane [ɑr'keɪn] *adj* : arcano, secreto, misterioso

arch¹ ['ɑrtʃ] *vt* : arquear — *vi* : formar un arco, arquearse

arch² *adj* **1** CHIEF : principal **2** MISCHIEVOUS : malicioso, pícaro

arch³ *n* : arco *m*

archaeological [,ɑrkiə'lɑdʒɪkəl] *or* **archeological** *adj* : arqueológico

archaeologist [,ɑrki'ɑlədʒɪst] *or* **archeologist** *n* : arqueólogo *m*, -ga *f*

archaeology *or* **archeology** [,ɑrki'ɑlədʒi] *n* : arqueología *f*

archaic [ɑr'keɪɪk] *adj* : arcaico — **archaically** [-ɪkli] *adv*

archangel ['ɑrk,eɪndʒəl] *n* : arcángel *m*

archbishop [ɑrtʃ'bɪʃəp] *n* : arzobispo *m*

archbishopric [ɑrtʃ'bɪʃəprɪk] *n* : arzobispado *m*

archdiocese [ɑrtʃ'daɪəsəs, -,si:z, -,si:s] *n* : arquidiócesis *f*, archidiócesis *f*

archer ['ɑrtʃər] *n* : arquero *m*, -ra *f*

archery ['ɑrtʃəri] *n* : tiro *m* al arco

archetypal [,ɑrkɪ'taɪpəl] *adj* : arquetípico

archetype ['ɑrkɪ,taɪp] *n* : arquetipo *m*

archipelago [,ɑrkə'pɛlə,go:, ,ɑrtʃə-] *n, pl* **-goes** *or* **-gos** [-go:z] : archipiélago *m*

architect ['ɑrkə,tɛkt] *n* : arquitecto *m*, -ta *f*

architectural [,ɑrkə'tɛktʃərəl] *adj* : arquitectónico — **architecturally** *adv*

architecture ['ɑrkə,tɛktʃər] *n* : arquitectura *f*

archive¹ ['ɑr,kaɪv] *vt* **archived; archiving** : archivar

archive² *n or* **archives** ['ɑr,kaɪvz] *npl* : archivo *m*

archivist ['ɑrkəvɪst, -,kaɪ-] *n* : archivero *m*, -ra *f*; archivista *mf*

archway ['ɑrtʃ,weɪ] *n* : arco *m*, pasadizo *m* abovedado

arctic ['ɑrktɪk, 'ɑrt-] *adj* **1** : ártico ⟨arctic regions : zonas árticas⟩ **2** FRIGID : glacial

arctic circle *n* : círculo *m* ártico

ardent ['ɑrdənt] *adj* **1** PASSIONATE : ardiente, fogoso, apasionado **2** FERVENT : ferviente, fervoroso — **ardently** *adv*

ardor ['ɑrdər] *n* : ardor *m*, pasión *f*, fervor *m*

arduous ['ɑrdʒuəs] *adj* : arduo, duro, riguroso — **arduously** *adv*

arduousness ['ɑrdʒuəsnəs] *n* : dureza *f*, rigor *m*

are → **be**

area ['æriə] *n* **1** SURFACE : área *f*, superficie *f* **2** REGION : área *f*, región *f*, zona *f* **3** FIELD : área *f*, terreno *m*, campo *m* (de conocimiento)

area code *n* : código *m* de la zona, prefijo *m Spain*

arena [ə'ri:nə] *n* **1** : arena *f*, estadio *m* ⟨sports arena : estadio deportivo⟩ **2** : arena *f*, ruedo *m* ⟨the political arena : el ruedo político⟩

aren't ['ɑrənt] *contraction of* ARE NOT → **be**

Argentine ['ɑrdʒən,taɪn, -,ti:n] *or* **Argentinean** *or* **Argentinian** [,ɑrdʒən'tɪniən] *n* : argentino *m*, -na *f* — **Argentine** *or* **Argentinean** *or* **Argentinian** *adj*

argon ['ɑr,gɑn] *n* : argón *m*

argot ['ɑrgət, -,go:] *n* : argot *m*

arguable ['ɑrgjuəbəl] *adj* : discutible — **arguably** [-bli] *adv*

argue ['ɑr,gju:] *v* **-gued; -guing** *vi* **1** REASON : argumentar, argüir, razonar ⟨to argue for something : abogar por algo, argumentar a favor de algo⟩ ⟨to argue against something : argumentar en contra de algo⟩ **2** DISPUTE : discutir, pelear(se), alegar ⟨to argue about something : discutir por algo, pelear(se) por algo⟩ — *vt* **1** SUGGEST : sugerir **2** MAINTAIN : alegar, argüir, sostener **3** DISCUSS : discutir, debatir

argument ['ɑrgjəmənt] *n* **1** REASONING : argumento *m*, razonamiento *m* **2** DISCUSSION : discusión *f*, debate *m* **3** QUARREL : pelea *f*, riña *f*, disputa *f*

argumentative [,ɑrgjə'mɛntəṭɪv] *adj* : discutidor

argyle ['ɑr,gaɪl] *n* : diseño *m* de rombos

aria ['æriə] *n* : aria *f*

arid ['ærəd] *adj* : árido

aridity [ə'rɪdəṭi, æ-] *n* : aridez *f*

Aries ['ɛri:z, -i,i:z] *n* **1** : Aries *m* (signo o constelación) **2** : Aries *mf* (persona)

arise [ə'raɪz] *vi* **arose** [ə'ro:z]; **arisen** [ə'rɪzən]; **arising 1** ASCEND : ascender, subir, elevarse **2** ORIGINATE : originarse, surgir, presentarse **3** GET UP : levantarse

aristocracy [,ærə'stɑkrəsi] *n, pl* **-cies** : aristocracia *f*

aristocrat [ə'rɪstə,kræt] *n* : aristócrata *mf*

aristocratic [ə,rɪstə'kræṭɪk] *adj* : aristocrático, noble

arithmetic¹ [,ærɪθ'mɛṭɪk] *or* **arithmetical** [-ṭɪkəl] *adj* : aritmético

arithmetic² [ə'rɪθmə,tɪk] *n* : aritmética *f*

ark ['ɑrk] *n* : arca *f*

arm¹ ['ɑrm] *vt* : armar — *vi* : armarse

arm² *n* **1** : brazo *m* (del cuerpo, de un sillón, de una máquina), manga *f* (de una prenda) ⟨he took her by the) arm : la tomó del brazo⟩ **2** BRANCH : rama *f*, sección *f* **3** WEAPON : arma *f* ⟨to take up arms : tomar las armas⟩ **4** ~ **in** ~ : del brazo **5** → **coat of arms**

armada [ɑrˈmɑdə, -ˈmeɪ-] *n* : armada *f*,
flota *f*
armadillo [ˌɑrməˈdɪlo] *n, pl* **-los** : armadillo *m*
armament [ˈɑrməmənt] *n* : armamento *m*
armband [ˈɑrmˌbænd] *n* : brazalete *m*
armchair [ˈɑrmˌtʃɛr] *n* : butaca *f*, sillón *m*
armed [ˈɑrmd] *adj* **1** : armado ⟨armed
robbery : robo a mano armada⟩ **2 ar-
med forces** : fuerzas *fpl* armadas **3** (*used
in combination*) : de brazos ⟨long-armed
: de brazos largos⟩ ⟨one-armed : manco⟩
Armenian [ɑrˈmiːniən] *n* : armenio *m*, -nia
f — **Armenian** *adj*
armistice [ˈɑrməstɪs] *n* : armisticio *m*
armor [ˈɑrmər] *n* : armadura *f*, coraza *f*
armored [ˈɑrmərd] *adj* : blindado,
acorazado
armory [ˈɑrməri] *n, pl* **-mories** : arsenal *m*
(almacén), armería *f* (museo), fábrica *f*
de armas
armpit [ˈɑrmˌpɪt] *n* : axila *f*, sobaco *m*
armrest [ˈɑrmˌrɛst] *n* : apoyabrazos *m*
army [ˈɑrmi] *n, pl* **-mies** **1** : ejército *m*
(militar) **2** MULTITUDE : legión *f*, multitud *f*, ejército *m*
aroma [əˈroːmə] *n* : aroma *f*
aromatic [ˌærəˈmæt̮ɪk] *adj* : aromático
around[1] [əˈraʊnd] *adv* **1** : en un círculo
⟨to go around (and around) : dar
vueltas⟩ ⟨to turn around : darse la
vuelta, voltearse⟩ ⟨the road goes around
the lake : la carretera bordea el lago⟩ **2**
: de circunferencia ⟨a tree three feet
around : un árbol de tres pies de circun-
ferencia⟩ **3** : alrededor ⟨for miles
around : por millas a la redonda⟩ ⟨all
around : por todos lados, todo alrede-
dor⟩ ⟨he looked around : miró a su alre-
dedor⟩ ⟨they crowded around to watch
: se aglomeraron para observar⟩ **4** : por
ahí ⟨they're around somewhere : deben
estar por ahí⟩ ⟨there was no one around
: no había nadie⟩ ⟨is your mother
around? : ¿está tu madre?⟩ ⟨I'll see you
around! : ¡nos vemos!⟩ **5** : por/en muchas partes ⟨to wander around : deam-
bular⟩ ⟨scattered around : esparci-
dos⟩ **6** APPROXIMATELY : más o menos,
aproximadamente ⟨around 5 o'clock : a
eso de las 5⟩ ⟨it's around 50 dollars
: cuesta unos 50 dólares⟩ **7 the wrong
way around** : al revés
around[2] *prep* **1** SURROUNDING : alrededor de, en torno a **2** THROUGH : por, en
⟨he traveled around Mexico : viajó por
México⟩ ⟨around the house : en casa⟩ **3**
: a la vuelta de ⟨around the corner : a la
vuelta de la esquina⟩ **4** NEAR : alrededor de, cerca de
arousal [əˈraʊzəl] *n* : excitación *f*
arouse [əˈraʊz] *vt* **aroused; arousing 1**
AWAKE : despertar **2** EXCITE : despertar, suscitar, excitar
arraign [əˈreɪn] *vt* : hacer comparecer
(ante un tribunal)
arraignment [əˈreɪnmənt] *n* : orden *m* de
comparecencia, acusación *f*
arrange [əˈreɪndʒ] *vt* **-ranged; -ranging 1**
ORDER : arreglar, poner en orden, dis-

poner **2** SETTLE : arreglar, fijar, concertar **3** ADAPT : arreglar, adaptar
arrangement [əˈreɪndʒmənt] *n* **1** ORDER
: arreglo *m*, orden *m* **2** ARRANGING
: disposición *f* ⟨floral arrangement : arreglo floral⟩ **3** AGREEMENT : arreglo *m*,
acuerdo *m*, convenio *m* **4 arrangements** *npl* : preparativos *mpl*, planes *mpl*
array[1] [əˈreɪ] *vt* **1** ORDER : poner en orden, presentar, formar **2** GARB : vestir,
ataviar, engalanar
array[2] *n* **1** ORDER : orden *m*, formación
f **2** ATTIRE : atavío *m*, galas *mpl* **3**
RANGE, SELECTION : selección *f*, serie *f*,
gama *f* ⟨an array of problems : una serie
de problemas⟩
arrears [əˈrɪrz] *npl* : atrasos *mpl* ⟨to be in
arrears : estar atrasado en los pagos⟩
arrest[1] [əˈrɛst] *vt* **1** APPREHEND : arrestar, detener **2** CHECK, STOP : detener,
parar
arrest[2] *n* **1** APPREHENSION : arresto *m*,
detención *f* ⟨under arrest : detenido⟩ **2**
STOPPING : paro *m*
arrival [əˈraɪvəl] *n* : llegada *f*, venida *f*,
arribo *m*
arrive [əˈraɪv] *vi* **-rived; -riving 1** COME
: llegar, arribar **2** SUCCEED : triunfar,
tener éxito
arrogance [ˈærəgənts] *n* : arrogancia *f*,
soberbia *f*, altanería *f*, altivez *f*
arrogant [ˈærəgənt] *adj* : arrogante, soberbio, altanero, altivo — **arrogantly**
adv
arrogate [ˈærəˌgeɪt] *vt* **-gated; -gating to
arrogate to oneself** : arrogarse
arrow [ˈæro] *n* : flecha *f*
arrowhead [ˈæroˌhɛd] *n* : punta *f* de flecha
arroyo [əˈrɔɪo] *n* : arroyo *m*
arsenal [ˈɑrsənəl] *n* : arsenal *m*
arsenic [ˈɑrsənɪk] *n* : arsénico *m*
arson [ˈɑrsən] *n* : incendio *m* premeditado
arsonist [ˈɑrsənɪst] *n* : incendiario *m*, -ria
f; pirómano *m*, -na *f*
art [ˈɑrt] *n* **1** : arte *m* **2** SKILL : destreza
f, habilidad *f*, maña *f* **3 arts** *npl* : letras
fpl (en la educación) **4 arts and crafts**
: artes y oficios **5 fine arts** : bellas artes
fpl
arterial [ɑrˈtɪriəl] *adj* : arterial
arteriosclerosis [ɑrˌtɪriosklərˈroːsɪs] *n* : arteriosclerosis *f*
artery [ˈɑrt̮əri] *n, pl* **-teries 1** : arteria
f **2** THOROUGHFARE : carretera *f* principal, arteria *f*
artful [ˈɑrtfəl] *adj* **1** INGENIOUS : ingenioso, diestro **2** CRAFTY : astuto,
taimado, ladino, artero — **artfully** *adv*
art gallery → **gallery**
arthritic [ɑrˈθrɪt̮ɪk] *adj* : artrítico
arthritis [ɑrˈθraɪt̮əs] *n, pl* **-tides**
[ɑrˈθrɪt̮əˌdiːz] : artritis *f*
arthropod [ˈɑrθrəˌpɑd] *n* : artrópodo *m*
artichoke [ˈɑrt̮əˌtʃoːk] *n* : alcachofa *f*
article [ˈɑrt̮ɪkəl] *n* **1** ITEM : artículo *m*,
objeto *m* **2** ESSAY : artículo *m* **3**
CLAUSE : artículo *m*, cláusula *f* **4** : artículo *m* ⟨definite article : artículo deter-
minado⟩

articulate¹ [ɑr'tɪkjə,leɪt] vt **-lated; -lating**
1 UTTER : articular, enunciar, expresar
2 CONNECT : articular (en anatomía)
articulate² [ɑr'tɪkjələt] adj **to be articulate** : poder articular palabras, expresarse bien
articulately [ɑr'tɪkjələtli] adv : elocuentemente, con fluidez
articulateness [ɑr'tɪkjələtnəs] n : elocuencia f, fluidez f
articulation [ɑr,tɪkjə'leɪʃən] n **1** JOINT : articulación f **2** UTTERANCE : articulación f, declaración f **3** ENUNCIATION : articulación f, pronunciación f
artifact ['ɑrtə,fækt] n : artefacto m
artifice ['ɑrtəfəs] n : artificio m
artificial [,ɑrtə'fɪʃəl] adj **1** SYNTHETIC : artificial, sintético **2** FEIGNED : artificial, falso, afectado
artificially [,ɑrtə'fɪʃəli] adv : artificialmente, con afectación
artillery [ɑr'tɪləri] n, pl **-leries** : artillería f
artisan ['ɑrtəzən, -sən] n : artesano m, -na f
artist ['ɑrtɪst] n : artista mf
artistic [ɑr'tɪstɪk] adj : artístico — **artistically** [-tɪkli] adv
artistry ['ɑrtəstri] n : maestría f, arte m
artless ['ɑrtləs] adj : sencillo, natural, ingenuo, cándido — **artlessly** adv
artlessness ['ɑrtləsnəs] n : ingenuidad f, candidez f
artwork ['ɑrt,wərk] n **1** : obra f de arte **2** WORKS : arte f, obra f **3** ILLUSTRATIONS : material m gráfico
arty ['ɑrti] or **artsy** ['ɑrtsi] adj **artier; -est** : pretenciosamente artístico
as¹ ['æz] adv **1** : tan, tanto ⟨this one's not as difficult : éste no es tan difícil⟩ ⟨he has a lot of time, but I don't have as much : él tiene mucho tiempo, pero yo no tengo tanto⟩ ⟨he was angry, but she was just as angry : él estaba enojado, pero ella estaba tan enojada como él⟩ **2** SUCH AS : como ⟨some trees, as oak and pine : algunos árboles, como el roble y el pino⟩
as² conj **1** LIKE : como, igual que ⟨(as) white as snow : blanca como la nieve⟩ ⟨she's as smart/guilty as he is : ella es tan inteligente/culpable como él⟩ ⟨she's Italian, as am I : es italiana, igual que yo⟩ ⟨she believes it, as do I : ella lo cree, y yo también⟩ ⟨twice as big as : el doble de grande que⟩ ⟨as soon as possible : lo más pronto posible⟩ **2** : como ⟨do (it) as I do : haz como yo⟩ ⟨knowing him as I do : conociéndolo como lo conozco⟩ ⟨as it happens . . . : da la casualidad de que . . .⟩ ⟨as is often/usually the case : como suele ocurrir⟩ ⟨as was to be expected : como era de esperar⟩ **3** WHEN, WHILE : cuando, mientras, a la vez que ⟨I saw it as I was leaving : lo vi cuando salía⟩ **4** BECAUSE : porque ⟨as I was tired, I stayed home : porque estaba cansada, me quedé en casa⟩ **5** THOUGH : aunque, por más que ⟨strange as it may appear : por extraño que parezca⟩ ⟨much as it pains me to say so : aunque me da pena decirlo⟩ ⟨try as he might

: por más que trataba⟩ **6** as for CONCERNING : en cuanto a **7** as if : como si ⟨it looks as if : parece que⟩ ⟨as if I weren't there : como si yo no estuviera ahí⟩ **8** as is : tal (y) como está ⟨it's being sold as is : se vende tal como está⟩ **9** as it is : tal (y) como está ⟨leave it as it is : déjalo tal como está⟩ **10** as it is ALREADY : ya ⟨we have too much to do as it is : ya tenemos demasiado que hacer⟩ **11** as of : a partir de **12** as to CONCERNING : en cuanto a ⟨I'm at a loss as to how to explain it : no sé como explicarlo⟩ **13** so as IN ORDER TO : para
as³ prep **1** : de ⟨I met her as a child : la conocí de pequeña⟩ ⟨he works as a secretary : trabaja de secretario⟩ **2** LIKE : como ⟨behave as a man : compórtate como un hombre⟩ ⟨I'm telling you this as a friend : te lo digo como amigo⟩
as⁴ pron : que ⟨in the same building as my brother : en el mismo edificio que mi hermano⟩
asbestos [æz'bɛstəs, æs-] n : asbesto m, amianto m
ascend [ə'sɛnd] vi : ascender, subir — vt : subir, subir a, escalar
ascendancy [ə'sɛndənsi] n : ascendiente m, predominio m
ascendant¹ [ə'sɛndənt] adj **1** RISING : ascendente **2** DOMINANT : superior, dominante
ascendant² n to be in the ascendant : estar en alza, ir ganando predominio
ascension [ə'sɛntʃən] n : ascensión f
ascent [ə'sɛnt] n **1** RISE : ascensión f, subida f, ascenso m **2** SLOPE : cuesta f, pendiente f
ascertain [,æsər'teɪn] vt : determinar, establecer, averiguar
ascetic¹ [ə'sɛtɪk] adj : ascético
ascetic² n : asceta mf
asceticism [ə'sɛtə,sɪzəm] n : ascetismo m
ascribable [ə'skraɪbəbəl] adj : atribuible, imputable
ascribe [ə'skraɪb] vt **-cribed; -cribing** : atribuir, imputar
aseptic [eɪ'sɛptɪk] adj : aséptico
asexual [,eɪ'sɛkʃuəl] adj : asexual
as for prep CONCERNING : en cuanto a, respecto a, para
ash ['æʃ] n **1** : ceniza f ⟨to reduce to ashes : reducir a cenizas⟩ **2** : fresno m (árbol)
ashamed [ə'ʃeɪmd] adj : avergonzado, abochornado, apenado — **ashamedly** [ə'ʃeɪmədli] adv
ashen ['æʃən] adj : lívido, ceniciento, pálido
ashore [ə'ʃor] adv **1** : en tierra **2** to go ashore : desembarcar
ashtray ['æʃ,treɪ] n : cenicero m
Ash Wednesday n : Miércoles m de Ceniza
Asian¹ ['eɪʒən, -ʃən] adj : asiático
Asian² n : asiático m, -ca f
aside [ə'saɪd] adv **1** : a un lado ⟨to step aside : hacerse a un lado⟩ **2** : de lado, aparte ⟨jesting aside : bromas aparte⟩ **3** to set aside : guardar, apartar, reservar

aside from *prep* **1** BESIDES : además de
2 EXCEPT : aparte de, menos
as if *conj* : como si
asinine ['æsən,aɪn] *adj* : necio, estúpido
ask ['æsk] *vt* **1** : preguntar ⟨to ask a question : hacer una pregunta⟩ ⟨ask him if
he's coming : pregúntale si viene⟩ **2** RE-
QUEST : pedir, solicitar ⟨to ask someone
(for) a favor, to ask a favor of someone
: pedirle un favor a alguien⟩ **3** INVITE
: invitar ⟨she asked us to the party : nos
invitó a la fiesta⟩ ⟨we asked them over
for dinner : los invitamos a cenar⟩ ⟨he
asked her out : la invitó a salir⟩ — *vi* **1**
INQUIRE : preguntar ⟨I asked about/af-
ter her children : pregunté por sus
niños⟩ **2** REQUEST : pedir ⟨we asked for
help : pedimos ayuda⟩ ⟨if you need help,
ask : si necesitas ayuda, pídela⟩ **3 to ask
for it/trouble** : buscársela
askance [ə'skænts] *adv* **1** SIDELONG : de
reojo, de soslayo **2** SUSPICIOUSLY : con
recelo, con desconfianza
askew [ə'skju:] *adj* : torcido, ladeado
asleep [ə'sli:p] *adj* **1** : dormido, durmiendo **2 to fall asleep** : quedarse dormido
as of *prep* : desde, a partir de
asparagus [ə'spærəgəs] *n* : espárrago *m*
aspect ['æ,spɛkt] *n* : aspecto *m*
aspen ['æspən] *n* : álamo *m* temblón
asperity [æ'spɛrəti, ə-] *n, pl* **-ties** : aspereza *f*
aspersion [ə'spərʒən] *n* : difamación *f*,
calumnia *f*
asphalt ['æs,fɔlt] *n* : asfalto *m*
asphyxia [æ'sfɪksiə, ə-] *n* : asfixia *f*
asphyxiate [æ'sfɪksi,eɪt] *v* **-ated; -ating** *vt*
: asfixiar — *vi* : asfixiarse
asphyxiation [æ,sfɪksi'eɪʃən] *n* : asfixia *f*
aspirant ['æspərənt, ə'spaɪrənt] *n* : aspirante *mf*, pretendiente *mf*
aspiration [,æspə'reɪʃən] *n* **1** DESIRE
: aspiración *f*, anhelo *m*, ambición *f* **2**
BREATHING : aspiración *f*
aspire [ə'spaɪr] *vi* **-pired; -piring** : aspirar
aspirin ['æsprən, 'æspə-] *n, pl* **aspirin** *or*
aspirins : aspirina *f*
ass ['æs] *n* **1** : asno *m* **2** IDIOT : imbécil
mf, idiota *mf*
assail [ə'seɪl] *vt* : atacar, asaltar
assailant [ə'seɪlənt] *n* : asaltante *mf*, atacante *mf*
assassin [ə'sæsən] *n* : asesino *m*, -na *f*
assassinate [ə'sæsən,eɪt] *vt* **-nated; -nat-
ing** : asesinar
assassination [ə,sæsən'eɪʃən] *n* : asesinato *m*
assault[1] [ə'sɔlt] *vt* : atacar, asaltar, agredir
assault[2] *n* : ataque *m*, asalto *m*, agresión *f*
assay[1] [æ'seɪ, 'æ,seɪ] *vt* : ensayar
assay[2] ['æ,seɪ, æ'seɪ] *n* : ensayo *m*
assemble [ə'sɛmbəl] *v* **-bled; -bling** *vt* **1**
GATHER : reunir, recoger, juntar **2**
CONSTRUCT : ensamblar, montar, construir — *vi* : reunirse, congregarse
assembly [ə'sɛmbli] *n, pl* **-blies 1** MEE-
TING : reunión *f* **2** CONSTRUCTING : ensamblaje *m*, montaje *m*
assembly line *n* : cadena *f* de montaje

assemblyman [ə'sɛmblimən] *n, pl* **-men**
[-mən, -,mɛn] : asambleísta *m*
assemblywoman [ə'sɛmbli,wʊmən] *n, pl*
-women [-,wɪmən] : asambleísta *f*
assent[1] [ə'sɛnt] *vi* : asentir, consentir
assent[2] *n* : asentimiento *m*, aprobación *f*
assert [ə'sərt] *vt* **1** AFFIRM : afirmar,
aseverar, mantener **2 to assert oneself**
: imponerse, hacerse valer
assertion [ə'sərʃən] *n* : afirmación *f*,
aseveración *f*, aserto *m*
assertive [ə'sərtɪv] *adj* : firme, enérgico
assertiveness [ə'sərtɪvnəs] *n* : seguridad *f*
en sí mismo
assess [ə'sɛs] *vt* **1** IMPOSE : gravar (un
impuesto), imponer **2** EVALUATE : evaluar, valorar, aquilatar
assessment [ə'sɛsmənt] *n* : evaluación *f*,
valoración *f*
assessor [ə'sɛsər] *n* : evaluador *m*, -dora
f; tasador *m*, -dora *f*
asset ['æ,sɛt] *n* **1** : ventaja *f*, recurso
m **2 assets** *npl* : bienes *mpl*, activo *m*
⟨assets and liabilities : activo y pasivo⟩
assiduous [ə'sɪdʒuəs] *adj* : diligente, aplicado, asiduo — **assiduously** *adv*
assign [ə'saɪn] *vt* **1** APPOINT : designar,
nombrar **2** ALLOT : asignar, señalar **3**
ATTRIBUTE : atribuir, dar, conceder
assignment [ə'saɪnmənt] *n* **1** TASK : función *f*, tarea *f*, misión *f* **2** HOMEWORK
: tarea *f*, asignación *f* PRi, deberes *mpl*
Spain **3** APPOINTMENT : nombramiento
m **4** ALLOCATION : asignación *f*
assimilate [ə'sɪmə,leɪt] *v* **-lated; -lating** *vt*
: asimilar — *vi* : adaptarse, integrarse
assimilation [ə,sɪmə'leɪʃən] *n* : asimilación *f*
assist[1] [ə'sɪst] *vt* : asistir, ayudar
assist[2] *n* : asistencia *f*, contribución *f*
assistance [ə'sɪstənts] *n* : asistencia *f*,
ayuda *f*, auxilio *m*
assistant [ə'sɪstənt] *n* : ayudante *mf*, asistente *mf*
associate[1] [ə'so:ʃi,eɪt, -si-] *v* **-ated; -ating**
vt **1** CONNECT, RELATE : asociar, relacionar **2 to be associated with** : estar
relacionado con, estar vinculado a — *vi*
to associate with : relacionarse con, frecuentar
associate[2] [ə'so:ʃiət, -siət] *n* : asociado *m*,
-da *f*; colega *mf*; socio *m*, -cia *f*
association [ə,so:ʃi'eɪʃən, -si-] *n* **1** OR-
GANIZATION : asociación *f*, sociedad *f* **2**
RELATIONSHIP : asociación *f*, relación *f*
as soon as *conj* : en cuanto, tan pronto
como
assorted [ə'sɔrtəd] *adj* : surtido
assortment [ə'sɔrtmənt] *n* : surtido *m*,
variedad *f*, colección *f*
assuage [ə'sweɪdʒ] *vt* **-suaged; -suag-
ing 1** EASE : aliviar, mitigar **2** CALM
: calmar, aplacar **3** SATISFY : saciar, satisfacer
assume [ə'su:m] *vt* **-sumed; -suming 1**
SUPPOSE : suponer, asumir **2** UNDER-
TAKE : asumir, encargarse de **3** TAKE
ON : adquirir, adoptar, tomar ⟨to assume
importance : tomar importancia⟩ **4**
FEIGN : adoptar, afectar, simular

assumed [ə'su:md] *adj* : fingido, falso ⟨an assumed air of confidence : un aire de falsa confianza⟩ ⟨an assumed name : un nombre falso/ficticio/supuesto, un seudónimo⟩

assumption [ə'sʌmpʃən] *n* : asunción *f*, presunción *f*

assurance [ə'ʃʊrənts] *n* **1** CERTAINTY : certidumbre *f*, certeza *f* **2** CONFIDENCE : confianza *f*, aplomo *m*, seguridad *f*

assure [ə'ʃʊr] *vt* **-sured; -suring** : asegurar, garantizar ⟨I assure you that I'll do it : te aseguro que lo haré⟩

assured [ə'ʃʊrd] *adj* **1** CERTAIN : seguro, asegurado **2** CONFIDENT : confiado, seguro de sí mismo

aster ['æstər] *n* : aster *m*

asterisk ['æstə‚rɪsk] *n* : asterisco *m*

astern [ə'stərn] *adv* **1** BEHIND : detrás, a popa **2** BACKWARDS : hacia atrás

asteroid ['æstə‚rɔɪd] *n* : asteroide *m*

asthma ['æzmə] *n* : asma *m*

asthmatic [æz'mætɪk] *adj* : asmático

as though → **as if**

astigmatism [ə'stɪgmə‚tɪzəm] *n* : astigmatismo *m*

as to *prep* **1** ABOUT : sobre, acerca de **2** → **according to**

astonish [ə'stɑnɪʃ] *vt* : asombrar, sorprender, pasmar

astonishing [ə'stɑnɪʃɪŋ] *adj* : asombroso, sorprendente, increíble — **astonishingly** *adv*

astonishment [ə'stɑnɪʃmənt] *n* : asombro *m*, estupefacción *f*, sorpresa *f*

astound [ə'staʊnd] *vt* : asombrar, pasmar, dejar estupefacto

astounding [ə'staʊndɪŋ] *adj* : asombroso, pasmoso — **astoundingly** *adv*

astraddle [ə'strædəl] *adv* : a horcajadas

astral ['æstrəl] *adj* : astral

astray [ə'streɪ] *adv & adj* : perdido, extraviado, descarriado

astride [ə'straɪd] *adv* : a horcajadas

astringency [ə'strɪndʒəntsi] *n* : astringencia *f*

astringent[1] [ə'strɪndʒənt] *adj* : astringente

astringent[2] *n* : astringente *m*

astrologer [ə'strɑlədʒər] *n* : astrólogo *m*, -ga *f*

astrological [‚æstrə'lɑdʒɪkəl] *adj* : astrológico

astrology [ə'strɑlədʒi] *n* : astrología *f*

astronaut ['æstrə‚nɔt] *n* : astronauta *mf*

astronautic [‚æstrə'nɔtɪk] *or* **astronautical** [-tɪkəl] *adj* : astronáutico

astronautics [‚æstrə'nɔtɪks] *ns & pl* : astronáutica *f*

astronomer [ə'strɑnəmər] *n* : astrónomo *m*, -ma *f*

astronomical [‚æstrə'nɑmɪkəl] *adj* **1** : astronómico **2** ENORMOUS : astronómico, enorme, gigantesco

astronomy [ə'strɑnəmi] *n, pl* **-mies** : astronomía *f*

astute [ə'stu:t, -'stju:t] *adj* : astuto, sagaz, perspicaz — **astutely** *adv*

astuteness [ə'stu:tnəs, -'stju:t-] *n* : astucia *f*, sagacidad *f*, perspicacia *f*

asunder [ə'sʌndər] *adv* : en dos, en pedazos ⟨to tear asunder : hacer pedazos⟩

as well as[1] *conj* : tanto como

as well as[2] *prep* BESIDES : además de, aparte de

as yet *adv* : aún, todavía

asylum [ə'saɪləm] *n* **1** REFUGE : refugio *m*, santuario *m*, asilo *m* **2** **insane asylum** : manicomio *m*

asymmetrical [‚eɪsə'mɛtrɪkəl] *or* **asymmetric** [-'mɛtrɪk] *adj* : asimétrico

asymmetry [‚eɪ'sɪmətri] *n* : asimetría *f*

at ['æt] *prep* **1** (*indicating location*) : en, a ⟨at the top : en lo alto⟩ ⟨at the rear : al fondo⟩ ⟨at Ann's house : en casa de Ana⟩ ⟨is she at home? : ¿está en casa?⟩ ⟨he was sitting at the table : estaba sentado a la mesa⟩ ⟨someone is knocking at the door : llaman a la puerta⟩ **2** (*indicating the recipient of an action, motion, or feeling*) ⟨she shouted at me : me gritó⟩ ⟨don't look at me! : ¡a mí no me mires!⟩ ⟨he's laughing at you : está riéndose de ti⟩ ⟨to be angry at someone : estar enojado con alguien⟩ **3** (*indicating a reaction or cause*) ⟨he laughed at the joke : se rió con el chiste⟩ ⟨to be surprised at something : sorprenderse por algo⟩ ⟨at the invitation of : por invitación de⟩ **4** (*indicating an activity or state*) ⟨children who are at play : niños que están jugando⟩ ⟨you're good at this : eres bueno para esto⟩ ⟨he's at peace now : ahora descansa en paz⟩ ⟨at peace/war : en paz/guerra⟩ ⟨to be at risk : peligrar⟩ **5** (*used for the symbol @*) : arroba ⟨at merriam-webster dot com : arroba merriam-webster punto com⟩ **6** (*indicating a rate or measure*) : a ⟨at 80 miles an hour : a 80 millas por hora⟩ ⟨they sell at a dollar each : se venden a un dólar cada uno⟩ **7** (*indicating an age or time*) : a ⟨at ten o'clock : a las diez⟩ ⟨at age 65 : a los 65 años (de edad)⟩ ⟨at last : por fin⟩ **8** **at it** (*while we're at it* : ya que estamos (en ello)⟩ ⟨they're at it again! : ¡ya empezaron otra vez!⟩

at all *adv* : en absoluto, para nada

ate → **eat**

atheism ['eɪθi‚ɪzəm] *n* : ateísmo *m*

atheist ['eɪθiɪst] *n* : ateo *m*, atea *f*

atheistic [‚eɪθi'ɪstɪk] *adj* : ateo

athlete ['æθ‚li:t] *n* : atleta *mf*

athletic [æθ'lɛtɪk] *adj* : atlético

athletics [æθ'lɛtɪks] *ns & pl* : atletismo *m*

Atlantic [ət'læntɪk, æt-] *adj* : atlántico

atlas ['ætləs] *n* : atlas *m*

ATM [‚eɪ‚ti:'ɛm] *n* : cajero *m* automático

atmosphere ['ætmə‚sfɪr] *n* **1** AIR : atmósfera *f*, aire *m* **2** AMBIENCE : ambiente *m*, atmósfera *f*, clima *m*

atmospheric [‚ætmə'sfɪrɪk, -'sfɛr-] *adj* : atmosférico — **atmospherically** [-ɪkli] *adv*

atoll ['æ‚tɔl, 'eɪ-, -‚tɑl] *n* : atolón *m*

atom ['ætəm] *n* **1** : átomo *m* **2** SPECK : ápice *m*, pizca *f*

atomic [ə'tɑmɪk] *adj* : atómico

atomic bomb *n* : bomba *f* atómica

atomizer ['ætə‚maɪzər] *n* : atomizador *m*, pulverizador *m* atone [ə'to:n] *vt* atoned; atoning to atone for : expiar

atonement [ə'to:nmənt] *n* : expiación *f*, desagravio *m*

atop¹ [ə'tɑp] *adj* : encima

atop² *prep* : encima de, sobre

atrium ['eitriəm] *n*, *pl* atria [-triə] *or* atriums 1 : atrio *m* 2 : aurícula *f* (del corazón)

atrocious [ə'tro:ʃəs] *adj* : atroz — atrociously *adv*

atrocity [ə'trɑsəti] *n*, *pl* -ties : atrocidad *f*

atrophy¹ ['ætrəfi] *vt* -phied; -phying : atrofiar

atrophy² *n*, *pl* -phies : atrofia *f*

at sign *n* (*used for the symbol* @) : arroba *f*

attach [ə'tætʃ] *vt* 1 FASTEN : sujetar, atar, amarrar, pegar 2 JOIN : juntar, adjuntar 3 ATTRIBUTE : dar, atribuir ⟨I attached little importance to it : le di poca importancia⟩ 4 SEIZE : embargar 5 to become attached to someone : encariñarse con alguien

attaché [ˌætəˈʃei, ˌæˌtæ-, əˌtæ-] *n* : agregado *m*, -da *f*

attaché case *n* : maletín *m*

attachment [ə'tætʃmənt] *n* 1 ACCESSORY : accesorio *m* 2 CONNECTION : conexión *f*, acoplamiento *m* 3 FONDNESS : apego *m*, cariño *m*, afición *f* 4 : adjunto *m* (en un email)

attack¹ [ə'tæk] *vt* 1 ASSAULT : atacar, asaltar, agredir 2 TACKLE : acometer, combatir, enfrentarse con

attack² *n* 1 : ataque *m* ⟨an attack on/against : un ataque a/contra⟩ ⟨to launch an attack : lanzar un ataque⟩ 2 : ataque *m* ⟨heart attack : ataque cardíaco, infarto⟩ ⟨panic/anxiety attack : ataque de pánico/ansiedad⟩

attacker [ə'tækər] *n* : asaltante *mf*

attain [ə'tein] *vt* 1 ACHIEVE : lograr, conseguir, alcanzar, realizar 2 REACH : alcanzar, llegar a

attainable [ə'teinəbəl] *adj* : realizable, asequible

attainment [ə'teinmənt] *n* : logro *m*, consecución *f*, realización *f*

attempt¹ [ə'tɛmpt] *vt* : intentar, tratar de

attempt² *n* : intento *m*, tentativa *f*

attend [ə'tɛnd] *vt* 1 : asistir a ⟨to attend a meeting : asistir a una reunión⟩ 2 : atender, ocuparse de, cuidar ⟨to attend a patient : atender a un paciente⟩ 3 HEED : atender a, hacer caso de 4 ACCOMPANY : acompañar

attendance [ə'tɛndənts] *n* 1 ATTENDING : asistencia *f* 2 TURNOUT : concurrencia *f*

attendant¹ [ə'tɛndənt] *adj* : concomitante, inherente

attendant² *n* : asistente *mf*, acompañante *mf*, guarda *mf*

attention [ə'tɛntʃən] *n* 1 : atención *f* ⟨I brought the problem to his attention : le informé del problema⟩ ⟨it has come to our attention that . . . : se nos ha informado que . . .⟩ ⟨to attract someone's attention : atraer la atención de alguien⟩ 2 to pay attention : prestar atención, hacer caso ⟨to pay attention to someone/something : prestarle atención a algo/alguien⟩ ⟨don't pay any attention to him : no le hagas caso⟩ ⟨she didn't pay attention to the rumors : no hizo caso de los rumores⟩ 3 to stand at attention : estar firme

attentive [ə'tɛntiv] *adj* : atento — attentively *adv*

attentiveness [ə'tɛntivnəs] *n* 1 THOUGHTFULNESS : cortesía *f*, consideración *f* 2 CONCENTRATION : atención *f*, concentración *f*

attest [ə'tɛst] *vt* : atestiguar, dar fe de

attestation [ˌæˌtsˈteiʃən] *n* : testimonio *m*

attic ['ætik] *n* : ático *m*, desván *m*, buhardilla *f*

attire¹ [ə'tair] *vt* -tired; -tiring : ataviar

attire² *n* : atuendo *m*, atavío *m*

attitude ['æt̬əˌtu:d, -ˌtju:d] *n* 1 FEELING : actitud *f* 2 POSTURE : postura *f*

attorney [ə'tərni] *n*, *pl* -neys : abogado *m*, -da *f*

attract [ə'trækt] *vt* 1 : atraer 2 to attract attention : llamar la atención

attraction [ə'trækʃən] *n* : atracción *f*, atractivo *m*

attractive [ə'træktiv] *adj* : atractivo, atrayente

attractively [ə'træktivli] *adv* : de manera atractiva, de buen gusto, hermosamente

attractiveness [ə'træktivnəs] *n* : atractivo *m*

attributable [ə'tribjut̬əbəl] *adj* : atribuible, imputable

attribute¹ [ə'triˌbju:t] *vt* -tributed; -tributing : atribuir

attribute² ['ætrəˌbju:t] *n* : atributo *m*, cualidad *f*

attribution [ˌætrəˈbju:ʃən] *n* : atribución *f*

attrition [ə'triʃən] *n* : desgaste *m* ⟨war of attrition : guerra de desgaste⟩

attune [ə'tu:n, -'tju:n] *vt* -tuned; -tuning 1 ADAPT : adaptar, adecuar 2 to be attuned to : estar en armonía con

ATV [ˌeiˌti:ˈvi:] → all-terrain vehicle

atypical [ˌeiˈtipikəl] *adj* : atípico

aubergine ['o:bərˌʒi:n] → eggplant

auburn ['ɔbərn] *adj* : castaño rojizo

auction¹ ['ɔkʃən] *vt* : subastar, rematar

auction² *n* : subasta *f*, remate *m*

auctioneer [ˌɔkʃəˈnir] *n* : subastador *m*, -dora *f*; rematador *m*, -dora *f*

audacious [ɔ'deiʃəs] *adj* : audaz, atrevido

audacity [ɔ'dæsəti] *n*, *pl* -ties : audacia *f*, atrevimiento *m*, descaro *m*

audible ['ɔdəbəl] *adj* : audible — audibly [-bli] *adv*

audience ['ɔdiənts] *n* 1 INTERVIEW : audiencia *f* 2 PUBLIC : audiencia *f*, público *m*, auditorio *m*, espectadores *mpl*

audio¹ ['ɔdiˌo:] *adj* : de sonido, de audio

audio² *n* : audio *m*

audiobook ['ɔdiˌo:ˌbʊk] *n* : audiolibro *m*

audiovisual [ˌɔdio'viʒuəl] *adj* : audiovisual

audit¹ ['ɔdət] *vt* 1 : auditar (finanzas) 2 : asistir como oyente a (una clase o un curso)

audit² *n* : auditoría *f*
audition¹ [ɔ'dɪʃən] *vi* : hacer una audición
audition² *n* : audición *f*
auditor ['ɔdətər] *n* **1** : auditor *m*, -tora *f* (de finanzas) **2** STUDENT : oyente *mf*
auditorium [ˌɔdə'toriəm] *n, pl* **-riums** *or* **-ria** [-riə] : auditorio *m*, sala *f*
auditory ['ɔdəˌtori] *adj* : auditivo
auger ['ɔgər] *n* : taladro *m*, barrena *f*
augment [ɔg'mɛnt] *vt* : aumentar, incrementar
augmentation [ˌɔgmən'teɪʃən] *n* : aumento *m*, incremento *m*
augmented reality *n* : realidad *f* aumentada
au gratin [ˌoː'grɑtən, -'græ-] *adj* : gratinado
augur¹ ['ɔgər] *vt* : augurar, presagiar — *vi* **to augur well** : ser de buen agüero
augur² *n* : augur *m*
augury ['ɔgjʊri, -gər-] *n, pl* **-ries** : augurio *m*, presagio *m*, agüero *m*
august [ɔ'gʌst] *adj* : augusto
August ['ɔgəst] *n* : agosto *m* ⟨they arrived on the 20th of August, they arrived on August 20th : llegaron el 20 de agosto⟩
auk ['ɔk] *n* : alca *f*
aunt ['ænt, 'ant] *n* : tía *f*
auntie ['ænti, 'anti] *n* : tita *f*
aura ['ɔrə] *n* : aura *f*
aural ['ɔrəl] *adj* : auditivo
auricle ['ɔrɪkəl] *n* : aurícula *f*
aurora borealis [ə'rorəˌbori'æləs] *n* : aurora *f* boreal
auspices ['ɔspəsəz, -ˌsiːz] *npl* : auspicios *mpl*
auspicious [ɔ'spɪʃəs] *adj* : prometedor, propicio, de buen augurio
austere [ɔ'stɪr] *adj* : austero, severo, adusto — **austerely** *adv*
austerity [ɔ'stɛrəti] *n, pl* **-ties** : austeridad *f*
Australian [ɔ'streɪljən] *n* : australiano *m*, -na *f* — **Australian** *adj*
Austrian ['ɔstriən] *n* : austriaco *m*, -ca *f* — **Austrian** *adj*
authentic [ə'θɛntɪk, ɔ-] *adj* : auténtico, genuino — **authentically** [-tɪkli] *adv*
authenticate [ə'θɛntɪˌkeɪt, ɔ-] *vt* **-cated; -cating** : autenticar, autentificar
authenticity [ɔˌθɛn'tɪsəti] *n* : autenticidad *f*
author ['ɔθər] *n* **1** WRITER : escritor *m*, -tora *f*; autor *m*, -tora *f* **2** CREATOR : autor *m*, -tora *f*; creador *m*, -dora *f*; artífice *mf*
authoritarian [ɔˌθɔrə'tɛriən, ə-] *adj* : autoritario
authoritative [ə'θɔrəˌteɪtɪv, ɔ-] *adj* **1** RELIABLE : fidedigno, autorizado **2** DICTATORIAL : autoritario, dictatorial, imperioso
authoritatively [ə'θɔrəˌteɪtɪvli, ɔ-] *adv* **1** RELIABLY : con autoridad **2** DICTATORIALLY : de manera autoritaria
authority [ə'θɔrəti, ɔ-] *n, pl* **-ties** **1** EXPERT : autoridad *f* **2** POWER : autoridad *f* **3** AUTHORIZATION : autorización *f* **4 the authorities** : las autoridades **5 on good authority** : de buena fuente ⟨he

has it on good authority that . . . : sabe de buena fuente que . . .⟩
authorization [ˌɔθərə'zeɪʃən] *n* : autorización *f*
authorize ['ɔθəˌraɪz] *vt* **-rized; -rizing** : autorizar, facultar
authorship ['ɔθərˌʃɪp] *n* : autoría *f*
autism ['ɔˌtɪzəm] *n* : autismo *m*
autistic [ɔ'tɪstɪk] *adj* : autista
auto ['ɔto] → **automobile**
auto- ['ɔto] *pref* **1** SELF- : auto- **2** : automático
autobiographical [ˌɔtoˌbaɪə'græfɪkəl] *adj* : autobiográfico
autobiography [ˌɔtobaɪ'ɑgrəfi] *n, pl* **-phies** : autobiografía *f*
autocorrect ['ɔˌtoːkə'rɛkt] *n* : autocorrector *m*, corrector *m* automático
autocracy [ɔ'tɑkrəsi] *n, pl* **-cies** : autocracia *f*
autocrat ['ɔtəˌkræt] *n* : autócrata *mf*
autocratic [ˌɔtə'krætɪk] *adj* : autocrático — **autocratically** [-tɪkli] *adv*
autograph¹ ['ɔtəˌgræf] *vt* : autografiar
autograph² *n* : autógrafo *m*
automaker ['ɔtoˌmeɪkər] *n* : fabricante *mf* de autos, automotriz *f*
automate ['ɔtəˌmeɪt] *vt* **-mated; -mating** : automatizar
automatic [ˌɔtə'mætɪk] *adj* : automático — **automatically** [-tɪkli] *adv*
automatic pilot → **autopilot**
automation [ˌɔtə'meɪʃən] *n* : automatización *f*
automaton [ɔ'tɑməˌtɑn] *n, pl* **-atons** *or* **-ata** [-tə, -ˌtɑ] : autómata *m*
automobile [ˌɔtəmo'biːl, -'moːˌbiːl] *n* : automóvil *m*, auto *m*, carro *m*, coche *m*
automotive [ˌɔtə'moːtɪv] *adj* : automotor
autonomous [ɔ'tɑnəməs] *adj* : autónomo — **autonomously** *adv*
autonomy [ɔ'tɑnəmi] *n, pl* **-mies** : autonomía *f*
autopilot ['ɔtoˌˌpaɪlət] *n* : piloto *m* automático
autopsy ['ɔˌtɑpsi, -təp-] *n, pl* **-sies** : autopsia *f*
autumn ['ɔtəm] *n* : otoño *m*
autumnal [ɔ'tʌmnəl] *adj* : otoñal
auxiliary¹ [ɔg'zɪljəri, -'zɪləri] *adj* : auxiliar
auxiliary² *n, pl* **-ries** : auxiliar *mf*, ayudante *mf*
avail¹ [ə'veɪl] *vt* **to avail oneself** : aprovecharse, valerse
avail² *n* **1** : provecho *m*, utilidad *f* **2 to no avail** : en vano **3 to be of no avail** : no servir de nada, ser inútil
availability [əˌveɪlə'bɪləti] *n, pl* **-ties** : disponibilidad *f*
available [ə'veɪləbəl] *adj* : disponible
avalanche ['ævəˌlæntʃ] *n* : avalancha *f*, alud *m*
avant–garde¹ [ˌɑˌvɑnt'gɑrd] *adj* : vanguardista
avant–garde² *n* : vanguardia *f* — **avant-gardist** [ˌɑˌvɑnt'gɑrdɪst] *n*
avarice ['ævərəs] *n* : avaricia *f*, codicia *f*
avaricious [ˌævə'rɪʃəs] *adj* : avaricioso, codicioso
avatar ['ævəˌtɑr] *n* : avatar *m*

avenge [ə'vɛndʒ] *vt* **avenged; avenging**
: vengar
avenue ['ævə,nuː, -,njuː] *n* **1** : avenida
f **2** MEANS : vía *f*, camino *m*
average¹ ['ævrɪdʒ, 'ævə-] *vt* **-aged; -aging**
1 : hacer un promedio de ⟨he averages 8
hours a day : hace un promedio de 8
horas diarias⟩ **2** : calcular el promedio
de, promediar (en matemáticas)
average² *adj* **1** MEAN : medio ⟨the average temperature : la temperatura me-
dia⟩ **2** ORDINARY : común, ordinario
⟨the average man : el hombre común⟩
average³ *n* : promedio *m*
averse [ə'vərs] *adj* : reacio, opuesto
aversion [ə'vərʒən] *n* : aversión *f*
avert [ə'vərt] *vt* **1** : apartar, desviar ⟨he
averted his eyes from the scene : apartó
los ojos de la escena⟩ **2** AVOID, PRE-
VENT : evitar, prevenir
aviary ['eɪvi,ɛri] *n, pl* **-aries** : pajarera *f*
aviation [,eɪvi'eɪʃən] *n* : aviación *f*
aviator ['eɪvi,eɪtər] *n* : aviador *m*, -dora *f*
avid ['ævɪd] *adj* **1** GREEDY : ávido, codicioso **2** ENTHUSIASTIC : ávido, entusiasta, ferviente — **avidly** *adv*
avocado [,ævə'kɑdo, ,ɑvə-] *n, pl* **-dos**
: aguacate *m*, palta *f*
avocation [,ævə'keɪʃən] *n* : pasatiempo *m*,
afición *f*
avoid [ə'vɔɪd] *vt* **1** SHUN : evitar, eludir **2** FORGO : evitar, abstenerse de ⟨I
always avoided gossip : siempre evitaba
los chismes⟩ **3** EVADE : evitar ⟨if I can
avoid it : si puedo evitarlo⟩
avoidable [ə'vɔɪdəbəl] *adj* : evitable
avoidance [ə'vɔɪdənts] *n* : el evitar
avoirdupois [,ævərdə'pɔɪz] *n* : sistema *m*
inglés de pesos y medidas
avow [ə'vaʊ] *vt* : reconocer, confesar
avowal [ə'vaʊəl] *n* : reconocimiento *m*,
confesión *f*
await [ə'weɪt] *vt* : esperar
awake¹ [ə'weɪk] *v* **awoke** [ə'woːk]; **awoken**
[ə'woːkən] *or* **awaked; awaking** : despertar
awake² *adj* : despierto
awaken [ə'weɪkən] → **awake¹**
award¹ [ə'wɔrd] *vt* : otorgar, conceder,
conferir
award² *n* **1** PRIZE : premio *m*, galardón
m **2** MEDAL : condecoración *f*
aware [ə'wær] *adj* : consciente ⟨to be
aware of : darse cuenta de, estar consciente de⟩
awareness [ə'wærnəs] *n* : conciencia *f*,
conocimiento *m*
awash [ə'wɔʃ] *adj* : inundado
away¹ [ə'weɪ] *adv* **1** : de aquí, de allí ⟨it's
10 miles away (from here) : queda/está a
10 millas (de aquí)⟩ ⟨she's away from the
office : está fuera de la oficina⟩ ⟨far
away from home : lejos de casa⟩ ⟨go

away! : ¡fuera de aquí!, ¡vete!⟩ ⟨he
walked away : se alejó (caminando)⟩
⟨she looked away : desvió la mirada⟩
⟨stay away from the dog : no te acerques
al perro⟩ **2** : en un lugar seguro ⟨she
tucked it away in a drawer : lo guardó en
un cajón⟩ ⟨the files are locked away
: los archivos están guardados bajo
llave⟩ **3** (*indicating a gradual diminish-
ing*) ⟨to fade away : desvanecerse,
apagarse⟩ ⟨to waste away (from illness)
: consumirse (por enfermedad)⟩ **4**
NONSTOP, STEADILY : sin parar, a un
ritmo constante ⟨she was typing away at
the computer : estaba tecleando en la
computadora⟩ **5** : fuera de casa (en deportes) ⟨they played at home and away
: jugaron en casa y fuera de casa⟩
away² *adj* **1** ABSENT : ausente ⟨away for
the week : ausente por la semana⟩ **2**
away game : partido *m* fuera de casa
awe¹ ['ɔ] *vt* **awed; awing** : abrumar, asombrar, impresionar
awe² *n* : asombro *m*
awesome ['ɔsəm] *adj* **1** IMPOSING : imponente, formidable **2** AMAZING
: asombroso
awestruck ['ɔ,strʌk] *adj* : asombrado
awful ['ɔfəl] *adj* **1** AWESOME : asombroso **2** DREADFUL : horrible, terrible,
atroz **3** ENORMOUS : enorme, tremendo
⟨an awful lot of people : muchísima
gente, la mar de gente⟩
awfully ['ɔfəli] *adv* **1** EXTREMELY : terriblemente, extremadamente **2** BADLY
: muy mal, espantosamente
awhile [ə'hwaɪl] *adv* : un rato, algún
tiempo
awkward ['ɔkwərd] *adj* **1** CLUMSY
: torpe, desmañado **2** EMBARRASSING
: embarazoso, delicado ⟨an awkward position : una situación embarazosa⟩ —
awkwardly *adv*
awkwardness ['ɔkwərdnəs] *n* **1** CLUMSI-
NESS : torpeza *f* **2** INCONVENIENCE
: incomodidad *f*
awl ['ɔl] *n* : punzón *m*
awning ['ɔnɪŋ] *n* : toldo *m*
awry [ə'raɪ] *adj* **1** ASKEW : torcido **2 to
go awry** : salir mal, fracasar
ax *or* **axe** ['æks] *n* : hacha *f*
axiom ['æksiəm] *n* : axioma *m*
axiomatic [,æksiə'mætɪk] *adj* : axiomático
axis ['æksɪs] *n, pl* **axes** [-,siːz] : eje *m*
axle ['æksəl] *n* : eje *m*
aye¹ ['aɪ] *adv* : sí
aye² *n* : sí *m*
azalea [ə'zeɪljə] *n* : azalea *f*
azimuth ['æzəməθ] *n* : azimut *m*, acimut
m
Aztec ['æz,tɛk] *n* : azteca *mf*
azure¹ ['æʒər] *adj* : azur, celeste
azure² *n* : azur *m*

B

b ['bi:] *n, pl* **b's** *or* **bs** ['bi:z]   **1** : segunda letra del alfabeto inglés   **2 B** : si *m* ⟨B sharp/flat : si sostenido/bemol⟩

babble¹ ['bæbəl] *vi* **-bled; -bling**   **1** PRATTLE : balbucear   **2** CHATTER : parlotear *fam*   **3** MURMUR : murmurar

babble² *n* : balbuceo *m* (de bebé), parloteo *m* (de adultos), murmullo *m* (de voces, de un arroyo)

babe ['beɪb] *n* → **baby³**

baboon [bæ'bu:n] *n* : babuino *m*

baby¹ ['beɪbi] *vt* **-bied; -bying** : mimar, consentir

baby² *adj*   **1** : de niño ⟨a baby carriage : un cochecito⟩ ⟨baby talk : habla infantil⟩   **2** TINY : pequeño, minúsculo

baby³ *n, pl* **-bies** : bebé *m*; niño *m*, -ña *f*; bebe *m*, -ba *f Arg, Uru*

babyhood ['beɪbi,hʊd] *n* : niñez *f*, primera infancia *f*

babyish ['beɪbiɪʃ] *adj* : infantil, pueril

baby–sit ['beɪbi,sɪt] *vi* **-sat** [-,sæt]; **-sitting** : cuidar niños, hacer de canguro *Spain*

baby–sitter ['beɪbi,sɪtər] *n* : niñero *m*, -ra *f*; canguro *mf Spain*

baccalaureate [,bækə'lɔriət] *n* : licenciatura *f*

bachelor ['bætʃələr] *n*   **1** : soltero *m*   **2** : licenciado *m*, -da *f* ⟨bachelor of arts degree : licenciatura en filosofía y letras⟩

back¹ ['bæk] *vt*   **1** *or* **to back up** SUPPORT : apoyar, respaldar   **2** *or* **to back up** REVERSE : dar marcha atrás a, dar reversa a *Col, Mex* (un vehículo)   **3** : estar detrás de, formar el fondo de ⟨trees back the garden : detrás del jardín hay unos árboles⟩   **4** : apostar por (un caballo, etc.)   **5** *or* **to back up** : acompañar (en música)   **6 to back up** : hacer una copia de seguridad de (archivos, etc.)   **7 to back up** BLOCK : atascar — *vi*   **1** *or* **to back away/up** : echarse atrás   **2** *or* **to back up** : dar marcha atrás, dar reversa *Col, Mex* (en un vehículo)   **3 to back off** : dejar a alguien en paz   **4 to back off/down** : volverse atrás, echarse para atrás   **5 to back off/out** RENEGE : volverse atrás, echarse para atrás, rajarse *fam*   **6 to back up** : hacer copias de seguridad

back² *adv*   **1** : atrás, hacia atrás, detrás ⟨to move back : moverse atrás⟩ ⟨to step back : dar un paso atrás⟩ ⟨to lean back : reclinarse⟩ ⟨it's two miles back : queda dos millas atrás⟩ ⟨back and forth : de acá para allá⟩   **2** AGO : atrás, antes, ya ⟨some years back : unos años atrás, ya unos años⟩ ⟨10 months back : hace diez meses⟩   **3** : de vuelta, de regreso ⟨we're back : estamos de vuelta⟩ ⟨I'll be back soon : vuelvo enseguida⟩ ⟨she ran back : volvió corriendo⟩ ⟨he never went back : nunca regresó⟩ ⟨I forgot to put it back : me olvidé de devolverlo a su lugar⟩   **4** : como respuesta, en cambio ⟨to call back : llamar de nuevo⟩ ⟨he smiled back at me : me devolvió la sonrisa⟩ ⟨she gave the money back : devolvió el dinero⟩

back³ *adj*   **1** REAR : de atrás, posterior, trasero   **2** OVERDUE : atrasado   **3** back pay : atrasos *mpl*

back⁴ *n*   **1** : espalda *f* (de un ser humano), lomo *m* (de un animal)   **2** : respaldo *m* (de una silla), espalda *f* (de ropa)   **3** REVERSE : reverso *m*, dorso *m*, revés *m* ⟨the back of an envelope : el reverso de un sobre⟩   **4** REAR : fondo *m*, parte *f* de atrás   **5** : defensa *mf* (en deportes)   **6 back to back** : espalda con espalda   **7 back to back** CONSECUTIVE : seguido   **8 back to front** BACKWARD : al revés   **9 behind someone's back** : a espaldas de alguien ⟨behind my back : a mis espaldas⟩   **10 in ∼** : en la parte de atrás, al fondo   **11 in back of** : detrás de   **12 out ∼** : detrás de la casa (etc.)   **13 to turn one's back on someone** : volverle la espalda a alguien

backache ['bæk,eɪk] *n* : dolor *m* de espalda

backbite ['bæk,baɪt] *v* **-bit** [-,bɪt]; **-bitten** [-,bɪtən]; **-biting** *vt* : calumniar, hablar mal de — *vi* : murmurar

backbone ['bæk,bo:n] *n*   **1** : columna *f* vertebral   **2** FIRMNESS : firmeza *f*, carácter *m*

backdrop ['bæk,drɑp] *n* : telón *m* de fondo

backer ['bækər] *n*   **1** SUPPORTER : partidario *m*, -ria *f*   **2** SPONSOR : patrocinador *m*, -dora *f*

backfire¹ ['bæk,faɪr] *vi* **-fired; -firing**   **1** : petardear (dícese de un automóvil)   **2** FAIL : fallar, salir el tiro por la culata

backfire² *n* : petardeo *m*, explosión *f*

background ['bæk,graʊnd] *n*   **1** : fondo *m* (de un cuadro, etc.) ⟨background color : color de fondo⟩ ⟨background noise/music : ruido/música de fondo⟩   **2** : segundo plano *m* ⟨a shy person who stays in the background : una persona tímida que permanece en (un) segundo plano⟩ ⟨the program runs in the background : el programa se ejecuta en segundo plano⟩   **3** *or* **background information** : antecedentes *mpl* (de una situación)   **4** : historial *m*, antecedentes *mpl* (de una persona) ⟨family background : historial familiar⟩ ⟨professional background : experiencia profesional⟩ ⟨background check : verificación de antecedentes⟩

backhand¹ ['bæk,hænd] *adv* : de revés, con el revés

backhand² *n* : revés *m*

backhanded ['bæk,hændəd] *adj*   **1** : dado con el revés, de revés   **2** INDIRECT : indirecto, ambiguo

backing ['bækɪŋ] *n*   **1** SUPPORT : apoyo *m*, respaldo *m*   **2** REINFORCEMENT : refuerzo *m*   **3** SUPPORTERS : partidarios *mpl*, -rias *fpl*

backlash ['bæk,læʃ] *n* : reacción *f* violenta

backlog [ˈbækˌlɔg] *n* : atraso *m*, trabajo *m* acumulado
backpack[1] [ˈbækˌpæk] *vi* : viajar con mochila
backpack[2] *n* : mochila *f*
backrest [ˈbækˌrɛst] *n* : respaldo *m*
backside [ˈbækˌsaɪd] *n* : trasero *m*
backslash [ˈbækˌslæʃ] *n* : barra *f* invertida, barra *f* inversa
backslide [ˈbækˌslaɪd] *vi* **-slid** [-ˌslɪd]; **-slid** *or* **-slidden** [-ˌslɪdən]; **-sliding** : recaer, reincidir
backstage [ˌbækˈsteɪʤ, ˈbækˌ-] *adv & adj* : entre bastidores
backstroke [ˈbækˌstro:k] *n* : estilo *m* espalda, estilo *m* dorso *Mex*
backtrack [ˈbækˌtræk] *vi* : dar marcha atrás, volverse atrás
backup [ˈbækˌʌp] *n* **1** SUPPORT : respaldo *m*, apoyo *m* **2** : copia *f* de seguridad (de un archivo, etc.)
backward[1] [ˈbækwərd] *or* **backwards** [-wərdz] *adv* **1** : hacia atrás **2** : de espaldas ⟨he fell backwards : se cayó de espaldas⟩ **3** : al revés ⟨you're doing it backwards : lo estás haciendo al revés⟩ **4 to bend over backwards** : hacer todo lo posible
backward[2] *adj* **1** : hacia atrás ⟨a backward glance : una mirada hacia atrás⟩ **2** RETARDED : retrasado **3** SHY : tímido **4** UNDERDEVELOPED : atrasado
backwardness [ˈbækwərdnəs] *n* : atraso *m* (dícese de una región), retraso *m* (dícese de una persona)
backwoods [ˌbækˈwʊdz] *npl* : monte *m*, región *f* alejada
backyard [ˌbækˈjɑrd] *n* : jardín *m* trasero
bacon [ˈbeɪkən] *n* : tocino *m*, tocineta *f* *Col, Ven*, bacon *m Spain*
bacterial [bækˈtɪriəl] *adj* : bacteriano
bacterium [bækˈtɪriəm] *n, pl* **-ria** [-iə] : bacteria *f*
bad[1] [ˈbæd] *adv* → **badly**
bad[2] *adj* **1** POOR : malo ⟨a bad example : un mal ejemplo⟩ ⟨a bad idea : una mala idea⟩ ⟨in bad shape : en malas condiciones⟩ **2** UNPLEASANT, UNFAVORABLE : malo ⟨bad news : malas noticias⟩ ⟨bad luck : mala suerte⟩ ⟨bad reviews : mala crítica⟩ ⟨a bad dream : una pesadilla⟩ ⟨it smells/tastes bad : huele/sabe mal⟩ **3** UNSUITABLE : malo ⟨bad lighting : mala iluminación⟩ ⟨you've come at a bad time : llegas en mal momento⟩ **4** INCORRECT, FAULTY : malo ⟨bad spelling : mala ortografía⟩ ⟨a bad check : un cheque sin fondos⟩ **5** ROTTEN : podrido ⟨to go bad : echarse a perder⟩ **6** UNHEALTHY, SERIOUS : malo, grave ⟨to have bad eyesight : tener mala vista⟩ ⟨a bad injury : una herida grave⟩ ⟨he's in bad health, his health is bad : está mal de salud⟩ **7** HARMFUL : malo, perjudicial **8** CORRUPT, EVIL : malo, corrupto ⟨the bad guys : los malos⟩ **9** NAUGHTY : malo, travieso **10 from bad to worse** : de mal en peor **11 to be bad about**

something : ser malo para algo **12 to be in a bad way** : estar mal **13 too bad!** : ¡qué lástima!
bad[3] *n* : lo malo ⟨the good and the bad : lo bueno y lo malo⟩
bade → **bid**
badge [ˈbæʤ] *n* : insignia *f*, botón *m*, chapa *f*
badger[1] [ˈbæʤər] *vt* : fastidiar, acosar, importunar
badger[2] *n* : tejón *m*
badly [ˈbædli] *adv* **1** : mal **2** URGENTLY : mucho, con urgencia **3** SEVERELY : gravemente
bad–mannered [ˈbædˈmænərd] *adj* : maleducado
badminton [ˈbædˌmɪntən, -ˌmɪt-] *n* : bádminton *m*
badness [ˈbædnəs] *n* : maldad *f*
bad–tempered [ˈbædˈtɛmpərd] *adj* : malhumorado
baffle [ˈbæfəl] *vi* **-fled; -fling 1** PERPLEX : desconcertar, confundir **2** FRUSTRATE : frustrar
bafflement [ˈbæfəlmənt] *n* : desconcierto *m*, confusión *f*
bag[1] [ˈbæg] *v* **bagged; bagging** *vi* SAG : formar bolsas — *vt* **1** : ensacar, poner en una bolsa **2** : cobrar (en la caza), cazar
bag[2] *n* **1** : bolsa *f*, saco *m* **2** HANDBAG : cartera *f*, bolso *m*, bolsa *f Mex* **3** SUITCASE : maleta *f*, valija *f* **4 to have bags under one's eyes** : tener ojeras
bagel [ˈbeɪgəl] *n* : rosquilla *f* de pan
baggage [ˈbægɪʤ] *n* : equipaje *m*
baggie [ˈbægi] *n* : bolsita *f* de plástico
baggy [ˈbægi] *adj* **baggier; -est** : holgado, ancho
bagpipe [ˈbægˌpaɪp] *n or* **bagpipes** [ˈbægˌpaɪps] *npl* : gaita *f*
baguette [bæˈgɛt] *n* : baguette *f*, barra *f* de pan *Mex, Spain*
bail[1] [ˈbeɪl] *vt* **1** : achicar (agua de un bote) **2 to bail out** : poner en libertad (de una cárcel) bajo fianza **3 to bail out** EXTRICATE : sacar de apuros — *vi* **1** *or* **to bail out** *fam* : largarse *fam*, rajarse *fam* ⟨when things got difficult, she bailed (out on us) : cuando las cosas se pusieron difíciles, nos dejó colgados⟩ **2 to bail out** : tirarse en paracaídas (de un avión)
bail[2] *n* : fianza *f*, caución *f*
bailiff [ˈbeɪləf] *n* : alguacil *mf*
bailiwick [ˈbeɪliˌwɪk] *n* : dominio *m*
bailout [ˈbeɪlˌaʊt] *n* : rescate *m* (financiero)
bait[1] [ˈbeɪt] *vt* **1** : cebar (un anzuelo o cepo) **2** HARASS : acosar
bait[2] *n* : cebo *m*, carnada *f*
bake[1] [ˈbeɪk] *vt* **baked; baking** : hornear, hacer al horno
bake[2] *n* : fiesta con platos hechos al horno
baker [ˈbeɪkər] *n* : panadero *m*, -ra *f*
baker's dozen *n* : docena *f* de fraile
bakery [ˈbeɪkəri] *n, pl* **-ries** : panadería *f*
bakeshop [ˈbeɪkˌʃɑp] *n* : pastelería *f*, panadería *f*

baking powder *n* : levadura *f* en polvo
baking soda → sodium bicarbonate
balaclava [ˌbælə'klɑvə, -'klæ-] *n* : pasamontañas *m*
balance¹ ['bælənts] *v* -anced; -ancing *vt* 1 : hacer el balance de (una cuenta) ⟨to balance the books : cuadrar las cuentas⟩ 2 EQUALIZE : balancear, equilibrar 3 HARMONIZE : armonizar — *vi* : balancearse
balance² *n* 1 SCALES : balanza *f*, báscula *f* 2 COUNTERBALANCE : contrapeso *m* 3 EQUILIBRIUM : equilibrio *m* ⟨to keep/lose one's balance : mantener/perder el equilibrio⟩ 4 REMAINDER : balance *m*, resto *m* 5 balance of trade : balanza comercial 6 balance of payments : balanza de pagos 7 to be/hang in the balance : estar en el aire
balanced ['bæləntst] *adj* : equilibrado, balanceado
balboa [bæl'bo:ə] *n* : balboa *f* (unidad monetaria)
balcony ['bælkəni] *n, pl* -nies 1 : balcón *m*, terraza *f* (de un edificio) 2 : galería *f* (de un teatro)
bald ['bɔld] *adj* 1 : calvo, pelado, pelón 2 PLAIN : simple, puro ⟨the bald truth : la pura verdad⟩
balding ['bɔldɪŋ] *adj* : quedándose calvo
baldly ['bɔldli] *adv* : sin reparos, sin rodeos, francamente
baldness ['bɔldnəs] *n* : calvicie *f*
bale¹ ['beɪl] *vt* baled; baling : empacar, hacer balas de
bale² *n* : bala *f*, fardo *m*, paca *f*
baleful ['beɪlfəl] *adj* 1 DEADLY : mortífero 2 SINISTER : siniestro, funesto, torvo ⟨a baleful glance : una mirada torva⟩
balk¹ ['bɔk] *vt* : obstaculizar, impedir — *vi* 1 : plantarse *fam* (dícese de un caballo, etc.) 2 to balk at : resistirse a, mostrarse reacio a
balk² *n* : obstáculo *m*
Balkan ['bɔlkən] *adj* : balcánico
balky ['bɔki] *adj* balkier; -est : reacio, obstinado, terco
ball¹ ['bɔl] *vt* : apelotonar, ovillar
ball² *n* 1 : pelota *f*, bola *f*, balón *m*, bollo *m* *Arg, Uru* ⟨ball of yarn : ovillo de lana⟩ 2 DANCE : baile *m* (de etiqueta) 3 : bola *f*, bola *f* mala (en béisbol) 4 : parte *f* anterior de la planta (de un pie) 5 balls *npl usu vulgar* : cojones *mpl, usu vulgar*; huevos *mpl, usu vulgar*; 6 balls *npl* GUTS : cojones *mpl, usu vulgar*; agallas *fpl fam* 7 on the ball : espabilado, alerta ⟨the ball is in your/his (etc.) court ⟨the ball is in your court : ahora te corresponde a ti⟩ 9 to drop the ball : cometer un gran error 10 to get/set/start the ball rolling : poner las cosas en marcha 11 to keep the ball rolling : mantener el impulso 12 to play ball : jugar al béisbol/baloncesto (etc.) 13 to play ball COOPERATE : cooperar
ballad ['bæləd] *n* : romance *m*, balada *f*
balladeer [ˌbælə'dɪr] *n* : cantante *mf* de baladas

ballast¹ ['bæləst] *vt* : lastrar
ballast² *n* : lastre *m*
ball bearing *n* : cojinete *m* de bola
ballerina [ˌbælə'ri:nə] *n* : bailarina *f* ⟨prima ballerina : primera bailarina⟩
ballet [bæ'leɪ, 'bæˌleɪ] *n* : ballet *m*
ballet dancer *n* : bailarín *m*, -rina *f*
ball game *n* : partido *m* de beisbol
ballistic [bə'lɪstɪk] *adj* : balístico
ballistics [bə'lɪstɪks] *ns & pl* : balística *f*
balloon¹ [bə'lu:n] *vi* 1 : viajar en globo 2 SWELL : hincharse, inflarse
balloon² *n* : globo *m*
balloonist [bə'lu:nɪst] *n* : aeróstata *mf*
ballot¹ ['bælət] *vi* : votar
ballot² *n* 1 : papeleta *f* (de voto), boleta *f* electoral 2 BALLOTING : votación *f* 3 VOTE : voto *m*
ballot box *n* : urna *f*
ballpoint pen ['bɔlˌpɔɪnt] *n* : bolígrafo *m*
ballroom ['bɔlˌru:m, -ˌrʊm] *n* : sala *f* de baile
ballyhoo ['bæliˌhu:] *n* : propaganda *f*, publicidad *f*, bombo *m fam*
balm ['bɑm, 'bɑlm] *n* : bálsamo *m*, ungüento *m*
balmy ['bɑmi, 'bɑl-] *adj* balmier; -est 1 MILD : templado, agradable 2 SOOTHING : balsámico 3 CRAZY : chiflado *fam*, chalado *fam*
baloney [bə'lo:ni] *n* NONSENSE : tonterías *fpl*, estupideces *fpl*
balsa ['bɔlsə] *n* : balsa *f*
balsam ['bɔlsəm] *n or* balsam fir : abeto *m* balsámico
Baltic ['bɔltɪk] *adj* : báltico
balustrade ['bæləˌstreɪd] *n* : balaustrada *f*
bam¹ ['bæm] *n* BANG : explosión *f*, estallido *m*, estampido *m*
bam² *interj* : ¡zas!
bamboo [bæm'bu:] *n* : bambú *m*
bamboozle [bæm'bu:zəl] *vt* -zled; -zling : engañar, embaucar
ban¹ ['bæn] *vt* banned; banning : prohibir, proscribir
ban² *n* : prohibición *f*, proscripción *f*
banal [bə'nɑl, bə'næl, 'beɪnəl] *adj* : banal, trivial
banality [bə'næləti] *n, pl* -ties : banalidad *f*, trivialidad *f*
banana [bə'nænə] *n* : banano *m*, plátano *m*, banana *f*, cambur *m Ven*, guineo *m Car*
band¹ ['bænd] *vt* 1 BIND : fajar, atar 2 to band together : unirse, juntarse
band² *n* 1 STRIP : banda *f*, cinta *f* (de un sombrero, etc.) 2 STRIPE : franja *f* 3 : banda *f* (de radiofrecuencia) 4 RING : anillo *m* 5 GROUP : banda *f*, grupo *m*, conjunto *m* ⟨jazz band : conjunto de jazz⟩
bandage¹ ['bændɪdʒ] *vt* -daged; -daging : vendar
bandage² *n* : vendaje *m*, venda *f*
Band–Aid ['bændˌeɪd] *trademark* se usa para una venda adhesiva
bandanna *or* bandana [bæn'dænə] *n* : pañuelo *m* (de colores)
bandit ['bændət] *n* : bandido *m*, -da *f*; bandolero *m*, -ra *f*

bandstand ['bænd,stænd] *n* : quiosco *m* de música

bandwagon ['bænd,wægən] *n* 1 : carroza *f* de músicos 2 **to jump on the bandwagon** : subirse al carro, seguir la moda

bandwidth ['bænd,wɪdθ] *n* : ancho *m* de banda

bandy ['bændi] *vt* **-died; -dying** 1 EXCHANGE : intercambiar 2 **to bandy about** : circular, propagar

bane ['beɪn] *n* 1 POISON : veneno *m* 2 RUIN : ruina *f*, pesadilla *f*

baneful ['beɪnfəl] *adj* : nefasto, funesto

bang¹ ['bæŋ] *vt* 1 STRIKE : golpear, darse ⟨he banged his elbow against the door : se dio con el codo en la puerta⟩ 2 SLAM : cerrar (la puerta) con/de un portazo 3 **to bang up** : rayar o abollar (algo), dejar (a alguien) con moretones — *vi* 1 SLAM : cerrarse de un golpe 2 **to bang on** : aporrear, golpear ⟨she was banging on the table : aporreaba la mesa⟩

bang² *adv* : directamente, exactamente

bang³ *n* 1 BLOW : golpe *m*, porrazo *m*, trancazo *m* 2 EXPLOSION : explosión *f*, estallido *m*, estampido *m* 3 SLAM : portazo *m* 4 **bangs** *npl* : flequillo *m*, fleco *m*

bang⁴ *interj* : ¡pum!

bangle ['bæŋgəl] *n* : brazalete *m*, pulsera *f*

banish ['bænɪʃ] *vt* 1 EXILE : desterrar, exiliar 2 EXPEL : expulsar

banishment ['bænɪʃmənt] *n* 1 EXILE : destierro *m*, exilio *m* 2 EXPULSION : expulsión *f*

banister ['bænəstər] *n* HANDRAIL : pasamanos *m*, barandilla *f*, barandal *m*

banjo ['bæn,dʒo:] *n*, *pl* **-jos** : banjo *m*

bank¹ ['bæŋk] *vt* 1 TILT : peraltar (una carretera), ladear (un avión) 2 HEAP : amontonar 3 : cubrir (un fuego) 4 : depositar (dinero en un banco) — *vi* 1 : ladearse (dícese de un avión) 2 : tener una cuenta (en un banco) 3 **to bank on** : contar con

bank² *n* 1 MASS : montón *m*, montículo *m*, masa *f* 2 : orilla *f*, ribera *f* (de un río) 3 : peralte *m* (de una carretera) 4 : banco *m* ⟨World Bank : Banco Mundial⟩ ⟨blood bank : banco de sangre⟩ 5 : banca *f* (en juegos)

bankbook ['bæŋk,bʊk] *n* : libreta *f* bancaria, libreta *f* de ahorros

banker ['bæŋkər] *n* : banquero *m*, -ra *f*

banking ['bæŋkɪŋ] *n* : banca *f*

banknote *n* : billete *m* de banco

bankrupt¹ ['bæŋ,krʌpt] *vt* : hacer quebrar, llevar a la quiebra, arruinar

bankrupt² *adj* 1 : en bancarrota, en quiebra 2 ~ **of** LACKING : carente de, falto de

bankrupt³ *n* : fallido *m*, -da *f*; quebrado *m*, -da *f*

bankruptcy ['bæŋ,krʌptsi] *n*, *pl* **-cies** : ruina *f*, quiebra *f*, bancarrota *f*

bank statement → statement

bank teller → teller

banner¹ ['bænər] *adj* : excelente

banner² *n* : estandarte *m*, bandera *f*

banns ['bænz] *npl* : amonestaciones *fpl*

banquet¹ ['bæŋkwət] *vi* : celebrar un banquete

banquet² *n* : banquete *m*

banter¹ ['bæntər] *vi* : bromear, hacer bromas

banter² *n* : bromas *fpl*

baptism ['bæp,tɪzəm] *n* : bautismo *m*

baptismal [bæp'tɪzməl] *adj* : bautismal

baptismal font → font

Baptist ['bæptɪst] *n* : bautista *mf*, baptista *mf* — **Baptist** *adj*

baptize [bæp'taɪz, 'bæp,taɪz] *vt* **-tized; -tizing** : bautizar

bar¹ ['bɑr] *vt* **barred; barring** 1 OBSTRUCT : obstruir, bloquear 2 EXCLUDE : excluir 3 PROHIBIT : prohibir 4 SECURE : atrancar, asegurar ⟨bar the door! : ¡atranca la puerta!⟩

bar² *n* 1 : barra *f*, barrote *m* (de una ventana), tranca *f* (de una puerta) ⟨behind bars : entre rejas⟩ 2 BARRIER : barrera *f*, obstáculo *m* 3 LAW : abogacía *f* 4 STRIPE : franja *f* 5 COUNTER : mostrador *m*, barra *f* 6 TAVERN : bar *m*, taberna *f* 7 MEASURE : compás *m* (en música)

bar³ *prep* 1 : excepto, con excepción de 2 **bar none** : sin excepción

barb ['bɑrb] *n* 1 POINT : púa *f*, lengüeta *f* 2 GIBE : pulla *f*

barbarian¹ [bɑr'bæriən] *adj* 1 : bárbaro 2 CRUDE : tosco, bruto

barbarian² *n* : bárbaro *m*, -ra *f*

barbaric [bɑr'bærɪk] *adj* 1 PRIMITIVE : primitivo 2 CRUEL : brutal, cruel

barbarity [bɑr'bærəti] *n*, *pl* **-ties** : barbaridad *f*

barbarous ['bɑrbərəs] *adj* 1 UNCIVILIZED : bárbaro 2 MERCILESS : despiadado, cruel

barbarously ['bɑrbərəsli] *adv* : bárbaramente

barbecue¹ ['bɑrbɪ,kju:] *vt* **-cued; -cuing** : asar a la parrilla

barbecue² *n* : barbacoa *f*, parrillada *f*

barbed ['bɑrbd] *adj* 1 : con púas ⟨barbed wire : alambre de púas⟩ 2 BITING : mordaz

barber ['bɑrbər] *n* : barbero *m*, -ra *f*

barbershop ['bɑrbər,ʃɑp] *n* : peluquería *f*, barbería *f*

barbiturate [bɑr'bɪtʃərət] *n* : barbitúrico *m*

bar code *n* : código *m* de barras

bard ['bɑrd] *n* : bardo *m*

bare¹ ['bær] *vt* **bared; baring** : desnudar

bare² *adj* 1 NAKED : desnudo 2 EXPOSED : descubierto, sin protección 3 EMPTY : desprovisto, vacío 4 MINIMUM : mero, mínimo ⟨the bare necessities : las necesidades mínimas⟩ 5 PLAIN : puro, sencillo

bareback ['bær,bæk] *or* **barebacked** [-,bækt] *adv* & *adj* : a pelo

barefaced ['bær,feɪst] *adj* : descarado

barefoot ['bær,fʊt] *or* **barefooted** [-,fʊtəd] *adv* & *adj* : descalzo

bareheaded ['bær'hɛdəd] *adv & adj* : sin sombrero, con la cabeza descubierta

barely ['bærli] *adv* : apenas, por poco

bareness ['bærnəs] *n* : desnudez *f*

barf¹ ['bɑrf] *v fam* → **vomit¹**

barf² *n fam* → **vomit²**

bargain¹ ['bɑrgən] *vi* HAGGLE : regatear, negociar — *vt* BARTER : trocar, cambiar

bargain² *n* **1** AGREEMENT : acuerdo *m*, convenio *m* ⟨to strike a bargain : cerrar un trato⟩ ⟨in/into the bargain : además, encima⟩ **2** : ganga *f* ⟨bargain price : precio de ganga⟩

bargaining *n* : regateo *m*, negociación *f*

barge¹ ['bɑrdʒ] *vi* **barged; barging 1** : mover con torpeza **2 to barge in** : entrometerse, interrumpir

barge² *n* : barcaza *f*, gabarra *f*

bar graph *n* : gráfico *m* de barras

baritone ['bærə,to:n] *n* : barítono *m*

bark¹ ['bɑrk] *vi* : ladrar — *vt or* **to bark out** : gritar ⟨to bark out an order : dar una orden a gritos⟩

bark² *n* **1** : ladrido *m* (de un perro) **2** : corteza *f* (de un árbol) **3** *or* **barque** : tipo de embarcación con velas de proa y popa

barley ['bɑrli] *n* : cebada *f*

barmaid ['bɑr,meɪd] *n* : camarera *f*

barman ['bɑr,mən] *n, pl* **-men** [-mən, -,mɛn] → **bartender**

barn ['bɑrn] *n* : granero *m* (para cosechas), establo *m* (para ganado)

barnacle ['bɑrnɪkəl] *n* : percebe *m*

barnyard ['bɑrn,jɑrd] *n* : corral *m*

barometer [bə'rɑmətər] *n* : barómetro *m*

barometric [,bærə'mɛtrɪk] *adj* : barométrico

baron ['bærən] *n* **1** : barón *m* **2** TYCOON : magnate *mf*

baroness ['bærənɪs, -nəs, -,nɛs] *n* : baronesa *f*

baronial [bə'ro:niəl] *adj* **1** : de barón **2** STATELY : señorial, majestuoso

baroque [bə'ro:k, -'rɑk] *adj* : barroco

barracks ['bærəks] *ns & pl* : cuartel *m*

barracuda [,bærə'ku:də] *n, pl* **-da** *or* **-das** : barracuda *f*

barrage [bə'rɑʒ, -'rɑdʒ] *n* **1** : descarga *f* (de artillería) **2** DELUGE : aluvión *m* ⟨a barrage of questions : un aluvión de preguntas⟩

barred ['bɑrd] *adj* : excluido, prohibido

barrel¹ ['bærəl] *v* **-reled** *or* **-relled; -reling** *or* **-relling** *vi* : ir disparado

barrel² *n* **1** : barril *m*, tonel *m* **2** : cañón *m* (de un arma de fuego), cilindro *m* (de una cerradura)

barren ['bærən] *adj* **1** STERILE : estéril (dícese de las plantas o la mujer), árido (dícese del suelo) **2** DESERTED : yermo, desierto

barrette [bɑ'rɛt, bə-] *n* : pasador *m*, broche *m* para el cabello

barricade¹ ['bærə,keɪd, ,bærə'-] *vt* **-caded; -cading** : cerrar con barricadas

barricade² *n* : barricada *f*

barrier ['bæriər] *n* **1** : barrera *f* **2** OBSTACLE : obstáculo *m*, impedimento *m*

barring ['bɑrɪŋ] *prep* : excepto, salvo, a excepción de

barrio ['bɑrio, 'bær-] *n* : barrio *m*

barroom ['bɑr,ru:m, -,rʊm] *n* : bar *m*

barrow ['bær,o:] → **wheelbarrow**

bartender ['bɑr,tɛndər] *n* : camarero *m*, -ra *f*; barman *m*

barter¹ ['bɑrtər] *vt* : cambiar, trocar

barter² *n* : trueque *m*, permuta *f*

basalt [bə'sɔlt, 'beɪ,-] *n* : basalto *m*

base¹ ['beɪs] *vt* **based; basing** : basar, fundamentar, establecer

base² *adj* **baser; basest 1** : de baja ley (dícese de un metal) **2** CONTEMPTIBLE : vil, despreciable

base³ *n, pl* **bases 1** : base *f* **2** : pie *m* (de una montaña, una estatua, etc.)

baseball ['beɪs,bɔl] *n* : beisbol *m*, béisbol *m*

baseball cap *n* : gorra *f* de visera, gorra *f* de beisbol

baseless ['beɪsləs] *adj* : infundado

basely ['beɪsli] *adv* : vilmente

basement ['beɪsmənt] *n* : sótano *m*

baseness ['beɪsnəs] *n* : vileza *f*, bajeza *f*

bash¹ ['bæʃ] *vt* : golpear violentamente

bash² *n* **1** BLOW : golpe *m*, porrazo *m*, madrazo *m Mex fam* **2** PARTY : fiesta *f*, juerga *f fam*

bashful ['bæʃfəl] *adj* : tímido, vergonzoso, penoso

bashfulness ['bæʃfəlnəs] *n* : timidez *f*

basic¹ ['beɪsɪk] *adj* **1** FUNDAMENTAL : básico, fundamental **2** RUDIMENTARY : básico, elemental **3** : básico (en química)

basic² *n* : fundamento *m*, rudimento *m*

basically ['beɪsɪkli] *adv* : fundamentalmente

basil ['beɪzəl, 'bæzəl] *n* : albahaca *f*

basilica [bə'sɪlɪkə] *n* : basílica *f*

basin ['beɪsən] *n* **1** WASHBOWL : palangana *f*, lavamanos *m*, lavabo *m* **2** : cuenca *f* (de un río)

basis ['beɪsəs] *n, pl* **bases** [-,si:z] **1** BASE : base *f*, pilar *m* **2** FOUNDATION : fundamento *m*, base *f* **3 on a weekly basis** : semanalmente

bask ['bæsk] *vi* : disfrutar, deleitarse ⟨to bask in the sun : disfrutar del sol⟩

basket ['bæskət] *n* : cesta *f*, cesto *m*, canasta *f*

basketball ['bæskət,bɔl] *n* : baloncesto *m*, basquetbol *m*, basket *m*

Basque ['bæsk, 'bɑsk] *n* : Basque *mf* — **Basque** *adj*

bas-relief [,bɑrɪ'li:f] *n* : bajorrelieve *m*

bass¹ ['beɪs] *adj* : de bajo (dícese de una voz, etc.) ⟨bass clef : clave de fa⟩ ⟨bass string : bordón⟩

bass² ['bæs] *n, pl* **bass** *or* **basses** : róbalo *m* (pesca)

bass³ ['beɪs] *n* **1** : bajo *m* (tono, voz, cantante) **2** → **bass guitar 3** → **double bass**

bass drum *n* : bombo *m*

basset hound ['bæsət,haʊnd] *n* : basset *m*

bass guitar *n* : bajo *m* (guitarra)

bassinet [,bæsə'nɛt] *n* : moisés *m*, cuna *f*

bassist ['beɪsɪst] *n* : bajista *mf*

bassoon [bə'su:n, bæ-] *n* : fagot *m*
bass viol ['beɪs'vaɪəl, -ˌoːl] → **double bass**
bastard[1] ['bæstərd] *adj* : bastardo
bastard[2] *n* **1** *usu offensive* : bastardo *m*,
-da *f* **2** *offensive* : hijo *m* de puta *sometimes offensive*; cabrón *m Mex*, *Spain offensive* **3** *sometimes offensive* : tipo *m*
⟨the poor bastard : el pobre diablo⟩
⟨what a lucky bastard! : ¡qué suertudo!⟩
bastardize ['bæstərˌdaɪz] *vt* **-ized; -izing**
DEBASE : degradar, envilecer
baste ['beɪst] *vt* **basted; basting 1**
STITCH : hilvanar **2** : bañar (con su jugo
durante la cocción)
bastion ['bæstʃən] *n* : bastión *m*, baluarte
m
bat[1] ['bæt] *vt* **batted; batting 1** HIT : batear **2 without batting an eye** : sin
pestañear
bat[2] *n* **1** : murciélago *m* (animal) **2**
: bate *m* ⟨baseball bat : bate de beisbol⟩
batch ['bætʃ] *n* : hornada *f*, tanda *f*, grupo
m, cantidad *f*
bate ['beɪt] *vt* **bated; bating 1** : aminorar, reducir **2 with bated breath**
: con ansiedad, aguantando la respiración
bath ['bæθ, 'baθ] *n*, *pl* **baths** ['bæðz,
'bæθs, 'baðz, 'baθs] **1** BATHING : baño
m ⟨to take a bath : bañarse⟩ **2** : baño *m*
(en fotografía, etc.) **3** BATHROOM
: baño *m*, cuarto *m* de baño **4** SPA
: balneario *m* **5** LOSS : pérdida *f*
bathe ['beɪð] *v* **bathed; bathing** *vt* **1**
WASH : bañar, lavar **2** SOAK : poner en
remojo **3** FLOOD : inundar ⟨to bathe
with light : inundar de luz⟩ — *vi*
: bañarse, ducharse
bather ['beɪðər] *n* : bañista *mf*
bathing suit → **swimsuit**
bathrobe ['bæθˌroːb] *n* : bata *f* (de baño)
bathroom ['bæθˌruːm, -ˌrʊm] *n* : baño *m*,
cuarto *m* de baño
bathroom tissue → **toilet paper**
bathtub ['bæθˌtʌb] *n* : bañera *f*, tina *f* (de
baño)
baton [bə'tɑn] *n* : batuta *f*, bastón *m*
battalion [bə'tæljən] *n* : batallón *m*
batten ['bætən] *vt* **to batten down the hatches** : cerrar las escotillas
batter[1] ['bætər] *v* **1** BEAT : aporrear, golpear **2** MISTREAT : maltratar
batter[2] *n* **1** : masa *f* para rebozar **2** HITTER : bateador *m*, -dora *f*
battered ['bætərd] *adj* **1** ABUSED
: maltratado **2** DAMAGED : maltrecho **3** INJURED : apaleado, aporreado
battering ram *n* : ariete *m*
battery ['bætəri] *n*, *pl* **-teries 1** : lesiones
fpl ⟨assault and battery : agresión con
lesiones⟩ **2** ARTILLERY : batería *f* **3**
: batería *f*, pila *f* (de electricidad) **4** SERIES : serie *f*
batting ['bætɪŋ] *n* **1** *or* **cotton batting**
: algodón *m* en láminas **2** : bateo *m* (en
beisbol)
battle[1] ['bætəl] *vi* **-tled; -tling** : luchar,
pelear
battle[2] *n* : batalla *f*, lucha *f*, pelea *f*

battle–ax ['bætəlˌæks] *n* : hacha *f* de
guerra
battlefield ['bætəlˌfiːld] *n* : campo *m* de
batalla
battleship ['bætəlˌʃɪp] *n* : acorazado *m*
batty ['bæti] *adj* **battier; -est** : chiflado
fam, chalado *fam*
bauble ['bɔbəl] *n* : chuchería *f*, baratija *f*
Bavarian [bə'verɪən] *n* : bávaro *m*, -ra *f* —
Bavarian *adj*
bawdiness ['bɔdinəs] *n* : picardía *f*
bawdy ['bɔdi] *adj* **bawdier; -est** : subido
de tono, verde, colorado *Mex*
bawl[1] ['bɔl] *vi* : llorar a gritos
bawl[2] *n* : grito *m*, alarido *m*
bawl out *vt* SCOLD : regañar
bay[1] ['beɪ] *vi* HOWL : aullar
bay[2] *adj* : castaño, zaino (dícese de los caballos)
bay[3] *n* **1** : bahía *f* ⟨Bay of Campeche
: Bahía de Campeche⟩ **2** *or* **bay horse**
: caballo *m* castaño **3** LAUREL : laurel
m (en cocina) ⟨bay leaf : hoja de laurel⟩ **4** HOWL : aullido *m* **5** : saliente *m*
⟨bay window : ventana en saliente⟩ **6**
COMPARTMENT : área *f*, compartimento
m **7 at ~** : acorralado
bayonet[1] [ˌbeɪə'nɛt, 'beɪəˌnɛt] *vt* **-neted;
-neting** : herir *o* matar) con bayoneta
bayonet[2] *n* : bayoneta *f*
bayou ['baɪˌuː, -ˌoː] *n* : pantano *m*
bazaar [bə'zɑr] *n* **1** : bazar *m* **2** SALE
: venta *f* benéfica
bazooka [bə'zuːkə] *n* : bazuca *f*
BB ['biːbi] *n* : balín *m*
bcc [ˌbiːˌsiː'siː] *vt* **bcc'd; bcc'ing** : enviarle
una copia oculta a (alguien), enviar una
copia oculta de (un mensaje)
be ['biː] *v* **was** ['wʌz, 'wɑz]; **were** ['wər];
been ['bɪn]; **being; am** ['æm]; **is** ['ɪz]; **are**
['ɑr] *vi* **1** (*expressing identity or category*)
: ser ⟨José is a doctor : José es doctor⟩
⟨I'm Ann's sister : soy la hermana de
Ann⟩ ⟨who is it? it's me : ¿quién es? soy
yo⟩ ⟨apes are mammals : los simios son
mamíferos⟩ ⟨if I were you : yo en tu
lugar, yo que tú⟩ **2** (*expressing a quality*)
: ser ⟨the dress is red : el vestido es rojo⟩
⟨she's very intelligent : ella es muy inteligente⟩ ⟨she's 10 years old : tiene 10 años⟩
⟨you're so silly! : ¡qué tonto eres!⟩ ⟨I
want you to be happy : quiero que seas
feliz⟩ **3** (*expressing origin or possession*)
: ser ⟨she's from Managua : es de Managua⟩ ⟨it's mine : es mío⟩ **4** (*expressing
location*) : estar, quedar ⟨he's not at
home : no está en casa⟩ ⟨the cups are on
the table : las tazas están en la mesa⟩ ⟨it's
ten miles away : está/queda diez millas
de aquí⟩ **5** EXIST : ser, existir ⟨to be or
not to be : ser, o no ser⟩ ⟨I think, therefore I am : pienso, luego existo⟩ **6**
COME, GO : estar, ir, venir ⟨have you
been to Paris? : ¿has estado en París?,
¿has ido a París?⟩ ⟨she's been and gone
: llegó y se fue⟩ **7** (*expressing a state of
being*) : estar, tener ⟨how are you?
: ¿cómo estás?⟩ ⟨I'm cold/hungry : tengo
frío/hambre⟩ ⟨they're sick : están enfermos⟩ ⟨she's angry : está enojada⟩ ⟨to be

frank : para serte franco⟩ **8** COST : ser, costar ⟨it's $5 : cuesta $5⟩ **9** EQUAL : ser (igual a) ⟨two plus two is four : dos más dos son cuatro⟩ **10** OCCUR : ser ⟨the concert is (on) Sunday : el concierto es el domingo⟩ — *v impers* **1** (*indicating time*) : ser ⟨it's eight o'clock : son las ocho⟩ ⟨it's Friday : hoy es viernes⟩ **2** (*indicating a condition*) : hacer, estar ⟨it's sunny : hace sol⟩ ⟨it's very dark in here : está muy oscuro aquí dentro⟩ **3** (*used with* there) : haber ⟨there's a book on the table : hay un libro en la mesa⟩ ⟨there was an accident : hubo un accidente⟩ ⟨there's someone at the door : llaman a la puerta⟩ — *v aux* **1** (*expressing progression*) : estar ⟨I'm working : estoy trabajando⟩ ⟨what were you saying? : ¿qué estabas diciendo?⟩ ⟨it's snowing : está nevando⟩ ⟨we've been waiting : hemos estado esperando⟩ **2** (*expressing future action*) ⟨I'm seeing him tonight : voy a verlo esta noche⟩ ⟨are you coming tomorrow? : ¿vienes mañana?⟩ ⟨she was never/not to see him again : nunca volvería a verlo⟩ ⟨the best is yet to come : lo mejor está por venir⟩ **3** (*used in passive constructions*) : ser ⟨it was finished yesterday : fue acabado ayer, se acabó ayer⟩ **4** (*expressing possibility*) : poderse ⟨can she be trusted? : ¿se puede confiar en ella?⟩ ⟨it was nowhere to be found : no se pudo encontrar por ninguna parte⟩ ⟨you're not to blame : no tienes la culpa⟩ **5** (*expressing obligation*) : deber ⟨you are to stay here : debes quedarte aquí⟩ ⟨he was to come yesterday : se esperaba que viniese ayer⟩ **6 to be oneself** : ser uno mismo ⟨be yourself : sé tú mismo⟩

beach[1] [ˈbiːtʃ] *vt* : hacer varar, hacer encallar

beach[2] *n* : playa *f*

beachcomber [ˈbiːtʃˌkoːmər] *n* : raquero *m*, -ra *f*

beachhead [ˈbiːtʃˌhɛd] *n* : cabeza *f* de playa

beacon [ˈbiːkən] *n* : faro *m*

bead[1] [ˈbiːd] *vi* : formarse en gotas

bead[2] *n* **1** : cuenta *f* **2** DROP : gota *f* **3** **beads** *npl* NECKLACE : collar *m*

beady [ˈbiːdi] *adj* **beadier; -est 1** : de forma de cuenta **2 beady eyes** : ojos *mpl* pequeños y brillantes

beagle [ˈbiːgəl] *n* : beagle *m*

beak [ˈbiːk] *n* : pico *m*

beaker [ˈbiːkər] *n* **1** CUP : taza *f* alta **2** : vaso *m* de precipitados (en un laboratorio)

beam[1] [ˈbiːm] *vi* **1** SHINE : brillar **2** SMILE : sonreír radiantemente — *vt* BROADCAST : transmitir, emitir

beam[2] *n* **1** : viga *f*, barra *f* **2** RAY : rayo *m*, haz *m* de luz **3** : haz *m* de radiofaro (para guiar pilotos, etc.)

bean [ˈbiːn] *n* **1** : habichuela *f*, frijol *m* **2 broad bean** : haba *f* **3 string bean** : judía *f*

bear[1] [ˈbær] *v* **bore** [ˈbor]; **borne** [ˈbɔrn]; **bearing** *vt* **1** CARRY : llevar, portar **2** : dar a luz a (un niño) **3** PRODUCE : dar (frutas, cosechas) **4** ENDURE, SUPPORT : soportar, resistir, aguantar **5** SHOW : llevar, tener ⟨to bear a resemblance to : tener una similitud con (algo), tener un parecido con (alguien)⟩ **6 to bear out** : corroborar — *vi* **1** TURN : doblar, dar la vuelta, girar ⟨bear right : doble a la derecha⟩ **2 to bear up** : resistir **3 to bear with** : tener paciencia con

bear[2] *n, pl* **bears** *or* **bear** : oso *m*, osa *f*

bearable [ˈbærəbəl] *adj* : soportable

beard [ˈbɪrd] *n* **1** : barba *f* **2** : arista *f* (de plantas)

bearded [ˈbɪrdəd] *adj* : barbudo, de barba

bearer [ˈbærər] *n* : portador *m*, -dora *f*

bearing [ˈbærɪŋ] *n* **1** CONDUCT, MANNERS : comportamiento *m*, modales *mpl* **2** SUPPORT : soporte *f* **3** SIGNIFICANCE : relación *f*, importancia *f* ⟨to have no bearing on : no tener nada que ver con⟩ **4** : cojinete *m*, rodamiento *m* (de una máquina) **5** COURSE, DIRECTION : dirección *f*, rumbo *m* ⟨to get one's bearings : orientarse⟩

beast [ˈbiːst] *n* **1** : bestia *f*, fiera *f* ⟨beast of burden : animal de carga⟩ **2** BRUTE : bruto *m*, -ta *f*; bestia *mf*

beastly [ˈbiːstli] *adj* : detestable, repugnante

beat[1] [ˈbiːt] *v* **beat; beaten** [ˈbiːtən] *or* **beat; beating** *vt* **1** STRIKE : golpear, pegar, darle una paliza (a alguien) **2** DEFEAT : vencer, derrotar (a un rival, etc.), batir (un récord) **3** : superar, ser mejor que ⟨nothing beats a nice, hot bath : no hay nada mejor que un baño caliente⟩ **4** AVOID : anticiparse a, evitar ⟨to beat the crowd : evitar el gentío⟩ **5** STIR, WHIP : batir (alas) **7 beat it!** *fam* : ¡lárgate! **8 it beats me** : no sé **9 to beat down** : echar abajo (una puerta) **10 to beat out** DEFEAT : vencer, derrotar **11 to beat up** : darle una paliza (a alguien) **12 to beat up on** : darle frecuentes palizas (a alguien) — *vi* **1** : batir **2** THROB : palpitar, latir **3 to beat down** : pegar fuerte, caer a plomo (dícese del sol)

beat[2] *adj* EXHAUSTED : derrengado, muy cansado ⟨I'm beat! : ¡estoy molido!⟩

beat[3] *n* **1** : golpe *m*, redoble *m* (de un tambor), latido *m* (del corazón) **2** RHYTHM : ritmo *m*, tiempo *m*

beater [ˈbiːtər] *n* : batidor *m*, -dora *f* **2** EGGBEATER : batidor *m*

beatific [ˌbiːəˈtɪfɪk] *adj* : beatífico

beating [ˈbiːtɪŋ] *n* **1** : paliza *f* **2** DEFEAT : derrota *f*

beau [ˈboː] *n, pl* **beaux** *or* **beaus** : pretendiente *m*, galán *m*

beautician [bjuːˈtɪʃən] *n* : esteticista *mf*

beautification [ˌbjuːtəfəˈkeɪʃən] *n* : embellecimiento *m*

beautiful [ˈbjuːtɪfəl] *adj* : hermoso, bello, lindo, precioso

beautifully [ˈbjuːtɪfəli] *adv* **1** ATTRACTIVELY : hermosamente **2** EXCELLENTLY : maravillosamente, excelentemente

beautify [ˈbjuːtəˌfaɪ] *vt* **-fied; -fying** : embellecer

beauty ['bju:ʈi] *n, pl* **-ties** : belleza *f*, hermosura *f*, beldad *f*
beauty shop *or* **beauty parlor** *or* **beauty salon** *n* : salón *m* de belleza
beauty spot *n* : lunar *m*
beaver ['bi:vər] *n* : castor *m*
because [bɪ'kʌz, -'kɔz] *conj* : porque
because of *prep* : por, a causa de, debido a
beck ['bɛk] *n* **to be at the beck and call of** : estar a la entera disposición de, estar sometido a la voluntad de
beckon ['bɛkən] *vi* **to beckon to someone** : hacerle señas a alguien
become [bɪ'kʌm] *v* **-came** [-'keɪm]; **-come; -coming** *vi* : hacerse, volverse, ponerse ⟨he became famous : se hizo famoso⟩ ⟨to become sad : ponerse triste⟩ ⟨to become accustomed to : acostumbrarse a⟩ — *vt* **1** BEFIT : ser apropiado para **2** SUIT : favorecer, quedarle bien (a alguien) ⟨that dress becomes you : ese vestido te favorece⟩
becoming [bɪ'kʌmɪŋ] *adj* **1** SUITABLE : apropiado **2** FLATTERING : favorecedor
bed¹ ['bɛd] *v* **bedded; bedding** *vt* : acostar — *vi* : acostarse
bed² *n* **1** : cama *f*, lecho *m* ⟨to make the bed : hacer la cama⟩ ⟨to go to bed : acostarse⟩ ⟨to be time for bed : ser hora de acostarse⟩ **2** : cauce *m* (de un río), fondo *m* (del mar) **3** : arriate *m* (para plantas) **4** LAYER, STRATUM : capa *f*, estrato *m* **5** : caja *f* (de una camioneta)
bed and breakfast *n* : pensión *f* con desayuno
bedbug ['bɛd,bʌg] *n* : chinche *f*
bedclothes ['bɛd,kloːðz, -,kloːz] *npl* : ropa *f* de cama, sábanas *fpl*
bedding ['bɛdɪŋ] *n* **1** → **bedclothes 2** : cama *f* (para animales)
bedeck [bɪ'dɛk] *vt* : adornar, engalanar
bedevil [bɪ'dɛvəl] *vt* **-iled** *or* **-illed; -iling** *or* **-illing** : acosar, plagar
bedlam ['bɛdləm] *n* : locura *f*, caos *m*, alboroto *m*
bedraggled [bɪ'drægəld] *adj* : desaliñado, despeinado
bedridden ['bɛd,rɪdən] *adj* : postrado en cama
bedrock ['bɛd,rɑk] *n* : lecho *m* de roca
bedroom ['bɛd,ruːm, -,rʊm] *n* : dormitorio *m*, habitación *f*, pieza *f*, recámara *f Col, Mex, Pan*
bedsheet → **sheet**
bedside table ['bɛd,saɪd-] *n* : mesita *f* de noche
bedspread ['bɛd,sprɛd] *n* : cubrecama *m*, colcha *f*, cobertor *m*
bedtime ['bɛd,taɪm] *n* : hora *f* de acostarse
bee ['bi:] *n* **1** : abeja *f* (insecto) **2** GATHERING : círculo *m*, reunión *f*
beech ['bi:tʃ] *n, pl* **beeches** *or* **beech** : haya *f*
beechnut ['bi:tʃ,nʌt] *n* : hayuco *m*
beef¹ ['bi:f] *vt* **to beef up** : fortalecer, reforzar — *vi* COMPLAIN : quejarse
beef² *n, pl* **beefs** ['bi:fs] *or* **beeves** ['bi:vz] : carne *f* de vaca, carne *f* de res *CA, Mex*

beefsteak ['bi:f,steɪk] *n* : filete *m*, bistec *m*
beehive ['bi:,haɪv] *n* : colmena *f*
beekeeper ['bi:,ki:pər] *n* : apicultor *m*, -tora *f*
beekeeping ['bi:,ki:pɪŋ] *n* : apicultura *f*
beeline ['bi:,laɪn] *n* **to make a beeline for** : ir derecho a, ir directo hacia
been → **be**
beep¹ ['bi:p] *v* : pitar
beep² *n* : pitido *m*
beeper ['bi:pər] *n* : buscapersonas *m*, busca *m Spain*
beer ['bɪr] *n* : cerveza *f*
beeswax ['bi:z,wæks] *n* : cera *f* de abejas
beet ['bi:t] *n* : remolacha *f*, betabel *m Mex*
beetle ['bi:ʈəl] *n* : escarabajo *m*
befall [bɪ'fɔl] *v* **-fell** [-'fɛl]; **-fallen** [-'fɔlən] *vt* : sucederle a, acontecerle a — *vi* : acontecer
befit [bɪ'fɪt] *vt* **-fitted; -fitting** : convenir a, ser apropiado para
before¹ [bɪ'for] *adv* **1** : antes ⟨before and after : antes y después⟩ **2** : anterior ⟨the month before : el mes anterior⟩
before² *conj* : antes que ⟨he would die before surrendering : moriría antes que rendirse⟩
before³ *prep* **1** : antes de ⟨before eating : antes de comer⟩ **2** : delante de, ante ⟨I stood before the house : estaba parada delante de la casa⟩ ⟨before the judge : ante el juez⟩
beforehand [bɪ'for,hænd] *adv* : antes, por adelantado, de antemano, con anticipación
befriend [bɪ'frɛnd] *vt* : hacerse amigo de
befuddle [bɪ'fʌdəl] *vt* **-dled; -dling** : aturdir, ofuscar, confundir
beg ['bɛg] *v* **begged; begging** *vt* **1** : mendigar, pedir (dinero, etc.) **2** : pedir, suplicar ⟨I begged him to go : le supliqué que fuera⟩ — *vi* **1** : mendigar, pedir limosna **2 to beg for** : implorar, suplicar ⟨she begged for mercy : imploró clemencia⟩
beget [bɪ'gɛt] *vt* **-got** [-'gɑt]; **-gotten** [-'gɑtən] *or* **-got; -getting** : engendrar
beggar ['bɛgər] *n* : mendigo *m*, -ga *f*; pordiosero *m*, -ra *f*
begin [bɪ'gɪn] *v* **-gan** [-'gæn]; **-gun** [-'gʌn]; **-ginning** *vt* : empezar, comenzar, iniciar ⟨she began to work, she began working : empezó a trabajar⟩ — *vi* **1** START : empezar, comenzar, iniciarse **2** ORIGINATE : nacer, originarse **3 to begin with** : en primer lugar, para empezar
beginner [bɪ'gɪnər] *n* : principiante *mf*
beginning [bɪ'gɪnɪŋ] *n* : principio *m*, comienzo *m* ⟨at the beginning of the week : a principios de la semana⟩
begone [bɪ'gɔn] *interj* : ¡fuera de aquí!
begonia [bɪ'goːnjə] *n* : begonia *f*
begrudge [bɪ'grʌʤ] *vt* **-grudged; -grudging 1** : dar/hacer (etc.) de mala gana ⟨he did the work, but he begrudged every minute of it : hizo el trabajo, pero de muy mala gana⟩ ⟨I don't begrudge the money I spent : no me molesta el dinero que gasté⟩ **2** (*indicating disapproval*)

⟨he begrudges (her) her success : a él le molesta que ella tenga éxito⟩

beguile [bɪ'gaɪl] *vt* **-guiled; -guiling 1** DECEIVE : engañar **2** AMUSE : divertir, entretener

behalf [bɪ'hæf, -'haf] *n* **1** : favor *m*, beneficio *m*, parte *f* **2 on behalf of** *or* **in behalf of** : de parte de, en nombre de

behave [bɪ'heɪv] *vi* **-haved; -having** : comportarse, portarse

behavior [bɪ'heɪvjər] *n* : comportamiento *m*, conducta *f*

behead [bɪ'hɛd] *vt* : decapitar

behest [bɪ'hɛst] *n* **1** : mandato *m*, orden *f* **2 at the behest of** : a instancia de

behind¹ [bɪ'haɪnd] *adv* : atrás, detrás ⟨to fall behind : quedarse atrás⟩

behind² *prep* **1** : atrás de, detrás de, tras ⟨behind the house : detrás de la casa⟩ ⟨one behind another : uno tras otro⟩ **2** : atrasado con, después de ⟨behind schedule : atrasado con el trabajo⟩ ⟨I arrived behind the others : llegué después de los otros⟩ **3** SUPPORTING : en apoyo de, detrás ⟨we're behind you all the way! : ¡tienes todo nuestro apoyo!⟩

behind³ [bɪ'haɪnd, 'bi:ˌhaɪnd] *n* : trasero *m*

behold [bɪ'hoːld] *vt* **-held; -holding** : contemplar

beholder [bɪ'hoːldər] *n* : observador *m*, -dora *f*

behoove [bɪ'hu:v] *vt* **-hooved; -hooving** : convenirle a, corresponderle a ⟨it behooves us to help him : nos conviene ayudarlo⟩

beige¹ [beɪʒ] *adj* : beige

beige² *n* : beige *m*

being ['bi:ɪŋ] *n* **1** EXISTENCE : ser *m*, existencia *f* **2** CREATURE : ser *m*, ente *m*

belabor [bɪ'leɪbər] *vt* **to belabor the point** : extenderse sobre el tema

belated [bɪ'leɪtəd] *adj* : tardío, retrasado

belch¹ ['bɛltʃ] *vi* **1** BURP : eructar **2** EXPEL : expulsar, arrojar

belch² *n* : eructo *m*

beleaguer [bɪ'li:gər] *vt* **1** BESIEGE : asediar, sitiar **2** HARASS : fastidiar, molestar

belfry ['bɛlfri] *n, pl* **-fries** : campanario *m*

Belgian ['bɛldʒən] *n* : belga *mf* — **Belgian** *adj*

belie [bɪ'laɪ] *vt* **-lied; -lying 1** MISREPRESENT : falsear, ocultar **2** CONTRADICT : contradecir, desmentir

belief [bə'li:f] *n* **1** TRUST : confianza *f* **2** CONVICTION : creencia *f*, convicción *f* **3** FAITH : fe *f*

believable [bə'li:vəbəl] *adj* : verosímil, creíble

believe [bə'li:v] *v* **-lieved; -lieving** *vt* : creer ⟨I don't believe it! : ¡no puedo creerlo!⟩ ⟨believe it or not : aunque no lo creas, lo creas o no⟩ ⟨I can't believe my eyes : si no lo veo, no lo creo⟩ ⟨you'd better believe it! : ¡ya lo creo!, ¡por supuesto!⟩ — *vi* : creer

believer [bə'li:vər] *n* **1** : creyente *mf* **2** : partidario *m*, -ria *f*; entusiasta *mf* ⟨she's a great believer in vitamins : ella es una gran partidaria de las vitaminas⟩

belittle [bɪ'lɪtəl] *vt* **-littled; -littling 1** DISPARAGE : menospreciar, denigrar, rebajar **2** MINIMIZE : minimizar, quitar importancia a

bell¹ ['bɛl] *vt* : ponerle un cascabel a

bell² *n* : campana *f*, cencerro *m* (para una vaca o cabra), cascabel *m* (para un gato), timbre *m* (de teléfono, de la puerta)

belle ['bɛl] *n* : belleza *f*, beldad *f*

bellhop ['bɛlˌhɑp] *n* : botones *m*

bellicose ['bɛlɪˌko:s] *adj* : belicoso *m*

belligerence [bə'lɪdʒərənts] *n* : agresividad *f*, beligerancia *f*

belligerent¹ [bə'lɪdʒərənt] *adj* : agresivo, beligerante

belligerent² *n* : beligerante *mf*

bellow¹ ['bɛˌlo:] *vi* : bramar, mugir — *vt* : gritar

bellow² *n* : bramido *m*, grito *m*

bellows ['bɛˌlo:z] *ns & pl* : fuelle *m*

bellwether ['bɛlˌwɛðər] *n* : líder *mf*

belly¹ ['bɛli] *vi* **-lied; -lying** SWELL : hincharse, inflarse

belly² *n, pl* **-lies** : abdomen *m*, vientre *m*, barriga *f*, panza *f*

bellyache¹ ['bɛliˌeɪk] *vi fam* → **grouse¹**

bellyache² → **stomachache**

belly button *n* : ombligo *m*

belong [bɪ'lɔŋ] *vi* **1** : pertenecer (a), ser propiedad (de) ⟨it belongs to her : pertenece a ella, es suyo, es de ella⟩ **2** : ser parte (de), ser miembro (de) ⟨he belongs to the club : es miembro del club⟩ **3** : deber estar, ir ⟨your coat belongs in the closet : tu abrigo va en el ropero⟩

belongings [bɪ'lɔŋɪŋz] *npl* : pertenencias *fpl*, efectos *mpl* personales

beloved¹ [bɪ'lʌvəd, -'lʌvd] *adj* : querido, amado

beloved² *n* : amado *m*, -da *f*; enamorado *m*, -da *f*; amor *m*

below¹ [bɪ'lo:] *adv* **1** : abajo ⟨the floor below : el piso de abajo⟩ ⟨the pilot looked at the ground below : el piloto miraba el suelo allá abajo⟩ ⟨from below : desde abajo⟩ **2** : más abajo ⟨as stated below : como se indica más abajo⟩ **3** UNDER, LOWER : más bajo ⟨children age 10 and below : niños menores de los 11 años⟩ **4** : abajo (en un navío) **5** : bajo cero (dícese de temperaturas)

below² *prep* **1** : abajo de, debajo de ⟨below the window : debajo de la ventana⟩ **2** : por debajo de, bajo ⟨below average : por debajo del promedio⟩ ⟨5 degrees below zero : 5 grados bajo cero⟩

belt¹ ['bɛlt] *vt* **1** : ceñir con un cinturón, ponerle un cinturón a **2** THRASH : darle una paliza a, darle un trancazo a

belt² *n* **1** : cinturón *m*, cinto *m* (para el talle) **2** BAND, STRAP : cinta *f*, correa *f*, banda *f Mex* **3** AREA : frente *m*, zona *f*

beltway ['bɛltˌweɪ] *n* : carretera *f* de circunvalación; periférico *m CA, Mex*; libramiento *m Mex*

bemoan [bɪ'mo:n] *vt* : lamentarse de

bemuse [bɪ'mju:z] *vt* **-mused; -musing 1** BEWILDER : confundir, desconcertar **2** ENGROSS : absorber

bench ['bɛntʃ] *n* **1** SEAT : banco *m*, escaño *m*, banca *f* **2** : estrado *m* (de un juez) **3** COURT : tribunal *m* **4** : banca *f* (en deportes)

bend¹ ['bɛnd] *v* **bent** ['bɛnt]; **bending** *vt* : torcer, doblar, curvar, flexionar — *vi* **1** : torcerse, agacharse ⟨to bend over : inclinarse⟩ **2** TURN : torcer, hacer una curva **3 on bended knee** : de rodillas, de hinojos

bend² *n* **1** TURN : vuelta *f*, recodo *m* **2** CURVE : curva *f*, ángulo *m*, codo *m*

beneath¹ [bɪ'ni:θ] *adv* : bajo, abajo, debajo

beneath² *prep* : bajo de, abajo de, por debajo de

benediction [,bɛnə'dɪkʃən] *n* : bendición *f*

benefactor ['bɛnə,fæktər] *n* : benefactor *m*, -tora *f*

benefactress ['bɛnə,fæktrɪs] *n* : benefactora *f*

beneficial [,bɛnə'fɪʃəl] *adj* : beneficioso, provechoso — **beneficially** *adv*

beneficiary [,bɛnə'fɪʃi,ɛri, -'fɪʃəri] *n, pl* **-ries** : beneficiario *m*, -ria *f*

benefit¹ ['bɛnəfɪt] *vt* : beneficiar — *vi* : beneficiarse

benefit² *n* **1** ADVANTAGE : beneficio *m*, ventaja *f*, provecho *m* **2** AID : asistencia *f*, beneficio *m* **3** : función *f* benéfica (para recaudar fondos)

benevolence [bə'nɛvələnts] *n* : bondad *f*, benevolencia *f*

benevolent [bə'nɛvələnt] *adj* : benévolo, bondadoso — **benevolently** *adv*

benign [bɪ'naɪn] *adj* **1** GENTLE, KIND : benévolo, amable **2** FAVORABLE : propicio, favorable **3** MILD : benigno ⟨a benign tumor : un tumor benigno⟩

bent ['bɛnt] *n* : aptitud *f*, inclinación *f*

benumb [bɪ'nʌm] *vt* : entumecer

bequeath [bɪ'kwi:θ, -'kwi:ð] *vt* : legar, dejar en testamento

bequest [bɪ'kwɛst] *n* : legado *m*

berate [bɪ'reɪt] *vt* **-rated; -rating** : reprender, regañar

bereaved¹ [bɪ'ri:vd] *adj* : que está de luto, afligido (por la muerte de alguien)

bereaved² *n* **the bereaved** : los deudos del difunto (o de la difunta)

bereavement [bɪ'ri:vmənt] *n* **1** SORROW : dolor *m*, pesar *m* **2** LOSS : pérdida *f*

bereft [bɪ'rɛft] *adj* : privado, desprovisto

beret [bə'reɪ] *n* : boina *f*

berm ['bərm] *n* : arcén *m*

Bermuda shorts [bər'mju:də-] *npl* : bermudas *fpl*

berry ['bɛri] *n, pl* **-ries** : baya *f*

berserk [bər'sərk, -'zərk] *adj* **1** : enloquecido **2 to go beserk** : volverse loco

berth¹ ['bərθ] *vi* : atracar

berth² *n* **1** DOCK : atracadero *m* **2** ACCOMMODATION : litera *f*, camarote *m* **3** POSITION : trabajo *m*, puesto *m*

beseech [bɪ'si:tʃ] *vt* **-seeched** *or* **-sought** [-'sɔt]; **-seeching** : suplicar, implorar, rogar

beset [bɪ'sɛt] *vt* **-set; -setting 1** HARASS : acosar **2** SURROUND : rodear

beside [bɪ'saɪd] *prep* : al lado de, junto a ⟨the car beside mine : el coche al lado

del mío⟩ ⟨that's beside the point : eso no tiene nada que ver, eso no viene al caso⟩

besides¹ [bɪ'saɪdz] *adv* **1** ALSO : además, también, aparte **2** MOREOVER : además, por otra parte

besides² *prep* **1** : además de, aparte de ⟨six others besides you : seis otros además de ti⟩ **2** EXCEPT : excepto, fuera de, aparte de

besiege [bɪ'si:dʒ] *vt* **-sieged; -sieging** : asediar, sitiar, cercar

besmirch [bɪ'smərtʃ] *vt* : ensuciar, mancillar

besotted [bɪ'sɑtəd] *adj* : enamorado

best¹ ['bɛst] *vt* : superar, ganar a

best² *adv (superlative of* WELL*)* : mejor ⟨as best I can : lo mejor que puedo⟩

best³ *adj (superlative of* GOOD*)* : mejor ⟨my best friend : mi mejor amigo⟩

best⁴ *n* **1 the best** : lo mejor, el mejor, la mejor, los mejores, las mejores **2 at ~** : a lo más **3 to do one's best** : hacer todo lo posible **4 to make the best of** ⟨I'll just have to make the best of it : tendré que arreglármelas como pueda⟩

best–case *adj* **a/the best–case scenario** : el mejor de los casos

bestial ['bɛstʃəl, 'bi:s-] *adj* **1** : bestial **2** BRUTISH : brutal, salvaje

bestie ['bɛsti] *n fam* : mejor amigo *m*, mejor amiga *f*

best man *n* : padrino *m*

bestow [bɪ'sto:] *vt* : conferir, otorgar, conceder

bestowal [bɪ'sto:əl] *n* : concesión *f*, otorgamiento *m*

best seller *n* : best-seller *m*

bet¹ ['bɛt] *v* **bet; betting** *vt* : apostar — *vi* **1 to bet on** : apostar a **2 you bet!** : ¡ya lo creo!, ¡por supuesto!

bet² *n* : apuesta *f*

beta ['beɪtə] *n* : beta *f* (software)

betoken [bɪ'to:kən] *vt* : denotar, ser indicio de

betray [bɪ'treɪ] *vt* **1** : traicionar ⟨to betray one's country : traicionar uno a su patria⟩ **2** DIVULGE, REVEAL : delatar, revelar ⟨to betray a secret : revelar un secreto⟩

betrayal [bɪ'treɪəl] *n* : traición *f*, delación *f*, revelación *f* ⟨betrayal of trust : abuso de confianza⟩

betrothal [bɪ'tro:ðəl, -'trɔ-] *n* : esponsales *mpl*, compromiso *m*

betrothed [bɪ'tro:ðd, -'trɔθt] *n* FIANCÉ : prometido *m*, -da *f*

better¹ ['bɛtər] *vt* **1** IMPROVE : mejorar **2** SURPASS : superar

better² *adv (comparative of* WELL*)* **1** : mejor **2** MORE : más ⟨better than 50 miles : más de 50 millas⟩

better³ *adj (comparative of* GOOD*)* **1** : mejor ⟨the weather is better today : hace mejor tiempo hoy⟩ ⟨I was sick, but now I'm better : estuve enfermo, pero ahora estoy mejor⟩ **2** : mayor ⟨the better part of a month : la mayor parte de un mes⟩

better⁴ *n* **1** : el mejor, la mejor ⟨the better of the two : el mejor de los dos⟩ **2 to**

get the better of : vencer a, quedar por encima de, superar

betterment [ˈbɛt̬ərmənt] *n* : mejoramiento *m*, mejora *f*

better off *adj* (*comparative of* WELL OFF) **1** : mejor ⟨to be better off : salir ganando, venirle mejor a uno⟩ **2** WEALTHIER : más adinerado

betting [ˈbɛt̬ɪŋ] *n* : apuestas *fpl*

bettor *or* **better** [ˈbɛt̬ər] *n* : apostador *m*, -dora *f*

between[1] [bɪˈtwiːn] *adv* **1** : en medio, por lo medio **2 in ～** : intermedio

between[2] *prep* : entre ⟨between the chair and the wall : entre la silla y la pared⟩ ⟨between now and then : de aquí a entonces⟩ ⟨between nine and ten o'clock : entre las nueve y las diez⟩ ⟨between five and ten people : entre cinco y diez personas⟩ ⟨between you and me : entre nosotros⟩ ⟨they divided it between them : se lo dividieron entre ellos/sí⟩ ⟨the difference between the two brands : la diferencia entre las dos marcas⟩ ⟨to choose between two options : escoger entre dos opciones⟩

bevel[1] [ˈbɛvəl] *v* **-eled** *or* **-elled; -eling** *or* **-elling** *vt* : biselar — *vi* INCLINE : inclinarse

bevel[2] *n* : bisel *m*

beverage [ˈbɛvrɪdʒ, ˈbɛvə-] *n* : bebida *f*

bevy [ˈbɛvi] *n*, *pl* **bevies** : grupo *m* (de personas), bandada *f* (de pájaros)

bewail [bɪˈweɪl] *vt* : lamentarse de, llorar

beware [bɪˈwær] *vi* **to beware of** : tener cuidado con ⟨beware of the dog! : ¡cuidado con el perro!⟩ — *vt* : guardarse de, cuidarse de

bewilder [bɪˈwɪldər] *vt* : desconcertar, dejar perplejo

bewilderment [bɪˈwɪldərmənt] *n* : desconcierto *m*, perplejidad *f*

bewitch [bɪˈwɪtʃ] *vt* **1** : hechizar, embrujar **2** CHARM : cautivar, encantar

bewitchment [bɪˈwɪtʃmənt] *n* : hechizo *m*

beyond[1] [biˈjɑnd] *adv* **1** FARTHER, LATER : más allá, más lejos (en el espacio), más adelante (en el tiempo) **2** MORE : más ⟨$50 and beyond : $50 o más⟩

beyond[2] *n* **the beyond** : el más allá, lo desconocido

beyond[3] *prep* **1** : más allá de ⟨beyond the frontier : más allá de la frontera⟩ **2** : fuera de ⟨beyond one's reach : fuera de su alcance⟩ **3** BESIDES : además de

BFF [ˌbiːˌɛfˈɛf] *n* (Best Friends Forever) : amigo *m* íntimo, amiga *f* íntima

bi- *pref* : bi-

biannual [ˌbaɪˈænjʊəl] *adj* : bianual — **biannually** *adv*

bias[1] [ˈbaɪəs] *vt* **-ased** *or* **-assed; -asing** *or* **-assing** **1** : predisponer, sesgar, influir en, afectar **2 to be biased against** : tener prejuicio contra

bias[2] *n* **1** : sesgo *m*, bies *m* (en la costura) **2** PREJUDICE : prejuicio *m* **3** TENDENCY : inclinación *f*, tendencia *f*

biased [ˈbaɪəst] *adj* : tendencioso, parcial

bib [ˈbɪb] *n* **1** : peto *m* **2** : babero *m* (para niños)

Bible [ˈbaɪbəl] *n* : Biblia *f*

biblical [ˈbɪblɪkəl] *adj* : bíblico

bibliographer [ˌbɪbliˈɑɡrəfər] *n* : bibliógrafo *m*, -fa *f*

bibliography [ˌbɪbliˈɑɡrəfi] *n*, *pl* **-phies** : bibliografía *f* — **bibliographic** [ˌbɪbliəˈɡræfɪk] *adj*

bicameral [ˌbaɪˈkæmərəl] *adj* : bicameral

bicarbonate [ˌbaɪˈkɑrbənət, -ˌneɪt] *n* : bicarbonato *m*

bicentennial [ˌbaɪsɛnˈtɛniəl] *n* : bicentenario *m*

biceps [ˈbaɪˌsɛps] *ns & pl* : bíceps *m*

bicker[1] [ˈbɪkər] *vi* : pelear, discutir, reñir

bicker[2] *n* : pelea *f*, riña *f*, discusión *f*

bicuspid [baɪˈkʌspɪd] *n* : premolar *m*

bicycle[1] [ˈbaɪsɪkəl, -ˌsɪ-] *vi* **-cled; -cling** : ir en bicicleta

bicycle[2] *n* : bicicleta *f*

bicycling [ˈbaɪsɪkəlɪŋ] *n* : ciclismo *m*

bicyclist [ˈbaɪsɪkəlɪst] *n* : ciclista *mf*

bid[1] [ˈbɪd] *vt* **bade** [ˈbæd, ˈbeɪd] *or* **bid; bidden** [ˈbɪdən] *or* **bid; bidding** **1** ORDER : pedir, mandar **2** INVITE : invitar **3** SAY : dar, decir ⟨to bid good evening : dar las buenas noches⟩ ⟨to bid farewell to : decir adiós a⟩ **4** : ofrecer (en una subasta), declarar (en juegos de cartas)

bid[2] *n* **1** OFFER : oferta *f* (en una subasta), declaración *f* (en juegos de cartas) **2** INVITATION : invitación *f* **3** ATTEMPT : intento *m*, tentativa *f*

bidder [ˈbɪdər] *n* : postor *m*, -tora *f*

bide [ˈbaɪd] *v* **bode** [ˈboːd] *or* **bided; bided; biding** *vt* : esperar, aguardar ⟨to bide one's time : esperar el momento oportuno⟩ — *vi* DWELL : morar, vivir

bidet [bɪˈdeɪ] *n* : bidé *m*, bidet *m*

biennial [baɪˈɛniəl] *adj* : bienal — **biennially** *adv*

bier [ˈbɪr] *n* **1** STAND : andas *fpl* **2** COFFIN : ataúd *m*, féretro *m*

bifocals [ˈbaɪˌfoːkəlz] *npl* : lentes *mpl* bifocales, bifocales *mpl* — **bifocal** [ˈbaɪˌfoːkəl] *adj*

big [ˈbɪɡ] *adj* **bigger; biggest** **1** LARGE : grande ⟨a big guy : un tipo grande⟩ ⟨a great big house : una casa grandísima⟩ ⟨a big group : un grupo grande/numeroso⟩ ⟨big words : palabras difíciles⟩ **2** (indicating degree) : to be a big eater : ser un comelón⟩ ⟨to be a big believer in something : ser un gran partidario de algo⟩ **3** IMPORTANT, MAJOR : importante, grande ⟨a big decision : una gran decisión⟩ **4** POPULAR : popular, famoso, conocido ⟨the next big thing : el próximo exitazo⟩ **5** KIND : generoso ⟨it was very big of him : fue muy generoso de su parte⟩ **6 to be big on** : ser entusiasta de

bigamist [ˈbɪɡəmɪst] *n* : bígamo *m*, -ma *f*

bigamous [ˈbɪɡəməs] *adj* : bígamo

bigamy [ˈbɪɡəmi] *n* : bigamia *f*

Big Dipper → dipper

big-headed [ˈbɪɡˈhɛdəd] *adj fam* : creído

bighorn [ˈbɪɡˌhɔrn] *n*, *pl* **-horn** *or* **-horns** *or* **bighorn sheep** : oveja *f* salvaje de las montañas

bight ['baɪt] *n* : bahía *f*, ensenada *f*, golfo *m*

bigot ['bɪgət] *n* : intolerante *mf*

bigoted ['bɪgətəd] *adj* : intolerante, prejuiciado, fanático

bigotry ['bɪgətri] *n*, *pl* **-tries** : intolerancia *f*

big picture *n* **to look at the big picture** : ver las cosas desde una perspectiva global

big shot *n* : pez *m* gordo *fam*, mandamás *mf*

big toe *n* : dedo *m* gordo (del pie)

bigwig ['bɪg,wɪg] → **big shot**

bike ['baɪk] *n* **1** : bicicleta *f*, bici *f fam* **2** : motocicleta *f*, moto *f*

bike lane *or* **bicycle lane** *n* : carril *m* para bicicletas

bikini [bə'ki:ni] *n* : bikini *m*

bilateral [baɪ'læt̬ərəl] *adj* : bilateral — **bilaterally** *adv*

bile ['baɪl] *n* **1** : bilis *f* **2** IRRITABILITY : mal genio *m*

bilingual [baɪ'lɪŋgwəl] *adj* : bilingüe

bilk ['bɪlk] *vt* : burlar, estafar, defraudar

bill¹ ['bɪl] *vt* : pasarle la cuenta a — *vi* : acariciar ⟨to bill and coo : acariciarse⟩

bill² *n* **1** LAW : proyecto *m* de ley, ley *f* **2** INVOICE : cuenta *f*, factura *f* **3** POSTER : cartel *m* **4** PROGRAM : programa *m* (del teatro) **5** : billete *m* ⟨a five-dollar bill : un billete de cinco dólares⟩ **6** BEAK : pico *m*

billboard ['bɪl,bɔrd] *n* : cartelera *f*

billet¹ ['bɪlət] *vt* : acuartelar, alojar

billet² *n* : alojamiento *m*

billfold ['bɪl,fo:ld] *n* : billetera *f*, cartera *f*

billiard ['bɪljərd] *adj* : de billar ⟨billiard ball : bola de billar⟩

billiards ['bɪljərdz] *n* : billar *m*

billion ['bɪljən] *n*, *pl* **billions** *or* **billion** : mil millones *mpl*

billionth ['bɪljənθ] *n* : milmillonésimo *m* — **billionth** *adj*

billow¹ ['bɪlo] *vi* : hincharse, inflarse

billow² *n* **1** WAVE : ola *f* **2** CLOUD : nube *f* ⟨a billow of smoke : un nube de humo⟩

billowy ['bɪlowi] *adj* : ondulante

billy goat ['bɪli,go:t] *n* : macho *m* cabrío

bimonthly [baɪ'mʌnθli] *adj* **1** SEMIMONTHLY : bimensual, quincenal **2** : bimestral

bin ['bɪn] *n* : cubo *m*, cajón *m*

binary ['baɪnəri, -,nɛri] *adj* : binario *m*

binational [,baɪ'næʃənəl] *adj* : binacional

bind ['baɪnd] *vt* **bound** ['baʊnd]; **binding 1** TIE : atar, amarrar **2** OBLIGATE : obligar **3** UNITE : aglutinar, ligar, unir **4** BANDAGE : vendar **5** : encuadernar (un libro)

binder ['baɪndər] *n* **1** FOLDER : carpeta *f* **2** : encuadernador *m*, -dora *f* (de libros)

binding ['baɪndɪŋ] *n* **1** : encuadernación *f* (de libros) **2** COVER : cubierta *f*, forro *m*

binge ['bɪndʒ] *n* : juerga *f*, parranda *f fam*

bingo ['bɪŋ,go:] *n*, *pl* **-gos** : bingo *m*

binocular [baɪ'nɑkjələr, bə-] *adj* : binocular

binoculars [bə'nɑkjələrz, baɪ-] *npl* : binoculares *mpl*

bio- *pref* : bio- ⟨biochemistry : bioquímica⟩

biochemical¹ [,baɪo'kɛmɪkəl] *adj* : bioquímico

biochemical² *n* : bioquímico *m*

biochemist [,baɪo'kɛmɪst] *n* : bioquímico *m*, -ca *f*

biochemistry [,baɪo'kɛməstri] *n* : bioquímica *f*

biodegradable [,baɪodɪ'greɪdəbəl] *adj* : biodegradable

biodiversity [,baɪodə'vərsət̬i, -daɪ-] *n*, *pl* **-ties** : biodiversidad *f*

biographer [baɪ'ɑgrəfər] *n* : biógrafo *m*, -fa *f*

biographical [,baɪə'græfɪkəl] *adj* : biográfico

biography [baɪ'ɑgrəfi, bi:-] *n*, *pl* **-phies** : biografía *f*

biologic [,baɪə'lɑdʒɪk] *or* **biological** [-dʒɪkəl] *adj* : biológico

biological weapon *n* : arma *f* biológica

biologist [baɪ'ɑlədʒɪst] *n* : biólogo *m*, -ga *f*

biology [baɪ'ɑlədʒi] *n* : biología *f*

biopsy ['baɪ,ɑpsi] *n*, *pl* **-sies** : biopsia *f*

biosphere ['baɪə,sfɪr] *n* : biosfera *f*, biósfera *f*

biotechnology [,baɪotɛk'nɑlədʒi] *n* : biotecnología *f* — **biotechnological** [,baɪo,tɛknə'lɑdʒɪkəl] *adj*

bipartisan [baɪ'pɑrt̬əzən, -sən] *adj* : bipartidista, de dos partidas

biped ['baɪ,pɛd] *n* : bípedo *m*

birch ['bərtʃ] *n* : abedul *m*

bird ['bərd] *n* : pájaro *m* (pequeño), ave *f* (grande)

birdbath ['bərd,bæθ, -,bɑθ] *n* : pila *f* para pájaros

bird dog *n* : perro *m*, -rra *f* de caza

bird of prey *n* : ave *f* rapaz, ave *f* de presa

birdseed ['bərd,si:d] *n* : alpiste *m*

bird's-eye ['bərdz,aɪ] *adj* **1** : visto desde arriba ⟨bird's-eye view : vista aérea⟩ **2** CURSORY : rápido, somero

birdwatching ['bərd,wɑtʃɪŋ] *n* : observación *f* de aves

biretta [bə'rɛt̬ə] *n* : birrete *m*

birth ['bərθ] *n* **1** : nacimiento *m*, parto *m* **2** ORIGIN : origen *m*, nacimiento *m*

birth certificate *n* : partida *f* de nacimiento, acta *f* de nacimiento, certificado *m* de nacimiento

birth control *n* : control *m* de natalidad

birthday ['bərθ,deɪ] *n* : cumpleaños *m*, aniversario *m* ⟨birthday boy/girl : cumpleañero/cumpleañera⟩

birthmark ['bərθ,mɑrk] *n* : mancha *f* de nacimiento

birthplace ['bərθ,pleɪs] *n* : lugar *m* de nacimiento

birthrate ['bərθ,reɪt] *n* : índice *m* de natalidad

birthright ['bərθ,raɪt] *n* : derecho *m* de nacimiento

biscuit ['bɪskət] *n* : bizcocho *m*

bisect ['baɪ,sɛkt, ,baɪ'-] *vt* : bisecar

bisexual [,baɪ'sɛkʃʊəl] *adj* : bisexual — **bisexuality** [,baɪ,sɛkʃʊ'æləti] *n*

bishop [ˈbɪʃəp] *n* 1 : obispo *m* 2 : alfil *m* (en ajedrez)

bishopric [ˈbɪʃəprɪk] *n* : obispado *m*

bison [ˈbaɪzən, -sən] *ns & pl* : bisonte *m*

bistro [ˈbiːstro, ˈbɪs-] *n*, *pl* **-tros** : bar *m*, restaurante *m* pequeño

bit [ˈbɪt] *n* 1 FRAGMENT, PIECE : pedazo *m*, trozo *m* ⟨he smashed it to bits : lo hizo pedazos⟩ 2 : freno *m*, bocado *m* (de una brida) 3 : broca *f* (de un taladro) 4 : bit *m* (de información) 5 : rato *m*, momento *m* ⟨stay a bit (longer) : quédate un ratito⟩ 6 SKETCH : sketch *m* (en teatro, etc.) 7 **a bit** SOMEWHAT : un poco 8 **a bit of** : un poco de 9 **bit by bit** : poco a poco 10 **every bit as . . . as** : tan . . . como 11 **quite a bit** : bastante

bitch¹ [ˈbɪtʃ] *vi* COMPLAIN : quejarse, reclamar

bitch² *n* 1 : perra *f* 2 *fam offensive* : bruja *f*; cabrona *f Spain, Mex offensive* 3 *fam* : cosa *f* difícil ⟨the exam was a bitch : el examen fue dificilísimo⟩ ⟨life's a bitch : la vida es dura⟩

Bitcoin [ˈbɪt.kɔɪn] *n* : bitcoin *m*

bite¹ [ˈbaɪt] *v* **bit** [ˈbɪt]; **bitten** [ˈbɪtən]; **biting** *vt* 1 : morder 2 STING : picar 3 PUNCTURE : punzar, pinchar 4 GRIP : agarrar 5 **to bite one's tongue** : morderse la lengua 6 **to bite someone's head off** : explotar, perder los estribos (sin provocación) 7 **to bite the bullet** : hacer de tripas corazón 8 **to bite the dust** : morder el polvo (dícese de una persona), pasar a mejor vida (dícese de una cosa) — *vi* 1 : morder ⟨that dog bites : ese perro muerde⟩ 2 STING : picar (dícese de un insecto), cortar (dícese del viento) 3 : picar ⟨the fish are biting now : ya están picando los peces⟩ 4 GRAB : agarrarse

bite² *n* 1 BITING : mordisco *m*, dentellada *f* 2 SNACK : bocado *m* ⟨a bite to eat : algo de comer⟩ 3 : picadura *f* (de un insecto), mordedura *f* (de un animal) 4 SHARPNESS : mordacidad *f*, penetración *f*

biting [ˈbaɪtɪŋ] *adj* 1 PENETRATING : cortante, penetrante 2 CAUSTIC : mordaz, sarcástico

bit part *n* : papel *m* secundario

bitter [ˈbɪtər] *adj* 1 ACRID : amargo, acre 2 PENETRATING : cortante, penetrante ⟨bitter cold : frío glacial⟩ 3 HARSH : duro, amargo ⟨to the bitter end : hasta el final⟩ 4 INTENSE, RELENTLESS : intenso, extremo, implacable ⟨bitter hatred : odio implacable⟩

bitterly [ˈbɪtərli] *adv* : amargamente

bitterness [ˈbɪtərnəs] *n* : amargura *f*

bittersweet [ˈbɪtərˌswiːt] *adj* : agridulce

bizarre [bəˈzɑr] *adj* : extraño, singular, estrafalario, estrambótico — **bizarrely** *adv*

blab [ˈblæb] *vi* **blabbed**; **blabbing** : parlotear *fam*, cotorrear *fam*

blabbermouth [ˈblæbərˌmaʊθ] *n fam* : bocón *m*, -cona *f fam*

black¹ [ˈblæk] *vt* : ennegrecer

black² *adj* 1 : negro (color, raza) 2 SOILED : sucio 3 DARK : oscuro, negro 4 WICKED : malvado, perverso, malo 5 GLOOMY : negro, sombrío, deprimente

black³ *n* 1 : negro *m* (color) 2 : negro *m*, -gra *f* (persona)

black-and-blue [ˌblækənˈbluː] *adj* : amoratado

blackball [ˈblækˌbɔl] *vt* 1 OSTRACIZE : hacerle el vacío a, aislar 2 BOYCOTT : boicotear

blackberry [ˈblækˌbɛri] *n*, *pl* **-ries** : mora *f*

blackbird [ˈblækˌbərd] *n* : mirlo *m*

blackboard [ˈblækˌbɔrd] *n* : pizarra *f*, pizarrón *m*

black box *n* : caja *f* negra

blacken [ˈblækən] *vt* 1 BLACK : ennegrecer 2 DEFAME : deshonrar, difamar, manchar

black eye *n* : ojo *m* morado

blackhead [ˈblækˌhɛd] *n* : espinilla *f*, punto *m* negro

black hole *n* : agujero *m* negro

blackish [ˈblækɪʃ] *adj* : negruzco

blackjack [ˈblækˌdʒæk] *n* 1 : cachiporra *f* (arma) 2 : veintiuna *f* (juego de cartas)

blacklist¹ [ˈblækˌlɪst] *vt* : poner en la lista negra

blacklist² *n* : lista *f* negra

blackmail¹ [ˈblækˌmeɪl] *vt* : chantajear, hacer chantaje a

blackmail² *n* : chantaje *m*

blackmailer [ˈblækˌmeɪlər] *n* : chantajista *mf*

blackness [ˈblæknəs] *n* : negrura *f*

blackout [ˈblækˌaʊt] *n* 1 : apagón *m* (de poder eléctrico) 2 FAINT : desmayo *m*, desvanecimiento *m*

black out *vt* : dejar sin luz — *vi* FAINT : perder el conocimiento, desmayarse

black sheep *n* : oveja *f* negra

blacksmith [ˈblækˌsmɪθ] *n* : herrero *m*

blacktop [ˈblækˌtɑp] *n* : asfalto *m*

bladder [ˈblædər] *n* : vejiga *f*

blade [ˈbleɪd] *n* : hoja *f* (de un cuchillo), cuchilla *f* (de un patín), pala *f* (de un remo o una hélice), brizna *f* (de hierba)

blamable [ˈbleɪməbəl] *adj* : culpable

blame¹ [ˈbleɪm] *vt* **blamed**; **blaming** : culpar, echar la culpa a

blame² *n* : culpa *f*

blameless [ˈbleɪmləs] *adj* : intachable, sin culpa, inocente — **blamelessly** *adv*

blameworthiness [ˈbleɪmˌwərðinəs] *n* : culpa *f*, culpabilidad *f*

blameworthy [ˈbleɪmˌwərði] *adj* : culpable, reprochable, censurable

blanch [ˈblæntʃ] *vt* WHITEN : blanquear — *vi* PALE : palidecer

bland [ˈblænd] *adj* : soso, insulso, desabrido ⟨a bland smile : una sonrisa insulsa⟩ ⟨a bland diet : una dieta fácil de digerir⟩

blandishments [ˈblændɪʃmənts] *npl* : lisonjas *fpl*, halagos *mpl*

blandly [ˈblændli] *adv* : de manera insulsa

blandness [ˈblændnəs] *n* : lo insulso, lo desabrido

blank¹ [ˈblæŋk] *vt* OBLITERATE : borrar

blank² *adj* 1 DAZED : perplejo, desconcertado 2 EXPRESSIONLESS : sin expre-

sión, inexpresivo **3** : en blanco (dícese de un papel), liso (dícese de una pared) **4** EMPTY : vacío, en blanco ⟨a blank stare : una mirada vacía⟩ ⟨his mind went blank : se quedó en blanco⟩
blank³ *n* **1** SPACE : espacio *m* en blanco **2** FORM : formulario *m* **3** CARTRIDGE : cartucho *m* de fogueo **4** *or* **blank key** : llave *f* ciega
blank check *n* **1** : cheque *m* en blanco **2** CARTE BLANCHE : carta *f* blanca
blanket¹ [ˈblæŋkət] *vt* : cubrir
blanket² *adj* : global
blanket³ *n* : manta *f*, cobija *f*, frazada *f*
blankly [ˈblæŋkli] *adv* : sin comprender
blankness [ˈblæŋknəs] *n* **1** PERPLEXITY : desconcierto *m*, perplejidad *f* **2** EMPTINESS : vacío *m*, vacuidad *f*
blare¹ [ˈblær] *vi* **blared; blaring** : resonar
blare² *n* : estruendo *m*
blarney [ˈblɑrni] *n* : labia *f* *fam*
blasé [blɑˈzeɪ] *adj* : displicente, indiferente
blaspheme [blæsˈfiːm, ˈblæsˌ-] *vi* **-phemed; -pheming** : blasfemar
blasphemer [blæsˈfiːmər, ˈblæsˌ-] *n* : blasfemo *m*, -ma *f*
blasphemous [ˈblæsfəməs] *adj* : blasfemo
blasphemy [ˈblæsfəmi] *n*, *pl* **-mies** : blasfemia *f*
blast¹ [ˈblæst] *vt* **1** BLOW UP : volar, hacer volar **2** ATTACK : atacar, arremeter contra
blast² *n* **1** GUST : ráfaga *f* **2** EXPLOSION : explosión *f*
blast–off [ˈblæstˌɔf] *n* : despegue *m*
blast off *vi* : despegar
blatant [ˈbleɪtənt] *adj* : descarado — **blatantly** [ˈbleɪtəntli] *adv*
blaze¹ [ˈbleɪz] *v* **blazed; blazing** *vi* SHINE : arder, brillar, resplandecer — *vt* MARK : marcar, señalar ⟨to blaze a trail : abrir un camino⟩
blaze² *n* **1** FIRE : fuego *m* **2** BRIGHTNESS : resplandor *m*, brillantez *f* **3** OUTBURST : arranque *m* ⟨a blaze of anger : un arranque de cólera⟩ **4** DISPLAY : alarde *m*, llamarada *f* ⟨a blaze of color : un derroche de color⟩
blazer [ˈbleɪzər] *n* : chaqueta *f* deportiva, blazer *m*
bleach¹ [ˈbliːtʃ] *vt* : blanquear, decolorar
bleach² *n* : lejía *f*, blanqueador *m*
bleachers [ˈbliːtʃərz] *ns & pl* : gradas *fpl*, tribuna *f* descubierta
bleak [ˈbliːk] *adj* **1** DESOLATE : inhóspito, sombrío, desolado **2** DEPRESSING : deprimente, triste, sombrío
bleakly [ˈbliːkli] *adv* : sombríamente
bleakness [ˈbliːknəs] *n* : lo inhóspito, lo sombrío
blear [ˈblɪr] *adj* : empañado, nublado
bleary [ˈblɪri] *adj* **1** : adormilado, fatigado **2** **bleary–eyed** : con los ojos nublados
bleat¹ [ˈbliːt] *vi* : balar
bleat² *n* : balido *m*
bleed [ˈbliːd] *v* **bled** [ˈblɛd]; **bleeding** *vi* **1** : sangrar **2** GRIEVE : sufrir, afligirse **3** EXUDE : exudar (dícese de una planta),

correrse (dícese de los colores) — *vt* **1** : sangrar (a una persona), purgar (frenos) **2 to bleed someone dry** : sacarle todo el dinero a alguien
blemish¹ [ˈblɛmɪʃ] *vt* : manchar, marcar
blemish² *n* : imperfección *f*, mancha *f*, marca *f*
blend¹ [ˈblɛnd] *vt* **1** MIX : mezclar **2** COMBINE : combinar, aunar
blend² *n* : mezcla *f*, combinación *f*
blender [ˈblɛndər] *n* : licuadora *f*
bless [ˈblɛs] *vt* **blessed** [ˈblɛst]; **blessing 1** : bendecir ⟨God bless you! : ¡que Dios te bendiga!⟩ ⟨you did the dishes? bless you! : ¿lavaste los trastes? ¡mil gracias!⟩ ⟨he's a little forgetful, bless his heart : es un poco olvidadizo, el pobre⟩ **2 bless you!** (*said to someone who has sneezed*) : ¡salud! **3 to bless with** : dotar de **4 to bless oneself** : santiguarse
blessed [ˈblɛsəd] *or* **blest** [ˈblɛst] *adj* : bienaventurado, bendito, dichoso
blessedly [ˈblɛsədli] *adv* : felizmente, alegremente, afortunadamente
blessing [ˈblɛsɪŋ] *n* **1** : bendición *f* **2** APPROVAL : aprobación *f*, consentimiento *m*
blew → blow
blight¹ [ˈblaɪt] *vt* : arruinar, infestar
blight² *n* **1** : añublo *m* **2** PLAGUE : peste *f*, plaga *f* **3** DECAY : deterioro *m*, ruina *f*
blimp [ˈblɪmp] *n* : dirigible *m*
blind¹ [ˈblaɪnd] *vt* **1** : cegar, dejar ciego **2** DAZZLE : deslumbrar
blind² *adj* **1** SIGHTLESS : ciego ⟨to go blind : quedarse ciego⟩ **2** INSENSITIVE : ciego, insensible, sin razón **3** CLOSED : sin salida ⟨blind alley : callejón sin salida⟩
blind³ *n* **1** : persiana *f* (para una ventana) **2** COVER : escondite *m*, escondrijo *m*
blind carbon copy *n* : copia *f* oculta
blind date *n* : cita *f* a ciegas
blinders [ˈblaɪndərz] *npl* : anteojeras *fpl*
blindfold¹ [ˈblaɪndˌfoːld] *vt* : vendar los ojos
blindfold² *n* : venda *f* (para los ojos)
blinding [ˈblaɪndɪŋ] *adj* : enceguecedor, cegador ⟨with blinding speed : con una rapidez inusitada⟩
blindly [ˈblaɪndli] *adv* : a ciegas, ciegamente
blindness [ˈblaɪndnəs] *n* : ceguera *f*
blind spot *n* **1** : ángulo *m* muerto (de un vehículo) **2** WEAKNESS : punto *m* débil
blink¹ [ˈblɪŋk] *vi* **1** WINK : pestañear, parpadear **2** : brillar intermitentemente
blink² *n* : pestañeo *m*, parpadeo *m*
blinker [ˈblɪŋkər] *n* : intermitente *m*, direccional *f*
bliss [ˈblɪs] *n* **1** HAPPINESS : dicha *f*, felicidad *f* absoluta **2** PARADISE : paraíso *m*
blissful [ˈblɪsfəl] *adj* : dichoso, feliz — **blissfully** *adv*
blister¹ [ˈblɪstər] *n* : ampollarse
blister² *n* : ampolla *f* (en la piel o una superficie), burbuja *f* (en una superficie)
blithe [ˈblaɪθ, ˈblaɪð] *adj* **blither; blithest 1** CAREFREE : despreocu-

pado **2** CHEERFUL : alegre, risueño —
blithely *adv*
blitz¹ [ˈblɪts] *vt* **1** BOMBARD : bombardear **2** : atacar con rapidez
blitz² *n* **1** : bombardeo *m* aéreo **2** CAM-
PAIGN : ataque *m*, acometida *f*
blizzard [ˈblɪzərd] *n* : tormenta *f* de nieve,
ventisca *f*
bloat [ˈbloːt] *vi* : hincharse, inflarse
blob [ˈblɑb] *n* : gota *f*, mancha *f*, borrón *m*
bloc [ˈblɑk] *n* : bloque *m*
block¹ [ˈblɑk] *vt* **1** OBSTRUCT : bloquear
(una calle, una arteria, etc.) ⟨you're
blocking my light : me estás tapando la
luz⟩ **2** *or* **to block up** CLOG : obstruir,
atascar, atorar (una tubería, etc.) **3** IM-
PEDE : bloquear, impedir **4** : bloquear
(en deportes) **5 to block in** : cerrarle el
paso a (un vehículo) **6 to block off** BAR-
RICADE : cortar (una calle) **7 to block
out** : tapar (el sol, etc.) **8 to block out**
FORGET, IGNORE : borrar de la mente
block² *n* **1** PIECE : bloque *m* ⟨building
blocks : cubos de construcción⟩ ⟨auc-
tion block : plataforma de subastas⟩
⟨starting block : taco de salida⟩ **2** OBS-
TRUCTION : obstrucción *f*, bloqueo *m*
⟨mental block : bloqueo mental⟩ **3**
: cuadra *f*, manzana *f* (de edificios) ⟨to
go around the block : dar la vuelta a la
cuadra⟩ **4** BUILDING : edificio *m* (de
apartamentos, oficinas, etc.) **5** SERIES,
GROUP : serie *f*, grupo *m* ⟨a block of
tickets : una serie de entradas⟩ **6 block
and tackle** : aparejo *m* de poleas
blockade¹ [blɑˈkeɪd] *vt* -aded; -ading
: bloquear
blockade² *n* : bloqueo *m*
blockage [ˈblɑkɪdʒ] *n* : bloqueo *m*, obstrucción *f*
blockbuster [ˈblɑkˌbʌstər] *n* : gran éxito
m (de taquilla)
blockhead [ˈblɑkˌhɛd] *n* : bruto *m*, -ta *f*;
estúpido *m*, -da *f*
block letters *npl* : letras *fpl* de molde/im-
prenta (mayúsculas)
blog [ˈblɔg, ˈblɑg] *n* : blog *m*, bitácora *f*
blond¹ *or* **blonde** [ˈblɑnd] *adj* : rubio,
güero *Mex*, claro (dícese de la madera)
blond² *or* **blonde** *n* : rubio *m*, -bia *f*; güero
m, -ra *f Mex*
blood [ˈblʌd] *n* **1** : sangre *f* ⟨to draw blood
: sacar sangre⟩ **2** LIFEBLOOD : vida *f*,
alma *f* **3** LINEAGE : linaje *m*, sangre *f*
⟨blood relatives : parientes consanguí-
neos⟩ **4 in cold blood** : a sangre fría
blood bank *n* : banco *m* de sangre
bloodbath [ˈblʌdˌbæθ, -ˌbɑθ] *n* : masacre
f, baño *m* de sangre
bloodcurdling [ˈblʌdˌkərdəlɪŋ] *adj* : espeluznante, aterrador
blood donor *n* : donador *m*, -dora *f* de
sangre; donante *mf* de sangre
blooded [ˈblʌdəd] *adj* : de sangre ⟨cold-
blooded animal : animal de sangre fría⟩
blood group *n* : grupo *m* sanguíneo
bloodhound [ˈblʌdˌhaʊnd] *n* : sabueso *m*
bloodless [ˈblʌdləs] *adj* **1** : incruento,
sin derramamiento de sangre **2** LIFE-
LESS : desanimado, insípido, sin vida

bloodmobile [ˈblʌdmoˌbiːl] *n* : unidad *f*
móvil para donantes de sangre
blood pressure *n* : tensión *f*, presión *f* (arterial)
bloodshed [ˈblʌdˌʃɛd] *n* : derramamiento
m de sangre
bloodshot [ˈblʌdˌʃɑt] *adj* : inyectado de
sangre
bloodstain [ˈblʌdˌsteɪn] *n* : mancha *f* de
sangre
bloodstained [ˈblʌdˌsteɪnd] *adj* : manchado de sangre
bloodstream [ˈblʌdˌstriːm] *n* : torrente *m*
sanguíneo, corriente *f* sanguínea
bloodsucker [ˈblʌdˌsʌkər] *n* : sanguijuela *f*
blood test *n* : análisis *m* de sangre
bloodthirsty [ˈblʌdˌθərsti] *adj* : sanguinario
blood transfusion *n* : transfusión *f* de
sangre
blood vessel *n* : vaso *m* sanguíneo
bloody [ˈblʌdi] *adj* **bloodier; -est** : ensangrentado, sangriento
bloom¹ [ˈbluːm] *vi* **1** FLOWER : florecer **2** MATURE : madurar
bloom² *n* **1** FLOWER : flor *f* ⟨to be in
bloom : estar en flor⟩ **2** FLOWERING
: floración *f* ⟨in full bloom : en plena flo-
ración⟩ **3** : rubor *m* (de la tez) ⟨in the
bloom of youth : en plena juventud, en
la flor de la vida⟩
bloomers [ˈbluːmərz] *npl* : bombachos
mpl
blooper [ˈbluːpər] *n* : metedura *f* de pata
fam
blossom¹ [ˈblɑsəm] *vi* : florecer, dar flor
blossom² *n* : flor *f*
blot¹ [ˈblɑt] *vt* **blotted; blotting 1** SPOT
: emborronar, borronear **2** DRY : secar
blot² *n* **1** STAIN : mancha *f*, borrón *m* **2**
BLEMISH : mancha *f*, tacha *f*
blotch¹ [ˈblɑtʃ] *vt* : emborronar, borronear
blotch² *n* : mancha *f*, borrón *m*
blotchy [ˈblɑtʃi] *adj* **blotchier; -est** : lleno
de manchas
blotter [ˈblɑtər] *n* : hoja *f* de papel secante, secante *m*
blouse [ˈblaʊs, ˈblaʊz] *n* : blusa *f*
blow¹ [ˈbloː] *v* **blew** [ˈbluː]; **blown** [ˈbloːn];
blowing *vi* **1** : soplar (dícese del
viento) **2** : agitarse (etc.) con el viento
⟨to blow open/shut : abrirse/cerrarse⟩
⟨to blow off/away : volar⟩ **3** SOUND
: sonar (dícese de un silbato, etc.) **4 to
blow off** *fam* : dejar plantado (a alguien)
fam, no ir a (una cita, etc.) **5 to blow
out** : fundirse (dícese de un fusible eléctrico), reventarse (dícese de una
llanta) **6 to blow over** : pasar, dispersarse (dícese de una tormenta) **7 to
blow over** : pasar, calmarse, caer en el
olvido (dícese de una situación) — *vt* **1**
: soplar, echar ⟨to blow smoke : echar
humo⟩ **2** SOUND : tocar, sonar **3**
SHAPE : soplar, dar forma a (vidrio,
etc.) **4** BUNGLE : echar a perder **5 to
blow one's nose** : sonarse la nariz
blow² *n* **1** PUFF : soplo *m*, soplido *m* **2**
GALE : vendaval *f* **3** HIT, STROKE : golpe

m **4** CALAMITY : golpe *m*, desastre *m* **5**
to come to blows : llegar a las manos
blow–dry ['bloː,draɪ] *n, pl* **-dries** : secado
m (de pelo)
blower ['bloːər] *n* FAN : ventilador *m*
blowout ['bloː,aʊt] *n* : reventón *m*
blowtorch ['bloː,tɔrtʃ] *n* : soplete *m*
blow up *vi* EXPLODE : estallar, hacer explosión — *vt* BLAST : volar, hacer volar
blubber¹ ['blʌbər] *vi* : lloriquear
blubber² *n* : esperma *f* de ballena
bludgeon ['blʌdʒən] *vt* : aporrear
blue¹ ['bluː] *adj* **bluer; bluest** **1** : azul **2**
MELANCHOLY : melancólico, triste
blue² *n* : azul *m*
bluebell ['bluː,bɛl] *n* : campanilla *f*
blueberry ['bluː,bɛri] *n, pl* **-ries** : arándano
m
bluebird ['bluː,bərd] *n* : azulejo *m*
blue cheese *n* : queso *m* azul
blue–collar ['bluː'kalər] *adj* : obrero
blueprint ['bluː,prɪnt] *n* **1** : plano *m*,
proyecto *m*, cianotipo *m* **2** PLAN : anteproyecto *m*, programa *m*
blues ['bluːz] *npl* **1** DEPRESSION : depresión *f*, melancolía *f* **2** : blues *m* ⟨to sing the blues : cantar blues⟩
bluff¹ ['blʌf] *vi* : hacer un farol, blofear
Col, Mex
bluff² *adj* **1** STEEP : escarpado **2** FRANK
: campechano, franco, directo
bluff³ *n* **1** : farol *m*; blof *m Col, Mex* **2**
CLIFF : acantilado *m*, risco *m*
bluing ['bluːɪŋ] *or* **blueing** *n* : añil *m*, azulete *m*
bluish ['bluːɪʃ] *adj* : azulado
blunder¹ ['blʌndər] *vi* **1** STUMBLE : tropezar, dar traspiés **2** ERR : cometer un error, tropezar, meter la pata *fam*
blunder² *n* : error *m*, fallo *m* garrafal,
metedura *f* de pata *fam*
blunderbuss ['blʌndər,bʌs] *n* : trabuco *m*
blunt¹ ['blʌnt] *vt* **1** : despuntar (un lápiz,
etc.), desafilar (un cuchillo, etc.) **2** : embotar (la mente, etc.), suavizar (críticas)
blunt² *adj* **1** DULL : desafilado, despuntado **2** DIRECT : directo, franco, categórico
bluntly ['blʌntli] *adv* : sin rodeos, francamente, bruscamente
bluntness ['blʌntnəs] *n* **1** DULLNESS
: falta *f* de filo **2** FRANKNESS : franqueza *f*
blur¹ ['blər] *vt* **blurred; blurring** : desdibujar, hacer borroso
blur² *n* **1** SMEAR : mancha *f*, borrón *m* **2**
: aspecto *m* borroso ⟨everything was just
a blur : todo se volvió borroso⟩
blurb ['blərb] *n* : propaganda *f*, nota *f*
publicitaria
blurred ['blərd] *adj* : borroso
blurry ['bləri] *adj* : borroso
blurt ['blərt] *vt* : espetar, decir impulsivamente
blush¹ ['blʌʃ] *vi* : ruborizarse, sonrojarse,
hacerse colorado
blush² *n* : rubor *m*, sonrojo *m*
bluster¹ ['blʌstər] *vi* **1** BLOW : soplar con
fuerza **2** BOAST : fanfarronear, echar
bravatas

bluster² *n* : fanfarronada *f*, bravatas *fpl*
blustery ['blʌstəri] *adj* : borrascoso, tempestuoso
boa ['boːə] *n* : boa *f*
boar ['bor] *n* : cerdo *m* macho, verraco *m*
board¹ ['bord] *vt* **1** : embarcarse en, subir
a bordo de (una nave o un avión), subir
a (un tren o carro) **2** LODGE : hospedar,
dar hospedaje con comidas a **3 to
board up** : cerrar con tablas
board² *n* **1** PLANK : tabla *f*, tablón *m* **2**
: tablero *m* ⟨chessboard : tablero de ajedrez⟩ **3** → **cardboard** **4** → **bulletin
board** **5** → **blackboard** **6** → **surfboard** **7** MEALS : comida *f* ⟨board and
lodging : comida y alojamiento⟩ **8** COMMITTEE, COUNCIL : junta *f*, consejo *m* **9
across the board** : en general, para todos **10 on ~** → **aboard** **11 on ~** ⟨to
get someone on board : conseguir el
apoyo de alguien⟩ ⟨to be on board
: apoyar algo, apoyar a alguien⟩
boarder ['bordər] *n* LODGER : huésped *m*,
-peda *f*
board game *n* : juego *m* de mesa
boardinghouse ['bordɪŋ,haʊs] *n* : casa *f*
de huéspedes
boarding school *n* : internado *m*
boardroom ['bord,ruːm, -,rʊm] *n* : sala *f*
de juntas
boardwalk ['bord,wɔk] *n* : paseo *m* marítimo
boast¹ ['boːst] *vi* : alardear, presumir, jactarse
boast² *n* : jactancia *f*, alarde *m*
boaster ['boːstər] *n* : presumido *m*, -da *f*;
fanfarrón *m*, -rrona *f fam*
boastful ['boːstfəl] *adj* : jactancioso, fanfarrón *fam*
boastfully ['boːstfəli] *adv* : de manera jactanciosa
boastfulness ['boːstfəlnəs] *n* : jactancia *f*
boat¹ ['boːt] *vt* : transportar en barco,
poner a bordo
boat² *n* : barco *m*, embarcación *f*, bote *m*,
barca *f*
boatman ['boːtmən] *n, pl* **-men** [-mən,
-,mɛn] : barquero *m*
boat person *n* : balsero *m*, -ra *f*
boatwoman ['boːt,wʊmən] *n, pl* **-women**
[-,wɪmən] : barquera *f*
bob¹ ['bab] *v* **bobbed; bobbing** *vi* **1**
: balancearse, mecerse ⟨to bob up and
down : subir y bajar⟩ **2** *or* **to bob up**
APPEAR : presentarse, surgir — *vt* **1**
: inclinar (la cabeza o el cuerpo) **2** CUT
: cortar, recortar ⟨she bobbed her hair
: se cortó el pelo⟩
bob² *n* **1** : inclinación *f* (de la cabeza, del
cuerpo), sacudida *f* **2** FLOAT : flotador
m, corcho *m* (de pesca) **3** : pelo *m* corto
bobbin ['babən] *n* : bobina *f*, carrete *m*
(de una máquina de coser)
bobby pin ['babi,pɪn] *n* : horquilla *f*
bobcat ['bab,kæt] *n* : lince *m* rojo
bobolink ['babə,lɪŋk] *n* : tordo *m* arrocero
bobsled ['bab,slɛd] *n* : bobsleigh *m*
bobwhite ['bab'ʰwaɪt] *n* : codorniz *m* (del
Nuevo Mundo)

bode[1] ['bo:d] *v* **boded; boding** *vt* : presagiar, augurar — *vi* **to bode well** : ser de buen agüero

bode[2] → **bide**

bodice ['badəs] *n* : corpiño *m*

bodied ['badid] *adj* : de cuerpo ⟨leanbodied : de cuerpo delgado⟩ ⟨able-bodied : no discapacitado⟩

bodiless ['badiləs, 'badələs] *adj* : incorpóreo

bodily[1] ['badəli] *adv* : en peso ⟨to lift someone bodily : levantar a alguien en peso⟩

bodily[2] *adj* : corporal, del cuerpo ⟨bodily harm : daños corporales⟩

body ['badi] *n, pl* **bodies** 1 : cuerpo *m*, organismo *m* 2 CORPSE : cadáver *m* 3 PERSON : persona *f*, ser *m* humano 4 : nave *f* (de una iglesia), carrocería (de un automóvil), fuselaje *m* (de un avión), casco *m* (de una nave) 5 COLLECTION, MASS : conjunto *m*, grupo *m*, masa *f* ⟨in a body : todos juntos, en masa⟩ 6 ORGANIZATION : organismo *m*, organización *f*

bodybuilding ['badi,bɪldɪŋ] *n* : culturismo *m*

bodyguard ['badi,ɡard] *n* : guardaespaldas *mf*

bodywork ['badi,wərk] *n* : carrocería *f*

bog[1] ['baɡ, 'bɔɡ] *v* **bogged; bogging** *vt* **to bog down** SWAMP : empantanar, inundar ⟨to get bogged down : quedar empantanado⟩ 2 STALL : estancar, paralizar — *vi* **to bog down** 1 STICK : embarrancar, empantanarse 2 STALL : estancarse, empantanarse

bog[2] *n* : lodazal *m*, ciénaga *f*, cenagal *m*

bogey ['bʊɡi, 'bo:-] *n* 1 : bogey *m* (en golf) 2 → **bugaboo**

bogeyman ['bʊɡi,mæn, 'bo:-] *n, pl* **-men** [-mən] : coco *m fam*; cuco *m Arg, Chile, Peru, Uru fam* ⟨the bogeyman will get you! : ¡viene el coco!⟩ ⟨he's the bogeyman of conservatives : es el coco de los conservativos⟩

boggle ['baɡəl] *vi* **-gled; -gling** : quedarse atónito, quedarse pasmado ⟨the mind boggles! : ¡es increíble!⟩

boggy ['baɡi, 'bɔ-] *adj* **boggier; -est** : cenagoso

bogus ['bo:ɡəs] *adj* : falso, fingido, falaz

bohemian [bo:'hi:miən] *n* : bohemio *m*, -mia *f* — **bohemian** *adj*

boil[1] ['bɔɪl] *vi* 1 : hervir 2 **to boil down to** : reducirse a 3 **to make one's blood boil** : hervirle la sangre a uno — *vt* 1 : hervir, hacer hervir ⟨to boil water : hervir agua⟩ 2 : cocer, hervir ⟨to boil potatoes : cocer papas⟩ 3 **to boil something down to** : reducir algo a

boil[2] *n* 1 BOILING : hervor *m* 2 : forúnculo *m* (en medicina)

boiler ['bɔɪlər] *n* : caldera *f*

boiling ['bɔɪlɪŋ] *adj* 1 : hirviendo 2 HOT : caliente ⟨I'm boiling : me muero de calor⟩

boiling point *n* : punto *m* de ebullición

boisterous ['bɔɪstərəs] *adj* : bullicioso, escandaloso — **boisterously** *adv*

bold[1] ['bo:ld] *adj* 1 COURAGEOUS : valiente 2 INSOLENT : insolente, descarado 3 DARING : atrevido, audaz — **boldly** *adv*

bold[2] → **boldface**

boldface ['bo:ld,feɪs] *or* **boldface type** *n* : negrita *f*

boldness ['bo:ldnəs] *n* 1 COURAGE : valor *m*, coraje *m* 2 INSOLENCE : atrevimiento *m*, insolencia *f*, descaro *m* 3 DARING : audacia *f*

bolero [bə'lɛro] *n, pl* **-ros** : bolero *m*

bolivar [bə'li:,var, 'baləvər] *n* : bolívar *m* (unidad monetaria)

Bolivian [bə'lɪviən] *n* : boliviano *m*, -na *f* — **Bolivian** *adj*

boliviano [bə,lɪvi'ano] *n* : boliviano *m* (unidad monetaria)

boll ['bo:l] *n* : cápsula *f* (del algodón)

boll weevil *n* : gorgojo *m* del algodón

bologna [bə'lo:ni] *n* : salchicha *f* ahumada

Bolshevik ['bo:lʃə,vɪk, 'bɔl-] *n* : bolchevique *nmf* — **Bolshevik** *adj*

bolster[1] ['bo:lstər] *vt* **-stered; -stering** : reforzar, reafirmar ⟨to bolster morale : levantar la moral⟩

bolster[2] *n* : cabezal *m*, almohadón *m*

bolt[1] ['bo:lt] *vt* 1 : atornillar, sujetar con pernos ⟨bolted to the floor : sujetado con pernos al suelo⟩ 2 : cerrar con pestillo, echar el cerrojo a ⟨to bolt the door : echar el cerrojo a la puerta⟩ 3 **to bolt down** : engullir ⟨she bolted down her dinner : engulló su comida⟩ — *vi* : echar a correr, salir corriendo ⟨he bolted from the room : salió corriendo de la sala⟩

bolt[2] *n* 1 LATCH : pestillo *m*, cerrojo *m* 2 : tornillo *m*, perno *m* ⟨nuts and bolts : tuercas y tornillos⟩ 3 : rollo *m* ⟨a bolt of cloth : un rollo de tela⟩ 4 **lightning bolt** : relámpago *m*, rayo *m*

bomb[1] ['bam] *vt* : bombardear

bomb[2] *n* 1 : bomba *f* 2 FAILURE : desastre *m*

bombard [bam'bard, bəm-] *vt* : bombardear

bombardment [bam'bardmənt] *n* : bombardeo *m*

bombast ['bam,bæst] *n* : grandilocuencia *f*, ampulosidad *f*

bombastic [bam'bæstɪk] *adj* : grandilocuente, ampuloso, bombástico

bomber ['bamər] *n* : bombardero *m*

bombing ['bamɪŋ] *n* : bombardeo *m*

bombproof ['bam,pru:f] *adj* : a prueba de bombas

bombshell ['bam,ʃɛl] *n* : bomba *f* ⟨a political bombshell : una bomba política⟩

bona fide ['bo:nə,faɪd, 'ba-:, ,bo:nə'faɪdi] *adj* 1 : de buena fe ⟨a bona fide offer : una oferta de buena fe⟩ 2 GENUINE : genuino, auténtico

bonanza [bə'nænzə] *n* : bonanza *f*

bon appétit ['bo:nəpə'ti:] *interj* : ¡buen provecho!

bonbon ['ban,ban] *n* : bombón *m*

bond[1] ['band] *vt* 1 INSURE : dar fianza a, asegurar 2 STICK : adherir, pegar — *vi* : adherirse, pegarse

bond[2] *n* 1 LINK, TIE : vínculo *m*, lazo *m* 2 BAIL : fianza *f*, caución *f* 3 : bono

m ⟨stocks and bonds : acciones y bonos⟩ **4 bonds** *npl* FETTERS : cadenas *fpl*
bondage [ˈbɑndɪd] *n* : esclavitud *f*
bondholder [ˈbɑndˌhoːldər] *n* : tenedor *m*, -dora *f* de bonos
bondsman [ˈbɑndzmən] *n, pl* **-men** [-mən, -ˌmn] **1** SLAVE : esclavo *m* **2** SURETY : fiador *m*, -dora *f*
bone[1] [ˈboːn] *vt* **boned; boning 1** : deshuesar **2 to bone up on** *fam* : estudiar
bone[2] *n* **1** : hueso *m* **2 to feel it in one's bones** : tener un presentimiento **3 to have a bone to pick with someone** : tener que arreglar cuentas con alguien **4 to the bone** : muchísimo ⟨it chilled me to the bone : se me heló la sangre⟩ **5 to throw someone a bone** : hacerle una pequeña concesión a alguien
boneless [ˈboːnləs] *adj* : sin huesos, sin espinas
boner [ˈboːnər] *n* : metedura *f* de pata, metida *f* de pata
bonfire [ˈbɑnˌfaɪr] *n* : hoguera *f*, fogata *f*, fogón *m*
bongo [ˈbɑŋGo, ˈbɔŋ-] *n* : bongó *m*, bongo *m*
bonito [bəˈniːꞯo] *n, pl* **-tos** *or* **-to** : bonito *m*
bonnet [ˈbɑnət] *n* : sombrero *m* (de mujer), gorra *f* (de niño)
bonus [ˈboːnəs] *n* **1** : prima *f*, bonificación *f* (pagado al empleado) **2** ADVANTAGE, BENEFIT : beneficio *m*, provecho *m*
bony [ˈboːni] *adj* **bonier, -est** : huesudo
boo[1] [ˈbuː] *vt* : abuchear
boo[2] *n, pl* **boos** : abucheo *m*
booby [ˈbuːbi] *n, pl* **-bies** FOOL : bobo *m*, -ba *f*; tonto *m*, -ta *f*
boogeyman [ˈbuGiˌmæn] *n, pl* **-men** [-mən, -ˌmen] → **bogeyman**
book[1] [ˈbʊk] *vt* : reservar ⟨to book a flight : reservar un vuelo⟩ — *vi* : hacer una reservación
book[2] *n* **1** : libro *m* **2 the Book** : la Biblia **3 by the book** : según las reglas
bookcase [ˈbʊkˌkeɪs] *n* **1** : estantería *f*, librero *m Mex*, biblioteca *f*
bookend [ˈbʊkˌɛnd] *n* : sujetalibros *m*
bookie [ˈbʊki] → **bookmaker**
bookish [ˈbʊkɪʃ] *adj* : libresco
bookkeeper [ˈbʊkˌkiːpər] *n* : tenedor *m*, -dora *f* de libros; contable *mf Spain*
bookkeeping [ˈbʊkˌkiːpɪŋ] *n* : contabilidad *f*, teneduría *f* de libros
booklet [ˈbʊklət] *n* : folleto *m*
bookmaker [ˈbʊkˌmeɪkər] *n* : corredor *m*, -dora *f* de apuestas
bookmark[1] [ˈbʊkˌmɑrk] *n* **1** : señalador *m* de libros, marcador *m* de libros **2** : marcador *m* (de Internet)
bookmark[2] *vt* : marcar (una página web)
bookseller [ˈbʊkˌslər] *n* : librero *m*, -ra *f*
bookshelf [ˈbʊkˌʃelf] *n, pl* **-shelves 1** : estante *m* **2 bookshelves** *npl* : estantería *f*
bookstore [ˈbʊkˌstor] *n* : librería *f*
bookworm [ˈbʊkˌwɔrm] *n* : ratón *m* de biblioteca *fam*

boom[1] [ˈbuːm] *vi* **1** THUNDER : tronar, resonar **2** FLOURISH, PROSPER : estar en auge, prosperar
boom[2] *n* **1** BOOMING : bramido *m*, estruendo *m* **2** FLOURISHING : auge *m* ⟨population boom : auge de población⟩
boomerang [ˈbuːməˌræŋ] *n* : bumerán *m*
boon[1] [ˈbuːn] *adj* **boon companion** : amigo *m*, -ga *f* del alma
boon[2] *n* : ayuda *f*, beneficio *m*, adelanto *m*
boondocks [ˈbuːnˌdɑks] *npl* : área *f* rural remota, región *f* alejada
boor [ˈbʊr] *n* : grosero *m*, -ra *f*
boorish [ˈbʊrɪʃ] *adj* : grosero
boost[1] [ˈbuːst] *vt* **1** LIFT : levantar, alzar **2** INCREASE : aumentar, incrementar **3** PROMOTE : promover, fomentar, hacer publicidad por
boost[2] *n* **1** THRUST : impulso *m*, empujón *m* **2** ENCOURAGEMENT : estímulo *m*, aliento *m* **3** INCREASE : aumento *m*, incremento *m*
booster [ˈbuːstər] *n* **1** SUPPORTER : partidario *m*, -ria *f* **2 booster rocket** : cohete *m* propulsor **3 booster shot** : vacuna *f* de refuerzo
boot[1] [ˈbuːt] *vt* KICK : dar una patada a, patear
boot[2] *n* **1** : bota *f*, botín *m* **2** KICK : puntapié *m*, patada *f*
bootee *or* **bootie** [ˈbuːꞯi] *n* : botita *f*, botín *m*
booth [ˈbuːθ] *n, pl* **booths** [ˈbuːðz, ˈbuːθs] : cabina *f* (de teléfono, de votar), caseta *f* (de información), barraca *f* (a una feria)
bootleg[1] [ˈbuːtˌlɛG] *adj* : pirata ⟨bootleg software : software pirata⟩
bootleg[2] *vt* : piratear (un video, etc.)
bootlegger [ˈbuːtˌlɛGər] *n* : contrabandista *mf* del alcohol
bootlegging [ˈbuːtˌlɛGɪŋ] *n* : piratería *f*
booty [ˈbuːꞯi] *n, pl* **-ties** : botín *m*
booze [ˈbuːz] *n fam* : alcohol *m*
border[1] [ˈbɔrdər] *vt* **1** EDGE : ribetear, bordear **2** BOUND : limitar con, lindar con — *vi* VERGE : rayar, lindar ⟨that borders on absurdity : eso raya en el absurdo⟩
border[2] *n* **1** EDGE : borde *m*, orilla *f* **2** TRIM : ribete *m* **3** FRONTIER : frontera *f*
borderline[1] [ˈbɔrdərˌlaɪn] *adj* : dudoso
borderline[2] *n* : límite *m*
bore[1] [ˈbor] *vt* **bored; boring 1** PIERCE : taladrar, perforar ⟨to bore metals : taladrar metales⟩ **2** OPEN : hacer, abrir ⟨to bore a tunnel : abrir un túnel⟩ **3** WEARY : aburrir
bore[2] → **bear**[1]
bore[3] *n* **1** : pesado *m*, -da *f* (persona aburrida) **2** TEDIOUSNESS : pesadez *f*, lo aburrido **3** DIAMETER : calibre *m*
bored [ˈbord] *adj* : aburrido ⟨to be bored stiff, to be bored to tears/death : aburrirse como una ostra⟩
boredom [ˈbordəm] *n* : aburrimiento *m*
boring [ˈborɪŋ] *adj* : aburrido, pesado
born [ˈbɔrn] *adj* **1** : nacido **2** : nato ⟨she's a born singer : es una cantante nata⟩ ⟨he's a born leader : nació para mandar⟩

borne *pp* → **bear**[1]
borough [ˈbəro] *n* : distrito *m* municipal
borrow [ˈbɑro] *vt* **1** : pedir prestado, tomar prestado **2** APPROPRIATE : apropiarse de, adoptar
borrower [ˈbɑrəwər] *n* : prestatario *m*, -ria *f*
borrowing [ˈbɑrəwɪŋ] *n* : préstamo *m* (en lingüística)
Bosnian [ˈbɑzniən, ˈbɔz-] *n* : bosnio *m*, -nia *f* — **Bosnian** *adj*
bosom[1] [ˈbʊzəm, ˈbu:-] *adj* : íntimo
bosom[2] *n* **1** CHEST : pecho *m* **2** BREAST : pecho *m*, seno *m* **3** CLOSENESS : seno *m* ⟨in the bosom of her family : en el seno de su familia⟩
bosomed [ˈbʊzəmd, ˈbu:-] *adj* : con busto ⟨big-bosomed : con mucho busto⟩
boss[1] [ˈbɔs] *vt* **1** SUPERVISE : dirigir, supervisar **2 to boss around** : mandonear *fam*, mangonear *fam*
boss[2] *n* : jefe *m*, -fa *f*; patrón *m*, -trona *f*
bossy [ˈbɔsi] *adj* **bossier; -est** : mandón *fam*, autoritario, dominante
bot [ˈbɑt] *n* : bot *m*
botanist [ˈbɑtənɪst] *n* : botánico *m*, -ca *f*
botany [ˈbɑtəni] *n* : botánica *f* — **botanical** [bəˈtænɪkəl] *adj*
botch[1] [ˈbɑtʃ] *vt* : hacer una chapuza de, estropear
botch[2] *n* : chapuza *f*
both[1] [ˈbo:θ] *adj* : ambos, ambas; los dos, las dos ⟨both classes : ambas clases, las dos clases⟩
both[2] *conj* : tanto como ⟨both Ann and her mother are tall : tanto Ana como su madre son altas⟩
both[3] *pron* : ambos ambas; los dos, las dos ⟨both of the women laughed : ambas mujeres rieron, las dos mujeres rieron⟩ ⟨we both went : fuimos los dos⟩ ⟨he knows both of my sisters : conoce a mis dos hermanas⟩
bother[1] [ˈbɑðər] *vt* **1** IRK : preocupar ⟨nothing's bothering me : nada me preocupa⟩ ⟨what's bothering him? : ¿qué le pasa?⟩ **2** PESTER : molestar, fastidiar — *vi* **to bother to** : molestarse en, tomar la molestia de
bother[2] *n* **1** TROUBLE : molestia *f*, problemas *mpl* **2** ANNOYANCE : molestia *f*, fastidio *m*
bothersome [ˈbɑðərsəm] *adj* : molesto, fastidioso
bottle[1] [ˈbɑtəl] *vt* **bottled; bottling** : embotellar, envasar
bottle[2] *n* : botella *f*, frasco *m*
bottleneck [ˈbɑtəlˌnɛk] *n* **1** : cuello *m* de botella (en un camino) **2** : embotellamiento *m*, atasco *m* (de tráfico) **3** OBSTACLE : obstáculo *m*
bottle opener *n* : abrebotellas *m*
bottom[1] [ˈbɑtəm] *adj* : más bajo, inferior, de abajo
bottom[2] *n* **1** : fondo *m* (de una caja, de una taza, del mar), pie *m* (de una escalera, una página, una montaña), asiento *m* (de una silla), parte *f* de abajo (de una pila) **2** CAUSE : origen *m*, causa *f* ⟨to get to the bottom of : llegar al fondo de⟩ **3** BUTTOCKS : trasero *m*, nalgas *fpl*
bottomless [ˈbɑtəmləs] *adj* : sin fondo, sin límites
bottom line *n* **1** : balance *m* final (en contabilidad) **2 the bottom line** : lo esencial, lo más importante **3 the bottom line** : el resultado final
botulism [ˈbɑtʃəˌlɪzəm] *n* : botulismo *m*
boudoir [bəˈdwɑr, bʊ-;, ˈbu:ˌ-, ˈbʊ-] *n* : tocador *m*
bough [ˈbaʊ] *n* : rama *f*
bought → **buy**[1]
bouillon [ˈbu:ˌjɑn;, ˈbʊlˌjɑn, -jən] *n* : caldo *m*
boulder [ˈbo:ldər] *n* : canto *m* rodado, roca *f* grande
boulevard [ˈbʊləˌvɑrd, ˈbu:-] *n* : bulevar *m*, boulevard *m*
bounce[1] [ˈbaʊnts] *v* **bounced; bouncing** *vt* **1** : hacer rebotar **2 to bounce a check** : emitir un cheque sin fondos — *vi* **1** : rebotar **2** : ser devuelto (dícese de un cheque)
bounce[2] *n* : rebote *m*
bouncer [ˈbaʊntsər] *n* : portero *m*; patovica *m Arg, Uru fam*; gorila *m Spain fam*
bouncy [ˈbaʊntsi] *adj* **bouncier; -est 1** LIVELY : vivo, exuberante, animado **2** RESILIENT : elástico, flexible **3** : que rebota (dícese de una pelota)
bound[1] [ˈbaʊnd] *vt* : delimitar, rodear — *vi* LEAP : saltar, dar brincos
bound[2] *adj* **1** OBLIGED : obligado **2** : encuadernado, empastado ⟨a book bound in leather : un libro encuadernado en cuero⟩ **3** DETERMINED : decidido, empeñado **4 to be bound to** : ser seguro que, tener que, no caber duda que ⟨it was bound to happen : tenía que suceder⟩ **5 bound for** : con rumbo a ⟨bound for Chicago : con rumbo a Chicago⟩ ⟨to be homeward bound : ir camino a casa⟩
bound[3] *n* **1** LIMIT : límite *m* **2** LEAP : salto *m*, brinco *m*
boundary [ˈbaʊndri, -dəri] *n, pl* **-aries** : límite *m*, línea *f* divisoria, linde *mf*
boundless [ˈbaʊndləs] *adj* : sin límites, infinito
bounteous [ˈbaʊntiəs] *adj* **1** GENEROUS : generoso **2** ABUNDANT : copioso, abundante — **bounteously** *adv*
bountiful [ˈbaʊntɪfəl] *adj* **1** GENEROUS, LIBERAL : pródigo, generoso **2** ABUNDANT : copioso, abundante
bounty [ˈbaʊnti] *n, pl* **-ties 1** GENEROSITY : generosidad *f* **2** REWARD : recompensa *f*
bouquet [bo:ˈkeɪ, bu:-] *n* **1** : ramo *m*, ramillete *m* **2** FRAGRANCE : bouquet *m*, aroma *m*
bourbon [ˈbərbən, ˈbʊr-] *n* : bourbon *m*, whisky *m* americano
bourgeois[1] [ˈbʊrʒˌwɑ, bʊrʒˈwɑ] *adj* : burgués
bourgeois[2] *n* : burgués *m*, -guesa *f*
bourgeoisie [ˌbʊrʒˌwɑˈzi] *n* : burguesía *f*
bout [ˈbaʊt] *n* **1** : encuentro *m*, combate *m* (en deportes) **2** ATTACK : ataque *m* (de una enfermedad) **3** PERIOD, SPELL : período *m* (de actividad)

boutique [bu:'ti:k] *n* : boutique *f*

bovine[1] ['bo:ˌvaɪn, -ˌvi:n] *adj* : bovino, vacuno

bovine[2] *n* : bovino *m*

bow[1] ['baʊ] *vi* **1** : hacer una reverencia, inclinarse **2** SUBMIT : ceder, resignarse, someterse — *vt* **1** LOWER : inclinar, bajar **2** BEND : doblar

bow[2] ['baʊ] *n* **1** BOWING : reverencia *f*, inclinación *f* **2** : proa *f* (de un barco)

bow[3] ['bo:] *vi* CURVE : arquearse, doblarse

bow[4] ['bo:] *n* **1** ARCH, CURVE : arco *m*, curva *f* **2** : arco *m* (arma o vara para tocar varios instrumentos de música) **3** : lazo *m*, moño *m* ⟨to tie a bow : hacer un moño⟩

bowel ['baʊəl] *n* **1** INTESTINE : intestino *m* ⟨to move one's bowels, to have a bowel movement : evacuar (el vientre)⟩ **2 the bowels** : las entrañas ⟨in the bowels of the earth : en las entrañas de la tierra⟩

bower ['baʊər] *n* : enramada *f*

bowl[1] ['bo:l] *vi* : jugar a los bolos

bowl[2] *n* : tazón *m*, cuenco *m*, bol *m* ⟨salad bowl : ensaladera⟩

bowler ['bo:lər] *n* : jugador *m*, -dora *f* de bolos

bowling ['bo:lɪŋ] *n* : bolos *mpl*

bowling alley *n* : bolera *f*, boliche *m*

bowling pin *n* : bolo *m*

bow tie *n* : corbata *f* de moño, pajarita *f* *Spain*

box[1] ['bɑks] *vt* **1** PACK : empaquetar, embalar, encajonar **2** SLAP : bofetear, cachetear — *vi* : boxear

box[2] *n* **1** CONTAINER : caja *f*, cajón *m* **2** COMPARTMENT : compartimiento *m*, palco *m* (en el teatro) **3** SLAP : bofetada *f*, cachetada *f*

boxcar ['bɑksˌkɑr] *n* : vagón *m* de carga, furgón *m*

boxer ['bɑksər] *n* **1** : boxeador *m*, -dora *f* **2 boxers** *pl* → **boxer shorts**

boxer shorts *n* : boxers *mpl*, calzoncillos *mpl*, calzones *mpl*

boxing ['bɑksɪŋ] *n* : boxeo *m*

box-office ['bɑks'ɔfəs] *adj* : taquillero

box office *n* : taquilla *f*, boletería *f*

box spring *n* : somier *m*

boy ['bɔɪ] *n* **1** : chico *m*, muchacho *m* **2** *or* **little boy** : niño *m*, chico *m* **3** SON : hijo *m*

boycott[1] ['bɔɪˌkɑt] *vt* : boicotear

boycott[2] *n* : boicot *m*

boyfriend ['bɔɪˌfrɛnd] *n* **1** FRIEND : amigo *m* **2** SWEETHEART : novio *m*

boyhood ['bɔɪˌhʊd] *n* : niñez *f*

boyish ['bɔɪɪʃ] *adj* : de niño, juvenil

bra ['brɑ] → **brassiere**

brace[1] ['breɪs] *v* **braced; bracing** *vt* **1** PROP UP, SUPPORT : apuntalar, apoyar, sostener **2** INVIGORATE : vigorizar **3** REINFORCE : reforzar — *vi* **to brace oneself** PREPARE : prepararse

brace[2] *n* **1** CLAMP, REINFORCEMENT : abrazadera *f*, refuerzo *m* **2** → **curly brace 3 braces** *npl* : aparatos *mpl* (de ortodoncia), frenos *mpl* *Mex*

bracelet ['breɪslət] *n* : brazalete *m*, pulsera *f*

bracken ['brækən] *n* : helecho *m*

bracket[1] ['brækət] *vt* **1** SUPPORT : asegurar, apuntalar **2** : poner entre corchetes **3** CATEGORIZE, GROUP : catalogar, agrupar

bracket[2] *n* **1** SUPPORT : soporte *m* **2** : corchete *m* (marca de puntuación) **3** CATEGORY, CLASS : clase *f*, categoría *f*

brackish ['brækɪʃ] *adj* : salobre

brad ['bræd] *n* : clavo *m* con cabeza pequeña, clavito *m*

brag[1] ['bræɡ] *vi* **bragged; bragging** : alardear, fanfarronear, jactarse

brag[2] *n* : alarde *m*, jactancia *f*, fanfarronada *f*

braggart ['bræɡərt] *n* : fanfarrón *m*, -rrona *f fam*; jactancioso *m*, -sa *f*

braid[1] ['breɪd] *vt* : trenzar

braid[2] *n* : trenza *f*

braille ['breɪl] *n* : braille *m*

brain[1] ['breɪn] *vt* : romper la crisma a, aplastar el cráneo a

brain[2] *n* **1** : cerebro *m* **2 brains** *npl* INTELLECT : inteligencia *f*, sesos *mpl*

brainchild ['breɪnˌtʃaɪld] *n* IDEA : creación *f*, invento *m*

brainless ['breɪnləs] *adj* : estúpido, tonto

brainstorm ['breɪnˌstɔrm] *n* : idea *f* brillante, idea *f* genial

brainy ['breɪni] *adj* **brainier; -est** : inteligente, listo

braise ['breɪz] *vt* **braised; braising** : cocer a fuego lento, estofar

brake[1] ['breɪk] *v* **braked; braking** : frenar

brake[2] *n* : freno *m*

bramble ['bræmbəl] *n* : zarza *f*, zarzamora *f*

bran ['bræn] *n* : salvado *m*

branch[1] ['bræntʃ] *vi* **1** : echar ramas (dícese de una planta) **2** *or* **to branch off** DIVERGE : ramificarse, separarse **3 to branch out** : diversificarse

branch[2] *n* **1** : rama *f* (de una planta) **2** EXTENSION : ramal *m* (de un camino, un ferrocarril, un río), brazo (de un río), rama *f* (de una familia o un campo de estudio), sucursal *f* (de una empresa), agencia *f* (del gobierno)

brand[1] ['brænd] *vt* **1** : marcar (ganado) **2** LABEL : tachar, tildar ⟨they branded him as a liar : lo tacharon de mentiroso⟩

brand[2] *n* **1** : marca *f* (de ganado) **2** STIGMA : estigma *m* **3** MAKE : marca *f*

brandish ['brændɪʃ] *vt* : blandir

brand-name ['brænd'neɪm] *adj* : de marca

brand name *n* : marca *f*

brand-new ['brænd'nu:, -'nju:] *adj* : nuevo, flamante

brandy ['brændi] *n, pl* **-dies** : brandy *m*

brash ['bræʃ] *adj* **1** IMPULSIVE : impulsivo, impetuoso **2** BRAZEN : excesivamente desenvuelto, descarado

brass ['bræs] *n* **1** : latón *m* **2** GALL, NERVE : descaro *m*, *f fam* **3** OFFICERS : mandamás *mpl fam* **4** : metal *m*, metales *mpl* (de una orquesta) : banda *f* de metales

brass band ['brɑ-] *n* : sostén *m*, **brassiere** *Col, Mex*

brassy ['bræsi] *adj* **brassier; -est** : dorado

brat ['bræt] *n disparaging* : mocoso *m*, -sa *f disparaging*; niño *m* mimado, niña *f* mimada

bravado [brə'vɑdo] *n, pl* **-does** *or* **-dos** : bravuconadas *fpl*, bravatas *fpl*

brave[1] ['breɪv] *vt* **braved; braving** : afrontar, hacer frente a

brave[2] *adj* **braver; bravest** : valiente, valeroso — **bravely** *adv*

brave[3] *n* : guerrero *m* (nativo americano)

bravery ['breɪvəri] *n* : valor *m*, valentía *f*

bravo ['brɑˌvoː] *n, pl* **-vos** : bravo *m*

brawl[1] ['brɔl] *vi* : pelearse, pegarse

brawl[2] *n* : pelea *f*, reyerta *f*

brawn ['brɔn] *n* : fuerza *f* muscular

brawny ['brɔni] *adj* **brawnier; -est** : musculoso

bray[1] ['breɪ] *vi* : rebuznar

bray[2] *n* : rebuzno *m*

brazen ['breɪzən] *adj* **1** : de latón **2** BOLD : descarado, directo

brazenly ['breɪzənli] *adv* : descaradamente, insolentemente

brazenness ['breɪzənnəs] *n* : descaro *m*, atrevimiento *m*

brazier ['breɪʒər] *n* : brasero *m*

Brazilian [brə'zɪljən] *n* : brasileño *m*, -ña *f* — **Brazilian** *adj*

Brazil nut [brə'zɪlˌnʌt] *n* : nuez *f* de Brasil

breach[1] ['briːtʃ] *vt* **1** PENETRATE : abrir una brecha en, penetrar **2** VIOLATE : infringir, violar

breach[2] *n* **1** VIOLATION : infracción *f*, violación *f* ⟨breach of trust : abuso de confianza⟩ ⟨breach of contract : incumplimiento de contrato⟩ **2** GAP, OPENING : brecha *f*

bread[1] ['brɛd] *vt* : empanar

bread[2] *n* : pan *m*

bread box *n* : panera *f*

breadstick ['brɛdˌstɪk] *n* : palito *m* de pan; grisín *m Arg, Uru*; colín *m Spain*

breadth ['brɛtθ] *n* : ancho *m*, anchura *f*

breadwinner ['brɛdˌwɪnər] *n* : sostén *m* de la familia

break[1] ['breɪk] *v* **broke** ['broːk]; **broken** ['broːkən]; **breaking** *vt* **1** : romper, quebrar (cristales, un hueso, etc.) ⟨to break something in two : partir algo en dos⟩ **2** : descomponer, romper (un aparato, etc.) **3** *or* **to break up** DIVIDE, SPLIT : dividir, separar (a abrir (la piel), salir a (la superficie) **5** : romper (el suelo) **6** VIOLATE : infringir, violar (la ley, etc.), romper (un contrato), faltar a (una promesa) ⟨to break the speed limit : exceder el límite de velocidad⟩ **7** SURPASS : batir (un récord), superar **8** CRUSH, RUIN : arruinar, deshacer, destrozar ⟨to break someone's spirit : quebrantar el espíritu de alguien⟩ **9** *or* **to break in** TAME : domar **10** : dar, comunicar ⟨to break the news to someone : darle la noticia a alguien⟩ : interrumpir, cortar **11** INTERRUPT, END : romper (el silencio), hacer (corto) circuito, perder (una concentración), perder (una costumbre), superar (un punto muerto

or **to break up** DISRUPT : romper (la monotonía, etc.) **13** SLOW : amortiguar (una caída) ⟨without breaking (one's) stride : sin cambiar el paso⟩ **14** SOLVE : esclarecer (un caso), descifrar (un código) **15** : cambiar ⟨to break a twenty : cambiar un billete de veinte dólares⟩ **16** **to break down** KNOCK DOWN : derribar, romper **17** **to break down** DIVIDE : desglosar (gastos, etc.), dividir **18** **to break in** : ablandar (zapatos) **19** **to break in** TRAIN : capacitar (a un nuevo empleado, etc.) **20** **to break off** : partir, romper, separar (un pedazo) **21** **to break open** : forzar (una puerta, etc.) **22** **to break someone of something** : quitarle a alguien la costumbre de hacer algo **23** **to break up** STOP : poner fin a, disolver (una manifestación, etc.), detener (una pelea) **24** **to break up** : hacer pedazos (algo), deshacer (grumos, etc.) — *vi* **1** : romperse, quebrarse ⟨my computer broke : se me rompió la computadora⟩ **2** DISSIPATE : disiparse **3** DIVIDE, SPLIT : dividirse **4** : desatarse (dícese de una tormenta), romper (dícese del día) **5** : romper (dícese de olas) **6** CHANGE : cambiar (dícese de la voz), acabarse (dícese del calor, etc.) **7** FALTER : entrecortarse (dícese de la voz) **8** : no poder resistir ⟨he broke under the strain : no pudo con el estrés⟩ **9** DECREASE : bajar ⟨my fever broke : me bajó la fiebre⟩ **10** PAUSE : parar, hacer una pausa **11** : divulgarse, revelarse ⟨the news broke : la noticia se divulgó⟩ **12** **to break away** : separarse **13** **to break down** SEPARATE : descomponerse **14** **to break down** MALFUNCTION : averiarse, descomponerse, estropearse **15** **to break down** : perder el control ⟨she broke down in tears : rompió a llorar⟩ **16** **to break even** : alcanzar su punto de equilibrio (financiero) **17** **to break free/loose** : soltarse **18** **to break in** : entrar (por la fuerza) **19** **to break into** : entrar a (una casa, etc.) para robar **20** **to break off** DETACH : romperse, desprenderse **21** **to break off** END : romper (relaciones, etc.) ⟨she broke off in the middle of a sentence : se detuvo en la mitad de una frase⟩ **22** **to break out** ERUPT : desencadenarse **23** **to break out in** : salirle a uno (un sarpullido, etc.) **24** **to break out of** : escaparse de **25** **to break through** : penetrar **26** **to break up** FRAGMENT : hacerse pedazos **27** **to break up** DISPERSE : disolverse **28** **to break up** : separarse ⟨they broke up : se separaron⟩ ⟨she broke up with him : rompió con él⟩

break[2] *n* **1** : ruptura *f*, rotura *f*, fractura *f* (de un hueso), claro *m* (entre las nubes), cambio *m* (del tiempo) **2** CHANCE : oportunidad *f* ⟨a lucky break : un golpe de suerte⟩ **3** REST : descanso *m* ⟨to take a break : tomar(se) un descanso⟩ **4** : corte *m*, pausa *f* ⟨commercial break : corte comercial/publicitaria, pausa publicitaria/comercial⟩

breakable ['breɪkəbəl] *adj* : quebradizo, frágil

breakage ['breɪkɪʤ] *n* **1** BREAKING : rotura *f* **2** DAMAGE : destrozos *mpl*, daños *mpl*

breakdown ['breɪk,daʊn] *n* **1** : avería *f* (de máquinas), interrupción *f* (de comunicaciones), fracaso *m* (de negociaciones) **2** ANALYSIS : análisis *m*, desglose *m* **3** *or* **nervous breakdown** : crisis *f* nerviosa

break down *vi* **1** : estropearse, descomponerse ⟨the machine broke down : la máquina se descompuso⟩ **2** FAIL : fracasar **3** CRY : echarse a llorar — *vt* **1** DESTROY : derribar, echar abajo **2** OVERCOME : vencer (la resistencia), disipar (sospechas) **3** ANALYZE : analizar, descomponer

breaker ['breɪkər] *n* **1** WAVE : ola *f* grande **2** : interruptor *m* automático (de electricidad)

breakfast¹ ['brɛkfəst] *vi* : desayunar

breakfast² *n* : desayuno *m*

break–in ['breɪk,ɪn] *n* : robo *m*

breakneck ['breɪk,nɛk] *adj* **at breakneck speed** : a una velocidad vertiginosa

break out *vi* **1** : salirse ⟨she broke out in spots : le salieron granos⟩ **2** ERUPT : estallar (dícese de una guerra, la violencia, etc.) **3** ESCAPE : fugarse, escaparse

breakthrough ['breɪk,θru:] *n* : avance *m* (importante)

breakup ['breɪk,əp] *n* **1** DIVISION : desintegración *f* **2** : ruptura *f*

break up *vt* **1** DIVIDE : dividir **2** : disolver (una muchedumbre, una pelea, etc.) — *vi* **1** BREAK : romperse **2** SEPARATE : deshacerse, separarse ⟨I broke up with him : terminé con él⟩

breakwater ['breɪk,wɔːtər, -,wɑː-] *n* : rompeolas *m*, malecón *m*, espigón *m*

breast ['brɛst] *n* **1** : pecho *m*, seno *m* (de una mujer) **2** CHEST : pecho *m*

breastbone ['brɛst,boːn] *n* : esternón *m*

breast–feed ['brɛst,fiːd] *vt* **-fed** [-,fɛd]; **-feeding** : amamantar, darle de mamar (a un niño)

breaststroke ['brɛst,stroːk] *adj* : estilo *m* (de) pecho, estilo *m* braza *Spain*

breath ['brɛθ] *n* **1** BREATHING : aliento *m* ⟨to hold one's breath : aguantar la respiración⟩ ⟨she was short of breath : le faltaba el aire⟩ **2** BREEZE : soplo *m* ⟨a breath of fresh air : un soplo de aire fresco⟩ **3 under one's breath** : entre dientes, en voz baja

breathe ['briːð] *v* **breathed; breathing** *vi* **1** : respirar **2** LIVE : vivir, respirar **3 to breathe in** : aspirar **4 to breathe out** : espirar — *vt* **1** : respirar, aspirar ⟨to breathe fresh air : respirar el aire fresco⟩ ⟨to breathe a sigh of relief : suspirar aliviado⟩ **2** UTTER : decir ⟨I won't breathe a word of this : no diré nada de esto⟩ **3 to breathe in** : aspirar (aire, etc.) **4 to breathe out** : espirar (aire, etc.)

breather ['briːðər] *n* : respiro *m*, resuello *m*

breathing ['briːðɪŋ] *n* : respiración *f*

breathless ['brɛθləs] *adj* : sin aliento, jadeante

breathlessly ['brɛθləsli] *adv* : entrecortadamente, jadeando

breathlessness ['brɛθləsnəs] *n* : dificultad *f* al respirar

breathtaking ['brɛθ,teɪkɪŋ] *adj* IMPRESSIVE : impresionante, imponente

breeches ['brɪtʃəz, 'briː-] *npl* : pantalones *mpl*, calzones *mpl*, bombachos *mpl*

breed¹ ['briːd] *v* **bred** ['brɛd]; **breeding** *vt* **1** : criar (animales) **2** ENGENDER : engendrar, producir ⟨familiarity breeds contempt : la confianza hace perder el respeto⟩ **3** RAISE, REAR : criar, educar — *vi* REPRODUCE : reproducirse

breed² *n* **1** : variedad *f* (de plantas), raza *f* (de animales) **2** CLASS : clase *f*, tipo *m*

breeder ['briːdər] *n* : criador *m*, -dora *f* (de animales); cultivador *m*, -dora *f* (de plantas)

breeze¹ ['briːz] *vi* **breezed; breezing** : pasar con ligereza ⟨to breeze in : entrar como si nada⟩

breeze² *n* : brisa *f*, soplo *m* (de aire)

breezy ['briːzi] *adj* **breezier; -est 1** AIRY, WINDY : aireado, ventoso **2** LIVELY : animado, alegre **3** NONCHALANT : despreocupado

brethren → **brother**

brevity ['brɛvəti] *n*, *pl* **-ties** : brevedad *f*, concisión *f*

brew¹ ['bruː] *vt* **1** : fabricar, elaborar (cerveza) **2** FOMENT : tramar, maquinar, fomentar — *vi* **1** : fabricar cerveza **2** : amenazar ⟨a storm is brewing : una tormenta amenaza⟩

brew² *n* **1** BEER : cerveza *f* **2** POTION : brebaje *m*

brewer ['bruːər] *n* : cervecero *m*, -ra *f*

brewery ['bruːəri, 'bruri] *n*, *pl* **-eries** : cervecería *f*

briar ['braɪər] → **brier**

bribe¹ ['braɪb] *vt* **bribed; bribing** : sobornar, cohechar, coimear *Arg, Chile, Peru*

bribe² *n* : soborno *m*, cohecho *m*, coima *f* *Arg, Chile, Peru*, mordida *f* *CA, Mex*

bribery ['braɪbəri] *n*, *pl* **-eries** : soborno *m*, cohecho *m*, coima *f*, mordida *f* *CA, Mex*

bric–a–brac ['brɪkə,bræk] *npl* : baratijas *fpl*, chucherías *fpl*

brick¹ ['brɪk] *vt* **to brick up** : tabicar, tapiar

brick² *n* : ladrillo *m*

bricklayer ['brɪk,leɪər] *n* : albañil *mf*

bricklaying ['brɪk,leɪɪŋ] *n* : albañilería *f*

bridal ['braɪdəl] *adj* : nupcial, de novia

bride ['braɪd] *n* : novia *f*

bridegroom ['braɪd,ɡruːm] *n* : novio *m*

bridesmaid ['braɪdz,meɪd] *n* : dama *f* de honor

bridge¹ ['brɪʤ] *vt* **bridged; bridging 1** : tender un puente sobre **2 to bridge the gap** : salvar las diferencias

bridge² *n* **1** : puente *m* **2** : caballete *m* (de la nariz) **3** : puente *m* de mando (de un barco) **4** : puente *m* (dental) **5** : bridge *m* (juego de naipes)

bridle¹ [ˈbraɪdəl] *v* **-dled; -dling** *vt* **1** : embridar (un caballo) **2** RESTRAIN : refrenar, dominar, contener — *vi* **to bridle at** : molestarse por, picarse por

bridle² *n* : brida *f*

brief¹ [ˈbriːf] *vt* : dar órdenes a, instruir

brief² *adj* : breve, sucinto, conciso

brief³ *n* **1** : resumen *m*, sumario *m* **2 briefs** *npl* : calzoncillos *mpl*

briefcase [ˈbriːfˌkeɪs] *n* : portafolio *m*, maletín *m*

briefing [ˈbriːfɪŋ] *n* : reunión *f* informativa

briefly [ˈbriːfli] *adv* : brevemente, por poco tiempo

brier [ˈbraɪər] *n* **1** BRAMBLE : zarza *f*, rosal *m* silvestre **2** HEATH : brezo *m* veteado

brig [ˈbrɪɡ] *n* **1** : bergantín *m* (barco) **2** : calabozo *m* (en un barco)

brigade [brɪˈɡeɪd] *n* : brigada *f*

brigadier [ˌbrɪɡəˈdɪr] *n* : brigadier *m*

brigadier general [ˌbrɪɡəˈdɪr] *n* : general *m* de brigada

brigand [ˈbrɪɡənd] *n* : bandolero *m*, -ra *f*; forajido *m*, -da *f*

bright [ˈbraɪt] *adj* **1** : brillante (dícese del sol, de los ojos), vivo (dícese de un color), claro, fuerte **2** CHEERFUL : alegre, animado ⟨bright and early : muy temprano⟩ **3** INTELLIGENT : listo, inteligente ⟨a bright idea : una idea luminosa⟩

brighten [ˈbraɪtən] *vt* **1** ILLUMINATE : iluminar **2** ENLIVEN : alegrar, animar — *vi* **1** : hacerse más brillante **2 to brighten up** : animarse, alegrarse, mejorar

brightly [ˈbraɪtli] *adv* : vivamente, intensamente, alegremente

brightness [ˈbraɪtnəs] *n* **1** LUMINOSITY : luminosidad *f*, brillantez *f*, resplandor *m*, brillo *m* **2** CHEERFULNESS : alegría *f*, ánimo *m*

brilliance [ˈbrɪljənts] *n* **1** BRIGHTNESS : resplandor *m*, fulgor *m*, brillo *m*, brillantez *f* **2** INTELLIGENCE : inteligencia *f*, brillantez *f*

brilliancy [ˈbrɪljənsi] → **brilliance**

brilliant [ˈbrɪljənt] *adj* : brillante

brilliantly [ˈbrɪljəntli] *adv* : brillantemente, con brillantez

brim¹ [ˈbrɪm] *vi* **brimmed; brimming 1** *or* **to brim over** : desbordarse, rebosar **2 to brim with tears** : llenarse de lágrimas

brim² *n* **1** : ala *f* (de un sombrero) **2** : borde *m* (de una taza o un vaso)

brimful [ˈbrɪmˈfʊl] *adj* : lleno hasta el borde, repleto, rebosante

brimless [ˈbrɪmləs] *adj* : sin ala

brimstone [ˈbrɪmˌstoːn] *n* : azufre *m*

brindled [ˈbrɪndəld] *adj* : manchado, pinto

brine [ˈbraɪn] *n* **1** : salmuera *f*, escabeche *m* (para encurtir) **2** OCEAN : océano *m*, mar *m*

bring [ˈbrɪŋ] *vt* **brought** [ˈbrɔt]; **bringing 1** : traer, llevar ⟨bring me some coffee : tráigame un café⟩ **2** ATTRACT : traer, atraer **3** : traer (problemas), conseguir (la paz), dar (alegría), obtener (ganancias) ⟨it brought him fame : lo lanzó a la fama⟩ ⟨it brought a smile to her face : la hizo sonreír⟩ **4** : llevar (a un estado) ⟨bring it to a boil : dejarlo hervir⟩ **5** YIELD : rendir, alcanzar ⟨to bring a good price : alcanzar un precio alto⟩ **6** : aportar (experiencia, etc.) **7** : presentar (cargos, etc.) **8** : llevar (a un tema) **9 to bring about** : ocasionar, provocar **10 to bring around** CONVINCE : convencer **11 to bring back** RETURN : devolver **12 to bring back** REINSTATE, REINTRODUCE : restablecer, reintroducir **13 to bring back** : traer (de otro lugar) **14 to bring back** : recordar, traer (recuerdos) **15 to bring down** LOWER : hacer bajar **16 to bring down** OVERTHROW : derrocar **17 to bring down** : derribar (a balazos, etc.) **18 to bring forth** PRODUCE : producir **19 to bring in** : invitar a (expertos), atraer (clientes) **20 to bring in** : ganar (dinero), obtener (ganancias) **21 to bring on** : provocar ⟨you brought this on yourself : te la buscaste⟩ **22 to bring oneself to** : animarse a (hacer algo) **23 to bring out** : sacar, publicar (un libro, etc.) **24 to bring out** EMPHASIZE : hacer resaltar **25 to bring to** REVIVE : resucitar **26 to bring up** REAR : criar **27 to bring up** MENTION : sacar, mencionar

brininess [ˈbraɪnɪnəs] *n* : salinidad *f*

brink [ˈbrɪŋk] *n* : borde *m*

briny [ˈbraɪni] *adj* **brinier; -est** : salobre

brisk [ˈbrɪsk] *adj* **1** LIVELY : rápido, enérgico, brioso **2** INVIGORATING : fresco, estimulante

brisket [ˈbrɪskət] *n* : falda *f*

briskly [ˈbrɪskli] *adv* : rápidamente, enérgicamente, con brío

briskness [ˈbrɪsknəs] *n* : brío *m*, rapidez *f*

bristle¹ [ˈbrɪsəl] *vi* **-tled; -tling 1** : erizarse, ponerse de punta **2** : enfurecerse, enojarse ⟨she bristled at the suggestion : se enfureció ante tal sugerencia⟩ **3** : estar plagado, estar repleto ⟨a city bristling with tourists : una ciudad repleta de turistas⟩

bristle² *n* : cerda *f* (de un animal), pelo *m* (de una planta)

bristly [ˈbrɪsəli] *adj* **bristlier; -est** : áspero y erizado

British¹ [ˈbrɪtɪʃ] *adj* : británico

British² *n* **the British** (*used with a plural verb*) : los británicos

brittle [ˈbrɪtəl] *adj* **brittler; brittlest** : frágil, quebradizo

brittleness [ˈbrɪtəlnəs] *n* : fragilidad *f*

broach [ˈbroːtʃ] *vt* BRING UP : mencionar, abordar, sacar

broad [ˈbrɔd] *adj* **1** WIDE : ancho **2** SPACIOUS : amplio, extenso **3** FULL : pleno ⟨in broad daylight : en pleno día⟩ **4** OBVIOUS : claro, evidente **5** TOLERANT : tolerante, liberal **6** GENERAL : general **7** ESSENTIAL : principal, esencial ⟨the broad outline : los rasgos esenciales⟩

broadband¹ [ˈbrɔdˌbænd] *adj* : de banda ancha

broadband² *n* : banda *f* ancha

broad bean n : haba f
broadcast[1] ['brɔd,kæst] vt -cast; -casting 1 SCATTER : esparcir, diseminar 2 CIRCULATE, SPREAD : divulgar, difundir, propagar 3 TRANSMIT : transmitir, emitir
broadcast[2] n 1 TRANSMISSION : transmisión f, emisión f 2 PROGRAM : programa m, emisión f
broadcaster ['brɔd,kæstər] n : presentador m, -dora f; locutor m, -tora f
broadcloth ['brɔd,klɔθ] n : paño m fino
broaden ['brɔdən] vt : ampliar, ensanchar
— vi : ampliarse, ensancharse
broadloom ['brɔd,lu:m] adj : tejido en telar ancho
broadly ['brɔdli] adv 1 GENERALLY : en general, aproximadamente 2 WIDELY : extensivamente
broad–minded ['brɔd'maɪndəd] adj : tolerante, de amplias miras
broad–mindedness [brɔd'maɪndədnəs] n : tolerancia f
broadside ['brɔd,saɪd] n 1 VOLLEY : andanada f 2 ATTACK : ataque m, invectiva f, andanada f
brocade [bro'keɪd] n : brocado m
broccoli ['brɑkəli] n : brócoli m
brochure [bro'ʃur] n : folleto m
brogue ['bro:G] n : acento m irlandés
broil[1] ['brɔɪl] vt : asar a la parrilla
broil[2] n : asado m
broiler ['brɔɪlər] n 1 GRILL : parrilla f 2 : pollo m para asar
broke[1] ['bro:k] → break[1]
broke[2] adj : pelado, arruinado ⟨to go broke : arruinarse, quebrar⟩
broken ['bro:kən] adj 1 DAMAGED, SHATTERED : roto, quebrado, fracturado 2 IRREGULAR, UNEVEN : accidentado, irregular, recortado 3 VIOLATED : roto, quebrantado 4 INTERRUPTED : interrumpido, discontinuo 5 CRUSHED : abatido, quebrantado ⟨a broken man : un hombre destrozado⟩ 6 IMPERFECT : mal ⟨to speak broken English : hablar el inglés con dificultad⟩
brokenhearted [,bro:kən'hɑrtəd] adj : descorazonado, desconsolado
broker[1] ['bro:kər] vt : hacer corretaje de
broker[2] n 1 : agente mf; corredor m, -dora f 2 → stockbroker
brokerage ['bro:kərɪdʒ] n : corretaje m, agencia f de corredores
bromine ['bro:,mi:n] n : bromo m
bronchial ['brɑŋkiəl] adj : bronquial
bronchitis [brɑn'kaɪtəs, brɑŋ-] n : bronquitis f
bronze[1] ['brɑnz] vt bronzed; bronzing : broncear
bronze[2] n : bronce m
brooch ['bro:tʃ, 'bru:tʃ] n : broche m, prendedor m
brood[1] ['bru:d] vt 1 INCUBATE : empollar, incubar 2 PONDER : sopesar, considerar — vi 1 INCUBATE : empollar 2 REFLECT : rumiar, reflexionar 3 WORRY : ponerse melancólico, inquietarse
brood[2] adj : de cría
brood[3] n : nidada f (de pájaros), camada f (de mamíferos)

brooder ['bru:dər] n 1 THINKER : pensador m, -dora f 2 INCUBATOR : incubadora f
brook[1] ['bruk] vt TOLERATE : tolerar, admitir
brook[2] n : arroyo m
broom ['bru:m, 'brum] n 1 : retama f, hiniesta f 2 : escoba f (para barrer)
broomstick ['bru:m,stɪk, 'brum-] n : palo m de escoba
broth ['brɔθ] n, pl **broths** ['brɔθs, 'brɔðz] : caldo m
brothel ['brɑθəl, 'brɔ-] n : burdel m
brother ['brʌðər] n, pl **brothers** also **brethren** ['brɔðrən, -ðərn] 1 : hermano m 2 KINSMAN : pariente m, familiar m
brotherhood ['brʌðər,hud] n 1 FELLOWSHIP : fraternidad f 2 ASSOCIATION : hermandad f
brother–in–law ['brʌðərɪn,lɔ] n, pl **brothers–in–law** : cuñado m
brotherly ['brʌðərli] adj : fraternal
brought → bring
brow ['braʊ] n 1 EYEBROW : ceja f 2 FOREHEAD : frente f 3 : cima f ⟨the brow of a hill : la cima de una colina⟩
browbeat ['braʊ,bi:t] vt -beat; -beaten [-,bi:tən] or -beat; -beating : intimidar
brown[1] ['braʊn] vt 1 : dorar (en cocina) 2 TAN : broncear — vi 1 : dorarse (en cocina) 2 TAN : broncearse
brown[2] adj : marrón, café, castaño (dícese del pelo), moreno (dícese de la piel)
brown[3] n : marrón m, café m
brown bread n 1 : pan m integral 2 : pan m negro (dulce)
brownie ['braʊni] n : bizcocho m de chocolate y nueces
brownish ['braʊnɪʃ] adj : pardo
brown rice n : arroz m integral
browse ['braʊz] v browsed; browsing vt 1 LOOK : mirar 2 : explorar (la Internet) — vi 1 GRAZE : pacer 2 LOOK : mirar, echar un vistazo 3 : navegar (en/por Internet)
browser ['braʊzər] or **Web browser** n : navegador m (web)
bruin ['bru:ɪn] n BEAR : oso m
bruise[1] ['bru:z] vt bruised; bruising 1 : contusionar, machucar, magullar (a una persona) 2 DAMAGE : magullar, dañar (frutas) 3 CRUSH : majar 4 HURT : herir (los sentimientos)
bruise[2] n : moretón m, cardenal m, magulladura f (dícese de frutas)
brunch ['brʌntʃ] n : combinación f de desayuno y almuerzo
brunet[1] or **brunette** [bru:'nɛt] adj : moreno
brunet[2] or **brunette** n : moreno m, -na f
brunt ['brʌnt] n to bear the brunt of : llevar el peso de, aguantar el mayor impacto de
brush[1] ['brʌʃ] vt 1 : cepillar ⟨I brushed my teeth : me cepillé los dientes⟩ 2 SWEEP : quitar, sacudir ⟨he brushed the dirt off his pants : se sacudió el polvo de los pantalones⟩ 3 PAINT, APPLY : pintar 4 GRAZE : rozar 5 to brush off DISREGARD : hacer caso omiso de (algo), no

hacerle caso (a alguien) — *vi* **to brush up (on)** : repasar, refrescar, dar un repaso a
brush² *n* **1** *or* **brushwood** [ˈbrʌʃˌwʊd] : broza *f* **2** SCRUB, UNDERBRUSH : maleza *f* **3** : cepillo *m*, pincel *m* (de artista), brocha *f* (de pintor) **4** TOUCH : roce *m* **5** SKIRMISH : escaramuza *f*
brush–off [ˈbrʌʃˌɔf] *n* **to give the brush–off to** : dar calabazas a
brushstroke [ˈbrʌʃˌstroːk] *n* : pincelada *f*
brusque [ˈbrʌsk] *adj* : brusco — **brusquely** *adv*
brusqueness [ˈbrʌsknəs] *n* : brusquedad *f*
brussels sprout [ˈbrʌsəlzˌspraʊt] *n* : col *f* de Bruselas
brutal [ˈbruːʈʈəl] *adj* : brutal, cruel, salvaje — **brutally** *adv*
brutality [bruːˈtæləʈiː] *n*, *pl* **-ties** : brutalidad *f*
brutalize [ˈbruːʈʈəlˌaɪz] *vt* **-ized; -izing** : brutalizar, maltratar
brute¹ [ˈbruːt] *adj* : bruto ⟨brute force : fuerza bruta⟩
brute² *n* **1** BEAST : bestia *f*, animal *m* **2** : bruto *m*, -ta *f*; bestia *mf* (persona)
brutish [ˈbruːʈiʃ] *adj* **1** : de animal **2** CRUEL : brutal, salvaje **3** STUPID : bruto, estúpido
bubble¹ [ˈbʌbəl] *vi* **-bled; -bling** : burbujear ⟨to bubble over with joy : rebosar de alegría⟩
bubble² *n* : burbuja *f*
bubble bath *n* **1** : baño *m* de espuma/burbujas **2** : espuma *f* de baño (jabón)
bubble gum *n* : chicle *m* (de) globo, chicle *m* (de) bomba
bubbly [ˈbʌbəli] *adj* **bubblier; -est 1** BUBBLING : burbujeante **2** LIVELY : vivaz, lleno de vida
bubonic plague [buːˈbɑnɪk-, ˈbjuː-] *n* : peste *f* bubónica
buccaneer [ˌbʌkəˈnɪr] *n* : bucanero *m*
buck¹ [ˈbʌk] *vi* **1** : corcovear (dícese de un caballo o un burro) **2** JOLT : dar sacudidas **3 to buck against** : resistirse a, rebelarse contra **4 to buck up** : animarse, levantar el ánimo — *vt* OPPOSE : oponerse a, ir en contra de
buck² *n*, *pl* **buck** *or* **bucks 1** : animal *m* macho, ciervo *m* (macho) **2** DOLLAR : dólar *m* **3 to pass the buck** *fam* : pasar la pelota *fam*
bucket [ˈbʌkət] *n* : balde *m*, cubo *m*, cubeta *f Mex*
bucketful [ˈbʌkətˌfʊl] *n* : balde *m* lleno
buckle¹ [ˈbʌkəl] *v* **-led; -ling** *vt* **1** FASTEN : abrochar **2** BEND, TWIST : combar, torcer — *vi* **1** BEND, TWIST : combarse, torcerse, doblarse (dícese de las rodillas) **2 to buckle down** : ponerse a trabajar con esmero **3 to buckle up** : abrocharse
buckle² *n* **1** : hebilla *f* **2** TWISTING : torcedura *f*
buckshot [ˈbʌkˌʃɑt] *n* : perdigón *m*
buckskin [ˈbʌkˌskɪn] *n* : gamuza *f*
buck tooth *n* : diente *m* saliente, diente *m* salido
bucktoothed [ˈbʌkˌtuːθt] *adj* : de dientes salientes, de dientes salidos

buckwheat [ˈbʌkˌhwiːt] *n* : alforfón *m*, trigo *m* sarraceno
bucolic [bjuːˈkɑlɪk] *adj* : bucólico
bud¹ [ˈbʌd] *v* **budded; budding** *vt* GRAFT : injertar — *vi* : brotar, hacer brotes
bud² *n* : brote *m*, yema *f*, capullo *m* (de una flor)
Buddhism [ˈbuːˌdɪzəm, ˈbʊ-] *n* : budismo *m*
Buddhist [ˈbuːdɪst, ˈbʊ-] *n* : budista *mf* — **Buddhist** *adj*
budding [ˈbʌdɪŋ] *adj* : en ciernes
buddy [ˈbʌdi] *n*, *pl* **-dies** *fam* : amigo *m*, -ga *f*; compinche *mf fam*; cuate *m*, -ta *f Mex fam*
budge [ˈbʌd] *vi* **budged; budging 1** MOVE : moverse, desplazarse **2** YIELD : ceder
budget¹ [ˈbʌd ət] *vt* : presupuestar (gastos), asignar (dinero) — *vi* : presupuestar, planear el presupuesto
budget² *n* : presupuesto
budgetary [ˈbʌd əˌteri] *adj* : presupuestario
buff¹ [ˈbʌf] *vt* POLISH : pulir, sacar brillo a, lustrar
buff² *adj* : beige, amarillento
buff³ *n* **1** : beige *m*, amarillento *m* **2** ENTHUSIAST : aficionado *m*, -da *f*; entusiasta *mf*
buffalo [ˈbʌfəˌloː] *n*, *pl* **-lo** *or* **-loes 1** : búfalo *m* **2** BISON : bisonte *m*
buffer [ˈbʌfər] *n* **1** BARRIER : barrera *f* ⟨buffer state : estado tapón⟩ **2** SHOCK ABSORBER : amortiguador *m*
buffet¹ [ˈbʌfət] *vt* : golpear, zarandear, sacudir
buffet² *n* BLOW : golpe *m*
buffet³ [ˌbʌˈfeɪ, ˌbuː-] *n* **1** : bufete *m*, bufé *m* (comida) **2** SIDEBOARD : aparador *m*
buffoon [ˌbʌˈfuːn] *n* : bufón *m*, -fona *f*; payaso *m*, -sa *f*
bug¹ [ˈbʌg] *vt* **bugged; bugging 1** PESTER : fastidiar, molestar **2** : ocultar micrófonos en
bug² *n* **1** INSECT : bicho *m*, insecto *m* **2** DEFECT : defecto *m*, falla *f*, problema *m* **3** GERM : microbio *m*, virus *m* **4** MICROPHONE : micrófono *m*
bugaboo [ˈbʌgəˌbuː] *n* : pesadilla *f*, terror *m*, coco *m*
bugbear [ˈbʌgˌbær] *n* : problema *m*, obstáculo *f*
buggy [ˈbʌgi] *n*, *pl* **-gies 1** : calesa *f* (tirada por caballos) **2** : cochecito *m* (para niños)
bugle [ˈbjuːgəl] *n* : clarín *m*, corneta *f*
bugler [ˈbjuːgələr] *n* : corneta *mf*
build¹ [ˈbɪld] *v* **built** [ˈbɪlt]; **building** *vt* **1** CONSTRUCT : construir, edificar, ensamblar, levantar **2** DEVELOP : desarrollar, elaborar, forjar **3** INCREASE : incrementar, aumentar — *vi* **1 to build on** : ampliar (conocimientos, etc.) **2 to build up** : aumentar, intensificar
build² *n* PHYSIQUE : físico *m*, complexión *f*
builder [ˈbɪldər] *n* : constructor *m*, -tora *f*; contratista *mf*
building [ˈbɪldɪŋ] *n* **1** EDIFICE : edificio *m* **2** CONSTRUCTION : construcción *f*

buildup ['bɪld‚ʌp] *n* : acumulación *f*
built–in ['bɪlt'ɪn] *adj* **1** : empotrado ⟨built-in cabinets : armarios empotrados⟩ **2** INHERENT : incorporado, intrínseco
built–up ['bɪlt‚ʌp] *adj* : urbanizado
bulb ['bʌlb] *n* **1** : bulbo *m* (de una planta), cabeza *f* (de ajo), cubeta *f* (de un termómetro) **2** LIGHTBULB : bombilla *f*, foco *m*, bombillo *m CA, Col, Ven*
bulbous ['bʌlbəs] *adj* : bulboso
Bulgarian [bʌl'gæriən, bʊl-] *n* **1** : búlgaro *m*, -ra *f* **2** : búlgaro *m* (idioma) — **Bulgarian** *adj*
bulge¹ ['bʌlD] *vi* **bulged; bulging** : abultar, sobresalir
bulge² *n* : bulto *m*, protuberancia *f*
bulk¹ ['bʌlk] *vt* : hinchar — *vi* EXPAND, SWELL : ampliarse, hincharse
bulk² *n* **1** SIZE, VOLUME : volumen *m*, tamaño *m* **2** FIBER : fibra *f* **3** MASS : mole *f* **4** **the bulk of** : la mayor parte de **5 in** ~ : en grandes cantidades
bulkhead ['bʌlk‚hɛd] *n* : mamparo *m*
bulky ['bʌlki] *adj* **bulkier; -est** : voluminoso, grande
bull¹ ['bʊl] *adj* : macho
bull² *n* **1** : toro *m*, macho *m* (de ciertas especies) **2** : bula *f* (papal) **3** DECREE : decreto *m*, edicto *m*
bulldog ['bʊl‚dɔG] *n* : bulldog *m*
bulldoze ['bʊl‚do:z] *vt* **-dozed; -dozing** **1** LEVEL : nivelar (el terreno), derribar (un edificio) **2** FORCE : forzar ⟨he bulldozed his way through : se abrió paso a codazos⟩
bulldozer ['bʊl‚do:zər] *n* : bulldozer *m*
bullet ['bʊlət] *n* : bala *f*
bulletin ['bʊlətən, -lətən] *n* **1** *or* **news bulletin** : boletín *m* informativo, boletín *m* de noticias **2** NEWSLETTER : boletín *m*
bulletin board *n* : tablón *m* de anuncios
bulletproof ['bʊlət‚pru:f] *adj* : antibalas, a prueba de balas
bullfight ['bʊl‚faɪt] *n* : corrida *f* (de toros)
bullfighter ['bʊl‚faɪtər] *n* : torero *m*, -ra *f*; matador *m*
bullfighting ['bʊl‚faɪtɪŋ] *n* : lidia *f*, toreo *m*
bullfrog ['bʊl‚frɔG] *n* : rana *f* toro
bullheaded ['bʊl'hɛdəd] *adj* : testarudo
bullion ['bʊljən] *n* : oro *m* en lingotes, plata *f* en lingotes
bullish ['bʊlɪʃ] *adj* : alcista
bullock ['bʊlək] *n* **1** STEER : buey *m*, toro *m* castrado **2** : toro *m* joven, novillo *m*
bullring ['bʊl‚rɪŋ] *n* : plaza *f* de toros, redondel *m*, ruedo *m*
bull's–eye ['bʊlz‚aɪ] *n, pl* **bull's–eyes** : diana *f*, blanco *m*
bully¹ ['bʊli] *vt* **-lied; -lying** : intimidar, amedrentar, mangonear
bully² *n, pl* **-lies** : matón *m*; bravucón *m*, -cona *f*
bullying ['bʊliɪŋ] *n* : bullying *m*, acoso *m* ⟨school bullying : bullying/acoso escolar⟩
bulrush ['bʊl‚rʌʃ] *n* : especie *f* de junco
bulwark ['bʊl‚wɔrk, -‚wɔrk;, 'bʌl‚wɔrk] *n* : baluarte *m*, bastión *f*
bum¹ ['bʌm] *v* **bummed; bumming** *vi* **to bum around** : vagabundear, vagar — *vt* : gorronear *fam*, sablear *fam*

bum² *adj* : inútil, malo ⟨a bum rap : una acusación falsa⟩
bum³ *n* **1** LOAFER : vago *m*, -ga *f* **2** HOBO, TRAMP : vagabundo *m*, -da *f*
bumblebee ['bʌmbəl‚bi:] *n* : abejorro *m*
bump¹ ['bʌmp] *vt* : chocar contra, golpear contra, dar ⟨to bump one's head : darse (un golpe) en la cabeza⟩ — *vi* **to bump into** MEET : encontrarse con, tropezarse con
bump² *n* **1** BULGE : bulto *m*, protuberancia *f* **2** IMPACT : golpe *m*, choque *m* **3** JOLT : sacudida *f*
bumper¹ ['bʌmpər] *adj* : extraordinario, récord ⟨a bumper crop : una cosecha abundante⟩
bumper² *n* : parachoques *mpl*
bumpkin ['bʌmpkən] *n* : palurdo *m*, -da *f*
bumpy ['bʌmpi] *adj* **bumpier; -est** : desigual, lleno de baches (dícese de un camino), agitado (dícese de un vuelo en avión)
bun ['bʌn] *n* **1** : bollo *m* (dulce) **2** ROLL : panecito *m* **3** CHIGNON : moño *m*, chongo *m Mex*
bunch¹ ['bʌntʃ] *vt* : agrupar, amontonar — *vi* **to bunch up** : amontonarse, agruparse, fruncirse (dícese de una tela)
bunch² *n* : grupo *m*, montón *m*, ramo *m* (de flores)
bundle¹ ['bʌndəl] *vt* **-dled; -dling** : liar, atar
bundle² *n* **1** : fardo *m*, atado *m*, bulto *m*, haz *m* (de palos) **2** PARCEL : paquete *m* **3** LOAD : montón *m* ⟨a bundle of money : un montón de dinero⟩
bungalow ['bʌŋGə‚lo:] *n* : tipo de casa de un solo piso
bungle¹ ['bʌŋGəl] *vt* **-gled; -gling** : echar a perder, malograr
bungle² *n* : chapuza *f*, desatino *m*
bungler ['bʌŋGələr] *n* : chapucero *m*, -ra *f*; inepto *m*, -ta *f*
bunion ['bʌnjən] *n* : juanete *m*
bunk¹ ['bʌŋk] *vi* : dormir (en una litera)
bunk² *n* **1** *or* **bunk bed** : litera *f* **2** NONSENSE : tonterías *fpl*, bobadas *fpl*
bunker ['bʌŋkər] *n* **1** : carbonera *f* (en un barco) **2** SHELTER : búnker *m*
bunny ['bʌni] *n, pl* **-nies** : conejo *m*, -ja *f*
buoy¹ ['bu:i, 'bɔɪ] *vt* **to buoy up** **1** : mantener a flote **2** CHEER, HEARTEN : animar, levantar el ánimo a
buoy² *n* : boya *f*
buoyancy ['bɔɪəntsi, 'bu:jən-] *n* **1** : flotabilidad *f* **2** OPTIMISM : confianza *f*, optimismo *m*
buoyant ['bɔɪənt, 'bu:jənt] *adj* : boyante, flotante
bur *or* **burr** ['bər] *n* : abrojo *m* (de una planta)
burden¹ ['bərdən] *vt* : cargar, oprimir
burden² *n* : carga *f*, peso *m*
burdensome ['bərdənsəm] *adj* : oneroso
bureau ['bjʊro] *n* **1** CHEST OF DRAWERS : cómoda *f* **2** DEPARTMENT : departamento *m* (del gobierno) **3** AGENCY : agencia *f* ⟨travel bureau : agencia de viajes⟩
bureaucracy [bjʊ'rɑkrəsi] *n, pl* **-cies** : burocracia *f*

bureaucrat [ˈbjʊrəˌkræt] n : burócrata mf
bureaucratic [ˌbjʊrəˈkrætɪk] adj : burocrático
burgeon [ˈbərɒ ən] vi : florecer, retoñar,
crecer
burger [ˈbərɡər] n 1 → **hamburger** 2
PATTY : hamburguesa f ⟨a turkey burger
: una hamburguesa de pavo⟩
burglar [ˈbərɡlər] n : ladrón m, -drona f
burglar alarm n : alarma f antirrobo
burglarize [ˈbərɡləˌraɪz] vt -**ized**; -**izing**
: robar
burglary [ˈbərɡləri] n, pl -**glaries** : robo m
burgle [ˈbərɡəl] vt -**gled**; -**gling** : robar
burgundy [ˈbərɡəndi] n, pl -**dies** : borgoña m, vino m de Borgoña
burial [ˈbɛriəl] n : entierro m, sepelio m
burlap [ˈbərˌlæp] n : arpillera f
burlesque[1] [bərˈlɛsk] vt -**lesqued**; -**lesqu-
ing** : parodiar
burlesque[2] n 1 PARODY : parodia f 2
REVUE : revista f (musical)
burly [ˈbərli] adj **burlier**; -**est** : fornido,
corpulento, musculoso
Burmese [ˌbərˈmiːz, -ˈmiːs] n : birmano
m, -na f — **Burmese** adj
burn[1] [ˈbərn] v **burned** [ˈbərnd, ˈbərnt] or
burnt [ˈbərnt]; **burning** vt 1 : quemar
(leña, etc.) ⟨to burn a candle : encender
una vela⟩ 2 : quemar (piel, ropa, etc.)
⟨I burned my hand : me quemé la mano⟩
⟨to burn a hole in something : quemar
algo (haciendo un agujero)⟩ 3 STING
: hacer escocer 4 OVERCOOK : quemar 5 CONSUME : usar, gastar ⟨a gas-
burning engine : un motor que funciona
con gas⟩ ⟨to burn (up) calories : quemar
calorías⟩ 6 CHEAT : estafar, timar 7
RECORD, WRITE : quemar (un DVD,
etc.) 8 or **to burn down** : quemar, incendiar (un edificio) 9 **to burn out**
: quemar (un motor, etc.) 10 **to burn up**
: quemar, incendiar ⟨the fire burned up
homes and forests : el incendio arrasó
con casas y bosques⟩ — vi 1 : arder
(dícese de un fuego o un edificio), quemarse ⟨I smell something burning
: huele a quemado⟩ ⟨the house burned
to the ground : la casa fue arrasada por
el incendio⟩ 2 : estar prendido, estar
encendido ⟨we left the lights burning
: dejamos las luces encendidas⟩ 3 STING
: arder ⟨ : quemarse (dícese de la
comida) 5 or **to burn up** : tener fiebre
⟨you're burning (up)! : ¡estás hirviendo!⟩ 6 : arder (dícese de las mejillas, etc.) 7 **to burn down** : incendiarse,
quemarse 8 **to burn off** : disiparse
(dícese de la niebla, etc.) 9 **to burn out**
: consumirse, apagarse 10 **to burn out**
: quemarse (dícese de un motor, etc.) 11
to burn out : quemarse, agotarse (dícese
de una persona) 12 **to burn to death**
: morir quemado 13 **to burn up** : desintegrarse (dícese de un asteroide, etc.) 14
to burn with : arder de ⟨he was burning
with jealousy : ardía de celos⟩
burn[2] n : quemadura f
burned out or **burnt out** adj 1 : con el
interior destruido (dícese de un edifi-

cio) 2 : quemado, agotado (dícese de
una persona)
burner [ˈbərnər] n : quemador m
burnish [ˈbərnɪʃ] vt : bruñir
burp[1] [ˈbərp] vi : eructar — vt : hacer
eructar
burp[2] n : eructo m
burr → **bur**
burrito [bəˈriːṭo] n, pl -**tos** : burrito m
burro [ˈbəro, ˈbʊr-] n, pl -**os** : burro m
burrow[1] [ˈbəro] vi 1 : cavar, hacer una
madriguera 2 **to burrow into** : hurgar
en — vt : cavar, excavar
burrow[2] n : madriguera f, conejera f (de
un conejo)
bursar [ˈbərsər] n : administrador m, -dora f
burst[1] [ˈbərst] v **burst**; **bursting** vi 1
: reventarse (dícese de una llanta o un
globo), estallar (dícese de obuses o
fuegos artificiales), romperse (dícese de
un dique) 2 **to burst in** : irrumpir en 3
to burst into (something) or **to burst
out in (something)** : empezar a (hacer
algo), echar a (hacer algo) ⟨to burst into
tears : echarse a llorar⟩ — vt : reventar
burst[2] n 1 EXPLOSION : estallido m, explosión f, reventón m (de una llanta) 2
OUTBURST : arranque m (de actividad,
de velocidad), arrebato m (de ira), salva
f (de aplausos)
bury [ˈberi] vt **buried**; **burying** 1 INTER
: enterrar, sepultar 2 HIDE : esconder,
ocultar 3 **to bury oneself in** : enfrascarse en
bus[1] [ˈbʌs] v **bused** or **bussed** [ˈbʌst];
busing or **bussing** [ˈbʌsɪŋ] vt : transportar en autobús — vi : viajar en autobús
bus[2] n : autobús m, bus m, camión m
Mex, colectivo m Arg, Bol, Peru
busboy [ˈbʌsˌbɔɪ] n : ayudante mf de camarero
bus driver n : chofer mf (de autobús);
conductor m, -tora f (de autobús);
busero m, -ra f CA; camionero m, -ra f
Mex; colectivero m, -ra f Arg
bush [ˈbʊʃ] n 1 SHRUB : arbusto m, mata
f 2 THICKET : maleza f, matorral m
bushel [ˈbʊʃəl] n : medida f de áridos igual
a 35.24 litros
bushing [ˈbʊʃɪŋ] n : cojinete m
bushy [ˈbʊʃi] adj **bushier**; -**est** : espeso,
poblado ⟨bushy eyebrows : cejas pobla-
das⟩
busily [ˈbɪzəli] adv : afanosamente, diligentemente
business [ˈbɪznəs, -nəz] n 1 OCCUPA-
TION : ocupación f, oficio m 2 DUTY,
MISSION : misión f, deber m, responsabilidad f 3 ESTABLISHMENT, FIRM : empresa f, firma f, negocio m, comercio
m 4 COMMERCE : negocios mpl, comercio m ⟨to go out of business : cerrar⟩ ⟨to
open for business : abrir al público⟩
⟨business hours : horas de atención al
público⟩ ⟨business meeting/trip : re-
unión/viaje de negocios⟩ 5 AFFAIR,
MATTER : asunto m, cuestión f, cosa f
⟨it's none of your business : no es asunto
tuyo⟩ ⟨to have no business doing something : no tener derecho a hacer algo⟩

business class *n* : clase *f* ejecutiva, clase *f* preferente *Spain*

business day *n* : día *m* hábil, día *m* laborable

businesslike ['bɪznəs,laɪk, -nəz-] *n* : profesional

businessman ['bɪznəs,mæn, -nəz-] *n, pl* **-men** [-mən, -,mɛn] : empresario *m*, hombre *m* de negocios

businesswoman ['bɪznəs,wʊmən, -nəz-] *n, pl* **-women** [-,wɪmən] : empresaria *f*, mujer *f* de negocios

bus shelter *n* : marquesina *f*

bus station *n* : estación *f* de autobús, terminal *f* de autobús

bus stop *n* : parada *f* de autobús

bust[1] ['bʌst] *vt* **1** BREAK, SMASH : romper, estropear, destrozar **2** TAME : domar, amansar (un caballo) — *vi* : romperse, estropearse

bust[2] *n* **1** : busto *m* (en la escultura) **2** BREASTS : pecho *m*, senos *mpl*, busto *m*

bustle[1] ['bʌsəl] *vi* **-tled; -tling to bustle about** : ir y venir, trajinar, ajetrearse

bustle[2] *n* **1** *or* **hustle and bustle** : bullicio *m*, ajetreo *m* **2** : polisón *m* (en la ropa femenina)

busy[1] ['bɪzi] *vt* **busied; busying to busy oneself with** : ocuparse con, ponerse a, entretenerse con

busy[2] *adj* **busier; -est 1** OCCUPIED : ocupado, atareado ⟨he's busy working : está ocupado en su trabajo⟩ ⟨the telephone was busy : el teléfono estaba ocupado⟩ **2** BUSTLING : concurrido, animado ⟨a busy street : una calle concurrida, una calle con mucho tránsito⟩

busybody ['bɪzi,badi] *n, pl* **-bodies** : entrometido *m*, -da *f*; metiche *mf fam*; metomentodo *mf*

busy signal *n* : tono *m* de ocupado, señal *f* de comunicando *Spain*

but[1] ['bʌt] *conj* **1** NEVERTHELESS : pero, no obstante, sin embargo ⟨I called her but she didn't answer : la llamé pero no contestó⟩ **2** EXCEPT : pero ⟨I'd do it, but I don't have time : lo haría pero no me da tiempo⟩ ⟨I had no choice but to leave : no tuve más remedio que irme⟩ ⟨they do nothing but argue : no hacen más que discutir⟩ **3** (*used for emphasis*) : pero ⟨but it's not fair! : ¡pero no es justo!⟩ **4** THAT : que ⟨there is no doubt but he is lazy : no cabe duda que es perezoso⟩ **5** WITHOUT : sin que **6** YET : pero ⟨he was poor but proud : era pobre pero orgulloso⟩ **7 but then** HOWEVER : pero

but[2] *prep* **1** EXCEPT : excepto, menos ⟨everyone but Charles : todos menos Charles⟩ ⟨no one but you would think that : sólo a ti te ocurriría eso⟩ ⟨we've had nothing but rain : no hace más que llover⟩ ⟨the last but one : el penúltimo⟩ **2 but for** : si no fuera por

butcher[1] ['bʊtʃər] *vt* **1** SLAUGHTER : matar (animales) **2** KILL : matar, asesinar, masacrar **3** BOTCH : estropear, hacer una chapuza

butcher[2] *n* **1** : carnicero *m*, -ra *f* **2** KILLER : asesino *m*, -na *f* **3** BUNGLER : chapucero *m*, -ra *f*

butcher shop *n* : carnicería *f*

butler ['bʌtlər] *n* : mayordomo *m*

butt[1] ['bʌt] *vt* **1** : embestir (con los cuernos), darle un cabezazo a **2** ABUT : colindar con, bordear — *vi* **to butt in 1** INTERRUPT : interrumpir **2** MEDDLE : entrometerse, meterse

butt[2] *n* **1** BUTTING : embestida *f* (de cuernos), cabezazo *m* **2** TARGET : blanco *m* ⟨the butt of their jokes : el blanco de sus bromas⟩ **3** BOTTOM, END : extremo *m*, culata *f* (de un rifle), colilla *f* (de un cigarrillo)

butte ['bju:t] *n* : colina *f* empinada y aislada

butter[1] ['bʌtər] *vt* **1** : untar con mantequilla **2 to butter up** : halagar

butter[2] *n* : mantequilla *f*

buttercup ['bʌtər,kʌp] *n* : ranúnculo *m*

butterfat ['bʌtər,fæt] *n* : grasa *f* de la leche

butterfly ['bʌtər,flaɪ] *n, pl* **-flies** : mariposa *f*

buttermilk ['bʌtər,mɪlk] *n* : suero *m* de mantequilla/manteca

butternut ['bʌtər,nʌt] *n* : nogal *m* ceniciento (árbol)

butterscotch ['bʌtər,skatʃ] *n* : caramelo *m* duro hecho con mantequilla

buttery ['bʌtəri] *adj* : mantecoso

buttock ['bʌtək, -,tak] *n* : nalga *f*

button[1] ['bʌtən] *vt* : abrochar, abotonar — *vi* : abrocharse, abotonarse

button[2] *n* : botón *m*

buttonhole[1] ['bʌtən,ho:l] *vt* **-holed; -holing** : acorralar

buttonhole[2] *n* : ojal *m*

buttress[1] ['bʌtrəs] *vt* : apoyar, reforzar

buttress[2] *n* **1** : contrafuerte *m* (en la arquitectura) **2** SUPPORT : apoyo *m*, sostén *m*

buxom ['bʌksəm] *adj* : con mucho busto, con mucho pecho

buy[1] ['baɪ] *v* **bought** ['bɔt]; **buying** *vt* **1** : comprar **2** BELIEVE : tragarse **3** BRIBE : comprar **4 to buy into** : comprar acciones de **5 to buy into** BELIEVE : tragarse **6 to buy off** BRIBE : tragarse **7 to buy out** : comprar la parte de **8 to buy time** : ganar tiempo **9 to buy up** : comprar (en grandes cantidades) — *vi* : comprar

buy[2] *n* BARGAIN : compra *f*, ganga *f*

buyer ['baɪər] *n* : comprador *m*, -ra *f*

buzz[1] ['bʌz] *vi* : zumbar (dícese de un insecto), sonar (dícese de un teléfono o un despertador)

buzz[2] *n* **1** : zumbido *m* (de insectos) **2** : murmullo *m*, rumor *m* (de voces)

buzzard ['bʌzərd] *n* VULTURE : buitre *m*, zopilote *m* CA, Mex

buzzer ['bʌzər] *n* : timbre *m*, chicharra *f*

buzzword ['bʌz,wərd] *n* : palabra *f* de moda

by[1] ['baɪ] *adv* **1** NEAR : cerca ⟨he lives close by : vive muy cerca⟩ **2** PAST : pasando ⟨the train went by : pasó el tren⟩ ⟨they rushed by : pasaron corriendo⟩

⟨as time goes by : con el paso del tiempo⟩ **3 by and by** : poco después, dentro de poco **4 by and large** : en general **5 to put by** : reservar, poner a un lado, apartar **6 to stop by** : pasar por casa, hacer una visita

by² *prep* **1** NEAR : cerca de, al lado de, junto a ⟨she was standing by the window : estaba parada al lado de la ventana⟩ **2** PAST : por, por delante de ⟨they walked by him : pasaron por delante de él⟩ **3** VIA : por ⟨she left by the back door : salió por la puerta trasera⟩ **4** (*indicating manner*) ⟨made by hand : hecho a mano⟩ ⟨he took her by the hand : la tomó de la mano⟩ ⟨you learn by making mistakes : uno aprende equivocándose⟩ ⟨I know her by sight/name : la conozco de vista/nombre⟩ ⟨she read by candlelight : leía a la luz de una vela⟩ ⟨to travel by train : viajar en tren⟩ ⟨to pay by credit card : pagar con tarjeta de crédito⟩ **5** (*indicating cause or agent*) ⟨built by the Romans : construido por los romanos⟩ ⟨a book by Borges : un libro de Borges⟩ ⟨I was surprised by the result : el resultado me sorprendió⟩ **6** AT : por ⟨stop/come by my house tonight : pásate por casa esta noche⟩ **7** DURING : de, durante ⟨by night : de noche⟩ **8** (*in expressions of time*) : para ⟨we'll be there by ten : estaremos allí para las diez⟩ ⟨by then : para entonces⟩ **9** : por ⟨I swear by all that's sacred : te lo juro por todo lo sagrado⟩ ⟨he said he'd do it, and by God, he did it! : dijo que lo haría y, efectivamente, lo hizo⟩ **10** : con ⟨what do you mean by

that? : ¿qué quieres decir con eso?⟩ **11** (*with numbers, rates, and amounts*) : por ⟨to pay by the hour : pagar por hora⟩ ⟨it was reduced by 10 percent : se redujo (en) un 10 por ciento⟩ ⟨by a narrow margin : por un estrecho margen⟩ ⟨10 feet by 20 feet : 10 pies por 20 pies⟩ ⟨divide 100 by 10 : dividir 100 por/entre 10⟩ **12** : según ⟨by my watch, it's ten o'clock : según mi reloj, son las diez⟩ ⟨that's fine by me : por mí no hay problema⟩ ⟨to play by the rules : respetar las reglas⟩ **13** : a ⟨little by little : poco a poco⟩ **14** : por ⟨one by one : uno por uno⟩ ⟨two by two : de dos en dos⟩ **15 by oneself** : solo

by and by *adv* : dentro de poco
bye ['baɪ] *interj fam* : ¡adiós!, ¡chao!, ¡hasta luego!
bygone¹ ['baɪˌɡɒn] *adj* : pasado
bygone² *n* **let bygones be bygones** : lo pasado, pasado está
bylaw *or* **byelaw** ['baɪˌlɔ] *n* : norma *f*, reglamento *m*
byline ['baɪˌlaɪn] *n* : data *f*
bypass¹ ['baɪˌpæs] *vt* : evitar
bypass² *n* **1** BELTWAY : carretera *f* de circunvalación **2** DETOUR : desvío *m*
by–product ['baɪˌprɑdəkt] *n* : subproducto *m*, producto *m* derivado
bystander ['baɪˌstændər] *n* : espectador *m*, -dora *f*
byte ['baɪt] *n* : byte *m*
byway ['baɪˌweɪ] *n* : camino *m* (apartado), carretera *f* secundaria
byword ['baɪˌwərd] *n* **1** PROVERB : proverbio *m*, refrán *m* **2 to be a byword for** : ser sinónimo de

C

c ['si:] *n, pl* **c's** *or* **cs** **1** : tercera letra del alfabeto inglés — **2 C** : do *m* ⟨C sharp/flat : do sostenido/bemol⟩
cab ['kæb] *n* **1** TAXI : taxi *m* **2** : cabina *f* (de un camión o una locomotora) **3** CARRIAGE : coche *m* de caballos
cabal [kəˈbɑl, -ˈbæl] *n* **1** INTRIGUE, PLOT : conspiración *f*, complot *m*, intriga *f* **2** : grupo *m* de conspiradores
cabaret [ˌkæbəˈreɪ] *n* : cabaret *m*
cabbage ['kæbɪdʒ] *n* : col *f*, repollo *m*
cabbie *or* **cabby** ['kæbi] *n* : taxista *mf*
cabin ['kæbən] *n* **1** HUT : cabaña *f*, choza *f*, barraca *f* **2** STATEROOM : camarote *m* **3** : cabina *f* (de un automóvil o avión)
cabinet ['kæbnət] *n* **1** CUPBOARD : armario *m* **2** : gabinete *m*, consejo *m* de ministros **3 medicine cabinet** : botiquín *m*
cabinetmaker ['kæbnətˌmeɪkər] *n* : ebanista *mf*
cable¹ ['keɪbəl] *vt* **-bled; -bling** : enviar un cable, telegrafiar
cable² *n* **1** : cable *m* (para colgar o sostener algo) **2** : cable *m* eléctrico **3** → **cable television**

cable car *n* **1** → **streetcar** **2** : funicular *m* (en una montaña), teleférico *m*
cable television *n* : cable *m*, televisión *f* por cable
caboose [kəˈbuːs] *n* : furgón *m* de cola, cabús *m Mex*
cabstand ['kæbˌstænd] *n* : parada *f* de taxis
cacao [kəˈkaʊ, -ˈkeɪoʊ] *n, pl* **cacaos** : cacao *m*
cache¹ ['kæʃ] *vt* **cached; caching** : esconder, guardar en un escondrijo
cache² *n* **1** : escondite *m*, escondrijo *m* ⟨cache of weapons : escondite de armas⟩ **2** : cache *m* ⟨cache memory : memoria cache⟩
cachet [kæˈʃeɪ] *n* : caché *m*, prestigio *m*
cackle¹ ['kækəl] *vi* **-led; -ling 1** CLUCK : cacarear **2** : reírse o carcajearse estridentemente ⟨he was cackling with delight : estaba carcajeándose de gusto⟩
cackle² *n* **1** : cacareo *m* (de una polla) **2** LAUGH : risa *f* estridente
cacophony [kæˈkɑfəni, -ˈkɔ-] *n, pl* **-nies** : cacofonía *f*

cactus ['kæktəs] *n, pl* **cacti** [-ˌtaɪ] *or* **-tuses** : cacto *m*, cactus *m*

cadaver [kə'dævər] *n* : cadáver *m*

cadaveric [kə'dævərɪk] *adj* : cadavérico (en medicina)

cadaverous [kə'dævərəs] *adj* : cadavérico

caddie¹ *or* **caddy** ['kædi] *vi* **caddied; caddying** : trabajar de caddie, hacer de caddie

caddie² *or* **caddy** *n, pl* **-dies** : caddie *mf*

caddy ['kædi] *n, pl* **-dies** : cajita *f* para té

cadence ['keɪdənts] *n* : cadencia *f*, ritmo *m*

cadenced ['keɪdənʌst] *adj* : cadencioso, rítmico

cadet [kə'dɛt] *n* : cadete *mf*

cadmium ['kædmiəm] *n* : cadmio *m*

cadre ['kæˌdreɪ, 'ka-, -ˌdri:] *n* : cuadro *m* (de expertos)

café [kæ'feɪ, kə-] *n* : café *m*, cafetería *f*

cafeteria [ˌkæfə'tɪriə] *n* : cafetería *f*, restaurante *m* de autoservicio

caffeinated ['kæfəˌneɪʊd] *adj* : con cafeína

caffeine [kæ'fi:n] *n* : cafeína *f*

cage¹ ['keɪD] *vt* **caged; caging** : enjaular

cage² *n* : jaula *f*

cagey ['keɪD i] *adj* **cagier; -est** **1** CAUTIOUS : cauteloso, reservado **2** SHREWD : astuto, vivo — **cagily** [-D əli] *adv*

cahoots [kə'hu:ts] *n* **to be in cahoots** *fam* : estar confabulado

caisson ['keɪˌsan, -sən] *n* **1** : cajón *m* de municiones **2** : cajón *m* hidráulico

cajole [kə'Ɖ oːl] *vt* **-joled; -joling** : engatusar

cake¹ ['keɪk] *v* **caked; caking** *vt* : cubrir ⟨caked with mud : cubierto de barro⟩ — *vi* : endurecerse

cake² *n* **1** : torta *f*, bizcocho *m*, pastel *m* **2** : pastilla *f* (de jabón) **3 to take the cake** : llevarse la palma, ser el colmo

calabash ['kæləˌbæʃ] *n* : calabaza *f*

calamari [ˌkɑlə'mari] *ns & pl* : calamares *mpl*

calamine ['kæləˌmaɪn] *n* : calamina *f* ⟨calamine lotion : loción de calamina⟩

calamitous [kə'læməʊs] *adj* : desastroso, catastrófico, calamitoso — **calamitously** *adv*

calamity [kə'læməʊi] *n, pl* **-ties** : desastre *m*, desgracia *f*, calamidad *f*

calcium ['kælsiəm] *n* : calcio *m*

calculate ['kælkjəˌleɪt] *v* **-lated; -lating** *vt* **1** COMPUTE : calcular, computar **2** ESTIMATE : calcular, creer **3** INTEND : planear, tener la intención de ⟨I calculated on spending $100 : planeaba gastar $100⟩ — *vi* : calcular, hacer cálculos

calculated ['kælkjəˌleɪʊd] *adj* **1** ESTIMATED : calculado **2** DELIBERATE : intencional, premeditado, deliberado

calculating ['kælkjəˌleɪʊŋ] *adj* SHREWD : calculador, astuto

calculation [ˌkælkjə'leɪʃən] *n* : cálculo *m*

calculator ['kælkjəˌleɪʊr] *n* : calculadora *f*

calculus ['kælkjələs] *n, pl* **-li** [-ˌlaɪ] **1** : cálculo *m* ⟨differential calculus : cálculo diferencial⟩ **2** TARTAR : sarro *m* (dental)

caldron ['kɔldrən] → **cauldron**

calendar ['kæləndər] *n* **1** : calendario *m* **2** SCHEDULE : calendario *m*, programa *m*, agenda *f*

calf ['kæf, 'kaf] *n, pl* **calves** ['kævz, 'kavz] **1** : becerro *m*, -rra *f*; ternero *m*, -ra *f* (de vacunos) **2** : cría *f* (de otros mamíferos) **3** : pantorrilla *f* (de la pierna)

calfskin ['kæfˌskɪn] *n* : piel *f* de becerro

caliber *or* **calibre** ['kæləbər] *n* **1** : calibre *m* ⟨a .38 caliber gun : una pistola de calibre .38⟩ **2** ABILITY : calibre *m*, valor *m*, capacidad *f*

calibrate ['kæləˌbreɪt] *vt* **-brated; -brating** : calibrar (armas), graduar (termómetros)

calibration [ˌkælə'breɪʃən] *n* : calibrado *m*, calibración *f*

calico ['kælɪˌkoː] *n, pl* **-coes** *or* **-cos** **1** : calicó *m*, percal *m* (estampado) **2** *or* **calico cat** : gato *m* manchado

calipers ['kæləpərz] *npl* : calibrador *m*

caliph *or* **calif** ['keɪləf, 'kæ-] *n* : califa *m*

calisthenics [ˌkæləs'θɛnɪks] *ns & pl* : calistenia *f*

calk ['kɔk] → **caulk**

call¹ ['kɔl] *vi* **1** CRY, SHOUT : llamar, gritar ⟨she called to me from upstairs : me llamó desde arriba⟩ **2** VISIT : hacer (una) visita, visitar **3** SING : cantar (dícese de las aves) — *vt* **4 to call back** : volver a llamar (por teléfono) **5 to call for** : exigir, requerir, necesitar ⟨it calls for patience : requiere mucha paciencia⟩ **6 to call for** SUMMON : llamar **7 to call for** DEMAND : pedir **8 to call in** : llamar ⟨to call in sick : reportarse enfermo⟩ **9 to call on** VISIT : visitar **10 to call on** IMPLORE : intimar, apelar — *vt* **1** SUMMON : llamar (un perro, un taxi, a una persona, etc.) ⟨he called her name : la llamó⟩ ⟨I was called away : tuve que ausentarme⟩ **2** *or* **to call up** TELEPHONE : llamar (por teléfono), telefonear ⟨she called me (up) at work : me llamó al trabajo⟩ ⟨he called 911 : llamó al 911⟩ **3** NAME : llamar ⟨what do you call this? : ¿cómo se llama esto?⟩ ⟨call me Kathy : llámeme Kathy⟩ ⟨to call someone names : insultar a alguien⟩ **4** ANNOUNCE, READ : anunciar, leer ⟨to call roll : pasar lista⟩ **5** CONSIDER : considerar ⟨call me crazy, but . . . : quizá esté loco, pero . . .⟩ ⟨give me a dollar and we'll call it even : dame un dólar y estamos en paz⟩ ⟨let's call it a day : basta por hoy⟩ **6** PREDICT : pronosticar **7** : convocar (elecciones, etc.) **8** CANCEL : cancelar (un partido) **9** : cobrar (un penal, etc.) **10 to call down** REPRIMAND : reprender, reñir **11 to call in a favor** : cobrar un favor **12 to call in an order** : llamar para hacer un pedido **13 to call into question/doubt** : poner en duda **14 to call off** CANCEL : cancelar **15 to call off** : llamar (un perro) **16 to call someone on something** *fam* ⟨he's rude, but no one calls him on it : es maleducado, pero nadie le dice nada⟩ **17 to call up** DRAFT : llamar a filas

call² *n* **1** SHOUT : grito *m*, llamada *f* **2** : grito *m* (de un animal), reclamo *m* (de un pájaro) **3** SUMMONS : llamada *f* ⟨call to action : llamada a la acción⟩ **4** DEMAND : llamado *m*, petición *f* **5** VISIT : visita *f* ⟨to pay a call on someone : hacerle una visita a alguien⟩ **6** DECISION : decisión *f* (en deportes) **7** ANNOUNCEMENT : llamada *f*, aviso *m* (para pasajeros, etc.) **8** : llamada *f* ⟨telephone/phone call : llamada (telefónica) ⟩ ⟨video call : videollamada⟩ ⟨to return someone's call : devolverle la llamada a alguien⟩ **9 to be on call** : estar de guardia

call center *n* : centro *m* de atención (telefónica), centro *m* de llamadas

caller ['kɔlər] *n* **1** VISITOR : visita *f* **2** : persona *f* que llama (por teléfono)

calligraphy [kə'lıɡrəfi] *n, pl* **-phies** : caligrafía *f*

calling ['kɔlɪŋ] *n* : vocación *f*, profesión *f*

calliope [kə'laɪə,pi:, 'kæli,o:p] : órgano *m* de vapor

callous ['kæləs] *adj* **1** CALLUSED : calloso, encallecido **2** UNFEELING : insensible, desalmado, cruel

callously ['kæləsli] *adv* : cruelmente, insensiblemente

callousness ['kæləsnəs] *n* : insensibilidad *f*, crueldad *f*

callow ['kælo] *adj* : inexperto, inmaduro

callus ['kæləs] *n* : callo *m*

callused ['kæləst] *adj* : encallecido, calloso

calm¹ ['kɑm, 'kɑlm] *vt* : tranquilizar, calmar, sosegar — *vi* **or to calm down** : tranquilizarse, calmarse ⟨calm down! : ¡tranquilízate!⟩

calm² *adj* **1** TRANQUIL : calmo, tranquilo, sereno, ecuánime **2** STILL : en calma (dícese del mar), sin viento (dícese del aire)

calm³ *n* : tranquilidad *f*, calma *f*

calmly ['kɑmli, 'kɑlm-] *adv* : con calma, tranquilamente

calmness ['kɑmnəs, 'kɑlm-] *n* : calma *f*, tranquilidad *f*

caloric [kə'lɔrık] *adj* : calórico (dícese de los alimentos), calorífico (dícese de la energía)

calorie ['kæləri] *n* : caloría *f*

calumniate [kə'lʌmni,eɪt] *vt* **-ated; -ating** : calumniar, difamar

calumny ['kæləmni] *n, pl* **-nies** : calumnia *f*, difamación *f*

calve ['kæv, 'kav] *vi* **calved; calving** : parir (dícese de los mamíferos)

calves → calf

calypso [kə'lıp,so:] *n, pl* **-sos** : calipso *m*

calyx ['keɪlıks, 'kæ-] *n, pl* **-lyxes** *or* **-lyces** [-lə,si:z] : cáliz *m*

cam ['kæm] *n* : leva *f*

camaraderie [,kɑm'rɑdəri, ,kæm-; ,kɑmə'rɑ-] *n* : compañerismo *m*, camaradería *f*

Cambodian [kæm'bo:diən] *n* : cambodiano *m*, -na *f* — **Cambodian** *adj*

camcorder ['kæm,kɔrdər] *n* : videocámara *f*

came → come

camel ['kæməl] *n* : camello *m*

cameo ['kæmi,o:] *n, pl* **-eos 1** : camafeo *m* **2** *or* **cameo performance** : actuación *f* especial

camera ['kæmrə, 'kæmərə] *n* : cámara *f*, máquina *f* fotográfica

cameraman ['kæmrə,mæn, 'kæmərə-] *n, pl* **-men** [-mən, -,mɛn] : cámara *m*

camerawoman ['kæmrə,wʊmən, 'kæmərə-] *n, pl* **-women** [,wɪmən] : cámara *f*

camouflage¹ ['kæmə,flɑʒ, -,flɑD] *vt* **-flaged; -flaging** : camuflajear, camuflar

camouflage² *n* : camuflaje *m*

camp¹ ['kæmp] *vi* : acampar, ir de camping

camp² *n* **1** : campamento *m* **2** FACTION : campo *m*, bando *m* ⟨in the same camp : del mismo bando⟩ **3 to pitch camp** : acampar, poner el campamento **4 to break camp** : levantar el campamento

campaign¹ [kæm'peɪn] *vi* : hacer (una) campaña

campaign² *n* : campaña *f*

campaigner [kæm'peɪnər] *n* : defensor *m*, -sora *f* ⟨civil rights campaigners : defensores de los derechos civiles⟩

campanile [,kæmpə'ni:,li:, -'ni:l] *n, pl* **-niles** *or* **-nili** [-'ni:,li:] : campanario *m*

camp bed *n* : cama *f* plegable

camper ['kæmpər] *n* **1** : campista *mf* (persona) **2** : cámper *m* (vehículo)

campfire ['kæmp,faɪr] *n* : fogata *f*, hoguera *f*, fogón *m*

campground ['kæmp,ɡraʊnd] *n* : campamento *m*, camping *m*

camphor ['kæmpfər] *n* : alcanfor *m*

camping ['kæmpɪŋ] *n* : camping *m*

campsite ['kæmp,saɪt] *n* : campamento *m*, camping *m*

campus ['kæmpəs] *n* : campus *m*, recinto *m* universitario

can¹ ['kæn] *v aux, past* **could** ['kʊd] *present s & pl* **can 1** (*referring to ability*) : poder ⟨I can't hear you : no te oigo⟩ ⟨I can do it myself : puedo hacerlo yo mismo⟩ ⟨I can't decide : no me decido⟩ ⟨it can withstand high temperatures : puede soportar altas temperaturas⟩ **2** (*referring to knowledge*) : saber ⟨he can already read and write : ya sabe leer y escribir⟩ **3** MAY : poder ⟨can I sit down? : ¿puedo sentarme?⟩ **4** (*expressing possibility*) : poder ⟨can/could you help me? : ¿podría ayudarme?⟩ ⟨sorry, I can't : lo siento pero no puedo⟩ ⟨I'll do what I can : haré lo que pueda⟩ ⟨she can't come : no puede venir⟩ ⟨he can be annoying : a veces es pesado⟩ ⟨it can get crowded : a veces se llena de gente⟩ ⟨it can't be! : ¡no puede ser!⟩ ⟨you can't be serious! : ¡no lo dirás en serio!⟩ ⟨where can they be? : ¿dónde estarán?⟩ ⟨we were as happy as can be : estábamos contentísimos⟩ **5** (*used to suggest or demand*) : poder ⟨why can't you be more romantic? : ¿por qué no puedes ser más romántico?⟩ ⟨you can always ask for help : siempre puedes pedir ayuda⟩ ⟨you can't leave so soon! : ¡no te vayas tan pronto!⟩ **6 no can do** *fam* : no puedo

can² ['kæn] *vt* **canned; canning 1** : enlatar, envasar ⟨to can tomatoes : enlatar tomates⟩ **2** DISMISS, FIRE : despedir, echar

can³ *n* : lata *f*, envase *m*, cubo *m* ⟨a can of beer : una lata de cerveza⟩ ⟨garbage can : cubo de basura⟩

Canadian [kə'neɪdiən] *n* : canadiense *mf* — **Canadian** *adj*

canal [kə'næl] *n* **1** : canal *m*, tubo *m* ⟨alimentary canal : tubo digestivo⟩ **2** : canal *m* ⟨Panama Canal : Canal de Panamá⟩

canapé ['kænəpi, -ˌpeɪ] *n* : canapé *m*

canary [kə'nɛri] *n, pl* **-naries** : canario *m*

cancel ['kæntsəl] *vt* **-celed** *or* **-celled; -celing** *or* **-celling 1** : cancelar **2 to cancel out** : anular

cancellation [ˌkæntsə'leɪʃən] *n* : cancelación *f*

cancer ['kænsər] *n* : cáncer *m*

Cancer *n* **1** : Cáncer *m* (signo o constelación) **2** : Cáncer *mf* (persona)

cancerous ['kæntsərəs] *adj* : canceroso

candelabrum [ˌkændə'lɑbrəm, -'læ-] *or* **candelabra** [-brə] *n, pl* **-bra** *or* **-bras** : candelabro *m*

candid ['kændɪd] *adj* **1** FRANK : franco, sincero, abierto **2** : natural, espontáneo (en la fotografía)

candidacy ['kændədəsi] *n, pl* **-cies** : candidatura *f*

candidate ['kændəˌdeɪt, -dət] *n* : candidato *m*, -ta *f*

candidly ['kændɪdli] *adv* : con franqueza

candied ['kændid] *adj* : confitado

candle ['kændəl] *n* : vela *f*, candela *f*, cirio *m* (ceremonial)

candlelight ['kændəlˌlaɪt] *n* **by** ∼ : a la luz de una vela

candlestick ['kændəlˌstɪk] *n* : candelero *m*

candor ['kændər] *n* : franqueza *f*

candy ['kændi] *n, pl* **-dies** : dulce *m*, caramelo *m*

cane¹ ['keɪn] *vt* **caned; caning 1** : tapizar (muebles) con mimbre **2** FLOG : azotar con una vara

cane² *n* **1** : bastón *m* (para andar), vara *f* (para castigar) **2** REED : caña *f*, mimbre *m* (para muebles)

canine¹ ['keɪˌnaɪn] *adj* : canino

canine² *n* **1** DOG : canino *m*; perro *m*, -rra *f* **2** *or* **canine tooth** : colmillo *m*, diente *m* canino

canister ['kænəstər] *n* : lata *f*, bote *m*

canker ['kæŋkər] *n* : úlcera *f* bucal

cannabis ['kænəbɪs] *n* : cannabis *m*

cannelloni [ˌkænə'lo:ni] *n* : canelones *mpl*

cannery ['kænəri] *n, pl* **-ries** : fábrica *f* de conservas

cannibal ['kænəbəl] *n* : caníbal *mf*; antropófago *m*, -ga *f*

cannibalism ['kænəbəˌlɪzəm] *n* : canibalismo *m*, antropofagia *f*

cannibalistic [ˌkænəbə'lɪstɪk] *adj* : antropófago, caníbal

cannily ['kænəli] *adv* : astutamente, sagazmente

cannon ['kænən] *n, pl* **-nons** *or* **-non** : cañón *m*

cannot (can not) ['kænˌɑt, kə'nɑt] → **can¹**

canny ['kæni] *adj* **-nier; -est** SHREWD : astuto, sagaz

canoe¹ [kə'nu:] *vt* **-noed; -noeing** : ir en canoa

canoe² *n* : canoa *f*, piragua *f*

canoeing [kə'nu:ɪŋ] *n* : piragüismo *m*

canoeist [kə'nu:ɪst] *or* **canoer** [kə'nu:ər] *n* : piragüista *mf*

canon ['kænən] *n* **1** : canon *m* ⟨canon law : derecho canónico⟩ **2** WORKS : canon *m* ⟨the canon of American literature : el canon de la literatura americana⟩ **3** : canónigo *m* (de una catedral) **4** STANDARD : canon *m*, norma *f*

canonical [kə'nɑnɪkəl] *adj* : canónico

canonize ['kænəˌnaɪz] *vt* **-ized; -izing** : canonizar

can opener *n* : abrelatas *m*

canopy ['kænəpi] *n, pl* **-pies** : dosel *m*, toldo *m*

cant¹ ['kænt] *vt* TILT : ladear, inclinar — *vi* **1** SLANT : ladearse, inclinarse, escorar (dícese de un buque) **2** : hablar insinceramente

cant² *n* **1** SLANT : plano *m* inclinado **2** JARGON : jerga *f* **3** : palabras *fpl* insinceras

can't ['kænt, 'kɑnt] *contraction of* CAN NOT → **can¹**

cantaloupe ['kæntəlˌo:p] *n* : melón *m*, cantalupo *m*

cantankerous [kæn'tæŋkərəs] *adj* : irritable, irascible — **cantankerously** *adv*

cantankerousness [kæn'tæŋkərəsnəs] *n* : irritabilidad *f*, irascibilidad *f*

cantata [kən'tɑtə] *n* : cantata *f*

canteen [kæn'ti:n] *n* **1** FLASK : cantimplora *f* **2** CAFETERIA : cantina *f*, comedor *m* **3** : club *m* para actividades sociales y recreativas

canter¹ ['kæntər] *vi* : ir a medio galope

canter² *n* : medio galope *m*

cantilever ['kæntəˌli:vər, -ˌlɛvər] *n* **1** : viga *f* voladiza **2 cantilever bridge** : puente *m* voladizo

canto ['kænˌto:] *n, pl* **-tos** : canto *m*

canton ['kæntən, -ˌtɑn] *n* : cantón *m*

Cantonese [ˌkæntən'i:z, -'i:s] *n* **1** : cantonés *m*, -nesa *f* **2** : cantonés *m* (idioma) — **Cantonese** *adj*

cantor ['kæntər] *n* : solista *mf*

canvas ['kænvəs] *n* **1** : lona *f* **2** SAILS : velas *fpl* (de un barco) **3** : lienzo *m*, tela *f* (de pintar) **4** PAINTING : pintura *f*, óleo *m*, cuadro *m*

canvass¹ ['kænvəs] *vt* **1** SOLICIT : solicitar votos o pedidos de, hacer campaña entre **2** SOUND OUT : sondear (opiniones, etc.)

canvass² *n* SURVEY : sondeo *m*, encuesta *f*

canyon ['kænjən] *n* : cañón *m*

cap¹ ['kæp] *vt* **capped; capping 1** COVER : tapar (un recipiente), enfundar (un diente), cubrir (una montaña) **2** CLIMAX : coronar, ser el punto culminante de ⟨to cap it all off : para colmo⟩ **3** LIMIT : limitar, poner un tope a

cap² *n* **1** : gorra *f*, gorro *m*, cachucha *f* *Mex* ⟨baseball cap : gorra de béisbol⟩ **2** COVER, TOP : tapa *f*, tapón *m* (de botellas), corcholata *f Mex* **3** LIMIT : tope *m*, límite *m*

capability [ˌkeɪpəˈbɪləti] *n*, *pl* **-ties** : capacidad *f*, habilidad *f*, competencia *f*

capable [ˈkeɪpəbəl] *adj* : competente, capaz, hábil — **capably** [-bli] *adv*

capacious [kəˈpeɪʃəs] *adj* : amplio, espacioso, de gran capacidad

capacity¹ [kəˈpæsəti] *adj* : completo, total ⟨a capacity crowd : un lleno completo⟩

capacity² *n*, *pl* **-ties** **1** ROOM, SPACE : capacidad *f*, cabida *f*, espacio *m* **2** CAPABILITY : habilidad *f*, competencia *f* **3** FUNCTION, ROLE : calidad *f*, función *f* ⟨in his capacity as ambassador : en su calidad de embajador⟩

cape [ˈkeɪp] *n* **1** : capa *f* **2** : cabo *m* ⟨Cape Horn : el Cabo de Hornos⟩

caper¹ [ˈkeɪpər] *vi* : dar saltos, correr y brincar

caper² *n* **1** : alcaparra *f* ⟨olives and capers : aceitunas y alcaparras⟩ **2** ANTIC, PRANK : broma *f*, travesura *f* **3** LEAP : brinco *m*, salto *m*

capful [ˈkæpˌfʊl] *n* : tapa *f*, tapita *f*

capillary¹ [ˈkæpəˌleri] *adj* : capilar

capillary² *n*, *pl* **-ries** : capilar *m*

capital¹ [ˈkæpətəl] *adj* **1** : capital ⟨capital punishment : pena capital⟩ **2** : mayúsculo (dícese de las letras) **3** : de capital ⟨capital assets : activo fijo⟩ ⟨capital gain : ganancia de capital, plusvalía⟩ **4** EXCELLENT : excelente, estupendo

capital² *n* **1** *or* **capital city** : capital *f*, sede *f* del gobierno **2** WEALTH : capital *m* **3** *or* **capital letter** : mayúscula *f* **4** : capitel *m* (de una columna)

capitalism [ˈkæpətəlˌɪzəm] *n* : capitalismo *m*

capitalist¹ [ˈkæpətəlɪst] *or* **capitalistic** [ˌkæpətəlˈɪstɪk] *adj* : capitalista

capitalist² *n* : capitalista *mf*

capitalization [ˌkæpətələˈzeɪʃən] *n* : capitalización *f*

capitalize [ˈkæpətəlˌaɪz] *v* **-ized; -izing** *vt* **1** FINANCE : capitalizar, financiar **2** : escribir con mayúscula — *vi* **to capitalize on** : sacar partido de, aprovechar

capitol [ˈkæpətəl] *n* : capitolio *m*

capitulate [kəˈpɪtʃəˌleɪt] *vi* **-lated; -lating** : capitular

capitulation [kəˌpɪtʃəˈleɪʃən] *n* : capitulación *f*

capon [ˈkeɪˌpɑn, -pən] *n* : capón *m*

cappuccino [ˌkɑpəˈtʃiːnoː] *n* : capuchino *m* (café)

caprice [kəˈpriːs] *n* : capricho *m*, antojo *m*

capricious [kəˈprɪʃəs, -ˈpriː-] *adj* : caprichoso — **capriciously** *adv*

Capricorn [ˈkæprɪˌkɔrn] *n* **1** : Capricornio *m* (signo o constelación) **2** : Capricornio *mf* (persona)

capsize [ˈkæpˌsaɪz, kæpˈsaɪz] *v* **-sized; -sizing** *vi* : volcar, volcarse — *vt* : hacer volcar

capsule [ˈkæpsəl, -ˌsuːl] *n* **1** : cápsula *f*

(en la farmacéutica y botánica) **2** **space capsule** : cápsula *f* espacial

captain¹ [ˈkæptən] *vt* : capitanear

captain² *n* **1** : capitán *m*, -tana *f* **2** HEADWAITER : jefe *m*, -fa *f* de comedor **3 captain of industry** : magnate *mf*

caption¹ [ˈkæpʃən] *vt* : ponerle una leyenda a (una ilustración), titular (un artículo), subtitular (una película)

caption² *n* **1** HEADING : titular *m*, encabezamiento *m* **2** : leyenda *f* (al pie de una ilustración) **3** SUBTITLE : subtítulo *m*

captivate [ˈkæptəˌveɪt] *vt* **-vated; -vating** CHARM : cautivar, hechizar, encantar

captivating [ˈkæptəˌveɪtɪŋ] *adj* : cautivador, hechicero, encantador

captive¹ [ˈkæptɪv] *adj* : cautivo

captive² *n* : cautivo *m*, -va *f*

captivity [kæpˈtɪvəti] *n* : cautiverio *m*

captor [ˈkæptər] *n* : captor *m*, -tora *f*

capture¹ [ˈkæpʃər] *vt* **-tured; -turing** **1** SEIZE : capturar, apresar **2** CATCH : captar ⟨to capture one's interest : captar el interés de uno⟩

capture² *n* : captura *f*, apresamiento *m*

car [ˈkɑr] *n* **1** AUTOMOBILE : automóvil *m*, carro *m*, coche *m* **2** : vagón *m*, coche *m* (de un tren) **3** : cabina *f* (de un ascensor)

carafe [kəˈræf, -ˈrɑf] *n* : garrafa *f*

caramel [ˈkɑrməl;, ˈkærəməl, -ˌmɛl] *n* **1** : caramelo *m*, azúcar *f* quemada **2** *or* **caramel candy** : caramelo *m*, dulce *m* de leche

carat [ˈkærət] *n* : quilate *m*

caravan [ˈkærəˌvæn] *n* : caravana *f*

caraway [ˈkærəˌweɪ] *n* : alcaravea *f*

carb [ˈkɑrb] *n fam* → **carbohydrate**

carbine [ˈkɑrˌbaɪn, -ˌbiːn] *n* : carabina *f*

carbohydrate [ˌkɑrboˈhaɪˌdreɪt, -drət] *n* : carbohidrato *m*, hidrato *m* de carbono

car bomb *n* : carro *m* bomba, coche *m* bomba, auto *m* bomba *Chile*

carbon [ˈkɑrbən] *n* **1** : carbono *m* **2** → **carbon paper** **3** → **carbon copy**

carbonated [ˈkɑrbəˌneɪtəd] *adj* : carbonatado (dícese del agua), gaseoso (dícese de las bebidas)

carbon copy *n* **1** : copia *f* al carbón **2** DUPLICATE : duplicado *m*, copia *f* exacta

carbon dioxide [-daɪˈɑkˌsaɪd] *n* : dióxido *m* de carbono

carbon footprint *n* : huella *f* de carbono

carbon monoxide [-məˈnɑkˌsaɪd] *n* : monóxido *m* de carbono

carbon paper *n* : papel *m* carbón

carburetor [ˈkɑrbəˌreɪtər, -bjə-] *n* : carburador *m*

carcass [ˈkɑrkəs] *n* : cuerpo *m* (de un animal muerto)

carcinogen [kɑrˈsɪnəʤ ən, ˈkɑrsənəˌʤ ɛn] *n* : carcinógeno *m*, cancerígeno *m*

carcinogenic [ˌkɑrsənoˈʤ ɛnɪk] *adj* : carcinogénico

carcinoma [ˌkɑrsəˈnoːmə] *n* : carcinoma *m*

card¹ [ˈkɑrd] *vt* : cardar (fibras)

card² *n* **1** : carta *f*, naipe *m* ⟨to play cards : jugar a las cartas⟩ ⟨a deck of cards

: una baraja⟩ **2** : tarjeta *f* ⟨birthday card : tarjeta de cumpleaños⟩ ⟨business card : tarjeta (de visita)⟩ **3** : tarjeta *f* (bancaria) ⟨credit/debit card : tarjeta de crédito/débito⟩ **4** : tarjeta *f* (de memoria, etc.) **5 to be in the cards** : estar escrito ⟨it just wasn't in the cards : estaba escrito que no iba a pasar⟩

cardboard [ˈkɑrdˌbord] *n* : cartón *m*, cartulina *f*

cardiac [ˈkɑrdiˌæk] *adj* : cardíaco, cardiaco

cardigan [ˈkɑrdɪɡən] *n* : cárdigan *m*, chaqueta *f* de punto

cardinal[1] [ˈkɑrdənəl] *adj* FUNDAMENTAL : cardinal, fundamental

cardinal[2] *n* : cardenal *m*

cardinal number *n* : número *m* cardinal

cardinal point *n* : punto *m* cardinal

cardiologist [ˌkɑrdiˈɑləʊ ɪst] *n* : cardiólogo *m*, -ga *f*

cardiology [ˌkɑrdiˈɑləʊ i] *n* : cardiología *f*

cardiopulmonary resuscitation [ˌkɑrdio ˈpʊlmənɛri-, -ˈpʌl-] *n* → **CPR**

cardiovascular [ˌkɑrdioˈvæskjələr] *adj* : cardiovascular

care[1] [ˈkær] *v* **cared; caring** *vi* **1** : importarle a uno ⟨they don't care : no les importa⟩ ⟨I could/couldn't care less : (no) me importa un bledo/comino⟩ ⟨see if I care! : ¡me tiene sin cuidado!⟩ ⟨who cares? : ¿y qué?, ¿qué importa?⟩ **2** LOVE : querer ⟨show her that you care (about her) : demuéstrale que la quieres⟩ **3** : preocuparse, inquietarse ⟨she cares about the poor : se preocupa por los pobres⟩ **4 to care for** TEND : cuidar (de), atender, encargarse de **5 to care for** LOVE : querer, sentir cariño por **6 to care for** LIKE : gustarle (algo a uno) ⟨I don't care for your attitude : tu actitud no me agrada⟩ — *vt* **1** WISH : desear, querer ⟨if you care to go : si deseas ir⟩ **2** : importarle a uno ⟨I don't care what happens to her : a mí no me importa lo que le pase⟩ ⟨for all I care, he can quit right now : por mí, puede renunciarse ahora mismo⟩ ⟨what does she care? : ¿a ella qué le importa?⟩

care[2] *n* **1** ANXIETY : inquietud *f*, preocupación *f* ⟨to be without a care in the world : no tener ninguna preocupación⟩ **2** CAREFULNESS : cuidado *m*, atención *f* ⟨handle with care : manejar con cuidado⟩ **3** : cargo *m*, cuidado *m* ⟨medical care : asistencia médica⟩ ⟨hair care : el cuidado del cabello/pelo⟩ ⟨the children are in my care : los niños están a mi cuidado/cargo⟩ **4 care of** : a casa de (en una carta) **5 take care!** : ¡cuídate! **6 to take care** : tener cuidado **7 to take care of** CARE FOR : cuidar (de), atender **8 to take care of** DEAL WITH : encargarse de

careen [kəˈriːn] *vi* **1** SWAY : oscilar, balancearse **2** CAREER : ir a toda velocidad

career[1] [kəˈrɪr] *vi* : ir a toda velocidad

career[2] *n* VOCATION : vocación *f*, profesión *f*, carrera *f*

carefree [ˈkærˌfriː, ˌkærˈ-] *adj* : despreocupado

careful [ˈkærfəl] *adj* **1** CAUTIOUS : cuidadoso, cauteloso ⟨be careful : ten cuidado⟩ ⟨you can't be too careful : toda prudencia es poca⟩ **2** PAINSTAKING : cuidadoso, esmerado, meticuloso ⟨after careful consideration : después de considerarlo detenidamente⟩

carefully [ˈkærfəli] *adv* : con cuidado, cuidadosamente

carefulness [ˈkærfəlnəs] *n* **1** CAUTION : cuidado *m*, cautela *f* **2** METICULOUSNESS : esmero *m*, meticulosidad *f*

caregiver [ˈkærˌɡɪvər] *n* : persona *f* que cuida a niños o enfermos

careless [ˈkærləs] *adj* : descuidado, negligente — **carelessly** *adv*

carelessness [ˈkærləsnəs] *n* : descuido *m*, negligencia *f*

caress[1] [kəˈrɛs] *vt* : acariciar

caress[2] *n* : caricia *f*

caret [ˈkærət] *n* : signo *m* de intercalación

caretaker [ˈkærˌteɪkər] *n* : conserje *mf*; velador *m*, -dora *f*

cargo [ˈkɑrˌɡoː] *n, pl* **-goes** *or* **-gos** : cargamento *m*, carga *f*

Caribbean [ˌkærəˈbiːən, kəˈrɪbiən] *adj* : caribeño ⟨the Caribbean Sea : el mar Caribe⟩

caribou [ˈkærəˌbuː] *n, pl* **-bou** *or* **-bous** : caribú *m*

caricature[1] [ˈkærɪkəˌtʃʊr] *vt* **-tured; -turing** : caricaturizar

caricature[2] *n* : caricatura *f*

caricaturist [ˈkærɪkəˌtʃʊrɪst] *n* : caricaturista *mf*

caries [ˈkærˌiːz] *ns & pl* : caries *f*

caring [ˈkærɪŋ] *n* **1** AFFECTIONATE : cariñoso, solícito **2** KIND : bondadoso

carjacking [ˈkɑrˌdʒækɪŋ] *n* : robo *m* de un vehículo (por asalto)

carmine [ˈkɑrmən, -ˌmaɪn] *n* : carmín *m*

carnage [ˈkɑrnɪdʒ] *n* : matanza *f*, carnicería *f*

carnal [ˈkɑrnəl] *adj* : carnal

carnation [kɑrˈneɪʃən] *n* : clavel *m*

carnival [ˈkɑrnəvəl] *n* : carnaval *m*, feria *f*

carnivore [ˈkɑrnəˌvor] *n* : carnívoro *m*

carnivorous [kɑrˈnɪvərəs] *adj* : carnívoro

carol[1] [ˈkærəl] *vi* **-oled** *or* **-olled; -oling** *or* **-olling** : cantar villancicos

carol[2] *n* : villancico *m*

caroler *or* **caroller** [ˈkærələr] *n* : persona *f* que canta villancicos

carom[1] [ˈkærəm] *vi* **1** REBOUND : rebotar ⟨the bullet caromed off the wall : la bala rebotó contra el muro⟩ **2** : hacer carambola (en billar)

carom[2] *n* : carambola *f*

carouse [kəˈrauz] *vt* **-roused; -rousing** : irse de parranda, irse de juerga

carousel *or* **carrousel** [ˌkærəˈsɛl, ˈkærəˌ-] *n* : carrusel *m*, tiovivo *m*

carouser [kəˈrauzər] *n* : juerguista *mf*

carp[1] [ˈkɑrp] *vi* **1** COMPLAIN : quejarse **2 to carp at** : criticar

carp[2] *n, pl* **carp** *or* **carps** : carpa *f*

carpenter [ˈkɑrpəntər] *n* : carpintero *m*, -ra *f*

carpentry [ˈkɑrpəntri] *n* : carpintería *f*

carpet[1] [ˈkɑrpət] *vt* : alfombrar

carpet² *n* : alfombra *f*

carpeting ['kɑrpətɪŋ] *n* : alfombrado *m*

carport ['kɑr,pɔrt] *n* : cochera *f*, garaje *m* abierto

carriage ['kærɪD] *n* **1** TRANSPORT : transporte *m* **2** POSTURE : porte *m*, postura *f* **3** *or* **horse–drawn carriage** : carruaje *m*, coche *m* **4** *or* **baby carriage** : cochecito *m*

carrier ['kæriər] *n* **1** : transportista *mf*, empresa *f* de transportes **2** : portador *m*, -dora *f* (de una enfermedad) **3** **aircraft carrier** : portaaviones *m*

carrier pigeon : paloma *f* mensajera

carrion ['kæriən] *n* : carroña *f*

carrot ['kærət] *n* : zanahoria *f*

carry ['kæri] *v* **-ried; -rying** *vt* **1** : llevar, cargar, transportar (cargamento) ⟨to carry a bag : cargar una bolsa⟩ ⟨to carry money : llevar dinero encima, traer dinero consigo⟩ **2** : llevar (sangre, agua, etc.) **3** HAVE : tener (una garantía, etc.), llevar (una advertencia) **4** BEAR : soportar, aguantar, resistir (peso) **5** STOCK : vender, tener en abasto **6** ENTAIL : llevar, implicar, acarrear **7** WIN, PASS : ganar (una elección o competición), aprobar (una moción) **8** : estar embarazada de (un hijo) **9** : portar, ser portador de (un virus, etc.) **10** : llevar (en matemáticas) **11 to be/get carried away** : pasarse, excederse ⟨to be/ get carried away by something : dejarse llevar por algo⟩ **12 to carry a tune** : cantar bien **13 to carry off** ACHIEVE : conseguir, lograr **14 to carry off** TAKE : llevarse **15 to carry on** CONTINUE : seguir con, continuar con **16 to carry on** CONDUCT : realizar, ejercer, mantener ⟨to carry on research : realizar investigaciones⟩ ⟨to carry on a correspondence : mantener una correspondencia⟩ **17 to carry oneself** : portarse, comportarse ⟨he carried himself honorably : se comportó dignamente⟩ **18 to carry out** COMPLETE : llevar a cabo, realizar, efectuar **19 to carry out** FULFILL : cumplir (una orden, etc.) **20 to carry through** SUSTAIN : sustentar, sostener — *vi* **1** : oírse, proyectarse ⟨her voice carries well : su voz se puede oír desde lejos⟩ **2 to carry on** CONTINUE : seguir, continuar **3 to carry on** : portarse de manera escandalosa o inapropiada ⟨it's embarrassing how he carries on : su manera de comportarse da vergüenza⟩

carryall ['kæri,ɔl] *n* : bolsa *f* de viaje

carsick ['kɑr,sɪk] *adj* : mareado (de ir en coche)

cart¹ ['kɑrt] *vt* : acarrear, llevar

cart² *n* : carreta *f*, carro *m*

carte blanche ['kɑrt'blɑnch] *n* : carta *f* blanca

cartel [kɑr'tɛl] *n* : cártel *m*

cartilage ['kɑrṱɪlɪD] *n* : cartílago *m*

cartographer [kɑr'tɑɡrəfər] *n* : cartógrafo *m*, -fa *f*

cartography [kɑr'tɑɡrəfi] *n* : cartografía *f*

carton ['kɑrtən] *n* : caja *f* de cartón

cartoon [kɑr'tu:n] *n* **1** : chiste *m* (gráfico), caricatura *f* ⟨a political cartoon : un chiste político⟩ **2** COMIC STRIP : tira *f* cómica, historieta *f* **3** : dibujo *m* animado ⟨to watch cartoons : mirar dibujos animados⟩

cartoonist [kɑr'tu:nɪst] *n* : caricaturista *mf*, dibujante *mf* (de chistes)

cartridge ['kɑrtrɪD] *n* : cartucho *m*

cartwheel ['kɑrt,ʍi:l] *n* : voltereta *f* lateral

carve ['kɑrv] *vt* **carved; carving 1** : tallar (madera), esculpir (piedra), grabar ⟨he carved his name in the bark : grabó su nombre en la corteza⟩ **2** SLICE : cortar, trinchar (carne) **3 to carve out** : hacerse, conquistar

carving ['kɑrvɪŋ] *n* : talla *f*, escultura *f* (de madera, piedra, etc.)

cascade¹ [kæs'keɪd] *vi* **-caded; -cading** : caer en cascada

cascade² *n* : cascada *f*, salto *m* de agua

case¹ ['keɪs] *vt* **cased; casing 1** BOX, PACK : embalar, encajonar **2** INSPECT : observar, inspeccionar (antes de cometer un delito)

case² *n* **1** : caso *m* ⟨an unusual case : un caso insólito⟩ ⟨a case of the flu : un caso de gripe⟩ ⟨a murder case : un caso de asesinato⟩ **2** BOX : caja *f* **3** CONTAINER : funda *f*, estuche *m* **4** SUITCASE : maleta *f*, valija *f* **5** ARGUMENT : argumento *m* ⟨to make a case for : presentar argumentos a favor de⟩ **6** : caso *m* (en gramática) **7 in any case** : de todos modos, en cualquier caso **8 in ∼** : como precaución ⟨just in case : por si acaso⟩ **9 in case of** : en caso de **10 in that case** : en ese caso

casement ['keɪsmənt] *n* : ventana *f* con bisagras

cash¹ ['kæʃ] *vt* : convertir en efectivo, cobrar, cambiar (un cheque) — *vi* **to cash in on** : sacar partido de

cash² *n* : efectivo *m*, dinero *m* en efectivo ⟨cash on delivery : entrega contra reembolso⟩ ⟨hard/cold cash : dinero contante y sonante⟩

cashew ['kæ,ʃu:, kə'ʃu:] *n* : anacardo *m*

cashier¹ [kæ'ʃɪr] *vt* : destituir, despedir

cashier² *n* : cajero *m*, -ra *f*

cashmere ['kæʒ,mɪr, 'kæʃ-] *n* : cachemir *m*

cash register *n* : caja *f* registradora

casing ['keɪsɪŋ] *n* **1** : caja *f*, cubierta *f* **2** : casquillo *m* (de una bala, etc.) **3** FRAME : marco *m* (de una puerta o ventana)

casino [kə'si:,no:] *n*, *pl* **-nos** : casino *m*

cask ['kæsk] *n* : tonel *m*, barrica *f*, barril *m*

casket ['kæskət] *n* COFFIN : ataúd *m*, féretro *m*

cassava [kə'sɑvə] *n* : mandioca *f*, yuca *f*

casserole ['kæsə,ro:l] *n* **1** : cazuela *f* **2** : guiso *m*, guisado *m* ⟨tuna casserole : guiso de atún⟩

cassette [kə'sɛt, kæ-] *n* : cassette *mf*

cassock ['kæsək] *n* : sotana *f*

cast¹ ['kæst] *vt* **cast; casting 1** THROW : tirar, echar, arrojar ⟨the die is cast : la suerte está echada⟩ **2** DIRECT : echar ⟨he cast a glance at the door : echó una mirada a la puerta⟩ **3** : depositar (un voto) **4** : asignar ⟨to cast a role : asignar un papel⟩ ⟨to cast someone as : asignarle a alguien el papel de⟩ **5** MOLD : moldear, fundir, vaciar **6** : proyectar (luz, etc.) ⟨to cast a shadow : proyectar una sombra⟩ ⟨to cast a shadow/pall on : ensombrecer⟩ **7 to be cast away** : quedarse varado (en un lugar remoto tras naufragar) **8 to cast adrift** : dejar a la deriva **9 to cast aside** : desechar (las preocupaciones, etc.) **10 to cast a spell on** : hechizar **11 to cast off** GET RID OF : deshacerse de **12 to cast out** EXPEL : expulsar — *vi* **1 to cast about/around for** : tratar de encontrar **2 to cast off** : desamarrar, soltar (las) amarras **3 to cast off** : cerrar (puntos) **4 to cast on** : montar puntos

cast² *n* **1** THROW : lance *m*, lanzamiento *m* **2** APPEARANCE : aspecto *m*, forma *f* **3** : elenco *m*, reparto *m* (de una obra de teatro) **4** MOLD : molde *m* **5** : yeso *m*, escayola *f Spain* (en medicina)

castanet [ˌkæstə'nɛt] *n* : castañuela *f*

castaway¹ ['kæstəˌweɪ] *adj* : náufrago

castaway² *n* : náufrago *m*, -ga *f*

caste ['kæst] *n* : casta *f*

caster ['kæstər] *n* : ruedita *f* (de un mueble)

castigate ['kæstəˌɡeɪt] *vt* **-gated; -gating** : castigar severamente, censurar, reprobar

Castilian [kæ'stɪljən] *n* **1** : castellano *m*, -na *f* **2** : castellano *m* (idioma) — **Castilian** *adj*

cast iron *n* : hierro *m* fundido

castle ['kæsəl] *n* **1** : castillo *m* **2** : torre *f* (en ajedrez)

cast–off ['kæstˌɔf] *adj* : desechado

castoff ['kæstˌɔf] *n* : desecho *m*

castor oil ['kæstər-] *n* : aceite *m* de ricino

castrate ['kæsˌtreɪt] *vt* **-trated; -trating** : castrar

castration [kæ'streɪʃən] *n* : castración *f*

casual ['kæʒuəl] *adj* **1** FORTUITOUS : casual, fortuito **2** INDIFFERENT : indiferente, despreocupado **3** INFORMAL : informal **4** IRREGULAR, OCCASIONAL : eventual, ocasional — **casually** ['kæʒʰuəli, 'kæʒəli] *adv*

casualness ['kæʒuəlnəs] *n* **1** INDIFFERENCE : indiferencia *f*, despreocupación *f* **2** INFORMALITY : informalidad *f*

casualty ['kæʒuəlti, 'kæʒəl-] *n, pl* **-ties 1** ACCIDENT : accidente *m* serio, desastre *m* **2** VICTIM : víctima *f*; baja *f*; herido *m*, -da *f*

cat ['kæt] *n* : gato *m*, -ta *f*

cataclysm ['kæɹəˌklɪzəm] *n* : cataclismo *m*

cataclysmal [ˌkæɹə'klɪzməl] *or* **cataclysmic** [ˌkæɹə'klɪzmɪk] *adj* : catastrófico

catacombs ['kæɹəˌkoːmz] *npl* : catacumbas *fpl*

Catalan ['kæɹələn, -ˌlæn] *n* **1** : catalán *m*, catalana *f* **2** : catalán *m* (idioma) — **Catalan** *adj*

catalog¹ *or* **catalogue** ['kæɹəˌlɔɡ] *vt* **-loged** *or* **-logued; -loging** *or* **-loguing** : catalogar

catalog² *n* : catálogo *m*

catalyst ['kæɹəl\st] *n* : catalizador *m*

catalytic converter [ˌkæɹəl'ɪtɪk-] *n* : catalizador *m*, convertidor *m* catalítico

catamaran [ˌkæɹəmə'ræn, 'kæɹəməˌræn] *n* : catamarán *m*

catapult¹ ['kæɹəˌpʌlt, -ˌpʊlt] *vt* : catapultar

catapult² *n* : catapulta *f*

cataract ['kæɹəˌrækt] *n* : catarata *f*

catarrh [kə'tɑr] *n* : catarro *m*

catastrophe [kə'tæstrəˌfiː] *n* : catástrofe *f*

catastrophic [ˌkæɹə'strɑfɪk] *adj* : catastrófico — **catastrophically** [-fɪkli] *adv*

catcall ['kætˌkɔl] *n* : rechifla *f*, abucheo *m*

catch¹ ['kætʃ, 'kɛtʃ] *v* **caught** ['kɔt]; **catching** *vt* **1** GRASP : agarrar, coger *Spain* **2** CAPTURE, TRAP : capturar, agarrar, atrapar, coger *Spain* **3** SURPRISE, INTERRUPT : agarrar, pillar *fam*, coger *Spain* ⟨they caught him red-handed : lo pillaron con las manos en la masa⟩ ⟨to catch by surprise : tomar por sorpresa⟩ ⟨we got caught in the rain : nos agarró la lluvia⟩ ⟨you've caught me at a bad time : llegas en mal momento⟩ ⟨I caught her just as she was leaving : llegué justo cuando ella salía⟩ **4** ENTANGLE : enganchar, enredar ⟨to get caught up in something : quedarse enredado en algo⟩ **5** MAKE : alcanzar (un tren, etc.) **6** TAKE : tomar (un tren, etc.) **7** : contagiarse de ⟨to catch a cold : contagiarse de un resfriado, resfriarse⟩ **8** ATTRACT : llamar (la atención), captar (el interés) **9** UNDERSTAND : captar ⟨if you catch my drift : si me entiendes⟩ **10** PERCEIVE : percibir ⟨to catch a glimpse of : alcanzar a ver⟩ **11** NOTICE, DETECT : darse cuenta de, detectar **12** : ver (una película), ir a (un concierto, etc.) — *vi* **1** GRASP : agarrar **2** HOOK : engancharse **3** IGNITE : prender, agarrar **4 to catch on** : hacerse popular **5 to catch on** LEARN : agarrarle la onda **6 to catch on** UNDERSTAND : entender, darse cuenta **7 to catch up** : ponerse al día ⟨to catch up on the news : ponerse al día con las noticias⟩ **8 to catch up to/ with** : alcanzar

catch² *n* **1** CATCHING : captura *f*, atrapada *f*, parada *f* (de una pelota) **2** : redada *f* (de pescado), presa *f* (de caza) ⟨he's a good catch : es un buen partido⟩ **3** LATCH : pestillo *m*, pasador *m* **4** DIFFICULTY, TRICK : problema *m*, trampa *f*, truco *m*

catcher ['kætʃər, 'kɛ-] *n* : catcher *mf*; receptor *m*, -tora *f* (en béisbol)

catching ['kætʃɪŋ, 'kɛ-] *adj* : contagioso

catchphrase ['kætʃˌfreɪz, 'kɛtʃ-] *n* : eslogan *m*, lema *m*

catchup ['kætʃəp, 'kɛ-] → **ketchup**

catchword ['kætʃˌwərd, 'kɛtʃ-] *n* : eslogan *m*, lema *m*

catchy ['kætʃi, 'kɛ-] *adj* **catchier; -est** : pegajoso ⟨a catchy song : una canción pegajosa⟩

catechism ['kæʈə,kızəm] *n* : catecismo *m*

categorical [,kæʈə'gɔrıkəl] *adj* : categórico, absoluto, rotundo — **categorically** [-kli] *adv*

categorize ['kæʈɪɡə,raız] *vt* **-rized; -rizing** : clasificar, catalogar

category ['kæʈə,ɡɔri] *n, pl* **-ries** : categoría *f*, género *m*, clase *f*

cater ['keıʈər] *vi* **1** : proveer servicio de alimentos (para fiestas, bodas, etc.) **2 to cater to** : atender a ⟨to cater to all tastes : atender a todos los gustos⟩ — *vt* : proveer servicio de alimentos para

catercorner¹ ['kæʈɪ,kɔrnər, 'kæʈə-, 'kıʈi-] *or* **cater-cornered** [-,kɔrnərd] *adv* : diagonalmente, en diagonal

catercorner² *or* **cater-cornered** *adj* : diagonal

caterer ['keıʈərər] *n* : proveedor *m*, -dora *f* de comida

catering ['keıʈərıŋ] *n* : servicio *m* de alimentos, catering *m*

caterpillar ['kæʈər,pılər] *n* : oruga *f*

catfish ['kæt,fıʃ] *n* : bagre *m*

catgut ['kæt,ɡʌt] *n* : cuerda *f* de tripa

catharsis [kə'θɑrsıs] *n, pl* **catharses** [-,si:z] : catarsis *f*

cathartic¹ [kə'θɑrʈık] *adj* : catártico

cathartic² *n* : purgante *m*

cathedral [kə'θi:drəl] *n* : catedral *f*

catheter ['kæθəʈər] *n* : catéter *m*, sonda *f*

cathode ['kæ,θo:d] *n* : cátodo *m*

catholic ['kæθəlık] *adj* **1** BROAD, UNIVERSAL : liberal, universal **2 Catholic** : católico

Catholic *n* : católico *m*, -ca *f*

Catholicism [kə'θɑlə,sızəm] *n* : catolicismo *m*

catlike ['kæt,laık] *adj* : felino

catnap¹ ['kæt,næp] *vi* **-napped; -napping** : tomarse una siestecita

catnap² *n* : siesta *f* breve, siestecita *f*

catnip ['kæt,nıp] *n* : nébeda *f*

catsup ['kɛtʃəp, 'kætsəp] → **ketchup**

cattail ['kæt,teıl] *n* : espadaña *f*, anea *f*

cattiness ['kæʈinəs] *n* : malicia *f*

cattle ['kæʈəl] *npl* : ganado *m*, reses *fpl*

cattleman ['kæʈəlmən, -,mæn] *n, pl* **-men** [-mən, -,mɛn] : ganadero *m*

catty ['kæʈi] *adj* **cattier; -est** : malicioso, malintencionado

catwalk ['kæt,wɔk] *n* : pasarela *f*

Caucasian¹ [kɔ'keıʒən] *adj* : caucásico

Caucasian² *n* : caucásico *m*, -ca *f*

caucus ['kɔkəs] *n* : junta *f* de políticos

caught → **catch**

cauldron ['kɔldrən] *n* : caldera *f*

cauliflower ['kɑlɪ,flauər, 'kɔ-] *n* : coliflor *f*

caulk¹ ['kɔk] *vt* : enmasillar (una grieta)

caulk² *n* : masilla *f*

causal ['kɔzəl] *adj* : causal — **causality** [kɔ'zæləʈi] *n*

cause¹ ['kɔz] *vt* **caused; causing** : causar, provocar, ocasionar

cause² *n* **1** ORIGIN : causa *f*, origen *m* **2** REASON : causa *f*, razón *f*, motivo *m* **3** LAWSUIT : litigio *m*, pleito *m* **4** MOVEMENT : causa *f*, movimiento *m*

causeless ['kɔzləs] *adj* : sin causa

causeway ['kɔz,weı] *n* : camino *m* elevado

caustic ['kɔstık] *adj* **1** CORROSIVE : cáustico, corrosivo **2** BITING : mordaz, sarcástico

cauterize ['kɔʈə,raız] *vt* **-ized; -izing** : cauterizar

caution¹ ['kɔʃən] *vt* : advertir

caution² *n* **1** WARNING : advertencia *f*, aviso *m* **2** CARE, PRUDENCE : precaución *f*, cuidado *m*, cautela *f*

cautionary ['kɔʃə,nɛri] *adj* : admonitorio ⟨cautionary tale : cuento moral⟩

cautious ['kɔʃəs] *adj* : cauteloso, cuidadoso, precavido

cautiously ['kɔʃəsli] *adv* : cautelosamente, con precaución

cautiousness ['kɔʃəsnəs] *n* : cautela *f*, precaución *f*

cavalcade [,kævəl'keıd, 'kævəl,-] *n* **1** : cabalgata *f* **2** SERIES : serie *f*

cavalier¹ [,kævə'lır] *adj* : altivo, desdeñoso — **cavalierly** *adv*

cavalier² *n* : caballero *m*

cavalry ['kævəlri] *n, pl* **-ries** : caballería *f*

cave¹ ['keıv] *vi* **caved; caving** *or* **to cave in** : derrumbarse

cave² *n* : cueva *f*

caveman ['keıv,mæn] *n, pl* **-men** [-mən, -,mɛn] : cavernícola *m*

cavern ['kævərn] *n* : caverna *f*

cavernous ['kævərnəs] *adj* : cavernoso — **cavernously** *adv*

cavewoman ['keıv,wumən] *n, pl* **-women** [-,wımən] : cavernícola *f*

caviar *or* **caviare** ['kævi,ɑr, 'kɑ-] *n* : caviar *m*

cavity ['kævəʈi] *n, pl* **-ties** **1** HOLE : cavidad *f*, hueco *m* **2** CARIES : caries *f*

cavort [kə'vɔrt] *vi* : brincar, hacer cabriolas

caw¹ ['kɔ] *vi* : graznar

caw² *n* : graznido *m*

cayenne pepper [,kaı'ɛn, ,keı-] *n* : pimienta *f* cayena, pimentón *m*

cc [,si:'si:] *vt* **cc'd; cc'ing** : enviarle una copia a (alguien), enviar una copia de (un email, etc.)

CD [,si:'di:] *n* : CD *m*, disco *m* compacto

CD-ROM [,si:,di:'ram] *n* : CD-ROM *m*

cease ['si:s] *v* **ceased; ceasing** *vt* : dejar de ⟨they ceased bickering : dejaron de discutir⟩ — *vi* : cesar, pasarse

cease-fire ['si:s'faır] *n* : alto *m* el fuego, cese *m* del fuego

ceaseless ['si:sləs] *adj* : incesante, continuo

cedar ['si:dər] *n* : cedro *m*

cede ['si:d] *vt* **ceded; ceding** : ceder, conceder

ceiling ['si:lıŋ] *n* **1** : techo *m*, cielo *m* raso **2** LIMIT : límite *m*, tope *m*

celebrant ['sɛləbrənt] *n* : celebrante *mf*, oficiante *mf*

celebrate ['sɛlə,breıt] *v* **-brated; -brating** *vt* **1** : celebrar, oficiar ⟨to celebrate Mass : celebrar la misa⟩ **2** : celebrar, festejar ⟨we're celebrating our anniversary : estamos celebrando nuestro aniversario⟩ **3** EXTOL : alabar, ensalzar, exaltar — *vi* : estar de fiesta, divertirse

celebrated ['sɛlə,breɪɾəd] *adj* : célebre, famoso, renombrado

celebration [,sɛlə'breɪʃən] *n* : celebración *f*, festejos *mpl*

celebrity [sə'lɛbrəɾi] *n*, *pl* **-ties** **1** RENOWN : fama *f*, renombre *m*, celebridad *f* **2** PERSONALITY : celebridad *f*, personaje *m*

celery ['sɛləri] *n*, *pl* **-eries** : apio *m*

celestial [sə'lɛstʃəl, -'lstiəl] *adj* **1** : celeste **2** HEAVENLY : celestial, paradisiaco

celibacy ['sɛləbəsi] *n* : celibato *m*

celibate[1] ['sɛləbət] *adj* : célibe

celibate[2] *n* : célibe *mf*

cell ['sɛl] *n* **1** : célula *f* (de un organismo) **2** : celda *f* (en una cárcel, etc.) **3** : elemento *m* (de una pila)

cellar ['sɛlər] *n* **1** BASEMENT : sótano *m* **2** : bodega *f* (de vinos)

cellist ['tʃɛlɪst] *n* : violonchelista *mf*

cello ['tʃɛ,lo:] *n*, *pl* **-los** : chelo *m*, violonchelo *m*

cellophane ['sɛlə,feɪn] *n* : celofán *m*

cell phone *n* : teléfono *m* celular

cellular ['sɛljələr] *adj* : celular

cellulite ['sɛljə,laɪt] *n* : celulitis *f*

celluloid ['sɛljə,lɔɪd] *n* : celuloide

cellulose ['sɛljə,lo:s] *n* : celulosa *f*

Celsius ['sɛlsiəs] *adj* : centígrado ⟨100 degrees Celsius : 100 grados centígrados⟩

Celt ['kɛlt, 'sɛlt] *n* : celta *mf*

Celtic[1] ['kɛltɪk, 'sɛl-] *adj* : celta

Celtic[2] *n* : celta *m*

cement[1] [sɪ'mɛnt] *vi* : unir o cubrir algo con cemento, cementar

cement[2] *n* **1** : cemento *m* **2** GLUE : pegamento *m*

cement mixer *n* : hormigonera *f*

cemetery ['sɛmə,tɛri] *n*, *pl* **-teries** : cementerio *m*, panteón *m*

censer ['sɛnsər] *n* : incensario *m*

censor[1] ['sɛnsər] *vt* : censurar

censor[2] *n* : censor *m*, -sora *f*

censorious [sɛn'soriəs] *adj* : de censura, crítico

censorship ['sɛntsər,ʃɪp] *n* : censura *f*

censure[1] ['sɛnʃər] *vt* **-sured; -suring** : censurar, criticar, reprobar — **censurable** [-tʃərəbəl] *adj*

censure[2] *n* : censura *f*, reproche *m* oficial

census ['sɛnsəs] *n* : censo *m*

cent ['sɛnt] *n* **1** : centavo *m* **2** : céntimo *m* (fracción del euro)

centaur ['sɛn,tɔr] *n* : centauro *m*

centavo [sɛn'tavo] *n* : centavo *m* (unidad monetaria)

centennial[1] [sɛn'tɛniəl] *adj* : del centenario

centennial[2] *n* : centenario *m*

center[1] ['sɛntər] *vt* **1** : centrar **2** CONCENTRATE : concentrar, fijar, enfocar — *vi* : centrarse, enfocarse

center[2] *n* **1** : centro *m* ⟨center of gravity : centro de gravedad⟩ **2** : centro *mf* (en futbol americano), pívot *mf* (en basquetbol)

centerpiece ['sɛntər,pi:s] *n* : centro *m* de mesa

centesimo [sɛn'tɛsə,mo] *n* : centésimo *m* (unidad monetaria)

centi- ['sɛntə] *pref* : centi-

centigrade ['sɛntə,ɡreɪd, 'san-] *adj* : centígrado

centigram ['sɛntə,ɡræm, 'san-] *n* : centigramo *m*

centime ['san,ti:m] *n* : céntimo *m* (unidad monetaria en varios países de habla francesa y portuguesa)

centimeter ['sɛntə,mi:tər, 'san-] *n* : centímetro *m*

centimo ['sɛntəmo] *n* : céntimo *m* (unidad monetaria en varios países de habla española y portuguesa)

centipede ['sɛntə,pi:d] *n* : ciempiés *m*

central ['sɛntrəl] *adj* **1** : céntrico, central ⟨in a central location : en un lugar céntrico⟩ **2** MAIN, PRINCIPAL : central, fundamental, principal

Central American[1] *adj* : centroamericano

Central American[2] *n* : centroamericano *m*, -na *f*

centralist ['sɛntrəlɪst] *n* : centralista *mf* — **centralist** *adj*

centralization [,sɛntrələ'zeɪʃən] *n* : centralización *f*

centralize ['sɛntrə,laɪz] *vt* **-ized; -izing** : centralizar

centrally ['sɛntrəli] *adv* **1 centrally heated** : con calefacción central **2 centrally located** : céntrico, en un lugar céntrico

centre ['sɛntər] → **center**

centrifugal force [sɛn'trɪfjəɡəl-, -'trɪfɪ-] *n* : fuerza *f* centrífuga

centrist ['sɛntrɪst] *n* : centrista *mf* — **centrist** *adj*

century ['sɛntʃəri] *n*, *pl* **-ries** : siglo *m*

CEO [,si:,i:'o:] *n* (chief executive officer) : director *m*, -tora *f* general (de una compañía)

ceramic[1] [sə'ræmɪk] *adj* : de cerámica

ceramic[2] *n* **1** : objeto *m* de cerámica, cerámica *f* **2 ceramics** *npl* : cerámica *f*

cereal[1] ['sɪriəl] *adj* : cereal

cereal[2] *n* : cereal *m*

cerebellum [,sɛrə'bɛləm] *n*, *pl* **-bellums** *or* **-bella** [-'bɛlə] : cerebelo *m*

cerebral [sə'ri:brəl, 'sɛrə-] *adj* : cerebral

cerebral palsy *n* : parálisis *f* cerebral

cerebrum [sə'ri:brəm, 'sɛrə-] *n*, *pl* **-brums** *or* **-bra** [-brə] : cerebro *m*

ceremonial[1] [,sɛrə'mo:niəl] *adj* : ceremonial

ceremonial[2] *n* : ceremonial *m*

ceremonious [,sɛrə'mo:niəs] *adj* **1** FORMAL : ceremonioso, formal **2** CEREMONIAL : ceremonial

ceremony ['sɛrə,mo:ni] *n*, *pl* **-nies** : ceremonia *f* ⟨without ceremony : sin ceremonias⟩ ⟨not to stand on ceremony : dejarse de ceremonias⟩

cerise [sə'ri:s] *n* : rojo *m* cereza

certain ['sərtən] *adj* **1** DEFINITE : cierto, determinado ⟨a certain percentage : un porcentaje determinado⟩ **2** TRUE : cierto, con certeza ⟨I don't know for certain : no sé exactamente⟩ **3** : cierto, alguno ⟨it has a certain charm : tiene cierta gracia⟩ **4** INEVITABLE : seguro, inevitable **5** ASSURED : seguro, asegu-

rado ⟨she's certain to do well : seguro que le irá bien⟩
certain² *pron* SOME : ciertos, algunos ⟨certain of my friends : algunos de mis amigos⟩
certainly ['sərtənli] *adv* **1** DEFINITELY : ciertamente, seguramente **2** OF COURSE : por supuesto
certainty ['sərtənti] *n, pl* **-ties** : certeza *f*, certidumbre *f*, seguridad *f*
certifiable [ˌsərtə'faɪəbəl] *adj* : certificable
certificate [sər'tɪfɪkət] *n* : certificado *m*, acta *f* ⟨birth certificate : partida/acta/ certificado de nacimiento⟩
certification [ˌsərtəfə'keɪʃən] *n* : certificación *f*
certified ['sərtəˌfaɪd] *adj* **1** ACCREDITED : acreditado, certificado, diplomado, titulado **2** VERIFIED : certificado **3** *fam* REAL : verdadero, auténtico
certify ['sərtəˌfaɪ] *vt* **-fied; -fying** **1** VERIFY : certificar, verificar, confirmar, constatar **2** ENDORSE : endosar, aprobar oficialmente **3** ACCREDIT, LICENSE : acreditar, autorizar
certitude ['sərtəˌtuːd, -ˌtjuːd] *n* : certeza *f*, certidumbre *f*
cervical ['sərvɪkəl] *adj* **1** : cervical (dícese del cuello) **2** : del cuello del útero
cervix ['sərvɪks] *n, pl* **-vices** [-və-ˌsiːz] *or* **-vixes** : cuello *m* del útero
cesarean¹ [sɪ'zæriən] *adj* : cesáreo
cesarean² *or* **cesarean section** *n* : cesárea *f*
cesium ['siːziəm] *n* : cesio *m*
cessation [sɛ'seɪʃən] *n* : cesación *f*, cese *m*
cesspool ['sɛsˌpuːl] *n* : pozo *m* séptico
chafe ['tʃeɪf] *v* **chafed; chafing** *vi* : enojarse, irritarse — *vt* : rozar
chaff ['tʃæf] *n* **1** : barcia *f*, granzas *fpl* **2 to separate the wheat from the chaff** : separar el grano de la paja
chagrin¹ [ʃə'ɡrɪn] *vt* : desilusionar, avergonzar
chagrin² *n* : desilusión *f*, disgusto *m*
chain¹ ['tʃeɪn] *vt* : encadenar
chain² *n* **1** : cadena *f* ⟨steel chain : cadena de acero⟩ ⟨restaurant chain : cadena de restaurantes⟩ **2** SERIES : serie *f* ⟨chain of events : serie de eventos⟩ **3 chains** *npl* FETTERS : grillos *mpl*
chain–smoke ['tʃeɪn'smoːk] *n* : fumar un cigarrillo tras otro
chair¹ ['tʃɛr] *vt* : presidir, moderar
chair² *n* **1** : silla *f* **2** CHAIRMANSHIP : presidencia *f* **3** → **chairman, chairwoman, chairperson 4** *or* **department chair** : catedrático *m*, -ca *f* (de una universidad)
chairlift ['tʃɛrˌlɪft] *n* : telesilla *mf*
chairman ['tʃɛrmən] *n, pl* **-men** [-mən, -ˌmɛn] : presidente *m*
chairmanship ['tʃɛrmənˌʃɪp] *n* : presidencia *f*
chairperson ['tʃɛrˌpərsən] *n* : presidente *mf*, presidenta *f*
chairwoman ['tʃɛrˌwʊmən] *n, pl* **-women** [-ˌwɪmən] : presidenta *f*

chalet [ʃæ'leɪ] *n* : chalet *m*, chalé *m*
chalice ['tʃælɪs] *n* : cáliz *m*
chalk¹ ['tʃɔk] *vt* : escribir con tiza
chalk² *n* **1** LIMESTONE : creta *f*, caliza *f* **2** : tiza *f*, gis *m Mex* (para escribir)
chalkboard ['tʃɔkˌbord] → **blackboard**
chalk up *vt* **1** ASCRIBE : atribuir, adscribir **2** SCORE : apuntarse, anotarse (una victoria, etc.)
chalky ['tʃɔki] *adj* **chalkier; -est** **1** PALE : pálido **2** POWDERY : polvoriento
challenge¹ ['tʃælɪnd] *vt* **-lenged; -lenging** **1** DISPUTE : disputar, cuestionar, poner en duda **2** DARE : desafiar, retar **3** STIMULATE : estimular, incentivar
challenge² *n* : reto *m*, desafío *m*
challenger ['tʃælɪnd ər] *n* : retador *m*, -dora *f*; contendiente *mf*
challenging ['tʃælɪnd ɪŋ] *adj* **1** DEMANDING : exigente **2** DEFIANT : desafiante, de desafío **3** STIMULATING : estimulante, provocador
chamber ['tʃeɪmbər] *n* **1** ROOM : cámara *f*, sala *f* ⟨the senate chamber : la cámara del senado⟩ **2** : recámara *f* (de un arma de fuego), cámara *f* (de combustión) **3** : cámara *f* ⟨chamber of commerce : cámara de comercio⟩ **4 chambers** *npl or* **judge's chambers** : despacho *m* del juez
chambermaid ['tʃeɪmbərˌmeɪd] *n* : camarera *f*
chamber music *n* : música *f* de cámara
chamber pot *n* : bacinica *f*
chameleon [kə'miːljən, -liən] *n* : camaleón *m*
chamois ['ʃæmi] *n, pl* **chamois** [-mi, -miz] : gamuza *f*
chamomile ['kæməˌmaɪl, -ˌmiːl] *n* **1** : manzanilla *f*, camomila *f* **2 chamomile tea** : manzanilla *f*
champ¹ ['tʃæmp, 'tʃɑmp] *vi* **1** : masticar ruidosamente **2 to champ at the bit** : impacientarse, comerle a uno la impaciencia
champ² ['tʃæmp] *n* : campeón *m*, -peona *f*
champagne [ʃæm'peɪn] *n* : champaña *m*, champán *m*
champion¹ ['tʃæmpiən] *vt* : defender, luchar por (una causa)
champion² *n* **1** ADVOCATE, DEFENDER : paladín *m*; campeón *m*, -peona *f*; defensor *m*, -sora *f* **2** WINNER : campeón *m*, -peona *f* ⟨world champion : campeón mundial⟩
championship ['tʃæmpiənˌʃɪp] *n* : campeonato *m*
chance¹ ['tʃænts] *v* **chanced; chancing** *vi* **1** HAPPEN : ocurrir por casualidad **2 to chance upon** : encontrar por casualidad — *vt* RISK : arriesgarse a (hacer algo) ⟨we can't chance it : no podemos arriesgarnos⟩
chance² *adj* : fortuito, casual ⟨a chance encounter : un encuentro casual⟩
chance³ *n* **1** FATE, LUCK : azar *m*, suerte *f*, fortuna *f* **2** OPPORTUNITY : oportunidad *f*, ocasión *f* **3** PROBABILITY : probabilidad *f*, posibilidad *f* **4** RISK : riesgo

m **5** : boleto *m* (de una rifa o lotería) **6**
by chance : por casualidad
chancellor [ˈtʃæntsələr] *n* **1** : canciller
m **2** : rector *m*, -tora *f* (de una universidad)
chancy [ˈtʃæntsi] *adj* **chancier; -est**
: riesgoso, arriesgado
chandelier [ˌʃændəˈlɪr] *n* : araña *f* de luces
change¹ [ˈtʃeɪndʒ] *v* **changed; changing**
vt **1** ALTER : cambiar ⟨to change one's
mind : cambiar de idea/opinión⟩ ⟨to
change direction : cambiar de direc-
ción⟩ **2** EXCHANGE, REPLACE : cambiar (pilas, etc.), cambiar de ⟨he changed
the subject : cambió de tema⟩ ⟨to
change jobs : cambiar de trabajo⟩ ⟨to
change places : cambiar de sitio⟩ **3**
: cambiar (dinero) ⟨can you change a
twenty? : ¿me puedes cambiar un billete
de veinte dólares?⟩ ⟨to change dollars
into yen : cambiar dólares a yen⟩ **4**
: cambiar ⟨I changed the baby, I changed
the baby's diaper : le cambié el pañal al
bebé⟩ ⟨to change the bed/sheets : cambiar las sábanas⟩ ⟨to change one's
clothes : cambiarse (de ropa)⟩ **5 to
change hands** : cambiar de manos/
dueño — *vi* **1** : cambiar ⟨you haven't
changed : no has cambiado⟩ **2** : cambiarse (de ropa) **3 to change over to**
: cambiar a (otro sistema, etc.)
change² *n* **1** ALTERATION : cambio *m* ⟨a
change for the better/worse : un cambio
para mejor/peor⟩ ⟨for a change : para
variar⟩ ⟨to make changes to : hacerle
cambios a⟩ **2** REPLACEMENT, EX-
CHANGE : cambio *m* ⟨an oil change : un
cambio de aceite⟩ ⟨a change of address
: un cambio de dirección⟩ ⟨a change of
scenery : un cambio de aire(s)⟩ ⟨a
change of clothes : una muda de
ropa⟩ **3** : cambio *m*, vuelto *m* ⟨two dollars change : dos dólares de vuelto⟩ ⟨do
you have change for a twenty? : ¿tienes
cambio de veinte dólares?⟩ **4** COINS
: cambio *m*, monedas *fpl* ⟨loose change
: dinero suelto⟩
changeable [ˈtʃeɪndʒəbəl] *adj* : cambiante, variable
changeless [ˈtʃeɪndʒləs] *adj* : invariable,
constante
changeover [ˈtʃeɪndʒˌoːvər] *n* : cambio *m*
changing [ˈtʃeɪndʒɪŋ] *adj* : cambiante,
variable
changing room *n* FITTING ROOM : probador *m*
changing table *n* : cambiador *m*
channel¹ [ˈtʃænəl] *vt* **-neled** *or* **-nelled;
-neling** *or* **-nelling** : encauzar, canalizar
channel² *n* **1** RIVERBED : cauce *m* **2**
STRAIT : canal *m*, estrecho *m* ⟨English
Channel : Canal de la Mancha⟩ **3**
COURSE, MEANS : vía *f*, conducto *m* ⟨the
usual channels : las vías normales⟩ **4**
: canal *m* (de televisión)
channel surfing *n* : zapping *m*
chant¹ [ˈtʃænt] *v* : salmodiar, cantar
chant² *n* **1** : salmodia *f* **2 Gregorian
chant** : canto *m* gregoriano
Chanukah [ˈxɑnəkə, ˈhɑ-] → **Hanukkah**

chaos [ˈkeɪˌɑs] *n* : caos *m*
chaotic [keɪˈɑʈɪk] *adj* : caótico — **chaoti-
cally** [-ɳkli] *adv*
chap *n* FELLOW : tipo *m*, hombre *m*
chapel [ˈtʃæpəl] *n* : capilla *f*
chaperon¹ *or* **chaperone** [ˈʃæpəˌroːn] *vt*
-oned; -oning : ir de chaperón, acompañar
chaperon² *or* **chaperone** *n* : chaperón *m*,
-rona *f*; acompañante *mf*
chaplain [ˈtʃæplɪn] *n* : capellán *m*
chapped [ˈtʃæpt] *adj* : agrietado ⟨chapped
lips : labios agrietados⟩
chapter [ˈtʃæptər] *n* **1** : capítulo *m* (de
un libro) **2** BRANCH : sección *f*, división
f (de una organización)
char [ˈtʃɑr] *v* **charred; charring** *vt* **1**
BURN : carbonizar **2** SCORCH : chamus-
car — *vi* **1** : carbonizarse **2** : chamuscarse
character [ˈkærɪktər] *n* **1** LETTER, SYM-
BOL : carácter *m* ⟨Chinese characters
: caracteres chinos⟩ **2** DISPOSITION
: carácter *m*, personalidad *f* ⟨of good
character : de buena reputación⟩ ⟨to
build character : forjar el carácter⟩ **3**
REPUTATION : carácter *m*, reputación *f*
⟨character attacks : ataques perso-
nales⟩ **4** NATURE, QUALITIES : carácter
m ⟨the national character : el carácter
nacional⟩ ⟨the character of the wine : el
carácter del vino⟩ ⟨the room has no
character : la habitación no tiene
carácter⟩ **5** : tipo *m*, personaje *m* peculiar ⟨he's quite a character! : ¡él es algo
serio!⟩ **6** : personaje *m* (ficticio) **7 to
be in character** : ser típico de alguien **8
to be out of character** : no ser típico de
alguien
characteristic¹ [ˌkærɪktəˈrɪstɪk] *adj* : característico, típico — **characteristically**
[-tɪkli] *adv*
characteristic² *n* : característica *f*
characterization [ˌkærɪktərəˈzeɪʃən] *n*
: caracterización *f*
characterize [ˈkærɪktəˌraɪz] *vt* **-ized; -iz-
ing** : caracterizar
charades [ʃəˈreɪdz] *ns & pl* : charada *f*
charcoal [ˈtʃɑrˌkoːl] *n* : carbón *m*
chard [ˈtʃɑrd] → **Swiss chard**
charge¹ [ˈtʃɑrdʒ] *v* **charged; charging**
vt **1** : cargar ⟨to charge the batteries
: cargar las pilas⟩ **2** ENTRUST : encomendar, encargar **3** COMMAND : ordenar,
mandar **4** ACCUSE : acusar ⟨charged
with robbery : acusado de robo⟩ **5**
: cargar a una cuenta, comprar a crédito
— *vi* **1** : cargar (contra el enemigo)
⟨charge! : ¡a la carga!⟩ **2** : cobrar ⟨they
charge too much : cobran demasiado⟩
charge² *n* **1** : carga *f* (eléctrica) **2**
: carga *f* (de dinamita, etc.) **3** BURDEN
: carga *f*, peso *m* **4** RESPONSIBILITY
: cargo *m*, responsabilidad *f* ⟨to take
charge of : hacerse cargo de⟩ ⟨to be in
charge : ser el responsable⟩ ⟨to be in
charge of : tener a su cargo⟩ **5** : persona *f* al cuidado de alguien ⟨her young
charges : los niños que están a su
cargo⟩ **6** ACCUSATION : cargo *m*,

acusación *f* ⟨to press charges : presentar cargos⟩ **7** COST : costo *m*, cargo *m*, precio *m* ⟨free of charge : gratis⟩ ⟨they gave it to us free of charge : nos lo regalaron gratuitamente⟩ **8** ATTACK : carga *f*, ataque *m* **9 to get a charge out of** ENJOY : disfrutar de, deleitarse con

chargeable ['tʃɑrdʒəbəl] *adj* **1** : perseguible (dícese de un delito) **2** ~ **to** : a cargo de (una cuenta)

charge card → **credit card**

charger ['tʃɑrdʒər] *n* : corcel *m*, caballo *m* (de guerra)

chariot ['tʃæriət] *n* : carro *m* (de guerra)

charisma [kə'rɪzmə] *n* : carisma *m*

charismatic [ˌkærəz'mætɪk] *adj* : carismático

charitable ['tʃærəṱəbəl] *adj* **1** GENEROUS : caritativo ⟨a charitable organization : una organización benéfica⟩ **2** KIND, UNDERSTANDING : generoso, benévolo, comprensivo — **charitably** [-bli] *adv*

charitableness ['tʃærəṱəbəlnəs] *n* : caridad *f*

charity ['tʃærəṱi] *n, pl* **-ties 1** GENEROSITY : caridad *f* **2** ALMS : caridad *f*, limosna *f* **3** : organización *f* benéfica, obra *f* de beneficencia

charlatan ['ʃɑrlətən] *n* : charlatán *m*, -tana *f*; farsante *mf*

charley horse ['tʃɑrliˌhɔrs] *n* : calambre *m*

charm¹ ['tʃɑrm] *vt* : encantar, cautivar, fascinar

charm² *n* **1** AMULET : amuleto *m*, talismán *m* **2** ATTRACTION : encanto *m*, atractivo *m* ⟨it has a certain charm : tiene cierto atractivo⟩ **3** : dije *m*, colgante *m* ⟨charm bracelet : pulsera de dijes⟩

charmer ['tʃɑrmər] *n* : persona *f* encantadora

charming ['tʃɑrmɪŋ] *adj* : encantador, fascinante

chart¹ ['tʃɑrt] *vt* **1** : trazar un mapa de, hacer un gráfico de **2** PLAN : trazar, planear ⟨to chart a course : trazar un derrotero⟩

chart² *n* **1** MAP : carta *f*, mapa *m* **2** DIAGRAM : gráfico *m*, cuadro *m*, tabla *f*

charter¹ ['tʃɑrṱər] *vt* **1** : establecer los estatutos de (una organización) **2** RENT : alquilar, fletar

charter² *adj* : chárter ⟨a charter flight : un vuelo chárter⟩

charter³ *n* **1** STATUTES : estatutos *mpl* **2** CONSTITUTION : carta *f*, constitución *f*

chartreuse [ʃɑr'truːz, -'truːs] *n* : color *m* verde-amarillo intenso

chary ['tʃæri] *adj* **charier; -est 1** WARY : cauteloso, precavido **2** SPARING : parco

chase¹ ['tʃeɪs] *vt* **chased; chasing 1** PURSUE : perseguir, ir a la caza de **2** DRIVE : ahuyentar, echar ⟨he chased the dog from the garden : ahuyentó al perro del jardín⟩ **3** : grabar (metales)

chase² *n* **1** PURSUIT : persecución *f*, caza *f* **2 the chase** HUNTING : caza *f*

chaser ['tʃeɪsər] *n* **1** PURSUER : perse-

guidor *m*, -dora *f* **2** : bebida *f* que se toma después de un trago de licor

chasm ['kæzəm] *n* : abismo *m*, sima *f*

chassis ['tʃæsi, 'ʃæsi] *n, pl* **chassis** [-siz] : chasis *m*, armazón *m*

chaste ['tʃeɪst] *adj* **chaster; -est 1** : casto **2** MODEST : modesto, puro **3** AUSTERE : austero, sobrio

chastely ['tʃeɪstli] *adv* : castamente

chasten ['tʃeɪsən] *vt* : castigar, sancionar

chasteness ['tʃeɪstnəs] *n* **1** MODESTY : modestia *f*, castidad *f* **2** AUSTERITY : sobriedad *f*, austeridad *f*

chastise ['tʃæsˌtaɪz, tʃæs'-] *vt* **-tised; -tising 1** REPRIMAND : reprender, corregir, reprobar **2** PUNISH : castigar

chastisement ['tʃæsˌtaɪzmənt, tʃæs'taɪz-, 'tʃæstəz-] *n* : castigo *m*, corrección *f*

chastity ['tʃæstəṱi] *n* : castidad *f*, decencia *f*, modestia *f*

chat¹ ['tʃæt] *vi* **chatted; chatting** : charlar, platicar

chat² *n* : charla *f*, plática *f*

château [ʃæ'toː] *n, pl* **-teaus** [-'toːz] *or* **-teaux** [-'toː, -'toːz] : mansión *f* campestre

chat room *n* : chat *m*, sala *f* de chat

chattel ['tʃæṱəl] *n* : bienes *fpl* muebles, enseres *mpl*

chatter¹ ['tʃæṱər] *vi* **1** : castañetear (dícese de los dientes) **2** GAB : parlotear *fam*, cotorrear *fam*

chatter² *n* **1** CHATTERING : castañeteo *m* (de dientes) **2** GABBING : parloteo *m fam*, cotorreo *m fam*, cháchara *f fam*

chatterbox ['tʃæṱərˌbaks] *n* : parlanchín *m*, -china *f*; charlatán *m*, -tana *f*; hablador *m*, -dora *f*

chatty ['tʃæṱi] *adj* **chattier; -est 1** TALKATIVE : parlanchín, charlatán **2** CONVERSATIONAL : familiar, conversador ⟨a chatty letter : una carta llena de noticias⟩

chauffeur¹ ['ʃoːfər, ʃoˈfər] *vi* : trabajar de chofer privado — *vt* : hacer de chofer para

chauffeur² *n* : chofer *m* privado

chauvinism ['ʃoːvəˌnɪzəm] *n* : chauvinismo *m*, patriotería *f*

chauvinist ['ʃoːvənɪst] *n* : chauvinista *mf*; patriotero *m*, -ra *f*

chauvinistic [ˌʃoːvəˈnɪstɪk] *adj* : chauvinista, patriotero

cheap¹ ['tʃiːp] *adv* : barato ⟨to sell cheap : vender barato⟩

cheap² *adj* **1** INEXPENSIVE : barato, económico **2** SHODDY : barato, mal hecho **3** STINGY : tacaño, agarrado *fam*, codo *Mex*

cheapen ['tʃiːpən] *vt* : degradar, rebajar

cheaply ['tʃiːpli] *adv* : barato, a precio bajo

cheapness ['tʃiːpnəs] *n* **1** : precio *m* bajo **2** STINGINESS : tacañería *f*

cheapskate ['tʃiːpˌskeɪt] *n* : tacaño *m*, -ña *f*; codo *m*, -da *f Mex*

cheat¹ ['tʃiːt] *vt* **1** : defraudar, estafar, engañar **2 to cheat on** : engañar (a un/una amante) — *vi* : hacer trampa

cheat² *n* **1** CHEATING : engaño *m*, fraude *m*, trampa *f* **2** → **cheater**

cheater ['tʃiːṭər] *n* : estafador *m*, -dora *f*; tramposo *m*, -sa *f*

check¹ ['tʃɛk] *vt* **1** VERIFY : verificar, comprobar (la ortografía, etc.) **2** INSPECT : revisar, chequear, inspeccionar **3** CONSULT : consultar, chequear ⟨let me check the files : déjame chequear los archivos⟩ **4** HALT : frenar, parar, detener **5** RESTRAIN : refrenar, contener, reprimir **6** MARK : marcar, señalar **7** *or* **to check in** : chequear, facturar (maletas, equipaje) **8** CHECKER : marcar con cuadros **9 to check off** : marcar (algo en una lista) **10 to check out** INVESTIGATE : investigar **11 to check out** *fam* LOOK AT : mirar **12 to check out** SIGN OUT : sacar (libros) **13 to check up** RING UP : cobrar (en una tienda) — *vi* **1** VERIFY : comprobar, verificar **2 to check back with** *fam* : volver a contactar ⟨I'll check back with you later : te llamaré/hablaré (etc.) más tarde⟩ **3 to check in** : registrarse (en un hotel) **4 to check into** INVESTIGATE : investigar **5 to check off on** APPROVE : aprobar **6 to check on** : ir a ver, visitar, llamar ⟨she checks on the patients regularly : visita a los pacientes regularmente⟩ **7 to check out** : pagar e irse (de un hotel) **8 to check out** SQUARE : cuadrar **9 to check up on** : vigilar, controlar **10 to check with** : consultar

check² *n* **1** HALT : detención *f* súbita, parada *f* **2** RESTRAINT : control *m*, freno *m* **3** INSPECTION : verificación *f*, comprobación *f*, inspección *f*, chequeo *m* ⟨she gave the list a quick check : le echó una ojeada a la lista⟩ ⟨security/background check : verificación de identidad/antecedentes⟩ ⟨system check : comprobación del sistema⟩ ⟨sound check : prueba de sonido⟩ **4** : cheque *m* ⟨to pay by check : pagar con cheque⟩ **5** VOUCHER : resguardo *m*, comprobante *m* **6** BILL : cuenta *f* (en un restaurante) **7** : jaque *m* (en ajedrez) **8** *or* **check mark** : marca *f* **9** *or* **check pattern** : dibujo *m* a/de cuadros

checkbook ['tʃɛk,bʊk] *n* : chequera *f*

checked *adj* : a/de cuadros

checker¹ ['tʃɛkər] *vt* : marcar con cuadros

checker² *n* **1** : pieza *f* (en el juego de damas) **2** : verificador *m*, -dora *f* **3** CASHIER : cajero *m*, -ra *f*

checkerboard ['tʃɛkər,bord] *n* : tablero *m* de damas

checkered *adj* **1** → **checked** **2** TROUBLED : accidentado

checkers ['tʃɛkərz] *n* : damas *fpl*

check–in ['tʃɛk,ɪn] *n* **1** : facturación *f* **2** *or* **check–in desk/counter** : mostrador *m* de facturación

checking account *n* : cuenta *f* corriente

checklist ['tʃɛk,lɪst] *n* : lista *f* de control

checkmate¹ ['tʃɛk,meɪt] *vt* **-mated; -mating** **1** : dar jaque mate a (en ajedrez) **2** THWART : frustrar, arruinar

checkmate² *n* : jaque mate *m*

checkout ['tʃɛk,aʊt] *n or* **checkout counter** : caja *f*

checkpoint ['tʃɛk,pɔɪnt] *n* : puesto *m* de control

checkroom ['tʃɛk,ruːm, -,rʊm] *n* : guardarropa *m*

checkup ['tʃɛk,ʌp] *n* : examen *m* médico, chequeo *m*

cheddar ['tʃɛdər] *n* : queso *m* Cheddar

cheek ['tʃiːk] *n* **1** : mejilla *f*, cachete *m* **2** IMPUDENCE : insolencia *f*, descaro *m*

cheekbone ['tʃiːk,boːn] *n* : pómulo *m*

cheeked ['tʃiːkt] *adj* (*used in combination*) : de mejillas ⟨rosy-cheeked : de mejillas sonrosadas⟩

cheeky ['tʃiːki] *adj* **cheekier; -est** : descarado, insolente, atrevido

cheep¹ ['tʃiːp] *vi* : piar

cheep² *n* : pío *m*

cheer¹ ['tʃɪr] *vt* **1** ENCOURAGE : alentar, animar **2** GLADDEN : alegrar, levantar el ánimo a **3** ACCLAIM : aclamar, vitorear, echar porras a

cheer² *n* **1** CHEERFULNESS : alegría *f*, buen humor *m*, jovialidad *f* **2** APPLAUSE : aclamación *f*, ovación *f*, aplausos *mpl* ⟨three cheers for the chief! : ¡viva el jefe!⟩ **3 cheers!** : ¡salud!

cheerful ['tʃɪrfəl] *adj* : alegre, de buen humor

cheerfully ['tʃɪrfəli] *adv* : alegremente, jovialmente

cheerfulness ['tʃɪrfəlnəs] *n* : buen humor *m*, alegría *f*

cheerily ['tʃɪrəli] *adv* : alegremente

cheeriness ['tʃɪrinəs] *n* : buen humor *m*, alegría *f*

cheerleader ['tʃɪr,liːdər] *n* : porrista *mf*

cheerless ['tʃɪrləs] *adj* BLEAK : triste, sombrío

cheery ['tʃɪri] *adj* **cheerier; -est** : alegre, de buen humor

cheese ['tʃiːz] *n* : queso *m*

cheeseburger ['tʃiːz,bərGər] *n* : hamburguesa *f* con queso

cheesecake ['tʃiːz,keɪk] *n* : tarta *f* de queso

cheesecloth ['tʃiːz,klɔθ] *n* : estopilla *f*

cheesy ['tʃiːzi] *adj* **cheesier; -est** **1** : a queso **2** : que contiene queso **3** CHEAP : barato, de mala calidad

cheetah ['tʃiːṭə] *n* : guepardo *m*

chef ['ʃɛf] *n* : chef *m*

chemical¹ ['kɛmɪkəl] *adj* : químico — **chemically** [-mɪkli] *adv*

chemical² *n* : sustancia *f* química

chemical weapon *n* : arma *f* química

chemise [ʃə'miːz] *n* **1** : camiseta *f*, prenda *f* interior de una pieza **2** : vestido *m* holgado

chemist ['kɛmɪst] *n* : químico *m*, -ca *f*

chemistry ['kɛmɪstri] *n*, *pl* **-tries** : química *f*

chemotherapy [,kiːmo'θɛrəpi, ,kɛmo-] *n*, *pl* **-pies** : quimioterapia *f*

cherish ['tʃɛrɪʃ] *vt* **1** VALUE : apreciar, valorar **2** HARBOR : abrigar, albergar

cherry ['tʃɛri] *n*, *pl* **-ries** **1** : cereza *f* (fruta) **2** : cerezo *m* (árbol)

cherub ['tʃɛrəb] *n* **1** *pl* **-ubim** ['tʃɛrə,bɪm, 'tʃɛrjə-] ANGEL : ángel *m*, querubín *m* **2**

pl **-ubs** : niño *m* regordete, niña *f* regordeta

cherubic [tʃə'ru:bɪk] *adj* : querúbico, angelical

chess ['tʃɛs] *n* : ajedrez *m*

chessboard ['tʃɛs,bord] *n* : tablero *m* de ajedrez

chessman ['tʃɛsmən, -,mæn] *n, pl* **-men** [-mən, -,mɛn] : pieza *f* de ajedrez

chest ['tʃɛst] *n* **1** : cofre *m*, baúl *m* **2** : pecho *m* ⟨chest pains : dolores de pecho⟩

chestnut ['tʃɛst,nʌt] *n* **1** : castaña *f* (fruto) **2** : castaño *m* (árbol)

chest of drawers *n* : cómoda *f*

chevron ['ʃɛvrən] *n* : galón *m* (de un oficial militar)

chew[1] ['tʃu:] *vt* **1** : masticar, mascar **2 to chew out** SCOLD : regañar **3 to chew the fat** CHAT : charlar, platicar **4 to chew up** : destrozar a mordiscos **5 to chew up** DESTROY : destrozar — *vi* **to chew on/over** THINK OVER : pensar

chew[2] *n* : algo que se masca (como tabaco)

chewing gum *n* : goma *f* de mascar, chicle *m*

chewy ['tʃu:i] *adj* **chewier; -est 1** : fibroso (dícese de las carnes o los vegetales) **2** : pegajoso, chicloso (dícese de los dulces)

chic[1] ['ʃi:k] *adj* : chic, elegante, de moda

chic[2] *n* : chic *m*, elegancia *f*

Chicana [tʃɪ'kɑnə] *n* : chicana *f*

Chicano [tʃɪ'kɑno] *n* : chicano *m*, -na *f* — **Chicano** *adj*

chick ['tʃɪk] *n* **1** : pollito *m*, -ta *f*; polluelo *m* **2** *fam, sometimes offensive* : chica *f*; mujer *f*

chicken[1] ['tʃɪkən] *adj* : miedoso, cobarde

chicken[2] *n* **1** FOWL : pollo *m* **2** COWARD : cobarde *mf*

chickenhearted ['tʃɪkən,hɑrtəd] *adj* : miedoso, cobarde

chicken out *vi fam* : acobardarse, rajarse

chicken pox *n* : varicela *f*

chickpea ['tʃɪk,pi:] *n* : garbanzo *m*

chicle ['tʃɪkəl] *n* : chicle *m* (resina)

chicory ['tʃɪkəri] *n, pl* **-ries 1** : endibia *f* (para ensaladas) **2** : achicoria *f* (aditivo de café)

chide ['tʃaɪd] *vt* **chid** ['tʃɪd] *or* **chided; chid** *or* **chidden** ['tʃɪdən] *or* **chided; chiding** ['tʃaɪdɪŋ] : regañar, reprender

chief[1] ['tʃi:f] *adj* : principal, capital ⟨chief negotiator : negociador en jefe⟩ — **chiefly** *adv*

chief[2] *n* : jefe *m*, -fa *f* ⟨fire/police chief : jefe de bomberos/policía⟩

chief executive officer *n* → CEO

chieftain ['tʃi:ftən] *n* : jefe *m*, -fa *f* (de una tribu)

chiffon [ʃɪ'fɑn, 'ʃɪ,-] *n* : chifón *m*

chigger ['tʃɪɡər] *n* : nigua *f*

chignon ['ʃi:n,jɑn, -,jɔn] *n* : moño *m*, chongo *m* *Mex*

child ['tʃaɪld] *n, pl* **children** ['tʃɪldrən] **1** BABY, YOUNGSTER : niño *m*, -ña *f*; criatura *f* **2 children** *npl* OFFSPRING : hijo *m*, -ja *f*; progenie *f*

childbearing[1] ['tʃaɪlbɛrɪŋ] *adj* : relativo al parto ⟨of childbearing age : en edad fértil⟩

childbearing[2] → **childbirth**

childbirth ['tʃaɪld,bərθ] *n* : parto *m*

childcare ['tʃaɪld,kær] *n* : cuidado *m* de los niños, puericultura *f*

childhood ['tʃaɪld,hʊd] *n* : infancia *f*, niñez *f*

childish ['tʃaɪldɪʃ] *adj* : infantil, inmaduro — **childishly** *adv*

childishness ['tʃaɪldɪʃnəs] *n* : inmadurez *f*

childless ['tʃaɪldləs] *adj* : sin hijos

childlike ['tʃaɪld,laɪk] *adj* : infantil, inocente ⟨a childlike imagination : una imaginación infantil⟩

childproof ['tʃaɪld,pru:f] *adj* : a prueba de niños

Chilean ['tʃɪliən, tʃɪ'leɪən] *n* : chileno *m*, -na *f* — **Chilean** *adj*

chili *or* **chile** *or* **chilli** ['tʃɪli] *n, pl* **chilies** *or* **chiles** *or* **chillies 1** *or* **chili pepper** : chile *m*, ají *m* **2** : chile *m* con carne

chill[1] ['tʃɪl] *v* : enfriar

chill[2] *adj* : frío, gélido ⟨a chill wind : un viento frío⟩

chill[3] *n* **1** CHILLINESS : fresco *m*, frío *m* **2** SHIVER : escalofrío *m* **3** DAMPER : enfriamiento *m*, frío *m* ⟨to cast a chill over : enfriar⟩

chilliness ['tʃɪlinəs] *n* : frío *m*, fresco *m*

chilly ['tʃɪli] *adj* **chillier; -est** : frío ⟨it's chilly tonight : hace frío esta noche⟩

chime[1] ['tʃaɪm] *v* **chimed; chiming** *vt* : hacer sonar (una campana) — *vi* : sonar una campana, dar campanadas

chime[2] *n* **1** BELLS : juego *m* de campanitas sintonizadas, carillón *m* **2** PEAL : tañido *m*, campanada *f*

chime in *vi* : meterse en una conversación

chimera *or* **chimaera** [kaɪ'mɪrə, kə-] *n* : quimera *f*

chimney ['tʃɪmni] *n, pl* **-neys** : chimenea *f*

chimney sweep *n* : deshollinador *m*, -dora *f*

chimp ['tʃɪmp, 'ʃɪmp] → **chimpanzee**

chimpanzee [,tʃɪm,pæn'zi:, ,ʃɪm-:, tʃɪm'pænzi, ʃɪm-] *n* : chimpancé *m*

chin ['tʃɪn] *n* : barbilla *f*, mentón *m*, barba *f*, pera *f Arg, Chile, Uru*

china ['tʃaɪnə] *n* **1** PORCELAIN : porcelana *f*, loza *f* **2** CROCKERY, TABLEWARE : loza *f*, vajilla *f*

chinchilla [tʃɪn'tʃɪlə] *n* : chinchilla *f*

Chinese[1] ['tʃaɪ'ni:z, -'ni:s] *adj* : chino

Chinese[2] *n* **1** : chino *m* (idioma) **2 the Chinese** (*used with a plural verb*) : los chinos

chink ['tʃɪŋk] *n* : grieta *f*, abertura *f*

chintz ['tʃɪnts] *n* : chintz *m*, chinz *m*

chip[1] ['tʃɪp] *v* **chipped; chipping** *vt* : desportillar, desconchar, astillar (madera) — *vi* : desportillarse, desconcharse, descascararse (dícese de la pintura, etc.)

chip[2] *n* **1** : astilla *f* (de madera o vidrio), lasca *f* (de piedra) ⟨he's a chip off the old block : de tal palo, tal astilla⟩ **2** : bocado *m* pequeño (en rodajas o rebanadas) ⟨tortilla chips : totopos, tortillitas

tostadas⟩ **3** : ficha *f* (de póker, etc.) **4**
NICK : mella *f* **5** : chip *m* ⟨memory chip
: chip de memoria⟩
chip in *v* CONTRIBUTE : contribuir
chipmunk ['tʃɪp,mʌŋk] *n* : ardilla *f* listada
chipotle [tʃə'po:tleɪ, tʃi-] *n* : chipotle *m*
chipper ['tʃɪpər] *adj* : alegre y vivaz
chiropodist [kə'rɑpədɪst, ʃə-] *n* : podólogo
m, -ga *f*
chiropody [kə'rɑpədi, ʃə-] *n* : podología *f*
chiropractic ['kaɪrə,præktɪk] *n* : quiropráctica *f*
chiropractor ['kaɪrə,præktər] *n* : quiropráctico *m*, -ca *f*
chirp¹ ['tʃərp] *vi* : gorjear (dícese de los
pájaros), chirriar (dícese de los grillos)
chirp² *n* : gorjeo *m* (de un pájaro), chirrido *m* (de un grillo)
chisel¹ ['tʃɪzəl] *vt* -eled *or* -elled; -eling *or*
-elling **1** : cincelar, tallar, labrar **2**
CHEAT : estafar, defraudar
chisel² *n* : cincel *m* (para piedras y metales), escoplo *m* (para madera), formón *m*
chiseler ['tʃɪzələr] *n* SWINDLER : estafador *m*, -dora *f*; fraude *mf*
chit ['tʃɪt] *n* : resguardo *m*, recibo *m*
chitchat ['tʃɪt,tʃæt] *n* : cotorreo *m*, charla
f
chivalric [ʃə'vælrɪk] → chivalrous
chivalrous ['ʃɪvəlrəs] *adj* **1** KNIGHTLY
: caballeresco, relativo a la caballería **2**
GENTLEMANLY : caballeroso, honesto,
cortés
chivalrousness ['ʃɪvəlrəsnəs] *n* : caballerosidad *f*, cortesía *f*
chivalry ['ʃɪvəlri] *n*, *pl* -ries **1**
KNIGHTHOOD : caballería *f* **2** CHIVAL-
ROUSNESS : caballerosidad *f*, nobleza *f*,
cortesía *f*
chive ['tʃaɪv] *n* : cebollino *m*
chloride ['klor,aɪd] *n* : cloruro *m*
chlorinate ['klorə,neɪt] *vt* -nated; -nating
: clorar
chlorination [,klorə'neɪʃən] *n* : cloración *f*
chlorine ['klor,i:n] *n* : cloro *m*
chloroform ['klorə,form] *n* : cloroformo
m
chlorophyll ['klorə,fɪl] *n* : clorofila *f*
chock–full ['tʃɑk'fʊl, 'tʃʌk-] *adj* : colmado, repleto
chocolate ['tʃɑkələt, 'tʃɔk-] *n* **1** : chocolate *m* **2** BONBON : bombón *m* **3**
: color *m* chocolate, marrón *m*
choice¹ ['tʃɔɪs] *adj* choicer; choicest : selecto, escogido, de primera calidad
choice² *n* **1** CHOOSING : elección *f*, selección *f* **2** OPTION : elección *f*, opción *f* ⟨I
have no choice : no tengo alternativa⟩ **3**
PREFERENCE : preferencia *f*, elección
f **4** VARIETY : surtido *m*, selección *f* ⟨a
wide choice : un gran surtido⟩
choir ['kwaɪr] *n* : coro *m*
choirboy ['kwaɪr,bɔɪ] *n* : niño *m* de coro
choke¹ ['tʃo:k] *v* choked; choking *vt* **1**
ASPHYXIATE, STRANGLE : sofocar, asfixiar, ahogar, estrangular **2** BLOCK
: tapar, obstruir — *vi* **1** SUFFOCATE
: asfixiarse, sofocarse, ahogarse ⟨to
choke on food : atragantarse con
comida⟩ **2** CLOG : taparse, obstruirse

choke² *n* **1** CHOKING : estrangulación
f **2** : choke *m*, estárter *m* (de un motor)
choker ['tʃo:kər] *n* : gargantilla *f*
cholera ['kɑlərə] *n* : cólera *m*
cholesterol [kə'lestə,rɔl] *n* : colesterol *m*
choose ['tʃu:z] *v* chose ['tʃo:z]; chosen
['tʃo:zən]; choosing *vt* **1** SELECT : escoger, elegir ⟨choose only one : escoja sólo
uno⟩ **2** DECIDE : decidir ⟨he chose to
leave : decidió irse⟩ **3** PREFER : preferir
⟨which one do you choose? : ¿cuál prefiere?⟩ — *vi* : escoger ⟨much to choose
from : mucho de donde escoger⟩
choosy *or* **choosey** ['tʃu:zi] *adj* choos-
ier; -est : exigente, remilgado
chop¹ ['tʃɑp] *vt* chopped; chopping **1**
MINCE : picar, cortar, moler (carne) **2**
to chop down : cortar, talar (un árbol)
chop² *n* **1** CUT : hachazo *m* (con una hacha), tajo *m* (con una cuchilla) **2** BLOW
: golpe *m* (penetrante) ⟨karate chop
: golpe de karate⟩ **3** : chuleta *f* ⟨pork
chops : chuletas de cerdo⟩
chopper ['tʃɑpər] → helicopter
choppy ['tʃɑpi] *adj* choppier; -est **1**
: agitado, picado (dícese del mar) **2** DIS-
CONNECTED : incoherente, inconexo
chops ['tʃɑps] *npl* **1** : quijada *f*, mandíbula *f*, boca *f* (de una persona) **2 to
lick one's chops** : relamerse
chopsticks ['tʃɑp,stɪks] *npl* : palillos *mpl*
choral ['korəl] *adj* : coral
chorale [kə'ræl, -'rɑl] *n* **1** : coral *f* (composición musical vocal) **2** CHOIR, CHO-
RUS : coral *f*, coro *m*
chord ['kord] *n* **1** : acorde *m* (en
música) **2** : cuerda *f* (en anatomía o
geometría)
chore ['tʃor] *n* **1** TASK : tarea *f* rutinaria **2** BOTHER, NUISANCE : lata *f*
fam, fastidio *m* **3** chores *npl* WORK
: quehaceres *mpl*, faenas *fpl*
choreograph ['koriə,Græf] *vt* : coreografiar
choreographer [,kori'ɑGrəfər] *n* : coreógrafo *m*, -fa *f*
choreographic [,koriə'Græfɪk] *adj*
: coreográfico
choreography [,kori'ɑGrəfi] *n*, *pl* -phies
: coreografía *f*
chorister ['korəstər] *n* : corista *mf*
chorizo [tʃə'ri:zo, -so] *n* : chorizo *m*
chortle¹ ['tʃortəl] *vi* -tled; -tling : reírse
(con satisfacción o júbilo)
chortle² *n* : risa *f* (de satisfacción o júbilo)
chorus¹ ['korəs] *vt* : corear
chorus² *n* **1** : coro *m* (grupo o composición musical) **2** REFRAIN : coro *m*,
estribillo *m*
chose → choose
chosen ['tʃo:zən] *adj* : elegido, selecto
chow ['tʃaʊ] *n* **1** FOOD : comida *f* **2**
: chow-chow *mf* (perro)
chowder ['tʃaʊdər] *n* : sopa *f* de pescado
Christ ['kraɪst] *n* **1** : Cristo *m* **2 for
Christ's sake** : ¡por Dios!
christen ['krɪsən] *vt* **1** BAPTIZE : bautizar **2** NAME : bautizar con el nombre de
Christendom ['krɪsəndəm] *n* : cristiandad
f

christening [ˈkrɪsənɪŋ] *n* : bautismo *m*, bautizo *m*

Christian¹ [ˈkrɪstʃən] *adj* : cristiano

Christian² *n* : cristiano *m*, -na *f*

Christianity [ˌkrɪstʃiˈænəʈi, ˌkrɪsˈtʃæ-] *n* : cristianismo *m*

Christian name *n* : nombre *m* de pila

Christmas [ˈkrɪsməs] *n* : Navidad *f* ⟨Christmas season : las Navidades⟩

Christmas carol *n* → **carol²**

Christmas eve *n* : Nochebuena *f*

chromatic [kroˈmæʈɪk] *adj* : cromático ⟨chromatic scale : escala cromática⟩

chrome [ˈkroːm] *n* : cromo *m* (metal)

chromium [ˈkroːmiəm] *n* : cromo *m* (elemento)

chromosome [ˈkroːməˌsoːm, -ˌzoːm] *n* : cromosoma *m*

chronic [ˈkrɑnɪk] *adj* : crónico — **chronically** [-nɪkli] *adv*

chronicle¹ [ˈkrɑnɪkəl] *vt* **-cled; -cling** : escribir (una crónica o historia)

chronicle² *n* : crónica *f*, historia *f*

chronicler [ˈkrɑnɪklər] *n* : historiador *m*, -dora *f*; cronista *mf*

chronological [ˌkrɑnəˈlɑɪkəl] *adj* : cronológico — **chronologically** [-kli] *adv*

chronology [krəˈnɑləʤi] *n, pl* **-gies** : cronología *f*

chronometer [krəˈnɑməʈər] *n* : cronómetro *m*

chrysalis [ˈkrɪsələs] *n, pl* **chrysalides** [krɪˈsæləˌdiːz] *or* **chrysalises** : crisálida *f*

chrysanthemum [krɪˈsænʈθəməm] *n* : crisantemo *m*

chubbiness [ˈtʃʌvbinəs] *n* : gordura *f*

chubby [ˈtʃʌvbi] *adj* **chubbier; -est** : gordito, regordete, rechoncho

chuck¹ [ˈtʃʌk] *vt* **1** TOSS : tirar, lanzar, aventar *Col, Mex* **2 to chuck under the chin** : hacer la mamola

chuck² *n* **1** PAT : mamola *f*, palmada *f* **2** TOSS : lanzamiento *m* **3** *or* **chuck steak** : corte *m* de carne de res

chuckle¹ [ˈtʃʌkəl] *vi* **-led; -ling** : reírse entre dientes

chuckle² *n* : risita *f*, risa *f* ahogada

chug [ˈtʃʌɡ] *vi* **chugged; chugging** : resoplar, traquetear

chum¹ [ˈtʃʌm] *vi* **chummed; chumming** : ser camaradas, ser cuates *Mex fam*

chum² *n* : amigo *m*, -ga *f*; camarada *mf*; compinche *mf fam*

chummy [ˈtʃʌmi] *adj* **chummier; -est** : amistoso ⟨they're very chummy : son muy amigos⟩

chump [ˈtʃʌmp] *n* : tonto *m*, -ta *f*; idiota *mf*

chunk [ˈtʃʌnk] *n* **1** PIECE : cacho *m*, pedazo *m*, trozo *m* **2** : cantidad *f* grande ⟨a chunk of money : mucho dinero⟩

chunky [ˈtʃʌnki] *adj* **chunkier; -est** **1** STOCKY : fornido, robusto **2** : que contiene pedazos

church [ˈtʃərtʃ] *n* **1** : iglesia *f* ⟨to go to church : ir a la iglesia⟩ **2** CHRISTIANS : iglesia *f*, conjunto *m* de fieles cristianos **3** DENOMINATION : confesión *f*, secta *f* **4** CONGREGATION : feligreses *mpl*, fieles *mpl*

churchgoer [ˈtʃərtʃˌɡoːər] *n* : practicante *mf*

churchyard [ˈtʃərtʃˌjɑrd] *n* : cementerio *m* (junto a una iglesia)

churn¹ [ˈtʃərn] *vt* **1** : batir (crema), hacer (mantequilla) **2** : agitar con fuerza, revolver **3 to churn out** : producir en masa — *vi* : agitarse, arremolinarse

churn² *n* : mantequera *f*

chute [ˈʃuːt] *n* : conducto *m* inclinado, vertedero *m* (para basuras)

chutney [ˈtʃʌtni] *n, pl* **-neys** : chutney *m*

chutzpah [ˈhʊtspə, ˈxʊt-, -ˌspɑ] *n* : descaro *m*, frescura *f*, cara *f fam*

cicada [səˈkeɪdə, -ˈkɑ-] *n* : cigarra *f*, chicharra *f*

cider [ˈsaɪdər] *n* **1** : jugo *m* (de manzana, etc.) **2 hard cider** : sidra *f*

cigar [sɪˈɡɑr] *n* : puro *m*, cigarro *m*

cigarette [ˌsɪɡəˈrɛt, ˈsɪɡəˌrɛt] *n* : cigarrillo *m*, cigarro *m*

cilantro [sɪˈlɑntroː, -ˈlæn-] *n* : cilantro *m*

cinch¹ [ˈsɪntʃ] *vt* **1** : cinchar (un caballo) **2** ASSURE : asegurar

cinch² *n* **1** : cincha *f* (para caballos) **2** : algo fácil o seguro ⟨it's a cinch : es bien fácil, es pan comido⟩

cinchona [sɪŋˈkoːnə] *n* : quino *m*

cinder [ˈsɪndər] *n* **1** EMBER : brasa *f*, ascua *f* **2 cinders** *npl* ASHES : cenizas *fpl*

cinema [ˈsɪnəmə] *n* : cine *m*

cinematic [ˌsɪnəˈmæʈɪk] *adj* : cinematográfico

cinematography [ˌsɪnəməˈtɑɡrəfi] *n* : cinematografía *f*

cinephile [ˈsɪnəˌfaɪl] *n* : cinéfilo *m*, -fila *f*

cinnamon [ˈsɪnəmən] *n* : canela *f*

cipher [ˈsaɪfər] *n* **1** ZERO : cero *m* **2** CODE : cifra *f*, clave *f*

circa [ˈsərkə] *prep* : alrededor de, hacia ⟨circa 1800 : hacia el año 1800⟩

circle¹ [ˈsərkəl] *v* **-cled; -cling** *vt* **1** : encerrar en un círculo, poner un círculo alrededor de **2** : girar alrededor de, dar vueltas a ⟨we circled the building twice : le dimos vueltas al edificio dos veces⟩ — *vi* : dar vueltas

circle² *n* **1** : círculo *m* **2** CYCLE : ciclo *m* ⟨to come full circle : volver al punto de partida⟩ **3** GROUP : círculo *m*, grupo *m* (social) **4 to have (dark) circles under one's eyes** : tener ojeras

circuit [ˈsərkət] *n* **1** BOUNDARY : circuito *m*, perímetro *m* (de una zona o un territorio) **2** TOUR : circuito *m*, recorrido *m*, tour *m* **3** : circuito *m* (eléctrico) ⟨a short circuit : un cortocircuito⟩

circuitous [ˌsərˈkjuːəʈəs] *adj* : sinuoso, tortuoso

circuitry [ˈsərkətri] *n, pl* **-ries** : sistema *m* de circuitos

circular¹ [ˈsərkjələr] *adj* ROUND : circular, redondo

circular² *n* : circular *f*

circulate [ˈsərkjəˌleɪt] *v* **-lated; -lating** *vi* : circular — *vt* **1** : circular (noticias, etc.) **2** DISSEMINATE : hacer circular, divulgar

circulation [ˌsərkjəˈleɪʃən] *n* : circulación *f*

circulatory [ˈsərkjələˌtori] *adj* : circulatorio

circumcise [ˈsərkəmˌsaɪz] *vt* **-cised; -cising** : circuncidar

circumcision [ˌsərkəmˈsɪʒən, ˈsərkəmˌ-] *n* : circuncisión *f*

circumference [sərˈkʌmpfrənts] *n* : circunferencia *f*

circumflex [ˈsərkəmˌflɛks] *n* : acento *m* circunflejo

circumlocution [ˌsərkəmloˈkjuːʃən] *n* : circunlocución *f*

circumnavigate [ˌsərkəmˈnævəˌɡeɪt] *vt* **-gated; -gating** : circunnavegar

circumscribe [ˈsərkəmˌskraɪb] *vt* **-scribed; -scribing 1** : circunscribir, trazar una figura alrededor de **2** LIMIT : circunscribir, limitar

circumspect [ˈsərkəmˌspɛkt] *adj* : circunspecto, prudente, cauto

circumstance [ˈsərkəmˌstænts] *n* **1** EVENT : circunstancia *f*, acontecimiento *m* **2 circumstances** *npl* SITUATION : circunstancias *fpl*, situación *f* ⟨under the circumstances : dadas las circunstancias⟩ ⟨under no circumstances : de ninguna manera, bajo ningún concepto⟩ **3 circumstances** *npl* : situación *f* económica

circumstantial [ˌsərkəmˈstæntʃəl] *adj* : circunstancial

circumvent [ˌsərkəmˈvɛnt] *vt* : evadir, burlar (una ley o regla), sortear (una responsabilidad o dificultad)

circumvention [ˌsərkəmˈvɛntʃən] *n* : evasión *f*

circus [ˈsərkəs] *n* : circo *m*

cirrhosis [səˈroːsɪs] *n*, *pl* **-rhoses** [-ˈroːˌsiːz] : cirrosis *f*

cis [ˈsɪs] → **cisgender**

cisgender [(ˌ)sɪsˈdʒɛndər] *adj* : cisgénero ⟨cisgender people : las personas cisgénero⟩

cistern [ˈsɪstərn] *n* : cisterna *f*, aljibe *m*

citadel [ˈsɪtədəl, -ˌdɛl] *n* FORTRESS : ciudadela *f*, fortaleza *f*

citation [saɪˈteɪʃən] *n* **1** SUMMONS : emplazamiento *m*, citación *f*, convocatoria *f* (judicial) **2** QUOTATION : cita *f* **3** COMMENDATION : elogio *m*, mención *f* (de honor)

cite [ˈsaɪt] *vt* **cited; citing 1** ARRAIGN, SUBPOENA : emplazar, citar, hacer comparecer (ante un tribunal) **2** QUOTE : citar **3** COMMEND : elogiar, honrar (oficialmente)

citizen [ˈsɪtəzən] *n* : ciudadano *m*, -na *f*

citizenry [ˈsɪtəzənri] *n*, *pl* **-ries** : ciudadanía *f*, conjunto *m* de ciudadanos

citizenship [ˈsɪtəzənˌʃɪp] *n* : ciudadanía *f* ⟨Nicaraguan citizenship : ciudadanía nicaragüense⟩

citrus [ˈsɪtrəs] *n*, *pl* **-rus** *or* **-ruses** : cítrico *m*

city [ˈsɪti] *n*, *pl* **cities** : ciudad *f*

civic [ˈsɪvɪk] *adj* : cívico

civic–minded [ˌsɪvɪkˈmaɪndəd] *adj* : cívico

civics [ˈsɪvɪks] *ns & pl* : civismo *m*

civil [ˈsɪvəl] *adj* **1** : civil ⟨civil law : derecho civil⟩ **2** POLITE : civil, cortés

civilian [səˈvɪljən] *n* : civil *mf* ⟨soldiers and civilians : soldados y civiles⟩

civility [səˈvɪləti] *n*, *pl* **-ties** : cortesía *f*, educación *f*

civilization [ˌsɪvələˈzeɪʃən] *n* : civilización *f*

civilize [ˈsɪvəˌlaɪz] *vt* **-lized; -lizing** : civilizar — **civilized** *adj*

civil liberties *npl* : derechos *mpl* civiles

civilly [ˈsɪvəli] *adv* : cortésmente

civil rights *npl* : derechos *mpl* civiles

civil servant *n* : funcionario *m*, -ria *f*

civil service *n* : administración *f* pública

civil war *n* : guerra *f* civil

clack¹ [ˈklæk] *vi* : tabletear

clack² *n* : tableteo *m*

clad [ˈklæd] *adj* **1** CLOTHED : vestido **2** COVERED : cubierto

claim¹ [ˈkleɪm] *vt* **1** DEMAND : reclamar, reivindicar ⟨she claimed her rights : reclamó sus derechos⟩ **2** MAINTAIN : afirmar, sostener ⟨they claim it's theirs : sostienen que es suyo⟩

claim² *n* **1** DEMAND : demanda *f*, reclamación *f* **2** DECLARATION : declaración *f*, afirmación *f* **3 to stake a claim** : reclamar, reivindicar

claimant [ˈkleɪmənt] *n* : demandante *mf* (ante un juez), pretendiente *mf* (al trono, etc.)

clairvoyance [klærˈvɔɪənts] *n* : clarividencia *f*

clairvoyant¹ [klærˈvɔɪənt] *adj* : clarividente

clairvoyant² *n* : clarividente *mf*

clam [ˈklæm] *n* : almeja *f*

clamber [ˈklæmbər] *vi* : treparse o subirse torpemente

clammy [ˈklæmi] *adj* **clammier; -est** : húmedo y algo frío

clamor¹ [ˈklæmər] *vi* : gritar, clamar

clamor² *n* : clamor *m*

clamorous [ˈklæmərəs] *adj* : clamoroso, ruidoso, estrepitoso

clamp¹ [ˈklæmp] *vt* : sujetar con abrazaderas

clamp² *n* : abrazadera *f*

clam up *vi fam* : callarse, negarse a hablar

clan [ˈklæn] *n* : clan *m*

clandestine [klænˈdɛstɪn] *adj* : clandestino, secreto

clang¹ [ˈklæŋ] *vi* : hacer resonar (dícese de un objeto metálico)

clang² *n* : ruido *m* metálico fuerte

clangor [ˈklæŋər, -ɡər] *n* : estruendo *m* metálico

clank¹ [ˈklæŋk] *vi* : producir un ruido metálico seco

clank² *n* : ruido *m* metálico seco

clap¹ [ˈklæp] *v* **clapped; clapping** *vt* **1** SLAP, STRIKE : golpear ruidosamente, dar una palmada ⟨to clap one's hands : batir palmas, dar palmadas⟩ **2** APPLAUD : aplaudir — *vi* APPLAUD : aplaudir

clap² *n* **1** SLAP : palmada *f*, golpecito *m* **2** NOISE : ruido *m* seco ⟨a clap of thunder : un trueno⟩

clapboard [ˈklæbərd, ˈklæpˌbord] *n* : tabla *f* de madera (para revestir muros)

clapper ['klæpər] *n* : badajo *m* (de una campana)

clapping ['klæpɪŋ] *n* : aplausos *mpl*

clarification [ˌklærəfə'keɪʃən] *n* : clarificación *f*

clarify ['klærəˌfaɪ] *vt* **-fied; -fying** **1** EXPLAIN : aclarar **2** : clarificar (un líquido)

clarinet [ˌklærə'nɛt] *n* : clarinete *m*

clarion ['klæriən] *adj* : claro y sonoro

clarity ['klærəti] *n* : claridad *f*, nitidez *f*

clash¹ ['klæʃ] *vi* **1** : sonar, chocarse ⟨the cymbals clashed : los platillos sonaron⟩ **2** : chocar, enfrentarse ⟨the students clashed with the police : los estudiantes se enfrentaron con la policía⟩ **3** CONFLICT : estar en conflicto, oponerse **4** : desentonar (dícese de los colores), coincidir (dícese de los datos)

clash² *n* **1** : ruido *m* (producido por un choque) **2** CONFLICT, CONFRONTATION : enfrentamiento *m*, conflicto *m*, choque *m*

clasp¹ ['klæsp] *vt* **1** FASTEN : sujetar, abrochar **2** EMBRACE, GRASP : agarrar, sujetar, abrazar

clasp² *n* **1** FASTENING : broche *m*, cierre *m* **2** EMBRACE, SQUEEZE : apretón *m*, abrazo *m*

class¹ ['klæs] *vt* : clasificar, catalogar

class² *n* **1** KIND, TYPE : clase *f*, tipo *m*, especie *f* **2** : clase *f*, rango *m* social ⟨the working class : la clase obrera⟩ **3** LESSON : clase *f*, curso *m* ⟨English class : clase de inglés⟩ ⟨to take a class : tomar/hacer un curso⟩ **4** : clase *f* ⟨he told the whole class : se lo dijo a toda la clase⟩ ⟨the class of '97 : la promoción del 97⟩ **5** STYLE : clase *f*, estilo *m* **6** : clase *f* (en un vuelo) ⟨business class : clase ejecutiva⟩

classic¹ ['klæsɪk] *adj* : clásico

classic² *n* : clásico *m*, obra *f* clásica

classical ['klæsɪkəl] *adj* : clásico — **classically** [-kli] *adv*

classicism ['klæsəˌsɪzəm] *n* : clasicismo *m*

classification [ˌklæsəfə'keɪʃən] *n* : clasificación *f*

classified ['klæsəˌfaɪd] *adj* **1** : clasificado ⟨classified ads : avisos clasificados⟩ **2** RESTRICTED : confidencial, secreto ⟨classified documents : documentos secretos⟩

classify ['klæsəˌfaɪ] *vt* **-fied; -fying** : clasificar, catalogar

classless ['klæsləs] *adj* : sin clases

classmate ['klæsˌmeɪt] *n* : compañero *m*, -ra *f* de clase

classroom ['klæsˌruːm] *n* : aula *f*, salón *m* de clase

classy ['klæsi] *adj* **classier; -est** : con clase

clatter¹ ['klætər] *vi* : traquetear, hacer ruido

clatter² *n* : traqueteo *m*, ruido *m*, estrépito *m*

clause ['klɔz] *n* : cláusula *f*

claustrophobia [ˌklɔstrə'foːbiə] *n* : claustrofobia *f*

claustrophobic [ˌklɔstrə'foːbɪk] *adj* : claustrofóbico

clavicle ['klævɪkəl] *n* : clavícula *f*

claw¹ ['klɔ] *v* : arañar

claw² *n* : garra *f*, uña *f* (de un gato), pinza *f* (de un crustáceo)

clay ['kleɪ] *n* : arcilla *f*, barro *m*

clean¹ ['kliːn] *vt* **1** *or* **to clean up** : limpiar ⟨to clean oneself up : lavarse⟩ **2** : limpiar (pescado, etc.) **3 to clean one's plate** : comérselo todo **4 to clean out** : limpiar y ordenar (un lugar) **5 to clean out** : dejar pelado, limpiar, robarle todo — *vi* **1** *or* **to clean up** : limpiar ⟨to clean up after dinner : lavar los platos/trastes⟩ ⟨I'm not cleaning up after you : no voy a limpiar lo que tú ensucias⟩ **2 to clean up** : hacerse su agosto, enriquecerse

clean² *adv* : limpio, limpiamente ⟨to play clean : jugar limpio⟩

clean³ *adj* **1** : limpio **2** UNADULTERATED : puro ⟨clean water : agua pura⟩ **3** IRREPROACHABLE : intachable, sin mancha ⟨to have a clean record : no tener antecedentes penales⟩ **4** GREEN : limpio ⟨clean energy : energía limpia⟩ **5** CLEAR, SHARP : claro, nítido ⟨clean lines : líneas sencillas/puras⟩ **6** DECENT : decente **7** COMPLETE : completo, absoluto ⟨a clean break with the past : un corte radical con el pasado⟩

cleaner ['kliːnər] *n* **1** : limpiador *m*, -dora *f* **2** : producto *m* de limpieza ⟨glass/window cleaner : limpiavidrios⟩ **3** DRY CLEANER : tintorería *f* ⟨the cleaner/cleaner's/cleaners : la tintorería⟩

cleaning ['kliːnɪŋ] *n* : limpieza *f*

cleanliness ['klɛnlinəs] *n* : limpieza *f*, aseo *m*

cleanly¹ ['kliːnli] *adv* : limpiamente, con limpieza

cleanly² ['klɛnli] *adj* **cleanlier; -est** : limpio, pulcro

cleanness ['kliːnnəs] *n* : limpieza *f*

cleanse ['klɛnz] *vt* **cleansed; cleansing** : limpiar, purificar

cleanser ['klɛnzər] *n* : limpiador *m*, purificador *m*

clean sweep *n* : barrida *f* (en una competencia)

clear¹ ['klɪr] *vt* **1** CLARIFY : aclarar, clarificar (un líquido) **2** : despejar (una superficie), desatascar (un tubo), desmontar (una selva) ⟨to clear the table : levantar la mesa⟩ ⟨to clear a path : abrir un camino⟩ ⟨to clear a space for : hacer lugar para⟩ ⟨to clear one's throat : carraspear, aclararse la voz⟩ **3** EMPTY, EVACUATE : vaciar, evacuar **4** EXONERATE : absolver, limpiar el nombre de **5** EARN : ganar, sacar (una ganancia de) **6** : pasar sin tocar ⟨he cleared the hurdle : saltó por encima de la valla⟩ **7** AUTHORIZE : autorizar **8 to clear away** : poner en su sitio **9 to clear off** : quitar de ⟨let me clear (the papers) off the table : déjame quitar los papeles de la mesa⟩ **10 to clear out** : ordenar **11 to clear up** RESOLVE : aclarar, resolver, esclarecer

— *vi* **1** DISPERSE : irse, despejarse, disiparse **2** : ser compensado (dícese de un cheque) **3 to clear up** : despejar (dícese del tiempo), mejorarse (dícese de una enfermedad)

clear² *adv* : claro, claramente

clear³ *adj* **1** BRIGHT : claro, lúcido **2** FAIR : claro, despejado **3** TRANSPARENT : transparente, translúcido **4** EVIDENT, UNMISTAKABLE : claro, evidente, obvio ⟨a clear explanation : una explicación clara⟩ ⟨is that clear?, do I make myself clear? : ¿está claro?⟩ ⟨I want to be clear : (quiero) que quede claro⟩ **5** SHARP : claro, nítido **6** CERTAIN : seguro ⟨to be clear on something : entender algo⟩ **7** ALERT : despejado, lúcido ⟨to have a clear head : estar despejado⟩ **8** : despejado (dícese de las vías, etc.) ⟨keep the area clear of clutter : mantener la zona libre de objetos⟩

clear⁴ *n* **1 in the clear** : inocente, libre de toda sospecha **2 in the clear** SAFE : fuera de peligro

clearance [ˈklɪrənʌs] *n* **1** CLEARING : despeje *m* **2** SPACE : espacio *m* (libre), margen *m* **3** AUTHORIZATION : autorización *f*, despacho *m* (de la aduana)

clear–cut [ˈklɪrˈkʌt] *adj* : bien definido

clearing [ˈklɪrɪŋ] *n* : claro *m* (de un bosque)

clearly [ˈklɪrli] *adv* **1** DISTINCTLY : claramente, directamente **2** OBVIOUSLY : obviamente, evidentemente

cleat [ˈkliːt] *n* **1** : taco *m* **2 cleats** *npl* : zapatos *mpl* deportivos (con tacos)

cleavage [ˈkliːvɪʤ] *n* **1** CLEFT : hendidura *f*, raja *f* **2** : escote *m* (del busto)

cleave¹ [ˈkliːv] *vi* **cleaved** [ˈkliːvd] *or* **clove** [ˈkloːv]; **cleaving** ADHERE : adherirse, unirse

cleave² *vt* **cleaved; cleaving** SPLIT : hender, dividir, partir

cleaver [ˈkliːvər] *n* : cuchilla *f* de carnicero

clef [ˈklɛf] *n* : clave *f*

cleft [ˈklɛft] *n* : hendidura *f*, raja *f*, grieta *f*

clemency [ˈklɛmənʦi] *n* : clemencia *f*

clement [ˈklɛmənt] *adj* **1** MERCIFUL : clemente, piadoso **2** MILD : clemente, apacible

clench [ˈklɛnʧ] *vt* **1** CLUTCH : agarrar **2** TIGHTEN : apretar (el puño, los dientes)

clergy [ˈklərʤi] *n, pl* **-gies** : clero *m*

clergyman [ˈklərʤimən] *n, pl* **-men** [-mən, -ˌmɛn] : clérigo *m*

cleric [ˈklɛrɪk] *n* : clérigo *m*, -ga *f*

clerical [ˈklɛrɪkəl] *adj* **1** : clerical ⟨a clerical collar : un alzacuello⟩ **2** : de oficina ⟨clerical staff : personal de oficina⟩

clerk¹ [ˈklərk, *Brit* ˈklɑrk] *vi* : trabajar de oficinista, trabajar de dependiente

clerk² *n* **1** : funcionario *m*, -ria *f* (de una oficina gubernamental) **2** : oficinista *mf*, empleado *m*, -da *f* de oficina **3** SALESPERSON : dependiente *m*, -ta *f*

clever [ˈklɛvər] *adj* **1** SKILLFUL : ingenioso, hábil **2** SMART : listo, inteligente, astuto

cleverly [ˈklɛvərli] *adv* **1** SKILLFULLY

: ingeniosamente, hábilmente **2** INTELLIGENTLY : inteligentemente

cleverness [ˈklɛvərnəs] *n* **1** SKILL : ingenio *m*, habilidad *f* **2** INTELLIGENCE : inteligencia *f*

clew [ˈkluː] → **clue**

cliché [kliˈʃeɪ] *n* : cliché *m*, tópico *m*

click¹ [ˈklɪk] *vt* **1** : chasquear (los dedos, etc.) ⟨to click one's heels : dar un taconazo⟩ **2** : hacer clic/click en (un botón, etc.) — *vi* **1** : hacer clic/click **2** SNAP : chasquear **3** SUCCEED : tener éxito **4** GET ALONG : congeniar, llevarse bien

click² *n* **1** : chasquido *m* (de los dedos, etc.) **2** : clic *m*, click *m* (de un botón, etc.)

client [ˈklaɪənt] *n* : cliente *m*, -ta *f*

clientele [ˌklaɪənˈtɛl, ˌkliː-] *n* : clientela *f*

cliff [ˈklɪf] *n* : acantilado *m*, precipicio *m*, risco *m*

climate [ˈklaɪmət] *n* : clima *m*

climatic [klaɪˈmætɪk, klə-] *adj* : climático

climax¹ [ˈklaɪˌmæks] *vi* : llegar al punto culminante, culminar — *vt* : ser el punto culminante de

climax² *n* : clímax *m*, punto *m* culminante

climb¹ [ˈklaɪm] *vt* : escalar, trepar a, subir a ⟨to climb a mountain : escalar una montaña⟩ — *vi* **1** RISE : subir, ascender ⟨prices are climbing : los precios están subiendo⟩ **2** : subirse, treparse ⟨to climb up a tree : treparse a un árbol⟩

climb² *n* : ascenso *m*, subida *f*

climber [ˈklaɪmər] *n* **1** : escalador *m*, -dora *f* ⟨a mountain climber : un alpinista⟩ **2** : trepadora *f* (planta)

climbing [ˈklaɪmɪŋ] *n* MOUNTAINEERING : montañismo *m*, alpinismo *m*

clinch¹ [ˈklɪnʧ] *vt* **1** FASTEN, SECURE : remachar (un clavo), afianzar, abrochar **2** SETTLE : decidir, cerrar ⟨to clinch the title : ganar el título⟩

clinch² *n* : abrazo *m*, clinch *m* (en el boxeo)

clincher [ˈklɪnʧər] *n* : argumento *m* decisivo

cling [ˈklɪŋ] *vi* **clung** [ˈklʌŋ]; **clinging 1** STICK : adherirse, pegarse **2** : aferrarse, agarrarse ⟨he clung to the railing : se aferró a la barandilla⟩

clingy [ˈklɪŋi] *adj* **clingier; -est 1** : ajustado, ceñido (dícese de la ropa) **2** : pegajoso (dícese de una persona)

clinic [ˈklɪnɪk] *n* : clínica *f*

clinical [ˈklɪnɪkəl] *adj* : clínico — **clinically** [-kli] *adv*

clink¹ [ˈklɪŋk] *vi* : tintinear

clink² *n* : tintineo *m*

clip¹ [ˈklɪp] *vt* **clipped; clipping 1** CUT : cortar, recortar **2** HIT : golpear, dar un puñetazo a **3** FASTEN : sujetar (con un clip)

clip² *n* **1** → **clippers 2** BLOW : golpe *m*, puñetazo *m* **3** PACE : paso *m* rápido **4** FASTENER : clip *m* ⟨a paper clip : un sujetapapeles⟩

clipper [ˈklɪpər] *n* **1** : clíper *m* (buque de vela) **2 clippers** *npl* : tijeras *fpl* ⟨nail clippers : cortaúñas⟩

clipping [ˈklɪpɪŋ] *n* **1** : recorte *m* (de un periódico) **2** BIT : pedazo *m*, trozo *m* (de uña, etc.), recorte *m* (de pasto, etc.)

clique [ˈkliːk, ˈklɪk] *n* : grupo *m* exclusivo, camarilla *f* (de políticos)

clitoris [ˈklɪt̬ərəs, klɪˈtɔrəs] *n, pl* **clitorides** [-ˈtɔrəˌdiːz] : clítoris *m*

cloak[1] [ˈkloːk] *vt* : encubrir, envolver (en un manto de)

cloak[2] *n* : capa *f*, capote *m*, manto *m* ⟨under the cloak of darkness : al amparo de la oscuridad⟩

cloakroom [ˈkloːkˌruːm, -ˌrʊm] *n* : guardarropa *m*

clobber [ˈklɑbər] *vt* : dar una paliza a

clock[1] [ˈklɑk] *vt* **1** : cronometrar **2 to clock in/out** : fichar (al entrar/salir)

clock[2] *n* **1** : reloj *m* (de pared), cronómetro *m* (en deportes o competencias) **2 around the clock** : las veinticuatro horas

clockmaker [ˈklɑkˌmeɪkər] *n* : relojero *m*, -ra *f*

clockmaking [ˈklɑkˌmeɪkɪŋ] *n* : relojería *f*

clockwise [ˈklɑkˌwaɪz] *adv & adj* : en la dirección de las manecillas del reloj

clockwork [ˈklɑkˌwərk] *n* : mecanismo *m* de relojería

clod [ˈklɑd] *n* **1** : terrón *m* **2** OAF : zoquete *mf*

clog[1] [ˈklɑg] *v* **clogged; clogging** *vt* **1** HINDER : estorbar, impedir **2** BLOCK : atascar, tapar — *vi* : atascarse, taparse

clog[2] *n* **1** OBSTACLE : traba *f*, impedimento *m*, estorbo *m* **2** : zueco *m* (zapato)

cloister [ˈklɔɪstər] *n* : claustro *m*

clone[1] [ˈkloːn] *vt* : clonar

clone[2] *n* **1** : clon *m* (de un organismo) **2** COPY : copia *f*, reproducción *f*

close[1] [ˈkloːz] *v* **closed; closing** *vt* **1** : cerrar (una puerta, un libro, un archivo, etc.) ⟨to close one's eyes : cerrar los ojos⟩ **2** *or* **to close up** : cerrar (una empresa, etc.) ⟨they close the store at five o'clock : cierran la tienda a las cinco⟩ **3** *or* **to close down** : cerrar (una empresa, etc.) ⟨they had to close the restaurant : tuvieron que cerrar el restaurante⟩ **4** *or* **to close off** : cerrar (una calle) **5** *or* **to close out** : cerrar (una cuenta) **6** *or* **to close out** END : concluir, terminar **7** : hacer, cerrar (un trato) **8** REDUCE : cerrar, reducir (una distancia) **9 to close up** : cerrar (una casa, etc.) — *vi* **1** : cerrarse, cerrar ⟨the door closed behind her : la puerta se cerró tras ella⟩ ⟨they close on Sundays : cierran los domingos⟩ **2** TERMINATE : concluirse, terminar **3 to close at (a price)** : cotizar a (un precio) al cierre **4 to close down** : cerrar (dícese de una empresa, etc.) **5 to close in** APPROACH : acercarse, aproximarse **6 to close on** : cerrar (un trato), cerrar la compra/venta (de una casa)

close[2] [ˈkloːs] *adv* : cerca, de cerca

close[3] *adj* **closer; closest 1** NEAR : cercano, próximo ⟨stay close to me : no te separes de mi lado⟩ ⟨don't get too close to the fire : no te acerques al fuego⟩ ⟨we

must be getting close by now : ya estaremos muy cerca⟩ ⟨Christmas is getting close : se acerca la Navidad⟩ ⟨at close range/quarters : de cerca⟩ ⟨to live in close quarters : vivir muy apretados⟩ **2** SIMILAR : parecido, similar ⟨they're close in age : tienen casi la misma edad⟩ ⟨close in size : de tamaño parecido⟩ ⟨to bear a close resemblance to : tener un gran parecido con/a⟩ **3** (*indicating approximation*) ⟨did I guess right? — no, but you're close : ¿acerté? — no, pero casi⟩ ⟨not even close : ni por asomo⟩ ⟨close, but no cigar : casi, pero no⟩ **4** (*indicating that something nearly did or didn't happen*) ⟨that was close!, that was a close one/call/shave! : ¡nos salvamos por los pelos!⟩ ⟨we won, but it was close : ganamos por los pelos⟩ **5** STRICT : estricto, detallado ⟨keep a close eye/watch on him : vigílalo bien⟩ ⟨to pay close attention to : prestar mucha atención a⟩ **6** STUFFY : de aire viciado o sofocante (dícese de un lugar) **7** TIGHT : apretado, entallado, ceñido ⟨it's a close fit : es muy apretado⟩ **8** : cercano ⟨close relatives : parientes cercanos⟩ **9** INTIMATE : íntimo ⟨close friends : amigos íntimos⟩ ⟨those close to the president : los allegados del presidente⟩ **10** ACCURATE : fiel, exacto **11** : reñido ⟨a close election : una elección muy reñida⟩ ⟨she came in a close second : quedó en segundo lugar por una diferencia mínima⟩ **12 to be close to** : estar a punto de, estar al borde de ⟨he was close to crying/tears : estaba a punto de llorar, estaba a punto de las lágrimas⟩ ⟨to close to death : estar al borde de la muerte⟩

close[4] [ˈkloːz] *n* : fin *m*, final *m*, conclusión *f*

close–knit [ˈkloːsˈnɪt] *adj* : unido, íntimo

closely [ˈkloːsli] *adv* : cerca, de cerca

closeness [ˈkloːsnəs] *n* **1** NEARNESS : cercanía *f*, proximidad *f* **2** INTIMACY : intimidad *f*

closet[1] [ˈklɑzət] *vt* **to be closeted with** : estar encerrado con

closet[2] *n* : armario *m*, guardarropa *f*, clóset *m*

close–up [ˈkloːsˌʌp] *n* : primer plano *m*

closure [ˈkloːʒər] *n* **1** CLOSING, END : cierre *m*, clausura *f*, fin *m* **2** FASTENER : cierre *m*

clot[1] [ˈklɑt] *v* **clotted; clotting** *vt* : coagular, cuajar — *vi* : cuajarse, coagularse

clot[2] *n* : coágulo *m*

cloth [ˈklɔθ] *n, pl* **cloths** [ˈklɔðz, ˈklɔθs] **1** FABRIC : tela *f* **2** RAG : trapo *m* **3** TABLECLOTH : mantel *m*

clothe [ˈkloːð] *vt* **clothed** *or* **clad** [ˈklæd]; **clothing** DRESS : vestir, arropar, ataviar

clothes [ˈkloːz, ˈkloːðz] *npl* **1** CLOTHING : ropa *f* **2** BEDCLOTHES : ropa *f* de cama

clothesline [ˈkloːzˌlaɪn] *n* : tendedero *m*

clothespin [ˈkloːzˌpɪn] *n* : pinza *f* (para la ropa)

clothing [ˈkloːðɪŋ] *n* : ropa *f*, indumentaria *f*

cloud[1] ['klaʊd] *vt* : nublar, oscurecer — *vi* **to cloud over** : nublarse

cloud[2] *n* **1** : nube *f* ⟨to have one's head in the clouds : andar en las nubes⟩ **2** : nube *f* (de polvo, etc.) **3** : nube *f* ⟨cloud computing : computación en la nube⟩

cloudburst ['klaʊd,bərst] *n* : chaparrón *m*, aguacero *m*

cloudiness ['klaʊdinəs] *n* : nubosidad *f*

cloudless ['klaʊdləs] *adj* : despejado, claro

cloudy ['klaʊdi] *adj* **cloudier; -est** : nublado, nuboso

clout[1] ['klaʊt] *vt* : bofetear, dar un tortazo a

clout[2] *n* **1** BLOW : golpe *m*, tortazo *m fam* **2** INFLUENCE : influencia *f*, palanca *f fam*

clove[1] ['klo:v] *n* **1** : diente *m* (de ajo) **2** : clavo *m* (especia)

clove[2] → **cleave**

cloven hoof ['klo:vən] *n* : pezuña *f* hendida

clover ['klo:vər] *n* : trébol *m*

cloverleaf ['klo:vər,li:f] *n, pl* **-leafs** or **-leaves** [-,li:vz] : intersección *f* en trébol

clown[1] ['klaʊn] *vi* : payasear, bromear ⟨stop clowning around : déjate de payasadas⟩

clown[2] *n* : payaso *m*, -sa *f*

clownish ['klaʊnɪʃ] *adj* **1** : de payaso **2** BOORISH : grosero — **clownishly** *adv*

cloying ['klɔɪɪŋ] *adj* : empalagoso, meloso

club[1] ['klʌb] *vt* **clubbed; clubbing** : aporrear, dar garrotazos a

club[2] *n* **1** CUDGEL : garrote *m*, porra *f* **2** : palo *m* ⟨golf club : palo de golf⟩ **3** : trébol *m*, basto *m* (en la baraja española) **4** ASSOCIATION : club *m*

clubfoot ['klʌb,fʊt] *n, pl* **-feet** : pie *m* deforme

clubhouse ['klʌb,haʊs] *n* : sede *f* de un club

cluck[1] ['klʌk] *vi* : cloquear, cacarear

cluck[2] *n* : cloqueo *m*, cacareo *m*

clue[1] ['klu:] *vt* **clued; clueing** or **cluing** or **to clue in** : dar una pista a, informar

clue[2] *n* : pista *f*, indicio *m*

clump[1] ['klʌmp] *vi* **1** : caminar con pisadas fuertes **2** LUMP : agruparse, aglutinarse — *vt* : amontonar

clump[2] *n* **1** : grupo *m* (de arbustos o árboles), terrón *m* (de tierra) **2** : pisada *f* fuerte

clumsily ['klʌmzəli] *adv* : torpemente, sin gracia

clumsiness ['klʌmzinəs] *n* : torpeza *f*

clumsy ['klʌmzi] *adj* **clumsier; -est 1** AWKWARD : torpe, desmañado **2** TACTLESS : carente de tacto, poco delicado

clung → **cling**

clunky ['klʌŋki] *adj* : torpe, poco elegante

cluster[1] ['klʌstər] *vt* : agrupar, juntar — *vi* : agruparse, apiñarse, arracimarse

cluster[2] *n* : grupo *m*, conjunto *m*, racimo *m* (de uvas)

clutch[1] ['klʌtʃ] *vt* : agarrar, asir — *vi* **to clutch at** : tratar de agarrar

clutch[2] *n* **1** GRASP, GRIP : agarre *m*, apretón *m* **2** : embrague *m*, clutch *m*

(de una máquina) **3 clutches** *npl* : garras *fpl* ⟨he fell into their clutches : cayó en sus garras⟩

clutter[1] ['klʌtər] *vt* : atiborrar o atestar de cosas, llenar desordenadamente

clutter[2] *n* : desorden *m*, revoltijo *m*

coach[1] ['ko:tʃ] *vt* : entrenar (atletas, artistas), preparar (alumnos)

coach[2] *n* **1** CARRIAGE : coche *m*, carruaje *m*, carroza *f* **2** : vagón *m* de pasajeros (de un tren) **3** BUS : autobús *m*, ómnibus *m* **4** : pasaje *m* aéreo de segunda clase **5** TRAINER : entrenador *m*, -dora *f*

coagulate [ko'ægjə,leɪt] *v* **-lated; -lating** *vt* : coagular, cuajar — *vi* : coagularse, cuajarse

coal ['ko:l] *n* **1** EMBER : ascua *f*, brasa *f* **2** : carbón *m* ⟨a coal mine : una mina de carbón⟩

coalesce [,ko:ə'lɛs] *vi* **-alesced; -alescing** : unirse

coalition [,ko:ə'lɪʃən] *n* : coalición *f*

coarse ['kors] *adj* **coarser; coarsest 1** : grueso (dícese de la arena o la sal), basto (dícese de las telas), áspero (dícese de la piel) **2** CRUDE, ROUGH : basto, tosco, ordinario **3** VULGAR : grosero — **coarsely** *adv*

coarsen ['korsən] *vt* : hacer áspero o basto — *vi* : volverse áspero o basto

coarseness ['korsnəs] *n* : aspereza *f*, tosquedad *f*

coast[1] ['ko:st] *vi* : deslizarse, rodar sin impulso

coast[2] *n* : costa *f*, litoral *m*

coastal ['ko:stəl] *adj* : costero

coaster ['ko:stər] *n* : posavasos *m*

coast guard *n* : guardia *f* costera, guardacostas *mpl*

coastline ['ko:st,laɪn] *n* : costa *f*

coat[1] ['ko:t] *vt* : cubrir, revestir, bañar (en un líquido)

coat[2] *n* **1** : abrigo *m* ⟨a sport coat : una chaqueta, un saco⟩ **2** : pelaje *m* (de animales) **3** LAYER : capa *f*, mano *f* (de pintura)

coat check *n* : guardarropa *m*

coat hanger *n* : percha *f*, gancho *m*

coating ['ko:tɪŋ] *n* : capa *f*

coat of arms *n* : escudo *m* de armas

coatrack ['ko:t,ræk] *n* : percha *f*, perchero *m*

coax ['ko:ks] *vt* : engatusar, persuadir

cob ['kab] → **corncob**

cobalt ['ko:,bɔlt] *n* : cobalto *m*

cobble ['kabəl] *vt* **cobbled; cobbling 1** : fabricar o remendar (zapatos) **2 to cobble together** : improvisar, hacer apresuradamente

cobbler ['kablər] *n* **1** SHOEMAKER : zapatero *m*, -ra *f* **2 fruit cobbler** : tarta *f* de fruta

cobblestone ['kabəl,sto:n] *n* : adoquín *m*

cobra ['ko:brə] *n* : cobra *f*

cobweb ['kab,wɛb] *n* : telaraña *f*

coca ['ko:kə] *n* : coca *f*

cocaine [ko:'keɪn, 'ko:,keɪn] *n* : cocaína *f*

cock[1] ['kak] *vt* **1** : ladear ⟨to cock one's head : ladear la cabeza⟩ **2** : montar, amartillar (un arma de fuego)

cock² *n* **1** ROOSTER : gallo *m* **2** FAUCET : grifo *m*, llave *f* **3** : martillo *m* (de un arma de fuego)

cockatoo ['kakə‚tu:] *n, pl* **-toos** : cacatúa *f*

cockeyed ['kak‚aɪd] *adj* **1** ASKEW : ladeado, torcido, chueco **2** ABSURD : disparatado, absurdo

cockfight ['kak‚faɪt] *n* : pelea *f* de gallos

cockiness ['kakinəs] *n* : arrogancia *f*

cockle ['kakəl] *n* : berberecho *m*

cockpit ['kak‚pɪt] *n* : cabina *f*

cockroach ['kak‚ro:tʃ] *n* : cucaracha *f*

cocktail ['kak‚teɪl] *n* **1** : coctel *m*, cóctel *m* **2** APPETIZER : aperitivo *m*

cocky ['kaki] *adj* **cockier; -est** : creído, engreído

cocoa ['ko:‚ko:] *n* **1** CACAO : cacao *m* **2** : cocoa *f*, chocolate *m* (bebida)

coconut ['ko:kə‚nʌt] *n* : coco *m*

cocoon [kə'ku:n] *n* : capullo *m*

cod ['kad] *n, pl* **cod** : bacalao *m*

coddle ['kadəl] *vt* **-dled; -dling** : mimar, consentir

code¹ ['ko:d] *vt* **coded; coding 1** EN-CODE : cifrar (mensajes, etc.) **2** EN-CODE : codificar (datos, etc.) **3** MARK : codificar

code² *n* **1** : código *m* ⟨civil code : código civil⟩ **2** : código *m*, clave *f* ⟨secret code : clave secreta⟩

codeine ['ko:‚di:n] *n* : codeína *f*

codex ['ko:‚dɛks] *n, pl* **-dexes** [-‚dɛksəz] *or* **-dices** [-də‚si:z] : códice *m*

codger ['kadʒər] *n* : viejo *m*, vejete *m*

codify ['kadə‚faɪ, 'ko:-] *vt* **-fied; -fying** : codificar

coeducational [‚ko:‚ɛdʒə'keɪʃənəl] *adj* : mixto

coefficient [‚ko:ə'fɪʃənt] *n* : coeficiente *m*

coerce [ko'ərs] *vt* **-erced; -ercing** : coaccionar, forzar, obligar

coercion [ko'ərʒən, -ʃən] *n* : coacción *f*

coercive [ko'ərsɪv] *adj* : coactivo

coexist [‚ko:ɪg'zɪst] *vi* : coexistir

coexistence [‚ko:ɪg'zɪstəns] *n* : coexistencia *f*

coffee ['kɔfi] *n* : café *m*

coffeemaker ['kɔfi‚meɪkər] *n* : cafetera *f*

coffeepot ['kɔfi‚pat] *n* : cafetera *f*

coffee table *n* : mesa *f* de centro

coffer ['kɔfər] *n* : cofre *m*

coffin ['kɔfən] *n* : ataúd *m*, féretro *m*

cog ['kag] *n* : diente *m* (de una rueda dentada)

cogent ['ko:dʒənt] *adj* : convincente, persuasivo

cogitate ['kadʒə‚teɪt] *vi* **-tated; -tating** : reflexionar, meditar, discurrir

cogitation [‚kadʒə'teɪʃən] *n* : reflexión *f*, meditación *f*

cognac ['ko:n‚jæk] *n* : coñac *m*

cognate ['kag‚neɪt] *adj* : relacionado, afín

cognition [kag'nɪʃən] *n* : cognición *f*

cognitive ['kagnətɪv] *adj* : cognitivo

cogwheel ['kag‚hwi:l] *n* : rueda *f* dentada

cohabit [‚ko:'hæbət] *vi* : cohabitar — **cohabitation** [‚ko:‚hæbə'teɪʃən] *n*

cohere [ko'hɪr] *vi* **-hered; -hering 1** AD-HERE : adherirse, pegarse **2** : ser coherente o congruente

coherence [ko'hɪrəns] *n* : coherencia *f*, congruencia *f*

coherent [ko'hɪrənt] *adj* : coherente, congruente — **coherently** *adv*

cohesion [ko'hi:ʒən] *n* : cohesión *f*

cohesive [ko'hi:sɪv, -zɪv] *adj* : cohesivo

cohort ['ko:‚hɔrt] *n* **1** : cohorte *f* (de soldados) **2** COMPANION : compañero *m*, -ra *f*; colega *mf*

coiffure [kwa'fjʊr] *n* : peinado *m*

coil¹ ['kɔɪl] *vt* : enrollar — *vi* : enrollarse, enroscarse

coil² *n* **1** : rollo *m* (de cuerda, etc.), espiral *f* (de humo) **2** : bobina *f* (eléctrica)

coin¹ ['kɔɪn] *vt* **1** MINT : acuñar (moneda) **2** INVENT : acuñar, crear, inventar ⟨to coin a phrase : como se suele decir⟩

coin² *n* : moneda *f*

coincide [‚ko:ɪn'saɪd, 'ko:ɪn‚saɪd] *vi* **-cided; -ciding** : coincidir

coincidence [ko'ɪntsədənts] *n* : coincidencia *f*, casualidad *f* ⟨what a coincidence! : ¡qué casualidad!⟩

coincident [ko'ɪntsədənt] *adj* : coincidente, concurrente

coincidental [ko‚ɪntsə'dɛntəl] *adj* : casual, accidental, fortuito

coitus ['ko:ətəs] *n* : coito *m*

coke ['ko:k] *n* : coque *m*

Coke ['ko:k] *trademark* se usa para un refresco de cola

cola ['ko:lə] *n* : refresco *m* de cola

colander ['kaləndər, 'kʌ-] *n* : colador *m*

cold¹ ['ko:ld] *adj* : frío ⟨it's cold out : hace frío⟩ ⟨a cold reception : una fría recepción⟩ ⟨in cold blood : a sangre fría⟩

cold² *n* **1** : frío *m* ⟨to feel the cold : sentir frío⟩ **2** : resfriado *m*, catarro *m* ⟨to catch a cold : resfriarse⟩

cold-blooded ['ko:ld'blʌdəd] *adj* **1** CRUEL : cruel, despiadado **2** : de sangre fría (dícese de los reptiles, etc.)

cold cuts *npl* : fiambres *mpl*

coldly ['ko:ldli] *adv* : fríamente, con frialdad

coldness ['ko:ldnəs] *n* : frialdad *f* (de una persona o una actitud), frío *m* (de la temperatura)

cold sore *n* : fuego *m*, calentura *f*

coleslaw ['ko:l‚slɔ] *n* : ensalada *f* de col

colic ['kalɪk] *n* : cólico *m*

coliseum [‚kalə'si:əm] *n* : coliseo *m*, arena *f*

collaborate [kə'læbə‚reɪt] *vi* **-rated; -rating** : colaborar

collaboration [kə‚læbə'reɪʃən] *n* : colaboración *f*

collaborator [kə'læbə‚reɪtər] *n* **1** COL-LEAGUE : colaborador *m*, -dora *f* **2** TRAITOR : colaboracionista *mf*

collage [kə'laʒ] *n* : collage *m*

collapse¹ [kə'læps] *vi* **-lapsed; -lapsing 1** : derrumbarse, desplomarse, hundirse ⟨the building collapsed : el edificio se derrumbó⟩ **2** FALL : desplomarse, caerse ⟨he collapsed on the bed : se desplomó en la cama⟩ ⟨to collapse with laughter : morirse de risa⟩ **3** FAIL : fracasar, quebrar, arruinarse **4** FOLD : plegarse

collapse² n **1** FALL : derrumbe m, desplome m **2** BREAKDOWN, FAILURE : fracaso m, colapso m (físico), quiebra f (económica)

collapsible [kə'læpsəbəl] adj : plegable

collar¹ ['kɑlər] vt : agarrar, atrapar

collar² n **1** : cuello m **2** : collar m (para un animal)

collarbone ['kɑlər,boːn] n : clavícula f

collate [kə'leɪt;, 'kɑ,leɪt, 'koː-] vt **-lated; -lating 1** COMPARE : cotejar, comparar **2** : ordenar, recopilar (páginas)

collateral¹ [kə'læt̬ərəl] adj : colateral

collateral² n : garantía f, fianza f, prenda f

colleague ['kɑ,liːg] n : colega mf; compañero m, -ra f

collect¹ [kə'lɛkt] vt **1** GATHER : recopilar, reunir, recoger ⟨she collected her thoughts : puso en orden sus ideas⟩ **2** : coleccionar, juntar ⟨to collect stamps : coleccionar timbres⟩ **3** : cobrar (una deuda), recaudar (un impuesto) **4** PICK UP : recoger, ir a buscar **5** DRAW : cobrar, percibir (un sueldo, etc.) — vi **1** ACCUMULATE : acumularse, juntarse **2** CONGREGATE : congregarse, reunirse

collect² adv & adj : por cobrar, a cobro revertido

collectible or **collectable** [kə'lɛktəbəl] adj : coleccionable

collection [kə'lɛkʃən] n **1** COLLECTING : colecta f (de contribuciones), cobro m (de deudas), recaudación f (de impuestos) **2** GROUP : colección f (de objetos), grupo m (de personas)

collective¹ [kə'lɛktɪv] adj : colectivo — **collectively** adv

collective² n : colectivo m

collector [kə'lɛktər] n **1** : coleccionista mf (de objetos) **2** : cobrador m, -dora f (de deudas)

college ['kɑlɪʤ] n **1** : universidad f **2** : colegio m (de electores o profesionales)

collegiate [kə'liːʤət] adj : universitario

collide [kə'laɪd] vi **-lided; -liding** : chocar, colisionar, estrellarse

collie ['kɑli] n : collie mf

collision [kə'lɪʒən] n : choque m, colisión f

colloquial [kə'loːkwiəl] adj : coloquial

colloquialism [kə'loːkwiə,lɪzəm] n : expresión f coloquial

collusion [kə'luː,ʒən] n : colusión f

cologne [kə'loːn] n : colonia f

Colombian [kə'lʌmbiən] n : colombiano m, -na f — **Colombian** adj

colon¹ ['koː,lən] n, pl **colons** or **cola** [-lə] : colon m (de los intestinos)

colon² n, pl **colons** : dos puntos mpl (signo ortográfico)

colón [kə'loːn] n, pl **-lones** [-'loː,neɪs] : colón m (unidad monetaria)

colonel ['kərnəl] n : coronel m

colonial¹ [kə'loːniəl] adj : colonial

colonial² n : colono m, -na f

colonist ['kɑlənɪst] n : colono m, -na f; colonizador m, -dora f

colonization [,kɑlənə'zeɪʃən] n : colonización f

colonize ['kɑlə,naɪz] vt **-nized; -nizing 1**

: establecer una colonia en **2** SETTLE : colonizar

colonnade [,kɑlə'neɪd] n : columnata f

colony ['kɑləni] n, pl **-nies** : colonia f

color¹ ['kʌlər] vt **1** : colorear, pintar **2** INFLUENCE : influir en, influenciar — vi BLUSH : sonrojarse, ruborizarse

color² n **1** : color m ⟨primary colors : colores primarios⟩ **2** INTEREST, VIVIDNESS : color m, colorido m ⟨local color : color local⟩

coloration [kʌlə'reɪʃən] n : coloración f

color-blind ['kʌlər,blaɪnd] adj : daltónico

color blindness n : daltonismo m

colored ['kʌlərd] adj **1** : de color **2** dated, now offensive : de color dated, now offensive; negro (dícese de las personas)

colorfast ['kʌlər,fæst] adj : que no se destiñe

colorful ['kʌlərfəl] adj **1** : lleno de colorido, de colores vivos **2** PICTURESQUE, STRIKING : pintoresco, llamativo

coloring ['kʌlərɪŋ] n **1** : color m, colorido m **2 food coloring** : colorante m

colorless ['kʌlərləs] adj **1** : incoloro, sin color **2** DULL : soso, aburrido

color scheme n : combinación f de colores, tonalidad f

colossal [kə'lɑsəl] adj : colosal

colossus [kə'lɑsəs] n, pl **-si** [-,saɪ] : coloso m

colt ['koːlt] n : potro m, potranco m

column ['kɑləm] n : columna f

columnist ['kɑləmnɪst, -ləmɪst] n : columnista mf

coma ['koːmə] n : coma m, estado m de coma

Comanche [kə'mæntʃi] n : comanche mf — **Comanche** adj

comatose ['koːmə,toːs, 'kɑ-] adj : comatoso, en estado de coma

comb¹ ['koːm] vt **1** : peinar (el pelo) **2** SEARCH : peinar, rastrear, registrar a fondo

comb² n **1** : peine m **2** : cresta f (de un gallo)

combat¹ [kəm'bæt, 'kɑm,bæt] vt **-bated** or **-batted; -bating** or **-batting** : combatir, luchar contra

combat² ['kɑm,bæt] n : combate m, lucha f

combatant [kəm'bæt̬ənt] n : combatiente mf

combative [kəm'bæt̬ɪv] adj : combativo

combination [,kɑmbə'neɪʃən] n : combinación f

combine¹ [kəm'baɪn] v **-bined; -bining** vt : combinar, aunar — vi : combinarse, mezclarse

combine² ['kɑm,baɪn] n **1** ALLIANCE : alianza f comercial o política **2** HARVESTER : cosechadora f

combustible [kəm'bʌstəbəl] adj : inflamable, combustible

combustion [kəm'bʌstʃən] n : combustión f

come ['kʌm] vi **came** ['keɪm]; **come**; **coming 1** APPROACH : venir, aproximarse ⟨here he comes : acá viene⟩ **2** ARRIVE : venir, llegar ⟨she came yesterday

: vino ayer⟩ ⟨did the mail come? : ¿llegó el correo?⟩ **3** : venir (a un lugar, una reunión, etc.) ⟨come with me : ven conmigo⟩ ⟨are you coming to the wedding? : ¿vienes a la boda?⟩ ⟨come (and) visit us! : ¡ven a visitarnos!⟩ ⟨I'm coming! : ¡voy!⟩ **4** HAPPEN : ocurrir, pasar ⟨to come at a bad time : llegar en mal momento⟩ **5** : venir ⟨it comes in three colors : viene en tres colores⟩ **6** : estar, ir (en una serie) ⟨*B* comes after *A* : la *B* va después de la *A*⟩ **7 come again?** : ¿cómo? **8 come on!** (*used to encourage or urge*) : ¡vamos! **9 come on!** (*expressing surprise, disbelief, etc.*) : ¡anda! **10 come to think of it** : ahora que lo pienso **11 come what may** : pase lo que pase **12 if it comes to that** : si es necesario **13 to be coming up** : acercarse (dícese de una fecha, etc.) ⟨her birthday is coming up : falta poco para su cumpleaños⟩ **14 to come about** HAPPEN : ocurrir, pasar **15 to come across** FIND : tropezar con, dar con **16 to come across as** : dar la impresión de ser, parecer ser **17 to come along** APPEAR, ARRIVE : aparecer, llegar **18 to come along** : venir con alguien ⟨would you like to come along? : ¿quieres venir conmigo?⟩ **19 to come along** PROGRESS : ir ⟨how's the project coming along? : ¿qué tal va el proyecto?⟩ **20 to come apart** : deshacerse **21 to come around** : convencerse al final **22 to come around** : venir, pasar ⟨why don't you come around to my place tonight? : ¿por qué no pasas por casa esta noche?⟩ **23 to come back** RETURN : volver ⟨come back here! : ¡vuelve acá!⟩ ⟨that style's coming back : ese estilo está volviendo⟩ **24 to come back** RETORT : replicar, contestar **25 to come between** : interponerse entre **26 to come by** STOP BY : pasar por casa **27 to come by** GET, OBTAIN : conseguir **28 to come clean** : confesar, desahogar la conciencia **29 to come down** : caer (dícese de la lluvia, etc.), bajar (dícese de los precios, etc.) **30 to come down hard on** : ser duro con **31 to come down to** : reducirse a **32 to come down with** : caer enfermo de **33 to come forward** : presentarse **34 to come from** : venir de (un lugar, etc.) **35 to come in** ENTER : entrar, pasar **36 to come in** ARRIVE : llegar **37 to come in** : desempeñar una función ⟨that's where you come in : ahí es donde entras tú⟩ ⟨to come in handy : venir bien, ser útil⟩ **38 to come into** ACQUIRE : adquirir ⟨to come into a fortune : heredar una fortuna⟩ **39 to come of** : resultar de **40 to come off** DETACH : soltarse, desprenderse **41 to come off** SUCCEED : tener éxito, ser un éxito **42 to come off as** : dar la impresión de ser, parecer ser **43 to come off well/poorly** : irle bien/mal a uno ⟨he came off poorly in the debate : le fue mal en el debate⟩ **44 to come on** TURN ON : encenderse **45 to come on** BEGIN : empe-

zar **46 to come on to someone** : insinuársele a alguien **47 to come out** : salir, aparecer, publicarse **48 to come out** : declararse ⟨to come out in favor of : declararse a favor de⟩ **49 to come out** : declararse homosexual **50 to come out and say** : decir sin rodeos **51 to come over** STOP BY : pasar por casa **52 to come over someone** : sobrevenirle (una emoción) a alguien ⟨I don't know what came over her : no sé qué le pasó⟩ **53 to come through** : pasar por, sobrevivir a **54 to come through** SHOW : ser evidente **55 to come through** : recibirse (dícese de una señal, etc.), llegar **56 to come to** REVIVE : recobrar el conocimiento, volver en sí **57 to come to** : llegar a (un lugar) **58 to come to** : llegar a, ascender a (una cantidad) **59 to come to** REACH : llegar a, alcanzar (un acuerdo, etc.) ⟨to come to an end : llegar a su fin⟩ ⟨to come to a boil : empezar a hervir⟩ **60 to come to** : ocurrírsele (a alguien) ⟨the answer came to me : la respuesta me vino, se me ocurrió la respuesta⟩ **61 to come to be/believe (etc.)** : llegar a ser/creer (etc.) **62 to come to pass** HAPPEN : acontecer **63 to come to terms** : llegar a un acuerdo **64 to come under** ⟨to come under attack/criticism : ser atacado/criticado⟩ ⟨to come under the control of : quedar bajo el control de⟩ **65 to come under** : ir bajo (una categoría, etc.) **66 to come undone** : desatarse, desabrocharse **67 to come up** ARISE : surgir **68 to come up** RISE, APPEAR : salir **69 to come up** : resultar, salir, quedar ⟨the shot came up short : el tiro se quedó corto⟩ ⟨to come up heads/tails : salir cara/cruz⟩ **70 to come up against** : enfrentarse a, tropezar con **71 to come up to someone** : acercarse a alguien **72 to come up with** : encontrar (una solución), idear (un plan), conseguir (dinero) ⟨we couldn't come up with a better idea : no se nos ocurrió nada mejor⟩ **73 to have it coming** : tenerlo merecido **74 what's coming to someone** ⟨one day he'll get what's coming to him : algún día recibirá su merecido⟩ **75 when it comes to** : en cuanto a, cuando se trata de ⟨when it comes to chess, he's the best : cuando se trata de ajedrez, él es el mejor⟩

comeback [ˈkʌmˌbæk] *n* **1** RETORT : réplica *f*, respuesta *f* **2** RETURN : retorno *m*, regreso *m* ⟨the champion announced his comeback : el campeón anunció su regreso⟩

comedian [kəˈmiːdiən] *n* : cómico *m*, -ca *f*; humorista *mf*

comedienne [kəˌmiːdiˈɛn] *n* : cómica *f*, humorista *f*

comedy [ˈkɑmədi] *n*, *pl* **-dies** : comedia *f*

comely [ˈkʌmli] *adj* **comelier; -est** : bello, bonito

comet [ˈkɑmət] *n* : cometa *m*

comfort[1] [ˈkʌmfərt] *vt* **1** CHEER : confortar, alentar **2** CONSOLE : consolar

comfort² *n* **1** CONSOLATION : consuelo *m* **2** WELL-BEING : confort *m*, bienestar *m* **3** CONVENIENCE : comodidad *f* ⟨the comforts of home : las comodidades del hogar⟩

comfortable [ˈkʌmpfərt̬əbəl, ˈkʌmpftə-] *adj* : cómodo, confortable — **comfortably** [ˈkʌmpfərt̬əbli, ˈkʌmpftə-] *adv*

comforter [ˈkʌmpfərt̬ər] *n* QUILT : edredón *m*, cobertor *m*

comic¹ [ˈkamɪk] *adj* : cómico, humorístico

comic² *n* **1** COMEDIAN : cómico *m*, -ca *f*; humorista *mf* **2** *or* **comic book** : historieta *f*, cómic *m*

comical [ˈkamɪkəl] *adj* : cómico, gracioso, chistoso

comic strip *n* : tira *f* cómica, historieta *f*

coming¹ [ˈkʌmɪŋ] *adj* : siguiente, próximo, que viene

coming² *n* **1** ARRIVAL : llegada *f* **2 comings and goings** : idas y venidas *fpl*

comma [ˈkamə] *n* : coma *f*

command¹ [kəˈmænd] *vt* **1** ORDER : ordenar, mandar **2** CONTROL, DIRECT : comandar, tener el mando de — *vi* **1** : dar órdenes **2** GOVERN : estar al mando *m*, gobernar

command² *n* **1** CONTROL, LEADERSHIP : mando *m*, control *m*, dirección *f* **2** ORDER : orden *f*, mandato *m* **3** MASTERY : maestría *f*, destreza *f*, dominio *m* **4** : tropa *f* asignada a un comandante

commandant [ˈkamən̩dɑnt, -̩dænt] *n* : comandante *mf*

commandeer [ˌkamənˈdɪr] *vt* : piratear, secuestrar (un vehículo, etc.)

commander [kəˈmændər] *n* : comandante *mf*

commanding [kəˈmændɪŋ] *adj* AUTHORITATIVE : autoritario, imperativo, imperioso

commandment [kəˈmændmənt] *n* : mandamiento *m*, orden *f* ⟨the Ten Commandments : los diez mandamientos⟩

commando [kəˈmændo:] *n* : comando *m*

commemorate [kəˈmɛmə̩reɪt] *vt* **-rated; -rating** : conmemorar

commemoration [kə̩mɛməˈreɪʃən] *n* : conmemoración *f*

commemorative [kəˈmɛmrət̬ɪv, -ˈmɛmə̩reɪt̬ɪv] *adj* : conmemorativo

commence [kəˈmɛnts] *v* **-menced; -mencing** *vt* : iniciar, comenzar — *vi* : iniciarse, comenzar

commencement [kəˈmɛntsmənt] *n* **1** BEGINNING : inicio *m*, comienzo *m* **2** : ceremonia *f* de graduación

commend [kəˈmɛnd] *vt* **1** ENTRUST : encomendar **2** RECOMMEND : recomendar **3** PRAISE : elogiar, alabar

commendable [kəˈmɛndəbəl] *adj* : loable, meritorio, encomiable

commendation [ˌkamənˈdeɪʃən, -̩mɛn-] *n* : elogio *m*, encomio *m*

commensurate [kəˈmɛntsərət, -ˈmɛntʃurət] *adj* : proporcionado ⟨commensurate with : en proporción a⟩

comment¹ [ˈkɑ̩mɛnt] *vi* **1** : hacer comentarios **2 to comment on** : comentar,

hacer observaciones sobre — **commenter** *n*

comment² *n* : comentario *m*, observación *f*

commentary [ˈkamən̩tɛri] *n, pl* **-taries** : comentario *m*, crónica *f* (deportiva)

commentator [ˈkamən̩teɪt̬ər] *n* **1** HOST, ANCHOR : comentarista *mf*, cronista *mf* (de deportes) **2** : comentarista *mf* ⟨political commentators : comentaristas políticos⟩

commerce [ˈkamərs] *n* : comercio *m*

commercial¹ [kəˈmərʃəl] *adj* : comercial — **commercially** *adv*

commercial² *n* : comercial *m*

commercialize [kəˈmərʃə̩laɪz] *vt* **-ized; -izing** : comercializar

commiserate [kəˈmɪzə̩reɪt] *vi* **-ated; -ating** : compadecerse, consolarse

commiseration [kə̩mɪzəˈreɪʃən] *n* : conmiseración *f*

commission¹ [kəˈmɪʃən] *vt* **1** : nombrar (un oficial) **2** : comisionar, encargar ⟨to commission a painting : encargar una pintura⟩

commission² *n* **1** : nombramiento *m* (al grado de oficial) **2** COMMITTEE : comisión *f*, comité *m* **3** COMMITTING : comisión *f*, realización *f* (de un acto) **4** PERCENTAGE : comisión *f* ⟨sales commissions : comisiones de venta⟩

commissioned officer *n* : oficial *mf*

commissioner [kəˈmɪʃənər] *n* **1** : comisionado *m*, -da *f*; miembro *m* de una comisión **2** : comisario *m*, -ria *f* (de policía, etc.)

commit [kəˈmɪt] *vt* **-mitted; -mitting** **1** ENTRUST : encomendar, confiar **2** CONFINE : internar (en un hospital), encarcelar (en una prisión) **3** PERPETRATE : cometer ⟨to commit a crime : cometer un crimen⟩ **4 to commit oneself** : comprometerse

commitment [kəˈmɪtmənt] *n* **1** RESPONSIBILITY : compromiso *m*, responsabilidad *f* **2** DEDICATION : dedicación *f*, devoción *f* ⟨commitment to the cause : devoción a la causa⟩

committee [kəˈmɪt̬i] *n* : comité *m*

commodious [kəˈmo:diəs] *adj* SPACIOUS : amplio, espacioso

commodity [kəˈmadət̬i] *n, pl* **-ties** : artículo *m* de comercio, mercancía *f*, mercadería *f*

commodore [ˈkamə̩dor] *n* : comodoro *m*

common¹ [ˈkamən] *adj* **1** PUBLIC : común, público ⟨the common good : el bien común⟩ **2** SHARED : común ⟨a common interest : un interés común⟩ **3** GENERAL : común, general ⟨it's common knowledge : todo el mundo lo sabe⟩ **4** ORDINARY : ordinario, común y corriente ⟨the common man : el hombre medio, el hombre de la calle⟩

common² *n* **1** : tierra *f* comunal **2 in ∼** : en común

common cold *n* : resfriado *m* común

common denominator *n* : denominador *m* común

commoner [ˈkamənər] *n* : plebeyo *m*, -ya *f*

common law *n* : derecho *m* consuetudinario

commonly [ˈkɑmənli] *adv* **1** FREQUENTLY : comúnmente, frecuentemente **2** USUALLY : normalmente

common noun *n* : nombre *m* común

commonplace¹ [ˈkɑmənˌpleɪs] *adj* : común, ordinario

commonplace² *n* : cliché *m*, tópico *m*

common sense *n* : sentido *m* común

commonwealth [ˈkɑmənˌwɛlθ] *n* : entidad *f* política ⟨the British Commonwealth : la Mancomunidad Británica⟩

commotion [kəˈmoːʃən] *n* **1** RUCKUS : alboroto *m*, jaleo *m*, escándalo *m* **2** STIR, UPSET : revuelo *m*, conmoción *f*

communal [kəˈmjuːnəl] *adj* : comunal

commune¹ [kəˈmjuːn] *vi* **-muned; -muning** : estar en comunión

commune² [ˈkɑˌmjuːn, kəˈmjuːn] *n* : comuna *f*

communicable [kəˈmjuːnɪkəbəl] *adj* CONTAGIOUS : transmisible, contagioso

communicate [kəˈmjuːnəˌkeɪt] *v* **-cated; -cating** *vt* **1** CONVEY : comunicar, expresar, hacer saber **2** TRANSMIT : transmitir (una enfermedad), contagiar — *vi* : comunicarse, expresarse

communication [kəˌmjuːnəˈkeɪʃən] *n* : comunicación *f*

communicative [kəˈmjuːnɪˌkeɪtɪv, -kətɪv] *adj* : comunicativo

communion [kəˈmjuːnjən] *n* **1** SHARING : comunión *f* **2 Communion** : comunión *f*, eucaristía *f*

communiqué [kəˈmjuːnəˌkeɪ, -ˌmjuːnəˈkeɪ] *n* : comunicado *m*

communism *or* **Communism** [ˈkɑmjəˌnɪzəm] *n* : comunismo *m*

communist¹ *or* **Communist** [ˈkɑmjəˌnɪst] *adj* : comunista ⟨the Communist Party : el Partido Comunista⟩

communist² *or* **Communist** *n* : comunista *mf*

communistic *or* **Communistic** [ˌkɑmjəˈnɪstɪk] *adj* : comunista

community¹ [kəˈmjuːnəti] *n*, *pl* **-ties** : comunidad *f*

community² *adj* : comunitario

commute [kəˈmjuːt] *v* **-muted; -muting** *vt* REDUCE : conmutar, reducir (una sentencia) — *vi* : viajar de la residencia al trabajo

commuter [kəˈmjuːtər] *n* : persona *f* que viaja diariamente al trabajo

compact¹ [kəmˈpækt, ˈkɑmˌpækt] *vt* : compactar, consolidar, comprimir

compact² [kəmˈpækt, ˈkɑmˌpækt] *adj* **1** DENSE, SOLID : compacto, macizo, denso **2** CONCISE : breve, conciso

compact³ [ˈkɑmˌpækt] *n* **1** AGREEMENT : acuerdo *m*, pacto *m* **2** : polvera *f*, estuche *m* de maquillaje **3** *or* **compact car** : auto *m* compacto

compact disc [ˈkɑmˌpæktˈdɪsk] *n* : disco *m* compacto, compact disc *m*

compactly [kəmˈpæktli, ˈkɑmˌpækt-] *adv* **1** DENSELY : densamente **2** CONCISELY : concisamente, brevemente

companion [kəmˈpænjən] *n* **1** COMRADE : compañero *m*, -ra *f*; acompañante *mf* **2** MATE : pareja *f* (de un zapato, etc.)

companionable [kəmˈpænjənəbəl] *adj* : sociable, amigable

companionship [kəmˈpænjənˌʃɪp] *n* : compañerismo *m*, camaradería *f*

company [ˈkʌmpəni] *n*, *pl* **-nies** **1** FIRM : compañía *f*, empresa *f* **2** GROUP : compañía *f* (de actores o soldados) **3** GUESTS : visita *f* ⟨we have company : tenemos visita⟩ **4** COMPANIONSHIP : compañía *f* ⟨to keep someone company : hacerle compañía a alguien⟩ ⟨I enjoy her company : me gusta estar con ella⟩ **5 to be in good company** : no ser el único

comparable [ˈkɑmpərəbəl] *adj* : comparable, parecido

comparative¹ [kəmˈpærətɪv] *adj* RELATIVE : comparativo, relativo — **comparatively** *adv*

comparative² *n* : comparativo *m*

compare¹ [kəmˈpær] *v* **-pared; -paring** *vt* : comparar — *vi* **to compare with** : poder comparar con, tener comparación con

compare² *n* : comparación *f* ⟨beyond compare : sin igual, sin par⟩

comparison [kəmˈpærəsən] *n* : comparación *f*

compartment [kəmˈpɑrtmənt] *n* : compartimento *m*, compartimiento *m*

compass [ˈkʌmpəs, ˈkɑm-] *n* **1** RANGE, SCOPE : alcance *m*, extensión *f*, límites *mpl* **2** : compás *m* (para trazar circunferencias) **3** : compás *m*, brújula *f* ⟨the points of the compass : los puntos cardinales⟩

compassion [kəmˈpæʃən] *n* : compasión *f*, piedad *f*, misericordia *f*

compassionate [kəmˈpæʃənət] *adj* : compasivo

compatibility [kəmˌpætəˈbɪləti] *n* : compatibilidad *f*

compatible [kəmˈpætəbəl] *adj* : compatible, afín

compatriot [kəmˈpeɪtriət, -ˈpæ-] *n* : compatriota *mf*; paisano *m*, -na *f*

compel [kəmˈpɛl] *vt* **-pelled; -pelling** : obligar, compeler

compelling [kəmˈpɛlɪŋ] *adj* **1** FORCEFUL : fuerte **2** ENGAGING : absorbente **3** PERSUASIVE : persuasivo, convincente

compendium [kəmˈpɛndiəm] *n*, *pl* **-diums** *or* **-dia** [-diə] : compendio *m*

compensate [ˈkɑmpənˌseɪt] *v* **-sated; -sating** *vi* **to compensate for** : compensar — *vt* : indemnizar, compensar

compensation [ˌkɑmpənˈseɪʃən] *n* : compensación *f*, indemnización *f*

compensatory [kəmˈpɛntsəˌtori] *adj* : compensatorio

compete [kəmˈpiːt] *vi* **-peted; -peting** : competir, contender, rivalizar

competence [ˈkɑmpətənts] *n* : competencia *f*, aptitud *f*

competency [ˈkɑmpətəntsi] → **competence**

competent [ˈkɑmpətənt] *adj* : competente, capaz

competition [ˌkɑmpə'tɪʃən] n : competencia f, concurso m

competitive [kəm'pɛt̬ət̬ɪv] adj : competitivo

competitively [kəm'pɛt̬ət̬ɪvli] adv : competitivamente ⟨competitively priced : a precios competitivos⟩

competitiveness [kəm'pɛt̬ət̬ɪvnəs] n : competitividad f

competitor [kəm'pɛt̬ət̬ər] n : competidor m, -dora f

compilation [ˌkɑmpə'leɪʃən] n : recopilación f, compilación f

compile [kəm'paɪl] vt -piled; -piling : compilar, recopilar

complacency [kəm'pleɪsəntsi] n : satisfacción f consigo mismo, suficiencia f

complacent [kəm'pleɪsənt] adj : satisfecho de sí mismo, suficiente

complain [kəm'pleɪn] vi 1 GRIPE : quejarse, regañar, rezongar 2 PROTEST : reclamar, protestar

complaint [kəm'pleɪnt] n 1 GRIPE : queja f 2 AILMENT : afección f, dolencia f 3 ACCUSATION : reclamo m, acusación f

complement[1] ['kɑmplə,mɛnt] vt : complementar

complement[2] ['kɑmpləmənt] n : complemento m

complementary [ˌkɑmplə'mɛntəri] adj : complementario

complete[1] [kəm'pli:t] vt -pleted; -pleting 1 : completar, hacer entero ⟨this piece completes the collection : esta pieza completa la colección⟩ 2 FINISH : completar, acabar, terminar ⟨she completed her studies : completó sus estudios⟩

complete[2] adj **completer; -est** 1 WHOLE : completo, entero, íntegro 2 FINISHED : terminado, acabado 3 TOTAL : completo, total, absoluto

completely [kəm'pli:tli] adv : completamente, totalmente

completion [kəm'pli:ʃən] n : finalización f, cumplimiento m

complex[1] [kɑm'plɛks, kəm-;, 'kɑm-ˌplɛks] adj : complejo, complicado

complex[2] ['kɑm,plɛks] n : complejo m

complexion [kəm'plɛkʃən] n : cutis m, tez f ⟨of dark complexion : de tez morena⟩

complexity [kəm'plɛksət̬i, kɑm-] n, pl -ties : complejidad f

compliance [kəm'plaɪənts] n : conformidad f ⟨in compliance with the law : conforme a la ley⟩

compliant [kəm'plaɪənt] adj : dócil, sumiso

complicate ['kɑmplə,keɪt] vt -cated; -cating : complicar

complicated ['kɑmplə,keɪt̬əd] adj : complicado

complication [ˌkɑmplə'keɪʃən] n : complicación f

complicity [kəm'plɪsət̬i] n, pl -ties : complicidad f

compliment[1] ['kɑmplə,mɛnt] vt : halagar, florear Mex

compliment[2] ['kɑmpləmənt] n 1 : halago m, cumplido m 2 **compliments** npl : saludos mpl ⟨give them my compliments : déles saludos de mi parte⟩

complimentary [ˌkɑmplə'mɛntəri] adj 1 FLATTERING : halagador, halagüeño 2 FREE : de cortesía, gratis

comply [kəm'plaɪ] vi -plied; -plying : cumplir, acceder, obedecer

component[1] [kəm'po:nənt, 'kɑm-ˌpo:-] adj : componente

component[2] n : componente m, elemento m, pieza f

compose [kəm'po:z] vt -posed; -posing 1 : componer, crear ⟨to compose a melody : componer una melodía⟩ 2 CALM : calmar, serenar ⟨to compose oneself : serenarse⟩ 3 CONSTITUTE : constar, componer ⟨to be composed of : constar de⟩ 4 : componer (un texto a imprimirse)

composed [kəm'po:zd] adj : tranquilo

composer [kəm'po:zər] n : compositor m, -tora f

composite[1] [kɑm'pɑzət, kəm-;, 'kɑmpəzət] adj : compuesto (de varias partes)

composite[2] n : compuesto m, mezcla f

composition [ˌkɑmpə'zɪʃən] n 1 MAKEUP : composición f 2 ESSAY : ensayo m, trabajo m

compost ['kɑm,po:st] n : abono m vegetal

composure [kəm'po:ʒər] n : compostura f, serenidad f

compote ['kɑm,po:t] n : compota f

compound[1] [kɑm'paʊnd, kəm-;, 'kɑm,paʊnd] vt 1 COMBINE, COMPOSE : combinar, componer 2 AUGMENT : agravar, aumentar ⟨to compound a problem : agravar un problema⟩

compound[2] ['kɑm,paʊnd;, kɑm'paʊnd, kəm-] adj : compuesto ⟨compound interest : interés compuesto⟩

compound[3] ['kɑm,paʊnd] n 1 MIXTURE : compuesto m, mezcla f 2 ENCLOSURE : recinto m (de residencias, etc.)

comprehend [ˌkɑmprɪ'hɛnd] vt 1 UNDERSTAND : comprender, entender 2 INCLUDE : comprender, incluir, abarcar

comprehensible [ˌkɑmprɪ'hɛntsəbəl] adj : comprensible

comprehension [ˌkɑmprɪ'hɛntʃən] n : comprensión f

comprehensive [ˌkɑmprɪ'hɛntsɪv] adj 1 INCLUSIVE : inclusivo, exhaustivo 2 BROAD : extenso, amplio

compress[1] [kəm'prɛs] vt : comprimir

compress[2] ['kɑm,prɛs] n : compresa f

compression [kəm'prɛʃən] n : compresión f

compressor [kəm'prɛsər] n : compresor m

comprise [kəm'praɪz] vt -prised; -prising 1 INCLUDE : comprender, incluir 2 : componerse de, constar de ⟨the installation comprises several buildings : la instalación está compuesta de varios edificios⟩

compromise[1] ['kɑmprə,maɪz] v -mised; -mising vi : transigir, avenirse — vt JEOPARDIZE : comprometer, poner en peligro

compromise² *n* : acuerdo *m* mutuo, compromiso *m*

comptroller [kən'tro:lər, 'kamp-ₜtro:-] *n* : contralor *m*, -lora *f*; interventor *m*, -tora *f*

compulsion [kəm'pʌlʃən] *n* **1** COERCION : coacción *f* **2** URGE : compulsión *f*, impulso *m*

compulsive [kəm'pʌlsɪv] *adj* : compulsivo

compulsory [kəm'pʌlsəri] *adj* : obligatorio

compunction [kəm'pʌŋkʃən] *n* **1** QUALM : reparo *m*, escrúpulo *m* **2** REMORSE : remordimiento *m*

computation [ₜkampjʊ'teɪʃən] *n* : cálculo *m*, cómputo *m*

compute [kəm'pju:t] *vt* **-puted; -puting** : computar, calcular

computer [kəm'pju:tər] *n* : computadora *f*, computador *m*, ordenador *m* Spain

computerization [kəmₜpju:tərə'zeɪʃən] *n* : informatización *f*

computerize [kəm'pju:təₜraɪz] *vt* **-ized; -izing** : computarizar, informatizar

computer programmer → programmer

computer programming → programming

computer science *n* : informática *f*

computing [kəm'pju:tɪŋ] *n* : informática *f*

comrade ['kamₜræd] *n* : camarada *mf*; compañero *m*, -ra *f*

con¹ ['kan] *vt* **conned; conning** SWINDLE : estafar, timar

con² *adv* : contra

con³ *n* : contra *m* ⟨the pros and cons : los pros y los contras⟩

concave [kan'keɪv, 'kanₜkeɪv] *adj* : cóncavo

conceal [kən'si:l] *vt* : esconder, ocultar, disimular

concealment [kən'si:lmənt] *n* : ocultación *f*

concede [kən'si:d] *vt* **-ceded; -ceding 1** ALLOW, GRANT : conceder **2** ADMIT : conceder, reconocer ⟨to concede defeat : reconocer la derrota⟩

conceit [kən'si:t] *n* : engreimiento *m*, presunción *f*

conceited [kən'si:təd] *adj* : presumido, engreído, presuntuoso

conceivable [kən'si:vəbəl] *adj* : concebible, imaginable

conceivably [kən'si:vəbli] *adv* : posiblemente, de manera concebible

conceive [kən'si:v] *v* **-ceived; -ceiving** *vi* : concebir, embarazarse — *vt* IMAGINE : concebir, imaginar

concentrate¹ ['kantsənₜtreɪt] *v* **-trated; -trating** *vt* : concentrar — *vi* : concentrarse

concentrate² *n* : concentrado *m*

concentration [ₜkantsən'treɪʃən] *n* : concentración *f*

concentration camp *n* : campo *m* de concentración

concentric [kən'sɛntrɪk] *adj* : concéntrico

concept ['kanₜsɛpt] *n* : concepto *m*, idea *f*

conception [kən'sɛpʃən] *n* **1** : concepción *f* (de un bebé) **2** IDEA : concepto *m*, idea *f*

conceptual [kən'sɛptʃəwəl] *adj* : conceptual — **conceptually** *adv*

conceptualize [kən'sɛptʃəwəₜlaɪz] *vt* **-ized; -izing** : conceptualizar, formarse un concepto de — **conceptualization** [kən'sɛptʃəwələ'zeɪʃən] *n*

concern¹ [kən'sərn] *vt* **1** : tratarse de, tener que ver con ⟨the novel concerns a sailor : la novela se trata de un marinero⟩ **2** INVOLVE : concernir, incumbir a, afectar ⟨that does not concern me : eso no me incumbe⟩

concern² *n* **1** AFFAIR : asunto *m* **2** WORRY : inquietud *f*, preocupación *f* **3** BUSINESS : negocio *m*

concerned [kən'sərnd] *adj* **1** ANXIOUS : preocupado, ansioso **2** INTERESTED, INVOLVED : interesado, afectado

concerning [kən'sərnɪŋ] *prep* REGARDING : con respecto a, acerca de, sobre

concert ['kanₜsərt] *n* **1** AGREEMENT : concierto *m*, acuerdo *m* **2** : concierto *m* (musical)

concerted [kən'sərtəd] *adj* : concertado, coordinado ⟨to make a concerted effort : coordinar los esfuerzos⟩

concerto [kən'tʃɛrto:] *n, pl* **-ti** [-ₜti, -ₜti:] *or* **-tos** : concierto *m* ⟨violin concerto : concierto para violín⟩

concession [kən'sɛʃən] *n* : concesión *f*

conch ['kaŋk, 'kantʃ] *n, pl* **conchs** ['kaŋks] *or* **conches** ['kantʃəz] : caracol *m* (animal), caracola *f* (concha)

conciliatory [kən'sɪliəₜtori] *adj* : conciliador, conciliatorio

concise [kən'saɪs] *adj* : conciso, breve — **concisely** *adv*

conclave ['kanₜkleɪv] *n* : cónclave *m*

conclude [kən'klu:d] *v* **-cluded; -cluding** *vt* **1** END : concluir, finalizar ⟨to conclude a meeting : concluir una reunión⟩ **2** DECIDE : concluir, llegar a la conclusión de — *vi* END : concluir, terminar

conclusion [kən'klu:ʒən] *n* **1** INFERENCE : conclusión *f* **2** END : fin *m*, final *m*

conclusive [kən'klu:sɪv] *adj* : concluyente, decisivo — **conclusively** *adv*

concoct [kən'kakt, kan-] *vt* **1** PREPARE : preparar, confeccionar **2** DEVISE : inventar, tramar

concoction [kən'kakʃən] *n* : invención *f*, mejunje *m*, brebaje *m*

concord ['kanₜkord, 'kaŋ-] *n* **1** HARMONY : concordia *f*, armonía *f* **2** AGREEMENT : acuerdo *m*

concordance [kən'kordənts] *n* : concordancia *f*

concourse ['kanₜkors] *n* : explanada *f*, salón *m* (para pasajeros)

concrete¹ [kan'kri:t, 'kanₜkri:t] *adj* **1** REAL : concreto ⟨concrete objects : objetos concretos⟩ **2** SPECIFIC : determinado, específico **3** : de concreto, de hormigón ⟨concrete walls : paredes de concreto⟩

concrete² ['kɑn‚kri:t, kɑn'kri:t] *n* : concreto *m*, hormigón *m*

concur [kən'kər] *vi* **concurred; concurring** **1** COINCIDE : concurrir, coincidir **2** AGREE : concurrir, estar de acuerdo

concurrence [kən'kərən/s] *n* **1** AGREEMENT : coincidencia *f* **2** COINCIDENCE : concurrencia *f*, concurso *m*, coincidencia *f*

concurrent [kən'kərənt] *adj* : concurrente, simultáneo

concussion [kən'kʌʃən] *n* : conmoción *f* cerebral

condemn [kən'dɛm] *vt* **1** CENSURE : condenar, reprobar, censurar **2** : declarar insalubre (alimentos), declarar ruinoso (un edificio) **3** SENTENCE : condenar ⟨condemned to death : condenado a muerte⟩

condemnation [‚kɑn‚dɛm'neɪʃən] *n* : condena *f*, reprobación *f*

condensation [‚kɑn‚dɛn'seɪʃən, -dən-] *n* : condensación *f*

condense [kən'dɛn/s] *v* **-densed; -densing** *vt* **1** ABRIDGE : condensar, resumir **2** : condensar (vapor, etc.) — *vi* : condensarse

condescend [‚kɑndɪ'sɛnd] *vi* **1** DEIGN : condescender, dignarse **2 to condescend to someone** : tratar a alguien con condescendencia

condescending [‚kɑndɪ'sɛndɪŋ] *adj* : condescendiente

condescension [‚kɑndɪ'sɛntʃən] *n* : condescendencia *f*

condiment ['kɑndəmənt] *n* : condimento *m*

condition¹ [kən'dɪʃən] *vt* **1** DETERMINE : condicionar, determinar **2** : acondicionar (el pelo o el aire), poner en forma (el cuerpo)

condition² *n* **1** STIPULATION : condición *f*, estipulación *f* ⟨on the condition that : a condición de que⟩ **2** STATE : condición *f*, estado *m* ⟨in good/poor condition : en buenas/malas condiciones⟩ ⟨he's in good condition : está en buena forma⟩ ⟨he's out of condition : no está en forma⟩ **3** **conditions** *npl* : condiciones *fpl*, situación *f* ⟨working conditions : condiciones del trabajo⟩

conditional [kən'dɪʃənəl] *adj* : condicional — **conditionally** *adv*

conditioner [kən'dɪʃənər] *n* : acondicionador *m*

condo ['kɑndo:] → **condominium**

condolence [kən'do:lən/s] *n* **1** SYMPATHY : condolencia *f* **2 condolences** *npl* : pésame *m*

condom ['kɑndəm] *n* : condón *m*

condominium [‚kɑndə'mɪniəm] *n, pl* **-ums** : condominio *m*

condone [kən'do:n] *vt* **-doned; -doning** : aprobar, perdonar, tolerar

condor ['kɑndər, -‚dɔr] *n* : cóndor *m*

conducive [kən'du:sɪv, -'dju:-] *adj* : propicio, favorable

conduct¹ [kən'dʌkt] *vt* **1** GUIDE : guiar, conducir ⟨to conduct a tour : guiar una visita⟩ **2** DIRECT : conducir, dirigir ⟨to conduct an orchestra : dirigir una orquesta⟩ **3** CARRY OUT : realizar, llevar a cabo ⟨to conduct an investigation : llevar a cabo una investigación⟩ **4** TRANSMIT : conducir, transmitir (calor, electricidad, etc.) **5 to conduct oneself** BEHAVE : conducirse, comportarse

conduct² ['kɑn‚dʌkt] *n* **1** MANAGEMENT : conducción *f*, dirección *f*, manejo *m* ⟨the conduct of foreign affairs : la conducción de asuntos exteriores⟩ **2** BEHAVIOR : conducta *f*, comportamiento *m*

conduction [kən'dʌkʃən] *n* : conducción *f*

conductivity [‚kɑn‚dʌk'tɪvəti] *n, pl* **-ties** : conductividad *f*

conductor [kən'dʌktər] *n* **1** : conductor *m*, -tora *f*; revisor *m*, -sora *f* (en un tren); cobrador *m*, -dora *f* (en un bus); director *m*, -tora *f* (de una orquesta) **2** : conductor *m* (de electricidad, etc.)

conduit ['kɑn‚du:ət, -‚dju:-] *n* : conducto *m*, canal *m*, vía *f*

cone ['ko:n] *n* **1** : piña *f* (fruto de las coníferas) **2** : cono *m* (en geometría) **3 ice–cream cone** : cono *m*, barquillo *m*, cucurucho *m*

confection [kən'fɛkʃən] *n* : dulce *m*

confectioner [kən'fɛkʃənər] *n* : confitero *m*, -ra *f*

confectionery [kən'fɛkʃə‚nɛri] *n, pl* **-eries 1** : dulces *mpl*, golosinas *fpl* **2** *or* **confectionery shop** : confitería *f* (tienda)

confederacy [kən'fɛdərəsi] *n, pl* **-cies** : confederación *f*

confederate¹ [kən'fɛdə‚reɪt] *v* **-ated; -ating** *vt* : unir, confederar — *vi* : confederarse, aliarse

confederate² [kən'fɛdərət] *adj* : confederado

confederate³ *n* : cómplice *mf*; aliado *m*, -da *f*

confederation [kən‚fɛdə'reɪʃən] *n* : confederación *f*, alianza *f*

confer [kən'fər] *v* **-ferred; -ferring** *vt* : conferir, otorgar — *vi* **to confer with** : consultar

conference ['kɑnfrən/s, -fərən/s] *n* : conferencia *f* ⟨press conference : conferencia de prensa⟩

confess [kən'fɛs] *vt* : confesar — *vi* **1** : confesar ⟨the prisoner confessed : el detenido confesó⟩ **2** : confesarse (en religión)

confession [kən'fɛʃən] *n* : confesión *f*

confessional [kən'fɛʃənəl] *n* : confesionario *m*

confessor [kən'fɛsər] *n* : confesor *m*

confetti [kən'fɛti] *n* : confeti *m*

confidant ['kɑnfə‚dɑnt, -‚dænt] *n* : confidente *mf*

confidante ['kɑnfə‚dɑnt, -‚dænt] *n* : confidente *f*

confide [kən'faɪd] *v* **-fided; -fiding** : confiar

confidence ['kɑnfədən/s] *n* **1** TRUST : confianza *f* **2** SELF-ASSURANCE : confianza *f* en sí mismo, seguridad *f* en sí mismo **3** SECRET : confidencia *f*, secreto *m*

confident ['kɑnfədənt] *adj* **1** SURE : seguro **2** SELF-ASSURED : confiado, seguro de sí mismo

confidential [ˌkɑnfə'dɛntʃəl] *adj* : confidencial — **confidentially** [ˌkɑnfə'dɛntʃəli] *adv*

confidentiality [ˌkɑnfəˌdɛntʃi'æləṭi] *n* : confidencialidad *f*

confidently ['kɑnfədəntli] *adv* : con seguridad, con confianza

configuration [kənˌfɪgjə'reɪʃən] *n* : configuración *f*

configure [kən'fɪgjər] *vt* : configurar (un sistema, etc.)

confine [kən'faɪn] *vt* -**fined**; -**fining** **1** LIMIT : confinar, restringir, limitar **2** IMPRISON : recluir, encarcelar, encerrar

confined [kən'faɪnd] *adj* SMALL : limitado ⟨confined spaces : espacios limitados⟩

confinement [kən'faɪnmənt] *n* : confinamiento *m*, reclusión *f*, encierro *m*

confines ['kɑnˌfaɪnz] *npl* : límites *mpl*, confines *mpl*

confirm [kən'fərm] *vt* **1** RATIFY : ratificar **2** VERIFY : confirmar, verificar **3** : confirmar (en religión)

confirmation [ˌkɑnfər'meɪʃən] *n* : confirmación *f*

confiscate ['kɑnfəˌskeɪt] *vt* -**cated**; -**cating** : confiscar, incautar, decomisar

confiscation [ˌkɑnfə'skeɪʃən] *n* : confiscación *f*, incautación *f*, decomiso *m*

conflagration [ˌkɑnflə'greɪʃən] *n* : conflagración *f*

conflict[1] [kən'flɪkt] *vi* : estar en conflicto, oponerse

conflict[2] ['kɑnˌflɪkt] *n* : conflicto *m* ⟨to be in conflict : estar en desacuerdo⟩

confluence ['kɑnˌfluːənʦ, kən'fluːənʦ] *n* : confluencia *f*

conform [kən'fɔrm] *vi* **1** ACCORD, COMPLY : ajustarse, adaptarse, conformarse ⟨it conforms with our standards : se ajusta a nuestras normas⟩ **2** CORRESPOND : corresponder, encajar ⟨to conform to the truth : corresponder a la verdad⟩

conformity [kən'fɔrməṭi] *n, pl* -**ties** : conformidad *f*

confound [kən'faʊnd, kɑn-] *vt* : confundir, desconcertar

confront [kən'frʌnt] *vt* : afrontar, enfrentarse a, encarar

confrontation [ˌkɑnfrən'teɪʃən] *n* : enfrentamiento *m*, confrontación *f*

confuse [kən'fjuːz] *vt* -**fused**; -**fusing** **1** PUZZLE : confundir, enturbiar **2** COMPLICATE : confundir, enredar, complicar ⟨to confuse the issue : complicar las cosas⟩

confused [kən'fjuːzd] *adj* **1** : confundido (dícese de una persona) **2** : confuso (dícese de una explicación, etc.)

confusing [kən'fjuːzɪŋ] *adj* : complicado, que confunde

confusion [kən'fjuːʒən] *n* **1** PERPLEXITY : confusión *f* **2** MESS, TURMOIL : confusión *f*, embrollo *m*, lío *m fam*

congeal [kən'ʤiːl] *vi* **1** FREEZE : congelarse **2** COAGULATE, CURDLE : coagularse, cuajarse

congenial [kən'ʤiːniəl] *adj* : agradable, simpático

congenital [kən'ʤɛnəṭəl] *adj* : congénito

congest [kən'ʤɛst] *vt* **1** : congestionar (en la medicina) **2** CROWD : abarrotar, atestar, congestionar (el tráfico) — *vi* : congestionarse

congested [kən'ʤɛstəd] *adj* : congestionado

congestion [kən'ʤɛstʃən] *n* : congestión *f*

conglomerate[1] [kən'glɑmərət] *adj* : conglomerado

conglomerate[2] [kən'glɑmərət] *n* : conglomerado *m*

conglomeration [kənˌglɑmə'reɪʃən] *n* : conglomerado *m*, acumulación *f*

Congolese [ˌkɑŋgə'liːz, -'liːs] *n* : congoleño *m*, -ña *f* — **Congolese** *adj*

congratulate [kən'græʤəˌleɪt, -'grætʃə-] *vt* -**lated**; -**lating** : felicitar

congratulation [kənˌgræʤə'leɪʃən, -ˌgrætʃə-] *n* : felicitación *f* ⟨congratulations! : ¡felicidades!, ¡enhorabuena!⟩

congregate ['kɑŋgrɪˌgeɪt] *vt* -**gated**; -**gating** *vt* : congregar, reunir — *vi* : congregarse, reunirse

congregation [ˌkɑŋgrɪ'geɪʃən] *n* **1** GATHERING : congregación *f*, fieles *mpl* (a un servicio religioso) **2** PARISHIONERS : feligreses *mpl*

congress ['kɑŋgrəs] *n* : congreso *m*

congressional [kən'grɛʃənəl, kɑn-] *adj* : del congreso

congressman ['kɑŋgrəsmən] *n, pl* -**men** [-mən, -ˌmɛn] : congresista *m*, diputado *m*

congresswoman ['kɑŋgrəsˌwʊmən] *n, pl* -**women** [-ˌwɪmən] : congresista *f*, diputada *f*

congruence [kən'gruːənʦ, 'kɑŋgrʊˌənʦ] *n* : congruencia *f*

congruent [kən'gruːənt, 'kɑŋgrʊənt] *adj* : congruente

conic ['kɑnɪk] → **conical**

conical ['kɑnɪkəl] *adj* : cónico

conifer ['kɑnəfər, 'ko:-] *n* : conífera *f*

coniferous [ko:'nɪfərəs, kə-] *adj* : conífero

conjecture[1] [kən'ʤɛktʃər] *v* -**tured**; -**turing** : conjeturar

conjecture[2] *n* : conjetura *f*, presunción *f*

conjugal ['kɑnʤɪgəl, kən'ʤuː-] *adj* : conyugal

conjugate ['kɑnʤəˌgeɪt] *vt* -**gated**; -**gating** : conjugar

conjugation [ˌkɑnʤə'geɪʃən] *n* : conjugación *f*

conjunction [kən'ʤʌŋkʃən] *n* : conjunción *f* ⟨in conjunction with : en combinación con⟩

conjunctivitis [kənˌʤʌŋkti'vaɪṭəs] *n* : conjuntivitis *f*

conjure ['kɑnʤər, 'kʌn-] *v* -**jured**; -**juring** *vt* **1** ENTREAT : rogar, suplicar **2** **to conjure up** : hacer aparecer (apariciones), evocar (memorias, etc.) — *vi* : practicar la magia

conjurer *or* **conjuror** ['kɑnʤərər, 'kʌn-] *n* : mago *m*, -ga *f*; prestidigitador *m*, -dora *f*

con man *n* : timador *m*

connect [kə'nɛkt] *vt* **1** JOIN, LINK : conectar (cables, etc.), comunicar (habitaciones) **2** RELATE : relacionar, asociar (ideas) ⟨evidence that connects him with the crime : evidencias que lo vinculan con el crimen⟩ — *vi* **1** : conectar, comunicarse ⟨to connect to the Internet : conectar a la Internet⟩ **2 to connect with someone** : sintonizar con alguien

connection [kə'nɛkʃən] *n* : conexión *f*, enlace *m* ⟨professional connections : relaciones profesionales⟩

connective [kə'nɛktɪv] *adj* : conectivo, conjuntivo ⟨connective tissue : tejido conjuntivo⟩ — **connectivity** *n*

connector [kə'nɛktər] *n* : conector *m*

connivance [kə'naɪvənts] *n* : connivencia *f*, complicidad *f*

connive [kə'naɪv] *vi* **-nived; -niving** CONSPIRE, PLOT : actuar en connivencia, confabularse, conspirar

connoisseur [ˌkɑnə'sər, -'sʊr] *n* : conocedor *m*, -dora *f*; entendido *m*, -da *f*

connotation [ˌkɑnə'teɪʃən] *n* : connotación *f*

connote [kə'noːt] *vt* **-noted; -noting** : connotar

conquer ['kɑŋkər] *vt* : conquistar, vencer

conqueror ['kɑŋkərər] *n* : conquistador *m*, -dora *f*

conquest ['kɑn,kwɛst, 'kɑŋ-] *n* : conquista *f*

conscience ['kɑntʃənts] *n* : conciencia *f*, consciencia *f* ⟨to have a clear conscience : tener la conciencia limpia⟩

conscientious [ˌkɑntʃi'ɛntʃəs] *adj* : concienzudo — **conscientiously** *adv*

conscious ['kɑntʃəs] *adj* **1** AWARE : consciente ⟨to become conscious of : darse cuenta de⟩ **2** ALERT, AWAKE : consciente **3** INTENTIONAL : intencional, deliberado

consciously ['kɑntʃəsli] *adv* INTENTIONALLY : intencionalmente, deliberadamente, a propósito

consciousness ['kɑntʃəsnəs] *n* **1** AWARENESS : conciencia *f*, consciencia *f* **2** : conocimiento *m* ⟨to lose consciousness : perder el conocimiento⟩

conscript¹ [kən'skrɪpt] *vt* : reclutar, alistar, enrolar

conscript² ['kɑn,skrɪpt] *n* : conscripto *m*, -ta *f*; recluta *mf*

conscription [kən'skrɪpʃən] *n* : conscripción *f*

consecrate ['kɑntsə,kreɪt] *vt* **-crated; -crating** : consagrar

consecration [ˌkɑntsə'kreɪʃən] *n* : consagración *f*, dedicación *f*

consecutive [kən'sɛkjətɪv] *adj* : consecutivo, seguido ⟨on five consecutive days : cinco días seguidos⟩

consecutively [kən'sɛkjətɪvli] *adv* : consecutivamente

consensus [kən'sɛntsəs] *n* : consenso *m*

consent¹ [kən'sɛnt] *vi* **1** AGREE : acceder, ponerse de acuerdo **2 to consent to do something** : consentir en hacer algo

consent² *n* : consentimiento *m*, permiso

m ⟨by common consent : de común acuerdo⟩

consequence ['kɑntsə,kwɛnts, -kwənts] *n* **1** RESULT : consecuencia *f*, secuela *f* **2** IMPORTANCE : importancia *f*, trascendencia *f*

consequent ['kɑntsəkwənt, -,kwɛnt] *adj* : consiguiente

consequential [ˌkɑntsə'kwɛntʃəl] *adj* **1** CONSEQUENT : consiguiente **2** IMPORTANT : importante, trascendente, trascendental

consequently ['kɑntsəkwəntli, -,kwɛnt-] *adv* : por consiguiente, por ende, por lo tanto

conservation [ˌkɑntsər'veɪʃən] *n* : conservación *f*, protección *f*

conservationist [ˌkɑntsər'veɪʃənɪst] *n* : conservacionista *mf*

conservatism [kən'sərvə,tɪzəm] *n* : conservadurismo *m*

conservative¹ [kən'sərvətɪv] *adj* **1** : conservador **2** CAUTIOUS : moderado, cauteloso ⟨a conservative estimate : un cálculo moderado⟩

conservative² *n* : conservador *m*, -dora *f*

conservatory [kən'sərvə,tori] *n, pl* **-ries** : conservatorio *m*

conserve¹ [kən'sərv] *vt* **-served; -serving** : conservar, preservar

conserve² ['kɑn,sərv] *n* PRESERVES : confitura *f*

consider [kən'sɪdər] *vt* **1** CONTEMPLATE : considerar, pensar en ⟨we'd considered attending : habíamos pensado en asistir⟩ **2** : considerar, tener en cuenta ⟨consider the consequences : considera las consecuencias⟩ **3** JUDGE, REGARD : considerar, estimar

considerable [kən'sɪdərəbəl] *adj* : considerable — **considerably** [-bli] *adv*

considerate [kən'sɪdərət] *adj* : considerado, atento

consideration [kən,sɪdə'reɪʃən] *n* : consideración *f* ⟨to take into consideration : tener en cuenta⟩

considering [kən'sɪdərɪŋ] *prep* : teniendo en cuenta, visto

consign [kən'saɪn] *vt* **1** COMMIT, ENTRUST : confiar, encomendar **2** TRANSFER : consignar, transferir **3** SEND : consignar, enviar (mercancía)

consignment [kən'saɪnmənt] *n* **1** : envío *m*, remesa *f* **2 on ~** : en consignación

consist [kən'sɪst] *vi* **1** LIE : consistir ⟨success consists in hard work : el éxito consiste en trabajar duro⟩ **2** : constar, componerse ⟨the set consists of 5 pieces : el juego se compone de 5 piezas⟩

consistency [kən'sɪstəntsi] *n, pl* **-cies** **1** : consistencia *f* (de una mezcla o sustancia) **2** COHERENCE : coherencia *f* **3** UNIFORMITY : regularidad *f*, uniformidad *f*

consistent [kən'sɪstənt] *adj* **1** COMPATIBLE : compatible, coincidente ⟨consistent with policy : coincidente con la política⟩ **2** UNIFORM : uniforme, constante, regular — **consistently** [kən'sɪstəntli] *adv*

consolation [ˌkɑntsəˈleɪʃə n] *n* **1** : consuelo *m* **2 consolation prize** : premio *m* de consolación

console[1] [kənˈsoːl] *vt* **-soled; -soling** : consolar

console[2] [ˈkɑnˌsoːl] *n* : consola *f*

consolidate [kənˈsɑləˌdeɪt] *vt* **-dated; -dating** : consolidar, unir

consolidation [kənˌsɑləˈdeɪʃən] *n* : consolidación *f*

consommé [ˌkɑntsəˈmeɪ] *n* : consomé *m*

consonant [ˈkɑntsənənt] *n* : consonante *m*

consort[1] [kənˈsɔrt] *vi* : asociarse, relacionarse, tener trato ⟨to consort with criminals : tener trato con criminales⟩

consort[2] [ˈkɑnˌsɔrt] *n* : consorte *mf*

consortium [kənˈsɔrʃəm] *n, pl* **-tia** [-ʃə] *or* **-tiums** [-ʃəmz] : consorcio *m*

conspicuous [kənˈspɪkjuəs] *adj* **1** OBVIOUS : visible, evidente **2** STRIKING : llamativo

conspicuously [kənˈspɪkjuəsli] *adv* : de manera llamativa

conspiracy [kənˈspɪrəsi] *n, pl* **-cies** : conspiración *f*, complot *m*, confabulación *f*

conspirator [kənˈspɪrətər] *n* : conspirador *m*, -dora *f*

conspire [kənˈspaɪr] *vi* **-spired; -spiring** : conspirar, confabularse

constable [ˈkɑntstəbəl, ˈkʌntstə-] *n* : agente *mf* de policía (en un pueblo)

constancy [ˈkɑntstəntsi] *n, pl* **-cies** : constancia *f*

constant[1] [ˈkɑntstənt] *adj* **1** FAITHFUL : leal, fiel **2** INVARIABLE : constante, invariable **3** CONTINUAL : constante, continuo

constant[2] *n* : constante *f*

constantly [ˈkɑntstəntli] *adv* : constantemente, continuamente

constellation [ˌkɑntstəˈleɪʃən] *n* : constelación *f*

consternation [ˌkɑntstərˈneɪʃən] *n* : consternación *f*

constipate [ˈkɑntstəˌpeɪt] *vt* **-pated; -pating** : estreñir

constipated [ˈkɑntstəˌpeɪtəd] *adj* : estreñido

constipation [ˌkɑntstəˈpeɪʃən] *n* : estreñimiento *m*, constipación *f* (de vientre)

constituency [kənˈstɪtʃuəntsi] *n, pl* **-cies** **1** : distrito *m* electoral **2** : residentes *mpl* de un distrito electoral

constituent[1] [kənˈstɪtʃuənt] *adj* **1** COMPONENT : constituyente, componente **2** : constituyente, constitutivo ⟨a constituent assembly : una asamblea constituyente⟩

constituent[2] *n* **1** COMPONENT : componente *m* **2** VOTER : elector *m*, -tora *f*; votante *mf*

constitute [ˈkɑntstəˌtuːt, -ˌtjuːt] *vt* **-tuted; -tuting** **1** ESTABLISH : constituir, establecer **2** COMPOSE, FORM : constituir, componer

constitution [ˌkɑntstəˈtuːʃən, -ˈtjuː-] *n* : constitución *f*

constitutional [ˌkɑntstəˈtuːʃənəl, -ˈtjuː-] *adj* : constitucional

constitutionality [ˌkɑntstəˌtuːʃəˈnæ-ləti, -ˌtjuː-] *n* : constitucionalidad *f*

constrain [kənˈstreɪn] *vt* **1** COMPEL : constreñir, obligar **2** CONFINE : constreñir, limitar, restringir **3** RESTRAIN : contener, refrenar

constraint [kənˈstreɪnt] *n* : restricción *f*, limitación *f*

constrict [kənˈstrɪkt] *vt* : estrechar, apretar, comprimir

constriction [kənˈstrɪkʃən] *n* : estrechamiento *m*, compresión *f*

construct [kənˈstrʌkt] *vt* : construir

construction [kənˈstrʌkʃən] *n* : construcción *f*

constructive [kənˈstrʌktɪv] *adj* : constructivo

construe [kənˈstruː] *vt* **-strued; -struing** : interpretar

consul [ˈkɑntsəl] *n* : cónsul *mf*

consular [ˈkɑntsələr] *adj* : consular

consulate [ˈkɑntsələt] *n* : consulado *m*

consult [kənˈsʌlt] *vt* : consultar — *vi* **to consult with** : consultar con, solicitar la opinión de

consultancy [kənˈsʌltəntsi] *n, pl* **-cies** : consultoría *f*

consultant [kənˈsʌltənt] *n* : consultor *m*, -tora *f*; asesor *m*, -sora *f*

consultation [ˌkɑntsəlˈteɪʃən] *n* : consulta *f*

consumable [kənˈsuːməbəl] *adj* : consumible

consume [kənˈsuːm] *vt* **-sumed; -suming** : consumir, usar, gastar

consumer [kənˈsuːmər] *n* : consumidor *m*, -dora *f*

consumerism [kənˈsuːməˌrɪzəm] *n* : consumismo *m*

consummate[1] [ˈkɑntsəˌmeɪt] *vt* **-mated; -mating** : consumar

consummate[2] [kənˈsʌmət, ˈkɑntsə-mət] *adj* : consumado, perfecto

consummation [ˌkɑntsəˈmeɪʃən] *n* : consumación *f*

consumption [kənˈsʌmpʃən] *n* USE : consumo *m*, uso *m* ⟨consumption of electricity : consumo de electricidad⟩

contact[1] [ˈkɑnˌtækt, kənˈ-] *vt* : ponerse en contacto con, contactar (con)

contact[2] [ˈkɑnˌtækt] *n* **1** TOUCHING : contacto *m* ⟨to come into contact with : entrar en contacto con⟩ **2** TOUCH : contacto *m*, comunicación *f* ⟨to lose contact with : perder contacto con⟩ **3** CONNECTION : contacto *m* (en negocios) **4** → **contact lens**

contact lens [ˈkɑnˌtæktˈlɛnz] *n* : lente *mf* de contacto, pupilente *m* *Mex*

contagion [kənˈteɪdʒən] *n* : contagio *m*

contagious [kənˈteɪdʒəs] *adj* : contagioso

contain [kənˈteɪn] *vt* **1** : contener **2 to contain oneself** : contenerse

container [kənˈteɪnər] *n* : recipiente *m*, envase *m*

containment [kənˈteɪnmənt] *n* : contención *f*

contaminant [kənˈtæmənənt] *n* : contaminante *m*

contaminate [kənˈtæməˌneɪt] *vt* **-nated; -nating** : contaminar

contamination [kən̩tæmə'neɪʃən] *n*
: contaminación *f*
contemplate ['kantəm̩pleɪt] *v* **-plated;**
-plating *vt* **1** VIEW : contemplar **2**
PONDER : contemplar, considerar **3**
CONSIDER, PROPOSE : proponerse,
proyectar, pensar en ⟨to contemplate a
trip : pensar en viajar⟩ — *vi* MEDITATE
: meditar
contemplation [ˌkantəm'pleɪʃən] *n* : contemplación *f*
contemplative [kən'tɛmplətɪv, 'kantəm-
ˌpleɪtɪv] *adj* : contemplativo
contemporaneous [kən̩tɛmpə'reɪniəs]
adj → **contemporary**[1]
contemporary[1] [kən'tɛmpəˌrɛri] *adj*
: contemporáneo
contemporary[2] *n, pl* **-raries** : contemporáneo *m*, -nea *f*
contempt [kən'tɛmpt] *n* **1** DISDAIN : desprecio *m*, desdén *m* ⟨to hold in contempt
: despreciar⟩ **2** : desacato *m* (ante un
tribunal)
contemptible [kən'tɛmptəbəl] *adj* : despreciable, vil
contemptuous [kən'tɛmptʃuəs] *adj* : despectivo, despreciativo, desdeñoso
contemptuously [kən'tɛmptʃuəsli] *adv*
: despectivamente, con desprecio
contend [kən'tɛnd] *vi* **1** STRUGGLE
: luchar, lidiar, contender ⟨to contend
with a problem : lidiar con un pro-
blema⟩ **2** COMPETE : competir ⟨to contend for a position : competir por un
puesto⟩ — *vt* **1** ARGUE, MAINTAIN
: argüir, sostener, afirmar ⟨he contended
that he was right : afirmó que tenía
razón⟩ **2** CONTEST : protestar contra
(una decisión, etc.), disputar
contender [kən'tɛndər] *n* : contendiente
mf; aspirante *mf*; competidor *m*, -dora *f*
content[1] [kən'tɛnt] *vt* SATISFY : contentar,
satisfacer
content[2] *adj* : conforme, contento, satisfecho
content[3] *n* CONTENTMENT : contento *m*,
satisfacción *f* ⟨to one's heart's content
: hasta quedar satisfecho, a más no
poder⟩
content[4] ['kanˌtɛnt] *n* **1** MEANING : contenido *m*, significado *m* **2** PROPORTION
: contenido *m*, proporción *f* ⟨fat content
: contenido de grasa⟩ **3 contents** *npl*
: contenido *m*, sumario *m* (de un libro)
⟨table of contents : índice de materias⟩
contented [kən'tɛntəd] *adj* : conforme,
satisfecho ⟨a contented smile : una sonrisa de satisfacción⟩
contentedly [kən'tɛntədli] *adv* : con satisfacción
contention [kən'tɛntʃən] *n* **1** DISPUTE
: disputa *f*, discusión *f* **2** COMPETITION
: competencia *f*, contienda *f* **3** OPINION
: argumento *m*, opinión *f*
contentious [kən'tɛntʃəs] *adj* **1** CON-
TROVERSIAL : controvertido **2** DEBA-
TED : discutido **3** ARGUMENTATIVE
: discutidor
contentment [kən'tɛntmənt] *n* : satisfacción *f*, contento *m*

contest[1] [kən'tɛst] *vt* : disputar, cuestionar, impugnar ⟨to contest a will : impugnar un testamento⟩
contest[2] ['kanˌtɛst] *n* **1** STRUGGLE : lucha *f*, contienda *f* **2** GAME : concurso *m*,
competencia *f*
contestable [kən'tɛstəbəl] *adj* : discutible, cuestionable
contestant [kən'tɛstənt] *n* : concursante
mf; competidor *m*, -dora *f*
context ['kanˌtɛkst] *n* : contexto *m*
contiguous [kən'tɪgjuəs] *adj* : contiguo
continent[1] ['kantənənt] *adj* : continente
continent[2] *n* : continente *m* — **continental** [ˌkantən'ɛntəl] *adj*
contingency [kən'tɪndʒəntsi] *n, pl* **-cies**
: contingencia *f*, eventualidad *f* ⟨contin-
gency plan : plan de emergencia⟩
contingent[1] [kən'tɪndʒənt] *adj* **1** POSSI-
BLE : contingente, eventual **2** ACCI-
DENTAL : fortuito, accidental **3 to be**
contingent on : depender de, estar sujeto a
contingent[2] *n* : contingente *m*
continual [kən'tɪnjuəl] *adj* : continuo,
constante — **continually** [kən-
'tɪnjuəli, -'tɪnjəli] *adv*
continuance [kən'tɪnjuənts] *n* **1** CON-
TINUATION : continuación *f* **2** DURA-
TION : duración *f* **3** : aplazamiento *m*
(de un proceso)
continuation [kən̩tɪnju'eɪʃən] *n* : continuación *f*, prolongación *f*
continue [kən'tɪnju:] *v* **-tinued; -tinuing**
vi **1** CARRY ON : continuar, seguir,
proseguir ⟨please continue : continúe,
por favor⟩ **2** ENDURE, LAST : continuar, prolongarse, durar **3** RESUME
: continuar, reanudarse — *vt* **1** : continuar, seguir ⟨she continued writing
: continuó escribiendo⟩ **2** RESUME
: continuar, reanudar **3** EXTEND, PRO-
LONG : continuar, prolongar
continuity [ˌkantə'nu:əti, -'nju:-] *n, pl*
-ties : continuidad *f*
continuous [kən'tɪnjuəs] *adj* : continuo
— **continuously** *adv*
contort [kən'tɔrt] *vt* : torcer, retorcer,
contraer (el rostro) — *vi* : contraerse,
demudarse
contortion [kən'tɔrʃən] *n* : contorsión *f*
contour ['kanˌtur] *n* **1** OUTLINE : contorno *m* **2 contours** *npl* SHAPE : forma
f, curvas *fpl* **3 contour map** : mapa *m*
topográfico
contraband ['kantrəˌbænd] *n* : contrabando *m*
contraception [ˌkantrə'sɛpʃən] *n* : anticoncepción *f*, contracepción *f*
contraceptive[1] [ˌkantrə'sɛptɪv] *adj* : anticonceptivo, contraceptivo
contraceptive[2] *n* : anticonceptivo *m*, contraceptivo *m*
contract[1] [kən'trækt, 1 *usu* 'kanˌtrækt]
vt **1** : contratar (servicios profesionales) **2** : contraer (una enfermedad,
una deuda) **3** TIGHTEN : contraer (un
músculo) **4** SHORTEN : contraer (una
palabra) — *vi* : contraerse, reducirse
contract[2] ['kanˌtrækt] *n* : contrato *m*

contraction [kən'trækʃən] n : contracción f

contractor ['kɑn₁træktər, kən'træk-] n : contratista mf

contractual [kən'træktʃuəl] adj : contractual — **contractually** adv

contradict [₁kɑntrə'dɪkt] vt : contradecir, desmentir

contradiction [₁kɑntrə'dɪkʃən] n : contradicción f

contradictory [₁kɑntrə'dɪktəri] adj : contradictorio

contralto [kən'træl₁to:] n, pl -tos : contralto m (voz), contralto mf (vocalista)

contraption [kən'træpʃən] n DEVICE : aparato m, artefacto m

contrary[1] ['kɑn₁trɛri, 2 often kən-'trɛri] adj 1 OPPOSITE : contrario, opuesto 2 BALKY, STUBBORN : terco, testarudo 3 contrary to : al contrario de, en contra de ⟨contrary to the facts : en contra de los hechos⟩

contrary[2] ['kɑn₁trɛri] n, pl -traries 1 OPPOSITE : lo contrario, lo opuesto 2 on the contrary : al contrario, todo lo contrario

contrast[1] [kən'træst] vi DIFFER : contrastar, diferir — vt COMPARE : contrastar, comparar

contrast[2] ['kɑn₁træst] n : contraste m

contravene [₁kɑntrə'vi:n] vt -vened; -vening : contravenir, infringir

contribute [kən'trɪbjət] v -uted; -uting vt : contribuir, aportar (dinero, bienes, etc.) — vi : contribuir

contribution [₁kɑntrə'bju:ʃən] n : contribución f

contributor [kən'trɪbjətər] n : contribuidor m, -dora f; colaborador m, -dora f (en periodismo)

contrite ['kɑn₁traɪt, kən'traɪt] adj REPENTANT : contrito, arrepentido

contrition [kən'trɪʃən] n : contrición f, arrepentimiento m

contrivance [kən'traɪvənts] n 1 DEVICE : aparato m, artefacto m 2 SCHEME : artimaña f, treta f, ardid m

contrive [kən'traɪv] vt -trived; -triving 1 DEVISE : idear, ingeniar, maquinar 2 MANAGE : lograr, ingeniárselas para ⟨she contrived a way out of the mess : se las ingenió para salir del enredo⟩

control[1] [kən'tro:l] vt -trolled; -trolling : controlar — **controllable** [kən-'tro:ləbəl] adj

control[2] n 1 : control m, dominio m, mando m ⟨to be under control : estar bajo control⟩ ⟨to be out of control : estar fuera de control⟩ ⟨he likes to be in control : le gusta mandar⟩ ⟨to be in control of : controlar⟩ ⟨to lose control : perder el control⟩ ⟨it's beyond my control : no está en mis manos⟩ ⟨for reasons beyond our control : por causas ajenas a nuestra voluntad⟩ 2 RESTRAINT : control m, limitación f ⟨birth control : control natal⟩ ⟨gun control : control de armas⟩ 3 : control m, dispositivo m de mando ⟨remote control : control remoto⟩

controller [kən'tro:lər, 'kɑn₁-] n 1 → comptroller 2 : controlador m, -dora f ⟨air traffic controller : controlador aéreo⟩

controversial [₁kɑntrə'vərʃəl, -siəl] adj : controvertido ⟨a controversial decision : una decisión controvertida⟩

controversy ['kɑntrə₁vərsi] n, pl -sies : controversia f

controvert ['kɑntrə₁vərt, ₁kɑntrə'-] vt : controvertir, contradecir

contusion [kən'tu:ʒən, -tju:-] n BRUISE : contusión f, moretón m

conundrum [kə'nʌndrəm] n RIDDLE : acertijo m, adivinanza f

convalesce [₁kɑnvə'lɛs] vi -lesced; -lescing : convalecer

convalescence [₁kɑnvə'lɛsənts] n : convalecencia f

convalescent[1] [₁kɑnvə'lɛsənt] adj : convaleciente

convalescent[2] n : convaleciente mf

convection [kən'vɛkʃən] n : convección f

convene [kən'vi:n] v -vened; -vening vt : convocar — vi : reunirse

convenience [kən'vi:njənts] n 1 : conveniencia f ⟨at your convenience : cuando le resulte conveniente⟩ 2 AMENITY : comodidad f ⟨modern conveniences : comodidades modernas⟩

convenience store n : tienda f de conveniencia

convenient [kən'vi:njənt] adj : conveniente, cómodo — **conveniently** adv

convent ['kɑnvənt, -₁vɛnt] n : convento m

convention [kən'vɛntʃən] n 1 PACT : convención f, convenio m, pacto m ⟨the Geneva Convention : la Convención de Ginebra⟩ 2 MEETING : convención f, congreso m 3 CUSTOM : convención f

conventional [kən'vɛntʃənəl] adj : convencional — **conventionally** adv

converge [kən'vərdʒ] vi -verged; -verging : converger, convergir

convergence [kən'vərdʒənts] n : convergencia f

convergent [kən'vərdʒənt] adj : convergente

conversant [kən'vərsənt] adj conversant with : versado en, experto en

conversation [₁kɑnvər'seɪʃən] n : conversación f

conversational [₁kɑnvər'seɪʃənəl] adj : familiar ⟨a conversational style : un estilo familiar⟩

conversationalist [₁kɑnvər'seɪʃənəlɪst] n : conversador m, -dora f

converse[1] [kən'vərs] vi -versed; -versing : conversar

converse[2] [kən'vərs, 'kɑn₁vərs] adj : contrario, opuesto, inverso

conversely [kən'vərsli, 'kɑn₁vərs-] adv : a la inversa

conversion [kən'vərʒən] n 1 CHANGE : conversión f, transformación f, cambio m 2 : conversión f (a una religión)

convert[1] [kən'vərt] vt 1 : convertir (a una religión o un partido) 2 CHANGE : convertir, cambiar — vi : convertirse

convert² [ˈkɑnˌvərt] *n* : converso *m*, -sa *f*

converter *or* **convertor** [kənˈvərtər] *n* : convertidor *m*

convertible¹ [kənˈvərtəbəl] *adj* : convertible

convertible² *n* : convertible *m*, descapotable *m*

convex [kɑnˈvɛks, ˈkɑnˌ-, kənˈ-] *adj* : convexo

convey [kənˈveɪ] *vt* **1** TRANSPORT : transportar, conducir **2** TRANSMIT : transmitir, comunicar, expresar (noticias, ideas, etc.)

conveyance [kənˈveɪənts] *n* **1** TRANSPORT : transporte *m*, transportación *f* **2** COMMUNICATION : transmisión *f*, comunicación *f* **3** TRANSFER : transferencia *f*, traspaso *m* (de una propiedad)

conveyor [kənˈveɪər] *n* : transportador *m*, -dora *f* ⟨conveyor belt : cinta transportadora⟩

convict¹ [kənˈvɪkt] *vt* : declarar culpable

convict² [ˈkɑnˌvɪkt] *n* : preso *m*, -sa *f*; presidiario *m*, -ria *f*; recluso *m*, -sa *f*

conviction [kənˈvɪkʃən] *n* **1** : condena *f* (de un acusado) **2** BELIEF : convicción *f*, creencia *f*

convince [kənˈvɪnts] *vt* **-vinced; -vincing** : convencer

convincing [kənˈvɪntsɪŋ] *adj* : convincente, persuasivo

convincingly [kənˈvɪntsɪŋli] *adv* : de forma convincente

convivial [kənˈvɪvjəl, -ˈvɪviəl] *adj* : jovial, festivo, alegre

conviviality [kənˌvɪviˈæləti] *n*, *pl* **-ties** : jovialidad *f*

convoke [kənˈvoːk] *vt* **-voked; -voking** : convocar

convoluted [ˈkɑnvəˌluːtəd] *adj* : intrincado, complicado

convoy [ˈkɑnˌvɔɪ] *n* : convoy *m*

convulse [kənˈvʌls] *v* **-vulsed; -vulsing** *vt* : convulsionar ⟨convulsed with laughter : muerto de risa⟩ — *vi* : sufrir convulsiones

convulsion [kənˈvʌlʃən] *n* : convulsión *f*

convulsive [kənˈvʌlsɪv] *adj* : convulsivo — **convulsively** *adv*

coo¹ [ˈkuː] *vi* : arrullar

coo² *n* : arrullo *m* (de una paloma)

cook¹ [ˈkʊk] *vi* : cocinar — *vt* **1** : preparar (comida) **2 to cook up** CONCOCT : inventar, tramar

cook² *n* : cocinero *m*, -ra *f*

cookbook [ˈkʊkˌbʊk] *n* : libro *m* de cocina

cookery [ˈkʊkəri] *n*, *pl* **-eries** : cocina *f*

cookie *or* **cooky** [ˈkʊki] *n*, *pl* **-ies** : galleta *f* (dulce)

cooking [ˈkʊkɪŋ] *n* **1** COOKERY : cocina *f* **2** : cocción *f*, cocimiento *m* ⟨cooking time : tiempo de cocción⟩

cookout [ˈkʊkˌaʊt] *n* : comida *f* al aire libre

cool¹ [ˈkuːl] *vt* : refrescar, enfriar — *vi* **1** : refrescarse, enfriarse ⟨the pie is cooling : el pastel se está enfriando⟩ **2** : calmarse, tranquilizarse ⟨his anger cooled : su ira se calmó⟩

cool² *adj* **1** : fresco, frío ⟨cool weather : tiempo fresco⟩ **2** CALM : tranquilo, sereno **3** ALOOF : frío, distante **4** *fam* EXCELLENT, TRENDY : muy en la onda *fam*; chévere *fam*; bacán *Chile, Ecua, Uru fam*; bacano *Col fam*; guay *Spain fam*; chido *Mex fam*

cool³ *n* **1** : fresco *m* ⟨the cool of the evening : el fresco de la tarde⟩ **2** COMPOSURE : calma *f*, serenidad *f*

coolant [ˈkuːlənt] *n* : refrigerante *m*

cooler [ˈkuːlər] *n* : nevera *f* portátil

coolly [ˈkuːlli] *adv* **1** CALMLY : con calma, tranquilamente **2** COLDLY : fríamente, con frialdad

coolness [ˈkuːlnəs] *n* **1** : frescura *f*, frescor *m* ⟨the coolness of the evening : el frescor de la noche⟩ **2** CALMNESS : tranquilidad *f*, serenidad *f* **3** COLDNESS, INDIFFERENCE : frialdad *f*, indiferencia *f*

coop¹ [ˈkuːp, ˈkʊp] *vt or* **to coop up** : encerrar ⟨cooped up in the house : encerrado en la casa⟩

coop² *n* : gallinero *m*

co–op [ˈkoːˌɑp] *n* → **cooperative²**

cooperate [koˈɑpəˌreɪt] *vi* **-ated; -ating** : cooperar, colaborar

cooperation [koˌɑpəˈreɪʃən] *n* : cooperación *f*, colaboración *f*

cooperative¹ [koˈɑpərətɪv] *adj* : cooperativo

cooperative² *n* : cooperativa *f*

co–opt [koˈɑpt] *vt* **1** : nombrar como miembro, cooptar **2** APPROPRIATE : apropiarse de

coordinate¹ [koˈɔrdənˌeɪt] *v* **-nated; -nating** *vt* : coordinar — *vi* : coordinarse, combinar, acordar

coordinate² [koˈɔrdənət] *adj* **1** COORDINATED : coordinado **2** EQUAL : igual, semejante

coordinate³ [koˈɔrdənət] *n* : coordenada *f*

coordination [koˌɔrdənˈeɪʃən] *n* : coordinación *f*

coordinator [koˈɔrdənˌeɪtər] *n* : coordinador *m*, -dora *f*

cop [ˈkɑp] *n* → **police officer**

cope [ˈkoːp] *vi* **coped; coping** **1** : arreglárselas **2 to cope with** : hacer frente a, poder con ⟨I can't cope with all this! : ¡no puedo con todo esto!⟩

copier [ˈkɑpiər] *n* : copiadora *f*, fotocopiadora *f*

copilot [ˈkoːˌpaɪlət] *n* : copiloto *m*

copious [ˈkoːpiəs] *adj* : copioso, abundante — **copiously** *adv*

copiousness [ˈkoːpiəsnəs] *n* : abundancia *f*

copper [ˈkɑpər] *n* : cobre *m*

coppery [ˈkɑpəri] *adj* : cobrizo

copse [ˈkɑps] *n* THICKET : soto *m*, matorral *m*

copulate [ˈkɑpjəˌleɪt] *vi* **-lated; -lating** : copular

copulation [ˌkɑpjəˈleɪʃən] *n* : cópula *f*, relaciones *fpl* sexuales

copy¹ [ˈkɑpi] *vt* **copied; copying** **1** DUPLICATE : hacer una copia de, duplicar, reproducir **2** IMITATE : copiar, imitar

copy² *n, pl* **copies** **1** : copia *f*, duplicado *m* (de un documento), reproducción *f* (de una obra de arte) **2** : ejemplar *m* (de un libro), número *m* (de una revista) **3** TEXT : manuscrito *m*, texto *m*

copycat [ˈkɑpiˌkæt] *n* : copión *m*, -piona *f*

copyright¹ [ˈkɑpiˌraɪt] *vt* : registrar los derechos de

copyright² *n* : derechos *mpl* de autor

coral¹ [ˈkɔrəl] *adj* : de coral ⟨a coral reef : un arrecife de coral⟩

coral² *n* : coral *m*

coral snake *n* : serpiente *f* de coral

cord [ˈkɔrd] *n* **1** ROPE, STRING : cuerda *f*, cordón *m*, cordel *m* **2** : cuerda *f*, cordón *m*, médula *f* (en la anatomía) ⟨vocal cords : cuerdas vocales⟩ **3** : cuerda *f* ⟨a cord of firewood : una cuerda de leña⟩ **4** *or* **electric cord** : cable *m* eléctrico

cordial¹ [ˈkɔrʤəl] *adj* : cordial — **cordially** *adv*

cordial² *n* : cordial *m*

cordiality [ˌkɔrʤiˈæləti] *n* : cordialidad *f*

cordless [ˈkɔrdləs] *adj* : inalámbrico

córdoba [ˈkɔrdəbə] *n* : córdoba *f* (unidad monetaria)

cordon¹ [ˈkɔrdən] *vt* **to cordon off** : acordonar

cordon² *n* : cordón *m*

corduroy [ˈkɔrdəˌrɔɪ] *n* **1** : pana *f* **2 corduroys** *npl* : pantalones *mpl* de pana

core¹ [ˈkor] *vt* **cored; coring** : quitar el corazón a (una fruta)

core² *n* **1** : corazón *m*, centro *m* (de algunas frutas) **2** CENTER : núcleo *m*, centro *m* **3** ESSENCE : núcleo *m*, meollo *m* ⟨to the core : hasta la médula⟩

coriander [ˈkoriˌændər] *n* : cilantro *m*

cork¹ [ˈkɔrk] *vt* : ponerle un corcho a

cork² *n* : corcho *m*

corkscrew [ˈkɔrkˌskru:] *n* : tirabuzón *m*, sacacorchos *m*

cormorant [ˈkɔrmərənt, -ˌrænt] *n* : cormorán *m*

corn¹ [ˈkɔrn] *vt* : conservar en salmuera ⟨corned beef : carne en conserva⟩

corn² *n* **1** GRAIN : grano *m* **2** : maíz *m*, choclo *m*, elote *m Mex* ⟨corn tortillas : tortillas de maíz⟩ **3** : callo *m* ⟨corn plaster : emplasto para callos⟩

corncob [ˈkɔrnˌkɑb] *n* : mazorca *f* (de maíz), choclo *m*, elote *m CA, Mex*

cornea [ˈkɔrniə] *n* : córnea *f*

corner¹ [ˈkɔrnər] *vt* **1** TRAP : acorralar, arrinconar **2** MONOPOLIZE : monopolizar, acaparar (un mercado) — *vi* : tomar una curva, doblar una esquina (en un automóvil)

corner² *n* **1** ANGLE : rincón *m*, esquina *f* (de una mesa, etc.), ángulo *m* (de una página) ⟨the corner of a room : el rincón de una habitación⟩ ⟨all corners of the world : todos los rincones del mundo⟩ **2** INTERSECTION : esquina *f* **3** BEND : curva *f* (en una carretera) **4** PREDICAMENT, IMPASSE : aprieto *m*, impasse *m* ⟨to be backed into a corner : estar acorralado⟩ **5 corner of the eye** : lagrimal *m*, rabillo *m* **6 corner of the mouth**

: comisura *f* de los labios **7 to cut corners** : economizar esfuerzos

corner kick *n* : córner *m*

cornerstone [ˈkɔrnərˌsto:n] *n* : piedra *f* angular

cornet [kɔrˈnɛt] *n* : corneta *f*

cornfield [ˈkɔrnˌfi:ld] *n* : maizal *m*; milpa *f CA, Mex*

cornflakes [ˈkɔrnˌfleɪks] *npl* : copos *mpl* de maíz

cornice [ˈkɔrnɪs] *n* : cornisa *f*

cornmeal [ˈkɔrnˌmi:l] *n* : harina *f* de maíz

cornstalk [ˈkɔrnˌstɔk] *n* : tallo *m* del maíz

cornstarch [ˈkɔrnˌstɑrtʃ] *n* : maicena *f*, almidón *m* de maíz

cornucopia [ˌkɔrnəˈko:piə, -njə-] *n* : cornucopia *f*

corny [ˈkɔrni] *adj* **cornier; -est** **1** SENTIMENTAL : sentimental, cursi **2** SILLY : tonto (dícese de un chiste, etc.)

corolla [kəˈrɑlə] *n* : corola *f*

corollary [ˈkɔrəˌlɛri] *n, pl* **-laries** : corolario *m*

corona [kəˈro:nə] *n* : corona *f* (del sol)

coronary¹ [ˈkɔrəˌnɛri] *adj* : coronario

coronary² *n, pl* **-naries** **1** : trombosis *f* coronaria **2** HEART ATTACK : infarto *m*, ataque *m* al corazón

coronation [ˌkɔrəˈneɪʃən] *n* : coronación *f*

coroner [ˈkɔrənər] *n* : médico *m* forense

corporal¹ [ˈkɔrpərəl] *adj* : corporal ⟨corporal punishment : castigos corporales⟩

corporal² *n* : cabo *m*

corporate [ˈkɔrpərət] *adj* : corporativo, empresarial

corporation [ˌkɔrpəˈreɪʃən] *n* : sociedad *f* anónima, corporación *f*, empresa *f*

corporeal [kɔrˈporiəl] *adj* **1** PHYSICAL : corpóreo **2** MATERIAL : material, tangible — **corporeally** *adv*

corps [ˈkor] *n, pl* **corps** [ˈkorz] : cuerpo *m* ⟨medical corps : cuerpo médico⟩ ⟨diplomatic corps : cuerpo diplomático⟩

corpse [ˈkorps] *n* : cadáver *m*

corpulence [ˈkɔrpjələnts] *n* : obesidad *f*, gordura *f*

corpulent [ˈkɔrpjələnt] *adj* : obeso, gordo

corpuscle [ˈkɔrˌpʌsəl] *n* : corpúsculo *m*, glóbulo *m* (sanguíneo)

corral¹ [kəˈræl] *vt* **-ralled; -ralling** : acorralar (ganado)

corral² *n* : corral *m*

correct¹ [kəˈrɛkt] *vt* **1** RECTIFY : corregir, rectificar **2** REPRIMAND : corregir, reprender

correct² *adj* **1** ACCURATE, RIGHT : correcto, exacto ⟨to be correct : estar en lo cierto⟩ **2** PROPER : correcto, apropiado

correction [kəˈrɛkʃən] *n* : corrección *f*

corrective [kəˈrɛktɪv] *adj* : correctivo

correctly [kəˈrɛktli] *adv* : correctamente

correctness [kəˈrɛk(t)nəs] *n* **1** ACCURACY : exactitud *f* **2** PROPRIETY : corrección *f*

correlate [ˈkɔrəˌleɪt] *vt* **-lated; -lating** : relacionar, poner en correlación

correlation [ˌkɔrəˈleɪʃən] *n* : correlación *f*

correspond [ˌkɔrəˈspɑnd] *vi* **1** MATCH : corresponder, concordar, coincidir **2** WRITE : corresponderse, escribirse

correspondence [ˌkɔrəˈspɑndənts] n
: correspondencia f
correspondent [ˌkɔrəˈspɑndənt] n : corresponsal mf
corresponding [kɔrəˈspɑndɪŋ, kɑr-] adj
: correspondiente
correspondingly [ˌkɔrəˈspɑndɪŋli] adv
: en consecuencia, de la misma manera
corridor [ˈkɔrədər, -ˌdɔr] n : corredor m,
pasillo m
corroborate [kəˈrɑbəˌreɪt] vt -rated; -rat-
ing : corroborar
corroboration [kəˌrɑbəˈreɪʃən] n : corroboración f
corrode [kəˈroːd] v -roded; -roding vt
: corroer — vi : corroerse
corrosion [kəˈroːʒən] n : corrosión f
corrosive [kəˈroːsɪv] adj : corrosivo
corrugate [ˈkɔrəˌgeɪt] vt -gated; -gating
: ondular, acanalar, corrugar
corrugated [ˈkɔrəˌgeɪtəd] adj : ondulado,
acanalado ⟨corrugated cardboard
: cartón ondulado⟩
corrupt¹ [kəˈrʌpt] vt 1 PERVERT : corromper, pervertir, degradar (información) 2 BRIBE : sobornar
corrupt² adj : corrupto, corrompido
corruptible [kəˈrʌptəbəl] adj : corruptible
corruption [kəˈrʌpʃən] n : corrupción f
corsage [kɔrˈsɑʒ, -ˈsɑʤ] n : ramillete m
que se lleva como adorno
corset [ˈkɔrsət] n : corsé m
cortex [ˈkɔrˌteks] n, pl -tices [ˈkɔrtəˌsiːz]
or -texes : corteza f ⟨cerebral cortex
: corteza cerebral⟩
cortisone [ˈkɔrtəˌsoːn, -zoːn] n : cortisona
f
cosmetic¹ [kɑzˈmetɪk] adj : cosmético
⟨cosmetic surgery : cirugía estética⟩
cosmetic² n : cosmético m
cosmic [ˈkɑzmɪk] adj 1 : cósmico ⟨cos-
mic ray : rayo cósmico⟩ 2 VAST : grandioso, inmenso, vasto
cosmonaut [ˈkɑzməˌnɔt] n : cosmonauta
mf
cosmopolitan¹ [ˌkɑzməˈpɑlətən] adj : cosmopolita
cosmopolitan² n : cosmopolita mf
cosmos [ˈkɑzməs, -ˌmoːs, -ˌmɑs] n : cosmos m, universo m
cost¹ [ˈkɔst] v cost; costing : costar
⟨how much does it cost? : ¿cuánto
cuesta?, ¿cuánto vale?⟩ — vi : costar
⟨these cost more : éstos cuestan más⟩
cost² n : costo m, precio m, coste m ⟨cost
of living : costo de vida⟩ ⟨victory at all
costs : victoria a toda costa⟩
co–star [ˈkoːˌstɑr] n : coprotagonista mf
Costa Rican¹ [ˌkɑstəˈriːkən] adj : costarricense
Costa Rican² n : costarricense mf
costly [ˈkɔstli] adj : costoso, caro
costume [ˈkɑsˌtuːm, -ˌtjuːm] n 1 : traje m
⟨national costume : traje típico⟩ 2 : disfraz m ⟨costume party : fiesta de dis-
fraces⟩ 3 OUTFIT : vestimenta f, traje m,
conjunto m
costume jewelry n : bisutería f
cosy [ˈkoːzi] → **cozy**
cot [ˈkɑt] n : catre m

coterie [ˈkoːtˌə,ri, ˌkoːˈtəˈ-] n : tertulia f, círculo m (social)
cottage [ˈkɑtɪʤ] n : casita f (de campo)
cottage cheese n : requesón m
cotton [ˈkɑtən] n : algodón m
cotton batting → **batting**
cotton candy n : algodón m de azúcar
cottonmouth [ˈkɑtənˌmaʊθ] → **moccasin**
cottonseed [ˈkɑtənˌsiːd] n : semilla f de
algodón
cotton swab → **swab**
cottontail [ˈkɑtənˌteɪl] n : conejo m de
cola blanca
couch¹ [ˈkaʊtʃ] vt : expresar, formular
⟨couched in strong language : expresado
en lenguaje enérgico⟩
couch² n SOFA : sofá m
couch potato n : haragán m, -gana f; vago
m, -ga f
cougar [ˈkuːgər] n : puma m
cough¹ [ˈkɔf] vi : toser
cough² n : tos f
could [ˈkʊd] → **can**
council [ˈkaʊntsəl] n 1 : concejo m ⟨city
council : concejo municipal, ayunta-
miento⟩ 2 MEETING : concejo m, junta
f 3 BOARD : consejo m 4 : concilio m
(eclesiástico)
councillor or **councilor** [ˈkaʊntsələr] n
: concejal m, -jala f
councilman [ˈkaʊntsəlmən] n, pl -men
[-mən, -ˌmɛn] : concejal m
councilwoman [ˈkaʊntsəlˌwʊmən] n, pl
-women [-ˌwɪmən] : concejala f
counsel¹ [ˈkaʊntsəl] v -seled or -selled;
-seling or -selling vt ADVISE : aconsejar,
asesorar, recomendar — vi CONSULT
: consultar
counsel² n 1 ADVICE : consejo m, recomendación f 2 CONSULTATION : consulta f 3 counsel ns & pl LAWYER : abogado m, -da f
counselor or **counsellor** [ˈkaʊntsələr] n
: consejero m, -ra f; consultor m, -tora f;
asesor m, -sora f
count¹ [ˈkaʊnt] vt 1 : contar 2 INCLUDE
: contar 3 CONSIDER : considerar
⟨count yourself (as) lucky : considérate
afortunado⟩ 4 to count down : contar
los días (etc.) que faltan 5 to count in/
out ⟨count me in : cuenta conmigo, yo
me apunto⟩ ⟨count me out : no cuentes
conmigo⟩ — vi 1 : contar ⟨to count out
loud : contar en voz alta⟩ 2 MATTER
: contar, valer, importar ⟨that's what
counts : eso es lo que cuenta⟩ 3 to
count on : contar con 4 to count
towards : contar para
count² n 1 COMPUTATION : cómputo m,
recuento m, cuenta f ⟨to lose count
: perder la cuenta⟩ 2 CHARGE : cargo m
⟨two counts of robbery : dos cargos de
robo⟩ 3 POINT : punto m, aspecto m
⟨you're wrong on all counts : se equivoca
en todo lo que dice⟩ 4 : conde m (noble)
countable [ˈkaʊntəbəl] adj : numerable
countdown [ˈkaʊntˌdaʊn] n : cuenta f
atrás
countenance¹ [ˈkaʊntənənts] vt -nanced;
-nancing : permitir, tolerar

countenance² *n* FACE : semblante *m*, rostro *m*

counter¹ [ˈkaʊntər] *vt* **1** → **counteract 2** OPPOSE : oponerse a, resistir — *vi* RETALIATE : responder, contraatacar

counter² *adv* **counter to** : contrario a, en contra de

counter³ *adj* : contrario, opuesto

counter⁴ *n* **1** PIECE : ficha *f* (de un juego) **2** : mostrador *m* (de un negocio), ventanilla *f* (en un banco) **3** : contador *m* (aparato) **4** COUNTERBALANCE : fuerza *f* opuesta, contrapeso *m*

counter- *pref* : contra- ⟨counterattack : contraataque⟩

counteract [ˌkaʊntərˈækt] *vt* : contrarrestar

counterattack [ˈkaʊntərəˌtæk] *n* : contraataque *m*

counterbalance¹ [ˌkaʊntərˈbælənts] *vt* **-anced; -ancing** : contrapesar

counterbalance² [ˈkaʊntərˌbælənts] *n* : contrapeso *m*

counterclockwise [ˌkaʊntərˈklɑk-ˌwaɪz] *adv & adj* : en el sentido opuesto al de las manecillas del reloj

counterfeit¹ [ˈkaʊntərˌfɪt] *vt* **1** : falsificar (dinero) **2** PRETEND : fingir, aparentar

counterfeit² *adj* : falso, inauténtico

counterfeit³ *n* : falsificación *f*

counterfeiter [ˈkaʊntərˌfɪtər] *n* : falsificador *m*, -dora *f*

countermand [ˈkaʊntərˌmænd, ˌkaʊntərˈ-] *vt* : contramandar

countermeasure [ˈkaʊntərˌmɛʒər] *n* : contramedida *f*

counterpart [ˈkaʊntərˌpɑrt] *n* : homólogo *m*, contraparte *f Mex*

counterpoint [ˈkaʊntərˌpɔɪnt] *n* : contrapunto *m*

counterproductive [ˌkaʊntərprəˈdʌktɪv] *adj* : contraproducente

counterrevolution [ˌkaʊntərˌrevə-ˈluːʃən] *n* : contrarrevolución *f*

counterrevolutionary¹ [ˌkaʊntərˌrevə-ˈluːʃənˌɛri] *adj* : contrarrevolucionario

counterrevolutionary² *n, pl* **-ries** : contrarrevolucionario *m*, -ria *f*

countersign [ˈkaʊntərˌsaɪn] *n* : contraseña *f*

countess [ˈkaʊntɪs] *n* : condesa *f*

countless [ˈkaʊntləs] *adj* : incontable, innumerable

country¹ [ˈkʌntri] *adj* : campestre, rural

country² *n, pl* **-tries 1** NATION : país *m*, nación *f*, patria *f* ⟨country of origin : país de origen⟩ ⟨love of one's country : amor a la patria⟩ **2** : campo *m* ⟨they left the city for the country : se fueron de la ciudad al campo⟩

countryman [ˈkʌntrimən] *n, pl* **-men** [-mən, -ˌmɛn] : compatriota *mf*; paisano *m*, -na *f*

countryside [ˈkʌntriˌsaɪd] *n* : campo *m*, campiña *f*

county [ˈkaʊnti] *n, pl* **-ties** : condado *m*

coup [ˈkuː] *n, pl* **coups** [ˈkuːz] **1** : golpe *m* maestro **2** → **coup d'état**

coup de grâce *or* **coup de grace** [ˌkuːdəˈgrɑs] *ns & pl* : tiro *m* de gracia, golpe *m* de gracia

coup d'état *or* **coup d'etat** [ˌkuːdeɪˈtɑ] *n, pl* **coups d'état** *or* **coups d'etat** [ˌkuːdeɪˈtɑ] : golpe *m* (de estado), cuartelazo *m*

coupe [ˈkuːp] *n* : cupé *m*

couple¹ [ˈkʌpəl] *vt* **-pled; -pling** : acoplar, enganchar, conectar

couple² *n* **1** PAIR : par *m* ⟨a couple of hours : un par de horas, unas dos horas⟩ **2** : pareja *f* ⟨a young couple : una pareja joven⟩

coupling [ˈkʌplɪŋ] *n* : acoplamiento *m*

coupon [ˈkuːˌpɑn, ˈkjuː-] *n* : cupón *m*

courage [ˈkərɪdʒ] *n* : valor *m*, valentía *f*, coraje *m*

courageous [kəˈreɪdʒəs] *adj* : valiente, valeroso

courageously [kəˈreɪdʒəsli] *adv* : con valor, con coraje

courier [ˈkʊriər, ˈkəriər] *n* : mensajero *m*, -ra *f*

course¹ [ˈkors] *vi* **coursed; coursing** : correr (a toda velocidad)

course² *n* **1** PROGRESS : curso *m*, transcurso *m* ⟨to run its course : seguir su curso⟩ ⟨to follow the normal course : seguir su curso normal⟩ ⟨in due course : a su debido tiempo⟩ ⟨in/during the course of : en/durante el transcurso de⟩ **2** DIRECTION : rumbo *m* (de un avión), derrota *f*, derrotero *m* (de un barco) ⟨to stay on course : mantener el rumbo⟩ ⟨to go off course : desviarse de su rumbo⟩ **3** PATH, WAY : camino *m*, vía *f* **4** : plato *m* (de una cena) ⟨the main course : el plato principal⟩ **5** : curso *m* (académico) **6** : pista *f* (de carreras, de esquí, de obstáculos), campo *m* (de golf) **7** **course of action** : línea *f* de conducta **8** **of course** : desde luego, por supuesto ⟨yes, of course! : ¡claro que sí!⟩

court¹ [ˈkort] *vt* WOO : cortejar, galantear

court² *n* **1** PALACE : palacio *m* **2** RETINUE : corte *f*, séquito *m* **3** COURTYARD : patio *m* **4** : cancha *f* (de tenis, baloncesto, etc.) **5** TRIBUNAL : corte *f*, tribunal *m* ⟨the Supreme Court : la Corte Suprema⟩

courteous [ˈkərtiəs] *adj* : cortés, atento, educado — **courteously** *adv*

courtesan [ˈkortəzən, ˈkər-] *n* : cortesana *f*

courtesy [ˈkərtəsi] *n, pl* **-sies** : cortesía *f*

courthouse [ˈkortˌhaʊs] *n* : palacio *m* de justicia, juzgado *m*

courtier [ˈkortiər, ˈkortjər] *n* : cortesano *m*, -na *f*

courtly [ˈkortli] *adj* **courtlier; -est** : distinguido, elegante, cortés

court–martial¹ [ˈkortˌmɑrʃəl] *vt* : someter a consejo de guerra

court–martial² *n, pl* **courts–martial** [ˈkortsˌmɑrʃəl] : consejo *m* de guerra

court order *n* : mandamiento *m* judicial

courtroom [ˈkortˌruːm] *n* : tribunal *m*, corte *f*

courtship [ˈkortˌʃɪp] *n* : cortejo *m*, noviazgo *m*

courtyard [ˈkortˌjɑrd] *n* : patio *m*

cousin [ˈkʌzən] *n* : primo *m*, -ma *f*

couture [ku:'tʊr] *n* : industria *f* de la moda ⟨haute couture : alta costura⟩

cove ['ko:v] *n* : ensenada *f*, cala *f*

covenant ['kʌvənənt] *n* : pacto *m*, contrato *m*

cover[1] ['kʌvər] *vt* **1** : cubrir, tapar ⟨cover your head : cúbrete la cabeza⟩ ⟨cover your eyes : tápate los ojos⟩ ⟨cover the pot : tapa la olla, ponle la tapa a la olla⟩ ⟨covered with mud : cubierto de lodo⟩ **2** : tratar (un tema), cubrir (noticias) **3** INSURE : cubrir, asegurar **4** GUARD, PROTECT : cubrir **5** : cubrir (gastos) **6** TRAVEL : recorrer, cubrir **7** **to cover one's ass/butt** *fam* : cubrirse las espaldas **8** **to cover up** : cubrir, tapar **9** **to cover up** HIDE : ocultar — *vi* **1** **to cover for** REPLACE : sustituir a **2** **to cover for** PROTECT : encubrir a

cover[2] *n* **1** SHELTER : cubierta *f*, abrigo *m*, refugio *m* ⟨to take cover : ponerse a cubierto⟩ ⟨under cover of darkness : al amparo de la oscuridad⟩ **2** LID, TOP : cubierta *f*, tapa *f* **3** : cubierta *f* (de un libro), portada *f* (de una revista) ⟨to read from cover to cover : leer de principio a fin⟩ **4** : funda *f* (protectora) **5** FRONT, FACADE : fachada *f* **6 covers** *npl* BEDCLOTHES : ropa *f* de cama, cobijas *fpl*, mantas *fpl*

coverage ['kʌvərɪdʒ] *n* : cobertura *f*

coveralls ['kʌvər,ɔlz] *npl* : overol *m* (con mangas)

covering ['kʌvərɪŋ] *n* : cubierta *f*

coverlet ['kʌvərlət] *n* : cobertor *m*

cover letter *n* : carta *f* de presentación

covert[1] ['ko:,vərt, 'kʌvərt] *adj* : encubierto, secreto ⟨covert operations : operaciones encubiertas⟩

covert[2] ['kʌvərt, 'ko:-] *n* THICKET : espesura *f*, maleza *f*

cover–up ['kʌvər,ʌp] *n* : encubrimiento *m* (de algo ilícito)

covet ['kʌvət] *vt* : codiciar

covetous ['kʌvətəs] *adj* : codicioso

covey ['kʌvi] *n*, *pl* **-eys** **1** : bandada *f* pequeña (de codornices, etc.) **2** GROUP : grupo *m*

cow[1] ['kaʊ] *vt* : intimidar, acobardar

cow[2] *n* : vaca *f*, hembra *f* (de ciertas especies)

coward ['kaʊərd] *n* : cobarde *mf*

cowardice ['kaʊərdɪs] *n* : cobardía *f*

cowardly ['kaʊərdli] *adj* : cobarde

cowbell ['kaʊ,bel] *n* : cencerro *m*, esquila *f*

cowboy ['kaʊ,bɔɪ] *n* : vaquero *m*, cowboy *m*

cower ['kaʊər] *vi* : encogerse (de miedo), acobardarse

cowgirl ['kaʊ,gərl] *n* : vaquera *f*

cowherd ['kaʊ,hərd] *n* : vaquero *m*, -ra *f*

cowhide ['kaʊ,haɪd] *n* : cuero *m*, piel *f* de vaca

cowl ['kaʊl] *n* : capucha *f* (de un monje)

cowlick ['kaʊ,lɪk] *n* : remolino *m*

coworker ['ko:,wərkər] *n* : colega *mf*; compañero *m*, -ra *f* de trabajo

cowpuncher ['kaʊ,pʌntʃər] → **cowboy**

cowslip ['kaʊ,slɪp] *n* : prímula *f*, primavera *f*

coxswain ['kɑksən, -,sweɪn] *n* : timonel *m*

coy ['kɔɪ] *adj* **1** SHY : tímido, cohibido **2** FLIRTATIOUS : coqueto

coyote [kaɪ'o:ṭi, 'kaɪ,o:t] *n*, *pl* **coyotes** *or* **coyote** : coyote *m*

cozy ['ko:zi] *adj* **cozier**; **-est** : acogedor, cómodo

CPR [,si:,pi:'ɑr] *n* (cardiopulmonary resuscitation) : resucitación *f* cardiopulmonar

CPU [,si:,pi:'ju:] *n* (central processing unit) : CPU *mf*, UPC *mf*, UCP *mf*

crab ['kræb] *n* : cangrejo *m*, jaiba *f*

crabby ['kræbi] *adj* **crabbier**; **-est** : gruñón, malhumorado

crabgrass ['kræb,græs] *n* : digitaria *f*, gramilla *f*

crack[1] ['kræk] *vt* **1** : chasquear, hacer restallar (un látigo, etc.) ⟨to crack one's knuckles : hacer crujir los nudillos⟩ **2** SPLIT : rajar, agrietar, resquebrajar **3** BREAK : romper (un huevo), cascar (nueces), forzar (una caja fuerte) **4** OPEN : abrir (un libro), dejar entreabierta (una puerta, etc.) **5** SOLVE : resolver, descifrar (un código) **6** **to crack a smile** : sonreír — *vi* **1** : restallar ⟨the whip cracked : el látigo restalló⟩ **2** SPLIT : rajarse, resquebrajarse, agrietarse **3** : quebrarse (dícese de la voz) **4** : dejar de resistirse (en un interrogatorio, etc.) ⟨he cracked under the strain : sufrió una crisis nerviosa⟩ **5** **to crack down on** : tomar medidas severas contra **6** **to crack up** : echarse a reír **7** **to get cracking** : ponerse manos a la obra

crack[2] *adj* FIRST-RATE : buenísimo, de primera

crack[3] *n* **1** : chasquido *m*, restallido *m*, estallido *m* (de un arma de fuego), crujido *m* (de huesos) ⟨a crack of thunder : un trueno⟩ **2** WISECRACK : chiste *m*, ocurrencia *f*, salida *f* **3** CREVICE : raja *f*, grieta *f*, fisura *f* **4** BLOW : golpe *m* **5** ATTEMPT : intento *m*

crackdown ['kræk,daʊn] *n* : medidas *fpl* enérgicas

crack down *vt* : tomar medidas enérgicas

cracker ['krækər] *n* : galleta *f* (de soda, etc.)

crackle[1] ['krækəl] *vi* **-led**; **-ling** : chisporrotear, crujir

crackle[2] *n* : crujido *m*

crackpot ['kræk,pɑt] *n* : excéntrico *m*, -ca *f*; chiflado *m*, -da *f*

crack–up ['kræk,ʌp] *n* **1** CRASH : choque *m*, estrellamiento *m* **2** BREAKDOWN : crisis *f* nerviosa

crack up *vt* **1** : estrellar (un vehículo) **2** : hacer reír **3** : elogiar ⟨it isn't all that it's cracked up to be : no es tan bueno como se dice⟩ — *vi* **1** : estrellarse **2** LAUGH : echarse a reír

cradle[1] ['kreɪdəl] *vt* **-dled**; **-dling** : acunar, mecer (a un niño)

cradle[2] *n* : cuna *f*

craft ['kræft] *n* **1** TRADE : oficio *m* ⟨the craft of carpentry : el oficio de carpintero⟩ **2** CRAFTSMANSHIP, SKILL : arte *m*, artesanía *f*, destreza *f* **3** CRAFTINESS

: astucia *f*, maña *f* **4** *pl usually* **craft BOAT** : barco *m*, embarcación *f* **5** *pl usually* **craft** AIRCRAFT : avión *m*, aeronave *f*

craftiness ['kræftinəs] *n* : astucia *f*, maña *f*

craftsman ['kræftsmən] *n, pl* **-men** [-mən, -ˌmɛn] : artesano *m*, -na *f*

craftsmanship ['kræftsmənˌʃɪp] *n* : artesanía *f*, destreza *f*

crafty ['kræfti] *adj* **craftier; -est** : astuto, taimado

crag ['kræg] *n* : peñasco *m*

craggy ['krægi] *adj* **craggier; -est** : peñascoso

cram ['kræm] *v* **crammed; cramming** *vt* **1** JAM : embutir, meter **2** STUFF : atiborrar, abarrotar ⟨crammed with people : atiborrado de gente⟩ — *vi* : estudiar a última hora, memorizar (para un examen)

cramp¹ ['kræmp] *vt* **1** : dar calambre en **2** RESTRICT : limitar, restringir, entorpecer ⟨to cramp someone's style : cortarle el vuelo a alguien⟩ — *vi or* **to cramp up** : acalambrarse

cramp² *n* **1** SPASM : calambre *m*, espasmo *m* (de los músculos) **2 cramps** *npl* : retorcijones *mpl* ⟨stomach cramps : retorcijones de estómago⟩

cranberry ['krænˌbɛri] *n, pl* **-berries** : arándano *m* (rojo y agrio)

crane¹ ['kreɪn] *vt* **craned; craning** : estirar ⟨to crane one's neck : estirar el cuello⟩

crane² *n* **1** : grulla *f* (ave) **2** : grúa *f* (máquina)

cranial ['kreɪniəl] *adj* : craneal, craneano

cranium ['kreɪniəm] *n, pl* **-niums** *or* **-nia** [-niə] : cráneo *m*

crank¹ ['kræŋk] *vt or* **to crank up** : arrancar (con una manivela)

crank² *n* **1** : manivela *f*, manubrio *m* **2** ECCENTRIC : excéntrico *m*, -ca *f*

cranky ['kræŋki] *adj* **crankier; -est** : irritable, malhumorado

cranny ['kræni] *n, pl* **-nies** : grieta *f* ⟨every nook and cranny : todos los rincones⟩

crash¹ ['kræʃ] *vi* **1** SMASH : caerse con estrépito, estrellarse **2** COLLIDE : estrellarse, chocar **3** BOOM, RESOUND : retumbar, resonar — *vt* **1** SMASH : estrellar **2 to crash a party** : colarse en una fiesta **3 to crash one's car** : tener un accidente

crash² *n* **1** DIN : estrépito *m* **2** COLLISION : choque *m*, colisión *f* ⟨car crash : accidente automovilístico⟩ **3** FAILURE : quiebra *f* (de un negocio), crac *m* (de la bolsa)

crash course *n* : curso *m* intensivo

crash helmet *n* : casco *m*

crass ['kræs] *adj* : grosero, de mal gusto

crate¹ ['kreɪt] *vt* **crated; crating** : empacar en un cajón

crate² *n* : cajón *m* (de madera)

crater ['kreɪtər] *n* : cráter *m*

cravat [krə'væt] *n* : corbata *f*

crave ['kreɪv] *vt* **craved; craving** : ansiar, apetecer, tener muchas ganas de

craven ['kreɪvən] *adj* : cobarde, pusilánime

craving ['kreɪvɪŋ] *n* : ansia *f*, antojo *m*, deseo *m*

crawfish ['krɔˌfɪʃ] → **crayfish**

crawl¹ ['krɔl] *vi* **1** CREEP : arrastrarse, gatear (dícese de un bebé) **2** TEEM : estar plagado

crawl² *n* **1** : paso *m* lento **2** : crol *m* (en natación)

crayfish ['kreɪˌfɪʃ] *n* **1** : ástaco *m* (de agua dulce) **2** : langostino *m* (de mar)

crayon ['kreɪˌɑn, -ən] *n* : crayón *m*

craze ['kreɪz] *n* : moda *f* pasajera, manía *f*

crazed ['kreɪzd] *adj* : enloquecido

crazily ['kreɪzəli] *adv* : locamente, erráticamente, insensatamente

craziness ['kreɪzinəs] *n* : locura *f*, demencia *f*

crazy ['kreɪzi] *adj* **crazier; -est 1** *usu offensive* INSANE : loco, demente ⟨to go crazy : volverse loco⟩ **2** ABSURD, FOOLISH : loco, insensato, absurdo **3** WEIRD, OUTLANDISH : extraño, raro **4** WILD : loco ⟨the team won and the crowd went crazy : el equipo ganó y el público se enloqueció⟩ **5 like crazy** : como loco **6 to be crazy about** : estar loco por **7 to drive/make someone crazy** : sacar a alguien de quicio

creak¹ ['kri:k] *vi* : chirriar, rechinar, crujir

creak² *n* : chirrido *m*, crujido *m*

creaky ['kri:ki] *adj* **creakier; -est** : chirriante, que cruje

cream¹ ['kri:m] *vt* **1** BEAT, MIX : batir, mezclar (azúcar y mantequilla, etc.) **2** : preparar (alimentos) con crema

cream² *n* **1** : crema *f*, nata *f* *Spain* (de leche) ⟨whipped cream : crema batida, nata montada⟩ **2** LOTION : crema *f*, loción *f* **3** ELITE : crema *f*, elite *f* ⟨the cream of the crop : la crema y nata, lo mejor⟩

cream cheese *n* : queso *m* crema

creamery ['kri:məri] *n, pl* **-eries** : fábrica *f* de productos lácteos

creamy ['kri:mi] *adj* **creamier; -est** : cremoso

crease¹ ['kri:s] *vt* **creased; creasing 1** : plegar, poner una raya en (pantalones) **2** WRINKLE : arrugar

crease² *n* : pliegue *m*, doblez *m*, raya *f* (de pantalones)

create [kri'eɪt] *vt* **-ated; -ating** : crear, hacer

creation [kri'eɪʃən] *n* : creación *f*

creative [kri'eɪtɪv] *adj* : creativo, original ⟨creative people : personas creativas⟩ ⟨a creative work : un obra original⟩

creatively [kri'eɪtɪvli] *adv* : creativamente, con originalidad

creativity [ˌkri:eɪˈtɪvəti] *n* : creatividad *f*

creator [kri'eɪtər] *n* : creador *m*, -dora *f*

creature ['kri:tʃər] *n* : ser *m* viviente, criatura *f*, animal *m*

créche ['krɛʃ, 'kreɪʃ] *n* : nacimiento *m*

credence ['kri:dəns] *n* : crédito *m*

credentials [krɪ'dɛntʃəlz] *npl* : referencias *fpl* oficiales, cartas *fpl* credenciales

credibility [ˌkrɛdə'bɪləti] *n* : credibilidad *f*

credible ['krɛdəbəl] *adj* : creíble
credit¹ ['krɛdɪt] *vt* **1** BELIEVE : creer, dar crédito a **2** : ingresar, abonar ⟨to credit $100 to an account : ingresar $100 en (una) cuenta⟩ **3** ATTRIBUTE : atribuir ⟨they credit the invention to him : a él se le atribuye el invento⟩
credit² *n* **1** : saldo *m* positivo, saldo *m* a favor (de una cuenta) **2** : crédito *m* ⟨to buy on credit : comprar a crédito⟩ ⟨credit card : tarjeta de crédito⟩ ⟨credit limit : límite de crédito⟩ ⟨credit history : historial crediticio⟩ **3** CREDENCE : crédito *m* ⟨I gave credit to everything he said : di crédito a todo lo que dijo⟩ **4** RECOGNITION : reconocimiento *m* ⟨he deserves all the credit : todo el mérito es suyo⟩ ⟨to get/take the credit for : llevarse/atribuirse el mérito de⟩ **5** : orgullo *m*, honor *m* ⟨she's a credit to the school : ella es el orgullo de la escuela⟩ **6** : crédito *m* ⟨a course worth three credits : un curso de tres créditos⟩ ⟨extra credit : puntos extras⟩ **7 credits** *npl* : créditos *mpl* (de una película)
creditable ['krɛdɪtəbəl] *adj* : encomiable, loable — **creditably** [-bli] *adv*
credit card *n* : tarjeta de crédito
creditor ['krɛdɪtər] *n* : acreedor *m*, -dora *f*
credo ['kri:do:, 'krei-] *n* : credo *m*
credulity [krɪ'du:ləti, -'dju:-] *n* : credulidad *f*
credulous ['krɛdʒələs] *adj* : crédulo
creed ['kri:d] *n* : credo *m*
creek ['kri:k, 'krɪk] *n* : arroyo *m*, riachuelo *m*
creel ['kri:l] *n* : nasa *f*, cesta *f* (de pescador)
creep¹ ['kri:p] *vi* **crept** ['krɛpt]; **creeping 1** CRAWL : arrastrarse, gatear **2** : moverse lentamente o sigilosamente ⟨he crept out of the house : salió sigilosamente de la casa⟩ **3** SPREAD : trepar (dícese de una planta)
creep² *n* **1** CRAWL : paso *m* lento **2** : asqueroso *m*, -sa *f* **3 creeps** *npl* : escalofríos *mpl* ⟨that gives me the creeps : eso me da escalofríos⟩
creeper ['kri:pər] *n* : planta *f* trepadora, trepadora *f*
creepy ['kri:pi] *adj* **1** SPOOKY : que da miedo, espeluznante **2** UNPLEASANT : asqueroso
cremate ['kri:,meɪt] *vt* **-mated; -mating** : cremar
cremation [krɪ'meɪʃən] *n* : cremación *f*
crematorium [,kri:mə'toriəm, ,krɛ-] *n* : crematorio *m*
Creole ['kri:,o:l] *n* **1** : criollo *m*, criolla *f* **2** : criollo *m* (idioma) — **Creole** *adj*
crepe *or* **crêpe** ['kreɪp] *n* **1** : crespón *m* (tela) **2** PANCAKE : crepe *mf*, crepa *f Mex*
crepe paper *n* : papel *m* crepé
crescendo [krɪ'ʃɛn,do:] *n, pl* **-dos** *or* **-does** : crescendo *m*
crescent ['krɛsənt] *n* : creciente *m*
crest ['krɛst] *n* **1** : cresta *f*, penacho *m* (de un ave) **2** PEAK, TOP : cresta *f* (de una ola), cima *f* (de una colina) **3** : emblema *m* (sobre un escudo de armas)

crestfallen ['krɛst,fɔlən] *adj* : alicaído, abatido
cretin ['kri:tən] *n* **1** *often offensive* : cretino *m*, -na *f* (en medicina) **2** : cretino *m*, -na *f*; imbécil *mf*
crevasse [krɪ'væs] *n* : grieta *f*, fisura *f*
crevice ['krɛvɪs] *n* : grieta *f*, hendidura *f*
crew ['kru:] *n* **1** : tripulación *f* (de una nave) **2** TEAM : equipo *m* (de trabajadores o atletas)
crew cut *n* : pelo *m* al rape, casquete *m* corto *Mex*
crib ['krɪb] *n* **1** MANGER : pesebre *m* **2** GRANARY : granero *m* **3** : cuna *f* (de un bebé)
crick ['krɪk] *n* : calambre *m*, espasmo *m* muscular
cricket ['krɪkət] *n* **1** : grillo *m* (insecto) **2** : críquet *m* (juego)
crime ['kraɪm] *n* **1** : crimen *m*, delito *m* ⟨to commit a crime : cometer un delito⟩ **2** : crimen *m*, delincuencia *f* ⟨organized crime : crimen organizado⟩
criminal¹ ['krɪmənəl] *adj* : criminal
criminal² *n* : criminal *mf*, delincuente *mf*
crimp ['krɪmp] *vt* : ondular, rizar (el pelo), arrugar (una tela, etc.)
crimson ['krɪmzən] *n* : carmesí *m*
cringe ['krɪndʒ] *vi* **cringed; cringing** : encogerse
crinkle¹ ['krɪŋkəl] *v* **-kled; -kling** *vt* : arrugar — *vi* : arrugarse
crinkle² *n* : arruga *f*
crinkly ['krɪŋkəli] *adj* : arrugado
cripple¹ ['krɪpəl] *vt* **-pled; -pling 1** DISABLE : lisiar, dejar inválido **2** INCAPACITATE : inutilizar, incapacitar
cripple² *n* *offensive* : lisiado *m*, -da *f offensive*
crisis ['kraɪsɪs] *n, pl* **crises** [-,si:z] : crisis *f*
crisp¹ ['krɪsp] *vt* : tostar, hacer crujiente
crisp² *adj* **1** CRUNCHY : crujiente, crocante **2** FIRM, FRESH : firme, fresco ⟨crisp lettuce : lechuga fresca⟩ **3** LIVELY : vivaz, alegre ⟨a crisp tempo : un ritmo alegre⟩ **4** INVIGORATING : fresco, vigorizante ⟨the crisp autumn air : el fresco aire otoñal⟩ — **crisply** *adv*
crisp³ *n* : postre *m* de fruta (con pedacitos de masa dulce por encima)
crispy ['krɪspi] *adj* **crispier; -est** : crujiente ⟨crispy potato chips : papitas crujientes⟩
crisscross ['krɪs,krɔs] *vt* : entrecruzar
criterion [kraɪ'tɪriən] *n, pl* **-ria** [-iə] : criterio *m*
critic ['krɪtɪk] *n* **1** : crítico *m*, -ca *f* (de las artes) **2** FAULTFINDER : detractor *m*, -tora *f*; criticón *m*, -cona *f*
critical ['krɪtɪkəl] *adj* : crítico
critically ['krɪtɪkli] *adv* : críticamente ⟨critically ill : gravemente enfermo⟩
criticism ['krɪtə,sɪzəm] *n* : crítica *f*
criticize ['krɪtə,saɪz] *vt* **-cized; -cizing 1** EVALUATE, JUDGE : criticar, analizar, evaluar **2** CENSURE : criticar, reprobar
critique [krɪ'ti:k] *n* : crítica *f*, evaluación *f*
croak¹ ['kro:k] *vi* : croar
croak² *n* : croar *m*, canto *m* (de la rana)

Croatian · cruel

Croatian [kro'eɪʃən] *n* : croata *mf* —
Croatian *adj*
crochet¹ [kro:'ʃeɪ] *v* : tejer al croché
crochet² *n* : croché *m*, crochet *m*
crock ['krɑk] *n* : vasija *f* de barro
crockery ['krɑkəri] *n* : vajilla *f* (de barro)
crocodile ['krɑkə,daɪl] *n* : cocodrilo *m*
crocus ['kro:kəs] *n, pl* **-cuses** : azafrán *m*
croissant [krə'sɑnt] *n* : croissant *m*
crone ['kro:n] *n* : vieja *f* bruja
crony ['kro:ni] *n, pl* **-nies** : amigote *m*
fam; compinche *mf fam*
crook¹ ['krʊk] *vt* : doblar (el brazo o el
dedo)
crook² *n* **1** STAFF : cayado *m* (de pastor),
báculo *m* (de obispo) **2** THIEF : ratero
m, -ra *f*; ladrón *m*, -drona *f*
crooked ['krʊkəd] *adj* **1** BENT : chueco,
torcido **2** DISHONEST : deshonesto
crookedness ['krʊkədnəs] *n* **1** : lo torcido, lo chueco **2** DISHONESTY : falta *f*
de honradez
croon ['kru:n] *v* : cantar suavemente
crop¹ ['krɑp] *v* **cropped; cropping** *vt* TRIM
: recortar, cortar — *vi* **to crop up** : aparecer, surgir ⟨these problems keep cropping up : estos problemas no cesan de
surgir⟩
crop² *n* **1** : buche *m* (de un ave o insecto) **2** WHIP : fusta *f* (de jinete) **3**
HARVEST : cosecha *f*, cultivo *m*
croquet [,kro:'keɪ] *n* : croquet *m*
croquette [,kro:'kɛt] *n* : croqueta *f*
cross¹ ['krɔs] *vt* **1** : cruzar, atravesar ⟨to
cross the street : cruzar la calle⟩ ⟨several
canals cross the city : varios canales
atraviesan la ciudad⟩ **2** : cruzar (los
brazos, los dedos, las piernas) **3** INTER-
BREED : cruzar (en genética) **4 cross
my heart** : te lo juro **5 to cross off/out**
: tachar ⟨he crossed his name off the list
: tachó su nombre de la planilla⟩ ⟨he
crossed off/out his name : tachó su nom-
bre⟩ **6 to cross one's mind** : ocurrírsele a uno **7 to cross paths** : cruzarse con alguien ⟨I crossed paths with
him, we crossed paths : me crucé con él⟩
cross² *adj* **1** : que atraviesa ⟨cross ventilation : ventilación que atraviesa un
cuarto⟩ **2** CONTRARY : contrario, opuesto
⟨cross purposes : objetivos opuestos⟩ **3**
ANGRY : enojado, de mal humor
cross³ *n* **1** : cruz *f* ⟨the sign of the cross
: la señal de la cruz⟩ **2** : cruza *f* (en
biología)
crossbar ['krɔs,bɑr] *n* : travesaño *m*,
tranca *f*
crossbones ['krɔs,bo:nz] *npl* **1** : huesos
mpl cruzados **2** → **skull**
crossbow ['krɔs,bo:] *n* : ballesta *f*
crossbreed ['krɔs,bri:d] *vt* **-bred** [-,brɛd];
-breeding : cruzar
cross–country ['krɔs'kʌntri] *n* : cross *m*
crosscurrent ['krɔs,kərənt] *n* : contracorriente *f*
cross–examination [,krɔsɪg,zæmə-
'neɪʃən] *n* : repreguntas *fpl*, interrogatorio *m*
cross–examine [,krɔsɪg'zæmən] *vt* **-ined;
-ining** : repreguntar

cross–eyed ['krɔs,aɪd] *adj* : bizco
crossfire ['krɔs,faɪr] *n* : fuego *m* cruzado
crossing ['krɔsɪŋ] *n* **1** INTERSECTION
: cruce *m*, paso *m* ⟨pedestrian crossing
: paso de peatones⟩ **2** VOYAGE : travesía
f (del mar)
cross–legged ['krɔs,lɛgəd] *adv* : con las
piernas cruzadas
crossly ['krɔsli] *adv* : con enojo, con enfado
crosspiece ['krɔs,pi:s] *n* : travesaño *m*
cross–reference [,krɔs'rɛfrənts, -'rɛfə-
rənts] *n* : referencia *f*, remisión *f*
crossroads ['krɔs,ro:dz] *n* : cruce *m*, encrucijada *f*, crucero *m Mex*
cross section *n* **1** SECTION : corte *m*
transversal **2** SAMPLE : muestra *f* representativa ⟨a cross section of the population : una muestra representativa de la
población⟩
crosswalk ['krɔs,wɔk] *n* : cruce *m* peatonal, paso *m* de peatones
crossways ['krɔs,weɪz] → **crosswise**
crosswise¹ ['krɔs,waɪz] *adv* : transversalmente, diagonalmente
crosswise² *adj* : transversal, diagonal
crossword ['krɔs,wərd] *or* **crossword
puzzle** *n* : crucigrama *m*
crotch ['krɑtʃ] *n* : entrepierna *f*
crotchety ['krɑtʃəti] *adj* CRANKY : malhumorado, irritable, enojadizo
crouch ['kraʊtʃ] *vi* : agacharse, ponerse
de cuclillas
croup ['kru:p] *n* : crup *m*
crouton ['kru:,tɑn] *n* : crutón *m*
crow¹ ['kro:] *vi* **1** : cacarear, cantar
(como un cuervo) **2** BRAG : alardear,
presumir
crow² *n* **1** : cuervo *m* (ave) **2** : cantar *m*
(del gallo)
crowbar ['kro:,bɑr] *n* : palanca *f*
crowd¹ ['kraʊd] *vi* : aglomerarse, amontonarse — *vt* : atestar, atiborrar, llenar
crowd² *n* : multitud *f*, muchedumbre *f*,
gentío *m*
crowded ['kraʊdəd] *adj* : repleto,
atestado, abarrotado
crown¹ ['kraʊn] *vt* : coronar
crown² *n* : corona *f*
crow's–feet *npl* : patas *fpl* de gallo
crucial ['kru:ʃəl] *adj* : crucial, decisivo
crucible ['kru:səbəl] *n* : crisol *m*
crucifix ['kru:sə,fɪks] *n* : crucifijo *m*
crucifixion [,kru:sə'fɪkʃən] *n* : crucifixión
f
crucify ['kru:sə,faɪ] *vt* **-fied; -fying** : crucificar
crude ['kru:d] *adj* **cruder; -est** **1** RAW,
UNREFINED : crudo, sin refinar ⟨crude
oil : petróleo crudo⟩ **2** VULGAR : grosero, de mal gusto **3** ROUGH : tosco,
burdo, rudo
crudely ['kru:dli] *adv* **1** VULGARLY
: groseramente **2** ROUGHLY : burdamente, de manera rudimentaria
crudity ['kru:dəti] *n, pl* **-ties** **1** VUL-
GARITY : grosería *f* **2** COARSENESS,
ROUGHNESS : tosquedad *f*, rudeza *f*
cruel ['kru:əl] *adj* **crueler** *or* **crueller;
cruelest** *or* **cruellest** : cruel

cruelly ['kru:əli] *adv* : cruelmente

cruelty ['kru:əlti] *n, pl* **-ties** : crueldad *f* ⟨the tyrant's cruelty : la crueldad del tirano⟩ ⟨the cruelties of war : las crueldades de la guerra⟩

cruet ['kru:ɪt] *n* : vinagrera *f*, aceitera *f*

cruise¹ ['kru:z] *vi* **cruised; cruising** 1 : hacer un crucero 2 : navegar o conducir a una velocidad constante ⟨cruising speed : velocidad de crucero⟩

cruise² *n* : crucero *m*

cruiser ['kru:zər] *n* 1 WARSHIP : crucero *m*, buque *m* de guerra 2 : patrulla *f* (de policía)

crumb ['krʌm] *n* : miga *f*, migaja *f* ⟨bread crumbs : migas de pan, pan rallado⟩

crumble ['krʌmbəl] *v* **-bled; -bling** *vt* : desmigajar, desmenuzar — *vi* : desmigajarse, desmoronarse, desmenuzarse

crumbly ['krʌmbli] *adj* : que se desmenuza fácilmente

crummy ['krʌmi] *adj* **crummier; -est** *fam* : malo

crumple ['krʌmpəl] *v* **-pled; -pling** *vt* RUMPLE : arrugar — *vi* 1 WRINKLE : arrugarse 2 COLLAPSE : desplomarse

crunch¹ ['krʌntʃ] *vt* 1 : ronzar (con los dientes) 2 : hacer crujir (con los pies, etc.) — *vi* : crujir

crunch² *n* : crujido *m*

crunchy ['krʌntʃi] *adj* **crunchier; -est** : crujiente

crusade¹ [kru:'seɪd] *vi* **-saded; -sading** : hacer una campaña (a favor de o contra algo)

crusade² *n* 1 : campaña *f* (de reforma, etc.) 2 **Crusade** : cruzada *f*

crusader [kru:'seɪdər] *n* 1 : cruzado *m* (en la Edad Media) 2 : campeón *m*, -peona *f* (de una causa)

crush¹ ['krʌʃ] *vt* 1 SQUASH : aplastar, apachurrar 2 GRIND, PULVERIZE : triturar, machacar 3 SUPPRESS : aplastar, suprimir 4 DEFEAT : darle una paliza a

crush² *n* 1 CROWD, MOB : gentío *m*, multitud *f*, aglomeración *f* 2 INFATUATION : enamoramiento *m*

crushing ['krʌʃɪŋ] *adj* : aplastante, abrumador

crust ['krʌst] *n* 1 : corteza *f*, costra *f* (de pan) 2 : tapa *f* de masa, pasta *f* (de un pastel) 3 LAYER : capa *f*, corteza *f* ⟨the earth's crust : la corteza terrestre⟩

crustacean [ˌkrʌs'teɪʃən] *n* : crustáceo *m*

crusty ['krʌsti] *adj* **crustier; -est** 1 : de corteza dura 2 CROSS, GRUMPY : enojado, malhumorado

crutch ['krʌtʃ] *n* : muleta *f*

crux ['krʌks, 'krʊks] *n, pl* **cruxes** : quid *m*, esencia *f*, meollo *m* ⟨the crux of the problem : el quid del problema⟩

cry¹ ['kraɪ] *vi* **cried; crying** 1 SHOUT : gritar 2 WEEP : llorar 3 **to cry for** DEMAND : pedir a gritos, clamar por 4 **to cry out** : gritar (de dolor, etc.) 5 **to cry out against** : clamar contra 6 **to cry over** : llorar por

cry² *n, pl* **cries** 1 SHOUT : grito *m* 2 WEEPING : llanto *m* 3 : chillido *m* (de un animal)

crybaby ['kraɪˌbeɪbi] *n, pl* **-bies** : llorón *m*, -rona *f*

crypt ['krɪpt] *n* : cripta *f*

cryptic ['krɪptɪk] *adj* : enigmático, críptico

cryptocurrency [ˌkrɪpto'kərəntsi] *n, pl* **-cies** : criptomoneda *f*, criptodivisa *f*

crystal ['krɪstəl] *n* : cristal *m*

crystalline ['krɪstəlɪn] *adj* : cristalino

crystallize ['krɪstəˌlaɪz] *v* **-lized; -lizing** *vt* : cristalizar, materializar ⟨to crystallize one's thoughts : cristalizar uno sus pensamientos⟩ — *vi* : cristalizarse

C–section ['si:ˌsɛkʃən] → **cesarean²**

cub ['kʌb] *n* : cachorro *m*

Cuban ['kju:bən] *n* : cubano *m*, -na *f* — **Cuban** *adj*

cubbyhole ['kʌbiˌho:l] *n* : chiribitil *m*

cube¹ ['kju:b] *vt* **cubed; cubing** 1 : elevar (un número) al cubo 2 : cortar en cubos

cube² *n* 1 : cubo *m* 2 **ice cube** : cubito *m* de hielo 3 **sugar cube** : terrón *m* de azúcar

cubic ['kju:bɪk] *adj* : cúbico

cubicle ['kju:bɪkəl] *n* : cubículo *m*

cuckoo¹ ['ku:ˌku:, 'kʊ-] *adj* : loco, chiflado

cuckoo² *n, pl* **-oos** : cuco *m*, cuclillo *m*

cucumber ['kju:ˌkʌmbər] *n* : pepino *m*

cud ['kʌd] *n* **to chew the cud** : rumiar

cuddle¹ ['kʌdəl] *v* **-dled; -dling** *vi* : abrazarse tiernamente, acurrucarse — *vt* : abrazar

cuddle² *n* : abrazo *m*

cudgel¹ ['kʌdʒəl] *vt* **-geled** *or* **-gelled; -geling** *or* **-gelling** : apalear, aporrear

cudgel² *n* : garrote *m*, porra *f*

cue¹ ['kju:] *vt* **cued; cuing** *or* **cueing** : darle el pie a, darle la señal a

cue² *n* 1 SIGNAL : señal *f*, pie *m* (en teatro), entrada *f* (en música) 2 : taco *m* (de billar)

cuff¹ ['kʌf] *vt* : bofetear, cachetear

cuff² *n* 1 : puño *m* (de una camisa), vuelta *f* (de pantalones) 2 SLAP : bofetada *f*, cachetada *f* 3 **cuffs** *npl* HANDCUFFS : esposas *fpl*

cuff link *n* : gemelo *m*

cuisine [kwɪ'zi:n] *n* : cocina *f* ⟨Mexican cuisine : la cocina mexicana⟩

cul–de–sac ['kʌldɪˌsæk] *n* : calle *f* sin salida

culinary ['kʌləˌnɛri, 'kju:lə-] *adj* : culinario

cull ['kʌl] *vt* : seleccionar

culminate ['kʌlməˌneɪt] *vi* **-nated; -nating** : culminar

culmination [ˌkʌlmə'neɪʃən] *n* : culminación *f*, punto *m* culminante

culpable ['kʌlpəbəl] *adj* : culpable

culprit ['kʌlprɪt] *n* : culpable *mf*

cult ['kʌlt] *n* : culto *m*

cultivate ['kʌltəˌveɪt] *vt* **-vated; -vating** 1 TILL : cultivar, labrar 2 FOSTER : cultivar, fomentar 3 REFINE : cultivar, refinar ⟨to cultivate the mind : cultivar la mente⟩

cultivation [ˌkʌltə'veɪʃən] *n* 1 : cultivo *m* ⟨under cultivation : en cultivo⟩ 2 CUL-

TURE, REFINEMENT : cultura f, refinamiento m

cultural ['kʌltʃərəl] *adj* : cultural — **culturally** *adv*

culture ['kʌltʃər] *n* **1** CULTIVATION : cultivo *m* **2** REFINEMENT : cultura f, educación f, refinamiento *m* **3** CIVILIZATION : cultura f, civilización f ⟨the Incan culture : la cultura inca⟩

cultured ['kʌltʃərd] *adj* **1** EDUCATED, REFINED : culto, educado, refinado **2** : de cultivo, cultivado ⟨cultured pearls : perlas de cultivo⟩

culvert ['kʌlvərt] *n* : alcantarilla f

cumbersome ['kʌmbərsəm] *adj* : torpe y pesado, difícil de manejar

cumin ['kʌmən] *n* : comino *m*

cumulative ['kju:mjələtɪv, -ˌleɪtɪv] *adj* : acumulativo

cumulus ['kju:mjələs] *n, pl* **-li** [-ˌlaɪ, -ˌli:] : cúmulo *m*

cunning[1] ['kʌnɪŋ] *adj* **1** CRAFTY : astuto, taimado **2** CLEVER : ingenioso, hábil **3** CUTE : mono, gracioso, lindo

cunning[2] *n* **1** SKILL : habilidad f **2** CRAFTINESS : astucia f, maña f

cup[1] ['kʌp] *vt* **cupped; cupping** : ahuecar (las manos)

cup[2] *n* **1** : taza f ⟨a cup of coffee : una taza de café⟩ **2** CUPFUL : taza f **3** : media pinta f (unidad de medida) **4** GOBLET : copa f **5** TROPHY : copa f, trofeo *m*

cupboard ['kʌbərd] *n* : alacena f, armario *m*

cupcake ['kʌpˌkeɪk] *n* : pastelito *m*

cupful ['kʌpˌfʊl] *n* : taza f

cupola ['kju:pələ, -ˌlo:] *n* : cúpula f

cur ['kər] *n* : perro *m* callejero, perro *m* corriente *Mex*

curate ['kjʊrət] *n* : cura *m*, párroco *m*

curator ['kjʊrˌeɪtər, kjʊ'reɪtər] *n* : conservador *m*, -dora f (de un museo); director *m*, -tora f (de un zoológico)

curb[1] ['kərb] *vt* : refrenar, restringir, controlar

curb[2] *n* **1** RESTRAINT : freno *m*, control *m* **2** : borde *m* de la acera

curd ['kərd] *n* : cuajada f

curdle ['kərdəl] *v* **-dled; -dling** *vi* : cuajarse — *vt* : cuajar ⟨to curdle one's blood : helarle la sangre a uno⟩

curdled ['kərdəld] *adj* : cortado (dícese de la leche, etc.)

cure[1] ['kjʊr] *vt* **cured; curing 1** HEAL : curar, sanar **2** REMEDY : remediar **3** PROCESS : curar (alimentos, etc.)

cure[2] *n* **1** RECOVERY : curación f, recuperación f **2** REMEDY : cura f, remedio *m*

curfew ['kərˌfju:] *n* : toque *m* de queda

curio ['kjʊriˌo:] *n, pl* **-rios** : curiosidad f, objeto *m* curioso

curiosity [ˌkjʊri'asəti] *n, pl* **-ties** : curiosidad f

curious ['kjʊriəs] *adj* **1** INQUISITIVE : curioso **2** STRANGE : curioso, raro

curl[1] ['kərl] *vt* **1** : rizar, ondular (el pelo) **2** COIL : enrollar **3** TWIST : torcer ⟨to curl one's lip : hacer una mueca⟩ —

vi **1** : rizarse, ondularse **2 to curl up** : acurrucarse (con un libro, etc.)

curl[2] *n* **1** RINGLET : rizo *m* **2** COIL : espiral f, rosca f

curler ['kərlər] *n* : rulo *m*

curlew ['kərˌlu:, 'kərlˌju:] *n, pl* **-lews** or **-lew** : zarapito *m*

curly ['kərli] *adj* **curlier; -est** : rizado, crespo

curly brace or **curly bracket** *n* : llave f (signo de puntuación)

currant ['kərənt] *n* **1** : grosella f (fruta) ⟨black currant : grosella negra⟩ ⟨red currant : grosella roja⟩ **2** RAISIN : pasa f de Corinto

currency ['kərəntsi] *n, pl* **-cies 1** PREVALENCE, USE : uso *m*, aceptación f, difusión f ⟨to be in currency : estar en uso⟩ **2** MONEY : moneda f, dinero *m*

current[1] ['kərənt] *adj* **1** PRESENT : actual ⟨current events : actualidades⟩ **2** PREVALENT : corriente, común — **currently** *adv*

current[2] *n* : corriente f

curriculum [kə'rɪkjələm] *n, pl* **-la** [-lə] : currículum *m*, currículo *m*, programa *m* de estudio

curriculum vitae ['vi:ˌtaɪ, 'vaɪti] *n, pl* **curricula vitae** : currículum *m*, currículo *m*

curry[1] ['kəri] *vt* **-ried; -rying 1** GROOM : almohazar (un caballo) **2** : condimentar con curry **3 to curry favor** : congraciarse (con alguien)

curry[2] *n, pl* **-ries** : curry *m*

curse[1] ['kərs] *v* **cursed; cursing** *vt* **1** DAMN : maldecir **2** INSULT : injuriar, insultar, decir malas palabras a **3** AFFLICT : afligir — *vi* : maldecir, decir malas palabras

curse[2] *n* **1** : maldición f ⟨to put a curse on someone : echarle una maldición a alguien⟩ **2** AFFLICTION : maldición f, aflicción f, cruz f

cursor ['kərsər] *n* : cursor *m*

cursory ['kərsəri] *adj* : rápido, superficial, somero

curt ['kərt] *adj* : cortante, brusco, seco — **curtly** *adv*

curtail [kər'teɪl] *vt* : acortar, limitar, restringir

curtailment [kər'teɪlmənt] *n* : restricción f, limitación f

curtain ['kərtən] *n* : cortina f (de una ventana), telón *m* (en un teatro)

curtness ['kərtnəs] *n* : brusquedad f, sequedad f

curtsy[1] or **curtsey** ['kərtsi] *vt* **-sied** or **-seyed; -sying** or **-seying** : hacer una reverencia

curtsy[2] or **curtsey** *n, pl* **-sies** or **-seys** : reverencia f

curvature ['kərvəˌtʃʊr] *n* : curvatura f

curve[1] ['kərv] *v* **curved; curving** *vi* : torcerse, describir una curva — *vt* : encorvar

curve[2] *n* : curva f

curvy ['kərvi] **curvier; -est** *adj* **1** : con muchas curvas, sinuoso **2** SHAPELY : curvilíneo

cushion[1] ['kʊʃən] *vt* **1** : poner cojines o almohadones a **2** SOFTEN : amortiguar, mitigar, suavizar ⟨to cushion a blow : amortiguar un golpe⟩

cushion² *n* **1** : cojín *m*, almohadón *m* **2** PROTECTION : colchón *m*, protección *f*

cusp ['kʌsp] *n* : cúspide *f* (de un diente), cuerno *m* (de la luna)

cuspid ['kʌspɪd] *n* : diente *m* canino, colmillo *m*

custard ['kʌstərd] *n* : natillas *fpl*

custodian [ˌkʌ'sto:diən] *n* : custodio *m*, -dia *f*; guardián, -diana *f*

custody ['kʌstədi] *n, pl* **-dies** : custodia *f*, cuidado *m* ⟨to be in custody : estar detenido⟩

custom¹ ['kʌstəm] *adj* : a la medida, a la orden

custom² *n* **1** : costumbre *f*, tradición *f* **2** **customs** *npl* : aduana *f* ⟨customs officer : agente de aduanas⟩

customarily [ˌkʌstə'mɛrəli] *adv* : habitualmente, normalmente, de costumbre

customary ['kʌstəˌmɛri] *adj* **1** TRADITIONAL : tradicional **2** USUAL : habitual, de costumbre

customer ['kʌstəmər] *n* : cliente *m*, -ta *f*

customize ['kʌstəˌmaɪz] *vt* **-ized; -izing** : adaptar (algo) a los requisitos de alguien, personalizar — **customization** [ˌkʌstəmə'zeɪʃən] *n*

custom–made ['kʌstəm'meɪd] *adj* : hecho a la medida

cut¹ ['kʌt] *v* **cut; cutting** *vt* **1** : cortar ⟨to cut paper : cortar papel⟩ ⟨to cut the meat into strips : cortar la carne en tiras⟩ ⟨cut the apple in half : cortar la manzana por la mitad⟩ ⟨to cut a hole in : hacer un agujero en⟩ ⟨to cut (off) a piece : cortar un trozo⟩ **2** : cortarse ⟨to cut one's finger : cortarse uno el dedo⟩ **3** TRIM : cortar, recortar ⟨to have one's hair cut : cortarse el pelo⟩ **4** INTERSECT : cruzar, atravesar **5** SHORTEN : acortar, abreviar **6** REDUCE : reducir, rebajar ⟨to cut prices : rebajar los precios⟩ **7** : cortar (en informática) ⟨to cut and paste : cortar y pegar⟩ **8** : cortar (una baraja) **9** : sacar (de un equipo, etc.) **10** SKIP : faltar a (clase) **11** TURN OFF : apagar **12** DILUTE : cortar (drogas) **13** cut it out! : ¡basta ya! **14** not to cut it : no ser lo suficientemente bueno **15** to cut a deal : hacer/cerrar un trato **16** to cut away : cortar **17** to cut back PRUNE : podar **18** to cut back REDUCE : reducir (gastos, etc.) **19** to cut down FELL : cortar, talar **20** to cut down REDUCE : reducir **21** to cut down KILL : matar **22** to cut in : cortar y mezclar (mantequilla, etc.) **23** to cut off : cortar (una rama, una pierna, etc.) **24** to cut off : cortar (el acceso, etc.) **25** to cut off INTERRUPT : interrumpir **26** to cut off ISOLATE : aislar **27** to cut off : cortarle el paso a (un vehículo, etc.) **28** to cut one's teeth : salirle los dientes a uno **29** to cut out CLIP : recortar **30** to cut out EXCLUDE : excluir **31** to cut up : cortar en pedazos — *vi* **1** : cortar, cortarse **2** to cut back : hacer economías **3** to cut down

: moderarse **4** to cut in : entrometerse **5** to cut in line : colarse **6** to cut up CLOWN AROUND : hacer payasadas

cut² *n* **1** : corte *m* ⟨a cut of meat : un corte de carne⟩ **2** SLASH : tajo *m*, corte *m*, cortadura *f* **3** REDUCTION : rebaja *f*, reducción *f* ⟨a cut in the rates : una rebaja en las tarifas⟩

cutaneous [kju'teɪniəs] *adj* : cutáneo

cutback ['kʌtˌbæk] *n* : recorte *m*, reducción *f*

cute ['kju:t] *adj* **cuter; cutest** : mono *fam*, lindo

cuticle ['kju:tɪkəl] *n* : cutícula *f*

cutlass ['kʌtləs] *n* : alfanje *m*

cutlery ['kʌtləri] *n* : cubiertos *mpl*

cutlet ['kʌtlət] *n* : chuleta *f*

cutoff ['kʌtˌɔf] *n* **1** INTERRUPTION : corte *m*, interrupción *f* **2** DEADLINE : fecha *f* límite, fecha *f* tope **3** **cutoffs** *npl* : shorts *mpl* de mezclilla

cut–rate ['kʌtˌreɪt] *adj* : a precio rebajado

cutter ['kʌtər] *n* **1** : cortadora *f* (implemento) **2** : cortador *m*, -dora *f* (persona) **3** : cúter *m* (embarcación)

cutthroat ['kʌtˌθro:t] *adj* : despiadado, desalmado ⟨cutthroat competition : competencia feroz⟩

cutting¹ ['kʌtɪŋ] *adj* **1** : cortante ⟨a cutting wind : un viento cortante⟩ **2** CAUSTIC : mordaz

cutting² *n* : esqueje *m* (de una planta)

cuttlefish ['kʌtəlˌfɪʃ] *n, pl* **-fish** *or* **-fishes** : jibia *f*, sepia *f*

cyanide ['saɪəˌnaɪd, -nɪd] *n* : cianuro *m*

cyber- ['saɪbər-] *pref* : ciber-

cyberbullying ['saɪbərˌbuliŋ] *n* : ciberacoso *m*

cybernetic [ˌsaɪbər'nɛtɪk] *adj* : cibernético

cycle¹ ['saɪkəl] *vi* **-cled; -cling** : andar en bicicleta, ir en bicicleta

cycle² *n* **1** : ciclo *m* ⟨life cycle : ciclo de vida, ciclo vital⟩ **2** BICYCLE : bicicleta *f* **3** MOTORCYCLE : motocicleta *f*

cyclic ['saɪklɪk, 'sɪ-] *or* **cyclical** [-klɪkəl] *adj* : cíclico

cycling ['saɪklɪŋ] *n* : ciclismo *m*

cyclist ['saɪklɪst] *n* : ciclista *mf*

cyclone ['saɪˌklo:n] *n* **1** : ciclón *m* **2** TORNADO : tornado *m*

cyclopedia *or* **cyclopaedia** [ˌsaɪklə'pi:diə] → **encyclopedia**

cylinder ['sɪləndər] *n* : cilindro *m*

cylindrical [sə'lɪndrɪkəl] *adj* : cilíndrico

cymbal ['sɪmbəl] *n* : platillo *m*, címbalo *m*

cynic ['sɪnɪk] *n* : cínico *m*, -ca *f*

cynical ['sɪnɪkəl] *adj* : cínico

cynicism ['sɪnəˌsɪzəm] *n* : cinismo *m*

cypress ['saɪprəs] *n* : ciprés *m*

cyst ['sɪst] *n* : quiste *m*

czar ['zɑr, 'sɑr] *n* : zar *m*

czarina [zɑ'ri:nə, sɑ-] *n* : zarina *f*

Czech ['tʃɛk] *n* **1** : checo *m*, -ca *f* **2** : checo *m* (idioma) — **Czech** *adj*

Czechoslovak [ˌtʃɛko'slo:ˌvɑk, -ˌvæk] *or* **Czechoslovakian** [-slo'vɑkiən, -'væ-] *n* : checoslovaco *m*, -ca *f* — **Czechoslovak** *or* **Czechoslovakian** *adj*

D

d ['di:] *n, pl* **d's** *or* **ds** ['di:z] **1** : cuarta letra del alfabeto inglés **2** : re *m* ⟨D sharp/flat : re sostenido/bemol⟩

dab¹ ['dæb] *vt* **dabbed; dabbing** : darle toques ligeros a, aplicar suavemente

dab² *n* **1** BIT : toque *m*, pizca *f*, poco *m* ⟨a dab of ointment : un toque de ungüento⟩ **2** PAT : toque *m* ligero, golpecito *m*

dabble ['dæbəl] *v* **-bled; -bling** *vt* SPATTER : salpicar — *vi* **1** SPLASH : chapotear **2** TRIFLE : jugar, interesarse superficialmente

dabbler ['dæbələr] *n* : diletante *mf*

dachshund ['dɑks,hʊnt, -,hʊnd;, 'dɑksənt, -sənd] *n* : perro *m* salchicha

dad ['dæd] *n* : papá *m fam*

daddy ['dædi] *n, pl* **-dies** : papi *m fam*

daddy longlegs [-'lɔŋ,lɛgz] *n, pl* **daddy longlegs** : segador *m* (insecto)

daffodil ['dæfə,dɪl] *n* : narciso *m*

daft ['dæft] *adj* : tonto, bobo

dagger ['dægər] *n* : daga *f*, puñal *m*

dahlia ['dæljə, 'dɑl-, 'dɑl-] *n* : dalia *f*

daily¹ ['deɪli] *adv* : a diario, diariamente

daily² *adj* : diario, cotidiano

daily³ *n, pl* **-lies** : diario *m*, periódico *m*

daintily ['deɪntəli] *adv* : delicadamente, con delicadeza

daintiness ['deɪntinəs] *n* : delicadeza *f*, finura *f*

dainty¹ ['deɪnti] *adj* **daintier; -est 1** DELICATE : delicado **2** FASTIDIOUS : remilgado, melindroso **3** DELICIOUS : exquisito, sabroso

dainty² *n, pl* **-ties** DELICACY : exquisitez *f*, manjar *m*

dairy¹ ['dæri] *adj* : lácteo ⟨dairy products : productos lácteos⟩

dairy² *n, pl* **-ries 1** *or* **dairy store** : lechería *f* **2** *or* **dairy farm** : granja *f* lechera **3** : (productos *mpl*) lácteos *mpl* ⟨she stopped eating dairy : dejó los lácteos⟩

dairymaid ['dæri,meɪd] *n* : lechera *f*

dairyman ['dærimən, -,mæn] *n, pl* **-men** [-mən, -,mɛn] : lechero *m*

dais ['deɪəs] *n* : tarima *f*, estrado *m*

daisy ['deɪzi] *n, pl* **-sies** : margarita *f*

dale ['deɪl] *n* : valle *m*

dally ['dæli] *vi* **-lied; -lying 1** TRIFLE : juguetear **2** DAWDLE : entretenerse, perder tiempo

dalmatian [dæl'meɪʃən, dɔl-] *n* : dálmata *m*

dam¹ ['dæm] *vt* **dammed; damming** : represar

dam² *n* **1** : represa *f*, dique *m* **2** : madre *f* (de animales domésticos)

damage¹ ['dæmɪʤ] *vt* **-aged; -aging** : dañar (un objeto o una máquina), perjudicar (la salud o una reputación)

damage² *n* **1** : daño *m*, perjuicio *m* ⟨to cause damage to : ocasionar daños a⟩ **2 damages** *npl* : daños y perjuicios *mpl*

damaging ['dæmədʒɪŋ] *adj* : perjudicial

damask ['dæməsk] *n* : damasco *m*

dame ['deɪm] *n* LADY : dama *f*, señora *f*

damn¹ ['dæm] *vt* **1** CONDEMN : condenar **2** CURSE : maldecir

damn² *or* **damned** ['dæmd] *adj* : condenado *fam*, maldito *fam*

damn³ *n* : pito *m*, bledo *m*, comino *m* ⟨it's not worth a damn : no vale un pito⟩ ⟨I don't give a damn : me importa un comino⟩

damnable ['dæmnəbəl] *adj* : condenable, detestable

damnation [dæm'neɪʃən] *n* : condenación *f*

damned¹ ['dæmd] *adv* VERY : muy

damned² *adj* **1** → **damnable 2** REMARKABLE : extraordinario

damning ['dæmɪŋ] *adj* : condenatorio

damp¹ ['dæmp] *vt* → **dampen**

damp² *adj* : húmedo

damp³ *n* MOISTURE : humedad *f*

dampen ['dæmpən] *vt* **1** MOISTEN : humedecer **2** DISCOURAGE : desalentar, desanimar

damper ['dæmpər] *n* **1** : regulador *m* de tiro (de una chimenea) **2** : sordina *f* (de un piano) **3 to put a damper on** : desanimar, apagar (el entusiasmo), enfriar

dampness ['dæmpnəs] *n* : humedad *f*

damsel ['dæmzəl] *n* : damisela *f*

dance¹ ['dænts] *v* **danced; dancing** : bailar

dance² *n* : baile *m*

dancer ['dæntsər] *n* : bailarín *m*, -rina *f*

dandelion ['dændəl,aɪən] *n* : diente *m* de león

dandruff ['dændrəf] *n* : caspa *f*

dandy¹ ['dændi] *adj* **dandier; -est** : excelente, magnífico, macanudo *fam*

dandy² *n, pl* **-dies 1** : dandi *m* **2** : algo *m* excelente ⟨this new program is a dandy : este programa nuevo es algo excelente⟩

Dane ['deɪn] *n* : danés *m*, -nesa *f*

danger ['deɪnʤər] *n* : peligro *m*

dangerous ['deɪnʤərəs] *adj* : peligroso

dangle ['dæŋgəl] *v* **-gled; -gling** *vi* HANG : colgar, pender — *vt* **1** SWING : hacer oscilar **2** PROFFER : ofrecer (como incentivo) **3 to keep someone dangling** : dejar a alguien en suspenso

Danish¹ ['deɪnɪʃ] *adj* : danés

Danish² *n* : danés *m* (idioma)

dank ['dæŋk] *adj* : frío y húmedo

dapper ['dæpər] *adj* : pulcro, atildado

dappled ['dæpəld] *adj* : moteado ⟨a dappled horse : un caballo rodado⟩

dare¹ ['dær] *v* **dared; daring** *vi* : osar, atreverse ⟨how dare you! : ¡cómo te atreves!⟩ — *vt* **1** CHALLENGE : desafiar, retar **2 to dare to do something** : atreverse a hacer algo, osar hacer algo

dare² *n* : desafío *m*, reto *m*

daredevil ['dær,dɛvəl] *n* : persona *f* temeraria

daring¹ ['dærɪŋ] *adj* : osado, atrevido, audaz

daring² *n* : arrojo *m*, coraje *m*, audacia *f*

dark¹ ['dɑrk] *adj* **1** : oscuro (dícese del ambiente o de los colores), moreno (dícese del pelo o de la piel) ⟨it's getting dark : está oscureciendo⟩ 2 SOMBER : sombrío, triste

dark² *n* 1 : oscuridad *f*, tinieblas *f* ⟨to be afraid of the dark : tenerle miedo a la oscuridad⟩ 2 NIGHT : noche ⟨before dark : antes del anochecer⟩

dark chocolate *n* : chocolate *m* oscuro, chocolate *m* amargo, chocolate *m* negro

darken ['dɑrkən] *vt* 1 DIM : oscurecer 2 SADDEN : entristecer — *vi* : ensombrecerse, nublarse

darkly ['dɑrkli] *adv* 1 DIMLY : oscuramente 2 GLOOMILY : tristemente 3 MYSTERIOUSLY : misteriosamente, enigmáticamente

darkness ['dɑrknəs] *n* : oscuridad *f*, tinieblas *f*

darkroom ['dɑrk,ru:m, -,rʊm] *n* : cuarto *m* oscuro

darling¹ ['dɑrlɪŋ] *adj* 1 BELOVED : querido, amado 2 CHARMING : encantador, mono *fam*

darling² *n* 1 BELOVED : querido *m*, -da *f*; amado *m*, -da *f*; cariño *m*, -ña *f* 2 FAVORITE : preferido *m*, -da *f*; favorito *m*, -ta *f*

darn¹ ['dɑrn] *vt* : zurcir

darn² *n* 1 : zurcido *m* 2 → **damn³**

dart¹ ['dɑrt] *vt* THROW : lanzar, tirar — *vi* DASH : lanzarse, precipitarse

dart² *n* 1 : dardo *m* 2 **darts** *npl* : juego *m* de dardos

dash¹ ['dæʃ] *vt* 1 SMASH : romper, estrellar 2 HURL : arrojar, lanzar 3 SPLASH : salpicar 4 FRUSTRATE : frustrar 5 **to dash off** : hacer (algo) rápidamente — *vi* 1 SMASH : romperse, estrellarse 2 DART : lanzarse, irse apresuradamente

dash² *n* 1 BURST, SPLASH : arranque *m*, salpicadura *f* (de aguas) 2 : guión *m* largo (signo de puntuación) 3 DROP : gota *f*, pizca *f* 4 VERVE : brío *m* 5 RACE : carrera *f* ⟨a 100-meter dash : una carrera de 100 metros⟩ 6 **to make a dash for it** : precipitarse (hacia), echarse a correr 7 → **dashboard**

dashboard ['dæʃ,bɔrd] *n* : tablero *m* de instrumentos

dashing ['dæʃɪŋ] *adj* : gallardo, apuesto

data ['deɪt̬ə, 'dæ-, 'dɑ-] *ns & pl* : datos *mpl*, información *f*

data bank *n* : banco *m* de datos

database ['deɪt̬ə,beɪs, 'dæ-, 'dɑ-] *n* : base *f* de datos

data processing *n* : procesamiento *m* de datos

date¹ ['deɪt] *v* **dated; dating** *vt* 1 : fechar (una carta, etc.), datar (un objeto) ⟨it was dated June 9 : estaba fechada el 9 de junio⟩ 2 : salir con ⟨she's dating my brother : sale con mi hermano⟩ — *vi* : datar

date² *n* 1 : fecha *f* ⟨to date : hasta la fecha⟩ 2 EPOCH, PERIOD : época *f*, período *m* 3 APPOINTMENT : cita *f* 4 COMPANION : acompañante *mf* 5 : dátil *m* (fruta)

dated ['deɪt̬əd] *adj* OUT-OF-DATE : anticuado, pasado de moda

datum ['deɪt̬əm, 'dæ-, 'dɑ-] *n*, *pl* **-ta** [-t̬ə] *or* **-tums** : dato *m*

daub¹ ['dɔb] *vt* : embadurnar

daub² *n* : mancha *f*

daughter ['dɔt̬ər] *n* : hija *f*

daughter–in–law ['dɔt̬ərɪn,lɔ] *n*, *pl* **daughters–in–law** : nuera *f*, hija *f* política

daunt ['dɔnt] *vt* : amilanar, acobardar, intimidar

daunting ['dɔntɪŋ] *adj* : desalentador

dauntless ['dɔntləs] *adj* : intrépido, impávido

dawdle ['dɔd̬əl] *vi* **-dled; -dling** 1 DALLY : demorarse, entretenerse, perder tiempo 2 LOITER : vagar, holgazanear, haraganear

dawn¹ ['dɔn] *vi* 1 : amanecer, alborear, despuntar ⟨Saturday dawned clear and bright : el sábado amaneció claro y luminoso⟩ 2 **to dawn on** : hacerse obvio ⟨it dawned on me that she was right : me di cuenta de que tenía razón⟩

dawn² *n* 1 DAYBREAK : amanecer *m*, alba *f* 2 BEGINNING : albor *m*, comienzo *m* ⟨the dawn of history : los albores de la historia⟩ 3 **from dawn to dusk** : de sol a sol

day ['deɪ] *n* 1 : día *m* ⟨the day after tomorrow : pasado mañana⟩ ⟨the day before yesterday : anteayer⟩ ⟨the other day : el otro día⟩ ⟨twice a day, two times a day : dos veces al día⟩ ⟨every day : todos los días⟩ ⟨all day : todo el día⟩ 2 DATE : fecha *f* ⟨what day is (it) today? : ¿qué día es hoy?⟩ 3 TIME : día *m*, tiempo *m* ⟨in those days : en aquellos tiempos⟩ ⟨in my day : en mis tiempos⟩ ⟨to the present day : hasta nuestros días⟩ ⟨to this day : hasta el día de hoy⟩ 4 WORKDAY : jornada *f* laboral 5 **any day now** SOON : cualquier día de estos 6 **in this day and age** : hoy (en) día 7 **one day** SOMEDAY : algún día 8 **the good old days** : los viejos tiempos 9 **these days** : hoy (en) día 10 **to make someone's day** : alegrarle el día a alguien

daybreak ['deɪ,breɪk] *n* : alba *f*, amanecer *m*

day care *n* : servicio *m* de guardería infantil

daydream¹ ['deɪ,dri:m] *vi* : soñar despierto, fantasear

daydream² *n* : ensueño *m*, ensoñación *f*, fantasía *f*

daylight ['deɪ,laɪt] *n* 1 : luz *f* del día ⟨in broad daylight : a plena luz del día⟩ 2 → **daybreak** 3 → **daytime**

daylight saving time *n* : hora *f* de verano

daytime ['deɪ,taɪm] *n* : horas *fpl* diurnas, día *m*

day–to–day *adj* : diario, cotidiano

daze¹ ['deɪz] *vt* **dazed; dazing** 1 STUN : aturdir 2 DAZZLE : deslumbrar, ofuscar

daze² *n* 1 : aturdimiento *m* 2 **in a daze** : aturdido, atontado

dazzle¹ ['dæzəl] *vt* **-zled; -zling** : deslumbrar, ofuscar

dazzle² *n* : resplandor *m*, brillo *m*

dazzling ['dæzəlɪŋ] *adj* : deslumbrante

de- *pref* : des-

deacon ['diːkən] *n* : diácono *m*

deaconess ['diːkənəs] *n* : diaconisa *f*

deactivate [diˈæktəˌveɪt] *vt* **-vated; -vating** : desactivar

dead¹ ['dɛd] *adv* **1** ABRUPTLY : repentinamente, súbitamente ⟨to stop dead : parar en seco⟩ **2** ABSOLUTELY : absolutamente ⟨I'm dead certain : estoy absolutamente seguro⟩ **3** DIRECTLY : justo ⟨dead ahead : justo adelante⟩

dead² *adj* **1** LIFELESS : muerto ⟨to drop dead : caerse muerto⟩ **2** NUMB : entumecido, dormido **3** INDIFFERENT : indiferente, frío **4** INACTIVE : inactivo ⟨a dead volcano : un volcán inactivo⟩ **5** : desconectado (dícese de un teléfono), descargado (dícese de una batería) **6** EXHAUSTED : agotado, derrengado, muerto **7** OBSOLETE : obsoleto, muerto ⟨a dead language : una lengua muerta⟩ **8** EXACT : exacto ⟨(in the) dead center : justo en el blanco⟩ **9** QUIET, SLOW : muerto (dícese de una fiesta, etc.), de poco movimiento (comercial) **10** : perdido ⟨if she catches you, you're dead : si te agarra, te mata⟩ **11** drop dead! : ¡vete al infierno! **12 to be caught dead in** ⟨I wouldn't be caught dead in that outfit : no me pondría ese conjunto ni muerta⟩

dead³ *n* **1 the dead** : los muertos **2 in the dead of night** : a las altas horas de la noche **3 in the dead of winter** : en pleno invierno

deadbeat ['dɛdˌbiːt] *n* **1** LOAFER : vago *m*, -ga *f*; holgazán *m*, -zana *f* **2** FREELOADER : gorrón *m*, -rrona *f fam*; gorrero *m*, -ra *f fam*

deaden ['dɛdən] *vt* **1** : atenuar (un dolor), entorpecer (sensaciones) **2** DULL : deslustrar **3** DISPIRIT : desanimar **4** MUFFLE : amortiguar, reducir (sonidos)

dead–end ['dɛdˈɛnd] *adj* **1** : sin salida ⟨dead-end street : calle sin salida⟩ **2** : sin futuro ⟨a dead-end job : un trabajo sin porvenir⟩

dead end *n* : callejón *m* sin salida

dead heat *n* : empate *m*

deadline ['dɛdˌlaɪn] *n* : fecha *f* límite, fecha *f* tope, plazo *m* (determinado)

deadlock¹ ['dɛdˌlɑk] *vt* : estancar — *vi* : estancarse, llegar a punto muerto

deadlock² *n* : punto *m* muerto, impasse *m*

deadly¹ ['dɛdli] *adv* : extremadamente, sumamente ⟨deadly serious : muy en serio⟩

deadly² *adj* **deadlier; -est 1** LETHAL : mortal, letal, mortífero **2** ACCURATE : certero, preciso ⟨with deadly aim : con puntería infalible⟩ **3** CAPITAL : capital ⟨the seven deadly sins : los siete pecados capitales⟩ **4** DULL : funesto, aburrido **5** EXTREME : extremo, absoluto ⟨a deadly calm : una calma absoluta⟩

deadpan¹ ['dɛdˌpæn] *adv* : de manera inexpresiva, sin expresión

deadpan² *adj* : inexpresivo, impasible

deaf ['dɛf] *adj* : sordo

deafen ['dɛfən] *vt* **-ened; -ening** : ensordecer

deafening ['dɛfənɪŋ] *adj* : ensordecedor

deaf–mute ['dɛf'mjuːt] *n often offensive* : sordomudo *m*, -da *f offensive*

deafness ['dɛfnəs] *n* : sordera *f*

deal¹ ['diːl] *v* **dealt; dealing** *vt* **1** *or* **to deal out** APPORTION : repartir ⟨to deal justice : repartir la justicia⟩ **2** DISTRIBUTE : repartir, dar (naipes) **3** DELIVER : asestar, propinar ⟨to deal a blow : asestar un golpe⟩ — *vi* **1** : dar, repartir (en juegos de naipes) **2 to deal in** : comerciar en, traficar con (drogas) **3 to deal with** CONCERN : tratar de, tener que ver con ⟨the book deals with poverty : el libro trata de la pobreza⟩ **4 to deal with** HANDLE : tratar (con), encargarse de **5 to deal with** TREAT : tratar ⟨the judge dealt with him severely : el juez lo trató con severidad⟩ **6 to deal with** ACCEPT : aceptar (una situación o desgracia)

deal² *n* **1** : reparto *m* (de naipes) **2** AGREEMENT, TRANSACTION : trato *m*, acuerdo *m*, transacción *f* ⟨to cut/make/strike a deal : hacer un trato⟩ **3** TREATMENT : trato *m* ⟨he got a raw deal : le hicieron una injusticia⟩ **4** BARGAIN : ganga *f*, oferta *f* ⟨she got a good deal on the car : consiguió el coche a un precio barato⟩ **5 a good/great deal** : mucho, una gran cantidad **6 big deal** : cosa *f* importante ⟨don't worry, it's no big deal : no te preocupes, no tiene importancia⟩ ⟨so what? big deal! : ¿a quién le importa?⟩ **7 the real deal** ⟨to be the real deal : ser auténtico, ser de verdad⟩

dealer ['diːlər] *n* : comerciante *mf*, traficante *mf*

dealership ['diːlərˌʃɪp] *n* : concesión *f*

dealings ['diːlɪŋz] *npl* **1** : relaciones *fpl* (personales) **2** TRANSACTIONS : negocios *mpl*, transacciones *fpl*

dean ['diːn] *n* **1** : deán *m* (del clero) **2** : decano *m*, -na *f* (de una facultad o profesión)

dear¹ ['dɪr] *adj* **1** ESTEEMED, LOVED : querido, estimado ⟨a dear friend : un amigo querido⟩ ⟨Dear Sir : Estimado Señor⟩ **2** COSTLY : caro, costoso

dear² *n* : querido *m*, -da *f*; amado *m*, -da *f*

dearly ['dɪrli] *adv* **1** : mucho ⟨I love them dearly : los quiero mucho⟩ **2** : caro ⟨to pay dearly : pagar caro⟩

dearth ['dərθ] *n* : escasez *f*, carestía *f*

death ['dɛθ] *n* **1** : muerte *f*, fallecimiento *m* ⟨to be the death of : matar⟩ **2** FATALITY : víctima *f* (mortal); muerto *m*, -ta *f* **3** END : fin *m* ⟨the death of civilization : el fin de la civilización⟩

deathbed ['dɛθˌbɛd] *n* : lecho *m* de muerte

deathblow ['dɛθˌbloː] *n* : golpe *m* mortal

death certificate *n* : certificado *m* de defunción, acta *f* de defunción

deathless ['dɛθləs] *adj* : eterno, inmortal

deathly ['dɛθli] *adj* : de muerte, sepulcral (dícese del silencio), cadavérico (dícese de la palidez)

death penalty *n* : pena *f* de muerte

death trap *n* : trampa *f* mortal, vehículo *m* (o edificio *m*, etc.) peligroso

debacle [dɪ'bɑkəl, -'bæ-] *n* : desastre *m*, debacle *m*, fiasco *m*

debar [di'bɑr] *vt* **-barred; -barring** : excluir, prohibir

debase [di'beɪs] *vt* **-based; -basing** : degradar, envilecer

debatable [di'beɪtəbəl] *adj* : discutible

debate[1] [di'beɪt] *vt* **-bated; -bating** : debatir, discutir

debate[2] *n* : debate *m*, discusión *f*

debauch [dɪ'bɔtʃ] *vt* : pervertir, corromper

debauchery [di'bɔtʃəri] *n, pl* **-eries** : libertinaje *m*, intemperancia *f*

debilitate [di'bɪlə,teɪt] *vt* **-tated; -tating** : debilitar

debility [di'bɪləti] *n, pl* **-ties** : debilidad *f*

debit[1] ['dɛbɪt] *vt* : adeudar, cargar, debitar

debit[2] *n* : débito *m*, cargo *m*, debe *m*

debit card *n* : tarjeta *f* de débito

debonair [,dɛbə'nær] *adj* : elegante y desenvuelto, apuesto

debris [də'bri:, deɪ-;, 'deɪ,bri:] *n, pl* **-bris** [-'bri:z, -,bri:z] **1** RUBBLE, RUINS : escombros *mpl*, ruinas *fpl*, restos *mpl* **2** RUBBISH : basura *f*, desechos *mpl*

debt ['dɛt] *n* **1** : deuda *f* ⟨to pay a debt : saldar una deuda⟩ **2** INDEBTEDNESS : endeudamiento *m*

debtor ['dɛtər] *n* : deudor *m*, -dora *f*

debunk [di'bʌŋk] *vt* DISCREDIT : desacreditar, desprestigiar

debut[1] [deɪ'bju:, 'deɪ,bju:] *vi* : debutar

debut[2] *n* **1** : debut *m* (de un actor), estreno *m* (de una obra) **2** : debut *m*, presentación *f* (en sociedad)

debutante ['dɛbju,tɑnt] *n* : debutante *f*

decade ['dɛ,keɪd, dɛ'keɪd] *n* : década *f*

decadence ['dɛkədənts] *n* : decadencia *f*

decadent ['dɛkədənt] *adj* : decadente

decaf[1] ['di:,kæf] → **decaffeinated**

decaf[2] *n* : café *m* descafeinado

decaffeinated [di'kæfə,neɪtəd] *adj* : descafeinado

decal ['di:,kæl, di'kæl] *n* : calcomanía *f*

decamp [di'kæmp] *vi* : irse, largarse *fam*

decanter [di'kæntər] *n* : licorera *f*, garrafa *f*

decapitate [di'kæpə,teɪt] *vt* **-tated; -tating** : decapitar

decay[1] [di'keɪ] *vi* **1** DECOMPOSE : descomponerse, pudrirse **2** DETERIORATE : deteriorarse **3** : cariarse (dícese de los dientes)

decay[2] *n* **1** DECOMPOSITION : descomposición *f* **2** DECLINE, DETERIORATION : decadencia *f*, deterioro *m* **3** : caries *f* (de los dientes)

decease[1] [di'si:s] *vi* **-ceased; -ceasing** : morir, fallecer

decease[2] *n* : fallecimiento *m*, defunción *f*, deceso *m*

deceased *n* : difunto *m*, -ta *f*

deceit [di'si:t] *n* **1** DECEPTION : engaño *m* **2** DISHONESTY : deshonestidad *f*

deceitful [di'si:tfəl] *adj* : falso, embustero, engañoso, mentiroso

deceitfully [di'si:tfəli] *adv* : con engaño, con falsedad

deceitfulness [di'si:tfəlnəs] *n* : falsedad *f*, engaño *m*

deceive [di'si:v] *vt* **-ceived; -ceiving** : engañar, burlar

deceiver [di'si:vər] *n* : impostor *m*, -tora *f*

decelerate [di'sɛlə,reɪt] *vi* **-ated; -ating** : reducir la velocidad, desacelerar

December [di'sɛmbər] *n* : diciembre *m* ⟨they arrived on the 18th of December, they arrived on December 18th : llegaron el 18 de diciembre⟩

decency ['disəntsi] *n, pl* **-cies** : decencia *f*, decoro *m*

decent ['di:sənt] *adj* **1** CORRECT, PROPER : decente, decoroso, correcto **2** CLOTHED : vestido, presentable **3** MODEST : púdico, modesto **4** ADEQUATE : decente, adecuado ⟨decent wages : paga adecuada⟩

decently ['di:səntli] *adv* : decentemente

decentralize [di'sɛntrə,laɪz] *v* **-lized** [-,laɪzd]; **-lizing** [-,laɪzɪŋ] *vt* : descentralizar — *vi* : descentralizarse

deception [di'sɛpʃən] *n* : engaño *m*

deceptive [di'sɛptɪv] *adj* : engañoso, falaz — **deceptively** *adv*

decibel ['dɛsəbəl, -,bɛl] *n* : decibelio *m*

decide [di'saɪd] *vt* **-cided; -ciding** *vt* **1** CONCLUDE : decidir, llegar a la conclusión de ⟨he decided what to do : decidió qué iba a hacer⟩ **2** DETERMINE : decidir, determinar ⟨one blow decided the fight : un solo golpe determinó la pelea⟩ **3** CONVINCE : decidir ⟨her pleas decided me to help : sus súplicas me decidieron a ayudarla⟩ **4** RESOLVE : resolver — *vi* : decidirse

decided [di'saɪdəd] *adj* **1** UNQUESTIONABLE : indudable **2** RESOLUTE : decidido, resuelto — **decidedly** *adv*

deciduous [di'sɪdʒuəs] *adj* : caduco, de hoja caduca

decimal[1] ['dɛsəməl] *adj* : decimal

decimal[2] *n* : número *m* decimal

decimal point *n* : punto *m* decimal, coma *f* decimal

decipher [di'saɪfər] *vt* : descifrar — **decipherable** [-əbəl] *adj*

decision [dɪ'sɪʒən] *n* : decisión *f*, determinación *f* ⟨to make a decision : tomar una decisión⟩

decisive [dɪ'saɪsɪv] *adj* **1** DECIDING : decisivo ⟨the decisive vote : el voto decisivo⟩ **2** CONCLUSIVE : decisivo, concluyente, contundente ⟨a decisive victory : una victoria contundente⟩ **3** RESOLUTE : decidido, resuelto, firme

decisively [dɪ'saɪsɪvli] *adv* : con decisión, de manera decisiva

decisiveness [dɪ'saɪsɪvnəs] *n* **1** FORCEFULNESS : contundencia *f* **2** RESOLUTION : firmeza *f*, decisión *f*, determinación *f*

deck[1] ['dɛk] *vt* **1** FLOOR : tumbar, derribar ⟨she decked him with one blow : lo tumbó de un solo golpe⟩ **2 to deck out** : adornar, engalanar

deck[2] *n* **1** : cubierta *f* (de un barco) **2** *or* **deck of cards** : baraja *f* (de naipes)

deck chair *n* : silla *f* de playa

declaim [di'kleɪm] *v* : declamar

declaration [,dɛklə'reɪʃən] *n* : declaración *f*, pronunciamiento *m* (oficial)

declare [dɪ'klær] *vt* -**clared; -claring** : declarar, manifestar ⟨to declare war : declarar la guerra⟩ ⟨they declared their support : manifestaron su apoyo⟩
declassify [dɪ'klæsə,faɪ] *vt* -**fied; -fying** : desclasificar
decline¹ [dɪ'klaɪn] *v* -**clined; -clining** *vi* 1 DESCEND : descender 2 DETERIORATE : deteriorarse, decaer ⟨her health is declining : su salud se está deteriorando⟩ 3 DECREASE : disminuir, decrecer, decaer 4 REFUSE : rehusar — *vt* 1 INFLECT : declinar 2 REFUSE, TURN DOWN : rehusar, rehusar
decline² *n* 1 DETERIORATION : decadencia *f*, deterioro *m* 2 DECREASE : disminución *f*, descenso *m* 3 SLOPE : declive *m*, pendiente *f*
decode [dɪ'ko:d] *vt* -**coded; -coding** : descifrar (un mensaje), descodificar (una señal)
decoder [dɪ'ko:dər] *n* : decodificador *m*
decompose [,di:kəm'po:z] *v* -**posed; -posing** *vt* 1 BREAK DOWN : descomponer 2 ROT : descomponer, pudrir — *vi* : descomponerse, pudrirse
decomposition [,di:,kɑmpə'zɪʃən] *n* : descomposición *f*
decongestant [,di:kən'dʒɛstənt] *n* : descongestionante *m*
decontaminate [,di:kən'tæmə,neɪt] *vt* -**nated; -nating** : descontaminar — **decontamination** [,di:kən,tæmə'neɪʃən] *n*
decor *or* **décor** [deɪ'kɔr, 'deɪ,kɔr] *n* : decoración *f*
decorate ['dɛkə,reɪt] *vt* -**rated; -rating** 1 ADORN : decorar, adornar 2 : condecorar ⟨he was decorated for bravery : lo condecoraron por valor⟩
decoration [,dɛkə'reɪʃən] *n* 1 ADORNMENT : decoración *f*, adorno *m* 2 : condecoración *f* (de honor)
decorative ['dɛkərətɪv, -,reɪ-] *adj* : decorativo, ornamental, de adorno
decorator ['dɛkə,reɪtər] *n* : decorador *m*, -dora *f*
decorum [dɪ'korəm] *n* : decoro *m*
decoy¹ ['di:,kɔɪ, dɪ'-] *vt* : atraer (con señuelo)
decoy² *n* : señuelo *m*, reclamo *m*
decrease¹ [dɪ'kri:s] *v* -**creased; -creasing** *vi* : decrecer, disminuir, bajar — *vt* : reducir, disminuir
decrease² ['di:,kri:s] *n* : disminución *f*, descenso *m*, bajada *f*
decree¹ [dɪ'kri:] *vt* -**creed; -creeing** : decretar
decree² *n* : decreto *m*
decrepit [dɪ'krɛpɪt] *adj* 1 FEEBLE : decrépito, débil 2 DILAPIDATED : deteriorado, ruinoso
decry [dɪ'kraɪ] *vt* -**cried; -crying** : censurar, criticar
dedicate ['dɛdɪ,keɪt] *vt* -**cated; -cating** 1 : dedicar ⟨she dedicated the book to Carlos : le dedicó el libro a Carlos⟩ 2 : consagrar, dedicar ⟨to dedicate one's life : consagrar uno su vida⟩
dedication [,dɛdɪ'keɪʃən] *n* 1 DEVOTION : dedicación *f*, devoción *f* 2 : dedicato-

ria *f* (de un libro, una canción, etc.) 3 CONSECRATION : dedicación *f*
deduce [dɪ'du:s, -'dju:s] *vt* -**duced; -ducing** : deducir, inferir
deduct [dɪ'dʌkt] *vt* : deducir, descontar, restar
deductible [dɪ'dʌktəbəl] *adj* : deducible
deduction [dɪ'dʌkʃən] *n* : deducción *f*
deed¹ ['di:d] *vt* : ceder, transferir
deed² *n* 1 ACT : acto *m*, acción *f*, hecho *m* ⟨a good deed : una buena acción⟩ 2 FEAT : hazaña *f*, proeza *f* 3 TITLE : escritura *f*, título *m*
deem ['di:m] *vt* : considerar, juzgar
deep¹ ['di:p] *adv* : hondo, profundamente ⟨to dig deep : cavar hondo⟩
deep² *adj* 1 : hondo, profundo ⟨the deep end : la parte honda⟩ ⟨a deep wound : una herida profunda⟩ ⟨take a deep breath : respire hondo⟩ 2 : de fondo, de profundidad ⟨the shelf is six inches deep : el estante mide seis pulgadas de fondo⟩ ⟨the lake is 50 meters deep : el lago tiene 50 metros de profundidad⟩ 3 INTENSE : profundo, intenso ⟨with deep regret : con profundo pesar⟩ 4 SERIOUS : grave, serio ⟨to be in deep trouble : estar en serios aprietos⟩ 5 DARK : intenso, subido ⟨deep red : rojo subido⟩ 6 LOW : profundo ⟨a deep tone : un tono profundo⟩ 7 ABSORBED : absorto ⟨deep in thought : absorto en la meditación⟩
deep³ *n* 1 **the deep** : lo profundo, el piélago 2 **the deep of night** : lo más profundo de la noche
deepen ['di:pən] *vt* 1 : ahondar, profundizar 2 INTENSIFY : intensificar — *vi* 1 : hacerse más profundo 2 INTENSIFY : intensificarse
deeply ['di:pli] *adv* : hondo, profundamente ⟨I'm deeply sorry : lo siento sinceramente⟩
deep–rooted ['di:p'ru:təd, -'ru-] *adj* : profundamente arraigado, enraizado
deep–seated ['di:p'si:təd] *adj* 1 → deep–rooted 2 : profundo (dícese de un miedo, etc.)
deer ['dɪr] *ns & pl* : ciervo *m*, venado *m*
deerskin ['dɪr,skɪn] *n* : piel *f* de venado
deface [dɪ'feɪs] *vt* -**faced; -facing** MAR : desfigurar
defamation [,dɛfə'meɪʃən] *n* : difamación *f*
defamatory [dɪ'fæmə,tori] *adj* : difamatorio
defame [dɪ'feɪm] *vt* -**famed; -faming** : difamar, calumniar
default¹ [dɪ'fɔlt, 'dɪ:,fɔlt] *vi* 1 : no cumplir (con una obligación), no pagar 2 : no presentarse (en un tribunal)
default² *n* 1 NEGLECT : omisión *f*, negligencia *f* 2 NONPAYMENT : impago *m*, falta *f* de pago 3 **to win by default** : ganar por abandono
defaulter [dɪ'fɔltər] *n* : moroso *m*, -sa *f*; rebelde *mf* (en un tribunal)
defeat¹ [dɪ'fi:t] *vt* 1 FRUSTRATE : frustrar 2 BEAT : vencer, derrotar
defeat² *n* : derrota *f*, rechazo *m* (de legislación), fracaso *m* (de planes, etc.)

defeatist [di'fi:tɪst] *n* : derrotista *mf* — **defeatist** *adj*

defecate ['dɛfɪ,keɪt] *vi* -cated; -cating : defecar

defect[1] [di'fɛkt] *vi* : desertar

defect[2] ['di:,fɛkt, di'fɛkt] *n* : defecto *m*

defection [di'fɛkʃən] *n* : deserción *f*

defective [di'fɛktɪv] *adj* 1 FAULTY : defectuoso 2 DEFICIENT : deficiente

defector [di'fɛktər] *n* : desertor *m*, -tora *f*

defend [di'fɛnd] *vt* : defender

defendant [di'fɛndənt] *n* : acusado *m*, -da *f*; demandado *m*, -da *f*

defender [di'fɛndər] *n* 1 ADVOCATE : defensor *m*, -sora *f* 2 : defensa *mf* (en deportes)

defense [di'fɛnts, 'di:,fɛnts] *n* : defensa *f*

defenseless [di'fɛntsləs] *adj* : indefenso

defenselessness [di'fɛntsləsnəs] *n* : indefensión *f*

defensive[1] [di'fɛntsɪv] *adj* : defensivo

defensive[2] *n* on the defensive : a la defensiva

defer [di'fər] *v* -ferred; -ferring *vt* POSTPONE : diferir, aplazar, posponer — *vi* to **defer to** : deferir a

deference ['dɛfərənts] *n* : deferencia *f*

deferential [,dɛfə'rɛntʃəl] *adj* : respetuoso

deferment [di'fərmənt] *n* : aplazamiento *m*

defiance [di'faɪənts] *n* : desafío *m*

defiant [di'faɪənt] *adj* : desafiante, insolente

deficiency [di'fɪʃəntsi] *n, pl* -cies : deficiencia *f*, carencia *f*

deficient [di'fɪʃənt] *adj* : deficiente, carente

deficit ['dɛfəsɪt] *n* : déficit *m*

defile [di'faɪl] *vt* -filed; -filing 1 DIRTY : ensuciar, manchar 2 CORRUPT : corromper 3 DESECRATE, PROFANE : profanar 4 DISHONOR : deshonrar

defilement [di'faɪlmənt] *n* 1 DESECRATION : profanación *f* 2 CORRUPTION : corrupción *f* 3 CONTAMINATION : contaminación *f*

define [di'faɪn] *vt* -fined; -fining 1 BOUND : delimitar, demarcar 2 CLARIFY : aclarar, definir 3 : definir ⟨to define a word : definir una palabra⟩

definite ['dɛfənɪt] *adj* 1 CERTAIN : definido, determinado 2 CLEAR : claro, explícito 3 UNQUESTIONABLE : seguro, incuestionable

definite article *n* : artículo *m* definido

definitely ['dɛfənɪtli] *adv* 1 DOUBTLESSLY : indudablemente, sin duda 2 DEFINITIVELY : definitivamente, seguramente

definition [,dɛfə'nɪʃən] *n* : definición *f*

definitive [di'fɪnətɪv] *adj* 1 CONCLUSIVE : definitivo, decisivo 2 AUTHORITATIVE : de autoridad, autorizado — **definitively** *adv*

deflate [di'fleɪt] *v* -flated; -flating *vt* 1 : desinflar (una llanta, etc.) 2 REDUCE : rebajar ⟨to deflate one's ego : bajarle los humos a uno⟩ — *vi* : desinflarse

deflation [di'fleɪʃən] *n* : deflación *f* (económica)

deflect [di'flɛkt] *vt* : desviar — *vi* : desviarse

deforestation [di,fɔrə'steɪʃən] *n* : deforestación *f*

deform [di'fɔrm] *vt* : deformar

deformation [,di:,fɔr'meɪʃən] *n* : deformación *f*

deformed [di'fɔrmd] *adj* : deforme

deformity [di'fɔrməti] *n, pl* -ties : deformidad *f*

defraud [di'frɔd] *vt* : estafar, defraudar

defray [di'freɪ] *vt* : sufragar, costear

defrost [di'frɔst] *vt* : descongelar, deshelar — *vi* : descongelarse, deshelarse

deft ['dɛft] *adj* : hábil, diestro — **deftly** *adv*

defunct [di'fʌŋkt] *adj* 1 DECEASED : difunto, fallecido 2 EXTINCT : extinto, fenecido

defuse [di'fju:z] *vt* : desactivar ⟨to defuse the situation : reducir las tensiones⟩

defy [di'faɪ] *vt* -fied; -fying 1 CHALLENGE : desafiar, retar 2 DISOBEY : desobedecer 3 RESIST : resistir, hacer imposible, hacer inútil ⟨to defy understanding/explanation : ser incomprensible/inexplicable⟩ ⟨to defy all reason : ir en contra de toda lógica⟩

degenerate[1] [di'dʒɛnə,reɪt] *vi* -ated; -ating : degenerar

degenerate[2] [di'dʒɛnərət] *adj* : degenerado

degeneration [di,dʒɛnə'reɪʃən] *n* : degeneración *f*

degenerative [di'dʒɛnərətɪv] *adj* : degenerativo

degradation [,dɛgrə'deɪʃən] *n* : degradación *f*

degrade [di'greɪd] *vt* -graded; -grading 1 : degradar, envilecer 2 to **degrade oneself** : rebajarse

degrading [di'greɪdɪŋ] *adj* : degradante

degree [di'gri:] *n* 1 EXTENT : grado *m* ⟨a third degree burn : una quemadura de tercer grado⟩ 2 : título *m* (de enseñanza superior) 3 : grado *m* (de un círculo, de la temperatura) 4 by **degrees** : gradualmente, poco a poco

dehydrate [di'haɪ,dreɪt] *v* -drated; -drating *vt* : deshidratar — *vi* : deshidratarse

dehydration [,di:haɪ'dreɪʃən] *n* : deshidratación *f*

deice [di:'aɪs] *vt* -iced; -icing : deshelar, descongelar

deify ['di:ə,faɪ, 'deɪ-] *vt* -fied; -fying : deificar

deign ['deɪn] *vi* : dignarse, condescender

deity ['di:əti, 'deɪ-] *n, pl* -ties 1 the **Deity** : Dios *m* 2 GOD, GODDESS : deidad *f*; dios *m*, diosa *f*

dejected [di'dʒɛktəd] *adj* : abatido, desalentado, desanimado

dejection [di'dʒɛkʃən] *n* : abatimiento *m*, desaliento *m*, desánimo *m*

delay[1] [di'leɪ] *vt* 1 POSTPONE : posponer, postergar 2 HOLD UP : retrasar, demorar — *vi* : tardar, demorar

delay[2] *n* 1 LATENESS : tardanza *f* 2 HOLDUP : demora *f*, retraso *m*

delectable [di'lɛktəbəl] *adj* 1 DELICIOUS : delicioso, exquisito 2 DELIGHTFUL : encantador

delegate¹ ['dɛlɪˌgeɪt] v -gated; -gating : delegar

delegate² ['dɛlɪgət, -ˌgeɪt] n : delegado m, -da f

delegation [ˌdɛlɪ'geɪʃən] n : delegación f

delete [dɪ'liːt] vt -leted; -leting 1 : suprimir, tachar, eliminar 2 : borrar (en informática)

delete key n : tecla f de borrar, tecla f de borrado

deletion [dɪ'liːʃən] n : supresión f, tachadura f, eliminación f

deli ['dɛli] → **delicatessen**

deliberate¹ [dɪ'lɪbəˌreɪt] v -ated; -ating vt : deliberar sobre, reflexionar sobre, considerar — vi : deliberar

deliberate² [dɪ'lɪbərət] adj 1 CONSIDERED : reflexionado, premeditado 2 INTENTIONAL : deliberado, intencional 3 SLOW : lento, pausado

deliberately [dɪ'lɪbərətli] adv 1 INTENTIONALLY : adrede, a propósito 2 SLOWLY : pausadamente, lentamente

deliberation [dɪˌlɪbə'reɪʃən] n 1 CONSIDERATION : deliberación f, consideración f 2 SLOWNESS : lentitud f

delicacy ['dɛlɪkəsi] n, pl -cies 1 : manjar m, exquisitez f ⟨caviar is a real delicacy : el caviar es un verdadero manjar⟩ 2 FINENESS : delicadeza f 3 FRAGILITY : fragilidad f

delicate ['dɛlɪkət] adj 1 SUBTLE : delicado ⟨a delicate fragrance : una fragancia delicada⟩ 2 DAINTY : delicado, primoroso, fino 3 FRAGILE : frágil 4 SENSITIVE : delicado ⟨a delicate matter : un asunto delicado⟩

delicately ['dɛlɪkətli] adv : delicadamente, con delicadeza

delicatessen [ˌdɛlɪkə'tɛsən] n : charcutería f, fiambrería f, salchichonería f Mex

delicious [dɪ'lɪʃəs] adj : delicioso, exquisito, rico — **deliciously** adv

delight¹ [dɪ'laɪt] vt : deleitar, encantar — vi **to delight in** : deleitarse con, complacerse en

delight² n 1 JOY : placer m, deleite m, gozo m 2 : encanto m ⟨your garden is a delight : su jardín es un encanto⟩

delighted [dɪ'laɪtəd] adj : encantado ⟨I'm delighted to meet you : estoy encantada de conocerlo⟩

delightful [dɪ'laɪtfəl] adj : delicioso, encantador

delightfully [dɪ'laɪtfəli] adv : de manera encantadora, de maravilla

delineate [dɪ'lɪniˌeɪt] vt -eated; -eating : delinear, trazar, bosquejar

delinquency [dɪ'lɪŋkwəntsi] n, pl -cies : delincuencia f

delinquent¹ [dɪ'lɪŋkwənt] adj 1 : delincuente 2 OVERDUE : vencido y sin pagar, moroso

delinquent² n : delincuente mf ⟨juvenile delinquent : delincuente juvenil⟩

delirious [dɪ'lɪriəs] adj : delirante ⟨delirious with joy : loco de alegría⟩

delirium [dɪ'lɪriəm] n : delirio m, desvarío m

deliver [dɪ'lɪvər] vt 1 FREE : liberar, librar 2 DISTRIBUTE : entregar, repartir

(periódicos, etc.) 3 : asistir en el parto de (un niño) 4 : pronunciar ⟨to deliver a speech : pronunciar un discurso⟩ 5 PROJECT : despachar, lanzar ⟨he delivered a fast ball : lanzó una pelota rápida⟩ 6 DEAL : propinar, asestar ⟨to deliver a blow : asestar un golpe⟩ — vi 1 : hacer entregas 2 : cumplir ⟨to deliver on one's promise : cumplir (con) su promesa⟩

deliverance [dɪ'lɪvərənts] n : liberación f, rescate m, salvación f

deliverer [dɪ'lɪvərər] n RESCUER : libertador m, -dora f; salvador m, -dora f

delivery [dɪ'lɪvəri] n, pl -eries 1 LIBERATION : liberación f 2 : entrega f, reparto m ⟨cash on delivery : entrega contra reembolso⟩ ⟨home delivery : servicio a domicilio⟩ 3 CHILDBIRTH : parto m, alumbramiento m 4 SPEECH : expresión f oral, modo m de hablar 5 THROW : lanzamiento m

dell ['dɛl] n : hondonada f, valle m pequeño

delta ['dɛltə] n : delta m

delude [dɪ'luːd] vt -luded; -luding 1 : engañar 2 **to delude oneself** : engañarse

deluge¹ ['dɛlˌjuːʤ, -ˌjuːʒ] vt -uged; -uging 1 FLOOD : inundar 2 OVERWHELM : abrumar ⟨deluged with requests : abrumado de pedidos⟩

deluge² n 1 FLOOD : inundación f 2 DOWNPOUR : aguacero m 3 BARRAGE : aluvión m

delusion [dɪ'luːʒən] n 1 : ilusión f (falsa) 2 **delusions of grandeur** : delirios mpl de grandeza

deluxe [dɪ'lʌks, -'lʊks] adj : de lujo

delve ['dɛlv] vi delved; delving 1 DIG : escarbar 2 **to delve into** PROBE : cavar en, ahondar en

demagogue ['dɛməˌgɑg] n : demagogo m, demagoga f

demand¹ [dɪ'mænd] vt : demandar, exigir, reclamar

demand² n 1 REQUEST : petición f, pedido m, demanda f ⟨by popular demand : a petición del público⟩ 2 CLAIM : reclamación f, exigencia f 3 MARKET : demanda f ⟨supply and demand : la oferta y la demanda⟩

demanding [dɪ'mændɪŋ] adj : exigente

demarcate [dɪ'mɑrˌkeɪt, 'diːˌmɑr-] vt -cated; -cating : demarcar, delimitar

demarcation [ˌdiːˌmɑr'keɪʃən] n : demarcación f, deslinde m

demean [dɪ'miːn] vt : degradar, rebajar

demeaning [dɪ'miːnɪŋ] adj : degradante

demeanor [dɪ'miːnər] n : comportamiento m, conducta f

demented [dɪ'mɛntəd] adj : demente, loco

dementia [dɪ'mɛnʧə] n : demencia f

demerit [dɪ'mɛrət] n : demérito m

demigod ['dɛmiˌgɑd, -ˌgɑd] n : semidiós m

demilitarize [dɪ'mɪlətəˌraɪz] vt -rized; -rizing : desmilitarizar

demise [dɪ'maɪz] n 1 DEATH : fallecimiento m, deceso m 2 END : hundimiento m, desaparición f (de una institución, etc.)

demitasse ['dɛmiˌtæs, -ˌtɑs] *n* : taza *f* pequeña (de café)

demo ['dɛmo] *n* **1** DEMONSTRATION : demostración *f* (de productos, etc.) **2** *or* **demo product/version** (etc.) : demo *f*, producto *m* (o versión *f*, etc.) de demostración **3** *or* **demo tape** : demo *f*, cinta *f* de demostración

demobilization [diˌmoːbələ'zeɪɫən] *n* : desmovilización *f*

demobilize [di'moːbəˌlaɪz] *vt* **-lized; -lizing** : desmovilizar

democracy [di'mɑkrəsi] *n*, *pl* **-cies** : democracia *f*

democrat ['dɛməˌkræt] *n* : demócrata *mf*

democratic [ˌdɛmə'krætɪk] *adj* : democrático — **democratically** [-ˌtɪkli] *adv*

democratize [di'mɑkrəˌtaɪz] *vt* **-tized; -tizing** : democratizar — **democratization** [di'mɑkrətə'zeɪɫən] *n*

demographic[1] [ˌdɛmə'græfɪk] *adj* : demográfico

demographic[2] *n* **1** : perfil *m* demográfico **2 demographics** *npl* : estadísticas *fpl* demográficas, demografía *f*

demography [di'mɑgrəfi] *n* : demografía *f*

demolish [di'mɑlɪʃ] *vt* **1** RAZE : demoler, derribar, arrasar **2** DESTROY : destruir, destrozar

demolition [ˌdɛmə'lɪɫən, ˌdiː-] *n* : demolición *f*, derribo *m*

demon ['diːmən] *n* : demonio *m*, diablo *m*

demoniac [di'moːniˌæk] *or* **demoniacal** [diːmə'naɪəkəl] → **demonic**

demonic [di'mɑnɪk] *adj* : demoníaco

demonstrably [di'mɑntstrəbli] *adv* : manifiestamente, claramente

demonstrate ['dɛmənˌstreɪt] *vt* **-strated; -strating 1** SHOW : demostrar **2** PROVE : probar, demostrar **3** EXPLAIN : explicar, ilustrar — *vi* : manifestarse ⟨to demonstrate for something : manifestarse a favor de algo⟩ ⟨to demonstrate against something : manifestarse en contra de algo⟩

demonstration [ˌdɛmən'streɪɫən] *n* **1** SHOW : muestra *f*, demostración *f* **2** RALLY : manifestación *f*

demonstrative [di'mɑntstrətɪv] *adj* **1** EFFUSIVE : efusivo, expresivo, demostrativo **2** : demostrativo (en lingüística) ⟨demonstrative pronoun : pronombre demostrativo⟩

demonstrator ['dɛmənˌstreɪtər] *n* PROTESTER : manifestante *mf*

demoralize [di'mɔrəˌlaɪz] *vt* **-ized; -izing** : desmoralizar

demoralizing [di'mɔrəˌlaɪzɪŋ] *adj* : desmoralizador, desmoralizante

demote [di'moːt] *vt* **-moted; -moting** : degradar, bajar de categoría

demotion [di'moːɫən] *n* : degradación *f*, descenso *m* de categoría

demur [di'mər] *vi* **-murred; -murring 1** OBJECT : oponerse **2 to demur at** : ponerle objeciones a (algo)

demure [di'mjʊr] *adj* : recatado, modesto — **demurely** *adv*

demystify [di'mɪstəˌfaɪ] *vt* **-fied; -fying** : desmitificar

den ['dɛn] *n* **1** LAIR : cubil *m*, madriguera *f* **2** HIDEOUT : guarida *f* **3** STUDY : estudio *m*, gabinete *m*

denature [di'neɪtʃər] *vt* **-tured; -turing** : desnaturalizar

dengue ['dɛŋgi, -ˌgeɪ] *n* : dengue *m*

denial [di'naɪəl] *n* **1** REFUSAL : rechazo *m*, denegación *f*, negativa *f* **2** REPUDIATION : negación *f* (de una creencia, etc.), rechazo *m*

denigrate ['dɛnɪˌgreɪt] *vt* **-grated; -grating** : denigrar

denim ['dɛnəm] *n* **1** : tela *f* vaquera, mezclilla *f* Chile, Mex **2 denims** *npl* → **jeans**

denizen ['dɛnəzən] *n* : habitante *mf*; morador *m*, -dora *f*

denomination [dɪˌnɑmə'neɪɫən] *n* **1** FAITH : confesión *f*, fe *f* **2** VALUE : denominación *f*, valor *m* (de una moneda)

denominator [dɪ'nɑməˌneɪtər] *n* : denominador *m*

denote [di'noːt] *vt* **-noted; -noting 1** INDICATE, MARK : indicar, denotar, señalar **2** MEAN : significar

denouement [ˌdeɪnuː'mɑ] *n* : desenlace *m*

denounce [di'naʊnts] *vt* **-nounced; -nouncing 1** CENSURE : denunciar, censurar **2** ACCUSE : denunciar, acusar, delatar

dense ['dɛnts] *adj* **denser; -est 1** THICK : espeso, denso ⟨dense vegetation : vegetación densa⟩ ⟨a dense fog : una niebla espesa⟩ **2** STUPID : estúpido, burro *fam*

densely ['dɛntsli] *adv* **1** THICKLY : densamente **2** STUPIDLY : torpemente

denseness ['dɛntsnəs] *n* **1** → **density 2** STUPIDITY : estupidez *f*

density ['dɛntsəti] *n*, *pl* **-ties** : densidad *f*

dent[1] ['dɛnt] *vt* : abollar, mellar

dent[2] *n* : abolladura *f*, mella *f*

dental ['dɛntəl] *adj* : dental

dental floss *n* : hilo *m* dental

dental surgeon *n* : odontólogo *m*, -ga *f*

dentifrice ['dɛntəfrɪs] *n* : dentífrico *m*, pasta *f* de dientes

dentist ['dɛntɪst] *n* : dentista *mf*

dentistry ['dɛntɪstri] *n* : odontología *f*

dentures ['dɛntɫərz] *npl* : dentadura *f* postiza

denude [di'nuːd, -'njuːd] *vt* **-nuded; -nuding** STRIP : desnudar, despojar

denunciation [diˌnʌntsi'eɪɫən] *n* : denuncia *f*, acusación *f*

deny [di'naɪ] *vt* **-nied; -nying 1** REFUTE : desmentir, negar **2** DISOWN, REPUDIATE : negar, renegar de **3** REFUSE : denegar **4 to deny oneself** : privarse, sacrificarse

deodorant [di'oːdərənt] *n* : desodorante *m*

deodorize [di'oːdəˌraɪz] *vt* **-ized; -izing** : eliminar los malos olores

depart [di'pɑrt] *vt* : salirse de — *vi* **1** LEAVE : salir, partir, irse **2** DIE : morir

department [di'pɑrtmənt] *n* **1** DIVISION : sección *f* (de una tienda, una organización, etc.), departamento *m* (de una empresa, una universidad, etc.), ministerio *m* (del gobierno) **2** PROVINCE,

SPHERE : esfera *f*, campo *m*, competencia *f*

departmental [dɪˌpɑrtˈmɛntəl, ˌdiː-] *adj* : departamental

department chair → **chair²**

department store *n* : grandes almacenes *mpl*

departure [dɪˈpɑrtʃər] *n* **1** LEAVING : salida *f*, partida *f* **2** DEVIATION : desviación *f*

depend [dɪˈpɛnd] *vi* **1** RELY : contar (con), confiar (en) ⟨depend on me! : ¡cuenta conmigo!⟩ **2 to depend on** : depender de ⟨success depends on hard work : el éxito depende de trabajar duro⟩ **3 that depends** : según, eso depende

dependable [dɪˈpɛndəbəl] *adj* : responsable, digno de confianza, fiable

dependence [dɪˈpɛndənts] *n* : dependencia *f*

dependency [dɪˈpɛndəntsi] *n, pl* **-cies 1** → **dependence 2** : posesión *f* (de una unidad política)

dependent¹ [dɪˈpɛndənt] *adj* : dependiente

dependent² *n* : persona *f* a cargo de alguien

depict [dɪˈpɪkt] *vt* **1** PORTRAY : representar **2** DESCRIBE : describir

depiction [dɪˈpɪkʃən] *n* : representación *f*, descripción *f*

deplete [dɪˈpliːt] *vt* **-pleted; -pleting 1** EXHAUST : agotar **2** REDUCE : reducir

depletion [dɪˈpliːʃən] *n* **1** EXHAUSTION : agotamiento *m* **2** REDUCTION : reducción *f*, disminución *f*

deplorable [dɪˈplorəbəl] *adj* **1** CONTEMPTIBLE : deplorable, despreciable **2** LAMENTABLE : lamentable

deplore [dɪˈplor] *vt* **-plored; -ploring 1** REGRET : deplorar, lamentar **2** CONDEMN : condenar, deplorar

deploy [dɪˈplɔɪ] *vt* : desplegar

deployment [dɪˈplɔɪmənt] *n* : despliegue *m*

deport [dɪˈport] *vt* **1** EXPEL : deportar, expulsar (de un país) **2 to deport oneself** BEHAVE : comportarse

deportation [ˌdiːˌporˈteɪʃən] *n* : deportación *f*

depose [dɪˈpoːz] *vt* **-posed; -posing** : deponer

deposit¹ [dɪˈpazət] *vt* **-ited; -iting** : depositar

deposit² *n* **1** : depósito *m* (en el banco) **2** DOWN PAYMENT : entrega *f* inicial **3** : depósito *m*, yacimiento *m* (en geología)

deposition [ˌdɛpəˈzɪʃən] *n* TESTIMONY : deposición *f*

depository [dɪˈpazəˌtori] *n, pl* **-ries** : almacén *m*, depósito *m*

depot [in sense 1 usu ˈdɛˌpoː, 2 usu ˈdiː-] *n* **1** STOREHOUSE : almacén *m*, depósito *m* **2** STATION, TERMINAL : terminal *mf*, estación *f* (de autobuses, ferrocarriles, etc.)

deprave [dɪˈpreɪv] *vt* **-praved; -praving** : depravar, pervertir

depraved [dɪˈpreɪvd] *adj* : depravado, degenerado

depravity [dɪˈprævəti] *n, pl* **-ties** : depravación *f*

depreciate [dɪˈpriːʃiˌeɪt] *v* **-ated; -ating** *vt* **1** DEVALUE : depreciar, devaluar **2** DISPARAGE : menospreciar, despreciar — *vi* : depreciarse, devaluarse

depreciation [dɪˌpriːʃiˈeɪʃən] *n* : depreciación *f*, devaluación *f*

depress [dɪˈprɛs] *vt* **1** PRESS, PUSH : apretar, presionar, pulsar **2** REDUCE : reducir, hacer bajar (precios, ventas, etc.) **3** SADDEN : deprimir, abatir, entristecer **4** DEVALUE : depreciar

depressant *n* : depresivo *m*

depressed [dɪˈprɛst] *adj* **1** DEJECTED : deprimido, abatido **2** : deprimido, en crisis (dícese de la economía)

depressing [dɪˈprɛsɪŋ] *adj* : deprimente, triste

depression [dɪˈprɛʃən] *n* **1** DESPONDENCY : depresión *f*, abatimiento *m* **2** : depresión (en una superficie) **3** RECESSION : depresión *f* económica, crisis *f*

deprivation [ˌdɛprəˈveɪʃən] *n* : privación *f*

deprive [dɪˈpraɪv] *vt* **-prived; -priving** : privar

depth [ˈdɛpθ] *n, pl* **depths** [ˈdɛpθs, ˈdɛps] **1** : profundidad *f* **2 depths** *npl* ⟨in the depths of winter : en pleno invierno⟩ ⟨in the depths of despair : en la más profunda desesperación⟩ **3 in depth** : a fondo **4 out of one's depth** : perdido ⟨I'm out of my depth : esto es demasiado difícil/especializado (etc.) para mí⟩

deputation [ˌdɛpjəˈteɪʃən] *n* : diputación *f*

deputize [ˈdɛpjuˌtaɪz] *vt* **-tized; -tizing** : nombrar como segundo

deputy [ˈdɛpjuti] *n, pl* **-ties** : suplente *mf*; sustituto *m*, -ta *f*

derail [dɪˈreɪl] *v* : descarrilar

derailment [dɪˈreɪlmənt] *n* : descarrilamiento *m*

derange [dɪˈreɪndʒ] *vt* **-ranged; -ranging 1** DISARRANGE : desarreglar, desordenar **2** DISTURB, UPSET : trastornar, perturbar **3** MADDEN : enloquecer, volver loco

deranged [dɪˈreɪndʒd] *adj* DISTURBED, INSANE : trastornado, perturbado

derangement [dɪˈreɪndʒmənt] *n* **1** DISTURBANCE, UPSET : trastorno *m* **2** INSANITY : locura *f*, perturbación *f* mental

derby [ˈdərbi] *n, pl* **-bies 1** : derby *m* ⟨the Kentucky Derby : el Derby de Kentucky⟩ **2** : sombrero *m* hongo, bombín *m*

deregulate [dɪˈrɛgjuˌleɪt] *vt* **-lated; -lating** : desregular

deregulation [dɪˌrɛgjuˈleɪʃən] *n* : desregulación *f*

derelict¹ [ˈdɛrəˌlɪkt] *adj* **1** ABANDONED : abandonado, en ruinas **2** REMISS : negligente, remiso

derelict² *n* **1** : propiedad *f* abandonada **2** VAGRANT : vagabundo *m*, -da *f*

deride [dɪˈraɪd] *vt* **-rided; -riding** : ridiculizar, burlarse de

derision [dɪ'rɪʒən] *n* : escarnio *m*, irrisión *f*, mofa *f*

derisive [dɪ'raɪsɪv] *adj* : burlón

derisory [dɪ'raɪsəri, -zə-] *adj* **1** → **derisive** **2** PALTRY, MEAGER : irrisorio, mísero ⟨a derisory price : un precio irrisorio⟩

derivation [ˌdɛrə'veɪʃən] *n* : derivación *f*

derivative[1] [dɪ'rɪvəṭɪv] *adj* **1** DERIVED : derivado **2** BANAL : carente de originalidad, banal

derivative[2] *n* : derivado *m*

derive [dɪ'raɪv] *v* **-rived; -riving** *vt* **1** OBTAIN : obtener, sacar **2** DEDUCE : deducir, inferir — *vi* : provenir, derivar, proceder

dermatologist [ˌdərmə'talədʒɪst] *n* : dermatólogo *m*, -ga *f*

dermatology [ˌdərmə'talədʒi] *n* : dermatología *f*

derogatory [dɪ'ragə,tori] *adj* : despectivo, despreciativo

derrick ['dɛrɪk] *n* **1** CRANE : grúa *f* **2** : torre *f* de perforación (sobre un pozo de petróleo)

descend [dɪ'sɛnd] *vt* : descender, bajar — *vi* **1** : descender, bajar ⟨he descended from the platform : descendió del estrado⟩ **2** DERIVE : descender, provenir **3** STOOP : rebajarse ⟨I descended to his level : me rebajé a su nivel⟩ **4 to descend upon** : caer sobre, invadir

descendant[1] [dɪ'sɛndənt] *adj* : descendente

descendant[2] *n* : descendiente *mf*

descent [dɪ'sɛnt] *n* **1** : bajada *f*, descenso *m* ⟨the descent from the mountain : el descenso de la montaña⟩ **2** ANCESTRY : ascendencia *f*, linaje *f* **3** SLOPE : pendiente *f*, cuesta *f* **4** FALL : caída *f* **5** ATTACK : incursión *f*, ataque *m*

describe [dɪ'skraɪb] *vt* **-scribed; -scribing** : describir

description [dɪ'skrɪpʃən] *n* : descripción *f*

descriptive [dɪ'skrɪptɪv] *adj* : descriptivo ⟨descriptive adjective : adjetivo calificativo⟩

desecrate ['dɛsɪ,kreɪt] *vt* **-crated; -crating** : profanar

desecration [ˌdɛsɪ'kreɪʃən] *n* : profanación *f*

desegregate [dɪ'sɛgrə,geɪt] *vt* **-gated; -gating** : eliminar la segregación racial de

desegregation [diˌsɛgrə'geɪʃən] *n* : eliminación *f* de la segregación racial

desert[1] [dɪ'zərt] *vt* : abandonar (una persona o un lugar), desertar de (una causa, etc.) — *vi* : desertar

desert[2] ['dɛzərt] *adj* : desierto ⟨a desert island : una isla desierta⟩

desert[3] *n* **1** [dɪ'zərt] : desierto *m* (en geografía) **2** [dɪ'zərt] → **deserts**

deserted [dɪ'zərṭəd] *adj* : desierto

deserter [dɪ'zərṭər] *n* : desertor *m*, -tora *f*

desertion [dɪ'zərʃən] *n* : abandono *m*, deserción *f* (militar)

deserts [dɪ'zərts] *npl* : merecido *m* ⟨to get one's just deserts : llevarse uno su merecido⟩

deserve [dɪ'zərv] *vt* **-served; -serving** : merecer

deservedly [dɪ'zərvədli] *adv* : merecidamente

deserving [dɪ'zərvɪŋ] *adj* : meritorio ⟨deserving of : digno de⟩

desiccate ['dɛsɪ,keɪt] *vt* **-cated; -cating** : desecar, deshidratar

design[1] [dɪ'zaɪn] *vt* **1** DEVISE : diseñar, concebir, idear **2** PLAN : proyectar **3** SKETCH : trazar, bosquejar

design[2] *n* **1** PLAN, SCHEME : plan *m*, proyecto *m* ⟨by design : a propósito, intencionalmente⟩ **2** SKETCH : diseño *m*, bosquejo *m* **3** PATTERN, STYLE : diseño *m*, estilo *m* **4 designs** *npl* INTENTIONS : propósitos *mpl*, designios *mpl*

designate ['dɛzɪg,neɪt] *vt* **-nated; -nating** **1** INDICATE, SPECIFY : indicar, especificar **2** APPOINT : nombrar, designar

designation [ˌdɛzɪg'neɪʃən] *n* **1** NAMING : designación *f* **2** NAME : denominación *f*, nombre *m* **3** APPOINTMENT : designación *f*, nombramiento *m*

designer[1] [dɪ'zaɪnər] *adj* : de diseño, de marca

designer[2] *n* : diseñador *m*, -dora *f*

desirability [dɪ,zaɪrə'bɪləṭi] *n*, *pl* **-ties** **1** ADVISABILITY : conveniencia *f* **2** ATTRACTIVENESS : atractivo *m*

desirable [dɪ'zaɪrəbəl] *adj* **1** ADVISABLE : conveniente, aconsejable **2** ATTRACTIVE : deseable, atractivo

desire[1] [dɪ'zaɪr] *vt* **-sired; -siring** **1** WANT : desear **2** REQUEST : rogar, solicitar

desire[2] *n* : deseo *m*, anhelo *m*, ansia *m*

desist [dɪ'sɪst, -'zɪst] *vi* **to desist from** : desistir de, abstenerse de

desk ['dɛsk] *n* : escritorio *m*, pupitre *m* (en la escuela)

desktop[1] ['dɛsk,tɑp] *adj* : de escritorio

desktop[2] *or* **desktop computer** *n* : computadora *f*, computador *m*, ordenador *m* *Spain* (no portátil)

desktop publishing *n* : autoedición *f*

desolate[1] ['dɛsə,leɪt, -zə-] *vt* **-lated; -lating** : devastar, desolar

desolate[2] ['dɛsələt, -zə-] *adj* **1** BARREN : desolado, desierto, yermo **2** DISCONSOLATE : desconsolado, desolado

desolation [ˌdɛsə'leɪʃən, -zə-] *n* : desolación *f*

despair[1] [dɪ'spær] *vi* : desesperar, perder las esperanzas

despair[2] *n* : desesperación *f*, desesperanza *f*

despairing *adj* : desesperado

desperate ['dɛspərət] *adj* **1** HOPELESS : desesperado, sin esperanzas **2** RASH : desesperado, precipitado **3** SERIOUS, URGENT : grave, urgente, apremiante ⟨a desperate need : una necesidad apremiante⟩

desperately ['dɛspərətli] *adv* : desesperadamente, urgentemente

desperation [ˌdɛspə'reɪʃən] *n* : desesperación *f*

despicable [dɪ'spɪkəbəl, 'dɛspɪ-] *adj* : vil, despreciable, infame

despise [di'spaɪz] *vt* -spised; -spising
: despreciar

despite [də'spaɪt] *prep* : a pesar de, aún con

despoil [di'spɔɪl] *vt* : saquear

despondency [di'spɑndən/si] *n* : desaliento *m*, desánimo *m*, depresión *f*

despondent [di'spɑndənt] *adj* : desalentado, desanimado

despot ['dɛspət, -ˌpɑt] *n* : déspota *mf*; tirano *m*, -na *f*

despotic [dɛs'pɑtɪk] *adj* : despótico

despotism ['dɛspəˌtɪzəm] *n* : despotismo
m

dessert [di'zərt] *n* : postre *m*

dessertspoon [di'zərtˌspuːn] *n* : cuchara *f*
de postre

destination [ˌdɛstə'neɪLən] *n* : destino *m*,
destinación *f*

destined ['dɛstənd] *adj* 1 FATED : predestinado 2 BOUND : destinado, con
destino (a), con rumbo (a)

destiny ['dɛstəni] *n, pl* -nies : destino *m*

destitute ['dɛstəˌtuːt, -ˌtjuːt] *adj* 1 LACK-
ING : carente, desprovisto 2 POOR
: indigente, en miseria

destitution [ˌdɛstə'tuːLən, -'tjuː-] *n* : indigencia *f*, miseria *f*

destroy [di'strɔɪ] *vt* 1 KILL : matar 2
DEMOLISH : destruir, destrozar

destroyer [di'strɔɪər] *n* : destructor *m*
(buque)

destruction [di'strʌkLən] *n* : destrucción
f, ruina *f*

destructive [di'strʌktɪv] *adj* : destructor,
destructivo

desultory ['dɛsəlˌtori] *adj* 1 AIMLESS
: sin rumbo, sin objeto 2 DISCON-
NECTED : inconexo

detach [di'tætʃ] *vt* : separar, quitar, desprender

detached [di'tætʃt] *adj* 1 SEPARATE
: separado, suelto 2 ALOOF : distante,
indiferente 3 IMPARTIAL : imparcial,
objetivo

detachment [di'tætʃmənt] *n* 1 SEPARA-
TION : separación *f* 2 DETAIL : destacamento *m* (de tropas) 3 ALOOFNESS
: reserva *f*, indiferencia *f* 4 IMPARTIAL-
ITY : imparcialidad *f*

detail[1] [di'teɪl, 'diːˌteɪl] *vt* : detallar, exponer en detalle

detail[2] *n* 1 : detalle *m*, pormenor *m* ⟨to
go into detail : entrar en detalles⟩ ⟨in
detail : con/en detalle, detallada-
mente⟩ 2 : destacamento *m* (de tropas)

detailed [di'teɪld, 'diːˌteɪld] *adj* : detallado, minucioso

detain [di'teɪn] *vt* 1 HOLD : detener 2
DELAY : entretener, demorar, retrasar

detect [di'tɛkt] *vt* : detectar, descubrir

detection [di'tɛkLən] *n* : descubrimiento
m

detective [di'tɛktɪv] *n* : detective *mf* ⟨pri-
vate detective : detective privado⟩ ⟨de-
tective novel : novela policial/policíaca⟩
⟨detective work : investigación⟩

detector [di'tɛktər] *n* : detector *m*

detention [di'tɛntLən] *n* : detención *m*

deter [di'tər] *vt* -terred; -terring : disuadir, impedir

detergent [di'tərdʒənt] *n* : detergente *m*

deteriorate [di'tɪriəˌreɪt] *vi* -rated; -rating
: deteriorarse, empeorar

deterioration [diˌtɪriə'reɪLən] *n* : deterioro
m, empeoramiento *m*

determinant[1] [di'tərmənənt] *adj* : determinante

determinant[2] *n* 1 : factor *m* determinante 2 : determinante *m* (en
matemáticas)

determination [diˌtərmə'neɪLən] *n* 1 DE-
CISION : determinación *f*, decisión *f* 2
RESOLUTION : resolución *f*, determinación *f* ⟨with grim determination : con
una firme resolución⟩

determine [di'tərmən] *vt* -mined; -min-
ing 1 ESTABLISH : determinar, establecer 2 SETTLE : decidir 3 FIND OUT
: averiguar 4 BRING ABOUT : determinar

determined [di'tərmənd] *adj* RESOLUTE
: decidido, resuelto

deterrence [di'tərən/s] *n* : disuasión *f*

deterrent [di'tərənt] *n* : medida *f* disuasiva

detest [di'tɛst] *vt* : detestar, odiar, aborrecer

detestable [di'tɛstəbəl] *adj* : detestable,
odioso, aborrecible

dethrone [di'θroːn] *vt* -throned; -throning
: destronar

detonate ['dɛtənˌeɪt] *v* -nated; -nating *vt*
: hacer detonar — *vi* : detonar, estallar

detonation [ˌdɛtə'neɪLən] *n* : detonación *f*

detonator ['dɛtənˌeɪtər] *n* : detonador *m*

detour[1] ['diːˌtʊr, di'tʊr] *vi* : desviarse

detour[2] *n* : desvío *m*, rodeo *m*

detox[1] ['diːˌtɑks, di'tɑks] *vt fam* : desintoxicar — *vi fam* : desintoxicarse

detox[2] *n fam* : desintoxicación *f* ⟨she's in
detox : está en el proceso de desintoxicación (de drogas, etc.)⟩

detoxify [di'tɑksəˌfaɪ] *vt* -fied; -fying
: desintoxicar — **detoxification**
[diˌtɑksəfə'keɪLən] *n*

detract [di'trækt] *vt* **to detract from** : restarle valor a, quitarle méritos a

detractor [di'træktər] *n* : detractor *m*,
-tora *f*

detriment ['dɛtrəmənt] *n* : detrimento *m*,
perjuicio *m*

detrimental [ˌdɛtrə'mɛntəl] *adj* : perjudicial — **detrimentally** *adv*

devaluation [diˌvæljuː'eɪLən] *n* : devaluación *f*

devalue [di'vælˌjuː] *vt* -ued; -uing : devaluar, depreciar

devastate ['dɛvəˌsteɪt] *vt* -tated; -tating
: devastar, arrasar, asolar

devastating ['dɛvəˌsteɪtɪŋ] *adj* 1 DE-
STRUCTIVE, PAINFUL : devastador 2
CUTTING, POWERFUL : demoledor,
aplastante, arrollador

devastation [ˌdɛvə'steɪLən] *n* : devastación *f*, estragos *mpl*

develop [di'vɛləp] *vt* 1 FORM, MAKE : desarrollar, elaborar, formar 2 : revelar
(en fotografía) 3 FOSTER : desarrollar,
fomentar 4 EXPLOIT : explotar (recursos), urbanizar (un área) 5 ACQUIRE
: adquirir ⟨to develop an interest : ad-

quirir un interés⟩ **6** CONTRACT : contraer (una enfermedad) — *vi* **1** GROW : desarrollarse **2** ARISE : aparecer, surgir

developed [dɪˈvɛləpt] *adj* : avanzado, desarrollado

developer [dɪˈvɛləpər] *n* **1** : inmobiliaria *f*, urbanizadora *f* **2** : revelador *m* (en fotografía)

developing [dɪˈvɛləpɪŋ] *adj* : en vías de desarrollo (dícese de países)

development [dɪˈvɛləpmənt] *n* **1** : desarrollo *m* ⟨physical development : desarrollo físico⟩ **2** : urbanización *f* (de un área), explotación *f* (de recursos), creación *f* (de inventos) **3** EVENT : acontecimiento *m*, suceso *m* ⟨to await developments : esperar acontecimientos⟩

deviant [ˈdiːviənt] *adj* : desviado, anormal

deviate [ˈdiːviˌeɪt] *v* **-ated; -ating** *vi* : desviarse, apartarse — *vt* : desviar

deviation [ˌdiːviˈeɪən] *n* : desviación *f*

device [dɪˈvaɪs] *n* **1** MECHANISM : dispositivo *m*, aparato *m*, mecanismo *m* **2** EMBLEM : emblema *m*

devil¹ [ˈdɛvəl] *vt* **-iled** *or* **-illed; -iling** *or* **-illing** **1** : sazonar con picante y especias **2** PESTER : molestar

devil² *n* **1** SATAN : el diablo, Satanás *m* **2** DEMON : diablo *m*, demonio *m* **3** FIEND : persona *f* diabólica; malvado *m*, -da *f* **4** FELLOW : persona *f* ⟨you lucky devil! : ¡vaya suerte que tienes!⟩ ⟨poor devil : pobre diablo⟩

devilish [ˈdɛvəlɪʃ] *adj* : diabólico

devilry [ˈdɛvəlri] *n, pl* **-ries** : diabluras *fpl*, travesuras *fpl*

devious [ˈdiːviəs] *adj* **1** CRAFTY : taimado, artero **2** WINDING : tortuoso, sinuoso

devise [dɪˈvaɪz] *vt* **-vised; -vising** **1** INVENT : idear, concebir, inventar **2** PLOT : tramar

devoid [dɪˈvɔɪd] *adj* ~ **of** : carente de, desprovisto de

devote [dɪˈvoːt] *vt* **-voted; -voting** **1** DEDICATE : consagrar, dedicar ⟨to devote one's life : dedicar uno su vida⟩ **2 to devote oneself** : dedicarse

devoted [dɪˈvoːt̬əd] *adj* **1** FAITHFUL : leal, fiel **2 to be devoted to someone** : tenerle mucho cariño a alguien

devotee [ˌdɛvəˈtiː, -ˈteɪ] *n* : devoto *m*, -ta *f*

devotion [dɪˈvoːʃən] *n* **1** DEDICATION : dedicación *f*, devoción *f* **2 devotions** PRAYERS : oraciones *fpl*, devociones *fpl*

devour [dɪˈvaʊər] *vt* : devorar

devout [dɪˈvaʊt] *adj* **1** PIOUS : devoto, piadoso **2** EARNEST, SINCERE : sincero, ferviente — **devoutly** *adv*

devoutness [dɪˈvaʊtnəs] *n* : devoción *f*, piedad *f*

dew [ˈduː, ˈdjuː] *n* : rocío *m*

dewlap [ˈduːˌlæp, ˈdjuː-] *n* : papada *f*

dew point *n* : punto *m* de condensación

dewy [ˈduːi, ˈdjuːi] *adj* **dewier; -est** : cubierto de rocío

dexterity [dɛkˈstɛrət̬i] *n, pl* **-ties** : destreza *f*, habilidad *f*

dexterous [ˈdɛkstrəs] *adj* : diestro, hábil

dexterously [ˈdɛkstrəsli] *adv* : con destreza, con habilidad, hábilmente

diabetes [ˌdaɪəˈbiːt̬iz] *n* : diabetes *f*

diabetic¹ [ˌdaɪəˈbɛt̬ɪk] *adj* : diabético

diabetic² *n* : diabético *m*, -ca *f*

diabolic [ˌdaɪəˈbɑlɪk] *or* **diabolical** [-lɪkəl] *adj* : diabólico, satánico

diacritic [ˌdaɪəˈkrɪt̬ɪk] *n* : diacrítico *m*

diacritical [ˌdaɪəˈkrɪt̬ɪkəl] *or* **diacritic** *adj* : diacrítico

diadem [ˈdaɪəˌdɛm, -dəm] *n* : diadema *f*

diagnose [ˈdaɪɪgˌnoːs, ˌdaɪɪgˈnoːs] *vt* **-nosed; -nosing** : diagnosticar

diagnosis [ˌdaɪɪgˈnoːsɪs] *n, pl* **-noses** [-ˈnoːˌsiːz] : diagnóstico *m*

diagnostic [ˌdaɪɪgˈnɑstɪk] *adj* : diagnóstico

diagonal¹ [daɪˈægənəl] *adj* : diagonal, en diagonal

diagonal² *n* : diagonal *f*

diagonally [daɪˈægənəli] *adv* : diagonalmente, en diagonal

diagram¹ [ˈdaɪəˌgræm] *vt* **-gramed** *or* **-grammed; -graming** *or* **-gramming** : hacer un diagrama de

diagram² *n* : diagrama *m*, gráfico *m*, esquema *m*

dial¹ [ˈdaɪl] *v* **dialed** *or* **dialled; dialing** *or* **dialling** : marcar, discar

dial² *n* : esfera *f* (de un reloj), dial *m* (de un radio), disco *m* (de un teléfono)

dialect [ˈdaɪəˌlɛkt] *n* : dialecto *m*

dialogue [ˈdaɪəˌlɔg] *n* : diálogo *m*

dial tone *n* : tono *m* (de marcar/marcado/discar)

diameter [daɪˈæmət̬ər] *n* : diámetro *m*

diamond [ˈdaɪmənd, ˈdaɪə-] *n* **1** : diamante *m*, brillante *m* ⟨a diamond necklace : un collar de brillantes⟩ **2** : rombo *m*, forma *f* de rombo **3** : diamante *m* (naipe) **4** INFIELD : cuadro *m*, diamante *m* (en béisbol)

diaper [ˈdaɪpər, ˈdaɪə-] *n* : pañal *m*

diaphragm [ˈdaɪəˌfræm] *n* : diafragma *m*

diarrhea [ˌdaɪəˈriːə] *n* : diarrea *f*

diary [ˈdaɪəri] *n, pl* **-ries** : diario *m*

diatribe [ˈdaɪəˌtraɪb] *n* : diatriba *f*

dice¹ [ˈdaɪs] *vt* **diced; dicing** : cortar en cubos

dice² *ns & pl* **1** → **die²** **2** : dados *mpl* (juego)

dicker [ˈdɪkər] *vt* : regatear

dictate¹ [ˈdɪkˌteɪt, dɪkˈteɪt] *v* **-tated; -tating** *vt* **1** : dictar ⟨to dictate a letter : dictar una carta⟩ **2** ORDER : mandar, ordenar — *vi* : dar órdenes

dictate² [ˈdɪkˌteɪt] *n* **1** : mandato *m*, orden *f* **2 dictates** *npl* : dictados *mpl* ⟨the dictates of conscience : los dictados de la conciencia⟩

dictation [dɪkˈteɪən] *n* : dictado *m*

dictator [ˈdɪkˌteɪt̬ər] *n* : dictador *m*, -dora *f*

dictatorial [ˌdɪktəˈtoriəl] *adj* : dictatorial — **dictatorially** *adv*

dictatorship [dɪkˈteɪt̬ərˌʃɪp, ˈdɪkˌ-] *n* : dictadura *f*

diction [ˈdɪkʃən] *n* **1** : lenguaje *m*, estilo *m* **2** ENUNCIATION : dicción *f*, articulación *f*

dictionary [ˈdɪkLə͵nɛri] *n, pl* **-naries** : diccionario *m*

did → **do**

didactic [daɪˈdæktɪk] *adj* : didáctico

die¹ [ˈdaɪ] *vi* **died** [ˈdaɪd]; **dying** [ˈdaɪɪŋ] **1** : morir, morirse **2** CEASE : morir, morirse ⟨a dying civilization : una civilización moribunda⟩ **3** STOP : apagarse, dejar de funcionar ⟨the motor died : el motor se apagó⟩ **4 to be dying for/to** : morirse por ⟨I'm dying for a coffee : me muero por un café⟩ ⟨I'm dying to leave : me muero por irme⟩ **5 to die away** FADE : irse apagando, disminuir (dícese de un sonido) **6 to die down** SUBSIDE : disminuir, amainar (dícese del viento, etc.), irse apagando (dícese de los aplausos, las llamas, etc.), calmarse (dícese de un escándalo, etc.) **7 to die laughing** : morirse de risa **8 to die of** : morir de, morirse de ⟨he died of old age : murió de viejo⟩ **9 to die out** : extinguirse

die² [ˈdaɪ] *n, pl* **dice** [ˈdaɪs] : dado *m*

die³ *n, pl* **dies** [ˈdaɪz] **1** STAMP : troquel *m*, cuño *m* **2** MOLD : matriz *f*, molde *m*

diehard [ˈdaɪ͵hɑrd] *adj* : fanático

diesel [ˈdiːzəl, -səl] *n* : diesel *m*

diet¹ [ˈdaɪət] *vi* : ponerse a régimen, hacer dieta

diet² *n* : régimen *m*, dieta *f*

dietary [ˈdaɪə͵tɛri] *adj* : alimenticio, dietético

dietitian *or* **dietician** [͵daɪəˈtɪʃən] *n* : dietista *mf*

differ [ˈdɪfər] *vi* **-ferred; -ferring 1** : diferir, diferenciarse **2** VARY : variar **3** DISAGREE : discrepar, diferir, no estar de acuerdo

difference [ˈdɪfrəns, ˈdɪfərəns] *n* **1** : diferencia *f* ⟨to tell/notice the difference : notar/ver la diferencia⟩ **2** DISCREPANCY : diferencia *f* ⟨to split the difference : dividirse la diferencia (en partes iguales)⟩ **3** DISAGREEMENT : diferencia *f*, desacuerdo *m* ⟨to resolve/settle one's differences : resolver/saldar sus diferencias⟩ **4 same difference!** : ¡es casi lo mismo! **5 to make a difference** MATTER : importar ⟨what difference does it make? : ¿qué importa?⟩ ⟨it makes no difference to me : me da igual⟩ **6 to make a difference in** AFFECT : afectar, influir en

different [ˈdɪfrənt, ˈdɪfərənt] *adj* : distinto, diferente

differential¹ [͵dɪfəˈrɛntʃəl] *adj* : diferencial

differential² *n* : diferencial *m*

differentiate [͵dɪfəˈrɛntʃi͵eɪt] *v* **-ated; -ating** *vt* **1** : hacer diferente **2** DISTINGUISH : distinguir, diferenciar — *vi* : distinguir

differentiation [͵dɪfə͵rɛntʃiˈeɪʃən] *n* : diferenciación *f*

differently [ˈdɪfrəntli, ˈdɪfərənt-] *adv* : de otra manera, de otro modo, distintamente

difficult [ˈdɪfɪ͵kʌlt] *adj* : difícil

difficulty [ˈdɪfɪ͵kʌlti] *n, pl* **-ties 1** : dificultad *f* **2** PROBLEM : problema *f*, dificultad *f*

diffidence [ˈdɪfədənts] *n* **1** SHYNESS : retraimiento *m*, timidez *f*, apocamiento *m* **2** RETICENCE : reticencia *f*

diffident [ˈdɪfədənt] *adj* **1** SHY : tímido, apocado, inseguro **2** RESERVED : reservado

diffuse¹ [dɪˈfjuːz] *v* **-fused; -fusing** *vt* : difundir, esparcir — *vi* : difundirse, esparcirse

diffuse² [dɪˈfjuːs] *adj* **1** WORDY : prolijo, verboso **2** WIDESPREAD : difuso

diffusion [dɪfˈjuːʒən] *n* : difusión *f*

dig¹ [ˈdɪg] *v* **dug** [ˈdʌg]; **digging** *vt* **1** : cavar, excavar ⟨to dig a hole : cavar un hoyo⟩ **2** EXTRACT : sacar ⟨to dig up potatoes : sacar papas del suelo⟩ **3** POKE, THRUST : clavar, hincar ⟨he dug me in the ribs : me dio un codazo en las costillas⟩ **4 to dig out** RETRIEVE, EXTRACT : sacar **5 to dig up** DISCOVER : descubrir, sacar a luz — *vi* **1** : cavar, excavar **2** *or* **to dig around** RUMMAGE : hurgar (en los bolsillos, etc.) ⟨I dug (around) in my purse for my keys : hurgué en el bolso buscando las llaves⟩ **3 to dig for** : buscar ⟨to dig for gold : buscar oro (cavando en el suelo)⟩ ⟨to dig for clues : buscar pistas, investigar⟩ **4 to dig in** : atrincherarse **5 to dig in** : empezar a comer ⟨dig in! : ¡a comer!⟩ **6 to dig into** POKE : clavarse en **7 to dig into** INVESTIGATE : investigar

dig² *n* **1** POKE : codazo *m* **2** GIBE : pulla *f* **3** EXCAVATION : excavación *f*

digest¹ [daɪˈdʒɛst, dɪ-] *vt* **1** ASSIMILATE : digerir, asimilar **2** : digerir (comida) **3** SUMMARIZE : compendiar, resumir

digest² [ˈdaɪ͵dʒɛst] *n* : compendio *m*, resumen *m*

digestible [daɪˈdʒɛstəbəl, dɪ-] *adj* : digerible

digestion [daɪˈdʒɛstʃən, dɪ-] *n* : digestión *f*

digestive [daɪˈdʒɛstɪv, dɪ-] *adj* : digestivo ⟨the digestive system : el sistema digestivo⟩

digit [ˈdɪdʒət] *n* **1** NUMERAL : dígito *m*, número *m* **2** FINGER, TOE : dedo *m*

digital [ˈdɪdʒətəl] *adj* : digital ⟨digital camera : cámara digital⟩ — **digitally** *adv*

digitalize [ˈdɪdʒətə͵laɪz] *vt* **-ized; -izing** : digitalizar

dignified [ˈdɪgnə͵faɪd] *adj* : digno, decoroso

dignify [ˈdɪgnə͵faɪ] *vt* **-fied; -fying** : dignificar, honrar

dignitary [ˈdɪgnə͵tɛri] *n, pl* **-taries** : dignatario *m*, -ria *f*

dignity [ˈdɪgnəti] *n, pl* **-ties** : dignidad *f*

digress [daɪˈgrɛs, də-] *vi* : desviarse del tema, divagar

digression [daɪˈgrɛʃən, də-] *n* : digresión *f*

dike *or* **dyke** [ˈdaɪk] *n* : dique *m*

dilapidated [dəˈlæpə͵deɪtəd] *adj* : ruinoso, desvencijado, destartalado

dilapidation [də͵læpəˈdeɪʃən] *n* : deterioro *m*, estado *m* ruinoso

dilate [daɪˈleɪt, ˈdaɪ͵leɪt] *v* **-lated; -lating** *vt* : dilatar — *vi* : dilatarse

dilemma [dɪ'lɛmə] *n* : dilema *m*
dilettante ['dɪlə,tɑnt, -,tænt] *n, pl* **-tantes** [-,tɑnts, -,tænts] *or* **-tanti** [,dɪlə'tɑnti, -'tæn-] : diletante *mf*
diligence ['dɪlədʒənts] *n* : diligencia *f*, aplicación *f*
diligent ['dɪlədʒənt] *adj* : diligente ⟨a diligent search : una búsqueda minuciosa⟩ — **diligently** *adv*
dill ['dɪl] *n* : eneldo *m*
dillydally ['dɪli,dæli] *vi* **-lied; -lying** : demorarse, perder tiempo
dilute [daɪ'luːt, də-] *vt* **-luted; -luting** : diluir, aguar
dilution [daɪ'luːLən, də-] *n* : dilución *f*
dim¹ ['dɪm] *v* **dimmed; dimming** *vt* : atenuar (la luz), nublar (la vista), borrar (la memoria), opacar (una superficie) — *vi* : oscurecerse, apagarse
dim² *adj* **dimmer; dimmest** **1** FAINT : oscuro, tenue (dícese de la luz), nublado (dícese de la vista), borrado (dícese de la memoria) **2** STUPID : tonto, torpe **3 to take a dim view of** : ver con malos ojos
dime ['daɪm] *n* : moneda *f* de diez centavos
dimension [də'mɛntLən, daɪ-] *n* **1** : dimensión *f* **2 dimensions** *npl* EXTENT, SCOPE : dimensiones *fpl*, extensión *f*, medida *f*
diminish [də'mɪnɪL] *vt* LESSEN : disminuir, reducir, aminar — *vi* DWINDLE, WANE : menguar, reducirse
diminutive [də'mɪnjuṯɪv] *adj* : diminutivo, minúsculo
dimly ['dɪmli] *adv* : indistintamente, débilmente
dimmer ['dɪmər] *n* : potenciómetro *m*, conmutador *m* de luces (en automóviles)
dimness ['dɪmnəs] *n* : oscuridad *f*, debilidad *f* (de la vista), imprecisión *f* (de la memoria)
dimple ['dɪmpəl] *n* : hoyuelo *m*
din ['dɪn] *n* : estrépito *m*, estruendo *m*
dine ['daɪn] *vi* **dined; dining** : cenar
diner ['daɪnər] *n* **1** : comensal *mf* (persona) **2** : vagón *m* restaurante (en un tren) **3** : cafetería *f*, restaurante *m* barato
dinghy ['dɪŋi, 'dɪŋgi, 'dɪŋki] *n, pl* **-ghies** : bote *m*
dinginess ['dɪndʒinəs] *n* **1** DIRTINESS : suciedad *f* **2** SHABBINESS : lo gastado, lo deslucido
dingy ['dɪndʒi] *adj* **dingier; -est** **1** DIRTY : sucio **2** SHABBY : gastado, deslucido
dining car *n* : coche *m* comedor (de un tren)
dining room *n* : comedor *m*
dinner ['dɪnər] *n* **1** : cena *f*, comida *f* **2** BANQUET : cena *f*, banquete *m*
dinner jacket *n* : esmoquin *m* (chaqueta)
dinosaur ['daɪnə,sɔr] *n* : dinosaurio *m*
dint ['dɪnt] *n* **by dint of** : a fuerza de
diocese ['daɪəsəs, -,siːz, -,siːs] *n, pl* **-ceses** ['daɪəsəsəz] : diócesis *f*
dip¹ ['dɪp] *v* **dipped; dipping** *vt* **1** DUNK, PLUNGE : sumergir, mojar, meter **2** LADLE : servir con cucharón **3** LOWER

: bajar, arriar (una bandera) — *vi* **1** DESCEND, DROP : bajar en picada, descender **2** SLOPE : bajar, inclinarse
dip² *n* **1** SWIM : chapuzón *m* **2** DROP : descenso *m*, caída *f* **3** SLOPE : cuesta *f*, declive *m* **4** SAUCE : salsa *f*
diphtheria [dɪf'θɪriə] *n* : difteria *f*
diphthong ['dɪf,θɔŋ] *n* : diptongo *m*
diploma [də'ploːmə] *n, pl* **-mas** : diploma *m*
diplomacy [də'ploːməsi] *n* **1** : diplomacia *f* **2** TACT : tacto *m*, discreción *f*
diplomat ['dɪplə,mæt] *n* **1** : diplomático *m*, -ca *f* (en relaciones internacionales) **2** : persona *f* diplomática
diplomatic [,dɪplə'mæṯɪk] *adj* : diplomático ⟨diplomatic immunity : inmunidad diplomática⟩
dipper ['dɪpər] *n* **1** LADLE : cucharón *m*, cazo *m* **2 Big Dipper** : Osa *f* Mayor **3 Little Dipper** : Osa *f* Menor
dipstick ['dɪp,stɪk] *n* : varilla *f* de medición (del aceite)
dire ['daɪr] *adj* **direr; direst** **1** HORRIBLE : espantoso, terrible, horrendo **2** EXTREME : extremo ⟨dire poverty : pobreza extrema⟩
direct¹ [də'rɛkt, daɪ-] *vt* **1** ADDRESS : dirigir, mandar **2** AIM, POINT : dirigir **3** GUIDE : indicarle el camino (a alguien), orientar **4** MANAGE : dirigir ⟨to direct a film : dirigir una película⟩ **5** COMMAND : ordenar, mandar
direct² *adv* : directamente
direct³ *adj* **1** STRAIGHT : directo **2** FRANK : franco
direct debit *n* : débito *m* automático
direct current *n* : corriente *f* continua
direction [də'rɛkLən, daɪ-] *n* **1** SUPERVISION : dirección *f* **2** INSTRUCTION, ORDER : instrucción *f*, orden *f* **3** COURSE : dirección *f*, rumbo *m* ⟨to change direction : cambiar de dirección⟩ **4 to ask directions** : pedir indicaciones
directional [də'rɛkLənəl, daɪ-] *adj* : direccional
directive [də'rɛktɪv, daɪ-] *n* : directiva *f*
directly [də'rɛktli, daɪ-] *adv* **1** STRAIGHT : directamente ⟨directly north : directamente al norte⟩ **2** FRANKLY : francamente **3** EXACTLY : exactamente, justo ⟨directly opposite : justo enfrente⟩ **4** IMMEDIATELY : en seguida, inmediatamente
directness [də'rɛktnəs, daɪ-] *n* : franqueza *f*
director [də'rɛktər, daɪ-] *n* **1** : director *m*, -tora *f* **2 board of directors** : junta *f* directiva, directorio *m*
directory [də'rɛktəri, daɪ-] *n, pl* **-ries** : guía *f*, directorio *m* ⟨telephone directory : directorio telefónico⟩ ⟨directory assistance : servicio de información (telefónica)⟩
dirge ['dərdʒ] *n* : canto *m* fúnebre
dirigible ['dɪrədʒəbəl, də'rɪdʒə-] *n* : dirigible *m*, zepelín *m*
dirt ['dərt] *n* **1** FILTH : suciedad *f*, mugre *f*, porquería *f* **2** SOIL : tierra *f*
dirt cheap *adj* : baratísimo, regalado

dirtiness ['dərtinəs] *n* : suciedad *f*
dirty¹ ['dərti] *vt* **dirtied; dirtying** : ensuciar, manchar
dirty² *adj* **dirtier; -est 1** SOILED, STAINED : sucio, manchado **2** DISHONEST : sucio, deshonesto ⟨a dirty player : un jugador tramposo⟩ ⟨a dirty trick : una mala pasada⟩ **3** INDECENT : indecente, cochino ⟨a dirty joke : un chiste verde⟩
dis- *pref* : des-
disability [,dɪsə'bɪləti] *n*, *pl* **-ties** : minusvalía *f*, discapacidad *f*, invalidez *f*
disable [dɪs'eɪbəl] *vt* **-abled; -abling** : dejar inválido, inutilizar, incapacitar
disabled [dɪs'eɪbəld] *adj* : minusválido, discapacitado
disabuse [,dɪsə'bjuːz] *vt* **-bused; -busing** : desengañar, sacar del error
disadvantage [,dɪsəd'væntɪdʒ] *n* : desventaja *f*
disadvantageous [,dɪs,æd,væn'teɪdʒəs] *adj* : desventajoso, desfavorable
disagree [,dɪsə'griː] *vi* **1** DIFFER : discrepar, no coincidir **2** DISSENT : disentir, discrepar, no estar de acuerdo ⟨I disagree (with you) : no estoy de acuerdo (contigo)⟩ **3 to disagree with someone** : sentarle mal a alguien (dícese de comida, etc.)
disagreeable [,dɪsə'griːəbəl] *adj* : desagradable
disagreement [,dɪsə'griːmənt] *n* **1** : desacuerdo *m* **2** DISCREPANCY : discrepancia *f* **3** ARGUMENT : discusión *f*, altercado *m*, disputa *f*
disallow [,dɪsə'laʊ] *vt* **1** : rechazar, desestimar **2** : anular (en deportes)
disappear [,dɪsə'pɪr] *vi* : desaparecer, desvanecerse ⟨to disappear from view : perderse de vista⟩
disappearance [,dɪsə'pɪrənts] *n* : desaparición *f*
disappoint [,dɪsə'pɔɪnt] *vt* : decepcionar, defraudar, fallar
disappointing [,dɪsə'pɔɪntɪŋ] *adj* : decepcionante
disappointment [,dɪsə'pɔɪntmənt] *n* : decepción *f*, desilusión *f*, chasco *m*
disapproval [,dɪsə'pruːvəl] *n* : desaprobación *f*
disapprove [,dɪsə'pruːv] *vi* **-proved; -proving** : desaprobar, estar en contra
disapprovingly [,dɪsə'pruːvɪŋli] *adv* : con desaprobación
disarm [dɪs'arm] *vt* : desarmar
disarmament [dɪs'arməmənt] *n* : desarme *m* ⟨nuclear disarmament : desarme nuclear⟩
disarrange [,dɪsə'reɪndʒ] *vt* **-ranged; -ranging** : desarreglar, desordenar
disarray [,dɪsə'reɪ] *n* : desorden *m*, confusión *f*, desorganización *f*
disassemble [,dɪsə'sɛmbəl] *v* **-bled; -bling** *vt* : desarmar, desmontar — *vi* : desarmarse, desmontarse
disassociate → **dissociate**
disaster [dɪ'zæstər] *n* : desastre *m*, catástrofe *f*
disastrous [dɪ'zæstrəs] *adj* : desastroso
disband [dɪs'bænd] *vt* : disolver — *vi* : disolverse, dispersarse

disbar [dɪs'bar] *vt* **-barred; -barring** : prohibir de ejercer la abogacía
disbelief [,dɪsbɪ'liːf] *n* : incredulidad *f*
disbelieve [,dɪsbɪ'liːv] *v* **-lieved; -lieving** : no creer, dudar
disburse [dɪs'bərs] *vt* **-bursed; -bursing** : desembolsar
disbursement [dɪs'bərsmənt] *n* : desembolso *m*
disc → **disk**
discard [dɪs'kard, 'dɪs,kard] *vt* : desechar, deshacerse de, botar — *vi* : descartarse (en juegos de naipes)
discern [dɪ'sərn, -'zərn] *vt* : discernir, distinguir, percibir
discernible [dɪ'sərnəbəl, -'zər-] *adj* : perceptible, visible
discerning [dɪ'sərnɪŋ, -'zər-] *adj* : refinado (dícese del gusto), perspicaz, sagaz
discernment [dɪ'sərnmənt, -'zərn-] *n* : discernimiento *m*, criterio *m*
discharge¹ [dɪs'tʃardʒ, 'dɪs,-] *v* **-charged; -charging 1** UNLOAD : descargar (carga), desembarcar (pasajeros) **2** SHOOT : descargar, disparar **3** FREE : liberar, poner en libertad **4** DISMISS : despedir **5** EMIT : despedir (humo, etc.), descargar (electricidad) **6** : cumplir con (una obligación), saldar (una deuda) — *vi* **1** : descargarse (dícese de una batería) **2** OOZE : supurar
discharge² ['dɪs,tʃardʒ, dɪs'-] *n* **1** EMISSION : descarga *f* (de electricidad), emisión *f* (de gases) **2** DISMISSAL : despido *m* (del empleo), baja *f* (del ejército) **3** SECRETION : secreción *f*
disciple [dɪ'saɪpəl] *n* : discípulo *m*, -la *f*
discipline¹ ['dɪsəplən] *vt* **-plined; -plining 1** PUNISH : castigar, sancionar (a los empleados) **2** CONTROL : disciplinar **3 to discipline oneself** : disciplinarse
discipline² *n* **1** FIELD : disciplina *f*, campo *m* **2** TRAINING : disciplina *f* **3** PUNISHMENT : castigo *m* **4** SELF-CONTROL : dominio *m* de sí mismo
disc jockey *n* : disc jockey *mf*
disclaim [dɪs'kleɪm] *vt* DENY : negar
disclose [dɪs'kloːz] *vt* **-closed; -closing** : revelar, poner en evidencia
disclosure [dɪs'kloːʒər] *n* : revelación *f*
disco ['dɪskoː] *n* **1** → **discotheque 2** *or* **disco music** : disco *f*, música *f* disco
discolor [dɪs'kʌlər] *vt* **1** BLEACH : decolorar **2** FADE : desteñir **3** STAIN : manchar — *vi* : decolorarse, desteñirse
discoloration [dɪs,kʌlə'reɪʃən] *n* STAIN : mancha *f*
discomfort [dɪs'kʌmfərt] *n* **1** PAIN : molestia *f*, malestar *m* **2** UNEASINESS : inquietud *f*
disconcert [,dɪskən'sərt] *vt* : desconcertar
disconcerting [,dɪskən'sərtɪŋ] *adj* : desconcertante
disconnect [,dɪskə'nɛkt] *vt* : desconectar
disconnected [,dɪskə'nɛktəd] *adj* : inconexo
disconsolate [dɪs'kantsələt] *adj* : desconsolado
discontent [,dɪskən'tɛnt] *n* : descontento *m*

discontented [ˌdɪskən'tɛntəd] *adj* : descontento

discontinue [ˌdɪskən'tɪn,ju:] *vt* **-ued; -uing** : suspender, descontinuar

discontinuity [dɪs,kɑntə'nu:əți, -'nju:-] *n*, *pl* **-ties** : discontinuidad *f*

discontinuous [ˌdɪskən'tɪnjəwəs] *adj* : discontinuo

discord ['dɪs,kord] *n* **1** STRIFE : discordia *f*, discordancia *f* **2** : disonancia *f* (en música)

discordant [dɪs'kɔrdənt] *adj* : discordante — **discordantly** *adv*

discotheque ['dɪskə,tɛk, ˌdɪskə'tɛk] *n* : discoteca *f*

discount¹ ['dɪs,kaʊnt, dɪs'-] *vt* **1** REDUCE : descontar, rebajar (precios) **2** DISREGARD : descartar, ignorar

discount² ['dɪs,kaʊnt] *n* : descuento *m*, rebaja *f*

discourage [dɪs'kərɪʤ] *vt* **-aged; -aging** **1** DISHEARTEN : desalentar, desanimar **2** DISSUADE : disuadir **3** DETER : impedir

discouragement [dɪs'kərɪʤmənt] *n* : desánimo *m*, desaliento *m*

discouraging [dɪs'kərəʤɪŋ] *adj* : desalentador

discourse¹ [dɪs'kors] *vi* **-coursed; -coursing** : disertar, conversar

discourse² ['dɪs,kors] *n* **1** TALK : conversación *f* **2** SPEECH, TREATISE : discurso *m*, tratado *m*

discourteous [dɪs'kərțiəs] *adj* : descortés — **discourteously** *adv*

discourtesy [dɪs'kərțəsi] *n*, *pl* **-sies** : descortesía *f*

discover [dɪs'kʌvər] *vt* : descubrir

discoverer [dɪs'kʌvərər] *n* : descubridor *m*, -dora *f*

discovery [dɪs'kʌvəri] *n*, *pl* **-ries** : descubrimiento *m*

discredit¹ [dɪs'krɛdət] *vt* **1** DISBELIEVE : no creer, dudar **2** : desacreditar, desprestigiar, poner en duda ⟨they discredited his research : desacreditaron sus investigaciones⟩

discredit² *n* **1** DISREPUTE : descrédito *m*, desprestigio *m* **2** DOUBT : duda *f*

discreet [dɪs'kri:t] *adj* : discreto — **discreetly** *adv*

discrepancy [dɪs'krɛpənʦi] *n*, *pl* **-cies** : discrepancia *f*

discretion [dɪs'krɛʧən] *n* **1** : discreción *f* **2** JUDGMENT : discernimiento *m*, criterio *m*

discretionary [dɪs'krɛʧə,nɛri] *adj* : discrecional

discriminate [dɪs'krɪmə,neɪt] *v* **-nated; -nating** *vt* DISTINGUISH : distinguir, discriminar, diferenciar — *vi* : discriminar ⟨to discriminate against women : discriminar a las mujeres⟩

discriminating [dɪs'krɪmə,neɪțɪŋ] *adj* : refinado (dícese del gusto), entendido (dícese de personas)

discrimination [dɪs,krɪmə'neɪʧən] *n* **1** PREJUDICE : discriminación *f* **2** DISCERNMENT : discernimiento *m*

discriminatory [dɪs'krɪmənə,tori] *adj* : discriminatorio

discus ['dɪskəs] *n*, *pl* **-cuses** [-kəsəz] : disco *m*

discuss [dɪs'kʌs] *vt* : hablar de, discutir, tratar (de)

discussion [dɪs'kʌLən] *n* : discusión *f*, debate *m*, conversación *f*

disdain¹ [dɪs'deɪn] *vt* : desdeñar, despreciar ⟨they disdained to reply : no se dignaron a responder⟩

disdain² *n* : desdén *m*

disdainful [dɪs'deɪnfəl] *adj* : desdeñoso — **disdainfully** *adv*

disease [dɪ'zi:z] *n* : enfermedad *f*, mal *m*, dolencia *f*

diseased [dɪ'zi:zd] *adj* : enfermo

disembark [ˌdɪsɪm'bark] *v* : desembarcar

disembarkation [dɪs,ɛm,bar'keɪLən] *n* : desembarco *m*, desembarque *m*

disembodied [ˌdɪsɪm'bɑdid] *adj* : incorpóreo

disenchant [ˌdɪsɪn'tʃænt] *vt* : desilusionar, desencantar, desengañar

disenchanted [ˌdɪsɪn'tʃæntəd] *adj* : desilusionado, desencantado

disenchantment [ˌdɪsɪn'tʃæntmənt] *n* : desencanto *m*, desilusión *f*

disenfranchise [dɪsɪn'fræn,tʃaɪz] *vt* **-chised; -chising** : privar del derecho a votar

disengage [ˌdɪsɪn'geɪʤ] *vt* **-gaged; -gaging** : soltar, desconectar (un mecanismo)

disentangle [ˌdɪsɪn'tæŋgəl] *vt* **-gled; -gling** UNTANGLE : desenredar, desenmarañar

disfavor [dɪs'feɪvər] *n* : desaprobación *f*

disfigure [dɪs'fɪgjər] *vt* **-ured; -uring** : desfigurar (a una persona), afear (un edificio, un área)

disgrace¹ [dɪ'skreɪs] *vt* **-graced; -gracing** : deshonrar

disgrace² *n* **1** DISHONOR : desgracia *f*, deshonra *f* **2** SHAME : vergüenza *f* ⟨he's a disgrace to his family : es una vergüenza para su familia⟩

disgraceful [dɪ'skreɪsfəl] *adj* : vergonzoso, deshonroso, ignominioso

disgracefully [dɪ'skreɪsfəli] *adv* : vergonzosamente

disgruntle [dɪs'grʌntəl] *vt* **-tled; -tling** : enfadar, contrariar

disgruntled [dɪs'grʌntəld] *adj* : descontento, contrariado

disguise¹ [dɪ'skaɪz] *vt* **-guised; -guising** **1** : disfrazar, enmascarar (el aspecto) **2** CONCEAL : encubrir, disimular

disguise² *n* : disfraz *m*

disgust¹ [dɪ'skʌst] *vt* : darle asco (a alguien), asquear, repugnar ⟨that disgusts me : eso me da asco⟩

disgust² *n* : asco *m*, repugnancia *f*

disgusting [dɪ'skʌstɪŋ] *adj* : asqueroso, repugnante — **disgustingly** *adv*

dish¹ ['dɪʃ] *vt* **1** *or* **to dish out/up** SERVE : servir **2** *or* **to dish out** DISPENSE : repartir (dinero, etc.), dar (consejos) **3** **to dish it out** : criticar

dish² *n* **1** : plato *m* ⟨the national dish : el plato nacional⟩ **2** PLATE : plato *m* ⟨to wash the dishes : lavar los platos⟩ **3** **serving dish** : fuente *f*

dishcloth ['dɪʃ‚klɔθ] n : paño m de cocina (para secar), trapo m de fregar (para lavar)

dishearten [dɪs'hɑrtən] vt : desanimar, desalentar

dishevel [dɪ'ʃɛvəl] vt **-eled** or **-elled; -eling** or **-elling** : desarreglar, despeinar (el pelo)

disheveled or **dishevelled** [dɪ'ʃɛvəld] adj : despeinado (dícese del pelo), desarreglado, desaliñado

dishonest [dɪ'sɑnəst] adj : deshonesto, fraudulento — **dishonestly** adv

dishonesty [dɪ'sɑnəsti] n, pl **-ties** : deshonestidad f, falta f de honradez

dishonor¹ [dɪ'sɑnər] vt : deshonrar

dishonor² n : deshonra f

dishonorable [dɪ'sɑnərəbəl] adj : deshonroso — **dishonorably** [-bli] adv

dishrag ['dɪʃ‚ræg] → **dishcloth**

dishtowel ['dɪʃ‚tauəl] → **dishcloth**

dishwasher ['dɪʃ‚wɔʃər] n : lavaplatos m, lavavajillas m

disillusion [‚dɪsə'lu:ʒən] vt : desilusionar, desencantar, desengañar

disillusionment [‚dɪsə'lu:ʒənmənt] n : desilusión f, desencanto m

disinclination [dɪs‚ɪnklə'neɪʃən, -‚ɪŋ-] n : aversión f

disinclined [‚dɪsɪn'klaɪnd] adv : poco dispuesto

disinfect [‚dɪsɪn'fɛkt] vt : desinfectar

disinfectant¹ [‚dɪsɪn'fɛktənt] adj : desinfectante

disinfectant² n : desinfectante m

disinherit [‚dɪsɪn'hɛrət] vt : desheredar

disintegrate [dɪs'ɪntə‚greɪt] v **-grated; -grating** vt : desintegrar, deshacer — vi : desintegrarse, deshacerse

disintegration [dɪs‚ɪntə'greɪʃən] n : desintegración f

disinterested [dɪs'ɪntərəstəd, -‚rɛs-] adj **1** INDIFFERENT : indiferente **2** IMPARTIAL : imparcial, desinteresado

disinterestedness [dɪs'ɪntərəstədnəs, -‚rɛs-] n : desinterés m

disjointed [dɪs'ʤɔɪntəd] adj : inconexo, incoherente

disk or **disc** ['dɪsk] n : disco m

diskette [‚dɪs'kɛt] n : diskette m, disquete m

dislike¹ [dɪs'laɪk] vt **-liked; -liking** : tenerle aversión a (algo), tenerle antipatía (a alguien), no gustarle (algo a uno)

dislike² n : aversión f, antipatía f ⟨to take a dislike to : tomarle antipatía a⟩

dislocate ['dɪslo‚keɪt, dɪs'lo:-] vt **-cated; -cating** : dislocar

dislocation [‚dɪslo'keɪʃən] n : dislocación f

dislodge [dɪs'lɑʤ] vt **-lodged; -lodging** : sacar, desalojar, desplazar

disloyal [dɪs'lɔɪəl] adj : desleal

disloyalty [dɪs'lɔɪəlti] n, pl **-ties** : deslealtad f

dismal ['dɪzməl] adj **1** GLOOMY : sombrío, lúgubre, tétrico **2** DEPRESSING : deprimente, triste

dismantle [dɪs'mæntəl] vt **-tled; -tling** : desmantelar, desmontar, desarmar

dismay¹ [dɪs'meɪ] vt : consternar

dismay² n : consternación f

dismember [dɪs'mɛmbər] vt : desmembrar

dismiss [dɪs'mɪs] vt **1** : dejar salir, darle permiso (a alguien) para retirarse **2** DISCHARGE : despedir, destituir **3** REJECT : descartar, desechar, rechazar

dismissal [dɪs'mɪsəl] n **1** : permiso m para retirarse **2** DISCHARGE : despido m (de un empleado), destitución f (de un funcionario) **3** REJECTION : rechazo m

dismount [dɪs'maunt] vi : desmontar, bajarse, apearse

disobedience [‚dɪsə'bi:diənts] n : desobediencia f — **disobedient** [-ənt] adj

disobey [‚dɪsə'beɪ] v : desobedecer

disorder¹ [dɪs'ɔrdər] vt : desordenar, desarreglar

disorder² n **1** DISARRAY : desorden m **2** UNREST : disturbios mpl, desórdenes mpl **3** AILMENT : afección f, indisposición f, dolencia f

disorderly [dɪs'ɔrdərli] adj **1** UNTIDY : desordenado, desarreglado **2** UNRULY : indisciplinado, alborotado **3** disorderly conduct : conducta f escandalosa

disorganization [dɪs‚ɔrgənə'zeɪʃən] n : desorganización f

disorganize [dɪs'ɔrgə‚naɪz] vt **-nized; -nizing** : desorganizar

disorient [dɪs'ori‚ɛnt] vt : desorientar

disown [dɪs'o:n] vt : renegar de, repudiar

disparage [dɪs'pærɪʤ] vt **-aged; -aging** : menospreciar, denigrar

disparagement [dɪs'pærɪʤmənt] n : menosprecio m

disparate ['dɪspərət, dɪs'pærət] adj : dispar, diferente

disparity [dɪs'pærəti] n, pl **-ties** : disparidad f

dispassionate [dɪs'pæLənət] adj : desapasionado, imparcial — **dispassionately** adv

dispatch¹ [dɪs'pætʃ] vt **1** SEND : despachar, enviar **2** KILL : despachar, matar **3** HANDLE : despachar

dispatch² n **1** SENDING : envío m, despacho m **2** MESSAGE : despacho m, reportaje m (de un periodista), parte m (en el ejército) **3** PROMPTNESS : prontitud f, rapidez f

dispel [dɪs'pɛl] vt **-pelled; -pelling** : disipar, desvanecer

dispensable [dɪ'spɛntsəbəl] adj : prescindible

dispensary [dɪ'spɛntsəri] n, pl **-ries** : dispensario m

dispensation [‚dɪspɛn'seɪʃən] n EXEMPTION : exención m, dispensa f

dispense [dɪs'pɛnts] v **-pensed; -pensing** vt **1** DISTRIBUTE : repartir, distribuir, dar **2** ADMINISTER, BESTOW : administrar (justicia), conceder (favores, etc.) **3** : preparar y despachar (medicamentos) — vi **to dispense with** : prescindir de

dispenser [dɪs'pɛntsər] n : dispensador m, distribuidor m automático

dispersal [dɪs'pərsəl] n : dispersión f

disperse [dɪs'pərs] v **-persed; -persing** vt : dispersar, diseminar — vi : dispersarse

dispersion [dɪˈspərʒən] *n* : dispersión *f*
dispirit [dɪˈspɪrət] *vt* : desalentar, desanimar
dispirited [dɪˈspɪrətəd] *adj* : desanimado
displace [dɪsˈpleɪs] *vt* **-placed; -placing** **1** : desplazar (un líquido, etc.) **2** REPLACE : reemplazar
displacement [dɪsˈpleɪsmənt] *n* **1** : desplazamiento *m* (de personas) **2** REPLACEMENT : sustitución *f*, reemplazo *m*
display¹ [dɪsˈpleɪ] *vt* : exponer, exhibir, mostrar
display² *n* **1** : muestra *f*, exposición *f*, alarde *m* **2** : visualizador *m* (de un aparato)
displease [dɪsˈpliːz] *vt* **-pleased; -pleasing** : desagradar a, disgustar, contrariar
displeasure [dɪsˈplɛʒər] *n* : desagrado *m*
disposable [dɪsˈpoːzəbəl] *adj* **1** : desechable ⟨disposable diapers : pañales desechables⟩ **2** AVAILABLE : disponible
disposal [dɪsˈpoːzəl] *n* **1** PLACEMENT : disposición *f*, colocación *f* **2** REMOVAL : eliminación *f* **3** → garbage disposal **4** to have at one's disposal : disponer de, tener a su disposición
dispose [dɪsˈpoːz] *v* **-posed; -posing** *vt* **1** ARRANGE : disponer, colocar **2** INCLINE : predisponer — *vi* **1** to dispose of DISCARD : desechar, deshacerse de **2** to dispose of HANDLE : despachar **3** to be disposed to do something : estar dispuesto a hacer algo
disposition [ˌdɪspəˈzɪʃən] *n* **1** ARRANGEMENT : disposición *f* **2** TENDENCY : predisposición *f*, inclinación *f* **3** TEMPERAMENT : temperamento *m*, carácter *m*
dispossess [ˌdɪspəˈzɛs] *vt* : desposeer
disproportion [ˌdɪsprəˈpɔrʃən] *n* : desproporción *f*
disproportionate [ˌdɪsprəˈpɔrʃənət] *adj* : desproporcionado — **disproportionately** *adv*
disprove [dɪsˈpruːv] *vt* **-proved; -proving** : rebatir, refutar
disputable [dɪsˈpjuːtəbəl, ˈdɪspjʊtəbəl] *adj* : discutible
dispute¹ [dɪsˈpjuːt] *v* **-puted; -puting** *vt* **1** QUESTION : discutir, cuestionar **2** OPPOSE : combatir, resistir — *vi* ARGUE, DEBATE : discutir
dispute² *n* **1** DEBATE : debate *m*, discusión *f* **2** QUARREL : disputa *f*, discusión *f*
disqualification [dɪsˌkwɑləfəˈkeɪʃən] *n* : descalificación *f*
disqualify [dɪsˈkwɑləˌfaɪ] *vt* **-fied; -fying** : descalificar, inhabilitar
disquiet¹ [dɪsˈkwaɪət] *vt* : inquietar
disquiet² *n* : ansiedad *f*, inquietud *f*
disregard¹ [ˌdɪsrɪˈgɑrd] *vt* : ignorar, no prestar atención a
disregard² *n* : indiferencia *f*
disrepair [ˌdɪsrɪˈpær] *n* : mal estado *m*
disreputable [dɪsˈrɛpjʊtəbəl] *adj* : de mala fama (dícese de una persona o un lugar), vergonzoso (dícese de la conducta)
disreputably [dɪsˈrɛpjʊtəbli] *adv* : vergonzosamente

disrepute [ˌdɪsrɪˈpjuːt] *n* : descrédito *m*, mala fama *f*, deshonra *f*
disrespect [ˌdɪsrɪˈspɛkt] *n* : falta *f* de respeto
disrespectful [ˌdɪsrɪˈspɛktfəl] *adj* : irrespetuoso — **disrespectfully** *adv*
disrobe [dɪsˈroːb] *v* **-robed; -robing** *vt* : desvestir, desnudar — *vi* : desvestirse, desnudarse
disrupt [dɪsˈrʌpt] *vt* : trastornar, perturbar
disruption [dɪsˈrʌpʃən] *n* : trastorno *m*
disruptive [dɪsˈrʌptɪv] *adj* : perjudicial, perturbador — **disruptively** *adv*
dissatisfaction [dɪsˌsætəsˈfækʃən] *n* : descontento *m*, insatisfacción *f*
dissatisfied [dɪsˈsætəsˌfaɪd] *adj* : descontento, insatisfecho
dissatisfy [dɪsˈsætəsˌfaɪ] *vt* **-fied; -fying** : no contentar, no satisfacer
dissect [dɪˈsɛkt] *vt* : disecar
dissection [dɪˈsɛkʃən] *n* : disección *f*
dissemble [dɪˈsɛmbəl] *v* **-bled; -bling** *vt* HIDE : ocultar, disimular — *vi* PRETEND : fingir, disimular
disseminate [dɪˈsɛməˌneɪt] *vt* **-nated; -nating** : diseminar, difundir, divulgar
dissemination [dɪˌsɛməˈneɪʃən] *n* : diseminación *f*, difusión *f*
dissension [dɪˈsɛntʃən] *n* : disensión *f*, desacuerdo *m*
dissent¹ [dɪˈsɛnt] *vi* : disentir
dissent² *n* : disentimiento *m*, disensión *f*, disenso *m*
dissertation [ˌdɪsərˈteɪʃən] *n* **1** DISCOURSE : disertación *f*, discurso *m* **2** THESIS : tesis *f*
disservice [dɪsˈsərvɪs] *n* : perjuicio *m*
dissident¹ [ˈdɪsədənt] *adj* : disidente
dissident² *n* : disidente *mf*
dissimilar [dɪˈsɪmələr] *adj* : distinto, diferente, disímil
dissipate [ˈdɪsəˌpeɪt] *vt* **-pated; -pating** **1** DISPERSE : disipar, dispersar **2** SQUANDER : malgastar, desperdiciar, derrochar, disipar
dissipation [ˌdɪsəˈpeɪʃən] *n* : libertinaje *m*
dissociate [dɪˈsoːʃiˌeɪt, -si-] *or* **disassociate** [ˌdɪsəˈsoːʃiˌeɪt, -si-] *v* **-ated** [-ˌeɪtəd]; **-ating** [-ˌeɪtɪŋ] *vt* : disociar ⟨to dissociate oneself : disociarse⟩ — *vi* : disociarse
dissociation [dɪˌsoːʃiˈeɪʃən, -si-] *n* : disociación *f*
dissolute [ˈdɪsəˌluːt] *adj* : disoluto
dissolution [ˌdɪsəˈluːʃən] *n* : disolución *f*
dissolve [dɪˈzɑlv] *v* **-solved; -solving** *vt* : disolver — *vi* : disolverse
dissonance [ˈdɪsənənts] *n* : disonancia *f*
dissuade [dɪˈsweɪd] *vt* **-suaded; -suading** : disuadir
distance¹ [ˈdɪstənts] *vt* **-tanced** [-təntst]; **-tancing** [-təntsɪŋ] to distance oneself : distanciarse
distance² *n* **1** : distancia *f* ⟨the distance between two points : la distancia entre dos puntos⟩ ⟨in the distance : a lo lejos⟩ **2** RESERVE : actitud *f* distante, reserva *f* ⟨to keep one's distance : guardar las distancias⟩

distant ['dɪstənt] *adj* **1** FAR : distante, lejano **2** REMOTE : distante, lejano, remoto **3** ALOOF : distante, frío
distantly ['dɪstəntli] *adv* **1** LOOSELY : aproximadamente, vagamente **2** COLDLY : fríamente, con frialdad
distaste [dɪs'teɪst] *n* : desagrado *m*, aversión *f*
distasteful [dɪs'teɪstfəl] *adj* : desagradable, de mal gusto
distemper [dɪs'tɛmpər] *n* : moquillo *m*
distend [dɪs'tɛnd] *vt* : dilatar, hinchar — *vi* : dilatarse, hincharse
distill [dɪ'stɪl] *vt* : destilar
distillation [ˌdɪstə'leɪLən] *n* : destilación *f*
distiller [dɪ'stɪlər] *n* : destilador *m*, -dora *f*
distillery [dɪ'stɪləri] *n, pl* **-ries** [-riz] : destilería *f*
distinct [dɪ'stɪŋkt] *adj* **1** DIFFERENT : distinto, diferente **2** CLEAR, UNMISTAKABLE : marcado, claro, evidente ⟨a distinct possibility : una clara posibilidad⟩
distinction [dɪ'stɪŋkLən] *n* **1** DIFFERENTIATION : distinción *f* **2** DIFFERENCE : diferencia *f* **3** EXCELLENCE : distinción *f*, excelencia *f* ⟨a writer of distinction : un escritor destacado⟩
distinctive [dɪ'stɪŋktɪv] *adj* : distintivo, característico — **distinctively** *adv*
distinctiveness [dɪ'stɪŋktɪvnəs] *n* : peculiaridad *f*
distinctly [dɪ'stɪŋktli] *adv* : claramente, con claridad
distinguish [dɪs'tɪŋgwɪL] *vt* **1** DIFFERENTIATE : distinguir, diferenciar **2** DISCERN : distinguir ⟨he distinguished the sound of the piano : distinguió el sonido del piano⟩ **3 to distinguish oneself** : señalarse, distinguirse — *vi* DISCRIMINATE : distinguir
distinguishable [dɪs'tɪŋgwɪLəbəl] *adj* : distinguible
distinguished [dɪs'tɪŋgwɪLt] *adj* : distinguido
distinguishing [dɪs'tɪŋgwɪLɪŋ] *adj* : distintivo
distort [dɪ'stɔrt] *vt* **1** MISREPRESENT : distorsionar, tergiversar **2** DEFORM : distorsionar, deformar
distortion [dɪ'stɔrLən] *n* : distorsión *f*, deformación *f*, tergiversación *f*
distract [dɪ'strækt] *vt* : distraer, entretener
distracted [dɪ'stræktəd] *adj* : distraído
distraction [dɪ'strækLən] *n* **1** INTERRUPTION : distracción *f*, interrupción *f* **2** CONFUSION : confusión *f* **3** AMUSEMENT : diversión *f*, entretenimiento *m*, distracción *f*
distraught [dɪ'strɔt] *adj* : afligido, turbado
distress¹ [dɪ'strɛs] *vt* : afligir, darle pena (a alguien), hacer sufrir
distress² *n* **1** SORROW : dolor *m*, angustia *f*, aflicción *f* **2** PAIN : dolor *m* **3 in** ∼ : en peligro
distressful [dɪ'strɛsfəl] *adj* : doloroso, penoso
distressing [dɪ'strɛsɪŋ] *adj* : angustioso

distribute [dɪ'strɪˌbjuːt, -bjʊt] *vt* **-uted; -uting** : distribuir, repartir
distribution [ˌdɪstrə'bjuːLən] *n* : distribución *f*, reparto *m*
distributive [dɪ'strɪbjʊtɪv] *adj* : distributivo
distributor [dɪ'strɪbjʊtər] *n* : distribuidor *m*, -dora *f*
district ['dɪsˌtrɪkt] *n* **1** REGION : región *f*, zona *f*, barrio *m* (de una ciudad) **2** : distrito *m* (zona política)
district attorney *n* : fiscal *mf* (del distrito)
distrust¹ [dɪs'trʌst] *vt* : desconfiar de
distrust² *n* : desconfianza *f*, recelo *m*
distrustful [dɪs'trʌstfəl] *adj* : desconfiado, receloso, suspicaz
disturb [dɪ'stərb] *vt* **1** BOTHER : molestar, perturbar ⟨sorry to disturb you : perdone la molestia⟩ **2** DISARRANGE : desordenar **3** WORRY : inquietar, preocupar **4 to disturb the peace** : alterar el orden público
disturbance [dɪ'stərbənʦ] *n* **1** COMMOTION : alboroto *m*, disturbio *m* **2** INTERRUPTION : interrupción *f*
disturbed [dɪ'stərbd] *adj* **1** : trastornado ⟨mentally/emotionally disturbed : con trastornos mentales/emocionales⟩ **2** WORRIED, UNSETTLED : inquieto, agitado
disturbing [dɪ'stərbɪŋ] *adj* : inquietante
disuse [dɪs'juːs] *n* : desuso *m*
disused [dɪs'juːzd] *adj* **1** ABANDONED : abandonado **2** ANTIQUATED : desusado
ditch¹ ['dɪtL] *vt* **1** : cavar zanjas en **2** DISCARD : deshacerse de, botar
ditch² *n* : zanja *f*, fosa *f*, cuneta *f* (en una carretera)
dither ['dɪðər] *n* **to be in a dither** : estar nervioso, ponerse como loco
ditto ['dɪtoː] *n, pl* **-tos** **1** : lo mismo, ídem *m* **2 ditto marks** : comillas *fpl*
ditty ['dɪti] *n, pl* **-ties** : canción *f* corta y simple
diurnal [dai'ərnəl] *adj* **1** DAILY : diario, cotidiano **2** : diurno ⟨a diurnal animal : un animal diurno⟩
diva ['diːvə] *n* : diva *f*
divan ['daɪˌvæn, dɪ'-] *n* : diván *m*
dive¹ ['daɪv] *vi* **dived** or **dove** ['doːv]; **dived; diving** **1** PLUNGE : tirarse al agua, zambullirse, dar un clavado **2** SUBMERGE : sumergirse **3** DROP : bajar en picada (dícese de un avión), caer en picada **4** : bucear, hacer submarinismo ⟨to dive for pearls : bucear buscando perlas⟩
dive² *n* **1** PLUNGE : zambullida *f*, clavado *m* (en el agua) **2** DESCENT : descenso *m* en picada **3** BAR, JOINT : antro *m*
diver ['daɪvər] *n* **1** : saltador *m*, -dora *f*; clavadista *mf* **2** : buceador *m*, -dora *f*; buzo *mf*; submarinista *mf*
diverge [də'vərʤ, dai-] *vi* **-verged; -verging** **1** SEPARATE : divergir, separarse **2** DIFFER : divergir, discrepar
divergence [də'vərʤənʦ, dai-] *n* : divergencia *f* — **divergent** [-ənt] *adj*
diverse [dai'vərs, də-, 'dai-vərs] *adj* : diverso, variado

diversification [daɪˌvərsəfəˈkeɪɫən, də-] *n* : diversificación *f*

diversify [daɪˈvərsəˌfaɪ, də-] *vt* **-fied; -fy-ing** : diversificar, variar

diversion [daɪˈvərʒən, də-] *n* **1** DEVIA-TION : desviación *f* **2** AMUSEMENT, DIS-TRACTION : diversión *f*, distracción *f*, entretenimiento *m*

diversity [daɪˈvərsəṭi, də-] *n, pl* **-ties** : diversidad *f*

divert [dəˈvərt, daɪ-] *vt* **1** DEFLECT : desviar **2** DISTRACT : distraer **3** AMUSE : divertir, entretener

divest [daɪˈvɛst, də-] *vt* **1** UNDRESS : desnudar, desvestir **2 to divest of** : despojar de

divide [dəˈvaɪd] *v* **-vided; -viding** *vt* **1** HALVE : dividir, partir por la mitad **2** SHARE : repartir, dividir ⟨to divide be-tween/among : dividir entre⟩ **3** : dividir (números) ⟨to divide by : dividir por⟩ — *vi* : dividirse, dividir (en matemáticas)

dividend [ˈdɪvəˌdɛnd, -dənd] *n* **1** : divi-dendo *m* (en finanzas) **2** ADVANTAGE, BENEFIT : beneficio *m*, provecho *m* ⟨to pay dividends : reportar beneficios⟩ **3** : dividendo *m* (en matemáticas)

divider [dɪˈvaɪdər] *n* **1** : separador *m* (para ficheros, etc.) **2** *or* **room divider** : mampara *f*, biombo *m*

divination [ˌdɪvəˈneɪɫən] *n* : adivinación *f*

divine[1] [dəˈvaɪn] *adj* **diviner; -est 1** : di-vino **2** SUPERB : divino, espléndido — **divinely** *adv*

divine[2] *n* : clérigo *m*, eclesiástico *m*

diving [ˈdaɪvɪŋ] *n* **1** : clavados *mpl* **2** : buceo *m*, submarinismo *m*

diving board *n* : trampolín *m*

divinity [dəˈvɪnəṭi] *n, pl* **-ties** : divinidad *f*

divisible [dɪˈvɪzəbəl] *adj* : divisible

division [dɪˈvɪʒən] *n* **1** DISTRIBUTION : división *f*, reparto *m* ⟨division of labor : distribución del trabajo⟩ **2** PART : di-visión *f*, sección *f* **3** : división *f* (en matemáticas)

divisive [dəˈvaɪsɪv] *adj* : divisivo

divisor [dɪˈvaɪzər] *n* : divisor *m*

divorce[1] [dəˈvors] *v* **-vorced; -vorcing** *vt* : divorciar — *vi* : divorciarse

divorce[2] *n* : divorcio *m*

divorcé [dɪˌvorˈseɪ, -ˈsiː;, -ˈvorˌ-] *n* : divor-ciado *m*

divorcée [dɪˌvorˈseɪ, -ˈsiː;, -ˈvorˌ-] *n* : di-vorciada *f*

divorced *adj* : divorciado

divulge [dəˈvʌldʒ, daɪ-] *vt* **-vulged; -vulg-ing** : revelar, divulgar

DIY[1] [ˌdiːˌaɪˈwaɪ] → **do-it-yourself**[1]

DIY[2] → **do-it-yourself**[2]

dizzily [ˈdɪzəli] *adv* : vertiginosamente

dizziness [ˈdɪzinəs] *n* : mareo *m*, vahído *m*, vértigo *m*

dizzy [ˈdɪzi] *adj* **dizzier; -est 1** : mareado ⟨I feel dizzy : estoy mareado⟩ **2** DIZZYING : vertiginoso ⟨a dizzy speed : una velocidad vertiginosa⟩

dizzying [ˈdɪziɪŋ] *adj* : vertiginoso

DNA [ˌdiːˌɛnˈeɪ] *n* (deoxyribonucleic acid) : ADN *m*

do[1] [ˈduː] *v* **did** [ˈdɪd]; **done** [ˈdʌn]; **doing; does** [ˈdʌz] *vt* **1** CARRY OUT, PERFORM : hacer, realizar, llevar a cabo ⟨she did her best : hizo todo lo posible⟩ ⟨I didn't do it! : ¡no fui yo!⟩ ⟨do something! : ¡haz algo!⟩ ⟨I did something to my knee : me lastimé la rodilla⟩ ⟨she did nothing to help : no hizo nada para ayudar⟩ ⟨I have nothing to do : no tengo nada que hacer⟩ ⟨are you doing anything tonight? : ¿haces algo esta noche?⟩ ⟨what can I do for you? : ¿en qué puedo servirle?⟩ ⟨to do the chores : hacer los quehaceres⟩ ⟨to do the right thing : hacer lo correcto⟩ ⟨to do someone a favor : hacerle un favor a alguien⟩ **2** : dedicarse a, trabajar en ⟨what do you do (for a living)? : ¿a qué te dedicas?⟩ **3** COMPLETE : hacer ⟨did you do your homework? : ¿hiciste la tarea?⟩ **4** PREPARE : hacer, preparar (comida) **5** ARRANGE : arreglar, peinar (el pelo) ⟨to do one's hair : peinarse⟩ ⟨to do one's makeup/face : maquillarse⟩ **6** GO : ir a (una velocidad) ⟨he was doing 90 (miles per hour) : iba a 90 millas por hora⟩ **7** VISIT : visitar (un lugar) **8** : hacer ⟨the change will do you good : el cambio te hará bien⟩ ⟨that color does nothing for you : ese color no te queda bien⟩ ⟨that song does nothing for me : esa canción no me dice nada⟩ **9** CREATE, PRODUCE : hacer **10** WASH, CLEAN : lavar, limpiar ⟨to do laundry : lavar la ropa⟩ **11** DECORATE : pintar, decorar **12 to do in** RUIN : estropear, arruinar **13 to do in** KILL : matar, liqui-dar *fam* **14 to do in** TIRE, EXHAUST : agotar **15 to do lunch/dinner (etc.)** : juntarse a almorzar/cenar (etc.) **16 to do over** : volver a hacer **17 to do up** FASTEN : atar, abrochar **18 what is/are ... doing ... ?** (*expressing surprise or annoyance*) ⟨what are you doing here? : ¿qué haces aquí?⟩ ⟨what is my coat do-ing on the floor? : ¿qué hace mi abrigo en el suelo?⟩ — *vi* **1** : hacer ⟨you did well : hiciste bien⟩ **2** FARE : estar, ir, an-dar ⟨how are you doing? : ¿cómo estás?, ¿cómo te va?⟩ **3** SERVE : servir, ser sufi-ciente, alcanzar ⟨this will do for now : esto servirá por el momento⟩ **4 could do with** ⟨I could do with a cup of coffee : un café no me vendría mal⟩ **5 to do away with** ABOLISH : abolir, suprimir **6 to do away with** KILL : eliminar, matar **7 to do by** TREAT : tratar ⟨he does well by her : él la trata bien⟩ **8 to do well to** : hacer bien en **9 to do without** MAN-AGE : arreglárselas **10 to do without something** : pasar sin algo, prescindir de algo **11 to have to do with** : tener que ver con ⟨that has nothing to do with it : eso no tiene nada que ver (con el asunto)⟩ ⟨I didn't have anything to do with it : no tuve nada que ver con eso⟩ **12 to want nothing to do with** : hacerle la cruz a — *v aux* **1** (*used in questions and negative statements*) ⟨do you know her? : ¿la conoces?⟩ ⟨I don't like that : a mí no me gusta eso⟩ ⟨I don't know : no sé⟩ ⟨do not touch : no tocar⟩ **2** (*used for emphasis*) ⟨I do hope you'll come : espero que vengas⟩ **3** (*used as a substitute verb to avoid repetition*) ⟨do you speak English? — yes, I do : ¿habla inglés? — sí⟩ ⟨so do I : yo también⟩

do² ['do:] *n* : do *m* (en el canto)

docile ['dɑsəl] *adj* : dócil, sumiso

dock¹ ['dɑk] *vt* **1** CUT : cortar **2** : descontar dinero de (un sueldo) — *vi* ANCHOR, LAND : fondear, atracar

dock² *n* **1** PIER : atracadero *m* **2** WHARF : muelle *m* **3** : banquillo *m* de los acusados (en un tribunal)

dockworker ['dɑk,wərkər] *n* : estibador *m*, -dora *f*

dockyard ['dɑk,jɑrd] *n* : astillero *m*

doctor¹ ['dɑktər] *vt* **1** TREAT : tratar, curar **2** ALTER : adulterar, alterar, falsificar (un documento)

doctor² *n* **1** : doctor *m*, -tora *f* ⟨Doctor of Philosophy : doctor en filosofía⟩ **2** PHYSICIAN : médico *m*, -ca *f*; doctor *m*, -tora *f*

doctorate ['dɑktərət] *n* : doctorado *m*

doctrine ['dɑktrɪn] *n* : doctrina *f*

document¹ ['dɑkjʊ,mɛnt] *vt* : documentar

document² ['dɑkjʊmənt] *n* : documento *m*

documentary¹ [,dɑkjʊ'mɛntəri] *adj* : documental

documentary² *n*, *pl* **-ries** : documental *m*

documentation [,dɑkjʊmən'teɪʒən] *n* : documentación *f*

dodge¹ ['dɑdʒ] *v* **dodged; dodging** *vt* : esquivar, eludir, evadir (impuestos) — *vi* : echarse a un lado

dodge² *n* **1** RUSE : truco *m*, treta *f*, artimaña *f* **2** EVASION : regate *m*, evasión *f*

doe ['do:] *n*, *pl* **does** *or* **doe** : gama *f*, cierva *f*

doer ['du:ər] *n* : hacedor *m*, -dora *f*

does → **do**

doesn't ['dʌzənt] *contraction of* DOES NOT → **do**

doff ['dɑf, 'dɔf] *vt* : quitarse ⟨to doff one's hat : quitarse el sombrero⟩

dog¹ ['dɔg, 'dɑg] *vt* **dogged; dogging** : seguir de cerca, perseguir, acosar ⟨to dog someone's footsteps : seguir los pasos de alguien⟩ ⟨dogged by bad luck : perseguido por la mala suerte⟩

dog² *n* **1** : perro *m*, -rra *f* **2** → **hot dog 3** (*offensive*) : mujer *f* fea **4 sick as a dog** : muy enfermo **5 to let sleeping dogs lie** : no remover el avispero

dogcatcher ['dɔg,kætʃər] *n* : perrero *m*, -ra *f*

dog–eared ['dɔg,ɪrd] *adj* : con las esquinas dobladas

dogged ['dɔgəd] *adj* : tenaz, terco, obstinado

doggy ['dɔgi] *n*, *pl* **doggies** : perrito *m*, -ta *f*

doghouse ['dɔg,haʊs] *n* : casita *f* de perro

dogma ['dɔgmə] *n* : dogma *m*

dogmatic [dɔg'mætɪk] *adj* : dogmático

dogmatism ['dɔgmə,tɪzəm] *n* : dogmatismo *m*

dogwood ['dɔg,wʊd] *n* : cornejo *m*

doily ['dɔɪli] *n*, *pl* **-lies** : pañito *m*

doings ['du:ɪŋz] *npl* : eventos *mpl*, actividades *fpl*

do–it–yourself¹ *n* : bricolaje *m*

do–it–yourself² *adj* : de bricolaje

doldrums ['do:ldrəmz, 'dɑl-] *npl* **1** : zona *f* de las calmas ecuatoriales **2 to be in the doldrums** : estar abatido (dícese de una persona), estar estancado (dícese de una empresa)

dole ['do:l] *n* **1** ALMS : distribución *f* a los necesitados, limosna *f* **2** : subsidios *mpl* de desempleo

doleful ['do:lfəl] *adj* : triste, lúgubre

dolefully ['do:lfəli] *adv* : con pesar, de manera triste

dole out *vt* **doled out; doling out** : repartir

doll ['dɑl, 'dɔl] *n* : muñeco *m*, -ca *f*

dollar ['dɑlər] *n* : dólar *m*

dolly ['dɑli] *n*, *pl* **-lies 1** → **doll 2** : plataforma *f* rodante

dolphin ['dɑlfən, 'dɔl-] *n* : delfín *m*

dolt ['do:lt] *n* : imbécil *mf*; tonto *m*, -ta *f*

domain [do'meɪn, də-] *n* **1** TERRITORY : dominio *m*, territorio *m* **2** FIELD : campo *m*, esfera *f*, ámbito *m* ⟨the domain of art : el ámbito de las artes⟩

dome ['do:m] *n* : cúpula *f*, bóveda *f*

domestic¹ [də'mɛstɪk] *adj* **1** HOUSEHOLD : doméstico, casero **2** : nacional, interno ⟨domestic policy : política interna⟩ **3** TAME : domesticado

domestic² *n* : empleado *m* doméstico, empleada *f* doméstica

domestically [də'mɛstɪkli] *adv* : domésticamente

domesticate [də'mɛstɪ,keɪt] *vt* **-cated; -cating** : domesticar

domicile ['dɑmə,saɪl, 'do:-;, 'dɑməsɪl] *n* : domicilio *m*

dominance ['dɑmənənts] *n* : dominio *m*, dominación *f*

dominant ['dɑmənənt] *adj* : dominante

dominate ['dɑmə,neɪt] *v* **-nated; -nating** : dominar

domination [,dɑmə'neɪʒən] *n* : dominación *f*

domineer [,dɑmə'nɪr] *vt* : dominar sobre, avasallar, tiranizar

domineering [,dɑmə'nɪrɪŋ] *adj* : dominante

Dominican¹ [də'mɪnɪkən] *adj* **1** : dominicano **2** : dominico (en religión)

Dominican² *n* **1** : dominicano *m*, -na *f* **2** : dominico *m*, -ca *f* (en religión)

dominion [də'mɪnjən] *n* **1** POWER : dominio *m* **2** DOMAIN, TERRITORY : dominio *m*, territorio *m*

domino ['dɑmə,no:] *n*, *pl* **-noes** *or* **-nos 1** : dominó *m* **2 dominoes** *npl* : dominó *m* (juego)

don ['dɑn] *vt* **donned; donning** : ponerse

donate ['do:,neɪt, do:'-] *vt* **-nated; -nating** : donar, hacer un donativo de

donation [do:'neɪʒən] *n* : donación *f*, donativo *m*

done¹ ['dʌn] → **do**

done² *adj* **1** FINISHED : terminado, acabado, concluido ⟨now I'm done : ya terminé⟩ **2** COOKED : cocinado **3 done in** : agotado, derrengado **4 done for** : perdido, frito *Arg, Chile, Peru, Uru fam*

donkey ['daŋki, 'dʌŋ-] *n, pl* **-keys** : burro *m*, asno *m*

donor ['do:nər] *n* : donante *mf*; donador *m*, -dora *f*

don't ['do:nt] *contraction of* DO NOT → **do**

donut → **doughnut**

doodle¹ ['du:dəl] *v* **-dled; -dling** : garabatear

doodle² *n* : garabato *m*

doom¹ ['du:m] *vt* : condenar ⟨to be doomed (to failure) : estar condenado al fracaso⟩

doom² *n* **1** JUDGMENT : sentencia *f*, condena *f* **2** DEATH : muerte *f* **3** FATE : destino *m* **4** RUIN : perdición *f*, ruina *f*

door ['dor] *n* **1** : puerta *f* ⟨there's someone at the door : llaman a la puerta⟩ ⟨to answer the door : abrir la puerta⟩ ⟨can you get the door for me? : ¿me abres/cierras la puerta?⟩ ⟨garage/refrigerator door : puerta del garaje/refrigerador⟩ **2** ENTRANCE : entrada *f*

doorbell ['dor,bɛl] *n* : timbre *m*

doorknob ['dor,nɑb] *n* : pomo *m*, perilla *f*

doorman ['dormən] *n, pl* **-men** [-mən, -,mɛn] : portero *m*

doormat ['dor,mæt] *n* : felpudo *m*

doorstep ['dor,stɛp] *n* : umbral *m*

doorstop ['dor,stɑp] *n* : tope *m* de puerta

doorway ['dor,weɪ] *n* : entrada *f*, portal *m*

do–over ['du:,o:vər] *n* : otra oportunidad *f*, otro intento *m*

dope¹ ['do:p] *vt* **doped; doping** : drogar, narcotizar

dope² *n* **1** DRUG : droga *f*, estupefaciente *m*, narcótico *m* **2** IDIOT : idiota *mf*; tonto *m*, -ta *f* **3** INFORMATION : información *f*

dopey ['do:pi] *adj* **1** GROGGY : atontado, grogui *fam* **2** FOOLISH : tonto **3** DRUGGED : drogado

doping *n* : doping *m* (en deportes)

dormant ['dormənt] *adj* : inactivo, latente

dormer ['dormər] *n* : buhardilla *f*

dormitory ['dormə,tori] *n, pl* **-ries** : dormitorio *m*, residencia *f* de estudiantes

dormouse ['dor,maʊs] *n* : lirón *m*

dorsal ['dorsəl] *adj* : dorsal — **dorsally** *adv*

dory ['dori] *n, pl* **-ries** : bote *m* de fondo plano

dosage ['do:sɪdʒ] *n* : dosis *f*

dose¹ ['do:s] *vt* **dosed; dosing** : medicinar

dose² *n* : dosis *f*

dossier ['dɔs,jeɪ, 'dɑs-] *n* : dossier *m*

dot¹ ['dɑt] *vt* **dotted; dotting 1** : poner el punto sobre (una letra) **2** SCATTER : esparcir, salpicar

dot² *n* : punto *m* ⟨at six on the dot : a las seis en punto⟩ ⟨dots and dashes : puntos y rayas⟩

dot–com ['dɑt,kɑm] *n* : puntocom *m*

dote ['do:t] *vi* **doted; doting** : chochear

double¹ ['dʌbəl] *v* **-bled; -bling** *vt* **1** : doblar, duplicar (una cantidad), redob-

lar (esfuerzos) **2** FOLD : doblar, plegar **3 to double one's fist** : apretar el puño — *vi* **1** : doblarse, duplicarse **2 to double over** : retorcerse

double² *adj* : doble — **doubly** *adv*

double³ *n* : doble *mf*

double–barreled *or* **double–barrelled** [,dʌbəl'bærəld] *adj* **1** : de dos cañones (dícese de un arma de fuego) **2** TWO-FOLD : doble

double bass *n* : contrabajo *m*

double bed *n* : cama *f* de matrimonio

double–breasted [,dʌbəl'brɛstəd] *adj* : cruzado

double–check [,dʌbəl'tʃɛk] *vt* : verificar dos veces

double chin *n* : papada *f*

double–click [,dʌbəl'klɪk] *vi* : hacer doble clic

double–cross [,dʌbəl'krɔs] *vt* : traicionar

double–crosser [,dʌbəl'krɔsər] *n* : traidor *m*, -dora *f*

double entendre ['dʌbəlɑn'tɑndrə] *n* : doble sentido *m*

double–glazed [,dʌbəl'gleɪzd] *n* : con doble acristalamiento

double–jointed [,dʌbəl'dʒɔintəd] *adj* : con articulaciones dobles

double–spaced [,dʌbəl'speɪst] *n* : a doble espacio

double–talk ['dʌbəl,tɔk] *n* : ambigüedades *fpl*, lenguaje *m* con doble sentido

doubt¹ ['daʊt] *vt* **1** QUESTION : dudar de, cuestionar **2** DISTRUST : desconfiar de **3** : dudar, creer poco probable ⟨I doubt it very much : lo dudo mucho⟩

doubt² *n* **1** UNCERTAINTY : duda *f*, incertidumbre *f* ⟨to cast/throw doubt on, to cast/throw/call into doubt, to raise doubts about : poner en duda/cuestión⟩ **2** DISTRUST : desconfianza *f* **3** SKEPTICISM : duda *f*, escepticismo *m* **4 beyond doubt** : sin lugar a duda ⟨beyond any/all doubt : fuera de toda duda⟩ ⟨beyond a reasonable doubt : más allá de toda duda razonable⟩ **5 in doubt** : en duda ⟨if/when in doubt : en/ante la duda⟩ ⟨the outcome remains in doubt : aún no se conoce el resultado⟩ **6 no doubt** DOUBTLESS : sin duda ⟨there's no doubt about it : no hay/cabe duda⟩ **7 without (a) doubt** : sin duda ⟨without a shadow of a doubt : sin el menor asomo de duda⟩

doubtful ['daʊtfəl] *adj* **1** QUESTIONABLE : dudoso **2** UNCERTAIN : dudoso, incierto

doubtfully ['daʊtfəli] *adv* : dudosamente, sin estar convencido

doubtless ['daʊtləs] *or* **doubtlessly** *adv* : sin duda

douche¹ ['du:ʃ] *vt* **douched; douching** : irrigar

douche² *n* : ducha *f*, irrigación *f*

dough ['do:] *n* : masa *f*

doughnut *or* **donut** ['do:,nʌt] *n* : rosquilla *f*, dona *f Mex*

doughty ['daʊti] *adj* **doughtier; -est** : fuerte, valiente

doughy ['do:i] *adj* **doughier; -est 1** : pastoso **2** PALE : pálido

dour ['daʊər, 'dʊr] *adj* **1** STERN : severo, adusto **2** SULLEN : hosco, taciturno — **dourly** *adv*

douse ['daʊs, 'daʊz] *vt* **doused; dousing** **1** DRENCH : empapar, mojar **2** EXTINGUISH : extinguir, apagar

dove[1] ['do:v] → **dive**

dove[2] ['dʌv] *n* : paloma *f*

dovetail ['dʌv,teɪl] *vi* : encajar, enlazar

dowdy ['daʊdi] *adj* **dowdier; -est** : sin gracia, poco elegante

dowel ['daʊəl] *n* : clavija *f*

down[1] ['daʊn] *vt* **1** FELL : tumbar, derribar, abatir **2** DEFEAT : derrotar

down[2] *adv* **1** DOWNWARD : hacia abajo ⟨to bend down : agacharse⟩ ⟨to fall down : caer, caerse⟩ ⟨to look down : mirar (hacia) abajo⟩ ⟨she came down to say hello : bajó a saludarnos⟩ ⟨put it down on the table : ponlo en la mesa⟩ ⟨they knocked the wall down : tiraron abajo la pared⟩ **2** BELOW : abajo ⟨we keep it down in the basement : lo guardamos abajo en el sótano⟩ ⟨what's going on down there? : ¿qué pasa allí abajo?⟩ **3** LOWERED : bajado ⟨keep down! : ¡no te levantes!⟩ **4** : a, hacia ⟨he went down to the store : fue a la tienda⟩ ⟨come down and see us! : ¡ven a visitarnos!⟩ **5** : hacia el sur ⟨we went down to Florida : fuimos a Florida⟩ **6** AWAY, OVER : hacia el fondo/lado (etc.) ⟨move down so I can sit : córrete un poco para que pueda sentarme⟩ **7** (*indicating reduction*) ⟨she turned the volume down : bajó el volumen⟩ **8** THOROUGHLY : bien, completamente ⟨to hose down : lavar (con manguera)⟩ **9** (*indicating restriction of motion*) ⟨tie it down : átalo⟩ **10** (*indicating following to a place or source*) ⟨were you able to track her down? : ¿pudiste localizarla?⟩ ⟨they couldn't pin down the cause : no pudieron averiguar la causa⟩ **11** (*indicating lesser importance in a series, etc.*) ⟨it's pretty far/low down on my list : no es muy importante para mí⟩ **12** : en el estómago ⟨to keep food down : retener comida⟩ **13 down to** INCLUDING : hasta ⟨down to the last detail : hasta el último detalle⟩ **14 down with . . . !** : abajo . . . ! ⟨down with racism! : ¡abajo el racismo!⟩ **15 to hand/pass down** : transmitir (cuentos, etc.), pasar ⟨it was handed down to me by my grandmother : lo heredé de mi abuela⟩ **16 to lie down** : acostarse, echarse **17 to put down** ⟨to put down money, to put down a deposit : pagar un depósito⟩ **18 to sit down** : sentarse **19 to take/write down** : apuntar, anotar

down[3] *adj* **1** DESCENDING : de bajada ⟨the down elevator : el ascensor de bajada⟩ **2** : abajo ⟨it's down on the bottom shelf : está en el estante de abajo⟩ ⟨it's further down : está más abajo⟩ ⟨I'm down here : estoy aquí abajo⟩ **3** LOWERED : bajado **4** REDUCED : reducido, rebajado ⟨attendance is down : la concurrencia ha disminuido⟩ ⟨to keep

prices down : mantener los precios bajos⟩ **5** DOWNCAST : abatido, deprimido ⟨to feel down : andar deprimido⟩ **6** INOPERATIVE : inoperante ⟨the system is down : el sistema no funciona⟩ **7** BEHIND : perdiendo ⟨they're down (by) ten points : van perdiendo por diez puntos⟩ **8** COMPLETED : hecho, acabado ⟨two down, one to go : dos menos, falta uno⟩

down[4] *n* **1** : plumón *m* **2 ups and downs** : altibajos *mpl*

down[5] *prep* **1** : (hacia) abajo ⟨down the mountain : montaña abajo⟩ ⟨I walked down the stairs : bajé por la escalera⟩ **2** ALONG : por, a lo largo de ⟨we ran down the beach : corrimos por la playa⟩ **3** : a través de ⟨down the years : a través de los años⟩

down–and–out *adj* : indigente

downcast ['daʊn,kæst] *adj* **1** SAD : triste, abatido **2 with downcast eyes** : con los ojos bajos, con los ojos mirando al suelo

downfall ['daʊn,fɔl] *n* : ruina *f*, perdición *f*

downgrade[1] ['daʊn,greɪd] *vt* **-graded; -grading** : bajar de categoría

downgrade[2] *n* : bajada *f*

downhearted ['daʊn'hɑrt̬əd] *adj* : desanimado, descorazonado

downhill ['daʊn'hɪl] *adv & adj* : cuesta abajo

download[1] ['daʊn,lo:d] *vt* : descargar, bajar (en informática)

download[2] *n* : descarga *f* (de archivos, etc.)

downloadable *adj* : descargable

down payment *n* : entrega *f* inicial

downplay ['daʊn,pleɪ] *vt* : minimizar

downpour ['daʊn,por] *n* : aguacero *m*, chaparrón *m*

downright[1] ['daʊn,raɪt] *adv* THOROUGHLY : absolutamente, completamente

downright[2] *adj* : patente, manifiesto, absoluto ⟨a downright refusal : un rechazo categórico⟩

downside ['daʊn,saɪd] *n* : desventaja *f*

downsize ['daʊn,saɪz] *vt* **-sized; -sizing** : recortar, reducir

downstairs[1] ['daʊn'stærz] *adv* : abajo

downstairs[2] ['daʊn'stærz] *adj* : del piso de abajo

downstairs[3] ['daʊn'stær, -,stærz] *n* : planta *f* baja

downstream ['daʊn'stri:m] *adv* : río abajo

Down syndrome *or* **Down's syndrome** *n* : síndrome *m* de Down

down–to–earth [,daʊntu'ərth] *adj* : práctico, realista

downtown[1] [,daʊn'taʊn] *adv* : hacia el centro, al centro, en el centro (de la ciudad)

downtown[2] *adj* : del centro (de la ciudad) ⟨downtown Chicago : el centro de Chicago⟩

downtown[3] [,daʊn'taʊn, 'daʊn,taʊn] *n* : centro *m* (de la ciudad)

downtrodden ['daʊn,trɑdən] *adj* : oprimido

downward ['daʊnwərd] *or* **downwards** [-wərdz] *adv & adj* : hacia abajo

downwind ['daʊn'wɪnd] *adv & adj* : en la dirección del viento

downy ['daʊni] *adj* **downier; -est** **1** : cubierto de plumón, plumoso **2** VELVETY : aterciopelado, velloso

dowry ['daʊri] *n, pl* **-ries** : dote *f*

doze¹ ['do:z] *vi* **dozed; dozing** : dormitar

doze² *n* : sueño *m* ligero, cabezada *f*

dozen ['dʌzən] *n, pl* **dozens** *or* **dozen** : docena *f* ⟨a dozen eggs : una docena de huevos⟩ ⟨ten dozen : diez docenas⟩ ⟨dozens (and dozens) : decenas, montones⟩

drab ['dræb] *adj* **drabber; drabbest** **1** BROWNISH : pardo **2** DULL, LACKLUSTER : monótono, gris, deslustrado

draft¹ ['dræft, 'draft] *vt* **1** CONSCRIPT : reclutar **2** COMPOSE, SKETCH : hacer el borrador de, redactar

draft² *adj* **1** : de barril ⟨draft beer : cerveza de barril⟩ **2** : de tiro ⟨draft horses : caballos de tiro⟩

draft³ *n* **1** HAULAGE : tiro *m* **2** DRINK, GULP : trago *m* **3** OUTLINE, SKETCH : bosquejo *m*, borrador *m*, versión *f* **4** : corriente *f* de aire, chiflón *m*, tiro *m* (de una chimenea) **5** CONSCRIPTION : conscripción *f* **6** bank draft : giro *m* bancario, letra *f* de cambio

draftee [dræf'ti:] *n* : recluta *mf*

draftsman ['dræftsmən] *n, pl* **-men** [-mən, -ˌmɛn] : dibujante *mf*

draftswoman ['dræfts.wʊmən] *n, pl* **-women** [-ˌwɪmən] : dibujante *f*

drafty ['dræfti] *adj* **draftier; -est** : con corrientes de aire

drag¹ ['dræg] *v* **dragged; dragging** *vt* **1** HAUL, TRAIL : arrastrar ⟨I could barely drag myself out of bed : me costó levantarme de la cama⟩ **2** DREDGE : dragar **3** INVOLVE : meter, involucrar ⟨don't drag me into this : no me metas en esto⟩ **4** to drag one's feet/heels : dar largas a algo ⟨they're still dragging their feet (on the issue) : siguen dando largas al asunto⟩ **5** to drag out PROLONG : alargar, dilatar — *vi* **1** TRAIL : arrastrarse **2** LAG : rezagarse **3** : hacerse pesado/largo ⟨the day dragged on : el día se hizo largo⟩

drag² *n* **1** RESISTANCE : resistencia *f* (aerodinámica) **2** HINDRANCE : traba *f*, estorbo *m* **3** BORE : pesadez *f*, plomo *m* *fam* **4** : chupada *f* (de un cigarrillo)

dragnet ['dræg.nɛt] *n* **1** : red *f* barredera (en pesca) **2** : operativo *m* policial de captura

dragon ['drægən] *n* : dragón *m*

dragonfly ['drægən.flaɪ] *n, pl* **-flies** : libélula *f*

drain¹ ['dreɪn] *vt* **1** EMPTY : vaciar, drenar **2** EXHAUST : agotar, consumir — *vi* **1** : escurrir, escurrirse ⟨the dishes are draining : los platos están escurriéndose⟩ **2** EMPTY : desaguar **3** to drain away : irse agotando

drain² *n* **1** : desagüe *m* **2** SEWER : alcantarilla *f* **3** GRATING : sumidero *m*, resumidero *m*, rejilla *f* **4** EXHAUSTION : agotamiento *m*, disminución *f* (de

energía, etc.) ⟨to be a drain on : agotar, consumir⟩ **5** to throw down the drain : tirar por la ventana

drainage ['dreɪnɪdʒ] *n* : desagüe *m*, drenaje *m*

drainpipe ['dreɪn.paɪp] *n* : tubo *m* de desagüe, caño *m*

drake ['dreɪk] *n* : pato *m* (macho)

drama ['drɑmə, 'dræ-] *n* **1** THEATER : drama *m*, teatro *m* **2** PLAY : obra *f* de teatro, drama *m*

dramatic [drə'mætɪk] *adj* : dramático — **dramatically** [-tɪkli] *adv*

dramatist ['dræmətɪst, 'drɑ-] *n* : dramaturgo *m*, -ga *f*

dramatization [ˌdræmətə'zeɪlən, ˌdrɑ-] *n* : dramatización *f*

dramatize ['dræmə.taɪz, 'drɑ-] *vt* **-tized; -tizing** : dramatizar

drank → **drink**

drape¹ ['dreɪp] *vt* **draped; draping** **1** COVER : cubrir (con tela) **2** HANG : disponer los pliegues de

drape² *n* **1** HANG : caída *f* **2** **drapes** *npl* : cortinas *fpl*

drapery ['dreɪpəri] *n, pl* **-eries** **1** CLOTH : pañería *f*, tela *f* para cortinas **2** **draperies** *npl* : cortinas *fpl*

drastic ['dræstɪk] *adj* **1** HARSH, SEVERE : drástico, severo **2** EXTREME : radical, excepcional — **drastically** [-tɪkli] *adv*

draught ['dræft, 'draft] *n* → **draft³**

draughty ['dræfti] → **drafty**

draw¹ ['drɔ] *v* **drew** ['dru:]; **drawn** ['drɔn]; **drawing** *vt* **1** PULL : tirar de, jalar, correr (cortinas) **2** ATTRACT : atraer ⟨to feel drawn to : sentirse atraído por⟩ ⟨to draw attention : llamar la atención⟩ **3** PROVOKE, ELICIT : provocar, suscitar (críticas, etc.) ⟨to draw cheers/applause : arrancar vítores/aplausos⟩ **4** INHALE : aspirar ⟨to draw breath : respirar⟩ **5** EXTRACT : sacar (agua, sangre, etc.) ⟨to draw a gun : sacar una pistola⟩ **6** TAKE : sacar ⟨to draw a number : sacar un número⟩ **7** WITHDRAW : retirar, sacar (dinero) ⟨he drew a hundred dollars from his account : sacó cien dólares de su cuenta⟩ **8** WRITE : hacer, extender (un cheque) **9** COLLECT : cobrar, percibir (un sueldo, etc.) **10** BEND : tensar (un arco) **11** SKETCH : dibujar, trazar ⟨to draw a picture : dibujar algo, hacer un dibujo⟩ **12** FORMULATE : sacar, formular, llegar a ⟨to draw a conclusion : llegar a una conclusión⟩ **13** MAKE : hacer (una distinción, una comparación) **14** to draw oneself up : erguirse **15** to draw out : hacer hablar (sobre algo), hacer salir de sí mismo **16** to draw out PROLONG : prolongar, alargar, extender **17** to draw up DRAFT : redactar — *vi* **1** SKETCH : dibujar **2** TUG : tirar, jalar **3** to draw away : alejarse **4** to draw near : acercarse **5** to draw on/upon USE : hacer uso de (información, etc.) **6** to draw to a close : terminar, finalizar **7** to draw up STOP : parar

draw² *n* **1** DRAWING, RAFFLE : sorteo *m* **2** TIE : empate *m* **3** ATTRACTION

: atracción *f*   **4** PUFF : chupada *f* (de un cigarrillo, etc.)

drawback ['drɔ,bæk] *n* : desventaja *f*, inconveniente *m*

drawbridge ['drɔ,brɪdʒ] *n* : puente *m* levadizo

drawer ['drɔr, 'drɔər] *n*   **1** ILLUSTRATOR : dibujante *mf*   **2** : gaveta *f*, cajón *m* (en un mueble)   **3 drawers** *npl* UNDERPANTS : calzones *mpl*

drawing ['drɔɪŋ] *n*   **1** LOTTERY : sorteo *m*, lotería *f*   **2** SKETCH : dibujo *m*, bosquejo *m*

drawing room *n* : salón *m*

drawl¹ ['drɔl] *vi* : hablar arrastrando las palabras

drawl² *n* : habla *f* lenta y con vocales prolongadas

dread¹ ['drɛd] *vt* : tenerle pavor a, temer

dread² *adj* : pavoroso, aterrado

dread³ *n* : pavor *m*, temor *m*

dreadful ['drɛdfəl] *adj*   **1** DREAD : pavoroso   **2** TERRIBLE : espantoso, atroz, terrible — **dreadfully** *adv*

dream¹ ['driːm] *v* **dreamed** ['drɛmpt, 'driːmd] *or* **dreamt** ['drɛmpt]; **dreaming** *vi*   **1** : soñar ⟨to dream about : soñar con⟩   **2** FANTASIZE : fantasear — *vt*   **1** : soñar   **2** IMAGINE : imaginarse   **3 to dream up** : inventar, idear

dream² *n*   **1** : sueño *m*, ensueño *m*   **2 bad dream** NIGHTMARE : pesadilla *f*

dreamer ['driːmər] *n* : soñador *m*, -dora *f*

dreamlike ['driːm,laɪk] *adj* : de ensueño

dreamy ['driːmi] *adj* **dreamier; -est**   **1** DISTRACTED : soñador, distraído   **2** DREAMLIKE : de ensueño   **3** MARVELOUS : maravilloso

drearily ['drɪrəli] *adv* : sombríamente

dreary ['drɪri] *adj* **drearier; -est** : deprimente, lóbrego, sombrío

dredge¹ ['drɛdʒ] *vt* **dredged; dredging**   **1** DIG : dragar   **2** COAT : espolvorear, enharinar

dredge² *n* : draga *f*

dredger ['drɛdʒər] *n* : draga *f*

dregs ['drɛgz] *npl*   **1** LEES : posos *mpl*, heces *fpl* (de un líquido)   **2** : heces *fpl*, escoria *f* ⟨the dregs of society : la escoria de la sociedad⟩

drench ['drɛntʃ] *vt* : empapar, mojar, calar

dress¹ ['drɛs] *vt*   **1** CLOTHE : vestir ⟨she was dressed in red : iba (vestida) de rojo⟩   **2** DECORATE : decorar, adornar   **3** : preparar (pollo o pescado), aliñar (ensalada)   **4** : curar, vendar (una herida)   **5** FERTILIZE : abonar (la tierra)   **6 to dress down** SCOLD : regañar   **7 to dress up** EMBELLISH : adornar, engalanar   **8 to dress up** DISGUISE : disfrazar — *vi*   **1** : vestirse ⟨to dress well/badly : vestir bien/mal⟩   **2 to dress down** : vestirse informalmente   **3 to dress up** : ataviarse, engalanarse, ponerse de etiqueta   **4 to dress up** : disfrazarse, vestirse ⟨we dressed up as ghosts : nos disfrazamos de fantasmas⟩

dress² *n*   **1** APPAREL : indumentaria *f*, ropa *f*   **2** : vestido *m*, traje *m* (de mujer)

dresser ['drɛsər] *n* : cómoda *f* con espejo

dressing ['drɛsɪŋ] *n*   **1** : vestirse *m*   **2** *or* **salad dressing** : aderezo *m*, aliño *m*   **3** STUFFING : relleno *m* (de pollo, etc.)   **4** : apósito *m*, vendaje *m*, gasa *f* (para una herida)

dressing gown *n* : bata *f*

dressing room *n*   **1** FITTING ROOM : probador *m*   **2** : camerino *m* (en un teatro)

dressing table *n* : tocador *m*

dressmaker ['drɛs,meɪkər] *n* : modista *mf*

dressmaking ['drɛs,meɪkɪŋ] *n* : costura *f*

dress rehearsal *n* : ensayo *m* general

dressy ['drɛsi] *adj* **dressier; -est** : de mucho vestir, elegante

drew → **draw**

dribble¹ ['drɪbəl] *vi* **-bled; -bling**   **1** DRIP : gotear   **2** DROOL : babear   **3** : driblar (en basquetbol)

dribble² *n*   **1** TRICKLE : goteo *m*, hilo *m*   **2** DROOL : baba *f*   **3** : drible *m* (en basquetbol)

drier → **dry**², **dryer**

driest *adj* → **dry**²

drift¹ ['drɪft] *vi*   **1** : dejarse llevar por la corriente, ir a la deriva (dícese de un bote), ir sin rumbo (dícese de una persona)   **2** ACCUMULATE : amontonarse, acumularse, apilarse

drift² *n*   **1** DRIFTING : deriva *f*   **2** HEAP, MASS : montón *m* (de arena, etc.), ventisquero *m* (de nieve)   **3** MEANING : sentido *m*

drifter ['drɪftər] *n* : vagabundo *m*, -da *f*

driftwood ['drɪft,wʊd] *n* : madera *f* flotante

drill¹ ['drɪl] *vt*   **1** BORE : perforar, taladrar   **2** INSTRUCT : instruir por repetición — *vi*   **1** TRAIN : entrenarse   **2 to drill for oil** : perforar en busca de petróleo

drill² *n*   **1** : taladro *m*, barrena *f*   **2** EXERCISE, PRACTICE : ejercicio *m*, instrucción *f*

drily → **dryly**

drink¹ ['drɪŋk] *v* **drank** ['dræŋk]; **drunk** ['drʌŋk] *or* **drank; drinking** *vt*   **1** IMBIBE : beber, tomar   **2 to drink up** ABSORB : absorber — *vi*   **1** : beber   **2** : beber alcohol, tomar

drink² *n*   **1** : bebida *f* ⟨food and drink : comida y bebida⟩   **2** : bebida *f* alcohólica ⟨to drive someone to drink : llevar a alguien a la bebida⟩

drinkable ['drɪŋkəbəl] *adj* : potable

drinker ['drɪŋkər] *n* : bebedor *m*, -dora *f*

drinking water *n* : agua *f* potable

drinking straw → **straw**

drip¹ ['drɪp] *vi* **dripped; dripping** : gotear, chorrear

drip² *n*   **1** DROP : gota *f*   **2** DRIPPING : goteo *m*

drip–dry ['drɪp,draɪ] *adj* : de lavar y poner

drippings *npl* : pringue *m*, jugo *m*

drive¹ ['draɪv] *v* **drove** ['droːv]; **driven** ['drɪvən]; **driving** *vt*   **1** : manejar, conducir (un vehículo) : llevar (en un automóvil) ⟨she drove me home : me llevó a casa⟩   **3** IMPEL : llevar, impulsar, impeler ⟨to drive someone to do something : llevar a alguien a hacer algo⟩   **4**

COMPEL : obligar, forzar **5** : arrear (ganado) **6** POWER : hacer funcionar **7** PROPEL : impeler, impulsar **8** : clavar, hincar ⟨to drive a stake into : clavar una estaca en⟩ **9** : hacer trabajar mucho, exigir mucho ⟨he drives himself too hard : se exige demasiado⟩ **10** : lanzar (una pelota) **11 to drive away/off/out** : ahuyentar, echar, expulsar **12 to drive back** REPEL : hacer retroceder **13 to drive crazy** : volver loco **14 to drive up/down** : hacer subir/bajar (dícese de precios, etc.) — *vi* **1** : manejar, conducir ⟨do you know how to drive? : ¿sabes manejar?⟩ **2** : viajar (en auto) **3 to drive at** : querer decir, insinuar **4 to drive away/off** : alejarse (en un auto) ⟨they drove off : su auto se alejó⟩

drive² *n* **1** RIDE : viaje *m*, paseo *m* (en un automóvil) ⟨a two-hour drive : un viaje de dos horas⟩ **2** CAMPAIGN : campaña *f* ⟨fund-raising drive : campaña para recaudar fondos⟩ **3** DRIVEWAY : camino *m* de entrada, entrada *f* **4** TRANSMISSION : transmisión *f* ⟨front-wheel drive : tracción delantera⟩ **5** ENERGY : dinamismo *m*, energía *f* **6** INSTINCT, NEED : instinto *m*, necesidad *f* básica **7** AMBITION, INITIATIVE : empuje *m*, iniciativa *f* **8** : disparo *m* fuerte, tiro *m* fuerte (en deportes) **9** : ofensiva *f* (militar) **10** STREET : calle *f* ⟨she lives on Oak Drive : vive en la calle Oak⟩ **11** : marcha *f* ⟨to put a car in/into drive : poner en marcha un auto⟩ **12** : unidad *f* ⟨flash drive : unidad (de memoria) flash⟩

drive–in *n* : autocine *m*

drivel ['drɪvəl] *n* : tontería *f*, estupidez *f*

driver ['draɪvər] *n* : conductor *m*, -tora *f*; chofer *m*

driveway ['draɪˌweɪ] *n* : camino *m* de entrada, entrada *f* (para coches)

driving ['draɪvɪŋ] *adj* : torrencial (dícese de la lluvia), que azota (dícese del viento) ⟨the driving force behind the reform : el principal impulsor de la reforma⟩

drizzle¹ ['drɪzəl] *vi* **-zled; -zling** : lloviznar, garuar

drizzle² *n* : llovizna *f*, garúa *f*

droll ['droːl] *adj* : cómico, gracioso, chistoso — **drolly** *adv*

dromedary ['drɑməˌderi] *n, pl* **-daries** : dromedario *m*

drone¹ ['droːn] *vi* **droned; droning** **1** BUZZ : zumbar **2** MURMUR : hablar con monotonía, murmurar

drone² *n* **1** : zángano *m* (abeja) **2** BUZZ, HUM : zumbido *m*, murmullo *m*

drool¹ ['druːl] *vi* : babear

drool² *n* : baba *f*

droop¹ ['druːp] *vi* **1** HANG : inclinarse (dícese de la cabeza), encorvarse (dícese de los escombros), marchitarse (dícese de las flores) **2** FLAG : decaer, flaquear ⟨his spirits drooped : se desanimó⟩

droop² *n* : inclinación *f*, caída *f*

drop¹ ['drɑp] *v* **dropped; dropping** *vt* **1** : dejar caer, soltar ⟨she dropped the glass : se le cayó el vaso⟩ **2** SEND : man-

dar ⟨drop me a line : mándame unas líneas⟩ **3** ABANDON : abandonar, dejar ⟨to drop the subject : cambiar de tema⟩ **4** LOWER : bajar ⟨he dropped his voice : bajó la voz⟩ **5** OMIT : omitir **6** REDUCE : reducir, rebajar (precios, etc.) **7** *fam* : perder (peso) **8** *fam* SPEND : gastar **9** : dejar caer (una noticia, etc.) ⟨to drop a hint : lanzar una indirecta⟩ **10 to drop off** : dejar ⟨I dropped her off at the store : la dejé en la tienda⟩ — *vi* **1** DRIP : gotear **2** FALL : caer(se) ⟨to drop to the ground : caer al suelo⟩ ⟨to drop out of sight : perderse de vista⟩ **3** *or* **to drop off** DECREASE, DESCEND : bajar, descender ⟨the wind dropped off : amainó el viento⟩ **4 to drop back/behind** : rezagarse, quedarse atrás **5 to drop by/in** : pasar ⟨he dropped by for a visit : pasó a visitarnos⟩ **6 to drop off** : quedarse dormido **7 to drop out (of something)** : abandonar algo ⟨he dropped out (of school) : abandonó los estudios⟩

drop² *n* **1** : gota *f* (de líquido) **2** DECLINE : caída *f*, bajada *f*, descenso *m* **3** INCLINE : caída *f*, pendiente *f* ⟨a 20-foot drop : una caída de 20 pies⟩ **4** SWEET : pastilla *f*, dulce *m* **5 drops** *npl* : gotas *fpl* (de medicina)

droplet ['drɑplət] *n* : gotita *f*

dropper ['drɑpər] *n* : gotero *m*, cuentagotas *m*

dross ['drɑs, 'drɔs] *n* : escoria *f*

drought ['draʊt] *n* : sequía *f*

drove¹ → **drive**

drove² ['droːv] *n* : multitud *f*, gentío *m*, manada *f* (de ganado) ⟨in droves : en manada⟩

drown ['draʊn] *vt* **1** : ahogar **2** INUNDATE : anegar, inundar **3 to drown out** : ahogar — *vi* : ahogarse

drowse¹ ['draʊz] *vi* **drowsed; drowsing** DOZE : dormitar

drowse² *n* : sueño *m* ligero, cabezada *f*

drowsiness ['draʊzinəs] *n* : somnolencia *f*, adormecimiento *m*

drowsy ['draʊzi] *adj* **drowsier; -est** : somnoliento, soñoliento

drub ['drʌb] *vt* **drubbed; drubbing** **1** BEAT, THRASH : golpear, apalear **2** DEFEAT : derrotar por completo

drudge¹ ['drʌdʒ] *vi* **drudged; drudging** : trabajar como esclavo, trabajar duro

drudge² *n* : esclavo *m*, -va *f* del trabajo

drudgery ['drʌdʒəri] *n, pl* **-eries** : trabajo *m* pesado

drug¹ ['drʌg] *vt* **drugged; drugging** : drogar, narcotizar

drug² *n* **1** MEDICATION : droga *f*, medicina *f*, medicamento *m* **2** NARCOTIC : narcótico *m*, estupefaciente *m*, droga *f*

drug addict → **addict**

druggist ['drʌgɪst] *n* : farmacéutico *m*, -ca *f*

drug pusher → **pusher**

drugstore ['drʌgˌstor] *n* : farmacia *f*, botica *f*, droguería *f*

drum¹ ['drʌm] *v* **drummed; drumming** *vt* **1** : meter a fuerza ⟨he drummed it into my head : me lo metió en la cabeza a fuerza⟩ **2 to drum up** : conseguir, obtener (apoyo, etc.) — *vi* : tocar el tambor

drum² *n* **1** : tambor *m* **2** : bidón *m* ⟨oil drum : bidón de petróleo⟩

drummer ['drʌmər] *n* : baterista *mf*

drumstick ['drʌmˌstɪk] *n* **1** : palillo *m* (de tambor), baqueta *f* **2** : muslo *m* de pollo

drunk¹ *pp* → **drink¹**

drunk² ['drʌŋk] *adj* : borracho, embriagado, ebrio

drunk³ *n* : borracho *m*, -cha *f*

drunkard ['drʌŋkərd] *n* : borracho *m*, -cha *f*

drunken ['drʌŋkən] *adj* : borracho, ebrio ⟨drunken driver : conductor ebrio⟩ ⟨drunken brawl : pleito de borrachos⟩

drunkenly ['drʌŋkənli] *adv* : como un borracho

drunkenness ['drʌŋkənnəs] *n* : borrachera *f*, embriaguez *f*, ebriedad *f*

dry¹ ['draɪ] *v* **dried; drying** *vt* : secar ⟨to dry the dishes : secar los platos⟩ ⟨to dry one's eyes : secarse las lágrimas⟩ — *vi* **1** *or* **to dry out/up** : secarse **2 to dry up** RUN OUT : agotarse

dry² *adj* **drier; driest 1** : seco ⟨the well went dry : el pozo se secó⟩ ⟨to have a dry mouth : tener la boca seca⟩ ⟨there was not a dry eye in the house : no hubo quien no llorara⟩ **2** THIRSTY : sediento **3** : donde la venta de bebidas alcohólicas está prohibida ⟨a dry county : un condado seco⟩ **4** : seco, sin alcohol ⟨a dry party : una fiesta seca⟩ **5** DULL : aburrido, árido ⟨a dry class : una clase aburrida⟩ **6** : sutil e irónico (dícese de un sentido de humor)

dry-clean ['draɪˌkliːn] *v* : limpiar en seco

dry cleaner *n* : tintorería *f* (servicio) ⟨the dry cleaner/cleaner's/cleaners : la tintorería⟩

dry cleaning *n* : limpieza *f* en seco

dryer ['draɪər] *n* **1** *or* **hair dryer** : secador *m*, secadora *f Mex* **2** *or* **clothes dryer** : secadora *f*

dry goods *npl* : artículos *mpl* de confección

dry ice *n* : hielo *m* seco

dryly ['draɪli] *adv* : secamente

dryness ['draɪnəs] *n* : sequedad *f*, aridez *f*

dual ['duːəl, 'djuː-] *adj* : doble

dualism ['duːəˌlɪzəm] *n* : dualismo *m*

duality [duːˈæləti] *n*, *pl* **-ties** : dualidad *f*

dub ['dʌb] *vt* **dubbed; dubbing 1** CALL : apodar **2** : doblar (una película), mezclar (una grabación)

dubious ['duːbiəs, 'djuː-] *adj* **1** UNCERTAIN : dudoso, indeciso **2** QUESTIONABLE : sospechoso, dudoso, discutible

dubiously ['duːbiəsli, 'djuː-] *adv* **1** UNCERTAINLY : dudosamente, con desconfianza **2** SUSPICIOUSLY : de modo sospechoso, con recelo

duchess ['dʌtʃəs] *n* : duquesa *f*

duck¹ ['dʌk] *vt* **1** LOWER : agachar, bajar (la cabeza) **2** PLUNGE : zambullir **3** EVADE : eludir, evadir — *vi* **to duck down** : agacharse

duck² *n*, *pl* **duck** *or* **ducks** : pato *m*, -ta *f*

duckling ['dʌklɪŋ] *n* : patito *m*, -ta *f*

duct ['dʌkt] *n* : conducto *m*

dud¹ ['dʌd] *adj* : que fracasa, que no funciona ⟨a dud movie : un fracaso de taquilla⟩ ⟨a dud grenade : una granada que no estalla⟩

dud² *n* **1** : fracaso *m* ⟨a box-office dud : un fracaso de taquilla⟩ **2** : cosa *f* que no funciona ⟨this match is a dud : este fósforo no prende⟩ **3 duds** *npl fam* : trapos *mpl fam*, ropa *f*

dude ['duːd, 'djuːd] *n* GUY : tipo *m*

due¹ ['duː, 'djuː] *adv* : justo a, derecho hacia ⟨due north : derecho hacia el norte⟩

due² *adj* **1** PAYABLE : pagadero, sin pagar ⟨the rent is due : hay que pagar el alquiler⟩ **2** APPROPRIATE : debido, apropiado ⟨after due consideration : con las debidas consideraciones⟩ ⟨with all due respect : con el debido respeto⟩ **3** EXPECTED : esperado ⟨the train is due soon : esperamos el tren muy pronto, el tren debe llegar pronto⟩ ⟨the movie is due out in April : la película sale en abril⟩ **4 due to** : debido a, por

due³ *n* **1 to give someone his (her) due** : darle a alguien su merecido **2 dues** *npl* : cuota *f*

duel¹ ['duːəl, 'djuː-] *vi* : batirse en duelo

duel² *n* : duelo *m*

duet [duˈɛt, djuˈ-] *n* : dúo *m*

due to *prep* : debido a

duffel bag *or* **duffle bag** *n* : bolso *m* (deportivo)

duffle coat *or* **duffel coat** *n* : chaqueta *f* de lana (con capucha), trenca *f Spain*

dug → **dig**

dugout ['dʌgˌaʊt] *n* **1** CANOE : piragua *f* **2** SHELTER : refugio *m* subterráneo

duke ['duːk, 'djuːk] *n* : duque *m*

dull¹ ['dʌl] *vt* **1** DIM : opacar, quitarle el brillo a, deslustrar **2** BLUNT : desafilar (un filo), despuntar (un lápiz, etc.) **3** BLUNT : entorpecer (los sentidos), embotar (la mente), aliviar (el dolor), amortiguar (sonidos)

dull² *adj* **1** STUPID : torpe, lerdo, lento **2** BLUNT : desafilado, despuntado **3** LACKLUSTER : sin brillo, deslustrado **4** BORING : aburrido, soso, pesado — **dully** *adv*

dullness ['dʌlnəs] *n* **1** STUPIDITY : estupidez *f* **2** MONOTONY : monotonía *f*, lo aburrido **3** : falta *f* de brillo **4** BLUNTNESS : falta *f* de filo

duly ['duːli, 'djuː-] *adv* PROPERLY : debidamente, a su debido tiempo

dumb ['dʌm] *adj* **1** *now often offensive* MUTE : mudo **2** STUPID : estúpido, tonto, bobo — **dumbly** *adv*

dumbbell ['dʌmˌbɛl] *n* **1** WEIGHT : pesa *f* **2** : estúpido *m*, -da *f*

dumbfound *or* **dumfound** [ˌdʌmˈfaʊnd] *vt* : dejar atónito, dejar sin habla

dummy¹ ['dʌmi] *adj* : falso, de imitación, artificial

dummy² *n*, *pl* **-mies 1** SHAM : imitación *f*, sustituto *m* **2** PUPPET : muñeco *m* **3** MANNEQUIN : maniquí *m* **4** IDIOT : tonto *m*, -ta *f*; idiota *mf*

dump¹ ['dʌmp] *vt* : descargar, verter

dump² *n* **1** : vertedero *m*, basural *m*, basurero *m*, botadero *m*, tiradero *m* *Mex* **2 down in the dumps** : triste, deprimido

dumpling ['dʌmplɪŋ] *n* : bola *f* de masa hervida

Dumpster *trademark* se usa para un contenedor de basura

dumpy ['dʌmpi] *adj* **dumpier; -est** : rechoncho, regordete

dun¹ ['dʌn] *vt* **dunned; dunning** : apremiar (a un deudor)

dun² *adj* : pardo (color)

dunce ['dʌnts] *n* : estúpido *m*, -da *f*; burro *m*, -rra *f fam*

dune ['duːn, 'djuːn] *n* : duna *f* (de arena)

dung ['dʌŋ] *n* **1** FECES : excrementos *mpl* **2** MANURE : estiércol *m*

dungarees [ˌdʌŋgəˈriːz] *n* **1** → **jeans 2** → **overalls**

dungeon ['dʌndʒən] *n* : mazmorra *f*, calabozo *m*

dunk ['dʌŋk] *vt* : mojar, ensopar

duo ['duːoː, 'djuː-] *n, pl* **duos** : dúo *m*, par *m*

dupe¹ ['duːp, djuːp] *vt* **duped; duping** : engañar, embaucar

dupe² *n* : inocentón *m*, -tona *f*; simple *mf*

duplex¹ ['duːˌpleks, 'djuː-] *adj* : doble

duplex² *n* : casa *f* de dos viviendas, dúplex *m*

duplicate¹ ['duːplɪˌkeɪt, 'djuː-] *vt* **-cated; -cating 1** COPY : duplicar, hacer copias de **2** REPEAT : repetir, reproducir

duplicate² ['duːplɪkət, 'djuː-] *adj* : duplicado ⟨a duplicate invoice : una factura por duplicado⟩

duplicate³ ['duːplɪkət, 'djuː-] *n* : duplicado *m*, copia *f*

duplication [ˌduːplɪˈkeɪʃən, ˌdjuː-] *n* **1** DUPLICATING : duplicación *f*, repetición *f* (de esfuerzos) **2** DUPLICATE : copia *f*, duplicado *m*

duplicity [dʊˈplɪsəti, ˌdjuː-] *n, pl* **-ties** : duplicidad *f*

durability [ˌdʊrəˈbɪləti, ˌdjʊr-] *n* : durabilidad *f* (de un producto), permanencia *f*

durable ['dʊrəbəl, 'djʊr-] *adj* : duradero

duration [dʊˈreɪən, djʊ-] *n* : duración *f*

duress [dʊˈrɛs, djʊ-] *n* : coacción *f*

during ['dʊrɪŋ, 'djʊr-] *prep* : durante

dusk ['dʌsk] *n* : anochecer *m*, crepúsculo *m*

dusky ['dʌski] *adj* **duskier; -est** : oscuro (dícese de los colores)

dust¹ ['dʌst] *vt* **1** : quitar el polvo de **2** SPRINKLE : espolvorear

dust² *n* : polvo *m*

dustcover ['dʌstˌkʌvər] *n* **1** : guardapolvo *m*, funda *f* **2** → **dust jacket**

duster ['dʌstər] *n* **1** *or* **dust cloth** : trapo

m de polvo **2** HOUSECOAT : guardapolvo *m* **3 feather duster** : plumero *m*

dust jacket *n* : sobrecubierta *f*

dustpan ['dʌstˌpæn] *n* : recogedor *m*

dusty ['dʌsti] *adj* **dustier; -est** : cubierto de polvo, polvoriento

Dutch¹ ['dʌtʃ] *adj* : holandés

Dutch² *n* **1** : holandés *m* (idioma) **2 the Dutch** (*used with a plural verb*) : los holandeses

Dutchman ['dʌtʃmən] *n, pl* **-men** [-mən, -ˌmɛn] : holandés *m* (persona)

Dutch treat *n* : invitación o pago a escote

Dutchwoman ['dʌtʃˌwʊmən] *n, pl* **-women** [-ˌwɪmən] : holandesa *f* (persona)

dutiful ['duːtɪfəl, 'djuː-] *adj* : motivado por sus deberes, responsable

duty ['duːti, 'djuː-] *n, pl* **-ties 1** OBLIGATION : deber *m*, obligación *f*, responsabilidad *f* **2** TAX : impuesto *m*, arancel *m*

duty–free [ˌduːtiˈfriː, ˌdjuː-] *adj* : libre de impuestos

duvet [duːˈveɪ, 'duːˌveɪ] *n* : edredón *m*, cobertor *m*

DVD [ˌdiːˌviːˈdiː] *n* : DVD *m* ⟨DVD player/recorder : reproductor/grabador de DVD⟩

dwarf¹ ['dwɔrf] *vt* **1** STUNT : arrestar el crecimiento de **2** : hacer parecer pequeño

dwarf² *n, pl* **dwarfs** ['dwɔrfs] *or* **dwarves** ['dwɔrvz] **1** : enano *m*, -na *f* (en cuentos) **2** *sometimes offensive* : enano *m*, -na *feminine sometimes offensive*

dwell ['dwɛl] *vi* **dwelled** *or* **dwelt** ['dwɛlt]; **dwelling 1** RESIDE : residir, morar, vivir **2 to dwell on** : pensar demasiado en, insistir en

dweller ['dwɛlər] *n* : habitante *mf*

dwelling ['dwɛlɪŋ] *n* : morada *f*, vivienda *f*, residencia *f*

dwindle ['dwɪndəl] *vi* **-dled; -dling** : menguar, reducirse, disminuir

dye¹ ['daɪ] *vt* **dyed; dyeing** : teñir

dye² *n* : tintura *f*, tinte *m*

dying → **die**

dyke → **dike**

dynamic [daɪˈnæmɪk] *adj* : dinámico

dynamics [daɪˈnæmɪks] *npl* : dinámica *f*

dynamite¹ ['daɪnəˌmaɪt] *vt* **-mited; -miting** : dinamitar

dynamite² *n* : dinamita *f*

dynamo ['daɪnəˌmoː] *n, pl* **-mos** : dínamo *m*, generador *m* de electricidad

dynasty ['daɪnəsti, -ˌnæs-] *n, pl* **-ties** : dinastía *f*

dysentery ['dɪsənˌtɛri] *n, pl* **-teries** : disentería *f*

dysfunction [dɪsˈfʌŋkən] *n* : disfunción *f* — **dysfunctional** [dɪsˈfʌŋkˌʃənəl] *adj*

dyslexia [dɪsˈlɛksiə] *n* : dislexia *f* — **dyslexic** [dɪsˈlɛksɪk] *adj*

dystrophy ['dɪstrəfi] *n, pl* **-phies 1** : distrofia *f* **2** → **muscular dystrophy**

E

e [ˈiː] *n, pl* **e's** *or* **es** [ˈiːz] **1** : quinta letra del alfabeto inglés **2 E** : mi *m* ⟨E sharp/flat : mi sostenido/bemol⟩

e- *pref* : electrónico ⟨e-mail : email, correo electrónico⟩

each[1] [ˈiːtʃ] *adv* : cada uno ⟨they cost $10 each : cuestan $10 cada uno⟩

each[2] *adj* : cada ⟨each student : cada estudiante⟩ ⟨each and every one : todos sin excepción⟩

each[3] *pron* **1** : cada uno, cada una ⟨each of us : cada uno de nosotros⟩ ⟨each of the cities : cada una de las ciudades⟩ **2 each other** : el uno al otro ⟨we are helping each other : nos ayudamos el uno al otro⟩ ⟨they all looked at each other : todos se miraron unos a otros⟩ ⟨they love each other : se quieren⟩

eager [ˈiːgər] *adj* **1** ENTHUSIASTIC : entusiasta, ávido, deseoso **2** ANXIOUS : ansioso, impaciente ⟨she's eager to meet you : está ansiosa de/por conocerte⟩ ⟨to be eager for change : tener deseos de cambio⟩

eagerly [ˈiːgərli] *adv* : con entusiasmo, ansiosamente

eagerness [ˈiːgərnəs] *n* : entusiasmo *m*, deseo *m*, impaciencia *f*

eagle [ˈiːgəl] *n* : águila *f*

ear [ˈɪr] *n* **1** : oído *m*, oreja *f* ⟨inner ear : oído interno⟩ ⟨big ears : orejas grandes⟩ **2 ear of corn** : mazorca *f*, choclo *m* **3 to play by ear** : tocar de oído **4 to play it by ear** : improvisar

earache [ˈɪrˌeɪk] *n* : dolor *m* de oído(s)

earbud [ˈɪrˌbʌd] *n* : auricular *m* de tapón

eardrum [ˈɪrˌdrʌm] *n* : tímpano *m*

earl [ˈərl] *n* : conde *m*

earldom [ˈərldəm] *n* : condado *m*

earliest [ˈərliəst] *n* **at the earliest** ⟨it won't happen until next year at the earliest : lo más pronto que podría ocurrir sería el año que viene⟩

earliness [ˈərlinəs] *n* : lo temprano

earlobe [ˈɪrˌloːb] *n* : lóbulo *m* de la oreja, perilla *f* de la oreja

early[1] [ˈərli] *adv* **earlier; -est 1** : temprano ⟨he arrived early : llegó temprano, llegó antes de la hora⟩ ⟨she bought the tickets a month early : compró las entradas con un mes de antelación⟩ **2** SOON : pronto ⟨why didn't you tell me earlier? : ¿por qué no me lo dijiste antes?⟩ ⟨as early as possible : lo más pronto posible, cuanto antes⟩ **3** (*long ago*) ⟨as early as the 1960's : ya en los años sesenta⟩ **4** *or* ∼ **on** : al principio ⟨early (on) in his career : al principio de su carrera⟩

early[2] *adj* **earlier; -est 1** (*referring to a beginning*) : primero ⟨the early stages/hours : las primeras etapas/horas⟩ ⟨the earliest example : el primer ejemplo⟩ ⟨in early May : a principios de mayo⟩ ⟨early in the morning : por la mañana temprano⟩ **2** (*referring to antiquity*) : primitivo, antiguo ⟨early man : el hombre primitivo⟩ ⟨early painting : la pintura antigua⟩ ⟨in earlier times : antiguamente, en épocas anteriores⟩ **3** (*referring to a designated time*) : temprano, antes de la hora, prematuro ⟨he was early : llegó temprano⟩ ⟨early fruit : frutas tempraneras⟩ ⟨an early death : una muerte prematura⟩ ⟨early retirement : jubilación anticipada⟩ ⟨an earlier version : una versión anterior⟩

earmark [ˈɪrˌmɑrk] *vt* : destinar ⟨funds earmarked for education : fondos destinados a la educación⟩

earn [ˈərn] *vt* **1** : ganar ⟨to earn money : ganar dinero⟩ **2** DESERVE : ganarse

earner [ˈərnər] *n or* **wage earner** : asalariado *m*, -da *f*

earnest[1] [ˈərnəst] *adj* : serio, sincero

earnest[2] *n* **in** ∼ : en serio, de verdad ⟨we began in earnest : empezamos de verdad⟩

earnestly [ˈərnəstli] *adv* **1** SERIOUSLY : con seriedad, en serio **2** FERVENTLY : de todo corazón

earnestness [ˈərnəstnəs] *n* : seriedad *f*, sinceridad *f*

earnings [ˈərnɪŋz] *npl* : ingresos *mpl*, ganancias *fpl*, utilidades *fpl*

earphone [ˈɪrˌfoːn] *n* : audífono *m*, auricular *m*

earplug [ˈɪrˌplʌg] *n* : tapón *m* para el oído

earring [ˈɪrˌrɪŋ] *n* : zarcillo *m*, arete *m*, aro *m Arg, Chile, Uru*, pendiente *m Spain*

earshot [ˈɪrˌʃɑt] *n* : alcance *m* del oído ⟨out of earshot : demasiado lejos para oír⟩

earth [ˈərθ] *n* **1** LAND, SOIL : tierra *f*, suelo *m* **2 the Earth** : la Tierra **3 on** ∼ : en el mundo ⟨what on earth . . . ? : ¿qué demonios/diablos . . . ?⟩

earthen [ˈərθən, -ðən] *adj* : de tierra, de barro

earthenware [ˈərθənˌwær, -ðən-] *n* : loza *f*, vajilla *f* de barro

earthly [ˈərθli] *adj* : terrenal, mundano

earthquake [ˈərθˌkweɪk] *n* : terremoto *m*, sismo *m*

earthworm [ˈərθˌwərm] *n* : lombriz *f* (de tierra)

earthy [ˈərθi] *adj* **earthier; -est 1** : terroso ⟨earthy colors : colores terrosos⟩ **2** DOWN-TO-EARTH : realista, práctico, llano **3** COARSE, CRUDE : basto, grosero, tosco ⟨earthy jokes : chistes groseros⟩

earwax [ˈɪrˌwæks] *n* → **wax**[2]

earwig [ˈɪrˌwɪg] *n* : tijereta *f*

ease[1] [ˈiːz] *v* **eased; easing** *vt* **1** ALLEVIATE : aliviar, calmar ⟨it eased her mind : la tranquilizó⟩ **2** REDUCE : paliar (un problema), reducir (tensiones), aligerar (una carga) **3** LOOSEN, RELAX : aflojar (una cuerda), relajar (restricciones) **4** : mover con cuidado ⟨I eased myself into the chair : me senté con cuidado en la silla⟩ — *vi* **1** : moverse con cuidado **2 to ease off/up** : calmarse (dícese del dolor), amainar (dícese del viento) **3 to ease up on** : aflojar (una cuerda), moderarse con (la comida, etc.), no ser tan duro con (alguien)

ease[2] *n* **1** CALM, RELIEF : tranquilidad *f*, comodidad *f*, desahogo *m* **2** FACILITY : facilidad *f* ⟨with ease : con facilidad⟩ **3 at** ~ : relajado, cómodo ⟨to put someone at ease : tranquilizar a alguien⟩ ⟨at ease! : ¡descansen!⟩

easel [ˈiːzəl] *n* : caballete *m*

easily [ˈiːzəli] *adv* **1** : fácilmente, con facilidad **2** UNQUESTIONABLY : con mucho, de lejos

easiness [ˈiːzinəs] *n* : facilidad *f*, soltura *f*

east[1] [ˈiːst] *adv* : al este ⟨to travel east : viajar hacia el este⟩

east[2] *adj* : este, del este, oriental ⟨east winds : vientos del este⟩

east[3] *n* **1** : este *m* **2 the East** : el Oriente

eastbound [ˈiːstˌbaʊnd] *adj* : que va hacia el este

Easter [ˈiːstər] *n* **1** : Pascua *f* (de Resurrección) **2** *or* **Easter Sunday** : Domingo *m* de Pascua, Domingo *m* de Resurrección

Easter egg *n* : huevo *m* de Pascua (pintado)

easterly [ˈiːstərli] *adv & adj* : del este

eastern [ˈiːstərn] *adj* **1** : Oriental, del Este ⟨Eastern Europe : Europa del Este⟩ **2** : oriental, este

Easterner [ˈiːstərnər] *n* : habitante *mf* del este

eastward [ˈiːstwərd] *adv & adj* : hacia el este

easy[1] [ˈiːzi] *adj* **easier; -est 1** : fácil ⟨easy to use : fácil de usar⟩ ⟨it's easy to see why : es fácil ver por qué⟩ ⟨to make something easier : facilitar algo⟩ **2** COMFORTABLE : fácil, cómodo **3** RELAXED : relajado **4 to be easy on the eye(s)** : ser agradable a la vista

easy[2] *adv* **easier; -est 1 to come easy** : ser fácil de conseguir **2 to go easy on** : no ser muy duro con (alguien), no pasarse con (algo) **3 to take it easy** RELAX : relajarse **4 to take it easy** CALM DOWN : tranquilizarse, calmarse

easy chair *n* : sillón *m*, butaca *f*

easygoing [ˌiːziˈɡoːɪŋ] *adj* : tolerante, poco exigente

eat [ˈiːt] *v* **ate** [ˈeɪt]; **eaten** [ˈiːtən]; **eating** *vt* **1** : comer ⟨eat it up! : ¡cómetelo!⟩ **2** CORRODE : corroer **3** *or* **to eat up** CONSUME : comerse (comida, ganancias), consumir (tiempo, recursos), gastar (combustible) — *vi* **1** : comer **2 to eat away at** *or* **to eat into** : comerse, consumir, corroer **3 to eat out** : comer fuera

eatable[1] [ˈiːtəbəl] *adj* : comestible, comible *fam*

eatable[2] *n* **1** : algo para comer **2 eatables** *npl* : comestibles *mpl*, alimentos *mpl*

eater [ˈiːtər] *n* : persona *f* o animal *m* que come ⟨a big eater : un comelón⟩ ⟨meat/plant eaters : carnívoros/herbívoros⟩

eaves [ˈiːvz] *npl* : alero *m*

eavesdrop [ˈiːvzˌdrɑp] *vi* **-dropped; -dropping** : escuchar a escondidas ⟨he was eavesdropping on us : nos escuchaba a escondidas⟩

eavesdropper [ˈiːvzˌdrɑpər] *n* : persona *f* que escucha a escondidas

ebb[1] [ˈɛb] *vi* **1** : bajar (dícese de la marea) **2** DECLINE : menguar, decaer, disminuir

ebb[2] *n* **1** : reflujo *m* (de la marea) **2** DECLINE : decadencia *f*, declive *m*, disminución *f* ⟨to be at a low ebb : tocar fondo⟩ **3 the ebb and flow** : el flujo y reflujo

ebony[1] [ˈɛbəni] *adj* **1** : de ébano **2** BLACK : de color ébano, negro

ebony[2] *n, pl* **-nies** : ébano *m*

e-book [ˈiːˌbʊk] *n* : libro *m* electrónico, e-book *m*

ebullience [ɪˈbʊljənts, -ˈbʌl-] *n* : efervescencia *f*, vivacidad *f*

ebullient [ɪˈbʊljənt, -ˈbʌl-] *adj* : efervescente, vivaz

eccentric[1] [ɪkˈsɛntrɪk] *adj* **1** : excéntrico ⟨an eccentric wheel : una rueda excéntrica⟩ **2** ODD, SINGULAR : excéntrico, extraño, raro — **eccentrically** [-trɪkli] *adv*

eccentric[2] *n* : excéntrico *m*, -ca *f*

eccentricity [ˌɛkˌsɛnˈtrɪsəti] *n, pl* **-ties** : excentricidad *f*

ecclesiastic [ɪˌkliːziˈæstɪk] *n* : eclesiástico *m*, clérigo *m*

ecclesiastical [ɪˌkliːziˈæstɪkəl] *or* **ecclesiastic** *adj* : eclesiástico — **ecclesiastically** *adv*

echelon [ˈɛləˌlɑn] *n* **1** : escalón *m* (de tropas o aviones) **2** LEVEL : nivel *m*, esfera *f*, estrato *m*

echo[1] [ˈɛˌkoː] *v* **echoed; echoing** *vi* : hacer eco, resonar — *vt* : repetir, hacerse eco de

echo[2] *n, pl* **echoes** : eco *m*

e-cigarette [ˈiːˌsɪɡəˈrɛt] → **electronic cigarette**

éclair [eɪˈklær, i-] *n* : pastel *m* relleno de crema

eclectic [ɛˈklɛktɪk, ɪ-] *adj* : ecléctico

eclipse[1] [ɪˈklɪps] *vt* **eclipsed; eclipsing** : eclipsar

eclipse[2] *n* : eclipse *m*

eco- [ˈiko] *pref* : eco-, ecológico, ecológicamente

eco-friendly [ˈikoˌfrɛndli] *adj* : ecológico

ecological [ˌiːkəˈlɑʤɪkəl, ˌɛkə-] *adj* : ecológico — **ecologically** *adv*

ecologist [iˈkɑləʤɪst, ɛ-] *n* : ecólogo *m*, -ga *f*

ecology [iˈkɑləʤi, ɛ-] *n, pl* **-gies** : ecología *f*

e-commerce [ˈiːˌkɑmərs] *n* : comercio *m* electrónico

economic [ˌiːkəˈnɑmɪk, ˌɛkə-] *adj* : económico

economical [ˌiːkəˈnɑmɪkəl, ˌɛkə-] *adj* : económicos — **economically** *adv*

economics [ˌiːkəˈnɑmɪks, ˌɛkə-] *n* **1** : economía *f* **2 the economics of** : el aspecto *m* económico de

economist [iˈkɑnəmɪst] *n* : economista *mf*

economize [iˈkɑnəˌmaɪz] *v* **-mized; -mizing** : economizar, ahorrar ⟨to economize on something : economizar algo⟩

economy [ɪˈkanəmi] *n, pl* **-mies** 1 : economía *f*, sistema *m* económico 2 THRIFT : economía *f*, ahorro *m*

ecosystem [ˈiːkoˌsɪstəm] *n* : ecosistema *m*

ecotourism [ˌiːkoˈtʊrˌɪzəm] *n* : ecoturismo *m*

ecru [ˈɛˌkruː, ˈeɪ-] *n* : color *m* crudo

ecstasy [ˈɛkstəsi] *n, pl* **-sies** 1 : éxtasis *m* 2 **Ecstasy** : éxtasis *m* (droga)

ecstatic [ɛkˈstætɪk, ɪk-] *adj* : extático ⟨to be ecstatic about : estar muy entusiasmado con⟩

ecstatically [ɛkˈstætɪkli, ɪk-] *adv* : con éxtasis, con gran entusiasmo

Ecuadoran [ˌɛkwəˈdorən] *or* **Ecuadorean** *or* **Ecuadorian** [-ˈdoriən] *n* : ecuatoriano *m*, -na *f* — **Ecuadorean** *or* **Ecuadorian** *adj*

ecumenical [ˌɛkjuˈmnnɪkəl] *adj* : ecuménico

eczema [ɪgˈziːmə, ˈɛgzəmə, ˈɛksə-] *n* : eczema *m*

edamame [ˌɛdəˈmameɪ] *n* : edamame *m*, habas *fpl* de soya/soja

eddy[1] [ˈɛdi] *vi* **eddied; eddying** : arremolinarse, formar remolinos

eddy[2] *n, pl* **-dies** : remolino *m*

edema [ɪˈdiːmə] *n* : edema *m*

Eden [ˈiːdən] *n* : Edén *m*

edge[1] [ˈɛdʒ] *v* **edged; edging** *vt* 1 BORDER : bordear, ribetear, orlar ⟨edged with lace : con borde de encaje⟩ 2 SHARPEN : afilar, aguzar 3 *or* **to edge one's way** : avanzar poco a poco 3 **to edge away/closer** : alejarse/acercarse poco a poco 4 **to edge out** : derrotar por muy poco — *vi* ADVANCE : ir avanzando (poco a poco)

edge[2] *n* 1 : borde *m* (de una cama, etc.), filo *m* (de un cuchillo), margen *m* (de una página) 2 BORDER : borde *m*, orilla *f*, margen *f* ⟨at the water's edge : a la orilla del agua⟩ 3 ADVANTAGE : ventaja *f* 4 **to be on edge** : tener los nervios de punta 5 **to be on the edge of** : estar al borde de (la guerra, etc.)

edgewise [ˈɛdʒˌwaɪz] *adv* SIDEWAYS : de lado, de canto

edginess [ˈɛdʒinəs] *n* : tensión *f*, nerviosismo *m*

edging [ˈɛdʒɪŋ] *n* : borde *m*

edgy [ˈɛdʒi] *adj* **edgier; -est** : tenso, nervioso

edible [ˈɛdəbəl] *adj* : comestible, comible *fam*

edict [ˈiːˌdɪkt] *n* : edicto *m*, mandato *m*, orden *f*

edification [ˌɛdəfəˈkeɪʃən] *n* : edificación *f*, instrucción *f*

edifice [ˈɛdəfɪs] *n* : edificio *m*

edify [ˈɛdəˌfaɪ] *vt* **-fied; -fying** : edificar

edit [ˈɛdɪt] *vt* 1 : editar (un texto, una película, etc.), corregir (un texto) 2 MANAGE : dirigir (un periódico, etc.) 3 *or* **to edit out** DELETE : recortar, cortar

edition [ɪˈdɪʃən] *n* : edición *f*

editor [ˈɛdɪtər] *n* 1 : editor *m*, -tora *f* (de libros, artículos, etc.); redactor *m*, -tora *f* (de artículos) 2 : director *m*, -tora *f* (de un periódico, etc.) 3 : editor *m*, -tora *f* (de una película, etc.) 4 : editor *m* (software)

editorial[1] [ˌɛdɪˈtoriəl] *adj* 1 : de redacción 2 : editorial ⟨an editorial comment : un comentario editorial⟩

editorial[2] *n* : editorial *m*

editorship [ˈɛdɪtərˌʃɪp] *n* : dirección *f*

educate [ˈɛdʒəˌkeɪt] *vt* **-cated; -cating** 1 TEACH : educar, enseñar 2 INSTRUCT : formar, educar, instruir 3 INFORM : informar, concientizar

educated [ˈɛdʒəˌkeɪtəd] *adj* : culto

education [ˌɛdʒəˈkeɪʃən] *n* : educación *f*

educational [ˌɛdʒəˈkeɪʃənəl] *adj* 1 : docente, de enseñanza ⟨an educational institution : una institución docente⟩ 2 PEDAGOGICAL : pedagógico 3 INSTRUCTIONAL : educativo, instructivo ⟨an educational film : una película educativa⟩

educator [ˈɛdʒəˌkeɪtər] *n* : educador *m*, -dora *f*

eel [ˈiːl] *n* : anguila *f*

eerie [ˈɪri] *adj* **eerier; -est** 1 SPOOKY : que da miedo, espeluznante 2 GHOSTLY : fantasmagórico

eerily [ˈɪrəli] *adv* : de manera extraña y misteriosa

efface [ɪˈfeɪs, ɛ-] *vt* **-faced; -facing** : borrar

effect[1] [ɪˈfɛkt] *vt* 1 CARRY OUT : efectuar, llevar a cabo 2 ACHIEVE : lograr, realizar

effect[2] *n* 1 RESULT : efecto *m*, resultado *m*, consecuencia *f* ⟨to no effect : sin resultado⟩ ⟨to have an effect : producir/surtir efecto⟩ 2 MEANING : sentido *m* ⟨something to that effect : algo por el estilo⟩ 3 INFLUENCE : efecto *m*, influencia *f* 4 **effects** *npl* : efectos *mpl* ⟨sound effects : efectos de sonido⟩ 5 **effects** *npl* BELONGINGS : efectos *mpl*, pertenencias *fpl* 6 **to come/go into effect** *or* **to take effect** : entrar en vigor 7 **for ~** : para impresionar ⟨he paused for effect : hizo una pausa dramática⟩ 8 **in ~** REALLY : en realidad, de hecho

effective [ɪˈfɛktɪv] *adj* 1 EFFECTUAL : efectivo, eficaz 2 OPERATIVE : vigente 3 REAL : efectivo

effectively [ɪˈfɛktɪvli] 1 : eficazmente, con eficacia 2 IN EFFECT : en realidad, de hecho

effectiveness [ɪˈfɛktɪvnəs] *n* : eficacia *f*, efectividad *f*

effectual [ɪˈfɛktʃuəl] *adj* : eficaz, efectivo — **effectually** *adv*

effeminate [əˈfɛmənət] *adj* : afeminado

effervesce [ˌɛfərˈvɛs] *vi* **-vesced; -vescing** 1 : estar en efervescencia, burbujear (dícese de líquidos) 2 : estar eufórico, estar muy animado (dícese de las personas)

effervescence [ˌɛfərˈvɛsənts] *n* : efervescencia *f* — **effervescent** [ˌɛfərˈvɛsənt] *adj*

effete [ɛˈfiːt, ɪ-] *adj* 1 WORN-OUT : desgastado, agotado 2 DECADENT : decadente 3 EFFEMINATE : afeminado

efficacious [ˌɛfəˈkeɪʃəs] *adj* : eficaz, efectivo

efficacy ['ɛfɪkəsi] *n, pl* **-cies** : eficacia *f*
efficiency [ɪ'fɪɪənsi] *n, pl* **-cies 1** : eficiencia *f* **2** YIELD : rendimiento *m*
efficient [ɪ'fɪɪənt] *adj* **1** : eficiente **2** : de alto rendimiento (dícese de una máquina) — **efficiently** *adv*
effigy ['ɛfədʒi] *n, pl* **-gies** : efigie *f*
effluent ['ɛ,flu:ənt, ɛ'flu:-] *n* : efluentes *mpl*
effort ['ɛfərt] *n* **1** EXERTION : esfuerzo *m* **2** ATTEMPT : tentativa *f*, intento *m* ⟨it's not worth the effort : no vale la pena⟩ ⟨to make an/the effort to do something : hacer un/el esfuerzo para hacer algo⟩ ⟨to make no effort to do something : no molestarse en hacer algo⟩
effortless ['ɛfərtləs] *adj* : sin esfuerzo, natural
effortlessly ['ɛfərtləsli] *adv* : sin esfuerzo
effrontery [ɪ'frʌntəri] *n, pl* **-teries** : insolencia *f*, desfachatez *f*, descaro *m*
effusive [ɪ'fju:sɪv, ɛ-] *adj* : efusivo — **effusively** *adv*
effusiveness [ɪ'fju:sɪvnəs, ɛ-] *n* : efusión *f*
EFL [,i:,ɛf'ɛl] *n* (English as a foreign language) : inglés *m* como lengua extranjera
egalitarian [ɪ,gælə'tæriən] *adj* : igualitario
egg[1] ['ɛg] *vt* **to egg on** : incitar, azuzar
egg[2] *n* **1** : huevo *m* ⟨egg white/yolk : clara/yema de huevo⟩ **2** OVUM : óvulo *m*
eggbeater ['ɛg,bi:tər] *n* : batidor *m* (de huevos)
eggnog ['ɛg,nɑg] *n* : ponche *m* de huevo, rompope *m CA, Mex*
eggplant ['ɛg,plænt] *n* : berenjena *f*
eggshell ['ɛg,ɪl] *n* : cascarón *m*
ego ['i:,go:] *n, pl* **egos 1** SELF-ESTEEM : amor *m* propio, ego *m* **2** SELF : ego *m*, yo *m*
egocentric [,i:go'sɛntrɪk] *adj* : egocéntrico
egoism ['i:go,wɪzəm] *n* : egoísmo *m*
egoist ['i:gowɪst] *n* : egoísta *mf*
egoistic [,i:,go'wɪstɪk] *adj* : egoísta
egotism ['i:gə,tɪzəm] *n* : egotismo *m*
egotist ['i:gətɪst] *n* : egotista *mf*
egotistic [,i:gə'tɪstɪk] *or* **egotistical** [-'tɪstɪkəl] *adj* : egotista — **egotistically** *adv*
egregious [ɪ'gri:dʒəs] *adj* : atroz, flagrante, mayúsculo — **egregiously** *adv*
egress ['i:,grɛs] *n* : salida *f*
egret ['i:,grət, -,grɛt] *n* : garceta *f*
Egyptian [ɪ'dʒɪpʃən] *n* **1** : egipcio *m*, -cia *f* **2** : egipcio *m* (idioma) — **Egyptian** *adj*
eh ['eɪ, 'ɛ] *interj* **1** WHAT : ¿eh?, ¿qué? **2** : ¿eh?, ¿no? ⟨pretty clever, eh? : qué listo, ¿no?⟩
eiderdown ['aɪdər,daʊn] *n* **1** : plumón *m* **2** COMFORTER : edredón *m*
eight[1] ['eɪt] *adj* : ocho ⟨she's eight (years old) : tiene ocho años⟩
eight[2] *n* : ocho *m* ⟨the eight of hearts : el ocho de corazones⟩
eight[3] *pron* : ocho ⟨there are eight of us : somos ocho⟩ ⟨it's eight (o'clock) : son las ocho⟩

eighteen[1] [eit'ti:n] *adj & pron* : dieciocho
eighteen[2] *n* : dieciocho *m*
eighteenth[1] [eɪt'ti:nθ] *adj* : decimoctavo
eighteenth[2] *n* **1** : decimoctavo *m*, -va *f* (en una serie) **2** : dieciochoavo *m*, dieciochoava parte *f*
eighth[1] ['eɪtθ] *adv* : en octavo lugar
eighth[2] *adj* : octavo
eighth[3] *n* **1** : octavo *m*, -va *f* (en una serie) ⟨(on) the eighth of May : el ocho de mayo⟩ **2** : octavo *m*, octava parte *f*
eight hundred[1] *adj & pron* : ochocientos
eight hundred[2] *n* : ochocientos *m*
eightieth[1] ['eɪtiəθ] *adj* : octogésimo
eightieth[2] *n* **1** : octogésimo *m*, -ma *f* (en una serie) **2** : ochentavo *m*, ochentava parte *f*
eighty[1] ['eɪti] *adj & pron* : ochenta
eighty[2] *n, pl* **eighties 1** : ochenta *m* **2 the eighties** : los ochenta
either[1] ['i:ðər, 'aɪ-] *adv* : tampoco ⟨she doesn't believe it and he doesn't, either : ella no lo cree y él tampoco⟩ ⟨me either! : ¡yo tampoco!⟩
either[2] *adj* **1** : cualquiera (de los dos) ⟨we can watch either movie : podemos ver cualquiera de las dos películas⟩ **2** : ninguno de los dos ⟨she wasn't in either room : no estaba en ninguna de las dos salas⟩ **3** EACH : cada ⟨on either side of : a cada lado de, a ambos lados de⟩
either[3] *pron* **1** : cualquiera (de los dos) ⟨either of the answers is correct : cualquiera de las dos respuestas es correcta⟩ **2** : ninguno (de los dos) ⟨which of the two do you want? I don't like either : ¿cuál de las dos quieres? no me gusta ninguna⟩ **3** : alguno ⟨is either of you interested? : ¿está alguno de ustedes (dos) interesado?⟩
either[4] *conj* **1** : o, u ⟨either David or Daniel could go : puede ir (o) David o Daniel⟩ **2** : ni ⟨he didn't call either yesterday or today : no llamó ni ayer ni hoy⟩
ejaculate [i'dʒækjə,leɪt] *v* **-lated; -lating** *vt* **1** : eyacular **2** EXCLAIM : exclamar — *vi* : eyacular
ejaculation [i,dʒækjə'leɪʃən] *n* **1** : eyaculación *f* (en fisiología) **2** EXCLAMATION : exclamación *f*
eject [i'dʒɛkt] *vt* **1** : expulsar (a alguien) **2** : expulsar (un CD, etc.), expeler (un gas) — *vi* : expulsarse
ejection [i'dʒɛkʃən] *n* : expulsión *f*
eke out ['i:k-] *vt* **eked out; eking out 1** STRETCH : estirar (provisiones, etc.) **2 to eke out a living** : ganarse la vida a duras penas
EKG [,i:,keɪ'dʒi:] *n, pl* **EKGs 1** → electrocardiogram **2** → electrocardiograph
elaborate[1] [i'læbə,reɪt] *v* **-rated; -rating** *vt* : elaborar (una teoría, etc.) — *vi* **to elaborate on** : ampliar, entrar en detalles sobre
elaborate[2] [i'læbərət] *adj* **1** DETAILED : detallado, minucioso, muy elaborado **2** COMPLICATED : complicado, muy elaborado — **elaborately** *adv*
elaboration [i,læbə'reɪʃən] *n* : elaboración *f*

elapse [i'læps] *vi* **elapsed; elapsing** : transcurrir, pasar

elastic[1] [i'læstɪk] *adj* **1** : elástico **2** : (de) elástico, elastizado (dícese de una cintura, etc.)

elastic[2] *n* **1** : elástico *m* **2** *or* **elastic band → rubber band**

elasticity [i,læs'tɪsəṭi, ,iː,læs-] *n*, *pl* **-ties** : elasticidad *f*

elated [i'leɪtəd] *adj* : eufórico

elation [i'leɪɫən] *n* : euforia *f*, júbilo *m*, alborozo *m*

elbow[1] ['ɛl,boː] *vt* : darle un codazo a

elbow[2] *n* : codo *m*

elder[1] ['ɛldər] *adj* : mayor

elder[2] *n* **1** : anciano *m*, -na *f* ⟨the tribal elders : los ancianos de la tribu⟩ **2** : miembro *m* del consejo (en varias religiones) **3** : mayor *mf* ⟨she's my elder by one year : es un año mayor que yo⟩

elderberry ['ɛldər,bɛri] *n*, *pl* **-berries** : baya *f* de saúco (fruta), saúco *m* (árbol)

elderly ['ɛldərli] *adj* : mayor, de edad, anciano ⟨the elderly : las personas mayores, los ancianos⟩

eldest ['ɛldəst] *adj* : mayor ⟨the eldest : el/la mayor, el/la de más edad⟩

elect[1] [i'lɛkt] *vt* **1** : elegir ⟨she was elected President : la eligieron Presidenta⟩ **2** : elegir (hacer algo)

elect[2] *adj* : electo ⟨the president-elect : el presidente electo⟩

elect[3] *npl* **the elect** : los elegidos *mpl*

election [i'lɛkɫən] *n* : elección *f* ⟨an election campaign : una campaña electoral⟩

elective[1] [i'lɛktɪv] *adj* **1** : electivo **2** OPTIONAL : facultativo, optativo

elective[2] *n* : asignatura *f* electiva

electoral [i'lɛktərəl] *adj* : electoral

electorate [i'lɛktərət] *n* : electorado *m*

electric [i'lɛktrɪk] *adj* **1** *or* **electrical** [-trɪkəl] : eléctrico **2** THRILLING : electrizante, emocionante

electric cord → cord

electrician [i,lɛk'trɪɫən] *n* : electricista *mf*

electricity [i,lɛk'trɪsəṭi] *n*, *pl* **-ties 1** : electricidad *f* **2** CURRENT : corriente *m* eléctrica

electric razor → razor

electric shock → shock[2]

electric socket → socket

electrification [i,lɛktrəfə'keɪɫən] *n* : electrificación *f*

electrify [i'lɛktrə,faɪ] *vt* **-fied; -fying 1** : electrificar **2** THRILL : electrizar, emocionar

electrocardiogram [i,lɛktro'kɑrdiə,græm] *n* : electrocardiograma *m*

electrocardiograph [i,lɛktro'kɑrdiə,græf] *n* : electrocardiógrafo *m*

electrocute [i'lɛktrə,kjuːt] *vt* **-cuted; -cuting** : electrocutar

electrocution [i,lɛktrə'kjuːɫən] *n* : electrocución *f*

electrode [i'lɛk,troːd] *n* : electrodo *m*

electrolysis [i,lɛk'trɑləsɪs] *n* : electrólisis *f*

electrolyte [i'lɛktrə,laɪt] *n* : electrolito *m*

electromagnet [i,lɛktro'mægnət] *n* : electroimán *m*

electromagnetic [i,lɛktromæg'nɛṭɪk] *adj* : electromagnético — **electromagnetically** [-ṭɪkli] *adv*

electromagnetism [i,lɛktro'mægnə,tɪzəm] *n* : electromagnetismo *m*

electron [i'lɛk,trɑn] *n* : electrón *m*

electronic [i,lɛk'trɑnɪk] *adj* : electrónico ⟨electronic devices : aparatos electrónicos⟩ — **electronically** [-nɪkli] *adv*

electronic cigarette *n* : cigarillo *m* electrónico, vaporizador *m*, vaporeador *m*

electronic mail *n* : correo *m* electrónico

electronics [i,lɛk'trɑnɪks] *n* **1** : electrónica *f* **2** : sistema *m* electrónico (de un aparato)

electroplate [i'lɛktrə,pleɪt] *vt* **-plated; -plating** : galvanizar mediante electrólisis

elegance ['ɛlɪgənts] *n* : elegancia *f*

elegant ['ɛlɪgənt] *adj* : elegante — **elegantly** *adv*

elegiac [,ɛlə'ʤaɪək] *adj* : elegíaco

elegy ['ɛləʤi] *n*, *pl* **-gies** : elegía *f*

element ['ɛləmənt] *n* **1** COMPONENT : elemento *m*, factor *m* ⟨the element of surprise : el factor sorpresa⟩ ⟨an element of risk : un factor de riesgo⟩ **2** : elemento *m* (en la química) **3** MILIEU : elemento *m*, medio *m* ⟨to be in one's element : estar en su elemento⟩ **4** GROUP : elemento *m*, grupo *m* ⟨criminal elements : elementos criminales⟩ **5 elements** *npl* RUDIMENTS : elementos *mpl* (básicos), rudimentos *mpl* **6 the elements** WEATHER : los elementos *mpl* **7** *or* **heating element** : resistencia *f*

elemental [,ɛlə'mɛntəl] *adj* **1** BASIC : elemental, primario **2** : elemental (dícese de los elementos químicos)

elementary [,ɛlə'mentri] *adj* **1** SIMPLE : elemental **2** : de enseñanza primaria ⟨elementary (school) teachers : maestros de enseñanza primaria⟩ ⟨elementary school/education : escuela/educación primaria⟩

elephant ['ɛləfənt] *n* : elefante *m*, -ta *f*

elevate ['ɛlə,veɪt] *vt* **-vated; -vating 1** RAISE : elevar, levantar, alzar **2** PROMOTE : elevar, ascender **3** UPLIFT : elevar, levantar (el espíritu, etc.) **4** INCREASE : aumentar, elevar (niveles, etc.)

elevation [,ɛlə'veɪɫən] *n* **1** : elevación *f* **2** ALTITUDE : altura *f*, altitud *f* **3** PROMOTION : ascenso *m*

elevator ['ɛlə,veɪṭər] *n* **1** : ascensor *m*, elevador *m* **2** *or* **freight elevator** : montacargas *m*

eleven[1] [ɪ'lɛvən] *adj & pron* : once

eleven[2] *n* : once *m*

eleventh[1] [ɪ'lɛvənθ] *adj* : undécimo

eleventh[2] *n* **1** : undécimo *m*, -ma *f* (en una serie) **2** : onceavo *m*, onceava parte *f*

elf ['ɛlf] *n*, *pl* **elves** ['ɛlvz] : elfo *m*, duende *m*

elfin ['ɛlfən] *adj* **1** : de elfo, menudo **2** ENCHANTING, MAGIC : mágico, encantador

elfish ['ɛlfɪɫ] *adj* **1** : de elfo **2** MISCHIEVOUS : travieso

elicit [ɪˈlɪsət] *vt* : provocar (una reacción), obtener (una respuesta)

eligibility [ˌɛləʤəˈbɪləti] *n, pl* **-ties** : elegibilidad *f*

eligible [ˈɛləʤəbəl] *adj* **1** QUALIFIED : que reúne los requisitos, elegible ⟨to be eligible for benefits : tener derecho a recibir prestaciones⟩ ⟨eligible voters : votantes habilitados⟩ **2** SUITABLE : idóneo ⟨an eligible bachelor : un buen partido⟩

eliminate [ɪˈlɪməˌneɪt] *vt* **-nated; -nating** **1** : eliminar **2** RULE OUT : eliminar, descartar

elimination [ɪˌlɪməˈneɪʃən] *n* : eliminación *f*

elite[1] [eɪˈliːt, i-] *n* : elite *f*, élite *f*

elite[2] *n* : de elite, de élite

elitist [eɪˈliːtɪst, i-] *n* : elitista *mf* — **elitist** *adj*

elixir [iˈlɪksər] *n* : elixir *m*

elk [ˈɛlk] *n* : alce *m* (de Europa), uapití *m* (de América)

ellipse [ɪˈlɪps, ɛ-] *n* : elipse *f*

ellipsis [ɪˈlɪpsəs, ɛ-] *n, pl* **-lipses** [-ˌsiːz] **1** : elipsis *f* **2** : puntos *mpl* suspensivos (en la puntuación)

elliptical [ɪˈlɪptɪkəl, ɛ-] *or* **elliptic** [-tɪk] *adj* : elíptico

elm [ˈɛlm] *n* : olmo *m*

elocution [ˌɛləˈkjuːʃən] *n* : elocución *f*

elongate [iˈlɔŋˌɡeɪt] *vt* **-gated; -gating** : alargar

elongation [ˌiːˌlɔŋˈɡeɪʃən] *n* : alargamiento *m*

elope [iˈloːp] *vi* **eloped; eloping** : fugarse

elopement [iˈloːpmənt] *n* : fuga *f*

eloquence [ˈɛləkwənts] *n* : elocuencia *f*

eloquent [ˈɛləkwənt] *adj* : elocuente — **eloquently** *adv*

El Salvadoran [ˌɛlˌsælvəˈdorən] *n* : salvadoreño *m*, -ña *f* — **El Salvadoran** *adj*

else[1] [ˈɛls] *adv* **1** (*indicating an alternative or addition*) ⟨how else? : ¿de qué otro modo?⟩ ⟨when else? : ¿a qué otra hora?, ¿en qué otro día? (etc.)⟩ ⟨where else? : ¿en qué otro lugar?⟩ ⟨to go someplace else : ir a otro sitio⟩ **2 or else** OTHERWISE : si no, de lo contrario

else[2] *adj* **1** OTHER : otro ⟨anyone else : cualquier otro⟩ ⟨someone else : otro, otra persona⟩ ⟨everyone else : todos los demás⟩ ⟨everything else : todo lo demás⟩ ⟨nobody else : ningún otro, nadie más⟩ ⟨somebody else : otra persona⟩ **2** MORE : más ⟨nothing else : nada más⟩ ⟨anything else? : ¿algo más?⟩ ⟨what else? : ¿qué más?⟩

elsewhere [ˈɛlsˌʍɛr] *adv* : en/a otra parte, en/a otro sitio/lugar ⟨to go elsewhere : ir a otro lugar⟩ ⟨elsewhere in the book : en otra parte del libro⟩

elucidate [iˈluːsəˌdeɪt] *vt* **-dated; -dating** : dilucidar, elucidar, esclarecer

elucidation [iˌluːsəˈdeɪʃən] *n* : elucidación *f*, esclarecimiento *m*

elude [iˈluːd] *vt* **eluded; eluding** : eludir, evadir

elusive [iˈluːsɪv] *adj* **1** : esquivo, escurridizo (dícese de una presa, etc.) ⟨an elusive goal : una meta difícil de alcan-

zar⟩ **2** : difícil de precisar (dícese de una cualidad, etc.)

elusively [iˈluːsɪvli] *adv* : de manera esquiva

elves → **elf**

em- → **en-**

'em [əm] → **them**

emaciate [iˈmeɪʃiˌeɪt] *vt* **-ated; -ating** : enflaquecer

e–mail[1] *or* **email** [ˈiːˌmeɪl] *vt* : enviarle/mandarle un email a (alguien), enviarle/mandarle un correo electrónico a (alguien), enviar/mandar (algo) por email, enviar/mandar (algo) por correo electrónico — *vi* : enviar/mandar un email, enviar/mandar un correo electrónico

e–mail[2] *or* **email** *n* : email *m*, correo *m* electrónico ⟨e-mail address : dirección de correo electrónico, dirección de email⟩

emanate [ˈɛməˌneɪt] *v* **-nated; -nating** *vi* : emanar, provenir, proceder — *vt* : emanar

emanation [ˌɛməˈneɪʃən] *n* : emanación *f*

emancipate [iˈmæntsəˌpeɪt] *vt* **-pated; -pating** : emancipar

emancipation [iˌmæntsəˈpeɪʃən] *n* : emancipación *f*

embalm [ɪmˈbɑm, ɛm-, -ˈbɑlm] *vt* : embalsamar

embankment [ɪmˈbæŋkmənt, ɛm-] *n* : terraplén *m*, muro *m* de contención

embargo[1] [ɪmˈbɑrɡo, ɛm-] *vt* **-goed; -going** : imponer un embargo sobre

embargo[2] *n, pl* **-goes** : embargo *m*

embark [ɪmˈbɑrk, ɛm-] *vt* : embarcar — *vi* **1** : embarcarse **2 to embark on** START : emprender, embarcarse en

embarkation [ˌɛmˌbɑrˈkeɪʃən] *n* : embarque *m*, embarco *m*

embarrass [ɪmˈbærəs, ɛm-] *vt* : avergonzar, abochornar ⟨you embarrassed me : me hiciste pasar vergüenza⟩

embarrassed [ɪmˈbærəst ɛm-] *adj* : embarazoso, violento ⟨I'm embarrassed (about it) : me da vergüenza⟩ ⟨an embarrassed silence : un silencio embarazoso⟩

embarrassing [ɪmˈbærəsɪŋ, ɛm-] *adj* : embarazoso, violento ⟨how embarrassing! : ¡qué vergüenza!⟩

embarrassment [ɪmˈbærəsmənt, ɛm-] *n* : vergüenza *f*, bochorno *m*, pena *f* ⟨to be an embarrassment to someone : ser una vergüenza para alguien⟩

embassy [ˈɛmbəsi] *n, pl* **-sies** : embajada *f*

embed [ɪmˈbɛd, ɛm-] *vt* **-bedded; -bedding** : incrustar, empotrar (en una pared, etc.), grabar (en la memoria) ⟨a firmly embedded belief : una creencia arraigada⟩

embellish [ɪmˈbɛlɪʃ, ɛm-] *vt* : adornar, embellecer

embellishment [ɪmˈbɛlɪʃmənt, ɛm-] *n* : adorno *m*

ember [ˈɛmbər] *n* : ascua *f*, brasa *f*

embezzle [ɪmˈbɛzəl, ɛm-] *vt* **-zled; -zling** : desfalcar, malversar

embezzlement [ɪmˈbɛzəlmənt, ɛm-] *n* : desfalco *m*, malversación *f*

embezzler [ɪm'bɛzələr, ɛm-] n : desfalcador m, -dora f; malversador m, -dora f
embitter [ɪm'bɪtər, ɛm-] vt : amargar
emblem ['ɛmbləm] n : emblema m, símbolo m
emblematic [ˌɛmblə'mætɪk] adj : emblemático, simbólico
embodiment [ɪm'bɑdɪmənt, ɛm-] n : encarnación f, personificación f
embody [ɪm'bɑdi, ɛm-] vt -bodied; -bodying 1 PERSONIFY : encarnar, personificar 2 INCLUDE : incorporar
embolism ['ɛmbəˌlɪzəm] n : embolia f
emboss [ɪm'bɑs, ɛm-, -'bɔs] vt : repujar (metal o cuero), grabar en relieve ⟨embossed lettering : caracteres en relieve⟩
embrace¹ [ɪm'breɪs, ɛm-] v -braced; -bracing vt 1 HUG : abrazar 2 ADOPT : adoptar, abrazar (una causa), aceptar (un cambio) 3 WELCOME : aprovechar (una oportunidad) 4 INCLUDE : abarcar — vi : abrazarse
embrace² n : abrazo m
embroider [ɪm'brɔɪdər, ɛm-] vt : bordar (una tela), adornar (una historia)
embroidery [ɪm'brɔɪdəri, ɛm-] n, pl -deries : bordado m
embroil [ɪm'brɔɪl, ɛm-] vt : enredar ⟨to become embroiled in something : enredarse en algo⟩
embryo ['ɛmbriˌoː] n, pl embryos : embrión m
embryonic [ˌɛmbri'ɑnɪk] adj : embrionario
emend [i'mɛnd] vt : enmendar, corregir
emendation [ˌiːˌmɛn'deɪɫən] n : enmienda f
emerald¹ ['ɛmrəld, 'ɛmə-] adj : verde esmeralda
emerald² n : esmeralda f
emerge [i'mərdʒ] vi emerged; emerging 1 : salir, emerger ⟨to emerge from : salir de⟩ 2 ARISE, DEVELOP : surgir 3 : revelarse (dícese de la verdad, etc.) 4 to emerge victorious : salir victorioso
emergence [i'mərdʒənʦ] n : aparición f, surgimiento m
emergency [i'mərdʒənʦi] n, pl -cies 1 : emergencia f ⟨in case of emergency : en caso de emergencia⟩ ⟨emergency exit/landing/vehicle : salida/aterrizaje/vehículo de emergencia⟩ 2 : urgencia f, emergencia f (en medicina)
emergency brake n HANDBRAKE : freno m de mano
emergency room n : sala f de urgencia(s), sala f de emergencia(s)
emergent [i'mərdʒənt] adj : emergente
emery ['ɛməri] n, pl -eries : esmeril m
emery board n : lima f de uñas (de esmeril)
emigrant ['ɛmɪgrənt] n : emigrante mf
emigrate ['ɛməˌgreɪt] vi -grated; -grating : emigrar
emigration [ˌɛmə'greɪɫən] n : emigración f
eminence ['ɛmənənʦ] n 1 PROMINENCE : eminencia f, prestigio m, renombre m 2 DIGNITARY : eminencia f; dignatario m, -ria f ⟨Your Eminence : Su Eminencia⟩
eminent ['ɛmənənt] adj : eminente, ilustre

eminently ['ɛmənəntli] adv : sumamente
emissary ['ɛməˌsɛri] n, pl -saries : emisario m, -ria f
emission [i'mɪɫən] n : emisión f
emit [i'mɪt] vt emitted; emitting : emitir, despedir, producir
emoji [i'moːdʒi] n, pl emoji or emojis : emoji m
emote [i'moːt] vi emoted; emoting : exteriorizar las emociones
emoticon [i'moʊtiˌkɑn] n : emoticono m, emoticón m
emotion [i'moːɫən] n : emoción f, sentimiento m
emotional [i'moːɫənəl] adj 1 : emocional, afectivo ⟨an emotional reaction : una reacción emocional⟩ 2 SENSITIVE : emotivo, sensible 3 MOVING : emotivo, conmovedor, emocionante 4 to get emotional : emocionarse
emotionally [i'moːɫənəli] adv : emocionalmente
empathize ['ɛmpəˌθaɪz] vi -thized; -thizing : sentir empatía ⟨to empathize with : identificarse con⟩
empathy ['ɛmpəθi] n : empatía f
emperor ['ɛmpərər] n : emperador m
emphasis ['ɛmfəsɪs] n, pl -phases [-ˌsiːz] 1 : énfasis m, hincapié m ⟨to put/place/lay emphasis on : poner énfasis en, hacer hincapié en⟩ 2 : acento m, énfasis m (en lingüística)
emphasize ['ɛmfəˌsaɪz] vt -sized; -sizing 1 : enfatizar, subrayar, recalcar 2 : acentuar, enfatizar (en lingüística) 3 ACCENTUATE : acentuar, (hacer) resaltar
emphatic [ɪm'fætɪk, ɛm-] adj 1 : enfático, enérgico, categórico ⟨an emphatic "no" : un "no" rotundo⟩ ⟨an emphatic victory : una victoria aplastante⟩ 2 to be emphatic about : poner mucho énfasis en — emphatically [-ɪkli] adv
empire ['ɛmˌpaɪr] n : imperio m
empirical [ɪm'pɪrɪkəl, ɛm-] adj : empírico — empirically [-ɪkli] adv
employ¹ [ɪm'plɔɪ, ɛm-] vt 1 USE : usar, utilizar, emplear 2 HIRE : contratar, emplear 3 : emplear, dar empleo a ⟨they employ 20 people : emplean a 20 personas⟩ 4 OCCUPY : ocupar, dedicar, emplear
employ² [ɪm'plɔɪ, ɛm-;, 'ɪm-, 'ɛmˌ-] n 1 : puesto m, cargo m, ocupación f 2 to be in the employ of : estar al servicio de, trabajar para
employee [ɪmˌplɔɪ'iː, ɛm-, -'plɔɪˌiː] n : empleado m, -da f
employer [ɪm'plɔɪər, ɛm-] n : patrón m, -trona f; empleador m, -dora f
employment [ɪm'plɔɪmənt, ɛm-] n : trabajo m, empleo m
employment agency n : agencia f de colocación, agencia f de trabajo
empower [ɪm'paʊər, ɛm-] vt : facultar, autorizar, conferirle poder a
empowerment [ɪm'paʊərmənt, ɛm-] n : autorización f
empress ['ɛmprəs] n : emperatriz f
emptiness ['ɛmptinəs] n : vacío m, vacuidad f

empty¹ [ˈɛmpti] *v* **-tied; -tying** *vt* : vaciar ⟨to empty (out) your pockets : vaciar sus bolsillos⟩ — *vi* **1** *or* **to empty out** : vaciarse (dícese de un lugar) **2 to empty into** : desaguar en (dícese de un río)

empty² *adj* **emptier; -est 1** : vacío **2** VACANT : desocupado, libre **3** MEANINGLESS : vacío, hueco, vano

empty³ *n, pl* **-ties** : envase *m* vacío

empty–handed [ˌɛmptiˈhændəd] *adj* : con las manos vacías

empty–headed [ˌɛmptiˈhɛdəd] *adj* : cabeza hueca, tonto

emu [ˈiːˌmjuː] *n* : emú *m*

emulate [ˈɛmjəˌleɪt] *vt* **-lated; -lating** : emular

emulation [ˌɛmjəˈleɪʃən] *n* : emulación *f*

emulsifier [ɪˈmʌlsəˌfaɪər] *n* : emulsionante *m*

emulsify [ɪˈmʌlsəˌfaɪ] *vt* **-fied; -fying** : emulsionar

emulsion [ɪˈmʌlʃən] *n* : emulsión *f*

en- *or* **em-** *pref* : en-, em- ⟨entangle : enredar⟩ ⟨empathy : empatía⟩

enable [ɪˈneɪbəl, ɛ-] *vt* **-abled; -abling 1** PERMIT : permitir, hacer posible, posibilitar ⟨to enable someone to do something : permitirle a alguien hacer algo⟩ **2** ACTIVATE : activar, habilitar

enact [ɪˈnækt, ɛ-] *vt* **1** : promulgar (un ley o decreto) **2** : representar (un papel en el teatro)

enactment [ɪˈnæktmənt, ɛ-] *n* : promulgación *f*

enamel¹ [ɪˈnæməl] *vt* **-eled** *or* **-elled; -eling** *or* **-elling** : esmaltar

enamel² *n* : esmalte *m*

enamor [ɪˈnæmər] *vt* **1** : enamorar **2 to be enamored of** : estar enamorado de (una persona), estar entusiasmado con (algo)

encamp [ɪnˈkæmp, ɛn-] *vi* : acampar

encampment [ɪnˈkæmpmənt, ɛn-] *n* : campamento *m*

encase [ɪnˈkeɪs, ɛn-] *vt* **-cased; -casing** : encerrar, revestir

-ence *suf* : -encia ⟨independence : independencia⟩

encephalitis [ɪnˌsfəˈlaɪtəs, ɛn-] *n, pl* **-litides** [ˈlɪtəˌdiːz] : encefalitis *f*

enchant [ɪnˈtʃænt, ɛn-] *vt* **1** BEWITCH : hechizar, encantar, embrujar **2** CHARM, FASCINATE : cautivar, fascinar, encantar

enchanting [ɪnˈtʃæntɪŋ, ɛn-] *adj* : encantador

enchanter [ɪnˈtʃæntər, ɛn-] *n* SORCERER : mago *m*, encantador *m*

enchantment [ɪnˈtʃæntmənt, ɛn-] *n* **1** SPELL : encanto *m*, hechizo *m* **2** CHARM : encanto *m*

enchantress [ɪnˈtʃæntrəs, ɛn-] *n* **1** SORCERESS : maga *f*, hechicera *f* **2** CHARMER : mujer *f* cautivadora

enchilada [ˌɛntʃɪˈlɑdə] *n* : enchilada *f*

encircle [ɪnˈsərkəl, ɛn-] *vt* **-cled; -cling** : rodear, ceñir, cercar

enclose [ɪnˈkloːz, ɛn-] *vt* **-closed; -closing 1** SURROUND : encerrar, cercar, rodear **2** INCLUDE : incluir, adjuntar,

acompañar ⟨please find enclosed : le(s) envío adjunto⟩

enclosure [ɪnˈkloːʒər, ɛn-] *n* **1** ENCLOSING : encierro *m* **2** : cercado *m* (de terreno), recinto *m* ⟨an enclosure for the press : un recinto para la prensa⟩ **3** : anexo *m* (de una carta), documento *m* adjunto

encode [ɪnˈkoːd, ɛn-] *vt* **1** : cifrar (mensajes, etc.) **2** : codificar (datos, etc.) **3** : codificar (tarjetas de crédito, etc.)

encompass [ɪnˈkʌmpəs, ɛn-, -ˈkɑm-] *vt* **1** SURROUND : circundar, rodear **2** INCLUDE : abarcar, comprender

encore [ˈɑnˌkor] *n* : bis *m* ⟨encore! : ¡otra!⟩

encounter¹ [ɪnˈkaʊntər, ɛn-] *vt* **1** MEET : encontrar, encontrarse con, toparse con, tropezar con **2** FIGHT : combatir, luchar contra

encounter² *n* : encuentro *m*

encourage [ɪnˈkərɪdʒ, ɛn-] *vt* **-aged; -aging 1** : animar, alentar ⟨she encouraged me to participate : me animó a participar⟩ **2** FOSTER : fomentar, promover

encouragement [ɪnˈkərɪdʒmənt, ɛn-] *n* : ánimo *m*, aliento *m*

encouraging [ɪnˈkərədʒɪŋ, ɛn-] *adj* : alentador, esperanzador

encroach [ɪnˈkroːtʃ, ɛn-] *vi* **to encroach on/upon** : invadir (territorio), abusar (derechos), quitar (tiempo)

encroachment [ɪnˈkroːtʃmənt, ɛn-] *n* : invasión *f*, usurpación *f*

encrust [ɪnˈkrʌst, ɛn-] *vt* **1** : recubrir con una costra **2** INLAY : incrustar ⟨encrusted with gems : incrustado de gemas⟩

encrypt [ɪnˈkrɪpt, ɛn-] *vt* : cifrar, encriptar (datos, etc.)

encumber [ɪnˈkʌmbər, ɛn-] *vt* **1** BLOCK : obstruir, estorbar **2** BURDEN : cargar, gravar

encumbrance [ɪnˈkʌmbrən*t*s, ɛn-] *n* : estorbo *m*, carga *f*, gravamen *m*

encyclopedia [ɪnˌsaɪkləˈpiːdiə, ɛn-] *n* : enciclopedia *f*

encyclopedic [ɪnˌsaɪkləˈpiːdɪk, ɛn-] *adj* : enciclopédico

end¹ [ˈɛnd] *vt* **1** STOP : terminar, poner fin a, acabar con **2** CONCLUDE : concluir, terminar — *vi* **1** : terminar(se), acabar, concluir(se) **2 to end up doing something** : acabar/terminar haciendo algo, acabar/terminar por hacer algo

end² *n* **1** : extremo *m* (de una cuerda, etc.), punta *f* (de un lápiz, etc.), final *m* (de una calle, etc.) ⟨I'm at the end of my rope : no puedo aguantar más⟩ **2** CONCLUSION : fin *m*, final *m* ⟨to bring something to an end : terminar algo, poner fin a algo⟩ ⟨to come to an end : llegar a su fin⟩ ⟨to put an end to : acabar con, poner fin a⟩ **3** AIM : fin *m*, objetivo *m* **4** : ala *f* (en fútbol americano) ⟨tight end : ala cerrada⟩ **5 at the end** : al fin, al final ⟨at the end of April : a fines/finales de abril⟩ **6 end to end** : juntados por los extremos **7 in the end** : al final **8 on end** : parado, (en posición) vertical ⟨my hair stood on end : se me pusieron los pelos de punta⟩ **9 on end** : sin parar ⟨he read for hours on end : pasaba horas enteras leyendo⟩

endanger [ɪn'deɪndʒər, ɛn-] *vt* : poner en peligro

endangered [ɪn'deɪndʒərd, ɛn-] *adj* : en peligro

endear [ɪn'dɪr, ɛn-] *vt* **to endear oneself to** : ganarse la simpatía de, granjearse el cariño de

endearing [ɪn'dɪrɪŋ, ɛn-] *adj* : encantador

endearment [ɪn'dɪrmənt, ɛn-] *n* : expresión *f* de cariño

endeavor[1] [ɪn'dɛvər, ɛn-] *vt* : intentar, esforzarse por ⟨he endeavored to improve his work : intentó mejorar su trabajo⟩

endeavor[2] *n* : intento *m*, esfuerzo *m*

ending ['ɛndɪŋ] *n* **1** CONCLUSION : final *m*, desenlace *m* **2** SUFFIX : sufijo *m*, terminación *f*

endive ['ɛn,daɪv, 'ɑn'di:v] *n* : endibia *f*, endivia *f*

endless ['ɛndləs] *adj* **1** INTERMINABLE : interminable, inacabable, sin fin ⟨endless hours : horas interminables⟩ ⟨endless prairie : praderas interminables⟩ ⟨an endless source of : una fuente inagotable de⟩ ⟨with endless patience : con paciencia infinita⟩ **2** COUNTLESS : innumerable, incontable ⟨endless possibilities : posibilidades infinitas⟩ ⟨endless questions : preguntas incesantes⟩

endlessly ['ɛndləsli] *adv* : interminablemente, eternamente, sin parar

endocrine ['ɛndəkrən, -,kraɪn, -,kri:n] *adj* : endocrino

endorse [ɪn'dɔrs, ɛn-] *vt* **-dorsed; -dorsing 1** SIGN : endosar, firmar **2** APPROVE, SUPPORT : aprobar, respaldar **3** PROMOTE : promocionar

endorsement [ɪn'dɔrsmənt, ɛn-] *n* **1** SIGNATURE : endoso *m*, firma *f* **2** APPROVAL, SUPPORT : aprobación *f*, aval *m*

endow [ɪn'daʊ, ɛn-] *vt* : dotar ⟨to be endowed with : estar dotado de⟩

endowment [ɪn'daʊmənt, ɛn-] *n* **1** FUNDING : dotación *f* **2** DONATION : donación *f*, legado *m* **3** ATTRIBUTE, GIFT : atributo *m*, dotes *fpl*

endurable [ɪn'dʊrəbəl, ɛn-, -'djʊr-] *adj* : tolerable, soportable

endurance [ɪn'dʊrənts, ɛn-, -'djʊr-] *n* : resistencia *f*, aguante *m*

endure [ɪn'dʊr, ɛn-, -'djʊr] *v* **-dured; -during** *vt* **1** BEAR : resistir, soportar, aguantar **2** TOLERATE : tolerar, soportar — *vi* LAST : durar, perdurar

enema ['ɛnəmə] *n* : enema *m*, lavativa *f*

enemy ['ɛnəmi] *n, pl* **-mies** : enemigo *m*, -ga *f*

energetic [,ɛnər'dʒɛtɪk] *adj* : enérgico, vigoroso — **energetically** [-tɪkli] *adv*

energize ['ɛnər,dʒaɪz] *vt* **-gized; -gizing 1** ACTIVATE : activar **2** INVIGORATE : vigorizar

energy ['ɛnərdʒi] *n, pl* **-gies 1** : energía *f* **2** EFFORT : energías *fpl*, esfuerzo *m*

enervate ['ɛnər,veɪt] *vt* **-vated; -vating** : enervar, debilitar

enfold [ɪn'fo:ld, ɛn-] *vt* : envolver

enforce [ɪn'fors, ɛn-] *vt* **-forced; -forcing 1** : hacer respetar, hacer cumplir (una ley, etc.) **2** IMPOSE : imponer ⟨to enforce one's will : imponer su voluntad⟩

enforcement [ɪn'forsmənt, ɛn-] *n* : imposición *f*

enfranchise [ɪn'fræn,tlaɪz, ɛn-] *vt* **-chised; -chising** : conceder el voto a

enfranchisement [ɪn'fræn,tlaɪzmənt, ɛn-] *n* : concesión *f* del voto

engage [ɪn'geɪdʒ, ɛn-] *v* **-gaged; -gaging** *vt* **1** ABSORB : captar (la atención, etc.) ⟨to engage someone in conversation : entablar conversación con alguien⟩ **2** : engranar ⟨to engage the clutch : embragar⟩ **3** HIRE : contratar **4** : entablar combate con (un enemigo) — *vi* **1** MESH, INTERLOCK : engranar **2 to engage in** PURSUE : dedicarse a (una actividad) **3 to engage in** INITIATE : entablar

engaged [ɪn'geɪdʒd, ɛn-] *adj* **1** BETROTHED : comprometido, prometido ⟨to get engaged (to someone) : comprometerse (con alguien), prometerse (a alguien)⟩ **2 to be engaged in** : dedicarse a (una actividad)

engagement [ɪn'geɪdʒmənt, ɛn-] *n* **1** APPOINTMENT : compromiso *m*, cita *f* **2** BETROTHAL : compromiso *m* (acto), noviazgo *m* (período) ⟨engagement ring : anillo de compromiso⟩

engaging [ɪn'geɪdʒɪŋ, ɛn-] *adj* : atractivo, encantador, interesante

engender [ɪn'dʒɛndər, ɛn-] *vt* **-dered; -dering** : engendrar

engine ['ɛndʒən] *n* **1** MOTOR : motor *m* **2** LOCOMOTIVE : locomotora *f*, máquina *f*

engineer[1] [,ɛndʒə'nɪr] *vt* **1** : diseñar, construir (un sistema, un mecanismo, etc.) **2** CONTRIVE : maquinar, tramar, fraguar

engineer[2] *n* **1** : ingeniero *m*, -ra *f* **2** : maquinista *mf* (de locomotoras)

engineering [,ɛndʒə'nɪrɪŋ] *n* : ingeniería *f*

English[1] ['ɪŋglɪl, 'ɪŋlɪl] *adj* : inglés ⟨the English language : la lengua inglesa⟩ ⟨an English teacher : un profesor de inglés⟩

English[2] *n* **1** : inglés *m* (idioma) **2 the English** (*used with a plural verb*) : los ingleses

Englishman ['ɪŋglɪlmən, 'ɪŋlɪl-] *n, pl* **-men** [-mən, -,mɛn] : inglés *m*

English muffin *n* : panecillo *m* (que se parte en dos y se come tostado)

Englishwoman ['ɪŋglɪl,wʊmən, 'ɪŋlɪl-] *n, pl* **-women** [-,wɪmən] : inglesa *f*

engrave [ɪn'greɪv, ɛn-] *vt* **-graved; -graving** : grabar

engraver [ɪn'greɪvər, ɛn-] *n* : grabador *m*, -dora *f*

engraving [ɪn'greɪvɪŋ, ɛn-] *n* : grabado *m*

engross [ɪn'gro:s, ɛn-] *vt* : absorber ⟨to be engrossed in something : estar absorto en algo⟩

engrossed [ɪn'gro:st, ɛn-] *adj* : absorto

engrossing [ɪn'gro:sɪŋ, ɛn-] *adj* : fascinante, absorbente

engulf [ɪn'gʌlf, ɛn-] vt : envolver, sepultar

enhance [ɪn'hænts, ɛn-] vt **-hanced; -hancing** : realzar, aumentar, mejorar

enhancement [ɪn'hæntsmənt, ɛn-] n : mejora f, realce m, aumento m

enigma [ɪ'nɪgmə] n : enigma m

enigmatic [ˌɛnɪg'mætɪk, ˌi:nɪg-] adj : enigmático — **enigmatically** [-tɪkli] adv

enjoin [ɪn'dʒɔɪn, ɛn-] vt **1** COMMAND : ordenar, imponer **2** FORBID : prohibir, vedar

enjoy [ɪn'dʒɔɪ, ɛn-] vt **1** : disfrutar, gozar de ⟨did you enjoy the book? : ¿te gustó el libro?⟩ ⟨to enjoy good health : gozar de buena salud⟩ **2 to enjoy oneself** : divertirse, pasarlo bien

enjoyable [ɪn'dʒɔɪəbəl, ɛn-] adj : agradable, placentero, divertido

enjoyment [ɪn'dʒɔɪmənt, ɛn-] n : placer m, goce m, disfrute m, deleite m

enlarge [ɪn'lɑrdʒ, ɛn-] v **-larged; -larging** vt : ampliar (una foto, etc.), agrandar (un espacio) — vi **1** : ampliarse **2 to enlarge upon** : extenderse sobre, entrar en detalles sobre

enlargement [ɪn'lɑrdʒmənt, ɛn-] n : expansión f, ampliación f (dícese de fotografías)

enlighten [ɪn'laɪtən, ɛn-] vt **1** INSTRUCT : ilustrar **2** : iluminar (en religión)

enlightenment [ɪn'laɪtənmənt, ɛn-] n **1** : ilustración f ⟨the Enlightenment : la Ilustración⟩ **2** CLARIFICATION : aclaración f

enlist [ɪn'lɪst, ɛn-] vt **1** ENROLL : alistar, reclutar **2** SECURE : conseguir ⟨to enlist the support of : conseguir el apoyo de⟩ — vi : alistarse

enlisted man [ɪn'lɪstəd, ɛn-] n : soldado m raso

enlistment [ɪn'lɪstmənt, ɛn-] n : alistamiento m, reclutamiento m

enliven [ɪn'laɪvən, ɛn-] vt : animar, alegrar, darle vida a

en masse [ɑn'mæs, -'mɑs, ɛn-] adv : en masa, masivamente

enmity ['ɛnməti] n, pl **-ties** : enemistad f, animadversión f

ennoble [ɪ'no:bəl, ɛ-] vt **-bled; -bling** : ennoblecer

ennui [ˌɑn'wi:] n : hastío m, tedio m, fastidio m, aburrimiento m

enormity [ɪ'nɔrməti] n, pl **-ties 1** ATROCITY : atrocidad f, barbaridad f **2** IMMENSITY : enormidad f, inmensidad f

enormous [ɪ'nɔrməs] adj : enorme, inmenso, tremendo — **enormously** adv

enough[1] [ɪ'nʌf] adv **1** : bastante, suficientemente ⟨it's small enough to fit in a briefcase : es lo bastante pequeño como para caber en un maletín⟩ **2** QUITE : bastante ⟨it seems simple enough : parece bastante sencillo⟩ **3 fair enough!** : ¡está bien!, ¡de acuerdo! **4 strangely/ oddly enough** : por extraño que parezca **5 sure enough** : en efecto, sin duda alguna **6 well enough** : muy bien, bastante bien

enough[2] adj : bastante, suficiente ⟨do we

have enough chairs? : ¿tenemos suficientes sillas?⟩

enough[3] pron : (lo) suficiente, (lo) bastante ⟨enough to eat : lo suficiente para comer⟩ ⟨it's more than enough : basta y sobra, es más que suficiente⟩ ⟨it's not enough : no basta⟩ ⟨I've had enough! : ¡estoy harto!, ¡está bueno ya!⟩ ⟨(that's) enough! : ¡basta ya!⟩

enquire [ɪn'kwaɪr, ɛn-], **enquiry** ['ɪn,kwaɪri, 'ɛn-, -kwəri;, ɪn'kwaɪri, ɛn'-] → **inquire, inquiry**

enrage [ɪn'reɪdʒ, ɛn-] vt **-raged; -raging** : enfurecer, encolerizar

enraged [ɪn'reɪdʒd, ɛn-] adj : enfurecido, furioso

enrapture [ɪn'ræptʃər, ɛn-] vt **-tured; -turing** : cautivar, arrobar

enrich [ɪn'rɪtʃ, ɛn-] vt : enriquecer

enrichment [ɪn'rɪtʃmənt, ɛn-] n : enriquecimiento m

enroll or **enrol** [ɪn'ro:l, ɛn-] v **-rolled; -rolling** vt : matricular, inscribir — vi : matricularse, inscribirse

enrollment [ɪn'ro:lmənt, ɛn-] n : matrícula f, inscripción f

en route [ɑ'ru:t, ɛn'raʊt] adv : de camino, por el camino

ensconce [ɪn'skɑnts, ɛn-] vt **-sconced; -sconcing** : acomodar, instalar, establecer cómodamente

ensemble [ɑn'sɑmbəl] n : conjunto m

enshrine [ɪn'ʃraɪn, ɛn-] vt **-shrined; -shrining** : conservar religiosamente, preservar

ensign ['ɛntsən, 'ɛn,saɪn] n **1** FLAG : enseña f, pabellón m **2** : alférez mf (de fragata)

enslave [ɪn'sleɪv, ɛn-] vt **-slaved; -slaving** : esclavizar

enslavement [ɪn'sleɪvmənt, ɛn-] n : esclavización f

ensnare [ɪn'snær, ɛn-] vt **-snared; -snaring** : atrapar

ensue [ɪn'su:, ɛn-] vi **-sued; -suing** : seguir, resultar ⟨in the ensuing weeks : en las semanas siguientes⟩

ensure [ɪn'ʊr, ɛn-] vt **-sured; -suring** : asegurar, garantizar

entail [ɪn'teɪl, ɛn-] vt : implicar, suponer, conllevar

entangle [ɪn'tæŋgəl, ɛn-] vt **-gled; -gling** : enredar

entanglement [ɪn'tæŋgəlmənt, ɛn-] n : enredo m

enter ['ɛntər] vt **1** : entrar en/a **2** JOIN : entrar en/a, incorporarse a, ingresar a **3** : entrar en/a (un debate, una profesión, etc.) **4** BEGIN : entrar en (una etapa, etc.) **5** RECORD : anotar, inscribir **6** INPUT : introducir, dar entrada a **7** : presentar (una queja, etc.) ⟨she entered a guilty plea : se declaró culpable⟩ **8** : presentarse a (un concurso, etc.), inscribirse en (una carrera, etc.) — vi **1** : entrar **2 to enter into** : entrar en, establecer (un acuerdo), entablar (negociaciones, etc.) **3 to enter into** AFFECT, INFLUENCE : incidir en, influir en

enterprise [ˈɛntərˌpraɪz] *n* **1** UNDER-
TAKING : empresa *f* **2** BUSINESS : empresa *f*, firma *f* **3** INITIATIVE : iniciativa
f, empuje *m*
enterprising [ˈɛntərˌpraɪzɪŋ] *adj* : emprendedor
entertain [ˌɛntərˈteɪn] *vt* **1** : recibir, agasajar ⟨to entertain guests : tener invita-
dos⟩ **2** CONSIDER : considerar, contemplar **3** AMUSE : entretener, divertir — *vi*
: tener invitados
entertainer [ˌɛntərˈteɪnər] *n* : artista *mf*
entertaining [ˌɛntərˈteɪnɪŋ] *adj* : entretenido, divertido
entertainment [ˌɛntərˈteɪnmənt] *n* **1** : entretenimiento *m*, diversión *f* **2** SHOW
: espectáculo *m*
enthrall *or* **enthral** [ɪnˈθrɔl, ɛn-] *vt*
-thralled; -thralling : cautivar, embelesar
enthuse [ɪnˈθuiz, ɛn-] *v* **-thused; -thusing**
vt **1** EXCITE : entusiasmar **2** : decir con
entusiasmo — *vi* **to enthuse over**
: hablar con entusiasmo sobre
enthusiasm [ɪnˈθuːziˌæzəm, ɛn-, -ˈθjuː-] *n*
: entusiasmo *m*
enthusiast [ɪnˈθuːziˌæst, ɛn-, -ˈθjuː-, -əst]
n : entusiasta *mf*; aficionado *m*, -da *f*
enthusiastic [ɪnˌθuːziˈæstɪk, ɛn-, -ˌθjuː-]
adj : entusiasta, aficionado ⟨to be enthusiastic about something : estar entusiasmado con algo⟩
enthusiastically [ɪnˌθuːziˈæstɪkli, ɛn-,
-ˌθjuː-] *adv* : con entusiasmo
entice [ɪnˈtaɪs, ɛn-] *vt* **-ticed; -ticing**
: atraer, tentar
enticement [ɪnˈtaɪsmənt, ɛn-] *n* : tentación *f*, atracción *f*, señuelo *m*
entire [ɪnˈtaɪr, ɛn-] *adj* : entero, completo
⟨the entire family : toda la familia⟩
entirely [ɪnˈtaɪrli, ɛn-] *adv* : completamente, totalmente
entirety [ɪnˈtaɪrti, ɛn-, -ˈtaɪrəti] *n, pl* **-ties**
: totalidad *f* ⟨in its entirety : en su totali-
dad⟩
entitle [ɪnˈtaɪtəl, ɛn-] *vt* **-tled; -tling** **1**
: titular, intitular ⟨a book entitled "My
Life" : un libro titulado "Mi vida"⟩ **2**
: dar derecho a ⟨it entitles you to participate : le da derecho a participar⟩ **3**
to be entitled to : tener derecho a
entitlement [ɪnˈtaɪtəlmənt, ɛn-] *n* RIGHT
: derecho *m*
entity [ˈɛntəti] *n, pl* **-ties** : entidad *f*, ente
m
entomologist [ˌɛntəˈmalədʒɪst] *n* : entomólogo *m*, -ga *f*
entomology [ˌɛntəˈmalədʒi] *n* : entomología *f*
entourage [ˌantuˈraʒ] *n* : séquito *m*
entrails [ˈɛnˌtreɪlz, -trəlz] *npl* : entrañas
fpl, vísceras *fpl*
entrance[1] [ɪnˈtræns, ɛn-] *vt* **-tranced;
-trancing** : encantar, embelesar, fascinar
entrance[2] [ˈɛntrənts] *n* **1** ENTERING : entrada *f* ⟨to make an entrance : entrar en
escena⟩ **2** ENTRY : entrada *f* ⟨the main
entrance : la entrada principal⟩ **3** AD-
MISSION : entrada *f*, ingreso *m* ⟨entrance
examination : examen de ingreso⟩

entrant [ˈɛntrənt] *n* : candidato *m*, -ta *f*
(en un examen); participante *mf* (en un
concurso)
entrap [ɪnˈtræp, ɛn-] *vt* **-trapped; -trap-
ping** : atrapar, entrampar, hacer caer en
una trampa
entrapment [ɪnˈtræpmənt, ɛn-] *n* : captura *f*
entreat [ɪnˈtriːt, ɛn-] *vt* : suplicar, rogar
entreaty [ɪnˈtriːti, ɛn-] *n, pl* **-treaties**
: ruego *m*, súplica *f*
entrée *or* **entree** [ˈanˌtreɪ, ˌanˈ-] *n* : plato
m principal
entrench [ɪnˈtrɛntʃ, ɛn-] *vt* **1** FORTIFY
: atrincherar (una posición militar) **2**
: consolidar, afianzar ⟨firmly entrenched
in his job : afianzado en su puesto⟩
entrepreneur [ˌantrəprəˈnər, -ˈnjʊr] *n*
: empresario *m*, -ria *f*
entrust [ɪnˈtrʌst, ɛn-] *vt* **to entrust something to someone** *or* **to entrust someone with something** : confiarle/encom-
endarle algo a alguien
entry [ˈɛntri] *n, pl* **-tries** **1** ENTRANCE
: entrada *f* ⟨a side entry : una entrada
lateral⟩ **2** ENTERING : entrada *f* ⟨after
her entry into politics : después de su
entrada en política⟩ **3** ADMISSION : entrada *f*, ingreso *m* **4** : entrada *f* (en un
diccionario, etc.), anotación *f* (en un diario), partida *f* (en contabilidad) **5** PAR-
TICIPANT : participante *mf*
entwine [ɪnˈtwaɪn, ɛn-] *vt* **-twined; -twin-
ing** : entrelazar, entretejer, entrecruzar
enumerate [ɪˈnuːməˌreɪt, ɛ-, -ˈnjuː-] *vt*
-ated; -ating **1** LIST : enumerar **2**
COUNT : contar, enumerar
enumeration [ɪˌnuːməˈreɪʃən, ɛ-, -ˌnjuː-] *n*
: enumeración *f*, lista *f*
enunciate [iˈnʌntsiˌeɪt, ɛ-] *vt* **-ated;
-ating** **1** STATE : enunciar, decir **2**
PRONOUNCE : articular, pronunciar
enunciation [iˌnʌntsiˈeɪʃən, ɛ-] *n* **1** STATE-
MENT : enunciación *f*, declaración *f* **2**
ARTICULATION : articulación *f*, pronunciación *f*, dicción *f*
envelop [ɪnˈvləp, ɛn-] *vt* : envolver, cubrir
envelope [ˈɛnvəˌloːp, ˈan-] *n* : sobre *m*
enviable [ˈɛnviəbəl] *adj* : envidiable
envious [ˈɛnviəs] *adj* : envidioso ⟨an envious look : una mirada de envidia⟩ ⟨to
be envious of : envidiar⟩ — **enviously**
adv
environment [ɪnˈvaɪrənmənt, ɛn-, -ˈva-
ɪərn-] *n* **1** : ambiente *m*, entorno *m* ⟨her
home environment : su ambiente/en-
torno familiar⟩ **2 the environment** : el
medio *m* ambiente
environmental [ɪnˌvaɪrənˈmɛntəl, ɛn-,
-ˌvaɪərn-] *adj* : ambiental, medioambiental ⟨environmental protection : protección del medio ambiente⟩
environmentalism [-ˌlɪzəm] *n* : ecologismo *m*
environmentalist [ɪnˌvaɪrənˈmɛntəlɪst,
ɛn-, -ˌvaɪərn-] *n* : ecologista *mf*
environmentally [ɪnˌvaɪrənˈmɛntəli, ɛn-,
-ˌvaɪərn-] *adv* : ecológicamente ⟨environ-
mentally friendly : verde, ecológico⟩
environs [ɪnˈvaɪrənz, ɛn-, -ˈvaɪərnz] *npl*

: alrededores *mpl*, entorno *m*, inmediaciones *fpl*

envisage [ɪn'vɪzɪʤ, ɛn-] *vt* **-aged; -aging** **1** IMAGINE : imaginarse, concebir **2** FORESEE : prever

envision [ɪn'vɪʒən, ɛn-] *vt* : imaginar

envoy ['ɛn,vɔɪ, 'ɑn-] *n* : enviado *m*, -da *f*

envy[1] ['ɛnvi] *vt* **-vied; -vying** : envidiar

envy[2] *n, pl* **envies** : envidia *f*

enzyme ['ɛn,zaɪm] *n* : enzima *f*

eon ['i:ən, i:,ɑn] → **aeon**

epaulet [,ɛpə'lɛt] *n* : charretera *f*

ephemeral [ɪ'fɛmərəl, -'fi:-] *adj* : efímero, fugaz

epic[1] ['ɛpɪk] *adj* : épico ⟨an epic film : una (película) épica⟩

epic[2] *n* : poema *m* épico, epopeya *f*

epicenter ['ɛpɪ,sɛntər] *n* : epicentro *m*

epicure ['ɛpɪ,kjʊr] *n* : epicúreo *m*, -rea *f*; gastrónomo *m*, -ma *f*

epicurean [,ɛpɪkjʊ'ri:ən, -'kjʊriən] *adj* : epicúreo

epidemic[1] [,ɛpə'dɛmɪk] *adj* : epidémico

epidemic[2] *n* : epidemia *f*

epidemiology [,ɛpə,di:mi'ɑləʤi] *n* : epidemiología *f* — **epidemiologic** [,ɛpə,di:miə'lɑʤɪk] *or* **epidemiological** [-'lɑʤɪkəl] *adj*

epigram ['ɛpə,græm] *n* : epigrama *m*

epilepsy ['ɛpə,lɛpsi] *n, pl* **-sies** : epilepsia *f*

epileptic[1] [,ɛpə'lɛptɪk] *adj* : epiléptico

epileptic[2] *n* : epiléptico *m*, -ca *f*

epilogue ['ɛpə,lɔg, -,lɑg] *n* : epílogo *m*

epiphany [ɪ'pɪfəni] *n, pl* **-nies** **1** **Epiphany** : Epifanía *f* **2 to have an epiphany** : tener una revelación

episcopal [ɪ'pɪskəpəl] *adj* : episcopal

Episcopalian [ɪ,pɪskə'peɪljən] *n* : episcopaliano *m*, -na *f*

episode ['ɛpə,so:d] *n* : episodio *m*

episodic [,ɛpə'sɑdɪk] *adj* : episódico

epistle [ɪ'pɪsəl] *n* : epístola *f*, carta *f*

epitaph ['ɛpə,tæf] *n* : epitafio *m*

epithet ['ɛpə,θɛt, -θət] *n* : epíteto *m*

epitome [ɪ'pɪt̬əmi] *n* **1** SUMMARY : epítome *m*, resumen *m* **2** EMBODIMENT : personificación *f*

epitomize [ɪ'pɪt̬ə,maɪz] *vt* **-mized; -mizing** **1** SUMMARIZE : resumir **2** EMBODY : ser la personificación de (dícese de una persona), ser representativo de

epoch ['ɛpək, 'ɛ,pɑk, 'i:,pɑk] *n* : época *f*, era *f*

epoxy [ɪ'pɑksi] *n, pl* **epoxies** : resina *f* epoxídica

equable ['ɛkwəbəl, 'i:-] *adj* **1** CALM, STEADY : ecuánime **2** UNIFORM : estable (dícese de la temperatura), constante (del clima), uniforme

equably ['ɛkwəbli, 'i:-] *adv* : con ecuanimidad

equal[1] ['i:kwəl] *vt* **equaled** *or* **equalled; equaling** *or* **equalling** **1** : ser igual a ⟨two plus three equals five : dos más tres es igual a cinco⟩ **2** MATCH : igualar

equal[2] *adj* **1** SAME : igual **2** ADEQUATE : adecuado, capaz ⟨she's equal to the task : es capaz de hacerlo⟩

equal[3] *n* : igual *mf*

equality [ɪ'kwɑlət̬i] *n, pl* **-ties** : igualdad *f*

equalize ['i:kwə,laɪz] *v* **-ized; -izing** *vt* **1** : igualar (oportunidades), equiparar (salarios) **2** : igualar (la presión) — *vi* **1** : igualar **2** *Brit* TIE : empatar (en deportes)

equalizer ['i:kwə,laɪzər] *n* : gol *m* del empate

equally ['i:kwəli] *adv* **1** : igualmente, por igual ⟨to treat everyone equally : tratar a todos (por) igual⟩ ⟨equally quickly : con la misma rapidez⟩ **2** EVENLY : por igual ⟨to divide equally : dividir en/a partes iguales⟩

equal opportunity employer *n* : empresa *f* con una política de igualdad de oportunidades

equal sign *n* : signo *m* de igual

equanimity [,i:kwə'nɪmət̬i, ,ɛ-] *n, pl* **-ties** : ecuanimidad *f*

equate [ɪ'kweɪt] *vt* **equated; equating** **1** : equiparar, identificar **2 to equate to** : equivaler a, ser igual a

equation [ɪ'kweɪʒən] *n* : ecuación *f*

equator [ɪ'kweɪt̬ər] *n* **the Equator** : el ecuador

equatorial [,i:kwə'toriəl, ,ɛ-] *adj* : ecuatorial

equestrian[1] [ɪ'kwɛstriən, ɛ-] *adj* : ecuestre

equestrian[2] *n* : jinete *mf*, caballista *mf*

equilateral [,i:kwə'læt̬ərəl, ,ɛ-] *adj* : equilátero

equilibrium [,i:kwə'lɪbriəm, ,ɛ-] *n, pl* **-riums** *or* **-ria** [-briə] : equilibrio *m*

equine ['i:,kwaɪn, 'ɛ-] *adj* : equino, hípico

equinox ['i:kwə,nɑks, 'ɛ-] *n* : equinoccio *m*

equip [ɪ'kwɪp] *vt* **equipped; equipping** **1** FURNISH : equipar ⟨to equip someone with something : proveer a alguien de algo⟩ **2** PREPARE : preparar

equipment [ɪ'kwɪpmənt] *n* : equipo *m* ⟨sports equipment : artículos deportivos⟩

equitable ['ɛkwət̬əbəl] *adj* : equitativo, justo, imparcial

equity ['ɛkwət̬i] *n, pl* **-ties** **1** FAIRNESS : equidad *f*, imparcialidad *f* **2** VALUE : valor *m* líquido

equivalence [ɪ'kwɪvələnts] *n* : equivalencia *f*

equivalent[1] [ɪ'kwɪvələnt] *adj* : equivalente ⟨to be equivalent to : equivaler a⟩

equivalent[2] *n* : equivalente *m*

equivocal [ɪ'kwɪvəkəl] *adj* **1** AMBIGUOUS : equívoco, ambiguo **2** QUESTIONABLE : incierto, dudoso, sospechoso

equivocate [ɪ'kwɪvə,keɪt] *vi* **-cated; -cating** : usar lenguaje equívoco, contestar con evasivas

equivocation [ɪ,kwɪvə'keɪʃən] *n* : evasiva *f*, subterfugio *m*

-er *suf* **1** : -ador *m*, -adora *f* ⟨worker : trabajador(a)⟩ ⟨adapter : adaptador⟩ **2** : más ⟨hotter : más caliente⟩

era ['ɪrə, 'ɛrə, 'i:rə] *n* : era *f*, época *f*

eradicate [ɪ'rædə,keɪt] *vt* **-cated; -cating** : erradicar

erase [ɪ'reɪs] *vt* **erased; erasing** : borrar

eraser [ɪ'reɪsər] *n* : goma *f* de borrar, borrador *m*

erasure [ɪˈreɪlər] n : tachadura f
ere¹ [ˈɛr] conj : antes de que
ere² prep 1 : antes de 2 ere long : dentro de poco
e–reader [ˈiːˌriːdər] n : lector m electrónico, lector m de libros electrónicos
erect¹ [ɪˈrɛkt] vt 1 CONSTRUCT : levantar, erigir (un monumento, etc.) 2 RAISE : levantar, armar
erect² adj : erguido, derecho, erecto
erection [ɪˈrɛklən] n 1 : erección f (en fisiología) 2 BUILDING : construcción f
ergonomics [ˌərgəˈnɑmɪks] npl : ergonomía f
ermine [ˈərmən] n : armiño m
erode [ɪˈroːd] v eroded; eroding vt : erosionar (el suelo), corroer (metales) ⟨to erode someone's confidence : minar la confianza de alguien⟩ — vi : erosionarse, corroerse ⟨his popular support eroded : perdió el apoyo popular⟩
erosion [ɪˈroːʒən] n 1 : erosión f, corrosión f 2 DETERIORATION : deterioro m
erotic [ɪˈrɑtɪk] adj : erótico — erotically [-tɪkli] adv
eroticism [ɪˈrɑtəˌsɪzəm] n : erotismo m
err [ˈɛr, ˈər] vi : equivocarse, errar
errand [ˈɛrənd] n : mandado m, encargo m, recado m Spain ⟨to run an errand (for somebody) : hacer(le) un mandado (a alguien)⟩
errant [ˈɛrənt] adj 1 WANDERING : errante 2 ASTRAY : descarriado
erratic [ɪˈrætɪk] adj 1 INCONSISTENT : errático, irregular, inconsistente 2 ECCENTRIC : excéntrico, raro
erratically [ɪˈrætɪkli] adv : erráticamente, de manera irregular
erroneous [ɪˈroːniəs, ɛ-] adj : erróneo — erroneously adv
error [ˈɛrər] n : error m, equivocación f ⟨to be in error : estar en un error⟩ ⟨to do something in error : hacer algo por equivocación⟩ ⟨to make an error : cometer un error⟩ ⟨spelling error : falta de ortografía⟩
ersatz [ˈɛrˌsɑts, ˈərˌsæts] adj : artificial, sustituto
erstwhile [ˈərstˌʍwaɪl] adj : antiguo
erudite [ˈɛrəˌdaɪt, ˈɛrjʊ-] adj : erudito, letrado
erudition [ˌɛrəˈdɪlən, ˌɛrjʊ-] n : erudición f
erupt [ɪˈrʌpt] vi 1 : hacer erupción, entrar en erupción (dícese de un volcán) 2 : estallar (dícese de la violencia, etc.)
eruption [ɪˈrʌplən] n 1 : erupción f 2 OUTBREAK : estallido m, brote m
eruptive [ɪˈrʌptɪv] adj : eruptivo
escalate [ˈɛskəˌleɪt] v -lated; -lating vt : intensificar (un conflicto), aumentar (precios) — vi : intensificarse, aumentar
escalation [ˌɛskəˈleɪlən] n : intensificación f, escalada f, aumento m, subida f
escalator [ˈɛskəˌleɪtər] n : escalera f mecánica
escapade [ˈɛskəˌpeɪd] n : aventura f
escape¹ [ɪˈskeɪp, ɛ-] v -caped; -caping vt 1 : escaparse de (la policía, etc.) ⟨the

name escapes me : el nombre se me escapa⟩ ⟨nothing escapes her (notice) : nada se le escapa⟩ 2 AVOID : escapar a, librarse de (un castigo), salvarse de (la muerte) — vi 1 : escaparse 2 SURVIVE : salvarse
escape² n 1 FLIGHT : fuga f, huida f, escapada f 2 LEAKAGE : escape m, fuga f 3 : escapatoria f, evasión f ⟨to have no escape : no tener escapatoria⟩ ⟨escape from reality : evasión de la realidad⟩
escapee [ɪˌskeɪˈpiː, ˌɛ-] n : fugitivo m, -va f
escapism [ɪˈskeɪpˌɪzəm] n : escapismo m — escapist [ɪˈskeɪpɪst] adj
escarole [ˈɛskəˌroːl] n : escarola f
escarpment [ɪsˈkɑrpmənt, ɛs-] n : escarpa f
eschew [ɛˈʃuː, ɪsˈtʃuː] vt : evitar, rehuir, abstenerse de
escort¹ [ɪˈskort, ɛ-] vt 1 : escoltar 2 : llevar (a un prisionero) 3 ACCOMPANY : acompañar
escort² [ˈɛsˌkort] n 1 : escolta f ⟨under armed/police escort : con escolta armada/policial⟩ 2 COMPANION : acompañante mf
escrow [ˈɛsˌkroː] n in escrow : en depósito, en custodia de un tercero
Eskimo [ˈɛskəˌmoː] n 1 now sometimes offensive : esquimal mf 2 : esquimal m (idioma) — Eskimo adj
ESL [ˌiːˌɛsˈɛl] n (English as a second language) : inglés m como lengua extranjera
esophagus [ɪˈsɑfəgəs, iː-] n, pl -gi [-ˌgaɪ, -ˌdʒaɪ] : esófago m
esoteric [ˌɛsəˈtɛrɪk] adj : esotérico, hermético
espadrille [ˈɛspəˌdrɪl] n : alpargata f Arg, Spain, Uru, Ven; sandalia f
especially [ɪˈspɛləli] adv 1 : especialmente, particularmente 2 SPECIFICALLY : expresamente, especialmente
espionage [ˈɛspiəˌnɑʒ, -ˌnɑdʒ] n : espionaje m
espouse [ɪˈspaʊz, ɛ-] vt espoused; espousing 1 MARRY : casarse con 2 ADOPT, ADVOCATE : apoyar, adherirse a, adoptar
espresso [ɛˈsprɛˌsoː] n, pl -sos : café m exprés
essay¹ [ˈɛseɪ, ˈɛˌseɪ] vt : intentar, tratar
essay² [ˈɛˌseɪ] n 1 ensayo m (publicado) 2 COMPOSITION, PAPER : redacción f, trabajo m 3 ATTEMPT : intento m
essayist [ˈɛˌseɪɪst] n : ensayista mf
essence [ˈɛsənts] n 1 CORE : esencia f, núcleo m, meollo m ⟨in essence : esencialmente⟩ 2 EXTRACT : esencia f, extracto m 3 PERFUME : esencia f, perfume m
essential¹ [ɪˈsɛntlʲəl] adj : esencial ⟨to be essential to : ser esencial para⟩ — essentially adv
essential² n : elemento m esencial ⟨the (bare) essentials : lo imprescindible⟩
-est suf : (el/la/los/las) más ⟨the biggest : el/la más grande, los/las más grandes⟩
establish [ɪˈstæblɪl, ɛ-] vt 1 FOUND : establecer, fundar 2 SET UP : establecer,

instaurar, instituir **3** PROVE : establecer, demostrar

established [ɪ'stæblɪʃt, ɛ-] *adj* **1** ACCEPTED : establecido **2** : de amplia trayectoria (dícese de una empresa, etc.) **3** OFFICIAL : oficial

establishment [ɪ'stæblɪʃmənt, ɛ-] *n* **1** ESTABLISHING : establecimiento *m*, fundación *f*, instauración *f* **2** BUSINESS : negocio *m*, establecimiento *m* **3 the Establishment** : la clase dirigente

estate [ɪ'steɪt, ɛ-] *n* **1** POSSESSIONS : bienes *mpl*, propiedad *f*, patrimonio *m* ⟨the estate of the deceased : la sucesión del difunto⟩ **2** PROPERTY : hacienda *f*, finca *f*, propiedad *f*

esteem¹ [ɪ'stiːm, ɛ-] *vt* : estimar, apreciar

esteem² *n* : estima *f*, aprecio *m*

esthetic [ɛs'θɛtɪk] → **aesthetic**

estimable ['ɛstəməbəl] *adj* : estimable

estimate¹ ['ɛstə,meɪt] *vt* **-mated; -mating** : calcular, estimar

estimate² ['ɛstəmət] *n* **1** : cálculo *m* aproximado ⟨to make an estimate : hacer un cálculo⟩ **2** ASSESSMENT : valoración *f*, estimación *f* **3** QUOTE : presupuesto *m*

estimation [ˌɛstə'meɪʃən] *n* **1** JUDGMENT : juicio *m*, opinión *f* ⟨in my estimation : en mi opinión, a mi juicio⟩ **2** ESTIMATE : cálculo *m* aproximado

estimator ['ɛstə,meɪtər] *n* : tasador *m*, -dora *f*

Estonian [ɛ'stoːniən] *n* : estonio *m*, -nia *f* — **Estonian** *adj*

estrange [ɪ'streɪndʒ, ɛ-] *vt* **-tranged; -tranging** : enajenar, apartar, alejar ⟨he is estranged from his wife : está separado de su mujer⟩

estrangement [ɪ'streɪndʒmənt, ɛ-] *n* : alejamiento *m*, distanciamiento *m*

estrogen ['ɛstrədʒən] *n* : estrógeno *m*

estrus ['ɛstrəs] *n* : celo *m*

estuary ['ɛstʃu,weri] *n*, *pl* **-aries** : estuario *m*

et cetera [ɛt'sɛtərə, -'sɛtrə] : etcétera

etch ['ɛtʃ] *v* : grabar al aguafuerte

etching ['ɛtʃɪŋ] *n* : aguafuerte *m*, grabado *m* al aguafuerte

eternal [ɪ'tərnəl, iː-] *adj* **1** EVERLASTING : eterno **2** INTERMINABLE : constante, incesante

eternally [ɪ'tərnəli, iː-] *adv* : eternamente, para siempre

eternity [ɪ'tərnəti, iː-] *n*, *pl* **-ties** : eternidad *f*

ethanol ['ɛθə,nɔl, -,noːl] *n* : etanol *m*

ether ['iːθər] *n* : éter *m*

ethereal [ɪ'θɪriəl, iː-] *adj* **1** CELESTIAL : etéreo, celeste **2** DELICATE : delicado

ethical ['ɛθɪkəl] *adj* : ético ⟨ethical code/question : código/cuestión de ética⟩ — **ethically** *adv*

ethics ['ɛθɪks] *ns & pl* **1** : ética *f* **2** MORALITY : ética *f*, moralidad *f*

Ethiopian [ˌiːθi'oːpiən] *n* : etíope *mf* — **Ethiopian** *adj*

ethnic ['ɛθnɪk] *adj* : étnico ⟨ethnic group : etnia, grupo étnico⟩ ⟨ethnic cleansing : limpieza étnica⟩

etiquette ['ɛtɪkət, -,kɛt] *n* : etiqueta *f*, protocolo *m*

etymological [ˌɛtəmə'lɑdʒɪkəl] *adj* : etimológico

etymology [ˌɛtə'mɑlədʒi] *n*, *pl* **-gies** : etimología *f*

eucalyptus [ˌjuːkə'lɪptəs] *n*, *pl* **-ti** [-,taɪ] *or* **-tuses** [-təsəz] : eucalipto *m*

Eucharist ['juːkərɪst] *n* : Eucaristía *f*

eulogize ['juːlə,dʒaɪz] *vt* **-gized; -gizing** : elogiar, encomiar

eulogy ['juːlədʒi] *n*, *pl* **-gies** : panegírico *m* (pronunciado en los funerales)

eunuch ['juːnək] *n* : eunuco *m*

euphemism ['juːfə,mɪzəm] *n* : eufemismo *m*

euphemistic [ˌjuːfə'mɪstɪk] *adj* : eufemístico

euphoria [jʊ'foriə] *n* : euforia *f*

euphoric [jʊ'forɪk] *adj* : eufórico

euro ['jʊr,oː] *n*, *pl* **euros** *or* **euro** : euro *m*

European¹ [ˌjʊrə'piːən] *adj* : europeo ⟨European Union : Unión Europea⟩

European² *n* : europeo *m*, -pea *f*

euthanasia [ˌjuːθə'neɪʒə, -ʒiə] *n* : eutanasia *f*

euthanize ['juːθə,naɪz] *n* **-nized; -nizing** : sacrificar (un perro, etc.)

evacuate [ɪ'vækjʊ,eɪt] *v* **-ated; -ating** *vt* VACATE : evacuar, desalojar — *vi* WITHDRAW : retirarse

evacuation [ɪ,vækjʊ'eɪʃən] *n* : evacuación *f*, desalojo *m*

evade [ɪ'veɪd] *vt* **evaded; evading** : eludir ⟨to evade taxes : evadir impuestos⟩

evaluate [ɪ'vælju,eɪt] *vt* **-ated; -ating** : evaluar, valorar, tasar

evaluation [ɪ,vælju'eɪʃən] *n* : evaluación *f*, valoración *f*, tasación *f*

evangelical [ˌiː,væn'dʒɛlɪkəl, ˌɛvən-] *adj* : evangélico

evangelism [ɪ'vændʒə,lɪzəm] *n* : evangelismo *m*

evangelist [ɪ'vændʒəlɪst] *n* **1** : evangelista *m* **2** PREACHER : predicador *m*, -dora *f*

evaporate [ɪ'væpə,reɪt] *vi* **-rated; -rating 1** VAPORIZE : evaporarse **2** VANISH : evaporarse, desvanecerse, esfumarse

evaporated milk *n* : leche *f* evaporada

evaporation [ɪ,væpə'reɪʃən] *n* : evaporación *f*

evasion [ɪ'veɪʒən] *n* : evasión *f*

evasive [ɪ'veɪsɪv] *adj* : evasivo

evasiveness [ɪ'veɪsɪvnəs] *n* : carácter *m* evasivo

eve ['iːv] *n* **1** : víspera *f* ⟨on the eve of the festivities : en vísperas de las festividades⟩ **2** → **evening**

even¹ ['iːvən] *vt* **1** LEVEL : allanar, nivelar, emparejar **2** EQUALIZE : igualar, equilibrar **3 to even out** : nivelar, emparejar — *vi* **to even out** : nivelarse, emparejarse

even² *adv* **1** : hasta, incluso ⟨even a child can do it : hasta un niño puede hacerlo⟩ ⟨he looked content, even happy : se le veía satisfecho, incluso feliz⟩ **2** (*in negative constructions*) : ni siquiera ⟨he didn't even try : ni siquiera lo intentó⟩ **3**

(*in comparisons*) : aún, todavía ⟨even better : aún mejor, todavía mejor⟩ **4 even if** : aunque **5 even so** : aun así **6 even though** : aun cuando, a pesar de que, aunque

even³ *adj* **1** SMOOTH : uniforme, liso, parejo **2** FLAT : plano, llano **3** EQUAL : igual, igualado ⟨an even score : un marcador igualado⟩ **4** REGULAR : regular, constante ⟨an even pace : un ritmo constante⟩ **5** EXACT : exacto, justo **6** : par ⟨even number : número par⟩ **7 to be even** : estar en paz, estar a mano **8 to get even** : desquitarse, vengarse

evening ['i:vnɪŋ] *n* **1** : tarde *f*, noche *f* ⟨good evening : buenas tardes/noches⟩ ⟨in the evening : por la noche⟩ ⟨evening class : clase nocturna⟩ **2** : velada *f* ⟨an evening of music : una velada musical⟩

evening gown *or* **evening dress** *n* : traje *m* de noche

evenings ['i:vnɪŋz] *adv* : por las noches

evenly ['i:vənli] *adv* **1** UNIFORMLY : de modo uniforme, de manera constante **2** FAIRLY : igualmente, equitativamente

evenness ['i:vənnəs] *n* : uniformidad *f*, igualdad *f*, regularidad *f*

event [ɪ'vɛnt] *n* **1** : acontecimiento *m*, suceso *m*, prueba *f* (en deportes) **2 in any event** *or* **at all events** : de cualquier modo **3 in the event that** : en caso de que

even–tempered ['i:vən'tɛmpərd] *adj* : ecuánime

eventful [ɪ'vɛntfəl] *adj* : lleno de incidentes, memorable

eventual [ɪ'vɛntʃʊəl] *adj* : final, consiguiente

eventuality [ɪˌvɛntʃʊ'æləti] *n, pl* **-ties** : eventualidad *f*

eventually [ɪ'vɛntʃʊəli] *adv* : finalmente, al fin, con el tiempo

ever ['ɛvər] *adv* **1** ALWAYS : siempre ⟨as ever : como siempre⟩ ⟨ever since (then) : desde entonces⟩ ⟨ever since we met : desde que nos conocimos⟩ **2** (*in questions*) : alguna vez, algún día ⟨have you ever been to Mexico? : ¿has estado en México alguna vez?⟩ ⟨do you ever plan to go back? : ¿piensas volver algún día?⟩ **3** (*in negative constructions*) : nunca ⟨doesn't he ever work? : ¿es que nunca trabaja?⟩ ⟨nobody ever helps me : nadie nunca me ayuda⟩ ⟨we hardly ever speak : casi nunca hablamos⟩ **4** (*in comparisons*) : nunca ⟨better than ever : mejor que nunca⟩ ⟨the best song I ever heard : la mejor canción que he oído nunca⟩ **5** (*as intensifier*) ⟨I'm ever so happy! : ¡estoy tan y tan feliz!⟩ ⟨he looks ever so angry : parece estar muy enojado⟩

evergreen¹ ['ɛvərˌgri:n] *adj* : de hoja perenne

evergreen² *n* : planta *f* de hoja perenne

everlasting [ˌɛvər'læstɪŋ] *adj* : eterno, perpetuo, imperecedero

evermore [ˌɛvər'mɔr] *adv* : eternamente

every ['ɛvri] *adj* **1** EACH : cada ⟨every time : cada vez⟩ ⟨every other house

: cada dos casas⟩ **2** ALL : todo ⟨every month : todos los meses⟩ ⟨every other year : un año sí y otro no, cada dos años⟩ ⟨every woman : toda mujer, todas las mujeres⟩ **3** COMPLETE : pleno, entero ⟨to have every confidence : tener plena confianza⟩ **4 every now and then** *or* **every once in a while** *or* **every so often** : de vez en cuando

everybody ['ɛvriˌbʌdi, -ˌbɑ-] *pron* : todos, todo el mundo

everyday [ˌɛvri'deɪ, 'ɛvriˌ-] *adj* : cotidiano, diario, corriente ⟨everyday clothes : ropa de todos los días⟩

everyone ['ɛvriˌwʌn] → **everybody**

everything ['ɛvriˌθɪŋ] *pron* : todo

everywhere ['ɛvriˌʰwɛr] *adv* : en todas partes, por todas partes, dondequiera ⟨I looked everywhere : busqué en/por todas partes⟩ ⟨everywhere we go : dondequiera que vayamos⟩

evict [ɪ'vɪkt] *vt* : desalojar, desahuciar

eviction [ɪ'vɪkLən] *n* : desalojo *m*, desahucio *m*

evidence ['ɛvədənʦ] *n* **1** INDICATIONS : indicios *mpl*, señales *mpl* ⟨to be in evidence : estar a la vista⟩ **2** PROOF : evidencia *f*, prueba *f* **3** TESTIMONY : testimonio *m*, declaración *f* ⟨to give evidence : declarar como testigo, prestar declaración⟩

evident ['ɛvidənt] *adj* : evidente, patente, manifiesto

evidently ['ɛvidəntli, ˌɛvi'dɛntli] *adv* **1** CLEARLY : claramente, obviamente **2** APPARENTLY : aparentemente, evidentemente, al parecer

evil¹ ['i:vəl, -vɪl] *adj* **eviler** *or* **eviller; evilest** *or* **evillest** : malvado (dícese de las personas), maligno (dícese de los espíritus), maléfico (dícese de las influencias) ⟨evil deeds : malas acciones, maldades⟩ ⟨an evil spell : una maldición⟩

evil² *n* **1** WICKEDNESS : mal *m*, maldad *f* **2** MISFORTUNE : desgracia *f*, mal *m*

evildoer [ˌi:vəl'duːər, ˌi:vɪl-] *n* : malhechor *m*, -chora *f*; malvado *m*, -da *f*

evil eye *n* **the evil eye** : el mal de ojo

evince [ɪ'vɪnʦ] *vt* **evinced; evincing** : mostrar, manifestar, revelar

eviscerate [ɪ'vɪsəˌreɪt] *vt* **-ated; -ating** : eviscerar

evocation [ˌiːvoˈkeɪLən, ˌɛ-] *n* : evocación *f*

evocative [iˈvɑkətɪv] *adj* : evocador

evoke [iˈvoːk] *vt* **evoked; evoking** : evocar, provocar

evolution [ˌɛvəˈluːLən, ˌi:-] *n* : evolución *f*, desarrollo *m*

evolutionary [ˌɛvəˈluːLəˌnɛri, ˌi:-] *adj* : evolutivo

evolve [iˈvɑlv] *vi* **evolved; evolving** : evolucionar, desarrollarse

ewe ['juː] *n* : oveja *f* (hembra)

ex ['ɛks] *n* : ex *mf*

ex- ['ɛks] *pref* : ex-, ex ⟨ex-wife : exesposa, ex esposa⟩

exacerbate [ɪgˈzæsərˌbeɪt] *vt* **-bated; -bating** : exacerbar

exact¹ [ɪgˈzækt, ɛ-] *vt* : exigir, imponer, arrancar

exact² *adj* : exacto, preciso
exacting [ɪg'zæktɪŋ, ɛg-] *adj* : exigente, riguroso
exactitude [ɪg'zæktə,tuːd, ɛg-, -,tjuːd] *n* : exactitud *f*, precisión *f*
exactly [ɪg'zæktli, ɛ-] *adv* : exactamente ⟨it's exactly six o'clock : son las seis en punto⟩ ⟨exactly! : ¡exacto!⟩
exaggerate [ɪg'zæʤə,reɪt, ɛg-] *v* **-ated; -ating** : exagerar
exaggerated [ɪg'zæʤə,reɪṭəd, ɛg-] *adj* : exagerado — **exaggeratedly** *adv*
exaggeration [ɪg,zæʤə'reɪʒən, ɛg-] *n* : exageración *f*
exalt [ɪg'zɔlt, ɛg-] *vt* : exaltar, ensalzar, glorificar
exaltation [,ɛg,zɔl'teɪʃən, ,ɛk,sɔl-] *n* : exaltación *f*
exam [ɪg'zæm, ɛg-] → **examination**
examination [ɪg,zæmə'neɪʃən, ɛg-] *n* **1** TEST : examen *m* **2** INSPECTION : inspección *f*, revisión *f* **3** : reconocimiento *m*, examen *m* (en medicina) **4** INVESTIGATION : examen *m*, estudio *m*
examine [ɪg'zæmən, ɛg-] *vt* **-ined; -ining 1** TEST : examinar **2** INSPECT : inspeccionar, revisar **3** : examinar, revisar (en medicina) **4** STUDY : examinar
example [ɪg'zæmpəl, ɛg-] *n* : ejemplo *m* ⟨for example : por ejemplo⟩ ⟨to set an example : dar ejemplo⟩ ⟨to make an example of someone : darle un castigo ejemplar a alguien⟩
exasperate [ɪg'zæspə,reɪt, ɛg-] *vt* **-ated; -ating** : exasperar, sacar de quicio
exasperation [ɪg,zæspə'reɪʃən, ɛg-] *n* : exasperación *f*
excavate ['ɛkskə,veɪt] *vt* **-vated; -vating** : excavar
excavation [,ɛkskə'veɪʃən] *n* : excavación *f*
excavator ['ɛkskə,veɪtər] *n* : excavadora *f*
exceed [ɪk'siːd, ɛk-] *vt* **1** : exceder de, sobrepasar (un límite, etc.) **2 to exceed expectations** : superar las expectativas **3 to exceed one's authority** : excederse en sus facultades
exceedingly [ɪk'siːdɪŋli, ɛk-] *adv* : extremadamente, sumamente
excel [ɪk'sɛl, ɛk-] *v* **-celled; -celling** *vi* : destacar, sobresalir ⟨to excel at/in something : destacar(se) en algo⟩ — *vt* : superar
excellence ['ɛksələnts] *n* : excelencia *f*
excellency ['ɛksələntsi] *n, pl* **-cies** : excelencia *f* ⟨His Excellency : Su Excelencia⟩
excellent ['ɛksələnt] *adj* : excelente, sobresaliente — **excellently** *adv*
except¹ [ɪk'sɛpt] *vt* : exceptuar, excluir
except² *conj* : pero, si no fuera por
except³ *prep* : excepto, menos, salvo ⟨everyone except Carlos : todos menos Carlos⟩
except for → **except³**
exception [ɪk'sɛpʃən] *n* **1** : excepción *f* **2 to take exception to** : ofenderse por, objetar a **3 with the exeption of** : a/con excepción de
exceptional [ɪk'sɛpʃənəl] *adj* : excepcional, extraordinario — **exceptionally** *adv*

excerpt¹ [ɛk'sərpt, ɛg'zərpt, 'ɛk,-, 'g,-] *vt* : escoger, seleccionar
excerpt² ['ɛk,sərpt, 'ɛg,zərpt] *n* : pasaje *m*, selección *f*
excess¹ ['ɛk,sɛs, ɪk'sɛs] *adj* **1** : excesivo, de sobra **2 excess baggage** : exceso *m* de equipaje
excess² [ɪk'sɛs, 'ɛk,sɛs] *n* **1** SUPERFLUITY : exceso *m*, superfluidad *f* ⟨an excess of energy : un exceso de energía⟩ **2** SURPLUS : excedente *m*, sobrante *m* ⟨in excess of : superior a⟩
excessive [ɪk'sɛsɪv, ɛk-] *adj* : excesivo, exagerado, desmesurado — **excessively** *adv*
exchange¹ [ɪks'tʃeɪnʤ, ɛks-;, 'ɛks-,tʃeɪnʤ] *vt* **-changed; -changing** : cambiar, intercambiar, canjear ⟨to exchange something for something : cambiar algo por algo⟩
exchange² *n* **1** : cambio *m*, intercambio *m*, canje *m* ⟨in exchange for : a cambio de⟩ **2 stock exchange** : bolsa *f* (de valores) **3** *or* **telephone exchange** : central *f* telefónica
exchangeable [ɪks'tʃeɪnʤəbəl, ɛks-] *adj* : canjeable
exchange rate *n* : tasa *f* de cambio
exchequer ['ɛks,tʃɛkər, ɪks'tʃɛkər] *n* TREASURY : erario *m*, tesoro *m*, fisco *m*
excise¹ [ɪk'saɪz, ɛk-] *vt* **-cised; -cising** : extirpar
excise² ['ɛk,saɪz] *n* **excise tax** : impuesto *m* interno, impuesto *m* sobre el consumo
excitability [ɪk,saɪtə'bɪləṭi, ɛk-] *n* : excitabilidad *f*
excitable [ɪk'saɪṭəbəl, ɛk-] *adj* : nervioso
excitation [,ɛk,saɪ'teɪʃən] *n* : excitación *f*
excite [ɪk'saɪt, ɛk-] *vt* **-cited; -citing 1** AROUSE, STIMULATE : excitar, mover, estimular **2** ANIMATE : entusiasmar, animar **3** EVOKE, PROVOKE : provocar, despertar, suscitar ⟨to excite curiosity : despertar la curiosidad⟩
excited [ɪk'saɪṭəd, ɛk-] *adj* **1** STIMULATED : excitado **2** ENTHUSIASTIC : entusiasmado, emocionado
excitedly [ɪk'saɪṭədli, ɛk-] *adv* : con excitación, con entusiasmo
excitement [ɪk'saɪtmənt, ɛk-] *n* **1** ENTHUSIASM : entusiasmo *m*, emoción *f* **2** AGITATION : agitación *f*, alboroto *m*, conmoción *f* **3** AROUSAL : excitación *f*
exciting [ɪk'saɪṭɪŋ, ɛk-] *adj* **1** : emocionante **2** AROUSING : excitante
exclaim [ɪks'kleɪm, ɛk-] *v* : exclamar
exclamation [,ɛksklə'meɪʃən] *n* : exclamación *f*
exclamation point *n* : signo *m* de admiración
exclude [ɪks'kluːd, ɛks-] *vt* **-cluded; -cluding 1** LEAVE OUT : excluir **2** RULE OUT : excluir, descartar **3** BAR : no admitir
excluding [ɪks'kluːdɪŋ, ɛks-] *prep* : excluyendo, sin incluir
exclusion [ɪks'kluːʒən, ɛks-] *n* : exclusión *f*
exclusive¹ [ɪks'kluːsɪv, ɛks-] *adj* **1** SOLE : exclusivo, único **2** SELECT : exclusivo, selecto **3 exclusive of** → **excluding**

exclusive² n : exclusiva f
exclusively [ɪks'klu:sɪvli, ɛks-] adv : exclusivamente, únicamente
exclusiveness [ɪks'klu:sɪvnəs, ɛks-] n : exclusividad f
excommunicate [ˌɛkskə'mju:nəˌkeɪt] vt -cated; -cating : excomulgar
excommunication [ˌɛkskəˌmju:nə'keɪlən] n : excomunión f
excrement ['ɛkskrəmənt] n : excremento m
excrete [ɪk'skri:t, ɛk-] vt -creted; -creting : excretar
excretion [ɪk'skri:lən, ɛk-] n : excreción f
excruciating [ɪk'skru:Liˌeɪtɪŋ, ɛk-] adj : insoportable, atroz, terrible — excruciatingly adv
exculpate ['ɛkskəlˌpeɪt] vt -pated; -pating : exculpar
excursion [ɪk'skərʒən, ɛk-] n 1 OUTING : excursión f, paseo m 2 DIGRESSION : digresión f
excusable [ɪk'skju:zəbəl, ɛk-] adj : disculpable
excuse¹ [ɪk'skju:z, ɛk-] vt -cused; -cusing 1 PARDON : disculpar, perdonar ⟨excuse me : con permiso, perdóneme, perdón⟩ 2 DISMISS : dejar salir ⟨may I be excused? : ¿puedo ir?⟩ 3 EXEMPT : disculpar, eximir 4 JUSTIFY : excusar, justificar 5 to excuse yourself : excusarse
excuse² [ɪk'skju:s, ɛk-] n 1 JUSTIFICATION : excusa f, justificación f 2 PRETEXT : pretexto m 3 to make excuses : poner excusas 4 to make one's excuses to someone : pedirle disculpas a alguien
execute ['ɛksɪˌkju:t] vt -cuted; -cuting 1 CARRY OUT : ejecutar, llevar a cabo, desempeñar 2 ENFORCE : ejecutar, cumplir (un testamento, etc.) 3 KILL : ejecutar, ajusticiar
execution [ˌɛksɪ'kju:lən] n 1 PERFORMANCE : ejecución f, desempeño m 2 IMPLEMENTATION : cumplimiento m 3 : ejecución f (por un delito)
executioner [ˌɛksɪ'kju:lənər] n : verdugo m
executive¹ [ɪg'zɛkjətɪv, ɛg-] adj : ejecutivo
executive² n : ejecutivo m, -va f
executor [ɪg'zɛkjətər, ɛg-] n : albacea mf, testamentario m, -ria f
executrix [ɪg'zɛkjəˌtrɪks, ɛg-] n, pl executrices [-ˌzɛkjə'traɪˌsi:z] or executrixes [-'zɛkjəˌtrɪksəz] : albacea f, testamentaria f
exemplary [ɪg'zɛmpləri, ɛg-] adj : ejemplar
exemplify [ɪg'zɛmpləˌfaɪ, ɛg-] vt -fied; -fying : ejemplificar, ilustrar, demostrar
exempt¹ [ɪg'zɛmpt, ɛg-] vt : eximir ⟨to exempt someone from something : eximir a alguien de algo⟩
exempt² adj : exento ⟨to be exempt from : estar exento de⟩
exemption [ɪg'zɛmplən, ɛg-] n : exención f
exercise¹ ['ɛksərˌsaɪz] v -cised; -cising vt 1 : ejercitar (el cuerpo) 2 : ejercitar

(un caballo), sacar a pasear (un perro) 3 USE : ejercer, hacer uso de ⟨to exercise caution/restraint : obrar con cautela/moderación⟩ — vi : hacer ejercicio
exercise² n 1 : ejercicio m ⟨to get exercise : hacer ejercicio⟩ ⟨arm exercises : ejercicios para los brazos⟩ 2 : ejercicio m ⟨math exercises : ejercicios de matemáticas⟩ 3 MANEUVER : ejercicio m, maniobra f 4 USE : ejercicio m 5 exercises npl CEREMONY : ceremonia f
exert [ɪg'zərt, ɛg-] vt 1 : ejercer, emplear 2 to exert oneself : esforzarse
exertion [ɪg'zərlən, ɛg-] n 1 USE : ejercicio m (de autoridad, etc.), uso m (de fuerza, etc.) 2 EFFORT : esfuerzo m, empeño m
exhalation [ˌɛksə'leɪlən, ˌɛkshə-] n : exhalación f
exhale [ɛks'heɪl] v -haled; -haling vt 1 : exhalar, espirar 2 EMIT : exhalar, despedir, emitir — vi : espirar
exhaust¹ [ɪg'zɔst, ɛg-] vt 1 DEPLETE : agotar 2 TIRE : cansar, fatigar, agotar 3 EMPTY : vaciar
exhaust² n 1 or exhaust fumes : gases mpl de escape 2 or exhaust pipe : tubo m de escape, caño m de escape Arg, Uru 3 or exhaust system : sistema m de escape
exhausted [ɪg'zɔstəd, ɛg-] adj : agotado, derrengado
exhausting [ɪg'zɔstɪŋ, ɛg-] adj : extenuante, agotador
exhaustion [ɪg'zɔstlən, ɛg-] n : agotamiento m
exhaustive [ɪg'zɔstɪv, ɛg-] adj : exhaustivo
exhibit¹ [ɪg'zɪbət, ɛg-] vt 1 DISPLAY : exhibir, exponer 2 PRODUCE, SHOW : mostrar, presentar
exhibit² n 1 OBJECT : objeto m expuesto 2 EXHIBITION : exposición f, exhibición f 3 EVIDENCE : prueba f instrumental 4 to be on exhibit : estar expuesto
exhibition [ˌɛksə'bɪlən] n 1 : exposición f, exhibición f 2 to make an exhibition of oneself : dar el espectáculo, hacer el ridículo
exhibitor [ɪg'zɪbətər] n : expositor m, -tora f
exhilarate [ɪg'zɪləˌreɪt, ɛg-] vt -rated; -rating 1 : animar mucho, llenar de alegría 2 STIMULATE : estimular
exhilaration [ɪgˌzɪlə'reɪlən, ɛg-] n : alegría f, regocijo m, júbilo m
exhort [ɪg'zɔrt, ɛg-] vt : exhortar
exhortation [ˌɛkˌsɔr'teɪlən, -sər-:, ˌɛgˌzɔr-] n : exhortación f
exhumation [ˌɛksju'meɪlən, -hju-:, ˌɛgzu-, -zju-] n : exhumación f
exhume [ɪg'zu:m, -'zju:m;, ɪks'ju:m, -'hju:m] vt -humed; -huming : exhumar, desenterrar
ex–husband ['ɛks'hʌzbənd] n : ex marido m
exigencies ['ɛksɪdʒənʦsiz, ɪg'zɪdʒənˌsi:z] npl : exigencias fpl
exile¹ ['ɛgˌzaɪl, 'ɛkˌsaɪl] vt exiled; exiling : exiliar, desterrar

exile² *n* **1** BANISHMENT : exilio *m*, destierro *m* **2** OUTCAST : exiliado *m*, -da *f*; desterrado *m*, -da *f*

exist [ɪɡ'zɪst, ɛɡ-] *vi* **1** BE : existir **2** LIVE : subsistir, vivir

existence [ɪɡ'zɪstənts, ɛɡ-] *n* : existencia *f*

existent [ɪɡ'zɪstənt, ɛɡ-] *adj* : existente

existing [ɪɡ'zɪstɪŋ] *adj* : existente

exit¹ ['ɛgzət, 'ɛksət] *vi* : salir, hacer mutis (en el teatro) — *vt* : salir de ⟨to exit the building : salir del edificio⟩ ⟨to exit a program : salir de un programa⟩

exit² *n* **1** DEPARTURE : salida *f*, partida *f* **2** EGRESS : salida *f* ⟨emergency exit : salida de emergencia⟩

exodus ['ɛksədəs] *n* : éxodo *m*

exonerate [ɪɡ'zɑnə,reɪt, ɛɡ-] *vt* **-ated; -ating** : exonerar, disculpar, absolver

exoneration [ɪɡ,zɑnə'reɪʃən, ɛɡ-] *n* : exoneración *f*

exorbitant [ɪɡ'zɔrbətənt, ɛɡ-] *adj* : exorbitante, excesivo

exorcise ['ɛk,sɔr,saɪz, -sər-] *vt* **-cised; -cising** : exorcizar

exorcism ['ɛksər,sɪzəm] *n* : exorcismo *m*

exotic¹ [ɪɡ'zɑtɪk, ɛɡ-] *adj* : exótico — **exotically** [-ɪkli] *adv*

exotic² *n* : planta *f* exótica

expand [ɪk'spænd, ɛk-] *vt* **1** ENLARGE : expandir, ampliar **2** BROADEN, EXTEND : ampliar, extender — *vi* **1** ENLARGE : ampliarse, extenderse **2** : expandirse, dilatarse (dícese de los metales, gases, etc.) **3 to expand on/upon** : extenderse en/sobre, explayarse en/sobre

expanse [ɪk'spænts, ɛk-] *n* : extensión *f*

expansion [ɪk'spæntʃən, ɛk-] *n* **1** ENLARGEMENT : expansión *f*, ampliación *f* **2** EXPANSE : extensión *f*

expansive [ɪk'spæntsɪv, ɛk-] *adj* **1** : expansivo **2** OUTGOING : expansivo, comunicativo **3** AMPLE : ancho, amplio — **expansively** *adv*

expatriate¹ [ɛks'peɪtri,eɪt] *vt* **-ated; -ating** : expatriar

expatriate² [ɛks'peɪtriət, -,eɪt] *adj* : expatriado

expatriate³ [ɛks'peɪtriət, -,eɪt] *n* : expatriado *m*, -da *f*

expect [ɪk'spkt, ɛk-] *vt* **1** SUPPOSE : suponer, imaginar ⟨I expect so : supongo que sí⟩ **2** ANTICIPATE : esperar ⟨we're expecting company : esperamos visita⟩ ⟨rain is expected : se pronostican lluvias⟩ ⟨I expect to win : espero ganar⟩ **3** COUNT ON, REQUIRE : contar con, esperar ⟨I expect you to come : cuento con que vengas⟩ ⟨we expected more of/from you : esperábamos otra cosa de ti⟩ — *vi* **to be expecting** : estar embarazada

expectancy [ɪk'spktəntsi, ɛk-] *n*, *pl* **-cies 1** : expectación *f*, expectativa *f* **2** → **life expectancy**

expectant [ɪk'spktənt, ɛk-] *adj* **1** ANTICIPATING : expectante **2** EXPECTING : futuro ⟨expectant mother : futura madre⟩

expectantly [ɪk'spktəntli, ɛk-] *adv* : con expectación

expectation [,ɛk,spk'teɪʃən] *n* **1** ANTICI-

PATION : expectación *f* ⟨to have every expectation of : tener muchas esperanzas de⟩ **2** EXPECTANCY : expectativa *f* ⟨it didn't live up to expectations : no estaba a la altura de las expectativas⟩

expedient¹ [ɪk'spi:diənt, ɛk-] *adj* : conveniente, oportuno

expedient² *n* : expediente *m*, recurso *m*

expedite ['ɛkspə,daɪt] *vt* **-dited; -diting 1** FACILITATE : facilitar, dar curso a **2** HASTEN : acelerar

expedition [,ɛkspə'dɪʃən] *n* : expedición *f*

expeditious [,ɛkspə'dɪʃəs] *adj* : pronto, rápido

expel [ɪk'spl, ɛk-] *vt* **-pelled; -pelling 1** : expulsar (a alguien) **2** : expulsar, expeler (aire, etc.)

expend [ɪk'spnd, ɛk-] *vt* **1** DISBURSE : gastar, desembolsar **2** CONSUME : consumir, agotar

expendable [ɪk'spndəbəl, ɛk-] *adj* : prescindible

expenditure [ɪk'spndɪtʃər, ɛk-, -,tʃʊr] *n* : gasto *m*

expense [ɪk'spnts, ɛk-] *n* **1** COST : gasto *m* **2 expenses** *npl* : gastos *mpl*, expensas *fpl* **3 at the expense of** : a costa de, a expensas de

expensive [ɪk'spntsɪv, ɛk-] *adj* : costoso, caro — **expensively** *adv*

experience¹ [ɪk'spɪriənts, ɛk-] *vt* **-enced; -encing** : experimentar (sentimientos), tener (dificultades), sufrir (una pérdida)

experience² *n* : experiencia *f*

experienced [ɪk'spɪriəntst, ɛk-] *adj* : con experiencia, experimentado

experiment¹ [ɪk'spɛrəmənt, ɛk-, -'spɪr-] *vi* **to experiment on/with** : experimentar con, hacer experimentos con

experiment² *n* : experimento *m*

experimental [ɪk,spɛrə'mntəl, ɛk-, -,spɪr-] *adj* : experimental — **experimentally** *adv*

experimentation [ɪk,spɛrəmən'teɪʃən, ɛk-, -,spɪr-] *n* : experimentación *f*

expert¹ ['ɛk,spərt, ɪk'spərt] *adj* : experto, de experto ⟨expert testimony : testimonio pericial⟩ ⟨expert at (doing) something : experto en (hacer) algo⟩ — **expertly** *adv*

expert² ['ɛk,spərt] *n* : experto *m*, -ta *f*; perito *m*, -ta *f*

expertise [,ɛkspər'ti:z] *n* : pericia *f*, competencia *f*

expiate ['ɛkspi,eɪt] *vt* **-ated; -ating** : expiar

expiation [,ɛkspi'eɪʃən] *n* : expiación *f*

expiration [,ɛkspə'reɪʃən] *n* **1** EXHALATION : exhalación *f*, espiración *f* **2** DEATH : muerte *f* **3** TERMINATION : vencimiento *m*, caducidad *f*

expire [ɪk'spaɪr, ɛk-] *vi* **-pired; -piring 1** EXHALE : espirar **2** DIE : expirar, morir **3** TERMINATE : caducar, vencer

explain [ɪk'spleɪn, ɛk-] *vt* **1** : explicar **2 to explain yourself** : explicarse — **explainable** [ɪk'spleɪnəbəl, ɛk-] *adj*

explanation [,ɛksplə'neɪʃən] *n* : explicación *f*

explanatory [ɪk'splænə,tori, ɛk-] *adj* : explicativo, aclaratorio

expletive [ˈɛkspləˌtɪv] n : improperio m, palabrota f fam, grosería f
explicable [ɛkˈsplɪkəbəl, ˈɛksplɪ-] adj : explicable
explicit [ɪkˈsplɪsət, ɛk-] adj : explícito, claro, categórico, rotundo — **explicitly** adv
explicitness [ɪkˈsplɪsətnəs, ɛk-] n : claridad f, carácter m explícito
explode [ɪkˈsploːd, ɛk-] v -ploded; -ploding vt 1 BURST : hacer explosionar, hacer explotar 2 REFUTE : rebatir, refutar, desmentir — vi 1 BURST : explotar, estallar, reventar 2 SKYROCKET : dispararse
exploit¹ [ɪkˈsplɔɪt, ɛk-] vt : explotar, aprovecharse de
exploit² [ˈɛkˌsplɔɪt] n : hazaña f, proeza f
exploitation [ˌɛkˌsplɔɪˈteɪʃən] n : explotación f
exploration [ˌɛkspləˈreɪʃən] n : exploración f
exploratory [ɪkˈsplɔrəˌtori, ɛk-] adj : exploratorio
explore [ɪkˈsplor, ɛk-] vt -plored; -ploring : explorar, investigar, examinar
explorer [ɪkˈsplorər, ɛk-] n : explorador m, -dora f
explosion [ɪkˈsploːʒən, ɛk-] n : explosión f, estallido m
explosive¹ [ɪkˈsploːsɪv, ɛk-] adj : explosivo, fulminante — **explosively** adv
explosive² n : explosivo m
exponent [ɪkˈspoːnənt, ˈɛkˌspoː-] n 1 : exponente m 2 ADVOCATE : defensor m, -sora f; partidario m, -ria f
exponential [ˌɛkspəˈnɛntʌl] adj : exponencial — **exponentially** adv
export¹ [ɛkˈsport, ˈɛkˌsport] vt : exportar
export² [ˈɛkˌsport] n 1 : artículo m de exportación 2 → exportation
exportation [ˌɛkˌsporˈteɪʃən] n : exportación f
exporter [ɛkˈsporʈər, ˈɛkˌspor-] n : exportador m, -dora f
expose [ɪkˈspoːz, ɛk-] vt -posed; -posing 1 : exponer (al peligro, a los elementos, a una enfermedad) 2 : exponer (una película a la luz) 3 DISCLOSE : revelar, develar, sacar a la luz 4 UNMASK : desenmascarar ⟨to expose someone as a fraud : demostrar que alguien es un farsante⟩
exposé or **expose** [ˌɛkspoˈzeɪ] n : exposición f (de hechos), revelación f (de un escándalo)
exposed [ɪkˈspoːzd, ɛk-] adj : expuesto, al descubierto ⟨exposed brick : ladrillo a la vista⟩
exposition [ˌɛkspəˈzɪʃən] n : exposición f
exposure [ɪkˈspoːʒər, ɛk-] n 1 : exposición f (a la luz, a enfermedades, etc.) 2 : congelación f (en medicina) 3 DISCLOSURE : revelación f 4 PUBLICITY : publicidad f 5 ORIENTATION : orientación f ⟨a room with a northern exposure : una sala orientada al norte⟩ 6 : exposición f (en fotografía)
expound [ɪkˈspaʊnd, ɛk-] vt : exponer, explicar — vi : hacer comentarios detallados

express¹ [ɪkˈsprɛs, ɛk-] vt 1 : expresar ⟨to express oneself : expresarse⟩ 2 : mandar/enviar (una carta, etc.) por correo expreso
express² adv : por correo expreso, por correo urgente
express³ adj 1 EXPLICIT : expreso, explícito 2 SPECIFIC : específico ⟨for that express purpose : con ese fin específico⟩ 3 RAPID : expreso, rápido — **expressly** adv
express⁴ n 1 or **express mail** : expreso m, correo m expreso/urgente 2 : expreso m, tren m expreso
expression [ɪkˈsprɛʃən, ɛk-] n 1 UTTERANCE : expresión f ⟨freedom of expression : libertad de expresión⟩ 2 : expresión f (en la matemática) 3 PHRASE : frase f, expresión f 4 LOOK : expresión f, cara f, gesto m ⟨with a sad expression : con un gesto de tristeza⟩
expressionless [ɪkˈsprɛʃənləs, ɛk-] adj : inexpresivo
expressive [ɪkˈsprɛsɪv, ɛk-] adj : expresivo
expressway [ɪkˈsprɛsˌweɪ, ɛk-] n : autopista f
expropriate [ɛkˈsproːpriˌeɪt] vt -ated; -ating : expropiar
expulsion [ɪkˈspʌlʃən, ɛk-] n : expulsión f
expurgate [ˈɛkspərˌgeɪt] vt -gated; -gating : expurgar
exquisite [ɛkˈskwɪzət, ˈɛkˌskwɪ-] adj 1 FINE : exquisito, primoroso ⟨in exquisite detail : con todo lujo de detalles⟩ 2 EXTREME : intenso (dícese del dolor, etc.), exquisito
exquisiteness [ɛkˈskwɪzətnəs, ˈɛkˌskwɪ-] n : exquisitez f
extant [ˈɛkstənt, ɛkˈstænt] adj : existente
extemporaneous [ɛkˌstɛmpəˈreɪniəs] adj : improvisado — **extemporaneously** adv
extend [ɪkˈstɛnd, ɛk-] vt 1 STRETCH : extender, tender 2 PROLONG : prolongar (una visita, etc.), prorrogar (un plazo) 3 ENLARGE : agrandar, ampliar 4 PROFFER : dar (una bienvenida), presentar (disculpas) ⟨to extend an invitation : invitar⟩ — vi : extenderse
extendable adj : extensible
extended [ɪkˈstɛndəd, ɛk-] adj LENGTHY : prolongado, largo ⟨extended warranty : garantía extendida⟩
extension [ɪkˈstɛntʌn, ɛk-] n 1 EXTENDING : extensión f, ampliación f (de un edificio), prórroga f (de un plazo), prolongación f (de una visita) 2 ADDITION, ANNEX : ampliación f, anexo m 3 LINE : extensión f, interno m
extension cord n : extensión f; alargador m; alargue m Arg, Uru
extensive [ɪkˈstɛntsɪv, ɛk-] adj 1 BROAD : extenso, amplio ⟨extensive damage : cuantiosos daños⟩ 2 THOROUGH : exhaustivo — **extensively** adv
extent [ɪkˈstɛnt, ɛk-] n 1 SIZE : extensión f, magnitud f 2 DEGREE, SCOPE : alcance m, grado m ⟨to a certain extent : hasta cierto punto⟩ ⟨to a great extent : en gran parte⟩

extenuate [ɪk'stɛnjəˌweɪt, ɛk-] vt **-ated; -ating** : atenuar, aminorar, mitigar ⟨extenuating circumstances : (circunstancias) atenuantes⟩
exterior[1] [ɛk'stɪriər] adj : exterior
exterior[2] n : exterior m
exterminate [ɪk'stərməˌneɪt, ɛk-] vt **-nated; -nating** : exterminar
extermination [ɪkˌstərmə'neɪʌən, ɛk-] n : exterminación f, exterminio m
exterminator [ɪk'stərməˌneɪt̬ər, ɛk-] n : exterminador m, -dora f de plagas; fumigador m, -dora f
external [ɪk'stərnəl, ɛk-] adj : externo, exterior — **externally** adv
extinct [ɪk'stɪŋkt, ɛk-] adj : extinto
extinction [ɪk'stɪŋkʌən, ɛk-] n : extinción f
extinguish [ɪk'stɪŋgwɪl, ɛk-] vt : extinguir, apagar
extinguisher [ɪk'stɪŋgwɪlər, ɛk-] n : extinguidor m, extintor m
extirpate ['ɛkstərˌpeɪt] vt **-pated; -pating** : extirpar, exterminar
extol [ɪk'stoːl, ɛk-] vt **-tolled; -tolling** : exaltar, ensalzar, alabar
extort [ɪk'stɔrt, ɛk-] vt : extorsionar
extortion [ɪk'stɔrlʌən, ɛk-] n : extorsión f
extra[1] ['ɛkstrə] adv **1** : extra, más, super ⟨extra special : super especial⟩ ⟨to pay extra for : pagar más/extra por⟩ **2** : excepcionalmente ⟨to be extra careful : tener especial cuidado⟩
extra[2] adj **1** ADDITIONAL : adicional, suplementario, de más ⟨to be/cost extra : no estar incluido en el precio⟩ ⟨at no extra charge : sin costo adicional⟩ **2** SUPERIOR : superior
extra[3] n **1** : extra m **2** : extra mf (en películas)
extra- pref : extra-
extract[1] [ɪk'strækt, ɛk-] vt : extraer, sacar
extract[2] ['ɛkˌstrækt] n **1** EXCERPT : pasaje m, selección f, trozo m **2** : extracto m ⟨vanilla extract : extracto de vainilla⟩
extraction [ɪk'strækʌən, ɛk-] n : extracción f
extractor [ɪk'stræktər, ɛk-] n : extractor m
extracurricular [ˌɛkstrəkə'rɪkjələr] adj : extracurricular
extradite ['ɛkstrəˌdaɪt] vt **-dited; -diting** : extraditar
extradition [ˌɛkstrə'dɪlʌən] n : extradición f
extramarital [ˌɛkstrə'mærət̬əl] adj : extramatrimonial
extraneous [ɛk'streɪniəs] adj **1** OUTSIDE : externo **2** SUPERFLUOUS : superfluo, ajeno — **extraneously** adv
extraordinary [ɪk'strɔrdənˌɛri, ˌɛkstrə'ɔrd-] adj : extraordinario, excepcional — **extraordinarily** [ɪkˌstrɔrdən'ɛrəli, ˌɛkstrəˌɔrd-] adv
extrapolate [ɪk'stræpəˌleɪt] v **-lated; -lating** vt : extrapolar — vi : hacer una extrapolación — **extrapolation** [ɪkˌstræpə'leɪlʌən]
extrasensory [ˌɛkstrə'sɛntsəri] adj : extrasensorial
extraterrestrial[1] [ˌɛkstrətə'rɛstriəl] adj : extraterrestre

extraterrestrial[2] n : extraterrestre mf
extravagance [ɪk'strævɪgənts, ɛk-] n **1** EXCESS : exceso m, extravagancia f **2** WASTEFULNESS : derroche m, despilfarro m **3** LUXURY : lujo m
extravagant [ɪk'strævɪgənt, ɛk-] adj **1** EXCESSIVE : excesivo, exagerado, extravagante **2** WASTEFUL : despilfarrador, derrochador, gastador **3** EXORBITANT : costoso, exorbitante
extravagantly [ɪk'strævɪgəntli, ɛk-] adv **1** LAVISHLY : a lo grande **2** EXCESSIVELY : exageradamente, desmesuradamente
extravaganza [ɪkˌstrævə'gænzə, ɛk-] n : gran espectáculo m
extreme[1] [ɪk'stri:m, ɛk-] adj **1** : extremo ⟨extreme cold : frío extremo⟩ ⟨of extreme importance : de suma importancia⟩ **2** : extremo, extremista ⟨extreme views : opiniones extremas⟩ **3** SEVERE, DRASTIC : extremo ⟨extreme conditions : condiciones extremas⟩ ⟨extreme measures : medidas excepcionales, medidas drásticas⟩ **4** : más lejos ⟨the extreme north : el extremo norte/septentrional⟩ **5** : extremo ⟨extreme sports : deportes extremos⟩
extreme[2] n **1** : extremo m **2 in the extreme** : en extremo, en sumo grado
extremely [ɪk'stri:mli, ɛk-] adv : sumamente, extremadamente, terriblemente ⟨extremely large : grandísimo⟩
extremist [ɪk'stri:mɪst, ɛk-] n : extremista mf — **extremist** adj
extremity [ɪk'strɛmət̬i, ɛk-] n, pl **-ties 1** EXTREME : extremo m **2 extremities** npl LIMBS : extremidades fpl
extricate ['ɛkstrəˌkeɪt] vt **-cated; -cating** : librar, sacar
extrovert ['ɛkstrəˌvərt] n : extrovertido m, -da f
extroverted ['ɛkstrəˌvərt̬əd] adj : extrovertido
extrude [ɪk'stru:d, ɛk-] vt **-truded; -truding** : extrudir, expulsar
exuberance [ɪg'zu:bərənts, ɛg-] n **1** JOYOUSNESS : euforia f, exaltación f **2** VIGOR : exuberancia f, vigor m
exuberant [ɪg'zu:bərənt, ɛg-] adj **1** JOYOUS : eufórico **2** LUSH : exuberante — **exuberantly** adv
exude [ɪg'zu:d, ɛg-] vt **-uded; -uding 1** OOZE : rezumar, exudar **2** EMANATE : emanar, irradiar
exult [ɪg'zʌlt, ɛg-] vi : exultar, regocijarse
exultant [ɪg'zʌltənt, ɛg-] adj : exultante, jubiloso — **exultantly** adv
exultation [ˌɛksəl'teɪlʌən, ˌɛgzəl-] n : exultación f, júbilo m, alborozo m
ex–wife ['ɛks'waɪf] n : ex esposa f
eye[1] ['aɪ] vt **eyed; eyeing** or **eying** : mirar, observar
eye[2] n **1** : ojo m **2** VISION : visión f, vista f, ojo m ⟨to have a good eye for bargains : tener un buen ojo para las gangas⟩ **3** GAZE : mirada f, ojeada f ⟨before my (very) eyes : ante mis propios ojos⟩ ⟨keep an eye on him : vigílalo⟩ ⟨keep an eye out for her : fíjate a ver si la ves⟩ ⟨don't take your eyes off the road : no

apartes la vista de la carretera⟩ **4** AT-TENTION : atención *f* ⟨to catch one's eye : llamar la atención⟩ **5** POINT OF VIEW : punto *m* de vista ⟨in the eyes of the law : según la ley⟩ **6** : ojo *m* (de una aguja, una papa, una tormenta)

eyeball ['aɪ₁bɔl] *n* : globo *m* ocular

eyebrow ['aɪ₁braʊ] *n* : ceja *f* ⟨to raise an eyebrow at : asombrarse ante⟩

eye-catching ['aɪ₁kætʃɪŋ, -₁ke-] *adj* : llamativo

eyed ['aɪd] *adj (used in combination)* : de ojos ⟨blue-eyed : de ojos azules⟩ ⟨wideeyed : con los ojos muy abiertos⟩ ⟨crosseyed : bizco⟩ ⟨one-eyed : tuerto⟩

eyedropper ['aɪ₁drɑpər] *n* : cuentagotas *f*

eyedrops ['aɪ₁drɑps] *npl* : colirio *m*

eyeglasses ['aɪ₁glæsəz] *npl* : anteojos *mpl*, lentes *mpl*, espejuelos *mpl*, gafas *fpl*

eyelash ['aɪ₁læʃ] *n* : pestaña *f*

eyelet ['aɪlət] *n* : ojete *m*

eyelid ['aɪ₁lɪd] *n* : párpado *m*

eyeliner ['aɪ₁laɪnər] *n* : delineador *m* (de ojos)

eye–opener ['aɪ₁o:pənər] *n* : revelación *f*, sorpresa *f*

eye–opening ['aɪ₁o:pənɪŋ] *adj* : revelador

eyepiece ['aɪ₁pi:s] *n* : ocular *m*

eye shadow *n* : sombra *f* de ojos

eyesight ['aɪ₁saɪt] *n* : vista *f*, visión *f*

eyesore ['aɪ₁sor] *n* : monstruosidad *f*, adefesio *m*

eyestrain ['aɪ₁streɪn] *n* : fatiga *f* visual, vista *f* cansada

eyetooth ['aɪ₁tu:θ] *n* : colmillo *m*

eyewitness ['aɪ'wɪtnəs] *n* : testigo *mf* ocular, testigo *mf* presencial

eyrie ['aɪri] → aerie

F

f ['ɛf] *n*, *pl* **f's** *or* **fs** ['ɛfs] **1** : sexta letra del alfabeto inglés **2 F** : fa *m* ⟨F sharp/flat : fa sostenido/bemol⟩ **3 F** : insuficiente *m* (calificación)

fa ['fɛ́] *n* : fa *m* (en el canto)

fable ['feɪbəl] *n* : fábula *f*

fabled ['feɪbəld] *adj* : legendario, fabuloso

fabric ['fæbrɪk] *n* **1** MATERIAL : tela *f*, tejido *m* **2** STRUCTURE : estructura *f* ⟨the fabric of society : la estructura de la sociedad⟩

fabricate ['fæbrɪ₁keɪt] *vt* **-cated; -cating** **1** CONSTRUCT, MANUFACTURE : construir, fabricar **2** INVENT : inventar (excusas o mentiras)

fabrication [₁fæbrɪ'keɪʃən] *n* **1** LIE : mentira *f*, invención *f* **2** MANUFACTURE : fabricación *f*

fabulous ['fæbjələs] *adj* **1** LEGENDARY : fabuloso, legendario **2** INCREDIBLE : increíble, fabuloso ⟨fabulous wealth : riqueza fabulosa⟩ **3** WONDERFUL : magnífico, estupendo, fabuloso — **fabulously** *adv*

facade [fə'séd] *n* : fachada *f*

face¹ ['feɪs] *v* **faced; facing** *vt* **1** LINE : recubrir (una superficie), forrar (ropa) **2** CONFRONT : enfrentarse a, afrontar, hacer frente a ⟨to face the music : afrontar las consecuencias⟩ ⟨to face the facts : aceptar la realidad⟩ **3** : estar de cara a, estar enfrente de ⟨she's facing her brother : está de cara a su hermano⟩ **4** OVERLOOK : dar a — *vi* : mirar (hacia), estar orientado (a) **5 to face up to** CONFRONT : hacer frente a

face² *n* **1** : cara *f*, rostro *m* ⟨he told me to my face : me lo dijo a la cara⟩ ⟨face to face : cara a cara⟩ **2** EXPRESSION : cara *f*, expresión *f* ⟨to make a face : poner mala cara⟩ ⟨he couldn't keep a straight face : no pudo aguantarse la risa⟩ ⟨to put on a brave face : no demostrar uno el miedo que tiene⟩ **3** GRIMACE : mueca

f ⟨to make faces : hacer muecas⟩ **4** APPEARANCE : fisonomía *f*, aspecto *m* ⟨the face of society : la fisonomía de la sociedad⟩ ⟨on the face of it : aparentemente, a primera vista⟩ **5** PERSON : cara *f* **6** PRESTIGE : prestigio *m* ⟨to lose face : desprestigiarse⟩ ⟨to save face : salvar las apariencias⟩ **7** FRONT, SIDE : cara *f* (de una moneda), esfera *f* (de un reloj), fachada *f* (de un edificio), pared *f* (de una montaña) **8** SURFACE : superficie *f*, faz *f* (de la tierra), cara *f* (de la luna) **9 in the face of** DESPITE : en medio de, en visto de, ante **10 to be/get in someone's face** *fam* : gritarle a alguien, regañarle a alguien **11 to fly in the face of** : hacer caso omiso de algo

facedown ['feɪs₁daʊn] *adv* : boca abajo

face–first [₁feɪs₁fərst] *adv* : de bruces

faceless ['feɪsləs] *adj* ANONYMOUS : anónimo

face–lift ['feɪs₁lɪft] *n* **1** : estiramiento *m* facial **2** RENOVATION : renovación *f*, remozamiento *m*

face–off ['feɪs₁ɔf] *n* : confrontación *f*, careo *m*

facet ['fæsət] *n* **1** : faceta *f* (de una piedra) **2** ASPECT : faceta *f*, aspecto *m*

facetious [fə'si:ʃəs] *adj* : gracioso, burlón, bromista

facetiously [fə'si:ʃəsli] *adv* : en tono de burla

facetiousness [fə'si:ʃəsnəs] *n* : jocosidad *f*

face–to–face *adv & adj* : cara a cara

faceup ['feɪs'ʌp] *adv* : boca arriba

face value *n* : valor *m* nominal

facial¹ ['feɪʃəl] *adj* : de la cara, facial

facial² *n* : tratamiento *m* facial, limpieza *f* de cutis

facile ['fæsəl] *adj* SUPERFICIAL : superficial, simplista

facilitate [fə'sɪlə₁teɪt] *vt* **-tated; -tating** : facilitar — **facilitator** [fə'sɪlə₁teɪtər] *n*

facility [fə'sɪləti] *n, pl* **-ties** 1 EASE : facilidad *f* 2 CENTER, COMPLEX : centro *m*, complejo *m* 3 **facilities** *npl* AMENITIES : comodidades *fpl*, servicios *mpl*

facing ['feɪsɪŋ] *n* 1 LINING : entretela *f* (de una prenda) 2 : revestimiento *m* (de un edificio)

facsimile [fæk'sɪməli] *n* : facsímil *m*

fact ['fækt] *n* 1 : hecho *m* ⟨as a matter of fact : de hecho⟩ 2 INFORMATION : información *f*, datos *mpl* ⟨facts and figures : datos y cifras⟩ 3 REALITY : realidad *f* ⟨in fact : en realidad⟩

faction ['fækʃən] *n* : facción *m*, bando *m*

factional ['fækʃənəl] *adj* : entre facciones

factor ['fæktər] *n* : factor *m*

factory ['fæktəri] *n, pl* **-ries** : fábrica *f*

factual ['fæktʃʊəl] *adj* : basado en hechos, objetivo

factually ['fæktʃʊəli] *adv* : en cuanto a los hechos

faculty ['fækəlti] *n, pl* **-ties** 1 : facultad *f* ⟨the faculty of sight : las facultades visuales, el sentido de la vista⟩ 2 APTITUDE : aptitud *f*, facilidad *f* 3 TEACHERS : cuerpo *m* docente

fad ['fæd] *n* : moda *f* pasajera, manía *f*

fade ['feɪd] *v* **faded; fading** *vi* 1 WITHER : debilitarse (dícese de las personas), marchitarse (dícese de las flores y las plantas) 2 DISCOLOR : desteñirse, decolorarse 3 DIM : apagarse (dícese de la luz), perderse (dícese de los sonidos), fundirse (dícese de las imágenes) 4 VANISH : desvanecerse, decaer — *vt* DISCOLOR : desteñir

fag ['fæg] *vt* **fagged; fagging** EXHAUST : cansar, fatigar

fagot *or* **faggot** ['fægət] *n* : haz *m* de leña

Fahrenheit ['færən,haɪt] *adj* : Fahrenheit

fail¹ ['feɪl] *vi* 1 WEAKEN : fallar, deteriorarse 2 STOP : fallar, detenerse ⟨his heart failed : le falló el corazón⟩ 3 : fracasar, fallar ⟨her plan failed : su plan fracasó⟩ ⟨the crops failed : se perdió la cosecha⟩ ⟨if all else fails : como último recurso⟩ 4 : quebrar ⟨a business about to fail : una empresa a punto de quebrar⟩ 5 **to fail in** : faltar a, no cumplir con ⟨to fail in one's duties : faltar a sus deberes⟩ — *vt* 1 FLUNK : reprobar (un examen) 2 : fallar ⟨words fail me : las palabras me fallan, no encuentro palabras⟩ 3 DISAPPOINT : fallar, decepcionar ⟨don't fail me! : ¡no me falles!⟩

fail² *n* : fracaso *m*

failing ['feɪlɪŋ] *n* : defecto *m*

failure ['feɪljər] *n* 1 : fracaso *m*, malogro *m* ⟨crop failure : pérdida de la cosecha⟩ ⟨heart failure : insuficiencia cardíaca⟩ ⟨engine failure : falla mecánica⟩ 2 BANKRUPTCY : bancarrota *f*, quiebra *f* 3 : fracaso *m* (persona) ⟨he was a failure as a manager : como gerente, fue un fracaso⟩

faint¹ ['feɪnt] *vi* : desmayarse

faint² *adj* 1 COWARDLY, TIMID : cobarde, tímido 2 DIZZY : mareado ⟨faint with hunger : desfallecido de hambre⟩ 3 SLIGHT : leve, ligero, vago ⟨I

haven't the faintest idea : no tengo la más mínima idea⟩ 4 INDISTINCT : tenue, indistinto, apenas perceptible

faint³ *n* : desmayo *m*

fainthearted ['feɪnt'hɑrtəd] *adj* : cobarde, pusilánime

faintly ['feɪntli] *adv* : débilmente, ligeramente, levemente

faintness ['feɪntnəs] *n* 1 INDISTINCTNESS : lo débil, falta *f* de claridad 2 FAINTING : desmayo *m*, desfallecimiento *m*

fair¹ ['fær] *adj* 1 ATTRACTIVE, BEAUTIFUL : bello, hermoso, atractivo 2 (*relating to weather*) : bueno, despejado 3 JUST : justo (dícese de personas, precios, etc.) ⟨fair elections : elecciones limpias⟩ ⟨one's fair share : lo que a uno le corresponde⟩ ⟨give her a fair chance : dale una oportunidad⟩ ⟨to be fair, . . . : en honor a la verdad, . . .⟩ 4 ADEQUATE : adecuado, aceptable ⟨fair to middling : mediano, regular⟩ ⟨he's in fair condition : se encuentra en estado estable⟩ ⟨a fair number : un buen número⟩ ⟨I have a fair idea of how it works : tengo una idea de como funciona⟩ ⟨they have a fair chance of winning : tienen (bastantes) posibilidades de ganar⟩ 5 BLOND, LIGHT : rubio (dícese del pelo), blanco (dícese de la tez) 6 **all's fair in love and war** : en el amor y en la guerra todo vale 7 **fair and square** : con todas las de la ley, en buena ley 8 **fair enough** : de acuerdo, me parece razonable 9 **fair's fair** : lo justo es justo 10 **fair game** : presa *f* fácil 11 **to play fair** : jugar limpio

fair² *n* : feria *f*

fairground ['fær,graʊnd] *n* : parque *m* de diversiones

fair–haired ['fær'hærd] *adj* : rubio

fairly ['færli] *adv* 1 IMPARTIALLY : imparcialmente, limpiamente, equitativamente 2 QUITE : bastante 3 MODERATELY : medianamente

fairness ['færnəs] *n* 1 IMPARTIALITY : imparcialidad *f*, justicia *f* 2 LIGHTNESS : blancura *f* (de la piel), lo rubio (del pelo)

fairy ['færi] *n, pl* **fairies** 1 : hada *f* 2 **fairy tale** : cuento *m* de hadas

fairyland ['færi,lænd] *n* 1 : país *m* de las hadas 2 : lugar *m* encantador

faith ['feɪθ] *n, pl* **faiths** ['feɪθs, 'feɪðz] 1 BELIEF : fe *f* 2 ALLEGIANCE : lealtad *f* 3 CONFIDENCE, TRUST : confianza *f*, fe *f* 4 RELIGION : religión *f*

faithful ['feɪθfəl] *adj* : fiel — **faithfully** *adv*

faithfulness ['feɪθfəlnəs] *n* : fidelidad *f*

faithless ['feɪθləs] *adj* 1 DISLOYAL : desleal 2 : infiel (en la religión) — **faithlessly** *adv*

faithlessness ['feɪθləsnəs] *n* : deslealtad *f*

fake¹ ['feɪk] *v* **faked; faking** *vt* 1 FALSIFY : falsificar, falsear 2 FEIGN : fingir — *vi* PRETEND : fingir 2 : hacer un engaño, hacer una finta (en deportes)

fake² *adj* : falso, fingido, postizo

fake³ *n* 1 IMITATION : imitación *f*, falsificación *f* 2 IMPOSTOR : impostor *m*,

faker · famously

-tora *f*; charlatán *m*, -tana *f*; farsante *mf* **3** FEINT : engaño *m*, finta *f* (en deportes)
faker ['feɪkər] *n* : impostor *m*, -tora *f*; charlatán *m*, -tana *f*; farsante *mf*
falcon ['fælkən, 'fɔl-] *n* : halcón *m*
fall¹ ['fɔl] *vi* **fell** ['fɛl]; **fallen** [fɔlən]; **falling 1** : caer, caerse ⟨the rain was falling : caía la lluvia⟩ ⟨a vase fell off the shelf : un jarrón se cayó del estante⟩ **2** : caerse, caer ⟨she tripped and fell down the stairs : tropezó y se cayó por las escaleras⟩ **3** HANG : caer **4** : caer (dícese de la noche) **5** DROP, LOWER : caer (dícese de los ingresos, etc.), bajar (dícese de los precios, las temperaturas, etc.), reducirse (dícese de la voz) ⟨her face fell : se le descompuso la cara⟩ **6** BECOME : volverse, quedarse ⟨to fall silent : callarse, quedarse callado⟩ ⟨to fall in love : enamorarse⟩ **7** : caer (ante un enemigo), rendirse ⟨the city fell : la ciudad se rindió⟩ **8** : caer ⟨to fall in battle : caer en combate⟩ **9** OCCUR : caer ⟨Christmas falls on a Friday : la Navidad cae en viernes⟩ **10 to fall (all) over oneself** to : desvivirse por **11 to fall apart** : deshacerse **12 to fall asleep** : dormirse, quedarse dormido **13 to fall away** : decaer, disminuir **14 to fall back** RETREAT : retirarse **15 to fall behind** : quedarse atrás **16 to fall behind on/with** : atrasarse en, retrasarse en **17 to fall down** : caerse **18 to fall down on the job** : no cumplir con su deber **19 to fall flat** : no ser bien recibido (dícese de un chiste, etc.), no dar resultado **20 to fall for** : enamorarse de **21 to fall for** BELIEVE : tragarse **22 to fall in** COLLAPSE : hundirse **23 to fall in** : formar filas **24 to fall into place** : ir bien, aclararse **25 to fall into the hands of** : caer en manos de **26 to fall in with** : juntarse con **27 to fall off** LESSEN : disminuir **28 to fall off** DETACH : desprenderse, caerse **29 to fall on** ATTACK : atacar, caer sobre **30 to fall out** : caerse (dícese del pelo, etc.) **31 to fall out** ARGUE : pelearse **32 to fall out** : romper filas **33 to fall out of favor** : caer en desgracia **34 to fall out of use** : caer en desuso **35 to fall over** : caerse **36 to fall sick** : caer enfermo, enfermarse **37 to fall through** : fracasar, caer en la nada **38 to fall to** : tocar a, corresponder a ⟨the task fell to him : le tocó a él hacerlo⟩
fall² *n* **1** TUMBLE : caída *f* ⟨to break one's fall : frenar uno su caída⟩ ⟨a fall of three feet : una caída de tres pies⟩ **2** FALLING : derrumbe *m* (de rocas), aguacero *m* (de lluvia), nevada *f* (de nieve), bajada *f* (de precios), disminución *f* (de cantidades) **3** AUTUMN : otoño *m* **4** DOWNFALL : caída *f*, ruina *f* **5 falls** *npl* WATERFALL : cascada *f*, catarata *f*
fallacious [fə'leɪləs] *adj* : erróneo, engañoso, falaz
fallacy ['fæləsi] *n, pl* **-cies** : falacia *f*
fall back *vi* **1** RETREAT : retirarse, replegarse **2 to fall back on** : recurrir a

fall guy *n* SCAPEGOAT : chivo *m* expiatorio
fallible ['fæləbəl] *adj* : falible
fallout ['fɔl,aʊt] *n* **1** : lluvia *f* radioactiva **2** CONSEQUENCES : secuelas *fpl*, consecuencias *fpl*
fallow¹ ['fæloː] *adj* **to lie fallow** : estar en barbecho
fallow² *n* : barbecho *m*
false ['fɔls] *adj* **falser; falsest 1** UNTRUE : falso ⟨true or false? : ¿verdadero o falso?⟩ ⟨a false name : un nombre falso/ficticio⟩ **2** ERRONEOUS, MISTAKEN : erróneo, equivocado ⟨false hopes : falsas expectativas⟩ ⟨false alarm : falsa alarma⟩ **3** FAKE : falso, postizo ⟨false teeth : dentadura postiza⟩ **4** UNFAITHFUL : infiel **5** INSINCERE, FEIGNED : falso **6** FRAUDULENT : fraudulento ⟨under false pretenses : por fraude⟩ **7 false move** : movimiento *m* en falso
falsehood ['fɔls,hʊd] *n* : mentira *f*, falsedad *f*
falsely ['fɔlsli] *adv* : falsamente, con falsedad
falseness ['fɔlsnəs] *n* : falsedad *f*
falsetto [fɔl'sɛtoː] *n, pl* **-tos** : falsete *m*
falsification [ˌfɔlsəfə'keɪʃən] *n* : falsificación *f*
falsify ['fɔlsə,faɪ] *vt* **-fied; fying** : falsificar, falsear
falsity ['fɔlsəti] *n, pl* **-ties** : falsedad *f*
falter ['fɔltər] *vi* **-tered; -tering 1** TOTTER : tambalearse **2** STAMMER : titubear, tartamudear **3** WAVER : vacilar
faltering ['fɔltərɪŋ] *adj* : titubeante, vacilante — **falteringly** *adv*
fame ['feɪm] *n* : fama *f*
famed ['feɪmd] *adj* : famoso, célebre, afamado
familial [fə'mɪljəl, -liəl] *adj* : familiar
familiar¹ [fə'mɪljər] *adj* **1** KNOWN : familiar, conocido ⟨to be familiar with : estar familiarizado con⟩ **2** INFORMAL : familiar, informal **3** INTIMATE : íntimo, de confianza **4** FORWARD : confianzudo, atrevido — **familiarly** *adv*
familiar² *n* : espíritu *m* guardián
familiarity [fəˌmɪli'ærəti, -ˌmɪl'jær-] *n, pl* **-ties 1** KNOWLEDGE : conocimiento *m*, familiaridad *f* **2** INFORMALITY, INTIMACY : confianza *f*, familiaridad *f* **3** FORWARDNESS : exceso *m* de confianza, descaro *m*
familiarize [fə'mɪljə,raɪz] *vt* **-ized; -izing 1** : familiarizar **2 to familiarize oneself** : familiarizarse
family ['fæmli, 'fæmə-] *n, pl* **-lies** : familia *f*
family name *n* SURNAME : apellido *m*
family room *n* : living *m*, sala *f* (informal)
family tree *n* : árbol *m* genealógico
famine ['fæmən] *n* : hambre *f*, hambruna *f*
famish ['fæmɪʃ] *vi* **to be famished** : estar famélico, estar hambriento, morir de hambre *fam*
famous ['feɪməs] *adj* : famoso
famously ['feɪməsli] *adv* **to get on famously** : llevarse de maravilla

fan¹ ['fæn] *vt* **fanned; fanning 1** : abanicar (a una persona), avivar (un fuego) **2** STIMULATE : avivar, estimular

fan² *n* **1** : ventilador *m*, abanico *m* **2** ADMIRER, ENTHUSIAST : aficionado *m*, -da *f*; entusiasta *mf*; admirador *m*, -dora *f*

fanatic¹ [fə'nætɪk] *or* **fanatical** [-ṭɪ-kəl] *adj* : fanático

fanatic² *n* : fanático *m*, -ca *f*

fanaticism [fə'næṭə͵sɪzəm] *n* : fanatismo *m*

fan belt *n* : correa *f* del ventilador

fanciful ['fænsɪfəl] *adj* **1** CAPRICIOUS : caprichoso, fantástico, extravagante **2** IMAGINATIVE : imaginativo — **fancifully** *adv*

fancy¹ ['fæntsi] *vt* **-cied; -cying 1** IMAGINE : imaginarse, figurarse ⟨fancy that! : ¡figúrate!, ¡imagínate!⟩ **2** CRAVE : apetecer, tener ganas de

fancy² *adj* **fancier; -est 1** ELABORATE : elaborado **2** LUXURIOUS : lujoso, elegante — **fancily** ['fæntsəli] *adv*

fancy³ *n, pl* **-cies 1** LIKING : gusto *m*, afición *f* **2** WHIM : antojo *m*, capricho *m* **3** IMAGINATION : fantasía *f*, imaginación *f*

fandango [fæn'dæŋgo] *n, pl* **-gos** : fandango *m*

fanfare ['fæn͵fær] *n* : fanfarria *f*

fang ['fæŋ] *n* : colmillo *m* (de un animal), diente *m* (de una serpiente)

fanlight ['fæn͵laɪt] *n* : tragaluz *m*

fantasia [fæn'teɪʒə, -ziə;, ͵fæntə-'zi:ə] *n* : fantasía *f*

fantasize ['fæntə͵saɪz] *vi* **-sized; -sizing** : fantasear

fantastic [fæn'tæstɪk] *adj* **1** UNBELIEVABLE : fantástico, increíble, extraño **2** ENORMOUS : fabuloso, inmenso ⟨fantastic sums : sumas fabulosas⟩ **3** WONDERFUL : estupendo, fantástico, bárbaro *fam*, macanudo *fam* — **fantastically** [-tɪkli] *adv*

fantasy ['fæntəsi] *n, pl* **-sies** : fantasía *f*

FAQ ['fæk, ͵ɛf͵eɪ'kju:] *n, pl* **FAQs** (frequently *a*sked *q*uestion, *f*requently *a*sked *q*uestions) : FAQ *m* (lista de preguntas)

far¹ ['fɑr] *adv* **farther** ['fɑrðər] *or* **further** ['fər-]; **farthest** *or* **furthest** [-ðəst] **1** : lejos ⟨far from here : lejos de aquí⟩ ⟨to go far : llegar lejos⟩ ⟨far away : a lo lejos⟩ ⟨in the far distant future : en un futuro lejano⟩ ⟨her birthday isn't far off/away : falta poco para su cumpleaños⟩ **2** MUCH : muy, mucho ⟨far bigger : mucho más grande⟩ ⟨far better : mucho mejor⟩ ⟨far different : muy distinto/diferente⟩ ⟨far too expensive : demasiado caro⟩ **3** (*indicating a particular point, degree, or extent*) ⟨we got as far as Chicago : llegamos hasta Chicago⟩ ⟨as far north as Toronto : tan al norte como Toronto⟩ ⟨to go so far as to say : decir tanto como⟩ ⟨as far as I know : que yo sepa⟩ **4** (*indicating an advanced point or extent*) : lejos ⟨to go far (in life) : llegar lejos (en la vida)⟩ ⟨not to go far enough : quedarse corto⟩ ⟨we've come too far to quit now

: hemos llegado demasiado lejos para dejarlo ahora⟩ ⟨we still have far to go : aún nos queda un largo camino por recorrer⟩ ⟨to take something too far : llevar algo demasiado lejos⟩ **5 as/so far as** WITH REGARD TO : en lo que respecta a **6 as/so far as** (*expressing an opinion*) ⟨as far as I'm concerned : en lo que a mí respecta, por mí⟩ **7 by far** : con mucho, de lejos ⟨it's by far the best : es con mucho el mejor⟩ **8 far and wide** : por todas partes **9 far from it!** : ¡todo lo contrario! **10 far off** : muy errado **11 so far** : hasta ahora, todavía

far² *adj* **farther** *or* **further**; **farthest** *or* **furthest 1** DISTANT, REMOTE : lejano, remoto ⟨the far horizon : el horizonte lejano⟩ ⟨the far reaches of outer space : los confines del espacio exterior⟩ ⟨the Far East : el Lejano Oriente, el Extremo Oriente⟩ ⟨in the far future : en el/un futuro lejano/remoto⟩ **2** : más lejano ⟨on the far side of the lake : en el otro lado del lago⟩ ⟨at the far end of the room : en el otro extremo de la sala⟩ **3 the far left/right** : la extrema izquierda/derecha (en la política)

faraway ['fɑrə͵weɪ] *adj* : remoto, lejano

farce ['fɑrs] *n* : farsa *f*

farcical ['fɑrsɪkəl] *adj* : absurdo, ridículo

fare¹ ['fær] *vi* **fared; faring** : ir, salir ⟨how did you fare? : ¿cómo te fue?⟩

fare² *n* **1** : pasaje *m*, billete *m*, boleto *m* ⟨half fare : medio pasaje⟩ **2** FOOD : comida *f*

farewell¹ [fær'wɛl] *adj* : de despedida

farewell² *n* : despedida *f*

far–fetched ['fɑr'fɛtʃt] *adj* : improbable, exagerado

farina [fə'ri:nə] *n* : harina *f*

farm¹ ['fɑrm] *vt* **1** : cultivar, labrar **2** : criar (animales) — *vi* : ser agricultor

farm² *n* : granja *f*, hacienda *f*, finca *f*, estancia *f*

farmer ['fɑrmər] *n* : agricultor *m*, granjero *m*

farmhand ['fɑrm͵hænd] *n* : peón *m*

farmhouse ['fɑrm͵haʊs] *n* : granja *f*, vivienda *f* del granjero, casa *f* de hacienda

farming ['fɑrmɪŋ] *n* : labranza *f*, cultivo *m*, crianza *f* (de animales)

farmland ['fɑrm͵lænd] *n* : tierras *fpl* de labranza

farmyard ['fɑrm͵jɑrd] *n* : corral *m*

far–off ['fɑr͵ɔf, -'ɔf] *adj* : remoto, distante, lejano

far–reaching ['fɑr'ri:tʃɪŋ] *adj* : de gran alcance

farsighted ['fɑr͵saɪṭəd] *adj* **1** : hipermétrope **2** JUDICIOUS : con visión de futuro, previsor, precavido

farsightedness ['fɑr͵saɪṭədnəs] *n* **1** : hipermetropía *f* **2** PRUDENCE : previsión *f*

fart¹ ['fɑrt] *vi often vulgar* : tirarse un pedo *fam*

fart² *n often vulgar* **1** : pedo *m fam* **2 old fart** : viejo *m*, -ja *f*

farther¹ ['fɑrðər] *adv* **1** AHEAD : más lejos (en el espacio), más adelante (en el tiempo) **2** MORE : más

farther² *adj* : más lejano, más remoto
farthermost ['fɑrðər,moːst] *adj* : (el) más lejano
farthest¹ ['fɑrðəst] *adv* **1** : lo más lejos ⟨I jumped farthest : salté lo más lejos⟩ **2** : lo más avanzado ⟨he progressed farthest : progresó al punto más avanzado⟩ **3** : más ⟨the farthest developed plan : el plan más desarrollado⟩
farthest² *adj* : más lejano
fascinate ['fæsən,eɪt] *vt* -nated; -nating : fascinar, cautivar
fascinating ['fæsən,eɪtɪŋ] *adj* : fascinante
fascination [,fæsən'eɪʃən] *n* : fascinación *f*
fascism ['fæʃ,ɪzəm] *n* : fascismo *m*
fascist¹ ['fæʃɪst] *adj* : fascista
fascist² *n* : fascista *mf*
fashion¹ ['fæʃən] *vt* : formar, moldear
fashion² *n* **1** MANNER : manera *f*, modo *m* **2** CUSTOM : costumbre *f* **3** STYLE : moda *f*
fashionable ['fæʃənəbəl] *adj* : de moda, chic
fashionably ['fæʃənəbli] *adv* : a la moda
fashion show *n* : desfile *m* de modelos
fast¹ ['fæst] *vi* : ayunar
fast² *adv* **1** SECURELY : firmemente, seguramente ⟨to hold fast : agarrarse bien⟩ **2** RAPIDLY : rápidamente, rápido, de prisa **3** to run fast : ir adelantado (dícese de un reloj) **4** SOUNDLY : profundamente ⟨fast asleep : profundamente dormido⟩
fast³ *adj* **1** SECURE : firme, seguro ⟨to make fast : amarrar (un barco)⟩ **2** FAITHFUL : leal ⟨fast friends : amigos leales⟩ **3** RAPID : rápido, veloz **4** : adelantado ⟨my watch is fast : tengo el reloj adelantado⟩ **5** DEEP : profundo ⟨a fast sleep : un sueño profundo⟩ **6** COLORFAST : inalterable, que no destiñe **7** DISSOLUTE : extravagante, disipado, disoluto
fast⁴ *n* : ayuno *m*
fasten ['fæsən] *vt* **1** ATTACH : sujetar, atar **2** FIX : fijar ⟨to fasten one's eyes on : fijar los ojos en⟩ **3** SECURE : abrochar (ropa o cinturones), atar (cordones), cerrar (una maleta) — *vi* : abrocharse, cerrar
fastener ['fæsənər] *n* : cierre *m*, sujetador *m*
fastening ['fæsənɪŋ] *n* : cierre *m*, sujetador *m*
fast food *n* : comida *f* rápida
fastidious [fæs'tɪdiəs] *adj* : quisquilloso, exigente — **fastidiously** *adv*
fat¹ ['fæt] *adj* **fatter; fattest 1** OBESE : gordo, obeso **2** THICK : grueso
fat² *n* : grasa *f*
fatal ['feɪţəl] *adj* **1** DEADLY : mortal **2** ILL-FATED : malhadado, fatal **3** MOMENTOUS : fatídico
fatalism ['feɪţəl,ɪzəm] *n* : fatalismo *m*
fatalist ['feɪţəlɪst] *n* : fatalista *mf*
fatalistic [,feɪţəl'ɪstɪk] *adj* : fatalista
fatality [feɪ'tæləţi, fə-] *n*, *pl* **-ties** : víctima *f* mortal
fatally ['feɪţəli] *adv* : mortalmente
fate ['feɪt] *n* **1** DESTINY : destino *m* **2** END, LOT : final *m*, suerte *f*

fated ['feɪţəd] *adj* : predestinado
fateful ['feɪtfəl] *adj* **1** MOMENTOUS : fatídico, aciago **2** PROPHETIC : profético — **fatefully** *adv*
father¹ ['fɑðər] *vt* : engendrar
father² *n* **1** : padre *m* ⟨my father and my mother : mi padre y mi madre⟩ ⟨Father Smith : el padre Smith⟩ **2 the Father** GOD : el Padre, Dios *m*
fatherhood ['fɑðər,hʊd] *n* : paternidad *f*
father-in-law ['fɑðərɪn,lɔ] *n*, *pl* **fathers-in-law** : suegro *m*
fatherland ['fɑðər,lænd] *n* : patria *f*
fatherless ['fɑðərləs] *adj* : huérfano de padre, sin padre
fatherly ['fɑðərli] *adj* : paternal
fathom¹ ['fæðəm] *vt* UNDERSTAND : entender, comprender
fathom² *n* : braza *f*
fatigue¹ [fə'tiːg] *vt* **-tigued; -tiguing** : fatigar, cansar
fatigue² *n* : fatiga *f*
fatness ['fætnəs] *n* : gordura *f* (de una persona o un animal), grosor *m* (de un objeto)
fatten ['fætən] *vt* : engordar, cebar
fattening ['fætnɪŋ] *adj* : que engorda
fatty ['fæţi] *adj* **fattier; -est** : graso, grasoso
fatuous ['fætʃʊəs] *adj* : necio, fatuo — **fatuously** *adv*
faucet ['fɔsət] *n* : llave *f*, canilla *f* *Arg*, *Uru*, grifo *m*
fault¹ ['fɔlt] *vt* : encontrar defectos a
fault² *n* **1** SHORTCOMING : defecto *m*, falta *f* **2** DEFECT : falta *f*, defecto *m*, falla *f* ⟨to find fault with : encontrarle defectos a, criticar⟩ **3** BLAME : culpa *f* ⟨to be at fault : tener la culpa⟩ **4** FRACTURE : falla *f* (geológica)
faultfinder ['fɔlt,faɪndər] *n* : criticón *m*, -cona *f*
faultfinding ['fɔlt,faɪndɪŋ] *n* : crítica *f*
faultless ['fɔltləs] *adj* : sin culpa, sin imperfecciones, impecable
faultlessly ['fɔltləsli] *adv* : impecablemente, perfectamente
faulty ['fɔlti] *adj* **faultier; -est** : defectuoso, imperfecto — **faultily** ['fɔltəli] *adv*
fauna ['fɔnə] *n* : fauna *f*
faux ['fo:] *adj* : de imitación
faux pas [,fo:'pɑ] *n*, *pl* **faux pas** [same or -'pɑz] : metedura *f* de pata *fam*
favor¹ ['feɪvər] *vt* **1** SUPPORT : estar a favor de, ser partidario de, apoyar **2** OBLIGE : hacerle un favor a **3** PREFER : preferir **4** RESEMBLE : parecerse a, salir a
favor² *n* : favor *m* ⟨in favor of : a favor de⟩ ⟨an error in his favor : un error a su favor⟩
favorable ['feɪvərəbəl] *adj* : favorable, propicio
favorably ['feɪvərəbli] *adv* : favorablemente, bien
favorite¹ ['feɪvərət] *adj* : favorito, preferido
favorite² *n* : favorito *m*, -ta *f*; preferido *m*, -da *f*
favoritism ['feɪvərə,tɪzəm] *n* : favoritismo *m*

fawn[1] ['fɔn] vi : adular, lisonjear
fawn[2] n : cervato m
fax[1] ['fæks] n : facsímil m, facsímile m
fax[2] vt **1** : mandarle un fax a **2** : enviar por fax
faze ['feɪz] vt **fazed; fazing** : desconcertar, perturbar
fear[1] ['fɪr] vt : temer, tener miedo de — vi : temer
fear[2] n : miedo m, temor m ⟨for fear of : por temor a⟩
fearful ['fɪrfəl] adj **1** FRIGHTENING : espantoso, aterrador, horrible **2** FRIGHTENED : temeroso, miedoso
fearfully ['fɪrfəli] adv **1** EXTREMELY : extremadamente, terriblemente **2** TIMIDLY : con temor
fearless ['fɪrləs] adj : intrépido, impávido
fearlessly ['fɪrləsli] adv : sin temor
fearlessness ['fɪrləsnəs] n : intrepidez f, impavidez f
fearsome ['fɪrsəm] adj : aterrador
feasibility [,fi:zə'bɪləti] n : viabilidad f, factibilidad f
feasible ['fi:zəbəl] adj : viable, factible, realizable
feast[1] ['fi:st] vi : banquetear — vt **1** : agasajar, festejar **2 to feast one's eyes on** : regalarse la vista con
feast[2] n **1** BANQUET : banquete m, festín m **2** FESTIVAL : fiesta f
feat ['fi:t] n : proeza f, hazaña f
feather[1] ['fɛðər] vt **to feather one's nest** : hacer su agosto
feather[2] n **1** : pluma f **2 a feather in one's cap** : un triunfo personal
feathered ['fɛðərd] adj : con plumas
feathery ['fɛðəri] adj **1** DOWNY : plumoso **2** LIGHT : liviano
feature[1] ['fi:tʃər] v **-tured; -turing** vt **1** IMAGINE : imaginarse **2** PRESENT : presentar — vi : figurar
feature[2] n **1** CHARACTERISTIC : característica f, rasgo m **2** : largometraje m (en el cine), artículo m (en un periódico), documental m (en la televisión) **3 features** npl : rasgos mpl, facciones fpl ⟨delicate features : facciones delicadas⟩
February ['fɛbjʊ,ri, 'fɛbʊ-, 'fɛbrʊ-] n : febrero m ⟨they arrived on the 21st of February, they arrived on February 21st : llegaron el 21 de febrero⟩
fecal ['fi:kəl] adj : fecal
feces ['fi:,si:z] npl : heces fpl, excrementos mpl
feckless ['fɛkləs] adj : irresponsable
fecund ['fɛkənd, 'fi:-] adj : fecundo
fecundity [fɪ'kʌndəti, fɛ-] n : fecundidad f
federal ['fɛdrəl, -dərəl] adj : federal
federalism ['fɛdrə,lɪzəm, -dərə-] n : federalismo m
federalist[1] ['fɛdrəlɪst, -dərə-] adj : federalista
federalist[2] n : federalista mf
federate ['fɛdə,reɪt] vt **-ated; -ating** : federar
federation [,fɛdə'reɪʃən] n : federación f
fedora [fɪ'dorə] n : sombrero m flexible de fieltro
fed up adj : harto
fee ['fi:] n **1** : honorarios mpl (a un

médico, un abogado, etc.) **2 entrance fee** : entrada f
feeble ['fi:bəl] adj **feebler; feeblest 1** WEAK : débil, endeble **2** INEFFECTIVE : flojo, pobre, poco convincente
feebleminded [,fi:bəl'maɪndəd] adj **1** often offensive : débil mental **2** FOOLISH, STUPID : imbécil, tonto
feebleness ['fi:bəlnəs] n : debilidad f
feebly ['fi:bli] adv : débilmente
feed[1] ['fi:d] v **fed** ['fɛd]; **feeding** vt **1** : dar de comer a, nutrir, alimentar (a una persona) **2** : alimentar (un fuego o una máquina), proveer (información), introducir (datos) — vi : comer, alimentarse
feed[2] n **1** NOURISHMENT : alimento m **2** FODDER : pienso m **3** : alimentación f ⟨paper feed : (mecanismo de) alimentación de papel⟩ **4** : transmisión f (de video, etc.) **5** : fuente f (de noticias), canal m (en una red social)
feedback ['fi:d,bæk] n **1** : retroalimentación f (electrónica) **2** RESPONSE : reacción f
feeder ['fi:dər] n : comedero m (para animales)
feel[1] ['fi:l] v **felt** ['fɛlt]; **feeling** vi **1** : sentirse, encontrarse ⟨I feel tired : me siento cansada⟩ ⟨he feels hungry/cold : tiene hambre/frío⟩ ⟨she feels like a fool : se siente como una idiota⟩ ⟨to feel like doing something : tener ganas de hacer algo⟩ **2** SEEM : parecer ⟨it feels like spring : parece primavera⟩ ⟨it feels like rain : parece que va a llover⟩ ⟨it feels smooth : es suave al tacto⟩ **3** THINK : parecerse, opinar, pensar ⟨how does he feel about that? : ¿qué opina él de eso?⟩ **4 to feel (around) for** : buscar a tientas **5 to feel for** PITY : compadecer — vt **1** TOUCH : tocar, palpar ⟨to feel one's way : tantear, ir a tientas⟩ **2** SENSE : sentir ⟨to feel the cold : sentir el frío⟩ **3** CONSIDER : sentir, creer, considerar ⟨I didn't feel it necessary to inform him : no creí necesario informarle⟩ **4 to feel out** : tantear **5 to feel up** fam : manosear, meterle mano a fam
feel[2] n **1** SENSATION, TOUCH : sensación f, tacto m **2** ATMOSPHERE : ambiente m, atmósfera f **3 to have a feel for** : tener un talento especial para
feeler ['fi:lər] n : antena f, tentáculo m
feeling ['fi:lɪŋ] n **1** SENSATION : sensación f, sensibilidad f **2** EMOTION : sentimiento m **3** HUNCH, INTUITION : sensación f **4** OPINION : opinión f **5 feelings** npl SENSIBILITIES : sentimientos mpl ⟨to hurt/spare someone's feelings : herir/no herir los sentimientos de alguien⟩ ⟨no hard feelings, right? : no me guardas rencor, ¿verdad?⟩ ⟨to have feelings for someone : tener sentimientos por alguien⟩
feet → **foot**
feign ['feɪn] vt : simular, aparentar, fingir
feint[1] ['feɪnt] vi : fintar, fintear
feint[2] n : finta f
felicitate [fɪ'lɪsə,teɪt] vt **-tated; -tating** : felicitar, congratular

felicitation [fɪˌlɪsəˈteɪlən] *n* : felicitación *f*
felicitous [fɪˈlɪsətəs] *adj* : acertado, oportuno
feline[1] [ˈfiːˌlaɪn] *adj* : felino
feline[2] *n* : felino *m*, -na *f*
fell[1] [ˈfɛl] *vt* : talar (un árbol), derribar (a una persona)
fell[2] → fall
fellow[1] [ˈfɛˌloː] *adj* ⟨his fellow students : sus compañeros de estudios⟩ ⟨fellow citizen : conciudadano, paisano⟩
fellow[2] *n* **1** COMPANION : compañero *m*, -ra *f*; camarada *mf* **2** ASSOCIATE : socio *m*, -cia *f* **3** MAN : tipo *m*, hombre *m*
fellowman [ˌfɛloˈmæn] *n, pl* **-men** : prójimo *m*, semejante *m*
fellowship [ˈfɛloˌʃɪp] *n* **1** COMPANIONSHIP : camaradería *f*, compañerismo *m* **2** ASSOCIATION : fraternidad *f* **3** GRANT : beca *f* (de investigación)
felon [ˈfɛlən] *n* : malhechor *m*, -chora *f*; criminal *mf*
felonious [fəˈloːniəs] *adj* : criminal
felony [ˈfɛləni] *n, pl* **-nies** : delito *m* grave
felt[1] [ˈfɛlt] *n* : fieltro *m*
felt[2] → feel
felt–tip [ˈfɛltˌtɪp] *or* **felt–tip pen** *n* : marcador *m*, rotulador *m* *Spain*
female[1] [ˈfiːˌmeɪl] *adj* : femenino
female[2] *n* **1** : hembra *f* (de animal) **2** WOMAN : mujer *f*
feminine [ˈfɛmənən] *adj* : femenino
femininity [ˌfɛməˈnɪnəti] *n* : feminidad *f*, femineidad *f*
feminism [ˈfɛməˌnɪzəm] *n* : feminismo *m*
feminist[1] [ˈfɛmənɪst] *adj* : feminista
feminist[2] *n* : feminista *mf*
femoral [ˈfɛmərəl] *adj* : femoral
femur [ˈfiːmər] *n, pl* **femurs** *or* **femora** [ˈfɛmərə] : fémur *m*
fence[1] [ˈfɛnts] *v* **fenced; fencing** *vt* : vallar, cercar — *vi* : hacer esgrima
fence[2] *n* : cerca *f*, valla *f*, cerco *m*, barda *f* *Mex*
fencer [ˈfɛntsər] *n* : esgrimista *mf*
fencing [ˈfɛntsɪŋ] *n* **1** : esgrima *m* (deporte) **2** : materiales *mpl* para cercas **3** ENCLOSURE : cercado *m*
fend [ˈfɛnd] *vt* **to fend off** : rechazar (un enemigo), parar (un golpe), eludir (una pregunta) — *vi* **to fend for oneself** : arreglárselas sólo, valerse por sí mismo
fender [ˈfɛndər] *n* : guardabarros *mpl*, salpicadera *f* *Mex*
fennel [ˈfɛnəl] *n* : hinojo *m*
ferment[1] [fərˈmɛnt] *v* : fermentar
ferment[2] [ˈfərˌmɛnt] *n* **1** : fermento *m* (en la química) **2** TURMOIL : agitación *f*, conmoción *f*
fermentation [ˌfərmənˈteɪlən, -ˌmɛn-] *n* : fermentación *f*
fern [ˈfərn] *n* : helecho *m*
ferocious [fəˈroːləs] *adj* : feroz — **ferociously** *adv*
ferociousness [fəˈroːləsnəs] *n* : ferocidad *f*
ferocity [fəˈrasəti] *n* : ferocidad *f*
ferret[1] [ˈfɛrət] *vi* SNOOP : hurgar, husmear — *vt* **to ferret out** : descubrir
ferret[2] *n* : hurón *m*

Ferris wheel [ˈfɛrɪs] *n* : noria *f*
ferry[1] [ˈfɛri] *vt* **-ried; -rying** : llevar, transportar
ferry[2] *n, pl* **-ries** : transbordador *m*, ferry *m*
ferryboat [ˈfɛriˌboːt] *n* : transbordador *m*, ferry *m*
fertile [ˈfərtəl] *adj* : fértil, fecundo
fertility [fərˈtɪləti] *n* : fertilidad *f*
fertilization [ˌfərtələˈzeɪlən] *n* : fertilización *f* (del suelo), fecundación (de un huevo)
fertilize [ˈfərtəlˌaɪz] *vt* **-ized; -izing** **1** : fecundar (un huevo) **2** : fertilizar, abonar (el suelo)
fertilizer [ˈfərtəlˌaɪzər] *n* : fertilizante *m*, abono *m*
fervent [ˈfərvənt] *adj* : ferviente, fervoroso, ardiente — **fervently** *adv*
fervid [ˈfərvɪd] *adj* : ardiente, apasionado — **fervidly** *adv*
fervor [ˈfərvər] *n* : fervor *m*, ardor *m*
fester [ˈfɛstər] *vi* : enconarse, supurar
festival [ˈfɛstəvəl] *n* : fiesta *f*, festividad *f*, festival *m*
festive [ˈfɛstɪv] *adj* : festivo — **festively** *adv*
festivity [fɛsˈtɪvəti] *n, pl* **-ties** : festividad *f*, celebración *f*
festoon[1] [fɛsˈtuːn] *vt* : adornar, engalanar
festoon[2] *n* GARLAND : guirnalda *f*
fetal [ˈfiːtəl] *adj* : fetal
fetch [ˈfɛtl] *vt* **1** BRING : traer, recoger, ir a buscar **2** REALIZE : realizar, venderse por ⟨the jewelry fetched $10,000 : las joyas se vendieron por $10,000⟩
fetching [ˈfɛtlɪŋ] *adj* : atractivo, encantador
fête[1] [ˈfeɪt, ˈfɛt] *vt* **fêted; fêting** : festejar, agasajar
fête[2] *n* : fiesta *f*
fetid [ˈfɛtəd] *adj* : fétido
fetish [ˈfɛtɪl] *n* : fetiche *m*
fetlock [ˈfɛtˌlak] *n* : espolón *m*
fetter [ˈfɛtər] *vt* : encadenar, poner grillos a
fetters [ˈfɛtərz] *npl* : grillos *mpl*, grilletes *mpl*, cadenas *fpl*
fettle [ˈfɛtəl] *n* **in fine fettle** : en buena forma, en plena forma
fetus [ˈfiːtəs] *n* : feto *m*
feud[1] [ˈfjuːd] *vi* : pelear, contender
feud[2] *n* : contienda *f*, enemistad *f* (heredada)
feudal [ˈfjuːdəl] *adj* : feudal
feudalism [ˈfjuːdəlˌɪzəm] *n* : feudalismo *m*
fever [ˈfiːvər] *n* : fiebre *f*, calentura *f*
feverish [ˈfiːvərɪl] *adj* **1** : afiebrado, con fiebre, febril **2** FRANTIC : febril, frenético
few[1] [ˈfjuː] *adj* **fewer; fewest** : pocos ⟨with few exceptions : con pocas excepciones⟩ ⟨a few times : varias veces⟩ ⟨fewer people : menos gente⟩ ⟨the fewest (number of) points : el menor número de puntos⟩
few[2] *pron* **fewer; fewest** **1** : pocos ⟨few (of them) were ready : pocos estaban listos⟩ ⟨the fewer, the better : cuantos menos mejor⟩ ⟨our group is the fewest in number : nuestro grupo tiene el menor

número de personas⟩ **2 a few** : algunos,
unos cuantos ⟨a few of the women came
: algunas de las mujeres vinieron⟩ ⟨I
read a few (of them) : leí algunos, leí
unos cuantos⟩ **3 few and far between**
: contados

fiancé [ˌfiːˌɑnˈseɪ, ˌfiːˈɑnˌseɪ] *n* : prometido
m, novio *m*

fiancée [ˌfiːˌɑnˈseɪ, ˌfiːˈɑnˌseɪ] *n* : pro-
metida *f*, novia *f*

fiasco [fiˈæsˌkoː] *n, pl* **-coes** : fiasco *m*,
fracaso *m*

fiat [ˈfiːˌɑt, -ˌæt, -ət;, ˈfaɪət, -ˌæt] *n* : decreto *m*, orden *m*

fib[1] [ˈfɪb] *vi* **fibbed; fibbing** *fam* : decir bolas

fib[2] *n fam* : bola *f fam*, mentira *f*

fibber [ˈfɪbər] *n* : mentirosillo *m*, -lla *f*;
cuentista *mf fam*

fiber *or* **fibre** [ˈfaɪbər] *n* : fibra *f*

fiberboard [ˈfaɪbərˌbord] *n* : cartón *m*
madera

fiberglass [ˈfaɪbərˌglæs] *n* : fibra *f* de vidrio

fibrous [ˈfaɪbrəs] *adj* : fibroso

fibula [ˈfɪbjələ] *n, pl* **-lae** [-ˌliː, -ˌlaɪ] *or* **-las**
: peroné *m*

fickle [ˈfɪkəl] *adj* : inconstante, voluble,
veleidoso

fickleness [ˈfɪkəlnəs] *n* : volubilidad *f*, inconstancia *f*, veleidad *f*

fiction [ˈfɪkʃən] *n* : ficción *f*

fictional [ˈfɪkʃənəl] *adj* : ficticio

fictitious [fɪkˈtɪʃəs] *adj* **1** IMAGINARY
: ficticio, imaginario **2** FALSE : falso,
ficticio

fiddle[1] [ˈfɪdəl] *vi* **-dled; -dling 1** : tocar el
violín **2 to fiddle with** : juguetear con,
toquetear

fiddle[2] *n* : violín *m*

fiddler [ˈfɪdlər, ˈfɪdələr] *n* : violinista *mf*

fiddlesticks [ˈfɪdəlˌstɪks] *interj* : ¡tonterías!

fidelity [fəˈdɛləti, faɪ-] *n, pl* **-ties** : fidelidad *f*

fidget[1] [ˈfɪdʒət] *vi* **1** : moverse, estarse inquieto **2 to fidget with** : juguetear con

fidget[2] *n* **1** : persona *f* inquieta **2 fid-
gets** *npl* RESTLESSNESS : inquietud *f*

fidgety [ˈfɪdʒəti] *adj* : inquieto

fiduciary[1] [fəˈduːʃiˌɛri, -ˈdjuː-, -ˌəri] *adj*
: fiduciario

fiduciary[2] *n, pl* **-ries** : fiduciario *m*, -ria *f*

field[1] [ˈfiːld] *vt* : interceptar y devolver
(una pelota), presentar (un candidato),
sortear (una pregunta)

field[2] *adj* : de campaña, de campo ⟨field
hospital : hospital de campaña⟩ ⟨field
goal : gol de campo⟩ ⟨field trip : viaje de
estudio⟩

field[3] *n* **1** : campo *m* (de cosechas, de
batalla, de magnetismo) **2** : campo *m*,
cancha *f* (en deportes) ⟨baseball field
: campo de beisbol⟩ ⟨left/right/center
field : jardín izquierdo/derecho/cen-
tral⟩ **3** : campo *m* (de trabajo), esfera *f*
(de actividades) ⟨the field of economics
: el campo de la economía⟩

fielder [ˈfiːldər] *n* : jugador *m*, -dora *f* de
campo; fildeador *m*, -dora *f*

field glasses *n* : binoculares *mpl*, gemelos *mpl*

field hockey *n* : hockey *m* sobre césped

fiend [ˈfiːnd] *n* **1** DEMON : demonio *m* **2**
EVILDOER : persona *f* maligna; malvado
m, -da *f* **3** FANATIC : fanático *m*, -ca *f*

fiendish [ˈfiːndɪʃ] *adj* : diabólico — **fiend-
ishly** *adv*

fierce [ˈfɪrs] *adj* **fiercer; -est 1** FERO-
CIOUS : fiero, feroz **2** HEATED : acalorado **3** INTENSE : intenso, violento,
fuerte — **fiercely** *adv*

fierceness [ˈfɪrsnəs] *n* **1** FEROCITY : ferocidad *f*, fiereza *f* **2** INTENSITY : intensidad *f*, violencia *f*

fieriness [ˈfaɪərinəs] *n* : pasión *f*, ardor *m*

fiery [ˈfaɪəri] *adj* **fierier; -est 1** BURNING
: ardiente, llameante **2** GLOWING : encendido **3** PASSIONATE : acalorado, ardiente, fogoso

fiesta [fiˈɛstə] *n* : fiesta *f*

fife [ˈfaɪf] *n* : pífano *m*

fifteen[1] [fɪfˈtiːn] *adj & pron* : quince

fifteen[2] *n* : quince *m*

fifteenth[1] [fɪfˈtiːnθ] *adj* : decimoquinto

fifteenth[2] *n* **1** : decimoquinto *m*, -ta *f* (en
una serie) **2** : quinceavo *m*, quinceava
parte *f*

fifth[1] [ˈfɪfθ] *adv* : en quinto lugar

fifth[2] *adj* : quinto ⟨(on) the fifth of June
: el cinco de junio⟩

fifth[3] *n* **1** : quinto *m*, -ta *f* (en una serie) **2** : quinto *m*, quinta parte *f* **3**
: quinta *f* (en la música) **4** *or* **fifth gear**
: quinta *f*

fiftieth[1] [ˈfɪftiəθ] *adj* : quincuagésimo

fiftieth[2] *n* **1** : quincuagésimo *m*, -ma *f* (en
una serie) **2** : cincuentavo *m*, cincuen-
tava parte *f*

fifty[1] [ˈfɪfti] *adj & pron* : cincuenta

fifty[2] *n, pl* **-ties** : cincuenta *m*

fifty–fifty[1] [ˌfɪftiˈfɪfti] *adv* : a medias, mitad
y mitad

fifty–fifty[2] *adj* **to have a fifty–fifty chance**
: tener un cincuenta por ciento de posibilidades

fig [ˈfɪg] *n* : higo *m*

fight[1] [ˈfaɪt] *v* **fought** [ˈfɔt]; **fighting** *vi* **1**
: luchar, combatir, pelear ⟨to fight to the
death : pelear a muerte⟩ ⟨to fight for
one's life : debatirse entre la vida y la
muerte⟩ **2 to fight back** : defenderse **3
to fight about/over** : discutir por **4 to
fight on** : seguir luchando — *vt* **1**
: luchar contra, combatir contra **2 to
fight back** SUPPRESS : reprimir, contener **3 to fight off** : rechazar, combatir

fight[2] *n* **1** COMBAT : lucha *f*, pelea *f*, combate *m* **2** MATCH : pelea *f*, combate *m*
(en boxeo) **3** QUARREL : disputa *f*, pelea
f, pleito *m*

fighter [ˈfaɪtər] *n* **1** COMBATANT : luchador *m*, -dora *f*; combatiente *mf* **2** BOXER
: boxeador *m*, -dora *f*

figment [ˈfɪgmənt] *n* **figment of the imagination** : producto *m* de la imaginación

figurative [ˈfɪgjərətɪv, -gə-] *adj* : figurado,
metafórico

figuratively [ˈfɪgjərətɪvli, -gə-] *adv* : en
sentido figurado, de manera metafórica

figure¹ ['fɪgjər, -gər] v **-ured; -uring** vt **1**
CALCULATE : calcular **2** ESTIMATE : figurarse, calcular ⟨he figured it was possible : se figuró que era posible⟩ **3 to figure in** : incluir en los cálculos **4 to figure out** : entender — vi **1** FEATURE,
STAND OUT : figurar, destacar **2 that figures!** : ¡obvio!, ¡no me extraña nada! **3
to figure on** : contar con, tener en
cuenta **4 to figure on doing something**
: pensar hacer algo
figure² n **1** DIGIT : número m, cifra f **2**
PRICE : precio m, cifra f **3** PERSONAGE
: figura f, personaje m **4** : figura f, tipo
m, físico m ⟨to have a good figure : tener
buen tipo, tener un buen físico⟩ **5** DE-
SIGN, OUTLINE : figura f **6 figures** npl
: aritmética f
figurehead ['fɪgjər‚hed, -gər-] n : testaferro m, líder mf sin poder
figure of speech n : figura f retórica, figura f de hablar
figure out vt **1** UNDERSTAND : entender **2** RESOLVE : resolver (un problema, etc.)
figurine [‚fɪgjəˈriːn] n : estatuilla f
filament ['fɪləmənt] n : filamento m
filbert ['fɪlbərt] n : avellana f
filch ['fɪltʃ] vt : hurtar, birlar fam
file¹ ['faɪl] v **filed; filing** vt **1** CLASSIFY
: clasificar **2** : archivar (documen-
tos) **3** SUBMIT : presentar ⟨to file
charges : presentar cargos⟩ **4** SMOOTH
: limar — vi : desfilar, entrar (o salir) en
fila
file² n **1** : lima f ⟨nail file : lima de
uñas⟩ **2** DOCUMENTS : archivo m **3**
LINE : fila f **4** : archivo m (de una computadora)
filial ['fɪliəl, 'fɪljəl] adj : filial
filibuster¹ ['fɪlə‚bʌstər] vi : practicar el obstruccionismo
filibuster² n : obstruccionismo m
filibusterer ['fɪlə‚bʌstərər] n : obstruccionista mf
filigree ['fɪlə‚griː] n : filigrana f
filing cabinet n : archivador m
Filipino [‚fɪləˈpiːnoː] n : filipino m, -na f —
Filipino adj
fill¹ ['fɪl] v **1** : llenar, ocupar ⟨to fill a cup
: llenar una taza⟩ ⟨to fill a room : ocupar
una sala⟩ **2** STUFF : rellenar **3** PLUG
: tapar, rellenar, empastar (un diente)
4 SATISFY : cumplir con, satisfacer **5** or
to fill in/out : rellenar, llenar ⟨fill (in) the
blanks : rellene los espacios⟩ ⟨to fill out
a form : rellenar un formulario⟩ **6 to fill
someone in on** : poner a alguien al corriente de **7 to fill up** : llenar (hasta
arriba) — vi or **to fill up** : llenarse ⟨her
eyes filled with tears : se le llenaron los
ojos de lágrimas⟩
fill² n **1** FILLING, STUFFING : relleno
m **2 to eat one's fill** : comer lo suficiente **3 to have one's fill of** : estar
harto de
filler ['fɪlər] n : relleno m
fillet¹ ['fɪlət, fɪˈleɪ, 'fɪ‚leɪ] vt : cortar en fi-
letes
fillet² n : filete m

fill in vt INFORM : informar, poner al corriente — vi **to fill in for** : reemplazar a
filling ['fɪlɪŋ] n **1** : relleno m **2** : empaste
m (de un diente)
filling station → **gas station**
filly ['fɪli] n, pl **-lies** : potra f, potranca f
film¹ ['fɪlm] vt : filmar — vi : rodar
film² n **1** COATING : capa f, película f **2**
: película f (fotográfica) **3** MOVIE
: película f, filme m
filmmaker ['fɪlm‚meɪkər] n : cineasta mf
filmy ['fɪlmi] adj **filmier; -est 1** GAUZY
: diáfano, vaporoso **2** : cubierto de una
película
filter¹ ['fɪltər] vt : filtrar
filter² n : filtro m
filth ['fɪlθ] n : mugre f, porquería f, roña f
filthiness ['fɪlθinəs] n : suciedad f
filthy ['fɪlθi] adj **filthier; -est 1** DIRTY
: mugriento, sucio **2** OBSCENE : obsceno, indecente
filtration [fɪlˈtreɪʃən] n : filtración f
fin ['fɪn] n **1** : aleta f **2** : alerón m (de un
automóvil o un avión)
finagle [fəˈneɪgəl] vt **-gled; -gling**
: arreglárselas para conseguir
final¹ ['faɪnəl] adj **1** DEFINITIVE : definitivo, final, inapelable **2** ULTIMATE : final **3** LAST : último, final
final² n **1** : final f (en deportes) **2 finals**
npl : exámenes mpl finales
finale [fɪˈnæli, -ˈnɑ-] n : final m ⟨grand finale : final triunfal⟩
finalist ['faɪnəlɪst] n : finalista mf
finality [faɪˈnæləṭi, fə-] n, pl **-ties** : finalidad f
finalize ['faɪnəl‚aɪz] vt **-ized; -izing** : finalizar
finally ['faɪnəli] adv **1** LASTLY : por
último, finalmente **2** EVENTUALLY
: por fin, al final **3** DEFINITIVELY : definitivamente
finance¹ [fəˈnænts, 'faɪ‚nænts] vt **-nanced;
-nancing** : financiar
finance² n **1** : finanzas fpl **2 finances**
npl RESOURCES : recursos mpl financie-
ros
financial [fəˈnæntʃəl, faɪ-] adj : financiero, económico
financially [fəˈnæntʃəli, faɪ-] adv
: económicamente
financier [‚fɪnənˈsɪr, ‚faɪ‚næn-] n : financiero m, -ra f; financista mf
financing [fəˈnæntsɪŋ, 'faɪ‚næntsɪŋ] n : financiación f, financiamiento m
finch ['fɪntʃ] n : pinzón m
find¹ ['faɪnd] vt found ['faʊnd]; **finding 1**
LOCATE : encontrar ⟨I can't find it : no
lo encuentro⟩ ⟨he was nowhere to be
found : no se lo encontraba por ninguna
parte⟩ **2** CHANCE UPON : encontrar
(por casualidad) ⟨I found a dollar : encontré un dólar⟩ **3** LEARN : encontrar,
descubrir ⟨to find the answer : encontrar la solución⟩ ⟨we found that . . .
: descubrimos que . . .⟩ **4** GET : encontrar, obtener ⟨to find the time to do
something : encontrar el tiempo para
hacer algo⟩ ⟨to find satisfaction in : obtener satisfacción de⟩ **5** PERCEIVE : en-

contrar ⟨I find it strange/difficult : lo encuentro raro/difícil, me resulta raro/difícil⟩ **6** DECLARE : declarar, hallar ⟨they found him guilty : lo declararon culpable⟩ **7 to find fault** : criticar **8 to find favor/approval** : ser bien recibido **9 to find oneself** ⟨she found herself in an unfamiliar place : se encontró en un lugar desconocido⟩ ⟨he found himself in a bad situation : se vio en apuros⟩ ⟨I found myself thinking about her : me di cuenta de que estaba pensando en ella⟩ **10 to find oneself** ⟨he left to find himself : se fue para encontrarse a sí mismo⟩ **11 to find one's way** : encontrar el camino, orientarse **12 to find out** : descubrir, averiguar

find² *n* : hallazgo *m*

finder ['faɪndər] *n* : descubridor *m*, -dora *f*

finding ['faɪndɪŋ] *n* **1** FIND : hallazgo *m* **2 findings** *npl* : conclusiones *fpl*

find out *vt* DISCOVER : descubrir, averiguar — *vi* LEARN : enterarse

fine¹ ['faɪn] *vt* **fined; fining** : multar

fine² *adj* **finer; finest** **1** PURE : puro (dícese del oro y de la plata) **2** THIN : fino, delgado **3** : fino ⟨fine sand : arena fina⟩ **4** SMALL : pequeño, minúsculo ⟨fine print : letras minúsculas⟩ **5** SUBTLE : sutil, delicado **6** EXCELLENT : excelente, magnífico, selecto **7** FAIR : bueno ⟨it's a fine day : hace buen tiempo⟩ **8** EXQUISITE : exquisito, delicado, fino **9 fine arts** : bellas artes *fpl*

fine³ *n* : multa *f*

finely ['faɪnli] *adv* **1** EXCELLENTLY : con arte **2** ELEGANTLY : elegantemente **3** PRECISELY : con precisión **4 to chop finely** : picar muy fino, picar en trozos pequeños

fineness ['faɪnnəs] *n* **1** EXCELLENCE : excelencia *f* **2** ELEGANCE : elegancia *f*, refinamiento *m* **3** DELICACY : delicadeza *f*, lo fino **4** PRECISION : precisión *f* **5** SUBTLETY : sutileza *f* **6** PURITY : ley *f* (de oro y plata)

finery ['faɪnəri] *n* : galas *fpl*, adornos *mpl*

finesse¹ [fə'nɛs] *vt* **-nessed; -nessing** : ingeniar

finesse² *n* **1** REFINEMENT : refinamiento *m*, finura *f* **2** TACT : delicadeza *f*, tacto *m*, diplomacia *f* **3** CRAFTINESS : astucia *f*

fine-tune ['faɪn'tu:n] *vt* **1** : poner a punto (un motor), ajustar **2** REFINE : afinar, ajustar

finger¹ ['fɪŋgər] *vt* **1** HANDLE : tocar, toquetear **2** ACCUSE : acusar, delatar

finger² *n* : dedo *m* ⟨to lay a finger on someone : ponerle a alguien la mano encima⟩ ⟨not to lift a finger : no mover un dedo, no hacer nada⟩ ⟨to point a finger at someone : culpar a alguien⟩ ⟨to put one's finger on it : dar en el clavo⟩ ⟨to work one's fingers to the bone : deslomarse trabajando⟩

fingerling ['fɪŋgərlɪŋ] *n* : pez *m* pequeño y joven

fingernail ['fɪŋgər,neɪl] *n* : uña *f*

fingerprint¹ ['fɪŋgər,prɪnt] *vt* : tomar las huellas digitales a

fingerprint² *n* : huella *f* digital

fingertip ['fɪŋgər,tɪp] *n* : punta *f* del dedo, yema *f* del dedo

finicky ['fɪnɪki] *adj* : maniático, melindroso, mañoso

finish¹ ['fɪnɪʃ] *vt* **1** COMPLETE : acabar, terminar **2** : aplicar un acabado a (muebles, etc.) **3** RUIN, DESTROY : acabar con **4 to finish off** : terminar **5 to finish up** : terminar — *vi* **1** : terminar **2 to finish up** : terminar, acabar

finish² *n* **1** END : fin *m*, final *m* **2** REFINEMENT : refinamiento *m* **3** : acabado *m* ⟨a glossy finish : un acabado brillante⟩

finish line *n* : línea *f* de meta

finite ['faɪ,naɪt] *adj* : finito

fink¹ ['fɪŋk] *vi fam* **to fink on someone** : delatar a alguien

fink² *n fam* : mequetrefe *mf fam*

Finn ['fɪn] *n* : finlandés *m*, -desa *f*

Finnish¹ ['fɪnɪʃ] *adj* : finlandés

Finnish² *n* : finlandés *m* (idioma)

fiord [fi'ɔrd] → **fjord**

fir ['fər] *n* : abeto *m*

fire¹ ['faɪr] *vt* **fired; firing** **1** IGNITE, KINDLE : encender **2** ENLIVEN : animar, avivar **3** DISMISS : despedir ⟨I was fired : me despidieron⟩ **4** SHOOT : disparar ⟨to fire a gun at someone : dispararle a alguien (con un arma de fuego)⟩ **5** BAKE : cocer (cerámica) **6 to fire off** : disparar (un arma, etc.) **7 to fire off** : lanzar (preguntas) **8 to fire up** ENERGIZE, MOTIVATE : entusiasmar **9 to fire up** START : arrancar, poner en marcha (un motor, etc.) — *vi* SHOOT : disparar ⟨to fire at someone : dispararle a alguien, disparar contra alguien⟩

fire² *n* **1** : fuego *m* **2** BURNING : incendio *m* ⟨forest fire : incendio forestal⟩ ⟨fire alarm : alarma contra incendios⟩ ⟨to be on fire : estar en llamas⟩ ⟨to catch (on) fire : prender fuego⟩ ⟨to set fire to : prenderle fuego a⟩ **3** ENTHUSIASM : ardor *m*, entusiasmo *m* **4** SHOOTING : fuego *m*, disparos *mpl* ⟨to open fire : abrir fuego⟩ ⟨to hold one's fire : hacer alto el fuego⟩ ⟨to come under enemy fire : ser sometido al fuego enemigo⟩ **5 to come under fire** : ser blanco de críticas

firearm ['faɪr,ɑrm] *n* : arma *f* de fuego

fireball ['faɪr,bɔl] *n* **1** : bola *f* de fuego **2** METEOR : bólido *m*

firebreak ['faɪr,breɪk] *n* : cortafuegos *m*

firebug ['faɪr,bʌg] *n* : pirómano *m*, -na *f*; incendiario *m*, -ria *f*

firecracker ['faɪr,krækər] *n* : petardo *m*

fire door *n* : puerta *f* cortafuegos

fire engine *n* : coche *m* de bomberos, autobomba *f*

fire escape *n* : escalera *f* de incendios

fire exit *n* : salida *f* de incendios

fire extinguisher *n* : extinguidor *m* de incendios

firefighter ['faɪr,faɪtər] *n* : bombero *m*, -ra *f*

firefly ['faɪr‚flaɪ] *n, pl* **-flies** : luciérnaga *f*
fireman ['faɪrmən] *n, pl* **-men** [-mən, -‚mɛn]
FIREFIGHTER : bombero *m*
fireplace ['faɪr‚pleɪs] *n* : hogar *m*, chimenea *f*
fireproof¹ ['faɪr‚pru:f] *vt* : hacer incombustible
fireproof² *adj* : incombustible, ignífugo
fireside¹ ['faɪr‚saɪd] *adj* : informal ⟨fireside chat : charla informal⟩
fireside² *n* **1** HEARTH : chimenea *f*, hogar *m* **2** HOME : hogar *m*, casa *f*
fire station *n* : estación *f* de bomberos
fire truck *n* → **fire engine**
firewall ['faɪr‚wɔl] *n* : cortafuegos *m*
firewood ['faɪr‚wʊd] *n* : leña *f*
fireworks ['faɪr‚wərks] *npl* : fuegos *mpl* artificiales, pirotecnia *f*
firing squad *n* : pelotón *m* de ejecución
firm¹ ['fərm] *vt or* **to firm up** : endurecer
firm² *adj* **1** VIGOROUS : fuerte, vigoroso **2** SOLID, UNYIELDING : firme, duro, sólido **3** UNCHANGING : firme, inalterable **4** RESOLUTE : firme, resuelto
firm³ *n* : empresa *f*, firma *f*, compañía *f*
firmament ['fərməmənt] *n* : firmamento *m*
firmly ['fərmli] *adv* : firmemente
firmness ['fərmnəs] *n* : firmeza *f*
first¹ ['fərst] *adv* **1** : primero ⟨finish your homework first : primero termina tu tarea⟩ ⟨first and foremost : ante todo⟩ ⟨first of all : en primer lugar⟩ **2** : por primera vez ⟨I saw it first in Boston : lo vi por primera vez en Boston⟩
first² *adj & pron* **1** : primero ⟨the first time : la primera vez⟩ ⟨the first of many : el primero de muchos, la primera de muchas⟩ ⟨at first sight : a primera vista⟩ ⟨in the first place : en primer lugar⟩ ⟨the first ten applicants : los diez primeros candidatos⟩ ⟨that's the first I've heard of it! : ¡(es la) primera noticia (que tengo)!, ¡ahora me entero!⟩ **2** FOREMOST : principal, primero ⟨first tenor : tenor principal⟩
first³ *n* **1** : primero *m*, -ra *f* ⟨the first of April : el primero/uno de abril⟩ **2** *or* **first base** : primera base *f* **3** *or* **first gear** : primera *f* **4** **at ~** : al principio
first aid *n* : primeros auxilios *mpl* ⟨first aid kit : botiquín⟩
firstborn *n* : primogénito *m*, -ta *f* — **firstborn** *adj*
first-class¹ ['fərst'klæs] *adv* : en primera ⟨to travel first-class : viajar en primera⟩
first-class² *adj* : de primera
first class *n* : primera clase *f*
firsthand¹ ['fərst'hænd] *adv* : directamente
firsthand² *adj* : de primera mano
first lady *n* : primera dama *f*
first lieutenant *n* : teniente *mf*; teniente primero *m*, teniente primera *f*
firstly ['fərstli] *adv* : primeramente, principalmente, en primer lugar
first name *n* : nombre *m* de pila
first-rate¹ ['fərst'reɪt] *adv* : muy bien
first-rate² *adj* : de primera, de primera clase
first sergeant *n* : sargento *mf*

firth ['fərθ] *n* : estuario *m*
fiscal ['fɪskəl] *adj* : fiscal — **fiscally** *adv*
fish¹ ['fɪʃ] *vi* **1** : pescar **2 to fish for** SEEK : buscar, rebuscar ⟨to fish for compliments : andar a la caza de cumplidos⟩ — *vt* : pescar
fish² *n, pl* **fish** *or* **fishes** : pez *m* (vivo), pescado *m* (para comer)
fishbowl ['fɪʃ‚bo:l] *n* : pecera *f*
fisherman ['fɪʃərmən] *n, pl* **-men** [-mən, ‚mɛn] : pescador *m*
fisherwoman ['fɪʃər‚wʊmən] *n, pl* **-women** [-‚wɪmən] : pescadora *f*
fishery ['fɪʃəri] *n, pl* **-eries** **1** → **fishing** **2** : zona *f* pesquera, pesquería *f*
fishhook ['fɪʃ‚hʊk] *n* : anzuelo *m*
fishing ['fɪʃɪŋ] *n* : pesca *f*, industria *f* pesquera
fishing pole *or* **fishing rod** *n* : caña *f* de pescar
fish market *n* : pescadería *f*
fish sticks *npl* : palitos *mpl* de pescado
fishy ['fɪʃi] *adj* **fishier; -est 1** : a pescado ⟨a fishy taste : un sabor a pescado⟩ **2** QUESTIONABLE : dudoso, sospechoso ⟨there's something fishy going on : aquí hay gato encerrado⟩
fission ['fɪʃən, -ʒən] *n* : fisión *f*
fissure ['fɪʃər] *n* : fisura *f*, hendidura *f*
fist ['fɪst] *n* : puño *m*
fist bump *n* : choque *m* de puños
fistful ['fɪst‚fʊl] *n* : puñado *m*
fisticuffs ['fɪstɪ‚kʌfs] *npl* : lucha *f* a puñetazos
fist pump *n* : acto *m* de batir un puño en el aire (para celebrar una victoria, etc.)
fit¹ ['fɪt] *v* **fitted; fitting** *vt* **1** MATCH : corresponder a, coincidir con ⟨the punishment fits the crime : el castigo corresponde al crimen⟩ **2** : quedar ⟨the dress doesn't fit me : el vestido no me queda⟩ **3** GO : caber, encajar ⟨her key fits the lock : su llave encaja en la cerradura⟩ **4** INSERT, INSTALL : poner, colocar **5** ADAPT : adecuar, ajustar, adaptar **6** *or* **to fit out** EQUIP : equipar **7 to fit in** : acomodar — *vi* **1** : quedar, entallar ⟨these pants don't fit : estos pantalones no me quedan⟩ **2** CONFORM : encajar, cuadrar **3 to fit in** : encajar, estar integrado **4 to fit in** : adaptarse (dícese de una persona)
fit² *adj* **fitter; fittest 1** SUITABLE : adecuado, apropiado, conveniente ⟨do as you see/think fit : haz lo que creas conveniente⟩ ⟨she didn't see fit to mention it : no juzgó necesario mencionarlo⟩ **2** QUALIFIED : calificado, competente **3** HEALTHY : sano, en forma ⟨to get/keep fit : ponerse/mantenerse en forma⟩
fit³ *n* **1** ATTACK : ataque *m*, acceso *m*, arranque *m* **2 to be a good fit** : quedar bien **3 to be a tight fit** : ser muy entallado (de ropa), estar apretado (de espacios)
fitful ['fɪtfəl] *adj* : irregular, intermitente — **fitfully** *adv*
fitness ['fɪtnəs] *n* **1** HEALTH : salud *f*, buena forma *f* (física) **2** SUITABILITY : idoneidad *f*

fitting[1] [ˈfɪtɪŋ] *adj* : adecuado, apropiado
fitting[2] *n* : accesorio *m*
fitting room *n* : probador *m*
five[1] [ˈfaɪv] *adj* : cinco ⟨the child is five (years old) : el niño tiene cinco años⟩
five[2] *n* : cinco *m* ⟨the five of hearts : el cinco de corazones⟩ ⟨it's five (o'clock) : son las cinco⟩
five[3] *pron* : cinco ⟨there are five of us : somos cinco⟩
five hundred[1] *adj & pron* : quinientos
five hundred[2] *n* : quinientos *m*
fiver [ˈfaɪvər] *n fam* : billete *m* de cinco dólares
fix[1] [ˈfɪks] *vt* **1** ATTACH, SECURE : sujetar, asegurar, fijar **2** ESTABLISH, SET : fijar (precios, fechas, etc.), concretar (planes, etc.) **3** : fijar (los ojos, la mirada, etc.) **4** REPAIR : arreglar, reparar **5** SOLVE : resolver, solucionar **6** PREPARE : preparar ⟨to fix dinner : preparar la cena⟩ **7** RIG : arreglar, amañar ⟨to fix a race : arreglar una carrera⟩ **8** ARRANGE : arreglar ⟨to fix one's hair/face : peinarse/maquillarse⟩ ⟨she fixed it so we won't have to pay : lo arregló para que no tengamos que pagar⟩ **9** PUNISH : castigar ⟨I'll fix him! : ¡se las verá conmigo!⟩ **10 to fix oneself up** : arreglarse **11 to fix someone up** : arreglarle una cita a alguien **12 to fix someone up** ⟨I'll fix you up : te lo arreglaré todo⟩ ⟨they fixed us up with a rental car : nos consiguió un auto/carro/coche de alquiler⟩ **13 to fix up** : arreglar (una casa, etc.)
fix[2] *n* **1** PREDICAMENT : aprieto *m*, apuro *m* **2** : posición *f* ⟨to get a fix on : establecer la posición de⟩
fixate [ˈfɪkˌseɪt] *vi* **-ated; -ating** : obsesionarse
fixation [fɪkˈseɪʒən] *n* : fijación *f*, obsesión *f*
fixed [ˈfɪkst] *adj* **1** STATIONARY : estacionario, inmóvil **2** UNCHANGING : fijo, inalterable **3** INTENT : fijo ⟨a fixed stare : una mirada fija⟩ **4 to be comfortably fixed** : estar en posición acomodada
fixedly [ˈfɪksədli] *adv* : fijamente
fixedness [ˈfɪksədnəs, ˈfɪkst-] *n* : rigidez *f*
fixture [ˈfɪkstʃər] *n* **1** : parte *f* integrante, elemento *m* fijo **2 fixtures** *npl* : instalaciones *fpl* (de una casa)
fizz[1] [ˈfɪz] *vi* : burbujear
fizz[2] *n* : efervescencia *f*
fizzle[1] [ˈfɪzəl] *vi* **-zled; -zling 1** FIZZ : burbujear **2** FAIL : fracasar
fizzle[2] *n* : fracaso *m*, fiasco *m*
fizzy [ˈfɪzi] *adj* **fizzier; -est** : gaseoso, efervescente
fjord [fiˈɔrd] *n* : fiordo *m*
flab [ˈflæb] *n* : gordura *f*
flabbergast [ˈflæbərˌgæst] *vt* : asombrar, pasmar, dejar atónito
flabby [ˈflæbi] *adj* **flabbier; -est** : blando, fofo, aguado *CA, Col, Mex*
flaccid [ˈflæksəd, ˈflæsəd] *adj* : fláccido
flag[1] [ˈflæg] *vi* **flagged; flagging 1** : hacer señales con banderas **2** WEAKEN : flaquear, desfallecer

flag[2] *n* : bandera *f*, pabellón *m*, estandarte *m*
flagon [ˈflægən] *n* : jarra *f* grande
flagpole [ˈflægˌpoːl] *n* : asta *f*, mástil *m*
flagrant [ˈfleɪɡrənt] *adj* : flagrante — **flagrantly** *adv*
flagship [ˈflægˌʃɪp] *n* : buque *m* insignia
flagstaff [ˈflægˌstæf] → **flagpole**
flagstone [ˈflægˌstoːn] *n* : losa *f*, piedra *f*
flail [ˈfleɪl] *vt* **1** : trillar (grano) **2** : sacudir, agitar (los brazos)
flair [ˈflær] *n* : don *m*, facilidad *f*
flak [ˈflæk] *ns & pl* **1** : fuego *m* antiaéreo **2** CRITICISM : críticas *fpl*
flake[1] [ˈfleɪk] *vi* **flaked; flaking** : desmenuzarse, pelarse (dícese de la piel)
flake[2] *n* : copo *m* (de nieve), escama *f* (de la piel), astilla *f* (de madera)
flamboyance [flæmˈbɔɪənts] *n* : extravagancia *f*
flamboyant [flæmˈbɔɪənt] *adj* : exuberante, extravagante, rimbombante
flame[1] [ˈfleɪm] *vi* **flamed; flaming 1** BLAZE : arder, llamear **2** GLOW : brillar, encenderse
flame[2] *n* BLAZE : llama *f* ⟨to burst into flames : estallar en llamas⟩ ⟨to go up in flame : incendiarse⟩
flamenco [fləˈmɛŋko] *n* : flamenco *m* (música o baile) — **flamenco** *adj*
flamethrower [ˈfleɪmˌθroːər] *n* : lanzallamas *m*
flamingo [fləˈmɪŋgo] *n, pl* **-gos** : flamenco *m*
flammable [ˈflæməbəl] *adj* : inflamable, flamable
flan [ˈflæn, ˈflɑn] *n* : flan *m*
flange [ˈflændʒ] *n* : reborde *m*, pestaña *f*
flank[1] [ˈflæŋk] *vt* **1** : flanquear (para defender o atacar) **2** BORDER, LINE : bordear
flank[2] *n* : ijada *f* (de un animal), costado *m* (de una persona), falda *f* (de una colina), flanco *m* (de un cuerpo de soldados)
flannel [ˈflænəl] *n* : franela *f*
flap[1] [ˈflæp] *v* **flapped; flapping** *vi* **1** : aletear ⟨the bird was flapping (its wings) : el pájaro aleteaba⟩ **2** FLUTTER : ondear, agitarse — *vt* : batir, agitar
flap[2] *n* **1** FLAPPING : aleteo *m* **2** : soplada *f* (de un sobre), hoja *f* (de una mesa), faldón *m* (de una chaqueta)
flapjack [ˈflæpˌdʒæk] → **pancake**
flare[1] [ˈflær] *vi* **flared; flaring 1** FLAME, SHINE : llamear, brillar **2** *or* **to flare up** : estallar, explotar (de cólera) ⟨tempers flared : se encendieron los ánimos⟩ **3 to flare up** : recrudecerse (dícese de una enfermedad)
flare[2] *n* **1** FLASH : destello *m* **2** SIGNAL : (luz *f* de) bengala *f* **3 solar flare** : erupción *f* solar
flare–up [ˈflærˌʌp] *n* **1** : llamarada *f* **2** OUTBREAK : estallido *m*, brote *m* **3** : empeoramiento *m* (de una enfermedad)
flash[1] [ˈflæʃ] *vi* **1** SHINE, SPARKLE : destellar, brillar, relampaguear **2** : pasar como un relámpago ⟨an idea

flashed through my mind : una idea me cruzó la mente como un relámpago⟩ — *vt* : despedir, lanzar (una luz), transmitir (un mensaje)

flash² *adj* SUDDEN : repentino

flash³ *n* 1 : destello *m* (de luz), fogonazo *m* (de una explosión) 2 **flash of lightning** : relámpago *m* 3 **in a flash** : de repente, de un abrir y cerrar los ojos

flashback ['flæʃˌbæk] *n* : flashback *m*

flash drive *n* : unidad *f* (de memoria) flash

flashiness ['flæʃinəs] *n* : ostentación *f*

flashlight ['flæʃˌlaɪt] *n* : linterna *f*

flash memory *n* : memoria *f* flash

flashy ['flæʃi] *adj* **flashier; -est** : llamativo, ostentoso

flask ['flæsk] *n* : frasco *m*

flat¹ ['flæt] *vt* **flatted; flatting** 1 FLATTEN : aplanar, achatar 2 : bajar de tono (en música)

flat² *adv* 1 EXACTLY : exactamente ⟨in ten minutes flat : en diez minutos exactos⟩ 2 : desafinado, demasiado bajo (en la música) ⟨to sing flat : cantar desafinado⟩ 3 HORIZONTALLY ⟨she fell flat on her back/face : cayó de espaldas/bruces⟩ ⟨lay the map flat on the desk : extiende el mapa sobre el escritorio⟩ 4 COMPLETELY : completamente ⟨I'm flat broke : estoy pelado⟩

flat³ *adj* **flatter; flattest** 1 EVEN, LEVEL : plano, llano 2 SMOOTH : liso 3 LOW : bajo (dícese de los zapatos, etc.) 4 SPREAD : tendido (dícese de una persona), extendido (dícese de una cosa) 5 DEFINITE : categórico, rotundo, explícito ⟨a flat refusal : una negativa categórica⟩ 6 : plano ⟨flat rate : tarifa plana⟩ 7 DULL : aburrido, soso, monótono (dícese de la voz) 8 DEFLATED : desinflado, pinchado, ponchado *Mex* 9 : bemol (en música) 10 : sin efervescencia 11 MATTE : mate

flat⁴ *n* 1 PLAIN : llano *m*, terreno *m* llano 2 : bemol *m* (en la música) 3 APARTMENT : apartamento *m*, departamento *m* 4 *or* **flat tire** : pinchazo *m*, ponchadura *f Mex* 5 **flats** *npl* : zapatos *mpl* bajos

flatbed ['flætˌbɛd] *n* : camión *m* de plataforma

flatcar ['flætˌkɑr] *n* : vagón *m* abierto

flatfish ['flætˌfɪʃ] *n* : platija *f*

flat–footed ['flætˌfʊtəd, ˌflæt'-] *adj* : de pies planos

flatly ['flætli] *adv* DEFINITELY : categóricamente, rotundamente

flatness ['flætnəs] *n* 1 EVENNESS : lo llano, lisura *f*, uniformidad *f* 2 DULLNESS : monotonía *f*

flat–out ['flæt'aʊt] *adj* 1 : frenético, a toda máquina ⟨a flat-out effort : un esfuerzo frenético⟩ 2 CATEGORICAL : descarado, rotundo, categórico

flatten ['flætən] *vt* : aplanar, achatar

flatter ['flætər] *vt* 1 OVERPRAISE : adular 2 COMPLIMENT : halagar 3 : favorecer ⟨the photo flatters you : la foto te favorece⟩

flatterer ['flætərər] *n* : adulador *m*, -dora *f*

flattering ['flætərɪŋ] *adj* 1 COMPLIMENTARY : halagador 2 BECOMING : favorecedor

flattery ['flætəri] *n, pl* **-ries** : halagos *mpl*

flatulence ['flætʃələnts] *n* : flatulencia *f*, ventosidad *f*

flatulent ['flætʃələnt] *adj* : flatulento

flatware ['flætˌwær] *n* : cubertería *f*, cubiertos *mpl*

flaunt¹ ['flɔnt] *vt* : alardear, hacer alarde de

flaunt² *n* : alarde *m*, ostentación *f*

flavor¹ ['fleɪvər] *vt* : dar sabor a, sazonar

flavor² *n* 1 : gusto *m*, sabor *m* 2 → **flavoring**

flavored ['fleɪvərd] *adj* : con sabor

flavorful ['fleɪvərfəl] *adj* : sabroso

flavoring ['fleɪvərɪŋ] *n* : condimento *m*, sazón *f* ⟨artificial flavoring : saborizante artificial⟩

flavorless ['fleɪvərləs] *adj* : sin sabor

flaw ['flɔ] *n* : falla *f*, defecto *m*, imperfección *f*

flawed ['flɔd] *adj* : imperfecto, con defectos

flawless ['flɔləs] *adj* : impecable, perfecto — **flawlessly** *adv*

flax ['flæks] *n* : lino *m*

flaxen ['flæksən] *adj* : rubio, blondo (dícese del pelo)

flay ['fleɪ] *vt* 1 SKIN : desollar, despellejar 2 VILIFY : criticar con dureza, vilipendiar

flea ['fli:] *n* : pulga *f*

flea market *n* : mercado *m* de pulgas, tianguis *m Mex*, mercadillo *m Spain*

fleck¹ ['flɛk] *vt* : salpicar

fleck² *n* : mota *f*, pinta *f*

fledgling ['flɛdʒlɪŋ] *n* : polluelo *m*, pollito *m*

flee ['fli:] *v* **fled** ['flɛd]; **fleeing** *vi* : huir, escapar(se) — *vt* : huir de

fleece¹ ['fli:s] *vt* **fleeced; fleecing** 1 SHEAR : esquilar, trasquilar 2 SWINDLE : estafar, defraudar

fleece² *n* : lana *f*, vellón *m*

fleet¹ ['fli:t] *vi* : moverse con rapidez

fleet² *adj* SWIFT : rápido, veloz

fleet³ *n* : flota *f*

fleet admiral *n* : almirante *mf*

fleeting ['fli:tɪŋ] *adj* : fugaz, breve

Fleming ['flɛmɪŋ] *n* : flamenco *m*, -ca *f*

Flemish ['flɛmɪʃ] *n* 1 **the Flemish** (*used with a plural verb*) : los flamencos *mpl* — 2 : flamenco *m* (idioma) — **Flemish** *adj*

flesh ['flɛʃ] *n* 1 : carne *f* (de seres humanos y animales) 2 : pulpa *f* (de frutas)

flesh out *vt* : desarrollar, darle cuerpo a

fleshy ['flɛʃi] *adj* **fleshier; -est** : gordo (dícese de las personas), carnoso (dícese de la fruta)

flew → **fly**

flex ['flɛks] *vt* : doblar, flexionar

flexibility [ˌflɛksə'bɪləti] *n, pl* **-ties** : flexibilidad *f*, elasticidad *f*

flexible ['flɛksəbəl] *adj* : flexible — **flexibly** [-bli] *adv*

flextime ['flɛksˌtaɪm] *n* : horario *m* flexible

flick¹ ['flɪk] *vt* : dar un capirotazo a (con el

dedo) ⟨to flick a switch : darle al interruptor⟩ — *vi* **1** FLIT : revolotear **2 to flick through** : hojear (un libro)

flick² *n* : coletazo *m* (de una cola), capirotazo *m* (de un dedo)

flicker¹ ['flɪkər] *vi* **1** FLUTTER : revolotear, aletear **2** BLINK, TWINKLE : parpadear, titilar

flicker² *n* **1** : parpadeo *m*, titileo *m* **2** HINT, TRACE : indicio *m*, rastro *m* ⟨a flicker of hope : un rayo de esperanza⟩

flier ['flaɪər] *n* **1** AVIATOR : aviador *m*, -dora *f* **2** CIRCULAR : folleto *m* publicitario, circular *f*

flight ['flaɪt] *n* **1** : vuelo *m* (de aves o aviones), trayectoria *f* (de proyectiles) **2** TRIP : vuelo *m* **3** FLOCK, SQUADRON : bandada *f* (de pájaros), escuadrilla *f* (de aviones) **4** ESCAPE : huida *f*, fuga *f* **5 flight of fancy** : ilusiones *fpl*, fantasía *f* **6 flight of stairs** : tramo *m*

flight attendant *n* : auxiliar *mf* de vuelo

flightless ['flaɪtləs] *adj* : no volador

flighty ['flaɪṭi] *adj* **flightier; -est** : caprichoso, frívolo

flimsy [flɪmzi] *adj* **flimsier; -est 1** LIGHT, THIN : ligero, fino **2** WEAK : endeble, poco sólido **3** IMPLAUSIBLE : pobre, flojo, poco convincente ⟨a flimsy excuse : una excusa floja⟩

flinch ['flɪntʃ] *vi* **1** WINCE : estremecerse **2** RECOIL : recular, retroceder

fling¹ ['flɪŋ] *vt* **flung** ['flʌŋ]; **flinging 1** THROW : lanzar, tirar, arrojar **2 to fling oneself** : lanzarse, tirarse, precipitarse

fling² *n* **1** THROW : lanzamiento *m* **2** ATTEMPT : intento *m* **3** AFFAIR : aventura *f* **4** BINGE : juerga *f*

flint ['flɪnt] *n* : pedernal *m*

flinty ['flɪnti] *adj* **flintier; -est 1** : de pedernal **2** STERN, UNYIELDING : severo, inflexible

flip¹ ['flɪp] *v* **flipped; flipping** *vt* **1** TOSS : tirar ⟨to flip a coin : echar a cara o cruz⟩ **2** OVERTURN : dar la vuelta a, voltear — *vi* **1** : moverse bruscamente **2 to flip through** : hojear (un libro)

flip² *adj* : insolente, descarado

flip³ *n* **1** FLICK : capirotazo *m*, golpe *m* ligero **2** SOMERSAULT : voltereta *f*

flip–flop ['flɪp‚flɑp] *n* **1** REVERSAL : giro *m* radical **2** THONG : chancla *f*, chancleta *f*

flippancy ['flɪpəntsi] *n*, *pl* -cies : ligereza *f*, falta *f* de seriedad

flippant ['flɪpənt] *adj* : ligero, frívolo, poco serio

flipper ['flɪpər] *n* : aleta *f*

flirt¹ ['flərt] *vi* **1** : coquetear, flirtear **2** TRIFLE : jugar ⟨to flirt with death : jugar con la muerte⟩

flirt² *n* : coqueto *m*, -ta *f*

flirtation [‚flər'teɪʃən] *n* : devaneo *m*, coqueteo *m*

flirtatious [‚flər'teɪʃəs] *adj* : insinuante, coqueto

flit ['flɪt] *vi* **flitted; flitting 1** : revolotear **2 to flit about** : ir y venir rápidamente

float¹ ['floːt] *vi* **1** : flotar **2** WANDER : vagar, errar — *vt* **1** : poner a flote, hacer flotar (un barco) **2** LAUNCH : hacer flotar (una empresa) **3** ISSUE : emitir (acciones en la bolsa)

float² *n* **1** : flotador *m*, corcho *m* (para pescar) **2** BUOY : boya *f* **3** : carroza *f* (en un desfile)

floating ['floːṭɪŋ] *adj* : flotante

flock¹ ['flɑk] *vi* **1** : moverse en rebaño **2** CONGREGATE : congregarse, reunirse

flock² *n* : rebaño *m* (de ovejas), bandada *f* (de pájaros)

floe ['floː] *n* : témpano *m* de hielo

flog ['flɑg] *vt* **flogged; flogging** : azotar, fustigar

flood¹ ['flʌd] *vt* : inundar, anegar

flood² *n* **1** INUNDATION : inundación *f* **2** TORRENT : avalancha *f*, diluvio *m*, torrente *m* ⟨a flood of tears : un mar de lágrimas⟩

floodgate ['flʌd‚geɪt] *n* : compuerta *f*, esclusa *f* ⟨to open the floodgates for/to : abrirle las puertas a, desatar una ola de⟩

flooding ['flʌdɪŋ] *n* : inundación *f*

floodlight ['flʌd‚laɪt] *n* : foco *m*

floodwater ['flʌd‚wɔṭər] *n* : crecida *f*, creciente *f*

floor¹ ['flor] *vt* **1** : solar, poner suelo a (una casa o una sala) **2** KNOCK DOWN : derribar, echar al suelo **3** NONPLUS : desconcertar, confundir, dejar perplejo

floor² *n* **1** : suelo *m*, piso *m* ⟨dance floor : pista *f* de baile⟩ **2** STORY : piso *m*, planta *f* ⟨ground floor : planta baja⟩ ⟨second floor : primer piso⟩ **3** : mínimo *m* (de sueldos, precios, etc.)

floorboard ['flor‚bord] *n* : tabla *f* del suelo, suelo *m*, piso *m*

flooring ['florɪŋ] *n* : entarimado *m*

floor show *n* : espectáculo *m* (en un cabaret, etc.)

floor tile → **tile²**

flop¹ ['flɑp] *vi* **flopped; flopping 1** FLAP : golpearse, agitarse **2** COLLAPSE : dejarse caer, desplomarse **3** FAIL : fracasar

flop² *n* **1** FAILURE : fracaso *m* **2 to take a flop** : caerse

floppy ['flɑpi] *adj* **floppier; -est 1** : blando, flexible **2 floppy disk** : diskette *m*, disquete *m*

flora ['florə] *n* : flora *f*

floral ['florəl] *adj* : floral, floreado

florid ['florɪd] *adj* **1** FLOWERY : florido **2** REDDISH : rojizo

florist ['florɪst] *n* : florista *mf*

floss¹ ['flɔs] *vi* : limpiarse los dientes con hilo dental

floss² *n* **1** : hilo *m* de seda (de bordar) **2** → **dental floss**

flotation [flo'teɪʃən] *n* : flotación *f*

flotilla [flo'tɪlə] *n* : flotilla *f*

flotsam ['flɑtsəm] *n* **1** : restos *mpl* flotantes (en el mar) **2 flotsam and jetsam** : desechos *mpl*, restos *mpl*

flounce¹ ['flaʊnts] *vi* **flounced; flouncing** : moverse haciendo aspavientos ⟨she flounced into the room : entró en la sala haciendo aspavientos⟩

flounce² *n* **1** RUFFLE : volante *m* **2** FLOURISH : aspaviento *m*

flounder [ˈflaʊndər] *vi* **1** STRUGGLE : forcejear **2** STUMBLE : no saber qué hacer o decir, perder el hilo (en un discurso)

flounder² *n, pl* **flounder** *or* **flounders** : platija *f*

flour¹ [ˈflaʊər] *vt* : enharinar

flour² *n* : harina *f*

flourish¹ [ˈflərɪʃ] *vi* THRIVE : florecer, prosperar, crecer (dícese de las plantas) — *vt* BRANDISH : blandir

flourish² *n* : floritura *f*, floreo *m*

flourishing [ˈflərɪʃɪŋ] *adj* : floreciente, próspero

flout [ˈflaʊt] *vt* : desobedecer (una regla, etc.) descaradamente

flow¹ [ˈfloː] *vi* **1** COURSE : fluir, manar, correr **2** CIRCULATE : circular, correr ⟨traffic is flowing smoothly : el tránsito está circulando con fluidez⟩

flow² *n* **1** FLOWING : flujo *m*, circulación *f* **2** STREAM : corriente *f*, chorro *m*

flow chart *n* : diagrama *m*, organigrama *m*

flower¹ [ˈflaʊər] *vi* : florecer, florear

flower² *n* : flor *f*

flowerbed [ˈflaʊərˌbɛd] *n* : arriate *m Mex, Spain*; cantero *m*

flowered [ˈflaʊərd] *adj* : florido, floreado

floweriness [ˈflaʊərinəs] *n* : floritura *f*

flowering¹ [ˈflaʊərɪŋ] *adj* : floreciente

flowering² *n* : floración *f*, florecimiento *m*

flowerpot [ˈflaʊərˌpɑt] *n* : maceta *f*, tiesto *m*, macetero *m*

flowery [ˈflaʊəri] *adj* **1** : florido **2** FLOWERED : floreado, de flores

flowing [ˈfloːɪŋ] *adj* : fluido, corriente

flown → fly

flu [ˈfluː] *n* : gripe *f*, gripa *f Col, Mex*

fluctuate [ˈflʌktʃuˌeɪt] *vi* -ated; -ating : fluctuar

fluctuation [ˌflʌktʃuˈeɪʃən] *n* : fluctuación *f*

flue [ˈfluː] *n* : tiro *m*, salida *f* de humos

fluency [ˈfluːəntsi] *n* : fluidez *f*, soltura *f*

fluent [ˈfluːənt] *adj* : fluido

fluently [ˈfluːəntli] *adv* : con soltura, con fluidez

fluff¹ [ˈflʌf] *vt* **1** : ahuecar (una almohada, etc.) **2** BUNGLE : echar a perder, equivocarse

fluff² *n* **1** FUZZ : pelusa *f* **2** DOWN : plumón *m*

fluffy [ˈflʌfi] *adj* **fluffier; -est 1** DOWNY : lleno de pelusa, velloso **2** SPONGY : esponjoso

fluid¹ [ˈfluːɪd] *adj* : fluido

fluid² *n* : fluido *m*, líquido *m*

fluidity [fluˈɪdəti] *n* : fluidez *f*

fluid ounce *n* : onza *f* líquida (29.57 mililitros)

fluke [ˈfluːk] *n* : golpe *m* de suerte, chiripa *f*, casualidad *f*

flummox [ˈflʌməks] *vt* CONFUSE : desconcertar

flung → fling

flunk [ˈflʌŋk] *vt* FAIL : reprobar — *vi* : salir reprobando

fluorescence [ˌflʊrˈɛsənts, ˌflɔr-] *n* : fluorescencia — **fluorescent** [ˌflʊrˈɛsənt, ˌflɔr-] *adj* ⟨fluorescent light : (luz) fluorescente⟩

fluoride [ˈflɔrˌaɪd, ˈflʊr-] *n* : fluoruro *m*

fluorine [ˈflɔrˌiːn] *n* : flúor *m*

flurry [ˈfləri] *n, pl* -ries **1** GUST : ráfaga *f* **2** SNOWFALL : nevisca *f* **3** BUSTLE : frenesí *m*, bullicio *m* **4** BARRAGE : aluvión *m*, oleada *f* ⟨a flurry of questions : un aluvión de preguntas⟩

flush¹ [ˈflʌl] *vt* **1** : limpiar con agua ⟨to flush the toilet : jalar la cadena⟩ **2** RAISE : hacer salir, levantar (en la caza) — *vi* BLUSH : ruborizarse, sonrojarse

flush² *adv* : al mismo nivel, a ras

flush³ *adj* **1** *or* **flushed** [ˈflʌlt] : colorado, rojo, encendido (dícese de la cara) **2** FILLED : lleno a rebosar **3** ABUNDANT : copioso, abundante **4** AFFLUENT : adinerado **5** ALIGNED, SMOOTH : alineado, liso **6 flush against** : pegado a, contra

flush⁴ *n* **1** FLOW, JET : chorro *m*, flujo *m* rápido **2** SURGE : arrebato *m*, arranque *m* ⟨a flush of anger : un arrebato de cólera⟩ **3** BLUSH : rubor *m*, sonrojo *m* **4** GLOW : resplandor *m*, flor *f* ⟨the flush of youth : la flor de la juventud⟩ ⟨in the flush of victory : en la euforia del triunfo⟩

fluster¹ [ˈflʌstər] *vt* : poner nervioso, aturdir

fluster² *n* : agitación *f*, confusión *f*

flute [ˈfluːt] *n* : flauta *f*

fluted [ˈfluːtəd] *adj* **1** GROOVED : acanalado **2** WAVY : ondulado

fluting [ˈfluːtɪŋ] *n* : estrías *fpl*

flutist [ˈfluːtɪst] *n* : flautista *mf*

flutter¹ [ˈflʌtər] *vi* **1** : revolotear (dícese de un pájaro), ondear (dícese de una bandera), palpitar con fuerza (dícese del corazón) **2 to flutter about** : ir y venir, revolotear — *vt* : sacudir, batir

flutter² *n* **1** FLUTTERING : revoloteo *m*, aleteo *m* **2** COMMOTION, STIR : revuelo *m*, agitación *f*

flux [ˈflʌks] *n* **1** : flujo *m* (en física y medicina) **2** CHANGE : cambio *m* ⟨to be in a state of flux : estar cambiando continuamente⟩

fly¹ [ˈflaɪ] *v* **flew** [ˈfluː]; **flown** [ˈfloːn]; **flying** *vi* **1** : volar ⟨the birds flew off/away : los pájaros se echaron a volar⟩ **2** TRAVEL : volar ⟨we flew to Europe : volamos a Europa, fuimos en avión a Europa⟩ **3** SOAR, SAIL : volar ⟨he tripped and went flying : se tropezó y salió volando⟩ ⟨clouds flew across the sky : las nubes pasaban rápido por el cielo⟩ ⟨bullets were flying in all directions : las balas silbaban en todas direcciones⟩ **4** : ondear (dícese de una bandera, etc.) **5** FLEE : huir, escapar **6** RUSH : correr, irse volando **7** : correr (dícese de rumores), lanzarse (dícese de insultos) **8** PASS : pasar (volando) ⟨how time flies! : ¡cómo pasa el tiempo!⟩ ⟨our vacation flew by : las vacaciones se nos pasaron volando⟩ **9 to fly open** : abrir de golpe

— *vt* **1** : pilotar (un avión), hacer volar (una cometa) **2** : transportar, llevar (en avión)

fly² *n*, *pl* **flies 1** : mosca *f* ⟨to drop like flies : caer como moscas⟩ **2** : bragueta *f* (de pantalones, etc.)

flyer → **flier**

flying saucer *n* : platillo *m* volador

flypaper ['flaɪˌpeɪpər] *n* : papel *m* matamoscas

flyswatter ['flaɪˌswɑt̬ər] *n* : matamoscas *m*

flywheel ['flaɪˌʍiːl] *n* : volante *m*

foal¹ ['foːl] *vi* : parir

foal² *n* : potro *m*, -tra *f*

foam¹ ['foːm] *vi* : hacer espuma

foam² *n* : espuma *f*

foam rubber *n* : goma *f* espuma, hule *m* espuma *Mex*

foamy ['foːmi] *adj* **foamier; -est** : espumoso

focal ['foːkəl] *adj* **1** : focal, central **2 focal point** : foco *m*, punto *m* de referencia

fo'c'sle ['foːksəl] → **forecastle**

focus¹ ['foːkəs] *v* **-cused** *or* **-cussed; -cusing** *or* **-cussing** *vt* **1** : enfocar (un instrumento) **2** CONCENTRATE : concentrar, centrar — *vi* : enfocar, fijar la vista

focus² *n*, *pl* **-ci** ['foːˌsaɪ, -ˌkaɪ] **1** : foco *m* ⟨to be in focus : estar enfocado⟩ **2** FOCUSING : enfoque *m* **3** CENTER : centro *m*, foco *m*

fodder ['fɑdər] *n* : pienso *m*, forraje *m*

foe ['foː] *n* : enemigo *m*, -ga *f*

fog¹ ['fɔɡ, 'fɑɡ] *v* **fogged; fogging** *vt* : empañar — *vi* **to fog up** : empañarse

fog² *n* : niebla *f*, neblina *f*

foggy ['fɔɡi, 'fɑ-] *adj* **foggier; -est** : nebuloso, brumoso

foghorn ['fɔɡˌhɔrn, 'fɑɡ-] *n* : sirena *f* de niebla

fogy ['foːɡi] *n*, *pl* **-gies** : carca *mf fam*, persona *f* chapada a la antigua

foible ['fɔɪbəl] *n* : flaqueza *f*, debilidad *f*

foil¹ ['fɔɪl] *vt* : frustrar, hacer fracasar

foil² *n* **1** : lámina *f* de metal, papel *m* de aluminio **2** CONTRAST : contraste *m*, complemento *m* **3** SWORD : florete *m* (en esgrima)

foist ['fɔɪst] *vt* : encajar, endilgar *fam*, colocar

fold¹ ['foːld] *vt* **1** BEND : doblar, plegar **2** CLASP : cruzar (brazos), enlazar (manos), plegar (alas) **3** EMBRACE : estrechar, abrazar **4 to fold in** : incorporar ⟨fold in the cream : incorpore la crema⟩ **5 to fold up** : doblar, plegar — *vi* **1** FAIL : fracasar, venirse abajo **2 to fold up** : doblarse, plegarse

fold² *n* **1** SHEEPFOLD : redil *m* (para ovejas) **2** FLOCK : rebaño *m* ⟨to return to the fold : volver al redil⟩ **3** CREASE : pliegue *m*, doblez *m*

-fold [ˌfoːld] *suf* **1** : (multiplicado) por ⟨to increase fourfold : multiplicarse por cuatro, cuadruplicarse⟩ ⟨there's been a tenfold increase in thefts : el número de robos se ha multiplicado por diez⟩ **2** (*indicating a number of parts*) ⟨a three-

fold problem : un problema que tiene tres aspectos⟩

folder ['foːldər] *n* **1** CIRCULAR : circular *f*, folleto *m* **2** BINDER : carpeta *f* **3** : carpeta *f*, directorio *m* (en informática)

foliage ['foːliɪd̠ʒ, -lɪd̠ʒ] *n* : follaje *m*

folio ['foːliˌoː] *n*, *pl* **-lios** : folio *m*

folk¹ ['foːk] *adj* : popular, folklórico ⟨folk customs : costumbres populares⟩ ⟨folk dance : danza folklórica⟩ ⟨folk music : (música) folk⟩

folk² *n*, *pl* **folk** *or* **folks 1** PEOPLE : gente *f* **2** : folk *m*, música *f* folk **3 folks** *npl* : familia *f*, padres *mpl*

folklore ['foːkˌlor] *n* : folklore *m*

folksy ['foːksi] *adj* **folksier; -est** : campechano

follicle ['fɑlɪkəl] *n* : folículo *m*

follow ['fɑlo] *vt* **1** : seguir (un camino, a una persona, etc.) **2** PURSUE : seguir, perseguir **3** : venir después de, seguir a (en una serie, etc.) **4** OBEY : seguir (instrucciones, etc.), cumplir (la ley, etc.) **5** MONITOR : seguir **6** UNDERSTAND : entender ⟨I don't follow you : no (te) entiendo⟩ **7 to follow suit** : hacer lo mismo **8 to follow up** : darle seguimiento a (un caso, etc.), seguir (una pista) — *vi* **1** : seguir **2** UNDERSTAND : entender **3 as follows** ⟨it reads as follows . . . : dice lo siguiente . . . , dice así . . .⟩ **4 it follows that . . .** : se deduce que . . . **5 to follow through** : continuar con algo **6 to follow through on/with** : continuar con (un plan, etc.), cumplir (una promesa, etc.) **7 to follow up** : dar seguimiento ⟨to follow up (on) a lead : seguir una pista⟩ ⟨he followed up with us later : nos contactó después⟩ ⟨she followed up with another best seller : después sacó otro best-seller⟩

follower ['fɑloər] *n* : seguidor *m*, -dora *f*

following¹ ['fɑloɪŋ] *adj* NEXT : siguiente

following² *n* FOLLOWERS : seguidores *mpl*

following³ *prep* AFTER : después de

follow–up ['fɑloˌʌp] *n* : continuación *f*, seguimiento *m*

folly ['fɑli] *n*, *pl* **-lies** : locura *f*, desatino *m*

foment [foˈmɛnt] *vt* : fomentar

fond ['fɑnd] *adj* **1** LOVING : cariñoso, tierno **2** PARTIAL : aficionado **3** FERVENT : ferviente, fervoroso

fondle ['fɑndəl] *vt* **-dled; -dling** : acariciar

fondly ['fɑndli] *adv* : cariñosamente, afectuosamente

fondness ['fɑndnəs] *n* **1** LOVE : cariño *m* **2** LIKING : afición *f*

fondue [fɑnˈduː, -ˈdjuː] *n* : fondue *f*

font ['fɑnt] *n* **1** *or* **baptismal font** : pila *f* bautismal **2** FOUNTAIN : fuente *f*

food ['fuːd] *n* : comida *f*, alimento *m*

food chain *n* : cadena *f* alimenticia

food poisoning *n* : intoxicación *f* alimenticia

food processor *n* : robot *m* de cocina

foodstuff ['fuːdˌstʌf] *n* : comestible *m*, producto *m* alimenticio

fool¹ ['fuːl] *vi* **1** JOKE : bromear, hacer el tonto ⟨I was only fooling : sólo estaba bromeando⟩ **2** *or* **to fool around** TOY

: jugar, juguetear ⟨don't fool (around) with the computer : no juegues con la computadora⟩ **3 to fool around** : perder el tiempo ⟨he fools around instead of working : pierde el tiempo en vez de trabajar⟩ **4 to fool around** : tener líos (amorosos) — *vt* DECEIVE : engañar, burlar ⟨he had me fooled : me tenía convencido⟩ ⟨he fooled me into thinking that . . . : me hizo creer que . . .⟩ ⟨stop fooling yourself! : ¡desengáñate!⟩

fool² *n* **1** IDIOT : idiota *mf*; tonto *m*, -ta *f*; bobo *m*, -ba *f* **2** JESTER : bufón *m*, -fona *f* **3 to make a fool of** : poner/dejar en ridículo, hacer quedar en ridículo ⟨to make a fool of oneself : hacer el ridículo, quedar en ridículo⟩

foolhardiness [ˈfuːlˌhɑrdinəs] *n* : imprudencia *f*

foolhardy [ˈfuːlˌhɑrdi] *adj* RASH : imprudente, temerario, precipitado

foolish [ˈfuːlɪʃ] *adj* **1** STUPID : insensato, estúpido **2** SILLY : idiota, tonto

foolishly [ˈfuːlɪʃli] *adv* : tontamente

foolishness [ˈfuːlɪʃnəs] *n* : insensatez *f*, estupidez *f*, tontería *f*

foolproof [ˈfuːlˌpruːf] *adj* : infalible

foot [ˈfʊt] *n*, *pl* **feet** [ˈfiːt] **1** : pie *m* ⟨to go on foot : ir a pie⟩ ⟨to be on one's feet : estar de pie⟩ **2 to get/start off on the wrong foot** : empezar con mal pie **3 to put one's best foot forward** : tratar de dejar una buena impresión **4 to put one's foot down** : no ceder **5 to put one's foot in one's mouth** : meter la pata **6 to stand on one's own two feet** : valerse por sí mismo **7 to think on one's feet** : pensar con rapidez

footage [ˈfʊtɪʤ] *n* : medida *f* en pies, metraje *m* (en el cine)

football [ˈfʊtˌbɔl] *n* : futbol *m* americano, fútbol *m* americano

footbridge [ˈfʊtˌbrɪʤ] *n* : pasarela *f*, puente *m* peatonal

foothills [ˈfʊtˌhɪlz] *npl* : estribaciones *fpl*

foothold [ˈfʊtˌhoːld] *n* **1** : punto *m* de apoyo **2 to gain a foothold** : afianzarse en una posición

footing [ˈfʊtɪŋ] *n* **1** BALANCE : equilibrio *m* **2** FOOTHOLD : punto *m* de apoyo **3** BASIS : base *f* ⟨on an equal footing : en igualdad⟩

footlights [ˈfʊtˌlaɪts] *npl* : candilejas *fpl*

footlocker [ˈfʊtˌlɑkər] *n* : baúl *m* pequeño, cofre *m*

footloose [ˈfʊtˌluːs] *adj* : libre y sin compromiso

footman [ˈfʊtmən] *n*, *pl* **-men** [-mən, -ˌmɛn] : lacayo *m*

footnote [ˈfʊtˌnoːt] *n* : nota *f* al pie de la página

footpath [ˈfʊtˌpæθ] *n* : sendero *m*, senda *f*, vereda *f*

footprint [ˈfʊtˌprɪnt] *n* : huella *f*

footrace [ˈfʊtˌreɪs] *n* : carrera *f* pedestre

footrest [ˈfʊtˌrɛst] *n* : apoyapiés *m*, reposapiés *m*

footstep [ˈfʊtˌstɛp] *n* **1** STEP : paso *m* **2** FOOTPRINT : huella *f*

footstool [ˈfʊtˌstuːl] *n* : taburete *m*, escabel *m*

footwear [ˈfʊtˌwær] *n* : calzado *m*

footwork [ˈfʊtˌwərk] *n* : juego *m* de piernas, juego *m* de pies

for¹ [ˈfɔr] *conj* : puesto que, porque

for² *prep* **1** (*indicating purpose*) : para, de, por ⟨the food for the party : la comida para la fiesta⟩ ⟨clothes for children : ropa para niños⟩ ⟨it's time for dinner : es la hora de comer⟩ ⟨to travel for pleasure : viajar por placer⟩ ⟨what's that for? : ¿para qué es/sirve eso?⟩ **2** (*indicating a recipient*) : para ⟨a gift for you : un regalo para ti⟩ **3** (*indicating an object of thoughts or feelings*) : por ⟨his admiration for her : su admiración por ella⟩ ⟨I feel sorry for him : le tengo lástima⟩ **4** BECAUSE OF : por ⟨for fear of : por miedo de⟩ ⟨to jump for joy : saltar de alegría⟩ **5** : por, en beneficio de ⟨he fought for his country : luchó por su patria⟩ ⟨I did it for you : lo hice por ti⟩ ⟨for your own good : por tu propio bien⟩ **6** (*indicating to whom a statement applies*) : para ⟨it's difficult for me : me es difícil, es difícil para mí⟩ ⟨it's time for us to go : es hora de irnos⟩ ⟨I'd hate for you to miss it : sería una lástima que te lo perdieras⟩ **7** IN FAVOR OF : a favor de **8** (*indicating a goal*) : para ⟨to study for a test : estudiar para un examen⟩ ⟨a cure for cancer : una cura para el cáncer⟩ ⟨for more information, call . . . : para más información, llame al . . .⟩ ⟨they ran for safety : corrieron para ponerse a salvo⟩ **9** TOWARDS, TO : para ⟨he left for the office : salió para la oficina⟩ ⟨the train for London : el tren para Londres⟩ **10** (*indicating correspondence or exchange*) : por, para ⟨I bought it for $5 : lo compré por $5⟩ ⟨a lot of trouble for nothing : mucha molestia para nada⟩ **11** AS FOR : para, con respecto a **12** (*indicating duration*) : por, durante ⟨he's going for two years : se va por dos años⟩ ⟨I spoke for ten minutes : hablé (durante) diez minutos⟩ ⟨she has known it for three months : lo sabe desde hace tres meses⟩ ⟨they won't arrive for hours yet : tardarán horas en llegar⟩ ⟨he drove for 100 miles : hizo 100 millas⟩ **13** (*indicating a particular time*) : para, por ⟨the wedding is planned for April : la boda está prevista para abril⟩ ⟨that's enough for now : basta por ahora⟩ **14** INSTEAD OF, ON BEHALF OF : por ⟨to speak for someone : hablar por alguien⟩ ⟨say hello for me : dales saludos de mi parte⟩ **15** (*indicating association*) : para ⟨he works for the university : trabaja para la universidad⟩ **16** (*used in listing items*) : para ⟨for one thing . . . : para empezar . . .⟩ **17** : para (una enfermedad) ⟨for colds and flu : para resfriados y gripe⟩ **18** (*indicating amount or value*) : por, de ⟨a check for $100 : un cheque por/de $100⟩ **19** (*indicating meaning*) ⟨The French word for "good" is "bon" : en francés la palabra "bon" significa "bueno"⟩ ⟨what's the word for "taxi" in Japanese? : ¿como se dice "taxi" en japonés?⟩ **20** (*used in comparisons*) : para ⟨he's tall for his age : es alto para su edad⟩ **21** (*used in comparing numbers or amounts*) : por ⟨for every dollar invested, there's a return of five dollars : por cada dólar invertido, hay un retorno de cinco dólares⟩ **22** (*used for emphasis*) : por ⟨for crying out loud! : ¡por el amor de Dios!⟩ **23** : para, con ocasión de ⟨a gift for his birthday : un regalo para su cumpleaños⟩ **24 for all** IN SPITE OF : a pesar de **25 for all** : por ⟨she can go now for all I care : por mí que se vaya ahora⟩ ⟨for all I know : que yo sepa⟩ **26 for breakfast/lunch/dinner (etc.)** ⟨we had eggs for breakfast : desayunamos huevos⟩ ⟨what's for dinner/dessert? : ¿qué hay de comer/postre?⟩ **27 in for** ⟨he's in for a surprise : se va a llevar una sorpresa⟩ **28 in for it** ⟨if mom finds out, you're in for it : si mamá se entera, te mata⟩ **29 not for** ⟨it's not for you to say she can't go : no te corresponde a ti decir que no vaya⟩

forage ['fɔrɪdʒ] *v* **-aged; -aging** *vi* : hurgar (en busca de alimento) — *vt* : buscar (provisiones)

foray ['fɔrˌeɪ] *n* : incursión *f*

forbear[1] [for'bær] *vi* **-bore** [-'bor]; **-borne** [-'born]; **-bearing 1** ABSTAIN : abstenerse **2** : tener paciencia

forbear[2] → **forbear**

forbearance [for'bærən*t*s] *n* **1** ABSTAINING : abstención *f* **2** PATIENCE : paciencia *f*

forbid [fər'bɪd] *vt* **-bade** [-'bæd, -'beɪd]; **-bidden** [-'bɪdən]; **-bidding 1** PROHIBIT : prohibir **2** PREVENT : impedir

forbidden [fər'bɪdən] *adj* : prohibido

forbidding [fər'bɪdɪŋ] *adj* **1** IMPOSING : imponente **2** DISAGREEABLE : desagradable, ingrato **3** GRIM : severo

force[1] ['fors] *vt* **forced; forcing 1** COMPEL : obligar, forzar **2** : forzar ⟨to force open the window : forzar la ventana⟩ ⟨to force a lock : forzar una cerradura⟩ **3** IMPOSE : imponer, obligar

force[2] *n* **1** : fuerza *f* ⟨brute force : fuerza bruta⟩ ⟨the force of gravity : la fuerza de la gravedad⟩ ⟨force of habit : la fuerza de la costumbre⟩ ⟨security forces : fuerzas de seguridad⟩ **2 by force** : por la fuerza **3 in force** : en vigor/vigencia

forced ['forst] *adj* : forzado, forzoso

forceful ['forsfəl] *adj* : fuerte, energético, contundente

forcefully ['forsfəli] *adv* : con energía, con fuerza

forcefulness ['forsfəlnəs] *n* : contundencia *f*, fuerza *f*

forceps ['forsəps, -ˌsɛps] *ns & pl* : fórceps *m*

forcible ['forsəbəl] *adj* **1** FORCED : forzoso **2** CONVINCING : contundente, convincente — **forcibly** [-bli] *adv*

ford[1] ['ford] *vt* : vadear

ford[2] *n* : vado *m*

fore[1] ['for] *adv* **1** FORWARD : hacia adelante **2 fore and aft** : de popa a proa

fore[2] *adj* **1** FORWARD : delantero, de adelante **2** FORMER : anterior

fore[3] *n* **1** : frente *m*, delantera *f* **2 to come to the fore** : empezar a destacar, saltar a primera plana

fore–and–aft ['forən'æft, -ənd-] *adj* : longitudinal

forearm ['for,arm] *n* : antebrazo *m*

forebear ['for,bær] *n* : antepasado *m*, -da *f*

foreboding [for'bo:dɪŋ] *n* : premonición *f*, presentimiento *m*

forecast[1] ['for,kæst] *vt* **-cast; -casting** : pronosticar, predecir

forecast[2] *n* : predicción *f*, pronóstico *m* ⟨weather forecast : pronóstico del tiempo, parte meteorológico⟩

forecastle ['fo:ksəl] *n* : castillo *m* de proa

foreclose [for'klo:z] *vt* **-closed; -closing** : ejecutar (una hipoteca)

forefather ['for,faðər] *n* : antepasado *m*, ancestro *m*

forefinger ['for,fɪŋɡər] *n* : índice *m*, dedo *m* índice

forefoot ['for,fʊt] *n* : pata *f* delantera

forefront ['for,frʌnt] *n* : frente *m*, vanguardia *f* ⟨in the forefront : a la vanguardia⟩

forego [for'go:] *vt* **-went; -gone; -going 1** PRECEDE : preceder **2** → **forgo**

foregoing [for'go:ɪŋ] *adj* : precedente, anterior

foregone [for'gɔn] *adj* : previsto ⟨a foregone conclusion : un resultado inevitable⟩

foreground ['for,graʊnd] *n* : primer plano *m*

forehand[1] ['for,hænd] *adj* : directo, derecho

forehand[2] *n* : golpe *m* del derecho

forehead ['forəd, 'for,hɛd] *n* : frente *f*

foreign ['forən] *adj* **1** : extranjero, exterior ⟨foreign countries : países extranjeros⟩ ⟨foreign trade : comercio exterior⟩ **2** ALIEN : ajeno, extraño ⟨foreign to their nature : ajeno a su carácter⟩ ⟨a foreign body : un cuerpo extraño⟩

foreigner ['forənər] *n* : extranjero *m*, -ra *f*

foreknowledge [for'nɑlɪdʒ] *n* : conocimiento *m* previo

foreleg ['for,lɛg] *n* : pata *f* delantera

foreman ['formən] *n*, *pl* **-men** [-mən, -ˌmɛn] : capataz *mf* ⟨foreman of the jury : presidente del jurado⟩

foremost[1] ['for,mo:st] *adv* : en primer lugar

foremost[2] *adj* : más importante, principal, grande

forenoon ['for,nu:n] *n* : mañana *m*

forensic [fə'rɛn*t*sɪk] *adj* **1** RHETORICAL : retórico, de argumentación **2** : forense ⟨forensic medicine : medicina forense⟩

foreordain [ˌforor'deɪn] *vt* : predestinar, predeterminar

forequarter ['for,kwɔrtər] *n* : cuarto *m* delantero

forerunner ['for,rʌnər] *n* : precursor *m*, -sora *f*

foresee [for'si:] *vt* **-saw; -seen; -seeing** : prever

foreseeable [for'si:əbəl] *adj* : previsible ⟨in the foreseeable future : en el futuro inmediato⟩

foreshadow [for'lædo:] *vt* : anunciar, prefigurar
foresight ['for,saɪt] *n* : previsión *f*
foresighted ['for,saɪt̬əd] *adj* : previsto
forest ['forəst] *n* : bosque *m* (en zonas templadas), selva *f* (en zonas tropicales)
forestall [for'stɔl] *vt* **1** PREVENT : prevenir, impedir **2** PREEMPT : adelantarse a
forested ['forəstəd] *adj* : arbolado
forester ['forəstər] *n* : silvicultor *m*, -tora *f*
forestland ['forəst,lænd] *n* : zona *f* boscosa
forest ranger → **ranger**
forestry ['forəstri] *n* : silvicultura *f*, ingeniería *f* forestal
foreswear → **forswear**
foretaste[1] ['for,teɪst] *vt* **-tasted; -tasting** : anticipar
foretaste[2] *n* : anticipo *m*
foretell [for'tɛl] *vt* **-told; -telling** : predecir, pronosticar, profetizar
forethought ['for,θɔt] *n* : previsión *f*, reflexión *f* previa
forever [for'ɛvər] *adv* **1** PERPETUALLY : para siempre, eternamente **2** CONTINUALLY : siempre, constantemente
forevermore [for,ɛvər'mor] *adv* : por siempre jamás
forewarn [for'wɔrn] *vt* : prevenir, advertir
forewoman ['for,wumən] *n, pl* **-women** [-,wimən] : capataz *f*, capataza *f* ⟨forewoman of the jury : presidente/presidenta del jurado⟩
foreword ['forwərd] *n* : prólogo *m*
forfeit[1] ['fɔrfət] *vt* : perder el derecho a
forfeit[2] *n* **1** FINE, PENALTY : multa *f* **2** : prenda *f* (en un juego)
forge[1] ['fordʒ] *v* **forged; forging** *vt* **1** : forjar (metal o un plan) **2** COUNTERFEIT : falsificar — *vi* **to forge ahead** : avanzar, seguir adelante
forge[2] *n* : forja *f*
forger ['fordʒər] *n* : falsificador *m*, -dora *f*
forgery ['fordʒəri] *n, pl* **-eries** : falsificación *f*
forget [fər'gɛt] *v* **-got** [-'gɑt]; **-gotten** [-'gɑt̬ən] *or* **-got; -getting** *vt* : olvidar — *vi* **to forget about** : olvidarse de, no acordarse de
forgetful [fər'gɛtfəl] *adj* : olvidadizo
forgetfulness [fər'gɛtfəlnəs] *n* : olvido *m*, mala memoria *f*
forget-me-not [fər'gɛtmi,nɑt] *n* : nomeolvides *mf*
forgettable [fər'gɛt̬əbəl] *adj* : poco memorable
forgivable [fər'gɪvəbəl] *adj* : perdonable
forgive [fər'gɪv] *vt* **-gave** [-'geɪv]; **-given** [-'gɪvən]; **-giving** : perdonar
forgiveness [fər'gɪvnəs] *n* : perdón *m*
forgiving [fər'gɪvɪŋ] *adj* : indulgente, comprensivo, clemente
forgo *or* **forego** [for'go:] *vt* **-went; -gone; -going** : privarse de, renunciar a
fork[1] ['fɔrk] *vi* : ramificarse, bifurcarse — *vt* **1** : levantar (con un tenedor, una horca, etc.) **2 to fork out/over** : desembolsar
fork[2] *n* **1** : tenedor *m* (utensilio de cocina) **2** PITCHFORK : horca *f*, horquilla

f **3** : bifurcación *f* (de un río o camino), horqueta *f* (de un árbol)
forked ['fɔrkt, 'fɔrkəd] *adj* : bífido, ahorquillado
forklift ['fɔrk,lɪft] *n* : carretilla *f* elevadora
forlorn [for'lorn] *adj* **1** DESOLATE : abandonado, desolado, desamparado **2** SAD : triste **3** DESPERATE : desesperado
forlornly [for'lornli] *adv* **1** SADLY : con tristeza **2** HALFHEARTEDLY : sin ánimo
form[1] ['fɔrm] *vt* **1** FASHION, MAKE : formar **2** DEVELOP : moldear, desarrollar **3** CONSTITUTE : constituir, formar **4** ACQUIRE : adquirir (un hábito), formar (una idea) — *vi* : tomar forma, formarse
form[2] *n* **1** SHAPE : forma *f*, figura *f* ⟨in the form of : en forma de⟩ **2** MANNER : manera *f*, forma *f* **3** DOCUMENT : formulario *m* ⟨tax form : formulario de declaración de renta⟩ ⟨to fill out a form : rellenar/llenar un formulario⟩ **4** : forma *f* ⟨in good form : en buena forma⟩ ⟨true to form : fiel a su costumbre⟩ **5** MOLD : molde *m* **6** KIND, VARIETY : clase *f*, tipo *m* ⟨some form of : algún tipo de⟩ **7** : forma *f* (en gramática) ⟨plural forms : formas plurales⟩
formal[1] ['fɔrməl] *adj* **1** CEREMONIOUS : formal, de etiqueta, ceremonioso **2** OFFICIAL : formal, oficial, de forma
formal[2] *n* **1** BALL : baile *m* formal, baile *m* de etiqueta **2** *or* **formal dress** : traje *m* de etiqueta
formaldehyde [for'mældə,haɪd] *n* : formaldehído *m*
formality [for'mæləti] *n, pl* **-ties** : formalidad *f*
formalize ['fɔrmə,laɪz] *vt* **-ized; -izing** : formalizar
formally ['fɔrməli] *adv* : formalmente
format[1] ['fɔr,mæt] *vt* **-matted; -matting** : formatear
format[2] *n* : formato *m*
formation [for'meɪʃən] *n* **1** FORMING : formación *f* **2** SHAPE : forma *f* **3 in formation** : en formación
formative ['fɔrmət̬ɪv] *adj* : formativo
former ['fɔrmər] *adj* **1** PREVIOUS : antiguo, anterior ⟨the former president : el antiguo presidente⟩ **2** : primero (de dos)
formerly ['fɔrmərli] *adv* : anteriormente, antes
formidable ['fɔrmədəbəl, for'mɪdə-] *adj* : formidable — **formidably** *adv*
formless ['fɔrmləs] *adj* : informe, amorfo
formula ['fɔrmjələ] *n, pl* **-las** *or* **-lae** [-,li:, -,laɪ] **1** : fórmula *f* **2 baby formula** : preparado *m* para biberón
formulate ['fɔrmjə,leɪt] *vt* **-lated; -lating** : formular, hacer
formulation [,fɔrmjə'leɪʃən] *n* : formulación *f*
fornicate ['fɔrnə,keɪt] *vi* **-cated; -cating** : fornicar
fornication [,fɔrnə'keɪʃən] *n* : fornicación *f*
forsake [fər'seɪk] *vt* **-sook** [-'suk]; **-saken** [-'seɪkən]; **-saking** **1** ABANDON : aban-

donar, desamparar **2** RELINQUISH : renunciar a

forswear [fɔr'swær] *v* **-swore; -sworn; -swearing** *vt* RENOUNCE : renunciar a — *vi* : perjurar

forsythia [fər'sıθiə] *n* : forsitia *f*

fort ['fort] *n* **1** STRONGHOLD : fuerte *m*, fortaleza *f*, fortín *m* **2** BASE : base *f* militar

forte ['fort, 'for,teı] *n* : fuerte *m*

forth ['forθ] *adv* **1** : adelante ⟨from this day forth : de hoy en adelante⟩ **2 and so forth** : etcétera

forthcoming [forθ'kʌmɪŋ, 'forθ,-] *adj* **1** COMING : próximo **2** DIRECT, OPEN : directo, franco, comunicativo

forthright ['forθ,raɪt] *adj* : directo, franco — **forthrightly** *adv*

forthrightness ['forθ,raɪtnəs] *n* : franqueza *f*

forthwith [forθ'wıθ, -'wıð] *adv* : inmediatamente, en el acto, enseguida

fortieth[1] ['fɔrţiəθ] *adj* : cuadragésimo

fortieth[2] *n* **1** : cuadragésimo *m*, -ma *f* (en una serie) **2** : cuarentavo *m*, cuarentava parte *f*

fortification [,fɔrţəfə'keɪʃən] *n* : fortificación *f*

fortify ['fɔrţə,faɪ] *vt* **-fied; -fying** : fortificar

fortitude ['fɔrţə,tu:d, -,tju:d] *n* : fortaleza *f*, valor *m*

fortnight ['fort,naɪt] *n* : quince días *mpl*, dos semanas *fpl*

fortnightly[1] ['fort,naɪtli] *adv* : cada quince días

fortnightly[2] *adj* : quincenal

fortress ['fortrəs] *n* : fortaleza *f*

fortuitous [fɔr'tu:əţəs, -'tju:-] *adj* : fortuito, accidental

fortunate ['fɔrtʃənət] *adj* : afortunado

fortunately ['fɔrtʃənətli] *adv* : afortunadamente, con suerte

fortune ['fɔrtʃən] *n* **1** : fortuna *f* ⟨to seek one's fortune : buscar uno su fortuna⟩ **2** LUCK : suerte *f*, fortuna *f* **3** DESTINY, FUTURE : destino *m*, buenaventura *f* **4** : dineral *m*, platal *m* ⟨she spent a fortune : se gastó un dineral⟩

fortune–teller ['fɔrtʃən,tɛlər] *n* : adivino *m*, -na *f*

fortune–telling ['fɔrtʃən,tɛlɪŋ] *n* : adivinación *f*

forty[1] ['fɔrţi] *adj & pron* : cuarenta

forty[2] *n, pl* **forties** : cuarenta *m*

forum ['forəm] *n, pl* **-rums** : foro *m*

forward[1] ['fɔrwərd] *vt* **1** PROMOTE : promover, adelantar, fomentar **2** SEND : remitir, enviar

forward[2] *adv* **1** : adelante, hacia adelante ⟨to go forward : irse adelante⟩ **2 from this day forward** : de aquí en adelante

forward[3] *adj* **1** : hacia adelante, delantero **2** BRASH : atrevido, descarado

forward[4] *n* : delantero *m*, -ra *f* (en deportes)

forwardness ['fɔrwərdnəs] *n* : atrevimiento *m*, descaro *m*

forwards ['fɔrwərdz] *adv* → **forward**[2]

fossil[1] ['fɑsəl] *adj* : fósil

fossil[2] *n* : fósil *m*

fossilize ['fɑsə,laɪz] *vt* **-ized; -izing** : fosilizar — *vi* : fosilizarse

foster[1] ['fɔstər] *vt* : promover, fomentar

foster[2] *adj* : adoptivo ⟨foster child : niño adoptivo⟩

fought → **fight**

foul[1] ['faʊl] *vi* : cometer faltas (en deportes) — *vt* **1** DIRTY, POLLUTE : contaminar, ensuciar **2** TANGLE : enredar

foul[2] *adv* **1** → **foully 2** : contra las reglas

foul[3] *adj* **1** REPULSIVE : asqueroso, repugnante **2** CLOGGED : atascado, obstruido **3** TANGLED : enredado **4** OBSCENE : obsceno **5** BAD : malo ⟨foul weather : mal tiempo⟩ **6** : antirreglamentario (en deportes)

foul[4] *n* : falta *f*, faul *m*

foully ['faʊli] *adv* : asquerosamente

foulmouthed ['faʊl,mæʊ.ðd, -,maʊθt] *adj* : malhablado

foulness ['faʊlnəs] *n* **1** DIRTINESS : suciedad *f* **2** INCLEMENCY : inclemencia *f* **3** OBSCENITY : obscenidad *f*, grosería *f*

foul play *n* : actos *mpl* criminales

foul shot *n* → **free throw**

foul–up ['faʊl,ʌp] *n* : lío *m*, confusión *f*, desastre *m*

foul up *vt* SPOIL : estropear, arruinar — *vi* BUNGLE : echar todo a perder

found[1] → **find**

found[2] ['faʊnd] *vt* : fundar, establecer

foundation [faʊn'deɪʃən] *n* **1** FOUNDING : fundación *f* **2** BASIS : fundamento *m*, base *f* **3** INSTITUTION : fundación *f* **4** : cimientos *mpl* (de un edificio) **5** *or* **foundation makeup** : base *f* de maquillaje

founder[1] ['faʊndər] *vi* SINK : hundirse, irse a pique

founder[2] *n* : fundador *m*, -dora *f*

founding ['faʊndɪŋ] *adj* : fundador ⟨the founding fathers : los fundadores⟩

foundling ['faʊndlɪŋ] *n* : expósito *m*, -ta *f*

foundry ['faʊndri] *n, pl* **-dries** : fundición *f*

fount ['faʊnt] *n* SOURCE : fuente *f*, origen *m*

fountain ['faʊntən] *n* **1** SPRING : fuente *f*, manantial *m* **2** SOURCE : fuente *f*, origen *m* **3** JET : chorro *m* (de agua), surtidor *m*

fountain pen *n* : pluma *f* fuente, estilográfica *f*

four[1] ['for] *adj* : cuatro ⟨the child is four (years old) : la niña tiene cinco años⟩

four[2] *n* **1** : cuatro *m* ⟨the four of hearts : el cuatro de corazones⟩ ⟨it's four o'clock : son las cuatro⟩ **2 on all fours** : a gatas

four[3] *pron* : cuatro ⟨there are four of us : somos cuatro⟩

four hundred[1] *adj & pron* : cuatrocientos

four hundred[2] *n* : cuatrocientos *m*

four–poster [,for'postər] *n* : cama *f* de (cuatro) columnas

fourscore ['for'skor] *adj* EIGHTY : ochenta

fourteen[1] [for'ti:n] *adj & pron* : catorce

fourteen[2] *n* : catorce *m*

fourteenth¹ [for'ti:nθ] *adj* : decimocuarto
fourteenth² *n* **1** : decimocuarto *m*, -ta *f* (en una serie) **2** : catorceavo *m*, catorceava parte *f*
fourth¹ ['forθ] *adv* : en cuarto lugar
fourth² *adj* : cuarto
fourth³ *n* **1** : cuarto *m*, -ta *f* (en una serie) ⟨(on) the fourth of August : el cuatro de agosto⟩ **2** : cuarto *m*, cuarta parte *f* **3** *or* **fourth gear** : cuarta *f*
fowl ['faʊl] *n, pl* **fowl** *or* **fowls 1** BIRD : ave *f* **2** CHICKEN : pollo *m*
fox¹ ['fɑks] *vt* **1** TRICK : engañar **2** BAFFLE : confundir
fox² *n, pl* **foxes** : zorro *m*, -ra *f*
foxglove ['fɑks,glʌv] *n* : dedalera *f*, digital *f*
foxhole ['fɑks,ho:l] *n* : hoyo *m* para atrincherarse, trinchera *f* individual
foxy ['fɑksi] *adj* **foxier; -est** SHREWD : astuto
foyer ['fɔɪər, 'fɔɪˌjeɪ] *n* : vestíbulo *m*
fracas ['freɪkəs, 'fræ-] *n, pl* **-cases** [-kəsəz] : altercado *m*, pelea *f*, reyerta *f*
fracking ['frækɪŋ] *n* : fracking *m*; fractura *f* hidráulica; fracturación *f* hidráulica; estimulación *f* hidráulica *Arg, Col*
fraction ['frækʃən] *n* **1** : fracción *f*, quebrado *m* **2** PORTION : porción *f*, parte *f*
fractional ['frækʃənəl] *adj* **1** : fraccionario **2** TINY : minúsculo, mínimo, insignificante
fractious ['frækʃəs] *adj* **1** UNRULY : rebelde **2** IRRITABLE : malhumorado, irritable
fracture¹ ['fræktʃər] *vt* **-tured; -turing** : fracturar
fracture² *n* **1** : fractura *f* (de un hueso) **2** CRACK : fisura *f*, grieta *f*, falla *f* (geológica)
fragile ['frædʒəl, -ˌdʒaɪl] *adj* : frágil
fragility [frə'dʒɪləti] *n, pl* **-ties** : fragilidad *f*
fragment¹ ['fræg,ment] *vt* : fragmentar — *vi* : fragmentarse, hacerse añicos
fragment² ['frægmənt] *n* : fragmento *m*, trozo *m*, pedazo *m*
fragmentary ['frægmənˌteri] *adj* : fragmentario, incompleto
fragmentation [ˌfrægmən'teɪʃən, -ˌmn-] *n* : fragmentación *f*
fragrance ['freɪgrənts] *n* : fragancia *f*, aroma *m*
fragrant ['freɪgrənt] *adj* : fragante, aromático — **fragrantly** *adv*
frail ['freɪl] *adj* : débil, delicado
frailty ['freɪlti] *n, pl* **-ties** : debilidad *f*, flaqueza *f*
frame¹ ['freɪm] *vt* **framed; framing 1** FORMULATE : formular, elaborar **2** BORDER : enmarcar, encuadrar **3** INCRIMINATE : incriminar
frame² *n* **1** BODY : cuerpo *m* **2** : armazón *f* (de un edificio, un barco, o un avión), bastidor *m* (de un automóvil), cuadro *m* (de una bicicleta), marco *m* (de un cuadro, una ventana, una puerta, etc.) **3 frames** *npl* : armazón *mf*, montura *f* (para anteojos) **4 frame of mind** : estado *m* de ánimo
framework ['freɪmˌwərk] *n* **1** SKELETON,

STRUCTURE : armazón *f*, estructura *f* **2** BASIS : marco *m*
franc ['fræŋk] *n* : franco *m*
franchise ['fræn,tlaɪz] *n* **1** LICENSE : licencia *f* exclusiva, concesión *f* (en comercio) **2** SUFFRAGE : sufragio *m*
franchisee [ˌfræn,tlaɪ'zi:, -tlə-] *n* : concesionario *m*, -ria *f*
Franciscan [fræn'sɪskən] *n* : franciscano *m*, -na *f* — **Franciscan** *adj*
frank¹ ['fræŋk] *vt* : franquear
frank² *adj* : franco, sincero, cándido — **frankly** *adv*
frank³ *n* : franqueo *m* (de correo)
frankfurter ['fræŋkfərtər, -ˌfər-] *or* **frankfurt** [-fərt] *n* : salchicha *f* (de Frankfurt, de Viena), perro *m* caliente
frankincense ['fræŋkən,sents] *n* : incienso *m*
frankness ['fræŋknəs] *n* : franqueza *f*, sinceridad *f*, candidez *f*
frantic ['fræntɪk] *adj* : frenético, desesperado — **frantically** *adv*
fraternal [frə'tərnəl] *adj* : fraterno, fraternal
fraternity [frə'tərnəti] *n, pl* **-ties** : fraternidad *f*
fraternization [ˌfrætərnə'zeɪlən] *n* : fraternización *f*, confraternización *f*
fraternize ['frætər,naɪz] *vi* **-nized; -nizing** : fraternizar, confraternizar
fraud ['frɔd] *n* **1** DECEPTION, SWINDLE : fraude *m*, estafa *f*, engaño *m* **2** IMPOSTOR : impostor *m*, -tora *f*; farsante *mf*
fraudulent ['frɔdʒələnt] *adj* : fraudulento — **fraudulently** *adv*
fraught ['frɔt] *adj* **fraught with** : lleno de, cargado de
fray¹ ['freɪ] *vt* **1** WEAR : desgastar, deshilachar **2** IRRITATE : crispar, irritar (los nervios) — *vi* : desgastarse, deshilacharse
fray² *n* : pelea *f* ⟨to join the fray : salir a la palestra⟩ ⟨to return to the fray : volver a la carga⟩
frazzle¹ ['fræzəl] *vt* **-zled; -zling 1** FRAY : desgastar, deshilachar **2** EXHAUST : agotar, fatigar
frazzle² *n* EXHAUSTION : agotamiento *m*
freak ['fri:k] *n* **1** ODDITY : ejemplar *m* anormal, fenómeno *m*, rareza *f* **2** ENTHUSIAST : entusiasta *mf*
freakish ['fri:kɪl] *adj* : extraño, estrafalario, raro
freak out *vi* : ponerse como loco — *vt* : darle un ataque (a alguien)
freckle¹ ['frekəl] *vi* **-led; -ling** : cubrirse de pecas
freckle² *n* : peca *f*
free¹ ['fri:] *vt* **freed; freeing 1** LIBERATE : libertar, liberar, poner en libertad **2** RELIEVE, RID : librar, eximir **3** RELEASE, UNTIE : desatar, soltar **4** UNCLOG : desatascar, destapar
free² *adv* **1** FREELY : libremente **2** GRATIS : gratuitamente, gratis
free³ *adj* **freer; freest 1** : gratuito, gratis ⟨free tickets : entradas gratuitas⟩ ⟨it's free : es gratis⟩ **2** : libre ⟨to set free : liberar, dejar/poner en libertad⟩ ⟨to get

free : escaparse〉 **3** PERMITTED : libre
〈to be free to do something : ser libre de
hacer algo〉 **4** : libre (dícese de un país,
etc.) 〈free speech : libertad de expre-
sión〉 〈free trade : libre comercio〉 **5**
EXEMPT : libre 〈tax-free : libre de im-
puestos〉 **6** VOLUNTARY : espontáneo,
voluntario, libre **7** UNOCCUPIED : libre,
desocupado 〈I'm free tomorrow
: mañana estoy libre〉 〈a free seat : un
asiento libre〉 〈he waved with his free
hand : nos saludó con su mano libre〉 **8**
LOOSE : suelto **9** : generoso 〈they were
very free with their money : fueron muy
generosos con su dinero〉 **10 for free**
: gratis **11 free from/of** : libre de
freeborn ['friː'bɔrn] *adj* : nacido libre
freedom ['friːdəm] *n* : libertad *f*
free enterprise *n* : libre empresa *f*
free–for–all ['friːfərˌɔl] *n* : pelea *f*, batalla
f campal
free gift *n* : obsequio *m*
freehand ['friːˌhænd] *adj* : a pulso, a
mano alzada
free kick *n* : tiro *m* libre
freelance[1] ['friːˌlænts] *vi* **-lanced; -lancing**
: trabajar por cuenta propia
freelance[2] *adj* : por cuenta propia, freelance
freelancer ['friːˌlæntsər] *n* : trabajador *m*,
-dora *f* por cuenta propia; freelance *mf*
freeload ['friːˌloːd] *vi* : gorronear *fam*,
gorrear *fam*
freeloader ['friːˌloːdər] *n* : gorrón *m*,
-rrona *f*; gorrero *m*, -ra *f*; vividor *m*,
-dora *f*
freely ['friːli] *adv* **1** FREE : libremente **2**
GRATIS : gratis, gratuitamente
Freemason ['friːˌmeɪsən] *n* : francmasón
m, masón *n*
Freemasonry ['friːˌmeɪsənri] *n* : francmasonería *f*, masonería *f*
free–range ['friːˌreɪndʒ] *adj* : de granja
freestanding ['friːˈstændɪŋ] *adj* : de pie,
no empotrado, independiente
free throw *n* : tiro *m* libre (en baloncesto)
freeway ['friːˌweɪ] *n* : autopista *f*
freewill ['friːˌwɪl] *adj* : de propia voluntad
free will *n* : libre albedrío *m*, propia voluntad *f*
freeze[1] ['friːz] *v* **froze** ['froːz]; **frozen**
['froːzən]; **freezing** *vi* **1** : congelarse, helarse 〈the water froze in the lake : el
agua se congeló en el lago〉 〈my blood
froze : se me heló la sangre〉 〈I'm freezing : me estoy helando〉 **2** STOP : quedarse inmóvil **3** : bloquearse (dícese de
una computadora) — *vt* : helar, congelar
(líquidos), congelar (alimentos, precios,
activos), bloquear (cuentas, etc.)
freeze[2] *n* **1** FROST : helada *f* **2** FREEZING
: congelación *f*, congelamiento *m*
freeze–dried ['friːz'draɪd] *adj* : liofilizado
freeze–dry ['friːz'draɪ] *vt* **-dried; -drying**
: liofilizar
freezer ['friːzər] *n* : congelador *m*
freezing ['friːzɪŋ] *adj* : helando 〈it's freezing! : ¡hace un frío espantoso!〉
freezing point *n* : punto *m* de congelación
freight[1] ['freɪt] *vt* : enviar como carga

freight[2] *n* **1** SHIPPING, TRANSPORT
: transporte *m*, porte *m*, flete *m* **2**
GOODS : mercancías *fpl*, carga *f*
freighter ['freɪtər] *n* : carguero *m*, buque
m de carga
freight train *n* : tren *m* de carga, tren *m* de
mercancías
French[1] ['frentʃ] *adj* : francés
French[2] *n* **1** : francés *m* (idioma) **2 the
French** (*used with a plural verb*) : los
franceses
French doors *npl* : puerta *f* ventana
French dressing *n* **1** : aderezo *m* cremoso con sabor a tomate **2** *Brit* VINAI-
GRETTE : vinagreta *f*
french fries ['frentʃˌfraɪz] *npl* : papas *fpl*
fritas, papas *fpl* a la francesa *Mexico, Colombia*
Frenchman ['frentʃmən] *n*, *pl* **-men** [-mən,
-ˌmen] : francés *m*
French toast *n* : torreja *f*, torrija *f* *Spain*
French windows *npl* → French doors
Frenchwoman ['frentʃˌwʊmən] *n*, *pl*
-women [-ˌwɪmən] : francesa *f*
frenemy ['frenəmi] *n*, *pl* **-mies**
: amienemigo *m*, -ga *f* *fam*
frenetic [frɪ'netɪk] *adj* : frenético — **fre-
netically** [-tɪkli] *adv*
frenzied ['frenzid] *adj* : frenesí
frenzy ['frenzi] *n*, *pl* **-zies** : frenesí *m*
frequency ['friːkwəntsi] *n*, *pl* **-cies** : frecuencia *f*
frequent[1] [fri'kwent, 'friːkwənt] *vt* : frecuentar
frequent[2] ['friːkwənt] *adj* : frecuente —
frequently *adv*
fresco ['frɛsˌkoː] *n*, *pl* **-coes** : fresco *m*
fresh ['frɛʃ] *adj* **1** : dulce 〈freshwater
: agua dulce〉 **2** PURE : puro **3** : fresco
〈fresh fruits : frutas frescas〉 **4** CLEAN,
NEW : limpio, nuevo 〈fresh clothes
: ropa limpia〉 〈fresh evidence : evidencia nueva〉 **5** REFRESHED : fresco, descansado **6** IMPERTINENT : descarado,
impertinente
freshen ['frɛʃən] *vt* : refrescar, arreglar —
vi **to freshen up** : arreglarse, lavarse
freshet ['frɛʃət] *n* : arroyo *m* desbordado
freshly ['frɛʃli] *adv* : recientemente, recién
freshman ['frɛʃmən] *n*, *pl* **-men** [-mən,
-ˌmen] : estudiante *mf* de primer año
universitario
freshness ['frɛʃnəs] *n* : frescura *f*
freshwater ['frɛʃˌwɔtər] *n* : agua *f* dulce
fret[1] ['frɛt] *vi* **fretted; fretting** : preocuparse, inquietarse
fret[2] *n* **1** VEXATION : irritación *f*, molestia *f* **2** WORRY : preocupación *f* **3**
: traste *m* (de un instrumento musical)
fretful ['frɛtfəl] *adj* : fastidioso, quejoso,
neurótico
fretfully ['frɛtfəli] *adv* : ansiosamente, fastidiosamente, inquieto
fretfulness ['frɛtfəlnəs] *n* : inquietud *f*, irritabilidad *f*
friar ['fraɪər] *n* : fraile *m*
friction ['frɪkʃən] *n* **1** RUBBING : fricción
f **2** CONFLICT : fricción *f*, roce *m*
Friday ['fraɪˌdeɪ, -di] *n* : viernes *m* 〈today
is Friday : hoy es viernes〉 〈(on) Friday

: el viernes⟩ ⟨(on) Fridays : los viernes⟩ ⟨last Friday : el viernes pasado⟩ ⟨next Friday : el viernes que viene⟩ ⟨every other Friday : cada dos viernes⟩ ⟨Friday afternoon/morning : viernes por la tarde/mañana⟩

fridge ['frɪdʒ] → **refrigerator**

fried ['fraɪd] *adj* : frito

friend[1] ['frɛnd] *n* : amigo *m*, -ga *f* ⟨to be/make friends with : ser/hacerse amigo de⟩

friend[2] *vt* : agregar (a alguien) a su lista de amigos ⟨he friended me on Facebook : me agregó (como amigo) en Facebook⟩

friendless ['frɛndləs] *adj* : sin amigos

friendliness ['frɛndlinəs] *n* : simpatía *f*, amabilidad *f*

friendly ['frɛndli] *adj* **friendlier; -est** **1** : simpático, amable, de amigo ⟨a friendly child : un niño simpático⟩ ⟨friendly advice : consejo de amigo⟩ **2** : agradable, acogedor ⟨a friendly atmosphere : un ambiente agradable⟩ **3** GOOD-NATURED : amigable, amistoso ⟨friendly competition : competencia amistosa⟩

friendship [frɛnd,ʃɪp] *n* : amistad *f*

frieze ['fri:z] *n* : friso *m*

frigate ['frɪgət] *n* : fragata *f*

fright ['fraɪt] *n* : miedo *m*, susto *m*

frighten ['fraɪtən] *vt* : asustar, espantar

frightened ['fraɪtənd] *adj* : asustado, temeroso

frightening ['fraɪtənɪŋ] *adj* : espantoso, aterrador

frightful ['fraɪtfəl] *adj* **1** → **frightening 2** TREMENDOUS : espantoso, tremendo

frightfully ['fraɪtfəli] *adv* : terriblemente, tremendamente

frigid ['frɪdʒɪd] *adj* : glacial, extremadamente frío

frigidity [frɪ'dʒɪdəti] *n* **1** COLDNESS : frialdad *f* **2** : frigidez *f* (sexual)

frill ['frɪl] *n* **1** RUFFLE : volante *m* **2** EMBELLISHMENT : floritura *f*, adorno *m*

frilly ['frɪli] *adj* **frillier; -est 1** RUFFLY : con volantes **2** OVERDONE : recargado

fringe[1] ['frɪndʒ] *vt* **fringed; fringing** : orlar, bordear

fringe[2] *n* **1** BORDER : fleco *m*, orla *f* **2** EDGE : periferia *f*, margen *m* **3** fringe benefits : incentivos *mpl*, extras *mpl*

Frisbee ['frɪzbi] *trademark* se usa para un disco volador que se lanza de un jugador a otro

frisk ['frɪsk] *vi* FROLIC : retozar, juguetear — *vt* SEARCH : cachear, registrar

friskiness ['frɪskinəs] *n* : vivacidad *f*

frisky ['frɪski] *adj* **friskier; -est** : retozón, juguetón

fritter[1] ['frɪtər] *vt* : desperdiciar, malgastar ⟨I frittered away the money : malgasté el dinero⟩

fritter[2] *n* : buñuelo *m*

frivolity [frɪ'vɑləti] *n, pl* **-ties** : frivolidad *f*

frivolous ['frɪvələs] *adj* : frívolo, de poca importancia

frivolously ['frɪvələsli] *adv* : frívolamente, a la ligera

frizz[1] ['frɪz] *vi* : rizarse, encresparse, ponerse chino *Mex*

frizz[2] *n* : rizos *mpl* muy apretados

frizzy ['frɪzi] *adj* **frizzier; -est** : rizado, crespo, chino *Mex*

fro ['fro:] *adv* **to and fro** : de aquí para allá, de un lado para otro

frock ['frɑk] *n* DRESS : vestido *m*

frog ['frɔg, 'frɑg] *n* **1** : rana *f* **2 to have a frog in one's throat** : tener carraspera

frogman ['frɔg,mæn, 'frɑg-, -mən] *n, pl* **-men** [-mən, -,mɛn] : hombre *m* rana, submarinista *mf*

frolic[1] ['frɑlɪk] *vi* **-icked; -icking** : retozar, juguetear

frolic[2] *n* FUN : diversión *f*

frolicsome ['frɑlɪksəm] *adj* : juguetón

from ['frʌm, 'frɑm] *prep* **1** (*indicating a starting, central, or lowest point*) : desde, de, a partir de ⟨from Cali to Bogota : de Cali a Bogotá⟩ ⟨where are you from? : ¿de dónde eres?⟩ ⟨he watched us from above : nos miraba desde arriba⟩ ⟨from that time onward : desde entonces⟩ ⟨from January to March : de enero a marzo, desde enero hasta marzo⟩ ⟨from tomorrow : a partir de mañana⟩ ⟨they cost from 5 to 10 dollars : cuestan entre 5 y 10 dólares⟩ ⟨to speak from the heart : hablar con el corazón⟩ **2** OFF, OUT OF : de ⟨she took it from the drawer : lo sacó del cajón⟩ **3** (*indicating a source or sender*) : de ⟨a letter from my friend : una carta de mi amiga⟩ ⟨a quote from Shakespeare : una cita de Shakespeare⟩ **4** (*indicating distance*) : de ⟨10 feet from the entrance : a 10 pies de la entrada⟩ ⟨we got separated from the group : nos vimos separados del grupo⟩ **5** (*indicating a cause*) : de ⟨red from crying : rojos de llorar⟩ ⟨he died from the cold : murió del frío⟩ **6** (*indicating material*) : de ⟨made from wood : (hecho) de madera⟩ **7** (*indicating blocking, removal, etc.*) : de ⟨to protect from : proteger de⟩ ⟨to provide relief from : aliviar⟩ ⟨to refrain from : abstenerse de⟩ ⟨to omit from : omitir de⟩ ⟨she was excluded from the club : no la admitieron en el club⟩ **8** (*indicating a change*) : de ⟨from bad to worse : de mal en peor⟩ **9** (*in mathematics*) : de ⟨to deduct something from something : deducir/descontar algo de algo⟩ ⟨to subtract 10 from 30 : restarle 10 a 30, restar 10 de 30⟩ **10** (*indicating alternatives*) : de ⟨to choose from (among) : elegir de (entre)⟩

frond ['frɑnd] *n* : fronda *f*, hoja *f*

front[1] ['frʌnt] *vi* **1** FACE : dar, estar orientado ⟨the house fronts north : la casa da al norte⟩ **2** : servir de pantalla ⟨he fronts for his boss : sirve de pantalla para su jefe⟩

front[2] *adj* : delantero, de adelante, primero ⟨the front row : la primera fila⟩ ⟨the front door : la puerta principal⟩ ⟨it appeared on the front page : salió en primera plana⟩

front[3] *n* **1** : frente *m*, parte *f* de adelante, delantera *f* ⟨the front of the class : el frente de la clase⟩ ⟨at the front of the

train : en la parte delantera del tren⟩ **2**
AREA, ZONE : frente *m*, zona *f* ⟨the
Eastern front : el frente oriental⟩ ⟨on
the educational front : en el frente de la
enseñanza⟩ **3** FACADE : fachada *f* (de
un edificio o una persona) **4** : frente *m*
(en meteorología)
frontage ['frʌntɪʤ] *n* : fachada *f*, frente *m*
frontal ['frʌntəl] *adj* : frontal, de frente
frontier [,frʌn'tɪr] *n* : frontera *f*
frontiersman [,frʌn'tɪrzmən] *n, pl* **-men**
[-mən, -,mɛn] : hombre *m* de la frontera
front–wheel drive ['frʌnt'ʰwiːl-] *n* : tracción *f* delantera
frost[1] ['frɔst] *vt* **1** FREEZE : helar **2** ICE
: bañar (pasteles)
frost[2] *n* **1** : helada *f* (en meteorología) **2**
: escarcha *f* ⟨frost on the window : escar-
cha en la ventana⟩
frostbite ['frɔst,baɪt] *n* : congelación *f*
frostbitten ['frɔst,bɪtən] *adj* : congelado
(dícese de una persona), quemado
(dícese de una planta)
frosting ['frɔstɪŋ] *n* ICING : baño *m*, glaseado *m*, betún *m* Mex
frosty ['frɔsti] *adj* **frostier; -est** **1** CHILLY
: helado, frío **2** COOL, UNFRIENDLY
: frío, glacial
froth ['frɔθ] *n, pl* **froths** ['frɔθs, 'frɔðz]
: espuma *f*
frothy ['frɔθi] *adj* **frothier; -est** : espumoso
frown[1] ['fraʊn] *vi* **1** : fruncir el ceño,
fruncir el entrecejo **2 to frown at** : mirar (algo) con ceño, mirar (a alguien)
con ceño **2 to frown on/upon** : desaprobar
frown[2] *n* : ceño *m* (fruncido)
froze → **freeze**
frozen → **freeze**
frugal ['fruːɡəl] *adj* : frugal, ahorrativo,
parco — **frugally** *adv*
frugality [fruˈɡæləti] *n* : frugalidad *f*
fruit[1] ['fruːt] *vi* : dar fruto
fruit[2] *n* **1** : fruta *f* (término genérico),
fruto *m* (término particular) **2 fruits**
npl REWARDS : frutos *mpl* ⟨the fruits of
his labor : los frutos de su trabajo⟩
fruitcake ['fruːt,keɪk] *n* : pastel *m* de frutas
fruitful ['fruːtfəl] *adj* : fructífero, provechoso
fruition [fruˈɪʃən] *n* **1** : cumplimiento *m*,
realización *f* **2 to bring to fruition** : realizar
fruitless ['fruːtləs] *adj* : infructuoso, inútil
— **fruitlessly** *adv*
fruit salad *n* : ensalada *f* de frutas
fruity ['fruːti] *adj* **fruitier; -est** : (con sabor) a fruta
frumpy ['frʌmpi] *adj* **frumpier; -est** : anticuado y sin atractivo
frustrate ['frʌs,treɪt] *vt* **-trated; -trating**
: frustrar
frustrating ['frʌs,treɪtɪŋ] *adj* : frustrante
— **frustratingly** *adv*
frustration [,frʌs'treɪʃən] *n* : frustración *f*
fry[1] ['fraɪ] *vt* **fried; frying** : freír
fry[2] *n, pl* **fries** **1** : fritura *f*, plato *m*
frito **2** : fiesta *f* en que se sirven fritu-

ras **3** *pl* **fry** : alevín *m* (pez) **4 fries** *npl*
→ **French fries**
frying pan *n* : sartén *mf*
fuchsia ['fjuːʃə] *n* **1** : fucsia *f* (planta) **2**
: fucsia *m* (color)
fuddle ['fʌdəl] *vt* **-dled; -dling** : confundir,
atontar
fuddy–duddy ['fʌdi,dʌdi] *n, pl* **-dies** : persona *f* chapada a la antigua, carca *mf*
fudge[1] ['fʌʤ] *vt* **fudged; fudging** **1** FAL-
SIFY : amañar, falsificar **2** DODGE : esquivar
fudge[2] *n* : dulce *m* blando de chocolate y
leche
fuel[1] ['fjuːəl] *vt* **-eled** *or* **-elled; -eling** *or*
-elling **1** : abastecer de combustible **2**
STIMULATE : estimular
fuel[2] *n* : combustible *m*; carburante *m*
(para motores)
fugitive[1] ['fjuːʤətɪv] *adj* **1** RUNAWAY
: fugitivo **2** FLEETING : efímero, pasajero, fugaz
fugitive[2] *n* : fugitivo *m*, -va *f*
fugue ['fjuːɡ] *n* : fuga *f*
fulcrum ['fʊlkrəm, 'fʌl-] *n, pl* **-crums** *or*
-cra [-krə] : fulcro *m*
fulfill *or* **fulfil** [fʊl'fɪl] *vt* **-filled; -filling** **1**
PERFORM : cumplir con, realizar, llevar
a cabo **2** SATISFY : satisfacer
fulfillment [fʊl'fɪlmənt] *n* **1** PERFOR-
MANCE : cumplimiento *m*, ejecución *f* **2**
SATISFACTION : satisfacción *f*, realización *f*
full[1] ['fʊl, 'fʌl] *adv* **1** VERY : muy ⟨full
well : muy bien, perfectamente⟩ **2** EN-
TIRELY : completamente ⟨she swung full
around : giró completamente⟩ **3** DI-
RECTLY : de lleno, directamente ⟨he
looked me full in the face : me miró directamente a la cara⟩
full[2] *adj* **1** FILLED : lleno ⟨a full glass
: un vaso lleno⟩ ⟨I'm full : estoy lleno⟩
⟨full of holes : lleno de agujeros⟩ **2**
COMPLETE : completo, detallado ⟨two
full weeks : dos semanas completas⟩ ⟨a
full report : un informe detallado⟩ **3**
MAXIMUM : todo, pleno ⟨at full speed : a
toda velocidad⟩ ⟨in full bloom : en plena
flor⟩ **4** PLUMP : redondo, llenito *fam*,
regordete *fam* ⟨a full face : una cara re-
donda⟩ ⟨a full figure : un cuerpo
llenito⟩ **5** AMPLE : amplio ⟨a full skirt
: una falda amplia⟩
full[3] *n* **1 to pay in full** : pagar en su totalidad **2 to the full** : al máximo
full–fledged ['fʊl'flɛʤd] *adj* : hecho y
derecho
full–length ['fʊl,lɛŋkθ] *adj* **1** : de cuerpo
entero (dícese de un espejo, etc.) **2**
: largo (dícese de un vestido, etc.) **3** : de
extensión normal ⟨full-length film : lar-
gometraje⟩
full moon *n* : luna *f* llena
fullness ['fʊlnəs] *n* **1** ABUNDANCE : plenitud *f*, abundancia *f* **2** : amplitud *f* (de
una falda)
full–scale ['fʊl,skeɪl] *adj* **1** : a escala natural **2** COMPLETE : total ⟨full-scale war
: guerra total⟩ ⟨a full-scale investigation
: una investigación rigurosa⟩

full–time¹ ['fʊl,taɪm] *adv* : a/de tiempo completo
full–time² *adj* : de tiempo completo
fully ['fʊli] *adv* **1** COMPLETELY : completamente, totalmente **2** : al menos, por lo menos ⟨fully half of them : al menos la mitad de ellos⟩
fulsome ['fʊlsəm] *adj* : excesivo, exagerado, efusivo
fumble¹ ['fʌmbəl] *v* **-bled; -bling** *vt* **1** : dejar caer, fumblear **2 to fumble one's way** : ir a tientas — *vi* **1** GROPE : hurgar, tantear **2 to fumble with** : manejar con torpeza
fumble² *n* : fumble *m* (en futbol americano)
fume¹ ['fju:m] *vi* **fumed; fuming 1** SMOKE : echar humo, humear **2** : estar furioso
fume² *n* : gas *m*, humo *m*, vapor *m*
fumigate ['fju:mə,geɪt] *vt* **-gated; -gating** : fumigar
fumigation [,fju:mə'geɪʃən] *n* : fumigación *m*
fun¹ ['fʌn] *adj* : divertido, entretenido
fun² *n* **1** AMUSEMENT : diversión *f*, entretenimiento *m* ⟨the party was really fun : la fiesta fue muy divertida⟩ ⟨for fun : por diversión⟩ **2** ENJOYMENT : disfrute *m* **3 to have fun** : divertirse **4 to make fun of** : reírse de, burlarse de
function¹ ['fʌŋkʃən] *vi* : funcionar, desempeñarse, servir
function² *n* **1** PURPOSE : función *f* **2** GATHERING : reunión *f* social, recepción *f* **3** CEREMONY : ceremonia *f*, acto *m*
functional ['fʌŋkʃənəl] *adj* : funcional — **functionally** *adv*
functionary ['fʌŋkʃə,neri] *n*, *pl* **-aries** : funcionario *m*, -ria *f*
fund¹ ['fʌnd] *vt* : financiar
fund² *n* **1** SUPPLY : reserva *f*, cúmulo *m* **2** : fondo *m* ⟨investment fund : fondo de inversiones⟩ **3 funds** *npl* RESOURCES : fondos *mpl*
fundamental¹ [,fʌndə'mentəl] *adj* **1** BASIC : fundamental, básico **2** PRINCIPAL : esencial, principal **3** INNATE : innato, intrínseco
fundamental² *n* : fundamento *m*
fundamentalism [,fʌndə'mentəl,ɪzəm] *n* : integrismo *m*, fundamentalismo *m*
fundamentalist [,fʌndə'mentəlɪst] *n* : integrista *mf*, fundamentalista *mf* — **fundamentalist** *adj*
fundamentally [,fʌndə'mentəli] *adv* : fundamentalmente, básicamente
funding ['fʌndɪŋ] *n* : financiación *f*
fund–raiser ['fʌnd,reɪzər] *n* : función *f* para recaudar fondos
funeral¹ ['fju:nərəl] *adj* **1** : funeral, funerario, fúnebre ⟨funeral procession : cortejo fúnebre⟩ **2 funeral home/parlor** : funeraria *f*
funeral² *n* : funeral *m*, funerales *mpl*
funereal [fju:'nɪriəl] *adj* : fúnebre
fungicide ['fʌndʒə,saɪd, 'fʌŋɡə-] *n* : fungicida *m*
fungus ['fʌŋɡəs] *n*, *pl* **fungi** ['fʌn,dʒaɪ, 'fʌŋ,ɡaɪ] : hongo *m*

funk ['fʌŋk] *n* **1** FEAR : miedo *m* **2** DEPRESSION : depresión *f*
funky ['fʌŋki] *adj* **funkier; -est** ODD, QUAINT : raro, extraño, original
funnel¹ ['fʌnəl] *vt* **-neled; -neling** CHANNEL : canalizar, encauzar
funnel² *n* **1** : embudo *m* **2** SMOKESTACK : chimenea *f* (de un barco o vapor)
funnies ['fʌniz] *npl* : tiras *fpl* cómicas
funny ['fʌni] *adj* **funnier; -est 1** AMUSING : divertido, cómico **2** STRANGE : extraño, raro
fur¹ ['fər] *adj* : de piel
fur² *n* **1** : pelaje *m*, piel *f* **2** : prenda *f* de piel
furbish ['fərbɪʃ] *vt* : pulir, limpiar
furious ['fjʊriəs] *adj* **1** ANGRY : furioso **2** FRANTIC : violento, frenético, vertiginoso (dícese de la velocidad)
furiously ['fjʊriəsli] *adv* **1** ANGRILY : furiosamente **2** FRANTICALLY : frenéticamente
furlong ['fər,lɔŋ] *n* : estadio *m* (201.2 m)
furlough¹ ['fər,lo:] *vt* : dar permiso a, dar licencia a
furlough² *n* LEAVE : permiso *m*, licencia *f*
furnace ['fərnəs] *n* : horno *m*
furnish ['fərnɪʃ] *vt* **1** SUPPLY : proveer, suministrar **2** : amueblar ⟨furnished apartment : departamento amueblado⟩
furnishings ['fərnɪʃɪŋz] *npl* **1** ACCESSORIES : accesorios *mpl* **2** FURNITURE : muebles *mpl*, mobiliario *m*
furniture ['fərnɪtʃər] *n* : muebles *mpl*, mobiliario *m*
furor ['fjʊr,ɔr, -ər] *n* **1** RAGE : furia *f*, rabia *f* **2** UPROAR : escándalo *m*, jaleo *m*, alboroto *m*
furrier ['fəriər] *n* : peletero *m*, -ra *f*
furrow¹ ['fəro:] *vt* **1** : surcar **2 to furrow one's brow** : fruncir el ceño
furrow² *n* **1** GROOVE : surco *m* **2** WRINKLE : arruga *f*, surco *m*
furry ['fəri] *adj* **furrier; -est** : peludo (dícese de un animal), peluche (dícese de un objeto)
further¹ ['fərðər] *vt* : promover, fomentar
further² *adv* **1** FARTHER : más lejos, más adelante **2** MOREOVER : además **3** MORE : más ⟨I'll consider it further in the morning : lo consideraré más en la mañana⟩
further³ *adj* **1** FARTHER : más lejano **2** ADDITIONAL : adicional, más
furtherance ['fərðərənts] *n* : promoción *f*, fomento *m*, adelantamiento *m*
furthermore ['fərðər,mor] *adv* : además
furthermost ['fərðər,mo:st] *adj* : más lejano, más distante
furthest ['fərðəst] → **farthest¹, farthest²**
furtive ['fərtɪv] *adj* : furtivo, sigiloso — **furtively** *adv*
furtiveness ['fərtɪvnəs] *n* STEALTH : sigilo *m*
fury ['fjʊri] *n*, *pl* **-ries 1** RAGE : furia *f*, ira *f* **2** VIOLENCE : furia *f*, furor *m*
fuse¹ ['fju:z] *or* **fuze** *vt* **fused** *or* **fuzed; fusing** *or* **fuzing** : equipar con un fusible
fuse² *v* **fused; fusing** *vt* **1** SMELT : fundir **2** MERGE : fusionar, fundir — *vi* : fundirse, fusionarse

fuse[3] *n* : fusible *m*
fuselage [ˈfjuːsəˌlɑʒ, -zə-] *n* : fuselaje *m*
fusillade [ˈfjuːsəˌlɑd, -ˌleɪd, ˌfjuːsəˈ-, -zə-] *n*
: descarga *f* de fusilería
fusion [ˈfjuːʒən] *n* : fusión *f*
fuss[1] [ˈfʌs] *vi* **1** WORRY : preocuparse **2**
to fuss with : juguetear con, toque-
tear **3 to fuss over** : mimar
fuss[2] *n* **1** COMMOTION : alboroto *m*,
escándalo *m* **2** ATTENTION : atenciones
fpl **3** COMPLAINT : quejas *fpl*
fussbudget [ˈfʌsˌbʌdʒət] *n* : quisquilloso
m, -sa *f*; melindroso *m*, -sa *f*
fussiness [ˈfʌsinəs] *n* **1** IRRITABILITY
: irritabilidad *f* **2** : lo recargado (dícese
de la decoración, etc.) **3** METICULOUS-
NESS : meticulosidad *f*
fussy [ˈfʌsi] *adj* **fussier; -est 1** IRRITA-
BLE : irritable, nervioso **2** OVERELABO-

RATE : recargado **3** METICULOUS : meticuloso **4** FASTIDIOUS : quisquilloso,
exigente
futile [ˈfjuːtəl, ˈfjuːˌtaɪl] *adj* : inútil, vano
futility [fjuˈtɪləti] *n, pl* **-ties** : inutilidad *f*
futon [ˈfuːˌtɑn] *n* : futón *m*
future[1] [ˈfjuːtʃər] *adj* : futuro
future[2] *n* : futuro *m* ⟨in the future : en el
futuro⟩ ⟨a job with a future : un trabajo
con futuro⟩
futuristic [ˌfjuːtʃəˈrɪstɪk] *adj* : futurista
fuze → **fuse**[1]
fuzz [ˈfʌz] *n* : pelusa *f*
fuzziness [ˈfʌzinəs] *n* **1** : vellosidad *f* **2**
INDISTINCTNESS : falta *f* de claridad
fuzzy [ˈfʌzi] *adj* **fuzzier; -est 1** FLUFFY,
FURRY : con pelusa, peludo **2** INDIS-
TINCT : indistinto, borroso ⟨a fuzzy image : una imagen borrosa⟩

G

g [ˈdʒiː] *n, pl* **g's** *or* **gs** [ˈdʒiːz] **1** : séptima
letra del alfabeto inglés — **2** : sol *m* ⟨G
sharp/flat : sol sostenido/bemol⟩
gab[1] [ˈgæb] *vi* **gabbed; gabbing** : charlar,
cotorrear *fam*, parlotear *fam*
gab[2] *n* CHATTER : cotorreo *m fam*, parloteo *m fam*
gabardine [ˈgæbərˌdiːn] *n* : gabardina *f*
gabby [ˈgæbi] *adj* **gabbier; -est** : hablador, parlanchín
gable [ˈgeɪbəl] *n* : gablete *m*, aguilón *m*
Gabonese [ˌgæbəˈniːz, -ˈniːs] *n* : gabonés
m, -nesa *f* — **Gabonese** *adj*
gad [ˈgæd] *vi* **gadded; gadding** WANDER
: deambular, vagar, callejear
gadfly [ˈgædˌflaɪ] *n, pl* **-flies 1** : tábano *m*
(insecto) **2** FAULTFINDER : criticón *m*,
-cona *f fam*
gadget [ˈgædʒət] *n* : artilugio *m*, aparato
m
gadgetry [ˈgædʒətri] *n* : artilugios *mpl*,
aparatos *mpl*
Gaelic [ˈgeɪlɪk, ˈgæ] *n* : gaélico *m* (idioma)
— **Gaelic** *adj*
gaff [ˈgæf] *n* **1** : garfio *m* **2** → **gaffe**
gaffe [ˈgæf] *n* : metedura *f* de pata *fam*
gag[1] [ˈgæg] *v* **gagged; gagging** *vt*
: amordazar ⟨to tie up and gag : atar y
amordazar⟩ — *vi* **1** CHOKE : atragantarse **2** RETCH : hacer arcadas
gag[2] *n* **1** : mordaza *f* (para la boca) **2**
JOKE : chiste *m*
gage → **gauge**
gaggle [ˈgægəl] *n* : bandada *f*, manada *f*
(de gansos)
gaiety [ˈgeɪəti] *n, pl* **-eties 1** MERRYMAK-
ING : juerga *f* **2** MERRIMENT : alegría *f*,
regocijo *m*
gaily [ˈgeɪli] *adv* : alegremente
gain[1] [ˈgeɪn] *vt* **1** ACQUIRE, OBTAIN : ganar, obtener, adquirir, conseguir ⟨to gain
knowledge : adquirir conocimientos⟩ ⟨to
gain a victory : obtener una victoria⟩ **2**
REACH : alcanzar, llegar a **3** INCREASE

: ganar, aumentar ⟨to gain weight : aumentar de peso⟩ **4** : adelantarse, ganar
⟨the watch gains two minutes a day : el
reloj se adelanta dos minutos por día⟩ **5**
to gain on someone : ganarle terreno a
alguien — *vi* **1** PROFIT : beneficiarse **2**
INCREASE : aumentar
gain[2] *n* **1** PROFIT : beneficio *m*, ganancia
f, lucro *m*, provecho *m* **2** INCREASE
: aumento *m*
gainful [ˈgeɪnfəl] *adj* : lucrativo, beneficioso, provechoso ⟨gainful employment
: trabajo remunerado⟩
gait [ˈgeɪt] *n* : paso *m*, andar *m*, manera *f*
de caminar
gal [ˈgæl] *n* : muchacha *f*
gala[1] [ˈgeɪlə, ˈgæ-, ˈgɑ-] *adj* : de gala
gala[2] *n* : gala *f*, fiesta *f*
galactic [gəˈlæktɪk] *adj* : galáctico
galaxy [ˈgæləksi] *n, pl* **-axies** : galaxia *f*
gale [ˈgeɪl] *n* **1** WIND : vendaval *f*, viento
m fuerte **2 gales of laughter** : carcajadas *fpl*
Galician [gəˈlɪʃən] *n* : gallego *m*, -ga *f* —
Galician *adj*
gall[1] [ˈgɔl] *vt* **1** CHAFE : rozar **2** IRRI-
TATE, VEX : irritar, molestar
gall[2] *n* **1** BILE : bilis *f*, hiel *f* **2** INSO-
LENCE : audacia *f*, insolencia *f*, descaro
m **3** SORE : rozadura *f* (de un caballo) **4** : agalla *f* (de una planta)
gallant [ˈgælənt] *adj* **1** BRAVE : valiente,
gallardo **2** CHIVALROUS, POLITE
: galante, cortés
gallantry [ˈgæləntri] *n, pl* **-ries** : galantería
f, caballerosidad *f*
gallbladder [ˈgɔlˌblædər] *n* : vesícula *f*
biliar
galleon [ˈgæljən] *n* : galeón *m*
gallery [ˈgæləri] *n, pl* **-leries 1** BALCONY
: galería *f* (para espectadores) **2** CORRI-
DOR : pasillo *m*, galería *f*, corredor *m* **3**
or **art gallery** : galería *f* (para exposicio-
nes)

galley ['gæli] *n, pl* **-leys** : galera *f*
gallium ['gæliəm] *n* : galio *m*
gallivant ['gælə,vænt] *vi* : callejear
gallon ['gælən] *n* : galón *m*
gallop¹ ['gæləp] *vi* : galopar
gallop² *n* : galope *m*
gallows ['gæ,lo:z] *n, pl* **-lows** *or* **-lowses** [-,lo:zəz] : horca *f*
gallstone ['gɔl,sto:n] *n* : cálculo *m* biliar
galore [gə'lor] *adj* : en abundancia ⟨bargains galore : muchísimas gangas⟩
galoshes [gə'lɑʃəz] *npl* : galochas *fpl*, chanclos *mpl*
galvanize ['gælvən,aɪz] *vt* **-nized; -nizing** 1 STIMULATE : estimular, excitar, impulsar 2 : galvanizar (metales)
Gambian ['gæmbiən] *n* : gambiano *m*, -na *f* — **Gambian** *adj*
gambit ['gæmbɪt] *n* 1 : gambito *m* (en ajedrez) 2 STRATAGEM : estratagema *f*, táctica *f*
gamble¹ ['gæmbəl] *v* **-bled; -bling** *vi* : jugar, arriesgarse — *vt* 1 BET, WAGER : apostar, jugarse 2 RISK : arriesgar
gamble² *n* 1 BET : apuesta *f* 2 RISK : riesgo *m*
gambler ['gæmblər] *n* : jugador *m*, -dora *f*
gambling ['gæmbəlɪŋ] *n* : juego *m*
gambol ['gæmbəl] *vi* **-boled** *or* **-bolled; -boling** *or* **-bolling** FROLIC : retozar, juguetear
game¹ ['geɪm] *adj* 1 READY : listo, dispuesto ⟨we're game for anything : estamos listos para lo que sea⟩ 2 LAME : cojo
game² *n* 1 : juego *m* ⟨card game : juego de cartas/naipes⟩ ⟨board game : juego de mesa⟩ ⟨video game : videojuego⟩ 2 MATCH : partido *m* (de fútbol, ajedrez, etc.), partida *f* (de ajedrez, etc.) 3 ROUND : juego *m* 4 : caza *f* ⟨big game : caza mayor⟩ 5 early in the game : al principio 6 late in the game : tarde ⟨it's a little late in the game for that : ya es tarde para eso⟩ 7 to be ahead of the game : llevar la delantera 8 to beat someone at their own game : vencer a alguien con sus propias armas 9 to be on/off one's game : estar/no estar en forma 10 to play games (with someone) : jugar con alguien, manipular a alguien
gamecock ['geɪm,kɑk] *n* : gallo *m* de pelea
gamekeeper ['geɪm,ki:pər] *n* : guardabosque *mf*
gamely ['geɪmli] *adv* : animosamente
gamer ['geɪmər] *n* : videojugador *m*, -dora *f*
gaming ['geɪmɪŋ] *n* 1 GAMBLING : juego *m* 2 : juegos *mpl* ⟨online gaming : juegos en línea⟩
gamma ray ['gæmə] *n* : rayo *m* gamma
gamut ['gæmət] *n* : gama *f*, espectro *m* ⟨to run the gamut : pasar por toda la gama⟩
gamy *or* **gamey** ['geɪmi] *adj* **gamier; -est** : con sabor de animal de caza, fuerte
gander ['gændər] *n* 1 : ganso *m* (animal) 2 GLANCE : mirada *f*, vistazo *m*, ojeada *f*

gang¹ ['gæŋ] *vi* **to gang up** : agruparse, unirse
gang² *n* : banda *f*, pandilla *f*
gangland ['gæŋ,lænd] *n* : hampa *f*
gangling ['gæŋglɪŋ] *adj* LANKY : larguirucho *fam*
ganglion ['gæŋgliən] *n, pl* **-glia** [-gliə] : ganglio *m*
gangplank ['gæŋ,plæŋk] *n* : pasarela *f*
gangrene ['gæŋ,ɑri:n, 'gæn-:, gæŋ'-, gæŋ'-] *n* : gangrena *f*
gangster ['gæŋstər] *n* : gángster *mf*
gangway ['gæŋ,weɪ] *n* 1 : pasarela *f* 2 **gangway!** : ¡abran paso!
gap ['gæp] *n* 1 BREACH, OPENING : espacio *m*, brecha *f*, abertura *f* 2 GORGE : desfiladero *m*, barranco *m* 3 : laguna *f* ⟨a gap in my education : una laguna en mi educación⟩ 4 INTERVAL : pausa *f*, intervalo *m* 5 DISPARITY : brecha *f*, disparidad *f*
gape¹ ['geɪp] *vi* **gaped; gaping** 1 OPEN : abrirse, estar abierto 2 STARE : mirar fijamente con la boca abierta, mirar boquiabierto
gape² *n* 1 OPENING : abertura *f*, brecha *f* 2 STARE : mirada *f* boquiabierta
garage¹ [gə'rɑʒ, -'rɑdʒ] *vt* **-raged; -raging** : dejar en un garaje
garage² *n* : garaje *m*, cochera *f*
garb¹ ['gɑrb] *vt* : vestir, ataviar
garb² *n* : vestimenta *f*, atuendo *f*
garbage ['gɑrbɪdʒ] *n* : basura *f*, desechos *mpl*
garbage can *n* : bote *m* de basura *CA, Mex*; basurero *m Mex*; caneca *f Col*; cubo *m* de (la) basura *Spain*; tacho *m* de basura *Arg, Chile, Ecua, Peru, Uru*; tarro *m* de (la) basura *Arg, Chile, CoRi, Uru*
garbage disposal *n* : trituradora *f* de basura
garbageman ['gɑrbɪdʒmən] *n, pl* **-men** [-mən, -,mɛn] : basurero *m*
garbage truck *n* : camión *m* de la basura
garble ['gɑrbəl] *vt* **-bled; -bling** : tergiversar, distorsionar
garbled ['gɑrbəld] *adj* : incoherente, incomprensible
garden¹ ['gɑrdən] *vi* : trabajar en el jardín
garden² *n* : jardín *m* ⟨vegetable garden : huerto⟩
garden center *n* : centro *m* de jardinería *f*
gardener ['gɑrdənər] *n* : jardinero *m*, -ra *f*
gardenia [gɑr'di:njə] *n* : gardenia *f*
gardening ['gɑrdənɪŋ] *n* : jardinería *f*
gargantuan [gɑr'gæntʃuən] *adj* : gigantesco, colosal
gargle¹ ['gɑrgəl] *vi* **-gled; -gling** : hacer gárgaras, gargarizar
gargle² *n* : gárgara *f*
gargoyle ['gɑr,gɔɪl] *n* : gárgola *f*
garish ['gærɪʃ] *adj* GAUDY : llamativo, chillón, charro — **garishly** *adv*
garland¹ ['gɑrlənd] *vt* : adornar con guirnaldas
garland² *n* : guirnalda *f*
garlic ['gɑrlɪk] *n* : ajo *m*
garment ['gɑrmənt] *n* : prenda *f*
garner ['gɑrnər] *vt* : recoger, cosechar
garnet ['gɑrnət] *n* : granate *m*

garnish[1] ['gɑrnɪʃ] *vt* : aderezar, guarnecer
garnish[2] *n* : aderezo *m*, guarnición *f*
garret ['gærət] *n* : buhardilla *f*, desván *m*
garrison[1] ['gærəsən] *vt* **1** QUARTER : acuartelar (tropas) **2** OCCUPY : guarnecer, ocupar (con tropas)
garrison[2] *n* **1** : guarnición *f* (ciudad) **2** FORT : fortaleza *f*, poste *m* militar
garrulous ['gærələs] *adj* : charlatán, parlanchín
garter ['gɑrtər] *n* : liga *f*
gas[1] ['gæs] *v* **gassed; gassing** *vt* : gasear — *vi* **to gas up** : llenar el tanque con gasolina
gas[2] *n, pl* **gases** ['gæsəz] **1** : gas *m* ⟨tear gas : gas lacrimógeno⟩ **2** → **gasoline**
gaseous ['gæʃəs, 'gæsiəs] *adj* : gaseoso
gash[1] ['gæʃ] *vt* : hacer un tajo en, cortar
gash[2] *n* : cuchillada *f*, tajo *m*
gasket ['gæskət] *n* : junta *f*
gas mask *n* : máscara *f* antigás
gasoline ['gæsə,li:n, ˌgæsə'-] *n* : gasolina *f*, nafta *f*, bencina *f* *Chile*
gasp[1] ['gæsp] *vi* **1** : boquear ⟨to gasp with surprise : gritar de asombro⟩ **2** PANT : jadear, respirar con dificultad
gasp[2] *n* **1** : boqueada *f* ⟨a gasp of surprise : un grito sofocado⟩ **2** PANTING : jadeo *m*
gas pedal *n* : acelerador *m*
gas station *n* : estación *f* de servicio; gasolinera *f*; bencinera *f* *Chile*; bomba *f* *Chile, CoRi, Ven*
gas tank *n* : tanque *m*, depósito *m* (de gasolina/bencina/nafta)
gastric ['gæstrɪk] *adj* : gástrico ⟨gastric juice : jugo gástrico⟩
gastronomic [ˌgæstrə'nɑmɪk] *adj* : gastronómico
gastronomy [gæs'trɑnəmi] *n* : gastronomía *f*
gate ['geɪt] *n* : portón *m*, verja *f*, puerta *f*
gatekeeper ['geɪt,ki:pər] *n* : guarda *mf*; guardián *m*, -diana *f*
gateway ['geɪt,weɪ] *n* : puerta *f* (de acceso), entrada *f*
gather ['gæðər] *vt* **1** ASSEMBLE, COLLECT : juntar, recoger, reunir ⟨to gather dust : acumular polvo⟩ **2** HARVEST : recoger, cosechar **3** : fruncir (una tela) **4** INFER : deducir, suponer — *vi* : reunirse, congregarse, acumularse
gathering ['gæðərɪŋ] *n* : reunión *f*
gauche ['go:ʃ] *adj* : torpe, falto de tacto
gaucho ['gaʊtʃo] *n* : gaucho *m*
gaudy ['gɔdi] *adj* **gaudier; -est** : chillón, llamativo
gauge[1] ['geɪdʒ] *vt* **gauged; gauging 1** MEASURE : medir **2** ESTIMATE, JUDGE : estimar, evaluar, juzgar
gauge[2] *n* **1** : indicador *m* ⟨pressure gauge : indicador de presión⟩ **2** CALIBER : calibre *m* **3** INDICATION : indicio *m*, muestra *f*
gaunt ['gɔnt] *adj* : demacrado, descarnado
gauntlet ['gɔntlət] *n* : guante *m* ⟨to run the gauntlet of : exponerse a⟩
gauze ['gɔz] *n* : gasa *f*
gauzy ['gɔzi] *adj* **gauzier; -est** : diáfano, vaporoso

gave → **give**
gavel ['gævəl] *n* : martillo *m* (de un juez, un subastador, etc.)
gawk ['gɔk] *vi* GAPE : mirar boquiabierto
gawker ['gɔkər] *n* : mirón *m*, -rona *f*
gawky ['gɔki] *adj* **gawkier; -est** : desmañado, torpe, desgarbado
gay[1] ['geɪ] *adj* **1** MERRY : alegre **2** BRIGHT, COLORFUL : vistoso, vivo **3** HOMOSEXUAL : homosexual
gay[2] *n* HOMOSEXUAL : homosexual *mf*
gaze[1] ['geɪz] *vi* **gazed; gazing** : mirar (fijamente)
gaze[2] *n* : mirada *f* (fija)
gazebo [gə'zi:bo] *n* : pabellón *m*, cenador *m*, glorieta *f*
gazelle [gə'zɛl] *n* : gacela *f*
gazette [gə'zɛt] *n* : gaceta *f*
gazetteer [ˌgæzə'tɪr] *n* : diccionario *m* geográfico
gazpacho [gəz'pɑtʃo, gə'spɑ-] *n* : gazpacho *m*
gear[1] ['gɪr] *vt* ADAPT, ORIENT : adaptar, ajustar, orientar ⟨a book geared to children : un libro adaptado a los niños⟩ — *vi* **to gear up** : prepararse
gear[2] *n* **1** CLOTHING : ropa *f* **2** BELONGINGS : efectos *mpl* personales **3** EQUIPMENT, TOOLS : equipo *m*, aparejo *m*, herramientas *fpl* ⟨fishing gear : aparejo de pescar⟩ ⟨landing gear : tren de aterrizaje⟩ **4** COGWHEEL : rueda *f* dentada **5** : marcha *f*, velocidad *f* (de un vehículo) ⟨to put in gear : poner en marcha⟩ ⟨to change gear(s) : cambiar de velocidad⟩
gearbox ['gɪr,bɑks] *n* : caja *f* de cambios
gearshift ['gɪr,ʃɪft] *n* TRANSMISSION : palanca *f* de cambio, palanca *f* de velocidad
geek ['gi:k] *n fam* **1** : intelectual *mf* (en general); fanático *m* -ca *f* (de algo específico) ⟨a computer geek : un genio informático⟩ **2** MISFIT : inadaptado *m*, -da *f*
geese → **goose**
Geiger counter ['gaɪgər,kaʊntər] *n* : contador *m* Geiger
gel ['dʒɛl] *n* : gel *m*
gelatin ['dʒɛlətən] *n* : gelatina *f*
gem ['dʒɛm] *n* : joya *f*, gema *f*, alhaja *f*
Gemini ['dʒɛmə,naɪ] *n* **1** : Géminis *m* (signo o constelación) **2** : Géminis *mf* (persona)
gemstone ['dʒɛm,sto:n] *n* : piedra *f* (semipreciosa o preciosa), gema *f*
gender ['dʒɛndər] *n* **1** SEX : sexo *m*, género *m* (de una persona) **2** : género *m* (en la gramática)
gender identity *n* : identidad *f* de género
gender–neutral *adj* : de género neutro
gene ['dʒi:n] *n* : gen *m*, gene *m*
genealogical [ˌdʒi:niə'lɑdʒɪkəl] *adj* : genealógico
genealogy [ˌdʒi:ni'ɑlədʒi, ˌdʒɛ-, -'æ-] *n, pl* **-gies** : genealogía *f*
genera → **genus**
general[1] ['dʒɛnrəl, 'dʒɛnə-] *adj* : general ⟨in general : en general, por lo general⟩ ⟨general election : elecciones generales⟩ ⟨general knowledge : cultura general⟩

general² n : general mf
generality [ˌʤɛnəˈrælət̬i] n, pl **-ties** : generalidad f
generalization [ˌʤɛnrələˈzeɪʃən, ˌʤɛnərə-] n : generalización f
generalize [ˈʤɛnrəˌlaɪz, ˈʤɛnərə-] v **-ized; -izing** : generalizar
generally [ˈʤɛnrəli, ˈʤɛnərə-] adv : generalmente, por lo general, en general
general practitioner n : médico m, -ca f de cabecera
generate [ˈʤɛnəˌreɪt] vt **-ated; -ating** : generar, producir
generation [ˌʤɛnəˈreɪʃən] n : generación f — **generational** [ˌʤɛnəˈreɪʃənəl] adj
generator [ˈʤɛnəˌreɪt̬ər] n : generador m
generic [ʤəˈnɛrɪk] adj : genérico
generosity [ˌʤɛnəˈrɑsət̬i] n, pl **-ties** : generosidad f
generous [ˈʤɛnərəs] adj **1** OPENHANDED : generoso, dadivoso, desprendido **2** ABUNDANT, AMPLE : abundante, amplio, generoso — **generously** adv
genetic [ʤəˈnɛt̬ɪk] adj : genético — **genetically** [-t̬ɪkli] adv
genetically modified adj : transgénico
geneticist [ʤəˈnɛt̬əsɪst] n : genetista mf
genetics [ʤəˈnɛt̬ɪks] n : genética f
genial [ˈʤiːniəl] adj GRACIOUS : simpático, cordial, afable — **genially** adv
geniality [ˌʤiːniˈælət̬i] n : simpatía f, afabilidad f
genie [ˈʤiːni] n : genio m
genital [ˈʤɛnət̬əl] adj : genital
genitals [ˈʤɛnət̬əlz] npl : genitales mpl
genius [ˈʤiːnjəs] n : genio m
genocide [ˈʤɛnəˌsaɪd] n : genocidio m
genre [ˈʒɑnrə, ˈʒɑr] n : género m
genteel [ʤɛnˈtiːl] adj : cortés, fino, refinado
gentile¹ [ˈʤɛnˌtaɪl] adj : gentil
gentile² n : gentil mf
gentility [ʤɛnˈtɪlət̬i] n, pl **-ties 1** : nobleza f (de nacimiento) **2** POLITENESS, REFINEMENT : cortesía f, refinamiento m
gentle [ˈʤɛnt̬əl] adj **gentler; gentlest 1** NOBLE : bien nacido, noble **2** DOCILE : dócil, manso **3** KINDLY : bondadoso, amable **4** MILD : suave, apacible ⟨a gentle breeze : una brisa suave⟩ **5** SOFT : suave (dícese de un sonido), ligero (dícese del tacto) **6** MODERATE : moderado, gradual ⟨a gentle slope : una cuesta gradual⟩
gentleman [ˈʤɛnt̬əlmən] n, pl **-men** [-mən, -ˌmɛn] : caballero m, señor m
gentlemanly [ˈʤɛnt̬əlmənli] adj : caballeroso
gentleness [ˈʤɛnt̬əlnəs] n : delicadeza f, suavidad f, ternura f
gentlewoman [ˈʤɛnt̬əlˌwʊmən] n, pl **-women** [-ˌwɪmən] : dama f, señora f
gently [ˈʤɛntli] adv **1** CAREFULLY, SOFTLY : con cuidado, suavemente, ligeramente **2** KINDLY : amablemente, con delicadeza
gentry [ˈʤɛntri] n, pl **-tries** : aristocracia f
genuflect [ˈʤɛnjʊˌflɛkt] vi : doblar la rodilla, hacer una genuflexión

genuflection [ˌʤɛnjʊˈflɛkʃən] n : genuflexión f
genuine [ˈʤɛnjuwən] adj **1** AUTHENTIC, REAL : genuino, verdadero, auténtico **2** SINCERE : sincero — **genuinely** adv
genus [ˈʤiːnəs] n, pl **genera** [ˈʤɛ-nərə] : género m
geographer [ʤiˈɑgrəfər] n : geógrafo m, -fa f
geographical [ˌʤiːəˈgræfɪkəl] or **geographic** [-fɪk] adj : geográfico — **geographically** [-fɪkli] adv
geography [ʤiˈɑgrəfi] n, pl **-phies** : geografía f
geologic [ˌʤiːəˈlɑʤɪk] or **geological** [-ʤɪkəl] adj : geológico — **geologically** [-ʤɪkli] adv
geologist [ʤiˈɑləʤɪst] n : geólogo m, -ga f
geology [ʤiˈɑləʤi] n : geología f
geometric [ˌʤiːəˈmɛtrɪk] or **geometrical** [-trɪkəl] adj : geométrico
geometry [ʤiˈɑmətri] n, pl **-tries** : geometría f
geopolitical [ˌʤiːopəˈlɪt̬ɪkəl] adj : geopolítico
Georgian [ˈʤɔrʤən] n **1** : georgiano m (idioma) **2** : georgiano m, -na f — **Georgian** adj
geranium [ʤəˈreɪniəm] n : geranio m
gerbil [ˈʤərbəl] n : jerbo m, gerbo m
geriatric [ˌʤɛriˈætrɪk] adj : geriátrico
geriatrics [ˌʤɛriˈætrɪks] n : geriatría f
germ [ˈʤərm] n **1** MICROORGANISM : microbio m, germen m **2** BEGINNING : germen m, principio m
German [ˈʤərmən] n **1** : alemán m, -mana f **2** : alemán m (idioma) — **German** adj
germane [ʤərˈmeɪn] adj : relevante, pertinente
Germanic [ʤərˈmænɪk] adj : germano
germanium [ʤərˈmeɪniəm] n : germanio m
German measles n : rubéola f
German shepherd n : pastor m alemán
germ cell n : célula f germen
germicide [ˈʤərməˌsaɪd] n : germicida m
germinate [ˈʤərməˌneɪt] v **-nated; -nating** vi : germinar — vt : hacer germinar
germination [ˌʤərməˈneɪʃən] n : germinación f
gerund [ˈʤɛrənd] n : gerundio m
gestation [ʤɛˈsteɪʃən] n : gestación f
gesticulate [ʤɛˈstɪkjəˌleɪt] vi **-lated; -lating** : gesticular — **gesticulation** [ʤɛ-ˌstɪkjəˈleɪʃən] n
gesture¹ [ˈʤɛstʃər] vi **-tured; -turing** : gesticular, hacer gestos
gesture² n **1** : gesto m, ademán m **2** SIGN, TOKEN : gesto m, señal f ⟨a gesture of friendship : una señal de amistad⟩
get [ˈgɛt] v **got** [ˈgɑt]; **got** or **gotten** [ˈgɑt̬ən]; **getting** v **1** OBTAIN : conseguir, obtener, adquirir ⟨to get a job : conseguir trabajo⟩ ⟨she got the dress on sale : compró el vestido rebajado⟩ ⟨to get someone's attention : atraer la atención de alguien⟩ ⟨to get a good night's sleep : dormir bien⟩ **2** RECEIVE : recibir ⟨to get a letter : recibir una carta⟩

⟨we've been getting a lot of rain : ha llovido mucho⟩ **3** EARN : ganar ⟨he gets $10 an hour : gana $10 por hora⟩ **4** FETCH : traer ⟨get me my book : tráeme el libro⟩ ⟨go (and) get your coat : vete a buscar tu abrigo⟩ **5** CATCH : tomar (un tren, etc.), agarrar (una pelota, etc.) **6** SEIZE, GRASP : agarrar ⟨he got me by the arm : me agarró del brazo⟩ **7** CAPTURE : agarrar, capturar **8** SEND : mandar, hacer llegar ⟨we got a message to her : le hicimos llegar un mensaje⟩ **9** TAKE : llevar ⟨we got him to the hospital : lo llevamos al hospital⟩ **10** : hacer ir/mover (etc.) ⟨he got them out of bed : los sacó de la cama⟩ ⟨we got ourselves through customs : pasamos por la aduana⟩ **11** : hacer progresar ⟨flattery will get you nowhere : con halagos no conseguirás nada⟩ **12** FIT : hacer entrar/pasar (etc.) ⟨can you get it into this box? : ¿puedes meterlo en esta caja?⟩ ⟨I can't get the key into the lock : la llave no entra en la cerradura⟩ ⟨can you get it through the door? : ¿va a pasar por la puerta?⟩ **13** CONTRACT : contagiarse de, contraer ⟨she got the measles from him : (a ella) le dio el sarampión⟩ **14** SUFFER, SUSTAIN : sufrir (una herida, etc.) **15** PREPARE : preparar (una comida) **16** : tener (una impresión, etc.) ⟨where did you get that idea? : ¿de dónde sacaste esa idea?⟩ **17** CAUSE, ELICIT : causar, provocar ⟨to get a laugh : hacer reír⟩ **18** (to cause to do something) ⟨I can't get them to behave : no puedo hacer que se porten bien⟩ ⟨I got him to agree : logré convencerlo⟩ ⟨she got the computer working, she got the computer to work : hizo funcionar la computadora⟩ **19** (to cause to be) ⟨I got my feet wet : me mojé los pies⟩ ⟨to get one's hair cut : cortarse el pelo⟩ ⟨he got himself ready to go : se preparará para ir⟩ ⟨let me get this straight : a ver si te entiendo⟩ **20** ANSWER : contestar (el teléfono), abrir (la puerta) **21** fam BOTHER : molestar, irritar ⟨what really gets me is . . . : lo que más me molesta es . . .⟩ **22** UNDERSTAND : entender ⟨now I get it! : ¡ya entiendo!⟩ ⟨I didn't get your name : no oí su nombre⟩ **23** NOTICE : notar, ver **24** STUMP : agarrar, pillar **25** TRICK : engañar **26** MOVE, SADDEN : conmover **27** RECEIVE : captar, recibir (un canal, etc.) **28** HIT : dar ⟨it got him in the leg : le dio en la pierna⟩ **29** KILL : matar, acabar con **30 to get across** : comunicar, hacer entender **31 to get back** : recuperar (dinero, etc.) **32 to get someone back** : vengarse de alguien **33 to get down** : bajar (de un estante, etc.) **34 to get down** SWALLOW : tragar **35 to get down** DEPRESS, SADDEN : deprimir **36 to get down** WRITE DOWN : anotar **37 to get in** SUBMIT, DELIVER : entregar **38 to get in** : hacer (un comentario, etc.), dar (un golpe, etc.) ⟨to get a word in edgewise : meter baza⟩ **39 to get in** : arreglárselas

para hacer ⟨we got in a visit to the museum : pudimos visitar el museo⟩ **40 to get into** : meter (a alguien) en (un asunto) ⟨to get oneself into trouble : meterse en un lío⟩ **41 to get off** REMOVE : quitar **42 to get off** : librar de, salvar de (un castigo) **43 to get off** SEND : mandar, enviar **44 to get out** EXTRACT, REMOVE : sacar, quitar **45 to get something out of someone** : sacarle algo a alguien **46 to get something over with** : quitarse algo de encima **47 to get through** : hacer llegar (un mensaje, etc.) **48 to get through** SUSTAIN : mantener, sustentar **49 to get through** LAST : alcanzar **50 to get together** COLLECT : juntar, reunir ⟨to get oneself together : organizarse⟩ **51 to get up** RAISE, LIFT : subir **52 to get up** MUSTER : armarse de (valor), cobrar (fuerzas) **53 to get up** : organizar (una petición, etc.) **54 to have got** : tener ⟨I've got a headache : tengo un dolor de cabeza⟩ **55 to have got to** : tener que ⟨you've got to come : tienes que venir⟩ — vi **1** BECOME : ponerse, volverse, hacerse ⟨to get angry : ponerse furioso, enojarse⟩ ⟨to get wet/dirty : mojarse/ensuciarse⟩ ⟨to get dressed : vestirse⟩ ⟨to get used to something : acostumbrarse a algo⟩ ⟨to get lost : perderse⟩ ⟨it's getting late : se hace tarde⟩ **2** GO, MOVE : ir, avanzar ⟨he didn't get far : no avanzó mucho⟩ **3** PROGRESS : progresar, avanzar ⟨now we're getting somewhere! : ¡ahora sí que estamos progresando!⟩ **4** ARRIVE : llegar ⟨to get home : llegar a casa⟩ ⟨she got to the last page : llegó a la última página⟩ **5 get out (of here)!** (expressing surprise or disbelief) : ¡anda!, ¡qué va! **6 to get across** COMMUNICATE : comunicarse, hacerse entender **7 to get after** fam NAG : estar encima de/a **8 to get ahead** : adelantarse, progresar **9 to get along** : llevarse bien (con alguien), congeniar **10 to get along** MANAGE : arreglárselas **11 to get along** PROGRESS : marchar, progresar **12 to get around** SPREAD, CIRCULATE : difundirse ⟨word got around that . . . : se corrió la voz de que . . .⟩ **13 to get around** CIRCUMVENT : evitar, vencer **14 to get around** WALK : caminar, andar **15 to get around** TRAVEL : viajar **16 to get around to doing something** : encontrar el tiempo para hacer algo **17 to get at** REACH : llegar a, alcanzar **18 to get at** DISCOVER : descubrir **19 to get at** IMPLY : insinuar **20 to get away** : salir ⟨I can't get away until later : no puedo salir hasta más tarde⟩ **21 to get away** ESCAPE : escaparse **22 to get away** : ir de vacaciones **23 to get away** MANAGE : arreglárselas (con/sin algo) **24 to get away with** ⟨to get away with a crime : salir impune de un delito⟩ ⟨how does he get away with being so rude? : ¿cómo se le permite ser tan grosero?⟩ **25 to get back** RETURN : volver **26 to get** back RETREAT : echarse atrás **27 to get back at someone** : vengarse de alguien **28 to get back to** : volver a, reanudar (una actividad) **29 to get back to** : volver a contactar **30 to get behind** : atrasarse **31 to get behind** SUPPORT : apoyar **32 to get by** MANAGE : arreglárselas **33 to get down to something** : ponerse a hacer algo **34 to get going** LEAVE : irse **35 to get going** : ponerse a hablar **36 to get going on something** : ponerse a hacer algo **37 to get in** ENTER : entrar ⟨it got in through the window : entró por la ventana⟩ **38 to get in** ARRIVE : llegar **39 to get in** : entrar, ser aceptado **40 to get into** : entrar en/a (una universidad, etc) **41 to get into** : meterse en (una situación) ⟨to get into trouble : meterse en un lío⟩ ⟨to get into an argument : empezar a discutir⟩ **42 to get into** : entusiasmarse con, interesarse en **43 to get into** : afectar a ⟨what's gotten into him? : ¿qué le pasa?⟩ **44 to get into** : llegar a (un lugar) **45 to get into** : ponerse ⟨I can't get into these jeans : estos jeans no me entran⟩ **46 to get in/into** BOARD : subir (a) **47 to get it** ⟨when mom finds out, you're going to get it! : cuando mamá se entere, ¡te mata!⟩ **48 to get off** : quedar impune ⟨to get off with a warning : librarse con sólo una amonestación⟩ **49 to get off** : salir (del trabajo) **50 to get off** : salirse de (un tema, etc.) **51 to get off (of)** EXIT : bajarse (de) **52 to get on** : llevarse bien (con alguien) **53 to get on** ⟨how are you getting on? : ¿qué tal te va?⟩ **54 to get on** SUCCEED : tener éxito **55 to get on** : ocuparse de ⟨I'll get right on it : lo haré ahora mismo⟩ **56 to get on/onto** MOUNT : montarse (a) **57 to get on/onto** BOARD : subirse (a) **58 to get onto** : empezar a hablar de (un tema) **59 to get on with** : seguir con (una actividad) **60 to get out** LEAVE : salir **61 to get out** LEAK : difundirse, filtrarse **62 to get out (of)** EXIT : bajarse (de) **63 to get out of** : escapar de **64 to get out of** : salvarse de **65 to get over** : recuperarse de (una enfermedad, etc.), superar (el miedo, etc.), aceptar (una situación), no guardar (rencor), olvidar a (un amante), consolarse de (una pérdida) **66 to get through** : sobrevivir (el invierno), superar (una crisis, etc.) **67 to get through** : aprobar (un examen) **68 to get through** : comunicar (por teléfono) **69 to get through** : hacer entender ⟨I think I finally got through (to him) : creo que por fin lo hice entender⟩ **70 to get through (with)** FINISH : terminar, acabar **71 to get to** BOTHER : molestar, irritar **72 to get to be** BECOME : llegar a ser **73 to get together** MEET : reunirse **74 to get together** UNITE : unirse, juntarse **75 to get up** : levantarse **76 to get up on** : subirse a **77 to get up to** : hacer (travesuras, etc.) **78 to get up to** REACH : alcanzar, llegar hasta — *v aux* ⟨I got

paid : me pagaron⟩ ⟨they got married : se casaron⟩

getaway [ˈɡɛtəˌweɪ] *n* ESCAPE : fuga *f*, huida *f*, escapada *f*

get–go [ˈɡɪtˌɡoː, ˈɡɛt-] *n* from the **get–go** : desde el primer momento

get–together [ˈɡɛttəˌɡɛðər] *n* : reunión *f* (informal)

geyser [ˈɡaɪzər] *n* : géiser *m*

Ghanaian [ɡɑˈniən, ˈɡæ-] *n* : ghanés *m*, -nesa *f* — **Ghanaian** *adj*

ghastly [ˈɡæstli] *adj* **ghastlier; -est 1** HORRIBLE : horrible, espantoso **2** PALE : pálido, cadavérico

gherkin [ˈɡərkən] *n* : pepinillo *m*

ghetto [ˈɡɛtoː] *n*, *pl* **-tos** *or* **-toes** : gueto *m*

ghost [ˈɡoːst] *n* **1** : fantasma *m*, espectro *m* **2 the Holy Ghost** : el Espíritu Santo

ghostly [ˈɡoːstli] *adv* : fantasmal

ghoul [ˈɡuːl] *n* **1** : demonio *m* (que come cadáveres) **2** : persona *f* de gustos macabros

GI [ˌʤiːˈaɪ] *n*, *pl* **GI's** *or* **GIs** : soldado *m* estadounidense

giant¹ [ˈʤaɪənt] *adj* : gigante, gigantesco, enorme

giant² *n* : gigante *m*, -ta *f*

gibberish [ˈʤɪbərɪʃ] *n* : galimatías *m*, jerigonza *f*

gibbon [ˈɡɪbən] *n* : gibón *m*

gibe¹ [ˈʤaɪb] *vi* **gibed; gibing** : mofarse, burlarse

gibe² *n* : pulla *f*, burla *f*, mofa *f*

giblets [ˈʤɪbləts] *npl* : menudos *mpl*, menudencias *fpl*

giddiness [ˈɡɪdinəs] *n* **1** DIZZINESS : vértigo *m*, mareo *m* **2** SILLINESS : frivolidad *f*, estupidez *f*

giddy [ˈɡɪdi] *adj* **giddier; -est 1** DIZZY : mareado, vertiginoso **2** FRIVOLOUS, SILLY : frívolo, tonto

gift [ˈɡɪft] *n* **1** TALENT : don *m*, talento *m*, dotes *fpl* **2** PRESENT : regalo *m*, obsequio *m*

gift card *n* : tarjeta *f* de regalo, tarjeta *f* regalo

gift certificate *n* : certificado *m* de regalo

gifted [ˈɡɪftəd] *adj* TALENTED : talentoso

gig¹ [ˈɡɪɡ] *n* : trabajo *m* (de duración limitada) ⟨to play a gig : tocar en un concierto⟩

gig² *n fam* : giga *mf fam*, gigabyte *m*

gigabyte [ˈʤɪɡəˌbaɪt, ˈɡɪ-] *n* : gigabyte *m*

gigantic [ʤaɪˈɡæntɪk] *adj* : gigantesco, enorme, colosal

giggle¹ [ˈɡɪɡəl] *vi* **-gled; -gling** : reírse tontamente

giggle² *n* : risita *f*, risa *f* tonta

gild [ˈɡɪld] *vt* **gilded** *or* **gilt** [ˈɡɪlt]; **gilding** : dorar

gill [ˈɡɪl] *n* : agalla *f*, branquia *f*

gilt¹ [ˈɡɪlt] *adj* : dorado

gilt² *n* : dorado *m*

gimlet [ˈɡɪmlət] *n* **1** : barrena *f* (herramienta) **2** : bebida *f* de vodka o ginebra y limón

gimmick [ˈɡɪmɪk] *n* **1** GADGET : artilugio *m* **2** CATCH : engaño *m*, trampa *f* **3** SCHEME, TRICK : ardid *m*, truco *m*

gin ['ʤɪn] *n* : ginebra *f* (bebida alcohólica)

ginger ['ʤɪnʤər] *n* : jengibre *m*

ginger ale *n* : gaseosa *f* de jengibre

gingerbread ['ʤɪnʤər,brɛd] *n* : pan *m* de jengibre

gingerly ['ʤɪnʤərli] *adv* : con cuidado, cautelosamente

gingham ['gɪnəm] *n* : guinga *f*

ginseng ['ʤɪn,sɪŋ, -,sɛŋ] *n* : ginseng *m*

giraffe [ʤə'ræf] *n* : jirafa *f*

gird ['gərd] *vt* **girded** *or* **girt** ['gərt]; **girding** **1** BIND : ceñir, atar **2** ENCIRCLE : rodear **3 to gird oneself** : prepararse

girder ['gərdər] *n* : viga *f*

girdle[1] ['gərdəl] *v* -**dled**; -**dling** **1** GIRD : ceñir, atar **2** SURROUND : rodear, circundar

girdle[2] *n* : faja *f*

girl ['gərl] *n* **1** : chica *f*, muchacha *f* **2** *or* **little girl** : niña *f*, chica *f* **3** SWEETHEART : novia *f* **4** DAUGHTER : hija *f*

girlfriend ['gərl,frɛnd] *n* : novia *f*, amiga *f*

girlhood ['gərl,hʊd] *n* : niñez *f*, juventud *f* (de una muchacha)

girlish ['gərlɪʃ] *adj* : de niña

girth ['gərθ] *n* **1** : circunferencia *f* (de un árbol, etc.), cintura *f* (de una persona) **2** CINCH : cincha *f* (para caballos, etc.)

gist ['ʤɪst] *n* : quid *m*, meollo *m*

give[1] ['gɪv] *v* **gave** ['geɪv]; **given** ['gɪvən]; **giving** *vt* **1** HAND : dar, entregar ⟨give it to me : dámelo⟩ **2** PRESENT : dar, regalar ⟨they gave him a gold watch : le regalaron un reloj de oro⟩ **3** DONATE : dar, donar ⟨to give blood : dar sangre⟩ ⟨to give money to charity : dar dinero a organizaciones benéficas⟩ **4** PAY : dar, pagar ⟨I'll give you $10 for the blue one : te daré $10 por el azul⟩ **5** : dar (un grito, un salto, etc.) ⟨she gave me a kiss : me dio un beso⟩ ⟨he gave us the signal : nos dio la señal⟩ **6** ADMINISTER : dar (un castigo, una inyección, etc.) **7** OFFER : dar ⟨he gave me his hand : me dio la mano⟩ ⟨she didn't give a reason : no dijo por qué⟩ **8** PROVIDE : dar ⟨to give one's word : dar uno su palabra⟩ ⟨she gave me a ride to work : me llevó a la oficina⟩ ⟨cows give milk : las vacas dan leche⟩ **9** ATTRIBUTE : dar ⟨to give credit to someone : darle el mérito a alguien⟩ **10** PRONOUNCE : dictar (una sentencia) **11** CAUSE : dar, causar, ocasionar ⟨to give trouble : causar problemas⟩ ⟨to give someone to understand : darle a entender a alguien⟩ **12** GRANT : dar, otorgar ⟨to give permission : dar permiso⟩ **13 to give away** : regalar **14 to give away** REVEAL : revelar **15 to give away** : llevar (una novia) al altar **16 to give away** BETRAY : delatar **17 to give back** RETURN : devolver **18 to give in (to)** : ceder (a) **19 to give off** EMIT : despedir **20 to give oneself (over) to** : entregarse a **21 to give out** DISTRIBUTE : distribuir **22 to give up** : dejar, renunciar a, abandonar ⟨to give up smoking : dejar de fumar⟩ — *vi* **1** : hacer regalos **2** *or* **to give way** YIELD : ceder, romperse ⟨it gave under

the weight of the crowd : cedió bajo el peso de la muchedumbre⟩ **3 to give in/ up** SURRENDER : rendirse, entregarse **4 to give out** RUN OUT : agotarse, acabarse

give[2] *n* FLEXIBILITY : flexibilidad *f*, elasticidad *f*

give–and–take *n* : toma y daca *m*

giveaway ['gɪvə,weɪ] *n* **1** : revelación *f* involuntaria **2** GIFT : regalo *m*, obsequio *m*

given ['gɪvən] *adj* **1** INCLINED : dado, inclinado ⟨he's given to quarreling : es muy dado a discutir⟩ **2** SPECIFIC : dado, determinado ⟨at a given time : en un momento dado⟩

given name *n* : nombre *m* de pila

give or take *adv* APPROXIMATELY : más o menos

gizzard ['gɪzərd] *n* : molleja *f*

glacial ['gleɪʃəl] *adj* : glacial — **glacially** *adv*

glacier ['gleɪʃər] *n* : glaciar *m*

glad ['glæd] *adj* **gladder; gladdest** **1** PLEASED : alegre, contento ⟨she was glad I came : se alegró de que haya venido⟩ ⟨glad to meet you! : ¡mucho gusto!⟩ **2** HAPPY, PLEASING : feliz, agradable ⟨glad tidings : buenas nuevas⟩ **3** WILLING : dispuesto, gustoso ⟨I'll be glad to do it : lo haré con mucho gusto⟩

gladden ['glædən] *vt* : alegrar

glade ['gleɪd] *n* : claro *m*

gladiator ['glædi,eɪtər] *n* : gladiador *m*

gladiolus [,glædi'oːləs] *n*, *pl* -**li** [-li, -,laɪ] : gladiolo *m*, gladíolo *m*

gladly ['glædli] *adv* : con mucho gusto

gladness ['glædnəs] *n* : alegría *f*, gozo *m*

glamor *or* **glamour** ['glæmər] *n* : atractivo *m*, hechizo *m*, encanto *m*

glamorous ['glæmərəs] *adj* : atractivo, encantador

glamping ['glæmpɪŋ] *n* : glamping *m fam*, camping *m* de lujo

glance[1] ['glænʦ] *vi* **glanced; glancing** **1** RICOCHET : rebotar ⟨it glanced off the wall : rebotó en la pared⟩ **2 to glance at** : mirar, echar un vistazo a **3 to glance away** : apartar los ojos

glance[2] *n* : mirada *f*, vistazo *m*, ojeada *f*

gland ['glænd] *n* : glándula *f*

glandular ['glænʤʊlər] *adj* : glandular

glare[1] ['glær] *vi* **glared; glaring** **1** SHINE : brillar, relumbrar **2** STARE : mirar con ira, lanzar una mirada feroz

glare[2] *n* **1** BRIGHTNESS : resplandor *m*, luz *f* deslumbrante **2** STARE : mirada *f* feroz

glaring ['glærɪŋ] *adj* **1** BRIGHT : deslumbrante, brillante **2** FLAGRANT, OBVIOUS : flagrante, manifiesto ⟨a glaring error : un error que salta a la vista⟩

glaringly ['glærɪŋli] *adv* ⟨to be glaringly obvious : saltar a la vista⟩

glass ['glæs] *n* **1** : vidrio *m*, cristal *m* (de una ventana etc.) **2** : vaso *m* ⟨a glass of milk : un vaso de leche⟩ **3 glasses** *npl* SPECTACLES : gafas *fpl*, anteojos *mpl*, lentes *mpl*, espejuelos *mpl*

glassblowing ['glæs,bloːɪŋ] *n* : soplado *m* del vidrio

glassful [ˈglæsˌfʊl] *n* : vaso *m*, copa *f*

glassware [ˈglæsˌwær] *n* : cristalería *f*

glassy [ˈglæsi] *adj* **glassier; -est** **1** : vítreo **2** : vidrioso ⟨glassy eyes : ojos vidriosos⟩

glaucoma [glaʊˈkoːmə, glɔ-] *n* : glaucoma *m*

glaze¹ [ˈgleɪz] *vt* **glazed; glazing** **1** : ponerle vidrios a (una ventana, etc.) **2** : vidriar (cerámica) **3** : glasear (papel, verduras, etc.)

glaze² *n* : vidriado *m*, glaseado *m*, barniz *m*

glazier [ˈgleɪʒər] *n* : vidriero *m*, -ra *f*

glazing [ˈgleɪzɪŋ] *n* : vidrios *mpl*, acristalamiento *m Spain* ⟨double-glazing : doble vidrio, doble acristalamiento⟩

gleam¹ [ˈgliːm] *vi* : brillar, destellar, relucir

gleam² *n* **1** LIGHT : luz *f* (oscura) **2** GLINT : destello *m* **3** GLIMMER : rayo *m*, vislumbre *f* ⟨a gleam of hope : un rayo de esperanza⟩

glean [ˈgliːn] *vt* : recoger, espigar

glee [ˈgliː] *n* : alegría *f*, júbilo *m*, regocijo *m*

gleeful [ˈgliːfəl] *adj* : lleno de alegría

glen [ˈglɛn] *n* : cañada *f*

glib [ˈglɪb] *adj* **glibber; glibbest** **1** : simplista ⟨a glib reply : una respuesta simplista⟩ **2** : con mucha labia (dícese de una persona)

glibly [ˈglɪbli] *adv* : con mucha labia

glide¹ [ˈglaɪd] *vi* **glided; gliding** : deslizarse (en una superficie), planear (en el aire)

glide² *n* : planeo *m*

glider [ˈglaɪdər] *n* **1** : planeador *m* (aeronave) **2** : mecedor *m* (tipo de columpio)

glimmer¹ [ˈglɪmər] *vi* : brillar con luz trémula

glimmer² *n* **1** : luz *f* trémula, luz *f* tenue **2** GLEAM : rayo *m*, vislumbre *f* ⟨a glimmer of understanding : un rayo de entendimiento⟩

glimpse¹ [ˈglɪmps] *vt* **glimpsed; glimpsing** : vislumbrar, entrever

glimpse² *n* : mirada *f* breve ⟨to catch a glimpse of : alcanzar a ver, vislumbrar⟩

glint¹ [ˈglɪnt] *vi* GLEAM, SPARKLE : destellar

glint² *n* **1** SPARKLE : destello *m*, centelleo *m* **2 to have a glint in one's eye** : chispearle los ojos a uno

glisten¹ [ˈglɪsən] *vi* : brillar, centellear

glisten² *n* : brillo *m*, centelleo *m*

glitch [ˈglɪtʃ] *n* **1** MALFUNCTION : mal funcionamiento *m* **2** SNAG : problema *m*, complicación *f*

glitter¹ [ˈglɪtər] *vi* **1** SPARKLE : destellar, relucir, brillar **2** FLASH : relampaguear ⟨his eyes glittered in anger : le relampagueaban los ojos de ira⟩

glitter² *n* **1** BRIGHTNESS : brillo *m* **2** : purpurina *f* (para decoración)

glitz [ˈglɪts] *n* : oropel *m*

gloat [ˈgloːt] *vi* **to gloat over** : regodearse en

glob [ˈglab] *n* : plasta *f*, masa *f*, grumo *m*

global [ˈgloːbəl] *adj* **1** FULL, COMPREHENSIVE : global **2** WORLDWIDE : global, mundial — **globally** *adv* —

globalization [ˌgloːbələˈzeɪʃən] *n*

global warming *n* : calentamiento *m* global

globe [ˈgloːb] *n* **1** SPHERE : esfera *f*, globo *m* **2** EARTH : globo *m*, Tierra *f* **3** : globo *m* terráqueo (modelo de la Tierra)

globe–trotter [ˈgloːbˌtratər] *n* : trotamundos *mf*

globule [ˈglaˌbjuːl] *n* : glóbulo *m*

gloom [ˈgluːm] *n* **1** DARKNESS : penumbra *f*, oscuridad *f* **2** MELANCHOLY : melancolía *f*, tristeza *f*

gloomily [ˈgluːməli] *adv* : tristemente

gloomy [ˈgluːmi] *adj* **gloomier; -est** **1** DARK : oscuro, tenebroso ⟨gloomy weather : tiempo gris⟩ **2** MELANCHOLY : melancólico **3** PESSIMISTIC : pesimista **4** DEPRESSING : deprimente, lúgubre

glorification [ˌgloːrəfəˈkeɪʃən] *n* : glorificación *f*

glorify [ˈgloːrəˌfaɪ] *vt* **-fied; -fying** : glorificar

glorious [ˈgloːriəs] *adj* **1** ILLUSTRIOUS : glorioso, ilustre **2** MAGNIFICENT : magnífico, espléndido, maravilloso — **gloriously** *adv*

glory¹ [ˈgloːri] *vi* **-ried; -rying** EXULT : exultar, regocijarse

glory² *n, pl* **-ries** **1** RENOWN : gloria *f*, fama *f*, honor *m* **2** PRAISE : gloria *f* ⟨glory to God : gloria a Dios⟩ **3** MAGNIFICENCE : magnificencia *f*, esplendor *m*, gloria *f* **4 to be in one's glory** : estar uno en su gloria

gloss¹ [ˈglɔs, ˈglas] *vt* **1** EXPLAIN : glosar, explicar **2** POLISH : lustrar, pulir **3 to gloss over** : quitarle importancia a, minimizar

gloss² *n* **1** SHINE : lustre *m*, brillo *m* **2** EXPLANATION : glosa *f*, explicación *f* breve **3** → **glossary**

glossary [ˈglɔsəri, ˈgla-] *n, pl* **-ries** : glosario *m*

glossy [ˈglɔsi, ˈgla-] *adj* **glossier; -est** : brillante, lustroso, satinado (dícese del papel)

glove [ˈglʌv] *n* : guante *m* ⟨boxing glove : guante de boxeo⟩

glove compartment *n* : guantera *f*

glow¹ [ˈgloː] *vi* **1** SHINE : brillar, resplandecer **2** BRIM : rebosar ⟨to glow with health : rebosar de salud⟩

glow² *n* **1** BRIGHTNESS : resplandor *m*, brillo *m*, luminosidad *f* **2** FEELING : sensación *f* (de bienestar), oleada *f* (de sentimiento) **3** INCANDESCENCE : incandescencia *f*

glower [ˈglaʊər] *vi* : fruncir el ceño

glowworm [ˈgloːˌwərm] *n* : luciérnaga *f*

glucose [ˈgluːˌkoːs] *n* : glucosa *f*

glue¹ [ˈgluː] *vt* **glued; gluing** *or* **glueing** : pegar con cola

glue² *n* : pegamento *m*, cola *f*

gluey [ˈgluːi] *adj* **gluier; -est** : pegajoso

glum [ˈglʌm] *adj* **glummer; glummest** **1** SULLEN : hosco, sombrío **2** DREARY, GLOOMY : sombrío, triste, melancólico

glut[1] [ˈglʌt] *vt* **glutted; glutting 1** SA-
TIATE : saciar, hartar **2** : inundar (el
mercado)
glut[2] *n* : exceso *m*, superabundancia *f*
glutinous [ˈgluːtənəs] *adj* STICKY : pegajoso, glutinoso
glutton [ˈglʌtən] *n* : glotón *m*, -tona *f*
gluttonous [ˈglʌtənəs] *adj* : glotón
gluttony [ˈglʌtəni] *n, pl* **-tonies** : glotonería *f*, gula *f*
glycerin *or* **glycerine** [ˈglɪsrən, ˈglɪ-] *n*
: glicerina *f*
gnarled [ˈnɑrld] *adj* **1** KNOTTY : nudoso **2** TWISTED : retorcido
gnash [ˈnæʃ] *vt* : hacer rechinar (los dientes)
gnat [ˈnæt] *n* : jején *m*
gnaw [ˈnɔ] *vt* : roer
gnome [ˈnoːm] *n* : gnomo *m*
gnu [ˈnuː, ˈnjuː] *n, pl* **gnu** *or* **gnus** : ñu *m*
go[1] [ˈgoː] *v* **went** [ˈwɛnt]; **gone** [ˈgɔn ˈgɑn];
going; goes [ˈgoːz] *vi* **1** : ir ⟨to go slow
: ir despacio⟩ ⟨to go shopping : ir de
compras⟩ ⟨to go to work : ir a trabajar⟩
⟨to go to school : ir a la escuela⟩ ⟨we
went to Spain : fuimos a España⟩ ⟨we
went to see a movie : fuimos a ver una
película⟩ ⟨you should go (to/and) see
her : deberías ir a verla⟩ ⟨we went up/
down to the mountains : fuimos a las
montañas, fuimos al norte/sur a ver las
montañas⟩ ⟨to go for a drive : ir a dar
una vuelta en coche⟩ ⟨to go on foot : ir
a pie⟩ **2** (*used figuratively*) : ir ⟨she'll go
far : llegará lejos⟩ ⟨I wouldn't go so far
as to say that . . . : no diría tanto como
que . . .⟩ ⟨this time he's gone too far
: esta vez se ha pasado⟩ ⟨to go a long
way towards : ayudar en gran medida
a⟩ **3** LEAVE : irse, marcharse, salir ⟨let's
go! : ¡vámonos!⟩ ⟨the train went on time
: el tren salió a tiempo⟩ **4** DISAPPEAR
: pasarse, irse ⟨her fear is gone : se le ha
pasado el miedo⟩ ⟨those days have gone
: esos días ya pasaron⟩ **5** DIE : morir **6**
EXTEND : ir, extenderse, llegar ⟨this
road goes to the river : este camino se
extiende hasta el río⟩ ⟨to go from top to
bottom : ir de arriba abajo⟩ **7** LEAD,
CONNECT : dar ⟨that door goes to the
cellar : esa puerta da al sótano⟩ **8**
FUNCTION : funcionar, marchar ⟨the car
won't go : el coche no funciona⟩ ⟨to get
something going : poner algo en mar-
cha⟩ **9** SELL : venderse ⟨it goes for $15
: se vende por $15⟩ **10** (*to be disposed
of*) ⟨that one can go : podemos deshacer-
nos de ése⟩ **11** FAIL : fallarse (dícese de
la vista, etc.), gastarse (dícese de pilas,
etc.), estropearse (dícese de un motor,
etc.) **12** GIVE WAY : ceder, romperse
(dícese de un dique, etc.) **13** PROGRESS
: ir, andar, seguir ⟨my exam went well
: me fue bien en el examen⟩ ⟨how did
the meeting go? : ¿qué tal la reunión?⟩ **14** BECOME : volverse, quedarse ⟨to go crazy : volverse loco⟩ ⟨he's
going bald : se está quedando calvo⟩
⟨the tire went flat : la llanta se desin-
fló⟩ **15** (*describing a condition*) ⟨to go

hungry : pasar hambre⟩ ⟨to go barefoot
: ir descalzo⟩ ⟨to go unnoticed : pasar
desapercibido⟩ **16** (*describing a story,
song, etc.*) ⟨how does the story go? : ¿qué
pasa en el cuento?⟩ ⟨how does the song
go? — it goes like this: . . . : ¿cómo es la
canción? — es así: . . .⟩ ⟨the legend goes
that . . . : cuenta la leyenda que . . . ,
según (dice) la leyenda . . .⟩ **17** FIT
: caber ⟨it will go through the door
: cabe por la puerta⟩ **18** : pasar (dícese
del tiempo) ⟨the time went quickly : el
tiempo pasó rápidamente⟩ **19** SOUND
: sonar **20 anything goes!** : ¡todo
vale! **21 to be good/ready to go** : estar
listo **22 to go** : faltar ⟨only 10 days to
go : faltan sólo 10 días⟩ ⟨we still have a
long way to go : aún nos queda mucho
camino por recorrer⟩ **23 to go** : para
llevar (dícese de comida, etc.) **24 to go
about** DO : hacer **25 to go about** AP-
PROACH, TACKLE : abordar, emprender **26 to go after** PURSUE : perseguir **27 to go against** : ir en contra
de **28 to go against** : jugar contra (en
deportes) **29 to go ahead** (*to proceed
without delay or hesitation*) ⟨go ahead
and start without me : empiecen sin mí⟩
⟨I went ahead and bought it : me decidí
y lo compré⟩ ⟨sure, go (right) ahead!
: ¡por supuesto!⟩ **30 to go ahead (with)**
: seguir adelante (con) **31 to go all out**
: hacer lo máximo ⟨he went all out for
his wife's birthday : en el cumpleaños de
su esposa tiró la casa por la ventana⟩ **32
to go along** PROCEED : ir, marchar **33
to go along** ACQUIESCE : acceder ⟨to go
along with something : acceder a algo,
aceptar algo⟩ ⟨to go along with someone
: cooperar con alguien⟩ **34 to go along
with** ⟨the stress that goes along with the
job : el estrés que conllea el tra-
bajo⟩ **35 to go around** : correr (dícese
de un rumor, etc.), circular ⟨there's a
bug going around : hay un virus dando
vueltas por ahí⟩ **36 to go around**
⟨there's enough/plenty to go around
: hay para todos⟩ **37 to go at** ATTACK
: atacar **38 to go at** : atacar, abordar
(un problema, etc.) **39 to go at it** AR-
GUE, FIGHT : discutir, pelearse **40 to go
away** LEAVE : irse **41 to go away** DIS-
APPEAR : desaparecer **42 to go back**
RETURN : volver (a un lugar, un tema,
etc.) ⟨he never went back : nunca
volvió⟩ ⟨to go back to school : volver a
la escuela⟩ **43 to go back** : remontarse
⟨the records go back to 1900 : los regis-
tros se remontan a 1900⟩ ⟨we go back a
long way : nos conocemos desde hace
muchos años⟩ **44 to go back on** : faltar
uno a (su promesa) **45 to go back to
(doing) something** : volver a hacer algo,
reanudar algo ⟨to go back to sleep
: volver a dormir⟩ ⟨she went back to
work : reanudó el trabajo⟩ ⟨afterwards
he went back to reading : después siguió
leyendo⟩ **46 to go bad** SPOIL : estropearse, echarse a perder **47 to go beyond**
: ir más allá de **48 to go by** PASS

: pasar   **49 to go by** : guiarse por (una regla, etc.), juzgar por (las apariencias, etc.)   **50 to go by** : hacerse llamar ⟨he goes by "Ed" : se hace llamar "Ed"⟩   **51 to go by** STOP BY : pasar por   **52 to go down** : hundirse (dícese de un barco), caer (dícese de un avión), caerse (dícese de una persona)   **53 to go down** DECREASE : bajar, disminuir   **54 to go down** : dejar de funcionar (dícese de un sistema, etc.)   **55 to go down** : caer (dícese de un gobierno, etc.)   **56 to go down** SET : ponerse (dícese del sol)   **57 to go down** : pasar (dícese de comida) ⟨it went down the wrong way : se me atragantó, se me fue por mal camino⟩   **58 to go down in history** → history   **59 to go down well/badly** : caer bien/mal, tener una buena/mala acogida   **60 to go for** : interesarse uno en, gustarle a uno (algo, alguien) ⟨I don't go for that : eso no me interesa⟩   **61 to go for** SELECT : decidirse por   **62 to go for** ACCEPT : aceptar   **63 to go for** ATTACK : atacar   **64 to go for** PURSUE : ir tras, ir a por *Spain*   **65 to go for** : ir por ⟨that goes for you, too! : ¡también va por ti!⟩   **66 to go in** : esconderse (dícese del sol o de la luna)   **67 to go in on** ⟨we both/all went in on the gift together : el regalo lo compramos a medias/entre todos⟩   **68 to go in for** LIKE : interesarse uno en, gustarle a uno (algo)   **69 to go into** : entrar en ⟨to go into action/effect : entrar en acción/vigor⟩ ⟨to go into hiding : esconderse⟩   **70 to go into** DISCUSS : entrar en   **71 to go into** LOOK INTO : investigar   **72 to go into** : dedicarse a (una profesión)   **73 to go off** : estallar, explotar (dícese de una bomba, etc.), dispararse (dícese de una pistola, etc.)   **74 to go off** SOUND : sonar   **75 to go off** : echarse a perder (dícese de la comida, etc.)   **76 to go off** TURN OFF : apagarse   **77 to go off on** *fam* SCOLD : regañar   **78 to go on** CONTINUE : seguir, continuar ⟨life goes on : la vida sigue⟩ ⟨we can't go on like this : no podemos seguir así⟩ ⟨we went on to Chicago : seguimos el viaje a Chicago, continuamos nuestro camino a Chicago⟩ ⟨she went on working : siguió trabajando⟩ ⟨she went on to say that . . . : pasó a decir que . . .⟩ ⟨to go on to become : llegar/pasar a ser⟩   **79 to go on** LAST : durar   **80 to go on** HAPPEN : pasar, ocurrir ⟨what's going on? : ¿qué pasa?⟩   **81 to go on** RAMBLE : no parar de hablar   **82 to go on** : guiarse por (pruebas, etc.)   **83 to go on (ahead)** : ir adelante, adelantarse   **84 to go out** LEAVE : salir   **85 to go out** : apagarse ⟨the power went out : se fue la electricidad⟩   **86 to go out** : bajar (dícese de la marea)   **87 to go out** : emitirse (dícese de un anuncio, etc.)   **88 to go out with** DATE : salir con   **89 to go over** EXAMINE, REVIEW : examinar, repasar   **90 to go over to** : pasarse a (la competencia, etc.)   **91 to go over to** APPROACH : acercarse a   **92 to go over well/badly** : caer bien/mal, tener una buena/mala acogida   **93 to go there** *fam* ⟨let's not go there : no quiero hablar/pensar de eso⟩   **94 to go through** PIERCE : penetrar, atravesar   **95 to go through** USE UP : gastar, agotar   **96 to go through** SEARCH : registrar, revolver en   **97 to go through** : pasar por (dificultades, etapas, etc.)   **98 to go through** PERFORM : hacer   **99 to go through** : ser aprobado (dícese de un proyecto de ley, etc.)   **100 to go through someone's head/mind** : pasársele por la cabeza/mente a alguien   **101 to go through with** : llevar a cabo   **102 to go to** : otorgarse a, transmitirse a ⟨the prize went to . . . : el premio se lo llevó . . .⟩   **103 to go to** (*to begin to be in*) ⟨to go to sleep : dormirse⟩ ⟨to go to war : entrar en guerra⟩   **104 to go together** MATCH : combinar, hacer juego, armonizar   **105 to go to show/prove** : demostrar   **106 to go to trouble/expense (etc.)** ⟨he went to a lot of trouble : se esmeró mucho⟩ ⟨they went to great expense : gastaron mucho⟩   **107 to go towards** : contribuir a   **108 to go under** FOUNDER : hundirse   **109 to go up** RISE, INCREASE : subir   **110 to go up** : levantarse (dícese de un edificio)   **111 to go up with** MATCH : armonizar con, hacer juego con, ir bien con   **112 to go with** CHOOSE : elegir, decidirse por   **113 to go without** MAKE DO : arreglárselas (sin algo)   **114 to go without something** : prescindir de algo — *v aux* **to be going to** : ir a ⟨I'm going to write a letter : voy a escribir una carta⟩ ⟨it's not going to last : no va a durar⟩

go² *n, pl* **goes**   **1** ATTEMPT : intento *m* ⟨to have a go at : intentar, probar⟩   **2** SUCCESS : éxito *m*   **3** ENERGY : energía *f*, empuje *m* ⟨to be on the go : no parar, no descansar⟩

goad¹ [ˈgoːd] *vt* : aguijonear (un animal), incitar (a una persona)

goad² *n* : aguijón *m*

go–ahead *n* APPROVAL : luz *f* verde

goal [ˈgoːl] *n*   **1** : portería *f*, arco *m*, marco *m* (en deportes)   **2** : gol *m* (en deportes) ⟨to score a goal : anotar un gol⟩   **3** AIM, OBJECTIVE : meta *m*, objetivo *m*

goalie [ˈgoːli] → **goalkeeper**

goalkeeper [ˈgoːl͜kiːpər] *n* : portero *m*, -ra *f*; guardameta *mf*; arquero *m*, -ra *f*

goalpost [ˈgoːl͜poːst] *n* : poste *m* (de la portería)

goaltender [ˈgoːl͜tɛndər] → **goalkeeper**

goat [ˈgoːt] *n*   **1** : cabra *f* (hembra)   **2** billy goat : macho *m* cabrío, chivo *m*

goatee [goːˈtiː] *n* : barbita *f* de chivo; perilla *f*; pera *f* *Arg, Chile, Uru*; piocha *f* *Mex*

goatskin [ˈgoːt͜skɪn] *n* : piel *f* de cabra

gob [ˈgɑb] *n* : masa *f*, grumo *m*

gobble [ˈgɑbəl] *v* **-bled; -bling** *vt* **to gobble up/down** : tragar, engullir — *vi* : hacer ruidos de pavo

gobbledygook [ˈɡabəldiˌɡuk, -ˌɡuːk] *n*
GIBBERISH : jerigonza *f*
go–between [ˈɡoːbɪˌtwiːn] *n* : intermediario *m*, -ria *f*; mediador *m*, -dora *f*
goblet [ˈɡablət] *n* : copa *f*
goblin [ˈɡablən] *n* : duende *m*, trasgo *m*
god [ˈɡad, ˈɡɔd] *n* 1 : dios *m* 2 God
: Dios *m*
godchild [ˈɡadˌtʃaɪld, ˈɡɔd-] *n, pl* -chil-
dren : ahijado *m*, -da *f*
goddaughter [ˈɡadˌdɔtər, ˈɡɔd-] *n* : ahi-
jada *f*
goddess [ˈɡadəs, ˈɡɔ-] *n* : diosa *f*
godfather [ˈɡadˌfaðər, ˈɡɔd-] *n* : padrino
m
godless [ˈɡadləs, ˈɡɔd-] *adj* : ateo
godlike [ˈɡadˌlaɪk, ˈɡɔd-] *adj* : divino
godly [ˈɡadli, ˈɡɔd-] *adj* **godlier; -est** 1
DIVINE : divino 2 DEVOUT, PIOUS
: piadoso, devoto, beato
godmother [ˈɡadˌmʌðər, ˈɡɔd-] *n* : madrina *f*
godparent [ˈɡadˌpærənt, ˈɡɔd-] *n* : padrino *m*, madrina *f* ⟨her godparents : sus
padrinos⟩
godsend [ˈɡadˌsɛnd, ˈɡɔd-] *n* : bendición
f, regalo *m* divino
godson [ˈɡadˌsʌn, ˈɡɔd-] *n* : ahijado *m*
goes → go
go–getter [ˈɡoːˌɡɛt̬ər] *n* : persona *f* ambi-
ciosa, buscavidas *mf fam*
goggle [ˈɡaɡəl] *vi* -gled; -gling : mirar
con ojos desorbitados
goggles [ˈɡaɡəlz] *npl* : gafas *fpl* (protecto-
ras), anteojos *mpl*
going [ˌɡoːɪŋ] *n* 1 DEPARTURE : salida *f*,
partida *f* 2 (*describing progress*) ⟨it's
been slow going : las cosas van despacio⟩
⟨it's going to be tough going : va a ser
difícil⟩ 3 **comings and goings** → coming²
goings–on [ˌɡoːɪŋzˈan, -ˈɔn] *npl* : sucesos
mpl, ocurrencias *fpl*
goiter [ˈɡɔɪt̬ər] *n* : bocio *m*
gold¹ [ˈɡoːld] *adj* 1 : (hecho) de oro 2
: dorado, de color oro
gold² *n* : oro *m*
golden [ˈɡoːldən] *adj* 1 : (hecho) de
oro 2 : dorado, de color oro ⟨golden
hair : pelo rubio⟩ 3 FLOURISHING,
PROSPEROUS : dorado, próspero ⟨golden
years : años dorados⟩ 4 FAVORABLE
: favorable, excelente ⟨a golden opportunity : una excelente oportunidad⟩
goldenrod [ˈɡoːldənˌrad] *n* : vara *f* de oro
golden rule *n* : regla *f* de oro
goldfinch [ˈɡoːldˌfɪntʃ] *n* : jilguero *m*
goldfish [ˈɡoːldˌfɪʃ] *n* : pez *m* de colores
gold mine *n* : mina *f* de oro
goldsmith [ˈɡoːldˌsmɪθ] *n* : orífice *mf*, orfebre *mf*
golf¹ [ˈɡalf, ˈɡɔlf] *vi* : jugar (al) golf
golf² *n* : golf *m*
golf ball *n* : pelota *f* de golf
golf cart *n* : carrito *m* de golf
golf club *n* 1 : palo *m* de golf (implemento) 2 : club *m* de golf (organización)
golf course *n* : campo *m* de golf, cancha *f*
de golf

golfer [ˈɡalfər, ˈɡɔl-] *n* : golfista *mf*
gondola [ˈɡandəl∂, ɡanˈdoːlə] *n* : góndola
f
gone [ˈɡɔn] *adj* 1 DEAD : muerto 2 PAST
: pasado, ido ⟨those days are gone : esos
días ya pasaron⟩ ⟨her fear is gone : se le
ha pasado el miedo⟩ 3 LOST : perdido,
desaparecido ⟨my car is gone! : ¡mi coche no está!⟩ 4 **to be far gone** : estar
muy avanzado 5 **to be gone on** : estar
loco por
goner [ˈɡɔnər] *n* **to be a goner** : estar en
las últimas
gong [ˈɡɔŋ, ˈɡaŋ] *n* : gong *m*
gonorrhea [ˌɡanəˈriːə] *n* : gonorrea *f*
good¹ [ˈɡud] *adv* 1 (*used as an intensifier*)
: bien ⟨a good strong rope : una cuerda
bien fuerte⟩ 2 WELL : bien
good² *adj* **better** [ˈbɛt̬ər]; **best** [ˈbɛst] 1
(*of high quality*) : bueno ⟨a good restaurant : un buen restaurante⟩ ⟨the book is
no good : el libro es malísimo⟩ ⟨in good
condition : en buenas condiciones⟩
⟨keep up the good work! : ¡buen trabajo!
sigue así⟩ 2 ACCEPTABLE : aceptable 3
PLEASANT : bueno, agradable ⟨good
weather : buen tiempo⟩ ⟨the sauce is
good : la salsa está buena⟩ ⟨that dress
looks good on you : ese vestido te queda
bien⟩ ⟨to have a good time : divertirse⟩
⟨have a good day! : ¡qué te vaya bien!⟩ 4
FORTUNATE : bueno ⟨good news : buenas noticias⟩ ⟨good luck : buena suerte⟩
⟨it's a good thing that . . . : menos mal
que . . .⟩ 5 SUITABLE : bueno ⟨a good
day for a picnic : un buen día para ir de
picnic⟩ ⟨these tires are no good : estas
llantas no sirven⟩ 6 SOUND : bueno,
sensato ⟨good advice : buenos consejos⟩
⟨with good reason : con razón⟩ 7 PROM-
ISING : bueno ⟨a good deal : un buen
negocio⟩ ⟨a good bet : una apuesta se-
gura⟩ 8 HEALTHY : bueno ⟨good for a
cold : bueno para los resfriados⟩ ⟨it's
good for you : es bueno para uno⟩ ⟨a
good diet : una buena alimentación⟩ ⟨to
be in good health : estar bien de salud⟩
⟨I'm not feeling very good : no me siento
bien⟩ 9 FULL : completo, entero ⟨a
good hour : una hora entera⟩ ⟨to get a
good night's sleep : dormir por la
noche⟩ 10 THOROUGH : bueno ⟨a good
kick : una buena patada⟩ ⟨take a good
look at it : míralo bien⟩ ⟨we had a good
laugh : nos reímos mucho⟩ 11 CON-
SIDERABLE : bueno, bastante ⟨a good
many people : muchísima gente, un
buen número de gente⟩ 12 ATTRAC-
TIVE, DESIRABLE : bueno ⟨a good salary/
price : un buen sueldo/precio⟩ 13 (referring to status) : bueno ⟨a good family
: una buena familia⟩ 14 APPROVING
: bueno ⟨good reviews : buena
crítica⟩ 15 KIND, VIRTUOUS : bueno,
amable ⟨she's a good person : es buena
gente⟩ ⟨that's good of you! : ¡qué amable!⟩ ⟨good deeds : buenas obras⟩ ⟨the
good guys : los buenos⟩ 16 CLOSE : íntimo ⟨we're good friends : somos muy
amigos⟩ 17 WELL-BEHAVED : bueno

⟨be good : sé bueno⟩ **18** LOYAL, FAITHFUL : bueno, fiel **19** (*within bounds*) : bueno (en deportes) **20** SKILLED : bueno, hábil ⟨to be good at : tener facilidad para⟩ ⟨a good cook : un buen cocinero⟩ ⟨he's good with children : es bueno con los niños⟩ **21** PLEASED, CHEERFUL : bueno ⟨in a good mood : de buen humor⟩ ⟨helping others makes me feel good : me siento bien ayudando a los demás⟩ **22** SATISFIED : satisfecho ⟨no thanks — I'm good : no, gracias — estoy bien⟩ **23** FRESH : fresco **24** FUNNY : gracioso ⟨she's always good for a laugh : es muy divertida⟩ ⟨he said he didn't know? that's a good one : ¿dijo que no lo sabía? no me hagas reír⟩ **25** (*in greetings*) : bueno ⟨good morning : buenos días⟩ ⟨good afternoon/evening : buenas tardes⟩ ⟨good night : buenas noches⟩ **26** (*used as a response*) ⟨I'm ready — good, let's go : estoy listo — bueno, vamos⟩ **27 as good as** NEARLY : casi **28 as good as it gets** *fam* ⟨this is as good as it gets : mejor imposible, no hay mejor⟩ **29 good and** (*used for emphasis*) ⟨good and hot : muy caliente⟩ ⟨I hit him good and hard : le pegué bien duro⟩ ⟨when I'm good and ready : cuando me dé la gana⟩ **30 good God/heavens!** : ¡Dios mío! **31 good old** : el bueno de, la buena de ⟨good old Carl : el bueno de Carl⟩ **32 to be good about** ⟨she's very good about calling us : nunca se olvida de llamarnos⟩ ⟨I'm trying to be better about exercising : estoy tratando de hacer más ejercicio⟩ **33 to be good for** *fam* ⟨he's good for the money : seguro que te pagará⟩ **34 to be good (for/until)** : valer (por/hasta) ⟨good for one free meal : vale por una comida gratis⟩ ⟨the car is good for a few more years : al carro le quedan unos años más⟩ **35 to be good to go** *fam* : estar listo **36 too good to be true** : demasiado bueno para ser cierto **37 to make good** : tener éxito **38 to make good on** : cumplir con

good³ *n* **1** RIGHT : bien *m* ⟨to do good : hacer el bien⟩ ⟨to be up to no good : estar tramando algo⟩ **2** GOODNESS : bondad *f* **3** BENEFIT : bien *m*, provecho *m* ⟨it's for your own good : es por tu propio bien⟩ ⟨for the common good : por el bien común⟩ **4 goods** *npl* PROPERTY : efectos *mpl* personales, posesiones *fpl* **5 goods** *npl* WARES : mercancía *f*, mercadería *f*, artículos *mpl* ⟨consumer goods : bienes de consumo⟩ **6 the ~** : para siempre **7 the good** : los buenos **8 to be in good with someone** *fam* : estar a bien con alguien **9 to be no good** : no servir (para nada) **10 to deliver the goods** *fam* : cumplir con lo prometido **11 to get/have the goods on** *fam* : obtener/tener pruebas contra

good–bye *or* **good–by** [gʊdˈbaɪ] *n* : adiós *m*

good–for–nothing [ˈgʊdfər͵nʌθɪŋ] *n*

: inútil *mf*; haragán *m*, -gana *f*; holgazán *m*, -zana *f*

Good Friday *n* : Viernes *m* Santo

good–hearted [ˈgʊdˈhɑrt̬əd] *adj* : bondadoso, benévolo, de buen corazón

good–looking [ˈgʊdˈlʊkɪŋ] *adj* : bello, bonito, guapo

goodly [ˈgʊdli] *adj* **goodlier; -est** : considerable, importante ⟨a goodly number : un número considerable⟩

good–natured [ˈgʊdˈneɪt̬ʃərd] *adj* : amigable, amistoso, bonachón *fam*

goodness [ˈgʊdnəs] *n* **1** : bondad *f* **2 thank goodness!** : ¡gracias a Dios!, ¡menos mal!

good–tempered [ˈgʊdˈtɛmpərd] *adj* : de buen genio

goodwill [͵gʊdˈwɪl] *n* **1** BENEVOLENCE : benevolencia *f*, buena voluntad *f* **2** : buen nombre *m* (de comercios), renombre *m* comercial

goody [ˈgʊdi] *n, pl* **goodies** : cosa *f* rica para comer, golosina *f*

gooey [ˈguːi] *adj* **gooier; gooiest** : pegajoso

goof¹ [ˈguːf] *vi fam* **1** *or* **to goof up** BLUNDER : cometer un error, equivocarse **2 to goof off** : holgazanear **3 to goof around** : hacer tonterías

goof² *n* **1** *fam* : bobo *m*, -ba *f*; tonto *m*, -ta *f* **2** BLUNDER : error *m*, planchazo *m fam*

goofy [ˈguːfi] *adj* **goofier; -est** SILLY : tonto, bobo

google *or* **Google** [ˈguːgəl] *vt* **-gled; -gling** (*Google*, trademark) : googlear

goose [ˈguːs] *n, pl* **geese** [ˈgiːs] : ganso *m*, -sa *f*; ánsar *m*; oca *f*

gooseberry [ˈguːs͵bɛriː, ˈguːz-] *n, pl* **-berries** : grosella *f* espinosa

goose bumps *npl* : carne *f* de gallina

gooseflesh [ˈguːs͵flɛʃ] → **goose bumps**

goose pimples → **goose bumps**

gopher [ˈgoːfər] *n* : taltuza *f*

gore¹ [ˈgor] *vt* **gored; goring** : cornear

gore² *n* BLOOD : sangre *f*

gorge¹ [ˈgɔrdʒ] *vt* **gorged; gorging** **1** SATIATE : saciar, hartar **2 to gorge oneself** : hartarse, atiborrarse, atracarse *fam*

gorge² *n* RAVINE : desfiladero *m*

gorgeous [ˈgɔrdʒəs] *adj* : hermoso, espléndido, magnífico

gorilla [gəˈrɪlə] *n* : gorila *m*

gory [ˈgori] *adj* **gorier; -est** BLOODY : sangriento

gosh [ˈgɑʃ, ˈgɔʃ] *interj* : ¡caramba!

gosling [ˈgɑzlɪŋ, ˈgɔz-] *n* : ansarino *m*

gospel [ˈgɑspəl] *n* **1** *or* **Gospel** : evangelio *m* ⟨the four Gospels : los cuatro evangelios⟩ **2 the gospel truth** : el evangelio, la pura verdad

gossamer [ˈgɑsəmər, ˈgɑzə-] *adj* : tenue, sutil ⟨gossamer wings : alas tenues⟩

gossip¹ [ˈgɑsɪp] *vi* : chismear, contar chismes

gossip² *n* **1** : chismoso *m*, -sa *f*; cotilla *mf Spain fam* (persona) **2** RUMOR : chisme *m*, rumor *m*

gossiper [ˈgɑsɪpər] *n* GOSSIP : chismoso *m*, -sa *f*; cotilla *mf Spain fam*

gossipy ['gɑsɪpi] *adj* : chismoso
got → **get**
Gothic ['gɑθɪk] *adj* : gótico
gotten → **get**
gouge[1] ['gaʊdʒ] *vt* **gouged; gouging 1**
: excavar **2** SWINDLE : estafar, extorsionar
gouge[2] *n* **1** CHISEL : formón *m* **2**
GROOVE : ranura *f*, hoyo *m* (hecho por
un formón)
goulash ['gu:ˌlɑʃ, -ˌlæʃ] *n* : estofado *m*,
guiso *m* al estilo húngaro
gourd ['gord, 'gʊrd] *n* : calabaza *f*
gourmand ['gʊrˌmɑnd] *n* **1** GLUTTON
: glotón *m*, -tona *f* **2** → **gourmet**
gourmet ['gʊrˌmeɪ, gʊr'meɪ] *n* : gourmet
mf; gastrónomo *m*, -ma *f*
gout ['gaʊt] *n* : gota *f*
govern ['gʌvərn] *vt* **1** RULE : gobernar **2** CONTROL, DETERMINE : determinar, controlar, guiar **3** RESTRAIN
: dominar (las emociones, etc.) — *vi*
: gobernar
governess ['gʌvərnəs] *n* : institutriz *f*
government ['gʌvərmənt] *n* : gobierno *m*
governmental [ˌgʌvər'mɛntəl] *adj* : gubernamental, gubernativo
governor ['gʌvənər, 'gʌvərnər] *n* **1**
: gobernador *m*, -dora *f* (de un estado,
etc.) **2** : regulador *m* (de una máquina)
governorship ['gʌvənərˌʃɪp, 'gʌvərnər-] *n*
: cargo *m* de gobernador
gown ['gaʊn] *n* **1** : vestido *m* ⟨evening
gown : traje de fiesta⟩ **2** : toga *f* (de
magistrados, clérigos, etc.)
GPS [ˌdʒiː'piː'ɛs] *n* (*Global Positioning
System*) : GPS *m*
grab[1] ['græb] *v* **grabbed; grabbing** *vt*
SNATCH : agarrar, arrebatar — *vi* : agarrarse
grab[2] *n* **1 to make a grab for** : tratar de
agarrar **2 up for grabs** : disponible, libre
grace[1] ['greɪs] *vt* **graced; gracing 1** HONOR : honrar **2** ADORN : adornar, embellecer
grace[2] *n* **1** : gracia *f* ⟨by the grace of
God : por la gracia de Dios⟩ **2** BLESSING : bendición *f* (de la mesa) **3** RESPITE : plazo *m*, gracia *f* ⟨a five days'
grace (period) : un plazo de cinco días,
un período de gracia de cinco días⟩ **4**
GRACIOUSNESS : gentileza *f*, cortesía *f* **5**
ELEGANCE : elegancia *f*, gracia *f* **6 to be
in the good graces of** : estar en buenas
relaciones con **7 with good grace** : de
buena gana
graceful ['greɪsfəl] *adj* : lleno de gracia,
garboso, grácil
gracefully ['greɪsfəli] *adv* : con gracia, con
garbo
gracefulness ['greɪsfəlnəs] *n* : gracilidad
f, apostura *f*, gallardía *f*
graceless ['greɪsləs] *adj* **1** DISCOURTEOUS : descortés **2** CLUMSY, INELEGANT : torpe, desgarbado, poco elegante
gracious ['greɪʃəs] *adj* : cortés, gentil,
cordial
graciously ['greɪʃəsli] *adv* : gentilmente
graciousness ['greɪʃəsnəs] *n* : gentileza *f*

gradation [greɪ'deɪʃən, grə-] *n* : gradación
f
grade[1] ['greɪd] *vt* **graded; grading 1**
SORT : clasificar **2** LEVEL : nivelar **3**
: calificar (exámenes, alumnos)
grade[2] *n* **1** QUALITY : categoría *f*, calidad
f **2** RANK : grado *m*, rango *m* (militar) **3** YEAR : grado *m*, curso *m*, año *m*
⟨sixth grade : el sexto grado⟩ **4** MARK
: nota *f*, calificación *f* (en educación) **5**
SLOPE : cuesta *f*, pendiente *f*, gradiente *f*
grade school → **elementary school**
gradient ['greɪdiənt] *n* : gradiente *f*
gradual ['grædʒuəl] *adj* : gradual, paulatino
gradually ['grædʒuəli, 'grædʒəli] *adv*
: gradualmente, poco a poco
graduate[1] ['grædʒuˌeɪt] *v* **-ated; -ating** *vi*
: graduarse, licenciarse — *vt* : graduar ⟨a
graduated thermometer : un termómetro graduado⟩
graduate[2] ['grædʒuət] *adj* : de postgrado
⟨graduate course : curso de postgrado⟩
graduate[3] *n* **1** : licenciado *m*, -da *f*; graduado *m*, -da *f* (de la universidad) **2**
: bachiller *mf* (de la escuela secundaria)
graduate student *n* : postgraduado *m*,
-da *f*
graduation [ˌgrædʒu'eɪʃən] *n* : graduación
f
graffiti [grə'fiːˌti, græ-] *npl* : pintadas *fpl*,
graffiti *mpl*
graft[1] ['græft] *vt* : injertar
graft[2] *n* **1** : injerto *m* ⟨skin graft : injerto
cutáneo⟩ **2** CORRUPTION : soborno *m*
(político), ganancia *f* ilegal
grain ['greɪn] *n* **1** : grano *m* ⟨a grain of
corn : un grano de maíz⟩ ⟨like a grain of
sand : como grano de arena⟩ **2** CEREALS
: cereales *mpl* **3** : veta *f*, vena *f*, grano *m*
(de madera) **4** SPECK, TRACE : pizca *f*,
ápice *m* ⟨a grain of truth : una pizca de
verdad⟩ **5** grano *m* (unidad de peso) **6**
to go against the grain ir a contrapelo
grainy ['greɪni] *adj* **grainier; -est** : granuloso, granulado, granular
gram ['græm] *n* : gramo *m*
grammar ['græmər] *n* : gramática *f*
grammar school → **elementary school**
grammatical [grə'mætɪkəl] *adj* : gramatical — **grammatically** [-kli] *adv*
gran ['græn] → **grandma**
granary ['greɪnəri, 'græ-] *n*, *pl* **-ries** : granero *m*
grand ['grænd] *adj* **1** FOREMOST
: grande **2** IMPRESSIVE : impresionante,
magnífico ⟨a grand view : una vista magnífica⟩ **3** LAVISH : grandioso, suntuoso,
lujoso ⟨to live in a grand manner : vivir
a lo grande⟩ **4** FABULOUS : fabuloso,
magnífico ⟨to have a grand time : pasarlo estupendamente, pasarlo en
grande⟩ **5 grand total** : total *m*, suma *f*
total
grandchild ['grændˌtʃaɪld] *n*, *pl* **-children**
: nieto *m*, -ta *f*
granddad ['grændˌdæd] → **grandpa**
granddaughter ['grændˌdɔtər] *n* : nieta *f*
grandeur ['grændʒər] *n* : grandiosidad *f*,
esplendor *m*

grandfather ['grænd,fɑðər] *n* : abuelo *m*
grandiose ['grændi,o:s, ,grændi'-] *adj* **1**
IMPOSING : imponente, grandioso **2**
POMPOUS : pomposo, presuntuoso
grandma ['græn,mɑ, -,mɔ] *n fam* : abuelita *f fam*, nana *f fam*, yaya *f fam*
grandmother ['grænd,mʌðər] *n* : abuela *f*
grandpa ['græm,pɑ, -,pɔ] *n fam* : abuelito *m fam*, yayo *m fam*
grandparents ['grænd,pærənts] *npl*
: abuelos *mpl*
grand piano *n* : piano *m* de cola
grandson ['grænd,sʌn] *n* : nieto *m*
grandstand ['grænd,stænd] *n* : tribuna *f*
granite ['grænɪt] *n* : granito *m*
granny ['græni] *n, pl* **-nies** → **grandma**
grant¹ ['grænt] *vt* **1** ALLOW : conceder
⟨to grant a request : conceder una petición⟩ **2** BESTOW : conceder, dar, otorgar ⟨to grant a favor : otorgar un favor⟩ **3** ADMIT : reconocer, admitir ⟨I'll grant that he's clever : reconozco que es listo⟩ **4 to take for granted** : dar (algo) por sentado
grant² *n* **1** GRANTING : concesión *f*, otorgamiento *m* **2** SCHOLARSHIP : beca *f* **3** SUBSIDY : subvención *f*
granular ['grænjʊlər] *adj* : granular
granulated ['grænjʊ,leɪtəd] *adj* : granulado
grape ['greɪp] *n* : uva *f*
grapefruit ['greɪp,fru:t] *n* : toronja *f*, pomelo *m*
grapevine ['greɪp,vaɪn] *n* **1** : vid *f*, parra *f* **2 through the grapevine** : por vías secretas ⟨I heard it through the grapevine : me lo contaron⟩
graph ['græf] *n* : gráfica *f*, gráfico *m*
graphic¹ ['græfɪk] *adj* VIVID : vívido, gráfico
graphic² *n* **1** GRAPH, CHART : gráfica *f*, gráfico *m* **2 graphics** *npl* : gráficos *mpl*, infografía *f*
graphically ['græfɪkli] *adv* : gráficamente
graphic arts *npl* : artes *fpl* gráficas
graphite ['græ,faɪt] *n* : grafito *m*
grapple ['græpəl] *v* **-pled; -pling** *vt* GRIP : agarrar (con un garfio) — *vi* STRUGGLE : forcejear, luchar (con un problema, etc.)
grasp¹ ['græsp] *vt* **1** GRIP, SEIZE : agarrar, asir **2** COMPREHEND : entender, comprender — *vi* **to grasp at** : aprovechar
grasp² *n* **1** GRIP : agarre *m* **2** CONTROL : control *m*, garras *fpl* **3** REACH : alcance *m* ⟨within your grasp : a su alcance⟩ **4** UNDERSTANDING : comprensión *f*, entendimiento *m*
grasping ['græspɪŋ] *adj* : avaricioso
grass ['græs] *n* **1** : hierba *f* (planta) **2** PASTURE : pasto *m*, zacate *m CA, Mex* **3** LAWN : césped *m*, pasto *m*
grasshopper ['græs,hɑpər] *n* : saltamontes *m*
grassland ['græs,lænd] *n* : pradera *f*
grassroots ['græs,ru:ts, -,rʊts] *adj* : de base ⟨at the grassroots level : a nivel de base⟩ ⟨a grassroots movement : un movimiento de base⟩

grass roots *npl* : las bases ⟨the party's grass roots : las bases del partido⟩
grassy ['græsi] *adj* **grassier; -est** : cubierto de hierba
grate¹ ['greɪt] *v* **grated; -ing** *vt* **1** : rallar (en cocina) **2** SCRAPE : rascar **3** **to grate one's teeth** : hacer rechinar los dientes — *vi* **1** RASP, SQUEAK : chirriar **2** IRRITATE : irritar ⟨it grates on me : me crispa⟩ ⟨to grate on one's nerves : crisparle los nervios a uno⟩
grate² *n* **1** : parrilla *f* (para cocinar) **2** GRATING : reja *f*, rejilla *f*, verja *f* (en una ventana)
grateful ['greɪtfəl] *adj* : agradecido
gratefully ['greɪtfəli] *adv* : con agradecimiento
gratefulness ['greɪtfəlnəs] *n* : gratitud *f*, agradecimiento *m*
grater ['greɪtər] *n* : rallador *m*
gratification [,grætəfə'keɪʃən] *n* : gratificación *f*
gratify ['grætə,faɪ] *vt* **-fied; -fying** **1** PLEASE : complacer **2** SATISFY : satisfacer, gratificar
grating ['greɪtɪŋ] *n* : reja *f*, rejilla *f*
gratis¹ ['grætəs, 'greɪ-] *adv* : gratis, gratuitamente
gratis² *adj* : gratis, gratuito
gratitude ['grætə,tu:d, -,tju:d] *n* : gratitud *f*, agradecimiento *m*
gratuitous [grə'tu:ətəs] *adj* UNWARRANTED : gratuito, injustificado — **gratuitously** [grə'tu:ətəsli] *adv*
gratuity [grə'tu:əti] *n, pl* **-ities** TIP : propina *f*
grave¹ ['greɪv] *adj* **graver; gravest** **1** IMPORTANT : grave, de mucha gravedad **2** SERIOUS, SOLEMN : grave, serio
grave² *n* : tumba *f*, sepultura *f*
gravel ['grævəl] *n* : grava *f*, gravilla *f*
gravelly ['grævəli] *adj* **1** : de grava **2** HARSH : áspero (dícese de la voz)
gravely ['greɪvli] *adv* : gravemente
gravestone ['greɪv,sto:n] *n* : lápida *f*
graveyard ['greɪv,jɑrd] *n* CEMETERY : cementerio *m*, panteón *m*, camposanto *m*
gravitate ['grævə,teɪt] *vi* **-tated; -tating** : gravitar
gravitation [,grævə'teɪʃən] *n* : gravitación *f*
gravitational [,grævə'teɪʃənəl] *adj* : gravitacional
gravity ['grævəti] *n, pl* **-ties** **1** SERIOUSNESS : gravedad *f*, seriedad *f* **2** : gravedad *f* ⟨the law of gravity : la ley de la gravedad⟩
gravy ['greɪvi] *n, pl* **-vies** : salsa *f* (preparada con el jugo de la carne asada)
gray¹ ['greɪ] *vt* : hacer gris — *vi* : encanecer, ponerse gris
gray² *adj* **1** : gris (dícese del color) **2** : cano, canoso ⟨gray hair : pelo canoso⟩ ⟨to go gray : volverse cano⟩ **3** DISMAL, GLOOMY : gris, triste
gray³ *n* : gris *m*
grayish ['greɪʃ] *adj* : grisáceo
graze ['greɪz] *v* **grazed; grazing** *vi* : pastar, pacer — *vt* **1** : pastorear (ganado) **2** BRUSH : rozar **3** SCRATCH : raspar

grease¹ ['griːs, 'griːz] *vt* greased; greasing : engrasar, lubricar
grease² ['griːs] *n* : grasa *f*
greasy ['griːsi, -zi] *adj* greasier; -est 1 : grasiento 2 OILY : graso, grasoso
great ['greɪt] *adj* 1 LARGE : grande ⟨a great mountain : una montaña grande⟩ ⟨a great crowd : una gran muchedumbre⟩ ⟨a great big house : una casa grandísima⟩ ⟨a great success : un gran éxito⟩ 2 EXTREME, INTENSE : grande, intenso, fuerte ⟨with great care/difficulty : con gran cuidado/dificultad⟩ ⟨in great pain : muy dolorido⟩ ⟨there's no great hurry : no hay prisa⟩ ⟨a great admirer of : un gran admirador de⟩ 3 IMPORTANT : grande ⟨a great poet : un gran poeta⟩ ⟨great works of art : grandes obras de arte⟩ 4 EXCELLENT, TERRIFIC : excelente, estupendo, fabuloso ⟨to have a great time : pasarlo en grande⟩ ⟨a great movie : una película estupenda⟩ ⟨he's great at soccer : juega muy bien al fútbol⟩ ⟨you look great! : ¡te ves muy bien!⟩ 5 : bis- ⟨great-grandson : bisabuelo/bisnieto⟩ ⟨great niece : sobrina nieta⟩ ⟨great-great-grandmother : tatarabuela⟩ 6 a great deal (of) : mucho, un montón (de) 7 a great while : mucho tiempo 8 great! : ¡qué bien!
great–aunt [ˌgreɪtˈænt, -ˈant] *n* : tía *f* abuela
greater ['greɪt̬ər] (*comparative of* GREAT) : mayor
greatest ['greɪt̬əst] (*superlative of* GREAT) : el mayor, la mayor
great–grandchild [ˌgreɪtˈgrænd-ˌtʃaɪld] *n*, *pl* -children [-ˌtʃɪldrən] : bisnieto *m*, -ta *f*
great–grandfather [ˌgreɪtˈgrænd-ˌfɑðər] *n* : bisabuelo *m*
great–grandmother [ˌgreɪtˈgrænd-ˌmʌðər] *n* : bisabuela *f*
greatly ['greɪtli] *adv* 1 MUCH : mucho, sumamente ⟨to be greatly improved : haber mejorado mucho⟩ 2 VERY : muy ⟨greatly superior : muy superior⟩
greatness ['greɪtnəs] *n* : grandeza *f*
great–uncle [ˌgreɪtˈʌŋkəl] *n* : tío *m* abuelo
grebe ['griːb] *n* : somorgujo *m*
greed ['griːd] *n* 1 AVARICE : avaricia *f*, codicia *f* 2 GLUTTONY : glotonería *f*, gula *f*
greedily ['griːdəli] *adv* : con avaricia, con gula
greediness ['griːdinəs] → greed
greedy ['griːdi] *adj* greedier; -est 1 AVARICIOUS : codicioso, avaricioso 2 GLUTTONOUS : glotón
Greek ['griːk] *n* 1 : griego *m*, -ga *f* 2 : griego *m* (idioma) — **Greek** *adj*
green¹ ['griːn] *adj* 1 : verde (dícese del color) 2 UNRIPE : verde, inmaduro 3 INEXPERIENCED : verde, novato
green² *n* 1 : verde *m* 2 greens *npl* VEGETABLES : verduras *fpl*
greenback ['griːnˌbæk] *n fam* : billete *m* (dinero)
green card *n* : permiso *m* de residencia y trabajo
greenery ['griːnəri] *n, pl* -eries : plantas *fpl* verdes, vegetación *f*

greengrocer ['griːnˌgroːsər] *n* : verdulero *m*, -ra *f*
greenhorn ['griːnˌhɔrn] *n* : novato *m*, -ta *f*
greenhouse ['griːnˌhaʊs] *n* : invernadero *m*
greenhouse effect : efecto *m* invernadero
greenish ['griːnɪʃ] *adj* : verdoso
Greenlander ['griːnləndər, -ˌlæn-] *n* : groenlandés *m*, -desa *f*
greenness ['griːnnəs] *n* 1 : verdor *m* 2 INEXPERIENCE : inexperiencia *f*
green thumb *n* to have a green thumb : tener buena mano para las plantas
greet ['griːt] *vt* 1 : saludar ⟨to greet a friend : saludar a un amigo⟩ 2 : acoger, recibir ⟨they greeted him with boos : lo recibieron con abucheos⟩
greeting ['griːt̬ɪŋ] *n* 1 : saludo *m* 2 greetings *npl* REGARDS : saludos *mpl*, recuerdos *mpl*
greeting card *n* : tarjeta *f* de felicitación
gregarious [grɪˈgæriəs] *adj* : gregario (dícese de los animales), sociable (dícese de las personas) — **gregariously** *adv*
gregariousness [grɪˈgæriəsnəs] *n* : sociabilidad *f*
gremlin ['gremlən] *n* : duende *m*
grenade [grəˈneɪd] *n* : granada *f*
Grenadian [grəˈneɪdiən] *n* : granadino *m*, -na *f* — **Grenadian** *adj*
grew → grow
grey → gray
greyhound ['greɪˌhaʊnd] *n* : galgo *m*
grid ['grɪd] *n* 1 GRATING : rejilla *f* 2 NETWORK : red *f* (de electricidad, etc.) 3 : cuadriculado *m* (de un mapa)
griddle ['grɪdəl] *n* : plancha *f*
griddle cake → pancake
gridiron ['grɪdˌaɪərn] *n* 1 GRILL : parrilla *f* 2 : campo *m* de futbol americano
gridlock ['grɪdˌlɑk] *n* : atasco *m* completo (de una red de calles)
grief ['griːf] *n* 1 SORROW : dolor *m*, pena *f* 2 ANNOYANCE, TROUBLE : problemas *mpl*, molestia *f*
grief–stricken *adj* : afligido, desconsolado
grievance ['griːvənts] *n* COMPLAINT : queja *f*
grieve ['griːv] *v* grieved; grieving *vt* DISTRESS : afligir, entristecer, apenar — *vi* 1 : sufrir, afligirse 2 to grieve for *or* to grieve over : llorar, lamentar
grievous ['griːvəs] *adj* 1 OPPRESSIVE : gravoso, opresivo, severo 2 GRAVE, SERIOUS : grave, severo, doloroso
grievously ['griːvəsli] *adv* : gravemente, de gravedad
grill¹ ['grɪl] *vt* 1 : asar (a la parrilla) 2 INTERROGATE : interrogar
grill² *n* 1 : parrilla *f* (para cocinar) 2 : parrillada *f* (comida) 3 : parrilla *f* (restaurante)
grille *or* **grill** ['grɪl] *n* : reja *f*, enrejado *m*
grim ['grɪm] *adj* grimmer; grimmest 1 CRUEL : cruel, feroz 2 STERN : adusto, severo ⟨a grim expression : un gesto severo⟩ 3 GLOOMY : sombrío, deprimente 4 SINISTER : macabro, sinies-

tro **5** UNYIELDING : inflexible, persistente ⟨with grim determination : con una voluntad de hierro⟩

grimace[1] ['grɪməs, grɪ'meɪs] *vi* **-maced; -macing** : hacer muecas

grimace[2] *n* : mueca *f*

grime ['graɪm] *n* : mugre *f*, suciedad *f*

grimly ['grɪmli] *adv* **1** STERNLY : severamente **2** RESOLUTELY : inexorablemente

grimy ['graɪmi] *adj* **grimier; -est** : mugriento, sucio

grin[1] ['grɪn] *vi* **grinned; grinning** : sonreír abiertamente

grin[2] *n* : sonrisa *f* abierta

grind[1] ['graɪnd] *v* **ground** ['graʊnd]; **grinding** *vt* **1** CRUSH : moler, machacar, triturar **2** SHARPEN : afilar **3** POLISH : pulir **4 to grind one's teeth** : rechinarle los dientes a uno **5 to grind down** OPPRESS : oprimir, agobiar — *vi* **1** : funcionar con dificultad, rechinar ⟨to grind to a halt : pararse poco a poco, llegar a un punto muerto⟩ **2** STUDY : estudiar mucho

grind[2] *n* : trabajo *m* pesado ⟨the daily grind : la rutina diaria⟩

grinder ['graɪndər] *n* : molinillo *m* ⟨coffee grinder : molinillo de café⟩

grindstone ['graɪnd,stoːn] *n* : piedra *m* de afilar

gringo ['grɪŋgo] *n often disparaging* : gringo *m*, -ga *feminine often disparaging*

grip[1] ['grɪp] *vt* **gripped; gripping 1** GRASP : agarrar, asir **2** HOLD, INTEREST : captar el interés de

grip[2] *n* **1** GRASP : agarre *m*, asidero *m* ⟨to have a firm grip on something : agarrarse bien de algo⟩ **2** CONTROL, HOLD : control *m*, dominio *m* ⟨to lose one's grip on : perder el control de⟩ ⟨inflation tightened its grip on the economy : la inflación se afianzó en su dominio de la economía⟩ ⟨to get a grip on oneself : controlarse, calmarse⟩ **3** UNDERSTANDING : comprensión *f*, entendimiento *m* ⟨to come to grips with : llegar a entender⟩ **4** HANDLE : asidero *m*, empuñadura *f* (de un arma)

gripe[1] ['graɪp] *v* **griped; griping** *vt* IRRITATE, VEX : irritar, fastidiar, molestar — *vi* COMPLAIN : quejarse, rezongar

gripe[2] *n* : queja *f*

grippe ['grɪp] *n* : influenza *f*, gripe *f*, gripa *f Col, Mex*

gripping ['grɪpɪŋ] *adj* : apasionante

grisly ['grɪzli] *adj* **grislier; -est** : horripilante, horroroso, truculento

grist ['grɪst] *n* : molienda *f* ⟨it's all grist for the mill : todo ayuda, todo es provechoso⟩

gristle ['grɪsəl] *n* : cartílago *m*

gristly ['grɪsli] *adj* **gristlier; -est** : duro, con mucho cartílago

grit[1] ['grɪt] *vt* **gritted; gritting** : hacer rechinar (los dientes, etc.)

grit[2] *n* **1** SAND : arena *f* **2** GRAVEL : grava *f* **3** COURAGE : valor *m*, coraje *m* **4 grits** *npl* : sémola *f* de maíz

gritty ['grɪti] *adj* **grittier; -est 1** : arenoso ⟨a gritty surface : una superficie arenosa⟩ **2** PLUCKY : valiente

grizzled ['grɪzəld] *adj* : entrecano

grizzly bear ['grɪzli] *n* : oso *m* pardo

groan[1] ['groːn] *vi* **1** MOAN : gemir, quejarse **2** CREAK : crujir

groan[2] *n* **1** MOAN : gemido *m*, quejido *m* **2** CREAK : crujido *m*

grocer ['groːsər] *n* : tendero *m*, -ra *f*

grocery ['groːsəri, -ʃəri] *n, pl* **-ceries 1** *or* **grocery store** : tienda *f* de comestibles, tienda *f* de abarrotes **2 groceries** *npl* : comestibles *mpl*, abarrotes *mpl*

groggy ['grɑgi] *adj* **groggier; -est** : atontado, grogui, tambaleante

groin ['grɔɪn] *n* : ingle *f*

grommet ['grɑmət, 'grʌ-] *n* : arandela *f*

groom[1] ['gruːm, 'grʊm] *vt* **1** : cepillar, almohazar (un animal) **2** : arreglar, cuidar ⟨well-groomed : bien arreglado⟩ **3** PREPARE : preparar

groom[2] *n* **1** : mozo *m*, -za *f* de cuadra **2** BRIDEGROOM : novio *m*

groove[1] ['gruːv] *vt* **grooved; grooving** : acanalar, hacer ranuras en, surcar

groove[2] *n* **1** FURROW, SLOT : ranura *f*, surco *m* **2** RUT : rutina *f*

grope ['groːp] *v* **groped; groping** *vi* : andar a tientas, tantear ⟨he groped for the switch : buscó el interruptor a tientas⟩ — *vt* **to grope one's way** : avanzar a tientas

gross[1] ['groːs] *vt* : tener entrada bruta de, recaudar en bruto

gross[2] *adj* **1** FLAGRANT : flagrante, grave ⟨a gross error : un error flagrante⟩ ⟨a gross injustice : una injusticia grave⟩ **2** FAT : muy gordo, obeso **3** : bruto ⟨gross national product : producto nacional bruto⟩ **4** COARSE, VULGAR : grosero, basto **5** *fam* DISGUSTING : asqueroso

gross[3] *n* **1** *pl* **gross** : gruesa *f* (12 docenas) **2** *or* **gross income** : ingresos *mpl* brutos

grossly ['groːsli] *adv* **1** EXTREMELY : extremadamente ⟨grossly unfair : totalmente injusto⟩ **2** CRUDELY : groseramente

grotesque [groːˈtɛsk] *adj* : grotesco

grotesquely [groːˈtɛskli] *adv* : de forma grotesca

grotto ['grɑtoː] *n, pl* **-toes** : gruta *f*

grouch[1] ['graʊtʃ] *vi* : refunfuñar, rezongar

grouch[2] *n* **1** COMPLAINT : queja *f* **2** GRUMBLER : gruñón *m*, -ñona *f*; cascarrabias *mf fam*

grouchy ['graʊtʃi] *adj* **grouchier; -est** : malhumorado, gruñón

ground[1] ['graʊnd] *vt* **1** BASE : fundar, basar **2** INSTRUCT : enseñar los conocimientos básicos a ⟨to be well grounded in : ser muy entendido en⟩ **3** : conectar a tierra (un aparato eléctrico) **4** : varar, hacer encallar (un barco) **5** : restringir (un avión o un piloto) a la tierra **6** *fam* : no dejar salir (como castigo)

ground[2] *n* **1** EARTH, SOIL : suelo *m*, tierra *f* ⟨to dig (in) the ground : cavar la tierra⟩ ⟨to fall to the ground : caerse al suelo⟩ **2** LAND, TERRAIN : terreno *m* ⟨high ground : terreno alto⟩ ⟨to be on solid/firm ground : pisar terreno firme⟩ **3** BASIS, REASON : razón *f*, motivo *m* ⟨grounds for complaint : motivos de queja⟩ **4** INFORMATION : información *f* ⟨we've covered a lot of ground : hemos abarcado muchos temas/puntos⟩ ⟨familiar ground : terreno conocido⟩ **5** VIEWS : terreno *m* ⟨to find a common/middle ground : encontrar un terreno común⟩ **6** BACKGROUND : fondo *m* **7** FIELD : campo *m*, plaza *f* ⟨parade ground : plaza de armas⟩ **8** : tierra *f* (para electricidad) **9** grounds *npl* PREMISES : recinto *m*, terreno *m* **10** grounds *npl* DREGS : posos *mpl* (de café) **11** from the ground up COMPLETELY : completamente, radicalmente **12** from the ground up FRESH : de cero ⟨to build/start from the ground up : construir/empezar de cero⟩ **13** into the ground ⟨he ran the business into the ground : llevó la empresa a la ruina⟩ ⟨she's working herself into the ground : se mata trabajando⟩ **14** to break new ground : abrir nuevos caminos **15** to gain/lose ground : ganar/perder terreno **16** to get off the ground : llegar a concretarse **17** to hold/stand one's ground : no ceder terreno

ground³ → grind

groundhog ['graʊnd,hɔg] *n* : marmota *f* (de América)

grounding ['graʊndɪŋ] *n* : conocimientos *mpl* básicos

groundless ['graʊndləs] *adj* : infundado

groundwork ['graʊnd,wərk] *n* **1** FOUNDATION : fundamento *m*, base *f* **2** PREPARATION : trabajo *m* preparatorio

group¹ ['gru:p] *vt* : agrupar

group² *n* : grupo *m*, agrupación *f*, conjunto *m*, compañía *f*

grouper ['gru:pər] *n* : mero *m*

grouse¹ ['graʊs] *vi* groused; grousing : quejarse, rezongar, refunfuñar

grouse² *n, pl* grouse *or* grouses : urogallo *m* (ave)

grout ['graʊt] *n* : lechada *f*

grove ['gro:v] *n* : bosquecillo *m*, arboleda *f*, soto *m*

grovel ['grɑvəl, 'grʌ-] *vi* -eled *or* -elled; -eling *or* -elling **1** CRAWL : arrastrarse **2** : humillarse, postrarse ⟨to grovel before someone : postrarse ante alguien⟩

grow ['gro:] *v* grew ['gru:]; grown ['gro:n]; growing *vi* **1** : crecer ⟨palm trees grow on the islands : en las islas crecen palmas⟩ ⟨my hair grows very fast : mi pelo crece muy rápido⟩ **2** DEVELOP, MATURE : desarrollarse, madurar **3** INCREASE : crecer, aumentar **4** BECOME : hacerse, volverse, ponerse ⟨she was growing angry : se estaba poniendo furiosa⟩ ⟨to grow dark : oscurecerse⟩ **5** to grow apart : distanciarse **6** to grow from : nacer de **7** to grow into BECOME : convertirse en **8** to grow on someone : empezar a gustarle a alguien **9** to grow out of : dejar atrás (las cosas de la niñez) **10** to grow to : llegar a ⟨I grew to love the city : aprendí a amar la ciudad⟩ **11** to grow up : hacerse mayor ⟨grow up! : ¡no seas niño!⟩ — *vt* **1** CULTIVATE, RAISE : cultivar **2** : dejar crecer ⟨to grow one's hair : dejarse crecer el pelo⟩ **3** EXPAND, DEVELOP : expansionar, desarrollar (una empresa, etc.)

grower ['gro:ər] *n* : cultivador *m*, -dora *f*

growl¹ ['graʊl] *vi* : gruñir (dícese de un animal), refunfuñar (dícese de una persona)

growl² *n* : gruñido *m*

grown ['gro:n] → grown-up¹

grown–up¹ ['gro:n,əp] *adj* : adulto, mayor

grown–up² *n* : adulto *m*, -ta *f*; persona *f* mayor

growth ['gro:θ] *n* **1** : crecimiento *m* ⟨to stunt one's growth : detener el crecimiento⟩ **2** INCREASE : aumento *m*, crecimiento *m*, expansión *f* **3** DEVELOPMENT : desarrollo *m* ⟨economic growth : desarrollo económico⟩ ⟨a five days' growth of beard : una barba de cinco días⟩ **4** LUMP, TUMOR : bulto *m*, tumor *m*

grub¹ ['grʌb] *vi* grubbed; grubbing **1** DIG : escarbar **2** RUMMAGE : hurgar, buscar **3** DRUDGE : trabajar duro

grub² *n* **1** : larva *f* ⟨beetle grub : larva del escarabajo⟩ **2** DRUDGE : esclavo *m*, -va *f* del trabajo **3** FOOD : comida *f*

grubby ['grʌbi] *adj* grubbier; -est : mugriento, sucio

grudge¹ ['grʌdʒ] *vt* grudged; grudging : dar/hacer (etc.) de mala gana ⟨I don't grudge the money I spent : no me molesta el dinero que gasté⟩

grudge² *n* : rencor *m*, resentimiento *m* ⟨to hold a grudge : guardar rencor⟩ ⟨to hold a grudge against someone for something : guardarle rencor a alguien por algo⟩

grueling *or* **gruelling** ['gru:lɪŋ, 'gru:ə-] *adj* : extenuante, agotador, duro

gruesome ['gru:səm] *adj* : horripilante, truculento, horroroso

gruff ['grʌf] *adj* **1** BRUSQUE : brusco ⟨a gruff reply : una respuesta brusca⟩ **2** HOARSE : ronco — **gruffly** *adv*

grumble¹ ['grʌmbəl] *vi* -bled; -bling **1** COMPLAIN : refunfuñar, rezongar, quejarse **2** RUMBLE : hacer un ruido sordo, retumbar (dícese del trueno)

grumble² *n* **1** COMPLAINT : queja *f* **2** RUMBLE : ruido *m* sordo, estruendo *m*

grumbler ['grʌmbələr] *n* : gruñón *m*, -ñona *f*

grumpy ['grʌmpi] *adj* grumpier; -est : malhumorado, gruñón

grungy ['grʌndʒi] *adj* : sucio

grunt¹ ['grʌnt] *vi* : gruñir

grunt² *n* : gruñido *m*

guacamole [,gwɑkə'mo:li] *n* : guacamole *m*, guacamol *m*

guanaco [gwə'nako] *n* : guanaco *m*

guano ['gwɑno] *n* : guano *m*

guarani [,gwɑrə'ni:] *n, pl* -nies *or* -nis : guaraní *m* (unidad monetaria)

Guarani [,gwɑrə'ni:] *n* **1** : guaraní *m* (idioma) **2** *pl* -ni *or* -nis : guaraní *mf* (persona)

guarantee¹ [ˌgærən'tiː] *vt* **-teed; -teeing 1** PROMISE : asegurar, prometer **2** : poner bajo garantía, garantizar (un producto o servicio)

guarantee² *n* **1** PROMISE : garantía *f*, promesa *f* ⟨lifetime guarantee : garantía de por vida⟩ **2** → **guarantor**

guarantor [ˌgærən'tɔr] *n* : garante *mf*; fiador *m*, -dora *f*

guaranty [ˌgærən'tiː] → **guarantee**

guard¹ ['gɑrd] *vt* **1** DEFEND, PROTECT : defender, proteger **2** : guardar, vigilar, custodiar ⟨to guard the frontier : vigilar la frontera⟩ ⟨she guarded my secret well : guardó bien mi secreto⟩ — *vi* **to guard against** : protegerse contra, evitar

guard² *n* **1** WATCHMAN : guarda *mf* ⟨security guard : guarda de seguridad⟩ **2** SOLDIERS : guardia *f* **3** VIGILANCE : guardia *f*, vigilancia *f* ⟨to be on guard : estar en guardia⟩ ⟨to let one's guard down : bajar la guardia⟩ ⟨to catch someone off guard : agarrar a alguien desprevenido⟩ ⟨to keep under guard : vigilar⟩ **4** SAFEGUARD : salvaguardia *f*, dispositivo *m* de seguridad (en una máquina) **5** PRECAUTION : precaución *f*, protección *f* **6** : guardia *mf* (en deportes)

guard dog *n* : perro *m* guardián

guarded ['gɑrdəd] *adj* : cauteloso

guardhouse ['gɑrd,haʊs] *n* : cuartel *m* de la guardia

guardian ['gɑrdiən] *n* **1** PROTECTOR : guardián *m*, -diana *f*; custodio *m*, -dia *f* ⟨guardian angel : ángel de la guarda⟩ **2** : tutor *m*, -tora *f* (de un niño)

guardianship ['gɑrdiən,ʃɪp] *n* : custodia *f*, tutela *f*

guardrail ['gɑrd,reɪl] *n* **1** : antepecho *m* (de un puente, etc.) **2** : barrera *f* de contención (de una carretera)

Guatemalan [ˌgwɑtə'mɑlən] *n* : guatemalteco *m*, -ca *f* — **Guatemalan** *adj*

guava ['gwɑvə] *n* : guayaba *f*

gubernatorial [ˌguːbənə'toriːəl, ˌgjuː-] *adj* : del gobernador

guerrilla *or* **guerilla** [gə'rɪlə] *n* : guerrillero *m*, -ra *f*

guess¹ ['gɛs] *vt* **1** CONJECTURE : adivinar, conjeturar ⟨guess what happened! : ¡adivina lo que pasó!⟩ **2** SUPPOSE : pensar, creer, suponer ⟨I guess so : supongo que sí⟩ **3** : adivinar correctamente, acertar ⟨to guess the answer : acertar la respuesta⟩ — *vi* : adivinar

guess² *n* : conjetura *f*, suposición *f*

guesswork ['gɛs,wərk] *n* : suposiciones *fpl*, conjeturas *fpl*

guest ['gɛst] *n* : huésped *mf*; invitado *m*, -da *f*

guffaw¹ [gə'fɔ] *vi* : reírse a carcajadas, carcajearse *fam*

guffaw² [gə'fɔ, 'gʌ,fɔ] *n* : carcajada *f*, risotada *f*

guidance ['gaɪdənts] *n* : orientación *f*, consejos *mpl*

guide¹ ['gaɪd] *vt* **guided; guiding 1** DIRECT, LEAD : guiar, dirigir, conducir **2** ADVISE, COUNSEL : aconsejar, orientar

guide² *n* : guía *f*

guidebook ['gaɪd,bʊk] *n* : guía *f* (para viajeros)

guide dog *n* : perro *m* guía, perro *m* lazarillo

guideline ['gaɪd,laɪn] *n* : pauta *f*, directriz *f*

guild ['gɪld] *n* : gremio *m*, sindicato *m*, asociación *f*

guile ['gaɪl] *n* : astucia *f*, engaño *m*

guileless ['gaɪlləs] *adj* : inocente, cándido, sin malicia

guillotine¹ ['gɪlə,tiːn, 'giːjəɹ-] *vt* **-tined; -tining** : guillotinar

guillotine² *n* : guillotina *f*

guilt ['gɪlt] *n* : culpa *f*, culpabilidad *f*

guilty ['gɪlti] *adj* **guiltier; -est** : culpable

guinea fowl ['gɪni] *n* : gallina *f* de Guinea

guinea pig *n* : conejillo *m* de Indias, cobaya *f*

guise ['gaɪz] *n* : apariencia *f*, aspecto *m*, forma *f*

guitar [gə'tɑr, gɪ-] *n* : guitarra *f*

guitarist [gə'tɑrɪst, gɪ-] *n* : guitarrista *mf*

gulch ['gʌltʃ] *n* : barranco *m*, quebrada *f*

gulf ['gʌlf] *n* **1** : golfo *m* ⟨the Gulf of Mexico : el Golfo de México⟩ **2** GAP : brecha *f* ⟨the gulf between generations : la brecha entre las generaciones⟩ **3** CHASM : abismo *m*

gull ['gʌl] *n* : gaviota *f*

gullet ['gʌlət] *n* : garganta *f*

gullible ['gʌlɪbəl] *adj* : crédulo

gully ['gʌli] *n, pl* **-lies** : barranco *m*, hondonada *f*

gulp¹ ['gʌlp] *vt* **1** : engullir, tragar ⟨he gulped down the whiskey : engulló el whisky⟩ **2** SUPPRESS : suprimir, reprimir, tragar ⟨to gulp down a sob : reprimir un sollozo⟩ — *vi* : tragar saliva, tener un nudo en la garganta

gulp² *n* : trago *m*

gum ['gʌm] *n* **1** CHEWING GUM : goma *f* de mascar, chicle *m* **2 gums** *npl* : encías *fpl*

gumbo ['gʌm,boː] *n* : sopa *f* de quingombó

gumdrop ['gʌm,drɑp] *n* : pastilla *f* de goma

gummy ['gʌmi] *adj* **gummier; -est** : gomoso

gumption ['gʌmpʃən] *n* : iniciativa *f*, agallas *fpl fam*

gun¹ ['gʌn] *vt* **gunned; gunning 1** *or* **to gun down** : matar a tiros, asesinar **2** : acelerar (rápidamente) ⟨to gun the engine : acelerar el motor⟩

gun² *n* **1** CANNON : cañón *m* **2** FIREARM : arma *f* de fuego **3** SPRAY GUN : pistola *f* **4 to jump the gun** : adelantarse, salir antes de tiempo

gunboat ['gʌn,boːt] *n* : cañonero *m*

gunfight ['gʌn,faɪt] *n* : tiroteo *m*, balacera *f*

gunfire ['gʌn,faɪr] *n* : disparos *mpl*

gunman ['gʌnmən] *n, pl* **-men** [-mən, -,mɛn] : pistolero *m*, gatillero *m Mex*

gunner ['gʌnər] *n* : artillero *m*, -ra *f*

gunnysack ['gʌni,sæk] *n* : saco *m* de yute

gunpoint ['gʌn,pɔɪnt] *n* **at ∼** : a punta de pistola

gunpowder ['gʌn,paʊdər] *n* : pólvora *f*

gunshot ['gʌnˌʃɑt] *n* : disparo *m*, tiro *m*, balazo *m*
gunsmith ['gʌnˌsmɪθ] *n* : armero *m*, -ra *f*
gunwale ['gʌnəl] *n* : borda *f*
guppy ['gʌpi] *n, pl* **-pies** : guppy *m*
gurgle[1] ['gərgəl] *vi* **-gled; -gling** **1** : borbotar, gorgotear (dícese de un líquido) **2** : gorjear (dícese de un niño)
gurgle[2] *n* **1** : borboteo *m*, gorgoteo *m* (de un líquido) **2** : gorjeo *m* (de un niño)
gush ['gʌʃ] *vi* **1** SPOUT : surgir, salir a chorros, chorrear **2** : hablar con entusiasmo efusivo ⟨she gushed with praise : se deshizo en elogios⟩
gust ['gʌst] *n* : ráfaga *f*, racha *f*
gusto ['gʌsˌtoː] *n, pl* **gustoes** : entusiasmo *m* ⟨with gusto : con deleite, con ganas⟩
gusty ['gʌsti] *adj* **gustier; -est** : racheado
gut[1] ['gʌt] *vt* **gutted; gutting** **1** EVISCERATE : limpiar (un pollo, un pescado, etc.) **2** : destruir el interior de (un edificio)
gut[2] *n* **1** INTESTINE : intestino *m* **2 guts** *npl* INNARDS : tripas *fpl fam*, entrañas *fpl* **3 guts** *npl* COURAGE : valentía *f*, agallas *fpl*
gutter ['gʌtər] *n* **1** : canal *mf*, canaleta *f* (de un techo) **2** : cuneta *f*, arroyo *m* (de una calle)
guttural ['gʌtərəl] *adj* : gutural
guy ['gʌi] *n* **1** → **guyline** **2** FELLOW : tipo *m*, hombre *m*

guyline ['gʌiˌlɑin] *n* : cable *m* tensor
guzzle ['gʌzəl] *vt* **-zled; -zling** : chupar, tragarse
gym ['dʒɪm] → **gymnasium**
gymnasium [dʒɪm'neɪziəm, -ʒəm] *n, pl* **-siums** *or* **-sia** [-ziːə, -ʒə] : gimnasio *m*
gymnast ['dʒɪmnəst, -ˌnæst] *n* : gimnasta *mf*
gymnastic [dʒɪm'næstɪk] *adj* : gimnástico
gymnastics [dʒɪm'næstɪks] *ns & pl* : gimnasia *f*
gynecologic [ˌgaɪnəkə'lɑdʒɪk, ˌdʒɪnə-] *or* **gynecological** [ˌgaɪnəkə'lɑdʒɪkəl, ˌdʒɪnə-] *adj* : ginecológico
gynecologist [ˌgaɪnə'kɑlədʒɪst, ˌdʒɪnə-] *n* : ginecólogo *m*, -ga *f*
gynecology [ˌgaɪnə'kɑlədʒi, ˌdʒɪnə-] *n* : ginecología *f*
gyp[1] ['dʒɪp] *vt* **gypped; gypping** *fam, now sometimes offensive* : estafar, timar
gyp[2] *n fam, now sometimes offensive* **1** SWINDLER : estafador *m*, -dora *f* **2** FRAUD, SWINDLE : estafa *f*, timo *m fam*
gypsum ['dʒɪpsəm] *n* : yeso *m*
Gypsy ['dʒɪpsi] *n, pl* **-sies** *sometimes offensive* : gitano *m*, -na *f*
gyrate ['dʒaɪˌreɪt] *vi* **-rated; -rating** : girar, rotar
gyration [dʒaɪ'reɪʃən] *n* : giro *m*, rotación *f*
gyroscope ['dʒaɪrəˌskoːp] *n* : giroscopio *m*, giróscopo *m*

H

h ['eɪtʃ] *n, pl* **h's** *or* **hs** ['eɪtʃəz] : octava letra del alfabeto inglés
ha ['hɑ] *interj* : ¡ja!
haberdashery ['hæbərˌdæʃəri] *n, pl* **-eries** : tienda *f* de ropa para caballeros
habit ['hæbɪt] *n* **1** CUSTOM : hábito *m*, costumbre *f* ⟨to break/kick a bad habit : perder una mala costumbre⟩ ⟨to be in the habit of doing something : acostumbrar/soler hacer algo, tener la costumbre de hacer algo⟩ ⟨she got into the habit of sleeping in : se le hizo costumbre dormir hasta tarde⟩ ⟨to make a habit of doing something : tomar el costumbre de hacer algo⟩ ⟨don't make a habit of it : que no se repita⟩ **2** : hábito *m* (de un monje o una religiosa) **3** ADDICTION : dependencia *f*, adicción *f* ⟨to have a drug habit : ser drogadicto⟩ ⟨to kick the habit : dejar el vicio⟩
habitable ['hæbɪtəbəl] *adj* : habitable
habitat ['hæbɪˌtæt] *n* : hábitat *m*
habitation [ˌhæbɪ'teɪʃən] *n* **1** OCCUPANCY : habitación *f* **2** RESIDENCE : residencia *f*, morada *f*
habit–forming ['hæbɪtˌfɔrmɪŋ] *adj* : que crea dependencia
habitual [hə'bɪtʃuəl] *adj* **1** CUSTOMARY : habitual, acostumbrado **2** INVETERATE : incorregible, empedernido — **habitually** *adv*

habituate [hə'bɪtʃuˌeɪt] *vt* **-ated; -ating** : habituar, acostumbrar
hack[1] ['hæk] *vt* **1** : cortar, tajear (a hachazos, etc.) ⟨to hack one's way : abrirse paso⟩ **2** : entrar en, hackear *fam* (un sistema, etc.) — *vi* **1** : hacer tajos **2** COUGH : toser **3 to hack into** : entrar en, hackear *fam*
hack[2] *n* **1** CHOP : hachazo *m*, tajo *m* **2** HORSE : caballo *m* de alquiler **3** WRITER : escritor *m*, -tora *f* a sueldo; escritorzuelo *m*, -la *f* **4** COUGH : tos *f* seca
hacker ['hækər] *n* : pirata *m* informático, pirata *f* informática; hacker *mf fam*
hackles ['hækəlz] *npl* **1** : pluma *f* erizada (de un ave), pelo *m* erizado (de un perro, etc.) **2 to get one's hackles up** : ponerse furioso
hackney ['hækni] *n, pl* **-neys** : caballo *m* de silla, caballo *m* de tiro
hackneyed ['hæknid] *adj* TRITE : trillado, gastado
hacksaw ['hækˌsɔ] *n* : sierra *f* para metales
had → **have**
haddock ['hædək] *ns & pl* : eglefino *m*
hadn't ['hædənt] *contraction of* HAD NOT → **have**
hag ['hæg] *n offensive* : bruja *f*, vieja *f* fea
haggard ['hægərd] *adj* : demacrado, macilento — **haggardly** *adv*

haggle ['hægəl] *vi* **-gled; -gling** : regatear

ha–ha *or* **ha ha** [ˌhɑ'hɑ, 'hɑ'hɑ] *interj* : ¡ja, ja!

hail¹ ['heɪl] *vt* **1** GREET : saludar **2** SUMMON : llamar ⟨to hail a taxi : llamar un taxi⟩ **3** WELCOME : aclamar — *vi* : granizar (en meteorología)

hail² *n* **1** : granizo *m* **2** BARRAGE : aluvión *m*, lluvia *f*

hail³ *interj* : ¡salve!

hailstone ['heɪlˌstoːn] *n* : granizo *m*, piedra *f* de granizo

hailstorm ['heɪlˌstɔrm] *n* : granizada *f*

hair ['hær] *n* **1** : pelo *m*, cabello *m* ⟨to get one's hair cut : cortarse el pelo⟩ **2** : vello *m* (en las piernas, etc.)

hairbreadth ['hærˌbrɛdθ] *or* **hairsbreadth** ['hærz-] *n* **by a hairbreadth** : por un pelo

hairbrush ['hærˌbrʌʃ] *n* : cepillo *m* (para el pelo)

haircut ['hærˌkʌt] *n* : corte *m* de pelo

hairdo ['hærˌduː] *n*, *pl* **-dos** : peinado *m*

hairdresser ['hærˌdrɛsər] *n* **1** : peluquero *m*, -ra *f* **2 the hairdresser's** : la peluquería

hairdressing ['hærˌdrɛsɪŋ] *n* : peluquería *f* (profesión o actividad)

haired ['hærd] *adj* (*used in combination*) : de pelo ⟨long-haired : de pelo largo⟩ ⟨red-haired : pelirrojo⟩

hairiness ['hærinəs] *n* : vellosidad *f*

hairless ['hærləs] *adj* : sin pelo, calvo, pelón

hairline ['hærˌlaɪn] *n* **1** : línea *f* delgada **2** : nacimiento *m* del pelo ⟨to have a receding hairline : tener entradas⟩

hairpiece ['hærˌpiːs] *n* : bisoñé *m*, peluquín *m*

hairpin ['hærˌpɪn] *n* : horquilla *f*

hair–raising ['hærˌreɪzɪŋ] *adj* : espeluznante

hair spray *n* : laca *f*, fijador *m* (para el pelo)

hairstyle ['hærˌstaɪl] *n* : peinado *m*

hairy ['hæri] *adj* **hairier; -est** : peludo, velludo

Haitian ['heɪʃən, 'heɪtiən] *n* : haitiano *m*, -na *f* — **Haitian** *adj*

hake ['heɪk] *n* : merluza *f*

hale¹ ['heɪl] *vt* **haled; haling** : arrastrar, halar ⟨to hale to court : arrastrar al tribunal⟩

hale² *adj* : saludable, robusto

half¹ ['hæf, 'haf] *adv* **1** PARTIALLY : medio, a medias ⟨half cooked : medio cocido⟩ ⟨half closed/open : entreabierto⟩ ⟨she was half asleep : estaba medio dormida⟩ **2** : medio ⟨half full : medio lleno⟩ ⟨it's half past eleven (o'clock) : son las once y media⟩ ⟨she's half Mexican : es medio mexicana⟩ **3 half off** : a mitad de precio

half² *adj* : medio, a medias ⟨a half hour : una media hora⟩ ⟨a half truth : una verdad a medias⟩

half³ *n*, *pl* **halves** ['hævz, 'havz] **1** : mitad *f* ⟨to cut in half, to cut into halves : cortar por la mitad⟩ **2** : tiempo *m* (en deportes)

half⁴ *pron* : la mitad ⟨half of my friends : la mitad de mis amigos⟩ ⟨do you want half? : ¿quieres la mitad?⟩ ⟨half a million people : medio millón de personas⟩

half brother *n* : medio hermano *m*, hermanastro *m*

halfhearted ['hæf'hɑrtəd] *adj* : sin ánimo, poco entusiasta

halfheartedly ['hæf'hɑrtədli] *adv* : con poco entusiasmo, sin ánimo

half–life ['hæfˌlaɪf] *n*, *pl* **half–lives** : media vida *f*

half–mast ['hæf'mæst] *n* **at** ~ : a media asta

half–moon ['hæfˌmuːn] *n*, *pl* **half–moons** : media luna *f*

half note *n* : blanca *f* (en música)

half–price ['hæf'praɪs] *adj & adv* : a mitad de precio ⟨a half-price sale : rebajas de 50 por ciento⟩

half price *n* : mitad *f* de precio ⟨to buy at half price, to pay half price for : comprar a mitad de precio⟩

half sister *n* : media hermana *f*, hermanastra *f*

halftime ['hæf'taɪm] *n* : descanso *m*, medio tiempo *m* (en deportes)

half–truth ['hæf'truːθ] *n* : verdad *f* a medias

halfway¹ ['hæf'weɪ] *adv* : a medio camino, a mitad de camino

halfway² *adj* : medio, intermedio ⟨a halfway point : un punto intermedio⟩

half–wit ['hæfˌwɪt] *n* : tonto *m*, -ta *f*; imbécil *mf*

half–witted ['hæf'wɪtəd] *adj* : estúpido

halibut ['hælɪbət] *ns & pl* : halibut *m*

hall ['hɔl] *n* **1** BUILDING : residencia *f* estudiantil, facultad *f* (de una universidad) **2** VESTIBULE : entrada *f*, vestíbulo *m*, zaguán *m* **3** CORRIDOR : corredor *m*, pasillo *m* **4** AUDITORIUM : sala *f*, salón *m* ⟨concert hall : sala de conciertos⟩ **5 city hall** : ayuntamiento *m*

hallelujah [ˌhælə'luːjə, ˌhɑ-] *interj* : ¡aleluya!

hallmark ['hɔlˌmɑrk] *n* : sello *m* (distintivo)

hallow ['hæˌloː] *vt* : santificar, consagrar

hallowed ['hæˌloːd, 'hæˌloːəd, 'hɑˌloːd] *adj* : sagrado

Halloween [ˌhælə'wiːn, ˌhɑ-] *n* : víspera *f* de Todos los Santos

hallucinate [hæ'luːsənˌeɪt] *vi* **-nated; -nating** : alucinar

hallucination [həˌluːsən'eɪʃən] *n* : alucinación *f*

hallucinatory [hə'luːsənəˌtori] *adj* : alucinante

hallucinogen [hə'luːsənədʒən] *n* : alucinógeno *m*

hallucinogenic [həˌluːsənə'dʒɛnɪk] *adj* : alucinógeno

hallway ['hɔlˌweɪ] *n* **1** ENTRANCE : entrada *f* **2** CORRIDOR : corredor *m*, pasillo *m*

halo ['heɪˌloː] *n*, *pl* **-los** *or* **-loes** : aureola *f*, halo *m*

halt¹ ['hɔlt] *vi* : detenerse, pararse — *vt* **1** STOP : detener, parar (a una persona) **2** INTERRUPT : interrumpir (una actividad)

halt² *n* **1** : alto *m*, parada *f* **2 to come to a halt** : pararse, detenerse

halter [ˈhɔltər] *n* **1** : cabestro *m*, ronzal *m* (para un animal) **2** : blusa *f* sin espalda

halting [ˈhɔltɪŋ] *adj* HESITANT : vacilante, titubeante — **haltingly** *adv*

halve [ˈhæv, ˈhav] *vt* **halved; halving 1** DIVIDE : partir por la mitad **2** REDUCE : reducir a la mitad

halves → **half**

ham [ˈhæm] *n* **1** : jamón *m* **2** : payaso *m*, -sa *f*; persona *f* graciosa **3** *or* **ham radio operator** : radioaficionado *m*, -da *f* **4 hams** *npl* HAUNCHES : ancas *fpl*

hamburger [ˈhæm‚bərgər] *or* **hamburg** [-‚bərg] *n* **1** : carne *f* molida **2** : hamburguesa *f* (emparedado)

hamlet [ˈhæmlət] *n* VILLAGE : aldea *f*, poblado *m*

hammer¹ [ˈhæmər] *vt* **1** STRIKE : clavar, golpear **2** NAIL : clavar, martillar **3** DEFEAT : darle una paliza a **4 to hammer out** NEGOTIATE : elaborar, negociar, llegar a — *vi* : martillar, golpear

hammer² *n* **1** : martillo *m* **2** : percusor *m*, percutor *m* (de un arma de fuego)

hammock [ˈhæmək] *n* : hamaca *f*

hamper¹ [ˈhæmpər] *vt* : obstaculizar, dificultar

hamper² *n* : cesto *m*, canasta *f*

hamster [ˈhæmpstər] *n* : hámster *m*

hamstring [ˈhæm‚strɪŋ] *vt* **-strung** [-‚strʌŋ]; **-stringing 1** : cortarle el tendón del corvejón a (un animal) **2** INCAPACITATE : incapacitar, inutilizar

hand¹ [ˈhænd] *vt* **1** : pasar, dar, entregar **2 to hand back** RETURN : devolver **3 to hand down** : dejar en herencia **4 to hand in** SUBMIT : entregar, presentar **5 to hand it to** *fam* : aplaudir, felicitar ⟨I've got to hand it to you — you did a great job! : ¡tengo que reconocer que hiciste muy bien!⟩ **6 to hand out** DISTRIBUTE : distribuir **7 to hand over** SURRENDER : entregar

hand² *n* **1** : mano *f* ⟨made by hand : hecho a mano⟩ ⟨hand in hand : tomados de la mano⟩ ⟨to hold hands : ir tomados de la mano⟩ ⟨to raise one's hand : levantar la mano⟩ ⟨to join hands : darse las manos⟩ **2** POINTER : manecilla *f*, aguja *f* (de un reloj o instrumento) **3** SIDE : lado *m* ⟨on the one hand . . . on the other hand . . . : por un lado . . . por otro lado . . .⟩ **4** HANDWRITING : letra *f*, escritura *f* **5** APPLAUSE : aplauso *m* ⟨let's give them all a hand! : ¡aplausos para todos!⟩ **6** : mano *f*, cartas *fpl* (en juegos de naipes) **7** WORKER : obrero *m*, -ra *f*; trabajador *m*, -dora *f* **8 hands** *npl* CONTROL : manos *fpl* ⟨to fall into the hands of : caer en manos de⟩ ⟨it's out of my hands : no está en mis manos⟩ **9 at hand** NEAR : a mano ⟨to keep close at hand : tener a mano⟩ ⟨the problem at hand : el problema más aciante⟩ **10 on hand** AVAILABLE : a mano, disponible **11 on hand** PRESENT, NEAR : presente, cerca **12 on one's hands** ⟨I had some time on my hands : tenía un rato libre⟩ ⟨she has all that work on her hands : tiene tanto trabajo que hacer⟩ **13 on one's hands and knees** : a gatas **14 out of hand** : descontrolado ⟨the situation is getting out of hand : la situación se les/nos (etc.) va de las manos⟩ **15 out of hand** IMMEDIATELY : sin miramientos **16 to ask for someone's hand (in marriage)** : pedir la mano de alguien **17 to give/lend a hand** : echar una mano **18 to go hand in hand** : ir de la mano **19 to have a hand in** : tener parte en **20 to have one's hands full** : estar muy ocupado **21 to have one's hands tied** : tener las manos atadas **22 to live from hand to mouth** : vivir al día **23 to try one's hand at** : probar a hacer **24 to wait on someone hand and foot** : hacerle de sirviente/sirvienta a alguien

handbag [ˈhænd‚bæg] *n* : cartera *f*, bolso *m*, bolsa *f Mex*

handball [ˈhænd‚bɔl] *n* : frontón *m*, pelota *f*

handbill [ˈhænd‚bɪl] *n* : folleto *m*, volante *m*

handbook [ˈhænd‚bʊk] *n* : manual *m*

handbrake [ˈhænd‚breɪk] *n* : freno *m* de mano

handcuff [ˈhænd‚kʌf] *vt* : esposar, ponerle esposas (a alguien)

handcuffs [ˈhænd‚kʌfs] *npl* : esposas *fpl*

handful [ˈhænd‚fʊl] *n* : puñado *m*

handgun [ˈhænd‚gʌn] *n* : pistola *f*, revólver *m*

handheld [ˈhænd‚hɛld] *adj* : de mano

handicap¹ [ˈhændi‚kæp] *vt* **-capped; -capping 1** : asignar un handicap a (en deportes) **2** HAMPER : obstaculizar, poner en desventaja

handicap² *n* **1** *sometimes offensive* DISABILITY : minusvalía *f*, discapacidad *f* **2** DISADVANTAGE : desventaja *f*, handicap *m* (en deportes)

handicapped [ˈhændi‚kæpt] *adj* *sometimes offensive* DISABLED : minusválido, discapacitado

handicraft [ˈhændi‚kræft] *n* : artesanía *f*

handily [ˈhændəli] *adv* EASILY : fácilmente, con facilidad

handiwork [ˈhændi‚wərk] *n* **1** WORK : trabajo *m* **2** CRAFTS : artesanías *fpl*

handkerchief [ˈhæŋkərtʃəf, -‚tʃiːf] *n*, *pl* **-chiefs** : pañuelo *m*

handle¹ [ˈhændəl] *v* **-dled; -dling** *vt* **1** TOUCH : tocar **2** MANAGE : tratar, manejar, despachar **3** SELL : comerciar con, vender — *vi* : responder, conducirse (dícese de un vehículo)

handle² *n* : asa *f*, asidero *m*, mango *m* (de un cuchillo, etc.), pomo *m* (de una puerta), tirador *m* (de un cajón)

handlebars [ˈhændəl‚bɑrz] *npl* : manubrio *m*, manillar *m*

handler [ˈhændələr] *n* : cuidador *m*, -dora *f*

handling [ˈhændəlɪŋ] *n* **1** MANAGEMENT : manejo *m* **2** TOUCHING : manoseo *m* **3 shipping and handling** : porte *m*, transporte *m*

handmade [ˈhænd‚meɪd] *adj* : hecho a mano

hand–me–downs ['hænd̩mi,daʊnz] *npl* : ropa *f* usada

handout ['hænd,aʊt] *n* **1** AID : dádiva *f*, limosna *f* **2** LEAFLET : folleto *m*

handpick ['hænd'pɪk] *vt* : seleccionar con cuidado

handrail ['hænd,reɪl] *n* : pasamanos *m*, barandilla *f*, barandal *m*

handsaw ['hænd,sɔ] *n* : serrucho *m*

hands down *adv* **1** EASILY : con facilidad **2** UNQUESTIONABLY : con mucho, de lejos

hands–free ['hændz'fri:] *adj* : (de) manos libres

handshake ['hænd,ʃeɪk] *n* : apretón *m* de manos

handsome ['hænʦəm] *adj* **handsomer; -est 1** ATTRACTIVE : apuesto, guapo, atractivo **2** GENEROUS : generoso **3** SIZABLE : considerable

handsomely ['hænʦəmli] *adv* **1** ELEGANTLY : elegantemente **2** GENEROUSLY : con generosidad

handspring ['hænd,sprɪŋ] *n* : voltereta *f*

handstand ['hænd,stænd] *n* **to do a handstand** : pararse de manos

hand–to–hand ['hændtə'hænd] *adj* : cuerpo a cuerpo

hand truck → **truck²**

handwriting ['hænd,raɪt̬ɪŋ] *n* : letra *f*, escritura *f*

handwritten ['hænd,rɪt̬ən] *adj* : escrito a mano

handy ['hændi] *adj* **handier; -est 1** NEARBY : a mano, cercano **2** USEFUL : útil, práctico **3** DEXTEROUS : hábil

handyman ['hændi,mæn] *n, pl* **-men** [-mən, -,mɛn] : hombre *m* que hace pequeños arreglos del hogar, manitas *m* *Spain*

handywoman ['hændi,wʊmən] *n, pl* **-women** [-,wɪmən] : mujer *f* que hace pequeños arreglos del hogar, manitas *f* *Spain*

hang¹ ['hæŋ] *v* **hung** ['hʌŋ]; **hanging** *vt* **1** SUSPEND : colgar, tender (ropa lavada), colocar (una pintura, etc.) **2** *past tense often* **hanged** EXECUTE : colgar, ahorcar **3 to hang one's head** : bajar la cabeza — *vi* **1** FALL : caer (dícese de las telas y la ropa) **2** DANGLE : colgar **3** HOVER : flotar, sostenerse en el aire **4** : ser ahorcado **5** DROOP : inclinarse **6 to hang around** *fam* : pasar el rato **7 to hang back** : quedar atrás **8 to hang in there** : seguir adelante **9 to hang on** : WAIT esperar **10 to hang on (to)** : agarrarse (a) **6 to hang out** *fam* : pasar el rato **11 to hang out with someone** : andar con alguien **12 to be hanging over one** *or* **to be hanging over one's head** : tener pendiente, quedarle a alguien por resolver/terminar (etc.) ⟨I can't relax with this test hanging over me : no puedo relajarme hasta que me quite de encima este examen⟩ **13 to hang tight** : seguir adelante **14 to hang tough** : mantenerse firme **15 to hang up** : colgar ⟨he hung up on me : me colgó⟩

hang² *n* **1** DRAPE : caída *f* **2 to get the hang of something** : agarrarle la onda a algo

hangar ['hæŋər, 'hæŋgər] *n* : hangar *m*

hanger ['hæŋər] *n* : percha *f*, gancho *m* (para ropa)

hang glider ['hæŋ,glaɪdər] *n* : ala *f* delta (vehículo), deslizador *m* Mex

hang gliding ['hæŋ,glaɪdɪŋ] *n* : ala *f* delta (deporte), aladeltismo *m*

hangman ['hæŋmən] *n, pl* **-men** [-mən, -,mɛn] : verdugo *m*

hangnail ['hæŋ,neɪl] *n* : padrastro *m*

hangout ['hæŋ,aʊt] *n* : lugar *m* popular, sitio *m* muy frecuentado

hangover ['hæŋ,oːvər] *n* : resaca *f*

hank ['hæŋk] *n* : madeja *f*

hanker ['hæŋkər] *vi* **to hanker for** : tener ansias de, tener ganas de

hankering ['hæŋkərɪŋ] *n* : ansia *f*, anhelo *m*

hankie *or* **hanky** ['hæŋki] *n, pl* **-kies** : pañuelo *m*

Hanukkah ['xɑnəkə, 'hɑ–] *n* : Janucá, Januká, Hanukkah

haphazard [hæp'hæzərd] *adj* : casual, fortuito, al azar — **haphazardly** *adv*

hapless ['hæpləs] *adj* UNFORTUNATE : desafortunado, desventurado — **haplessly** *adv*

happen ['hæpən] *vi* **1** OCCUR : pasar, ocurrir, suceder, tener lugar **2** BEFALL : pasar, acontecer ⟨what happened to her? : ¿qué le ha pasado?⟩ **3** CHANCE : resultar, ocurrir por casualidad ⟨it happened that I wasn't home : resulta que estaba fuera de casa⟩ ⟨he happens to be right : da la casualidad de que tiene razón⟩

happening ['hæpənɪŋ] *n* : suceso *m*, acontecimiento *m*

happiness ['hæpinəs] *n* : felicidad *f*, dicha *f*

happy ['hæpi] *adj* **happier; -est 1** JOYFUL : feliz, contento, alegre ⟨I'm happy for you : me alegro por ti⟩ ⟨a happy smile : una sonrisa de alegría⟩ **2** FORTUNATE : afortunado, feliz — **happily** [-pəli] *adv*

happy–go–lucky ['hæpigo:'lʌki] *adj* : despreocupado

harangue¹ [hə'ræŋ] *vt* **-rangued; -ranguing** : arengar

harangue² *n* : arenga *f*

harass [hə'ræs, 'hærəs] *vt* **1** BESIEGE, HOUND : acosar, asediar, hostigar **2** ANNOY : molestar

harassment [hə'ræsmənt, 'hærəsmənt] *n* : acoso *m*, hostigamiento *m* ⟨sexual harassment : acoso sexual⟩

harbinger ['hɑrbɪnʤər] *n* **1** HERALD : heraldo *m*, precursor *m* **2** OMEN : presagio *m*

harbor¹ ['hɑrbər] *vt* **1** SHELTER : dar refugio a, albergar **2** CHERISH, KEEP : abrigar, guardar, albergar ⟨to harbor doubts : guardar dudas⟩

harbor² *n* **1** REFUGE : refugio *m* **2** PORT : puerto *m*

hard¹ ['hɑrd] *adv* **1** FORCEFULLY : fuerte, con fuerza ⟨the wind blew hard : el viento

sopló fuerte⟩ **2** STRENUOUSLY : duro, mucho ⟨to work hard : trabajar duro⟩ **3 to take something hard** : tomarse algo muy mal, estar muy afectado por algo
hard² *adj* **1** FIRM, SOLID : duro, firme, sólido **2** DIFFICULT : difícil, arduo **3** SEVERE : severo, duro ⟨a hard winter : un invierno severo⟩ **4** UNFEELING : insensible, duro **5** DILIGENT : diligente ⟨to be a hard worker : ser muy trabajador⟩ **6** FORCEFUL : fuerte (dícese de un golpe, etc.) **7** HARSH : fuerte (dícese de una luz), definido (dícese de una línea) **8 hard liquor** : bebidas *fpl* fuertes **9 hard water** : agua *f* dura **10 to be hard on** *fam* CRITICIZE, PUNISH : ser duro con **11 to be hard on** *fam* HARM : ser malo para **12 to be hard on** *fam* STRESS : ser difícil para **13 to be hard up** *fam* : estar/andar mal de dinero **14 to be hard up for** *fam* : andar escaso de **15 to have a hard time** *fam* : pasarlo mal **16 to have a hard time with/doing something** *fam* : costarle a uno hacer algo **17 to learn the hard way** *fam* : aprender a las malas **18 to do something the hard way** *fam* : complicar las cosas
hardback [ˈhɑrdˌbæk] *n* : libro *m* de tapa dura
hardball [ˈhɑrdˌbɔl] *n* **1** → **baseball 2 to play hardball** : ser agresivo, jugar sucio
hard–boiled [ˈhɑrdˌbɔild] *adj* : duro (dícese de un huevo)
hard copy *n* : copia *f* impresa
hardcover¹ [ˈhɑrdˌkʌvər] *adj* : de pasta dura, de tapa dura
hardcover² *n* : libro *m* de pasta/tapa dura
hard disk *n* : disco *m* duro
hard drive 1 → **hard disk 2** : (unidad *f* de) disco *m* duro
harden [ˈhɑrdən] *vt* **1** SOLIDIFY, CONGEAL : endurecer **2** : endurecer, hacer duro (a una persona) ⟨to harden someone's heart : endurecerle el corazón a alguien⟩ **3** : reforzar, fortalecer (la determinación, etc.) — *vi* **1** SOLIDIFY, CONGEAL : endurecerse **2** : reforzarse, fortalecerse **3** : endurecerse, hacerse duro (dícese de la voz, etc.)
hard–fought [ˈhɑrdˈfɔt] *adj* : muy reñido
hardheaded [ˌhɑrdˈhɛdəd] *adj* **1** STUBBORN : testarudo, terco **2** REALISTIC : realista, práctico — **hardheadedly** *adv*
hard–hearted [ˌhɑrdˈhɑrtəd] *adj* : despiadado, insensible — **hard–heartedly** *adv*
hard–heartedness [ˌhɑrdˈhɑrtədnəs] *n* : dureza *f* de corazón
hardly [ˈhɑrdli] *adv* **1** SCARCELY : apenas, casi ⟨I hardly knew her : apenas la conocía⟩ ⟨hardly ever : casi nunca⟩ **2** NOT : difícilmente, poco, no ⟨they can hardly blame me! : ¡difícilmente pueden echarme la culpa!⟩ ⟨it's hardly likely : es poco probable⟩
hardness [ˈhɑrdnəs] *n* **1** FIRMNESS : dureza *f* **2** DIFFICULTY : dificultad *f* **3** SEVERITY : severidad *f*
hardship [ˈhɑrdˌʃɪp] *n* : dificultad *f*, privación *f*

hardware [ˈhɑrdˌwær] *n* **1** : ferretería *f* **2** : hardware *m* (de una computadora)
hardware store *n* : ferretería *f*
hardwired [ˈhɑrdˌwaɪrd] *adj* **1** : integrado (dícese de un sistema, etc.) **2** : mentalmente programado
hardwood [ˈhɑrdˌwʊd] *n* : madera *f* dura, madera *f* noble
hardworking [ˈhɑrdˈwərkɪŋ] *adj* : trabajador
hardy [ˈhɑrdi] *adj* **hardier; -est** : fuerte, robusto, resistente (dícese de las plantas) — **hardily** [-dəli] *adv*
hare [ˈhær] *n, pl* **hare** *or* **hares** : liebre *f*
harebrained [ˈhærˌbreɪnd] *adj* : estúpido, absurdo, disparatado
harem [ˈhærəm] *n* : harén *m*
hark [ˈhɑrk] *vi* **1** (*used only in the imperative*) LISTEN : escuchar **2 hark back** RETURN : volver **3 hark back** RECALL : recordar
harlequin [ˈhɑrlɪkən, -kwən] *n* : arlequín *m*
harlot [ˈhɑrlət] *n* : ramera *f*
harm¹ [ˈhɑrm] *vt* : hacerle daño a, perjudicar
harm² *n* **1** : daño *m*, perjuicio *m* ⟨I meant no harm : no lo dije/hice (etc.) con mala intención⟩ ⟨to do more harm than good : hacer más mal/daño que bien⟩ ⟨there's no harm in asking : con preguntar no se pierde nada⟩ **2 in harm's way** : en peligro **3 no harm done** *fam* : no fue nada, no pasó nada
harmful [ˈhɑrmfəl] *adj* : dañino, perjudicial — **harmfully** *adv*
harmless [ˈhɑrmləs] *adj* : inofensivo, inocuo — **harmlessly** *adv*
harmlessness [ˈhɑrmləsnəs] *n* : inocuidad *f*
harmonic [hɑrˈmɑnɪk] *adj* : armónico — **harmonically** [-nɪkli] *adv*
harmonica [hɑrˈmɑnɪkə] *n* : armónica *f*
harmonious [hɑrˈmoːniəs] *adj* : armonioso — **harmoniously** *adv*
harmonize [ˈhɑrməˌnaɪz] *v* **-nized; -nizing** : armonizar
harmony [ˈhɑrməni] *n, pl* **-nies** : armonía *f*
harness¹ [ˈhɑrnəs] *vt* **1** : enjaezar (un animal) **2** UTILIZE : utilizar, aprovechar
harness² *n* : arreos *mpl*, guarniciones *fpl*, arnés *m*
harp¹ [ˈhɑrp] *vi* **to harp on** : insistir sobre, machacar sobre
harp² *n* : arpa *m*
harpist [ˈhɑrpɪst] *n* : arpista *mf*
harpoon¹ [hɑrˈpuːn] *vt* : arponear
harpoon² *n* : arpón *m*
harpsichord [ˈhɑrpsɪˌkɔrd] *n* : clavicémbalo *m*
harrow¹ [ˈhærˌoː] *vt* **1** CULTIVATE : gradar, labrar (la tierra) **2** TORMENT : atormentar
harrow² *n* : grada *f*, rastra *f*
harry [ˈhæri] *vt* **-ried; -rying** HARASS : acosar, hostigar
harsh [ˈhɑrʃ] *adj* **1** ROUGH : áspero **2** SEVERE : duro, severo **3** : discordante (dícese de los sonidos) — **harshly** *adv*

harshness ['hɑrʃnəs] *n* **1** ROUGHNESS : aspereza *f* **2** SEVERITY : dureza *f*, severidad *f*
harvest¹ ['hɑrvəst] *v* : cosechar
harvest² *n* **1** HARVESTING : siega *f*, recolección *f* **2** CROP : cosecha *f*
harvester ['hɑrvəstər] *n* : segador *m*, -dora *f*; cosechadora *f* (máquina)
has → have
has–been ['hæz,bɪn, -,bɛn] *n* : vieja gloria *f*
hash¹ ['hæʃ] *vt* **1** MINCE : picar **2 to hash over** DISCUSS : discutir, repasar
hash² *n* **1** : picadillo *m* (comida) **2** JUMBLE : revoltijo *m*, fárrago *m*
hashish ['hæ,ʃiːʃ, hæˈʃiːʃ] *n* : hachís *m*
hashtag ['hæʃ,tæg] *n* : hashtag *m*, etiqueta *f* (en las redes sociales)
hasn't ['hæzənt] *contraction of* HAS NOT → has
hasp ['hæsp] *n* : picaporte *m*, pestillo *m*
hassle¹ ['hæsəl] *vt* **-sled; -sling** : fastidiar, molestar
hassle² *n* **1** ARGUMENT : discusión *f*, disputa *f*, bronca *f* **2** FIGHT : pelea *f*, riña *f* **3** BOTHER, TROUBLE : problemas *mpl*, lío *m*
hassock ['hæsək] *n* **1** CUSHION : almohadón *m*, cojín *m* **2** FOOTSTOOL : escabel *m*
haste ['heɪst] *n* **1** : prisa *f*, apuro *m* **2 to make haste** : darse prisa, apurarse
hasten ['heɪsən] *vt* : acelerar, precipitar — *vi* : apresurarse, apurarse
hasty ['heɪsti] *adj* **hastier; -est 1** HURRIED, QUICK : rápido, apresurado, apurado **2** RASH : precipitado — **hastily** [-təli] *adv*
hat ['hæt] *n* : sombrero *m*
hatch¹ ['hætʃ] *vt* **1** : incubar, empollar (huevos) **2** DEVISE : idear, tramar — *vi* : salir del cascarón
hatch² *n* : escotilla *f*
hatchback ['hætʃ,bæk] *n* **1** : hatchback *m* (automóvil) **2** : puerta *f* trasera
hatchery ['hætʃəri] *n, pl* **-ries** : criadero *m*
hatchet ['hætʃət] *n* : hacha *f*
hatchway ['hætʃ,weɪ] *n* : escotilla *f*
hate¹ ['heɪt] *vt* **hated; hating** : odiar, aborrecer, detestar
hate² *n* : odio *m*
hateful ['heɪtfəl] *adj* : odioso, aborrecible, detestable — **hatefully** *adv*
hatred ['heɪtrəd] *n* : odio *m*
hatter ['hætər] *n* : sombrerero *m*, -ra *f*
haughtiness ['hɔtinəs] *n* : altanería *f*, altivez *f*
haughty ['hɔti] *adj* **haughtier; -est** : altanero, altivo — **haughtily** [-təli] *adv*
haul¹ ['hɔl] *vt* **1** DRAG, PULL : arrastrar, jalar **2** TRANSPORT : transportar
haul² *n* **1** PULL : tirón *m*, jalón *m* **2** CATCH : redada *f* **3** JOURNEY : viaje *m*, trayecto *m* ⟨it's a long haul : es un trayecto largo⟩
haulage ['hɔlɪʤ] *n* : transporte *m*, tiro *m*
hauler ['hɔlər] *n* : transportista *mf*
haunch ['hɔntʃ] *n* **1** HIP : cadera *f* **2 haunches** *npl* HINDQUARTERS : ancas *fpl*, cuartos *mpl* traseros

haunt¹ ['hɔnt] *vt* **1** : rondar, habitar (dícese de un fantasma) **2** FREQUENT : frecuentar, rondar **3** PREOCCUPY : perseguir, obsesionar
haunt² *n* : guarida *f* (de animales o ladrones), lugar *m* predilecto
haunted ['hɔntəd] *adj* : embrujado, encantado (dícese de una casa, etc.)
haunting ['hɔntɪŋ] *adj* : inolvidable (por ser hermoso o triste) — **hauntingly** *adv*
haute ['oːt] *adj* **1** : de moda, de categoría **2 haute couture** [,oːtkuˈtur] : alta costura *f* **3 haute cuisine** [,oːtkwiˈziːn] : alta cocina *f*
have ['hæv, in sense 7 as an auxiliary verb usu 'hæf] *v* **had** ['hæd]; **having; has** ['hæz, in sense 7 as an auxiliary verb usu 'hæs] *vt* **1** POSSESS : tener ⟨she has long hair : tiene el pelo largo⟩ ⟨they have three children : tienen tres hijos⟩ ⟨do you have change? : ¿tienes cambio?⟩ ⟨you can have it : te lo doy⟩ **2** OBTAIN : conseguir ⟨I must have it! : ¡no puedo sin ello!⟩ **3** (*indicating availability*) : tener ⟨when you have a minute : cuando tengas un momento⟩ **4** : tener (en casa) ⟨we have guests : tenemos visita⟩ **5** EXPERIENCE, UNDERGO : tener ⟨I have a toothache : tengo un dolor de muelas⟩ ⟨to have surgery : operarse⟩ ⟨to have a good time : pasarlo bien⟩ **6** : tener (una idea, una opinión, etc.) **7** INCLUDE : tener, incluir ⟨April has 30 days : abril tiene 30 días⟩ **8** CONSUME : comer, tomar **9** RECEIVE : tener, recibir ⟨he had my permission : tenía mi permiso⟩ **10** ALLOW : permitir, tolerar ⟨I won't have it! : ¡no lo permitiré!⟩ **11** HOLD : hacer ⟨to have a party : dar una fiesta⟩ ⟨to have a meeting : celebrar una reunión⟩ **12** DO : hacer ⟨to have a nap : echarse una siesta⟩ ⟨to have a look at : mirar⟩ ⟨I'll have a talk with him : hablaré con él⟩ **13** HOLD : tener ⟨he had me in his power : me tenía en su poder⟩ ⟨she had me by the arm : me tenía agarrado del brazo⟩ **14** BEAR : tener (niños) **15** (*indicating causation*) ⟨she had a dress made : mandó hacer un vestido⟩ ⟨to have one's hair cut : cortarse el pelo⟩ ⟨have her call me : dile que me llame⟩ ⟨he had it ready : lo tenía listo⟩ **16** (*indicating loss, damage, etc.*) ⟨she had her car stolen : le robaron el auto⟩ **17 to be had** : ser engañado ⟨I've been had! : ¡me han engañado!⟩ **18 to be had** ⟨there were none to be had : no había disponibles⟩ **19 to have back** ⟨can I have my book back? : ¿me puedes devolver el libro?⟩ **20 to have back** : volver a invitar ⟨we must have you back : tienes que volver a visitarnos⟩ **21 to have back** ⟨it's good to have you back! : ¡qué gusto volver a verte por aquí!⟩ **22 to have it easy/rough (etc.)** : tenerlo todo muy fácil/difícil (etc.) **23 to have it in for** : tenerle manía a **24 to have it in one** : ser capaz ⟨she doesn't have it in her to be cruel : no es capaz de ser cruel⟩ **25 to have it out (with)**

: aclarar(le) las cosas (a) **26 to have off**
: tener (un día, etc.) libre **27 to have on**
WEAR : llevar **28 to have over** : invitar
(a casa) **29 to have on one** : tener/lle-
var encima ⟨I don't have it on me : no lo
tengo encima⟩ **30 to have with one**
: traer (a alguien), tener/llevar (algo) encima — *v aux* **1** : haber ⟨she has been
very busy : ha estado muy ocupada⟩
⟨I've lived here three years : hace tres
años que vivo aquí⟩ **2** (*used in tags*)
⟨you've finished, haven't you?⟩ **3 to have got** (*used in
the present tense*) *fam* : tener ⟨I've got an
idea : tengo una idea⟩ ⟨we've got to
leave : tenemos que salir⟩ **4 you've got
me!** : ¡no sé!, ¡ni idea! **5 to have had it**
: no dar para más (dícese de una cosa) **6
to have had it (with someone/some-
thing)** : estar harto (de alguien/algo) **7
to have to** : deber, tener que ⟨we have to
leave : tenemos que salir⟩

haven ['heɪvən] *n* : refugio *m*
havoc ['hævək] *n* **1** DESTRUCTION : estragos *mpl*, destrucción *f* **2** CHAOS, DIS-
ORDER : desorden *m*, caos *m*
Hawaiian¹ [həˈwaɪən] *adj* : hawaiano
Hawaiian² *n* : hawaiano *m*, -na *f*
hawk¹ ['hɔk] *vt* : pregonar, vender (mercancías) en la calle
hawk² *n* : halcón *m*
hawker ['hɔkər] *n* : vendedor *m*, -dora *f*
ambulante
hawthorn ['hɔˌθɔrn] *n* : espino *m*
hay ['heɪ] *n* : heno *m*
hay fever *n* : fiebre *f* del heno
hayloft ['heɪˌlɔft] *n* : pajar *m*
hayseed ['heɪˌsiːd] *n* : palurdo *m*, -da *f*
haystack ['heɪˌstæk] *n* : almiar *m*
haywire ['heɪˌwaɪr] *adj* : descompuesto,
desbaratado ⟨to go haywire : estro-
pearse⟩
hazard¹ ['hæzərd] *vt* : arriesgar, aventurar
hazard² *n* **1** DANGER : peligro *m*, riesgo
m **2** CHANCE : azar *m*
hazardous ['hæzərdəs] *adj* : arriesgado,
peligroso
haze¹ ['heɪz] *vt* **hazed; hazing** : abrumar,
acosar
haze² *n* : bruma *f*, neblina *f*
hazel ['heɪzəl] *n* **1** : avellano *m* (árbol) **2**
: color *m* avellana
hazelnut ['heɪzəlˌnʌt] *n* : avellana *f*
haziness ['heɪzinəs] *n* **1** MISTINESS
: nebulosidad *f* **2** VAGUENESS : vaguedad *f*
hazy ['heɪzi] *adj* **hazier; -est** **1** MISTY
: brumoso, neblinoso, nebuloso **2**
VAGUE : vago, confuso
he ['hiː] *pron* : él
head¹ ['hɛd] *vt* **1** LEAD : encabezar **2** DI-
RECT : dirigir — *vi* : dirigirse
head² *adj* MAIN : principal ⟨the head office : la oficina central, la sede⟩ ⟨head of
state/government : jefe de estado/go-
bierno⟩
head³ *n* **1** : cabeza *f* ⟨from head to foot
: de pies a cabeza⟩ ⟨to stand on one's
head : pararse de cabeza⟩ ⟨to nod one's
head : asentir con la cabeza⟩ **2** MIND

: mente *f*, cabeza *f* ⟨use your head! : ¡usa
la cabeza!⟩ ⟨to add in one's head : sumar
mentalmente⟩ ⟨it's all in your head : es
pura imaginación tuya⟩ ⟨to come into
one's head : venirle a la cabeza⟩ ⟨to enter one's head : pasársele por la cabeza⟩
⟨to put something out of your head
: sacarse algo de la cabeza⟩ ⟨don't put
ideas in his head! : ¡no le metas ideas a la
cabeza!⟩ ⟨she's gotten it into her head
that . . . : se le ha metido en la cabeza
que . . .⟩ **3** TIP, TOP : cabeza *f* (de un
clavo, un martillo, etc.), cabecera *f* (de
una mesa o un río), punta *f* (de una flecha), flor *m* (de un repollo, etc.), encabezamiento *m* (de una carta, etc.),
espuma *f* (de cerveza) **4** DIRECTOR,
LEADER : director *m*, -tora *f*; jefe *m*, -fa
f; cabeza *f* (de una familia) ⟨head of
state/government : jefe de Estado/go-
bierno⟩ **5** : cara *f* (de una moneda)
⟨heads or tails : cara o cruz⟩ **6** : cabeza
f ⟨500 head of cattle : 500 cabezas de ga-
nado⟩ ⟨$10 a head : $10 por cabeza⟩ **7
to come to a head** : llegar a un punto
crítico **8 heads or/nor tails** ⟨I can't
make heads nor tails of it : para mí no
tiene ni pies ni cabeza⟩ **9 heads will
roll** : van a rodar cabezas **10 over one's
head** ⟨it's over my head : no alcanzo a
entenderlo⟩ ⟨the joke went over his
head : no entendió el chiste⟩ **11 to be
head over heels (in love)** : estar perdidamente enamorado **12 to be out of
one's head** : estar como una cabra **13
to go to someone's head** : subírsele a la
cabeza a alguien **14 to have a good
head on one's shoulders** : tener cabeza **15 to hold one's head high** : ir
con la cabeza bien alta **16 to keep/lose
one's head** : mantener/perder la
calma **17 to keep one's head above
water** : mantenerse a flote **18 to keep
one's head down** : mantenerse al margen **19 to rear its (ugly) head** : aparecer
headache ['hɛdˌeɪk] *n* : dolor *m* de cabeza, jaqueca *f*
headband ['hɛdˌbænd] *n* : cinta *f* del pelo
headboard ['hɛdˌbɔrd] *n* : cabecera *f*
headdress ['hɛdˌdrɛs] *n* : tocado *m*
headfirst ['hɛdˈfərst] *adv* : de cabeza
headgear ['hɛdˌgɪr] *n* : gorro *m*, casco *m*,
sombrero *m*
heading ['hɛdɪŋ] *n* **1** DIRECTION : dirección *f* **2** TITLE : encabezamiento *m*, título *m* **3** : membrete *m* (de una carta)
headland ['hɛdlənd, -ˌlænd] *n* : cabo *m*
headlight ['hɛdˌlaɪt] *n* : faro *m*, foco *m*,
farol *m* Mex
headline ['hɛdˌlaɪn] *n* : titular *m*
headlong¹ ['hɛdˈlɔŋ] *adv* **1** HEADFIRST
: de cabeza **2** HASTILY : precipitadamente
headlong² ['hɛdˌlɔŋ] *adj* : precipitado
headmaster ['hɛdˌmæstər] *n* : director *m*
headmistress ['hɛdˌmɪstrəs, -ˈmɪs-] *n* : directora *f*
head-on ['hɛdˈɑn, -ˈɔn] *adv & adj* : de
frente

headphones ['hɛd,foːnz] *npl* : audífonos *mpl*, cascos *mpl*

headquarters ['hɛd,kwɔrtərz] *ns & pl* 1 SEAT : oficina *f* central, sede *f* 2 : cuartel *m* general (de los militares)

headrest ['hɛd,rɛst] *n* : apoyacabezas *m*

headroom ['hɛd,ruːm, -,rʊm] *n* : espacio *m* libre entre la cabeza y el techo (de un coche, etc.)

headset ['hɛd,sɛt] *n* : audífonos *mpl*, cascos *mpl*

headship ['hɛd,ʃɪp] *n* : dirección *f*

head start *n* : ventaja *f*

headstone ['hɛd,stoːn] *n* : lápida *f*

headstrong ['hɛd'strɔŋ] *adj* : testarudo, obstinado, empecinado

heads-up ['hɛdz'ʌp] *n fam* WARNING : aviso *m* ⟨to give someone a heads-up : avisarle/advertirle a alguien⟩

headwaiter ['hɛd'weɪtər] *n* : jefe *m*, -fa *f* de comedor

headwaters ['hɛd,wɔtərz, -,wɑ-] *npl* : cabecera *f*

headway ['hɛd,weɪ] *n* : progreso *m* ⟨to make headway against : avanzar contra⟩

heady ['hɛdi] *adj* **headier; -est** 1 INTOXICATING : embriagador, excitante 2 SHREWD : astuto, sagaz

heal ['hiːl] *vt* : curar, sanar — *vi* 1 : sanar, curarse 2 to heal up : cicatrizarse

healer ['hiːlər] *n* 1 : curandero *m*, -dera *f* 2 : curador *m*, -dora *f* (cosa)

health ['hɛlθ] *n* : salud *f* ⟨health care : asistencia médica⟩ ⟨health center : centro sanitario⟩ ⟨health food : alimentos naturales⟩

healthful ['hɛlθfəl] *adj* : saludable, salubre — **healthfully** *adv*

healthiness ['hɛlθinəs] *n* : lozanía *f*

healthy ['hɛlθi] *adj* **healthier; -est** : sano, bien — **healthily** [-θəli] *adv*

heap¹ ['hiːp] *vt* 1 PILE : amontonar, apilar 2 SHOWER : colmar

heap² *n* : montón *m*, pila *f*

hear ['hɪr] *v* **heard** ['hərd]; **hearing** *vt* 1 : oír ⟨do you hear me? : ¿me oyes?⟩ ⟨I can't hear myself think : no puedo pensar con tanto ruido⟩ 2 HEED : oír, prestar atención a 3 LEARN : oír, enterarse de 4 to hear out : escuchar hasta el final — *vi* 1 : oír ⟨to hear about : oír hablar de⟩ 2 to hear from : tener noticias de 3 to hear of : oír hablar de ⟨I've heard of him : lo conozco de oídas⟩ 4 not to hear of : no permitir ⟨I won't hear of it! : ¡no lo permitiré!, ¡ni hablar!⟩ 5 not/never to hear the end of ⟨I'll never hear the end of it, she'll never let me hear the end of it : nunca me lo dejará olvidar⟩

hearing ['hɪrɪŋ] *n* 1 : oído *m* ⟨hard of hearing : duro de oído⟩ 2 : vista *f* (en un tribunal) 3 ATTENTION : consideración *f*, oportunidad *f* de expresarse 4 EARSHOT : alcance *m* del oído

hearing aid *n* : audífono *m*

hearken ['hɑrkən] *vt* : escuchar

hearsay ['hɪr,seɪ] *n* : rumores *mpl*

hearse ['hərs] *n* : coche *m* fúnebre

heart ['hɑrt] *n* 1 : corazón *m* ⟨heart rate : ritmo cardíaco⟩ ⟨heart disease : enfer-

medades cardíacas⟩ ⟨heart surgery : cirugía cardíaca⟩ ⟨heart murmur : soplo en el corazón⟩ 2 CENTER, CORE : corazón *m*, centro *m* ⟨the heart of the matter : el meollo del asunto⟩ 3 FEELINGS : corazón *m*, sentimientos *mpl* ⟨a broken heart : un corazón destrozado⟩ ⟨to have a good heart : tener buen corazón⟩ ⟨to take something to heart : tomarse algo a pecho⟩ ⟨from the heart : con toda sinceridad⟩ ⟨to be close to one's heart : significar mucho a alguien⟩ ⟨with a light heart : con el corazón alegre⟩ ⟨with a heavy heart : deprimido, acongojado⟩ ⟨my heart sank : se me cayó el alma a los pies⟩ 4 COURAGE : valor *m*, corazón *m* ⟨to take heart : animarse, cobrar ánimos⟩ 5 : corazón *m* (naipe) 6 at heart : en el fondo 7 by heart : de memoria 8 to one's heart's content : a voluntad, todo lo que quiere

heartache ['hɑrt,eɪk] *n* : pena *f*, angustia *f*

heart attack *n* : infarto *m*, ataque *m* al corazón

heartbeat ['hɑrt,biːt] *n* : latido *m* (del corazón)

heartbreak ['hɑrt,breɪk] *n* : congoja *f*, angustia *f*

heartbreaker ['hɑrt,breɪkər] *n* : rompecorazones *mf*

heartbreaking ['hɑrt,breɪkɪŋ] *adj* : desgarrador, que parte el corazón

heartbroken ['hɑrt,broːkən] *adj* : desconsolado, destrozado

heartburn ['hɑrt,bərn] *n* : acidez *f* estomacal

hearten ['hɑrtən] *vt* : alentar, animar

heartfelt ['hɑrt,fɛlt] *adj* : sentido

hearth ['hɑrθ] *n* : hogar *m*, chimenea *f*

heartily ['hɑrtəli] *adv* 1 ENTHUSIASTICALLY : de buena gana, con entusiasmo 2 TOTALLY : totalmente, completamente

heartless ['hɑrtləs] *adj* : desalmado, despiadado, cruel

heart of palm *n* : palmito *m*

heartsick ['hɑrt,sɪk] *adj* : abatido, desconsolado

heartstrings ['hɑrt,strɪŋz] *npl* : fibras *fpl* del corazón

heartwarming ['hɑrt,wɔrmɪŋ] *adj* : conmovedor, emocionante

hearty ['hɑrti] *adj* **heartier; -est** 1 CORDIAL, WARM : cordial, caluroso 2 STRONG : fuerte ⟨to have a hearty appetite : ser de buen comer⟩ 3 SUBSTANTIAL : abundante, sustancioso ⟨a hearty breakfast : un desayuno abundante⟩

heat¹ ['hiːt] *vt* : calentar

heat² *n* 1 WARMTH : calor *m* 2 HEATING : calefacción *f* 3 EXCITEMENT : calor *m*, entusiasmo *m* ⟨in the heat of the moment : en el calor del momento⟩ 4 ESTRUS : celo *m*

heated ['hiːt̬əd] *adj* 1 WARMED : calentado 2 IMPASSIONED : acalorado, apasionado

heater ['hiːt̬ər] *n* : calentador *m*, estufa *f*, calefactor *m*

heath ['hiːθ] *n* 1 MOOR : páramo *m* 2 HEATHER : brezo *m*

heathen¹ ['hi:ðən] *adj often offensive* : pagano

heathen² *n, pl* **-thens** *or* **-then** *often offensive* : pagano *m*, -na *f*; infiel *mf*

heather ['hɛðər] *n* : brezo *m*

heating ['hi:tɪŋ] *n* : calefacción *f*

heat wave *n* : ola *f* de calor

heave¹ ['hi:v] *v* **heaved** *or* **hove** ['ho:v]; **heaving** *vt* **1** LIFT, RAISE : levantar con esfuerzo **2** HURL : lanzar, tirar **3 to heave a sigh** : echar un suspiro, suspirar — *vi* **1** : subir y bajar, palpitar (dícese del pecho) **2 to heave up** RISE : levantarse

heave² *n* **1** EFFORT : gran esfuerzo *m* (para levantar algo) **2** THROW : lanzamiento *m*

heaven ['hɛvən] *n* **1** : cielo *m* ⟨for heaven's sake : por Dios⟩ **2 heavens** *npl* SKY : cielo *m* ⟨the heavens opened up : empezó a llover a cántaros⟩

heavenly ['hɛvənli] *adj* **1** : celestial, celeste **2** DELIGHTFUL : divino, encantador

heavily ['hɛvəli] *adv* **1** : mucho, muy ⟨heavily salted foods : comidas muy saladas⟩ ⟨he relies heavily on her : depende mucho de ella⟩ ⟨to smoke/drink heavily : fumar/beber mucho⟩ **2** LABORIOUSLY : pesadamente

heaviness ['hɛvinəs] *n* : peso *m*, pesadez *f*

heavy ['hɛvi] *adj* **heavier; -est 1** WEIGHTY : pesado ⟨to be heavy : pesar mucho, ser pesado⟩ ⟨how heavy is it? : ¿cuánto pesa?⟩ **2** DENSE, THICK : denso, espeso, grueso ⟨a heavy coat : un grueso abrigo⟩ ⟨a heavy beard : una barba poblada⟩ **3** LARGE, HIGH : grande, alto ⟨heavy turnout : alta concurrencia⟩ **4** INTENSE : intenso ⟨heavy traffic : denso tráfico⟩ ⟨heavy trading : mucha actividad (en la bolsa, etc.)⟩ **5** FORCEFUL : fuerte **6** SEVERE : severo ⟨heavy losses : grandes pérdidas⟩ **7** SERIOUS, IMPORTANT : serio, importante **8** PROFOUND : profundo ⟨to be a heavy sleeper : tener el sueño pesado⟩ **9** FILLING : pesado, fuerte **10** SLUGGISH : lento, tardo **11** STOUT : corpulento

heavy–duty ['hɛvi'du:ṭi, -'dju:-] *adj* : muy resistente, fuerte

heavyweight ['hɛvi,weɪt] *n* : peso *m* pesado (en deportes)

Hebrew¹ ['hi:,bru:] *adj* : hebreo

Hebrew² *n* **1** : hebreo *m*, -brea *f* **2** : hebreo *m* (idioma)

heck ['hɛk] *n* : ¡caramba!, ¡caray! ⟨a heck of a lot : un montón⟩ ⟨what the heck is . . . ? : ¿que diablos es . . . ?⟩

heckle ['hɛkəl] *vt* **-led; -ling** : interrumpir (a un orador)

hectare ['hɛk,tær] *n* : hectárea *f*

hectic ['hɛktɪk] *adj* : agitado, ajetreado — **hectically** [-tɪkli] *adv*

he'd ['hi:d] *contraction of* HE HAD *or* HE WOULD → **have, would**

hedge¹ ['hɛʤ] *v* **hedged; hedging** *vt* **1** : cercar con un seto **2 to hedge one's bet** : cubrirse — *vi* **1** : dar rodeos, contestar con evasivas **2 to hedge against** : cubrirse contra, protegerse contra

hedge² *n* **1** : seto *m* vivo **2** SAFEGUARD : salvaguarda *f*, protección *f*

hedgehog ['hɛʤ,hɔg, -hɑg] *n* : erizo *m*

heed¹ ['hi:d] *vt* : prestar atención a, hacer caso de

heed² *n* : atención *f*

heedless ['hi:dləs] *adj* : descuidado, despreocupado, inconsciente ⟨to be heedless of : hacer caso omiso de⟩ — **heedlessly** *adv*

heel¹ ['hi:l] *vi* : inclinarse

heel² *n* **1** : talón *m* (del pie), tacón *m* (de calzado) **2 to be close/hard/hot on the heels of** : ir pisándole los talones (a alguien), seguir (algo) inmediatamente **3 to cool one's heels** *fam* : esperar **4 to dig one's heels in** : no ceder

heft ['hɛft] *vt* : sopesar

hefty ['hɛfti] *adj* **heftier; -est** : robusto, fornido, pesado

hegemony [hɪ'ʤɛməni] *n, pl* **-nies** : hegemonía *f*

heifer ['hɛfər] *n* : novilla *f*

height ['haɪt] *n* **1** PEAK : cumbre *f*, cima *f*, punto *m* alto ⟨at the height of her career : en la cumbre de su carrera⟩ ⟨the height of stupidity : el colmo de la estupidez⟩ **2** : estatura *f* (de una persona), altura *f* (de un objeto) **3** ALTITUDE : altura *f*

heighten ['haɪtən] *vt* **1** : hacer más alto **2** INTENSIFY : aumentar, intensificar — *vi* : aumentarse, intensificarse

heinous ['heɪnəs] *adj* : atroz, abominable, nefando

heir ['ær] *n* : heredero *m*, -ra *f*

heiress ['ærəs] *n* : heredera *f*

heirloom ['ær,lu:m] *n* : reliquia *f* de familia

heist ['haɪst] *n* : golpe *m*, asalto *m*, atraco *m* ⟨to pull a heist : dar un golpe⟩

held → **hold**

helicopter ['hɛlə,kɑptər] *n* : helicóptero *m*

heliport ['hɛlə,pɔrt] *n* : helipuerto *m*

helium ['hi:liəm] *n* : helio *m*

helix ['hi:lɪks] *n, pl* **helices** ['hɛlə,si:z, 'hi:-] *or* **helixes** ['hi:lɪksəz] : hélice *f*

hell ['hɛl] *n* **1** : infierno *m* **2** (*referring to a bad situation*) ⟨a living hell : un auténtico infierno⟩ ⟨to go through hell : vivir un infierno, pasar las de Caín⟩ ⟨all hell broke loose : se armó la gorda⟩ **3** *fam* (*used for emphasis*) ⟨she was mad as hell : estaba que echaba chispas⟩ ⟨a/one hell of a (nice) guy : un tipo genial⟩ ⟨it hurts like hell : duele muchísimo⟩ ⟨to run like hell : correr como loco⟩ ⟨what (in) the hell . . . ? : ¿que diablos/demonios . . . ?⟩ ⟨you scared the hell out of me! : ¡qué susto me pegaste!⟩ **4 come hell or high water** *fam* : sea como sea, pase lo que pase **5 go to hell!** *fam* : ¡vete al infierno! **6 (just) for the hell of it** *fam* : sólo por divertirse **7 like hell** *fam* : malísimo ⟨you look like hell : tienes muy mala cara⟩ **8 like hell I did/will (etc.)!** *fam* : ¡y un cuerno! **9 there will be hell to pay** *fam* : se va a armar la gorda **10 to catch hell** *fam* ⟨she caught hell from the boss : el jefe le echó la bronca⟩ **11 to give someone hell** *fam* : echarle la bronca a alguien **12 to raise hell** *fam* : armar un buen lío, armar jarana

he'll [ˈhiːl, ˈhɪl] *contraction of* HE SHALL *or* HE WILL → **shall, will**

hellhole [ˈhɛlˌhoːl] *n* : infierno *m*

hellish [ˈhɛlɪʃ] *adj* : horroroso, infernal

hello [həˈloː, hɛ-] *interj* : ¡hola!

helm [ˈhɛlm] *n* **1** : timón *m* **2 to take the helm** : tomar el mando

helmet [ˈhɛlmət] *n* : casco *m*

help¹ [ˈhɛlp] *vt* **1** : ayudar ⟨can I help you? : ¿en qué puedo servirle?⟩ **2** ALLEVIATE : aliviar **3** SERVE : servir ⟨help yourself! : ¡sírvete!⟩ **4** AVOID : evitar ⟨it can't be helped : no lo podemos evitar, no hay más remedio⟩ ⟨I couldn't help smiling : no pude menos que sonreír⟩ **5 to help out** : echarle una mano a — *vi* **1** : ayudar ⟨I was only trying to help : sólo quería ayudar⟩ **2 to help out** : echar una mano

help² *n* **1** ASSISTANCE : ayuda *f* ⟨help! : ¡socorro!, ¡auxilio!⟩ ⟨to call for help : pedir ayuda⟩ ⟨to go for help : ir a buscar ayuda⟩ ⟨she was a big help : me ayudó mucho⟩ ⟨she's no help : no me ayuda en absoluto⟩ ⟨thanks for your help : gracias por ayudarme⟩ ⟨help menu/screen : menú/pantalla de ayuda⟩ **2** STAFF : personal *m* (en una oficina), servicio *m* doméstico ⟨help wanted : se necesita personal⟩

help desk *n* : servicio *m* de asistencia (técnica), soporte *m* técnico

helper [ˈhɛlpər] *n* : ayudante *mf*

helpful [ˈhɛlpfəl] *adj* **1** OBLIGING : servicial, amable, atento **2** USEFUL : útil, práctico — **helpfully** *adv*

helpfulness [ˈhɛlpfəlnəs] *n* **1** KINDNESS : bondad *f*, amabilidad *f* **2** USEFULNESS : utilidad *f*

helping [ˈhɛlpɪŋ] *n* : porción *f*

helpless [ˈhɛlpləs] *adj* **1** POWERLESS : incapaz, impotente **2** DEFENSELESS : indefenso

helplessly [ˈhɛlpləsli] *adv* : en vano, inútilmente

helplessness [ˈhɛlpləsnəs] *n* POWERLESSNESS : incapacidad *f*, impotencia *f*

helter-skelter [ˌhɛltərˈskɛltər] *adv* : atropelladamente, precipitadamente

hem¹ [ˈhɛm] *vt* **hemmed; hemming 1** : hacerle el dobladillo a **2 to hem in** : encerrar

hem² *n* : dobladillo *m*

he-man [ˈhiːˌmæn] *n, pl* **-men** [-mən, -ˌmɛn] : macho *m*, machote *m*

hematoma [ˌhiːməˈtoːmə] *n* : hematoma *m*

hemisphere [ˈhɛməˌsfɪr] *n* : hemisferio *m*

hemispheric [ˌhɛməˈsfɪrɪk, -ˈsfɪr-] *or* **hemispherical** [-ɪkəl] *adj* : hemisférico

hemline [ˈhɛmˌlaɪn] *n* : bajo *m* (de un vestido, etc.)

hemlock [ˈhɛmˌlɑk] *n* : cicuta *f*

hemoglobin [ˈhiːməˌgloːbən] *n* : hemoglobina *f*

hemophilia [ˌhiːməˈfɪliə] *n* : hemofilia *f*

hemophiliac [ˌhiːməˈfɪliˌæk] *n* : hemofílico *m*, -ca *f* — **hemophiliac** *adj*

hemorrhage¹ [ˈhɛmərɪdʒ] *vi* **-rhaged; -rhaging** : sufrir una hemorragia

hemorrhage² *n* : hemorragia *f*

hemorrhoids [ˈhɛməˌrɔɪdz, ˈhɛm-ˌrɔɪdz] *npl* : hemorroides *fpl*, almorranas *fpl*

hemp [ˈhɛmp] *n* : cáñamo *m*

hen [ˈhɛn] *n* : gallina *f*

hence [ˈhɛnts] *adv* **1** : de aquí, de ahí ⟨10 years hence : de aquí a 10 años⟩ ⟨a dog bit me, hence my dislike of animals : un perro me mordió, de ahí mi aversión a los animales⟩ **2** THEREFORE : por lo tanto, por consiguiente

henceforth [ˈhɛntsˌforθ, ˌhɛntsˈ-] *adv* : de ahora en adelante

henchman [ˈhɛntʃmən] *n, pl* **-men** [-mən, -ˌmɛn] : secuaz *mf*, esbirro *m*

henpeck [ˈhɛnˌpɛk] *vt* : dominar (al marido)

hepatitis [ˌhɛpəˈtaɪtəs] *n, pl* **-titides** [-ˈtɪtəˌdiːz] : hepatitis *f*

her¹ [ˈhər, ər] *adj* : su, sus, de ella ⟨her house : su casa, la casa de ella⟩

her² *pron* **1** (*used as direct object*) : la ⟨I saw her yesterday : la vi ayer⟩ ⟨I like her : me gusta⟩ **2** (*used as indirect object*) : le, se ⟨he gave her the book : le dio el libro⟩ ⟨he sent it to her : se lo mandó⟩ **3** (*used as object of a preposition*) : ella ⟨we did it for her : lo hicimos por ella⟩ ⟨taller than her : más alto que ella⟩

herald¹ [ˈhɛrəld] *vt* ANNOUNCE : anunciar, proclamar

herald² *n* **1** MESSENGER : heraldo *m* **2** HARBINGER : precursor *m*

heraldic [hɛˈrældɪk, hə-] *adj* : heráldico

heraldry [ˈhɛrəldri] *n, pl* **-ries** : heráldica *f*

herb [ˈərb, ˈhərb] *n* : hierba *f*

herbal [ˈərbəl, ˈhər-] *adj* : herbario

herbicide [ˈərbəˌsaɪd, ˈhər-] *n* : herbicida *m*

herbivore [ˈərbəˌvor, ˈhər-] *n* : herbívoro *m*

herbivorous [ˌərˈbɪvərəs, ˌhər-] *adj* : herbívoro

herculean [ˌhərkjəˈliːən, ˌhərˈkjuː-liən] *adj* : hercúleo, sobrehumano

herd¹ [ˈhərd] *vt* : reunir en manada, conducir en manada — *vi* : ir en manada (dícese de los animales), apiñarse (dícese de la gente)

herd² *n* : manada *f*

herder [ˈhərdər] → **herdsman**

herdsman [ˈhərdzmən] *n, pl* **-men** [-mən, -ˌmɛn] : vaquero *m* (de ganado), pastor *m* (de ovejas)

here [ˈhɪr] *adv* **1** : aquí, acá ⟨come here! : ¡ven acá!⟩ ⟨right here : aquí mismo⟩ ⟨she's not here : no está⟩ **2** NOW : en este momento, ahora, ya ⟨here he comes : ya viene⟩ ⟨here it's three o'clock (already) : ahora son las tres⟩ **3** : en este punto ⟨here we agree : estamos de acuerdo en este punto⟩ **4 here and now** : ahora mismo, en este mismo momento **5 here and there** : aquí y allá **6 here (you are/go)!** : ¡toma! **7 the here**

and now : el presente, el momento **8 to be neither here nor there** : no venir al caso

hereabouts [ˈhɪrəˌbaʊts] *or* **hereabout** [-ˌbaʊt] *adv* : por aquí (cerca)

hereafter[1] [hɪrˈæftər] *adv* **1** : de aquí en adelante, a continuación **2** : en el futuro

hereafter[2] *n* **the hereafter** : el más allá

hereby [hɪrˈbaɪ] *adv* : por este medio

hereditary [həˈrɛdəˌteri] *adj* : hereditario

heredity [həˈrɛdəˌti] *n* : herencia *f*

herein [hɪrˈɪn] *adv* : aquí

hereof [hɪrˈʌv] *adv* : de aquí

hereon [hɪrˈɑn, -ˈɔn] *adv* : sobre esto

heresy [ˈhɛrəsi] *n, pl* **-sies** : herejía *f*

heretic [ˈhɛrəˌtɪk] *n* : hereje *mf*

heretical [həˈrɛtɪkəl] *adj* : herético

hereto [hɪrˈtuː] *adv* : a esto

heretofore [ˈhɪrtəˌfor] *adv* HITHERTO : hasta ahora

hereunder [hɪrˈʌndər] *adv* : a continuación, abajo

hereupon [hɪrəˈpɑn, -ˈpɔn] *adv* : con esto, en ese momento

herewith [hɪrˈwɪθ] *adv* : adjunto

heritage [ˈhɛrətɪdʒ] *n* : patrimonio *m* (nacional)

hermaphrodite [hərˈmæfrəˌdaɪt] *n* : hermafrodita *mf*

hermetic [hərˈmɛtɪk] *adj* : hermético — **hermetically** [-tɪkli] *adv*

hermit [ˈhərmət] *n* : ermitaño *m*, -ña *f*; eremita *mf*

hernia [ˈhərniə] *n, pl* **-nias** *or* **-niae** [-niˌiː, -niˌaɪ] : hernia *f*

hero [ˈhiːˌroː, ˈhɪrˌoː] *n, pl* **-roes** **1** : héroe *m* **2** PROTAGONIST : protagonista *mf*

heroic [hɪˈroːɪk] *adj* : heroico — **heroically** [-ɪkli] *adv*

heroics [hɪˈroːɪks] *npl* : actos *mpl* heroicos

heroin [ˈhɛroən] *n* : heroína *f*

heroine [ˈhɛroən] *n* **1** : heroína *f* **2** PROTAGONIST : protagonista *f*

heroism [ˈhɛroˌɪzəm] *n* : heroísmo *m*

heron [ˈhɛrən] *n* : garza *f*

herpes [ˈhərˌpiːz] *n* : herpes *m*

herring [ˈhɛrɪŋ] *n, pl* **-ring** *or* **-rings** : arenque *m*

hers [ˈhərz] *pron* : suyo, de ella ⟨these suitcases are hers : estas maletas son suyas⟩ ⟨hers are bigger : los de ella son más grandes⟩

herself [hərˈsɪf] *pron* **1** (*used reflexively*) : se ⟨she dressed herself : se vistió⟩ **2** (*used emphatically*) : ella misma ⟨she fixed it herself : lo arregló ella misma, lo arregló por sí sola⟩

hertz [ˈhərts, ˈhrts] *ns & pl* : hercio *m*

he's [ˈhiːz] *contraction of* HE IS *or* HE HAS → be, have

hesitancy [ˈhɛzəˌtənsi] *n, pl* **-cies** : vacilación *f*, titubeo *m*, indecisión *f*

hesitant [ˈhɛzəˌtənt] *adj* : titubeante, vacilante — **hesitantly** *adv*

hesitate [ˈhɛzəˌteɪt] *vi* **-tated; -tating** : vacilar, titubear

hesitation [ˌhɛzəˈteɪʃən] *n* : vacilación *f*, indecisión *f*, titubeo *m*

heterogeneous [ˌhɛtərəˈdʒiːniəs, -njəs] *adj* : heterogéneo

heterosexual[1] [ˌhɛtəroˈsɛkʃuəl] *adj* : heterosexual

heterosexual[2] *n* : heterosexual *mf*

heterosexuality [ˌhɛtəroˌsɛkʃuˈæləti] *n* : heterosexualidad *f*

hew [ˈhjuː] *v* **hewed; hewed** *or* **hewn** [ˈhjuːn]; **hewing** *vt* **1** CUT : cortar, talar (árboles) **2** SHAPE : labrar, tallar — *vi* CONFORM : conformarse, ceñirse

hex[1] [ˈhɛks] *vt* : hacerle un maleficio (a alguien)

hex[2] *n* : maleficio *m*

hexagon [ˈhɛksəˌɡɑn] *n* : hexágono *m*

hexagonal [hɛkˈsæɡənəl] *adj* : hexagonal

hey [ˈheɪ] *interj* : ¡eh!, ¡oye!

heyday [ˈheɪˌdeɪ] *n* : auge *m*, apogeo *m*

hi [ˈhaɪ] *interj* : ¡hola!

hiatus [haɪˈeɪtəs] *n* **1** : hiato *m* **2** PAUSE : pausa *f*

hibernate [ˈhaɪbərˌneɪt] *vi* **-nated; -nating** : hibernar, invernar

hibernation [ˌhaɪbərˈneɪʃən] *n* : hibernación *f*

hiccup[1] [ˈhɪkəp] *vi* **-cuped; -cuping** : hipar, tener hipo

hiccup[2] *n* : hipo *m* ⟨to have the hiccups : tener hipo⟩

hick [ˈhɪk] *n* BUMPKIN : palurdo *m*, -da *f*

hickory [ˈhɪkəri] *n, pl* **-ries** : nogal *m* americano

hidden [ˈhɪdən] *adj* : oculto

hide[1] [ˈhaɪd] *v* **hid** [ˈhɪd]; **hidden** [ˈhɪdən] *or* **hid; hiding** *vt* **1** : esconder ⟨to be in hiding : estar escondido⟩ **2** : ocultar (los sentimientos, etc.) **3** SCREEN : tapar, no dejar ver — *vi* : esconderse

hide[2] *n* : piel *f*, cuero *m* ⟨to save one's hide : salvar el pellejo⟩

hide-and-seek [ˈhaɪdəndˈsiːk] *n* **to play hide-and-seek** : jugar a las escondidas

hidebound [ˈhaɪdˌbaʊnd] *adj* : rígido, conservador

hideous [ˈhɪdiəs] *adj* : horrible, horroroso, espantoso — **hideously** *adv*

hideout [ˈhaɪdˌaʊt] *n* : guarida *f*, escondrijo *m*

hiding [ˈhaɪdɪŋ] *n* **1** *chiefly Brit fam* : paliza *f* **2 to be in hiding** : estar escondido

hierarchical [ˌhaɪəˈrɑrkɪkəl] *adj* : jerárquico

hierarchy [ˈhaɪəˌrɑrki] *n, pl* **-chies** : jerarquía *f*

hieroglyphic [ˌhaɪərəˈɡlɪfɪk] *n* : jeroglífico *m*

hi-fi [ˈhaɪˈfaɪ] *n* **1** → **high fidelity** **2** : equipo *m* de alta fidelidad

high[1] [ˈhaɪ] *adv* **1** : alto ⟨to aim high : apuntar alto⟩ **2 high and low** : por todas partes **3 to leave high and dry** : dejar tirado

high[2] *adj* **1** TALL : alto ⟨a high wall : un muro alto⟩ ⟨it's two feet high : tiene dos pies de altura⟩ ⟨waist-high : que llega hasta la cintura⟩ ⟨the highest mountain : la montaña más alta⟩ **2** ELEVATED : alto, elevado ⟨high ground : terreno elevado⟩ ⟨high prices : precios elevados⟩ ⟨high blood pressure : presión alta⟩ ⟨at a

high rate of speed : a gran velocidad⟩ 3
GREAT : grande ⟨a high number : un
número grande⟩ ⟨high hopes : grandes
esperanzas⟩ 4 GOOD, FAVORABLE
: bueno, favorable ⟨in high esteem : en
gran estima⟩ ⟨on a high note : con una
nota de optimismo⟩ ⟨the high point of
the trip : el mejor momento del viaje⟩ 5
STRONG : fuerte ⟨high winds : fuertes
vientos⟩ 6 : alto ⟨high society : alta so-
ciedad⟩ ⟨high-ranking : alto, de alto
rango⟩ ⟨the high life : la gran vida⟩ 7
: alto (en música) 8 : pleno ⟨in high
summer : en pleno verano⟩ 9 INTOXI-
CATED : borracho, drogado
high³ n 1 : récord m, punto m máximo
⟨to reach an all-time high : batir el ré-
cord⟩ 2 : zona f de alta presión (en meteorología) 3 or **high gear** : directa f 4
on high : en las alturas
highbrow ['haɪˌbraʊ] n : intelectual mf
high chair n : silla f alta (para bebé), periquera f Mex, trona f Spain
high-definition ['haɪˌdefəˈnɪLən] adj : de
alta definición (dícese de una televisión)
high-end ['haɪˈɛnd] : de lujo
higher ['haɪər] adj : superior ⟨higher education : enseñanza superior⟩
high fidelity n : alta fidelidad f
high-flown ['haɪˈfloːn] adj : altisonante
high-handed ['haɪˈhændəd] adj : arbitrario
high-heeled ['haɪˈhiːld] adj : de tacón alto
highlands ['haɪləndz] npl : tierras fpl
altas, altiplano m
high-level ['haɪˈlɛvəl] adj : de alta nivel
highlight¹ ['haɪˌlaɪt] vt 1 EMPHASIZE : destacar, poner en relieve, subrayar 2 : ser
el punto culminante de
highlight² n : punto m culminante
highlighter ['haɪˌlaɪtər] n : marcador m,
rotulador m Spain
highly ['haɪli] adv 1 VERY : muy, sumamente 2 FAVORABLY : muy bien ⟨to
speak highly of : hablar muy bien de⟩
⟨to think highly of : tener en mucho a⟩
highness ['haɪnəs] n 1 HEIGHT : altura
f 2 **Highness** : Alteza f ⟨Your Royal
Highness : Su Alteza Real⟩
high-pitched ['haɪˈpɪtLt] adj : agudo
high-rise ['haɪˌraɪz] adj : alto, de muchas
plantas
high school n : escuela f superior, escuela
f secundaria
high seas npl : alta mar f
high-speed ['haɪˈspiːd] adj : de alta velocidad
high-spirited ['haɪˈspɪrətəd] adj : vivaz,
muy animado, brioso
high-strung [ˌhaɪˈstrʌŋ] adj : nervioso
high-tech ['haɪˈtɛk] adj : de alta tecnología
high-tension ['haɪˈtɛntLən] adj : de alta
tensión
high-voltage ['haɪˈvoːltɪdʒ] adj : de alto
voltaje
highway ['haɪˌweɪ] n : carretera f
highwayman ['haɪˌweɪmən] n, pl -men
[- mən, -ˌmɛn] : salteador m (de caminos), bandido m
hijab [hiˈdʒɑb] n : hiyab m, hijab m

hijack¹ ['haɪˌdʒæk] vt : secuestrar
hijack² n : secuestro m
hijacker ['haɪˌdʒækər] n : secuestrador m,
-dora f
hike¹ ['haɪk] v **hiked; hiking** vi : hacer una
caminata — vt RAISE : subir
hike² n 1 : caminata f, excursión f 2 IN-
CREASE : subida f (de precios)
hiker ['haɪkər] n : excursionista mf
hilarious [hɪˈlæriəs, haɪ-] adj : muy divertido, hilarante
hilarity [hɪˈlærəti, haɪ-] n : hilaridad f
hill ['hɪl] n 1 : colina f, cerro m 2 SLOPE
: cuesta f, pendiente f
hillbilly ['hɪlˌbɪli] n, pl **-lies** often disparaging + offensive : palurdo m, -da f (de las
montañas)
hillock ['hɪlək] n : loma f, altozano m,
otero m
hillside ['hɪlˌsaɪd] n : ladera f, cuesta f
hilltop ['hɪlˌtɑp] n : cima f, cumbre f
hilly ['hɪli] adj **hillier; -est** : montañoso,
accidentado
hilt ['hɪlt] n : puño m, empuñadura f
him ['hɪm, əm] pron 1 (used as direct object) : lo ⟨I found him : lo encontré⟩ 2
(used as indirect object) : le, se ⟨we gave
him a present : le dimos un regalo⟩ ⟨I
sent it to him : se lo mandé⟩ 3 (used as
object of a preposition) : él ⟨she was
thinking of him : pensaba en él⟩
⟨younger than him : más joven que él⟩
himself [hɪmˈsɛlf] pron 1 (used reflexively) : se ⟨he washed himself : se
lavó⟩ 2 (used emphatically) : él mismo
⟨he did it himself : lo hizo él mismo, lo
hizo por sí solo⟩
hind¹ ['haɪnd] adj : trasero, posterior
⟨hind legs : patas traseras⟩
hind² n : cierva f
hinder ['hɪndər] vt : dificultar, impedir,
estorbar
Hindi ['hɪndiː] n : hindi m
hindquarters ['haɪndˌkwɔrtərz] npl : cuartos mpl traseros
hindrance ['hɪndrənts] n : estorbo m,
obstáculo m, impedimento m
hindsight ['haɪndˌsaɪt] n : retrospectiva f
⟨with the benefit of hindsight : en retrospectiva, con la perspectiva que da la
experiencia⟩
Hindu¹ ['hɪnˌduː] adj : hindú
Hindu² n : hindú mf
Hinduism ['hɪnduˌɪzəm] n : hinduismo m
hinge¹ ['hɪndʒ] v **hinged; hinging** vt : unir
con bisagras — vi **to hinge on/upon**
: depender de
hinge² n : bisagra f, gozne m
hint¹ ['hɪnt] vt : insinuar, dar a entender —
vi : soltar indirectas
hint² n 1 INSINUATION : insinuación f,
indirecta f 2 TIP : consejo m, sugerencia
f 3 TRACE : pizca f, indicio m
hinterland ['hɪntərˌlænd, -lənd] n : interior m (de un país)
hip ['hɪp] n : cadera f
hip-hop ['hɪpˌhɑp] n : hip-hop m
hippie ['hɪpi] n : hippie mf, hippy mf
hippo ['hɪpoː] n, pl **hippos** → **hippopotamus**

hippopotamus [ˌhɪpə'paṭəməs] *n, pl* **-muses** *or* **-mi** [-ˌmaɪ] : hipopótamo *m*

hire¹ ['haɪr] *vt* **hired; hiring** **1** EMPLOY : contratar, emplear **2** RENT : alquilar, arrendar

hire² *n* **1** RENT : alquiler *m* ⟨for hire : se alquila⟩ **2** WAGES : paga *f*, sueldo *m* **3** EMPLOYEE : empleado *m*, -da *f*

his¹ ['hɪz, ɪz] *adj* : su, sus, de él ⟨his hat : su sombrero, el sombrero de él⟩

his² *pron* : suyo, de él ⟨the decision is his : la decisión es suya⟩ ⟨it's his, not hers : es de él, no de ella⟩

Hispanic¹ [hɪ'spænɪk] *adj* : hispano, hispánico

Hispanic² *n* : hispano *m*, -na *f*; hispánico *m*, -ca *f*

hiss¹ ['hɪs] *vi* : sisear, silbar — *vt* : decir entre dientes

hiss² *n* : siseo *m*, silbido *m*

historian [hɪ'stɔriən] *n* : historiador *m*, -dora *f*

historic [hɪ'stɔrɪk] *or* **historical** [-ɪkəl] *adj* : histórico — **historically** [-ɪkli] *adv*

history ['hɪstəri] *n, pl* **-ries** **1** : historia *f* **2** RECORD : historial *m* ⟨family history : historial personal⟩ **3 to go down in history** : pasar a la historia **4 to go down in history** : hacer historia

histrionics [ˌhɪstri'anɪks] *ns & pl* : histrionismo *m*

hit¹ ['hɪt] *v* **hit; hitting** *vt* **1** STRIKE : golpear (algo), pegarle a (alguien), batear (una pelota) ⟨he hit the dog : le pegó al perro⟩ **2** : chocar contra, dar con, dar en (el blanco) ⟨the car hit a tree : el coche chocó contra un árbol⟩ ⟨it hit me in the face : me dio en la cara⟩ ⟨he hit his head against the door : se dio con la cabeza contra la puerta⟩ **3** *fam* OPERATE : apretar (un botón), darle a (un freno, un interruptor, etc.) **4** ATTACK : atacar **5** AFFECT : afectar ⟨the news hit us hard : la noticia nos afectó mucho⟩ **6** ENCOUNTER : tropezar con, toparse con ⟨to hit a snag : tropezar con un obstáculo⟩ **7** : ocurrírsele a uno ⟨it hit me that . . . : se me ocurrió que . . . , me di cuenta de que . . .⟩ **8** REACH : llegar a, alcanzar ⟨the price hit $10 a pound : el precio alcanzó los $10 dólares por libra⟩ ⟨to hit the headlines : ser noticia⟩ **9** ARRIVE AT : llegar a ⟨to hit town : llegar a la ciudad⟩ ⟨let's hit the beach! : ¡vamos a la playa!⟩ **10** MAKE : hacer ⟨to hit a home run : hacer un jonrón⟩ **11 to hit it off** (with) : congeniar (con) **12 to hit someone up for something** : pedirle algo a alguien **13 to hit the ceiling/roof** *fam* : poner el grito en el cielo **14 to hit the hay/sack** *fam* : irse al catre, acostarse **15 to hit the nail on the head** *fam* : dar en el clavo **16 to hit the road** *fam* : ponerse en marcha — *vi* **1** : golpear **2 to hit back** : devolver el golpe **3 to hit on** *fam* : tratar de ligarse a **4 to hit on/upon** : dar con (una solución, etc.)

hit² *n* **1** BLOW : golpe *m* **2** : impacto *m* (de un arma) **3** SUCCESS : éxito *m* **4** : visita *f* (a un sitio Web)

hit–and–run [ˌhɪtən'rʌn] *adj* **1** : en que el conductor culpable se da a la fuga (dícese de un accidente de tránsito) **2** : fugitivo (dícese de un conductor)

hitch¹ ['hɪtʃ] *vt* **1** : mover con sacudidas **2** ATTACH : enganchar, atar, amarrar **3 to hitch up** : subirse (los pantalones, etc.) — *vi* → **hitchhike**

hitch² *n* **1** JERK : tirón *m*, jalón *m* **2** OBSTACLE : obstáculo *m*, impedimento *m*, tropiezo *m*

hitchhike ['hɪtʃˌhaɪk] *vi* **-hiked; -hiking** : hacer autostop, ir de aventón *Col, Mex fam*

hitchhiker ['hɪtʃˌhaɪkər] *n* : autostopista *mf*

hither ['hɪðər] *adv* : acá, por aquí

hitherto ['hɪðərˌtu:, ˌhɪðər'-] *adv* : hasta ahora

hit man *n* : sicario *m*, -ria *f*; asesino *m*, -na *f*

hitter ['hɪṭər] *n* BATTER : bateador *m*, -dora *f*

HIV [ˌeɪtiˌaɪ'vi:] *n* (*human immunodeficiency virus*) : VIH *m*, virus *m* del sida ⟨HIV negative/positive : VIH negativo/positivo⟩

hive ['haɪv] *n* **1** : colmena *f* **2** SWARM : enjambre *m* **3** : lugar *m* muy activo ⟨a hive of activity : un hervidero de actividad⟩

hives ['haɪvz] *ns & pl* : urticaria *f*

hoard¹ ['hɔrd] *vt* : acumular, atesorar

hoard² *n* : tesoro *m*, reserva *f*, provisión *f*

hoarfrost ['hɔrˌfrɔst] *n* : escarcha *f*

hoarse ['hɔrs] *adj* **hoarser; hoarsest** : ronco — **hoarsely** *adv*

hoarseness ['hɔrsnəs] *n* : ronquera *f*

hoary ['hɔri] *adj* **hoarier; -est** **1** : cano, canoso **2** OLD : vetusto, antiguo

hoax¹ ['ho:ks] *vt* : engañar, embaucar, bromear

hoax² *n* : engaño *m*, broma *f*

hobble¹ ['habəl] *v* **-bled; -bling** *vi* LIMP : cojear, renguear

hobble² *n* LIMP : cojera *f*, rengo *m*

hobby ['habi] *n, pl* **-bies** : pasatiempo *m*, afición *f*

hobgoblin ['habˌgablən] *n* : duende *m*

hobnail ['habˌneɪl] *n* : tachuela *f*

hobnob ['habˌnab] *vi* **-nobbed; -nobbing** : codearse

hobo ['ho:ˌbo:] *n, pl* **-boes** : vagabundo *m*, -da *f*

hock¹ ['hak] *vt* PAWN : empeñar

hock² *n* **in hock** : empeñado

hockey ['haki] *n* : hockey *m*

hodgepodge ['hadʒˌpadʒ] *n* : mezcolanza *f*

hoe¹ ['ho:] *vt* **hoed; hoeing** : remover con una azada

hoe² *n* : azada *f*

hog¹ ['hɔg, 'hag] *vt* **hogged; hogging** : acaparar, monopolizar

hog² *n* **1** PIG : cerdo *m*, -da *f* **2** GLUTTON : glotón *m*, -tona *f*

hogshead ['hɔgzˌhed, 'hagz-] *n* : tonel *m*

hoist¹ ['hɔɪst] *vt* : levantar, alzar, izar (una bandera, una vela)

hoist² *n* : grúa *f*

hold[1] ['ho:ld] *v* **held** ['hɛld]; **holding** *vt* **1**
POSSESS : tener ⟨to hold office : ocupar
un puesto⟩ **2** RESTRAIN : detener, controlar ⟨to hold one's temper : controlar
su mal genio⟩ **3** CLASP, GRASP : agarrar, coger ⟨to hold hands : agarrarse de
la mano⟩ ⟨hold it tightly : agárralo
fuerte⟩ **4** CARRY : llevar, tener (en la
mano o las manos) **5** : sujetar, mantener fijo ⟨hold this nail for me : su-
jétame este clavo⟩ ⟨hold it upright
: mantenlo derecho⟩ ⟨hold the door
: sostén la puerta⟩ **6** CONTAIN : dar cabida a, tener capacidad para (personas,
etc.), tener una capacidad de (litros,
etc.) **7** *or* **to hold in store** : deparar **8**
SUPPORT : aguantar, sostener **9** RE-
GARD : considerar, tener ⟨he held me
responsible : me consideró respon-
sable⟩ **10** CONDUCT : celebrar (una reunión, una elección), realizar (un
evento), mantener (una conversación) **11** KEEP, RESERVE : guardar **12** MAINTAIN : mantener **13** DE-
TAIN : detener **14 to hold against**
: tomar en cuenta, guardar rencor
por **15 to hold back** REPRESS, CONTAIN
: reprimir, contener **16 to hold back**
WITHHOLD : retener, ocultar (información) **17 to hold down** : conservar
(un trabajo) **18 to hold in** CONTAIN
: contener **19 to hold off** RESIST : resistir **20 to hold one's liquor** : ser de
buen beber **21 to hold one's tongue**
: callarse **22 to hold out** : extender, tender (la mano, etc.), dar (esperanzas) **23
to hold over** POSTPONE : postergar, aplazar **24 to hold up** DELAY : retrasar **25
to hold up** LIFT : levantar **26 to hold
up** *fam* ROB : robarle (a alguien), atracar, asaltar — *vi* **1** : aguantar, resistir
⟨the rope will hold : la cuerda re-
sistirá⟩ **2** : ser válido, valer ⟨my offer
still holds : mi oferta todavía es
válida⟩ **3 to hold forth** : perorar, arengar **4 to hold off** WAIT : esperar, aguantar **5 to hold off (on)** DELAY : retrasar **6 to hold on** WAIT : esperar,
aguantar **7 to hold on to** : agarrarse
a **8 to hold out** LAST : aguantar, durar **9 to hold out** RESIST : resistir **10 to
hold out for** AWAIT : esperar (algo mejor) **11 to hold to** : mantenerse firme
en **12 to hold together** : mantenerse
unidos **13 to hold up** : aguantar ⟨how
are you holding up? : ¿cómo estás?,
¿cómo no estás llevando?⟩ **14 to hold
with** : estar de acuerdo con
hold[2] *n* **1** GRIP : agarre *m*, llave *f* (en deportes) **2** CONTROL : control *m*, dominio
m ⟨to get hold of oneself : controlarse⟩ **3**
DELAY : demora *f* **4** : bodega *f* (en un
barco o un avión) **5 on hold** DELAYED
: suspendido ⟨to put on hold : suspender
temporalmente⟩ **6 on hold** : en espera
(en el teléfono) ⟨to be/put on hold : estar/
poner en espera⟩ **7 no holds barred** : sin
restricciones **8 to get hold of** : conseguir,
localizar **9 to take hold** : establecerse **10
to take hold of** GRASP : agarrar

holder ['ho:ldər] *n* : poseedor *m*, -dora *f*;
titular *mf*
holdings ['ho:ldɪŋz] *npl* : propiedades *fpl*
holdup ['ho:ld,ʌp] *n* **1** ROBBERY : atraco
m **2** DELAY : retraso *m*, demora *f*
hole ['ho:l] *n* : agujero *m*, hoyo *m*
holiday ['hɑlə,deɪ] *n* **1** : día *m* feriado,
fiesta *f* ⟨happy holidays : felices fies-
tas⟩ **2** VACATION : vacaciones *fpl*
holiness ['ho:linəs] *n* **1** : santidad *f* **2**
His Holiness : Su Santidad
holistic [ho:'lɪstɪk] *adj* : holístico
holler[1] ['hɑlər] *vi* : gritar, chillar
holler[2] *n* : grito *m*, chillido *m*
hollow[1] ['hɑ,lo:] *vt or* **to hollow out**
: ahuecar
hollow[2] *adj* **hollower; -est 1** : hueco,
hundido (dícese de las mejillas, etc.),
cavernoso (dícese de un sonido) **2**
EMPTY, FALSE : vacío, falso
hollow[3] *n* **1** CAVITY : hueco *m*, depresión
f, cavidad *f* **2** VALLEY : hondonada *f*,
valle *m*
hollowness ['hɑ,lonəs] *n* **1** HOLLOW
: hueco *m*, cavidad *f* **2** FALSENESS
: falsedad *f* **3** EMPTINESS : vacuidad *f*
holly ['hɑli] *n, pl* **-lies** : acebo *m*
holocaust ['hɑlə,kɔst, 'ho:-, 'hɔ-] *n* : holocausto *m*
hologram ['ho:lə,græm, 'hɑ-] *n* : holograma *m*
holster ['ho:lstər] *n* : pistolera *f*
holy ['ho:li] *adj* **holier; -est** : santo, sagrado
Holy Ghost → **Holy Spirit**
holy orders → **order**[2]
Holy Spirit *n* **the Holy Spirit** : el Espíritu
Santo
homage ['ɑmɪdʒ, 'hɑ-] *n* : homenaje *m*
home ['ho:m] *n* **1** : hogar *m*, casa *f* ⟨home
sweet home : hogar dulce hogar⟩ ⟨there's
no place like home : como en casa no se
está en ningún sitio⟩ ⟨to leave home : irse
de casa⟩ ⟨to hit close to home : tocar muy
de cerca⟩ **2** HOUSE, RESIDENCE : casa *f*,
domicilio *m* ⟨to own one's own home
: tener casa propia⟩ ⟨a home away from
home : una segunda casa⟩ **3** SEAT : sede
f **4** HABITAT : hábitat *m* **5** INSTITUTION
: residencia *f*, asilo *m* **6** → **home plate 7
at home** : en casa ⟨is Julia at home? : ¿está
Julia (en casa)?⟩ **8 at home** : cómodo
⟨make yourself at home : estás en tu
casa⟩ **9 to play at home** : jugar en casa
homebody ['ho:m,bɑdi] *n, pl* **-dies** : persona *f* hogareña
homecoming ['ho:m,kʌmɪŋ] *n* : regreso *m*
(a casa)
home game *n* : partido *m* en casa
homegrown ['ho:m'gro:n] *adj* **1** : de cosecha propia **2** LOCAL : local
homeland ['ho:m,lænd] *n* : patria *f*, tierra
f natal, terruño *m*
homeless ['ho:mləs] *adj* : sin hogar, sin
techo
homely ['ho:mli] *adj* **homelier; -est 1**
DOMESTIC : casero, hogareño **2** UGLY
: feo, poco atractivo
homemade ['ho:m'meɪd] *adj* : casero,
hecho en casa

homemaker ['hoːmˌmeɪkər] *n* : ama *f* de casa, persona *f* que se ocupa de la casa
homeopathy [ˌhoːmiˈɑpəθi] *n* : homeopatía *f* — **homeopathic** *adj*
home page *n* : página *f* de inicio
home plate *n* : base *f* del bateador
home run *n* : jonrón *m*
homesick ['hoːmˌsɪk] *adj* : nostálgico ⟨to be homesick : echar de menos a la familia⟩
homesickness ['hoːmˌsɪknəs] *n* : nostalgia *f*, morriña *f*
homespun ['hoːmˌspʌn] *adj* : simple, sencillo
homestead ['hoːmˌstɛd] *n* : estancia *f*, hacienda *f*
hometown ['hoːmˌtaʊn] *n* : ciudad *f* natal, pueblo *m* natal
homeward[1] ['hoːmwərd] *or* **homewards** [-wərdz] *adv* : de vuelta a casa, hacia casa
homeward[2] *adj* : de vuelta, de regreso
homework ['hoːmˌwərk] *n* : tarea *f*, deberes *mpl Spain*, asignación *f PRi*
homey ['hoːmi] *adj* **homier; -est** : hogareño
homicidal [ˌhɑməˈsaɪdəl, ˌhoː-] *adj* : homicida
homicide ['hɑməˌsaɪd, 'hoː-] *n* : homicidio *m*
homily ['hɑməli] *n, pl* **-lies** : homilía *f*
hominy ['hɑməni] *n* : maíz *m* descascarado
homogeneity [ˌhoːmədʒəˈniːəṭi, -'neɪ-] *n, pl* **-ties** : homogeneidad *f*
homogeneous [ˌhoːməˈdʒiːniəs, -njəs] *adj* : homogéneo — **homogeneously** *adv*
homogenize [hoːˈmɑdʒəˌnaɪz, hə-] *vt* **-nized; -nizing** : homogeneizar
homograph ['hɑməˌɡræf, 'hoː-] *n* : homógrafo *m*
homologous [hoːˈmɑləɡəs, hə-] *adj* : homólogo
homonym ['hɑməˌnɪm, 'hoː-] *n* : homónimo *m*
homophone ['hɑməˌfoːn, 'hoː-] *n* : homófono *m*
homosexual[1] [ˌhoːməˈsɛkɫʊəl] *adj* : homosexual
homosexual[2] *n* : homosexual *mf*
homosexuality [ˌhoːməˌsɛkɫʊˈæləṭi] *n* : homosexualidad *f*
honcho ['hɑnˌtɫoː] *n* : pez *m* gordo ⟨the head honcho : el jefe⟩
Honduran [hɑnˈdʊrən, -'djʊr-] *n* : hondureño *m*, -ña *f* — **Honduran** *adj*
hone ['hoːn] *vt* **honed; honing** : afilar
honest ['ɑnəst] *adj* : honesto, honrado — **honestly** *adv*
honesty ['ɑnəsti] *n, pl* **-ties** : honestidad *f*, honradez *f*
honey ['hʌni] *n, pl* **-eys** : miel *f*
honeybee ['hʌniˌbiː] *n* : abeja *f*
honeycomb ['hʌniˌkoːm] *n* : panal *m*
honeymoon[1] ['hʌniˌmuːn] *vi* : pasar la luna de miel
honeymoon[2] *n* : luna *f* de miel
honeysuckle ['hʌniˌsʌkəl] *n* : madreselva *f*
honk[1] ['hɑŋk, 'hɔŋk] *vi* **1** : graznar (dícese del ganso) **2** : tocar la bocina (dícese de un vehículo), pitar
honk[2] *n* : graznido *m* (del ganso), bocinazo *m* (de un vehículo)
honor[1] ['ɑnər] *vt* **1** RESPECT : honrar **2** : cumplir con ⟨to honor one's word : cumplir con su palabra⟩ **3** : aceptar (un cheque, etc.)
honor[2] *n* **1** : honor *m* ⟨in honor of : en honor de⟩ ⟨a man of honor : un hombre de honor/palabra⟩ ⟨guest of honor : invitado de honor⟩ **2 honors** *npl* AWARDS : honores *mpl*, condecoraciones *fpl* **3 on my honor** : juro por mi honor **4 to do someone the honor of** : hacerle a alguien el honor de **5 to do the honors** : hacer los honores **6 Your Honor** : Su Señoría
honorable ['ɑnərəbəl] *adj* : honorable, honroso — **honorably** [-bli] *adv*
honorary ['ɑnəˌrɛri] *adj* : honorario
hood ['hʊd] *n* **1** : capucha *f* **2** : capó *m*, bonete *m Car* (de un automóvil)
hooded ['hʊdəd] *adj* : encapuchado
hoodie ['hʊdi] *n* : sudadera *f* (con capucha); buzo *m Arg, Col*
hoodlum ['hʊdləm, 'huːd-] *n* THUG : maleante *mf*, matón *m*
hoodwink ['hʊdˌwɪŋk] *vt* : engañar
hoof ['hʊf, 'huːf] *n, pl* **hooves** ['hʊvz, 'huːvz] *or* **hoofs** : pezuña *f*, casco *m*
hoofed ['hʊft, 'huːft] *adj* : ungulado
hook[1] ['hʊk] *vt* **1** : enganchar **2** CATCH : pescar **3 to hook up** CONNECT : conectar (algo a algo) **4 to hook up** *fam* ⟨don't worry — I'll hook you up to be preocupes, te lo arreglaré todo⟩ — *vi* **1** : abrocharse, engancharse **2 to hook up** *fam* MEET : reunirse **3 to hook up** *fam* JOIN, UNITE : juntarse, unirse **4 to hook up** *fam* : tener sexo
hook[2] *n* **1** : gancho *m*, percha *f* **2 to let someone off the hook** : dejar a alguien ir sin castigo
hooked ['hʊkt] *adj* **1** : en forma de gancho **2 to be hooked on** : estar enganchado a
hooker ['hʊkər] *n* : prostituta *f*, fulana *f fam*
hookworm ['hʊkˌwərm] *n* : anquilostoma *m*
hooligan ['huːlɪɡən] *n* : gamberro *m*, -rra *f*
hoop ['huːp] *n* : aro *m*
hooray [hʊˈreɪ] → **hurrah**
hoot[1] ['huːt] *vi* **1** SHOUT : gritar **2** : ulular (dícese de un búho), tocar la bocina (dícese de un vehículo), silbar (dícese de un tren o un barco) **3** *or* **to hoot with laughter** : reírse a carcajadas
hoot[2] *n* **1** : ululato *m* (de un búho), silbido *m* (de un tren), bocinazo *m* (de un vehículo) **2** GUFFAW : carcajada *f*, risotada *f* **3 I don't give a hoot** : me vale un comino, me importa un pito
hop[1] ['hɑp] *vi* **hopped; hopping** : brincar, saltar
hop[2] *n* **1** LEAP : salto *m*, brinco *m* **2** FLIGHT : vuelo *m* corto **3** : lúpulo *m* (planta)

hope¹ ['ho:p] *v* **hoped; hoping** *vi* : esperar
— *vt* : esperar que ⟨we hope she comes : esperamos que venga⟩ ⟨I hope so/not : espero que sí/no⟩
hope² *n* : esperanza *f* ⟨to have high hopes of : tener muchas esperanzas de⟩ ⟨to get one's hopes up : hacerse ilusiones⟩ ⟨in the hope of : con la esperanza de⟩ ⟨in the hope that : con la esperanza de que⟩
hopeful ['ho:pfəl] *adj* : esperanzado
hopefully ['ho:pfəli] *adj* **1** : con esperanza ⟨"it's a good sign," she said hopefully : "es buena señal," dijo esperanzada⟩ **2** ⟨hopefully, it won't rain : ojalá no llueva, espero que no llueva⟩ ⟨the rain will hopefully continue : se espera que las lluvias continúen⟩
hopeless ['ho:pləs] *adj* **1** DESPAIRING : desesperado **2** IMPOSSIBLE : imposible ⟨a hopeless case : un caso perdido⟩
hopelessly ['ho:pləsli] *adv* **1** : sin esperanzas, desesperadamente **2** COMPLETELY : totalmente, completamente **3** IMPOSSIBLY : imposiblemente
hopelessness ['ho:pləsnəs] *n* : desesperanza *f*
hopper ['hapər] *n* : tolva *f*
hopping¹ *adv* **to be hopping mad** : estar furioso
hopping² *adj* BUSY : animado, concurrido
hopscotch ['hap,skatʃ] *n* : tejo *m*
horde ['hord] *n* : horda *f*, multitud *f*
horizon [hə'raɪzən] *n* : horizonte *m*
horizontal [,hɔrə'zantəl] *adj* : horizontal
— **horizontally** *adv*
hormone ['hor,mo:n] *n* : hormona *f* —
hormonal [hor'mo:nəl] *adj*
horn ['horn] *n* **1** : cuerno *m* (de un toro, una vaca, etc.) **2** : cuerno *m*, trompa *f* (instrumento musical) **3** : bocina *f*, claxon *m* (de un vehículo)
horned ['hornd, 'hornəd] *adj* : cornudo, astado, con cuernos
hornet ['hornət] *n* : avispón *m*
horny ['horni] *adj* **hornier; -est 1** CALLOUS : calloso **2** LUSTFUL *fam* : caliente *fam*
horoscope ['hɔrə,sko:p] *n* : horóscopo *m*
horrendous [hɔ'rɛndəs] *adj* : horrendo, horroroso, atroz
horrible ['hɔrəbəl] *adj* : horrible, espantoso, horroroso — **horribly** [-bli] *adv*
horrid ['hɔrɪd] *adj* : horroroso, horrible — **horridly** *adv*
horrific [hɔ'rɪfɪk] *adj* : terrorífico, horroroso
horrify ['hɔrə,faɪ] *vt* **-fied; -fying** : horrorizar
horrifying ['hɔrə,faɪɪŋ] *adj* : horripilante, horroroso
horror ['hɔrər] *n* : horror *m*
hors d'oeuvre [ɔr'dərv] *n*, *pl* **hors d'oeuvres** [-'dərvz] : entremés *m*
horse ['hɔrs] *n* **1** : caballo *m* **2 a horse of a different color** : harina de otro costal **3 from the horse's mouth** ⟨I heard it straight from the horse's mouth : me lo dijo él mismo, me lo dijo ella misma⟩ **4 hold your horses** : un momentito

horseback ['hɔrs,bæk] *n* **on ~** : a caballo
horseback riding *n* : equitación *f*
horse chestnut *n* : castaña *f* de Indias
horsefly ['hɔrs,flaɪ] *n*, *pl* **-flies** : tábano *m*
horsehair ['hɔrs,hær] *n* : crin *f*
horseman ['hɔrsmən] *n*, *pl* **-men** [-mən, -,mɛn] : jinete *m*, caballista *m*
horsemanship ['hɔrsmən,ʃɪp] *n* : equitación *f*
horseplay ['hɔrs,pleɪ] *n* : payasadas *fpl*
horsepower ['hɔrs,pauər] *n* : caballo *m* de fuerza
horse racing *n* : carreras *fpl* de caballos
horseradish ['hɔrs,rædɪʃ] *n* : rábano *m* picante
horseshoe ['hɔrs,ʃu:] *n* : herradura *f*
horsewhip ['hɔrs,ʰwɪp] *vt* **-whipped; -whipping** : azotar
horsewoman ['hɔrs,wumən] *n*, *pl* **-women** [-,wɪmən] : amazona *f*, jinete *f*, caballista *f*
horsey *or* **horsy** ['hɔrsi] *adj* **horsier; -est** : relacionado a los caballos, caballar
horticultural [,hɔrtə'kʌltɛrəl] *adj* : hortícola
horticulture ['hɔrtə,kʌltɛr] *n* : horticultura *f*
hose¹ ['ho:z] *vt* **hosed; hosing** : regar o lavar con manguera
hose² *n* **1** *pl* **hose** SOCKS : calcetines *mpl*, medias *fpl* **2** *pl* **hose** STOCKINGS : medias *fpl* **3** *pl* **hoses** : manguera *f*, manga *f* .
hosiery ['ho:ʒəri, 'ho:ʒə-] *n* : calcetería *f*, medias *fpl*
hospice ['haspəs] *n* : centro *m* de cuidados paliativos
hospitable [ha'spɪtəbəl, 'has,pɪ-] *adj* : hospitalario — **hospitably** [-bli] *adv*
hospital ['has,pɪtəl] *n* : hospital *m*
hospitality [,haspə'tæləti] *n*, *pl* **-ties** : hospitalidad *f*
hospitalization [,has,pɪtələ'zeɪʃən] *n* : hospitalización *f*
hospitalize ['has,pɪtəl,aɪz] *vt* **-ized; -izing** : hospitalizar
host¹ ['ho:st] *vt* : presentar (un programa de televisión, etc.)
host² *n* **1** : anfitrión *m*, -triona *f* (en la casa, a un evento); presentador *m*, -dora *f* (de un programa de televisión, etc.) **2** *or* **host organism** : huésped *m* **3** TROOPS : huestes *fpl* **4** MULTITUDE : multitud *f* ⟨for a host of reasons : por muchas razones⟩ **5** EUCHARIST : hostia *f*, Eucaristía *f*
hostage ['hastɪdʒ] *n* : rehén *m*
hostel ['hastəl] *n* : albergue *m* juvenil
hostess ['ho:stɪs] *n* : anfitriona *f* (en la casa), presentadora *f* (de un programa)
hostile ['hastəl, -,taɪl] *adj* : hostil — **hostilely** *adv*
hostility [has'tɪləti] *n*, *pl* **-ties** : hostilidad *f*
hot ['hat] *adj* **hotter; hottest 1** : caliente, cálido, caluroso ⟨hot water : agua caliente⟩ ⟨a hot climate : un clima cálido⟩ ⟨a hot day : un día caluroso⟩ ⟨it's hot in here : hace calor aquí dentro⟩ **2** ARDENT, FIERY : ardiente, acalorado ⟨to

have a hot temper : tener mal genio⟩ **3**
SPICY : picante **4** FRESH : reciente,
nuevo ⟨hot news : noticias de última
hora⟩ ⟨hot off the press : de último mo-
mento⟩ **5** EAGER : ávido **6** STOLEN
: robado **7** *fam* SEXY : guapo, bueno
fam **8 hot and bothered** *or* **hot under
the collar** : enojado — **hotly** *adv*
hot air *n* : palabrería *f*
hotbed ['hɑt,bɛd] *n* **1** : semillero *m* (de
plantas) **2** : hervidero *m*, semillero *m*
(de crimen, etc.)
hot chocolate *n* COCOA : chocolate *m*,
cocoa *f*, cacao *m* (bebida)
hot dog *n* : perro *m* caliente; pancho *m*
Arg, Uru
hotel [ho:'tɛl] *n* : hotel *m*
hotelier [ho:'tɛljər, ,o:təl'jeɪ] *n* : hotelero
m, -ra *f*
hot flash *n* : bochorno *m*, sofoco *m* (de la
menopausia)
hothead ['hɑt,hɛd] *n* : exaltado *m*, -da *f*
hotheaded ['hɑt'hɛdəd] *adj* : exaltado
hothouse ['hɑt,haʊs] *n* : invernadero *m*
hot plate *n* : placa *f* (de cocina)
hot rod *n* : coche *m* con motor modi-
ficado
hot tub *n* : bañera *f* de hidromasaje
hot water *n* **to get into hot water** : meterse en un lío
hot–water bottle *n* : bolsa *f* de agua caliente
hound[1] ['haʊnd] *vt* : acosar, perseguir
hound[2] *n* : perro *m* (de caza)
hour ['aʊər] *n* **1** : hora *f* ⟨on the hour : a
la hora en punto⟩ ⟨60 miles an/per hour
: 60 millas por hora⟩ ⟨by the hour : por
hora(s)⟩ ⟨at all hours : a todas horas⟩
⟨until all hours : hasta las tantas, hasta
muy tarde⟩ ⟨open 24 hours (a day)
: abierto 24 horas (al día)⟩ **2 hours** *npl*
: horas *pl*, horario *m* (de una empresa,
etc.) **3 the wee hours** ⟨in/until the wee
hours (of the morning/night) : a/hasta
las altas horas de la madrugada/noche⟩
hourglass ['aʊər,glæs] *n* : reloj *m* de
arena
hourly ['aʊərli] *adv & adj* : cada hora, por
hora
house[1] ['haʊz] *vt* **housed; housing** : albergar, alojar, hospedar
house[2] ['haʊs] *n, pl* **houses** ['haʊzəz,
-səz] **1** HOME : casa *f* ⟨come (over) to my
house : ven a mi casa⟩ ⟨house pet : animal doméstico⟩ ⟨house painter : pintor
de casas⟩ **2** : cámara *f* (del gobierno) **3**
BUSINESS : casa *f*, empresa *f* **4 on the
house** : gratis ⟨it's on the house : invita
la casa⟩ **5 to bring the house down**
: ser muy aplaudido **6 to clean house**
: limpiar la casa **7 to get/put/set one's
house in order** : poner sus asuntos en
orden, ordenar sus asuntos **8 to keep
house** : ocuparse de la casa **9 to play
house** : jugar a las casitas **10 to set up
house** : poner casa
houseboat ['haʊs,bo:t] *n* : casa *f* flotante
housebroken   ['haʊs,bro:kən]   *adj*
: enseñado
housecoat ['haʊs,ko:t] *n* : bata *f*,
guardapolvo *m*

housefly ['haʊs,flaɪ] *n, pl* **-flies** : mosca *f*
común
household[1] ['haʊs,ho:ld] *adj* **1** DOMES-
TIC : doméstico, de la casa **2** FAMILIAR
: conocido por todos
household[2] *n* : casa *f*, familia *f*
householder ['haʊs,ho:ldər] *n* : dueño *m*,
-ña *f* de casa
housekeeper ['haʊs,ki:pər] *n* : ama *f* de
llaves
housekeeping ['haʊs,ki:pɪŋ] *n* : gobierno
m de la casa, quehaceres *mpl* domésticos
housemaid ['haʊs,meɪd] *n* : criada *f*, mucama *f*, muchacha *f*, sirvienta *f*
houseplant ['haʊs,plænt] *n* : planta *f* de
interior
housewarming ['haʊs,wɔrmɪŋ] *n* : fiesta *f*
de estreno de una casa
housewife ['haʊs,waɪf] *n, pl* **-wives** : ama
f de casa
housework ['haʊs,wɔrk] *n* : faenas *fpl*
domésticas, quehaceres *mpl* domésticos
housing ['haʊzɪŋ] *n* **1** HOUSES : vivienda
f **2** COVERING : caja *f* protectora
hove → **heave**
hovel ['hʌvəl, 'hɑ-] *n* : casucha *f*, tugurio
m
hover ['hʌvər, 'hɑ-] *vi* **1** : cernerse, sostenerse en el aire **2 to hover about**
: rondar
hovercraft ['hʌvər,kræft] *n* : aerodeslizador *m*
how ['haʊ] *adv* **1** : cómo ⟨how are you?
: ¿cómo estás?⟩ ⟨I don't know how to fix
it : no sé cómo arreglarlo⟩ ⟨how do I
look? : ¿cómo estoy?⟩ ⟨how big is it?
: ¿cómo es de grande?, ¿qué tan grande
es?⟩ ⟨how bad is it? : ¿de qué gravedad
es?, ¿qué tan grave es?⟩ ⟨how do you do
: mucho gusto⟩ **2** (*used for emphasis*)
: qué ⟨how beautiful! : ¡qué bonito!⟩
⟨how right you are! : ¡cuánta razón
tiene!⟩ ⟨I can't tell you how grateful I
am : no puedo decirte lo agradecida que
estoy⟩ **3** : cuánto ⟨how old are you?
: ¿cuántos años tienes?⟩ ⟨how many
people are here? : ¿cuánta gente está
aquí?⟩ **4 and how!** : ¡y cómo! **5 how
about . . . ?** : ¿qué te parece . . . ? **6 how
come?** *fam* : ¿cómo es eso?, ¿por
qué? **7 how come . . . ?** *fam* : ¿cómo es
que . . . ?, ¿por qué . . . ? **8 how much**
: cuánto **9 how so?** : ¿por qué dice(s)
eso? **10 how's that?** *fam* : ¿qué?,
¿cómo?
however[1] [haʊ'ɛvər] *adv* **1** : por mucho
que, por más que ⟨however hot it is : por
mucho calor que haga⟩ **2** NEVERTHE-
LESS : sin embargo, no obstante
however[2] *conj* : comoquiera que, de cualquier manera que
howl[1] ['haʊl] *vi* : aullar
howl[2] *n* : aullido *m*, alarido *m*
hub ['hʌb] *n* **1** CENTER : centro *m* **2**
: cubo *m* (de una rueda)
hubbub ['hʌ,bʌb] *n* : algarabía *f*, alboroto
m, jaleo *m*
hubcap ['hʌb,kæp] *n* : tapacubos *m*
huckster ['hʌkstər] *n* : buhonero *m*, -ra *f*;
vendedor *m*, -dora *f* ambulante

huddle¹ [ˈhʌdəl] *vi* **-dled; -dling** **1** : apiñarse, amontonarse **2 to huddle together** : acurrucarse

huddle² *n* : grupo *m* (cerrado) ⟨to go into a huddle : discutir en secreto⟩

hue [ˈhjuː] *n* : color *m*, tono *m*

huff [ˈhʌf] *n* : enojo *m*, enfado *m* ⟨to be in a huff : estar enojado⟩

huffy [ˈhʌfi] *adj* **huffier; -est** : enojado, enfadado

hug¹ [ˈhʌg] *vt* **hugged; hugging** **1** EMBRACE : abrazar **2** : ir pegado a ⟨the road hugs the river : el camino está pegado al río⟩

hug² *n* : abrazo *m*

huge [ˈhjuːdʒ] *adj* **huger; hugest** : inmenso, enorme — **hugely** *adv*

hugeness [ˈhjuːdʒnəs] *n* : lo grande

huh [ˈhʌ] *interj* **1** WHAT : ¿eh?, ¿qué? **2** : ¿eh?, ¿no? ⟨not bad, huh? : no está mal, ¿eh?⟩ **3** (*expressing surprise or disbelief*) : ¡vaya!, ¡anda! **4** (*expressing disapproval*) : ¡bah!

hulk [ˈhʌlk] *n* **1** : persona *f* fornida **2** : casco *m* (barco), armatoste *m* (edificio, etc.)

hulking [ˈhʌlkɪŋ] *adj* : grande, pesado

hull¹ [ˈhʌl] *vt* : pelar

hull² *n* **1** HUSK : cáscara *f* **2** : casco *m* (de un barco, un avión, etc.)

hullabaloo [ˈhʌləbəˌluː] *n, pl* **-loos** : alboroto *m*, jaleo *m*

hum¹ [ˈhʌm] *v* **hummed; humming** *vi* **1** BUZZ : zumbar **2** : estar muy activo, moverse ⟨to hum with activity : bullir de actividad⟩ — *vt* : tararear (una melodía)

hum² *n* : zumbido *m*, murmullo *m*

human¹ [ˈhjuːmən, ˈjuː-] *adj* : humano ⟨human rights : derechos humanos⟩ — **humanly** *adv*

human² *n* : humano *m*

human being *n* : ser *m* humano

humane [hjuːˈmeɪn, juː-] *adj* : humano, humanitario — **humanely** *adv*

humanism [ˈhjuːməˌnɪzəm, ˈjuː-] *n* : humanismo *m*

humanist¹ [ˈhjuːmənɪst, ˈjuː-] *n* : humanista *mf*

humanist² *or* **humanistic** [ˌhjuːməˈnɪstɪk, ˌjuː-] *adj* : humanístico

humanitarian¹ [hjuːˌmænəˈtriən, juː-] *adj* : humanitario

humanitarian² *n* : humanitario *m*, -ria *f*

humanity [hjuːˈmænəṭi, juː-] *n, pl* **-ties** : humanidad *f*

humanize [ˈhjuːməˌnaɪz, ˈjuː-] *vt* **-ized; -izing** : humanizar

humankind [ˈhjuːmənˈkaɪnd, ˈjuː-] *n* : género *m* humano

humble¹ [ˈhʌmbəl] *vt* **-bled; -bling** **1** : humillar **2 to humble oneself** : humillarse

humble² *adj* **humbler; humblest** : humilde, modesto — **humbly** [ˈhʌmbli] *adv*

humbug [ˈhʌmˌbʌg] *n* **1** FRAUD : charlatán *m*, -tana *f*; farsante *mf* **2** NONSENSE : patrañas *fpl*, tonterías *fpl*

humdrum [ˈhʌmˌdrʌm] *adj* : monótono, rutinario

humid [ˈhjuːməd, ˈjuː-] *adj* : húmedo

humidifier [hjuːˈmɪdəˌfaɪər, juː-] *n* : humidificador *m*

humidify [hjuːˈmɪdəˌfaɪ, juː-] *vt* **-fied; -fying** : humidificar

humidity [hjuːˈmɪdəṭi, juː-] *n, pl* **-ties** : humedad *f*

humiliate [hjuːˈmɪliˌeɪt, juː-] *vt* **-ated; -ating** : humillar

humiliating [hjuːˈmɪliˌeɪtɪŋ, juː-] *adj* : humillante

humiliation [hjuːˌmɪliˈeɪʔən, juː-] *n* : humillación *f*

humility [hjuːˈmɪləṭi, juː-] *n* : humildad *f*

hummingbird [ˈhʌmɪŋˌbərd] *n* : colibrí *m*, picaflor *m*

hummock [ˈhʌmək] *n* : montículo *m*

humor¹ [ˈhjuːmər, ˈjuː-] *vt* : seguir el humor a, complacer

humor² *n* : humor *m*

humorist [ˈhjuːmərɪst, ˈjuː-] *n* : humorista *mf*

humorless [ˈhjuːmərləs, ˈjuː-] *adj* : sin sentido del humor ⟨a humorless smile : una sonrisa forzada⟩

humorous [ˈhjuːmərəs, ˈjuː-] *adj* : humorístico, cómico — **humorously** *adv*

hump [ˈhʌmp] *n* : joroba *f*, giba *f*

humpback [ˈhʌmpˌbæk] *n* **1** HUMP, HUNCHBACK : joroba *f*, giba *f* **2** *offensive* HUNCHBACK : jorobado *m*, -da *f*; giboso *m*, -sa *f* (persona) **3** *or* **humpback whale** : ballena *f* jorobada , yubarta *f*

humpbacked [ˈhʌmpˌbækt] *adj* : jorobado, giboso

humus [ˈhjuːməs, ˈjuː-] *n* : humus *m*

hunch¹ [ˈhʌntʃ] *vt* : encorvar — *vi or* **to hunch up** : encorvarse

hunch² *n* PREMONITION : presentimiento *m*

hunchback [ˈhʌntʃˌbæk] *n* **1** HUMP, HUMPBACK : joroba *f*, giba *f* **2** *offensive* HUMPBACK : jorobado *m*, -da *f*; giboso *m*, -sa *f* (persona)

hunchbacked [ˈhʌntʃˌbækt] *adj* : jorobado, giboso

hundred¹ [ˈhʌndrəd] *adj* : cien, ciento

hundred² *n, pl* **-dreds** *or* **-dred** **1** : cien *m*, ciento *m* ⟨a/one hundred : cien⟩ ⟨a/one hundred (and) one : ciento uno⟩ ⟨hundreds of people : cientos de personas⟩ ⟨hundreds of times : cientos de veces⟩ **2** : billete *m* de cien dólares

hundredth¹ [ˈhʌndrədθ] *adv* : en centésimo lugar

hundredth² *adj* : centésimo

hundredth³ *n* **1** : centésimo *m*, -ma *f* (en una serie) **2** : centésimo *m*, centésima parte *f*

hundredweight [ˈhʌndrədˌweɪt] *n* : quintal *m*

hung → hang

Hungarian [hʌŋˈgæriən] *n* **1** : húngaro *m*, -ra *f* **2** : húngaro *m* (idioma) — **Hungarian** *adj*

hunger¹ [ˈhʌŋgər] *vi* **1** : tener hambre **2 to hunger after/for** : ansiar, anhelar

hunger² *n* : hambre *m*

hungrily [ˈhʌŋgrəli] *adv* : ávidamente

hungry [ˈhʌŋgri] *adj* **hungrier; -est** **1** : hambriento **2 to be hungry** : tener hambre

hunk ['hʌŋk] *n* : trozo *m*, pedazo *m*
hunt¹ ['hʌnt] *vt* **1** PURSUE : cazar **2 to hunt for** : buscar
hunt² *n* **1** PURSUIT : caza *f*, cacería *f* **2** SEARCH : búsqueda *f*, busca *f*
hunter ['hʌntər] *n* : cazador *m*, -dora *f*
hunting ['hʌntɪŋ] *n* : caza *f* ⟨to go hunting : ir de caza⟩
hurdle¹ ['hərdəl] *vt* **-dled; -dling** : saltar, salvar (un obstáculo)
hurdle² *n* : valla *f* (en deportes), obstáculo *m*
hurl ['hərl] *vt* : arrojar, tirar, lanzar
hurrah [hʊ'rɑ, -'rɔ] *interj* : ¡hurra!
hurricane ['hərə,keɪn] *n* : huracán *m*
hurried ['hərid] *adj* : apresurado, precipitado
hurriedly ['hərədli] *adv* : apresuradamente, de prisa
hurry¹ ['həri] *v* **-ried; -rying** *vi* : apurarse, darse prisa, apresurarse — *vt* : apurar, darle prisa (a alguien)
hurry² *n* : prisa *f*, apuro *f*
hurt¹ ['hərt] *v* **hurt; hurting** *vt* **1** INJURE : hacer daño a, herir, lastimar ⟨to hurt oneself : hacerse daño⟩ **2** DISTRESS, OFFEND : hacer sufrir, ofender, herir — *vi* : doler ⟨my foot hurts : me duele el pie⟩
hurt² *n* **1** INJURY : herida *f* **2** DISTRESS, PAIN : dolor *m*, pena *f*
hurtful ['hərtfəl] *adj* : hiriente, doloroso
hurtle ['hərtəl] *vi* **-tled; -tling** : lanzarse, precipitarse
husband¹ ['hʌzbənd] *vt* : economizar, bien administrar
husband² *n* : esposo *m*, marido *m*
husbandry ['hʌzbəndri] *n* **1** MANAGEMENT, THRIFT : economía *f*, buena administración *f* **2** AGRICULTURE : agricultura *f* ⟨animal husbandry : cría de animales⟩
hush¹ ['hʌʃ] *vt* **1** SILENCE : hacer callar, acallar **2** CALM : calmar, apaciguar
hush² *n* : silencio *m*
hush–hush ['hʌʃ,hʌʃ, ,hʌʃ'hʌʃ] *adj* : muy secreto, confidencial
husk¹ ['hʌsk] *vt* : descascarar
husk² *n* : cáscara *f*
huskily ['hʌskəli] *adv* : con voz ronca
husky¹ ['hʌski] *adj* **huskier; -est 1** HOARSE : ronco **2** BURLY : fornido
husky² *n*, *pl* **-kies** : perro *m*, -rra *f* esquimal
hustle¹ ['həsəl] *v* **-tled; -tling** *vt* : darle prisa (a alguien), apurar ⟨they hustled me in : me hicieron entrar a empujones⟩ — *vi* : apurarse, ajetrearse
hustle² *n or* **hustle and bustle** : bullicio *m*, ajetreo *m*
hut ['hʌt] *n* : cabaña *f*, choza *f*, barraca *f*, bohío *m*
hutch ['hʌtʃ] *n* **1** CUPBOARD : alacena *f* **2 rabbit hutch** : conejera *f*
hyacinth ['haɪə,sɪnθ] *n* : jacinto *m*
hybrid¹ ['haɪbrɪd] *adj* : híbrido
hybrid² *n* : híbrido *m*
hydrant ['haɪdrənt] *n* : boca *f* de riego, hidrante *m CA, Col* ⟨fire hydrant : boca de incendios⟩

hydraulic [haɪ'drɔlɪk] *adj* : hidráulico — **hydraulically** *adv*
hydrocarbon [,haɪdro'kɑrbən] *n* : hidrocarburo *m*
hydrochloric acid [,haɪdro'klorɪk] *n* : ácido *m* clorhídrico
hydroelectric [,haɪdroɪ'lɛktrɪk] *adj* : hidroeléctrico
hydrofoil ['haɪdrə,fɔɪl] *n* : hidroala *m*, aliscafo *m*
hydrogen ['haɪdrədʒən] *n* : hidrógeno *m*
hydrogen bomb *n* : bomba *f* de hidrógeno
hydrogen peroxide *n* : agua *f* oxigenada, peróxido *m* de hidrógeno
hydrophobia [,haɪdrə'fo:biə] *n* : hidrofobia *f*, rabia *f*
hydroplane ['haɪdrə,pleɪn] *n* : hidroplano *m*
hyena [haɪ'i:nə] *n* : hiena *f*
hygiene ['haɪ,dʒi:n] *n* : higiene *f*
hygienic [haɪ'dʒɛnɪk, -'dʒi:-;, ,haɪ-dʒi'nɪk] *adj* : higiénico — **hygienically** [-nɪkli] *adv*
hygienist [haɪ'dʒi:nɪst, -'dʒɛ-;, 'haɪ-,dʒi:-] *n* : higienista *mf*
hygrometer [haɪ'grɑmətər] *n* : higrómetro *m*
hymn ['hɪm] *n* : himno *m*
hymnal ['hɪmnəl] *n* : himnario *m*
hype¹ ['haɪp] *n* : bombo *m* publicitario
hype² *vt* **hyped; hyping** : promocionar con bombos y platillos
hyperactive [,haɪpər'æktɪv] *adj* : hiperactivo
hyperactivity [,haɪpər,æk'tɪvəti] *n*, *pl* **-ties** : hiperactividad *f*
hyperbole [haɪ'pərbəli] *n* : hipérbole *f*
hyperbolic [,haɪpər'bɑlɪk] *adj* : hiperbólico
hypercritical [,haɪpər'krɪtəkəl] *adj* : hipercrítico
hyperlink ['haɪpər,lɪŋk] *n* : hiperenlace *m*
hypermarket ['haɪpər,mɑrkət] *n* : hipermercado *m*
hypersensitivity [,haɪpər,sɛntsə'tɪ-vəti] *n* : hipersensibilidad *f*
hypertension ['haɪpər,tɛntʃən] *n* : hipertensión *f*
hyphen ['haɪfən] *n* : guión *m*
hyphenate ['haɪfən,eɪt] *vt* **-ated; -ating** : escribir con guión
hypnosis [hɪp'no:sɪs] *n*, *pl* **-noses** [-,si:z] : hipnosis *f*
hypnotic [hɪp'nɑtɪk] *adj* : hipnótico, hipnotizador
hypnotism ['hɪpnə,tɪzəm] *n* : hipnotismo *m*
hypnotist ['hɪpnə,tɪst] *n* : hipnotizador *m*, -dora *f*
hypnotize ['hɪpnə,taɪz] *vt* **-tized; -tizing** : hipnotizar
hypochondria [,haɪpə'kɑndriə] *n* : hipocondría *f*
hypochondriac [,haɪpə'kɑndri,æk] *n* : hipocondríaco *m*, -ca *f*
hypocrisy [hɪp'ɑkrəsi] *n*, *pl* **-sies** : hipocresía *f*
hypocrite ['hɪpə,krɪt] *n* : hipócrita *mf*
hypocritical [,hɪpə'krɪtɪkəl] *adj* : hipócrita
hypodermic¹ [,haɪpə'dərmɪk] *adj* : hipodérmico
hypodermic² *n* : aguja *f* hipodérmica

hypotenuse [haɪ'patən,u:s, -,u:z, -,ju:s, -ju:z] n : hipotenusa f
hypothermia [,haɪpo'θərmiə] n : hipotermia f
hypothesis [haɪ'paθəsɪs] n, pl -eses [-,si:z] : hipótesis f
hypothetical [,haɪpə'θɛţɪkəl] adj : hipotético — hypothetically [-ţɪkli] adv

hysterectomy [,hɪstə'rɛktəmi] n, pl -mies : histerectomía f
hysteria [hɪs'tɛriə, -'tɪr-] n : histeria f, histerismo m
hysterical [hɪs'tɛrɪkəl] adj : histérico — hysterically [-ɪkli] adv
hysterics [hɪs'tɛrɪks] n : histeria f, histerismo m

I

i ['aɪ] n, pl i's or is ['aɪz] : novena letra del alfabeto inglés
I ['aɪ] pron : yo
Iberian [aɪ'bɪriən] adj : ibérico
-ible suf : -ible
ice¹ ['aɪs] v iced; icing vt 1 FREEZE : congelar, helar 2 CHILL : enfriar 3 to ice a cake : bañar un pastel — vi : helarse, congelarse
ice² n 1 : hielo m ⟨ice cube : cubito de hielo⟩ 2 SHERBET : sorbete m; nieve f Cuba, Mex, PRi
iceberg ['aɪs,bərg] n : iceberg m
icebox ['aɪs,baks] → refrigerator
icebreaker ['aɪs,breɪkər] n : rompehielos m
ice cap n : casquete m glaciar ⟨polar ice cap : casquete polar⟩
ice–cold ['aɪs'ko:ld] adj : helado
ice cream n : helado m, mantecado m PRi
ice–cream soda → soda
ice hockey n : hockey m sobre hielo
Icelander ['aɪs,lændər, -lən-] n : islandés m, -desa f
Icelandic¹ [aɪs'lændɪk] adj : islandés
Icelandic² n : islandés m (idioma)
ice–skate ['aɪs,skeɪt] vi -skated; -skating : patinar
ice skater n : patinador m, -dora f
icicle ['aɪ,sɪkəl] n : carámbano m
icily ['aɪsəli] adv : fríamente, con frialdad ⟨he stared at me icily : me fijó la mirada con mucha frialdad⟩
icing ['aɪsɪŋ] n : baño m, glaseado m, betún m Mex
icon ['aɪ,kan, -kən] n : icono m
iconoclasm [aɪ'kanə,klæzəm] n : iconoclasia f
iconoclast [aɪ'kanə,klæst] n : iconoclasta mf
icy ['aɪsi] adj icier; -est 1 : cubierto de hielo ⟨an icy road : una carretera cubierta de hielo⟩ 2 FREEZING : helado, gélido, glacial 3 ALOOF : frío, distante
id ['ɪd] n : id m
I'd ['aɪd] contraction of I SHOULD or I HAD or I WOULD → should, have, would
ID ['aɪ'di:] n, pl ID's or IDs → identification
ID card → identification card
idea [aɪ'di:ə] n : idea f ⟨to have an idea about something : tener idea de algo⟩ ⟨to have no idea : no tener (ni) idea⟩ ⟨to get the idea : captar la idea⟩ ⟨that's not a bad idea : no es mala idea⟩

ideal¹ [aɪ'di:əl] adj : ideal
ideal² n : ideal m
idealism [aɪ'di:ə,lɪzəm] n : idealismo m
idealist [aɪ'di:əlɪst] n : idealista mf
idealistic [aɪ,di:ə'lɪstɪk] adj : idealista
idealistically [aɪ,di:ə'lɪstɪkli] adv : con idealismo
idealization [aɪ,di:ələ'zeɪlən] n : idealización f
idealize [aɪ'di:ə,laɪz] vt -ized; -izing : idealizar
ideally [aɪ'di:əli] adv : perfectamente
identical [aɪ'dɛntɪkəl] adj : idéntico — identically [-ţɪkli] adv
identifiable [aɪ,dɛntə'faɪəbəl] adj : identificable
identification [aɪ,dɛntəfə'keɪlən] n : identificación f
identification card n : carnet m (de identidad), cédula f de identidad, tarjeta f de identificación/identidad
identify [aɪ'dɛntə,faɪ] v -fied; -fying vt : identificar — vi to identify with : identificarse con
identity [aɪ'dɛntəţi] n, pl -ties : identidad f
identity card → identification card
identity theft n : robo m de identidad, suplantación f de identidad
ideological [,aɪdiə'laʤɪkəl, ,ɪ-] adj : ideológico — ideologically [-ʤɪkli] adv
ideologue ['aɪdi:ə,lɔg, -,lɑg] n : ideólogo m, -ga f
ideology [,aɪdi'aləʤi, ,ɪ-] n, pl -gies : ideología f
idiocy ['ɪdiəsi] n, pl -cies 1 dated, now offensive : idiotez f 2 NONSENSE : estupidez f, tontería f
idiom ['ɪdiəm] n 1 LANGUAGE : lenguaje m 2 EXPRESSION : modismo m, expresión f idiomática
idiomatic [,ɪdiə'mæţɪk] adj : idiomático
idiosyncrasy [,ɪdio'sɪŋkrəsi] n, pl -sies : idiosincrasia f
idiosyncratic [,ɪdiosɪn'kræţɪk] adj : idiosincrásico — idiosyncratically [-ţɪkli] adv
idiot ['ɪdiət] n 1 dated, now offensive : idiota mf (en medicina) dated, now offensive 2 FOOL : idiota mf; tonto m, -ta f; imbécil mf fam
idiotic [,ɪdi'aţɪk] adj : estúpido, idiota
idiotically [,ɪdi'aţɪkli] adv : estúpidamente
idle¹ ['aɪdəl] v idled; idling vi 1 LOAF : holgazanear, flojear, haraganear 2 : andar al ralentí (dícese de un au-

tomóvil), marchar en vacío (dícese de una máquina) — *vt* : dejar sin trabajo

idle² *adj* **idler; idlest 1** VAIN : frívolo, vano, infundado ⟨idle curiosity : pura curiosidad⟩ **2** INACTIVE : inactivo, parado, desocupado **3** LAZY : holgazán, haragán, perezoso

idleness ['aɪdəlnəs] *n* **1** INACTIVITY : inactividad *f*, ociosidad *f* **2** LAZINESS : holgazanería *f*, flojera *f*, pereza *f*

idler ['aɪdələr] *n* : haragán *m*, -gana *f*; holgazán *m*, -zana *f*

idly ['aɪdəli] *adv* : ociosamente

idol ['aɪdəl] *n* : ídolo *m*

idolater *or* **idolator** [aɪ'dɑlətər] *n* : idólatra *mf*

idolatrous [aɪ'dɑlətrəs] *adj* : idólatra

idolatry [aɪ'dɑlətri] *n*, *pl* **-tries** : idolatría *f*

idolize ['aɪdə,laɪz] *vt* **-ized; -izing** : idolatrar

idyll ['aɪdəl] *n* : idilio *m*

idyllic [aɪ'dɪlɪk] *adj* : idílico

if ['ɪf] *conj* **1** : si ⟨I would do it if I could : lo haría si pudiera⟩ ⟨if so : si es así⟩ ⟨as if : como si⟩ ⟨if I were you : yo que tú⟩ ⟨if not : si no, de lo contrario⟩ ⟨if only it were true! : ¡si fuera verdad!⟩ **2** WHETHER : si ⟨I don't know if they're ready : no sé si están listos⟩ **3** THOUGH : aunque, si bien ⟨it's pretty, if somewhat old-fashioned : es lindo aunque algo anticuado⟩

igloo ['ɪ,glu:] *n*, *pl* **-loos** : iglú *m*

ignite [ɪg'naɪt] *v* **-nited; -niting** *vt* : prenderle fuego a, encender — *vi* : prender, encenderse

ignition [ɪg'nɪʃən] *n* **1** IGNITING : ignición *f*, encendido *m* **2** *or* **ignition switch** : encendido *m*, arranque *m* ⟨to turn on the ignition : arrancar el motor⟩

ignoble [ɪg'no:bəl] *adj* : innoble — **ignobly** *adv*

ignominious [,ɪgnə'mɪniəs] *adj* : ignominioso, deshonroso — **ignominiously** *adv*

ignominy ['ɪgnə,mɪni] *n*, *pl* **-nies** : ignominia *f*

ignoramus [,ɪgnə'reɪməs] *n* : ignorante *mf*; bestia *mf*; bruto *m*, -ta *f*

ignorance ['ɪgnərənts] *n* : ignorancia *f*

ignorant ['ɪgnərənt] *adj* **1** : ignorante **2 to be ignorant of** : no ser consciente de, desconocer, ignorar

ignorantly ['ɪgnərəntli] *adv* : ignorantemente, con ignorancia

ignore [ɪg'nor] *vt* **-nored; -noring** : ignorar, hacer caso omiso de (algo), no hacer caso de (algo), no hacerle caso (a alguien)

iguana [ɪ'gwɑnə] *n* : iguana *f*, garrobo *f* CA

il- → **in-**

ilk ['ɪlk] *n* : tipo *m*, clase *f*, índole *f*

ill¹ ['ɪl] *adv* worse ['wərs]; worst ['wərst] : mal ⟨to speak ill of : hablar mal de⟩ ⟨he can ill afford to fail : mal puede permitirse el lujo de fracasar⟩

ill² *adj* worse; worst **1** SICK : enfermo **2** BAD : malo ⟨ill luck : mala suerte⟩

ill³ *n* **1** EVIL : mal *m* **2** MISFORTUNE : mal *m*, desgracia *f* **3** AILMENT : enfermedad *f*

I'll ['aɪl] *contraction of* I SHALL *or* I WILL → **shall, will**

ill–advised ['ɪləd'vaɪzd] *adj* : poco aconsejable, imprudente

ill at ease *adj* : incómodo

ill–bred ['ɪl'bred] *adj* : malcriado

illegal [ɪl'li:gəl] *adj* : ilegal — **illegally** *adv*

illegality [ɪli'gæləti] *n* : ilegalidad *f*

illegibility [ɪl,lɛʤə'bɪləti] *n*, *pl* **-ties** : ilegibilidad *f*

illegible [ɪl'lɛʤəbəl] *adj* : ilegible — **illegibly** [-bli] *adv*

illegitimacy [,ɪli'ʤɪtəməsi] *n* : ilegitimidad *f*

illegitimate [,ɪli'ʤɪtəmət] *adj* **1** BASTARD : ilegítimo, bastardo **2** UNLAWFUL : ilegítimo, ilegal — **illegitimately** *adv*

ill–fated ['ɪl'feɪtəd] *adj* : malhadado, infortunado, desventurado

ill–gotten ['ɪl'gɑtən] *adj* : mal habido

illicit [ɪl'lɪsət] *adj* : ilícito — **illicitly** *adv*

illiteracy [ɪl'lɪtərəsi] *n*, *pl* **-cies** : analfabetismo *m*

illiterate¹ [ɪl'lɪtərət] *adj* : analfabeto

illiterate² *n* : analfabeto *m*, -ta *f*

ill–mannered [,ɪl'mænərd] *adj* : descortés, maleducado

ill–natured [,ɪl'neɪtɭərd] *adj* : desagradable, de mal genio

ill–naturedly [,ɪl'neɪtɭərdli] *adv* : desagradablemente

illness ['ɪlnəs] *n* : enfermedad *f*

illogical [ɪl'lɑʤɪkəl] *adj* : ilógico — **illogically** [-kli] *adv*

ill–tempered [,ɪl'tempərd] → **ill–natured**

ill–treat [,ɪl'tri:t] *vt* : maltratar

ill–treatment [,ɪl'tri:tmənt] *n* : maltrato *m*

illuminate [ɪ'lu:mə,neɪt] *vt* **-nated; -nating 1** : iluminar, alumbrar **2** ELUCIDATE : esclarecer, elucidar

illumination [ɪ,lu:mə'neɪʃən] *n* **1** LIGHTING : iluminación *f*, luz *f* **2** ELUCIDATION : esclarecimiento *m*, elucidación *f*

ill–use ['ɪl'ju:z] → **ill–treat**

illusion [ɪ'lu:ʒən] *n* : ilusión *f*

illusory [ɪ'lu:səri, -zəri] *adj* : engañoso, ilusorio

illustrate ['ɪləs,treɪt] *v* **-trated; -trating** : ilustrar

illustration [,ɪlə'streɪʃən] *n* **1** PICTURE : ilustración *f* **2** EXAMPLE : ejemplo *m*, ilustración *f*

illustrative [ɪ'lʌstrətɪv, 'ɪlə,streɪtɪv] *adj* : ilustrativo — **illustratively** *adv*

illustrator ['ɪlə,streɪtər] *n* : ilustrador *m*, -dora *f*; dibujante *mf*

illustrious [ɪ'lʌstriəs] *adj* : ilustre, eminente, glorioso

illustriousness [ɪ'lʌstriəsnəs] *n* : eminencia *f*, prestigio *m*

ill will *n* : animosidad *f*, malquerencia *f*, mala voluntad *f*

IM ['aɪ'em] *v* **IM'd; IM'ing** (*i*nstant *m*essage) *vt* : enviarle un mensaje instantáneo a — *vi* : enviar un mensaje instantáneo

I'm ['aɪm] *contraction of* I AM → **be**

im- → **in-**

image¹ ['ɪmɪʤ] *vt* **-aged; -aging** : imaginar, crear una imagen de

image² *n* : imagen *f*

imagery [ˈɪmɪdʒri] *n, pl* **-eries 1** IMAGES : imágenes *fpl* **2** : imaginería *f* (en el arte)

imaginable [ɪˈmædʒənəbəl] *adj* : imaginable — **imaginably** [-bli] *adv*

imaginary [ɪˈmædʒəˌneri] *adj* : imaginario

imagination [ɪˌmædʒəˈneɪʃən] *n* : imaginación *f*

imaginative [ɪˈmædʒənətɪv, -əˌneɪtɪv] *adj* : imaginativo — **imaginatively** *adv*

imagine [ɪˈmædʒən] *vt* **-ined; -ining 1** : imaginar(se) ⟨try to imagine it : trata de imaginarlo⟩ ⟨imagine that! : ¡imagínate!⟩ ⟨I can't imagine why : no me imagino por qué⟩ **2** : imaginar, creer (equivocadamente) ⟨she imagines herself to be charming : se cree encantadora⟩ ⟨you're imagining things : son imaginaciones tuyas⟩ **3** BELIEVE : imaginarse, creer ⟨I imagine so : me imagino que sí⟩

imbalance [ɪmˈbælənts] *n* : desajuste *m*, desbalance *m*, desequilibrio *m*

imbecile¹ [ˈɪmbəsəl, -ˌsɪl] *or* **imbecilic** [ˌɪmbəˈsɪlɪk] *adj* : imbécil, estúpido

imbecile² *n* **1** *dated, now offensive* : imbécil *mf* (en medicina) *dated, now offensive* **2** FOOL : idiota *mf*; imbécil *mf fam*; estúpido *m*, -da *f*

imbecility [ˌɪmbəˈsɪləti] *n, pl* **-ties 1** *dated, now offensive* : imbecilidad *f* (en medicina) **2** FOOLISHNESS : imbecilidad *f*

imbibe [ɪmˈbaɪb] *v* **-bibed; -bibing** *vt* **1** DRINK : beber **2** ABSORB : absorber, embeber — *vi* : beber

imbue [ɪmˈbjuː] *vt* **-bued; -buing** : imbuir

imitate [ˈɪməˌteɪt] *vt* **-tated; -tating** : imitar, remedar

imitation¹ [ˌɪməˈteɪʃən] *adj* : de imitación, artificial

imitation² *n* : imitación *f*

imitative [ˈɪməˌteɪtɪv] *adj* : imitativo, imitador, poco original

imitator [ˈɪməˌteɪtər] *n* : imitador *m*, -dora *f*

immaculate [ɪˈmækjələt] *adj* **1** PURE : inmaculado, puro **2** FLAWLESS : impecable, intachable — **immaculately** *adv*

immaterial [ˌɪməˈtɪriəl] *adj* **1** INCORPOREAL : incorpóreo **2** UNIMPORTANT : irrelevante, sin importancia

immature [ˌɪməˈtʊr, -ˈtjʊr, -ˈtʊr] *adj* : inmaduro, verde (dícese de la fruta)

immaturity [ˌɪməˈtʊrəti, -ˈtjʊr-, -ˈtʊr-] *n, pl* **-ties** : inmadurez *f*, falta *f* de madurez

immeasurable [ɪˈmeʒərəbəl] *adj* : inconmensurable, incalculable — **immeasurably** [-bli] *adv*

immediacy [ɪˈmiːdiəsi] *n* : inmediatez *f*

immediate [ɪˈmiːdiət] *adj* **1** INSTANT : inmediato, instantáneo ⟨immediate relief : alivio instantáneo⟩ **2** DIRECT : inmediato, directo ⟨the immediate cause of death : la causa directa de la muerte⟩ **3** URGENT : urgente, apremiante **4** CLOSE : cercano, próximo, inmediato ⟨her immediate family : sus familiares más cercanos⟩ ⟨in the immediate vicinity : en los alrededores, en las inmediaciones⟩

immediately [ɪˈmiːdiətli] *adv* : inmediatamente, enseguida

immemorial [ˌɪməˈmoriəl] *adj* : inmemorial

immense [ɪˈmɛnts] *adj* : inmenso, enorme — **immensely** *adv*

immensity [ɪˈmɛntsəti] *n, pl* **-ties** : inmensidad *f*

immerse [ɪˈmərs] *vt* **-mersed; -mersing 1** SUBMERGE : sumergir **2 to immerse oneself in** : enfrascarse en

immersion [ɪˈmərʒən] *n* **1** : inmersión *f* (en un líquido) **2** : absorción *f* (en una actividad)

immigrant [ˈɪmɪɡrənt] *n* : inmigrante *mf*

immigrate [ˈɪməˌɡreɪt] *vi* **-grated; -grating** : inmigrar

immigration [ˌɪməˈɡreɪʃən] *n* : inmigración *f*

imminence [ˈɪmənənts] *n* : inminencia *f*

imminent [ˈɪmənənt] *adj* : inminente — **imminently** *adv*

immobile [ɪˈmoːbəl] *adj* **1** FIXED, IMMOVABLE : inmovible, fijo **2** MOTIONLESS : inmóvil

immobility [ˌɪmoˈbɪləti] *n, pl* **-ties** : inmovilidad *f*

immobilize [ɪˈmoːbəˌlaɪz] *vt* **-lized; -lizing** : inmovilizar, paralizar — **immobilization** *n*

immoderate [ɪˈmɑdərət] *adj* : inmoderado, desmesurado, desmedido, excesivo — **immoderately** *adv*

immodest [ɪˈmɑdəst] *adj* **1** INDECENT : inmodesto, indecente, impúdico **2** CONCEITED : inmodesto, presuntuoso, engreído — **immodestly** *adv*

immodesty [ɪˈmɑdəsti] *n* : inmodestia *f*

immoral [ɪˈmɔrəl] *adj* : inmoral

immorality [ˌɪmoˈrælət̮i, ˌɪmə-] *n, pl* **-ties** : inmoralidad *f*

immorally [ɪˈmɔrəli] *adv* : de manera inmoral

immortal¹ [ɪˈmɔrt̮əl] *adj* : inmortal

immortal² *n* : inmortal *mf*

immortality [ˌɪˌmɔrˈtælət̮i] *n* : inmortalidad *f*

immortalize [ɪˈmɔrt̮əlˌaɪz] *vt* **-ized; -izing** : inmortalizar

immovable [ɪˈmuːvəbəl] *adj* **1** FIXED : fijo, inmovible **2** UNYIELDING : inflexible

immune [ɪˈmjuːn] *adj* **1** : inmune ⟨immune to smallpox : inmune a la viruela⟩ **2** EXEMPT : exento, inmune

immune system *n* : sistema *m* inmunológico

immunity [ɪˈmjuːnət̮i] *n, pl* **-ties 1** : inmunidad *f* **2** EXEMPTION : exención *f*

immunization [ˌɪmjunəˈzeɪʃən] *n* : inmunización *f*

immunize [ˈɪmjuˌnaɪz] *vt* **-nized; -nizing** : inmunizar

immunology [ˌɪmjuˈnɑlədʒi] *n* : inmunología *f*

immutable [ɪˈmjuːt̮əbəl] *adj* : inmutable

imp [ˈɪmp] *n* RASCAL : diablillo *m*; pillo *m*, -lla *f*

impact¹ [ɪmˈpækt] *vt* **1** STRIKE : chocar con, impactar **2** AFFECT : afectar, impactar, impresionar — *vi* **1** STRIKE : hacer impacto, golpear **2 to impact on** : tener un impacto sobre

impact² [ˈɪmˌpækt] *n* **1** COLLISION : impacto *m*, choque *m*, colisión *f* **2** EFFECT : efecto *m*, impacto *m*, consecuencias *fpl*
impacted [ɪmˈpæktəd] *adj* : impactado, incrustado (dícese de los dientes)
impair [ɪmˈpær] *vt* : perjudicar, dañar, afectar
impairment [ɪmˈpærmənt] *n* : perjuicio *m*, daño *m*
impala [ɪmˈpɑlə, -ˈpæ-] *n, pl* **impalas** *or* **impala** : impala *m*
impale [ɪmˈpeɪl] *vt* **-paled; -paling** : empalar
impalpable [ɪmˈpælpəbəl] *adj* : impalpable, intangible
impanel [ɪmˈpænəl] *vt* **-eled** *or* **-elled; -eling** *or* **-elling** : elegir (un jurado)
impart [ɪmˈpɑrt] *vt* **1** CONVEY : impartir, dar, conferir **2** DISCLOSE : revelar, divulgar
impartial [ɪmˈpɑrtəl] *adj* : imparcial — **impartially** *adv*
impartiality [ɪmˌpɑrtiˈæləti] *n, pl* **-ties** : imparcialidad *f*
impassable [ɪmˈpæsəbəl] *adj* : infranqueable, intransitable — **impassably** [-bli] *adv*
impasse [ˈɪmˌpæs] *n* **1** DEADLOCK : impasse *m*, punto *m* muerto **2** DEAD END : callejón *m* sin salida
impassioned [ɪmˈpæʃənd] *adj* : apasionado, vehemente
impassive [ɪmˈpæsɪv] *adj* : impasible, indiferente
impassively [ɪmˈpæsɪvli] *adv* : impasiblemente, sin emoción
impatience [ɪmˈpeɪʃənts] *n* : impaciencia *f*
impatient [ɪmˈpeɪʃənt] *adj* : impaciente — **impatiently** *adv*
impeach [ɪmˈpiːtʃ] *vt* : destituir (a un funcionario) de su cargo
impeachment [ɪmˈpiːtʃmənt] *n* **1** ACCUSATION : acusación *f* **2** DISMISSAL : destitución *f*
impeccable [ɪmˈpɛkəbəl] *adj* : impecable — **impeccably** [-bli] *adv*
impecunious [ˌɪmpɪˈkjuːniəs] *adj* : falto de dinero
impede [ɪmˈpiːd] *vt* **-peded; -peding** : impedir, dificultar, obstaculizar
impediment [ɪmˈpɛdəmənt] *n* **1** HINDRANCE : impedimento *m*, obstáculo *m* **2** speech impediment : defecto *m* del habla
impel [ɪmˈpɛl] *vt* **-pelled; -pelling** : impeler
impending [ɪmˈpɛndɪŋ] *adj* : inminente
impenetrable [ɪmˈpɛnətrəbəl] *adj* **1** : impenetrable ⟨an impenetrable forest : una selva impenetrable⟩ **2** INSCRUTABLE : incomprensible, inescrutable, impenetrable — **impenetrably** [-bli] *adv*
imperative¹ [ɪmˈpɛrətɪv] *adj* **1** AUTHORITATIVE : imperativo, imperioso **2** NECESSARY : imprescindible — **imperatively** *adv*
imperative² *n* : imperativo *m*
imperceptible [ˌɪmpərˈsɛptəbəl] *adj* : imperceptible — **imperceptibly** [-bli] *adv*

imperfect [ɪmˈpərfɪkt] *adj* : imperfecto, defectuoso — **imperfectly** *adv*
imperfection [ˌɪmpərˈfɛkʃən] *n* : imperfección *f*, defecto *m*
imperial [ɪmˈpɪriəl] *adj* **1** : imperial **2** SOVEREIGN : soberano **3** IMPERIOUS : imperioso, señorial
imperialism [ɪmˈpɪriəˌlɪzəm] *n* : imperialismo *m*
imperialist¹ [ɪmˈpɪriəlɪst] *adj* : imperialista
imperialist² *n* : imperialista *mf*
imperialistic [ɪmˌpɪriːəˈlɪstɪk] *adj* : imperialista
imperil [ɪmˈpɛrəl] *vt* **-iled** *or* **-illed; -iling** *or* **-illing** : poner en peligro
imperious [ɪmˈpɪriəs] *adj* : imperioso — **imperiously** *adv*
imperishable [ɪmˈpɛrɪləbəl] *adj* : imperecedero
impermanent [ɪmˈpərmənənt] *adj* : pasajero, inestable, efímero — **impermanently** *adv*
impermeable [ɪmˈpərmiəbəl] *adj* : impermeable
impersonal [ɪmˈpərsənəl] *adj* : impersonal — **impersonally** *adv*
impersonate [ɪmˈpərsənˌeɪt] *vt* **-ated; -ating** : hacerse pasar por, imitar
impersonation [ɪmˌpərsənˈeɪʃən] *n* : imitación *f*
impersonator [ɪmˈpərsənˌeɪtər] *n* : imitador *m*, -dora *f*
impertinence [ɪmˈpərtənənts] *n* : impertinencia *f*
impertinent [ɪmˈpərtənənt] *adj* **1** IRRELEVANT : impertinente, irrelevante **2** INSOLENT : impertinente, insolente
impertinently [ɪmˈpərtənəntli] *adv* : con impertinencia, impertinentemente
imperturbable [ˌɪmpərˈtərbəbəl] *adj* : imperturbable
impervious [ɪmˈpərviəs] *adj* **1** IMPENETRABLE : impermeable **2** INSENSITIVE : insensible ⟨impervious to criticism : insensible a la crítica⟩
impetuous [ɪmˈpɛtʃuəs] *adj* : impetuoso, impulsivo
impetuously [ɪmˈpɛtʃuəsli] *adv* : de manera impulsiva, impetuosamente
impetus [ˈɪmpətəs] *n* : ímpetu *m*, impulso *m*
impiety [ɪmˈpaɪəti] *n, pl* **-ties** : impiedad *f*
impinge [ɪmˈpɪndʒ] *vi* **-pinged; -pinging 1 to impinge on** AFFECT : afectar a, incidir en **2 to impinge on** VIOLATE : violar, vulnerar
impious [ˈɪmpiəs, ɪmˈpaɪəs] *adj* : impío, irreverente
impish [ˈɪmpɪʃ] *adj* MISCHIEVOUS : pícaro, travieso
impishly [ˈɪmpɪʃli] *adv* : con picardía
implacable [ɪmˈplækəbəl] *adj* : implacable — **implacably** [-bli] *adv*
implant¹ [ɪmˈplænt] *vt* **1** INCULCATE, INSTILL : inculcar, implantar **2** INSERT : implantar, insertar
implant² [ˈɪmˌplænt] *n* : implante *m* (de pelo), injerto *m* (de piel)
implantation [ˌɪmˌplænˈteɪʃən] *n* : implantación *f*

implausibility [ɪm,plɔzə'bɪləti] *n, pl* **-ties** : inverosimilitud *f*

implausible [ɪm'plɔzəbəl] *adj* : inverosímil, poco convincente

implement[1] ['ɪmplə,mnt] *vt* : poner en práctica, implementar

implement[2] ['ɪmpləmənt] *n* : utensilio *m*, instrumento *m*, implemento *m*

implementation [,ɪmpləmən'teɪLən] *n* : implementación *f*, ejecución *f*, cumplimiento *m*

implicate ['ɪmplə,keɪt] *vt* **-cated; -cating** : implicar, involucrar

implication [,ɪmplə'keɪLən] *n* **1** CONSEQUENCE : implicación *f*, consecuencia *f* **2** INFERENCE : insinuación *f*, inferencia *f*

implicit [ɪm'plɪsət] *adj* **1** IMPLIED : implícito, tácito **2** ABSOLUTE : absoluto, completo ⟨implicit faith : fe ciega⟩ — **implicitly** *adv*

implied [ɪm'plaɪd] *adj* : implícito, tácito

implode [ɪm'plo:d] *vi* **-ploded; -ploding** : implosionar

implore [ɪm'plor] *vt* **-plored; -ploring** : implorar, suplicar

implosion [ɪm'plo:ʒən] *n* : implosión *f*

imply [ɪm'plaɪ] *vt* **-plied; -plying** **1** SUGGEST : insinuar, dar a entender **2** INVOLVE : implicar, suponer ⟨rights imply obligations : los derechos implican unas obligaciones⟩

impolite [,ɪmpə'laɪt] *adj* : descortés, maleducado

impoliteness [,ɪmpə'laɪtnəs] *n* : descortesía *f*, falta *f* de educación

impolitic [ɪm'palə,tɪk] *adj* : imprudente, poco político

imponderable[1] [ɪm'pandərəbəl] *adj* : imponderable

imponderable[2] *n* : imponderable *m*

import[1] [ɪm'port] *vt* **1** SIGNIFY : significar **2** : importar ⟨to import foreign cars : importar autos extranjeros⟩ **3** : importar (en informática)

import[2] ['ɪm,port] *n* **1** SIGNIFICANCE : importancia *f*, significación *f* **2** → **importation**

importance [ɪm'portənts] *n* : importancia *f*

important [ɪm'portənt] *adj* : importante

importantly [ɪm'portəntli] *adv* **1** : con importancia **2 more importantly** : lo que es más importante

importation [,ɪm,por'teɪLən] *n* : importación *f*

importer [ɪm'portər] *n* : importador *m*, -dora *f*

importune [,ɪmpər'tu:n, -'tju:n;, ɪm'portLən] *vt* **-tuned; -tuning** : importunar, implorar

impose [ɪm'po:z] *v* **-posed; -posing** *vt* : imponer ⟨to impose a tax : imponer un impuesto⟩ — *vi* **to impose on** : abusar de, molestar ⟨to impose on her kindness : abusar de su bondad⟩

imposing [ɪm'po:zɪŋ] *adj* : imponente, impresionante

imposition [,ɪmpə'zɪLən] *n* : imposición *f*

impossibility [ɪm,pasə'bɪləti] *n, pl* **-ties** : imposibilidad *f*

impossible [ɪm'pasəbəl] *adj* **1** : imposible ⟨an impossible task : una tarea imposible⟩ ⟨to make life impossible for : hacerle la vida imposible a⟩ **2** UNACCEPTABLE : inaceptable

impossibly [ɪm'pasəbli] *adv* : imposiblemente, increíblemente

impostor *or* **imposter** [ɪm'pastər] *n* : impostor *m*, -tora *f*

impotence ['ɪmpətənts] *n* : impotencia *f*

impotency ['ɪmpətəntsi] → **impotence**

impotent ['ɪmpətənt] *adj* : impotente

impound [ɪm'paʊnd] *vt* : incautar, embargar, confiscar

impoverish [ɪm'pavərɪL] *vt* : empobrecer

impoverished [ɪm'pavərɪLt] *adj* : empobrecido

impoverishment [ɪm'pavərɪLmənt] *n* : empobrecimiento *m*

impracticable [ɪm'præktɪkəbəl] *adj* : impracticable

impractical [ɪm'præktɪkəl] *adj* : poco práctico

imprecise [,ɪmprɪ'saɪs] *adj* : impreciso

imprecisely [,ɪmprɪ'saɪsli] *adv* : con imprecisión

impreciseness [,ɪmprɪ'saɪsnəs] → **imprecision**

imprecision [,ɪmprɪ'sɪʒən] *n* : imprecisión *f*, falta de precisión *f*

impregnable [ɪm'prɛgnəbəl] *adj* : inexpugnable, impenetrable, inconquistable

impregnate [ɪm'prɛg,neɪt] *vt* **-nated; -nating** **1** FERTILIZE : fecundar **2** PERMEATE, SATURATE : impregnar, empapar, saturar

impresario [,ɪmprə'sari,o, -'sær-] *n, pl* **-rios** : empresario *m*, -ria *f*

impress [ɪm'prɛs] *vt* **1** IMPRINT : imprimir, estampar **2** : impresionar, causar impresión a ⟨I was not impressed : no me hizo buena impresión⟩ **3 to impress (something) on someone** : recalcarle (algo) a alguien — *vi* : impresionar, hacer una impresión

impression [ɪm'prɛLən] *n* **1** IMPRINT : marca *f*, huella *f*, molde *m* (de los dientes) **2** EFFECT : impresión *f*, efecto *m*, impacto *m* ⟨to make a good/bad impression on someone : causarle (una) buena/mala impresión a alguien⟩ **3** PRINTING : impresión *f* **4** NOTION : impresión *f*, noción *f* ⟨to give the impression that : dar la impresión de que⟩ ⟨to have the impression that, to be under the impression that : tener la impresión de que⟩

impressionable [ɪm'prɛLənəbəl] *adj* : impresionable

impressionism [ɪm'prɛLə,nɪzəm] *n* : impresionismo *m*

impressionist [ɪm'prɛLənɪst] *n* : impresionista *mf* — **impressionist** *adj*

impressive [ɪm'prɛsɪv] *adj* : impresionante — **impressively** *adv*

impressiveness [ɪm'prɛsɪvnəs] *n* : calidad de ser impresionante

imprint[1] [ɪm'prɪnt, 'ɪm,-] *vt* : imprimir, estampar

imprint[2] ['ɪm,prɪnt] *n* : marca *f*, huella *f*

imprison [ɪm'prɪzən] *vt* **1** JAIL : encarcelar, aprisionar **2** CONFINE : recluir, encerrar
imprisonment [ɪm'prɪzənmənt] *n* : encarcelamiento *m*
improbability [ɪm,prabə'bɪləti] *n, pl* **-ties** : improbabilidad *f*, inverosimilitud *f*
improbable [ɪm'prabəbəl] *adj* : improbable, inverosímil
impromptu[1] [ɪm'pramp,tuː, -,tjuː] *adv* : sin preparación, espontáneamente
impromptu[2] *adj* : espontáneo, improvisado
impromptu[3] *n* : improvisación *f*
improper [ɪm'prapər] *adj* **1** INCORRECT : incorrecto, impropio **2** INDECOROUS : indecoroso
improperly [ɪm'prapərli] *adv* : incorrectamente, indebidamente
impropriety [,ɪmprə'praɪəti] *n, pl* **-eties** **1** INDECOROUSNESS : indecoro *m*, falta *f* de decoro **2** ERROR : impropiedad *f*, incorrección *f*
improve [ɪm'pruːv] *v* **-proved; -proving** : mejorar
improvement [ɪm'pruːvmənt] *n* : mejoramiento *m*, mejora *f*
improvidence [ɪm'pravədənts] *n* : imprevisión *f*
improvisation [ɪm,pravə'zeɪʃən, ,ɪmprəvə-] *n* : improvisación *f*
improvise ['ɪmprə,vaɪz] *v* **-vised; -vising** : improvisar
imprudence [ɪm'pruːdənts] *n* : imprudencia *f*, indiscreción *f*
imprudent [ɪm'pruːdənt] *adj* : imprudente, indiscreto
impudence ['ɪmpjədənts] *n* : insolencia *f*, descaro *m*
impudent ['ɪmpjədənt] *adj* : insolente, descarado — **impudently** *adv*
impugn [ɪm'pjuːn] *vt* : impugnar
impulse ['ɪm,pʌls] *n* **1** : impulso *m* **2 on impulse** : sin reflexionar
impulsive [ɪm'pʌlsɪv] *adj* : impulsivo — **impulsively** *adv*
impulsiveness [ɪm'pʌlsɪvnəs] *n* : impulsividad *f*
impunity [ɪm'pjuːnəti] *n* **1** : impunidad *f* **2 with impunity** : impunemente
impure [ɪm'pjʊr] *adj* **1** : impuro ⟨impure thoughts : pensamientos impuros⟩ **2** CONTAMINATED : con impurezas, impuro
impurity [ɪm'pjʊrəti] *n, pl* **-ties** : impureza *f*
impute [ɪm'pjuːt] *vt* **-puted; -puting** ATTRIBUTE : imputar, atribuir
in[1] ['ɪn] *adv* **1** INSIDE : dentro, adentro ⟨let's go in : vamos adentro⟩ ⟨the burglars broke in through the window : los ladrones entraron por la ventana⟩ **2** (*to or towards a place*) ⟨they flew in yesterday : llegaron ayer (en avión)⟩ ⟨she leaned farther in : se inclinó más (hacia adelante)⟩ **3** (*indicating a union*) ⟨mix the flour in : añade la harina⟩ **4** (*indicating containment*) ⟨to shut in : encerrar⟩ **5** PARTICIPATING ⟨count me in : yo me apunto⟩ **6** (*to a job or position*)

⟨she was voted in : fue elegida, ganó las elecciones⟩ **7** COLLECTED ⟨the crops are in : las cosechas ya están recogidas⟩ ⟨are all the votes in? : ¿tenemos todos los votos?⟩ ⟨the results are in : se conocen los resultados⟩ **8** (*within bounds*) : dentro (en deportes) **9 in that** : en el sentido de que **10 to be in** : estar ⟨is Linda in? : ¿está Linda?⟩ **11 to be in** : estar en poder ⟨the Democrats are in : los demócratas están en el poder⟩ **12 to be in for** ⟨they're in for a treat : les va a encantar⟩ ⟨he's in for a surprise : se va a llevar una sorpresa⟩ **13 to be in on** : participar en, tomar parte en **14 to be in with someone** : ser muy amigo de alguien **15 to get in good/bad with someone** : quedar bien/mal con alguien
in[2] *adj* **1** INSIDE : interior ⟨the in part : la parte interior⟩ **2** FASHIONABLE : de moda
in[3] *prep* **1** (*indicating location or position*) ⟨in the lake : en el lago⟩ ⟨a pain in the leg : un dolor en la pierna⟩ ⟨in the sun : al sol⟩ ⟨in the rain : bajo la lluvia⟩ **2** (*with superlatives*) : de ⟨the best in the world : el mejor del mundo⟩ **3** INTO : en, a ⟨he broke it in pieces : lo rompió en pedazos⟩ ⟨she went in the house : se metió a la casa⟩ **4** DURING : por, en, durante ⟨in the afternoon : por la tarde⟩ **5** WITHIN : dentro de ⟨I'll be back in a week : vuelvo dentro de una semana⟩ **6** (*indicating belonging*) : en, de ⟨she plays in a band : toca en una banda⟩ ⟨the first scene in the movie : la primera escena de la película⟩ **7** (*indicating manner or form*) : en, con, de ⟨in Spanish : en español⟩ ⟨written in pencil : escrito con lápiz⟩ ⟨in this way : de esta manera⟩ ⟨in some respects : en algún sentido⟩ ⟨in a circle : en un círculo⟩ ⟨in height : de altura⟩ ⟨in theory : en teoría⟩ ⟨she was in uniform : llevaba uniforme⟩ ⟨she was (dressed) in blue : iba (vestido) de azul⟩ **8** (*indicating states or circumstances*) ⟨to be in luck : tener suerte⟩ ⟨to be in love : estar enamorado⟩ ⟨to be in a hurry : tener prisa⟩ ⟨to be/get in trouble : estar/meterse en un lío⟩ **9** (*indicating purpose*) : en ⟨in reply : en respuesta, como réplica⟩ **10** (*with regard to*) : en ⟨do you believe in ghosts? : ¿crees en los fantasmas?⟩ **11** : en (un campo) ⟨he works in insurance : trabaja en seguros⟩ **12** (*in approximations*) ⟨she's in her thirties : tiene treinta y tantos años⟩ ⟨in the 1940's : en los años cuarenta⟩ **13** (*indicating a ratio*) : de ⟨one in five : uno de cada cinco⟩
in[4] *n* **ins and outs** : pormenores *mpl*
in- *or* **im-** *or* **il-** *pref* : in-, im-, i- ⟨inexact : inexacto⟩ ⟨imperfect : imperfecto⟩ ⟨illegal : ilegal⟩
inability [,ɪnə'bɪləti] *n, pl* **-ties** : incapacidad *f*
inaccessibility [,ɪnɪk,sɛsə'bɪləti] *n, pl* **-ties** : inaccesibilidad *f*
inaccessible [,ɪnɪk'sɛsəbəl] *adj* : inaccesible

inaccuracy [ɪn'ækjərəsi] *n, pl* **-cies** 1 : inexactitud *f* 2 MISTAKE : error *m*
inaccurate [ɪn'ækjərət] *n* : inexacto, erróneo, incorrecto
inaccurately [ɪn'ækjərətli] *adv* : incorrectamente, con inexactitud
inaction [ɪn'ækɪən] *n* : inactividad *f*, inacción *f*
inactive [ɪn'æktɪv] *adj* : inactivo
inactivity [ˌɪnˌæk'tɪvəti] *n, pl* **-ties** : inactividad *f*, ociosidad *f*
inadequacy [ɪn'ædɪkwəsi] *n, pl* **-cies** 1 INSUFFICIENCY : insuficiencia *f* 2 INCOMPETENCE : ineptitud *f*, incompetencia *f*
inadequate [ɪn'ædɪkwət] *adj* 1 INSUFFICIENT : insuficiente, inadecuado 2 INCOMPETENT : inepto, incompetente
inadmissible [ˌɪnæd'mɪsəbəl] *adj* : inadmisible
inadvertent [ˌɪnəd'vərtənt] *adj* : inadvertido, involuntario — **inadvertently** *adv*
inadvisable [ˌɪnæd'vaɪzəbəl] *adj* : desaconsejable
inalienable [ɪn'eɪljənəbəl, -'eɪliənə-] *adj* : inalienable
inane [ɪ'neɪn] *adj* **inaner; -est** : estúpido, idiota, necio
inanimate [ɪn'ænəmət] *adj* : inanimado, exánime
inanity [ɪ'nænəti] *n, pl* **-ties** 1 STUPIDITY : estupidez *f* 2 NONSENSE : idiotez *f*, disparate *m*
inapplicable [ɪn'æplɪkəbəl, ˌɪnə-'plɪkəbəl] *adj* IRRELEVANT : inaplicable, irrelevante
inappropriate [ˌɪnə'proːpriət] *adj* : inapropiado, inadecuado, impropio
inappropriateness [ˌɪnə'proːpriətnəs] *n* : lo inapropiado, impropiedad *f*
inapt [ɪn'æpt] *adj* 1 UNSUITABLE : inadecuado, inapropiado 2 INEPT : inepto
inarticulate [ˌɪnɑr'tɪkjələt] *adj* : inarticulado, incapaz de expresarse
inarticulately [ˌɪnɑr'tɪkjələtli] *adv* : inarticuladamente
inasmuch as [ˌɪnæz'mʌtˌæz] *conj* : ya que, dado que, puesto que
inattention [ˌɪnə'tɛntɪən] *n* : falta *f* de atención, distracción *f*
inattentive [ˌɪnə'tɛntɪv] *adj* : distraído, despistado
inattentively [ˌɪnə'tɛntɪvli] *adv* : distraídamente, sin prestar atención
inaudible [ɪn'ɔdəbəl] *adj* : inaudible
inaudibly [ɪn'ɔdəbli] *adv* : de forma inaudible
inaugural[1] [ɪ'nɔgjərəl, -gərəl] *adj* : inaugural, de investidura
inaugural[2] *n* 1 *or* **inaugural address** : discurso *m* de investidura 2 INAUGURATION : investidura *f* (de una persona)
inaugurate [ɪ'nɔgjəˌreɪt, -gə-] *vt* **-rated; -rating** 1 BEGIN : inaugurar 2 INDUCT : investir ⟨to inaugurate the president : investir al presidente⟩
inauguration [ɪˌnɔgjə'reɪɪən, -gə-] *n* 1 : inauguración *f* (de un edificio, un sistema, etc.) 2 : investidura *f* (de una persona)

inauspicious [ˌɪnɔ'spɪləs] *adj* : desfavorable, poco propicio
inauthentic [ˌɪnɔ'θɛntɪk] *adj* : inauténtico
inborn ['ɪnˌbɔrn] *adj* 1 CONGENITAL, INNATE : innato, congénito 2 HEREDITARY : hereditario
inbound ['ɪnˌbaʊnd] *adj* : que llega, de llegada
in—box ['ɪnˌbɑks] *n* : bandeja *f* de entrada
inbred ['ɪnˌbrɛd] *adj* 1 : engendrado por endogamia 2 INNATE : innato
inbreed ['ɪnˌbriːd] *vt* **-bred; -breeding** : engendrar por endogamia
inbreeding ['ɪnˌbriːdɪŋ] *n* : endogamia *f*
Inca ['ɪŋkə] *n* : inca *mf*
incalculable [ɪn'kælkjələbəl] *adj* : incalculable — **incalculably** [-bli] *adv*
Incan ['ɪŋkən] *adj* : incaico
incandescence [ˌɪnkən'dɛsənts] *n* : incandescencia *f*
incandescent [ˌɪnkən'dɛsənt] *adj* 1 : incandescente 2 BRILLIANT : brillante
incantation [ˌɪnˌkæn'teɪɪən] *n* : conjuro *m*, ensalmo *m*
incapable [ɪn'keɪpəbəl] *adj* : incapaz
incapacitate [ˌɪnkə'pæsəˌteɪt] *vt* **-tated; -tating** : incapacitar
incapacity [ˌɪnkə'pæsəti] *n, pl* **-ties** : incapacidad *f*
incarcerate [ɪn'kɑrsəˌreɪt] *vt* **-ated; -ating** : encarcelar
incarceration [ɪnˌkɑrsə'reɪɪən] *n* : encarcelamiento *m*, encarcelación *f*
incarnate[1] [ɪn'kɑrˌneɪt] *vt* **-nated; -nating** : encarnar
incarnate[2] [ɪn'kɑrnət, -ˌneɪt] *adj* : encarnado
incarnation [ˌɪnˌkɑr'neɪɪən] *n* : encarnación *f*
incendiary[1] [ɪn'sɛndiˌri] *adj* : incendiario
incendiary[2] *n, pl* **-aries** : incendiario *m*, -ria *f*; pirómano *m*, -na *f*
incense[1] [ɪn'sɛnts] *vt* **-censed; -censing** : indignar, enfadar, enfurecer
incense[2] ['ɪnˌsɛnts] *n* : incienso *m*
incentive [ɪn'sɛntɪv] *n* : incentivo *m*, aliciente *m*, motivación *f*, acicate *m*
inception [ɪn'sɛpɪən] *n* : comienzo *m*, principio *m*
incessant [ɪn'sɛsənt] *adj* : incesante, continuo — **incessantly** *adv*
incest ['ɪnˌsɛst] *n* : incesto *m*
incestuous [ɪn'sɛstɪʊəs] *adj* : incestuoso
inch[1] ['ɪntɪ] *v* : avanzar poco a poco
inch[2] *n* 1 : pulgada *f* 2 **every inch** : absoluto, seguro ⟨every inch a winner : un seguro ganador⟩ 3 **within an inch of** : a punto de
incidence ['ɪntsədənts] *n* 1 FREQUENCY : frecuencia *f*, índice *m* ⟨a high incidence of crime : un alto índice de crímenes⟩ 2 **angle of incidence** : ángulo *m* de incidencia
incident[1] ['ɪntsədənt] *adj* : incidente
incident[2] *n* : incidente *m*, incidencia *f*, episodio *m* (en una obra de ficción)
incidental[1] [ˌɪntsə'dɛntəl] *adj* 1 SECONDARY : incidental, secundario 2 ACCIDENTAL : casual, fortuito

incidental² *n* **1** : algo incidental **2 incidentals** *npl* : imprevistos *mpl*
incidentally [ˌɪntsəˈdɛntəli, -ˈdɛntli] *adv* **1** BY CHANCE : incidentalmente, casualmente **2** BY THE WAY : a propósito, por cierto
incinerate [ɪnˈsɪnəˌreɪt] *vt* **-ated; -ating** : incinerar
incinerator [ɪnˈsɪnəˌreɪtər] *n* : incinerador *m*
incipient [ɪnˈsɪpiənt] *adj* : incipiente, naciente
incise [ɪnˈsaɪz] *vt* **-cised; -cising** **1** ENGRAVE : grabar, cincelar, inscribir **2** : hacer una incisión en
incision [ɪnˈsɪʒən] *n* : incisión *f*
incisive [ɪnˈsaɪsɪv] *adj* : incisivo, penetrante
incisively [ɪnˈsaɪsɪvli] *adv* : con agudeza
incisor [ɪnˈsaɪzər] *n* : incisivo *m*
incite [ɪnˈsaɪt] *vt* **-cited; -citing** : incitar, instigar
incitement [ɪnˈsaɪtmənt] *n* : incitación *f*
inclemency [ɪnˈklɛməntsi] *n, pl* **-cies** : inclemencia *f*
inclement [ɪnˈklɛmənt] *adj* : inclemente, tormentoso
inclination [ˌɪnkləˈneɪʃən] *n* **1** PROPENSITY : inclinación *f*, tendencia *f* **2** DESIRE : deseo *m*, ganas *fpl* **3** BOW : inclinación *f*
incline¹ [ɪnˈklaɪn] *v* **-clined; -clining** *vi* **1** SLOPE : inclinarse **2** TEND : inclinarse, tender ⟨he is inclined to be late : tiende a llegar tarde⟩ — *vt* **1** LOWER : inclinar, bajar ⟨to incline one's head : bajar la cabeza⟩ **2** SLANT : inclinar **3** PREDISPOSE : predisponer
incline² [ˈɪnˌklaɪn] *n* : inclinación *f*, pendiente *f*
inclined [ɪnˈklaɪnd] *adj* **1** SLOPING : inclinado **2** PRONE : prono, dispuesto, dado
inclose, inclosure → **enclose, enclosure**
include [ɪnˈkluːd] *vt* **-cluded; -cluding** : incluir, comprender
including [ɪnˈkluːdɪŋ] *prep* : incluyendo ⟨including tax : (con) impuestos incluidos⟩ ⟨without including expenses : sin incluir los gastos⟩ ⟨up to and including . . . : hasta . . . inclusive⟩
inclusion [ɪnˈkluːʒən] *n* : inclusión *f*
inclusive [ɪnˈkluːsɪv] *adj* : inclusivo
incognito [ˌɪnkagˈniːˌto, ɪnˈkagnə-ˌtoː] *adv & adj* : de incógnito
incoherence [ˌɪnkoˈhɪrənts, -ˈhɛr-] *n* : incoherencia *f*
incoherent [ˌɪnkoˈhɪrənt, -ˈhɛr-] *adj* : incoherente — **incoherently** *adv*
incombustible [ˌɪnkəmˈbʌstəbəl] *adj* : incombustible
income [ˈɪnˌkʌm] *n* : ingresos *mpl*, entradas *fpl*
income tax *n* : impuesto *m* sobre la renta
incoming [ˈɪnˌkʌmɪŋ] *adj* **1** ARRIVING : que se recibe (dícese del correo), que llega (dícese de las personas), ascendente (dícese de la marea) **2** NEW : nuevo, entrante ⟨the incoming president : el nuevo presidente⟩ ⟨the incoming year : el año entrante⟩
incommunicado [ˌɪnkəˌmjuːnəˈkado] *adj* : incomunicado

incomparable [ɪnˈkampərəbəl] *adj* : incomparable, sin igual
incompatibility [ˌɪnkəmˌpætəˈbɪləti] *n, pl* **-ties** : incompatibilidad *f*
incompatible [ˌɪnkəmˈpætəbəl] *adj* : incompatible
incompetence [ɪnˈkampətənts] *n* : incompetencia *f*, impericia *f*, ineptitud *f*
incompetent [ɪnˈkampətənt] *n* : incompetente *mf*; inepto *m*, -ta *f* — **incompetent** *adj*
incomplete [ˌɪnkəmˈpliːt] *adj* : incompleto — **incompletely** *adv*
incomprehensible [ˌɪnˌkampriˈhɛntsəbəl] *adj* : incomprensible
incomprehension [ˌɪnˌkampriˈhɛntɪən] *n* : incomprensión *f*
inconceivable [ˌɪnkənˈsiːvəbəl] *adj* **1** INCOMPREHENSIBLE : incomprensible **2** UNBELIEVABLE : inconcebible, increíble
inconceivably [ˌɪnkənˈsiːvəbli] *adv* : inconcebiblemente, increíblemente
inconclusive [ˌɪnkənˈkluːsɪv] *adj* : no concluyente, no decisivo
incongruity [ˌɪnkənˈgruːəti, -ˌkan-] *n, pl* **-ties** : incongruencia *f*
incongruous [ɪnˈkaŋgruəs] *adj* : incongruente, inapropiado, fuera de lugar
incongruously [ɪnˈkaŋgruəsli] *adv* : de manera incongruente, inapropiadamente
inconsequential [ˌɪnˌkansəˈkwɛntɪəl] *adj* : intrascendente, de poco importancia
inconsiderable [ˌɪnkənˈsɪdərəbəl] *adj* : insignificante
inconsiderate [ˌɪnkənˈsɪdərət] *adj* : desconsiderado, sin consideración — **inconsiderately** *adv*
inconsistency [ˌɪnkənˈsɪstəntsi] *n, pl* **-cies** : inconsecuencia *f*, inconsistencia *f*
inconsistent [ˌɪnkənˈsɪstənt] *adj* : inconsecuente, inconsistente
inconsolable [ˌɪnkənˈsoːləbəl] *adj* : inconsolable — **inconsolably** [-bli] *adv*
inconspicuous [ˌɪnkənˈspɪkjuəs] *adj* : discreto, no conspicuo, que no llama la atención
inconspicuously [ˌɪnkənˈspɪkjuəsli] *adv* : discretamente, sin llamar la atención
incontestable [ˌɪnkənˈtɛstəbəl] *adj* : incontestable, indiscutible — **incontestably** [-bli] *adv*
incontinence [ɪnˈkantənənts] *n* : incontinencia *f*
incontinent [ɪnˈkantənənt] *adj* : incontinente
inconvenience¹ [ˌɪnkənˈviːnjənts] *vt* **-nienced; -niencing** : importunar, incomodar, molestar
inconvenience² *n* : incomodidad *f*, molestia *f*
inconvenient [ˌɪnkənˈviːnjənt] *adj* : inconveniente, importuno, incómodo — **inconveniently** *adv*
incorporate [ɪnˈkɔrpəˌreɪt] *vt* **-rated; -rating** **1** INCLUDE : incorporar, incluir **2** : incorporar, constituir en sociedad (dícese de un negocio)
incorporation [ɪnˌkɔrpəˈreɪʃən] *n* : incorporación *f*

incorporeal [ˌɪnˌkɔr'poriəl] *adj* : incorpóreo

incorrect [ˌɪnkə'rɛkt] *adj* **1** INACCURATE : incorrecto **2** WRONG : equivocado, erróneo **3** IMPROPER : impropio — **incorrectly** *adv*

incorrigible [ɪn'kɔrədʒəbəl] *adj* : incorregible

incorruptible [ˌɪnkə'rʌptəbəl] *adj* : incorruptible

increase¹ [ɪn'kri:s, 'ɪnˌkri:s] *v* **-creased; -creasing** *vi* GROW : aumentar, crecer, subir (dícese de los precios) — *vt* AUGMENT : aumentar, acrecentar

increase² ['ɪnˌkri:s, ɪn'kri:s] *n* : aumento *m*, incremento *m*, subida *f* (de precios)

increasing [ɪn'kri:sɪŋ, 'ɪnˌkri:sɪŋ] *adj* : creciente

increasingly [ɪn'kri:sɪŋli] *adv* : cada vez más

incredible [ɪn'krɛdəbəl] *adj* : increíble — **incredibly** [-bli] *adv*

incredulity [ˌɪnkrɪ'du:ləti, -'dju:-] *n* : incredulidad *f*

incredulous [ɪn'krɛdʒələs] *adj* : incrédulo, escéptico

incredulously [ɪn'krɛdʒələsli] *adv* : con incredulidad

increment ['ɪŋkrəmənt, 'ɪn-] *n* : incremento *m*, aumento *m*

incremental [ˌɪŋkrə'mɛntəl, ˌɪn-] *adj* : de incremento

incriminate [ɪn'krɪməˌneɪt] *vt* **-nated; -nating** : incriminar

incrimination [ɪnˌkrɪmə'neɪʃən] *n* : incriminación *f*

incriminatory [ɪn'krɪmənəˌtori] *adj* : incriminatorio

incubate ['ɪŋkjuˌbeɪt, 'ɪn-] *v* **-bated; -bating** *vt* : incubar, empollar — *vi* : incubar(se), empollar

incubation [ˌɪŋkju'beɪʃən, ˌɪn-] *n* : incubación *f*

incubator ['ɪŋkjuˌbeɪtər, 'ɪn-] *n* : incubadora *f*

inculcate [ɪn'kʌlˌkeɪt, 'ɪnˌkʌl-] *vt* **-cated; -cating** : inculcar

incumbency [ɪn'kʌmbəntsi] *n, pl* **-cies 1** OBLIGATION : incumbencia *f* **2** : mandato *m* (en la política)

incumbent¹ [ɪn'kʌmbənt] *adj* : obligatorio

incumbent² *n* : titular *mf*

incur [ɪn'kər] *vt* **incurred; incurring** : provocar (al enojo), incurrir en (gastos, obligaciones)

incurable [ɪn'kjurəbəl] *adj* : incurable, sin remedio

incursion [ɪn'kərʒən] *n* : incursión *f*

indebted [ɪn'dɛtəd] *adj* **1** : endeudado **2 to be indebted to** : estar en deuda con, estarle agradecido a

indebtedness [ɪn'dɛtədnəs] *n* : endeudamiento *m*

indecency [ɪn'di:səntsi] *n, pl* **-cies** : indecencia *f*

indecent [ɪn'di:sənt] *adj* : indecente — **indecently** *adv*

indecipherable [ˌɪndɪ'saɪfərəbəl] *adj* : indescifrable

indecision [ˌɪndɪ'sɪʒən] *n* : indecisión *f*, irresolución *f*

indecisive [ˌɪndɪ'saɪsɪv] *adj* **1** INCONCLUSIVE : indeciso, que no es decisivo **2** IRRESOLUTE : indeciso, irresoluto, vacilante **3** INDEFINITE : indefinido — **indecisively** *adv*

indecorous [ɪn'dɛkərəs, ˌɪndɪ'korəs] *adj* : indecoroso — **indecorously** *adv*

indecorousness [ɪn'dkərəsnəs, ˌɪndɪ'korəs-] *n* : indecoro *m*

indeed [ɪn'di:d] *adv* **1** (*emphasizing the truth of a statement*) : efectivamente ⟨yes, indeed : sí, efectivamente⟩ ⟨it's a very serious problem indeed : esto sí que es un problema muy grave⟩ ⟨thank you very much indeed : muchísimas gracias⟩ **2** (*expressing surprise or doubt*) ⟨indeed? : ¿ah, sí?, ¿de veras?, ¡no me digas!⟩ **3** (*strengthening a previous statement*) ⟨it is possible — indeed, probable — that . . . : es posible, e incluso probable, que . . .⟩ **4** (*emphasizing that one does not know the answer*) ⟨how can we help them? how, indeed! : ¿cómo podemos ayudarlos? ¡buena pregunta!⟩

indefatigable [ˌɪndɪ'fætɪgəbəl] *adj* : incansable, infatigable — **indefatigably** [-bli] *adv*

indefensible [ˌɪndɪ'fɛntsəbəl] *adj* **1** VULNERABLE : indefendible, vulnerable **2** INEXCUSABLE : inexcusable

indefinable [ˌɪndɪ'faɪnəbəl] *adj* : indefinible

indefinite [ɪn'dɛfənət] *adj* **1** : indefinido, indeterminado **2** : indefinido (en lingüística) ⟨indefinite pronouns/articles : pronombres/artículos indefinidos⟩ **3** VAGUE : vago, impreciso

indefinitely [ɪn'dɛfənətli] *adv* : indefinidamente, por un tiempo indefinido

indelible [ɪn'dɛləbəl] *adj* : indeleble, imborrable — **indelibly** [-bli] *adv*

indelicacy [ɪn'dɛləkəsi] *n* : falta *f* de delicadeza

indelicate [ɪn'dɛlɪkət] *adj* **1** IMPROPER : indelicado, indecoroso **2** TACTLESS : indiscreto, falto de tacto

indemnify [ɪn'dɛmnəˌfaɪ] *vt* **-fied; -fying 1** INSURE : asegurar **2** COMPENSATE : indemnizar, compensar

indemnity [ɪn'dɛmnəti] *n, pl* **-ties 1** INSURANCE : indemnidad *f* **2** COMPENSATION : indemnización *f*

indent [ɪn'dɛnt] *vt* : sangrar (un párrafo)

indentation [ˌɪnˌdɛn'teɪʃən] *n* **1** NOTCH : muesca *f*, mella *f* **2** INDENTING : sangría *f* (de un párrafo)

indenture¹ [ɪn'dɛntⱢər] *vt* **-tured; -turing** : ligar por contrato

indenture² *n* : contrato de aprendizaje

independence [ˌɪndə'pɛndən(t)s] *n* : independencia *f*

Independence Day *n* : día *m* de la Independencia (4 de julio en los EEUU.)

independent¹ [ˌɪndə'pɛndənt] *adj* : independiente — **independently** *adv*

independent² *n* : independiente *mf*

in–depth *adj* : a fondo, exhaustivo

indescribable [ˌɪndɪ'skraɪbəbəl] *adj* : indescriptible, incalificable — **indescribably** [-bli] *adv*

indestructible [ˌɪndɪ'strʌktəbəl] *adj* : indestructible

indeterminate [ˌɪndɪ'tərmənət] *adj* 1 VAGUE : vago, impreciso, indeterminado 2 INDEFINITE : indeterminado, indefinido

index[1] ['ɪnˌdɛks] *vt* 1 : ponerle un índice a (un libro o una revista) 2 : incluir en un índice ⟨all proper names are indexed : todos los nombres propios están incluidos en el índice⟩ 3 INDICATE : indicar, señalar 4 REGULATE : indexar, indiciar ⟨to index prices : indiciar los precios⟩

index[2] *n, pl* **-dexes** *or* **-dices** ['ɪndəˌsiːz] 1 : índice *m* (de un libro, de precios) 2 INDICATION : indicio *m*, índice *m*, señal *f* ⟨an index of her character : una señal de su carácter⟩

index finger *n* FOREFINGER : dedo *m* índice

Indian ['ɪndiən] *n* 1 : indio *m*, -dia *f* 2 *often offensive* → Native American — **Indian** *adj*

indicate ['ɪndəˌkeɪt] *vt* **-cated; -cating** 1 POINT OUT : indicar, señalar 2 SHOW, SUGGEST : ser indicio de, ser señal de 3 EXPRESS : expresar, señalar 4 REGISTER : marcar, poner (una medida, etc.)

indication [ˌɪndə'keɪʃən] *n* : indicio *m*, señal *f*

indicative [ɪn'dɪkətɪv] *adj* : indicativo

indicator ['ɪndəˌkeɪtər] *n* : indicador *m*

indict [ɪn'daɪt] *vt* : acusar, procesar (por un crimen)

indictment [ɪn'daɪtmənt] *n* : acusación *f*

indifference [ɪn'dɪfrənts, -'dɪfə-] *n* : indiferencia *f*

indifferent [ɪn'dɪfrənt, -'dɪfə-] *adj* 1 UNCONCERNED : indiferente 2 MEDIOCRE : mediocre

indifferently [ɪn'dɪfrəntli, -'dɪfə-] *adv* 1 : con indiferencia, indiferentemente 2 SO-SO : de modo regular, más o menos

indigence ['ɪndɪdʒənts] *n* : indigencia *f*

indigenous [ɪn'dɪdʒənəs] *adj* : indígena, nativo

indigent ['ɪndɪdʒənt] *adj* : indigente, pobre

indigestible [ˌɪndaɪ'dʒɛstəbəl, -dɪ-] *adj* : difícil de digerir

indigestion [ˌɪndaɪ'dʒɛstʃən, -dɪ-] *n* : indigestión *f*, empacho *m*

indignant [ɪn'dɪgnənt] *adj* : indignado

indignantly [ɪn'dɪgnəntli] *adv* : con indignación

indignation [ˌɪndɪg'neɪʃən] *n* : indignación *f*

indignity [ɪn'dɪgnəti] *n, pl* **-ties** : indignidad *f*

indigo ['ɪndɪˌgoː] *n, pl* **-gos** *or* **-goes** : añil *m*, índigo *m*

indirect [ˌɪndə'rɛkt, -daɪ-] *adj* : indirecto — **indirectly** *adv*

indiscernible [ˌɪndɪ'sərnəbəl, -'zər-] *adj* : imperceptible

indiscreet [ˌɪndɪ'skriːt] *adj* : indiscreto — **indiscreetly** *adv*

indiscretion [ˌɪndɪ'skrɛʃən] *n* : indiscreción *f*

indiscriminate [ˌɪndɪ'skrɪmənət] *adj* : indiscriminado

indiscriminately [ˌɪndɪ'skrɪmənətli] *adv* : sin discriminación, sin discernimiento

indispensable [ˌɪndɪ'spɛntsəbəl] *adj* : indispensable, necesario, imprescindible — **indispensably** [-bli] *adv*

indisposed [ˌɪndɪ'spoːzd] *adj* 1 ILL : indispuesto, enfermo 2 AVERSE, DISINCLINED : opuesto, reacio ⟨to be indisposed toward working : no tener ganas de trabajar⟩

indisputable [ˌɪndɪ'spjuːtəbəl, ɪn'dɪspjuːtə-] *adj* : indiscutible, incuestionable, incontestable — **indisputably** [-bli] *adv*

indistinct [ˌɪndɪ'stɪŋkt] *adj* : indistinto — **indistinctly** *adv*

indistinctness [ˌɪndɪ'stɪŋktnəs] *n* : falta *f* de claridad

indistinguishable [ˌɪndɪ'stɪŋgwɪləbəl] *adj* : indistinguible

individual[1] [ˌɪndə'vɪdʒuəl] *adj* 1 PERSONAL : individual, personal ⟨individual traits : características personales⟩ 2 SEPARATE : individual, separado 3 PARTICULAR : particular, propio

individual[2] *n* : individuo *m*

individualism [ˌɪndə'vɪdʒəwəˌlɪzəm] *n* : individualismo *m*

individualist [ˌɪndə'vɪdʒuəlɪst] *n* : individualista *mf*

individualistic [ˌɪndəˌvɪdʒuə'lɪstɪk] *adj* : individualista

individuality [ˌɪndəˌvɪdʒu'æləti] *n, pl* **-ties** : individualidad *f*

individualize [ˌɪndə'vɪdʒuəˌlaɪz] *vt* **-ized; -izing** : individualizar

individually [ˌɪndə'vɪdʒuəli, -dʒəli] *adv* : individualmente

indivisible [ˌɪndɪ'vɪzəbəl] *adj* : indivisible

indoctrinate [ɪn'daktrəˌneɪt] *vt* **-nated; -nating** 1 TEACH : enseñar, instruir 2 PROPAGANDIZE : adoctrinar

indoctrination [ɪnˌdaktrə'neɪʃən] *n* : adoctrinamiento *m*

indolence ['ɪndələnts] *n* : indolencia *f*

indolent ['ɪndələnt] *adj* : indolente

indomitable [ɪn'damətəbəl] *adj* : invencible, indomable, indómito — **indomitably** [-bli] *adv*

Indonesian [ˌɪndo'niːʒən, -ʒən] *n* : indonesio *m*, -sia *f* — **Indonesian** *adj*

indoor ['ɪn'dor] *adj* : interior (dícese de las plantas), para estar en casa (dícese de la ropa), cubierto (dícese de las piscinas, etc.), bajo techo (dícese de los deportes)

indoors ['ɪn'dorz] *adv* : adentro, dentro

indubitable [ɪn'duːbətəbəl, -'djuː-] *adj* : indudable, incuestionable, indiscutible

indubitably [ɪn'duːbətəbli, -'djuː-] *adv* : indudablemente

induce [ɪn'duːs, -'djuːs] *vt* **-duced; -ducing** 1 PERSUADE : persuadir, inducir 2 CAUSE : inducir, provocar ⟨to induce labor : provocar un parto⟩

inducement [ɪn'duːsmənt, -'djuː-] *n* 1 INCENTIVE : incentivo *m*, aliciente *m* 2 : inducción *f*, provocación *f* (de un parto)

induct [ɪn'dʌkt] *vt* **1** INSTALL : instalar, investir **2** ADMIT : admitir (como miembro) **3** CONSCRIPT : reclutar (al servicio militar)

inductee [ˌɪn‚dʌk'tiː] *n* : recluta *mf*, conscripto *m*, -ta *f*

induction [ɪn'dʌkʃən] *n* **1** INTRODUCTION : iniciación *f*, introducción *f* **2** : inducción *f* (en la lógica o la electricidad)

inductive [ɪn'dʌktɪv] *adj* : inductivo

indulge [ɪn'dʌldʒ] *v* **-dulged; -dulging** *vt* **1** GRATIFY : gratificar, satisfacer **2** SPOIL : consentir, mimar — *vi* **to indulge in** : permitirse

indulgence [ɪn'dʌldʒənʃ] *n* **1** SATISFYING : satisfacción *f*, gratificación *f* **2** HUMORING : complacencia *f*, indulgencia *f* **3** SPOILING : consentimiento *m* **4** : indulgencia *f* (en la religión)

indulgent [ɪn'dʌldʒənt] *adj* : indulgente, consentido — **indulgently** *adv*

industrial [ɪn'dʌstriəl] *adj* : industrial — **industrially** *adv*

industrialist [ɪn'dʌstriəlɪst] *n* : industrial *mf*

industrialization [ɪn‚dʌstriələ'zeɪ-ʃən] *n* : industrialización *f*

industrialize [ɪn'dʌstriə‚laɪz] *vt* **-ized; -izing** : industrializar

industrious [ɪn'dʌstriəs] *adj* : diligente, industrioso, trabajador

industriously [ɪn'dʌstriəsli] *adv* : con diligencia, con aplicación

industriousness [ɪn'dʌstriəsnəs] *n* : diligencia *f*, aplicación *f*

industry ['ɪndəstri] *n*, *pl* **-tries 1** DILIGENCE : diligencia *f*, aplicación *f* **2** : industria *f* ⟨the steel industry : la industria siderúrgica⟩

inebriated [ɪ'niːbri‚eɪtəd] *adj* : ebrio, embriagado

inebriation [ɪ‚niːbri'eɪʃən] *n* : ebriedad *f*, embriaguez *f*

inedible [ɪn'ɛdəbəl] *adj* : incomible

ineffable [ɪn'ɛfəbəl] *adj* : inefable — **ineffably** [-bli] *adv*

ineffective [ˌɪnɪ'fɛktɪv] *adj* **1** INEFFECTUAL : ineficaz, inútil **2** INCAPABLE : incompetente, ineficiente, incapaz

ineffectively [ˌɪnɪ'fɛktɪvli] *adv* : ineficazmente, infructuosamente

ineffectual [ˌɪnɪ'fɛktʃuəl] *adj* : inútil, ineficaz — **ineffectually** *adv*

inefficiency [ˌɪnɪ'fɪʃənʃi] *n*, *pl* **-cies** : ineficiencia *f*, ineficacia *f*

inefficient [ˌɪnɪ'fɪʃənt] *adj* **1** : ineficiente, ineficaz **2** INCAPABLE, INCOMPETENT : incompetente, incapaz — **inefficiently** *adv*

inelegance [ɪn'ɛləgənʃ] *n* : inelegancia *f*

inelegant [ɪn'ɛləgənt] *adj* : inelegante, poco elegante

ineligibility [ɪn‚ɛlədʒə'bɪləti] *n* : inelegibilidad *f*

ineligible [ɪn'ɛlədʒəbəl] *adj* : inelegible

inept [ɪ'nɛpt] *adj* : inepto ⟨inept at : incapaz para⟩

ineptitude [ɪ'nɛptə‚tuːd, -‚tjuːd] *n* : ineptitud *f*, incompetencia *f*, incapacidad *f*

inequality [ˌɪnɪ'kwɑləti] *n*, *pl* **-ties** : desigualdad *f*

inequitable [ɪn'ɛkwətəbəl] *adj* : inequitativo

inequity [ɪn'ɛkwəti] *n*, *pl* **-ties** : inequidad *f*

inert [ɪ'nərt] *adj* **1** INACTIVE : inerte, inactivo **2** SLUGGISH : lento

inertia [ɪ'nərlə] *n* : inercia *f*

inescapable [ˌɪnɪ'skeɪpəbəl] *adj* : inevitable, ineludible — **inescapably** [-bli] *adv*

inessential [ˌɪnɪ'sɛnʃəl] *adj* : que no es esencial, innecesario

inestimable [ɪn'ɛstəməbəl] *adj* : inestimable, inapreciable

inevitability [ɪn‚ɛvətə'bɪləti] *n*, *pl* **-ties** : inevitabilidad *f*

inevitable [ɪn'ɛvətəbəl] *adj* : inevitable — **inevitably** [-bli] *adv*

inexact [ˌɪnɪg'zækt] *adj* : inexacto

inexactly [ˌɪnɪg'zæktli] *adv* : sin exactitud

inexcusable [ˌɪnɪk'skjuːzəbəl] *adj* : inexcusable, imperdonable — **inexcusably** [-bli] *adv*

inexhaustible [ˌɪnɪg'zɔstəbəl] *adj* **1** INDEFATIGABLE : infatigable, incansable **2** ENDLESS : inagotable — **inexhaustibly** [-bli] *adv*

inexorable [ɪn'ɛksərəbəl] *adj* : inexorable — **inexorably** [-bli] *adv*

inexpensive [ˌɪnɪk'spɛnʃɪv] *adj* : barato, económico

inexperience [ˌɪnɪk'spɪriənʃ] *n* : inexperiencia *f*

inexperienced [ˌɪnɪk'spɪriənʃt] *adj* : inexperto, novato

inexplicable [ˌɪnɪk'splɪkəbəl] *adj* : inexplicable — **inexplicably** [-bli] *adv*

inexpressible [ˌɪnɪk'sprɛsəbəl] *adj* : inexpresable, inefable

inextricable [ˌɪnɪk'strɪkəbəl, ɪ'nɛk-‚strɪ-] *adj* : inextricable — **inextricably** [-bli] *adv*

infallibility [ɪn‚fælə'bɪləti] *n* : infalibilidad *f*

infallible [ɪn'fæləbəl] *adj* : infalible — **infallibly** [-bli] *adv*

infamous ['ɪnfəməs] *adj* : infame — **infamously** *adv*

infamy ['ɪnfəmi] *n*, *pl* **-mies** : infamia *f*

infancy ['ɪnfənʃi] *n*, *pl* **-cies** : infancia *f*

infant ['ɪnfənt] *n* : bebé *m*; niño *m*, -ña *f*

infantile ['ɪnfən‚taɪl, -təl, -‚tiːl] *adj* : infantil, pueril

infantile paralysis → **poliomyelitis**

infantry ['ɪnfəntri] *n*, *pl* **-tries** : infantería *f*

infatuated [ɪn'fætʃu‚eɪtəd] *adj* **to be infatuated with** : estar encaprichado con

infatuation [ɪn‚fætʃu'eɪʃən] *n* : encaprichamiento *m*, enamoramiento *m*

infect [ɪn'fɛkt] *vt* : infectar, contagiar

infection [ɪn'fɛkʃən] *n* : infección *f*, contagio *m*

infectious [ɪn'fɛkʃəs] *adj* : infeccioso, contagioso

infer [ɪn'fər] *vt* **inferred; inferring 1** DEDUCE : deducir, inferir **2** SURMISE : concluir, suponer, tener entendido **3** IMPLY : sugerir, insinuar

inference ['ɪnfərənʃ] *n* : deducción *f*, inferencia *f*, conclusión *f*

inferior[1] [ɪn'fɪriər] *adj* : inferior, malo
inferior[2] *n* : inferior *mf*
inferiority [ɪn,fɪri'ɔrəti] *n, pl* **-ties** : inferioridad *f* ⟨inferiority complex : complejo de inferioridad⟩
infernal [ɪn'fərnəl] *adj* **1** : infernal ⟨infernal fires : fuegos infernales⟩ **2** DIABOLICAL : infernal, diabólico **3** DAMNABLE : maldito, condenado
inferno [ɪn'fər,no:] *n, pl* **-nos** : infierno *m*
infertile [ɪn'fərtəl, -,taɪl] *adj* : estéril, infecundo
infertility [,ɪnfər'tɪləti] *n* : esterilidad *f*, infecundidad *f*
infest [ɪn'fɛst] *vt* : infestar, plagar
infestation [,ɪn,fɛs'teɪlən] *n* : infestación *f*, plaga *f*
infidel ['ɪnfədəl, -,dɛl] *n* : infiel *mf*
infidelity [,ɪnfə'dɛləti, -faɪ-] *n, pl* **-ties 1** UNFAITHFULNESS : infidelidad *f* **2** DISLOYALTY : deslealtad *f*
infield ['ɪn,fi:ld] *n* : cuadro *m*, diamante *m*
infighting ['ɪn,faɪtɪŋ] *n* : disputas *fpl* internas, luchas *fpl* internas
infiltrate [ɪn'fɪl,treɪt, 'ɪnfɪl-] *v* **-trated; -trating** *vt* : infiltrar — *vi* : infiltrarse
infiltration [,ɪnfɪl'treɪlən] *n* : infiltración *f*
infiltrator [ɪn'fɪl,treɪtər, 'ɪnfɪl-] *n* : infiltrado *m*, -da *f*
infinite ['ɪnfənət] *adj* **1** LIMITLESS : infinito, sin límites **2** VAST : infinito, vasto, extenso
infinitely ['ɪnfənətli] *adv* : infinitamente
infinitesimal [,ɪn,fɪnə'tɛsəməl] *adj* : infinitesimal — **infinitesimally** *adv*
infinitive [ɪn'fɪnətɪv] *n* : infinitivo *m*
infinity [ɪn'fɪnəti] *n, pl* **-ties 1** : infinito *m* (en matemáticas, etc.) **2** : infinidad *f* ⟨an infinity of stars : una infinidad de estrellas⟩
infirm [ɪn'fərm] *adj* **1** FEEBLE : enfermizo, endeble **2** INSECURE : inseguro
infirmary [ɪn'fərməri] *n, pl* **-ries** : enfermería *f*, hospital *m*
infirmity [ɪn'fərməti] *n, pl* **-ties 1** FRAILTY : debilidad *f* **2** AILMENT : enfermedad *f*, dolencia *f* ⟨the infirmities of age : los achaques de la vejez⟩
inflame [ɪn'fleɪm] *v* **-flamed; -flaming** *vt* **1** KINDLE : inflamar, encender **2** : inflamar (una herida) **3** STIR UP : encender, provocar, inflamar — *vi* : inflamarse
inflammable [ɪn'flæməbəl] *adj* **1** FLAMMABLE : inflamable **2** IRASCIBLE : irascible, explosivo
inflammation [,ɪnflə'meɪlən] *n* : inflamación *f*
inflammatory [ɪn'flæmə,tori] *adj* : inflamatorio, incendiario
inflatable [ɪn'fleɪtəbəl] *adj* : inflable
inflate [ɪn'fleɪt] *vt* **-flated; -flating** : inflar, hinchar
inflation [ɪn'fleɪlən] *n* : inflación *f*
inflationary [ɪn'fleɪlə,nɛri] *adj* : inflacionario, inflacionista
inflect [ɪn'flɛkt] *vt* **1** CONJUGATE, DECLINE : conjugar, declinar **2** MODULATE : modular (la voz)
inflection [ɪn'flɛklən] *n* : inflexión *f*

inflexibility [ɪn,flɛksə'bɪləti] *n, pl* **-ties** : inflexibilidad *f*
inflexible [ɪn'flɛksɪbəl] *adj* : inflexible
inflict [ɪn'flɪkt] *vt* **1** : infligir, causar, imponer **2 to inflict oneself on** : imponer uno su presencia (a alguien)
infliction [ɪn'flɪklən] *n* : imposición *f*
influence[1] ['ɪn,flu:ənts, ɪn'flu:ənts] *vt* **-enced; -encing** : influenciar, influir en
influence[2] *n* **1** : influencia *f*, influjo *m* ⟨to exert influence over : ejercer influencia sobre⟩ ⟨the influence of gravity : el influjo de la gravedad⟩ **2 under the influence** : bajo la influencia del alcohol, embriagado
influential [,ɪnflu'ɛntləl] *adj* : influyente
influenza [,ɪnflu'ɛnzə] *n* : gripe *f*, influenza *f*, gripa *f Col, Mex*
influx ['ɪn,flʌks] *n* : afluencia *f* (de gente), entrada *f* (de mercancías), llegada *f* (de ideas)
info ['ɪnfo] *n fam* → **information**
inform [ɪn'fɔrm] *vt* : informar, notificar, avisar — *vi* **to inform on** : delatar, denunciar
informal [ɪn'fɔrməl] *adj* **1** UNCEREMONIOUS : sin ceremonia, sin etiqueta **2** CASUAL : informal, familiar (dícese del lenguaje) **3** UNOFFICIAL : informal, extraoficial
informality [,ɪnfɔr'mæləti, -fər-] *n, pl* **-ties** : informalidad *f*, familiaridad *f*, falta *f* de ceremonia
informally [ɪn'fɔrməli] *adv* : sin ceremonias, de manera informal, informalmente
informant [ɪn'fɔrmənt] *n* : informante *mf*; informador *m*, -dora *f*
information [,ɪnfər'meɪlən] *n* : información *f*
informational [,ɪnfər'meɪlənəl] *adj* : informativo
information technology *n* : informática *f*
informative [ɪn'fɔrmətɪv] *adj* : informativo, instructivo
informer [ɪn'fɔrmər] *n* : informante *mf*; informador *m*, -dora *f*
infraction [ɪn'fræklən] *n* : infracción *f*, violación *f*, transgresión *f*
infrared [,ɪnfrə'rɛd] *adj* : infrarrojo
infrastructure ['ɪnfrə,strʌktlər] *n* : infraestructura *f*
infrequent [ɪn'fri:kwənt] *adj* : infrecuente, raro
infrequently [ɪn'fri:kwəntli] *adv* : raramente, con poca frecuencia
infringe [ɪn'frɪnʤ] *v* **-fringed; -fringing** *vt* : infringir, violar — *vi* **to infringe on** : abusar de, violar
infringement [ɪn'frɪnʤmənt] *n* **1** VIOLATION : violación *f* (de la ley), incumplimiento *m* (de un contrato) **2** ENCROACHMENT : usurpación *f* (de derechos, etc.)
infuriate [ɪn'fjʊri,eɪt] *vt* **-ated; -ating** : enfurecer, poner furioso
infuriating [ɪn'fjʊri,eɪtɪŋ] *adj* : indignante, exasperante
infuse [ɪn'fju:z] *vt* **-fused; -fusing 1** INSTILL : infundir **2** STEEP : hacer una infusión de

infusion [ɪn'fjuːʒən] *n* : infusión *f*
ingenious [ɪn'dʒiːnjəs] *adj* : ingenioso —
  ingeniously *adv*
ingenue *or* **ingénue** ['ɑndʒəˌnuː, 'æn-ː,
  'æʒə-, 'ɑ-] *n* : ingenua *f*
ingenuity [ˌɪndʒə'nuːəti, -'njuː-] *n, pl* **-ities**
  : ingenio *m*
ingenuous [ɪn'dʒenjuəs] *adj* 1 FRANK
  : cándido, franco 2 NAIVE : ingenuo —
  ingenuously *adv*
ingenuousness [ɪn'dʒenjuəsnəs] *n* 1
  FRANKNESS : candidez *f*, candor *m* 2
  NAÏVETÉ : ingenuidad *f*
ingest [ɪn'dʒest] *vt* : ingerir
ingestion [ɪn'dʒestLən] *n* : ingestión *f*
inglorious [ɪn'gloriəs] *adj* : deshonroso,
  ignominioso
ingot ['ɪŋgət] *n* : lingote *m*
ingrained [ɪn'greɪnd] *adj* : arraigado
ingrate ['ɪnˌgreɪt] *n* : ingrato *m*, -ta *f*
ingratiate [ɪn'greɪLiˌeɪt] *vt* **-ated; -ating**
  : conseguir la benevolencia de ⟨to ingratiate oneself with someone : congraciarse con alguien⟩
ingratiating [ɪn'greɪLiˌeɪtɪŋ] *adj* : halagador, zalamero, obsequioso
ingratitude [ɪn'grætəˌtuːd, -ˌtjuːd] *n* : ingratitud *f*
ingredient [ɪn'griːdiənt] *n* : ingrediente *m*,
  componente *m*
ingrown ['ɪnˌgroːn] *adj* 1 : crecido hacia
  adentro 2 **ingrown toenail** : uña *f* en-
  carnada
inhabit [ɪn'hæbət] *vt* : vivir en, habitar,
  ocupar
inhabitable [ɪn'hæbətəbəl] *adj* : habitable
inhabitant [ɪn'hæbətənt] *n* : habitante *mf*
inhalant [ɪn'heɪlənt] *n* : inhalante *m*
inhalation [ˌɪnhə'leɪLən, ˌɪnə-] *n* : inhalación *f*
inhale [ɪn'heɪl] *v* **-haled; -haling** *vt* : inhalar, aspirar — *vi* : inspirar
inhaler [ɪn'heɪlər] *n* : inhalador *m*
inhere [ɪn'hɪr] *vi* **-hered; -hering** : ser inherente
inherent [ɪn'hɪrənt, -'hɛr-] *adj* : inherente,
  intrínseco — **inherently** *adv*
inherit [ɪn'hɛrət] *vt* : heredar
inheritance [ɪn'hɛrətənts] *n* : herencia *f*
inheritor [ɪn'hɛrətər] *n* : heredero *m*, -ra
  f
inhibit [ɪn'hɪbət] *vt* IMPEDE : inhibir, impedir
inhibition [ˌɪnhə'bɪLən, ˌɪnə-] *n* : inhibición *f*, cohibición *f*
inhospitable [ˌɪnhɑ'spɪtəbəl, -'hɑsˌpɪ-] *adj*
  : inhóspito
inhuman [ɪn'hjuːmən, -'juː-] *adj* : inhumano, cruel — **inhumanly** *adv*
inhumane [ˌɪnhju'meɪn, -juː-] *adj* INHU-
  MAN : inhumano, cruel
inhumanity [ˌɪnhju'mænəti, -juː-] *n, pl*
  -ties : inhumanidad *f*, crueldad *f*
inimical [ɪ'nɪmɪkəl] *adj* 1 UNFAVORABLE
  : adverso, desfavorable 2 HOSTILE
  : hostil — **inimically** *adv*
inimitable [ɪ'nɪmətəbəl] *adj* : inimitable
iniquitous [ɪ'nɪkwətəs] *adj* : inicuo, malvado
iniquity [ɪ'nɪkwəti] *n, pl* **-ties** : iniquidad *f*

initial¹ [ɪ'nɪLəl] *vt* **-tialed** *or* **-tialled; -tial-
  ing** *or* **-tialling** : poner las iniciales a, firmar con las iniciales
initial² *adj* : inicial, primero — **initially** *adv*
initial³ *n* : inicial *f*
initiate¹ [ɪ'nɪLiˌeɪt] *vt* **-ated; -ating** 1 BE-
  GIN : comenzar, iniciar 2 INDUCT : instruir 3 INTRODUCE : introducir, instruir
initiate² [ɪ'nɪLiət] *n* : iniciado *m*, -da *f*
initiation [ɪˌnɪLi'eɪLən] *n* : iniciación *f*
initiative [ɪ'nɪLətɪv] *n* : iniciativa *f*
initiatory [ɪ'nɪLiəˌtori] *adj* 1 INTRODUC-
  TORY : introductorio 2 : de iniciación
  ⟨initiatory rites : ritos de iniciación⟩
inject [ɪn'dʒekt] *vt* : inyectar
injection [ɪn'dʒekLən] *n* : inyección *f*
injudicious [ˌɪndʒʊ'dɪLəs] *adj* : imprudente, indiscreto, poco juicioso
injunction [ɪn'dʒʌŋkLən] *n* 1 ORDER : orden *f*, mandato *m* 2 COURT ORDER
  : mandamiento *m* judicial
injure ['ɪndʒər] *vt* **-jured; -juring** 1
  WOUND : herir, lesionar 2 HURT : lastimar, dañar, herir 3 **to injure oneself**
  : hacerse daño
injurious [ɪn'dʒʊriəs] *adj* : perjudicial ⟨in-
  jurious to one's health : perjudicial a la
  salud⟩
injury ['ɪndʒəri] *n, pl* **-ries** 1 WRONG
  : mal *m*, injusticia *f* 2 DAMAGE, HARM
  : herida *f*, daño *m*, perjuicio *m*
injustice [ɪn'dʒʌstəs] *n* : injusticia *f*
ink¹ ['ɪŋk] *vt* : entintar
ink² *n* : tinta *f*
inkjet printer ['ɪŋkˌdʒet-] *n* : impresora *f*
  de inyección de tinta
inkling ['ɪŋklɪŋ] *n* : presentimiento *m*, indicio *m*, sospecha *f*
ink pad *n* : tampón *m* (para entintar)
inkwell ['ɪŋkˌwel] *n* : tintero *m*
inky ['ɪŋki] *adj* 1 : manchado de tinta 2
  BLACK : negro, impenetrable ⟨inky darkness : negra oscuridad⟩
inland¹ ['ɪnˌlænd, -lənd] *adv* : hacia el interior, tierra adentro
inland² *adj* : interior
inland³ *n* : interior *m*
in–law ['ɪnˌlɔ] *n* 1 : pariente *m* político 2
  in–laws *npl* : suegros *mpl*
inlay¹ [ɪn'leɪ, 'ɪnˌleɪ] *vt* **-laid** [-'leɪd, -ˌleɪd];
  -laying : incrustar
inlay² ['ɪnˌleɪ] *n* 1 : incrustación *f* 2
  : empaste *m* (de un diente)
inlet ['ɪnˌlet, -lət] *n* : cala *f*, ensenada *f*,
  brazo *m* del mar
in–line skate ['ɪnˌlaɪn-] *n* : patín *m* en
  línea
inmate ['ɪnˌmeɪt] *n* : paciente *mf* (en un
  hospital); preso *m*, -sa *f* (en una prisión);
  interno *m*, -na *f* (en un asilo)
in memoriam [ˌɪnmə'moriəm] *prep* : en
  memoria de
inmost ['ɪnˌmoːst] → **innermost**
inn ['ɪn] *n* 1 : posada *f*, hostería *f*, fonda
  f 2 TAVERN : taberna *f*
innards ['ɪnərdz] *npl* : entrañas *fpl*, tripas
  fpl fam
innate [ɪ'neɪt] *adj* 1 INBORN : innato 2
  INHERENT : inherente

inner [ˈɪnər] *adj* : interior, interno
inner city *n* : barrios *mpl* pobres (en el centro de una ciudad)
innermost [ˈɪnərˌmoːst] *adj* : más íntimo, más profundo
innersole [ˈɪnərˈsoːl] → **insole**
inner tube → **tube**
inning [ˈɪnɪŋ] *n* : entrada *f*
innkeeper [ˈɪnˌkiːpər] *n* : posadero *m*, -ra *f*
innocence [ˈɪnəsənts] *n* : inocencia *f*
innocent[1] [ˈɪnəsənt] *adj* : inocente — **innocently** *adv*
innocent[2] *n* : inocente *mf*
innocuous [ɪˈnɑkjəwəs] *adj* **1** HARMLESS : inocuo **2** INOFFENSIVE : inofensivo
innovate [ˈɪnəˌveɪt] *vi* **-vated; -vating** : innovar
innovation [ˌɪnəˈveɪʃən] *n* : innovación *f*, novedad *f*
innovative [ˈɪnəˌveɪtɪv] *adj* : innovador
innovator [ˈɪnəˌveɪtər] *n* : innovador *m*, -dora *f*
innuendo [ˌɪnjuˈɛndo] *n, pl* **-dos** *or* **-does** : insinuación *f*, indirecta *f*
innumerable [ɪˈnuːmərəbəl, -ˈnjuː-] *adj* : innumerable
inoculate [ɪˈnɑkjəˌleɪt] *vt* **-lated; -lating** : inocular
inoculation [ɪˌnɑkjəˈleɪʃən] *n* : inoculación *f*
inoffensive [ˌɪnəˈfɛntsɪv] *adj* : inofensivo
inoperable [ɪnˈɑpərəbəl] *adj* : inoperable
inoperative [ɪnˈɑpərətɪv, -ˌreɪ-] *adj* : inoperante
inopportune [ɪnˌɑpərˈtuːn, -ˈtjuːn] *adj* : inoportuno — **inopportunely** *adv*
inordinate [ɪnˈɔrdənət] *adj* : excesivo, inmoderado, desmesurado — **inordinately** *adv*
inorganic [ˌɪnˌɔrˈɡænɪk] *adj* : inorgánico
inpatient [ˈɪnˌpeɪʃənt] *n* : paciente *mf* hospitalizado
input[1] [ˈɪnˌpʊt] *vt* **inputted** *or* **input; inputting** : entrar (datos, información)
input[2] *n* **1** CONTRIBUTION : aportación *f*, contribución *f* **2** ENTRY : entrada *f* (de datos) **3** ADVICE, OPINION : consejos *mpl*, opinión *f*
inquest [ˈɪnˌkwɛst] *n* INQUIRY, INVESTIGATION : investigación *f*, pesquisa *f* (judicial), indagatoria *f*
inquire [ɪnˈkwaɪr] *v* **-quired; -quiring** *vt* : preguntar, informarse de, inquirir ⟨he inquired how to get in : preguntó como entrar⟩ — *vi* **1** ASK : preguntar, informarse ⟨to inquire about : informarse sobre⟩ ⟨to inquire after (someone) : preguntar por (alguien)⟩ **2 to inquire into** INVESTIGATE : investigar, inquirir sobre
inquiringly [ɪnˈkwaɪrɪŋli] *adv* : inquisitivamente
inquiry [ˈɪnˌkwaɪri, ɪnˈkwaɪri;, ˈɪnkwəri, ˈɪŋ-] *n, pl* **-ries 1** QUESTION : pregunta *f* ⟨to make inquiries about : pedir información sobre⟩ **2** INVESTIGATION : investigación *f*, inquisición *f*, pesquisa *f*
inquisition [ˌɪnkwəˈzɪʃən, ˌɪŋ-] *n* **1** : inquisición *f*, interrogatorio *m*, investigación *f* **2 the Inquisition** : la Inquisición *f*

inquisitive [ɪnˈkwɪzətɪv] *adj* : inquisidor, inquisitivo, curioso — **inquisitively** *adv*
inquisitiveness [ɪnˈkwɪzətɪvnəs] *n* : curiosidad *f*
inquisitor [ɪnˈkwɪzətər] *n* : inquisidor *m*, -dora *f*; interrogador *m*, -dora *f*
inroad [ˈɪnˌroːd] *n* **1** ENCROACHMENT, INVASION : invasión *f*, incursión *f* **2 to make inroads into** : ocupar parte de (un tiempo), agotar parte de (ahorros, recursos), invadir (un territorio)
insane [ɪnˈseɪn] *adj* **1** MAD : loco, demente ⟨to go insane : volverse loco⟩ ⟨to drive someone insane : volver loco a alguien⟩ **2** ABSURD : absurdo, insensato ⟨an insane scheme : un proyecto insensato⟩
insanely [ɪnˈseɪnli] *adv* : como un loco ⟨insanely suspicious : loco de recelo⟩
insanity [ɪnˈsænəti] *n, pl* **-ties 1** MADNESS : locura *f* **2** FOLLY : locura *f*, insensatez *f*
insatiable [ɪnˈseɪʃəbəl] *adj* : insaciable — **insatiably** [-bli] *adv*
inscribe [ɪnˈskraɪb] *vt* **-scribed; -scribing 1** ENGRAVE : inscribir, grabar **2** ENROLL : inscribir **3** DEDICATE : dedicar (un libro)
inscription [ɪnˈskrɪpʃən] *n* : inscripción *f* (en un monumento), dedicación *f* (en un libro), leyenda *f* (de una ilustración, etc.)
inscrutable [ɪnˈskruːt̬əbəl] *adj* : inescrutable, misterioso — **inscrutably** [-bli] *adv*
inseam [ˈɪnˌsiːm] *n* : entrepierna *f*
insect [ˈɪnˌsɛkt] *n* : insecto *m*
insecticidal [ɪnˌsɛktəˈsaɪdəl] *adj* : insecticida
insecticide [ɪnˈsɛktəˌsaɪd] *n* : insecticida *m*
insecure [ˌɪnsɪˈkjʊr] *adj* : inseguro, poco seguro
insecurely [ˌɪnsɪˈkjʊrli] *adv* : inseguramente
insecurity [ˌɪnsɪˈkjʊrəti] *n, pl* **-ties** : inseguridad *f*
inseminate [ɪnˈsɛməˌneɪt] *vt* **-nated; -nating** : inseminar
insemination [ɪnˌsɛməˈneɪʃən] *n* : inseminación *f*
insensibility [ɪnˌsɛntsəˈbɪləti] *n, pl* **-ties** : insensibilidad *f*
insensible [ɪnˈsɛntsəbəl] *adj* **1** UNCONSCIOUS : inconsciente, sin conocimiento **2** NUMB : insensible, entumecido **3** UNAWARE : inconsciente
insensitive [ɪnˈsɛntsətɪv] *adj* : insensible
insensitivity [ɪnˌsɛntsəˈtɪvəti] *n, pl* **-ties** : insensibilidad *f*
inseparable [ɪnˈsɛpərəbəl] *adj* : inseparable
insert[1] [ɪnˈsərt] *vt* **1** : insertar, introducir, poner, meter ⟨insert your key in the lock : mete tu llave en la cerradura⟩ **2** INTERPOLATE : interpolar, intercalar
insert[2] [ˈɪnˌsərt] *n* : inserción *f*, hoja *f* insertada (en una revista, etc.)
insertion [ɪnˈsərʃən] *n* : inserción *f*
inshore[1] [ˈɪnˈlor] *adv* : hacia la costa
inshore[2] *adj* : cercano a la costa, costero ⟨inshore fishing : pesca costera⟩

inside¹ [ɪn'saɪd, 'ɪn,saɪd] *adv* : adentro, dentro ⟨to run inside : correr para adentro⟩ ⟨inside and out : por dentro y por fuera⟩
inside² *adj* **1** : interior, de adentro, de dentro ⟨the inside lane : el carril interior⟩ **2** : confidencial ⟨inside information : información confidencial⟩
inside³ *n* **1** : interior *m*, parte *f* de adentro ⟨the inside of the house : el interior de la casa⟩ **2 insides** *npl* BELLY, GUTS : tripas *fpl fam* **3 inside out** : al/del revés ⟨to turn something inside out : darle la vuelta a algo, volver/poner algo al/del revés, voltear algo⟩
inside⁴ *prep* **1** INTO : al interior de **2** WITHIN : dentro de **3** (*referring to time*) : en menos de ⟨inside an hour : en menos de una hora⟩
inside of *prep* INSIDE : dentro de
insider [ɪn'saɪdər] *n* : persona *f* enterada
insidious [ɪn'sɪdiəs] *adj* : insidioso — **insidiously** *adv*
insidiousness [ɪn'sɪdiəsnəs] *n* : insidia *f*
insight ['ɪn,saɪt] *n* : perspicacia *f*, penetración *f*
insightful [ɪn'saɪtfəl] *adj* : perspicaz
insignia [ɪn'sɪgniə] *or* **insigne** [-,ni:] *n, pl* **-nia** *or* **-nias** : insignia *f*, enseña *f*
insignificance [,ɪnsɪg'nɪfɪkən/s] *n* : insignificancia *f*
insignificant [,ɪnsɪg'nɪfɪkənt] *adj* : insignificante
insincere [,ɪnsɪn'sɪr] *adj* : insincero, poco sincero
insincerely [,ɪnsɪn'sɪrli] *adv* : con poca sinceridad
insincerity [,ɪnsɪn'serəti, -'sɪr-] *n, pl* **-ties** : insinceridad *f*
insinuate [ɪn'sɪnju,eɪt] *vt* **-ated; -ating** : insinuar
insinuation [ɪn,sɪnju'eɪlən] *n* : insinuación *f*
insipid [ɪn'sɪpəd] *adj* : insípido
insist [ɪn'sɪst] *v* : insistir
insistence [ɪn'sɪstən/s] *n* : insistencia *f*
insistent [ɪn'sɪstənt] *adj* : insistente — **insistently** *adv*
insofar as [,ɪnso'fɑræz] *conj* : en la medida en que, en tanto que, en cuanto a
insole ['ɪn,soːl] *n* : plantilla *f*
insolence ['ɪntsələn/s] *n* : insolencia *f*
insolent ['ɪntsələnt] *adj* : insolente
insolubility [ɪn,salju'bɪləti] *n* : insolubilidad *f*
insoluble [ɪn'saljubəl] *adj* : insoluble
insolvency [ɪn'salvən/si] *n, pl* **-cies** : insolvencia *f*
insolvent [ɪn'salvənt] *adj* : insolvente
insomnia [ɪn'samniə] *n* : insomnio *m*
insomniac [ɪn'samni,æk] *n* : insomne *mf* — **insomniac** *adj*
insomuch as [,ɪnso'mʌtɬæz] → **inasmuch as**
insomuch that *conj* SO : así que, de manera que
inspect [ɪn'spɛkt] *vt* : inspeccionar, examinar, revisar
inspection [ɪn'spɛkɬən] *n* : inspección *f*, examen *m*, revisión *f*, revista *f* (de tropas)

inspector [ɪn'spɛktər] *n* : inspector *m*, -tora *f*
inspiration [,ɪntspə'reɪlən] *n* : inspiración *f*
inspirational [,ɪntspə'reɪlənəl] *adj* : inspirador
inspire [ɪn'spaɪr] *v* **-spired; -spiring** **1** INHALE : inhalar, aspirar **2** STIMULATE : estimular, animar, inspirar **3** INSTILL : inspirar, infundir — *vi* : inspirar
instability [,ɪntstə'bɪləti] *n, pl* **-ties** : inestabilidad *f*
install [ɪn'stɔl] *vt* **-stalled; -stalling** **1** : instalar ⟨to install a fan : montar un abanico⟩ **2** INDUCT : instalar, investir ⟨to install the new president : instalar el presidente nuevo⟩ **3 to install oneself** : instalarse
installation [,ɪntstə'leɪlən] *n* : instalación *f*
installment [ɪn'stɔlmənt] *n* **1** : plazo *m*, cuota *f* ⟨to pay in four installments : pagar a cuatro plazos⟩ **2** : entrega *f* (de una publicación o telenovela) **3** INSTALLATION : instalación *f*
instance ['ɪntstən/s] *n* **1** INSTIGATION : instancia *f* **2** EXAMPLE : ejemplo *m* ⟨for instance : por ejemplo⟩ **3** OCCASION : instancia *f*, caso *m*, ocasión *f* ⟨he prefers, in this instance, to remain anonymous : en este caso prefiere quedarse anónimo⟩
instant¹ ['ɪntstənt] *adj* **1** IMMEDIATE : inmediato, instantáneo ⟨an instant reply : una respuesta inmediata⟩ **2** : instantáneo ⟨instant coffee : café instantáneo⟩
instant² *n* : momento *m*, instante *m*
instantaneous [,ɪntstən'teɪniəs] *adj* : instantáneo
instantaneously [,ɪntstən'teɪniəsli] *adv* : instantáneamente, al instante
instantly ['ɪntstəntli] *adv* : al instante, instantáneamente
instant message *n* : mensaje *m* instantáneo
instant messaging *n* : mensajería *f* instantánea
instead [ɪn'stɛd] *adv* **1** : en cambio, en lugar de eso, en su lugar ⟨Dad was going, but Mom went instead : papá iba a ir, pero mamá fue en su lugar⟩ **2** RATHER : al contrario
instead of *prep* : en vez de, en lugar de
instep ['ɪn,stɛp] *n* : empeine *m*
instigate ['ɪntstə,geɪt] *vt* **-gated; -gating** INCITE, PROVOKE : instigar, incitar, provocar, fomentar
instigation [,ɪntstə'geɪlən] *n* : instancia *f*, incitación *f*
instigator ['ɪntstə,geɪtər] *n* : instigador *m*, -dora *f*; incitador *m*, -dora *f*
instill [ɪn'stɪl] *vt* **-stilled; -stilling** : inculcar, infundir
instinct ['ɪn,stɪŋkt] *n* **1** TALENT : instinto *m*, don *m* ⟨an instinct for the right word : un don para escoger la palabra apropiada⟩ **2** : instinto *m* ⟨maternal instincts : instintos maternales⟩
instinctive [ɪn'stɪŋktɪv] *adj* : instintivo
instinctively [ɪn'stɪŋktɪvli] *adv* : instintivamente, por instinto

instinctual [ɪn'stɪŋktɯəl] *adj* : instintivo

institute¹ ['ɪnˌstəˌtuːt, -ˌtjuːt] *vt* **-tuted;
-tuting 1** ESTABLISH : establecer, instituir, fundar **2** INITIATE : iniciar, empezar, entablar

institute² *n* : instituto *m*

institution [ˌɪnˌstə'tuːʒən, -'tjuː-] *n* **1** ESTABLISHING : institución *f*, establecimiento *m* **2** CUSTOM : institución *f*, tradición *f* ⟨the institution of marriage : la institución del matrimonio⟩ **3** ORGANIZATION : institución *f*, organismo *m* **4** ASYLUM : asilo *m*

institutional [ˌɪnˌstə'tuːʒənəl, -'tjuː-] *adj* : institucional

institutionalize [ˌɪnˌstə'tuːʒənəˌlaɪz, -'tjuː-] *vt* **-ized; -izing 1** : institucionalizar ⟨institutionalized values : valores institucionalizados⟩ **2** : internar ⟨institutionalized orphans : huérfanos internados⟩

instruct [ɪn'strʌkt] *vt* **1** TEACH, TRAIN : instruir, adiestrar, enseñar **2** COMMAND : mandar, ordenar, dar instrucciones a

instruction [ɪn'strʌkʃən] *n* **1** TEACHING : instrucción *f*, enseñanza *f* **2** COMMAND : orden *f*, instrucción *f* **3** **instructions** *npl* DIRECTIONS : instrucciones *fpl*, modo *m* de empleo

instructional [ɪn'strʌkʃənəl] *adj* : instructivo, educativo

instructive [ɪn'strʌktɪv] *adj* : instructivo

instructor [ɪn'strʌktər] *n* : instructor *m*, -tora *f*

instrument ['ɪnˌstrəmənt] *n* **1** : instrumento *m* (musical) **2** TOOL, DEVICE : instrumento *m* **3** MEANS : instrumento *m*

instrumental [ˌɪnˌstrə'mɛntəl] *adj* : instrumental

instrumentalist [ˌɪnˌstrə'mɛntəlɪst] *n* : instrumentista *mf*

insubordinate [ˌɪnsə'bɔrdənət] *adj* : insubordinado

insubordination [ˌɪnsəˌbɔrdən'eɪʒən] *n* : insubordinación *f*

insubstantial [ˌɪnsəb'stæntʃəl] *adj* : insustancial, poco nutritivo (dícese de una comida), poco sólido (dícese de una estructura o un argumento)

insufferable [ɪn'sʌfərəbəl] *adj* UNBEARABLE : insufrible, intolerable, inaguantable, insoportable — **insufferably** [-bli] *adv*

insufficiency [ˌɪnsə'fɪləntsi] *n, pl* **-cies** : insuficiencia *f*

insufficient [ˌɪnsə'fɪʃənt] *adj* : insuficiente — **insufficiently** *adv*

insular ['ɪnˌsʊlər, -sjʊ-] *adj* **1** : isleño (dícese de la gente), insular (dícese del clima) ⟨insular residents : residentes de la isla⟩ **2** NARROW-MINDED : de miras estrechas

insularity [ˌɪnˌsʊ'lærəti, -sjʊ-] *n* : insularidad *f*

insulate ['ɪnˌsəˌleɪt] *vt* **-lated; -lating** : aislar

insulation [ˌɪnˌsə'leɪʒən] *n* : aislamiento *m*

insulator ['ɪnˌsəˌleɪtər] *n* : aislador *m* (pieza), aislante *m* (material)

insulin ['ɪntsələn] *n* : insulina *f*

insult¹ [ɪn'sʌlt] *vt* : insultar, ofender, injuriar

insult² ['ɪnˌsʌlt] *n* : insulto *m*, injuria *f*, agravio *m*

insulting [ɪn'sʌltɪŋ] *adj* : ofensivo, injurioso, insultante

insultingly [ɪn'sʌltɪŋli] *adv* : ofensivamente, de manera insultante

insurance [ɪn'ʊrənts, 'ɪnˌʊr-] *n* : seguro *m* ⟨life insurance : seguro de vida⟩ ⟨insurance company/policy : compañía/póliza de seguros⟩

insure [ɪn'ʊr] *vt* **-sured; -suring 1** UNDERWRITE : asegurar **2** ENSURE : asegurar, garantizar

insured [ɪn'ʊrd] *n* : asegurado *m*, -da *f*

insurer [ɪn'ʊrər] *n* : asegurador *m*, -dora *f*

insurgent¹ [ɪn'sərʤənt] *adj* : insurgente

insurgent² *n* : insurgente *mf*

insurmountable [ˌɪnsər'maʊntəbəl] *adj* : insuperable, insalvable — **insurmountably** [-bli] *adv*

insurrection [ˌɪnsə'rɛkʃən] *n* : insurrección *f*, levantamiento *m*, alzamiento *m*

intact [ɪn'tækt] *adj* : intacto

intake ['ɪnˌteɪk] *n* **1** OPENING : entrada *f*, toma *f* ⟨fuel intake : toma de combustible⟩ **2** : entrada *f* (de agua o aire), consumo *m* (de sustancias nutritivas) **3** **intake of breath** : inhalación *f*

intangible [ɪn'tænʤəbəl] *adj* : intangible, impalpable — **intangibly** [-bli] *adv*

integer ['ɪntɪʤər] *n* : entero *m*

integral ['ɪntɪgrəl] *adj* : integral, esencial

integrate ['ɪntəˌgreɪt] *v* **-grated; -grating** *vt* **1** UNITE : integrar, unir **2** DESEGREGATE : eliminar la segregación de — *vi* : integrarse

integration [ˌɪntə'greɪʒən] *n* : integración *f*

integrity [ɪn'tɛgrəti] *n* : integridad *f*

intellect ['ɪntəlˌɛkt] *n* : intelecto *m*, inteligencia *f*, capacidad *f* intelectual

intellectual¹ [ˌɪntə'lɛktɯəl] *adj* : intelectual — **intellectually** *adv*

intellectual² *n* : intelectual *mf*

intelligence [ɪn'tɛləʤənts] *n* **1** : inteligencia *f* **2** INFORMATION, NEWS : inteligencia *f*, información *f*, noticias *fpl*

intelligent [ɪn'tɛləʤənt] *adj* : inteligente — **intelligently** *adv*

intelligentsia [ɪnˌtɛlə'ʤɛnʃə, -'gɛn-] *ns & pl* : intelectualidad *f*

intelligibility [ɪnˌtɛləʤə'bɪləti] *n* : inteligibilidad *f*

intelligible [ɪn'tɛləʤəbəl] *adj* : inteligible, comprensible — **intelligibly** [-bli] *adv*

intemperance [ɪn'tɛmpərənts] *n* : inmoderación *f*, intemperancia *f*

intemperate [ɪn'tɛmpərət] *adj* : excesivo, inmoderado, desmedido

intend [ɪn'tɛnd] *vt* **1** (*indicating goal or purpose*) : querer, tener la intención de ⟨I didn't intend to hurt you : no quería hacerte daño⟩ ⟨no insult was intended : no fue mi intención ofender⟩ ⟨it was intended as a warning : pretendía servir de advertencia⟩ ⟨she intended for him to

come : su intención era que viniera⟩ ⟨I
intended it as a joke : lo dije en broma⟩
⟨a film intended to educate : una
película tendiente a educar⟩ **2** MEAN,
SIGNIFY : querer decir **3** PLAN : pensar,
tener planeado, proyectar, proponerse
⟨what do you intend to do? : ¿qué piensas hacer?⟩ ⟨I intend to finish by Thursday : me propongo acabar para el
jueves⟩ ⟨if all goes as intended : si todo
va según lo planeado⟩ **4 to be intended
for** : ser para, ir dirigido a (un público,
etc.), estar destinado a (un fin), estar diseñado para (un uso)
intended [ɪnˈtɛndəd] *adj* **1** PLANNED
: previsto, proyectado **2** INTENTIONAL
: intencional, deliberado
intense [ɪnˈtɛnts] *adj* **1** EXTREME : intenso,
extremo ⟨intense pain : dolor intenso⟩ **2**
: profundo, intenso ⟨to my intense relief
: para mi alivio profundo⟩ ⟨intense enthusiasm : entusiasmo ardiente⟩
intensely [ɪnˈtɛntsli] *adv* : sumamente,
profundamente, intensamente
intensification [ɪnˌtɛntsəfəˈkeɪʃən] *n* : intensificación *f*
intensifier [ɪnˈtɛntsəˌfaɪər] *n* : intensificador *m* (en lingüística)
intensify [ɪnˈtɛntsəˌfaɪ] *v* **-fied; -fying** *vt* **1**
STRENGTHEN : intensificar, redoblar ⟨to
intensify one's efforts : redoblar uno sus
esfuerzos⟩ **2** SHARPEN : intensificar,
agudizar (dolor, ansiedad) — *vi* : intensificarse, hacerse más intenso
intensity [ɪnˈtɛntsəti] *n, pl* **-ties** : intensidad *f*
intensive [ɪnˈtɛntsɪv] *adj* : intensivo ⟨in-
tensive care : cuidados intensivos⟩ —
intensively *adv*
intent¹ [ɪnˈtɛnt] *adj* **1** FIXED : concentrado, fijo ⟨an intent stare : una mirada
fija⟩ **2 intent on** *or* **intent upon** : resuelto a, atento a
intent² *n* **1** PURPOSE : intención *f*,
propósito *m* **2 for all intents and purposes** : a todos los efectos, prácticamente
intention [ɪnˈtɛntʃən] *n* : intención *f*,
propósito *m*
intentional [ɪnˈtɛntʃənəl] *adj* : intencional, deliberado
intentionally [ɪnˈtɛntʃənəli] *adv* : a
propósito, adrede
intently [ɪnˈtɛntli] *adv* : atentamente, fijamente
inter [ɪnˈtər] *vt* **-terred; -terring** : enterrar,
inhumar
inter- *pref* inter-
interact [ˌɪntərˈækt] *vi* : interactuar, actuar recíprocamente, relacionarse
interaction [ˌɪntərˈækʃən] *n* : interacción
f, interrelación *f*
interactive [ˌɪntərˈæktɪv] *adj* : interactivo
interbreed [ˌɪntərˈbriːd] *v* **-bred** [-ˈbrɛd];
-breeding *vt* : cruzar — *vi* : cruzarse
intercede [ˌɪntərˈsiːd] *vi* **-ceded; -ceding**
: interceder
intercept [ˌɪntərˈsɛpt] *vt* : interceptar
interception [ˌɪntərˈsɛpʃən] *n* : intercepción *f*

intercession [ˌɪntərˈsɛʃən] *n* : intercesión
f
interchange¹ [ˌɪntərˈtʃeɪndʒ] *vt* **-changed;
-changing** : intercambiar
interchange² [ˈɪntərˌtʃeɪndʒ] *n* **1** EX-
CHANGE : intercambio *m*, cambio *m* **2**
JUNCTION : empalme *m*, enlace *m* de
carreteras
interchangeable [ˌɪntərˈtʃeɪndʒəbəl] *adj*
: intercambiable
intercity [ˈɪntərˌsɪti] *adj* : interurbano
intercollegiate [ˌɪntərkəˈliːdʒət, -dʒiət] *adj*
: interuniversitario
intercom [ˈɪntərˌkɑm] *n* : interfono *m*
Spain, interfón *m Mex*
interconnect [ˌɪntərkəˈnɛkt] *vt* **1** : conectar, interconectar (en tecnología) **2** RE-
LATE : interrelacionar — *vi* **1** : conectar **2** : interrelacionarse
intercontinental [ˌɪntərˌkɑntənˈnɛtəl] *adj*
: intercontinental
intercourse [ˈɪntərˌkors] *n* **1** RELATIONS
: relaciones *fpl*, trato *m* **2** COPULATION
: acto *m* sexual, relaciones *fpl* sexuales,
coito *m*
interdenominational [ˌɪntərdɪˌnɑmə-
ˈneɪʃənəl] *adj* : interconfesional
interdepartmental [ˌɪntərdɪˌpɑrt-ˈmɛntəl,
-ˌdiː-] *adj* : interdepartamental
interdependence [ˌɪntərdɪˈpɛndənts] *n*
: interdependencia *f*
interdependent [ˌɪntərdɪˈpɛndənt] *adj*
: interdependiente
interdict [ˌɪntərˈdɪkt] *vt* **1** PROHIBIT
: prohibir **2** : cortar (las líneas de comunicación o provisión del enemigo)
interdisciplinary [ˌɪntərˈdɪsəpləˌnɛri] *adj*
: interdisciplinario
interest¹ [ˈɪntrəst, -təˌrɛst] *vt* : interesar
interest² *n* **1** SHARE, STAKE : interés *m*,
participación *f* **2** BENEFIT : provecho *m*,
beneficio *m*, interés *m* ⟨in the public interest : en el interés público⟩ **3** CHARGE
: interés *m*, cargo *m* ⟨compound interest
: interés compuesto⟩ ⟨interest rate : tasa
de interés⟩ **4** CURIOSITY : interés *m*, curiosidad *f* ⟨to take an interest in : interesarse por⟩ ⟨to lose interest : perder in-
terés⟩ **5** COLOR : color *m*, interés *m*
⟨places of local interest : lugares de color
local⟩ **6** HOBBY : afición *f*
interested [ˈɪntrəstəd, -təˌrɛstəd] *adj* : interesado
interesting [ˈɪntrəstɪŋ, -təˌrɛstɪŋ] *adj* : interesante — **interestingly** *adv*
interface [ˈɪntərˌfeɪs] *n* **1** : interfaz *f*, interfase *f* **2** : punto *m* de contacto (en la
física, etc.)
interfere [ˌɪntərˈfɪr] *vi* **-fered; -fering** **1**
INTERPOSE : interponerse, hacer inter-
ferencia ⟨to interfere with a play : obstruir una jugada⟩ **2** MEDDLE : entrometerse, interferir, intervenir **3 to
interfere with** DISRUPT : afectar (una
actividad), interferir (la transmisión de
una señal) **4 to interfere with** TOUCH
: tocar ⟨someone interfered with my papers : alguien tocó mis papeles⟩
interference [ˌɪntərˈfɪrənts] *n* : interferencia *f*, intromisión *f*

intergalactic [ˌɪntərgəˈlæktɪk] *adj* : intergaláctico

intergovernmental [ˌɪntərˌgʌvərˈmentəl, -vərn-] *adj* : intergubernamental

interim[1] [ˈɪntərəm] *adj* : interino, provisional

interim[2] *n* **1** : interín *m*, intervalo *m* **2 in the interim** : en el interín, mientras tanto

interior[1] [ɪnˈtɪriər] *adj* : interior

interior[2] *n* : interior *m*

interject [ˌɪntərˈdʒɛkt] *vt* : interponer, agregar

interjection [ˌɪntərˈdʒɛklən] *n* **1** : interjección *f* (en lingüística) **2** EXCLAMATION : exclamación *f* **3** INTERRUPTION : interrupción *f*

interlace [ˌɪntərˈleɪs] *vt* -**laced; -lacing** **1** INTERWEAVE : entrelazar **2** INTERSPERSE : intercalar

interlock [ˌɪntərˈlɑk] *vt* **1** UNITE : trabar, unir **2** ENGAGE : engranar — *vi* : entrelazarse, trabarse

interloper [ˌɪntərˈloːpər] *n* **1** INTRUDER : intruso *m*, -sa *f* **2** MEDDLER : entrometido *m*, -da *f*

interlude [ˈɪntərˌluːd] *n* **1** INTERVAL : intervalo *m*, intermedio *m* (en el teatro) **2** : interludio *m* (en música)

intermarriage [ˌɪntərˈmærɪdʒ] *n* **1** : matrimonio *m* mixto (entre miembros de distintas razas o religiones) **2** : matrimonio *m* entre miembros del mismo grupo

intermarry [ˌɪntərˈmæri] *vi* -**married; -marrying** **1** : casarse (con miembros de otros grupos) **2** : casarse entre sí (con miembros del mismo grupo)

intermediary[1] [ˌɪntərˈmiːdiˌɛri] *adj* : intermediario

intermediary[2] *n, pl* -**aries** : intermediario *m*, -ria *f*

intermediate[1] [ˌɪntərˈmiːdiət] *adj* : intermedio

intermediate[2] *n* GO-BETWEEN : intermediario *m*, -ria *f*; mediador *m*, -dora *f*

interment [ɪnˈtərmənt] *n* : entierro *m*

interminable [ɪnˈtərmənəbəl] *adj* : interminable, constante — **interminably** [-bli] *adv*

intermingle [ˌɪntərˈmɪŋgəl] *vt* -**mingled; -mingling** : entremezclar, mezclar — *vi* : entremezclarse

intermission [ˌɪntərˈmɪlən] *n* : intermisión *f*, intervalo *m*, intermedio *m*

intermittent [ˌɪntərˈmɪtənt] *adj* : intermitente — **intermittently** *adv*

intermix [ˌɪntərˈmɪks] *vt* : entremezclar

intern[1] [ˈɪnˌtərn, ɪnˈtərn] *vt* : confinar (durante la guerra) — *vi* : servir de interno, hacer las prácticas

intern[2] [ˈɪnˌtərn] *n* : interno *m*, -na *f*

internal [ɪnˈtərnəl] *adj* : interno, interior ⟨internal bleeding : hemorragia interna⟩ ⟨internal affairs : asuntos interiores, asuntos domésticos⟩ — **internally** *adv*

international [ˌɪntərˈnæɫənəl] *adj* : internacional — **internationally** *adv*

internationalize [ˌɪntərˈnæɫənəˌlaɪz] *vt* -**ized; -izing** : internacionalizar

internecine [ˌɪntərˈnɛˌsiːn, ɪnˈtərnəˌsiːn] *adj* : intestino, interno

Internet [ˈɪntərˌnɛt] *n* : Internet *mf*

Internet café *n* : cibercafé *m*

Internet service provider → ISP

internist [ˈɪnˌtərnɪst] *n* : internista *mf*

internment [ɪˈtərnmənt] *n* : internamiento *m*

interpersonal [ˌɪntərˈpərsənəl] *adj* : interpersonal

interplay [ˈɪntərˌpleɪ] *n* : interacción *f*, juego *m*

interpolate [ɪnˈtərpəˌleɪt] *vt* -**lated; -lating** : interpolar

interpose [ˌɪntərˈpoːz] *v* -**posed; -posing** *vt* : interponer, interrumpir con — *vi* : interponerse

interpret [ɪnˈtərprət] *vt* : interpretar

interpretation [ɪnˌtərprəˈteɪlən] *n* : interpretación *f*

interpretative [ɪnˈtərprəˌteɪtɪv] *adj* : interpretativo

interpreter [ɪnˈtərprəˌtər] *n* : intérprete *mf*

interpretive [ɪnˈtərprəˌtɪv] *adj* : interpretativo

interracial [ˌɪntərˈreɪləl] *adj* : interracial

interrelate [ˌɪntərɪˈleɪt] *v* -**related; -relating** : interrelacionar

interrelationship [ˌɪntərɪˈleɪlənˌlɪp] *n* : interrelación *f*

interrogate [ɪnˈtɛrəˌgeɪt] *vt* -**gated; -gating** : interrogar, someter a un interrogatorio

interrogation [ɪnˌtɛrəˈgeɪlən] *n* : interrogatorio *m*, interrogación *f*

interrogative[1] [ˌɪntəˈrɑgətɪv] *adj* : interrogativo

interrogative[2] *n* : interrogativo *m*

interrogator [ɪnˈtɛrəˌgeɪtər] *n* : interrogador *m*, -dora *f*

interrogatory [ˌɪntəˈrɑgəˌtori] *adj* → **interrogative**[1]

interrupt [ˌɪntəˈrʌpt] *v* : interrumpir

interruption [ˌɪntəˈrʌplən] *n* : interrupción *f*

intersect [ˌɪntərˈsɛkt] *vt* : cruzar, cortar — *vi* : cruzarse (dícese de los caminos), intersecarse (dícese de las líneas o figuras), cortarse

intersection [ˌɪntərˈsɛklən] *n* : intersección *f*, cruce *m*

intersperse [ˌɪntərˈspərs] *vt* -**spersed; -spersing** : intercalar, entremezclar

interstate [ˌɪntərˈsteɪt] *adj* : interestatal

interstellar [ˌɪntərˈstɛlər] *adj* : interestelar

interstice [ɪnˈtərstəs] *n, pl* -**stices** [-stəˌsiːz, -stəsəz] : intersticio *m*

intertwine [ˌɪntərˈtwaɪn] *vi* -**twined; -twining** : entrelazarse

interval [ˈɪntərvəl] *n* : intervalo *m*

intervene [ˌɪntərˈviːn] *vi* -**vened; -vening** **1** ELAPSE : transcurrir, pasar ⟨the intervening years : los años intermediarios⟩ **2** INTERCEDE : intervenir, interceder, mediar

intervention [ˌɪntərˈvɛntlən] *n* : intervención *f*

interview[1] [ˈɪntərˌvjuː] *vt* : entrevistar — *vi* : hacer entrevistas

interview[2] *n* : entrevista *f*

interviewer ['ɪntər,vju:ər] *n* : entrevistador *m*, -dora *f*
interweave [,ɪntər'wi:v] *v* **-wove** [-'wo:v]; **-woven** [-'wo:vən]; **-weaving** *vt* : entretejer, entrelazar — *vi* INTERTWINE : entrelazarse, entretejerse
interwoven [,ɪntər'wo:vən] *adj* : entretejido
intestate [ɪn'tɛs,teɪt, -tət] *adj* : intestado
intestinal [ɪn'tɛstənəl] *adj* : intestinal
intestine [ɪn'tɛstən] *n* **1** : intestino *m* **2 small intestine** : intestino *m* delgado **3 large intestine** : intestino *m* grueso
intimacy ['ɪntəməsi] *n*, *pl* **-cies 1** CLOSENESS : intimidad *f* **2** FAMILIARITY : familiaridad *f*
intimate[1] ['ɪntə,meɪt] *vt* **-mated; -mating** : insinuar, dar a entender
intimate[2] ['ɪntəmət] *adj* **1** CLOSE : íntimo, de confianza ⟨intimate friends : amigos íntimos⟩ **2** PRIVATE : íntimo, privado ⟨intimate clubs : clubes íntimos⟩ **3** INNERMOST, SECRET : íntimo, secreto ⟨intimate fantasies : fantasías secretas⟩
intimate[3] *n* : amigo *m* íntimo, amiga *f* íntima
intimidate [ɪn'tɪmə,deɪt] *vt* **-dated; -dating** : intimidar
intimidation [ɪn,tɪmə'deɪɪən] *n* : intimidación *f*
into ['ɪn,tu:] *prep* **1** (*indicating motion*) : en, a, contra, dentro de ⟨she got into bed : se metió en la cama⟩ ⟨to get into a plane : subir a un avión⟩ ⟨he crashed into the wall : chocó contra la pared⟩ ⟨looking into the sun : mirando al sol⟩ ⟨staring into space : mirando al vacío⟩ **2** (*indicating state or condition*) : a, en ⟨to burst into tears : echarse a llorar⟩ ⟨the water turned into ice : el agua se convirtió en hielo⟩ ⟨to translate into English : traducir al inglés⟩ **3** (*indicating time*) ⟨far into the night : hasta bien entrada la noche⟩ ⟨he's well into his eighties : tiene los ochenta bien cumplidos⟩ **4** (*in mathematics*) ⟨3 into 12 is 4 : 12 dividido por 3 es 4⟩ **5** *fam* (*indicating interest or involvement*) ⟨he's really into sports : le ha dado fuerte por los deportes⟩
intolerable [ɪn'tɑlərəbəl] *adj* : intolerable — **intolerably** [-bli] *adv*
intolerance [ɪn'tɑlərənts] *n* : intolerancia *f*
intolerant [ɪn'tɑlərənt] *adj* : intolerante
intonation [,ɪnto'neɪɪən] *n* : entonación *f*
intone [ɪn'to:n] *vt* **-toned; -toning** : entonar
intoxicant [ɪn'tɑksɪkənt] *n* : bebida *f* alcohólica
intoxicate [ɪn'tɑksə,keɪt] *vt* **-cated; -cating** : emborrachar, embriagar
intoxicated [ɪn'tɑksə,keɪtəd] *adj* : borracho, embriagado
intoxicating [ɪn'tɑksə,keɪtɪŋ] *adj* : embriagador
intoxication [ɪn,tɑksə'keɪɪən] *n* : embriaguez *f*
intractable [ɪn'træktəbəl] *adj* : obstinado, intratable

intramural [,ɪntrə'mjʊrəl] *adj* : interno, dentro de la universidad
intransigence [ɪn'trænsədʒənts, -'trænzə-] *n* : intransigencia *f*
intransigent [ɪn'trænsədʒənt, -'trænzə-] *adj* : intransigente
intransitive [ɪn'trænsətɪv, -'trænzə-] *adj* : intransitivo
intrauterine device [,ɪntrə'ju:tərən-] *n* : dispositivo *m* intrauterino, DIU *m*
intravenous [,ɪntrə'vi:nəs] *adj* : intravenoso — **intravenously** *adv*
intrepid [ɪn'trɛpəd] *adj* : intrépido
intricacy ['ɪntrɪkəsi] *n*, *pl* **-cies** : complejidad *f*, lo intrincado
intricate ['ɪntrɪkət] *adj* : intrincado, complicado — **intricately** *adv*
intrigue[1] [ɪn'tri:g] *v* **-trigued; -triguing** : intrigar
intrigue[2] ['ɪn,tri:g, ɪn'tri:g] *n* : intriga *f*
intriguing [ɪn'tri:gɪŋ] *adj* : intrigante, fascinante
intrinsic [ɪn'trɪnzɪk, -'trɪntsɪk] *adj* : intrínseco, esencial — **intrinsically** [-zɪkli, -sɪ-] *adv*
intro ['ɪntro] *n fam* → **introduction**
introduce [,ɪntrə'du:s, -'dju:s] *vt* **-duced; -ducing 1** : presentar ⟨let me introduce my father : permítame presentar a mi padre⟩ ⟨to introduce oneself : presentarse⟩ **2** : introducir (algo nuevo), lanzar (un producto), presentar (una ley), proponer (una idea o un tema)
introduction [,ɪntrə'dʌkɪən] *n* : introducción *f*, presentación *f*
introductory [,ɪntrə'dʌktəri] *adj* : introductorio, preliminar, de introducción
introspection [,ɪntrə'spɛkɪən] *n* : introspección *f*
introspective [,ɪntrə'spɛktɪv] *adj* : introspectivo — **introspectively** *adv*
introvert ['ɪntrə,vərt] *n* : introvertido *m*, -da *f*
introverted ['ɪntrə,vərtəd] *adj* : introvertido
intrude [ɪn'tru:d] *v* **-truded; -truding** *vi* **1** INTERFERE : inmiscuirse, entrometerse **2** DISTURB, INTERRUPT : molestar, estorbar, interrumpir — *vt* : introducir por fuerza
intruder [ɪn'tru:dər] *n* : intruso *m*, -sa *f*
intrusion [ɪn'tru:ʒən] *n* : intrusión *f*
intrusive [ɪn'tru:sɪv] *adj* : intruso
intuit [ɪn'tu:ɪt, -'tju:-] *vt* : intuir
intuition [,ɪntʊ'ɪɪən, -tju-] *n* : intuición *f*
intuitive [ɪn'tu:ətɪv, -'tju:-] *adj* : intuitivo — **intuitively** *adv*
inundate ['ɪnən,deɪt] *vt* **-dated; -dating** : inundar
inundation [,ɪnən'deɪɪən] *n* : inundación *f*
inure [ɪ'nʊr, -'njʊr] *vt* **-ured; -uring** : acostumbrar, habituar
invade [ɪn'veɪd] *vt* **-vaded; -vading** : invadir
invader [ɪn'veɪdər] *n* : invasor *m*, -sora *f*
invalid[1] [ɪn'væləd] *adj* : inválido, nulo
invalid[2] ['ɪnvələd] *adj* : inválido, discapacitado
invalid[3] ['ɪnvələd] *n* : inválido *m*, -da *f*
invalidate [ɪn'vælə,deɪt] *vt* **-dated; -dating** : invalidar

invalidity [ˌɪnvəˈlɪdət̬i] *n, pl* **-ties** : invalidez *f*, falta de validez *f*

invaluable [ɪnˈvæljəbəl, -ˈvæljʊə-] *adj* : invalorable, inestimable, inapreciable

invariable [ɪnˈværiəbəl] *adj* : invariable, constante — **invariably** [-bli] *adv*

invasion [ɪnˈveɪʒən] *n* : invasión *f*

invasive [ɪnˈveɪsɪv] *adj* : invasivo

invective [ɪnˈvɛktɪv] *n* : invectiva *f*, improperio *m*

inveigh [ɪnˈveɪ] *vi* **to inveigh against** : arremeter contra, lanzar invectivas contra

inveigle [ɪnˈveɪgəl, -ˈviː-] *vt* **-gled; -gling** : engatusar, embaucar, persuadir con engaños

invent [ɪnˈvɛnt] *vt* : inventar

invention [ɪnˈvɛntən] *n* : invención *f*, invento *m*

inventive [ɪnˈvɛntɪv] *adj* : inventivo

inventiveness [ɪnˈvɛntɪvnəs] *n* : ingenio *m*, inventiva *f*

inventor [ɪnˈvɛntər] *n* : inventor *m*, -tora *f*

inventory¹ [ˈɪnvənˌtɔri] *vt* **-ried; -rying** : inventariar

inventory² *n, pl* **-ries** **1** LIST : inventario *m* **2** STOCK : existencias *fpl*

inverse¹ [ɪnˈvərs, ˈɪnˌvərs] *adj* : inverso — **inversely** *adv*

inverse² *n* : inverso *m*

inversion [ɪnˈvərʒən] *n* : inversión *f*

invert [ɪnˈvərt] *vt* : invertir

invertebrate¹ [ɪnˈvərt̬əbrət, -ˌbreɪt] *adj* : invertebrado

invertebrate² *n* : invertebrado *m*

invest [ɪnˈvɛst] *vt* **1** AUTHORIZE : investir, autorizar **2** CONFER : conferir **3** : invertir, dedicar ⟨he invested his savings in stocks : invirtió sus ahorros en acciones⟩ ⟨to invest one's time : dedicar uno su tiempo⟩

investigate [ɪnˈvɛstəˌgeɪt] *v* **-gated; -gating** : investigar

investigation [ɪnˌvɛstəˈgeɪʃən] *n* : investigación *f*, estudio *m*

investigative [ɪnˈvɛstəˌgeɪt̬ɪv] *adj* : investigador

investigator [ɪnˈvɛstəˌgeɪt̬ər] *n* : investigador *m*, -dora *f*

investiture [ɪnˈvɛstəˌtʊr, -tɫər] *n* : investidura *f*

investment [ɪnˈvɛstmənt] *n* : inversión *f*

investor [ɪnˈvɛstər] *n* : inversor *m*, -sora *f*; inversionista *mf*

inveterate [ɪnˈvɛt̬ərət] *adj* **1** DEEP-SEATED : inveterado, enraizado **2** HABITUAL : empedernido, incorregible

invidious [ɪnˈvɪdiəs] *adj* **1** OBNOXIOUS : repugnante, odioso **2** UNJUST : injusto — **invidiously** *adv*

invigorate [ɪnˈvɪgəˌreɪt] *vt* **-rated; -rating** : vigorizar, animar

invigorating [ɪnˈvɪgəˌreɪt̬ɪŋ] *adj* : vigorizante, estimulante

invincibility [ɪnˌvɪnsəˈbɪləti] *n* : invencibilidad *f*

invincible [ɪnˈvɪntsəbəl] *adj* : invencible — **invincibly** [-bli] *adv*

inviolable [ɪnˈvaɪələbəl] *adj* : inviolable

inviolate [ɪnˈvaɪələt] *adj* : inviolado, puro

invisibility [ɪnˌvɪzəˈbɪləti] *n* : invisibilidad *f*

invisible [ɪnˈvɪzəbəl] *adj* : invisible — **invisibly** [-bli] *adv*

invitation [ˌɪnvəˈteɪʃən] *n* : invitación *f*

invite [ɪnˈvaɪt] *vt* **-vited; -viting** **1** ATTRACT : atraer, tentar ⟨a book that invites interest : un libro que atrae el interés⟩ **2** PROVOKE : provocar, buscar ⟨to invite trouble : buscarse problemas⟩ **3** ASK : invitar ⟨we invited them for dinner : los invitamos a cenar⟩ **4** SOLICIT : solicitar, buscar (preguntas, comentarios, etc.)

inviting [ɪnˈvaɪt̬ɪŋ] *adj* : atractivo, atrayente

invocation [ˌɪnvəˈkeɪʃən] *n* : invocación *f*

invoice¹ [ˈɪnˌvɔɪs] *vt* **-voiced; -voicing** : facturar

invoice² *n* : factura *f*

invoke [ɪnˈvoːk] *vt* **-voked; -voking** **1** : invocar, apelar a ⟨she invoked our aid : apeló a nuestra ayuda⟩ **2** CITE : invocar, citar ⟨to invoke a precedent : invocar un precedente⟩ **3** CONJURE UP : hacer aparecer, invocar

involuntary [ɪnˈvɑlənˌteri] *adj* : involuntario — **involuntarily** [ɪn-ˌvɑlənˈtrɛli] *adv*

involve [ɪnˈvɑlv] *vt* **-volved; -volving** **1** ENGAGE : ocupar (con una tarea, etc.) **2** IMPLICATE : involucrar, enredar, implicar ⟨to be involved in a crime : estar involucrado en un crimen⟩ **3** CONCERN : concernir, afectar **4** CONNECT : conectar, relacionar **5** ENTAIL, INCLUDE : suponer, incluir, consistir en ⟨what does the job involve? : ¿en qué consiste el trabajo?⟩ **6** **to be involved with someone** : tener una relación (amorosa) con alguien

involved [ɪnˈvɑlvd] *adj* **1** COMPLEX, INTRICATE : complicado, complejo **2** CONCERNED : interesado, afectado

involvement [ɪnˈvɑlvmənt] *n* **1** PARTICIPATION : participación *f*, complicidad *f* **2** RELATIONSHIP : relación *f*

invulnerable [ɪnˈvʌlnərəbəl] *adj* : invulnerable

inward¹ [ˈɪnwərd] *or* **inwards** [-wərdz] *adv* : hacia adentro, hacia el interior

inward² *adj* INSIDE : interior, interno

inwardly [ˈɪnwərdli] *adv* **1** MENTALLY, SPIRITUALLY : por dentro **2** INTERNALLY : internamente, interiormente **3** PRIVATELY : para sus adentros, para sí

iodine [ˈaɪəˌdaɪn, -dən] *n* : yodo *m*, tintura *f* de yodo

ion [ˈaɪən, ˈaɪˌɑn] *n* : ion *m*

ionic [aɪˈɑnɪk] *adj* : iónico

ionize [ˈaɪəˌnaɪz] *v* **ionized; ionizing** : ionizar

ionosphere [aɪˈɑnəˌsfɪr] *n* : ionosfera *f*

iota [aɪˈoːt̬ə] *n* : pizca *f*, ápice *m*

IOU [ˌaɪˌoˈjuː] *n* : pagaré *m*, vale *m*

IPA [ˌaɪˌpiːˈeɪ] *n* (*International Phonetic Alphabet*) : AFI *m*

IQ [ˌaɪˈkjuː] *n* (*intelligence quotient*) : CI *m*, coeficiente *m* intelectual

Iranian [ɪˈreɪniən, -ˈræ-, -ˈrɑ-;, aɪˈ-] *n* : iraní *mf* — **Iranian** *adj*

Iraqi [ɪ'rɑki:] *n* : iraquí *mf* — **Iraqi** *adj*
irascibility [ɪ,ræsə'bɪləti] *n* : irascibilidad *f*
irascible [ɪ'ræsəbəl] *adj* : irascible
irate [aɪ'reɪt] *adj* : furioso, airado, iracundo — **irately** *adv*
ire ['aɪr] *n* : ira *f*, cólera *f*
iridescence [,ɪrə'dɛsənts] *n* : iridiscencia *f*
iridescent [,ɪrə'dɛsənt] *adj* : iridiscente
iridium [ɪ'rɪdiəm] *n* : iridio *m*
iris ['aɪrəs] *n*, *pl* **irises** *or* **irides** ['aɪrə,di:z, 'ɪr-] **1** : iris *m* (del ojo) **2** : lirio *m* (planta)
Irish[1] ['aɪrɪl] *adj* : irlandés
Irish[2] **1** : irlandés *m* (idioma) **2 the Irish** (*used with a plural verb*) : los irlandeses
Irishman ['aɪrɪlmən] *n*, *pl* **-men** : irlandés *m*
Irishwoman ['aɪrɪl,wʊmən] *n*, *pl* **-women** : irlandesa *f*
irk ['ərk] *vt* : fastidiar, irritar, preocupar
irksome ['ərksəm] *adj* : irritante, fastidioso — **irksomely** *adv*
iron[1] ['aɪərn] *v* **1** : planchar **2 to iron out** : resolver
iron[2] *n* **1** : hierro *m*, fierro *m* ⟨a will of iron : una voluntad de hierro, una voluntad férrea⟩ **2** : plancha *f* (para planchar la ropa)
ironclad ['aɪərn'klæd] *adj* **1** : acorazado, blindado **2** STRICT : riguroso, estricto
ironic [aɪ'rɑnɪk] *or* **ironical** [-nɪkəl] *adj* : irónico — **ironically** [-kli] *adv*
ironing ['aɪərnɪŋ] *n* **1** PRESSING : planchada *f* **2** : ropa *f* para planchar
ironing board *n* : tabla *f* (de planchar)
ironwork ['aɪərn,wərk] *n* **1** : obra *f* de hierro **2 ironworks** *npl* : fundición *f*
irony ['aɪrəni] *n*, *pl* **-nies** : ironía *f*
irradiate [ɪ'reɪdi,eɪt] *vt* **-ated; -ating** : irradiar, radiar
irradiation [ɪ,reɪdi'eɪʃən] *n* : irradiación *f*, radiación *f*
irrational [ɪ'ræʃənəl] *adj* : irracional — **irrationally** *adv*
irrationality [ɪ,ræʃə'næləti] *n*, *pl* **-ties** : irracionalidad *f*
irreconcilable [ɪ,rɛkən'saɪləbəl] *adj* : irreconciliable
irrecoverable [,ɪrɪ'kʌvərəbəl] *adj* : irrecuperable — **irrecoverably** [-bli] *adv*
irredeemable [,ɪrɪ'di:məbəl] *adj* **1** : irredimible (dícese de un bono) **2** HOPELESS : irremediable, irreparable
irrefutable [,ɪrɪ'fju:təbəl, ɪɪ'refjə-] *adj* : irrefutable
irregular[1] [ɪ'rɛgjələr] *adj* : irregular — **irregularly** *adv*
irregular[2] *n* **1** : soldado *m* irregular **2 irregulars** *npl* : artículos *mpl* defectuosos
irregularity [ɪ,rɛgjə'lærəti] *n*, *pl* **-ties** : irregularidad *f*
irrelevance [ɪ'rɛləvənts] *n* : irrelevancia *f*
irrelevant [ɪ'rɛləvənt] *adj* : irrelevante
irreligious [,ɪrɪ'lɪdʒəs] *adj* : irreligioso
irreparable [ɪ'rɛpərəbəl] *adj* : irreparable
irreplaceable [,ɪrɪ'pleɪsəbəl] *adj* : irreemplazable, insustituible
irrepressible [,ɪrɪ'presəbəl] *adj* : incontenible, incontrolable

irreproachable [,ɪrɪ'pro:tləbəl] *adj* : irreprochable, intachable
irresistible [,ɪrɪ'zɪstəbəl] *adj* : irresistible — **irresistibly** [-bli] *adv*
irresolute [ɪ'rɛzə,lu:t] *adj* : irresoluto, indeciso
irresolutely [ɪ'rɛzə,lu:tli, -,rzə'lu:t-] *adv* : de manera indecisa
irresolution [ɪ,rɛzə'lu:lən] *n* : irresolución *f*
irrespective of [,ɪrɪ'spɛktɪvəv] *prep* : sin tomar en consideración, sin tener en cuenta
irresponsibility [,ɪrɪ,spantsə'bɪləti] *n*, *pl* **-ties** : irresponsabilidad *f*, falta *f* de responsabilidad
irresponsible [,ɪrɪ'spantsəbəl] *adj* : irresponsable — **irresponsibly** [-bli] *adv*
irretrievable [,ɪrɪ'tri:vəbəl] *adj* IRRECOVERABLE : irrecuperable
irreverence [ɪ'rɛvərənts] *n* : irreverencia *f*, falta *f* de respeto
irreverent [ɪ'rɛvərənt] *adj* : irreverente, irrespetuoso
irreversible [,ɪrɪ'vərsəbəl] *adj* : irreversible
irrevocable [ɪ'rɛvəkəbəl] *adj* : irrevocable — **irrevocably** [-bli] *adv*
irrigate ['ɪrə,geɪt] *vt* **-gated; -gating** : irrigar, regar
irrigation [,ɪrə'geɪlən] *n* : irrigación *f*, riego *m*
irritability [,ɪrətə'bɪləti] *n*, *pl* **-ties** : irritabilidad *f*
irritable ['ɪrətəbəl] *adj* : irritable, colérico
irritably ['ɪrətəbli] *adv* : con irritación
irritant[1] ['ɪrətənt] *adj* : irritante
irritant[2] *n* : agente *m* irritante
irritate ['ɪrə,teɪt] *vt* **-tated; -tating 1** ANNOY : irritar, molestar **2** : irritar (en medicina)
irritating ['ɪrə,teɪtɪŋ] *adj* : irritante
irritatingly ['ɪrə,teɪtɪŋli] *adv* : de modo irritante, fastidiosamente
irritation [,ɪrə'teɪlən] *n* : irritación *f*
is → **be**
-ish [,ɪl] *suf* ALMOST, APPROXIMATELY ⟨grayish : grisáceo⟩ ⟨she's fiftyish : tiene unos cincuenta años⟩
Islam [ɪs'lɑm, ɪz-, -'læm;, 'ɪs,lɑm, 'ɪz-, -,læm] *n* : el Islam
Islamic [ɪs'lɑmɪk, ɪz-, -'læ-] *adj* : islámico
Islamism [ɪs'lɑ,mɪzəm, ɪz-, -'læ-;, 'ɪzlə-] *n* : islamismo *m* — **Islamist** *n*
island ['aɪlənd] *n* : isla *f*
islander ['aɪləndər] *n* : isleño *m*, -ña *f*
isle ['aɪl] *n* : isla *f*, islote *m*
islet ['aɪlət] *n* : islote *m*
isn't ['ɪzənt] *contraction of* IS NOT → **be**
isolate ['aɪsə,leɪt] *vt* **-lated; -lating** : aislar
isolated ['aɪsə,leɪtəd] *adj* : aislado, solo
isolation [,aɪsə'leɪlən] *n* : aislamiento *m*
isometric [,aɪsə'mɛtrɪk] *adj* : isométrico
isometrics [,aɪsə'mɛtrɪks] *ns* & *pl* : isometría *f*
isosceles [aɪ'sɑsə,li:z] *adj* : isósceles
isotope ['aɪsə,to:p] *n* : isótopo *m*
ISP [,aɪ,ɛs'pi:] *n* (Internet service provider) : PSI *m*, proveedor *m* de servicios de Internet

Israeli [ɪz'reɪli] *n* : israelí *mf* — **Israeli** *adj*
issue¹ ['ɪˌʃuː] *v* -**sued**; -**suing** *vi* **1**
EMERGE : emerger, salir, fluir **2** DES-
CEND : descender (dícese de los padres o
antepasados específicos) **3** EMANATE,
RESULT : emanar, surgir, resultar —
vt **1** EMIT : emitir **2** DISTRIBUTE
: emitir, distribuir (to issue a new stamp
: emitir un sello nuevo) **3** PUBLISH
: publicar
issue² *n* **1** EMERGENCE, FLOW : emergencia *f*, flujo *m* **2** PROGENY : descendencia *f*, progenie *f* **3** OUTCOME, RE-
SULT : desenlace *m*, resultado *m*,
consecuencia *f* **4** MATTER, QUESTION
: asunto *m*, cuestión *f* (to avoid the issue
: evitar el tema) (to make an issue of
something : darle demasiada importancia a algo) **5** PUBLICATION : publicación *f*, distribución *f*, emisión *f* **6**
: número *m* (de un periódico o una revista)
isthmus ['ɪsməs] *n* : istmo *m*
it ['ɪt] *pron* **1** (*as subject; generally omitted*) : él, ella, ello (it's a big building : es
un edificio grande) (who was it? : ¿quién
era?) (one more and that's it : uno más y
se acabó) **2** (*as indirect object*) : le (I'll
give it some water : voy a darle agua)
(give it time : dale tiempo) **3** (*as direct
object*) : lo, la (give it to me : dámelo) (I
don't understand it : no lo entiendo)
(stop it! : ¡basta!) **4** (*as object of a preposition; generally omitted*) : él, ella, ello
(behind it : detrás, detrás de él) **5** (*in
impersonal constructions*) (it's raining
: está lloviendo) (what time is it? : ¿qué
hora es?) (it's 8 o'clock : son las ocho)
(it's hot/cold : hace calor/frío) **6** (*as the
implied subject or object of a verb*) (it is
necessary to study : es necesario estudiar) (it's good to see you : (me) da gusto
verte) (it is known/said that . . . : se
sabe/dice que . . .) (it would seem so
: eso parece) (to give it all one's got : dar
lo mejor de sí)
Italian [ɪ'tælien, aɪ-] *n* **1** : italiano *m*, -na
f **2** : italiano *m* (idioma) — **Italian** *adj*
italic¹ [ɪ'tælɪk, aɪ-] *adj* : en cursiva, en bastardilla

italic² *n* : cursiva *f*, bastardilla *f*
italicize [ɪ'tæləˌsaɪz, aɪ-] *vt* -**cized**; -**cizing**
: poner en cursiva
itch¹ ['ɪtʃ] *vi* **1** : picar (her arm itched : le
pica el brazo) **2** : morirse (they were
itching to go outside : se morían por
salir) — *vt* : dar picazón, hacer picar
itch² *n* **1** ITCHING : picazón *f*, picor *m*,
comezón *f* **2** RASH : sarpullido *m*, erupción *f* **3** DESIRE : ansia *f*, deseo *m*
itchiness ['ɪtʃinəs] *n* ITCHING : picazón *f*,
picor *m*, comezón *f*
itchy ['ɪtʃi] *adj* **itchier**; -**est** : que pica, que
da comezón
it'd ['ɪtəd] *contraction of* IT HAD *or* IT
WOULD → **have**, **would**
item ['aɪtəm] *n* **1** OBJECT : artículo *m*,
pieza *f* (item of clothing : prenda de vestir) **2** : punto *m* (en una agenda),
número *m* (en el teatro), ítem *m* (en un
documento) **3 news item** : noticia *f*
itemization [ˌaɪtəməˈzeɪlən] *n* : desglose
m
itemize ['aɪtəˌmaɪz] *vt* -**ized**; -**izing** : detallar, enumerar, listar
itinerant [aɪ'tɪnərənt] *adj* : itinerante, ambulante
itinerary [aɪ'tɪnəˌrɛri] *n, pl* -**aries** : itinerario *m*
it'll ['ɪtəl] *contraction of* IT SHALL *or* IT
WILL → **shall**, **will**
its ['ɪts] *adj* : su, sus (its kennel : su perrera) (a city and its inhabitants : una
ciudad y sus habitantes)
it's ['ɪts] *contraction of* IT IS *or* IT HAS →
be, **have**
itself [ɪt'sɛlf] *pron* **1** (*used reflexively*) : se
(the cat gave itself a bath : el gato se
bañó) **2** (*used for emphasis*) : (él)
mismo, (ella) misma, sí (mismo), solo
(he is courtesy itself : es la misma cortesía) (in and of itself : por sí mismo) (it
opened by itself : se abrió solo)
IUD [ˌaɪˌjuːˈdiː] *n* (intrauterine *d*evice)
: DIU *m*, dispositivo *m* intrauterino
I've ['aɪv] *contraction of* I HAVE → **have**
ivory ['aɪvəri] *n, pl* -**ries** **1** : marfil *m* **2**
: color *m* de marfil
ivy ['aɪvi] *n, pl* **ivies** **1** : hiedra *f*, yedra
f **2** → **poison ivy**

J

j ['dʒeɪ] *n, pl* **j's** *or* **js** ['dʒeɪz] : décima letra
del alfabeto inglés
jab¹ ['dʒæb] *v* **jabbed**; **jabbing** *vt* **1**
PUNCTURE : clavar, pinchar **2** POKE
: dar, golpear (con la punta de algo) (he
jabbed me in the ribs : me dio un codazo
en las costillas) — *vi* **to jab at** : dar, golpear
jab² *n* **1** PRICK : pinchazo *m* **2** POKE
: golpe *m* abrupto
jabber ['dʒæbər] *v* : farfullar
jack¹ ['dʒæk] *vt* **to jack up** **1** : levantar (con
un gato) **2** INCREASE : subir, aumentar

jack² *n* **1** : gato *m*, cric *m* (hydraulic
jack : gato hidráulico) **2** FLAG : pabellón *m* **3** SOCKET : enchufe *m* hembra **4** : jota *f*, valet *m* (jack of hearts
: jota de corazones) **5 jacks** *npl* : cantillos *mpl*
jackal ['dʒækəl] *n* : chacal *m*
jackass ['dʒækˌæs] *n* : asno *m*, burro *m*
jacket ['dʒækət] *n* **1** : chaqueta *f* **2** COVER
: sobrecubierta *f* (de un libro), carátula *f*
(de un disco)
jackhammer ['dʒækˌhæmər] *n* : martillo
m neumático

jack–in–the–box [ˈʤækɪndəˌbɑks] *n*
: caja *f* de sorpresa
jackknife¹ [ˈʤækˌnaɪf] *vi* **-knifed; -knifing**
: doblarse como una navaja, plegarse
jackknife² *n* : navaja *f*
jack–of–all–trades *n* : persona *f* que sabe
un poco de todo, persona *f* de muchos
oficios
jack–o'–lantern [ˈʤækəˌlæntərn] *n* : linterna *f* hecha de una calabaza
jackpot [ˈʤækˌpɑt] *n* **1** : primer premio
m, gordo *m* **2 to hit the jackpot**
: sacarse la lotería, sacarse el gordo
jackrabbit [ˈʤækˌræbət] *n* : liebre *f*
grande de Norteamérica
Jacuzzi [ʤəˈkuːzi] *trademark* se usa para
una bañera de hidromasaje
jade [ˈʤeɪd] *n* : jade *m*
jaded [ˈʤeɪdəd] *adj* **1** TIRED : agotado **2**
BORED : hastiado
jagged [ˈʤægəd] *adj* : dentado, mellado
jaguar [ˈʤægˌwɑr, ˈʤægjuˌwɑr] *n* : jaguar
m
jai alai [ˈhaɪˌlaɪ] *n* : jai alai *m*, pelota *f*
vasca
jail¹ [ˈʤeɪl] *vt* : encarcelar
jail² *n* : cárcel *f*
jailbreak [ˈʤeɪlˌbreɪk] *n* : fuga *f*, huida *f*
(de la cárcel)
jailer *or* **jailor** [ˈʤeɪlər] *n* : carcelero *m*, -ra
f
jalapeño [ˌhɑləˈpeɪnjo, ˌhæ-, -ˈpiːno] *n*
: jalapeño *m*
jalopy [ʤəˈlɑpi] *n, pl* **-lopies** : cacharro *m*
fam, carro *m* destartalado
jalousie [ˈʤæləsi] *n* : celosía *f*
jam¹ [ˈʤæm] *v* **jammed; jamming** *vt* **1**
CRAM : apiñar, embutir, atiborrar
⟨jammed with people : atestado de
gente⟩ **2** STICK, THRUST : meter **3**
BLOCK : atascar, atorar **4** : interferir
(una señal, etc.) **5 to jam on the brakes**
: frenar en seco — *vi* **1** : atascarse,
atrancarse, bloquearse (dícese de un mecanismo) ⟨the copier has jammed : la
fotocopiadora se ha bloqueado/atas-
cado⟩ **2** PLAY *fam* : tocar
jam² *n* **1** *or* **traffic jam** : atasco *m*, embotellamiento *m* (de tráfico) **2** PRE-
DICAMENT : lío *m*, aprieto *m*, apuro
m **3** : mermelada *f* ⟨strawberry jam
: mermelada de fresa⟩
Jamaican [ʤəˈmeɪkən] *n* : jamaiquino *m*,
-na *f*; jamaicano *m*, -na *f* — **Jamaican**
adj
jamb [ˈʤæm] *n* : jamba *f*
jamboree [ˌʤæmbəˈriː] *n* : fiesta *f* grande
jam–packed *adj* : repleto, hasta el tope
(dícese de un recipiente), atestado (de
gente)
jangle¹ [ˈʤæŋgəl] *v* **-gled; -gling** *vi* : hacer
un ruido metálico — *vt* **1** : hacer sonar **2**
to jangle one's nerves : irritar, crispar
jangle² *n* : ruido *m* metálico
janitor [ˈʤænətər] *n* : portero *m*, -ra *f*;
conserje *mf*
January [ˈʤænjuˌeri] *n* : enero *m* ⟨they
arrived on January 12th, they arrived on
the 12th of January : llegaron el 12 de
enero⟩

Japanese¹ [ˌʤæpəˈniːz, -ˈniːs] *adj* : japonés
Japanese² *n* **1** : japonés *m* (idioma) **2**
the Japanese (*used with a plural verb*)
: los japoneses
jar¹ [ˈʤɑr] *v* **jarred; jarring** *vi* **1** GRATE
: chirriar **2** CLASH : desentonar **3**
SHAKE : sacudirse **4 to jar on** : crispar,
enervar — *vt* JOLT : sacudir
jar² *n* **1** GRATING : chirrido *m* **2** JOLT
: vibración *f*, sacudida *f* **3** : tarro *m*,
bote *m*, pote *m* ⟨a jar of honey : un tarro
de miel⟩
jargon [ˈʤɑrgən] *n* : jerga *f*
jasmine [ˈʤæzmən] *n* : jazmín *m*
jasper [ˈʤæspər] *n* : jaspe *m*
jaundice [ˈʤɔndɪs] *n* : ictericia *f*
jaundiced [ˈʤɔndɪst] *adj* **1** : ictérico **2**
EMBITTERED, RESENTFUL : amargado,
resentido, negativo ⟨with a jaundiced
eye : con una actitud de cinismo⟩
jaunt [ˈʤɔnt] *n* : excursión *f*, paseo *m*
jauntily [ˈʤɔntəli] *adv* : animadamente
jauntiness [ˈʤɔntinəs] *n* : animación *f*,
vivacidad *f*
jaunty [ˈʤɔnti] *adj* **jauntier; -est 1**
SPRIGHTLY : animado, alegre **2** RAKISH
: desenvuelto, desenfadado
java [ˈʤɑvə] *n fam* → **coffee**
Javanese [ˌʤɑvəˈniːz, ˌʤæ-, -ˈniːs] *n* **1**
: javanés *m* (idioma) **2** : javanés *m*,
-nesa *f* — **Javanese** *adj*
javelin [ˈʤævələn] *n* : jabalina *f*
jaw¹ [ˈʤɔ] *vi* GAB : cotorrear *fam*, parlotear *fam*
jaw² *n* **1** : mandíbula *f*, quijada *f* **2**
: mordaza *f* (de una herramienta) **3 the**
jaws of death : las garras *f* de la muerte
jawbone [ˈʤɔˌboːn] *n* : mandíbula *f*
jay [ˈʤeɪ] *n* : arrendajo *m*, chara *f Mex*,
azulejo *m Mex*
jaybird [ˈʤeɪˌbərd] → **jay**
jaywalk [ˈʤeɪˌwɔk] *vi* : cruzar la calle sin
prudencia
jaywalker [ˈʤeɪˌwɔkər] *n* : peatón *m* imprudente
jazz¹ [ˈʤæz] *vt* **to jazz up** : animar, alegrar
jazz² *n* : jazz *m*
jazzy [ˈʤæzi] *adj* **jazzier; -est 1** : con
ritmo de jazz **2** FLASHY SHOWY : llamativo, ostentoso
jealous [ˈʤɛləs] *adj* : celoso, envidioso —
jealously *adv*
jealousy [ˈʤɛləsi] *n* : celos *mpl*, envidia *f*
jeans [ˈʤiːnz] *npl* : jeans *mpl*; vaqueros
mpl; tejanos *mpl*; pantalones *mpl* de
mezclilla *Chile, Mex*
jeep [ˈʤiːp] *n* : jeep *m* (vehículo militar)
Jeep *trademark* se usa para un camión
pequeño
jeer¹ [ˈʤɪr] *vi* **1** BOO : abuchear **2** SCOFF
: mofarse, burlarse — *vt* RIDICULE : mofarse de, burlarse de
jeer² *n* **1** : abucheo *m* **2** TAUNT : mofa *f*,
burla *f*
Jehovah [ʤɪˈhoːvə] *n* : Jehová *m*
jell [ˈʤɛl] *vi* **1** SET : gelificarse, cuajar **2**
FORM : cuajar, formarse (una idea, etc.)
Jell–O [ˈʤɛˌloː] *trademark* se usa para gelatina con sabor a frutas, etc.

jelly *n, pl* **-lies** **1** : jalea *f* **2** GELATIN : gelatina *f*

jellyfish [ˈDɛliˌfɪʃ] *n* : medusa *f*

jeopardize [ˈDɛpərˌdaɪz] *vt* **-dized; -dizing** : arriesgar, poner en peligro

jeopardy [ˈDɛpərdi] *n* : peligro *m*, riesgo *m*

jerk¹ [ˈDərk] *vt* **1** JOLT : sacudir **2** TUG, YANK : darle un tirón a — *vi* JOLT : dar sacudidas ⟨the train jerked along : el tren iba moviéndose a sacudidas⟩

jerk² *n* **1** TUG : tirón *m*, jalón *m* **2** JOLT : sacudida *f* brusca **3** FOOL : estúpido *m*, -da *f*; idiota *mf*

jerkin [ˈDərkən] *n* : chaqueta *f* sin mangas, chaleco *m*

jerky¹ [ˈDərki] *adj* **jerkier; -est** **1** : espasmódico (dícese de los movimientos) **2** CHOPPY : inconexo (dícese de la prosa) — **jerkily** [-kəli] *adv*

jerky² *n* : cecina *f*; tasajo *m*; charqui *m* *Chile, Peru*

jerry–built [ˈDɛriˌbɪlt] *adj* : mal construido, chapucero

jersey [ˈDərzi] *n, pl* **-seys** : jersey *m*

jest¹ [ˈDɛst] *vi* : bromear

jest² *n* : broma *f*, chiste *m*

jester [ˈDɛstər] *n* : bufón *m*, -fona *f*

Jesuit [ˈDɛzuət] *n* : jesuita *m* — **Jesuit** *adj*

Jesus [ˈDiːzəs, -zəz] *n* **1** : Jesús *m* **2 Jesus Christ** : Jesucristo *m* **3 Jesus (Christ)!** *fam* : ¡por Dios!

jet¹ [ˈDɛt] *v* **jetted; jetting** *vt* SPOUT : arrojar a chorros — *vi* **1** GUSH : salir a chorros, chorrear **2** FLY : viajar en avión, volar

jet² *n* **1** STREAM : chorro *m* **2** *or* **jet airplane** : avión *m* a reacción, reactor *m* **3** : azabache *m* (mineral)

jet–black *adj* : negro azabache

jet black *n* : negro *m* azabache

jet engine *n* : reactor *m*, motor *m* a reacción

jet lag *n* : desfase *m* (de) horario

jet–propelled *adj* : a reacción

jetsam [ˈDɛtsəm] *n* **flotsam and jetsam** : restos *mpl*, desechos *mpl*

jettison [ˈDɛtəsən] *vt* **1** : echar al mar **2** DISCARD : desechar, deshacerse de

jetty [ˈDɛti] *n, pl* **-ties** **1** PIER, WHARF : embarcadero *m*, muelle *m* **2** BREAKWATER : malecón *m*, rompeolas *m*

Jew [ˈDuː] *n* : judío *m*, -día *f*

jewel [ˈDuːəl] *n* **1** : joya *f*, alhaja *f* **2** GEM : piedra *f* preciosa, gema *f* **3** : rubí *m* (de un reloj) **4** TREASURE : joya *f*, tesoro *m*

jeweler *or* **jeweller** [ˈDuːələr] *n* : joyero *m*, -ra *f*

jewelry [ˈDuːəlri] *n* : joyas *fpl*, alhajas *fpl* ⟨jewelry store : joyería⟩ ⟨jewelry box : alhajero, joyero⟩

Jewish [ˈDuːɪʃ] *adj* : judío

jibe [ˈDaɪb] *vi* **jibed; jibing** AGREE : concordar

jicama [ˈhiːkəmə] *n* : jícama *f*

jiffy [ˈDɪfi] *n, pl* **-fies** : santiamén *m*, segundo *m*, momento *m*

jig¹ [ˈDɪɡ] *vi* **jigged; jigging** : bailar la giga

jig² *n* **1** : giga *f* **2 the jig is up** : se acabó la fiesta

jigger [ˈDɪɡər] *n* : medida *f* de 1 a 2 onzas (para licores)

jiggle¹ [ˈDɪɡəl] *v* **-gled; -gling** *vt* : agitar o sacudir ligeramente — *vi* : agitarse, vibrar

jiggle² *n* : sacudida *f*, vibración *f*

jigsaw [ˈDɪɡˌsɔ] *n* **1** : sierra *f* de vaivén **2 jigsaw puzzle** : rompecabezas *m*

jihad [Dɪˈhɑːd] *n* : yihad *mf*, jihad *mf* — **jihadist** [Dɪˈhɑːdɪst] *n*

jilt [ˈDɪlt] *vt* : dejar plantado, dar calabazas a

jimmy¹ [ˈDɪmi] *vt* **-mied; -mying** : forzar con una palanqueta

jimmy² *n, pl* **-mies** : palanqueta *f*

jingle¹ [ˈDɪŋɡəl] *v* **-gled; -gling** *vi* : tintinear — *vt* : hacer sonar

jingle² *n* **1** TINKLE : tintineo *m*, retintín *m* **2** : canción *f* rimada

jingoism [ˈDɪŋɡoˌɪzəm] *n* : jingoísmo *m*, patriotería *f*

jingoistic [ˌDɪŋɡoˈɪstɪk] *or* **jingoist** [ˈDɪŋɡoɪst] *adj* : jingoísta, patriotero

jinx¹ [ˈDɪŋks] *vt* : traer mala suerte a, salar *CoRi, Mex*

jinx² *n* **1** : cenizo *m*, -za *f* **2 to put a jinx on** : echarle el mal de ojo a

jitters [ˈDɪɾərz] *npl* : nervios *mpl* ⟨he got the jitters : se puso nervioso⟩

jittery [ˈDɪɾəri] *adj* : nervioso

Jivaro [ˈhiːvəˌroː] *n* : jíbaro *m*, -ra *f*

job [ˈDɑb] *n* **1** : trabajo *m* ⟨he did odd jobs for her : le hizo algunos trabajos⟩ **2** CHORE, TASK : tarea *f*, quehacer *m* **3** EMPLOYMENT : trabajo *m*, empleo *m*, puesto *m*

jobber [ˈDɑbər] *n* MIDDLEMAN : intermediario *m*, -ria *f*

jobless [ˈDɑbləs] *adj* : desempleado

jock [ˈDɑk] *n* : deportista *mf*, atleta *mf*

jockey¹ [ˈDɑki] *v* **-eyed; -eying** *vt* **1** MANIPULATE : manipular **2** MANEUVER : maniobrar — *vi* **to jockey for position** : maniobrar para conseguir algo

jockey² *n, pl* **-eys** : jockey *mf*

jocose [Doˈkoːs] *adj* : jocoso

jocular [ˈDɑkjələr] *adj* : jocoso — **jocularly** *adv*

jocularity [ˌDɑkjʊˈlærəɾi] *n* : jocosidad *f*

jodhpurs [ˈDɑdpərz] *npl* : pantalones *mpl* de montar

joe [ˈDoː] *n fam* **1** GUY, FELLOW : tipo *m* *fam* ⟨an average joe : un hombre cualquiera⟩ **2** → **coffee**

jog¹ [ˈDɑɡ] *v* **jogged; jogging** *vt* **1** NUDGE : dar, empujar, codear **2 to jog one's memory** : refrescar la memoria — *vi* **1** RUN : correr despacio, trotar, hacer footing (como ejercicio) **2** TRUDGE : andar a trote corto

jog² *n* **1** PUSH, SHAKE : empujoncito *m*, sacudida *f* leve **2** TROT : trote *m* corto, footing *m* (en deportes) **3** TWIST : recodo *m*, vuelta *f*, curva *f*

jogger [ˈDɑɡər] *n* : persona *f* que hace footing

jogging [ˈDɑɡɪŋ] *n* : footing *m*, jogging *m*

john [ˈʤɑn] *n fam* TOILET : inodoro *m*

join¹ [ˈʤɔɪn] *vt* **1** CONNECT, LINK : unir, juntar ⟨to join in marriage : unir en matrimonio⟩ ⟨to join hands : tomarse de la mano⟩ **2** ADJOIN : lindar con, colindar con **3** MEET : reunirse con, encontrarse con ⟨we joined them for lunch : nos reunimos con ellos para almorzar⟩ ⟨may I join you? : ¿puedo sentarme aquí?⟩ **4** ACCOMPANY : acompañar **5** : hacerse socio de (una organización), afiliarse a (un partido), entrar en (una empresa) ⟨to join the ranks of : sumarse a las filas de⟩ — *vi* **1** UNITE : unirse **2** MERGE : empalmar (dícese de las carreteras), confluir (dícese de los ríos) **3** : hacerse socio, afiliarse, entrar **4 to join in** PARTICIPATE : participar, tomar parte **5 to join up** ENLIST : enrolarse, alistarse

join² *n* JUNCTURE : juntura *f*, unión *f*

joiner [ˈʤɔɪnər] *n* **1** CARPENTER : carpintero *m*, -ra *f* **2** : persona *f* que se une a varios grupos

joint¹ [ˈʤɔɪnt] *adj* : conjunto, colectivo, mutuo ⟨a joint effort : un esfuerzo conjunto⟩ ⟨a joint account : una cuenta conjunta⟩ — **jointly** *adv*

joint² *n* **1** : articulación *f*, coyuntura *f* ⟨out of joint : dislocado⟩ **2** ROAST : asado *m* **3** JUNCTURE : juntura *f*, unión *f* **4** DIVE : antro *m*, tasca *f* **5** *fam* : porro *m*

joist [ˈʤɔɪst] *n* : viga *f*

joke¹ [ˈʤoːk] *vi* **joked; joking** : bromear

joke² *n* **1** STORY : chiste *m* **2** PRANK : broma *f*

joker [ˈʤoːkər] *n* **1** PRANKSTER : bromista *mf* **2** : comodín *m* (en los naipes)

jokingly [ˈʤoːkɪŋli] *adv* : en broma

jollity [ˈʤɑləti] *n, pl* **-ties** MERRIMENT : alegría *f*, regocijo *m*

jolly [ˈʤɑli] *adj* **jollier; -est** : alegre, jovial

jolt¹ [ˈʤoːlt] *vi* JERK : dar tumbos, dar sacudidas — *vt* : sacudir

jolt² *n* **1** JERK : sacudida *f* brusca **2** SHOCK : golpe *m* (emocional)

jonquil [ˈʤɑŋkwɪl] *n* : junquillo *m*

Jordanian [ʤɔrˈdeɪniən] *n* : jordano *m*, -na *f* — **Jordanian** *adj*

josh [ˈʤɑʃ] *vt* TEASE : tomarle el pelo (a alguien) — *vi* JOKE : bromear

jostle [ˈʤɑsəl] *v* **-tled; -tling** *vi* **1** SHOVE : empujar, dar empellones **2** CONTEND : competir — *vt* **1** SHOVE : empujar **2 to jostle one's way** : abrirse paso a empellones

jot¹ [ˈʤɑt] *vt* **jotted; jotting** : anotar, apuntar ⟨jot it down : apúntalo⟩

jot² *n* BIT : ápice *m*, jota *f*, pizca *f*

jounce¹ [ˈʤaʊnts] *v* **jounced; jouncing** *vt* JOLT : sacudir — *vi* : dar tumbos, dar sacudidas

jounce² *n* JOLT : sacudida *f*, tumbo *m*

journal [ˈʤɜrnəl] *n* **1** DIARY : diario *m* **2** PERIODICAL : revista *f*, publicación *f* periódica **3** NEWSPAPER : periódico *m*, diario *m*

journalism [ˈʤɜrnəlˌɪzəm] *n* : periodismo *m*

journalist [ˈʤɜrnəlɪst] *n* : periodista *mf*

journalistic [ˌʤɜrnəlˈɪstɪk] *adj* : periodístico

journey¹ [ˈʤɜrni] *vi* **-neyed; -neying** : viajar

journey² *n, pl* **-neys** : viaje *m*

journeyman [ˈʤɜrnimən] *n, pl* **-men** [-mən, -ˌmn] : oficial *m*

joust¹ [ˈʤaʊst] *vi* : justar

joust² *n* : justa *f*

jovial [ˈʤoːviəl] *adj* : jovial — **jovially** *adv*

joviality [ˌʤoːviˈæləti] *n* : jovialidad *f*

jowl [ˈʤaʊl] *n* **1** JAW : mandíbula *f* **2** CHEEK : mejilla *f*, cachete *m*

joy [ˈʤɔɪ] *n* **1** HAPPINESS : gozo *m*, alegría *f*, felicidad *f* **2** DELIGHT : placer *m*, deleite *m* ⟨the child is a real joy : el niño es un verdadero placer⟩

joyful [ˈʤɔɪfəl] *adj* : gozoso, alegre, feliz — **joyfully** *adv*

joyless [ˈʤɔɪləs] *adj* : sin alegría, triste

joyous [ˈʤɔɪəs] *adj* : alegre, feliz, eufórico — **joyously** *adv*

joyousness [ˈʤɔɪəsnəs] *n* : alegría *f*, felicidad *f*, euforia *f*

joyride [ˈʤɔɪˌraɪd] *n* **1** : paseo *m* en coche a alta velocidad **2** : paseo *m* en un coche robado

joyriding [ˈʤɔɪˌraɪdɪŋ] *n* **to go joyriding** **1** : pasear en coche a alta velocidad (por diversión) **2** : pasear en un coche robado

joystick [ˈʤɔɪˌstɪk] *n* : joystick *m*

jubilant [ˈʤuːbələnt] *adj* : jubiloso, alborozado — **jubilantly** *adv*

jubilation [ˌʤuːbəˈleɪʃən] *n* : júbilo *m*

jubilee [ˈʤuːbəˌliː] *n* **1** : quincuagésimo aniversario *m* **2** CELEBRATION : celebración *f*, festejos *mpl*

Judaic [ʤuˈdeɪɪk] *adj* : judaico

Judaism [ˈʤuːdəˌɪzəm, ˈʤuːdi-, ˈʤuːˌdeɪ-] *n* : judaísmo *m*

judge¹ [ˈʤʌʤ] *vt* **judged; judging** **1** ASSESS : evaluar, juzgar **2** DEEM : juzgar, considerar **3** TRY : juzgar (ante el tribunal) **4 judging by** : a juzgar por ⟨judging by the results : a juzgar por los resultados⟩

judge² *n* **1** : juez *mf*, jueza *f* **2** : jurado *mf* (en una competencia) **3 to be a good judge of** : saber juzgar a, entender mucho de

judge's chambers → **chamber**

judgment *or* **judgement** [ˈʤʌʤmənt] *n* **1** RULING : fallo *m*, sentencia *f* **2** OPINION : opinión *f* **3** DISCERNMENT : juicio *m*, discernimiento *m* ⟨against my better judgment, I agreed to go : aunque me pareció mala idea, consentí en ir⟩

judgmental [ˌʤʌʤˈmntəl] *adj* : crítico — **judgmentally** *adv*

judicature [ˈʤuːdɪkəˌtʃʊr] *n* : judicatura *f*

judicial [ʤʊˈdɪʃəl] *adj* : judicial — **judicially** *adv*

judiciary¹ [ʤʊˈdɪʃiˌri, -ˈdɪʃəri] *adj* : judicial

judiciary² *n* **1** JUDICATURE : judicatura *f* **2** : poder *m* judicial

judicious [ʤʊˈdɪʃəs] *adj* SOUND, WISE : juicioso, sensato — **judiciously** *adv*

judo [ˈʤuːˌdoː] *n* : judo *m*

jug ['ᴅ vɢ] *n* **1** : jarra *f*, jarro *m*, cántaro *m* **2** JAIL : cárcel *f*, chirona *f fam*

juggernaut ['ᴅ vɢər͵nɔt] *n* : gigante *m*, fuerza *f* irresistible ⟨a political juggernaut : un gigante político⟩

juggle ['ᴅ vɢəl] *v* **-gled; -gling** *vt* **1** : hacer juegos malabares con **2** MANIPULATE : manipular, jugar con — *vi* : hacer juegos malabares

juggler ['ᴅ vɢələr] *n* : malabarista *mf*

jugular ['ᴅ vɢjulər] *adj* : yugular ⟨jugular vein : vena yugular⟩

juice ['ᴅ u:s] *n* **1** : jugo *m* (de carne, de frutas) *m*, zumo *m* (de frutas) **2** ELECTRICITY : electricidad *f*, luz *f*

juicer ['ᴅ u:sər] *n* : exprimidor *m*

juiciness ['ᴅ u:sinəs] *n* : jugosidad *f*

juicy ['ᴅ u:si] *adj* **juicier; -est 1** SUCCULENT : jugoso, suculento **2** PROFITABLE : jugoso, lucrativo **3** RACY : picante

jukebox ['ᴅ u:k͵bɑks] *n* : rocola *f*, máquina *f* de discos

julep ['ᴅ u:ləp] *n* : bebida *f* hecha con whisky americano y menta

July [ᴅ ʊ'lai] *n* **1** : julio *m* ⟨they arrived on July 29th, they arrived on the 29th of July : llegaron el 29 de julio⟩ **2 the Fourth of July** INDEPENDENCE DAY : el 4 de julio (día festivo en los EEUU)

jumble[1] ['ᴅ vmbəl] *vt* **-bled; -bling** : mezclar, revolver

jumble[2] *n* : revoltijo *m*, fárrago *m*, embrollo *m*

jumbo[1] ['ᴅ vm͵bo:] *adj* : gigante, enorme, de tamaño extra grande

jumbo[2] *n, pl* **-bos** : coloso *m*, cosa *f* de tamaño extra grande

jump[1] ['ᴅ vmp] *vi* **1** LEAP : saltar, brincar **2** START : levantarse de un salto, sobresaltarse **3** MOVE, SHIFT : moverse, pasar ⟨to jump from job to job : pasar de un empleo a otro⟩ **4** INCREASE, RISE : dar un salto, aumentarse de golpe, subir bruscamente **5** BUSTLE : animarse, ajetrearse **6 to jump at** : no dejar escapar (una oportunidad) **7 to jump in** : meterse (en una conversación, etc.) **8 to jump on** ATTACK, CRITICIZE : atacar, criticar **9 to jump on** SCOLD : regañar, reprender, reñir **10 to jump out at** POUNCE ON : abalanzarse sobre **11 to jump out at** : llamar la atención de ⟨it jumps out at you : salta a la vista⟩ **12 to jump to conclusions** : sacar conclusiones precipitadas — *vt* **1** : saltar ⟨to jump a fence : saltar una valla⟩ **2** SKIP : saltarse **3** ATTACK : atacar, asaltar **5 to jump the gun** : precipitarse

jump[2] *n* **1** LEAP : salto *m* **2** : sobresalto *m*, respingo *m* **3** INCREASE : subida *f* brusca, aumento *m* **4** ADVANTAGE : ventaja *f* ⟨we got the jump on them : les llevamos la ventaja⟩

jumper ['ᴅ vmpər] *n* **1** : saltador *m*, -dora *f* (en deportes) **2** : jumper *m*, vestido *m* sin mangas

jumper cables *npl* : cables *mpl* de arranque, cables *mpl* pasacorriente *Mex*

jump-start *vt* : arrancar haciendo puente

jumpy ['ᴅ vmpi] *adj* **jumpier; -est** : asustadizo, nervioso

junction ['ᴅ vŋkʃən] *n* **1** JOINING : unión *f* **2** : cruce *m* (de calles), empalme *m* (de un ferrocarril), confluencia *f* (de ríos)

juncture ['ᴅ vŋktʃər] *n* **1** UNION : juntura *f*, unión *f* **2** MOMENT POINT : coyuntura *f* ⟨at this juncture : en esta coyuntura, en este momento⟩

June ['ᴅ u:n] *n* : junio *m* ⟨they arrived on the 15th of June, they arrived on June 15th : llegaron el 15 de junio⟩

jungle ['ᴅ vŋɢəl] *n* : jungla *f*, selva *f*

junior[1] ['ᴅ u:njər] *adj* **1** YOUNGER : más joven ⟨John Smith, Junior : John Smith, hijo⟩ **2** SUBORDINATE : subordinado, subalterno

junior[2] *n* **1** : persona *f* de menor edad ⟨she's my junior : es menor que yo⟩ **2** SUBORDINATE : subalterno *m*, -na *f*; subordinado *m*, -da *f* **3** : estudiante *mf* de penúltimo año

junior high school *n* : primer ciclo *m* de la educación secundaria en los EEUU

juniper ['ᴅ u:nəpər] *n* : enebro *m*

junk[1] ['ᴅ vŋk] *vt* : echar a la basura

junk[2] *n* **1** RUBBISH : desechos *mpl*, desperdicios *mpl* **2** STUFF : trastos *mpl fam*, cachivaches *mpl fam* **3 piece of junk** : cacharro *m*, porquería *f*

junket ['ᴅ vŋkət] *n* : viaje *m* (pagado con dinero público)

junk food *n* : comida *f* basura, comida *f* chatarra

junkie ['ᴅ vŋki] *n* : drogadicto *m*, -ta *f*

junk mail *n* : correo *m* basura, propaganda *f*

junta ['hʊntə, 'ᴅ vn-, 'hvn-] *n* : junta *f* militar

Jupiter ['ᴅ u:pəṭər] *n* : Júpiter *m*

jurisdiction [͵ᴅ ʊrəs'dɪkʃən] *n* : jurisdicción *f* — **jurisdictional** [͵ᴅ ʊrəs'dɪkʃənəl] *adj*

jurisprudence [͵ᴅ ʊrəs'pru:dənts] *n* : jurisprudencia *f*

jurist ['ᴅ ʊrɪst] *n* : jurista *mf*; magistrado *m*, -da *f*

juror ['ᴅ ʊrər] *n* : jurado *m*, -da *f*

jury ['ᴅ ʊri] *n, pl* **-ries** : jurado *m*

just[1] ['ᴅ vst] *adv* **1** EXACTLY : justo, precisamente, exactamente ⟨it was just what she hoped for : fue exactamente lo que esperaba⟩ ⟨it is just what I need : es justo lo que necesito⟩ ⟨just as/when : justo cuando⟩ **2** POSSIBLY : posiblemente ⟨it just might work : tal vez resulte⟩ **3** BARELY : justo, apenas ⟨just in time : justo a tiempo⟩ ⟨I had just enough time : tenía el tiempo justo⟩ ⟨just over an hour : una hora larga, una hora y pico⟩ ⟨we just missed the plane : perdimos el avión por un pelo⟩ ⟨we just missed each other : no nos vimos por poco⟩ ⟨it's just around the corner : está a la vuelta de la esquina⟩ **4** ONLY : sólo, solamente, nada más ⟨just us : sólo nosotros⟩ ⟨just one more : sólo uno más⟩ ⟨she's just a child : es sólo una niña⟩ ⟨just for fun : sólo por diversión⟩ ⟨just a moment/minute, please : un momento, por favor⟩

⟨I'm just kidding : (sólo) estoy bromeando⟩ ⟨she's not just my friend, she's my lawyer : además de ser mi amiga, es mi abogada⟩ **5** (*used for emphasis*) ⟨it's just horrible! : ¡qué horrible!⟩ ⟨I just don't understand it : simplemente no lo entiendo⟩ ⟨I just knew it! : ¡ya me lo sospechaba!⟩ ⟨just imagine! : ¡imagínate!⟩ ⟨just tell him how you feel! : ¿por qué no le dices lo que sientes?⟩ ⟨don't just stand there — do something! : no te quedes ahí parado — ¡haz algo!⟩ **6 to have just done something** : acabar de hacer algo ⟨he just called : acaba de llamar⟩ **7 just about** ALMOST : casi **8 just about to** : al punto de **9 just as ... as** : tan ... como ⟨just as good as : tan bueno como⟩ **10 just as soon** RATHER ⟨I'd just as soon stay home : prefiero quedarme en casa⟩ **11 just as well (that)** : menos mal (que) **12 just like that** : de repente **13 just now** : hace un momento ⟨I saw him just now : acabo de verlo⟩ **14 just now** RIGHT NOW : ahora mismo **15 just so** PERFECT : perfecto **16 just the thing** ⟨just the thing for

you : justo lo que necesitas⟩ **17 just yet** ⟨are you ready? — not just yet : ¿estás lista? — casi⟩ ⟨don't buy it just yet : no lo compres ahora mismo⟩
just² *adj* : justo — **justly** *adv*
justice [ˈdʒʌstɪs] *n* **1** : justicia *f* ⟨to do justice to : hacerle justicia a⟩ **2** JUDGE : juez *mf*, jueza *f*
justice of the peace *n* : juez *mf* de paz, jueza *f* de paz
justification [ˌdʒʌstəfəˈkeɪʃən] *n* : justificación *f*
justify [ˈdʒʌstəˌfaɪ] *vt* **-fied; -fying** : justificar — **justifiable** [ˌdʒʌstəˈfaɪəbəl] *adj*
jut [ˈdʒʌt] *vi* **jutted; jutting** : sobresalir
jute [ˈdʒuːt] *n* : yute *m*
juvenile¹ [ˈdʒuːvəˌnaɪl, -vənəl] *adj* **1** : juvenil ⟨juvenile delinquent : delincuente juvenil⟩ ⟨juvenile court : tribunal de menores⟩ **2** CHILDISH : infantil
juvenile² *n* : menor *mf*
juxtapose [ˈdʒʌkstəˌpoːz] *vt* **-posed; -posing** : yuxtaponer
juxtaposition [ˌdʒʌkstəpəˈzɪʃən] *n* : yuxtaposición *f*

K

k [ˈkeɪ] *n, pl* **k's** *or* **ks** [ˈkeɪz] : undécima letra del alfabeto inglés
kabob [kəˈbɑb] → **kebab**
kaiser [ˈkaɪzər] *n* : káiser *m*
kale [ˈkeɪl] *n* : col *f* rizada
kaleidoscope [kəˈlaɪdəˌskoːp] *n* : calidoscopio *m*
kamikaze [ˌkɑmɪˈkɑzi] *n* : kamikaze *m* — **kamikaze** *adj*
kangaroo [ˌkæŋɡəˈruː] *n, pl* **-roos** : canguro *m*
karaoke [ˌkæriˈoːki] *n* : karaoke *m*
karat [ˈkærət] *n* : quilate *m*
karate [kəˈrɑti] *n* : karate *m*
katydid [ˈkeɪtiˌdɪd] *n* : saltamontes *m*
kayak [ˈkaɪˌæk] *n* : kayac *m*, kayak *m*
kebab [kəˈbɑb] *n* : kebab *m*
keel¹ [ˈkiːl] *vi* **to keel over** : volcar (dícese de un barco), desplomarse (dícese de una persona)
keel² *n* : quilla *f*
keen [ˈkiːn] *adj* **1** SHARP : afilado, filoso ⟨a keen blade : una hoja afilada⟩ **2** PENETRATING : cortante, penetrante ⟨a keen wind : un viento cortante⟩ **3** ENTHUSIASTIC : entusiasta **4** ACUTE : agudo, fino ⟨keen hearing : oído fino⟩ ⟨keen intelligence : inteligencia aguda⟩
keenly [ˈkiːnli] *adv* **1** ENTHUSIASTICALLY : con entusiasmo **2** INTENSELY : vivamente, profundamente ⟨keenly aware of : muy consciente de⟩
keenness [ˈkiːnnəs] *n* **1** SHARPNESS : lo afilado, lo filoso **2** ENTHUSIASM : entusiasmo *m* **3** ACUTENESS : agudeza *f*
keep¹ [ˈkiːp] *v* **kept** [ˈkɛpt]; **keeping** *vt* **1** RETAIN : guardar, conservar, quedarse con ⟨do you want to keep these papers?

: ¿quieres guardar estos papeles?⟩ ⟨he kept the money : se quedó con el dinero⟩ ⟨to keep one's cool : mantener la calma⟩ **2** : mantener ⟨keep me informed : mantenme informado⟩ ⟨she keeps herself fit : se mantiene en forma⟩ ⟨he kept his coat on : se quedó con el abrigo puesto⟩ ⟨to keep something a secret : mantener algo en secreto⟩ **3** DETAIN : retener, detener ⟨I won't keep you any longer : no te entretengo más⟩ ⟨what kept you? : ¿por qué tardaste?⟩ **4** (*with a present participle*) ⟨don't keep her waiting : no la hagas esperar⟩ ⟨he kept the company going : mantuvo la compañía a flote⟩ **5** : cumplir (su palabra), acudir a (una cita) **6** PRESERVE : guardar ⟨to keep a secret : guardar un secreto⟩ ⟨he kept it to himself : no se lo contó a nadie⟩ **7** HIDE : ocultar ⟨he kept it from her : se lo ocultó, no se lo dijo⟩ **8** OBSERVE : observar (una fiesta) **9** STORE : guardar **10** RESERVE : guardar **11** GUARD : guardar, cuidar **12** : llevar, escribir (un diario, etc.) **13** SUPPORT : mantener (una familia) **14** RAISE : criar (animales) **15** : mantener (a un amante) **16 to keep after (school)** : hacer quedar después de clase **17 to keep back** : no dejar acercarse a **18 to keep back** : hacer repetir un año (a un estudiante) **19 to keep back** HIDE, REPRESS : ocultar, retener **20 to keep company** : hacerle compañía a **21 to keep company with** : andar en compañía de **22 to keep down** : mantener bajo ⟨to keep prices down : mantener los precios bajos⟩ **23**

to **keep down** : retener (en el estómago) **24 to keep in** : no dejar salir **25 to keep in** CONTAIN : contener **26 to keep it down** : no hacer tanto ruido **27 to keep off** : no dejar pisar, tocar, etc. ⟨keep the dog off the sofa : no dejes que el perro se suba al sofá⟩ **28 to keep off** : hacer evitar (un tema) **29 to keep weight off** ⟨he has kept the weight off : ha mantenido el peso (tras adelgazar)⟩ **30 to keep on** : mantener (a un empleado) en el puesto **31 to keep down** BLOCK : no dejar pasar **32 to keep up** CONTINUE : seguir con **33 to keep up** MAINTAIN : mantener **34 to keep up one's end of something** : cumplir (con) su parte de algo — *vi* **1** REMAIN, STAY : mantener ⟨to keep quiet : mantener silencio⟩ ⟨to keep still : estarse quieto⟩ ⟨to keep calm : mantener la calma⟩ ⟨she likes to keep busy : le gusta estar ocupada⟩ **2** : conservarse (dícese de los alimentos) ⟨the soup will keep for a week : la sopa se conserva una semana⟩ **3** *or* **to keep on** (*with a present participle*) CONTINUE : seguir, no dejar de ⟨keep going straight : sigue todo recto⟩ ⟨he keeps on pestering us : no deja de molestarnos⟩ **4 to keep after** NAG : estarle encima a ⟨he kept after me to quit smoking : me estaba encima para que deje de fumar⟩ **5 to keep at it** PERSIST : seguir dándole **6 to keep back** : no acercarse **7 to keep down** : no levantarse **8 to keep from** : abstenerse de ⟨I couldn't keep from laughing : no pude contener la risa⟩ **9 to keep off** : no pisar (el césped, etc.) **10 to keep off** AVOID : evitar (un tema) **11 to keep on** CONTINUE : seguir, continuar ⟨the rain kept on : seguía lloviendo⟩ **12 to keep out (of)** : no entrar (en) ⟨the sign says "keep out" : el letrero dice "prohibido el paso"⟩ ⟨to keep out of an argument : no meterse en una discusión⟩ **13 to keep to** : no apartarse de (un camino, etc.), quedarse dentro de (una casa, etc.) **14 to keep to** : ceñirse a (las reglas, un tema, etc.) **15 to keep to oneself** : ser muy reservado **16 to keep up** CONTINUE : seguir, continuar ⟨the rain kept up : seguía lloviendo⟩ **17 to keep up** : mantenerse al tanto/corriente (de las noticias, etc.) **18 to keep up (with)** : seguir/mantener el ritmo (de) ⟨I can't keep up (with him) : no puedo seguir su ritmo, no puedo seguirle el ritmo⟩ ⟨to keep up with the Joneses : no ser menos que el vecino⟩ **19 to keep up with someone** : mantener contacto con alguien
keep² *n* **1** TOWER : torreón *m* (de un castillo), torre *f* del homenaje **2** SUSTENANCE : manutención *f*, sustento *m* **3 for keeps** : para siempre
keeper ['ki:pər] *n* **1** : guarda *mf* (en un zoológico); conservador *m*, -dora *f* (en un museo) **2** GAMEKEEPER : guardabosque *mf*
keeping ['ki:pɪŋ] *n* **1** CONFORMITY : conformidad *f*, acuerdo *m* ⟨in keeping with

: de acuerdo con⟩ **2** CARE : cuidado *m* ⟨in the keeping of : al cuidado de⟩
keepsake ['ki:p,seɪk] *n* : recuerdo *m*
keg ['kɛɡ] *n* : barril *m*
kelp ['kɛlp] *n* : alga *f* marina
ken ['kɛn] *n* **1** SIGHT : vista *f*, alcance *m* de la vista **2** UNDERSTANDING : comprensión *f*, alcance *m* del conocimiento ⟨it's beyond his ken : no lo puede entender⟩
kennel ['kɛnəl] *n* : caseta *f* para perros, perrera *f*
Kenyan ['kɛnjən, 'ki:n-] *n* : keniano *m*, -na *f* — **Kenyan** *adj*
kept → **keep**
kerchief ['kərtʃəf, -,tʃi:f] *n* : pañuelo *m*
kernel ['kərnəl] *n* **1** : almendra *f* (de semillas y nueces) **2** : grano *m* (de cereales) **3** CORE : meollo *m* ⟨a kernel of truth : un fondo de verdad⟩
kerosene *or* **kerosine** ['kɛrə,si:n, ,kɛrə'-] *n* : queroseno *m*, kerosén *m*, kerosene *m*
ketchup ['kɛtʃəp, 'kæ-] *n* : salsa *f* catsup
kettle ['kɛt̬əl] *n* **1** : hervidor *m*, pava *f* *Arg, Bol, Chile* **2** → **teakettle**
kettledrum ['kɛt̬əl,drʌm] *n* : timbal *m*
key¹ ['ki:] *vt* **1** ATTUNE : adaptar, adecuar **2 to key up** : poner nervioso, inquietar
key² *adj* : clave, fundamental
key³ *n* **1** : llave *f* **2** SOLUTION : clave *f*, soluciones *fpl* **3** : tecla *f* (de un piano o una máquina) **4** : tono *m*, tonalidad *f* (en la música) **5** ISLET, REEF : cayo *m*, islote *m*
keyboard ['ki:,bord] *n* : teclado *m*
key chain *n* : llavero *m*
keyhole ['ki:,ho:l] *n* : bocallave *f*, ojo *m* (de una cerradura)
keynote¹ ['ki:,no:t] *vt* **-noted; -noting** **1** : establecer la tónica de (en música) **2** : pronunciar el discurso principal de
keynote² *n* **1** : tónica *f* (en música) **2** : idea *f* fundamental
keypad ['ki:,pæd] *n* : teclado *m* numérico
key ring *n* : llavero *m*
keystroke ['ki:,stro:k] *n* : pulsación *f* (de tecla)
khaki ['kæki, 'kɑ-] *n* : caqui *m*
khan ['kɑn, 'kæn] *n* : kan *m*
kibbutz [kə'bʊts, -'bu:ts] *n, pl* **-butzim** [-,bʊt'si:m, -,bu:t-] : kibutz *m*
kibitz ['kɪbɪts] *vi* : dar consejos molestos
kibitzer ['kɪbɪtsər, kɪ'bɪt-] *n* : persona *f* que da consejos molestos
kick¹ ['kɪk] *vi* **1** : dar patadas (dícese de una persona), cocear (dícese de un animal) **2** PROTEST : patalear, protestar **3** RECOIL : dar un culatazo (dícese de un arma de fuego) **4 to kick around** *fam* : andar dando vueltas (por), viajar (por) **5 to kick back** *fam* : relajarse **6 to kick in** *fam* : arrancar (dícese de un motor, etc.), hacer efecto (dícese de drogas), tener efecto (dícese de una ley) **7 to kick off** BEGIN : empezar, iniciar **8 to kick off** : hacer el saque inicial (en deportes) — *vt* **1** : patear, darle una patada (a alguien) ⟨to kick someone when they're down : pegarle a alguien en el

suelo⟩ 2 : dejar, perder (un vicio) 3 **to kick around** *fam* : considerar, barajar (ideas, etc.) 4 **to kick in** *fam* CONTRIBUTE : contribuir, poner 5 **to kick off** : empezar 6 **to kick oneself** *fam* : castigarse, culparse 7 **to kick out** EJECT : echar 8 **to kick up** : levantar (polvo, etc.) 9 **to kick up a fuss** *fam* : armar una bronca

kick² *n* 1 : patada *f*, puntapié *m*, coz *f* (de un animal) 2 RECOIL : culatazo *m* (de un arma de fuego) 3 : fuerza *f* ⟨a drink with a kick : una bebida fuerte⟩ 4 **to get a kick out of** : disfrutar de, deleitarse con

kicker ['kɪkər] *n* : pateador *m*, -dora *f* (en deportes)

kickoff ['kɪk,ɔf] *n* : saque *m* (inicial)

kid¹ ['kɪd] *v* **kidded; kidding** *vt* 1 FOOL : engañar 2 TEASE : tomarle el pelo (a alguien) 3 **to kid oneself** : hacerse ilusiones — *vi* JOKE : bromear ⟨I'm only kidding : lo digo en broma⟩

kid² *n* 1 : chivo *m*, -va *f*; cabrito *m*, -ta *f* 2 CHILD : chico *m*, -ca *f*; niño *m*, -ña *f*

kidder ['kɪdər] *n* : bromista *mf*

kiddingly ['kɪdɪŋli] *adv* : en broma

kidnap ['kɪd,næp] *vt* **-napped** *or* **-naped** [-,næpt]; **-napping** *or* **-naping** [-,næpɪŋ] : secuestrar, raptar

kidnapper *or* **kidnaper** ['kɪd,næpər] *n* : secuestrador *m*, -dora *f*; raptor *m*, -tora *f*

kidnapping ['kɪd,næpɪŋ] *n* : secuestro *m*

kidney ['kɪdni] *n, pl* **-neys** : riñón *m*

kidney bean *n* : frijol *m*

kill¹ ['kɪl] *vt* 1 : matar 2 END : acabar con, poner fin a 3 **to kill off** : matar 4 **to kill time** : matar el tiempo

kill² *n* 1 KILLING : matanza *f* 2 PREY : presa *f*

killer ['kɪlər] *n* : asesino *m*, -na *f*

killer whale *n* : orca *f*

killing ['kɪlɪŋ] *n* 1 : asesinato *m* (de alguien), matanza *f* (de un animal) 2 **to make a killing** : enriquecerse, hacer una fortuna

killjoy ['kɪl,dʒɔɪ] *n* : aguafiestas *mf*

kiln ['kɪl, 'kɪln] *n* : horno *m*

kilo ['kiː,loː] *n, pl* **-los** : kilo *m*

kilobyte ['kɪlə,baɪt] *n* : kilobyte *m*

kilocycle ['kɪlə,saɪkəl] *n* : kilociclo *m*

kilogram ['kɪlə,ɡræm, 'kiː-] *n* : kilogramo *m*

kilohertz ['kɪlə,hərts] *n* : kilohertzio *m*

kilometer [kɪ'lɑmətər, 'kɪlə,miː-] *n* : kilómetro *m*

kilowatt ['kɪlə,wɑt] *n* : kilovatio *m*

kilt ['kɪlt] *n* : falda *f* escocesa

kilter ['kɪltər] *n* 1 ORDER : buen estado *m* 2 **out of kilter** : descompuesto, estropeado

kimono [kə'moːno, -nə] *n, pl* **-nos** : kimono *m*, quimono *m*

kin ['kɪn] *n* : familiares *mpl*, parientes *mpl*

kind¹ ['kaɪnd] *adj* : amable, bondadoso, benévolo

kind² *n* 1 ESSENCE : esencia *f* ⟨a difference in degree, not in kind : una diferencia cuantitativa y no cualitativa⟩ 2 CAT-EGORY : especie *f*, género *m* 3 TYPE : clase *f*, tipo *m*, índole *f* ⟨they're two of a kind : son tal para cual⟩ ⟨of all kinds : de todo tipo⟩

kindergarten ['kɪndər,ɡɑrtən, -dən] *n* : kinder *m*, kindergarten *m*, jardín *m* de infantes, jardín *m* de niños *Mex*

kindhearted [,kaɪnd'hɑrtəd] *adj* : bondadoso, de buen corazón

kindle ['kɪndəl] *v* **-dled; -dling** *vt* 1 IGNITE : encender 2 AROUSE : despertar, suscitar — *vi* : encenderse

kindliness ['kaɪndlinəs] *n* : bondad *f*

kindling ['kɪndlɪŋ, 'kɪndlən] *n* : astillas *fpl*, leña *f*

kindly¹ ['kaɪndli] *adv* 1 AMIABLY : amablemente, bondadosamente 2 COURTEOUSLY : cortésmente, con cortesía ⟨we kindly ask you not smoke : les rogamos que no fumen⟩ 3 PLEASE : por favor 4 **to take kindly to** : aceptar de buena gana

kindly² *adj* **kindlier; -est** : bondadoso, amable

kindness ['kaɪndnəs] *n* : bondad *f*

kind of *adv* SOMEWHAT : un tanto, algo

kindred¹ ['kɪndrəd] *adj* SIMILAR : similar, afín ⟨kindred spirits : almas gemelas⟩

kindred² *n* 1 FAMILY : familia *f*, parentela *f* 2 → **kin**

kinfolk ['kɪn,foːk] *or* **kinfolks** [-,foːks] *npl* → **kin**

king ['kɪŋ] *n* : rey *m*

kingdom ['kɪŋdəm] *n* : reino *m*

kingfisher ['kɪŋ,fɪʃər] *n* : martín *m* pescador

kingly ['kɪŋli] *adj* **kinglier; -est** : regio, real

king–size ['kɪŋ,saɪz] *or* **king–sized** [-,saɪzd] *adj* : de tamaño muy grande, extra largo (dícese de cigarrillos)

kink ['kɪŋk] *n* 1 : rizo *m* (en el pelo), vuelta *f* (en una cuerda) 2 CRAMP : calambre *m* ⟨to have a kink in the neck : tener tortícolis⟩

kinky ['kɪŋki] *adj* **kinkier; -est** : rizado (dícese del pelo), enroscado (dícese de una cuerda)

kinship ['kɪn,ʃɪp] *n* : parentesco *m*

kinsman ['kɪnzmən] *n, pl* **-men** [-mən, -,mɛn] : familiar *m*, pariente *m*

kinswoman ['kɪnz,wʊmən] *n, pl* **-women** [-,wɪmən] : familiar *f*, pariente *f*

kiosk ['kiː,ɑsk] *n* : quiosco *m*

kipper ['kɪpər] *n* : arenque *m* ahumado

kiss¹ ['kɪs] *vt* : besar — *vi* : besarse

kiss² *n* : beso *m* ⟨to blow someone a kiss : tirarle un beso a alguien⟩

kit ['kɪt] *n* 1 SET : juego *m*, kit *m* 2 CASE : estuche *m*, caja *f* 3 **first–aid kit** : botiquín *m* 4 → **tool kit** 5 **travel kit** : neceser *m*

kitchen ['kɪtʃən] *n* : cocina *f*

kitchenette [,kɪtʃə'nɛt] *n* : cocineta *f*

kite ['kaɪt] *n* : cometa *f*, papalote *m Mex* ⟨to fly a kite : hacer volar una cometa⟩

kith ['kɪθ] *n* : amigos *mpl* ⟨kith and kin : amigos y parientes⟩

kitten ['kɪtən] *n* : gatito *m*, -ta *f*

kitty ['kɪti] *n, pl* **-ties** 1 FUND, POOL

: bote *m*, fondo *m* común 2 CAT : gato *m*, gatito *m*

kitty–corner ['kɪɾɪ,kɔrnər] *or* **kitty–cornered** [-nərd] → **catercorner**

kiwi ['ki:,wi:] *or* **kiwifruit** ['ki:,wi:,fru:t] *n* : kiwi *m*

Kleenex ['kli:,nɛks] *trademark* se usa para un pañuelo de papel

kleptomania [,klɛptə'meɪniə] *n* : cleptomanía *f*

kleptomaniac [,klɛptə'meɪni,æk] *n* : cleptómano *m*, -na *f*

klutz ['klʌts] *n* : torpe *mf*

knack ['næk] *n* : maña *f*, facilidad *f* ⟨to have a knack for something : tener habilidad para algo⟩ ⟨to get the knack of something : agarrarle la onda a algo⟩

knapsack ['næp,sæk] *n* : mochila *f*, morral *m*

knave ['neɪv] *n* : bellaco *m*, pícaro *m*

knead ['ni:d] *vt* 1 : amasar, sobar 2 MASSAGE : masajear

knee ['ni:] *n* : rodilla *f*

kneecap ['ni:,kæp] *n* : rótula *f*

kneel ['ni:l] *vi* **knelt** ['nɛlt] *or* **kneeled** ['ni:ld]; **kneeling** : arrodillarse, ponerse de rodillas

knell ['nɛl] *n* : doble *m*, toque *m* ⟨death knell : toque de difuntos⟩

knew → **know**

knickers ['nɪkərz] *npl* : pantalones *mpl* bombachos de media pierna

knickknack ['nɪk,næk] *n* : chuchería *f*, baratija *f*

knife[1] ['naɪf] *vt* **knifed** ['naɪft]; **knifing** : acuchillar, apuñalar

knife[2] *n, pl* **knives** ['naɪvz] : cuchillo *m*

knight[1] ['naɪt] *vt* : conceder el título de *Sir* a

knight[2] *n* 1 : caballero *m* ⟨knight errant : caballero andante⟩ 2 : caballo *m* (en ajedrez) 3 : uno que tiene el título de *Sir*

knighthood ['naɪt,hʊd] *n* 1 : caballería *f* 2 : título *m* de *Sir*

knightly ['naɪtli] *adj* : caballeresco

knit[1] ['nɪt] *v* **knit** *or* **knitted** ['nɪɾəd]; **knitting** *vt* 1 UNITE : unir, enlazar 2 : tejer ⟨to knit a sweater : tejer un suéter⟩ 3 to knit one's brows : fruncir el ceño — *vi* 1 : tejer 2 : soldarse (dícese de los huesos)

knit[2] *n* : prenda *f* tejida

knitter ['nɪɾər] *n* : tejedor *m*, -dora *f*

knitwear ['nɪt,wær] *n* : ropa *f* de punto

knob ['nɑb] *n* 1 LUMP : bulto *m*, protuberancia *f* 2 HANDLE : perilla *f*, tirador *m*, botón *m*

knobbed ['nɑbd] *adj* 1 KNOTTY : nudoso 2 : que tiene perilla o botón

knobby ['nɑbi] *adj* **knobbier; -est** 1 KNOTTY : nudoso 2 **knobby knees** : rodillas *fpl* huesudas

knock[1] ['nɑk] *vt* 1 HIT, RAP : golpear, golpetear 2 : hacer chocar ⟨they knocked heads : se dieron en la cabeza⟩ 3 CRITICIZE : criticar 4 to knock around *fam* BEAT : pegarle a 5 to knock back *fam* DRINK : beberse, tomarse 6 to knock dead *fam* STUN : dejar boquiabierto 7 to knock down : derribar, echar abajo (una puerta, etc.), tirar al suelo (a una persona) 8 to knock off *fam* KILL : asesinar, liquidar *fam* 9 to knock off *fam* : quitar (puntos, etc.) ⟨he knocked 10% off the price : rebajó el precio un 10%⟩ 10 to knock off *fam* RIP OFF : copiar (un diseño, etc.) ilegalmente 11 knock it off! *fam* : ¡basta ya!, ¡déjala! 12 to knock out : dejar sin sentido, dejar fuera de combate (en el boxeo) 13 to knock out ELIMINATE : eliminar 14 to knock out DESTROY : destruir (un edificio, etc.) ⟨the storm knocked out the power : la tormenta nos dejó sin luz⟩ 15 to knock oneself out *fam* : matarse (trabajando, etc.) ⟨go ahead — knock yourself out! : ¡adelante!, ¡disfruta!⟩ 16 to knock over OVERTURN : tirar, volcar 17 to knock over *fam* ROB : robar 18 to knock up *fam* : dejar embarazada — *vi* 1 RAP : dar un golpe, llamar (a la puerta) 2 COLLIDE : darse, chocar 3 to knock around in *fam* : viajar por 4 to knock off *fam* : salir del trabajo ⟨to knock off early : salir temprano⟩

knock[2] *n* : golpe *m*, llamada *f* (a la puerta), golpeteo *m* (de un motor)

knocker ['nɑkər] *n* : aldaba *f*, llamador *m*

knock–kneed ['nɑk'ni:d] *adj* : patizambo

knockout ['nɑk,aʊt] *n* 1 : nocaut *m*, knockout *m* (en deportes) 2 to be a knockout *fam* : estar bueno *fam*, ser muy guapo

knoll ['no:l] *n* : loma *f*, otero *m*, montículo *m*

knot[1] ['nɑt] *v* **knotted; knotting** *vt* : anudar — *vi* : anudarse

knot[2] *n* 1 : nudo *m* (en cordel o madera), nódulo *m* (en los músculos) 2 CLUSTER : grupo *m* 3 : nudo *m* (unidad de velocidad)

knotty ['nɑɾi] *adj* **knottier; -est** 1 GNARLED : nudoso 2 COMPLEX : espinoso, enredado, complejo

know ['no:] *v* **knew** ['nu:, 'nju:]; **known** ['no:n]; **knowing** *vt* 1 : saber ⟨he knows French/the answer : sabe francés/la respuesta⟩ ⟨I might/should have known that . . . : debería haber sabido que . . .⟩ ⟨he made it known that . . . : hizo saber que . . .⟩ ⟨she let me know that . . . : me avisó que . . .⟩ ⟨to know something for a fact : constarse que algo es así⟩ 2 : conocer (a una persona, un lugar) ⟨do you know Julia? : ¿conoces a Julia?⟩ ⟨she knows the city well : conoce bien la ciudad⟩ ⟨he's better known as . . . : es más conocido por el nombre de . . .⟩ ⟨to be known for : conocerse por⟩ 3 RECOGNIZE : reconocer 4 DISCERN, DISTINGUISH : distinguir, discernir 5 before you know it : antes de que te des cuenta 6 for all I know : que yo sepa 7 God/heaven (only) knows : quién sabe 8 if you know what I mean : si me entiendes 9 not to know the first thing about : no saber nada de, no tener ni idea de 10 to know how to do something

: saber hacer algo **11 to know something inside out** *or* **to know something like the back of your hand** : saberse algo al dedillo **12 to know what's best** : saber lo que es lo mejor — *vi* **1** : saber ⟨yes, I know : sí, lo sé⟩ ⟨how should I know? : ¿qué sé yo?⟩ **2 to know best** : saber lo que es lo mejor **3 to know better** ⟨you're old enough to know better : a tu edad no debes hacer eso⟩ ⟨she doesn't know any better : es demasiado joven/novata (etc.) para saber lo que hace⟩ ⟨you know better than to ask : ya deberías saber que es mejor no preguntar⟩ **4 you know** (*used for emphasis*) ⟨you know, we really have to go : bueno, ya es hora de irnos⟩ ⟨it's cold out, you know : hace frío, ¿eh?⟩ **5 you know** (*expressing uncertainty*) ⟨we're going to, you know, hang out : vamos a . . . pues nada, pasar el rato⟩ **6 you never know** : nunca se sabe

knowable ['noːəbəl] *adj* : conocible
know–how ['noːˌhaʊ] *n* EXPERTISE : pericia *f*
knowing ['noːɪŋ] *adj* **1** KNOWLEDGEABLE : informado ⟨a knowing look : una mirada de complicidad⟩ **2** ASTUTE : astuto **3** DELIBERATE : deliberado, intencional
knowingly ['noːɪŋli] *adv* **1** : con complicidad ⟨she smiled knowingly : sonrió con una mirada de complicidad⟩ **2** DE-

LIBERATELY : a sabiendas, adrede, a propósito
know–it–all ['noːɪˌt̬ˌɔl] *n* : sabelotodo *mf fam*
knowledge ['nɑlɪɖ] *n* **1** AWARENESS : conocimiento *m* **2** LEARNING : conocimientos *mpl*, saber *m*
knowledgeable ['nɑlɪɖ əbəl] *adj* : informado, entendido, enterado
known ['noːn] *adj* : conocido, familiar
knuckle ['nʌkəl] *n* : nudillo *m*
KO[1] [ˌkeɪˈoː, 'keɪˌoː] *vt* **KO'd; KO'ing** KNOCK OUT : noquear (en deportes)
KO[2] *n* KNOCKOUT : nocaut *m*, knockout *m* (en deportes)
koala [koˈwɑlə] *n* : koala *m*
Koran [kəˈrɑn, -ˈræn] *n* **the Koran** : el Corán
Korean [kəˈriːən] *n* **1** : coreano *m*, -na *f* **2** : coreano *m* (idioma) — **Korean** *adj*
kosher ['koːʃər] *adj* : aprobado por la ley judía
kowtow [ˌkaʊˈtaʊ, 'kaʊˌtaʊ] *vi* **to kowtow to** : humillarse ante, doblegarse ante
krypton ['krɪpˌtɑn] *n* : criptón *m*
kudos ['kjuːˌdɑs, 'kuː-, -ˌdoːz] *n* : fama *f*, renombre *m*
kumquat ['kʌmˌkwɑt] *n* : naranjita *f* china
Kurd ['kʊrd, 'kərd] *n* : kurdo *m*, -da *f*
Kurdish ['kʊrdɪʃ, 'kər-] *adj* : kurdo
Kuwaiti [kʊˈweɾi] *n* : kuwaití *mf* —
Kuwaiti *adj*

L

l ['ɛl] *n, pl* **l's** *or* **ls** ['lz] : duodécima letra del alfabeto inglés
la ['lɑ] *n* : la *m* (en el canto)
lab ['læb] → **laboratory**
label[1] ['leɪbəl] *vt* **-beled** *or* **-belled; -beling** *or* **-belling** **1** : etiquetar, poner etiqueta a **2** BRAND, CATEGORIZE : calificar, tildar, tachar ⟨they labeled him as a fraud : lo calificaron de farsante⟩
label[2] *n* **1** : etiqueta *f*, rótulo *m* **2** DESCRIPTION : calificación *f*, descripción *f* **3** BRAND : marca *f*
labial ['leɪbiəl] *adj* : labial
labor[1] ['leɪbər] *vi* **1** WORK : trabajar **2** STRUGGLE : avanzar penosamente (dícese de una persona), funcionar con dificultad (dícese de un motor) **3 to labor under a delusion** : hacerse ilusiones, tener una falsa impresión — *vt* BELABOR : insistir en, extenderse sobre
labor[2] *n* **1** EFFORT, WORK : trabajo *m*, esfuerzos *mpl* **2** : parto *m* ⟨to be in labor : estar de parto⟩ **3** TASK : tarea *f*, labor *m* **4** WORKERS : mano *f* de obra
laboratory ['læbrəˌtori, ləˈbɔrə-] *n, pl* **-ries** : laboratorio *m*
Labor Day *n* : Día *m* del Trabajo
laborer ['leɪbərər] *n* : peón *m*; trabajador *m*, -dora *f*
laborious [ləˈboriəs] *adj* : laborioso, difícil

laboriously [ləˈboriəsli] *adv* : laboriosamente, trabajosamente
labor union → **union**
labyrinth ['læbəˌrɪnθ] *n* : laberinto *m*
labyrinthine [ˌlæbəˈrɪnθən, -ˌθaɪn, -ˌθiːn] *adj* : laberíntico
lace[1] ['leɪs] *vt* **laced; lacing** **1** TIE : acordonar, atar los cordones de **2** : adornar de encaje ⟨I laced the dress in white : adorné el vestido de encaje blanco⟩ **3** SPIKE : echar licor a
lace[2] *n* **1** : encaje *m* **2** SHOELACE : cordón *m* (de zapatos), agujeta *f Mex*
lacerate ['læsəˌreɪt] *vt* **-ated; -ating** : lacerar
laceration [ˌlæsəˈreɪʃən] *n* : laceración *f*
lack[1] ['læk] *vt* : carecer de, no tener ⟨she lacks patience : carece de paciencia⟩ — *vi* : faltar ⟨they lack for nothing : no les falta nada⟩
lack[2] *n* : falta *f*, carencia *f*
lackadaisical [ˌlækəˈdeɪzɪkəl] *adj* : apático, indiferente, lánguido — **lackadaisically** [-kli] *adv*
lackey ['læki] *n, pl* **-eys** **1** FOOTMAN : lacayo *m* **2** TOADY : adulador *m*, -dora *f*
lackluster ['lækˌlʌstər] *adj* **1** DULL : sin brillo, apagado, deslustrado **2** MEDIOCRE : deslucido, mediocre
laconic [ləˈkɑnɪk] *adj* : lacónico — **laconically** [-nɪkli] *adv*

lacquer[1] [ˈlækər] *vt* : laquear, pintar con laca
lacquer[2] *n* : laca *f*
lacrosse [ləˈkrɔs] *n* : lacrosse *m*
lacy [ˈleɪsi] *adj* **lacier; -est** : de encaje, como de encaje
lad [ˈlæd] *n* : muchacho *m*, niño *m*
ladder [ˈlædər] *n* : escalera *f*
laden [ˈleɪdən] *adj* : cargado
ladle[1] [ˈleɪdəl] *vt* **-dled; -dling** : servir con cucharón
ladle[2] *n* : cucharón *m*, cazo *m*
lady [ˈleɪdi] *n, pl* **-dies** **1** : señora *f*, dama *f* **2** WOMAN : mujer *f*
ladybird [ˈleɪdiˌbərd] → **ladybug**
ladybug [ˈleɪdiˌbʌg] *n* : mariquita *f*
lag[1] [ˈlæg] *vi* **lagged; lagging to lag behind** **1** : quedarse atrás, quedarse rezagado, ir a la zaga ⟨she lagged behind (the group) : se quedó atrás (del grupo), iba a la zaga (del grupo)⟩ ⟨we lag behind other countries : quedamos rezagados con respecto a otros países, vamos a la zaga de los otros países⟩ **2** : atrasarse, retrasarse (con respecto a un programa, etc.)
lag[2] *n* **1** DELAY : retraso *m*, demora *f* **2** INTERVAL : lapso *m*, intervalo *m*
lager [ˈlɑgər] *n* : cerveza *f* rubia
laggard[1] [ˈlægərd] *adj* : retardado, retrasado
laggard[2] *n* : rezagado *m*, -da *f*
lagoon [ləˈguːn] *n* : laguna *f*
laid → **lay**[1]
laid–back [ˈleɪdˈbæk] *adj* : tranquilo, relajado
lain *pp* → **lie**[1]
lair [ˈlær] *n* : guarida *f*, madriguera *f*
laissez–faire [ˌlɛˌseɪˈfær, ˌleɪˌzeɪ-] *n* : liberalismo *m* económico
laity [ˈleɪəti] *n* **the laity** : los laicos, el laicado
lake [ˈleɪk] *n* : lago *m*
lama [ˈlɑmə] *n* : lama *m*
lamb [ˈlæm] *n* **1** : cordero *m*, borrego *m* (animal) **2** : carne *f* de cordero
lambaste [læmˈbeɪst] *or* **lambast** [-ˈbæst] *vt* **-basted; -basting** **1** BEAT, THRASH : golpear, azotar, darle una paliza (a alguien) **2** CENSURE : arremeter contra, censurar
lame[1] [ˈleɪm] *vt* **lamed; laming** : lisiar, hacer cojo
lame[2] *adj* **lamer; lamest** **1** : cojo, renco, rengo **2** WEAK : pobre, débil, poco convincente ⟨a lame excuse : una excusa débil⟩
lame duck *n* : persona *f* sin poder ⟨a lame-duck President : un presidente saliente⟩
lamely [ˈleɪmli] *adv* : sin convicción
lameness [ˈleɪmnəs] *n* **1** : cojera *f*, renquera *f* **2** : falta *f* de convicción, debilidad *f*, pobreza *f* ⟨the lameness of her response : la pobreza de su respuesta⟩
lament[1] [ləˈmɛnt] *vt* **1** MOURN : llorar, llorar por **2** DEPLORE : lamentar, deplorar — *vi* : llorar
lament[2] *n* : lamento *m*
lamentable [ˈlæməntəbəl, ləˈmɛntə-] *adj*

: lamentable, deplorable — **lamentably** [-bli] *adv*
lamentation [ˌlæmənˈteɪʃən] *n* : lamentación *f*, lamento *m*
laminate[1] [ˈlæməˌneɪt] *vt* **-nated; -nating** : laminar
laminate[2] [ˈlæmənət] *n* : laminado *m*
laminated [ˈlæməˌneɪtəd] *adj* : laminado
lamp [ˈlæmp] *n* : lámpara *f*
lampoon[1] [læmˈpuːn] *vt* : satirizar
lampoon[2] *n* : sátira *f*
lamppost [ˈlæmpˌpoːst] *n* : farol *m*, farola *f*
lamprey [ˈlæmpri] *n, pl* **-preys** : lamprea *f*
lampshade [ˈlæmpˌʃeɪd] *n* : pantalla *f* (de lámpara)
lance[1] [ˈlænts] *vt* **lanced; lancing** : sajar
lance[2] *n* : lanza *f*
lance corporal *n* : cabo *m* interino, soldado *m* de primera clase
land[1] [ˈlænd] *vt* **1** : desembarcar (pasajeros de un barco), hacer aterrizar (un avión) **2** CATCH : pescar, sacar (un pez) del agua **3** GAIN, SECURE : conseguir, ganar ⟨to land a job : conseguir empleo⟩ **4** DELIVER : dar, asestar ⟨he landed a punch : asestó un puñetazo⟩ — *vi* **1** : aterrizar, tomar tierra, atracar ⟨the plane just landed : el avión acaba de aterrizar⟩ ⟨the ship landed an hour ago : el barco atracó hace una hora⟩ **2** ALIGHT : posarse, aterrizar ⟨to land on one's feet : caer de pie⟩ **3** FALL : caer **4** END UP, WIND UP : ir a parar
land[2] *n* **1** GROUND : tierra *f* ⟨dry land : tierra firme⟩ **2** TERRAIN : terreno *m* **3** NATION : país *m*, nación *f* **4** DOMAIN : mundo *m*, dominio *m* ⟨the land of dreams : el mundo de los sueños⟩
landfill [ˈlændˌfɪl] *n* : vertedero *m* (de basuras)
landing [ˈlændɪŋ] *n* **1** : aterrizaje *m* (de aviones), desembarco *m* (de barcos) **2** : descanso *m*, descansillo *m* *Spain* (de una escalera)
landing field *n* : campo *m* de aterrizaje
landing pad *n* : plataforma *f* de aterrizaje
landing strip → **airstrip**
landlady [ˈlændˌleɪdi] *n, pl* **-dies** : casera *f*, dueña *f*, arrendadora *f*
landless [ˈlændləs] *adj* : sin tierra
landlocked [ˈlændˌlɑkt] *adj* : sin salida al mar
landlord [ˈlændˌlɔrd] *n* : dueño *m*, casero *m*, arrendador *m*
landlubber [ˈlændˌlʌbər] *n* : marinero *m* de agua dulce
landmark [ˈlændˌmɑrk] *n* **1** : señal *f* (geográfica), punto *m* de referencia **2** MILESTONE : hito *m* ⟨a landmark in our history : un hito en nuestra historia⟩ **3** MONUMENT : monumento *m* histórico
landowner [ˈlændˌoːnər] *n* : hacendado *m*, -da *f*; terrateniente *mf*
landscape[1] [ˈlændˌskeɪp] *vt* **-scaped; -scaping** : ajardinar
landscape[2] *n* : paisaje *m*
landscaper [ˈlændˌskeɪpər] *n* : paisajista *mf*
landscaping [ˈlændˌskeɪpɪŋ] *n* : paisajismo *m*

landslide [ˈlændˌslaɪd] *n* **1** : desprendimiento *m* de tierras, derrumbe *m* **2 landslide victory** : victoria *f* arrolladora

landward [ˈlændwərd] *adv* : en dirección de la tierra, hacia tierra

lane [ˈleɪn] *n* **1** PATH, WAY : camino *m*, sendero *m* **2** : carril *m* (de una carretera)

language [ˈlæŋɡwɪd] *n* **1** : idioma *m*, lengua *f* ⟨the English language : el idioma inglés⟩ **2** : lenguaje *m* ⟨body language : lenguaje corporal⟩

languid [ˈlæŋɡwɪd] *adj* : lánguido — **languidly** *adv*

languish [ˈlæŋɡwɪʃ] *vi* **1** WEAKEN : languidecer, debilitarse **2** PINE : consumirse, suspirar (por) ⟨to languish for love : suspirar por el amor⟩ ⟨he languished in prison : estuvo pudriéndose en la cárcel⟩

languor [ˈlæŋɡər] *n* : languidez *f*

languorous [ˈlæŋɡərəs] *adj* : lánguido — **languorously** *adv*

lank [ˈlæŋk] *adj* **1** THIN : delgado, larguirucho *fam* **2** LIMP : lacio

lanky [ˈlæŋki] *adj* **lankier; -est** : delgado, larguirucho *fam*

lanolin [ˈlænələn] *n* : lanolina *f*

lantern [ˈlæntərn] *n* : linterna *f*, farol *m*

Laotian [leɪˈoːʃən, ˈlaʊʃən] *n* : laosiano *m*, -na *f* — **Laotian** *adj*

lap¹ [ˈlæp] *v* **lapped; lapping** *vt* **1** FOLD : plegar, doblar **2** WRAP : envolver **3** : lamer, besar ⟨waves were lapping the shore : las olas lamían la orilla⟩ **4 to lap up** : beber a lengüetadas (como un gato) — *vi* OVERLAP : traslaparse

lap² *n* **1** : falda *f*, regazo *m* (del cuerpo) **2** OVERLAP : traslapo *m* **3** : vuelta *f* (en deportes) **4** STAGE : etapa *f* (de un viaje)

lapdog [ˈlæpˌdɔɡ] *n* : perro *m* faldero

lapel [ləˈpɛl] *n* : solapa *f*

Lapp [ˈlæp] *n* : lapón *m*, -pona *f* — **Lapp** *adj*

lapse¹ [ˈlæps] *vi* **lapsed; lapsing 1** FALL, SLIP : caer ⟨to lapse into bad habits : caer en malos hábitos⟩ ⟨to lapse into unconsciousness : perder el conocimiento⟩ ⟨to lapse into silence : quedarse callado⟩ **2** FADE : decaer, desvanecerse ⟨her dedication lapsed : su dedicación se desvaneció⟩ **3** CEASE : cancelarse, perderse **4** ELAPSE : transcurrir, pasar **5** EXPIRE : caducar

lapse² *n* **1** SLIP : lapsus *m*, desliz *m*, falla *f* ⟨a lapse of memory : una falla de memoria⟩ **2** INTERVAL : lapso *m*, intervalo *m*, período *m* **3** EXPIRATION : caducidad *f*

laptop¹ [ˈlæpˌtɑp] *adj* : portátil, laptop

laptop² *n* : laptop *m*

larcenous [ˈlɑrsənəs] *adj* : de robo

larceny [ˈlɑrsəni] *n, pl* **-nies** : robo *m*, hurto *m*

larch [ˈlɑrtʃ] *n* : alerce *m*

lard [ˈlɑrd] *n* : manteca *f* de cerdo

larder [ˈlɑrdər] *n* : despensa *f*, alacena *f*

large [ˈlɑrd] *adj* **larger; largest 1** BIG : grande **2** COMPREHENSIVE : amplio, extenso **3 by and large** : por lo ge-

neral **4 at large** : en general ⟨society at large : la sociedad en general⟩ **5 at large** FREE : prófugo, suelto ⟨the criminal is still at large : el criminal permanece prófugo⟩ **6 at large** : general, que habla/escribe (etc.) de diversos temas

largely [ˈlɑrdli] *adv* : en gran parte, en su mayoría

largeness [ˈlɑrdnəs] *n* : lo grande

largesse *or* **largess** [lɑrˈʒɛs, -ˈdʒɛs] *n* : generosidad *f*, largueza *f*

lariat [ˈlæriət] *n* : lazo *m*

lark [ˈlɑrk] *n* **1** FUN : diversión *f* ⟨what a lark! : ¡qué divertido!⟩ **2** : alondra *f* (pájaro)

larva [ˈlɑrvə] *n, pl* **-vae** [-ˌviː, -ˌvaɪ] : larva *f* — **larval** [-vəl] *adj*

laryngitis [ˌlærənˈdʒaɪtəs] *n* : laringitis *f*

larynx [ˈlærɪŋks] *n, pl* **-rynges** [ləˈrɪnˌdʒiːz] *or* **-ynxes** [ˈlærɪŋksəz] : laringe *f*

lasagna [ləˈzɑnjə] *n* : lasaña *f*

lascivious [ləˈsɪviəs] *adj* : lascivo

lasciviousness [ləˈsɪviəsnəs] *n* : lascivia *f*, lujuria *f*

laser [ˈleɪzər] *n* : láser *m*

laser disc *n* : disco *m* láser

laser printer *n* : impresora *f* láser

lash¹ [ˈlæʃ] *vt* **1** WHIP : azotar **2** BIND : atar, amarrar

lash² *n* **1** WHIP : látigo *m* **2** STROKE : latigazo *m* **3** EYELASH : pestaña *f*

lass [ˈlæs] *or* **lassie** [ˈlæsi] *n* : muchacha *f*, chica *f*

lasso¹ [ˈlæˌsoː, læˈsuː] *vt* : lazar

lasso² *n, pl* **-sos** *or* **-soes** : lazo *m*, reata *f* *Mex*

last¹ [ˈlæst] *vi* **1** CONTINUE : durar ⟨how long will it last? : ¿cuánto durará?⟩ **2** ENDURE : aguantar, durar **3** SURVIVE : durar, sobrevivir **4** SUFFICE : durar, bastar — *vt* ` **1** : durar ⟨it will last you a lifetime : te durará toda la vida⟩ **2 to last out** : aguantar

last² *adv* **1** : en último lugar, al último ⟨we came in last : llegamos en último lugar⟩ **2** : por última vez, la última vez ⟨I saw him last in Bogota : lo vi por última vez en Bogotá⟩ **3** FINALLY : por último, en conclusión ⟨last but not least : por último, pero no por ello menos importante⟩

last³ *adj* **1** FINAL : último, final **2** PREVIOUS : pasado ⟨last year : el año pasado⟩

last⁴ *n* **1** : el último, la última, lo último ⟨at last : por fin, al fin, finalmente⟩ **2** : horma *f* (de zapatero)

last–ditch [ˈlæstˈdɪtʃ] *adj* : desesperado, último

lasting [ˈlæstɪŋ] *adj* : perdurable, duradero, estable

lastly [ˈlæstli] *adv* : por último, finalmente

last–minute [ˈlæstˈmɪnət] *adj* : de última hora

latch¹ [ˈlætʃ] *vt* **1** : cerrar con picaporte **2 to latch on to** *or* **to latch onto** GRAB : agarrarse de **3 to latch on to** *or* **to latch onto** : pegarse a (alguien), abrazar (una costumbre, etc.)

latch[2] *n* : picaporte *m*, pestillo *m*, pasador *m*

late[1] [ˈleɪt] *adv* **later; latest** **1** : tarde ⟨to arrive late : llegar tarde⟩ ⟨to sleep late : dormir hasta tarde⟩ ⟨I'm running late : voy a llegar tarde⟩ **2** : a última hora, a finales ⟨late in the evening : a últimas horas de la tarde⟩ ⟨late in the month : a finales del mes⟩ **3** RECENTLY : recién, últimamente ⟨as late as last year : todavía en el año pasado⟩ **4 of late** → **lately**

late[2] *adj* **later; latest** **1** TARDY : tardío ⟨I'm sorry I'm late : perdón por llegar tarde⟩ ⟨I was two hours late : llegué dos horas tarde⟩ ⟨the plane was two hours late : el avión llegó con dos horas de retraso⟩ ⟨we had a late start : salimos tarde⟩ ⟨the train's late arrival/departure : el retraso en la llegada/salida del tren⟩ **2** : avanzado ⟨because of the late hour : a causa de la hora avanzada⟩ ⟨he's in his late thirties : tiene cerca de cuarenta años⟩ **3** DECEASED : difunto, fallecido **4** RECENT : reciente, último ⟨our late quarrel : nuestra última pelea⟩ **5 it's getting late** : se hace tarde **6 late in the day** : tarde ⟨it's a little late in the day for an apology : ya es un poco tarde para pedir disculpas⟩

latecomer [ˈleɪtˌkʌmər] *n* : rezagado *m*, -da *f*

lately [ˈleɪtli] *adv* : recientemente, últimamente

lateness [ˈleɪtnəs] *n* **1** DELAY : retraso *m*, atraso *m*, tardanza *f* **2** : lo avanzado (de la hora)

latent [ˈleɪtənt] *adj* : latente — **latently** *adv*

later[1] [ˈleɪtər] *adv* **1** : más tarde, después ⟨she returned later : volvió más tarde⟩ ⟨later in the week : a finales de la semana⟩ **2 later on** : más tarde, después **3 no later than** : a más tardar **4 see you later!** : ¡hasta luego!

later[2] *adj* **1** : posterior, ulterior ⟨his later works : sus obras posteriores⟩ ⟨in her later years : en su madurez⟩ **2 at a later time/date** : más tarde, más adelante

lateral [ˈlæʈərəl] *adj* : lateral — **laterally** *adv*

latest[1] [ˈleɪtəst] *adj* : último

latest[2] *n* **1** : lo último **2 at the latest** : a más tardar

latex [ˈleɪˌtɛks] *n, pl* **-tices** [ˈleɪʈəˌsiːz, ˈlæʈə-] *or* **-texes** : látex *m*

lath [ˈlæθ, ˈlæð] *n, pl* **laths** *or* **lath** : listón *m*

lathe [ˈleɪð] *n* : torno *m*

lather[1] [ˈlæðər] *vt* : enjabonar — *vi* : espumar, hacer espuma

lather[2] *n* **1** : espuma *f* (de jabón) **2** : sudor *m* (de caballo) **3 to get into a lather** : ponerse histérico

Latin[1] *adj* : latino

Latin[2] *n* **1** : latín *m* (idioma) **2** → **Latin American**

Latin–American [ˈlæʈənəˈmrikən] *adj* : latinoamericano

Latin American *n* : latinoamericano *m*, -na *f*

latitude [ˈlæʈəˌtuːd, -ˌtjuːd] *n* : latitud *f*

latrine [ləˈtriːn] *n* : letrina *f*

latte [ˈlɑˌteɪ] *n* : café *m* con leche

latter [ˈlæʈər] *adj* **1** SECOND : segundo **2** LAST : último **3 the latter** : éste, ésta, éstos *pl*, éstas *pl*

lattice [ˈlæʈəs] *n* : enrejado *m*, celosía *f*

Latvian [ˈlætviən] *n* : letón *m*, -tona *f* — **Latvian** *adj*

laud[1] [ˈlɔd] *vt* : alabar, loar

laud[2] *n* : alabanza *f*, loa *f*

laudable [ˈlɔdəbəl] *adj* : loable — **laudably** [-bli] *adv*

laugh[1] [ˈlæf] *vi* **1** : reír, reírse **2 to laugh at** : reírse de — *vt* **to laugh off** : tomar en/a broma

laugh[2] *n* **1** LAUGHTER : risa *f* **2** JOKE : chiste *m*, broma *f* ⟨he did it for a laugh : lo hizo en broma, lo hizo para divertirse⟩

laughable [ˈlæfəbəl] *adj* : risible, de risa

laughingstock [ˈlæfɪŋˌstɑk] *n* : hazmerreír *m*

laughter [ˈlæftər] *n* : risa *f*, risas *fpl*

launch[1] [ˈlɔntʃ] *vt* **1** HURL : lanzar **2** : botar (un barco) **3** START : iniciar, empezar **4** : lanzar, abrir (un programa)

launch[2] *n* **1** : lancha *f* (bote) **2** LAUNCHING : lanzamiento *m*

launchpad [ˈlɔntʃˌpæd] *n* : plataforma *f* de lanzamiento

launder [ˈlɔndər] *vt* **1** : lavar y planchar (ropa) **2** : blanquear, lavar (dinero)

launderer [ˈlɔndərər] *n* : lavandero *m*, -ra *f*

laundress [ˈlɔndrəs] *n* : lavandera *f*

laundry [ˈlɔndri] *n, pl* **laundries** **1** : ropa *f* sucia, ropa *f* para lavar ⟨to do the laundry : lavar la ropa⟩ **2** : lavandería *f* (servicio de lavar)

laureate [ˈlɔriət] *n* : laureado *m*, -da *f* ⟨poet laureate : poeta laureado⟩

laurel [ˈlɔrəl] *n* **1** : laurel *m* (planta) **2 laurels** *npl* : laureles *mpl* ⟨to rest on one's laurels : dormirse uno en sus laureles⟩

lava [ˈlɑvə, ˈlæ-] *n* : lava *f*

lavatory [ˈlævəˌtori] *n, pl* **-ries** : baño *m*, cuarto *m* de baño

lavender [ˈlævəndər] *n* : lavanda *f*, espliego *m*

lavish[1] [ˈlævɪʃ] *vt* : prodigar (a), colmar (de)

lavish[2] *adj* **1** EXTRAVAGANT : pródigo, generoso, derrochador **2** ABUNDANT : abundante **3** LUXURIOUS : lujoso, espléndido

lavishly [ˈlævɪʃli] *adv* : con generosidad, espléndidamente ⟨to live lavishly : vivir a lo grande⟩

lavishness [ˈlævɪʃnəs] *n* : generosidad *f*, esplendidez *f*

law [ˈlɔ] *n* **1** : ley *f* ⟨to break the law : violar la ley⟩ **2** : derecho *m* ⟨criminal law : derecho criminal⟩ ⟨to study law : estudiar derecho⟩ ⟨law school : facultad de Derecho⟩ **3** : abogacía *f* ⟨to practice law : ejercer la abogacía⟩ **4** PRINCIPLE : ley *f* ⟨the laws of physics : las leyes de la física⟩ **5** RULE : ley *f* (en religión, etc.) **6 the law** POLICE : policía *f* ⟨to be in trouble with the law : tener problemas con la ley⟩

law–abiding ['lɔǝ,baɪdɪŋ] *adj* : observante de la ley

lawbreaker ['lɔ,breɪkǝr] *n* : infractor *m*, -tora *f* de la ley

lawful ['lɔfǝl] *adj* : legal, legítimo, lícito — **lawfully** *adv*

lawgiver ['lɔ,ɡɪvǝr] *n* : legislador *m*, -dora *f*

lawless ['lɔlǝs] *adj* : anárquico, ingobernable — **lawlessly** *adv*

lawlessness ['lɔlǝsnǝs] *n* : anarquía *f*, desorden *m*

lawmaker ['lɔ,meɪkǝr] *n* : legislador *m*, -dora *f*

lawman ['lɔmǝn] *n, pl* **-men** [-mǝn, -,mɛn] : agente *m* del orden

lawn ['lɔn] *n* : césped *m*, pasto *m*

lawn mower *n* : cortadora *f* de césped

lawsuit ['lɔ,su:t] *n* : pleito *m*, litigio *m*, demanda *f*

lawyer ['lɔɪǝr, 'lɔjǝr] *n* : abogado *m*, -da *f*

lax ['læks] *adj* : laxo, relajado — **laxly** *adv*

laxative ['læksǝṭɪv] *n* : laxante *m*

laxity ['læksǝṭi] *n* : relajación *f*, descuido *m*, falta *f* de rigor

lay¹ ['leɪ] *v* **laid** ['leɪd]; **laying** *vt* **1** PLACE PUT : poner, colocar ⟨she laid it on the table : lo puso en la mesa⟩ ⟨to lay a hand/finger on someone : ponerle a alguien la mano encima⟩ **2** INSTALL : poner, colocar (ladrillos, etc.), tender (vías, cables, etc.) ⟨to lay the foundation : poner los cimientos⟩ **3** PREPARE : preparar ⟨to lay a trap : tender una trampa⟩ ⟨the best-laid plans : los planes mejor trazados⟩ **4** BET : apostar **5** PLACE : poner (énfasis, etc.) ⟨to lay the blame on : echarle la culpa a⟩ **6 to be laid over** : hacer escala **7 to be laid up** : estar enfermo, tener que guardar cama **8 to lay aside** : dejar a un lado **9 to lay aside/by** SAVE : guardar, ahorrar **10 to lay down** IMPOSE ESTABLISH : imponer, establecer **11 to lay down** : dejar, deponer (armas) **12 to lay eggs** : poner huevos **13 to lay in** STOCK : comprar, proveerse de **14 to lay it on (thick)** : exagerar, cargar las tintas **15 to lay out** PRESENT : presentar, exponer ⟨he laid out his plan : presentó su proyecto⟩ **16 to lay off** : despedir (a un empleado) **17 to lay out** DESIGN : diseñar (el trazado de) **18 to lay up** STORE : guardar, almacenar — *vi* **1 to lay into** ATTACK : arremeter contra **2 to lay off** : dejar (un vicio) **3 to lay off** : dejar en paz ⟨lay off him! : ¡déjalo en paz!⟩ ⟨lay off! : ¡basta ya!⟩ **4 to lay over** : hacer escala

lay² → **lie¹**

lay³ *adj* SECULAR : laico, lego

lay⁴ *n* **1** : disposición *f*, configuración *f* ⟨the lay of the land : la configuración del terreno⟩ **2** BALLAD : romance *m*, balada *f*

layer ['leɪǝr] *n* **1** : capa *f* (de pintura, etc.), estrato *m* (de roca) **2** : gallina *f* ponedora

layman ['leɪmǝn] *n, pl* **-men** [-mǝn, -,mɛn] **1** : laico *m*, lego *m*, seglar *mf* (en religión) **2** : profano *m*, -na *f*; lego *m*, -ga *f* ⟨in layman's terms : en lenguaje sencillo⟩

layoff ['leɪ,ɔf] *n* : despido *m*

layout ['leɪ,aut] *n* : disposición *f*, distribución *f* (de una casa, etc.), trazado *m* (de una ciudad)

layover ['leɪ,o:vǝr] *n* STOPOVER : escala *f*

layperson ['leɪ,pǝrsǝn] *n* **1** : laico *m*, -ca *f*; lego *m*, -ga *f*; seglar *mf* (en religión) **2** : profano *m*, -na *f*; lego *m*, -ga *f*

laywoman ['leɪ,wumǝn] *n, pl* **-women** [-,wɪmǝn] : laica *f*, lega *f*

laziness ['leɪzinǝs] *n* : pereza *f*, flojera *f*

laze ['leɪz] *v* **lazed; lazing** *vi or* **to laze around** : holgazanear — *vt* **to laze away** ⟨she lazed away the afternoon : pasó la tarde holgazaneando⟩

lazy ['leɪzi] *adj* **lazier; -est** : perezoso, holgazán — **lazily** ['leɪzǝli] *adv*

lazybones ['leɪzi,bo:nz] *n* : gandul *m*, -dula *f*

LCD [,ɛl,si:'di:] *n* (*l*iquid *c*rystal *d*isplay) : LCD *m*, pantalla *f* de cristal líquido

leach ['li:tʃ] *vt* : filtrar

lead¹ ['li:d] *v* **led** ['lɛd]; **leading** *vt* **1** GUIDE : conducir, llevar, guiar **2** DIRECT : dirigir **3** HEAD : encabezar, ir al frente de **4** : llevar (una vida) **5 to lead on** : engañar — *vi* **1 to lead to** : conducir a, llevar a **2 to lead to** : dar a (dícese de una puerta) **3** : ir a la cabeza, ir en cabeza (en una competición, etc.) ⟨they're leading by 20 points : van ganando por 20 puntos, tienen 20 puntos de ventaja⟩ **4 to lead to** : resultar en, llevar a ⟨it only leads to trouble : sólo resulta en problemas⟩ **5 to lead up to** PRECEDE : preceder a **6 to lead up to** INTRODUCE : introducir

lead² *n* **1** : delantera *f*, primer lugar *m* ⟨to take the lead : tomar la delantera⟩ ⟨to be in the lead : ir a la cabeza, ir en cabeza⟩ ⟨to follow someone's lead : seguir el ejemplo de alguien⟩ **2** *or* **lead actor** : primer actor *m*, primera actriz *f* **3** *or* **lead guitarist** : guitarrista *mf* principal **4** *or* **lead role** : papel *m* principal **5** *or* **lead singer** : cantante *mf* principal **6** *or* **lead story** : artículo *m* principal **7** CLUE : pista *f* **8** : correa *f* (de un perro)

lead³ ['lɛd] *n* **1** : plomo *m* (metal) **2** : mina *f* (de lápiz) **3 lead poisoning** : saturnismo *m*

leaden ['lɛdǝn] *adj* **1** : plomizo ⟨a leaden sky : un cielo plomizo⟩ **2** HEAVY : pesado

leader ['li:dǝr] *n* : jefe *m*, -fa *f*; líder *mf*; dirigente *mf*; gobernante *mf*

leadership ['li:dǝr,ʃɪp] *n* : mando *m*, dirección *f*

leading ['li:dɪŋ] *adj* **1** IMPORTANT : principal, importante ⟨a leading expert : un destacado experto⟩ **2** FOREMOST : principal, más importante ⟨the leading cause of death : la principal causa de muerte⟩

leaf¹ ['li:f] *vi* **1** : echar hojas (dícese de un

árbol) **2 to leaf through** : hojear (un libro)

leaf² *n, pl* **leaves** [ˈliːvz] **1** : hoja *f* (de
plantas o libros) **2 to turn over a new
leaf** : hacer borrón y cuenta nueva

leafless [ˈliːfləs] *adj* : sin hojas, pelado

leaflet [ˈliːflət] *n* : folleto *m*

leafy [ˈliːfi] *adj* **leafier; -est** : frondoso

league¹ [ˈliːɡ] *v* **leagued; leaguing** *vt*
: aliar, unir — *vi* : aliarse, unirse

league² *n* **1** : legua *f* (medida de distancia) **2** ASSOCIATION : alianza *f*, sociedad
f, liga *f*

leak¹ [ˈliːk] *vt* **1** : perder, dejar escapar (un
líquido o un gas) **2** : filtrar (información) — *vi* **1** : gotear, escaparse, fugarse (dícese de un líquido o un gas) **2**
: hacer agua (dícese de un bote) **3** : filtrarse, divulgarse (dícese de información)

leak² *n* **1** HOLE : agujero *m* (en recipien-
tes), gotera *f* (en un tejado) **2** ESCAPE
: fuga *f*, escape *m* **3** : filtración *f* (de información)

leakage [ˈliːkɪd] *n* : escape *m*, fuga *f*

leaky [ˈliːki] *adj* **leakier; -est** : agujereado
(dícese de un recipiente), que hace agua
(dícese de un bote), con goteras (dícese
de un tejado)

lean¹ [ˈliːn] *vi* **1** BEND : inclinarse,
ladearse **2** RECLINE : reclinarse **3**
RELY : apoyarse (en), depender (de) **4**
INCLINE TEND : inclinarse, tender — *vt*
: apoyar

lean² *adj* **1** THIN : delgado, flaco **2** : sin
grasa, magro (dícese de la carne)

leaning [ˈliːnɪŋ] *n* TENDENCY : inclinación
f

leanness [ˈliːnnəs] *n* : delgadez *f*

lean–to [ˈliːnˌtuː] *n* : cobertizo *m*

leap¹ [ˈliːp] *vi* **leaped** [ˈliːpt, ˈlɛpt] *or* **leapt;
leaping** : saltar, brincar

leap² *n* : salto *m*, brinco *m*

leap year *n* : año *m* bisiesto

learn [ˈlərn] *vt* **1** : aprender ⟨to learn to
sing : aprender a cantar⟩ **2** MEMORIZE
: aprender de memoria **3** DISCOVER
: saber, enterarse de — *vi* **1** : aprender
⟨to learn from experience : aprender por
experiencia⟩ **2** FIND OUT : enterarse,
saber

learned [ˈlərnəd] *adj* : erudito

learner [ˈlərnər] *n* : principiante *mf*, estudiante *mf*

learning [ˈlərnɪŋ] *n* : erudición *f*, saber *m*

lease¹ [ˈliːs] *vt* **leased; leasing** : arrendar

lease² *n* : contrato *m* de arrendamiento

leash *n* : traílla *f*

least¹ [ˈliːst] *adv* : menos ⟨when least expected : cuando menos se espera⟩

least² *adj* (*superlative of* LITTLE) : menor,
más mínimo

least³ *n* **1 at least** : al menos, por lo menos **2 the least** : lo menos ⟨it's the least
I can do : es lo menos que puedo hacer⟩
⟨it doesn't bother me in the least : no me
molesta para nada⟩ **3 to say the least**
: por no decir más

leather [ˈlɛðər] *n* : cuero *m*

leathery [ˈlɛðəri] *adj* : curtido (dícese de
la piel), correoso (dícese de la carne)

leave¹ [ˈliːv] *v* **left** [ˈlɛft]; **leaving** *vt* **1** DE-
PART : salir(se) de, ir(se) de ⟨she left the
office/party : salió de la oficina/fiesta⟩
⟨I left home after high school : me fui de
casa después de terminar el colegio⟩ **2**
: dejar ⟨we left her doing her work : la
dejamos trabajando⟩ **3** : dejar (que alguien haga algo) ⟨leave the dishes for me
: deja los trastes, los lavaré después⟩ ⟨we
left all the arrangements to him : dejamos que él lo arreglara todo⟩ ⟨I'll leave
it (up) to you (to decide) : te dejo a ti
decidir⟩ ⟨leave it to me! : ¡yo me encargo!⟩ ⟨leave it to her to arrive early
: llegó temprano, como siempre⟩ **4**
ABANDON : dejar (uno a su familia, etc.)
⟨they left me to clean up : se fueron y
me tocó a mí limpiar⟩ **5** QUIT, GIVE UP
: dejar (un trabajo, etc.) **6** *or* **to leave
behind** FORGET : dejar, olvidarse (en
casa, etc.) **7** *or* **to leave behind** : dejar
⟨she left her home/family (behind)
: dejó (atrás) su hogar/a su familia⟩ ⟨to
leave the past behind : dejar atrás el
pasado⟩ **8** DEPOSIT : dejar ⟨leave it on
the table/with me : déjalo en la mesa/
conmigo⟩ ⟨I left him at the airport : lo
dejé en el aeropuerto⟩ ⟨to leave a message : dejar un mensaje⟩ **9** : dejar (en
un estado) ⟨I left the lights on : dejé las
luces encendidas⟩ ⟨he was left paralyzed
: se quedó paralizado⟩ **10** ALLOW, RE-
SERVE : dejar (espacio, etc.) **11** : dejar
(una marca, etc.) **12** BEQUEATH : dejar,
legar **13** : dejar ⟨he left (behind) a wife
and child : dejó esposa y un hijo⟩ **14 to
be left** : quedar ⟨it's all I have left : es
todo lo que me queda⟩ **15 to be left
over** : sobrar **16 to be/get left behind**
: quedarse atrás **17 to leave off** : dejar
de, parar de **18 to leave off/out** OMIT
: omitir, excluir — *vi* : irse, salir, partir,
marcharse ⟨she left yesterday morning
: se fue ayer por la mañana⟩ ⟨they left
for Paris : salieron para París⟩

leave² *n* **1** PERMISSION : permiso *m* ⟨by
your leave : con su permiso⟩ **2** *or* **leave
of absence** : permiso *m*, licencia *f* ⟨ma-
ternity leave : licencia por materni-
dad⟩ **3 to take one's leave** : despedirse

leaven [ˈlɛvən] *n* : levadura *f*

leaves → **leaf²**

leaving [ˈliːvɪŋ] *n* **1** : salida *f*, partida *f* **2**

leavings *npl* : restos *mpl*, sobras *fpl*

Lebanese [ˌlɛbəˈniːz, -ˈniːs] *n* : libanés *m*,
-nesa *f* — **Lebanese** *adj*

lecherous [ˈlɛtʃərəs] *adj* : lascivo, libidinoso — **lecherously** *adv*

lechery [ˈlɛtʃəri] *n* : lascivia *f*, lujuria *f*

lectern [ˈlɛktərn] *n* : atril *m*

lecture¹ [ˈlɛktʃər] *v* **-tured; -turing** *vi* : dar
clase, dictar clase, dar una conferencia
— *vt* SCOLD : sermonear, echar una reprimenda a, regañar

lecture² *n* **1** : conferencia *f* **2** REPRI-
MAND : reprimenda *f*

lecturer [ˈlɛktʃərər] *n* **1** SPEAKER : conferenciante *mf* **2** TEACHER : profesor
m, -sora *f*

led → **lead¹**

LED [ˌɛlˌiː'diː] *n* (*l*ight-*e*mitting *d*iode) : LED *m*, led *m*
ledge ['lɛD] *n* : repisa *f* (de una pared), antepecho *m* (de una ventana), saliente *m* (de una montaña)
ledger ['lɛD ər] *n* : libro *m* mayor, libro *m* de contabilidad
lee[1] ['liː] *adj* : de sotavento
lee[2] *n* : sotavento *m*
leech ['liːtʃ] *n* : sanguijuela *f*
leek ['liːk] *n* : puerro *m*
leer[1] ['lɪr] *vi* : mirar con lascivia
leer[2] *n* : mirada *f* lasciva
leery ['lɪri] *adj* : receloso
lees ['liːz] *npl* : posos *mpl*, heces *fpl*
leeward[1] ['liːwərd, 'luːərd] *adj* : de sotavento
leeward[2] *n* : sotavento *m*
leeway ['liːˌweɪ] *n* : libertad *f*, margen *m*
left[1] ['lɛft] *adv* : hacia la izquierda
left[2] → **leave**[1]
left[3] *adj* : izquierdo
left[4] *n* : izquierda *f* ⟨on the left : a la izquierda⟩
left–click ['lɛft'klɪk] *vi* : hacer clic/click izquierdo — *vt* : hacer clic/click izquierdo en
left–hand ['lɛft'hand] *adj* 1 : de la izquierda 2 → **left-handed**
left–handed ['lɛft'handəd] *adj* 1 : zurdo (dícese de una persona) 2 : con doble sentido ⟨a left-handed compliment : un cumplido a medias⟩
leftist ['lɛftɪst] *n* : izquierdista *mf* — **leftist** *adj*
leftover ['lɛftˌoːvər] *adj* : sobrante, que sobra
leftovers ['lɛftˌoːvərz] *npl* : restos *mpl*, sobras *fpl*
left wing *n* **the left wing** : la izquierda
left–winger ['lɛft'wɪŋər] *n* : izquierdista *mf*
leg ['lɛG] *n* 1 : pierna *f* (de una persona, de carne, de ropa), pata *f* (de un animal, de muebles) 2 STAGE : etapa *f* (de un viaje), vuelta *f* (de una carrera)
legacy ['lɛGəsi] *n*, *pl* **-cies** : legado *m*, herencia *f*
legal ['liːGəl] *adj* 1 : legal, jurídico ⟨legal advisor : asesor jurídico⟩ ⟨the legal profession : la abogacía⟩ 2 LAWFUL : legítimo, legal ⟨legal tender : moneda de curso legal⟩
legalistic [ˌliːGə'lɪstɪk] *adj* : legalista
legality [li'GæləDi] *n*, *pl* **-ties** : legalidad *f*
legalize ['liːGəˌlaɪz] *vt* **-ized; -izing** : legalizar
legally ['liːGəli] *adv* : legalmente
legate ['lɛGət] *n* : legado *m*
legation [lɪ'GeɪʃƏn] *n* : legación *f*
legend ['lɛD ənd] *n* 1 STORY : leyenda *f* 2 INSCRIPTION : leyenda *f*, inscripción *f* 3 : signos *mpl* convencionales (en un mapa)
legendary ['lɛD ənˌdɛri] *adj* : legendario
legerdemain [ˌlɛD ərdə'meɪn] → **sleight of hand**
leggings ['lɛGɪŋz, 'lɛGənz] *npl* : mallas *fpl*
legibility [ˌlɛD ə'bɪləDi] *n* : legibilidad *f*
legible ['lɛD əbəl] *adj* : legible

legibly ['lɛD əbli] *adv* : de manera legible
legion ['liːD ən] *n* : legión *f*
legionnaire [ˌliːD ə'nær] *n* : legionario *m*, -ria *f*
legislate ['lɛD əsˌleɪt] *vi* **-lated; -lating** : legislar
legislation [ˌlɛD əs'leɪʃən] *n* : legislación *f*
legislative ['lɛD əsˌleɪDɪv] *adj* : legislativo, legislador
legislator ['lɛD əsˌleɪDər] *n* : legislador *m*, -dora *f*
legislature ['lɛD əsˌleɪtʃər] *n* : asamblea *f* legislativa
legitimacy [lɪ'D ɪDəməsi] *n* : legitimidad *f*
legitimate [lɪ'D ɪDəmət] *adj* 1 VALID : legítimo, válido, justificado 2 LAWFUL : legítimo, legal
legitimately [lɪ'D ɪDəmətli] *adv* : legítimamente
legitimize [lɪ'D ɪDəˌmaɪz] *vt* **-mized; -mizing** : legitimar, hacer legítimo
legume ['lɛˌGjuːm, lɪ'Gjuːm] *n* : legumbre *f*
leisure ['liːʒər, 'lɛ-] *n* 1 : ocio *m*, tiempo *m* libre ⟨a life of leisure : una vida de ocio⟩ 2 **to take one's leisure** : reposar 3 **at your leisure** : cuando te venga bien, cuando tengas tiempo
leisurely ['liːʒərli, 'lɛ-] *adj* & *adv* : lento, sin prisas
lemming ['lɛmɪŋ] *n* : lemming *m*
lemon ['lɛmən] *n* : limón *m*
lemonade [ˌlɛmə'neɪd] *n* : limonada *f*
lemony ['lɛməni] *adj* : a limón
lempira [lɛm'pɪrə] *n* : lempira *f* (unidad monetaria)
lend ['lɛnd] *vt* **lent** ['lɛnt]; **lending** 1 : prestar ⟨to lend money : prestar dinero⟩ 2 GIVE : dar ⟨it lends force to his criticism : da fuerza a su crítica⟩ ⟨to lend a hand to someone : echarle una mano a alguien⟩ 3 **to lend oneself to** : prestarse a
length ['lɛŋkθ] *n* 1 : longitud *f*, largo *m* ⟨10 feet in length : 10 pies de largo⟩ 2 DURATION : duración *f* 3 : trozo *m* (de madera), corte *m* (de tela) 4 **to go to any lengths** : hacer todo lo posible 5 **at ~** : extensamente ⟨to speak at length : hablar largo y tendido⟩ 6 **at ~** FINALLY : por fin
lengthen ['lɛŋkθən] *vt* 1 : alargar ⟨can they lengthen the dress? : ¿se puede alargar el vestido?⟩ 2 EXTEND, PROLONG : prolongar, extender — *vi* : alargarse, crecer ⟨the days are lengthening : los días están creciendo⟩
lengthways ['lɛŋkθˌweɪz] → **lengthwise**
lengthwise ['lɛŋkθˌwaɪz] *adv* : a lo largo, longitudinalmente
lengthy ['lɛŋkθi] *adj* **lengthier; -est** 1 OVERLONG : largo y pesado 2 EXTENDED : prolongado, largo
leniency ['liːniənsi] *n*, *pl* **-cies** : lenidad *f*, indulgencia *f*
lenient ['liːniənt] *adj* : indulgente, poco severo
leniently ['liːniəntli] *adv* : con lenidad, con indulgencia
lens ['lɛnz] *n* 1 : cristalino *m* (del ojo) 2 : lente *mf* (de un instrumento o una cámara) 3 → **contact lens**

lent → **lend**

Lent [ˈlɛnt] n : Cuaresma f

lentil [ˈlɛntəl] n : lenteja f

Leo [ˈliːoː] n **1** : Leo m (signo o constelación) **2** : Leo mf (persona)

leopard [ˈlɛpərd] n : leopardo m

leotard [ˈliːəˌtɑrd] n : leotardo m, malla f

leper [ˈlɛpər] n : leproso m, -sa f

leprechaun [ˈlɛprəˌkɑn] n : duende m (irlandés)

leprosy [ˈlɛprəsi] n : lepra f — **leprous** [ˈlɛprəs] adj

lesbian[1] [ˈlɛzbiən] adj : lesbiano

lesbian[2] n : lesbiana f

lesbianism [ˈlɛzbiəˌnɪzəm] n : lesbianismo m

lesion [ˈliːʒən] n : lesión f

less[1] [ˈlɛs] adv (comparative of LITTLE[1]) : menos ⟨the less you know, the better : cuanto menos sepas, mejor⟩ ⟨less and less : cada vez menos⟩

less[2] adj (comparative of LITTLE[2]) : menos ⟨less than three : menos de tres⟩ ⟨less money : menos dinero⟩ ⟨nothing less than perfection : nada menos que la perfección⟩

less[3] pron : menos ⟨I'm earning less : estoy ganando menos⟩

less[4] prep : menos ⟨one month less two days : un mes menos dos días⟩

-less [ləs] suf : sin

lessee [lɛˈsiː] n : arrendatario m, -ria f

lessen [ˈlɛsən] vt : disminuir, reducir — vi : disminuir, reducirse

lesser [ˈlɛsər] adj : menor ⟨to a lesser degree : en menor grado⟩

lesson [ˈlɛsən] n **1** CLASS : clase f, curso m **2** : lección f ⟨the lessons of history : las lecciones de la historia⟩

lessor [ˈlɛˌsɔr, lˈsɔr] n : arrendador m, -dora f

lest [ˈlɛst] conj : para (que) no ⟨lest we forget : para que no olvidemos⟩

let [ˈlɛt] v let; letting vt **1** ALLOW : dejar, permitir ⟨let me see it : déjame verlo⟩ ⟨let it chill : dejarlo enfriar⟩ ⟨let him in/out : déjalo entrar/salir⟩ **2** MAKE : hacer ⟨let me know : házmelo saber, avísame⟩ ⟨let them wait! : ¡que esperen!⟩ **3** RENT : alquilar **4** (used in the first person plural imperative) ⟨let's go! : ¡vamos!, ¡vámonos!⟩ ⟨let us pray : oremos⟩ **5** let alone : ni mucho menos, (y) menos aún ⟨I can barely understand it, let alone explain it : apenas puedo entenderlo, ni mucho menos explicarlo⟩ **6** to let down LOWER : bajar **7** to let down DISAPPOINT : fallar ⟨to let someone down gently : suavizarle el golpe a alguien⟩ **8** to let go RELEASE, FREE : soltar ⟨let me go! : ¡suéltame!⟩ **9** to let oneself go : dejarse, abandonarse **10** to let in on ⟨to let someone in on a secret : contarle un secreto a alguien⟩ **11** to let off FORGIVE : perdonar ⟨they let him off the hook : no dejaron ir sin castigo⟩ ⟨they let her off lightly : la dieron un leve castigo⟩ **12** to let off : echar (vapor), hacer estallar (un petardo, etc.) **13** to let oneself in for : exponerse a (críticas), buscarse (problemas) ⟨I didn't know what I was letting myself in for : no sabía en la que me estaba metiendo⟩ **14** to let out REVEAL : revelar **15** to let out : soltar (un grito, etc.) **16** to let out : ensanchar (un vestido, etc.) — vi **1** to let go RELAX : soltarse el pelo **2** to let go (of) : soltar ⟨let go (of me)! : ¡suéltame!⟩ **3** to let on REVEAL, SHOW : revelar, demostrar ⟨don't let on! : ¡no digas nada!⟩ ⟨he didn't let on that he knew : hizo como si no lo supiera⟩ **4** to let on PRETEND, SEEM : fingir, parecer **5** to let out END : terminar ⟨school lets out in June : el año escolar termina en junio⟩ **6** to let up ABATE : amainar, disminuir ⟨the pace never lets up : el ritmo nunca disminuye⟩ **7** to let up STOP : parar **8** to let up on : soltar (un freno, etc.), no ser tan duro con (alguien)

letdown [ˈlɛtˌdaʊn] n : chasco m, decepción f

lethal [ˈliːθəl] adj : letal — **lethally** adv

lethargic [lɪˈθɑrDɪk] adj : letárgico

lethargy [ˈlɛθərDi] n : letargo m

let's [ˈlɛts] contraction of LET US → **let**

letter[1] [ˈlɛtər] vt : marcar con letras, inscribir letras en

letter[2] n **1** : letra f (del alfabeto) **2** : carta f ⟨a letter to my mother : una carta a mi madre⟩ **3 letters** npl ARTS : letras fpl **4** to the letter : al pie de la letra

letter bomb n : carta f bomba

letterhead [ˈlɛtərˌhɛd] n **1** : membrete m (de una carta) **2** : papel m con membrete

lettering [ˈlɛtərɪŋ] n : letra f

lettuce [ˈlɛtəs] n : lechuga f

letup [ˈlɛtˌʌp] n LULL : pausa f, respiro m

leukemia [luˈkiːmiə] n : leucemia f

levee [ˈlɛvi] n : dique m

level[1] [ˈlɛvəl] v -eled or -elled; -eling or -elling vt **1** or to level off FLATTEN : nivelar, aplanar **2** AIM : apuntar (una pistola), dirigir (una acusación) **3** RAZE : rasar, arrasar — vi **1** to level off/out : estabilizarse (dícese de los precios, etc.), nivelarse (dícese de un avión), allanarse (dícese del paisaje) **2** to level with someone : ser sincero con alguien

level[2] adj **1** EVEN : llano, plano, parejo **2** CALM : tranquilo ⟨to keep a level head : no perder la cabeza⟩

level[3] n : nivel m

leveler [ˈlɛvələr] n : nivelador m, -dora f

levelheaded [ˈlɛvəlˈhɛdəd] adj : sensato, equilibrado

levelly [ˈlɛvəli] adv CALMLY : con ecuanimidad f, con calma

levelness [ˈlɛvəlnəs] n : uniformidad f

lever [ˈlɛvər, ˈliː-] n : palanca f

leverage [ˈlɛvərɪdʒ, ˈliː-] n **1** : apalancamiento m (en física) **2** INFLUENCE : influencia f, palanca f fam

leviathan [lɪˈvaɪəθən] n : leviatán m, gigante m

levitate [ˈlɛvəˌteɪt] vi -tated; -tating : levitar — vt : hacer levitar

levity ['lɛvəṭi] *n* : ligereza *f*, frivolidad *f*

levy[1] ['lɛvi] *vt* **levied; levying 1** IMPOSE : imponer, exigir, gravar (un impuesto) **2** COLLECT : recaudar (un impuesto)

levy[2] *n*, *pl* **levies** : impuesto *m*, gravamen *m*

lewd ['lu:d] *adj* : lascivo — **lewdly** *adv*

lewdness ['lu:dnəs] *n* : lascivia *f*

lexical ['lɛksikəl] *adj* : léxico

lexicographer [ˌlɛksə'kɑɡrəfər] *n* : lexicógrafo *m*, -fa *f*

lexicographical [ˌlɛksəko'ɡræfıkəl] *or* **lexicographic** [-'ɡræfık] *adj* : lexicográfico

lexicography [ˌlɛksə'kɑɡrəfi] *n* : lexicografía *f*

lexicon ['lɛksıˌkɑn] *n*, *pl* **-ica** [-kə] *or* **-icons** : léxico *m*

liability [ˌlaɪə'bıləṭi] *n*, *pl* **-ties 1** RESPONSIBILITY : responsabilidad *f* **2** SUSCEPTIBILITY : propensión *f* **3** DRAWBACK : desventaja *f* **4 liabilities** *npl* DEBTS : deudas *fpl*, pasivo *m*

liable ['laɪəbəl] *adj* **1** RESPONSIBLE : responsable **2** SUSCEPTIBLE : propenso **3** PROBABLE : probable ⟨it's liable to happen : es probable que suceda⟩

liaison ['li:əˌzɑn, li'eɪ-] *n* **1** CONNECTION : enlace *m*, relación *f* **2** AFFAIR : amorío *m*, aventura *f*

liar ['laɪər] *n* : mentiroso *m*, -sa *f*; embustero *m*, -ra *f*

libel[1] ['laɪbəl] *vt* **-beled** *or* **-belled; -beling** *or* **-belling** : difamar, calumniar

libel[2] *n* : difamación *f*, calumnia *f*

libelous *or* **libellous** ['laɪbələs] *adj* : difamatorio, calumnioso, injurioso

liberal[1] ['lıbrəl, 'lıbərəl] *adj* **1** TOLERANT : liberal, tolerante **2** GENEROUS : generoso **3** ABUNDANT : abundante **4 liberal arts** : humanidades *fpl*, artes *fpl* liberales

liberal[2] *n* : liberal *mf*

liberalism ['lıbrəˌlızəm, 'lıbərə-] *n* : liberalismo *m*

liberality [ˌlıbə'ræləṭi] *n*, *pl* **-ties** : liberalidad *f*, generosidad *f*

liberalize ['lıbrəˌlaɪz, 'lıbərə-] *vt* **-ized; -izing** : liberalizar

liberally ['lıbrəli, 'lıbərə-] *adv* **1** GENEROUSLY : generosamente **2** ABUNDANTLY : abundantemente **3** FREELY : libremente

liberate ['lıbəˌreɪt] *vt* **-ated; -ating** : liberar, libertar

liberation [ˌlıbə'reɪʃən] *n* : liberación *f*

liberator ['lıbəˌreɪṭər] *n* : libertador *m*, -dora *f*

Liberian [laɪ'bıriən] *n* : liberiano *m*, -na *f* — **Liberian** *adj*

libertarian [ˌlıbər'tɛriən] *adj & n* : libertario *m*, -ria *f*

libertine ['lıbərˌti:n] *n* : libertino *m*, -na *f*

liberty ['lıbərṭi] *n*, *pl* **-ties 1** : libertad *f* **2 to take the liberty of** : tomarse la libertad de **3 to take liberties with** : tomarse confianzas con, tomarse libertades con

libido [lə'bi:do:, -'baɪ-] *n*, *pl* **-dos** : libido *f* — **libidinous** [lə'bıdənəs] *adj*

Libra ['li:brə] *n* **1** : Libra *m* (signo o constelación) **2** : Libra *mf* (persona)

librarian [laɪ'brɛriən] *n* : bibliotecario *m*, -ria *f*

library ['laɪˌbrɛri] *n*, *pl* **-braries** : biblioteca *f*

librettist [lı'brɛnɪst] *n* : libretista *mf*

libretto [lı'brɛṭo] *n*, *pl* **-tos** *or* **-ti** [-'ṭi:] : libreto *m*

Libyan ['lıbiən] *n* : libio *m*, -bia *f* — **Libyan** *adj*

lice → **louse**

license[1] ['laɪsənts] *vt* **licensed; licensing** : licenciar, autorizar, dar permiso a

license[2] *or* **licence** *n* **1** PERMISSION : licencia *f*, permiso *m* **2** PERMIT : licencia *f*, carnet *m* *Spain* ⟨driver's license : licencia de conducir⟩ **3** FREEDOM : libertad *f* **4** LICENTIOUSNESS : libertinaje *m*

licensed *adj* CERTIFIED : autorizado, certificado, licenciado ⟨a licensed physician : un médico certificado⟩ ⟨a licensed driver : un conductor con licencia⟩

license plate *n* : placa *f* de matrícula; chapa *f* Arg, Uru; patente *f* Arg, Chile, Uru

licentious [laɪ'sɛntʃəs] *adj* : licencioso, disoluto — **licentiously** *adv*

licentiousness [laɪ'sɛntʃəsnəs] *n* : libertinaje *m*

lichen ['laɪkən] *n* : liquen *m*

licit ['lısət] *adj* : lícito

lick[1] ['lık] *vt* **1** : lamer **2** BEAT : darle una paliza (a alguien)

lick[2] *n* **1** : lamida *f*, lengüetada *f* ⟨a lick of paint : una mano de pintura⟩ **2** BIT : pizca *f*, ápice *m* **3 a lick and a promise** : una lavada a la carrera

licorice ['lıkərıʃ, -rəs] *n* : regaliz *m*, dulce *m* de regaliz

lid ['lıd] *n* **1** COVER : tapa *f* **2** EYELID : párpado *m*

lie[1] ['laɪ] *vi* **lay** ['leɪ]; **lain** ['leɪn]; **lying** ['laɪıŋ] **1** *or* **to lie down** : acostarse, echarse, tumbarse, tenderse ⟨I lay down on the bed : me acosté en la cama⟩ ⟨lie on your back : acuéstate boca arriba⟩ ⟨he was lying unconscious on the floor : estaba tendido en el suelo sin sentido⟩ ⟨to take something lying down : dejar pasar algo sin protestar⟩ **2** : estar, estar situado, encontrarse ⟨the book lay on the table : el libro estaba en la mesa⟩ ⟨the city lies to the south : la ciudad se encuentra al sur⟩ ⟨there were papers lying around : había papeles tirados por todos lados⟩ **3** CONSIST : consistir **4 to lie ahead** AWAIT : estar por venir **5 to lie around** RELAX : holgazanear **6 to lie back** : reclinarse **7 to lie down on the job** : no cumplir **8 to lie in/with** : residir en ⟨the power lies in the people : el poder reside en el pueblo⟩ **9 to lie low** : tratar de no llamar la atención

lie[2] *vi* **lied; lying** ['laɪıŋ] : mentir

lie[3] *n* **1** UNTRUTH : mentira *f* ⟨to tell lies : decir mentiras⟩ **2** POSITION : posición *f*

liege ['li:ɖ] *n* : señor *m* feudal

lien ['li:n, 'li:ən] *n* : derecho *m* de retención

lieu ['lu:] *n* **in lieu of** : en lugar de

lieutenant [lu:'tɛnənt] *n* : teniente *mf*

life ['laɪf] *n, pl* **lives** ['laɪvz] **1** : vida *f* ⟨plant life : la vida vegetal⟩ **2** EXISTENCE : vida *f* ⟨early/late in life : en la juventud/vejez⟩ ⟨later in life : a una edad más avanzada⟩ ⟨I've lived here my whole/entire life, I've lived here all my life : siempre he vivido aquí⟩ ⟨never in my life : (jamás) en la vida⟩ ⟨life of crime : vida delictiva⟩ ⟨way of life : estilo de vida⟩ **3** BIOGRAPHY : biografía *f*, vida *f* **4** DURATION : duración *f*, vida *f* **5** LIVELINESS : vivacidad *f*, animación *f* **6** *or* **life imprisonment** : cadena *f* perpetua **7 a matter of life and death** : una cuestión de vida o muerte **8 as big as life** : en carne y hueso **9 for dear life** : desesperadamente **10 for the life of me** : por nada del mundo **11 not on your life** : ni pensarlo **12 that's life** : así es la vida **13 the life of the party** : el alma de la fiesta **14 to bring back to life** : resucitar **15 to come to life** : animarse **16 to claim/take someone's life** : matar a alguien **17 to frighten/scare the life out of** : darle/pegarle un susto mortal a **18 to lose one's life** : perder la vida **19 to risk life and limb** : arriesgar la vida **20 to save someone's life** : salvarse la vida **21 to take one's own life** : suicidarse **22 true to life** : verosímil

lifeblood ['laɪf,blʌd] *n* : parte *f* vital, sustento *m*

lifeboat ['laɪf,bo:t] *n* : bote *m* salvavidas

life cycle *n* : ciclo *m* vital

life expectancy *n* : esperanza *f* de vida, expectativa *f* de vida, expectativas *fpl* de vida

lifeguard ['laɪf,ɡɑrd] *n* : socorrista *mf*; salvavidas *mf*; bañero *m*, -ra *f Arg, Uru*

life insurance *n* : seguro *m* de vida

life jacket *n* : chaleco *m* salvavidas

lifeless ['laɪfləs] *adj* : sin vida, muerto

lifelike ['laɪf,laɪk] *adj* : que parece vivo, natural, verosímil

lifeline ['laɪf,laɪn] *n* **1** : cuerda *f* de salvamento **2** : sustento *m*

lifelong ['laɪf'lɔŋ] *adj* : de toda la vida ⟨a lifelong friend : un amigo de toda la vida⟩

life preserver *n* : salvavidas *m*

lifesaver ['laɪf,seɪvər] *n* **1** : salvación *f* **2** → **lifeguard**

lifesaving ['laɪf,seɪvɪŋ] *n* : socorrismo *m*

life sentence *n* : cadena *f* perpetua

life–size ['laɪf'saɪz] *or* **life–sized** ['laɪf'saɪzd] *adj* : de tamaño natural

lifespan ['laɪf,spæn] *n* : vida *f*

lifestyle ['laɪf,staɪl] *n* : estilo *m* de vida

lifetime ['laɪf,taɪm] *n* : vida *f*, curso *m* de la vida

lift¹ ['lɪft] *vt* **1** RAISE : levantar, alzar, subir **2** END : levantar ⟨to lift a ban : levantar una prohibición⟩ — *vi* **1** RISE : levantarse, alzarse **2** CLEAR UP : despejar ⟨the fog lifted : se disipó la niebla⟩

lift² *n* **1** LIFTING : levantamiento *m*, alzamiento *m* **2** BOOST : impulso *m*, estímulo *m* **3 to give someone a lift** : llevar en coche a alguien

liftoff ['lɪft,ɔf] *n* : despegue *m*

ligament ['lɪɡəmənt] *n* : ligamento *m*

ligature ['lɪɡə,tʃʊr, -tʃər] *n* : ligadura *f*

light¹ ['laɪt] *v* **lit** ['lɪt] *or* **lighted; lighting** *vt* **1** ILLUMINATE : iluminar, alumbrar **2** IGNITE : encender, prenderle fuego a — *vi* : encenderse, prender

light² *vi* **lighted** *or* **lit** ['lɪt]; **lighting 1** LAND, SETTLE : posarse **2** DISMOUNT : bajarse, apearse

light³ ['laɪt] *adv* **1** LIGHTLY : suavemente, ligeramente **2 to travel light** : viajar con poco equipaje

light⁴ *adj* **1** LIGHTWEIGHT : ligero, liviano, poco pesado **2** EASY : fácil, ligero, liviano ⟨light reading : lectura fácil⟩ ⟨light work : trabajo liviano⟩ **3** GENTLE, MILD : fino, suave, leve ⟨a light breeze : una brisa suave⟩ ⟨a light rain : una lluvia fina⟩ **4** DELICATE : leve, ligero ⟨she wore light makeup : llevaba poco maquillaje⟩ **5** LOW : bajo ⟨light turnout : baja asistencia⟩ ⟨light trading : poco movimiento (en los mercados)⟩ ⟨traffic was light : había poco tráfico⟩ **6** MINOR, SUPERFICIAL : de poca importancia, superficial **7** BRIGHT : brillante (dícese de una luz), luminosa (dícese de una habitación) ⟨to be light out : ser de día⟩ ⟨to get light out : amanecer⟩ **8** PALE : claro (dícese de los colores), rubio (dícese del pelo) **9** *or* **lite** : light

light⁵ *n* **1** ILLUMINATION : luz *f* **2** DAYLIGHT : luz *f* del día **3** DAWN : amanecer *m*, madrugada *f* **4** LAMP : lámpara *f* ⟨to turn off the light : apagar la luz⟩ **5** ASPECT : aspecto *m* ⟨in a new light : con otros ojos⟩ ⟨to show in a good/bad light : dar una imagen positiva/negativa a⟩ ⟨in (the) light of : en vista de, a la luz de⟩ **6** MATCH : fósforo *m*, cerillo *m* **7 the light at the end of the tunnel** : la luz al final del túnel **8 the light of someone's life** : la niña de los ojos de alguien **9 to be out like a light** : dormirse como un tronco **10 to bring to light** : sacar a (la) luz **11 to cast/shed/throw light on** : arrojar luz sobre **12 to come to light** : salir a (la) luz **13 to see the light** : abrir los ojos

lightbulb ['laɪt,bʌlb] *n* : bombilla *f*; foco *m*; bombillo *m CA, Col, Ven*; bombita *f Arg, Uru*

lighten ['laɪtən] *vt* **1** ILLUMINATE : iluminar, dar más luz a **2** : aclararse (el pelo) **3** : aligerar (una carga, etc.) **4** RELIEVE : aliviar **5** GLADDEN : alegrar ⟨it lightened his heart : alegró su corazón⟩

lighter ['laɪtər] *n* : encendedor *m*

light–headed ['laɪt,hɛ'dəd] *adj* : mareado

lighthearted ['laɪt,hɑrtəd] *adj* : alegre, despreocupado, desenfadado — **lightheartedly** *adv*

lightheartedness ['laɪt,hɑrtədnəs] *n* : desenfado *m*, alegría *f*

lighthouse ['laɪt,haʊs] *n* : faro *m*

lighting ['laɪtɪŋ] *n* : iluminación *f*

lightly ['laɪtli] *adv* **1** GENTLY : suavemente **2** SLIGHTLY : ligeramente **3** FRIVOLOUSLY : a la ligera **4 to let off lightly** : tratar con indulgencia

lightness ['laɪtnəs] *n* **1** BRIGHTNESS : luminosidad *f*, claridad *f* **2** GENTLENESS : ligereza *f*, suavidad *f*, delicadeza *f* **3** : ligereza *f*, liviandad *f* (de peso)

lightning ['laɪtnɪŋ] *n* : relámpago *m*, rayo *m*

lightning bug → **firefly**

lightproof ['laɪt,pru:f] *adj* : impenetrable por la luz, opaco

lightweight¹ ['laɪt,weɪt] *adj* : ligero, liviano, de poco peso

lightweight² *n* : peso *m* ligero (en deportes)

light–year ['laɪt,jɪr] *n* : año *m* luz

likable *or* **likeable** ['laɪkəbəl] *adj* : simpático, agradable

like¹ ['laɪk] *v* **liked; liking** *vt* **1** : gustarle (algo a uno) ⟨he likes rice : le gusta el arroz⟩ ⟨she doesn't like flowers : a ella no le gustan las flores⟩ ⟨I like you : me caes bien⟩ **2** WANT : querer, desear ⟨I'd like a hamburger : quiero una hamburguesa⟩ ⟨he would like more help : le gustaría tener más ayuda⟩ ⟨I'd like to come : quiero venir⟩ ⟨I'd like to think (that) . . . : quiero creer que . . .⟩ — *vi* : querer ⟨do as you like : haz lo que quieras⟩ ⟨if you like : si quieres, si te parece⟩ ⟨whenever you like : cuando quieras⟩

like² *adj* : parecido, semejante, similar

like³ *n* **1** PREFERENCE : preferencia *f*, gusto *m* **2 the like** : cosa *f* parecida, cosas *fpl* por el estilo ⟨I've never seen the like : nunca he visto cosa parecida⟩

like⁴ *conj* **1** AS IF : como si ⟨they looked at me like I was crazy : se me quedaron mirando como si estuviera loca⟩ **2** AS : como, igual que ⟨she doesn't love you like I do : ella no te quiere como yo⟩

like⁵ *prep* **1** : como, parecido a ⟨she acts like my mother : se comporta como mi madre⟩ ⟨he looks like me : se parece a mí⟩ **2** : propio de, típico de ⟨that's just like her : eso es muy típico de ella⟩ **3** : como ⟨animals like cows : animales como vacas⟩ **4 like this like that** : así ⟨do it like that : hazlo así⟩

-like ['laɪk] *suf* **1** : como, parecido a ⟨cat-like : como un gato, parecido a un gato, felino⟩ **2** : propio de ⟨ladylike : propio de una dama⟩

likelihood ['laɪkli,hʊd] *n* : probabilidad *f* ⟨in all likelihood : con toda probabilidad⟩

likely¹ ['laɪkli] *adv* : probablemente ⟨most likely he's sick : lo más probable es que esté enfermo⟩ ⟨they're likely to come : es probable que vengan⟩

likely² *adj* **likelier; -est 1** PROBABLE : probable ⟨to be likely to : ser muy probable que⟩ **2** SUITABLE : apropiado, adecuado **3** BELIEVABLE : verosímil, creíble **4** PROMISING : prometedor

liken ['laɪkən] *vt* : comparar

likeness ['laɪknəs] *n* **1** SIMILARITY : se-

mejanza *f*, parecido *m* **2** PORTRAIT : retrato *m*

likewise ['laɪk,waɪz] *adv* **1** SIMILARLY : de la misma manera, asimismo **2** ALSO : también, además, asimismo

liking ['laɪkɪŋ] *n* **1** FONDNESS : afición *f* (por una cosa), simpatía *f* (por una persona) **2** TASTE : gusto *m* ⟨is it to your liking? : ¿te gusta?⟩ ⟨to take a liking to : tomarle el gusto a algo⟩

lilac ['laɪlək, -,læk, -,lɑk] *n* : lila *f* — **lilac** *adj*

lilt ['lɪlt] *n* : cadencia *f*, ritmo *m* alegre

lily ['lɪli] *n, pl* **lilies 1** : lirio *m*, azucena *f* **2 lily of the valley** : lirio *m* de los valles, muguete *m*

lily pad *n* : hoja *f* grande (de un nenúfar)

lima bean ['laɪmə] *n* : frijol *m* de media luna

limb ['lɪm] *n* **1** APPENDAGE : miembro *m*, extremidad *f* **2** BRANCH : rama *f*

limber¹ ['lɪmbər] *vi or* **to limber up** : calentarse, prepararse

limber² *adj* : ágil (dícese de las personas), flexible (dícese de los objetos)

limbo ['lɪm,bo:] *n, pl* **-bos 1** : limbo *m* (en religión) **2** OBLIVION : olvido *m* ⟨the project is in limbo : el proyecto ha caído en el olvido⟩

lime ['laɪm] *n* **1** : cal *f* (óxido) **2** : lima *f* (fruta), limón *m* verde *Mex*

limelight ['laɪm,laɪt] *n* **to be in the limelight** : ser el centro de atención, estar en el candelero

limerick ['lɪmərɪk] *n* : poema *m* jocoso de cinco versos

limestone ['laɪm,sto:n] *n* : piedra *f* caliza, caliza *f*

limit¹ ['lɪmət] *vt* : limitar, restringir

limit² *n* **1** MAXIMUM : límite *m*, máximo *m* ⟨speed limit : límite de velocidad⟩ **2 limits** *npl* : límites *mpl*, confines *mpl* ⟨city limits : límites de la ciudad⟩ **3 that's the limit!** : ¡eso es el colmo!

limitation [,lɪmə'teɪʃən] *n* : limitación *f*, restricción *f*

limited ['lɪmətəd] *adj* : limitado, restringido

limitless ['lɪmətləs] *adj* : ilimitado, sin límites

limousine ['lɪmə,zi:n, ,lɪmə'-] *n* : limusina *f*

limp¹ ['lɪmp] *vi* : cojear

limp² *adj* **1** FLACCID : fláccido **2** LANK : lacio (dícese del pelo) **3** WEAK : débil ⟨to feel limp : sentirse desfallecer, sentirse sin fuerzas⟩

limp³ *n* : cojera *f*

limpet ['lɪmpət] *n* : lapa *f*

limpid ['lɪmpəd] *adj* : límpido, claro

limply ['lɪmpli] *adv* : sin fuerzas

limpness ['lɪmpnəs] *n* : flaccidez *f*, debilidad *f*

limy ['laɪmi] *adj* : calizo

linden ['lɪndən] *n* : tilo *m*

line¹ ['laɪn] *v* **lined; lining** *vt* **1** : forrar, cubrir ⟨to line a dress : forrar un vestido⟩ ⟨to line the walls : cubrir las paredes⟩ **2** MARK : rayar, trazar líneas en **3** BORDER : bordear **4** *or* **to line up** ALIGN : alinear **5 to line up** : organizar — *vi* **to line up** : ponerse en fila, hacer cola

line² *n* **1** MARK : línea *f*, raya *f* ⟨straight line : (línea) recta⟩ ⟨dotted line : línea de puntos⟩ **2** BOUNDARY : línea *f*, límite *m* ⟨dividing line : línea divisoria⟩ ⟨property line : límite de la propiedad⟩ ⟨to draw the line : fijar límites⟩ ⟨to draw the line at something : no tolerar algo⟩ **3** ROW : fila *f*, hilera *f* **4** QUEUE : cola *f* ⟨to wait in line : hacer cola⟩ **5 lines** *npl* SILHOUETTE : líneas *fpl* **6** CORD, ROPE : cuerda *f* **7** → **pipeline 8** WIRE : cable *m* ⟨power line : cable eléctrico⟩ **9** : línea *f* (de teléfono) ⟨the line is busy : está ocupado⟩ ⟨the boss is on the line : te llama el jefe⟩ **10** : línea *f* (de texto), verso *m* (de poesía) **11** NOTE : nota *f*, líneas *fpl* ⟨drop me a line : mándame unas líneas⟩ **12 lines** *npl* : diálogo *m* (de un actor) **13** COMMENT : comentario *m* **14** WRINKLE : línea *f*, arruga *f* (de la cara) **15** PATH : línea *f* ⟨line of fire : línea de fuego⟩ **16** SERVICE : línea *f* ⟨bus line : línea de autobuses⟩ **17** : línea *f*, cadena *f* ⟨production line : línea de producción⟩ **18** SERIES : serie *f* (de problemas, etc.) **19** LINEAGE : línea *f*, linaje *m* **20** MANNER : línea *f* ⟨line of inquiry : línea de investigación⟩ ⟨to take a firm line on : ponerse firme sobre⟩ **21** POSITION : línea *f* ⟨the party line : la línea del partido⟩ **22** OCCUPATION : ocupación *f*, rama *f*, especialidad *f* **23 lines** *npl* RANKS : líneas *fpl*, filas *fpl* ⟨behind enemy lines : tras las líneas enemigas⟩ **24** RANGE : línea *f* ⟨product line : línea de productos⟩ **25** AGREEMENT : conformidad *f* ⟨to be in line with : estar conforme con⟩ ⟨to fall into line : conformarse⟩ **26 along the line** ⟨somewhere along the line : en algún momento⟩ **27 along the lines of** : por el estilo de **28 down the line** : en el futuro **29 in line** ⟨he's in line for a promotion : lo consideran para un ascenso⟩ ⟨first/next in line to succeed the President : primero en la línea de sucesión a la presidencia⟩ **30 in line** ⟨to keep someone in line : mantener a alguien a raya⟩ **31 on the line** ENDANGERED : en peligro **32 out of line** DISRESPECTFUL : fuera de lugar (dícese de un comentario) ⟨you're out of line : te has pasado de la raya⟩ **33 to lay it on the line** : no andarse con rodeos **34 to read between the lines** : leer entre líneas

lineage [ˈlɪniɪɪd] *n* : linaje *m*, abolengo *m*

lineal [ˈlɪniəl] *adj* : en línea directa

lineaments [ˈlɪniəmənts] *npl* : facciones *fpl* (de la cara), rasgos *mpl*

linear [ˈlɪniər] *adj* : lineal

lined [ˈlaɪnd] *adj* **1** : de rayas (dícese de papel, etc.) **2** WRINKLY : arrugado (dícese de la cara)

linen [ˈlɪnən] *n* **1** : lino *m* **2** *or* **bed linen** : ropa *f* de cama **3** *or* **table linen** : mantelería *f*

liner [ˈlaɪnər] *n* **1** LINING : forro *m* **2** SHIP : buque *m*, transatlántico *m*

lineup [ˈlaɪnˌəp] *n* **1** : fila *f* de sospechosos **2** : formación *f* (en deportes) **3** ALIGNMENT : alineación *f*

linger [ˈlɪŋɡər] *vi* **1** TARRY : quedarse, entretenerse, rezagarse **2** PERSIST : persistir, sobrevivir

lingerie [ˌlɑnD əˈreɪ, ˌlænʒəˈriː] *n* : ropa *f* íntima femenina, lencería *f*

lingo [ˈlɪŋɡo] *n*, *pl* **-goes 1** LANGUAGE : idioma *m* **2** JARGON : jerga *f*

linguist [ˈlɪŋɡwɪst] *n* : lingüista *mf*

linguistic [lɪŋˈɡwɪstɪk] *adj* : lingüístico

linguistics [lɪŋˈɡwɪstɪks] *n* : lingüística *f*

liniment [ˈlɪnəmənt] *n* : linimento *m*

lining [ˈlaɪnɪŋ] *n* : forro *m*

link¹ [ˈlɪŋk] *vt* : unir, enlazar, conectar — *vi* **to link up** : unirse, conectar

link² *n* **1** : eslabón *m* (de una cadena) **2** BOND : conexión *f*, lazo *m*, vínculo *m* **3** HYPERLINK : enlace *m*, vínculo *m*

linkage [ˈlɪŋkɪD] *n* : conexión *f*, unión *f*, enlace *m*

links [ˈlɪŋks] *n* : campo *m* de golf, cancha *f* de golf

linoleum [ləˈnoːliəm] *n* : linóleo *m*

lint [ˈlɪnt] *n* : pelusa *f*

lintel [ˈlɪntəl] *n* : dintel *m*

lion [ˈlaɪən] *n* : león *m*

lioness [ˈlaɪənɪs] *n* : leona *f*

lionize [ˈlaɪəˌnaɪz] *vt* **-ized; -izing** : tratar a una persona como muy importante

lip [ˈlɪp] *n* **1** : labio *m* **2** : pico *m* (de una jarra), borde *m* (de una taza)

lip-read [ˈlɪpˌriːd] *vi* : leer los labios

lipreading [ˈlɪpˌriːdɪŋ] *n* : lectura *f* de los labios

lipstick [ˈlɪpˌstɪk] *n* : lápiz *m* labial, barra *f* de labios

liquefy [ˈlɪkwəˌfaɪ] *v* **-fied; -fying** *vt* : licuar — *vi* : licuarse

liqueur [lɪˈkʊr, -ˈkər, -ˈkjʊr] *n* : licor *m*

liquid¹ [ˈlɪkwəd] *adj* : líquido

liquid² *n* : líquido *m*

liquidate [ˈlɪkwəˌdeɪt] *vt* **-dated; -dating** : liquidar

liquidation [ˌlɪkwəˈdeɪʃən] *n* : liquidación *f*

liquidity [lɪkˈwɪdət‖] *n* : liquidez *f*

liquor [ˈlɪkər] *n* : alcohol *m*, bebidas *fpl* alcohólicas, licor *m*

lisp¹ [ˈlɪsp] *vi* : cecear

lisp² *n* : ceceo *m*

lissome [ˈlɪsəm] *adj* **1** FLEXIBLE : flexible **2** LITHE : ágil y grácil

list¹ [ˈlɪst] *vt* **1** ENUMERATE : hacer una lista de, enumerar **2** INCLUDE : poner en una lista, incluir — *vi* : escorar (dícese de un barco)

list² *n* : lista *f* ⟨he's first/last on the list : es el primero/último de la lista⟩

listen [ˈlɪsən] *vi* **1** : escuchar, oír **2 to listen to** HEED : escuchar, prestar atención a, hacer caso de (algo), hacerle caso (a alguien) **3 to listen to reason** : atender a razones

listener [ˈlɪsənər] *n* : oyente *mf*, persona *f* que sabe escuchar

listless [ˈlɪstləs] *adj* : lánguido, apático — **listlessly** *adv*

listlessness [ˈlɪstləsnəs] *n* : apatía *f*, languidez *f*, desgana *f*

lit ['lɪt] → light
litany ['lɪtəni] n, pl -nies : letanía f
liter ['liːtər] n : litro m
literacy ['lɪtərəsi] n : alfabetismo m
literal ['lɪtərəl] adj : literal — literally adv
literary ['lɪtə,rri] adj : literario
literate ['lɪtərət] adj : alfabetizado
literature ['lɪtərə,tʃʊr, -tʃər] n : literatura f
lithe ['laɪð, 'laɪθ] adj : ágil y grácil
lithesome ['laɪðsəm, 'laɪθ-] → lissome
lithium ['lɪθiəm] n : litio m
lithograph ['lɪθə,ɡræf] n : litografía f
lithographer [lɪ'θɑɡrəfər, 'lɪθə-,ɡræfər] n
  : litógrafo m, -fa f
lithography [lɪ'θɑɡrəfi] n : litografía f
lithosphere ['lɪθə,sfɪr] n : litosfera f
Lithuanian [,lɪθə'weɪniən] n 1 : lituano
  m (idioma) 2 : lituano m, -na f —
  Lithuanian adj
litigant ['lɪtɪɡənt] n : litigante mf
litigate ['lɪtə,ɡeɪt] vi -gated; -gating : litigar
litigation [,lɪtə'ɡeɪʃən] n : litigio m
litmus ['lɪtməs] n : tornasol m
litmus paper n : papel m de tornasol
litmus test n : prueba f decisiva
litter¹ ['lɪtər] vt : tirar basura en, ensuciar
  — vi : tirar basura
litter² n 1 : camada f, cría f ⟨a litter of
  kittens : una cría de gatitos⟩ 2 STRETCHER : camilla f 3 RUBBISH : basura f 4
  : arena f higiénica (para gatos)
little¹ ['lɪtəl] adv less ['lɛs]; least ['liːst]
  1 : poco ⟨she sings very little : canta muy
  poco⟩ 2 little did I know that . . . : no
  tenía la menor idea de que . . . 3 as little
  as possible : lo menos posible
little² adj littler or less ['lɛs] or lesser
  ['lɛsər]; littlest or least ['liːst] 1 SMALL
  : pequeño 2 : poco ⟨they speak little
  Spanish : hablan poco español⟩ ⟨little by
  little : poco a poco⟩ ⟨a little bit : un
  poco⟩ ⟨a little while : un ratito⟩ 3 TRIVIAL : sin importancia, trivial
little³ n 1 : poco m ⟨little has changed
  : poco ha cambiado⟩ 2 a little : un
  poco, algo ⟨it's a little surprising : es algo
  sorprendente⟩
Little Dipper → dipper
little person n, pl little people 1 : persona f pequeña; enano m, -na f 2 the
  little people : la gente común
liturgical [lə'tərdʒɪkəl] adj : litúrgico —
  liturgically [-kli] adv
liturgy ['lɪtərdʒi] n, pl -gies : liturgia f
livable ['lɪvəbəl] adj : habitable
live¹ ['lɪv] v lived; living vi 1 EXIST : vivir
  ⟨as long as I live : mientras viva⟩ ⟨to live
  from day to day : vivir al día⟩ ⟨long live
  the Queen/King! : ¡viva el rey/la
  reina!⟩ 2 : llevar una vida, vivir ⟨he
  lived simply : llevó una vida sencilla⟩
  ⟨they lived happily ever after : vivieron
  felices (y comieron perdices)⟩ 3 SUBSIST : vivir, mantenerse ⟨to live within/
  beyond one's means : vivir dentro/fuera
  de sus posibilidades⟩ 4 RESIDE : vivir,
  residir ⟨where do you live? : ¿dónde
  vives?⟩ 5 live and let live : vive y deja
  vivir a los demás 6 to live down ⟨they'll

never let you live it down, you'll never
  live it down : nunca te dejarán olvidarlo⟩ 7 to live off : vivir de (algo), vivir a costa de (alguien) 8 to live on : vivir de (un sueldo, etc.), alimentarse de
  (comida) ⟨they live on less than a dollar
  a day : viven con menos de un dólar por
  día⟩ 9 to live on PERSIST : permanecer 10 to live out one's life : vivir
  toda su vida 11 to live through SURVIVE : sobrevivir 12 to live together
  : vivir juntos 13 to live up to : estar a la
  altura de (las expectativas, etc.) 14 to
  live up to : cumplir (su palabra, etc.) 15
  to live with : vivir con (alguien) 16 to
  live with ACCEPT : aceptar — vt : llevar,
  vivir ⟨he lived a simple life : llevó una
  vida sencilla⟩ ⟨to live the good life : vivir
  la buena vida⟩
live² ['laɪv] adj 1 LIVING : vivo 2 BURNING : encendido ⟨a live coal : una
  brasa⟩ 3 : con corriente ⟨live wires
  : cables con corriente⟩ 4 : cargado, sin
  estallar ⟨a live bomb : una bomba sin
  estallar⟩ 5 CURRENT : de actualidad ⟨a
  live issue : un asunto de actualidad⟩ 6
  : en vivo, en directo ⟨a live interview
  : una entrevista en vivo⟩
livelihood ['laɪvli,hʊd] n : sustento m, vida
  f, medio m de vida
liveliness ['laɪvlinəs] n : animación f, vivacidad f
livelong ['lɪv'lɔŋ] adj : entero, completo
lively ['laɪvli] adj livelier; -est : animado,
  vivaz, vivo, enérgico
liven ['laɪvən] vt : animar — vi : animarse
liver ['lɪvər] n : hígado m
livery ['lɪvəri] n, pl -eries : librea f
lives → life
livestock ['laɪv,stɑk] n : ganado m
livestream¹ ['laɪv,striːm] vi : hacer (un)
  streaming en vivo
livestream² : streaming m en vivo
live wire n : persona f vivaz y muy activa
livid ['lɪvəd] adj 1 BLACK-AND-BLUE
  : amoratado 2 PALE : lívido 3 ENRAGED : furioso
living¹ ['lɪvɪŋ] adj : vivo
living² n to make a living : ganarse la vida
living room n : living m, sala f de estar
lizard ['lɪzərd] n : lagarto m
llama ['lɑmə, 'jɑ-] n : llama f
load¹ ['loːd] vt 1 : cargar, embarcar (vehículos, cargamento, etc.) 2 : embarcar
  (pasajeros) 3 : cargar (una pistola,
  etc.) 4 : cargar (un programa, etc.) 5
  : cargar, sobrecargar ⟨she loaded (up)
  her plate with food : llenó el plato de
  comida⟩ 6 to load down with BURDEN
  : cargar de ⟨to be loaded down with debt
  : estar agobiado por las deudas⟩ — vi
  : cargar 2 to load up on : pasarse con
  (la comida, etc.)
load² n 1 CARGO : carga f 2 WEIGHT
  : peso m 3 BURDEN : carga f, peso m 4
loads npl : montón m, cantidad f
  ⟨loads of work : un montón de trabajo⟩
loaded ['loːdəd] adj 1 : cargado (dícese
  de una pistola, una cámara, etc.) 2
  WEIGHTED : cargado ⟨loaded dice : da-

dos cargados⟩ **3** : cargado (de conotaciones) ⟨a loaded question : una pregunta capciosa⟩ **4** RICH : muy rico **5** *fam* DRUNK : borracho, chupado *fam* **6 to be loaded with** : estar repleto de

loaf¹ ['lo:f] *vi* : holgazanear, flojear, haraganear

loaf² *n, pl* **loaves** ['lo:vz] **1** : pan *m*, pan *m* de molde, barra *f* de pan **2 meat loaf** : pan *m* de carne

loafer ['lo:fər] *n* : holgazán *m*, -zana *f*; haragán *m*, -gana *f*; vago *m*, -ga *f*

loan¹ ['lo:n] *vt* : prestar

loan² *n* : préstamo *m*, empréstito *m* (del banco)

loanword ['lo:n₁wərd] *n* : préstamo *m*, barbarismo *m*

loath ['lo:θ, 'lo:ð] *adj* : poco dispuesto ⟨I am loath to say it : me resisto a decirlo⟩

loathe ['lo:ð] *vt* **loathed; loathing** : odiar, aborrecer

loathing ['lo:ðɪŋ] *n* : aversión *f*, odio *m*, aborrecimiento *m*

loathsome ['lo:θsəm, 'lo:ð-] *adj* : odioso, repugnante

lob¹ ['lab] *vt* **lobbed; lobbing** : hacerle un globo (a otro jugador)

lob² *n* : globo *m* (en deportes)

lobby¹ ['labi] *v* **-bied; -bying** *vt* : presionar, ejercer presión sobre — *vi* **to lobby for** : presionar para (lograr algo)

lobby² *n, pl* **-bies 1** FOYER : vestíbulo *m* **2** LOBBYISTS : grupo *m* de presión, lobby *m*

lobbyist ['labiist] *n* : miembro *m* de un lobby

lobe ['lo:b] *n* : lóbulo *m*

lobed ['lo:bd] *adj* : lobulado

lobotomy [lə'baᴅəmi, lo-] *n, pl* **-mies** : lobotomía *f*

lobster ['labstər] *n* : langosta *f*

local¹ ['lo:kəl] *adj* : local

local² *n* **1** : anestesia *f* local **2 the locals** : los vecinos del lugar, los habitantes

locale [lo'kæl] *n* : lugar *m*, escenario *m*

locality [lo'kæləᴛi] *n, pl* **-ties** : localidad *f*

localization [₁lo:kələ'zeɪʃən] *n* POSITION : localización *f*

localize ['lo:kə₁laɪz] *vt* **-ized; -izing** : localizar

locally ['lo:kəli] *adv* : en la localidad, en la zona

locate ['lo:₁keɪt, lo'keɪt] *v* **-cated; -cating** *vt* **1** POSITION : situar, ubicar **2** FIND : localizar, ubicar — *vi* SETTLE : establecerse

location [lo'keɪʃən] *n* **1** POSITION : posición *f*, emplazamiento *m*, ubicación *f* **2** PLACE : lugar *m*, sitio *m*

loch ['lak] *n* : lago *m*

lock¹ ['lak] *vt* **1** FASTEN : cerrar (con llave) **2** CONFINE : encerrar ⟨they locked me in the room : me encerraron en la habitación⟩ **3** IMMOBILIZE : bloquear (una rueda) **4 to lock away/up** : encerrar (a alguien), guardar (algo) bajo llave **5 to lock out** : dejar fuera a, cerrar la puerta a ⟨I locked myself out : me quedé fuera (sin llaves)⟩ — *vi* **1** *or* **to lock up** : cerrar (con llave) **2** : ce-

rrarse (dícese de una puerta) **3** : trabarse, bloquearse (dícese de una rueda) **4 to lock horns** : chocar, pelearse **5 to lock on/onto** TARGET : fijar (el blanco)

lock² *n* **1** : mechón *m* (de pelo) **2** FASTENER : cerradura *f*, cerrojo *m*, chapa *f* **3** : esclusa *f* (de un canal)

locker ['lakər] *n* : armario *m*, cajón *m* con llave, lócker *m*

locker room *n* : vestuario *m*; camarín *m* *Chile, Peru, Uru*

locket ['lakət] *n* : medallón *m*, guardapelo *m*, relicario *m*

lockjaw ['lak₁jɔ] *n* : tétano *m*

lockout ['lak₁aʊt] *n* : cierre *m* patronal

locksmith ['lak₁smɪθ] *n* : cerrajero *m*, -ra *f*

lockup ['lak₁ʌp] *n* JAIL : cárcel *f*

locomotion [₁lo:kə'mo:ʃən] *n* : locomoción *f*

locomotive¹ [₁lo:kə'mo:ᴛɪv] *adj* : locomotor

locomotive² *n* : locomotora *f*

locust ['lo:kəst] *n* **1** : langosta *f*, chapulín *m* *CA, Mex* **2** CICADA : cigarra *f*, chicharra *f* **3** : acacia *f* blanca (árbol)

locution [lo'kju:ʃən] *n* : locución *f*

lode ['lo:d] *n* : veta *f*, vena *f*, filón *m*

lodestar ['lo:d₁star] *n* : estrella *f* polar

lodestone ['lo:d₁sto:n] *n* : piedra *f* imán

lodge¹ ['laᴅ] *v* **lodged; lodging** *vt* **1** HOUSE : hospedar, alojar **2** FILE : presentar ⟨to lodge a complaint : presentar una demanda⟩ — *vi* **1** : posarse, meterse ⟨the bullet lodged in the door : la bala se incrustó en la puerta⟩ **2** STAY : hospedarse, alojarse

lodge² *n* **1** : pabellón *m*, casa *f* de campo ⟨hunting lodge : refugio de caza⟩ **2** : madriguera *f* (de un castor) **3** : logia *f* ⟨Masonic lodge : logia masónica⟩

lodger ['laᴅ ər] *n* : inquilino *m*, -na *f*; huésped *m*, -peda *f*

lodging ['laᴅ ɪŋ] *n* **1** : alojamiento *m* **2 lodgings** *npl* ROOMS : habitaciones *fpl*

loft ['lɔft] *n* **1** ATTIC : desván *m*, ático *m*, buhardilla *f* **2** : piso *m* superior (de un depósito comercial) ⟨a converted loft : un depósito convertido en apartamentos⟩ **3** HAYLOFT : pajar *m* **4** : galería *f* ⟨choir loft : galería del coro⟩

loftily ['lɔftəli] *adv* : altaneramente, con altivez

loftiness ['lɔftinəs] *n* **1** NOBILITY : nobleza *f* **2** ARROGANCE : altanería *f*, arrogancia *f* **3** HEIGHT : altura *f*, elevación *f*

lofty ['lɔfti] *adj* **loftier; -est 1** NOBLE : noble, elevado **2** HAUGHTY : altivo, arrogante, altanero **3** HIGH : majestuoso, elevado

log¹ ['lɔG, 'laG] *vi* **logged; logging 1** : talar (árboles) **2** RECORD : registrar, anotar **3 to log in** *or* **to log on** : entrar (al sistema), iniciar (la) sesión **4 to log off** *or* **to log out** : salir (del sistema), cerrar (la) sesión

log² *n* **1** : tronco *m*, leño *m* **2** RECORD : diario *m*

logarithm [ˈlɔɡəˌrɪðəm, ˈlɑ-] *n* : logaritmo *m*

logger [ˈlɔɡər, ˈlɑ-] *n* : leñador *m*, -dora *f*

loggerhead [ˈlɔɡərˌhd, ˈlɑ-] *n* **1** : tortuga *f* boba **2 to be at loggerheads** : estar en pugna, estar en desacuerdo

logic [ˈlɑɖɪk] *n* : lógica *f* — **logical** [ˈlɑɖɪkəl] *adj* — **logically** [-kli] *adv*

login [ˈlɔɡˌɪn, ˈlɑɡ-] *n* **1** *or* **logon** [ˈlɔɡˌɔn, ˈlɑɡˌɑn] : inicio *m* de sesión, login *m* **2** *or* **login credentials** : login *m*, credenciales *fpl* de acceso/usuario

logistic [ləˈɖɪstɪk, lo-] *adj* : logístico

logistics [ləˈɖɪstɪks, lo-] *ns & pl* : logística *f*

logo [ˈloːˌɡoː] *n*, *pl* **logos** [-ˌɡoːz] : logotipo *m*

loin [ˈlɔɪn] *n* **1** : lomo *m* ⟨pork loin : lomo de cerdo⟩ **2 loins** *npl* : lomos *mpl* ⟨to gird one's loins : prepararse para la lucha⟩

loincloth [ˈlɔɪnˌklɔθ] *n* : taparrabos *m*

loiter [ˈlɔɪtər] *vi* : vagar, perder el tiempo

loll [ˈlɑl] *vi* **1** SLOUCH : repantigarse **2** IDLE : holgazanear, hacer el vago

lollipop *or* **lollypop** [ˈlɑliˌpɑp] *n* : dulce *m* en palito, chupete *m* Chile, Peru, paleta *f* CA, Mex

Londoner [ˈlʌndənər] *n* : londinense *mf*

lone [ˈloːn] *adj* **1** SOLITARY : solitario **2** ONLY : único

loneliness [ˈloːnlinəs] *n* : soledad *f*

lonely [ˈloːnli] *adj* **lonelier; -est 1** SOLITARY : solitario, aislado **2** LONESOME : solo ⟨to feel lonely : sentirse muy solo⟩

loner [ˈloːnər] *n* : solitario *m*, -ria *f*; recluso *m*, -sa *f*

lonesome [ˈloːnsəm] *adj* : solo, solitario

long¹ [ˈlɔŋ] *vi* **1 to long for** : añorar, desear, anhelar **2 to long to** : anhelar, estar deseando ⟨they longed to see her : estaban deseando verla, tenían muchas ganas de verla⟩

long² *adv* **1** : mucho, mucho tiempo ⟨it didn't take long : no llevó mucho tiempo⟩ ⟨will it last long? : ¿va a durar mucho?⟩ ⟨will you be long? : ¿tardarás mucho?⟩ ⟨a (little) bit longer : un poco más (tiempo)⟩ ⟨I didn't have long enough to visit : no me alcanzó el tiempo para visitar⟩ **2 all day long** : todo el día **3 as/so long as** IF : mientras, con tal (de) que **4 as/so long as** SINCE : ya que **5 as/so long as** WHILE : mientras **6 before long** : antes de poco **7 long ago** : hace mucho tiempo **8 long before/after** : mucho antes/después **9 long gone** ⟨that building is long gone : ese edificio se desapareció hace mucho⟩ **10 long since** : hace mucho **11 no longer** *or* **(not) any longer** ⟨it's no longer needed : ya no hace falta⟩ ⟨I can't wait any longer : no puedo esperar más⟩ **12 so long!** : ¡hasta luego!, ¡adiós!

long³ *adj* **longer** [ˈlɔŋɡər]; **longest** [ˈlɔŋɡəst] **1** (*indicating length*) : largo ⟨long hair : pelo largo⟩ ⟨the dress is too long : el vestido es demasiado largo⟩ ⟨the book is two hundred pages long : el libro tiene doscientas páginas⟩ ⟨a long way

from : bastante lejos de⟩ **2** (*indicating time*) : largo, prolongado ⟨a long illness : una enfermedad prolongada⟩ ⟨a long walk : un paseo largo⟩ ⟨a long time ago : hace mucho (tiempo)⟩ ⟨I've known him for a long time : lo conozco desde hace mucho⟩ ⟨the drive is five hours long : el viaje dura cinco horas⟩ ⟨at long last : por fin⟩ ⟨in the long run : a la larga⟩ **3 to be long on** : estar cargado de

long⁴ *n* **1 before long** : dentro de poco **2 the long and (the) short of it** : lo esencial, lo fundamental

long–distance [ˈlɔŋˈdɪstənts] *adj* **1** : de larga distancia ⟨long-distance call : llamada de larga distancia, llamada interurbana⟩ ⟨long-distance trip : viaje de largo recorrido⟩ ⟨long-distance runner : fondista⟩ **2** : a larga distancia ⟨long-distance romance : una relación a (larga) distancia⟩

longevity [lɑnˈɖvəti] *n* : longevidad *f*

long–haired [ˈlɔŋˈhærd] *adj* : melenudo

longhand [ˈlɔŋˌhænd] *n* : escritura *f* a mano, escritura *f* cursiva

long–haul [ˈlɔŋˈhɔl] *adj* : de larga distancia

longing [ˈlɔŋɪŋ] *n* : vivo deseo *m*, ansia *f*, anhelo *m*

longingly [ˈlɔŋɪŋli] *adv* : ansiosamente, con ansia

longitude [ˈlɑndʒəˌtuːd, -ˌtjuːd] *n* : longitud *f*

longitudinal [ˌlɑndʒəˈtuːdənəl, -ˈtjuː-] *adj* : longitudinal — **longitudinally** *adv*

long jump *n* : salto *m* de longitud, salto *m* (en) largo

long–lived [ˈlɔŋˈlɪvd, -ˈlaɪvd] *adj* : longevo

long–range [ˈlɔŋˈreɪndʒ] *adj* **1** : de largo alcance (dícese de un avión, etc.) **2** : a largo plazo (dícese de un plan, etc.)

longshoreman [ˈlɔŋˈʃormən] *n*, *pl* **-men** [-mən, -ˌmɛn] : estibador *m*, -dora *f*

longshorewoman [ˈlɔŋˈʃorˌwʊmən] *n*, *pl* **-women** [-ˌwɪmən] : cargadora *f*

long–standing [ˈlɔŋˈstændɪŋ] *adj* : de larga data

long–suffering [ˈlɔŋˈsʌfərɪŋ] *adj* : paciente, sufrido

long–term [ˈlɔŋˈtərm] *adj* : a largo plazo (dícese de un plan, etc.)

long–winded [ˈlɔŋˈwɪndəd] *adj* : prolijo

look¹ [ˈlʊk] *vi* **1** : mirar ⟨to look out the window : mirar por la ventana⟩ ⟨to look ahead/back : mirar hacia adelante/atrás⟩ ⟨look around you : mira a tu alrededor⟩ ⟨look! there he is : ¡mira! ahí está⟩ **2** INVESTIGATE : buscar, mirar ⟨look in the closet : busca en el clóset⟩ ⟨look before you leap : mira lo que haces⟩ **3** SEEM : parecer ⟨he looks happy : parece estar contento⟩ ⟨you look very nice! : ¡estás guapísima!⟩ ⟨she looked (to be) about forty : parecía tener alrededor de cuarenta años⟩ **4** (*used to warn, express anger, etc.*) ⟨look, it's not going to work : mira, no va a funcionar⟩ ⟨now look what you've done! : ¡mira lo que has hecho!⟩ ⟨(now) look here! : ¡oye!⟩ **5** FACE, POINT : dar a **6 to look**

after TAKE CARE OF : cuidar, cuidar de (personas o animales), encargarse de (una empresa, etc.) **7 to look ahead** : mirar hacia el futuro **8 to look around** EXPLORE : mirar, echar un vistazo a **9 to look around for** : buscar **10 to look as if/though** : parecer que ⟨it looks as if it will rain : parece que va llover⟩ **11 to look at** : mirar **12 to look at** CONSIDER : considerar **13 to look at** EXAMINE : examinar **14 to look at** FACE : estar frente a, enfrentarse a (problemas, etc.) **15 to look back** : mirar hacia el pasado **16 to look down on** : despreciar, menospreciar **17 to look for** EXPECT : esperar **18 to look for** SEEK : buscar **19 to look forward to** ANTICIPATE : estar ansioso de (hacer algo), estar ansioso de que llegue(n) (una fecha, etc.) **20 to look in on** : ir a ver (a alguien) **21 to look into** INVESTIGATE : investigar **22 to look like** : parecer, parecerse ⟨it looks like a large bird : parece un pájaro grande⟩ ⟨it looks like (it will) rain : parece que va a llover⟩ ⟨I look like my mother : me parezco a mi madre⟩ **23 to look on** WATCH : mirar **24 to look on** CONSIDER : considerar ⟨I look on her as a friend : la considero una amiga⟩ ⟨he looked on his accomplishments with pride : sus logros le llenaba de orgullo⟩ **25 to look out** : tener cuidado **26 to look out for** WATCH FOR : estar alerta por **27 to look out for** PROTECT : mirar por ⟨she only looks out for number one : sólo piensa en sí misma⟩ **28 to look the other way** : hacer la vista gorda **29 to look through** : hojear (una revista, etc.) **30 to look to . . . for . . .** ⟨to look to someone for something : recurrir a alguien para hacer algo⟩ ⟨they looked to history for an answer : buscaron la solución en la historia⟩ **31 to look up** IMPROVE : mejorar **32 to look up to** ADMIRE : respetar, admirar — *vt* **1** : mirar ⟨look what I found! : ¡mira lo que encontré!⟩ **2** HOPE, EXPECT : esperar ⟨we look to have a good year, we're looking to have a good year : esperamos tener un buen año⟩ **3 to look over/through** EXAMINE : revisar **4 to look up** : buscar (en un diccionario, etc.) **5 to look up** CALL, VISIT : llamar, visitar

look² *n* **1** GLANCE : mirada *f* ⟨to take a look at : mirar⟩ **2** EXPRESSION : cara *f* ⟨a look of disapproval : una cara de desaprobación⟩ **3** ASPECT : aspecto *m*, apariencia *f*, aire *m* **4 looks** *npl* : belleza *f*

looker ['lʊkər] *n* **to be a looker** : ser guapísimo

looking ['lʊkɪŋ] *adj (used in combination)* : de aspecto ⟨nice-looking : (de aspecto) atractivo⟩

lookout ['lʊk,aʊt] *n* **1** : centinela *mf*, vigía *mf* **2 to be on the lookout for** : estar al acecho de, andar a la caza de

loom¹ ['lu:m] *vi* **1** : aparecer, surgir ⟨the city loomed up in the distance : la ciu-

dad surgió en la distancia⟩ **2** MENACE, APPROACH : amenazar, ser inminente **3 to loom large** : cobrar mucha importancia

loom² *n* : telar *m*

loon ['lu:n] *n* : somorgujo *m*, somormujo *m*

loony *or* **looney** ['lu:ni] *adj* **loonier; -est** : loco, chiflado *fam*

loop¹ ['lu:p] *vt* **1** : hacer lazadas con **2 to loop around** : pasar alrededor de — *vi* **1** : rizar el rizo (dícese de un avión) **2** : serpentear (dícese de una carretera)

loop² *n* **1** : lazada *f* (en hilo o cuerda) **2** BEND : curva *f* **3** CIRCUIT : circuito *m* cerrado **4** : rizo *m* (en la aviación) ⟨to loop the loop : rizar el rizo⟩

loophole ['lu:p,ho:l] *n* : escapatoria *f*, pretexto *m*

loose¹ ['lu:s] *vt* **loosed; loosing 1** RELEASE : poner en libertad, soltar **2** UNTIE : deshacer, desatar **3** DISCHARGE, UNLEASH : descargar, desatar

loose² → **loosely**

loose³ *adj* **looser; -est 1** INSECURE : flojo, suelto, poco seguro ⟨a loose tooth : un diente flojo⟩ **2** ROOMY : suelto, holgado ⟨loose clothing : ropa holgada⟩ **3** OPEN : suelto, abierto ⟨loose soil : suelo suelto⟩ ⟨a loose weave : una tejida abierta⟩ **4** FREE : suelto ⟨to break loose : soltarse⟩ ⟨to let loose : soltar⟩ ⟨loose sheets of paper : papeles sueltos⟩ ⟨loose change : dinero suelto⟩ **5** SLACK : flojo, flexible **6** APPROXIMATE : libre, aproximado ⟨a loose translation : una traducción aproximada⟩

loosely ['lu:sli] *adv* **1** : sin apretar **2** ROUGHLY : aproximadamente, más o menos

loose–leaf ['lu:s'li:f] *adj* : de hojas sueltas

loosen ['lu:sən] *vt* **1** : aflojar **2 to loosen up** RELAX : relajar — *vi* **1** : aflojarse **2 to loosen up** RELAX : relajarse

looseness ['lu:snəs] *n* **1** : holgura *f* (de ropa) **2** IMPRECISION : imprecisión *f*

loot¹ ['lu:t] *vt* : saquear, robar

loot² *n* : botín *m*

looter ['lu:tər] *n* : saqueador *m*, -dora *f*

lop ['lɑp] *vt* **lopped; lopping** : cortar, podar

lope¹ ['lo:p] *vi* **loped; loping** : correr a paso largo

lope² *n* : paso *m* largo

lopsided ['lɑp,saɪdəd] *adj* **1** CROOKED : torcido, chueco, ladeado **2** ASYMMETRICAL : asimétrico

loquacious [lo'kweɪʃəs] *adj* : locuaz

lord ['lɔrd] *n* **1** : señor *m*, noble *m* **2** : lord *m* (en la Gran Bretaña) **3 the Lord** : el Señor **4 (good) Lord!** : ¡Dios mío!

lordly ['lɔrdli] *adj* **lordlier; -est** HAUGHTY : arrogante, altanero

lordship ['lɔrd,ʃɪp] *n* : señoría *f*

Lord's Supper *n* : Eucaristía *f*

lore ['lor] *n* : saber *m* popular, tradición *f*

lose ['lu:z] *v* **lost** ['lɔst]; **losing** ['lu:zɪŋ] *vt* **1** MISLAY : perder ⟨I lost my umbrella : perdí mi paraguas⟩ **2** : perder (un partido, etc.) **3** (*to fail to keep*) : perder ⟨to lose blood : perder sangre⟩ ⟨to lose one's appetite : perder el apetito⟩ ⟨to lose track of the time : perder la noción del tiempo⟩ ⟨to have nothing to lose : no tener nada que perder⟩ ⟨to lose sight of : perder de vista⟩ **4** : perder (dinero) **5** (*to be deprived of*) : perder ⟨they lost everything : lo perdieron todo⟩ ⟨we lost power : se cortó la luz⟩ ⟨to lose one's voice : quedarse afónico⟩ ⟨she lost her husband : perdió a su esposo⟩ ⟨we're sorry to lose you! : ¡qué pena que te vayas!⟩ **6** (*to gradually have less of*) : perder (peso, interés, etc.) **7** : perder (valor) **8** WASTE : perder ⟨there's no time to lose : no hay tiempo que perder⟩ **9** : perder (la calma, el control, etc.) ⟨to lose one's temper : perder los estribos, enojarse, enfadarse⟩ ⟨to lose one's nerve : perder el valor⟩ **10** : costar, hacer perder ⟨the errors lost him his job : los errores le costaron su empleo⟩ **11** : atrasar ⟨my watch loses 5 minutes a day : mi reloj se atrasa 5 minutos por día⟩ **12** CONFUSE : confundir **13** GET RID OF : deshacerse de **14** GET AWAY FROM : deshacerse de **15 to lose oneself** : perderse, ensimismarse **16 to lose one's way** : perderse — *vi* : perder ⟨we lost to the other team : perdimos contra el otro equipo⟩

loser ['luːzər] *n* : perdedor *m*, -dora *f*

loss ['lɔs] *n* **1** LOSING : pérdida *f* ⟨loss of memory : pérdida de memoria⟩ ⟨to sell at a loss : vender con pérdida⟩ ⟨to cut one's losses : reducir las pérdidas (económicas)⟩ ⟨to be at a loss to : no saber cómo⟩ ⟨to be at a loss for words : no saber qué decir⟩ **2** DEFEAT : derrota *f*, juego *m* perdido **3 losses** *npl* DEATHS : muertos *mpl*

lost ['lɔst] *adj* **1** : perdido ⟨a lost cause : una causa perdida⟩ ⟨lost in thought : absorto⟩ **2 to get lost** : perderse **3 to make up for lost time** : recuperar el tiempo perdido

lot ['lɑt] *n* **1** DRAWING : sorteo *m* ⟨by lot : por sorteo⟩ **2** SHARE : parte *f*, porción *f* **3** FATE : suerte *f* **4** LAND, PLOT : terreno *m*, solar *m*, lote *m*, parcela *f* ⟨parking lot : estacionamiento⟩ **5 a lot** : mucho ⟨I liked it a lot : me gustó mucho⟩ ⟨she doesn't travel a lot : no viaja mucho⟩ **6 a lot** *or* **lots** : mucho ⟨a lot better : mucho mejor⟩ ⟨thanks a lot : muchas gracias⟩ ⟨there's lots to do : hay mucho que hacer⟩ **7 a lot of** *or* **lots of** : mucho, un montón de, bastante ⟨lots of books : un montón de libros, muchos libros⟩ ⟨a lot of people : mucha gente⟩

loth ['loːθ, 'loːð] → **loath**

lotion ['loːʃən] *n* : loción *f*

lottery ['lɑtəri] *n, pl* **-teries** : lotería *f*

lotus ['loːtəs] *n* : loto *m*

loud¹ ['laud] *adv* : alto, fuerte ⟨out loud : en voz alta⟩

loud² *adj* **1** : alto, fuerte ⟨a loud voice : una voz alta⟩ **2** NOISY : ruidoso ⟨a loud party : una fiesta ruidosa⟩ **3** FLASHY : llamativo, chillón

loudly ['laudli] *adv* : alto, fuerte, en voz alta

loudmouth ['laud,mauθ] *n* : bocón *m*, -cona *f*

loudness ['laudnəs] *n* : volumen *m*, fuerza *f* (del ruido)

loudspeaker ['laud,spiːkər] *n* : altavoz *m*, altoparlante *m*

lounge¹ ['launᴅ] *vi* **lounged; lounging** : holgazanear, gandulear

lounge² *n* : salón *m*, sala *f* de estar

louse ['laus] *n, pl* **lice** ['lais] : piojo *m*

lousy ['lauzi] *adj* **lousier; -est** **1** : piojoso, lleno de piojos **2** BAD : pésimo, muy malo

lout ['laut] *n* : bruto *m*, patán *m*

louver *or* **louvre** ['luːvər] *n* : persiana *f*, listón *m* de persiana

lovable ['lʌvəbəl] *adj* : adorable, amoroso, encantador

love¹ ['lʌv] *v* **loved; loving** *vt* **1** : querer, amar ⟨I love you : te quiero⟩ **2** ENJOY : encantarle a alguien, ser (muy) aficionado a, gustarle mucho a uno (algo) ⟨she loves flowers : le encantan las flores⟩ ⟨he loves golf : es muy aficionado al golf⟩ ⟨I'd love to go with you : me gustaría mucho acompañarte⟩ — *vi* : querer, amar

love² *n* **1** : amor *m*, cariño *m* ⟨to be in love with : estar enamorado de⟩ ⟨to fall in love with : enamorarse de⟩ ⟨to fall out of love with : dejar de querer a⟩ ⟨love affair : aventura⟩ ⟨love life : vida amorosa⟩ **2** ENTHUSIASM, INTEREST : amor *m*, afición *m*, gusto *m* ⟨love of music : afición a la música⟩ **3** BELOVED : amor *m*; amado *m*, -da *f*; enamorado *m*, -da *f* ⟨yes, my love : sí, mi amor⟩ **4** REGARDS : recuerdos *mpl* ⟨Love, Brian : cariños, Brian⟩ **5 love at first sight** : amor a primera vista **6 no/little love lost** ⟨there is no love lost between them : no se pueden ver⟩ **7 not for love or money** : por nada del mundo **8 to make love** : hacer el amor

loveless ['lʌvləs] *adj* : sin amor

loveliness ['lʌvlinəs] *n* : belleza *f*, hermosura *f*

lovelorn ['lʌv,lɔrn] *adj* : herido de amor, perdidamente enamorado

lovely ['lʌvli] *adj* **lovelier; -est** : hermoso, bello, lindo, precioso

lover ['lʌvər] *n* : amante *mf* (de personas); aficionado *m*, -da *f* (a alguna actividad)

loving ['lʌvɪŋ] *adj* : amoroso, cariñoso

lovingly ['lʌvɪŋli] *adv* : cariñosamente

low¹ ['loː] *vi* : mugir

low² *adv* : bajo, profundo ⟨to aim low : apuntar bajo⟩ ⟨to lie low : mantenerse escondido⟩ ⟨to turn the lights down low : bajar las luces⟩

low³ *adj* **lower** ['loːər]; **lowest** **1** : bajo ⟨a low building : un edificio bajo⟩ ⟨a low bow : una profunda reverencia⟩ **2** : bajo ⟨low temperatures/speeds : bajas temperaturas/velocidades⟩ ⟨low-calorie/low-fat : bajo en calorías/grasas⟩ **3** SHALLOW : bajo, poco profundo **4** WEAK, GENTLE : flojo (dícese del viento), tenue (dícese de la luz) ⟨over low heat : a fuego lento⟩ **5** SOFT : bajo, suave ⟨in a low voice : en voz baja⟩ **6** DEEP : grave, profundo (dícese de la voz, etc.) **7** HUMBLE : humilde, modesto **8** DEPRESSED : deprimido, bajo de moral **9** INFERIOR : bajo, inferior **10** UNFAVORABLE : mal ⟨she has a low opinion of him : tiene un mal concepto de él⟩ **11** LOW-CUT : escotado **12 to be low on** : tener poco de, estar escaso de ⟨we're low on gas : nos queda muy poca gasolina⟩

low⁴ *n* **1** : punto *m* bajo ⟨to reach an all-time low : estar más bajo que nunca⟩ **2** *or* **low gear** : primera velocidad *f* **3** : mugido *m* (de una vaca)

lowbrow ['lo:ˌbraʊ] *n* : persona *f* inculta

low-class ['lo:'klæs] *adj* → **lower-class**

low-cut ['lo:'kʌt] *adj* : escotado

lower¹ ['lo:ər] *vt* **1** DROP : bajar ⟨to lower one's voice : bajar la voz⟩ **2** : arriar, bajar ⟨to lower the flag : arriar la bandera⟩ **3** REDUCE : reducir, bajar **4 to lower oneself** : rebajarse

lower² ['lo:ər] *adj* : inferior, más bajo, de abajo

lowercase¹ [ˌlo:ər'keɪs] *adj* : minúsculo

lowercase² *n* **in lowercase** : en minúsculas

lower-class [ˌlo:ər'klæs] *adj* : de clase baja

lower class *n* : clase *f* baja

low-key ['lo:'ki:] *adj* : informal, sin ceremonias

lowland ['lo:lənd, -ˌlænd] *n* : tierras *fpl* bajas

lowliness ['lo:linəs] *n* : humildad *f*, bajeza *f*

lowly ['lo:li] *adj* **lowlier; -est** : humilde, modesto

loyal ['lɔɪəl] *adj* : leal, fiel — **loyally** *adv*

loyalist ['lɔɪəlɪst] *n* : partidario *m*, -ria *f* del régimen

loyalty ['lɔɪəlti] *n, pl* **-ties** : lealtad *f*, fidelidad *f*

loyalty card *n* : tarjeta *f* de cliente

lozenge ['lazənɪ] *n* : pastilla *f*

LSD [ˌɛlˌɛs'di:] *n* : LSD *m*

lubricant ['lu:brɪkənt] *n* : lubricante *m*

lubricate ['lu:brɪˌkeɪt] *vt* **-cated; -cating** : lubricar — **lubrication** [ˌlu:brɪ'keɪʃən] *n*

lucid ['lu:səd] *adj* : lúcido, claro — **lucidly** *adv*

lucidity [lu:'sɪdəti] *n* : lucidez *f*

luck ['lʌk] *n* **1** : suerte *f* ⟨hard luck : mala suerte⟩ **2 as luck would have it** : quiso la suerte que **3 good luck!** : ¡(buena) suerte! **4 the luck of the draw** ⟨to depend on the luck of the draw : ser cuestión de suerte⟩ **5 to be down on one's luck** : estar de mala racha **6 to be in luck** : estar de suerte **7 to be out of luck** : no estar de suerte **8 to have bad luck** : tener mala suerte **9 to press/push one's luck** : desafiar a la suerte **10 to try one's luck** : probar suerte **11 with any luck** : con un poco de suerte

luckily ['lʌkəli] *adv* : afortunadamente, por suerte

luckless ['lʌkləs] *adj* : desafortunado

lucky ['lʌki] *adj* **luckier; -est 1** : afortunado, que tiene suerte ⟨a lucky woman : una mujer afortunada⟩ **2** FORTUITOUS : fortuito, de suerte **3** OPPORTUNE : oportuno **4** : de (la) suerte ⟨lucky number : número de la suerte⟩

lucrative ['lu:krəṭɪv] *adj* : lucrativo, provechoso — **lucratively** *adv*

ludicrous ['lu:dəkrəs] *adj* : ridículo, absurdo — **ludicrously** *adv*

ludicrousness ['lu:dəkrəsnəs] *n* : ridiculez *f*, absurdo *m*

lug ['lʌɡ] *vt* **lugged; lugging** : arrastrar, transportar con dificultad

luggage ['lʌɡɪʤ] *n* : equipaje *m*

lugubrious [lʊ'ɡu:briəs] *adj* : lúgubre — **lugubriously** *adv*

lukewarm ['lu:k'wɔrm] *adj* **1** TEPID : tibio **2** HALFHEARTED : poco entusiasta

lull¹ ['lʌl] *vt* **1** CALM, SOOTHE : calmar, sosegar **2 to lull to sleep** : arrullar, adormecer

lull² *n* : calma *f*, pausa *f*

lullaby ['lʌləˌbaɪ] *n, pl* **-bies** : canción *f* de cuna, arrullo *m*, nana *f*

lumbago [ˌlʌm'beɪɡo] *n* : lumbago *m*

lumbar ['lʌmbər, -ˌbɑr] *adj* : lumbar

lumber¹ ['lʌmbər] *vt* : aserrar (madera) — *vi* : moverse pesadamente

lumber² *n* : madera *f*

lumberjack ['lʌmbərˌʤæk] *n* : leñador *m*, -dora *f*

lumberyard ['lʌmbərˌjɑrd] *n* : almacén *m* de maderas

luminary ['lu:məˌnɛri] *n, pl* **-naries** : lumbrera *f*, luminaria *f*

luminescence [ˌlu:mə'nɛsənts] *n* : luminiscencia *f* — **luminescent** [-'nɛs-ənt] *adj*

luminosity [ˌlu:mə'nɑsəṭi] *n, pl* **-ties** : luminosidad *f*

luminous ['lu:mənəs] *adj* : luminoso — **luminously** *adv*

lump¹ ['lʌmp] *vt or* **to lump together** : juntar, agrupar, amontonar — *vi* CLUMP : agruparse, aglutinarse

lump² *n* **1** GLOB : grumo *m* **2** PIECE : pedazo *m*, trozo *m*, terrón *m* ⟨a lump of coal : un trozo de carbón⟩ ⟨a lump of sugar : un terrón de azúcar⟩ **3** SWELLING : bulto *m*, hinchazón *f*, protuberancia *f* **4 to have a lump in one's throat** : tener un nudo en la garganta

lump sum *n* : cantidad *f* global, pago *m* único

lumpy ['lʌmpi] *adj* **lumpier; -est 1** : lleno de grumos (dícese de una salsa) **2** UNEVEN : desigual, disparejo

lunacy ['lu:nəsi] *n, pl* **-cies** : locura *f*

lunar ['lu:nər] *adj* : lunar

lunatic¹ ['lu:nəˌtɪk] *adj sometimes offensive* : lunático, loco

lunatic² *n sometimes offensive* : loco *m*, -ca *f*

lunch¹ ['lʌntʃ] *vi* : almorzar, comer

lunch² *n* : almuerzo *m*, comida *f*, lonche *m Mex*

luncheon ['lʌntʃən] n 1 : comida f, almuerzo m 2 **luncheon meat** : fiambres fpl

lunchroom ['lʌntʃ,ru:m, -,rʊm] n : merendero m, cafetería f

lunchtime ['lʌntʃ,taɪm] n : hora f del almuerzo

lung ['lʌŋ] n : pulmón m

lunge[1] ['lʌnD] vi **lunged; lunging** 1 THRUST : atacar (en la esgrima) 2 **to lunge forward** : arremeter, lanzarse

lunge[2] n 1 : arremetida f, embestida f 2 : estocada f (en la esgrima)

lurch[1] ['lərtʃ] vi 1 PITCH : cabecear, dar bandazos, dar sacudidas 2 STAGGER : tambalearse

lurch[2] n 1 : sacudida f, bandazo m (de un vehículo) 2 : tambaleo m (de una persona)

lure[1] ['lʊr] vt **lured; luring** : atraer

lure[2] n 1 ATTRACTION : atractivo m 2 ENTICEMENT : señuelo m, aliciente m 3 BAIT : cebo m artificial (en la pesca)

lurid ['lʊrəd] adj 1 GRUESOME : espeluznante, horripilante 2 SENSATIONAL : sensacionalista, chocante 3 GAUDY : chillón

lurk ['lərk] vi : estar al acecho

luscious ['lʌʃəs] adj 1 DELICIOUS : delicioso, exquisito 2 SEDUCTIVE : seductor, cautivador

lush ['lʌʃ] adj 1 LUXURIANT : exuberante, lozano 2 LUXURIOUS : suntuoso, lujoso — **lushness** ['lʌʃnəs] n

lust[1] ['lʌst] vi **to lust after** : desear (a una persona), codiciar (riquezas, etc.)

lust[2] n 1 LASCIVIOUSNESS : lujuria f, lascivia f 2 CRAVING : deseo m, ansia f, anhelo m

luster or **lustre** ['lʌstər] n 1 GLOSS, SHEEN : lustre m, brillo m 2 SPLENDOR : lustre m, esplendor m

lusterless ['lʌstərləs] adj : deslustrado, sin brillo

lustful ['lʌstfəl] adj : lujurioso, lascivo, lleno de deseo

lustrous ['lʌstrəs] adj : brillante, brilloso, lustroso

lusty ['lʌsti] adj **lustier; -est** : fuerte, robusto, vigoroso — **lustily** ['lʌstəli] adv

lute ['lu:t] n : laúd m

luxuriance [,lʌg'ʒʊriənts, ,lʌk'ʃʊr-] n : lozanía f, exuberancia f

luxuriant [,lʌg'ʒʊriənt, ,lʌk'ʃʊr-] adj 1 : exuberante, lozano (dícese de las plantas) 2 : abundante y hermoso (dícese del pelo) — **luxuriantly** adv

luxuriate [,lʌg'ʒʊri,eɪt, ,lʌk'ʃʊr-] vi **-ated; -ating** 1 : disfrutar 2 **to luxuriate in** : deleitarse con

luxurious [,lʌg'ʒʊriəs, ,lʌk'ʃʊr-] adj : lujoso, suntuoso — **luxuriously** adv

luxury ['lʌkʃəri, 'lʌgʒə-] n, pl **-ries** : lujo m

-ly [li] suf : -mente ⟨frequently : frecuentemente⟩

lye ['laɪ] n : lejía f

lying → **lie**[1], **lie**[2]

lymph ['lɪmpf] n : linfa f

lymphatic [lɪm'fæɪk] adj : linfático

lynch ['lɪntʃ] vt : linchar

lynx ['lɪŋks] n, pl **lynx** or **lynxes** : lince m

lyre ['laɪr] n : lira f

lyric[1] ['lɪrɪk] adj : lírico

lyric[2] n 1 : poema m lírico 2 **lyrics** npl : letra f (de una canción)

lyrical ['lɪrɪkəl] adj : lírico, elocuente

lyricist ['lɪrɪsɪst] n : letrista mf

M

m ['ɛm] n, pl **m's** or **ms** ['ɛmz] : decimotercera letra del alfabeto inglés

ma'am ['mæm] → **madam**

macabre [mə'kɑb, -'kɑbər, -'kɑbrə] adj : macabro

macadam [mə'kædəm] n : macadán m

macaroni [,mækə'roni] n : macarrones mpl

macaroon [,mækə'ru:n] n : macarrón m, mostachón m

macaw [mə'kɔ] n : guacamayo m

mace ['meɪs] n 1 : maza f (arma o símbolo) 2 : macis f (especia)

machete [mə'ʃɛti] n : machete m

machination [,mækə'neɪʃən, ,mæʃə-] n : maquinación f, intriga f

machine[1] [mə'ʃi:n] vt **-chined; -chining** : trabajar a máquina

machine[2] n 1 : máquina f ⟨machine shop : taller de máquinas⟩ 2 : aparato m, maquinaria f (en política)

machine gun n : ametralladora f

machinery [mə'ʃi:nəri] n, pl **-eries** 1 : maquinaria f 2 WORKS : mecanismo m

machinist [mə'ʃi:nɪst] n : maquinista mf

machismo [mɑ'tʃi:zmo:] n : machismo m, masculinidad f

macho ['mɑtʃo:] adj : machote, macho

mackerel ['mækərəl] n, pl **-el** or **-els** : caballa f

mad ['mæd] adj **madder; maddest** 1 INSANE : loco, demente 2 RABID : rabioso 3 FOOLISH : tonto, insensato 4 ANGRY : enojado, furioso 5 CRAZY : loco ⟨I'm mad about you : estoy loco por ti⟩

Madagascan [,mædə'Gæskən] n : malgache mf — **Madagascan** adj

madam ['mædəm] n, pl **mesdames** [meɪ'dɑm, -'dæm] : señora f

madcap[1] ['mæd,kæp] adj ZANY : alocado, disparatado

madcap[2] n : alocado m, -da f

madden ['mædən] vt : enloquecer, enfurecer

maddening ['mædənɪŋ] adj : enloquecedor, exasperante ⟨I find it maddening : me saca de quicio⟩

made → **make**[1]
made-to-measure *adj* : hecho a la medida
made-up *adj* **1** : maquillado **2** INVENTED : inventado
madhouse ['mæd,haʊs] *n fam* **1** : INSANE ASYLUM *now often offensive* : manicomio *m fam* **2** (*used figuratively*) : manicomio *m fam*, casa *f* de locos
madly ['mædli] *adv* : como un loco, locamente
madman ['mæd,mæn, -mən] *n, pl* -**men** [-mən, -,mɛn] : loco *m*, demente *m*
madness ['mædnəs] *n* : locura *f*, demencia *f*
madwoman ['mæd,wʊmən] *n, pl* -**women** [-,wɪmən] : loca *f*, demente *f*
maelstrom ['meɪlstrəm] *n* : remolino *m*, vorágine *f*
maestro ['maɪ,stroː] *n, pl* -**stros** *or* -**stri** [-,striː] : maestro *m*
Mafia ['mɑfiə] *n* : Mafia *f*
mafioso [,mɑfi'oːso] *n* : mafioso *m*, -sa *f*
magazine ['mæɡə,ziːn] *n* **1** STOREHOUSE : almacén *m*, polvorín *m* (de explosivos) **2** PERIODICAL : revista *f* **3** : cargador *m* (de un arma de fuego)
magenta [mə'Dɛntə] *n* : magenta *f*, color *m* magenta
maggot ['mæɡət] *n* : gusano *m*
Magi ['meɪ,dʒaɪ, 'mæ-] *npl* **the Magi** : los Reyes Magos
magic[1] ['mædʒɪk] *or* **magical** ['mædʒɪkəl] *adj* : mágico
magic[2] *n* : magia *f*
magically ['mædʒɪkli] *adv* : mágicamente ⟨they magically appeared : aparecieron como por arte de magia⟩
magician [mə'dʒɪʃən] *n* **1** SORCERER : mago *m*, -ga *f* **2** CONJURER : prestidigitador *m*, -dora *f*; mago *m*, -ga *f*
magistrate ['mædʒə,streɪt] *n* : magistrado *m*, -da *f*
magma ['mæɡmə] *n* : magma *m*
magnanimity [,mæɡnə'nɪmə'ti] *n, pl* -**ties** : magnanimidad *f*
magnanimous [mæɡ'nænəməs] *adj* : magnánimo, generoso — **magnanimously** *adv*
magnate ['mæɡ,neɪt, -nət] *n* : magnate *mf*
magnesium [mæɡ'niːziəm, -ʒəm] *n* : magnesio *m*
magnet ['mæɡnət] *n* : imán *m*
magnetic [mæɡ'nɛtɪk] *adj* : magnético — **magnetically** [-tɪkli] *adv*
magnetic field *n* : campo *m* magnético
magnetism ['mæɡnə,tɪzəm] *n* : magnetismo *m*
magnetize ['mæɡnə,taɪz] *vt* -**tized**; -**tizing 1** : magnetizar, imantar **2** ATTRACT : magnetizar, atraer
magnification [,mæɡnəfə'keɪʃən] *n* : aumento *m*, ampliación *f*
magnificence [mæɡ'nɪfəsənts] *n* : magnificencia *f*
magnificent [mæɡ'nɪfəsənt] *adj* : magnífico — **magnificently** *adv*
magnify ['mæɡnə,faɪ] *vt* -**fied**; -**fying 1** ENLARGE : ampliar **2** EXAGGERATE : magnificar, exagerar

magnifying glass *n* : lupa *f*
magnitude ['mæɡnə,tuːd, -,tjuːd] *n* **1** GREATNESS : magnitud *f*, grandeza *f* **2** QUANTITY : cantidad *f* **3** IMPORTANCE : magnitud *f*, envergadura *f*
magnolia [mæɡ'noːljə] *n* : magnolia *f* (flor), magnolio *m* (árbol)
magpie ['mæɡ,paɪ] *n* : urraca *f*
maguey [mə'ɡeɪ] *n* : maguey *m*
mahogany [mə'hɑɡəni] *n, pl* -**nies** : caoba *f*
maid ['meɪd] *n* **1** MAIDEN : doncella *f* **2** *or* **maidservant** ['meɪd,sərvənt] : sirvienta *f*, muchacha *f*, mucama *f*, criada *f*
maiden[1] ['meɪdən] *adj* **1** UNMARRIED : soltera **2** FIRST : primero ⟨maiden voyage : primera travesía⟩
maiden[2] *n* : doncella *f*
maiden name *n* : nombre *m* de soltera
mail[1] ['meɪl] *vt* : enviar por correo, echar al correo
mail[2] *n* **1** : correo *m* **2** : malla *f* ⟨coat of mail : cota de malla⟩
mailbox ['meɪl,bɑks] *n* : buzón *m*
mailing list *n* : lista *f* de correo(s), lista *f* de direcciones
mailman ['meɪl,mæn, -mən] *n, pl* -**men** [-mən, -,mn] : cartero *m*
mail order *n* : venta *f* por correo
maim ['meɪm] *vt* : mutilar, desfigurar, lisiar
main[1] ['meɪn] *adj* : principal, central ⟨the main office : la oficina central⟩ ⟨main course : plato principal/fuerte⟩ ⟨main road : carretera principal⟩
main[2] *n* **1** HIGH SEAS : alta mar *f* **2** : tubería *f* principal (de agua o gas), cable *m* principal (de un circuito) **3 with might and main** : con todas sus fuerzas
mainframe ['meɪn,freɪm] *n* : mainframe *m*, computadora *f* central
mainland ['meɪn,lænd, -lənd] *n* : continente *m*
mainly ['meɪnli] *adv* **1** PRINCIPALLY : principalmente, en primer lugar **2** MOSTLY : principalmente, en la mayor parte
mainstay ['meɪn,steɪ] *n* : pilar *m*, sostén *m* principal
mainstream[1] ['meɪn,striːm] *adj* : dominante, corriente, convencional
mainstream[2] *n* : corriente *f* principal
maintain [meɪn'teɪn] *vt* **1** SERVICE : dar mantenimiento a (una máquina) **2** PRESERVE : mantener, conservar ⟨to maintain silence : guardar silencio⟩ **3** SUPPORT : mantener, sostener **4** ASSERT : mantener, sostener, afirmar
maintenance ['meɪntənənts] *n* : mantenimiento *m*
maize ['meɪz] *n* : maíz *m*
majestic [mə'dʒɛstɪk] *adj* : majestuoso — **majestically** [-tɪkli] *adv*
majesty ['mædʒəsti] *n, pl* -**ties 1** : majestad *f* ⟨Your Majesty : su Majestad⟩ **2** SPLENDOR : majestuosidad *f*, esplendor *m*
major[1] ['meɪdʒər] *vi* -**jored**; -**joring** : especializarse
major[2] *adj* **1** GREATER : mayor **2** NOTEWORTHY : mayor, notable **3** SERIOUS : grave **4** : mayor (en la música)

major³ *n* **1** : mayor *mf*, comandante *mf* (en las fuerzas armadas) **2** : especialidad *f* (universitaria)

Majorcan [mə'Dɔrkən, mə-, -'jɔr-] *n* : mallorquín *m*, -quina *f* — **Majorcan** *adj*

major general *n* : general *mf* de división

majority [mə'Dɔrəṭi] *n, pl* **-ties 1** ADULTHOOD : mayoría *f* de edad **2** : mayoría *f*, mayor parte *f* ⟨the vast majority : la inmensa mayoría⟩

make¹ ['meɪk] *v* **made** ['meɪd]; **making** *vt* **1** CREATE, PRODUCE : hacer, fabricar (máquinas, etc.), promulgar (leyes) ⟨she made a dress : hizo un vestido⟩ ⟨to make a fire : hacer un fuego⟩ ⟨to make a movie : hacer una película⟩ ⟨the milk is made into cheese : con la leche se hace queso⟩ ⟨to be made from : hacerse de⟩ ⟨made (out) of stone : hecho de piedra⟩ **2** CAUSE, PRODUCE : hacer (ruido, etc.) ⟨to make trouble : hacer problemas⟩ ⟨to make a mistake : cometer un error⟩ ⟨to make room for : hacer lugar para⟩ **3** ARRANGE : hacer (planes, etc.) ⟨to make an appointment : hacer/pedir/concertar una cita, pedir hora⟩ **4** PREPARE : hacer (una cama, etc.), preparar (una comida, etc.) **5** RENDER : hacer, poner ⟨it makes him nervous : lo pone nervioso⟩ ⟨it made me happy : me hizo feliz, me alegró⟩ ⟨it made me sad : me dio pena⟩ ⟨it made her famous : la hizo famosa⟩ **6** : hacer, convertir en ⟨it'll make a man of you : te hará hombre⟩ ⟨to make a fool of : dejar en ridículo⟩ ⟨to make a big deal of : hacer un problema por⟩ ⟨to make a mess of things : meter la pata⟩ ⟨wait — make that a cheeseburger : o mejor, dame una hamburguesa con queso⟩ **7** BE, BECOME : ser ⟨you'll make a fine doctor : serás una médica buenísima⟩ **8** EQUAL : ser ⟨two plus two makes four : dos y dos son cuatro⟩ ⟨that makes two of us! : ¡ya somos dos!⟩ **9** SCORE : hacer, marcar **10** PERFORM : hacer ⟨to make a gesture : hacer un gesto⟩ ⟨to make a speech : pronunciar un discurso⟩ **11** : no perder (un vuelo, etc.), cumplir con (una fecha de entrega) **12** REACH : llegar a (un lugar, etc.) ⟨they made the finals : llegaron a las finales⟩ **13** ATTEND : asistir a **14** COMPEL : hacer, forzar, obligar **15** EARN : hacer (dinero, amigos) ⟨to make a living : ganarse la vida⟩ **16 to make do (with something)** : arreglárselas (con algo) **17 to make into** : convertir en **18 to make it** SUCCEED : tener éxito en la vida **19 to make it** SURVIVE : vivir, sobrevivir **20 to make it** : llegar ⟨we made it home safely : llegamos bien a casa⟩ ⟨I'm glad you could make it! : ¡me alegro de que hayas podido venir!⟩ **21 to make it up to someone** ⟨I'll make it up to you : te lo compensaré⟩ **22 to make of** : pensar de ⟨I don't know what to make of him/it : no sé qué pensar de él/ello⟩ ⟨I can't make anything of it : no lo entiendo⟩ **23 to make or break** : ser el éxito o la ruina de **24 to make out** DISCERN : distin-

guir **25 to make out** : comprender, entender (a alguien) **26 to make out** WRITE : hacer (una lista, etc.) ⟨to make a check out to : extender un cheque a nombre de⟩ **27 to make out** PORTRAY : pintar, hacer parecer **28 to make over** : transformar, maquillar (a alguien), redecorar (una habitación) **29 to make someone's day** : alegrarle el día a alguien **30 to make up** INVENT : inventar **31 to make up** PREPARE : preparar **32 to make up** FORM : formar, constituir **33 to make up** : compensar (tiempo) **34 to make up one's mind** : decidirse — *vi* **1** HEAD : ir, dirigirse ⟨we made for home : nos fuimos a casa⟩ **2 to make away with** : escaparse con **3 to make do** : arreglárselas **4 to make for** HEAD FOR : dirigirse a **5 to make for** PROMOTE : contribuir a **6 to make good** REPAY : pagar **7 to make good** SUCCEED : tener éxito **8 to make off** : salir corriendo **9 to make off with** : escaparse con **10 to make out** *fam* : besuquearse ⟨to make out with someone : besar y acariciar a alguien⟩ **11 to make up for** : compensar

make² *n* BRAND : marca *f*

make–believe¹ [ˌmeɪkbəˈliːv] *adj* : imaginario

make–believe² *n* : fantasía *f*, invención *f* ⟨a world of make-believe : un mundo de ensueño⟩

make out *vt* **1** WRITE : hacer (un cheque) **2** DISCERN : distinguir, divisar **3** UNDERSTAND : comprender, entender — *vi* : arreglárselas ⟨how did you make out? : ¿qué tal te fue?⟩

makeover ['meɪkˌoːvər] *n* **1** : cambio *m* de imagen **2** REMODELING : reformas *fpl*, remodelación *f*

maker ['meɪkər] *n* : fabricante *mf*

makeshift ['meɪkˌʃɪft] *adj* : provisional, improvisado

makeup ['meɪkˌʌp] *n* **1** COMPOSITION : composición *f* **2** CHARACTER : carácter *m*, temperamento *m* **3** COSMETICS : maquillaje *m*

make up *vt* **1** INVENT : inventar **2** : recuperar ⟨she made up the time : recuperó las horas perdidas⟩ — *vi* RECONCILE : hacer las paces, reconciliarse

making ['meɪkɪŋ] *n* **1** : creación *f*, producción *f* ⟨in the making : en ciernes⟩ **2 to have the makings of** : tener madera de (dícese de personas), tener los ingredientes para

maladjusted [ˌmæləˈdʒʌstəd] *adj* : inadaptado

maladjustment [ˌmæləˈdʒʌstmənt] *n* : desajuste *m*

malady ['mælədi] *n, pl* **-dies** : dolencia *f*, enfermedad *f*, mal *m*

malaise [məˈleɪz, mæ-] *n* : malestar *m*

malaria [məˈlɛriə] *n* : malaria *f*, paludismo *m*

Malawian [məˈlɑwiən] *n* : malauiano *m*, -na *f* — **Malawian** *adj*

Malay [məˈleɪ, ˈmeɪˌleɪ] *n* **1** *or* **Malayan** [məˈleɪən, meɪ-;, ˈmeɪˌleɪən] : malayo *m*,

-ya *f* 2 : malayo *m* (idioma) — **Malay** *or* **Malayan** *adj*

Malaysian [mə'leɪʒən, -ʃən] *n* : malasio *m*, -sia *f*; malaisio *m*, -sia *f* — **Malaysian** *adj*

male[1] ['meɪl] *adj* 1 : macho 2 MASCULINE : masculino

male[2] *n* : macho *m* (de animales o plantas), varón *m* (de personas)

malefactor ['mælə,fæktər] *n* : malhechor *m*, -chora *f*

maleness ['meɪlnəs] *n* : masculinidad *f*

malevolence [mə'levələnts] *n* : malevolencia *f*

malevolent [mə'levələnt] *adj* : malévolo

malformation [,mælfɔr'meɪʃən] *n* : malformación *f*

malformed [mæl'fɔrmd] *adj* : mal formado, deforme

malfunction[1] [mæl'fʌŋkʃən] *vi* : funcionar mal

malfunction[2] *n* : mal funcionamiento *m*

malice ['mælɪs] *n* 1 : malicia *f*, malevolencia *f* 2 **with malice aforethought** : con premeditación

malicious [mə'lɪʃəs] *adj* : malicioso, malévolo — **maliciously** *adv*

malign[1] [mə'laɪn] *vt* : calumniar, difamar

malign[2] *adj* : maligno

malignancy [mə'lɪɡnəntsi] *n, pl* **-cies** : malignidad *f*

malignant [mə'lɪɡnənt] *adj* : maligno

malinger [mə'lɪŋɡər] *vi* : fingirse enfermo

malingerer [mə'lɪŋɡərər] *n* : uno que se finge enfermo

mall ['mɔl] *n* 1 PROMENADE : alameda *f*, paseo *m* (arbolado) 2 : centro *m* comercial ⟨shopping mall : galería comercial⟩

mallard ['mælərd] *n, pl* **-lard** *or* **-lards** : pato *m* real, ánade *mf* real

malleable ['mæliəbəl] *adj* : maleable

mallet ['mælət] *n* : mazo *m*

malnourished [mæl'nərɪʃt] *adj* : desnutrido, malnutrido

malnutrition [,mælnu'trɪʃən, -nju-] *n* : desnutrición *f*, malnutrición *f*

malodorous [mæl'o:dərəs] *adj* : maloliente

malpractice [,mæl'præktəs] *n* : mala práctica *f*, negligencia *f*

malt ['mɔlt] *n* : malta *f*

maltreat [mæl'tri:t] *vt* : maltratar

malware ['mæl,wær] *n* : malware *m*

mama *or* **mamma** ['mɑmə] *n* : mamá *f*

mambo ['mɑmbo] *n* : mambo *m*

mammal ['mæməl] *n* : mamífero *m*

mammalian [mə'meɪliən, mæ-] *adj* : mamífero

mammary ['mæməri] *adj* 1 : mamario 2 **mammary gland** : glándula mamaria

mammogram ['mæmə,ɡræm] *n* : mamografía *f*

mammoth[1] ['mæməθ] *adj* : colosal, gigantesco

mammoth[2] *n* : mamut *m*

man[1] ['mæn] *vt* **manned; manning** : tripular (un barco o avión), encargarse de (un servicio)

man[2] *n, pl* **men** ['mɛn] 1 PERSON : hombre *m*, persona *f* ⟨the man in the street

: el hombre de la calle⟩ ⟨to a man : todos sin excepción⟩ ⟨every man for himself : sálvese quien pueda⟩ ⟨to be one's own man : ser independiente⟩ 2 MALE : hombre *m* 3 MANKIND : humanidad *f* 4 HUSBAND, BOYFRIEND : marido *m*, novio *m* 5 **men** *npl* : trabajadores *mpl* (de una empresa), soldados *mpl* (en el ejército) 6 **hey, man** *fam* : hola amigo

manacles ['mænɪkəlz] *npl* HANDCUFFS : esposas *fpl*

manage ['mænɪD] *v* **-aged; -aging** *vt* 1 HANDLE : controlar, manejar 2 DIRECT : administrar, dirigir ⟨to manage one's life : organizar uno su vida⟩ 3 CONTRIVE : lograr, ingeniárselas para ⟨I managed to do it : pude hacerlo⟩ — *vi* COPE : arreglárselas

manageable ['mænɪD əbəl] *adj* : manejable

management ['mænɪD mənt] *n* 1 DIRECTION : administración *f*, gestión *f*, dirección *f* 2 HANDLING : manejo *m* 3 MANAGERS : dirección *f*, gerencia *f*

manager ['mænɪD ər] *n* : director *m*, -tora *f*; gerente *mf*; administrador *m*, -dora *f*

managerial [,mænə'D ɪriəl] *adj* : directivo, gerencial

managing director *n* : director *m* gerente, directora *f* gerente

manatee ['mænə,ti:] *n* : manatí *m*

mandarin ['mændərən] *n* 1 : mandarín *m* 2 *or* **mandarin orange** : mandarina *f*

mandate ['mæn,deɪt] *n* : mandato *m*

mandatory ['mændə,tori] *adj* : obligatorio

mandible ['mændəbəl] *n* : mandíbula *f*

mandolin [,mændə'lɪn, 'mændələn] *n* : mandolina *f*

mane ['meɪn] *n* : crin *f* (de un caballo), melena *f* (de un león o una persona)

maneuver[1] [mə'nu:vər, -'nju:-] *vt* 1 PLACE, POSITION : maniobrar, posicionar, colocar 2 MANIPULATE : manipular, maniobrar — *vi* : maniobrar

maneuver[2] *n* : maniobra *f*

manfully ['mænfəli] *adj* : valientemente

manganese ['mæŋɡə,ni:z, -,ni:s] *n* : manganeso *m*

mange ['meɪnD] *n* : sarna *f*

manger ['meɪnD ər] *n* : pesebre *m*

mangle ['mæŋɡəl] *vt* **-gled; -gling** 1 CRUSH, DESTROY : aplastar, despedazar, destrozar 2 MUTILATE : mutilar ⟨to mangle a text : mutilar un texto⟩

mango ['mæŋ,ɡo:] *n, pl* **-goes** : mango *m*

mangrove ['mæn,ɡro:v, 'mæŋ-] *n* : mangle *m*

mangy ['meɪnD i] *adj* **mangier; -est** 1 : sarnoso 2 SHABBY : gastado

manhandle ['mæn,hændəl] *vt* **-dled; -dling** : maltratar, tratar con poco cuidado

manhole ['mæn,ho:l] *n* : boca *f* de alcantarilla

manhood ['mæn,hʊd] *n* 1 : madurez *f* (de un hombre) 2 COURAGE, MANLINESS : hombría *f*, valor *m* 3 MEN : hombres *mpl*

manhunt ['mæn,hʌnt] *n* : búsqueda *f* (de un criminal)

mania ['meɪniə, -njə] *n* : manía *f*
maniac ['meɪni,æk] *n* : maníaco *m*, -ca *f*; maniático *m*, -ca *f*
maniacal [mə'naɪəkəl] *adj fam* : maníaco, maniaco
manic ['mænɪk] *adj* : maníaco, maniaco
manicure[1] ['mænə,kjʊr] *vt* **-cured; -curing 1** : hacer la manicura a **2** TRIM : recortar
manicure[2] *n* : manicura *f*
manicurist ['mænə,kjʊrɪst] *n* : manicuro *m*, -ra *f*
manifest[1] ['mænə,fɛst] *vt* : manifestar
manifest[2] *adj* : manifiesto, patente — **manifestly** *adv*
manifestation [,mænəfə'steɪʃən] *n* : manifestación *f*
manifesto [,mænə'fɛs,to:] *n, pl* **-tos** *or* **-toes** : manifiesto *m*
manifold[1] ['mænə,fo:ld] *adj* : diverso, variado
manifold[2] *n* : colector *m* (de escape)
manioc ['mæni,ak] *n* : mandioca *f*, yuca *f*
manipulate [mə'nɪpjə,leɪt] *vt* **-lated; -lating** : manipular
manipulation [mə,nɪpjə'leɪʃən] *n* : manipulación *f*
manipulative [mə'nɪpjə,leɪɾɪv, -ləɾɪv] *adj* : manipulador
manipulator [mə'nɪpjə,leɪɾər] *n* : manipulador *m*, -dora *f*
mankind ['mæn'kaɪnd, -,kaɪnd] *n* : género *m* humano, humanidad *f*
manliness ['mænlinəs] *n* : hombría *f*, masculinidad *f*
manly ['mænli] *adj* **manlier; -est** : varonil, viril
man–made ['mæn'meɪd] *adj* : artificial ⟨man-made fabrics : telas sintéticas⟩
manna ['mænə] *n* : maná *m*
mannequin ['mænɪkən] *n* **1** DUMMY : maniquí *m* **2** MODEL : modelo *mf*
manner ['mænər] *n* **1** KIND, SORT : tipo *m*, clase *f* **2** WAY : manera *f*, modo *m* **3** STYLE : estilo *m* (artístico) **4 manners** *npl* CUSTOMS : costumbres *fpl* **5 manners** *npl* ETIQUETTE : modales *mpl*, educación *f*, etiqueta *f* ⟨good manners : buenos modales⟩
mannered ['mænərd] *adj* **1** AFFECTED, ARTIFICIAL : amanerado, afectado **2 well–mannered** : educado, cortés **3** → **ill-mannered**
mannerism ['mænə,rɪzəm] *n* : peculiaridad *f*, gesto *m* particular
mannish ['mænɪʃ] *adj* : masculino, hombruno
man–of–war [,mænə'wɔr, -əv'wɔr] *n, pl* **men–of–war** [,mɛn-] WARSHIP : buque *m* de guerra
manor ['mænər] *n* **1** : casa *f* solariega, casa *f* señorial **2** ESTATE : señorío *m*
manpower ['mæn,paʊər] *n* : personal *m*, mano *f* de obra
mansion ['mæntʃən] *n* : mansión *f*
manslaughter ['mæn,slɔɾər] *n* : homicidio *m* sin premeditación
mantel ['mæntəl] *n* : repisa *f* de chimenea
mantelpiece ['mæntəl,pi:s] → **mantel**

mantis ['mæntəs] *n, pl* **-tises** *or* **-tes** ['mæn,ti:z] : mantis *f* religiosa
mantle ['mæntəl] *n* : manto *m*
manual[1] ['mænjʊəl] *adj* : manual — **manually** *adv*
manual[2] *n* : manual *m*
manufacture[1] [,mænjə'fæktʃər] *vt* **-tured; -turing** : fabricar, manufacturar, confeccionar (ropa), elaborar (comestibles)
manufacture[2] *n* : manufactura *f*, fabricación *f*, confección *f* (de ropa), elaboración *f* (de comestibles)
manufacturer [,mænjə'fæktʃərər] *n* : fabricante *m*; manufacturero *m*, -ra *f*
manure [mə'nʊr, -'njʊr] *n* : estiércol *m*
manuscript ['mænjə,skrɪpt] *n* : manuscrito *m*
many[1] ['mɛni] *adj* **more** ['mor]; **most** ['mo:st] **1** : muchos ⟨for many years : durante muchos años⟩ ⟨many years ago : hace muchos años⟩ ⟨so/too many ideas : tantas/demasiadas ideas⟩ ⟨I don't have that many employees : no tengo tantos empleados⟩ ⟨a good/great many people : muchísima gente⟩ ⟨one of her many interests : uno de sus muchos intereses⟩ **2 as many** ⟨I have as many books as she does : tengo tantos libros como ella⟩ ⟨take as many books as you want : llévate cuantos libros quieras⟩ ⟨we saw three plays in as many days : vimos tres obras en el mismo número de días⟩ **3 how many** : cuántos, cuántas ⟨how many people were there? : ¿cuánta gente había?⟩
many[2] *pron* **1** : muchos ⟨many of them : muchos de ellos⟩ ⟨many of the novels : muchas de las novelas⟩ ⟨some stayed, but many left : algunos se quedaron, pero muchos se fueron⟩ ⟨I don't have that many : no tengo tantos⟩ **2 as many as** ⟨I have as many as she does : tengo tantos como ella⟩ ⟨as many as a hundred people : hasta cien personas⟩ ⟨take as many as you want : llévate cuantas quieras⟩ **3 many a/an** ⟨many a time : muchas veces⟩ **4 the many** : la mayoría
map[1] ['mæp] *vt* **mapped; mapping 1** : trazar el mapa de **2** PLAN : planear, proyectar ⟨to map out a program : planear un programa⟩
map[2] *n* : mapa *m*
maple ['meɪpəl] *n* : arce *m*
mar ['mɑr] *vt* **marred; marring 1** SPOIL : estropear, echar a perder **2** DEFACE : desfigurar
maraca [mə'rɑkə] *n* : maraca *f*
maraschino [,mærə'ski:no:, -'ʃi:-] *n, pl* **-nos** : cereza *f* al marrasquino
marathon ['mærə,θɑn] *n* **1** RACE : maratón *m* **2** CONTEST : competencia *f* de resistencia
maraud [mə'rɔd] *vi* : merodear
marauder [mə'rɔdər] *n* : merodeador *m*, -dora *f*
marble ['mɑrbəl] *n* **1** : mármol *m* **2** : canica *f*, bolita *f* ⟨to play marbles : jugar a las canicas⟩
march[1] ['mɑrtʃ] *vi* **1** : marchar, desfilar ⟨they marched past the grandstand

: desfilaron ante la tribuna⟩ **2** : caminar con resolución ⟨she marched right up to him : se le acercó sin vacilación⟩
march² *n* **1** MARCHING : marcha *f* **2** PASSAGE : paso *m* (del tiempo) **3** PROGRESS : avance *m*, progreso *m* **4** : marcha *f* (en música)
March ['mɑrtʃ] *n* : marzo *m* ⟨they arrived on the 13th of March, they arrived on March 13th : llegaron el trece de marzo⟩
marchioness ['mɑrʃənɪs] *n* : marquesa *f*
Mardi Gras ['mɑrdi,ɡrɑ] *n* : martes *m* de Carnaval
mare ['mær] *n* : yegua *f*
margarine ['mɑrdʒ ərən] *n* : margarina *f*
margarita [,mɑrɡə'ri:tə] *n* : margarita *f* (cóctel)
margin ['mɑrdʒ ən] *n* : margen *m*
marginal ['mɑrdʒ ənəl] *adj* **1** : marginal **2** MINIMAL : mínimo — **marginally** *adv*
marginalization [,mɑrdʒ ənələ'zeɪʃən] *n* : marginación *f*
mariachi [,mɑri'ɑtʃi, ,mæ-] *n* **1** *or* **mariachi band** : mariachi *m* (grupo) **2** *or* **mariachi musician** : mariachi *m* (músico) **3** **mariachi music** : mariachi *m*, música *f* de mariachi
marigold ['mærə,ɡo:ld] *n* : maravilla *f*, caléndula *f*
marijuana *or* **marihuana** [,mærə'hwɑnə] *n* : marihuana *f*
marimba [mə'rɪmbə] *n* : marimba *f*
marina [mə'ri:nə] *n* : puerto *m* deportivo
marinade [,mærə'nɑd] *n* : adobo *m*, marinada *f*
marinate ['mærə,neɪt] *vt* **-nated; -nating** : marinar
marine¹ [mə'ri:n] *adj* **1** : marino ⟨marine life : vida marina⟩ **2** NAUTICAL : náutico, marítimo **3** : de la infantería de marina
marine² *n* : soldado *m* de marina
mariner ['mærɪnər] *n* : marinero *m*, marino *m*
marionette [,mæriə'nɛt] *n* : marioneta *f*, títere *m*
marital ['mærətəl] *adj* **1** : matrimonial **2** **marital status** : estado *m* civil
maritime ['mærə,taɪm] *adj* : marítimo
marjoram ['mɑrdʒ ərəm] *n* : mejorana *f*
mark¹ ['mɑrk] *vt* **1** : marcar **2** MAR : dejar marca en **3** CHARACTERIZE : caracterizar **4** SIGNAL : señalar, marcar **5** GRADE : corregir (exámenes, etc.) **6** **mark my words!** : ¡acuérdate de lo que te digo! **7** **to mark down** : rebajar **8** **to mark off** : demarcar, delimitar **9** **to mark up** : anotar (un manuscrito, etc.) **10** **to mark up** : aumentar el precio de
mark² *n* **1** TARGET : blanco *m* ⟨to miss the mark, to be wide of the mark : no dar en el blanco⟩ **2** : marca *f*, señal *f* ⟨put a mark where you left off : pon una señal donde terminaste⟩ **3** INDICATION : señal *f*, indicio *m* ⟨a mark of respect : una señal de respeto⟩ **4** GRADE : nota *f* **5** LEVEL : nivel *m* ⟨to reach the halfway mark : llegar al ecuador⟩ ⟨we've

topped the one million dollar mark : hemos superado el millón de dólares⟩ **6** IMPRINT : huella *f*, marca *f* **7** BLEMISH : marca *f*, imperfección *f* **8** **on your mark(s), get set, go!** : en sus marcas, listos, ¡ya!; en sus marcas, listos, ¡fuera! *Mex*; preparados, listos, ¡ya! *Spain* **9** **to fall short of the mark** : quedarse corto **10** **to make/leave one's mark** : dejar su impronta **11** **to miss the mark** ERR, FAIL : errar, fracasar
marked ['mɑrkt] *adj* : marcado, notable — **markedly** ['mɑrkədli] *adv*
marker ['mɑrkər] *n* : marcador *m*
market¹ ['mɑrkət] *vt* : poner en venta, comercializar
market² *n* **1** MARKETPLACE : mercado *m* ⟨the open market : el mercado libre⟩ **2** DEMAND : demanda *f*, mercado *m* **3** STORE : tienda *f* **4** → **stock market**
marketable ['mɑrkətəbəl] *adj* : vendible
marketing ['mɑrkətɪŋ] *n* : mercadotecnia *f*, mercadeo *m*
marketplace ['mɑrkət,pleɪs] *n* : mercado *m*
market research *n* : estudio *m* de mercado
marking *n* **1** : corrección *f* (de exámenes, etc.) **2** : marca *f*, señal *f* **3** : pinta *f*, mancha *f* (de un animal) **4** **to have all the markings of** : tener madera de (dícese de personas), tener los ingredientes para
marksman ['mɑrksmən] *n, pl* **-men** [-mən, -,mɪn] : tirador *m*
marksmanship ['mɑrksmən,ʃɪp] *n* : puntería *f*
markswoman ['mɑrks,wʊmən] *n, pl* **-women** [-,wɪmən] : tiradora *f*
marmalade ['mɑrmə,leɪd] *n* : mermelada *f*
marmoset ['mɑrmə,sɛt] *n* : tití *m*
marmot ['mɑrmət] *n* : marmota *f*
maroon¹ [mə'ru:n] *vt* : abandonar, aislar
maroon² *n* : rojo *m* oscuro, granate *m*
marquee [mɑr'ki:] *n* : marquesina *f*
marquess ['mɑrkwɪs] *or* **marquis** ['mɑrkwɪs, mɑr'ki:] *n, pl* **-quesses** *or* **-quises** [-'ki:z, -'ki:zəz] *or* **-quis** [-'ki:, -'ki:z] : marqués *m*
marquise [mɑr'ki:z] → **marchioness**
marriage ['mærɪdʒ] *n* **1** : matrimonio *m* **2** WEDDING : casamiento *m*, boda *f*
marriageable ['mærɪdʒ əbəl] *adj* **of marriageable age** : de edad de casarse
marriage certificate : certificado *m* de matrimonio, acta *f* de matrimonio
married ['mærid] *adj* **1** : casado **2** **to get married** : casarse
marrow ['mæro:] *n* : médula *f*, tuétano *m*
marry ['mæri] *vt* **-ried; -rying** **1** : casar ⟨the priest married them : el cura los casó⟩ **2** : casarse con ⟨she married John : se casó con John⟩
Mars ['mɑrz] *n* : Marte *m*
marsh ['mɑrʃ] *n* **1** : pantano *m* **2** **salt marsh** : marisma *f*
marshal¹ ['mɑrʃəl] *vt* **-shaled** *or* **-shalled; -shaling** *or* **-shalling** **1** : poner en orden, reunir **2** USHER : conducir
marshal² *n* **1** : maestro *m* de ceremonias **2** : mariscal *m* (en el ejército); jefe

m, -fa *f* (de la policía, de los bomberos, etc.)
marshmallow [ˈmɑrʃˌmɛloː, -ˌmælo:] *n* : malvavisco *m*
marshy [ˈmɑrʃi] *adj* **marshier; -est** : pantanoso
marsupial [mɑrˈsuːpiəl] *n* : marsupial *m*
mart [ˈmɑrt] *n* MARKET : mercado *m*
marten [ˈmɑrtən] *n, pl* **-ten** *or* **-tens** : marta *f*
martial [ˈmɑrʃəl] *adj* : marcial ⟨martial arts : artes marciales⟩ ⟨martial law : ley marcial⟩
Martian [ˈmɑrʃən] *n* : marciano *m*, -na *f* — **Martian** *adj*
martin [ˈmɑrtən] *n* **1** SWALLOW : golondrina *f* **2** SWIFT : vencejo *m*
martyr[1] [ˈmɑrtər] *vt* : martirizar
martyr[2] *n* : mártir *mf*
martyrdom [ˈmɑrtərdəm] *n* : martirio *m*
marvel[1] [ˈmɑrvəl] *vi* **-veled** *or* **-velled; -veling** *or* **-velling** : maravillarse
marvel[2] *n* : maravilla *f*
marvelous [ˈmɑrvələs] *or* **marvellous** *adj* : maravilloso — **marvelously** *adv*
Marxism [ˈmɑrkˌsɪzəm] *n* : marxismo *m*
Marxist[1] [ˈmɑrksɪst] *adj* : marxista
Marxist[2] *n* : marxista *mf*
marzipan [ˈmɑrtsəˌpan, ˈmɑrzəˌpæn] *n* : mazapán *m*
mascara [mæsˈkærə] *n* : rímel *m*, rimel *m*
mascot [ˈmæsˌkɑt, -kət] *n* : mascota *f*
masculine [ˈmæskjələn] *adj* : masculino
masculinity [ˌmæskjəˈlɪnəṭi] *n* : masculinidad *f*
mash[1] [ˈmæʃ] *vt* **1** : hacer puré de (papas, etc.) **2** CRUSH : aplastar, majar
mash[2] *n* **1** FEED : afrecho *m* **2** : malta *f* (para hacer bebidas alcohólicas) **3** PASTE, PULP : papilla *f*, pasta *f*
mask[1] [ˈmæsk] *vt* **1** CONCEAL, DISGUISE : enmascarar, ocultar **2** COVER : cubrir, tapar
mask[2] *n* **1** : máscara *f*, careta *f*, mascarilla *f* (de un cirujano o dentista) **2** *or* **facial mask** : mascarilla *f* (facial)
masochism [ˈmæsəˌkɪzəm, ˈmæzə-] *n* : masoquismo *m*
masochist [ˈmæsəˌkɪst, ˈmæzə-] *n* : masoquista *mf*
masochistic [ˌmæsəˈkɪstɪk, ˌmæzə-] *adj* : masoquista
mason [ˈmeɪsən] *n* **1** BRICKLAYER : albañil *mf* **2** *or* **stonemason** [ˈstoːnˌ-] : mampostero *m*, cantero *m* **3** **Mason** → **freemason**
Masonic [məˈsɑnɪk] *adj* : masónico
masonry [ˈmeɪsənri] *n, pl* **-ries 1** BRICKLAYING : albañilería *f* **2** *or* **stonemasonry** [ˈstoːnˌ-] : mampostería *f*
masquerade[1] [ˌmæskəˈreɪd] *vi* **-aded; -ading 1** : disfrazarse (de), hacerse pasar (por) **2** : asistir a una mascarada
masquerade[2] *n* **1** : mascarada *f*, baile *m* de disfraces **2** FACADE : farsa *f*, fachada *f*
mass[1] [ˈmæs] *vi* : concentrarse, juntarse en masa — *vt* : concentrar
mass[2] *n* **1** : masa *f* ⟨atomic mass : masa atómica⟩ **2** BULK : mole *f*, volumen *m* **3** MULTITUDE : cantidad *f*, montón *m*

(de cosas), multitud *f* (de gente) **4 the masses** : las masas, el pueblo, el populacho
Mass [ˈmæs] *n* : misa *f*
massacre[1] [ˈmæsɪkər] *vt* **-cred; -cring** : masacrar
massacre[2] *n* : masacre *f*
massage[1] [məˈsɑʒ, -ˈsɑd] *vt* **-saged; -saging** : masajear
massage[2] *n* : masaje *m*
masseur [mæˈsər] *n* : masajista *m*
masseuse [mæˈsøz, -ˈsuːz] *n* : masajista *f*
massive [ˈmæsɪv] *adj* **1** BULKY : voluminoso, macizo **2** HUGE : masivo, enorme — **massively** *adv*
mass media *npl* : medios *mpl* de comunicación masiva; medios *mpl* de comunicación de masas
mass–produce *vt* : producir en masa, fabricar en serie
mass production *n* : producción *f* en masa, fabricación *f* en serie
mass transit *n* : transporte *m* público
mast [ˈmæst] *n* : mástil *m*, palo *m*
master[1] [ˈmæstər] *vt* **1** SUBDUE : dominar **2** : llegar a dominar ⟨she mastered French : llegó a dominar el francés⟩
master[2] *n* **1** TEACHER : maestro *m*, profesor *m* **2** EXPERT : experto *m*, -ta *f*; maestro *m*, -tra *f* **3** : amo *m* (de animales o esclavos), señor *m* (de la casa) **4**
master's degree : maestría *f*
masterful [ˈmæstərfəl] *adj* **1** IMPERIOUS : autoritario, imperioso, dominante **2** SKILLFUL : magistral — **masterfully** *adv*
masterly [ˈmæstərli] *adj* : magistral
mastermind[1] [ˈmæstərˌmaɪnd] *n* : cerebro *m*, artífice *mf*
mastermind[2] *vt* : ser el cerebro de, planear, organizar
masterpiece [ˈmæstərˌpiːs] *n* : obra *f* maestra
masterwork [ˈmæstərˌwərk] → **masterpiece**
mastery [ˈmæstəri] *n* **1** DOMINION : dominio *m*, autoridad *f* **2** SUPERIORITY : superioridad *f* **3** EXPERTISE : maestría *f*
masticate [ˈmæstəˌkeɪt] *v* **-cated; -cating** : masticar
mastiff [ˈmæstɪf] *n* : mastín *m*
mastodon [ˈmæstəˌdɑn] *n* : mastodonte *m*
masturbate [ˈmæstərˌbeɪt] *vi* **-bated; -bating** : masturbarse
masturbation [ˌmæstərˈbeɪʃən] *n* : masturbación *f*
mat[1] [ˈmæt] *v* **matted; matting** *vt* TANGLE : enmarañar — *vi* : enmarañarse
mat[2] *n* **1** : estera *f* **2** TANGLE : maraña *f* **3** PAD : colchoneta *f* (de gimnasia) **4** *or* **matt** *or* **matte** [ˈmæt] FRAME : marco *m* (de cartón)
mat[3] → **matte**
matador [ˈmæṭəˌdɔr] *n* : matador *m*
match[1] [ˈmætʃ] *vt* **1** PIT : enfrentar, oponer **2** EQUAL, FIT : igualar, corresponder a, coincidir con **3** : combinar con, hacer juego con ⟨her shoes match her dress : sus zapatos hacen juego con su vestido⟩ — *vi* **1** CORRESPOND : con-

cordar, coincidir **2** : hacer juego ⟨with a tie to match : con una corbata que hace juego⟩
match² *n* **1** EQUAL : igual *mf* ⟨he's no match for her : no puede competir con ella⟩ **2** FIGHT, GAME : partido *m*, combate *m* (en boxeo) **3** MARRIAGE : matrimonio *m*, casamiento *m* **4** : fósforo *m*, cerilla *f*, cerillo *m* (*in various countries*) ⟨he lit a match : encendió un fósforo⟩ **5 to be a good match** : hacer buena pareja (dícese de las personas), hacer juego (dícese de la ropa)
matchbox ['mætʃˌbɑks] *n* : caja *f* de cerillas
matchless ['mætʃləs] *adj* : sin igual, sin par
matchmaker ['mætʃˌmeɪkər] *n* : casamentero *m*, -ra *f*
mate¹ ['meɪt] *v* **mated; mating** *vi* **1** FIT : encajar **2** PAIR : emparejarse **3** (*relating to animals*) : aparearse, copular — *vt* : aparear, acoplar (animales)
mate² *n* **1** COMPANION : compañero *m*, -ra *f*; camarada *mf* **2** : macho *m*, hembra *f* (de animales) **3** : oficial *mf* (de un barco) ⟨first mate : primer oficial⟩ **4** : compañero *m*, -ra *f*; pareja *f* (de un zapato, etc.)
maté ['mɑˌteɪ] *n* : yerba *f*, mate *m*
material¹ [mə'tɪriəl] *adj* **1** PHYSICAL : material, físico ⟨the material world : el mundo material⟩ ⟨material needs : necesidades materiales⟩ **2** IMPORTANT : importante, esencial **3 material evidence** : prueba *f* sustancial
material² *n* **1** : material *m* **2** CLOTH : tejido *m*, tela *f*
materialism [mə'tɪriəˌlɪzəm] *n* : materialismo *m*
materialist [mə'tɪriəlɪst] *n* : materialista *mf*
materialistic [məˌtɪriə'lɪstɪk] *adj* : materialista
materialize [mə'tɪriəˌlaɪz] *v* **-ized; -izing** *vt* : materializar, hacer aparecer — *vi* : materializarse, aparecer
maternal [mə'tərnəl] *adj* MOTHERLY : maternal — **maternally** *adv*
maternity¹ [mə'tərnəti] *adj* : de maternidad ⟨maternity clothes : ropa de futura mamá⟩ ⟨maternity leave : licencia por maternidad⟩
maternity² *n*, *pl* **-ties** : maternidad *f*
math ['mæθ] → **mathematics**
mathematical [ˌmæθə'mætɪkəl] *adj* : matemático — **mathematically** *adv*
mathematician [ˌmæθəmə'tɪʃən] *n* : matemático *m*, -ca *f*
mathematics [ˌmæθə'mætɪks] *ns & pl* : matemáticas *fpl*, matemática *f*
matinee *or* **matinée** [ˌmætən'eɪ] *n* : matiné *f*
matriarch ['meɪtriˌɑrk] *n* : matriarca *f*
matriarchy ['meɪtriˌɑrki] *n*, *pl* **-chies** : matriarcado *m*
matriculate [mə'trɪkjəˌleɪt] *v* **-lated; -lating** *vt* : matricular — *vi* : matricularse
matriculation [məˌtrɪkjə'leɪʃən] *n* : matrícula *f*, matriculación *f*

matrimony ['mætrəˌmoːni] *n* : matrimonio *m* — **matrimonial** [ˌmætrə'moːniəl] *adj*
matrix ['meɪtrɪks] *n*, *pl* **-trices** ['meɪtrəˌsiːz, 'mæ-] *or* **-trixes** ['meɪtrɪksəz] : matriz *f*
matron ['meɪtrən] *n* : matrona *f*
matronly ['meɪtrənli] *adj* : de matrona, matronal
matte ['mæt] *adj* : mate, de acabado mate
matter¹ ['mætər] *vi* : importar ⟨it doesn't matter : no importa⟩
matter² *n* **1** QUESTION : asunto *m*, cuestión *f* ⟨a matter of taste/opinion/time : una cuestión de gusto/opiniones/tiempo⟩ **2** SUBSTANCE : materia *f*, sustancia *f* **3 matters** *npl* CIRCUMSTANCES : situación *f*, cosas *fpl* ⟨to make matters worse : para colmo de males⟩ **4 as a matter of course** : automáticamente **5 as a matter of fact** : en efecto, en realidad **6 for that matter** : de hecho **7 no matter how much** : por mucho que **8 the fact/truth of the matter** : la verdad **9 to be no laughing matter** : no ser motivo de risa **10 to be the matter** : pasar ⟨what's the matter? : ¿qué pasa?⟩
matter–of–fact [ˌmætərəv'fækt] *adj* : práctico, realista
mattress ['mætrəs] *n* : colchón *m*
mature¹ [mə'tʊr, -'tjʊr, -'tʊr] *vi* **-tured; -turing** **1** : madurar **2** : vencer ⟨when does the loan mature? : ¿cuándo vence el préstamo?⟩
mature² *adj* **maturer; -est** **1** : maduro **2** DUE : vencido
maturity [mə'tʊrəti, -'tjʊr-, -'tʊr-] *n* : madurez *f*
maudlin ['mɔdlɪn] *adj* : sensiblero
maul¹ ['mɔl] *vt* **1** BEAT : golpear, pegar **2** MANGLE : mutilar **3** MANHANDLE : maltratar
maul² *n* MALLET : mazo *m*
Mauritanian [ˌmɔrə'teɪniən] *n* : mauritano *m*, -na *f* — **Mauritanian** *adj*
mausoleum [ˌmɔsə'liːəm, ˌmɔzə-] *n*, *pl* **-leums** *or* **-lea** [-'liːə] : mausoleo *m*
mauve ['moːv, 'mɔv] *n* : malva *m*
maven *or* **mavin** ['meɪvən] *n* EXPERT : experto *m*, -ta *f*
maverick ['mævrɪk, 'mævə-] *n* **1** : ternero *m* sin marcar **2** NONCONFORMIST : inconformista *mf*, disidente *mf*
maw ['mɔ] *n* : fauces *fpl*
mawkish ['mɔkɪʃ] *adj* : sensiblero
maxim ['mæksəm] *n* : máxima *f*
maximize ['mæksəˌmaɪz] *vt* **-mized; -mizing** **1** : maximizar, llevar al máximo **2** : maximizar (en informática)
maximum¹ ['mæksəməm] *adj* : máximo
maximum² *n*, *pl* **-ma** ['mæksəmə] *or* **-mums** : máximo *m*
may ['meɪ] *v aux*, *past* **might** ['maɪt] *present s & pl* **may** **1** (*expressing permission*) : poder ⟨you may go : puedes ir⟩ ⟨if I may : si me lo permites⟩ **2** (*expressing possibility or probability*) : poder ⟨you may be right : puede que tengas razón⟩ ⟨it may happen occasionally : puede pasar de vez en cuando⟩ ⟨be that as it may : sea como

sea⟩ **3** (*expressing desires, intentions, or contingencies*) ⟨may the best man win : que gane el mejor⟩ ⟨I laugh that I may not weep : me río para no llorar⟩ ⟨come what may : pase lo que pase⟩

May ['meɪ] *n* : mayo *m* ⟨they arrived on the 20th of May, they arrived on May 20th : llegaron el 20 de mayo⟩

Maya ['maɪə] *or* **Mayan** ['maɪən] *n* : maya *mf* — **Maya** *or* **Mayan** *adj*

maybe ['meɪbi] *adv* PERHAPS : quizás, tal vez

mayfly ['meɪˌflaɪ] *n, pl* **-flies** : efímera *f*

mayhem ['meɪˌhɛm, 'meɪəm] *n* **1** MUTILATION : mutilación *f* **2** DEVASTATION : estragos *mpl*

mayonnaise ['meɪəˌneɪz] *n* : mayonesa *f*

mayor ['meɪər, 'mɛr] *n* : alcalde *m*, -desa *f*

mayoral ['meɪərəl, 'mɛrəl] *adj* : de alcalde

maze ['meɪz] *n* : laberinto *m*

me ['miː] *pron* **1** : me ⟨she called me : me llamó⟩ ⟨give it to me : dámelo⟩ **2** (*after a preposition*) : mí ⟨for me : para mí⟩ ⟨with me : conmigo⟩ **3** (*after conjunctions and verbs*) : yo ⟨it's me : soy yo⟩ ⟨as big as me : tan grande como yo⟩ **4** (*emphatic use*) : yo ⟨me, too! : ¡yo también!⟩ ⟨who, me? : ¿quién, yo?⟩

meadow ['mɛdoː] *n* : prado *m*, pradera *f*

meadowland ['mɛdoˌlænd] *n* : pradera *f*

meadowlark ['mɛdoˌlark] *n* : pájaro *m* cantor con el pecho amarillo

meager *or* **meagre** ['miːgər] *adj* **1** THIN : magro, flaco **2** POOR SCANTY : exiguo, escaso, pobre

meagerly ['miːgərli] *adv* : pobremente

meagerness ['miːgərnəs] *n* : escasez *f*, pobreza *f*

meal ['miːl] *n* **1** : comida *f* ⟨a hearty meal : una comida sustanciosa⟩ **2** : harina *f* (de maíz, etc.)

mealtime ['miːlˌtaɪm] *n* : hora *f* de comer

mean[1] ['miːn] *vt* **meant** ['mɛnt]; **meaning 1** INTEND : querer, pensar, tener la intención de ⟨I didn't mean to do it : lo hice sin querer⟩ ⟨what do you mean to do? : ¿qué piensas hacer?⟩ ⟨I don't mean you any harm : no quiero hacerte daño⟩ ⟨she meant for him to come : su intención era que viniera⟩ **2** : querer decir ⟨what do you mean? : ¿qué quieres decir?⟩ ⟨if you know what I mean : si me entiendes⟩ ⟨I meant it : lo dije en serio⟩ ⟨she meant it as a compliment : lo dijo como un cumplido⟩ **3** SIGNIFY : querer decir, significar ⟨what does that mean? : ¿qué quiere decir eso?⟩ ⟨that means nothing to me : no significa nada para mí⟩ ⟨that means trouble : eso supone problemas⟩ **4** : importar ⟨health means everything : lo que más importa es la salud⟩ ⟨she means the world to me : ella es muy importante para mí⟩ **5 to mean well** : tener buenas intenciones

mean[2] *adj* **1** HUMBLE : humilde **2** NEGLIGIBLE : despreciable ⟨it's no mean feat : no es poca cosa⟩ **3** STINGY : mezquino, tacaño **4** CRUEL : malo, cruel ⟨to be mean to someone : tratar mal a alguien⟩ **5** AVERAGE, MEDIAN : medio

mean[3] *n* **1** MIDPOINT : término *m* medio **2** AVERAGE : promedio *m*, media *f* aritmética **3 means** *npl* WAY : medio *m*, manera *f*, vía *f* **4 means** *npl* RESOURCES : medios *mpl*, recursos *mpl* **5 by all means** : por supuesto, cómo no **6 by means of** : por medio de **7 by no means** : de ninguna manera, de ningún modo

meander [miˈændər] *vi* **-dered; -dering 1** WIND : serpentear **2** WANDER : vagar, andar sin rumbo fijo

meaning ['miːnɪŋ] *n* **1** : significado *m*, sentido *m* ⟨double meaning : doble sentido⟩ **2** INTENT : intención *f*, propósito *m*

meaningful ['miːnɪŋfəl] *adj* : significativo — **meaningfully** *adv*

meaningless ['miːnɪŋləs] *adj* : sin sentido

meanness ['miːnnəs] *n* **1** CRUELTY : crueldad *f*, mezquindad *f* **2** STINGINESS : tacañería *f*

meantime[1] ['miːnˌtaɪm] *adv* → **meanwhile**[1]

meantime[2] *n* **1** : interín *m* **2 in the meantime** : entretanto, mientras tanto

meanwhile[1] ['miːnˌhwaɪl] *adv* : entretanto, mientras tanto

meanwhile[2] *n* → **meantime**[2]

measles ['miːzəlz] *ns & pl* : sarampión *m*

measly ['miːzli] *adj* **measlier; -est** : miserable, mezquino

measurable ['mɛʒərəbəl, 'meɪ-] *adj* : mensurable — **measurably** [-bli] *adv*

measure[1] ['mɛʒər, 'meɪ-] *v* **-sured; -suring** : medir ⟨he measured the table : midió la mesa⟩ ⟨it measures 15 feet tall : mide 15 pies de altura⟩

measure[2] *n* **1** AMOUNT : medida *f*, cantidad *f* ⟨in large measure : en gran medida⟩ ⟨a full measure : una cantidad exacta⟩ ⟨a measure of proficiency : una cierta competencia⟩ ⟨for good measure : de ñapa, por añadidura⟩ **2** DIMENSIONS, SIZE : medida *f*, tamaño *m* **3** RULER : regla *f* ⟨tape measure : cinta métrica⟩ **4** MEASUREMENT : medida *f* ⟨cubic measure : medida de capacidad⟩ **5** MEASURING : medición *f* **6 measures** *npl* : medidas *fpl* ⟨security measures : medidas de seguridad⟩

measureless ['mɛʒərləs, 'meɪ-] *adj* : inmensurable

measurement ['mɛʒərmənt, 'meɪ-] *n* **1** MEASURING : medición *f* **2** DIMENSION : medida *f*

measure up *vi* **to measure up to** : estar a la altura de

meat ['miːt] *n* **1** FOOD : comida *f* **2** : carne *f* ⟨meat and fish : carne y pescado⟩ **3** SUBSTANCE : sustancia *f*, esencia *f* ⟨the meat of the story : la sustancia del cuento⟩

meatball ['miːtˌbɔl] *n* : albóndiga *f*

meaty ['miːti] *adj* **meatier; -est** : con mucha carne, carnoso

mechanic [mɪˈkænɪk] *n* : mecánico *m*, -ca *f*

mechanical [mɪˈkænɪkəl] *adj* : mecánico — **mechanically** *adv*

mechanics [mɪˈkænɪks] *ns & pl* **1** : mecánica *f* ⟨fluid mechanics : la mecánica de fluidos⟩ **2** MECHANISMS : mecanismos *mpl*, aspectos *mpl* prácticos

mechanism ['mɛkə,nɪzəm] *n* : mecanismo *m*

mechanization [,mɛkənə'zeɪLən] *n* : mecanización *f*

mechanize ['mɛkə,naɪz] *vt* **-nized; -nizing** : mecanizar

medal ['mɛdəl] *n* : medalla *f*, condecoración *f*

medalist ['mɛdəlɪst] *or* **medallist** *n* : medallista *mf*

medallion [mə'dæljən] *n* : medallón *m*

meddle ['mɛdəl] *vi* **-dled; -dling** : meterse, entrometerse

meddler ['mɛdələr] *n* : entrometido *m*, -da *f*

meddlesome ['mɛdəlsəm] *adj* : entrometido

media ['mi:diə] *npl* : medios *mpl* de comunicación ⟨social media : redes/medios sociales⟩

median¹ ['mi:diən] *adj* : medio

median² *n* : valor *m* medio

mediate ['mi:di,eɪt] *vi* **-ated; -ating** : mediar

mediation [,mi:di'eɪLən] *n* : mediación *f*

mediator ['mi:di,eɪtər] *n* : mediador *m*, -dora *f*

medical ['mɛdɪkəl] *adj* : médico

medicate ['mɛdə,keɪt] *vt* **-cated; -cating** : medicar ⟨medicated powder : polvos medicinales⟩

medication [,mɛdə'keɪLən] *n* **1** TREATMENT : tratamiento *m*, medicación *f* **2** MEDICINE : medicamento *m* ⟨to be on medication : estar medicado⟩

medicinal [mə'dɪsənəl] *adj* : medicinal

medicine ['mɛdəsən] *n* **1** MEDICATION : medicina *f*, medicamento *m* **2** : medicina *f* ⟨he's studying medicine : estudia medicina⟩

medicine man *n* : hechicero *m*

medieval *or* **mediaeval** [mɪ'di:vəl, ,mi:-, ,m-, -di'i:vəl] *adj* : medieval

mediocre [,mi:di'o:kər] *adj* : mediocre

mediocrity [,mi:di'akrəti] *n*, *pl* **-ties** : mediocridad *f*

meditate ['mɛdə,teɪt] *vi* **-tated; -tating** : meditar

meditation [,mɛdə'teɪLən] *n* : meditación *f*

meditative ['mɛdə,teɪtɪv] *adj* : meditabundo

Mediterranean [,mɛdətə'reɪniən] *adj* : mediterráneo

medium¹ ['mi:diəm] *adj* : mediano ⟨of medium height : de estatura mediana, de estatura regular⟩ ⟨medium-sized : de tamaño mediano⟩

medium² *n*, *pl* **-diums** *or* **-dia** ['mi:-diə] **1** MEAN : punto *m* medio, término *m* medio ⟨happy medium : justo medio⟩ **2** MEANS : medio *m* **3** SUBSTANCE : medio *m*, sustancia *f* ⟨a viscous medium : un medio viscoso⟩ **4** : medio *m* de comunicación **5** : medio *m* (artístico) **6** *pl* **mediums** : médium *mf* (persona)

medley ['mɛdli] *n*, *pl* **-leys** : popurrí *m* (de canciones)

meek ['mi:k] *adj* **1** LONG-SUFFERING : paciente, sufrido **2** SUBMISSIVE : sumiso, dócil, manso

meekly ['mi:kli] *adv* : dócilmente

meekness ['mi:knəs] *n* : mansedumbre *f*, docilidad *f*

meet¹ ['mi:t] *v* **met** ['mɛt]; **meeting** *vt* **1** ENCOUNTER : encontrarse con ⟨he met me at the park : nos encontramos en el parque⟩ **2** JOIN : unirse con **3** CONFRONT : enfrentarse a **4** ENCOUNTER : encontrar **5** SATISFY : satisfacer, cumplir con ⟨to meet costs : cubrir los gastos⟩ **6** REACH : alcanzar (una meta, etc.) **7** MATCH : igualar **8** : conocer ⟨I met his sister : conocí a su hermana⟩ **9 to meet someone halfway** : llegar a un arreglo con alguien **10 to meet someone's eyes/gaze** : mirarlo a la cara a alguien — *vi* **1** : encontrarse ⟨I hope we meet again : espero que nos volvamos a encontrar⟩ **2** ASSEMBLE : reunirse, congregarse **3** COMPETE, BATTLE : enfrentarse **4** : conocerse **5** JOIN : unirse **6** : encontrarse (dícese de los ojos) **7** : cerrarse (dícese de una chaqueta, etc.), tocar (dícese de dos extremos) **8 to meet up** : encontrarse **9 to meet with** : reunirse con **10 to meet with** RECEIVE : ser recibido con

meet² *n* : encuentro *m*

meeting ['mi:tɪŋ] *n* **1** : reunión *f* ⟨to open the meeting : abrir la sesión⟩ **2** ENCOUNTER : encuentro *m* **3** : entrevista *f* (formal)

meetinghouse ['mi:tɪŋ,haʊs] *n* : iglesia *f* (de ciertas confesiones protestantes)

megabyte ['mɛgə,baɪt] *n* : megabyte *m*

megahertz ['mɛgə,hərts, -,hrts] *n* : megahercio *m*

megaphone ['mɛgə,fo:n] *n* : megáfono *m*

megaton ['mɛgə,tʌn] *n* : megatón *m*

megawatt ['mɛgə,wat] *n* : megavatio *m*

melancholy¹ ['mɛlən,kali] *adj* : melancólico, triste, sombrío

melancholy² *n*, *pl* **-cholies** : melancolía *f*

melanoma [,mɛlə'no:mə] *n*, *pl* **-mas** : melanoma *m*

meld ['mɛld] *vt* : fusionar, unir — *vi* : fusionarse, unirse

melee ['meɪ,leɪ, meɪ'leɪ] *n* BRAWL : reyerta *f*, riña *f*, pelea *f*

meliorate ['mi:ljə,reɪt, 'mi:liə-] → **ameliorate**

mellow¹ ['mɛlo:] *vt* : suavizar, endulzar — *vi* : suavizarse, endulzarse

mellow² *adj* **1** RIPE : maduro **2** MILD : apacible ⟨a mellow character : un carácter apacible⟩ ⟨mellow wines : vinos añejos⟩ **3** : suave, dulce ⟨mellow colors : colores suaves⟩ ⟨mellow tones : tonos dulces⟩

mellowness ['mɛlonəs] *n* : suavidad *f*, dulzura *f*

melodic [mə'ladɪk] *adj* : melódico — **melodically** [-dɪkli] *adv*

melodious [mə'lo:diəs] *adj* : melodioso — **melodiously** *adv*

melodiousness [mə'lo:diəsnəs] *n* : calidad *f* de melódico

melodrama [ˈmɛləˌdrɑmə, -ˌdræ-] *n* : melodrama *m*

melodramatic [ˌmɛlədrəˈmæṭɪk] *adj* : melodramático — **melodramatically** [-ṭɪkli] *adv*

melody [ˈmɛlədi] *n*, *pl* **-dies** : melodía *f*, tonada *f*

melon [ˈmɛlən] *n* : melón *m*

melt [ˈmɛlt] *vt* **1** : derretir, disolver **2** SOFTEN : ablandar ⟨it melted his heart : ablandó su corazón⟩ **3 to melt down** : fundir — *vi* **1** : derretirse, disolverse **2** SOFTEN : ablandarse **3** DISAPPEAR : desvanecerse, esfumarse ⟨the clouds melted away : las nubes se desvanecieron⟩

melting point *n* : punto *m* de fusión

member [ˈmɛmbər] *n* **1** LIMB : miembro *m* **2** : miembro *m* (de un grupo); socio *m*, -cia *f* (de un club) **3** PART : miembro *m*, parte *f*

membership [ˈmɛmbərˌʃɪp] *n* **1** : membresía *f* ⟨application for membership : solicitud de entrada⟩ **2** MEMBERS : membresía *f*, miembros *mpl*, socios *mpl*

membrane [ˈmɛmˌbreɪn] *n* : membrana *f* — **membranous** [ˈmɛmbrə-nəs] *adj*

memento [mɪˈmɛnˌtoː] *n*, *pl* **-tos** *or* **-toes** : recuerdo *m*

memo [ˈmɛmoː] *n*, *pl* **memos** : memorándum *m*

memoirs [ˈmɛmˌwɑrz] *npl* : memorias *fpl*, autobiografía *f*

memorabilia [ˌmɛmərəˈbiliə, -ˈbɪljə] *npl* **1** : objetos *mpl* de interés histórico **2** MEMENTOS : recuerdos *mpl*

memorable [ˈmɛmərəbəl] *adj* : memorable, notable — **memorably** [-bli] *adv*

memorandum [ˌmɛməˈrændəm] *n*, *pl* **-dums** *or* **-da** [-də] : memorándum *m*

memorial[1] [məˈmoriəl] *adj* : conmemorativo

memorial[2] *n* : monumento *m* conmemorativo

Memorial Day *n* : el último lunes de mayo (observado en Estados Unidos como día feriado para conmemorar a los caídos en guerra)

memorialize [məˈmoriəˌlaɪz] *vt* **-ized; -izing** COMMEMORATE : conmemorar

memorization [ˌmɛmərəˈzeɪʃən] *n* : memorización *f*

memorize [ˈmɛməˌraɪz] *vt* **-rized; -rizing** : memorizar, aprender de memoria

memory [ˈmɛmri, ˈmɛmə-] *n*, *pl* **-ries** **1** : memoria *f* ⟨he has a good memory : tiene buena memoria⟩ **2** RECOLLECTION : recuerdo *m* **3** COMMEMORATION : memoria *f*, conmemoración *f* **4** : memoria *f* (en informática)

men → **man**[2]

menace[1] [ˈmɛnəs] *vt* **-aced; -acing** **1** THREATEN : amenazar **2** ENDANGER : poner en peligro

menace[2] *n* : amenaza *f*

menacing [ˈmɛnəsɪŋ] *adj* : amenazador, amenazante

menagerie [məˈnædʒəri, -ˈnæʒəri] *n* : colección *f* de animales salvajes

mend[1] [ˈmɛnd] *vt* **1** CORRECT : enmendar, corregir ⟨to mend one's ways : en-

mendarse⟩ **2** REPAIR : remendar, arreglar, reparar — *vi* HEAL : curarse

mend[2] *n* : remiendo *m*

mendicant [ˈmɛndɪkənt] *n* BEGGAR : mendigo *m*, -ga *f*

menhaden [mɛnˈheɪdən, mən-] *ns & pl* : pez *m* de la misma familia que los arenques

menial[1] [ˈmiːniəl] *adj* : servil, bajo

menial[2] *n* : sirviente *m*, -ta *f*

meningitis [ˌmɛnənˈdʒaɪṭəs] *n*, *pl* **-gitides** [-ˈdʒɪṭəˌdiːz] : meningitis *f*

menopausal [ˌmɛnəˈpɔzəl] *adj* : menopáusico

menopause [ˈmɛnəˌpɔz] *n* : menopausia *f*

menorah [məˈnorə] *n* : candelabro *m* (usado en los oficios religiosos judíos)

men's room *n* : servicios *mpl* de caballeros

menstrual [ˈmɛnstruəl] *adj* : menstrual

menstruate [ˈmɛnstruˌeɪt] *vi* **-ated; -ating** : menstruar

menstruation [ˌmɛnstruˈeɪʃən] *n* : menstruación *f*

menswear [ˈmɛnzˌwær] *n* : ropa *f* de caballero

-ment [mənt] *suf* : -miento ⟨entertainment : entretenimiento⟩

mental [ˈmɛnṭəl] *adj* : mental ⟨mental hospital : hospital psiquiátrico⟩ ⟨mental block : bloqueo mental⟩ — **mentally** *adv*

mentality [mɛnˈtæləṭi] *n*, *pl* **-ties** : mentalidad *f*

mental retardation [ˌriːˌtɑrˈdeɪʃən] *n* *dated, now sometimes offensive* : retraso *m* mental *dated, now sometimes offensive*

menthol [ˈmɛnˌθɔl, -ˌθoːl] *n* : mentol *m* — **mentholated** [ˌmɛnθəˌleɪṭəd] *adj*

mention[1] [ˈmɛnṭʃən] *vt* : mencionar, mentar, referirse a ⟨don't mention it! : ¡de nada!, ¡no hay de qué!⟩

mention[2] *n* : mención *f*

mentor [ˈmɛnˌtɔr, ˈmɛntər] *n* : mentor *m*

menu [ˈmɛnˌjuː] *n* **1** : menú *m*, carta *f* (en un restaurante) **2** : menú *m* (en informática)

meow[1] [miˈaʊ] *vi* : maullar

meow[2] *n* : maullido *m*, miau *m*

mercantile [ˈmərkənˌtiːl, -ˌtaɪl] *adj* : mercantil

mercenary[1] [ˈmərsəneˌri] *adj* : mercenario

mercenary[2] *n*, *pl* **-naries** : mercenario *m*, -ria *f*

merchandise [ˈmərʧənˌdaɪz, -ˌdaɪs] *n* : mercancía *f*, mercadería *f*

merchandiser [ˈmərʧənˌdaɪzər] *n* : comerciante *mf*; vendedor *m*, -dora *f*

merchant [ˈmərʧənt] *n* : comerciante *mf*

merchant marine *n* : marina *f* mercante

merciful [ˈmərsɪfəl] *adj* : misericordioso, clemente

mercifully [ˈmərsɪfli] *adv* **1** : con misericordia, con compasión **2** FORTUNATELY : afortunadamente

merciless [ˈmərsɪləs] *adj* : despiadado — **mercilessly** *adv*

mercurial [ˌmərˈkjuriəl] *adj* TEMPERAMENTAL : temperamental, volátil

mercury [ˈmərkjəri] *n*, *pl* **-ries** : mercurio *m*

Mercury *n* : Mercurio *m*

mercy ['mərsi] *n, pl* **-cies 1** CLEMENCY : misericordia *f*, clemencia *f* **2** BLESSING : bendición *f*

mere ['mɪr] *adj, superlative* **merest** : mero, simple

merely ['mɪrli] *adv* : solamente, simplemente

merengue [mə'rɛŋˌgeɪ] *n* : merengue *m* (música o baile)

merge ['mərdʒ] *v* **merged; merging** *vi* : unirse, fusionarse (dícese de las compañías), confluir (dícese de los ríos, las calles, etc.) — *vt* : unir, fusionar, combinar

merger ['mərdʒər] *n* : unión *f*, fusión *f*

meridian [mə'rɪdiən] *n* : meridiano *m*

meringue [mə'ræŋ] *n* : merengue *m*

merit[1] ['mɛrət] *vt* : merecer, ser digno de

merit[2] *n* : mérito *m*, valor *m*

meritorious [ˌmɛrə'toriəs] *adj* : meritorio

mermaid ['mərˌmeɪd] *n* : sirena *f*

merriment ['mɛrɪmənt] *n* : alegría *f*, júbilo *m*, regocijo *m*

merry ['mɛri] *adj* **merrier; -est** : alegre — **merrily** ['mɛrəli] *adv*

merry–go–round ['mɛriɡoˌraʊnd] *n* : carrusel *m*, tiovivo *m*

merrymaker ['mɛriˌmeɪkər] *n* : juerguista *mf*

merrymaking ['mɛriˌmeɪkɪŋ] *n* : juerga *f*

mesa ['meɪsə] *n* : mesa *f*

mesdames → **madam, Mrs.**

mesh[1] ['mɛʃ] *vi* **1** ENGAGE : engranar (dícese de las piezas mecánicas) **2** TANGLE : enredarse **3** COORDINATE : coordinarse, combinar

mesh[2] *n* **1** : malla *f* ⟨wire mesh : malla metálica⟩ **2** NETWORK : red *f* **3** MESHING : engranaje *m* ⟨in mesh : engranado⟩

mesmerize ['mɛzməˌraɪz] *vt* **-ized; -izing 1** HYPNOTIZE : hipnotizar **2** FASCINATE : cautivar, embelesar, fascinar

mess[1] ['mɛs] *vt* **1 to mess up** DISARRANGE : desordenar, desarreglar **2 to mess up** BUNGLE : echar a perder — *vi* **1 to mess around** HANG OUT : pasar el rato, entretenerse **2 to mess around** : tener líos (amorosos) **3 to mess (around) with** : tocar, jugar con ⟨don't mess with my things! : ¡no toques mis cosas!⟩ **4 to mess with** PROVOKE : meterse con

mess[2] *n* **1** : rancho *m* (para soldados, etc.) **2** DISORDER : desorden *m* ⟨your room is a mess : tienes el cuarto hecho un desastre⟩ **3** CONFUSION, TURMOIL : confusión *f*, embrollo *m*, lío *m fam*

message[1] ['mɛsɪdʒ] *v* **-saged; -saging** : mensajear

message[2] *n* : mensaje *m*, recado *m*

messaging ['mɛsɪdʒɪŋ] *n* : mensajería *f*

messenger ['mɛsəndʒər] *n* : mensajero *m*, -ra *f*

Messiah [mə'saɪə] *n* : Mesías *m*

Messrs. → **Mr.**

messy ['mɛsi] *adj* **messier; -est** UNTIDY : desordenado, sucio — **messily** *adv*

mestizo [mɛ'stiːzo] *n* : mestizo *m*, -za *f*; ladino *m*, -na *f* CA, Mex — **mestizo** *adj*

met → **meet**

metabolic [ˌmɛtə'balɪk] *adj* : metabólico

metabolism [mə'tæbəˌlɪzəm] *n* : metabolismo *m*

metabolize [mə'tæbəˌlaɪz] *vt* **-lized; -lizing** : metabolizar

metal ['mɛtəl] *n* : metal *m*

metallic [mə'tælɪk] *adj* : metálico

metallurgical [ˌmɛtəl'ərdʒɪkəl] *adj* : metalúrgico

metallurgy ['mɛtəlˌərdʒi] *n* : metalurgia *f*

metalwork ['mɛtəlˌwərk] *n* : objeto *m* de metal

metalworker ['mɛtəlˌwərkər] *n* : metalúrgico *m*, -ca *f*

metalworking ['mɛtəlˌwərkɪŋ] *n* : metalistería *f*

metamorphosis [ˌmɛtə'mɔrfəsɪs] *n, pl* **-phoses** [-ˌsiːz] : metamorfosis *f*

metaphor ['mɛtəˌfor, -fər] *n* : metáfora *f*

metaphoric [ˌmɛtə'fɔrɪk] *or* **metaphorical** [-ɪkəl] *adj* : metafórico

metaphysical [ˌmɛtə'fɪzəkəl] *adj* : metafísico

metaphysics [ˌmɛtə'fɪzɪks] *n* : metafísica *f*

mete ['miːt] *vt* **meted; meting** ALLOT : repartir, distribuir ⟨to mete out punishment : imponer castigos⟩

meteor ['miːtiər, -tiˌɔr] *n* : meteoro *m*

meteoric [ˌmiːti'ɔrɪk] *adj* : meteórico

meteorite ['miːtiəˌraɪt] *n* : meteorito *m*

meteorologic [ˌmiːtiˌɔrə'ladʒɪk] *or* **meteorological** [-'ladʒɪkəl] *adj* : meteorológico

meteorologist [ˌmiːtiə'ralədʒɪst] *n* : meteorólogo *m*, -ga *f*

meteorology [ˌmiːtiə'ralədʒi] *n* : meteorología *f*

meter ['miːtər] *n* **1** : metro *m* ⟨it measures 2 meters : mide 2 metros⟩ **2** : contador *m*, medidor *m* (de electricidad, etc.) ⟨parking meter : parquímetro⟩ **3** : metro *m* (en literatura o música)

methane ['mɛˌθeɪn] *n* : metano *m*

method ['mɛθəd] *n* : método *m*

methodical [mə'θadɪkəl] *adj* : metódico — **methodically** *adv*

Methodist ['mɛθədɪst] *n* : metodista *mf* — **Methodist** *adj*

methodology [ˌmɛθə'dalədʒi] *n, pl* **-gies** : metodología *f*

meticulous [mə'tɪkjələs] *adj* : meticuloso — **meticulously** *adv*

meticulousness [mə'tɪkjələsnəs] *n* : meticulosidad *f*

metric ['mɛtrɪk] *or* **metrical** [-trɪkəl] *adj* : métrico

metric system *n* : sistema *m* métrico

metro ['mɛtro] *n* SUBWAY : metro *m*; subterráneo *m Arg, Uru*

metronome ['mɛtrəˌnoːm] *n* : metrónomo *m*

metropolis [mə'trapələs] *n* : metrópoli *f*, metrópolis *f*

metropolitan [ˌmɛtrə'palətən] *adj* : metropolitano

mettle ['mɛtəl] *n* : temple *m*, valor *m* ⟨on one's mettle : dispuesto a mostrar su valía⟩

Mexican ['mɛksɪkən] *n* : mexicano *m*, -na *f* — **Mexican** *adj*

mezzanine ['mɛzə,ni:n, ,mɛzə'ni:n] *n* **1** : entrepiso *m* **2** : primer piso *m* (de un teatro)

mi ['mi:] *n* : mi *m* (en el canto)

miasma [maɪ'æzmə] *n* : miasma *m*

mica ['maɪkə] *n* : mica *f*

mice → **mouse**

micro ['maɪkro] *adj* : muy pequeño, microscópico

micro- *pref* : micro-

microbe ['maɪ,kro:b] *n* : microbio *m*

microbiology [,maɪkrobaɪ'ɑlədʒi] *n* : microbiología *f*

microchip ['maɪkro,tʃɪp] *n* : microchip *m*

microcomputer ['maɪkrokəm,pju:tər] *n* : microcomputadora *f*

microcosm ['maɪkro,kɑzəm] *n* : microcosmos *m*

microfilm ['maɪkro,fɪlm] *n* : microfilm *m*

micrometer ['maɪkro,mi:tər] *n* : micrómetro *m*

microorganism [,maɪkro'ɔrgə,nɪzəm] *n* : microorganismo *m*, microbio *m*

microphone ['maɪkrə,fo:n] *n* : micrófono *m*

microprocessor [,maɪkro'prɑ'sɛsər] *n* : microprocesador *m*

microscope ['maɪkrə,sko:p] *n* : microscopio *m*

microscopic [,maɪkrə'skɑpɪk] *adj* : microscópico

microwave ['maɪkrə,weɪv] *n* **1** : microonda *f* **2** *or* **microwave oven** : microondas *m*

mid ['mɪd] *adj* : medio ⟨mid morning : a media mañana⟩ ⟨in mid-August : a mediados de agosto⟩ ⟨in mid ocean : en alta mar⟩

midair ['mɪd'ær] *n* in ~ : en el aire ⟨to catch in midair : agarrar al vuelo⟩

midday ['mɪd'deɪ] *n* NOON : mediodía *m*

middle[1] ['mɪdəl] *adj* **1** CENTRAL : medio, del medio, de en medio **2** INTERMEDIATE : intermedio, mediano ⟨middle age : la mediana edad⟩

middle[2] *n* **1** CENTER : medio *m*, centro *m* ⟨fold it down the middle : dóblalo por la mitad⟩ **2** in the middle of : en medio de (un espacio), a mitad de (una actividad) ⟨in the middle of the month : a mediados del mes⟩

Middle Ages *npl* : Edad *f* Media

middle–class *adj* : de clase media

middle class *n* : clase *f* media

middleman ['mɪdəl,mæn] *n, pl* **-men** [-mən, -,mɛn] : intermediario *m*, -ria *f*

middle school *n* : colegio *m* para niños de 10 a 14 años

middling ['mɪdlɪŋ, -lən] *adj* **1** MEDIUM, MIDDLE : mediano **2** MEDIOCRE : mediocre, regular

midfielder ['mɪd,fi:ldər] *n* : mediocampista *mf*

midge ['mɪdʒ] *n* : mosca *f* pequeña

midget ['mɪdʒət] *n* **1** *sometimes offensive* : enano *m*, -na *f* (persona) *sometimes offensive* **2** : cosa *f* diminuta

midland ['mɪdlənd, -,lænd] *n* : región *f* central (de un país)

midnight ['mɪd,naɪt] *n* : medianoche *f*

midpoint ['mɪd,pɔɪnt] *n* : punto *m* medio, término *m* medio

midriff ['mɪd,rɪf] *n* : diafragma *m*

midshipman ['mɪd,ʃɪpmən, ,mɪd'ʃɪp-] *n, pl* **-men** [-mən, -,mɛn] : guardiamarina *m*

midst[1] ['mɪdst] *n* : medio *m* ⟨in our midst : entre nosotros⟩ ⟨in the midst of : en medio de⟩

midst[2] *prep* : entre

midstream ['mɪd'stri:m, -,stri:m] *n* : medio *m* de la corriente ⟨in the midstream of his career : en medio de su carrera⟩

midsummer ['mɪd'sʌmər, -,sʌ-] *n* : pleno verano *m*

midtown ['mɪd,taʊn] *n* : centro *m* (de una ciudad)

midway ['mɪd,weɪ] *adv* HALFWAY : a mitad de camino

midweek ['mɪd,wi:k] *n* : medio *m* de la semana ⟨in midweek : a media semana⟩

midwife ['mɪd,waɪf] *n, pl* **-wives** [-,waɪvz] : partera *f*, comadrona *f*

midwinter ['mɪd'wɪntər, -,wɪn-] *n* : pleno invierno *m*

midyear ['mɪd,jɪr] *n* : medio *m* del año ⟨at midyear : a mediados del año⟩

mien ['mi:n] *n* : aspecto *m*, porte *m*, semblante *m*

miff ['mɪf] *vt* : ofender

might[1] ['maɪt] (*used to express permission or possibility or as a polite alternative to* **may**) → **may** ⟨it might be true : podría ser verdad⟩ ⟨might I speak with Sarah? : ¿se puede hablar con Sarah?⟩

might[2] *n* : fuerza *f*, poder *m*

mightily ['maɪtəli] *adv* : con mucha fuerza, poderosamente

mighty[1] ['maɪti] *adv* VERY : muy ⟨mighty good : muy bueno, buenísimo⟩

mighty[2] *adj* **mightier; -est** **1** POWERFUL : poderoso, potente **2** GREAT : grande, imponente

migraine ['maɪ,greɪn] *n* : jaqueca *f*, migraña *f*

migrant ['maɪgrənt] *n* : trabajador *m*, -dora *f* ambulante

migrate ['maɪ,greɪt] *vi* **-grated; -grating** : emigrar, migrar

migration [maɪ'greɪlən] *n* : migración *f*

migratory ['maɪgrə,tori] *adj* : migratorio

mike ['maɪk] *n fam* → **microphone**

mild ['maɪld] *adj* **1** GENTLE : apacible, suave ⟨a mild disposition : un temperamento suave⟩ **2** LIGHT : leve, ligero ⟨a mild punishment : un castigo leve, un castigo poco severo⟩ **3** TEMPERATE : templado (dícese del clima) — **mildly** *adv*

mildew[1] ['mɪl,du:, -,dju:] *vi* : enmohecerse

mildew[2] *n* : moho *m*

mildness ['maɪldnəs] *n* : suavidad *f*

mile ['maɪl] *n* : milla *f*

mileage ['maɪlɪdʒ] *n* **1** ALLOWANCE : viáticos *mpl* (pagados por milla recorrida) **2** : distancia *f* recorrida (en millas), kilometraje *m*

milestone ['maɪl,sto:n] *n* LANDMARK : hito *m*, jalón *m* ⟨a milestone in his life : un hito en su vida⟩

milieu [mi:'lju:, -'ljø] *n, pl* **-lieus** *or* **-lieux**

[-'juːz, -'jø] SURROUNDINGS : entorno *m*, medio *m*, ambiente *m*

militancy ['mɪlətəntsi] *n, pl* **-cies** : militancia *f*

militant¹ ['mɪlətənt] *adj* : militante, combativo

militant² *n* : militante *mf*

militarism ['mɪlətə,rɪzəm] *n* : militarismo *m*

militaristic [,mɪlətə'rɪstɪk] *adj* : militarista

militarize ['mɪlətə,raɪz] *vt* **-rized; -rizing** : militarizar

military¹ ['mɪlə,teri] *adj* : militar

military² *n* **the military** : las fuerzas armadas

militia [mə'lɪlə] *n* : milicia *f*

milk¹ ['mɪlk] *vt* **1** : ordeñar (una vaca, etc.) **2** EXPLOIT : explotar

milk² *n* **1** : leche *f* **2** : leche *f* (de una planta)

milk chocolate *n* : chocolate *m* con leche

milkman ['mɪlk,mæn, -mən] *n, pl* **-men** [-mən, -,mɛn] : lechero *m*

milk of magnesia *n* : leche *f* de magnesia

milk shake *n* : batido *m*, licuado *m*

milkweed ['mɪlk,wiːd] *n* : algodoncillo *m*

milky ['mɪlki] *adj* **milkier; -est** : lechoso

Milky Way *n* : Vía *f* Láctea

mill¹ ['mɪl] *vt* : moler (granos), acordonar (monedas) — *vi* **to mill about/around** : arremolinarse

mill² *n* **1** : molino *m* (para moler granos) **2** FACTORY : fábrica *f* ⟨textile mill : fábrica textil⟩ **3** GRINDER : molinillo *m*

millennial¹ [mə'lɛniəl] *adj* : milenario

millennial² *n* : milenario *m*, -ria *f*; milenial *mf* (persona nacida entre 1980 y 2000)

millennium [mə'lɛniəm] *n, pl* **-nia** [-niə] *or* **-niums** : milenio *m*

miller ['mɪlər] *n* : molinero *m*, -ra *f*

millet ['mɪlət] *n* : mijo *m*

milligram ['mɪlə,ɡræm] *n* : miligramo *m*

milliliter ['mɪlə,liːţər] *n* : mililitro *m*

millimeter ['mɪlə,miːţər] *n* : milímetro *m*

milliner ['mɪlənər] *n* : sombrerero *m*, -ra *f* (de señoras)

millinery ['mɪlə,neri] *n* : sombreros *mpl* de señora

million¹ ['mɪljən] *adj* **a million** : un millón de

million² *n, pl* **millions** *or* **million** : millón *m*

millionaire [,mɪljə'nær, 'mɪljə,nær] *n* : millonario *m*, -ria *f*

millionth¹ ['mɪljənθ] *adj* : millonésimo

millionth² *n* : millonésimo *m*

millipede ['mɪlə,piːd] *n* : milpiés *m*

millstone ['mɪl,stoːn] *n* : rueda *f* de molino, muela *f*

mime¹ ['maɪm] *v* **mimed; miming** *vt* MIMIC : imitar, remedar — *vi* PANTOMIME : hacer la mímica

mime² *n* **1** : mimo *mf* **2** PANTOMIME : pantomima *f*

mimeograph ['mɪmiə,ɡræf] *n* : mimeógrafo *m*

mimic¹ ['mɪmɪk] *vt* **-icked; -icking** : imitar, remedar

mimic² *n* : imitador *m*, -dora *f*

mimicry ['mɪmɪkri] *n, pl* **-ries** : mímica *f*, imitación *f*

minaret [,mɪnə'rɛt] *n* : alminar *m*, minarete *m*

mince ['mɪnts] *v* **minced; mincing** *vt* **1** CHOP : picar, moler (carne) **2** **not to mince one's words** : no tener uno pelos en la lengua — *vi* : caminar de manera afectada

mincemeat ['mɪnts,miːt] *n* : mezcla *f* de fruta picada, sebo, y especias

mind¹ ['maɪnd] *vt* **1** TEND : cuidar, atender ⟨mind the children : cuida a los niños⟩ **2** OBEY : obedecer **3** : preocuparse por, sentirse molestado por ⟨I don't mind his jokes : sus bromas no me molestan⟩ ⟨if you don't mind my saying so : si me permites⟩ ⟨never mind him : no le hagas caso⟩ **4** : tener cuidado con ⟨mind the ladder! : ¡cuidado con la escalera!⟩ **5 never mind** LET ALONE : ni mucho menos, (y) menos aún ⟨I can barely understand it, never mind explain it : apenas puedo entenderlo, ni mucho menos explicarlo⟩ — *vi* **1** OBEY : obedecer **2** CARE : importarle a uno ⟨I don't mind : no me importa, me es igual⟩ — **3 never mind** : no importa, no se preocupe

mind² *n* **1** : mente *f* ⟨the mind and the body : la mente y el cuerpo⟩ ⟨it's all in your mind : es pura imaginación tuya⟩ ⟨what's on your mind? : ¿qué te preocupa?⟩ **2** INTENTION : intención *f*, propósito *m* **3** : razón *f* ⟨he's out of his mind : está loco⟩ **4** OPINION : opinión *f* ⟨in/to my mind : a mi parecer⟩ **5** INTELLECT : mente *f* ⟨she has a brilliant mind : tiene una mente brillante⟩ **6** ATTENTION : atención *f* ⟨pay him no mind : no le hagas caso⟩ **7 at/in the back of one's mind** : en el fondo **8 great minds think alike** : los genios pensamos igual **9 state of mind** : estado *m* de ánimo **10 to be of one mind** *or* **to be of the same mind** : estar de acuerdo **11 to be of two minds about** : estar indeciso sobre **12 to blow someone's mind** *fam* : maravillar a alguien **13 to call/bring to mind** : recordar, traer a la memoria **14 to change one's mind** : cambiar de opinión **15 to change someone's mind** : hacerle a alguien cambiar de opinión **16 to come/leap/spring to mind** : ocurrírsele a alguien **17 to cross someone's mind** : pasársele a alguien por la cabeza **18 to give someone a piece of one's mind** : cantarle las cuarentas a alguien **19 to have a good mind to** *or* **to have half a mind to** : tener ganas de (regañar a alguien, etc.) **20 to have a mind of one's own** : ser independiente **21 to have in mind** : tener (algo, a alguien) en mente, tener pensado (hacer algo) ⟨what did you have in mind? : ¿qué tenías en mente?⟩ **22 to have one's mind set on** : estar empeñado en **23 to keep an open mind** : mantener la mente abierta **24 to keep/bear in mind** : tener en cuenta **25 to keep**

one's mind on : concentrarse en **26 to lose one's mind** : perder la razón **27 to make up one's mind** : decidirse **28 to put/set one's mind to** : poner empeño en **29 to put someone in mind of something** : recordarle algo a alguien **30 to speak one's mind** : hablar sin rodeos **31 to take a load/weight off one's mind** : quitarse un peso de encima

minded [ˈmaɪndəd] *adj* **1** (*used in combination*) ⟨narrow-minded : de mentalidad cerrada⟩ ⟨health-minded : preocupado por la salud⟩ **2** INCLINED : inclinado

mindful [ˈmaɪndfəl] *adj* AWARE : consciente — **mindfully** *adv*

mindless [ˈmaɪndləs] *adj* **1** SENSELESS : estúpido, sin sentido ⟨mindless violence : violencia sin sentido⟩ **2** HEEDLESS : inconsciente

mindlessly [ˈmaɪndləsli] *adv* **1** SENSELESSLY : sin sentido **2** HEEDLESSLY : inconscientemente

mine[1] [ˈmaɪn] *vt* **mined; mining 1** : extraer (oro, etc.) **2** : minar (con artefactos explosivos)

mine[2] *n* : mina *f* ⟨gold mine : mina de oro⟩

mine[3] *pron* : mío ⟨that one's mine : ése es el mío, ésa es la mía⟩ ⟨some friends of mine : unos amigos míos⟩

minefield [ˈmaɪnˌfiːld] *n* : campo *m* de minas

miner [ˈmaɪnər] *n* : minero *m*, -ra *f*

mineral [ˈmɪnərəl] *n* : mineral *m* — **mineral** *adj*

mineralogy [ˌmɪnəˈrɑlədʒi, -ˈræ-] *n* : mineralogía *f*

mine shaft → **shaft**

mingle [ˈmɪŋgəl] *v* **-gled; -gling** *vt* MIX : mezclar — *vi* **1** MIX : mezclarse **2** CIRCULATE : circular

mini- *pref* : mini-

miniature[1] [ˈmɪniəˌtʊr, ˈmɪniˌtʊr, -tɪər] *adj* : en miniatura, diminuto

miniature[2] *n* : miniatura *f*

minibus [ˈmɪniˌbʌs] *n* : microbús *m*; pesera *f Mex*; buseta *f Col, CoRi, Ecua, Ven*

minicomputer [ˈmɪnɪkəmˌpjuːtər] *n* : minicomputadora *f*

minimal [ˈmɪnəməl] *adj* : mínimo

minimally [ˈmɪnəməli] *adv* : en grado mínimo

minimize [ˈmɪnəˌmaɪz] *vt* **-mized; -mizing 1** : minimizar (un riesgo, etc.) **2** : minimizar (en informática)

minimum[1] [ˈmɪnəməm] *adj* : mínimo

minimum[2] *n, pl* **-ma** [ˈmɪnəmə] *or* **-mums** : mínimo *m*

mining [ˈmaɪnɪŋ] *n* : minería *f*

miniseries [ˈmɪniˌsɪriːz] *n* : miniserie *f*

miniskirt [ˈmɪniˌskərt] *n* : minifalda *f*

minister[1] [ˈmɪnəstər] *vi* **to minister to** : cuidar (de), atender a

minister[2] *n* **1** : pastor *m*, -tora *f* (de una iglesia) **2** : ministro *m*, -tra *f* (en política)

ministerial [ˌmɪnəˈstɪriəl] *adj* : ministerial

ministry [ˈmɪnəstri] *n, pl* **-tries 1** : ministerio *m* (en política) **2** : sacerdocio *m*

(en el catolicismo), clerecía *f* (en el protestantismo)

minivan [ˈmɪniˌvæn] *n* : minivan *f*

mink [ˈmɪŋk] *n, pl* **mink** *or* **minks** : visón *m*

minnow [ˈmɪnoʊ] *n, pl* **-nows** : pececillo *m* de agua dulce

minor[1] [ˈmaɪnər] *adj* : menor

minor[2] *n* **1** : menor *mf* (de edad) **2** : asignatura *f* secundaria (de estudios)

minority [məˈnɔrəti, maɪ-] *n, pl* **-ties** : minoría *f*

minstrel [ˈmɪnstrəl] *n* : juglar *m*, trovador *m* (en el medioevo)

mint[1] [ˈmɪnt] *vt* : acuñar

mint[2] *adj* : sin usar ⟨in mint condition : como nuevo⟩

mint[3] *n* **1** : menta *f* ⟨mint tea : té de menta⟩ **2** : pastilla *f* de menta **3** : casa *f* de la moneda ⟨the U.S. Mint : la casa de la moneda de los EEUU⟩ **4** FORTUNE : dineral *m*, fortuna *f*

minuet [ˌmɪnjuˈet] *n* : minué *m*

minus[1] [ˈmaɪnəs] *n* **1** : cantidad *f* negativa **2 minus sign** : signo *m* de menos

minus[2] *prep* **1** : menos ⟨four minus two : cuatro menos dos⟩ **2** WITHOUT : sin ⟨minus his hat : sin su sombrero⟩

minuscule *or* **miniscule** [ˈmɪnəsˌkjuːl, mɪˈnʌs-] *adj* : minúsculo

minute[1] [maɪˈnuːt, mɪ-, -ˈnjuːt] *adj* **minuter; -est 1** TINY : diminuto, minúsculo **2** DETAILED : minucioso

minute[2] [ˈmɪnət] *n* **1** : minuto *m* **2** MOMENT : momento *m* ⟨at any minute : en cualquier momento⟩ **3 minutes** *npl* : actas *fpl* (de una reunión) **4 at the last minute** : a último momento, a última hora **5 hang/hold on a minute** *or* **wait a minute** : espera un momento **6 just a minute** : un momento **7 this minute** : ahora mismo, inmediatamente

minute hand *n* : minutero *m*

minutely [maɪˈnuːtli, mɪ-, -ˈnjuːt-] *adv* : minuciosamente

miracle [ˈmɪrɪkəl] *n* : milagro *m*

miraculous [məˈrækjələs] *adj* : milagroso — **miraculously** *adv*

mirage [mɪˈrɑʒ, *chiefly Brit* ˈmɪrˌɑʒ] *n* : espejismo *m*

mire[1] [ˈmaɪr] *vi* **mired; miring** : atascarse

mire[2] *n* **1** MUD : barro *m*, lodo *m* **2** : atolladero *m* ⟨stuck in a mire of debt : agobiado por la deuda⟩

mirror[1] [ˈmɪrər] *vt* : reflejar

mirror[2] *n* : espejo *m*

mirth [ˈmərθ] *n* : alegría *f*, regocijo *m*

mirthful [ˈmərθfəl] *adj* : alegre, regocijado

misadventure [ˌmɪsədˈventʃər] *n* : malaventura *f*, desventura *f*

misanthrope [ˈmɪsənˌθroːp] *n* : misántropo *m*, -pa *f*

misanthropic [ˌmɪsənˈθrɑpɪk] *adj* : misantrópico

misanthropy [mɪˈsænθrəpi] *n* : misantropía *f*

misapprehend [ˌmɪsˌæprəˈhend] *vt* : entender mal

misapprehension [ˌmɪsˌæprəˈhentʃən] *n* : malentendido *m*

misappropriate [ˌmɪsəˈproːpriˌeɪt] vt -ated; -ating : malversar
misappropriation [ˌmɪsəˌproːpriˈeɪlən] n : malversación f
misbegotten [ˌmɪsbɪˈɡɑtən] adj 1 ILLE-GITIMATE : ilegítimo 2 : mal concebido ⟨misbegotten laws : leyes mal concebidas⟩
misbehave [ˌmɪsbɪˈheɪv] vi -haved; -having : portarse mal
misbehavior [ˌmɪsbɪˈheɪvjər] n : mala conducta f
miscalculate [mɪsˈkælkjəˌleɪt] v -lated; -lating : calcular mal
miscalculation [mɪsˌkælkjəˈleɪlən] n : error m de cálculo, mal cálculo m
miscarriage [ˌmɪsˈkærɪʤ, ˈmɪsˌkærɪʤ] n 1 : aborto m 2 FAILURE : fracaso m, malogro m ⟨a miscarriage of justice : una injusticia, un error judicial⟩
miscarry [ˌmɪsˈkæri, ˈmɪsˌkæri] vi -ried; -rying 1 ABORT : abortar 2 FAIL : malograrse, fracasar
miscellaneous [ˌmɪsəˈleɪniəs] adj : misceláneo
miscellany [ˈmɪsəˌleɪni] n, pl -nies : miscelánea f
mischance [mɪsˈtʃænts] n : desgracia f, infortunio m, mala suerte f
mischief [ˈmɪstʃəf] n : diabluras fpl, travesuras fpl
mischievous [ˈmɪstʃəvəs] adj : travieso, pícaro
mischievously [ˈmɪstʃəvəsli] adv : de manera traviesa
misconception [ˌmɪskənˈsɛplən] n : concepto m erróneo, idea f falsa
misconduct [mɪsˈkɑndəkt] n : mala conducta f
misconstrue [ˌmɪskənˈstruː] vt -strued; -struing : malinterpretar
misdeed [mɪsˈdiːd] n : fechoría f
misdemeanor [ˌmɪsdɪˈmiːnər] n : delito m menor
miser [ˈmaɪzər] n : avaro m, -ra f; tacaño m, -ña f
miserable [ˈmɪzərəbəl] adj 1 UNHAPPY : triste, desdichado 2 WRETCHED : miserable, desgraciado ⟨a miserable hut : una choza miserable⟩ 3 UNPLEASANT : desagradable, malo ⟨miserable weather : tiempo malísimo⟩ 4 CONTEMPTIBLE : despreciable, mísero ⟨for a miserable $10 : por unos míseros diez dólares⟩
miserably [ˈmɪzərəbli] adv 1 SADLY : tristemente 2 WRETCHEDLY : miserablemente, lamentablemente 3 UNFORTUNATELY : desgraciadamente
miserly [ˈmaɪzərli] adj : avaro, tacaño
misery [ˈmɪzəri] n, pl -eries : miseria f, sufrimiento m
misfire [mɪsˈfaɪr] vi -fired; -firing : fallar
misfit [ˈmɪsˌfɪt] n : inadaptado m, -da f
misfortune [mɪsˈfɔrtlən] n : desgracia f, desventura f, infortunio m
misgiving [mɪsˈɡɪvɪŋ] n : duda f, recelo m
misguided [mɪsˈɡaɪdəd] adj : desacertado, equivocado, mal informado
mishap [ˈmɪsˌhæp] n : contratiempo m, percance m, accidente m

misinform [ˌmɪsɪnˈfɔrm] vt : informar mal
misinterpret [ˌmɪsɪnˈtərprət] vt : malinterpretar
misinterpretation [ˌmɪsɪnˌtərprəˈteɪlən] n : mala interpretación f, malentendido m
misjudge [mɪsˈʤʌʤ] vt -judged; -judging : juzgar mal
mislay [mɪsˈleɪ] vt -laid [-ˈleɪd]; -laying : extraviar, perder
mislead [mɪsˈliːd] vt -led [-ˈlɛd]; -leading : engañar
misleading [mɪsˈliːdɪŋ] adj : engañoso
mismanage [mɪsˈmænɪʤ] vt -aged; -aging : administrar mal
mismanagement [mɪsˈmænɪʤmənt] n : mala administración f
misnomer [mɪsˈnoːmər] n : nombre m inapropiado
misogynist [mɪˈsɑʤənɪst] n : misógino m
misogyny [məˈsɑʤəni] n : misoginia f
misplace [mɪsˈpleɪs] vt -placed; -placing : extraviar, perder
misprint [ˈmɪsˌprɪnt, mɪsˈ-] n : errata f, error m de imprenta
mispronounce [ˌmɪsprəˈnaʊnts] vt -nounced; -nouncing : pronunciar mal
mispronunciation [ˌmɪsprəˌnʌntsiˈeɪlən] n : pronunciación f incorrecta
misquote [mɪsˈkwoːt] vt -quoted; -quoting : citar incorrectamente
misread [mɪsˈriːd] vt -read [-ˈrɛd]; -reading 1 : leer mal ⟨she misread the sentence : leyó mal la frase⟩ 2 MISUNDERSTAND : malinterpretar ⟨they misread his intention : malinterpretaron su intención⟩
misrepresent [ˌmɪsˌrprɪˈzɛnt] vt : distorsionar, falsear, tergiversar
miss[1] [ˈmɪs] vt 1 : errar, faltar ⟨to miss the target : no dar en el blanco⟩ 2 : no encontrar, perder ⟨they missed each other : no se encontraron⟩ ⟨I missed the plane : perdí el avión⟩ 3 : echar de menos, extrañar ⟨we miss him a lot : lo echamos mucho de menos⟩ 4 OVERLOOK : pasar por alto ⟨to miss the point : no entender algo⟩ ⟨you can't miss it : no puedes dejar de verlo⟩ 5 : no enterarse de (una noticia), no oír (palabras habladas) 6 : perderse (una oportunidad, etc.) 7 PASS UP : pasar por alto 8 : faltar a (una reunión, etc.) 9 AVOID : evitar ⟨they just missed hitting the tree : por muy poco chocan contra el árbol⟩ 10 OMIT : saltarse ⟨he missed breakfast : se saltó el desayuno⟩ 11 to be missing : faltarle (algo a uno) ⟨he's missing two teeth : le faltan dos dientes⟩ 12 to miss out on : perderse (una oportunidad, etc.)
miss[2] n 1 : fallo m (de un tiro, etc.) 2 FAILURE : fracaso m 3 : señorita f ⟨Miss Jones called us : nos llamó la señorita Jones⟩ ⟨excuse me, miss : perdone, señorita⟩
misshapen [mɪsˈleɪpən] adj : deforme
missile [ˈmɪsəl] n 1 : misil m ⟨guided missile : misil guiado⟩ 2 PROJECTILE : proyectil m
missing [ˈmɪsɪŋ] adj 1 ABSENT : ausente ⟨who's missing? : ¿quién falta?⟩ 2 LOST

: perdido, desaparecido ⟨missing persons : los desaparecidos⟩

mission ['mɪʃən] *n* **1** : misión *f* (mandada por una iglesia) **2** DELEGATION : misión *f*, delegación *f*, embajada *f* **3** TASK : misión *f*

missionary¹ ['mɪʃəˌnɛri] *adj* : misionero

missionary² *n, pl* **-aries** : misionero *m*, -ra *f*

missive ['mɪsɪv] *n* : misiva *f*

misspell [mɪs'spɛl] *vt* : escribir mal

misspelling [mɪs'spɛlɪŋ] *n* : falta *f* de ortografía

misstep ['mɪsˌstɛp] *n* : traspié *m*, tropezón *m*

mist ['mɪst] *n* **1** HAZE : neblina *f*, niebla *f* **2** SPRAY : rocío *m*

mistake¹ [mɪ'steɪk] *vt* **-took** [-'stʊk]; **-taken** [-'steɪkən]; **-taking 1** MISINTERPRET : malinterpretar **2** CONFUSE : confundir ⟨he mistook her for Clara : la confundió con Clara⟩

mistake² *n* **1** MISUNDERSTANDING : malentendido *m*, confusión *f* **2** ERROR : error *m* ⟨I made a mistake : me equivoqué, cometí un error⟩

mistaken [mɪ'steɪkən] *adj* WRONG : equivocado — **mistakenly** *adv*

mister ['mɪstər] *n* : señor *m* ⟨watch out, mister : cuidado, señor⟩

mistiness ['mɪstinəs] *n* : nebulosidad *f*

mistletoe ['mɪsəlˌtoː] *n* : muérdago *m*

mistreat [mɪs'triːt] *vt* : maltratar

mistreatment [mɪs'triːtmənt] *n* : maltrato *m*, abuso *m*

mistress ['mɪstrəs] *n* **1** : dueña *f*, señora *f* (de una casa) **2** LOVER : amante *f*

mistrust¹ [mɪs'trʌst] *vt* : desconfiar de

mistrust² *n* : desconfianza *f*

mistrustful [mɪs'trʌstfəl] *adj* : desconfiado

misty ['mɪsti] *adj* **mistier; -est 1** : neblinoso, nebuloso **2** TEARFUL : lloroso

misunderstand [ˌmɪsˌʌndər'stænd] *vt* **-stood** [-'stʊd]; **-standing 1** : entender mal **2** MISINTERPRET : malinterpretar ⟨don't misunderstand me : no me malinterpretes⟩

misunderstanding [ˌmɪsˌʌndər'stændɪŋ] *n* **1** MISINTERPRATION : malentendido *m* **2** DISAGREEMENT, QUARREL : disputa *f*, discusión *f*

misuse¹ [mɪs'juːz] *vt* **-used; -using 1** : emplear mal **2** ABUSE, MISTREAT : abusar de, maltratar

misuse² [mɪs'juːs] *n* **1** : mal empleo *m*, mal uso *m* **2** WASTE : derroche *m*, despilfarro *m* **3** ABUSE : abuso *m*

mite ['maɪt] *n* **1** : ácaro *m* **2** BIT : poco *m* ⟨a wee tired : un poquito cansado⟩

miter *or* **mitre** ['maɪtər] *n* **1** : mitra *f* (de un obispo) **2** *or* **miter joint** : inglete *m*

mitigate ['mɪtəˌgeɪt] *vt* **-gated; -gating** : mitigar, aliviar

mitigation [ˌmɪtə'geɪʃən] *n* : mitigación *f*, alivio *m*

mitosis [maɪ'toːsɪs] *n, pl* **-toses** [-ˌsiːz] : mitosis *f*

mitt ['mɪt] *n* **1** : manopla *f*, guante *m* (de béisbol) **2** HAND : mano *f*, manaza *f*

mitten ['mɪtən] *n* : manopla *f*

mix¹ ['mɪks] *vt* **1** COMBINE : mezclar **2** STIR : remover, revolver **3 to mix up** CONFUSE : confundir **4 to mix up** COMBINE : mezclar — *vi* : mezclarse

mix² *n* : mezcla *f*

mixed *adj* : mezclado, variado

mixed–up *adj* **1** CONFUSED, TROUBLED : confundido, con problemas **2** CONFUSING : confuso

mixer ['mɪksər] *n* **1** : batidora *f* (de la cocina) **2 cement mixer** : hormigonera *f*

mixture ['mɪkstʃər] *n* : mezcla *f*

mix–up ['mɪksˌʌp] *n* CONFUSION : confusión *f*, lío *m* fam

mnemonic [nɪ'manɪk] *adj* : mnemónico

moan¹ ['moːn] *vi* : gemir

moan² *n* : gemido *m*

moat ['moːt] *n* : foso *m*

mob¹ ['mab] *vt* **mobbed; mobbing 1** ATTACK : atacar en masa **2** HOUND : acosar, rodear

mob² *n* **1** THRONG : multitud *f*, turba *f*, muchedumbre *f* **2** GANG : pandilla *f*

mobile¹ ['moːbəl, -ˌbiːl, -ˌbaɪl] *adj* : móvil ⟨mobile home : caravana, casa rodante⟩

mobile² ['moːˌbiːl] *n* : móvil *m*

mobile phone → cell phone

mobility [moːˈbɪləti] *n* : movilidad *f*

mobilize ['moːbəˌlaɪz] *vt* **-lized; -lizing** : movilizar

moccasin ['makəsən] *n* **1** : mocasín *m* **2** *or* **water moccasin** : serpiente *f* venenosa de Norteamérica

mocha ['moːkə] *n* **1** : mezcla *f* de café y chocolate **2** : color *m* chocolate

mock¹ ['mak, 'mɔk] *vt* **1** RIDICULE : burlarse de, mofarse de **2** MIMIC : imitar, remedar (de manera burlona)

mock² *adj* **1** SIMULATED : simulado **2** PHONY : falso

mockery ['makəri, 'mɔ-] *n, pl* **-eries 1** JEER TAUNT : burla *f*, mofa *f* ⟨to make a mockery of : burlarse de⟩ **2** FAKE : imitación *f* (burlona)

mockingbird ['makɪŋˌbərd, 'mɔ-] *n* : sinsonte *m*

mode ['moːd] *n* **1** FORM : modo *m*, forma *f* **2** MANNER : modo *m*, manera *f*, estilo *m* **3** FASHION : moda *f*

model¹ ['madəl] *v* **-eled** *or* **-elled; -eling** *or* **-elling** *vt* SHAPE : modelar — *vi* : trabajar de modelo

model² *adj* **1** EXEMPLARY : modelo, ejemplar ⟨a model student : un estudiante modelo⟩ **2** MINIATURE : en miniatura

model³ *n* **1** PATTERN : modelo *m* **2** MINIATURE : modelo *m*, miniatura *f* **3** EXAMPLE : modelo *m*, ejemplo *m* **4** MANNEQUIN : modelo *mf* **5** DESIGN : modelo *m* ⟨the '97 model : el modelo '97⟩

modem ['moːdəm, -ˌdɛm] *n* : módem *m*

moderate¹ ['madəˌreɪt] *v* **-ated; -ating** *vt* : moderar, temperar — *vi* **1** CALM : moderarse, calmarse **2** : fungir como moderador (en un debate, etc.)

moderate² ['madərət] *adj* : moderado

moderate³ ['madərət] *n* : moderado *m*, -da *f*

moderately ['mɑdərətli] *adv* **1** : con moderación **2** FAIRLY : medianamente

moderation [ˌmɑdə'reɪʃən] *n* : moderación *f*

moderator ['mɑdəˌreɪtər] *n* : moderador *m*, -dora *f*

modern ['mɑdərn] *adj* : moderno

modernism ['mɑdərˌnɪzəm] *n* : modernismo *m*

modernist ['mɑdərnɪst] *n* : modernista *mf* — **modernist** *adj*

modernity [mə'dərnəti] *n* : modernidad *f*

modernization [ˌmɑdərnə'zeɪʃən] *n* : modernización *f*

modernize ['mɑdərˌnaɪz] *v* -ized; -izing *vt* : modernizar — *vi* : modernizarse

modest ['mɑdəst] *adj* **1** HUMBLE : modesto **2** DEMURE : recatado, pudoroso **3** MODERATE : modesto, moderado — **modestly** *adv*

modesty ['mɑdəsti] *n* : modestia *f*

modicum ['mɑdɪkəm] *n* : mínimo *m*, pizca *f*

modification [ˌmɑdəfə'keɪʃən] *n* : modificación *f*

modifier ['mɑdəˌfaɪər] *n* : modificante *m*, modificador *m*

modify ['mɑdəˌfaɪ] *vt* -fied; -fying : modificar, calificar (en gramática)

modish ['mo:dɪʃ] *adj* STYLISH : a la moda, de moda

modular ['mɑdʒələr] *adj* : modular

modulate ['mɑdʒəˌleɪt] *vt* -lated; -lating : modular

modulation [ˌmɑdʒə'leɪʃən] *n* : modulación *f*

module ['mɑˌdʒu:l] *n* : módulo *m*

mogul ['mo:gəl] *n* : magnate *mf*; potentado *m*, -da *f*

moist ['mɔɪst] *adj* : húmedo

moisten ['mɔɪsən] *vt* : humedecer

moistness ['mɔɪstnəs] *n* : humedad *f*

moisture ['mɔɪstʃər] *n* : humedad *f*

moisturize ['mɔɪstʃəˌraɪz] *vt* -ized; -izing : humedecer (el aire), hidratar (la piel)

moisturizer ['mɔɪstʃəˌraɪzər] *n* : crema *f* hidratante, crema *f* humectante

molar ['mo:lər] *n* : muela *f*, molar *m*

molasses [mə'læsəz] *n* : melaza *f*

mold[1] ['mo:ld] *vt* : moldear, formar (carácter, etc.) — *vi* : enmohecerse ⟨the bread will mold : el pan se enmohecerá⟩

mold[2] *n* **1** FORM : molde *m* ⟨to break the mold : romper el molde⟩ **2** FUNGUS : moho *m*

molder ['mo:ldər] *vi* CRUMBLE : desmoronarse

molding ['mo:ldɪŋ] *n* : moldura *f* (en arquitectura)

moldy ['mo:ldi] *adj* **moldier; -est** : mohoso

mole ['mo:l] *n* **1** : lunar *m* (en la piel) **2** : topo *m* (animal)

molecule ['mɑlɪˌkju:l] *n* : molécula *f* — **molecular** [mə'lɛkjələr] *adj*

molehill ['mo:l,hɪl] *n* **to make a mountain out of a molehill** : ahogarse en un vaso de agua

molest [mə'lɛst] *vt* **1** ANNOY, DISTURB : molestar **2** : abusar (sexualmente)

mollify ['mɑləˌfaɪ] *vt* -fied; -fying : apaciguar, aplacar

mollusk *or* **mollusc** ['mɑləsk] *n* : molusco *m*

mollycoddle ['mɑliˌkɑdəl] *vt* -dled; -dling PAMPER : consentir, mimar

molt ['mo:lt] *vi* : mudar, hacer la muda

molten ['mo:ltən] *adj* : fundido

mom ['mɑm, 'mʌm] *n* : mamá *f*

moment ['mo:mənt] *n* **1** INSTANT : momento *m* ⟨one moment, please : un momento, por favor⟩ **2** TIME : momento *m* ⟨from that moment : desde entonces⟩ **3** **at any moment** : de un momento a otro **4** **at the moment** : de momento, actualmente **5** **for the moment** : de momento, por el momento **6** **the moment of truth** : la hora de la verdad

momentarily [ˌmo:mən'tɛrəli] *adv* **1** : momentáneamente **2** SOON : dentro de poco, pronto

momentary ['mo:mənˌtɛri] *adj* : momentáneo

momentous [mo'mɛntəs] *adj* : de suma importancia, fatídico

momentum [mo'mɛntəm] *n, pl* **-ta** [-tə] *or* **-tums** **1** : momento *m* (en física) **2** IMPETUS : ímpetu *m*, impulso *m*

mommy ['mɑmi, 'mʌ-] *n* : mami *f*

monarch ['mɑˌnɑrk, -nərk] *n* : monarca *mf*

monarchist ['mɑˌnɑrkɪst, -nər-] *n* : monárquico *m*, -ca *f*

monarchy ['mɑˌnɑrki, -nər-] *n, pl* **-chies** : monarquía *f*

monastery ['mɑnəˌstɛri] *n, pl* **-teries** : monasterio *m*

monastic [mə'næstɪk] *adj* : monástico — **monastically** [-tɪkli] *adv*

Monday ['mʌnˌdeɪ, -di] *n* : lunes *m* ⟨today is Monday : hoy es lunes⟩ ⟨(on) Monday : el lunes⟩ ⟨(on) Mondays : los lunes⟩ ⟨last Monday : el lunes pasado⟩ ⟨next Monday : el lunes que viene⟩ ⟨every other Monday : cada dos lunes⟩ ⟨Monday afternoon/morning : lunes por la tarde/mañana⟩

monetary ['mɑnəˌtɛri, 'mʌnə-] *adj* : monetario

money ['mʌni] *n, pl* **-eys** *or* **-ies** ['mʌniz] **1** : dinero *m*, plata *f* ⟨to make/lose money : ganar/perder dinero⟩ **2 monies** *npl* : sumas *fpl* de dinero **3 for my money** : en mi opinión, para mí **4 money talks** : poderoso caballero es don Dinero **5 on the money** : exacto, correcto

money changer [-'tʃeɪndʒər] *n* : cambista *mf* (de dinero)

moneyed ['mʌnid] *adj* : adinerado

moneylender ['mʌniˌlɛndər] *n* : prestamista *mf*

money order *n* : giro *m* postal

Mongol ['mɑŋgəl, -ˌgo:l] → **Mongolian**

Mongolian [mɑn'go:liən, mɑŋ-] *n* : mongol *m*, -gola *f* — **Mongolian** *adj*

mongoose ['mɑnˌgu:s, 'mɑŋ-] *n, pl* **-gooses** : mangosta *f*

mongrel ['mɑŋgrəl, 'mʌn-] *n* **1** : perro *m* mestizo, perro *m* corriente *Mex* **2** HYBRID : híbrido *m*

monitor[1] ['manəṭər] *vt* : controlar, monitorear

monitor[2] *n* **1** : ayudante *mf* (en una escuela) **2** : monitor *m* (de una computadora, etc.)

monk ['mʌŋk] *n* : monje *m*

monkey[1] ['mʌŋki] *vi* **-keyed; -keying 1 to monkey around** : hacer payasadas, payasear **2 to monkey with** : juguetear con

monkey[2] *n, pl* **-keys** : mono *m*, -na *f*

monkeyshines ['mʌŋki,ʃaɪnz] *npl* PRANKS : picardías *fpl*, travesuras *fpl*

monkey wrench *n* → **wrench**[2]

monocle ['manɪkəl] *n* : monóculo *m*

monogamous [mə'nagəməs] *adj* : monógamo

monogamy [mə'nagəmi] *n* : monogamia *f*

monogram[1] ['manə,græm] *vt* **-grammed; -gramming** : marcar con monograma ⟨monogrammed towels : toallas con monograma⟩

monogram[2] *n* : monograma *m*

monograph ['manə,græf] *n* : monografía *f*

monolingual [,manə'lɪŋgwəl] *adj* : monolingüe

monolith ['manə,lɪθ] *n* : monolito *m*

monolithic [,manə'lɪθɪk] *adj* : monolítico

monologue ['manə,lɔg] *n* : monólogo *m*

monopolize [mə'napə,laɪz] *vt* **-lized; -lizing** : monopolizar

monopoly [mə'napəli] *n, pl* **-lies** : monopolio *m*

monosyllabic [,manəsə'læbɪk] *adj* : monosilábico

monosyllable ['manə,sɪləbəl] *n* : monosílabo *m*

monotheism ['manoθi:,ɪzəm] *n* : monoteísmo *m* — **monotheist** *n*

monotheistic [,manoθi:'ɪstɪk] *adj* : monoteísta

monotone ['manə,to:n] *n* : voz *f* monótona

monotonous [mə'natənəs] *adj* : monótono — **monotonously** *adv*

monotony [mə'natəni] *n* : monotonía *f*, uniformidad *f*

monsignor [man'si:njər] *n* : monseñor *m*

monsoon [man'su:n] *n* : monzón *m*

monster ['manstər] *n* : monstruo *m*

monstrosity [man'strasəṭi] *n, pl* **-ties** : monstruosidad *f*

monstrous ['manstrəs] *adj* : monstruoso — **monstrously** *adv*

montage [man'taʒ] *n* : montaje *m*

month ['mʌnθ] *n* : mes *m*

monthly[1] ['mʌnθli] *adv* : mensualmente

monthly[2] *adj* : mensual

monthly[3] *n, pl* **-lies** : publicación *f* mensual

monument ['manjəmənt] *n* : monumento *m*

monumental [,manjə'mɛntəl] *adj* : monumental — **monumentally** *adv*

moo[1] ['mu:] *vi* : mugir

moo[2] *n* : mugido *m*

mood ['mu:d] *n* : humor *m* ⟨to be in a good mood : estar de buen humor⟩ ⟨to be in the mood for : tener ganas de⟩ ⟨to be in no mood for : no estar para⟩

moodiness ['mu:dinəs] *n* **1** SADNESS : melancolía *f*, tristeza *f* **2** : cambios *mpl* de humor, carácter *m* temperamental

moody ['mu:di] *adj* **moodier; -est 1** GLOOMY : melancólico, deprimido **2** TEMPERAMENTAL : temperamental, de humor variable

moon ['mu:n] *n* : luna *f*

moonbeam ['mu:n,bi:m] *n* : rayo *m* de luna

moonlight[1] ['mu:n,laɪt] *vi* : estar pluriempleado

moonlight[2] *n* : claro *m* de luna, luz *f* de la luna

moonlit ['mu:n,lɪt] *adj* : iluminado por la luna ⟨a moonlit night : una noche de luna⟩

moonshine ['mu:n,ʃaɪn] *n* **1** MOONLIGHT : luz *f* de la luna **2** NONSENSE : disparates *mpl*, tonterías *fpl* **3** : whisky *m* destilado ilegalmente

moor[1] ['mur, 'mɔr] *vt* : amarrar

moor[2] *n* : páramo *m*

Moor ['mur] *n* : moro *m*, -ra *f*

mooring ['murɪŋ, 'mɔr-] *n* DOCK : atracadero *m*

Moorish ['murɪʃ] *adj* : moro

moose ['mu:s] *ns & pl* : alce *m* (norteamericano)

moot ['mu:t] *adj* DEBATABLE : discutible

mop[1] ['map] *v* **mopped; mopping** *vt* **1** : trapear **2 to mop up** : limpiar (un líquido) **3 to mop up** FINISH : terminar, acabar — *vi* **1** : trapear el suelo **2 to mop up** FINISH : terminar, acabar

mop[2] *n* : trapeador *m*

mope ['mo:p] *vi* **moped; moping** : andar deprimido, quedar abatido

moped ['mo:,pɛd] *n* : ciclomotor *m*

moraine [mə'reɪn] *n* : morena *f*

moral[1] ['mɔrəl] *adj* : moral ⟨moral judgment : juicio moral⟩ ⟨moral support : apoyo moral⟩ — **morally** *adv*

moral[2] *n* **1** : moraleja *f* (de un cuento, etc.) **2 morals** *npl* : moral *f*, moralidad *f*

morale [mə'ræl] *n* : moral *f*

moralist ['mɔrəlɪst] *n* : moralista *mf*

moralistic [,mɔrə'lɪstɪk] *adj* : moralista

morality [mə'ræləṭi] *n, pl* **-ties** : moralidad *f*

morass [mə'ræs] *n* **1** SWAMP : ciénaga *f*, pantano *m* **2** CONFUSION, MESS : lío *m* *fam*, embrollo *m*

moratorium [,mɔrə'toriəm] *n, pl* **-riums** *or* **-ria** [-iə] : moratoria *f*

moray ['mɔr,eɪ, mə'reɪ] *n* : morena *f*

morbid ['mɔrbɪd] *adj* **1** : mórbido, morboso (en medicina) **2** GRUESOME : morboso, horripilante

morbidity [mɔr'bɪdəṭi] *n, pl* **-ties** : morbosidad *f*

more[1] ['mor] *adv* **1** : más ⟨what more can I say? : ¿qué más puedo decir?⟩ ⟨you need to exercise more : debes hacer más ejercicio⟩ ⟨more important : más importante⟩ ⟨once more : una vez más⟩ ⟨more and more difficult : cada vez más difícil⟩ **2 more or less** : más o menos **3 more than** VERY : muy, bastante ⟨I'm more than happy to help you : te ayudo encantado⟩ **4 more than a little** ⟨I was more than a little surprised : me sorprendió bastante⟩

more² *adj* : más ⟨nothing more than that : nada más que eso⟩ ⟨more than a hundred : más de cien⟩ ⟨more work : más trabajo⟩

more³ *n* : más *m* ⟨the more you eat, the more you want : cuanto más comes, tanto más quieres⟩

more⁴ *pron* **1** : más ⟨more were found : se encontraron más⟩ ⟨I don't want any more : no quiero más⟩ ⟨it costs more : cuesta más⟩ ⟨no more, no less : ni más ni menos⟩ ⟨more and more of them : un número cada vez mayor de ellos⟩ ⟨and what's more : y lo que es más⟩ ⟨we see more of each other now : ahora nos vemos más⟩ **2 more of** : más bien ⟨it's more of a maroon than a red : es más bien granate que rojo⟩

morello [mə'rɛlo] *n* : guinda *f*

moreover [mor'o:vər] *adv* : además

mores ['mɔr,eɪz, -i:z] *npl* CUSTOMS : costumbres *fpl*, tradiciones *fpl*

morgue ['mɔrg] *n* : morgue *f*

moribund ['mɔrə,bʌnd] *adj* : moribundo

Mormon ['mɔrmən] *n* : mormón *m*, -mona *f* — **Mormon** *adj*

morn ['mɔrn] → **morning**

morning ['mɔrnɪŋ] *n* : mañana *f* ⟨good morning! : ¡buenos días!⟩

morning sickness *n* : náuseas *fpl* matutinas (del embarazo)

Moroccan [mə'rɑkən] *n* : marroquí *mf* — **Moroccan** *adj*

moron ['mor,ɑn] *n* **1** *dated, now offensive* : retrasado *m*, -da *f* mental *dated, now offensive* **2** DUNCE : estúpido *m*, -da *f*; tonto *m*, -ta *f*

morose [mə'ro:s] *adj* : hosco, sombrío — **morosely** *adv*

moroseness [mə'ro:snəs] *n* : malhumor *m*

morphine ['mɔr,fi:n] *n* : morfina *f*

morphology [mɔr'fɑlədʒi] *n*, *pl* **-gies** : morfología *f*

morrow ['mɑro:] *n* : día *m* siguiente

Morse code ['mɔrs] *n* : código *m* morse

morsel ['mɔrsəl] *n* **1** BITE : bocado *m* **2** FRAGMENT : pedazo *m*

mortadella [,mɔrtə'dɛlə] *n* : mortadela *f*

mortal¹ ['mɔrtəl] *adj* : mortal ⟨mortal blow : golpe mortal⟩ ⟨mortal fear : miedo mortal⟩ — **mortally** *adv*

mortal² *n* : mortal *mf*

mortality [mɔr'tæləti] *n* : mortalidad *f*

mortar ['mɔrtər] *n* **1** : mortero *m*, molcajete *m* *Mex* ⟨mortar and pestle : mortero y maja⟩ **2** : mortero *m* ⟨mortar shell : granada de mortero⟩ **3** CEMENT : mortero *m*, argamasa *f*

mortarboard ['mɔrtər,bord] *n* : bonete *m*, birrete *m*

mortgage¹ ['mɔrgɪdʒ] *vt* **-gaged; -gaging** : hipotecar

mortgage² *n* : hipoteca *f*

mortification [,mɔrtəfə'keɪʃən] *n* **1** : mortificación *f* **2** HUMILIATION : humillación *f*, vergüenza *f*

mortify ['mɔrtə,faɪ] *vt* **-fied; -fying 1** : mortificar (en religión) **2** HUMILIATE : humillar, avergonzar

mortuary ['mɔrtuₐ,wɛri] *n*, *pl* **-aries** FUNERAL HOME : funeraria *f*

mosaic [mo'zeɪɪk] *n* : mosaico *m*

Moslem ['mɑzləm] → **Muslim**

mosque ['mɑsk] *n* : mezquita *f*

mosquito [mə'ski:ṭo] *n*, *pl* **-toes** : mosquito *m*, zancudo *m*

moss ['mɔs] *n* : musgo *m*

mossy ['mɔsi] *adj* **mossier; -est** : musgoso

most¹ ['mo:st] *adv* : más ⟨the most interesting book : el libro más interesante⟩ ⟨most certainly : con toda seguridad⟩ ⟨most often : más a menudo⟩

most² *adj* **1** : la mayoría de, la mayor parte de ⟨most people : la mayoría de la gente⟩ **2** GREATEST : más (dícese de los números), mayor (dícese de las cantidades) ⟨the most ability : la mayor capacidad⟩

most³ *n* : más *m*, máximo *m* ⟨the most I can do : lo más que puedo hacer⟩ ⟨he did the most : hizo más que nadie⟩ ⟨three weeks at (the) most : tres semanas como máximo⟩ ⟨to make the most of something : sacar el mejor provecho/partido posible de algo⟩

most⁴ *pron* : la mayoría, la mayor parte ⟨most will go : la mayoría irá⟩ ⟨most of : la mayoría de⟩ ⟨most of the time : la mayor parte del tiempo⟩

mostly ['mo:stli] *adv* MAINLY : en su mayor parte, principalmente

mote ['mo:t] *n* SPECK : mota *f*

motel [mo'tɛl] *n* : motel *m*

moth ['mɔθ] *n* : palomilla *f*, polilla *f*

mothball ['mɔθ,bɔl] *n* : bola *f* de naftalina

mother¹ ['mʌðər] *vt* **1** BEAR : dar a luz a **2** PROTECT : cuidar de, proteger

mother² *n* : madre *f*

motherhood ['mʌðər,hʊd] *n* : maternidad *f*

mother–in–law ['mʌðərɪn,lɔ] *n*, *pl* **mothers–in–law** : suegra *f*

motherland ['mʌðər,lænd] *n* : patria *f*

motherly ['mʌðərli] *adj* : maternal

mother–of–pearl [,mʌðərəv'pərl] *n* : nácar *m*, madreperla *f*

mother–to–be *n* : futura madre *f*

mother tongue *n* : lengua *f* materna

motif [mo'ti:f] *n* : motivo *m*

motion¹ ['mo:ʃən] *vt* : hacerle señas (a alguien) ⟨she motioned us to come in : nos hizo señas para que entráramos⟩

motion² *n* **1** MOVEMENT : movimiento *m* ⟨to set in motion : poner en marcha⟩ **2** PROPOSAL : moción *f* ⟨to second a motion : apoyar una moción⟩

motionless ['mo:ʃənləs] *adj* : inmóvil, quieto

motion picture *n* MOVIE : película *f*

motivate ['mo:tə,veɪt] *vt* **-vated; -vating** : motivar, mover, inducir

motivation [,mo:tə'veɪʃən] *n* : motivación *f*

motive¹ ['mo:ṭɪv] *adj* : motor ⟨motive power : fuerza motriz⟩

motive² n : motivo m, móvil m

motley [ˈmɑtli] adj : abigarrado, variopinto

motor¹ [ˈmoːt̬ər] vi : viajar en coche

motor² n : motor m

motorbike [ˈmoːt̬ərˌbaɪk] n : motocicleta f (pequeña), moto f

motorboat [ˈmoːt̬ərˌboːt] n : bote m a motor, lancha f motora

motorcar [ˈmoːt̬ərˌkɑr] n : automóvil m

motorcycle [ˈmoːt̬ərˌsaɪkəl] n : motocicleta f

motorcycling [ˈmoːt̬ərˌsaɪklɪŋ] n : motociclismo m

motorcyclist [ˈmoːt̬ərˌsaɪklɪst] n : motociclista mf

motorist [ˈmoːt̬ərɪst] n : automovilista mf, motorista mf

motorized [ˈmoːt̬əraɪzd] adj : motorizado

motor racing n : carreras fpl de coches

motor vehicle → vehicle

mottled [ˈmɑt̬əld] adj : manchado, moteado ⟨mottled skin : piel manchada⟩ ⟨a mottled surface : una superficie moteada⟩

motto [ˈmɑt̬oː] n, pl **-toes** : lema m

mould [ˈmoːld] → **mold**

mound [ˈmaʊnd] n 1 PILE : montón m 2 KNOLL : montículo m 3 burial mound : túmulo m

mount¹ [ˈmaʊnt] vt 1 : montar a (un caballo), montar en (una bicicleta), subir a 2 : montar (artillería, etc.) — vi INCREASE : aumentar

mount² n 1 SUPPORT : soporte m 2 HORSE : caballería f, montura f 3 MOUNTAIN : monte m, montaña f

mountain [ˈmaʊnt̬ən] n 1 : montaña f 2 to make a mountain out of a molehill → molehill

mountain bike n : bicicleta f de montaña

mountaineer [ˌmaʊnt̬ənˈɪr] n : alpinista mf; montañero m, -ra f

mountaineering [ˌmaʊnt̬ənˈɪrɪŋ] n : montañismo m, alpinismo m

mountainous [ˈmaʊnt̬ənəs] adj : montañoso

mountaintop [ˈmaʊnt̬ənˌtɑp] n : cima f, cumbre f

mourn [ˈmorn] vt : llorar (por), lamentar ⟨to mourn the death of : llorar la muerte de⟩ — vi : llorar, estar de luto

mourner [ˈmornər] n : doliente mf

mournful [ˈmornfəl] adj 1 SORROWFUL : lloroso, plañidero, triste 2 GLOOMY : deprimente — **mournfully** adv

mourning [ˈmornɪŋ] n : duelo m, luto m

mouse [ˈmaʊs] n, pl **mice** [ˈmaɪs] 1 : ratón m, -tona f 2 : ratón m (de una computadora)

mouse pad n : alfombrilla f de/para ratón, almohadilla f de/para ratón

mousetrap [ˈmaʊsˌtræp] n : ratonera f

mousse [ˈmuːs] n : mousse mf

moustache [ˈmʌˌstæʃ, məˈstæʃ] → **mustache**

mouth¹ [ˈmaʊð] vt 1 : decir con poca sinceridad, repetir sin comprensión 2 : articular en silencio ⟨she mouthed the words : formó las palabras con los labios⟩

mouth² [ˈmaʊθ] n : boca f (de una persona o un animal), entrada f (de un túnel), desembocadura f (de un río)

mouthed [ˈmaʊðd, ˈmaʊθt] adj (used in combination) : de boca ⟨a large-mouthed jar : un tarro de boca grande⟩

mouthful [ˈmaʊθˌfʊl] n : bocado m (de comida), bocanada f (de líquido o humo)

mouth organ n → **harmonica**

mouthpiece [ˈmaʊθˌpiːs] n : boquilla f (de un instrumento musical)

mouth-to-mouth resuscitation or **mouth-to-mouth** n : respiración f boca a boca, el boca a boca

mouthwash [ˈmaʊθˌwɔl, -ˌwɑl] n : enjuague m bucal

mouth-watering [ˈmaʊθˌwɔt̬ərɪŋ, -ˌwɑ-] n : delicioso

movable [ˈmuːvəbəl] or **moveable** adj : movible, móvil

move¹ [ˈmuːv] v **moved; moving** vi 1 GO : ir ⟨to move closer : acercarse⟩ ⟨to move forward/back : echarse (hacia) adelante/atrás⟩ 2 RELOCATE : mudarse, trasladarse 3 STIR : moverse ⟨don't move! : ¡no te muevas!⟩ 4 ACT : actuar 5 to move aside : hacerse a un lado 6 to move along PROCEED : circular 7 to move away LEAVE : marcharse 8 to move away STEP BACK : apartarse 9 to move heaven and earth : hacer todo lo posible 10 to move in : mudarse (a un lugar) ⟨to move in with someone : irse a vivir con alguien⟩ 11 to move on LEAVE : marcharse 12 to move on CONTINUE : pasar 13 to move out : mudarse (de un lugar) 14 to move over : hacer sitio 15 to move up : subir — vt 1 : mover ⟨he kept moving his feet : no dejaba de mover los pies⟩ ⟨move it forward/back : muévalo hacia adelante/atrás⟩ ⟨move it over there : ponlo allí⟩ 2 RELOCATE : trasladar 3 INDUCE, PERSUADE : inducir, persuadir, mover 4 TOUCH : conmover ⟨it moved him to tears : lo hizo llorar⟩ 5 PROPOSE : proponer 6 to move along : dispersar, hacer circular 7 to move up : adelantar (una fecha)

move² n 1 MOVEMENT : movimiento m 2 RELOCATION : mudanza f (de casa), traslado m 3 STEP : paso m ⟨a good move : un paso acertado⟩

movement [ˈmuːvmənt] n : movimiento m

mover [ˈmuːvər] n : persona f que hace mudanzas

movie [ˈmuːvi] n 1 : película f 2 **movies** npl : cine m

movie theater n : cine m

moving [ˈmuːvɪŋ] adj 1 : en movimiento ⟨a moving target : un blanco móvil⟩ 2 TOUCHING : conmovedor, emocionante

mow¹ [ˈmoː] vt **mowed; mowed** or **mown** [ˈmoːn]; **mowing** 1 : cortar (la hierba) 2 **mow down** SHOOT : acribillar

mow² [ˈmaʊ] n : pajar m

mower [ˈmoːər] → **lawn mower**

MP3 [ˌɛmˌpiːˈθriː] n : MP3 m

Mr. [ˈmɪstər] n, pl **Messrs.** [ˈmɛsərz] : señor m

Mrs. ['mɪsəz, -səs, esp South 'mɪzəz, -zəs] *n, pl* **Mesdames** [meɪ'dɑm, -'dæm] : señora *f*

Ms. ['mɪz] *n* : señora *f*, señorita *f*

much¹ ['mʌtʃ] *adv* **more** ['mor]; **most** ['moːst] **1** : mucho ⟨I'm much happier : estoy mucho más contenta⟩ ⟨she talks as much as I do : habla tanto como yo⟩ ⟨do you travel much? : ¿viajas mucho?⟩ ⟨I like it very much : me gusta mucho⟩ ⟨thank you very much : muchas gracias⟩ **2** VERY : muy ⟨he's not much good at golf : no es muy bueno para el golf⟩ **3** NEARLY : casi ⟨the town looks much the same : el pueblo no ha cambiado mucho, el pueblo es casi igual que antes⟩ **4** LONG : mucho ⟨not much before noon : poco antes del mediodía⟩ **5 as much** : lo mismo ⟨she'd do as much for me : haría lo mismo para mí⟩ ⟨I thought as much : ya me lo imaginaba⟩ **6 as much as** : tanto como **7 as much as** NEARLY : casi **8 much as** ALTHOUGH : aunque **9 very much** (*used for emphasis*) ENTIRELY, UNQUESTIONABLY : totalmente, indudablemente

much² *adj* **more; most** : mucho ⟨there isn't much difference : no hay mucha diferencia⟩ ⟨he doesn't know much French : no sabe mucho francés⟩ ⟨she wasn't much help : no nos ayudó mucho⟩ ⟨was there much food? : ¿había mucha comida?⟩ ⟨we spent so much money : gastamos tanto dinero⟩ ⟨too much time : demasiado tiempo⟩ ⟨it was all too much for him : no podía con todo⟩

much³ *pron* **1** : mucho ⟨I don't need much : no necesito mucho⟩ ⟨there was food, but not much : había comida, pero poca cantidad⟩ ⟨I don't see much of them : no los veo mucho⟩ ⟨it doesn't amount to much : no es gran cosa⟩ ⟨much of the time : una buena parte del tiempo⟩ ⟨too much : demasiado⟩ **2 as much as** : tanto como **3 not much of a** ⟨he's not much of a cook : no cocina muy bien⟩ ⟨it wasn't much of a vacation : mis vacaciones no fueron nada especial⟩ **4 not much on** ⟨she's not much on studying : no estudia mucho⟩ ⟨he's not much on looks : no es muy guapo⟩

mucilage ['mjuːsəlɪdʒ] *n* : mucílago *m*

muck ['mʌk] *n* **1** MANURE : estiércol *m* **2** DIRT, FILTH : mugre *f*, suciedad *f* **3** MIRE, MUD : barro *m*, fango *m*, lodo *m*

mucous ['mjuːkəs] *adj* : mucoso ⟨mucous membrane : membrana mucosa⟩

mucus ['mjuːkəs] *n* : mucosidad *f*

mud ['mʌd] *n* : barro *m*, fango *m*, lodo *m*

muddle¹ ['mʌdəl] *v* **-dled; -dling** *vt* **1** CONFUSE : confundir (a alguien) **2** *or to* **muddle up** MIX UP : confundir ⟨I always get them muddled up in my mind : siempre los confundo⟩ — *vi* : andar confundido ⟨to muddle through : arreglárselas⟩

muddle² *n* : confusión *f*, embrollo *m*, lío *m*

muddleheaded [ˌmʌdəl'hɛdəd, 'mʌdəlˌ-] *adj* CONFUSED : confuso, despistado

muddy¹ ['mʌdi] *vt* **-died; -dying** : llenar de barro

muddy² *adj* **muddier; -est** : barroso, fangoso, lodoso, enlodado ⟨you're all muddy : estás cubierto de barro⟩

mudguard ['mʌdˌgɑrd] *n* : guardabarros *m*

muff¹ ['mʌf] *vt* BUNGLE : echar a perder, fallar (un tiro, etc.)

muff² *n* : manguito *m*

muffin ['mʌfən] *n* : magdalena *f*

muffle ['mʌfəl] *vt* **-fled; -fling 1** ENVELOP : cubrir, tapar **2** DEADEN : amortiguar (un sonido)

muffler ['mʌflər] *n* **1** SCARF : bufanda *f* **2** : silenciador *m*; mofle *m CA, Mex* (de un automóvil)

mug¹ ['mʌg] *v* **mugged; mugging** *vi* : posar (con afectación), hacer muecas ⟨mugging for the camera : haciendo muecas para la cámara⟩ — *vt* ASSAULT : asaltar, atracar

mug² *n* CUP : tazón *m*

mugger ['mʌgər] *n* : atracador *m*, -dora *f*

mugginess ['mʌginəs] *n* : bochorno *m*

mugging ['mʌgiŋ] *n* : atraco *m*

muggy ['mʌgi] *adj* **muggier; -est** : bochornoso

mulatto [muˈlɑto, -ˈlæ-] *n, pl* **-toes** *or* **-tos** *now sometimes offensive* : mulato *m*, -ta *f*

mulberry ['mʌlˌbɛri] *n, pl* **-ries** : morera *f* (árbol), mora *f* (fruta)

mulch¹ ['mʌltʃ] *vt* : cubrir con pajote

mulch² *n* : pajote *m*

mule ['mjuːl] *n* **1** : mula *f* **2** : obstinado *m*, -da *f*; terco *m*, -ca *f*

mulish ['mjuːlɪʃ] *adj* : obstinado, terco

mull ['mʌl] *vt* **to mull over** : reflexionar sobre

mullet ['mʌlət] *n, pl* **-let** *or* **-lets** : mújol *m*

multi- [ˌmʌlti-, ˌmʌltaɪ-] *pref* : multi-

multicolored [ˌmʌltiˈkʌlərd, ˌmʌltaɪ-] *adj* : multicolor, abigarrado

multicultural [ˌmʌltiˈkʌltʃərəl] *adj* : multicultural — **multiculturalism** [ˌmʌltiˈkʌltʃərəˌlɪzəm] *n*

multidisciplinary [ˌmʌltiˈdɪsəpləˌnɛri] *adj* : multidisciplinario

multifaceted [ˌmʌltiˈfæsətəd, ˌmʌltaɪ-] *adj* : multifacético

multifamily [ˌmʌltiˈfæmli, ˌmʌltaɪ-] *adj* : multifamiliar

multifarious [ˌmʌltəˈfæriəs] *adj* DIVERSE : diverso, variado

multilateral [ˌmʌltiˈlætərəl, ˌmʌltaɪ-] *adj* : multilateral

multimedia [ˌmʌltiˈmiːdiə, ˌmʌltaɪ-] *adj* : multimedia

multimillionaire [ˌmʌltiˌmɪljəˈnær, ˌmʌltaɪ-, -ˈmɪljəˌnær] *adj* : multimillonario

multinational [ˌmʌltiˈnæɫənəl, ˌmʌltaɪ-] *adj* : multinacional

multiple¹ ['mʌltəpəl] *adj* : múltiple

multiple² *n* : múltiplo *m*

multiple sclerosis [skləˈroːsɪs] *n* : esclerosis *f* múltiple

multiplex ['mʌltəˌplɛks] *n* : multicine *m*

multiplication [ˌmʌltəpləˈkeɪʃən] *n* : multiplicación *f*

multiplicity [ˌmʌltəˈplɪsəti] *n, pl* **-ties** : multiplicidad *f*

multiply ['mʌltə,plaɪ] v **-plied; -plying** vt : multiplicar — vi : multiplicarse

multipurpose [,mʌlti'pərpəs, ,mʌltaɪ-] adj : multiuso

multistory [,mʌlti'stori, ,mʌltaɪ-] adj : de varias plantas, de varios pisos

multitask ['mʌlti,tæsk] vi : hacer multitarea

multitasking ['mʌlti,tæskɪŋ] n : multitarea f

multitude ['mʌltə,tu:d, -,tju:d] n **1** CROWD : multitud f, muchedumbre f **2** HOST : multitud f, gran cantidad f ⟨a multitude of ideas : numerosas ideas⟩

multivitamin [,mʌlti'vaɪtəmən, ,mʌltaɪ-] adj : multivitamínico

mum¹ ['mʌm] adj SILENT : callado

mum² n → **chrysanthemum**

mumble¹ ['mʌmbəl] v **-bled; -bling** vt : mascullar, musitar — vi : mascullar, hablar entre dientes, murmurar

mumble² n **to speak in a mumble** : hablar entre dientes

mummy ['mʌmi] n, pl **-mies** : momia f

mumps ['mʌmps] ns & pl : paperas fpl

munch ['mʌntʃ] v : mascar, masticar

mundane [,mʌn'deɪn, 'mʌn,-] adj **1** EARTHLY, WORLDLY : mundano, terrenal **2** COMMONPLACE : rutinario, ordinario

municipal [mju'nɪsəpəl] adj : municipal

municipality [mjʊ,nɪsə'pæləti] n, pl **-ties** : municipio m

munitions [mjʊ'nɪlənz] npl : municiones fpl

mural¹ ['mjʊrəl] adj : mural

mural² n : mural m

murder¹ ['mərdər] vt : asesinar, matar — vi : matar

murder² n : asesinato m, homicidio m

murderer ['mərdərər] n : asesino m, -na f; homicida mf

murderess ['mərdərəs] n : asesina f, homicida f

murderous ['mərdərəs] adj : asesino, homicida

murk ['mərk] n DARKNESS : oscuridad f, tinieblas fpl

murkiness ['mərkinəs] n : oscuridad f, tenebrosidad f

murky ['mərki] adj **murkier; -est** : oscuro, tenebroso

murmur¹ ['mərmər] vi **1** DRONE : murmurar **2** GRUMBLE : refunfuñar, regañar, rezongar — vt MUMBLE : murmurar

murmur² n **1** COMPLAINT : queja f **2** DRONE : murmullo m, rumor m

muscle¹ ['mʌsəl] vi **-cled; -cling** : meterse ⟨to muscle in on : meterse por la fuerza en, entrometerse en⟩

muscle² n **1** : músculo m **2** STRENGTH : fuerza f

muscular ['mʌskjələr] adj **1** : muscular ⟨muscular tissue : tejido muscular⟩ **2** BRAWNY : musculoso

muscular dystrophy n : distrofia f muscular

musculature ['mʌskjələ,tlʊr, -tlər] n : musculatura f

muse¹ ['mju:z] vi **mused; musing** PON-DER, REFLECT : cavilar, meditar, reflexionar

muse² n : musa f

museum [mjʊ'zi:əm] n : museo m

mush ['mʌl] n **1** : gachas fpl (de maíz) **2** SENTIMENTALITY : sensiblería f

mushroom¹ ['mʌl,ru:m, -,rʊm] vi GROW, MULTIPLY : crecer rápidamente, multiplicarse

mushroom² n : hongo m, champiñón m, seta f, callampa f Chile

mushy ['mʌli] adj **mushier; -est 1** SOFT : blando **2** MAWKISH : sensiblero

music ['mju:zɪk] n : música f

musical¹ ['mju:zɪkəl] adj : musical, de música ⟨musical instrument : instrumento musical⟩ — **musically** adv

musical² n : comedia f musical

music box n : cajita f de música

musician [mjʊ'zɪlən] n : músico m, -ca f

musk ['mʌsk] n : almizcle m

musket ['mʌskət] n : mosquete m

musketeer [,mʌskə'tɪr] n : mosquetero m

muskrat ['mʌsk,ræt] n, pl **-rat** or **-rats** : rata f almizclera

Muslim¹ ['mʌzləm, 'mʊs-, 'mʊz-] adj : musulmán

Muslim² n : musulmán m, -mana f

muslin ['mʌzlən] n : muselina f

muss¹ ['mʌs] vt : desordenar, despeinar (el pelo)

muss² n : desorden m

mussel ['mʌsəl] n : mejillón m

must¹ ['mʌst] v aux **1** (expressing obligation or necessity) : deber, tener que ⟨you must stop : debes parar⟩ ⟨we must obey : tenemos que obedecer⟩ **2** (expressing probability) : deber (de), haber de ⟨you must be tired : debes de estar cansado⟩ ⟨it must be late : ha de ser tarde⟩

must² n **1** : necesidad f ⟨to be a must : ser imprescindible⟩ **2** : mosto m

mustache ['mʌ,stæl, mʌ'stæl] n : bigote m, bigotes mpl

mustang ['mʌ,stæŋ] n : caballo m mesteño

mustard ['mʌstərd] n : mostaza f

muster¹ ['mʌstər] vt **1** ASSEMBLE : reunir **2 to muster up** : armarse de, cobrar (valor, fuerzas, etc.)

muster² n **1** INSPECTION : revista f (de tropas) ⟨it didn't pass muster : no resistió un examen minucioso⟩ **2** COLLECTION : colección f

mustiness ['mʌstinəs] n : lo mohoso

musty ['mʌsti] adj **mustier; -est** : mohoso, que huele a moho, que huele a encerrado

mutant¹ ['mju:tənt] adj : mutante

mutant² n : mutante m

mutate ['mju:,teɪt] vi **-tated; -tating 1** : mutar (genéticamente) **2** CHANGE : transformarse

mutation [mju:'teɪlən] n : mutación f (genética)

mute¹ ['mju:t] vt **muted; muting** MUFFLE : amortiguar, ponerle sordina a (un instrumento musical)

mute² adj **muter; mutest** : mudo — **mutely** adv

mute³ *n* **1** *sometimes offensive* : mudo *m*, -da *f* (persona) **2** : sordina *f* (para un instrumento musical)

muted *adj* **1** : apagado (dícese de colores, la voz, etc.), sordo (dícese de sonidos) **2** RESTRAINED, WEAK : contenido, débil

mutilate ['mjuːt̬ə‚leɪt] *vt* **-lated; -lating** : mutilar

mutilation [‚mjuːt̬ə'leɪ‚ən] *n* : mutilación *f*

mutineer [‚mjuːt̬ən'ɪr] *n* : amotinado *m*, -da *f*

mutinous ['mjuːt̬ənəs] *adj* : amotinado

mutiny¹ ['mjuːt̬əni] *vi* **-nied; -nying** : amotinarse

mutiny² *n, pl* **-nies** : amotinamiento *m*, motín *m*

mutt ['mʌt] *n* MONGREL : perro *m* mestizo, perro *m* corriente *Mex*

mutter ['mʌt̬ər] *vi* **1** MUMBLE : mascullar, hablar entre dientes, murmurar **2** GRUMBLE : refunfuñar, regañar, rezongar

mutton ['mʌt̬ən] *n* : carne *f* de carnero

mutual ['mjuːtʃʊəl] *adj* **1** : mutuo ⟨mutual respect : respeto mutuo⟩ **2** COMMON : común ⟨a mutual friend : un amigo común⟩

mutually ['mjuːtʃʊəli, -tʃəli] *adv* **1** : mutuamente ⟨mutually beneficial : mutuamente beneficioso⟩ **2** JOINTLY : conjuntamente

muzzle¹ ['mʌzəl] *vt* **-zled; -zling** : ponerle un bozal a (un animal), amordazar

muzzle² *n* **1** SNOUT : hocico *m* **2** : bozal *m* (para un perro, etc.) **3** : boca *f* (de un arma de fuego)

my¹ ['maɪ] *adj* : mi ⟨my parents : mis padres⟩

my² *interj* : ¡caramba!, ¡Dios mío!

myopia [maɪ'oː‚piə] *n* : miopía *f*

myopic [maɪ'oː‚pɪk, -'ɑ-] *adj* : miope

myriad¹ ['mɪriəd] *adj* INNUMERABLE : innumerable

myriad² *n* : miríada *f*

myrrh ['mər] *n* : mirra *f*

myrtle ['mərt̬əl] *n* : mirto *m*, arrayán *m*

myself [maɪ'sɛlf] *pron* **1** (*used reflexively*) : me ⟨I washed myself : me lavé⟩ **2** (*used for emphasis*) : yo mismo, yo misma ⟨I did it myself : lo hice yo mismo⟩

mysterious [mɪ'stɪriəs] *adj* : misterioso — **mysteriously** *adv*

mysteriousness [mɪ'stɪriəsnəs] *n* : lo misterioso

mystery ['mɪstəri] *n, pl* **-teries** : misterio *m*

mystic¹ ['mɪstɪk] *adj* : místico

mystic² *n* : místico *m*, -ca *f*

mystical ['mɪstɪkəl] *adj* : místico — **mystically** *adv*

mysticism ['mɪstə‚sɪzəm] *n* : misticismo *m*

mystify ['mɪstə‚faɪ] *vt* **-fied; -fying** : dejar perplejo, confundir

mystique [mɪ'stiːk] *n* : aura *f* de misterio

myth ['mɪθ] *n* : mito *m*

mythic ['mɪθɪk] *adj* : mítico

mythical ['mɪθɪkəl] *adj* : mítico

mythological [‚mɪθə'lɑdʒɪkəl] *adj* : mitológico

mythology [mɪ'θɑlədʒi] *n, pl* **-gies** : mitología *f*

N

n ['ɛn] *n, pl* **n's** *or* **ns** ['ɛnz] : decimocuarta letra del alfabeto inglés

nab ['næb] *vt* **nabbed; nabbing** : prender, pillar *fam*, pescar *fam*

nadir ['neɪdər, 'neɪ‚dɪr] *n* : nadir *m*, punto *m* más bajo

nag¹ ['næg] *v* **nagged; nagging** *vi* **1** COMPLAIN : quejarse, rezongar **2 to nag at** HASSLE : molestar, darle (la) lata (a alguien) — *vt* **1** PESTER : molestar, fastidiar **2** SCOLD : regañar, estarle encima a *fam*

nag² *n* **1** GRUMBLER : gruñón *m*, -ñona *f* **2** HORSE : jamelgo *m*

nail¹ ['neɪl] *vt* : clavar, sujetar con clavos

nail² *n* **1** FINGERNAIL : uña *f* ⟨nail file : lima (de uñas)⟩ ⟨nail polish : laca de uñas⟩ **2** : clavo *m* ⟨to hit the nail on the head : dar en el clavo⟩

naive *or* **naïve** [nɑ'iːv] *adj* **naiver; -est** **1** INGENUOUS : ingenuo, cándido **2** GULLIBLE : crédulo

naively [nɑ'iːvli] *adv* : ingenuamente

naïveté [‚nɑ‚iːvə'teɪ, nɑ'iːvə‚-] *n* : ingenuidad *f*

naked ['neɪkəd] *adj* **1** UNCLOTHED : desnudo **2** UNCOVERED : desenvainado (dícese de una espada), pelado (dícese de los árboles), expuesto al aire (dícese de una llama) **3** OBVIOUS, PLAIN : manifiesto, puro, desnudo ⟨the naked truth : la pura verdad⟩ **4 to the naked eye** : a simple vista

nakedly ['neɪkədli] *adv* : manifiestamente

nakedness ['neɪkədnəs] *n* : desnudez *f*

name¹ ['neɪm] *vt* **named; naming** **1** CALL : llamar, bautizar, ponerle nombre a ⟨they named the baby after his father : le pusieron al niño el nombre de su padre⟩ **2** MENTION : mentar, mencionar, dar el nombre de ⟨they have named a suspect : han dado el nombre de un sospechoso⟩ **3** APPOINT : nombrar **4 to name a price** : fijar un precio

name² *adj* PROMINENT : de renombre, de prestigio

name³ *n* **1** : nombre *m* ⟨what is your name? : ¿cómo se llama?⟩ ⟨my name is Ted : me llamo Ted⟩ ⟨first name : nombre de pila⟩ ⟨middle name : segundo nombre⟩ ⟨last name : apellido⟩ ⟨full name : nombre completo, nombre y apellido(s)⟩ ⟨she wasn't mentioned by name : no dieron su nombre⟩ **2** EPITHET : epíteto *m* ⟨to call somebody names : insultar a alguien⟩ **3** REPUTA-

TION : fama *f*, reputación *f* ⟨to make a name for oneself : darse a conocer, hacerse famoso⟩ ⟨to have a good name : tener buena fama⟩ **5 in all/everything but name** : a todos los efectos **6 in name only** : sólo de nombre **7 in the name of** : en nombre de **8 to drop names** : mencionar a gente importante

name–brand ['neɪm,brænd] *adj* : de marca conocida

name brand *n* : marca *f* conocida

nameless ['neɪmləs] *adj* **1** ANONYMOUS : anónimo **2** INDESCRIBABLE : indecible, indescriptible

namelessly ['neɪmləsli] *adv* : anónimamente

namely ['neɪmli] *adv* : a saber

namesake ['neɪm,seɪk] *n* : tocayo *m*, -ya *f*; homónimo *m*, -ma *f*

Namibian [nə'mɪbiən] *n* : namibio *m*, -bia *f* — **Namibian** *adj*

nanny ['næni] *n, pl* **nannies** : niñera *f*; nana *f* CA, Col, Mex, Ven

nanotechnology [,nænoʊtɛk'nɑlədʒi] *n, pl* **-gies** : nanotecnología *f*

nap¹ ['næp] *vi* **napped; napping** **1** : dormir, dormir la siesta **2 to be caught napping** : estar desprevenido

nap² *n* **1** SLEEP : siesta *f* ⟨to take a nap : echarse una siesta⟩ **2** FUZZ, PILE : pelo *m*, pelusa *f* (de telas)

nape ['neɪp, 'næp] *n* : nuca *f*, cerviz *f*, cogote *m*

naphtha ['næfθə] *n* : nafta *f*

napkin ['næpkən] *n* : servilleta *f*

narcissism ['nɑrsə,sɪzəm] *n* : narcisismo *m*

narcissist ['nɑrsəsɪst] *n* : narcisista *mf*

narcissistic [,nɑrsə'sɪstɪk] *adj* : narcisista

narcissus [nɑr'sɪsəs] *n, pl* **-cissus** *or* **-cissuses** *or* **-cissi** [-'sɪ,saɪ, -,si:] : narciso *m*

narcotic¹ [nɑr'kɑtɪk] *adj* : narcótico

narcotic² *n* : narcótico *m*, estupefaciente *m*

narrate ['nær,eɪt] *vt* **-rated; -rating** : narrar, relatar

narration [næ'reɪlən] *n* : narración *f*

narrative¹ ['nærətɪv] *adj* : narrativo

narrative² *n* : narración *f*, narrativa *f*, relato *m*

narrator ['nær,eɪtər] *n* : narrador *m*, -dora *f*

narrow¹ ['nær,oʊ] *vi* : estrecharse, angostarse ⟨the river narrowed : el río se estrechó⟩ — *vt* **1** : estrechar, angostar **2** LIMIT : restringir, limitar ⟨to narrow the search : limitar la búsqueda⟩

narrow² *adj* **1** : estrecho, angosto **2** LIMITED : estricto, limitado ⟨in the narrowest sense of the word : en el sentido más estricto de la palabra⟩ **3 to have a narrow escape** : escapar por un pelo

narrowly ['næroʊli] *adv* **1** BARELY : por poco **2** CLOSELY : de cerca

narrow–minded [,næroʊ'maɪndəd] *adj* : de miras estrechas

narrowness ['næroʊnəs] *n* : estrechez *f*

narrows ['næroʊz] *npl* STRAIT : estrecho *m*

nasal ['neɪzəl] *adj* : nasal

nasally ['neɪzəli] *adv* **1** : por la nariz **2** : con voz nasal

nastily ['næstəli] *adv* : con maldad, cruelmente

nastiness ['næstinəs] *n* : porquería *f*

nasty ['næsti] *adj* **nastier; -est** **1** FILTHY : sucio, mugriento **2** OBSCENE : obsceno **3** MEAN, SPITEFUL : malo, malicioso **4** UNPLEASANT : desagradable, feo **5** REPUGNANT : asqueroso, repugnante ⟨a nasty smell : un olor asqueroso⟩

natal ['neɪtəl] *adj* : natal

nation ['neɪlən] *n* : nación *f*

national¹ ['næLənəl] *adj* : nacional

national² *n* : ciudadano *m*, -na *f*; nacional *mf*

national anthem *n* : himno *m* nacional

nationalism ['næLənə,lɪzəm] *n* : nacionalismo *m*

nationalist¹ ['næLənəlɪst] *adj* : nacionalista

nationalist² *n* : nacionalista *mf*

nationalistic [,næLənə'lɪstɪk] *adj* : nacionalista

nationality [,næLə'næləti] *n, pl* **-ties** : nacionalidad *f*

nationalization [,næLənələ'zeɪlən] *n* : nacionalización *f*

nationalize ['næLənə,laɪz] *vt* **-ized; -izing** : nacionalizar

nationally ['næLənəli] *adv* : a escala nacional, a nivel nacional

national park *n* : parque *m* nacional

nationwide ['neɪlən'waɪd] *adj* : en toda la nación, por todo el país

native¹ ['neɪtɪv] *adj* **1** INNATE : innato **2** : natal ⟨her native city : su ciudad natal⟩ ⟨native speaker : hablante nativo/nativa⟩ ⟨native language : lengua materna⟩ **3** INDIGENOUS : indígena, autóctono

native² *n* **1** ABORIGINE : nativo *m*, -va *f*; indígena *mf* **2** : natural *m* ⟨he's a native of Mexico : es natural de México⟩

Native American *n* : nativo *m* americano, nativa *f* americana; indígena *m* (americano), indígena *f* (americana) — **Native American** *adj*

nativity [nə'tɪvəti, neɪ-] *n, pl* **-ties** **1** BIRTH : navidad *f* **2 the Nativity** : la Natividad, la Navidad

natty ['næti] *adj* **nattier; -est** : elegante, garboso

natural¹ ['nætlərəl] *adj* **1** : natural, de la naturaleza ⟨natural woodlands : bosques naturales⟩ ⟨natural childbirth : parto natural⟩ **2** INNATE : innato, natural **3** UNAFFECTED : natural, sin afectación **4** LIFELIKE : natural, vivo

natural² *n* **to be a natural** : tener un talento innato (para algo)

natural gas *n* : gas *m* natural

natural history *n* : historia *f* natural

naturalism ['nætlərə,lɪzəm] *n* : naturalismo *m*

naturalist ['nætlərəlɪst] *n* : naturalista *mf* — **naturalist** *adj*

naturalistic [,nætlərə'lɪstɪk] *adj* : naturalista

naturalization [,nætlərələ'zeɪlən] *n* : naturalización *f*

naturalize ['nætlərə,laɪz] *vt* **-ized; -izing** : naturalizar

naturally [ˈnætʃərəli] *adv* **1** INHERENTLY : naturalmente, intrínsecamente **2** UNAFFECTEDLY : de manera natural **3** OF COURSE : por supuesto, naturalmente

naturalness [ˈnætʃərəlnəs] *n* : naturalidad *f*

natural science *n* : ciencias *fpl* naturales

nature [ˈneɪtʃər] *n* **1** : naturaleza *f* ⟨the laws of nature : las leyes de la naturaleza⟩ **2** KIND, SORT : índole *f*, clase *f* ⟨things of this nature : cosas de esta índole⟩ **3** DISPOSITION : carácter *m*, natural *m*, naturaleza *f* ⟨it is his nature to be friendly : es de natural simpático⟩ ⟨human nature : la naturaleza humana⟩

naught [ˈnɔt] *n* **1** : nada *f* ⟨to come to naught : reducirse a nada, fracasar⟩ **2** ZERO : cero *m*

naughtily [ˈnɔt̬əli] *adv* : traviesamente, con malicia

naughtiness [ˈnɔt̬inəs] *n* : mala conducta *f*, travesuras *fpl*, malicia *f*

naughty [ˈnɔt̬i] *adj* **naughtier; -est 1** MISCHIEVOUS : travieso, pícaro **2** RISQUÉ : picante, subido de tono

nausea [ˈnɔziə, ˈnɔlə] *n* **1** SICKNESS : náuseas *fpl* **2** DISGUST : asco *m*

nauseate [ˈnɔziˌeɪt, -ʒi-, -si-, -li-] *vt* **-ated; -ating 1** SICKEN : darle náuseas (a alguien) **2** DISGUST : asquear, darle asco (a alguien)

nauseating *adj* : nauseabundo, repugnante

nauseatingly [ˈnɔziˌeɪtɪŋli, -ʒi-, -si-, -li-] *adv* : hasta el punto de dar asco ⟨nauseatingly sweet : tan dulce que da asco⟩

nauseous [ˈnɔləs, -ʒiəs] *adj* **1** SICK : mareado, con náuseas **2** SICKENING : nauseabundo

nautical [ˈnɔtɪkəl] *adj* : náutico

nautilus [ˈnɔt̬ələs] *n, pl* **-luses** *or* **-li** [-ˌlaɪ, -ˌliː] : nautilo *m*

Navajo [ˈnævəˌhoː, ˈnɑ-] *n* : navajo *m*, -ja *f* — **Navajo** *adj*

naval [ˈneɪvəl] *adj* : naval

nave [ˈneɪv] *n* : nave *f*

navel [ˈneɪvəl] *n* : ombligo *m*

navigability [ˌnævɪɡəˈbɪləti] *n* : navegabilidad *f*

navigable [ˈnævɪɡəbəl] *adj* : navegable

navigate [ˈnævəˌɡeɪt] *v* **-gated; -gating** *vi* : navegar — *vt* **1** STEER : gobernar (un barco), pilotar (un avión) **2** : navegar por (un río, etc.)

navigation [ˌnævəˈɡeɪlən] *n* : navegación *f*

navigator [ˈnævəˌɡeɪtər] *n* : navegante *mf*

navy [ˈneɪvi] *n, pl* **-vies 1** FLEET : flota *f* **2** : marina *f* de guerra, armada *f* ⟨the United States Navy : la armada de los Estados Unidos⟩ **3** *or* **navy blue** : azul *m* marino

nay[1] [ˈneɪ] *adv* : no

nay[2] *n* : no *m*, voto *m* en contra

Nazi [ˈnɑtsi, ˈnæt-] *n* : nazi *mf*

Nazism [ˈnɑtˌsɪzəm, ˈnæt-] *or* **Naziism** [ˈnɑtsiˌɪzəm, ˈnæt-] *n* : nazismo *m*

Neanderthal [niˈændərˌθɔl, -ˌtɔl] *n* **1** *or* **Neanderthal man** : Neandertal *m*, hombre *m* de Neandertal **2** *fam* : neandertal *m*

near[1] [ˈnɪr] *vt* **1** : acercarse a ⟨the ship is nearing port : el barco se está acercando al puerto⟩ **2** : estar a punto de ⟨she is nearing graduation : está a punto de graduarse⟩

near[2] *adv* **1** CLOSE : cerca ⟨my family lives quite near : mi familia vive muy cerca⟩ ⟨the day of the wedding was drawing near : se acercaba el día de la boda⟩ **2** NEARLY : casi ⟨near perfect/impossible : casi perfecto/imposible⟩ **3** (as) near as I can tell/figure : según parece, por lo visto **4** nowhere near → nowhere[1]

near[3] *adj* **1** CLOSE : cercano, próximo ⟨the nearest pharmacy : la farmacia más cercana/próxima⟩ ⟨in the near future : en un/el futuro próximo/cercano⟩ **2** CLOSER : más cercano, más próximo ⟨the near side/end : el lado/extremo más cercano/próximo, el lado/extremo de acá⟩ **3** (*close to or similar to being*) ⟨they had a near win : perdieron por poco⟩ ⟨a near miracle : casi un milagro⟩ ⟨the nearest thing to : lo más parecido a⟩ **4** : cercano (dícese de un pariente) **5** : cercano (de grado, etc.) ⟨his nearest rival : su más cercano rival⟩ **6** near and dear ⟨my nearest and dearest friend : mi amigo más íntimo⟩ **7** to the nearest ⟨it's rounded to the nearest dollar : se redondea al dólar más cercano⟩

near[4] *prep* : cerca de ⟨near the store : cerca de la tienda⟩ ⟨she lives near here : vive cerca de aquí, vive aquí cerca⟩ ⟨it was near midnight : era casi medianoche⟩ ⟨near the end : casi al final⟩ ⟨near death : al borde de la muerte⟩ ⟨to go near someone/something : acercarse a alguien/algo⟩

nearby[1] [ˌnɪrˈbaɪ, ˈnɪrˌbaɪ] *adv* : cerca

nearby[2] *adj* : cercano

nearly [ˈnɪrli] *adv* **1** ALMOST : casi ⟨nearly asleep : casi dormido⟩ **2** not nearly : ni con mucho, ni mucho menos ⟨it was not nearly so bad as I had expected : no fue ni con mucho tan malo como esperaba⟩

nearness [ˈnɪrnəs] *n* : proximidad *f*

nearsighted [ˈnɪrˌsaɪtəd] *adj* : miope, corto de vista

nearsightedly [ˈnɪrˌsaɪtədli] *adv* : con miopía

nearsightedness [ˈnɪrˌsaɪtədnəs] *n* : miopía *f*

neat [ˈniːt] *adj* **1** CLEAN, ORDERLY : ordenado, pulcro, limpio **2** UNDILUTED : solo, sin diluir **3** SIMPLE, TASTEFUL : sencillo y de buen gusto **4** CLEVER : hábil, ingenioso ⟨a neat trick : un truco ingenioso⟩ **5** GREAT, TERRIFIC : genial, estupendo

neaten [ˈniːtən] *vt* : arreglar, ordenar, poner en orden — *vi* to neaten up : poner las cosas en orden

neatly [ˈniːtli] *adv* **1** TIDILY : ordenadamente **2** CLEVERLY : ingeniosamente

neatness [ˈniːtnəs] *n* : pulcritud *f*, limpieza *f*, orden *m*

nebula ['nɛbjʊlə] *n, pl* **-lae** [-ˌliː, -ˌlaɪ] : nebulosa *f*

nebulous ['nɛbjʊləs] *adj* : nebuloso, vago

necessarily [ˌnɛsəˈsɛrəli] *adv* : necesariamente, forzosamente

necessary[1] ['nɛsəˌsɛri] *adj* **1** INEVITABLE : inevitable **2** COMPULSORY : necesario, obligatorio **3** ESSENTIAL : imprescindible, preciso, necesario

necessary[2] *n, pl* **-saries** : lo esencial, lo necesario

necessitate [nɪˈsɛsəˌteɪt] *vt* **-tated; -tating** : necesitar, requerir

necessity [nɪˈsɛsəti] *n, pl* **-ties 1** NEED : necesidad *f* **2** REQUIREMENT : requisito *m* indispensable **3** POVERTY : indigencia *f*, necesidad *f* **4** INEVITABILITY : inevitabilidad *f*

neck[1] ['nɛk] *vi* : besuquearse

neck[2] *n* **1** : cuello *m* (de una persona), pescuezo *m* (de un animal) **2** COLLAR : cuello *m* **3** : cuello *m* (de una botella), mástil *m* (de una guitarra)

necklace ['nɛkləs] *n* : collar *m*

neckline ['nɛkˌlaɪn] *n* : escote *m*

necktie ['nɛkˌtaɪ] *n* : corbata *f*

nectar ['nɛktər] *n* : néctar *m*

nectarine [ˌnɛktəˈriːn] *n* : nectarina *f*

née *or* **nee** ['neɪ] *adj* : de soltera ⟨Mrs. Smith, née Whitman : la señora Smith, de soltera Whitman⟩

need[1] ['niːd] *vt* **1** : necesitar ⟨I need your help : necesito su ayuda⟩ ⟨I need money : me falta dinero⟩ **2** REQUIRE : requerir, exigir ⟨that job needs patience : ese trabajo exige paciencia⟩ **3 to need to** : tener que ⟨he needs to study : tiene que estudiar⟩ ⟨they need to be scolded : hay que reprenderlos⟩ — *v aux* **1** MUST : tener que, deber ⟨need you shout? : ¿tienes que gritar?⟩ **2 to be needed** : hacer falta ⟨you needn't worry : no hace falta que te preocupes, no hay por qué preocuparse⟩

need[2] *n* **1** NECESSITY : necesidad *f* ⟨in case of need : en caso de necesidad⟩ **2** LACK : falta *f* ⟨the need for better training : la falta de mejor capacitación⟩ ⟨to be in need : necesitar⟩ **3** POVERTY : necesidad *f*, indigencia *f* **4 needs** *npl* : requisitos *mpl*, carencias *fpl*

needful ['niːdfəl] *adj* : necesario

needle[1] ['niːdəl] *vt* **-dled; -dling** : pinchar

needle[2] *n* **1** : aguja *f* ⟨to thread a needle : enhebrar una aguja⟩ ⟨knitting needle : aguja de tejer⟩ **2** POINTER : aguja *f*, indicador *m*

needlepoint ['niːdəlˌpɔɪnt] *n* **1** LACE : encaje *m* de mano **2** EMBROIDERY : bordado *m*

needless ['niːdləs] *adj* : innecesario

needlessly ['niːdləsli] *adv* : sin ninguna necesidad, innecesariamente

needlework ['niːdəlˌwərk] *n* : bordado *m*

needn't ['niːdənt] *contraction of* NEED NOT → **need**

needy[1] ['niːdi] *adj* **needier; -est** : necesitado

needy[2] *n* **the needy** : los necesitados *mpl*

nefarious [nɪˈfæriəs] *adj* : nefario, nefando, infame

negate [nɪˈgeɪt] *vt* **-gated; -gating 1** DENY : negar **2** NULLIFY : invalidar, anular

negation [nɪˈgeɪlən] *n* : negación *f*

negative[1] ['nɛgətɪv] *adj* : negativo

negative[2] *n* **1** : negación *f* (en lingüística) **2** : negativa *f* ⟨to answer in the negative : contestar con una negativa⟩ **3** : término *m* negativo (en matemáticas) **4** : negativo *m*, imagen *f* en negativo (en fotografía)

negatively ['nɛgətɪvli] *adv* : negativamente

neglect[1] [nɪˈglɛkt] *vt* **1** : desatender, descuidar ⟨to neglect one's health : descuidar la salud⟩ **2** : no cumplir con, faltar a ⟨to neglect one's obligations : faltar uno a sus obligaciones⟩ ⟨he neglected to tell me : omitió decírmelo⟩

neglect[2] *n* **1** : negligencia *f*, descuido *m*, incumplimiento *m* ⟨through neglect : por negligencia⟩ ⟨neglect of duty : incumplimiento del deber⟩ **2 in a state of neglect** : abandonado, descuidado

neglected [nɪˈglɛktəd] *adj* : abandonado, descuidado

neglectful [nɪˈglɛktfəl] *adj* : descuidado *m*

negligee [ˌnɛgləˈʒeɪ] *n* : negligé *m*

negligence ['nɛglɪdʒənts] *n* : descuido *m*, negligencia *f*

negligent ['nɛglɪdʒənt] *adj* : negligente, descuidado — **negligently** *adv*

negligible ['nɛglɪdʒəbəl] *adj* : insignificante, despreciable

negotiable [nɪˈgoːʃəbəl, -ʃiə-] *adj* : negociable

negotiate [nɪˈgoːʃiˌeɪt] *v* **-ated; -ating** *vi* : negociar — *vt* **1** : negociar, gestionar ⟨to negotiate a treaty : negociar un trato⟩ **2** : salvar, franquear ⟨they negotiated the obstacles : salvaron los obstáculos⟩ ⟨to negotiate a turn : tomar una curva⟩

negotiation [nɪˌgoːʃiˈeɪlən, -siˈeɪ-] *n* : negociación *f*

negotiator [nɪˈgoːʃiˌeɪtər, -siˌeɪ-] *n* : negociador *m*, -dora *f*

Negro ['niːˌgroː] *n, pl* **-groes** *dated, now sometimes offensive* : negro *m*, -gra *f*

neigh[1] ['neɪ] *vi* : relinchar

neigh[2] *n* : relincho *m*

neighbor[1] ['neɪbər] *vt* : ser vecino de, estar junto a ⟨her house neighbors mine : su casa está junto a la mía⟩ — *vi* : estar cercano, lindar, colindar ⟨her land neighbors on mine : sus tierras lindan con las mías⟩

neighbor[2] *n* **1** : vecino *m*, -na *f* **2 love thy neighbor** : ama a tu prójimo

neighborhood ['neɪbərˌhʊd] *n* **1** : barrio *m*, vecindad *f*, vecindario *m* **2 in the neighborhood of** : alrededor de, cerca de

neighboring ['neɪbərɪŋ] *adj* : vecino

neighborly ['neɪbərli] *adv* : amable, de buena vecindad

neither[1] ['niːðər, 'naɪ-] *adj* : ninguno (de los dos)

neither² *conj* **1** : ni ⟨neither asleep nor awake : ni dormido ni despierto⟩ **2** NOR : ni (tampoco) ⟨I'm not asleep — neither am I : no estoy dormido — ni yo tampoco⟩

neither³ *pron* : ninguno ⟨which do you want? neither : ¿cuál quieres? ninguno⟩ ⟨neither of the two sisters : ninguna de las dos hermanas⟩

nemesis ['nɛməsɪs] *n, pl* **-eses** [-ˌsiːz] **1** RIVAL : rival *mf* **2** RETRIBUTION : justo castigo *m*

neologism [ni'aləˌdʒɪzəm] *n* : neologismo *m*

neon¹ ['niːˌɑn] *adj* : de neón ⟨neon sign : letrero de neón⟩

neon² *n* : neón *m*

neophyte ['niːəˌfaɪt] *n* : neófito *m*, -ta *f*

Nepali [nə'pɔli, -'pɑ-, -'pæ-] *n* : nepalés *m*, -lesa *f* — **Nepali** *adj*

nephew ['nɛˌfjuː, *chiefly Brit* 'nɛˌvjuː] *n* : sobrino *m*

nepotism ['nɛpəˌtɪzəm] *n* : nepotismo *m*

Neptune ['nɛpˌtuːn, -ˌtjuːn] *n* : Neptuno *m*

nerd ['nərd] *n* : ganso *m*, -sa *f*

nerve ['nərv] *n* **1** : nervio *m* **2** COURAGE : coraje *m*, valor *m*, fuerza *f* de la voluntad ⟨to lose one's nerve : perder el valor⟩ **3** AUDACITY, GALL : atrevimiento *m*, descaro *m* ⟨of all the nerve!, some/what nerve! : ¡qué descaro!⟩ ⟨you have a lot of nerve! : ¡qué cara tienes!⟩ **4 nerves** *npl* : nervios *mpl* ⟨to be a bag/bundle of nerves : ser un manojo de nervios⟩ ⟨to calm one's nerves : calmarse (los nervios)⟩ ⟨to get on someone's nerves : crisparle los nervios a alguien⟩ ⟨to have a (bad) case of nerves : estar nerviosísimo⟩ ⟨to have nerves of steel : tener nervios de acero⟩ ⟨to have one's nerves on edge : tener los nervios de punta⟩ ⟨a war of nerves : una guerra de nervios⟩ **5 to hit/strike/touch a nerve** : poner el dedo en la llaga

nerve–racking *or* **nerve–wracking** ['nərvˌrækɪŋ] *adj* : estresante, desesperante, angustioso

nervous ['nərvəs] *adj* **1** : nervioso ⟨the nervous system : el sistema nervioso⟩ **2** EXCITABLE : nervioso ⟨to get nervous : excitarse, ponerse nervioso⟩ **3** FEARFUL : miedoso, temeroso

nervous breakdown *n* → **breakdown**

nervously ['nərvəsli] *adv* : nerviosamente

nervousness ['nərvəsnəs] *n* : nerviosismo *m*, nerviosidad *f*, ansiedad *f*

nervy ['nərvi] *adj* **nervier; -est 1** COURAGEOUS : valiente **2** IMPUDENT : atrevido, descarado, fresco *fam* **3** NERVOUS : nervioso

nest¹ ['nɛst] *vi* : anidar

nest² *n* **1** : nido *m* (de un ave), avispero *m* (de una avispa), madriguera *f* (de un animal) **2** REFUGE : nido *m*, refugio *m* **3** SET : juego *m* ⟨a nest of tables : un juego de mesitas⟩

nestle ['nɛsəl] *vi* **-tled; -tling** : acurrucarse, arrimarse cómodamente

net¹ ['nɛt] *vt* **netted; netting 1** CATCH : pescar, atrapar con una red **2** CLEAR : ganar neto ⟨they netted $5000 : ganaron $5000 netos⟩ **3** YIELD : producir neto

net² *adj* : neto ⟨net weight : peso neto⟩ ⟨net gain : ganancia neta⟩

net³ *n* : red *f*, malla *f*

nether ['nɛðər] *adj* **1** : inferior, más bajo **2 the nether regions** : el infierno

nettle¹ ['nɛt̮əl] *vt* **-tled; -tling** : irritar, provocar, molestar

nettle² *n* : ortiga *f*

network ['nɛtˌwərk] *n* **1** SYSTEM : red *f* ⟨social network : red social⟩ **2** CHAIN : cadena *f* ⟨a network of supermarkets : una cadena de supermercados⟩

neural ['nʊrəl, 'njʊr-] *adj* : neural

neuralgia [nʊ'rældʒə, nju-] *n* : neuralgia *f*

neuritis [nʊ'raɪt̮əs, nju-] *n, pl* **-ritides** [-'rɪt̮əˌdiːz] *or* **-ritises** : neuritis *f*

neurological [ˌnʊrə'lɑdʒɪkəl, ˌnjʊr-] *or* **neurologic** [ˌnʊrə'lɑdʒɪk, ˌnjʊr-] *adj* : neurológico

neurologist [nʊ'ralədʒɪst, nju-] *n* : neurólogo *m*, -ga *f*

neurology [nʊ'ralədʒi, nju-] *n* : neurología *f*

neurosis [nʊ'roːsɪs, nju-] *n, pl* **-roses** [-ˌsiːz] : neurosis *f*

neurotic¹ [nʊ'rɑt̮ɪk, nju-] *adj* : neurótico

neurotic² *n* : neurótico *m*, -ca *f*

neuter¹ ['nuːt̮ər, 'njuː-] *vt* : castrar

neuter² *adj* : neutro

neutral¹ ['nuːtrəl, 'njuː-] *adj* **1** IMPARTIAL : neutral, imparcial ⟨to remain neutral : permanecer neutral⟩ **2** : neutro ⟨a neutral color : un color neutro⟩ **3** : neutro (en la química o la electricidad)

neutral² *n* : punto *m* muerto (de un automóvil)

neutrality [nuː'træləti, nju-] *n* : neutralidad *f*

neutralization [ˌnuːtrələ'zeɪlə[n](o), ˌnju-] *n* : neutralización *f*

neutralize ['nuːtrəˌlaɪz, 'njuː-] *vt* **-ized; -izing** : neutralizar

neutron ['nuːˌtrɑn, 'njuː-] *n* : neutrón *m*

never ['nɛvər] *adv* **1** : nunca, jamás ⟨he never studies : nunca estudia⟩ **2 never again** : nunca más, nunca jamás **3 never mind** : no importa

never–ending ['nɛvər'ɛndɪŋ] *adj* ENDLESS : interminable, inacabable, sin fin

nevermore [ˌnɛvər'mor] *adv* : nunca más

nevertheless [ˌnɛvərðə'lɛs] *adv* : sin embargo, no obstante

new ['nuː, 'njuː] *adj* **1** : nuevo ⟨a new dress : un vestido nuevo⟩ **2** RECENT : nuevo, reciente ⟨what's new? : ¿qué hay de nuevo?⟩ ⟨a new arrival : un recién llegado⟩ **3** DIFFERENT : nuevo, distinto ⟨this problem is new : este problema es distinto⟩ ⟨new ideas : ideas nuevas⟩ **4 like new** : como nuevo

newborn ['nuːˌbɔrn, 'njuː-] *adj* : recién nacido

newcomer ['nuːˌkʌmər, 'njuː-] *n* : recién llegado *m*, recién llegada *f*

newfangled ['nuː'fæŋɡəld, 'njuː-] *adj* : novedoso

newfound ['nuːˌfaʊnd, 'njuː-] *adj* : recién descubierto

newly ['nu:li, 'nju:-] *adv* : recién, recientemente
newlywed ['nu:li‚wɛd, 'nju:-] *n* : recién
casado *m*, -da *f*
new moon *n* : luna *f* nueva
newness ['nu:nəs, 'nju:-] *n* : novedad *f*
news ['nu:z, 'nju:z] *n* 1 INFORMATION
: noticias *fpl* ⟨good/bad news : buenas/
malas noticias⟩ ⟨to break the news to
someone : darle la noticia a alguien⟩
⟨further news : más noticias⟩ ⟨that's
news to me! : ¡(es la) primera noticia (que
tengo)!⟩ ⟨no news is good news : (el) que
no haya noticias es (una) buena noti-
cia⟩ 2 : noticias *fpl* ⟨local/international
news : noticias locales/internacionales⟩
⟨to be in the news : salir en las noti-
cias⟩ 3 NEWSCAST : noticias *fpl*, noticiero *m*, informativo *m*, noticiario *m* ⟨the
nightly news : el noticiero nocturno⟩ ⟨I
saw it on the news : lo vi en las noticias⟩
newscast ['nu:z‚kæst, 'nju:z-] *n* : noticiero *m*, informativo *m*, noticiario *m*
newscaster ['nu:z‚kæstər, 'nju:z-] *n* : presentador *m*, -dora *f*; locutor *m*, -tora *f*
newsgroup ['nu:z‚gru:p, 'nju:z-] *n* : grupo
m de noticias
newsletter ['nu:z‚lɛtər, 'nju:z-] *n* : boletín
m informativo
newsman ['nu:zmən, 'nju:z-, -‚mæn] *n, pl*
-men [-mən, -‚mɛn] : periodista *m*, reportero *m*
newspaper ['nu:z‚peɪpər, 'nju:z-] *n* 1
: periódico *m*, diario *m* ⟨newspaper articles : artículos periodísticos⟩ ⟨newspa-
per reporter : periodista⟩ 2 : papel *m* de
periódico
newspaperman ['nu:z‚peɪpər‚mæn, 'nju:z-]
n, pl **-men** [-mən, -‚mɛn] 1 REPORTER
: periodista *m*, reportero *m* 2 : dueño *m*
de un periódico
newsprint ['nu:z‚prɪnt, 'nju:z-] *n* : papel *m*
de prensa
newsstand ['nu:z‚stænd, 'nju:z-] *n* : quiosco *m*, puesto *m* de periódicos
newswoman ['nu:z‚wʊmən, 'nju:z-] *n, pl*
-women [-‚wɪmən] : periodista *f*, reportera *f*
newsworthy ['nu:z‚wərði, 'nju:z-] *adj* : de
interés periodístico
newsy ['nu:zi:, 'nju:-] *adj* **newsier; -est**
: lleno de noticias
newt ['nu:t, 'nju:t] *n* : tritón *m*
New Testament *n* : Nuevo Testamento *m*
New Year *n* : Año *m* Nuevo
New Year's Day *n* : día *m* del Año Nuevo
New Year's Eve *n* : noche *f* de Fin de Año,
Nochevieja *f*
New Yorker [nu:'jɔrkər, nju:-] *n* : neo-
yorquino *m*, -na *f*
New Zealander [nu:'zi:ləndər, nju:-] *n*
: neozelandés *m*, -desa *f*
next¹ ['nɛkst] *adv* 1 AFTERWARD
: después, luego ⟨what will you do next?
: ¿qué harás después?⟩ 2 NOW
: después, ahora, entonces ⟨next I will
sing a song : ahora voy a cantar una can-
ción⟩ 3 : la próxima vez ⟨when next we
meet : la próxima vez que nos encontre-
mos⟩

next² *adj* 1 ADJACENT : contiguo, de al
lado 2 COMING : que viene, próximo
⟨next Friday : el viernes que viene⟩ 3
FOLLOWING : siguiente ⟨the next year
: el año siguiente⟩
next–door ['nɛkst'dor] *adj* : de al lado
next–of–kin *n, pl* **next–of–kin** : familiar
m más cercano, pariente *m* más cercano
next to¹ *adv* ALMOST : casi, prácticamente
⟨next to impossible : casi imposible⟩
next to² *prep* : junto a, al lado de
nexus ['nɛksəs] *n* : nexo *m*
nib ['nɪb] *n* : plumilla *f*
nibble¹ ['nɪbəl] *v* **-bled; -bling** *vt* : pellizcar, mordisquear, picar — *vi* : picar
nibble² *n* : mordisco *m*
Nicaraguan [‚nɪkə'rɑgwən] *n* : nicaragüense *mf* — **Nicaraguan** *adj*
nice ['naɪs] *adj* **nicer; nicest** 1 REFINED
: pulido, refinado 2 SUBTLE : fino, sutil 3 PLEASING : agradable, bueno,
lindo ⟨nice weather : buen tiempo⟩ 4
RESPECTABLE : bueno, decente 5 **nice
and** : bien, muy ⟨nice and hot : bien ca-
liente⟩ ⟨nice and slow : despacito⟩
nicely ['naɪsli] *adv* 1 KINDLY : amablemente 2 POLITELY : con buenos modales 3 ATTRACTIVELY : de buen gusto
niceness ['naɪsnəs] *n* : simpatía *f*, amabilidad *f*
nicety ['naɪsəti] *n, pl* **-ties** 1 DETAIL,
SUBTLETY : sutileza *f*, detalle *m* 2 **nice-
ties** *npl* : lujos *mpl*, detalles *mpl*
niche ['nɪtʃ] *n* 1 RECESS : nicho *m*, hornacina *f* 2 : nicho *m*, hueco *m* ⟨to make
a niche for oneself : hacerse un hueco,
encontrarse una buena posición⟩
nick¹ ['nɪk] *vt* : cortar, hacer una muesca en
nick² *n* 1 CUT : corte *m*, muesca *f* 2 **in
the nick of time** : en el momento crítico,
justo a tiempo
nickel ['nɪkəl] *n* 1 : níquel *m* 2 : moneda
f de cinco centavos
nickname¹ ['nɪk‚neɪm] *vt* **-named; -nam-
ing** : apodar
nickname² *n* : apodo *m*, mote *m*, sobrenombre *m*
nicotine ['nɪkə‚ti:n] *n* : nicotina *f*
niece ['ni:s] *n* : sobrina *f*
Nigerian [naɪ'dʒɪriən] *n* : nigeriano *m*, -na
f — **Nigerian** *adj*
niggardly ['nɪgərdli] *adj* : mezquino,
tacaño
niggling ['nɪgəlɪn] *adj* 1 PETTY : insignificante 2 PERSISTENT : constante,
persistente ⟨a niggling doubt : una duda
constante⟩
nigh¹ ['naɪ] *adv* 1 NEARLY : casi 2 **to
draw nigh** : acercarse, avecinarse
nigh² *adj* : cercano, próximo
night¹ ['naɪt] *adj* : nocturno, de la noche
⟨the night sky : el cielo nocturno⟩ ⟨night
shift : turno de la noche⟩
night² *n* 1 EVENING : noche *f* ⟨at night
: de noche⟩ ⟨last night : anoche⟩ ⟨to-
morrow night : mañana por la noche⟩ 2
DARKNESS : noche *f*, oscuridad *f* ⟨night
fell : cayó la noche⟩
nightclothes ['naɪt‚klo:ðz, -‚klo:z] *npl*
: ropa *f* de dormir

nightclub ['naɪt,klʌb] *n* : cabaret *m*; club *m* nocturno; boliche *m Arg, Uru*
night crawler ['naɪt,krɔlər] *n* EARTH-WORM : lombriz *f* (de tierra)
nightdress ['naɪt,drɛs] → **nightgown**
nightfall ['naɪt,fɔl] *n* : anochecer *m*
nightgown ['naɪt,gaʊn] *n* : camisón *m* (de noche)
nightie ['naɪti] *n* : camisón *m* corto (de noche)
nightingale ['naɪtən,geɪl, 'naɪtɪŋ-] *n* : ruiseñor *m*
nightlife ['naɪt,laɪf] *n* : vida *f* nocturna
nightly[1] ['naɪtli] *adv* : cada noche, todas las noches
nightly[2] *adj* : de todas las noches
nightmare ['naɪt,mær] *n* : pesadilla *f*
nightmarish ['naɪt,mærɪʃ] *adj* : de pesadilla
night owl *n* : noctámbulo *m*, -la *f*
night school *n* : escuela *f* nocturna, clases *fpl* nocturnas
nightshade ['naɪt,ʃeɪd] *n* : hierba *f* mora
nightshirt ['naɪt,ʃərt] *n* : camisa *f* de dormir
nightstick ['naɪt,stɪk] *n* : porra *f*
night table *or* **nightstand** ['naɪt,stænd] *n* : mesita *f*, mesilla *f Spain* (de noche)
nighttime ['naɪt,taɪm] *n* : noche *f*
nihilism ['naɪə,lɪzəm] *n* : nihilismo *m*
nil ['nɪl] *n* : nada *f*, cero *m*
nimble ['nɪmbəl] *adj* **nimbler; -blest 1** AGILE : ágil **2** CLEVER : hábil, ingenioso
nimbleness ['nɪmbəlnəs] *n* : agilidad *f*
nimbly ['nɪmbli] *adv* : con agilidad, ágilmente
nincompoop ['nɪnkəm,puːp, 'nɪŋ-] *n* FOOL : tonto *m*, -ta *f*; bobo *m*, -ba *f*
nine[1] ['naɪn] *adj* **1** : nueve ⟨he's nine (years old) : tiene nueve años⟩ **2 nine times out of ten** : casi siempre
nine[2] *n* : nueve *m* ⟨the nine of hearts : el nueve de corazones⟩
nine[3] *pron* : nueve ⟨it's nine (o'clock) : son las nueve⟩ ⟨there are nine of us : somos nueve⟩
nine hundred[1] *adj* : novecientos
nine hundred[2] *n* : novecientos *m*
ninepins ['naɪn,pɪnz] *n* : bolos *mpl*
nineteen[1] ['naɪn'tiːn] *adj & pron* : diecinueve
nineteen[2] *n* : diecinueve *m*
nineteenth[1] ['naɪn'tiːnθ] *adj* : decimonoveno, decimonono ⟨the nineteenth century : el siglo diecinueve⟩
nineteenth[2] *n* **1** : decimonoveno *m*, -na *f*; decimonono *m*, -na *f* (en una serie) **2** : diecinueveavo *m*, diecinueveava parte *f*
ninetieth[1] ['naɪnt̬iəθ] *adj* : nonagésimo
ninetieth[2] *n* **1** : nonagésimo *m*, -ma *f* (en una serie) **2** : noventavo *m*, noventava parte *f*
ninety[1] ['naɪnt̬i] *adj & pron* : noventa
ninety[2] *n, pl* **-ties** : noventa *m*
ninny ['nɪni] *n, pl* **ninnies** FOOL : tonto *m*, -ta *f*; bobo *m*, -ba *f*
ninth[1] ['naɪnθ] *adv* : en noveno lugar
ninth[2] *adj* : noveno
ninth[3] *n* **1** : noveno *m*, -na *f* (en una serie) ⟨(on) the ninth of June : el nueve de junio⟩ **2** : noveno *m*, novena parte *f*

nip[1] ['nɪp] *vt* **nipped; nipping 1** PINCH : pellizcar **2** BITE : morder, mordisquear **3 to nip in the bud** : cortar de raíz
nip[2] *n* **1** TANG : sabor *m* fuerte **2** PINCH : pellizco *m* **3** NIBBLE : mordisco *m* **4** SWALLOW : trago *m*, traguito *m* **5 there's a nip in the air** : hace fresco
nipple ['nɪpəl] *n* : pezón *m* (de una mujer), tetilla *f* (de un hombre)
nippy ['nɪpi] *adj* **nippier; -est 1** SHARP : fuerte, picante **2** CHILLY : frío ⟨it's nippy today : hoy hace frío⟩
nit ['nɪt] *n* : liendre *f*
nitrate ['naɪ,treɪt] *n* : nitrato *m*
nitric acid ['naɪtrɪk] *n* : ácido *m* nítrico
nitrogen ['naɪtrədʒən] *n* : nitrógeno *m*
nitroglycerin *or* **nitroglycerine** [,naɪtro-'glɪsərən] *n* : nitroglicerina *f*
nitwit ['nɪt,wɪt] *n* : zonzo *m*, -za *f*; bobo *m*, -ba *f*
no[1] ['noː] *adv* : no ⟨are you leaving? — no : ¿te vas? — no⟩ ⟨no less than : no menos de⟩ ⟨to say no : decir que no⟩ ⟨like it or no : quieras o no quieras⟩
no[2] *adj* **1** : ninguno ⟨it's no trouble : no es ningún problema⟩ ⟨she has no money : no tiene dinero⟩ ⟨with little or no experience : con poca o ninguna experiencia⟩ ⟨the sign says "no smoking" : el letrero dice "no fumar"⟩ ⟨there's no arguing with him : no se puede discutir con él⟩ **2** (*indicating a small amount*) ⟨we'll be there in no time : enseguida llegamos⟩ **3** (*expressing that someone or something is not the kind of person or thing being described*) ⟨he's no liar : no es mentiroso⟩ ⟨that's no excuse : eso no es ninguna excusa⟩
no[3] *n, pl* **noes** *or* **nos** ['noːz] **1** DENIAL : no *m* ⟨I won't take no for an answer : no aceptaré un no por respuesta⟩ **2** : voto *f* en contra ⟨the noes have it : se ha rechazado la moción⟩
nobility [noˈbɪlət̬i] *n* : nobleza *f*
noble[1] ['noːbəl] *adj* **nobler; -blest 1** ILLUSTRIOUS : noble, glorioso **2** ARISTOCRATIC : noble **3** STATELY : majestuoso, magnífico **4** LOFTY : noble, elevado ⟨noble sentiments : sentimientos elevados⟩
noble[2] *n* : noble *mf*, aristócrata *mf*
nobleman ['noːbəlmən] *n, pl* **-men** [-mən, -,mɛn] : noble *m*, aristócrata *m*
nobleness ['noːbəlnəs] *n* : nobleza *f*
noblewoman ['noːbəl,wʊmən] *n, pl* **-women** [-,wɪmən] : noble *f*, aristócrata *f*
nobly ['noːbli] *adv* : noblemente
nobody[1] ['noːbədi, -,bɑdi] *n, pl* **-bodies** : don nadie *m* ⟨he's a mere nobody : es un don nadie⟩
nobody[2] *pron* : nadie
nocturnal [nɑkˈtərnəl] *adj* : nocturno
nocturne ['nɑk,tərn] *n* : nocturno *m*
nod[1] ['nɑd] *v* **nodded; nodding** *vi* **1** : saludar con la cabeza, asentir con la cabeza **2 to nod off** : dormirse, quedarse dormido — *vt* : inclinar (la cabeza) ⟨to nod one's head in agreement : asentir con la cabeza⟩
nod[2] *n* : saludo *m* con la cabeza, señal *m* con la cabeza, señal *m* de asentimiento

node ['no:d] *n* : nudo *m* (de una planta)
nodule ['nɑˌdʒu:l] *n* : nódulo *m*
noel [no'ɛl] *n* **1** CAROL : villancico *m* de Navidad **2 Noel** CHRISTMAS : Navidad *f*
noes → **no³**
noise *n* : ruido *m*
noiseless ['nɔɪzləs] *adj* : silencioso, sin ruido
noiselessly ['nɔɪzləsli] *adv* : silenciosamente
noisemaker ['nɔɪzˌmeɪkər] *n* : matraca *f*
noisiness ['nɔɪzinəs] *n* : ruido *m*
noisy ['nɔɪzi] *adj* **noisier; -est** : ruidoso — **noisily** ['nɔɪzəli] *adv*
nomad¹ ['no:ˌmæd] → **nomadic**
nomad² *n* : nómada *mf*
nomadic [no'mædɪk] *adj* : nómada
nomenclature ['no:mənˌkleɪtʃər] *n* : nomenclatura *f*
nominal ['nɑmənəl] *adj* **1** : nominal ⟨the nominal head of his party : el jefe nominal de su partido⟩ **2** TRIFLING : insignificante
nominally ['nɑmənəli] *adv* : sólo de nombre, nominalmente
nominate ['nɑməˌneɪt] *vt* **-nated; -nating 1** PROPOSE : proponer (como candidato), nominar **2** APPOINT : nombrar
nomination [ˌnɑmə'neɪʃən] *n* **1** PROPOSAL : propuesta *f*, postulación *f* **2** APPOINTMENT : nombramiento *m*
nominative¹ ['nɑmənəˌtɪv] *adj* : nominativo
nominative² *n or* **nominative case** : nominativo *m*
nominee [ˌnɑmə'ni:] *n* : candidato *m*, -ta *f*
non- [ˌnɑn] *pref* : no ⟨non-smoker : no fumador⟩
nonaddictive [ˌnɑnə'dɪktɪv] *adj* : que no crea dependencia
nonalcoholic [ˌnɑnˌælkə'hɔlɪk] *adj* : sin alcohol, no alcohólico
nonaligned [ˌnɑnə'laɪnd] *adj* : no alineado
nonbeliever [ˌnɑnbə'li:vər] *n* : no creyente *mf*
nonbreakable [ˌnɑn'breɪkəbəl] *adj* : irrompible
nonce ['nɑnts] *n* **for the nonce** : por el momento
nonchalance [ˌnɑnʃə'lɑnts] *n* : indiferencia *f*, despreocupación *f*
nonchalant [ˌnɑnʃə'lɑnt] *adj* : indiferente, despreocupado, impasible
nonchalantly [ˌnɑnʃə'lɑntli] *adv* : con aire despreocupado, con indiferencia
noncombatant [ˌnɑnkəm'bætənt, -'kɑmbə-] *n* : no combatiente *mf*
noncommissioned officer [ˌnɑnkə'mɪlənd] *n* : suboficial *mf*
noncommittal [ˌnɑnkə'mɪtəl] *adj* : evasivo, que no se compromete
nonconductor [ˌnɑnkən'dʌktər] *n* : aislante *m*
nonconformist [ˌnɑnkən'fɔrmɪst] *n* : inconformista *mf*, inconforme *mf*
nonconformity [ˌnɑnkən'fɔrməti] *n* : inconformidad *f*, no conformidad *f*
noncontagious [ˌnɑnkən'teɪdʒəs] *adj* : no contagioso

nondenominational [ˌnɑndɪˌnamə'neɪlənəl] *adj* : no sectario
nondescript [ˌnɑndɪ'skrɪpt] *adj* : anodino, soso
nondiscriminatory [ˌnɑndɪ'skrɪmənəˌtori] *adj* : no discriminatorio
nondrinker [ˌnɑn'drɪŋkər] *n* : abstemio *m*, -mia *f*
none¹ ['nʌn] *adv* : de ninguna manera, de ningún modo, nada ⟨he was none too happy : no se sintió nada contento⟩ ⟨I'm none the worse for it : no estoy peor por ello⟩ ⟨none too soon : a buena hora⟩
none² *pron* **1** (*not one*) : ninguno ⟨there's none left : no queda ninguno/ninguna⟩ ⟨none of the cities : ninguna de las ciudades⟩ ⟨do you have any ideas? none whatsoever : ¿se te ocurre algo? no, nada⟩ **2** (*no amount or part*) : nada, ninguna parte ⟨there's none left : no queda nada⟩ ⟨none of it makes any sense : no tiene ningún sentido⟩ ⟨it's none of your business : no es asunto tuyo⟩ **3 to have none of** : no permitir, no aceptar **4 ∼ but** : sólo, solamente **5 none other than** : ni más ni menos que **6 second to none** : insuperable
nonentity [ˌnɑn'entəti] *n, pl* **-ties** : persona *f* insignificante, nulidad *f*
nonessential [ˌnɑnɪ'sɛntʃəl] *adj* : secundario, no esencial
nonessentials [ˌnɑnɪ'sɛntʃəlz] *npl* : cosas *fpl* secundarias, cosas *fpl* accesorias
nonetheless [ˌnʌnðə'lɛs] *adv* : sin embargo, no obstante
nonexistence [ˌnɑnɪg'zɪstənts] *n* : inexistencia *f*
nonexistent [ˌnɑnɪg'zɪstənt] *adj* : inexistente
nonfat [ˌnɑn'fæt] *adj* : sin grasa
nonfattening [ˌnɑn'fætənɪŋ] *adj* : que no engorda
nonfiction [ˌnɑn'fɪkʃən] *n* : no ficción *f*
nonflammable [ˌnɑn'flæməbəl] *adj* : no inflamable
nonintervention [ˌnɑnˌɪntər'vɛntʃən] *n* : no intervención *f*
noninvasive [ˌnɑnɪn'veɪsɪv] *adj* : no invasivo
nonmalignant [ˌnɑnmə'lɪgnənt] *adj* : no maligno, benigno
nonnegotiable [ˌnɑnnɪ'goːʃəbəl, -ʃiə-] *adj* : no negociable
nonpareil¹ [ˌnɑnpə'rɛl] *adj* : sin parangón, sin par
nonpareil² *n* : persona *f* sin igual, cosa *f* sin par
nonpartisan [ˌnɑn'pɑrtəzən, -sən] *adj* : imparcial
nonpaying [ˌnɑn'peɪɪŋ] *adj* : que no paga
nonpayment [ˌnɑn'peɪmənt] *n* : impago *m*, falta *f* de pago
nonperson [ˌnɑn'pərsən] *n* : persona *f* sin derechos
nonplus [ˌnɑn'plʌs] *vt* **-plussed; -plussing** : confundir, desconcertar, dejar perplejo
nonprescription [ˌnɑnprɪ'skrɪpʃən] *adj* : disponible sin receta del médico
nonproductive [ˌnɑnprə'dʌktɪv] *adj* : improductivo

nonprofit [ˌnɑnˈprɑfət] *adj* : sin fines lucrativos

nonproliferation [ˌnɑnprəˌlɪfəˈreɪʃən] *adj* : no proliferación

nonresident [ˌnɑnˈrɛzədənt, -ˌdɛnt] *n* : no residente *mf*

nonscheduled [ˌnɑnˈskɛˌdʒuːld] *adj* : no programado, no regular

nonsectarian [ˌnɑnˌsɛkˈtæriən] *adj* : no sectario

nonsense [ˈnɑnˌsɛnʦ, ˈnɑnʦənʦ] *n* : tonterías *fpl*, disparates *mpl*

nonsensical [nɑnˈsɛnʦɪkəl] *adj* ABSURD : absurdo, disparatado — **nonsensically** [-kli] *adv*

nonsmoker [ˌnɑnˈsmoːkər] *n* : no fumador *m*, -dora *f*; persona *f* que no fuma

nonsmoking [nɑnˈsmoːkɪŋ] *adj* **1** → **nosmoking 2** : que no fuma, no fumador (dícese de una persona)

nonstandard [ˌnɑnˈstændərd] *adj* : no regular, no estándar

nonstick [ˌnɑnˈstɪk] *adj* : antiadherente

nonstop[1] [ˌnɑnˈstɑp] *adv* : sin parar ⟨he talked nonstop : habló sin parar⟩

nonstop[2] *adj* : directo, sin escalas ⟨nonstop flight : vuelo directo⟩

nonsupport [ˌnɑnsəˈpɔrt] *n* : falta *f* de manutención

nontaxable [ˌnɑnˈtæksəbəl] *adj* : exento de impuestos

nontoxic [ˌnɑnˈtɑksɪk] *adj* : no tóxico

nontransferable [ˌnɑnˌtrænʦˈfərəbəl] *adj* : intransferible

nonviolence [ˌnɑnˈvaɪlənʦ, -ˈvaɪə-] *n* : no violencia *f*

nonviolent [ˌnɑnˈvaɪlənt, -ˈvaɪə-] *adj* : pacífico, no violento

noodle [ˈnuːdəl] *n* : fideo *m*, tallarín *m*

nook [ˈnʊk] *n* : rincón *m*, recoveco *m*, escondrijo *m* ⟨in every nook and cranny : en todos los rincones⟩

noon [ˈnuːn] *n* : mediodía *m*

noonday [ˈnuːnˌdeɪ] *n* : mediodía *m* ⟨the noonday sun : el sol de mediodía⟩

no one *pron* NOBODY : nadie

noontime [ˈnuːnˌtaɪm] *n* : mediodía *m*

noose [ˈnuːs] *n* **1** LASSO : lazo *m*, cuerda *f* (con un nudo corredizo) **2 hangman's noose** : soga *f*

nope [ˈnoːp] *adv fam* → **no**[1]

nor [ˈnɔr] *conj* : ni ⟨neither good nor bad : ni bueno ni malo⟩ ⟨nor I! : ¡ni yo tampoco!⟩

Nordic [ˈnɔrdɪk] *adj* : nórdico

norm [ˈnɔrm] *n* **1** STANDARD : norma *f*, modelo *m* **2** CUSTOM, RULE : regla *f* general, lo normal

normal [ˈnɔrməl] *adj* : normal — **normally** *adv*

normalcy [ˈnɔrməlsi] *n* : normalidad *f*

normality [nɔrˈmæləti] *n* : normalidad *f*

normalization [ˌnɔrmələˈzeɪʃən] *n* : normalización *f*, regularización *f*

normalize [ˈnɔrməˌlaɪz] *vt* : normalizar

Norse [ˈnɔrs] *adj* : nórdico

north[1] [ˈnɔrθ] *adv* : al norte

north[2] *adj* : norte, del norte ⟨the north coast : la costa del norte⟩

north[3] *n* **1** : norte *m* **2 the North** : el Norte *m*

North American *n* : norteamericano *m*, -na *f* — **North American** *adj*

northbound[1] [ˈnɔrθˌbaʊnd] *adv* : con rumbo al norte

northbound[2] *adj* : que va hacia el norte

northeast[1] [nɔrθˈiːst] *adv* : hacia el nordeste

northeast[2] *adj* : nordeste, del nordeste

northeast[3] *n* : nordeste *m*, noreste *m*

northeasterly[1] [nɔrθˈiːstərli] *adv* : hacia el nordeste

northeasterly[2] *adj* : nordeste, del nordeste

northeastern [nɔrθˈiːstərn] *adj* : nordeste, del nordeste

northerly[1] [ˈnɔrðərli] *adv* : hacia el norte

northerly[2] *adj* : del norte ⟨a northerly wind : un viento del norte⟩

northern [ˈnɔrðərn] *adj* : norte, norteño, septentrional

Northerner [ˈnɔrðərnər] *n* : norteño *m*, -ña *f*

northern lights → **aurora borealis**

North Pole : Polo *m* Norte

North Star *n* : estrella *f* polar

northward [ˈnɔrθwərd] *adv & adj* : hacia el norte

northwest[1] [nɔrθˈwɛst] *adv* : hacia el noroeste

northwest[2] *adj* : del noroeste

northwest[3] *n* : noroeste *m*

northwesterly[1] [nɔrθˈwɛstərli] *adv* : hacia el noroeste

northwesterly[2] *adj* : del noroeste

northwestern [nɔrθˈwɛstərn] *adj* : noroeste, del noroeste

Norwegian [nɔrˈwiːdʒən] *n* **1** : noruego *m*, -ga *f* **2** : noruego *m* (idioma) — **Norwegian** *adj*

nose[1] [ˈnoːz] *v* **nosed; nosing** *vt* **1** SMELL : olfatear **2** : empujar con el hocico ⟨the dog nosed open the bag : el perro abrió el saco con el hocico⟩ **3** EDGE, MOVE : mover poco a poco — *vi* **1** PRY : entrometerse, meter las narices **2** EDGE : avanzar poco a poco

nose[2] *n* **1** : nariz *f* (de una persona), hocico *m* (de un animal) ⟨to blow one's nose : sonarse las narices⟩ **2** SMELL : olfato *m*, sentido *m* del olfato **3** FRONT : parte *f* delantera, nariz *f* (de un avión), proa *f* (de un barco) **4 to be right on the nose** : dar en el clavo **5 to follow one's nose** : dejarse guiar por el instinto **6 to look down one's nose at someone** : mirar a alguien por encima del hombro **7 to pay through the nose** : pagar un ojo de la cara **8 to poke/stick one's nose in** : meter las narices en **9 to turn up one's nose at** : hacerle ascos a **10 to win by a nose** : ganar por un pelo **11 under one's nose** : delante de las narices

nosebleed [ˈnoːzˌbliːd] *n* : hemorragia *f* nasal

nosed [ˈnoːzd] *adj* : de nariz ⟨big-nosed : de nariz grande, narigón⟩

nosedive [ˈnoːzˌdaɪv] *n* **1** : descenso *m* en picada (de un avión) **2** : caída *f* súbita (de precios, etc.)

nose–dive ['no:z,daɪv] *vi* : descender en picada, caer en picada

no–smoking *adj* : de no fumar, de/para no fumadores (dícese de un área, etc.)

nostalgia [nɑ'stældʒə, nə-] *n* : nostalgia *f*

nostalgic [nɑ'stældʒɪk, nə-] *adj* : nostálgico

nostril ['nɑstrəl] *n* : ventana *f* de la nariz

nostrum ['nɑstrəm] *n* : panacea *f*

nosy *or* **nosey** ['no:zi] *adj* **nosier; -est** : entrometido

not ['nɑt] *adv* **1** (*used to form a negative*) : no ⟨she is not tired : no está cansada⟩ ⟨not many came : no vinieron muchos⟩ ⟨not to say something would be wrong : no decir nada sería injusto⟩ ⟨not at all : en absoluto⟩ ⟨not a chance : de ninguna manera⟩ ⟨not only . . . but also . . . : no sólo . . . sino también . . .⟩ **2** (*used to replace a negative clause*) : no ⟨are we going or not? : ¿vamos a ir o no?⟩ ⟨of course not! : ¡claro que no!⟩ ⟨I hope/think not : espero/creo que no⟩ ⟨believe it or not : aunque no lo creas⟩ **3** : menos de ⟨not six inches away : a menos de seis pulgadas⟩ ⟨not all of us agree : no todos estamos de acuerdo⟩

notable¹ ['no:təbəl] *adj* **1** NOTEWORTHY : notable, de notar **2** DISTINGUISHED, PROMINENT : distinguido, destacado

notable² *n* : persona *f* importante, personaje *m*

notably ['no:təbli] *adv* : notablemente, particularmente

notarize ['no:tə,raɪz] *vt* **-rized; -rizing** : autenticar, autorizar

notary ['no:təri] *or* **notary public** *n, pl* **notaries** *or* **notaries public** *or* **notary publics** : notario *m*, -ria *f*; escribano *m*, -na *f*

notation [no'teɪʃən] *n* **1** NOTE : anotación *f*, nota *f* **2** : notación *f* ⟨musical notation : notación musical⟩

notch¹ ['nɑtʃ] *vt* : hacer una muesca en, cortar

notch² *n* : muesca *f*, corte *m*

note¹ ['no:t] *vt* **noted; noting** **1** NOTICE : notar, observar, tomar nota de **2** RECORD : anotar, apuntar

note² *n* **1** : nota *f* (musical) **2** COMMENT : nota *f*, comentario *m* **3** ANNOTATION : nota *f*, apunte *m* ⟨to take notes : tomar notas/apuntes⟩ ⟨to compare notes : cambiar impresiones⟩ ⟨I'll make a note of it : lo apuntaré⟩ **4** LETTER : nota *f*, cartita *f* ⟨to leave a note : dejar una nota⟩ **5** PROMINENCE : prestigio *m* ⟨a musician of note : un músico destacado⟩ **6** ATTENTION : atención *f* ⟨to take note of : tomar nota de, prestar atención a⟩ **7** TOUCH : nota *f*, dejo *m* **8 on a high note** : con una nota de optimismo

notebook ['no:t,bʊk] *n* **1** : libreta *f*, cuaderno *m* **2** : notebook *m* (computadora)

noted ['no:təd] *adj* EMINENT : renombrado, eminente, celebrado

notepad ['no:t,pæd] *n* : bloc *m* de notas

notepaper ['no:t,peɪpər] *n* : papel *m* de escribir

noteworthy ['no:t,wərði] *adj* : notable, de notar, de interés

nothing¹ ['nʌθɪŋ] *adv* **1** : de ninguna manera ⟨nothing daunted, we carried on : sin amilanarnos, seguimos adelante⟩ **2 nothing like** : no . . . en nada ⟨he's nothing like his brother : no se parece en nada a su hermano⟩

nothing² *n* **1** NOTHINGNESS : nada *f* **2** ZERO : cero *m* **3** : persona *f* de poca importancia, cero *m* **4** TRIFLE : nimiedad *f*

nothing³ *pron* : nada ⟨there's nothing better : no hay nada mejor⟩ ⟨there's nothing like . . . : no hay nada como . . .⟩ ⟨there's nothing to it : es facilísimo⟩ ⟨nothing else : nada más⟩ ⟨nothing but : solamente⟩ ⟨they're nothing but trouble : no traen más que problemas⟩ ⟨they mean nothing to me : ellos me son indiferentes⟩ ⟨I got it for nothing : me lo dieron gratis⟩ ⟨it was all for nothing : todo fue en vano⟩ ⟨are you hurt? it's nothing : ¿te hiciste daño? no es nada⟩ ⟨he's nothing if not polite : es muy cortés⟩

nothingness ['nʌθɪŋnəs] *n* **1** VOID : vacío *m*, nada *f* **2** NONEXISTENCE : inexistencia *f* **3** TRIFLE : nimiedad *f*

notice¹ ['no:tɪs] *vt* **-ticed; -ticing** : notar, observar, advertir, darse cuenta de

notice² *n* **1** NOTIFICATION : aviso *m*, notificación *f* ⟨at/on short notice, at a moment's notice : con poca antelación⟩ ⟨until further notice : hasta nuevo aviso⟩ ⟨without notice : sin previo aviso⟩ ⟨to give notice : presentar la renuncia⟩ **2** ATTENTION : atención *f* ⟨to take notice of : prestar atención a⟩ ⟨to make someone sit up and take notice : hacer que alguien preste atención⟩

noticeable ['no:tɪsəbəl] *adj* : evidente, perceptible — **noticeably** [-bli] *adv*

notification [,no:təfə'keɪʃən] *n* : notificación *f*, aviso *m*

notify ['no:tə,faɪ] *vt* **-fied; -fying** : notificar, avisar

notion ['no:ʃən] *n* **1** IDEA : idea *f*, noción *f* **2** WHIM : capricho *m*, antojo *m* **3 notions** *npl* : artículos *mpl* de mercería

notoriety [,no:tə'raɪəti] *n* : mala fama *f*, notoriedad *f*

notorious [no'to:riəs] *adj* : de mala fama, célebre, bien conocido

notwithstanding¹ [,nɑtwɪθ'stændɪŋ, -wɪð-] *adv* NEVERTHELESS : no obstante, sin embargo

notwithstanding² *conj* : a pesar de que

notwithstanding³ *prep* : a pesar de, no obstante

nougat ['nu:gət] *n* : turrón *m*

nought ['nɔt, 'nɑt] → **naught**

noun ['naʊn] *n* : nombre *m*, sustantivo *m*

nourish ['nərɪʃ] *vt* **1** FEED : alimentar, nutrir, sustentar **2** FOSTER : fomentar, alentar

nourishing ['nərɪʃɪŋ] *adj* : alimenticio, nutritivo

nourishment ['nərɪʃmənt] *n* : nutrición *f*, alimento *m*, sustento *m*

novel[1] [ˈnɑvəl] *adj* : original, novedoso
novel[2] *n* : novela *f*
novelist [ˈnɑvəlɪst] *n* : novelista *mf*
novelty [ˈnɑvəlt̬i] *n, pl* **-ties** **1** : novedad *f* **2 novelties** *npl* TRINKETS : baratijas *fpl*, chucherías *fpl*
November [noˈvɛmbər] *n* : noviembre *m* ⟨they arrived on the 18th of November, they arrived on November 18th : llegaron el 18 de noviembre⟩
novena [noˈviːnə] *n* : novena *f*
novice [ˈnɑvɪs] *n* : novato *m*, -ta *f*; principiante *mf*; novicio *m*, -cia *f*
novocaine [ˈnoːvəˌkeɪn] *n* : novocaína *f*
now[1] [ˈnɑu] *adv* **1** PRESENTLY : ahora, ya, actualmente ⟨from now on : de ahora en adelante⟩ ⟨for now : por ahora⟩ ⟨for several months now : desde hace varios meses⟩ ⟨between now and . . . , from now until . . . : de aquí a . . .⟩ ⟨long before now : ya hace tiempo⟩ ⟨now or never : ahora o nunca⟩ **2** SOON : dentro de poco, pronto ⟨any day now : cualquier día de estos⟩ ⟨they'll be here any minute now : estarán por caer⟩ **3** : ahora, como están las cosas ⟨do you believe me now? : ¿ahora me crees?⟩ **4** IMMEDIATELY : ahora (mismo), inmediatamente ⟨do it right now! : ¡hazlo ahora mismo!⟩ **5** THEN : ya, entonces ⟨now they were ready : ya estaban listos⟩ **6** (*used to introduce a statement, a question, a command, or a transition*) ⟨now hear this! : ¡presten atención!⟩ ⟨now what do you think of that? : ¿qué piensas de eso?⟩ **7** now and then : de vez en cuando **8** now, now : vamos, vamos
now[2] *n* (*indicating the present time*) ⟨until now : hasta ahora⟩ ⟨by now : ya⟩ ⟨ten years from now : dentro de 10 años⟩
now[3] *conj* now that : ahora que, ya que
nowadays [ˈnɑuəˌdeɪz] *adv* : hoy en día, actualmente, en la actualidad
nowhere[1] [ˈnoːˌʍɛr] *adv* **1** : en ninguna parte, a ningún lado ⟨nowhere to be found : en ninguna parte, por ningún lado⟩ ⟨you're going nowhere : no estás yendo a ningún lado, no estás yendo a ninguna parte⟩ **2 nowhere near** : ni con mucho, nada cerca ⟨it's nowhere near here : no está nada cerca de aquí⟩ ⟨it's nowhere near finished : no está terminado ni mucho menos⟩
nowhere[2] *n* **1** : ninguna parte *f* **2 out of nowhere** : de la nada
noxious [ˈnɑkʃəs] *adj* : nocivo, dañino, tóxico
nozzle [ˈnɑzəl] *n* : boca *f*, boquilla *f*
nth [ˈɛnθ] *adj* **1** : enésimo ⟨for the nth time : por enésima vez⟩ **2 to the nth degree** EXTREMELY : al máximo, sumamente
nuance [ˈnuːˌɑns, ˈnjuː-] *n* : matiz *m*
nub [ˈnʌb] *n* **1** KNOB, LUMP : protuberancia *f*, nudo *m* **2** GIST : quid *m*, meollo *m*
nuclear [ˈnuːkliər, ˈnjuː-] *adj* : nuclear
nucleus [ˈnuːkliəs, ˈnjuː-] *n, pl* **-clei** [-kliˌaɪ] : núcleo *m*
nude[1] [ˈnuːd, ˈnjuːd] *adj* **nuder; nudest** : desnudo
nude[2] *n* : desnudo *m*

nudge[1] [ˈnʌʤ] *vt* **nudged; nudging** : darle con el codo (a alguien)
nudge[2] *n* : toque *m* que se da con el codo
nudism [ˈnuːˌdɪzəm, ˈnjuː-] *n* : nudismo *m*
nudist [ˈnuːdɪst, ˈnjuː-] *n* : nudista *mf*
nudity [ˈnuːdət̬i, ˈnjuː-] *n* : desnudez *f*
nugget [ˈnʌɡət] *n* : pepita *f*
nuisance [ˈnuːsənts, ˈnjuː-] *n* **1** BOTHER : fastidio *m*, molestia *f*, lata *f* **2** PEST : pesado *m*, -da *f fam*
nuke[1] [ˈnuːk, ˈnjuːk] *vt* **nuked; nuking** *fam* **1** : atacar con armas nucleares **2** : cocinar en el microondas
nuke[2] *n fam* : arma *m* nuclear
null [ˈnʌl] *adj* : nulo ⟨null and void : nulo y sin efecto⟩
nullify [ˈnʌləˌfaɪ] *vt* **-fied; -fying** : invalidar, anular
nullity [ˈnʌlət̬i] *n, pl* **-ties** : nulidad *f*
numb[1] [ˈnʌm] *vt* : entumecer, adormecer
numb[2] *adj* : entumecido, dormido ⟨numb with fear : paralizado de miedo⟩
number[1] [ˈnʌmbər] *vt* **1** COUNT, INCLUDE : contar, incluir **2** : numerar ⟨number the pages : numera las páginas⟩ **3** TOTAL : ascender a, sumar
number[2] *n* **1** : número *m* ⟨in round numbers : en números redondos⟩ **2** *or* **telephone number** *or* **phone number** : número *m* (de teléfono) **3 a number of** : varios, unos pocos, unos cuantos **4 any number of** : una cantidad de **5 to look out for number one** : pensar ante todo en el propio interés
numberless [ˈnʌmbərləs] *adj* : innumerable, sin número
numbness [ˈnʌmnəs] *n* : entumecimiento *m*
numeral [ˈnuːmərəl, ˈnjuː-] *n* : número *m* ⟨Roman numeral : número romano⟩
numerator [ˈnuːməˌreɪt̬ər, ˈnjuː-] *n* : numerador *m*
numeric [nʊˈmɛrɪk, njuː-] *adj* : numérico
numerical [nʊˈmɛrɪkəl, njuː-] *adj* : numérico — **numerically** [-kli] *adv*
numerous [ˈnuːmərəs, ˈnjuː-] *adj* : numeroso
numismatics [ˌnuːməzˈmæt̬ɪks, ˌnjuː-] *n* : numismática *f*
numskull [ˈnʌmˌskʌl] *n* : tonto *m*, -ta *f*; mentecato *m*, -ta *f*; zoquete *m fam*
nun [ˈnʌn] *n* : monja *f*
nuptial [ˈnʌpʃəl] *adj* : nupcial
nuptials [ˈnʌpʃəlz] *npl* WEDDING : nupcias *fpl*, boda *f*
nurse[1] [ˈnərs] *vt* **nursed; nursing** **1** SUCKLE : amamantar **2** : cuidar (de), atender ⟨to nurse the sick : cuidar a los enfermos⟩ ⟨to nurse a cold : curarse de un resfriado⟩
nurse[2] *n* **1** : enfermero *m*, -ra *f* **2** → **nursemaid**
nursemaid [ˈnərsˌmeɪd] *n* : niñera *f*
nursery [ˈnərsəri] *n, pl* **-eries** **1** *or* **day nursery** : guardería *f* **2** : vivero *m* (de plantas)
nursery rhyme *n* : canción *f* infantil
nursery school *n* : parvulario *m*
nursing [ˈnərsɪŋ] *n* : profesión *f* de enfermero

nursing home *n* : hogar *m* de ancianos, clínica *f* de reposo
nurture[1] ['nərtɬər] *vt* **-tured; -turing** **1** FEED, NOURISH : nutrir, alimentar **2** EDUCATE : criar, educar **3** FOSTER : alimentar, fomentar
nurture[2] *n* **1** UPBRINGING : crianza *f*, educación *f* **2** FOOD : alimento *m*
nut ['nʌt] *n* **1** : nuez *f* **2** : tuerca *f* ⟨nuts and bolts : tuercas y tornillos⟩ **3** LUNATIC : loco *m*, -ca *f*; chiflado *m*, -da *f* *fam* **4** ENTHUSIAST : fanático *m*, -ca *f*; entusiasta *mf*
nutcracker ['nʌt,krækər] *n* : cascanueces *m*
nuthatch ['nʌt,hætɬ] *n* : trepador *m*
nutmeg ['nʌt,mɛg] *n* : nuez *f* moscada
nutria ['nu:triə, 'nju:-] *n* : nutria *f*
nutrient ['nu:triənt, 'nju:-] *n* : nutriente *m*, alimento *m* nutritivo
nutriment ['nu:trəmənt, 'nju:-] *n* : nutrimento *m*

nutrition [nʊ'trɪɬən, nju-] *n* : nutrición *f*
nutritional [nʊ'trɪɬənəl, nju-] *adj* : alimenticio
nutritionist [nʊ'trɪɬənɪst, nju-] *n* : nutricionista *mf*
nutritious [nʊ'trɪɬəs, nju-] *adj* : nutritivo, alimenticio
nuts ['nʌts] *adj* **1** FANATICAL : fanático **2** CRAZY : loco, chiflado *fam*
nutshell ['nʌt,ɬɛl] *n* **1** : cáscara *f* de nuez **2 in a nutshell** : en pocas palabras
nutty ['nʌt̬i] *adj* **nuttier; -est** : loco, chiflado *fam*
nuzzle ['nʌzəl] *v* **-zled; -zling** *vi* NESTLE : acurrucarse, arrimarse — *vt* : acariciar con el hocico
nylon ['nai,lan] *n* **1** : nilón *m* **2 nylons** *npl* : medias *fpl* de nilón
nymph ['nɪmpf] *n* : ninfa *f*

O

o ['o:] *n*, *pl* **o's** *or* **os** ['o:z] **1** : decimoquinta letra del alfabeto inglés **2** ZERO : cero *m*
O ['o:] → **oh**
oaf ['o:f] *n* : zoquete *m*; bruto *m*, -ta *f*
oafish ['o:fɪʃ] *adj* : torpe, lerdo
oak ['o:k] *n*, *pl* **oaks** *or* **oak** : roble *m*
oaken ['o:kən] *adj* : de roble
oar ['or] *n* : remo *m*
oarlock ['or,lak] *n* : tolete *m*
oasis [o'eɪsɪs] *n*, *pl* **oases** [-,si:z] : oasis *m*
oat ['o:t] *n* : avena *f*
oath ['o:θ] *n*, *pl* **oaths** ['o:ðz, 'o:θs] **1** : juramento *m* ⟨to take an oath : prestar juramento⟩ **2** SWEARWORD : mala palabra *f*, palabrota *f*
oatmeal ['o:t,mi:l] *n* : avena *f* ⟨instant oatmeal : avena instantánea⟩
obdurate ['abdurət, -dju-] *adj* : inflexible, firme, obstinado
obedience [o'bi:diənts] *n* : obediencia *f*
obedient [o'bi:diənt] *adj* : obediente — **obediently** *adv*
obelisk ['abə,lɪsk] *n* : obelisco *m*
obese [o'bi:s] *adj* : obeso
obesity [o'bi:səti] *n* : obesidad *f*
obey [o'beɪ] *v* **obeyed; obeying** : obedecer ⟨to obey the law : cumplir la ley⟩
obfuscate ['abfə,skeɪt] *vt* **-cated; -cating** : ofuscar, confundir
obituary [ə'bɪtʃu,ɛri] *n*, *pl* **-aries** : obituario *m*, necrología *f*
object[1] [əb'dʒɛkt] *vt* : objetar — *vi* : oponerse, poner reparos, hacer objeciones
object[2] ['abdʒɪkt] *n* **1** : objeto *m* **2** OBJECTIVE, PURPOSE : objetivo *m*, propósito *m* **3** : complemento *m* (en gramática)
objection [əb'dʒɛkɬən] *n* : objeción *f*
objectionable [əb'dʒɛkɬənəbəl] *adj* : ofensivo, indeseable — **objectionably** [-bli] *adv*
objective[1] [əb'dʒɛktɪv] *adj* **1** IMPARTIAL

: objetivo, imparcial **2** : de complemento, directo (en gramática)
objective[2] *n* **1** : objetivo *m* **2** *or* **objective case** : acusativo *m*
objectively [əb'dʒɛktɪvli] *adv* : objetivamente
objectivity [,ab,dʒɛk'tɪvət̬i] *n*, *pl* **-ties** : objetividad *f*
objector [əb'dʒɛktər] *n* : objetor *m*, -tora *f* ⟨conscientious objector : objetor de conciencia⟩
obligate ['ablə,geɪt] *vt* **-gated; -gating** : obligar
obligation [,ablə'geɪɬən] *n* : obligación *f*
obligatory [ə'blɪgə,tori] *adj* : obligatorio
oblige [ə'blaɪdʒ] *vt* **obliged; obliging** **1** COMPEL : obligar **2** : hacerle un favor (a alguien), complacer ⟨to oblige a friend : hacerle un favor a un amigo⟩ **3 to be much obliged** : estar muy agradecido
obliging [ə'blaɪdʒɪŋ] *adj* : servicial, complaciente — **obligingly** *adv*
oblique [o'bli:k] *adj* **1** SLANTING : oblicuo **2** INDIRECT : indirecto — **obliquely** *adv*
obliterate [ə'blɪt̬ə,reɪt] *vt* **-ated; -ating** **1** ERASE : obliterar, borrar **2** DESTROY : destruir, eliminar
obliteration [ə,blɪt̬ə'reɪɬən] *n* : obliteración *f*
oblivion [ə'blɪviən] *n* : olvido *m*
oblivious [ə'blɪviəs] *adj* : inconsciente — **obliviously** *adv*
oblong[1] ['a,blɔŋ] *adj* : oblongo
oblong[2] *n* : figura *f* oblonga, rectángulo *m*
obnoxious [ab'nakɬəs, əb-] *adj* : repugnante, odioso — **obnoxiously** *adv*
oboe ['o:,bo:] *n* : oboe *m*
oboist ['o,boɪst] *n* : oboe *mf*
obscene [ab'si:n, əb-] *adj* : obsceno, indecente — **obscenely** *adv*

obscenity [ab'sɛnəţi, əb-] *n, pl* **-ties** : obscenidad *f*

obscure¹ [ab'skjʊr, əb-] *vt* **-scured; -scuring** **1** CLOUD, DIM : oscurecer, nublar **2** HIDE : ocultar

obscure² *adj* **1** DIM : oscuro **2** REMOTE, SECLUDED : recóndito **3** VAGUE : oscuro, confuso, vago **4** UNKNOWN : desconocido ⟨an obscure poet : un poeta desconocido⟩ — **obscurely** *adv*

obscurity [ab'skjʊrəţi, əb-] *n, pl* **-ties** : oscuridad *f*

obsequious [əb'si:kwiəs] *adj* : servil, excesivamente atento

observable [əb'zərvəbəl] *adj* : observable, perceptible

observance [əb'zərvənts] *n* **1** FULFILLMENT : observancia *f*, cumplimiento *m* **2** PRACTICE : práctica *f*

observant [əb'zərvənt] *adj* : observador

observation [ˌabsər'veɪʊ̃n, -zər-] *n* : observación *f*

observatory [əb'zərvəˌtori] *n, pl* **-ries** : observatorio *m*

observe [əb'zərv] *v* **-served; -serving** *vt* **1** OBEY : observar, obedecer **2** CELEBRATE : celebrar, guardar (una práctica religiosa) **3** WATCH : observar, mirar **4** REMARK : observar, comentar — *vi* LOOK : mirar

observer [əb'zərvər] *n* : observador *m*, -dora *f*

obsess [əb'sɛs] *vt* : obsesionar

obsession [ab'sɛʊ̃n, əb-] *n* : obsesión *f*

obsessive [ab'sɛsɪv, əb-] *adj* : obsesivo — **obsessively** *adv*

obsolescence [ˌabsə'lɛsənts] *n* : obsolescencia *f*

obsolescent [ˌabsə'lɛsənt] *adj* : obsolescente ⟨to become obsolescent : caer en desuso⟩

obsolete [ˌabsə'li:t, 'absəˌ-] *adj* : obsoleto, anticuado

obstacle ['abstɪkəl] *n* : obstáculo *m*, impedimento *m*

obstetric [əb'stɛtrɪk] *or* **obstetrical** [-trɪkəl] *adj* : obstétrico

obstetrician [ˌabstə'trɪʊ̃n] *n* : obstetra *mf*; tocólogo *m*, -ga *f*

obstetrics [əb'stɛtrɪks] *ns & pl* : obstetricia *f*, tocología *f*

obstinacy ['abstənəsi] *n, pl* **-cies** : obstinación *f*, terquedad *f*

obstinate ['abstənət] *adj* : obstinado, terco — **obstinately** *adv*

obstreperous [əb'strɛpərəs] *adj* **1** CLAMOROUS : ruidoso, clamoroso **2** UNRULY : rebelde, indisciplinado

obstruct [əb'strʌkt] *vt* : obstruir, bloquear

obstruction [əb'strʌkʊ̃n] *n* : obstrucción *f*, bloqueo *m*

obstructive [əb'strʌktɪv] *adj* : obstructor

obtain [əb'teɪn] *vt* : obtener, conseguir — *vi* PREVAIL : imperar, prevalecer

obtainable [əb'teɪnəbəl] *adj* : obtenible, asequible

obtrusive [əb'tru:sɪv] *adj* **1** IMPERTINENT, MEDDLESOME : impertinente, entrometido **2** PROTRUDING : prominente

obtuse [ab'tu:s, əb-, -'tju:s] *adj* : obtuso, torpe

obtuse angle *n* : ángulo obtuso

obvious ['abviəs] *adj* : obvio, evidente, manifiesto

obviously ['abviəsli] *adv* **1** CLEARLY : obviamente, evidentemente **2** OF COURSE : claro, por supuesto

occasion¹ [ə'keɪʒən] *vt* : ocasionar, causar

occasion² *n* **1** OPPORTUNITY : oportunidad *f*, ocasión *f* **2** CAUSE : motivo *m*, razón *f* **3** INSTANCE : ocasión *f* **4** EVENT : ocasión *f*, acontecimiento *m* **5 on ~** : de vez en cuando, ocasionalmente

occasional [ə'keɪʒənəl] *adj* : ocasional

occasionally [ə'keɪʒənəli] *adv* : de vez en cuando, ocasionalmente

occult¹ [ə'kʌlt, 'aˌkʌlt] *adj* **1** HIDDEN, SECRET : oculto, secreto **2** ARCANE : arcano, esotérico

occult² *n* **the occult** : las ciencias ocultas

occupancy ['akjəpəntsi] *n, pl* **-cies** : ocupación *f*, habitación *f*

occupant ['akjəpənt] *n* : ocupante *mf*

occupation [ˌakjə'peɪʊ̃n] *n* : ocupación *f*, profesión *f*, oficio *m*

occupational [ˌakjə'peɪʊ̃nəl] *adj* : ocupacional

occupier ['akjəˌpaɪər] *n* : ocupante *mf*

occupy ['akjəˌpaɪ] *vt* **-pied; -pying** : ocupar

occur [ə'kər] *vi* **occurred; occurring** **1** EXIST : encontrarse, existir **2** HAPPEN : ocurrir, acontecer, suceder, tener lugar **3** : ocurrirse ⟨it occurred to him that . . . : se le ocurrió que . . .⟩

occurrence [ə'kərənts] *n* : acontecimiento *m*, suceso *m*, ocurrencia *f*

ocean ['o:ʊ̃n] *n* : océano *m*

oceanic [ˌo:Li'ænɪk] *adj* : oceánico

oceanography [ˌo:Lə'nagrəfi] *n* : oceanografía *f* — **oceanographic** *adj*

ocelot ['asəˌlat, 'o:-] *n* : ocelote *m*

ocher *or* **ochre** ['o:kər] *n* : ocre *m*

o'clock [ə'klak] *adv* (*used in telling time*) ⟨it's ten o'clock : son las diez⟩ ⟨at six o'clock : a las seis⟩

octagon ['aktəˌgan] *n* : octágono *m*

octagonal [ak'tægənəl] *adj* : octagonal

octave ['aktɪv] *n* : octava *f*

October [ak'to:bər] *n* : octubre *m* ⟨they arrived on the 13th of October, they arrived on October 13th : llegaron el 13 de octubre⟩

octopus ['aktəˌpʊs, -pəs] *n, pl* **-puses** *or* **-pi** [-ˌpaɪ] : pulpo *m*

ocular ['akjələr] *adj* : ocular

oculist ['akjəlɪst] *n* **1** OPHTHALMOLOGIST : oftalmólogo *m*, -ga *f*; oculista *mf* **2** OPTOMETRIST : optometrista *mf*

odd ['ad] *adj* **1** : sin pareja, suelto ⟨an odd sock : un calcetín sin pareja⟩ **2** UNEVEN : impar ⟨odd numbers : números impares⟩ **3** : y pico, y tantos ⟨forty-odd years ago : hace cuarenta y pico años⟩ **4** : alguno, uno que otro ⟨odd jobs : algunos trabajos⟩ **5** STRANGE : extraño, raro

oddball ['adˌbɔl] *n* : excéntrico *m*, -ca *f*; persona *f* rara

oddity [ˈɑdət̬i] *n, pl* **-ties** : rareza *f*, cosa *f* rara

oddly [ˈɑdli] *adv* : de manera extraña

oddness [ˈɑdnəs] *n* : rareza *f*, excentricidad *f*

odds [ˈɑdz] *npl* **1** CHANCES : probabilidades *fpl* ⟨against all odds : contra viento y marea⟩ **2** : puntos *mpl* de ventaja (de una apuesta) **3 to be at odds** : estar en desacuerdo

odds and ends *npl* : costillas *fpl*, cosas *fpl* sueltas, cachivaches *mpl*

ode [ˈoːd] *n* : oda *f*

odious [ˈoːdiəs] *adj* : odioso — **odiously** *adv*

odometer [oˈdɑmət̬ər] *n* : cuentakilómetros *m*, odómetro *m*

odor [ˈoːdər] *n* : olor *m*

odorless [ˈoːdərləs] *adj* : inodoro, sin olor

odyssey [ˈɑdəsi] *n, pl* **-seys** : odisea *f*

o'er [ˈoːr] → **over**

of [ˈʌv, ˈɑv] *prep* **1** FROM : de ⟨a man of the city : un hombre de la ciudad⟩ **2** (*indicating a quality or characteristic*) : de ⟨a woman of great ability : una mujer de gran capacidad⟩ ⟨a boy of twelve : un niño de doce años⟩ ⟨her husband of 30 years : su marido, con quien lleva 30 años de casada⟩ **3** (*describing behavior*) : de parte de (alguien) ⟨that was very nice of you : fue muy amable de tu parte⟩ **4** (*indicating cause*) : de ⟨he died of the flu : murió de la gripe⟩ **5** BY : de ⟨the works of Shakespeare : las obras de Shakespeare⟩ **6** (*indicating contents, material, or quantity*) : de ⟨a house of wood : una casa de madera⟩ ⟨a glass of water : un vaso de agua⟩ ⟨thousands of people : miles de personas⟩ **7** (*indicating belonging or connection*) : de ⟨the front of the house : el frente de la casa⟩ ⟨a friend of mine : un amigo mío⟩ ⟨the President of the United States : el presidente de los Estados Unidos⟩ ⟨the best of intentions : las mejores intenciones⟩ **8** (*indicating belonging to a group*) : de ⟨one of my friends : uno de mis amigos⟩ ⟨the four of us went : fuimos los cuatro⟩ ⟨two of which : dos de los/las cuales⟩ **9** ABOUT : sobre, de ⟨tales of the West : los cuentos del Oeste⟩ **10** (*indicating a particular example*) : de ⟨the city of Caracas : la ciudad de Caracas⟩ **11** FOR : por, a ⟨love of country : amor por la patria⟩ **12** (*indicating time or date*) ⟨five minutes of ten : las diez menos cinco⟩ ⟨the eighth of April : el ocho de abril⟩

off¹ [ˈɔf] *adv* **1** (*indicating change of position or state*) ⟨to march off : marcharse⟩ ⟨he dozed off : se puso a dormir⟩ **2** (*indicating distance in space or time*) ⟨some miles off : a varias millas⟩ ⟨the holiday is three weeks off : faltan tres semanas para la fiesta⟩ **3** (*indicating removal*) ⟨the knob came off : se le cayó el pomo⟩ ⟨he took off his coat : se quitó el abrigo⟩ **4** (*indicating termination*) ⟨shut the television off : apaga la televisión⟩ ⟨to finish off : terminar, acabar⟩ **5** (*indicating suspension of work*) ⟨to take a day off : tomarse un día de descanso⟩ **6 off and on** : de vez en cuando

off² *adj* **1** FARTHER : más remoto, distante ⟨the off side of the building : el lado distante del edificio⟩ **2** STARTED : empezado ⟨to be off on a spree : irse de juerga⟩ **3** OUT : apagado ⟨the light is off : la luz está apagada⟩ **4** CANCELED : cancelado, suspendido **5** INCORRECT : erróneo, incorrecto **6** REMOTE : remoto, lejano ⟨an off chance : una posibilidad remota⟩ **7** FREE : libre ⟨I'm off today : hoy estoy libre⟩ **8** SPOILED : estropeado, cortado **9 to be well off** : vivir con desahogo, tener bastante dinero

off³ *prep* **1** (*indicating physical separation*) : de ⟨she took it off the table : lo tomó de la mesa⟩ ⟨a shop off the main street : una tienda al lado de la calle principal⟩ **2** : a la costa de, a expensas de ⟨he lives off his sister : vive a expensas de su hermana⟩ **3** (*indicating the suspension of an activity*) ⟨to be off duty : estar libre⟩ ⟨he's off liquor : ha dejado el alcohol⟩ **4** BELOW : por debajo de ⟨he's off his game : está por debajo de su juego normal⟩

offal [ˈɔfəl] *n* **1** RUBBISH, WASTE : desechos *mpl*, desperdicios *mpl* **2** VISCERA : vísceras *fpl*, asaduras *fpl*

off-balance [ˈɔfˈbælənts] *adj* : desequilibrado

off-color [ˈɔfˈkʌlər] *adj* : subido de tono, pícaro, picante

offend [əˈfɛnd] *vt* **1** VIOLATE : violar, atentar contra **2** HURT : ofender ⟨to be easily offended : ser muy susceptible⟩

offender [əˈfɛndər] *n* : delincuente *mf*; infractor *m*, -tora *f*

offense *or* **offence** [əˈfɛnts, ˈɔˌfɛnts] *n* **1** INSULT : ofensa *f*, injuria *f*, agravio *m* ⟨to take offense : ofenderse⟩ **2** ASSAULT : ataque *m* **3** : ofensiva *f* (en deportes) **4** CRIME, INFRACTION : infracción *f*, delito *m*

offensive¹ [əˈfɛntsɪv, ˈɔˌfɛnt-] *adj* : ofensivo — **offensively** *adv*

offensive² *n* : ofensiva *f*

offer¹ [ˈɔfər] *vt* **1** : ofrecer ⟨they offered him the job : le ofrecieron el puesto⟩ **2** PROPOSE : proponer, sugerir **3** SHOW : ofrecer, mostrar ⟨to offer resistance : ofrecer resistencia⟩

offer² *n* : oferta *f*, ofrecimiento *m*, propuesta *f*

offering [ˈɔfərɪŋ] *n* : ofrenda *f*

offhand¹ [ˈɔfˈhænd] *adv* : sin preparación, sin pensarlo

offhand² *adj* **1** IMPROMPTU : improvisado **2** ABRUPT : brusco

office [ˈɔfəs] *n* **1** : cargo *m* ⟨to run for office : presentarse como candidato⟩ **2** : oficina *f*, despacho *m*, gabinete *m* (en la casa)

officeholder [ˈɔfəsˌhoːldər] *n* : titular *mf*

office hours *n* : horas *fpl* de oficina

officer [ˈɔfəsər] *n* **1** → **police officer** **2** OFFICIAL : oficial *mf*; funcionario *m*, -ria *f*; director *m*, -tora *f* (en una empresa) **3** COMMISSIONED OFFICER : oficial *mf*

office worker *n* : oficinista *mf*

official[1] [ə'fɪlɪəl] *adj* : oficial — **officially** *adv*

official[2] *n* : funcionario *m*, -ria *f*; oficial *mf*

officiate [ə'fɪlɪˌeɪt] *v* **-ated; -ating** *vi* **1** : arbitrar (en deportes) **2 to officiate at** : oficiar, celebrar — *vt* : arbitrar

officious [ə'fɪləs] *adj* : oficioso

offing ['ɔfɪŋ] *n* **in the offing** : en perspectiva

off–key ['ɔf'kiː] *adj* : desafinado

off–line ['ɔf'laɪn] *adj* : fuera de línea

off–peak ['ɔf'piːk] *adj* : fuera de las horas pico

off–putting ['ɔfˌpʊtɪŋ] *adj* : desagradable, repelente

offset ['ɔfˌsɛt] *vt* **-set; -setting** : compensar

offshoot ['ɔfˌʃuːt] *n* **1** OUTGROWTH : producto *m*, resultado *m* **2** BRANCH, SHOOT : retoño *m*, rama *f*, vástago *m* (de una planta)

offshore[1] ['ɔf'ʃɔr] *adv* : a una distancia de la costa

offshore[2] *adj* **1** : de (la) tierra ⟨an offshore wind : un viento que sopla de tierra⟩ **2** : (de) costa afuera, cercano a la costa ⟨an offshore island : una isla costera⟩

offside ['ɔf'saɪd] *adj* : fuera de juego (en deportes)

offspring ['ɔfˌsprɪŋ] *ns & pl* **1** YOUNG : crías *fpl* (de los animales) **2** PROGENY : prole *f*, progenie *f*

off–white ['ɔf'hwaɪt] *adj* : blancuzco

often ['ɔfən, 'ɔftən] *adv* : muchas veces, a menudo, seguido

oftentimes ['ɔfənˌtaɪmz, 'ɔftən-] *or* **oftentimes** ['ɔftˌtaɪmz] → **often**

ogle ['oːgəl] *vt* **ogled; ogling** : comerse con los ojos, quedarse mirando a

ogre ['oːgər] *n* : ogro *m*

oh ['oː] *interj* : ¡oh!, ¡ah!, ¡ay! ⟨oh, of course : ah, por supuesto⟩ ⟨oh no! : ¡ay no!⟩ ⟨oh really? : ¿de veras?⟩

ohm ['oːm] *n* : ohm *m*, ohmio *m*

oil[1] ['ɔɪl] *vt* : lubricar, engrasar, aceitar

oil[2] *n* **1** : aceite *m* **2** PETROLEUM : petróleo *m* **3** *or* **oil painting** : óleo *m*, pintura *f* al óleo **4** *or* **oil paint(s)** : óleo *m*

oilcan ['ɔɪlˌkæn] *n* : aceitera *f*

oilcloth ['ɔɪlˌklɔθ] *n* : hule *m*

oiliness ['ɔɪlinəs] *n* : lo aceitoso

oil rig → **rig**[2]

oilskin ['ɔɪlˌskɪn] *n* **1** : hule *m* **2 oilskins** *npl* : impermeable *m*

oil slick *n* : marea *f* negra

oil well *n* : pozo *m* petrolero

oily ['ɔɪli] *adj* **oilier; -est** : aceitoso, grasiento, grasoso ⟨oily fingers : dedos grasientos⟩

ointment ['ɔɪntmənt] *n* : ungüento *m*, pomada *f*

OK[1] [ˌoː'keɪ] *vt* **OK'd** *or* **okayed** [ˌoː'keɪd]; **OK'ing** *or* **okaying** APPROVE, AUTHORIZE : dar el visto bueno a, autorizar, aprobar

OK[2] *or* **okay** [ˌoː'keɪ] *adv* **1** WELL : bien **2** YES : sí, por supuesto

OK[3] *adj* : bien ⟨he's OK : está bien⟩ ⟨it's OK with me : estoy de acuerdo⟩

OK[4] *n* : autorización *f*, visto *m* bueno

okra ['oːkrə, South also -kri] *n* : quingombó *m*

old[1] ['oːld] *adj* **1** ANCIENT : antiguo ⟨old civilizations : civilizaciones antiguas⟩ **2** FAMILIAR : viejo ⟨old friends : viejos amigos⟩ ⟨the same old story : la misma historia de siempre⟩ **3** (*indicating a certain age*) ⟨how old is he? : ¿cuántos años tiene?⟩ ⟨he's ten years old : tiene diez años (de edad)⟩ ⟨he's a year older than I am : es un año mayor que yo⟩ ⟨she's my older sister : es mi hermana mayor⟩ ⟨our oldest daughter : nuestra hija mayor⟩ **4** AGED : viejo, anciano ⟨an old woman : una anciana⟩ **5** FORMER : antiguo ⟨her old neighborhood : su antiguo barrio⟩ **6** WORN-OUT : viejo, gastado **7 any old** *fam* : cualquier

old[2] *n* **1 the old** : los viejos, los ancianos **2 in the days of old** : antaño, en los tiempos antiguos

old age *n* : vejez *f*

olden ['oːldən] *adj* : de antaño, de antigüedad

old–fashioned ['oːld'fæʃənd] *adj* : anticuado, pasado de moda

old maid *n offensive* SPINSTER : solterona *f*

Old Testament *n* : Antiguo Testamento *m*

old–time ['oːld'taɪm] *adj* : antiguo

old–timer ['oːld'taɪmər] *n* **1** VETERAN : veterano *m*, -na *f* **2** *or* **oldster** : anciano *m*, -na *f*

old–world ['oːld'wərld] *adj* : pintoresco (de antaño)

oleander ['oːliˌændər] *n* : adelfa *f*

oleomargarine [ˌoːlio'mɑrdʒərən] → **margarine**

olfactory [al'fæktəri, ol-] *adj* : olfativo

oligarchy ['ɑləˌgɑrki, 'oːlə-] *n*, *pl* **-chies** : oligarquía *f*

olive ['ɑlɪv, -ləv] *n* **1** : aceituna *f*, oliva *f* (fruta) **2** : olivo *m* (árbol) **3** *or* **olive green** : color *m* aceituna, verde *m* oliva

olive oil *n* : aceite *m* de oliva

Olmec ['ɑlˌmɛk, 'oːl-] *n* : olmeca *mf* — **Olmec** *adj*

Olympiad [ə'lɪmpiˌæd, oː-] *n* : olimpiada *f*

Olympic [ə'lɪmpɪk, oː-] *adj* : olímpico

Olympic Games *npl* : Juegos *mpl* Olímpicos

Olympics [ə'lɪmpɪks, oː-] *npl* : olimpiadas *fpl*

Omani [oː'mɑni, -'mæ-] *n* : omaní *mf* — **Omani** *adj*

ombudsman ['ɑmˌbʊdzmən, ɑm-'bʊdz-] *n*, *pl* **-men** [-mən, -ˌmɛn] : ombudsman *m*

omelet *or* **omelette** ['ɑmlət, 'ɑmə-] *n* : omelette *mf*, tortilla *f* (de huevo)

omen ['oːmən] *n* : presagio *m*, augurio *m*, agüero *m*

ominous ['ɑmənəs] *adj* : ominoso, agorero, de mal agüero

ominously ['ɑmənəsli] *adv* : de manera amenazadora

omission [oː'mɪlən] *n* : omisión *f*

omit [oː'mɪt] *vt* **omitted; omitting 1** LEAVE OUT : omitir, excluir **2** NEGLECT

: omitir ⟨they omitted to tell us : omitieron decírnoslo⟩

omnipotence [am'nɪpətənts] *n* : omnipotencia *f* — **omnipotent** [am-'nɪpətənt] *adj*

omnipresence [ˌɑmnɪ'prɛzənts] *n* : omnipresencia *f*

omnipresent [ˌɑmnɪ'prɛzənt] *adj* : omnipresente

omniscient [ɑm'nɪlənt] *adj* : omnisciente

omnivorous [ɑm'nɪvərəs] *adj* **1** : omnívoro **2** AVID : ávido, voraz

on¹ ['ɑn, 'ɔn] *adv* **1** (*indicating contact with a surface*) ⟨put the top on : pon la tapa⟩ ⟨he has a hat on : lleva un sombrero puesto⟩ **2** (*indicating forward movement*) ⟨from that moment on : a partir de ese momento⟩ ⟨farther on : más adelante⟩ **3** (*indicating operation or an operating position*) ⟨turn the light on : prende la luz⟩

on² *adj* **1** (*being in operation*) ⟨the radio is on : el radio está prendido⟩ **2** (*taking place*) ⟨the game is on : el juego ha comenzado⟩ **3 to be on to** : estar enterado de

on³ *prep* **1** (*indicating location or position*) : en, sobre, encima de ⟨on the table : en/sobre la mesa, encima de la mesa⟩ ⟨shadows on the wall : sombras en la pared⟩ ⟨on foot/horseback : a pie/caballo⟩ ⟨on one's hands and knees : a gatas⟩ ⟨she kissed him on the cheek : lo besó en la mejilla⟩ ⟨on page 102 : en la página 102⟩ ⟨on a Web site : en un sitio web⟩ **2** BY, BESIDE : junto a, al lado de ⟨a house on the lake : una casa junto al lago⟩ **3** AT, TO : a la derecha⟩ **4** ABOARD IN : en, a ⟨on the plane : en el avión⟩ ⟨he got on the train : subió al tren⟩ **5** (*indicating time*) ⟨she worked on Saturdays : trabajaba los sábados⟩ ⟨every hour on the hour : cada hora en punto⟩ **6** (*indicating means or agency*) : por ⟨he cut himself on a tin can : se cortó con una lata⟩ ⟨to talk on the telephone : hablar por teléfono⟩ **7** (*indicating source*) : de ⟨to live on a salary : vivir de un sueldo⟩ ⟨it runs on diesel : funciona con diesel⟩ ⟨based on fact : basado en hechos reales⟩ **8** ACCORDING TO : de, según ⟨on good authority : de buena fuente⟩ **9** (*indicating a state or process*) : en ⟨on fire : en llamas⟩ ⟨on the increase : en aumento⟩ ⟨on sale : rebajado⟩ **10** (*indicating connection or membership*) : en ⟨on a committee : en una comisión⟩ **11** (*indicating an activity*) ⟨on vacation : de vacaciones⟩ ⟨on a diet : a dieta⟩ **12** ABOUT, CONCERNING : sobre ⟨a book on insects : un libro sobre insectos⟩ ⟨reflect on that : reflexiona sobre eso⟩ **13** : tomando ⟨to be on medication : tomar medicamentos⟩ ⟨to be on drugs : drogarse⟩ **14** *on that fam* ⟨don't worry — I'm on it : no te preocupes, yo me encargo de eso⟩ **15 on one** : encima ⟨I don't have it on me : no lo llevo/tengo encima⟩ **16 on someone** : por cuenta de alguien ⟨drinks are on the house : invita la casa⟩

once¹ ['wʌnts] *adv* **1** : una vez ⟨once a month : una vez al mes⟩ ⟨once and for all : de una vez por todas⟩ ⟨once in a while : de vez en cuando⟩ ⟨once or twice : alguna que otra vez⟩ ⟨for once : por una vez⟩ **2** EVER : alguna vez **3** FORMERLY : antes, anteriormente

once² *adj* FORMER : antiguo

once³ *n* **1** : una vez **2 (all) at ~** : de una vez, de un golpe, de un tirón **3 at ~** SIMULTANEOUSLY : al mismo tiempo, simultáneamente **4 at ~** IMMEDIATELY : inmediatamente, en seguida

once⁴ *conj* : una vez que, tan pronto como

once–over [ˌwʌnts'oːvər, 'wʌntsˌ-] *n* **to give someone the once–over** : echarle un vistazo a alguien

oncoming ['ɑnˌkʌmɪŋ, 'ɔn-] *adj* : que viene

one¹ ['wʌn] *adj* **1** (*being a single unit*) : un, una ⟨he only wants one apple : sólo quiere una manzana⟩ **2** (*being a particular one*) : un, una ⟨he arrived early one morning : llegó temprano una mañana⟩ **3** (*being the same*) : mismo, misma ⟨they're all members of one team : todos son miembros del mismo equipo⟩ ⟨one and the same thing : la misma cosa⟩ **4** SOME : alguno, alguna; un, una ⟨I'll see you again one day : algún día te veré otra vez⟩ ⟨at one time or another : en una u otra ocasión⟩

one² *n* **1** : uno *m* (número) **2** (*indicating the first of a set or series*) ⟨from day one : desde el primer momento⟩ **3** (*indicating a single person or thing*) ⟨the one (girl) on the right : la de la derecha⟩ ⟨he has the one but needs the other : tiene uno pero necesita el otro⟩

one³ *pron* **1** : uno ⟨it's one (o'clock) : es la una⟩ ⟨one of his friends : una de sus amigas⟩ ⟨one never knows : uno nunca sabe, nunca se sabe⟩ ⟨to cut one's finger : cortarse el dedo⟩ **2 one and all** : todos, todo el mundo **3 one another** : el uno al otro, se ⟨they loved one another : se amaban⟩ **4 that one** : aquél, aquella **5 which one?** : ¿cuál?

one–handed [ˌwʌn'hændəd] *adj & adv* : con una sola mano

one–on–one [ˌwʌnɑn'wʌn, -ɑn-] *adj* : uno a uno — **one–on–one** *adv*

onerous ['ɑnərəs, 'oːnə-] *adj* : oneroso, gravoso

oneself [ˌwʌn'sɛlf] *pron* **1** (*used reflexively or for emphasis*) : se, sí mismo, uno mismo ⟨to control oneself : controlarse⟩ ⟨to talk to oneself : hablarse a sí mismo⟩ ⟨to do it oneself : hacérselo uno mismo⟩ **2 by ~** : solo

one–sided ['wʌn'saɪdəd] *adj* **1** : de un solo lado **2** LOPSIDED : asimétrico **3** BIASED : parcial, tendencioso **4** UNILATERAL : unilateral

onetime ['wʌnˌtaɪm] *adj* FORMER : antiguo

one–way ['wʌn'weɪ] *adj* **1** : de sentido único, de una sola dirección ⟨a one-way street : una calle de sentido único⟩ **2**

: de ida, sencillo ⟨a one-way ticket : un boleto de ida⟩

one–way mirror *n* : espejo *m* polarizado

ongoing [ˈɑnˌgoːɪŋ] *adj* **1** CONTINUING : en curso, corriente **2** DEVELOPING : en desarrollo

onion [ˈʌnjən] *n* : cebolla *f*

online [ˈɔnˈlaɪn, ˈɑn-] *adj & adv* : en línea, online

onlooker [ˈɔnˌlʊkər, ˈɑn-] *n* : espectador *m*, -dora *f*, circunstante *mf*

only¹ [ˈoːnli] *adv* **1** MERELY : sólo, solamente, nomás ⟨for only two dollars : por tan sólo dos dólares⟩ ⟨only once : sólo una vez, no más de una vez⟩ ⟨I only did it to help : lo hice por ayudar nomás⟩ **2** SOLELY : únicamente, sólo, solamente ⟨only he knows it : solamente él lo sabe⟩ ⟨only because you asked me to : sólo porque tú me lo pediste⟩ **3** ASSUMING : sólo, solamente ⟨I'll go only if he goes with me : iré sólo si él me acompaña⟩ **4** (*indicating a result*) ⟨it will only cause him problems : no hará más que crearle problemas⟩ **5** (*used for emphasis*) ⟨I only hope it will work! : ¡espero que resulte!⟩ **6** (*indicating that something was recent*) ⟨it seems like only yesterday : parece que fue ayer⟩ **7 if only** : ojalá, por lo menos ⟨if only it were true! : ¡ojalá sea cierto!⟩ ⟨if he could only dance : si por lo menos pudiera bailar⟩ **8 not only . . . but also . . .** : no sólo . . . sino también **9 only just** BARELY : apenas ⟨we've only just begun : acabamos de empezar⟩ ⟨I only just missed the flight : perdí el vuelo por un pelo⟩

only² *adj* : único ⟨an only child : un hijo único⟩ ⟨the only chance : la única oportunidad⟩

only³ *conj* BUT : pero ⟨I would go, only I'm sick : iría, pero estoy enfermo⟩

onset [ˈɑnˌsɛt] *n* : comienzo *m*, llegada *f*

onslaught [ˈɑnˌslɔt, ˈɔn-] *n* : arremetida *f*, embestida *f*, embate *m*

onto [ˈɑnˌtuː, ˈɔn-] *prep* **1** : sobre **2** (*indicating knowledge or awareness*) ⟨the police are onto them : la policía anda tras ellos⟩ ⟨I think you're onto something : creo que has dado con algo interesante/importante⟩ ⟨the scientists were onto something big : los científicos estaban a punto de descubrir algo importante⟩

onus [ˈoːnəs] *n* : responsabilidad *f*, carga *f*

onward¹ [ˈɑnwərd, ˈɔn-] *or* **onwards** *adv* FORWARD : adelante, hacia adelante

onward² *adj* : hacia adelante

onyx [ˈɑnɪks] *n* : ónix *m*

oops [ˈʊps, ˈwʊps] *interj* : ¡huy! ⟨oops! I goofed : ¡huy! me equivoqué⟩

ooze¹ [ˈuːz] *v* **oozed; oozing** *vi* : rezumar — *vt* **1** : rezumar **2** EXUDE : irradiar, rebosar ⟨to ooze confidence : irradiar confianza⟩

ooze² *n* SLIME : cieno *m*, limo *m*

opacity [oˈpæsəti] *n, pl* **-ties** : opacidad *f*

opal [ˈoːpəl] *n* : ópalo *m*

opaque [oˈpeɪk] *adj* **1** : opaco **2** UNCLEAR : poco claro

open¹ [ˈoːpən] *vt* **1** : abrir ⟨open the door : abre la puerta⟩ ⟨open your books : abran sus libros⟩ **2** UNCOVER : abrir, destapar (una botella, etc.) **3** UNFOLD : abrir, desplegar **4** CLEAR : abrir (un camino, etc.) **5** INAUGURATE : abrir (una tienda), inaugurar (una exposición, etc.) **6** INITIATE : iniciar, entablar, abrir ⟨to open the meeting : abrir la sesión⟩ ⟨to open a discussion : entablar un debate⟩ ⟨to open a document : abrir un documento⟩ **7 to open fire (on)** : abrir fuego (sobre) **8 to open up** : abrir — *vi* **1** : abrirse **2** BEGIN : empezar, comenzar **3 to open onto** : dar a **4 to open up** : abrirse **5 to open up** : abrir (dícese de una empresa, etc.)

open² *adj* **1** : abierto ⟨an open window : una ventana abierta⟩ **2** FRANK : abierto, franco, directo ⟨to be open with : ser sincero/franco con⟩ **3** UNCOVERED : abierto, descubierto ⟨an open box : una caja abierta⟩ **4** EXTENDED : abierto, extendido ⟨with open arms : con los brazos abiertos⟩ **5** UNRESTRICTED : libre, abierto ⟨in the open air : al aire libre⟩ ⟨open to the public : abierto al público⟩ ⟨open admission : entrada libre⟩ ⟨an open letter : una carta abierta⟩ **6** : abierto (dícese de una tienda, etc.) **7** UNDECIDED : pendiente, por decidir, sin resolver ⟨an open question : una cuestión pendiente⟩ **8** AVAILABLE : vacante, libre ⟨the job is open : el puesto está vacante⟩ **9** EXPOSED, VULNERABLE : expuesto, vulnerable ⟨he has left himself open to criticism : se ha expuesto a las críticas⟩ ⟨to be open to abuse : prestarse al abuso⟩ ⟨to be open to doubt/question : ser discutible⟩

open³ *n* **in the open** **1** OUTDOORS : al aire libre **2** KNOWN : conocido, sacado a la luz

open–air [ˈoːpənˈær] *adj* OUTDOOR : al aire libre

open–and–shut [ˈoːpənəndˈʃʌt] *adj* : claro, evidente ⟨an open-and-shut case : un caso muy claro⟩

opener [ˈoːpənər] *n* : destapador *m*, abrelatas *m*, abridor *m*

openhanded [ˌoːpənˈhændəd] *adj* : generoso, liberal

open–heart [ˈoːpənˈhɑrt] *adj* : de corazón abierto

openhearted [ˌoːpənˈhɑrtəd] *adj* **1** FRANK : franco, sincero **2** : generoso, de gran corazón

opening [ˈoːpənɪŋ] *n* **1** BEGINNING : comienzo *m*, principio *m*, apertura *f* **2** APERTURE : abertura *f*, brecha *f*, claro *m* (en el bosque) **3** OPPORTUNITY : oportunidad *f*

openly [ˈoːpənli] *adv* **1** FRANKLY : abiertamente, francamente **2** PUBLICLY : públicamente, declaradamente

open–minded [ˌoːpənˈmaɪndəd] *adj* : sin prejuicios, de actitud abierta

open–mouthed [ˌoːpənˈmaʊðd, -ˈmaʊθt] *adj* : boquiabierto

openness [ˈoːpənnəs] *n* : franqueza *f*

opera ['ɑprə, 'ɑpərə] *n* 1 : ópera *f* 2 → opus

opera glasses *npl* : gemelos *mpl* de teatro

operate ['ɑpə,reɪt] *v* -ated; -ating *vi* 1 ACT, FUNCTION : operar, funcionar, actuar 2 **to operate on (someone)** : operar a (alguien) — *vt* 1 WORK : operar, manejar, hacer funcionar (una máquina) 2 MANAGE : manejar, administrar (un negocio)

operatic [,ɑpə'rætɪk] *adj* : operístico

operating room *n* : quirófano *m*

operation [,ɑpə'reɪʃən] *n* 1 FUNCTIONING : funcionamiento *m* 2 USE : uso *m*, manejo *m* (de máquinas) 3 SURGERY : operación *f*, intervención *f* quirúrgica

operational [,ɑpə'reɪʃənəl] *adj* : operacional, de operación

operative ['ɑpərətɪv, -,reɪ-] *adj* 1 OPERATING : vigente, en vigor 2 WORKING : operativo 3 SURGICAL : quirúrgico

operator ['ɑpə,reɪtər] *n* : operador *m*, -dora *f*

operetta [,ɑpə'rɛtə] *n* : opereta *f*

ophthalmologist [,ɑf,θæl'mɑlədʒɪst, -θə'mɑ-] *n* : oftalmólogo *m*, -ga *f*

ophthalmology [,ɑf,θæl'mɑlədʒi, -θə'mɑ-] *n* : oftalmología *f*

opiate ['o:piət, -pi,eɪt] *n* : opiato *m*

opine [o'paɪn] *v* : opinar

opinion [ə'pɪnjən] *n* : opinión *f*

opinionated [ə'pɪnjə,neɪtəd] *adj* : testarudo, dogmático

opinion poll *n* SURVEY : sondeo *m*, encuesta *f* de opinión

opium ['o:piəm] *n* : opio *m*

opossum [ə'pɑsəm] *n* : zarigüeya *f*, oposum *m*

opponent [ə'po:nənt] *n* : oponente *mf*; opositor *m*, -tora *f*; contrincante *mf* (en deportes)

opportune [,ɑpər'tu:n, -'tju:n] *adj* : oportuno — **opportunely** *adv*

opportunism [,ɑpər'tu:,nɪzəm, -'tju:-] *n* : oportunismo *m*

opportunist [,ɑpər'tu:nɪst, -'tju:-] *n* : oportunista *mf*

opportunistic [,ɑpərtu'nɪstɪk, -tju-] *adj* : oportunista *mf*

opportunity [,ɑpər'tu:nəti, -'tju:-] *n, pl* -ties : oportunidad *f*, ocasión *f*, chance *m*, posibilidades *fpl*

oppose [ə'po:z] *vt* -posed; -posing 1 : ir en contra de, oponerse a ⟨good opposes evil : el bien se opone al mal⟩ 2 COMBAT : luchar contra, combatir, resistir

opposite[1] ['ɑpəzət] *adv* : enfrente

opposite[2] *adj* 1 FACING : de enfrente ⟨the opposite side : el lado de enfrente⟩ 2 CONTRARY : opuesto, contrario ⟨in opposite directions : en direcciones contrarias⟩ ⟨the opposite sex : el sexo opuesto, el otro sexo⟩

opposite[3] *n* : lo contrario, lo opuesto

opposite[4] *prep* : enfrente de, frente a

opposition [,ɑpə'zɪʃən] *n* 1 : oposición *f*, resistencia *f* 2 **in opposition to** AGAINST : en contra de

oppress [ə'prɛs] *vt* 1 PERSECUTE : opri-

mir, perseguir 2 BURDEN : oprimir, agobiar

oppression [ə'prɛʃən] *n* : opresión *f*

oppressive [ə'prɛsɪv] *adj* 1 HARSH : opresivo, severo 2 STIFLING : agobiante, sofocante ⟨oppressive heat : calor sofocante⟩

oppressor [ə'prɛsər] *n* : opresor *m*, -sora *f*

opprobrium [ə'pro:briəm] *n* : oprobio *m*

opt ['ɑpt] *vi* 1 : optar 2 **to opt for** : optar por 3 **to opt in** : decidir participar 4 **to opt into** : decidir participar en 5 **to opt out (of)** : decidir no participar (en)

optic ['ɑptɪk] *or* **optical** [-tɪkəl] *adj* : óptico

optical disk *n* : disco *m* óptico

optician [ɑp'tɪʃən] *n* : óptico *m*, -ca *f*

optics ['ɑptɪks] *npl* : óptica *f*

optimal ['ɑptəməl] *adj* : óptimo

optimism ['ɑptə,mɪzəm] *n* : optimismo *m*

optimist ['ɑptəmɪst] *n* : optimista *mf*

optimistic [,ɑptə'mɪstɪk] *adj* : optimista

optimistically [,ɑptə'mɪstɪkli] *adv* : con optimismo, positivamente

optimum[1] ['ɑptəməm] *adj* → **optimal**

optimum[2] *n, pl* -ma ['ɑptəmə] : lo óptimo, lo ideal

option ['ɑpʃən] *n* : opción *f* ⟨she has no option : no tiene más remedio⟩

optional ['ɑpʃənəl] *adj* : facultativo, optativo

optometrist [ɑp'tɑmətrɪst] *n* : optometrista *mf*

optometry [ɑp'tɑmətri] *n* : optometría *f*

opulence ['ɑpjələnts] *n* : opulencia *f*

opulent ['ɑpjələnt] *adj* : opulento

opus ['o:pəs] *n, pl* **opera** ['o:pərə, 'ɑpə-] : opus *m*, obra *f* (de música)

or ['ɔr] *conj* 1 (*indicating an alternative*) : o (**u** *before words beginning with o or ho*) ⟨coffee or tea : café o té⟩ ⟨one day or another : un día u otro⟩ 2 (*following a negative*) : ni ⟨he didn't have his keys or his wallet : no llevaba ni sus llaves ni su billetera⟩

oracle ['ɔrəkəl] *n* : oráculo *m*

oral ['ɔrəl] *adj* : oral — **orally** *adv*

orange ['ɔrɪndʒ] *n* 1 : naranja *f*, china *f* PRi (fruto) 2 : naranja *m* (color), color *m* de china PRi

orangeade [,ɔrɪndʒ'eɪd] *n* : naranjada *f*

orangutan [ə'ræŋə,tæn, -'ræŋgə-, -,tæn] *n* : orangután *m*

oration [ə'reɪʃən] *n* : oración *f*, discurso *m*

orator ['ɔrətər] *n* : orador *m*, -dora *f*

oratorio [,ɔrə'tori,o:] *n, pl* -rios : oratorio *m*

oratory ['ɔrə,tori] *n, pl* -ries : oratoria *f*

orb ['ɔrb] *n* : orbe *m*

orbit[1] ['ɔrbət] *vt* 1 CIRCLE : girar alrededor de, orbitar 2 : poner en órbita (un satélite, etc.) — *vi* : orbitar

orbit[2] *n* : órbita *f*

orbital ['ɔrbətəl] *adj* : orbital

orca ['ɔrkə] *n* : orca *f*

orchard ['ɔrtʃərd] *n* : huerto *m*

orchestra ['ɔrkəstrə] *n* : orquesta *f*

orchestral [ɔr'kɛstrəl] *adj* : orquestal

orchestrate ['ɔrkə,streɪt] *vt* **-trated; -trating 1** : orquestar, instrumentar (en música) **2** ORGANIZE : arreglar, organizar

orchestration [,ɔrkə'streɪʃən] *n* : orquestación *f*

orchid ['ɔrkɪd] *n* : orquídea *f*

ordain [ɔr'deɪn] *vt* **1** : ordenar (en religión) **2** DECREE : decretar, ordenar

ordeal [ɔr'di:l, 'ɔr,di:l] *n* : prueba *f* dura, experiencia *f* terrible

order¹ ['ɔrdər] *vt* **1** ORGANIZE : arreglar, ordenar, poner en orden **2** COMMAND : ordenar, mandar **3** REQUEST : pedir, encargar ⟨to order a meal : pedir algo de comer⟩ — *vi* : hacer un pedido

order² *n* **1** : orden *f* ⟨a religious order : una orden religiosa⟩ **2** COMMAND : orden *f*, mandato *m* ⟨to give an order : dar una orden⟩ ⟨to give the order to do something : dar orden de hacer algo⟩ ⟨by order of : por orden de⟩ **3** REQUEST : orden *f*, pedido *m* ⟨purchase order : orden de compra⟩ ⟨to place/take an order : hacer/tomar un pedido⟩ ⟨to be on order : estar pedido⟩ **4** SERVING : porción *f*, ración *f* ⟨an order of fries : una porción de papas fritas⟩ **5** ARRANGEMENT : orden *m* ⟨in chronological order : por orden cronológico⟩ ⟨out of order : desordenado⟩ ⟨everything seems to be in order : parece que todo está en orden⟩ **6** DISCIPLINE : orden *m* ⟨law and order : el orden público⟩ ⟨to keep order : mantener el orden⟩ **7 in order for** : para que ⟨in order for this to work : para que esto funcione⟩ **8 in order that** : para que ⟨in order that others might live : para que otros puedan vivir⟩ **9 in order to** : para **10 in (working) order** : funcionando **11 out of order** BROKEN : descompuesto, averiado **12 orders** *npl or* **holy orders** : órdenes *fpl* sagradas

orderliness ['ɔrdərlinəs] *n* : orden *m*

orderly¹ ['ɔrdərli] *adj* **1** METHODICAL : ordenado, metódico **2** PEACEFUL : pacífico, disciplinado

orderly² *n, pl* **-lies 1** : ordenanza *m* (en el ejército) **2** : camillero *m* (en un hospital)

ordinal ['ɔrdənəl] *n or* **ordinal number** : ordinal *m*, número *m* ordinal

ordinance ['ɔrdənənts] *n* : ordenanza *f*, reglamento *m*

ordinarily [,ɔrdən'erəli] *adv* : ordinariamente, por lo general

ordinary ['ɔrdən,eri] *adj* **1** NORMAL, USUAL : normal, usual **2** AVERAGE : común y corriente, normal **3** MEDIOCRE : mediocre, ordinario

ordination [,ɔrdən'eɪʃən] *n* : ordenación *f*

ordnance ['ɔrdnənts] *n* : artillería *f*

ore ['or] *n* : mineral *m* (metálico), mena *f*

oregano [ə'regə,no:] *n* : orégano *m*

organ ['ɔrgən] *n* **1** : órgano *m* (instrumento) **2** : órgano *m* (del cuerpo) **3** PERIODICAL : publicación *f* periódica, órgano *m*

organic [ɔr'gænɪk] *adj* : orgánico — **organically** *adv*

organism ['ɔrgə,nɪzəm] *n* : organismo *m*

organist ['ɔrgənɪst] *n* : organista *mf*

organization [,ɔrgənə'zeɪʃən] *n* **1** ORGANIZING : organización *f* **2** BODY : organización *f*, organismo *m*

organizational [,ɔrgənə'zeɪʃənəl] *adj* : organizativo

organize ['ɔrgə,naɪz] *vt* **-nized; -nizing** : organizar, arreglar, poner en orden

organizer ['ɔrgə,naɪzər] *n* : organizador *m*, -dora *f*

orgasm ['ɔr,gæzəm] *n* : orgasmo *m*

orgy ['ɔrʤi] *n, pl* **-gies** : orgía *f*

orient ['ori,ɛnt] *vt* : orientar

Orient *n* **the Orient** : el Oriente

oriental [,ori'ɛntəl] *adj dated, now usu offensive when used of people* : del Oriente, oriental *dated, now sometimes offensive when used of people*

Oriental *n dated, now usu offensive* : oriental *masculine or feminine dated, now sometimes offensive*

orientation [,oriən'teɪʃən] *n* : orientación *f*

orifice ['ɔrəfəs] *n* : orificio *m*

origin ['ɔrəʤən] *n* **1** ANCESTRY : origen *m*, ascendencia *f* **2** SOURCE : origen *m*, raíz *f*, fuente *f*

original¹ [ə'rɪʤənəl] *adj* : original

original² *n* : original *m*

originality [ə,rɪʤə'næləti] *n* : originalidad *f*

originally [ə'rɪʤənəli] *adv* **1** AT FIRST : al principio, originariamente **2** CREATIVELY : originalmente, con originalidad

originate [ə'rɪʤə,neɪt] *v* **-nated; -nating** *vt* : originar, iniciar, crear — *vi* **1** BEGIN : originarse, empezar **2** COME : provenir, proceder, derivarse

originator [ə'rɪʤə,neɪtər] *n* : creador *m*, -dora *f*; inventor *m*, -tora *f*

oriole ['ori,o:l, -iəl] *n* : oropéndola *f*

ornament¹ ['ɔrnəmənt] *vt* : adornar, decorar, ornamentar

ornament² *n* : ornamento *m*, adorno *m*, decoración *f*

ornamental [,ɔrnə'mɛntəl] *adj* : ornamental, de adorno, decorativo

ornamentation [,ɔrnəmən'teɪʃən, -mɛn-] *n* : ornamentación *f*

ornate [ɔr'neɪt] *adj* : elaborado, recargado

ornery ['ɔrnəri, 'ɑrnəri] *adj* **ornerier; -est** : de mal genio, malhumorado

ornithologist [,ɔrnə'θɑləʤɪst] *n* : ornitólogo *m*, -ga *f*

ornithology [,ɔrnə'θɑləʤi] *n, pl* **-gies** : ornitología *f*

orphan¹ ['ɔrfən] *vt* : dejar huérfano

orphan² *n* : huérfano *m*, -na *f*

orphanage ['ɔrfənɪʤ] *n* : orfelinato *m*, orfanato *m*

orthodontics [,ɔrθə'dɑntɪks] *n* : ortodoncia *f*

orthodontist [,ɔrθə'dɑntɪst] *n* : ortodoncista *mf*

orthodox ['ɔrθə,dɑks] *adj* : ortodoxo

orthodoxy ['ɔrθə,dɑksi] *n, pl* **-doxies** : ortodoxia *f*

orthographic [,ɔrθə'græfɪk] *adj* : ortográfico

orthography [ɔr'θɑgrəfi] *n, pl* **-phies** SPELL-ING : ortografía *f*

orthopedic [ˌɔrθə'piːdɪk] *adj* : ortopédico

orthopedics [ˌɔrθə'piːdɪks] *ns & pl* : ortopedia *f*

orthopedist [ˌɔrθə'piːdɪst] *n* : ortopedista *mf*

oscillate ['ɑsəˌleɪt] *vi* **-lated; -lating** : oscilar

oscillation [ˌɑsə'leɪʃən] *n* : oscilación *f*

osmosis [ɑz'moːsɪs, ɑs-] *n* : ósmosis *f*, osmosis *f*

osprey ['ɑspri, -ˌpreɪ] *n* : pigargo *m*

ostensible [ɑ'stɛntsəbəl] *adj* APPARENT : aparente, ostensible — **ostensibly** [-bli] *adv*

ostentation [ˌɑstən'teɪʃən] *n* : ostentación *f*, boato *m*

ostentatious [ˌɑstən'teɪʃəs] *adj* : ostentoso — **ostentatiously** *adv*

osteopath ['ɑstiəˌpæθ] *n* : osteópata *f*

osteopathy [ˌɑsti'ɑpəθi] *n* : osteopatía *f*

osteoporosis [ˌɑstiopə'roːsɪs] *n, pl* **-roses** [-ˌsiːz] : osteoporosis *f*

ostracism ['ɑstrəˌsɪzəm] *n* : ostracismo *m*

ostracize ['ɑstrəˌsaɪz] *vt* **-cized; -cizing** : condenar al ostracismo, marginar, aislar

ostrich ['ɑstrɪtʃ, 'ɔs-] *n* : avestruz *m*

other¹ ['ʌðər] *adv* **other than** : aparte de, fuera de

other² *adj* **1** : otro ⟨the other boys : los otros muchachos⟩ ⟨smarter than other people : más inteligente que los demás⟩ ⟨on the other hand : por otra parte, por otro lado⟩ **2 every other** : cada dos ⟨every other day : cada dos días⟩

other³ *pron* **1** : otro ⟨one in front of the other : uno tras otro⟩ ⟨either one or the other : uno u otro⟩ ⟨myself and three others : yo y tres otros/más⟩ ⟨this class and three others : esta clase y tres otras/más⟩ ⟨from one extreme to the other : de un extremo al otro⟩ ⟨somewhere or other : en alguna parte⟩ ⟨somehow or other : de alguna manera⟩ **2 the others** : los otros, los demás ⟨this class and the others : esta clase y las otras⟩

otherwise¹ ['ʌðərˌwaɪz] *adv* **1** DIFFERENTLY : de otro modo, de manera distinta ⟨he could not act otherwise : no pudo actuar de manera distinta⟩ **2** : eso aparte, por lo demás ⟨I'm dizzy, but otherwise I'm fine : estoy mareado pero, por lo demás, estoy bien⟩ **3** OR ELSE : de lo contrario, si no ⟨do what I tell you, otherwise you'll be sorry : haz lo que te digo, de lo contrario, te arrepentirás⟩

otherwise² *adj* : diferente, distinto ⟨the facts are otherwise : la realidad es diferente⟩

otitis [o'taɪtəs] *n* : otitis *f*

otter ['ɑtər] *n* : nutria *f*

Ottoman ['ɑtəmən] *n* **1** : otomano *m*, -na *f* **2** : otomana *f* (mueble) — **Ottoman** *adj*

ouch ['aʊtʃ] *interj* : ¡ay!, ¡huy!

ought ['ɔt] *v aux* : deber ⟨you ought to take care of yourself : deberías cuidarte⟩

oughtn't ['ɔtənt] *contraction of* OUGHT NOT → **ought**

ounce ['aʊnts] *n* : onza *f*

our ['ɑr, 'aʊr] *adj* : nuestro

ours ['aʊrz, 'ɑrz] *pron* : nuestro ⟨a cousin of ours : un primo nuestro, una prima nuestra⟩

ourselves [ɑr'sɛlvz, aʊr-] *pron* **1** (*used reflexively*) : nos, nosotros, nosotras ⟨we amused ourselves : nos divertimos⟩ ⟨we were always thinking of ourselves : siempre pensábamos en nosotros⟩ **2** (*used for emphasis*) : nosotros mismos, nosotras mismas ⟨we did it ourselves : lo hicimos nosotros mismos⟩

oust ['aʊst] *vt* : desbancar, expulsar

ouster ['aʊstər] *n* : expulsión *f* (de un país, etc.), destitución *f* (de un puesto)

out¹ ['aʊt] *vi* : revelarse, hacerse conocido

out² *adv* **1** (*indicating direction or movement*) OUTSIDE : para afuera ⟨she opened the door and looked out : abrió la puerta y miró para afuera⟩ ⟨he went out to the garden : salió al jardín⟩ ⟨she took the dog out : sacó al perro⟩ **2** (*indicating location*) OUTSIDE : fuera, afuera ⟨out in the garden : afuera en el jardín⟩ ⟨it's sunny out : hace sol⟩ ⟨your shirt is hanging out : tienes la camisa afuera⟩ **3** (*indicating outward movement*) ⟨they flew out yesterday : salieron ayer (en avión)⟩ ⟨out to sea : mar adentro⟩ **4** (*indicating distance*) ⟨they live out in the country : viven en el campo⟩ **5** (*indicating omission*) ⟨you left out a comma : omitiste una coma⟩ ⟨count me out : no cuentes conmigo⟩ **6** (*indicating removal, loss, or incorrect placement*) ⟨they voted him out : no lo reeligieron⟩ ⟨his hair is falling out : se le está cayendo el pelo⟩ ⟨she threw out her shoulder : se lastimó el hombro⟩ **7** (*indicating drawing from a group*) ⟨she picked out a shirt : escogió una camisa⟩ **8** (*indicating a location away from home or work*) : fuera, afuera ⟨to eat out : comer afuera⟩ ⟨he asked her out : la invitó a salir⟩ **9** (*indicating loss of control or possession*) ⟨they let the secret out : sacaron el secreto a la luz⟩ **10** (*indicating ending or stopping*) ⟨his money ran out : se le acabó el dinero⟩ ⟨to turn out the light : apagar la luz⟩ **11** (*indicating completion*) ⟨to fill out a form : rellenar un formulario⟩ **12** ALOUD : en voz alta, en alto ⟨to cry out : gritar⟩ **13** UNCONSCIOUS : inconsciente **14** : abiertamente homosexual **15** → **out-of-bounds 16 to be out for** : estar buscando (venganza, etc.) **17 to be out to** : querer (vengarse, etc.) ⟨he's out to get me : me la tiene jurada⟩

out³ *adj* **1** EXTERNAL : externo, exterior **2** OUTLYING : alejado, distante ⟨the out islands : las islas distantes⟩ **3** ABSENT : ausente **4** UNFASHIONABLE : fuera de moda **5** EXTINGUISHED : apagado **6 to be out and about** : estar andando por ahí

out⁴ *prep* **1** (*used to indicate an outward movement*) : por ⟨I looked out the window : miré por la ventana⟩ ⟨she ran out the door : corrió por la puerta⟩ **2 → out of**

out–and–out [ˈaʊtənˈaʊt] *adj* UTTER : redomado, absoluto

outback [ˈaʊtˌbæk] *n* **the outback** : el interior (de Australia)

outboard motor [ˈaʊtˌbord] *n* : motor *m* fuera de borde

outbound [ˈaʊtˌbaʊnd] *adj* : que sale, de salida

out–box [ˈaʊtˌbɑks] *n* : bandeja *f* de salida

outbreak [ˈaʊtˌbreɪk] *n* : brote *m* (de una enfermedad), comienzo *m* (de guerra), ola *f* (de violencia), erupción *f* (de granos)

outbuilding [ˈaʊtˌbɪldɪŋ] *n* : edificio *m* anexo

outburst [ˈaʊtˌbərst] *n* : arranque *m*, arrebato *m*

outcast [ˈaʊtˌkæst] *n* : marginado *m*, -da *f*; paria *mf*

outcome [ˈaʊtˌkʌm] *n* : resultado *m*, desenlace *m*, consecuencia *f*

outcry [ˈaʊtˌkraɪ] *n*, *pl* **-cries** : clamor *m*, protesta *f*

outdated [ˌaʊtˈdeɪtəd] *adj* : anticuado, fuera de moda

outdistance [ˌaʊtˈdɪstənts] *vt* **-tanced; -tancing** : aventajar, dejar atrás

outdo [ˌaʊtˈduː] *vt* **-did** [-ˈdɪd]; **-done** [-ˈdʌn]; **-doing; -does** [-ˈdʌz] : superar

outdoor [ˈaʊtˈdor] *adj* : al aire libre ⟨outdoor sports : deportes al aire libre⟩ ⟨outdoor clothing : ropa de calle⟩

outdoors¹ [ˈaʊtˈdorz] *adv* : afuera, al aire libre

outdoors² *n* : aire *m* libre

outer [ˈaʊtər] *adj* **1** : exterior, externo **2 outer space** : espacio *m* exterior

outermost [ˈaʊtərˌmoːst] *adj* : más remoto, más exterior, extremo

outfield [ˈaʊtˌfiːld] *n* **the outfield** : los jardines

outfielder [ˈaʊtˌfiːldər] *n* : jardinero *m*, -ra *f*

outfit¹ [ˈaʊtˌfɪt] *vt* **-fitted; -fitting** EQUIP : equipar

outfit² *n* **1** EQUIPMENT : equipo *m* **2** COSTUME, ENSEMBLE : traje *m*, conjunto *m* **3** GROUP : conjunto *m*

outgo [ˈaʊtˌgoː] *n*, *pl* **outgoes** : gasto *m*

outgoing [ˈaʊtˌgoːɪŋ] *adj* **1** OUTBOUND : que sale **2** DEPARTING : saliente ⟨an outgoing president : un presidente saliente⟩ **3** EXTROVERTED : extrovertido, expansivo

outgrow [ˌaʊtˈgroː] *vt* **-grew** [-ˈgruː]; **-grown** [-ˈgroːn]; **-growing 1** : crecer más que ⟨that tree outgrew all the others : ese árbol creció más que todos los otros⟩ **2 to outgrow one's clothes** : quedarle pequeña la ropa a uno

outgrowth [ˈaʊtˌgroːθ] *n* **1** OFFSHOOT : brote *m*, vástago *m* (de una planta) **2** CONSEQUENCE : consecuencia *f*, producto *m*, resultado *m*

outing [ˈaʊtɪŋ] *n* : excursión *f*

outlandish [aʊtˈlændɪʃ] *adj* : descabellado, muy extraño

outlast [ˌaʊtˈlæst] *vt* : durar más que

outlaw¹ [ˈaʊtˌlɔ] *vt* : hacerse ilegal, declarar fuera de la ley, prohibir

outlaw² *n* : bandido *m*, -da *f*; bandolero *m*, -ra *f*; forajido *m*, -da *f*

outlay [ˈaʊtˌleɪ] *n* : gasto *m*, desembolso *m*

outlet [ˈaʊtˌlɛt, -lət] *n* **1** EXIT : salida *f*, escape *m* ⟨electrical outlet : toma de corriente⟩ **2** RELIEF : desahogo *m* **3** MARKET : mercado *m*, salida *f*

outline¹ [ˈaʊtˌlaɪn] *vt* **-lined; -lining 1** SKETCH : diseñar, esbozar, bosquejar **2** DEFINE EXPLAIN : perfilar, delinear, explicar ⟨she outlined our responsibilities : delineó nuestras responsabilidades⟩

outline² *n* **1** PROFILE : perfil *m*, silueta *f*, contorno *m* **2** SKETCH : bosquejo *m*, boceto *m* **3** SUMMARY : esquema *m*, resumen *m*, sinopsis *m* ⟨an outline of world history : un esquema de la historia mundial⟩

outlive [ˌaʊtˈlɪv] *vt* **-lived; -living** : sobrevivir a

outlook [ˈaʊtˌlʊk] *n* **1** VIEW : vista *f*, panorama *f* **2** POINT OF VIEW : punto *m* de vista **3** PROSPECTS : perspectivas *fpl*

outlying [ˈaʊtˌlaɪŋ] *adj* : alejado, distante, remoto ⟨the outlying areas : las afueras⟩

outmoded [ˌaʊtˈmoːdəd] *adj* : pasado de moda, anticuado

outnumber [ˌaʊtˈnʌmbər] *vt* : superar en número a, ser más numeroso de

out of *prep* **1** (*indicating direction or movement from within*) : de, por ⟨we ran out of the house : salimos corriendo de la casa⟩ ⟨to look out of the window : mirar por la ventana⟩ **2** (*being beyond the limits of*) ⟨out of control : fuera de control⟩ ⟨to be out of sight : desaparecer de vista⟩ **3** OF : de ⟨one out of four : uno de cada cuatro⟩ **4** (*indicating absence or loss*) : sin ⟨out of money : sin dinero⟩ ⟨we're out of matches : nos hemos quedado sin fósforos⟩ **5** BECAUSE OF : por ⟨out of curiosity : por curiosidad⟩ **6** FROM : de ⟨made out of plastic : hecho de plástico⟩

out–of–bounds [ˌaʊtəvˈbaʊndz] *adj* : fuera de juego

out–of–date [ˌaʊtəvˈdeɪt] *adj* : anticuado, obsoleto, pasado de moda

out–of–door [ˌaʊtəvˈdor] *or* **out–of–doors** [-ˈdorz] **→ outdoor**

out–of–doors *n* **→ outdoors²**

out–of–the–way [ˌaʊtəvðəˈweɪ] *adj* : alejado, distante, remoto

outpatient [ˈaʊtˌpeɪʃənt] *n* : paciente *m* externo, paciente *f* externa

outpost [ˈaʊtˌpoːst] *n* : puesto *m* avanzado

output¹ [ˈaʊtˌpʊt] *vt* **-putted** *or* **-put; -putting** : producir

output² *n* : producción *f* (de una fábrica), rendimiento *m* (de una máquina), productividad *f* (de una persona)

outrage¹ [ˈaʊtˌreɪʤ] *vt* **-raged; -raging 1** INSULT : ultrajar, injuriar **2** INFURIATE : indignar, enfurecer

outrage² *n* **1** ATROCITY : atropello *m*, atrocidad *f*, atentado *m* **2** SCANDAL : escándalo *m* **3** ANGER : ira *f*, furia *f*

outrageous [ˌaʊtˈreɪʤəs] *adj* **1** SCANDALOUS : escandaloso, ofensivo, atroz **2**

UNCONVENTIONAL : poco convencional, extravagante **3** EXORBITANT : exorbitante, excesivo (dícese de los precios, etc.)

outright[1] [ˌaʊtˈraɪt] *adv* **1** COMPLETELY : por completo, totalmente ⟨to sell outright : vender por completo⟩ ⟨he refused it outright : lo rechazó rotundamente⟩ **2** DIRECTLY : directamente, sin reserva **3** INSTANTLY : al instante, en el acto

outright[2] [ˈaʊtˌraɪt] *adj* **1** COMPLETE : completo, absoluto, categórico ⟨an outright lie : una mentira absoluta⟩ **2** : sin reservas ⟨an outright gift : un regalo sin reservas⟩

outset [ˈaʊtˌsɛt] *n* : comienzo *m*, principio *m*

outshine [ˌaʊtˈʃaɪn] *vt* **-shone** [-ˈʃoːn, -ˈʃɑn] *or* **-shined; -shining** : eclipsar

outside[1] [ˌaʊtˈsaɪd, ˈaʊtˌ-] *adv* : fuera, afuera

outside[2] *adj* **1** : exterior, externo ⟨the outside edge : el borde exterior⟩ ⟨outside influences : influencias externas⟩ **2** REMOTE : remoto ⟨an outside chance : una posibilidad remota⟩

outside[3] *n* **1** EXTERIOR : parte *f* de afuera, exterior *m* **2** MOST : máximo *m* ⟨three weeks at the outside : tres semanas como máximo⟩ **3 from the outside** : desde afuera, desde fuera

outside[4] *prep* : fuera de, afuera de ⟨outside my window : fuera de mi ventana⟩ ⟨outside regular hours : fuera del horario normal⟩ ⟨outside the law : afuera de la ley⟩

outside of *prep* **1** → **outside**[4] **2** → **besides**[2]

outsider [ˌaʊtˈsaɪdər] *n* : forastero *m*, -ra *f*

outsize [ˈaʊtˌsaɪz] *also* **outsized** [ˈaʊtˌsaɪzd] *adj* : enorme

outskirts [ˈaʊtˌskərts] *npl* : afueras *fpl*, alrededores *mpl*

outsmart [ˌaʊtˈsmɑrt] → **outwit**

outsource [ˈaʊtˌsors] *vt* : externalizar

outsourcing [ˈaʊtˌsorsɪŋ] *n* : externalización *f*

outspoken [ˌaʊtˈspoːkən] *adj* : franco, directo

outstanding [ˌaʊtˈstændɪŋ] *adj* **1** UNPAID : pendiente **2** NOTABLE : destacado, notable, excepcional, sobresaliente

outstandingly [ˌaʊtˈstændɪŋli] *adv* : excepcionalmente

outstretched [ˌaʊtˈstrɛtʃt] *adj* : extendido

outstrip [ˌaʊtˈstrɪp] *vt* **-stripped** *or* **-stript** [-ˈstrɪpt]; **-stripping** **1** : aventajar, dejar atrás ⟨he outstripped the other runners : aventajó a los otros corredores⟩ **2** SURPASS : aventajar, sobrepasar

outward[1] [ˈaʊtwərd] *or* **outwards** [-wərdz] *adv* : hacia afuera, hacia el exterior

outward[2] *adj* **1** : hacia afuera ⟨an outward flow : un flujo hacia afuera⟩ **2** : externo ⟨outward beauty : belleza externa⟩

outwardly [ˈaʊtwərdli] *adv* **1** EXTERNALLY : exteriormente **2** APPARENTLY : aparentemente ⟨outwardly friendly : aparentemente simpático⟩

outweigh [ˌaʊtˈweɪ] *vt* **1** : pesar más que **2** : ser mayor que ⟨the benefit outweighs the risk : el beneficio es mayor que el riesgo⟩

outwit [ˌaʊtˈwɪt] *vt* **-witted; -witting** : ser más listo que

ova → **ovum**

oval[1] [ˈoːvəl] *adj* : ovalado, oval

oval[2] *n* : óvalo *m*

ovarian [oˈværiən] *adj* : ovárico

ovary [ˈoːvəri] *n, pl* **-ries** : ovario *m*

ovation [oˈveɪʃən] *n* : ovación *f*

oven [ˈʌvən] *n* : horno *m*

over[1] [ˈoːvər] *adv* **1** (*indicating movement across*) ⟨he flew over to London : voló a Londres⟩ ⟨come on over! : ¡ven acá!⟩ ⟨we crossed over to the other side : cruzamos al otro lado⟩ **2** (*indicating movement from an upright position*) ⟨to fall over : caerse⟩ ⟨to push someone over : tirar a alguien al suelo⟩ **3** (*indicating reversal of position*) ⟨to turn/flip something over : darle la vuelta a algo, voltear algo⟩ ⟨roll over, please : date la vuelta, por favor⟩ **4** (*indicating an additional amount*) ⟨the show ran 10 minutes over : el espectáculo terminó 10 minutos tarde⟩ ⟨there's a lot of food left over : sobra/queda mucha comida⟩ ⟨women 65 and over : mujeres de 65 años en adelante⟩ ⟨parties of six or over : grupos de seis o más⟩ **5** (*indicating a later time*) ⟨to sleep over : quedarse a dormir⟩ ⟨some money to tide him over : un poco de dinero para sacarlo del apuro⟩ **6** (*indicating covering*) ⟨the sky clouded over : se nubló⟩ **7** THOROUGHLY : bien ⟨read it over : léelo bien⟩ **8** ABOVE, OVERHEAD : por encima **9** (*indicating repetition*) ⟨over and over : una y otra vez⟩ ⟨to start over : volver a empezar⟩ ⟨twice over : dos veces⟩ ⟨many times over : muchas veces⟩ **10 all over** EVERYWHERE : por todas partes **11 over (and done) with** ⟨I want to get this over (and done) with : quiero quitarme esto de encima⟩ **12 over and out** (*in radio transmissions*) : cambio y corto/fuera, corto y cambio

over[2] *adj* **1** HIGHER, UPPER : superior **2** REMAINING : sobrante, que sobra **3** ENDED : terminado, acabado ⟨the work is over : el trabajo está terminado⟩

over[3] *prep* **1** ABOVE : encima de, arriba de, sobre ⟨over the fireplace : encima de la chimenea⟩ ⟨the hawk flew over the hills : el halcón voló sobre los cerros⟩ **2** : más de ⟨over $50 : más de $50⟩ **3** ALONG : por, sobre ⟨to glide over the ice : deslizarse sobre el hielo⟩ **4** (*indicating motion through a place or thing*) ⟨they showed me over the house : me mostraron la casa⟩ **5** ACROSS : por encima de, sobre ⟨he jumped over the ditch : saltó por encima de la zanja⟩ ⟨we crossed over the border : cruzamos la frontera⟩ **6** BEYOND : más allá de ⟨just over that hill : un poco más allá de esa colina⟩ **7** OFF : por ⟨she fell over the side of the boat : se cayó por la borda del barco⟩ **8** (*indicating direction*) : por ⟨it's over here somewhere : está por acá⟩ ⟨look over there! : ¡mira allí!⟩ **9** UPON : sobre ⟨a cape over my shoulders : una capa sobre los hombros⟩ ⟨she hit him over the head : le dio en la cabeza⟩ **10** ON : por ⟨to speak over the phone : hablar por teléfono⟩ ⟨over the radio : por la radio⟩ **11** DURING : en, durante ⟨over the past 25 years : durante los últimos 25 años⟩ **12** PAST, THROUGH : terminado con ⟨we're over the worst of it : hemos pasado lo peor⟩ **13** BECAUSE OF : por ⟨they fought over the money : se pelearon por el dinero⟩ ⟨to laugh over something : reírse por algo⟩ **14** CONCERNING : sobre **15** (*indicating comparison*) ⟨to be an improvement over : ser mejor que⟩ ⟨to choose one thing over another : elegir una cosa en lugar de otra⟩ ⟨to have an advantage over : tener una ventaja sobre⟩ **16** DESPITE : a pesar de (objeciones, etc.) **17** (*indicating omission*) ⟨to skip over something : saltarse algo⟩ **18** (*referring to power or authority*) : por encima de, sobre ⟨those over you : los que están por encima de ti⟩ ⟨to have control over : tener control sobre⟩ **19 all over** ⟨there was water all over the floor : había agua por todo el suelo⟩ ⟨all over the place : por todas partes⟩ **20 over and above** : además de

over- *pref* : demasiado, excesivamente

overabundance [ˌoːvərə'bʌndənts] *n* : superabundancia *f*

overabundant [ˌoːvərə'bʌndənt] *adj* : superabundante

overactive [ˌoːvər'æktɪv] *adj* : hiperactivo

overall [ˌoːvər'ɔl] *adj* : total, global, de conjunto

overalls ['oːvərˌɔlz] *npl* : overol *m*

overawe [ˌoːvər'ɔ] *vt* **-awed; -awing** : intimidar, impresionar

overbearing [ˌoːvər'bærɪŋ] *adj* : dominante, imperioso, prepotente

overblown [ˌoːvər'bloːn] *adj* **1** INFLATED : inflado, exagerado **2** BOMBASTIC : grandilocuente, rimbombante

overboard ['oːvərˌbord] *adv* : por la borda, al agua

overburden [ˌoːvər'bərdən] *vt* : sobrecargar, agobiar

overcast ['oːvərˌkæst] *adj* CLOUDY : nublado

overcharge [ˌoːvər'tʃɑrdʒ] *vt* **-charged; -charging** : cobrarle de más (a alguien)

overcoat ['oːvərˌkoːt] *n* : abrigo *m*

overcome [ˌoːvər'kʌm] *v* **-came** [-'keɪm]; **-come; -coming** *vt* **1** CONQUER : vencer, derrotar, superar **2** OVERWHELM : abrumar, agobiar — *vi* : vencer

overconfidence [ˌoːvər'kɑnfədənts] *n* : exceso *m* de confianza

overconfident [ˌoːvər'kɑnfədənt] *adj* : demasiado confiado

overcook [ˌoːvər'kʊk] *vt* : recocer, cocer demasiado

overcrowded [ˌoːvər'kraʊdəd] *adj* **1** PAC-

KED : abarrotado, atestado de gente **2** OVERPOPULATED : superpoblado

overcrowding [ˌoːvər'kraʊdɪŋ] *n* **1** : hacinamiento *m*, masificación *f* *Spain* **2** OVERPOPULATION : superpoblación *f*

overdo [ˌoːvər'duː] *vt* **-did** [-'dɪd]; **-done** [-'dʌn]; **-doing; -does** [-'dʌz] **1** : hacer demasiado **2** EXAGGERATE : exagerar **3** OVERCOOK : recocer

overdose ['oːvərˌdoːs] *n* : sobredosis *f*

overdraft ['oːvərˌdræft] *n* : sobregiro *m*, descubierto *m*

overdraw [ˌoːvər'drɔ] *vt* **-drew** [-'druː]; **-drawn** [-'drɔn]; **-drawing** **1** : sobregirar ⟨my account is overdrawn : tengo la cuenta en descubierto⟩ **2** EXAGGERATE : exagerar

overdue [ˌoːvər'duː] *adj* **1** UNPAID : vencido y sin pagar **2** TARDY : de retraso, tardío

overeat [ˌoːvər'iːt] *vi* **-ate** [-'eɪt]; **-eaten** [-'iːtən]; **-eating** : comer demasiado

overelaborate [ˌoːvərɪ'læbərət] *adj* : recargado

overestimate [ˌoːvər'ɛstəˌmeɪt] *vt* **-mated; -mating** : sobreestimar

overexcited [ˌoːvərɪk'saɪtəd] *adj* : sobreexcitado

overexpose [ˌoːvərɪk'spoːz] *vt* **-posed; -posing** : sobreexponer

overfeed [ˌoːvər'fiːd] *vt* **-fed** [-'fɛd]; **-feeding** : sobrealimentar

overflow¹ [ˌoːvər'floː] *vt* **1** : desbordar **2** INUNDATE : inundar — *vi* : desbordarse, rebosar

overflow² ['oːvərˌfloː] *n* **1** : derrame *m*, desbordamiento *m* (de un río) **2** SURPLUS : exceso *m*, excedente *m*

overfly [ˌoːvər'flaɪ] *vt* **-flew** [-'fluː]; **-flown** [-'floːn]; **-flying** : sobrevolar

overgrown [ˌoːvər'groːn] *adj* **1** : cubierto ⟨overgrown with weeds : cubierto de malas hierbas⟩ **2** : demasiado grande

overhand¹ ['oːvərˌhænd] *adv* : por encima de la cabeza

overhand² *adj* : por lo alto (tirada)

overhang¹ [ˌoːvər'hæŋ] *v* **-hung** [-'hʌŋ]; **-hanging** *vt* **1** : sobresalir por encima de **2** THREATEN : amenazar — *vi* : sobresalir

overhang² ['oːvərˌhæŋ] *n* : saliente *mf*

overhaul [ˌoːvər'hɔl] *vt* **1** : revisar ⟨to overhaul an engine : revisar un motor⟩ **2** OVERTAKE : adelantar

overhead¹ [ˌoːvər'hɛd] *adv* : por encima, arriba, por lo alto

overhead² ['oːvərˌhɛd] *adj* : de arriba

overhead³ ['oːvərˌhɛd] *n* : gastos *mpl* generales

overhear [ˌoːvər'hɪr] *vt* **-heard** [-'hərd]; **-hearing** : oír por casualidad

overheat [ˌoːvər'hiːt] *vt* : recalentar, sobrecalentar, calentar demasiado

overjoyed [ˌoːvər'dʒɔɪd] *adj* : rebosante de alegría

overkill ['oːvərˌkɪl] *n* : exceso *m*, excedente *m*

overland¹ ['oːvərˌlænd, -lənd] *adv* : por tierra

overland² *adj* : terrestre, por tierra

overlap¹ [ˌoːvərˈlæp] *v* **-lapped; -lapping** *vt* : traslapar — *vi* : traslaparse, solaparse

overlap² [ˈoːvərˌlæp] *n* : traslapo *m*

overlay¹ [ˌoːvərˈleɪ] *vt* **-laid** [-ˈleɪd]; **-laying** : recubrir, revestir

overlay² [ˈoːvərˌleɪ] *n* : revestimiento *m*

overload [ˌoːvərˈloːd] *vt* : sobrecargar

overlong [ˌoːvərˈlɔŋ] *adj* : excesivamente largo, largo y pesado

overlook [ˌoːvərˈlʊk] *vt* **1** INSPECT : inspeccionar, revisar **2** : tener vista a, dar a ⟨a house overlooking the valley : una casa que tiene vista al valle⟩ **3** MISS : pasar por alto **4** EXCUSE : dejar pasar, disculpar

overly [ˈoːvərli] *adv* : demasiado

overnight¹ [ˌoːvərˈnaɪt] *adv* **1** : por la noche, durante la noche **2** : de la noche a la mañana ⟨we can't do it overnight : no podemos hacerlo de la noche a la mañana⟩

overnight² [ˈoːvərˌnaɪt] *adj* **1** : de noche ⟨an overnight stay : una estancia de una noche⟩ ⟨an overnight bag : una bolsa de viaje⟩ **2** SUDDEN : repentino

overpass [ˈoːvərˌpæs] *n* : paso *m* elevado, paso *m* a desnivel *Mex*

overpay [ˌoːvərˈpeɪ] *v* **-paid** [-ˈpeɪd]; **-paying** *vt* : pagarle demasiado a (alguien) — *vi* : pagar demasiado

overpopulated [ˌoːvərˈpɑpjəˌleɪt̬əd] *adj* : superpoblado, sobrepoblado

overpopulation [ˌoːvərˌpɑpjəˈleɪʃən] *n* : superpoblación *f*, sobrepoblación *f*

overpower [ˌoːvərˈpaʊər] *vt* **1** CONQUER, SUBDUE : vencer, superar **2** OVERWHELM : abrumar, agobiar ⟨overpowered by the heat : sofocado por el calor⟩

overpraise [ˌoːvərˈpreɪz] *vt* **-praised; -praising** : adular

overprotective [ˌoːvərprəˈtɛktɪv] *adj* : sobreprotector

overrate [ˌoːvərˈreɪt] *vt* **-rated; -rating** : sobrevalorar, sobrevaluar

overreact [ˌoːvərriˈækt] *vi* : reaccionar de forma exagerada

override [ˌoːvərˈraɪd] *vt* **-rode** [-ˈroːd]; **-ridden** [-ˈrɪdən]; **-riding** **1** : predominar sobre, contar más que ⟨hunger overrode our manners : el hambre predominó sobre los modales⟩ **2** ANNUL : anular, invalidar ⟨to override a veto : anular un veto⟩

overripe [ˌoːvərˈraɪp] *adj* : pasado

overrule [ˌoːvərˈruːl] *vt* **-ruled; -ruling** : anular (una decisión), desautorizar (una persona), denegar (un pedido)

overrun [ˌoːvərˈrʌn] *v* **-ran** [-ˈræn]; **-running** *vt* **1** INVADE : invadir **2** INFEST : infestar, plagar **3** EXCEED : exceder, rebasar — *vi* : rebasar el tiempo previsto

overseas¹ [ˌoːvərˈsiːz] *adv* : en el extranjero ⟨to travel overseas : viajar al extranjero⟩

overseas² [ˈoːvərˌsiːz] *adj* : extranjero, exterior

oversee [ˌoːvərˈsiː] *vt* **-saw** [-ˈsɔ]; **-seen** [-ˈsiːn]; **-seeing** SUPERVISE : supervisar

overseer [ˈoːvərˌsiːər] *n* : supervisor *m*, -sora *f*; capataz *mf*

oversell [ˌoːvərˈsɛl] *vt* : sobrevender

overshadow [ˌoːvərˈlæˌdoː] *vt* **1** DARKEN : oscurecer, ensombrecer **2** ECLIPSE, OUTSHINE : eclipsar

overshoe [ˈoːvərˌʃuː] *n* : chanclo *m*

overshoot [ˌoːvərˈʃuːt] *vt* **-shot** [-ˈʃɑt]; **-shooting** : pasarse de ⟨to overshoot the mark : pasarse de la raya⟩

oversight [ˈoːvərˌsaɪt] *n* : descuido *m*, inadvertencia *f*

oversleep [ˌoːvərˈsliːp] *vi* **-slept** [-ˈslɛpt]; **-sleeping** : no despertarse a tiempo, quedarse dormido

overspread [ˌoːvərˈsprɛd] *vt* **-spread; -spreading** : extenderse sobre

overstaffed [ˌoːvərˈstæft] *adj* : con exceso de personal

overstate [ˌoːvərˈsteɪt] *vt* **-stated; -stating** EXAGGERATE : exagerar

overstatement [ˌoːvərˈsteɪtmənt] *n* : exageración *f*

overstep [ˌoːvərˈstɛp] *vt* **-stepped; -stepping** EXCEED : sobrepasar, traspasar, exceder

overt [oːˈvərt, ˈoːˌvərt] *adj* : evidente, manifiesto, patente

overtake [ˌoːvərˈteɪk] *vt* **-took** [-ˈtʊk]; **-taken** [-ˈteɪkən]; **-taking** : pasar, adelantar, rebasar *Mex*

overthrow¹ [ˌoːvərˈθroː] *vt* **-threw** [-ˈθruː]; **-thrown** [-ˈθroːn]; **-throwing** **1** OVERTURN : dar la vuelta a, volcar **2** DEFEAT, TOPPLE : derrocar, derribar, deponer

overthrow² [ˈoːvərˌθroː] *n* : derrocamiento *m*, caída *f*

overtime [ˈoːvərˌtaɪm] *n* **1** : horas *fpl* extras (de trabajo) **2** : prórroga *f*; alargue *m Arg, Chile, Uru* (en deportes)

overtly [oːˈvərtli, ˈoːˌvərt-] *adv* OPENLY : abiertamente

overtone [ˈoːvərˌtoːn] *n* **1** : armónico *m* (en música) **2** HINT SUGGESTION : tinte *m*, insinuación *f*

overture [ˈoːvərˌtʃʊr, -tʃər] *n* **1** PROPOSAL : propuesta *f* **2** : obertura *f* (en música)

overturn [ˌoːvərˈtərn] *vt* **1** UPSET : dar la vuelta a, volcar **2** NULLIFY : anular, invalidar — *vi* TURN OVER : volcar, dar un vuelco

overuse [ˌoːvərˈjuːz] *vt* **-used; -using** : abusar de

overview [ˈoːvərˌvjuː] *n* : resumen *m*, visión *f* general

overweening [ˌoːvərˈwiːnɪŋ] *adj* **1** ARROGANT : arrogante, soberbio **2** IMMODERATE : desmesurado

overweight [ˌoːvərˈweɪt] *adj* : demasiado gordo, demasiado pesado

overwhelm [ˌoːvərˈʰwɛlm] *vt* **1** CRUSH, DEFEAT : aplastar, arrollar **2** SUBMERGE : inundar, sumergir **3** OVERPOWER : abrumar, agobiar ⟨overwhelmed by remorse : abrumado de remordimiento⟩

overwhelming [ˌoːvərˈʰwɛlmɪŋ] *adj* **1** CRUSHING : abrumador, apabullante **2** SWEEPING : arrollador, aplastante ⟨an overwhelming majority : una mayoría aplastante⟩

overwork [ˌoːvərˈwərk] vt **1** : hacer trabajar demasiado **2** OVERUSE : abusar de — vi : trabajar demasiado

overwrought [ˌoːvərˈrɔt] adj : alterado, sobreexcitado

ovoid [ˈoːˌvɔɪd] or **ovoidal** [oˈvɔɪdəl] adj : ovoide

ovulate [ˈɑvjəˌleɪt, ˈoː-] vi **-lated; -lating** : ovular

ovulation [ˌɑvjəˈleɪlən, ˌoː-] n : ovulación f

ovum [ˈoːvəm] n, pl **ova** [-və] : óvulo m

ow [ˈaʊ] interj : ¡ay!, ¡huy!, ¡uy!

owe [ˈoː] vt **owed; owing** : deber ⟨you owe me $10 : me debes $10⟩ ⟨he owes his wealth to his father : le debe su riqueza a su padre⟩

owing to prep : debido a

owl [ˈaʊl] n : búho m, lechuza f, tecolote m Mex

own¹ [ˈoːn] vt **1** POSSESS : poseer, tener, ser dueño de **2** ADMIT : reconocer, admitir — vi **to own up** : reconocer (algo), admitir (algo)

own² adj : propio, personal, particular ⟨his own car : su propio coche⟩

own³ pron **1** (used with a possessive) ⟨the book is his own : el libro es suyo, el libro lo escribió él⟩ ⟨money of your own : tu/su propio dinero⟩ ⟨I want an apartment to call my own : quiero un apartamento para mí solo⟩ ⟨she has a style all her own : tiene un estilo muy particular⟩ ⟨to each his own : cada uno a lo suyo⟩ **2 on one's own** : solo ⟨we did it on our own : lo hicimos solos⟩ ⟨they left her on her own : la dejaron sola⟩

owner [ˈoːnər] n : dueño m, -ña f; propietario m, -ria f

ownership [ˈoːnərˌʃɪp] n : propiedad f

ox [ˈɑks] n, pl **oxen** [ˈɑksən] : buey m

oxidation [ˌɑksəˈdeɪlən] n : oxidación f

oxide [ˈɑkˌsaɪd] n : óxido m

oxidize [ˈɑksəˌdaɪz] vt **-dized; -dizing** : oxidar

oxygen [ˈɑksɪʤən] n : oxígeno m

oxygenate [ˈɑksɪʤəˌneɪt] vt **-nated; -nating** : oxigenar

oyster [ˈɔɪstər] n : ostra f, ostión m Mex

ozone [ˈoːˌzoːn] n : ozono m ⟨ozone layer : capa de ozono⟩

P

p [ˈpiː] n, pl **p's** or **ps** [ˈpiːz] : decimosexta letra del alfabeto inglés

PA [ˌpiːˈeɪ] n (public address system) : altavoces mpl, altoparlantes mpl

pace¹ [ˈpeɪs] v **paced; pacing** vi : caminar, ir y venir — vt **1** : caminar por ⟨she paced the floor : caminaba de un lado a otro del cuarto⟩ **2 to pace a runner** : marcarle el ritmo a un corredor

pace² n **1** STEP : paso m **2** RATE : paso m, ritmo m ⟨to set the pace : marcar el paso, marcar la pauta⟩

pacemaker [ˈpeɪsˌmeɪkər] n : marcapasos m

pacific [pəˈsɪfɪk] adj : pacífico

pacifier [ˈpæsəˌfaɪər] n : chupete m, chupón m, mamila f Mex

pacifism [ˈpæsəˌfɪzəm] n : pacifismo m

pacifist [ˈpæsəfɪst] n : pacifista mf

pacify [ˈpæsəˌfaɪ] vt **-fied; -fying** **1** SOOTHE : apaciguar, pacificar **2** : pacificar (un país, una región, etc.) — **pacification** n

pack¹ [ˈpæk] vt **1** PACKAGE : empaquetar, embalar, envasar **2** : empacar, meter en una maleta) ⟨to pack one's bags : hacer las maletas⟩ **3** FILL : llenar, abarrotar ⟨a packed theater : un teatro abarrotado⟩ **4** TAMP : apisonar (tierra), compactar (nieve) ⟨firmly packed brown sugar : azúcar morena bien compacta⟩ **5 to pack in** LEAVE : dejar **6 to pack in/into** : meter en ⟨they packed us all into one room : nos metieron a todos en una sala⟩ ⟨to pack them in : atraer una multitud⟩ **7 to pack it in** fam QUIT, STOP : parar **8 to pack off** SEND : mandar **9 to pack up** : recoger, guardar (para llevar) — vi or **to pack up** : empacar, hacer las maletas

pack² n **1** BUNDLE : bulto m, fardo m **2** BACKPACK : mochila f **3** PACKAGE : paquete m, cajetilla f (de cigarrillos, etc.) **4** : manada f (de lobos, etc.), jauría f (de perros) ⟨a pack of thieves : una pandilla de ladrones⟩ **5** : baraja f (de naipes)

package¹ [ˈpækɪʤ] vt **-aged; -aging** : empaquetar, embalar

package² n : paquete m, bulto m

packaging [ˈpækɪʤɪŋ] n **1** : embalaje m **2** WRAPPING : envoltorio m

packer [ˈpækər] n : empacador m, -dora f

packet [ˈpækət] n : paquete m

packing [ˈpækɪŋ] n : embalaje m

pact [ˈpækt] n : pacto m, acuerdo m

pad¹ [ˈpæd] vt **padded; padding** **1** FILL, STUFF : rellenar, acolchar (una silla, una pared) **2** : meter paja en, rellenar ⟨to pad a speech : rellenar un discurso⟩

pad² n **1** CUSHION : almohadilla f ⟨a shoulder pad : una hombrera⟩ **2** TABLET : bloc m (de papel) **3** → lily pad **4** → ink pad **5** → launchpad **6** → landing pad

padding [ˈpædɪŋ] n **1** FILLING : relleno m **2** : paja f (en un discurso, etc.)

paddle¹ [ˈpædəl] v **-dled; -dling** vt **1** : hacer avanzar (una canoa) con canalete **2** HIT : azotar, darle nalgadas a (con una pala o paleta) — vi **1** : remar (en una canoa) **2** SPLASH : chapotear, mojarse los pies

paddle² n **1** : canalete m, zagual m (de una canoa, etc.) **2** : pala f, paleta f (en deportes)

paddock [ˈpædək] n **1** PASTURE : potrero m **2** : paddock m, cercado m (en un hipódromo)

paddy ['pædi] n, pl -dies : arrozal m
padlock¹ ['pæd,lɑk] vt : cerrar con candado
padlock² n : candado m
paella [pɑ'ɛlə, -'eɪljə, -'eɪə] n : paella f
pagan¹ ['peɪgən] adj : pagano
pagan² n : pagano m, -na f
paganism ['peɪgən,ɪzəm] n : paganismo m
page¹ ['peɪʤ] vt paged; paging : llamar por altavoz
page² n 1 BELLHOP : botones m 2 : página f (de un libro, etc.) ⟨page six : la página seis⟩
pageant ['pæʤənt] n 1 SPECTACLE : espectáculo m 2 PROCESSION : desfile m
pageantry ['pæʤəntri] n : pompa f, fausto m
pager ['peɪʤər] n BEEPER : buscapersonas m
pagoda [pə'go:də] n : pagoda f
paid → pay
pail ['peɪl] n : balde m, cubo m, cubeta f Mex
pailful ['peɪl,fʊl] n : balde m, cubo m, cubeta f Mex
pain¹ ['peɪn] vt : doler
pain² n 1 PENALTY : pena f ⟨under pain of death : so pena de muerte⟩ 2 SUFFERING : dolor m, malestar m, pena f (mental) 3 pains npl EFFORT : esmero m, esfuerzo m ⟨to take pains : esmerarse⟩ 4 ANNOYANCE : molestia f, fastidio m ⟨he's a pain in the neck : es un pesado⟩
painful ['peɪnfəl] adj : doloroso — painfully adv
painkiller ['peɪn,kɪlər] n : analgésico m
painless ['peɪnləs] adj : indoloro, sin dolor
painlessly ['peɪnləsli] adv : sin dolor
painstaking ['peɪn,steɪkɪŋ] adj : esmerado, cuidadoso, meticuloso — painstakingly adv
paint¹ ['peɪnt] v : pintar
paint² n : pintura f
paintbrush ['peɪnt,brʌʃ] n : pincel m (de un artista), brocha f (para pintar casas, etc.)
painter ['peɪntər] n : pintor m, -tora f
painting ['peɪntɪŋ] n : pintura f
pair¹ ['pær] vt : emparejar, poner en parejas — vi : emparejarse
pair² n : par m (de objetos), pareja f (de personas o animales) ⟨a pair of scissors : unas tijeras⟩
pajamas [pə'ʤɑməz, -'ʤæ-] npl : pijama m, piyama mf
Pakistani [,pækɪ'stæni, ,pɑkɪ'stɑni] n : paquistaní mf — Pakistani adj
pal ['pæl] n : amigo m, -ga f; compinche mf fam; chamo m, -ma feminine Venezuela familiar; cuate m, -ta f Mex
palace ['pæləs] n : palacio m
palatable ['pælətəbəl] adj : sabroso
palate ['pælət] n 1 : paladar m (de la boca) 2 TASTE : paladar m, gusto m
palatial [pə'leɪʃəl] adj : suntuoso, espléndido
palaver [pə'lævər, -'lɑ-] n : palabrería f

pale¹ ['peɪl] v paled; paling vi : palidecer — vt : hacer pálido
pale² adj paler; palest 1 : pálido ⟨to turn pale : palidecer, ponerse pálido⟩ 2 : claro (dícese de los colores)
paleness ['peɪlnəs] n : palidez f
paleontologist [,peɪli,ɑn'talədʒɪst] n : paleontólogo m, -ga f
paleontology [,peɪli,ɑn'talədʒi] n : paleontología f
Palestinian [,pælə'stɪniən] n : palestino m, -na f — Palestinian adj
palette ['pælət] n : paleta f (para mezclar pigmentos)
palisade [,pælə'seɪd] n 1 FENCE : empalizada f, estacada f 2 CLIFFS : acantilado m
pall¹ ['pɔl] vi : perder su sabor, dejar de gustar
pall² n 1 : paño m funerario (sobre un ataúd) 2 COVER : cortina f (de humo, etc.) 3 to cast a pall over : ensombrecer
pallbearer ['pɔl,bɛrər] n : portador m, -dora f del féretro
pallet ['pælət] n 1 BED : camastro m 2 PLATFORM : plataforma f de carga
palliative ['pæli,eɪtɪv, 'pæljətɪv] adj : paliativo ⟨palliative care : cuidados paliativos⟩
pallid ['pæləd] adj : pálido
pallor ['pælər] n : palidez f
palm¹ ['pɑm, 'pɑlm] vt 1 CONCEAL : escamotear (un naipe, etc.) 2 to palm off : encajar, endilgar fam ⟨he palmed it off on me : me lo endilgó⟩
palm² n 1 or palm tree : palmera f 2 : palma f (de la mano)
palmistry ['pɑməstri, 'pɑlmə-] n : quiromancia f
Palm Sunday n : Domingo m de Ramos
palomino [,pælə'mi:,no:] n, pl -nos : caballo m de color dorado
palpable ['pælpəbəl] adj : palpable — palpably [-bli] adv
palpitate ['pælpə,teɪt] vi -tated; -tating : palpitar
palpitation [,pælpə'teɪʃən] n : palpitación f
palsy ['pɔlzi] n, pl -sies 1 : parálisis f 2 → cerebral palsy
paltry ['pɔltri] adj paltrier; -est : mísero, mezquino, insignificante ⟨a paltry excuse : una mala excusa⟩
pampas ['pæmpəz, 'pɑmpəs] npl : pampa f
pamper ['pæmpər] vt : mimar, consentir, chiquear Mex
pamphlet ['pæmpflət] n : panfleto m, folleto m
pan¹ ['pæn] vt panned; panning CRITICIZE : poner por los suelos — vi 1 to pan for gold : cribar el oro con batea, lavar oro 2 to pan out : resultar, salir
pan² n 1 : cacerola f, cazuela f 2 frying pan : sartén mf, freidera f Mex
pan- pref : pan- ⟨panacea : panacea⟩
panacea [,pænə'si:ə] n : panacea f
Panamanian [,pænə'meɪniən] n : panameño m, -ña f — Panamanian adj

pancake ['pæn,keɪk] *n* : panqueque *m*
pancreas ['pæŋkriəs, 'pæn-] *n* : páncreas *m*
panda ['pændə] *n* : panda *mf*
pandemonium [,pændə'moːniəm] *n* : pandemonio *m*, pandemónium *m*
pander ['pændər] *vi* **to pander to** : satisfacer, complacer (a alguien) ⟨to pander to popular taste : satisfacer el gusto popular⟩
pane ['peɪn] *n* : cristal *m*, vidrio *m*
panel[1] ['pænəl] *vt* **-eled** *or* **-elled; -eling** *or* **-elling** : adornar con paneles
panel[2] *n* **1** : lista *f* de nombres (de un jurado, etc.) **2** GROUP : grupo *m*, panel *m* (de discusión), jurado *m* (de un concurso, etc.) **3** : panel *m* (de una pared, etc.) **4** : tablero *m* ⟨control panel : tablero de control⟩
paneling ['pænəlɪŋ] *n* : paneles *mpl*
pang ['pæŋ] *n* : puntada *f*, punzada *f*
panhandler ['pæn,hændlər] *n* : mendigo *m*, -ga *f*
panic[1] ['pænɪk] *v* **-icked; -icking** *vt* : llenar de pánico — *vi* : ser presa de pánico
panic[2] *n* : pánico *m*
panicky ['pænɪki] *adj* : presa del pánico
panic–stricken *adj* : presa del pánico ⟨to be panic-stricken : ser presa del pánico⟩
panini [pə'niːni] *n*, *pl* **-ni** *or* **-nis** : panini *m*
panorama [,pænə'ræmə, -'rɑ-] *n* : panorama *m*
panoramic [,pænə'ræmɪk, -'rɑ-] *adj* : panorámico
pansexual [,pæn'sɛkʃuəl] *adj* : pansexual ⟨pansexual people : las personas pansexuales⟩
pansy ['pænzi] *n*, *pl* **-sies** : pensamiento *m*
pant[1] ['pænt] *vi* : jadear, resoplar
pant[2] *adj* : del pantalón
pant[3] *n* : jadeo *m*, resoplo *m*
pantaloons [,pæntə'luːnz] → **pants**
pantheon ['pænθiˌɑn, -ən] *n* : panteón *m*
panther ['pænθər] *n* : pantera *f*
panties ['pæntiz] *npl* : calzones *mpl*; pantaletas *fpl Mex, Ven*; bombacha *f Arg, Uru*; panties *mfpl CA, Car*; bragas *fpl Spain*
pantomime[1] ['pæntəˌmaɪm] *v* **-mimed; -miming** *vt* : representar mediante la pantomima — *vi* : hacer la mímica
pantomime[2] *n* : pantomima *f*
pantry ['pæntri] *n*, *pl* **-tries** : despensa *f*
pants ['pænts] *npl* **1** TROUSERS : pantalón *m*, pantalones *mpl* **2** → **panties**
pantsuit ['pænt,suːt] *n* : traje *m* pantalón
panty hose ['pænti] *ns & pl* : medias *fpl*, panties *mfpl Spain*, pantimedias *fpl Mex*
pap ['pæp] *n* : papilla *f* (para bebés, etc.)
papa ['pɑpə] *n* : papá *m*
papal ['peɪpəl] *adj* : papal
papaya [pə'paɪə] *n* : papaya *f* (fruta)
paper[1] ['peɪpər] *vt* WALLPAPER : empapelar
paper[2] *adj* : de papel
paper[3] *n* **1** : papel *m* ⟨a piece of paper : un papel⟩ **2** DOCUMENT : papel *m*, documento *m* **3** NEWSPAPER : periódico *m*, diario *m* **4** ESSAY : ensayo *m*

paperback ['peɪpərˌbæk] *n* : libro *m* en rústica
paper clip *n* : clip *m*, sujetapapeles *m*
paperweight ['peɪpərˌweɪt] *n* : pisapapeles *m*
paperwork ['peɪpərˌwərk] *n* : papeleo *m*
papery ['peɪpəri] *adj* : parecido al papel
papier–mâché [,peɪpərmə'leɪ, ˌpæˌpjeɪmæ'leɪ] *n* : papel *m* maché
paprika [pə'priːkə, pæ-] *n* : pimentón *m*, paprika *f*
Pap smear ['pæp-] *n* : Papanicolau *m*
papyrus [pə'paɪrəs] *n*, *pl* **-ruses** *or* **-ri** [-ri, -ˌraɪ] : papiro *m*
par ['pɑr] *n* **1** VALUE : valor *m* (nominal), par *f* ⟨below par : debajo de la par⟩ **2** EQUALITY : igualdad *f* ⟨to be on a par with : estar al mismo nivel que⟩ **3** : par *m* (en golf)
parable ['pærəbəl] *n* : parábola *f*
parabola [pə'ræbələ] *n* : parábola *f* (en matemáticas)
parachute[1] ['pærəˌʃuːt] *vi* **-chuted; -chuting** : lanzarse en paracaídas
parachute[2] *n* : paracaídas *m*
parachutist ['pærəˌʃuːtɪst] *n* : paracaidista *mf*
parade[1] [pə'reɪd] *vi* **-raded; -rading** **1** MARCH : desfilar **2** SHOW OFF : pavonearse, lucirse
parade[2] *n* **1** PROCESSION : desfile *m* **2** DISPLAY : alarde *m*
paradigm ['pærəˌdaɪm] *n* : paradigma *m*
paradise ['pærəˌdaɪs, -ˌdaɪz] *n* : paraíso *m*
paradox ['pærəˌdɑks] *n* : paradoja *f*
paradoxical [ˌpærə'dɑksɪkəl] *adj* : paradójico — **paradoxically** *adv*
paraffin ['pærəfən] *n* : parafina *f*
paragliding ['pærəˌglaɪdɪŋ] *n* : parapente *m*
paragon ['pærəˌgɑn, -gən] *n* : dechado *m*
paragraph[1] ['pærəˌgræf] *vt* : dividir en párrafos
paragraph[2] *n* : párrafo *m*, acápite *m*
Paraguayan [ˌpærə'gwaɪən, -'gweɪ-] *n* : paraguayo *m*, -ya *f* — **Paraguayan** *adj*
parakeet ['pærəˌkiːt] *n* : periquito *m*
paralegal [ˌpærə'liːgəl] *n* : asistente *mf* de abogado
parallel[1] ['pærəˌlɛl, -ləl] *vt* **1** MATCH, RESEMBLE : ser paralelo a, ser análogo a, corresponder con **2** : extenderse en línea paralela con ⟨the road parallels the river : el camino se extiende a lo largo del río⟩
parallel[2] *adj* : paralelo
parallel[3] *n* **1** : línea *f* paralela, superficie *f* paralela **2** : paralelo *m* (en geografía) **3** SIMILARITY : paralelismo *m*, semejanza *f*
parallelogram [ˌpærə'lɛləˌgræm] *n* : paralelogramo *m*
paralysis [pə'ræləsɪs] *n*, *pl* **-yses** [-ˌsiːz] : parálisis *f*
paralyze ['pærəˌlaɪz] *vt* **-lyzed; -lyzing** : paralizar
paramedic [ˌpærə'mɛdɪk] *n* : paramédico *m*, -ca *f*
parameter [pə'ræmətər] *n* : parámetro *m*
paramount ['pærəˌmaʊnt] *adj* : supremo ⟨of paramount importance : de suma importancia⟩

paranoia [ˌpærə'nɔɪə] *n* : paranoia *f*
paranoid ['pærə,nɔɪd] *adj* : paranoico
paranormal [ˌpærə'nɔrməl] *adj* : paranormal
parapet ['pærəpət, -ˌpɛt] *n* : parapeto *m*
paraphernalia [ˌpærəfə'neɪljə, -fər-] *ns & pl* : parafernalia *f*
paraphrase[1] ['pærə,freɪz] *vt* **-phrased; -phrasing** : parafrasear
paraphrase[2] *n* : paráfrasis *f*
paraplegic[1] [ˌpærə'pli:dʒɪk] *adj* : parapléjico
paraplegic[2] *n* : parapléjico *m*, -ca *f*
parasite ['pærə,saɪt] *n* : parásito *m*
parasitic [ˌpærə'sɪtɪk] *adj* : parasitario
parasol ['pærə,sɔl] *n* : sombrilla *f*, quitasol *m*, parasol *m*
paratrooper ['pærə,tru:pər] *n* : paracaidista *mf* (militar)
parboil ['par,bɔɪl] *vt* : sancochar, cocer a medias
parcel[1] ['parsəl] *vt* **-celed** *or* **-celled; -celing** *or* **-celling** *or* **to parcel out** : repartir, parcelar (tierras)
parcel[2] *n* **1** LOT : parcela *f*, lote *m* **2** PACKAGE : paquete *m*, bulto *m*
parch ['partʃ] *vt* : resecar
parched *adj* **1** DRY : muy seco, quemado **2** THIRSTY : seco
parchment ['partʃmənt] *n* : pergamino *m*
pardon[1] ['pardən] *vt* **1** FORGIVE : perdonar, disculpar ⟨pardon me! : ¡perdone!, ¡disculpe la molestia!⟩ **2** REPRIEVE : indultar (a un delincuente)
pardon[2] *n* **1** FORGIVENESS : perdón *m* **2** REPRIEVE : indulto *m*
pardonable ['pardənəbəl] *adj* : perdonable
pare ['pær] *vt* **pared; paring 1** PEEL : pelar **2** TRIM : recortar **3** REDUCE : reducir ⟨he pared it (down) to 50 pages : lo redujo a 50 páginas⟩
parent ['pærənt] *n* **1** : madre *f*, padre *m* **2 parents** *npl* : padres *mpl*
parentage ['pærəntɪdʒ] *n* : linaje *m*, abolengo *m*, origen *m*
parental [pə'rɛntəl] *adj* : de los padres
parenthesis [pə'rɛnθəsɪs] *n, pl* **-theses** [-ˌsi:z] : paréntesis *m*
parenthetic [ˌpærən'θɛtɪk] *or* **parenthetical** [-tɪkəl] *adj* : parentético — **parenthetically** [-tɪkli] *adv*
parenthood ['pærənt,hʊd] *n* : paternidad *f*
parfait [par'feɪ] *n* : postre *m* elaborado con frutas y helado
pariah [pə'raɪə] *n* : paria *m*
parish ['pærɪʃ] *n* : parroquia *f*
parishioner [pə'rɪʃənər] *n* : feligrés *m*, -gresa *f*
parity ['pærəti] *n, pl* **-ties** : paridad *f*
park[1] ['park] *vt* : estacionar, parquear, aparcar *Spain* — *vi* : estacionarse, parquearse, aparcar *Spain*
park[2] *n* : parque *m*
parka ['parkə] *n* : parka *f*
parking ['parkɪŋ] *n* : estacionamiento *m*, aparcamiento *m Spain*
parking lot *n* : estacionamiento *m*, parking *m*, aparcamiento *m Spain* (lugar)
parking meter *n* : parquímetro *m*

parking ticket *n* : multa *f* (de parquímetro o por estacionarse mal)
parkour [par'kʊr] *n* : parkour *m*
parkway ['park,weɪ] *n* : carretera *f* ajardinada, bulevar *m*
parley[1] ['parli] *vi* : parlamentar, negociar
parley[2] *n, pl* **-leys** : negociación *f*, parlamento *m*
parliament ['parləmənt, 'parljə-] *n* : parlamento *m*
parliamentary [ˌparlə'mɛntəri, ˌparljə-] *adj* : parlamentario
parlor ['parlər] *n* **1** : sala *f*, salón *m* (en una casa) **2** : salón *m* ⟨beauty parlor : salón de belleza⟩ **3 funeral parlor** : funeraria *f*
parochial [pə'ro:kiəl] *adj* **1** : parroquial **2** PROVINCIAL : pueblerino, de miras estrechas
parody[1] ['pærədi] *vt* **-died; -dying** : parodiar
parody[2] *n, pl* **-dies** : parodia *f*
parole [pə'ro:l] *n* : libertad *f* condicional
paroxysm ['pærək,sɪzəm, pə'rak-] *n* : paroxismo *m*
parquet ['par,keɪ, par'keɪ] *n* : parquet *m*, parqué *m*
parrakeet → parakeet
parrot ['pærət] *n* : loro *m*, papagayo *m*
parry[1] ['pæri] *v* **-ried; -rying** *vi* : parar un golpe — *vt* EVADE : esquivar (una pregunta, etc.)
parry[2] *n, pl* **-ries** : parada *f*
parsimonious [ˌparsə'mo:niəs] *adj* : tacaño, mezquino
parsley ['parsli] *n* : perejil *m*
parsnip ['parsnɪp] *n* : chirivía *f*
parson ['parsən] *n* : pastor *m*, -tora *f*; clérigo *m*
parsonage ['parsənɪdʒ] *n* : rectoría *f*, casa *f* del párroco
part[1] ['part] *vi* **1** SEPARATE : separarse, despedirse ⟨we should part as friends : debemos separarnos amistosamente⟩ **2** OPEN : abrirse ⟨the curtains parted : las cortinas se abrieron⟩ **3 to part with** : deshacerse de — *vt* **1** SEPARATE : separar **2 to part one's hair** : hacerse la raya, peinarse con raya
part[2] *n* **1** SECTION, SEGMENT : parte *f*, sección *f* ⟨for the better part of a year : durante casi un año⟩ ⟨in the latter part of the century : hacia finales de siglo⟩ ⟨the western part of the state : la parte oeste del estado⟩ ⟨the best/worst part is that . . . : lo mejor/peor es que . . .⟩ **2** PIECE : pieza *f* (de una máquina, etc.) **3** ROLE : papel *m* (en teatro, etc.) ⟨to play a part : hacer un papel⟩ ⟨to look the part : tener el aspecto para el papel⟩ **4** ROLE, INFLUENCE : papel *m* ⟨to play a part : jugar un papel⟩ ⟨to want no part of/in : no querer tener nada que ver con⟩ **5** : raya *f* (del pelo) **6 for my/his (etc.) part** : por mi/su (etc.) parte **7 for the most part** MOSTLY : en su mayoría, en su mayor parte **8 for the most part** USUALLY : en general **9 in part** : en parte **10 in these parts** : por aquí **11 on the part of** : de/por parte de **12 to**

take part (in) : tomar parte (en), participar (en)
partake [pɑr'teɪk, pər-] vi **-took** [-'tʊk]; **-taken** [-'teɪkən]; **-taking** 1 to partake of CONSUME : comer, beber, tomar 2 to partake in : participar en (una actividad, etc.)
partial ['pɑrʃəl] adj 1 BIASED : parcial, tendencioso 2 INCOMPLETE : parcial, incompleto 3 to be partial to : ser aficionado a
partiality [ˌpɑrʃi'æləti] n, pl **-ties** : parcialidad f
partially ['pɑrʃəli] adv : parcialmente
participant [pər'tɪsəpənt, pɑr-] n : participante mf
participate [pər'tɪsəˌpeɪt, pɑr-] vi **-pated**; **-pating** : participar
participation [pərˌtɪsə'peɪlən, pɑr-] n : participación f
participle ['pɑrtəˌsɪpəl] n : participio m
particle ['pɑrtɪkəl] n : partícula f
particular¹ [pɑr'tɪkjələr] adj 1 SPECIFIC : particular, en particular ⟨this particular person : esta persona en particular⟩ 2 SPECIAL : particular, especial ⟨with particular emphasis : con un énfasis especial⟩ 3 FUSSY : exigente, maniático ⟨to be very particular : ser muy especial⟩ ⟨I'm not particular : me da igual⟩
particular² n 1 DETAIL : detalle m, sentido m 2 in particular : en particular, en especial
particularly [pɑr'tɪkjələrli] adv 1 ESPECIALLY : particularmente, especialmente 2 SPECIFICALLY : específicamente, en especial
partisan ['pɑrtəzən, -sən] n 1 ADHERENT : partidario m, -ria f 2 GUERRILLA : partisano m, -na f; guerrillero m, -ra f
partition¹ [pər'tɪlən, pɑr-] vt : dividir ⟨to partition off (a room) : dividir (una habitación) con un tabique⟩
partition² n 1 DISTRIBUTION : partición f, división f, reparto m 2 DIVIDER : tabique m, mampara f, biombo m
partly ['pɑrtli] adv : en parte, parcialmente
partner ['pɑrtnər] n 1 COMPANION : compañero m, -ra f 2 : pareja f (en un juego, etc.) ⟨dancing partner : pareja de baile⟩ 3 MATE : pareja f; compañero m, -ra f ⟨(marital) partner : cónyuge⟩ 4 : socio m, -cia f; asociado m, -da f ⟨business/senior partner : socio comercial/mayoritario⟩
partnership ['pɑrtnərˌlɪp] n 1 ASSOCIATION : asociación f, compañerismo m 2 : sociedad f (de negociantes) ⟨to form a partnership : asociarse⟩
part of speech : categoría f gramatical
partridge ['pɑrtrɪdʒ] n, pl **-tridge** or **-tridges** : perdiz f
part–time¹ ['pɑrt'taɪm] adv : medio tiempo, a tiempo parcial
part–time² adj : de medio tiempo, a tiempo parcial
party ['pɑrti] n, pl **-ties** 1 : partido m (político) 2 PARTICIPANT : parte f, par-

ticipante mf 3 GROUP : grupo m (de personas) 4 GATHERING : fiesta f ⟨to throw a party : dar una fiesta⟩
parvenu ['pɑrvəˌnuː, -ˌnjuː] n : advenedizo m, -za f
pass¹ ['pæs] vi 1 : pasar, cruzarse ⟨a plane passed overhead : pasó un avión⟩ ⟨we passed in the hallway : nos cruzamos en el pasillo⟩ 2 CEASE : pasarse ⟨the pain passed : se pasó el dolor⟩ 3 ELAPSE : pasar, transcurrir 4 PROCEED : pasar ⟨let me pass : déjame pasar⟩ 5 HAPPEN : pasar, ocurrir 6 : pasar, aprobar (en un examen) 7 or to pass down : pasar ⟨the throne passed to his son : el trono pasó a su hijo⟩ 8 to pass as : pasar por 9 to pass away/on DIE : fallecer, morir 10 to pass by : pasar 11 to pass out FAINT : desmayarse — vt 1 : pasar por (un lugar) 2 OVERTAKE : pasar, adelantar 3 SPEND : pasar (tiempo) 4 HAND : pasar ⟨pass me the salt : pásame la sal⟩ 5 : aprobar (un examen) 6 : aprobar (a un estudiante) 7 APPROVE : aprobar (una ley) 8 to let pass OVERLOOK, IGNORE : pasar por alto, dejar pasar 9 to pass by : escapársele a (alguien) ⟨don't let life pass you by : no dejes que la vida se te pase⟩ 10 to pass off as : hacer pasar por ⟨to pass oneself off as : hacerse pasar por⟩ 11 to pass on TRANSMIT, RELAY : pasar 12 to pass over SKIP, OMIT : pasar por alto 13 to pass up DECLINE : dejar pasar 14 to pass the time : pasar el rato
pass² n 1 CROSSING, GAP : paso m, desfiladero m, puerto m ⟨mountain pass : puerto de montaña⟩ 2 PERMIT : pase m, permiso m 3 : pase m (en deportes) 4 SITUATION : situación f (difícil) ⟨how did we come to such a pass? : ¿cómo llegamos a tal extremo?⟩
passable ['pæsəbəl] adj 1 ADEQUATE : adecuado, pasable 2 : transitable (dícese de un camino, etc.)
passably ['pæsəbli] adv : pasablemente
passage ['pæsɪdʒ] n 1 PASSING : paso m ⟨the passage of time : el paso del tiempo⟩ 2 PASSAGEWAY : pasillo m (dentro de un edificio), pasaje m (entre edificios) 3 VOYAGE : travesía f (por el mar), viaje m ⟨to grant safe passage : dar un salvoconducto⟩ 4 SECTION : pasaje m (en música o literatura) 5 APPROVAL : aprobación f (de un proyecto de ley, etc.)
passageway ['pæsɪdʒˌweɪ] n : pasillo m, pasadizo m, corredor m
passbook ['pæsˌbʊk] n BANKBOOK : libreta f de ahorros
passé [pæ'seɪ] adj : pasado de moda
passenger ['pæsəndʒər] n : pasajero m, -ra f
passerby [ˌpæsər'baɪ, 'pæsər,-] n, pl **passersby** : transeúnte mf
passing¹ adj 1 : que pasa ⟨he saw a passing train : vio un tren que pasaba⟩ ⟨with each passing day/year : con cada día/año que pasa⟩ 2 TRANSIENT : pasajero 3

CURSORY : somero ⟨to make a passing reference to : referirse de pasada⟩ 4 SLIGHT, SUPERFICIAL : ligero (dícese de un parecido), superficial (dícese de un conocimiento, un interés, etc.) 5 SATISFACTORY : satisfactorio ⟨to get a passing grade : aprobar (en un examen, etc.)⟩

passing² ['pæsɪŋ] n 1 DEATH : fallecimiento m 2 PASSAGE, MOVEMENT : paso m (del tiempo, etc.) 3 PASSAGE, APPROVAL : aprobación f 4 in passing : de pasada

passion ['pæʒən] n : pasión f, ardor m

passionate ['pæʒənət] adj 1 IRASCIBLE : irascible, iracundo 2 ARDENT : apasionado, ardiente, ferviente, fogoso

passionately ['pæʒənətli] adv : apasionadamente, fervientemente, con pasión

passionflower ['pæʒən,flauər] n : pasionaria f, pasiflora f

passive¹ ['pæsɪv] adj : pasivo — **passively** adv

passive² n : voz f pasiva (en gramática)

Passover ['pæs,o:vər] n : Pascua f (en el judaísmo)

passport ['pæs,port] n : pasaporte m

password ['pæs,wərd] n : contraseña f

past¹ ['pæst] adv : por delante ⟨he drove past : pasamos en coche⟩

past² adj 1 AGO : hace ⟨10 years past : hace 10 años⟩ 2 LAST : último ⟨the past few months : los últimos meses⟩ 3 BYGONE : pasado ⟨in past times : en tiempos pasados⟩ 4 : pasado (en gramática)

past³ n : pasado m

past⁴ prep 1 BY : por, por delante de ⟨he ran past the house : pasó por la casa corriendo⟩ 2 BEYOND : más allá de ⟨just past the corner : un poco más allá de la esquina⟩ ⟨we went past the exit : pasamos la salida⟩ 3 AFTER : después de ⟨past noon : después del mediodía⟩ ⟨half past two : las dos y media⟩

pasta ['pɑstə, 'pæs-] n : pasta f

paste¹ ['peɪst] vt **pasted; pasting** 1 : pegar (con engrudo) 2 : pegar (en un documento electrónico)

paste² n 1 : pasta f ⟨tomato paste : pasta de tomate⟩ 2 : engrudo m (para pegar)

pasteboard ['peɪst,bord] n : cartón m, cartulina f

pastel [pæ'stɛl] n : pastel m — **pastel** adj

pasteurization [,pæstʃərə'zeɪʃən, ,pæstjə-] n : pasteurización f

pasteurize ['pæstʃə,raɪz, 'pæstjə-] vt **-ized; -izing** : pasteurizar

pastime ['pæs,taɪm] n : pasatiempo m

pastor ['pæstər] n : pastor m, -tora f

pastoral ['pæstərəl] adj : pastoral

past participle n : participio m pasado

pastry ['peɪstri] n, pl **-ries** 1 DOUGH : pasta f, masa f 2 **pastries** npl : pasteles mpl

pasture¹ ['pæstʃər] v **-tured; -turing** vi GRAZE : pacer, pastar — vt : apacentar, pastar

pasture² n : pastizal m, potrero m, pasto m

pasty ['peɪsti] adj **pastier; -est** 1 : pastoso (en consistencia) 2 PALLID : pálido

pat¹ ['pæt] vt **patted; patting** : dar palmaditas a, tocar

pat² adv : de memoria ⟨to have down pat : saberse de memoria⟩

pat³ adj 1 APT : apto, apropiado 2 GLIB : fácil 3 UNYIELDING : firme ⟨to stand pat : mantenerse firme⟩

pat⁴ n 1 TAP : golpecito m, palmadita f ⟨a pat on the back : una palmadita en la espalda⟩ 2 CARESS : caricia f 3 : porción f ⟨a pat of butter : una porción de mantequilla⟩

patch¹ ['pætʃ] vt 1 MEND, REPAIR : remendar, parchar, ponerle un parche a 2 **to patch together** IMPROVISE : confeccionar, improvisar 3 **to patch up** : arreglar ⟨they patched things up : hicieron las paces⟩

patch² n 1 : parche m, remiendo m (para la ropa) ⟨eye patch : parche para el ojo⟩ 2 PIECE : mancha f, trozo m ⟨a patch of sky : un trozo de cielo⟩ 3 PLOT : parcela f, terreno m ⟨cabbage patch : parcela de repollos⟩ 4 : período m ⟨to go through a bad/rough patch : pasar una mala racha⟩ 5 : parche m (para el software)

patchwork ['pætʃ,wərk] n : labor f de retazos

patchy ['pætʃi] adj **patchier; -est** 1 IRREGULAR : irregular, desigual 2 INCOMPLETE : parcial, incompleto

pâté [pɑ'teɪ, pæ-] n : paté m

patent¹ ['pætənt] vt : patentar

patent² ['pætənt, 'peɪt-] adj 1 OBVIOUS : patente, evidente 2 ['pæt-] PATENTED : patentado

patent³ ['pætənt] n : patente f

patent leather ['pætənt-] n : charol m

patently ['pætəntli] adv : patentemente, evidentemente

paternal [pə'tərnəl] adj 1 FATHERLY : paternal 2 : paterno ⟨paternal grandfather : abuelo paterno⟩

paternity [pə'tərnəti] n : paternidad f ⟨paternity leave : licencia por paternidad⟩

path ['pæθ, 'pɑθ] n 1 TRACK, TRAIL : camino m, sendero m, senda f 2 COURSE, ROUTE : recorrido m, trayecto m, trayectoria f

pathetic [pə'θɛtɪk] adj : patético — **pathetically** [-tɪkli] adv

pathological [,pæθə'lɑdʒɪkəl] adj : patológico

pathologist [pə'θɑlədʒɪst] n : patólogo m, -ga f

pathology [pə'θɑlədʒi] n, pl **-gies** : patología f

pathos ['peɪ,θɑs, 'pæ-, -,θɔs] n : patetismo m

pathway ['pæθ,weɪ] n : camino m, sendero m, senda f, vereda f

patience ['peɪʃəns] n : paciencia f

patient¹ ['peɪʃənt] adj : paciente — **patiently** adv

patient² n : paciente mf

patina [pə'ti:nə, 'pætənə] n : pátina f

patio ['pæti,o:] n, pl **-tios** : patio m

patriarch ['peɪtri,ɑrk] n : patriarca m

patriarchy ['peɪtri,ɑrki] n, pl **-chies** : patriarcado m

patrimony ['pætrə,mo:ni] *n, pl* **-nies** : patrimonio *m*

patriot ['peɪtriət] *n* : patriota *mf*

patriotic [,peɪtri'atɪk] *adj* : patriótico — **patriotically** *adv*

patriotism ['peɪtriə,tɪzəm] *n* : patriotismo *m*

patrol[1] [pə'tro:l] *v* **-trolled; -trolling** : patrullar

patrol[2] *n* : patrulla *f*

patrol car *n* : patrulla *f*, patrullero *m* (automóvil)

patrolman [pə'tro:lmən] *n, pl* **-men** [-mən, -,mɛn] : policía *mf*, guardia *mf*

patron ['peɪtrən] *n* **1** SPONSOR : patrocinador *m*, -dora *f* **2** CUSTOMER : cliente *m*, -ta *f* **3** *or* **patron saint** : patrono *m*, -na *f*

patronage ['peɪtrənɪdʒ, 'pæ-] *n* **1** SPONSORSHIP : patrocinio *m* **2** CLIENTELE : clientela *f* **3** : influencia *f* (política)

patronize ['peɪtrə,naɪz, 'pæ-] *vt* **-ized; -izing 1** SPONSOR : patrocinar **2** : ser cliente de (un negocio) **3** : tratar con condescendencia

patronizing *adj* : condescendiente

patter[1] ['pætər] *vi* TAP : golpetear, tamborilear (dícese de la lluvia)

patter[2] *n* **1** TAPPING : golpeteo *m*, tamborileo *m* (de la lluvia), correteo *m* (de pies) **2** CHATTER : palabrería *f*, parloteo *m fam*

pattern[1] ['pætərn] *vt* **1** BASE : basar (en un modelo) **2 to pattern after** : hacer imitación de

pattern[2] *n* **1** MODEL : modelo *m*, patrón *m* (de costura) **2** DESIGN : diseño *m*, dibujo *m*, estampado *m* (de tela) **3** NORM, STANDARD : pauta *f*, norma *f*, patrón *m*

patty ['pæti] *n, pl* **-ties** : porción *f* de carne picada (u otro alimento) en forma de ruedita ⟨a hamburger patty : una hamburguesa⟩ ⟨a turkey patty : una hamburguesa de pavo⟩

paucity ['pɔsəti] *n* : escasez *f*

paunch ['pɔntʃ] *n* : panza *f*, barriga *f*

pauper ['pɔpər] *n* : pobre *mf*, indigente *mf*

pause[1] ['pɔz] *vi* **paused; pausing** : hacer una pausa, pararse (brevemente)

pause[2] *n* : pausa *f*

pave ['peɪv] *vt* **paved; paving** : pavimentar ⟨to pave with stones : empedrar⟩

pavement ['peɪvmənt] *n* : pavimento *m*, empedrado *m*

pavilion [pə'vɪljən] *n* : pabellón *m*

paving ['peɪvɪŋ] → **pavement**

paw[1] ['pɔ] *vt* : tocar, manosear, sobar

paw[2] *n* : pata *f*, garra *f*, zarpa *f*

pawn[1] ['pɔn] *vt* : empeñar, prendar

pawn[2] *n* **1** PLEDGE, SECURITY : prenda *f* **2** PAWNING : empeño *m* **3** : peón *m* (en ajedrez)

pawnbroker ['pɔn,bro:kər] *n* : prestamista *mf*

pawnshop ['pɔn,ʃɑp] *n* : casa *f* de empeños, monte *m* de piedad

pay[1] ['peɪ] *v* **paid** ['peɪd]; **paying** *vt* **1** : pagar ⟨she paid the bill/rent : pagó la cuenta/renta⟩ ⟨he paid $200 for the bike

: pagó $200 por la bici⟩ ⟨they paid her to mow the lawn : la pagaron para cortar el pasto⟩ **2 to pay attention** : poner atención, prestar atención, hacer caso **3 to pay a visit** : hacer una visita **4 to pay back** : pagar (un préstamo), devolver (dinero) ⟨she paid them back : les devolvió el dinero⟩ ⟨I'll pay you back for what you did! : ¡me las pagarás!⟩ **5 to pay off** SETTLE : saldar, cancelar (una deuda, etc.) **6 to pay one's respects** : presentar uno sus respetos — *vi* **1** : pagar ⟨to pay in cash : pagar en efectivo⟩ ⟨the job pays well : el trabajo está bien pagado⟩ **2** : valer la pena ⟨crime doesn't pay : no hay crimen sin castigo⟩ **3 to pay for** : pagar ⟨he paid for our dinner : nos pagó la comida⟩ ⟨she paid dearly for her mistakes : pagó caro sus errores⟩ ⟨you'll pay for this! : ¡me las pagarás!⟩ **4 to pay one's (own) way** ⟨she paid her way through college : se pagó los estudios⟩ ⟨he paid his own way at dinner : pagó su parte de la cena⟩ **5 to pay up** : pagar

pay[2] *n* : paga *f*

payable ['peɪəbəl] *adj* DUE : pagadero

paycheck ['peɪ,tʃɛk] *n* : sueldo *m*, cheque *m* del sueldo

payday ['peɪ,deɪ] *n* : día *m* de pago/paga

payee [peɪ'i:] *n* : beneficiario *m*, -ria *f* (de un cheque, etc.)

payer ['peɪər] *n* : pagador *m*, -dora *f*

payment ['peɪmənt] *n* **1** : pago *m* **2** INSTALLMENT : plazo *m*, cuota *f* **3** REWARD : recompensa *f*

payoff ['peɪ,ɔf] *n* **1** REWARD : recompensa *f* **2** PROFIT : ganancia *f* **3** BRIBE : soborno *m*

pay phone *n* : teléfono *m* público

payroll ['peɪ,ro:l] *n* : nómina *f*

PC [,pi:'si:] *n, pl* **PCs** *or* **PC's** : PC *mf*, computadora *f* personal

PDA [,pi:,di:'eɪ] *n, pl* **PDAs** *or* **PDA's** (personal *digital* assistant) : PDA *m*

pea ['pi:] *n* : chícharo *m*, guisante *m*, arveja *f*

peace ['pi:s] *n* **1** : paz *f* ⟨peace treaty : tratado de paz⟩ ⟨peace and tranquillity : paz y tranquilidad⟩ **2** ORDER : orden *m* (público)

peaceable ['pi:səbəl] *adj* : pacífico — **peaceably** [-bli] *adv*

peaceful ['pi:sfəl] *adj* **1** PEACEABLE : pacífico **2** CALM, QUIET : tranquilo, sosegado — **peacefully** *adv*

peacemaker ['pi:s,meɪkər] *n* : conciliador *m*, -dora *f*; mediador *m*, -dora *f*

peacetime ['pi:s,taɪm] *n* : tiempos *mpl* de paz

peach ['pi:tʃ] *n* : durazno *m*, melocotón *m*

peacock ['pi:,kɑk] *n* : pavo *m* real

peak[1] ['pi:k] *vi* : alcanzar su nivel máximo

peak[2] *adj* : máximo

peak[3] *n* **1** POINT : punta *f* **2** CREST, SUMMIT : cima *f*, cumbre *f* **3** APEX : cúspide *f*, apogeo *m*, nivel *m* máximo

peaked ['pi:kəd] *adj* SICKLY : pálido

peal[1] ['pi:l] *vi* : repicar

peal[2] *n* : repique *m*, tañido *m* (de campanada) ⟨peals of laughter : carcajadas⟩

peanut ['pi:ˌnʌt] *n* : maní *m*, cacahuate *m Mex*, cacahuete *m Spain*

peanut butter *n* : mantequilla/crema *f* de maní, manteca *f* de maní *Arg*, crema/ mantequilla *f* de cacahuate *Mex*, mantequilla/crema *f* de cacahuete *Spain*

pear ['pær] *n* : pera *f*

pearl ['pərl] *n* : perla *f*

pearly ['pərli] *adj* **pearlier; -est** : nacarado

peasant ['pɛzənt] *n* : campesino *m*, -na *f*

peat ['pi:t] *n* : turba *f*

pebble ['pɛbəl] *n* : guijarro *m*, piedrecita *f*, piedrita *f*

pecan [pɪ'kɑn, -'kæn, 'pi:ˌkæn] *n* : pacana *f*, nuez *f Mex*

peck¹ ['pɛk] *vt* : picar, picotear

peck² *n* **1** : medida *f* de áridos equivalente a 8.810 litros **2** : picotazo *m* (de un pájaro) ⟨a peck on the cheek : un besito en la mejilla⟩

pectoral ['pɛktərəl] *adj* : pectoral

peculiar [pɪ'kju:ljər] *adj* **1** DISTINCTIVE : propio, peculiar, característico ⟨peculiar to this area : propio de esta zona⟩ **2** STRANGE : extraño, raro — **peculiarly** *adv*

peculiarity [pɪˌkju:l'jærəˌti, -ˌkju:li'ær-] *n*, *pl* **-ties 1** DISTINCTIVENESS : peculiaridad *f* **2** ODDITY, QUIRK : rareza *f*, idiosincrasia *f*, excentricidad *f*

pecuniary [pɪ'kju:niˌɛri] *adj* : pecuniario

pedagogical [ˌpɛdə'gɑʤɪkəl, -'go:-] *or* **pedagogic** [ˌpɛdə'gɑʤɪk, -'go:-] *adj* : pedagógico

pedagogy ['pɛdəˌgo:ʤi, -ˌgɑ-] *n* : pedagogía *f*

pedal¹ ['pɛdəl] *v* **-aled** *or* **-alled; -aling** *or* **-alling** *vi* : pedalear — *vt* : darle a los pedales de

pedal² *n* : pedal *m*

pedant ['pɛdənt] *n* : pedante *mf*

pedantic [pɪ'dæntɪk] *adj* : pedante

pedantry ['pɛdəntri] *n*, *pl* **-ries** : pedantería *f*

peddle ['pɛdəl] *vt* **-dled; -dling** : vender (en las calles)

peddler ['pɛdlər] *n* : vendedor *m*, -dora *f* ambulante; mercachifle *m*

pedestal ['pɛdəstəl] *n* : pedestal *m*

pedestrian¹ [pə'dɛstriən] *adj* **1** COMMONPLACE : pedestre, ordinario **2** : de peatón, peatonal ⟨pedestrian crossing : paso de peatones⟩

pedestrian² *n* : peatón *m*, -tona *f*

pediatric [ˌpi:di'ætrɪk] *adj* : pediátrico

pediatrician [ˌpi:diə'trɪʃən] *n* : pediatra *mf*

pediatrics [ˌpi:di'ætrɪks] *ns & pl* : pediatría *f*

pedigree ['pɛdəˌgri:] *n* **1** FAMILY TREE : árbol *m* genealógico **2** LINEAGE : pedigrí *m* (de un animal), linaje *m* (de una persona)

pee¹ ['pi:] *vi fam* URINATE : hacer pipí *fam*

pee² *n fam* : pipí *m fam* ⟨to take a pee : hacer pipí⟩

peek¹ ['pi:k] *vi* **1** PEEP : espiar, mirar furtivamente **2** GLANCE : echar un vistazo

peek² *n* **1** : miradita *f* (furtiva) **2** GLANCE : vistazo *m*, ojeada *f*

peel¹ ['pi:l] *vt* **1** : pelar (fruta, etc.) **2** *or* **to peel away** : quitar — *vi* : pelarse (dícese de la piel), desconcharse (dícese de la pintura)

peel² *n* : cáscara *f*

peeler ['pi:lər] *n* : pelador *m*, pelapapas *mpl*

peep¹ ['pi:p] *vi* **1** PEEK : espiar, mirar furtivamente **2** CHEEP : piar **3 to peep out** SHOW : asomarse

peep² *n* **1** CHEEP : pío *m* (de un pajarito) **2** GLANCE : vistazo *m*, ojeada *f*

peer¹ ['pɪr] *vi* : mirar detenidamente, mirar con atención

peer² *n* **1** EQUAL : par *m*, igual *mf* ⟨peer group : grupo paritario⟩ **2** NOBLE : noble *mf*

peerage ['pɪrɪʤ] *n* : nobleza *f*

peerless ['pɪrləs] *adj* : sin par, incomparable

peeve¹ ['pi:v] *vt* **peeved; peeving** : fastidiar, irritar, molestar

peeve² *n* : queja *f*

peevish ['pi:vɪʃ] *adj* : quejoso, fastidioso — **peevishly** *adv*

peevishness ['pi:vɪʃnəs] *n* : irritabilidad *f*

peg¹ ['pɛg] *vt* **pegged; pegging 1** PLUG : tapar (con una clavija) **2** FASTEN, FIX : sujetar (con estaquillas) **3 to peg out** MARK : marcar (con estaquillas)

peg² *n* : estaquilla *f* (para clavar), clavija *f* (para tapar)

pejorative [pɪ'ʤɔrətɪv] *adj* : peyorativo — **pejoratively** *adv*

pelican ['pɛlɪkən] *n* : pelícano *m*

pellagra [pə'lægrə, -'leɪ-] *n* : pelagra *f*

pellet ['pɛlət] *n* **1** BALL : bolita *f* ⟨food pellet : bolita de comida⟩ **2** SHOT : perdigón *m*

pell–mell ['pɛl'mɛl] *adv* : desordenadamente, atropelladamente

pelt¹ ['pɛlt] *vt* **1** THROW : lanzar, tirar (algo a alguien) **2 to pelt with stones** : apedrear — *vi* **1** BEAT : golpear con fuerza ⟨the rain was pelting down : llovía a cántaros⟩ **2** : ir a todo correr

pelt² *n* : piel *f*, pellejo *m*

pelvic ['pɛlvɪk] *adj* : pélvico

pelvis ['pɛlvɪs] *n*, *pl* **-vises** *or* **-ves** ['pɛlˌvi:z] : pelvis *f*

pen¹ ['pɛn] *vt* **penned; penning 1** *or* **pen in** : encerrar (animales) **2** WRITE : escribir

pen² *n* **1** CORRAL : corral *m*, redil *m* (para ovejas) **2** : pluma *f* ⟨fountain pen : pluma fuente⟩ ⟨ballpoint pen : bolígrafo⟩

penal ['pi:nəl] *adj* : penal

penalize ['pi:nəlˌaɪz, 'pɛn-] *vt* **-ized; -izing** : penalizar, sancionar, penar

penalty ['pɛnəlti] *n*, *pl* **-ties 1** PUNISHMENT : pena *f*, castigo *m* **2** DISADVANTAGE : desventaja *f*, castigo *m*, penalty *m* (en deportes) **3** FINE : multa *f*

penance ['pɛnənts] *n* : penitencia *f*

pence → penny

penchant ['pɛntʃənt] *n* : inclinación *f*, afición *f*

pencil[1] ['pɛntsəl] *vt* **-ciled** *or* **-cilled; -cil-ing** *or* **-cilling** : escribir con lápiz, dibujar con lápiz
pencil[2] *n* : lápiz *m*
pencil case *n* : estuche *m* (para lápices)
pencil sharpener *n* : sacapuntas *m*
pencil skirt *n* : falda *f* de tubo
pendant ['pɛndənt] *n* : colgante *m*
pending[1] ['pɛndɪŋ] *adj* : pendiente
pending[2] *prep* **1** DURING : durante **2** AWAITING : en espera de
pendulum ['pɛndʒələm, -djʊləm] *n* : péndulo *m*
penetrate ['pɛnə̩treɪt] *vt* **-trated; -trating** : penetrar
penetrating ['pɛnə̩treɪtɪŋ] *adj* : penetrante, cortante
penetration [ˌpɛnə'treɪʃən] *n* : penetración *f*
penguin ['pɛŋgwɪn, 'pɛn-] *n* : pingüino *m*
penicillin [ˌpɛnə'sɪlən] *n* : penicilina *f*
peninsula [pə'nɪntsələ, -'nɪntʊlə] *n* : península *f*
penis ['pi:nəs] *n, pl* **-nes** [-ˌni:z] *or* **-nises** : pene *m*
penitence ['pɛnətənts] *n* : arrepentimiento *m*, penitencia *f*
penitent[1] ['pɛnətənt] *adj* : arrepentido, penitente
penitent[2] *n* : penitente *mf*
penitentiary [ˌpɛnə'tɛntʃəri] *n, pl* **-ries** : penitenciaría *f*, prisión *m*, presidio *m*
penknife ['pɛnˌnaɪf] *n* : navaja *f*
penmanship ['pɛnmənˌʃɪp] *n* : escritura *f*, caligrafía *f*
pen name *n* : seudónimo *m*
pennant ['pɛnənt] *n* : gallardete *m* (de un barco), banderín *m*
penniless ['pɛniləs] *adj* : sin un centavo
penny ['pɛni] *n, pl* **-nies** *or* **pence** ['pɛnts] **1** : penique *m* (del Reino Unido) **2** *pl* **-nies** CENT : centavo *m* (de los Estados Unidos)
pen pal *n* : amigo *m*, -ga *f* por correspondencia
pension[1] ['pɛnʃən] *vt or* **to pension off** : jubilar
pension[2] *n* : pensión *m*, jubilación *f*
pensioner ['pɛnʃənər] *n* : pensionista *mf*
pensive ['pɛntsɪv] *adj* : pensativo, meditabundo — **pensively** *adv*
pentagon ['pɛntəˌɡɑn] *n* : pentágono *m*
pentagonal [pɛn'tægənəl] *adj* : pentagonal
penthouse ['pɛntˌhaʊs] *n* : ático *m*, penthouse *m*
pent–up ['pɛnt'ʌp] *adj* : encerrado ⟨pent-up feelings : emociones reprimidas⟩
penultimate [pɪ'nʌltəmət] *adj* : penúltimo
penury ['pɛnjəri] *n* : penuria *f*, miseria *f*
peon ['pi:ˌɑn, -ən] *n, pl* **-ons** *or* **-ones** [pɛɪ'o:ni:z] : peón *m*
peony ['pi:əni] *n, pl* **-nies** : peonía *f*
people[1] ['pi:pəl] *vt* **-pled; -pling** : poblar
people[2] *ns & pl* **1** **people** *npl* : gente *f*, personas *fpl* ⟨people like him : él le cae bien a la gente⟩ ⟨many people : mucha gente, muchas personas⟩ ⟨young/old people : los jóvenes/ancianos⟩ **2** *pl* **peoples** : pueblo *m* ⟨the Cuban people : el pueblo cubano⟩

pep[1] ['pɛp] *vt* **pepped; pepping** *or* **to pep up** : animar
pep[2] *n* : energía *f*, vigor *m*
pepper[1] ['pɛpər] *vt* **1** : añadir pimienta a **2** RIDDLE : acribillar (a balazos) **3** SPRINKLE : salpicar ⟨peppered with quotations : salpicado de citas⟩
pepper[2] *n* **1** : pimienta *f* (condimento) **2** : pimiento *m*, pimentón *m* (fruta) **3** → **chili**
peppermint ['pɛpərˌmɪnt] *n* : menta *f*
pepper shaker → **shaker**
peppery ['pɛpəri] *adj* : picante
peppy ['pɛpi] *adj* **peppier; -est** : lleno de energía, vivaz
pep rally *n* : reunión *f* (para animar a un equipo antes de un partido)
pep talk *n* : plática *f*, charla *f* (para animar a un equipo, etc.) ⟨to give someone a pep talk : animar a alguien⟩
peptic ['pɛptɪk] *adj* **peptic ulcer** : úlcera *f* estomacal
per ['pər] *prep* **1** : por ⟨miles per hour : millas por hora⟩ **2** ACCORDING TO : según ⟨per his specifications : según sus especificaciones⟩
per annum [pər'ænəm] *adv* : al año, por año
percale [ˌpər'keɪl, 'pər-ˌ;, ˌpər'kæl] *n* : percal *m*
per capita [pər'kæpɪtə] *adv & adj* : per cápita
perceive [pər'si:v] *vt* **-ceived; -ceiving 1** REALIZE : percatarse de, concientizarse de, darse cuenta de **2** NOTE : percibir, notar
percent[1] [pər'sɛnt] *adv* : por ciento
percent[2] *n, pl* **-cent** *or* **-cents 1** : por ciento ⟨10 percent of the population : el 10 por ciento de la población⟩ **2** → **percentage**
percentage [pər'sɛntɪdʒ] *n* : porcentaje *m*
perceptible [pər'sɛptəbəl] *adj* : perceptible — **perceptibly** [-bli] *adv*
perception [pər'sɛpʃən] *n* **1** : percepción *f* ⟨color perception : la percepción de los colores⟩ **2** INSIGHT : perspicacia *f* **3** IDEA : idea *f*, imagen *f*
perceptive [pər'sɛptɪv] *adj* : perspicaz
perceptively [pər'sɛptɪvli] *adv* : con perspicacia
perch[1] ['pərtʃ] *vi* **1** ROOST : posarse **2** SIT : sentarse (en un sitio elevado) — *vt* PLACE : posar, colocar
perch[2] *n* **1** ROOST : percha *f* (para los pájaros) **2** *pl* **perch** *or* **perches** : perca *f* (pez)
percolate ['pərkəˌleɪt] *vi* **-lated; -lating** : colarse, filtrarse ⟨percolated coffee : café filtrado⟩
percolator ['pərkəˌleɪtər] *n* : cafetera *f* de filtro
percussion [pər'kʌʃən] *n* **1** STRIKING : percusión *f* **2** *or* **percussion instruments** : instrumentos *mpl* de percusión
peremptory [pə'rɛmptəri] *adj* : perentorio
perennial[1] [pə'rɛniəl] *adj* **1** : perenne, vivaz ⟨perennial flowers : flores perennes⟩ **2** RECURRENT : perenne, con-

tinuo ⟨a perennial problem : un problema eterno⟩
perennial[2] *n* : planta *f* perenne, planta *f* vivaz
perfect[1] [pər'fɛkt] *vt* : perfeccionar
perfect[2] ['pərfɪkt] *adj* : perfecto — **perfectly** *adv*
perfection [pər'fɛkɪən] *n* : perfección *f*
perfectionism [pər'fɛkɪə,nɪzəm] *n* : perfeccionismo *m*
perfectionist [pər'fɛkɪənɪst] *n* : perfeccionista *mf*
perfidious [pər'fɪdiəs] *adj* : pérfido
perforate ['pərfə,reɪt] *vt* -rated; -rating : perforar
perforation [,pərfə'reɪɪən] *n* : perforación *f*
perform [pər'fɔrm] *vt* **1** CARRY OUT : realizar, hacer, desempeñar **2** PRESENT : representar, dar (una obra teatral, etc.) — *vi* **1** : actuar (en una obra teatral), cantar (en una ópera, etc.), tocar (en un concierto, etc.), bailar (en un ballet, etc.) **2** : funcionar
performance [pər'fɔrmənts] *n* **1** EXECUTION : ejecución *f*, realización *f*, desempeño *m*, rendimiento *m* **2** INTERPRETATION : interpretación *f* ⟨his performance of Hamlet : su interpretación de Hamlet⟩ **3** PRESENTATION : representación *f* (de una obra teatral), función *f*
performer [pər'fɔrmər] *n* : artista *mf*; actor *m*, -triz *f*; intérprete *mf* (de música)
perfume[1] [pər'fju:m, 'pər,-] *vt* -fumed; -fuming : perfumar
perfume[2] ['pər,fju:m, pər'-] *n* : perfume *m*
perfunctory [pər'fʌŋktəri] *adj* : mecánico, superficial, somero
perhaps [pər'hæps] *adv* : tal vez, quizá, quizás, a lo mejor ⟨perhaps so/not : tal vez sí/no⟩ ⟨perhaps he didn't know : quizá(s) no lo sabía⟩ ⟨perhaps I'm wrong : a lo mejor me equivoco⟩ ⟨perhaps I can go tomorrow : quizá(s) pueda ir mañana⟩
peril ['pɛrəl] *n* : peligro *m*
perilous ['pɛrələs] *adj* : peligroso — **perilously** *adv*
perimeter [pə'rɪmətər] *n* : perímetro *m*
period ['pɪriəd] *n* **1** : punto *m* (en puntuación) **2** : período *m* ⟨a two-hour period : un período de dos horas⟩ **3** STAGE : época *f* (histórica), fase *f*, etapa *f* **4** MENSTRUATION : período *m*, regla *f* ⟨to have one's period : tener el período, tener la regla⟩ **5** : hora *f* (de clase)
periodic [,pɪri'ɑdɪk] *or* **periodical** [-dɪkəl] *adj* : periódico — **periodically** [-dɪkli] *adv*
periodical [,pɪri'ɑdɪkəl] *n* : publicación *f* periódica, revista *f*
peripheral [pə'rɪfərəl] *adj* : periférico
periphery [pə'rɪfəri] *n, pl* -eries : periferia *f*
periscope ['pɛrə,sko:p] *n* : periscopio *m*
perish ['pɛrɪʃ] *vi* DIE : perecer, morirse
perishable[1] ['pɛrɪʃəbəl] *adj* : perecedero
perishable[2] *n* : producto *m* perecedero
perjure ['pərdʒər] *vt* -jured; -juring (*used in law*) **to perjure oneself** : perjurar, perjurarse

perjury ['pərdʒəri] *n* : perjurio *m*
perk[1] ['pərk] *vt* **1** : levantar (las orejas, etc.) **2** *or* **to perk up** FRESHEN : arreglar — *vi* **to perk up** : animarse, reanimarse
perk[2] *n* : extra *m*
perky ['pərki] *adj* **perkier; -est** : animado, alegre, lleno de vida
perm ['pərm] *n* : permanente *f*
permanence ['pərmənənts] *n* : permanencia *f*
permanent[1] ['pərmənənt] *adj* : permanente — **permanently** *adv*
permanent[2] *n* : permanente *f*
permeability [,pərmiə'bɪləti] *n* : permeabilidad *f*
permeable ['pərmiəbəl] *adj* : permeable
permeate ['pərmi,eɪt] *v* -ated; -ating *vt* **1** PENETRATE : penetrar, impregnar **2** PERVADE : penetrar, difundirse por — *vi* : penetrar
permissible [pər'mɪsəbəl] *adj* : permisible, lícito
permission [pər'mɪʃən] *n* : permiso *m*
permissive [pər'mɪsɪv] *adj* : permisivo
permissiveness [pər'mɪsɪvnəs] *adj* : permisividad *f*
permit[1] [pər'mɪt] *vt* -mitted; -mitting : permitir, dejar ⟨weather permitting : si el tiempo lo permite⟩
permit[2] ['pər,mɪt, pər'-] *n* : permiso *m*, licencia *f*
permutation [,pərmju'teɪʃən] *n* : permutación *f*
pernicious [pər'nɪʃəs] *adj* : pernicioso
peroxide [pə'rɑk,saɪd] *n* **1** : peróxido *m* **2** → hydrogen peroxide
perpendicular[1] [,pərpən'dɪkjələr] *adj* **1** VERTICAL : vertical **2** : perpendicular ⟨perpendicular lines : líneas perpendiculares⟩ — **perpendicularly** *adv*
perpendicular[2] *n* : perpendicular *f*
perpetrate ['pərpə,treɪt] *vt* -trated; -trating : perpetrar, cometer (un delito)
perpetrator ['pərpə,treɪtər] *n* : autor *m*, -tora *f* (de un delito)
perpetual [pər'pɛtʃuəl] *adj* **1** EVERLASTING : perpetuo, eterno **2** CONTINUAL : perpetuo, continuo, constante
perpetually [pər'pɛtʃuəli, -tʃəli] *adv* : para siempre, eternamente
perpetuate [pər'pɛtʃu,eɪt] *vt* -ated; -ating : perpetuar
perpetuity [,pərpə'tu:əti, -'tju:-] *n, pl* -ties : perpetuidad *f*
perplex [pər'plɛks] *vt* : dejar perplejo, confundir
perplexed [pər'plɛkst] *adj* : perplejo
perplexity [pər'plɛksəti] *n, pl* -ties : perplejidad *f*, confusión *f*
per se [pər'seɪ] *adv* : per se, de por sí, en sí
persecute ['pərsɪ,kju:t] *vt* -cuted; -cuting : perseguir
persecution [,pərsɪ'kju:ʃən] *n* : persecución *f*
persecutor ['pərsɪ,kju:tər] *n* : perseguidor *m*, -dora *f*
perseverance [,pərsə'vɪrənts] *n* : perseverancia *f*

persevere [ˌpərsə'vɪr] *vi* **-vered; -vering**
: perseverar
Persian ['pərʒən] *n* **1** : persa *mf* **2**
: persa *m* (idioma) — **Persian** *adj*
persist [pər'sɪst] *vi* : persistir
persistence [pər'sɪstənts] *n* **1** CONTI-
NUATION : persistencia *f* **2** TENACITY
: perseverancia *f*, tenacidad *f*
persistent [pər'sɪstənt] *adj* : persistente
— **persistently** *adv*
person ['pərsən] *n* **1** *pl* **people** *or* **persons** HUMAN, INDIVIDUAL : persona *f*,
individuo *m*, ser *m* humano **2** : persona
f (en gramática) **3 in person** : en persona
personable ['pərsənəbəl] *adj* : agradable
personage ['pərsənɪʤ] *n* : personaje *m*
personal ['pərsənəl] *adj* **1** OWN, PRIVATE
: personal, particular, privado ⟨for personal reasons : por razones personales⟩ **2**
: en persona ⟨to make a personal appearance : presentarse en persona, hacerse
acto de presencia⟩ **3** : íntimo, personal
⟨personal hygiene : higiene personal⟩ **4**
INDISCREET, PRYING : indiscreto, personal
personal assistant *n* : secretario *m*, -ria *f*
personal
personal computer *n* : computadora *f*
personal, ordenador *m* personal *Spain*
personality [ˌpərsən'æləti] *n, pl* **-ties 1**
DISPOSITION : personalidad *f*, temperamento *m* **2** CELEBRITY : personalidad *f*,
personaje *m*, celebridad *f*
personalize ['pərsənəˌlaɪz] *vt* **-ized; -izing**
: personalizar
personally ['pərsənəli] *adv* **1** : personalmente, en persona ⟨I'll do it personally
: lo haré personalmente⟩ **2** : como persona ⟨personally she's very amiable
: como persona es muy amable⟩ **3**
: personalmente ⟨personally, I don't believe it : yo, personalmente, no me lo
creo⟩
personification [pərˌsɑnəfə'keɪʃən] *n*
: personificación *f*
personify [pər'sɑnəˌfaɪ] *vt* **-fied; -fying**
: personificar
personnel [ˌpərsən'ɛl] *n* : personal *m*
perspective [pər'spɛktɪv] *n* : perspectiva *f*
perspicacious [ˌpərspə'keɪʃəs] *adj* : perspicaz
perspicacity [ˌpərspə'kæsəti] *n* : clarividencia *f*, perspicacia *f*
perspiration [ˌpərspə'reɪʃən] *n* : transpiración *f*, sudor *m*
perspire [pər'spaɪr] *vi* **-spired; -spiring**
: transpirar, sudar
persuade [pər'sweɪd] *vt* **-suaded; -suad-
ing** : persuadir, convencer
persuasion [pər'sweɪʒən] *n* : persuasión *f*
persuasive [pər'sweɪsɪv, -zɪv] *adj* : persuasivo — **persuasively** *adv*
persuasiveness [pər'sweɪsɪvnəs, -zɪv-] *n*
: persuasión *f*
pert ['pərt] *adj* **1** SAUCY : descarado, impertinente **2** JAUNTY : alegre, animado
⟨a pert little hat : un sombrero coqueto⟩
pertain [pər'teɪn] *vi* **1** BELONG
: pertenecer (a) **2** RELATE : estar relacionado (con)

pertinence ['pərtənənts] *n* : pertinencia *f*
pertinent ['pərtənənt] *adj* : pertinente
perturb [pər'tərb] *vt* : perturbar
perusal [pə'ru:zəl] *n* : lectura *f* cuidadosa
peruse [pə'ru:z] *vt* **-rused; -rusing 1**
READ : leer con cuidado **2** SCAN : recorrer con la vista ⟨he perused the newspaper : echó un vistazo al periódico⟩
Peruvian [pə'ru:viən] *n* : peruano *m*, -na *f*
— **Peruvian** *adj*
pervade [pər'veɪd] *vt* **-vaded; -vading**
: penetrar, difundirse por
pervasive [pər'veɪsɪv, -zɪv] *adj* : penetrante
perverse [pər'vərs] *adj* **1** CORRUPT : perverso, corrompido **2** STUBBORN : obstinado, porfiado, terco (sin razón) — **per-
versely** *adv*
perversion [pər'vərʒən] *n* : perversión *f*
perversity [pər'vərsəti] *n, pl* **-ties 1** COR-
RUPTION : corrupción *f* **2** STUBBORN-
NESS : obstinación *f*, terquedad *f*
pervert[1] [pər'vərt] *vt* **1** DISTORT : pervertir, distorsionar **2** CORRUPT : pervertir,
corromper
pervert[2] ['pərˌvərt] *n* : pervertido *m*, -da *f*
peseta [pə'seɪt̬ə] *n* : peseta *f*
pesky ['pɛski] *adj* : molestoso, molesto
peso ['peɪˌso:] *n, pl* **-sos** : peso *m* (unidad
monetaria)
pessimism ['pɛsəˌmɪzəm] *n* : pesimismo
m
pessimist ['pɛsəmɪst] *n* : pesimista *mf*
pessimistic [ˌpɛsə'mɪstɪk] *adj* : pesimista
pest ['pɛst] *n* **1** NUISANCE : peste *f*; la-
toso *m*, -sa *f fam* ⟨to be a pest : dar (la)
lata⟩ **2** : insecto *m* nocivo, animal *m*
nocivo ⟨the squirrels were pests : las ar-
dillas eran una plaga⟩
pester ['pɛstər] *vt* **-tered; -tering** : molestar, fastidiar
pesticide ['pɛstəˌsaɪd] *n* : pesticida *m*
pestilence ['pɛstələnts] *n* : pestilencia *f*,
peste *f*
pestle ['pɛsəl, 'pɛstəl] *n* : mano *f* de
mortero, mazo *m*, maja *f*
pet[1] ['pɛt] *vt* **petted; petting** : acariciar
pet[2] *n* **1** : animal *m* doméstico, mascota *f*
⟨pet store : tienda de mascotas⟩ ⟨pet food
: alimento para mascotas⟩ **2** FAVORITE
: favorito *m*, -ta *f*
pet[3] *adj* : preferido, favorito ⟨her pet theory : su teoría preferida⟩ ⟨his pet project
: su proyecto favorito⟩ ⟨pet name
: apodo (cariñoso)⟩
petal ['pɛt̬əl] *n* : pétalo *m*
peter ['pi:t̬ər] *vi* **to peter out** : agotarse,
apagarse, disminuir (poco a poco)
petite [pə'ti:t] *adj* : pequeña, menuda,
chiquita
petition[1] [pə'tɪʃən] *vt* : peticionar
petition[2] *n* : petición *f*
petitioner [pə'tɪʃənər] *n* : peticionario *m*,
-ria *f*
petrify ['pɛtrəˌfaɪ] *vt* **-fied; -fying** : petrificar
petroleum [pə'tro:liəm] *n* : petróleo *m*
petroleum jelly *n* : vaselina *f*
petticoat ['pɛt̬iˌko:t] *n* : enagua *f*, fondo *m*
Mex

pettiness ['pɛtinəs] *n* **1** INSIGNIFICANCE : insignificancia *f* **2** MEANNESS : mezquindad *f*

petty ['pɛti] *adj* **pettier; -est** **1** MINOR : menor ⟨petty cash : dinero para gastos menores⟩ **2** INSIGNIFICANT : insignificante, trivial, nimio **3** MEAN : mezquino

petty officer *n* : suboficial *mf*

petulance ['pɛtɭələnʦ] *n* : irritabilidad *f*, mal genio *m*

petulant ['pɛtɭələnt] *adj* : irritable, de mal genio

petunia [pɪ'tu:njə, -'tju:-] *n* : petunia *f*

pew ['pju:] *n* : banco *m* (de iglesia)

pewter ['pju:t̬ər] *n* : peltre *m*

pH [ˌpi:'eɪtɭ] *n* : pH *m*

phallic ['fælɪk] *adj* : fálico

phallus ['fæləs] *n*, *pl* **-li** ['fæˌlaɪ] *or* **-luses** : falo *m*

phantasy ['fæntəsi] → **fantasy**

phantom ['fæntəm] *n* : fantasma *m*

pharaoh ['fɛrˌo:, 'feɪˌro:] *n* : faraón *m*

pharmaceutical [ˌfɑrmə'su:t̬ɪkəl] *adj* : farmacéutico

pharmacist ['fɑrməsɪst] *n* : farmacéutico *m*, -ca *f*

pharmacology [ˌfɑrmə'kɑləʤi] *n* : farmacología *f*

pharmacy ['fɑrməsi] *n*, *pl* **-cies** : farmacia *f*

pharynx ['færɪŋks] *n*, *pl* **pharynges** [fə'rɪnˌʤi:z] : faringe *f*

phase¹ ['feɪz] *vt* **phased; phasing** **1** SYNCHRONIZE : sincronizar, poner en fase **2** STAGGER : escalonar **3 to phase in** : introducir progresivamente **4 to phase out** : retirar progresivamente, dejar de producir

phase² *n* **1** : fase *f* (de la luna, etc.) **2** STAGE : fase *f*, etapa *f*

pheasant ['fɛzənt] *n*, *pl* **-ant** *or* **-ants** : faisán *m*

phenomenal [fɪ'nɑmənəl] *adj* : extraordinario, excepcional

phenomenon [fɪ'nɑməˌnɑn, -nən] *n*, *pl* **-na** [-nə] *or* **-nons** **1** : fenómeno *m* **2** *pl* **-nons** PRODIGY : fenómeno *m*, prodigio *m*

phew ['fju:] *interj* : ¡uf!

philanthropic [ˌfɪlən'θrɑpɪk] *adj* : filantrópico

philanthropist [fə'lænθrəpɪst] *n* : filántropo *m*, -pa *f*

philanthropy [fə'lænθrəpi] *n*, *pl* **-pies** : filantropía *f*

philately [fə'lætəli] *n* : filatelia *f*

philharmonic [ˌfɪlər'mɑnɪk] *n* : filarmónica *f*

philosopher [fə'lɑsəfər] *n* : filósofo *m*, -fa *f*

philosophic [ˌfɪlə'sɑfɪk] *or* **philosophical** [-fɪkəl] *adj* : filosófico — **philosophically** [-kli] *adv*

philosophize [fə'lɑsəˌfaɪz] *vi* **-phized; -phizing** : filosofar

philosophy [fə'lɑsəfi] *n*, *pl* **-phies** : filosofía *f*

phishing ['fɪlɪŋ] *n* : phishing *m*, suplantación *f* de identidad (en Internet)

phlegm ['flɛm] *n* : flema *f*

phlegmatic [flɛg'mætɪk] *adj* : flemático

phlox ['flɑks] *n*, *pl* **phlox** *or* **phloxes** : polemonio *m*

phobia ['fo:biə] *n* : fobia *f*

phoenix ['fi:nɪks] *n* : fénix *m*

phone¹ ['fo:n] *v* → **telephone¹**

phone² *n* → **telephone²**

phone book *n* : guía *f* telefónica

phone call → **call²**

phone card *n* : tarjeta *f* telefónica

phoneme ['fo:ˌni:m] *n* : fonema *m*

phone number → **number²**

phonetic [fə'nɛtɪk] *adj* : fonético

phonetics [fə'nɛtɪks] *n* : fonética *f*

phonics ['fɑnɪks] *n* : método *m* fonético de aprender a leer

phony¹ *or* **phoney** ['fo:ni] *adj* **phonier; -est** : falso

phony² *or* **phoney** *n*, *pl* **-nies** : farsante *mf*; charlatán *m*, -tana *f*

phosphate ['fɑsˌfeɪt] *n* : fosfato *m*

phosphorescence [ˌfɑsfə'rɛsənts] *n* : fosforescencia *f*

phosphorescent [ˌfɑsfə'rɛsənt] *adj* : fosforescente — **phosphorescently** *adv*

phosphorus ['fɑsfərəs] *n* : fósforo *m*

photo ['fo:ˌto:] *n*, *pl* **-tos** : foto *f*

photocopier ['fo:t̬oˌkɑpiər] *n* : fotocopiadora *f*

photocopy¹ ['fo:t̬oˌkɑpi] *vt* **-copied; -copying** : fotocopiar

photocopy² *n, pl* **-copies** : fotocopia *f*

photoelectric [ˌfo:toɪ'lɛktrɪk] *adj* : fotoeléctrico

photogenic [ˌfo:tə'ʤɛnɪk] *adj* : fotogénico

photograph¹ ['fo:təˌgræf] *vt* : fotografiar

photograph² *n* : fotografía *f*, foto *f* ⟨to take a photograph of : tomarle una fotografía a, tomar una fotografía de⟩

photographer [fə'tɑgrəfər] *n* : fotógrafo *m*, -fa *f*

photographic [ˌfo:tə'græfɪk] *adj* : fotográfico — **photographically** [-fɪkli] *adv*

photography [fə'tɑgrəfi] *n* : fotografía *f*

photojournalist [ˌfo:to'ʤərnəlɪst] *n* : reportero *m* gráfico, reportera *f* gráfica

photoshop *or* **Photoshop** ['fo:t̬oˌʃɑp] *vt* (*Photoshop*, trademark) : editar (con un editor de imágenes)

photosynthesis [ˌfo:to'sɪnθəsɪs] *n* : fotosíntesis *f*

phrasal verb *n* : verbo *m* con partícula(s)

phrase¹ ['freɪz] *vt* **phrased; phrasing** : expresar

phrase² *n* : frase *f*, locución *f* ⟨to coin a phrase : para decirlo así⟩

phrase book *n* : guía *f* de conversación

phylum ['faɪləm] *n*, *pl* **-la** [-lə] : phylum *m*

phys ed ['fɪz'ɛd] *n fam* → **physical education**

physical¹ ['fɪzɪkəl] *adj* **1** : físico ⟨physical laws : leyes físicas⟩ **2** MATERIAL : material, físico **3** BODILY : físico, corpóreo — **physically** [-kli] *adv*

physical² *n* CHECKUP : chequeo *m*, reconocimiento *m* médico

physical education *n* : educación *f* física

physical therapist *n* : fisioterapeuta *mf*

physical therapy *n* : fisioterapia *f*
physician [fə'zıʃən] *n* : médico *m*, -ca *f*
physicist ['fızəsıst] *n* : físico *m*, -ca *f*
physics ['fızıks] *ns & pl* : física *f*
physiognomy [ˌfızı'ɑgnəmi] *n, pl* **-mies**
: fisonomía *f*
physiological ['fızıə'lɑʤıkəl] *or* **physiologic** [-ʤık] *adj* : fisiológico
physiologist [ˌfızi'ɑləʤıst] *n* : fisiólogo
m, -ga *f*
physiology [ˌfızi'ɑləʤi] *n* : fisiología *f*
physique [fə'zi:k] *n* : físico *m*
pi ['paı] *n, pl* **pis** ['paız] : pi *f*
pianist [pi'ænıst, 'pi:ənıst] *n* : pianista *mf*
piano [pi'æno:] *n, pl* **-anos** : piano *m*
piazza [pi'æzə, -'ɑtsə] *n, pl* **-zas** *or* **-ze**
[-'ɑt,seı] : plaza *f*
picador ['pıkə,dɔr] *n* : picador *m*, -dora *f*
picaresque [ˌpıkə'rɛsk, ˌpi:-] *adj* : picaresco
picayune [ˌpıki'ju:n] *adj* : trivial, nimio,
insignificante
piccolo ['pıkə,lo:] *n, pl* **-los** : flautín *m*
pick¹ ['pık] *vt* 1 SELECT : escoger, elegir
⟨pick a card : elige una carta⟩ 2 : quitar, sacar (poco a poco) ⟨to pick meat
off the bones : quitar pedazos de carne
de los huesos⟩ 3 : recoger, arrancar
(frutas, flores, etc.) 4 PROVOKE : provocar ⟨to pick a fight : buscar pelea⟩ 5
: hurgarse (la nariz), escarbar (los dientes) 6 to pick a lock : forzar una cerradura 7 to pick out CHOOSE : escoger 8
to pick out IDENTIFY : identificar, distinguir 9 to pick someone's pocket
: robarle a alguien la cartera (etc.) del
bolsillo 10 to pick up LIFT : levantar 11 to pick up TIDY : ordenar (una
habitación, etc.), recoger (juguetes,
etc.) 12 to pick up FETCH : (ir a) recoger 13 to pick up LOAD : recoger (pasajeros), cargar 14 to pick up BUY, GET
: comprar, conseguir 15 to pick up
LEARN : aprender (un idioma, etc.), adquirir (una costumbre) 16 to pick up
RESUME : continuar 17 to pick up
: captar (una señal) 18 to pick up DE-
TECT : detectar 19 to pick up speed
: ganar velocidad 20 to pick up the
pace : ir/trabajar (etc.) más rápido 21
to pick up the tab/bill/check : cargar
con la cuenta — *vi* 1 NIBBLE : picar,
picotear 2 to pick and choose : ser
exigente 3 to pick at : tocar, rascarse
(una herida, etc.) 4 to pick on TEASE
: mofarse de, atormentar 5 to pick up
IMPROVE : mejorar 6 to pick up : levantarse (dícese del viento), acelerarse
(dícese de un ritmo, etc.) 7 to pick up
ANSWER : contestar (el teléfono) 8 to
pick up TIDY : ordenar ⟨pick up after
yourself : ordena lo que has desorde-
nado⟩ 9 to pick up RESUME : continuar
⟨let's pick up where we left off : re-
tomemos donde lo dejamos⟩ 10 to pick
up on : darse cuenta de
pick² *n* 1 CHOICE : selección *f* 2 BEST
: lo mejor ⟨the pick of the crop : la
crema y nata⟩ 3 → pickax 4 : púa *f*
(para una guitarra, etc.)

pickax ['pık,æks] *n* : pico *m*, zapapico *m*,
piqueta *f*
pickerel ['pıkərəl] *n, pl* **-el** *or* **-els** : lucio
m pequeño
picket¹ ['pıkət] *v* : piquetear
picket² *n* 1 STAKE : estaca *f* 2 STRIKER
: huelguista *mf*, integrante *mf* de un piquete
picketer ['pıkətər] *n* : piquete *nm*
pickle¹ ['pıkəl] *vt* **-led; -ling** : encurtir, escabechar
pickle² *n* 1 BRINE : escabeche *m* 2
GHERKIN : pepinillo *m* (encurtido) 3
JAM, TROUBLE : lío *m*, apuro *m*
pickpocket ['pık,pɑkət] *n* : carterista *mf*
pickup ['pık,əp] *n* 1 IMPROVEMENT : mejora *f* 2 *or* **pickup truck** : camioneta *f*
picky ['pıki] *adj* : quisquilloso, melindroso, mañoso ⟨he's a picky eater : es
muy quisquilloso para comer⟩
picnic¹ ['pık,nık] *vi* **-nicked; -nicking** : ir
de picnic
picnic² *n* : picnic *m*
pictorial [pık'toriəl] *adj* : pictórico
picture¹ ['pıktʃər] *vt* **-tured; -turing** 1
DEPICT : representar 2 IMAGINE : imaginarse ⟨can you picture it? : ¿te lo puedes imaginar?⟩
picture² *n* 1 : cuadro *m* (pintado o dibu-
jado), ilustración *f*, fotografía *f* 2 DE-
SCRIPTION : descripción *f* 3 IMAGE
: imagen *f* ⟨he's the picture of his father
: es la viva imagen de su padre⟩ 4
MOVIE : película *f* 5 IMAGE : imagen *f*
(de una pantalla) 6 : idea *f* ⟨now I get
the picture : ahora lo entiendo⟩ 7 : situación *f* ⟨the economic picture : la situación económica⟩ ⟨marriage never
entered the picture : nunca pensaron en
casarse⟩ ⟨her old boyfriend is back in
the picture : ha vuelto a salir con su
antiguo novio⟩ 8 → big picture
picturesque [ˌpıktʃə'rɛsk] *adj* : pintoresco
pie ['paı] *n* : pastel *m* (con fruta o carne),
empanada *f* (con carne)
piece¹ ['pi:s] *vt* **pieced; piecing** 1 PATCH
: parchar, arreglar 2 to piece together
: construir pieza por pieza
piece² *n* 1 FRAGMENT : pedazo *m* ⟨to
rip/tear something to pieces : hacer pedazos algo, romper algo en pedazos⟩ ⟨to
fall to pieces : hacerse pedazos⟩ ⟨in
pieces : en pedazos⟩ ⟨in one piece : in-
tacto⟩ 2 SEGMENT : pedazo *m*, trozo *m*
(de pan, carne, cordel, etc.) 3 COMPO-
NENT : pieza *f* ⟨a three-piece suit : un
traje de tres piezas⟩ 4 UNIT : pieza *f* ⟨a
piece of fruit : una (pieza de) fruta⟩ ⟨a
piece of clothing : una prenda⟩ ⟨a piece
of paper : un papel⟩ 5 (*indicating an
instance of something*) ⟨a piece of advice
: un consejo⟩ ⟨a piece of news : una no-
ticia⟩ ⟨a nice piece of work : un buen
trabajo⟩ 6 WORK : obra *f*, pieza *f* (de
música, etc.) 7 (*in board games*) : ficha
f, pieza *f*, figura *f* (en ajedrez) 8 ARTI-
CLE : artículo *m* 9 COIN : moneda *f*,
pieza *f* 10 *fam* GUN : pistola *f* 11 *fam*
DISTANCE : trecho *m* 12 in one piece

SAFE : sano y salvo **13 to fall/go to pieces** : venirse abajo **14 to give someone a piece of one's mind** : cantarle las cuarenta a alguien **15 to pick up the pieces** : sacarse las castañas del fuego **16 to pieces** : mucho, muy ⟨she was thrilled to pieces : estaba contentísima⟩ ⟨he loves her to pieces : la quiere muchísimo⟩

piecemeal¹ ['piːsˌmiːl] *adv* : poco a poco, por partes

piecemeal² *adj* : hecho poco a poco, poco sistemático

piecework ['piːsˌwərk] *n* : trabajo *m* a destajo

pied ['paɪd] *adj* : pío

pier ['pɪr] *n* **1** : pila *f* (de un puente) **2** WHARF : muelle *m*, atracadero *m*, embarcadero *m* **3** PILLAR : pilar *m*

pierce ['pɪrs] *vt* **pierced; piercing 1** PENETRATE : atravesar, traspasar, penetrar (en) ⟨the bullet pierced his leg : la bala le atravesó la pierna⟩ ⟨to pierce one's heart : traspasarle el corazón a uno⟩ **2** PERFORATE : perforar, agujerear (las orejas, etc.) **3 to pierce the silence** : desgarrar el silencio

piety ['paɪəti] *n, pl* **-eties** : piedad *f*

pig ['pɪg] *n* **1** HOG, SWINE : cerdo *m*, -da *f*; puerco *m*, -ca *f* **2** SLOB : persona *f* desaliñada; cerdo *m*, -da *f* **3** GLUTTON : glotón *m*, -tona *f* **4** *or* **pig iron** : lingote *m* de hierro

pigeon ['pɪdʒən] *n* : paloma *f*

pigeonhole ['pɪdʒənˌhoːl] *n* : casilla *f*

piggish ['pɪgɪʃ] *adj* **1** GREEDY : glotón **2** DIRTY : cochino, sucio

piggyback ['pɪgiˌbæk] *adv & adj* : a cuestas

piggy bank *n* : alcancía *f*

pigheaded ['pɪgˌhɛdəd] *adj* : terco, obstinado

piglet ['pɪglət] *n* : cochinillo *m*; lechón *m*, -chona *f*

pigment ['pɪgmənt] *n* : pigmento *m*

pigmentation [ˌpɪgmənˈteɪʃən] *n* : pigmentación *f*

pigmy → **pygmy**

pig out *vi* **to pig out (on)** : darse un atracón (de)

pigpen ['pɪgˌpɛn] *n* : chiquero *m*, pocilga *f*

pigsty ['pɪgˌstaɪ] → **pigpen**

pigtail ['pɪgˌteɪl] *n* : coleta *f*, trenza *f*

pike ['paɪk] *n, pl* **pike** *or* **pikes 1** : lucio *m* (pez) **2** LANCE : pica *f* **3** → **turnpike**

pile¹ ['paɪl] *v* **piled; piling** *vt* : amontonar, apilar — *vi* **to pile up** : amontonarse, acumularse

pile² *n* **1** STAKE : pilote *m* **2** HEAP : montón *m*, pila *f* **3** NAP : pelo *m* (de telas)

pileup ['paɪlˌʌp] *n* : choque *m* en cadena

piles ['paɪlz] *npl* HEMORRHOIDS : hemorroides *fpl*, almorranas *fpl*

pilfer ['pɪlfər] *vt* : robar (cosas pequeñas), ratear

pilgrim ['pɪlgrəm] *n* : peregrino *m*, -na *f*

pilgrimage ['pɪlgrəmɪdʒ] *n* : peregrinación *f*

pill ['pɪl] *n* : pastilla *f*, píldora *f* ⟨to be on the pill, to be on birth control pills : tomar la píldora (anticonceptiva)⟩

pillage¹ ['pɪlɪdʒ] *vt* **-laged; -laging** : saquear

pillage² *n* : saqueo *m*

pillar ['pɪlər] *n* : pilar *m*, columna *f*

pillory ['pɪləri] *n, pl* **-ries** : picota *f*

pillow ['pɪloː] *n* : almohada *f*

pillowcase ['pɪloːˌkeɪs] *n* : funda *f*

pilot¹ ['paɪlət] *vt* : pilotar, pilotear

pilot² *n* : piloto *mf*

pilot light *n* : piloto *m*

pimento [pəˈmɛnˌtoː] → **pimiento**

pimiento [pəˈmɛnˌtoː, -ˈmjɛn-] *n, pl* **-tos** : pimiento *m* morrón

pimp ['pɪmp] *n* : proxeneta *m*

pimple ['pɪmpəl] *n* : grano *m*

pimply ['pɪmpəli] *adj* **pimplier; -est** : cubierto de granos

pin¹ ['pɪn] *vt* **pinned; pinning 1** FASTEN : prender, sujetar (con alfileres) **2** HOLD, IMMOBILIZE : inmovilizar, sujetar **3 to pin one's hopes on** : poner sus esperanzas en **4 to pin down** : identificar, determinar, definir

pin² *n* **1** : alfiler *m* ⟨safety pin : alfiler de gancho⟩ ⟨a bobby pin : una horquilla⟩ **2** BROOCH : alfiler *m*, broche *m*, prendedor *m* **3** → **bowling pin**

pinafore ['pɪnəˌfor] *n* : delantal *m*

piñata [pinˈjɑtə] *n* : piñata *f*

pinball ['pɪnˌbol] *n* : pinball *m*

pincer ['pɪnˌsər] *n* **1** CLAW : pinza *f* (de una langosta, etc.) **2 pincers** *npl* : pinzas *fpl*, tenazas *fpl*, tenaza *f*

pinch¹ ['pɪntʃ] *vt* **1** : pellizcar ⟨she pinched my cheek : me pellizcó el cachete⟩ **2** STEAL : robar — *vi* : apretar ⟨my shoes pinch : me aprietan los zapatos⟩

pinch² *n* **1** EMERGENCY : emergencia *f* ⟨in a pinch : en caso necesario⟩ **2** PAIN : dolor *m*, tormento *m* **3** SQUEEZE : pellizco *m* (con los dedos) **4** BIT : pizca *f*, pellizco *m* ⟨a pinch of cinnamon : una pizca de canela⟩

pinch hitter *n* **1** SUBSTITUTE : sustituto *m*, -ta *f* **2** : bateador *m* emergente (en beisbol)

pincushion ['pɪnˌkʊʃən] *n* : acerico *m*, alfiletero *m*

pine¹ ['paɪn] *vi* **pined; pining 1 to pine away** : languidecer, consumirse **2 to pine for** : añorar, suspirar por

pine² *n* **1** : pino *m* (árbol) **2** : madera *f* de pino

pineapple ['paɪnˌæpəl] *n* : piña *f*, ananá *m*, ananás *m*

pine cone *n* : piña *f*

ping ['pɪŋ] *n* : sonido *m* metálico

Ping-Pong ['pɪŋˌpɑŋ, -ˌpɔŋ] *trademark* se usa para tenis de mesa

pinion¹ ['pɪnjən] *vt* : sujetar los brazos de, inmovilizar

pinion² *n* : piñón *m*

pink¹ ['pɪŋk] *adj* : rosa, rosado

pink² *n* **1** : clavelito *m* (flor) **2** : rosa *m*, rosado *m* (color) **3 to be in the pink** : estar en plena forma, rebosar de salud

pinkeye ['pɪŋk‚aɪ] *n* : conjuntivitis *f* aguda
pinkie *or* **pinky** ['pɪŋki] *n* : meñique *m*
pinkish ['pɪŋkɪl] *adj* : rosáceo
pinnacle ['pɪnɪkəl] *n* **1** : pináculo *m* (de un edificio) **2** PEAK : cima *f*, cumbre *f* (de una montaña) **3** ACME : pináculo *m*, cúspide *f*, apogeo *m*
pinpoint ['pɪn‚pɔɪnt] *vt* : precisar, localizar con precisión
pint ['paɪnt] *n* : pinta *f*
pinto ['pɪn‚to:] *n, pl* **pintos** : caballo *m* pinto
pinworm ['pɪn‚wərm] *n* : oxiuro *m*
pioneer[1] [‚paɪə'nɪr] *vt* : promover, iniciar, introducir
pioneer[2] *n* : pionero *m*, -ra *f*
pious ['paɪəs] *adj* **1** DEVOUT : piadoso, devoto **2** SANCTIMONIOUS : beato, santurrón — **piously** ['paɪəsli] *adv*
pip ['pɪp] *n* : pepita *f*
pipe[1] ['paɪp] *v* **piped; piping** *vi* : hablar en voz chillona — *vt* **1** PLAY : tocar (el caramillo o la flauta) **2** : conducir por tuberías ⟨to pipe water : transportar el agua por tubería⟩
pipe[2] *n* **1** : caramillo *m* (instrumento musical) **2** BAGPIPE : gaita *f* **3** : tubo *m*, caño *m* ⟨gas pipes : tubería de gas⟩ **4** : pipa *f* (para fumar)
pipe dream *n* : quimera *f*, sueño *m* imposible
pipeline ['paɪp‚laɪn] *n* **1** : conducto *m*, oleoducto *m* (para petróleo), gasoducto *m* (para gas) **2** CONDUIT : vía *f* (de información, etc.)
piper ['paɪpər] *n* : músico *m*, -ca *f* que toca el caramillo o la gaita
piping ['paɪpɪŋ] *n* **1** : música *f* del caramillo o de la gaita **2** TRIM : cordoncillo *m*, ribete *m* con cordón
piping hot *adj* : muy caliente
piquant ['pi:kənt, 'pɪkwənt] *adj* **1** SPICY : picante **2** INTRIGUING : intrigante, estimulante
pique[1] ['pi:k] *vt* **piqued; piquing 1** IRRITATE : picar, irritar **2** AROUSE : despertar (la curiosidad, etc.)
pique[2] *n* : pique *m*, resentimiento *m*
piracy ['paɪrəsi] *n, pl* **-cies** : piratería *f*
piranha [pə'rɑnə, -'rɑnjə, -'rænjə] *n* : piraña *f*
pirate[1] ['paɪrət] *n* : pirata *mf*
pirate[2] *vt* **-rated; -rating** : piratear (software, etc.)
pirouette [‚pɪrə'wɛt] *n* : pirueta *f*
pis → **pi**
Pisces ['paɪ‚si:z, 'pɪ-‚, 'pɪs‚keɪs] *n* **1** : Piscis *m* (signo o constelación) **2** : Piscis *mf* (persona)
piss[1] ['pɪs] *vi usu vulgar* : mear *usu vulgar* — *vt fam* **to piss off** ANGER : enojar, enfadar
piss[2] *n usu vulgar* **1** URINE : meados *mpl, usu vulgar*; pipí *m fam*; pis *m fam* **2** **to take a piss** : mear *usu vulgar*, hacer pipí/pis *fam*
pistachio [pə'stæʃi‚o:, -'stɑ-] *n, pl* **-chios** : pistacho *m*
pistil ['pɪstəl] *n* : pistilo *m*
pistol ['pɪstəl] *n* : pistola *f*

piston ['pɪstən] *n* : pistón *m*, émbolo *m*
pit[1] ['pɪt] *v* **pitted; pitting** *vt* **1** : marcar de hoyos, picar (una superficie) **2** : deshuesar (una fruta) **3** **to pit against** : enfrentar a, oponer a — *vi* : quedar marcado
pit[2] *n* **1** HOLE : fosa *f*, hoyo *m* ⟨a bottomless pit : un pozo sin fondo⟩ **2** MINE : mina *f* **3** : foso *m* ⟨orchestra pit : foso orquestal⟩ **4** POCKMARK : marca *f* (en la cara), cicatriz *f* de viruela **5** STONE : hueso *m*, pepa *f* (de una fruta) **6** **pit of the stomach** : boca *f* del estómago
pita ['pi:tə] *or* **pita bread** *n* : pita *f*; pan *m* pita; pan *m* árabe *Arg, Ven, Uru*
pitch[1] ['pɪtʃ] *vt* **1** SET UP : montar, armar (una tienda) **2** THROW : lanzar, arrojar **3** ADJUST, SET : dar el tono de (un discurso, un instrumento musical) — *vi* **1** *or* **to pitch forward** FALL : caerse **2** LURCH : cabecear (dícese de un barco o un avión), dar bandazos **3** **to pitch in** : arrimar el hombro
pitch[2] *n* **1** LURCHING : cabezada *f*, cabeceo *m* (de un barco o un avión) **2** SLOPE : (grado de) inclinación *f*, pendiente *f* **3** : tono *m* (en música) ⟨perfect pitch : oído absoluto⟩ **4** THROW : lanzamiento *m* **5** DEGREE : grado *m*, nivel *m*, punto *m* ⟨the excitement reached a high pitch : la excitación llegó a un punto culminante⟩ **6** *or* **sales pitch** : presentación *f* (de un vendedor) **7** TAR : pez *f*, brea *f*
pitch–black ['pɪtʃ'blæk] *adj* : muy oscuro, oscuro como boca de lobo *fam*
pitcher ['pɪtʃər] *n* **1** JUG : jarra *f*, jarro *m*, cántaro *m*, pichel *m* **2** : lanzador *m*, -dora *f* (en béisbol, etc.)
pitchfork ['pɪtʃ‚fɔrk] *n* : horquilla *f*, horca *f*
piteous ['pɪtiəs] *adj* : lastimoso, lastimero — **piteously** *adv*
pitfall ['pɪt‚fɔl] *n* : peligro *m* (poco obvio), dificultad *f*
pith ['pɪθ] *n* **1** : médula *f* (de una planta) **2** CORE : meollo *m*, entraña *f*
pithy ['pɪθi] *adj* **pithier; -est** : conciso y sustancioso ⟨pithy comments : comentarios sucintos⟩
pitiable ['pɪtiəbəl] → **pitiful**
pitiful ['pɪtɪfəl] *adj* **1** LAMENTABLE : lastimero, lastimoso, lamentable **2** CONTEMPTIBLE : despreciable, lamentable — **pitifully** [-fli] *adv*
pitiless ['pɪtiləs] *adj* : despiadado — **pitilessly** *adv*
pittance ['pɪtənts] *n* : miseria *f*
pituitary [pə'tu:ə‚teri, -'tju:-] *adj* : pituitario
pity[1] ['pɪti] *vt* **pitied; pitying** : compadecer, compadecerse de
pity[2] *n, pl* **pities 1** COMPASSION : compasión *f*, piedad *f* **2** SHAME : lástima *f*, pena *f* ⟨what a pity! : ¡qué lástima!⟩
pivot[1] ['pɪvət] *vi* **1** : girar sobre un eje **2** **to pivot on** : girar sobre, depender de
pivot[2] *n* : pivote *m*
pivotal ['pɪvətəl] *adj* : fundamental, central

pixie *or* **pixy** [ˈpɪksi] *n, pl* **pixies** : elfo *m*, hada *f*

pizza [ˈpiːtsə] *n* : pizza *f*

pizzazz *or* **pizazz** [pəˈzæz] *n* **1** GLAMOR : encanto *m* **2** VITALITY : animación *f*, vitalidad *f*

pizzeria [ˌpiːtsəˈriːə] *n* : pizzería *f*

placard [ˈplækərd, -ˌkɑrd] *n* POSTER : cartel *m*, póster *m*, afiche *m*

placate [ˈpleɪˌkeɪt, ˈplæ-] *vt* **-cated; -cating** : aplacar, apaciguar

place[1] [ˈpleɪs] *vt* **placed; placing** **1** PUT SET : poner, colocar ⟨she carefully placed the book on the table : colocó el libro con cuidado sobre la mesa⟩ **2** SITUATE : situar, ubicar, emplazar ⟨to be well placed : estar bien situado⟩ ⟨to place in a job : colocar en un trabajo⟩ **3** IDENTIFY RECALL : identificar, ubicar, recordar ⟨I can't place him : no lo ubico⟩ **4 to place an order** : hacer un pedido

place[2] *n* **1** SPACE : sitio *m*, lugar *m* ⟨there's no place to sit : no hay sitio para sentarse⟩ **2** LOCATION : lugar *m*, sitio *m*, parte *f* ⟨place of work : lugar de trabajo⟩ ⟨faraway places : lugares remotos⟩ ⟨all over the place : por todas partes⟩ **3** HOME : casa *f* ⟨our summer place : nuestra casa de verano⟩ **4** POSITION, SPOT : lugar *m*, sitio *m* ⟨everything in its place : todo en su lugar⟩ ⟨to hold in place : sujetar⟩ ⟨I got distracted and lost my place : me distraje y ya no sé por donde iba⟩ **5** SEAT, SPOT : asiento *m*, sitio *m* ⟨she changed places with him : le cambió el asiento⟩ ⟨would you hold/save my place? : ¿me guardas el asiento?⟩ **6** *or* **place setting** : cubierto *m* **7** RANK : lugar *m*, puesto *m* ⟨he took first place : ganó el primer lugar⟩ **8** JOB : puesto *m* **9** ROLE : lugar *m*, papel *m* ⟨to trade places with someone : cambiarse por alguien, cambiarle el lugar a alguien⟩ ⟨put yourself in my place : ponte en mi lugar⟩ ⟨she put him in his place : le puso en su lugar⟩ **10** : lugar *m* ⟨the ones/tens place : el lugar de las unidades/decenas⟩ ⟨a decimal place : un decimal⟩ **11 in place** : en marcha ⟨to put a plan/system in place : poner en marcha un plan/sistema⟩ **12 in place of** : en lugar de **13 in the first place** : para empezar **14 in the first/second place** : en primer/segundo lugar **15 out of place** : fuera de lugar **16 to go places** : tener éxito, llegar lejos **17 to take place** : tener lugar **18 to take the place of** : sustituir a

placebo [pləˈsiːˌboː] *n, pl* **-bos** : placebo *m*

place mat *n* : individual *m*, mantel *m* individual

placement [ˈpleɪsmənt] *n* : colocación *f*

placenta [pləˈsɛntə] *n, pl* **-tas** *or* **-tae** [-ti, -ˌtaɪ] : placenta *f*

placid [ˈplæsəd] *adj* : plácido, tranquilo — **placidly** *adv*

plagiarism [ˈpleɪdʒəˌrɪzəm] *n* : plagio *m*

plagiarist [ˈpleɪdʒərɪst] *n* : plagiario *m*, -ria *f*

plagiarize [ˈpleɪdʒəˌraɪz] *vt* **-rized; -rizing** : plagiar

plague[1] [ˈpleɪɡ] *vt* **plagued; plaguing** **1** AFFLICT : plagar, afligir ⟨plagued with problems : plagado de problemas⟩ **2** DISTRESS : acosar, atormentar ⟨plagued by doubts : acosado por dudas⟩

plague[2] *n* **1** : plaga *f* (de insectos, etc.) **2** : peste *f* (en medicina)

plaid[1] [ˈplæd] *adj* : escocés, de cuadros ⟨a plaid skirt : una falda escocesa⟩

plaid[2] *n* TARTAN : tela *f* escocesa, tartán *m*

plain[1] [ˈpleɪn] *adj* **1** SIMPLE, UNADORNED : liso, sencillo, sin adornos **2** CLEAR : claro ⟨in plain language : en palabras claras⟩ ⟨to make something plain : dejar algo (en) claro⟩ **3** FRANK : franco, puro ⟨the plain truth : la pura verdad⟩ **4** HOMELY : ordinario, poco atractivo **5 in plain sight** : a la vista de todos

plain[2] *n* : llanura *f*, llano *m*, planicie *f*

plainclothes [ˈpleɪnˈkloːz, -ˈkloːðz] *adj* : de civil; de paisano; de particular *Arg, Uru* (dícese de un policía, etc.)

plainly [ˈpleɪnli] *adv* **1** CLEARLY : claramente **2** FRANKLY : francamente, con franqueza **3** SIMPLY : sencillamente

plaintiff [ˈpleɪntɪf] *n* : demandante *mf*

plaintive [ˈpleɪntɪv] *adj* MOURNFUL : lastimero, plañidero

plait[1] [ˈpleɪt, ˈplæt] *vt* **1** PLEAT : plisar **2** BRAID : trenzar

plait[2] *n* **1** PLEAT : pliegue *m* **2** BRAID : trenza *f*

plan[1] [ˈplæn] *v* **planned; planning** *vt* **1** : planear, proyectar, planificar ⟨to plan a trip : planear un viaje⟩ ⟨to plan a city : planificar una ciudad⟩ **2** INTEND : tener planeado, proyectar — *vi* : hacer planes

plan[2] *n* **1** DIAGRAM : plano *m*, esquema *m* **2** SCHEME : plan *m*, proyecto *m*, programa *m* ⟨to draw up a plan : elaborar un proyecto⟩

plane[1] [ˈpleɪn] *vt* **planed; planing** : cepillar (madera)

plane[2] *adj* : plano

plane[3] *n* **1** : plano *m* (en matemáticas, etc.) **2** LEVEL : nivel *m* **3** : cepillo *m* (de carpintero) **4** → **airplane**

planet [ˈplænət] *n* : planeta *f*

planetarium [ˌplænəˈtɛriəm] *n, pl* **-iums** *or* **-ia** [-iə] : planetario *m*

planetary [ˈplænəˌtɛri] *adj* : planetario

plank [ˈplæŋk] *n* **1** BOARD : tablón *m*, tabla *f* **2** : artículo *m*, punto *m* (de una plataforma política)

plankton [ˈplæŋktən] *n* : plancton *m*

planner [ˈplænər] *n* : planificador *m*, -dora *f* ⟨wedding planner : organizador de bodas⟩ ⟨financial planner : asesor financiero⟩

plant[1] [ˈplænt] *vt* **1** : plantar, sembrar (semillas) ⟨planted with flowers : plantado de flores⟩ **2** PLACE : plantar, colocar ⟨to plant an idea : inculcar una idea⟩

plant[2] *n* **1** : planta *f* ⟨leafy plants : plantas frondosas⟩ **2** FACTORY : planta *f*, fábrica *f* ⟨hydroelectric plant : planta hidroeléctrica⟩ **3** MACHINERY : maquinaria *f*, equipo *m*

plantain ['plæntən] *n* **1** : llantén *m* (mala hierba) **2** : plátano *m*, plátano *m* macho *Mex* (fruta)

plantation [plæn'teɪlən] *n* : plantación *f*, hacienda *f* ⟨a coffee plantation : un cafetal⟩

planter ['plæntər] *n* **1** : hacendado *m*, -da *f* (de una hacienda) **2** FLOWERPOT : tiesto *m*, maceta *f*

plaque ['plæk] *n* **1** TABLET : placa *f* **2** : placa *f* (dental)

plasma ['plæzmə] *n* : plasma *m*

plaster[1] ['plæstər] *vt* **1** : enyesar, revocar (con yeso) **2** COVER : cubrir, llenar ⟨a wall plastered with notices : una pared cubierta de avisos⟩

plaster[2] *n* **1** : yeso *m*, revoque *m* (para paredes, etc.) **2** : escayola *f*, yeso *m* (en medicina) **3 plaster of Paris** ['pærɪs] : yeso *m* mate

plastered ['plæstərd] *adj* INTOXICATED : colocado

plastic[1] ['plæstɪk] *adj* **1** : de plástico **2** PLIABLE : plástico, flexible

plastic[2] *n* : plástico *m*

plasticity [plæ'stɪsəti] *n, pl* **-ties** : plasticidad *f*

plastic surgery *n* : cirugía *f* plástica

plastic wrap *n* : papel *m* film

plate[1] ['pleɪt] *vt* **plated; plating** : chapar (en metal)

plate[2] *n* **1** PLAQUE, SHEET : placa *f* ⟨a steel plate : una placa de acero⟩ **2** UTENSILS : vajilla *f* (de metal) ⟨silver plate : vajilla de plata⟩ **3** DISH : plato *m* **4** DENTURES : dentadura *f* postiza **5** ILLUSTRATION : lámina *f* (en un libro) **6 license plate** : matrícula *f*, placa *f* de matrícula

plateau [plæ'to:] *n, pl* **-teaus** *or* **-teaux** [-'to:z] : meseta *f*

platform ['plæt,fɔrm] *n* **1** STAGE : plataforma *f*, estrado *m*, tribuna *f* **2** : andén *m* (de una estación de ferrocarril) **3 political platform** : plataforma *f* política, programa *m* electoral

plating ['pleɪtɪŋ] *n* **1** : enchapado *m* **2 silver plating** : plateado *m*

platinum ['plætənəm] *n* : platino *m*

platitude ['plætə,tu:d, -,tju:d] *n* : lugar *m* común, perogrullada *f*

platonic [plə'tɑnɪk] *adj* : platónico

platoon [plə'tu:n] *n* : sección *f* (en el ejército)

platter ['plætər] *n* : fuente *f*

platypus ['plætɪpəs, -,pʊs] *n, pl* **platypuses** *or* **platypi** [-,paɪ, -,pi:] : ornitorrinco *m*

plausibility [,plɔzə'bɪləti] *n, pl* **-ties** : credibilidad *f*, verosimilitud *f*

plausible ['plɔzəbəl] *adj* : creíble, convincente, verosímil — **plausibly** [-bli] *adv*

play[1] ['pleɪ] *vi* **1** : jugar ⟨the children were playing in the yard : los niños jugaban en el jardín⟩ ⟨she plays on the basketball team : juega con el equipo de baloncesto⟩ ⟨he plays for the Red Sox : juega para los Red Sox⟩ ⟨we play for fun : jugamos por diversión⟩ ⟨they're playing against the Yankees : juegan

contra los Yanquis⟩ ⟨it's your turn to play : te toca a ti jugar⟩ ⟨to play with a doll : jugar con una muñeca⟩ ⟨to play with an idea : darle vueltas a una idea⟩ **2** *or* **to play around** FIDDLE, TOY : jugar, juguetear ⟨don't play (around) with your food : no juegues con la comida⟩ **3** *or* **to play around** JOKE : bromear, hacer el tonto ⟨I was only playing (around) : sólo estaba bromeando⟩ **4** : tocar ⟨to play in a band : tocar en un grupo⟩ **5** : sonar (en la radio, etc.) **6** : actuar (en una obra de teatro) **7** SHOW ⟨what's playing at the movies/theatre? : ¿qué dan/ponen en el cine?⟩ **8** BEHAVE ⟨to play fair/dirty : jugar limpio/sucio⟩ ⟨to play by the rules : respetar las reglas⟩ **9** ACT : hacerse ⟨to play dumb/dead : hacerse el tonto/muerto⟩ **10 to play along (with someone)** : seguirle la corriente a alguien, hacerle el juego a alguien **11 to play around** : perder el tiempo ⟨he plays around instead of working : pierde el tiempo en vez de trabajar⟩ **12 to play around** : tener líos (amorosos) **13 to play for time** STALL : tratar de ganar tiempo **14 to play hard to get** : hacerse (de) rogar **15 to play into** SUPPORT : dar crédito a **16 to play into the hands of** : dárselo en bandeja a **17 to play off** COMPLEMENT : complementar **18 to play on** EXPLOIT : explotar, aprovecharse de **19 to play out** DEVELOP UNFOLD : desarrollarse, desenvolverse — *vt* **1** : jugar (un deporte, etc.), jugar a (un juego), jugar contra (un contrincante) ⟨he wouldn't play her at chess : no quiso jugar (al) ajedrez con ella⟩ ⟨the Yankees are playing the Red Sox : los Yanquis juegan contra los Red Sox⟩ ⟨he plays shortstop : juega de/ como torpedero⟩ ⟨to play house : jugar a las casitas, jugar a papás y mamás⟩ **2** : tirar (una carta), mover (una pieza), tirar/patear (etc.) (una pelota) ⟨to play a shot : hacer un tiro⟩ **3** : tocar (música o un instrumento), tocar en (un lugar) **4** : poner (un DVD, etc.), poner/pasar (una canción en la radio, etc.) ⟨he plays his music too loud : pone la música demasiado alta/fuerte⟩ **5** SHOW : dar, poner (una película) **6** : jugar a (la lotería, etc.) **7** PERFORM : interpretar, hacer el papel de (un carácter), representar (una obra de teatro) ⟨she plays the lead : hace el papel principal⟩ **8** CARRY OUT : jugar, desempeñar ⟨she played an important role in the negotiations : jugó un papel importante en las negociaciones⟩ **9** ACT : hacerse ⟨to play the fool : hacerse el tonto⟩ **10** BEHAVE ⟨to play it cool : (actuar) como si nada⟩ ⟨to play it safe : ir a la segura, ir a lo seguro⟩ **11** MANIPULATE : manipular ⟨to play someone for a fool : engañar a alguien⟩ **12** : hacer, gastar ⟨he played a joke on her : le hizo/gastó una broma⟩ ⟨to play a dirty trick on : jugarle una mala pasada a⟩ **13 to play back** : poner (una grabación) **14 to play down** : minimizar **15 to play God** : jugar a ser Dios **16 to play out** : realizar, vivir (un sueño, etc.) ⟨this scene plays itself out every day : esta situación ocurre cada día⟩ **17 to play up** EMPHASIZE : resaltar

play² *n* **1** GAME, RECREATION : juego *m* ⟨children at play : niños jugando⟩ ⟨a play on words : un juego de palabras⟩ **2** ACTION : juego *m* ⟨rain held up play for an hour : el partido tuvo una hora de retraso por lluvia⟩ ⟨the ball is in play : la pelota está en juego⟩ ⟨to bring into play : poner en juego⟩ **3** DRAMA : obra *f* de teatro, pieza *f* (de teatro) ⟨to put on a play : presentar/representar una obra⟩ **4** MOVEMENT : juego *m* (de la luz, una brisa, etc.) **5** SLACK : juego *m* ⟨there's not enough play in the wheel : la rueda no da lo suficiente⟩

playacting ['pleɪˌæktɪŋ] *n* : actuación *f*, teatro *m*

playboy ['pleɪˌbɔɪ] *n* : playboy *m*

player ['pleɪər] *n* **1** : jugador *m*, -dora *f* (en un juego) **2** ACTOR : actor *m*, actriz *f* **3** MUSICIAN : músico *m*, -ca *f* **4** : reproductor *m* (de DVD, etc.)

playful ['pleɪfəl] *adj* **1** FROLICSOME : juguetón **2** JOCULAR : jocoso — **playfully** *adv*

playfulness ['pleɪfəlnəs] *n* : lo juguetón, jocosidad *f*, alegría *f*

playground ['pleɪˌɡraʊnd] *n* : patio *m* de recreo, jardín *m* para jugar

playgroup ['pleɪˌɡruːp] *n* : grupo *m* de recreo para niños

playhouse ['pleɪˌhaʊs] *n* **1** THEATER : teatro *m* **2** : casita *f* de juguete

playing card *n* : naipe *m*, carta *f*

playing field *n* : campo *m* de juego

playmate ['pleɪˌmeɪt] *n* : compañero *m*, -ra *f* de juego

play–off ['pleɪˌɔf] *n* : desempate *m*

playpen ['pleɪˌpɛn] *n* : corral *m* (para niños)

playroom ['pleɪˌruːm] *n* : cuarto *m* de juegos

plaything ['pleɪˌθɪŋ] *n* : juguete *m*

playtime ['pleɪˌtaɪm] *n* : hora *f* de recreo

playwright ['pleɪˌraɪt] *n* : dramaturgo *m*, -ga *f*

plaza ['plæzə, 'plɑ-] *n* **1** SQUARE : plaza *f* **2 shopping plaza** MALL : centro *m* comercial

plea ['pliː] *n* **1** : acto *m* de declararse ⟨he entered a plea of guilty : se declaró culpable⟩ **2** APPEAL : ruego *m*, súplica *f*

plead ['pliːd] *v* **pleaded** *or* **pled** ['plɛd]; **pleading** *vi* **1** : declararse (culpable o inocente) **2 to plead for** : suplicar, implorar **3 to plead with** : implorarle, suplicarle (a alguien) — *vt* **1** : alegar, pretextar ⟨he pleaded illness : pretextó la enfermedad⟩ **2 to plead a case** : defender un caso

pleasant ['plɛzənt] *adj* : agradable, grato, bueno — **pleasantly** *adv*

pleasantness ['plɛzəntnəs] *n* : lo agradable, amenidad *f*

pleasantries ['plɛzəntriz] *npl* : cumplidos *mpl*, cortesías *fpl* ⟨to exchange pleasantries : intercambiar cumplidos⟩

please¹ ['pliːz] *v* **pleased; pleasing** *vt* **1** GRATIFY : complacer ⟨please yourself! : ¡cómo quieras!⟩ **2** SATISFY : contentar, satisfacer — *vi* **1** SATISFY : complacer, agradar ⟨anxious to please : deseoso de complacer⟩ **2** LIKE : querer ⟨do as you please : haz lo que quieras, haz lo que te parezca⟩

please² *adv* : por favor

pleased ['pliːzd] *adj* : contento, satisfecho, alegre ⟨to be pleased about/with : estar contento por/con⟩ ⟨pleased to meet you! : ¡mucho gusto!⟩

pleasing ['pliːzɪŋ] *adj* : agradable — **pleasingly** *adv*

pleasurable ['plɛʒərəbəl] *adj* PLEASANT : agradable

pleasure ['plɛʒər] *n* **1** WISH : deseo *m*, voluntad *f* ⟨at your pleasure : cuando guste⟩ **2** ENJOYMENT : placer *m*, disfrute *m*, goce *m* ⟨with pleasure : con mucho gusto⟩ **3** : placer *m*, gusto *m* ⟨it's a pleasure to be here : me da gusto estar aquí⟩ ⟨the pleasures of reading : los placeres de leer⟩

pleat¹ ['pliːt] *vt* : plisar

pleat² *n* : pliegue *m*

plebeian [plɪ'biən] *adj* : ordinario, plebeyo

pledge¹ ['plɛʤ] *vt* **pledged; pledging 1** PAWN : empeñar, prendar **2** PROMISE : prometer, jurar

pledge² *n* **1** SECURITY : garantía *f*, prenda *f* **2** PROMISE : promesa *f*

plenteous ['plɛntiəs] *adj* : copioso, abundante

plentiful ['plɛntɪfəl] *adj* : abundante — **plentifully** [-fli] *adv*

plenty ['plɛnti] *n* : abundancia *f* ⟨plenty of time : tiempo de sobra⟩ ⟨plenty of visitors : muchos visitantes⟩

plethora ['plɛθərə] *n* : plétora *f*

pleurisy ['plʊrəsi] *n* : pleuresía *f*

plexiglass ['plɛksɪˌɡlæs] *n* (*Plexiglas*, trademark) : acrílico *m*, plexiglás *m Spain*

pliable ['plaɪəbəl] *adj* : flexible, maleable

pliant ['plaɪənt] → **pliable**

pliers ['plaɪərz] *npl* : alicates *mpl*, pinzas *fpl*

plight ['plaɪt] *n* : situación *f* difícil, apuro *m*

plod ['plɑd] *vi* **plodded; plodding 1** TRUDGE : caminar pesadamente y lentamente **2** DRUDGE : trabajar laboriosamente

plonk → **plunk**

plot¹ ['plɑt] *v* **plotted; plotting** *vt* **1** DEVISE : tramar **2 to plot out** : trazar, determinar (una posición, etc.) — *vi* CONSPIRE : conspirar

plot² *n* **1** LOT : terreno *m*, parcela *f*, lote *m* **2** STORY : argumento *m* (en el teatro), trama *f* (en un libro, etc.) **3** CONSPIRACY, INTRIGUE : complot *m*, intriga *f*

plotter ['plɑtər] *n* : conspirador *m*, -dora *f*; intrigante *mf*

plow[1] *or* **plough** [ˈplaʊ] *vt* **1** : arar (la tierra) **2 to plow the seas** : surcar los mares

plow[2] *or* **plough** *n* **1** : arado *m* **2** → **snowplow**

plowshare [ˈplaʊˌʃɛr] *n* : reja *f* del arado

ploy [ˈplɔɪ] *n* : estratagema *f*, maniobra *f*

pluck[1] [ˈplʌk] *vt* **1** PICK : arrancar **2** : desplumar (un pollo, etc.) — *vi* **to pluck at** : tirar de

pluck[2] *n* **1** TUG : tirón *m* **2** COURAGE, SPIRIT : valor *m*, ánimo *m*

plucky [ˈplʌki] *adj* **pluckier; -est** : valiente, animoso

plug[1] [ˈplʌg] *vt* **plugged; plugging 1** BLOCK : tapar **2** PROMOTE : hacerle publicidad a, promocionar **3 to plug in** : enchufar

plug[2] *n* **1** STOPPER : tapón *m* **2** : enchufe *m* (eléctrico) **3** ADVERTISEMENT : publicidad *f*, propaganda *f*

plum [ˈplʌm] *n* **1** : ciruela *f* (fruta) **2** : color *m* ciruela **3** PRIZE : premio *m*, algo muy atractivo

plumage [ˈpluːmɪdʒ] *n* : plumaje *m*

plumb[1] [ˈplʌm] *vt* **1** : aplomar ⟨to plumb a wall : aplomar una pared⟩ **2** SOUND : sondear, sondar

plumb[2] *adv* **1** VERTICALLY : a plomo, verticalmente **2** EXACTLY : justo, exactamente **3** COMPLETELY : completamente, absolutamente ⟨plumb crazy : loco de remate⟩

plumb[3] *adj* : a plomo

plumb[4] *n or* **plumb line** : plomada *f*

plumber [ˈplʌmər] *n* : plomero *m*, -ra *f*; fontanero *m*, -ra *f*

plumbing [ˈplʌmɪŋ] *n* **1** : plomería *f*, fontanería *f* (trabajo del plomero) **2** PIPES : cañería *f*, tubería *f*

plume [ˈpluːm] *n* **1** FEATHER : pluma *f* **2** TUFT : penacho *m* (en un sombrero, etc.)

plumed [ˈpluːmd] *adj* : con plumas ⟨white-plumed birds : aves de plumaje blanco⟩

plummet [ˈplʌmət] *vi* : caer en picada, desplomarse

plump[1] [ˈplʌmp] *vi or* **to plump down** : dejarse caer (pesadamente)

plump[2] *adv* **1** STRAIGHT : a plomo **2** DIRECTLY : directamente, sin rodeos ⟨he ran plump into the door : dio de cara con la puerta⟩

plump[3] *adj* : llenito *fam*, regordete *fam*, rechoncho *fam*

plumpness [ˈplʌmpnəs] *n* : gordura *f*

plunder[1] [ˈplʌndər] *vi* : saquear, robar

plunder[2] *n* : botín *m*

plunderer [ˈplʌndərər] *n* : saqueador *m*, -dora *f*

plunge[1] [ˈplʌndʒ] *v* **plunged; plunging** *vt* **1** IMMERSE : sumergir **2** THRUST : hundir, clavar — *vi* **1** DIVE : zambullirse (en el agua) **2** : meterse precipitadamente o violentamente ⟨they plunged into war : se enfrascaron en una guerra⟩ ⟨he plunged into depression : cayó en la depresión⟩ **3** DESCEND : descender en picada ⟨the road plunges dizzily : la calle desciende vertiginosamente⟩

plunge[2] *n* **1** DIVE : zambullida *f* **2** DROP : descenso *m* abrupto ⟨the plunge in prices : el desplome de los precios⟩

plunger [ˈplʌndʒər] *n* : desatorador *m*, desatascador *m* *Spain*, destapacaños *m* *Mex*, bomba *f* (destapacaños) *Mex*, sopapa *f* *Arg*

plunk [ˈplʌŋk] *or* **plonk** [ˈplɑŋk] *vt* **1** : dejar caer **2 to plunk down** : gastar (dinero) — *vi* **to plunk down** : dejarse caer

pluperfect [ˌpluːˈpərfɪkt] *n* : pluscuamperfecto *m*

plural[1] [ˈplʊrəl] *adj* : plural

plural[2] *n* : plural *m*

plurality [plʊˈræləti] *n*, *pl* **-ties** : pluralidad *f*

pluralize [ˈplʊrəˌlaɪz] *vt* **-ized; -izing** : pluralizar

plus[1] [ˈplʌs] *adj* **1** POSITIVE : positivo ⟨a plus factor : un factor positivo⟩ **2** (*indicating a quantity in addition*) ⟨a grade of C plus : una calificación entre C y B⟩ ⟨a salary of $30,000 plus : un sueldo de más de $30,000⟩

plus[2] *n* **1** *or* **plus sign** : más *m*, signo *m* de más **2** ADVANTAGE : ventaja *f*

plus[3] *prep* : más (en matemáticas)

plus[4] *conj* AND : y

plush[1] [ˈplʌʃ] *adj* **1** : afelpado **2** LUXURIOUS : lujoso

plush[2] *n* : felpa *f*, peluche *m*

plushy [ˈplʌʃi] *adj* **plushier; -est** : lujoso

plus–size [ˈplʌsˌsaɪz] *adj* : de talla grande

Pluto [ˈpluːˌtoː] *n* : Plutón *m*

plutocracy [pluːˈtɑkrəsi] *n*, *pl* **-cies** : plutocracia *f*

plutonium [pluːˈtoːniəm] *n* : plutonio *m*

ply[1] [ˈplaɪ] *v* **plied; plying** *vt* **1** USE, WIELD : manejar ⟨to ply an ax : manejar un hacha⟩ **2** PRACTICE : ejercer ⟨to ply a trade : ejercer un oficio⟩ **3 to ply with questions** : acosar con preguntas

ply[2] *n*, *pl* **plies 1** LAYER : chapa *f* (de madera), capa *f* (de papel) **2** STRAND : cabo *m* (de hilo, etc.)

plywood [ˈplaɪˌwʊd] *n* : contrachapado *m*

PMS [ˌpiːˌɛmˈɛs] → **premenstrual syndrome**

pneumatic [nʊˈmætɪk, njʊ-] *adj* : neumático

pneumonia [nʊˈmoːnjə, njʊ-] *n* : pulmonía *f*, neumonía *f*

poach [ˈpoːtʃ] *vt* **1** : cocer a fuego lento ⟨to poach an egg : escalfar un huevo⟩ **2 to poach game** : cazar ilegalmente — *vi* : cazar ilegalmente

poacher [ˈpoːtʃər] *n* : cazador *m* furtivo, cazadora *f* furtiva

P.O. Box *n* (*Post Office Box*) : apartado *m* postal, casilla *f* de correos *Arg*

pock [ˈpɑk] *n* **1** PUSTULE : pústula *f* **2** → **pockmark**

pocket[1] [ˈpɑkət] *vt* **1** : meterse en el bolsillo ⟨he pocketed the pen : se metió la pluma en el bolsillo⟩ **2** STEAL : embolsarse

pocket[2] *n* **1** : bolsillo *m*, bolsa *f Mex* ⟨a coat pocket : el bolsillo de un abrigo⟩ ⟨air pockets : bolsas/baches de aire⟩ **2**

CENTER : foco *m*, centro *m* ⟨a pocket of resistance : un foco de resistencia⟩

pocketbook [ˈpɑkətˌbʊk] *n* **1** PURSE : cartera *f*, bolso *m*, bolsa *f Mex* **2** MEANS : recursos *mpl*

pocketknife [ˈpɑkətˌnaɪf] *n, pl* **-knives** : navaja *f*

pocket money *n* : dinero *m* de bolsillo

pocket–size [ˈpɑkətˌsaɪz] *adj* : de bolsillo

pockmark [ˈpɑkˌmɑrk] *n* : cicatriz *f* de viruela, viruela *f*

pod [ˈpɑd] *n* : vaina *f* ⟨pea pod : vaina de guisantes⟩

podcast [ˈpɑdˌkæst] *n* : podcast *m*

podiatrist [pəˈdaɪətrɪst, po-] *n* : podólogo *m*, -ga *f*

podiatry [pəˈdaɪətri, po-] *n* : podología *f*, podiatría *f*

podium [ˈpoːdiəm] *n, pl* **-diums** *or* **-dia** [-diə] : podio *m*, estrado *m*, tarima *f*

poem [ˈpoːəm] *n* : poema *m*, poesía *f*

poet [ˈpoːət] *n* : poeta *mf*

poetess [ˈpoːətəs] *n* : poetisa *f*

poetic [poˈɛtɪk] *or* **poetical** [-tɪkəl] *adj* : poético

poetry [ˈpoːətri] *n* : poesía *f*

pogrom [ˈpoːɡrəm, pəˈɡrɑm, ˈpɑɡrəm] *n* : pogrom *m*

poignancy [ˈpɔɪnjənʦi] *n, pl* **-cies** : lo conmovedor

poignant [ˈpɔɪnjənt] *adj* **1** PAINFUL : penoso, doloroso ⟨poignant grief : profundo dolor⟩ **2** TOUCHING : conmovedor, emocionante

poinsettia [pɔɪnˈsɛtiə, -ˈsɛtə] *n* : flor *f* de Nochebuena

point[1] [ˈpɔɪnt] *vt* **1** : apuntar (una pistola, etc.), señalar con (el dedo) **2** DIRECT : encaminar ⟨can you point me towards the highway? : ¿me puedes indicar cómo llegar a la carretera?⟩ **3** INDICATE : señalar, indicar ⟨to point the way : señalar el camino⟩ **4** SHARPEN : afilar (la punta de) **5 to point out** : señalar, indicar — *vi* **1** : señalar (con el dedo) **2** : apuntar ⟨the needle points north : la aguja apunta hacia el norte⟩ **3** : apuntar (en una pantalla, etc.) ⟨to point and click : apuntar y hacer clic⟩ **4 to point at/to** : señalar (con el dedo) **5 to point to REFERENCE** : señalar **6 to point to/ toward** INDICATE : señalar, indicar

point[2] *n* **1** ITEM : punto *m* ⟨the main points : los puntos principales⟩ **2** : argumento *m*, observación *f* ⟨what's your point? : ¿qué quieres decir?⟩ ⟨that's a good point : es cierto⟩ ⟨point taken : te entiendo⟩ ⟨to have a point : tener razón⟩ ⟨to make a point : hacer una observación⟩ ⟨to get one's point across : hacerse entender⟩ **3 the point** (*indicating the chief idea or meaning*) ⟨to get to the point : ir al grano⟩ ⟨to be beside the point : no venir al caso⟩ ⟨to stick to the point : no salirse del tema⟩ **4** PURPOSE : fin *m*, propósito *m* ⟨there's no point to it : no vale la pena, no sirve para nada⟩ ⟨to make a point of doing something : proponerse hacer algo⟩ **5** QUALITY : cualidad *f* ⟨her good points : sus bue-

nas cualidades⟩ ⟨it's not his strong point : no es su (punto) fuerte⟩ **6** PLACE : punto *m*, lugar *m* ⟨points of interest : puntos interesantes⟩ **7** : punto *m* (en una escala) ⟨boiling point : punto de ebullición⟩ **8** MOMENT : momento *m*, coyuntura *f* ⟨at this point : en este momento⟩ **9** TIP : punta *f* **10** HEADLAND : punta *f*, cabo *m* **11** PERIOD : punto *m* (marca de puntuación) **12** UNIT : punto *m* ⟨he scored 15 points : ganó 15 puntos⟩ ⟨shares fell 10 points : las acciones bajaron 10 enteros⟩ **13** → **decimal point** **14 compass points** : puntos *mpl* cardinales **15 sore point** : asunto *m* delicado

point–blank[1] [ˈpɔɪntˈblæŋk] *adv* **1** : a quemarropa ⟨to shoot point-blank : disparar a quemarropa⟩ **2** BLUNTLY, DIRECTLY : a bocajarro, sin rodeos, francamente

point–blank[2] *adj* **1** : a quemarropa ⟨point-blank shots : disparos a quemarropa⟩ **2** BLUNT DIRECT : directo, franco

pointed [ˈpɔɪntəd] *adj* **1** POINTY : puntiagudo **2** PERTINENT : atinado **3** CONSPICUOUS : marcado, manifiesto

pointedly [ˈpɔɪntədli] *adv* : intencionadamente, directamente

pointer [ˈpɔɪntər] *n* **1** STICK : puntero *m* (para maestros, etc.) **2** INDICATOR, NEEDLE : indicador *m*, aguja *f* **3** : perro *m* de muestra **4** HINT, TIP : consejo *m*

pointless [ˈpɔɪntləs] *adj* : inútil, ocioso, vano ⟨it's pointless to continue : no tiene sentido continuar⟩

point of view *n* : perspectiva *f*, punto *m* de vista

pointy [ˈpɔɪnti] *adj* : puntiagudo

poise[1] [ˈpɔɪz] *vt* **poised; poising** BALANCE : equilibrar, balancear

poise[2] *n* : aplomo *m*, compostura *f*

poison[1] [ˈpɔɪzən] *vt* **1** : envenenar, intoxicar **2** CORRUPT : corromper

poison[2] *n* : veneno *m*

poisoning *n* : envenenamiento *m*

poison ivy *n* : hiedra *f* venenosa

poisonous [ˈpɔɪzənəs] *adj* : venenoso, tóxico, ponzoñoso

poke[1] [ˈpoːk] *v* **poked; poking** *vt* **1** JAB : golpear (con la punta de algo), dar ⟨he poked me with his finger : me dio con el dedo⟩ **2** THRUST : introducir, asomar ⟨I poked my head out the window : asomé la cabeza por la ventana⟩ — *vi* **1 to poke around** RUMMAGE : hurgar **2 to poke along** DAWDLE : demorarse, entretenerse **3 to poke out of** : asomar por, sobresalir por

poke[2] *n* : golpe *m* abrupto (con la punta de algo)

poker [ˈpoːkər] *n* **1** : atizador *m* (para el fuego) **2** : póker *m*, poker *m* (juego de naipes)

poky [ˈpoːki] *adj fam* **1** SLOW : lento **2** TINY : diminuto

polar [ˈpoːlər] *adj* : polar

polar bear *n* : oso *m* blanco

Polaris [poˈlærɪs, -ˈlɑr-] → **North Star**

polarize [ˈpoːləˌraɪz] *vt* **-ized; -izing** : polarizar

Polaroid ['poːlǝˌrɔɪd] *trademark* se usa para una cámara que produce fotos reveladas o para las fotos así producidas
pole ['poːl] *n* 1 : palo *m*, poste *m*, vara *f* ⟨telephone pole : poste de teléfonos⟩ 2 : polo *m* ⟨the South Pole : el Polo Sur⟩ 3 : polo *m* (eléctrico o magnético)
Pole ['poːl] *n* : polaco *m*, -ca *f*
polecat ['poːlˌkæt] *n, pl* **polecats** *or* **polecat** 1 : turón *m* (de Europa) 2 SKUNK : mofeta *f*, zorrillo *m*
polemical [pǝ'lɛmɪkǝl] *adj* : polémico
polemics [pǝ'lɛmɪks] *ns & pl* : polémica *f*
polestar ['poːlˌstɑr] → **North Star**
pole vault *n* : salto *m* con/de pértiga, salto *m* con/de garrocha
police[1] [pǝ'liːs] *vt* **-liced; -licing** : mantener el orden en ⟨to police the streets : patrullar las calles⟩
police[2] *ns & pl* 1 : policía *f* (organización) 2 POLICE OFFICERS : policías *mfpl*
police car *n* : patrulla *f*, patrullero *m*
police force *n* : fuerza *f* policial, cuerpo *m* policial
policeman [pǝ'liːsmǝn] *n, pl* **-men** [-mǝn, -ˌmɛn] : policía *m*
police officer *n* : policía *mf*, agente *mf* de policía
police station *n* : comisaría *f*
policewoman [pǝ'liːsˌwʊmǝn] *n, pl* **-women** [-ˌwɪmǝn] : policía *f*, mujer *f* policía
policy ['pɑlǝsi] *n, pl* **-cies** 1 : política *f* ⟨foreign policy : política exterior⟩ 2 *or* **insurance policy** : póliza *f* de seguros, seguro *m*
polio[1] ['poːliˌoː] *adj* : de polio ⟨polio vaccine : vacuna contra la polio⟩
polio[2] *n* → **poliomyelitis**
poliomyelitis [ˌpoːliˌoːˌmaɪǝ'laɪtǝs] *n* : poliomielitis *f*, polio *f*
polish[1] ['pɑlɪʃ] *vt* 1 : pulir, lustrar, sacar brillo a ⟨to polish one's nails : pintarse las uñas⟩ 2 REFINE : pulir, perfeccionar 3 **to polish off** : despacharse (comida)
polish[2] *n* 1 LUSTER : brillo *m*, lustre *m* 2 REFINEMENT : refinamiento *m* 3 : betún *m* (para zapatos), cera *f* (para suelos y muebles), esmalte *m* (para las uñas)
Polish[1] ['poːlɪʃ] *adj* : polaco
Polish[2] *n* : polaco *m* (idioma)
polite [pǝ'laɪt] *adj* **politer; -est** : cortés, correcto, educado
politely [pǝ'laɪtli] *adv* : cortésmente, correctamente, con buenos modales
politeness [pǝ'laɪtnǝs] *n* : cortesía *f*
politic ['pɑlǝˌtɪk] *adj* : diplomático, prudente
political [pǝ'lɪtɪkǝl] *adj* : político — **politically** [-ˌtɪkli] *adv*
politically correct *adj* : políticamente correcto
politician [ˌpɑlǝ'tɪʃǝn] *n* : político *m*, -ca *f*
politics ['pɑlǝˌtɪks] *ns & pl* : política *f*
polka ['poːlkǝ, 'poːkǝ] *n* : polka *f*
polka dot ['poːkǝˌdɑt] *n* : lunar *m* (en un diseño)

poll[1] ['poːl] *vt* 1 : obtener (votos) ⟨she polled over 1000 votes : obtuvo más de 1000 votos⟩ 2 CANVASS : encuestar, sondear — *vi* : obtener votos
poll[2] *n* 1 SURVEY : encuesta *f*, sondeo *m* 2 **polls** *npl* : urnas *fpl* ⟨to go to the polls : acudir a las urnas, ir a votar⟩
pollen ['pɑlǝn] *n* : polen *m*
pollinate ['pɑlǝˌneɪt] *vt* **-nated; -nating** : polinizar
pollination [ˌpɑlǝ'neɪɬǝn] *n* : polinización *f*
polling place *n* : centro *m* de votación
pollster ['poːlstǝr] *n* : encuestador *m*, -dora *f*
pollutant [pǝ'luːtǝnt] *n* : contaminante *m*
pollute [pǝ'luːt] *vt* **-luted; -luting** : contaminar
pollution [pǝ'luːɬǝn] *n* : contaminación *f*
pollywog *or* **polliwog** ['pɑliˌwɔg] *n* TADPOLE : renacuajo *m*
polo ['poːlˌloː] *n* 1 : polo *m* (deporte) 2 *or* **polo shirt** : polo *m*
poltergeist ['poːltǝrˌgaɪst] *n* : fantasma *m* travieso
polyester ['pɑliˌɛstǝr, ˌpɑli'-] *n* : poliéster *m*
polygamist [pǝ'lɪgǝmɪst] *n* : polígamo *m*, -ma *f*
polygamous [pǝ'lɪgǝmǝs] *adj* : polígamo
polygamy [pǝ'lɪgǝmi] *n* : poligamia *f*
polygon ['pɑliˌgɑn] *n* : polígono *m* — **polygonal** [pǝ'lɪgǝnǝl] *adj*
polymer ['pɑlǝmǝr] *n* : polímero *m*
Polynesian [ˌpɑlǝ'niːʒǝn, -lǝn] *n* : polinesio *m*, -sia *f* — **Polynesian** *adj*
polytheism ['pɑliˌθiːˌɪzǝm] *n* : politeísmo *m*
polyunsaturated [ˌpɑliˌʌn'sætɫǝ-ˌreɪʈǝd] *adj* : poliinsaturado
pomegranate ['pɑmǝˌgrænǝt, 'pɑm-ˌgrænǝt] *n* : granada *f* (fruta)
pommel[1] ['pʌmǝl] *vt* → **pummel**
pommel[2] ['pʌmǝl, 'pɑ-] *n* 1 : pomo *m* (de una espada) 2 : perilla *f* (de una silla de montar)
pomp ['pɑmp] *n* 1 SPLENDOR : pompa *f*, esplendor *m* 2 OSTENTATION : boato *m*, ostentación *f*
pom–pom ['pɑmˌpɑm] *n* : borla *f*, pompón *m*
pomposity [pɑm'pɑsǝʈi] *n, pl* **-ties** : pomposidad *f*
pompous ['pɑmpǝs] *adj* : pomposo — **pompously** *adv*
poncho ['pɑnˌtʃoː] *n, pl* **-chos** : poncho *m*
pond ['pɑnd] *n* : charca *f* (natural), estanque *m* (artificial)
ponder ['pɑndǝr] *vt* : reflexionar, considerar — *vi* **to ponder over** : reflexionar sobre, sopesar
ponderous ['pɑndǝrǝs] *adj* : pesado
pontiff ['pɑntɪf] *n* POPE : pontífice *m*
pontificate [pɑn'tɪfǝˌkeɪt] *vi* **-cated; -cating** : pontificar
pontoon [pɑn'tuːn] *n* : pontón *m*
pony ['poːni] *n, pl* **-nies** : poni *m*, poney *m*, jaca *f*
ponytail ['poːniˌteɪl] *n* : cola *f* de caballo, coleta *f*

poodle ['pu:dəl] *n* : caniche *m*
pool[1] ['pu:l] *vt* : mancomunar (recursos), hacer un fondo común de (dinero) — *vi* : encharcarse
pool[2] *n* 1 : charca *f* ⟨a swimming pool : una piscina⟩ 2 PUDDLE : charco *m* 3 RESERVE SUPPLY : fondo *m* común (de recursos), reserva *f* 4 : billar *m* (juego)
poop[1] ['pu:p] *vi fam* : hacerse caca — *vt fam* **to poop one's pants/diaper** (etc.) : hacerse caca
poop[2] *n fam* : caca *f*
poor ['pʊr, 'pɔr] *adj* 1 : pobre ⟨poor people : los pobres⟩ 2 SCANTY : pobre, escaso ⟨poor attendance : baja asistencia⟩ 3 UNFORTUNATE : pobre ⟨poor thing! : ¡pobrecito!⟩ 4 BAD : malo ⟨to be in poor health : estar mal de salud⟩
poorly ['pʊrli, 'pɔr-] *adv* : mal
pop[1] ['pɑp] *v* **popped; popping** *vi* 1 BURST : reventarse, estallar 2 : saltar (dícese de un corcho) 3 : ir, venir, o aparecer abruptamente ⟨he popped into the house : se metió en la casa⟩ ⟨a menu pops up : aparece un menú⟩ 4 **to pop out** PROTRUDE : salirse, saltarse ⟨my eyes popped out of my head : se me saltaban los ojos⟩ 5 **to pop the question** *fam* : proponerle matrimonio a alguien — *vt* 1 BURST : reventar 2 : sacar o meter abruptamente ⟨he popped it into his mouth : se lo metió en la boca⟩ ⟨she popped her head out the window : sacó la cabeza por la ventana⟩
pop[2] *adj* : popular ⟨pop music : música popular⟩ ⟨pop star : estrella de música popular⟩
pop[3] *n* 1 : estallido *m* pequeño (de un globo, etc.) 2 SODA : refresco *m*, gaseosa *f*
popcorn ['pɑp,kɔrn] *n* : palomitas *fpl* (de maíz)
pope ['po:p] *n* : papa *m* ⟨Pope John : el Papa Juan⟩
poplar ['pɑplər] *n* : álamo *m*
poplin ['pɑplɪn] *n* : popelín *m*, popelina *f*
poppy ['pɑpi] *n, pl* **-pies** : amapola *f*
Popsicle ['pɑp,sɪkəl] *trademark* se usa para una paleta helada
populace ['pɑpjələs] *n* 1 MASSES : pueblo *m* 2 POPULATION : población *f*
popular ['pɑpjələr] *adj* 1 : popular ⟨the popular vote : el voto popular⟩ 2 COMMON : generalizado, común ⟨popular beliefs : creencias generalizadas⟩ 3 : popular, de gran popularidad ⟨a popular singer : un cantante popular⟩
popularity [,pɑpjə'lærəṭi] *n* : popularidad *f*
popularize ['pɑpjələ,raɪz] *vt* **-ized; -izing** : popularizar
popularly ['pɑpjələrli] *adv* : popularmente, vulgarmente
populate ['pɑpjə,leɪt] *vt* **-lated; -lating** : poblar
population [,pɑpjə'leɪʃən] *n* : población *f*
populist ['pɑpjəlɪst] *n* : populista *mf* — **populist** *adj*
populous ['pɑpjələs] *adj* : populoso

pop–up ['pɑp,ʌp] *n* : ventana *f* emergente (de una página web)
porcelain ['pɔrsələn] *n* : porcelana *f*
porch ['pɔrtʃ] *n* : porche *m*
porcupine ['pɔrkjə,paɪn] *n* : puerco *m* espín
pore[1] ['pɔr] *vi* **pored; poring** 1 GAZE : mirar (con atención) 2 **to pore over** : leer detenidamente, estudiar
pore[2] *n* : poro *m*
pork ['pɔrk] *n* : carne *f* de cerdo, carne *f* de puerco ⟨pork chop : chuleta de cerdo⟩
pornographic [,pɔrnə'græfɪk] *adj* : pornográfico
pornography [pɔr'nɑgrəfi] *n* : pornografía *f*
porous ['pɔrəs] *adj* : poroso
porpoise ['pɔrpəs] *n* 1 : marsopa *f* 2 DOLPHIN : delfín *m*
porridge ['pɔrɪdʒ] *n* : sopa *f* espesa de harina, gachas *fpl*
port[1] ['pɔrt] *adj* : de babor ⟨on the port side : a babor⟩
port[2] *n* 1 HARBOR : puerto *m* 2 ORIFICE : orificio *m* (de una válvula, etc.) 3 : puerto *m* (de una computadora) 4 PORTHOLE : portilla *f* 5 *or* **port side** : babor *m* (de un barco) 6 : oporto *m* (vino)
portable ['pɔrṭəbəl] *adj* : portátil
portal ['pɔrṭəl] *n* : portal *m*
portend [pɔr'tɛnd] *vt* : presagiar, augurar
portent ['pɔr,tɛnt] *n* : presagio *m*, augurio *m*
portentous [pɔr'tɛntəs] *adj* : profético, que presagia
porter ['pɔrṭər] *n* : maletero *m*, mozo *m* (de estación)
portfolio [pɔrt'fo:li,o] *n, pl* **-lios** 1 FOLDER : cartera *f* (para llevar papeles), carpeta *f* 2 : cartera *f* (diplomática) 3 **investment portfolio** : cartera de inversiones
porthole ['pɔrt,ho:l] *n* : portilla *f* (de un barco), ventanilla *f* (de un avión)
portico ['pɔrṭɪ,ko] *n, pl* **-coes** *or* **-cos** : pórtico *m*
portion[1] ['pɔrʃən] *vt* DISTRIBUTE : repartir
portion[2] *n* PART, SHARE : porción *f*, parte *f*
portly ['pɔrtli] *adj* **portlier; -est** : corpulento
portrait ['pɔrtrət, -,treɪt] *n* : retrato *m*
portray [pɔr'treɪ] *vt* 1 DEPICT : representar, retratar 2 DESCRIBE : describir 3 PLAY : interpretar (un personaje)
portrayal [pɔr'treɪəl] *n* 1 REPRESENTATION : representación *f* 2 PORTRAIT : retrato *m*
Portuguese[1] [,pɔrtʃə'gi:z, -'gi:s] *adj* : portugués
Portuguese[2] *n* 1 : portugués *m* (idioma) 2 **the Portuguese** (*used with a plural verb*) : los portugueses
pose[1] ['po:z] *v* **posed; posing** *vt* PRESENT : plantear (una pregunta, etc.), representar (una amenaza) — *vi* 1 : posar (para una foto, etc.) 2 **to pose as** : hacerse pasar por

pose² *n* **1** : pose *f* ⟨to strike a pose : asumir una pose⟩ **2** PRETENSE : pose *f*, afectación *f*

posh ['paʃ] *adj* : elegante, de lujo

position¹ [pə'zɪʃən] *vt* : colocar, situar, ubicar

position² *n* **1** LOCATION : posición *f*, ubicación *f* **2** : posición *f*, postura *f* (del cuerpo) **3** OPINION, STANCE : posición *f*, postura *f*, planteamiento *m* **4** STATUS : posición *f* (en una jerarquía) **5** JOB : puesto *m* **6** : posición *f* (en un equipo) **7** SITUATION : situación *f* ⟨to be in no position to do something : no estar en condiciones de hacer algo⟩

positive ['pazətɪv] *adj* **1** DEFINITE : incuestionable, inequívoco ⟨positive evidence : pruebas irrefutables⟩ **2** CONFIDENT : seguro **3** : positivo (en gramática, matemáticas, y física) **4** AFFIRMATIVE : positivo, afirmativo ⟨a positive response : una respuesta positiva⟩

positively ['pazətɪvli] *adv* **1** FAVORABLY : favorablemente **2** OPTIMISTICALLY : positivamente **3** DEFINITELY : definitivamente, en forma concluyente **4** (*used for emphasis*) : realmente, verdaderamente ⟨it's positively awful! : ¡es verdaderamente malo!⟩

posse ['pasi] *n* **1** : partida *f*, patrulla *f* **2** *fam* GANG, ENTOURAGE : grupo *m* de amigos/seguidores (etc.) **3** *fam* GROUP : grupo *m*

possess [pə'zɛs] *vt* **1** HAVE, OWN : poseer, tener **2** SEIZE : apoderarse de ⟨he was possessed by fear : el miedo se apoderó de él⟩

possession [pə'zɛʃən] *n* **1** POSSESSING : posesión *f* **2** : posesión *f* (por un demonio, etc.) **3 possessions** *npl* PROPERTY : bienes *mpl*, propiedad *f*

possessive¹ [pə'zɛsɪv] *adj* **1** : posesivo (en gramática) **2** JEALOUS : posesivo, celoso

possessive² *n* *or* **possessive case** : posesivo *m*

possessor [pə'zɛsər] *n* : poseedor *m*, -dora *f*

possibility [ˌpasə'bɪləti] *n*, *pl* **-ties** : posibilidad *f*

possible ['pasəbəl] *adj* : posible ⟨as soon as possible : lo antes posible⟩ ⟨as much as possible : lo más posible⟩ ⟨if possible : si es posible⟩

possibly ['pasəbli] *adv* **1** CONCEIVABLY : posiblemente ⟨it can't possibly be true! : ¡no puede ser!⟩ ⟨I can't possibly do that : me es imposible, no puedo hacerlo de ninguna manera⟩ **2** PERHAPS : quizás, posiblemente

possum ['pasəm] → **opossum**

post¹ ['po:st] *vt* **1** MAIL : echar al correo, mandar por correo **2** : postear *fam*, publicar en la red **3** ANNOUNCE : anunciar ⟨they've posted the grades : han anunciado las notas⟩ **4** AFFIX : fijar, poner (noticias, etc.) **5** STATION : apostar **6 to keep (someone) posted** : tener al corriente (a alguien)

post² *n* **1** POLE : poste *m*, palo *m* **2** STATION : puesto *m* **3** CAMP : puesto *m* (militar) **4** JOB, POSITION : puesto *m*, empleo *m*, cargo *m* **5** : post *m*, posteo *m*, mensaje *m* en Internet

post- ['po:st] *pref* : pos-, post- ⟨postpone : posponer⟩ ⟨postgraduate : postgraduado⟩

postage ['po:stɪdʒ] *n* : franqueo *m*

postage stamp → **stamp²**

postal ['po:stəl] *adj* : postal

postcard ['po:stˌkɑrd] *n* : postal *f*, tarjeta *f* postal

postdate [ˌpo:st'deɪt] *vt* **-dated; -dating** : posfechar

poster ['po:stər] *n* : póster *m*, cartel *m*, afiche *m*

posterior¹ [pɑ'stɪriər, po-] *adj* : posterior

posterior² *n* BUTTOCKS : trasero *m*, nalgas *fpl*, asentaderas *fpl*

posterity [pɑ'stɛrəti] *n* : posteridad *f*

postgraduate¹ [ˌpo:st'grædʒuət] *adj* : de postgrado

postgraduate² *n* : postgraduado *m*, -da *f*

posthaste ['po:st'heɪst] *adv* : a toda prisa

posthumous ['pastləməs] *adj* : póstumo — **posthumously** *adv*

Post–it ['po:stˌɪt] *trademark* se usa para un papelito con borde adhesivo

postman ['po:stmən, -ˌmæn] *n*, *pl* **-men** [-mən, -ˌmɛn] → **mailman**

postmark¹ ['po:stˌmɑrk] *vt* : matasellar

postmark² *n* : matasellos *m*

postmaster ['po:stˌmæstər] *n* : administrador *m*, -dora *f* de correos

postmodern [ˌpo:st'mɑdərn] *adj* : posmoderno

postmortem [ˌpo:st'mɔrtəm] *n* : autopsia *f*

postnatal [ˌpo:st'neɪtəl] *adj* : postnatal

postnatal depression → **postpartum depression**

post office *n* : correo *m*, oficina *f* de correos

post office box → **P.O. Box**

postoperative [ˌpo:st'ɑpərətɪv, -ˌreɪ-] *adj* : posoperatorio

postpaid [ˌpo:st'peɪd] *adv* : con franqueo pagado

postpartum depression [ˌpo:st'pɑrtəm-] *n* : depresión *f* posparto

postpone [ˌpo:st'po:n] *vt* **-poned; -poning** : postergar, aplazar, posponer

postponement [ˌpo:st'po:nmənt] *n* : postergación *f*, aplazamiento *m*

postscript ['po:stˌskrɪpt] *n* : postdata *f*, posdata *f*

postulate ['pastləˌleɪt] *vt* **-lated; -lating** : postular

posture¹ ['pastlər] *vi* **-tured; -turing** : posar, asumir una pose

posture² *n* : postura *f*

postwar [ˌpo:st'wɔr] *adj* : de (la) posguerra

posy ['po:zi] *n*, *pl* **-sies** **1** FLOWER : flor *f* **2** BOUQUET : ramo *m*, ramillete *m*

pot¹ ['pat] *vt* **potted; potting** : plantar (en una maceta)

pot² *n* **1** : olla *f* (de cocina) **2 pots and pans** : cacharros *mpl* **3 to go to pot** : echarse a perder

potable ['po:ṭəbəl] *adj* : potable
potash ['pɑt,æl] *n* : potasa *f*
potassium [pə'tæsiəm] *n* : potasio *m*
potato [pə'teiṭo] *n, pl* **-toes** : papa *f*, patata *f Spain*
potato chips *npl* : papas *fpl* fritas (de bolsa)
potbellied ['pɑt,bɛlid] *adj* : panzón, barrigón *fam*
potbelly ['pɑt,bɛli] *n* : panza *f*, barriga *f*
potency ['po:ṭəntsi] *n, pl* **-cies** **1** POWER : fuerza *f*, potencia *f* **2** EFFECTIVENESS : eficacia *f*
potent ['po:ṭənt] *adj* **1** POWERFUL : potente, poderoso **2** EFFECTIVE : eficaz ⟨a potent medicine : una medicina bien fuerte⟩
potential¹ [pə'tɛntɭəl] *adj* : potencial, posible
potential² *n* **1** : potencial *m* ⟨growth potential : potencial de crecimiento⟩ ⟨a child with potential : un niño que promete⟩ **2** : potencial *m* (eléctrico) — **potentially** *adv*
potful ['pɑt,ful] *n* : contenido *m* de una olla ⟨a potful of water : una olla de agua⟩
pothole ['pɑt,ho:l] *n* : bache *m*
potion ['po:ɭən] *n* : brebaje *m*, poción *f*
potluck ['pɑt,lʌk] *n* **to take potluck** : tomar lo que haya
potpourri [,po:pu'ri:] *n* : popurrí *m*
potshot ['pɑt,ɭɑt] *n* **1** : tiro *m* al azar ⟨to take potshots at : disparar al azar a⟩ **2** CRITICISM : crítica *f* (hecha al azar)
potter¹ ['pɑṭər] *n* : alfarero *m*, -ra *f*
potter² → **putter**
pottery ['pɑṭəri] *n, pl* **-teries** : cerámica *f*
potty ['pɑṭi] *n fam* **1** : bacinica *f* (para niños) **2 to go potty** : hacer pipí, hacer popó
pouch ['pautʃ] *n* **1** BAG : bolsa *f* pequeña **2** : bolsa *f* (de un animal)
poultice ['po:lṭəs] *n* : emplasto *m*, cataplasma *f*
poultry ['po:ltri] *n* : aves *fpl* de corral
pounce ['pauntʃ] *vi* **pounced; pouncing** : abalanzarse
pound¹ ['paund] *vt* **1** CRUSH : machacar, machucar, majar **2** BEAT : golpear, machacar ⟨she pounded the lessons into them : les machacaba las lecciones⟩ ⟨he pounded home his point : les hizo entender su razonamiento⟩ — *vi* **1** BEAT : palpitar (dícese del corazón) **2** RESOUND : retumbar, resonar **3** : andar con paso pesado ⟨we pounded through the mud : caminamos pesadamente por el barro⟩
pound² *n* **1** : libra *f* (unidad de peso) **2** : libra *f* (unidad monetaria) **3 dog pound** : perrera *f*
pour ['por] *vt* **1** : echar, verter, servir (bebidas) ⟨pour it into a pot : viértalo en una olla⟩ **2** : proveer con abundancia ⟨they poured money into it : le invirtieron mucho dinero⟩ **3 to pour out** : dar salida a ⟨he poured out his feelings to her : se desahogó con ella⟩ — *vi* **1** FLOW : manar, fluir, salir ⟨blood was

pouring from the wound : la sangre le manaba de la herida⟩ ⟨people poured out of the subway : la gente salía del metro a raudales⟩ ⟨the orders came pouring in : había un aluvión de pedidos⟩ **2 it's pouring (outside)** : está lloviendo a cántaros
pout¹ ['paut] *vi* : hacer pucheros
pout² *n* : puchero *m*
poverty ['pɑvərṭi] *n* : pobreza *f*, indigencia *f*
poverty–stricken *adj* : necesitado, paupérrimo
powder¹ ['paudər] *vt* **1** : empolvar ⟨to powder one's face : empolvarse la cara⟩ **2** PULVERIZE : pulverizar
powder² *n* : polvo *m*, polvos *mpl*
powdery ['paudəri] *adj* : polvoriento, como polvo
power¹ ['pauər] *vt* : impulsar, propulsar
power² *n* **1** CONTROL, AUTHORITY : poder *m*, autoridad *f* ⟨executive powers : poderes ejecutivos⟩ ⟨power struggle : lucha por el poder⟩ ⟨to have power over somebody : tener poder sobre alguien⟩ ⟨to come to power : llegar al poder⟩ ⟨to be in power : estar en el poder⟩ **2** ABILITY : capacidad *f*, poder *m* ⟨the power of speech : el habla⟩ ⟨I'll do everything in my power : haré todo lo que pueda⟩ ⟨it's not within my power : no está en mis manos⟩ **3** : potencia *f* (política) ⟨foreign powers : potencias extranjeras⟩ **4** STRENGTH : fuerza *f*, poder *m* ⟨the power of love : la fuerza del amor⟩ **5** : potencia *f* (en física y matemáticas) **6** : electricidad *f*, luz *f* ⟨power failure : corte de luz, corte de energía eléctrica, apagón⟩
powerboat ['pauər,bo:t] *n* **1** → **motorboat 2** → **speedboat**
powerful ['pauərfəl] *adj* : poderoso, potente — **powerfully** *adv*
powerhouse ['pauər,haus] *n* : persona *f* dinámica
powerless ['pauərləs] *adj* : impotente
powerlessness ['pauərləsnəs] *n* : impotencia *f*
power plant *n* : central *f* eléctrica
powwow ['pau,wau] *n* : conferencia *f*
pox ['pɑks] *n, pl* **pox** *or* **poxes** **1** CHICKEN POX : varicela *f* **2** SYPHILIS : sífilis *f*
PR ['pi:'ɑr] → **public relations**
practicable ['præktɪkəbəl] *adj* : practicable, viable, factible
practical ['præktɪkəl] *adj* : práctico
practicality [,præktɪ'kæləṭi] *n, pl* **-ties** : factibilidad *f*, viabilidad *f*
practical joke *n* : broma *f* (pesada)
practically ['præktɪkli] *adv* **1** : de manera práctica **2** ALMOST : casi, prácticamente
practice¹ *or* **practise** ['præktəs] *vt* **-ticed** *or* **-tised; -ticing** *or* **-tising 1** : practicar, ensayar, entrenar ⟨he practiced his German on us : practicó el alemán con nosotros⟩ ⟨to practice politeness : practicar la cortesía⟩ **2** : ejercer ⟨to practice medicine : ejercer la medicina⟩
practice² *n* **1** USE : práctica *f* ⟨to put into practice : poner en práctica⟩ **2**

CUSTOM : costumbre *f* ⟨it's a common practice here : por aquí se acostumbra hacerlo⟩ 3 TRAINING : práctica *f* ⟨she's out of practice : le falta práctica⟩ ⟨practice makes perfect : la práctica hace al maestro⟩ 4 : ejercicio *m* (de una profesión)

practitioner [præk'tɪɪənər] *n* 1 : profesional *mf* 2 **general practitioner** : médico *m*, -ca *f*

pragmatic [præg'mæt̬ɪk] *adj* : pragmático — **pragmatically** *adv*

pragmatism ['prægmə,tɪzəm] *n* : pragmatismo

prairie ['prɛri] *n* : pradera *f*, llanura *f*

praise[1] ['prɛɪz] *vt* **praised; praising** : elogiar, alabar ⟨to praise God : alabar a Dios⟩

praise[2] *n* : elogio *m*, alabanza *f*

praiseworthy ['prɛɪz,wərði] *adj* : digno de alabanza, loable

prance[1] ['præns] *vi* **pranced; prancing** 1 : hacer cabriolas, cabriolar ⟨a prancing horse : un caballo haciendo cabriolas⟩ 2 SWAGGER : pavonearse

prance[2] *n* : cabriola *f*

prank ['præŋk] *n* : broma *f*, travesura *f*

prankster ['præŋkstər] *n* : bromista *mf*

prattle[1] ['præt̬əl] *vt* **-tled; -tling** : parlotear *fam*, cotorrear *fam*, balbucear (como un niño)

prattle[2] *n* : parloteo *m fam*, cotorreo *m fam*, cháchara *f fam*

prawn ['prɔn] *n* : langostino *m*, camarón *m*, gamba *f*

pray ['prɛɪ] *vt* ENTREAT : rogar, suplicar — *vi* : rezar

prayer ['prɛr] *n* 1 : plegaria *f*, oración *f* ⟨to say one's prayers : orar, rezar⟩ ⟨the Lord's Prayer : el Padrenuestro⟩ 2 PRAYING : rezo *m*, oración *f* ⟨to kneel in prayer : arrodillarse para rezar⟩

praying mantis → **mantis**

pre- [,pri] *pref* 1 : antes de 2 : con antelación

preach ['pri:tʃ] *vi* : predicar — *vt* ADVOCATE : abogar por ⟨to preach cooperation : promover la cooperación⟩

preacher ['pri:tʃər] *n* 1 : predicador *m*, -dora *f* 2 MINISTER : pastor *m*, -tora *f*

preamble ['pri:,æmbəl] *n* : preámbulo *m*

prearrange [,pri:ə'rɛɪndʒ] *vt* **-ranged; -ranging** : arreglar de antemano

precarious [prɪ'kæriəs] *adj* : precario — **precariously** *adv*

precariousness [prɪ'kæriəsnəs] *n* : precariedad *f*

precaution [prɪ'kɔʃən] *n* : precaución *f*

precautionary [prɪ'kɔʃə,neri] *adj* : preventivo, cautelar, precautorio

precede [prɪ'si:d] *v* **-ceded; -ceding** : preceder a

precedence ['prɛsədənts, prɪ'si:dənts] *n* : precedencia *f*

precedent ['prɛsədənt] *n* : precedente *m*

precept ['pri:,sɛpt] *n* : precepto *m*

precinct ['pri:,sɪŋkt] *n* 1 DISTRICT : distrito *m* (policial, electoral, etc.) 2 **precincts** *npl* PREMISES : recinto *m*, predio *m*, límites *mpl* (de una ciudad)

precious ['prɛɪəs] *adj* 1 : precioso ⟨precious gems : piedras preciosas⟩ 2 DEAR : querido 3 AFFECTED : afectado

precipice ['prɛsəpəs] *n* : precipicio *m*

precipitate [prɪ'sɪpə,tɛɪt] *v* **-tated; -tating** *vt* 1 HASTEN, PROVOKE : precipitar, provocar 2 HURL : arrojar 3 : precipitar (en química) — *vi* : precipitarse (en química), condensarse (en meteorología)

precipitation [prɪ,sɪpə'tɛɪʃən] *n* 1 HASTE : precipitación *f*, prisa *f* 2 : precipitaciones *fpl* (en meteorología)

precipitous [prɪ'sɪpət̬əs] *adj* 1 HASTY, RASH : precipitado 2 STEEP : escarpado, empinado ⟨a precipitous drop : una caída vertiginosa⟩

précis [prɛɪ'si:] *n*, *pl* **précis** [-'si:z] : resumen *m*

precise [prɪ'sɑɪs] *adj* 1 DEFINITE : preciso, explícito 2 EXACT : exacto, preciso ⟨precise calculations : cálculos precisos⟩ — **precisely** *adv*

preciseness [prɪ'sɑɪsnəs] *n* : precisión *f*, exactitud *f*

precision [prɪ'sɪʒən] *n* : precisión *f*

preclude [prɪ'klu:d] *vt* **-cluded; -cluding** : evitar, impedir, excluir (una posibilidad, etc.)

precocious [prɪ'ko:ʃəs] *adj* : precoz — **precociously** *adv*

precocity [prɪ'kɑsət̬i] *n* : precocidad *f*

preconceived [,pri:kən'si:vd] *adj* : preconcebido

preconception [,pri:kən'spʃən] *n* : idea *f* preconcebida

precondition [,pri:kən'dɪʃən] *n* : precondición *f*, condición *f* previa

precook [,pri:'kʊk] *vt* : precocinar

precursor [prɪ'kərsər] *n* : precursor *m*, -sora *f*

predator ['prɛdət̬ər] *n* : depredador *m*, -dora *f*

predatory ['prɛdə,tori] *adj* : depredador

predecessor ['prɛdə,sesər, 'pri:-] *n* : antecesor *m*, -sora *f*; predecesor *m*, -sora *f*

predestination [prɪ,dɛstə'nɛɪʃən] *n* : predestinación *f*

predestine [prɪ'dɛstən] *vt* **-tined; -tining** : predestinar

predetermine [,pri:dɪ'tərmən] *vt* **-mined; -mining** : predeterminar

predicament [prɪ'dɪkəmənt] *n* : apuro *m*, aprieto *m*

predicate[1] ['prɛdə,kɛɪt] *vt* **-cated; -cating** 1 AFFIRM : afirmar, aseverar 2 **to be predicated on** : estar basado en

predicate[2] ['prɛdɪkət] *n* : predicado *m*

predict [prɪ'dɪkt] *vt* : pronosticar, predecir

predictable [prɪ'dɪktəbəl] *adj* : previsible — **predictably** [-bli] *adv*

prediction [prɪ'dɪkʃən] *n* : pronóstico *m*, predicción *f*

predilection [,prɛdəl'ɛkʃən, ,pri:-] *n* : predilección *f*

predispose [,pri:dɪ'spo:z] *vt* **-posed; -posing** : predisponer

predisposition [,pri:,dɪspə'zɪʃən] *n* : predisposición *f*

predominance [prɪ'dɑmənənts] *n* : predominio *m*

predominant · presage

predominant [pri'dɑmənənt] *adj* : predominante — **predominantly** *adv*
predominate [pri'dɑmə,neɪt] *vi* -nated;
-nating 1 : predominar (en cantidad) 2
PREVAIL : prevalecer
preeminence [pri'ɛmənənts] *n* : preeminencia *f*
preeminent [pri'ɛmənənt] *adj* : preeminente
preeminently [pri'ɛmənəntli] *adv* : especialmente
preempt [pri'ɛmpt] *vt* 1 APPROPRIATE
: apoderarse de, apropiarse de 2 : reemplazar (un programa de televisión,
etc.) 3 FORESTALL : adelantarse a (un
ataque, etc.)
preemptive [pri'ɛmptɪv] *adj* : preventivo
preen ['pri:n] *vt* : arreglarse (el pelo, las
plumas, etc.)
prefabricated [,pri:'fæbrə,keɪtəd] *adj*
: prefabricado
preface ['prɛfəs] *n* : prefacio *m*, prólogo
m
prefatory ['prɛfə,tori] *adj* : preliminar
prefect ['pri:,fɛkt] *n* 1 : prefecto *m* (oficial) 2 : monitor *m*, -tora *f* (estudiante)
prefer [pri'fər] *vt* -ferred; -ferring 1
: preferir ⟨I prefer coffee : prefiero
café⟩ 2 to prefer charges against
: presentar cargos contra
preferable ['prɛfərəbəl] *adj* : preferible
preferably ['prɛfərəbli] *adv* : preferentemente, de preferencia
preference ['prɛfrənts, 'prɛfər-] *n* : preferencia *f*, gusto *m*
preferential [,prɛfə'rɛntɪəl] *adj* : preferencial, preferente
prefigure [pri'fɪgjər] *vt* -ured; -uring FORE-
SHADOW : prefigurar, anunciar
prefix ['pri:,fɪks] *n* : prefijo *m*
pregnancy ['prɛgnəntsi] *n, pl* -cies : embarazo *m*, preñez *f*
pregnant ['prɛgnənt] *adj* 1 : embarazada
(dícese de una mujer), preñada (dícese
de un animal) 2 MEANINGFUL : significativo
preheat [,pri:'hi:t] *vt* : precalentar
prehensile [pri'hɛntsəl, -'hɛn,saɪl] *adj*
: prensil
prehistoric [,pri:hɪs'tɔrɪk] *or* prehistori-
cal [-ɪkəl] *adj* : prehistórico
prejudge [,pri:'dʒʌdʒ] *vt* -judged; -judging
: prejuzgar
prejudice[1] ['prɛdʒədəs] *vt* -diced; -dic-
ing 1 DAMAGE : perjudicar 2 BIAS
: predisponer, influir en
prejudice[2] *n* 1 DAMAGE : perjuicio *m* (en
derecho) 2 BIAS : prejuicio *m*
prelate ['prɛlət] *n* : prelado *m*
preliminary[1] [pri'lɪmə,nɛri] *adj* : preliminar
preliminary[2] *n, pl* -naries 1 : preámbulo
m, preludio *m* 2 preliminaries *npl*
: preliminares *mpl*
prelude ['prɛ,lu:d, 'prɛl,ju:d;, 'preɪ,lu:d,
'pri:-] *n* : preludio *m*
premarital [,pri:'mærətəl] *adj* : prematrimonial
premature [,pri:mə'tʊr, -'tjʊr, -'tʊr] *adj*
: prematuro — **prematurely** *adv*

premeditate [pri'mɛdə,teɪt] *vt* -tated; -tat-
ing : premeditar
premeditation [pri,mɛdə'teɪʃən] *n* : premeditación *f*
premenstrual [pri'mɛntstruəl] *adj* : premenstrual
premenstrual syndrome *n* : síndrome *m*
premenstrual, SPM *m*
premier[1] [pri'mɪr, -'mjɪr;, 'pri:miər] *adj*
: principal
premier[2] *n* PRIME MINISTER : primer ministro *m*, primera ministra *f*
premiere[1] [prɪ'mjɛr, -'mɪr] *vt* -miered;
-miering : estrenar
premiere[2] *n* : estreno *m*
premise ['prɛmɪs] *n* 1 : premisa *f* ⟨the
premise of his arguments : la premisa de
sus argumentos⟩ 2 premises *npl* : recinto *m*, local *m*
premium ['pri:miəm] *n* 1 BONUS : prima
f 2 SURCHARGE : recargo *m* ⟨to sell at a
premium : vender (algo) muy caro⟩ 3
insurance premium : prima *f* (de seguros) 4 to set a premium on : darle un
gran valor (a algo)
premonition [,pri:mə'nɪʃən, ,prɛmə-] *n*
: presentimiento *m*, premonición *f*
prenatal [,pri:'neɪtəl] *adj* : prenatal
preoccupation [pri,ɑkjə'peɪʃən] *n* : preocupación *f*
preoccupied [pri'ɑkjə,paɪd] *adj* : abstraído, ensimismado, preocupado
preoccupy [pri'ɑkjə,paɪ] *vt* -pied; -pying
: preocupar
preparation [,prɛpə'reɪʃən] *n* 1 PREPAR-
ING : preparación *f* 2 MIXTURE : preparado *m* ⟨a preparation for burns : un
preparado para quemaduras⟩ 3 preparations *npl* ARRANGEMENTS : preparativos *mpl*
preparatory [pri'pærə,tori] *adj* : preparatorio
preparatory school → prep school
prepare [pri'pær] *v* -pared; -paring *vt*
: preparar — *vi* : prepararse
prepay [,pri:'peɪ] *vt* -paid; -paying : pagar
por adelantado
preponderance [pri'pɑndərənts] *n* : preponderancia *f*
preponderant [pri'pɑndərənt] *adj* : preponderante — **preponderantly** *adv*
preposition [,prɛpə'zɪʃən] *n* : preposición
f
prepositional [,prɛpə'zɪʃənəl] *adj* : preposicional
prepossessing [,pri:pə'zɛsɪŋ] *adj* : atractivo, agradable
preposterous [pri'pɑstərəs] *adj* : absurdo, ridículo
prep school ['prɛp-] *n* : escuela *f* secundaria privada
prerecorded [,pri:rɪ'kɔrdəd] *adj* : pregrabado
prerequisite[1] [pri'rɛkwəzət] *adj* : necesario, esencial
prerequisite[2] *n* : condición *f* necesario,
requisito *m* previo
prerogative [pri'rɑgətɪv] *n* : prerrogativa *f*
presage ['prɛsɪdʒ, pri'seɪdʒ] *vt* -saged;
-saging : presagiar

preschool [ˈpriːˌskuːl] *adj* : preescolar
preschooler [ˈpriːˌskuːlər] *n* : párvulo *m*, -la *f*; estudiante *mf* de preescolar
prescient [ˈprɛʃiənt] *adj* : profético
prescribe [priˈskraɪb] *vt* **-scribed; -scrib-ing** **1** ORDAIN : prescribir, ordenar **2** : recetar (medicinas, etc.)
prescription [priˈskrɪpʃən] *n* : receta *f*
presence [ˈprɛzənts] *n* : presencia *f*
presence of mind *n* : aplomo *m*
present¹ [priˈzɛnt] *vt* **1** INTRODUCE : presentar ⟨to present oneself : presentarse⟩ **2** : presentar (una obra de teatro, etc.) **3** GIVE : entregar (un regalo, etc.), regalar, obsequiar **4** SHOW : presentar, ofrecer ⟨it presents a lovely view : ofrece una vista muy linda⟩
present² [ˈprɛzənt] *adj* **1** : actual ⟨present conditions : condiciones actuales⟩ **2** : presente ⟨all the students were present : todos los estudiantes estaban presentes⟩
present³ [ˈprɛzənt] *n* **1** GIFT : regalo *m*, obsequio *m* **2** : presente *m* ⟨at present : en este momento⟩ **3** *or* **present tense** : presente *m*
presentable [priˈzɛntəbəl] *adj* : presentable
presentation [ˌpriːˌzɛnˈteɪʃən, ˌprɛzən-] *n* : presentación *f* ⟨presentation ceremony : ceremonia de entrega⟩
present-day [ˈprɛzəntˈdeɪ] *adj* : actual, de hoy en día
presenter [priˈzɛntər] *n* : presentador *m*, -dora *f*
presentiment [priˈzɛntəmənt] *n* : presentimiento *m*, premonición *f*
presently [ˈprɛzəntli] *adv* **1** SOON : pronto, dentro de poco **2** NOW : actualmente, ahora
present participle *n* : participio *m* presente, participio *m* activo
preservation [ˌprɛzərˈveɪʃən] *n* : conservación *f*, preservación *f*
preservative [priˈzərvətɪv] *n* : conservante *m*
preserve¹ [priˈzərv] *vt* **-served; -serv-ing** **1** PROTECT : proteger, preservar **2** : conservar (los alimentos, etc.) **3** MAINTAIN : conservar, mantener
preserve² *n* **1** *or* **preserves** *npl* : conserva *f* ⟨peach preserves : duraznos en conserva⟩ **2** : coto *m* ⟨game preserve : coto de caza⟩
preside [priˈzaɪd] *vi* **-sided; -siding** **1 to preside over** : presidir ⟨he presided over the meeting : presidió la reunión⟩ **2 to preside over** : supervisar ⟨she presides over the department : dirige el departamento⟩
presidency [ˈprɛzədəntsi] *n, pl* **-cies** : presidencia *f*
president [ˈprɛzədənt] *n* : presidente *m*, -ta *f*
presidential [ˌprɛzəˈdɛntʃəl] *adj* : presidencial
press¹ [ˈprɛs] *vt* **1** PUSH : apretar (un botón, etc.) **2** SQUEEZE : apretar, prensar (frutas, flores, etc.) **3** IRON : planchar (ropa) **4** URGE : instar, apremiar ⟨he pressed me to come : insistió en

que viniera⟩ **5** STRESS : recalcar ⟨to press the point/issue : insistir⟩ **6** IMPOSE : imponer **7 to press charges against** : demandar a **8 to press the flesh** *fam* : estrechar manos — *vi* **1** PUSH : apretar ⟨press hard : aprieta con fuerza⟩ **2** CROWD : apiñarse **3** : abrirse paso ⟨I pressed through the crowd : me abrí paso entre el gentío⟩ **4** URGE : presionar **5 to press ahead/on/forward** : seguir adelante **6 to press for** DEMAND : exigir, presionar para
press² *n* **1** CROWD : multitud *f* **2** : imprenta *f*, prensa *f* ⟨to go to press : entrar en prensa⟩ **3** URGENCY : urgencia *f*, prisa *f* **4** PRINTER, PUBLISHER : imprenta *f*, editorial *f* **5 the press** : la prensa ⟨freedom of the press : libertad de prensa⟩
press conference *n* : conferencia *f* de prensa, rueda *f* de prensa
pressing [ˈprɛsɪŋ] *adj* URGENT : urgente
press release *n* : boletín *m* de prensa
pressure¹ [ˈprɛʃər] *vt* **-sured; -suring** : presionar, apremiar
pressure² *n* **1** : presión *f* ⟨to be under pressure : estar bajo presión⟩ **2** → **blood pressure**
pressure cooker *n* : olla *f* a presión
pressure group *n* : grupo *m* de presión
pressurize [ˈprɛʃəˌraɪz] *vt* **-ized; -izing** : presurizar
prestige [prɛˈstiːʒ, -ˈstiːdʒ] *n* : prestigio *m*
prestigious [prɛˈstɪdʒəs] *adj* : prestigioso
presto [ˈprɛsˌtoː] *adv* : de pronto
presumably [priˈzuːməbli] *adv* : es de suponer, supuestamente ⟨presumably, he's guilty : supone que es culpable⟩
presume [priˈzuːm] *vt* **-sumed; -suming** **1** ASSUME, SUPPOSE : suponer, asumir, presumir **2 to presume to** : atreverse a, osar
presumption [priˈzʌmpʃən] *n* **1** AUDACITY : atrevimiento *m*, osadía *f* **2** ASSUMPTION : presunción *f*, suposición *f*
presumptuous [priˈzʌmptʃuəs] *adj* : descarado, atrevido
presuppose [ˌpriːsəˈpoːz] *vt* **-posed; -posing** : presuponer
preteen [ˈpriːˈtiːn] *n* : preadolescente *nmf*
pretend [priˈtɛnd] *vt* **1** CLAIM : pretender ⟨I won't pretend to understand it : no voy a pretender comprenderlo⟩ **2** FEIGN : fingir, simular ⟨to pretend to do something : fingir hacer algo⟩ ⟨he pretended everything was fine : fingía que todo estaba bien⟩ ⟨she pretended not to hear me : hacía como si no me oyera⟩ — *vi* : fingir
pretender [priˈtɛndər] *n* : pretendiente *mf* (al trono, etc.)
pretense *or* **pretence** [ˈpriːˌtɛnts, priˈtɛnts] *n* **1** CLAIM : afirmación *f* (falsa), pretensión *f* **2** FEIGNING : fingimiento *m*, simulación *f* ⟨to make a pretense of doing something : fingir hacer algo⟩ ⟨a pretense of order : una apariencia de orden⟩ **3** PRETEXT : pretexto *m* ⟨under false pretenses : con pretextos falsos, de manera fraudulenta⟩

pretension [prɪ'tɛntɫən] *n* **1** CLAIM : pretensión *f*, afirmación *f* **2** ASPIRATION : aspiración *f*, ambición *f* **3** PRETENTIOUSNESS : pretensiones *fpl*, presunción *f*

pretentious [prɪ'tɛntɫəs] *adj* : pretencioso

pretentiousness [prɪ'tɛntɫəsnəs] *n* : presunción *f*, pretensiones *fpl*

preterit ['prɛţərət] *nm* : pretérito *m*

pretext ['priːˌtɛkst] *n* : pretexto *m*, excusa *f*

prettily ['prɪtəli] *adv* : atractivamente

prettiness ['prɪţinəs] *n* : lindeza *f*

pretty[1] ['prɪţi] *adv* : bastante, bien ⟨it's pretty obvious : está bien claro⟩ ⟨it's pretty much the same : es más o menos igual⟩

pretty[2] *adj* **prettier; -est** : bonito, lindo, guapo ⟨a pretty girl : una muchacha guapa⟩ ⟨what a pretty dress! : ¡qué vestido más lindo!⟩

pretzel ['prɛtsəl] *n* : galleta *f* salada (en forma de nudo)

prevail [prɪ'veɪl] *vi* **1** TRIUMPH : prevalecer **2** PREDOMINATE : predominar **3 to prevail upon** : persuadir, convencer ⟨I prevailed upon her to sing : la convencí para que cantara⟩

prevailing [prɪ'veɪlɪŋ] *adj* : imperante, prevaleciente

prevalence ['prɛvələnts] *n* : preponderancia *f*, predominio *m*

prevalent ['prɛvələnt] *adj* **1** COMMON : común y corriente, general **2** WIDESPREAD : extendido

prevaricate [prɪ'værəˌkeɪt] *vi* **-cated; -cating** LIE : mentir

prevarication [prɪˌværə'keɪɫən] *n* : mentira *f*

prevent [prɪ'vɛnt] *vt* **1** AVOID : prevenir, evitar ⟨steps to prevent war : medidas para evitar la guerra⟩ **2** HINDER : impedir

preventable [prɪ'vɛntəbəl] *adj* : evitable

preventative [prɪ'vɛntətɪv] → **preventive**

prevention [prɪ'vɛntɫən] *n* : prevención *f*

preventive [prɪ'vɛntɪv] *adj* : preventivo

preview ['priːˌvju] *n* : preestreno *m*

previous ['priːviəs] *adj* : previo, anterior ⟨previous knowledge : conocimientos previos⟩ ⟨the previous day : el día anterior⟩ ⟨in the previous year : en el año pasado⟩

previously ['priːviəsli] *adv* : antes

prewar [ˌpriː'wɔr] *adj* : de antes de la guerra

prey ['preɪ] *n, pl* **preys** : presa *f*

prey on *vt* **1** : cazar, alimentarse de ⟨it preys on fish : se alimenta de peces⟩ **2 to prey on one's mind** : hacer presa en alguien, atormentar a alguien

price[1] ['praɪs] *vt* **priced; pricing** : poner un precio a ⟨to be reasonably/competitively priced : tener precios razonables/competitivos⟩

price[2] *n* **1** : precio *m* ⟨to pay the price for something : pagar el precio de algo⟩ ⟨price tag : etiqueta de precio⟩ ⟨price range : gama de precios⟩ ⟨to go up/down in price : subir/bajar de precio⟩

⟨price cut : rebaja en el precio⟩ **2 at any price** : a toda costa

priceless ['praɪsləs] *adj* : inestimable, inapreciable

pricey ['praɪsi] *adj* : caro

prick[1] ['prɪk] *vt* **1** : pinchar **2 to prick up one's ears** : levantar las orejas — *vi* : pinchar

prick[2] *n* **1** STAB : pinchazo *m* ⟨a prick of conscience : un remordimiento⟩ **2** → **pricker**

pricker ['prɪkər] *n* THORN : espina *f*

prickle[1] ['prɪkəl] *vi* **-led; -ling** : sentir un cosquilleo, tener un hormigueo

prickle[2] *n* **1** : espina *f* (de una planta) **2** TINGLE : cosquilleo *m*, hormigueo *m*

prickly ['prɪkəli] *adj* **1** THORNY : espinoso **2** : que pica ⟨a prickly sensation : un hormigueo⟩

prickly pear *n* **1** : nopal *m*, tuna *f* (planta) **2** : tuna *f*, higo *m* chumbo (fruta)

pride[1] ['praɪd] *vt* **prided; priding** : estar orgulloso de ⟨to pride oneself on : preciarse de, enorgullecerse de⟩

pride[2] *n* : orgullo *m*

priest ['priːst] *n* : sacerdote *m*, cura *m*

priestess ['priːstɪs] *n* : sacerdotisa *f*

priesthood ['priːstˌhʊd] *n* : sacerdocio *m*

priestly ['priːstli] *adj* : sacerdotal

prig ['prɪg] *n* : mojigato *m*, -ta *f*; gazmoño *m*, -ña *f*

prim ['prɪm] *adj* **primmer; primmest 1** PRISSY : remilgado **2** PRUDISH : mojigato, gazmoño

prima ballerina ['priːmə-] *n* : prima bailarina *f*

prima donna [ˌprɪmə'dɑnə, ˌpriː-] *n* : divo *m*, diva *f*

primarily [praɪ'mɛrəli] *adv* : principalmente, fundamentalmente

primary[1] ['praɪˌmɛri, 'praɪməri] *adj* **1** FIRST : primario **2** PRINCIPAL : principal **3** BASIC : fundamental

primary[2] *n, pl* **-ries** : elección *f* primaria

primary color *n* : color *m* primario

primary school → **elementary school**

primate *n* **1** ['praɪˌmeɪt, -mət] : primado *m* (obispo) **2** [-ˌmeɪt] : primate *m* (animal)

prime[1] ['praɪm] *vt* **primed; priming 1** : cebar ⟨to prime a pump : cebar una bomba⟩ **2** PREPARE : preparar (una superficie para pintar) **3** COACH : preparar (a un testigo, etc.)

prime[2] *adj* **1** CHIEF, MAIN : principal, primero **2** EXCELLENT : de primera (categoría), excelente

prime[3] *n* **the prime of one's life** : la flor de la vida

prime minister *n* : primer ministro *m*, primera ministra *f*

prime number *n* : número *m* primo

primer[1] ['prɪmər] *n* **1** READER : cartilla *f* **2** MANUAL : manual *m*

primer[2] ['praɪmər] *n* **1** : cebo *m* (para explosivos) **2** : base *f* (de pintura)

prime time *n* : horas *fpl* de mayor audiencia

primeval [praɪ'miːvəl] *adj* : primitivo, primigenio

primitive [ˈprɪmətɪv] *adj* : primitivo
primly [ˈprɪmli] *adv* : mojigatamente
primness [ˈprɪmnəs] *n* : mojigatería *f*, gazmoñería *f*
primordial [praɪˈmɔrdiəl] *adj* : primordial, fundamental
primp [ˈprɪmp] *vi* : arreglarse, acicalarse
primrose [ˈprɪmˌroːz] *n* : primavera *f*, prímula *f*
prince [ˈprɪnts] *n* : príncipe *m*
princely [ˈprɪntsli] *adj* : principesco
princess [ˈprɪntsəs, ˈprɪnˌsɛs] *n* : princesa *f*
principal[1] [ˈprɪntsəpəl] *adj* : principal — **principally** *adv*
principal[2] *n* **1** PROTAGONIST : protagonista *mf* **2** : director *m*, -tora *f* (de una escuela) **3** CAPITAL : principal *m*, capital *m* (en finanzas)
principality [ˌprɪntsəˈpæləti] *n*, *pl* **-ties** : principado *m*
principle [ˈprɪntsəpəl] *n* **1** : principio *m* ⟨it's against my principles : va en contra de mis principios⟩ ⟨it's a matter of principle : es una cuestión de principios⟩ **2 as a matter of principle** : por principio **3 in principle** : en principio **4 on principle** : por principio
print[1] [ˈprɪnt] *vt* **1** : imprimir (libros, etc.) **2** : publicar **3** : estampar (tela) **4 to print out** : imprimir — *vi* : escribir con letra de molde/imprenta
print[2] *n* **1** IMPRESSION : marca *f*, huella *f*, impresión *f* **2** : texto *m* impreso ⟨to be out of print : estar agotado⟩ **3** LETTERING : letra *f* **4** ENGRAVING : grabado *m* **5** : copia *f* (en fotografía) **6** : estampado *m* (de tela)
printer [ˈprɪntər] *n* **1** : impresor *m*, -sora *f* (persona) **2** : impresora *f* (máquina)
printing [ˈprɪntɪŋ] *n* **1** : imprenta *f* (acto) ⟨the third printing : la tercera tirada⟩ **2** : imprenta *f* (profesión) **3** LETTERING : letras *fpl* de molde
printing press *n* : prensa *f*
print out *vt* : imprimir (de una computadora)
printout [ˈprɪntˌaʊt] *n* : copia *f* impresa (de una computadora)
prior[1] [ˈpraɪər] *adj* **1** : previo ⟨prior engagement/commitment : compromiso previo⟩ ⟨without prior notice : sin previo aviso⟩ **2 prior to** : antes de
prior[2] *n* : prior *m*
prioress [ˈpraɪərəs] *n* : priora *f*
priority [praɪˈɔrəti] *n*, *pl* **-ties** : prioridad *f*
priory [ˈpraɪəri] *n*, *pl* **-ries** : priorato *m*
prism [ˈprɪzəm] *n* : prisma *m*
prison [ˈprɪzən] *n* : prisión *f*, cárcel *f* ⟨he's in prison : está preso, está en la cárcel⟩ ⟨they put him in prison : lo encarcelaron, lo metieron en la cárcel⟩ ⟨a prison sentence : una pena de prisión⟩ ⟨she was sentenced to ten years in prison : fue condenada a diez años de prisión⟩
prisoner [ˈprɪzənər] *n* : preso *m*, -sa *f*; recluso *m*, -sa *f* ⟨prisoner of war : prisionero de guerra⟩
prison warden → **warden**
prissy [ˈprɪsi] *adj* **prissier; -est** : remilgado, melindroso

pristine [ˈprɪsˌtiːn, prɪsˈ-] *adj* : puro, prístino
privacy [ˈpraɪvəsi] *n*, *pl* **-cies** : privacidad *f*
private[1] [ˈpraɪvət] *adj* **1** PERSONAL : privado, particular ⟨private property : propiedad privada⟩ **2** INDEPENDENT : privado, independiente ⟨private studies : estudios privados⟩ **3** SECRET : secreto **4** SECLUDED : aislado, privado **5** SHY : reservado — **privately** *adv*
private[2] *n* : soldado *m* raso
private detective → **private investigator**
private enterprise → **free enterprise**
private eye *fam* → **private investigator**
private investigator *n* : investigador *m* privado, investigadora *f* privada, detective *m* privado, detective *f* privada
private school *n* : escuela *f* privada
privation [praɪˈveɪʃən] *n* : privación *f*
privatize [ˈpraɪvəˌtaɪz] *vt* **-ized; -izing** : privatizar
privilege [ˈprɪvlɪdʒ, ˈprɪvə-] *n* : privilegio *m*
privileged [ˈprɪvlɪdʒd, ˈprɪvə-] *adj* : privilegiado
privy[1] [ˈprɪvi] *adj* **to be privy to** : estar enterado de
privy[2] *n*, *pl* **privies** : excusado *m*, retrete *m* (exterior)
prize[1] [ˈpraɪz] *vt* **prized; prizing** : valorar, apreciar
prize[2] *adj* **1** : premiado ⟨a prize stallion : un semental premiado⟩ **2** OUTSTANDING : de primera, excepcional
prize[3] *n* **1** AWARD : premio *m* ⟨third prize : el tercer premio⟩ **2** : joya *f*, tesoro *m* ⟨he's a real prize : es un tesoro⟩
prizefighter [ˈpraɪzˌfaɪtər] *n* : boxeador *m*, -dora *f* profesional
prizewinner [ˈpraɪzˌwɪnər] *n* : premiado *m*, -da *f*
prizewinning [ˈpraɪzˌwɪnɪŋ] *adj* : premiado, galardonado
pro[1] [ˈproː] *adv* : a favor
pro[2] *adj* → **professional**[1]
pro[3] *n* **1** : pro *m* ⟨the pros and cons : los pros y los contras⟩ **2** → **professional**[2]
pro- *pref* : pro-
probability [ˌprɑbəˈbɪləti] *n*, *pl* **-ties** : probabilidad *f*
probable [ˈprɑbəbəl] *adj* : probable — **probably** [-bli] *adv*
probate[1] [ˈproːˌbeɪt] *vt* **-bated; -bating** : autenticar (un testamento)
probate[2] *n* : autenticación *f* (de un testamento)
probation [proˈbeɪʃən] *n* **1** : período *m* de prueba (para un empleado, etc.) **2** : libertad *f* condicional (para un preso) ⟨to put someone on probation : dejar/poner a alguien en libertad condicional⟩
probationary [proˈbeɪʃəˌnɛri] *adj* : de prueba
probe[1] [ˈproːb] *vt* **probed; probing 1** : sondar (en medicina y tecnología) **2** INVESTIGATE : investigar, sondear
probe[2] *n* **1** : sonda *f* (en medicina, etc.) ⟨space probe : sonda espacial⟩ **2** INVESTIGATION : investigación *f*, sondeo *m*

probity ['proːbəti] *n* : probidad *f*
problem[1] ['probləm] *adj* : difícil
problem[2] *n* : problema *m*
problematic [ˌprobləˈmætɪk] *or* **problematical** [-ˌtɪkəl] *adj* : problemático
proboscis [prəˈbasɪs] *n, pl* **-cises** *also* **-cides** [-səˌdiːz] : trompa *f*, probóscide *f*
procedural [prəˈsiːdʒərəl] *adj* : de procedimiento
procedure [prəˈsiːdʒər] *n* : procedimiento *m* ⟨administrative procedures : trámites administrativos⟩
proceed [proˈsiːd] *vi* **1** : proceder ⟨to proceed to do something : proceder a hacer algo⟩ **2** CONTINUE : continuar, proseguir, seguir ⟨he proceeded to the next phase : pasó a la segunda fase⟩ **3** ADVANCE : avanzar ⟨as the conference proceeded : mientras seguía avanzando la conferencia⟩ ⟨the road proceeds south : la calle sigue hacia el sur⟩
proceeding [proˈsiːdɪŋ] *n* **1** PROCEDURE : procedimiento *m* **2 proceedings** *npl* EVENTS : acontecimientos *mpl* **3 proceedings** *npl* MINUTES : actas *fpl* (de una reunión, etc.)
proceeds ['proːˌsiːdz] *npl* : ganancias *fpl*
process[1] ['proˌsɛs, 'proː-] *vt* : procesar, tratar
process[2] *n, pl* **-cesses** ['proˌsɛsəz, 'proː-, -səsəz, -səˌsiːz] **1** : proceso *m* ⟨the process of elimination : el proceso de eliminación⟩ **2** METHOD : proceso *m*, método *m* ⟨manufacturing processes : procesos industriales⟩ **3** : acción *f* judicial ⟨due process of law : el debido proceso (de la ley)⟩ **4** SUMMONS : citación *f* **5** PROJECTION : protuberancia *f* (anatómica) **6 in the process of** : en vías de ⟨in the process of repair : en reparaciones⟩
processing *n* : procesamiento *m* (en informática)
procession [prəˈsɛlən] *n* : procesión *f*, desfile *m* ⟨a funeral procession : un cortejo fúnebre⟩
processional [prəˈsɛlənəl] *n* : himno *m* para una procesión
processor ['proˌsɛsər, 'proː-, -səsər] *n* **1** : procesador *m* (de una computadora) **2 food processor** : procesador *m* de alimentos
proclaim [proˈkleɪm] *vt* : proclamar
proclamation [ˌprokləˈmeɪlən] *n* : proclamación *f*
proclivity [proˈklɪvəti] *n, pl* **-ties** : proclividad *f*
procrastinate [prəˈkræstəˌneɪt] *vi* **-nated; -nating** : demorar, aplazar las responsabilidades
procrastination [prəˌkræstəˈneɪlən] *n* : aplazamiento *m*, demora *f*, dilación *f*
procreate ['proːkriˌeɪt] *vi* **-ated; -ating** : procrear
procreation [ˌproːkriˈeɪlən] *n* : procreación *f*
proctor[1] ['proktər] *vt* : supervisar (un examen)
proctor[2] *n* : supervisor *m*, -sora *f* (de un examen)

procure [prəˈkjʊr] *vt* **-cured; -curing 1** OBTAIN : procurar, obtener **2** BRING ABOUT : provocar, lograr, conseguir
procurement [prəˈkjʊrmənt] *n* : obtención *f*
prod[1] ['prod] *vt* **prodded; prodding 1** JAB, POKE : pinchar, golpear (con la punta de algo) **2** GOAD : incitar, estimular
prod[2] *n* **1** JAB, POKE : golpe *m* (con la punta de algo), pinchazo *m* **2** STIMULUS : estímulo *m* **3 cattle prod** : picana *f*, aguijón *m*
prodigal[1] ['prodɪgəl] *adj* SPENDTHRIFT : pródigo, despilfarrador, derrochador
prodigal[2] *n* : pródigo *m*, -ga *f*; derrochador *m*, -dora *f*
prodigious [prəˈdɪdʒəs] *adj* **1** MARVELOUS : prodigioso, maravilloso **2** HUGE : enorme, vasto ⟨prodigious sums : muchísimo dinero⟩ — **prodigiously** *adv*
prodigy ['prodədʒi] *n, pl* **-gies** : prodigio *m* ⟨child prodigy : niño prodigio⟩
produce[1] [prəˈduːs, -ˈdjuːs] *vt* **-duced; -ducing 1** EXHIBIT : presentar, mostrar **2** YIELD : producir **3** CAUSE : producir, causar **4** CREATE : producir ⟨to produce a poem : escribir un poema⟩ **5** : poner en escena (una obra de teatro), producir (una película)
produce[2] ['proˌduːs, 'proː-, -ˌdjuːs] *n* : productos *mpl* agrícolas
producer [prəˈduːsər, -ˈdjuː-] *n* : productor *m*, -tora *f*
product ['proˌdʌkt] *n* : producto *m*
production [prəˈdʌklən] *n* : producción *f*
productive [prəˈdʌktɪv] *adj* : productivo
productivity [ˌproːˌdʌkˈtɪvəti, ˌproː-] *n* : productividad *f*
profane[1] [proˈfeɪn] *vt* **-faned; -faning** : profanar
profane[2] *adj* **1** SECULAR : profano **2** IRREVERENT : irreverente, impío
profanity [proˈfænəti] *n, pl* **-ties 1** IRREVERENCE : irreverencia *f*, impiedad *f* **2** : blasfemias *fpl*, obscenidades *fpl* ⟨don't use profanity : no digas blasfemias⟩
profess [prəˈfɛs] *vt* **1** DECLARE : declarar, manifestar **2** CLAIM : pretender **3** : profesar (una religión, etc.)
professedly [prəˈfɛsədli] *adv* **1** OPENLY : declaradamente **2** ALLEGEDLY : supuestamente
profession [prəˈfɛlən] *n* : profesión *f*
professional[1] [prəˈfɛlənəl] *adj* : profesional — **professionally** *adv*
professional[2] *n* : profesional *mf*
professionalism [prəˈfɛlənəˌlizəm] *n* : profesionalismo *m*
professor [prəˈfɛsər] *n* : profesor *m* (universitario), profesora *f* (universitaria); catedrático *m*, -ca *f*
professorship [prəˈfɛsərˌlɪp] *n* : cátedra *f*
proffer ['profər] *vt* **-fered; -fering** : ofrecer, dar
proficiency [prəˈfɪləntsi] *n* : competencia *f*, capacidad *f*
proficient [prəˈfɪlənt] *adj* : competente, experto — **proficiently** *adv*

profile ['pro:ˌfaɪl] *n* : perfil *m* ⟨a portrait in profile : un retrato de perfil⟩ ⟨to keep a low profile : no llamar la atención, hacerse pasar desapercibido⟩

profit¹ ['prɑfət] *vi* : sacar provecho (de), beneficiarse (de)

profit² *n* **1** ADVANTAGE : provecho *m*, partido *m*, beneficio *m* **2** GAIN : beneficio *m*, utilidad *f*, ganancia *f* ⟨to make a profit : sacar beneficios⟩

profitability [ˌprɑfətəˈbɪləti] *n* : rentabilidad *f*

profitable ['prɑfətəbəl] *adj* : rentable, lucrativo — **profitably** [-bli] *adv*

profitless ['prɑfətləs] *adj* : infructuoso, inútil

profligate ['prɑflɪɡət, -ˌɡeɪt] *adj* **1** DISSOLUTE : disoluto, licencioso **2** SPENDTHRIFT : despilfarrador, derrochador, pródigo

profound [prəˈfaʊnd] *adj* : profundo

profoundly [prəˈfaʊndli] *adv* : profundamente, en profundidad

profundity [prəˈfʌndəti] *n, pl* **-ties** : profundidad *f*

profuse [prəˈfju:s] *adj* **1** COPIOUS : profuso, copioso **2** LAVISH : pródigo — **profusely** *adv*

profusion [prəˈfju:ʒən] *n* : abundancia *f*, profusión *f*

progenitor [proˈdʒɛnətər] *n* : progenitor *m*, -tora *f*

progeny ['prɑdʒəni] *n, pl* **-nies** : progenie *f*

progesterone [proˈdʒɛstəˌroːn] *n* : progesterona *f*

prognosis [prɑɡˈnoːsɪs] *n, pl* **-noses** [-ˌsiːz] : pronóstico *m* (médico)

program¹ ['proːˌɡræm, -ɡrəm] *vt* **-grammed** *or* **-gramed; -gramming** *or* **-graming** : programar

program² *n* : programa *m*

programmable ['proːˌɡræməbəl] *adj* : programable

programmer ['proːˌɡræmər] *n* : programador *m*, -dora *f*

programming ['proːˌɡræmɪŋ] *n* : programación *f*

progress¹ [prəˈɡrɛs] *vi* **1** PROCEED : progresar, adelantar **2** IMPROVE : mejorar

progress² ['prɑɡrəs, -ˌɡrɛs] *n* **1** ADVANCE : progreso *m*, adelanto *m*, avance *m* ⟨to make progress : hacer progresos⟩ **2** BETTERMENT : mejora *f*, mejoramiento *m*

progression [prəˈɡrɛʒən] *n* **1** ADVANCE : avance *m* **2** SEQUENCE : desarrollo *m* (de eventos)

progressive [prəˈɡrɛsɪv] *adj* **1** : progresista ⟨a progressive society : una sociedad progresista⟩ **2** : progresivo ⟨a progressive disease : una enfermedad progresiva⟩ **3** *or* **Progressive** : progresista (en política) **4** : progresivo (en gramática)

progressively [prəˈɡrɛsɪvli] *adv* : progresivamente, poco a poco

prohibit [proˈhɪbət] *vt* : prohibir

prohibition [ˌproːəˈbɪʃən, ˌproːhə-] *n* : prohibición *f*

prohibitive [proˈhɪbətɪv] *adj* : prohibitivo

project¹ [prəˈdʒɛkt] *vt* **1** PLAN : proyectar, planear **2** : proyectar (imágenes, misiles, etc.) — *vi* PROTRUDE : sobresalir, salir

project² ['prɑˌdʒɛkt, -dʒɪkt] *n* : proyecto *m*, trabajo *m* (de un estudiante) ⟨research project : proyecto de investigación⟩

projectile [prəˈdʒɛktəl, -ˌtaɪl] *n* : proyectil *m*

projection [prəˈdʒɛkʃən] *n* **1** PLAN : plan *m*, proyección *f* **2** : proyección *f* (de imágenes, misiles, etc.) **3** PROTRUSION : saliente *m*

projectionist [prəˈdʒɛkʃənɪst] *n* : proyeccionista *mf*; operador *m*, -dora *f*

projector [prəˈdʒɛktər] *n* : proyector *m*

proletarian¹ [ˌproːləˈtɛriən] *adj* : proletario

proletarian² *n* : proletario *m*, -ria *f*

proletariat [ˌproːləˈtɛriət] *n* : proletariado *m*

proliferate [prəˈlɪfəˌreɪt] *vi* **-ated; -ating** : proliferar

proliferation [prəˌlɪfəˈreɪʃən] *n* : proliferación *f*

prolific [prəˈlɪfɪk] *adj* : prolífico

prologue ['proːˌlɔɡ] *n* : prólogo *m*

prolong [prəˈlɔŋ] *vt* : prolongar

prolongation [ˌproːˌlɔŋˈɡeɪʃən] *n* : prolongación *f*

prom ['prɑm] *n* : baile *m* formal (de un colegio)

promenade¹ [ˌprɑməˈneɪd, -ˈnɑd] *vi* **-naded; -nading** : pasear, pasearse, dar un paseo

promenade² *n* : paseo *m*

prominence ['prɑmənənts] *n* **1** PROJECTION : prominencia *f* **2** EMINENCE : eminencia *f*, prestigio *m*

prominent ['prɑmənənt] *adj* **1** OUTSTANDING : prominente, destacado **2** PROJECTING : prominente, saliente

prominently ['prɑmənəntli] *adv* : destacadamente, prominentemente

promiscuity [ˌprɑmɪsˈkju:əti] *n, pl* **-ties** : promiscuidad *f*

promiscuous [prəˈmɪskjuəs] *adj* : promiscuo — **promiscuously** *adv*

promise¹ ['prɑməs] *v* **-ised; -ising** : prometer

promise² *n* **1** : promesa *f* ⟨he kept his promise : cumplió su promesa⟩ **2 to show promise** : prometer

promising ['prɑməsɪŋ] *adj* : prometedor

promissory ['prɑməˌsori] *adj* : que promete ⟨a promissory note : un pagaré⟩

promontory ['prɑmənˌtori] *n, pl* **-ries** : promontorio *m*

promote [prəˈmoːt] *vt* **-moted; -moting** **1** : ascender (a un alumno o un empleado) **2** ADVERTISE : promocionar, hacerle publicidad a **3** FURTHER : promover, fomentar

promoter [prəˈmoːtər] *n* : promotor *m*, -tora *f*; empresario *m*, -ria *f* (en deportes)

promotion [prəˈmoːʃən] *n* **1** : ascenso *m* (de un alumno o un empleado) **2** FURTHERING : promoción *f*, fomento *m* **3**

ADVERTISING : publicidad *f*, propaganda *f*

promotional [prə'moːlᵊnəl] *adj* : promocional

prompt[1] ['prɑmpt] *vt* **1** INDUCE : provocar (una cosa), inducir (a una persona) ⟨curiosity prompted me to ask you : la curiosidad me indujo a preguntarle⟩ **2** : apuntar (a un actor, etc.)

prompt[2] *adj* : pronto, rápido ⟨prompt payment : pago puntual⟩

prompter ['prɑmptər] *n* : apuntador *m*, -dora *f* (en teatro)

promptly ['prɑmptli] *adv* : inmediatamente, rápidamente

promptness ['prɑmptnəs] *n* : prontitud *f*, rapidez *f*

promulgate ['prɑməl,geɪt] *vt* -gated; -gating : promulgar

prone ['proːn] *adj* **1** LIABLE : propenso, proclive ⟨accident-prone : propenso a los accidentes⟩ **2** : boca abajo, decúbito prono ⟨in a prone position : en decúbito prono⟩

prong ['prɔŋ] *n* : punta *f*, diente *m*

pronoun ['proː,naʊn] *n* : pronombre *m*

pronounce [prə'naʊnʦ] *vt* -nounced; -nouncing **1** : pronunciar ⟨how do you pronounce your name? : ¿cómo se pronuncia su nombre?⟩ **2** DECLARE : declarar **3 to pronounce sentence** : dictar sentencia, pronunciar un fallo

pronounced [prə'naʊnʦt] *adj* MARKED : pronunciado, marcado

pronouncement [prə'naʊnʦmənt] *n* : declaración *f*

pronunciation [prə,nʌnʦi'eɪlən] *n* : pronunciación *f*

proof[1] ['pruːf] *adj* : a prueba ⟨proof against tampering : a prueba de manipulación⟩

proof[2] *n* : prueba *f*

proofread ['pruːf,riːd] *v* -read; -reading *vt* : corregir — *vi* : corregir pruebas

proofreader ['pruːf,riːdər] *n* : corrector *m*, -tora *f* (de pruebas)

prop[1] ['prɑp] *vt* propped; propping **1 to prop against** : apoyar contra **2 to prop up** SUPPORT : apoyar, apuntalar, sostener **3 to prop up** SUSTAIN : alentar (a alguien), darle ánimo (a alguien)

prop[2] *n* **1** SUPPORT : puntal *m*, apoyo *m*, soporte *m* **2** : accesorio *m* (en teatro)

propaganda [,prɑpə'gændə, ,proː-] *n* : propaganda *f*

propagandize [,prɑpə'gæn,daɪz, ,proː-] *v* -dized; -dizing *vt* : someter a propaganda — *vi* : hacer propaganda

propagate ['prɑpə,geɪt] *v* -gated; -gating *vi* : propagarse — *vt* : propagar

propagation [,prɑpə'geɪlən] *n* : propagación *f*

propane ['proː,peɪn] *n* : propano *m*

propel [prə'pɛl] *vt* -pelled; -pelling : impulsar, propulsar, impeler

propellant *or* **propellent** [prə'pɛlənt] *n* : propulsor *m*

propeller [prə'pɛlər] *n* : hélice *f*

propensity [prə'pɛnʦəti] *n*, *pl* -ties : propensión *f*, tendencia *f*, inclinación *f*

proper ['prɑpər] *adj* **1** RIGHT, SUITABLE : apropiado, adecuado **2** : propio, mismo ⟨the city proper : la propia ciudad⟩ **3** CORRECT : correcto **4** GENTEEL : fino, refinado, cortés **5** OWN, SPECIAL : propio — **properly** *adv*

proper noun *or* **proper name** *n* : nombre *m* propio

property ['prɑpərti] *n*, *pl* -ties **1** CHARACTERISTIC : característica *f*, propiedad *f* **2** POSSESSIONS : propiedad *f* **3** BUILDING : inmueble *m* **4** LAND, LOT : terreno *m*, lote *m*, parcela *f* **5** PROP : accesorio *m* (en teatro)

prophecy ['prɑfəsi] *n*, *pl* -cies : profecía *f*, vaticinio *m*

prophesy ['prɑfə,saɪ] *v* -sied; -sying *vt* **1** FORETELL : profetizar (como profeta) **2** PREDICT : profetizar, predecir, vaticinar — *vi* : hacer profecías

prophet ['prɑfət] *n* : profeta *m*

prophetic [prə'fɛtɪk] *or* **prophetical** [-tɪkəl] *adj* : profético — **prophetically** [-tɪkli] *adv*

propitiate [proː'pɪliˌeɪt] *vt* -ated; -ating : propiciar

propitious [prə'pɪləs] *adj* : propicio

proponent [prə'poːnənt] *n* : defensor *m*, -sora *f*; partidario *m*, -ria *f*

proportion[1] [prə'porⱡən] *vt* : proporcionar ⟨well-proportioned : de buenas proporciones⟩

proportion[2] *n* **1** RATIO : proporción *f* **2** SYMMETRY : proporción *f*, simetría *f* ⟨out of proportion : desproporcionado⟩ ⟨to keep things in proportion : no exagerar⟩ ⟨you're blowing things out of proportion : estás exagerando⟩ **3** PART, SHARE : parte *f* **4 proportions** *npl* SIZE : dimensiones *fpl*

proportional [prə'porⱡənəl] *adj* : proporcional — **proportionally** *adv*

proportionate [prə'porⱡənət] *adj* : proporcional — **proportionately** *adv*

proposal [prə'poːzəl] *n* **1** PROPOSITION : propuesta *f*, proposición *f* ⟨marriage proposal : propuesta de matrimonio⟩ **2** PLAN : proyecto *m*, propuesta *f*

propose [prə'poːz] *v* -posed; -posing *vi* : proponer matrimonio — *vt* **1** INTEND : pensar, proponerse **2** SUGGEST : proponer

proposition [,prɑpə'zɪlən] *n* **1** PROPOSAL : proposición *f*, propuesta *f* **2** STATEMENT : proposición *f*

propound [prə'paʊnd] *vt* : proponer, exponer

proprietary [prə'praɪəˌtɛri] *adj* : propietario, patentado

proprietor [prə'praɪətər] *n* : propietario *m*, -ria *f*

propriety [prə'praɪəti] *n*, *pl* -eties **1** DECORUM : decencia *f*, decoro *m* **2 proprieties** *npl* CONVENTIONS : convenciones *fpl*, cánones *mpl* sociales

propulsion [prə'pʌlⱡən] *n* : propulsión *f*

prosaic [proː'zeɪk] *adj* : prosaico

proscribe [proː'skraɪb] *vt* -scribed; -scribing : proscribir

prose ['proːz] *n* : prosa *f*

prosecute [ˈprɑsɪˌkjuːt] vt **-cuted; -cuting 1** CARRY OUT : llevar a cabo **2** : procesar, enjuiciar ⟨prosecuted for fraud : procesado por fraude⟩

prosecution [ˌprɑsɪˈkjuːlən] n **1** : procesamiento m ⟨the prosecution of forgers : el procesamiento de falsificadores⟩ **2** PROSECUTORS : acusación f ⟨witness for the prosecution : testigo de cargo⟩

prosecutor [ˈprɑsɪˌkjuːlər] n : acusador m, -dora f; fiscal mf

prospect¹ [ˈprɑˌspɛkt] vi : prospectar (el terreno) ⟨to prospect for gold : buscar oro⟩

prospect² n **1** VISTA : vista f, panorama m **2** OPPORTUNITY : posibilidad f, perspectiva f ⟨he has few prospects for employment : tiene pocas posibilidades/perspectivas de empleo⟩ **3** POSSIBILITY : posibilidad f ⟨the prospect of going to war : la posibilidad de entrar en guerra⟩ **4** CANDIDATE : candidato m, -ta f **5 in prospect** : en perspectiva

prospective [prəˈspɛktɪv, ˈprɑˌspɛk-] adj **1** EXPECTANT : futuro ⟨prospective mother : futura madre⟩ **2** POTENTIAL : potencial, posible ⟨prospective employee : posible empleado⟩

prospector [ˈprɑˌspɛktər, prɑˈspɛk-] n : prospector m, -tora f; explorador m, -dora f

prospectus [prəˈspɛktəs] n : prospecto m

prosper [ˈprɑspər] vi : prosperar

prosperity [prɑˈspɛrəti] n : prosperidad f

prosperous [ˈprɑspərəs] adj : próspero

prostate [ˈprɑˌsteɪt] n : próstata f

prosthesis [prɑsˈθiːsɪs, ˈprɑsθə-] n, pl **-theses** [-ˌsiːz] : prótesis f

prostitute¹ [ˈprɑstəˌtuːt, -ˌtjuːt] vt **-tuted; -tuting 1** : prostituir **2 to prostitute oneself** : prostituirse

prostitute² n : prostituto m, -ta f

prostitution [ˌprɑstəˈtuːlən, -ˈtjuː-] n : prostitución f

prostrate¹ [ˈprɑˌstreɪt] vt **-trated; -trating 1** : postrar **2 to prostrate oneself** : postrarse

prostrate² adj : postrado

prostration [prɑˈstreɪlən] n : postración f

protagonist [proˈtæɡənɪst] n : protagonista mf

protect [prəˈtɛkt] vt : proteger

protection [prəˈtɛklən] n : protección f

protective [prəˈtɛktɪv] adj : protector

protector [prəˈtɛktər] n **1** : protector m, -tora f (persona) **2** GUARD : protector m (aparato)

protectorate [prəˈtɛktərət] n : protectorado m

protégé [ˈproːtəˌʒeɪ] n : protegido m, -da f

protein [ˈproːˌtiːn] n : proteína f

protest¹ [proˈtɛst, prə-] vt **1** ASSERT : afirmar, declarar **2** : protestar ⟨they protested the decision : protestaron (por) la decisión⟩ — vi **to protest against** : protestar contra

protest² [ˈproːˌtɛst] n **1** DEMONSTRATION : manifestación f (de protesta) ⟨a public protest : una manifestación pública⟩ **2** COMPLAINT : queja f, protesta f

Protestant [ˈprɑtəstənt] n : protestante mf

Protestantism [ˈprɑtəstənˌtɪzəm] n : protestantismo m

protester [proˈtɛstər, prə-] n : manifestante mf

protocol [ˈproːtəˌkɔl] n : protocolo m

proton [ˈproːˌtɑn] n : protón m

protoplasm [ˈproːtəˌplæzəm] n : protoplasma m

prototype [ˈproːtəˌtaɪp] n : prototipo m

protract [proˈtrækt] vt : prolongar

protractor [proˈtræktər] n : transportador m (instrumento)

protrude [proˈtruːd] vi **-truded; -truding** : salir, sobresalir

protrusion [proˈtruːʒən] n : protuberancia f, saliente m

protuberance [proˈtuːbərənts, -ˈtjuː-] n : protuberancia f

proud [ˈpraʊd] adj **1** HAUGHTY : altanero, orgulloso, arrogante **2** : orgulloso ⟨she was proud of her work : estaba orgullosa de su trabajo⟩ ⟨too proud to beg : demasiado orgulloso para rogar⟩ **3** GLORIOUS : glorioso — **proudly** adv

provable [ˈpruːvəbəl] adj : comprobable

prove [ˈpruːv] v **proved** or **proven** [ˈpruːvən]; **proving** vt **1** TEST : probar **2** DEMONSTRATE : probar, demostrar ⟨this proves her guilt, this proves that she is guilty : esto prueba/demuestra que es culpable⟩ ⟨you've already proven your point : ya sé que tienes razón⟩ **3** (show someone/something to be) ⟨can you prove him wrong? : ¿puedes demostrar que está equivocado?⟩ ⟨evidence that proves her guilty : pruebas que demuestran que es culpable⟩ ⟨it has been proven effective : se ha demostrado ser eficaz⟩ — vi **1** : resultar ⟨it proved effective : resultó eficaz⟩ **2 to prove oneself** : demostrar sus cualidades

Provençal [ˌproːvanˈsɑl, ˌprɑvən-] n **1** : provenzal mf **2** : provenzal m (idioma) — **Provençal** adj

proverb [ˈprɑˌvərb] n : proverbio m, refrán m

proverbial [prəˈvərbiəl] adj : proverbial

provide [prəˈvaɪd] v **-vided; -viding** vt **1** STIPULATE : estipular **2 to provide with** : proveer de, proporcionar — vi **1** : proveer ⟨the Lord will provide : el Señor proveerá⟩ **2 to provide for** SUPPORT : mantener **3 to provide for** ANTICIPATE : hacer previsiones para, prever

provided [prəˈvaɪdəd] or **provided that** conj : con tal (de) que, siempre que

providence [ˈprɑvədənts] n **1** PRUDENCE : previsión f, prudencia f **2** or **Providence** : providencia f ⟨divine providence : la Divina Providencia⟩ **3 Providence** GOD : Providencia f

provident [ˈprɑvədənt] adj **1** PRUDENT : previsor, prudente **2** FRUGAL : frugal, ahorrativo

providential [ˌprɑvəˈdɛntIəl] adj : providencial

provider [prəˈvaɪdər] n **1** PURVEYOR : proveedor m, -dora f **2** BREADWINNER : sostén m (económico) providing that → provided

province ['prɑvɪnts] *n* 1 : provincia *f* (de un país) ⟨to live in the provinces : vivir en las provincias⟩ 2 FIELD, SPHERE : campo *m*, competencia *f* ⟨it's not in my province : no es de mi competencia⟩

provincial [prə'vɪntɪəl] *adj* 1 : provincial ⟨provincial government : gobierno provincial⟩ 2 : provinciano, pueblerino ⟨a provincial mentality : una mentalidad provinciana⟩

provision[1] [prə'vɪʒən] *vt* : aprovisionar, abastecer

provision[2] *n* 1 PROVIDING : provisión *f*, suministro *m* 2 STIPULATION : condición *f*, salvedad *f*, estipulación *f* 3 **provisions** *npl* : despensa *f*, víveres *mpl*, provisiones *fpl*

provisional [prə'vɪʒənəl] *adj* : provisional, provisorio — **provisionally** *adv*

proviso [prə'vaɪ,zo:] *n, pl* -sos *or* -soes : condición *f*, salvedad *f*, estipulación *f*

provocation [,prɑvə'keɪʃən] *n* : provocación *f*

provocative [prə'vɑkətɪv] *adj* 1 INCITING : provocador 2 SUGGESTIVE : provocativo, insinuante 3 INTRIGUING : que hace pensar

provoke [prə'vo:k] *vt* -voked; -voking : provocar

prow ['praʊ] *n* : proa *f*

prowess ['praʊəs] *n* 1 VALOR : valor *m*, valentía *f* 2 SKILL : habilidad *f*, destreza *f*

prowl ['praʊl] *vi* : merodear, rondar — *vt* : rondar por

prowler ['praʊlər] *n* : merodeador *m*, -dora *f*

proximity [prɑk'sɪmət̬i] *n* : proximidad *f*

proxy ['prɑksi] *n, pl* **proxies** 1 : poder *m* (de actuar en nombre de alguien) ⟨by proxy : por poder⟩ 2 AGENT : apoderado *m*, -da *f*; representante *mf*

prude ['pru:d] *n* : mojigato *m*, -ta *f*; gazmoño *m*, -ña *f*

prudence ['pru:dənts] *n* 1 SHREWDNESS : prudencia *f*, sagacidad *f* 2 CAUTION : prudencia *f*, cautela *f* 3 THRIFT : frugalidad *f*

prudent ['pru:dənt] *adj* 1 SHREWD : prudente, sagaz 2 CAUTIOUS, FARSIGHTED : prudente, previsor, precavido 3 THRIFTY : frugal, ahorrativo — **prudently** *adv*

prudery ['pru:dəri] *n, pl* -eries : mojigatería *f*, gazmoñería *f*

prudish ['pru:dɪʃ] *adj* : mojigato, gazmoño

prune[1] ['pru:n] *vt* **pruned; pruning** : podar (arbustos, etc.), acortar (un texto), recortar (gastos, etc.)

prune[2] *n* : ciruela *f* pasa

prurient ['prʊriənt] *adj* : lascivo

pry ['praɪ] *v* **pried; prying** *vi* : curiosear, huronear ⟨to pry into other people's business : meterse uno en lo que no le importa⟩ — *vt or* **to pry open** : abrir (con una palanca), apalancar

psalm ['sɑm, 'sɑlm] *n* : salmo *m*

pseudonym ['su:də,nɪm] *n* : seudónimo *m*

psoriasis [sə'raɪəsɪs] *n* : soriasis *f*, psoriasis *f*

psyche ['saɪki] *n* : psique *f*, psiquis *f*

psychedelic[1] [,saɪkə'dɛlɪk] *adj* : psicodélico

psychedelic[2] *n* : droga *f* psicodélica

psychiatric [,saɪki'ætrɪk] *adj* : psiquiátrico, siquiátrico

psychiatrist [sə'kaɪətrɪst, saɪ-] *n* : psiquiatra *mf*, siquiatra *mf*

psychiatry [sə'kaɪətri, saɪ-] *n* : psiquiatría *f*, siquiatría *f*

psychic[1] ['saɪkɪk] *adj* 1 : psíquico, síquico (en psicología) 2 CLAIRVOYANT : clarividente

psychic[2] *n* : vidente *mf*, clarividente *mf*

psychoanalysis [,saɪkoə'næləsɪs] *n, pl* -yses : psicoanálisis *m*, sicoanálisis *m*

psychoanalyst [,saɪko'ænəlɪst] *n* : psicoanalista *mf*, sicoanalista *mf*

psychoanalytic [,saɪko,ænəl'ɪt̬ɪk] *adj* : psicoanalítico, sicoanalítico

psychoanalyze [,saɪko'ænə,laɪz] *vt* -lyzed; -lyzing : psicoanalizar, sicoanalizar

psychological [,saɪkə'lɑd͡ʒɪkəl] *adj* : psicológico, sicológico — **psychologically** *adv*

psychologist [saɪ'kɑləd͡ʒɪst] *n* : psicólogo *m*, -ga *f*; sicólogo *m*, -ga *f*

psychology [saɪ'kɑləd͡ʒi] *n, pl* -gies : psicología *f*, sicología *f*

psychopath ['saɪkə,pæθ] *n* : psicópata *mf*, sicópata *mf*

psychopathic [,saɪkə'pæθɪk] *adj* : psicopático, sicopático

psychosis [saɪ'ko:sɪs] *n, pl* -choses [-'ko:,si:z] : psicosis *f*, sicosis *f*

psychosomatic [,saɪkəsə'mæt̬ɪk] *adj* : psicosomático, sicosomático

psychotherapist [,saɪko'θɛrəpɪst] *n* : psicoterapeuta *mf*, sicoterapeuta *mf*

psychotherapy [,saɪko'θɛrəpi] *n, pl* -pies : psicoterapia *f*, sicoterapia *f*

psychotic[1] [saɪ'kɑt̬ɪk] *adj* : psicótico, sicótico

psychotic[2] *n* : psicótico *m*, -ca *f*; sicótico *m*, -ca *f*

pub ['pʌb] *n* : cervecería *f*, taberna *m*, bar *m*

puberty ['pju:bərt̬i] *n* : pubertad *f*

pubic ['pju:bɪk] *adj* : pubiano, púbico

public[1] ['pʌblɪk] *adj* 1 : público ⟨public opinion : opinión pública⟩ ⟨a public figure : un personaje público⟩ 2 **to go public** : salir a la bolsa, comenzar/empezar a cotizar en (la) bolsa (dícese de una empresa) 3 **to go public with** REVEAL : revelar — **publicly** *adv*

public[2] *n* : público *m*

publication [,pʌblə'keɪʃən] *n* : publicación *f*

publicist ['pʌbləsɪst] *n* : publicista *mf*

publicity [pə'blɪsət̬i] *n* : publicidad *f*

publicize ['pʌblə,saɪz] *vt* -cized; -cizing : publicitar

public relations *npl* : relaciones *fpl* públicas

public school *n* : escuela *f* pública

public–spirited *adj* : de espíritu cívico

public transit *n* : transporte *m* público
publish ['pʌblɪʃ] *vt* : publicar
publisher ['pʌblɪʃər] *n* : casa *f* editorial
(compañía); editor *m*, -tora *f* (persona)
publishing ['pʌblɪʃɪŋ] *n* : industria *f* editorial
pucker¹ ['pʌkər] *vt* : fruncir, arrugar — *vi*
: arrugarse
pucker² *n* : arruga *f*, fruncido *m*
pudding ['pʊdɪŋ] *n* : budín *m*, pudín *m*
puddle ['pʌdəl] *n* : charco *m*
pudgy ['pʌdʒi] *adj* pudgier; -est : regordete *fam*, rechoncho *fam*, gordinflón
fam
puerile ['pjʊrəl] *adj* : pueril
Puerto Rican¹ [ˌpwɛrtəˈriːkən, ˌpɔrtə-] *adj*
: puertorriqueño
Puerto Rican² *n* : puertorriqueño *m*, -ña *f*
puff¹ ['pʌf] *vi* 1 BLOW : soplar 2 PANT
: resoplar, jadear 3 to puff up SWELL
: hincharse — *vt* 1 BLOW : soplar ⟨to
puff smoke : echar humo⟩ 2 INFLATE
: inflar, hinchar ⟨to puff out one's
cheeks : inflar las mejillas⟩
puff² *n* 1 GUST : soplo *m*, ráfaga *f*, bocanada *f* (de humo) 2 DRAW : chupada *f* a
un cigarrillo) 3 SWELLING : hinchazón
f 4 cream puff : pastelito *m* de crema 5
powder puff : borla *f*
puff pastry *n* : hojaldre *m*
puffy ['pʌfi] *adj* puffier; -est 1 SWOLLEN
: hinchado, inflado 2 SPONGY : esponjoso, suave
pug ['pʌg] *n* 1 : doguillo *m* (perro) 2 *or*
pug nose : nariz *f* achatada
pugnacious [ˌpʌgˈneɪʃəs] *adj* : pugnaz,
agresivo
pug–nosed ['pʌgˌnoːzd] *adj* : de nariz
chata
puke ['pjuːk] *vi* puked; puking *fam*
: vomitar, devolver
pull¹ ['pʊl, 'pʌl] *vt* 1 DRAW, TUG : tirar de,
jalar 2 EXTRACT : sacar, extraer ⟨to pull
teeth : sacar muelas⟩ ⟨to pull a gun on
someone : amenazar a alguien con una
pistola⟩ 3 TEAR : desgarrarse (un
músculo, etc.) 4 DO : hacer (una broma,
un turno, etc.) ⟨to pull a heist : dar un
golpe⟩ ⟨to pull an all-nighter : trasnochar (estudiando, etc.)⟩ 5 to pull a fast
one on DECEIVE : engañar, jugarle una
mala pasada a 6 to pull apart SEPARATE, TEAR : separar, hacer pedazos 7
to pull aside : llevar aparte, llevar a un
lado 8 to pull down : bajar, echar abajo,
derribar (un edificio) 9 to pull in ATTRACT : atraer (clientes, etc.) ⟨to pull in
votes : conseguir votos⟩ 10 to pull off
REMOVE : sacar, quitar 11 to pull off
ACHIEVE : conseguir, lograr 12 to pull
oneself together : calmarse, tranquilizarse 13 to pull out EXTRACT : sacar,
arrancar 14 to pull out RECALL, WITHDRAW : retirar 15 to pull over : parar
⟨he was pulled over for speeding : lo
pararon por exceso de velocidad⟩ 16 to
pull through SUSTAIN : sacar adelante 17 to pull up RAISE : levantar,
subir 18 to pull up STOP : parar (un vehículo) — *vi* 1 DRAW, TUG : tirar, ja-

lar 2 (*indicating movement of a vehicle
in a specific direction*) ⟨he pulled off the
highway : salió de la carretera⟩ ⟨they
pulled in front of us : se nos metieron
delante⟩ ⟨to pull to a stop : pararse⟩ 3
to pull ahead : tomar la delantera 4 to
pull at : tirar, dar tirones de 5 to pull
away : alejarse 6 to pull back : echarse
atrás 7 to pull for : apoyar a, alentar 8
to pull on : tirar de, jalar 9 to pull on
DON : ponerse 10 to pull out LEAVE
: salir, arrancar (en un vehículo) 11 to
pull out WITHDRAW : retirarse 12 to
pull over : hacerse a un lado (en un vehículo) 13 to pull through SURVIVE,
ENDURE : sobrevivir, salir adelante 14
to pull together COOPERATE : trabajar
juntos, cooperar 15 to pull up STOP
: parar (en un vehículo)
pull² *n* 1 TUG : tirón *m*, jalón *m* ⟨he gave
it a pull : le dio un tirón⟩ 2 ATTRACTION
: atracción *f*, fuerza *f* ⟨the pull of gravity
: la fuerza de la gravedad⟩ 3 INFLUENCE
: influencia *f* 4 HANDLE : tirador *m* (de
un cajón, etc.) 5 bell pull : cuerda *f*
pullet ['pʊlət] *n* : polla *f*, gallina *f* (joven)
pulley ['pʊli] *n*, *pl* -leys : polea *f*
pullover ['pʊlˌoːvər] *n* : suéter *m*
pulmonary ['pʊlməˌnɛri, 'pʌl-] *adj* : pulmonar
pulp ['pʌlp] *n* 1 : pulpa *f* (de una fruta,
etc.) 2 MASH : papilla *f*, pasta *f* ⟨wood
pulp : pasta de papel, pulpa de papel⟩
⟨to beat to a pulp : hacer papilla (a alguien)⟩ 3 : pulpa *f* (de los dientes)
pulpit ['pʊlˌpɪt] *n* : púlpito *m*
pulsate ['pʌlˌseɪt] *vi* -sated; -sating 1
BEAT : latir, palpitar 2 VIBRATE : vibrar
pulsation [ˌpʌlˈseɪʃən] *n* : pulsación *f*
pulse ['pʌls] *n* : pulso *m*
pulverize ['pʌlvəˌraɪz] *vt* -ized; -izing
: pulverizar
puma ['puːmə, 'pjuː-] *n* : puma *m*; león *m*,
leona *f* (*in various countries*)
pumice ['pʌməs] *n* : piedra *f* pómez
pummel ['pʌməl] *vt* -meled; -meling
: aporrear, apalear
pump¹ ['pʌmp] *vt* 1 : bombear ⟨to pump
water : bombear agua⟩ ⟨to pump (up) a
tire : inflar una llanta⟩ 2 : mover (una
manivela, un pedal, etc.) de arriba abajo
⟨to pump someone's hand : darle un
fuerte apretón de manos a alguien⟩ 3 to
pump iron : hacer pesas 4 to pump out
: sacar, vaciar (con una bomba) 5 to
pump out CHURN OUT : producir (en
masa) — *vi* : bombear
pump² *n* 1 : bomba *f* ⟨water pump
: bomba de agua⟩ 2 SHOE : zapato *m* de
tacón
pumpernickel ['pʌmpərˌnɪkəl] *n* : pan *m*
negro de centeno
pumpkin ['pʌmpkɪn, 'pʌŋkən] *n* : calabaza *f*, zapallo *m* *Arg, Chile, Peru, Uru*
pun¹ ['pʌn] *vi* punned; punning : hacer
juegos de palabras
pun² *n* : juego *m* de palabras, albur *m*
Mex
punch¹ ['pʌntʃ] *vt* 1 HIT : darle un
puñetazo (a alguien), golpear ⟨she

punched him in the nose : le dio un puñetazo en la nariz⟩ **2** PERFORATE : perforar (papel, etc.), picar (un boleto)

punch² *n* **1** : perforadora *f* ⟨paper punch : perforadora de papel⟩ **2** BLOW : golpe *m*, puñetazo *m* **3** : ponche *m* ⟨fruit punch : ponche de frutas⟩

punch line *n* : remate *m*

punctilious [pəŋk'tɪliəs] *adj* : puntilloso

punctual ['pʌŋktɬʊəl] *adj* : puntual

punctuality [ˌpʌŋktɬʊ'æləti] *n* : puntualidad *f*

punctually ['pʌŋktɬʊəli] *adv* : puntualmente, a tiempo

punctuate ['pʌŋktɬʊˌeɪt] *vt* **-ated; -ating** : puntuar

punctuation [ˌpʌŋktɬʊ'eɪɬən] *n* : puntuación *f*

punctuation mark *n* : signo *m* de puntuación

puncture¹ ['pʌŋktɬər] *vt* **-tured; -turing** : pinchar, punzar, perforar, ponchar *Mex*

puncture² *n* : pinchazo *m*, ponchadura *f* *Mex*

pundit ['pʌndɪt] *n* : experto *m*, -ta *f*

pungency ['pʌndʒənʦi] *n* : acritud *f*, acrimonia *f*

pungent ['pʌndʒənt] *adj* : acre

punish ['pʌnɪʃ] *vt* : castigar

punishable ['pʌnɪɬəbəl] *adj* : punible

punishment ['pʌnɪɬmənt] *n* : castigo *m*

punitive ['pju:nəṭɪv] *adj* : punitivo

punk¹ ['pʌŋk] *adj* : punk

punk² *n* **1** *or* **punk rock** : punk *m* (música) **2** *or* **punk rocker** : punk *mf* **3** HOODLUM : matón *m*, maleante *mf*

punt¹ ['pʌnt] *vt* : impulsar (un barco) con una pértiga — *vi* : despejar (en deportes)

punt² *n* **1** : batea *f* (barco) **2** : patada *f* de despeje (en deportes)

puny ['pju:ni] *adj* **punier; -est** : enclenque, endeble

pup ['pʌp] *n* : cachorro *m*, -rra *f* (de un perro); cría *f* (de otros animales)

pupa ['pju:pə] *n*, *pl* **-pae** [-pi, -ˌpaɪ] *or* **-pas** : crisálida *f*, pupa *f*

pupil ['pju:pəl] *n* **1** : alumno *m*, -na *f* (de colegio) **2** : pupila *f* (del ojo)

puppet ['pʌpət] *n* : títere *m*, marioneta *f*

puppeteer [ˌpʌpə'tɪr] *n* : titiritero *m*, -ra *f*

puppy ['pʌpi] *n*, *pl* **-pies** : cachorro *m*, -rra *f*

purchase¹ ['pərtɬəs] *vt* **-chased; -chasing** : comprar — **purchaser** *n*

purchase² *n* **1** PURCHASING : compra *f*, adquisición *f* **2** : compra *f* ⟨last-minute purchases : compras de última hora⟩ **3** GRIP : agarre *m*, asidero *m* ⟨she got a firm purchase on the wheel : se agarró bien del volante⟩

purchase order *n* : orden *f* de compra

pure ['pjʊr] *adj* **purer; purest** : puro

purebred ['pjʊrˌbred] *adj* : de pura raza

puree¹ [pjʊ'reɪ, -'ri:] *vt* **-reed; -reeing** : hacer un puré con

puree² *n* : puré *m*

purely ['pjʊrli] *adv* **1** WHOLLY : puramente, completamente ⟨purely by

chance : por pura casualidad⟩ **2** SIMPLY : sencillamente, meramente

purgative ['pərgəṭɪv] *n* : purgante *m*

purgatory ['pərgəˌtori] *n*, *pl* **-ries** : purgatorio *m*

purge¹ ['pərdʒ] *vt* **purged; purging** : purgar

purge² *n* : purga *f*

purification [ˌpjʊrəfə'keɪɬən] *n* : purificación *f*

purifier ['pjʊrəˌfaɪər] *n* : purificador *m*

purify ['pjʊrəˌfaɪ] *vt* **-fied; -fying** : purificar

puritan ['pjʊrəṭən] *n* : puritano *m*, -na *f* — **puritan** *adj*

puritanical [ˌpjuːrə'tænɪkəl] *adj* : puritano

purity ['pjʊrəṭi] *n* : pureza *f*

purl¹ ['pərl] *v* : tejer al revés, tejer del revés

purl² *n* : punto *m* del revés

purloin [pər'lɔɪn, 'pərˌlɔɪn] *vt* : hurtar, robar

purple ['pərpəl] *n* : morado *m*, color *m* púrpura

purport [pər'port] *vt* : pretender ⟨to purport to be : pretender ser⟩

purpose ['pərpəs] *n* **1** INTENTION : propósito *m*, intención *f* ⟨on purpose : a propósito, adrede⟩ ⟨for a purpose : por una razón⟩ ⟨for all practical purposes : a efectos prácticos⟩ **2** FUNCTION : función *f* ⟨to serve a purpose : servir de algo⟩ **3** RESOLUTION : resolución *f*, determinación *f* ⟨to have a sense of purpose : tener un norte en la vida⟩

purposeful ['pərpəsfəl] *adj* : determinado, decidido, resuelto

purposefully ['pərpəsfəli] *adv* : decididamente, resueltamente

purposely ['pərpəsli] *adv* : intencionadamente, a propósito, adrede

purr¹ ['pər] *vi* : ronronear

purr² *n* : ronroneo *m*

purse¹ ['pərs] *vt* **pursed; pursing** : fruncir ⟨to purse one's lips : fruncir la boca⟩

purse² *n* **1** HANDBAG : cartera *f*, bolso *m*, bolsa *f Mex* ⟨a change purse : un monedero⟩ **2** FUNDS : fondos *mpl* **3** PRIZE : premio *m*

purser ['pərsər] *n* : sobrecargo *mf*

pursue [pər'su:] *vt* **-sued; -suing** **1** CHASE : perseguir **2** SEEK : buscar, tratar de encontrar ⟨to pursue pleasure : buscar el placer⟩ **3** FOLLOW : seguir ⟨the road pursues a northerly course : el camino sigue hacia el norte⟩ **4** : dedicarse a ⟨to pursue a hobby : dedicarse a un pasatiempo⟩

pursuer [pər'su:ər] *n* : perseguidor *m*, -dora *f*

pursuit [pər'su:t] *n* **1** CHASE : persecución *f* **2** SEARCH : búsqueda *f*, busca *f* **3** ACTIVITY : actividad *f*, pasatiempo *m*

purveyor [pər'veɪər] *n* : proveedor *m*, -dora *f*

pus ['pʌs] *n* : pus *m*

push¹ ['pʊʃ] *vt* **1** : empujar ⟨he pushed the chair back/forward : empujó la silla hacia atrás/adelante⟩ ⟨she pushed him

aside : lo apartó (de un empujón)⟩ **2**
PRESS : apretar, pulsar (un botón,
etc.) **3** PRESSURE, URGE : presionar ⟨to
push someone to do something : empujar a alguien a hacer algo⟩ ⟨to push
someone too hard : exigir demasiado de
alguien⟩ **4** STRESS : recalcar ⟨to push
the point/issue : insistir⟩ **5** PROVOKE,
PESTER : provocar, fastidiar ⟨don't push
him too far : no lo provoques⟩ **6** FORCE
: hacer cambiar ⟨to push prices up/down
: hacer subir/bajar los precios⟩ **7** PRO-
MOTE : promocionar **8** : pasar (drogas) **9** APPROACH : rayar, rozar (una
edad, un número, un límite) **10 to push
around** BULLY : intimidar, mangonear **11 to push back** : aplazar,
postergar (una fecha) **12 to push it (too
far)** : pasarse **13 to push through**
: conseguir que se apruebe **14 to push
one's luck** : tentar a la suerte **15 to
push over** : echar abajo, tirar al suelo —
vi **1** : empujar **2** INSIST : insistir, presionar **3 to push ahead/forward/on**
: seguir adelante **4 to push for** DE-
MAND : exigir, presionar para **5 to push
off** LEAVE : marcharse, irse, largarse *fam*
push² *n* **1** SHOVE : empujón *m* **2** DRIVE
: empuje *m*, energía *f*, dinamismo *m* **3**
EFFORT : esfuerzo *m*
push–button [ˈpʊlˈbʌtən] *adj* : de botones
pusher [ˈpʊlər] *n* : camello *m fam*
push–up [ˈpʊlˌʌp] *n* : flexión *f*
pushy [ˈpʊli] *adj* **pushier; -est** : mandón,
prepotente
pussy [ˈpʊsi] *n, pl* **pussies** : gatito *m*, -ta
f; minino *m*, -na *f*
pussy willow *n* : sauce *m* blanco
pustule [ˈpʌsˌtʃuːl] *n* : pústula *f*
put [ˈpʊt] *v* **put; putting** *vt* **1** PLACE
: poner, colocar ⟨put it on the table
: ponlo en la mesa⟩ ⟨put the car in the
garage : guarda el auto en el garaje⟩ ⟨she
put her arms around me : me abrazó⟩ **2**
INSERT : meter **3** : poner (en cierto estado) ⟨it put her in a good mood : la
puso de buen humor⟩ ⟨to put into effect
: poner en práctica⟩ **4** IMPOSE : imponer ⟨they put a tax on it : lo gravaron
con un impuesto⟩ **5** SUBJECT : someter,
poner ⟨to put to the test : poner a
prueba⟩ ⟨to put to death : ejecutar⟩ **6**
EXPRESS : expresar, decir ⟨he put it simply : lo dijo sencillamente⟩ **7** APPLY
: aplicar ⟨to put one's mind to something
: proponerse hacer algo⟩ **8** SET : poner
⟨I put him to work : lo puse a traba-
jar⟩ **9** ATTACH : dar ⟨to put a high value
on : dar gran valor a⟩ **10** PRESENT
: presentar, exponer ⟨to put a question
to someone : hacerle una pregunta a al-
guien⟩ **11 to put across/over** : comunicar (un mensaje, etc.) **12 to put oneself across/over as** : dar la impresión de
ser **13 to put aside** : dejar a un lado **14
to put aside** RESERVE : guardar, reservar **15 to put at** : calcular en ⟨they put
the number of deaths at 3,000 : calculan
en 3000 la cifra de muertos⟩ **16 to put
away** SAVE : guardar **17 to put back/**

away : volver a su sitio **18 to put before**
: presentar a **19 to put behind one**
: olvidar ⟨to put the past behind you
: olvidar el pasado⟩ **20 to put down** DE-
POSIT : dejar (en el suelo, etc.) **21 to put
down** SUPPRESS : aplastar, suprimir **22
to put down** *fam* DISPARAGE : menospreciar **23 to put down** ATTRIBUTE
: atribuir ⟨she put it down to luck : lo
atribuyó a la suerte⟩ **24 to put down**
: dejar (un depósito) **25 to put down**
WRITE DOWN : escribir, apuntar **26 to
put down** INSTALL, LAY : poner, colocar **27 to put down** EUTHANIZE : sacrificar **28 to put forth/forward** PROPOSE
: proponer, presentar **29 to put in** IN-
VEST : dedicar (tiempo), invertir (dinero)
⟨to put in a lot of effort : esforzarse
mucho⟩ **30 to put in** DO : hacer, trabajar (horas extras, etc.) ⟨to put in one's
time : cumplir su condena⟩ **31 to put in**
PRESENT : presentar, hacer (una oferta,
etc.) **32 to put in** INSTALL : instalar **33
to put in** MAKE : hacer (una llamada,
etc.) ⟨to put in an appearance : hacer
acto de presencia⟩ **34 to put in** INTER-
JECT : hacer (un comentario) **35 to put
in a good word for** RECOMMEND, PRAISE
: recomendar, hablar bien de **36 to put
into** INVEST : dedicar (tiempo) a, invertir
(dinero) en ⟨to put effort into something
: esforzarse en algo⟩ ⟨to put thought into
something : pensar algo⟩ **37 to put off**
DEFER : aplazar, posponer **38 to put off**
STALL, DISTRACT : hacer esperar, distraer **39 to put off** DISSUADE, DISCOUR-
AGE : disuadir, desalentar ⟨it put him off
his food : le quitó las ganas de
comer⟩ **40 to put on** DON : ponerse
(ropa, etc.) **41 to put on** ASSUME : afectar, adoptar ⟨to put on a brave face
: ponerle buena cara a algo/alguien⟩ **42
to put on** ADD, INCREASE : añadir, aumentar ⟨to put on weight : engordar,
ganar peso⟩ **43 to put on** PRODUCE
: presentar (una obra de teatro, etc.) **44
to put on** TURN ON, START : encender
(luces, etc.), poner (música) ⟨to put the
water on (to boil) : poner el agua a calen-
tar⟩ **45 to put money (etc.) on** : apostar dinero (etc.) por **46 to put on**
: poner en (una lista, un menú, etc.) **47
to put on** : poner a (régimen, etc.),
recetarle (medicina) a **48 to put on (the
phone)** ⟨put Dad on (the phone)
: pásame a papá⟩ **49 to put someone
on** *fam* TEASE : tomarle el pelo a alguien **50 to put out** : apagar (llamas,
luces, etc.) **51 to put out** BOTHER, IN-
CONVENIENCE : molestar, incomodar **52
to put out** : sacar (la basura, etc.) **53 to
put out** DISPLAY : disponer **54 to put
out** EXTEND : extender, tender (la
mano) **55 to put out** PRODUCE : producir **56 to put out** RELEASE, ISSUE
: sacar (un álbum, etc.), publicar (un estudio, etc.), emitir (un aviso, etc.) ⟨to put
word out that . . . : hacer correr la voz
que . . .⟩ **57 to put something/one over
on** TRICK : engañar **58 to put through**

: pasar (una llamada) **59 to put through**
: hacer pasar (dificultades, etc.) ⟨she put
us through hell : nos hizo pasar las de
Caín⟩ **60 to put someone through college** : pagarle los estudios a alguien **61
to put together** COMBINE : reunir, juntar **62 to put together** PREPARE : preparar, hacer **63 to put together** ASSEM-
BLE : armar, montar **64 to put up** RAISE
: subir, levantar (la mano, etc.), izar (una
bandera) ⟨to put up one's hair : recoger
el pelo⟩ **65 to put up** PRESERVE : hacer
conserva de **66 to put up** LODGE : alojar **67 to put up** BUILD, ERECT, ASSEM-
BLE : construir, levantar, montar **68 to
put up** HANG : poner, colgar **69 to put
up** : oponer ⟨to put up a fight/struggle
: oponer resistencia⟩ ⟨to put up a fuss
: armar un lío⟩ **70 to put up** OFFER UP
: ofrecer ⟨to put up for sale : poner a la
venta⟩ ⟨to put up for adoption : dar en
adopción⟩ **71 to put up** PRESENT : presentar (argumentos), hacer (una propuesta) **72 to put up** PROVIDE : poner
(dinero), ofrecer (una recompensa) **73
to put someone up to something** : incitar a alguien a algo, animar a alguien a
hacer algo — vi **1 to put forth** : echar,
extender **2 to put in for** REQUEST : solicitar (una promoción, etc.) **3 to put to
sea** : hacerse a la mar **4 to put up with**
: aguantar, soportar
putrefy [ˈpjuːtrəˌfaɪ] v **-fied; -fying** vt : pudrir — vi : pudrirse
putrid [ˈpjuːtrɪd] adj : putrefacto, pútrido

putter [ˈpʌtər] vi or **to putter around** : entretenerse
putty[1] [ˈpʌti] vt **-tied; -tying** : poner masilla en
putty[2] n, pl **-ties** : masilla f
puzzle[1] [ˈpʌzəl] vt **-zled; -zling 1** CON-
FUSE : confundir, dejar perplejo **2 to
puzzle out** : dar vueltas a, tratar de resolver
puzzle[2] n **1** : rompecabezas m ⟨a crossword puzzle : un crucigrama⟩ **2** MYS-
TERY : misterio m, enigma m
puzzlement [ˈpʌzəlmənt] n : desconcierto
m, perplejidad f
puzzling adj : desconcertante
pygmy [ˈpɪgmi] adj : enano, pigmeo
Pygmy n, pl **-mies** : pigmeo m, -mea f
pylon [ˈpaɪˌlɑn, -lən] n **1** : torre f de conducta eléctrica **2** : pilón m (de un puente)
pyramid [ˈpɪrəˌmɪd] n : pirámide f
pyre [ˈpaɪr] n : pira f
pyromania [ˌpaɪroˈmeɪniə] n : piromanía
f
pyromaniac [ˌpaɪroˈmeɪniˌæk] n : pirómano m, -na f
pyrotechnics [ˌpaɪroˈtɛknɪks] npl **1** FIRE-
WORKS : fuegos mpl artificiales **2**
DISPLAY, SHOW : espectáculo m, muestra
f de virtuosismo ⟨computer pyrotechnics : efectos especiales hechos por
computadora⟩ — **pyrotechnic** adj
Pyrrhic [ˈpɪrɪk] adj : pírrico
python [ˈpaɪˌθɑn, -θən] n : pitón f, serpiente f pitón

Q

q [ˈkjuː] n, pl **q's** or **qs** [ˈkjuːz] : deci-
moséptima letra del alfabeto inglés
Q–tips [ˈkjuːˌtɪps] trademark se usa para
hisopos
quack[1] [ˈkwæk] vi : graznar
quack[2] n **1** : graznido m (de pato) **2**
CHARLATAN : curandero m, -ra f; matasanos m fam
quad [ˈkwɑd] → quadrangle 1
quadrangle [ˈkwɑˌdræŋgəl] n **1** COURT-
YARD : patio m interior (de una universidad, etc.) **2** → quadrilateral
quadrant [ˈkwɑdrənt] n : cuadrante m
quadrilateral [ˌkwɑdrəˈlætərəl] n
: cuadrilátero m
quadruple[1] [kwɑˈdruːpəl, -ˈdrʌ-; ˈkwɑdrə-]
v **-pled; -pling** vt : cuadruplicar — vi
: cuadruplicarse
quadruple[2] adj : cuádruple
quadruplet [kwɑˈdruːplət, -ˈdrʌ-; ˈkwɑdrə-]
n : cuatrillizo m, -za f
quagmire [ˈkwægˌmaɪr, ˈkwɑg-] n **1**
: lodazal m, barrizal m **2** PREDICAMENT
: atolladero m
quail [ˈkweɪl] n, pl **quail** or **quails** : codorniz f
quaint [ˈkweɪnt] adj **1** ODD : extraño, curioso **2** PICTURESQUE : pintoresco —
quaintly adv

quake[1] [ˈkweɪk] vi **quaked; quaking**
: temblar
quake[2] n : temblor m, terremoto m
Quaker [ˈkweɪkər] n : cuáquero m, -ra f
— **Quaker** adj
qualification [ˌkwɑləfəˈkeɪʃən] n **1** LIMITA-
TION, RESERVATION : reserva f, limitación
f ⟨without qualification : sin reservas⟩ **2**
REQUIREMENT : requisito m **3 qualifica-
tions** npl ABILITY : aptitud f, capacidad f
qualified [ˈkwɑləˌfaɪd] adj **1** : capacitado, habilitado ⟨to be qualified to
: ser capacitado para⟩ ⟨she's qualified
for the job : cumple los requisitos para el
puesto⟩ **2** LIMITED : limitado
qualifier [ˈkwɑləˌfaɪər] n **1** : clasificado
m, -da f (en deportes) **2** : calificativo m
(en gramática)
qualify [ˈkwɑləˌfaɪ] v **-fied; -fying** vt **1**
: matizar ⟨to qualify a statement : matizar una declaración⟩ **2** : calificar (en
gramática) **3** : habilitar, capacitar ⟨the
certificate qualified her to teach : el certificado la habilitó para enseñar⟩ —
vi **1** : obtener el título, recibirse ⟨to
qualify as an engineer : recibirse de in-
geniero⟩ **2** : tener derecho ⟨to qualify
for assistance : tener derecho a recibir
ayuda⟩ **3** : clasificarse (en deportes)

qualitative ['kwɑlə,teɪtɪv] *adj* : cualitativo
quality ['kwɑləti] *n, pl* **-ties** **1** NATURE : carácter *m* **2** ATTRIBUTE : cualidad *f* **3** GRADE : calidad *f* ⟨of good quality : de buena calidad⟩
qualm ['kwɑm, 'kwɑlm, 'kwɔm] *n* **1** MIS-GIVING : duda *f*, aprensión *f* **2** RESERVA-TION, SCRUPLE : escrúpulo *m*, reparo *m*
quandary ['kwɑndri] *n, pl* **-ries** : dilema *m*
quantify ['kwɑntəfaɪ] *vt* **-fied; -fying** : cuantificar
quantitative ['kwɑntə,teɪtɪv] *adj* : cuantitativo
quantity ['kwɑntəti] *n, pl* **-ties** : cantidad *f*
quantum¹ ['kwɑntəm] *n* : cuanto *m* (en física)
quantum² *adj* : cuántico ⟨quantum theory : teoría cuántica⟩
quarantine¹ ['kwɔrən,ti:n] *vt* **-tined; -tining** : poner en cuarentena
quarantine² *n* : cuarentena *f*
quarrel¹ ['kwɔrəl] *vi* **-reled** *or* **-relled; -reling** *or* **-relling** : pelearse, reñir, discutir
quarrel² *n* : pelea *f*, riña *f*, disputa *f*
quarrelsome ['kwɔrəlsəm] *adj* : pendenciero, discutidor
quarry¹ ['kwɔri] *vt* **quarried; quarrying** **1** EXTRACT : extraer (mármol, etc.) **2** EX-CAVATE : excavar (un cerro, etc.)
quarry² *n, pl* **quarries** **1** : cantera *f* **2** PREY : presa *f*
quart ['kwɔrt] *n* : cuarto *m* de galón
quarter¹ ['kwɔrtər] *vt* **1** : dividir en cuatro partes **2** LODGE : alojar, acuartelar (tropas)
quarter² *adj* : cuarto ⟨a quarter hour/mile : un cuarto de hora/milla⟩
quarter³ *n* **1** : cuarto *m*, cuarta parte *f* ⟨a foot and a quarter : un pie y cuarto⟩ ⟨a quarter after three : las tres y cuarto⟩ **2** : moneda *f* de 25 centavos, cuarto *m* de dólar **3** DISTRICT : barrio *m* ⟨business quarter : barrio comercial⟩ **4** PLACE : parte *f* ⟨from all quarters : de todas partes⟩ ⟨at close quarters : de muy cerca⟩ **5** MERCY : clemencia *f*, cuartel *m* ⟨to give no quarter : no dar cuartel⟩ **6 quarters** *npl* LODGING : alojamiento *m*, cuartel *m* (militar)
quarterback ['kwɔrtər,bæk] *n* : mariscal *m* de campo
quarterfinal [,kwɔrtər'faɪnəl] *n* : cuarto *m* de final
quarterly¹ ['kwɔrtərli] *adv* : cada tres meses, trimestralmente
quarterly² *adj* : trimestral
quarterly³ *n, pl* **-lies** : publicación *f* trimestral
quartermaster ['kwɔrtər,mæstər] *n* : intendente *mf*
quarter note *n* : negra *f* (en música)
quartet [kwɔr'tɛt] *n* : cuarteto *m*
quartz ['kwɔrts] *n* : cuarzo *m*
quash ['kwɑʃ, 'kwɔʃ] *vt* **1** ANNUL : anular **2** QUELL : sofocar, aplastar
quasi- ['kweɪ,zaɪ, 'kwɑzi] *pref* : cuasi-
quaver¹ ['kweɪvər] *vi* **1** SHAKE : temblar ⟨her voice was quavering : le temblaba la voz⟩ **2** TRILL : trinar

quaver² *n* : temblor *m* (de la voz)
quay ['ki:, 'keɪ, 'kweɪ] *n* : muelle *m*
queasiness ['kwi:zinəs] *n* : mareo *m*, náusea *f*
queasy ['kwi:zi] *adj* **queasier; -est** : mareado
quebracho *or* **quebracho tree** [keɪ'brɑtʃo:, kɪ-] *n* : quebracho *m*
queen ['kwi:n] *n* : reina *f*
queenly ['kwi:nli] *adj* **queenlier; -est** : de reina, regio
queer¹ ['kwɪr] *adj* **1** : extraño, raro, curioso **2** *sometimes disparaging + offensive* : queer
queer² *n sometimes disparaging + offensive* : queer *mf*
quell ['kwɛl] *vt* : aplastar, sofocar
quench ['kwɛntʃ] *vt* **1** EXTINGUISH : apagar, sofocar **2** SATISFY : saciar, satisfacer (la sed)
query¹ ['kwɪri, 'kwɛr-] *vt* **-ried; -rying** **1** ASK : preguntar, interrogar ⟨to query someone about something : preguntarle a alguien sobre algo⟩ **2** QUESTION, CHALLENGE : cuestionar
query² *n, pl* **-ries** **1** QUESTION : pregunta *f* **2** DOUBT : duda *f*
quesadilla [,keɪsə'di:ə] *n* : quesadilla *f*
quest¹ ['kwɛst] *v* : buscar
quest² *n* : búsqueda *f*
question¹ ['kwɛstʃən] *vt* **1** ASK : preguntar **2** DOUBT : poner en duda, cuestionar **3** INTERROGATE : interrogar — *vi* INQUIRE : preguntar, preguntar
question² *n* **1** QUERY : pregunta *f* ⟨to ask a question : hacer una pregunta⟩ **2** ISSUE : cuestión *f*, asunto *m*, problema *f* **3** POSSIBILITY : posibilidad *f* ⟨it's out of the question : es absolutamente imposible⟩ **4** DOUBT : duda *f* ⟨without question : sin duda⟩ ⟨to call into question : poner en duda⟩ ⟨there's no question about it : no cabe duda⟩ **5 in question** : en cuestión ⟨the book in question : el libro en cuestión⟩
questionable ['kwɛstʃənəbəl] *adj* : cuestionable
questioner ['kwɛstʃənər] *n* : interrogador *m*, -dora *f*
questioning¹ ['kwɛstʃənɪŋ] *adj* : inquisitivo
questioning² *n* INTERROGATION : interrogatorio *m*, interrogación *f*
question mark *n* : signo *m* de interrogación
questionnaire [,kwɛstʃə'nær] *n* : cuestionario *m*
quetzal [kɛt'sɑl] *n, pl* **-zals** *or* **-zales** **1** : quetzal *m* (pájaro) **2** : quetzal *m* (unidad monetaria)
queue¹ ['kju:] *vi* **queued; queuing** *or* **queueing** : hacer cola
queue² *n* LINE : cola *f*, fila *f*
quibble¹ ['kwɪbəl] *vi* **-bled; -bling** : quejarse por nimiedades ⟨to quibble about : quejarse por⟩ ⟨to quibble over : discutir sobre⟩
quibble² *n* : queja *f* (menor)
quiche ['ki:ʃ] *n* : quiche *f* (pastel)
quick¹ ['kwɪk] *adv* : rápidamente

quick² *adj* **1** RAPID : rápido ⟨make it quick : date prisa⟩ ⟨a quick fix : una solución rápida⟩ ⟨she was quick to criticize us : se apresuró a criticarnos⟩ **2** ALERT, CLEVER : listo, vivo, agudo ⟨to have a quick wit/mind : ser muy agudo⟩ **3 a quick temper** : un genio vivo

quick³ *n* **1** FLESH : carne *f* viva **2 to cut someone to the quick** : herir a alguien en lo más vivo

quicken [ˈkwɪkən] *vt* **1** REVIVE : resucitar **2** AROUSE : estimular, despertar **3** HASTEN : acelerar (el paso, etc.)

quickly [ˈkwɪkli] *adv* : rápidamente, rápido

quickness [ˈkwɪknəs] *n* : rapidez *f*

quicksand [ˈkwɪkˌsænd] *n* : arena *f* movediza

quick–tempered [ˈkwɪkˈtɛmpərd] *adj* : de genio vivo

quick–witted [ˈkwɪkˈwɪt̬əd] *adj* : agudo

quid [ˈkwɪd] *n fam* POUND : libra *f* (unidad monetaria)

quiet¹ [ˈkwaɪət] *vt* **1** SILENCE : hacer callar, acallar **2** CALM : calmar, tranquilizar — *vi* **to quiet down** : calmarse, tranquilizarse

quiet² *adv* : silenciosamente

quiet³ *adj* **1** : silencioso ⟨a quiet voice : una voz baja⟩ **2** CALM : tranquilo ⟨a quiet life : una vida tranquila⟩ **3** : callado ⟨be quiet! : ¡cállate!⟩ ⟨to keep quiet about : no decir nada de⟩ **4** MILD : sosegado, suave ⟨a quiet disposition : un temperamento sosegado⟩ **5** UNOBTRUSIVE : discreto **6** SECLUDED : aislado ⟨a quiet nook : un rincón aislado⟩ — **quietly** *adv*

quiet⁴ *n* **1** CALM : calma *f*, tranquilidad *f* **2** SILENCE : silencio *m*

quietness [ˈkwaɪətnəs] *n* : suavidad *f* (de la voz, etc.), quietud *f* (de un lugar, etc.)

quietude [ˈkwaɪəˌtuːd, -ˌtjuːd] *n* : quietud *f*, reposo *m*

quill [ˈkwɪl] *n* **1** : púa *f* (de un puerco espín) **2** : pluma *f* de ave (para escribir)

quilt¹ [ˈkwɪlt] *vt* : acolchar

quilt² *n* : colcha *f*, edredón *m*

quince [ˈkwɪnt̮s] *n* : membrillo *m*

quinine [ˈkwaɪˌnaɪn] *n* : quinina *f*

quintessence [kwɪnˈtɛsənts] *n* : quintaesencia *f*

quintessential [ˌkwɪntəˈsɛtl̩əl] *adj* : arquetípico

quintet [kwɪnˈtɛt] *n* : quinteto *m*

quintuple [kwɪnˈtuːpəl, -ˈtjuː-, -ˈtʌ-;, ˈkwɪntə-] *adj* : quíntuplo

quintuplet [kwɪnˈtʌplət, -ˈtuː-, -ˈtjuː-;, ˈkwɪntə-] *n* : quintillizo *m*, -za *f*

quip¹ [ˈkwɪp] *vi* **quipped; quipping** : bromear

quip² *n* : ocurrencia *f*, salida *f*

quirk [ˈkwərk] *n* : peculiaridad *f*, rareza *f* ⟨a quirk of fate : un capricho del destino⟩

quirky [ˈkwərki] *adj* **quirkier; -est** : peculiar, raro

quit [ˈkwɪt] *v* **quit; quitting** *vt* : dejar, abandonar ⟨to quit smoking : dejar de fumar⟩ ⟨quit complaining! : ¡deja de quejarte!⟩ ⟨quit it! : ¡basta ya!⟩ — *vi* **1** STOP : parar **2** RESIGN : dimitir, renunciar

quite [ˈkwaɪt] *adv* **1** VERY : muy, bastante ⟨quite near : bastante cerca⟩ ⟨quite ill : muy enfermo⟩ **2** COMPLETELY : completamente, totalmente ⟨I'm not quite sure : no estoy del todo seguro⟩ **3** EXACTLY : exactamente ⟨there's nothing quite like Paris : no hay como París⟩ **4** (*used as an intensifier*) ⟨that's quite enough! : ¡basta ya!⟩ ⟨that's quite all right : no fue nada⟩ ⟨I haven't seen her in quite a while : hace bastante tiempo que no la veo⟩ ⟨quite a few things : muchas cosas⟩ ⟨quite a lot/bit of money : bastante dinero⟩ ⟨quite a surprise : una gran sorpresa⟩ ⟨quite an experience : toda una experiencia⟩

quits [ˈkwɪts] *adj* **to call it quits** : quedar en paz

quitter [ˈkwɪt̬ər] *n* : derrotista *mf*

quiver¹ [ˈkwɪvər] *vi* : temblar, estremecerse, vibrar

quiver² *n* **1** : carcaj *m*, aljaba *f* (para flechas) **2** TREMBLING : temblor *m*, estremecimiento *m*

quixotic [kwɪkˈsɑt̬ɪk] *adj* : quijotesco

quiz¹ [ˈkwɪz] *vt* **quizzed; quizzing 1** QUESTION : interrogar **2** TEST : hacerle una prueba a, examinar

quiz² *n, pl* **quizzes** : examen *m* corto, prueba *f*

quizzical [ˈkwɪzɪkəl] *adj* CURIOUS : curioso, interrogativo

quorum [ˈkworəm] *n* : quórum *m*

quota [ˈkwoːt̬ə] *n* : cuota *f*, cupo *m*

quotable [ˈkwoːt̬əbəl] *adj* : citable

quotation [kwoˈteɪ̯ən] *n* **1** CITATION : cita *f* **2** ESTIMATE : presupuesto *m*, estimación *f* **3** PRICE : cotización *f*

quotation marks *npl* : comillas *fpl*

quote¹ [ˈkwoːt] *vt* **quoted; quoting 1** CITE : citar (un pasaje, a un autor, etc.) ⟨don't quote me on that : no lo repitas⟩ ⟨he said, (and I) quote, . . . : dijo textualmente: . . .⟩ **2** : cotizar (en finanzas)

quote² *n* **1** → **quotation 2 quotes** *npl* → **quotation marks 3** ESTIMATE : presupuesto *m*

quotient [ˈkwoːlənt] *n* : cociente *m*

quotidian [kwoˈtɪdiən] *adj* : cotidiano

Quran *or* **Qur'an** → **Koran**

R

r ['ɑr] n, pl r's or rs ['ɑrz] : decimoctava letra del alfabeto inglés

rabbi ['ræ,baɪ] n : rabino m, -na f

rabbit ['ræbət] n, pl -bit or -bits : conejo m, -ja f

rabble ['ræbəl] n 1 MASSES : populacho m 2 RIFFRAFF : chusma f, gentuza f

rabid ['ræbɪd] adj 1 : rabioso, afectado con la rabia 2 FURIOUS : furioso 3 FANATIC : fanático

rabies ['reɪbiːz] ns & pl : rabia f

raccoon [ræ'kuːn] n, pl -coon or -coons : mapache m

race¹ ['reɪs] vi raced; racing 1 : correr, competir (en una carrera) 2 RUSH : ir a toda prisa, ir corriendo

race² n 1 CURRENT : corriente f (de agua) 2 : carrera f ⟨dog race : carrera de perros⟩ ⟨the presidential race : la carrera presidencial⟩ 3 : raza f ⟨all races and creeds : todas las razas y religiones⟩ ⟨the human race : el género humano⟩

race car n : carro/auto/coche m de carreras

race course n : pista f (de carreras)

racehorse ['reɪs,hɔrs] n : caballo m de carreras

racer ['reɪsər] n : corredor m, -dora f

racetrack ['reɪs,træk] n : pista f (de carreras)

racial ['reɪʃəl] adj : racial ⟨racial discrimination : discriminación racial⟩ — racially adv

racing ['reɪsɪŋ] n : carreras fpl

racing shell → shell²

racism ['reɪ,sɪzəm] n : racismo m

racist ['reɪsɪst] n : racista mf

rack¹ ['ræk] vt 1 : atormentar ⟨racked with pain : atormentado por el dolor⟩ 2 to rack one's brains : devanarse los sesos

rack² n SHELF, STAND : estante m ⟨a luggage/roof rack : un portaequipajes, una baca⟩ ⟨a coatrack : un perchero, una percha⟩

racket ['rækət] n 1 or racquet : raqueta f (en deportes) 2 DIN : estruendo m, bulla f, jaleo m fam 3 SWINDLE : estafa f, timo m fam

racketeer [,rækə'tɪr] n : estafador m, -dora f

racy ['reɪsi] adj racier; -est : subido de tono, picante

radar ['reɪ,dɑr] n : radar m

radial ['reɪdiəl] adj : radial

radiance ['reɪdiənts] n : resplandor m

radiant ['reɪdiənt] adj : radiante — radiantly adv

radiate ['reɪdi,eɪt] v -ated; -ating vt : irradiar (calor), emitir (luz) ⟨to radiate happiness : rebosar de alegría⟩ — vi 1 : irradiar 2 or to radiate out SPREAD : extenderse, salir (de un centro)

radiation [,reɪdi'eɪʃən] n : radiación f

radiator ['reɪdi,eɪʈər] n : radiador m

radical¹ ['rædɪkəl] adj : radical — radically [-kli] adv

radical² n : radical mf

radicalism ['rædɪkə,lɪzəm] n : radicalismo m

radii → radius

radio¹ ['reɪdi,oː] v : llamar por radio, transmitir por radio

radio² n, pl -dios : radio m (aparato), radio f (emisora, radiodifusión)

radioactive ['reɪdio'æktɪv] adj : radiactivo, radioactivo

radioactivity [,reɪdio,æk'tɪvəʈi] n, pl -ties : radiactividad f, radioactividad f

radio-controlled adj : teledirigido

radiologist [,reɪdi'ɑləʤɪst] n : radiólogo m, -ga f

radiology [,reɪdi'ɑləʤi] n : radiología f

radio station n : emisora f

radish ['rædɪʃ] n : rábano m

radium ['reɪdiəm] n : radio m

radius ['reɪdiəs] n, pl radii [-di,aɪ] : radio m

radon ['reɪ,dɑn] n : radón m

raffle¹ ['ræfəl] vt -fled; -fling : rifar, sortear

raffle² n : rifa f, sorteo m

raft ['ræft] n 1 : balsa f ⟨rubber rafts : balsas de goma⟩ 2 LOT, SLEW : montón m

rafter ['ræftər] n : par m, viga f

rafting ['ræftɪŋ] n : rafting m

rag ['ræg] n 1 CLOTH : trapo m ⟨rag doll : muñeca de trapo⟩ 2 rags npl TATTERS : harapos mpl, andrajos mpl

ragamuffin ['rægə,mʌfən] n : pilluelo m, -la f

rage¹ ['reɪʤ] vi raged; raging 1 : estar furioso, rabiar ⟨to rage against : clamar contra⟩ 2 : seguir de manera violenta ⟨the wind was raging : el viento bramaba⟩ ⟨the debate raged on : el debate continuaba desenfrenado⟩

rage² n 1 ANGER : furia f, ira f, cólera f ⟨to fly into a rage : enfurecerse⟩ 2 FAD : moda f, furor m

ragged ['rægəd] adj 1 UNEVEN : irregular, desigual 2 TORN : hecho jirones 3 TATTERED : andrajoso, harapiento

ragtime ['ræg,taɪm] n : ragtime m

raid¹ ['reɪd] vt 1 : invadir, hacer una incursión en ⟨raided by enemy troops : invadido por tropas enemigas⟩ 2 : asaltar, atracar ⟨the gang raided the warehouse : la pandilla asaltó el almacén⟩ 3 : allanar, hacer una redada en ⟨police raided the house : la policía allanó la vivienda⟩

raid² n 1 : invasión f (militar) 2 : asalto m (por delincuentes) 3 : redada f, batida f, allanamiento m (por la policía)

raider ['reɪdər] n 1 ATTACKER : asaltante mf; invasor m, -sora f 2 corporate raider : tiburón m

rail¹ ['reɪl] vi 1 to rail against REVILE : denostar contra 2 to rail at SCOLD : regañar, reprender

rail² n 1 BAR : barra f, barrera f 2 HANDRAIL : pasamanos m, barandilla f 3

TRACK : riel *m* (para ferrocarriles) **4** RAILROAD : ferrocarril *m*

railing ['reɪlɪŋ] *n* **1** : baranda *f* (de un balcón, etc.) **2** RAILS : verja *f*

raillery ['reɪləri] *n, pl* **-leries** : bromas *fpl*

railroad ['reɪl,ro:d] *n* : ferrocarril *m*

railroad tie → **tie²**

railroad track → **track²**

railway ['reɪl,weɪ] → **railroad**

raiment ['reɪmənt] *n* : vestiduras *fpl*

rain¹ ['reɪn] *vi* **1** : llover ⟨it's raining : está lloviendo⟩ **2 to rain down** : llover ⟨insults rained down on him : le llovieron los insultos⟩

rain² *n* : lluvia *f*

rainbow ['reɪn,bo:] *n* : arco *m* iris

raincoat ['reɪn,ko:t] *n* : impermeable *m*

raindrop ['reɪn,drɑp] *n* : gota *f* de lluvia

rainfall ['reɪn,fɔl] *n* : lluvia *f*, precipitación *f*

rain forest *n* : bosque *m* tropical

rainstorm ['reɪn,stɔrm] *n* : temporal *m* (de lluvia)

rainwater ['reɪn,wɔtər] *n* : agua *f* de lluvia

rainy ['reɪni] *adj* **rainier; -est** : lluvioso

raise¹ ['reɪz] *vt* **raised; raising 1** LIFT : levantar, subir, alzar ⟨to raise someone's spirits : levantarle el ánimo a alguien⟩ **2** ERECT : levantar, erigir **3** COLLECT : recaudar ⟨to raise money : recaudar dinero⟩ **4** REAR : criar ⟨she raised her two children : crió a sus dos niños⟩ **5** GROW : cultivar **6** INCREASE : aumentar, subir ⟨to raise one's voice : levantar la voz⟩ **7** PROMOTE : ascender **8** PROVOKE : provocar ⟨it raised a laugh : provocó una risa⟩ **9** BRING UP : sacar (temas, objeciones, etc.)

raise² *n* : aumento *m*

raisin ['reɪzən] *n* : pasa *f*

raja *or* **rajah** ['rɑʤə, -,ʤɑ, -,ʒɑ] *n* : rajá *m*

rake¹ ['reɪk] *v* **raked; raking** *vt* **1** : rastrillar ⟨to rake (up) leaves : rastrillar las hojas⟩ **2** SWEEP : barrer ⟨raked with gunfire : barrido con balas⟩ **3 to rake it in** : hacer mucho dinero — *vi* **to rake through** : revolver, hurgar en

rake² *n* **1** : rastrillo *m* **2** LIBERTINE : libertino *m*, -na *f*; calavera *m*

rakish ['reɪkɪʃ] *adj* **1** JAUNTY : desenvuelto, desenfadado **2** DISSOLUTE : libertino, disoluto

rally¹ ['ræli] *v* **-lied; -lying** *vi* **1** MEET, GATHER : reunirse, congregarse **2** RECOVER : recuperarse **3 to rally against** : unirse en contra de **4 to rally around** : juntarse para apoyar (algo/a alguien) **5 to rally for/behind** : unirse a favor de — *vt* **1** ASSEMBLE : reunir (tropas, etc.) **2** RECOVER : recobrar (la fuerza, etc.)

rally² *n, pl* **-lies** : reunión *f*, mitin *m*, manifestación *f*

ram¹ ['ræm] *v* **rammed; ramming** *vt* **1** DRIVE : hincar, clavar ⟨he rammed it into the ground : lo hincó en la tierra⟩ **2** SMASH : estrellar, embestir — *vi* COLLIDE : chocar (contra), estrellarse

ram² *n* **1** : carnero *m* (animal) **2 battering ram** : ariete *m*

RAM ['ræm] *n* : RAM *f*, memoria *f* de acceso aleatorio

Ramadan ['rɑmə,dɑn] *n* : Ramadán *m*

ramble¹ ['ræmbəl] *vi* **-bled; -bling 1** WANDER : pasear, deambular **2 to ramble on** : divagar, perder el hilo **3** SPREAD : trepar (dícese de una planta)

ramble² *n* : paseo *m*, excursión *f*

rambler ['ræmblər] *n* **1** WALKER : excursionista *mf* **2** ROSE : rosa *f* trepadora

rambling ['ræmblɪŋ] *adj* **1** : laberíntico **2** DISJOINTED : inconexo, incoherente

rambunctious [ræm'bʌŋkləs] *adj* UNRULY : alborotado

ramification [,ræməfə'keɪʒən] *n* : ramificación *f*

ramp ['ræmp] *n* : rampa *f*

rampage¹ ['ræm,peɪʤ, ræm'peɪʤ] *vi* **-paged; -paging** : andar arrasando todo, correr destrozando

rampage² ['ræm,peɪʤ] *n* : alboroto *m*, frenesí *m* (de violencia)

rampant ['ræmpənt] *adj* : desenfrenado

rampart ['ræm,pɑrt] *n* : terraplén *m*, muralla *f*

ramrod ['ræm,rɑd] *n* : baqueta *f*

ramshackle ['ræm,ʃækəl] *adj* : destartalado

ran → **run**

ranch¹ ['ræntʃ] *vi* : trabajar en una hacienda *f* — *vt* : criar (ganado)

ranch² *n* **1** : hacienda *f*, rancho *m*, finca *f* ganadera **2** *or* **ranch house** : casa *f* (en una hacienda) **3** *or* **ranch house** : casa *f* de una sola planta

ranch dressing *n* : aderezo *m* a base de leche de manteca, mayonesa, y hierbas

rancher ['ræntʃər] *n* : estanciero *m*, -ra *f*; ranchero *m*, -ra *f*

rancid ['rænsɪd] *adj* : rancio

rancor ['ræŋkər] *n* : rencor *m* — **rancorous** ['ræŋkərəs] *adj*

random ['rændəm] *adj* **1** : fortuito, aleatorio **2 at ~** : al azar — **randomly** *adv*

random-access memory *n* : memoria *f* de acceso aleatorio, RAM *f*

rang → **ring**

range¹ ['reɪnʤ] *v* **ranged; ranging** *vt* ARRANGE : alinear, ordenar, arreglar — *vi* **1** ROAM : deambular **2** EXTEND : extenderse ⟨the results range widely : los resultados se extienden mucho⟩ **3** VARY : variar ⟨discounts range from 20% to 40% : los descuentos varían entre 20% y 40%⟩

range² *n* **1** ROW : fila *f*, hilera *f* ⟨a mountain range : una cordillera⟩ **2** GRASSLAND : pradera *f*, pampa *f* **3** STOVE : cocina *f* **4** VARIETY : variedad *f*, gama *f* **5** SPHERE : ámbito *m*, esfera *f*, campo *m* **6** REACH : registro *m* (de la voz), alcance *m* (de un arma de fuego) ⟨out of range : fuera del alcance⟩ ⟨at close range : de cerca⟩ **7 shooting range** : campo *m* de tiro

ranger ['reɪnʤər] *n or* **forest ranger** : guardabosque *m*

rangy ['reɪnʤi] *adj* **rangier; -est** : alto y delgado

rank[1] [ˈræŋk] vt **1** RANGE : alinear, ordenar, poner en fila **2** CLASSIFY : clasificar — vi **1 to rank above** : ser superior a **2 to rank among** : encontrarse entre, figurar entre

rank[2] adj **1** SMELLY : fétido, maloliente **2** OUTRIGHT : completo, absoluto ⟨a rank injustice : una injusticia manifiesta⟩

rank[3] n **1** LINE, ROW : fila f ⟨to close ranks : cerrar filas⟩ **2** GRADE, POSITION : grado m, rango m (militar) ⟨to pull rank : abusar de su autoridad⟩ **3** CLASS : categoría f, clase f **4 ranks** npl : soldados mpl rasos

rank and file n **1** RANKS : soldados mpl rasos **2** : bases fpl (de un partido, etc.)

rankle [ˈræŋkəl] v **-kled; -kling** vi : doler — vt : irritar, herir

ransack [ˈrænˌsæk] vt : revolver, desvalijar, registrar de arriba abajo

ransom[1] [ˈræntsəm] vt : rescatar, pagar un rescate por

ransom[2] n : rescate m

ransomware [ˈræntsəmˌwær] n : ransomware m, virus m de secuestro de datos

rant [ˈrænt] vi or **to rant and rave** : despotricar, desvariar

rap[1] [ˈræp] v **rapped; rapping** vt **1** KNOCK : golpetear, dar un golpe en **2** CRITICIZE : criticar — vi **1** CHAT : charlar, cotorrear fam **2** KNOCK : dar un golpe

rap[2] n **1** BLOW, KNOCK : golpe m, golpecito m **2** CHAT : charla f **3** or **rap music** : rap m **4 to take the rap** : pagar el pato fam

rapacious [rəˈpeɪləs] adj GREEDY : avaricioso, codicioso

rape[1] [ˈreɪp] vt **raped; raping** : violar

rape[2] n **1** : colza f (planta) **2** : violación f (de una persona)

rapid [ˈræpɪd] adj : rápido — **rapidly** adv

rapidity [rəˈpɪdəti] n : rapidez f

rapids [ˈræpɪdz] npl : rápidos mpl

rapier [ˈreɪpiər] n : estoque m

rapist [ˈreɪpɪst] n : violador m, -dora f

rapper [ˈræpər] n : cantante mf de rap; rapero m, -ra f

rapport [ræˈpor] n : relación f armoniosa, entendimiento m

rapprochement [ˌræˌproːˈmɑnt] n : acercamiento m, aproximación f

rapt [ˈræpt] adj : absorto, embelesado

rapture [ˈræptʃər] n : éxtasis m

rapturous [ˈræptʃərəs] adj : extasiado, embelesado

rare [ˈrær] adj **rarer; rarest 1** FINE : excelente, excepcional ⟨a rare talent : un talento excepcional⟩ **2** UNCOMMON : raro, poco común **3** : poco cocido (dícese de la carne)

rarefy [ˈrærəˌfaɪ] vt **-fied; -fying** : enrarecer

rarely [ˈrærli] adv SELDOM : pocas veces, rara vez

raring [ˈrærən, -ɪŋ] adj : lleno de entusiasmo, con muchas ganas

rarity [ˈrærəti] n, pl **-ties** : rareza f

rascal [ˈræskəl] n : pillo m, -lla f; pícaro m, -ra f

rash[1] [ˈræʃ] adj : imprudente, precipitado — **rashly** adv

rash[2] n : sarpullido m, erupción f

rashness [ˈræʃnəs] n : precipitación f

rasp[1] [ˈræsp] vt **1** SCRAPE : raspar **2** : decir en voz áspera — vi : hacer un ruido áspero

rasp[2] n : escofina f

raspberry [ˈræzˌbɛri] n, pl **-ries** : frambuesa f

rat [ˈræt] n : rata f

ratchet [ˈrætʃət] n : trinquete m

rate[1] [ˈreɪt] vt **rated; rating 1** CONSIDER, REGARD : considerar, estimar **2** DESERVE : merecer

rate[2] n **1** SPEED, PACE : velocidad f, ritmo m ⟨at this rate : a este paso⟩ **2** : índice m, tasa f ⟨birth rate : índice de natalidad⟩ ⟨interest rate : tasa de interés⟩ **3** CHARGE, PRICE : precio m, tarifa f **4 at any rate** ANYWAY : de todos modos **5 at any rate** AT LEAST : al menos, por lo menos

rather [ˈræðər, ˈrɑ-, ˈrɑ-] adv **1** (indicating preference) ⟨she would rather stay : preferiría quedarse⟩ ⟨I'd rather not : mejor que no⟩ **2** (indicating preciseness) ⟨my father, or rather, my stepfather : mi padre, o mejor dicho mi padrastro⟩ **3** INSTEAD : sino que, más que, al contrario ⟨I'm not pleased; rather, I'm disappointed : no estoy satisfecho, sino desilusionado⟩ **4** SOMEWHAT : algo, un tanto ⟨rather strange : un poco extraño⟩ **5** QUITE : bastante ⟨rather difficult : bastante difícil⟩ **6** ~ **than** INSTEAD OF : en vez de

ratification [ˌrætəfəˈkeɪʃən] n : ratificación f

ratify [ˈrætəˌfaɪ] vt **-fied; -fying** : ratificar

rating [ˈreɪtɪŋ] n **1** STANDING : clasificación f, posición f **2 ratings** npl : índice m de audiencia

ratio [ˈreɪʃio] n, pl **-tios** : proporción f, relación f

ration[1] [ˈræʃən, ˈreɪʃən] vt : racionar

ration[2] n **1** : ración f **2 rations** npl PROVISIONS : víveres mpl

rational [ˈræʃənəl] adj **1** : racional **2** REASONABLE : razonable, racional — **rationally** adv — **rationality** [ˌræʃəˈnæləti] n

rationale [ˌræʃəˈnæl] n **1** EXPLANATION : explicación f **2** BASIS : base f, razones fpl

rationalize [ˈræʃənəˌlaɪz] vt **-ized; -izing** : racionalizar — **rationalization** [ˌræʃənələˈzeɪʃən] n

rat race n : competencia f laboral (excesiva)

rattle[1] [ˈrætəl] v **-tled; -tling** vi **1** CLATTER : traquetear, hacer ruido **2 to rattle on** CHATTER : parlotear fam — vt **1** : hacer sonar, agitar ⟨the wind rattled the door : el viento sacudió la puerta⟩ **2** DISCONCERT, WORRY : desconcertar, poner nervioso **3 to rattle off** : despachar, recitar, decir de corrido

rattle[2] n **1** CLATTER : traqueteo m, ruido m **2** : sonajero m (para bebés) **3** : cascabel m (de una culebra)

rattler [ˈrætələr] → **rattlesnake**

rattlesnake ['ræt̬əlˌsneɪk] *n* : serpiente *f* de cascabel

ratty ['ræt̬i] *adj* **rattier; -est** : raído, andrajoso

raucous ['rɔkəs] *adj* **1** HOARSE : ronco **2** BOISTEROUS : escandaloso, bullicioso — **raucously** *adv*

ravage¹ ['rævɪdʒ] *vt* **-aged; -aging** : devastar, arrasar, hacer estragos

ravage² *n* : destrozo *m*, destrucción *f* ⟨the ravages of war : los estragos de la guerra⟩

rave ['reɪv] *vi* **raved; raving 1** : delirar, desvariar **2 to rave about** : hablar con entusiasmo sobre, entusiasmarse por

ravel ['rævəl] *v* **-eled** *or* **-elled; -eling** *or* **-elling** *vt* UNRAVEL : desenredar, desenmarañar — *vi* FRAY : deshilacharse

raven ['reɪvən] *n* : cuervo *m*

ravenous ['rævənəs] *adj* : hambriento, voraz — **ravenously** *adv*

ravine [rə'viːn] *n* : barranco *m*, quebrada *f*

ravings ['reɪvɪŋz] *npl* : desvaríos *mpl*, delirios *mpl*

ravioli [ˌrævi'oːli] *ns & pl* : raviolis *mpl*, ravioles *mpl*

ravish ['rævɪʃ] *vt* **1** PLUNDER : saquear **2** ENCHANT : embelesar, cautivar, encantar

ravishing ['rævɪʃɪŋ] *adj* : deslumbrante, impresionante (dícese de la belleza, etc.)

raw ['rɔ] *adj* **rawer; rawest 1** : crudo ⟨raw meat : carne cruda⟩ **2** UNTREATED : sin tratar, sin refinar, puro ⟨raw data : datos en bruto⟩ ⟨raw materials : materias primas⟩ **3** INEXPERIENCED : novato, inexperto **4** SORE, CHAFED : en carne viva **5** : frío y húmedo ⟨a raw day : un día crudo⟩ **6** UNFAIR : injusto ⟨a raw deal : un trato injusto, una injusticia⟩

rawhide ['rɔˌhaɪd] *n* : cuero *m* sin curtir

ray ['reɪ] *n* **1** : rayo *m* (de la luz, etc.) ⟨a ray of hope : un resquicio de esperanza⟩ **2** : raya *f* (pez)

rayon ['reɪˌɑn] *n* : rayón *m*

raze ['reɪz] *vt* **razed; razing** : arrasar, demoler

razor ['reɪzər] *n* **1** *or* **straight razor** : navaja *f* de afeitar **2** *or* **safety razor** : maquinilla *f* de afeitar, rastrillo *m* *Mex* **3** *or* **electric razor** SHAVER : afeitadora *f*, rasuradora *f* **4** *or* **razor blade** : hoja *f* de afeitar, cuchilla *f* de afeitar

re ['reɪ] *n* : re *m* (en el canto)

re- [ˌriː] *pref* : re-

reach¹ ['riːtʃ] *vt* **1** EXTEND : extender, alargar ⟨to reach out one's hand : extender la mano⟩ **2** : alcanzar ⟨I couldn't reach the apple : no pude alcanzar la manzana⟩ **3** : llegar a/hasta ⟨the shadow reached the wall : la sombra llegó hasta la pared⟩ **4** CONTACT : contactar, ponerse en contacto con — *vi* **1** *or* **to reach out** : extender la mano **2** STRETCH : extenderse **3 to reach for** : tratar de agarrar

reach² *n* : alcance *m*, extensión *f* ⟨within reach : a mi/tu (etc.) alcance⟩ ⟨within reach of : al alcance de⟩ ⟨out of reach : fuera de mi/tu (etc.) alcance⟩

react [ri'ækt] *vi* : reaccionar

reaction [ri'ækʃən] *n* : reacción *f*

reactionary¹ [ri'ækʃəˌneri] *adj* : reaccionario

reactionary² *n, pl* **-ries** : reaccionario *m*, -ria *f*

reactivate [ri'æktəˌveɪt] *vt* **-vated; -vating** : reactivar — **reactivation** *n*

reactor [ri'æktər] *n* : reactor *m* ⟨nuclear reactor : reactor nuclear⟩

read¹ ['riːd] *v* **read** ['rɛd]; **reading** *vt* **1** : leer ⟨to read a story : leer un cuento⟩ **2** INTERPRET : interpretar ⟨it can be read two ways : se puede interpretar de dos maneras⟩ **3** : decir, poner ⟨the sign read "No smoking" : el letrero decía "No Fumar"⟩ **4** : marcar ⟨the thermometer reads 70° : el termómetro marca 70°⟩ **5 to read aloud/out** : leer en voz alta **6 to read between the lines** : leer entre las líneas **7 to read into something** : buscarle el significado a algo ⟨don't read too much into it : no le des demasiada importancia⟩ **8 to read through/over** : leer (del principio al fin) **9 to read up on** : documentarse sobre — *vi* **1** : leer ⟨he can read : sabe leer⟩ **2** SAY : decir ⟨the list reads as follows : la lista dice lo siguiente⟩

read² *n* **to be a good read** : ser una lectura amena

readable ['riːdəbəl] *adj* : legible

reader ['riːdər] *n* : lector *m*, -tora *f*

readership ['riːdərˌʃɪp] *n* : lectores *mpl*

readily ['rɛdəli] *adv* **1** WILLINGLY : de buena gana, con gusto **2** EASILY : fácilmente, con facilidad

readiness ['rɛdinəs] *n* **1** WILLINGNESS : buena disposición *f* **2 to be in readiness** : estar preparado

reading ['riːdɪŋ] *n* : lectura *f*

readjust [ˌriːə'dʒʌst] *vt* : reajustar — *vi* : volverse a adaptar

readjustment [ˌriːə'dʒʌstmənt] *n* : reajuste *m*

readout ['riːdˌaʊt] *n* : lectura *f* (en informática)

ready¹ ['rɛdi] *vt* **readied; readying** : preparar

ready² *adj* **readier; -est 1** PREPARED : listo, preparado ⟨they'll be ready soon : enseguida están listos⟩ ⟨to be ready to : estar listo para⟩ ⟨to make ready : prepararse⟩ **2** WILLING : dispuesto ⟨ready and willing : dispuesto a todo⟩ **3** : a punto de ⟨ready to cry : a punto de llorar⟩ **4** AVAILABLE : disponible ⟨ready cash/money : efectivo⟩ **5** QUICK : vivo, agudo ⟨a ready wit : un ingenio agudo⟩

ready–made ['rɛdi'meɪd] *adj* : preparado, confeccionado

reaffirm [ˌriːə'fərm] *vt* : reafirmar

real¹ ['riːl] *adv fam* VERY : muy ⟨we had a real good time : lo pasamos muy bien⟩

real² *adj* **1** : inmobiliario ⟨real property : bien inmueble, bien raíz⟩ **2** GENUINE : auténtico, genuino **3** ACTUAL, TRUE : real, verdadero ⟨a real friend : un verdadero amigo⟩ **4 for real** SERIOUSLY : de veras, de verdad **5 for real** GEN-

UINE, TRUE : auténtico, verdadero **6 for real** SINCERE : sincero ⟨is that guy for real? : ¿nos está tomando el pelo?⟩ **7 get real!** *fam* : ¡no te engañes! **8 to keep it real** *fam* : ser sincero, no darse aires

real³ [reɪˈɑl] *n, pl* **reais** [ˈreɪɪ] *or* **reis** [ˈreɪɪ] : real *m* (unidad monetaria)

real estate *n* : propiedad *f* inmobiliaria, bienes *mpl* raíces

real estate agent *n* : agente *m* inmobiliario, agente *f* inmobiliaria

realign [ˌriːəˈlaɪn] *vt* : realinear — **realignment** [ˌriːəˈlaɪnmənt] *n*

realism [ˈriːəˌlɪzəm] *n* : realismo *m*

realist [ˈriːəlɪst] *n* : realista *mf*

realistic [ˌriːəˈlɪstɪk] *adj* : realista

realistically [ˌriːəˈlɪstɪkli] *adv* : de manera realista

reality [riˈæləti] *n, pl* **-ties** : realidad *f*

reality TV *or* **reality television** *n* : telerrealidad *f*

realizable [ˌriːəˈlaɪzəbəl] *adj* : realizable, asequible

realization [ˌriːələˈzeɪlən] *n* : realización *f*

realize [ˈriːəˌlaɪz] *vt* **-ized; -izing 1** UNDERSTAND : darse cuenta de, saber **2** FULFILL : realizar (sueños, etc.) ⟨my worst fears were realized : mis mayores temores se hicieron realidad⟩ **3** ACCOMPLISH : realizar, llevar a cabo **4** EARN : obtener, realizar

really [ˈrɪli, ˈriː-] *adv* **1** ACTUALLY : de verdad, en realidad ⟨really good : buenísimo⟩ **2** TRULY : verdaderamente, realmente ⟨I really don't care : la verdad es que no me importa⟩ **3** FRANKLY : francamente, en serio

realm [ˈrɛlm] *n* **1** KINGDOM : reino *m* **2** SPHERE : esfera *f*, campo *m*

Realtor [ˈriːltər, -ˌtɔr] *service mark* se usa para un agente inmobiliario autorizado

ream [ˈriːm] *n* **1** : resma *f* (de papel) **2 reams** *npl* LOADS : montones *mpl*

reap [ˈriːp] *v* : cosechar

reaper [ˈriːpər] *n* **1** : cosechador *m*, -dora *f* (persona) ⟨the Grim Reaper : la muerte⟩ **2** : cosechadora *f* (máquina)

reappear [ˌriːəˈpɪr] *vi* : reaparecer

reappearance [ˌriːəˈpɪrənts] *n* : reaparición *f*

rear¹ [ˈrɪr] *vt* **1** LIFT, RAISE : levantar **2** BREED, BRING UP : criar — *vi or* **to rear up** : encabritarse

rear² *adj* : trasero, posterior, de atrás

rear³ *n* **1** BACK : parte *f* de atrás ⟨to bring up the rear : cerrar la marcha⟩ **2** *or* **rear end** : trasero *m*

rear admiral *n* : contraalmirante *mf*

rearrange [ˌriːəˈreɪndʒ] *vt* **-ranged; -ranging** : colocar de otra manera, volver a arreglar, reorganizar

rearview mirror [ˈrɪrˌvjuː-] *n* : retrovisor *m*

reason¹ [ˈriːzən] *vt* THINK : pensar — *vi* : razonar ⟨I can't reason with her : no puedo razonar con ella⟩ — **reasoned** [ˈriːzənd] *adj*

reason² *n* **1** CAUSE, GROUND : razón *f*, motivo *m* ⟨the reason for his trip : el mo-

tivo de su viaje⟩ ⟨for this reason : por esta razón, por lo cual⟩ ⟨for no (good) reason : sin razón⟩ ⟨he's the champion for a reason : por algo es el campeón⟩ ⟨the reason why : la razón por la cual, el porqué⟩ ⟨to have reason to : tener motivos para⟩ **2** SENSE : razón *f* ⟨to listen to reason, to see reason : avenirse a razones⟩ ⟨to stand to reason : ser lógico⟩ ⟨within reason : dentro de lo razonable⟩

reasonable [ˈriːzənəbəl] *adj* **1** SENSIBLE : razonable **2** INEXPENSIVE : barato, económico

reasonably [ˈriːzənəbli] *adv* **1** SENSIBLY : razonablemente **2** FAIRLY : bastante

reasoning [ˈriːzənɪŋ] *n* : razonamiento *m*, raciocinio *m*, argumentos *mpl*

reassess [ˌriːəˈsɛs] *vt* : revaluar, reconsiderar

reassurance [ˌriːəˈʃʊrənts] *n* : consuelo *m*, palabras *fpl* alentadoras

reassure [ˌriːəˈʃʊr] *vt* **-sured; -suring** : tranquilizar

reassuring [ˌriːəˈʃʊrɪŋ] *adj* : tranquilizador

reawaken [ˌriːəˈweɪkən] *vt* : volver a despertar, reavivar

rebate [ˈriːˌbeɪt] *n* : reembolso *m*, devolución *f*

rebel¹ [rɪˈbɛl] *vi* **-belled; -belling** : rebelarse, sublevarse

rebel² [ˈrɛbəl] *adj* : rebelde

rebel³ [ˈrɛbəl] *n* : rebelde *mf*

rebellion [rɪˈbɛljən] *n* : rebelión *f*

rebellious [rɪˈbɛljəs] *adj* : rebelde

rebelliousness [rɪˈbɛljəsnəs] *n* : rebeldía *f*

rebirth [ˌriːˈbərθ] *n* : renacimiento *m*

reboot [riˈbuːt] *vt* : reiniciar (una computadora)

reborn [riːˈbɔrn] *adj* **to be reborn** : renacer

rebound¹ [ˈriːˌbaʊnd, rɪˈbaʊnd] *vi* : rebotar

rebound² [ˈriːˌbaʊnd] *n* : rebote *m*

rebuff¹ [rɪˈbʌf] *vt* : desairar, rechazar

rebuff² *n* : desaire *m*, rechazo *m*

rebuild [ˌriːˈbɪld] *vt* **-built** [-ˈbɪlt]; **-building** : reconstruir

rebuke¹ [rɪˈbjuːk] *vt* **-buked; -buking** : reprender, regañar

rebuke² *n* : reprimenda *f*, reproche *m*

rebut [rɪˈbʌt] *vt* **-butted; -butting** : rebatir, refutar

rebuttal [rɪˈbʌtəl] *n* : refutación *f*

recalcitrant [rɪˈkælsətrənt] *adj* : recalcitrante

recall¹ [rɪˈkɔl] *vt* **1** : llamar, retirar ⟨recalled to active duty : llamado al servicio activo⟩ **2** REMEMBER : recordar, acordarse de **3** REVOKE : revocar

recall² [rɪˈkɔl, ˈriːˌkɔl] *n* **1** : retirada *f* (de personas o mercancías) **2** MEMORY : memoria *f* ⟨to have total recall : poder recordar todo⟩

recant [rɪˈkænt] *vt* : retractarse de — *vi* : retractarse, renegar

recap¹ [ˈriːˌkæp] *v* **-capped; -capping** *fam* → **recapitulate**

recap² [ˈriːˌkæp] *n* SUMMARY : resumen *m*

recapitulate [ˌriːkəˈpɪtləˌleɪt] *v* **-lated; -lating** : resumir, recapitular

recapture [ˌri:'kæptʃər] *vt* **-tured; -turing 1** : volver a capturar **2** REGAIN : recuperar

recast [ri:'kæst] *vt* **-cast; -casting 1** : cambiar el reparto de (una película, etc.), cambiarle el papel a (un actor) **2** REWRITE : refundir

recede [rɪ'si:d] *vi* **-ceded; -ceding 1** WITHDRAW : retirarse, retroceder **2** FADE : desvanecerse, alejarse **3** SLANT : inclinarse **4 to have a receding hairline** : tener entradas

receipt [rɪ'si:t] *n* **1** : recibo *m*, boleta *f*, ticket *m* **2 receipts** *npl* : ingresos *mpl*, entradas *fpl*

receivable [rɪ'si:vəbəl] *adj* **accounts receivable** : cuentas por cobrar

receive [rɪ'si:v] *vt* **-ceived; -ceiving 1** GET : recibir (una carta, un golpe, etc.) **2** WELCOME : acoger, recibir ⟨to receive guests : tener invitados⟩ **3** : recibir, captar (señales de radio)

receiver [rɪ'si:vər] *n* **1** : receptor *m*, -tora *f* (en futbol americano) **2** : receptor *m* (de radio o televisión) **3** *or* **telephone receiver** : auricular *m*

recent ['ri:sənt] *adj* : reciente — **recently** *adv*

receptacle [rɪ'sɛptɪkəl] *n* : receptáculo *m*, recipiente *m*

reception [rɪ'sɛpʃən] *n* : recepción *f* ⟨reception desk : recepción⟩ ⟨reception area : vestíbulo⟩

receptionist [rɪ'sɛpʃənɪst] *n* : recepcionista *mf*

receptive [rɪ'sɛptɪv] *adj* : receptivo — **receptivity** [ˌri:ˌsɛp'tɪvəti] *n*

receptiveness [rɪ'sɛptɪvnəs] *n* : receptividad *f*

recess[1] ['ri:ˌsɛs, rɪ'sɛs] *vt* ADJOURN : suspender, levantar

recess[2] *n* **1** ALCOVE : hueco *m*, nicho *m* **2** BREAK : receso *m*, descanso *m*, recreo *m* (en el colegio)

recessed ['ri:ˌsɛst, rɪ'sɛst] *adj* : empotrado

recession [rɪ'sɛʃən] *n* : recesión *f*, depresión *f* económica

recessive [rɪ'sɛsɪv] *adj* : recesivo

recharge [ˌri:'tʃɑrdʒ] *vt* **-charged; -charging** : recargar

rechargeable [ˌri:'tʃɑrdʒəbəl] *adj* : recargable

recidivism [rɪ'sɪdəˌvɪzəm] *n* : reincidencia *f*

recidivist [rɪ'sɪdəvɪst] *n* : reincidente *mf* — **recidivist** *adj*

recipe ['rɛsəˌpi:] *n* : receta *f*

recipient [rɪ'sɪpiənt] *n* : recipiente *mf*

reciprocal [rɪ'sɪprəkəl] *adj* : recíproco

reciprocate [rɪ'sɪprəˌkeɪt] *vi* **-cated; -cating** : reciprocar

reciprocity [ˌrɛsə'prɑsəti] *n*, *pl* **-ties** : reciprocidad *f*

recital [rɪ'saɪtəl] *n* **1** PERFORMANCE : recital *m* **2** ENUMERATION : relato *m*, enumeración *f*

recitation [ˌrɛsə'teɪʃən] *n* : recitación *f*

recite [rɪ'saɪt] *vt* **-cited; -citing 1** : recitar (un poema, etc.) **2** LIST : enumerar

reckless ['rɛkləs] *adj* : imprudente, temerario — **recklessly** *adv*

recklessness ['rɛkləsnəs] *n* : imprudencia *f*, temeridad *f*

reckon ['rɛkən] *vt* **1** *fam* THINK, SUPPOSE : creer ⟨I reckon so : creo que sí⟩ **2** CALCULATE : calcular, contar **3** CONSIDER : considerar **4 to reckon on/with** : contar con **5 to reckon with** : enfrentarse a ⟨they'll have me to reckon with : se las verán conmigo⟩ ⟨to be a force to be reckoned with : ser algo/alguien de temer⟩

reckoning ['rɛkənɪŋ] *n* **1** CALCULATION : cálculo *m* **2** SETTLEMENT : ajuste *m* de cuentas ⟨day of reckoning : día del juicio final⟩

reclaim [rɪ'kleɪm] *vt* **1** : ganar (tierra) ⟨to reclaim marshy land : sanear las tierras pantanosas⟩ **2** RECOVER : recobrar, reciclar ⟨to reclaim old tires : reciclar llantas desechadas⟩ **3** REGAIN : reclamar, recuperar ⟨to reclaim one's rights : reclamar uno sus derechos⟩

recline [rɪ'klaɪn] *vi* **-clined; -clining 1** LEAN : reclinarse **2** REPOSE : recostarse

reclining [rɪ'klaɪnɪŋ] *adj* : reclinable

recluse ['rɛˌklu:s, rɪ'klu:s] *n* : solitario *m*, -ria *f*

recognition [ˌrɛkɪg'nɪʃən] *n* : reconocimiento *m*

recognizable ['rɛkəgˌnaɪzəbəl] *adj* : reconocible

recognize ['rɛkɪgˌnaɪz] *vt* **-nized; -nizing** : reconocer

recoil[1] [rɪ'kɔɪl] *vi* : retroceder, dar un culatazo

recoil[2] ['ri:ˌkɔɪl, rɪ'-] *n* : retroceso *m*, culatazo *m*

recollect [ˌrɛkə'lɛkt] *v* : recordar

recollection [ˌrɛkə'lɛkʃən] *n* : recuerdo *m*

recommend [ˌrɛkə'mɛnd] *vt* **1** : recomendar **2** ADVISE, COUNSEL : aconsejar, recomendar

recommendation [ˌrɛkəmən'deɪʃən] *n* : recomendación *f*

recompense[1] ['rɛkəmˌpɛnts] *vt* **-pensed; -pensing** : indemnizar, recompensar

recompense[2] *n* : indemnización *f*, compensación *f*

reconcile ['rɛkənˌsaɪl] *v* **-ciled; -ciling 1** : reconciliar (personas), conciliar (ideas, etc.) **2 to reconcile oneself to** : resignarse a — *vi* MAKE UP : reconciliarse, hacer las paces

reconciliation [ˌrɛkənˌsɪli'eɪʃən] *n* : reconciliación *f* (con personas), conciliación *f* (con ideas, etc.)

recondition [ˌri:kən'dɪʃən] *vt* : reacondicionar

reconnaissance [rɪ'kɑnəzənts, -sənts] *n* : reconocimiento *m*

reconnoiter *or* **reconnoitre** [ˌri:kə'nɔɪtər, ˌrɛkə-] *v* **-tered** *or* **-tred; -tering** *or* **-tring** *vt* : reconocer — *vi* : hacer un reconocimiento

reconquer [ˌri:'kɑŋkər] *vt* : reconquistar

reconquest [ˌri:'kɑnˌkwɛst, -'kɑŋ-] *n* : reconquista *f*

reconsider [ˌri:kən'sɪdər] *vt* : reconsiderar, repensar

reconsideration [ˌriːkənˌsɪdəˈreɪʃən] *n* : reconsideración *f*

reconstruct [ˌriːkənˈstrʌkt] *vt* : reconstruir

reconstruction [ˌriːkənˈstrʌkʃən] *n* : reconstrucción *f*

reconstructive [ˌriːkənˈstrʌktɪv] *adj* : reconstructivo

record[1] [rɪˈkɔrd] *vt* **1** WRITE DOWN : anotar, apuntar **2** REGISTER : registrar, hacer constar **3** INDICATE : marcar (una temperatura, etc.) **4** : grabar (audio o video)

record[2] [ˈrɛkərd] *adj* : récord

record[3] [ˈrɛkərd] *n* **1** DOCUMENT : registro *m*, documento *m* oficial **2** HISTORY : historial *m* ⟨a good academic record : un buen historial académico⟩ ⟨criminal record : antecedentes penales⟩ **3** : récord *m* ⟨the world record : el récord mundial⟩ **4** : disco *m* (de música, etc.) **5 for the record** : que conste **6 off the record** : extraoficialmente **7 on record** ⟨he is on record as saying . . . : dijo públicamente que . . .⟩ **8 on record** : registrado ⟨the highest on record : el más alto registrado⟩ **9 on the record** : oficialmente **10 to set the record straight** : poner las cosas en su lugar

recorder [rɪˈkɔrdər] *n* **1** : flauta *f* dulce (instrumento de viento) **2 tape recorder** : grabadora *f*

recording [rɪˈkɔrdɪŋ] *n* : grabación *f*

record player *n* : tocadiscos *m*

recount[1] [rɪˈkaʊnt] *vt* **1** NARRATE : narrar, relatar **2** : volver a contar (votos, etc.)

recount[2] [ˈriːˌkaʊnt, ˌrɪ-] *n* : recuento *m*

recoup [rɪˈkuːp] *vt* : recuperar, recobrar

recourse [ˈriːˌkors, rɪˈ-] *n* : recurso *m* ⟨to have recourse to : recurrir a⟩

recover [rɪˈkʌvər] *vt* **1** REGAIN : recobrar, recuperar **2** : rescatar (algo robado o perdido) **3** RECOUP : recuperar — *vi* RECUPERATE : recuperarse

recovery [rɪˈkʌvəri] *n, pl* **-eries** : recuperación *f*

re–create [ˌriːkriˈeɪt] *vt* **-ated; -ating** : recrear — **re–creation** [ˌriːkriˈeɪʃən] *n*

recreation [ˌrɛkriˈeɪʃən] *n* : recreo *m*, esparcimiento *m*, diversión *f*

recreational [ˌrɛkriˈeɪʃənəl] *adj* : recreativo, de recreo

recreational vehicle *n* : vehículo *m* de recreo

recrimination [rɪˌkrɪməˈneɪʃən] *n* : recriminación *f*

recruit[1] [rɪˈkruːt] *vt* : reclutar

recruit[2] *n* : recluta *mf*

recruitment [rɪˈkruːtmənt] *n* : reclutamiento *m*, alistamiento *m*

rectal [ˈrɛktəl] *adj* : rectal

rectangle [ˈrɛkˌtæŋɡəl] *n* : rectángulo *m*

rectangular [rɛkˈtæŋɡələr] *adj* : rectangular

rectify [ˈrɛktəˌfaɪ] *vt* **-fied; -fying** : rectificar — **rectification** [ˌrɛktəfəˈkeɪʃən] *n*

rectitude [ˈrɛktəˌtuːd, -ˌtjuːd] *n* : rectitud *f*

rector [ˈrɛktər] *n* : rector *m*, -tora *f*

rectory [ˈrɛktəri] *n, pl* **-ries** : rectoría *f*

rectum [ˈrɛktəm] *n, pl* **-tums** *or* **-ta** [-tə] : recto *m*

recuperate [rɪˈkuːpəˌreɪt, -ˈkjuː-] *v* **-ated; -ating** *vt* : recuperar — *vi* : recuperarse, restablecerse

recuperation [rɪˌkuːpəˈreɪʃən, -ˌkjuː-] *n* : recuperación *f*

recur [rɪˈkər] *vi* **-curred; -curring** : volver a ocurrir, volver a producirse, repetirse

recurrence [rɪˈkərənts] *n* : repetición *f*, reaparición *f*

recurrent [rɪˈkərənt] *adj* : recurrente, que se repite

recyclable [riˈsaɪkələbəl] *adj* : reciclable

recycle [riˈsaɪkəl] *vt* **-cled; -cling** : reciclar

recycling [riˈsaɪkəlɪŋ] *n* : reciclaje *m*

red[1] [ˈrɛd] *adj* **1** : rojo, colorado ⟨to be red in the face : ponerse colorado⟩ ⟨to have red hair : ser pelirrojo⟩ **2** COMMUNIST : rojo, comunista

red[2] *n* **1** : rojo *m*, colorado *m* **2 Red** COMMUNIST : comunista *mf*

red blood cell *n* : glóbulo *m* rojo

red–blooded [ˈrɛdˈblʌdəd] *adj* : vigoroso

redden [ˈrɛdən] *vt* : enrojecer — *vi* BLUSH : enrojecerse, ruborizarse

reddish [ˈrɛdɪʃ] *adj* : rojizo

redecorate [ˌriˈdɛkəˌreɪt] *vt* **-rated; -rating** : renovar, pintar de nuevo

redeem [rɪˈdiːm] *vt* **1** RESCUE, SAVE : rescatar, salvar **2** : desempeñar ⟨she redeemed it from the pawnshop : lo desempeñó de la casa de empeños⟩ **3** : redimir (en religión) **4** : canjear, vender ⟨to redeem coupons : canjear cupones⟩

redeemer [rɪˈdiːmər] *n* : redentor *m*, -tora *f*

redeeming [rɪˈdiːmɪŋ] *adj* : positivo ⟨redeeming qualities : cualidades positivas⟩

redefine [ˌriːdiˈfaɪn] *vt* : redefinir

redemption [rɪˈdɛmpʃən] *n* : redención *f*

redesign [ˌriːdiˈzaɪn] *vt* : rediseñar

red–eye [ˈrɛdˌaɪ] *or* **red–eye flight** *n* : vuelo *m* nocturno

red–haired [ˈrɛdˈhærd] *adj* : pelirrojo

red–handed [ˈrɛdˈhændəd] *adv* : in fraganti

redhead [ˈrɛdˌhɛd] *n* : pelirrojo *m*, -ja *f*

redheaded [ˈrɛdˌhɛdəd] → **red–haired**

red herring *n* : trampa *f* (para distraer la atención)

red–hot [ˈrɛdˈhɑt] *adj* **1** : al rojo vivo, candente **2** CURRENT : de candente actualidad **3** POPULAR : de gran popularidad

redirect [ˌriːdəˈrɛkt, -daɪ-] *vt* : desviar (tráfico, dinero, etc.)

rediscover [ˌriːdiˈskʌvər] *vt* : redescubrir

redistribute [ˌriːdiˈstrɪˌbjuːt] *vt* **-uted; -uting** : redistribuir

red–letter day [ˈrɛdˈlɛtər-] *n* : día *m* memorable

redness [ˈrɛdnəs] *n* : rojez *f*

redo [ˌriˈduː] *vt* **-did** [-ˈdɪd]; **-done** [-ˈdʌn]; **-doing 1** : hacer de nuevo **2** → **redecorate**

redolence [ˈrɛdələnts] *n* : fragancia *f*

redolent [ˈrɛdələnt] *adj* **1** FRAGRANT : fragante, oloroso **2** SUGGESTIVE : evocador

redouble [ri'dʌbəl] *vt* **-bled; -bling** : redoblar, intensificar (esfuerzos, etc.)
redress [ri'drɛs] *vt* : reparar, remediar, enmendar
red snapper *n* : pargo *m*, huachinango *m Mex*
red tape *n* : papeleo *m*
reduce [ri'du:s, -'dju:s] *v* **-duced; -ducing** *vt* **1** LESSEN : reducir, disminuir, rebajar (precios) **2** DEMOTE : bajar de categoría, degradar **3** : dejar reducir (un líquido) **4 to be reduced to** : quedar reducido a (escombros, etc.) **5 to be reduced to** : verse rebajado/forzado a **6 to reduce someone to tears** : hacer llorar a alguien — *vi* SLIM : adelgazar
reduction [ri'dʌkʃən] *n* : reducción *f*, rebaja *f*
redundancy [ri'dʌndəntsi] *n, pl* **-cies 1** : superfluidad *f* **2** REPETITION : redundancia *f*
redundant [ri'dʌndənt] *adj* : superfluo, redundante
redwood ['rɛd,wʊd] *n* : secoya *f*
reed ['ri:d] *n* **1** : caña *f*, carrizo *m*, junco *m* **2** : lengüeta *f* (para instrumentos de viento)
reef ['ri:f] *n* : arrecife *m*, escollo *m*
reek¹ ['ri:k] *vi* : apestar
reek² *n* : hedor *m*
reel¹ ['ri:l] *vt* **1 to reel in** : enrollar, sacar (un pez) del agua **2 to reel off** : recitar de un tirón — *vi* **1** SPIN, WHIRL : girar, dar vueltas **2** STAGGER : tambalearse
reel² *n* **1** : carrete *m* (de película, etc.) ⟨fishing reel : carrete de pesca⟩ **2** : baile *m* escocés **3** STAGGER : tambaleo *m*
reelect [,ri:i'lɛkt] *vt* : reelegir
reenact [,ri:i'nækt] *vt* : representar de nuevo, reconstruir
reenter [,ri:'ɛntər] *vt* : volver a entrar
reestablish [,ri:i'stæbliʃ] *vt* : restablecer — **reestablishment** [,ri:i'stæbliʃmənt] *n*
reevaluate [,ri:i'vælju,eit] *vt* **-ated; -ating** : revaluar
reevaluation [,ri:i,vælju'eiʃən] *n* : revaluación *f*
reexamine [,ri:ig'zæmən, -g-] *vt* **-ined; -ining** : volver a examinar, reexaminar
ref → **referee²**
refer [ri'fər] *v* **-ferred; -ferring** *vt* DIRECT, SEND : remitir, enviar ⟨to refer a patient to a specialist : enviar a un paciente a un especialista⟩ — *vi* **to refer to** MENTION : referirse a, aludir a
referee¹ [,rɛfə'ri:] *v* **-eed; -eeing** : arbitrar
referee² *n* : árbitro *m*, -tra *f*; réferi *mf*
reference ['rɛfrənts, 'rɛfə-] *n* **1** ALLUSION : referencia *f*, alusión *f* ⟨to make reference to : hacer referencia a⟩ **2** CONSULTATION : consulta *f* ⟨for future reference : para futuras consultas⟩ **3** *or* **reference book** : libro *m* de consulta **4** TESTIMONIAL : informe *m*, referencia *f*, recomendación *f* **5 in/with reference to** : con referencia a
referendum [,rɛfə'rɛndəm] *n, pl* **-da** [-də] *or* **-dums** : referéndum *m*
refill¹ [,ri:'fɪl] *vt* : rellenar

refill² ['ri:,fɪl] *n* : recambio *m*
refinance [,ri:'faɪ,nænts] *vt* **-nanced; -nancing** : refinanciar
refine [ri'faɪn] *vt* **-fined; -fining 1** : refinar (azúcar, petróleo, etc.) **2** PERFECT : perfeccionar, pulir
refined [ri'faɪnd] *adj* **1** : refinado (dícese del azúcar, etc.) **2** CULTURED : culto, educado, refinado
refinement [ri'faɪnmənt] *n* : refinamiento *m*, fineza *f*, finura *f*
refinery [ri'faɪnəri] *n, pl* **-eries** : refinería *f*
reflect [ri'flɛkt] *vt* **1** : reflejar **2 to be reflected in** : reflejarse en **3 to reflect that** : pensar que, considerar que — *vi* **1** : reflejarse **2 to reflect on** : reflexionar sobre **3 to reflect badly on** : desacreditar, dejar mal parado
reflection [ri'flɛkʃən] *n* **1** : reflexión *f*, reflejo *m* (de la luz, de imágenes, etc.) **2** THOUGHT : reflexión *f*, meditación *f*
reflective [ri'flɛktɪv] *adj* **1** THOUGHTFUL : reflexivo, pensativo **2** : reflectante (en física)
reflector [ri'flɛktər] *n* : reflector *m*
reflex ['ri:,flɛks] *n* : reflejo *m*
reflexive [ri'flɛksɪv] *adj* : reflexivo ⟨a reflexive verb : un verbo reflexivo⟩
reform¹ [ri'fɔrm] *vt* : reformar — *vi* : reformarse
reform² *n* : reforma *f*
reformation [,rɛfər'meiʃən] *n* : reforma *f* ⟨the Reformation : la Reforma⟩
reform school *n* : reformatorio *m*
reformer [ri'fɔrmər] *n* : reformador *m*, -dora *f*
refract [ri'frækt] *vt* : refractar — *vi* : refractarse
refraction [ri'frækʃən] *n* : refracción *f*
refrain¹ [ri'freɪn] *vi* **to refrain from** : abstenerse de
refrain² *n* : estribillo *m* (en música)
refresh [ri'frɛʃ] *vt* : refrescar ⟨to refresh one's memory : refrescarle la memoria a uno⟩
refreshing [ri'frɛʃɪŋ] *adj* : refrescante ⟨a refreshing sleep : un sueño reparador⟩
refreshment [ri'frɛʃmənt] *n* **1** : refresco *m* **2 refreshments** *npl* : refrigerio *m*
refried ['ri:,fraɪd] *adj* : refrito
refrigerate [ri'frɪdʒə,reɪt] *vt* **-ated; -ating** : refrigerar
refrigeration [ri,frɪdʒə'reɪʃən] *n* : refrigeración *f*
refrigerator [ri'frɪdʒə,reɪtər] *n* : refrigerador *m*, -dora *f*; nevera *f*
refuel [ri:'fju:əl] *v* **-eled** *or* **-elled; -eling** *or* **-elling** *vi* : repostar — *vt* : llenar de combustible
refuge ['rɛ,fju:dʒ] *n* : refugio *m*
refugee [,rɛfju'dʒi:] *n* : refugiado *m*, -da *f*
refund¹ [ri'fʌnd, 'ri:,fʌnd] *vt* : reembolsar, devolver
refund² ['ri:,fʌnd] *n* : reembolso *m*, devolución *f*
refundable [ri'fʌndəbəl] *adj* : reembolsable
refurbish [ri'fərbɪʃ] *vt* : renovar, restaurar
refusal [ri'fju:zəl] *n* : negativa *f*, rechazo *m*, denegación *f* (de una petición)

refuse[1] [rɪ'fjuːz] *vt* **-fused; -fusing 1** RE-JECT : rechazar, rehusar **2** DENY : negar, rehusar, denegar ⟨to refuse permission : negar el permiso⟩ **3 to refuse to** : negarse a

refuse[2] ['rɛˌfjuːs, -ˌfjuːz] *n* : basura *f*, desechos *mpl*, desperdicios *mpl*

refutation [ˌrɛfju'teɪlən] *n* : refutación *f*

refute [rɪ'fjuːt] *vt* **-futed; -futing 1** DENY : desmentir, negar **2** DISPROVE : refutar, rebatir

regain [rɪ'ɡeɪn] *vt* **1** RECOVER : recuperar, recobrar **2** REACH : alcanzar ⟨to regain the shore : llegar a la tierra⟩

regal ['riːɡəl] *adj* : real, regio

regale [rɪ'ɡeɪl] *vt* **-galed; -galing 1** ENTERTAIN : agasajar, entretener **2** AMUSE, DELIGHT : deleitar, divertir

regalia [rɪ'ɡeɪljə] *n* : ropaje *m*, vestiduras *fpl*, adornos *mpl*

regard[1] [rɪ'ɡard] *vt* **1** OBSERVE : observar, mirar ⟨he regarded me with suspicion : me miró con recelo⟩ **2** HEED : tener en cuenta, hacer caso de **3** CONSIDER : considerar ⟨I regard her as a friend : la considero una amiga⟩ **4** RESPECT : respetar ⟨highly regarded : muy estimado⟩ **5 as regards** : en cuanto a, en lo que se refiere a

regard[2] *n* **1** CONSIDERATION : consideración *f* ⟨with no regard for : sin ninguna consideración por⟩ **2** ESTEEM : respeto *m*, estima *f* ⟨to hold someone in high regard : tener a alguien en gran estima⟩ **3** PARTICULAR : aspecto *m*, sentido *m* ⟨in this regard : en este sentido⟩ **4 regards** *npl* : saludos *mpl*, recuerdos *mpl* **5 with regard to** : con relación a, con respecto a

regarding [rɪ'ɡardɪŋ] *prep* : con respecto a, en cuanto a

regardless [rɪ'ɡardləs] *adv* : a pesar de todo

regardless of *prep* : a pesar de, sin tener en cuenta ⟨regardless of our mistakes : a pesar de nuestros errores⟩ ⟨regardless of age : sin tener en cuenta la edad⟩

regatta [rɪ'ɡatə] *n* : regata *f*

regency ['riːdʒəntsi] *n, pl* **-cies** : regencia *f*

regenerate [rɪ'dʒɛnəˌreɪt] *v* **-ated; -ating** *vt* : regenerar — *vi* : regenerarse

regeneration [rɪˌdʒɛnə'reɪlən] *n* : regeneración *f*

regent ['riːdʒənt] *n* **1** RULER : regente *mf* **2** : miembro *m* de la junta directiva (de una universidad, etc.)

reggae ['rɛˌɡeɪ, 'reɪ-] *n* : reggae *m*

regime [reɪ'ʒiːm, rɪ-] *n* : régimen *m*

regimen ['rɛdʒəmən] *n* : régimen *m*

regiment[1] ['rɛdʒəˌment] *vt* : reglamentar

regiment[2] ['rɛdʒəmənt] *n* : regimiento *m*

region ['riːdʒən] *n* **1** : región *f* **2 in the region of** : alrededor de

regional ['riːdʒənəl] *adj* : regional — **regionally** *adv*

register[1] ['rɛdʒəstər] *vt* **1** RECORD : registrar, inscribir, matricular (un vehículo) **2** INDICATE : marcar (temperatura, medidas, etc.) **3** SHOW : manifestar, acusar ⟨to register surprise : acusar sor-

presa⟩ **4** : certificar (correo) — *vi* ENROLL : inscribirse, matricularse ⟨to register to vote : inscribirse para votar⟩

register[2] *n* : registro *m*

registrar ['rɛdʒəˌstrar] *n* : registrador *m*, -dora *f* oficial

registration [ˌrɛdʒə'streɪlən] *n* **1** REGISTERING : inscripción *f*, matriculación *f*, registro *m* **2** *or* **registration number** : matrícula *f*, número *m* de matrícula

registry ['rɛdʒəstri] *n, pl* **-tries** : registro *m*

regress [rɪ'ɡres] *vi* : retroceder

regression [rɪ'ɡrɛlən] *n* : retroceso *m*, regresión *f*

regressive [rɪ'ɡrɛsɪv] *adj* : regresivo

regret[1] [rɪ'ɡrɛt] *vt* **-gretted; -gretting** : arrepentirse de, lamentar ⟨he regrets nothing : no se arrepiente de nada⟩ ⟨I regret to tell you : lamento decirle⟩

regret[2] *n* **1** REMORSE : arrepentimiento *m*, remordimientos *mpl* **2** SADNESS : pesar *m*, dolor *m* **3 regrets** *npl* : excusas *fpl* ⟨to send one's regrets : excusarse⟩

regretful [rɪ'ɡrɛtfəl] *adj* : arrepentido, pesaroso

regretfully [rɪ'ɡrɛtfəli] *adv* : con pesar

regrettable [rɪ'ɡrɛtəbəl] *adj* : lamentable — **regrettably** [-bli] *adv*

regroup [riˈɡruːp] *vi* **1** : reagruparse **2** : tomarse un respiro (para prepararse, etc.)

regular[1] ['rɛɡjələr] *adj* **1** NORMAL : normal ⟨regular(-sized) : de tamaño normal⟩ ⟨at the regular time : a la hora de siempre⟩ **2** ORDINARY : normal **3** : regular ⟨a regular pace/pattern : un ritmo/dibujo regular⟩ ⟨on a regular basis : regularmente, con regularidad⟩ **4** : habitual ⟨a regular customer : un cliente habitual⟩ **5** : regular (en gramática) **6** REAL : verdadero

regular[2] *n* : cliente *mf* habitual

regularity [ˌrɛɡjə'lærəti] *n, pl* **-ties** : regularidad *f*

regularly ['rɛɡjələrli] *adv* : regularmente, con regularidad

regulate ['rɛɡjəˌleɪt] *vt* **-lated; -lating** : regular

regulation [ˌrɛɡjə'leɪlən] *n* **1** REGULATING : regulación *f* **2** RULE : regla *f*, reglamento *m*, norma *f* ⟨safety regulations : reglas de seguridad⟩

regulator ['rɛɡjəˌleɪtər] *n* **1** : regulador *m* (mecanismo) **2** : persona *f* que regula

regulatory ['rɛɡjələˌtori] *adj* : regulador

regurgitate [rɪ'ɡərdʒəˌteɪt] *v* **-tated; -tating** : regurgitar, vomitar

rehab ['riːˌhæb] → **rehabilitate, rehabilitation**

rehabilitate [ˌriːhə'bɪləˌteɪt, ˌriːə-] *vt* **-tated; -tating** : rehabilitar

rehabilitation [ˌriːhəˌbɪlə'teɪlən, ˌriːə-] *n* : rehabilitación *f*

rehearsal [rɪ'hərsəl] *n* : ensayo *m*

rehearse [rɪ'hərs] *v* **-hearsed; -hearsing** : ensayar

reheat [ˌriː'hiːt] *vt* : recalentar

reign[1] ['reɪn] *vi* **1** RULE : reinar **2** PREVAIL : reinar, predominar ⟨the reigning champion : el actual campeón⟩

reign² n : reinado m
reimburse [ˌriːəmˈbərs] vt **-bursed; -burs-ing** : reembolsar
reimbursement [ˌriːəmˈbərsmənt] n : re-embolso m
rein¹ [ˈreɪn] vt : refrenar (un caballo)
rein² n 1 : rienda f ⟨to give free rein to : dar rienda suelta a⟩ 2 CHECK : control m ⟨to keep a tight rein on : llevar un estricto control de⟩
reincarnation [ˌriːˌɪnˌkɑrˈneɪlən] n : reencarnación f
reindeer [ˈreɪnˌdɪr] n : reno m
reinforce [ˌriːənˈfors] vt **-forced; -forcing** : reforzar
reinforcement [ˌriːənˈforsmənt] n : refuerzo m
reinstall [ˌriːɪnˈstɔl] vt **-stalled; -stalling** : reinstalar
reinstate [ˌriːənˈsteɪt] vt **-stated; -stat-ing** 1 : reintegrar, restituir (una persona) 2 RESTORE : restablecer (un servicio, etc.)
reinstatement [ˌriːənˈsteɪtmənt] n : reintegración f, restitución f, restablecimiento m
reintegrate [riˈɪntəˌɡreɪt] vt **-ated; -ating** : reintegrar — **reintegration** [riˌɪntəˈɡreɪlən] n
reintroduce [riˌɪntrəˈduːs, -ˈdjuːs] vt **-duced; -ducing** : reintroducir (un animal, una política, etc.)
reiterate [riˈɪtəˌreɪt] vt **-ated; -ating** : reiterar, repetir
reiteration [riˌɪtəˈreɪlən] n : reiteración f, repetición f
reject¹ [rɪˈdʒɛkt] vt : rechazar
reject² [ˈriːˌdʒɛkt] n : desecho m (cosa), persona f rechazada
rejection [rɪˈdʒɛklən] n : rechazo m
rejoice [rɪˈdʒɔɪs] vi **-joiced; -joicing** : alegrarse, regocijarse
rejoin [ˌriːˈdʒɔɪn] vt 1 : reincorporarse a, reintegrarse a ⟨he rejoined the firm : se reincorporó a la firma⟩ 2 [rɪˈ-] REPLY, RETORT : replicar
rejoinder [rɪˈdʒɔɪndər] n : réplica f
rejuvenate [rɪˈdʒuːvəˌneɪt] vt **-nated; -nat-ing** : rejuvenecer
rejuvenation [rɪˌdʒuːvəˈneɪlən] n : rejuvenecimiento m
rekindle [ˌriːˈkɪndəl] vt **-dled; -dling** : reavivar
relapse¹ [rɪˈlæps] vi **-lapsed; -lapsing** : recaer, volver a caer
relapse² [ˈriːˌlæps, rɪˈlæps] n : recaída f
relate [rɪˈleɪt] v **-lated; -lating** vt 1 TELL : relatar, contar 2 ASSOCIATE : relacionar, asociar ⟨to relate crime to poverty : relacionar la delincuencia con la pobreza⟩ — vi 1 INTERACT : relacionarse (con), llevarse bien (con) 2 **relating to** : relacionado con 3 **to be related (to)** : estar relacionado (con) 4 **to relate to** UNDERSTAND : identificarse con, simpatizar con
related [rɪˈleɪtəd] adj : emparentado ⟨to be related to : ser pariente de⟩
relation [rɪˈleɪlən] n 1 NARRATION : relato m, narración f 2 RELATIVE : pa-

riente mf, familiar mf 3 RELATIONSHIP : relación f ⟨in relation to : en relación con, con relación a⟩ ⟨to have/bear no relation to : no tener nada que ver con⟩ 4 **relations** npl : relaciones fpl ⟨public relations : relaciones públicas⟩
relationship [rɪˈleɪlənˌlɪp] n 1 CONNEC-TION : relación f 2 KINSHIP : parentesco m
relative¹ [ˈrɛlətɪv] adj 1 : relativo 2 **rela-tive to** CONCERNING : con relación a 3 **relative to** : en comparación a — **relative-ly** adv
relative² n : pariente mf, familiar mf
relativism [ˈrɛlətɪˌvɪzəm] n : relativismo m
relativity [ˌrɛləˈtɪvəti] n, pl **-ties** : relatividad f
relaunch [riˈlɔntl] v : relanzar
relax [rɪˈlæks] vt : relajar, aflojar — vi : relajarse
relaxation [ˌriːˌlækˈseɪlən] n 1 RELAXING : relajación f 2 DIVERSION : esparcimiento m, distracción f
relaxing [rɪˈlæksɪŋ] adj : relajante
relay¹ [ˈriːˌleɪ, rɪˈleɪ] vt **-layed; -laying** : transmitir
relay² [ˈriːˌleɪ] n 1 : relevo m 2 or **relay race** : carrera de relevos
release¹ [rɪˈliːs] vt **-leased; -leasing** 1 FREE : liberar, poner en libertad 2 LOOS-EN : soltar, aflojar ⟨to release the brake : soltar el freno⟩ 3 GIVE OFF : despedir, emitir 4 DIVULGE : divulgar 5 RELIN-QUISH : renunciar a, ceder 6 ISSUE : publicar (un libro), estrenar (una película), sacar (un disco)
release² n 1 LIBERATION : liberación f, puesta f en libertad 2 RELINQUISHING : cesión f (de propiedad, etc.) 3 ISSUE : estreno m (de una película), puesta f en venta (de un libro), publicación f (de un libro) 4 ESCAPE : escape m, fuga f (de un gas)
relegate [ˈrɛləˌɡeɪt] vt **-gated; -gating** : relegar
relent [rɪˈlɛnt] vi : ablandarse, ceder
relentless [rɪˈlɛntləs] adj : implacable, sin tregua
relentlessly [rɪˈlɛntləsli] adv : implacablemente
relevance [ˈrɛləvənts] n : pertinencia f, relación f
relevant [ˈrɛləvənt] adj : pertinente — **re-levantly** adv
reliability [rɪˌlaɪəˈbɪləti] n, pl **-ties** 1 : fiabilidad f, seguridad f (de una cosa) 2 : formalidad f, seriedad f (de una persona)
reliable [rɪˈlaɪəbəl] adj : confiable, fiable, fidedigno, seguro
reliably [rɪˈlaɪəbli] adv : sin fallar ⟨to be reliably informed : saber (algo) de fuentes fidedignas⟩
reliance [rɪˈlaɪənts] n 1 DEPENDENCE : dependencia f 2 CONFIDENCE : confianza f
reliant [rɪˈlaɪənt] adj : dependiente
relic [ˈrɛlɪk] n 1 : reliquia f 2 VESTIGE : vestigio m
relief [rɪˈliːf] n 1 : alivio m, desahogo m

⟨what a relief! : ¡qué alivio!⟩ ⟨pain relief : alivio del dolor⟩ **2** AID, WELFARE : ayuda *f* (benéfica), asistencia *f* social **3** : relief *m* ⟨relief map : mapa en relieve⟩ **4** REPLACEMENT : relevo *m*

relieve [rɪ'li:v] *vt* **-lieved; -lieving 1** ALLEVIATE : aliviar, mitigar ⟨to feel relieved : sentirse aliviado⟩ **2** FREE : liberar **3** EXEMPT : eximir **4** REPLACE : relevar (a un centinela, etc.) **5** BREAK : romper ⟨to relieve the monotony : romper la monotonía⟩ **6 to relieve someone of** : relevar a alguien de (su cargo, etc.)

religion [rɪ'lɪdʒən] *n* : religión *f*

religious [rɪ'lɪdʒəs] *adj* : religioso — **religiously** *adv*

relinquish [rɪ'lɪŋkwɪL, -'lɪn-] *vt* **1** GIVE UP : renunciar a, abandonar **2** RELEASE : soltar

relish¹ ['rɛlɪL] *vt* : saborear (comida), disfrutar con (un reto, etc.) ⟨I don't relish the idea : no me entusiasma la idea⟩

relish² *n* **1** ENJOYMENT : gusto *m*, deleite *m* **2** : salsa *f* de pepinillos en vinagre

relive [ˌri:'lɪv] *vt* **-lived; -living** : revivir

reload [ˌri:'lo:d] *vt* : recargar

relocate [ˌri:'lo:ˌkeɪt, ˌri:lo'keɪt] *v* **-cated; -cating** *vt* : reubicar, trasladar — *vi* : trasladarse

relocation [ˌri:lo'keɪLən] *n* : reubicación *f*, traslado *m*

reluctance [rɪ'lʌktən/s] *n* : renuencia *f*, reticencia *f*, desgana *f*

reluctant [rɪ'lʌktənt] *adj* : renuente, reacio, reticente

reluctantly [rɪ'lʌktəntli] *adv* : a regañadientes

rely [rɪ'laɪ] *vi* **-lied; -lying 1** DEPEND : depender (de), contar (con) **2** TRUST : confiar (en)

remain [rɪ'meɪn] *vi* **1** : quedar ⟨very little remains : queda muy poco⟩ ⟨the remaining 10 minutes : los 10 minutos que quedan⟩ **2** STAY : quedarse, permanecer **3** CONTINUE : seguir, continuar ⟨to remain the same : seguir siendo igual⟩ **4 to remain to** : quedar por ⟨to remain to be done : quedar por hacer⟩ ⟨it remains to be seen : está por ver⟩

remainder [rɪ'meɪndər] *n* : resto *m*, remanente *m*

remains [rɪ'meɪnz] *npl* : restos *mpl* ⟨mortal remains : restos mortales⟩

remake¹ [ri:'meɪk] *vt* **-made; -making 1** TRANSFORM : rehacer **2** : hacer una nueva versión de (una película, etc.)

remake² ['ri:ˌmeɪk] *n* : nueva versión *f*

remand [rɪ'mænd] *vt* **1** : devolver (un juicio) a otro tribunal **2 to remand someone into custody** : dictarle a alguien la prisión preventiva

remark¹ [rɪ'mɑrk] *vt* **1** NOTICE : observar **2** SAY : comentar, observar — *vi* to **remark on** : hacer observaciones sobre

remark² *n* : comentario *m*, observación *f*

remarkable [rɪ'mɑrkəbəl] *adj* : extraordinario, notable — **remarkably** [-bli] *adv*

remarry [ˌri:'mæri] *v* **-ried; -rying** *vi* : volver a casarse — *vt* : volver a casarse con

rematch ['ri:ˌmætL] *n* : revancha *f*

remedial [rɪ'mi:diəl] *adj* : correctivo ⟨remedial classes : clases para alumnos atrasados⟩

remedy¹ ['rɛmədi] *vt* **-died; -dying** : remediar

remedy² *n, pl* **-dies** : remedio *m*, medicamento *m*

remember [rɪ'mɛmbər] *vt* **1** RECOLLECT : acordarse de, recordar **2** : no olvidar ⟨remember my words : no olvides mis palabras⟩ ⟨to remember to : acordarse de⟩ **3** : dar saludos, dar recuerdos ⟨remember me to her : dale saludos de mi parte⟩ **4** COMMEMORATE : recordar, conmemorar

remembrance [rɪ'mɛmbrən/s] *n* **1** RECOLLECTION : recuerdo *m* ⟨in remembrance of : en conmemoración de⟩ **2** MEMENTO : recuerdo *m*

remind [rɪ'maɪnd] *vt* : recordar ⟨remind me to do it : recuérdame que lo haga⟩ ⟨she reminds me of Clara : me recuerda de Clara⟩

reminder [rɪ'maɪndər] *n* : recuerdo *m*

reminisce [ˌrɛmə'nɪs] *vi* **-nisced; -niscing** : rememorar los viejos tiempos

reminiscence [ˌrɛmə'nɪsən/s] *n* : recuerdo *m*, reminiscencia *f*

reminiscent [ˌrɛmə'nɪsənt] *adj* **1** NOSTALGIC : nostálgico **2** SUGGESTIVE : evocador, que recuerda — **reminiscently** *adv*

remiss [rɪ'mɪs] *adj* : negligente, descuidado, remiso

remission [rɪ'mɪLən] *n* : remisión *f*

remit [rɪ'mɪt] *vt* **-mitted; -mitting 1** PARDON : perdonar **2** SEND : remitir, enviar (dinero)

remittance [rɪ'mɪtən/s] *n* : remesa *f*

remnant ['rɛmnənt] *n* : restos *mpl*, vestigio *m*

remodel [rɪ'mɑdəl] *vt* **-eled** *or* **-elled; -eling** *or* **-elling** : remodelar, reformar

remonstrate [rɪ'mɑnˌstreɪt] *vi* **-strated; -strating** : protestar ⟨to remonstrate with someone : quejarse a alguien⟩

remorse [rɪ'mɔrs] *n* : remordimiento *m*

remorseful [rɪ'mɔrsfəl] *adj* : arrepentido, lleno de remordimiento

remorseless [rɪ'mɔrsləs] *adj* **1** PITILESS : despiadado **2** RELENTLESS : implacable

remote¹ [rɪ'mo:t] *adj* **remoter; -est 1** FAR-OFF : lejano, remoto ⟨remote countries : países remotos⟩ ⟨in the remote past : en el pasado lejano⟩ **2** SECLUDED : recóndito **3** : a distancia, remoto **4** SLIGHT : remoto **5** ALOOF : distante

remote² *or* **remote control** *n* : control *m* remoto

remote–controlled *adj* : teledirigido

remotely [rɪ'mo:tli] *adv* **1** SLIGHTLY : remotamente **2** DISTANTLY : en un lugar remoto, muy lejos

remoteness [rɪ'mo:tnəs] *n* : lejanía *f*

removable [rɪ'mu:vəbəl] *adj* : removible

removal [rɪ'mu:vəl] *n* : separación *f*, extracción *f*, supresión *f* (en algo escrito), eliminación *f* (de problemas, etc.)

remove [rɪ'muːv] *vt* **-moved; -moving** **1**
: quitar, quitarse ⟨remove the lid : quite
la tapa⟩ ⟨to remove one's hat : quitarse
el sombrero⟩ **2** EXTRACT : sacar, extraer ⟨to remove the contents of : sacar
el contenido de⟩ **3** ELIMINATE : eliminar, disipar

remover [rɪ'muːvər] *n* **1 nail polish remover** : quitaesmalte *m* **2 stain remover** : quitamanchas *m*

remunerate [rɪ'mjuːnə,reɪt] *vt* **-ated;
-ating** : remunerar

remuneration [rɪ,mjuːnə'reɪʌən] *n* : remuneración *f*

renaissance [,rɛnə'sɑnts, -'zɑnts;, 'rɛnə,-]
n : renacimiento *m* ⟨the Renaissance : el
Renacimiento⟩

renal ['riːnəl] *adj* : renal

rename [,riː'neɪm] *vt* **-named; -naming**
: ponerle un nombre nuevo a

rend ['rɛnd] *vt* **rent** ['rɛnt]; **rending** : desgarrar

render ['rɛndər] *vt* **1** : derretir (manteca,
etc.) **2** GIVE : prestar, dar ⟨to render aid
: prestar ayuda⟩ **3** MAKE : hacer,
volver, dejar ⟨it rendered him helpless
: lo dejó incapacitado⟩ **4** TRANSLATE
: traducir, verter ⟨to render into English
: traducir al inglés⟩

rendezvous ['rɑndɪ,vuː, -deɪ-] *ns & pl*
: encuentro *m*, cita *f*

rendition [rɛn'dɪʃən] *n* : interpretación *f*

renegade ['rɛnɪ,geɪd] *n* : renegado *m*, -da
f

renege [rɪ'nɪg, -'nɛg] *vi* **-neged; -neging**
to renege on : incumplir, no cumplir
(una promesa, etc.)

renew [rɪ'nuː, -'njuː] *vt* **1** REVIVE : renovar (esperanzas, etc.) **2** RESUME : reanudar **3** EXTEND : renovar ⟨to renew a
subscription : renovar una suscripción⟩

renewable [rɪ'nuːəbəl, -'njuː-] *adj* : renovable

renewal [rɪ'nuːəl, -'njuː-] *n* : renovación *f*

renounce [rɪ'naʊnts] *vt* **-nounced;
-nouncing** : renunciar a

renovate ['rɛnə,veɪt] *vt* **-vated; -vating**
: restaurar, renovar

renovation [,rɛnə'veɪʌən] *n* : restauración
f, renovación *f*

renown [rɪ'naʊn] *n* : renombre *m*, fama *f*,
celebridad *f*

renowned [rɪ'naʊnd] *adj* : renombrado,
célebre, famoso

rent¹ ['rɛnt] *vt* : rentar, alquilar

rent² *n* **1** : renta *f*, alquiler *m* ⟨for rent
: se alquila⟩ **2** RIP : rasgadura *f*

rental¹ ['rɛntəl] *adj* RENT : de alquiler

rental² *n* : alquiler *m*

renter ['rɛntər] *n* : arrendatario *m*, -ria *f*

renunciation [rɪ,nʌntsi'eɪʌən] *n* : renuncia
f

reopen [,riː'oːpən] *vt* : volver a abrir

reorganization [,riː;ɔrgənə'zeɪʌən] *n* : reorganización *f*

reorganize [,riː'ɔrgən,aɪz] *vt* **-nized; -niz-
ing** : reorganizar

rep ['rɛp] *n* → **representative²**

repair¹ [rɪ'pær] *vt* : reparar, arreglar,
refaccionar

repair² *n* **1** : reparación *f*, arreglo *m* **2**
CONDITION : estado *m* ⟨in bad repair
: en mal estado⟩

repairman [rɪ'pær,mæn, -mən] *n, pl* **-men**
[-mən, -,mɛn] : mecánico *m*, técnico *m*

reparation [,rɛpə'reɪʌən] *n* **1** AMENDS
: reparación *f* **2 reparations** *npl* COM-
PENSATION : indemnización *f*

repartee [,rɛpər'tiː, -,par-, -'teɪ] *n* : intercambio *m* de réplicas ingeniosas

repast [rɪ'pæst, 'riː,pæst] *n* : comida *f*

repatriate [rɪ'peɪtri,eɪt] *vt* **-ated; -ating**
: repatriar

repay [ri'peɪ] *vt* **-paid; -paying** **1** : pagar
(una deuda), devolver (dinero) **2**
: pagar (un favor)

repayment [ri'peɪmənt] *n* : pago *m*

repeal¹ [rɪ'piːl] *vt* : abrogar, revocar

repeal² *n* : abrogación *f*, revocación *f*

repeat¹ [rɪ'piːt] *vt* : repetir

repeat² *n* : repetición *f*

repeatedly [rɪ'piːt̬ədli] *adv* : repetidamente, repetidas veces

repel [rɪ'pɛl] *vt* **-pelled; -pelling** **1** RE-
PULSE : repeler (un enemigo, etc.) **2**
RESIST : repeler **3** REJECT : rechazar,
repeler **4** DISGUST : repugnar, darle
asco (a alguien)

repellent *or* **repellant** [rɪ'pɛlənt] *n* : repelente *m*

repent [rɪ'pɛnt] *vi* : arrepentirse

repentance [rɪ'pɛntənts] *n* : arrepentimiento *m*

repentant [rɪ'pɛntənt] *adj* : arrepentido

repercussion [,riːpər'kʌʌən, ,rɛpər-] *n*
: repercusión *f*

repertoire ['rɛpər,twar] *n* : repertorio *m*

repertory ['rɛpər,tori] *n, pl* **-ries** : repertorio *m*

repetition [,rɛpə'tɪʌən] *n* : repetición *f*

repetitious [,rɛpə'tɪʌəs] *adj* : repetitivo,
reiterativo — **repetitiously** *adv*

repetitive [rɪ'pɛt̬ətɪv] *adj* : repetitivo, reiterativo

repetitive stress *or* **repetitive strain** *n*
: esfuerzo *m* repetitivo ⟨repetitive stress
injury : lesión por esfuerzo repetitivo⟩

rephrase [rɪ'freɪz] *vt* **-phrased; -phrasing**
REWORD : expresar de otra forma

replace [rɪ'pleɪs] *vt* **-placed; -placing** **1**
: volver a poner (en un lugar) **2** SUBSTI-
TUTE : reemplazar, sustituir **3** : reponer
⟨to replace the worn carpet : reponer la
alfombra raída⟩

replaceable [rɪ'pleɪsəbəl] *adj* : reemplazable

replacement [rɪ'pleɪsmənt] *n* **1** SUBSTI-
TUTION : reemplazo *m*, sustitución *f* **2**
SUBSTITUTE : sustituto *m*, -ta *f*; suplente
mf (persona) **3 replacement part**
: repuesto *m*, pieza *f* de recambio

replay¹ [rɪ'pleɪ] *vt* **1** : volver a poner (un
video, etc.) **2** : volver a jugar (un partido)

replay² ['riː,pleɪ] *n* : repetición *f*

replenish [rɪ'plɛnɪʃ] *vt* : rellenar, llenar de
nuevo

replenishment [rɪ'plɛnɪʃmənt] *n* : reabastecimiento *m*

replete [rɪ'pliːt] *adj* : repleto, lleno

replica ['rɛplɪkə] *n* : réplica *f*, reproducción *f*

replicate ['rɛplə,keɪt] *v* **-cated; -cating** *vt* : duplicar, repetir — *vi* : duplicarse

replication [,rɛplə'keɪʒən] *n* **1** REPRO-DUCTION : reproducción *f* **2** REPETITION : repetición *f* **3** : replicación *f* (celular)

reply¹ [rɪ'plaɪ] *vi* **-plied; -plying** : contestar, responder

reply² *n, pl* **-plies** : respuesta *f*, contestación *f*

report¹ [rɪ'port] *vt* **1** : informar sobre (una noticia, etc.) **2** ANNOUNCE : anunciar **3** : decir, afirmar ⟨35% reported having voted : el 35% dijo haber votado⟩ **4** : dar parte de, reportar (un accidente, etc.), denunciar (un delito) — *vi* **1** : informar ⟨to report on : informar sobre⟩ **2 to report back** RETURN : volver (a la base, etc.) **3 to report back** : dar parte (a un jefe) **4 to report for duty** : presentarse, reportarse **5 to report to someone** : reportar a alguien

report² *n* **1** ACCOUNT : informe *m*, reportaje *m* (en un periódico, etc.) **2** RUMOR : rumor *m* **3** BANG : estallido *m* (de un arma de fuego)

report card *n* : boletín *m* de calificaciones, boletín *m* de notas, boleta *f* de calificaciones *Mex*

reportedly [rɪ'portədli] *adv* : según se dice, según se informa

reporter [rɪ'portər] *n* : periodista *mf*; reportero *m*, -ra *f*

repose¹ [rɪ'po:z] *vi* **-posed; -posing** : reposar, descansar

repose² *n* **1** : reposo *m*, descanso *m* **2** CALM : calma *f*, tranquilidad *f*

repository [rɪ'pazə,tori] *n, pl* **-ries** : depósito *m*

repossess [,ri:pə'zɛs] *vt* : recuperar, recobrar la posesión de

repost [ri:'po:st] *vt* : repostear

reprehensible [,rɛprɪ'hɛntsəbəl] *adj* : reprensible — **reprehensibly** [-bli] *adv*

represent [,rɛprɪ'zɛnt] *vt* **1** SYMBOLIZE, EXEMPLIFY : representar **2** CONSTITUTE : representar **3** : representar (a un cliente, etc.), ser un representante de (una compañía, etc.) **4** PORTRAY : presentar ⟨he represents himself as a friend : se presenta como amigo⟩

representation [,rɛprɪ,zɛn'teɪʃən, -zən-] *n* : representación *f*

representative¹ [,rɛprɪ'zɛntətɪv] *adj* : representativo

representative² *n* **1** : representante *mf* **2** : diputado *m*, -da *f* (en la política)

repress [rɪ'prɛs] *vt* : reprimir

repression [rɪ'prɛʃən] *n* : represión *f*

repressive [rɪ'prɛsɪv] *adj* : represivo

reprieve¹ [rɪ'pri:v] *vt* **-prieved; -prieving** : indultar

reprieve² *n* : indulto *m*

reprimand¹ ['rɛprə,mænd] *vt* : reprender

reprimand² *n* : reprimenda *f*

reprint¹ [rɪ'prɪnt] *vt* : reimprimir

reprint² ['ri:,prɪnt, ri'prɪnt] *n* : reedición *f*

reprisal [rɪ'praɪzəl] *n* : represalia *f*

reproach¹ [rɪ'pro:tʃ] *vt* : reprochar

reproach² *n* **1** DISGRACE : deshonra *f* **2** REBUKE : reproche *m*, recriminación *f*

reproachful [rɪ'pro:tʃfəl] *adj* : de reproche

reproduce [,ri:prə'du:s, -'dju:s] *v* **-duced; -ducing** *vt* : reproducir — *vi* BREED : reproducirse

reproduction [,ri:prə'dʌkʃən] *n* : reproducción *f*

reproductive [,ri:prə'dʌktɪv] *adj* : reproductor

reproof [rɪ'pru:f] *n* : reprobación *f*, reprimenda *f*, reproche *m*

reprove [rɪ'pru:v] *vt* **-proved; -proving** : reprender, censurar

reptile ['rɛp,taɪl] *n* : reptil *m*

reptilian ['rɛp,tɪliən] *n* : reptil

republic [rɪ'pʌblɪk] *n* : república *f*

republican¹ [rɪ'pʌblɪkən] *adj* : republicano

republican² *n* : republicano *m*, -na *f* — **Republicanism** [rɪ'pʌblɪkə,nɪzəm] *n*

repudiate [rɪ'pju:di,eɪt] *vt* **-ated; -ating** **1** REJECT : rechazar **2** DISOWN : repudiar, renegar de

repudiation [rɪ,pju:di'eɪʃən] *n* : rechazo *m*, repudio *m*

repugnance [rɪ'pʌgnənts] *n* : repugnancia *f*

repugnant [rɪ'pʌgnənt] *adj* : repugnante, asqueroso

repulse¹ [rɪ'pʌls] *vt* **-pulsed; -pulsing** **1** REPEL : repeler **2** REBUFF : desairar, rechazar

repulse² *n* : rechazo *m*

repulsive [rɪ'pʌlsɪv] *adj* : repulsivo, repugnante, asqueroso — **repulsively** *adv*

reputable ['rɛpjətəbəl] *adj* : acreditado, de buena reputación

reputation [,rɛpjə'teɪʃən] *n* : reputación *f*, fama *f*

repute [rɪ'pju:t] *n* : reputación *f*, fama *f*

reputed [rɪ'pju:təd] *adj* : reputado, supuesto ⟨she's reputed to be the best : tiene fama de ser la mejor⟩

reputedly [rɪ'pju:tədli] *adv* : supuestamente, según se dice

request¹ [rɪ'kwɛst] *vt* : pedir, solicitar, rogar ⟨to request information : solicitar/pedir información⟩ ⟨as requested : conforme a lo solicitado⟩

request² *n* : petición *f*, solicitud *f*, pedido *m*

requiem ['rɛkwiəm, 'reɪ-] *n* : réquiem *m*

require [rɪ'kwaɪr] *vt* **-quired; -quiring** **1** CALL FOR, DEMAND : requerir, exigir ⟨if required : si se requiere⟩ ⟨to require that something be done : exigir que algo se haga⟩ **2** NEED : necesitar, requerir

requirement [rɪ'kwaɪrmənt] *n* **1** NECESSITY : necesidad *f* **2** DEMAND : requisito *m*, demanda *f*

requisite¹ ['rɛkwəzɪt] *adj* : esencial, necesario

requisite² *n* : requisito *m*, necesidad *f*

requisition¹ [,rɛkwə'zɪʃən] *vt* : requisar

requisition² *n* : requisa *f*

reread [,ri:'ri:d] *vt* **-read** [-'rɛd]; **-reading** : releer

reroute [,ri:'ru:t, -'raʊt] *vt* **-routed; -routing** : desviar

rerun[1] [riː'rʌn] *vt* **-ran; -run; -running** : reponer (un programa televisivo)

rerun[2] ['riːˌrʌn] *n* **1** : reposición *f* (de un programa televisivo) **2** REPEAT : repetición *f*

resale ['riːˌseɪl, ˌriː'seɪl] *n* : reventa *f*

reschedule [riː'skɛˌʤuːl, -ʤəl, esp Brit -'lɛdˌjuːl] *vt* **-duled; -duling** : cambiar la hora/fecha de (una cita, etc.)

rescind [rɪ'sɪnd] *vt* **1** CANCEL : rescindir, cancelar **2** REPEAL : abrogar, revocar

rescue[1] ['rɛsˌkjuː] *vt* **-cued; -cuing** : rescatar, salvar

rescue[2] *n* : rescate *m*

rescuer ['rɛsˌkjuːər] *n* : salvador *m*, -dora *f*

research[1] [rɪ'sərtʃ, 'riːˌsərtʃ] *v* : investigar

research[2] *n* : investigación *f*

researcher [rɪ'sərtʃər, 'riːˌ-] *n* : investigador *m*, -dora *f*

resell [riː'sɛl] *vt* **-sold** [-'soːld]; **-selling** : revender

resemblance [rɪ'zɛmblənts] *n* : semejanza *f*, parecido *m*

resemble [rɪ'zɛmbəl] *vt* **-sembled; -sembling** : parecerse a, asemejarse a

resent [rɪ'zɛnt] *vt* : molestarse por (algo), ofenderse por (algo), guardarle rencor a (alguien)

resentful [rɪ'zɛntfəl] *adj* : resentido, rencoroso — **resentfully** *adv*

resentment [rɪ'zɛntmənt] *n* : resentimiento *m*

reservation [ˌrɛzər'veɪʃən] *n* **1** : reservación *f*, reserva *f* ⟨to make a reservation : hacer una reservación⟩ **2** DOUBT, MISGIVING : reserva *f*, duda *f* ⟨without reservations : sin reservas⟩ **3** : reserva *f* (de indios americanos)

reserve[1] [rɪ'zərv] *vt* **-served; -serving** : reservar

reserve[2] *n* **1** STOCK : reserva *f* ⟨to keep in reserve : guardar en reserva⟩ **2** RESTRAINT : reserva *f*, moderación *f* **3 reserves** *npl* : reservas *fpl* (militares)

reserved [rɪ'zərvd] *adj* : reservado

reservoir ['rɛzərˌvwɑr, -ˌvwɔr, -ˌvɔr] *n* : embalse *m*

reset [ˌriː'sɛt] *vt* **-set; -setting** : poner en hora (un reloj), poner a cero (un temporizador), reiniciar (una computadora), borrar (una contraseña)

reside [rɪ'zaɪd] *vi* **-sided; -siding 1** DWELL : residir **2** LIE : radicar, residir ⟨the power resides in the presidency : el poder radica en la presidencia⟩

residence ['rɛzədənts] *n* : residencia *f*

resident[1] ['rɛzədənt] *adj* : residente

resident[2] *n* : residente *mf*

residential [ˌrɛzə'dɛntʃəl] *adj* : residencial

residual [rɪ'zɪʤuəl] *adj* : residual

residue ['rɛzəˌduː, -ˌdjuː] *n* : residuo *m*, resto *m*

resign [rɪ'zaɪn] *vt* **1** QUIT : dimitir, renunciar **2 to resign oneself** : aguantarse, resignarse

resignation [ˌrɛzɪg'neɪʃən] *n* : resignación *f*

resilience [rɪ'zɪljənts] *n* **1** : capacidad *f*

de recuperación, adaptabilidad *f* **2** ELASTICITY : elasticidad *f*

resiliency [rɪ'zɪljəntsi] → **resilience**

resilient [rɪ'zɪljənt] *adj* **1** STRONG : resistente, fuerte **2** ELASTIC : elástico

resin ['rɛzən] *n* : resina *f*

resist [rɪ'zɪst] *vt* **1** : resistir (el calor, la tentación, etc.) **2** OPPOSE : oponerse a — *vi* **1** OPPOSE : resistir **2** : resistirse ⟨I couldn't resist : no me pude resistir⟩

resistance [rɪ'zɪstənts] *n* : resistencia *f*

resistant [rɪ'zɪstənt] *adj* : resistente

resolute ['rɛzəˌluːt] *adj* : firme, resuelto, decidido

resolutely ['rɛzəˌluːtli, ˌrɛzə'-] *adv* : resueltamente, firmemente

resolution [ˌrɛzə'luːʃən] *n* **1** SOLUTION : solución *f* **2** RESOLVE : resolución *f*, determinación *f* **3** DECISION : propósito *m*, decisión *f* ⟨New Year's resolutions : propósitos para el Año Nuevo⟩ **4** MOTION, PROPOSAL : moción *f*, resolución *f* (legislativa)

resolve[1] [rɪ'zɑlv] *vt* **-solved; -solving 1** SOLVE : resolver, solucionar **2** DECIDE : resolver ⟨she resolved to get more sleep : resolvió dormir más⟩

resolve[2] *n* : resolución *f*, determinación *f*

resonance ['rɛzənənts] *n* : resonancia *f*

resonant ['rɛzənənt] *adj* : resonante

resort[1] [rɪ'zɔrt] *vi* **to resort to** : recurrir a ⟨to resort to force : recurrir a la fuerza⟩

resort[2] *n* **1** RECOURSE : recurso *m* ⟨as a last resort : como último recurso⟩ **2** HANGOUT : lugar *m* popular, lugar *m* muy frecuentado **3** : lugar *m* de vacaciones ⟨tourist resort : centro turístico⟩

resound [rɪ'zaʊnd] *vi* : retumbar, resonar

resounding [rɪ'zaʊndɪŋ] *adj* **1** RESONANT : resonante **2** ABSOLUTE, CATEGORICAL : rotundo, tremendo ⟨a resounding success : un éxito rotundo⟩

resource ['riːˌsors, rɪ'sors] *n* **1** RESOURCEFULNESS : ingenio *m*, recursos *mpl* **2 resources** *npl* : recursos *mpl* ⟨natural resources : recursos naturales⟩ **3 resources** *npl* MEANS : recursos *mpl*, medios *mpl*, fondos *mpl*

resourceful [rɪ'sorsfəl, -'zors-] *adj* : ingenioso

resourcefulness [rɪ'sorsfəlnəs, -'zors-] *n* : ingenio *m*, recursos *mpl*, inventiva *f*

respect[1] [rɪ'spɛkt] *vt* : respetar, estimar

respect[2] *n* **1** REFERENCE : relación *f*, respecto *m* ⟨with respect to : en lo que respecta a⟩ **2** ESTEEM : respeto *m* **3** DETAIL, PARTICULAR : aspecto *m*, sentido *m*, respecto *m* ⟨in some respects : en algunos aspectos⟩ ⟨in this/that respect : en este/ese sentido⟩ **4 respects** *npl* : respetos *mpl* ⟨to pay one's respects : presentar uno sus respetos⟩

respectability [rɪˌspɛktə'bɪləti] *n* : respetabilidad *f*

respectable [rɪ'spɛktəbəl] *adj* **1** PROPER : respetable, decente **2** CONSIDERABLE : considerable, respetable ⟨a respectable amount : una cantidad respetable⟩ — **respectably** [-bli] *adv*

respectful [rɪ'spɛktfəl] *adj* : respetuoso — **respectfully** *adv*

respectfulness [rɪ'spɛktfəlnəs] *n* : respetuosidad *f*

respective [rɪ'spɛktɪv] *adj* : respectivo ⟨their respective homes : sus casas respectivas⟩ — **respectively** *adv*

respiration [ˌrɛspə'reɪʃən] *n* : respiración *f*

respirator ['rɛspəˌreɪʃər] *n* : respirador *m*

respiratory ['rɛspərəˌtori, rɪ'spaɪrə-] *adj* : respiratorio

respite ['rɛspɪt, rɪ'spaɪt] *n* : respiro *m*, tregua *f*

resplendent [rɪ'splɛndənt] *adj* : resplandeciente — **resplendently** *adv*

respond [rɪ'spand] *vi* **1** ANSWER : contestar, responder **2** REACT : responder, reaccionar ⟨to respond to treatment : responder al tratamiento⟩

response [rɪ'spanʦ] *n* : respuesta *f*

responsibility [rɪˌspanʦə'bɪləʈi] *n, pl* **-ties** : responsabilidad *f*

responsible [rɪ'spanʦəbəl] *adj* **1** : responsable **2 to be responsible for** CAUSE : ser el/la responsable de (dícese de una persona), ser la causa de **3 to be responsible for** MANAGE : ser responsable de (algo), tener (a alguien) a su cargo **4 to be responsible to** : ser responsable ante **5 to hold someone responsible for** : hacer responsable a alguien de — **responsibly** [-bli] *adv*

responsive [rɪ'spanʦɪv] *adj* **1** ANSWERING : que responde **2** SENSITIVE : sensible, receptivo

responsiveness [rɪ'spanʦɪvnəs] *n* : receptividad *f*, sensibilidad *f*

rest¹ ['rɛst] *vi* **1** : descansar ⟨to rest comfortably : descansar cómodamente⟩ **2** STOP : pararse, detenerse **3** DEPEND : basarse (en), descansar (sobre), depender (de) ⟨the decision rests with her : la decisión pesa sobre ella⟩ **4 to rest easy** : quedarse tranquilo **5 to rest on** : apoyarse en, descansar sobre ⟨to rest on one's arm : apoyarse en el brazo⟩ — *vt* **1** RELAX : descansar **2** SUPPORT : apoyar **3 to rest one's eyes on** : fijar la mirada en

rest² *n* **1** RELAXATION : descanso *m*, reposo *m* ⟨to get some rest : descansar⟩ **2** BREAK : descanso *m* **3** SUPPORT : soporte *m*, apoyo *m* **4** : silencio *m* (en música) **5** REMAINDER : resto *m* ⟨the rest (of us/them) : los demás⟩ **6 to come to rest** : pararse

rest area → **rest stop**

restart [rɪ'start] *vt* **1** : volver a empezar **2** RESUME : reanudar **3** : volver a arrancar (un motor), reiniciar (una computadora) — *vi* **1** : reanudarse **2** : volver a arrancar

restate [ˌri:'steɪt] *vt* **-stated; -stating** : replantear (una pregunta, etc.), repetir

restatement [ˌri:'steɪtmənt] *n* : repetición *f*

restaurant ['rɛstəˌrant, -rənt] *n* : restaurante *m*

restful ['rɛstfəl] *adj* **1** RELAXING : relajante **2** PEACEFUL : tranquilo, sosegado

rest home → **nursing home**

restitution [ˌrɛstə'tu:ʃən, -'tju:-] *n* : restitución *f*

restive ['rɛstɪv] *adj* : inquieto, nervioso

restless ['rɛstləs] *adj* **1** FIDGETY : inquieto, agitado **2** IMPATIENT : impaciente **3** SLEEPLESS : desvelado ⟨a restless night : una noche en blanco⟩

restlessly ['rɛstləsli] *adv* : nerviosamente

restlessness ['rɛstləsnəs] *n* : inquietud *f*, agitación *f*

restoration [ˌrɛstə'reɪʃən] *n* : restauración *f*, restablecimiento *m*

restore [rɪ'stor] *vt* **-stored; -storing** **1** RETURN, GIVE BACK : devolver, restituir **2** REESTABLISH : restablecer (el orden, etc.), recuperar (la confianza, la salud, etc.), restaurar (una monarquía, etc.) **3** REPAIR : restaurar

restrain [rɪ'streɪn] *vt* **1** : refrenar, contener **2 to restrain oneself** : contenerse

restrained [rɪ'streɪnd] *adj* : comedido, templado, contenido

restraint [rɪ'streɪnt] *n* **1** RESTRICTION : restricción *f*, limitación *f*, control *m* **2** CONFINEMENT : encierro *m* **3** RESERVE : reserva *f*, control *m* de sí mismo

restrict [rɪ'strɪkt] *vt* : restringir, limitar, constreñir

restricted [rɪ'strɪktəd] *adj* **1** LIMITED : limitado, restringido **2** CLASSIFIED : secreto, confidencial

restriction [rɪ'strɪkʃən] *n* : restricción *f*

restrictive [rɪ'strɪktɪv] *adj* : restrictivo — **restrictively** *adv*

restroom ['rɛstˌru:m, -ˌrʊm] *n* : servicios *mpl*, baño *m*

restructure [rɪ'strʌktʃər] *vt* **-tured; -turing** : reestructurar

rest stop *n* : área *f* de descanso (en una carretera)

result¹ [rɪ'zʌlt] *vi* : resultar ⟨to result in : resultar en, tener por resultado⟩ ⟨to result from : resultar de⟩

result² *n* : resultado *m*, consecuencia *f* ⟨as a result of : como consecuencia de⟩

resultant [rɪ'zʌltənt] *adj* : resultante

resume [rɪ'zu:m] *v* **-sumed; -suming** *vt* : reanudar — *vi* : reanudarse

résumé *or* **resume** *or* **resumé** ['rɛzəˌmeɪ, ˌrɛzə'-] *n* **1** SUMMARY : resumen *m* **2** CURRICULUM VITAE : currículum *m*, currículo *m*

resumption [rɪ'zʌmpʃən] *n* : reanudación *f*

resurface [ˌri:'sərfəs] *v* **-faced; -facing** *vt* : pavimentar (una carretera) de nuevo — *vi* **1** : volver a salir a la superficie **2** REAPPEAR : resurgir, reaparecer

resurgence [rɪ'sərdʒənʦ] *n* : resurgimiento *m*

resurrect [ˌrɛzə'rɛkt] *vt* : resucitar, desempolvar

resurrection [ˌrɛzə'rɛkʃən] *n* : resurrección *f*

resuscitate [rɪ'sʌsəˌteɪt] *vt* **-tated; -tating** : resucitar, revivir

resuscitation [rɪˌsʌsə'teɪʃən] *n* : reanimación *f*, resucitación *f*

retail¹ ['ri:ˌteɪl] *vt* : vender al por menor, vender al detalle

retail² *adv* : al por menor, al detalle
retail³ *adj* : detallista, minorista ⟨retail price : precio de venta al público⟩
retail⁴ *n* : venta *f* al detalle, venta *f* al por menor
retailer ['ri:ˌteɪlər] *n* : detallista *mf*, minorista *mf*
retain [rɪ'teɪn] *vt* : retener, conservar, guardar
retainer [rɪ'teɪnər] *n* **1** SERVANT : criado *m*, -da *f* **2** ADVANCE : anticipo *m*
retaliate [rɪ'tæliˌeɪt] *vi* **-ated; -ating** : responder, contraatacar, tomar represalias
retaliation [rɪˌtæli'eɪʃən] *n* : represalia *f*, retaliación *f*
retard [rɪ'tɑrd] *vt* : retardar, retrasar
retardation → **mental retardation**
retarded [rɪ'tɑrdəd] *adj dated, now usu offensive* : retrasado *dated, now usu offensive*
retch ['rɛtʃ] *vi* : hacer arcadas
retention [rɪ'tɛntʃən] *n* : retención *f*
retentive [rɪ'tɛntɪv] *adj* : retentivo
rethink [ri:'θɪŋk] *vt* **-thought; -thinking** : reconsiderar, repensar
reticence ['rɛtəsənts] *n* : reticencia *f*
reticent ['rɛtəsənt] *adj* : reticente
retina ['rɛtənə] *n, pl* **-nas** *or* **-nae** [-əni, -ənˌaɪ] : retina *f*
retinue ['rɛtənˌu:, -ˌju:] *n* : séquito *m*, comitiva *f*, cortejo *m*
retire [rɪ'taɪr] *vi* **-tired; -tiring 1** RETREAT, WITHDRAW : retirarse, retraerse **2** : retirarse, jubilarse (de su trabajo) **3** : acostarse, irse a dormir
retiree [rɪˌtaɪ'ri:] *n* : jubilado *m*, -da *f*
retirement [rɪ'taɪrmənt] *n* : jubilación *f*
retiring [rɪ'taɪrɪŋ] *adj* SHY : retraído
retort¹ [rɪ'tɔrt] *vt* : replicar
retort² *n* : réplica *f*
retrace [ˌri:'treɪs] *vt* **-traced; -tracing** : volver sobre, desandar ⟨to retrace one's steps : volver uno sobre sus pasos⟩
retract [rɪ'trækt] *vt* **1** TAKE BACK, WITHDRAW : retirar, retractarse de **2** : retraer (las garras) — *vi* : retractarse
retractable [rɪ'træktəbəl] *adj* : retractable
retraction [rɪ'trækʃən] *n* : retracción *f*, retractación *f*
retrain [ˌri:'treɪn] *vt* : reciclar, reconvertir
retreat¹ [rɪ'tri:t] *vi* : retirarse, batirse en retirada
retreat² *n* **1** : retirada *f* ⟨to beat a hasty retreat : salir huyendo⟩ **2** REFUGE : retiro *m* (espiritual), refugio *m*
retrial [ˌri:'traɪəl] *n* : nuevo juicio *m*
retribution [ˌrɛtrə'bju:ʃən] *n* : castigo *m*
retrieval [rɪ'tri:vəl] *n* : recuperación *f* ⟨beyond retrieval : irrecuperable⟩ ⟨data retrieval : recuperación de datos⟩
retrieve [rɪ'tri:v] *vt* **-trieved; -trieving 1** RECOVER : recuperar **2** FETCH : ir a buscar, cobrar (la caza)
retriever [rɪ'tri:vər] *n* : perro *m* cobrador
retroactive [ˌrɛtro'æktɪv] *adj* : retroactivo — **retroactively** *adv*
retrograde ['rɛtrəˌgreɪd] *adj* : retrógrado
retrospect ['rɛtrəˌspɛkt] *n* **in retrospect** : mirando hacia atrás, retrospectivamente

retrospective [ˌrɛtrə'spɛktɪv] *adj* : retrospectivo
return¹ [rɪ'tɔrn] *vi* **1** : volver, regresar ⟨to return home : regresar a casa⟩ **2** REAPPEAR : reaparecer, resurgir **3** REVERT : volver (a un estado anterior) **4** : volver (a una actividad, un tema, etc.) **5** ANSWER : responder **6** : emitir (un veredicto) — *vt* **1** REPLACE, RESTORE : devolver, volver (a poner), restituir ⟨to return something to its place : volver a poner algo en su lugar⟩ **2** YIELD : producir, redituar, rendir **3** REPAY : devolver, corresponder a ⟨to return a compliment : devolver un cumplido⟩
return² *adj* : de vuelta
return³ *n* **1** RETURNING : regreso *m*, vuelta *f*, retorno *m* **2** *or* **tax return** : declaración *f* de impuestos, declaración *f* de la renta **3** YIELD : rédito *m*, rendimiento *m*, ganancia *f* **4 returns** *npl* DATA, RESULTS : resultados *mpl*, datos *mpl* **5 in return (for)** : a cambio (de)
retweet [rɪ'twi:t] *vt* : retuitear
reunion [ri'ju:njən] *n* : reunión *f*, reencuentro *m*
reunite [ˌri:ju'naɪt] *v* **-nited; -niting** *vt* : (volver a) reunir — *vi* : (volver a) reunirse
reusable [ri'ju:zəbəl] *adj* : reutilizable
reuse [ri'ju:z] *vt* **-used; -using** : reutilizar, usar de nuevo
rev¹ ['rɛv] *v* **-revved; -revving** *vt* **1** *or* **to rev up** : acelerar (un motor) **2 to rev up** : impulsar (la economía), acelerar (un proceso, etc.) — *vi* **to rev up** : prepararse
rev² *n* : revolución *f* (de un motor)
revamp [ˌri'væmp] *vt* : renovar
reveal [rɪ'vi:l] *vt* **1** DIVULGE : revelar, divulgar ⟨to reveal a secret : revelar un secreto⟩ **2** SHOW : manifestar, mostrar, dejar ver
revealing [rɪ'vi:lɪŋ] *adj* : revelador
reveille ['rɛvəli] *n* : toque *m* de diana
revel¹ ['rɛvəl] *vi* **-eled** *or* **-elled; -eling** *or* **-elling 1** CAROUSE : ir de juerga **2 to revel in** : deleitarse en
revel² *n* : juerga *f*, parranda *f fam*
revelation [ˌrɛvə'leɪʃən] *n* : revelación *f*
reveler *or* **reveller** ['rɛvələr] *n* : juerguista *mf*
revelry ['rɛvəlri] *n, pl* **-ries** : juerga *f*, parranda *f fam*, jarana *f fam*
revenge¹ [rɪ'vɛndʒ] *vt* **-venged; -venging to revenge oneself on** : vengarse de
revenge² *n* : venganza *f* ⟨to take (one's) revenge on : vengarse de⟩ ⟨in revenge for : como venganza por⟩
revenue ['rɛvəˌnu:, -ˌnju:] *n* : ingresos *mpl*, rentas *fpl*
reverberate [rɪ'vərbəˌreɪt] *vi* **-ated; -ating** : reverberar
reverberation [rɪˌvərbə'reɪʃən] *n* : reverberación *f*
revere [rɪ'vɪr] *vt* **-vered; -vering** : reverenciar, venerar
reverence ['rɛvərənts] *n* : reverencia *f*, veneración *f*
reverend ['rɛvərənd] *adj* : reverendo ⟨the

Reverend John Chapin : el reverendo John Chapin⟩
reverent ['rɛvərənt] *adj* : reverente — **reverently** *adv*
reverie ['rɛvəri] *n, pl* **-eries** : ensueño *m*
reversal [rɪ'vərsəl] *n* **1** INVERSION : inversión *f* (del orden normal) **2** CHANGE : cambio *m* total **3** SETBACK : revés *m*, contratiempo *m*
reverse[1] *n* [rɪ'vərs] *v* **-versed; -versing** *vt* **1** INVERT : invertir (el orden, los roles, etc.) **2** CHANGE : cambiar totalmente **3** UNDO : reparar (daño, etc.), revertir ⟨to reverse a trend : revertir una tendencia⟩ **4** ANNUL : revocar, revertir — *vi* : dar marcha atrás
reverse[2] *adj* **1** : inverso ⟨in reverse order : en orden inverso⟩ ⟨the reverse side : el reverso⟩ **2** OPPOSITE : contrario, opuesto
reverse[3] *n* **1** BACK : reverso *m*, dorso *m*, revés *m* **2** SETBACK : revés *m*, contratiempo *m* **3** the reverse : lo contrario, lo opuesto **4** *or* **reverse gear** : marcha *f* atrás; reversa *f Col, Mex* ⟨to put a car in reverse : dar marcha atrás, dar reversa⟩
reversible [rɪ'vərsəbəl] *adj* : reversible
reversion [rɪ'vərʒən] *n* : reversión *f*, vuelta *f*
revert [rɪ'vərt] *vi* **1** : revertir (a un propietario) **2** : volver (a un estado anterior)
review[1] [rɪ'vju:] *vt* **1** REEXAMINE : volver a examinar, repasar (una lección) **2** CRITICIZE : reseñar, hacer una crítica de **3** EXAMINE : examinar, analizar ⟨to review one's life : examinar su vida⟩ **4** to review the troops : pasar revista a las tropas
review[2] *n* **1** INSPECTION : revista *f* (de tropas) **2** ANALYSIS, OVERVIEW : resumen *m*, análisis *m* ⟨a review of current affairs : un análisis de las actualidades⟩ **3** CRITICISM : reseña *f*, crítica *f* (de un libro, etc.) **4** : repaso *m* (para un examen) **5** REVUE : revista *f* (musical)
reviewer [rɪ'vju:ər] *n* : crítico *m*, -ca *f*
revile [rɪ'vaɪl] *vt* **-viled; -viling** : injuriar, denostar
revise [rɪ'vaɪz] *vt* **-vised; -vising** : revisar, corregir, refundir ⟨to revise a dictionary : corregir un diccionario⟩
revision [rɪ'vɪʒən] *n* : revisión *f*
revitalize [rɪ'vaɪtə,laɪz] *vt* **-ized; -izing** : resucitar, revitalizar
revival [rɪ'vaɪvəl] *n* **1** : renacimiento *m* (de ideas, etc.), restablecimiento *m* (de costumbres, etc.), reactivación *f* (de la economía) **2** : reanimación *f*, resucitación *f* (en medicina) **3** *or* **revival meeting** : asamblea *f* evangelista
revive [rɪ'vaɪv] *v* **-vived; -viving** *vt* **1** REAWAKEN : reavivar, reanimar, reactivar (la economía), resucitar (a un paciente) **2** REESTABLISH : restablecer — *vi* **1** : renacer, reanimarse, reactivarse **2** COME TO : recobrar el sentido, volver en sí
revoke [rɪ'vo:k] *vt* **-voked; -voking** : revocar — **revocation** [,rɛvə'keɪʃən, rɪ,vo:-] *n*
revolt[1] [rɪ'vo:lt] *vi* **1** REBEL : rebelarse,

sublevarse **2** to revolt at : sentir repugnancia por — *vt* DISGUST : darle asco (a alguien), repugnar
revolt[2] *n* REBELLION : rebelión *f*, revuelta *f*, sublevación *f*
revolting [rɪ'vo:ltɪŋ] *adj* : asqueroso, repugnante
revolution [,rɛvə'lu:ʃən] *n* : revolución *f*
revolutionary[1] [,rɛvə'lu:ʃəne,ri] *adj* : revolucionario
revolutionary[2] *n, pl* **-aries** : revolucionario *m*, -ria *f*
revolutionize [,rɛvə'lu:ʃən,aɪz] *vt* **-ized; -izing** : cambiar radicalmente, revolucionar
revolve [rɪ'vɑlv] *v* **-volved; -volving** *vt* ROTATE : hacer girar — *vi* **1** ROTATE : girar ⟨to revolve around : girar alrededor de⟩ **2** to revolve in one's mind : darle vueltas en la cabeza a alguien
revolver [rɪ'vɑlvər] *n* : revólver *m*
revolving [rɪ'vɑlvɪŋ] *adj* : giratorio ⟨revolving door : puerta giratoria⟩
revue [rɪ'vju:] *n* : revista *f* (musical)
revulsion [rɪ'vʌlʃən] *n* : repugnancia *f*
reward[1] [rɪ'wɔrd] *vt* : recompensar, premiar
reward[2] *n* : recompensa *f*
rewarding [rɪ'wɔrdɪŋ] *adj* **1** : gratificante **2** PROFITABLE : rentable
rewarm [ri'wɔrm] *vt* : recalentar
rewind [,ri:'waɪnd] *vt* : rebobinar
reword [,ri:'wərd] *vt* REPHRASE : expresar de otra forma
rewrite [,ri:'raɪt] *vt* **-wrote; -written; -writing** : escribir de nuevo, volver a escribir
rhapsody ['ræpsədi] *n, pl* **-dies** : elogio *m* excesivo ⟨to go into rhapsodies over : extasiarse por⟩ **2** : rapsodia *f* (en música)
rhea ['ri:ə] *n* : ñandú *m*
rhetoric ['rɛtərɪk] *n* : retórica *f*
rhetorical [rɪ'tɔrɪkəl] *adj* : retórico ⟨rhetorical question : pregunta retórica⟩
rheumatic [ru'mætɪk] *adj* : reumático
rheumatism ['ru:mə,tɪzəm, 'rʊ-] *n* : reumatismo *m*
rhinestone ['raɪn,sto:n] *n* : diamante *m* de imitación
rhino ['raɪ,no:] *n, pl* **rhino** *or* **rhinos** → **rhinoceros**
rhinoceros [raɪ'nɑsərəs] *n, pl* **-eroses** *or* **-eros** *or* **-eri** [-,raɪ] : rinoceronte *m*
rhododendron [,ro:də'dɛndrən] *n* : rododendro *m*
rhombus ['rɑmbəs] *n, pl* **-buses** *or* **-bi** [-,baɪ, -,bi] : rombo *m*
rhubarb ['ru:,bɑrb] *n* : ruibarbo *m*
rhyme[1] ['raɪm] *vi* **rhymed; rhyming** : rimar
rhyme[2] *n* **1** : rima *f* **2** VERSE : verso *m* (en rima)
rhythm ['rɪðəm] *n* : ritmo *m*
rhythmic ['rɪðmɪk] *or* **rhythmical** [-mɪkəl] *adj* : rítmico — **rhythmically** [-mɪkli] *adv*
rib[1] ['rɪb] *vt* **ribbed; ribbing** **1** : hacer en canalé ⟨a ribbed sweater : un suéter en canalé⟩ **2** TEASE : tomarle el pelo (a alguien)

rib² *n* **1** : costilla *f* (de una persona o un animal) **2** : nervio *m* (de una bóveda o una hoja), varilla *f* (de un paraguas), canalé *m* (de una prenda tejida)

ribald ['rɪbəld] *adj* : escabroso, procaz

ribbon ['rɪbən] *n* **1** : cinta *f* **2 to tear to ribbons** : hacer jirones

rib cage *n* : caja *f* torácica

rice ['raɪs] *n* : arroz *m*

rich ['rɪtʃ] *adj* **1** WEALTHY : rico **2** SUMPTUOUS : suntuoso, lujoso **3** : pesado ⟨rich foods : comidas pesadas⟩ **4** ABUNDANT : abundante **5** : vivo, intenso ⟨rich colors : colores vivos⟩ **6** FERTILE : fértil, rico

riches ['rɪtʃəz] *npl* : riquezas *fpl*

richly ['rɪtʃli] *adv* **1** SUMPTUOUSLY : suntuosamente, ricamente **2** ABUNDANTLY : abundantemente **3 richly deserved** : bien merecido

richness ['rɪtʃnəs] *n* : riqueza *f*

rickets ['rɪkəts] *n* : raquitismo *m*

rickety ['rɪkəti] *adj* : desvencijado, destartalado

rickshaw ['rɪk,ʃɔ] *n* : rickshaw *m*

ricochet¹ ['rɪkə,ʃeɪ] *vi* **-cheted** [-,ʃeɪd] *or* **-chetted** [-,ʃɛtəd]; **-cheting** [-,ʃeɪɪŋ] *or* **-chetting** [-,ʃɛtɪŋ] : rebotar

ricochet² *n* : rebote *m*

rid ['rɪd] *vt* **rid; ridding 1** FREE : librar ⟨to rid the city of thieves : librar la ciudad de ladrones⟩ **2 to get rid of** *or* **to rid oneself of** : deshacerse de, desembarazarse de

riddance ['rɪdənts] *n* : libramiento *m* ⟨good riddance! : ¡adiós y buen viaje!, ¡vete con viento fresco!⟩

riddle¹ ['rɪdəl] *vt* **-dled; -dling** : acribillar ⟨riddled with bullets : acribillado a balazos⟩ ⟨riddled with errors : lleno de errores⟩

riddle² *n* : acertijo *m*, adivinanza *f*

ride¹ ['raɪd] *v* **rode** ['roːd]; **ridden** ['rɪdən]; **riding** *vt* **1** : montar, ir, andar ⟨to ride a horse : montar a caballo⟩ ⟨to ride a bicycle : montar/andar en bicicleta⟩ ⟨to ride the bus/train : ir en autobús/tren⟩ **2** : recorrer ⟨he rode 5 miles : recorrió 5 millas⟩ ⟨we rode the trails : recorrimos los senderos⟩ **3** TEASE : burlarse de, ridiculizar **4 to ride out** WEATHER : capear ⟨they rode out the storm : capearon el temporal⟩ **5 to ride the waves** : surcar los mares — *vi* **1** : montar a caballo, cabalgar **2** TRAVEL : ir, viajar (en coche, en bicicleta, etc.) **3** RUN : andar, marchar ⟨the car rides well : el coche anda bien⟩ **4 to be riding high** : estar encantado de la vida **5 to be riding on** : depender de **6 to be riding for a fall** : ir camino al desastre **7 to let something ride** *fam* : dejar pasar algo **8 to ride herd on** *fam* : vigilar **9 to ride shotgun** *fam* : ir en el asiento del pasajero delantero **10 to ride up** : subírsele (dícese de la ropa)

ride² *n* **1** : paseo *m*, vuelta *f* (en coche, en bicicleta, a caballo) ⟨to go for a ride : dar una vuelta⟩ ⟨to give someone a ride : llevar en coche a alguien⟩ **2** : aparato

m, juego *m* (en un parque de diversiones)

rider ['raɪdər] *n* **1** : jinete *mf* ⟨the rider fell off his horse : el jinete se cayó de su caballo⟩ **2** CYCLIST : ciclista *mf* **3** MOTORCYCLIST : motociclista *mf* **4** CLAUSE : cláusula *f* añadida

ridge ['rɪdʒ] *n* **1** CHAIN : cadena *f* (de montañas o cerros) **2** : caballete *m* (de un techo), cresta *f* (de una ola o una montaña), cordoncillo *m* (de telas)

ridicule¹ ['rɪdə,kjuːl] *vt* **-culed; -culing** : burlarse de, mofarse de, ridiculizar

ridicule² *n* : burlas *fpl*

ridiculous [rə'dɪkjələs] *adj* : ridículo, absurdo

ridiculously [rə'dɪkjələsli] *adv* : de forma ridícula

rife ['raɪf] *adj* : abundante, común ⟨to be rife with : estar plagado de⟩

riffraff ['rɪf,ræf] *n* : chusma *f*, gentuza *f*

rifle¹ ['raɪfəl] *v* **-fled; -fling** *vt* RANSACK : desvalijar, saquear — *vi* **to rifle through** : revolver

rifle² *n* : rifle *m*, fusil *m*

rift ['rɪft] *n* **1** FISSURE : grieta *f*, fisura *f* **2** BREAK : ruptura *f* (entre personas), división *f* (dentro de un grupo)

rig¹ ['rɪg] *vt* **rigged; rigging 1** : aparejar (un barco) **2** EQUIP : equipar **3** FIX : amañar (una elección, etc.) **4 to rig up** CONSTRUCT : construir, erigir **5 to rig oneself out as** : vestirse de

rig² *n* **1** : aparejo *m* (de un barco) **2** *or* **oil rig** : torre *f* de perforación, plataforma *f* petrolífera

rigamarole → **rigmarole**

rigging ['rɪgɪŋ, -gən] *n* : jarcia *f*, aparejo *m*

right¹ ['raɪt] *vt* **1** FIX, RESTORE : reparar **2** STRAIGHTEN : enderezar

right² *adv* **1** PRECISELY : justo ⟨right here : aquí mismo⟩ ⟨right on time : a la hora exacta⟩ **2** DIRECTLY, STRAIGHT : derecho, directamente ⟨to go right home : ir derecho a casa⟩ ⟨come right this way : pase por aquí⟩ **3** CORRECTLY : correctamente ⟨to guess right : acertar⟩ **4** WELL : bien ⟨to eat right : comer bien⟩ ⟨nothing is going right : nada está saliendo bien⟩ **5** IMMEDIATELY : inmediatamente ⟨right after class : inmediatamente después de la clase⟩ ⟨I'll be right with you : enseguida lo atiendo⟩ **6** COMPLETELY : completamente ⟨to feel right at home : sentirse completamente cómodo⟩ ⟨right from the start : desde el principio⟩ **7** : a la derecha ⟨to turn right : girar a la derecha⟩ **8** ~ **away** : enseguida **9** ~ **now** IMMEDIATELY : ahora mismo **10** ~ **now** PRESENTLY : en este momento

right³ *adj* **1** MORAL : justo ⟨to be right : ser justo⟩ ⟨to do the right thing : hacer lo correcto⟩ ⟨you were right to forgive him : hiciste bien en perdonarlo⟩ **2** CORRECT : correcto ⟨the right answer : la respuesta correcta⟩ ⟨you're right : tienes razón⟩ ⟨you know him, right? : lo conoces, ¿verdad?⟩ ⟨that's right : así es⟩ **3** APPROPRIATE : apropiado, adecuado

⟨the right man for the job : el hombre indicado para el trabajo⟩ ⟨the right moment : el momento oportuno⟩ ⟨if the price is right : si está bien de precio⟩ **4** (*used for emphasis*) : bien, bueno ⟨right — let's go : bueno, vamos⟩ **5** (*used ironically*) ⟨it's true! yeah, right : ¡es verdad! sí, claro⟩ **6** : derecho ⟨the right hand : la mano derecha⟩ **7** : bien ⟨I don't feel right : no me siento bien⟩ ⟨he's not in his right mind : no está bien de la cabeza⟩ **8 right side** : derecho *m* ⟨right side up : con el derecho para arriba⟩ ⟨right side out : del/al derecho⟩

right⁴ *n* **1** GOOD : bien *m* ⟨you did right : hiciste bien⟩ ⟨to know right from wrong : saber la diferencia entre el bien y el mal⟩ **2** : derecha *f* ⟨on the right : a la derecha⟩ **3** : derecho *m* ⟨to have a right to : tener derecho a⟩ ⟨the right to vote : el derecho a votar⟩ ⟨women's rights : los derechos de la mujer⟩ **4 rights** *npl* : derechos *mpl* ⟨television rights : derechos televisivos⟩ **5 to take/make a right** : girar a la derecha ⟨take the next right : gire en la próxima a la derecha⟩ **6 the Right** : la derecha (en la política)

right angle *n* : ángulo *m* recto

right–click ['raɪt'klɪk] *vi* : hacer clic/click derecho — *vt* : hacer clic/click derecho en

righteous ['raɪtʃəs] *adj* : recto, honrado — **righteously** *adv*

righteousness ['raɪtʃəsnəs] *n* : rectitud *f*, honradez *f*

rightful ['raɪtfəl] *adj* **1** JUST : justo **2** LAWFUL : legítimo — **rightfully** *adv*

right–hand ['raɪt'hænd] *adj* **1** : situado a la derecha **2** RIGHT-HANDED : para la mano derecha, con la mano derecha **3 right–hand man** : brazo *m* derecho

right–handed ['raɪt'hændəd] *adj* **1** : diestro ⟨a right-handed pitcher : un lanzador diestro⟩ **2** : para la mano derecha, con la mano derecha **3** CLOCKWISE : en la dirección de las manecillas del reloj

rightist ['raɪtɪst] *n* : derechista *mf* — **rightist** *adj*

rightly ['raɪtli] *adv* **1** JUSTLY : justamente, con razón **2** PROPERLY : debidamente, apropiadamente **3** CORRECTLY : correctamente

right–of–way ['raɪtə'weɪ, -əv-] *n, pl* **rights–of–way 1** : preferencia (del tráfico) **2** ACCESS : derecho *m* de paso

right triangle *n* : triángulo *m* rectángulo

rightward ['raɪtwərd] *adj* : a la derecha, hacia la derecha

right–wing ['raɪt'wɪŋ] *adj* : derechista

right wing *n* **the right wing** : la derecha

right–winger ['raɪt'wɪŋər] *n* : derechista *mf*

rigid ['rɪdʒɪd] *adj* : rígido — **rigidly** *adv*

rigidity [rɪ'dʒɪdəṭi] *n, pl* **-ties** : rigidez *f*

rigmarole ['rɪgmə,ro:l, 'rɪgə-] *n* **1** NONSENSE : galimatías *m*, disparates *mpl* **2** PROCEDURES : trámites *mpl*

rigor ['rɪgər] *n* : rigor *m*

rigor mortis [,rɪgər'mɔrṭəs] *n* : rigidez *f* cadavérica

rigorous ['rɪgərəs] *adj* : riguroso — **rigorously** *adv*

rile ['raɪl] *vt* **riled; riling** : irritar

rill ['rɪl] *n* : riachuelo *m*

rim ['rɪm] *n* **1** EDGE : borde *m* **2** : llanta *f*, rin *m Col, Mex* (de una rueda) **3** FRAME : montura *f* (de anteojos)

rime ['raɪm] *n* : escarcha *f*

rind ['raɪnd] *n* : corteza *f*

ring¹ ['rɪŋ] *v* **rang** ['ræŋ]; **rung** ['rʌŋ]; **ringing** *vi* **1** : sonar ⟨the doorbell rang : sonó el timbre⟩ ⟨to ring for : llamar⟩ **2** RESOUND : resonar **3** SEEM : parecer ⟨to ring true : parecer cierto⟩ **4 to ring out** : sonar, oírse — *vt* **1** : tocar, hacer sonar (un timbre, una alarma, etc.) ⟨the name rings a bell : el nombre me suena⟩ **2** SURROUND : cercar, rodear **3 to ring up** : cobrar (compras) **4 to ring in the New Year** : recibir el Año Nuevo

ring² *n* **1** : anillo *m*, sortija *f* ⟨wedding ring : anillo de matrimonio⟩ **2** BAND : aro *m*, anillo *m* ⟨key ring : llavero⟩ **3** CIRCLE : círculo *m* **4** ARENA : arena *f*, ruedo *m* ⟨a boxing ring : un cuadrilátero, un ring⟩ **5** GANG : banda *f* (de ladrones, etc.) **6** SOUND : timbre *m*, sonido *m* **7** CALL : llamada *f* (por teléfono)

ringer ['rɪŋər] *n* **to be a dead ringer for** : ser un vivo retrato de

ringing ['rɪŋɪŋ] *adj* **1** : de timbre, de campana (dícese de un sonido) **2** LOUD : sonoro **3** RESOUNDING : categórico

ringleader ['rɪŋ,li:dər] *n* : cabecilla *mf*

ringlet ['rɪŋlət] *n* : sortija *f*, rizo *m*

ringtone ['rɪŋ,to:n] *n* : tono *m* de llamada, ringtone *m*

ringworm ['rɪŋ,wərm] *n* : tiña *f*

rink ['rɪŋk] *n* : pista *f* ⟨skating rink : pista de patinaje⟩

rinse¹ ['rɪn*t*s] *vt* **rinsed; rinsing** : enjuagar ⟨to rinse out one's mouth : enjuagarse la boca⟩

rinse² *n* : enjuague *m*

riot¹ ['raɪət] *vi* : amotinarse

riot² *n* : motín *m*, tumulto *m*, alboroto *m*

rioter ['raɪəṭər] *n* : alborotador *m*, -dora *f*

riotous ['raɪəṭəs] *adj* **1** UNRULY, WILD : desenfrenado, alborotado **2** ABUNDANT : abundante

rip¹ ['rɪp] *v* **ripped; ripping** *vt* **1** : rasgar, arrancar, desgarrar **2 to rip apart** : destruir **3 to rip up** : hacer pedazos — *vi* : rasgarse, desgarrarse

rip² *n* : rasgón *m*, desgarrón *m*

ripe ['raɪp] *adj* **riper; ripest 1** MATURE : maduro ⟨ripe fruit : fruta madura⟩ **2** READY : listo, preparado

ripen ['raɪpən] *v* : madurar

ripeness ['raɪpnəs] *n* : madurez *f*

rip–off ['rɪp,ɔf] *n* **1** THEFT : robo *m* **2** SWINDLE : estafa *f*, timo *m fam* **3** COPY : copia *f* (plagiada)

rip off *vt* **1** : rasgar, arrancar, desgarrar **2** SWINDLE *fam* : estafar, timar

ripple¹ ['rɪpəl] *v* **-pled; -pling** *vi* : rizarse, ondear, ondular — *vt* : rizar

ripple² *n* : onda *f*, ondulación *f*

rise¹ ['raɪz] *vi* **rose** ['ro:z]; **risen** ['rɪzən]; **rising 1** GET UP : levantarse ⟨to rise to

rise · rocker

one's feet : ponerse de pie⟩ **2** : elevarse, alzarse ⟨the mountains rose to the west : las montañas se elevaron al oeste⟩ **3** : salir (dícese del sol y de la luna) **4** : subir (dícese de las aguas, del humo, etc.) ⟨the river rose : las aguas del río subieron de nivel⟩ ⟨let the dough rise : dejar subir la masa⟩ ⟨my spirits rose : me animé⟩ **5** INCREASE : aumentar, subir **6** ORIGINATE : nacer, proceder **7 to rise in rank** : ascender **8 to rise to the occasion** : estar a la altura de las circunstancias **9 to rise up** REBEL : sublevarse, rebelarse

rise² *n* **1** ASCENT : ascensión *f*, subida *f* **2** ORIGIN : origen *m* **3** ELEVATION : elevación *f* **4** INCREASE : subida *f*, aumento *m*, alzamiento *m* ⟨on the rise : en alza, en ascenso⟩ **5** SLOPE : pendiente *f*, cuesta *f* **6 to get a rise out of** PROVOKE : provocar, fastidiar **7 to give rise to** CAUSE : causar, dar origen a

riser ['raɪzər] *n* **1** : contrahuella *f* (de una escalera) **2 early riser** : madrugador *m*, -dora *f* **3 late riser** : dormilón *m*, -lona *f*

risk¹ ['rɪsk] *vt* : arriesgar, arriesgarse ⟨to risk one's life : arriesgar la vida⟩ ⟨to risk losing : arriesgarse a perder⟩ ⟨I won't risk it : no me arriesgo⟩

risk² *n* : riesgo *m*, peligro *m* ⟨at risk : en peligro⟩ ⟨at your own risk : por su cuenta y riesgo⟩ ⟨to take a risk : arriesgarse⟩ ⟨to run the risk of : arriesgarse a, correr el riesgo de⟩ ⟨at the risk of : a riesgo de⟩

risky ['rɪski] *adj* **riskier; -est** : arriesgado, peligroso, riesgoso

risqué [rɪ'skeɪ] *adj* : escabroso, picante, subido de tono

rite ['raɪt] *n* : rito *m*

ritual¹ ['rɪtʃuəl] *adj* : ritual — **ritually** *adv*

ritual² *n* : ritual *m*

rival¹ ['raɪvəl] *vt* **-valed** *or* **-valled; -valing** *or* **-valling** : rivalizar con, competir con

rival² *adj* : competidor, rival

rival³ *n* : rival *mf*; competidor *m*, -dora *f*

rivalry ['raɪvəlri] *n, pl* **-ries** : rivalidad *f*

river ['rɪvər] *n* : río *m*

riverbank ['rɪvər,bæŋk] *n* : ribera *f*, orilla *f*

riverbed ['rɪvər,bɛd] *n* : cauce *m*, lecho *m*

riverside ['rɪvər,saɪd] *n* : ribera *f*, orilla *f*

rivet¹ ['rɪvət] *vt* **1** : remachar **2** FIX : fijar (los ojos, etc.) **3** FASCINATE : fascinar, cautivar

rivet² *n* : remache *m*

riveting ['rɪvətɪŋ] *adj* : fascinante

rivulet ['rɪvjələt] *n* : arroyo *m*, riachuelo *m* ⟨rivulets of sweat : gotas de sudor⟩

roach ['roːtʃ] → **cockroach**

road ['roːd] *n* **1** : carretera *f*, calle *f*, camino *m* ⟨road map : mapa de rutas⟩ ⟨road rage : agresividad al volante⟩ ⟨road safety : seguridad vial⟩ ⟨road trip : viaje en coche (de larga distancia)⟩ ⟨to hit the road : ponerse en marcha⟩ ⟨I've been on the road since six : llevo viajando desde las seis⟩ **2** PATH : camino *m*, sendero *m*, vía *f* ⟨on the road to a solution : en vías de una solución⟩

roadblock ['roːd,blɑk] *n* : control *m*

roadrunner ['roːd,rʌnər] *n* : correcaminos *m*

roadside ['roːd,saɪd] *n* : borde *m* de la carretera

road sign *n* : señal *f* de tráfico, señal *f* de tránsito

roadway ['roːd,weɪ] *n* : carretera *f*, calzada *f*

roadwork ['roːd,wərk] *n* : obras *fpl* (viales)

roam ['roːm] *vi* : vagar, deambular, errar — *vt* : vagar por

roar¹ ['ror] *vi* : rugir, bramar ⟨to roar with laughter : reírse a carcajadas⟩ — *vt* : decir a gritos

roar² *n* **1** : rugido *m*, bramido *m* (de un animal) **2** DIN : clamor *m* (de gente), fragor *m* (del trueno), estruendo *m* (del tráfico, etc.)

roaring ['rorɪŋ] *adj* **1** THUNDEROUS : estruendoso, atronador **2** ACTIVE, STRONG : vivo (dícese de un fuego), caudaloso (dícese de un río), pujante (dícese de la economía) ⟨a roaring success : un gran éxito⟩

roast¹ ['roːst] *vt* : asar (carne, papas), tostar (café, nueces) — *vi* : asarse

roast² *adj* **1** : asado ⟨roast chicken : pollo asado⟩ **2 roast beef** : rosbif *m*

roast³ *n* : asado *m*

roaster ['roːstər] *n* **1** : asador *m* (para carne), tostador *m* (para café) **2** : pollo *m* (para asar)

rob ['rɑb] *v* **robbed; robbing** *vt* **1** STEAL : robar **2** DEPRIVE : privar, quitar — *vi* : robar

robber ['rɑbər] *n* : ladrón *m*, -drona *f*

robbery ['rɑbəri] *n, pl* **-beries** : robo *m*

robe¹ ['roːb] *vt* **robed; robing** : vestirse

robe² *n* **1** : toga *f* (de magistrados, etc.), sotana *f* (de eclesiásticos) ⟨robe of office : traje de ceremonias⟩ **2** BATHROBE : bata *f*

robin ['rɑbən] *n* : petirrojo *m*

robot ['roː,bɑt, -bət] *n* : robot *m* — **robotic** [roː'bɑtɪk] *adj*

robotics [roː'bɑtɪks] *ns & pl* : robótica *f*

robust [roː'bʌst, 'roː,bʌst] *adj* : robusto, fuerte — **robustly** *adv*

robustness [roː'bʌstnəs, 'roː,bʌst-] *n* : robustez *f*, lozanía *f*

rock¹ ['rɑk] *vt* **1** : acunar (a un niño), mecer (una cuna) **2** SHAKE : sacudir **3** SHOCK : sacudir, conmocionar — *vi* SWAY : mecerse, balancearse

rock² *n* **1** : roca *f* (sustancia) ⟨rock climbing : escalada en roca⟩ **2** STONE : piedra *f* **3** ROCKING : balanceo *m* **4** *or* **rock music** : rock *m*, música *f* rock ⟨a rock band : una banda de rock⟩ **5 on the rocks** : con hielo **6 to be on the rocks** : andar mal

rock and roll *n* : rock and roll *m*

rock bottom *n* **to hit/reach rock bottom** : tocar fondo

rocker ['rɑkər] *n* **1** : balancín *m* **2** *or* **rocking chair** : mecedora *f*, balancín *m* **3 to be off one's rocker** : estar chiflado, estar loco

rocket[1] [ˈrɑkət] *vi* : dispararse, subir rápidamente

rocket[2] *n* : cohete *m*

rocking horse *n* : caballito *m* (de balancín)

rock salt *n* : sal *f* gema

rocky [ˈrɑki] *adj* **rockier; -est** **1** : rocoso, pedregoso **2** UNSTEADY : inestable

rod [ˈrɑd] *n* **1** BAR : barra *f*, varilla *f*, vara *f* (de madera) ⟨a fishing rod : una caña (de pescar)⟩ **2** : medida *f* de longitud equivalente a 5.03 metros (5 yardas)

rode → **ride**[1]

rodent [ˈroːdənt] *n* : roedor *m*

rodeo [ˈroːdiˌoː, roˈdeɪˌoː] *n, pl* **-deos** : rodeo *m*

roe [ˈroː] *n* : hueva *f*

rogue [ˈroːg] *n* SCOUNDREL : pícaro *m*, -ra *f*; pillo *m*, -lla *f*

roguish [ˈroːgɪʃ] *adj* : pícaro, travieso

role [ˈroːl] *n* : papel *m*, función *f*, rol *m*

role model *n* : modelo *m* de conducta

roll[1] [ˈroːl] *vi* **1** : rodar (dícese de una pelota, etc.) **2** SLIP : resbalar **3** : ir (en un vehículo) ⟨to roll to a stop : detenerse poco a poco⟩ ⟨to roll up : llegar⟩ **4** SWAY : balancearse **5** : tronar (dícese del trueno), redoblar (dícese de un tambor) **6** FILM : rodar **7** *or* **to get rolling** : ponerse en marcha **8** *or* **to roll over** : darse la vuelta ⟨to roll (over) onto one's back/stomach : ponerse boca arriba/abajo⟩ **9** *or* **to roll over** OVERTURN : volcarse **10** *or* **to roll up** CURL : enrollarse ⟨he rolled up into a ball : se hizo una bola⟩ **11 to be rolling in it** : ser ricachón **12 to roll around** THRASH : revolcarse **13 to roll around** : llegar (dícese de una fecha, etc.) **14 to roll by/ past** : pasar — *vt* **1** : hacer rodar (una pelota, etc.) ⟨to roll the dice : echar los dados⟩ ⟨to roll one's eyes : poner los ojos en blanco⟩ **2** *fam* : hacer volcar ⟨he rolled his car : se volcó (en su auto)⟩ **3** : liar (un cigarrillo) **4** *or* **to roll up** : enrollar ⟨to roll something (up) into a ball : hacer una bola de algo⟩ **5** *or* **to roll out** FLATTEN : estirar (masa), laminar (metales) **6 to roll back** : rebajar (precios) **7 to roll back** : revertir (cambios, etc.) ⟨to roll back the clock : volver atrás⟩ **8 to roll down/up** : bajar/subir (una ventanilla, etc.) **9 to roll out** : lanzar (un producto) **10 to roll the cameras** : rodar **11 to roll up one's sleeves** : arremangarse

roll[2] *n* **1** LIST : lista *f* ⟨to call the roll : pasar lista⟩ ⟨to have on the roll : tener inscrito⟩ **2** BUN : panecito *m*, bolillo *m* *Mex* **3** : rollo *m* (de papel, de tela, etc.) ⟨a roll of film : un carrete⟩ ⟨a roll of bills : un fajo⟩ **4** : redoble *m* (de tambores), retumbo *m* (del trueno, etc.) **5** ROLLING, SWAYING : balanceo *m*

roller [ˈroːlər] *n* **1** : rodillo *m* **2** CURLER : rulo *m*

Rollerblade [ˈroːlərˌbleɪd] *trademark* se usa para patines en línea

roller coaster [ˈroːlərˌkoːstər] *n* : montaña *f* rusa

roller–skate [ˈroːlərˌskeɪt] *vi* **-skated; -skating** : patinar (sobre ruedas)

roller skate *n* : patín *m* (de ruedas)

rollicking [ˈrɑlɪkɪŋ] *adj* : animado, alegre

rolling [ˈroːlɪŋ] *adj* : ondulante

rolling pin *n* : rodillo *m*

ROM [ˈrɑm] *n* : ROM *f*

Roman[1] [ˈroːmən] *adj* : romano

Roman[2] *n* : romano *m*, -na *f*

Roman Catholic *n* : católico *m*, -ca *f* — **Roman Catholic** *adj*

Roman Catholicism *n* : catolicismo *m*

romance[1] [roˈmænts, ˈroːˌmænts] *vi* **-manced; -mancing** FANTASIZE : fantasear

romance[2] *n* **1** : romance *m*, novela *f* de caballerías **2** : novela *f* de amor, novela *f* romántica **3** AFFAIR : romance *m*, amorío *m*

Romanian [rʊˈmeɪniən, ro-] *n* **1** : rumano *m*, -na *f* **2** : rumano *m* (idioma) — **Romanian** *adj*

Roman numeral *n* : número *m* romano

romantic [roˈmæntɪk] *adj* : romántico — **romantic** *n* — **romantically** [-tɪkli] *adv*

romanticism [roˈmæntəˌsɪzəm] *n* : romanticismo *m*

romp[1] [ˈrɑmp] *vi* FROLIC : retozar, juguetear

romp[2] *n* : retozo *m*

roof[1] [ˈruːf, ˈrʊf] *vt* : techar

roof[2] *n, pl* **roofs** [ˈruːfs, ˈrʊfs;, ˈruːvz, ˈrʊvz] **1** : techo *m*, tejado *m*, techado *m* **2 roof of the mouth** : paladar *m*

roofing [ˈruːfɪn, ˈrʊfɪŋ] *n* : techumbre *f*

roof rack *n* : portaequipajes *m*

rooftop [ˈruːfˌtɑp, ˈrʊf-] *n* ROOF : tejado *m*

rook[1] [ˈrʊk] *vt* CHEAT : defraudar, estafar, timar

rook[2] *n* **1** : grajo *m* (ave) **2** : torre *f* (en ajedrez)

rookie [ˈrʊki] *n* : novato *m*, -ta *f*

room[1] [ˈruːm, ˈrʊm] *vi* LODGE : alojarse, hospedarse

room[2] *n* **1** SPACE : espacio *m*, sitio *m*, lugar *m* ⟨to make room for : hacer lugar para⟩ **2** : cuarto *m*, habitación *f* (en una casa), sala *f* (para reuniones, etc.) **3** BEDROOM : dormitorio *m*, habitación *f*, pieza *f* **4** (*indicating possibility or opportunity*) ⟨room for improvement : posibilidad de mejorar⟩ ⟨there's no room for error : no hay lugar para errores⟩

room divider → **divider**

roomer [ˈruːmər, ˈrʊmər] *n* : inquilino *m*, -na *f*

roomie [ˈruːmi] *n fam* → **roommate**

rooming house *n* : pensión *f*

roommate [ˈruːmˌmeɪt, ˈrʊm-] *n* : compañero *m*, -ra *f* de cuarto

room service *n* : servicio *m* de habitaciones, servicio *m* a la habitación

roomy [ˈruːmi, ˈrʊmi] *adj* **roomier; -est** **1** SPACIOUS : espacioso, amplio **2** LOOSE : suelto, holgado ⟨a roomy blouse : una blusa holgada⟩

roost[1] [ˈruːst] *vi* : posarse, dormir (en una percha)

roost[2] *n* : percha *f*

rooster [ˈruːstər, ˈrʊs-] *n* : gallo *m*

root[1] ['ruːt, 'rʊt] vi **1** : arraigar (en botánica) **2** : hozar (dícese de los cerdos) ⟨to root around in : hurgar en⟩ **3 to be rooted in** : estar basado en, tener su origen en **4 to be rooted to** : no poder moverse de (su silla, etc.) **5 to root for** : apoyar a, alentar — vt **to root out** : desarraigar (plantas), extirpar (problemas, etc.)

root[2] n **1** : raíz f (de una planta) **2** ORIGIN : origen m, raíz f **3** CORE : centro m, núcleo m ⟨to get to the root of the matter : ir al centro del asunto⟩ **4 to put down roots** SETTLE : afincarse **5 to take root** : arraigar, enraizar, echar raíces

root beer n : refresco m hecho de raíces e hierbas

rootless ['ruːtləs, 'rʊt-] adj : desarraigado

rope[1] ['roːp] vt **roped; roping 1** TIE : amarrar, atar **2** LASSO : lazar **3 to rope in/ into** ⟨they roped me into driving : me agarraron para manejar⟩ ⟨I didn't want to go, but I was roped in : no quería ir, pero me arrastraron⟩ **4 to rope off** : acordonar

rope[2] n : soga f, cuerda f

rosary ['roːzəri] n, pl **-ries** : rosario m

rose[1] → **rise**[1]

rose[2] ['roːz] adj : rosa, color de rosa

rose[3] n **1** : rosal m (planta), rosa f (flor) **2** : rosa m (color)

rosé [roːˈzeɪ] n : vino m rosado

rosebush ['roːzˌbʊʃ] n : rosal m

rosemary ['roːzˌmeri] n, pl **-maries** : romero m

rosette [roːˈzɛt] n : escarapela f (hecho de cintas), roseta f (en arquitectura)

Rosh Hashanah [ˌrɑʃhɑˈʃɑnə, ˌroːʃ-] n : el Año Nuevo judío

rosin ['rɑzən] n : colofonia f

roster ['rɑstər] n : lista f

rostrum ['rɑstrəm] n, pl **-trums** or **-tra** [-trə] : tribuna f, estrado m

rosy ['roːzi] adj **rosier; -est 1** : sonrosado, de color rosa **2** PROMISING : prometedor

rot[1] ['rɑt] v **rotted; rotting** vi : pudrirse, descomponerse — vt : pudrir, descomponer

rot[2] n : putrefacción f, descomposición f, podredumbre f

rotary[1] ['roːtəri] adj : rotativo, rotatorio

rotary[2] n, pl **-ries 1** : máquina f rotativa **2** TRAFFIC CIRCLE : rotonda f, glorieta f

rotate ['roːˌteɪt] v **-tated; -tating** vi REVOLVE : girar, rotar — vt **1** TURN : hacer girar, darle vueltas a **2** ALTERNATE : alternar

rotation [roːˈteɪʃən] n : rotación f

rote ['roːt] n **to learn by rote** : aprender de memoria

rotisserie [roːˈtɪsri, -ˈtɪsəri] n SPIT : asador m

rotor ['roːtər] n : rotor m

rotten ['rɑtən] adj **1** PUTRID : podrido, putrefacto **2** CORRUPT : corrompido **3** BAD : malo ⟨a rotten day : un día malísimo⟩

rottenness ['rɑtənnəs] n : podredumbre f

rotund [roːˈtʌnd] adj **1** ROUNDED : redondeado **2** PLUMP : regordete fam, llenito fam

rotunda [roːˈtʌndə] n : rotonda f

rouge ['ruːʒ, 'ruːdʒ] n : colorete m

rough[1] ['rʌf] vt **1** ROUGHEN : poner áspero **2 to rough out** : esbozar, bosquejar **3 to rough up** BEAT : darle una paliza (a alguien) **4 to rough it** : vivir sin comodidades

rough[2] adj **1** COARSE : áspero, basto **2** UNEVEN : desigual, escabroso, accidentado (dícese del terreno) **3** : agitado (dícese del mar), tempestuoso (dícese del tiempo), violento (dícese del viento) **4** VIOLENT : violento, brutal ⟨a rough neighborhood : un barrio peligroso⟩ **5** DIFFICULT : duro, difícil **6** CRUDE : rudo, tosco, burdo ⟨a rough cottage : una casita tosca⟩ ⟨a rough draft : un borrador⟩ ⟨a rough sketch : un bosquejo⟩ **7** APPROXIMATE : aproximado ⟨a rough idea : una idea aproximada⟩

rough[3] n **1 the rough** : el rough (en golf) **2 in the rough** : en borrador

roughage ['rʌfɪdʒ] n : fibra f (dietética)

roughen ['rʌfən] vt : poner áspero — vi : ponerse áspero

roughly ['rʌfli] adv **1** : bruscamente ⟨to treat roughly : maltratar⟩ **2** CRUDELY : burdamente **3** APPROXIMATELY : aproximadamente, más o menos

roughneck ['rʌfˌnɛk] n : matón m

roughness ['rʌfnəs] n : rudeza f, aspereza f

roulette [ruːˈlɛt] n : ruleta f

round[1] ['raʊnd] vt **1** TURN : doblar ⟨to round the corner : dar la vuelta a la esquina⟩ **2** : redondear ⟨she rounded the edges : redondeó los bordes⟩ **3 to round off** : redondear (un número) **4 to round off/out** COMPLETE : rematar, terminar **5 to round up** GATHER : reunir (a personas), rodear (ganado), hacer una redada de (delincuentes) ⟨to round up suspects : detener a los sospechosos⟩ **6 to round up/down** : redondear (un número) por exceso/defecto

round[2] adv → **around**[1]

round[3] adj **1** CIRCULAR, SPHERICAL : redondo ⟨a round table/face : una mesa/ cara redonda⟩ **2** CYLINDRICAL : circular, cilíndrico **3** CURVED : redondeado ⟨round shoulders : espaldas cargadas⟩ **4 round number** : número m redondo **5 round trip** : viaje m de ida y vuelta

round[4] n **1** CIRCLE : círculo m ⟨cucumber rounds : rodajas de pepino⟩ **2** SERIES : serie f, sucesión f ⟨a round of talks : una ronda de negociaciones⟩ **3** : asalto m (en boxeo), recorrido m (en golf), vuelta f (en varios juegos) **4** : salva f (de aplausos) **5** : ronda f (de bebidas) **6** or **round of ammunition** : disparo m, cartucho m **7 rounds** npl : recorridos mpl (de un cartero), rondas fpl (de un vigilante), visitas fpl (de un médico) ⟨to make the rounds : hacer visitas⟩

round[5] *prep* → **around**[2]

roundabout ['raʊndə,baʊt] *adj* : indirecto ⟨to speak in a roundabout way : hablar con rodeos⟩

roundly ['raʊndli] *adv* 1 THOROUGHLY : completamente 2 BLUNTLY : francamente, rotundamente 3 VIGOROUSLY : con vigor

roundness ['raʊndnəs] *n* : redondez *f*

round–shouldered ['raʊnd,ʃoːldərd] *adj* : cargado de hombros

round–trip ['raʊnd,trɪp] *adj* : de ida y vuelta

roundup ['raʊnd,ʌp] *n* 1 : rodeo *m* (de animales), redada *f* (de delincuentes, etc.) 2 SUMMARY : resumen *m*

roundworm ['raʊnd,wərm] *n* : lombriz *f* intestinal

rouse ['raʊz] *vt* **roused; rousing** 1 AWAKE : despertar 2 EXCITE : excitar ⟨it roused him to fury : lo enfureció⟩

rout[1] ['raʊt] *vt* 1 DEFEAT : derrotar, aplastar 2 **to rout out** : hacer salir

rout[2] *n* 1 DISPERSAL : desbandada *f*, dispersión *f* 2 DEFEAT : derrota *f* aplastante

route[1] ['ruːt, 'raʊt] *vt* **routed; routing** : dirigir, enviar, encaminar

route[2] *n* : camino *m*, ruta *f*, recorrido *m*

router ['raʊtər] *n* : router *m* (en informática)

routine[1] [ruː'tiːn] *adj* : rutinario — **routinely** *adv*

routine[2] *n* : rutina *f*

rove ['roːv] *v* **roved; roving** *vi* : vagar, errar — *vt* : errar por

rover ['roːvər] *n* 1 : vagabundo *m*, -da *f* 2 : explorador *m* (robot)

row[1] ['roː] *vt* 1 : avanzar a remo ⟨to row a boat : remar⟩ 2 : llevar a remo ⟨he rowed me to shore : me llevó hasta la orilla⟩ — *vi* : remar

row[2] ['raʊ] *n* 1 : paseo *m* en barca ⟨to go for a row : salir a remar⟩ 2 LINE, RANK : fila *f*, hilera *f* 3 SERIES : serie *f* ⟨three days in a row : tres días seguidos⟩ 4 RACKET : estruendo *m*, bulla *f* 5 QUARREL : pelea *f*, riña *f*

rowboat ['roː,boːt] *n* : bote *m* de remos

rowdiness ['raʊdinəs] *n* : bulla *f*

rowdy[1] ['raʊdi] *adj* **rowdier; -est** : escandaloso, alborotador

rowdy[2] *n, pl* **-dies** : alborotador *m*, -dora *f*

rower ['roːər] *n* : remero *m*, -ra *f*

row house *n* : casa *f* adosada

royal[1] ['rɔɪəl] *adj* : real — **royally** *adv*

royal[2] *n* : persona *f* de linaje real, miembro de la familia real

royalist ['rɔɪəlɪst] *n* : realista *mf* — **royalism** ['rɔɪə,lɪzəm] *n* — **royalist** *adj*

royalty ['rɔɪəlti] *n, pl* **-ties** 1 : realeza *f* (posición) 2 : miembros *mpl* de la familia real 3 **royalties** *npl* : derechos *mpl* de autor

rub[1] ['rʌb] *v* **rubbed; rubbing** *vt* 1 : frotar, restregar, friccionar ⟨to rub one's hands together : frotarse las manos⟩ ⟨rub the lotion into your skin : frote la loción en la piel⟩ 2 CHAFE

: rozar 3 POLISH : frotar, pulir 4 SCRUB : fregar 5 **to rub elbows with** : codearse con 6 **to rub off on** ⟨the ink rubbed off on my fingers : se me mancharon los dedos de tinta⟩ ⟨his enthusiasm rubbed off on me : me contagió con su entusiasmo⟩ 7 **to rub someone the wrong way** *fam* : crispar a alguien 8 **to rub something in (someone's face)** *fam* : restregarle (en la cara) algo a alguien ⟨you don't have to rub it in : no tienes que restregármelo⟩ — *vi* **to rub against** : rozar

rub[2] *n* 1 RUBBING : fricción *f*, friega *f* 2 **the rub** : el problema

rubber ['rʌbər] *n* 1 : goma *f*, caucho *m*, hule *m* *Mex* 2 **rubbers** *npl* OVERSHOES : chanclos *mpl*

rubber band *n* : goma *f* (elástica), gomita *f*

rubber–stamp ['rʌbər'stæmp] *vt* 1 APPROVE : aprobar, autorizar 2 STAMP : sellar

rubber stamp *n* : sello *m* (de goma)

rubbery ['rʌbəri] *adj* : gomoso

rubbish ['rʌbɪʃ] *n* : basura *f*, desechos *mpl*, desperdicios *mpl*

rubble ['rʌbəl] *n* : escombros *mpl*, ripio *m*

rubella [ruː'belə] *n* : rubéola *f*

ruble ['ruːbəl] *n* : rublo *m*

ruby ['ruːbi] *n, pl* **-bies** 1 : rubí *m* (gema) 2 : color *m* de rubí

rucksack ['rʌk,sæk, 'rʊk-] *n* BACKPACK : mochila *f*

ruckus ['rʌkəs] *n* COMMOTION : alboroto *m*, bullicio *m*

rudder ['rʌdər] *n* : timón *m*

ruddy ['rʌdi] *adj* **ruddier; -est** : rubicundo (dícese del rostro, etc.), sanguíneo (dícese de la complexión)

rude ['ruːd] *adj* **ruder; rudest** 1 CRUDE : tosco, rústico 2 IMPOLITE : grosero, descortés, maleducado 3 ABRUPT : brusco ⟨a rude awakening : una sorpresa desagradable⟩

rudely ['ruːdli] *adv* : groseramente

rudeness ['ruːdnəs] *n* 1 IMPOLITENESS : grosería *f*, descortesía *f*, falta *f* de educación 2 ROUGHNESS : tosquedad *f* 3 SUDDENNESS : brusquedad *f*

rudiment ['ruːdəmənt] *n* : rudimento *m*, noción *f* básica ⟨the rudiments of Spanish : los rudimentos del español⟩

rudimentary [,ruːdə'mentəri] *adj* : rudimentario, básico

rue ['ruː] *vt* **rued; ruing** : lamentar, arrepentirse de

rueful ['ruːfəl] *adj* 1 PITIFUL : lastimoso 2 REGRETFUL : arrepentido, pesaroso

ruffian ['rʌfiən] *n* : matón *m*

ruffle[1] ['rʌfəl] *vt* **-fled; -fling** 1 AGITATE : agitar, rizar (agua) 2 RUMPLE : arrugar (ropa), despeinar (pelo) 3 ERECT : erizar (plumas) 4 VEX : alterar, irritar, perturbar 5 : fruncir volantes en (tela)

ruffle[2] *n* FLOUNCE : volante *m*

ruffly ['rʌfəli] *adj* : con volantes

rug ['rʌg] *n* : alfombra *f*, tapete *m*

rugby ['rʌgbi] *n* : rugby *m*

rugged ['rʌgəd] *adj* **1** ROUGH, UNEVEN : accidentado, escabroso ⟨rugged mountains : montañas accidentadas⟩ **2** HARSH : duro, severo **3** ROBUST, STURDY : robusto, fuerte

ruin¹ ['ru:ən] *vt* **1** DESTROY : destruir, arruinar **2** BANKRUPT : arruinar, hacer quebrar

ruin² *n* **1** : ruina *f* ⟨to fall into ruin : caer en ruinas⟩ **2** : ruina *f*, perdición *f* ⟨to be the ruin of : ser la perdición de⟩ **3 ruins** *npl* : ruinas *fpl*, restos *mpl* ⟨the ruins of the ancient temple : las ruinas del templo antiguo⟩

ruinous ['ru:ənəs] *adj* : ruinoso

rule¹ ['ru:l] *v* **ruled; ruling** *vt* **1** CONTROL, GOVERN : gobernar (un país), controlar (las emociones) **2** DECIDE : decidir, fallar ⟨the judge ruled that . . . : el juez falló que . . .⟩ **3** DRAW : trazar con una regla **4 to rule out** EXCLUDE : descartar — *vi* **1** GOVERN : gobernar, reinar **2** PREVAIL : prevalecer, imperar **3 to rule against** : fallar en contra de **4 to rule in favor of** : fallar a favor de **5 to rule on** : fallar en

rule² *n* **1** REGULATION : regla *f*, norma *f* ⟨to follow/break the rules : seguir/violar las reglas⟩ ⟨to be against the rules : ir en contra de las reglas⟩ **2** CUSTOM, HABIT : regla *f* general ⟨as a rule : por lo general⟩ **3** GOVERNMENT : gobierno *m*, dominio *m* ⟨to be under the rule of : estar bajo el dominio de⟩ **4** RULER : regla *f* (para medir)

ruler ['ru:lər] *n* **1** LEADER, SOVEREIGN : gobernante *mf*; soberano *m*, -na *f* **2** : regla *f* (para medir)

ruling ['ru:lɪŋ] *n* : resolución *f*, fallo *m*

rum ['rʌm] *n* : ron *m*

Rumanian [ru'meɪniən] → **Romanian**

rumba ['rʌmbə, 'rʊm-, 'ru:m-] *n* : rumba *f*

rumble¹ ['rʌmbəl] *vi* **-bled; -bling** : retumbar, hacer ruidos (dícese del estómago)

rumble² *n* : estruendo *m*, ruido *m* sordo, retumbo *m*

ruminant¹ ['ru:mənənt] *adj* : rumiante

ruminant² *n* : rumiante *m*

ruminate ['ru:mə,neɪt] *vt* **-nated; -nating** **1** : rumiar (en zoología) **2** REFLECT : reflexionar, rumiar

rummage ['rʌmɪʤ] *vi* **-maged; -maging** : hurgar ⟨to rummage (around) in, to rummage through : hurgar en⟩

rummage sale *n* : venta *f* de beneficencia (de objetos de segunda mano)

rummy ['rʌmi] *n* : rummy *m* (juego de naipes)

rumor¹ ['ru:mər] *vt* : rumorear ⟨it is rumored that . . . : se rumorea que . . . , se dice que . . .⟩ ⟨her rumored resignation : su rumoreada dimisión⟩

rumor² *n* : rumor *m*

rump ['rʌmp] *n* **1** : ancas *fpl*, grupa *f* (de un animal) **2** : cadera *f* ⟨rump steak : filete de cadera⟩

rumple ['rʌmpəl] *vt* **-pled; -pling** : arrugar (ropa, etc.), despeinar (pelo)

run¹ ['rʌn] *v* **ran** ['ræn]; **run; running** *vi* **1** : correr ⟨she ran to catch the bus : corrió para alcanzar el autobús⟩ ⟨run and fetch the doctor : corre a buscar al médico⟩ ⟨he ran to the store : salió rápido a la tienda⟩ ⟨to run after someone/something : correr tras alguien/algo⟩ **2** : circular, correr ⟨the train runs between Detroit and Chicago : el tren circula entre Detroit y Chicago⟩ ⟨to run on time : ser puntual⟩ **3** FUNCTION : funcionar, ir ⟨the engine runs on gasoline : el motor funciona con gasolina⟩ ⟨with the motor running : con el motor en marcha⟩ ⟨to run smoothly : ir bien⟩ **4** FLOW : correr, ir **5** LAST : durar ⟨the movie runs for two hours : la película dura dos horas⟩ ⟨the contract runs for three years : el contrato es válido por tres años⟩ **6** : desteñir, despintar (dícese de los colores) **7** EXTEND : correr, extenderse ⟨the path runs along the lake : el sendero bordea el lago⟩ **8** TRAVEL, SPREAD : correr, extenderse **9 to run away** : salir corriendo ⟨to run away from : fugarse de⟩ ⟨to run away from home : escaparse de casa⟩ **10 to run down** : agotarse, gastarse (dícese de pilas, etc.) **11 to run for office** : postularse, presentarse (como candidato) **12 to run out** : acabarse ⟨time is running out : se acaba el tiempo⟩ ⟨I ran out of money : se me acabó el dinero⟩ **13 to run over** OVERFLOW : rebosar — *vt* **1** : correr ⟨to run 10 miles : correr 10 millas⟩ ⟨to run errands : hacer los mandados⟩ ⟨to run out of town : hacer salir del pueblo⟩ **2** PASS : pasar ⟨she ran her fingers through her hair : se pasó la mano por el pelo⟩ **3** DRIVE : llevar (en coche) **4** OPERATE : hacer funcionar (un motor, etc.) **5** PERFORM : realizar (un análisis, etc.) **6** : echar ⟨to run water over : echarle agua a⟩ ⟨to run the water/faucet : abrir la llave (del agua)⟩ **7** MANAGE : dirigir, llevar (un negocio, etc.) **8** EXTEND : tender (un cable, etc.) **9 to run across** : encontrarse con **10 to run a risk** : correr un riesgo **11 to run down** USE UP : gastar, agotar **12 to run down/over** : atropellar **13 to run into** : encontrar **14 to run off** PRINT : tirar, sacar **15 to run through** : repasar, ensayar **16 to run up** : incurrir en **17 to run up against** : tropezar con

run² *n* **1** : carrera *f* ⟨at a run : a la carrera, corriendo⟩ ⟨to go for a run : ir a correr⟩ ⟨to make a run for it : huir corriendo⟩ ⟨to be on the run : estar fugitivo⟩ **2** TRIP : vuelta *f*, paseo *m* (en coche), viaje *m* (en avión) **3** SERIES : serie *f* ⟨a run of disappointments : una serie de desilusiones⟩ ⟨in the long run : a la larga⟩ ⟨in the short run : a corto plazo⟩ **4** DEMAND : gran demanda *f* ⟨a run on the banks : una corrida bancaria⟩ **5** (*used for theatrical productions and films*) ⟨to have a long run : mantenerse mucho tiempo en la cartelera⟩ **6** TYPE : tipo *m* ⟨the average run of students : el tipo más común de estudiante〉 **7** : carrera *f* (en béisbol) **8** : carrera *f* (en una media) **9 to have the run of** : tener libre acceso de (una casa, etc.) **10 ski run** : pista *f* (de esquí)

runaway[1] ['rʌnə,weɪ] *adj* **1** FUGITIVE : fugitivo **2** UNCONTROLLABLE : incontrolable, fuera de control 〈runaway inflation : inflación desenfrenada〉 〈a runaway success : un éxito aplastante〉

runaway[2] *n* : fugitivo *m*, -va *f*

rundown ['rʌn,daʊn] *n* SUMMARY : resumen *m*

run–down ['rʌn'daʊn] *adj* **1** DILAPIDATED : ruinoso, destartalado **2** SICKLY, TIRED : cansado, débil

rung[1] *pp* → **ring**[1]

rung[2] ['rʌŋ] *n* : peldaño *m*, escalón *m*

run–in ['rʌn,ɪn] *n* : disputa *f*, altercado *m*

runner ['rʌnər] *n* **1** RACER : corredor *m*, -dora *f* **2** MESSENGER : mensajero *m*, -ra *f* **3** TRACK : riel *m* (de un cajón, etc.) **4** : patín *m* (de un trineo), cuchilla *f* (de un patín) **5** : estolón *m* (planta)

runner–up [,rʌnər'ʌp] *n, pl* **runners–up** : subcampeón *m*, -peona *f*

running ['rʌnɪŋ] *adj* **1** FLOWING : corriente 〈running water : agua corriente〉 **2** CONTINUOUS : continuo 〈a running battle : una lucha continua〉 **3** CONSECUTIVE : seguido 〈six days running : por seis días seguidos〉

runny ['rʌni] *adj* **runnier; -est 1** WATERY : caldoso **2 to have a runny nose** : moquear

run–of–the–mill [,rʌnəvðə'mɪl] *adj* : normal y corriente, común

runt ['rʌnt] *n* : animal *m* pequeño 〈the runt of the litter : el más pequeño de la camada〉

runway ['rʌn,weɪ] *n* : pista *f* de aterrizaje

rupee [ru:'pi:, 'ru:,-] *n* : rupia *f*

rupture[1] ['rʌptʃər] *v* **-tured; -turing** *vt* **1** BREAK, BURST : romper, reventar **2** : causar una hernia en — *vi* : reventarse

rupture[2] *n* **1** BREAK : ruptura *f* **2** HERNIA : hernia *f*

rural ['rʊrəl] *adj* : rural, campestre

ruse ['ru:s, 'ru:z] *n* : treta *f*, ardid *m*, estratagema *f*

rush[1] ['rʌʃ] *vi* **1** : correr, ir de prisa 〈to rush around : correr de un lado a otro〉 〈to rush off/in/out : irse/entrar/salir corriendo〉 〈let's not rush into it : no nos precipitemos〉 **2** FLOW : correr con fuerza — *vt* **1** HURRY : apresurar, apurar

〈don't rush me : no me apures〉 〈to rush something : hacer algo apresuradamente〉 〈she rushed me into making a decision : me hizo tomar una decisión apresurada〉 **2** : llevar o enviar urgentemente 〈he was rushed to the hospital : fue trasladado de urgencia al hospital〉 **3** ATTACK : abalanzarse sobre, asaltar

rush[2] *adj* : urgente

rush[3] *n* **1** HASTE : prisa *f*, apuro *m* 〈there's no rush : no hay ninguna prisa〉 〈to be in a rush : tener prisa, estar/ir apurado〉 **2** SURGE : ráfaga *f* (de aire), torrente *m* (de aguas), avalancha *f* (de gente) **3** DEMAND : demanda *f* 〈a rush on sugar : una gran demanda para el azúcar〉 **4** : carga *f* (en futbol americano) **5** : junco *m* (planta)

rush hour *n* : hora *f* pico

russet ['rʌsət] *n* : color *m* rojizo

Russian ['rʌʃən] *n* **1** : ruso *m*, -sa *f* **2** : ruso *m* (idioma) — **Russian** *adj*

rust[1] ['rʌst] *vi* : oxidarse — *vt* : oxidar

rust[2] *n* **1** : herrumbre *f*, orín *m*, óxido *m* (en los metales) **2** : roya *f* (en las plantas)

rustic[1] ['rʌstɪk] *adj* : rústico, campestre

rustic[2] *n* : rústico *m*, -ca *f*; campesino *m*, -na *f*

rustle[1] ['rʌsəl] *v* **rustled; rustling** *vt* **1** : hacer susurrar, hacer crujir 〈to rustle a newspaper : hacer crujir un periódico〉 **2** STEAL : robar (ganado) **3 to rustle up** : improvisar (una comida), conseguir (información, etc.) — *vi* : susurrar, crujir

rustle[2] *n* : murmullo *m*, susurro *m*, crujido *m*

rustler ['rʌsələr] *n* : ladrón *m*, -drona *f* de ganado

rustproof ['rʌst,pru:f] *adj* : inoxidable

rusty ['rʌsti] *adj* **rustier; -est** : oxidado, herrumbroso

rut ['rʌt] *n* **1** GROOVE, TRACK : rodada *f*, surco *m* **2 to be in a rut** : ser esclavo de la rutina

ruthless ['ru:θləs] *adj* : despiadado, cruel — **ruthlessly** *adv*

ruthlessness ['ru:θləsnəs] *n* : crueldad *f*, falta *f* de piedad

RV [,ɑr'vi:] → **recreational vehicle**

Rwandan [rʊ'ɑndən] *n* : ruandés *m*, -desa *f* — **Rwandan** *adj*

rye ['raɪ] *n* **1** : centeno *m* **2** *or* **rye bread** : pan *m* de centeno **3** *or* **rye whiskey** : whisky *m* de centeno

S

s ['ɛs] *n, pl* **s's** *or* **ss** ['ɛsəz] : decimonovena letra del alfabeto inglés

Sabbath ['sæbəθ] *n* **1** : sábado *m* (en el judaísmo) **2** : domingo *m* (en el cristianismo)

sabbatical [sə'bæṭɪkəl] *n* : sabático *m*

saber ['seɪbər] *n* : sable *m*

sable ['seɪbəl] *n* **1** BLACK : negro *m* **2** : marta *f* cebellina (animal)

sabotage[1] ['sæbə,tɑʒ] *vt* **-taged; -taging** : sabotear

sabotage[2] *n* : sabotaje *m*

saboteur [,sæbə'tər] *n* : saboteador *m*, -dora *f*

sac ['sæk] *n* : saco *m* (anatómico)

saccharin ['sækərən] *n* : sacarina *f*
saccharine ['sækərən, -ˌriːn, -ˌraɪn] *adj* : meloso, empalagoso
sachet [sæ'ʃeɪ] *n* : bolsita *f* (perfumada)
sack¹ ['sæk] *vt* **1** FIRE : echar (del trabajo), despedir **2** PLUNDER : saquear
sack² *n* BAG : saco *m*
sacrament ['sækrəmənt] *n* : sacramento *m*
sacramental [ˌsækrə'mɛntəl] *adj* : sacramental
sacred ['seɪkrəd] *adj* **1** RELIGIOUS : sagrado, sacro ⟨sacred texts : textos sagrados⟩ **2** HOLY : sagrado **3** sacred to : consagrado a
sacrifice¹ ['sækrəˌfaɪs] *vt* **-ficed; -ficing 1** : sacrificar **2 to sacrifice oneself** : sacrificarse
sacrifice² *n* : sacrificio *m*
sacrilege ['sækrəlɪʤ] *n* : sacrilegio *m*
sacrilegious [ˌsækrə'lɪʤəs, -'liː-] *adj* : sacrílego
sacrosanct ['sækroˌsæŋkt] *adj* : sacrosanto
sad ['sæd] *adj* **sadder; saddest** : triste — **sadly** *adv*
sadden ['sædən] *vt* : entristecer
saddle¹ ['sædəl] *vt* **-dled; -dling 1** : ensillar **2 to saddle someone with something** : cargar a alguien con algo, endilgarle algo a alguien
saddle² *n* : silla *f* (de montar)
saddlebag ['sædəlˌbæg] *n* : alforja *f*
sadism ['seɪˌdɪzəm, 'sæ-] *n* : sadismo *m*
sadist ['seɪdɪst, 'sæ-] *n* : sádico *m*, -ca *f*
sadistic [sə'dɪstɪk] *adj* : sádico — **sadistically** [-tɪkli] *adv*
sadness ['sædnəs] *n* : tristeza *f*
safari [sə'fɑri, -'fær-] *n* : safari *m*
safe¹ ['seɪf] *adj* **safer; safest 1** UNHARMED : ileso ⟨safe and sound : sano y salvo⟩ **2** SECURE, PROTECTED : seguro **3** : seguro (dícese de vehículos, actividades, etc.) ⟨have a safe trip! : ¡(que tengas un) buen viaje!⟩ **4** : seguro (dícese de medicamentos, etc.) ⟨safe to eat/drink : comestible/potable⟩ **5** PROTECTIVE : seguro ⟨a safe place : un lugar seguro⟩ ⟨at a safe distance : a una distancia prudencial⟩ **6** : seguro (dícese de inversiones, etc.) **7** CAREFUL : prudente ⟨a safe driver : un conductor responsable⟩ **8 (it's) better (to be) safe than sorry** : más vale prevenir que curar **9 it's safe to say that . . .** *or* **it's a safe bet that . . .** : se puede decir, sin temor a equivocarse, que . . . **10 to be on the safe side** : para mayor seguridad **11 to play it safe** : ir a la segura
safe² *n* : caja *f* fuerte
safe–conduct ['seɪf'kɑnˌdʌkt] *n* : salvoconducto *m*
safe–deposit box *n* : caja *f* de seguridad
safeguard¹ ['seɪfˌgɑrd] *vt* : salvaguardar, proteger
safeguard² *n* : salvaguarda *f*, protección *f*
safekeeping ['seɪf'kiːpɪŋ] *n* : custodia *f*, protección *f* ⟨to put into safekeeping : poner en buen recaudo⟩
safely ['seɪfli] *adv* **1** UNHARMED : sin incidentes, sin novedades ⟨they landed safely : aterrizaron sin novedades⟩ **2** SECURELY : con toda seguridad, sin peligro **3** : sin temor a equivocarse ⟨one can safely say that . . . : se puede decir, sin temor a equivocarse, que . . .⟩
safety ['seɪfti] *n*, *pl* **-ties** : seguridad *f*
safety belt *n* : cinturón *m* de seguridad
safety net *n* **1** : red *f* de seguridad **2** : protección *f*
safety pin *n* : alfiler *m* de gancho, alfiler *m* de seguridad, imperdible *m* *Spain*
safety razor → **razor**
saffron ['sæfrən] *n* : azafrán *m*
sag¹ ['sæg] *vi* **sagged; sagging 1** DROOP, SINK : combarse, hundirse, inclinarse **2** : colgar, caer ⟨his jowls sagged : le colgaban las mejillas⟩ **3** FLAG : flaquear, decaer ⟨his spirits sagged : se le flaqueó el ánimo⟩
sag² *n* : comba *f*
saga ['sɑgə, 'sæ-] *n* : saga *f*
sagacious [sə'geɪʃəs] *adj* : sagaz
sage¹ ['seɪʤ] *adj* **sager; sagest** : sabio — **sagely** *adv*
sage² *n* **1** : sabio *m*, -bia *f* **2** : salvia *f* (planta)
sagebrush ['seɪʤˌbrʌʃ] *n* : artemisa *f*
Sagittarius [ˌsæʤə'tɛriəs] *n* **1** : Sagitario *m* (signo o constelación) **2** : Sagitario *mf* (persona)
said → **say**
sail¹ ['seɪl] *vi* **1** : navegar (en un barco) **2** : ir/marchar (etc.) fácilmente ⟨we sailed right in : entramos sin ningún problema⟩ ⟨she sailed through the exam : aprobó/pasó el examen sin problemas⟩ — *vt* **1** : gobernar (un barco) **2 to sail the seas** : cruzar los mares
sail² *n* **1** : vela *f* (de un barco) **2** : viaje *m* en velero ⟨to go for a sail : salir a navegar⟩
sailboat ['seɪlˌboːt] *n* : velero *m*, barco *m* de vela
sailfish ['seɪlˌfɪʃ] *n* : pez *m* vela
sailing ['seɪlɪŋ] *n* **1** : navegación *f* (de un barco de vela) **2** : vela *f* (deporte)
sailing ship *n* : barco *m* de vela
sailor ['seɪlər] *n* : marinero *m*
saint ['seɪnt, before a name ˌseɪnt, or sənt] *n* : santo *m*, -ta *f* ⟨Saint Francis : San Francisco⟩ ⟨Saint Rose : Santa Rosa⟩
saintliness ['seɪntlinəs] *n* : santidad *f*
saintly ['seɪntli] *adj* **saintlier; -est** : santo
sake ['seɪk] *n* **1** BENEFIT : bien *m* ⟨for the children's sake : por el bien de los niños⟩ **2** (*indicating an end or a purpose*) ⟨art for art's sake : el arte por el arte⟩ ⟨let's say, for argument's sake, . . . : pongamos que . . .⟩ **3 for goodness' sake!** : ¡por (el amor de) Dios!
salable *or* **saleable** ['seɪləbəl] *adj* : vendible
salacious [sə'leɪʃəs] *adj* : salaz — **salaciously** *adv*
salad ['sæləd] *n* : ensalada *f*
salad dressing → **dressing**
salamander ['sæləˌmændər] *n* : salamandra *f*
salami [sə'lɑmi] *n* : salami *m*

salary ['sæləri] *n, pl* **-ries** : sueldo *m*
sale ['seɪl] *n* **1** SELLING : venta *f* **2** : liquidación *f*, rebajas *fpl* ⟨on sale : de rebaja⟩ **3 sales** *npl* : ventas *fpl* ⟨to work in sales : trabajar en ventas⟩
salesman ['seɪlzmən] *n, pl* **-men** [-mən, -ˌmɛn] **1** : vendedor *m*, dependiente *m* (en una tienda) **2 traveling salesman** : viajante *m*, representante *m*
salesperson ['seɪlzˌpərsən] *n* : vendedor *m*, -dora *f*; dependiente *m*, -ta *f* (en una tienda)
sales pitch → **pitch**[2]
saleswoman ['seɪlzˌwʊmən] *n, pl* **-women** [-ˌwɪmən] **1** : vendedora *f*, dependienta *f* (en una tienda) **2 traveling saleswoman** : viajante *f*, representante *f*
salient ['seɪljənt] *adj* : saliente, sobresaliente
saline ['seɪˌli:n, -ˌlaɪn] *adj* : salino
salinity [ˌseɪˈlɪnəti, sə-] *n* : salinidad *f*
saliva [səˈlaɪvə] *n* : saliva *f*
salivary ['sæləˌvɛri] *adj* : salival ⟨salivary gland : glándula salival⟩
salivate ['sæləˌveɪt] *vi* **-vated; -vating** : salivar
sallow ['sælo] *adj* : amarillento
sally[1] ['sæli] *vi* **-lied; -lying** SET OUT : salir, hacer una salida
sally[2] *n, pl* **-lies** **1** : salida *f* (militar), misión *f* **2** QUIP : salida *f*, ocurrencia *f*
salmon ['sæmən] *ns & pl* **1** : salmón *m* (pez) **2** : color *m* salmón
salon [səˈlɑn, 'sæˌlɑn, sæˈlõ] *n* : salón *m* ⟨beauty salon : salón de belleza⟩
saloon [səˈlu:n] *n* **1** HALL : salón *m* (en un barco) **2** BARROOM : bar *m*
salsa ['solsə, 'sɑl-] *n* : salsa *f* mexicana, salsa *f* picante
salt[1] ['sɔlt] *vt* : salar, echarle sal a
salt[2] *adj* : salado
salt[3] *n* : sal *f*
saltiness ['sɔltinəs] *adj* : lo salado, salinidad *f*
salt shaker → **shaker**
saltwater ['sɔltˌwɔtər, -ˌwɑ-] *adj* : de agua salada
salty ['sɔlti] *adj* **saltier; -est** : salado
salubrious [səˈlu:briəs] *adj* : salubre
salutary ['sæljəˌtɛri] *adj* : saludable, salubre
salutation [ˌsæljəˈteɪʃən] *n* : saludo *m*, salutación *f*
salute[1] [səˈlu:t] *v* **-luted; -luting** *vt* **1** : saludar (con gestos o ceremonias) **2** ACCLAIM : reconocer, aclamar — *vi* : hacer un saludo
salute[2] *n* **1** : saludo *m* (gesto), salva *f* (de cañonazos) **2** TRIBUTE : reconocimiento *m*, homenaje *m*
Salvadoran [ˌsælvəˈdorən] → **El Salvadoran**
salvage[1] ['sælvɪdʒ] *vt* **-vaged; -vaging** : salvar, rescatar
salvage[2] *n* **1** SALVAGING : salvamento *m*, rescate *m* **2** : objetos *mpl* salvados
salvation [sælˈveɪʃən] *n* : salvación *f*
salve[1] ['sæv, 'sav] *vt* **salved; salving** : calmar, apaciguar ⟨to salve one's conscience : aliviarse la conciencia⟩

salve[2] *n* : ungüento *m*
salvo ['sælˌvo:] *n, pl* **-vos** *or* **-voes** : salva *f*
samba ['sæmbə, 'sɑ-] *n* : samba *f*
same[1] ['seɪm] *adj* **1** : mismo ⟨he and I are from the same town : él y yo somos del mismo pueblo⟩ ⟨the same exact day, the exact/very same day : el mismísimo día⟩ ⟨they're one and the same person : son la misma persona⟩ ALIKE, IDENTICAL : igual ⟨I have the same shirt : tengo una camisa igual a la tuya⟩ ⟨they're spelled the same way : se escriben igual⟩ **3** (*indicating repetition*) : mismo ⟨the same thing happened yesterday : ayer pasó lo mismo⟩ **4** (*indicating a shared characteristic*) : mismo ⟨they're the same age : tienen la misma edad⟩ ⟨she has the same eyes as her father : tiene los mismos ojos de su padre⟩ **5 the same old** ⟨it's always the same old thing : siempre pasa lo mismo⟩ ⟨the same old story : la misma historia de siempre⟩ **6 the same thing** ⟨it amounts to the same thing : viene a ser lo mismo⟩
same[2] *pron* **1 the same** : lo mismo ⟨it's all the same to me : me da lo mismo, me da igual⟩ ⟨the same to you! : ¡igualmente!⟩ ⟨the same goes for you : también va por ti⟩ ⟨you should do the same : deberías hacer lo mismo⟩ ⟨they're one and the same : son la misma persona/cosa⟩ ⟨I could say the same : podría decir lo mismo⟩ **2 the same** : igual ⟨the two cars are the same : los dos coches son iguales⟩ **3 the same** : igual (que antes) ⟨things are still the same : las cosas siguen igual⟩ ⟨he was never quite the same again : ya no era el mismo de antes⟩ **4 all/just the same** : de todos modos **5 same here** *fam* : yo también, a mí también
sameness ['seɪmnəs] *n* **1** SIMILARITY : identidad *f*, semejanza *f* **2** MONOTONY : monotonía *f*
same-sex ['seɪmˈsɛks] *adj* : del mismo sexo ⟨same-sex marriage : el matrimonio entre personas del mismo sexo⟩
sample[1] ['sæmpəl] *vt* **-pled; -pling** : probar
sample[2] *n* : muestra *f*, prueba *f*
sampler ['sæmplər] *n* **1** : dechado *m* (de bordado) **2** COLLECTION : colección *f* **3** ASSORTMENT : surtido *m*
sanatorium [ˌsænəˈtoriəm] *n, pl* **-riums** *or* **-ria** [-iə] : sanatorio *m*
sanctify ['sæŋktəˌfaɪ] *vt* **-fied; -fying** : santificar
sanctimonious [ˌsæŋktəˈmoniəs] *adj* : beato, santurrón
sanction[1] ['sæŋkʃən] *vt* : sancionar, aprobar
sanction[2] *n* **1** AUTHORIZATION : sanción *f*, autorización *f* **2 sanctions** *npl* : sanciones *fpl* ⟨to impose sanctions on : imponer sanciones a⟩
sanctity ['sæŋktəti] *n, pl* **-ties** : santidad *f*
sanctuary ['sæŋktʃuˌɛri] *n, pl* **-aries** **1** : presbiterio *m* (en una iglesia) **2** REFUGE : refugio *m*, asilo *m*

sand¹ ['sænd] *vt* : lijar (madera)
sand² *n* : arena *f*
sandal ['sændəl] *n* : sandalia *f*
sandalwood ['sændəl,wʊd] *n* : sándalo *m*
sandbank ['sænd,bæŋk] *n* : banco *m* de arena
sandbar ['sænd,bɑr] *n* : banco *m* de arena
sandbox ['sænd,bɑks] *n* : cajón *m* de arena
sand castle *n* : castillo *m* de arena
sand dune *n* → **dune**
sandpaper ['sænd,peɪpər] *n* : papel *m* de lija
sandstone ['sænd,sto:n] *n* : arenisca *f*
sandstorm ['sænd,stɔrm] *n* : tormenta *f* de arena
sandwich¹ ['sænd,wɪtʃ] *vt* : intercalar, encajonar, meter (entre dos cosas)
sandwich² *n* : sandwich *m*, emparedado *m*, bocadillo *m Spain*
sandy ['sændi] *adj* **sandier; -est** : arenoso
sane ['seɪn] *adj* **saner; sanest** **1** : cuerdo **2** SENSIBLE : sensato, razonable
sang → **sing**
sangria [,sæn'gri:ə, ,sæn-] *n* : sangría *f*
sanguine ['sæŋgwən] *adj* **1** RUDDY : sanguíneo, rubicundo **2** HOPEFUL : optimista
sanitarium [,sænə'teriəm] *n, pl* **-iums** *or* **-ia** [-iə] → **sanatorium**
sanitary ['sænəteri] *adj* **1** : sanitario ⟨sanitary measures : medidas sanitarias⟩ **2** HYGIENIC : higiénico **3 sanitary napkin** : compresa *f*, paño *m* higiénico
sanitation [,sænə'teɪʃən] *n* : sanidad *f*
sanitize ['sænə,taɪz] *vt* **-tized; -tizing** **1** : desinfectar **2** EXPURGATE : expurgar
sanity ['sænəti] *n* : cordura *f*, razón *f* ⟨to lose one's sanity : perder el juicio⟩
sank → **sink**
Santa Claus ['sæntə,klɔz] *n* : Papá Noel, San Nicolás
sap¹ ['sæp] *vt* **sapped; sapping** **1** UNDERMINE : socavar **2** WEAKEN : minar, debilitar
sap² *n* **1** : savia *f* (de una planta) **2** SUCKER : inocentón *m*, -tona *f*
sapling ['sæplɪŋ] *n* : árbol *m* joven
sapphire ['sæ,faɪr] *n* : zafiro *m*
Saran Wrap [sə'ræn-] *trademark* se usa para papel film
sarcasm ['sɑr,kæzəm] *n* : sarcasmo *m*
sarcastic [sɑr'kæstɪk] *adj* : sarcástico — **sarcastically** [-tɪkli] *adv*
sarcophagus [sɑr'kɑfəgəs] *n, pl* **-gi** [-,gaɪ, -,dʒaɪ] : sarcófago *m*
sardine [sɑr'di:n] *n* : sardina *f*
sardonic [sɑr'dɑnɪk] *adj* : sardónico — **sardonically** [-nɪkli] *adv*
sari ['sɑri] *n* : sari *m*
sarsaparilla [,sæspə'rɪlə, ,sɑrs-] *n* : zarzaparrilla *f*
sash ['sæʃ] *n* **1** : faja *f* (de un vestido), fajín *m* (de un uniforme) **2** *pl* **sash** : marco *m* (de una ventana)
sassafras ['sæsə,fræs] *n* : sasafrás *m*
sassy ['sæsi] *adj* **sassier; -est** **1** *fam* IMPERTINENT : fresco, descarado, impertinente **2** STYLISH : moderno, llamativo **3** VIVACIOUS : vivaz

sat → **sit**
Satan ['seɪtən] *n* : Satanás *m*, Satán *m*
satanic [sə'tænɪk, seɪ-] *adj* : satánico — **satanically** [-nɪkli] *adv*
satchel ['sætʃəl] *n* : cartera *f*, saco *m*
sate ['seɪt] *vt* **sated; sating** : saciar
satellite ['sætə,laɪt] *n* : satélite *m* ⟨spy satellite : satélite espía⟩
satellite dish *n* : antena *m* parabólica
satiate ['seɪʃi,eɪt] *vt* **-ated; -ating** : saciar, hartar
satin ['sætən] *n* : raso *m*, satín *m*, satén *m*
satire ['sæ,taɪr] *n* : sátira *f*
satiric [sə'tɪrɪk] *or* **satirical** [-ɪkəl] *adj* : satírico
satirize ['sætə,raɪz] *vt* **-rized; -rizing** : satirizar
satisfaction [,sætəs'fækʃən] *n* : satisfacción *f*
satisfactory [,sætəs'fæktəri] *adj* : satisfactorio, bueno — **satisfactorily** [-rəli] *adv*
satisfy ['sætəs,faɪ] *v* **-fied; -fying** *vt* **1** PLEASE : satisfacer, contentar **2** CONVINCE : convencer **3** FULFILL : satisfacer, cumplir con, llenar **4** SETTLE : pagar, saldar (una cuenta) — *vi* SUFFICE : bastar
satisfying ['sætəs,faɪɪŋ] *adj* : satisfactorio
saturate ['sætʃə,reɪt] *vt* **-rated; -rating** **1** SOAK : empapar **2** FILL : saturar
saturation [,sætʃə'reɪʃən] *n* : saturación *f*
Saturday ['sætər,deɪ, -di] *n* : sábado *m* ⟨today is Saturday : hoy es sábado⟩ ⟨(on) Saturday : el sábado⟩ ⟨(on) Saturdays : los sábados⟩ ⟨last Saturday : el sábado pasado⟩ ⟨next Saturday : el sábado que viene⟩ ⟨every other Saturday : cada dos sábados⟩ ⟨Saturday afternoon/morning : sábado por la tarde/mañana⟩
Saturn ['sætərn] *n* : Saturno *m*
satyr ['seɪtər, 'sæ-] *n* : sátiro *m*
sauce ['sɔs] *n* : salsa *f*
saucepan ['sɔs,pæn] *n* : cacerola *f*, cazo *m*, cazuela *f*
saucer ['sɔsər] *n* : platillo *m*
sauciness ['sɔsinəs] *n* : descaro *m*, frescura *f*
saucy ['sɔsi] *adj* **saucier; -est** IMPUDENT : descarado, fresco *fam* — **saucily** *adv*
Saudi ['saʊdi, 'sɔ-] → **Saudi Arabian**
Saudi Arabian *n* : saudita *mf*, saudí *mf* — **Saudi Arabian** *adj*
sauna ['sɔnə, 'saʊnə] *n* : sauna *mf*
saunter ['sɔntər, 'sɑn-] *vi* : pasear, pasearse
sausage ['sɔsɪdʒ] *n* : salchicha *f*, embutido *m*
sauté [sɔ'teɪ, so:-] *vt* **-téed** *or* **-téd; -téing** : saltear, sofreír
savage¹ ['sævɪdʒ] *adj* **1** *offensive* PRIMITIVE : salvaje **2** : salvaje, feroz — **savagely** *adv*
savage² *n* **1** *offensive* : salvaje *mf* **2** BEAST, BRUTE : salvaje *mf*
savagery ['sævɪdʒri] *n, pl* **-ries** **1** FEROCITY : ferocidad *f* **2** ATROCITY : salvajada *f*, atrocidad *f*, crueldad *f* ⟨the savageries of war : las atrocidades de la guerra⟩

savanna [sə'vænə] *n* : sabana *f*
save¹ ['seɪv] *v* **saved; saving** *vt* **1** RES-
CUE : salvar, rescatar ⟨she saved him
from drowning : lo salvó de morir aho-
gado⟩ ⟨you really saved my bacon/hide/
neck/skin! : ¡me salvaste el pellejo!⟩ **2**
PRESERVE : salvar, preservar, conservar
⟨he hopes to save his job : espera salvar
su trabajo⟩ **3** KEEP : guardar, ahorrar
(dinero), almacenar (alimentos) ⟨to save
one's strength : guardarse las fuerzas⟩ **4**
: guardar (en informática) **5** ECONO-
MIZE : ahorrar (tiempo, espacio, combustible, etc.) **6** SPARE : ahorrar ⟨you
saved me a trip : me ahorraste el viaje⟩ **7**
to save someone's life : salvarle la vida
a alguien **8 to save the day** : salvar la
situación — *vi* : ahorrar ⟨to save for the
future : ahorrar para el futuro⟩ ⟨you'll
save on insurance : ahorrarás dinero en
tu seguro⟩
save² *prep* EXCEPT : salvo, excepto, menos
savings ['seɪvɪŋz] *n* : ahorros *mpl*
savings account *n* : cuenta *f* de ahorro(s)
savings bank *n* : caja *f* de ahorros
savior ['seɪvjər] *n* **1** : salvador *m*, -dora
f **2 the Savior** : el Salvador *m*
savor¹ ['seɪvər] *vt* : saborear
savor² *n* : sabor *m*
savory ['seɪvəri] *adj* : sabroso
saw¹ → **see**
saw² ['sɔ] *v* **sawed; sawed** *or* **sawn**
['sɔn]; **sawing** : serrar, cortar (con sierra)
saw³ *n* : sierra *f*
sawdust ['sɔˌdʌst] *n* : aserrín *m*, serrín *m*
sawhorse ['sɔˌhɔrs] *n* : caballete *m*, burro
m (en carpintería)
sawmill ['sɔˌmɪl] *n* : aserradero *m*
sax ['sæks] *n* : saxo *m fam* (instrumento)
saxophone ['sæksəˌfoːn] *n* : saxofón *m* —
saxophonist ['sæksəˌfoːnɪst] *n*
say¹ ['seɪ] *v* **said** ['sed]; **saying; says** ['sɛz]
vt **1** EXPRESS, UTTER : decir, expresar
⟨to say yes/no : decir que sí/no⟩ ⟨to say
again : repetir⟩ ⟨to say one's prayers
: rezar⟩ ⟨she didn't say a word : no dijo
ni una palabra⟩ **2** INDICATE : marcar
(dícese de un reloj), poner (dícese de un
letrero, etc.) **3** EXPRESS, REVEAL
: decir, revelar ⟨her face says it all : su
cara lo dice todo⟩ **4** OPINE : decir ⟨so
they say : eso dicen⟩ **5** KNOW : decir,
saber ⟨it's hard to say why : es difícil
decir por qué⟩ **6** COMMAND : decir,
mandar ⟨what she says goes : lo que ella
dice va a misa⟩ ⟨do as I say : haz lo que
te digo⟩ ⟨whatever you say : lo que tú
digas⟩ **7** PRONOUNCE : decir, pronunciar **8** SUPPOSE : suponer, decir **9 if I
say so myself** : modestia aparte **10 no
sooner said than done** : dicho y
hecho **11 that goes without saying** : ni
que decir tiene **12 that is to say** : es
decir **13 that said, . . .** : dicho
esto, . . . **14 to say the least** : y me
quedo corto **15 when all is said and
done** : al fin y al cabo **16 you can say
that again!** *fam* : ¡y tanto! **17 you said

it!** : ¡de acuerdo! — *vi* **1** : decir ⟨I
couldn't say : no podría decirte⟩ **2 I'll
say!** : ¡tú tanto! **3 you don't say!** : ¡no
me digas!
say² *n*, *pl* **says** ['seɪz] : voz *f*, opinión *f* ⟨to
have no say : no tener ni voz ni voto⟩ ⟨to
have one's say : dar uno su opinión⟩
saying ['seɪɪŋ] *n* : dicho *m*, refrán *m*
scab ['skæb] *n* **1** : costra *f*, postilla *f* (en
una herida) **2** STRIKEBREAKER
: rompehuelgas *mf*, esquirol *mf*
scabbard ['skæbərd] *n* : vaina *f* (de una
espada), funda *f* (de un puñal, etc.)
scabby ['skæbi] *adj* **scabbier; -est** : lleno
de costras
scaffold ['skæfəld, -ˌfoːld] *n* **1** *or* **scaffolding** : andamio *m* (para obreros, etc.) **2**
: patíbulo *m*, cadalso *m* (para ejecuciones)
scald ['skɔld] *vt* **1** BURN : escaldar **2**
HEAT : calentar (hasta el punto de ebullición)
scale¹ ['skeɪl] *v* **scaled; scaling** *vt* **1** : escamar (un pescado) **2** CLIMB : escalar
(un muro, etc.) **3 to scale down** : reducir — *vi* WEIGH : pesar ⟨he scaled in at
200 pounds : pesó 200 libras⟩
scale² *n* **1** *or* **scales** *npl* : balanza *f*,
báscula *f* (para pesar), baremo *m* ⟨bath-
room scale : báscula de baño⟩ ⟨kitchen
scale : balanza de cocina⟩ ⟨to tip the
scales in one's favor : inclinar la balanza
a su favor⟩ **2** : escama *f* (de un pez,
etc.) **3** EXTENT : escala *f*, proporción *f*
⟨on a worldwide scale : a escala mundial⟩
⟨large-scale production : producción a
gran escala⟩ **4** RANGE : escala *f* ⟨wage
scale : escala salarial⟩ **5** : escala *f* (en
cartografía, etc.) ⟨to draw to scale : dibujar a escala⟩ **6** : escala *f* (en música)
scallion ['skæljən] *n* : cebollino *m*, cebolleta *f*
scallop ['skɑləp, 'skæ-] *n* **1** : vieira *f*
(molusco) **2** : festón *m* (decoración)
scalp¹ ['skælp] *vt* **1** : arrancar la cabellera a **2** : revender (ilegalmente)
scalp² *n* : cuero *m* cabelludo
scalpel ['skælpəl] *n* : bisturí *m*, escalpelo
m
scalper ['skælpər] *n* : revendedor *m*,
-dora *f* (de entradas)
scaly ['skeɪli] *adj* **scalier; -est** : escamoso
scam ['skæm] *n* : estafa *f*, timo *m fam*,
chanchullo *m fam*
scamp ['skæmp] *n* : bribón *m*, -bona *f*;
granuja *mf*; travieso *m*, -sa *f*
scamper ['skæmpər] *vi* : corretear
scan¹ ['skæn] *vt* **scanned; scanning 1**
: escandir (versos) **2** SCRUTINIZE : escudriñar, escrutar ⟨to scan the horizon
: escudriñar el horizonte⟩ **3** PERUSE
: echarle un vistazo a (un periódico,
etc.) **4** EXPLORE : explorar (con radar),
hacer un escáner de (en ecografía) **5**
: escanear (una imagen)
scan² *n* **1** : ecografía *f*, examen *m* ultrasónico, escáner *m* (en medicina) **2** : imagen *f* escaneada (en una computadora)
scandal ['skændəl] *n* **1** DISGRACE, OUT-
RAGE : escándalo *m* **2** GOSSIP : habladurías *fpl*, chismes *mpl*

scandalize ['skændəl͵aɪz] *vt* **-ized; -izing** : escandalizar

scandalous ['skændələs] *adj* : de escándalo

Scandinavian[1] [͵skændə'neɪviən] *adj* : escandinavo

Scandinavian[2] *n* : escandinavo *m*, -va *f*

scanner ['skænər] *n* : escáner *m*, scanner *m*

scant ['skænt] *adj* : escaso

scanty ['skænti] *adj* **scantier; -est** : exiguo, escaso ⟨a scanty meal : una comida insuficiente⟩ — **scantily** [-təli] *adv*

scapegoat ['skeɪp͵goːt] *n* : chivo *m* expiatorio, cabeza *f* de turco

scapula ['skæpjələ] *n, pl* **-lae** [-͵liː, -͵laɪ] *or* **-las** → **shoulder blade**

scar[1] ['skɑr] *v* **scarred; scarring** *vt* : dejar una cicatriz en — *vi* : cicatrizar

scar[2] *n* : cicatriz *f*, marca *f*

scarab ['skærəb] *n* : escarabajo *m*

scarce ['skɛrs] *adj* **scarcer; -est** : escaso

scarcely ['skɛrsli] *adv* **1** BARELY : apenas **2** : ni mucho menos, ni nada que se le parezca ⟨he's scarcely an expert : ciertamente no es experto⟩

scarcity ['skɛrsəti] *n, pl* **-ties** : escasez *f*

scare[1] ['skɛr] *vt* **scared; scaring 1** : asustar, espantar **2 to scare away/off** : ahuyentar

scare[2] *n* **1** FRIGHT : susto *m*, sobresalto *m* **2** ALARM : pánico *m*

scarecrow ['skɛr͵kroː] *n* : espantapájaros *m*, espantajo *m*

scared ['skɛrd] *n* : asustado ⟨to be scared stiff, to be scared to death : estar muerto de miedo⟩ ⟨I'm scared of snakes : las culebras me dan miedo⟩

scarf ['skɑrf] *n, pl* **scarves** ['skɑrvz] *or* **scarfs 1** MUFFLER : bufanda *f* **2** KERCHIEF : pañuelo *m*

scarlet ['skɑrlət] *n* : escarlata *f* — **scarlet** *adj*

scarlet fever *n* : escarlatina *f*

scary ['skɛri] *adj* **scarier; -est** : espantoso, pavoroso

scathing ['skeɪðɪŋ] *adj* : mordaz, cáustico

scatter ['skætər] *vt* : esparcir, desparramar — *vi* DISPERSE : dispersarse

scatterbrained ['skætər͵breɪnd] *adj* : atolondrado, despistado, alocado

scavenge ['skævəndʒ] *v* **-venged; -venging** *vt* : rescatar (de la basura); pepenar *CA, Mex* — *vi* : rebuscar, hurgar en la basura ⟨to scavenge for food : andar buscando comida⟩

scavenger ['skævəndʒər] *n* **1** : persona *f* que rebusca en las basuras; pepenador *m*, -dora *f CA, Mex* **2** : carroñero *m*, -ra *f* (animal)

scenario [sə'næri͵oː, -'nɑr-] *n, pl* **-ios 1** PLOT : argumento *m* (en teatro), guión *m* (en cine) **2** SITUATION : situación *f* hipotética ⟨in the worst-case scenario : en el peor de los casos⟩

scene ['siːn] *n* **1** : escena *f* (en una obra de teatro) **2** SCENERY : decorado *m* (en el teatro) ⟨behind the scenes : entre bastidores⟩ **3** VIEW : escena *f* **4** LOCALE, LOCATION : escena *f*, escenario *m* ⟨the scene where the movie was filmed : el lugar donde la película se filmó⟩ ⟨the scene of the crime : la escena del crimen⟩ ⟨police are on/at the scene : los policías están en el lugar⟩ **5** COMMOTION, FUSS : escándalo *m*, escena *f* ⟨to make a scene : armar un escándalo⟩ **6 to set the scene** : describir el escenario (de un cuento, etc.) **7 to set the scene for** : crear un ambiente propicio para

scenery ['siːnəri] *n, pl* **-eries 1** : decorado *m* (en el teatro) **2** LANDSCAPE : paisaje *m*

scenic ['siːnɪk] *adj* : pintoresco

scent[1] ['sɛnt] *vt* **1** SMELL : oler, olfatear **2** PERFUME : perfumar **3** SENSE : sentir, percibir

scent[2] *n* **1** ODOR : olor *m*, aroma *m* **2** : olfato *m* ⟨a dog with a keen scent : un perro con un buen olfato⟩ **3** PERFUME : perfume *m*

scented ['sɛntəd] *adj* : perfumado

scepter ['sɛptər] *n* : cetro *m*

sceptic ['skɛptɪk] → **skeptic**

schedule[1] ['skɛ͵dʒuːl, -dʒəl, esp Brit 'ʃɛd͵juːl] *vt* **-uled; -uling** : planear, programar

schedule[2] *n* **1** PLAN : programa *m*, plan *m* ⟨on schedule : según lo previsto⟩ ⟨behind schedule : atrasado, con retraso⟩ **2** TIMETABLE : horario *m*

schematic[1] [skɪ'mætɪk] *adj* : esquemático

schematic[2] *n* : plano *m*, esquema *m*

scheme[1] ['skiːm] *vi* **schemed; scheming** : intrigar, conspirar

scheme[2] *n* **1** PLAN : plan *m*, proyecto *m* **2** PLOT, TRICK : intriga *f*, ardid *m* **3** FRAMEWORK : esquema *m* ⟨a color scheme : una combinación de colores⟩

schemer ['skiːmər] *n* : intrigante *mf*

schism ['sɪzəm, 'skɪ-] *n* : cisma *m*

schizophrenia [͵skɪtsə'friːniə, ͵skɪzə-, -'frɛ-] *n* : esquizofrenia *f*

schizophrenic [͵skɪtsə'frɛnɪk, ͵skɪzə-] *n* : esquizofrénico *m*, -ca *f* — **schizophrenic** *adj*

scholar ['skɑlər] *n* **1** STUDENT : escolar *mf*; alumno *m*, -na *f* **2** EXPERT : especialista *mf*

scholarly ['skɑlərli] *adj* : erudito

scholarship ['skɑlər͵ʃɪp] *n* **1** LEARNING : erudición *f* **2** GRANT : beca *f*

scholastic [skə'læstɪk] *adj* : académico

school[1] ['skuːl] *vt* : instruir, enseñar

school[2] *n* **1** : escuela *f*, colegio *m* (institución) ⟨to go to school : ir a la escuela⟩ ⟨school district : distrito escolar⟩ ⟨law/medical school : facultad de derecho/medicina⟩ **2** : estudiantes y profesores (de una escuela) **3** : escuela *f* (en pintura, etc.) ⟨the Flemish school : la escuela flamenca⟩ **4 school of fish** : banco *m*, cardumen *m*

schoolbook ['skuːl͵bʊk] *n* : libro *m* de texto

schoolboy ['skuːl͵bɔɪ] *n* : escolar *m*, colegial *m*

schoolchild ['skuːl͵tʃaɪld] *n* : colegial *m*, -giala *f*; escolar *mf*

schoolgirl ['skuːl͵gərl] *n* : escolar *f*, colegiala *f*

schoolhouse ['sku:l₁haʊs] *n* : escuela *f*

schooling ['sku:lɪŋ] *n* : educación *f* escolar

schoolmate ['sku:l₁meɪt] *n* : compañero *m*, -ra *f* de escuela

schoolroom ['sku:l₁ru:m, -₁rʊm] → **classroom**

schoolteacher ['sku:l₁ti:tʃər] *n* : maestro *m*, -tra *f*; profesor *m*, -sora *f*

schoolwork ['sku:l₁wərk] *n* : trabajo *m* escolar

schooner ['sku:nər] *n* : goleta *f*

science ['saɪənts] *n* : ciencia *f*

science fiction *n* : ciencia ficción *f*

scientific [₁saɪən'tɪfɪk] *adj* : científico — **scientifically** [-fɪkli] *adv*

scientist ['saɪəntɪst] *n* : científico *m*, -ca *f*

sci–fi ['saɪ'faɪ] *fam* → **science fiction**

scintillating ['sɪntə₁leɪtɪŋ] *adj* : chispeante, brillante

scissors ['sɪzərz] *npl* : tijeras *fpl*

sclerosis [sklə'ro:səs] *n*, *pl* **-roses** : esclerosis *f*

scoff ['skɑf] *vi* **to scoff at** : burlarse de, mofarse de

scold ['sko:ld] *vt* : regañar, reprender, reñir

scoop¹ ['sku:p] *vt* **1** : sacar (con pala o cucharón) **2 to scoop out** HOLLOW : vaciar, ahuecar

scoop² *n* **1** : pala *f* (para harina, etc.), cucharón *m* (para helado, etc.) **2** : bola *f* (de helado), cucharada *f*

scoot ['sku:t] *vi* : ir rápidamente ⟨she scooted around the corner : volvió la esquina a toda prisa⟩

scooter ['sku:tər] *n* : patineta *f*, monopatín *m*, patinete *m*

scope ['sko:p] *n* **1** RANGE : alcance *m*, ámbito *m*, extensión *f* **2** OPPORTUNITY : posibilidades *fpl*, libertad *f*

scorch ['skɔrtʃ] *vt* : chamuscar, quemar — *vi* : chamuscarse, quemarse

score¹ ['skor] *v* **scored; scoring** *vt* **1** RECORD : anotar **2** MARK, SCRATCH : marcar, rayar **3** : marcar, meter (en deportes) **4** GAIN : ganar, apuntarse **5** GRADE : calificar (exámenes, etc.) **6** : instrumentar, orquestar (música) — *vi* **1** : marcar (en deportes) **2** : obtener una puntuación (en un examen)

score² *n*, *pl* **scores 1** *or pl* **score** TWENTY : veintena *f* **2** LINE, SCRATCH : línea *f*, marca *f* **3** : resultado *m* (en deportes) ⟨what's the score? : ¿cómo va el marcador?⟩ ⟨to keep score : anotar los tantos⟩ **4** GRADE, POINTS : calificación *f* (en un examen), puntuación *f* (en un concurso) **5** ACCOUNT : cuenta *f* ⟨to settle a score : ajustar una cuenta⟩ ⟨on that score : a ese respecto⟩ **6** : partitura *f* (musical)

scoreboard ['skor₁bord] *n* : marcador *m*, tanteador *m*, pizarra *f*

scorer ['skorər] *n* : anotador *m*, -dora *f*; goleador *m*, -dora *f* (de fútbol, etc.) ⟨the team's top scorer : el máximo anotador del equipo⟩

scorn¹ ['skɔrn] *vt* : despreciar, menospreciar, desdeñar

scorn² *n* : desprecio *m*, menosprecio *m*, desdén *m*

scornful ['skɔrnfəl] *adj* : desdeñoso, despreciativo — **scornfully** *adv*

Scorpio ['skɔrpi₁o:] *n* **1** : Escorpio *m*, Escorpión *m* (signo o constelación) **2** : Escorpio *mf*, Escorpión *mf* (persona)

scorpion ['skɔrpiən] *n* : alacrán *m*, escorpión *m*

Scot ['skɑt] *n* : escocés *m*, -cesa *f*

Scotch¹ ['skɑtʃ] *adj* → **Scottish¹**

Scotch² *npl* **the Scotch** (*used with a plural verb*) : los escoceses

Scotch³ *trademark* se usa para un tipo de cinta adhesiva

scot–free ['skɑt'fri:] *adj* **to get off scot–free** : salir impune, quedar sin castigo

Scots ['skɑts] *n* : escocés *m* (idioma)

Scottish¹ ['skɑtɪʃ] *adj* : escocés

Scottish² *n* → **Scots**

scoundrel ['skaʊndrəl] *n* : sinvergüenza *mf*; bellaco *m*, -ca *f*

scour ['skaʊər] *vt* **1** EXAMINE, SEARCH : registrar (un área), revisar (documentos, etc.) **2** SCRUB : fregar, restregar

scourge¹ ['skərdʒ] *vt* **scourged; scourging** : azotar

scourge² *n* : azote *m*

scout¹ ['skaʊt] *vi* **1** RECONNOITER : reconocer **2 to scout around for** : explorar en busca de

scout² *n* **1** : explorador *m*, -dora *f* **2** *or* **talent scout** : cazatalentos *mf*

scowl¹ ['skaʊl] *vi* : fruncir el ceño

scowl² *n* : ceño *m* fruncido

scrabble ['skræbəl] *vi* **scrabbled; -bling** : escarbar/hurgar (etc.) frenéticamente ⟨they scrabbled in the dirt : escarbaban en el suelo⟩ ⟨she scrabbled around in her handbag : hurgaba en el bolso⟩ ⟨he scrabbled at the rock : intentó agarrarse a la roca⟩

scram ['skræm] *vi* **scrammed; scramming** : largarse

scramble¹ ['skræmbəl] *v* **scrambled; -bling** *vi* **1** : trepar, gatear (apresuradamente) ⟨he scrambled over the fence : se trepó a la cerca con rapidez⟩ **2** : hacer/ir (etc.) frenéticamente ⟨we scrambled for cover : corrimos a ponernos a cubierto⟩ **3** STRUGGLE : pelearse (por) ⟨they scrambled for seats : se pelearon por los asientos⟩ — *vt* **1** JUMBLE : mezclar **2** ENCODE, ENCRYPT : codificar, cifrar, encriptar **3 to scramble eggs** : hacer huevos revueltos

scramble² *n* : rebatiña *f*, pelea *f*

scrambled eggs *npl* : huevos *mpl* revueltos

scrap¹ ['skræp] *v* **scrapped; scrapping** *vt* DISCARD : desechar — *vi* FIGHT : pelearse

scrap² *n* **1** FRAGMENT : pedazo *m*, trozo *m* ⟨a scrap of paper : un pedacito de papel, un papelito⟩ ⟨scraps of fabric : retazos⟩ **2** FIGHT : pelea *f* **3** *or* **scrap metal** : chatarra *f* **4 scraps** *npl* LEFTOVERS : restos *mpl*, sobras *fpl*

scrapbook ['skræp₁bʊk] *n* : álbum *m* de recortes

scrape¹ ['skreɪp] *v* **scraped; scraping**
vt **1** GRAZE, SCRATCH : rozar, rascar ⟨to
scrape one's knee : rasparse la ro-
dilla⟩ **2** CLEAN : raspar (con un
cuchillo, etc.) **3 to scrape off** : raspar
(pintura, etc.) **4 to scrape up/together**
: juntar, reunir poco a poco — *vi* **1** RUB
: rozar **2 to scrape by/along**
: arreglárselas, ir tirando **3 to scrape
by/through** ⟨he just barely scraped by
on the exam : aprobó el examen por los
pelos⟩
scrape² *n* **1** SCRAPING : raspadura *f* **2**
SCRATCH : rasguño *m* **3** PREDICAMENT
: apuro *m*, aprieto *m*
scraping ['skreɪpɪŋ] *n* SHAVING : raspadura *f*
scrap paper *n* : papel para borrador, papel usado
scratch¹ ['skrætʃ] *vt* **1** : rascarse (la cabeza, etc.) ⟨to scratch an itch : ras-
carse⟩ **2** : arañar, rasguñar (con las
uñas, etc.) **3** MARK : rayar, marcar **4
to scratch out** : tachar — *vi* **1** : rascarse **2** : arañar **3** : rayar **4 to scratch
at** : arañar, rasguñar (una puerta, etc.)
scratch² *n* **1** : rasguño *m*, arañazo *m* (en
la piel) **2** MARK : raya *f*, rayón *m* (en un
mueble, etc.) **3** : sonido *m* rasposo ⟨I
heard a scratch at the door : oí como
que raspaban a la puerta⟩ **4 from** ~
⟨to start from scratch : empezar desde
cero⟩ ⟨I made the cake from scratch : el
pastel lo hice yo⟩ **5 to be up to scratch**
: dar la talla
scratchy ['skrætʃi] *adj* **scratchier; -est**
: áspero, que pica ⟨a scratchy sweater
: un suéter que pica⟩
scrawl¹ ['skrɔl] *v* : garabatear
scrawl² *n* : garabato *m*
scrawny ['skrɔni] *adj* **scrawnier; -est**
: flaco, escuálido
scream¹ ['skri:m] *vi* : chillar, gritar
scream² *n* : chillido *m*, grito *m*
screech¹ ['skri:tʃ] *vi* : chillar (dícese de las
personas o de los animales), chirriar
(dícese de los frenos, etc.)
screech² *n* **1** : chillido *m*, grito *m* (de
una persona o un animal) **2** : chirrido
m (de frenos, etc.)
screen¹ ['skri:n] *vt* **1** SHIELD : proteger **2** CONCEAL : tapar, ocultar **3** TEST
: someter (a un paciente) a pruebas preventivas o de detección ⟨to screen for
drugs/cancer : someter a una prueba de
(detección de) drogas/cáncer⟩ **4** IN-
SPECT : revisar (equipaje, etc.) **5** SELECT
: seleccionar (candidatos, etc.), filtrar
(llamadas, etc.) **6** SIEVE : cribar **7**
: emitir (un programa de televisión),
proyectar (una película)
screen² *n* **1** PARTITION : biombo *m*, pantalla *f* **2** SIEVE : criba *f* **3** : pantalla *f*
(de un televisor, una computadora,
etc.) **4** MOVIES : cine *m* **5** *or* **window
screen** : ventana *f* de tela metálica
screening ['skri:nɪŋ] *n* **1** : proyección *f*
(de una película), emisión *f* (de un programa de televisión) **2** TESTING : acto *m*
de hacer pruebas médicas (preventivas o

de drogas) **3** INSPECTION : control *m*
(de pasajeros, equipaje), selección *f* (de
candidatos)
screenplay ['skri:nˌpleɪ] *n* SCRIPT : guión
m
screen saver *n* : protector *m* de pantalla,
salvapantallas *m*
screw¹ ['skru:] *vt* **1** : atornillar (un tornillo) **2** : atornillar, sujetar (con tornillos) **3** : enroscar (una tapa) **4** *or* **to
screw over** *fam* CHEAT, DECEIVE : estafar, engañar **5 to screw someone out
of something** *fam* : quitarle algo a alguien (injustamente) — *vi* **1 to screw
around** *fam* TOY : jugar, juguetear **2 to
screw around** *fam* : perder el tiempo **3
to screw around** *fam* : tener líos (amorosos) **4 to screw in** : atornillarse **5 to
screw up** *fam* : meter la pata
screw² *n* **1** : tornillo *m* (para fijar
algo) **2** TWIST : vuelta *f* **3** PROPELLER
: hélice *f*
screwdriver ['skru:ˌdraɪvər] *n* : destornillador *m*, desarmador *m* Mex
scribble¹ ['skrɪbəl] *v* **-bled; -bling** : garabatear
scribble² *n* : garabato *m*
scribe ['skraɪb] *n* : escriba *m*
scrimmage ['skrɪmɪdʒ] *n* : escaramuza *f*
scrimp ['skrɪmp] *vi* **1 to scrimp on** : escatimar **2 to scrimp and save** : hacer
economías
script ['skrɪpt] *n* **1** HANDWRITING : letra
f, escritura *f* **2** : guión *m* (de una
película, etc.)
scriptural ['skrɪptʃərəl] *adj* : bíblico
scripture ['skrɪptʃər] *n* **1** : escritos *mpl*
sagrados (de una religión) **2 the Scriptures** *npl* : las Sagradas Escrituras
scriptwriter ['skrɪptˌraɪtər] *n* : guionista
mf, libretista *mf*
scroll¹ ['skro:l] *n* **1** : rollo *m* (de pergamino, etc.) **2** : voluta *f* (adorno en
arquitectura)
scroll² *vi* : desplazarse (en informática) —
vt : desplazar (en informática)
scrotum ['skro:təm] *n, pl* **scrota** [-ʈə] *or*
scrotums : escroto *m*
scrounge ['skraʊndʒ] *v* **scrounged;
scrounging** *vt* **1** BUM, SPONGE : gorrear *fam*, sablear *fam* (dinero) **2** *or* **to
scrounge up** : conseguir, encontrar —
vi **1 to scrounge off** : vivir a costa
de **2 to scrounge around for** : buscar,
andar a la busca de
scrounger ['skraʊndʒər] *n* : gorrón *m*,
-rrona *f*
scrub¹ ['skrʌb] *vt* **scrubbed; scrubbing**
: restregar, fregar
scrub² *n* **1** THICKET, UNDERBRUSH
: maleza *f*, matorral *m*, matorrales
mpl **2** SCRUBBING : fregado *m*, restregadura *f*
scrubby ['skrʌbi] *adj* **scrubbier; -est 1**
STUNTED : achaparrado **2** : cubierto de
maleza
scruff ['skrʌf] *n* **by the scruff of the neck**
: por el cogote, por el pescuezo
scruffy ['skrʌfi] *adj* **scruffier; -est** : dejado, desaliñado

scrumptious ['skrʌmpfəs] *adj* : delicioso, muy rico

scruple ['skru:pəl] *n* : escrúpulo *m*

scrupulous ['skru:pjələs] *adj* : escrupuloso — **scrupulously** *adv*

scrutinize ['skru:tən,aɪz] *vt* **-nized; -nizing** : escrutar, escudriñar

scrutiny ['skru:təni] *n*, *pl* **-nies** : escrutinio *m*, inspección *f*

scuba ['sku:bə] *n* **1** *or* **scuba gear** : equipo *m* de submarinismo **2 scuba diver** : submarinista *mf* **3 scuba diving** : submarinismo *m*

scuff ['skʌf] *vt* : rayar, raspar ⟨to scuff one's feet : arrastrar los pies⟩

scuffle¹ ['skʌfəl] *vi* **-fled; -fling 1** TUSSLE : pelearse **2** SHUFFLE : caminar arrastrando los pies

scuffle² *n* **1** TUSSLE : refriega *f*, pelea *f* **2** SHUFFLE : arrastre *m* de los pies

sculpt ['skʌlpt] *v* : esculpir

sculptor ['skʌlptər] *n* : escultor *m*, -tora *f*

sculptural ['skʌlptfərəl] *adj* : escultórico

sculpture¹ ['skʌlptfər] *vt* **-tured; -turing** : esculpir

sculpture² *n* : escultura *f*

scum ['skʌm] *n* **1** FROTH : espuma *f*, nata *f* **2** : verdín *m* (encima de un líquido)

scurrilous ['skərələs] *adj* : difamatorio, calumnioso, injurioso

scurry ['skəri] *vi* **-ried; -rying** : corretear

scurvy ['skərvi] *n* : escorbuto *m*

scuttle¹ ['skʌtəl] *v* **-tled; -tling** *vt* : hundir (un barco) — *vi* SCAMPER : corretear

scuttle² *n* : cubo *m* (para carbón)

scythe ['saɪð] *n* : guadaña *f*

sea¹ ['si:] *adj* : del mar

sea² *n* **1** : mar *mf* ⟨the Black Sea : el Mar Negro⟩ ⟨on the high seas : en alta mar⟩ ⟨heavy seas : mar gruesa, mar agitada⟩ **2** MASS : mar *m*, multitud *f* ⟨a sea of faces : un mar de rostros⟩

sea bass [-'bæs] *n* : lubina *f*

seabed ['si:,bɛd] *n* : fondo *m* del mar

seabird ['si:,bərd] *n* : ave *f* marina

seaboard ['si:,bord] *n* : litoral *m*

seacoast ['si:,ko:st] *n* : costa *f*, litoral *m*

seafarer ['si:,færər] *n* : marinero *m*

seafaring¹ ['si:,færɪŋ] *adj* : marinero

seafaring² *n* : navegación *f*

seafood ['si:,fu:d] *n* : mariscos *mpl*

seafront ['si:,frʌnt] *n* : paseo *m* marítimo ⟨a restaurant on the seafront : un restaurante frente al mar⟩

seagull ['si:,gʌl] *n* : gaviota *f*

sea horse ['si:,hors] *n* : hipocampo *m*, caballito *m* de mar

seal¹ ['si:l] *vt* **1** CLOSE : sellar, cerrar ⟨to seal a letter : cerrar una carta⟩ ⟨to seal an agreement : sellar un acuerdo⟩ **2 to seal off** : acordonar, cerrar **3 to seal up** : tapar, rellenar (una grieta, etc.)

seal² *n* **1** : foca *f* (animal) **2** : sello *m* ⟨seal of approval : sello de aprobación⟩ **3** CLOSURE : cierre *m*, precinto *m*

sea level *n* : nivel *m* del mar

sea lion *n* : león *m* marino

sealskin ['si:l,skɪn] *n* : piel *f* de foca

seam¹ ['si:m] *vt* **1** STITCH : unir con costuras **2** MARK : marcar

seam² *n* **1** STITCHING : costura *f* **2** LODE, VEIN : veta *f*, filón *m*

seaman ['si:mən] *n*, *pl* **-men** [-mən, -ˌmɛn] **1** SAILOR : marinero *m* **2** : marino *m* (en la armada)

seamless ['si:mləs] *adj* **1** : sin costuras, de una pieza **2** : perfecto ⟨a seamless transition : una transición fluida⟩

seamstress ['si:mpstrəs] *n* : costurera *f*

seamy ['si:mi] *adj* **seamier; -est** : sórdido

séance ['seɪ,ɑnts] *n* : sesión *f* de espiritismo

seaplane ['si:,pleɪn] *n* : hidroavión *m*

seaport ['si:,port] *n* : puerto *m* marítimo

sear ['sɪr] *vt* **1** PARCH, WITHER : secar, resecar **2** SCORCH : chamuscar, quemar

search¹ ['sərtf] *vt* : registrar (un edificio, un área), cachear (a una persona), buscar en — *vi* **to search for** : buscar

search² *n* **1** : búsqueda *f*, registro *m* (de un edificio, etc.), cacheo *m* (de una persona) **2 in search of** : en busca de

search engine *n* : buscador *m*

searching ['sərtfɪŋ] *adj* : inquisitivo, penetrante

searchlight ['sərtf,laɪt] *n* : reflector *m*

seashell ['si:,fel] *n* : concha *f* (marina)

seashore ['si:,for] *n* : orilla *f* del mar

seasick ['si:,sɪk] *adj* : mareado ⟨to get seasick : marearse⟩

seasickness ['si:,sɪknəs] *n* : mareo *m*

seaside → **seacoast**

season¹ ['si:zən] *vt* **1** FLAVOR, SPICE : sazonar, condimentar **2** CURE : curar, secar (madera)

season² *n* **1** : estación *f* (del año) **2** : temporada *f* ⟨baseball season : la temporada de beisbol⟩ ⟨the holiday season : las fiestas⟩ ⟨in season : en temporada⟩ ⟨out of season : fuera de temporada⟩ **3** HEAT, ESTRUS : celo *m*

seasonable ['si:zənəbəl] *adj* **1** : propio de la estación (dícese del tiempo, de las temperaturas, etc.) **2** TIMELY : oportuno

seasonal ['si:zənəl] *adj* : estacional — **seasonally** *adv*

seasoned ['si:zənd] *adj* **1** SPICED : condimentado, sazonado **2** EXPERIENCED : veterano ⟨a seasoned veteran : un veterano avezado⟩ **3** : curado, seco ⟨seasoned wood : madera curada/seca⟩

seasoning ['si:zənɪŋ] *n* : condimento *m*, sazón *f*

season ticket *n* : abono *m*

seat¹ ['si:t] *vt* **1** SIT : sentar ⟨please be seated : siéntense, por favor⟩ **2** HOLD : tener cabida para ⟨the stadium seats 40,000 : el estadio tiene 40,000 asientos⟩

seat² *n* **1** : asiento *m*, plaza *f* (en un vehículo) ⟨take a seat : tome asiento⟩ **2** : asiento *m* (de una silla) **3** BOTTOM : fondillos *mpl* (de la ropa), trasero *m* (del cuerpo) **4** : sede *f* (de un gobierno, del poder, etc.), centro *m* (de enseñanza, etc.)

seat belt *n* : cinturón *m* de seguridad

seating ['si:tɪŋ] *n* **1** : asientos *mpl* ⟨is there enough seating for everyone? : ¿hay asientos para todos?⟩ ⟨seating capacity : aforo⟩ ⟨the seating plan/arrangement for the wedding reception : el plano de mesas para el banquete de bodas⟩ **2** SITTING : turno *m*

sea urchin *n* : erizo *m* de mar

seawall [ˈsiːˌwɑl] *n* : rompeolas *m*, dique *m* marítimo

seawater [ˈsiːˌwɔt̬ər, -ˌwɑ-] *n* : agua *f* de mar

seaweed [ˈsiːˌwiːd] *n* : alga *f* marina

seaworthy [ˈsiːˌwərði] *adj* : en condiciones de navegar

secede [sɪˈsiːd] *vi* **-ceded; -ceding** : separarse (de una nación, etc.)

seclude [sɪˈkluːd] *vt* **-cluded; -cluding** : aislar

seclusion [sɪˈkluːʒən] *n* : aislamiento *m*

second¹ [ˈsɛkənd] *vt* : secundar, apoyar (una moción)

second² *or* **secondly** [ˈsɛkəndli] *adv* : en segundo lugar

second³ *adj* **1** : segundo ⟨her second husband : su segundo marido⟩ ⟨the second house on the left : la segunda casa a la izquierda⟩ ⟨he took second place : ganó el segundo lugar⟩ **2** : otro ⟨a second chance/time : otra oportunidad/vez⟩ **3 every second** EVERY OTHER : cada dos ⟨every second month : cada dos meses⟩

second⁴ *n* **1** : segundo *m*, -da *f* (en una serie) ⟨the second of July : el dos de julio⟩ **2** : segundo *m*, ayudante *m* (en deportes) **3** MOMENT : segundo *m*, momento *m* **4** *or* **second base** : segunda base *f* **5** *or* **second gear** : segunda *f* (de un automóvil) **6 seconds** *npl* : segunda ración *f* ⟨to have seconds : repetir⟩ ⟨who wants seconds? : ¿quién quiere más?⟩

secondary [ˈsɛkənˌdri] *adj* : secundario

secondary school *n* : escuela *f* de enseñanza secundaria

second–class [ˈsɛkəndˈklæs] *adj* : de segunda clase/categoría, mediocre

secondhand [ˈsɛkəndˈhænd] *adj* : de segunda mano

second lieutenant *n* : alférez *mf*, subteniente *mf*

second–rate [ˈsɛkəndˈreɪt] *adj* : mediocre, de segunda categoría

second thought *n* **1** : duda *f* ⟨later he had second thoughts about going : luego le entró la duda sobre si ir o no⟩ ⟨don't give it a second thought : no tiene importancia, no te preocupes⟩ **2 on second thought** : pensándolo bien **3 without a second thought** : sin pensarlo dos veces

secrecy [ˈsiːkrəsi] *n*, *pl* **-cies** : secreto *m*

secret¹ [ˈsiːkrət] *adj* **1** : secreto ⟨to keep a secret : guardar un secreto⟩ ⟨to make no secret of something : no ocultar/esconder algo⟩ ⟨in secret : en secreto⟩ **2** → **secretive** — **secretly** *adv*

secret² *n* : secreto *m*

secretarial [ˌsɛkrəˈtriəl] *adj* : de secretario, de oficina

secretariat [ˌsɛkrəˈtriət] *n* : secretaría *f*, secretariado *m*

secretary [ˈsɛkrəˌtri] *n*, *pl* **-taries** **1** : secretario *m*, -ria *f* (en una oficina, etc.) **2** : ministro *m*, -tra *f*; secretario *m*, -ria *f* ⟨Secretary of State : Secretario de Estado⟩

secrete [sɪˈkriːt] *vt* **-creted; -creting** **1** : secretar, segregar (en fisiología) **2** HIDE : ocultar

secretion [sɪˈkriːʃən] *n* : secreción *f*

secretive [ˈsiːkrət̬ɪv, sɪˈkriːt̬ɪv] *adj* : reservado, callado, secreto

sect [ˈsɛkt] *n* : secta *f*

sectarian [sɛkˈtriən] *adj* : sectario

section¹ [ˈsɛkʃən] *vt* **1** : dividir **2 to section off** : separar

section² *n* : sección *f*, parte *f* (de un mueble, etc.), sector *m* (de la población), barrio *m* (de una ciudad)

sectional [ˈsɛkʃənəl] *adj* **1** : en sección, en corte ⟨a sectional diagram : un gráfico en corte⟩ **2** FACTIONAL : de grupo, entre facciones **3** : modular ⟨sectional furniture : muebles modulares⟩

sector [ˈsɛktər] *n* : sector *m*

secular [ˈsɛkjələr] *adj* **1** : secular, laico ⟨secular life : la vida secular⟩ **2** : seglar (dícese de los sacerdotes, etc.)

secure¹ [sɪˈkjur] *vt* **-cured; -curing** **1** FASTEN : asegurar (una puerta, etc.), sujetar **2** GET : conseguir

secure² *adj* **securer; -est** : seguro — **securely** *adv*

security [sɪˈkjʊrət̬i] *n*, *pl* **-ties** **1** SAFETY : seguridad *f* **2** GUARANTEE : garantía *f* **3 securities** *npl* : valores *mpl*

security guard *n* : guardia *mf* de seguridad, guarda *mf* de seguridad

sedan [sɪˈdæn] *n* **1** *or* **sedan chair** : silla *f* de manos **2** : sedán *m* (automóvil)

sedate¹ [sɪˈdeɪt] *vt* **-dated; -dating** : sedar

sedate² *adj* : sosegado — **sedately** *adv*

sedation [sɪˈdeɪʃən] *n* : sedación *f*

sedative¹ [ˈsɛdət̬ɪv] *adj* : sedante

sedative² *n* : sedante *m*, calmante *m*

sedentary [ˈsɛdənˌteri] *adj* : sedentario

sedge [ˈsɛdʒ] *n* : juncia *f*

sediment [ˈsɛdəmənt] *n* : sedimento *m* (geológico), poso *m* (en un líquido) — **sedimentary** [ˌsɛdəˈmentəri] *adj* — **sedimentation** [ˌsɛdəmənˈteɪʃən] *n*

sedition [sɪˈdɪʃən] *n* : sedición *f*

seditious [sɪˈdɪʃəs] *adj* : sedicioso

seduce [sɪˈduːs, -ˈdjuːs] *vt* **-duced; -ducing** : seducir

seduction [sɪˈdʌkʃən] *n* : seducción *f*

seductive [sɪˈdʌktɪv] *adj* : seductor, seductivo

seducer [sɪˈduːsər, -ˈdjuː-] *n* : seductor *m*, -tora *f*

see¹ [ˈsiː] *v* **saw** [ˈsɔ]; **seen** [ˈsiːn]; **seeing** *vt* **1** : ver ⟨I saw a dog : vi un perro⟩ ⟨see you later! : ¡hasta luego!⟩ ⟨I'll believe it when I see it : hasta que no lo vea, no lo creo⟩ ⟨so I see : ya veo⟩ ⟨did you see the game? : ¿viste el partido?⟩ ⟨see below : ver más abajo, véase más abajo⟩ **2** ASCERTAIN : ver ⟨see who's at the door : ve a abrir (la puerta)⟩ ⟨let's wait and see what happens : esperemos a ver qué pasa⟩ **3** READ : leer **4** EXPERIENCE : ver, conocer **5** UNDERSTAND

: ver, entender **6** CONSIDER : ver ⟨as I see it : a mi entender⟩ **7** IMAGINE : imaginar **8** FORESEE : ver **9** ENSURE : asegurarse ⟨see that it's correct : asegúrese de que sea correcto⟩ **10** MEET, VISIT : ver **11** CONSULT : ver **12** ACCOMPANY : acompañar ⟨to see someone to the door : acompañar a alguien a la puerta⟩ **13 to be seeing someone** : salir con alguien **14 to see in someone** ⟨what does she see in him? : ¿qué le ve?⟩ **15 to see off** : despedir, despedirse de **16 to see out/through** COMPLETE : terminar **17 to see through** HELP : sacar adelante — *vi* **1** : ver ⟨seeing is believing : ver para creer⟩ **2** UNDERSTAND : entender, ver ⟨now I see! : ¡ya entiendo!⟩ **3** ASCERTAIN : ver ⟨can I go? we'll see : ¿puedo ir? vamos a ver⟩ ⟨you'll see : ya verás⟩ **4** CONSIDER : ver ⟨let's see : vamos a ver⟩ **5 see here!** : ¡oye!, ¡mira! **6 to see about** : ocuparse de (algo) **7 we'll see about that!** : ¡ya veremos! **8 to see after/to** : ocuparse de **9 to see through** : calar (a alguien)

see² *n* : sede *f* ⟨the Holy See : la Santa Sede⟩

seed¹ ['si:d] *vt* **1** SOW : sembrar **2** : quitarle las semillas a

seed² *n, pl* **seed** *or* **seeds 1** : semilla *f*, pepita *f* (de una fruta) **2** SOURCE : germen *m*, semilla *f*

seedless ['si:dləs] *adj* : sin semillas

seedling ['si:dlɪŋ] *n* : plantón *m*

seedpod ['si:d,pɑd] → **pod**

seedy ['si:di] *adj* **seedier; -est 1** : lleno de semillas **2** SHABBY : raído (dícese de la ropa) **3** RUN-DOWN : ruinoso (dícese de los edificios, etc.), sórdido

Seeing Eye *trademark* se usa para un perro guía

seek ['si:k] *v* **sought** ['sɔt]; **seeking** *vt* **1** : buscar ⟨to seek an answer : buscar una solución⟩ **2** REQUEST : solicitar, pedir **3 to seek to** : tratar de, intentar de — *vi* SEARCH : buscar

seem ['si:m] *vi* : parecer

seeming ['si:mɪŋ] *adj* : aparente, ostensible

seemingly ['si:mɪŋli] *adv* : aparentemente, según parece

seemly ['si:mli] *adj* **seemlier; -est** : apropiado, decoroso

seep ['si:p] *vi* : filtrarse

seer ['si:ər] *n* : vidente *mf*, clarividente *mf*

seesaw¹ ['si:,sɔ] *vi* **1** : jugar en un subibaja **2** VACILLATE : vacilar, oscilar

seesaw² *n* : balancín *m*, subibaja *m*

seethe ['si:ð] *vi* **seethed; seething 1** : bullir, hervir **2 to seethe with anger** : rabiar, estar furioso

segment ['sɛgmənt] *n* : segmento *m*

segmented ['sɛg,mɛntəd, sɛg'mɛn-] *adj* : segmentado

segregate ['sɛgrɪ,geɪt] *vt* **-gated; -gating** : segregar

segregation [,sɛgrɪ'geɪʃən] *n* : segregación *f*

seismic ['saɪzmɪk, 'saɪs-] *adj* : sísmico

seismograph ['saɪzmə,græf, 'saɪs-] *n* : sismógrafo *m*

seize ['si:z] *v* **seized; seizing** *vt* **1** CAPTURE : capturar, tomar, apoderarse de **2** ARREST : detener **3** CLUTCH, GRAB : agarrar, coger, aprovechar (una oportunidad) **4 to be seized with** : estar sobrecogido por — *vi or* **to seize up** : agarrotarse

seizure ['si:ʒər] *n* **1** CAPTURE : toma *f*, captura *f* **2** ARREST : detención *f* **3** : ataque *m* ⟨an epileptic seizure : un ataque epiléptico⟩

seldom ['sɛldəm] *adv* : pocas veces, rara vez, casi nunca

select¹ [sə'lɛkt] *vt* : escoger, elegir, seleccionar (a un candidato, etc.)

select² *adj* : selecto

selection [sə'lɛkʃən] *n* : selección *f*, elección *f*

selective [sə'lɛktɪv] *adj* : selectivo

selenium [sə'li:niəm] *n* : selenio *m*

self ['sɛlf] *n, pl* **selves** ['sɛlvz] **1** : ser *m*, persona *f* ⟨the self : el yo⟩ ⟨with his whole self : con todo su ser⟩ ⟨her own self : su propia persona⟩ **2** SIDE : lado (de la personalidad) ⟨his better self : su lado bueno⟩

self- [,sɛlf] *pref* : auto-

self–addressed [,sɛlfə'drst] *adj* : con la dirección del remitente ⟨include a self-addressed envelope : incluya un sobre con su nombre y dirección⟩

self–appointed [,sɛlfə'pɔɪntəd] *adj* : autoproclamado, autonombrado

self–assurance [,sɛlfə'ʃʊrənts] *n* : seguridad *f* en sí mismo

self–assured [,sɛlfə'ʃʊrd] *adj* : seguro de sí mismo

self–care [,sɛlf'kær] *n* : cuidado *m* personal

self–centered [,sɛlf'sɛntərd] *adj* : egocéntrico

self–confidence [,sɛlf'kɑnfədənts] *n* : confianza *f* en sí mismo

self–confident [,sɛlf'kɑnfədənt] *adj* : seguro de sí mismo

self–conscious [,sɛlf'kɑntʃəs] *adj* : cohibido, tímido

self–consciously [,sɛlf'kɑntʃəsli] *adv* : de manera cohibida

self–consciousness [,sɛlf'kɑntʃəsnəs] *n* : vergüenza *f*, timidez *f*

self–contained [,sɛlfkən'teɪnd] *adj* **1** INDEPENDENT : independiente **2** RESERVED : reservado

self–control [,sɛlfkən'tro:l] *n* : autocontrol *m*, control *m* de sí mismo

self–defense [,sɛlfdɪ'fɛnts] *n* : defensa *f* propia, defensa *f* personal ⟨to act in self-defense : actuar en defensa propia⟩ ⟨self-defense class : clase de defensa personal⟩

self–denial [,sɛlfdɪ'naɪəl] *n* : abnegación *f*

self–destructive [,sɛlfdɪ'strʌktɪv] *adj* : autodestructivo — **self–destruction** *n*

self–determination [,sɛlfdɪ,tərmə'neɪʃən] *n* : autodeterminación *f*

self–discipline [,sɛlf'dɪsəplən] *n* : autodisciplina *f*

self–employed [ˌsɛlfɪm'plɔɪd] *adj* : que trabaja por cuenta propia, autónomo

self–esteem [ˌsɛlfɪ'stiːm] *n* : autoestima *f*, amor *m* propio

self–evident [ˌsɛlf'ɛvədənt] *adj* : evidente, manifiesto

self–explanatory [ˌsɛlfɪk'splænəˌtori] *adj* : fácil de entender, evidente

self–expression [ˌsɛlfɪk'sprɪʃən] *n* : expresión *f* personal

self–government [ˌsɛlf'ɡʌvərmənt, -vərn-] *n* : autogobierno *m*

self–help [ˌsɛlf'hɛlp] *n* : autoayuda *f*

selfie ['sɛlfi] *n, pl* **-fies** : selfie *m*, selfi *m*, autofoto *f*

self–important [ˌsɛlfɪm'pɔrtənt] *adj* **1** VAIN : vanidoso, presumido **2** ARROGANT : arrogante

self–indulgent [ˌsɛlfɪn'dʌldʒənt] *adj* : que se permite excesos

self–inflicted [ˌsɛlfɪn'flɪktəd] *adj* : autoinfligido

self–interest [ˌsɛlf'ɪntrəst, -təˌrst] *n* : interés *m* personal

selfish ['sɛlfɪʃ] *adj* : egoísta

selfishly ['sɛlfɪʃli] *adv* : de manera egoísta

selfishness ['sɛlfɪʃnəs] *n* : egoísmo *m*

selfless ['sɛlfləs] *adj* UNSELFISH : desinteresado

self–made [ˌsɛlf'meɪd] *adj* : próspero gracias a sus propios esfuerzos

self–pity [ˌsɛlf'pɪti] *n, pl* **-ties** : autocompasión *f*

self–portrait [ˌsɛlf'pɔrtrət] *n* : autorretrato *m*

self–proclaimed [ˌsɛlfpro'kleɪmd] *adj* : autoproclamado

self–propelled [ˌsɛlfpro'pɛld] *adj* : autopropulsado

self–reliance [ˌsɛlfrɪ'laɪənts] *n* : independencia *f*, autosuficiencia *f*

self–respect [ˌsɛlfrɪ'spɛkt] *n* : autoestima *f*, amor *m* propio

self–restraint [ˌsɛlfrɪ'streɪnt] *n* : autocontrol *m*, moderación *f*

self–righteous [ˌsɛlf'raɪtʃəs] *adj* : santurrón, moralista

self–sacrifice [ˌsɛlf'sækrəˌfaɪs] *n* : abnegación *f*

self–sacrificing [ˌsɛlf'sækrəˌfaɪsɪŋ] *adj* : abnegado

selfsame ['sɛlfˌseɪm] *adj* : mismo

self–satisfaction [ˌsɛlfˌsætəs'fækʃən] *n* : suficiencia *f*

self–satisfied [ˌsɛlf'sætəsˌfaɪd] *adj* : ufano *fam*

self–seeking [ˌsɛlf'siːkɪŋ] *adj* : interesado

self–service [ˌsɛlf'sɚvɪs] *adj* **1** : de autoservicio **2 self–service restaurant** : autoservicio *m*

self–sufficiency [ˌsɛlfsə'fɪʃəntsi] *n* : autosuficiencia *f*

self–sufficient [ˌsɛlfsə'fɪʃənt] *adj* : autosuficiente

self–taught [ˌsɛlf'tɔt] *adj* : autodidacta

sell ['sɛl] *v* **sold** ['soːld]; **selling** *vt* **1** : vender ⟨to sell someone something, to sell something to someone : venderle algo a alguien⟩ **2 to sell at a loss** : vender con pérdidas **3 to sell off** : liquidar **4 to sell on** ⟨can you sell them on the project? : ¿puedes convencerles de los méritos del proyecto?⟩ ⟨she's not sold on the idea : la idea no la convence⟩ **5 to sell out** BETRAY : vender, traicionar a **6 to sell short** UNDERESTIMATE : subestimar, menospreciar — *vi* **1** : venderse ⟨this car sells well : este coche se vende bien⟩ **2 to sell out** : agotarse (dícese de entradas, etc.) **3 to sell out** : venderse (dícese de un músico, etc.)

seller ['sɛlər] *n* : vendedor *m*, -dora *f*

selves → **self**

semantic [sɪ'mæntɪk] *adj* : semántico

semantics [sɪ'mæntɪks] *ns & pl* : semántica *f*

semaphore ['sɛməˌfor] *n* : semáforo *m*

semblance ['sɛmblənts] *n* : apariencia *f*

semen ['siːmən] *n* : semen *m*

semester [sə'mɛstər] *n* : semestre *m*

semi- [ˌsɛmi, 'sɛmaɪ] *pref* : semi-

semiannual [ˌsɛmi'ænjʊəl, 'sɛmaɪ-] *adj* : semestral

semicircle ['sɛmiˌsɚkəl, 'sɛˌmaɪ-] *n* : semicírculo *m*

semicolon ['sɛmiˌkoːlən, 'sɛˌmaɪ-] *n* : punto y coma *m*

semiconductor ['sɛmikənˌdʌktər, 'sɛˌmaɪ-] *n* : semiconductor *m*

semifinal ['sɛmiˌfaɪnəl, 'sɛˌmaɪ-] *n* : semifinal *f*

semimonthly ['sɛmiˌmʌnθli, 'sɛˌmaɪ-] *adj* : bimensual, quincenal

seminar ['sɛməˌnɑr] *n* : seminario *m*

seminary ['sɛməˌnɛri] *n, pl* **-naries** : seminario *m*

semiprecious ['sɛmi'prɛʃəs, 'sɛˌmaɪ-] *adj* : semiprecioso

Semite ['sɛˌmaɪt] *n* : semita *mf* — **Semitic** [sə'mɪtɪk] *adj*

semolina [ˌsɛmə'liːnə] *n* : sémola *f*

senate ['sɛnət] *n* : senado *m*

senator ['sɛnətər] *n* : senador *m*, -dora *f*

send ['sɛnd] *vt* **sent** ['sɛnt]; **sending 1** : mandar, enviar ⟨to send a letter : mandar una carta⟩ ⟨to send word : avisar, mandar decir⟩ ⟨he was sent to prison : lo mandaron a la cárcel, lo encarcelaron⟩ **2** PROPEL : mandar, lanzar ⟨he sent it into left field : lo mandó al jardín izquierdo⟩ ⟨it sent a shiver down my spine : me dio un escalofrío⟩ ⟨to send up dust : levantar polvo⟩ **3 to send away for** : pedir (por correo) **4 to send back** RETURN : devolver, mandar de vuelta **5 to send for** SUMMON : mandar llamar **6 to send for** REQUEST : pedir (ayuda, refuerzos, etc.) **7 to send in** SUBMIT : enviar, mandar, presentar **8 to send in** : enviar, mandar (tropas, etc.) **9 to send into a rage** : poner furioso **10 to send off** : mandar, enviar (por correo, etc.) **11 to send on** : enviar por adelantado **12 to send out** : enviar, mandar (invitaciones, etc.) **13 to send out** EMIT : emitir

sender ['sɛndər] *n* : remitente *mf* (de una carta, etc.)

send–off ['sɛndˌɔf] *n* FAREWELL : despedida *f*

Senegalese [ˌsɛnəgəˈliːz, -ˈliːs] *n* : senegalés *m*, -lesa *f* — **Senegalese** *adj*

senile [ˈsiːˌnaɪl] *adj* : senil

senility [sɪˈnɪləti] *n* : senilidad *f*

senior[1] [ˈsiːnjər] *adj* **1** ELDER : mayor ⟨John Doe, Senior : John Doe, padre⟩ **2** : superior (en rango), más antiguo (en años de servicio) ⟨a senior official : un alto oficial⟩

senior[2] *n* **1** : superior *m* (en rango) **2** **to be someone's senior** : ser mayor que alguien ⟨she's two years my senior : me lleva dos años⟩

senior citizen *n* : persona *f* de la tercera edad

seniority [ˌsiːˈnjɔrəti] *n* : antigüedad *f* (en años de servicio)

sensation [sɛnˈseɪʃən] *n* : sensación *f*

sensational [sɛnˈseɪʃənəl] *adj* : que causa sensación ⟨sensational stories : historias sensacionalistas⟩

sensationalism [sɛnˈseɪʃənəˌlɪzəm] *n* : sensacionalismo *m*

sensationalist [sɛnˈseɪʃənəlɪst] *or* **sensationalistic** [sɛnˌseɪʃənəˈlɪstɪk] *adj* : sensacionalista

sense[1] [ˈsɛns] *vt* **sensed; sensing** : sentir ⟨he sensed danger : se dio cuenta del peligro⟩

sense[2] *n* **1** MEANING : sentido *m*, significado *m* **2** : sentido *m* ⟨the sense of smell : el sentido del olfato⟩ **3** : sentido *m* ⟨sense of humor : sentido del humor⟩ ⟨sense of duty : sentido del deber⟩ ⟨sense of direction : sentido de la orientación⟩ **4** FEELING : sensación *f* ⟨a huge sense of relief : un gran alivio⟩ ⟨his sense of accomplishment : su satisfacción (por haber logrado algo)⟩ **5** WISDOM : sensatez *f*, tino *m* ⟨he had the (good) sense to leave : tuvo la sensatez de retirarse⟩ ⟨common sense : sentido común⟩ ⟨to come to one's senses : entrar en razón⟩ ⟨there's no sense in arguing : no tiene sentido discutir⟩ **6** **to make sense** : tener sentido **7** **to make sense of** : entender

senseless [ˈsɛntsləs] *adj* **1** MEANINGLESS : sin sentido, sin razón **2** UNCONSCIOUS : inconsciente

senselessly [ˈsɛntsləsli] *adv* : sin sentido

sensibility [ˌsɛntsəˈbɪləti] *n, pl* **-ties** : sensibilidad *f*

sensible [ˈsɛntsəbəl] *adj* **1** PERCEPTIBLE : sensible, perceptible **2** AWARE : consciente **3** REASONABLE : sensato ⟨a sensible man : un hombre sensato⟩ ⟨sensible shoes : zapatos prácticos⟩ — **sensibly** [-bli] *adv*

sensibleness [ˈsɛntsəbəlnəs] *n* : sensatez *f*, solidez *f*

sensitive [ˈsɛntsətɪv] *adj* **1** : sensible, delicado ⟨sensitive skin : piel sensible⟩ **2** TOUCHY : susceptible, sensible ⟨to be sensitive to criticism : ser susceptible a las críticas⟩ ⟨to be sensitive about something : tener complejo por algo, preocuparse mucho por algo⟩ **3** AWARE : sensibilizado ⟨sensitive to something : sensibilizado sobre/con algo, sensibilizado frente a algo⟩ **4** : de mucha sensibilidad (dícese de un artista, una interpretación, etc.) **5** DELICATE : delicado **6** CONTROVERSIAL : controvertido **7** CONFIDENTIAL : confidencial

sensitiveness [ˈsɛntsətɪvnəs] → **sensitivity**

sensitivity [ˌsɛntsəˈtɪvəti] *n, pl* **-ties** : sensibilidad *f*

sensitize [ˈsɛntsəˌtaɪz] *vt* **-tized; -tizing** : sensibilizar

sensor [ˈsɛnˌsɔr, ˈsɛntsər] *n* : sensor *m*

sensory [ˈsɛntsəri] *adj* : sensorial

sensual [ˈsɛntʃʊəl] *adj* : sensual — **sensually** *adv*

sensuality [ˌsɛntʃəˈwæləti] *n, pl* **-ties** : sensualidad *f*

sensuous [ˈsɛntʃʊəs] *adj* : sensual

sent → **send**

sentence[1] [ˈsɛntəns, -ˌənz] *vt* **-tenced; -tencing** : sentenciar

sentence[2] *n* **1** JUDGMENT : sentencia *f* **2** : oración *f*, frase *f* (en gramática)

sentient [ˈsɛntʃənt, -ʃiənt] *adj* : sensitivo, sensible

sentiment [ˈsɛntəmənt] *n* **1** BELIEF : opinión *f* **2** FEELING : sentimiento *m* **3** → **sentimentality**

sentimental [ˌsɛntəˈmɛntəl] *adj* : sentimental

sentimentality [ˌsɛntəˌmɛnˈtæləti] *n, pl* **-ties** : sentimentalismo *m*, sensiblería *f*

sentinel [ˈsɛntənəl] *n* : centinela *mf*, guardia *mf*

sentry [ˈsɛntri] *n, pl* **-tries** : centinela *mf*

separate[1] [ˈsɛpəˌreɪt] *v* **-rated; -rating** *vt* **1** DETACH, SEVER : separar **2** DISTINGUISH : diferenciar, distinguir — *vi* PART : separarse

separate[2] [ˈsɛprət, ˈsɛpə-] *adj* **1** INDIVIDUAL : separado, aparte ⟨a separate state : un estado separado⟩ ⟨in a separate envelope : en un sobre aparte⟩ **2** DISTINCT : distinto

separately [ˈsɛprətli, ˈsɛpə-] *adv* : por separado, separadamente, aparte

separation [ˌsɛpəˈreɪʃən] *n* : separación *f*

sepia [ˈsiːpiə] *n* : color *m* sepia

September [sɛpˈtɛmbər] *n* : septiembre *m*, setiembre *m* ⟨they arrived on the 30th of September, they arrived on September 30th : llegaron el 30 de septiembre⟩

septic [ˈsɛptɪk] *adj* : séptico ⟨septic tank : fosa séptica⟩

sepulchre [ˈsɛpəlkər] *n* : sepulcro *m*

sequel [ˈsiːkwəl] *n* **1** CONSEQUENCE : secuela *f*, consecuencia *f* **2** : continuación *f* (de una película, etc.)

sequence [ˈsiːkwənts] *n* **1** SERIES : serie *f*, sucesión *f*, secuencia *f* (matemática o música) **2** ORDER : orden *m*

sequester [sɪˈkwɛstər] *vt* : aislar

sequin [ˈsiːkwən] *n* : lentejuela *f*

sequoia [sɪˈkwɔɪə] *n* : secoya *f*, secuoya *f*

sera → **serum**

Serb [ˈsərb] *or* **Serbian** [ˈsərbiən] *n* **1** : serbio *m*, -bia *f* **2** : serbio *m* (idioma) — **Serb** *or* **Serbian** *adj*

Serbo–Croatian [ˌsərbokroˈeɪʃən] *n* : serbocroata *m* (idioma) — **Serbo–Croatian** *adj*

serenade[1] [ˌsɛrə'neɪd] *vt* **-naded; -nading**
: darle una serenata (a alguien)
serenade[2] *n* : serenata *f*
serene [sə'riːn] *adj* : sereno — **serenely**
adv
serendipity [ˌsɛrən'dɪpəti] *n* : suerte *f*, fortuna *f* (de descubrir algo bueno por pura casualidad)
serenity [sə'rɛnəti] *n* : serenidad *f*
serf ['sərf] *n* : siervo *m*, -va *f*
serge ['sərdʒ] *n* : sarga *f*
sergeant ['sɑrdʒənt] *n* : sargento *mf*
serial[1] ['sɪriəl] *adj* : seriado
serial[2] *n* : serie *f*, serial *m* (de radio o televisión), publicación *f* por entregas
serially ['sɪriəli] *adv* : en serie
serial number *n* : número *m* de serie
series ['sɪrˌiːz] *n, pl* **series** : serie *f*, sucesión *f*
serious ['sɪriəs] *adj* **1** SOBER : serio **2** DEDICATED, EARNEST : serio, dedicado ⟨to be serious about something : tomar algo en serio⟩ **3** GRAVE : serio, grave ⟨serious problems : problemas graves⟩
seriously ['sɪriəsli] *adv* **1** EARNESTLY : seriamente, con seriedad, en serio ⟨to take seriously : tomar an serio⟩ **2** SEVERELY : gravemente ⟨seriously ill : gravemente enfermo⟩
seriousness ['sɪriəsnəs] *n* : seriedad *f*, gravedad *f*
sermon ['sərmən] *n* : sermón *m*
serpent ['sərpənt] *n* : serpiente *f*
serrated [sə'reɪtəd, 'sɛrˌeɪtəd] *adj* : dentado, serrado
serum ['sɪrəm] *n, pl* **serums** *or* **sera** ['sɪrə] : suero *m*
servant ['sərvənt] *n* : criado *m*, -da *f*; sirviente *m*, -ta *f*
serve ['sərv] *v* **served; serving** *vi* **1** : servir ⟨to serve in the navy : servir en la armada⟩ ⟨to serve on a jury : ser miembro de un jurado⟩ **2** DO, FUNCTION : servir ⟨to serve as : servir de, servir como⟩ **3** : sacar (en deportes) — *vt* **1** : servir ⟨to serve God : servir a Dios⟩ **2** HELP : servir ⟨it serves no purpose : no sirve para nada⟩ ⟨it serves you right : te lo mereces⟩ **3** : servir (comida o bebida) ⟨dinner is served : la cena está servida⟩ **4** SUPPLY : abastecer **5** CARRY OUT : cumplir, hacer ⟨to serve time : servir una pena⟩ **6 to serve a summons** : entregar una citación
server ['sərvər] *n* **1** : camarero *m*, -ra *f*; mesero *m*, -ra *f* (en un restaurante) **2** *or* **serving dish** : fuente *f* (para servir comida) **3** : servidor *m* (en informática)
service[1] ['sərvəs] *vt* **-viced; -vicing 1** MAINTAIN : darle mantenimiento a (una máquina), revisar **2** REPAIR : arreglar, reparar
service[2] *n* **1** HELP, USE : servicio *m* ⟨to do someone a service : hacerle un servicio a alguien⟩ ⟨at your service : a sus órdenes⟩ ⟨out of service : no funcionar⟩ **2** CEREMONY : oficio *m* (religioso) **3** DEPARTMENT, SYSTEM : servicio *m* ⟨social services : servicios sociales⟩ ⟨train service : servicio de trenes⟩ **4** SET

: juego *m*, servicio *m* ⟨tea service : juego de té⟩ **5** MAINTENANCE : mantenimiento *m*, revisión *f*, servicio *m* **6** : servicio *m* (en un restaurante, etc.) ⟨customer service : atención al cliente⟩ **7** : saque *m* (en deportes) **8 armed services** : fuerzas *fpl* armadas
serviceable ['sərvəsəbəl] *adj* **1** USEFUL : útil **2** DURABLE : duradero
service charge *n* : servicio *m*
serviceman ['sərvəsˌmæn, -mən] *n, pl* **-men** [-mən, -ˌmɛn] : militar *m*
service station → **gas station**
servicewoman ['sərvəsˌwʊmən] *n, pl* **-women** [-ˌwɪmən] : militar *f*
servile ['sərvəl, -ˌvaɪl] *adj* : servil
servility [sər'vɪləti] *n* : servilismo *m*
serving ['sərvɪŋ] *n* HELPING : porción *f*, ración *f*
servitude ['sərvəˌtuːd, -ˌtjuːd] *n* : servidumbre *f*
sesame ['sɛsəmi] *n* : ajonjolí *m*, sésamo *m*
session ['sɛʃən] *n* : sesión *f*
set[1] ['sɛt] *v* **set; setting** *vt* **1** *or* **to set down** PLACE : poner, colocar ⟨set the books (down) on the table : pon los libros en la mesa⟩ **2** INSTALL : poner, colocar (ladrillos, etc.) **3** MOUNT : engarzar, montar (un diamante, etc.) **4** ESTABLISH : fijar (una fecha, un precio, etc.), establecer (reglas, un récord, etc.) ⟨to set (oneself) a goal : fijarse una meta⟩ ⟨to set a precedent : sentar precedente⟩ ⟨to set a good/bad example : dar buen/mal ejemplo⟩ **5** PREPARE : tender (una trampa), poner (un freno de mano, etc.) ⟨to set the table : poner la mesa⟩ **6** ADJUST : poner (un reloj, etc.) **7** (*indicating the causing of a certain condition*) ⟨to set fire to : prenderle fuego a⟩ ⟨she set it free : lo soltó⟩ **8** MAKE, START : poner, hacer ⟨I set them working : los puse a trabajar⟩ ⟨it set me (to) thinking : me hizo pensar⟩ ⟨to set something in motion : poner algo en marcha⟩ **9** : ambientar ⟨the book is set in Chicago : el libro está ambientado en Chicago⟩ **10** : componer (un hueso roto, etc.) **11** : tensar (la mandíbula, la boca, etc.) **12** : marcar (el pelo) **13** : componer (texto) **14 to set about** BEGIN : comenzar **15 to set aside** RESERVE : reservar, dejar de lado **16 to set back** DELAY : retrasar, atrasar **17 to set off** PROVOKE : provocar **18 to set off** EXPLODE : hacer estallar (una bomba, etc.) **19 to set out** INTEND : proponerse **20 to set up** ASSEMBLE : montar, armar **21 to set up** ERECT : levantar, erigir **22 to set up** ESTABLISH : establecer, fundar, montar (un negocio) **23 to set up** CAUSE : armar ⟨they set up a clamor : armaron un alboroto⟩ — *vi* **1** SOLIDIFY : fraguar (dícese del cemento, etc.), cuajar (dícese de la gelatina, etc.) **2** : ponerse (dícese del sol o de la luna) **3 to set in** BEGIN : comenzar, empezar **4 to set off/forth** : salir **5 to set out** : salir (de viaje)
set[2] *adj* **1** ESTABLISHED, FIXED : fijo, es

tablecido **2** RIGID : inflexible ⟨to be set in one's ways : tener costumbres muy arraigadas⟩ **3** READY : listo, preparado

set³ *n* **1** COLLECTION : juego *m* ⟨a set of dishes : un juego de platos, una vajilla⟩ ⟨a tool set : una caja de herramientas⟩ **2** *or* **stage set** : decorado *m* (en el teatro), plató *m* (en el cine) **3** APPARATUS : aparato *m* ⟨a television set : un televisor⟩ **4** : conjunto *m* (en matemáticas)

setback [ˈsɛtˌbæk] *n* : revés *m*, contratiempo *m*

settee [sɛˈtiː] *n* : sofá *m*

setter [ˈsɛt̬ər] *n* **1** : setter *mf* ⟨Irish setter : setter irlandés⟩ **2** (*one that establishes*) ⟨record setter : persona que establece un récord⟩ ⟨style setter : persona que inicia una moda⟩

setting [ˈsɛt̬ɪŋ] *n* **1** : posición *f*, ajuste *m* (de un control) **2** : montura *f* (de una gema) **3** SCENE : escenario *m* (de una novela, etc.) **4** SURROUNDINGS : ambiente *m*, entorno *m*, marco *m*

settle [ˈsɛt̬əl] *v* **settled; settling** *vi* **1** ALIGHT, LAND : posarse (dícese de las aves, una mirada, etc.), depositarse (dícese del polvo) **2** SINK : asentarse (dícese de los edificios) **3** : acomodarse ⟨he settled into the chair : se arrellanó en la silla⟩ **4** : resolver una disputa ⟨they settled out of court : resolvieron extrajudicialmente su disputa⟩ **5** DECIDE : decidir (un asunto) ⟨that settles it : ya está decidido⟩ **6** : instalarse (en una casa), establecerse (en una ciudad o región) **7 to settle down** : calmarse, tranquilizarse ⟨settle down! : ¡tranquilízate!, ¡cálmate!⟩ **8 to settle down** : sentar cabeza, hacerse sensato ⟨to marry and settle down : casarse y sentar cabeza⟩ **9 to settle for** : conformarse con **10 to settle in** : instalarse (en una casa, etc.), adaptarse (a un trabajo, etc.) **11 to settle up** : arreglar las cuentas — *vt* **1** ARRANGE, DECIDE : fijar, decidir, acordar (planes, etc.) **2** RESOLVE : resolver, solucionar ⟨to settle an argument : resolver una discusión⟩ **3** PAY : pagar ⟨to settle an account : saldar una cuenta⟩ **4** CALM : calmar (los nervios), asentar (el estómago) **5** : acomodar, poner ⟨he settled the baby into its crib : puso al bebé en su cuna⟩ **6** COLONIZE : colonizar **7 to settle oneself** : acomodarse, hacerse cómodo

settlement [ˈsɛt̬əlmənt] *n* **1** PAYMENT : pago *m*, liquidación *f* **2** COLONY : asentamiento *m* **3** RESOLUTION : acuerdo *m*

settler [ˈsɛt̬lər] *n* : poblador *m*, -dora *f*; colono *m*, -na *f*

setup [ˈsɛt̬ˌʌp] *n* **1** ASSEMBLY : montaje *m*, ensamblaje *m* **2** ARRANGEMENT : disposición *f* **3** PREPARATION : preparación *f* **4** TRAP, TRICK : encerrona *f*

seven¹ [ˈsɛvən] *adj* : siete ⟨he's seven (years old) : tiene siete años⟩

seven² *n* : siete *m* ⟨the seven of hearts : siete de corazones⟩

seven³ *pron* : siete ⟨there are seven of us : somos siete⟩ ⟨it's seven (o'clock) : son las siete⟩

seven hundred¹ *adj & pron* : setecientos

seven hundred² *n* : setecientos *m*

seventeen¹ [ˌsɛvənˈtiːn] *adj & pron* : diecisiete

seventeen² *n* : diecisiete *m*

seventeenth¹ [ˌsɛvənˈtiːnθ] *adj* : decimoséptimo

seventeenth² *n* **1** : decimoséptimo *m*, -ma *f* (en una serie) **2** : diecisieteavo *m*, diecisieteava parte *f*

seventh¹ [ˈsɛvənθ] *adv* : en séptimo lugar

seventh² *adj* : séptimo

seventh³ *n* **1** : séptimo *m*, -ma *f* (en una serie) **2** : séptimo *m*, séptima parte *f*

seventieth¹ [ˈsɛvəntiəθ] *adj* : septuagésimo

seventieth² *n* **1** : septuagésimo *m*, -ma *f* (en una serie) **2** : setentavo *m*, setentava parte *f*, septuagésima parte *f*

seventy¹ [ˈsɛvənt̬i] *adj & pron* : setenta

seventy² *n, pl* **-ties** : setenta *m*

sever [ˈsɛvər] *vt* **-ered; -ering** : cortar, romper

several¹ [ˈsɛvrəl, ˈsɛvə-] *adj* **1** DISTINCT : distinto **2** SOME : varios ⟨several weeks : varias semanas⟩

several² *pron* : varios ⟨several of the novels : varias de las novelas⟩

severance [ˈsɛvrənts, ˈsɛvə-] *n* **1** : ruptura *f* (de relaciones, etc.) **2 severance pay** : indemnización *f* (por despido)

severe [səˈvɪr] *adj* **severer; -est** **1** STRICT : severo **2** AUSTERE : sobrio, austero **3** SERIOUS : grave ⟨a severe wound : una herida grave⟩ ⟨severe aches : dolores fuertes⟩ **4** DIFFICULT : duro, difícil — **severely** *adv*

severity [səˈvrət̬i] *n* **1** HARSHNESS : severidad *f* **2** AUSTERITY : sobriedad *f*, austeridad *f* **3** SERIOUSNESS : gravedad *f* (de una herida, etc.)

sew [ˈsoː] *v* **sewed; sewn** [ˈsoːn] *or* **sewed; sewing** : coser

sewage [ˈsuːɪdʒ] *n* : aguas *fpl* negras, aguas *fpl* residuales

sewer¹ [ˈsoːər] *n* : uno que cose

sewer² [ˈsuːər] *n* : alcantarilla *f*, cloaca *f*

sewing [ˈsoːɪŋ] *n* : costura *f*

sewing machine *n* : máquina *f* de coser

sex [ˈsɛks] *n* **1** : sexo *m* ⟨the opposite sex : el sexo opuesto⟩ **2** COPULATION : relaciones *fpl* sexuales ⟨sex education : educación sexual⟩

sexism [ˈsɛkˌsɪzəm] *n* : sexismo *m*

sexist¹ [ˈsɛksɪst] *adj* : sexista

sexist² *n* : sexista *mf*

sextant [ˈsɛkstənt] *n* : sextante *m*

sextet [sɛkˈstɛt] *n* : sexteto *m*

sexton [ˈsɛkstən] *n* : sacristán *m*

sexual [ˈsɛkʃuəl] *adj* : sexual ⟨sexual intercourse : relaciones sexuales⟩ ⟨sexual discrimination/harassment : discriminación/acoso sexual⟩ — **sexually** *adv*

sexuality [ˌsɛkʃuˈæləti] *n* : sexualidad *f*

sexy [ˈsɛksi] *adj* **sexier; -est** : sexy

sh *or* **ssh** *or* **sssh** [ʃ, often prolonged] *interj* : chis!, chist!

shabbily ['ʃæbəli] *adv* **1** : pobremente ⟨shabbily dressed : pobremente vestido⟩ **2** UNFAIRLY : mal, injustamente
shabbiness ['ʃæbinəs] *n* **1** : lo gastado (de ropa, etc.) **2** : lo mal vestido (de personas) **3** UNFAIRNESS : injusticia *f*
shabby ['ʃæbi] *adj* **shabbier; -est 1** : gastado (dícese de la ropa, etc.) **2** : mal vestido (dícese de las personas) **3** UNFAIR : malo, injusto ⟨shabby treatment : mal trato⟩
shack ['ʃæk] *n* : choza *f*, rancho *m*
shackle[1] ['ʃækəl] *vt* **-led; -ling** : ponerle grilletes (a alguien)
shackle[2] *n* : grillete *m*
shad ['ʃæd] *n* : sábalo *m*
shade[1] ['ʃeɪd] *v* **shaded; shading** *vt* **1** SHELTER : proteger (del sol o de la luz) **2** *or* **to shade in** : matizar los colores de — *vi* : convertirse gradualmente ⟨his irritation shaded into rage : su irritación iba convirtiéndose en furia⟩
shade[2] *n* **1** : sombra *f* ⟨to give shade : dar sombra⟩ **2** : tono *m* (de un color) **3** NUANCE : matiz *m* **4** : pantalla *f* (de una lámpara), persiana *f* (de una ventana)
shadow[1] ['ʃædo:] *vt* **1** DARKEN : ensombrecer **2** TRAIL : seguir de cerca, seguirle la pista (a alguien)
shadow[2] *n* **1** : sombra *f* **2** DARKNESS : oscuridad *f* **3** TRACE : sombra *f*, atisbo *m*, indicio *m* ⟨without a shadow of a doubt : sin sombra de duda, sin lugar a dudas⟩ **4 to cast a shadow over** : ensombrecer
shadowy ['ʃædowi] *adj* **1** INDISTINCT : vago, indistinto **2** DARK : oscuro
shady ['ʃeɪdi] *adj* **shadier; -est 1** : sombreado (dícese de un lugar), que da sombra (dícese de un árbol) **2** DISREPUTABLE : sospechoso (dícese de una persona), turbio (dícese de un negocio, etc.)
shaft ['ʃæft] *n* **1** : asta *f* (de una lanza), astil *m* (de una flecha), mango *m* (de una herramienta) **2** *or* **mine shaft** : pozo *m*
shaggy ['ʃægi] *adj* **shaggier; -est 1** HAIRY : peludo ⟨a shaggy dog : un perro peludo⟩ **2** UNKEMPT : enmarañado, despeinado (dícese del pelo, de las barbas, etc.)
shake[1] ['ʃeɪk] *v* **shook** ['ʃʊk]; **shaken** ['ʃeɪkən]; **shaking** *vt* **1** : sacudir, agitar, hacer temblar ⟨he shook his head : negó con la cabeza⟩ **2** WEAKEN : debilitar, hacer flaquear ⟨it shook her faith : debilitó su confianza⟩ **3** UPSET : afectar, alterar **4 to shake hands with someone** : darle/estrecharle la mano a alguien **5 to shake off** : deshacer **6 to shake up** : reestructurar, reorganizar — *vi* : temblar, sacudirse ⟨to shake with fear : temblar de miedo⟩
shake[2] *n* : sacudida *f*, apretón *m* (de manos)
shaker ['ʃeɪkər] *n* **1 salt shaker** : salero *m* **2 pepper shaker** : pimentero *m* **3 cocktail shaker** : coctelera *f*
shake–up ['ʃeɪkˌʌp] *n* : reorganización *f*
shakily ['ʃeɪkəli] *adv* : temblorosamente

shaky ['ʃeɪki] *adj* **shakier; -est 1** SHAKING : tembloroso **2** UNSTABLE : poco firme, inestable **3** PRECARIOUS : precario, incierto **4** QUESTIONABLE : dudoso, cuestionable ⟨shaky arguments : argumentos discutibles⟩
shale ['ʃeɪl] *n* : esquisto *m*
shall ['ʃæl] *v aux, past* **should** ['ʃʊd] *present s & pl* **shall 1** (*used formally to express a command*) ⟨you shall do as I say : harás lo que te digo⟩ ⟨there shall be no talking during the test : se prohíbe hablar durante el examen⟩ **2** (*used formally to request an opinion*) ⟨shall I call a taxi? : ¿quiere que llame un taxi?⟩ **3** (*used formally to express futurity*) ⟨we shall see : ya veremos⟩ ⟨when shall we expect you? : ¿cuándo te podemos esperar?⟩ ⟨I shall not mention it, I shan't mention it : no lo mencionaré⟩ **4** (*used formally to express determination*) ⟨you shall have the money : tendrás el dinero⟩
shallow ['ʃælo:] *adj* **1** : poco profundo (dícese del agua, etc.) **2** SUPERFICIAL : superficial
shallows ['ʃælo:z] *npl* : bajío *m*, bajos *mpl*
sham[1] ['ʃæm] *v* **shammed; shamming** : fingir
sham[2] *adj* : falso, fingido
sham[3] *n* **1** FAKE, PRETENSE : farsa *f*, simulación *f*, imitación *f* **2** FAKER : impostor *m*, -tora *f*; farsante *mf*
shamble ['ʃæmbəl] *vi* **-bled; -bling** : caminar arrastrando los pies
shambles ['ʃæmbəlz] *ns & pl* : caos *m*, desorden *m*, confusión *f*
shame[1] ['ʃeɪm] *vt* **shamed; shaming 1** : avergonzar ⟨he was shamed by their words : sus palabras le dieron vergüenza⟩ **2** DISGRACE : deshonrar
shame[2] *n* **1** : vergüenza *f* ⟨to have no shame : no tener vergüenza⟩ **2** DISGRACE : vergüenza *f*, deshonra *f* **3** PITY : lástima *f*, pena *f* ⟨what a shame! : ¡qué pena!⟩
shamefaced ['ʃeɪmˌfeɪst] *adj* : avergonzado
shameful ['ʃeɪmfəl] *adj* : vergonzoso — **shamefully** *adv*
shameless ['ʃeɪmləs] *adj* : descarado, desvergonzado — **shamelessly** *adv*
shampoo[1] [ʃæmˈpu:] *vt* : lavar (el pelo)
shampoo[2] *n, pl* **-poos** : champú *m*
shamrock ['ʃæmˌrak] *n* : trébol *m*
shank ['ʃæŋk] *n* : parte *f* baja de la pierna
shan't ['ʃænt] *contraction of* SHALL NOT → **shall**
shanty ['ʃænti] *n, pl* **-ties** : choza *f*, rancho *m*
shantytown ['ʃæntiˌtaʊn] *n* : barriada *f*, cinturón *m* de miseria, ciudad *f* perdida *Mex*, villa *f* miseria *Arg*, villa *f* de emergencia *Arg*, pueblo *m* joven *Peru*, población *f* callampa *Chile*, barrio *m* de invasión *Col*, barrio *m* de chabolas *Spain*
shape[1] ['ʃeɪp] *v* **shaped; shaping** *vt* **1** : dar forma a, modelar (arcilla, etc.), tallar (madera, piedra), formar (carácter) ⟨to be shaped like : tener forma de⟩ **2**

DETERMINE : decidir, determinar — *vi or* **to shape up** : tomar forma

shape² *n* **1** : forma *f*, figura *f* ⟨in the shape of a circle : en forma de círculo⟩ ⟨to take shape : tomar forma⟩ **2** CONDITION : estado *m*, condiciones *fpl*, forma *f* (física) ⟨to be in good shape : estar en forma⟩ ⟨to be in bad shape : no estar en forma⟩ ⟨to get in shape : ponerse en forma⟩

-shaped [ˌʃeɪpt] *suf* : en forma de

shapeless [ˈʃeɪpləs] *adj* : informe

shapely [ˈʃeɪpli] *adj* **shapelier; -est** : curvilíneo, bien proporcionado

shard [ˈʃɑrd] *n* : fragmento *m*, casco *m* (de cerámica, etc.)

share¹ [ˈʃɛr] *v* **shared; sharing** *vt* **1** APPORTION : dividir, repartir **2** : compartir ⟨they share a room : comparten una habitación⟩ — *vi* : compartir

share² *n* **1** PORTION : parte *f*, porción *f* ⟨one's fair share : lo que le corresponde a uno⟩ **2** : acción *f* (en una compañía) ⟨to hold shares : tener acciones⟩

sharecropper [ˈʃɛrˌkrɑpər] *n* : aparcero *m*, -ra *f*

shareholder [ˈʃɛrˌhoːldər] *n* : accionista *mf*

shark [ˈʃɑrk] *n* : tiburón *m*

sharp¹ [ˈʃɑrp] *adv* : en punto ⟨at two o'clock sharp : a las dos en punto⟩

sharp² *adj* **1** : afilado, filoso ⟨a sharp knife : un cuchillo afilado⟩ **2** PENETRATING : cortante, fuerte **3** CLEVER : agudo, listo, perspicaz **4** ACUTE : agudo ⟨sharp eyesight : vista aguda⟩ **5** HARSH, SEVERE : duro, severo, agudo ⟨a sharp rebuke : una reprimenda mordaz⟩ ⟨to have a sharp tongue : tener una lengua afilada⟩ **6** STRONG : fuerte ⟨sharp cheese : queso fuerte⟩ **7** ABRUPT : brusco, repentino **8** DISTINCT : nítido, definido ⟨a sharp image : una imagen bien definida⟩ **9** ANGULAR : anguloso (dícese de la cara) **10** : sostenido (en música)

sharp³ *n* : sostenido *m* (en música)

sharpen [ˈʃɑrpən] *vt* : afilar, aguzar ⟨to sharpen a pencil : sacarle punta a un lápiz⟩ ⟨to sharpen one's wits : aguzar el ingenio⟩

sharpener [ˈʃɑrpənər] *n* : afilador *m* (para cuchillos, etc.), sacapuntas *m* (para lápices)

sharply [ˈʃɑrpli] *adv* **1** ABRUPTLY : bruscamente **2** DISTINCTLY : claramente, marcadamente

sharpness [ˈʃɑrpnəs] *n* **1** : lo afilado (de un cuchillo, etc.) **2** ACUTENESS : agudeza *f* (de los sentidos o de la mente) **3** INTENSITY : intensidad *f*, agudeza *f* (de dolores, etc.) **4** HARSHNESS : dureza *f*, severidad *f* **5** ABRUPTNESS : brusquedad *f* **6** CLARITY : nitidez *f*

sharpshooter [ˈʃɑrpˌʃuːtər] *n* : tirador *m*, -dora *f* de primera

shatter [ˈʃætər] *vt* **1** : hacer añicos ⟨to shatter the silence : romper el silencio⟩ **2 to be shattered by** : quedar destrozado por — *vi* : hacerse añicos, romperse en pedazos

shave¹ [ˈʃeɪv] *v* **shaved; shaved** *or* **shaven** [ˈʃeɪvən]; **shaving** *vt* **1** : afeitar, rasurar ⟨she shaved her legs : se rasuró las piernas⟩ ⟨they shaved (off) his beard : le afeitaron la barba⟩ **2** SLICE : cortar (en pedazos finos) — *vi* : afeitarse, rasurarse

shave² *n* : afeitada *f*, rasurada *f*

shaver [ˈʃeɪvər] *n* : afeitadora *f*, máquina *f* de afeitar, rasuradora *f*

shaving [ˈʃeɪvɪŋ] *n* : viruta *f* ⟨wood shavings : virutas de madera⟩

shaving cream *n* : crema *f* de afeitar

shawl [ˈʃɔl] *n* : chal *m*, mantón *m*, rebozo *m*

she [ˈʃiː] *pron* : ella

sheaf [ˈʃiːf] *n, pl* **sheaves** [ˈʃiːvz] : gavilla *f* (de cereales), haz *m* (de flechas), fajo *m* (de papeles)

shear [ˈʃɪr] *vt* **sheared; sheared** *or* **shorn** [ˈʃorn]; **shearing** **1** : esquilar, trasquilar ⟨to shear sheep : trasquilar ovejas⟩ **2** CUT : cortar (el pelo, etc.)

shears [ˈʃɪrz] *npl* : tijeras *fpl* (grandes)

sheath [ˈʃiːθ] *n, pl* **sheaths** [ˈʃiːðz, ˈʃiːθs] : funda *f*, vaina *f*

sheathe [ˈʃiːð] *vt* **sheathed; sheathing** : envainar, enfundar

shed¹ [ˈʃd] *vt* **shed; shedding** **1** : derramar (sangre o lágrimas) **2** EMIT : emitir (luz) ⟨to shed light on : aclarar⟩ **3** DISCARD : mudar (la piel, etc.) ⟨to shed one's clothes : quitarse uno la ropa⟩

shed² *n* : cobertizo *m*

she'd [ˈʃiːd] *contraction of* SHE HAD *or* SHE WOULD → **have, would**

sheen [ˈʃiːn] *n* : brillo *m*, lustre *m*

sheep [ˈʃiːp] *ns & pl* : oveja *f*

sheepdog [ˈʃiːpˌdɔg] *n* : perro *m* pastor

sheepfold [ˈʃiːpˌfoːld] *n* : redil *m*

sheepish [ˈʃiːpɪʃ] *adj* : avergonzado

sheepskin [ˈʃiːpˌskɪn] *n* : piel *f* de oveja, piel *f* de borrego

sheer¹ [ˈʃɪr] *adv* **1** COMPLETELY : completamente, totalmente **2** VERTICALLY : verticalmente

sheer² *adj* **1** TRANSPARENT : vaporoso, transparente **2** ABSOLUTE, UTTER : puro ⟨by sheer luck : por pura suerte⟩ **3** STEEP : escarpado, vertical

sheet [ˈʃiːt] *n* **1** *or* **bedsheet** [ˈbɛd-ˌʃiːt] : sábana *f* **2** : hoja *f* (de papel) **3** : capa *f* (de hielo, etc.) **4** : lámina *f*, placa *f* (de vidrio, metal, etc.), plancha *f* (de metal, madera, etc.) ⟨baking sheet : placa de horno⟩

sheikh *or* **sheik** [ˈʃiːk, ˈʃeɪk] *n* : jeque *m*

shelf [ˈʃɛlf] *n, pl* **shelves** [ˈʃɛlvz] **1** : estante *m*, anaquel *m* (en una pared) **2** : banco *m*, arrecife *m* (en geología) ⟨continental shelf : plataforma continental⟩

shell¹ [ˈʃɛl] *vt* **1** : pelar (nueces, etc.) **2** BOMBARD : bombardear

shell² *n* **1** SEASHELL : concha *f* **2** : cáscara *f* (de huevos, nueces, etc.), vaina *f* (de chícharos, etc.), caparazón *m* (de crustáceos, tortugas, etc.) **3** : cartucho *m*, casquillo *m* (de a .45 caliber shell : un cartucho calibre .45⟩ **4** *or* **racing shell** : bote *m* (para hacer regatas de remos)

she'll [ˈʃiːl, ˈʃɪl] *contraction of* SHE SHALL *or* SHE WILL → **shall, will**

shellac¹ [ʃəˈlæk] *vt* -lacked; -lacking 1 : laquear (madera, etc.) 2 DEFEAT : darle una paliza (a alguien), derrotar

shellac² *n* : laca *f*

shellfish [ˈʃɛl,fɪʃ] *n* : marisco *m*

shelter¹ [ˈʃɛltər] *vt* 1 PROTECT : proteger, abrigar 2 HARBOR : dar refugio a, albergar

shelter² *n* : refugio *m*, abrigo *m* ⟨to take shelter : refugiarse⟩

shelve [ˈʃɛlv] *vt* **shelved; shelving** 1 : poner en estantes 2 DEFER : dar carpetazo a

shenanigans [ʃəˈnænɪɡənz] *npl* 1 TRICKERY : artimañas *fpl* 2 MISCHIEF : travesuras *fpl*

shepherd¹ [ˈʃɛpərd] *vt* 1 : cuidar (ovejas, etc.) 2 GUIDE : conducir, guiar

shepherd² *n* : pastor *m*

shepherdess [ˈʃɛpərdəs] *n* : pastora *f*

sherbet [ˈʃərbət] *or* **sherbert** [-bərt] *n* : sorbete *m*; nieve *f Cuba, Mex, PRi*

sheriff [ˈʃɛrɪf] *n* : sheriff *mf*

sherry [ˈʃɛri] *n, pl* **-ries** : jerez *m*

she's [ˈʃiːz] *contraction of* SHE IS *or* SHE HAS → **be, have**

Shia *or* **Shi'a** [ˈʃiːˌɑ] *n* 1 : chiismo *m* 2 *pl* **Shia** *or* **Shi'a** *or* **Shias** *or* **Shi'as** SHIITE : chií *mf*, chiita *mf*

shield¹ [ˈʃiːld] *vt* 1 PROTECT : proteger 2 CONCEAL : ocultar ⟨to shield one's eyes : taparse los ojos⟩

shield² *n* 1 : escudo *m* (armadura) 2 PROTECTION : protección *f*, blindaje *m* (de un cable)

shier, shiest → shy

shift¹ [ˈʃɪft] *vt* 1 CHANGE : cambiar ⟨to shift gears : cambiar de velocidad⟩ 2 MOVE : mover 3 TRANSFER : transferir ⟨to shift the blame : echarle la culpa (a otro)⟩ — *vi* 1 CHANGE : cambiar 2 MOVE : moverse 3 **to shift for oneself** : arreglárselas solo

shift² *n* 1 CHANGE, TRANSFER : cambio *m* ⟨a shift in priorities : un cambio de prioridades⟩ 2 : turno *m* ⟨night shift : turno de noche⟩ 3 DRESS : vestido *m* (suelto) 4 → **gearshift**

shiftless [ˈʃɪftləs] *adj* : perezoso, vago, holgazán

shifty [ˈʃɪfti] *adj* **shiftier; -est** : taimado, artero ⟨a shifty look : una mirada huidiza⟩

Shiite *or* **Shi'ite** [ˈʃiːˌaɪt] *n* SHIA : chií *mf*, chiita *mf* — **Shiite** *or* **Shi'ite** *adj*

shilling [ˈʃɪlɪŋ] *n* : chelín *m*

shimmer [ˈʃɪmər] *vi* GLIMMER : brillar con luz trémula

shin¹ [ˈʃɪn] *vi* **shinned; shinning** : trepar, subir ⟨she shinned up the pole : subió al poste⟩

shin² *n* : espinilla *f*, canilla *f*

shine¹ [ˈʃaɪn] *v* **shone** [ˈʃoːn] *or* **shined; shining** *vi* 1 : brillar, relucir ⟨the stars were shining : las estrellas brillaban⟩ 2 EXCEL : brillar, lucirse — *vt* 1 : alumbrar ⟨he shined the flashlight at it : lo alumbró con la linterna⟩ 2 POLISH : sacarle brillo a, lustrar

shine² *n* : brillo *m*, lustre *m*

shingle¹ [ˈʃɪŋɡəl] *vt* -gled; -gling : techar

shingle² *n* : tablilla *f* (para techar)

shingles [ˈʃɪŋɡəlz] *npl* : herpes *m*

shinny [ˈʃɪni] *vi* -nied; -nying → **shin¹**

shiny [ˈʃaɪni] *adj* **shinier; -est** : brillante

ship¹ [ˈʃɪp] *vt* **shipped; shipping** 1 LOAD : embarcar (en un barco) 2 SEND : transportar (en barco), enviar ⟨to ship by air : enviar por avión⟩

ship² *n* 1 : barco *m*, buque *m* 2 → **spaceship**

shipboard [ˈʃɪp,bord] *n* **on** ~ : a bordo

shipbuilder [ˈʃɪp,bɪldər] *n* : constructor *m*, -tora *f* naval

shipment [ˈʃɪpmənt] *n* 1 SHIPPING : transporte *m*, embarque *m* 2 : envío *m*, remesa *f* ⟨a shipment of medicine : un envío de medicina⟩

shipper [ˈʃɪpər] *n* : exportador *m*, -dora *f*

shipping [ˈʃɪpɪŋ] *n* 1 SHIPS : barcos *mpl*, embarcaciones *fpl* 2 TRANSPORTATION : transporte *m* (de mercancías)

shipshape [ˈʃɪpˌʃeɪp] *adj* : ordenado

shipwreck¹ [ˈʃɪp,rɛk] *vt* **to be shipwrecked** : naufragar

shipwreck² *n* : naufragio *m*

shipyard [ˈʃɪp,jɑrd] *n* : astillero *m*

shirk [ˈʃərk] *vt* : eludir, rehuir ⟨to shirk one's responsibilities : esquivar uno sus responsabilidades⟩

shirt [ˈʃərt] *n* : camisa *f*

shiver¹ [ˈʃɪvər] *vi* 1 : tiritar (de frío) 2 TREMBLE : estremecerse, temblar

shiver² *n* : escalofrío *m*, estremecimiento *m*

shoal [ˈʃoːl] *n* : banco *m*, bajío *m*

shock¹ [ˈʃɑk] *vt* 1 UPSET : conmover, conmocionar 2 STARTLE : asustar, sobresaltar 3 SCANDALIZE : escandalizar 4 : darle una descarga eléctrica a

shock² *n* 1 COLLISION, JOLT : choque *m*, sacudida *f* 2 UPSET : shock *m*, choque *m*, golpe *m* (emocional) ⟨she's in for a shock : se va a llevar un shock⟩ ⟨it came as a shock to me : me sorprendió/afectó mucho⟩ 3 : shock *m*, choque *m* (en medicina) ⟨to be in shock : estar en estado de shock⟩ 4 *or* **electric shock** : descarga *f* eléctrica, calambre *m* 5 SHEAVES : gavillas *fpl* 6 **shock of hair** : mata *f* de pelo

shock absorber *n* : amortiguador *m*

shocker [ˈʃɑkər] *n* : bomba *f*, bombazo *m*

shocking [ˈʃɑkɪŋ] *adj* 1 : chocante 2 **shocking pink** : rosa *m* estridente

shoddy [ˈʃɑdi] *adj* **shoddier; -est** : de mala calidad ⟨a shoddy piece of work : un trabajo chapucero⟩

shoe¹ [ˈʃuː] *vt* **shod** [ˈʃɑd]; **shoeing** : herrar (un caballo)

shoe² *n* 1 : zapato *m* ⟨the shoe industry : la industria del calzado⟩ 2 HORSESHOE : herradura *f* 3 **brake shoe** : zapata *f*

shoehorn [ˈʃuːˌhɔrn] *n* : calzador *m*

shoelace [ˈʃuːˌleɪs] *n* : cordón *m* (de zapatos)

shoemaker [ˈʃuːˌmeɪkər] *n* : zapatero *m*, -ra *f*

shoe polish *n* : betún *m*, grasa *f Mex*
shoeshine ['ʃuː,ʃaɪn] *n* : acto *m* de limpiar o lustrar los zapatos ⟨shoeshine boy/girl : limpiabotas, lustrabotas, bolero/bolera⟩
shoe store *n* : zapatería *f*
shone → **shine**
shoo ['ʃuː] *vt* **to shoo away/off/out** (etc.) : espantar, mandar a otra parte
shook → **shake**
shoot[1] ['ʃuːt] *v* **shot** ['ʃɑt]; **shooting** *vt* **1** : disparar, tirar ⟨to shoot a bullet/pistol : disparar una bala/pistola⟩ **2** : pegarle un tiro a, darle un balazo a, balacear, balear ⟨he shot her : le pegó un tiro⟩ ⟨to shoot oneself : pegarse un tiro⟩ ⟨to shoot and kill, to shoot dead/down : matar a balazos⟩ **3** THROW : lanzar (una pelota, una mirada, etc.) **4** SCORE : anotar ⟨to shoot a basket : encestar⟩ **5** PLAY : jugar a (los dados, etc.) **6** PHOTOGRAPH : fotografiar **7** FILM : filmar **8 to shoot down** : derribar (un avión) **9 to shoot down** DEFEAT : echar por tierra **10 to shoot oneself in the foot** *fam* : crearse problemas — *vi* **1** : disparar (con un arma de fuego) **2** DART : ir rápidamente ⟨it shot past : pasó como una bala⟩ **3** : disparar (en deportes) **4 to shoot for** : poner como objetivo ⟨let's shoot for Monday : intentémoslo para el lunes⟩ **5 to shoot up** : pincharse, inyectarse **6 to shoot up** INCREASE : dispararse
shoot[2] *n* : brote *m*, retoño *m*, vástago *m*
shooting ['ʃuːtɪŋ] *n* : baleo *m*, tiroteo *m* ⟨shooting death : asesinato (con arma de fuego)⟩
shooting star *n* : estrella *f* fugaz
shoot-out ['ʃuːt,aʊt] *n* : balacera *f*, baleo *m*, tiroteo *m*
shop[1] ['ʃɑp] *vi* **shopped; shopping** : hacer compras ⟨to go shopping : ir de compras⟩
shop[2] *n* **1** WORKSHOP : taller *m* **2** STORE : tienda *f*
shopkeeper ['ʃɑp,kiːpər] *n* : tendero *m*, -ra *f*
shoplift ['ʃɑp,lɪft] *vi* : hurtar mercancía (de una tienda) — *vt* : hurtar (de una tienda)
shoplifter ['ʃɑp,lɪftər] *n* : ladrón *m*, -drona *f* (que roba en una tienda)
shopper ['ʃɑpər] *n* : comprador *m*, -dora *f*
shopping bag *n* : bolsa *f* (para las compras)
shopping cart *n* : carrito/carro *m* de compras; carrito *m* de la compra *Mex, Spain*; carro *m* de la compra *Spain*
shopping center *or* **shopping plaza** *n* : centro *m* comercial
shopping mall *n* : centro *m* comercial
shop window *n* : vitrina *f*, escaparate *m*, aparador *m*
shore[1] ['ʃor] *vt* **shored; shoring** : apuntalar ⟨they shored up the wall : apuntalaron la pared⟩
shore[2] *n* **1** : orilla *f* (del mar, etc.) **2** PROP : puntal *m*

shoreline ['ʃor,laɪn] *n* : orilla *f*
shorn → **shear**
short[1] ['ʃort] *v* → **short-circuit**
short[2] *adv* **1** ABRUPTLY : repentinamente, súbitamente ⟨the car stopped short : el carro se paró en seco⟩ ⟨the sight of it brought me up short : lo que vi me hizo parar en seco⟩ **2 to be running short** ⟨the food is running short, we're running short on food : se nos está acabando la comida⟩ **3 to cut short** : interrumpir **4 to fall short** : no alcanzar, quedarse corto ⟨to fall short of expectations : no estar a la altura de las expectativas⟩ **5 to stop short of doing something** : no llegar a hacer algo
short[3] *adj* **1** : corto (de medida), bajo (de estatura) ⟨a short distance away : a poca distancia⟩ **2** BRIEF : corto ⟨short and sweet : corto y bueno⟩ ⟨a short time ago : hace poco⟩ ⟨a short delay : una pequeña demora⟩ ⟨on short notice : con poca antelación⟩ **3** ABBREVIATED : abreviado ⟨to be short for : ser una forma breve de⟩ **4** CURT : brusco, cortante, seco **5** : corto (de dinero, etc.) ⟨I'm one dollar short : me falta un dólar⟩ ⟨to be short on/of time : andar corto de tiempo⟩ ⟨to be short of breath : quedarse sin aliento⟩ **6 nothing short of** : nada menos que, ni más ni menos que
short[4] *n* **1 shorts** *npl* : shorts *mpl*, pantalones *mpl* cortos **2 short circuit 3** : cortometraje *m* (en el cine) **4 for short** : para abreviar **5 in short** : en resumen
shortage ['ʃortɪdʒ] *n* : falta *f*, escasez *f*, carencia *f*
shortbread ['ʃort,brɛd] *n* : galleta *f* dulce de mantequilla, harina, y azúcar
shortcake ['ʃort,keɪk] *n* : tarta *f* de fruta
shortchange ['ʃort'tʃeɪndʒ] *vt* **-changed; -changing** : darle mal el cambio (a alguien)
short-circuit *vt* : provocar un cortocircuito en — *vi* **1** : provocar un cortocircuito **2** : hacer cortocircuito ⟨the lamp short-circuited : la lámpara hizo cortocircuito⟩
short circuit *n* : cortocircuito *m*, corto *m* (eléctrico)
shortcoming ['ʃort,kʌmɪŋ] *n* : defecto *m*
shortcut ['ʃort,kʌt] *n* **1** : atajo *m* ⟨to take a shortcut : cortar camino⟩ **2** : alternativa *f* fácil, método *m* rápido
shorten ['ʃortən] *vt* : acortar — *vi* : acortarse
shortfall ['ʃort,fɔl] *n* : déficit *m*
shorthand ['ʃort,hænd] *n* : taquigrafía *f*
short list *n* : lista *f* de candidatos finales
short-lived ['ʃort'lɪvd, -'laɪvd] *adj* : efímero
shortly ['ʃortli] *adv* **1** BRIEFLY : brevemente ⟨to put it shortly : para decirlo en pocas palabras⟩ **2** SOON : dentro de poco
shortness ['ʃortnəs] *n* **1** : lo corto ⟨shortness of stature : estatura baja⟩ **2** BREVITY : brevedad *f* **3** CURTNESS : brusquedad *f* **4** SHORTAGE : falta *f*, escasez *f*, carencia *f*

shortsighted [ˈʃɔrtˌsaɪtəd] → **nearsighted**

short–sleeved [ˈʃɔrtˌsliːvd] *adj* : de manga corta

short–staffed [ˈʃɔrtˌstæft] *adj* **to be short–staffed** : faltarle personal a

shortstop [ˈʃɔrtˌstɑp] *n* : torpedero *m*, -ra *f*; parador *m*, -dora *f* en corto *Car*, *Mex*, *Ven*

short story *n* : cuento *m*

short–tempered [ˈʃɔrtˌtɛmpərd] *adj* : de mal genio

short–term [ˈʃɔrtˌtərm] *adj* : a corto plazo

shorty [ˈʃɔrti] *n* : enano *m*, -na *f*, *often disparaging*; petiso *m*, -sa *f* (persona)

shot [ˈʃɑt] *n* **1** : disparo *m*, tiro *m* ⟨to fire a shot : disparar⟩ **2** PELLETS : perdigones *mpl* **3** : tiro *m* (en deportes) **4** ATTEMPT : intento *m*, tentativa *f* ⟨to have/take a shot at : hacer un intento por⟩ **5** CHANCE : posibilidad *f*, chance *m* ⟨we have a shot at winning : tenemos posibilidades de ganar⟩ ⟨a long shot : una posibilidad remota⟩ **6** PHOTOGRAPH : foto *f* **7** INJECTION : inyección *f* **8** : trago *m* (de licor) **9** MARKSMAN : tirador *m*, -dora *f* ⟨a good/poor shot : un buen/mal tirador⟩

shotgun [ˈʃɑtˌgʌn] *n* : escopeta *f*

shot put *n* : lanzamiento *m* de bala

should [ˈʃʊd] *v aux* (*past of* **shall**) **1** (*expressing a condition*) ⟨if he should die : si muriera⟩ ⟨if they should call, tell me : si llaman, dímelo⟩ **2** (*indicating what is proper, required, or desirable*) ⟨they should be punished : deberían ser castigados⟩ ⟨what time should we meet? : ¿a qué hora nos encontramos?⟩ **3** (*indicating a preferred thing that did not happen*) ⟨I should have realized : tendría que haberme dado cuenta⟩ ⟨he shouldn't have said it : no debería haberlo dicho⟩ **4** (*expressing polite thanks*) ⟨you shouldn't have gone to all that trouble! : ¡no deberías haberte molestado tanto!⟩ **5** (*expressing a wish*) ⟨you should have seen her face! : ¡tendrías que haber visto la cara que puso!⟩ **6** (*requesting an opinion*) ⟨what should I do? : ¿qué hago?⟩ **7** (*expressing a feeling about someone's words or behavior*) ⟨(it's) funny you should say that — I was just thinking the same thing : ¡qué casualidad! estaba pensando lo mismo⟩ **8** (*emphasizing a belief, thought, or hope*) ⟨I should hope so/not! : ¡faltaría más!⟩ **9** (*expressing probability*) ⟨they should arrive soon : deben (de) llegar pronto⟩ ⟨why should he lie? : ¿porqué ha de mentir?⟩

shoulder[1] [ˈʃoːldər] *vt* **1** JOSTLE : empujar (con el hombro) **2** : ponerse al hombro (una mochila, etc.) **3** : cargar con (la responsabilidad, etc.)

shoulder[2] *n* **1** : hombro *m* ⟨to shrug one's shoulders : encogerse los hombros⟩ **2** : arcén *m*; banquina *f Arg*, *Uru*; berma *f Chile*, *Col*, *Ecua*, *Peru* (de una carretera)

shoulder bag *n* HANDBAG : cartera *f*, bolso *m*, bolsa *f Mex* (con correa)

shoulder blade *n* : omóplato *m*, omoplato *m*, escápula *f*

shoulder–length *n* : hasta los hombros

shoulder strap *n* : tirante *m*

shouldn't [ˈʃʊdənt] *contraction of* SHOULD NOT → **should**

shout[1] [ˈʃaʊt] *v* : gritar, vocear

shout[2] *n* : grito *m*

shove[1] [ˈʃʌv] *v* **shoved; shoving** : empujar bruscamente

shove[2] *n* : empujón *m*, empellón *m*

shovel[1] [ˈʃʌvəl] *vt* -**veled** *or* -**velled**; -**veling** *or* -**velling** **1** : mover con (una) pala ⟨they shoveled the dirt out : sacaron la tierra con palas⟩ **2** DIG : cavar (con una pala)

shovel[2] *n* : pala *f*

show[1] [ˈʃoː] *v* **showed; shown** [ˈʃoːn] *or* **showed; showing** *vt* **1** PRESENT, DISPLAY : mostrar, enseñar ⟨I showed him the photo : le mostré la foto⟩ **2** REVEAL : demostrar, manifestar, revelar ⟨he showed himself to be a coward : se reveló como cobarde⟩ ⟨to show signs of : dar muestras/señales/indicios de⟩ ⟨to show one's feelings : demostrar uno sus emociones⟩ **3** TEACH : enseñar ⟨show me how to do it : enséñame cómo hacerlo⟩ ⟨to show someone who's boss : demostrarle a alguien quién manda⟩ ⟨I'll show him! : ¡ya lo verá!⟩ **4** PROVE : demostrar, probar ⟨it just goes to show that . . . : esto demuestra que . . .⟩ **5** DEPICT : representar ⟨the photo shows children playing : la foto es de unos niños jugando⟩ **6** DISPLAY, READ : marcar **7** INDICATE : indicar **8** CONDUCT, LEAD : llevar, conducir ⟨to show someone the way : conducir a alguien⟩ ⟨to show someone out : acompañar a alguien a la puerta⟩ ⟨they showed us around their house : nos mostraron su casa⟩ **9** : proyectar (una película), dar (un programa de televisión) **10 to show off** : lucirse con **11 to show off** ACCENTUATE : hacer resaltar **12 to show up** EMBARRASS : hacer quedar mal — *vi* **1** : notarse, verse ⟨the stain doesn't show : la mancha no se ve⟩ **2** APPEAR : aparecer, dejarse ver **3 to show off** : lucirse

show[2] *n* **1** : demostración *f* ⟨a show of force/strength : una demostración de fuerza⟩ **2** EXHIBITION : exposición *f*, exhibición *f* ⟨flower show : exposición de flores⟩ ⟨to be on show : estar expuesto⟩ **3** : espectáculo *m* (teatral), programa *m* (de televisión, etc.) ⟨to go to a show : ir al teatro⟩ **4** APPEARANCE : apariencia *f* ⟨she put on a show of sympathy : fingió compasión⟩ ⟨his friendliness was all show : su simpatía era puro teatro⟩ **5 to run the show** : ser el/la que manda

show business *n* : mundo *m* del espectáculo

showcase [ˈʃoːˌkeɪs] *n* : vitrina *f*

showdown [ˈʃoːˌdaʊn] *n* : confrontación *f* (decisiva)

shower[1] [ˈʃaʊər] *vt* **1** SPRAY : regar, mojar **2** HEAP : colmar ⟨they showered him with gifts : lo colmaron de regalos, le llovieron los regalos⟩ — *vi* **1** BATHE : ducharse, darse una ducha **2** RAIN : llover

shower² *n* **1** : chaparrón *m*, chubasco *m* ⟨a chance of showers : una posibilidad de chaparrones⟩ **2** : ducha *f* ⟨to take a shower : ducharse⟩ **3** PARTY : fiesta *f* ⟨a bridal shower : una despedida de soltera⟩

shower cap *n* : gorro *m* de ducha

showing [' ʃ o u ɪ ŋ] *n* : exposición *f*

show–off [' ʃ o u ˌ ɔ f] *n* : fanfarrón *m*, -rrona *f*

show off *vt* : hacer alarde de, ostentar — *vi* : lucirse

showroom [' ʃ o u ˌ r u ː m, -ˌ r ʊ m] *n* : sala *f* de exposición

show up *vi* APPEAR : aparecer — *vt* EXPOSE : revelar

showy [' ʃ o ː i] *adj* **showier; -est** : llamativo, ostentoso — **showily** *adv*

shrank → **shrink**

shrapnel [' ʃ r æ p n ə l] *ns & pl* : metralla *f*

shred¹ [' ʃ r ɛ d] *vt* **shredded; shredding** : hacer trizas, desmenuzar (con las manos), triturar (con una máquina) ⟨to shred vegetables : cortar verduras en tiras⟩

shred² *n* **1** STRIP : tira *f*, jirón *m* (de tela) ⟨to tear to shreds : hacer trizas⟩ **2** BIT : pizca *f* ⟨not a shred of evidence : ni la más mínima prueba⟩ ⟨not a shred of truth : ni pizca de verdad⟩

shredder *n* : trituradora *f* ⟨paper shredder : trituradora de papel⟩

shrew [' ʃ r u ː] *n* **1** : musaraña *f* (animal) **2** : mujer *f* regañona

shrewd [' ʃ r u ː d] *adj* : astuto, inteligente, sagaz — **shrewdly** *adv*

shrewdness [' ʃ r u ː d n ə s] *n* : astucia *f*

shriek¹ [' ʃ r i ː k] *vi* : chillar, gritar

shriek² *n* : chillido *m*, alarido *m*, grito *m*

shrill [' ʃ r ɪ l] *adj* : agudo, estridente

shrilly [' ʃ r ɪ l i] *adv* : agudamente

shrimp [' ʃ r ɪ m p] *n* **1** : camarón *m*; langostino *m*; gamba *f Arg, Uru, Spain* **2** *usu disparaging* : enano *m*, -na *f*, *often disparaging*; petiso *m*, -sa *f* (persona)

shrine [' ʃ r a ɪ n] *n* **1** TOMB : sepulcro *m* (de un santo) **2** SANCTUARY : lugar *m* sagrado, santuario *m*

shrink [' ʃ r ɪ ŋ k] *vi* **shrank** [' ʃ r æ ŋ k] *or* **shrunk** [' ʃ r ʌ ŋ k]; **shrunk** *or* **shrunken** [' ʃ r ʌ ŋ k ə n]; **shrinking 1** RECOIL : retroceder ⟨he shrank back : se echó para atrás⟩ **2** : encogerse (dícese de la ropa) **3 to shrink from** AVOID : eludir

shrinkage [' ʃ r ɪ ŋ k ɪ ʤ] *n* : encogimiento *m* (de ropa, etc.), contracción *f*, reducción *f*

shrivel [' ʃ r ɪ v ə l] *vi* **-veled** *or* **-velled; -veling** *or* **-velling** : arrugarse, marchitarse

shroud¹ [' ʃ r a ʊ d] *vt* : envolver

shroud² *n* **1** : sudario *m*, mortaja *f* **2** VEIL : velo *m* ⟨wrapped in a shroud of mystery : envuelto en un aura de misterio⟩

shrub [' ʃ r ʌ b] *n* : arbusto *m*, mata *f*

shrubbery [' ʃ r ʌ b ə r i] *n*, *pl* **-beries** : arbustos *mpl*, matas *fpl*

shrug [' ʃ r ʌ g] *vi* **shrugged; shrugging** : encogerse de hombros — *vt* **to shrug off** DISMISS : hacer caso omiso de

shrunk → **shrink**

shuck [' ʃ ʌ k] *vt* : pelar (mazorcas, etc.), abrir (almejas, etc.)

shudder¹ [' ʃ ʌ d ə r] *vi* : estremecerse

shudder² *n* : estremecimiento *m*, escalofrío *m*

shuffle¹ [' ʃ ʌ f ə l] *v* **-fled; -fling** *vt* MIX : mezclar, revolver, barajar (naipes) — *vi* : caminar arrastrando los pies

shuffle² *n* **1** : acto *m* de revolver ⟨each player gets a shuffle : a cada jugador le toca barajar⟩ **2** JUMBLE : revoltijo *m* **3** : el arrastrar los pies

shun [' ʃ ʌ n] *vi* **shunned; shunning** : evitar, esquivar, eludir

shunt [' ʃ ʌ n t] *vt* : desviar, cambiar de vía (un tren)

shut [' ʃ ʌ t] *v* **shut; shutting** *vt* **1** CLOSE : cerrar (una puerta, los ojos, un libro, etc.) ⟨shut the lid : tápalo⟩ **2 to shut away/in** : encerrar **3 to shut down** CLOSE : cerrar (un negocio, etc.) **4 to shut down** TURN OFF : apagar **5 to shut off** TURN OFF : cortar (la electricidad), apagar (las luces, etc.) **6 to shut off** ISOLATE : aislar **7 to shut out** EXCLUDE : excluir, dejar fuera a (personas), no dejar que entre (luz, ruido, etc.) **8 to shut up** CLOSE : cerrar **9 to shut up** CONFINE : encerrar **10 to shut up** *fam* SILENCE : callar — *vi* **1** : cerrarse **2 to shut down** : cerrar, cerrar sus puertas (dícese de una empresa) **3 to shut up** *fam* : callarse ⟨shut up! : ¡cállate (la boca)!⟩

shut–in [' ʃ ʌ t ˌ ɪ n] *n* : inválido *m*, -da *f* (que no puede salir de casa)

shutter [' ʃ ʌ t ə r] *n* **1** : contraventana *f*, postigo *m* (de una ventana o puerta) **2** : obturador *m* (de una cámara)

shuttle¹ [' ʃ ʌ t ə l] *v* **-tled; -tling** *vt* : transportar ⟨she shuttled him back and forth : lo llevaba de acá para allá⟩ — *vi* : ir y venir

shuttle² *n* **1** : lanzadera *f* (para tejer) **2** : vehículo *m* que hace recorridos cortos **3** → **space shuttle**

shuttlecock [' ʃ ʌ t ə l ˌ k ɑ k] *n* : volante *m*

shy¹ [' ʃ a ɪ] *vi* **shied; shying** : retroceder, asustarse

shy² *adj* **shier** *or* **shyer** [' ʃ a ɪ ə r]; **shiest** *or* **shyest** [' ʃ a ɪ ə s t] **1** TIMID : tímido **2** WARY : cauteloso ⟨he's not shy about asking : no vacila en preguntar⟩ **3** SHORT : corto (de dinero, etc.) ⟨I'm two dollars shy : me faltan dos dólares⟩

shyly [' ʃ a ɪ l i] *adv* : tímidamente

shyness [' ʃ a ɪ n ə s] *n* : timidez *f*

Siamese¹ [ˌ s a ɪ ə ' m i ː z, -' m i ː s] *adj* : siamés ⟨Siamese twins : hermanos siameses⟩

Siamese² *n* **1** : siamés *m*, -mesa *f* **2** : siamés *m* (idioma) **3** *or* **Siamese cat** : gato *m* siamés

sibling [' s ɪ b l ɪ ŋ] *n* : hermano *m*, hermana *f*

Sicilian [s ə ' s ɪ l j ə n] *n* : siciliano *m*, -na *f* — **Sicilian** *adj*

sick · sign

sick ['sɪk] *adj* **1** : enfermo ⟨the baby is sick : el bebé está enfermo⟩ **2** NAUSEOUS : mareado, con náuseas ⟨to get sick : vomitar⟩ **3** : para uso de enfermos ⟨sick day : día de permiso (por enfermedad)⟩ **4 to be sick (and tired) of** : estar harto de, estar hasta la coronilla de

sickbed ['sɪk,bɛd] *n* : lecho *m* de enfermo

sicken ['sɪkən] *vt* **1** : poner enfermo **2** REVOLT : darle asco (a alguien) — *vi* : enfermar(se), caer enfermo

sickening ['sɪkənɪŋ] *adj* : asqueroso, repugnante, nauseabundo

sickle ['sɪkəl] *n* : hoz *f*

sick leave *n* : baja *f* por enfermedad

sickly ['sɪkli] *adj* **sicklier; -est 1** : enfermizo **2** → **sickening**

sickness ['sɪknəs] *n* **1** : enfermedad *f* **2** NAUSEA : náuseas *fpl*

side¹ ['saɪd] *n* **1** : lado *m* (de un lago, una cama, una frontera, etc.) ⟨by the side of the road : al lado de la calle⟩ ⟨the far side : el otro lado⟩ ⟨on the left-hand side : a mano izquierda⟩ ⟨on both sides : a ambos lados⟩ ⟨on either side : a cada lado⟩ ⟨from side to side : de un lado a otro⟩ ⟨side by side : uno al lado del otro⟩ ⟨they attacked from all sides : atacaron desde todos los frentes⟩ ⟨there are mountains on all sides : todo alrededor hay montañas⟩ **2** : lado *m*, cara *f* (de una moneda, una caja, etc.) ⟨this side up : este lado hacia arriba⟩ **3** : falda *f* (de una montaña) **4** : lado *m*, costado *m* (de una persona), ijada *f* (de un animal) **5** *or* **side dish** : guarnición *f*, acompañamiento *m* ⟨with a side of fries : con papas fritas (como guarnición)⟩ **6** : lado *m*, parte *f* ⟨he's on my side : está de mi parte⟩ ⟨to take sides : tomar partido⟩ ⟨to listen to both sides (of the story) : escuchar las dos campanas⟩ **7** : aspecto *m* ⟨to look on the bright side : ver el aspecto positivo⟩ **8 on the side** SEPARATELY : aparte **9 on the side** : como segundo trabajo **10 on the side** ⟨a lover on the side : un/una amante (de una persona casada)⟩

side² *v* **sided; siding** *vt* : instalar revestimiento exterior en — *vi* **1 to side against** : ponerse en contra de **2 to side with** : ponerse de parte de

sideboard ['saɪd,bord] *n* : aparador *m*

sideburns ['saɪd,bərnz] *npl* : patillas *fpl*

sided ['saɪdəd] *adj* : que tiene lados ⟨one-sided : de un lado⟩

side effect *n* : efecto *m* secundario

sideline ['saɪd,laɪn] *n* **1** : línea *f* de banda (en deportes) **2** : actividad *f* suplementaria (en negocios) **3 to be on the sidelines** : estar al margen

sidelong ['saɪd,lɔŋ] *adj* : de reojo, de soslayo

sideshow ['saɪd,ʃoː] *n* : espectáculo *m* secundario, atracción *f* secundaria

sidestep ['saɪd,stɛp] *v* **-stepped; -stepping** *vi* : dar un paso hacia un lado — *vt* AVOID : esquivar, eludir

side street *n* : calle *f* lateral

sidetrack ['saɪd,træk] *vt* : desviar (una conversación, etc.), distraer (a una persona)

sidewalk ['saɪd,wɔk] *n* : acera *f*; vereda *f*; andén *m CA, Col*; banqueta *f Mex*

sideways¹ ['saɪd,weɪz] *adv* **1** : hacia un lado ⟨it leaned sideways : se inclinaba hacia un lado⟩ **2** : de lado, de costado ⟨lie sideways : acuéstese de costado⟩

sideways² *adj* : hacia un lado ⟨a sideways glance : una mirada de reojo⟩

siding ['saɪdɪŋ] *n* : revestimiento *m* exterior (de un edificio)

sidle ['saɪdəl] *vi* **-dled; -dling** : moverse furtivamente

siege ['siːdʒ, 'siːʒ] *n* : sitio *m* ⟨to be under siege : estar sitiado⟩

siesta [si:'ɛstə] *n* : siesta *f*

sieve ['sɪv] *n* : tamiz *m*, cedazo *m*, criba *f* (en mineralogía)

sift ['sɪft] *vt* **1** : tamizar, cerner ⟨sift the flour : tamice la harina⟩ **2** *or* **to sift through** : examinar cuidadosamente, pasar por el tamiz

sifter ['sɪftər] *n* : tamiz *m*, cedazo *m*

sigh¹ ['saɪ] *vi* : suspirar

sigh² *n* : suspiro *m*

sight¹ ['saɪt] *vt* : ver (a una persona), divisar (la tierra, un barco)

sight² *n* **1** EYESIGHT : vista *f* (facultad) **2** VIEW : vista *f* ⟨out of sight : fuera de vista⟩ ⟨to come into sight : aparecer⟩ ⟨in plain sight : a plena vista⟩ **3** : algo visto ⟨it's a familiar sight : se ve con frecuencia⟩ ⟨she's a sight for sore eyes : da gusto verla⟩ **4** : lugar *m* de interés (para turistas, etc.) **5** : mira *f* (de un rifle, etc.) **6** GLIMPSE : mirada *f* breve ⟨at first sight : a primera vista⟩ ⟨I know him by sight : lo conozco de vista⟩ ⟨I caught sight of her : la divisé, alcancé a verla⟩ ⟨to lose sight of : perder de vista⟩ ⟨he faints at the sight of blood : cuando ve sangre se desmaya⟩ ⟨to shoot on sight : disparar sin previo aviso⟩

sighting ['saɪtɪŋ] *n* : avistamiento *m*

sightless ['saɪtləs] *adj* : invidente, ciego

sightseeing ['saɪt,siːɪŋ] *n* : acto *m* de visitar los lugares de interés ⟨to go sightseeing : hacer turismo⟩ ⟨sightseeing tour : excursión, tour⟩

sightseer ['saɪt,siːər] *n* : turista *mf*

sign¹ ['saɪn] *vt* **1** : firmar ⟨to sign a check : firmar un cheque⟩ **2** *or* **to sign on/up** HIRE : contratar (a un empleado), fichar (a un jugador) **3 to sign in/out** : registrar la entrada/salida de — *vi* **1** : hacer una seña ⟨she signed for him to stop : le hizo una seña para que se parara⟩ **2** : comunicarse por señas **3 to sign for** : firmar el recibo de **4 to sign in/out** : firmar el registro (al entrar/salir), registrar la entrada/salida **5 to sign off** : despedirse (en una carta, etc.) **6 to sign off (on)** APPROVE : dar el visto bueno (a) **7 to sign up** : inscribirse, matricularse

sign² *n* **1** SYMBOL : símbolo *m*, signo *m* ⟨minus sign : signo de menos⟩ ⟨sign of the zodiac : signo del zodíaco⟩ **2** GES-

TURE : seña *f*, señal *f*, gesto *m* **3** : letrero *m*, cartel *m* ⟨neon sign : letrero de neón⟩ **4** TRACE : señal *f*, indicio *m*

signage ['saɪnɪdʒ] *n* : señalización *f*

signal[1] ['sɪgnəl] *vt* **-naled** *or* **-nalled; -naling** *or* **-nalling** **1** : hacerle señas (a alguien) ⟨she signaled me to leave : me hizo señas para que saliera⟩ **2** INDICATE : señalar, indicar — *vi* : hacer señas, comunicar por señas

signal[2] *adj* NOTABLE : señalado, notable

signal[3] *n* : señal *f*

signatory ['sɪgnə,tori] *n, pl* **-ries** : firmante *mf*; signatario *m*, -ria *f*

signature ['sɪgnə,tʃʊr] *n* : firma *f*

signer ['saɪnər] *n* : firmante *mf*

signet ['sɪgnət] *n* : sello *m*

significance [sɪg'nɪfɪkənts] *n* **1** MEANING : significado *m* **2** IMPORTANCE : importancia *f*

significant [sɪg'nɪfɪkənt] *adj* **1** IMPORTANT : importante **2** MEANINGFUL : significativo — **significantly** *adv*

signify ['sɪgnə,faɪ] *vt* **-fied; -fying** **1** : indicar ⟨he signified his desire for more : haciendo señas indicó que quería más⟩ **2** MEAN : significar

sign language *n* : lenguaje *m* por señas

signpost ['saɪn,po:st] *n* : poste *m* indicador

silence[1] ['saɪlənts] *vt* **-lenced; -lencing** : silenciar, acallar

silence[2] *n* : silencio *m*

silencer ['saɪləntsər] *n* : silenciador *m*

silent ['saɪlənt] *adj* **1** : callado ⟨to remain silent : quedarse callado, guardar silencio⟩ **2** QUIET, STILL : silencioso **3** MUTE : mudo ⟨a silent letter : una letra muda⟩

silently ['saɪləntli] *adv* : silenciosamente, calladamente

silhouette[1] [,sɪlə'wɛt] *vt* **-etted; -etting** : destacar la silueta de ⟨it was silhouetted against the sky : se perfilaba contra el cielo⟩

silhouette[2] *n* : silueta *f*

silica ['sɪlɪkə] *n* : sílice *f*

silicon ['sɪlɪkən, -,kɑn] *n* : silicio *m* ⟨silicon chip : chip de silicio⟩

silk ['sɪlk] *n* : seda *f*

silk–cotton tree *n* : ceiba *f*

silken ['sɪlkən] *adj* **1** : de seda ⟨a silken veil : un velo de seda⟩ **2** SILKY : sedoso ⟨silken hair : cabellos sedosos⟩

silkworm ['sɪlk,wərm] *n* : gusano *m* de seda

silky ['sɪlki] *adj* **silkier; -est** : sedoso

sill ['sɪl] *n* : alféizar *m* (de una ventana), umbral *m* (de una puerta)

silliness ['sɪlinəs] *n* : tontería *f*, estupidez *f*

silly ['sɪli] *adj* **sillier; -est** : tonto, estúpido, ridículo

silo ['saɪ,lo:] *n, pl* **silos** : silo *m*

silt ['sɪlt] *n* : cieno *m*

silver[1] ['sɪlvər] *adj* **1** : de plata ⟨a silver spoon : una cuchara de plata⟩ **2** → **silvery**

silver[2] *n* **1** : plata *f* **2** COINS : monedas *fpl* **3** → **silverware** **4** : color *m* plata

silver–plated ['sɪlvər'pleɪtəd] *adj* : plateado

silversmith ['sɪlvər,smɪθ] *n* : orfebre *mf*

silverware ['sɪlvər,wær] *n* **1** : artículos *mpl* de plata, platería *f* **2** FLATWARE : cubertería *f*

silvery ['sɪlvəri] *adj* : plateado

similar ['sɪmələr] *adj* : similar, parecido, semejante

similarity [,sɪmə'lærəti] *n, pl* **-ties** : semejanza *f*, parecido *m*

similarly ['sɪmələrli] *adv* : de manera similar

simile ['sɪmə,li:] *n* : símil *m*

simmer ['sɪmər] *v* : hervir a fuego lento

simper[1] ['sɪmpər] *vi* : sonreír como un tonto

simper[2] *n* : sonrisa *f* tonta

simple ['sɪmpəl] *adj* **simpler; simplest** **1** INNOCENT : inocente **2** PLAIN : sencillo, simple **3** EASY : simple, sencillo, fácil **4** STRAIGHTFORWARD : simple ⟨the simple truth : la pura verdad⟩ **5** NAIVE : ingenuo, simple

simpleminded [,sɪmpəl'maɪndəd] *adj* : simple (dícese de una persona)

simpleton ['sɪmpəltən] *n* : bobo *m*, -ba *f*; tonto *m*, -ta *f*

simplicity [sɪm'plɪsəti] *n* : simplicidad *f*, sencillez *f*

simplification [,sɪmpləfə'keɪʃən] *n* : simplificación *f*

simplify ['sɪmplə,faɪ] *vt* **-fied; -fying** : simplificar

simplistic [sɪm'plɪsətɪk] *n* : simplista

simply ['sɪmpli] *adv* **1** PLAINLY : sencillamente **2** SOLELY : simplemente, sólo **3** REALLY : absolutamente

simulate ['sɪmjə,leɪt] *vt* **-lated; -lating** : simular

simulation [,sɪmjə'leɪʃən] *n* : simulación *f*

simultaneous [,saɪməl'teɪniəs] *adj* : simultáneo — **simultaneously** *adv*

sin[1] ['sɪn] *vi* **sinned; sinning** : pecar

sin[2] *n* : pecado *m*

since[1] ['sɪnts] *adv* **1** : desde entonces ⟨they've been friends ever since : desde entonces han sido amigos⟩ ⟨she's since become mayor : más tarde se hizo alcalde⟩ **2** AGO : hace ⟨he's long since dead : murió hace mucho⟩

since[2] *conj* **1** : desde que ⟨since he was born : desde que nació⟩ **2** INASMUCH AS : ya que, puesto que, dado que

since[3] *prep* : desde

sincere [sɪn'sɪr] *adj* **-cerer; -est** : sincero — **sincerely** *adv*

sincerity [sɪn'sɛrəti] *n* : sinceridad *f*

sinew ['sɪn,ju:, 'sɪ,nu:] *n* **1** TENDON : tendón *m*, nervio *m* (en la carne) **2** POWER : fuerza *f*

sinewy ['sɪnjʊi, 'sɪnʊi] *adj* **1** STRINGY : fibroso **2** STRONG, WIRY : fuerte, nervudo

sinful ['sɪnfəl] *adj* : pecador (dícese de las personas), pecaminoso

sing ['sɪŋ] *v* **sang** ['sæŋ] *or* **sung** ['sʌŋ]; **sung; singing** : cantar

singe ['sɪndʒ] *vt* **singed; singeing** : chamuscar, quemar

singer ['sɪŋər] *n* : cantante *mf*
singer–songwriter ['sɪŋər'sɔŋ,raɪtər] *n* : cantautor *m*, -tora *f*
single¹ ['sɪŋgəl] *vt* **-gled; -gling** *or* **to single out 1** SELECT : escoger **2** DISTINGUISH : señalar
single² *adj* **1** UNMARRIED : soltero ⟨a single parent : un padre soltero, una madre soltera⟩ **2** SOLE : solo ⟨a single survivor : un solo sobreviviente⟩ ⟨every single one : cada uno, todos⟩
single³ *n* **1** : soltero *m*, -ra *f* ⟨for married couples and singles : para los matrimonios y los solteros⟩ **2** *or* **single room** : habitación *f* individual **3** DOLLAR : billete *m* de un dólar
single file¹ *adv* : en fila india
single file² *n* **in single file** : solo a fila india
single–handed ['sɪŋgəl'hændəd] *adj* : sin ayuda, solo
single–minded ['sɪŋgəl'maɪndəd] *adj* : resuelto
singly ['sɪŋgli] *adv* : individualmente, uno por uno
singular¹ ['sɪŋgjələr] *adj* **1** : singular (en gramática) **2** OUTSTANDING : singular, sobresaliente **3** STRANGE : singular, extraño
singular² *n* : singular *m*
singularity [,sɪŋgjə'lærəti] *n, pl* **-ties** : singularidad *f*
singularly ['sɪŋgjələrli] *adv* : singularmente
sinister ['sɪnəstər] *adj* : siniestro
sink¹ ['sɪŋk] *v* **sank** ['sæŋk] *or* **sunk** ['sʌŋk]; **sunk; sinking** *vi* **1** : hundirse (dícese de un barco, etc.) ⟨his foot sank into the mud : su pie se hundió en el barro⟩ **2** DROP, FALL : descender, caer ⟨to sink into a chair : dejarse caer en una silla⟩ ⟨her heart sank : se le cayó el alma a los pies⟩ ⟨I had the sinking feeling that . . . : tenía un mal presentimiento de que . . .⟩ **3** DECREASE : bajar ⟨the company's stock sank : las acciones de la compañía cayeron en picada⟩ ⟨his voice sank to a whisper : su voz se redujo a un susurro⟩ **4** FOUNDER : hundirse, irse a pique (dícese de una compañía, etc.) **5** STOOP : rebajarse (a hacer algo) ⟨to sink so/that low : caer tan bajo⟩ **6 to sink in** : hacer mella — *vt* **1** : hundir (un barco, etc.) **2** EXCAVATE : excavar (un pozo para minar), perforar (un pozo de agua) **3** PLUNGE, STICK : clavar, hincar **4** INVEST : invertir (fondos) **5** : meter (en deportes) ⟨to sink a basket : encestar⟩
sink² *n* **1** *or* **kitchen sink** : fregadero *m*; lavaplatos *m* *Chile, Col, Mex* **2** *or* **bathroom sink** : lavabo *m*, lavamanos *m* **3** WEIGHT : plomo *m*, plomada *f*
sinker ['sɪŋkər] *n* WEIGHT : plomada *f*, plomo *m*
sinner ['sɪnər] *n* : pecador *m*, -dora *f*
sinuous ['sɪnjuəs] *adj* : sinuoso — **sinuously** *adv*
sinus ['saɪnəs] *n* : seno *m*
sip¹ ['sɪp] *v* **sipped; sipping** *vt* : sorber — *vi* : beber a sorbos

sip² *n* : sorbo *m*
siphon¹ ['saɪfən] *vt* : sacar con sifón
siphon² *n* : sifón *m*
sir ['sər] *n* **1** (*in titles*) : sir *m* **2** (*as a form of address*) : señor *m* ⟨Dear Sir : Muy señor mío⟩ ⟨yes sir! : ¡sí, señor!⟩
sire¹ ['saɪr] *vt* **sired; siring** : engendrar, ser el padre de
sire² *n* : padre *m*
siren ['saɪrən] *n* : sirena *f*
sirloin ['sər,lɔɪn] *n* : solomillo *m*
sirup → **syrup**
sissy ['sɪsi] *n, pl* **-sies** *fam* + *disparaging* : mariquita *f* *fam* + *disparaging*
sister ['sɪstər] *n* **1** : hermana *f* **2 Sister** : hermana *f*, Sor *f* ⟨Sister Mary : Sor María⟩
sisterhood ['sɪstər,hʊd] *n* **1** : condición *f* de ser hermana **2** : sociedad *f* de mujeres
sister–in–law ['sɪstərɪn,lɔ] *n, pl* **sisters–in–law** : cuñada *f*
sisterly ['sɪstərli] *adj* : de hermana
sit ['sɪt] *v* **sat** ['sæt]; **sitting** *vi* **1** : sentarse ⟨he sat down : se sentó⟩ ⟨he sat (down) in the chair : se sentó en la silla⟩ **2** : estar sentado ⟨she was sitting in the chair : estaba sentada en la silla⟩ ⟨they sat across from me : estaban sentados frente a mí⟩ **3** ROOST : posarse **4** : sesionar ⟨the legislature is sitting : la legislatura está en sesión⟩ **5** POSE : posar (para un retrato) **6** LIE, REST : estar (ubicado) ⟨the house sits on a hill : la casa está en una colina⟩ ⟨it was sitting right in front of me : lo tenía delante de las narices⟩ **7 to sit around** : relajarse, no hacer nada **8 to sit back** : relajarse **9 to sit in for** : sustituir a **10 to sit in on** : asistir a (como observador) **11 to sit on** : darle largas a (algo) **12 to sit out** ENDURE : aguantar **13 to sit out** : no participar en ⟨I'll sit this one out : no voy a bailar/jugar (etc.) esta vez⟩ **14 to sit through** : aguantar (un discurso, etc.) **15 to sit tight** : esperar **16 to sit up** : incorporarse **17 to sit up** : quedarse levantado ⟨we sat up talking : nos quedamos hablando hasta muy tarde⟩ — *vt* SEAT : sentar, colocar ⟨I sat him on the sofa : lo senté en el sofá⟩
sitcom ['sɪt,kɑm] → **situation comedy**
site ['saɪt] *n* **1** : sitio *m*, lugar *m* (en general), emplazamiento *m*, ubicación *f* (de un edificio, etc.) ⟨construction/building site : obra⟩ **2** SCENE : lugar *m*, escena *f* (de un accidente, etc.), escenario *m* (de una batalla) **3** → **Web site**
sitter ['sɪtər] *n* → **baby-sitter**
sitting ['sɪtɪŋ] *n* **1** : turno *m* (de cena, etc.) **2** : sesión *f*
sitting room → **living room**
situate ['sɪtʃu,eɪt] *vt* **-ated; -ating 1** ESTABLISH, LOCATE : situar, ubicar **2** PLACE : poner, colocar
situated ['sɪtʃu,eɪtəd] *adj* LOCATED : ubicado, situado
situation [,sɪtʃu'eɪʃən] *n* **1** LOCATION : situación *f*, ubicación *f*, emplazamiento *m* **2** CIRCUMSTANCES : situación *f* **3** JOB : empleo *m*

situation comedy *n* : comedia *f* de situación

six[1] [ˈsɪks] *adj* : seis ⟨she's six (years old) : tiene seis años⟩

six[2] *n* : seis *m* ⟨the six of hearts : el seis de corazones⟩

six[3] *pron* : seis ⟨there are six of us : somos seis⟩ ⟨it's six (o'clock) : son las seis⟩

six–gun [ˈsɪksˌgʌn] *n* : revólver *m* (con seis cámaras)

six hundred[1] *adj & pron* : seiscientos

six hundred[2] *n* : seiscientos *m*

six–shooter [ˈsɪksˌʃuːtər] → **six-gun**

sixteen[1] [sɪksˈtiːn] *adj & pron* : dieciséis

sixteen[2] *n* : dieciséis *m*

sixteenth[1] [sɪksˈtiːnθ] *adj* : decimosexto

sixteenth[2] *n* **1** : decimosexto *m*, -ta *f* (en una serie) **2** : dieciseisavo *m*, dieciseisava parte *f*

sixth[1] [ˈsɪksθ, ˈsɪkst] *adv* : en sexto lugar

sixth[2] *adj* : sexto

sixth[3] *n* **1** : sexto *m*, -ta *f* (en una serie) **2** : sexto *m*, sexta parte *f*

sixtieth[1] [ˈsɪkstiəθ] *adj* : sexagésimo

sixtieth[2] *n* **1** : sexagésimo *m*, -ma *f* (en una serie) **2** : sesentavo *m*, sesentava parte *f*

sixty[1] [ˈsɪksti] *adj & pron* : sesenta

sixty[2] *n, pl* **-ties** : sesenta *m*

sizable *or* **sizeable** [ˈsaɪzəbəl] *adj* : considerable

size[1] [ˈsaɪz] *vt* **sized; sizing** **1** : clasificar según el tamaño **2 to size up** : evaluar, apreciar

size[2] *n* **1** DIMENSIONS : tamaño *m*, talla *f* (de ropa), número *m* (de zapatos) **2** MAGNITUDE : magnitud *f*

sized [ˈsaɪzd] *adj* (*used in combination*) : de tamaño ⟨large-sized : (de tamaño) grande⟩

sizzle [ˈsɪzəl] *vi* **-zled; -zling** : chisporrotear

skate[1] [ˈskeɪt] *vi* **skated; skating** : patinar

skate[2] *n* **1** : patín *m* ⟨roller skate : patín de ruedas⟩ **2** : raya *f* (pez)

skateboard [ˈskeɪtˌbord] *n* : monopatín *m*, patineta *f*, skateboard *m*

skateboarding [ˈskeɪtˌbordɪŋ] *n* : monopatinaje *m*, skateboarding *m*

skater [ˈskeɪtər] *n* : patinador *m*, -dora *f*

skating [ˈskeɪtɪŋ] *n* : patinaje *m*

skating rink *n* : pista *f* de patinaje

skein [ˈskeɪn] *n* : madeja *f*

skeletal [ˈskɛlətəl] *adj* **1** : óseo (en anatomía) **2** EMACIATED : esquelético

skeleton [ˈskɛlətən] *n* **1** : esqueleto *m* (anatómico) **2** FRAMEWORK : armazón *mf*

skeleton key *n* : llave *f* maestra

skeptic [ˈskɛptɪk] *n* : escéptico *m*, -ca *f*

skeptical [ˈskɛptɪkəl] *adj* : escéptico

skepticism [ˈskɛptəˌsɪzəm] *n* : escepticismo *m*

sketch[1] [ˈskɛtʃ] *vt* : bosquejar — *vi* : hacer bosquejos

sketch[2] *n* **1** DRAWING, OUTLINE : esbozo *m*, bosquejo *m* **2** ESSAY : ensayo *m*

sketchy [ˈskɛtʃi] *adj* **sketchier; -est** : incompleto, poco detallado

skewer[1] [ˈskjuːər] *vt* : ensartar (carne, etc.)

skewer[2] *n* : brocheta *f*, broqueta *f*

ski[1] [ˈskiː] *vi* **skied; skiing** : esquiar

ski[2] *n, pl* **skis** : esquí *m*

ski boot *n* : bota *f* de esquiar

skid[1] [ˈskɪd] *vi* **skidded; skidding** : derrapar, patinar

skid[2] *n* : derrape *m*, patinazo *m*

skier [ˈskiːər] *n* : esquiador *m*, -dora *f*

skiing [ˈskiːɪŋ] *n* : esquí *m*

ski jump *n* : trampolín *m* (de esquí)

ski lift *n* : telesquí *m*, telesilla *f*

skill [ˈskɪl] *n* **1** DEXTERITY : habilidad *f*, destreza *f* **2** CAPABILITY : capacidad *f*, arte *m*, técnica *f* ⟨organizational skills : la capacidad para organizar⟩

skilled [ˈskɪld] *adj* : hábil, experto

skillet [ˈskɪlət] *n* : sartén *mf*

skillful [ˈskɪlfəl] *adj* : hábil, diestro

skillfully [ˈskɪlfəli] *adv* : con habilidad, con destreza

skim[1] [ˈskɪm] *v* **skimmed; skimming** *vt* **1** : espumar (sopa, etc.), quitar (grasa, etc.) ⟨I skimmed the broth to remove the fat, I skimmed the fat off/from the broth : le quité la grasa al caldo⟩ **2** : echarle un vistazo a (un libro, etc.) **3** : pasar rozando (una superficie) **4** *or* **to skim off** : embolsarse (dinero) — *vi* **to skim through/over** : echarle un vistazo a (un libro, etc.)

skim[2] *adj* : descremado ⟨skim milk : leche descremada⟩

ski mask *n* : pasamontañas *m*

skimp [ˈskɪmp] *vi* **to skimp on** : escatimar

skimpy [ˈskɪmpi] *adj* **skimpier; -est** : exiguo, escaso, raquítico

skin[1] [ˈskɪn] *vt* **skinned; skinning** : despellejar, desollar

skin[2] *n* **1** : piel *f*, cutis *m* (de la cara) ⟨dark skin : piel morena⟩ **2** RIND : piel *f*

skin–deep [ˈskɪnˈdiːp] *adj* : superficial

skin diving *n* : buceo *m*, submarinismo *m*

skinflint [ˈskɪnˌflɪnt] *n* : tacaño *m*, -ña *f*

skinhead [ˈskɪnˌhɛd] *n* : cabeza *mf* rapada

skinned [ˈskɪnd] *adj* (*used in combination*) : de piel ⟨tough-skinned : de piel dura⟩

skinny [ˈskɪni] *adj* **skinnier; -est** : flaco

skip[1] [ˈskɪp] *v* **skipped; skipping** *vi* : ir dando brincos — *vt* : saltarse

skip[2] *n* : brinco *m*, salto *m*

skipper [ˈskɪpər] *n* : capitán *m*, -tana *f*

ski pole *n* : bastón *m* (de esquí)

skirmish[1] [ˈskərmɪʃ] *vi* : escaramuzar

skirmish[2] *n* : escaramuza *f*, refriega *f*

skirt[1] [ˈskərt] *vt* **1** BORDER : bordear **2** EVADE : evadir, esquivar

skirt[2] *n* : falda *f*, pollera *f*

skit [ˈskɪt] *n* : sketch *m* (teatral)

skittish [ˈskɪtɪʃ] *adj* : asustadizo, nervioso

skulk [ˈskʌlk] *vi* : merodear

skull [ˈskʌl] *n* **1** : cráneo *m*, calavera *f* **2** **skull and crossbones** : calavera *f* (bandera pirata)

skullcap [ˈskʌlˌkæp] *n* : casquete *m*

skunk [ˈskʌŋk] *n* : zorrillo *m*, mofeta *f*

sky [ˈskaɪ] *n, pl* **skies** : cielo *m*

skylark [ˈskaɪˌlɑrk] *n* : alondra *f*

skylight ['skaɪˌlaɪt] *n* : claraboya *f*, tragaluz *m*

skyline ['skaɪˌlaɪn] *n* : horizonte *m*

skyrocket ['skaɪˌrɑkət] *vi* : dispararse

skyscraper ['skaɪˌskreɪpər] *n* : rascacielos *m*

slab ['slæb] *n* : losa *f* (de piedra), tabla *f* (de madera), pedazo *m* grueso (de pan, etc.)

slack[1] ['slæk] *adj* **1** CARELESS : descuidado, negligente **2** LOOSE : flojo **3** SLOW : de poco movimiento

slack[2] *n* **1** : parte *f* floja ⟨to take up the slack : tensar (una cuerda, etc.)⟩ **2 slacks** *npl* : pantalones *mpl*

slacken ['slækən] *vt* : aflojar — *vi* : aflojarse

slacker ['slækər] *n* : vago *m*, -ga *f*; holgazán *m*, -zana *f*

slackness ['slæknəs] *n* **1** LOOSENESS : soltura *f* **2** LAXITY : laxitud *f*

slag ['slæg] *n* : escoria *f*

slain → **slay**

slake ['sleɪk] *vt* **slaked; slaking** : saciar (la sed), satisfacer (la curiosidad)

slam[1] ['slæm] *v* **slammed; slamming** *vt* **1** : cerrar de golpe ⟨he slammed the door : dio un portazo⟩ **2** : tirar o dejar caer de golpe ⟨he slammed down the book : dejó caer el libro de un golpe⟩ — *vi* **1** : cerrarse de golpe **2 to slam into** : chocar contra

slam[2] *n* : golpe *m*, portazo *m* (de una puerta)

slam dunk *n* : clavada *f*, mate *m*, donqueo *m*

slander[1] ['slændər] *vt* : calumniar, difamar

slander[2] *n* : calumnia *f*, difamación *f*

slanderous ['slændərəs] *adj* : difamatorio, calumnioso

slang ['slæŋ] *n* : argot *m*, jerga *f*

slant[1] ['slænt] *vi* : inclinarse, ladearse — *vt* **1** SLOPE : inclinar **2** ANGLE : sesgar, orientar, dirigir ⟨a story slanted towards youth : un artículo dirigido a los jóvenes⟩

slant[2] *n* **1** INCLINE : inclinación *f* **2** PERSPECTIVE : perspectiva *f*, enfoque *m*

slap[1] ['slæp] *vt* **slapped; slapping** **1** : bofetear, cachetear ⟨she slapped him in/across the face, she slapped his face : le dio una bofetada⟩ ⟨to slap someone on the back : darle una palmada a alguien en la espalda⟩ **2** : golpear (dícese de las olas, etc.) **3** : tirar (con fuerza) ⟨she slapped the book (down) on the desk : tiró el libro en el escritorio⟩ **4** : poner (rápidamente) ⟨he slapped some butter on the bread : le puso mantequilla al pan⟩ ⟨she slapped some paint on it : le dio una pasada rápida de pintura⟩ **5 to slap around** : darle palizas a **6 to slap together** : preparar de prisa **7 to slap with** : ponerle (una multa, etc.)

slap[2] *n* **1** : bofetada *f*, cachetada *f*, palmada *f* **2 slap in the face** INSULT : bofetada *f*

slapdash ['slæpˌdæʃ] *adj* : chapucero

slapstick ['slæpˌstɪk] *n* : payasadas *fpl*, bufonadas *fpl*

slash[1] ['slæʃ] *vt* **1** GASH : cortar, hacer un tajo en **2** REDUCE : reducir, rebajar (precios)

slash[2] *n* **1** : tajo *m*, corte *m* **2 or forward slash** : diagonal *f*, barra *f* (oblicua)

slat ['slæt] *n* : tablilla *f*, listón *m*

slate ['sleɪt] *n* **1** : pizarra *f* ⟨a slate roof : un techo de pizarra⟩ **2** : lista *f* de candidatos (políticos)

slaughter[1] ['slɔtər] *vt* **1** BUTCHER : matar (animales) **2** MASSACRE : masacrar (personas)

slaughter[2] *n* **1** : matanza *f* (de animales) **2** MASSACRE : masacre *f*, carnicería *f*

slaughterhouse ['slɔtərˌhaʊs] *n* : matadero *m*

Slav ['slɑv, 'slæv] *n* : eslavo *m*, -va *f*

slave[1] ['sleɪv] *vi* **slaved; slaving** : trabajar como un burro

slave[2] *n* : esclavo *m*, -va *f*

slaver ['slævər, 'sleɪ-] *vi* : babear

slavery ['sleɪvəri] *n* : esclavitud *f*

Slavic ['slɑvɪk, 'slæ-] *adj* : eslavo

slavish ['sleɪvɪʃ] *adj* **1** SERVILE : servil **2** IMITATIVE : poco original

slay ['sleɪ] *vt* **slew** ['slu:]; **slain** ['sleɪn]; **slaying** : asesinar, matar

slayer ['sleɪər] *n* : asesino *m*, -na *f*

sleazy ['sli:zi] *adj* **sleazier; -est** **1** SHODDY : chapucero, de mala calidad **2** DILAPIDATED : ruinoso **3** DISREPUTABLE : de mala fama

sled[1] ['slɛd] *v* **sledded; sledding** *vi* : ir en trineo — *vt* : transportar en trineo

sled[2] *n* : trineo *m*

sledge ['slɛdʒ] *n* **1** : trineo *m* (grande) **2** → **sledgehammer**

sledgehammer ['slɛdʒˌhæmər] *n* : almádena *f*; combo *m* *Chile, Peru*

sleek[1] ['sli:k] *vt* SLICK : alisar

sleek[2] *adj* : liso y brillante

sleep[1] ['sli:p] *vi* **slept** ['slɛpt]; **sleeping** **1** : dormir **2 to sleep in** : levantarse tarde **3 to sleep together** : acostarse, tener relaciones **4 to sleep with** : acostarse con

sleep[2] *n* **1** : sueño *m* **2** : legañas *fpl* (en los ojos) **3 to go to sleep** : dormirse

sleeper ['sli:pər] *n* **1** : durmiente *mf* ⟨to be a light sleeper : tener el sueño ligero⟩ **2 or sleeping car** : coche *m* cama, coche *m* dormitorio

sleepily ['sli:pəli] *adv* : de manera somnolienta

sleepiness ['sli:pinəs] *n* : somnolencia *f*

sleeping bag *n* : saco *m* de dormir

sleeping pill *n* : pastilla *f* para dormir

sleepless ['sli:pləs] *adj* : sin dormir, desvelado ⟨to have a sleepless night : pasar la noche en blanco⟩

sleepwalk ['sli:pˌwɔk] *vi* : caminar dormido

sleepwalker ['sli:pˌwɔkər] *n* : sonámbulo *m*, -la *f*

sleepwalking ['sli:pˌwɔkɪŋ] *n* : sonambulismo *m*

sleepy ['sli:pi] *adj* **sleepier; -est** **1** DROWSY : somnoliento, soñoliento ⟨to be sleepy : tener sueño⟩ **2** LETHARGIC : aletargado, letárgico

sleet[1] ['sli:t] *vi* **to be sleeting** : caer aguanieve

sleet[2] *n* : aguanieve *f*

sleeve ['sli:v] *n* : manga *f* (de una camisa, etc.)

sleeveless ['sli:vləs] *adj* : sin mangas

sleigh[1] ['sleɪ] *vi* : ir en trineo

sleigh[2] *n* : trineo *m* (tirado por caballos)

sleight of hand [ˌslaɪtəv'hænd] : prestidigitación *f*, juegos *mpl* de manos

slender ['slɛndər] *adj* **1** SLIM : esbelto, delgado **2** SCANTY : exiguo, escaso ⟨a slender hope : una esperanza lejana⟩

sleuth ['slu:θ] *n* : detective *mf*, sabueso *m*

slew → **slay**

slice[1] ['slaɪs] *vt* **sliced; slicing** : cortar

slice[2] *n* : rebanada *f*, tajada *f*, lonja *f* (de carne, etc.), rodaja *f* (de una verdura, fruta, etc.), trozo *m* (de pastel, etc.)

slicer ['slaɪsər] *n* : cortadora *f* (de fiambres, etc.), rebanadora *f* (de pan)

slick[1] ['slɪk] *vt* : alisar

slick[2] *adj* **1** SLIPPERY : resbaladizo, resbaloso **2** CRAFTY : astuto, taimado

slicker ['slɪkər] *n* : impermeable *m*

slide[1] ['slaɪd] *v* **slid** ['slɪd]; **sliding** ['slaɪdɪŋ] *vi* **1** SLIP : resbalar **2** GLIDE : deslizarse **3** DECLINE : bajar ⟨to let things slide : dejar pasar las cosas⟩ — *vt* : correr, deslizar

slide[2] *n* **1** SLIDING : deslizamiento *m* **2** SLIP : resbalón *m* **3** : tobogán *m* (para niños) **4** TRANSPARENCY : diapositiva *f* (fotográfica) **5** DECLINE : descenso *m*

slider ['slaɪdər] *n* **1** (*in baseball*) : slider *m* **2** : hamburguesa *f* pequeña, sandwich *m* pequeño

slier, sliest → **sly**

slight[1] ['slaɪt] *vt* : desairar, despreciar

slight[2] *adj* **1** SLENDER : esbelto, delgado **2** FLIMSY : endeble **3** TRIFLING : leve, insignificante ⟨a slight pain : un leve dolor⟩ **4** SMALL : pequeño, ligero ⟨not in the slightest : en absoluto⟩

slight[3] *n* SNUB : desaire *m*

slightly ['slaɪtli] *adv* : ligeramente, un poco

slim[1] ['slɪm] *v* **slimmed; slimming** : adelgazar

slim[2] *adj* **slimmer; slimmest 1** SLENDER : esbelto, delgado **2** SCANTY : exiguo, escaso

slime ['slaɪm] *n* **1** : baba *f* (secretada por un animal) **2** MUD, SILT : fango *m*, cieno *m*

slimy ['slaɪmi] *adj* **slimier; -est** : viscoso

sling[1] ['slɪŋ] *vt* **slung** ['slʌŋ]; **slinging 1** THROW : lanzar, tirar **2** HANG : colgar

sling[2] *n* **1** : honda *f* (arma) **2** : cabestrillo *m* ⟨my arm is in a sling : llevo el brazo en cabestrillo⟩

slingshot ['slɪŋˌʃɑt] *n* : tiragomas *m*, resortera *f Mex*

slink ['slɪŋk] *vi* **slunk** ['slʌŋk]; **slinking** : caminar furtivamente

slip[1] ['slɪp] *v* **slipped; slipping** *vi* **1** STEAL : ir sigilosamente ⟨to slip away : escabullirse⟩ ⟨to slip out the door : escaparse

por la puerta⟩ ⟨an error slipped through : se deslizó un error⟩ **2** SLIDE : resbalarse, deslizarse ⟨he slipped and fell : se resbaló y se cayó⟩ **3** FALL, LAPSE : caer ⟨she slipped into a coma : cayó en coma⟩ **4** WORSEN, DECLINE : empeorar, bajar ⟨I must be slipping : voy perdiendo facultades⟩ **5 to let slip** : dejar escapar **6 to slip off** *or* **to slip out of** TAKE OFF : quitarse (una prenda) **7 to slip on/into** PUT ON : ponerse (una prenda) **8 to slip through one's fingers** : escaparse de las manos **9 to slip up** : meter la pata — *vt* **1** PUT : meter, poner **2** PASS : pasar ⟨she slipped me a note : me pasó una nota⟩ **3** ESCAPE : escaparse de **4 to slip one's mind** : olvidársele a uno

slip[2] *n* **1** PIER : atracadero *m* **2** MISHAP : percance *m*, contratiempo *m* **3** MISTAKE : error *m*, desliz *m* ⟨a slip of the tongue : un lapsus⟩ **4** PETTICOAT : enagua *f* **5** : injerto *m*, esqueje *m* (de una planta) **6** RECEIPT, TICKET : recibo *m*, boleta *f*, ticket *m* **7 slip of paper** : papelito *m* **8 to give someone the slip** : dar esquinazo a alguien

slipknot ['slɪpˌnɑt] *n* : nudo *m* corredizo

slipper ['slɪpər] *n* : zapatilla *f*, pantufla *f*

slipperiness ['slɪpərinəs] *n* **1** : lo resbaloso, lo resbaladizo **2** CRAFTINESS : astucia *f*

slippery ['slɪpəri] *adj* **slipperier; -est 1** : resbaloso, resbaladizo ⟨a slippery road : un camino resbaloso⟩ **2** TRICKY : artero, astuto, taimado **3** ELUSIVE : huidizo, escurridizo

slipshod ['slɪpˌʃɑd] *adj* : descuidado, chapucero

slipup *n* ERROR : patinazo *m*

slip up *vi* : equivocarse

slit[1] ['slɪt] *vt* **slit; slitting** : cortar, abrir por lo largo

slit[2] *n* **1** OPENING : abertura *f*, rendija *f* **2** CUT : corte *m*, raja *f*, tajo *m*

slither ['slɪðər] *vi* : deslizarse

sliver ['slɪvər] *n* : astilla *f*

slob ['slɑb] *n* : persona *f* desaliñada ⟨what a slob! : ¡qué cerdo!⟩

slobber[1] ['slɑbər] *vi* : babear

slobber[2] *n* : baba *f*

slog[1] ['slɑg] *vi* : trabajar duro

slog[2] *n* : trabajo *m* largo y arduo

slogan ['slo:gən] *n* : lema *m*, eslogan *m*

sloop ['slu:p] *n* : balandra *f*

slop[1] ['slɑp] *v* **slopped; slopping** *vt* : derramar — *vi* : derramarse

slop[2] *n* : bazofia *f*

slope[1] ['slo:p] *vi* **sloped; sloping** : inclinarse ⟨the road slopes upward : el camino sube (en pendiente)⟩

slope[2] *n* : inclinación *f*, pendiente *f*, declive *m*

sloppiness ['slɑpinəs] *n* : falta *f* de cuidado (en el trabajo, etc.), desaliño *m* (de aspecto)

sloppy ['slɑpi] *adj* **sloppier; -est 1** : que chorrea ⟨a sloppy kiss : un beso baboso⟩ **2** : descuidado (en el trabajo, etc.), desaliñado (de aspecto)

slot ['slɑt] *n* 1 : ranura *f* 2 *or* **time slot** : espacio *m* (de un programa de televisión, etc.)

sloth ['slɔθ, 'sloːθ] *n* 1 LAZINESS : pereza *f* 2 : perezoso *m* (animal)

slot machine *n* : tragamonedas *mf*, tragaperras *mf Spain*

slotted spoon ['slɑtəd-] *n* : espumadera *f*

slouch[1] ['slaʊtʃ] *vi* : andar con los hombros caídos, repantigarse (en un sillón)

slouch[2] *n* 1 SLUMPING : mala postura *f* 2 BUNGLER, IDLER : haragán *m*, -gana *f*; inepto *m*, -ta *f* ⟨to be no slouch : no quedarse atrás⟩

slough[1] ['slʌf] *vt* : mudar de (piel)

slough[2] ['sluː, 'slaʊ] *n* SWAMP : ciénaga *f*

Slovak ['sloːˌvɑk, -ˌvæk] *or* **Slovakian** [sloːˈvɑkiən, -ˈvæ-] *n* : eslovaco *m*, -ca *f* — **Slovak** *or* **Slovakian** *adj*

Slovene ['sloːˌviːn] *or* **Slovenian** [sloːˈviːniən] *n* : esloveno *m*, -na *f* — **Slovene** *or* **Slovenian** *adj*

slovenliness ['slɑvənlinəs, 'slʌv-] *adj* : falta *f* de cuidado (en el trabajo, etc.), desaliño *m* (de aspecto)

slovenly ['slɑvənli, 'slʌv-] *adj* : descuidado (en el trabajo, etc.), desaliñado (de aspecto)

slow[1] ['sloː] *vt* : retrasar, reducir la marcha de — *vi* : ir más despacio

slow[2] *adv* : despacio, lentamente

slow[3] *adj* 1 : lento ⟨a slow process : un proceso lento⟩ 2 : atrasado ⟨my watch is slow : mi reloj está atrasado, mi reloj se atrasa⟩ 3 SLUGGISH : lento, poco activo 4 STUPID : lento, torpe, corto de alcances

slow cooker [-ˈkʊkər] *n* : olla *f* de cocción lenta, olla *f* de cocimiento lento

slowly ['sloːli] *adv* : lentamente, despacio

slow motion *n* : cámara *f* lenta ⟨in slow motion : a cámara lenta⟩

slowness ['sloːnəs] *n* : lentitud *f*, torpeza *f*

slow-witted ['sloːˈwɪtəd] *adj* : limitado, lento, lerdo

sludge ['slʌdʒ] *n* : aguas *fpl* negras, aguas *fpl* residuales

slug[1] ['slʌg] *vt* **slugged; slugging** : pegarle un porrazo a (alguien)

slug[2] *n* 1 : babosa *f* (molusco) 2 BULLET : bala *f* 3 TOKEN : ficha *f* 4 BLOW : porrazo *m*, puñetazo *m*

sluggish ['slʌgɪʃ] *adj* : aletargado, lento

sluice[1] ['sluːs] *vt* **sluiced; sluicing** : lavar en agua corriente

sluice[2] *n* : canal *m*

slum ['slʌm] *n* : barriada *f*, barrio *m* bajo

slumber[1] ['slʌmbər] *vi* : dormir

slumber[2] *n* : sueño *m*

slump[1] ['slʌmp] *vi* 1 DECLINE, DROP : disminuir, bajar 2 SLOUCH : encorvarse, dejarse caer (en una silla, etc.)

slump[2] *n* : bajón *m*, declive *m* (económico)

slung → sling

slunk → slink

slur[1] ['slər] *vt* **slurred; slurring** : ligar (notas musicales), tragarse (las palabras)

slur[2] *n* 1 : ligado *m* (en música), mala pronunciación *f* (de las palabras) 2 ASPERSION : calumnia *f*, difamación *f*

slurp[1] ['slərp] *vi* : beber o comer haciendo ruido — *vt* : sorber ruidosamente

slurp[2] *n* : sorbo *m* (ruidoso)

slush ['slʌʃ] *n* : nieve *f* medio derretida

slut ['slʌt] *n disparaging + offensive* : fulana *f disparaging*, ramera *f*

sly ['slaɪ] *adj* **slier** ['slaɪər]; **sliest** ['slaɪəst] 1 CUNNING : astuto, taimado 2 UNDERHANDED : solapado — **slyly** *adv*

slyness ['slaɪnəs] *n* : astucia *f*

smack[1] ['smæk] *vi* **to smack of** : oler a, saber a — *vt* 1 KISS : besar, plantarle un beso (a alguien) 2 SLAP : pegarle una bofetada (a alguien) 3 **to smack one's lips** : relamerse

smack[2] *adv* : justo, exactamente ⟨smack in the face : en plena cara⟩

smack[3] *n* 1 TASTE, TRACE : sabor *m*, indicio *m* 2 : chasquido *m* (de los labios) 3 SLAP : bofetada *f* 4 KISS : beso *m*

small ['smɔl] *adj* 1 : pequeño, chico ⟨a small house : una casa pequeña⟩ ⟨small change : monedas de poco valor⟩ 2 TRIVIAL : pequeño, insignificante

smallness ['smɔlnəs] *n* : pequeñez *f*

smallpox ['smɔlˌpɑks] *n* : viruela *f*

small talk *n* **to make small talk** : hablar de cosas sin importancia

smart[1] ['smɑrt] *vi* 1 STING : escocer, picar, arder 2 HURT : dolerse, resentirse ⟨to smart under a rejection : dolerse ante un rechazo⟩

smart[2] *adj* 1 BRIGHT : listo, vivo, inteligente 2 STYLISH : elegante — **smartly** *adv*

smart[3] *n* 1 PAIN : escozor *m*, dolor *m* 2 **smarts** *npl* : inteligencia *f*

smarten up ['smɑrtənˌʌp] *vt* : atildar, arreglar — *vi* : atildarse, arreglarse

smartness ['smɑrtnəs] *n* 1 INTELLIGENCE : inteligencia *f* 2 ELEGANCE : elegancia *f*

smartphone ['smɑrtˌfoːn] *n* : smartphone *m*, teléfono *m* inteligente

smash[1] ['smæʃ] *vt* 1 BREAK : romper, quebrar, hacer pedazos 2 WRECK : destrozar, arruinar 3 CRASH : estrellar, chocar — *vi* 1 SHATTER : hacerse pedazos, hacerse añicos 2 COLLIDE, CRASH : estrellarse, chocar ⟨to smash against/ into something : chocar contra algo⟩

smash[2] *n* 1 BLOW : golpe *m* 2 COLLISION : choque *m* 3 BANG, CRASH : estrépito *m* 4 HIT, SUCCESS : exitazo *m*

smattering ['smætərɪŋ] *n* 1 : nociones *fpl* ⟨she has a smattering of programming : tiene nociones de programación⟩ 2 : un poco, unos cuantos ⟨a smattering of spectators : unos cuantos espectadores⟩

smear[1] ['smɪr] *vt* 1 DAUB : embadurnar, untar (mantequilla, etc.) 2 SMUDGE : emborronar 3 SLANDER : calumniar, difamar

smear[2] *n* 1 SMUDGE : mancha *f* 2 SLANDER : calumnia *f*

smell[1] ['smɛl] *v* **smelled** *or* **smelt** ['smɛlt]; **smelling** *vt* : oler, olfatear ⟨to smell danger : olfatear el peligro⟩ — *vi* : oler ⟨to smell good : oler bien⟩

smell² *n* **1** : olfato *m*, sentido *m* del olfato **2** ODOR : olor *m*

smelly ['smɛli] *adj* **smellier; -est** : maloliente

smelt¹ ['smɛlt] *vt* : fundir

smelt² *n, pl* **smelts** *or* **smelt** : eperlano *m* (pez)

smidgen ['smɪdʒən] *or* **smidge** ['smɪdʒ] *or* **smidgeon** ['smɪdʒən] *n* BIT : poquito *m*

smile¹ ['smaɪl] *vi* **smiled; smiling** : sonreír

smile² *n* : sonrisa *f*

smiley face ['smaɪli-] *n* : carita *f* sonriente (emoticono o dibujo)

smirk¹ ['smərk] *vi* : sonreír con suficiencia

smirk² *n* : sonrisa *f* satisfecha

smite ['smaɪt] *vt* **smote** ['smo:t]; **smitten** ['smɪtən] *or* **smote; smiting** **1** STRIKE : golpear **2** AFFLICT : afligir

smith ['smɪθ] *n* : herrero *m*, -ra *f*

smithereens [ˌsmɪðəˈriːnz] *npl* : añicos *mpl*

smithy ['smɪθi] *n, pl* **smithies** : herrería *f*

smock ['smɑk] *n* : bata *f*, blusón *m*

smog ['smɑg, 'smɔg] *n* : smog *m*

smoke¹ ['smo:k] *v* **smoked; smoking** *vi* **1** : echar humo, humear ⟨a smoking chimney : una chimenea que echa humo⟩ **2** : fumar ⟨I don't smoke : no fumo⟩ — *vt* : ahumar (carne, etc.)

smoke² *n* : humo *m*

smoked ['smo:kt] *adj* : ahumado

smoke detector [dɪˈtɛktər] *n* : detector *m* de humo

smoker ['smo:kər] *n* : fumador *m*, -dora *f*

smokescreen ['smo:kˌskri:n] *n* : cortina *f* de humo

smoke signal *n* : señal *f* de humo

smokestack ['smo:kˌstæk] *n* : chimenea *f*

smoky ['smo:ki] *adj* **smokier; -est** **1** SMOKING : humeante **2** : a humo ⟨a smoky flavor : un sabor a humo⟩ **3** : lleno de humo ⟨a smoky room : un cuarto lleno de humo⟩

smolder ['smo:ldər] *vi* **1** : arder sin llama **2** : arder (en el corazón) ⟨his anger smoldered : su rabia ardía⟩

smooch ['smu:tʃ] *vi* : besuquearse

smooth¹ ['smu:ð] *vt* **1** : alisar ⟨she smoothed (down/back) her hair : alisó el pelo⟩ ⟨he smoothed (out) the tablecloth : alisó los pliegues del mantel⟩ **2** SPREAD : extender ⟨smooth the cream on/onto/over your skin : extienda la crema sobre la piel⟩ **3 to smooth away/over** REMOVE : allanar (dificultades, etc.) ⟨to smooth things over : limar asperezas⟩ **4 to smooth the way for** *or* **to smooth a path for** : allanarle el camino a

smooth² *adj* **1** : liso (dícese de una superficie) ⟨smooth skin : piel lisa⟩ **2** : suave (dícese de un movimiento) ⟨a smooth landing : un aterrizaje suave⟩ **3** : sin grumos ⟨a smooth sauce : una salsa sin grumos⟩ **4** : fluido ⟨smooth writing : escritura fluida⟩

smoothly ['smu:ðli] *adv* **1** GENTLY, SOFTLY : suavemente **2** EASILY : con facilidad, sin problemas

smoothness ['smu:ðnəs] *n* : suavidad *f*

smother ['smʌðər] *vt* **1** SUFFOCATE : ahogar, sofocar **2** COVER : cubrir **3** SUPPRESS : contener — *vi* : asfixiarse

smudge¹ ['smʌdʒ] *v* **smudged; smudging** *vt* : emborronar — *vi* : correrse

smudge² *n* : mancha *f*, borrón *m*

smug ['smʌg] *adj* **smugger; smuggest** : suficiente, pagado de sí mismo

smuggle ['smʌgəl] *vt* **-gled; -gling** : contrabandear, pasar de contrabando

smuggler ['smʌgələr] *n* : contrabandista *mf*

smuggling ['smʌgəlɪŋ] *n* : contrabando *m* (acto)

smugly ['smʌgli] *adv* : con suficiencia

smut ['smʌt] *n* **1** SOOT : tizne *m*, hollín *m* **2** OBSCENITY : obscenidad *f*, inmundicia *f*

smutty ['smʌti] *adj* **smuttier; -est** **1** SOOTY : tiznado **2** OBSCENE : obsceno, indecente

snack ['snæk] *n* : refrigerio *m*, bocado *m*, tentempié *m fam* ⟨an afternoon snack : una merienda⟩

snack bar *n* : cafetería *f*

snag¹ ['snæg] *v* **snagged; snagging** *vt* : enganchar — *vi* : engancharse

snag² *n* : problema *m*, inconveniente *m*

snail ['sneɪl] *n* : caracol *m*

snake ['sneɪk] *n* : culebra *f*, serpiente *f*

snakebite ['sneɪkˌbaɪt] *n* : mordedura *f* de serpiente

snap¹ ['snæp] *v* **snapped; snapping** *vi* **1** BREAK : romperse, quebrarse (haciendo un chasquido) ⟨the branch snapped : la rama se rompió⟩ **2** : intentar morder (dícese de un perro, etc.) **3** : hablar con severidad ⟨he snapped at me! : ¡me gritó!⟩ **4** : moverse de un golpe ⟨the trap snapped shut : la trampa se cerró de golpe⟩ ⟨the branch snapped back : la rama se volvió de golpe⟩ ⟨the pieces snap together : las piezas se encajan⟩ **5 to snap out of** *fam* : salir de (la depresión, el ensueño, etc.) ⟨snap out of it! : ¡anímate!, ¡espabílate!⟩ **6 to snap to it** *fam* : moverse, apurarse — *vt* **1** BREAK : partir (en dos), quebrar **2** : hacer (algo) de un golpe ⟨she snapped it open : lo abrió de golpe⟩ **3** RETORT : decir bruscamente **4** CLICK : chasquear ⟨to snap one's fingers : chasquear los dedos⟩ **5 to snap up** : no dejar escapar

snap² *n* **1** CLICK, CRACK : chasquido *m* **2** FASTENER : broche *m* **3** CINCH : cosa *f* fácil ⟨it's a snap : es facilísimo⟩

snapdragon ['snæpˌdrægən] *n* : dragón *m* (flor)

snapper ['snæpər] → **red snapper**

snappy ['snæpi] *adj* **snappier; -est** **1** FAST : rápido ⟨make it snappy! : ¡date prisa!⟩ **2** LIVELY : vivaz **3** CHILLY : frío **4** STYLISH : elegante

snapshot ['snæpˌʃɑt] *n* : instantánea *f*

snare¹ ['snær] *vt* **snared; snaring** : atrapar

snare² *n* : trampa *f*, red *f*

snare drum *n* : tambor *m* con bordón

snarl¹ ['snɑrl] *vi* **1** TANGLE : enmarañar, enredar **2** GROWL : gruñir

snarl² n **1** TANGLE : enredo m, maraña f **2** GROWL : gruñido m

snatch¹ ['snætʃ] vt : arrebatar

snatch² n : fragmento m

sneak¹ ['sni:k] vi : ir a hurtadillas ⟨to sneak in/out : entrar/salir a escondidas⟩ ⟨to sneak away : escabullirse⟩ — vt : hacer furtivamente ⟨to sneak a look : mirar con disimulo⟩ ⟨he sneaked a smoke : fumó un cigarrillo a escondidas⟩

sneak² n : soplón m, -plona f

sneaker ['sni:kərz] npl : tenis m, zapatilla f ⟨a pair of sneakers : un par de tenis/zapatillas⟩

sneaky ['sni:ki] adj **sneakier; -est** : solapado

sneer¹ ['snɪr] vi : sonreír con desprecio

sneer² n : sonrisa f de desprecio

sneeze¹ ['sni:z] vi **sneezed; sneezing** : estornudar

sneeze² n : estornudo m

snicker¹ ['snɪkər] vi : reírse (disimuladamente)

snicker² n : risita f

snide ['snaɪd] adj : sarcástico

sniff¹ ['snɪf] vi **1** SMELL : oler, husmear (dícese de los animales) **2 to sniff at** : despreciar, desdeñar — vt **1** SMELL : oler **2 to sniff out** : olerse, husmear

sniff² n **1** SNIFFING : aspiración f por la nariz **2** SMELL : olor m

sniffle ['snɪfəl] vi **-fled; -fling** : respirar con la nariz congestionada

sniffles ['snɪfəlz] npl : resfriado m

snigger¹ ['snɪgər] → **snicker¹**

snigger² → **snicker²**

snip¹ ['snɪp] vt **snipped; snipping** : cortar (con tijeras)

snip² n : tijeretada f, recorte m

snipe¹ ['snaɪp] vi **sniped; sniping** : disparar

snipe² n, pl **snipes** or **snipe** : agachadiza f

sniper ['snaɪpər] n : francotirador m, -dora f

snippet ['snɪpət] n : fragmento m (de un texto, etc.)

snitch¹ ['snɪtʃ] v fam vi : cantar (a la policía, etc.) ⟨to snitch on someone : acusar/delatar a alguien⟩ — vt STEAL : robar

snitch² n fam : chivato m, -ta f

snivel ['snɪvəl] vi **-veled** or **-velled; -veling** or **-velling 1** → **snuffle 2** WHINE : lloriquear

snob ['snab] n : esnob mf, snob mf

snobbery ['snabəri] n, pl **-beries** : esnobismo m

snobbish ['snabɪʃ] adj : esnob, snob

snobbishness ['snabɪʃnəs] n : esnobismo m

snoop¹ ['snu:p] vi : husmear, curiosear

snoop² n : fisgón m, -gona f

snooty ['snu:ʈi] adj **snootier; -est** fam HAUGHTY : esnob, snob, altanero, altivo

snooze¹ ['snu:z] vi **snoozed; snoozing** : dormitar

snooze² n : siestecita f, siestita f

snore¹ ['snor] vi **snored; snoring** : roncar

snore² n : ronquido m

snorkel¹ ['snorkəl] vi : bucear con esnórquel

snorkel² n : esnórquel m, snorkel m, tubo m respiratorio/respirador

snort¹ ['snort] vi : bufar, resoplar

snort² n : bufido m, resoplo m

snot ['snat] n : mocos mpl

snotty ['snaʈi] adj **snottier; -est 1** → **snooty 2** : lleno de mocos

snout ['snaʊt] n : hocico m, morro m

snow¹ ['sno:] vi **1** : nevar ⟨I'm snowed in : estoy aislado por la nieve⟩ **2 to be snowed under** : estar inundado

snow² n : nieve f

snowball¹ ['sno:,bɔl] vi : aumentar, agravarse (rápidamente)

snowball² n : bola f de nieve

snowboard ['sno:,bord] n : snowboard m

snowboarding ['sno:,bordɪŋ] n : snowboard m (deporte)

snowcapped ['sno:,kæpt] adj : nevado

snowdrift ['sno:,drɪft] n : ventisquero m

snowdrop ['sno:,drap] n : campanilla f blanca

snowfall ['sno:,fɔl] n : nevada f

snowflake ['sno:,fleɪk] n : copo m de nieve

snowman ['sno:,mæn] n, pl **-men** [-mən, -,men] : muñeco m de nieve

snowplow ['sno:,plaʊ] n : quitanieves m

snowshoe ['sno:,ʃu:] n : raqueta f (para nieve)

snowstorm ['sno:,stɔrm] n : tormenta f de nieve, ventisca f

snow-white adj : blanco como la nieve

snowy ['sno:i] adj **snowier; -est** : nevoso ⟨a snowy road : un camino nevado⟩

snub¹ ['snʌb] vt **snubbed; snubbing** : desairar

snub² n : desaire m

snub-nosed ['snʌb,no:zd] adj : de nariz respingada

snuff¹ ['snʌf] vt **1** : apagar (una vela) **2** : sorber (algo) por la nariz

snuff² n : rapé m

snuffle ['snʌfəl] vi **-fled; -fling** : respirar con la nariz congestionada

snug ['snʌg] adj **snugger; snuggest 1** COMFORTABLE : cómodo **2** TIGHT : ajustado, ceñido ⟨snug pants : pantalones ajustados⟩

snuggle ['snʌgəl] vi **-gled; -gling** : acurrucarse ⟨to snuggle up to someone : arrimársele a alguien⟩

snugly ['snʌgli] adv **1** COMFORTABLY : cómodamente **2** : de manera ajustada ⟨the shirt fits snugly : la camisa queda ajustada⟩

so¹ ['so:] adv **1** (indicating a stated or suggested degree) : tan, tanto ⟨he'd never been so happy : nunca había estado tan contento⟩ ⟨she was so tired that she almost fell asleep : estaba tan cansada que casi se durmió⟩ ⟨would you be so kind as to help me? : ¿tendría la amabilidad de ayudarme?⟩ ⟨it's not so much a science as an art : no es tanto una ciencia como un arte⟩ ⟨all the more so because : tanto más cuanto que⟩ ⟨never more so than : nunca más que⟩ **2** VERY : tan, tanto ⟨it's so much fun : es tan divertido⟩ ⟨I'm so glad to meet you : me alegro tanto de conocerte⟩ ⟨he loves her so : la quiere tanto⟩ ⟨not so long ago : no hace mucho tiempo⟩ ⟨thank you so much : muchísimas gracias⟩ **3** ALSO : también ⟨so do I : yo también⟩ **4** THUS : así, de esta manera ⟨and so it began : y así empezó⟩ ⟨it so happened that . . . : resultó que . . .⟩ **5** (*used for emphasis*) *fam* ⟨it's so not fair : es totalmente injusto⟩ ⟨I so wanted to go : tenía tantas ganas de ir⟩ **6** CONSEQUENTLY : por lo tanto **7 and so forth/on** : etcétera **8 so much for** (*indicating that something has ended*) ⟨so much for that idea : hasta ahí llegó esa idea⟩ **9 so much so (that)** : tanto es así que **10 without so much as** : sin siquiera

so² *adj* : cierto, verdad ⟨it's not so : no es cierto, no es verdad⟩ ⟨is that so? : ¿ah, sí?⟩

so³ *conj* **1** THEREFORE : así que ⟨he didn't answer, so I called again : no contestó, así que lo llamé otra vez⟩ **2 or so that** : para que, así que, de manera que ⟨move over so I can sit down : córrete para que pueda sentarme⟩ ⟨we left early so that we would arrive on time : salimos temprano para llegar a tiempo⟩ **3 so what?** : ¿y qué?

so⁴ *pron* **1** (*referring to something indicated or suggested*) ⟨do you think so? : ¿tú crees?⟩ ⟨so it would seem : eso/así parece⟩ ⟨I told her so : se lo dije⟩ ⟨he's ready, or he says : según dice, está listo⟩ ⟨do it like so : hazlo así⟩ ⟨so be it : así sea⟩ ⟨if so : si es así⟩ ⟨I'm afraid so : me temo que sí⟩ **2 or so** : más o menos ⟨a week or so : una semana, más o menos⟩

soak¹ ['so:k] *vi* : estar en remojo — *vt* **1** : poner en remojo **2** DRENCH : empapar **3 to soak up** ABSORB : absorber

soak² *n* : remojo *m*

so-and-so *n* : fulano *m*, -na *f*

soap¹ ['so:p] *vt* : enjabonar

soap² *n* **1** : jabón *m* **2** → **soap opera**

soap opera *n* : culebrón *m*, telenovela *f*

soapsuds ['so:p,sʌdz] → **suds**

soapy ['so:pi] *adj* **soapier; -est** : jabonoso ⟨a soapy taste : un gusto a jabón⟩ ⟨a soapy texture : una textura de jabón⟩

soar ['sor] *vi* **1** FLY : volar **2** RISE : remontar el vuelo (dícese de las aves) ⟨her hopes soared : su esperanza renació⟩ ⟨prices are soaring : los precios están subiendo vertiginosamente⟩

sob¹ ['sɑb] *vi* **sobbed; sobbing** : sollozar

sob² *n* : sollozo *m*

sober¹ ['so:bər] *adj* **1** : sobrio ⟨he's not sober enough to drive : está demasiado borracho para manejar⟩ **2** SERIOUS : serio

sober² *vi* **1** SADDEN : entristecer **2 to sober up** : pasársele la borrachera

soberly ['so:bərli] *adv* **1** : sobriamente **2** SERIOUSLY : seriamente

sobriety [sə'braɪəti, so-] *n* **1** : sobriedad *f*

⟨sobriety test : prueba de alcoholemia⟩ **2** SERIOUSNESS : seriedad *f*

so-called ['so:'kɔld] *adj* : supuesto, presunto ⟨the so-called experts : los expertos, así llamados⟩

soccer ['sɑkər] *n* : futbol *m*, fútbol *m*

sociability [,so:ʃə'bɪləti] *n* : sociabilidad *f*

sociable ['so:ʃəbəl] *adj* : sociable

social¹ ['so:ʃəl] *adj* : social — **socially** *adv*

social² *n* : reunión *f* social

socialism ['so:ʃə,lɪzəm] *n* : socialismo *m*

socialist¹ ['so:ʃəlɪst] *adj* : socialista

socialist² *n* : socialista *mf*

socialize ['so:ʃə,laɪz] *v* **-ized; -izing** *vt* **1** NATIONALIZE : nacionalizar **2** : socializar (en psicología) — *vi* : alternar, circular ⟨to socialize with friends : alternar con amigos⟩

social media *ns & pl* : redes *fpl* sociales, medios *mpl* sociales

social networking *n* : establecimiento *m* y mantenimiento *m* de una red de contactos en línea ⟨a social networking site : un sitio de redes sociales⟩

social security *n* : seguridad *f* social

social work *n* : asistencia *f* social

social worker *n* : asistente *m*, -ta *f* social

society [sə'saɪəti] *n, pl* **-eties 1** COMPANIONSHIP : compañía *f* **2** : sociedad *f* ⟨a democratic society : una sociedad democrática⟩ ⟨high society : alta sociedad⟩ **3** ASSOCIATION : sociedad *f*, asociación *f*

socioeconomic [,so:sio,i:kə'nɑmɪk, -,ɛkə-] *adj* : socioeconómico

sociological [,so:siə'lɑdʒɪkəl] *adj* : sociológico

sociologist [,so:si'ɑlədʒɪst] *n* : sociólogo *m*, -ga *f*

sociology [,so:si'ɑlədʒi] *n* : sociología *f*

sock¹ ['sɑk] *vt* : pegar, golpear, darle un puñetazo a

sock² *n* **1** *pl* **socks** *or* **sox** ['sɑks] : calcetín *m*, media *f* ⟨shoes and socks : zapatos y calcetines⟩ **2** *pl* **socks** ['sɑks] PUNCH : puñetazo *m*

socket ['sɑkət] *n* **1** *or* **electric socket** : enchufe *m*, toma *f* de corriente **2** : glena *f* (de una articulación) ⟨shoulder socket : glena del hombro⟩ **3 eye socket** : órbita *f*, cuenca *f*

sod¹ ['sɑd] *vt* **sodded; sodding** : cubrir de césped

sod² *n* TURF : césped *m*, tepe *m*

soda ['so:də] *n* **1** *or* **soda water** : soda *f* **2** *or* **soda pop** : gaseosa *f*; refresco *m*; fresco *m*; soda *f* CA, Car **3** *or* **ice-cream soda** : refresco *m* con helado

sodden ['sɑdən] *adj* SOGGY : empapado

sodium ['so:diəm] *n* : sodio *m*

sodium bicarbonate *n* : bicarbonato *m* de soda

sodium chloride → **salt**

sofa ['so:fə] *n* : sofá *m*

soft ['sɔft] *adj* **1** : blando ⟨a soft pillow : una almohada blanda⟩ **2** SMOOTH : suave (dícese de las texturas, de los sonidos, etc.) **3** NONALCOHOLIC : no alcohólico ⟨a soft drink : un refresco⟩

softball ['sɔft,bɔl] *n* : softbol *m*

soft–boiled ['sɔft'bɔɪld] *adj* : pasado por agua

soften ['sɔfən] *vt* : ablandar (algo sólido), suavizar (la piel, un golpe, etc.), amortiguar (un impacto) — *vi* : ablandarse, suavizarse

softener ['sɔfənər] *n* : suavizante *m*

softly ['sɔftli] *adv* : suavemente ⟨she spoke softly : habló en voz baja⟩

softness ['sɔftnəs] *n* **1** : blandura *f*, lo blando (de una almohada, de la mantequilla, etc.) **2** SMOOTHNESS : suavidad *f*

soft–spoken ['sɔft'spokən] *adj* : de voz suave

software ['sɔft,wær] *n* : software *m*

soggy ['sɑgi] *adj* **soggier; -est** : empapado

soil¹ ['sɔɪl] *vt* : ensuciar — *vi* : ensuciarse

soil² *n* **1** DIRTINESS : suciedad *f* **2** DIRT, EARTH : suelo *m*, tierra *f* **3** COUNTRY : patria *f* ⟨her native soil : su tierra natal⟩

sojourn¹ ['so:ˌdʒərn, so:'dʒərn] *vi* : pasar una temporada

sojourn² *n* : estadía *f*, estancia *f*, permanencia *f*

sol ['so:l] *n* **1** : sol *m* (en el canto) **2** : sol *m* (unidad monetaria)

solace ['sɑləs] *n* : consuelo *m*

solar ['so:lər] *adj* : solar ⟨the solar system : el sistema solar⟩ ⟨solar energy/power : energía solar⟩

sold → **sell**

solder¹ ['sɑdər, 'sɔ-] *vt* : soldar

solder² *n* : soldadura *f*

soldier¹ ['so:ldʒər] *vi* : servir como soldado

soldier² *n* : soldado *mf*

sole¹ ['so:l] *adj* : único

sole² *n* **1** : suela *f* (de un zapato) **2** : lenguado *m* (pez)

solely ['so:li] *adv* : únicamente, sólo

solemn ['sɑləm] *adj* : solemne, serio — **solemnly** *adv*

solemnity [sə'lɛmnəti] *n, pl* **-ties** : solemnidad *f*

sol–fa [ˌso:l'fɑ] *n* : solfeo *m*

solicit [sə'lɪsət] *vt* : solicitar

solicitous [sə'lɪsətəs] *adj* : solícito

solicitude [sə'lɪsəˌtu:d, -ˌtju:d] *n* : solicitud *f*

solid¹ ['sɑləd] *adj* **1** : macizo ⟨a solid rubber ball : una bola maciza de caucho⟩ **2** CUBIC : tridimensional **3** COMPACT : compacto, denso **4** STURDY : sólido **5** CONTINUOUS : seguido, continuo ⟨two solid hours : dos horas seguidas⟩ ⟨a solid line : una línea continua⟩ **6** UNANIMOUS : unánime **7** DEPENDABLE : serio, fiable **8** PURE : macizo, puro ⟨solid gold : oro macizo⟩

solid² *n* : sólido *m*

solidarity [ˌsɑlə'dærəti] *n* : solidaridad *f*

solidify [sə'lɪdəˌfaɪ] *v* **-fied; -fying** *vt* : solidificar — *vi* : solidificarse

solidity [sə'lɪdəti] *n, pl* **-ties** : solidez *f*

solidly ['sɑlədli] *adv* **1** : sólidamente **2** UNANIMOUSLY : unánimemente

soliloquy [sə'lɪləkwi] *n, pl* **-quies** : soliloquio *m*

solitaire ['sɑləˌter] *n* : solitario *m*

solitary ['sɑləˌteri] *adj* **1** ALONE : solitario **2** SECLUDED : apartado, retirado **3** SINGLE : solo

solitude ['sɑləˌtu:d, -ˌtju:d] *n* : soledad *f*

solo¹ ['so:ˌlo:] *vi* : volar en solitario (dícese de un piloto)

solo² *adv & adj* : en solitario, a solas

solo³ *n, pl* **solos** : solo *m*

soloist ['so:loɪst] *n* : solista *mf*

solstice ['sɑlstɪs] *n* : solsticio *m*

soluble ['sɑljəbəl] *adj* : soluble

solution [sə'lu:tən] *n* : solución *f*

solve ['sɑlv] *vt* **solved; solving** : resolver, solucionar

solvency ['sɑlvəntsi] *n* : solvencia *f*

solvent ['sɑlvənt] *n* : solvente *m*

somber ['sɑmbər] *adj* **1** DARK : sombrío, oscuro ⟨somber colors : colores oscuros⟩ **2** GRAVE : sombrío, serio **3** MELANCHOLY : sombrío, lúgubre

sombrero [səm'brɛrˌo:] *n, pl* **-ros** : sombrero *m* (mexicano)

some¹ ['sʌm] *adv* **1** : unos, unas ⟨some 80 people came, 80-some people came : unas 80 personas vinieron⟩ **2** : un poco ⟨he helped me some *fam* : me ayudó un poco⟩ ⟨I need to work on it some more : necesito pulirlo un poco más⟩

some² *adj* **1** : un, algún ⟨some lady stopped me : una mujer me detuvo⟩ ⟨some distant galaxy : alguna galaxia lejana⟩ ⟨there must be some mistake : debe de haber algún error⟩ **2** : algo de, un poco de ⟨he drank some water : tomó (un poco de) agua⟩ **3** : unos ⟨do you want some apples? : ¿quieres unas manzanas?⟩ ⟨some years ago : hace varios años⟩ **4** *fam (expressing approval)* ⟨that was some game! : ¡vaya partido!⟩ **5** *fam (expressing disapproval)* ⟨you've got some nerve! : ¡qué cara tienes!⟩ ⟨some friend he is! : ¡qué clase de amigo!⟩

some³ *pron* **1** : algunos ⟨some went, others stayed : algunos se fueron, otros se quedaron⟩ ⟨some of my friends : algunos de mis amigos⟩ ⟨some of the movies : algunas de las películas⟩ **2** : un poco, algo ⟨there's some left : queda un poco⟩ ⟨some of the cake : parte del pastel⟩ ⟨I have gum; do you want some? : tengo chicle, ¿quieres?⟩

somebody ['sʌmbədi, -ˌbɑdi] *pron* : alguien

someday ['sʌmˌdeɪ] *adv* : algún día

somehow ['sʌmˌhaʊ] *adv* **1** : de alguna manera, de algún modo ⟨I'll do it somehow : lo haré de alguna manera⟩ **2** : por alguna razón ⟨somehow I don't trust her : por alguna razón no me fío de ella⟩

someone ['sʌmˌwʌn] *pron* : alguien

someplace ['sʌmˌpleɪs] → **somewhere**

somersault¹ ['sʌmərˌsɔlt] *vi* : dar volteretas, dar un salto mortal

somersault² *n* : voltereta *f*, salto *m* mortal

something ['sʌmθɪŋ] *pron* : algo ⟨I want something else : quiero otra cosa⟩ ⟨she's writing a novel or something : está escribiendo una novela o no sé qué⟩

sometime ['sʌmˌtaɪm] *adv* : algún día, en algún momento ⟨sometime next month : durante el mes que viene⟩

sometimes ['sʌmˌtaɪmz] *adv* : a veces, algunas veces, de vez en cuando

somewhat ['sʌmˌhwʌt, -ˌhwɑt] *adv* : algo, un tanto

somewhere ['sʌmˌhwɛr] *adv* **1** (*indicating location*) : en algún lugar ⟨it must be somewhere else : estará en otra parte⟩ **2** (*indicating destination*) : a algún lugar ⟨she went somewhere else : fue a otra parte⟩ **3** APPROXIMATELY : alrededor de ⟨somewhere around a thousand dollars : alrededor de mil dólares⟩ ⟨he's somewhere in his thirties : tiene unos treinta años, tiene treinta y tantos/pico⟩

son ['sʌn] *n* : hijo *m*

sonar ['soːˌnɑr] *n* : sonar *m*

sonata [sə'nɑt̬ə] *n* : sonata *f*

song ['sɔŋ] *n* : canción *f*, canto *m* (de un pájaro)

songbird ['sɔŋˌbərd] *n* : pájaro *m* cantor

songbook ['sɔŋˌbʊk] *n* : cancionero *m*

songwriter ['sɔŋˌraɪt̬ər] *n* : compositor *m*, -tora *f*

sonic ['sɑnɪk] *adj* **1** : sónico **2 sonic boom** : estampido *m* sónico

son–in–law ['sʌnɪnˌlɔ] *n, pl* **sons–in–law** : yerno *m*, hijo *m* político

sonnet ['sɑnət] *n* : soneto *m*

son of a bitch *n, pl* **sons of bitches** *sometimes offensive* : hijo *m* de puta *sometimes offensive*

sonorous ['sɑnərəs, sə'norəs] *adj* : sonoro

soon ['suːn] *adv* **1** : pronto, dentro de poco ⟨he'll arrive soon : llegará pronto⟩ **2** QUICKLY : pronto ⟨as soon as possible : lo más pronto posible⟩ ⟨the sooner the better : cuanto antes mejor⟩ **3** : de buena gana ⟨I'd sooner walk : prefiero caminar⟩

soot ['sʊt, 'suːt, 'sʌt] *n* : hollín *m*, tizne *m*

soothe ['suːð] *vt* **soothed; soothing 1** CALM : calmar, tranquilizar **2** RELIEVE : aliviar

soothsayer ['suːˌθeɪˌseɪər] *n* : adivino *m*, -na *f*

sooty ['sʊt̬i, 'suː-, 'sʌ-] *adj* **sootier; -est** : cubierto de hollín, tiznado

sop¹ ['sɑp] *vt* **sopped; sopping 1** DIP : mojar, SOAK : empapar **3 to sop up** : rebañar, absorber

sop² *n* **1** CONCESSION : concesión *f* **2** BRIBE : soborno *m*

sophisticated [sə'fɪstɪˌkeɪt̬əd] *adj* **1** : sofisticado **2** COMPLEX : complejo

sophistication [səˌfɪstə'keɪlən] *n* **1** COMPLEXITY : complejidad *f* **2** : sofisticación *f*

sophomore ['sɑfˌmor, 'sɑfəˌmor] *n* : estudiante *mf* de segundo año

sophistry ['sɑfəstri] *n* : sofistería *f*

soporific [ˌsɑpə'rɪfɪk, ˌso:-] *adj* : soporífero

soprano [sə'præˌno:] *n, pl* **-nos** : soprano *mf*

sorbet [ˌsor'beɪ] *n* : sorbete *m*

sorcerer ['sorsərər] *n* : hechicero *m*, brujo *m*, mago *m*

sorceress ['sorsərəs] *n* : hechicera *f*, bruja *f*, maga *f*

sorcery ['sorsəri] *n* : hechicería *f*, brujería *f*

sordid ['sordɪd] *adj* : sórdido

sore¹ ['sor] *adj* **sorer; sorest 1** PAINFUL : dolorido, doloroso ⟨I have a sore throat : me duele la garganta⟩ **2** ACUTE, SEVERE : extremo, grande ⟨in sore straits : en grandes apuros⟩ **3** ANGRY : enojado, enfadado

sore² *n* : llaga *f*

sorely ['sorli] *adv* : muchísimo ⟨it was sorely needed : se necesitaba urgentemente⟩ ⟨she was sorely missed : la echaban mucho de menos⟩

soreness ['sornəs] *n* : dolor *m*

sorghum ['sorgəm] *n* : sorgo *m*

sorority [sə'rorət̬i] *n, pl* **-ties** : hermandad *f* (de estudiantes femeninas)

sorrel ['sorəl] *n* **1** : alazán *m* (color o animal) **2** : acedera *f* (hierba)

sorrow ['sɑrˌo:] *n* : pesar *m*, dolor *m*, pena *f*

sorrowful ['sɑrəfəl] *adj* : triste, afligido, apenado

sorrowfully ['sɑrəfəli] *adv* : con tristeza

sorry ['sɑri] *adj* **sorrier; -est 1** PITIFUL : lastimero, lastimoso ⟨to be a sorry sight : tener un aspecto lamentable/horrible⟩ **2 to be sorry** : sentir, lamentar ⟨I'm sorry : lo siento⟩ ⟨I'm sorry to have to tell you that . . . : siento tener que decirte que . . .⟩ ⟨I'm sorry, but I disagree : lo siento, pero no estoy de acuerdo⟩ ⟨I'm sorry to disturb you : siento molestarlo⟩ **3 to feel sorry for** : compadecer ⟨I feel sorry for him : me da pena⟩ ⟨to feel sorry for oneself : lamentarse de su suerte⟩

sort¹ ['sort] *vt* **1** : dividir en grupos **2** CLASSIFY : clasificar **3 to sort out** ORGANIZE : poner en orden **4 to sort out** RESOLVE : resolver

sort² *n* **1** KIND : tipo *m*, clase *f* ⟨a sort of writer : una especie de escritor⟩ ⟨all sorts of : todo tipo de⟩ **2** NATURE : índole *f* **3 of the sort** ⟨I said nothing of the sort : no dije nada semejante⟩ **4 of sorts** *or* **of a sort** ⟨he's a poet of sorts : es poeta, si se le puede llamar así⟩ **5 out of sorts** : de mal humor **6 sort of** : más o menos **7 sort of a** : una especie de

sortie ['sorti, sor'tiː] *n* : salida *f*

SOS [ˌɛsˌoː'ɛs] *n* : SOS *m*

so–so ['soːˌso:] *adj & adv* : así así, de modo regular

soufflé [su'fleɪ] *n* : suflé *m*

sought → seek

soul ['soːl] *n* **1** SPIRIT : alma *f* **2** ESSENCE : esencia *f* **3** PERSON : persona *f*, alma *f*

soulful ['soːlfəl] *adj* : conmovedor, lleno de emoción

sound¹ ['saʊnd] *vt* **1** : sondar (en navegación) **2** *or* **to sound out** PROBE : sondear **3** : hacer sonar, tocar (una trompeta, etc.) — *vi* **1** : sonar ⟨the alarm sounded : la alarma sonó⟩ **2** SEEM : parecer

sound² *adj* **1** HEALTHY : sano ⟨safe and sound : sano y salvo⟩ ⟨of sound mind and body : en pleno uso de sus facultades⟩ **2** FIRM, SOLID : sólido **3** SENSIBLE : lógico, sensato **4** DEEP : profundo ⟨a sound sleep : un sueño profundo⟩

sound³ *adv* : profundamente ⟨sound asleep : profundamente dormido⟩

sound⁴ *n* **1** : sonido *m* ⟨the speed of sound : la velocidad del sonido⟩ **2** NOISE : sonido *m*, ruido *m* ⟨I heard a sound : oí un sonido⟩ **3** CHANNEL : brazo *m* de mar, canal *m* (ancho)

soundless ['saʊndləs] *adj* : sordo

soundlessly ['saʊndləsli] *adv* : silenciosamente

soundly ['saʊndli] *adv* **1** SOLIDLY : sólidamente **2** SENSIBLY : lógicamente, sensatamente **3** DEEPLY : profundamente ⟨sleeping soundly : durmiendo profundamente⟩

soundness ['saʊndnəs] *n* **1** SOLIDITY : solidez *f* **2** SENSIBLENESS : sensatez *f*, solidez *f*

soundproof ['saʊnd,pru:f] *adj* : insonorizado

sound system *n* : equipo *m* de sonido

soundtrack ['saʊnd,træk] *n* : banda *f* sonora

sound wave *n* : onda *f* sonora

soup ['su:p] *n* : sopa *f*

sour¹ ['saʊər] *vi* : agriarse, cortarse (dícese de la leche) — *vt* : agriar, cortar (leche)

sour² *adj* **1** ACID : agrio, ácido (dícese de la fruta, etc.), cortado (dícese de la leche) **2** DISAGREEABLE : desagradable, agrio

source ['sors] *n* : fuente *f*, origen *m*, nacimiento *m* (de un río)

sourness ['saʊərnəs] *n* : acidez *f*

soursop ['saʊər,sɑp] *n* : guanábana *f*

south¹ ['saʊθ] *adv* : al sur, hacia el sur ⟨the window looks south : la ventana mira al sur⟩ ⟨she continued south : continuó hacia el sur⟩

south² *adj* : sur, del sur ⟨the south entrance : la entrada sur⟩ ⟨South America : Sudamérica, América del Sur⟩

south³ *n* : sur *m*

South African *n* : sudafricano *m*, -na *f* — **South African** *adj*

South American¹ *adj* : sudamericano, suramericano

South American² *n* : sudamericano *m*, -na *f*; suramericano *m*, -na *f*

southbound ['saʊθ,baʊnd] *adj* : con rumbo al sur

southeast¹ [saʊ'θi:st] *adj* : sureste, sudeste, del sureste

southeast² *n* : sureste *m*, sudeste *m*

southeasterly [saʊ'θi:stərli] *adv & adj* **1** : del sureste (dícese del viento) **2** : hacia el sureste

southeastern [saʊ'θi:stərn] *adj* → **southeast¹**

southerly ['sʌðərli] *adv & adj* : del sur

southern ['sʌðərn] *adj* : sur, sureño, meridional, austral ⟨a southern city : una ciudad del sur del país, una ciudad meridional⟩ ⟨the southern side : el lado sur⟩

Southerner ['sʌðərnər] *n* : sureño *m*, -ña *f*

South Pole : Polo *m* Sur

southward ['saʊθwərd] *or* **southwards** [-wərdz] *adv & adj* : hacia el sur

southwest¹ [saʊθ'wɛst, as a nautical term often saʊ'wɛst] *adj* : suroeste, sudoeste, del suroeste

southwest² *n* : suroeste *m*, sudoeste *m*

southwesterly [saʊθ'wɛstərli] *adv & adj* **1** : del suroeste (dícese del viento) **2** : hacia el suroeste

southwestern [saʊθ'wɛstərn] *adj* → **southwest¹**

souvenir [,su:və'nɪr, 'su:və,-] *n* : recuerdo *m*, souvenir *m*

sovereign¹ ['sɑvərən] *adj* : soberano

sovereign² *n* **1** : soberano *m*, -na *f* (monarca) **2** : soberano *m* (moneda)

sovereignty ['sɑvərənti] *n, pl* **-ties** : soberanía *f*

Soviet ['so:vi,ɛt, 'sɑ-, -viət] *adj* : soviético

sow¹ ['so:] *vt* **sowed**; **sown** ['so:n] *or* **sowed**; **sowing** **1** PLANT : sembrar **2** SCATTER : esparcir

sow² ['saʊ] *n* : cerda *f*

sox → **sock**

soy ['sɔɪ] *n* : soya *f*, soja *f*

soybean ['sɔɪ,bi:n] *n* : soya *f*, soja *f*

spa ['spɑ] *n* : balneario *m*

space¹ ['speɪs] *vt* **spaced**; **spacing** : espaciar

space² *n* **1** PERIOD : espacio *m*, lapso *m*, período *m* **2** ROOM : espacio *m*, sitio *m*, lugar *m* ⟨is there space for me? : ¿hay sitio para mí?⟩ **3** : espacio *m* ⟨blank space : espacio en blanco⟩ **4** : espacio *m* (en física) **5** PLACE : plaza *f*, sitio *m* ⟨to reserve space : reservar plazas⟩ ⟨parking space : sitio para estacionarse⟩

spacecraft ['speɪs,kræft] *n* : nave *f* espacial

spaceflight ['speɪs,flaɪt] *n* : vuelo *m* espacial

spaceman ['speɪsmən, -,mæn] *n, pl* **-men** [-mən, -,mɛn] : astronauta *m*, cosmonauta *m*

spaceship ['speɪs,ʃɪp] *n* : nave *f* espacial

space shuttle *n* : transbordador *m* espacial

space station *n* : estación *f* espacial

space suit *n* : traje *m* espacial

spacious ['speɪʃəs] *adj* : espacioso, amplio

spade¹ ['speɪd] *v* **spaded**; **spading** *vt* : palear — *vi* : usar una pala

spade² *n* **1** SHOVEL : pala *f* **2** : pica *f* (naipe)

spaghetti [spə'gɛti] *n* : espagueti *m*, espaguetis *mpl*, spaghetti *mpl*

spam¹ ['spæm] *vt* **spammed**; **spamming** : enviarle spam a

spam² *n* : spam *m*, correo *m* electrónico no solicitado

Spam *trademark* se usa para un tipo de carne enlatada

span¹ ['spæn] *vt* **spanned**; **spanning** : abarcar (un período de tiempo), extenderse sobre (un espacio)

span² *n* **1** : lapso *m*, espacio *m* (de tiempo) ⟨life span : duración de la vida⟩ **2** : luz *f* (entre dos soportes)

spangle ['spæŋgəl] *n* : lentejuela *f*
Spaniard ['spænjərd] *n* : español *m*, -ñola *f*
spaniel ['spænjəl] *n* : spaniel *m*
Spanish[1] ['spænɪʃ] *adj* : español
Spanish[2] *n* **1** : español *m* (idioma) **2 the Spanish** (*used with a plural verb*) : los españoles
spank ['spæŋk] *vt* : darle nalgadas (a alguien)
spar[1] ['spɑr] *vi* **sparred; sparring** : entrenarse (en boxeo)
spar[2] *n* : palo *m*, verga *f* (de un barco)
spare[1] ['spær] *vt* **spared; sparing 1** : perdonar ⟨to spare someone's life : perdonarle la vida a alguien⟩ ⟨to spare someone's feelings : no herir los sentimientos de alguien⟩ ⟨the fire spared their house : su casa se salvó del fuego⟩ **2** SAVE : ahorrar, evitar ⟨he spared us the trouble/embarrassment : nos ahorró la molestia/vergüenza⟩ ⟨spare me the details : ahórrate los detalles⟩ ⟨she was spared (from) punishment : se libró del castigo⟩ **3** : prescindir de ⟨I can't spare her : no puedo prescindir de ella⟩ ⟨I can't spare the time : no me da el tiempo⟩ ⟨can you spare a dollar? : ¿me das un dólar?⟩ ⟨can you spare a minute? : ¿tienes un momento?⟩ **4** STINT : escatimar ⟨they spared no expense : no repararon en gastos⟩ **5 to spare** : de sobra
spare[2] *adj* **sparer; sparest 1** : de repuesto, de recambio ⟨spare tire : llanta de repuesto⟩ **2** EXCESS, EXTRA : de más, de sobra, libre ⟨spare time : tiempo libre⟩ ⟨spare room : cuarto de huéspedes⟩ **3** LEAN : delgado
spare[3] *n* or **spare part** : repuesto *m*, recambio *m*
sparing ['spærɪŋ] *adj* : parco, económico — **sparingly** *adv*
spark[1] ['spɑrk] *vi* : chispear, echar chispas — *vt* PROVOKE : despertar, provocar ⟨to spark interest : despertar interés⟩
spark[2] *n* **1** : chispa *f* ⟨to throw off sparks : echar chispas⟩ **2** GLIMMER, TRACE : destello *m*, pizca *f*
sparkle[1] ['spɑrkəl] *vi* **-kled; -kling 1** FLASH, SHINE : destellar, centellear, brillar **2** : estar muy animado (dícese de una conversación, etc.)
sparkle[2] *n* : destello *m*, centelleo *m*
sparkler ['spɑrklər] *n* : luz *f* de bengala
spark plug *n* : bujía *f*
sparrow ['spæro:] *n* : gorrión *m*
sparse ['spɑrs] *adj* **sparser; sparsest** : escaso — **sparsely** *adv*
spasm ['spæzəm] *n* **1** : espasmo *m* (muscular) **2** BURST, FIT : arrebato *m*
spasmodic [spæz'mɑdɪk] *adj* **1** : espasmódico **2** SPORADIC : irregular, esporádico — **spasmodically** [-dɪkli] *adv*
spastic ['spæstɪk] *adj* : espástico
spat[1] → **spit**[1]
spat[2] ['spæt] *n* : discusión *f*, disputa *f*, pelea *f*
spate ['speɪt] *n* : avalancha *f*, torrente *m*

spatial ['speɪʃəl] *adj* : espacial
spatter[1] ['spætər] *v* : salpicar
spatter[2] *n* : salpicadura *f*
spatula ['spætʃələ] *n* : espátula *f*, paleta *f* (para servir)
spawn[1] ['spɔn] *vi* : desovar — *vt* GENERATE : generar, producir
spawn[2] *n* : hueva *f*
spay ['speɪ] *vt* : esterilizar (una perra, etc.)
speak ['spi:k] *v* **spoke** ['spo:k]; **spoken** ['spo:kən]; **speaking** *vi* **1** TALK : hablar ⟨to speak to/with someone : hablar con alguien⟩ ⟨who's speaking? : ¿de parte de quien?⟩ ⟨so to speak : por así decirlo⟩ ⟨generally speaking : por lo general, generalmente⟩ ⟨they're not speaking (to each other) : no se hablan⟩ ⟨she spoke at the conference : habló en el congreso⟩ ⟨she spoke well of you : habló bien de ti⟩ **2 to be spoken for** : estar reservado (dícese de un asiento, etc.), estar comprometido (dícese de una persona) **3 to speak for** : hablar en nombre de ⟨speak for yourself! : ¡habla por ti mismo!⟩ **4 to speak of** SIGNIFICANT : significante, que merece comentario ⟨there's been no progress to speak of : no han avanzado nada⟩ **5 to speak of** MENTION : mencionar ⟨(and) speaking of which . . . . : a propósito . . .⟩ **6 to speak out** : hablar claramente **7 to speak out against** : denunciar **8 to speak up** : hablar en voz alta **9 to speak up for** : defender — *vt* **1** SAY : decir ⟨she spoke her mind : habló con franqueza⟩ **2** : hablar (un idioma)
speaker ['spi:kər] *n* **1** : hablante *mf* ⟨a native speaker : un hablante nativo⟩ **2** : orador *m*, -dora *f* ⟨the keynote speaker : el orador principal⟩ **3** LOUDSPEAKER : altavoz *m*, altoparlante *m*
spear[1] ['spɪr] *vt* : atravesar con una lanza
spear[2] *n* : lanza *f*
spearhead[1] ['spɪr,hɛd] *vt* : encabezar
spearhead[2] *n* : punta *f* de lanza
spearmint ['spɪrmɪnt] *n* : menta *f* verde
special ['spɛʃəl] *adj* : especial ⟨nothing special : nada en especial, nada en particular⟩ — **specially** *adv*
special delivery *n* : correo *m* urgente
special effects *npl* : efectos *mpl* especiales
specialist ['spɛʃəlɪst] *n* : especialista *mf*
specialization [,spɛʃələ'zeɪʃən] *n* : especialización *f*
specialize ['spɛʃə,laɪz] *vi* **-ized; -izing** : especializarse
specialty ['spɛʃəlti] *n*, *pl* **-ties** : especialidad *f*
species ['spi:,ʃi:z, -,si:z] *ns & pl* : especie *f*
specific [spɪ'sɪfɪk] *adj* : específico, determinado — **specifically** [-fɪkli] *adv*
specification [,spɛsəfə'keɪʃən] *n* : especificación *f*
specify ['spɛsə,faɪ] *vt* **-fied; -fying** : especificar
specimen ['spɛsəmən] *n* **1** SAMPLE : espécimen *m*, muestra *f* **2** EXAMPLE : espécimen *m*, ejemplar *m*
speck ['spɛk] *n* **1** SPOT : manchita *f* **2** BIT, TRACE : mota *f*, pizca *f*, ápice *m*

speckled ['spɛkəld] *adj* : moteado
spectacle ['spɛktɪkəl] *n* **1** : espectáculo *m* **2 spectacles** *npl* GLASSES : lentes *fpl*, gafas *fpl*, anteojos *mpl*, espejuelos *mpl*
spectacular [spɛk'tækjələr] *adj* : espectacular
spectator ['spɛk,teɪţər] *n* : espectador *m*, -dora *f*
specter *or* **spectre** ['spɛktər] *n* : espectro *m*, fantasma *m*
spectrum ['spɛktrəm] *n, pl* **spectra** [-trə] *or* **spectrums 1** : espectro *m* (de colores, etc.) **2** RANGE : gama *f*, abanico *m*
speculate ['spɛkjə,leɪt] *vi* **-lated; -lating 1** : especular (en finanzas) **2** WONDER : preguntarse, hacer conjeturas
speculation [,spɛkjə'leɪʒən] *n* : especulación *f*
speculative ['spɛkjə,leɪţɪv] *adj* : especulativo
speculator ['spɛkjə,leɪţər] *n* : especulador *m*, -dora *f*
speech ['spiːţʃ] *n* **1** : habla *f*, modo *m* de hablar, expresión *f* **2** ADDRESS : discurso *m*
speechless ['spiːţʃləs] *adj* : enmudecido, estupefacto
speed¹ ['spiːd] *v* **sped** ['spɛd] *or* **speeded; speeding** *vi* **1** : ir a toda velocidad, correr a toda prisa ⟨he sped off : se fue a toda velocidad⟩ **2** : conducir a exceso de velocidad — *vt* **to speed up** : acelerar
speed² *n* **1** SWIFTNESS : rapidez *f* **2** VELOCITY : velocidad *f*
speedboat ['spiːd,boːt] *n* : lancha *f* motora (rápida), deslizador *m*
speed bump *n* : badén *m*
speeding ['spiːdɪŋ] *n* : exceso *m* de velocidad ⟨he was stopped/ticketed for speeding : lo pararon/multaron por exceso de velocidad⟩
speed limit *n* : velocidad *f* máxima, límite *m* de velocidad
speedometer [spɪ'dɑməţər] *n* : velocímetro *m*
speedup ['spiːd,ʌp] *n* : aceleración *f*
speedy ['spiːdi] *adj* **speedier; -est** : rápido — **speedily** [-dəli] *adv*
spell¹ ['spɛl] *vt* **1** : escribir, deletrear (verbalmente) ⟨how do you spell it? : ¿cómo se escribe?, ¿cómo se deletrea?⟩ **2** MEAN : significar ⟨that could spell trouble : eso puede significar problemas⟩ **3** RELIEVE : relevar **4 to spell out** EXPLAIN : explicar en detalle — *vi* : escribir correctamente, deletrear (verbalmente)
spell² *n* **1** TURN : turno *m* **2** PERIOD, TIME : período *m* (de tiempo) ⟨a dry spell : un período de sequía⟩ ⟨a cold spell : una ola de frío⟩ **3** : condición *f* pasajera ⟨a fainting spell : un desmayo⟩ ⟨a dizzy spell : un mareo⟩ **4** ENCHANTMENT : encanto *m*, hechizo *m*, maleficio *m*
spellbinding ['spɛl,baɪndɪŋ] *adj* : hipnotizador
spellbound ['spɛl,baʊnd] *adj* : embelesado
spell–check¹ ['spɛl,tʃɛk] *vt* : corregir (la ortografía de), pasar el corrector ortográfico a

spell–check² *n* : corrección *f* ortográfica
spellchecker ['spɛl,tʃɛkər] *n* : corrector *m* ortográfico
speller ['spɛlər] *n* : persona *f* que escribe ⟨she's a good speller : tiene buena ortografía⟩
spelling ['spɛlɪŋ] *n* : ortografía *f*
spend ['spɛnd] *vt* **spent** ['spɛnt]; **spending 1** : gastar (dinero, etc.) **2** PASS : pasar (el tiempo) ⟨to spend time on : dedicar tiempo a⟩
spendthrift ['spɛnd,θrɪft] *n* : derrochador *m*, -dora *f*; despilfarrador *m*, -dora *f*
sperm ['spərm] *n, pl* **sperm** *or* **sperms** : esperma *mf*
sperm whale *n* : cachalote *m*
spew ['spjuː] *vi* : salir a chorros — *vt* : vomitar, arrojar (lava, etc.)
sphere ['sfɪr] *n* : esfera *f*
spherical ['sfɪrɪkəl, 'sfɛr-] *adj* : esférico
sphinx ['sfɪŋks] *n* : esfinge *f*
spice¹ ['spaɪs] *vt* **spiced; spicing 1** SEASON : condimentar, sazonar **2** *or* **to spice up** : salpimentar, hacer más interesante
spice² *n* **1** : especia *f* **2** FLAVOR, INTEREST : sabor *m* ⟨the spice of life : la sal de la vida⟩
spick–and–span ['spɪkənd'spæn] *adj* : limpio y ordenado
spiciness ['spaɪsinəs] *n* : picante *m*, lo picante
spicy ['spaɪsi] *adj* **spicier; -est 1** SPICED : condimentado, sazonado **2** HOT : picante **3** RACY : picante
spider ['spaɪdər] *n* : araña *f*
spiderweb ['spaɪdər,wɛb] *n* : telaraña *f*, tela *f* de araña
spiel ['spiːl] *n* : rollo *m*, perorata *f*
spigot ['spɪgət, -kət] *n* : llave *f*; grifo *m*; canilla *f Arg, Uru*
spike¹ ['spaɪk] *vt* **spiked; spiking 1** FASTEN : clavar (con clavos grandes) **2** PIERCE : atravesar **3** : añadir alcohol a ⟨he spiked her drink with rum : le puso ron a la bebida⟩
spike² *n* **1** : clavo *m* grande **2** CLEAT : clavo *m* **3** : remache *m* (en voleibol) **4** PEAK : pico *m*
spill¹ ['spɪl] *vt* **1** SHED : derramar, verter ⟨to spill blood : derrame sangre⟩ **2** DIVULGE : revelar, divulgar — *vi* : derramarse
spill² *n* **1** SPILLING : derrame *m*, vertido *m* ⟨oil spill : derrame de petróleo⟩ **2** FALL : caída *f*
spin¹ ['spɪn] *v* **spun** ['spʌn]; **spinning** *vi* **1** : hilar **2** TURN : girar ⟨the car spun out of control : el auto giró fuera de control⟩ ⟨he spun around to look at me : se dio la vuelta para mirarme⟩ **3** REEL : dar vueltas ⟨my head is spinning : la cabeza me está dando vueltas⟩ — *vt* **1** : hilar (hilo, etc.) **2** : tejer ⟨to spin a web : tejer una telaraña⟩ **3** TWIRL : hacer girar **4** : darle un sesgo positivo a (en política) **5 to spin a yarn/tale** : contar un cuento **6 to spin one's wheels** *fam* STAGNATE : estancarse
spin² *n* : vuelta *f*, giro *m* ⟨to go for a spin : dar una vuelta (en coche)⟩

spinach ['spɪnɪtʃ] *n* : espinacas *fpl*, espinaca *f*

spinal ['spaɪnəl] *adj* : espinal

spinal column *n* BACKBONE : columna *f* vertebral

spinal cord *n* : médula *f* espinal

spindle ['spɪndəl] *n* **1** : huso *m* (para hilar) **2** : eje *m* (de un mecanismo)

spindly ['spɪndli] *adj* : larguirucho *fam*, largo y débil (dícese de una planta)

spin doctor *n* : portavoz *mf*

spine ['spaɪn] *n* **1** BACKBONE : columna *f* vertebral, espina *f* dorsal **2** QUILL : púa *f* (de un animal) **3** THORN : espina *f* **4** : lomo *m* (de un libro)

spineless ['spaɪnləs] *adj* **1** : sin púas, sin espinas **2** INVERTEBRATE : invertebrado **3** WEAK : débil (de carácter)

spinster ['spɪnstər] *n* : soltera *f*

spiny ['spaɪni] *adj* spinier; -est : con púas (dícese de los animales), espinoso (dícese de las plantas)

spiral[1] ['spaɪrəl] *vi* -raled *or* -ralled; -raling *or* -ralling : ir en espiral

spiral[2] *adj* : espiral, en espiral ⟨a spiral staircase : una escalera de caracol⟩

spiral[3] *n* : espiral *f*

spire ['spaɪr] *n* : aguja *f*

spirit[1] ['spɪrət] *vt* **to spirit away** : hacer desaparecer

spirit[2] *n* **1** : espíritu *m* ⟨body and spirit : cuerpo y espíritu⟩ **2** GHOST : espíritu *m*, fantasma *m* **3** MOOD : espíritu *m*, humor *m* ⟨in the spirit of friendship : en el espíritu de amistad⟩ ⟨to be in good spirits : estar de buen humor⟩ **4** ENTHUSIASM, VIVACITY : espíritu *m*, ánimo *m*, brío *m* **5** spirits *npl* : licores *mpl*

spirited ['spɪrətəd] *adj* : animado, enérgico

spiritless ['spɪrətləs] *adj* : desanimado

spiritual[1] ['spɪrɪtʃʊəl, -tʃəl] *adj* : espiritual — **spiritually** *adv*

spiritual[2] *n* : espiritual *m* (canción)

spiritualism ['spɪrɪtʃʊəˌlɪzəm, -tʃə-] *n* : espiritismo *m*

spiritualist ['spɪrɪtʃʊəlɪst, -tʃə-] *n* : médium *mf*, espiritista *mf*

spirituality [ˌspɪrɪtʃʊˈæləti] *n, pl* -ties : espiritualidad *f*

spit[1] ['spɪt] *v* spit *or* spat ['spæt]; spitting : escupir

spit[2] *n* **1** SALIVA : saliva *f* **2** ROTISSERIE : asador *m* **3** POINT : lengua *f* (de tierra)

spite[1] ['spaɪt] *vt* spited; spiting : fastidiar, molestar

spite[2] *n* **1** : despecho *m*, rencor *m* **2 in spite of** : a pesar de (que), pese a (que)

spiteful ['spaɪtfəl] *adj* : malicioso, rencoroso

spitting image *n* **to be the spitting image of** : ser el vivo retrato de

spittle ['spɪtəl] *n* : saliva *f*

splash[1] ['splæʃ] *vt* : salpicar — *vi* **1** : salpicar **2 to splash around** : chapotear

splash[2] *n* **1** SPLASHING : salpicadura *f* **2** SQUIRT : chorrito *m* **3** SPOT : mancha *f*

splatter ['splætər] → **spatter**

splay ['spleɪ] *vt* : extender (hacia afuera)

⟨to splay one's fingers : abrir los dedos⟩ — *vi* : extenderse (hacia afuera)

spleen ['spliːn] *n* **1** : bazo *m* (órgano) **2** ANGER, SPITE : ira *f*, rencor *m*

splendid ['splendəd] *adj* : espléndido — **splendidly** *adv*

splendor ['splendər] *n* : esplendor *m*

splice[1] ['splaɪs] *vt* spliced; splicing : empalmar, unir

splice[2] *n* : empalme *m*, unión *f*

splint ['splɪnt] *n* : tablilla *f*

splinter[1] ['splɪntər] *vt* : astillar — *vi* : astillarse

splinter[2] *n* : astilla *f*

split[1] ['splɪt] *v* split; splitting *vt* **1** CLEAVE : partir, hender ⟨to split wood : partir madera⟩ **2** BURST : romper, rajar ⟨to split open : abrir⟩ **3** DIVIDE, SHARE : dividir, repartir — *vi* **1** : partirse (dícese de la madera, etc.) **2** BURST, CRACK : romperse, rajarse **3** *or* **to split up** : dividirse

split[2] *n* **1** CRACK : rajadura *f* **2** TEAR : rotura *f* **3** DIVISION : división *f*, escisión *f*

splurge[1] ['splərdʒ] *v* splurged; splurging *vt* : derrochar — *vi* : derrochar dinero

splurge[2] *n* : derroche *m*

splutter ['splʌtər] *vi* **1** : balbucear (dícese de una persona) **2** SPUTTER : petardear (dícese de un motor)

spoil[1] ['spɔɪl] *vt* **1** PILLAGE : saquear **2** RUIN : estropear, arruinar **3** PAMPER : consentir, mimar — *vi* : estropearse, echarse a perder

spoil[2] *n* PLUNDER : botín *m*

spoiled ['spɔɪld, 'spɔɪlt] *adj* **1** : estropeado, cortado (dícese de la comida) **2** PAMPERED : consentido

spoilsport ['spɔɪlˌsport] *n* : aguafiestas *mf*

spoke[1] → **speak**

spoke[2] ['spoːk] *n* : rayo *m* (de una rueda)

spoken → **speak**

spokesman ['spoːksmən] *n, pl* -men [-mən] : portavoz *mf*; vocero *m*, -ra *f*

spokesperson ['spoːksˌpərsən] *n* : portavoz *mf*; vocero *m*, -ra *f*

spokeswoman ['spoːksˌwʊmən] *n, pl* -women [-ˌwɪmən] : portavoz *f*, vocera *f*

sponge[1] ['spʌndʒ] *vt* sponged; sponging **1** : limpiar con una esponja **2** BUM, SCROUNGE : gorrear *fam*, sablear *fam* (dinero) — *vi* **to sponge off someone** : vivir a costa de alguien

sponge[2] *n* : esponja *f*

sponge cake *n* : bizcocho *m*

sponger ['spʌndʒər] *n* : gorrero *m*, -ra *f* *fam*; vividor *m*, -dora *f*; sanguijuela *f*; arrimado *m*, -da *f* Mex *fam*

spongy ['spʌndʒi] *adj* spongier; -est : esponjoso

sponsor[1] ['spɑntsər] *vt* : patrocinar, auspiciar, apadrinar (a una persona)

sponsor[2] *n* : patrocinador *m*, -dora *f*; padrino *m*, madrina *f*

sponsorship ['spɑntsərˌʃɪp] *n* : patrocinio *m*

spontaneity [ˌspɑntəˈniːəti, -ˈneɪ-] *n* : espontaneidad *f*

spontaneous [spɑn'teɪnɪəs] *adj* : espontáneo — **spontaneously** *adv*

spoof ['spu:f] *n* : burla *f*, parodia *f*

spook[1] ['spu:k] *vt* : asustar

spook[2] *n* : fantasma *m*, espíritu *m*, espectro *m*

spooky ['spu:ki] *adj* **spookier; -est** : que da miedo, espeluznante

spool ['spu:l] *n* : carrete *m*, bobina *f*

spoon[1] ['spu:n] *vt* : comer, servir, o echar con cuchara

spoon[2] *n* : cuchara *f*

spoonful ['spu:n,fʊl] *n* : cucharada *f* ⟨by the spoonful : a cucharadas⟩

spoor ['spʊr, 'spor] *n* : rastro *m*, pista *f*

sporadic [spə'rædɪk] *adj* : esporádico — **sporadically** [-dɪkli] *adv*

spore ['spor] *n* : espora *f*

sport[1] ['sport] *vi* FROLIC : retozar, juguetear — *vt* SHOW OFF : lucir, ostentar

sport[2] *n* **1** : deporte *m* ⟨outdoor sports : deportes al aire libre⟩ **2** JEST : broma *f* **3 to be a good sport** : tener espíritu deportivo

sporting ['sportɪŋ] *adj* : deportivo ⟨a sporting chance : buenas posibilidades⟩

sports car *n* : carro *m* sport, auto *m* sport, coche *m* deportivo

sports center *n* : centro *m* deportivo

sportsman ['sportsmən] *n*, *pl* **-men** [-mən, -,mɛn] : deportista *m*

sportsmanship ['sportsmən,ʃɪp] *n* : espíritu *m* deportivo, deportividad *f* Spain

sportswear ['sports,wær] *n* : ropa *f* deportiva

sportswoman ['sports,wʊmən] *n*, *pl* **-women** [-,wɪmən] : deportista *f*

sport–utility vehicle *n* → SUV

sporty ['sporti] *adj* **sportier; -est** : deportivo

spot[1] ['spɑt] *v* **spotted; spotting** *vt* **1** STAIN : manchar **2** RECOGNIZE, SEE : ver, reconocer ⟨to spot an error : descubrir un error⟩ — *vi* : mancharse

spot[2] *adj* : hecho al azar ⟨a spot check : un vistazo, un control aleatorio⟩

spot[3] *n* **1** STAIN : mancha *f* **2** DOT : punto *m* **3** PIMPLE : grano *m* ⟨to break out in spots : salirle granos a alguien⟩ **4** PREDICAMENT : apuro *m*, aprieto *m*, lío *m* ⟨in a tight spot : en apuros⟩ **5** PLACE : lugar *m*, sitio *m* ⟨to be on the spot : estar en el lugar⟩

spotless ['spɑtləs] *adj* : impecable, inmaculado — **spotlessly** *adv*

spotlight[1] ['spɑt,laɪt] *vt* **-lighted** *or* **-lit** [-,lɪt]; **-lighting 1** LIGHT : iluminar (con un reflector) **2** HIGHLIGHT : destacar, poner en relieve

spotlight[2] *n* **1** : reflector *m*, foco *m* **2 to be in the spotlight** : ser el centro de atención

spotty ['spɑti] *adj* **spottier; -est** : irregular, desigual

spouse ['spaʊs] *n* : cónyuge *mf*

spout[1] ['spaʊt] *vt* **1** : lanzar chorros de **2** DECLAIM : declamar — *vi* : salir a chorros

spout[2] *n* **1** : pico *m* (de una jarra, etc.) **2** STREAM : chorro *m*

sprain[1] ['spreɪn] *vt* : sufrir un esguince en

sprain[2] *n* : esguince *m*, torcedura *f*

sprawl[1] ['sprɔl] *vi* **1** LIE : tumbarse, echarse, despatarrarse **2** EXTEND : extenderse

sprawl[2] *n* **1** : postura *f* despatarrada **2** SPREAD : extensión *f*, expansión *f*

spray[1] ['spreɪ] *vt* : rociar (una superficie), pulverizar (un líquido)

spray[2] *n* **1** BOUQUET : ramillete *m* **2** MIST : rocío *m* **3** ATOMIZER : atomizador *m*, pulverizador *m*

spray gun *n* : pistola *f*

spread[1] ['sprɛd] *v* **spread; spreading** *vt* **1** *or* **to spread out** : desplegar, extender **2** SCATTER, STREW : esparcir **3** SMEAR : untar (mantequilla, etc.) **4** DISSEMINATE : difundir, sembrar, propagar — *vi* **1** : difundirse, correr, propagarse **2** EXTEND : extenderse

spread[2] *n* **1** EXTENSION : extensión *f*, difusión *f* (de noticias, etc.), propagación *f* (de enfermedades, etc.) **2** : colcha *f* (para una cama), mantel *m* (para una mesa) **3** PASTE : pasta *f* ⟨cheese spread : pasta de queso⟩

spreadsheet ['sprɛd,ʃi:t] *n* : hoja *f* de cálculo

spree ['spri] *n* **1** : acción *f* desenfrenada ⟨to go on a shopping spree : comprar como loco⟩ **2** BINGE : parranda *f*, juerga *f* ⟨on a spree : de parranda, de juerga⟩

sprig ['sprɪg] *n* : ramita *f*, ramito *m*

sprightly ['spraɪtli] *adj* **sprightlier; -est** : vivo, animado ⟨with a sprightly step : con paso ligero⟩

spring[1] ['sprɪŋ] *v* **sprang** ['spræŋ] *or* **sprung** ['sprʌŋ]; **sprung; springing** *vi* **1** LEAP : saltar **2** : mover rápidamente ⟨the lid sprang shut : la tapa se cerró de un golpe⟩ ⟨he sprang to his feet : se paró de un salto⟩ **3 to spring up** : brotar (dícese de las plantas), surgir **4 to spring from** : surgir de — *vt* **1** RELEASE : soltar (de repente) ⟨to spring the news on someone : sorprender a alguien con las noticias⟩ ⟨to spring a trap : hacer saltar una trampa⟩ **2** ACTIVATE : accionar (un mecanismo) **3 to spring a leak** : hacer agua

spring[2] *n* **1** SOURCE : fuente *f*, origen *m* **2** : manantial *m*, fuente *f* ⟨hot spring : fuente termal⟩ **3** : primavera *f* ⟨spring and summer : la primavera y el verano⟩ **4** : resorte *m*, muelle *m* (de metal, etc.) **5** LEAP : salto *m*, brinco *m* **6** RESILIENCE : elasticidad *f*

springboard ['sprɪŋ,bord] *n* : trampolín *m*

spring cleaning *n* : limpieza *f* a fondo

springtime ['sprɪŋ,taɪm] *n* : primavera *f*

springy ['sprɪŋi] *adj* **springier; -est 1** RESILIENT : elástico **2** LIVELY : enérgico

sprinkle[1] ['sprɪŋkəl] *vt* **-kled; -kling** : rociar (con agua), espolvorear (con azúcar, etc.), salpicar

sprinkle[2] *n* : llovizna *f*

sprinkler ['sprɪŋkələr] *n* : rociador *m*, aspersor *m*

sprint[1] ['sprɪnt] *vi* : echar la carrera, esprintar (en deportes)

sprint[2] *n* : esprint *m* (en deportes)

sprinter ['sprɪntər] *n* : esprínter *mf*

sprite ['spraɪt] *n* : hada *f*, elfo *m*

sprocket ['sprɑkət] *n* : diente *m* (de una rueda dentada)

sprout[1] ['spraʊt] *vi* : brotar

sprout[2] *n* : brote *m*, retoño *m*, vástago *m*

spruce[1] ['spru:s] *v* **spruced; sprucing** *vt* : arreglar — *vi or* **to spruce up** : arreglarse, acicalarse

spruce[2] *adj* **sprucer; sprucest** : pulcro, arreglado

spruce[3] *n* : picea *f* (árbol)

spry ['spraɪ] *adj* **sprier** *or* **spryer** ['spraɪər]; **spriest** *or* **spryest** ['spraɪəst] : ágil, activo

spun → **spin**

spunk ['spʌŋk] *n* : valor *m*, coraje *m*, agallas *fpl fam*

spunky ['spʌŋki] *adj* **spunkier; -est** : animoso, corajudo

spur[1] ['spər] *vt* **spurred; spurring** *or* **to spur on** : espolear (un caballo), motivar (a una persona, etc.)

spur[2] *n* **1** : espuela *f*, acicate *m* **2** STIMULUS : acicate *m* **3** : espolón *m* (de un gallo) **4** : ramal *m* (de una línea de ferrocarril)

spurious ['spjʊriəs] *adj* : espurio

spurn ['spərn] *vt* : desdeñar, rechazar

spurt[1] ['spərt] *vt* SQUIRT : lanzar un chorro de — *vi* SPOUT : salir a chorros

spurt[2] *n* **1** : actividad *f* repentina ⟨a spurt of energy : una explosión de energía⟩ ⟨to do in spurts : hacer por rachas⟩ **2** JET : chorro *m* (de agua, etc.)

sputter[1] ['spʌtər] *vi* **1** JABBER : farfullar **2** : petardear (dícese de un motor)

sputter[2] *n* : petardeo *m* (de un motor)

spy[1] ['spaɪ] *v* **spied; spying** *vt* SEE : ver, divisar — *vi* : espiar ⟨to spy on someone : espiar a alguien⟩

spy[2] *n* : espía *mf*

squab ['skwɑb] *n, pl* **squabs** *or* **squab** : pichón *m*

squabble[1] ['skwɑbəl] *vi* **-bled; -bling** : reñir, pelearse, discutir

squabble[2] *n* : riña *f*, pelea *f*, discusión *f*

squad ['skwɑd] *n* : pelotón *m* (militar), brigada *f* (de policías), cuadrilla *f* (de obreros, etc.)

squadron ['skwɑdrən] *n* : escuadrón *m* (de militares), escuadrilla *f* (de aviones), escuadra *f* (de naves)

squalid ['skwɑlɪd] *adj* : miserable

squall ['skwɔl] *n* **1** : aguacero *m* tormentoso, chubasco *m* tormentoso **2 snow squall** : tormenta *f* de nieve

squalor ['skwɑlər] *n* : miseria *f*

squander ['skwɑndər] *vt* : derrochar (dinero, etc.), desaprovechar (una oportunidad, etc.), desperdiciar (talentos, energías, etc.)

square[1] ['skwær] *vt* **squared; squaring 1** : cuadrar **2** : elevar al cuadrado (en matemáticas) **3** CONFORM : conciliar (con), ajustar (con) **4** SETTLE : saldar (una cuenta) ⟨I squared it with him : lo arreglé con él⟩

square[2] *adj* **squarer; -est 1** : cuadrado ⟨a square house : una casa cuadrada⟩ **2** : a escuadra, en ángulo recto (en carpintería, etc.) **3** : cuadrado (en matemáticas) ⟨a square mile : una milla cuadrada⟩ **4** HONEST : justo ⟨a square deal : un buen acuerdo⟩ ⟨fair and square : en buena lid⟩

square[3] *n* **1** : escuadra *f* (instrumento) **2** : cuadrado *m*, cuadro *m* ⟨to fold into squares : plegar en cuadrados⟩ **3** : plaza *f* (de una ciudad) **4** : cuadrado *m* (en matemáticas)

squarely ['skwærli] *adv* **1** EXACTLY : exactamente, directamente, justo **2** HONESTLY : honradamente, justamente

square root *n* : raíz *f* cuadrada

squash[1] ['skwɑʃ, 'skwɔʃ] *vt* **1** CRUSH : aplastar **2** SUPPRESS : acallar (protestas), sofocar (una rebelión)

squash[2] *n* **1** *pl* **squashes** *or* **squash** : calabaza *f* (vegetal) **2** *or* **squash racquets** : squash *m* (deporte)

squat[1] ['skwɑt] *vi* **squatted; squatting 1** CROUCH : agacharse, ponerse en cuclillas **2** : ocupar un lugar sin derecho

squat[2] *adj* **squatter; squattest** : bajo y ancho, rechoncho *fam* (dícese de una persona)

squat[3] *n* **1** : posición *f* en cuclillas, flexión *f* (en deportes) **2** : ocupación *f* ilegal (de un lugar)

squatter ['skwɑtər] *n* : okupa *mf*

squawk[1] ['skwɔk] *vi* : graznar (dícese de las aves), chillar

squawk[2] *n* : graznido *m* (de un ave), chillido *m*

squeak[1] ['skwi:k] *vi* : chillar (dícese de un animal), chirriar (dícese de un objeto)

squeak[2] *n* : chillido *m*, chirrido *m*

squeaky ['skwi:ki] *adj* **squeakier; -est** : chirriante ⟨a squeaky voice : una voz chillona⟩

squeal[1] ['skwi:l] *vi* **1** : chillar (dícese de las personas o los animales), chirriar (dícese de los frenos, etc.) **2** PROTEST : quejarse **3** *fam* SNITCH : cantar (a la policía, etc.) ⟨to squeal on someone : acusar/delatar a alguien⟩

squeal[2] *n* **1** : chillido *m* (de una persona o un animal) **2** SCREECH : chirrido *m* (de frenos, etc.)

squeamish ['skwi:mɪʃ] *adj* : impresionable, sensible ⟨he's squeamish about cockroaches : las cucarachas le dan asco⟩

squeeze[1] ['skwi:z] *vt* **squeezed; squeezing 1** PRESS : apretar, exprimir (naranjas, etc.) **2** EXTRACT : extraer (jugo, etc.) **3** : meter

squeeze[2] *n* : apretón *m*

squelch ['skwɛltʃ] *vt* : aplastar (una rebelión, etc.)

squid ['skwɪd] *n, pl* **squid** *or* **squids** : calamar *m*

squint[1] ['skwɪnt] *vi* : mirar con los ojos entornados

squint[2] *adj or* **squint–eyed** ['skwɪnt̩aɪd] : bizco

squint[3] *n* : estrabismo *m*
squire ['skwaɪr] *n* : hacendado *m*, -da *f*; terrateniente *mf*
squirm ['skwərm] *vi* : retorcerse
squirrel ['skwərəl] *n* : ardilla *f*
squirt[1] ['skwərt] *vt* : lanzar un chorro de — *vi* SPURT : salir a chorros
squirt[2] *n* : chorrito *m*
stab[1] [stæb] *vt* **stabbed; stabbing 1** KNIFE : acuchillar, apuñalar **2** STICK : clavar (con una aguja, etc.), golpear (con el dedo, etc.)
stab[2] *n* **1** : puñalada *f*, cuchillada *f* **2** JAB : pinchazo *m* (con una aguja, etc.), golpe *m* (con un dedo, etc.) **3 to take a stab at** : intentar
stability [stə'bɪləṭi] *n, pl* **-ties** : estabilidad *f*
stabilize ['steɪbə,laɪz] *v* **-lized; -lizing** *vt* : estabilizar — *vi* : estabilizarse — **stabilization** *n* — **stabilizer** *n*
stable[1] ['steɪbəl] *vt* **-bled; -bling** : poner (ganado) en un establo, poner (caballos) en una caballeriza
stable[2] *adj* **stabler; -blest 1** FIXED, STEADY : fijo, sólido, estable **2** LASTING : estable, perdurable ⟨a stable government : un gobierno estable⟩ **3** : estacionario (en medicina), equilibrado (en psicología)
stable[3] *n* : establo *m* (para ganado), caballeriza *f* o cuadra *f* (para caballos)
staccato [stə'kɑṭo:] *adj* : staccato
stack[1] ['stæk] *vt* **1** PILE : amontonar, apilar **2** COVER : cubrir, llenar ⟨he stacked the table with books : cubrió la mesa de libros⟩
stack[2] *n* **1** PILE : montón *m*, pila *f* **2** SMOKESTACK : chimenea *f*
stadium ['steɪdiəm] *n, pl* **-dia** [-diə] *or* **-diums** : estadio *m*
staff[1] ['stæf] *vt* : proveer de personal
staff[2] *n, pl* **staffs** ['stæfs, 'stævz] *or* **staves** ['stævz, 'steɪvz] **1** : bastón *m* (de mando), báculo *m* (de obispo) **2** *pl* **staffs** PERSONNEL : personal *m* **3** *or* **stave** : pentagrama *m* (en música)
stag[1] ['stæg] *adv* : solo, sin pareja ⟨to go stag : ir solo⟩
stag[2] *adj* : sólo para hombres
stag[3] *n, pl* **stags** *or* **stag** : ciervo *m*, venado *m*
stage[1] ['steɪʤ] *vt* **staged; staging** : poner en escena (una obra de teatro)
stage[2] *n* **1** PLATFORM : estrado *m*, tablado *m*, escenario *m* (de un teatro) **2** PHASE, STEP : fase *f*, etapa *f* ⟨stage of development : fase de desarrollo⟩ ⟨in stages : por etapas⟩ **3 the stage** : el teatro *m*
stagecoach ['steɪʤ,ko:tʃ] *n* : diligencia *f*
stage fright *n* : miedo *m* escénico, pánico *m* escénico
stage set → **set**[3]
stagger[1] ['stægər] *vi* TOTTER : tambalearse — *vt* **1** ALTERNATE : alternar, escalonar (turnos de trabajo) **2** : hacer tambalear ⟨to be staggered by : quedarse estupefacto por⟩
stagger[2] *n* : tambaleo *m*

staggering ['stægərɪŋ] *adj* : asombroso
stagnant ['stægnənt] *adj* : estancado
stagnate ['stæg,neɪt] *vi* **-nated; -nating** : estancarse
stagnation [stæg'neɪʃən] *n* : estancamiento *m*
staid ['steɪd] *adj* : serio, sobrio
stain[1] ['steɪn] *vt* **1** DISCOLOR : manchar **2** DYE : teñir (madera, etc.) **3** SULLY : manchar, empañar
stain[2] *n* **1** SPOT : mancha *f* **2** DYE : tinte *m*, tintura *f* **3** BLEMISH : mancha *f*, mácula *f*
stained glass *n* : vidrio *m* de color ⟨stained-glass window : vidriera, vitral⟩
stainless ['steɪnləs] *adj* : sin mancha ⟨stainless steel : acero inoxidable⟩
stair ['stær] *n* **1** STEP : escalón *m*, peldaño *m* **2 stairs** *npl* : escalera *f*, escaleras *fpl*
staircase ['stær,keɪs] *n* : escalera *f*, escaleras *fpl*
stairway ['stær,weɪ] *n* : escalera *f*, escaleras *fpl*
stairwell ['stær,wɛl] *n* : caja *f*, hueco *m* (de la escalera)
stake[1] ['steɪk] *vt* **staked; staking 1** : estacar, marcar con estacas (una propiedad) **2** BET : jugarse, apostar **3 to stake a claim to** : reclamar, reivindicar
stake[2] *n* **1** POST : estaca *f* **2** BET : apuesta *f* ⟨to be at stake : estar en juego⟩ **3** INTEREST, SHARE : interés *m*, participación *f*
stalactite [stə'læk,taɪt] *n* : estalactita *f*
stalagmite [stə'læg,maɪt] *n* : estalagmita *f*
stale ['steɪl] *adj* **staler; stalest** : viejo ⟨stale bread : pan duro⟩ ⟨stale news : viejas noticias⟩
stalemate ['steɪl,meɪt] *n* : punto *m* muerto, impasse *m*
stalk[1] ['stɔk] *vt* : acechar — *vi* : caminar rígidamente (por orgullo, ira, etc.)
stalk[2] *n* : tallo *m* (de una planta)
stall[1] ['stɔl] *vt* **1** : parar (un motor) **2** DELAY : entretener (a una persona), demorar — *vi* **1** : pararse (dícese de un motor) **2** DELAY : demorar, andar con rodeos ⟨to stall for time : tratar de ganar tiempo⟩
stall[2] *n* **1** : compartimiento *m* (de un establo) **2** : puesto *m* (en un mercado, etc.)
stallion ['stæljən] *n* : caballo *m* semental
stalwart ['stɔlwərt] *adj* **1** STRONG : fuerte ⟨a stalwart supporter : un firme partidario⟩ **2** BRAVE : valiente, valeroso
stamen ['steɪmən] *n* : estambre *m*
stamina ['stæmənə] *n* : resistencia *f*
stammer[1] ['stæmər] *vi* : tartamudear, titubear
stammer[2] *n* : tartamudeo *m*, titubeo *m*
stamp[1] ['stæmp] *vt* **1** : pisotear (con los pies) ⟨to stamp one's feet : patear, dar una patada⟩ **2** IMPRESS, IMPRINT : sellar (una factura, etc.), acuñar (monedas) **3** : franquear, ponerle estampillas a (correo) **4 to stamp out** : aplastar, sofocar, erradicar
stamp[2] *n* **1** : sello *m* (para documentos, etc.) **2** DIE : cuño *m* (para monedas) **3**

or **postage stamp** : sello *m*, estampilla *f*, timbre *m CA, Mex*

stampede¹ [stæmˈpiːd] *vi* **-peded; -peding** : salir en estampida

stampede² *n* : estampida *f*

stance [ˈstænts] *n* : postura *f*

stanch [ˈstɔntʃ, ˈstɑntʃ] *vt* : detener, estancar (un líquido)

stand¹ [ˈstænd] *v* **stood** [ˈstʊd]; **standing** *vi* **1** : estar de pie, estar parado ⟨I was standing on the corner : estaba parada en la esquina⟩ ⟨to stand still : estarse quieto⟩ ⟨to stand in line : hacer cola⟩ ⟨to stand around waiting/watching : quedarse esperando/mirando (sin hacer nada)⟩ **2** MOVE : ponerse, pararse ⟨stand beside me : ponte a mi lado⟩ ⟨stand aside/back! : ¡apártate!⟩ **3** *or* to **stand up** : levantarse, pararse, ponerse de pie ⟨she stood up and left : se paró y se fue⟩ ⟨to stand up straight : ponerse derecho⟩ **4** (*indicating a specified position or location*) ⟨they stand third in the country : ocupan el tercer lugar en el país⟩ **5** (*referring to an opinion*) ⟨how does he stand on the matter? : ¿cuál es su postura respecto al asunto?⟩ **6** BE : estar ⟨the house stands on a hill : la casa está en una colina⟩ ⟨I won't stand in your way : no te lo voy a impedir⟩ **7** REMAIN : estar ⟨the machines are standing idle : las máquinas están paradas⟩ ⟨as things stand : tal (y) como están las cosas⟩ **8** CONTINUE : seguir ⟨the order still stands : el mandato sigue vigente⟩ **9** MEASURE : medir ⟨he stands six feet two (inches tall) : mide seis pies y dos pulgadas⟩ **10 to stand by** : estar listo, estar disponible **11 to stand by** SUPPORT : apoyar **12 to stand by** HONOR : cumplir con (una promesa, etc.) **13 to stand down** : bajar las armas (dícese de un soldado), retirarse (dícese de un ejército) **14 to stand firm** : mantenerse firme **15 to stand for** SIGNIFY, REPRESENT : significar, representar **16 to stand for** ALLOW : permitir **17 to stand guard** : hacer la guardia **18 to stand in (for)** : sustituir (a) **19 to stand on end** : ponerse de punta, pararse (dícese de los pelos) **20 to stand out** : resaltar **21 to stand out** EXCEL : destacarse **22 to stand up for** DEFEND : defender **23 to stand up to** WITHSTAND : resistir **24 to stand up to** CONFRONT : hacerle frente a — *vt* **1** PLACE, SET : poner, colocar ⟨he stood them in a row : los colocó en hilera⟩ **2** TOLERATE : aguantar, soportar ⟨he can't stand her : no la puede tragar⟩ **3** WITHSTAND : resistir **4** USE : beneficiarse de ⟨you could stand a nap : una siesta te vendría bien⟩ **5 to stand someone up** : dejar plantado a alguien

stand² *n* **1** RESISTANCE : resistencia *f* ⟨to make a stand against : resistir a⟩ **2** BOOTH, STALL : stand *m*, puesto *m*, quiosco *m* (para vender periódicos, etc.) **3** BASE : pie *m*, base *f* **4** : grupo *m* (de árboles, etc.) **5** POSITION : posición *f*, postura *f* **6 stands** *npl* GRANDSTAND : tribuna *f*

standard¹ [ˈstændərd] *adj* **1** ESTABLISHED : estándar, oficial ⟨standard measures : medidas oficiales⟩ ⟨standard English : el inglés estándar⟩ **2** NORMAL : normal, estándar, común **3** CLASSIC : estándar, clásico ⟨a standard work : una obra clásica⟩

standard² *n* **1** BANNER : estandarte *m* **2** CRITERION : criterio *m* **3** RULE : estándar *m*, norma *f*, regla *f* **4** LEVEL : nivel *m* ⟨standard of living : nivel de vida⟩ **5** SUPPORT : poste *m*, soporte *m*

standard-bearer [ˈstændərdˌbærər] *n* : abanderado *m*, -da *f*

standardization [ˌstændərdəˈzeɪlən] *n* : estandarización *f*

standardize [ˈstændərˌdaɪz] *vt* **-ized; -izing** : estandarizar

standard time *n* : hora *f* oficial

standby [ˈstændˌbaɪ] *n* **1** BACKUP ⟨we bought another as a standby : compramos otro de reserva/emergencia⟩ **2 to be on standby** : estar a la espera de órdenes, etc. ⟨the passengers who are on standby : los pasajeros que están en la lista de espera⟩

stand by *vt* : atenerse a, cumplir con (una promesa, etc.) — *vi* **1** : mantenerse aparte ⟨to stand by and do nothing : mirar sin hacer nada⟩ **2** : estar preparado, estar listo (para un anuncio, un ataque, etc.)

stand for *vt* **1** REPRESENT : significar **2** PERMIT, TOLERATE : permitir, tolerar

stand-in [ˈstændˌɪn] *n* : doble *m*, sustituto *m*, -ta *f*

standing¹ [ˈstændɪŋ] *adj* **1** : de pie, parado ⟨in a standing position : en posición parada, (en posición) de pie⟩ **2** STAGNANT : estancado **3** ACTIVE : en pie (dícese de una oferta, etc.), fijo (dícese de un pedido) **4** PERMANENT : permanente

standing² *n* **1** POSITION, RANK : posición *f* **2** DURATION : duración *f*

stand out *vi* **1** : destacar(se) ⟨she stands out from the rest : se destaca entre los otros⟩ **2 to stand out against** RESIST : oponerse a

standpoint [ˈstændˌpɔɪnt] *n* : punto *m* de vista

standstill [ˈstændˌstɪl] *n* **1** STOP : detención *f*, paro *m* ⟨to come to a standstill : pararse⟩ **2** DEADLOCK : punto *m* muerto, impasse *m*

stand up *vt* : dejar plantado ⟨he stood me up again : otra vez me dejó plantado⟩ — *vi* **1** ENDURE : durar, resistir **2 to stand up for** : defender **3 to stand up to** : hacerle frente (a alguien)

stank → stink

stanza [ˈstænzə] *n* : estrofa *f*

staple¹ [ˈsteɪpəl] *vt* **-pled; -pling** : engrapar, grapar

staple² *adj* : principal, básico ⟨a staple food : un alimento básico⟩

staple³ *n* **1** : producto *m* principal, producto *m* de primera necesidad **2** : grapa *f*, broche *m Arg* (para engrapar papeles)

stapler [ˈsteɪplər] *n* : engrapadora *f*, grapadora *f*

star¹ ['stɑr] *v* **starred; starring** *vt* **1** : marcar con una estrella o un asterisco **2** FEATURE : estar protagonizado por — *vi* : tener el papel principal ⟨to star in : protagonizar⟩

star² *n* **1** : estrella *f* (en astronomía) **2** : estrella *f* (medalla, etc.), asterisco *m* (símbolo) **3** CELEBRITY : estrella *f* ⟨rock/movie star : estrella de rock/cine⟩ ⟨the star of the movie : el protagonista de la película⟩ ⟨our star player : la estrella de nuestro equipo⟩

starboard ['stɑrbərd] *n* : estribor *m*

starch¹ ['stɑrtʃ] *vt* : almidonar

starch² *n* : almidón *m*, fécula *f* (comida)

starchy ['stɑrtʃi] *adj* **starchier; -est** : lleno de almidón

stardom ['stɑrdəm] *n* : estrellato *m*

stare¹ ['stær] *vi* **stared; staring** : mirar fijamente

stare² *n* : mirada *f* fija

starfish ['stɑrˌfɪʃ] *n* : estrella *f* de mar

stark¹ ['stɑrk] *adv* : completamente ⟨stark raving mad : loco de remate⟩ ⟨stark naked : completamente desnudo⟩

stark² *adj* **1** ABSOLUTE : absoluto **2** BARREN, DESOLATE : desolado, desierto **3** BARE : desnudo **4** HARSH : severo, duro

starlight ['stɑrˌlaɪt] *n* : luz *f* de las estrellas

starling ['stɑrlɪŋ] *n* : estornino *m*

starry ['stɑri] *adj* **starrier; -est** : estrellado

start¹ ['stɑrt] *vi* **1** JUMP : sobresaltarse, dar un respingo **2** BEGIN : empezar, comenzar ⟨let's get started : empecemos⟩ ⟨she started (off/out) by thanking us : empezó por agradecernos⟩ ⟨he started (off/out) as a receptionist : empezó como recepcionista⟩ ⟨young couples who are just starting off/out : parejas jóvenes que acaban de casarse⟩ **3** *or* **to start off/out** SET OUT : salir (de viaje, etc.) **4** *or* **to start up** : arrancar (dícese de un motor, etc.) **5** **to start from scratch** : empezar desde cero **6** **to start in** : empezar ⟨after a break he started in again : tras un descanso empezó otra vez⟩ **7** **to start over** : volver a empezar, empezar de nuevo — *vt* **1** BEGIN : empezar, comenzar, iniciar ⟨I started cleaning, I started to clean : empecé a limpiar⟩ ⟨she started (off/out) her speech with a joke : empezó su discurso con una broma⟩ **2** CAUSE : empezar (una discusión, etc.), provocar (un incendio, etc.), causar **3** SET : hacer, poner ⟨her questions started me thinking : sus preguntas me hicieron pensar⟩ ⟨I started them working : los puse a trabajar⟩ ⟨he started us (off) with some questions : para empezar nos hizo unas preguntas⟩ **4** ESTABLISH : fundar, montar, establecer ⟨to start (up) a business : montar un negocio⟩ **5** : arrancar, poner en marcha, encender ⟨to start (up) the car : arrancar el auto/carro/coche⟩ **6** **to start a family** : tener hijos **7** **to start over** : volver a empezar, empezar de nuevo

start² *n* **1** JUMP : sobresalto *m*, respingo *m* **2** BEGINNING : principio *m*, comienzo *m* ⟨to get an early start : salir temprano⟩

starter ['stɑrtər] *n* **1** : participante *mf* (en una carrera, etc.); jugador *m* titular, jugadora *f* titular (en beisbol, etc.) **2** APPETIZER : entremés *m*, aperitivo *m* **3** *or* **starter motor** : motor *m* de arranque

starting point *n* : punto *m* de partida

startle ['stɑrtəl] *vt* **-tled; -tling** : asustar, sobresaltar

start–up ['stɑrtˈʌp] *adj* : de puesta en marcha

starvation [stɑrˈveɪʃən] *n* : inanición *f*, hambre *f*

starve ['stɑrv] *v* **starved; starving** *vi* **1** : morirse de hambre ⟨starving children : niños hambrientos/famélicos⟩ **2** **to be starved/starving** *fam* ⟨I'm starved/starving! : ¡me muero de hambre!⟩ **3** **to be starved/starving for** *or* **to be starved of** : estar hambriento/sediento de (atención, cariño, etc.) — *vt* : privar de comida

stash ['stæʃ] *vt* : esconder, guardar (en un lugar secreto)

stat ['stæt] → **statistic**

state¹ ['steɪt] *vt* **stated; stating** **1** REPORT : puntualizar, exponer (los hechos, etc.) ⟨state your name : diga su nombre⟩ **2** ESTABLISH, FIX : establecer, fijar

state² *n* **1** CONDITION : estado *m*, condición *f* ⟨a liquid state : un estado líquido⟩ ⟨state of mind : estado de ánimo⟩ ⟨in a bad state : en malas condiciones⟩ **2** NATION : estado *m*, nación *f* **3** : estado *m* (dentro de un país) ⟨the States : los Estados Unidos⟩

stateliness ['steɪtlinəs] *n* : majestuosidad *f*

stately ['steɪtli] *adj* **statelier; -est** : majestuoso

statement ['steɪtmənt] *n* **1** DECLARATION : declaración *f*, afirmación *f* **2** *or* **bank statement** : estado *m* de cuenta

stateroom ['steɪtˌruːm, -ˌrʊm] *n* : camarote *m*

statesman ['steɪtsmən] *n*, *pl* **-men** [-mən, -ˌmɛn] : estadista *mf*

static¹ ['stætɪk] *adj* : estático

static² *n* : estática *f*, interferencia *f*

station¹ ['steɪʃən] *vt* : apostar, estacionar

station² *n* **1** : estación *f* (de trenes, etc.) **2** RANK, STANDING : condición *f* (social) **3** : canal *m* (de televisión), estación *f* o emisora *f* (de radio) **4** → **police station** **5** → **fire station**

stationary ['steɪʃəˌnɛri] *adj* **1** IMMOBILE : estacionario, inmovible **2** UNCHANGING : inmutable, inalterable

stationery ['steɪʃəˌnɛri] *n* : papel y sobres (para correspondencia) ⟨stationery store : papelería⟩

station wagon *n* : camioneta *f* ranchera, camioneta *f* guayín *Mex*

statistic [stəˈtɪstɪk] *n* : estadística *f* ⟨according to statistics : según las estadísticas⟩

statistical [stəˈtɪstɪkəl] *adj* : estadístico

statistician [ˌstætəˈstɪʃən] *n* : estadístico *m*, -ca *f*

statue ['stæˌtʃuː] *n* : estatua *f*

statuesque [ˌstætʊ'ɛsk] *adj* : escultural
statuette [ˌstætʊ'ɛt] *n* : estatuilla *f*
stature ['stætʃər] *n* **1** HEIGHT : estatura *f*, talla *f* **2** PRESTIGE : talla *f*, prestigio *m*
status ['steɪtəs, 'stæ-] *n* : condición *f*, situación *f*, estatus *m* (social) ⟨marital status : estado civil⟩
status quo [-'kwo:] *n* : statu quo *m*
status symbol *n* : símbolo *m* de estatus
statute ['stæˌtʃuːt] *n* : ley *f*, estatuto *m*
statutory ['stæˌtʃəˌtori] *adj* : estatutario
staunch ['stɔntʃ] *adj* : acérrimo, incondicional, leal ⟨a staunch supporter : un partidario incondicional⟩ — **staunchly** *adv*
stave ['steɪv] *vt* **staved** *or* **stove** ['sto:v]; **staving** **1 to stave in** : romper **2 to stave off** : evitar (un ataque), prevenir (un problema)
staves → staff
stay¹ ['steɪ] *vi* **1** REMAIN : quedarse, permanecer ⟨she stayed after class : se quedó después de clase⟩ ⟨stay out of my room! : ¡no entres a/en mi cuarto!⟩ ⟨stay off the grass : no pisar el césped⟩ ⟨he stayed in the city : permaneció en la ciudad⟩ **2** CONTINUE : seguir, quedarse ⟨it stayed cloudy : seguía nublado⟩ ⟨to stay awake : mantenerse despierto⟩ ⟨stay in touch! : ¡mantente en contacto!⟩ ⟨they stayed friends : siguieron siendo amigos⟩ **3** LODGE : hospedarse, alojarse (en un hotel, etc.) **4 to stay away from** : no acercarse a (una persona, un lugar) ⟨I stay away from coffee : no puedo tomar café⟩ **5 to stay in** : quedarse en casa **6 to stay off** AVOID : evitar (un tema, etc.) ⟨to stay off drugs : no volver a tomar drogas⟩ **7 to stay on** : permanecer, quedarse (en un trabajo, etc.) **8 to stay out** : quedarse fuera **9 to stay out of** : no meterse en (problemas, una discusión, etc.) **10 to stay over** : quedarse a dormir **11 to stay up (late)** : quedarse levantado (hasta tarde) — *vt* **1** HALT : detener, suspender (una ejecución, etc.) **2 to stay the course** : aguantar hasta el final
stay² *n* **1** SOJOURN : estadía *f*, estancia *f*, permanencia *f* **2** SUSPENSION : suspensión *f* (de una sentencia) **3** SUPPORT : soporte *m*
stead ['stɛd] *n* **1** : lugar *m* ⟨she went in his stead : fue en su lugar⟩ **2 to stand (someone) in good stead** : ser muy útil a, servir de mucho a
steadfast ['stɛdˌfæst] *adj* : firme, resuelto ⟨a steadfast friend : un fiel amigo⟩ ⟨a steadfast refusal : una negativa categórica⟩
steadily ['stɛdəli] *adv* **1** CONSTANTLY : continuamente, sin parar **2** FIRMLY : con firmeza **3** FIXEDLY : fijamente
steady¹ ['stɛdi] *v* **steadied; steadying** *vt* : sujetar ⟨she steadied herself : recobró el equilibrio⟩ — *vi* : estabilizarse
steady² *adj* **steadier; -est** **1** FIRM, SURE : seguro, firme ⟨to have a steady hand : tener buen pulso⟩ **2** FIXED, REGULAR : fijo ⟨a steady income : ingresos fi-

jos⟩ **3** CALM : tranquilo, ecuánime ⟨she has steady nerves : es imperturbable⟩ **4** DEPENDABLE : responsable, fiable **5** CONSTANT : constante
steak ['steɪk] *n* : bistec *m*; filete *m*; churrasco *m*; bife *m Arg, Chile, Uru*
steal ['stiːl] *v* **stole** ['sto:l]; **stolen** ['sto:lən]; **stealing** *vt* : robar, hurtar — *vi* **1** : robar, hurtar **2** : ir sigilosamente ⟨to steal away : escabullirse⟩
stealth ['stɛlθ] *n* : sigilo *m*
stealthily ['stɛlθəli] *adv* : furtivamente
stealthy ['stɛlθi] *adj* **stealthier; -est** : furtivo, sigiloso
steam¹ ['stiːm] *vi* **1** : echar vapor ⟨to steam away/along (etc.) : moverse echando vapor⟩ **2 to steam up** : empañarse — *vt* **1** : cocer al vapor (en cocina) **2 to steam open** : abrir con vapor **3 to steam up** : empañar
steam² *n* **1** : vapor *m* **2 to let off steam** : desahogarse
steamboat ['stiːmˌbo:t] → steamship
steamed *adj* **1** : cocido al vapor **2** IRATE : furioso
steam engine *n* : motor *m* de vapor
steamer ['stiːmər] *n* **1** → steamship **2** : vaporera, olla vaporera (en cocina) **3** : almeja *f* de Nueva Inglaterra
steaming *adj* **1** *or* **steaming hot** : muy caliente **2** *or* **steaming mad** : furioso
steamroller ['stiːmˌro:lər] *n* : apisonadora *f*
steamship ['stiːmˌʃɪp] *n* : vapor *m*, barco *m* de vapor
steamy ['stiːmi] *adj* **steamier; -est** **1** : lleno de vapor **2** EROTIC : erótico ⟨a steamy romance : un tórrido romance⟩
steed ['stiːd] *n* : corcel *m*
steel¹ ['stiːl] *vt* **to steel oneself** : armarse de valor
steel² *adj* : de acero
steel³ *n* : acero *m*
steely ['stiːli] *adj* **steelier; -est** : como acero ⟨a steely gaze : una mirada fría⟩ ⟨steely determination : determinación férrea⟩
steep¹ ['stiːp] *vt* : remojar, dejar (té, etc.) en infusión
steep² *adj* **1** : empinado, escarpado ⟨a steep cliff : un precipicio escarpado⟩ **2** CONSIDERABLE : considerable, marcado **3** EXCESSIVE : excesivo ⟨steep prices : precios muy altos⟩
steeple ['stiːpəl] *n* : aguja *f*, campanario *m*
steeplechase ['stiːpəlˌtʃeɪs] *n* : carrera *f* de obstáculos
steeply ['stiːpli] *adv* : abruptamente
steer¹ ['stɪr] *vt* **1** : manejar, conducir (un automóvil), gobernar (un barco) **2** GUIDE : dirigir, guiar — *vi* **to steer clear of** : evitar (algo, a alguien)
steer² *n* : buey *m*
steering ['stɪrɪŋ] *n* : dirección *f*
steering wheel → wheel
stein ['staɪn] *n* : jarra *f* (para cerveza)
stellar ['stɛlər] *adj* : estelar
stem¹ ['stɛm] *v* **stemmed; stemming** *vt* : detener, contener, parar ⟨to stem the

tide : detener el curso⟩ — *vi* **to stem from** : provenir de, ser el resultado de
stem² *n* : tallo *m* (de una planta)
stem cell *n* : célula *f* madre
stench [ˈstɛntʃ] *n* : hedor *m*, mal olor *m*
stencil¹ [ˈstɛntsəl] *vt* **-ciled** *or* **-cilled; -ciling** *or* **-cilling** : marcar utilizando una plantilla
stencil² *n* : plantilla *f* (para marcar)
stenographer [stəˈnɑɡrəfər] *n* : taquígrafo *m*, -fa *f*
stenographic [ˌstɛnəˈɡræfɪk] *adj* : taquigráfico
stenography [stəˈnɑɡrəfi] *n* : taquigrafía *f*
step¹ [ˈstɛp] *v* **stepped; stepping** *vi* **1** : dar un paso ⟨step this way, please : pase por aquí, por favor⟩ ⟨step aside : apártate⟩ ⟨to step forward/back : dar un paso (hacia) adelante/atrás⟩ ⟨he stepped outside : salió⟩ ⟨step right up! : ¡acérquense!⟩ **2 to step back** : distanciarse **3 to step down** RESIGN : renunciar **4 to step in** INTERVENE : intervenir **5 to step on** : pisar **6 to step out** *fam* : salir **7 to step up** INCREASE : aumentar **8 to step up** *fam* : mejorarse, esforzarse más — *vt* **1 to step up** INCREASE : aumentar **2 to step up** *fam* IMPROVE : mejorar
step² *n* **1** : paso *m* ⟨to take a step : dar un paso⟩ **2** : paso *m* (distancia) ⟨a few steps away : a unos pasos⟩ **3** : paso *m* (sonido) **4** FOOTPRINT : huella *f* **5** STAIR : escalón *m*, peldaño *m* **6** RUNG : escalón *m*, travesaño *m* **7** RANK, DEGREE : peldaño *m*, escalón *m* ⟨a step up : un ascenso⟩ **8** MEASURE, MOVE : medida *f*, paso *m* ⟨to take steps : tomar medidas⟩ **9** STAGE : paso *m* ⟨step by step : paso a paso⟩ **10** STRIDE : paso *m* ⟨with a quick step : con paso rápido⟩ **11 to be a/one step ahead of** : llevarle ventaja a **12 to be in step** : llevar el paso **13 to watch one's step** : mirar uno donde camina **14 to watch one's step** BEWARE : andarse con cuidado
stepbrother [ˈstɛpˌbrʌðər] *n* : hermanastro *m*
stepchild [ˈstɛpˌtʃaɪld] *n* : hijastro *m*, -tra *f*; entenado *m*, -da *f Mex*
stepdaughter [ˈstɛpˌdɔtər] *n* : hijastra *f*
stepfather [ˈstɛpˌfɑðər, -ˌfɑ-] *n* : padrastro *m*
stepladder [ˈstɛpˌlædər] *n* : escalera *f* de tijera
stepmother [ˈstɛpˌmʌðər] *n* : madrastra *f*
steppe [ˈstɛp] *n* : estepa *f*
stepping-stone [ˈstɛpɪŋˌstoːn] *n* : **1** : piedra *f* (para cruzar un arroyo, etc.) **2** : trampolín *m* (al éxito)
stepsister [ˈstɛpˌsɪstər] *n* : hermanastra *f*
stepson [ˈstɛpˌsʌn] *n* : hijastro *m*
step up *vt* INCREASE : aumentar
stereo¹ [ˈstɛriˌoː, ˈstɪr-] *adj* : estéreo
stereo² *n, pl* **stereos** : estéreo *m*
stereophonic [ˌstɛrioˈfɑnɪk, ˌstɪr-] *adj* : estereofónico
stereotype¹ [ˈstɛrioˌtaɪp, ˈstɪr-] *vt* **-typed; -typing** : estereotipar
stereotype² *n* : estereotipo *m*

sterile [ˈstɛrəl] *adj* : estéril
sterility [stəˈrɪləti] *n* : esterilidad *f*
sterilization [ˌstɛrələˈzeɪlən] *n* : esterilización *f*
sterilize [ˈstɛrəˌlaɪz] *vt* **-ized; -izing** : esterilizar
sterling [ˈstərlɪŋ] *adj* **1** : de ley ⟨sterling silver : plata de ley⟩ **2** EXCELLENT : excelente
stern¹ [ˈstərn] *adj* : severo, adusto — **sternly** *adv*
stern² *n* : popa *f*
sternness [ˈstərnnəs] *n* : severidad *f*
sternum [ˈstərnəm] *n, pl* **sternums** *or* **sterna** [-nə] : esternón *m*
steroid [ˈstɪrˌɔɪd, ˈstɛr-] *n, pl* **steroids** : esteroide *m*
stethoscope [ˈstɛθəˌskoːp] *n* : estetoscopio *m*
stevedore [ˈstiːvəˌdor] *n* : estibador *m*, -dora *f*
stew¹ [ˈstuː, ˈstjuː] *vt* : estofar, guisar — *vi* **1** : cocer (dícese de la carne, etc.) **2** FRET : preocuparse
stew² *n* **1** : estofado *m*, guiso *m* **2 to be in a stew** : estar agitado
steward [ˈstuːərd, ˈstjuː-] *n* **1** MANAGER : administrador *m* **2** : auxiliar *m* de vuelo (en un avión), camarero *m* (en un barco)
stewardess [ˈstuːərdəs, ˈstjuː-] *n* **1** MANAGER : administradora *f* **2** : camarera *f* (en un barco) **3** : auxiliar *f* de vuelo, azafata *f*, aeromoza *f* (en un avión)
stick¹ [ˈstɪk] *v* **stuck** [ˈstʌk]; **sticking** *vt* **1** STAB : clavar **2** ATTACH : pegar **3** PUT : poner, meter ⟨she stuck the letter under the door : metió la carta por debajo de la puerta⟩ ⟨stick 'em up! : ¡manos arriba!, ¡arriba las manos!⟩ **4 to stick it to** : darle duro a **5 to stick out** : sacar (la lengua, etc.), extender (la mano) **6 to stick out** ENDURE : aguantar en **7 to stick someone with** : endilgarle (una responsabilidad) a alguien, dejar a alguien solo con (una persona) — *vi* **1** ADHERE : pegarse, adherirse **2** JAM : atascarse ⟨the door sticks : la puerta se atasca⟩ ⟨the song stuck in my head/mind : la canción se me grabó en la cabeza/mente⟩ **3 to stick around** : quedarse **4 to stick by** : no abandonar **5 to stick out** PROJECT : sobresalir (de una superficie), asomar (por detrás o debajo de algo) **6 to stick out** STAND OUT : resaltar **7 to stick to** : no abandonar, no desviarse de ⟨stick to your guns : manténgase firme⟩ ⟨to stick to the rules : atenerse a las reglas⟩ ⟨to stick to one's word : cumplir uno con su palabra⟩ **8 to stick up** : estar parado (dícese del pelo, etc.), sobresalir (de una superficie) **9 to stick up for** : defender **10 to stick with** : serle fiel a (una persona), seguir con (una cosa) ⟨I'll stick with what I know : prefiero lo conocido⟩
stick² *n* **1** BRANCH, TWIG : ramita *f* **2** : palo *m*, vara *f* ⟨a walking stick : un bastón⟩
sticker [ˈstɪkər] *n* : etiqueta *f* adhesiva

stick–in–the–mud *n* : aguafiestas *mf*

stickler ['stɪklər] *n* : persona *f* exigente ⟨to be a stickler for : insistir mucho en⟩

sticky ['stɪki] *adj* **stickier; -est** **1** ADHESIVE : pegajoso, adhesivo **2** MUGGY : bochornoso **3** DIFFICULT : difícil

stiff ['stɪf] *adj* **1** RIGID : rígido, tieso ⟨a stiff dough : una masa firme⟩ **2** : agarrotado, entumecido ⟨stiff muscles : músculos entumecidos⟩ **3** STILTED : acartonado, poco natural **4** STRONG : fuerte (dícese del viento, etc.) **5** DIFFICULT, SEVERE : severo, difícil, duro

stiffen ['stɪfən] *vt* **1** STRENGTHEN : fortalecer, reforzar (tela, etc.) **2** : hacer más duro (un castigo, etc.) — *vi* **1** HARDEN : endurecerse **2** : entumecerse (dícese de los músculos)

stiffly ['stɪfli] *adv* **1** RIGIDLY : rígidamente **2** COLDLY : con frialdad

stiffness ['stɪfnəs] *n* **1** RIGIDITY : rigidez *f* **2** COLDNESS : frialdad *f* **3** SEVERITY : severidad *f*

stifle ['staɪfəl] *vt* **-fled; -fling** SMOTHER, SUPPRESS : sofocar, reprimir, contener ⟨to stifle a yawn : reprimir un bostezo⟩

stifling ['staɪfəlɪŋ] *adj* : sofocante

stigma ['stɪgmə] *n, pl* **stigmata** [stɪg'mɑtə, 'stɪgmətə] *or* **stigmas** : estigma *m*

stigmatize ['stɪgmə,taɪz] *vt* **-tized; -tizing** : estigmatizar

stile ['staɪl] *n* : escalones *mpl* para cruzar un cerco

stiletto [stə'lɛ,to:] *n, pl* **-tos** *or* **-toes** : estilete *m*

still[1] ['stɪl] *vt* CALM : pacificar, apaciguar — *vi* : pacificarse, apaciguarse

still[2] *adv* **1** QUIETLY : quieto ⟨sit still! : ¡quédate quieto!⟩ **2** : de todos modos, aún, todavía ⟨she still lives there : aún vive allí⟩ ⟨it's still the same : sigue siendo lo mismo⟩ **3** IN ANY CASE : de todos modos, aún así ⟨he still has doubts : aún así le quedan dudas⟩ ⟨I still prefer that you stay : de todos modos prefiero que te quedes⟩

still[3] *adj* **1** MOTIONLESS : quieto, inmóvil **2** SILENT : callado

still[4] *n* **1** SILENCE : quietud *f*, calma *f* **2** : alambique *m* (para destilar alcohol)

stillborn ['stɪl,bɔrn] *adj* : nacido muerto

still life *n* : naturaleza *f* muerta, bodegón *m*

stillness ['stɪlnəs] *n* : calma *f*, silencio *m*

stilt ['stɪlt] *n* : zanco *m*

stilted ['stɪltəd] *adj* : afectado, poco natural

stimulant ['stɪmjələnt] *n* : estimulante *m* — **stimulant** *adj*

stimulate ['stɪmjə,leɪt] *vt* **-lated; -lating** : estimular

stimulation [,stɪmjə'leɪlʌn] *n* **1** STIMULATING : estimulación *f* **2** STIMULUS : estímulo *m*

stimulus ['stɪmjələs] *n, pl* **-li** [-,laɪ] **1** : estímulo *m* **2** INCENTIVE : acicate *m*

sting[1] ['stɪŋ] *v* **stung** ['stʌŋ]; **stinging** *vt* **1** : picar ⟨a bee stung him : le picó una abeja⟩ **2** HURT : hacer escocer (físicamente), herir (emocionalmente) — *vi* **1** : picar (dícese de las abejas, etc.) **2** SMART : escocer, arder

sting[2] *n* : picadura *f* (herida), escozor *m* (sensación)

stinger ['stɪŋər] *n* : aguijón *m* (de una abeja, etc.)

stinginess ['stɪndʒinəs] *n* : tacañería *f*

stingy ['stɪndʒi] *adj* **stingier; -est** **1** MISERLY : tacaño, avaro **2** PALTRY : mezquino, mísero

stink[1] ['stɪŋk] *vi* **stank** ['stæŋk] *or* **stunk** ['stʌŋk]; **stunk; stinking** : apestar, oler mal

stink[2] *n* : hedor *m*, mal olor *m*, peste *f*

stint[1] ['stɪnt] *vt* : escatimar ⟨to stint oneself of : privarse de⟩ — *vi* **to stint on** : escatimar

stint[2] *n* : período *m*

stipend ['staɪ,pɛnd, -pənd] *n* : estipendio *m*

stipulate ['stɪpjə,leɪt] *vt* **-lated; -lating** : estipular

stipulation [,stɪpjə'leɪlʌn] *n* : estipulación *f*

stir[1] ['stər] *v* **stirred; stirring** *vt* **1** AGITATE : mover, agitar **2** MIX : revolver, remover **3** INCITE : incitar, impulsar, motivar **4** *or* **to stir up** AROUSE : despertar (memorias, etc.), provocar (ira, etc.) — *vi* : moverse, agitarse

stir[2] *n* **1** MOTION : movimiento *m* **2** COMMOTION : revuelo *m*

stirrup ['stərəp, 'stɪr-] *n* : estribo *m*

stitch[1] ['stɪtl] *vt* : coser, bordar (para decorar) — *vi* : coser

stitch[2] *n* **1** : puntada *f* **2** TWINGE : punzada *f*, puntada *f*

stock[1] ['stɑk] *vt* : surtir, abastecer, vender — *vi* **to stock up** : abastecerse

stock[2] *n* **1** SUPPLY : reserva *f*, existencias *fpl* (en comercio) ⟨to be out of stock : estar agotadas las existencias⟩ **2** SECURITIES : acciones *fpl*, valores *mpl* **3** LIVESTOCK : ganado *m* **4** ANCESTRY : linaje *m*, estirpe *f* **5** BROTH : caldo *m* **6** **to take stock (of)** : evaluar

stockade [stɑ'keɪd] *n* : estacada *f*

stockbroker ['stɑk,bro:kər] *n* : corredor *m*, -dora *f* de bolsa

stock exchange *n* : bolsa *f*

stockholder ['stɑk,ho:ldər] *n* : accionista *mf*

stocking ['stɑkɪŋ] *n* : media *f* ⟨a pair of stockings : unas medias⟩

stock market *n* : mercado *m* de valores, bolsa *f* de valores

stockpile[1] ['stɑk,paɪl] *vt* **-piled; -piling** : acumular, almacenar

stockpile[2] *n* : reservas *fpl*

stocky ['stɑki] *adj* **stockier; -est** : robusto, fornido

stockyard ['stɑk,jɑrd] *n* : corral *m*

stodgy ['stɑdʒi] *adj* **stodgier; -est** **1** DULL : aburrido, pesado **2** OLD-FASHIONED : anticuado

stoic[1] ['sto:ɪk] *or* **stoical** [-ɪkəl] *adj* : estoico — **stoically** [-ɪkli] *adv*

stoic[2] *n* : estoico *m*, -ca *f*

stoicism ['sto:ə,sɪzəm] *n* : estoicismo *m*

stoke ['sto:k] *vt* **stoked; stoking** : atizar (un fuego), echarle carbón a (un horno)

stole¹ → **steal**
stole² ['sto:l] *n* : estola *f*
stolen → **steal**
stolid ['stɑlɪd] *adj* : impasible, imperturbable — **stolidly** *adv*
stomach¹ ['stʌmɪk] *vt* : aguantar, soportar
stomach² *n* **1** : estómago *m* **2** BELLY : vientre *m*, barriga *f*, panza *f* **3** DESIRE : ganas *fpl* ⟨he had no stomach for a fight : no quería pelea⟩
stomachache ['stʌmɪk,eɪk] *n* : dolor *m* de estómago
stomp ['stɑmp, 'stɔmp] *vt* : pisotear — *vi* : pisar fuerte
stone¹ ['sto:n] *vt* **stoned; stoning** : apedrear, lapidar
stone² *n* **1** : piedra *f* **2** PIT : hueso *m*, pepa *f* (de una fruta)
Stone Age *n* : Edad *f* de Piedra
stoned ['sto:nd] *adj fam* : drogado
stonemason → **mason**
stonemasonry → **masonry**
stony ['sto:ni] *adj* **stonier; -est 1** ROCKY : pedregoso **2** UNFEELING : insensible, frío ⟨a stony stare : una mirada glacial⟩
stood → **stand**
stool ['stu:l] *n* **1** SEAT : taburete *m*, banco *m* **2** FOOTSTOOL : escabel *m* **3** FECES : deposición *f* de heces
stoop¹ ['stu:p] *vi* **1** CROUCH : agacharse **2 to stoop to** : rebajarse a
stoop² *n* **1** : espaldas *fpl* encorvadas ⟨to have a stoop : ser encorvado⟩ **2** : entrada *f* (de una casa)
stop¹ ['stɑp] *v* **stopped; stopping** *vt* **1** *or* **to stop up** PLUG : tapar **2** PREVENT : impedir, evitar ⟨she stopped me from leaving : me impidió que saliera⟩ **3** HALT : parar, detener ⟨I was stopped by the police : me paró un policía⟩ ⟨he stopped the car : paró el carro⟩ **4** CEASE, QUIT : dejar de ⟨he stopped talking : dejó de hablar⟩ ⟨stop it! : ¡basta!⟩ **5** END : terminar (una pelea, etc.), detener (una hemorragia) ⟨we must stop the violence : tenemos que poner fin a la violencia⟩ **6 to stop (payment on) a check** : dar orden de no pago (a un cheque) — *vi* **1** HALT : detenerse, parar ⟨she stopped to watch : se detuvo a mirar⟩ ⟨we stopped for gas : paramos a poner gasolina⟩ ⟨he stopped dead : paró en seco⟩ ⟨stop! who goes there? : ¡alto! ¿quién va?⟩ **2** : detenerse, parar ⟨let's stop and take a break : paremos para descansar⟩ ⟨to stop to consider something : detenerse a pensar en algo⟩ **3** : pararse (dícese de un motor, etc.) ⟨his heart stopped : se le paró el corazón⟩ **4** CEASE, END : cesar, terminar ⟨the rain won't stop : no deja de llover⟩ **5** STAY : quedarse ⟨I can't stop for long : no puedo quedarme mucho tiempo⟩ **6 to stop by/in** : pasar a ver, visitar **7 to stop off** : hacer una parada **8 to stop over** : parar, quedarse **9 to stop over** : hacer escala (dícese de un avión)
stop² *n* **1** STOPPER : tapón *m* **2** HALT : parada *f*, alto *m* ⟨to come to a stop : pararse, detenerse⟩ ⟨to put a stop to

: poner fin a⟩ **3** : parada *f* ⟨bus stop : parada de autobús⟩
stopgap ['stɑp,gæp] *n* : arreglo *m* provisorio
stoplight ['stɑp,laɪt] *n* : semáforo *m*
stopover ['stɑp,o:vər] *n* LAYOVER : escala *f*
stoppage ['stɑpɪʤ] *n* : acto *m* de parar ⟨a work stoppage : un paro⟩
stopper ['stɑpər] *n* : tapón *m*
stopwatch ['stɑp,wɑtʃ] *n* : cronómetro *m*
storage ['storɪʤ] *n* : almacenamiento *m*, almacenaje *m*
storage battery *n* : acumulador *m*
store¹ ['stor] *vt* **stored; storing** : guardar, almacenar
store² *n* **1** RESERVE, SUPPLY : reserva *f* **2** SHOP : tienda *f* ⟨grocery store : tienda de comestibles⟩
storehouse ['stor,haʊs] *n* : almacén *m*, depósito *m*
storekeeper ['stor,ki:pər] *n* : tendero *m*, -ra *f*
storeroom ['stor,ru:m, -,rʊm] *n* : almacén *m*, depósito *m*
stork ['stork] *n* : cigüeña *f*
storm¹ ['storm] *vi* **1** : llover o nevar tormentosamente **2** RAGE : ponerse furioso, vociferar **3 to storm out** : salir echando pestes — *vt* ATTACK : asaltar
storm² *n* **1** : tormenta *f*, tempestad *f* **2** UPROAR : alboroto *m*, revuelo *m*, escándalo *m* ⟨a storm of abuse : un torrente de abusos⟩
stormy ['stormi] *adj* **stormier; -est** : tormentoso — **stormily** *adv*
story ['stori] *n, pl* **stories 1** NARRATIVE, TALE : cuento *m*, relato *m* ⟨a bedtime story : un cuento para dormir⟩ **2** ACCOUNT : historia *f*, relato *m* ⟨it's a long story : es largo de contar⟩ ⟨to make a long story short : en pocas palabras⟩ **3** ARTICLE : artículo *m* **4** TALE, LIE : cuento *m*, mentira *f* **5** INFORMATION : información *f* ⟨what's his story? : ¿qué me puedes contar de él?⟩ ⟨the story behind the changes : la razón de los cambios⟩ **6** : piso *m*, planta *f* (de un edificio) ⟨first story : planta baja⟩
stout ['staʊt] *adj* **1** FIRM, RESOLUTE : firme, resuelto **2** STURDY : fuerte, robusto, sólido **3** FAT : corpulento, gordo
stoutness ['staʊtnəs] *n* **1** FIRMNESS : firmeza *f* **2** STURDINESS : fuerza *f*, robustez *f*, solidez *f* **3** FATNESS : corpulencia *f*, gordura *f*
stove¹ ['sto:v] *n* : cocina *f* (para cocinar), estufa *f* (para calentar)
stove² → **stave¹**
stow ['sto:] *vt* **1** STORE : poner, meter, guardar **2** LOAD : cargar — *vi* **to stow away** : viajar de polizón
stowaway ['sto:ə,weɪ] *n* : polizón *m*
straddle ['strædəl] *vt* **-dled; -dling** : sentarse a horcajadas sobre
straggle ['strægəl] *vi* **-gled; -gling** : rezagarse, quedarse atrás
straggler ['strægələr] *n* : rezagado *m*, -da *f*

straight¹ ['streɪt] *adv* **1** : derecho, directamente ⟨go straight, then turn right : sigue derecho, luego gira a la derecha⟩ **2** HONESTLY : honestamente ⟨to go straight : enmendarse⟩ **3** CLEARLY : con claridad **4** FRANKLY : francamente, con franqueza

straight² *adj* **1** : recto (dícese de las líneas, etc.), derecho (dícese de algo vertical), lacio (dícese del pelo) **2** HONEST, JUST : honesto, justo **3** NEAT, ORDERLY : arreglado, ordenado **4** : solo (dícese de una bebida alcohólica)

straightaway [ˌstreɪtə'weɪ] *adv* : inmediatamente

straighten ['streɪtən] *vt* **1** *or* **to straighten out** : enderezar, poner derecho **2 to straighten out/up** NEATEN : arreglar, ordenar ⟨he straightened up the house : arregló la casa⟩ ⟨I straightened out my papers : ordené los papeles⟩ **3 to straighten out** FIX : arreglar, resolver (problemas, etc.), poner (la vida) en orden **4 to straighten out** : enderezar, meter en vereda (a un niño rebelde, etc.) **5 to straighten out** ENLIGHTEN : aclararle las dudas (a alguien) — *vi* **1 to straighten up** : ponerse derecho **2 to straighten up/out** IMPROVE : enderezarse

straightforward [streɪt'fɔrwərd] *adj* **1** FRANK : franco, sincero **2** CLEAR, PRECISE : puro, simple, claro

straight razor → **razor**

strain¹ ['streɪn] *vt* **1** EXERT : forzar (la vista, la voz), esforzar ⟨to strain oneself : hacer un gran esfuerzo⟩ **2** FILTER : colar, filtrar **3** INJURE : lastimarse, hacerse daño en ⟨to strain a muscle : sufrir un esguince⟩ — *vi* **to strain to do something** : esforzarse por hacer algo

strain² *n* **1** LINEAGE : linaje *m*, abolengo *m* **2** STREAK, TRACE : veta *f* **3** VARIETY : tipo *m*, variedad *f* **4** STRESS : tensión *f*, presión *f* **5** SPRAIN : esguince *m*, torcedura *f* (del tobillo, etc.) **6 strains** *npl* TUNE : melodía *f*, acordes *mpl*, compases *fpl*

strained ['streɪnd] *adj* **1** FORCED : forzado **2** ANXIOUS : preocupado **3** TIRED : cansado **4** TENSE : tenso

strainer ['streɪnər] *n* : colador *m*

strait ['streɪt] *n* **1** : estrecho *m* **2 straits** *npl* DISTRESS : aprietos *mpl*, apuros *mpl* ⟨in dire straits : en serios aprietos⟩

straitened ['streɪtənd] *adj* **in straitened circumstances** : en apuros económicos

straitjacket ['streɪtˌʤækət] *n* : camisa *f* de fuerza

strand¹ ['strænd] *vt* **1** : varar **2 to be left stranded** : quedar(se) varado, quedar colgado ⟨they left me stranded : me dejaron abandonado⟩

strand² *n* **1** : hebra *f* (de hilo, etc.) ⟨a strand of hair : un pelo⟩ **2** BEACH : playa *f*

strange ['streɪnʤ] *adj* **stranger; -est 1** QUEER, UNUSUAL : extraño, raro **2** UNFAMILIAR : desconocido, nuevo

strangely ['streɪnʤli] *adv* ODDLY : de manera extraña ⟨to behave strangely : portarse de una manera rara⟩ ⟨strangely, he didn't call : curiosamente, no llamó⟩

strangeness ['streɪnʤnəs] *n* **1** ODDNESS : rareza *f* **2** UNFAMILIARITY : lo desconocido

stranger ['streɪnʤər] *n* : desconocido *m*, -da *f*; extraño *m*, -ña *f*

strangle ['stræŋɡəl] *vt* **-gled; -gling** : estrangular

strangler ['stræŋɡlər] *n* : estrangulador *m*, -dora *f*

strangulation [ˌstræŋɡjə'leɪʒən] *n* : estrangulamiento *m*

strap¹ ['stræp] *vt* **strapped; strapping 1** FASTEN : sujetar con una correa **2** FLOG : azotar (con una correa)

strap² *n* **1** : correa *f* **2 shoulder strap** : tirante *m*

strapless ['stræpləs] *n* : sin tirantes

strapping ['stræpɪŋ] *adj* : robusto, fornido

stratagem ['strætəʤəm, -ˌʤɛm] *n* : estratagema *f*, artimaña *f*

strategic [strə'ti:ʤɪk] *adj* : estratégico

strategist ['strætəʤɪst] *n* : estratega *mf*

strategy ['strætəʤi] *n, pl* **-gies** : estrategia *f*

stratified ['strætəˌfaɪd] *adj* : estratificado

stratosphere ['strætəˌsfɪr] *n* : estratosfera *f*

stratospheric [ˌstrætə'sfɪrɪk, -'sfɛr-] *adj* : estratosférico

stratum ['streɪtəm, 'stræ-] *n, pl* **strata** [- t̬ə] : estrato *m*, capa *f*

straw ['strɔ] *n* **1** : paja *f* ⟨the last straw : el colmo⟩ **2** *or* **drinking straw** : pajita *f*, popote *m* Mex

strawberry ['strɔˌbɛri] *n, pl* **-ries** : fresa *f*

stray¹ ['streɪ] *vi* **1** WANDER : alejarse, extraviarse ⟨the cattle strayed away : el ganado se descarrió⟩ **2** DIGRESS : desviarse, divagar

stray² *adj* : perdido, callejero (dícese de un perro o un gato), descarriado (dícese del ganado)

stray³ *n* : animal *m* perdido, animal *m* callejero

streak¹ ['stri:k] *vt* : hacer rayas en ⟨blue streaked with grey : azul veteado con gris⟩ — *vi* : ir como una flecha

streak² *n* **1** : raya *f*, veta *f* (en mármol, queso, etc.), mechón *m* (en el pelo) **2** : rayo *m* (de luz) **3** TRACE : veta *f* **4** : racha *f* ⟨a streak of luck : una racha de suerte⟩

stream¹ ['stri:m] *vi* : correr, salir a chorros ⟨tears streamed from his eyes : las lágrimas brotaban de sus ojos⟩ — *vt* **1** : derramar, dejar correr ⟨to stream blood : derramar sangre⟩ **2** : transmitir (audio o video) en streaming **3** : ver (video) o escuchar (audio) en streaming

stream² *n* **1** BROOK : arroyo *m*, riachuelo *m* **2** RIVER : río *m* **3** FLOW : corriente *f*, chorro *m* **4** SERIES : serie *f*, sarta *f*

streamer ['stri:mər] *n* **1** PENNANT : banderín *m* **2** RIBBON : serpentina *f* (de papel), cinta *f* (de tela)

streaming[1] ['stri:mɪŋ] *adj* : de streaming ⟨streaming video : video en streaming⟩

streaming[2] *n* : streaming *m*

streamline ['stri:mˌlaɪn] *vt* : racionalizar (un proceso, etc.)

streamlined ['stri:mˌlaɪnd] *adj* **1** : aerodinámico (dícese de los automóviles, etc.) **2** EFFICIENT : eficiente, racionalizado

street ['stri:t] *n* : calle *f*

streetcar ['stri:tˌkɑr] *n* : tranvía *m*

streetlight ['stri:tˌlaɪt] *or* **streetlamp** ['stri:tˌlæmp] *n* : farol *m*, farola *f*

strength ['strɛŋkθ] *n* **1** : fuerza *f* ⟨with all her strength : con toda(s) su(s) fuerza(s)⟩ ⟨to save one's strength : reservar uno sus energías⟩ **2** POWER : poder *m*, fuerza *f* ⟨economic/military strength : poder económico/militar⟩ ⟨there is strength in numbers : la unión hace la fuerza⟩ **3** FORTITUDE : fortaleza *f* ⟨strength of character : fortaleza/fuerza de carácter⟩ **4** SOLIDITY, TOUGHNESS : solidez *f*, resistencia *f*, dureza *f* (de un material) **5** INTENSITY : intensidad *f* (de emociones, etc.), fuerza *f* (del viento, etc.), lo fuerte (de un sabor, etc.) **6** CONCENTRATION : concentración *f* ⟨full strength : sin diluir⟩ **7** POTENCY : potencia *f* (de un medicamento) ⟨full/maximum strength : máxima potencia⟩ **8** : fuerte *m*, punto *m* fuerte ⟨strengths and weaknesses : virtudes y defectos⟩ **9** NUMBER : número *m*, complemento *m* ⟨in full strength : en gran número⟩

strengthen ['strɛŋkθən] *vt* **1** : fortalecer (los músculos, el espíritu, etc.) **2** REINFORCE : reforzar **3** INTENSIFY : intensificar, redoblar (esfuerzos, etc.) — *vi* **1** : fortalecerse, hacerse más fuerte **2** INTENSIFY : intensificarse

strenuous ['strɛnjuəs] *adj* **1** VIGOROUS : vigoroso, enérgico **2** ARDUOUS : duro, riguroso

strenuously ['strɛnjuəsli] *adv* : vigorosamente, duro

stress[1] ['strɛs] *vt* **1** : someter a tensión (física) **2** EMPHASIZE : enfatizar, recalcar **3** to stress out : estresar

stress[2] *n* **1** : tensión *f* (en un material) **2** EMPHASIS : énfasis *m*, acento *m* (en lingüística) **3** TENSION : tensión *f* (nerviosa), estrés *m*

stressful ['strɛsfəl] *adj* : estresante

stretch[1] ['strɛtʃ] *vt* **1** : estirar (un suéter, un cable, etc.), extender (un lienzo, etc.), desplegar (alas) ⟨to stretch one's legs : estirar las piernas, caminar⟩ **2** to stretch the truth : forzar la verdad, exagerar — *vi* **1** *or* to stretch out : estirarse **2** REACH : extenderse **3** to stretch back (in time) : remontarse

stretch[2] *n* **1** STRETCHING : extensión *f*, estiramiento *m* (de músculos) **2** ELASTICITY : elasticidad *f* **3** EXPANSE : tramo *m*, trecho *m* ⟨the home stretch : la recta final⟩ **4** PERIOD : período *m* (de tiempo)

stretcher ['strɛtʃər] *n* : camilla *f*

strew ['stru:] *vt* **strewed**; **strewed** *or* **strewn** ['stru:n]; **strewing 1** SCATTER : esparcir (semillas, etc.), desparramar (papeles, etc.) **2** to strew with : cubrir de

stricken ['strɪkən] *adj* **stricken with** : aquejado de (una enfermedad), afligido por (tristeza, etc.)

strict ['strɪkt] *adj* : estricto — **strictly** *adv*

strictness ['strɪktnəs] *n* : severidad *f*, lo estricto

stricture ['strɪktʃər] *n* : crítica *f*, censura *f*

stride[1] ['straɪd] *vi* **strode** ['stro:d]; **stridden** ['strɪdən]; **striding** : ir dando trancos, ir dando zancadas

stride[2] *n* : tranco *m*, zancada *f*

strident ['straɪdənt] *adj* : estridente

strife ['straɪf] *n* : conflictos *mpl*, disensión *f*

strike[1] ['straɪk] *v* **struck** ['strʌk]; **striking** *vt* **1** HIT : golpear, pegarle (a una persona) ⟨the bullet struck him in the leg : la bala lo alcanzó en la pierna⟩ **2** HIT : chocar contra, dar contra ⟨the car struck a tree : el carro chocó contra un árbol⟩ **3** DELETE : suprimir, tachar **4** COIN, MINT : acuñar (monedas) **5** : dar (la hora) **6** AFFLICT : sobrevenir ⟨he was stricken with a fever : le sobrevino una fiebre⟩ **7** IMPRESS : impresionar, parecer ⟨her voice struck me : su voz me impresionó⟩ ⟨it struck him as funny : le pareció chistoso⟩ **8** : ocurrírsele a ⟨it struck me that . . . : se me ocurrió que . . .⟩ **9** : encender (un fósforo) **10** FIND : descubrir (oro, petróleo) **11** ADOPT : adoptar (una pose, etc.) **12** : tocar (en música) **13** REACH : llegar a, alcanzar (un acuerdo, etc.) **14 to strike a blow** : pegar un golpe **15 to strike down** : fulminar **16 to strike out** : tachar (palabras, etc.) **17 to strike up** : entablar (una conversación, una amistad), empezar a tocar (una canción) — *vi* **1** HIT : golpear ⟨to strike against : chocar contra⟩ **2** ATTACK : atacar **3** : declararse en huelga **4 to strike back at** : devolverle el golpe a **5 to strike out** : poncharse (en beisbol) **6 to strike out** FAIL : fracasar **7 to strike out at** ATTACK : arremeter contra **8 to strike out for** : emprender el camino hacia **9 to strike out on one's own** : emprender algo solo

strike[2] *n* **1** BLOW : golpe *m* **2** : huelga *f*, paro *m* ⟨to be on strike : estar en huelga⟩ **3** ATTACK : ataque *m*

strikebreaker ['straɪkˌbreɪkər] *n* : rompehuelgas *mf*, esquirol *mf*

strike out *vi* **1** HEAD : salir (para) **2** : ser ponchado (en béisbol) ⟨the batter struck out : poncharon al bateador⟩

striker ['straɪkər] *n* : huelguista *mf*

strike up *vt* START : entablar, empezar

striking ['straɪkɪŋ] *adj* : notable, sorprendente, llamativo ⟨a striking beauty : una belleza imponente⟩ — **strikingly** *adv*

string[1] ['strɪŋ] *vt* **strung** ['strʌŋ]; **stringing 1** THREAD : ensartar ⟨to string beads : ensartar cuentas⟩ **2** HANG : colgar (con un cordel)

string[2] *n* **1** : cordel *m*, cuerda *f* **2** SERIES : serie *f*, sarta *f* (de insultos, etc.) **3**

strings *npl* : cuerdas *fpl* (en música) **4**
strings *npl* : influencias *fpl* ⟨to pull strings : utilizar sus influencias⟩ **5**
strings *npl* : compromisos *mpl* ⟨with no strings attached : sin compromiso(s)⟩
string bean *n* : judía *f*, ejote *m Mex*
stringent [ˈstrɪndʒənt] *adj* : estricto, severo
stringy [ˈstrɪŋi] *adj* **stringier; -est** : fibroso
strip¹ [ˈstrɪp] *v* **stripped; stripping** *vt* : quitar (ropa, pintura, etc.), desnudar, despojar — *vi* UNDRESS : desnudarse
strip² *n* : tira *f* ⟨a strip of land : una faja⟩
stripe¹ [ˈstraɪp] *vt* **striped** [ˈstraɪpt]; **striping** : marcar con rayas o listas
stripe² *n* **1** : raya *f*, lista *f* **2** BAND : franja *f*
striped [ˈstraɪpt, ˈstraɪpəd] *adj* : a rayas, de rayas, rayado, listado
strive [ˈstraɪv] *vi* **strove** [ˈstroːv]; **striven** [ˈstrɪvən] *or* **strived; striving 1 to strive for** : luchar por lograr **2 to strive to** : esforzarse por
strode → stride
stroke¹ [ˈstroːk] *vt* **stroked; stroking** : acariciar
stroke² *n* **1** : apoplejía *f*, derrame *m* cerebral (en medicina) **2** : pincelada *f*, trazo *m* (en el arte) **3** : estilo *m* (de nadar) **4** : movimiento *m*, batir *m* (de alas), brazada *f* (al nadar), remada *f* (al remar) **5** CARESS : caricia *f* **6** : golpe *m* (en beisbol, etc.) **7** ACT : golpe *m* ⟨in one stroke : de un golpe⟩ ⟨a stroke of genius/inspiration : una genialidad/inspiración⟩ **8** : golpe *m* ⟨a stroke of luck : un golpe de suerte⟩ **9** : campanada *f* (de un reloj)
stroll¹ [ˈstroːl] *vi* : pasear, pasearse, dar un paseo
stroll² *n* : paseo *m*
stroller [ˈstroːlər] *n* : cochecito *m* (para niños)
strong [ˈstrɔŋ] *adj* **1** : fuerte ⟨strong arms : brazos fuertes⟩ ⟨strong winds : vientos fuertes⟩ ⟨a strong odor : un olor fuerte⟩ ⟨strong coffee/medicine : café/medicina fuerte⟩ ⟨strong language : lenguaje fuerte⟩ ⟨a strong candidate/leader : un candidato/líder fuerte⟩ ⟨strong opposition : fuerte oposición⟩ ⟨of strong character : de carácter fuerte⟩ ⟨his strong point : su (punto) fuerte⟩ **2** DURABLE : resistente, fuerte **3** HEALTHY : sano **4** NOTICEABLE : marcado **5** FIRM : firme (dícese de convicciones, etc.) **6** PERSUASIVE : poderoso, convincente **7** CONCENTRATED : concentrado (dícese de detergente, etc.) **8** : con mucho aumento (dícese de lentes) **9** (*with numbers*) ⟨an organization five hundred people strong : una organización de quinientas personas⟩
strongbox [ˈstrɔŋˌbaks] *n* : caja *f* fuerte
stronghold [ˈstrɔŋˌhoːld] *n* : fortaleza *f*, fuerte *m*, bastión *m* ⟨a cultural stronghold : un baluarte de la cultura⟩
strongly [ˈstrɔŋli] *adv* **1** POWERFULLY : fuerte, con fuerza **2** STURDILY

: fuertemente, sólidamente **3** INTENSELY : intensamente, profundamente ⟨to feel strongly about something : tener ideas muy claras sobre algo⟩ ⟨to feel/believe strongly that . . . : estar totalmente convencido de que . . . , tener la convicción de que . . .⟩ ⟨I am strongly tempted : me siento muy tentada⟩ **4** WHOLEHEARTEDLY : totalmente ⟨I strongly agree : estoy totalmente de acuerdo⟩ ⟨I strongly disagree : estoy totalmente en desacuerdo⟩ **5** EMPHATICALLY : enérgicamente ⟨to criticize strongly : criticar duramente⟩ ⟨a strongly worded letter : una carta muy dura⟩ ⟨I strongly advise that you see a doctor : le recomiendo encarecidamente que vaya a un médico⟩ **6 to smell/taste strongly of** : oler/saber fuertemente a
struck → strike¹
structural [ˈstrʌktʃərəl] *adj* : estructural
structure¹ [ˈstrʌktʃər] *vt* **-tured; -turing** : estructurar
structure² *n* **1** BUILDING : construcción *f* **2** ARRANGEMENT, FRAMEWORK : estructura *f*
struggle¹ [ˈstrʌgəl] *vi* **-gled; -gling 1** CONTEND : forcejear (físicamente), luchar, contender **2** : hacer con dificultad ⟨she struggled forward : avanzó con dificultad⟩
struggle² *n* : lucha *f*, pelea *f* (física)
strum [ˈstrʌm] *vt* **strummed; strumming** : rasguear
strung → string¹
strut¹ [ˈstrʌt] *vi* **strutted; strutting** : pavonearse
strut² *n* **1** : pavoneo *m* ⟨he walked with a strut : se pavoneaba⟩ **2** : puntal *m* (en construcción, etc.)
stub¹ [ˈstʌb] *vt* **stubbed; stubbing 1 to stub one's toe** : darse en el dedo (del pie) **2 to stub out** : apagarse
stub² *n* : colilla *f* (de un cigarrillo), cabo *m* (de un lápiz, etc.), talón *m* (de un cheque)
stubble [ˈstʌbəl] *n* **1** : rastrojo *m* (de plantas) **2** BEARD : barba *f*
stubborn [ˈstʌbərn] *adj* **1** OBSTINATE : terco, obstinado, empecinado **2** PERSISTENT : pertinaz, persistente — **stubbornly** *adv*
stubbornness [ˈstʌbərnnəs] *n* **1** OBSTINACY : terquedad *f*, obstinación *f* **2** PERSISTENCE : persistencia *f*
stubby [ˈstʌbi] *adj* **stubbier; -est** : corto y grueso ⟨stubby fingers : dedos regordetes⟩
stucco [ˈstʌkoː] *n, pl* **stuccos** *or* **stuccoes** : estuco *m*
stuck → stick¹
stuck–up [ˈstʌkˈʌp] *adj* : engreído, creído *fam*
stud¹ [ˈstʌd] *vt* **studded; studding** : tachonar, salpicar
stud² *n* **1** *or* **stud horse** : semental *m* **2** : montante *m* (en construcción) **3** HOBNAIL : tachuela *f*, tachón *m*
student [ˈstuːdənt, ˈstjuː-] *n* : estudiante *mf*; alumno *m*, -na *f* (de un colegio)

studied ['stʌdɪd] *adj* : intencionado, premeditado

studio ['stu:di,o:, 'stju:-] *n, pl* **studios** : estudio *m*

studious ['stu:diəs, 'stju:-] *adj* : estudioso — **studiously** *adv*

study[1] ['stʌdi] *v* **studied; studying** **1** : estudiar **2** EXAMINE : examinar, estudiar

study[2] *n, pl* **studies** **1** STUDYING : estudio *m* **2** OFFICE : estudio *m*, gabinete *m* (en una casa) **3** RESEARCH : investigación *f*, estudio *m*

stuff[1] ['stʌf] *vt* : rellenar, llenar, atiborrar ⟨a stuffed toy : un juguete de peluche⟩

stuff[2] *n* **1** POSSESSIONS : cosas *fpl* ⟨my stuff : mis cosas⟩ **2** SUPPLIES, EQUIPMENT : cosas *fpl* ⟨baby stuff : cosas para bebés⟩ **3** *fam* : cosa *f*, cosas *fpl* ⟨some sticky stuff : una cosa pegajosa⟩ ⟨this stuff really works! : ¡esto funciona de maravilla!⟩ ⟨they're giving away free stuff : están regalando cosas⟩ ⟨and stuff (like that) : y cosas por el estilo⟩ **4** (*referring to something heard, read, etc.*) *fam* ⟨this is fascinating stuff : esto es fascinante⟩ ⟨the stuff he said isn't true : lo que dijo no es verdad⟩ **5** (*referring to behavior*) *fam* : cosas *fpl* ⟨she does stuff to bug me : hace cosas para fastidiarme⟩ ⟨how can he get away with that stuff? : ¿cómo es que siempre se sale con la suya?⟩ **6** ESSENCE : esencia *f* **7 to know your stuff** : ser experto

stuffing ['stʌfɪŋ] *n* : relleno *m*

stuffy ['stʌfi] *adj* **stuffier; -est** **1** CLOSE : viciado, cargado ⟨a stuffy room : una sala mal ventilada⟩ ⟨stuffy weather : tiempo bochornoso⟩ **2** : tapado (dícese de la nariz) **3** STODGY : pesado, aburrido

stumble[1] ['stʌmbəl] *vi* **-bled; -bling** **1** TRIP : tropezar, dar un traspié **2** FLOUNDER : quedarse sin saber qué hacer o decir **3 to stumble across** *or* **to stumble upon** : dar con, tropezar con

stumble[2] *n* : tropezón *m*, traspié *m*

stumbling block *n* : obstáculo *m*

stump[1] ['stʌmp] *vt* : dejar perplejo ⟨to be stumped : no tener respuesta⟩

stump[2] *n* **1** : muñón *m* (de un brazo o una pierna) **2** *or* **tree stump** : cepa *f*, tocón *m* **3** STUB : cabo *m*

stun ['stʌn] *vt* **stunned; stunning** **1** : aturdir (con un golpe) **2** ASTONISH, SHOCK : dejar estupefacto, dejar atónito, aturdir

stung → **sting**[1]

stunk → **stink**[1]

stunning ['stʌnɪŋ] *adj* **1** ASTONISHING : asombroso, pasmoso, increíble **2** STRIKING : imponente, impresionante (dícese de la belleza)

stunt[1] ['stʌnt] *vt* : atrofiar

stunt[2] *n* : proeza *f* (acrobática)

stupefy ['stu:pə,faɪ, 'stju:-] *vt* **-fied; -fying** **1** : aturdir, atontar (con drogas, etc.) **2** AMAZE : dejar estupefacto, dejar atónito

stupendous [stʊ'pɛndəs, stju-] *adj* **1** MARVELOUS : estupendo, maravilloso **2**

TREMENDOUS : tremendo — **stupendously** *adv*

stupid ['stu:pəd, 'stju:-] *adj* **1** IDIOTIC, SILLY : tonto, bobo, estúpido **2** DULL, OBTUSE : lento, torpe, lerdo

stupidity [stʊ'pɪdəti, stju-] *n* : tontería *f*, estupidez *f*

stupidly ['stu:pədli, 'stju:-] *adv* **1** IDIOTICALLY : estúpidamente, tontamente **2** DENSELY : torpemente

stupor ['stu:pər, 'stju:-] *n* : estupor *m*

sturdily ['stərdəli] *adv* : sólidamente

sturdiness ['stərdinəs] *n* : solidez *f* (de muebles, etc.), robustez *f* (de una persona)

sturdy ['stərdi] *adj* **sturdier; -est** : fuerte, robusto, sólido

sturgeon ['stərdʒən] *n* : esturión *m*

stutter[1] ['stʌtər] *vi* : tartamudear

stutter[2] *n* STAMMER : tartamudeo *m*

sty ['staɪ] *n* **1** *pl* **sties** PIGPEN : chiquero *m*, pocilga *f* **2** *or* **stye** *pl* **sties** *or* **styes** : orzuelo *m* (en el ojo)

style[1] ['staɪl] *vt* **styled; styling** **1** NAME : llamar **2** : peinar (pelo), diseñar (vestidos, etc.) ⟨carefully styled prose : prosa escrita con gran esmero⟩

style[2] *n* **1** : estilo *m* ⟨that's just his style : él es así⟩ ⟨to live in style : vivir a lo grande⟩ **2** FASHION : moda *f*

stylish ['staɪlɪʃ] *adj* : de moda, elegante, chic

stylishly ['staɪlɪʃli] *adv* : con estilo

stylishness ['staɪlɪʃnəs] *n* : estilo *m*

stylist ['staɪlɪst] *n* : estilista *mf*

stylize ['staɪ,laɪz, 'staɪə-] *vt* : estilizar

stylus ['staɪləs] *n, pl* **styli** ['staɪ,laɪ] **1** PEN : estilo *m* **2** NEEDLE : aguja *f* (de un tocadiscos)

stymie ['staɪmi] *vt* **-mied; -mieing** : obstaculizar

suave ['swɑv] *adj* : fino, urbano

sub[1] ['sʌb] *vi* **subbed; subbing** → **substitute**[1]

sub[2] *n* **1** → **substitute**[2] **2** → **submarine**

sub- [,sʌb] *pref* : sub-

subcommittee ['sʌbkə,mɪti] *n* : subcomité *m*

subconscious[1] [səb'kɑntləs] *adj* : subconsciente — **subconsciously** *adv*

subconscious[2] *n* : subconsciente *m*

subcontract [,sʌb'kɑn,trækt] *vt* : subcontratar

subcontractor [,sʌb'kɑn,træktər] *n* : subcontratista *mf*

subculture ['sʌb,kʌltʃər] *n* : subcultura *f*

subdivide [,sʌbdə'vaɪd, 'sʌbdə,vaɪd] *vt* **-vided; -viding** : subdividir

subdivision ['sʌbdə,vɪʒən] *n* : subdivisión *f*

subdue [səb'du:, -'dju:] *vt* **-dued; -duing** **1** OVERCOME : sojuzgar (a un enemigo), vencer, superar **2** CONTROL : dominar **3** SOFTEN : suavizar, atenuar (luz, etc.), moderar (lenguaje)

subgroup ['sʌb,gru:p] *n* : subgrupo *m*

subhead ['sʌb,hɛd] *or* **subheading** [-,hɛdɪŋ] *n* : subtítulo *m*

subhuman [,sʌb'hju:mən, -'ju:-] *adj* : infrahumano

subject¹ [səb'dʒɛkt] *vt* **1** CONTROL, DOM-INATE : controlar, dominar **2** : someter ⟨they subjected him to pressure : lo sometieron a presiones⟩

subject² ['sʌbdʒɪkt] *adj* **1** : subyugado, sometido ⟨a subject nation : una nación subyugada⟩ **2** PRONE : sujeto, propenso ⟨subject to colds : sujeto a resfriarse⟩ **3 subject to** : sujeto a ⟨subject to congressional approval : sujeto a la aprobación del congreso⟩

subject³ ['sʌbdʒɪkt] *n* **1** : súbdito *m*, -ta *f* (de un gobierno) **2** *or* **subject matter** TOP-IC : tema *m* **3** : sujeto *m* (en gramática)

subjection [səb'dʒɛklən] *n* : sometimiento *m*

subjective [səb'dʒɛktɪv] *adj* : subjetivo — **subjectively** *adv*

subjectivity [ˌsʌbˌdʒɛk'tɪvəti] *n* : subjetividad *f*

subjugate ['sʌbdʒɪˌgeɪt] *vt* **-gated; -gating** : subyugar, someter, sojuzgar

subjunctive [səb'dʒʌŋktɪv] *n* : subjuntivo *m* — **subjunctive** *adj*

sublet ['sʌbˌlɛt] *vt* **-let; -letting** : subarrendar

sublimate ['sʌbləˌmeɪt] *vt* **-mated; -mating** : sublimar — **sublimation** [ˌsʌbləˈmeɪlən] *n*

sublime [sə'blaɪm] *adj* : sublime

sublimely [sə'blaɪmli] *adv* **1** : de manera sublime **2** UTTERLY : absolutamente, completamente

submarine¹ ['sʌbməˌriːn, ˌsʌbmə'-] *adj* : submarino

submarine² *n* : submarino *m*

submachine gun [ˌsʌbmə'liːn-] *n* : metralleta *f*

submerge [səb'mərdʒ] *v* **-merged; -merging** *vt* : sumergir — *vi* : sumergirse

submission [səb'mɪlən] *n* **1** YIELDING : sumisión *f* **2** PRESENTATION : presentación *f*

submissive [səb'mɪsɪv] *adj* : sumiso, dócil

submissiveness [səb'mɪsɪvnəs] *n* : sumisión *f*

submit [səb'mɪt] *v* **-mitted; -mitting** *vi* YIELD : rendirse ⟨to submit to : someterse a⟩ — *vt* PRESENT : presentar

subnormal [ˌsʌb'nɔrməl] *adj* : por debajo de lo normal

subordinate¹ [sə'bɔrdənˌeɪt] *vt* **-nated; -nating** : subordinar

subordinate² [sə'bɔrdənət] *adj* : subordinado ⟨a subordinate clause : una oración subordinada⟩

subordinate³ *n* : subordinado *m*, -da *f*; subalterno *m*, -na *f*

subordination [səˌbɔrdən'eɪlən] *n* : subordinación *f*

subpoena¹ [sə'piːnə] *vt* **-naed; -naing** : citar

subpoena² *n* : citación *f*, citatorio *m*

subscribe [səb'skraɪb] *vi* **-scribed; -scribing 1** : suscribirse ⟨a una revista, etc.⟩ **2 to subscribe to** : suscribir (una opinión, etc.), estar de acuerdo con

subscriber [səb'skraɪbər] *n* : suscriptor *m*, -tora *f* (de una revista, etc.); abonado *m*, -da *f* (de un servicio)

subscription [səb'skrɪplən] *n* : suscripción *f*

subsection ['sʌbˌsɛklən] *n* : inciso *m* (de un artículo, etc.)

subsequent ['sʌbsɪkwənt, -səˌkwɛnt] *adj* : subsiguiente ⟨subsequent to : posterior a⟩

subsequently ['sʌbˌsɪkwɛntli, -kwənt-] *adv* : posteriormente

subservient [səb'sərviənt] *adj* : servil

subside [səb'saɪd] *vi* **-sided; -siding 1** SINK : hundirse, descender **2** ABATE : calmarse (dícese de las emociones), amainar (dícese del viento, etc.)

subsidiary¹ [səb'sɪdiˌɛri] *adj* : secundario

subsidiary² *n, pl* **-ries** : filial *f*, subsidiaria *f*

subsidize ['sʌbsəˌdaɪz] *vt* **-dized; -dizing** : subvencionar, subsidiar

subsidy ['sʌbsədi] *n, pl* **-dies** : subvención *f*, subsidio *m*

subsist [səb'sɪst] *vi* : subsistir, mantenerse, vivir

subsistence [səb'sɪstənts] *n* : subsistencia *f*

substance ['sʌbstənts] *n* **1** ESSENCE : sustancia *f*, esencia *f* **2** : sustancia *f* ⟨a toxic substance : una sustancia tóxica⟩ **3** WEALTH : riqueza *f* ⟨a woman of substance : una mujer acaudalada⟩

substandard [ˌsʌb'stændərd] *adj* : inferior, deficiente

substantial [səb'stæntləl] *adj* **1** ABUNDANT : sustancioso ⟨a substantial meal : una comida sustanciosa⟩ **2** CONSIDERABLE : considerable, apreciable **3** SOLID, STURDY : sólido

substantially [səb'stæntləli] *adv* : considerablemente

substantiate [səb'stæntlɪˌeɪt] *vt* **-ated; -ating** : confirmar, probar, justificar

substitute¹ ['sʌbstəˌtuːt, -ˌtjuːt] *v* **-tuted; -tuting** *vt* : sustituir — *vi* **to substitute for** : sustituir

substitute² *n* **1** : sustituto *m*, -ta *f*; suplente *mf* (persona) **2** : sucedáneo *m* ⟨sugar substitute : sucedáneo de azúcar⟩

substitute teacher *n* : profesor *m*, -sora *f* suplente

substitution [ˌsʌbstə'tuːlən, -'tjuː-] *n* : sustitución *f*

subterfuge ['sʌbtərˌfjuːdʒ] *n* : subterfugio *m*

subterranean [ˌsʌbtə'reɪniən] *adj* : subterráneo

subtitle ['sʌbˌtaɪtəl] *n* : subtítulo *m*

subtle ['sʌtəl] *adj* **subtler; subtlest 1** DELICATE, ELUSIVE : sutil, delicado **2** CLEVER : sutil, ingenioso

subtlety ['sʌtəlti] *n, pl* **-ties** : sutileza *f*

subtly ['sʌtəli] *adv* : sutilmente

subtotal ['sʌbˌtoːtəl] *m* : subtotal *m*

subtract [səb'trækt] *vt* : restar, sustraer

subtraction [səb'træklən] *n* : resta *f*, sustracción *f*

suburb ['sʌˌbərb] *n* : municipio *m* periférico, suburbio *m*

suburban [sə'bərbən] *adj* : de las afueras (de una ciudad), suburbano

suburbia [sə'bərbiə] *n* : municipios *mpl* periféricos, suburbios *mpl*

subversion [səb'vərʒən] *n* : subversión *f*
subversive [səb'vərsɪv] *adj* : subversivo
subvert [səb'vərt] *vt* : subvertir
subway ['sʌb,weɪ] *n* : metro *m*; subterráneo *m Arg, Uru*
succeed [sək'si:d] *vt* FOLLOW : suceder a — *vi* **1** : tener éxito (dícese de las personas), dar resultado (dícese de los planes, etc.) ⟨she succeeded in finishing : logró terminar⟩ ⟨to succeed in life : triunfar en la vida⟩ **2** : subir, acceder ⟨to succeed to the throne : subir/acceder al trono⟩ — *vt* **1** : suceder a (algo) **2** : suceder (a alguien)
success [sək'sɛs] *n* : éxito *m*
successful [sək'sɛsfəl] *adj* : exitoso, logrado — **successfully** *adv*
succession [sək'sɛɪən] *n* : sucesión *f* ⟨in succession : sucesivamente⟩
successive [sək'sɛsɪv] *adj* : sucesivo, consecutivo — **successively** *adv*
successor [sək'sɛsər] *n* : sucesor *m*, -sora *f*
succinct [sək'sɪŋkt, sə'sɪŋkt] *adj* : sucinto — **succinctly** *adv*
succor[1] ['sʌkər] *vt* : socorrer
succor[2] *n* : socorro *m*
succotash ['sʌkə,tæʃ] *n* : guiso *m* de maíz y frijoles
succulent[1] ['sʌkjələnt] *adj* : suculento, jugoso
succulent[2] *n* : suculenta *f* (planta)
succumb [sə'kʌm] *vi* : sucumbir
such[1] ['sʌtʃ] *adj* **1** (*used for emphasis*) : tan ⟨she's such a nice person! : ¡es tan amable!⟩ ⟨it's been such a long time! : ¡(hace) tanto tiempo!⟩ ⟨it's such a long trip : es un viaje tan largo, es un viaje larguísimo⟩ ⟨such tall buildings! : ¡qué edificios más grandes!⟩ ⟨he's not in such good shape : anda un poco mal⟩ **2** (*indicating degree*) : tan ⟨I've never seen such a large cat! : ¡nunca he visto un gato tan grande como ése!⟩ **3 such as** : como ⟨animals such as cows and sheep : animales como vacas y ovejas⟩
such[2] *adj* **1** : tal ⟨there's no such thing : no existe tal cosa⟩ ⟨there's no such person here : no hay nadie aquí con ese nombre⟩ ⟨in such cases : en tales casos⟩ ⟨to such a degree : hasta tal punto⟩ **2** (*indicating degree*) : tal . . . que, tanto . . . que ⟨where are you off to in such a rush? : ¿adónde vas con tanta prisa?⟩ ⟨I'm such a fool! : ¡qué tonto soy!⟩ **3 such that** : tal . . . que, tanto . . . que ⟨her excitement was such that . . . : tal/tanto era su entusiasmo que . . .⟩
such[3] *pron* **1** : tal ⟨such was the result : tal fue el resultado⟩ ⟨he's a child, and acts as such : es un niño, y se porta como tal⟩ **2** : algo o alguien semejante ⟨books, papers and such : libros, papeles y cosas por el estilo⟩
such–and–such *adj* : tal, cual ⟨at such-and-such (a) time : a tal tiempo⟩
suck ['sʌk] *vt* **1** : chupar **2** : aspirar (dícese de las máquinas) **3** SUCKLE : mamar **4** *fam* : apestar, ser una lata ⟨this sucks : qué lata⟩ **5** *fam* : ser malísimo ⟨I

suck at sports : soy malísimo en los deportes⟩ **6 to suck on** : chupar **7 to suck up to** : dar coba a — *vt* **1** : sorber (bebidas), chupar (dulces, etc.) **2** PULL, DRAG : arrastrar **3** *or* **to suck up** ABSORB : absorber **4 to suck in** : meter (la panza), aspirar (aire) **5 to be/get sucked in** : dejarse engañar **6 to be/get sucked into** : verse envuelto en (un asunto)
sucker ['sʌkər] *n* **1** : ventosa *f* (de un insecto, etc.) **2** : chupón *m* (de una planta) **3** → **lollipop 4** FOOL : tonto *m*, -ta *f*; idiota *mf*
suckle ['sʌkəl] *v* **-led; -ling** *vt* : amamantaɪ — *vi* : mamar
suckling ['sʌklɪŋ] *n* : lactante *mf*
sucrose ['su:,kro:s, -,kro:z] *n* : sacarosa *f*
suction ['sʌkʃən] *n* : succión *f*
Sudanese[1] [,su:də'ni:z, -'i:s] *adj* : sudanés
Sudanese[2] *n* **the Sudanese** (*used with a plural verb*) : los sudaneses
sudden ['sʌdən] *adj* **1** : repentino, súbito ⟨all of a sudden : de pronto, de repente⟩ **2** UNEXPECTED : inesperado, improviso **3** ABRUPT, HASTY : precipitado, brusco
suddenly ['sʌdənli] *adv* **1** : de repente, de pronto **2** ABRUPTLY : bruscamente
suddenness ['sʌdənnəs] *n* **1** : lo repentino **2** ABRUPTNESS : brusquedad *f* **3** HASTE : lo precipitado
suds ['sʌdz] *npl* : espuma *f* (de jabón)
sue ['su:] *v* **sued; suing** *vt* : demandar — *vi* **to sue for** : demandar por (daños, etc.)
suede ['sweɪd] *n* : ante *m*, gamuza *f*
suet ['su:ət] *n* : sebo *m*
suffer ['sʌfər] *vi* : sufrir — *vt* **1** : sufrir, padecer (dolores, etc.) **2** PERMIT : permitir, dejar
sufferer ['sʌfərər] *n* : persona que padece (una enfermedad, etc.)
suffering ['sʌfərɪŋ] *n* : sufrimiento *m*
suffice [sə'faɪs] *vi* **-ficed; -ficing** : ser suficiente, bastar
sufficient [sə'fɪlənt] *adj* : suficiente
sufficiently [sə'fɪləntli] *adv* : (lo) suficientemente, bastante
suffix ['sʌ,fɪks] *n* : sufijo *m*
suffocate ['sʌfə,keɪt] *v* **-cated; -cating** *vt* : asfixiar, ahogar — *vi* : asfixiarse, ahogarse
suffocation [,sʌfə'keɪʃən] *n* : asfixia *f*, ahogo *m*
suffrage ['sʌfrɪʤ] *n* : sufragio *m*, derecho *m* al voto
suffuse [sə'fju:z] *vt* **-fused; -fusing** : impregnar (de olores, etc.), bañar (de luz), teñir (de colores), llenar (de emociones)
sugar[1] ['ʊgər] *vt* : azucarar
sugar[2] *n* : azúcar *mf*
sugarcane ['ʊgər,keɪn] *n* : caña *f* de azúcar
sugary ['ʊgəri] *adj* **1** : azucarado ⟨sugary desserts : postres azucarados⟩ **2** SACCHARINE : empalagoso
suggest [səg'ʤɛst, sə-] *vt* **1** PROPOSE : sugerir **2** IMPLY : indicar, dar a entender
suggestible [səg'ʤɛstəbəl, sə-] *adj* : influenciable

suggestion [sǝg'ʤɛstLǝn, sǝ-] *n* **1** PRO-
POSAL : sugerencia *f* **2** INDICATION
: indicio *m* **3** INSINUATION : insinuación *f*
suggestive [sǝg'ʤɛstɪv, sǝ-] *adj* : insinuante — **suggestively** *adv*
suicidal [ˌsuːǝ'saɪdǝl] *adj* : suicida
suicide ['suːǝˌsaɪd] *n* **1** : suicidio *m*
(acto) **2** : suicida *mf* (persona)
suit[1] ['suːt] *vt* **1** ADAPT : adaptar **2** BEFIT
: convenir a, ser apropiado a **3** BECOME
: favorecer, quedarle bien (a alguien)
⟨the dress suits you : el vestido te queda
bien⟩ **4** PLEASE : agradecer, satisfacer,
convenirle bien (a alguien) ⟨does Friday
suit you? : ¿le conviene el viernes?⟩
⟨suit yourself! : ¡como quieras!⟩
suit[2] *n* **1** LAWSUIT : pleito *m*, litigio *m* **2**
: traje *m* (ropa) **3** : palo *m* (de naipes)
suitability [ˌsuːtǝ'bɪlǝti] *n* : idoneidad *f*, lo
apropiado
suitable ['suːtǝbǝl] *adj* : apropiado, idóneo — **suitably** [-bli] *adv*
suitcase ['suːtˌkeɪs] *n* : maleta *f*, valija *f*,
petaca *f Mex*
suite ['swiːt, for 2 also 'suːt] *n* **1** : suite *f*
(de habitaciones) **2** SET : juego *m* (de
muebles)
suitor ['suːtǝr] *n* : pretendiente *m*
sulfur ['sʌlfǝr] *n* : azufre *m*
sulfuric acid [ˌsʌl'fjʊrɪk] *adj* : ácido *m*
sulfúrico
sulk[1] ['sʌlk] *vi* : estar de mal humor, enfurruñarse *fam*
sulk[2] *n* : mal humor *m*
sulky ['sʌlki] *adj* **sulkier; -est** : malhumorado, taimado *Chile*
sullen ['sʌlǝn] *adj* **1** MOROSE : hosco,
taciturno **2** DREARY : sombrío, deprimente
sullenly ['sʌlǝnli] *adv* **1** MOROSELY
: hoscamente **2** GLOOMILY : sombríamente
sully ['sʌli] *vt* **sullied; sullying** : manchar,
empañar
sultan ['sʌltǝn] *n* : sultán *m*
sultry ['sʌltri] *adj* **sultrier; -est 1** : bochornoso ⟨sultry weather : tiempo sofocante, tiempo bochornoso⟩ **2** SENSUAL
: sensual, seductor
sum[1] ['sʌm] *vt* **summed; summing 1**
: sumar (números) **2** → **sum up**
sum[2] *n* **1** AMOUNT : suma *f*, cantidad
f **2** TOTAL : suma *f*, total *f* **3** : suma *f*,
adición *f* (en matemáticas)
sumac ['ʃuːˌmæk, 'suː-] *n* : zumaque *m*
summarize ['sʌmǝˌraɪz] *v* **-rized; -rizing**
: resumir, compendiar
summary[1] ['sʌmǝri] *adj* **1** CONCISE
: breve, conciso **2** IMMEDIATE : inmediato ⟨a summary dismissal : un despido
inmediato⟩ — **summarily** *adv*
summary[2] *n, pl* **-ries** : resumen *m*, compendio *m*
summation [sǝ'meɪLǝn] *n* : resumen *m*
summer ['sʌmǝr] *n* : verano *m*
summertime ['sʌmǝrˌtaɪm] *n* : verano *m*,
estío *m*
summery ['sʌmǝri] *adj* : veraniego
summit ['sʌmǝt] *n* **1** : cumbre *f*, cima *f*

(de una montaña) **2** *or* **summit conference** : cumbre *f*
summon ['sʌmǝn] *vt* **1** CALL : convocar
(una reunión, etc.), llamar (a una persona) **2** : citar (en derecho) **3 to summon up** : armarse de (valor, etc.) ⟨to
summon up one's strength : reunir fuer-
zas⟩
summons ['sʌmǝnz] *n, pl* **summonses 1**
SUBPOENA : citación *f*, citatorio *m*
Mex **2** CALL : llamada *f*, llamamiento *m*
sumptuous ['sʌmptʃʊǝs] *adj* : suntuoso
— **sumptuously** *adv*
sum up *vt* **1** SUMMARIZE : resumir **2**
EVALUATE : evaluar — *vi* : recapitular
sun[1] ['sʌn] *vt* **sunned; sunning 1** : poner
al sol **2 to sun oneself** : asolearse, tomar el sol
sun[2] *n* **1** : sol *m* **2** SUNSHINE : luz *f* del
sol
sunbathe ['sʌnˌbeɪð] *vi* **-bathed; -bathing**
: asolearse, tomar el sol
sunbeam ['sʌnˌbiːm] *n* : rayo *m* de sol
sunblock ['sʌnˌblɑk] *n* : filtro *m* solar
sunburn[1] ['sʌnˌbǝrn] *vi* **-burned** [-ˌbǝrnd]
or **-burnt** [-ˌbǝrnt]; **-burning** : quemarse
por el sol
sunburn[2] *n* : quemadura *f* de sol
sundae ['sʌnˌdeɪ, -di] *n* : postre *m* de helado (con jarabe, crema batida, etc.)
Sunday ['sʌnˌdeɪ, -di] *n* : domingo *m* ⟨to-
day is Sunday : hoy es domingo⟩ ⟨(on)
Sunday : el domingo⟩ ⟨(on) Sundays
: los domingos⟩ ⟨last Sunday : el domingo pasado⟩ ⟨next Sunday : el domingo que viene⟩ ⟨every other Sunday
: cada dos domingos⟩ ⟨Sunday after-
noon/morning : domingo por la tarde/
mañana⟩
sundial ['sʌnˌdaɪl] *n* : reloj *m* de sol
sundown ['sʌnˌdaʊn] → **sunset**
sundries ['sʌndriz] *npl* : artículos *mpl* diversos
sundry ['sʌndri] *adj* : varios, diversos
sunflower ['sʌnˌflaʊǝr] *n* : girasol *m*, mirasol *m*
sung → **sing**
sunglasses ['sʌnˌglæsǝz] *npl* : gafas *fpl* de
sol, lentes *mpl* de sol
sunk → **sink**[1]
sunken ['sʌŋkǝn] *adj* : hundido
sunlight ['sʌnˌlaɪt] *n* : sol *m*, luz *f* del sol
Sunni ['sʊni] *n* : sunita *mf*
sunny ['sʌni] *adj* **sunnier; -est** : soleado
sunrise ['sʌnˌraɪz] *n* : salida *f* del sol
sunroof ['sʌnˌruːf] *n* : techo *m* corredizo
sunscreen ['sʌnˌskriːn] *n* : filtro *m* solar
sunset ['sʌnˌsɛt] *n* : puesta *f* del sol
sunshine ['sʌnˌʃaɪn] *n* : sol *m*, luz *f* del sol
sunspot ['sʌnˌspɑt] *n* : mancha *f* solar
sunstroke ['sʌnˌstroːk] *n* : insolación *f*
suntan ['sʌnˌtæn] *n* : bronceado *m* ⟨sun-
tan lotion : bronceador⟩
suntanned ['sʌnˌtænd] *adj* : bronceado
sup ['sʌp] *vi* **supped; supping** : cenar
super ['suːpǝr] *adj* : súper ⟨super!
: ¡fantástico!⟩
super- [ˌsuːpǝr] *pref* : super-
superb [sʊ'pǝrb] *adj* : magnífico, espléndido — **superbly** *adv*

supercilious [ˌsuːpərˈsɪliəs] *adj* : altivo, altanero, desdeñoso

supercomputer [ˈsuːpərkəmˌpjuːtər] *n* : supercomputadora *f*

superficial [ˌsuːpərˈfɪʃəl] *adj* : superficial — **superficially** *adv* — **superficiality** *n*

superfluous [suˈpərfluəs] *adj* : superfluo — **superfluity** *n*

superhighway [ˈsuːpərˌhaɪˌweɪ, ˌsuːpərˈ-] *n* : autopista *f*

superhuman [ˌsuːpərˈhjuːmən] *adj* **1** SUPERNATURAL : sobrenatural **2** HERCULEAN : sobrehumano

superimpose [ˌsuːpərɪmˈpoːz] *vt* **-posed; -posing** : superponer, sobreponer

superintend [ˌsuːpərɪnˈtɛnd] *vt* : supervisar

superintendent [ˌsuːpərɪnˈtɛndənt] *n* : portero *m*, -ra *f* (de un edificio); director *m*, -tora *f* (de una escuela, etc.); superintendente *mf* (de policía)

superior¹ [suˈpɪriər] *adj* **1** BETTER : superior **2** HAUGHTY : altivo, altanero

superior² *n* : superior *m*

superiority [suˌpɪriˈɔrət̬i] *n*, *pl* **-ties** : superioridad *f*

superlative¹ [suˈpərlət̬ɪv] *adj* **1** : superlativo (en gramática) **2** SUPREME : supremo **3** EXCELLENT : excelente, excepcional

superlative² *n* : superlativo *m*

supermarket [ˈsuːpərˌmɑrkət] *n* : supermercado *m*

supernatural [ˌsuːpərˈnætʃərəl] *adj* : sobrenatural

supernaturally [ˌsuːpərˈnætʃərəli] *adv* : de manera sobrenatural

superpower [ˈsuːpərˌpaʊər] *n* : superpotencia *f*

supersede [ˌsuːpərˈsiːd] *vt* **-seded; -seding** : suplantar, reemplazar, sustituir

supersonic [ˌsuːpərˈsɑnɪk] *adj* : supersónico

superstar [ˈsuːpərˌstɑr] *n* : superestrella *f*

superstition [ˌsuːpərˈstɪʃən] *n* : superstición *f*

superstitious [ˌsuːpərˈstɪʃəs] *adj* : supersticioso

superstore [ˈsuːpərˌstor] *n* : hipermercado *m*

superstructure [ˈsuːpərˌstrʌktʃər] *n* : superestructura *f*

supervise [ˈsuːpərˌvaɪz] *vt* **-vised; -vising** : supervisar, dirigir

supervision [ˌsuːpərˈvɪʒən] *n* : supervisión *f*, dirección *f*

supervisor [ˈsuːpərˌvaɪzər] *n* : supervisor *m*, -sora *f*

supervisory [ˌsuːpərˈvaɪzəri] *adj* : de supervisor

supine [suˈpaɪn] *adj* **1** : en decúbito supino, en decúbito dorsal **2** ABJECT, INDIFFERENT : indiferente, apático

supper [ˈsʌpər] *n* : cena *f*, comida *f*

supplant [səˈplænt] *vt* : suplantar

supple [ˈsʌpəl] *adj* **suppler; supplest** : flexible

supplement¹ [ˈsʌpləˌmɛnt] *vt* : complementar, completar

supplement² [ˈsʌpləmənt] *n* **1** : complemento *m* ⟨dietary supplement : complemento alimenticio⟩ **2** : suplemento *m* (de un libro o periódico)

supplementary [ˌsʌpləˈmɛntəri] *adj* : suplementario

supplicate [ˈsʌpləˌkeɪt] *v* **-cated; -cating** *vi* : rezar — *vt* : suplicar

supplier [səˈplaɪər] *n* : proveedor *m*, -dora *f*; abastecedor *m*, -dora *f*

supply¹ [səˈplaɪ] *vt* **-plied; -plying** : suministrar, proveer de, proporcionar

supply² *n*, *pl* **-plies 1** PROVISION : provisión *f*, suministro *m* ⟨supply and demand : la oferta y la demanda⟩ **2** STOCK : reserva *f*, existencias *fpl* (de un negocio) **3** **supplies** *npl* PROVISIONS : provisiones *fpl*, víveres *mpl*, despensa *f*

support¹ [səˈport] *vt* **1** BACK : apoyar, respaldar **2** MAINTAIN : mantener, sostener, sustentar **3** PROP UP : sostener, apoyar, apuntalar, soportar

support² *n* **1** : apoyo *m* (moral), ayuda *f* (económica) **2** PROP : soporte *m*, apoyo *m*

supporter [səˈportər] *n* : partidario *m*, -ria *f*

supportive [səˈportɪv] *adj* : que apoya ⟨his family is very supportive : su familia lo apoya mucho⟩

suppose [səˈpoːz] *vt* **-posed; -posing 1** ASSUME : suponer, imaginarse ⟨(let's) suppose that . . . : supongamos que . . .⟩ **2** BELIEVE : suponer, creer ⟨I suppose so/not : supongo que sí/no⟩ **3** (*used in polite requests*) ⟨I don't suppose you could help me? : ¿tú no podrías ayudarme?⟩ **4 to be supposed to** (*indicating expectation or intention*) ⟨he's supposed to arrive today : se supone que llegue hoy⟩ ⟨it was supposed to be a surprise : se suponía que iba a ser una sorpresa⟩ ⟨what's that supposed to mean? : ¿qué quieres decir con eso?⟩ **5 to be supposed to** (*indicating obligation or permission*) ⟨I'm supposed to study : (se supone que) tengo que estudiar⟩ ⟨you're not supposed to go : no deberías ir⟩ **6 to be supposed to** (*indicating what others say*) ⟨she's supposed to be the best : dicen que es la mejor⟩

supposed [səˈpoːzd, -ˈpoːzəd] *adj* : supuesto — **supposedly** [səˈpoːzədli] *adv*

supposition [ˌsʌpəˈzɪʃən] *n* : suposición *f*

suppository [səˈpɑzəˌtori] *n*, *pl* **-ries** : supositorio *m*

suppress [səˈprɛs] *vt* **1** SUBDUE : sofocar, suprimir, reprimir (una rebelión, etc.) **2** : suprimir, ocultar (información) **3** REPRESS : reprimir, contener ⟨to suppress a yawn : reprimir un bostezo⟩

suppression [səˈprɛʃən] *n* **1** SUBDUING : represión *f* **2** : supresión *f* (de información) **3** REPRESSION : represión *f*, inhibición *f*

supremacy [suˈprɛməsi] *n*, *pl* **-cies** : supremacía *f*

supreme [suˈpriːm] *adj* : supremo

Supreme Being *n* : Ser *m* Supremo

supremely [sʊ'priːmli] *adv* : totalmente, sumamente

surcharge ['sər,tlɑrdʒ] *n* : recargo *m*

sure¹ ['lʊr] *adv* 1 ALL RIGHT : por supuesto, claro 2 (*used as an intensifier*) ⟨it sure is hot! : ¡hace tanto calor!⟩ ⟨she sure is pretty! : ¡qué linda es!⟩

sure² *adj* **surer; -est** 1 : seguro ⟨a sure sign : una clara señal⟩ ⟨a sure method : un método seguro⟩ ⟨it's a sure thing that . . . : seguro que . . .⟩ 2 **for sure** ⟨to know for sure : saber a ciencia cierta, saber con certeza⟩ ⟨for sure! : ¡ya lo creo!⟩ ⟨that's for sure : eso es seguro⟩ 3 **to be sure** ⟨to be sure (about/of something) : estar seguro (de algo)⟩ ⟨to be sure that . . . : estar seguro de que . . .⟩ ⟨to be sure of oneself : estar seguro de sí mismo⟩ ⟨I'm not sure why : no sé por qué⟩ ⟨be sure to call! : ¡no dejes de llamar!⟩ 4 **to make sure** ⟨he made sure (that) the door was locked : se aseguró de que la puerta estaba cerrada con llave⟩ ⟨make sure to call! : ¡no dejes de llamar!⟩ ⟨make sure it doesn't happen again : que no vuelva a pasar⟩

surely ['lʊrli] *adv* 1 CERTAINLY : seguramente 2 (*used as an intensifier*) ⟨you surely don't mean that! : ¡no me digas que estás hablando en serio!⟩

sureness ['lʊrnəs] *n* : certeza *f*, seguridad *f*

surety ['lʊrəṭi] *n, pl* **-ties** : fianza *f*, garantía *f*

surf¹ ['sərf] *vi* : hacer surf — *vt* : navegar ⟨to surf the Web : navegar por/en la web⟩

surf² *n* 1 WAVES : oleaje *m* 2 FOAM : espuma *f*

surface¹ ['sərfəs] *v* **-faced; -facing** *vi* : salir a la superficie — *vt* : revestir (una carretera)

surface² *n* 1 : superficie *f* 2 **on the surface** : en apariencia

surfboard ['sərf,bord] *n* : tabla *f* de surf, tabla *f* de surfing

surfeit ['sərfət] *n* : exceso *m*

surfer ['sərfər] *n* : surfista *mf* ⟨Internet surfers : internautas⟩

surfing ['sərfɪŋ] *n* : surf *m*, surfing *m*

surge¹ ['sərdʒ] *vi* **surged; surging** 1 : hincharse (dícese del mar), levantarse (dícese de las olas) 2 SWARM : salir en tropel (dícese de la gente, etc.)

surge² *n* 1 : oleaje *m* (del mar), oleada *f* (de gente) 2 FLUSH : arranque *m*, arrebato *m* (de ira, etc.) 3 INCREASE : aumento *m* (súbito)

surgeon ['sərdʒən] *n* : cirujano *m*, -na *f*

surgery ['sərdʒəri] *n, pl* **-geries** : cirugía *f*

surgical ['sərdʒɪkəl] *adj* : quirúrgico — **surgically** [-kli] *adv*

surly ['sərli] *adj* **surlier; -est** : hosco, arisco

surmise¹ [sər'maɪz] *vt* **-mised; -mising** : conjeturar, suponer, concluir

surmise² *n* : conjetura *f*

surmount [sər'maʊnt] *vt* 1 OVERCOME : superar, vencer, salvar 2 CLIMB : escalar 3 CAP, TOP : coronar

surname ['sər,neɪm] *n* : apellido *m*

surpass [sər'pæs] *vt* : superar, exceder, rebasar, sobrepasar

surplus ['sər,plʌs] *n* : excedente *m*, sobrante *m*, superávit *m* (de dinero)

surprise¹ [sə'praɪz, sər-] *vt* **-prised; -prising** : sorprender

surprise² *n* : sorpresa *f* ⟨to take by surprise : sorprender⟩

surprising [sə'praɪzɪŋ, sər-] *adj* : sorprendente — **surprisingly** *adv*

surreal [sə'riːl] *adj* : surrealista

surrealism [sə'riːə,lɪzəm] *n* : surrealismo *m*

surrealist [sə'riːəlɪst] *n* : surrealista *mf*

surrealistic [sə,riːə'lɪstɪk] *adj* : surrealista

surrender¹ [sə'rɛndər] *vt* 1 : entregar, rendir 2 **to surrender oneself** : entregarse — *vi* : rendirse

surrender² *n* : rendición *m* (de una ciudad, etc.), entrega *f* (de posesiones)

surreptitious [,sərəp'tɪləs] *adj* : subrepticio — **surreptitiously** *adv*

surrogate ['sərəgət, -,ɡeɪt] *n* 1 : sustituto *m* 2 *or* **surrogate mother** : madre *f* de alquiler

surround [sə'raʊnd] *vt* : rodear

surroundings [sə'raʊndɪŋz] *npl* : ambiente *m*, entorno *m*

surveillance [sər'veɪlən*t*s, -'veɪljən*t*s, -'veɪən*t*s] *n* : vigilancia *f*

survey¹ [sər'veɪ] *vt* **-veyed; -veying** 1 : medir (un terreno) 2 EXAMINE : inspeccionar, examinar, revisar 3 POLL : hacer una encuesta de, sondear

survey² ['sər,veɪ] *n, pl* **-veys** 1 INSPECTION : inspección *f*, revisión *f* 2 : medición *f* (de un terreno) 3 POLL : encuesta *f*, sondeo *m*

surveyor [sər'veɪər] *n* : agrimensor *m*, -sora *f*

survival [sər'vaɪvəl] *n* : supervivencia *f*, sobrevivencia *f*

survive [sər'vaɪv] *v* **-vived; -viving** *vi* : sobrevivir — *vt* OUTLIVE : sobrevivir a

survivor [sər'vaɪvər] *n* : superviviente *mf*, sobreviviente *mf*

susceptibility [sə,sɛptə'bɪləṭi] *n, pl* **-ties** : vulnerabilidad *f*, propensión *f* (a enfermedades, etc.)

susceptible [sə'sɛptəbəl] *adj* 1 VULNERABLE : vulnerable, sensible ⟨susceptible to flattery : sensible a halagos⟩ 2 PRONE : propenso ⟨susceptible to colds : propenso a resfriarse⟩

suspect¹ [sə'spɛkt] *vt* 1 DISTRUST : dudar de 2 : sospechar (algo), sospechar de (una persona) 3 IMAGINE, THINK : imaginarse, creer

suspect² ['sʌs,pɛkt, sə'spɛkt] *adj* : sospechoso, dudoso, cuestionable

suspect³ ['sʌs,pɛkt] *n* : sospechoso *m*, -sa *f*

suspend [sə'spɛnd] *vt* : suspender

suspenders [sə'spɛndərz] *npl* : tirantes *mpl*

suspense [sə'spɛn*t*s] *n* : incertidumbre *f*, suspenso *m* (en una película, etc.)

suspenseful [sə'spɛn*t*sfəl] *adj* : de suspenso

suspension [sə'spɛntɫən] *n* : suspensión *f*
suspension bridge *n* : puente *m* colgante
suspicion [sə'spɪʃən] *n* **1** : sospecha *f* **2** TRACE : pizca *f*, atisbo *m*
suspicious [sə'spɪʃəs] *adj* **1** QUESTIONABLE : sospechoso, dudoso **2** DISTRUSTFUL : suspicaz, desconfiado
suspiciously [sə'spɪʃəsli] *adv* : de modo sospechoso, con recelo
sustain [sə'steɪn] *vt* **1** NOURISH : sustentar **2** PROLONG : sostener **3** SUFFER : sufrir **4** SUPPORT, UPHOLD : apoyar, respaldar, sostener
sustainable [sə'steɪnəbəl] *adj* : sostenible
sustenance ['sʌstənənts] *n* **1** NOURISHMENT : sustento *m* **2** SUPPORT : sostén *m*
suture ['su:tɫər] *n* : sutura *f*
SUV [ˌɛsˌju:'vi:] *n* : SUV *m*, vehículo *m* deportivo utilitario
svelte ['sfɛlt] *adj* : esbelto
swab[1] ['swɑb] *vt* **swabbed; swabbing 1** CLEAN : lavar, limpiar **2** : aplicar a (con hisopo)
swab[2] *n* **cotton swab** : hisopo *m*, bastoncillo *m*, cotonete *m Mex*
swaddle ['swɑdəl] *vt* **-dled; -dling** ['swɑdəlɪŋ] : envolver (en pañales)
swagger[1] ['swægər] *vi* : pavonearse
swagger[2] *n* : pavoneo *m*
swallow[1] ['swɑlo:] *vt* **1** : tragar (comida, etc.) **2** ENGULF : tragarse, envolver **3** REPRESS : tragarse (insultos, etc.) — *vi* : tragar
swallow[2] *n* **1** : golondrina *f* (pájaro) **2** GULP : trago *m*
swam → **swim**[1]
swamp[1] ['swɑmp] *vt* : inundar ⟨to swamp with : inundar de⟩
swamp[2] *n* : pantano *m*, ciénaga *f*
swampy ['swɑmpi] *adj* **swampier; -est** : pantanoso, cenagoso
swan ['swɑn] *n* : cisne *f*
swap[1] ['swɑp] *vt* **swapped; swapping** : cambiar, intercambiar ⟨to swap places : cambiarse de sitio⟩
swap[2] *n* : cambio *m*, intercambio *m*
swarm[1] ['swɔrm] *vi* : enjambrar
swarm[2] *n* : enjambre *m*
swarthy ['swɔrði, -θi] *adj* **swarthier; -est** : moreno
swashbuckling ['swɑɪˌbʌklɪŋ] *adj* : de aventurero
swastika ['swɑstɪskə] *n* : esvástica *f*
swat[1] ['swɑt] *vt* **swatted; swatting** : aplastar (un insecto), darle una palmada (a alguien)
swat[2] *n* : palmada *f* (con la mano), golpe *m* (con un objeto)
swatch ['swɑtʃ] *n* : muestra *f*
swath ['swɑθ, 'swɔθ] *or* **swathe** ['swɑð, 'swɔð, 'sweɪð] *n* : franja *f* (de grano segado)
swathe ['swɑð, 'swɔð, 'sweɪð] *vt* **swathed; swathing** : envolver
swatter ['swɑtər] → **flyswatter**
sway[1] ['sweɪ] *vi* : balancearse, mecerse — *vt* INFLUENCE : influir en, convencer
sway[2] *n* **1** SWINGING : balanceo *m* **2** INFLUENCE : influjo *m*

swear ['swær] *v* **swore** ['swor]; **sworn** ['sworn]; **swearing** *vi* **1** VOW : jurar ⟨I could have sworn it was true : habría jurado que era verdad⟩ **2** CURSE : decir palabrotas — *vt* **1** : jurar ⟨I couldn't swear to it : no me atrevería a jurarlo⟩ **2 to swear in** : juramentar (a un testigo), investir (a un oficial)
swearword ['swær,wərd] *n* : mala palabra *f*, palabrota *f*
sweat[1] ['swɛt] *vi* **sweat** *or* **sweated; sweating 1** PERSPIRE : sudar, transpirar **2** OOZE : rezumar **3 to sweat over** : sudar la gota gorda por
sweat[2] *n* : sudor *m*, transpiración *f*
sweater ['swɛtər] *n* : suéter *m*, buzo *m Uru*
sweatpants ['swɛt,pænts] *n* : pantalón *m* de ejercicio, jogging *m Arg*, pants *m Mex*
sweatshirt ['swɛt,ʃərt] *n* : sudadera *f*; buzo *m Arg, Col*; polerón *m Chile* (camisa)
sweatsuit ['swɛt,su:t] *n* : sudadera *f*; buzo *m Chile, Peru*; jogging *m Arg*; pants *m Mex*; chándal *m Spain* (traje)
sweaty ['swɛti] *adj* **sweatier; -est** : sudoroso, sudado, transpirado
Swede ['swi:d] *n* : sueco *m*, -ca *f*
Swedish[1] ['swi:dɪʃ] *adj* : sueco
Swedish[2] *n* **1** : sueco *m* (idioma) **2 the Swedish** (*used with a plural verb*) : los suecos
sweep[1] ['swi:p] *v* **swept** ['swɛpt]; **sweeping** *vt* **1** : barrer (el suelo, etc.), limpiar (la suciedad, etc.) ⟨he swept the books aside : apartó los libros de un manotazo⟩ **2** *or* **to sweep through** : extenderse por (dícese del fuego, etc.), azotar (dícese de una tormenta) ⟨a craze that's sweeping the nation : una moda que está haciendo furor en todo el país⟩ **3** DRAG : barrer, arrastrar **4** : recorrer ⟨her gaze swept the class : recorrió la clase con la mirada⟩ **5** SEARCH : peinar **6** : ir (dramáticamente) ⟨she swept into the room : entró a lo grande en la habitación⟩ **7** DEFEAT : barrer con (un rival, etc.) **8** : barrer en, arrasar en (elecciones, etc.) ⟨the team swept the series : el equipo barrió en la serie⟩ **9 to sweep aside** DISMISS : desechar **10 to sweep up** : recoger — *vi* **1** : barrer, limpiar **2** : extenderse (en una curva), describir una curva ⟨the sun swept across the sky : el sol describía una curva en el cielo⟩ **3 to sweep up** : barrer
sweep[2] *n* **1** : barrido *m*, barrida *f* (con una escoba) **2** : movimiento *m* circular **3** SCOPE : alcance *m*
sweeper ['swi:pər] *n* : barrendero *m*, -ra *f*
sweeping ['swi:pɪŋ] *adj* **1** WIDE : amplio (dícese de un movimiento) **2** EXTENSIVE : extenso, radical **3** INDISCRIMINATE : indiscriminado, demasiado general **4** OVERWHELMING : arrollador, aplastante
sweepstakes ['swi:p,steɪks] *ns & pl* **1** : carrera *f* (en que el ganador se lleva el premio entero) **2** LOTTERY : lotería *f*

sweet[1] ['swi:t] *adj* **1** : dulce ⟨sweet desserts : postres dulces⟩ **2** FRESH : fresco **3** : sin sal (dícese de la mantequilla, etc.) **4** PLEASANT : dulce, agradable **5** DEAR : querido

sweet[2] *n* : dulce *m*

sweet–and–sour *adj* : agridulce

sweeten ['swi:tən] *vt* : endulzar

sweetener ['swi:tənər] *n* : endulzante *m*

sweetheart ['swi:t,hɑrt] *n* : novio *m*, -via *f* ⟨thanks, sweetheart : gracias, cariño⟩

sweetly ['swi:tli] *adv* : dulcemente

sweetness ['swi:tnəs] *n* : dulzura *f*

sweet potato *n* : batata *f*, boniato *m*

swell[1] ['swɛl] *vi* **swelled; swelled** *or* **swollen** ['swo:lən, 'swʌl-]; **swelling 1** *or* **to swell up** : hincharse ⟨her ankle swelled : se le hinchó el tobillo⟩ **2** *or* **to swell out** : inflarse, hincharse (dícese de las velas, etc.) **3** INCREASE : aumentar, crecer

swell[2] *n* **1** : oleaje *m* (del mar) **2** → **swelling**

swelling ['swɛlɪŋ] *n* : hinchazón *f*

swelter ['swɛltər] *vi* : sofocarse de calor

swept → **sweep**[1]

swerve[1] ['swərv] *vi* **swerved; swerving** : virar bruscamente

swerve[2] *n* : viraje *m* brusco

swift[1] ['swɪft] *adj* **1** FAST : rápido, veloz **2** SUDDEN : repentino, súbito — **swiftly** *adv*

swift[2] *n* : vencejo *m* (pájaro)

swiftness ['swɪftnəs] *n* : rapidez *f*, velocidad *f*

swig[1] ['swɪg] *vi* **swigged; swigging** : tomar a tragos, beber a tragos

swig[2] *n* : trago *m*

swill[1] ['swɪl] *vt* : chupar, beber a tragos grandes

swill[2] *n* **1** SLOP : bazofia *f* **2** GARBAGE : basura *f*

swim[1] ['swɪm] *vi* **swam** ['swæm]; **swum** ['swʌm]; **swimming 1** : nadar **2** FLOAT : flotar **3** REEL : dar vueltas ⟨his head was swimming : la cabeza le daba vueltas⟩

swim[2] *n* : baño *m*, chapuzón *m* ⟨to go for a swim : ir a nadar⟩

swimmer ['swɪmər] *n* : nadador *m*, -dora *f*

swimming ['swɪmɪŋ] *n* : natación *f* ⟨to go swimming : ir a nadar⟩

swimming pool *n* : piscina *f*

swimming trunks *n* : traje *m* de baño; malla *f Arg, Uru*; bañador *m Spain* (de hombre)

swimsuit ['swɪm,su:t] *n* : traje *m* de baño; malla *f* de baño *Arg, Uru*; bañador *m Spain*

swindle[1] ['swɪndəl] *vt* **-dled; -dling** : estafar, timar

swindle[2] *n* : estafa *f*, timo *m fam*

swindler ['swɪndələr] *n* : estafador *m*, -dora *f*; timador *m*, -dora *f*

swine ['swaɪn] *ns & pl* : cerdo *m*, -da *f*

swing[1] ['swɪŋ] *v* **swung** ['swʌŋ]; **swinging** *vt* **1** : describir una curva con ⟨she swung the ax at the tree : le dio al árbol con el hacha⟩ ⟨he swung himself (up) into the truck : se subió al camión⟩ **2** : balancear (los brazos, etc.), hacer osci-

lar **3** SUSPEND : colgar **4** MANAGE : arreglar ⟨he'll come if he can swing it : vendrá si puede arreglarlo⟩ ⟨I can't swing a new car : no me alcanza para comprar un auto nuevo⟩ — *vi* **1** SWAY : balancearse (dícese de los brazos, etc.), oscilar (dícese de un objeto), columpiarse, mecerse (en un columpio) **2** SWIVEL : girar (en un pivote) ⟨the door swung shut : la puerta se cerró⟩ **3** CHANGE : virar, cambiar (dícese de las opiniones, etc.) **4** : intentar darle a algo/alguien ⟨he swung at me : intentó pegarme⟩ ⟨she swung (at the ball) but missed : bateó pero no conectó⟩ **5 to swing by** *fam* : pasar (por) ⟨I'll swing by later : pasaré a verte luego⟩ ⟨he'll swing by the store on his way home : pasará por la tienda de camino a casa⟩ **6 to swing into action** : entrar en acción

swing[2] *n* **1** SWINGING : vaivén *m*, balanceo *m* **2** CHANGE, SHIFT : viraje *m*, movimiento *m* **3** : columpio *m* (para niños) **4 to take a swing at someone** : intentar pegarle a alguien

swipe[1] ['swaɪp] *vt* **swiped; swiping 1** STRIKE : dar, pegar (con un movimiento amplio) **2** WIPE : limpiar **3** STEAL : birlar *fam*, robar

swipe[2] *n* BLOW : golpe *m*

swirl[1] ['swərl] *vi* : arremolinarse

swirl[2] *n* **1** EDDY : remolino *m* **2** SPIRAL : espiral *f*

swish[1] ['swɪʃ] *vt* : mover (produciendo un sonido) ⟨she swished her skirt : movía la falda⟩ — *vi* : moverse (produciendo un sonido) ⟨the cars swished by : se oían pasar los coches⟩

swish[2] *n* : silbido *m* (de un látigo, etc.), susurro *m* (de agua), crujido *m* (de ropa, etc.)

Swiss[1] ['swɪs] *adj* : suizo

Swiss[2] *n* **the Swiss** (*used with a plural verb*) : los suizos

swiss chard *n* : acelga *f*

switch[1] ['swɪtʃ] *vt* **1** LASH, WHIP : azotar **2** CHANGE : cambiar de **3** EXCHANGE : intercambiar **4 to switch on** : encender, prender **5 to switch off** : apagar — *vi* **1** : moverse de un lado al otro **2** CHANGE : cambiar **3** SWAP : intercambiarse

switch[2] *n* **1** WHIP : vara *f* **2** CHANGE, SHIFT : cambio *m* **3** : interruptor *m*, llave *f* (de la luz, etc.)

switchblade ['swɪtʃ,bleɪd] *n* : navaja *f* de muelle

switchboard ['swɪtʃ,bord] *n* : conmutador *m*, centralita *f*

swivel[1] ['swɪvəl] *vi* **-veled** *or* **-velled; -veling** *or* **-velling** : girar (sobre un pivote)

swivel[2] *n* : base *f* giratoria

swollen *pp* → **swell**[1]

swoon[1] ['swu:n] *vi* : desvanecerse, desmayarse

swoon[2] *n* : desvanecimiento *m*, desmayo *m*

swoop[1] ['swu:p] *vi* : abatirse (dícese de las aves), descender en picada (dícese de un avión)

swoop² *n* : descenso *m* en picada
sword ['sɔrd] *n* : espada *f*
swordfish ['sɔrd,fɪʃ] *n* : pez *m* espada
swore, sworn → **swear**
swum *pp* → **swim¹**
swung → **swing¹**
sycamore ['sɪkə,mor] *n* : sicomoro *m*
sycophant ['sɪkəfənt, -,fænt] *n* : adulador *m*, -dora *f*
syllabic [sə'læbɪk] *adj* : silábico
syllable ['sɪləbəl] *n* : sílaba *f*
syllabus ['sɪləbəs] *n, pl* **-bi** [-,baɪ] *or* **-buses** : programa *m* (de estudios)
symbol ['sɪmbəl] *n* : símbolo *m*
symbolic [sɪm'bɑlɪk] *adj* : simbólico — **symbolically** [-kli] *adv*
symbolism ['sɪmbə,lɪzəm] *n* : simbolismo *m*
symbolize ['sɪmbə,laɪz] *vt* **-ized; -izing** : simbolizar
symmetrical [sə'mɛtrɪkəl] *or* **symmetric** [-trɪk] *adj* : simétrico — **symmetrically** [-trɪkli] *adv*
symmetry ['sɪmətri] *n, pl* **-tries** : simetría *f*
sympathetic [,sɪmpə'θɛt̬ɪk] *adj* **1** PLEASING : agradable **2** RECEPTIVE : receptivo, favorable **3** COMPASSIONATE, UNDERSTANDING : comprensivo, compasivo
sympathetically [,sɪmpə'θɛt̬ɪkli] *adv* : con compasión, con comprensión
sympathize ['sɪmpə,θaɪz] *vi* **-thized; -thizing** : compadecer ⟨I sympathize with you : te compadezco⟩
sympathizer ['sɪmpə,θaɪzər] *n* : simpatizante *mf*
sympathy ['sɪmpəθi] *n, pl* **-thies 1** COMPASSION : compasión *f* **2** UNDERSTANDING : comprensión *f* **3** AGREEMENT : solidaridad *f* ⟨in sympathy with : de acuerdo con⟩ **4** CONDOLENCES : pésame *m*, condolencias *fpl*
symphonic [sɪm'fɑnɪk] *adj* : sinfónico
symphony ['sɪmpfəni] *n, pl* **-nies 1** : sinfonía *f* **2** *or* **symphony orchestra** : orquesta *f* sinfónica
symposium [sɪm'po:ziəm] *n, pl* **-sia** [-ziə] *or* **-siums** : simposio *m*
symptom ['sɪmptəm] *n* : síntoma *m*
symptomatic [,sɪmptə'mæt̬ɪk] *adj* : sintomático

synagogue ['sɪnə,gɑg, -,gɔg] *n* : sinagoga *f*
sync ['sɪŋk] *n* : sincronización *f* ⟨in sync : sincronizado⟩
synchronize ['sɪŋkrə,naɪz, 'sɪn-] *v* **-nized; -nizing** *vi* : estar sincronizado — *vt* : sincronizar
syncopate ['sɪŋkə,peɪt, 'sɪn-] *vt* **-pated; -pating** : sincopar
syncopation [,sɪŋkə'peɪʃən, ,sɪn-] *n* : síncopa *f*
syndicate¹ ['sɪndə,keɪt] *vi* **-cated; -cating** : formar una asociación
syndicate² ['sɪndɪkət] *n* : asociación *f*, agrupación *f*
syndrome ['sɪn,dro:m] *n* : síndrome *m*
synonym ['sɪnə,nɪm] *n* : sinónimo *m*
synonymous [sə'nɑnəməs] *adj* : sinónimo
synopsis [sə'nɑpsɪs] *n, pl* **-opses** [-,si:z] : sinopsis *f*
syntactic [sɪn'tæktɪk] *adj* : sintáctico
syntax ['sɪn,tæks] *n* : sintaxis *f*
synthesis ['sɪnθəsɪs] *n, pl* **-theses** [-,si:z] : síntesis *f*
synthesize ['sɪnθə,saɪz] *vt* **-sized; -sizing** : sintetizar
synthesizer ['sɪnθə,saɪzər] *n* : sintetizador *m*
synthetic¹ [sɪn'θɪt̬ɪk] *adj* : sintético, artificial — **synthetically** [-t̬ɪkli] *adv*
synthetic² *n* : producto *m* sintético
syphilis ['sɪfələs] *n* : sífilis *f*
Syrian ['sɪriən] *n* : sirio *m*, -ria *f* — **Syrian** *adj*
syringe [sə'rɪndʒ, 'sɪrɪndʒ] *n* : jeringa *f*, jeringuilla *f*
syrup ['sərəp, 'sɪrəp] *n* : jarabe *m*, almíbar *m* (de azúcar y agua)
system ['sɪstəm] *n* **1** METHOD : sistema *m*, método *m* **2** APPARATUS : sistema *m*, instalación *f*, aparato *m* ⟨electrical system : instalación eléctrica⟩ ⟨digestive system : aparato digestivo⟩ **3** BODY : organismo *m*, cuerpo *m* ⟨diseases that affect the whole system : enfermedades que afectan el organismo entero⟩ **4** NETWORK : red *f*
systematic [,sɪstə'mæt̬ɪk] *adj* : sistemático — **systematically** [-t̬ɪkli] *adv*
systematize ['sɪstəmə,taɪz] *vt* **-tized; -tizing** : sistematizar
systemic [sɪs'tɛmɪk] *adj* : sistémico
systems analyst *n* : analista *mf* de sistemas (en informática)

T

t ['ti:] *n, pl* **t's** *or* **ts** ['ti:z] : vigésima letra del alfabeto inglés
tab¹ ['tæb] *n* **1** FLAP, TAG : lengüeta *f* (de un sobre, una caja, etc.), etiqueta *f* (de ropa) **2** : pestaña *f* (de un navegador, etc.) **3** BILL, CHECK : cuenta *f* **4** *or* **tab key** : tabulador *m*, tecla *f* Tab **5 to keep tabs on** : tener bajo vigilancia
tab² *vi* **tabbed; tabbing** : usar el tabulador, usar la tecla Tab
tabby ['tæbi] *n, pl* **-bies 1** *or* **tabby cat** : gato *m* atigrado **2** : gata *f*

tabernacle ['tæbər,nækəl] *n* : tabernáculo *m*
table ['teɪbəl] *n* **1** : mesa *f* ⟨a table for two : una mesa para dos⟩ ⟨table lamp : lámpara de mesa⟩ **2** LIST : tabla *f* ⟨multiplication table : tabla de multiplicar⟩ **3 table of contents** : índice *m* de materias
tableau [tæ'blo:, 'tæ,-] *n, pl* **-leaux** [-'blo:z, -,blo:z] : retablo *m*, cuadro *m* vivo (en teatro)
tablecloth ['teɪbəl,klɔθ] *n* : mantel *m*

tablespoon ['teɪbəl,spuːn] *n* 1 : cuchara *f* (de mesa) 2 → **tablespoonful**

tablespoonful ['teɪbəl,spuːn,fʊl] *n* : cucharada *f*

tablet ['tæblət] *n* 1 PLAQUE : placa *f* 2 PAD : bloc *m* (de papel) 3 PILL : tableta *f*, pastilla *f*, píldora *f* ⟨an aspirin tablet : una tableta de aspirina⟩ 4 : tableta *f*, tablet *f* (computadora)

table tennis *n* : tenis *m* de mesa

tableware ['teɪbəl,wær] *n* : vajillas *fpl*, cubiertos *mpl* (de mesa)

tabloid ['tæ,blɔɪd] *n* : tabloide *m*

taboo[1] [tə'buː, tæ-] *adj* : tabú

taboo[2] *n* : tabú *m*

tabular ['tæbjələr] *adj* : tabular

tabulate ['tæbjə,leɪt] *vt* -**lated**; -**lating** : tabular

tabulator ['tæbjə,leɪtər] *n* : tabulador *m*

tacit ['tæsɪt] *adj* : tácito, implícito — **tacitly** *adv*

taciturn ['tæsɪ,tərn] *adj* : taciturno

tack[1] ['tæk] *vt* 1 : sujetar con tachuelas 2 **to tack on** ADD : añadir, agregar

tack[2] *n* 1 : tachuela *f* 2 COURSE : rumbo *m* ⟨to change tack : cambiar de rumbo⟩

tackle[1] ['tækəl] *vt* -**led**; -**ling** 1 : taclear (en futbol americano) 2 CONFRONT : abordar, enfrentar, emprender (un problema, un trabajo, etc.)

tackle[2] *n* 1 EQUIPMENT, GEAR : equipo *m*, aparejo *m* 2 : aparejo *m* (de un buque) 3 : tacleada *f* (en futbol americano)

tacky ['tæki] *adj* **tackier**; -**est** 1 STICKY : pegajoso 2 CHEAP, GAUDY : de mal gusto, naco *Mex*

taco ['tako] *n, pl* **tacos** : taco *m*

tact ['tækt] *n* : tacto *m*, delicadeza *f*, discreción *f*

tactful ['tæktfəl] *adj* : discreto, diplomático, de mucho tacto

tactfully ['tæktfəli] *adv* : discretamente, con mucho tacto

tactic ['tæktɪk] *n* : táctica *f*

tactical ['tæktɪkəl] *adj* : táctico, estratégico

tactics ['tæktɪks] *ns & pl* : táctica *f*, estrategia *f*

tactile ['tæktəl, -,taɪl] *adj* : táctil

tactless ['tæktləs] *adj* : indiscreto, poco delicado

tactlessly ['tæktləsli] *adv* : rudamente, sin tacto

tadpole ['tæd,poːl] *n* : renacuajo *m*

taffeta ['tæfətə] *n* : tafetán *m*; tafeta *f Arg, Mex, Uru*

taffy ['tæfi] *n, pl* -**fies** : caramelo *m* de melaza, chicloso *m Mex*

tag[1] ['tæg] *v* **tagged**; **tagging** *vt* 1 LABEL : etiquetar 2 TAIL : seguir de cerca 3 TOUCH : tocar (en varios juegos) — *vi* **to tag along** : pegarse, acompañar

tag[2] *n* 1 LABEL : etiqueta *f* 2 SAYING : dicho *m*, refrán *m*

tail[1] ['teɪl] *vt* FOLLOW : seguir de cerca, pegarse

tail[2] *n* 1 : cola *f*, rabo *m* (de un animal) 2 : cola *f*, parte *f* posterior ⟨a comet's tail : la cola de un cometa⟩ 3 **tails**

npl : cruz *f* (de una moneda) ⟨heads or tails : cara o cruz⟩ 4 **tails** *npl* → **tailcoat**

tailcoat ['teɪl,koːt] *n* : frac *m*

tailed ['teɪld] *adj* 1 : que tiene cola 2 (*used in combination*) : de cola ⟨long-tailed : de cola larga⟩

tail end *n* 1 : final *m*, últimos momentos *mpl* (de un espectáculo, etc.), cola *f* (de un grupo, etc.)

tailgate[1] ['teɪl,geɪt] *vi* -**gated**; -**gating** : seguir a un vehículo demasiado de cerca

tailgate[2] *n* : puerta *f* trasera (de un vehículo)

taillight ['teɪl,laɪt] *n* : luz *f* trasera (de un vehículo), calavera *f Mex*

tailor[1] ['teɪlər] *vt* 1 : confeccionar o alterar (ropa) 2 ADAPT : adaptar, ajustar

tailor[2] *n* : sastre *m*, -tra *f*

tailor–made *adj* : hecho a la medida

tailpipe ['teɪl,paɪp] *n* : tubo *m* de escape

tailspin ['teɪl,spɪn] *n* : barrena *f*

taint[1] ['teɪnt] *vt* : contaminar, corromper

taint[2] *n* : corrupción *f*, impureza *f*

take[1] ['teɪk] *v* **took** ['tʊk]; **taken** ['teɪkən]; **taking** *vt* 1 GRASP : tomar, agarrar ⟨to take by the hand : tomar de la mano⟩ ⟨to take the bull by the horns : tomar al toro por los cuernos⟩ 2 BRING, CARRY : llevar, sacar, cargar ⟨take them with you : llévalos contigo⟩ ⟨take this note to your teacher : lleva esta nota a tu maestro⟩ ⟨I took her to school : la llevé a la escuela⟩ ⟨she took him aside : lo llevó aparte⟩ 3 REMOVE, EXTRACT : sacar, extraer ⟨take a beer from the fridge : saca una cerveza de la nevera⟩ ⟨to take blood : sacar sangre⟩ 4 CATCH : tomar, agarrar ⟨taken by surprise : tomado por sorpresa⟩ 5 CAPTURE, SEIZE : tomar ⟨to take someone prisoner : hacer/tomar a alguien prisionero⟩ ⟨to take someone hostage : tomar a alguien como rehén⟩ ⟨to take control of : tomar el control de⟩ 6 CAPTIVATE : encantar, fascinar 7 REMOVE, STEAL : llevarse ⟨someone took the painting : alguien se llevó la pintura⟩ ⟨he took it from her : se lo quitó⟩ ⟨to take someone's life : quitarle la vida a alguien⟩ 8 (*indicating selection*) ⟨I'll take the fish : dame el pescado⟩ ⟨I'll take it : me lo llevo⟩ ⟨take your pick : escoge el que quieras⟩ ⟨do you take cream in your coffee? : ¿le pones crema al café?⟩ 9 NEED, REQUIRE : tomar, requerir ⟨it will take a month to complete : llevará un mes terminarlo⟩ ⟨these things take time : estas cosas toman tiempo⟩ ⟨will it take long? : ¿tardará mucho (tiempo)?⟩ ⟨what size do you take? : ¿qué talla usas?⟩ ⟨it takes diesel : usa diesel⟩ 10 BORROW : tomar (una frase, etc.) ⟨to take one's inspiration from : inspirarse en⟩ 11 OCCUPY : ocupar ⟨to take a seat : tomar asiento⟩ ⟨this seat is taken : este asiento está ocupado⟩ ⟨to take the place of : ocupar el lugar de⟩ 12 INGEST : tomar, ingerir ⟨take two pills : tome dos píldoras⟩ ⟨to take drugs : drogarse⟩ 13 : tomar, coger (un tren, un autobús, etc.) 14 TRAVEL : tomar (un camino) **15** BEAR, ENDURE : soportar, aguantar (dolores, etc.), resistir (el frío, etc.) ⟨I can't take it anymore : no puedo más⟩ ⟨she can't take a joke : no sabe aguantar una broma⟩ ⟨to take something well/badly : llevar algo bien/mal⟩ **16** ACCEPT : aceptar (un cheque, un cliente, un trabajo, etc.), seguir (consejos), cargar con (la culpa, la responsabilidad) ⟨take it or leave it : tómalo o déjalo⟩ ⟨take it from me : hazme caso⟩ **17** ADOPT : adoptar (una perspectiva, etc.) **18** INTERPRET : tomar, interpretar ⟨don't take it the wrong way : no te lo tomes a mal, no me malinterpretes⟩ **19** FEEL : sentir ⟨to take offense : ofenderse⟩ ⟨to take pride in : sentirse orgulloso de⟩ **20** SUPPOSE : suponer ⟨I take it that . . . : supongo que . . .⟩ **21** CONSIDER : mirar (como ejemplo) **22** (*indicating an action or an undertaking*) ⟨to take a walk : dar un paseo⟩ ⟨to take a class : tomar una clase⟩ ⟨to take a picture : sacar una foto⟩ ⟨to take a right/left : girar a la derecha/izquierda⟩ **23** MEASURE, RECORD : tomar ⟨to take someone's temperature : tomarle la temperatura a alguien⟩ ⟨to take notes : tomar apuntes⟩ **24** EXACT ⟨to take a toll on : afectar⟩ ⟨to take revenge : vengarse⟩ **25** WIN : ganar **26 to be taken sick/ill** : caer enfermo **27 to take aback** : sorprender, desconcertar **28 to take a lot out of someone** : agotar a alguien **29 to take apart** : desmontar **30 to take away** REMOVE : quitar **31 take it away!** : ¡adelante!, ¡vamos! (dícese a un cantante, etc.) **32 to take back** : retirar (palabras, etc.) **33 to take back** RETURN : devolver **34 to take back** RECLAIM : llevarse **35 to take back** : aceptar la devolución de (mercancía), dejar regresar (a un amante) **36 to take down** NOTE : tomar nota de **37 to take down** DISASSEMBLE : desmontar **38 to take down** REMOVE : quitar **39 to take down** LOWER : bajar **40 to take for** : tomar por **41 to take in** : recoger (a un perro, etc.) **42 to take in** : detener, llevar a la comisaría **43 to take in** : hacer (dinero) **44 to take in** : tomarle a, achicar (un vestido, etc.) **45 to take in** INCLUDE : incluir, abarcar **46 to take in** ATTEND, VISIT : ir a (una película, etc.), visitar (un museo, etc.) **47 to take in** GRASP, UNDERSTAND : captar, entender **48 to take in** DECEIVE : engañar **49 to take it upon oneself (to do something)** : encargarse (de hacer algo) **50 to take note/notice of** : notar, prestarle atención a **51 to take off** REMOVE : quitar ⟨take off your hat : quítate el sombrero⟩ ⟨take your hands off me! : ¡quítame las manos de encima!⟩ **52 to take off** : tomar (el día, etc.) libre **53 to take someone off (of)** : hacerle a alguien dejar (un proyecto, etc.) **54 to take on** TACKLE : abordar, enfrentar (problemas, etc.) **55 to take on** UNDERTAKE : encargarse de, emprender (una tarea), asumir

(una responsabilidad) **56 to take on** ACCEPT : tomar (como un cliente, etc.) **57 to take on** CONTRACT : contratar (trabajadores) **58 to take on** ASSUME : adoptar, asumir, adquirir ⟨the neighborhood took on a dingy look : el barrio asumió una apariencia deprimente⟩ **59 to take out** REMOVE, WITHDRAW, EXTRACT : sacar ⟨take the trash out : saca la basura⟩ ⟨they took her tonsils out : la operaron de las amígdalas⟩ **60 to take out** OBTAIN : sacar **61 to take out** : sacar (libros, etc.) **62 to take out** : llevar (a cenar, etc.), sacar (a pasear, etc.) **63 to take out** DESTROY : eliminar **64 to take it out on someone** : desquitarse con alguien, agarrársela con alguien **65 to take over** SEIZE : apoderarse de **66 to take over** : hacerse cargo de (una compañía, etc.), asumir (una responsabilidad) **67 to take over** RELIEVE : sustituir, relevar **68 to take place** HAPPEN : tener lugar, suceder, ocurrir **69 to take shape/form** : tomar forma **70 to take something to something** ⟨he took an axe to the tree : empezó a cortar el árbol con un hacha⟩ **71 to take up** LIFT : levantar **72 to take up** SHORTEN : acortar (una falda, etc.) **73 to take up** BEGIN : empezar, dedicarse a (un pasatiempo, etc.) **74 to take up** OCCUPY : ocupar (espacio), llevar (tiempo) **75 to take up** PURSUE : volver a (una cuestión, un asunto) **76 to take up** CONTINUE : seguir con **77 to take someone up on** : aceptarle la invitación (etc.) a alguien — *vi* **1** : agarrar (dícese de un tinte), prender (dícese de una vacuna) **2 to take after** : parecerse a, salir a **3 to take away from** : restarle valor/atractivo (etc.) a **4 to take off** : despegar (dícese de un avión, etc.) **5 to take off** *fam* LEAVE : irse **6 to take over** : asumir el mando **7 to take to** : aficionarse a (un pasatiempo), adaptarse a (una situación), tomarle simpatía a (alguien) ⟨he doesn't take kindly to criticism : no le gusta nada que lo critiquen⟩ **8 to take to** START : empezar a, acostumbrarse a (hacer algo)

take² *n* **1** PROCEEDS : recaudación *f*, ingresos *mpl*, ganancias *fpl* **2** : toma *f* (de un rodaje o una grabación)
takeoff ['teɪkˌɔf] *n* **1** PARODY : parodia *f* **2** : despegue *m* (de un avión o cohete)
takeout ['teɪkˌaʊt] *n* : comida *f* para llevar
takeover ['teɪkˌoːvər] *n* : toma *f* (de poder o de control), adquisición *f* (de una empresa por otra)
taker ['teɪkər] *n* : persona *f* interesada ⟨available to all takers : disponible a cuantos estén interesados⟩
takings ['teɪkɪŋz] *n* EARNINGS : recaudación *f*
talc ['tælk] *n* : talco *m*
talcum powder ['tælkəm] *n* : talco *m*, polvos *mpl* de talco
tale ['teɪl] *n* **1** ANECDOTE, STORY : cuento *m*, relato *m*, anécdota *f* **2** FALSEHOOD : cuento *m*, mentira *f*

talent ['tælənt] *n* : talento *m*, don *m*
talented ['tæləntəd] *adj* : talentoso
talent scout → **scout**[2]
talisman ['tælɪsmən, -lɪz-] *n, pl* **-mans**
: talismán *m*
talk[1] ['tɔk] *vi* **1** : hablar ⟨he talks for hours : se pasa horas hablando⟩ **2** CHAT
: charlar, platicar **3 to talk about/of**
: hablar de **4 to talk back** : contestar
(de manera impertinente) **5 to talk down to** : hablarle en tono condescendiente a — *vt* **1** SPEAK : hablar ⟨to talk French : hablar francés⟩ ⟨to talk business : hablar de negocios⟩ **2 to talk into**
⟨I talked him into coming : lo convencí de que viniera⟩ **3 to talk out of** ⟨she talked me out of it : me convenció de que no lo hiciera⟩ **4 to talk over** DISCUSS : hablar de, discutir
talk[2] *n* **1** CONVERSATION : charla *f*, plática *f*, conversación *f* **2** GOSSIP, RUMOR : chisme *m*, rumores *mpl* **3** SPEECH : charla *f*
talkative ['tɔkəṭɪv] *adj* : locuaz, parlanchín, charlatán
talker ['tɔkər] *n* : conversador *m*, -dora *f*; hablador *m*, -dora *f*
talk show *n* : programa *m* de entrevistas
tall ['tɔl] *adj* : alto ⟨how tall is he?
: ¿cuánto mide?⟩
tallow ['tælo:] *n* : sebo *m*
tall tale *adj* : cuento *m* chino
tally[1] ['tæli] *v* **-lied; -lying** *vt* RECKON : contar, hacer una cuenta de — *vi* MATCH
: concordar, corresponder, cuadrar
tally[2] *n, pl* **-lies** : cuenta *f* ⟨to keep a tally
: llevar la cuenta⟩
talon ['tælən] *n* : garra *f* (de un ave de rapiña)
tamale [tə'mɑli] *n* : tamal *m*
tamarind ['tæmərənd] *n* : tamarindo *m*
tambourine [ˌtæmbə'riːn] *n* : pandero *m*, pandereta *f*
tame[1] ['teɪm] *vt* **tamed; taming** : domar, amansar, domesticar
tame[2] *adj* **tamer; -est** **1** DOMESTICATED
: domesticado, manso **2** DOCILE
: manso, dócil **3** DULL : aburrido, soso
tamely ['teɪmli] *adv* : mansamente, dócilmente
tamer ['teɪmər] *n* : domador *m*, -dora *f*
tamp ['tæmp] *vt* : apisonar
tamper ['tæmpər] *vi* **to tamper with**
: adulterar (una sustancia), forzar (un sello, una cerradura), falsear (documentos), manipular (una máquina)
tampon ['tæmˌpɑn] *n* : tampón *m*
tan[1] ['tæn] *v* **tanned; tanning** *vt* **1** : curtir (pieles) **2** : broncear — *vi* : broncearse
tan[2] *n* **1** SUNTAN : bronceado *m* ⟨to get a tan : broncearse⟩ **2** : color *m* canela, color *m* café con leche
tandem[1] ['tændəm] *adv or* **in tandem** : en tándem
tandem[2] *n* : tándem *m* (bicicleta)
tang ['tæŋ] *n* : sabor *m* fuerte
tangent ['tændʒənt] *n* : tangente *f* ⟨to go off on a tangent : irse por la tangente⟩
tangerine ['tændʒəˌriːn, ˌtændʒə'-] *n*
: mandarina *f*

tangible ['tændʒəbəl] *adj* : tangible, palpable — **tangibly** [-bli] *adv*
tangle[1] ['tæŋgəl] *v* **-gled; -gling** *vt* : enredar, enmarañar — *vi* : enredarse
tangle[2] *n* : enredo *m*, maraña *f*
tango[1] ['tæŋˌgoː] *vi* : bailar el tango
tango[2] *n, pl* **-gos** : tango *m*
tangy ['tæŋi] *adj* **tangier; -est** : que tiene un sabor fuerte
tank ['tæŋk] *n* **1** : tanque *m*; depósito *m*; bombona *f* *Spain, Ven* ⟨fuel tank : depósito de combustibles⟩
tankard ['tæŋkərd] *n* : jarra *f*
tanker ['tæŋkər] *n* : buque *m* cisterna, camión *m* cisterna, avión *m* cisterna ⟨an oil tanker : un petrolero⟩
tanner ['tænər] *n* : curtidor *m*, -dora *f*
tannery ['tænəri] *n, pl* **-neries** : curtiduría *f*, tenería *f*
tannin ['tænən] *n* : tanino *m*
tantalize ['tæntəˌlaɪz] *vt* **-lized; -lizing**
: tentar, atormentar (con algo inasequible)
tantalizing ['tæntəˌlaɪzɪŋ] *adj* : tentador, seductor
tantamount ['tæntəˌmaʊnt] *adj* : equivalente
tantrum ['tæntrəm] *n* : rabieta *f*, berrinche *m* ⟨to throw a tantrum : hacer un berrinche⟩
tap[1] ['tæp] *vt* **tapped; tapping** **1** : ponerle una espita a, sacar líquido de (un barril, un tanque, etc.) **2** : intervenir, pinchar *fam* (un teléfono) **3** PAT, TOUCH : tocar, golpear ligeramente ⟨he tapped me on the shoulder : me tocó en el hombro⟩
tap[2] *n* **1** FAUCET : llave *f*, grifo *m* ⟨beer on tap : cerveza de barril⟩ **2** : extracción *f* (de líquido) ⟨a spinal tap : una punción lumbar⟩ **3** PAT, TOUCH : golpecito *m*, toque *m*
tape[1] ['teɪp] *vt* **taped; taping** **1** : sujetar o arreglar con cinta adhesiva **2** RECORD
: grabar (en cinta)
tape[2] *n* **1** : cinta *f* (adhesiva, magnética, etc.) **2** → **tape measure**
tape measure *n* : cinta *f* métrica
taper[1] ['teɪpər] *vi* **1** : estrecharse gradualmente ⟨its tail tapers towards the tip : su cola va estrechándose hacia la punta⟩ **2** *or* **to taper off** : disminuir gradualmente
taper[2] *n* **1** CANDLE : vela *f* larga y delgada **2** TAPERING : estrechamiento *m* gradual
tape recorder *n* : grabadora *f*, grabador *m* (de cinta)
tapestry ['tæpəstri] *n, pl* **-tries** : tapiz *m*
tapeworm ['teɪpˌwərm] *n* : solitaria *f*, tenia *f*
tapioca [ˌtæpi'oːkə] *n* : tapioca *f*
tapir ['teɪpər] *n* : tapir *m*
tar[1] ['tɑr] *vt* **tarred; tarring** : alquitranar
tar[2] *n* : alquitrán *m*, brea *f*, chapopote *m* *Mex*
tarantula [tə'ræntʃələ, -'ræntələ] *n*
: tarántula *f*
tardiness ['tɑrdinəs] *n* : tardanza *f*, retraso *m*
tardy ['tɑrdi] *adj* **tardier; -est** LATE : tardío, de retraso

target[1] ['tɑrgət] *vt* : fijar como objetivo, dirigir, destinar

target[2] *n* **1** : blanco *m* ⟨target practice : tiro al blanco⟩ **2** GOAL, OBJECTIVE : meta *f*, objetivo *m*

tariff ['tærɪf] *n* DUTY : tarifa *f*, arancel *m*

tarmac ['tɑr,mæk] *n* pista *f* (de un aeropuerto)

Tarmac ['tɑr,mæk] *trademark* se usa para un tipo de pavimento

tarnish[1] ['tɑrnɪʃ] *vt* **1** DULL : deslustrar **2** SULLY : empañar, manchar (una reputación, etc.) — *vi* : deslustrarse

tarnish[2] *n* : deslustre *m*

taro ['tɑro, 'ter-] *n* : taro *m*, malanga *f*

tarpaulin [tɑr'pɔlən, 'tɑrpə-] *n* : lona *f* (impermeable)

tarragon ['tærə,gɑn, -gən] *n* : estragón *m*

tarry[1] ['tæri] *vi* **-ried; -rying** : demorarse, entretenerse

tarry[2] ['tɑri] *adj* **1** : parecido al alquitrán **2** : cubierto de alquitrán

tart[1] ['tɑrt] *adj* **1** SOUR : ácido, agrio **2** CAUSTIC : mordaz, acrimonioso — **tartly** *adv*

tart[2] *n* : tartaleta *f*

tartan ['tɑrtən] *n* : tartán *m*

tartar ['tɑrtər] *n* **1** : tártaro *m* ⟨tartar sauce : salsa tártara⟩ **2** : sarro *m* (dental)

tartness ['tɑrtnəs] *n* **1** SOURNESS : acidez *f* **2** ACRIMONY, SHARPNESS : mordacidad *f*, acrimonia *f*, acritud *f*

task ['tæsk] *n* : tarea *f*, trabajo *m*

taskmaster ['tæsk,mæstər] *n* **to be a hard taskmaster** : ser exigente, ser muy estricto

tassel ['tæsəl] *n* : borla *f*

taste[1] ['teɪst] *v* **tasted; tasting** *vt* : probar (alimentos), degustar, catar (vinos) ⟨taste this soup : prueba esta sopa⟩ — *vi* : saber ⟨this tastes good : esto sabe bueno⟩

taste[2] *n* **1** SAMPLE : prueba *f*, bocado *m* (de comida), trago *m* (de bebidas) **2** FLAVOR : gusto *m*, sabor *m* **3** : gusto *m* ⟨she has good taste : tiene buen gusto⟩ ⟨in bad taste : de mal gusto⟩

taste bud *n* : papila *f* gustativa

tasteful ['teɪstfəl] *adj* : de buen gusto

tastefully ['teɪstfəli] *adv* : con buen gusto

tasteless ['teɪstləs] *adj* **1** FLAVORLESS : sin sabor, soso, insípido **2** : de mal gusto ⟨a tasteless joke : un chiste de mal gusto⟩

taster ['teɪstər] *n* : degustador *m*, -dora *f*; catador *m*, -dora *f* (de vinos)

tastiness ['teɪstinəs] *n* : lo sabroso

tasty ['teɪsti] *adj* **tastier; -est** : sabroso, gustoso

tatter ['tætər] *n* **1** SHRED : tira *f*, jirón *m* (de tela) **2 tatters** *npl* : andrajos *mpl*, harapos *mpl* ⟨to be in tatters : estar por los suelos⟩

tattered ['tætərd] *adj* : andrajoso, en jirones

tattle ['tætəl] *vi* **-tled; -tling 1** CHATTER : parlotear *fam*, cotorrear *fam* **2 to tattle on someone** : acusar a alguien

tattletale ['tætəl,teɪl] *n* : soplón *m*, -plona *f fam*

tattoo[1] [tæ'tu:] *vt* : tatuar

tattoo[2] *n* : tatuaje *m* ⟨to get a tattoo : tatuarse⟩

tatty ['tæti] *adj* **tattier; -est** SHABBY, WORN : gastado

taught → **teach**

taunt[1] ['tɔnt] *vt* MOCK : mofarse de, burlarse de

taunt[2] *n* : mofa *f*, burla *f*

Taurus ['tɔrəs] *n* **1** : Tauro *m* (signo o constelación) **2** : Tauro *mf* (persona)

taut ['tɔt] *adj* : tirante, tenso — **tautly** *adv*

tautness ['tɔtnəs] *n* : tirantez *f*, tensión *f*

tavern ['tævərn] *n* : taberna *f*

tawdry ['tɔdri] *adj* **tawdrier; -est** : chabacano, vulgar

tawny ['tɔni] *adj* **tawnier; -est** : leonado

tax[1] ['tæks] *vt* **1** : gravar, cobrar un impuesto sobre **2** CHARGE : acusar ⟨they taxed him with neglect : fue acusado de incumplimiento⟩ **3 to tax someone's strength** : ponerle a prueba las fuerzas (a alguien)

tax[2] *n* **1** : impuesto *m*, tributo *m* ⟨tax collector : recaudador de impuestos⟩ ⟨tax evasion : evasión de impuestos⟩ **2** BURDEN : carga *f*

taxable ['tæksəbəl] *adj* : sujeto a un impuesto

taxation [tæk'seɪʃən] *n* : impuestos *mpl*

tax-exempt ['tæksɪg'zempt, -ɛg-] *adj* : libre de impuestos

taxi[1] ['tæksi] *vi* **taxied; taxiing** *or* **taxying; taxis** *or* **taxies 1** : ir en taxi **2** : rodar sobre la pista de aterrizaje (dícese de un avión)

taxi[2] *n*, *pl* **taxis** : taxi *m*, libre *m Mex*

taxicab ['tæksi,kæb] *n* → **taxi**[2]

taxidermist ['tæksə,dərmɪst] *n* : taxidermista *mf*

taxidermy ['tæksə,dərmi] *n* : taxidermia *f*

taxi driver *n* : taxista *mf*

taxpayer ['tæks,peɪər] *n* : contribuyente *mf*, causante *mf Mex*

tax return → **return**[3]

TB [,ti:'bi:] → **tuberculosis**

tea ['ti:] *n* **1** : té *m* (planta y bebida) **2** : merienda *f*, té *m* (comida)

tea bag *n* : bolsita *f* de té

teach ['ti:tʃ] *v* **taught** ['tɔt]; **teaching** *vt* : enseñar, dar clases de ⟨she teaches math : da clases de matemáticas⟩ ⟨she taught me everything I know : me enseñó todo lo que sé⟩ — *vi* : enseñar, dar clases

teacher ['ti:tʃər] *n* : maestro *m*, -tra *f* (de enseñanza primaria); profesor *m*, -sora *f* (de enseñanza secundaria)

teaching ['ti:tʃɪŋ] *n* : enseñanza *f*

teacup ['ti:,kʌp] *n* : taza *f* para té

teak ['ti:k] *n* : teca *f*

teakettle ['ti:,ketəl] *n* : tetera *f*

teal ['ti:l] *n*, *pl* **teal** *or* **teals 1** : cerceta *f* (pato) **2** *or* **teal blue** : azul *m* verdoso oscuro

team[1] ['ti:m] *vi* *or* **to team up 1** : formar un equipo (en deportes) **2** COLLABORATE : asociarse, juntarse, unirse

team[2] *adj* : de equipo

team[3] *n* **1** : tiro *m* (de caballos), yunta *f*

(de bueyes o mulas) **2** : equipo *m* (en deportes, etc.)

teammate ['ti:m‚meɪt] *n* : compañero *m*, -ra *f* de equipo

teamster ['ti:mstər] *n* : camionero *m*, -ra *f*

teamwork ['ti:m‚wərk] *n* : trabajo *m* en equipo, cooperación *f*

teapot ['ti:‚pɑt] *n* : tetera *f*

tear[1] ['tær] *v* **tore** ['tor]; **torn** ['torn]; **tearing** *vt* **1** RIP : desgarrar, romper, rasgar (tela) ⟨to tear to pieces : hacer pedazos⟩ ⟨to tear apart : desgarrar⟩ **2** *or* **to tear apart** DIVIDE : dividir **3** REMOVE : arrancar ⟨torn from his family : arrancado de su familia⟩ **4 to tear down** : derribar **5 to tear off** : arrancar (un pedazo, etc.) **6 to tear out** : arrancar (una página, etc.) **7 to tear up** : hacer pedazos — *vi* **1** RIP : desgarrarse, romperse **2** RUSH : ir a gran velocidad ⟨she went tearing down the street : se fue como rayo por la calle⟩ **3 to tear into** ATTACK : arremeter contra

tear[2] *n* : desgarradura *f*, rotura *f*, desgarro *m* (muscular)

tear[3] ['tɪr] *n* : lágrima *f*

teardrop ['tɪr‚drɑp] *n* → **tear**[3]

tearful ['tɪrfəl] *adj* : lloroso, triste — **tearfully** *adv*

tear gas *n* : gas *m* lacrimógeno

tearoom ['ti:‚ru:m, -‚rʊm] *n* : salón *m* de té, confitería *f*

tease[1] ['ti:z] *vt* **teased; teasing 1** MOCK : burlarse de, mofarse de **2** ANNOY : irritar, fastidiar

tease[2] *n* **1** TEASING : burla *f*, mofa *f* **2** : bromista *mf*; guasón *m*, -sona *f*

teaspoon ['ti:‚spu:n] *n* **1** : cucharita *f* **2** → **teaspoonful**

teaspoonful ['ti:‚spu:n‚fʊl] *n*, *pl* **-spoonfuls** [-‚fʊlz] *or* **-spoonsful** [-‚spu:nz‚fʊl] : cucharadita *f*

teat ['ti:t] *n* : tetilla *f*

technical ['tɛknɪkəl] *adj* : técnico — **technically** [-kli] *adv*

technicality [‚tɛknə'kæləti] *n*, *pl* **-ties** : detalle *m* técnico

technician [tɛk'nɪʃən] *n* : técnico *m*, -ca *f*

technique [tɛk'ni:k] *n* : técnica *f*

technological [‚tɛknə'lɑʤɪkəl] *adj* : tecnológico

technology [tɛk'nɑləʤi] *n*, *pl* **-gies** : tecnología *f*

teddy bear ['tɛdi] *n* : oso *m* de peluche

tedious ['ti:diəs] *adj* : aburrido, pesado, monótono — **tediously** *adv*

tediousness ['ti:diəsnəs] *n* : lo aburrido, lo pesado

tedium ['ti:diəm] *n* : tedio *m*, pesadez *f*

tee ['ti:] *n* : tee *m* (en golf)

teem ['ti:m] *vi* **to teem with** : estar repleto de, estar lleno de

teen ['ti:n] → **teenager**

teenage ['ti:n‚eɪʤ] *or* **teenaged** [-eɪʤd] *adj* : adolescente, de adolescencia

teenager ['ti:n‚eɪʤər] *n* : adolescente *mf*

teens ['ti:nz] *npl* : adolescencia *f*

teepee → **tepee**

teeter[1] ['ti:tər] *vi* : balancearse, tambalearse

teeter[2] *or* **teeter–totter** ['ti:tər-‚tɑtər] *n* → **seesaw**

teeth → **tooth**

teethe ['ti:ð] *vi* **teethed; teething** : formársele a uno los dientes ⟨the baby's teething : le están saliendo los dientes al niño⟩

teetotal ['ti:'to:təl] *adj* : abstemio

teetotaler ['ti:'to:tələr] *n* : abstemio *m*, -mia *f*

Teflon ['tɛ‚flɑn] *trademark* se usa para un revestimiento antiadherente

telecast[1] ['tɛlə‚kæst] *vt* **-cast; -casting** : televisar, transmitir por televisión

telecast[2] *n* : transmisión *f* por televisión

telecommunication [‚tɛləkə‚mju:nə'keɪʃən] *n* : telecomunicación *f*

teleconference ['tɛli‚kɑnfrənts, -fərənts] *n* : teleconferencia *f*

telegram ['tɛlə‚græm] *n* : telegrama *m*

telegraph[1] ['tɛlə‚græf] *v* : telegrafiar

telegraph[2] *n* : telégrafo *m*

telemarketing [‚tɛlə'markətɪŋ] *n* : telemárketing *m*

telepathic [‚tɛlə'pæθɪk] *adj* : telepático — **telepathically** [-θɪkli] *adv*

telepathy [tə'lɛpəθi] *n* : telepatía *f*

telephone[1] ['tɛlə‚fo:n] *v* **-phoned; -phoning** *vt* : llamar por teléfono a, telefonear — *vi* : telefonear

telephone[2] *n* : teléfono *m*

telephone book → **phone book**

telephone call → **call**[2]

telephone directory → **phone book**

telephone exchange → **exchange**[2]

telephone number → **number**[2]

telephone receiver → **receiver**

telescope[1] ['tɛlə‚sko:p] *vi* **-scoped; -scoping** : plegarse (como un telescopio)

telescope[2] *n* : telescopio *m*

telescopic [‚tɛlə'skɑpɪk] *adj* : telescópico

televise ['tɛlə‚vaɪz] *vt* **-vised; -vising** : televisar

television ['tɛlə‚vɪʒən] *n* : televisión *f*

tell ['tɛl] *v* **told** ['to:ld]; **telling** *vt* **1** : decir, contar ⟨he told us the story : nos contó la historia⟩ ⟨he told us what happened : nos contó qué pasó⟩ ⟨she told me the news : me dio la noticia⟩ ⟨tell me all about it : cuéntamelo todo⟩ ⟨tell her that . . . : dile que . . .⟩ ⟨tell her hello for me : dale saludos de mi parte⟩ **2** INFORM : decir ⟨tell me when they get here : dime cuando lleguen⟩ ⟨I won't tell anyone : no se lo diré a nadie⟩ ⟨I'm telling Mom! : ¡se lo voy a decir a mamá!⟩ **3** INSTRUCT : decir ⟨do what I tell you : haz lo que te digo⟩ ⟨they told her to wait : le dijeron que esperara⟩ **4** RELATE : contar ⟨to tell a story : contar una historia⟩ ⟨to tell a lie : decir una mentira⟩ **5** DISCERN : discernir, notar ⟨I can't tell the difference : no noto la diferencia⟩ ⟨I could tell that she was lying : me di cuenta de que estaba mintiendo⟩ **6** : indicar, señalar ⟨the evidence tells us that . . . : las pruebas nos indican que . . .⟩ **7 all told** : en total **8**

don't tell me : no me digas **9 I'll tell you what** (*introducing a suggestion*) : hagamos así **10 I told you so** : te lo dije **11 to tell apart** : distinguir **12 to tell it like it is** *fam* : contar/decir las cosas como son **13 to tell off** *fam* : regañar **14 to tell (you) the truth** : a decir verdad **15 you're telling me!** : ¡a mí me lo vas a decir! — *vi* **1** SAY : decir ⟨I won't tell : no voy a decírselo a nadie⟩ **2** KNOW : saber ⟨you never can tell : nunca se sabe⟩ ⟨as far as I can tell : según parece⟩ **3** SHOW : notarse, hacerse sentir ⟨the strain is beginning to tell : la tensión se empieza a notar⟩ **4 to tell on** : denunciar

teller ['tɛlər] *n* **1** NARRATOR : narrador *m*, -dora *f* **2** *or* **bank teller** : cajero *m*, -ra *f*

telltale ['tɛl,teɪl] *adj* : revelador

temerity [tə'mɛrəti] *n, pl* **-ties** : temeridad *f*

temp¹ ['tɛmp] *n* : empleado *m*, -da *f* temporal

temp² *vi* : hacer trabajo temporal

temper¹ ['tɛmpər] *vt* **1** MODERATE : moderar, temperar **2** ANNEAL : templar (acero, etc.)

temper² *n* **1** DISPOSITION : carácter *m*, genio *m* **2** HARDNESS : temple *m*, dureza *f* (de un metal) **3** COMPOSURE : calma *f*, serenidad *f* ⟨to lose one's temper : perder los estribos⟩ **4** RAGE : furia *f* ⟨to fly into a temper : ponerse furioso⟩

temperament ['tɛmpərmənt, -prə-, -pərə-] *n* : temperamento *m*

temperamental [,tɛmpər'mɛntəl, -prə-, -pərə-] *adj* : temperamental

temperance ['tɛmprənts] *n* : templanza *f*, temperancia *f*

temperate ['tɛmpərət] *adj* : templado (dícese del clima, etc.), moderado

temperature ['tɛmpər,tʃur, -prə-, -pərə-, -tʃər] *n* **1** : temperatura *f* **2** FEVER : calentura *f*, fiebre *f*

tempest ['tɛmpəst] *n* **1** : tempestad *f* **2 a tempest in a teapot** : una tormenta en un vaso de agua

tempestuous [tɛm'pɛstʃuəs] *adj* : tempestuoso

template ['tɛmplət] *n* : plantilla *f*

temple ['tɛmpəl] *n* **1** : templo *m* (en religión) **2** : sien *f* (en anatomía)

tempo ['tɛm,po:] *n, pl* **-pi** [-,pi:] *or* **-pos** : ritmo *m*, tempo *m* (en música)

temporal ['tɛmpərəl] *adj* : temporal

temporarily [,tɛmpə'rɛrəli] *adv* : temporalmente, provisionalmente

temporary ['tɛmpə,rɛri] *adj* : temporal, provisional, provisorio

tempt ['tɛmpt] *vt* : tentar

temptation [tɛmp'teɪʃən] *n* : tentación *f*

tempter ['tɛmptər] *n* : tentador *m*

temptress ['tɛmptrəs] *n* : tentadora *f*

ten¹ ['tɛn] *adj* : diez ⟨she's ten (years old) : tiene diez años⟩

ten² *n* **1** : diez *m* (número) ⟨the ten of hearts : el diez de corazones⟩ **2** : decena *f* ⟨tens of thousands : decenas de millares⟩

ten³ *pron* : diez ⟨there are ten of us : somos diez⟩ ⟨it's ten (o'clock) : son las diez⟩

tenable ['tɛnəbəl] *adj* : sostenible, defendible

tenacious [tə'neɪʃəs] *adj* : tenaz — **tenaciously** [tə'neɪʃəsli] *adv*

tenacity [tə'næsəti] *n* : tenacidad *f*

tenancy ['tɛnəntsi] *n, pl* **-cies** : tenencia *f*, inquilinato *m* (de un inmueble)

tenant ['tɛnənt] *n* : inquilino *m*, -na *f*; arrendatario *m*, -ria *f*

tend ['tɛnd] *vt* : atender, cuidar (de), ocuparse de — *vi* : tender ⟨it tends to benefit the consumer : tiende a beneficiar al consumidor⟩

tendency ['tɛndəntsi] *n, pl* **-cies** : tendencia *f*, proclividad *f*, inclinación *f*

tender¹ ['tɛndər] *vt* : entregar, presentar ⟨I tendered my resignation : presenté mi renuncia⟩

tender² *adj* **1** : tierno, blando ⟨tender steak : bistec tierno⟩ **2** AFFECTIONATE, LOVING : tierno, cariñoso, afectuoso **3** DELICATE : tierno, sensible, delicado

tender³ *n* **1** OFFER : propuesta *f*, oferta *f* (en negocios) **2 legal tender** : moneda *f* de curso legal

tenderize ['tɛndə,raɪz] *vt* **-ized; -izing** : ablandar (carnes)

tenderloin ['tɛndr,lɔɪn] *n* : lomo *f* (de res o de puerco)

tenderly ['tɛndərli] *adv* : tiernamente, con ternura

tenderness ['tɛndərnəs] *n* : ternura *f*

tendon ['tɛndən] *n* : tendón *m*

tendril ['tɛndrɪl] *n* : zarcillo *m*

tenement ['tɛnəmənt] *n* : casa *f* de vecindad

tenet ['tɛnət] *n* : principio *m*

tennis ['tɛnəs] *n* : tenis *m* ⟨tennis ball/court/match/racket : pelota/cancha/partido/raqueta de tenis⟩ ⟨tennis player : tenista⟩

tenor ['tɛnər] *n* **1** PURPORT : tenor *m*, significado *m* **2** : tenor *m* (en música)

tenpins ['tɛn,pɪnz] *npl* : bolos *mpl*, boliche *m*

tense¹ ['tɛnts] *v* **tensed; tensing** *vt* : tensar — *vi* : tensarse, ponerse tenso

tense² *adj* **tenser; tensest 1** TAUT : tenso, tirante **2** NERVOUS : tenso, nervioso

tense³ *n* : tiempo *m* (de un verbo)

tensely ['tɛnt*s*li] *adv* : tensamente

tenseness ['tɛntsnəs] → **tension**

tension ['tɛntʃən] *n* **1** TAUTNESS : tensión *f*, tirantez *f* **2** STRESS : tensión *f*, nerviosismo *m*, estrés *m*

tent ['tɛnt] *n* : tienda *f* de campaña

tentacle ['tɛntɪkəl] *n* : tentáculo *m*

tentative ['tɛntətɪv] *adj* **1** HESITANT : indeciso, vacilante **2** PROVISIONAL : sujeto a cambios, provisional

tentatively ['tɛntətɪvli] *adv* : provisionalmente

tenth¹ ['tɛnθ] *adv* : en décimo lugar

tenth² *adj* : décimo

tenth³ *n* **1** : décimo *m*, -ma *f* (en una serie) **2** : décimo *m*, décima parte *f*

tenuous ['tɛnjʊəs] *adj* : tenue, débil ⟨tenuous reasons : razones poco convincentes⟩

tenuously ['tɛnjʊəsli] *adv* : ligeramente, débilmente

tenure ['tɛnjər] *n* : tenencia *f* (de un cargo o una propiedad), titularidad *f* (de un puesto académico)

tepee ['ti:ˌpi:] *n* : tipi *m*

tepid ['tɛpɪd] *adj* : tibio

tequila [təˈki:lə] *n* : tequila *m*

term¹ ['tərm] *vt* : calificar de, llamar, nombrar

term² *n* **1** PERIOD : término *m*, plazo *m*, período *m* **2** : término *m* (en matemáticas) **3** WORD : término *m*, vocablo *m* ⟨a term of endearment : un apelativo cariñoso⟩ ⟨medical terms : términos médicos⟩ **4 terms** *npl* CONDITIONS : términos *mpl*, condiciones *fpl* **5 terms** *npl* RELATIONS : relaciones *fpl* ⟨to be on good terms with : tener buenas relaciones con⟩ **6 in terms of** : con respecto a, en cuanto a **7 to come to terms with** : aceptar

terminal¹ ['tərmənəl] *adj* : terminal

terminal² *n* **1** : terminal *m*, polo *m* (en electricidad) **2** : terminal *m* (de una computadora) **3** STATION : terminal *f*, estación *f* (de transporte público)

terminate ['tərməˌneɪt] *v* **-nated; -nating** *vi* : terminar(se), concluirse — *vt* : terminar, poner fin a

termination [ˌtərməˈneɪʃən] *n* : cese *m*, terminación *f*

terminology [ˌtərməˈnɑlədʒi] *n, pl* **-gies** : terminología *f*

terminus ['tərmənəs] *n, pl* **-ni** [-ˌnaɪ] *or* **-nuses 1** END : término *m*, fin *m* **2** : terminal *f* (de transporte público)

termite ['tərˌmaɪt] *n* : termita *f*

tern ['tərn] *n* : golondrina *f* de mar

terrace¹ ['tɛrəs] *vt* **-raced; -racing** : formar en terrazas, disponer en bancales

terrace² *n* **1** PATIO : terraza *f*, patio *m* **2** : terraplén *m*, terraza *f*, bancal *m* (en agricultura)

terra–cotta [ˌtɛrəˈkɑtə] *n* : terracota *f*

terrain [təˈreɪn] *n* : terreno *m*

terrapin ['tɛrəpɪn] *n* : galápago *m* norteamericano

terrestrial [təˈrɛstriəl] *adj* : terrestre

terrible ['tɛrəbəl] *adj* : atroz, horrible, terrible

terribly ['tɛrəbli] *adv* **1** BADLY : muy mal **2** EXTREMELY : terriblemente, extremadamente

terrier ['tɛriər] *n* : terrier *mf*

terrific [təˈrɪfɪk] *adj* **1** FRIGHTFUL : aterrador **2** EXTRAORDINARY : extraordinario, excepcional **3** EXCELLENT : excelente, estupendo

terrify ['tɛrəˌfaɪ] *vt* **-fied; -fying** : aterrorizar, aterrar, espantar

terrifying ['tɛrəˌfaɪɪŋ] *adj* : espantoso, aterrador

territory ['tɛrəˌtori] *n, pl* **-ries** : territorio *m* — **territorial** [ˌtɛrəˈtoriəl] *adj*

terror ['tɛrər] *n* : terror *m*

terrorism ['tɛrərˌɪzəm] *n* : terrorismo *m*

terrorist¹ ['tɛrərɪst] *adj* : terrorista

terrorist² *n* : terrorista *mf*

terrorize ['tɛrərˌaɪz] *vt* **-ized; -izing** : aterrorizar

terry ['tɛri] *n, pl* **-ries** *or* **terry cloth** : (tela de) toalla *f*

terse ['tərs] *adj* **terser; tersest** : lacónico, conciso, seco — **tersely** *adv*

tertiary ['tərʃiˌɛri] *adj* : terciario

test¹ ['tɛst] *vt* **1** : examinar (estudiantes, etc.), evaluar (conocimientos, etc.) **2** : hacerle un análisis a, hacerle una prueba a, someter a pruebas ⟨to test someone for drugs/cancer : hacerle a alguien pruebas de drogas/cáncer⟩ **3** : analizar ⟨to test soil for lead : analizar tierra para detectar la presencia de plomo⟩ **4** : probar, experimentar (productos, etc.) **5** CHALLENGE, TRY : poner a prueba ⟨you're testing my patience : estás poniendo a prueba mi paciencia⟩ — *vi* : hacer pruebas

test² *n* : prueba *f*, examen *m*, test *m* ⟨to put to the test : poner a prueba⟩

testament ['tɛstəmənt] *n* **1** WILL : testamento *m* **2** : Testamento *m* (en la Biblia) ⟨the Old Testament : el Antiguo Testamento⟩

tester ['tɛstər] *n* **1** : probador *m*, -dora *f*; verificador *m*, -dora *f* (persona) **2** : verificador *m* (aparato)

testicle ['tɛstɪkəl] *n* : testículo *m*

testify ['tɛstəˌfaɪ] *v* **-fied; -fying** *vi* : testificar, atestar, testimoniar — *vt* : testificar

testimonial [ˌtɛstəˈmoːniəl] *n* **1** REFERENCE : recomendación *f* **2** TRIBUTE : homenaje *m*, tributo *m*

testimony ['tɛstəˌmoːni] *n, pl* **-nies** : testimonio *m*, declaración *f*

test tube *n* : probeta *f*, tubo *m* de ensayo

testy ['tɛsti] *adj* **testier; -est** : irritable

tetanus ['tɛtənəs] *n* : tétano *m*, tétanos *m*

tête–à–tête [ˌtɛtəˈtɛt, ˌteɪtəˈteɪt] *n* : conversación *f* en privado

tether¹ ['tɛðər] *vt* : atar (con una cuerda), amarrar

tether² *n* : atadura *f*, cadena *f*, correa *f*

text¹ ['tɛkst] *n* **1** : texto *m* **2** TOPIC : tema *m* **3** → **textbook** **4** *or* **text message** : mensaje *m* de texto, SMS *m*

text² *vi* : mandar un mensaje de texto, mensajear *fam*, textear *fam* — *vt* : mandarle un mensaje de texto a, mensajear *fam*, textear *fam*

textbook ['tɛkstˌbʊk] *n* : libro *m* de texto

texting ['tɛkstɪŋ] *or* **text messaging** *n* : mensajería *f* de texto

textile ['tɛkˌstaɪl, 'tɛkstəl] *n* : textil *m*, tela *f* ⟨the textile industry : la industria textil⟩

textual ['tɛkstʃʊəl] *adj* : textual

texture ['tɛkstʃər] *n* : textura *f*

Thai ['taɪ] *n* **1** : tailandés *m*, -desa *f* **2** : tailandés *m* (idioma) — **Thai** *adj*

than¹ ['ðæn] *conj* : que, de ⟨it's worth more than that : vale más que eso⟩ ⟨more than you think : más de lo que piensas⟩

than² *prep* : que, de ⟨you're better than he is : eres mejor que él⟩ ⟨more than once : más de una vez⟩

thank [ˈθæŋk] *vt* : agradecer, darle (las) gracias (a alguien) ⟨thank you! : ¡gracias!⟩ ⟨I thanked her for the present : le di las gracias por el regalo⟩ ⟨I thank you for your help : le agradezco su ayuda⟩

thankful [ˈθæŋkfəl] *adj* : agradecido

thankfully [ˈθæŋkfəli] *adv* **1** GRATEFULLY : con agradecimiento **2** FORTUNATELY : afortunadamente, por suerte ⟨thankfully, it's over : se acabó, gracias a Dios⟩

thankfulness [ˈθæŋkfəlnəs] *n* : agradecimiento *m*, gratitud *f*

thankless [ˈθæŋkləs] *adj* : ingrato ⟨a thankless task : un trabajo ingrato⟩

thanks [ˈθæŋks] *npl* **1** : agradecimiento *m* **2 thanks!** : ¡gracias!

Thanksgiving [θæŋksˈɡɪvɪŋ, ˈθæŋksˌ-] *n* : el día de Acción de Gracias (fiesta estadounidense)

that¹ [ˈðæt] *adv* (*in negative constructions*) : tan ⟨it's not that expensive : no es tan caro⟩ ⟨not that much : no tanto⟩

that² *adj*, *pl* **those** : ese, esa, aquel, aquella ⟨do you see those children? : ¿ves a aquellos niños?⟩

that³ *conj & pron* : que ⟨he said that he was afraid : dijo que tenía miedo⟩ ⟨the book that he wrote : el libro que escribió⟩

that⁴ *pron*, *pl* **those** [ˈðoːz] **1** : ese/ése, esa/ésa, eso ⟨that's my father : ese/ése es mi padre⟩ ⟨those are the ones he likes : esos/ésos son los que le gustan⟩ ⟨what's that? : ¿qué es eso?⟩ ⟨why did you do that? : ¿por qué hiciste eso?⟩ ⟨that's impossible : (eso) es imposible⟩ ⟨is that so? : ¿de veras?, ¿ah, sí?⟩ ⟨after that : después, luego⟩ **2 those** *pl* (*referring to a group of people*) : those who came : los que vinieron⟩ ⟨there are those who say . . . : hay quien dice . . .⟩ **3** (*referring to more distant objects or times*) : aquel/aquél, aquella/aquélla, aquello ⟨those are maples and these are elms : aquellos/aquéllos son arces y estos/éstos son olmos⟩ ⟨that came to an end : aquello se acabó⟩ **4 at that** ALSO, MOREOVER : además **5 at that** THEREUPON : al decir/oír (etc.) eso **6 at that** : sin decir más ⟨let's leave it at that : dejémoslo ahí⟩ **7 for all that** : a pesar de ello **8 that is (to say)** : o sea, es decir **9 that's it** ⟨that's it — it's finished : ya está (terminado)⟩ ⟨that's it — I'm leaving! : ¡se acabó! ¡me voy!⟩ ⟨do it like this — that's it! : hazlo así — ¡eso así!⟩

thatch¹ [ˈθætʃ] *vt* : cubrir o techar con paja, hojas, etc.

thatch² *n* : paja *f*, hojas *fpl* (para techos)

thaw¹ [ˈθɔ] *vt* : descongelar — *vi* : derretirse (dícese de la nieve), descongelarse (dícese de los alimentos)

thaw² *n* : deshielo *m*

the¹ [ðə, before vowel sounds usu ði:] *adv* **1** (*used to indicate comparison*) : the sooner the better : cuanto más pronto, mejor⟩ ⟨she likes this one the best : éste es el que más le gusta⟩ **2** (*used as a conjunction*) : cuanto ⟨the more I learn, the less I understand : cuanto más aprendo, menos entiendo⟩

the² *art* : el, la, los, las, lo ⟨the gloves : los guantes⟩ ⟨the girl : la chica⟩ ⟨the winter : el invierno⟩ ⟨the worst part : lo peor⟩ ⟨forty cookies to the box : cuarenta galletas por caja⟩ ⟨today is the ninth : hoy es nueve⟩ ⟨the 18th of august : el 18 de agosto⟩ ⟨William the Conqueror : Guillermo el Conquistador⟩ ⟨the French : los franceses⟩ ⟨the Smiths : los Smith⟩ ⟨the Mississippi River : el río Mississippi⟩ ⟨the English language : la lengua inglesa, el idioma inglés⟩

theater *or* **theatre** [ˈθiːəʔ̩ər] *n* **1** : teatro *m* (edificio) **2** DRAMA : teatro *m*, drama *m*

theatrical [θiˈætrɪkəl] *adj* : teatral, dramático

thee [ˈði:] *pron* : te, ti

theft [ˈθeft] *n* : robo *m*, hurto *m*

their [ˈðɛr] *adj* : su ⟨their friends : sus amigos⟩

theirs [ˈðɛrz] *pron* : (el) suyo, (la) suya, (los) suyos, (las) suyas ⟨they came for theirs : vinieron por el suyo⟩ ⟨theirs is bigger : la suya es más grande, la de ellos es más grande⟩ ⟨a brother of theirs : un hermano suyo, un hermano de ellos⟩

them [ˈðɛm] *pron* **1** (*as a direct object*) : los *Spain sometimes* les, las ⟨I know them : los conozco⟩ **2** (*as indirect object*) : les, se ⟨I sent them a letter : les mandé una carta⟩ ⟨give it to them : dáselo (a ellos)⟩ **3** (*as object of a preposition*) : ellos, ellas ⟨go with them : ve con ellos⟩ **4** (*for emphasis*) : ellos, ellas ⟨I wasn't expecting them : no los esperaba a ellos⟩

thematic [θiˈmætɪk] *adj* : temático

theme [ˈθiːm] *n* **1** SUBJECT, TOPIC : tema *m* **2** COMPOSITION : composición *f*, trabajo *m* (escrito) **3** : tema *m* (en música)

theme park *n* : parque *m* temático

themselves [ðəmˈsɛlvz, ðɛm-] *pron* **1** (*as a reflexive*) : se, sí ⟨they enjoyed themselves : se divirtieron⟩ ⟨they divided it among themselves : lo repartieron entre sí, se lo repartieron⟩ **2** (*for emphasis*) : ellos mismos, ellas mismas ⟨they built it themselves : ellas mismas lo construyeron⟩

then¹ [ˈðɛn] *adv* **1** : entonces, en ese tiempo ⟨I was sixteen then : tenía entonces dieciséis años⟩ ⟨by/since/until then : para/desde/hasta entonces⟩ **2** NEXT : después, luego ⟨we'll go to Toronto, then to Winnipeg : iremos a Toronto, y luego a Winnipeg⟩ **3** BESIDES, FURTHERMORE : además, aparte ⟨then there's the tax : y aparte está el impuesto⟩ **4** : entonces, en ese caso ⟨if you like music, then you should attend : si te gusta la música, entonces deberías asistir⟩ ⟨it's true, then? : ¿entonces es cierto?⟩ ⟨OK, then, I'll see you later : hasta luego, entonces⟩ ⟨you're sure? all right, then : ¿estás seguro? bueno, está bien⟩ **5 then and there** : en el momento

then² *adj* : entonces ⟨the then governor of Georgia : el entonces gobernador de Georgia⟩

thence ['ðɛnts, 'ðnts] *adv* : de ahí, de ahí en adelante

theologian [ˌθi:ə'lo:dʒkəl] *n* : teólogo *m*, -ga *f*

theological [ˌθi:ə'lɑdʒɪkəl] *adj* : teológico

theology [θi'ɑlədʒi] *n, pl* **-gies** : teología *f*

theorem ['θi:ərəm, 'θɪrəm] *n* : teorema *m*

theoretical [ˌθi:ə'rɛṭɪkəl] *adj* : teórico — **theoretically** *adv*

theorist ['θi:ərɪst] *n* : teórico *m*, -ca *f*

theorize ['θi:ə,raɪz] *vi* **-rized; -rizing** : teorizar

theory ['θi:əri, 'θɪri] *n, pl* **-ries** : teoría *f*

therapeutic [ˌθɛrə'pju:ṭɪk] *adj* : terapéutico — **therapeutically** *adv*

therapist ['θɛrəpɪst] *n* : terapeuta *mf*

therapy ['θɛrəpi] *n, pl* **-pies** : terapia *f*

there[1] ['ðær] *adv* **1** : ahí, allí, allá ⟨stand over there : párate ahí⟩ ⟨we can walk there : podemos ir a pie⟩ ⟨over there : por allí/allá⟩ ⟨out/in there : ahí fuera/dentro⟩ ⟨who's there? : ¿quién es?⟩ ⟨is Mom there? : ¿está mamá?⟩ ⟨there it is : ahí está⟩ ⟨there you are/go : aquí tienes, toma⟩ ⟨ . . . and there you have it! : ¡ . . . y ya está!⟩ ⟨that clock there : ese reloj que ves allí⟩ ⟨you there! : ¡oye, tú!⟩ ⟨hello there! : ¡hola!⟩ **2** : ahí, en esto, en eso ⟨there is where we disagree : en eso es donde no estamos de acuerdo⟩ **3** THEN : entonces ⟨from there : de ahí, a partir de ese momento⟩ **4 to be out there** EXIST : existir **5 to have been there** (*referring to an experience*) ⟨I've been there myself : yo también he pasado por eso⟩

there[2] *pron* **1** (*introducing a sentence or clause*) ⟨there comes a time to decide : llega un momento en que uno tiene que decidir⟩ **2 there is/are** : hay ⟨there are many children here : aquí hay muchos niños⟩ ⟨are there a lot of errors? : ¿hay muchos errores?⟩ ⟨there's a good hotel downtown : hay un buen hotel en el centro⟩ ⟨there was no way to know : no había manera de saberlo⟩

thereabouts [ˌðærə'bauts, 'ðærə-] *or* **thereabout** [-'baut, -ˌbaut] *adv* **or thereabouts** : por ahí, más o menos ⟨at five o'clock or thereabouts : por ahí de las cinco⟩

thereafter [ðær'æftər] *adv* : después ⟨shortly thereafter : poco después⟩

thereby [ðær'baɪ, 'ðær,baɪ] *adv* : de tal modo, de esa manera, así

therefore ['ðær,for] *adv* : por lo tanto, por consiguiente

therein [ðær'ɪn] *adv* **1** : allí adentro, ahí adentro ⟨the contents therein : lo que allí se contiene⟩ **2** : allí, en ese aspecto ⟨therein lies the problem : allí está el problema⟩

thereof [ðær'ʌv, -'ɑv] *adv* : de eso, de esto

thereupon ['ðærə,pɑn, -,pɔn;, ˌðærə'pɑn, -'pɔn] *adv* : acto seguido, inmediatamente (después)

therewith [ðær'wɪð, -'wɪθ] *adv* : con eso, con ello

thermal ['θərməl] *adj* **1** : térmico (en física) **2** HOT : termal

thermodynamics [ˌθərmodaɪ'næmɪks] *ns & pl* : termodinámica *f*

thermometer [θər'mɑməṭər] *n* : termómetro *m*

thermos ['θərməs] *n* : termo *m*

thermostat ['θərmə,stæt] *n* : termostato *m*

thesaurus [θɪ'sɔrəs] *n, pl* **-sauri** [-'sɔr,aɪ] *or* **-sauruses** [-'sɔrəsəz] : diccionario *m* de sinónimos

these → **this**

thesis ['θi:sɪs] *n, pl* **theses** ['θi:,si:z] : tesis *f*

they ['ðeɪ] *pron* : ellos, ellas ⟨they are here : están aquí⟩ ⟨they don't know : ellos no saben⟩

they'd ['ðeɪd] *contraction of* THEY HAD *or* THEY WOULD → **have, would**

they'll ['ðeɪl, 'ðel] *contraction of* THEY SHALL *or* THEY WILL → **shall, will**

they're ['ðər] *contraction of* THEY ARE → **be**

they've ['ðeɪv] *contraction of* THEY HAVE → **have**

thiamine ['θaɪəmɪn, -,mi:n] *n* : tiamina *f*

thick[1] ['θɪk] *adj* **1** : grueso ⟨a thick plank : una tabla gruesa⟩ **2** : espeso, denso ⟨thick syrup : jarabe espeso⟩ — **thickly** *adv*

thick[2] *n* **1 in the thick of** : en medio de ⟨in the thick of the battle : en lo más reñido de la batalla⟩ **2 through thick and thin** : a las duras y a las maduras

thicken ['θɪkən] *vt* : espesar (un líquido) — *vi* : espesarse

thickener ['θɪkənər] *n* : espesante *m*

thicket ['θɪkət] *n* : matorral *m*, maleza *f*, espesura *f*

thickness ['θɪknəs] *n* : grosor *m*, grueso *m*, espesor *m*

thickset ['θɪk'sɛt] *adj* STOCKY : robusto, fornido

thick-skinned ['θɪk'skɪnd] *adj* : poco sensible, que no se ofende fácilmente

thief ['θi:f] *n, pl* **thieves** ['θi:vz] : ladrón *m*, -drona *f*

thieve ['θi:v] *v* **thieved; thieving** : hurtar, robar

thievery ['θi:vəri] *n* : hurto *m*, robo *m*, latrocinio *m*

thigh ['θaɪ] *n* : muslo *m*

thighbone ['θaɪ,bo:n] *n* : fémur *m*

thimble ['θɪmbəl] *n* : dedal *m*

thin[1] ['θɪn] *v* **thinned; thinning** *vt* : hacer menos denso, diluir, aguar (un líquido), enrarecer (un gas) — *vi* : diluirse, aguarse (dícese de un líquido), enrarecerse (dícese de un gas)

thin[2] *adj* **thinner; thinnest 1** LEAN, SLIM : delgado, esbelto, flaco **2** SPARSE : ralo, escaso ⟨a thin beard : una barba rala⟩ **3** WATERY : claro, aguado, diluido **4** FINE : delgado, fino ⟨thin slices : rebanadas finas⟩

thing ['θɪŋ] *n* **1** MATTER, FACT, IDEA : cosa *f* ⟨don't talk about those things : no hables de esas cosas⟩ ⟨how are things? : ¿cómo van las cosas?⟩ ⟨the main thing : lo principal⟩ ⟨the thing is . . . : el caso es que . . .⟩ ⟨to think things over : pensarlo (bien)⟩ ⟨for one thing, . . . : para empezar, . . .⟩ ⟨I said no such thing! : ¡no dije tal/semejante cosa!⟩ **2** ACT, EVENT : cosa *f* ⟨the flood was a terrible thing : la inundación fue una cosa terrible⟩ ⟨it's a good thing that . . . : menos mal que . . .⟩ ⟨to do the right thing : hacer lo correcto⟩ **3** OBJECT : cosa *f* ⟨don't forget your things : no olvides tus cosas⟩ ⟨baby things : cosas para bebés⟩ ⟨there's no such thing : no existe (tal cosa)⟩ ⟨I can't see a thing : no puedo ver nada⟩ ⟨I have just the thing for you : tengo justo lo que necesitas⟩ **4 as things stand** : tal como están las cosas **5 a thing or two** : unas cuantas cosas **6 first/last thing** : a primera/última hora ⟨I'll do it first thing tomorrow : lo haré mañana a primera hora⟩ **7 it's (just) one of those things** : son cosas de la vida **8 of all things** ⟨he's learning jousting, of all things! : ¡está aprendiendo a justar! ¿te lo imaginas?⟩ **9 to have another thing coming** : estar muy equivocado

thingamajig [ˈθɪŋəməˌdʒɪɡ] *or* **thingamabob** [ˈθɪŋəməˌbɑb] *n fam* : cosa *f*, vaina *f fam*, chisme *m Spain fam*

think[1] [ˈθɪŋk] *v* **thought** [ˈθɔt]; **thinking** *vt* **1** PLAN : pensar, creer ⟨he thinks (that) he'll return early : pienso regresar temprano⟩ ⟨I think (that) I'll call her : creo que la llamaré⟩ **2** BELIEVE : creer, opinar ⟨I think (that) I can go : creo que puedo ir⟩ ⟨I think so : creo que sí⟩ ⟨I don't think so : creo que no⟩ ⟨what do you think? : ¿qué opinas?⟩ ⟨who does she think she is? : ¿quién se cree?⟩ **3** PONDER : pensar ⟨"how odd," he thought : qué raro — pensó⟩ ⟨what were you thinking? : ¿en qué pensabas?⟩ **4** REMEMBER : acordarse de ⟨I didn't think to ask : no se me ocurrió preguntar⟩ **5 to think better of** : cambiar de idea **6 to think nothing of** ⟨she thinks nothing of running 10 miles : correr 10 millas no le parece nada extraño⟩ ⟨think nothing of it : de nada, no hay de qué⟩ **7 to think out/through** : pensar bien, estudiar **8 to think over** CONSIDER : pensar **9 to think up** : idear, inventar ⟨we've thought up a plan : se nos ha ocurrido un plan⟩ — *vi* **1** : pensar ⟨let me think : déjame pensar⟩ **2 to think about/of** : pensar en ⟨I was just thinking about/of you when you called : pensaba en ti justo cuando llamaste⟩ **3 to think about/of** WEIGH : pensar (en) ⟨think about it : piénsalo⟩ ⟨I'm thinking about/of buying it : estoy pensando en comprarlo⟩ **4 to think about/of** : pensar en ⟨think about/of your family! : ¡piensa en tu familia!⟩ **5 to think about/of** : pensar de ⟨what did you think about/of the book? : ¿qué pensaste del libro?, ¿qué te pareció el libro?⟩ **6 to think again** : pensar dos veces **7 to think ahead** : ser previsor **8 to think aloud** : pensar en voz alta **9 to think back** : recordar **10 to think of** REMEMBER : acordarse de **11 to think of** : idear,

inventar ⟨we'll think of something : algo se nos ocurrirá⟩ **12 to think poorly of** : pensar mal de **13 to think twice** : pensárselo dos veces **14 to think well of** : tener buena opinión de

think[2] *n* **1 to have a think about** : pensar **2 to have another think coming** : estar muy equivocado

thinker [ˈθɪŋkər] *n* : pensador *m*, -dora *f*

thinly [ˈθɪnli] *adv* **1** LIGHTLY : ligeramente **2** SPARSELY : escasamente ⟨thinly populated : poco populado⟩ **3** BARELY : apenas

thinness [ˈθɪnnəs] *n* : delgadez *f*

thin-skinned [ˈθɪnˈskɪnd] *adj* : susceptible, muy sensible

third[1] [ˈθərd] *or* **thirdly** [-li] *adv* : en tercer lugar ⟨she came in third : llegó en tercer lugar⟩

third[2] *adj* : tercero ⟨the third day : el tercer día⟩

third[3] *n* **1** : tercero *m*, -ra *f* (en una serie) ⟨the third of June : el tres de junio⟩ **2** : tercero *m*, tercera parte *f* **3** *or* **third base** : tercera base *f* **4** *or* **third gear** : tercera *f*

third world *n* *sometimes offensive* **the Third World** : el Tercer Mundo *m*

thirst[1] [ˈθərst] *vi* **1** : tener sed **2 to thirst for** DESIRE : tener sed de, estar sediento de

thirst[2] *n* : sed *f*

thirsty [ˈθərsti] *adj* **thirstier, -est** : sediento, que tiene sed ⟨I'm thirsty : tengo sed⟩

thirteen[1] [ˌθərˈtiːn] *adj & pron* : trece

thirteen[2] *n* : trece *m*

thirteenth[1] [ˌθərˈtiːnθ] *adj* : décimo tercero

thirteenth[2] *n* **1** : decimotercero *m*, -ra *f* (en una serie) **2** : treceavo *m*, treceava parte *f*

thirtieth[1] [ˈθərtiəθ] *adj* : trigésimo

thirtieth[2] *n* **1** : trigésimo *m*, -ma *f* (en una serie) **2** : treintavo *m*, treintava parte *f*

thirty[1] [ˈθərti] *adj & pron* : treinta

thirty[2] *n, pl* **thirties** : treinta *m*

this[1] [ˈðɪs] *adv* : así, a tal punto ⟨this big : así de grande⟩

this[2] *adj, pl* **these** [ˈðiːz] : este ⟨these things : estas cosas⟩ ⟨read this book : lee este libro⟩

this[3] *pron, pl* **these** : este/éste, esta/ésta, esto ⟨what's this? : ¿qué es esto?⟩ ⟨this wasn't here yesterday : esto no estaba aquí ayer⟩ ⟨this is for you : esto es para ti⟩ ⟨those magazines and these : aquellas revistas y estas/éstas⟩ ⟨these aren't the files I need : estos/éstos no son los archivos que necesito⟩

thistle [ˈθɪsəl] *n* : cardo *m*

thong [ˈθɔŋ] *n* **1** STRAP : correa *f*, tira *f* **2** FLIP-FLOP : chancla *f*, chancleta *f*

thorax [ˈθɔrˌæks] *n, pl* **-raxes** *or* **-races** [ˈθɔrəˌsiːz] : tórax *m*

thorn [ˈθɔrn] *n* : espina *f*

thorny [ˈθɔrni] *adj* **thornier; -est** : espinoso

thorough [ˈθəro] *adj* **1** CONSCIENTIOUS

: concienzudo, meticuloso **2** COMPLETE : absoluto, completo — **thoroughly** *adv*

thoroughbred ['θəro,brɛd] *adj* : de pura sangre (dícese de un caballo)

Thoroughbred *n or* **Thoroughbred horse** : pura sangre *mf*

thoroughfare ['θərə,fær] *n* : vía *f* pública, carretera *f*

thoroughness ['θərənəs] *n* : esmero *m*, meticulosidad *f*

those → **that**

thou ['ðaʊ] *pron* : tú

though¹ ['ðo:] *adv* **1** HOWEVER, NEVERTHELESS : sin embargo, no obstante **2** **as ~** : como si ⟨as though nothing had happened : como si nada hubiera pasado⟩

though² *conj* : aunque, a pesar de ⟨though it was raining, we went out : salimos a pesar de la lluvia⟩

thought¹ → **think**

thought² ['θɔt] *n* **1** THINKING : pensamiento *m*, ideas *fpl* ⟨Western thought : el pensamiento occidental⟩ **2** COGITATION : pensamiento *m*, reflexión *f*, raciocinio *m* **3** IDEA : idea *f*, ocurrencia *f* ⟨it was just a thought : fue sólo una idea⟩

thoughtful ['θɔtfəl] *adj* **1** PENSIVE : pensativo, meditabundo **2** CONSIDERATE : considerado, atento, cortés — **thoughtfully** *adv*

thoughtfulness ['θɔtfəlnəs] *n* : consideración *f*, atención *f*, cortesía *f*

thoughtless ['θɔtləs] *adj* **1** CARELESS : descuidado, negligente **2** INCONSIDERATE : desconsiderado — **thoughtlessly** *adv*

thoughtlessness *n* **1** CARELESSNESS : descuido *m*, irreflexión *f*, imprevisión *f* **2** : falta *f* de consideración

thousand¹ ['θaʊzənd] *adj & pron* : mil

thousand² *n, pl* **-sands** *or* **-sand** : mil *m*

thousandth¹ ['θaʊzənθ] *adj* : milésimo

thousandth² *n* **1** : milésimo *m*, -ma *f* (en una serie) **2** : milésimo *m*, milésima parte *f*

thrash ['θræʃ] *vt* **1** → **thresh** **2** BEAT : golpear, azotar, darle una paliza (a alguien) **3** FLAIL : sacudir, agitar bruscamente

thread¹ ['θrɛd] *vt* **1** : enhilar, enhebrar (una aguja) **2** STRING : ensartar (cuentas en un hilo) **3 to thread one's way** : abrirse paso

thread² *n* **1** : hilo *m*, hebra *f* ⟨needle and thread : aguja e hilo⟩ ⟨the thread of an argument : el hilo de un debate⟩ **2** : rosca *f*, filete *m* (de un tornillo)

threadbare ['θrɛd'bær] *adj* **1** SHABBY, WORN : raído, gastado **2** TRITE : trillado, tópico, manido

threat ['θrɛt] *n* : amenaza *f*

threaten ['θrɛtən] *v* : amenazar

threatening ['θrɛtənɪŋ] *adj* : amenazador — **threateningly** *adv*

three¹ ['θri:] *adj* : tres ⟨he's three (years old) : tiene tres años⟩

three² *n* : tres *m* ⟨the three of hearts : el tres de corazones⟩

three³ *pron* : tres ⟨there are three of us

: somos tres⟩ ⟨it's three (o'clock) : son las tres⟩

3–D ['θri:'di:] *adj* → **three-dimensional**

three–dimensional ['θri:də'mɛntʃənəl] *adj* : tridimensional

threefold ['θri:,fo:ld] *adj* TRIPLE : triple

three hundred¹ *adj & pron* : trescientos

three hundred² *n* : trescientos *m*

three–piece suit *n* : terno *m*, tresillo *m*

threescore ['θri:'skor] *adj* SIXTY : sesenta

thresh ['θrɛʃ] *vt* : trillar (grano)

thresher ['θrɛʃər] *n* : trilladora *f*

threshold ['θrɛʃ,ho:ld, -,o:ld] *n* : umbral *m*

threw → **throw¹**

thrice ['θraɪs] *adv* : tres veces

thrift ['θrɪft] *n* : economía *f*, frugalidad *f*

thriftless ['θrɪftləs] *adj* : despilfarrador, manirroto

thrifty ['θrɪfti] *adj* **thriftier; -est** : económico, frugal — **thriftily** ['θrɪftəli] *adv*

thrill¹ ['θrɪl] *vt* : emocionar — *vi* **to thrill to** : dejarse conmover por, estremecerse con

thrill² *n* : emoción *f*

thriller ['θrɪlər] *n* **1** : evento *m* emocionante **2** : obra *f* de suspenso

thrilling ['θrɪlɪŋ] *adj* : emocionante, excitante

thrive ['θraɪv] *vi* **throve** ['θro:v] *or* **thrived; thriven** ['θrɪvən] **1** FLOURISH : florecer, crecer abundantemente **2** PROSPER : prosperar

throat ['θro:t] *n* : garganta *f*

throaty ['θro:ti] *adj* **throatier; -est** : ronco (dícese de la voz)

throb¹ ['θrɑb] *vi* **throbbed; throbbing** : palpitar, latir (dícese del corazón), vibrar (dícese de un motor, etc.)

throb² *n* : palpitación *f*, latido *m*, vibración *f*

throe ['θro:] *n* **1** PAIN, SPASM : espasmo *m*, dolor *m* ⟨the throes of childbirth : los dolores de parto⟩ **2 throes** *npl* : lucha *f* larga y ardua ⟨in the throes of : en el medio de⟩

thrombosis [θrɑm'bo:səs] *n* : trombosis *f*

throne ['θro:n] *n* : trono *m*

throng¹ ['θrɔŋ] *vt* CROWD : atestar, atiborrar, llenar — *vi* : aglomerarse, amontonarse

throng² *n* : muchedumbre *f*, gentío *m*, multitud *f*

throttle¹ ['θrɑtəl] *vt* **-tled; -tling** **1** STRANGLE : estrangular, ahogar **2 to throttle down** : desacelerar un motor

throttle² *n* **1** : válvula *f* reguladora **2 at full throttle** : a toda máquina

through¹ ['θru:] *adv* **1** : a través, de un lado a otro ⟨let them through : déjenlos pasar⟩ **2** : de principio a fin ⟨she read the book through : leyó el libro de principio a fin⟩ **3** COMPLETELY : completamente ⟨soaked through : completamente empapado⟩

through² *adj* **1** DIRECT : directo ⟨a through train : un tren directo⟩ **2** FINISHED : terminado, acabado ⟨we're through : hemos terminado⟩

through[3] *prep* **1** : a través de, por ⟨through the door : por la puerta⟩ ⟨a road through the woods : un camino que atraviesa el bosque⟩ **2** BETWEEN : entre ⟨a path through the trees : un sendero entre los árboles⟩ **3** BECAUSE OF : a causa de, como consecuencia de **4** DURING : por, durante ⟨through the night : durante la noche⟩ **5** : a, hasta ⟨from Monday through Friday : de lunes a viernes⟩ **6** (*indicating completion*) ⟨she's been through a lot : ha pasado muchas dificultades⟩ ⟨we're through the worst of it : hemos pasado lo peor⟩ **7** VIA : a través de, por ⟨I got the job through her cousin : conseguí el trabajo a través de su primo⟩

throughout[1] [θru:'aut] *adv* **1** EVERYWHERE : por todas partes **2** THROUGH : desde el principio hasta el fin de (algo)

throughout[2] *prep* **1** : en todas partes de, a través de ⟨throughout the United States : en todo Estados Unidos⟩ **2** : de principio a fin de, durante ⟨throughout the winter : durante todo el invierno⟩

throve → **thrive**

throw[1] ['θro:] *v* **threw** ['θru:]; **thrown** ['θro:n]; **throwing** *vt* **1** TOSS : tirar; lanzar; echar; arrojar; aventar *Col, Mex* ⟨to throw a ball : tirar una pelota⟩ **2** : desmontar (a un jinete) **3** CAST : proyectar ⟨it threw a long shadow : proyectó una sombra larga⟩ **4** to throw a party : dar una fiesta **5** to throw in : dar de ñapa **6** to throw into confusion : desconcertar **7** to throw away/out DISCARD : botar, tirar (a la basura) **8** to throw out REJECT : rechazar **9** to throw out EJECT : echar **10** to throw up VOMIT : vomitar, devolver (comida, etc.) — *vi* to throw up VOMIT : vomitar, devolver

throw[2] *n* TOSS : tiro *m*, tirada *f*, lanzamiento *m*, lance *m* (de dados)

thrower ['θro:ər] *n* : lanzador *m*, -dora *f*

thrush ['θrʌʃ] *n* : tordo *m*, zorzal *m*

thrust[1] ['θrʌst] *vt* **thrust**; **thrusting 1** SHOVE : empujar bruscamente **2** PLUNGE, STAB : apuñalar, clavar ⟨he thrust a dagger into her heart : la apuñaló en el corazón⟩ **3** to thrust one's way : abrirse paso **4** to thrust upon : imponer a

thrust[2] *n* **1** PUSH, SHOVE : empujón *m*, empellón *m* **2** LUNGE : estocada *f* (en esgrima) **3** IMPETUS : ímpetu *m*, impulso *m*, propulsión *f* (de un motor)

thud[1] ['θʌd] *vi* **thudded**; **thudding** : producir un ruido sordo

thud[2] *n* : ruido *m* sordo (que produce un objeto al caer)

thug ['θʌg] *n* : matón *m*

thumb[1] ['θʌm] *vt* : hojear (con el pulgar)

thumb[2] *n* : pulgar *m*, dedo *m* pulgar

thumbnail ['θʌm,neɪl] *n* **1** : uña *f* del pulgar **2** : thumbnail *m*, miniatura *f*

thumbtack ['θʌm,tæk] *n* : tachuela *f*, chinche *f*

thump[1] ['θʌmp] *vt* POUND : golpear, aporrear — *vi* : latir con vehemencia (dícese del corazón)

thump[2] *n* THUD : ruido *m* sordo

thunder[1] ['θʌndər] *vi* **1** : tronar ⟨it rained and thundered all night : llovió y tronó durante la noche⟩ **2** BOOM : retumbar, bramar, resonar — *vt* ROAR, SHOUT : decir a gritos, vociferar

thunder[2] *n* : truenos *mpl*

thunderbolt ['θʌndər,bo:lt] *n* : rayo *m*

thunderclap ['θʌndər,klæp] *n* : trueno *m*

thunderous ['θʌndərəs] *adj* : atronador, ensordecedor, estruendoso

thundershower ['θʌndər,ʃauər] *n* : lluvia *f* con truenos y relámpagos

thunderstorm ['θʌndər,stɔrm] *n* : tormenta *f* con truenos y relámpagos

thunderstruck ['θʌndər,strʌk] *adj* : atónito

Thursday ['θərz,deɪ, -di] *n* : jueves *m* ⟨today is Thursday : hoy es jueves⟩ ⟨(on) Thursday : el jueves⟩ ⟨(on) Thursdays : los jueves⟩ ⟨last Thursday : el jueves pasado⟩ ⟨next Thursday : el jueves que viene⟩ ⟨every other Thursday : cada dos jueves⟩ ⟨Thursday afternoon/morning : jueves por la tarde/mañana⟩

thus ['ðʌs] *adv* **1** : así, de esta manera **2** SO : hasta (cierto punto) ⟨the weather's been nice thus far : hasta ahora ha hecho buen tiempo⟩ **3** HENCE : por consiguiente, por lo tanto

thwart ['θwɔrt] *vt* : frustrar

thy ['ðaɪ] *adj* : tu

thyme ['taɪm, 'θaɪm] *n* : tomillo *m*

thyroid ['θaɪ,rɔɪd] *n or* **thyroid gland** : tiroides *mf*, glándula *f* tiroidea ⟨thyroid hormone : hormona tiroidea⟩

thyself [ðaɪ'sɛlf] *pron* : ti, ti mismo

ti ['ti:] *n* : si *m* (en el canto)

tiara [ti'ærə, -'ɑr-] *n* : diadema *f*

Tibetan [tə'bɛtən] *n* **1** : tibetano *m*, -na *f* **2** : tibetano *m* (idioma) — **Tibetan** *adj*

tibia ['tɪbiə] *n, pl* **-iae** [-bi,i:] : tibia *f*

tic ['tɪk] *n* : tic *m*

tick[1] ['tɪk] *vi* **1** : hacer tictac **2** OPERATE, RUN : operar, andar (dícese de un mecanismo) ⟨what makes him tick? : ¿qué es lo que lo mueve?⟩ — *vt or* **to tick off** CHECK : marcar

tick[2] *n* **1** : tictac *m* (de un reloj) **2** CHECK : marca *f* **3** : garrapata *f* (insecto)

ticket[1] ['tɪkət] *vt* LABEL : etiquetar

ticket[2] *n* **1** : boleto *m*, boleta *f*, entrada *f* (de un espectáculo), pasaje *m* (de avión, tren, etc.) **2** SLATE : lista *f* de candidatos

ticket collector *n* : revisor *m*, -sora *f*

ticket office *n* : taquilla *f*

tickle[1] ['tɪkəl] *v* **-led**; **-ling** *vt* **1** AMUSE : divertir, hacerle gracia (a alguien) **2** : hacerle cosquillas (a alguien) ⟨don't tickle me! : ¡no me hagas cosquillas!⟩ — *vi* : picar

tickle[2] *n* : cosquilleo *m*, cosquillas *fpl*, picor *m* (en la garganta)

ticklish ['tɪkəlɪʃ] *adj* **1** : cosquilloso (dícese de una persona) **2** DELICATE, TRICKY : delicado, peliagudo

tick–tock *n* : tictac *m*

tidal ['taɪdəl] *adj* : de marea, relativo a la marea

tidal wave *n* : maremoto *m*

tidbit ['tɪd͵bɪt] *n* **1** BITE, SNACK : bocado *m*, golosina *f* **2** : dato *m* o noticia *f* interesante ⟨useful tidbits of information : informaciones útiles⟩

tide[1] ['taɪd] *vt* **tided; tiding** *or* **to tide over** : proveer lo necesario para aguantar una dificultad ⟨this money will tide you over until you find work : este dinero te mantendrá hasta que encuentres empleo⟩

tide[2] *n* **1** : marea *f* **2** CURRENT : corriente *f* (de eventos, opiniones, etc.)

tidily ['taɪdəli] *adv* : ordenadamente

tidiness ['taɪdinəs] *n* : aseo *m*, limpieza *f*, orden *m*

tidings ['taɪdɪŋz] *npl* : nuevas *fpl*

tidy[1] ['taɪdi] *vt* **-died; -dying** : asear, limpiar, poner en orden — *vi* **to tidy up** : poner las cosas en orden

tidy[2] *adj* **tidier; -est 1** CLEAN, NEAT : limpio, aseado, en orden **2** SUBSTANTIAL : grande, considerable ⟨a tidy sum : una suma considerable⟩

tie[1] ['taɪ] *v* **tied; tying** *or* **tieing** *vt* **1** : atar, amarrar ⟨to tie a knot : atar un nudo⟩ ⟨to tie one's shoelaces : atarse los cordones⟩ **2** BIND,[s] UNITE : ligar, atar **3** : empatar ⟨they tied the score : empataron el marcador⟩ **4 to be fit to be tied** : estar hecho una furia **5 to tie down/up** : atar **6 to tie in with** : relacionar con **7 to tie up** : ocupar (a alguien), inmovilizar (dinero), atascar (tráfico) — *vi* **1** : empatar ⟨the two teams were tied : los dos equipos empataron⟩ **2 to tie in with** : relacionarse con

tie[2] *n* **1** : ligadura *f*, cuerda *f*, cordón *m* (para atar algo) **2** BOND, LINK : atadura *f*, ligadura *f*, vínculo *m*, lazo *m* ⟨family ties : lazos familiares⟩ **3** *or* **railroad tie** : traviesa *f* **4** DRAW : empate *m* (en deportes) **5** NECKTIE : corbata *f*

tiebreaker ['taɪ͵breɪkər] *n* : desempate *m*

tier ['tɪr] *n* : hilera *f*, escalón *m*

tiff ['tɪf] *n* : disgusto *m*, disputa *f*

tiger ['taɪgər] *n* : tigre *m*

tight[1] ['taɪt] *adv* TIGHTLY : bien, fuerte ⟨shut it tight : ciérralo bien⟩

tight[2] *adj* **1** : bien cerrado, hermético ⟨a tight seal : un cierre hermético⟩ **2** STRICT : estricto, severo **3** TAUT : tirante, tenso **4** SNUG : apretado, ajustado, ceñido ⟨a tight dress : un vestido ceñido⟩ **5** DIFFICULT : difícil ⟨to be in a tight spot : estar en un aprieto⟩ **6** STINGY : apretado, avaro, agarrado *fam* **7** CLOSE : reñido ⟨a tight game : un juego reñido⟩ **8** SCARCE : escaso ⟨money is tight : escasea el dinero⟩

tighten ['taɪtən] *vt* : tensar (una cuerda, etc.), apretar (un nudo, un tornillo, etc.), apretarse (el cinturón), reforzar (las reglas)

tightfisted ['taɪt'fɪstəd] *adj* STINGY : apretado, avaro, agarrado *fam*

tightly ['taɪtli] *adv* : bien, fuerte

tightness ['taɪtnəs] *n* : lo apretado, lo tenso, tensión *f*

tightrope ['taɪt͵ro:p] *n* : cuerda *f* floja

tights ['taɪts] *npl* : leotardo *m*, malla *f*

tightwad ['taɪt͵wɑd] *n* : avaro *m*, -ra *f*; tacaño *m*, -ña *f*

tigress ['taɪgrəs] *n* : tigresa *f*

tilde ['tɪldə] *n* : tilde *mf*

tile[1] ['taɪl] *vt* **tiled; tiling** : embaldosar (un piso), revestir de azulejos (una pared), tejar (un techo)

tile[2] *n* **1** *or* **floor tile** : losa *f*, baldosa *f*, mosaico *m Mex* (de un piso) **2** : azulejo *m* (de una pared) **3** : teja *f* (de un techo)

till[1] ['tɪl] *vt* : cultivar, labrar

till[2] *n* : caja *f*, caja *f* registradora

till[3] *prep & conj* → **until**

tiller ['tɪlər] *n* **1** : cultivador *m*, -dora *f* (de la tierra) **2** : caña *f* del timón (de un barco)

tilt[1] ['tɪlt] *vt* : ladear, inclinar — *vi* : ladearse, inclinarse

tilt[2] *n* **1** SLANT : inclinación *f* **2 at full tilt** : a toda velocidad

timber ['tɪmbər] *n* **1** : madera *f* (para construcción) **2** BEAM : viga *f*

timberland ['tɪmbər͵lænd] *n* : bosque *m* maderero

timbre ['tæmbər, 'tɪm-] *n* : timbre *m*

time[1] ['taɪm] *vt* **timed; timing 1** SCHEDULE : fijar la hora de, calcular el momento oportuno para **2** CLOCK : cronometrar, medir el tiempo de (una competencia, etc.)

time[2] *n* **1** : tiempo *m* ⟨the passing of time : el paso del tiempo⟩ ⟨she doesn't have time : no tiene tiempo⟩ **2** MOMENT : tiempo *m*, momento *m* ⟨this is not the time to bring it up : no es el momento de sacar el tema⟩ ⟨it can wait until another time : podemos dejarlo para otro momento⟩ ⟨since that time : desde entonces⟩ **3** : vez *f* ⟨he called you three times : te llamó tres veces⟩ ⟨three times greater : tres veces mayor⟩ ⟨this time : esta vez⟩ ⟨one more time : una vez más⟩ **4** AGE : tiempo *m*, era *f* ⟨in your grandparents' time : en el tiempo de tus abuelos⟩ ⟨it was before your time : fue antes de que nacieras⟩ **5** TEMPO : tiempo *m*, ritmo *m* (en música) **6** : hora *f* (del día), época *f* (del año) ⟨what time is it? : ¿qué hora es?⟩ ⟨do you have the time? : ¿tienes hora?⟩ ⟨it's time for dinner : es hora de comer⟩ ⟨at the usual time : a la hora acostumbrada⟩ ⟨during work time : en horas de trabajo⟩ ⟨local time : hora local⟩ ⟨arrival/departure time : hora de llegada/salida⟩ **7** WHILE : tiempo *m*, rato *m* ⟨a short/long time ago : hace poco/mucho tiempo⟩ ⟨for (quite) some time now : desde hace mucho tiempo⟩ ⟨he watched us the whole/entire time : nos miraba (durante) todo el tiempo⟩ **8** EXPERIENCE : rato *m*, experiencia *f* ⟨we had a nice time together : pasamos juntos un rato agradable⟩ ⟨to have a rough time : pasarlo mal⟩ ⟨have a good time! : ¡que se diviertan!⟩ **9 against time** : contra el reloj **10 ahead of one's time** ⟨she was ahead of her time : se adelantó a su época⟩ **11 ahead of time** ⟨I prepared it ahead of time : lo preparé con antelación⟩ ⟨she handed it in ahead of time : lo entregó antes de tiempo⟩ ⟨he showed up ahead of time : apareció antes de la hora⟩ **12 all in good time** : todo a su debido tiempo **13 all the time** ALWAYS, OFTEN : todo el tiempo **14 all the time** THROUGHOUT : (durante) todo el tiempo **15 at all times** : siempre, en todo momento **16 (at) any time** : en cualquier momento **17 at a time** SIMULTANEOUSLY : al mismo tiempo, a la vez ⟨one at a time : uno por uno, de a uno⟩ ⟨two at a time : de dos en dos⟩ ⟨one thing at a time : una cosa por vez⟩ ⟨one step at a time : paso por paso⟩ **18 at a time** : sin parar ⟨he read for hours at a time : pasaba horas enteras leyendo⟩ ⟨she disappears for months at a time : desaparece por meses⟩ **19 at no time** : en ningún momento **20 at the same time** CONVERSELY : al mismo tiempo **21 at the same time** SIMULTANEOUSLY : al mismo tiempo, a la vez **22 at times** SOMETIMES : a veces **23 behind the times** OUTDATED : anticuado **24 each and every time** : cada vez **25 each/every time** : cada vez **26 for a time** : (por) un tiempo **27 for the time being** : por el momento, de momento **28 from time to time** OCCASIONALLY : de vez en cuando **29 in good time** : con tiempo **30 in no time** : enseguida, en un santiamén **31 in time** PUNCTUALLY : a tiempo **32 in time** EVENTUALLY : con el tiempo **33 it's about time** : ya es hora, ya va siendo hora ⟨it's about time (that) you got here : ya era hora de que llegaras⟩ **34 most of the time** : la mayor parte del tiempo **35 on time** : a tiempo **36 over time** : con el paso del tiempo **37 time after time** : una y otra vez **38 time flies** : el tiempo pasa volando **39 time marches on** : el tiempo pasa **40 time off** : tiempo *m* libre, vacaciones *fpl* **41 to buy time** : ganar tiempo **42 to give someone a hard time** : mortificar a alguien **43 to have time on one's hands** : sobrarle el tiempo a uno **44 to keep time** : marcar la hora (dícese de un reloj) **45 to keep time** : seguir/marcar el ritmo (en música) **46 to lose time** : atrasar (dícese de un reloj) **47 to make good time** : ir adelantado (en un viaje, etc.) **48 to make time for** : encontrar tiempo para **49 to pass the time** : pasar el rato **50 to serve/do time** : cumplir una condena **51 to take one's time** : tomarse tiempo ⟨take your time : tómate todo el tiempo que necesites⟩ ⟨you sure took your time! : tardaste mucho⟩ **52 to take the time to** : tomar el tiempo para/de **53 to take time** : tomar tiempo, tomarse tiempo ⟨these things take time : estas cosas toman tiempo⟩ ⟨take all the time you need : tómate todo el tiempo que necesites⟩ **54 to waste time** : perder el tiempo

time bomb *n* : bomba *f* de tiempo, bomba *f* de relojería *Spain*

timekeeper ['taɪmˌkiːpər] *n* : cronometrador *m*, -dora *f*

timeless ['taɪmləs] *adj* : eterno

time limit *n* : plazo *m*

timely ['taɪmli] *adj* **timelier; -est** : oportuno

timepiece ['taɪmˌpiːs] *n* : reloj *m*

timer ['taɪmər] *n* : temporizador *m*, cronómetro *m*

times ['taɪmz] *prep* : por ⟨3 times 4 is 12 : 3 por 4 son 12⟩

timeshare ['taɪmˌʃer] *n* : multipropiedad *f*, tiempo *m* compartido

time slot → **slot**

timetable ['taɪmˌteɪbəl] *n* : horario *m*

time zone *n* : huso *m* horario

timid ['tɪmɪd] *adj* : tímido — **timidly** *adv*

timidity [tə'mɪdəti] *n* : timidez *f*

timorous ['tɪmərəs] *adj* : timorato, miedoso

timpani ['tɪmpəni] *npl* : timbales *mpl*

tin ['tɪn] *n* **1** : estaño *m* (elemento), hojalata *f* (metal) **2** CAN, BOX : lata *f*, bote *m*, envase *m*

tincture ['tɪŋktʃər] *n* : tintura *f*

tinder ['tɪndər] *n* : yesca *f*

tine ['taɪn] *n* : diente *m* (de un tenedor, etc.)

tinfoil ['tɪnˌfɔɪl] *n* : papel *m* (de) aluminio

tinge[1] ['tɪndʒ] *vt* **tinged; tingeing** *or* **tinging** ['tɪndʒɪŋ] TINT : matizar, teñir ligeramente

tinge[2] *n* **1** TINT : matiz *m*, tinte *m* sutil **2** TOUCH : dejo *m*, sensación *f* ligera

tingle[1] ['tɪŋgəl] *vi* **-gled; -gling** : sentir (un) hormigueo, sentir (un) cosquilleo

tingle[2] *n* : hormigueo *m*, cosquilleo *m*

tinker ['tɪŋkər] *vi* **to tinker with** : arreglar con pequeños ajustes, toquetear (con intento de arreglar)

tinkle[1] ['tɪŋkəl] *vi* **-kled; -kling** : tintinear

tinkle[2] *n* : tintineo *m*

tinplate ['tɪn'pleɪt] *n* : hojalata *f*

tinsel ['tɪntsəl] *n* : oropel *m*

tint[1] ['tɪnt] *vt* : teñir, colorear

tint[2] *n* : tinte *m*

tiny ['taɪni] *adj* **tinier; -est** : diminuto, minúsculo

tip[1] ['tɪp] *v* **tipped; tipping** *vt* **1** *or* **to tip over** : volcar, voltear, hacer caer **2** TILT : ladear, inclinar ⟨to tip one's hat : saludar con el sombrero⟩ **3** TAP : tocar, golpear ligeramente **4** : darle una propina (a un mesero, etc.) ⟨I tipped him $5 : le di $5 de propina⟩ **5** : adornar o cubrir la punta de ⟨wings tipped in red : alas que tienen las puntas rojas⟩ **6 to tip off** : avisar a, dar información a (la policía, etc.) — *vi* **1** TILT : ladearse, inclinarse **2 to tip over** : volcarse, caerse

tip[2] *n* **1** END, POINT : punta *f*, extremo *m* ⟨on the tip of one's tongue : en la punta de la lengua⟩ **2** GRATUITY : propina *f* **3** ADVICE, INFORMATION : consejo *m*, información *f* (confidencial)

tip–off ['tɪpˌɔf] *n* **1** SIGN : indicación *f*, señal *f* **2** TIP : información *f* (confidencial)

tipple ['tɪpəl] *vi* **-pled; -pling** : tomarse unas copas

tipsy [ˈtɪpsi] *adj* **tipsier; -est** : achispado
tiptoe[1] [ˈtɪpˌtoː] *vi* **-toed; -toeing** : caminar de puntillas
tiptoe[2] *adv* : de puntillas
tiptoe[3] *n* : punta *f* del pie
tip–top[1] [ˈtɪpˈtɑp, -ˌtɑp] *adj* EXCELLENT : excelente
tip–top[2] *n* SUMMIT : cumbre *f*, cima *f*
tirade [ˈtaɪˌreɪd] *n* : diatriba *f*
tire[1] [ˈtaɪr] *v* **tired; tiring** *vt* : cansar — *vi* : cansarse
tire[2] *n* : llanta *f*, neumático *m*, goma *f*
tired [ˈtaɪrd] *adj* : cansado ⟨to get tired : cansarse⟩
tiredness *n* : cansancio *m*
tireless [ˈtaɪrləs] *adj* : incansable, infatigable — **tirelessly** *adv*
tiresome [ˈtaɪrsəm] *adj* : fastidioso, pesado, tedioso — **tiresomely** *adv*
tissue [ˈtɪˌʃuː] *n* **1** : pañuelo *m* de papel **2** : tejido *m* ⟨lung tissue : tejido pulmonar⟩
tissue paper *n* : papel *m* de seda
titanic [taɪˈtænɪk, tə-] *adj* GIGANTIC : titánico, gigantesco
titanium [taɪˈteɪniəm, tə-] *n* : titanio *m*
titillate [ˈtɪtəlˌeɪt] *vt* **-lated; -lating** : excitar, estimular placenteramente
title[1] [ˈtaɪt̬əl] *vt* **-tled; -tling** : titular, intitular
title[2] *n* : título *m*
titter[1] [ˈtɪt̬ər] *vi* GIGGLE : reírse tontamente
titter[2] *n* : risita *f*, risa *f* tonta
titular [ˈtɪt̬ələr] *adj* : titular
tizzy [ˈtɪzi] *n, pl* **tizzies** : estado *m* agitado o nervioso ⟨I'm all in a tizzy : estoy todo alterado⟩
TNT [ˌtiːˌɛnˈtiː] *n* : TNT *m*
to[1] [ˈtuː] *adv* **1** : a un estado consciente ⟨to come to : volver en sí⟩ **2 to and fro** : de aquí para allá, de un lado para otro
to[2] *prep* **1** (*indicating a place or activity*) : a ⟨to go to the doctor : ir al médico⟩ ⟨I'm going to John's : voy a casa de John⟩ ⟨we went to lunch : fuimos a almorzar⟩ **2** TOWARD : a, hacia ⟨two miles to the south : dos millas hacia el sur⟩ ⟨to the right : a la derecha⟩ ⟨she ran to her mother : corrió a su mamá⟩ **3** UP TO : hasta, a ⟨to a degree : hasta cierto grado⟩ ⟨from head to toe : de pies a cabeza⟩ ⟨the water was up to my waist : el agua me llegaba a la cintura⟩ **4** (*in expressions of time*) ⟨it's quarter to seven : son las siete menos cuarto⟩ **5** UNTIL : a, hasta ⟨from May to December : de mayo a diciembre⟩ **6** (*indicating belonging or association*) : de, con ⟨the key to the lock : la llave del candado⟩ ⟨he's married to my sister : está casado con mi hermana⟩ **7** (*indicating recipient*) : a ⟨I gave it to the boss : se lo di a la jefa⟩ ⟨she spoke to his parents : habló con sus padres⟩ ⟨listen to me : escúchame⟩ **8** (*indicating response or result*) : a ⟨dancing to the rhythm : bailando al compás⟩ ⟨to my surprise : para mi sorpresa⟩ ⟨the answer to your question : la respuesta a su pregunta⟩ ⟨to my surprise : para mi sor-

presa⟩ **9** (*indicating comparison or proportion*) : a ⟨it's similar to mine : es parecido al mío⟩ ⟨they won 4 to 2 : ganaron 4 a 2⟩ **10** (*indicating agreement or conformity*) : a, de acuerdo con ⟨made to order : hecho a la orden⟩ ⟨to my knowledge : a mi saber⟩ **11** (*indicating opinion or viewpoint*) : a, para ⟨it's agreeable to all of us : nos parece bien a todos⟩ ⟨it seemed odd to us : nos pareció raro⟩ ⟨it's news to me : no lo sabía⟩ ⟨it means nothing to him : para él no significa nada⟩ **12** (*indicating inclusion*) : en cada, por ⟨twenty to the box : veinte por caja⟩ **13** (*indicating joining or touching*) : a ⟨he tied it to a tree : lo ató a un árbol⟩ ⟨apply salve to the wound : póngale ungüento a la herida⟩ **14** (*used to form the infinitive*) ⟨to understand : entender⟩ ⟨to go away : irse⟩ ⟨I didn't mean to (do it) : lo hice sin querer⟩ **15 (all) to one-self** : para sí sólo
toad [ˈtoːd] *n* : sapo *m*
toadstool [ˈtoːdˌstuːl] *n* : hongo *m* (no comestible)
toady [ˈtoːdi] *n, pl* **toadies** : adulador *m*, -dora *f*
toast[1] [ˈtoːst] *vt* **1** : tostar (pan) **2** : brindar por ⟨to toast the victors : brindar por los vencedores⟩ **3** WARM : calentar ⟨to toast oneself : calentarse⟩
toast[2] *n* **1** : pan *m* tostado, tostadas *fpl* **2** : brindis *m* ⟨to propose a toast : proponer un brindis⟩
toaster [ˈtoːstər] *n* : tostador *m*
tobacco [təˈbæko:] *n, pl* **-cos** : tabaco *m*
toboggan[1] [təˈbɑgən] *vi* : deslizarse en tobogán
toboggan[2] *n* : tobogán *m*
today[1] [təˈdeɪ] *adv* **1** : hoy ⟨she arrives today : hoy llega⟩ **2** NOWADAYS : hoy en día
today[2] *n* : hoy *m* ⟨today is a holiday : hoy es día de fiesta⟩
toddle [ˈtɑdəl] *vi* **-dled; -dling** : hacer pininos, hacer pinitos
toddler [ˈtɑdələr] *n* : niño *m* pequeño, niña *f* pequeña (que comienza a caminar)
to–do [təˈduː] *n, pl* **to–dos** [-ˈduːz] FUSS : lío *m*, alboroto *m*
toe[1] [ˈtoː] *vt* **toed; toeing to toe the line** : acatar la disciplina
toe[2] *n* : dedo *m* del pie
TOEFL [ˈtoːfəl] *trademark* se usa para un examen que evalúa el dominio del inglés de personas que estudian este idioma como lengua extranjera
toenail [ˈtoːˌneɪl] *n* : uña *f* del pie
toffee *or* **toffy** [ˈtɔfi, ˈtɑ-] *n, pl* **toffees** *or* **toffies** : caramelo *m* elaborado con azúcar y mantequilla
toga [ˈtoːgə] *n* : toga *f*
together [təˈgɛðər] *adv* **1** : juntamente, juntos (el uno con el otro) ⟨Susan and Sarah work together : Susan y Sarah trabajan juntas⟩ **2** ~ **with** : junto con
togetherness [təˈgɛðərnəs] *n* : unión *f*, compañerismo *m*
togs [ˈtɑgz, ˈtɔgz] *npl* : ropa *f*

toil[1] ['tɔɪl] *vi* : trabajar arduamente

toil[2] *n* : trabajo *m* arduo

toilet ['tɔɪlət] *n* **1** : arreglo *m* personal **2** BATHROOM : (cuarto de) baño *m*, servicios *mpl* (públicos), sanitario *m* Col, Mex, Ven **3** : inodoro *m* ⟨to flush the toilet : jalar la cadena⟩

toilet paper *n* : papel *m* higiénico

toiletries ['tɔɪlətriz] *npl* : artículos *mpl* de tocador

token[1] ['to:kən] *adj* : simbólico

token[2] *n* **1** PROOF, SIGN : prueba *f*, muestra *f*, señal *m* **2** SYMBOL : símbolo *m* **3** SOUVENIR : recuerdo *m* **4** : ficha *f* (para reconocer público, etc.) **5 by the same token** : del mismo modo

told → **tell**

tolerable ['tɑlərəbəl] *adj* : tolerable — **tolerably** [-bli] *adv*

tolerance ['tɑlərənts] *n* : tolerancia *f*

tolerant ['tɑlərənt] *adj* : tolerante — **tolerantly** *adv*

tolerate ['tɑlə,reɪt] *vt* **-ated; -ating 1** ACCEPT : tolerar, aceptar **2** BEAR, ENDURE : tolerar, aguantar, soportar

toleration [,tɑlə'reɪʃən] *n* : tolerancia *f*

toll[1] ['to:l] *vt* : tañer, sonar (una campana) — *vi* : sonar, doblar (dícese de las campanas)

toll[2] *n* **1** : peaje *m* (de una carretera, un puente, etc.) **2** CASUALTIES : pérdida *f*, número *m* de víctimas **3** TOLLING : tañido *m* (de campanas)

tollbooth ['to:l,bu:θ] *n* : caseta *f* de peaje; caseta *f* de cobro CA, Mex

toll–free ['to:l'fri:] *adj* : gratuito

tollgate ['to:l,geɪt] *n* : barrera *f* de peaje

tomahawk ['tɑmə,hɔk] *n* : hacha *f* de guerra (de los indígenas norteamericanos)

tomato [tə'meɪto, -'mɑ-] *n, pl* **-toes** : tomate *m*

tomb ['tu:m] *n* : sepulcro *m*, tumba *f*

tomboy ['tɑm,bɔɪ] *n* : marimacho *mf*; niña *f* que se porta como muchacho

tombstone ['tu:m,sto:n] *n* : lápida *f*

tomcat ['tɑm,kæt] *n* : gato *m* (macho)

tome ['to:m] *n* : tomo *m*

tomorrow[1] [tə'mɑro] *adv* : mañana

tomorrow[2] *n* : mañana *m*

tom–tom ['tɑm,tɑm] *n* : tam-tam *m*

ton ['tən] *n* : tonelada *f*

tone[1] ['to:n] *vt* **toned; toning 1** *or* **to tone down** : atenuar, suavizar, moderar **2** *or* **to tone up** STRENGTHEN : tonificar, vigorizar

tone[2] *n* : tono *m* ⟨in a friendly tone : en tono amistoso⟩ ⟨a grayish tone : un tono grisáceo⟩

tongs ['tɑŋz, 'tɔŋz] *npl* : tenazas *fpl*

tongue ['tʌŋ] *n* **1** : lengua *f* **2** LANGUAGE : lengua *f*, idioma *m*

tongue–tied ['tʌŋ,taɪd] *adj* **to get tongue-tied** : trabársele la lengua a uno

tongue–twister ['tʌŋ,twɪstər] *n* : trabalenguas *m*

tonic[1] ['tɑnɪk] *adj* : tónico

tonic[2] *n* **1** : tónico *m* **2** *or* **tonic water** : tónica *f*

tonight[1] [tə'naɪt] *adv* : esta noche

tonight[2] *n* : esta noche *f*

tonnage ['tʌnɪdʒ] *n* : tonelaje *m*

tonsil ['tɑntsəl] *n* : amígdala *f*, angina *f* Mex

tonsillitis [,tɑntsə'laɪtəs] *n* : amigdalitis *f*, anginas *fpl* Mex

too ['tu:] *adv* **1** ALSO : también **2** EXCESSIVELY : demasiado ⟨it's too hot in here : aquí hace demasiado calor⟩

took → **take**[1]

tool[1] ['tu:l] *vt* **1** : fabricar, confeccionar (con herramientas) **2** EQUIP : instalar maquinaria en (una fábrica)

tool[2] *n* : herramienta *f*

toolbar ['tu:l,bɑr] *n* : barra *f* de herramientas

toolbox ['tu:l,bɑks] *n* : caja *f* de herramientas

tool kit *n* : juego *m* de herramientas

toot[1] ['tu:t] *vt* : sonar (un claxon o un pito)

toot[2] *n* : pitido *m*, bocinazo *m* (de un claxon)

tooth ['tu:θ] *n, pl* **teeth** ['ti:θ] **1** : diente *m* **2 like pulling teeth** : casi imposible **3 long in the tooth** : viejo **4 to grit one's teeth** : apretar los dientes, aguantarse **5 to have a sweet tooth** : ser goloso, gustarle mucho los dulces a uno **6 to lie through one's teeth** : mentir descaradamente **7 tooth and nail** : a ultranza, a capa y espada **8 to set someone's teeth on edge** : crispar/erizar a alguien **9 to sink one's teeth into** : clavar los dientes en **10 to sink/get one's teeth into** : hincarle el diente a (una actividad, etc.)

toothache ['tu:θ,eɪk] *n* : dolor *m* de muelas

toothbrush ['tu:θ,brʌʃ] *n* : cepillo *m* de dientes

toothed ['tu:θt] *adj* **1** : dentado **2** (*used in combination*) : de dientes ⟨bucktoothed : de dientes salientes⟩

toothless ['tu:θləs] *adj* : desdentado

toothpaste ['tu:θ,peɪst] *n* : pasta *f* de dientes, crema *f* dental, dentífrico *m*

toothpick ['tu:θ,pɪk] *n* : palillo *m* (de dientes), mondadientes *m*

top[1] ['tɑp] *vt* **topped; topping 1** COVER : cubrir, coronar **2** SURPASS : sobrepasar, superar **3** CLEAR : pasar por encima de **4** : encabezar (una lista, etc.) ⟨to top the charts : ser el número uno en las listas de éxitos⟩ **5 to top off** END : terminar ⟨to top it all off : para colmo⟩ **6 to top off** : llenar hasta arriba (un depósito, un vaso, etc.)

top[2] *adj* : superior ⟨the top shelf : la repisa superior⟩ ⟨one of the top lawyers : uno de los mejores abogados⟩

top[3] *n* **1** : parte *f* superior, cumbre *f*, cima *f* (de un monte, etc.) ⟨to climb to the top : subir a la cumbre⟩ ⟨from top to bottom : de arriba abajo⟩ **2** COVER : tapa *f*, cubierta *f* **3** : trompo *m* (juguete) **4 at the top of one's lungs/voice** : a voz en grito/cuello, a grito pelado **5 on top of** : encima de **6 on top of** BESIDES : además de **7 on top of the world** : muy alegre **8 over the top** : exagerado **9 to be on top of** CONTROL

: controlar, tener controlado **10 to be/ stay on top of** : estar/mantenerse al día en (las noticias, etc.) **11 to come out on top** : salir ganando

topaz [ˈtoːˌpæz] *n* : topacio *m*

topcoat [ˈtɑpˌkoːt] *n* : sobretodo *m*, abrigo *m*

top hat *n* : sombrero *m* de copa

topic [ˈtɑpɪk] *n* : tema *m*, tópico *m*

topical [ˈtɑpɪkəl] *adj* : de interés actual

topless [ˈtɑpləs] *adj* : sin camisa

topmost [ˈtɑpˌmoːst] *adj* : más alto

top-notch [ˈtɑpˈnɑtʃ] *adj* : de lo mejor, de primera categoría

topographic [ˌtɑpəˈɡræfɪk] *or* **topographical** [-fɪkəl] *adj* : topográfico

topography [təˈpɑɡrəfi] *n, pl* **-phies** : topografía *f*

topple [ˈtɑpəl] *v* **-pled; -pling** *vi* : caerse, venirse abajo — *vt* : volcar, derrocar (un gobierno, etc.)

top secret *adj* : ultrasecreto

topsoil [ˈtɑpˌsɔil] *n* : capa *f* superior del suelo

topsy-turvy [ˌtɑpsiˈtərvi] *adv & adj* : patas arriba, al revés

torch [ˈtɔrtʃ] *n* : antorcha *f*

tore → **tear**[1]

torment[1] [tɔrˈmɛnt, ˈtɔrˌ-] *vt* : atormentar, torturar, martirizar

torment[2] [ˈtɔrˌmɛnt] *n* : tormento *m*, suplicio *m*, martirio *m*

tormentor [tɔrˈmɛntər] *n* : atormentador *m*, -dora *f*

torn *pp* → **tear**[1]

tornado [tɔrˈneɪdo] *n, pl* **-does** *or* **-dos** : tornado *m*

torpedo[1] [tɔrˈpiːdo] *vt* : torpedear

torpedo[2] *n, pl* **-does** : torpedo *m*

torpid [ˈtɔrpɪd] *adj* **1** SLUGGISH : aletargado **2** APATHETIC : apático

torpor [ˈtɔrpər] *n* : letargo *m*, apatía *f*

torrent [ˈtɔrənt] *n* : torrente *m*

torrential [təˈrɛntʃəl, tə-] *adj* : torrencial

torrid [ˈtɔrɪd] *adj* : tórrido

torso [ˈtɔrˌsoː] *n, pl* **-sos** *or* **-si** [-ˌsiː] : torso *m*

tortilla [tɔrˈtiːjə] *n* : tortilla *f* (de maíz)

tortoise [ˈtɔrtəs] *n* : tortuga *f* (terrestre)

tortoiseshell [ˈtɔrtəsˌʃɛl] *n* : carey *m*, concha *f*

tortuous [ˈtɔrtʃuəs] *adj* : tortuoso

torture[1] [ˈtɔrtʃər] *vt* **-tured; -turing** : torturar, atormentar

torture[2] *n* : tortura *f*, tormento *m* ⟨it was sheer torture! : ¡fue un verdadero suplicio!⟩

torturer [ˈtɔrtʃərər] *n* : torturador *m*, -dora *f*

toss[1] [ˈtɔs, ˈtɑs] *vt* **1** AGITATE, SHAKE : sacudir, agitar ⟨to toss a salad : mezclar una ensalada⟩ **2** THROW : tirar, echar, lanzar ⟨to toss a coin : echarlo a cara o cruz⟩ **3 to toss away/out** DISCARD : botar, tirar (a la basura) **4 to toss back** *fam* : tomarse **5 to toss off** : escribir (rápidamente) **6 to toss out** REJECT : rechazar **7 to toss out** EJECT : echar — *vi* : sacudirse ⟨to toss and turn : dar vueltas⟩

toss[2] *n* THROW : lanzamiento *m*, tiro *m*, tirada *f*, lance *m* (de dados, etc.)

toss-up [ˈtɔsˌʌp] *n* : posibilidad *f* igual ⟨it's a toss-up : quizá sí, quizá no⟩

tot [ˈtɑt] *n* : pequeño *m*, -ña *f*

total[1] [ˈtoːtəl] *vt* **-taled** *or* **-talled; -taling** *or* **-talling 1** *or* **to total up** ADD : sumar, totalizar **2** AMOUNT TO : ascender a, llegar a **3** *fam* WRECK : destrozar (un automóvil)

total[2] *adj* : total, completo, absoluto — **totally** *adv*

total[3] *n* : total *m*

totalitarian [toːˌtæləˈtɛriən] *adj* : totalitario

totalitarianism [toːˌtæləˈtɛriəˌnɪzəm] *n* : totalitarismo *m*

totality [toːˈtæləti] *n, pl* **-ties** : totalidad *f*

tote [ˈtoːt] *vt* **toted; toting** : cargar, llevar

totem [ˈtoːtəm] *n* : tótem *m*

totter [ˈtɑtər] *vi* : tambalearse

touch[1] [ˈtʌtʃ] *vt* **1** FEEL, HANDLE : tocar, tentar **2** AFFECT, MOVE : conmover, afectar, tocar ⟨his gesture touched our hearts : su gesto nos tocó el corazón⟩ **3 to touch up** : retocar — *vi* **1** : tocar ⟨do not touch : no tocar⟩ **2** : tocarse ⟨our hands touched : nuestras manos se tocaron⟩ **3 to touch down** : aterrizar **4 to touch on** : tocar (un tema)

touch[2] *n* **1** : tacto *m* (sentido) **2** DETAIL : toque *m*, detalle *m* ⟨a touch of color/humor : un toque de color/humor⟩ ⟨the finishing touches : los toques finales⟩ **3** BIT : pizca *f*, gota *f*, poco *m* **4** ABILITY : habilidad *f* ⟨to lose one's touch : perder la habilidad⟩ **5** CONTACT : contacto *m*, comunicación *f* ⟨to keep/stay in touch : mantenerse en contacto⟩ ⟨to lose touch : perder el contacto⟩ **6 out of touch** : desconectado (de la realidad, etc.)

touch-and-go *adj* : poco seguro, poco cierto ⟨it was touch-and-go for a while : no sabíamos qué pasaría⟩

touchdown [ˈtʌtʃˌdaʊn] *n* : touchdown *m* (en futbol americano)

touching [ˈtʌtʃɪŋ] *adj* MOVING : conmovedor

touchline [ˈtʌtʃˌlaɪn] *n* : banda *f*, línea *f* de banda (en fútbol)

touchscreen [ˈtʌtʃˈskriːn] *n* : pantalla *f* táctil

touchstone [ˈtʌtʃˌstoːn] *n* : piedra *f* de toque

touch-up [ˈtʌtʃˌʌp] *n* : retoque *m*

touchy [ˈtʌtʃi] *adj* **touchier; -est 1** : sensible, susceptible (dícese de una persona) **2** : delicado ⟨a touchy subject : un tema delicado⟩

tough[1] [ˈtʌf] *adj* **1** STRONG : fuerte, resistente (dícese de materiales) **2** LEATHERY : correoso ⟨a tough steak : un bistec duro⟩ **3** HARDY : fuerte, robusto (dícese de una persona) **4** STRICT : severo, exigente **5** DIFFICULT : difícil **6** STUBBORN : terco, obstinado

tough[2] *n* : matón *m*, persona *f* ruda y brusca

toughen [ˈtʌfən] *vt* : fortalecer, endurecer — *vi* : endurecerse, hacerse más fuerte

toughness ['tʌfnəs] *n* : dureza *f*

toupee [tu:'peɪ] *n* : peluquín *m*, bisoñé *m*

tour¹ ['tʊr] *vt* : tomar una excursión, viajar — *vt* : recorrer, hacer una gira por

tour² *n* 1 : gira *f*, tour *m*, excursión *f* 2 **tour of duty** : período *m* de servicio

tourism ['tʊrˌɪzəm] *n* : turismo *m*

tourist ['tʊrɪst, 'tɔr-] *n* : turista *mf*

tournament ['tɜrnəmənt, 'tʊr-] *n* : torneo *m*

tourniquet ['tɜrnɪkət, 'tʊr-] *n* : torniquete *m*

tousle ['taʊzəl] *vt* **-sled; -sling** : desarreglar, despeinar (el cabello)

tout ['taʊt] *vt* : promocionar, elogiar (con exageración)

tow¹ ['to:] *vt* : remolcar

tow² *n* : remolque *m*

toward ['tord, tə'wɔrd] *or* **towards** ['tordz, tə'wɔrdz] *prep* 1 (*indicating direction*) : hacia, rumbo a ⟨heading toward town : dirigiéndose rumbo al pueblo⟩ ⟨efforts towards peace : esfuerzos hacia la paz⟩ 2 (*indicating time*) : alrededor de ⟨toward midnight : alrededor de la medianoche⟩ 3 REGARDING : hacia, con respecto a ⟨his attitude toward life : su actitud hacia la vida⟩ 4 FOR : para, como pago parcial de (una compra o deuda)

towel ['taʊəl] *n* 1 : toalla *f* 2 **to throw in the towel** : tirar la toalla

tower¹ ['taʊər] *vi* **to tower over** : descollar sobre, elevarse sobre, dominar

tower² *n* : torre *f*

towering ['taʊərɪŋ] *adj* : altísimo, imponente

town ['taʊn] *n* : pueblo *m*, ciudad *f* (pequeña)

town hall *n* : ayuntamiento *m*

township ['taʊnˌʃɪp] *n* : municipio *m*

tow truck ['to:ˌtrʌk] *n* : grúa *f*

toxic ['tɑksɪk] *adj* : tóxico

toxicity [tɑk'sɪsəti] *n*, *pl* **-ties** : toxicidad *f*

toxin ['tɑksɪn] *n* : toxina *f*

toy¹ ['tɔɪ] *vi* : juguetear, jugar

toy² *adj* : de juguete ⟨a toy rifle : un rifle de juguete⟩

toy³ *n* : juguete *m*

trace¹ ['treɪs] *vt* **traced; tracing** 1 : calcar (un dibujo, etc.) 2 OUTLINE : delinear, trazar (planes, etc.) 3 TRACK : describir (un curso, una historia) 4 FIND : localizar, ubicar

trace² *n* 1 SIGN, TRACK : huella *f*, rastro *m*, indicio *m*, vestigio *m* ⟨he disappeared without a trace : desapareció sin dejar rastro⟩ 2 BIT, HINT : pizca *f*, ápice *m*, dejo *m*

trachea ['treɪkiə] *n*, *pl* **-cheae** [-kiˌiː] : tráquea *f*

tracing paper *n* : papel *m* de calcar

track¹ ['træk] *vt* 1 TRAIL : seguir la pista de, rastrear 2 : dejar huellas de ⟨he tracked mud all over : dejó huellas de lodo por todas partes⟩ 3 **to track down** : localizar

track² *n* 1 : rastro *m*, huella *f* (de animales), pista *f* (de personas) 2 PATH : pista *f*, sendero *m*, camino *m* 3 *or* **rail-**

road track : vía *f* (férrea) 4 → **racetrack** 5 : oruga *f* (de un tanque, etc.) 6 : atletismo *m* (deporte) 7 **the wrong side of the tracks** : los barrios bajos 8 **to be on the right/wrong track** : ir bien/mal encaminado, ir por buen/mal camino 9 **to be on track** : ir bien encaminado 10 **to cover one's tracks** : no dejar rastros 11 **to get back on track** : volver a encarrilarse 12 **to get/go off track** : desviarse del tema/plan (etc.) 13 **to keep track of** : llevar la cuenta de 14 **to lose track of** : perder la cuenta de ⟨I lost track of the time : no me di cuenta de la hora⟩ 15 **to throw someone off the track** : despistar a alguien

track–and–field ['trækənd'fi:ld] *adj* : de pista y campo

tracksuit ['trækˌsu:t] *n* : sudadera *f*; buzo *m* Chile, Peru; jogging *m* Arg; pants *m* Mex; chándal *m* Spain (traje)

tract ['trækt] *n* 1 AREA : terreno *m*, extensión *f*, área *f* 2 : tracto *m* ⟨digestive tract : tracto digestivo⟩ 3 PAMPHLET : panfleto *m*, folleto *m*

traction ['trækʃən] *n* : tracción *f*

tractor ['træktər] *n* 1 : tractor *m* (vehículo agrícola) 2 TRUCK : camión *m* (con remolque)

trade¹ ['treɪd] *v* **traded; trading** *vi* 1 : comerciar, negociar 2 EXCHANGE : hacer un cambio 3 **to trade on** : explotar — *vt* 1 EXCHANGE : cambiar, intercambiar, canjear ⟨we traded seats : nos cambiamos de asiento⟩ ⟨I'll trade (you) a cookie for a chocolate : te cambio una galleta por un chocolate⟩ 2 **to trade in** : entregar en/como parte de pago

trade² *n* 1 OCCUPATION : oficio *m*, profesión *f*, ocupación *f* ⟨a carpenter by trade : carpintero de oficio⟩ 2 COMMERCE : comercio *m*, industria *f* ⟨free trade : libre comercio⟩ ⟨the book trade : la industria del libro⟩ 3 EXCHANGE : intercambio *m*, canje *m*

trade–in ['treɪdˌɪn] *n* : artículo *m* que se canjea por otro

trademark ['treɪdˌmark] *n* 1 : marca *f* ⟨registered trademark : marca registrada⟩ 2 : sello *m* característico (de un grupo, una persona, etc.)

trader ['treɪdər] *n* : negociante *mf*, tratante *mf*, comerciante *mf*

tradesman ['treɪdzmən] *n*, *pl* **-men** [-mən, -ˌmɛn] 1 CRAFTSMAN : artesano *m*, -na *f* 2 SHOPKEEPER : tendero *m*, -ra *f*; comerciante *mf*

tradition [trə'dɪʃən] *n* : tradición *f*

traditional [trə'dɪʃənəl] *adj* : tradicional — **traditionally** *adv*

traffic¹ ['træfɪk] *vi* **trafficked; trafficking** : traficar (con)

traffic² *n* 1 COMMERCE : tráfico *m*, comercio *m* ⟨the drug traffic : el narcotráfico⟩ 2 : tráfico *m*, tránsito *m*, circulación *f* (de vehículos, etc.)

traffic circle *n* : rotonda *f*, glorieta *f*

traffic jam → **jam²**

trafficker ['træfɪkər] *n* : traficante *mf*

traffic light *n* : semáforo *m*, luz *f* (de tránsito)

tragedy ['trædʒədi] *n, pl* **-dies** : tragedia *f*

tragic ['trædʒɪk] *adj* : trágico — **tragically** *adv*

trail[1] ['treɪl] *vi* **1** DRAG : arrastrarse **2** LAG : quedarse atrás, retrasarse **3 to trail away** *or* **to trail off** : disminuir, menguar, desvanecerse — *vt* **1** DRAG : arrastrar **2** PURSUE : perseguir, seguir la pista de

trail[2] *n* **1** TRACK : rastro *m*, huella *f*, pista *f* ⟨a trail of blood : un rastro de sangre⟩ **2** : cola *f*, estela *f* (de un meteoro) **3** PATH : sendero *m*, camino *m*, vereda *f*

trailer ['treɪlər] *n* **1** : remolque *m*, tráiler *m* (de un camión) **2** : caravana *f* (vivienda ambulante)

train[1] ['treɪn] *vt* **1** : adiestrar, entrenar (atletas), capacitar (trabajadores), amaestrar (animales) **2** POINT : apuntar (un arma, etc.) — *vi* : entrenar(se) (físicamente), prepararse (profesionalmente) ⟨she's training at the gym : se está entrenando en el gimnasio⟩

train[2] *n* **1** : cola *f* (de un vestido) **2** RETINUE : cortejo *m*, séquito *m* **3** SERIES : serie *f* (de eventos) **4** : tren *m* ⟨passenger train : tren de pasajeros⟩ **5** : tren *m* (mecanismo) ⟨drive train : tren motriz⟩ **6 train of thought** : hilo *m* de razonamiento

trainee [treɪ'ni:] *n* : aprendiz *m*, -diza *f*

trainer ['treɪnər] *n* : entrenador *m*, -dora *f*

training ['treɪnɪŋ] *n* : adiestramiento *m*, entrenamiento *m* (físico), capacitación *f* (de trabajadores)

traipse ['treɪps] *vi* **traipsed; traipsing** : andar de un lado para otro, vagar

trait ['treɪt] *n* : rasgo *m*, característica *f*

traitor ['treɪtər] *n* : traidor *m*, -dora *f*

traitorous ['treɪtərəs] *adj* : traidor

trajectory [trə'dʒɛktəri] *n, pl* **-ries** : trayectoria *f*

tramp[1] ['træmp] *vi* : caminar (a paso pesado) — *vt* : deambular por, vagar por ⟨to tramp the streets : vagar por las calles⟩

tramp[2] *n* **1** VAGRANT : vagabundo *m*, -da *f* **2** HIKE : caminata *f*

trample ['træmpəl] *vt* **-pled; -pling** : pisotear, hollar

trampoline [ˌtræmpə'li:n, 'træmpəˌ-] *n* : trampolín *m*, cama *f* elástica

trance ['trænts] *n* : trance *m*

tranquil ['træŋkwəl] *adj* : calmo, tranquilo, sereno — **tranquilly** *adv*

tranquilize ['træŋkwəˌlaɪz] *vt* **-ized; -izing** : tranquilizar

tranquilizer ['træŋkwəˌlaɪzər] *n* : tranquilizante *m*

tranquillity *or* **tranquility** [træŋ'kwɪləti] *n* : sosiego *m*, tranquilidad *f*

trans ['trænts, 'trænz] *adj* **1** TRANSGENDER : trans, transgénero **2** TRANSEXUAL : trans, transexual

transact [træn'zækt] *vt* : negociar, gestionar, hacer (negocios)

transaction [træn'zækʃən] *n* **1** : transacción *f*, negocio *m*, operación *f* **2 transactions** *npl* RECORDS : actas *fpl*

transatlantic [ˌtræntsət'læntɪk, ˌtrænz-] *adj* : transatlántico

transcend [træn'sɛnd] *vt* : trascender, sobrepasar

transcendent [træn'sɛndənt] *adj* : trascendente — **transcendence** [træn'sɛndənts] *n*

transcendental [ˌtræntsɛn'dɛntəl, -sən-] *adj* : trascendental ⟨transcendental meditation : meditación trascendental⟩

transcribe [træn'skraɪb] *vt* **-scribed; -scribing** : transcribir

transcript ['trænˌskrɪpt] *n* : copia *f* oficial

transcription [træn'skrɪpʃən] *n* : transcripción *f*

transfer[1] [træn/s'fər, 'træn/sˌfər] *v* **-ferred; -ferring** *vt* **1** : trasladar (a una persona), transferir (fondos) **2** : transferir, traspasar, ceder (propiedad) **3** PRINT : imprimir (un diseño) — *vi* **1** MOVE : trasladarse, cambiarse **2** CHANGE : transbordar, cambiar (de un transporte a otro) ⟨he transfers at E Street : hace transbordo en la calle E⟩

transfer[2] ['træn/sˌfər] *n* **1** TRANSFERRING : transferencia *f* (de fondos, de propiedad, etc.), traslado *m* (de una persona) **2** DECAL : calcomanía *f* **3** : boleto *m* (para cambiar de un avión, etc., a otro)

transferable [træn/s'fərəbəl] *adj* : transferible

transference [træn/s'fərənts] *n* : transferencia *f*

transfigure [træn/s'fɪgjər] *vt* **-ured; -uring** : transfigurar, transformar

transfix [træn/s'fɪks] *vt* **1** PIERCE : traspasar, atravesar **2** IMMOBILIZE : paralizar

transform [træn/s'fɔrm] *vt* : transformar

transformation [ˌtræn/sfər'meɪʃən] *n* : transformación *f*

transformer [træn/s'fɔrmər] *n* : transformador *m*

transfusion [træn/s'fju:ʒən] *n* : transfusión *f*

transgender [træn/s'dʒɛndər, trænz-] *adj* : transgénero ⟨transgender people : las personas transgénero⟩

transgress [træn/s'grɛs, trænz-] *vt* : transgredir, infringir — **transgression** [træn/s'grɛʃən, trænz-] *n* — **transgressor** [træn/s'grɛsər, trænz-] *n*

transient[1] ['trænʃənt, 'trænsiənt] *adj* : pasajero, transitorio — **transiently** *adv*

transient[2] *n* : transeúnte *mf*

transistor [træn'zɪstər, -'sɪs-] *n* : transistor *m*

transit ['træn/sɪt, 'trænzɪt] *n* **1** PASSAGE : pasaje *m*, tránsito *m* ⟨in transit : en tránsito⟩ **2** TRANSPORTATION : transporte *m* (público)

transition [træn'sɪʒən, -'zɪʃ-] *n* : transición *f*

transitional [træn'sɪʃənəl, -'zɪʃ-] *adj* : de transición

transitive ['træn/sətɪv, 'trænzə-] *adj* : transitivo

transitory ['trænɾsə,tori, 'trænzə-] adj : transitorio

translatable [trænɾs'leɪţəbəl, trænz-] adj : traducible

translate [trænɾs'leɪt, trænz-:, 'trænɾsₗ-, 'trænz-] vt **-lated; -lating** : traducir

translation [trænɾs'leɪʃən, trænz-] n : traducción f

translator [trænɾs'leɪţər, trænz-:, 'trænɾsₗ-, 'trænzₗ-] n : traductor m, -tora f

translucent [trænɾs'lu:sənt, trænz-] adj : translúcido

transmissible [trænɾs'mɪsəbəl, trænz-] adj : transmisible

transmission [trænɾs'mɪʃən, trænz-] n : transmisión f

transmit [trænɾs'mɪt, trænz-] vt **-mitted; -mitting** : transmitir

transmitter [trænɾs'mɪţər, trænz-:, 'trænɾsₗ-, 'trænzₗ-] n : transmisor m, emisor m

transom ['trænɾsəm] n : montante m (de una puerta), travesaño m (de una ventana)

transparency [trænɾs'pærəntsi] n, pl **-cies** : transparencia f

transparent [trænɾs'pærənt] adj 1 : transparente, traslúcido ⟨a transparent fabric : una tela transparente⟩ 2 OBVIOUS : transparente, obvio, claro — **transparently** adv

transpiration [,trænɾspə'reɪʃən] n : transpiración f

transpire [trænɾs'paɪr] vi **-spired; -spiring** 1 : transpirar (en biología y botánica) 2 TURN OUT : resultar 3 HAPPEN : suceder, ocurrir, tener lugar

transplant[1] [trænɾs'plænt] vt : trasplantar

transplant[2] ['trænɾs,plænt] n : trasplante m

transport[1] [trænɾs'port, 'trænɾsₗ-] vt 1 CARRY : transportar, acarrear 2 ENRAPTURE : transportar

transport[2] ['trænɾs,port] n 1 TRANSPORTATION : transporte m, transportación f 2 RAPTURE : éxtasis m 3 or **transport ship** : buque m de transporte (de personal militar)

transportation [,trænɾspər'teɪʃən] n : transporte m, transportación f

transpose [trænɾs'po:z] vt **-posed; -posing** : trasponer, trasladar, transportar (una composición musical)

transsexual [trænɾs'sɛkʃuəl] n : transexual mf — **transsexual** adj

transverse [trænɾs'vərs, trænz-] adj : transversal, transverso, oblicuo — **transversely** adv

transvestite [trænɾs'vɛstaɪt, trænz-] n : travesti mf, travestí mf — **transvestite** adj

trap[1] ['træp] vt **trapped; trapping** : atrapar, apresar (en una trampa)

trap[2] n : trampa f ⟨to set a trap : tender una trampa⟩

trapdoor ['træp'dor] n : trampilla f

trapeze [træ'pi:z] n : trapecio m

trapezoid ['træpə,zɔɪd] n : trapezoide m, trapecio m

trapper ['træpər] n : trampero m, -ra f; cazador m, -dora f (que usa trampas)

trappings ['træpɪŋz] npl 1 : arreos mpl, jaeces mpl (de un caballo) 2 ADORNMENTS : adornos mpl, pompa f

trash ['træʃ] n : basura f

trash can → **garbage can**

trashy ['træʃi] adj : de pacotilla

trauma ['trɔmə, 'trau-] n : trauma m

traumatic [trə'mæţɪk, trɔ-, trau-] adj : traumático

travel[1] ['trævəl] vi **-eled** or **-elled; -eling** or **-elling** 1 JOURNEY : viajar 2 GO, MOVE : desplazarse, moverse, ir ⟨the waves travel at uniform speed : las ondas se desplazan a una velocidad uniforme⟩

travel[2] n or **travels** npl : viajes mpl

travel agency n : agencia f de viajes

travel agent n : agente mf de viajes

traveler or **traveller** ['trævələr] n : viajero m, -ra f

traveler's check or **traveller's check** n : cheque m de viajero

traverse [trə'vərs, træ'vərs, 'trævərs] vt **-versed; -versing** CROSS : atravesar, extenderse a través de, cruzar

travesty ['trævəsti] n, pl **-ties** : parodia f

trawl[1] ['trɔl] vi : pescar con red de arrastre, rastrear

trawl[2] n or **trawl net** : red f de arrastre

trawler ['trɔlər] n : barco m de pesca (utilizado para rastrear)

tray ['treɪ] n : bandeja f, charola f Bol, Mex, Peru

treacherous ['trɛtʃərəs] adj 1 TRAITOROUS : traicionero, traidor 2 DANGEROUS : peligroso

treacherously ['trɛtʃərəsli] adv : a traición

treachery ['trɛtʃəri] n, pl **-eries** : traición f

tread[1] ['trɛd] v **trod** ['trɑd]; **trodden** ['trɑdən] or **trod; treading** vt TRAMPLE : pisotear, hollar — vi 1 WALK : caminar, andar 2 **to tread on** : pisar

tread[2] n 1 STEP : paso m, andar m 2 : banda f de rodadura (de un neumático, etc.) 3 : escalón m (de una escalera)

treadle ['trɛdəl] n : pedal m (de una máquina)

treadmill ['trɛd,mɪl] n 1 : rueda f de andar 2 ROUTINE : rutina f

treason ['tri:zən] n : traición f (a la patria, etc.)

treasure[1] ['trɛʒər, 'treɪ-] vt **-sured; -suring** : apreciar, valorar

treasure[2] n : tesoro m

treasurer ['trɛʒərər, 'treɪ-] n : tesorero m, -ra f

treasury ['trɛʒəri, 'treɪ-] n, pl **-suries** : sorería f, tesoro m

treat[1] ['tri:t] vt 1 DEAL WITH : tratar (un asunto) ⟨the article treats of poverty : el artículo trata de la pobreza⟩ 2 HANDLE : tratar (a una persona), manejar (un objeto) ⟨to treat something as a joke : tomar(se) algo a broma⟩ 3 INVITE : invitar, convidar ⟨he treated me to a meal : me invitó a comer⟩ 4 : tratar, atender (en medicina) 5 PROCESS : tratar ⟨to

treat sewage : tratar las aguas negras⟩ —
treatable [ˈtriːʈəbəl] *adj*
treat² *n* : gusto *m*, placer *m* ⟨it was a treat
to see you : fue un placer verte⟩ ⟨it's my
treat : yo invito⟩
treatise [ˈtriːʈɪs] *n* : tratado *m*, estudio *m*
treatment [ˈtriːtmənt] *n* : trato *m*, tratamiento *m* (médico)
treaty [ˈtriːʈi] *n, pl* **-ties** : tratado *m*, convenio *m*
treble¹ [ˈtrɛbəl] *vt* **-bled; -bling** : triplicar
treble² *adj* 1 → **triple** 2 : de tiple, soprano
(en música) 3 **treble clef** : clave *f* de sol
treble³ *n* : tiple *m*, parte *f* de soprano
tree [ˈtriː] *n* : árbol *m*
treeless [ˈtriːləs] *adj* : carente de árboles
tree–lined [ˈtriːˌlaɪnd] *adj* : bordeado de
árboles
tree stump → **stump²**
trek¹ [ˈtrɛk] *vi* **trekked; trekking** : hacer
un viaje largo y difícil
trek² *n* : viaje *m* largo y difícil
trellis [ˈtrɛlɪs] *n* : enrejado *m*, celosía *f*
tremble [ˈtrɛmbəl] *vi* **-bled; -bling** : temblar
tremendous [trɪˈmɛndəs] *adj* : tremendo
— **tremendously** *adv*
tremor [ˈtrɛmər] *n* : temblor *m*
tremulous [ˈtrɛmjələs] *adj* : trémulo, tembloroso
trench [ˈtrɛntʃ] *n* 1 DITCH : zanja *f* 2
: trinchera *f* (militar)
trenchant [ˈtrɛntʃənt] *adj* : cortante,
mordaz
trend¹ [ˈtrɛnd] *vi* : tender, inclinarse
trend² *n* 1 TENDENCY : tendencia *f* 2
FASHION : moda *f*
trendy [ˈtrɛndi] *adj* **trendier; -est** : de
moda
trepidation [ˌtrɛpəˈdeɪʃən] *n* : inquietud *f*,
ansiedad *f*
trespass¹ [ˈtrɛspəs, -ˌpæs] *vi* 1 SIN : pecar, transgredir 2 : entrar ilegalmente
(en propiedad ajena)
trespass² *n* 1 SIN : pecado *m*, transgresión *f* ⟨forgive us our trespasses
: perdónanos nuestras deudas⟩ 2 : entrada *f* ilegal (en propiedad ajena)
tress [ˈtrɛs] *n* : mechón *m*
trestle [ˈtrɛsəl] *n* 1 : caballete *m*
(armazón) 2 *or* **trestle bridge** : puente
m de caballete
tri- [ˈtraɪ] *pref* : tri-
triad [ˈtraɪˌæd] *n* : tríada *f*
trial¹ [ˈtraɪəl] *adj* : de prueba ⟨trial period
: período de prueba⟩
trial² *n* 1 : juicio *m*, proceso *m* ⟨to stand
trial : ser sometido a juicio⟩ 2 AFFLIC-
TION : aflicción *f*, tribulación *f* 3 TEST
: prueba *f*, ensayo *m* ⟨by trial and error
: por ensayo y error⟩
triangle [ˈtraɪˌæŋgəl] *n* : triángulo *m*
triangular [traɪˈæŋgjələr] *adj* : triangular
tribal [ˈtraɪbəl] *adj* : tribal
tribe [ˈtraɪb] *n* : tribu *f*
tribesman [ˈtraɪbzmən] *n, pl* **-men** [-mən,
-ˌmɛn] : miembro *m* de una tribu
tribulation [ˌtrɪbjəˈleɪʃən] *n* : tribulación *f*
tribunal [traɪˈbjuːnəl, trɪ-] *n* : tribunal *m*,
corte *f*

tributary [ˈtrɪbjəˌtɛri] *n, pl* **-taries** : afluente *m*
tribute [ˈtrɪbˌjuːt] *n* : tributo *m*
trick¹ [ˈtrɪk] *vt* : engañar, embaucar
trick² *n* 1 RUSE : trampa *f*, treta *f*, artimaña *f* 2 PRANK : broma *f* ⟨we played a
trick on her : le gastamos una broma⟩ 3
: truco *m* ⟨magic tricks : trucos de ma-
gia⟩ ⟨the trick is to wait five minutes : el
truco está en esperar cinco minutos⟩ 4
MANNERISM : peculiaridad *f*, manía *f* 5
: baza *f* (en juegos de naipes) 6 **to do
the trick** *fam* : servir como solución
trickery [ˈtrɪkəri] *n* : engaños *mpl*, trampas *fpl*
trickle¹ [ˈtrɪkəl] *vi* **-led; -ling** : gotear,
chorrear
trickle² *n* : goteo *m*, hilo *m*
trickster [ˈtrɪkstər] *n* : estafador *m*, -dora
f; embaucador *m*, -dora *f*
tricky [ˈtrɪki] *adj* **trickier; -est** 1 SLY : astuto, taimado 2 DIFFICULT : delicado,
peliagudo, difícil
tricolor [ˈtraɪˌkʌlər] *adj* : tricolor
tricycle [ˈtraɪsəkəl, -ˌsɪkəl] *n* : triciclo *m*
trident [ˈtraɪdənt] *n* : tridente *m*
triennial [ˌtraɪˈɛniəl] *adj* : trienal
trifle¹ [ˈtraɪfəl] *vi* **-fled; -fling** : jugar,
juguetear
trifle² *n* : nimiedad *f*, insignificancia *f*
trifling [ˈtraɪflɪŋ] *adj* : trivial, insignificante
trigger¹ [ˈtrɪgər] *vt* : causar, provocar
trigger² *n* : gatillo *m*
trigonometry [ˌtrɪgəˈnɑmətri] *n* : trigonometría *f*
trill¹ [ˈtrɪl] *vi* QUAVER : trinar, gorjear — *vt*
: vibrar ⟨to trill the r : vibrar la *r*⟩
trill² *n* 1 QUAVER : trino *m*, gorjeo *m* 2
: vibración *f* (en fonética)
trillion [ˈtrɪljən] *n* : billón *m*
trilogy [ˈtrɪlədʒi] *n, pl* **-gies** : trilogía *f*
trim¹ [ˈtrɪm] *vt* **trimmed; trimming** 1 DEC-
ORATE : adornar, decorar 2 CUT : recortar 3 REDUCE : recortar, reducir ⟨to
trim the excess : recortar el exceso⟩
trim² *adj* **trimmer; trimmest** 1 SLIM : esbelto 2 NEAT : limpio y arreglado, bien
cuidado
trim³ *n* 1 CONDITION : condición *f*, estado *m* ⟨to keep in trim : mantenerse en
buena forma⟩ 2 CUT : recorte *m* 3
TRIMMING : adornos *mpl*
trimester [ˌtraɪˈmɛstər] *n* : trimestre *m*
trimming [ˈtrɪmɪŋ] *n* : adornos *mpl*, accesorios *mpl*
Trinity [ˈtrɪnəʈi] *n* : Trinidad *f*
trinket [ˈtrɪŋkət] *n* : chuchería *f*, baratija *f*
trio [ˈtriːˌoː] *n, pl* **trios** : trío *m*
trip¹ [ˈtrɪp] *v* **tripped; tripping** *vi* 1 : caminar (a paso ligero) 2 STUMBLE : tro-
pezar 3 **to trip up** ERR : equivocarse,
cometer un error — *vt* 1 : hacerle una
zancadilla (a alguien) ⟨you tripped me
on purpose! : ¡me hiciste la zancadilla a
propósito!⟩ 2 ACTIVATE : activar (un
mecanismo) 3 **to trip up** : hacer equivocar (a alguien)
trip² *n* 1 JOURNEY : viaje *m* ⟨to take a
trip : hacer un viaje⟩ 2 STUMBLE
: tropiezo *m*, traspié *m*

tripartite [traɪˈpɑrˌtaɪt] *adj* : tripartito
tripe [ˈtraɪp] *n* **1** : mondongo *m*, callos *mpl*, pancita *f Mex* **2** TRASH : porquería *f*
triple[1] [ˈtrɪpəl] *vt* **-pled; -pling** : triplicar
triple[2] *adj* : triple
triple[3] *n* : triple *m*
triplet [ˈtrɪplət] *n* **1** : terceto *m* (en poesía, música, etc.) **2** : trillizo *m*, -za *f* (persona)
triplicate [ˈtrɪplɪkət] *n* : triplicado *m*
tripod [ˈtraɪˌpɑd] *n* : trípode *m*
trite [ˈtraɪt] *adj* **triter; tritest** : trillado, tópico, manido
triumph[1] [ˈtraɪəmpf] *vi* : triunfar
triumph[2] *n* : triunfo *m*
triumphal [traɪˈʌmpfəl] *adj* : triunfal
triumphant [traɪˈʌmpfənt] *adj* : triunfante, triunfal — **triumphantly** *adv*
triumvirate [traɪˈʌmvərət] *n* : triunvirato *m*
trivet [ˈtrɪvət] *n* : salvamanteles *m*
trivia [ˈtrɪviə] *ns & pl* : trivialidades *fpl*, nimiedades *fpl*
trivial [ˈtrɪviəl] *adj* : trivial, intrascendente, insignificante
triviality [ˌtrɪviˈæləti] *n*, *pl* **-ties** : trivialidad *f*
trod, trodden → **tread**[1]
troll [ˈtroːl] *n* : duende *m* o gigante *m* de cuentos folklóricos
trolley [ˈtrɑli] *n*, *pl* **-leys** : tranvía *m*
trombone [trɑmˈboːn] *n* : trombón *m*
trombonist [trɑmˈboːnɪst] *n* : trombón *m*
troop[1] [ˈtruːp] *vi* : desfilar, ir en tropel
troop[2] *n* **1** : escuadrón *m* (de caballería) **2** GROUP : grupo *m*, banda *f* (de personas) **3 troops** *npl* SOLDIERS : tropas *fpl*, soldados *mpl*
trooper [ˈtruːpər] *n* **1** : soldado *m* (de caballería) **2** : policía *m* montado **3** : policía *m* (estatal)
trophy [ˈtroːfi] *n*, *pl* **-phies** : trofeo *m*
tropic[1] [ˈtrɑpɪk] *or* **tropical** [-pɪkəl] *adj* : tropical
tropic[2] *n* **1** : trópico *m* ⟨tropic of Cancer : trópico de Cáncer⟩ **2 the tropics** : el trópico
trot[1] [ˈtrɑt] *vi* **trotted; trotting** : trotar
trot[2] *n* : trote *m*
troubadour [ˈtruːbəˌdɔr] *n* : trovador *m*, -dora *f*
trouble[1] [ˈtrʌbəl] *v* **-bled; -bling** *vt* **1** DISTURB, WORRY : molestar, perturbar, inquietar **2** AFFLICT : afligir, afectar — *vi* : molestarse, hacer un esfuerzo ⟨they didn't trouble to come : no se molestaron en venir⟩
trouble[2] *n* **1** PROBLEMS : problemas *mpl*, dificultades *fpl* ⟨to be in trouble : estar en un aprieto⟩ ⟨heart trouble : problemas de corazón⟩ **2** EFFORT : molestia *f*, esfuerzo *m* ⟨to take the trouble : tomarse la molestia⟩ ⟨it's not worth the trouble : no vale la pena⟩
troublemaker [ˈtrʌbəlˌmeɪkər] *n* : agitador *m*, -dora *f*; alborotador *m*, -dora *f*
troubleshooter [ˈtrʌbəlˌfuːʈər] *n* : persona *f* que resuelve problemas
troublesome [ˈtrʌbəlsəm] *adj* : proble-

mático, dificultoso — **troublesomely** *adv*
trough [ˈtrɔf] *n*, *pl* **troughs** [ˈtrɔfs, ˈtrɔvz] **1** : comedero *m*, bebedero *m* (de animales) **2** CHANNEL, HOLLOW : depresión *f* (en el suelo), seno *m* (de olas)
trounce [ˈtraʊnʦ] *vt* **trounced; trouncing 1** THRASH : apalear, darle una paliza (a alguien) **2** DEFEAT : derrotar contundentemente
troupe [ˈtruːp] *n* : troupe *f*
trouser [ˈtraʊzər] *adj* : del pantalón
trousers [ˈtraʊzərz] *npl* : pantalón *m*, pantalones *mpl*
trousseau [ˈtruːˌsoː, truˈsoː] *n* : ajuar *m*
trout [ˈtraʊt] *ns & pl* : trucha *f*
trowel [ˈtraʊəl] *n* **1** : llana *f*, paleta *f* (de albañil) **2** : desplantador *m* (de jardinero)
truant [ˈtruːənt] *n* : alumno *m*, -na *f* que falta a clase sin permiso
truce [ˈtruːs] *n* : tregua *f*, armisticio *m*
truck[1] [ˈtrʌk] *vt* : transportar en camión
truck[2] *n* **1** : camión *m* (vehículo automóvil), carro *m* (manual) ⟨truck driver : camionero⟩ **2** *or* **hand truck** : carretilla *f*, carro *m* (para llevar cajones, etc.) **3** DEALINGS : tratos *mpl* ⟨to have no truck with : no tener nada que ver con⟩
trucker [ˈtrʌkər] *n* : camionero *m*, -ra *f*
truculent [ˈtrʌkjələnt] *adj* : agresivo, beligerante
trudge [ˈtrʌʤ] *vi* **trudged; trudging** : caminar a paso pesado
true[1] [ˈtruː] *vt* **trued; trueing** : aplomar (algo vertical), nivelar (algo horizontal), centrar (una rueda)
true[2] *adv* **1** TRUTHFULLY : lealmente, sinceramente **2** ACCURATELY : exactamente, certeramente
true[3] *adj* **truer; truest 1** LOYAL : fiel, leal **2** : cierto, verdadero, verídico ⟨it's true : es cierto, es la verdad⟩ ⟨a true story : una historia verídica⟩ **3** GENUINE : auténtico, genuino — **truly** *adv*
true–blue [ˈtruːˈbluː] *adj* LOYAL : leal, fiel
truffle [ˈtrʌfəl] *n* : trufa *f*
truism [ˈtruːˌɪzəm] *n* : perogrullada *f*, verdad *f* obvia
trump[1] [ˈtrʌmp] *vt* : matar (en juegos de naipes)
trump[2] *n* : triunfo *m* (en juegos de naipes)
trumped–up [ˈtrʌmptˈʌp] *adj* : inventado, fabricado ⟨trumped-up charges : falsas acusaciones⟩
trumpet[1] [ˈtrʌmpət] *vi* **1** : sonar una trompeta **2** : berrear, bramar (dícese de un animal) — *vt* : proclamar a los cuatro vientos
trumpet[2] *n* : trompeta *f*
trumpeter [ˈtrʌmpəʈər] *n* : trompetista *mf*
truncate [ˈtrʌŋˌkeɪt, ˈtrʌn-] *vt* **-cated; -cating** : truncar
trundle [ˈtrʌndəl] *v* **-dled; -dling** *vi* : rodar lentamente — *vt* : hacer rodar, empujar lentamente
trunk [ˈtrʌŋk] *n* **1** : tronco *m* (de un árbol o del cuerpo) **2** : trompa *f* (de un ele-

fante) **3** CHEST : baúl *m* **4** : maletero *m*, baúl *m* (*in various countries*), cajuela *f Mex* (de un auto) **5** trunks *npl* → **swimming trunks**

truss¹ ['trʌs] *vt* : atar (con fuerza)

truss² *n* **1** FRAMEWORK : armazón *m* (de una estructura) **2** : braguero *m* (en medicina)

trust¹ ['trʌst] *vi* : confiar, esperar ⟨to trust in God : confiar en Dios⟩ — *vt* **1** ENTRUST : confiar, encomendar **2** : confiar en, tenerle confianza a ⟨I trust you : te tengo confianza⟩

trust² *n* **1** CONFIDENCE : confianza *f* **2** HOPE : esperanza *f*, fe *f* **3** CREDIT : crédito *m* ⟨to sell on trust : fiar⟩ **4** : fideicomiso *m* ⟨to hold in trust : guardar en fideicomiso⟩ **5** : trust *m* (consorcio empresarial) **6** CUSTODY : responsabilidad *f*, custodia *f*

trustee [ˌtrʌs'tiː] *n* : fideicomisario *m*, -ria *f*; fiduciario *m*, -ria *f*

trustful ['trʌstfəl] *adj* : confiado — **trustfully** *adv*

trustworthiness ['trəst,wərðinəs] *n* : integridad *f*, honradez *f*

trustworthy ['trəst,wərði] *adj* : digno de confianza, confiable

trusty ['trəsti] *adj* **trustier; -est** : fiel, confiable

truth ['truːθ] *n, pl* **truths** ['truːðz, 'truːθs] : verdad *f*

truthful ['truːθfəl] *adj* : sincero, veraz — **truthfully** *adv*

truthfulness ['truːθfəlnəs] *n* : sinceridad *f*, veracidad *f*

try¹ ['traɪ] *v* **tried; trying** *vt* **1** : enjuiciar, juzgar, procesar ⟨he was tried for murder : fue procesado por homicidio⟩ **2** : probar ⟨did you try the salad? : ¿probaste la ensalada?⟩ **3** TEST : tentar, poner a prueba ⟨to try one's patience : tentarle la paciencia a uno⟩ **4** ATTEMPT : tratar (de), intentar **5** *or* **to try on** : probarse (ropa) **6** **to try out** : poner a prueba — *vi* **1** : tratar, intentar **2** **to try out (for)** : presentarse a una prueba (para)

try² *n, pl* **tries** : intento *m*, tentativa *f*

tryout ['traɪˌaʊt] *n* : prueba *f*

tsar ['zɑr, 'tsɑr, 'sɑr] → **czar**

T-shirt ['tiːˌʃərt] *n* : camiseta *f*

tub ['tʌb] *n* **1** CASK : cuba *f*, barril *m*, tonel *m* **2** CONTAINER : envase *m* (de plástico, etc.) ⟨a tub of margarine : un envase de margarina⟩ **3** BATHTUB : tina *f* (de baño), bañera *f*

tuba ['tuːbə, 'tjuː-] *n* : tuba *f*

tube ['tuːb, 'tjuːb] *n* **1** PIPE : tubo *m* **2** : tubo *m* (de dentífrico, etc.) **3** *or* **inner tube** : cámara *f* **4** : tubo *m* (de un aparato electrónico) **5** : trompa *f* (en anatomía) **6** (*Brit*) SUBWAY : metro *m*; subterráneo *m Arg, Uru* **7** **the tube** *fam* : la tele *fam*

tubeless ['tuːbləs, 'tjuːb-] *adj* : sin cámara (dícese de una llanta)

tuber ['tuːbər, 'tjuː-] *n* : tubérculo *m*

tubercular [tʊ'bərkjələr, tjʊ-] → **tuberculous**

tuberculosis [tʊˌbərkjə'loːsɪs, tjʊ-] *n, pl* **-loses** [-ˌsiːz] : tuberculosis *f*

tuberculous [tʊ'bərkjələs, tjʊ-] *adj* : tuberculoso

tuberous ['tuːbərəs, 'tjuː-] *adj* : tuberoso

tubing ['tuːbɪŋ, 'tjuː-] *n* : tubería *f*

tubular ['tuːbjələr, 'tjuː-] *adj* : tubular

tuck¹ ['tʌk] *vt* **1** PLACE, PUT : meter, colocar ⟨tuck in your shirt : métete la camisa⟩ **2** : guardar, esconder ⟨to tuck away one's money : guardar uno bien su dinero⟩ **3** *or* **to tuck in** COVER : arropar (a un niño en la cama)

tuck² *n* : pliegue *m*, alforza *f*

Tuesday ['tuːzˌdeɪ, 'tjuːz-, -di] *n* : martes *m* ⟨today is Tuesday : hoy es martes⟩ ⟨(on) Tuesday : el martes⟩ ⟨(on) Tuesdays : los martes⟩ ⟨last Tuesday : el martes pasado⟩ ⟨next Tuesday : el martes que viene⟩ ⟨every other Tuesday : cada dos martes⟩ ⟨Tuesday afternoon/morning : martes por la tarde/mañana⟩

tuft ['tʌft] *n* : penacho *m* (de plumas), copete *m* (de pelo)

tug¹ ['tʌg] *v* **tugged; tugging** *vi* : tirar, jalar, dar un tirón — *vt* : jalar, arrastrar, remolcar (con un barco)

tug² *n* **1** : tirón *m*, jalón *m* **2** → **tugboat**

tugboat ['tʌgˌboːt] *n* : remolcador *m*

tug-of-war [ˌtʌgə'wɔr] *n, pl* **tugs-of-war** **1** : juego *m* de tirar de la cuerda **2** : lucha *f*

tuition [tu'ɪʃən] *n or* **tuition fees** : tasas *fpl* de matrícula, colegiatura *f Mex*

tulip ['tuːlɪp, 'tjuː-] *n* : tulipán *m*

tulle ['tuːl] *n* : tul *m*

tumble¹ ['tʌmbəl] *v* **-bled; -bling** *vi* **1** : dar volteretas (en acrobacia) **2** FALL : caerse, venirse abajo — *vt* **1** TOPPLE : volcar **2** TOSS : hacer girar

tumble² *n* : voltereta *f*, caída *f*

tumbledown ['tʌmbəl'daʊn] *adj* : en ruinas

tumbler ['tʌmblər] *n* **1** ACROBAT : acróbata *mf*, saltimbanqui *mf* **2** GLASS : vaso *m* (de mesa) **3** : clavija *f* (de una cerradura)

tummy ['tʌmi] *n, pl* **-mies** BELLY : panza *f*, vientre *m*

tumor ['tuːmər, 'tjuː-] *n* : tumor *m*

tumult ['tuːˌmʌlt, 'tjuː-] *n* : tumulto *m*, alboroto *m*

tumultuous [tʊ'mʌltʃuəs, tjuː-] *adj* : tumultuoso

tuna ['tuːnə, 'tjuː-] *n, pl* **-na** *or* **-nas** : atún *m*

tundra ['tʌndrə] *n* : tundra *f*

tune¹ ['tuːn, 'tjuːn] *v* **tuned; tuning** *vt* **1** ADJUST : ajustar, hacer más preciso, afinar (un motor) **2** : afinar (un instrumento musical) **3** : sintonizar (un radio o televisor) — *vi* **to tune in** : sintonizar (con una emisora)

tune² *n* **1** MELODY : tonada *f*, canción *f*, melodía *f* **2** **in tune** : afinado (dícese de un instrumento o de la voz), sintonizado, en sintonía

tuneful ['tuːnfəl, 'tjuːn-] *adj* : armonioso, melódico

tuner ['tu:nər, 'tju:-] *n* : afinador *m*, -dora *f* (de instrumentos); sintonizador *m* (de un radio o un televisor)

tune–up *n* : afinado *m*, afinación *f*, puesta *f* a punto

tungsten ['tʌŋkstən] *n* : tungsteno *m*

tunic ['tu:nɪk, 'tju:-] *n* : túnica *f*

tuning fork *n* : diapasón *m*

Tunisian [tu:'ni:ʒən, tju:'nɪziən] *n* : tunecino *m*, -na *f* — **Tunisian** *adj*

tunnel[1] ['tʌnəl] *vi* **-neled** *or* **-nelled; -neling** *or* **-nelling** : hacer un túnel

tunnel[2] *n* : túnel *m*

turban ['tərbən] *n* : turbante *m*

turbid ['tərbɪd] *adj* : turbio

turbine ['tərbən, -ˌbaɪn] *n* : turbina *f*

turbulence ['tərbjələnts] *n* : turbulencia *f*

turbulent ['tərbjələnt] *adj* : turbulento — **turbulently** *adv*

tureen [tə'ri:n, tjʊ-] *n* : sopera *f*

turf ['tərf] *n* SOD : tepe *m*

turgid ['tərdʒɪd] *adj* **1** SWOLLEN : turgente **2** : ampuloso, hinchado ⟨turgid style : estilo ampuloso⟩

Turk ['tərk] *n* : turco *m*, -ca *f*

turkey ['tərki] *n, pl* **-keys** : pavo *m*

Turkish[1] ['tərkɪʃ] *adj* : turco

Turkish[2] *n* : turco *m* (idioma)

turmoil ['tərˌmɔɪl] *n* : agitación *f*, desorden *m*, confusión *f*

turn[1] ['tərn] *vt* **1** : girar, voltear, volver ⟨to turn one's head : voltear la cabeza⟩ ⟨she turned her chair toward the fire : giró su asiento hacia la hoguera⟩ **2** ROTATE, SPIN : darle vuelta(s) a, hacer girar ⟨turn the handle : dale vuelta a la manivela⟩ **3** FLIP : darle vuelta a, dar vuelta, voltear ⟨to turn the page : darle vuelta a la página/hoja, voltear/pasar la hoja/página⟩ ⟨to turn face up/down : volver boca arriba/abajo⟩ **4** SET : poner (un termostato, etc.) **5** SPRAIN, WRENCH : torcer, dislocar **6** DIRECT : dirigir (los esfuerzos, la atención, etc.) ⟨to turn one's mind/thoughts to : ponerse a pensar en⟩ **7** UPSET : revolver (el estómago) **8** TRANSFORM : convertir ⟨to turn water into wine : convertir el agua en vino⟩ **9** SHAPE : tornear (en carpintería) **10 to turn against** : poner (a alguien) en contra de **11 to turn a profit** : obtener ganancias/beneficios **12 to turn around** SPIN : hacer girar **13 to turn around** FLIP : dar la vuelta a, dar vuelta, voltear **14 to turn away** : no dejar/permitir entrar **15 to turn back** : hacer volver **16 to turn down** REFUSE, REJECT : rehusar, rechazar ⟨they turned down our invitation : rehusaron nuestra invitación⟩ **17 to turn down** LOWER : bajar (el volumen) **18 to turn in** : entregar ⟨to turn in one's work : entregar uno su trabajo⟩ ⟨they turned in the suspect : entregaron al sospechoso⟩ **19 to turn off/out** : apagar (la luz, la radio, etc.) **20 to turn on** : prender (la luz, etc.), encender (un motor, etc.) **21 to turn on** : interesarle a, excitar (sexualmente) **22 to turn on to** : despertarle el interés por **23 to turn out** EVICT, EXPEL : expulsar, echar, desalojar **24 to turn out** PRODUCE : producir **25 to turn over** TRANSFER : entregar, transferir (un cargo, una responsabilidad) **26 to turn over** FLIP : voltear, darle la vuelta a ⟨turn the pancake over : voltea el panqueque⟩ **27 to turn over** CONSIDER : considerar ⟨I kept turning the problem over in my mind : el problema me estaba dando vueltas en la cabeza⟩ **28 to turn up** : subir (el volumen) — *vi* **1** ROTATE, SPIN : girar, dar vueltas **2** : girar, doblar, dar una vuelta (en un vehículo) ⟨turn left : gira/dobla a la izquierda⟩ ⟨to turn around : dar la media vuelta⟩ ⟨turn onto Main : toma la calle Main⟩ **3** : volverse, darse la vuelta, voltearse ⟨to turn towards : volverse hacia⟩ ⟨I turned (around) and left : di media vuelta y me fui⟩ **4** BECOME : hacerse, volverse, ponerse ⟨it got cold (out) : (el tiempo) se volvió frío⟩ ⟨she turned red : se puso colorado, se sonrojó⟩ ⟨he turned 80 : cumplió los 80⟩ **5** CHANGE : cambiar (dícese de la marea, etc.) **6** SOUR : agriarse, cortarse (dícese de la leche) **7 to turn against** : volverse en contra de **8 to turn away** : volverse (de espaldas), darse la vuelta, voltearse **9 to turn back** RETURN : volverse **10 to turn in** : acostarse, irse a la cama **11 to turn into** : convertirse en **12 to turn off** : salir (de una carretera), desviarse de ⟨turn off at/onto Main : toma (la calle) Main⟩ ⟨turn off (of) First onto Main : sal de First tomando Main⟩ **13 to turn on** ATTACK : atacar (inesperadamente) **14 to turn out** : concurrir, presentarse ⟨many turned out to vote : muchos concurrieron a votar⟩ **15 to turn out** PROVE, RESULT : resultar **16 to turn over** : darse (la) vuelta (dícese de una persona, etc.), volcarse (dícese de un vehículo) **17 to turn over** START : arrancar **18 to turn to** : recurrir a ⟨they have no one to turn to : no tienen quien les ayude⟩ ⟨to turn to violence : recurrir a la violencia⟩ **19 to turn up** APPEAR : aparecer, presentarse **20 to turn up** HAPPEN : ocurrir, suceder (inesperadamente)

turn[2] *n* **1** : vuelta *f*, giro *m* ⟨give it a turn : dale vuelta⟩ ⟨a sudden turn : una vuelta repentina⟩ **2** CHANGE : cambio *m* ⟨to take a turn for the better/worse : mejorar/empeorar⟩ ⟨turn of events : giro de los acontecimientos⟩ **3** INTERSECTION : bocacalle *f* ⟨we took a wrong turn : nos equivocamos de calle/salida (etc.), dimos una vuelta equivocada⟩ **4** CURVE : curva *f* (en un camino) **5** : turno *m* ⟨they're awaiting their turn : están esperando su turno⟩ ⟨whose turn is it? : ¿a quién le toca?⟩ ⟨to take turns : turnarse⟩ **6 at every turn** : a cada paso **7 in turn** : sucesivamente **8 in turn** LIKEWISE : a su vez **9 one good turn deserves another** : favor por favor se paga **10 out of turn** : fuera de lugar **11 the turn of the century** : el final del siglo

turnaround ['tərnə,raʊnd] *n* PROCESSING : procesamiento *m*
turncoat ['tərn,ko:t] *n* : traidor *m*, -dora *f*
turning point *n* : momento *m* decisivo
turnip ['tərnəp] *n* : nabo *m*
turnout ['tərn,aʊt] *n* : concurrencia *f*
turnover ['tərn,o:vər] *n* **1** : empanada *f* (salada o dulce) **2** : volumen *m* (de ventas) **3** : rotación *f* (de personal) ⟨a high turnover : un alto nivel de rotación⟩
turnpike ['tərn,paɪk] *n* : carretera *f* de peaje
turnstile ['tərn,staɪl] *n* : torniquete *m* (de acceso)
turntable ['tərn,teɪbəl] *n* : tornamesa *mf*
turpentine ['tərpən,taɪn] *n* : aguarrás *m*, trementina *f*
turquoise ['tər,kɔɪz, -,kwɔɪz] *n* : turquesa *f*
turret ['tərət] *n* **1** TOWER : torre *f* pequeña **2** : torreta *f* (de un tanque, un avión, etc.)
turtle ['tərtəl] *n* : tortuga *f* (marina)
turtledove ['tərtəl,dʌv] *n* : tórtola *f*
turtleneck ['tərtəl,nɛk] *n* : cuello *m* de tortuga, cuello *m* alto
tusk ['tʌsk] *n* : colmillo *m*
tussle¹ ['tʌsəl] *vi* **-sled; -sling** SCUFFLE : pelearse, reñir
tussle² *n* : riña *f*, pelea *f*
tutelage ['tu:tl̩ɪdʒ, 'tju:-] *n* : tutela *f*
tutor¹ ['tu:tər, 'tju:-] *vt* : darle clases particulares (a alguien)
tutor² *n* : tutor *m*, -tora *f*; maestro *m*, -tra *f* (particular)
tutorial [,tu:'toriəl, ,tju:-] *n* **1** : tutorial *m* **2** : clase *f* (individual o con un pequeño grupo de estudiantes)
tuxedo [,tək'si:,do:] *n*, *pl* **-dos** *or* **-does** : esmoquin *m*, smoking *m* (traje)
TV [,ti:'vi:, 'ti:,vi:] → television
twain ['tweɪn] *n* : dos *m*
twang¹ ['twæŋ] *vt* : pulsar la cuerda de (una guitarra) — *vi* : hablar en tono nasal
twang² *n* **1** : tañido *m* (de una cuerda de guitarra) **2** : tono *m* nasal (de voz)
tweak¹ ['twi:k] *vt* : pellizcar
tweak² *n* : pellizco *m*
tweed ['twi:d] *n* : tweed *m*
tweet¹ ['twi:t] *vi* **1** : piar **2** : tuitear, twittear (en la red social Twitter) — *vt* : tuitear, twittear (en la red social Twitter)
tweet² *n* **1** : gorjeo *m*, pío *m* **2** : tuit *m*, tweet *m* (en la red social Twitter)
tweezers ['twi:zərz] *npl* : pinzas *fpl*
twelfth¹ ['twɛlfθ] *adj* : duodécimo
twelfth² *n* **1** : duodécimo *m*, -ma *f* (en una serie) **2** : doceavo *m*, doceava parte *f*
twelve¹ ['twɛlv] *adj & pron* : doce
twelve² *n* : doce *m*
twentieth¹ ['twʌntiəθ, 'twɛn-] *adj* : vigésimo
twentieth² *n* **1** : vigésimo *m*, -ma *f* (en una serie) **2** : veinteavo *m*, veinteava parte *f*
twenty¹ ['twʌnti, 'twɛn-] *adj & pron* : veinte
twenty² *n*, *pl* **-ties** : veinte *m*
twice ['twaɪs] *adv* : dos veces ⟨twice a day : dos veces al día⟩ ⟨it costs twice as much : cuesta el doble⟩
twig ['twɪg] *n* : ramita *f*

twilight ['twaɪ,laɪt] *n* : crepúsculo *m*
twill ['twɪl] *n* : sarga *f*, tela *f* cruzada
twin¹ ['twɪn] *adj* **1** : gemelo, mellizo **2** : doble, gemelo ⟨twin city : ciudad hermana⟩ ⟨twin-engine plane : avión bimotor⟩
twin² *n* : gemelo *m*, -la *f*; mellizo *m*, -za *f*
twin bed *n* : cama *f* individual
twine¹ ['twaɪn] *v* **twined; twining** *vt* : entrelazar, entrecruzar — *vi* : enroscarse (alrededor de algo)
twine² *n* : cordel *m*, cuerda *f*, mecate *m* CA, Mex, Ven
twinge¹ ['twɪndʒ] *vi* **twinged; twinging** *or* **twingeing** : punzada *f*, dolor *m* agudo
twinge² *n* : punzada *f*, dolor *m* agudo
twinkle¹ ['twɪŋkəl] *vi* **-kled; -kling 1** : centellear, titilar (dícese de las estrellas o de la luz) **2** : chispear, brillar (dícese de los ojos)
twinkle² *n* : centelleo *m* (de las estrellas), brillo *m* (de los ojos)
twirl¹ ['twərl] *vt* : girar, darle vueltas a — *vi* : girar, dar vueltas (rápidamente)
twirl² *n* : giro *m*, vuelta *f*
twist¹ ['twɪst] *vt* **1** : torcer, retorcer ⟨he twisted my arm : me torció el brazo⟩ **2** DISTORT : tergiversar — *vi* : retorcerse, enroscarse, serpentear (dícese de un río, un camino, etc.)
twist² *n* **1** BEND : vuelta *f*, recodo *m* (en el camino, el río, etc.) **2** TURN : giro *m* ⟨give it a twist : hazlo girar⟩ **3** SPIRAL : espiral *f* ⟨a twist of lemon : una rodajita de limón⟩ **4** : giro *m* inesperado (de eventos, etc.)
twisted ['twɪstəd] *adj* : retorcido ⟨a twisted mind : una mente retorcida⟩
twister ['twɪstər] *n* **1** → tornado **2** → waterspout
twitch¹ ['twɪtʃ] *vi* : moverse nerviosamente, contraerse espasmódicamente (dícese de un músculo)
twitch² *n* : espasmo *m*, sacudida *f* ⟨a nervous twitch : un tic nervioso⟩
twitter¹ ['twɪtər] *vi* CHIRP : gorjear, cantar (dícese de los pájaros)
twitter² *n* : gorjeo *m*
two¹ ['tu:] *adj* : dos ⟨she's two (years old) : tiene dos años⟩
two² *n*, *pl* **twos** : dos *m* ⟨the two of hearts : el dos de corazones⟩
two³ *pron* : dos ⟨there are two of us : somos dos⟩ ⟨it's two (o'clock) : son las dos⟩
two-faced ['tu:'feɪst] *adj* : hipócrita
twofold¹ ['tu:'fo:ld] *adv* : al doble
twofold² ['tu:,fo:ld] *adj* : doble
two hundred¹ *adj & pron* : doscientos
two hundred² *n* : doscientos *m*
two-piece ['tu:'pi:s] *adj* : de dos piezas
twosome ['tu:səm] *n* COUPLE : pareja *f*
two-tone ['tu:'to:n] *adj* : bicolor
two-way *adj* **1** : de doble sentido, de doble dirección (dícese de una calle) **2** MUTUAL : mutuo **3** : bidireccional
two-way mirror → one-way mirror
tycoon [taɪ'ku:n] *n* : magnate *mf*
tying → tie¹
type¹ ['taɪp] *v* **typed; typing** *vt* **1** TYPEWRITE : escribir a máquina, pasar (un

texto) a máquina **2** CATEGORIZE : categorizar, identificar — *vi* : escribir a máquina

type² *n* **1** KIND : tipo *m*, clase *f*, categoría *f* **2** : tipo *m* (de imprenta) ⟨italic type : bastardilla, cursiva⟩

typeface ['taɪpˌfeɪs] *n* : tipo *m* de imprenta

typewrite ['taɪpˌraɪt] *v* **-wrote; -written** : escribir a máquina

typewriter ['taɪpˌraɪtər] *n* : máquina *f* de escribir

typhoid¹ ['taɪˌfɔɪd, taɪ'-] *adj* : relativo al tifus o a la tifoidea

typhoid² *n or* **typhoid fever** : tifoidea *f*

typhoon [taɪ'fu:n] *n* : tifón *m*

typhus ['taɪfəs] *n* : tifus *m*

typical ['tɪpɪkəl] *adj* : típico, característico — **typically** *adv*

typify ['tɪpəˌfaɪ] *vt* **-fied; -fying** : ser típico o representativo de (un grupo, una clase, etc.)

typing ['taɪpɪŋ] *n* : mecanografía *f*

typist ['taɪpɪst] *n* : mecanógrafo *m*, -fa *f*

typographer [taɪ'pɑgrəfər] *n* : tipógrafo *m*, -fa *f*

typographic [ˌtaɪpə'græfɪk] *or* **typographical** [-fɪkəl] *adj* : tipográfico — **typographically** [-fɪkli] *adv*

typography [taɪ'pɑgrəfi] *n* : tipografía *f*

tyrannical [tə'rænɪkəl, taɪ-] *adj* : tiránico — **tyrannically** [-nɪkli] *adv*

tyrannize ['tɪrəˌnaɪz] *vt* **-nized; -nizing** : tiranizar

tyranny ['tɪrəni] *n, pl* **-nies** : tiranía *f*

tyrant ['taɪrənt] *n* : tirano *m*, -na *f*

Tyrolean [tə'ro:liən, taɪ-] *adj* : tirolés

tzar ['zɑr, 'tsɑr, 'sɑr] → **czar**

U

u ['ju:] *n, pl* **u's** *or* **us** ['ju:z] : vigésima primera letra del alfabeto inglés

ubiquitous [ju:'bɪkwətəs] *adj* : ubicuo, omnipresente

udder ['ʌdər] *n* : ubre *f*

UFO [ˌju:ˌef'o:, 'ju:ˌfo:] *n, pl* **UFO's** *or* **UFOs** (*u*nidentified *f*lying *o*bject) : ovni *m*, OVNI *m*

Ugandan [ju:'gændən, -'gɑn-:, u:'gɑn-] *n* : ugandés *m*, -desa *f* — **Ugandan** *adj*

ugliness ['ʌglinəs] *n* : fealdad *f*

ugly ['ʌgli] *adj* **uglier; -est 1** UNATTRACTIVE : feo **2** DISAGREEABLE : desagradable, feo ⟨ugly weather : tiempo feo⟩ ⟨to have an ugly temper : tener mal genio⟩

Ukrainian [ju:'kreɪniən, -'kraɪ-] *n* **1** : ucraniano *m*, -na *f* **2** : ucraniano *m* (idioma) — **Ukrainian** *adj*

ukulele [ˌju:kə'leɪli] *n* : ukelele *m*

ulcer ['ʌlsər] *n* : úlcera *f* (interna), llaga *f* (externa)

ulcerate ['ʌlsəˌreɪt] *vi* **-ated; -ating** : ulcerarse

ulcerous ['ʌlsərəs] *adj* : ulceroso

ulna ['ʌlnə] *n* : cúbito *m*

ulterior [ˌʌl'tɪriər] *adj* : oculto ⟨ulterior motive : motivo oculto, segunda intención⟩

ultimate ['ʌltəmət] *adj* **1** FINAL : último, final **2** SUPREME : supremo, máximo **3** FUNDAMENTAL : fundamental, esencial

ultimately ['ʌltəmətli] *adv* **1** FINALLY : por último, finalmente **2** EVENTUALLY : a la larga, con el tiempo

ultimatum [ˌʌltə'meɪtəm, -'mɑ-] *n, pl* **-tums** *or* **-ta** [-tə] : ultimátum *m*

ultra- [ˌʌltrə] *pref* : ultra-, super-

ultrasonic [ˌʌltrə'sɑnɪk] *adj* : ultrasónico

ultrasound ['ʌltrəˌsaʊnd] *n* **1** : ultrasonido *m* **2** : ecografía *f* (técnica o imagen)

ultraviolet [ˌʌltrə'vaɪələt] *adj* : ultravioleta

umbilical cord [ˌʌm'bɪlɪkəl] *n* : cordón *m* umbilical

umbrage ['ʌmbrɪdʒ] *n* **to take umbrage at** : ofenderse por

umbrella [ˌʌm'brelə] *n* **1** : paraguas *m* **2** **beach umbrella** : sombrilla *f*

umpire¹ ['ʌmˌpaɪr] *v* **-pired; -piring** : arbitrar

umpire² *n* : árbitro *m*, -tra *f*

umpteen [ˌʌmp'ti:n] *adj* : miles de, un millón de

umpteenth [ˌʌmp'ti:nθ] *adj* : enésimo ⟨for the umpteenth time : por enésima vez⟩

un- [ˌʌn] *pref* : in-, im-, ir-, i-, des-, poco, no ⟨uncertain : incierto⟩ ⟨unforeseeable : imprevisible⟩ ⟨unreasonable : irrazonable⟩ ⟨unlimited : ilimitado⟩ ⟨unfavorable : desfavorable⟩ ⟨uncommon : poco común⟩ ⟨unresolved : no resuelto⟩ ⟨to uncurl : desenrollar⟩

unable [ˌʌn'eɪbəl] *adj* : incapaz ⟨to be unable to : no poder⟩

unabridged [ˌʌnə'brɪdʒd] *adj* : íntegro

unacceptable [ˌʌnɪk'septəbəl] *adj* : inaceptable

unaccompanied [ˌʌnə'kʌmpənid] *adj* : solo, sin acompañamiento (en música)

unaccountable [ˌʌnə'kaʊntəbəl] *adj* : inexplicable, incomprensible — **unaccountably** [-bli] *adv*

unaccustomed [ˌʌnə'kʌstəmd] *adj* **1** UNUSUAL : desacostumbrado, inusual **2** UNUSED : inhabituado ⟨unaccustomed to noise : inhabituado al ruido⟩

unacquainted [ˌʌnə'kweɪntəd] *adj* **to be unacquainted with** : desconocer, ignorar

unadorned [ˌʌnə'dɔrnd] *adj* : sin adornos, puro y simple

unadulterated [ˌʌnə'dʌltəˌreɪtəd] *adj* **1** PURE : puro ⟨unadulterated food : comida pura⟩ **2** ABSOLUTE : completo, absoluto

unaffected [ˌʌnə'fɛktəd] *adj* **1** : no afectado, indiferente **2** NATURAL : sin afectación, natural

unaffectedly [ˌʌnəˈfɛktədli] *adv* : de manera natural

unafraid [ˌʌnəˈfreɪd] *adj* : sin miedo

unaided [ˌʌnˈeɪdəd] *adj* : sin ayuda, solo

unalterable [ˌʌnˈɔltərəbəl] *adj* : inalterable

unambiguous [ˌʌnæmˈbɪgjuəs] *adj* : inequívoco

unanimity [ˌjuːnəˈnɪməṭi] *n* : unanimidad *f*

unanimous [juˈnænəməs] *adj* : unánime — **unanimously** *adv*

unannounced [ˌʌnəˈnaʊnst] *adj* : sin dar aviso

unanswerable [ˌʌnˈænɬsərəbəl] *adj* **1** : incontestable **2** IRREFUTABLE : irrefutable, irrebatible

unanswered [ˌʌnˈænɬsərd] *adj* : sin contestar

unappealing [ˌʌnəˈpiːlɪŋ] *adj* : desagradable

unarmed [ˌʌnˈɑrmd] *adj* : sin armas, desarmado

unashamed [ˌʌnəˈʃeɪmd] *adj* : sin vergüenza ⟨he's unashamed of his patriotism : no tiene reparos en demostrar su patriotismo⟩

unassailable [ˌʌnəˈseɪləbəl] *adj* IRREFUTABLE : irrefutable, irrebatible

unassisted [ˌʌnəˈsɪstəd] *adj* : sin ayuda

unassuming [ˌʌnəˈsuːmɪŋ] *adj* : modesto, sin pretensiones

unattached [ˌʌnəˈtætʃt] *adj* **1** LOOSE : suelto **2** INDEPENDENT : independiente **3** : solo (ni casado ni prometido)

unattainable [ˌʌnəˈteɪnəbəl] *adj* : inalcanzable, inasequible

unattended [ˌʌnəˈtɛndəd] *adj* : desatendido

unattractive [ˌʌnəˈtræktɪv] *adj* : poco atractivo

unauthorized [ˌʌnˈɔθəˌraɪzd] *adj* : sin autorización, no autorizado

unavailable [ˌʌnəˈveɪləbəl] *adj* : no disponible

unavoidable [ˌʌnəˈvɔɪdəbəl] *adj* : inevitable, ineludible — **unavoidably** *adv*

unaware¹ [ˌʌnəˈwær] *adv* → **unawares**

unaware² *adj* : inconsciente

unawares [ˌʌnəˈwærz] *adv* **1** : por sorpresa ⟨to catch someone unawares : agarrar a alguien desprevenido⟩ **2** UNINTENTIONALLY : inconscientemente, inadvertidamente

unbalance [ˌʌnˈbælənɬs] *vt* : desequilibrar

unbalanced [ˌʌnˈbælənɬst] *adj* : desequilibrado

unbearable [ˌʌnˈbærəbəl] *adj* : insoportable, inaguantable — **unbearably** [-bli] *adv*

unbeatable [ˌʌnˈbiːṭəbəl] *adj* : insuperable

unbeaten [ˌʌnˈbiːtən] *adj* : invicto

unbecoming [ˌʌnbɪˈkʌmɪŋ] *adj* **1** UNSEEMLY : impropio, indecoroso **2** UNFLATTERING : poco favorecedor

unbeknownst [ˌʌbɪˈnoʊnɬst] *adj* **unbeknownst to** : sin el conocimiento de

unbelievable [ˌʌnbəˈliːvəbəl] *adj* : increíble — **unbelievably** [-bli] *adv*

unbend [ˌʌnˈbɛnd] *vi* **-bent** [-ˈbɛnt]; **-bending** RELAX : relajarse

unbending [ˌʌnˈbɛndɪŋ] *adj* : inflexible

unbiased [ˌʌnˈbaɪəst] *adj* : imparcial, objetivo

unblock [ˌʌnˈblɑk] *vt* : desatascar, destapar (cañería, etc.)

unbolt [ˌʌnˈboːlt] *vt* : abrir el cerrojo de, descorrer el pestillo de

unborn [ˌʌnˈbɔrn] *adj* : aún no nacido, que va a nacer

unbosom [ˌʌnˈbuzəm, -ˈbuː-] *vt* : revelar, divulgar

unbreakable [ˌʌnˈbreɪkəbəl] *adj* : irrompible

unbreathable [ˌʌˈbriːðəbəl] *adj* : irrespirable

unbridled [ˌʌnˈbraɪdəld] *adj* : desenfrenado

unbroken [ˌʌnˈbroːkən] *adj* **1** INTACT : intacto, sano **2** CONTINUOUS : continuo, ininterrumpido

unbuckle [ˌʌnˈbʌkəl] *vt* **-led; -ling** : desabrochar

unburden [ˌʌnˈbərdən] *vt* **1** UNLOAD : descargar **2 to unburden oneself** : desahogarse

unbutton [ˌʌnˈbʌtən] *vt* : desabrochar, desabotonar

uncalled-for [ˌʌnˈkɔldˌfɔr] *adj* : inapropiado, innecesario

uncanny [ənˈkæni] *adj* **uncannier; -est 1** STRANGE : extraño **2** EXTRAORDINARY : raro, extraordinario — **uncannily** [-ˈkænəli] *adv*

uncaring [ˌʌnˈkærɪŋ] *adj* : indiferente

unceasing [ˌʌnˈsiːsɪŋ] *adj* : incesante, continuo — **unceasingly** *adv*

unceremonious [ˌʌnˌserəˈmoːniəs] *adj* **1** INFORMAL : sin ceremonia, sin pompa **2** ABRUPT : abrupto, brusco — **unceremoniously** *adv*

uncertain [ˌʌnˈsərtən] *adj* **1** INDEFINITE : indeterminado **2** UNSURE : incierto, dudoso **3** CHANGEABLE : inestable, variable ⟨uncertain weather : tiempo inestable⟩ **4** HESITANT : indeciso **5** VAGUE : poco claro

uncertainly [ˌʌnˈsərtənli] *adv* : dudosamente, con desconfianza

uncertainty [ˌʌnˈsərtənṭi] *n, pl* **-ties** : duda *f*, incertidumbre *f*

unchain [ˌʌnˈtʃeɪn] *vt* : desencadenar

unchangeable [ˌʌnˈtʃeɪndʒəbəl] *adj* : inalterable, inmutable

unchanged [ˌʌnˈtʃeɪndʒd] *adj* : sin cambiar

unchanging [ˌʌnˈtʃeɪndʒɪŋ] *adj* : inalterable, inmutable, firme

uncharacteristic [ˌʌnˌkærɪktəˈrɪstɪk] *adj* : inusual, desacostumbrado

uncharged [ˌʌnˈtʃɑrdʒd] *adj* : sin carga (eléctrica)

uncharitable [ˌʌnˈtʃærəṭəbəl] *adj* : poco caritativo

unchecked [ˌʌnˈtʃɛkt] *adj* : sin freno, sin obsáculos

uncivilized [ˌʌnˈsɪvəˌlaɪzd] *adj* **1** BARBAROUS : incivilizado, bárbaro **2** WILD : salvaje

uncle [ˈʌŋkəl] *n* : tío *m*

unclean [ˌʌnˈkliːn] *adj* **1** IMPURE : impuro **2** DIRTY : sucio

unclear [ˌʌnˈklɪr] *adj* : confuso, borroso, poco claro

Uncle Sam [ˈsæm] *n* : el Tío Sam

unclog [ˌʌnˈklɑg] *vt* -clogged; -clogging : desatascar, destapar

unclothed [ˌʌnˈkloːðd] *adj* : desnudo

uncluttered [ˌʌnˈklʌt̬ərd] *adj* : despejado (dícese de una habitación, etc.)

uncoil [ˌʌnˈkɔɪl] *vi* : desenroscarse — *vt* : desenroscar

uncomfortable [ˌʌnˈkʌmpfərt̬əbəl] *adj* **1** : incómodo (dícese de una silla, etc.) **2** UNEASY : inquieto, incómodo — **uncomfortably** *adv*

uncommitted [ˌʌnkəˈmɪt̬əd] *adj* : sin compromisos

uncommon [ˌʌnˈkɑmən] *adj* **1** UNUSUAL : raro, poco común **2** REMARKABLE : excepcional, extraordinario

uncommonly [ˌʌnˈkɑmənli] *adv* : extraordinariamente

uncommunicative [ˌʌnkəˈmjuːnɪˌkeɪtɪv, -kətɪv] *adj* : poco comunicativo

uncomplaining [ˌʌkəmˈpleɪnɪŋ] *adj* : que no se queja

uncomplicated [ˌʌˈkɑmpləˌkeɪt̬əd] *adj* : sencillo ⟨he's an uncomplicated person : no es una persona complicada⟩

uncompromising [ˌʌnˈkɑmprəˌmaɪzɪŋ] *adj* : inflexible, intransigente

unconcerned [ˌʌnkənˈsərnd] *adj* : indiferente — **unconcernedly** [-ˈsərnədli] *adv*

unconditional [ˌʌnkənˈdɪʃənəl] *adj* : incondicional — **unconditionally** *adv*

unconnected [ˌʌnkəˈnɛktəd] *adj* **1** UNRELATED : no relacionado, sin conexión **2** DISCONNECTED : desconectado

unconscious¹ [ˌʌnˈkɑntʃəs] *adj* : inconsciente — **unconsciously** *adv*

unconscious² *n* : inconsciente *m*

unconsciousness [ˌʌnˈkɑntʃəsnəs] *n* : inconsciencia *f*

unconstitutional [ˌʌnˌkɑntʃstəˈtuːʃənəl, -ˈtjuː-] *adj* : inconstitucional — **unconstitutionality** *n*

uncontrollable [ˌʌnkənˈtroːləbəl] *adj* : incontrolable, incontenible — **uncontrollably** [-bli] *adv*

uncontrolled [ˌʌnkənˈtroːld] *adj* : incontrolado

unconventional [ˌʌnkənˈvɛntʃənəl] *adj* : poco convencional

unconvinced [ˌʌnkənˈvɪntst] *adj* : no convencido, escéptico

unconvincing [ˌʌnkənˈvɪntsɪŋ] *adj* : poco convincente

uncoordinated [ˌʌnkoˈɔrdənˌeɪt̬əd] *adj* **1** : no coordinado **2** CLUMSY : torpe

uncork [ˌʌnˈkɔrk] *vt* : descorchar

uncorroborated [ˌʌnkəˈrɑbəˌreɪt̬əd] *adj* : no corroborado

uncountable [ˌʌnˈkaʊntəbəl] *adj* : no contable

uncouple [ˌʌnˈkʌpəl] *vt* : desenganchar

uncouth [ˌʌnˈkuːθ] *adj* CRUDE, ROUGH : grosero, rudo

uncover [ˌʌnˈkʌvər] *vt* **1** : destapar (un objeto), dejar al descubierto **2** EXPOSE, REVEAL : descubrir, revelar, exponer

uncultivated [ˌʌnˈkʌltəˌveɪt̬əd] *adj* : inculto

uncultured [ˌʌnˈkʌltʃərd] *adj* : inculto

uncurl [ˌʌnˈkərl] *vt* UNROLL : desenrollar — *vi* : desenrollarse

uncut [ˌʌnˈkʌt] *adj* **1** : sin cortar ⟨uncut grass : hierba sin cortar⟩ **2** : sin tallar, en bruto ⟨an uncut diamond : un diamante en bruto⟩ **3** UNABRIDGED : completo, íntegro

undamaged [ˌʌnˈdæmɪdʒd] *adj* : intacto, no dañado

undaunted [ˌʌnˈdɔntəd] *adj* : impávido

undecided [ˌʌndiˈsaɪdəd] *adj* **1** IRRESOLUTE : indeciso, irresoluto **2** UNRESOLVED : pendiente, no resuelto

undefeated [ˌʌndiˈfiːt̬əd] *adj* : invicto

undefined [ˌʌndiˈfaɪnd] *adj* : indefinido

undemanding [ˌʌndiˈmændɪŋ] *adj* : que exige poco

undeniable [ˌʌndiˈnaɪəbəl] *adj* : innegable — **undeniably** [-bli] *adv*

under¹ [ˈʌndər] *adv* **1** LESS : menos ⟨$10 or under : $10 o menos⟩ **2** UNDERWATER : debajo del agua **3** : bajo los efectos de la anestesia

under² *adj* **1** LOWER : (más) bajo, inferior **2** SUBORDINATE : inferior **3** : insuficiente ⟨an under dose of medicine : una dosis insuficiente de medicina⟩

under³ *prep* **1** BELOW, BENEATH : debajo de, abajo de ⟨under the table : abajo de la mesa⟩ ⟨we walked under the arch : pasamos por debajo del arco⟩ ⟨under the sun : bajo el sol⟩ **2** : menos de ⟨in under 20 minutes : en menos de 20 minutos⟩ **3** : bajo (un nombre, una categoría, etc.) **4** (*indicating rank or authority*) : bajo ⟨under the command of : bajo las órdenes de⟩ **6** SUBJECT TO : bajo ⟨under suspicion : bajo sospecha⟩ ⟨he's under stress : está estresado, sufre de estrés⟩ ⟨under the influence of alcohol : bajo los efectos del alcohol⟩ ⟨under the circumstances : dadas las circunstancias⟩ ⟨I was under the impression that . . . : tenía la impresión de que . . .⟩ **7** : en (una condición) ⟨under arrest : detenido⟩ ⟨under construction : en construcción⟩ ⟨it's under discussion : se está discutiendo⟩ **8** ACCORDING TO : según, de acuerdo con, conforme a ⟨under the present laws : según las leyes actuales⟩

under- [ˌʌndər] *pref* **1** : sub-, abajo ⟨underside : parte de abajo⟩ ⟨underlying : subyacente⟩ **2** : sub-, insuficientemente ⟨underdeveloped : subdesarrollado⟩ ⟨underestimate : subestimar⟩

underage [ˌʌndərˈeɪdʒ] *adj* : menor de edad

underarm¹ [ˈʌndərˌɑrm] *adj* : de axila, para las axilas ⟨underarm deodorant : desodorante⟩

underarm² [ˈʌndərˌɑrm] *n* ARMPIT : axila *f*, sobaco *m*

underbrush [ˈʌndərˌbrəʃ] *n* : maleza *f*

undercarriage [ˈʌndərˌkærɪdʒ] *n* **1** CHASSIS : chassis *m*, armazón *m* **2** : tren *f* de aterrizaje (de un avión)

undercharge [ˌʌndə'tʃɑrdʒ] *vt* : cobrarle de menos a

underclass ['ʌndərˌklæs] *n* : clases *fpl* marginadas

underclothes ['ʌndərˌkloːz, -ˌkloːðz] → **underwear**

underclothing ['ʌndərˌkloːðɪŋ] → **underwear**

undercoat ['ʌndərˌkoːt] *n* : primera capa *f* (de pintura)

undercooked [ˌʌndər'kʊkt] *adj* : medio crudo, poco cocinado ⟨it's a little undercooked : le falta un poco de cocción⟩

undercover [ˌʌndər'kʌvər] *adj* : secreto, clandestino

undercurrent ['ʌndərˌkərənt] *n* 1 : corriente *f* submarina 2 UNDERTONE : corriente *f* oculta, trasfondo *m*

undercut [ˌʌndər'kʌt] *vt* -**cut**; -**cutting** : vender más barato que

underdeveloped [ˌʌndərdɪ'vɛləpt] *adj* : subdesarrollado, atrasado

underdevelopment [ˌʌndərdɪ'vɛləpmənt] *n* : subdesarrollo *m*

underdog ['ʌndərˌdɔg] *n* : persona *f* que tiene menos posibilidades

underdone [ˌʌndər'dʌn] *adj* RARE : poco cocido

underestimate [ˌʌndər'ɛstəˌmeɪt] *vt* -**mated**; -**mating** : subestimar, menospreciar

underexpose [ˌʌndərɪk'spoːz] *vt* : subexponer (en fotografía)

underexposure [ˌʌndərɪk'spoːʒər] *vt* : subexposición *f*

underfoot [ˌʌndər'fʊt] *adv* 1 : bajo los pies ⟨to trample underfoot : pisotear⟩ 2 to be **underfoot** : estorbar ⟨they're always underfoot : están siempre estorbando⟩

undergarment ['ʌndərˌgɑrmənt] *n* : prenda *f* íntima

undergo [ˌʌndər'goː] *vt* -**went** [-'wɛnt]; -**gone** [-'gɔn]; -**going** : sufrir, experimentar ⟨to undergo an operation : someterse a una intervención quirúrgica⟩

undergraduate [ˌʌndər'grædʒuət] *n* : estudiante *m* universitario, estudiante *f* universitaria

underground[1] [ˌʌndər'graʊnd] *adv* 1 : bajo tierra 2 SECRETLY : clandestinamente, en secreto ⟨to go underground : pasar a la clandestinidad⟩

underground[2] ['ʌndərˌgraʊnd] *adj* 1 SUBTERRANEAN : subterráneo 2 SECRET : secreto, clandestino

underground[3] ['ʌndərˌgraʊnd] *n* : movimiento *m* o grupo *m* clandestino

undergrowth ['ʌndərˌgroːθ] *n* : maleza *f*, broza *f*

underhand[1] ['ʌndərˌhænd] *adv* 1 SECRETLY : de manera clandestina 2 or **underhanded** : sin levantar el brazo por encima del hombro (en deportes)

underhand[2] *adj* 1 SLY : solapado 2 : por debajo del hombro (en deportes)

underhanded [ˌʌndər'hændəd] *adj* 1 SLY : solapado 2 SHADY : turbio, poco limpio

underlie [ʌndər'laɪ] *vt* -**lay**; -**lain**; -**lying** : subyacer en/a

underline ['ʌndərˌlaɪn] *vt* -**lined**; -**lining** 1 : subrayar 2 EMPHASIZE : subrayar, acentuar, hacer hincapié en

underling ['ʌndərlɪŋ] *n* : subordinado *m*, -da *f*; inferior *mf*

underlying [ˌʌndər'laɪɪŋ] *adj* 1 : subyacente ⟨the underlying rock : la roca subyacente⟩ 2 FUNDAMENTAL : fundamental, esencial

undermine [ˌʌndər'maɪn] *vt* -**mined**; -**mining** 1 : socavar (una estructura, etc.) 2 SAP, WEAKEN : minar, debilitar

underneath[1] [ˌʌndər'niːθ] *adv* : debajo, abajo ⟨the part underneath : la parte de abajo⟩

underneath[2] *prep* : debajo de, abajo de

undernourished [ˌʌndər'nərɪʃt] *adj* : desnutrido

underpaid [ˌʌndər'peɪd] *adj* : mal pagado

underpants ['ʌndərˌpænts] *npl* : calzoncillos *mpl*, calzones *mpl*

underpass ['ʌndərˌpæs] *n* : paso *m* a desnivel

underpay [ˌʌndər'peɪ] *v* -**paid** [-'peɪd]; -**paying** *vt* : pagarle mal a (alguien) — *vi* : pagar mal

underprivileged [ˌʌndər'prɪvlɪdʒd] *adj* : desfavorecido

underrate [ˌʌndər'reɪt] *vt* -**rated**; -**rating** : subestimar, menospreciar

underscore ['ʌndərˌskor] *vt* -**scored**; -**scoring** → **underline**

undersea[1] [ˌʌndər'siː] *or* **underseas** [-'siːz] *adv* : bajo la superficie del mar

undersea[2] *adj* : submarino

undersecretary [ˌʌndər'sɛkrəˌtɛri] *n, pl* -**ries** : subsecretario *m*, -ria *f*

undersell [ˌʌndər'sɛl] *vt* -**sold**; -**selling** : vender más barato que

undeserved [ˌʌndɪ'zərvd] *adj* : inmerecido

undershirt ['ʌndərˌʃərt] *n* : camiseta *f*

undershorts ['ʌndərˌʃɔrts] *npl* : calzoncillos *mpl*

underside ['ʌndərˌsaɪd, ˌʌndər'saɪd] *n* : parte *f* de abajo

undersigned ['ʌndərˌsaɪnd] *n* the under-**signed** : el abajo firmante, la abajo firmante, los abajo firmantes, las abajo firmantes

undersized [ˌʌndər'saɪzd] *adj* : más pequeño de lo normal

understand [ˌʌndər'stænd] *v* -**stood** [-'stʊd]; -**standing** *vt* 1 COMPREHEND : comprender, entender ⟨I don't understand it : no lo entiendo⟩ ⟨that's understood : eso se comprende⟩ ⟨to make oneself understood : hacerse entender⟩ 2 BELIEVE : entender ⟨to give someone to understand : dar a alguien a entender⟩ 3 INFER : tener entendido ⟨I understand that she's leaving : tengo entendido que se va⟩ — *vi* : comprender, entender

understandable [ˌʌndər'stændəbəl] *adj* : comprensible

understanding[1] [ˌʌndər'stændɪŋ] *adj* : comprensivo, compasivo

understanding[2] *n* 1 GRASP : comprensión *f*, entendimiento *m* 2 SYMPATHY

: comprensión *f* (mutua) **3** INTERPRE-
TATION : interpretación *f* ⟨it's my understanding that . . . : tengo la impresión de
que . . . , tengo entendido que . . .⟩ **4**
AGREEMENT : acuerdo *m*, arreglo *m*
understate [ˌʌndərˈsteɪt] *vt* **-stated; -stat-
ing** : minimizar, subestimar
understatement [ˌʌndərˈsteɪtmənt] *n* : atenuación *f* ⟨that's an understatement
: decir sólo eso es quedarse corto⟩
understudy [ˈʌndərˌstʌdi] *n, pl* **-dies** : sobresaliente *mf*, suplente *mf* (en el teatro)
undertake [ˌʌndərˈteɪk] *vt* **-took** [-ˈtʊk];
-taken [-ˈteɪkən]; **-taking 1** : emprender
(una tarea), asumir (una responsabilidad) **2** PROMISE : comprometerse (a
hacer algo)
undertaker [ˈʌndərˌteɪkər] *n* : director *m*,
-tora *f* de funeraria
undertaking [ˈʌndərˌteɪkɪŋ, ˌʌndər'-] *n* **1**
ENTERPRISE, TASK : empresa *f*, tarea *f* **2**
PLEDGE : promesa *f*, garantía *f*
undertone [ˈʌndərˌtoːn] *n* **1** : voz *f* baja
⟨to speak in an undertone : hablar en
voz baja⟩ **2** HINT, UNDERCURRENT
: trasfondo *m*, matiz *m*
undertow [ˈʌndərˌtoː] *n* : resaca *f*
undervalue [ˌʌndərˈvælˌjuː] *vt* **-ued; -uing**
: menospreciar, subestimar
underwater[1] [ˌʌndərˈwɔtər, -ˈwɑ-] *adv*
: debajo (del agua)
underwater[2] *adj* : submarino
under way [ˌʌndərˈweɪ] *adv* : en marcha,
en camino ⟨to get under way : ponerse
en marcha⟩
underwear [ˈʌndərˌwær] *n* : ropa *f* interior, ropa *f* íntima
underworld [ˈʌndərˌwərld] *n* **1** HELL : infierno *m* **2 the underworld** CRIMINALS
: la hampa, los bajos fondos
underwrite [ˈʌndərˌraɪt, ˌʌndər'-] *vt* **-wrote**
[-ˌroːt, -ˈroːt]; **-written** [-ˌrɪtən, -ˈrɪtən];
-writing 1 INSURE : asegurar **2** FI-
NANCE : financiar **3** BACK, ENDORSE
: suscribir, respaldar
underwriter [ˈʌndərˌraɪtər, ˌʌndər'-] *n* IN-
SURER : asegurador *m*, -dora *f*
undeserving [ˌʌndiˈzərvɪŋ] *adj* : indigno
undesirable[1] [ˌʌndiˈzaɪrəbəl] *adj* : indeseable
undesirable[2] *n* : indeseable *mf*
undeveloped [ˌʌndiˈvɛləpt] *adj* : sin desarrollar, sin revelar (dícese de una
película)
undies [ˈʌndiːz] → **underwear**
undignified [ˌʌnˈdɪgnəfaɪd] *adj* : indecoroso
undiluted [ˌʌndaɪˈluːtəd, -də-] *adj* : sin diluir, concentrado
undisciplined [ˌʌnˈdɪsəplənd] *adj* : indisciplinado
undiscovered [ˌʌndɪˈskʌvərd] *adj* : no
descubierto
undisputed [ˌʌndɪˈspjuːtəd] *adj* : indiscutible
undisturbed [ˌʌndɪˈstərbd] *adj* : tranquilo
(dícese de una persona), sin tocar (dícese
de un objeto)
undivided [ˌʌndɪˈvaɪdəd] *adj* : íntegro,
completo

undo [ˌʌnˈduː] *vt* **-did** [-ˈdɪd]; **-done**
[-ˈdʌn]; **-doing 1** UNFASTEN : desabrochar, desatar, abrir **2** ANNUL : anular **3** REVERSE : deshacer, reparar
(daños, etc.) **4** RUIN : arruinar, destruir
undoing [ˌʌnˈduːɪŋ] *n* : ruina *f*, perdición *f*
undoubted [ˌʌnˈdaʊtəd] *adj* : cierto, indudable — **undoubtedly** *adv*
undress [ˌʌnˈdrɛs] *vt* : desvestir, desabrigar,
desnudar — *vi* : desvestirse, desnudarse
undue [ˌʌnˈduː, -ˈdjuː] *adj* : excesivo, indebido — **unduly** *adv*
undulate [ˈʌndʒəˌleɪt] *vi* **-lated; -lating**
: ondular
undulation [ˌʌndʒəˈleɪʃən] *n* : ondulación *f*
undying [ˌʌnˈdaɪɪŋ] *adj* : perpetuo, imperecedero
unearth [ˌʌnˈərθ] *vt* **1** EXHUME : desenterrar, exhumar **2** DISCOVER : descubrir
unearthly [ˌʌnˈərθli] *adj* **unearthlier; -est**
: sobrenatural, de otro mundo
unease [ˌʌnˈiːz] *n* : inquietud *f*
uneasily [ˌʌnˈiːzəli] *adv* : inquietamente,
con inquietud
uneasiness [ˌʌnˈiːzinəs] *n* : inquietud *f*
uneasy [ˌʌnˈiːzi] *adj* **uneasier; -est 1**
AWKWARD : incómodo **2** WORRIED
: preocupado, inquieto **3** RESTLESS : inquieto, agitado
uneducated [ˌʌnˈɛdʒəˌkeɪtəd] *adj* : inculto, sin educación
unemotional [ˌʌniˈmoːʃənəl] *adj* **1** COLD
: frío, indiferente **2** IMPARTIAL : imparcial, objetivo
unemployed [ˌʌnɪmˈplɔɪd] *adj* : desempleado
unemployment [ˌʌnɪmˈplɔɪmənt] *n* : desempleo *m*
unending [ˌʌnˈɛndɪŋ] *adj* ENDLESS : interminable, inacabable, sin fin
unenthusiastic [ˌʌnɪnˌθuːziˈæstɪk, -ɛn-,
-ˌθjuː-] *adj* : poco entusiasta, tibio
unenviable [ˌʌnˈɛnviəbəl] *adj* : nada envidiable
unequal [ˌʌnˈiːkwəl] *adj* **1** : desigual **2**
INADEQUATE : incapaz, incompetente
⟨to be unequal to a task : no estar a la
altura de una tarea⟩
unequaled *or* **unequalled** [ˌʌnˈiːkwəld]
adj : sin igual
unequivocal [ˌʌniˈkwɪvəkəl] *adj* : inequívoco, claro — **unequivocally** *adv*
unerring [ˌʌnˈɛrɪŋ, -ˈər-] *adj* : infalible
unethical [ˌʌnˈɛθɪkəl] *adj* : poco ético
uneven [ˌʌnˈiːvən] *adj* **1** ODD : impar
(dícese de un número) **2** : desigual, disparejo, desnivelado (dícese de una superficie) ⟨uneven terrain : terreno acciden-
tado⟩ **3** IRREGULAR : irregular,
desigual, disparejo **4** UNEQUAL
: desigual — **unevenly** [ˌʌnˈiːvənli] *adv*
unevenness [ˌʌnˈiːvənnəs] *n* **1** : lo
desigual, lo desnivelado (de una superficie) **2** IRREGULARITY : irregularidad
f **3** : lo desigual (de una contienda, etc.)
uneventful [ˌʌnɪˈvɛntfəl] *adj* : sin incidentes, tranquilo
unexpected [ˌʌnɪkˈspɛktəd] *adj* : imprevisto, inesperado — **unexpectedly** *adv*

unexplored [ˌʌnɪkˈsplord] adj : inexplorado

unfailing [ˌʌnˈfeɪlɪŋ] adj 1 CONSTANT : constante 2 INEXHAUSTIBLE : inagotable 3 SURE : a toda prueba, indefectible

unfair [ˌʌnˈfær] adj : injusto — **unfairly** adv

unfairness [ˌʌnˈfærnəs] n : injusticia f

unfaithful [ˌʌnˈfeɪθfəl] adj : desleal, infiel — **unfaithfully** adv

unfaithfulness [ˌʌnˈfeɪθfəlnəs] n : infidelidad f, deslealtad f

unfamiliar [ˌʌnfəˈmɪljər] adj 1 STRANGE : desconocido, extraño ⟨an unfamiliar place : un lugar nuevo⟩ 2 **to be unfamiliar with** : no estar familiarizado con, desconocer

unfamiliarity [ˌʌnfəˌmɪliˈærəti] n : falta f de familiaridad

unfashionable [ˌʌnˈfæʃənəbəl] adj : fuera de moda

unfasten [ˌʌnˈfæsən] vt : desabrochar, desatar (una cuerda, etc.), abrir (una puerta)

unfavorable [ˌʌnˈfeɪvərəbəl] adj : desfavorable, mal — **unfavorably** [-bli] adv

unfeeling [ˌʌnˈfiːlɪŋ] adj : insensible — **unfeelingly** adv

unfinished [ˌʌnˈfɪnɪʃd] adj : inacabado, incompleto

unfit [ˌʌnˈfɪt] adj 1 UNSUITABLE : inadecuado, impropio 2 UNSUITED : no apto, incapaz 3 : incapacitado (físicamente) ⟨to be unfit : no estar en forma⟩

unflagging [ˌʌnˈflæɡɪŋ] adj : inagotable

unflappable [ˌʌnˈflæpəbəl] adj : imperturbable

unflattering [ˌʌnˈflætərɪŋ] adj : poco favorecedor

unfold [ˌʌnˈfoːld] vt 1 EXPAND : desplegar, desdoblar, extender ⟨to unfold a map : desplegar un mapa⟩ 2 DISCLOSE, REVEAL : revelar, exponer (un plan, etc.) — vi 1 DEVELOP : desarrollarse, desenvolverse ⟨the story unfolded : el cuento se desarrollaba⟩ 2 EXPAND : extenderse, desplegarse

unforeseeable [ˌʌnforˈsiːəbəl] adj : imprevisible

unforeseen [ˌʌnforˈsiːn] adj : imprevisto

unforgettable [ˌʌnfərˈɡɛtəbəl] adj : inolvidable, memorable — **unforgettably** [-bli] adv

unforgivable [ˌʌnfərˈɡɪvəbəl] adj : imperdonable

unfortunate¹ [ˌʌnˈfɔrtʃənət] adj 1 UNLUCKY : desgraciado, infortunado, desafortunado ⟨how unfortunate! : ¡qué mala suerte!⟩ 2 INAPPROPRIATE : inoportuno ⟨an unfortunate comment : un comentario poco feliz⟩

unfortunate² n : desgraciado m, -da f

unfortunately [ˌʌnˈfɔrtʃənətli] adv : desafortunadamente

unfounded [ˌʌnˈfaʊndəd] adj : infundado

unfreeze [ˌʌnˈfriːz] v **-froze** [-ˈfroːz]; **-frozen** [-ˈfroːzən]; **-freezing** vt : descongelar — vi : descongelarse

unfriend [ˌʌnˈfrɛnd] vt : eliminar (a alguien) de sus amigos (en una red social)

unfriendliness [ˌʌnˈfrɛndlinəs] n : hostilidad f, antipatía f

unfriendly [ˌʌnˈfrɛndli] adj **unfriendlier**; **-est** : poco amistoso, hostil

unfulfilled [ˌʌnfʊlˈfɪld] adj 1 UNSATISFIED : insatisfecho 2 : no realizado

unfurl [ˌʌnˈfərl] vt : desplegar, desdoblar — vi : desplegarse

unfurnished [ˌʌnˈfərnɪʃt] adj : desamueblado

ungainly [ˌʌnˈɡeɪnli] adj : desgarbado

ungodly [ˌʌnˈɡɑːdli, -ˈɡɑd-] adj 1 IMPIOUS : impío 2 OUTRAGEOUS : atroz, terrible ⟨at an ungodly hour : a una hora intempestiva⟩

ungovernable [ˌʌnˈɡʌvərnəbəl] adj : ingobernable

ungracious [ˌʌnˈɡreɪʃəs] adj : descortés

ungrateful [ˌʌnˈɡreɪtfəl] adj : desagradecido, ingrato — **ungratefully** adv

ungratefulness [ˌʌnˈɡreɪtfəlnəs] n : ingratitud f

unguarded [ˌʌnˈɡɑrdəd] adj 1 CARELESS : irreflexivo, desprevenido 2 UNPROTECTED : sin vigilancia, no vigilado

unhappily [ˌʌnˈhæpəli] adv 1 SADLY : tristemente 2 UNFORTUNATELY : desafortunadamente, lamentablemente

unhappiness [ˌʌnˈhæpinəs] n : infelicidad f, tristeza f, desdicha f

unhappy [ˌʌnˈhæpi] adj **unhappier**; **-est** 1 UNFORTUNATE : desafortunado, desventurado 2 MISERABLE, SAD : infeliz, triste, desdichado 3 INOPPORTUNE : inoportuno, poco feliz

unharmed [ˌʌnˈhɑrmd] adj : salvo, ileso

unhealthy [ˌʌnˈhɛlθi] adj **unhealthier**; **-est** 1 UNWHOLESOME : insalubre, malsano, nocivo a la salud ⟨an unhealthy climate : un clima insalubre⟩ 2 SICKLY : de mala salud, enfermizo

unheard-of [ˌʌnˈhərdəv] adj : sin precedente, inaudito, insólito

unhelpful [ˌʌnˈhɛlpfəl] adj : poco servicial (dícese de personas), inútil (dícese de consejos, etc.)

unhinge [ˌʌnˈhɪndʒ] vt **-hinged**; **-hinging** 1 : desquiciar (una puerta, etc.) 2 DISRUPT, UNSETTLE : trastornar, perturbar

unhitch [ˌʌnˈhɪtʃ] vt : desenganchar

unholy [ˌʌnˈhoːli] adj **unholier**, **-est** 1 : profano, impío 2 UNGODLY : atroz, terrible

unhook [ˌʌnˈhʊk] vt 1 : desenganchar, descolgar (de algo) 2 UNDO : desabrochar

unhurried [ˌʌnˈhərid] adj : lento, sin prisas

unhurt [ˌʌnˈhərt] adj : ileso

unhygienic [ˌʌnhaɪˈdʒɛnɪk, -ˈdʒiː-; -ˌhaɪdiˈɛnɪk] adj : antihigiénico

unicorn [ˈjuːnəˌkɔrn] n : unicornio m

unidentified [ˌʌnaɪˈdɛntəˌfaɪd] adj : no identificado ⟨unidentified flying object : objeto volador no identificado⟩

unification [ˌjuːnəfəˈkeɪʃən] n : unificación f

uniform¹ [ˈjuːnəˌfɔrm] adj : uniforme, homogéneo, constante — **uniformly** adv

uniform² *n* : uniforme *m*
uniformed [ˈjuːnəˌfɔrmd] *adj* : uniformado
uniformity [ˌjuːnəˈfɔrməṱi] *n*, *pl* **-ties** : uniformidad *f*
unify [ˈjuːnəˌfaɪ] *vt* **-fied; -fying** : unificar, unir
unilateral [ˌjuːnəˈlæṱərəl] *adj* : unilateral — **unilaterally** *adv*
unimaginable [ˌvnɪˈmæɒ ənəbəl] *adj* : inimaginable, inconcebible
unimaginative [ˌvnɪˈmæɒ ənəṱɪv, -ə,nerṱɪv] *adj* : poco imaginativo
unimportant [ˌvnɪmˈpɔrtənt] *adj* : intrascendente, insignificante, sin importancia
unimpressive [ˌvnɪmˈprɛsɪv] *adj* : mediocre
uninformed [ˌvnɪnˈfɔrmd] *adj* : no enterado
uninhabitable [ˌvnɪnˈhæbəṱəbəl] *adj* : inhabitable
uninhabited [ˌvnɪnˈhæbəṱəd] *adj* : deshabitado, desierto, despoblado
uninhibited [ˌvnɪnˈhɪbəṱəd] *adj* : desenfadado, desinhibido, sin reservas
uninjured [ˌvnˈɪnɒ ərd] *adj* : ileso
unintelligent [ˌvnɪnˈtɛlɒ ənt] *adj* : poco inteligente
unintelligible [ˌvnɪnˈtɛlɒ əbəl] *adj* : ininteligible, incomprensible
unintentional [ˌvnɪnˈtɛntʃənəl] *adj* : no deliberado, involuntario
unintentionally [ˌvnɪnˈtɛntʃənəli] *adv* : involuntariamente, sin querer
uninterested [ˌvnˈɪntəˌrɛstəd, -trəstəd] *adj* : indiferente
uninteresting [ˌvnˈɪntəˌrɛstɪŋ, -trəstɪŋ] *adj* : poco interesante, sin interés
uninterrupted [ˌvnˌɪntəˈrvptəd] *adj* : ininterrumpido, continuo
uninvited [ˌvnɪnˈvaɪṱəd] *adj* : no invitado ⟨she showed up uninvited : vino sin que nadie la invitara⟩
uninviting [ˌvnɪnˈvaɪṱɪŋ] *adj* : poco acogedor (dícese de una casa, etc.), poco atractivo
union [ˈjuːnjən] *n* **1** : unión *f* **2** *or* **labor union** : sindicato *m*, gremio *m*
unionism [ˈjuːnjəˌnɪzəm] *n* : sindicalismo *m* — **unionist** [ˈjuːnjənɪst] *n*
unionize [ˈjuːnjəˌnaɪz] *v* **-ized; -izing** *vt* : sindicalizar, sindicar — *vi* : sindicalizarse
unique [juˈniːk] *adj* **1** SOLE : único, solo **2** UNUSUAL : extraordinario
uniquely [juˈniːkli] *adv* **1** EXCLUSIVELY : exclusivamente **2** EXCEPTIONALLY : excepcionalmente
uniqueness [juˈniːknəs] *n* : singularidad *f*
unison [ˈjuːnəsən, -zən] *n* **1** : unísono *m* (en música) **2** CONCORD : acuerdo *m*, armonía *f*, concordia *f* **3 in ~** SIMULTANEOUSLY : simultáneamente, al unísono
unit [ˈjuːnɪt] *n* **1** : unidad *f* **2** : módulo *m* (de un mobiliario)
unitary [ˈjuːnəˌteri] *adj* : unitario
unite [juˈnaɪt] *v* **united; uniting** *vt* : unir, juntar, combinar — *vi* : unirse, juntarse
unity [ˈjuːnəṱi] *n*, *pl* **-ties** **1** UNION : unidad *f*, unión *f* **2** HARMONY : armonía *f*, acuerdo *m*

universal [ˌjuːnəˈvərsəl] *adj* **1** GENERAL : general, universal ⟨a universal rule : una regla universal⟩ **2** WORLDWIDE : universal, mundial — **universality** *n* — **universally** *adv*
universe [ˈjuːnəˌvərs] *n* : universo *m*
university [ˌjuːnəˈvərsəṱi] *n*, *pl* **-ties** : universidad *f*
unjust [ˌvnˈɒ vst] *adj* : injusto — **unjustly** *adv*
unjustifiable [ˌvnˌɒ vstəˈfaɪəbəl] *adj* : injustificable — **unjustifiably** *adv*
unjustified [ˌvnˈɒ vstəˌfaɪd] *adj* : injustificado
unkempt [ˌvnˈkɛmpt] *adj* : descuidado, desaliñado, despeinado (dícese del pelo)
unkind [ˌvnˈkaɪnd] *adj* : poco amable, cruel — **unkindly** *adv*
unkindness [ˌvnˈkaɪndnəs] *n* : crueldad *f*, falta *f* de amabilidad
unknowing [ˌvnˈnoːɪŋ] *adj* : inconsciente, ignorante — **unknowingly** *adv*
unknown [ˌvnˈnoːn] *adj* : desconocido
unlawful [ˌvnˈlɔfəl] *adj* : ilícito, ilegal — **unlawfully** *adv*
unleaded [ˌvnˈlɛdəd] *adj* : sin plomo
unleash [ˌvnˈliːʃ] *vt* : soltar, desatar
unless [ənˈlɛs] *conj* : a menos que, salvo que, a no ser que
unlike¹ [ˌvnˈlaɪk] *adj* **1** DIFFERENT : diferente, distinto **2** UNEQUAL : desigual
unlike² *prep* **1** : diferente de, distinto de ⟨unlike the others : distinto a los demás⟩ **2** : a diferencia de ⟨unlike her sister, she is shy : a diferencia de su hermana, es tímida⟩
unlikelihood [ˌvnˈlaɪkliˌhʊd] *n* : improbabilidad *f*
unlikely [ˌvnˈlaɪkli] *adj* **unlikelier; -est 1** IMPROBABLE : improbable, poco probable **2** UNPROMISING : poco prometedor
unlimited [ˌvnˈlɪməṱəd] *adj* : ilimitado
unlisted [ənˈlɪstəd] *adj* : que no aparece en la guía telefónica
unload [ˌvnˈloːd] *vt* **1** REMOVE : descargar, desembarcar (mercancías o pasajeros) **2** : descargar (un avión, un camión, etc.) **3** DUMP : deshacerse de — *vi* : descargar (dícese de un avión, un camión, etc.)
unlock [ˌvnˈlɑk] *vt* **1** : abrir (con llave) **2** DISCLOSE, REVEAL : revelar
unluckily [ˌvnˈlvkəli] *adv* : desgraciadamente
unlucky [ˌvnˈlvki] *adj* **unluckier; -est 1** : de mala suerte, desgraciado, desafortunado ⟨an unlucky year : un año de mala suerte⟩ **2** INAUSPICIOUS : desfavorable, poco propicio **3** REGRETTABLE : lamentable
unmanageable [ˌvnˈmænɪɒ əbəl] *adj* : difícil de controlar, poco manejable, ingobernable
unmanned [ˌvnˈmænd] *adj* : no tripulado, sin tripulación
unmarried [ˌvnˈmærid] *adj* : soltero
unmask [ˌvnˈmæsk] *vt* EXPOSE : desenmascarar
unmerciful [ˌvnˈmərsɪfəl] *adj* MERCILESS : despiadado — **unmercifully** *adv*

unmistakable [ˌʌnmɪˈsteɪkəbəl] *adj* : evidente, inconfundible, obvio — **unmistakably** [-bli] *adv*

unmotivated [ˌʌnˈmoːṱoˌveɪṱəd] *adj* : inmotivado

unmoved [ˌʌnˈmuːvd] *adj* : impasible ⟨to be unmoved by : permanecer impasible ante⟩

unnatural [ˌʌnˈnætʃərəl] *adj* **1** ABNORMAL, UNUSUAL : anormal, poco natural, poco normal **2** AFFECTED : afectado, forzado ⟨an unnatural smile : una sonrisa forzada⟩ **3** PERVERSE : perverso, antinatural

unnecessary [ˌʌnˈnɛsəˌsɛri] *adj* : innecesario — **unnecessarily** [-ˌnɛsəˈsɛrəli] *adv*

unnerve [ˌʌnˈnərv] *vt* -**nerved; -nerving** : turbar, desconcertar, poner nervioso

unnoticed [ˌʌnˈnoːṱəst] *adj* : inadvertido ⟨to go unnoticed : pasar inadvertido⟩

unobjectionable [ˌʌnəbˈʤɛkʃənəbəl] *adj* : inobjetable

unobstructed [ˌʌnəbˈstrʌktəd] *adj* : libre, despejado

unobtainable [ˌʌnəbˈteɪnəbəl] *adj* : inasequible

unobtrusive [ˌʌnəbˈstruːsɪv] *adj* : discreto

unoccupied [ˌʌnˈɑkjəˌpaɪd] *adj* **1** IDLE : desempleado, desocupado **2** EMPTY : desocupado, libre, deshabitado

unofficial [ˌʌnəˈfɪʃəl] *adj* : extraoficial, no oficial, oficioso

unopened [ˌʌnˈoːpənd] *adj* : sin abrir

unorganized [ˌʌnˈɔrgəˌnaɪzd] *adj* : desorganizado

unorthodox [ˌʌnˈɔrθəˌdɑks] *adj* : poco ortodoxo, poco convencional

unpack [ˌʌnˈpæk] *vt* : desempacar — *vi* : desempacar, deshacer las maletas

unpaid [ˌʌnˈpeɪd] *adj* : no remunerado, no retribuido ⟨an unpaid bill : una cuenta pendiente⟩

unparalleled [ˌʌnˈpærəˌlɛld] *adj* : sin igual

unpatriotic [ˌʌnˌpeɪtriˈɑṱɪk] *adj* : antipatriótico

unpayable [ˌʌnˈpeɪəbəl] *adj* : impagable

unpleasant [ˌʌnˈplɛzənt] *adj* : desagradable — **unpleasantly** *adv*

unplug [ˌʌnˈplʌɡ] *vt* -**plugged; -plugging 1** UNCLOG : destapar, desatascar **2** DISCONNECT : desconectar, desenchufar

unpolished [ˌʌnˈpɑlɪʃt] *adj* IMPERFECT : poco pulido

unpopular [ˌʌnˈpɑpjələr] *adj* : impopular, poco popular

unprecedented [ˌʌnˈprɛsəˌdɛntəd] *adj* : sin precedentes, inaudito, nuevo

unpredictable [ˌʌnpriˈdɪktəbəl] *adj* : impredecible

unprejudiced [ˌʌnˈprɛdʒədəst] *adj* : imparcial, objetivo

unprepared [ˌʌnpriˈpærd] *adj* : no preparado ⟨an unprepared speech : un discurso improvisado⟩

unpretentious [ˌʌnpriˈtɛntʃəs] *adj* : modesto, sin pretensiones

unprincipled [ˌʌnˈprɪntʃəpəld] *adj* : sin principios, carente de escrúpulos

unproductive [ˌʌnprəˈdʌktɪv] *adj* : improductivo

unprofessional [ˌʌnprəˈfɛʃənəl] *adj* : poco profesional

unprofitable [ˌʌnˈprɑfəṱəbəl] *adj* : no rentable, poco provechoso

unpromising [ˌʌnˈprɑməsɪŋ] *adj* : poco prometedor

unprotected [ˌʌnprəˈtɛktəd] *adj* : sin protección, desprotegido

unproven [ˌʌnˈpruːvən] *adj* : no demostrado

unprovoked [ˌʌnprəˈvoːkt] *adj* : no provocado

unpublished [ˌʌnˈpʌblɪʃt] *adj* : inédito

unpunished [ˌʌnˈpʌnɪʃt] *adj* : impune ⟨to go unpunished : escapar sin castigo⟩

unqualified [ˌʌnˈkwɑləˌfaɪd] *adj* **1** : no calificado, sin título **2** COMPLETE : completo, absoluto ⟨an unqualified denial : una negación incondicional⟩

unquestionable [ˌʌnˈkwɛstʃənəbəl] *adj* : incuestionable, indudable, indiscutible — **unquestionably** [-bli] *adv*

unquestioning [ˌʌnˈkwɛstʃənɪŋ] *adj* : incondicional, absoluto, ciego

unravel [ˌʌnˈrævəl] *v* -**eled** *or* -**elled; -eling** *or* -**elling** *vt* **1** DISENTANGLE : desenmarañar, desenredar **2** SOLVE : aclarar, desenmarañar, desentrañar — *vi* : deshacerse

unreachable [ˌʌnˈriːtʃəbəl] *adj* : inalcanzable

unreadable [ˌʌnˈriːdəbəl] *adj* **1** ILLEGIBLE : ilegible **2** : difícil de leer

unreal [ˌʌnˈriːl] *adj* : irreal

unrealistic [ˌʌnˌriːəˈlɪstɪk] *adj* : poco realista

unreasonable [ˌʌnˈriːzənəbəl] *adj* **1** IRRATIONAL : poco razonable, irrazonable, irracional **2** EXCESSIVE : excesivo ⟨unreasonable prices : precios excesivos⟩

unreasonably [ˌʌnˈriːzənəbli] *adv* **1** IRRATIONALLY : irracionalmente, de manera irrazonable **2** EXCESSIVELY : excesivamente

unrecognizable [ˌʌnˈrɛkəɡˌnaɪzəbəl] *adj* : irreconocible

unrefined [ˌʌnriˈfaɪnd] *adj* **1** : no refinado, sin refinar (dícese del azúcar, de la harina, etc.) **2** : poco refinado, inculto (dícese de una persona)

unrelated [ˌʌnriˈleɪṱəd] *adj* : no relacionado, inconexo

unrelenting [ˌʌnriˈlɛntɪŋ] *adj* **1** STERN : severo, inexorable **2** CONSTANT, RELENTLESS : constante, implacable

unreliable [ˌʌnriˈlaɪəbəl] *adj* : que no es de fiar, de poca confianza, inestable (dícese del tiempo)

unrepeatable [ˌʌnriˈpiːṱəbəl] *adj* : irrepetible

unrepentant [ˌʌnriˈpɛntənt] *adj* : impenitente

unrepresentative [ˌʌnˌrɛprɪˈzɛntəṱɪv] *adj* : poco representativo

unrequited [ˌʌnriˈkwaɪṱəd] *adj* : no correspondido

unreserved [ˌʌnrɪˈzərvd] *adv* **1** UNLIMITED : sin reservas **2** : sin reservar unresolved [ˌʌnri'zɑlvd] *adj* : pendiente, no resuelto

unresponsive [ˌʌnrɪ'spɑntsɪv] *adj* **1** : indiferente **2** : insensible, inconsciente (en medicina)

unrest [ˌʌn'rɛst] *n* : inquietud *f*, malestar *m* ⟨political unrest : disturbios políticos⟩

unrestrained [ˌʌnri'streɪnd] *adj* : desenfrenado, incontrolado

unrestricted [ˌʌnri'strɪktəd] *adj* : sin restricción ⟨unrestricted access : libre acceso⟩

unrewarding [ˌʌnri'wɔrdɪŋ] *adj* THANKLESS : ingrato

unripe [ˌʌn'raɪp] *adj* : inmaduro, verde

unrivaled *or* unrivalled [ˌʌn'raɪvəld] *adj* : incomparable

unroll [ˌʌn'roːl] *vt* : desenrollar — *vi* : desenrollarse

unruffled [ˌʌn'rʌfəld] *adj* **1** SERENE : sereno, tranquilo **2** SMOOTH : tranquilo, liso ⟨unruffled waters : aguas tranquilas⟩

unruliness [ˌʌn'ruːlinəs] *n* : indisciplina *f*

unruly [ˌʌn'ruːli] *adj* : indisciplinado, díscolo, rebelde

unsafe [ˌʌn'seɪf] *adj* : inseguro

unsaid [ˌʌn'sɛd] *adj* : sin decir ⟨to leave unsaid : quedar por decir⟩

unsalted [ˌʌn'sɔltəd] *adj* : sin sal

unsanitary [ˌʌn'sænəˌteri] *adj* : antihigiénico

unsatisfactory [ˌʌnˌsætəs'fæktəri] *adj* : insatisfactorio

unsatisfied [ˌʌn'sætəsˌfaɪd] *adj* : insatisfecho

unsavory [ˌʌn'seɪvəri] *adj* : desagradable

unscathed [ˌʌn'skeɪðd] *adj* UNHARMED : ileso

unscheduled [ˌʌn'skɛˌɪuːld] *adj* : no programado, imprevisto

unscientific [ˌʌnˌsaɪən'tɪfɪk] *adj* : poco científico

unscramble [ˌʌn'skræmbəl] *vt* : descifrar, descodificar (una señal, etc.)

unscrew [ˌʌn'skruː] *vt* **1** : quitar (una tapa, etc.) **2** : destornillar

unscrupulous [ˌʌn'skruːpjələs] *adj* : inescrupuloso, sin escrúpulos — unscrupulously *adv*

unseal [ˌʌn'siːl] *vt* : abrir, quitarle el sello a

unseasonable [ˌʌn'siːzənəbəl] *adj* **1** : extemporáneo ⟨unseasonable rain : lluvia extemporánea⟩ **2** UNTIMELY : extemporáneo, inoportuno

unseat [ˌʌn'siːt] *vt* : derribar, derrocar

unseemly [ˌʌn'siːmli] *adj* unseemlier; -est **1** INDECOROUS : indecoroso **2** INAPPROPRIATE : impropio, inapropiado

unseen [ˌʌn'siːn] *adj* **1** UNNOTICED : inadvertido **2** INVISIBLE : oculto, invisible

unselfish [ˌʌn'sɛlfɪʃ] *adj* : generoso, desinteresado — unselfishly *adv*

unselfishness [ˌʌn'sɛlfɪʃnəs] *n* : generosidad *f*, desinterés *m*

unsentimental [ˌʌnˌsɛntə'mɛntəl] *adj* : poco sentimental

unsettle [ˌʌn'sɛtəl] *vt* -tled; -tling DISTURB : trastornar, alterar, perturbar

unsettled [ˌʌn'sɛtəld] *adj* **1** CHANGEABLE : inestable, variable ⟨unsettled weather : tiempo inestable⟩ **2** DISTURBED : agitado, inquieto ⟨unsettled waters : aguas agitadas⟩ **3** UNDECIDED : pendiente (dícese de un asunto), indeciso (dícese de una persona) **4** UNPAID : sin saldar, pendiente **5** UNINHABITED : despoblado, no colonizado

unsettling [ˌʌn'sɛtlɪŋ] *adj* : inquietante

unshakable [ˌʌn'ʃeɪkəbəl] *adj* : inquebrantable

unshaped [ˌʌn'ʃeɪpt] *adj* : sin forma, informe

unshaven [ˌʌn'ʃeɪvən] *adj* : sin afeitar, sin rasurar

unsheathe [ˌʌn'ʃiːð] *vt* : desenvainar

unsightly [ˌʌn'saɪtli] *adj* UGLY : feo, de aspecto malo

unsigned [ˌʌn'saɪnd] *adj* : sin firmar

unskilled [ˌʌn'skɪld] *adj* : no calificado

unsmiling [ˌʌn'smaɪlɪŋ] *adj* : de aspecto serio

unsnap [ˌʌn'snæp] *vt* -snapped; -snapping : desabrochar

unsociable [ˌʌn'soːʃəbəl] *adj* : poco sociable

unsolicited [ˌʌnsə'lɪsəˌɪəd] *adj* : no solicitado

unsolved [ˌʌn'sɔlvd] *adj* : no resuelto, sin resolver

unsophisticated [ˌʌnsə'fɪstəˌkeɪtəd] *adj* **1** NAIVE : ingenuo, de poco mundo **2** SIMPLE : simple, poco sofisticado, rudimentario

unsound [ˌʌn'saʊnd] *adj* **1** UNHEALTHY : enfermizo, de mala salud **2** : poco sólido, defectuoso (dícese de una estructura, etc.) **3** INVALID : inválido, erróneo **4 of unsound mind** : mentalmente incapacitado

unspeakable [ˌʌn'spiːkəbəl] *adj* **1** INDESCRIBABLE : indecible, inexpresable, incalificable **2** HEINOUS : atroz, nefando, abominable — unspeakably [-bli] *adv*

unspecified [ˌʌn'spɛsəˌfaɪd] *adj* : indeterminado, sin especificar

unspoiled [ˌʌn'spɔɪld] *adj* **1** : conservado, sin estropear (dícese de un lugar) **2** : que no está mimado (dícese de un niño)

unspoken [ˌʌn'spoːkən] *adj* TACIT : tácito

unstable [ˌʌn'steɪbəl] *adj* **1** CHANGEABLE : variable, inestable, cambiable ⟨an unstable pulse : un pulso irregular⟩ **2** UNSTEADY : inestable, poco sólido (dícese de una estructura)

unsteadily [ˌʌn'stɛdəli] *adv* : de modo inestable

unsteadiness [ˌʌn'stɛdinəs] *n* : inestabilidad *f*, inseguridad *f*

unsteady [ˌʌn'stɛdi] *adj* **1** UNSTABLE : inestable, variable **2** SHAKY : tembloroso

unstoppable [ˌʌn'stɑpəbəl] *adj* : irrefrenable, incontenible

unsubscribe [ˌʌnsəb'skraɪb] *vi* -scribed; -scribing : darse de baja, cancelar la suscripción

unsubstantiated [ˌʌnsəbˈstæntʃiˌeɪtəd] *adj* : no corroborado, no demostrado

unsuccessful [ˌʌnsəkˈsɛsfəl] *adj* : fracasado, infructuoso

unsuitable [ˌʌnˈsuːʈəbəl] *adj* : inadecuado, impropio, inapropiado ⟨an unsuitable time : una hora inconveniente⟩

unsuited [ˌʌnˈsuːʈəd] *adj* : inadecuado, inepto

unsung [ˌʌnˈsʌŋ] *adj* : olvidado

unsure [ˌʌnˈʃʊr] *adj* : incierto, dudoso

unsurpassed [ˌʌnsərˈpæst] *adj* : sin par, sin igual

unsuspecting [ˌʌnsəˈspɛktɪŋ] *adj* : desprevenido, desapercibido, confiado

unsweetened [ˌʌnˈswiːtənd] *adj* : sin endulzar

unsympathetic [ˌʌnˌsɪmpəˈθɛʈɪk] *adj* : poco comprensivo, indiferente

untamed [ˌʌnˈteɪmd] *adj* : indómito, agreste

untangle [ˌʌnˈtæŋɡəl] *vt* -gled; -gling : desenmarañar, desenredar

untapped [ˌʌnˈtæpt] *adj* : sin explotar

untenable [ˌʌnˈtɛnəbəl] *adj* : insostenible

unthinkable [ˌʌnˈθɪŋkəbəl] *adj* : inconcebible, impensable

unthinking [ˌʌnˈθɪŋkɪŋ] *adj* : irreflexivo, inconsciente — **unthinkingly** *adv*

untidiness [ˌʌnˈtaɪdinəs] *n* : desarreglo *m*

untidy [ˌʌnˈtaɪdi] *adj* 1 SLOVENLY : desaliñado 2 DISORDERLY : desordenado, desarreglado — **untidily** *adv*

untie [ˌʌnˈtaɪ] *vt* -tied; -tying *or* -tieing : desatar, deshacer

until¹ [ˌʌnˈtɪl] *prep* : hasta ⟨until now : hasta ahora⟩

until² *conj* : hasta que ⟨until they left : hasta que salieron⟩ ⟨don't answer until you're sure : no contestes hasta que (no) estés seguro⟩

untimely [ˌʌnˈtaɪmli] *adj* 1 PREMATURE : prematuro ⟨an untimely death : una muerte prematura⟩ 2 INOPPORTUNE : inoportuno, intempestivo

untold [ˌʌnˈtoːld] *adj* 1 : nunca dicho ⟨the untold secret : el secreto sin contar⟩ 2 INCALCULABLE : incalculable, indecible

untouchable [ˌʌnˈtʌtʃəbəl] *adj* : intocable

untouched [ˌʌnˈtʌtʃt] *adj* 1 INTACT : intacto, sin tocar, sin probar (dícese de la comida) 2 UNAFFECTED : insensible, indiferente

untoward [ˌʌnˈtɔrd, -ˈtoːərd, -tə-ˈwɔrd] *adj* 1 : indecoroso, impropio (dícese del comportamiento) 2 ADVERSE, UNFORTUNATE : desafortunado, adverso ⟨untoward effects : efectos perjudiciales⟩ 3 UNSEEMLY : indecoroso

untrained [ˌʌnˈtreɪnd] *adj* : inexperto, no capacitado

untreated [ˌʌnˈtriːʈəd] *adj* : no tratado (dícese de una enfermedad, etc.), sin tratar (dícese de un material)

untroubled [ˌʌnˈtrʌbəld] *adj* : tranquilo ⟨to be untroubled by : no estar afectado por⟩

untrue [ˌʌnˈtruː] *adj* 1 UNFAITHFUL : infiel 2 FALSE : falso

untrustworthy [ˌʌnˈtrʌstˌwərði] *adj* : de poca confianza (dícese de una persona), no fidedigno (dícese de la información)

untruth [ˌʌnˈtruːθ, ˈʌnˌ-] *n* : mentira *f*, falsedad *f*

untruthful [ˌʌnˈtruːθfəl] *adj* : mentiroso, falso

unusable [ˌʌnˈjuːzəbəl] *adj* : inútil, inservible

unused [ˌʌnˈjuːzd, in sense 1 usu -ˈjuːst] *adj* 1 UNACCUSTOMED : inhabituado 2 NEW : nuevo 3 IDLE : no utilizado (dícese de la tierra) 4 REMAINING : restante ⟨the unused portion : la porción restante⟩

unusual [ˌʌnˈjuːʒəl] *adj* : inusual, poco común, raro

unusually [ˌʌnˈjuːʒəli, -ˈjuːʒəli] *adv* : excepcionalmente, extraordinariamente, fuera de lo común

unveil [ˌʌnˈveɪl] *vt* 1 REVEAL : revelar 2 : develar, descubrir (una estatua, etc.)

unwanted [ˌʌnˈwɑntəd] *adj* : superfluo, de sobre

unwarranted [ˌʌnˈwɔrəntəd] *adj* : injustificado

unwary [ˌʌnˈwæri] *adj* : incauto

unwashed [ˌʌnˈwɔʃt, -ˈwɑʃt] *adj* : sin lavar, sucio

unwavering [ˌʌnˈweɪvərɪŋ] *adj* : firme, inquebrantable ⟨an unwavering gaze : una mirada fija⟩

unwed [ˌʌnˈwɛd] *adj* : soltero

unwelcome [ˌʌnˈwɛlkəm] *adj* : importuno, molesto

unwell [ˌʌnˈwɛl] *adj* : enfermo, mal

unwholesome [ˌʌnˈhoːlsəm] *adj* 1 UNHEALTHY : malsano, insalubre 2 PERNICIOUS : pernicioso 3 LOATHSOME : repugnante, muy desagradable

unwieldy [ˌʌnˈwiːldi] *adj* CUMBERSOME : difícil de manejar, torpe y pesado

unwilling [ˌʌnˈwɪlɪŋ] *adj* : poco dispuesto ⟨to be unwilling to : no estar dispuesto a⟩

unwillingly [ˌʌnˈwɪlɪŋli] *adv* : a regañadientes, de mala gana

unwillingness [ˌʌnˈwɪlɪŋnəs] *n* : desgana *f*, renuencia *f*

unwind [ˌʌnˈwaɪnd] *v* -wound [-ˈwaʊnd]; -winding *vt* UNROLL : desenrollar — *vi* 1 : desenrollarse 2 RELAX : relajarse

unwise [ˌʌnˈwaɪz] *adj* : imprudente, desacertado, poco aconsejable

unwisely [ˌʌnˈwaɪzli] *adv* : imprudentemente

unwitting [ˌʌnˈwɪʈɪŋ] *adj* 1 UNAWARE : inconsciente 2 INADVERTENT : involuntario, inadvertido ⟨an unwitting mistake : un error inadvertido⟩ — **unwittingly** *adv*

unworkable [ˌʌnˈwərkəbəl] *adj* : impracticable

unworthiness [ˌʌnˈwərðinəs] *n* : falta *f* de valía

unworthy [ˌʌnˈwərði] *adj* 1 UNDESERVING : indigno ⟨to be unworthy of : no ser digno de⟩ 2 UNMERITED : inmerecido

unwrap [ˌʌnˈræp] *vt* -**wrapped; -wrapping**
: desenvolver, deshacer
unwritten [ˌʌnˈrɪtən] *adj* : no escrito
unyielding [ˌʌnˈjiːldɪŋ] *adj* : firme, inflexible, rígido
unzip [ˌʌnˈzɪp] *vt* -**zipped; -zipping** : abrir el cierre de
up¹ [ˈʌp] *v* **upped** [ˈʌpt]; **upping; ups** *vt*
INCREASE : aumentar, subir ⟨they upped the prices : aumentaron los precios⟩ —
vi **to up and** : agarrar *y fam* ⟨she up and left : agarró y se fue⟩
up² *adv* **1** ABOVE : arriba, en lo alto ⟨up in the mountains : arriba en las montañas⟩ ⟨put it up on the shelf : ponlo en el estante⟩ ⟨we keep it up in the attic : lo guardamos arriba en el desván⟩ ⟨what's going on up there? : ¿qué pasa allí arriba?⟩ **2** UPWARDS : hacia arriba ⟨push it up : empújalo hacia arriba⟩ ⟨pull up your pants : súbete los pantalones⟩ ⟨the sun came up : el sol salió⟩ ⟨prices went up : los precios subieron⟩ ⟨she called up to me : me llamó desde abajo⟩ ⟨he looked up at the sky : miró al cielo⟩ **3** (*indicating an upright position*) ⟨to sit up : ponerse derecho⟩ **4** (*indicating a waking state*) ⟨they got up late : se levantaron tarde⟩ ⟨I stayed up all night : pasé toda la noche sin dormir⟩ **5** (*indicating a usable state*) ⟨we set up the equipment : instalamos el equipo⟩ **6** (*indicating closure*) ⟨I sealed up the package : precinté el paquete⟩ **7** (*indicating activity or excitement*) ⟨they stirred up the crowd : incitaron a la muchedumbre⟩ **8** (*indicating greater or higher volume or intensity*) ⟨to speak up : hablar más fuerte⟩ ⟨to speed up : acelerar⟩ **9** (*indicating a northerly direction*) ⟨the climate up north : el clima del norte⟩ ⟨I'm going up to Canada : voy para Canadá⟩ ⟨come up and see us! : ¡ven a visitarnos!⟩ **10** (*indicating the appearance or existence of something*) ⟨the book turned up : el libro apareció⟩ **11** (*indicating consideration*) ⟨she brought the matter up : mencionó el asunto⟩ **12** COMPLETELY : completamente ⟨eat it up : cómetelo todo⟩ **13** : en pedazos ⟨he tore it up : lo rompió en pedazos⟩ **14** (*indicating approaching and stopping*) ⟨the car pulled up to the curb : el carro paró al borde de la acera⟩ ⟨he walked up to her : se le acercó⟩ **15** (*indicating advancement or progress*) ⟨we moved up to the front of the line : nos pusimos al principio de la fila⟩ ⟨she has moved up in the company : ha ascendido en la compañía⟩ ⟨to grow up : hacerse mayor⟩ **16** (*indicating greater importance in a series, etc.*) ⟨it's pretty far/high up on my list : es muy importante para mí⟩ **17** (*indicating an even score*) ⟨the game was 10 up : empataron a 10⟩ **18 to be one up on someone** : tener ventaja sobre alguien **19 up and down** : de arriba abajo
up³ *adj* **1** (*above the horizon*) ⟨the sun is up : ha salido el sol⟩ **2** (*above a surface*) ⟨the tulips are up : los tulipanes han salido⟩ **3** (*in a high or higher position*) ⟨it's up on the top shelf : está en el estante de arriba⟩ ⟨it's further up : está más arriba⟩ ⟨I'm up here : estoy aquí arriba⟩ **4** (*in a forward place or position*) ⟨we were up near the stage : estábamos cerca del escenario⟩ ⟨the table was up against the wall : la mesa estaba contra la pared⟩ **5** (*above a normal or former level*) ⟨prices are up : los precios han aumentado⟩ ⟨the river is up : las aguas están altas⟩ **6** (*equal to a given level*) ⟨it wasn't up to our expectations : no estuvo a la altura de lo que esperábamos⟩ ⟨I've had it up to here with your nonsense! : ¡estoy hasta las narices de tus tonterías!⟩ **7** : despierto, levantado ⟨up all night : despierto toda la noche⟩ **8** BUILT : construido ⟨the house is up : la casa está construida⟩ **9** OPEN : abierto ⟨the windows are up : las ventanas están abiertas⟩ **10** (*moving or going upward*) ⟨the up staircase : la escalera para subir⟩ **11** ABREAST : enterado, al día, al corriente ⟨to be up on the news : estar al corriente de las noticias⟩ **12** PREPARED : preparado ⟨we were up for the test : estuvimos preparados para el examen⟩ **13** CAPABLE : capaz ⟨she's up to the task : es capaz de hacerlo⟩ **14** FUNCTIONING : funcionando ⟨the system is back up, the system is up and running again : el sistema ha vuelto a funcionar⟩ **15** AHEAD : ganando ⟨they're up (by) ten points : van ganando por diez puntos⟩ **16** FINISHED : terminado, acabado ⟨time is up : se ha terminado el tiempo permitido⟩ **17 to be up** : pasar ⟨what's up? : ¿qué pasa?⟩ **18 to be up and about** : estar levantado **19 to be up against** : enfrentarse a **20 to be up to something** : estar tramando algo
up⁴ *prep* **1** (*to, toward, or at a higher point of*) ⟨he went up the stairs : subió la escalera⟩ **2** (*to or toward the source of*) ⟨to go up the river : ir río arriba⟩ **3** ALONG : a lo largo, por ⟨up the coast : a lo largo de la costa⟩ ⟨just up the way : un poco más adelante⟩ ⟨up and down the city : por toda la ciudad⟩
up–and–coming *adj* : prometedor
upbraid [ˌʌpˈbreɪd] *vt* : reprender, regañar
upbringing [ˈʌpˌbrɪŋɪŋ] *n* : crianza *f*, educación *f*
upcoming [ˌʌpˈkʌmɪŋ] *adj* : próximo
update¹ [ˌʌpˈdeɪt] *vt* -**dated; -dating** : poner al día, poner al corriente, actualizar
update² [ˈʌpˌdeɪt] *n* : actualización *f*, puesta *f* al día
upend [ˌʌpˈɛnd] *vt* **1** : poner vertical **2** OVERTURN : volcar
upgrade¹ [ˈʌpˌɡreɪd, ˌʌpˈ-] *vt* -**graded; -grading 1** PROMOTE : ascender **2** IMPROVE : mejorar
upgrade² [ˈʌpˌɡreɪd] *n* **1** SLOPE : cuesta *f*, pendiente *f* **2** RISE : aumento *m* de categoría (de un puesto), ascenso *m* (de un empleado) **3** IMPROVEMENT : mejoramiento *m*

upheaval [ˌʌp'hiːvəl] *n* **1** : levantamiento *m* (en geología) **2** DISTURBANCE, UPSET : trastorno *m*, agitación *f*, conmoción *f*

uphill¹ [ˌʌp'hɪl] *adv* : cuesta arriba

uphill² ['ʌpˌhɪl] *adj* **1** ASCENDING : en subida **2** DIFFICULT : difícil, arduo

uphold [ˌʌp'hoːld] *vt* **-held; -holding 1** SUPPORT : sostener, apoyar, mantener **2** RAISE : levantar **3** CONFIRM : confirmar (una decisión judicial)

upholster [ˌʌp'hoːlstər] *vt* : tapizar

upholsterer [ˌʌp'hoːlstərər] *n* : tapicero *m*, -ra *f*

upholstery [ˌʌp'hoːlstəri] *n, pl* **-steries** : tapicería *f*

upkeep ['ʌpˌkiːp] *n* : mantenimiento *m*

upland ['ʌplənd, -ˌlænd] *n* : altiplanicie *f*, altiplano *m*

uplift¹ [ˌʌp'lɪft] *vt* **1** RAISE : elevar, levantar **2** ELEVATE : elevar, animar (el espíritu, la mente, etc.)

uplift² ['ʌpˌlɪft] *n* : elevación *f*

uplifting ['ʌpˌlɪftɪŋ] *adj* : inspirador

upload [ˌʌp'loʊd, 'ʌpˌloʊd] *vt* : cargar, subir (un archivo, etc.)

upon [ə'pɔn, ə'pɑn] *prep* : en, sobre ⟨upon the desk : sobre el escritorio⟩ ⟨upon leaving : al salir⟩ ⟨questions upon questions : pregunta tras pregunta⟩

upper¹ ['ʌpər] *adj* **1** HIGHER : superior **2** : alto (en geografía) ⟨the upper Mississippi : el alto Mississippi⟩

upper² *n* : parte *f* superior (del calzado, etc.)

uppercase¹ [ˌʌpər'keɪs] *adj* : mayúsculo

uppercase² *n* **in uppercase** : en mayúsculas

upper-class [ˌʌpər'klæs] *adj* : de clase alta

upper class *n* : clase *f* alta

upper hand *n* : ventaja *f*, dominio *m*

uppermost ['ʌpərˌmoːst] *adj* : más alto ⟨it was uppermost in his mind : era lo que más le preocupaba⟩

upright¹ ['ʌpˌraɪt] *adj* **1** VERTICAL : vertical **2** ERECT : erguido, derecho **3** JUST : recto, honesto, justo

upright² *n* : montante *m*, poste *m*, soporte *m*

uprising ['ʌpˌraɪzɪŋ] *n* : insurrección *f*, revuelta *f*, alzamiento *m*

uproar ['ʌpˌror] *n* COMMOTION : alboroto *m*, jaleo *m*, escándalo *m*

uproarious [ˌʌp'roriəs] *adj* **1** CLAMOROUS : estrepitoso, clamoroso **2** HILARIOUS : muy divertido, hilarante — **uproariously** *adv*

uproot [ˌʌp'ruːt, -'rʊt] *vt* : desarraigar

upset¹ [ˌʌp'sɛt] *vt* **-set; -setting 1** OVERTURN : volcar **2** SPILL : derramar **3** DISTURB : perturbar, disgustar, inquietar, alterar **4** SICKEN : sentar mal a ⟨it upsets my stomach : me sienta mal al estómago⟩ **5** DISRUPT : trastornar, desbaratar (planes, etc.) **6** DEFEAT : derrotar (en deportes)

upset² *adj* **1** DISPLEASED, DISTRESSED : disgustado, alterado **2 to have an upset stomach** : estar mal del estómago, estar descompuesto (de estómago)

upset³ ['ʌpˌsɛt] *n* **1** OVERTURNING : vuelco *m* **2** DISRUPTION : trastorno *m* (de planes, etc.) **3** DEFEAT : derrota *f* (en deportes)

upshot ['ʌpˌʃɑt] *n* : resultado *m* final

upside-down [ˌʌpˌsaɪd'daʊn] *adj* : al revés

upside down [ˌʌpˌsaɪd'daʊn] *adv* **1** : al revés **2** : en confusión, en desorden

upstairs¹ [ˌʌp'stærz] *adv* : arriba, en el piso superior

upstairs² ['ʌpˌstærz, ˌʌp'-] *adj* : de arriba

upstairs³ ['ʌpˌstærz, ˌʌp'-] *ns & pl* : piso *m* de arriba, planta *f* de arriba

upstanding [ˌʌp'stændɪŋ, 'ʌpˌ-] *adj* HONEST, UPRIGHT : honesto, íntegro, recto

upstart ['ʌpˌstart] *n* : advenedizo *m*, -za *f*

upstream ['ʌp'striːm] *adv* : río arriba

upsurge ['ʌpˌsərD] *n* : aumento *m* apreciable

upswing ['ʌpˌswɪŋ] *n* : alza *f*, mejora *f* notable ⟨to be on the upswing : estar mejorándose⟩

uptight [ˌʌp'taɪt] *adj* : tenso, nervioso

up to *prep* **1** : hasta ⟨up to a year : hasta un año⟩ ⟨in mud up to my ankles : en barro hasta los tobillos⟩ **2 to be up to** : estar a la altura de ⟨I'm not up to going : no estoy en condiciones de ir⟩ **3 to be up to** : depender de ⟨it's up to the director : depende del director⟩

up-to-date [ˌʌptə'deɪt] *adj* **1** CURRENT : corriente, al día ⟨to keep up-to-date : mantenerse al corriente⟩ **2** MODERN : moderno

uptown ['ʌp'taʊn] *adv* : hacia la parte alta de la ciudad, hacia el distrito residencial

upturn ['ʌpˌtərn] *n* : mejora *f*, auge *m* (económico)

upward¹ ['ʌpwərd] *or* **upwards** [-wərdz] *adv* **1** : hacia arriba **2 ~ of** : más de

upward² *adj* : ascendente, hacia arriba

upwind [ˌʌp'wɪnd] *adv & adj* : contra el viento

uranium [jʊ'reɪniəm] *n* : uranio *m*

Uranus [jʊ'reɪnəs, 'jʊrənəs] *n* : Urano *m*

urban ['ərbən] *adj* : urbano

urbane [ˌər'beɪn] *adj* : urbano, cortés

urchin ['ərtʃən] *n* **1** SCAMP : granuja *mf*; pillo *m*, -lla *f* **2 sea urchin** : erizo *m* de mar

urethra [jʊ'riːθrə] *n, pl* **-thras** *or* **-thrae** [-ˌθriː] : uretra *f*

urge¹ ['ərD] *vt* **urged; urging 1** PRESS : instar, apremiar, insistir ⟨we urged him to come : insistimos en que viniera⟩ **2** ADVOCATE : recomendar, abogar por **3 to urge on** : animar, alentar

urge² *n* : impulso *m*, ganas *fpl*, compulsión *f*

urgency ['ərD əntsi] *n, pl* **-cies** : urgencia *f*

urgent ['ərD ənt] *adj* **1** PRESSING : urgente, apremiante **2** INSISTENT : insistente **3 to be urgent** : urgir

urgently ['ərD əntli] *adv* : urgentemente

urinal ['jʊrənəl, esp Brit jʊ'raɪnəl] *n* : orinal *m*

urinary ['jʊrəˌneri] *adj* : urinario

urinate ['jʊrəˌneɪt] *vi* **-nated; -nating** : orinar

urination [ˌjʊrəˈneɪʃən] *n* : orinación *f*
urine [ˈjʊrən] *n* : orina *f*
urn [ˈərn] *n* 1 VASE : urna *f* 2 : recipiente *m* (para servir café, etc.)
Uruguayan [ˌʊrəˈɡwaɪən, ˌjʊr-, -ˈɡweɪ-] *n* : uruguayo *m*, -ya *f* — **Uruguayan** *adj*
us [ˈʌs] *pron* 1 (*as direct object*) : nos ⟨they were visiting us : nos visitaban⟩ 2 (*as indirect object*) : nos ⟨he gave us a present : nos dio un regalo⟩ 3 (*as object of preposition*) : nosotros, nosotras ⟨stay with us : quédese con nosotros⟩ ⟨both of us : nosotros dos⟩ ⟨all/some of us : todos/algunos de nosotros⟩ 4 (*for emphasis*) : nosotros, nosotras ⟨it's us! : ¡somos nosotros!⟩
usable [ˈjuːzəbəl] *adj* : utilizable
usage [ˈjuːsɪd, -zɪd] *n* 1 HABIT : costumbre *f*, hábito *m* 2 USE : uso *m*
use[1] [ˈjuːz] *v* **used** [ˈjuːzd, in phrase "used to" usually ˈjuːstu:]; **using** *vt* 1 EMPLOY, UTILIZE : usar, utilizar, emplear ⟨can I use your phone? : ¿puedo usar tu teléfono?⟩ ⟨they use traditional methods : utilizan métodos tradicionales⟩ ⟨use your head! : ¡usa la cabeza!⟩ ⟨we used a contractor : contratamos a un contratista⟩ ⟨use this to clean it : usa esto para limpiarlo, límpialo con esto⟩ ⟨he uses it as an office : lo usa de/como oficina⟩ ⟨she used the money for college : usó el dinero para pagar la matrícula (universitaria)⟩ 2 CONSUME : consumir (electricidad, etc.), tomar (drogas, etc.) 3 EXPLOIT : usar, utilizar ⟨he used his friends to get ahead : usó a sus amigos para mejorar su posición⟩ 4 TREAT : tratar ⟨they used the horse cruelly : maltrataron al caballo⟩ 5 STAND : beneficiarse de ⟨you could use a nap : una siesta te vendría bien⟩ 6 **to use up** : agotar, consumir, gastar — *vi* (*used in the past with* **to** *to indicate a former fact or state*) : soler, acostumbrar ⟨winters used to be colder : los inviernos solían ser más fríos, los inviernos eran más fríos⟩ ⟨she used to dance : acostumbraba bailar⟩
use[2] [ˈjuːs] *n* 1 : uso *m*, empleo *m*, utilización *f* ⟨ready for use : listo para usar⟩ ⟨the use of seat belts : el uso de los cinturones de seguridad⟩ ⟨to wear down from/with use : desgastarse por el uso⟩ 2 USEFULNESS : utilidad *f* ⟨to be of use : ser útil⟩ ⟨to be of no use : no servir (para nada)⟩ ⟨it's no use! : ¡es inútil!⟩ 3 : uso *m* ⟨a tool with many uses : una herramienta con muchos usos⟩ ⟨to find a use for : encontrarle uso a⟩ 4 : uso *m* ⟨to have the use of : poder usar, tener acceso a⟩ ⟨for member use only : para uso exclusivo de los socios⟩ 5 : uso *m* (de las piernas, etc.) 6 **to be in use** : usarse, estar en uso (dícese de máquinas, palabras, etc.) ⟨the room is in use : la sala está ocupada⟩ 7 **to fall out of use** : caer en desuso 8 **to have**

no use for : no necesitar ⟨she has no use for poetry : a ella no le gusta la poesía⟩ 9 **to make use of** : servirse de, aprovechar 10 **to put to (good) use** : hacer (buen) uso de
used [ˈjuːzd] *adj* 1 SECONDHAND : usado, de segunda mano ⟨used cars : coches usados⟩ 2 ACCUSTOMED : acostumbrado ⟨used to the heat : acostumbrado al calor⟩
useful [ˈjuːsfəl] *adj* : útil, práctico — **usefully** *adv*
usefulness [ˈjuːsfəlnəs] *n* : utilidad *f*
useless [ˈjuːsləs] *adj* : inútil — **uselessly** *adv*
uselessness [ˈjuːsləsnəs] *n* : inutilidad *f*
user [ˈjuːzər] *n* : usuario *m*, -ria *f*
user–friendly *adj* : fácil de usar
user name *n* : nombre *m* de usuario
usher[1] [ˈvʃər] *vt* 1 ESCORT : acompañar, conducir 2 **to usher in** : hacer pasar (a alguien) ⟨to usher in a new era : anunciar una nueva época⟩
usher[2] *n* : acomodador *m*, -dora *f*
usherette [ˌʌʃəˈrɛt] *n* : acomodadora *f*
usual [ˈjuːʒʊəl] *adj* 1 NORMAL : usual, normal 2 CUSTOMARY : acostumbrado, habitual, de costumbre 3 ORDINARY : ordinario, típico
usually [ˈjuːʒʊəli, ˈjuːʒəli] *adv* : usualmente, normalmente
usurp [jʊˈsərp, -ˈzərp] *vt* : usurpar
usurper [jʊˈsərpər, -ˈzər-] *n* : usurpador *m*, -dora *f*
usury [ˈjuːʒəri] *n* : usura *f*
utensil [jʊˈtɛntsəl] *n* 1 : utensilio *m* (de cocina) 2 IMPLEMENT : implemento *m*, útil *m* (de labranza, etc.)
uterine [ˈjuːtə̩raɪn, -rən] *adj* : uterino
uterus [ˈjuːtərəs] *n, pl* **uteri** [-ˌraɪ] : útero *m*, matriz *f*
utilitarian [juːˌtɪləˈtɛriən] *adj* : utilitario
utility [juːˈtɪləti] *n, pl* **-ties** 1 USEFULNESS : utilidad *f* 2 **public utility** : empresa *f* de servicio público
utilization [ˌjuːtələˈzeɪʃən] *n* : utilización *f*
utilize [ˈjuːtə̩laɪz] *vt* **-lized; -lizing** : utilizar, hacer uso de
utmost[1] [ˈvtˌmoːst] *adj* 1 FARTHEST : extremo, más lejano 2 GREATEST : sumo, mayor ⟨of the utmost importance : de suma importancia⟩
utmost[2] *n* : lo más posible ⟨to the utmost : al máximo⟩
utopia [jʊˈtoːpiə] *n* : utopía *f*
utopian [jʊˈtoːpiən] *adj* : utópico
utter[1] [ˈvtər] *vt* : decir, articular, pronunciar (palabras)
utter[2] *adj* : absoluto — **utterly** *adv*
utterance [ˈvtərənts] *n* : declaración *f*, articulación *f*
U–turn [ˈjuːˌtərn] *n* 1 : giro *m* en U, vuelta *f* en U, cambio *m* de sentido 2 *fam* ABOUT-FACE, REVERSAL : giro *m* de 180 grados
uvula [ˈjuːvjələ] *n* : campanilla *f*

V

v ['vi:] *n, pl* **v's** *or* **vs** ['vi:z] : vigésima segunda letra del alfabeto inglés

vacancy ['veɪkənʦi] *n, pl* **-cies** **1** EMPTINESS : vacío *m*, vacuidad *f* **2** : vacante *f*, puesto *m* vacante ⟨to fill a vacancy : ocupar un puesto⟩ **3** : habitación *f* libre (en un hotel) ⟨no vacancies : completo⟩

vacant ['veɪkənt] *adj* **1** EMPTY : libre, desocupado (dícese de los edificios, etc.) **2** : vacante (dícese de los puestos) **3** BLANK : vacío, ausente ⟨a vacant stare : una mirada ausente⟩

vacate ['veɪˌkeɪt] *vt* **-cated; -cating** : desalojar, desocupar

vacation[1] [veɪ'keɪʃən, və-] *vi* : pasar las vacaciones, vacacionar *Mex*

vacation[2] *n* : vacaciones *fpl* ⟨to be on vacation : estar de vacaciones⟩

vacationer [veɪ'keɪʃənər, və-] *n* : turista *mf*, veraneante *mf*, vacacionista *mf CA, Mex*

vaccinate ['væksə,neɪt] *vt* **-nated; -nating** : vacunar

vaccination [,væksə'neɪʃən] *n* : vacunación *f*

vaccine [væk'si:n, 'væk,-] *n* : vacuna *f*

vacillate ['væsə,leɪt] *vi* **-lated; -lating** **1** HESITATE : vacilar **2** SWAY : oscilar

vacillation [,væsə'leɪʃən] *n* : indecisión *f*, vacilación *f*

vacuous ['vækjuəs] *adj* **1** EMPTY : vacío **2** INANE : vacuo, necio, estúpido

vacuousness ['vækjuəsnəs] *n* : vacuidad *f*

vacuum[1] ['væ,kju:m, -kjəm] *vt* : limpiar con aspiradora, pasar la aspiradora por

vacuum[2] *n, pl* **vacuums** *or* **vacua** ['vækjuə] : vacío *m*

vacuum cleaner *n* : aspiradora *f*

vagabond[1] ['vægə,band] *adj* : vagabundo

vagabond[2] *n* : vagabundo *m*, -da *f*

vagary ['veɪɡəri, və'ɡɛri] *n, pl* **-ries** : capricho *m*

vagina [və'ɒ aɪnə] *n, pl* **-nae** [-,ni:, -,naɪ] *or* **-nas** : vagina *f*

vagrancy ['veɪɡrənʦi] *n, pl* **-cies** : vagancia *f*

vagrant[1] ['veɪɡrənt] *adj* : vagabundo

vagrant[2] *n* : vagabundo *m*, -da *f*

vague ['veɪɡ] *adj* **vaguer; vaguest** **1** IMPRECISE : vago, impreciso ⟨a vague feeling : una sensación indefinida⟩ ⟨I haven't the vaguest idea : no tengo la más remota idea⟩ **2** UNCLEAR : borroso, poco claro ⟨a vague outline : un perfil indistinto⟩ **3** ABSENTMINDED : distraído

vaguely ['veɪɡli] *adv* : vagamente, de manera imprecisa

vagueness ['veɪɡnəs] *n* : vaguedad *f*, imprecisión *f*

vain ['veɪn] *adj* **1** WORTHLESS : vano **2** FUTILE : vano, inútil ⟨in vain : en vano⟩ **3** CONCEITED : vanidoso, presumido

vainly ['veɪnli] *adv* : en vano, vanamente, inútilmente

valance ['vælənʦ, 'veɪ-] *n* **1** FLOUNCE : volante *m* (de una cama, etc.) **2** : galería *f* de cortina (sobre una ventana)

vale ['veɪl] *n* : valle *m*

valedictorian [,vælə,dɪk'toriən] *n* : estudiante *mf* que pronuncia el discurso de despedida en ceremonia de graduación

valedictory [,vælə'dɪktəri] *adj* : de despedida

valentine ['vælən,taɪn] *n* : tarjeta *f* que se manda el Día de los Enamorados (el 14 de febrero)

Valentine's Day *n* : Día *m* de los Enamorados

valet ['væ,leɪ, væ'leɪ, 'vælət] *n* : ayuda *m* de cámara

valiant ['væljənt] *adj* : valiente, valeroso

valiantly ['væljəntli] *adv* : con valor, valientemente

valid ['væləd] *adj* : válido

validate ['vælə,deɪt] *vt* **-dated; -dating** : validar, dar validez a

validity [və'lɪdəʈi, væ-] *n* : validez *f*

valise [və'li:s] *n* : maleta *f* (de mano)

Valium ['væliəm, 'væljəm] *trademark* se usa para una droga que reduce la ansiedad y el estrés

valley ['væli] *n, pl* **-leys** : valle *m*

valor ['vælər] *n* : valor *m*, valentía *f*

valuable[1] ['væljuəbəl, 'væljəbəl] *adj* **1** EXPENSIVE : costoso, de valor **2** WORTHWHILE : valioso, apreciable

valuable[2] *n* : objeto *m* de valor

valuation [,vælju'eɪʃən] *n* **1** APPRAISAL : valoración *f*, tasación *f* **2** VALUE : valuación *f*

value[1] ['væl,ju:] *vt* **-ued; -uing** **1** APPRAISE : valorar, avaluar, tasar **2** APPRECIATE : valorar, apreciar

value[2] *n* **1** : valor *m* ⟨of little value : de poco valor⟩ ⟨to be a good value : estar bien de precio, tener buen precio⟩ ⟨at face value : en su sentido literal⟩ **2** **values** *npl* : valores *mpl* (morales), principios *mpl*

valueless ['vælju:ləs] *adj* : sin valor

valve ['vælv] *n* : válvula *f*

vampire ['væm,paɪr] *n* **1** : vampiro *m* **2** *or* **vampire bat** : vampiro *m*

van[1] ['væn] → **vanguard**

van[2] *n* : furgoneta *f*, camioneta *f*

vandal ['vændəl] *n* : vándalo *m*

vandalism ['vændəl,ɪzəm] *n* : vandalismo *m*

vandalize ['vændəl,aɪz] *vt* : destrozar, destruir, estropear

vane ['veɪn] *n or* **weather vane** : veleta *f*

vanguard ['væn,ɡard] *n* : vanguardia *f*

vanilla [və'nɪlə, -'nɛ-] *n* : vainilla *f*

vanish ['vænɪʃ] *vi* : desaparecer, disiparse, desvanecerse

vanity ['vænəʈi] *n, pl* **-ties** **1** : vanidad *f* **2** *or* **vanity table** : tocador *m*

vanquish ['væŋkwɪʃ, 'væn-] *vt* : vencer, conquistar

vantage point ['væntɪɒ] *n* : posición *f* ventajosa

vape ['veɪp] v **vaped; vaping** : vapear
vapid ['væpəd, 'veɪ-] adj : insípido, insulso
vapor ['veɪpər] n : vapor m
vaporize ['veɪpə,raɪz] v **-rized; -rizing** vt
: vaporizar — vi : vaporizarse, evaporarse
vaporizer ['veɪpə,raɪzər] n : vaporizador
m
variability [,vɛriə'bɪləʈi] n, pl **-ties** : variabilidad f
variable[1] ['vɛriəbəl] adj : variable ⟨vari-
able cloudiness : nubosidad variable⟩
variable[2] n : variable f, factor m
variance ['vɛriənʦ] n **1** DISCREPANCY
: varianza f, discrepancia f **2** DISAGREE-
MENT : desacuerdo m ⟨at variance with
: en desacuerdo con⟩
variant[1] ['vɛriənt] adj : variante, divergente
variant[2] n : variante f
variation [,vɛri'eɪʃən] n : variación f, diferencias fpl
varicose ['værə,ko:s] adj : varicoso
varicose veins npl : varices fpl, várices fpl
varied ['vɛrid] adj : variado, dispar, diferente
variegated ['vɛriə,ɡeɪʈɪd] adj : abigarrado,
multicolor
variety [və'raɪəʈi] n, pl **-ties 1** DIVERSITY
: diversidad f, variedad f **2** ASSORTMENT
: surtido m ⟨for a variety of reasons
: por diversas razones⟩ **3** SORT : clase
f **4** BREED : variedad f (de plantas)
various ['vɛriəs] adj : varios, diversos
varnish[1] ['vɑrnɪʃ] vt : barnizar
varnish[2] n : barniz f
varsity ['vɑrsəʈi] n, pl **-ties** : equipo m universitario
vary ['vɛri] v **varied; varying** vt : variar,
diversificar — vi **1** CHANGE : variar,
cambiar **2** DEVIATE : desviarse
vascular ['væskjələr] adj : vascular
vase ['veɪs, 'veɪz, 'vɑz] n : jarrón m, florero m
Vaseline ['væsə,li:n, ,væsə'li:n] trademark
se usa para vaselina
vassal ['væsəl] n : vasallo m, -lla f
vast ['væst] adj : inmenso, enorme, vasto
vastly ['væstli] adv : enormemente
vastness ['væstnəs] n : vastedad f, inmensidad f
vat ['væt] n : cuba f, tina f
vaudeville ['vɔdvəl, -ˌvɪl;, 'vɔdə,vɪl] n
: vodevil m
vault[1] ['vɔlt] vi LEAP : saltar
vault[2] n **1** JUMP : salto m ⟨pole vault
: salto de pértiga, salto con garrocha⟩ **2**
DOME : bóveda f **3** : bodega f (para
vino), bóveda f de seguridad (de un
banco) **4** CRYPT : cripta f
vaulted ['vɔltəd] adj : abovedado
vaunted ['vɔntəd] adj : cacareado,
alardeado ⟨a much vaunted wine : un
vino muy alardeado⟩
VCR [,vi:,si:'ɑr] n : video m, videocasetera
f
veal ['vi:l] n : ternera f, carne f de ternera
veer ['vɪr] vi : virar (dícese de un barco),
girar (dícese de un coche), torcer (dícese
de un camino)

vegan ['vi:ɡən] n : vegetariano m estricto,
vegetariana f estricta
vegetable[1] ['vɛɡ təbəl, 'vɛɡ əʈə-] adj : vegetal
vegetable[2] n **1** : vegetal m ⟨the vegetable kingdom : el reino vegetal⟩ **2** : verdura f, hortaliza f (para comer)
vegetarian [,vɛɡ ə'tɛriən] n : vegetariano
mf — **vegetarian** adj — **vegetarianism**
n
vegetate ['vɛɡ ə,teɪt] vi **-tated; -tating**
: vegetar
vegetation [,vɛɡ ə'teɪʃən] n : vegetación f
vegetative ['vɛɡ ə,teɪʈɪv] adj : vegetativo
veggie ['vɛɡ i] n fam VEGETABLE : verdura f, hortaliza f (para comer)
vehemence ['vi:əmənʦ] n : intensidad f,
vehemencia f
vehement ['vi:əmənt] adj : intenso, vehemente
vehemently ['vi:əməntli] adv : vehementemente, con vehemencia
vehicle ['vi:əkəl, 'vi:,hɪkəl] n **1** or **motor
vehicle** : vehículo m **2** MEDIUM : vehículo m, medio m
vehicular [vi'hɪkjələr, və-] adj : vehicular
⟨vehicular homicide : muerte por atro-
pello⟩
veil[1] ['veɪl] vt **1** CONCEAL : velar, disimular **2** : cubrir con un velo ⟨to veil one's
face : cubrirse con un velo⟩
veil[2] n : velo m ⟨bridal veil : velo de no-
via⟩
vein ['veɪn] n **1** : vena f (en anatomía,
botánica, etc.) **2** LODE : veta f, vena f,
filón m **3** STYLE : vena f ⟨in a humorous vein : en vena humorística⟩
veined ['veɪnd] adj : veteado (dícese del
queso, de los minerales, etc.)
Velcro ['vɛl,kro:] trademark se usa para
un tipo de cierre de nilón
velocity [və'lɑsəʈi] n, pl **-ties** : velocidad f
velour [və'lʊr] or **velours** [-'lʊrz] n : velour m
velvet[1] ['vɛlvət] adj **1** : de terciopelo **2**
→ **velvety**
velvet[2] n : terciopelo m
velvety ['vɛlvəʈi] adj : aterciopelado
venal ['vi:nəl] adj : venal
vend ['vɛnd] vt : vender
vendetta [vɛn'dɛʈə] n : vendetta f
vending machine n : máquina f expendedora
vendor ['vɛndər] n : vendedor m, -dora f;
puestero m, -ra f
veneer n **1** : enchapado m, chapa f **2**
APPEARANCE : apariencia f, barniz m ⟨a
veneer of culture : un barniz de cultura⟩
venerable ['vɛnərəbəl] adj : venerable
venerate ['vɛnə,reɪt] vt **-ated; -ating** : venerar
veneration [,vɛnə'reɪʃən] n : veneración f
venereal disease [və'nɪriəl] n : enfermedad f venérea
venetian blind [və'ni:ʃən] n : persiana f
(de lamas)
Venezuelan [,vɛnə'zweɪlən, -zʊ'eɪ-] n
: venezolano m, -na f — **Venezuelan** adj
vengeance ['vɛnd ənʦ] n : venganza f ⟨to
take vengeance on : vengarse de⟩

vengeful ['vɛnɒ fəl] *adj* : vengativo
venial ['vi:niəl] *adj* : venial ⟨a venial sin : un pecado venial⟩
venison ['vɛnəsən, -zən] *n* : venado *m*, carne *f* de venado
venom ['vɛnəm] *n* 1 : veneno *m* 2 MALICE : veneno *m*, malevolencia *f*
venomous ['vɛnəməs] *adj* : venenoso
vent¹ ['vɛnt] *vt* : desahogar, dar salida a ⟨to vent one's feelings : desahogarse⟩
vent² *n* 1 OPENING : abertura *f* (de escape), orificio *m* 2 *or* **air vent** : respiradero *m*, rejilla *f* de ventilación 3 OUTLET : desahogo *m* ⟨to give vent to one's anger : desahogar la ira⟩
ventilate ['vɛntəl,eɪt] *vt* **-lated; -lating** : ventilar
ventilation [,vɛntəl'eɪʃən] *n* : ventilación *f*
ventilator ['vɛntəl,eɪtər] *n* : ventilador *m*
ventricle ['vɛntrɪkəl] *n* : ventrículo *m*
ventriloquism [vɛn'trɪlə,kwɪzəm] *n* : ventriloquia *f*
ventriloquist [vɛn'trɪlə,kwɪst] *n* : ventrílocuo *m*, -cua *f*
venture¹ ['vɛntʃər] *v* **-tured; -turing** *vt* 1 RISK : arriesgar 2 OFFER : aventurar ⟨to venture an opinion : aventurar una opinión⟩ — *vi* : arriesgarse, atreverse, aventurarse
venture² *n* 1 UNDERTAKING : empresa *f* 2 GAMBLE, RISK : aventura *f*, riesgo *m*
venturesome ['vɛntʃərsəm] *adj* 1 ADVENTUROUS : audaz, atrevido 2 RISKY : arriesgado
venue ['vɛn,ju:] *n* 1 PLACE : lugar *m* 2 : jurisdicción *f* (en derecho)
Venus ['vi:nəs] *n* : Venus *m*
veracity [və'ræsəti] *n, pl* **-ties** : veracidad *f*
veranda *or* **verandah** [və'rændə] *n* : terraza *f*, veranda *f*
verb ['vərb] *n* : verbo *m*
verbal ['vərbəl] *adj* : verbal
verbalize ['vərbə,laɪz] *vt* **-ized; -izing** : expresar con palabras, verbalizar
verbally ['vərbəli] *adv* : verbalmente, de palabra
verbatim¹ [vər'beɪtəm] *adv* : palabra por palabra, textualmente
verbatim² *adj* : literal, textual
verbose [vər'bo:s] *adj* : verboso, prolijo
verdant ['vərdənt] *adj* : verde, verdeante
verdict ['vərdɪkt] *n* 1 : veredicto *m* (de un jurado) 2 JUDGMENT, OPINION : juicio *m*, opinión *f*
verge¹ ['vərɒ] *vi* **verged; verging** : estar al borde, rayar ⟨it verges on madness : raya en la locura⟩
verge² *n* 1 EDGE : borde *m* 2 **to be on the verge of** : estar a pique de, estar al borde de, estar a punto de
verification [,vɛrəfə'keɪʃən] *n* : verificación *f*
verify ['vɛrə,faɪ] *vt* **-fied; -fying** : verificar, comprobar, confirmar
veritable ['vɛrətəbəl] *adj* : verdadero — **veritably** [-bli] *adv*
vermicelli [,vərmə'tʃɛli, -'sɛli] *n* : fideos *mpl* finos
vermin ['vərmən] *ns & pl* : alimañas *fpl*, bichos *mpl*, sabandijas *fpl*

vermouth [vər'mu:θ] *n* : vermut *m*
vernacular¹ [vər'nækjələr] *adj* : vernáculo
vernacular² *n* : lengua *f* vernácula
vernal ['vərnəl] *adj* : vernal
versatile ['vərsəɒl] *adj* : versátil
versatility [,vərsə'tɪləti] *n* : versatilidad *f*
verse ['vərs] *n* 1 LINE, STANZA : verso *m*, estrofa *f* 2 POETRY : poesía *f* 3 : versículo *m* (en la Biblia)
versed ['vərst] *adj* : versado ⟨to be well versed in : ser muy versado en⟩
version ['vərʒən] *n* : versión *f*
versus ['vərsəs] *prep* : versus
vertebra ['vərtəbrə] *n, pl* **-brae** [-,breɪ, -,bri:] *or* **-bras** : vértebra *f*
vertebrate¹ ['vərtəbrət, -,breɪt] *adj* : vertebrado
vertebrate² *n* : vertebrado *m*
vertex ['vər,tɛks] *n, pl* **vertices** ['vərtə,si:z] 1 : vértice *m* (en matemáticas y anatomía) 2 SUMMIT, TOP : ápice *m*, cumbre *f*, cima *f*
vertical¹ ['vərtɪkəl] *adj* : vertical — **vertically** *adv*
vertical² *n* : vertical *f*
vertigo ['vərtɪ,ɡo:] *n, pl* **-goes** *or* **-gos** : vértigo *m*
verve ['vərv] *n* : brío *m*
very¹ ['vɛri] *adv* 1 EXTREMELY : muy, sumamente ⟨very few : muy pocos⟩ ⟨very much : mucho⟩ ⟨I am very sorry : lo siento mucho⟩ 2 (*used for emphasis*) ⟨at the very least : por lo menos, como mínimo⟩ ⟨the very same dress : el mismo vestido⟩ ⟨a room of my very own : mi propio cuarto⟩ ⟨(on) the very next day : al día siguiente⟩
very² *adj* **verier; -est** 1 EXACT, PRECISE : mismo, exacto ⟨at that very moment : en ese mismo momento⟩ ⟨it's the very thing : es justo lo que hacía falta⟩ 2 BARE, MERE : solo, mero ⟨the very thought of it : sólo pensarlo⟩ 3 EXTREME : extremo, de todo ⟨at the very top : arriba de todo⟩
vesicle ['vɛsikəl] *n* : vesícula *f*
vespers ['vɛspərz] *npl* : vísperas *fpl*
vessel ['vɛsəl] *n* 1 CONTAINER : vasija *f*, recipiente *m* 2 BOAT, CRAFT : nave *f*, barco *m*, buque *m* 3 : vaso *m* ⟨blood vessel : vaso sanguíneo⟩
vest¹ ['vɛst] *vt* 1 CONFER : conferir ⟨to vest authority in : conferirle la autoridad a⟩ 2 CLOTHE : vestir
vest² *n* 1 : chaleco *m* 2 UNDERSHIRT : camiseta *f*
vestibule ['vɛstə,bju:l] *n* : vestíbulo *m*
vestige ['vɛstɪɒ] *n* : vestigio *m*, rastro *m*
vestments ['vɛstmənts] *npl* : vestiduras *fpl*
vestry ['vɛstri] *n, pl* **-tries** : sacristía *f*
vet ['vɛt] *n* 1 → **veterinarian** 2 → **veteran²**
veteran¹ ['vɛtɒrən, 'vɛtrən] *adj* : veterano
veteran² *n* : veterano *m*, -na *f*
Veterans Day *n* : día *m* del Armisticio (celebrado el 11 de noviembre en los Estados Unidos)
veterinarian [,vɛtɒrə'nɛriən, ,vɛtɒ-] *n* : veterinario *m*, -ria *f*

veterinary [ˈvɛtˠərəˌnɛri] *adj* : veterinario
veto¹ [ˈviːˌtˠo] *vt* **1** FORBID : prohibir **2** : vetar ⟨to veto a bill : vetar un proyecto de ley⟩
veto² *n, pl* **-toes 1** : veto *m* ⟨the power of veto : el derecho de veto⟩ **2** BAN : veto *m*, prohibición *f*
vex [ˈvɛks] *vt* : contrariar, molestar, irritar
vexation [vɛkˈseɪʃən] *n* : contrariedad *f*, irritación *f*
via [ˈvaɪə, ˈviːə] *prep* : por, vía
viability [ˌvaɪəˈbɪlətˠi] *n* : viabilidad *f*
viable [ˈvaɪəbəl] *adj* : viable
viaduct [ˈvaɪəˌdʌkt] *n* : viaducto *m*
vial [ˈvaɪəl] *n* : frasco *m*
vibrant [ˈvaɪbrənt] *adj* **1** LIVELY : vibrante, animado, dinámico **2** BRIGHT : fuerte, vivo (dícese de los colores)
vibrate [ˈvaɪˌbreɪt] *vi* **-brated; -brating 1** OSCILLATE : vibrar, oscilar **2** THRILL : bullir ⟨to vibrate with excitement : bullir de emoción⟩
vibration [vaɪˈbreɪʃən] *n* : vibración *f*
vibrator [ˈvaɪˌbreɪtˠər] *n* : vibrador *m*
vicar [ˈvɪkər] *n* : vicario *m*, -ria *f*
vicarious [vaɪˈkæriːəs, vɪ-] *adj* : indirecto — **vicariously** *adv*
vice [ˈvaɪs] *n* : vicio *m*
vice- [ˈvaɪs] *pref* : vice-
vice admiral *n* : vicealmirante *mf*
vice president *n* : vicepresidente *m*, -ta *f*
viceroy [ˈvaɪsˌrɔɪ] *n* : virrey *m*, -rreina *f*
vice versa [ˌvaɪsɪˈvərsə, ˌvaɪsˈvər-] *adv* : viceversa
vicinity [vəˈsɪnətˠi] *n, pl* **-ties 1** NEIGHBORHOOD : vecindad *f*, inmediaciones *fpl* **2** NEARNESS : proximidad *f*
vicious [ˈvɪʃəs] *adj* **1** DEPRAVED : depravado, malo **2** SAVAGE : malo, fiero, salvaje ⟨a vicious dog : un perro feroz⟩ **3** MALICIOUS : malicioso
vicious circle *n* : círculo *m* vicioso
viciously [ˈvɪʃəsli] *adv* : con saña, brutalmente
viciousness [ˈvɪʃəsnəs] *n* : brutalidad *f*, ferocidad *f* (de un animal), malevolencia *f* (de un comentario, etc.)
vicissitude [vəˈsɪsəˌtuːd, vaɪ-, -ˌtjuːd] *n* : vicisitud *f*
victim [ˈvɪktəm] *n* : víctima *f*
victimize [ˈvɪktəˌmaɪz] *vt* **-mized; -mizing** : tomar como víctima; perseguir; victimizar *Arg, Mex*
victor [ˈvɪktər] *n* : vencedor *m*, -dora *f*
Victorian [vɪkˈtoːriən] *adj* : victoriano
victorious [vɪkˈtoːriəs] *adj* : victorioso — **victoriously** *adv*
victory [ˈvɪktəri] *n, pl* **-ries** : victoria *f*, triunfo *m*
video¹ [ˈvɪdiˌoː] *adj* : de video ⟨video recording : grabación de video⟩
video² *n* : video *m*
video camera *n* : videocámara *f*
videocassette [ˌvɪdiokəˈsɛt] *n* : videocasete *m*, videocassette *m*
videocassette recorder → VCR
videoconferencing [ˌvɪdioˈkɑnfrənˌsɪŋ] *n* : uso *m* de videoconferencias — **videoconference** [ˌvɪdioˈkɑnfrənˌs, -ˈkɑnfərənˌs] *n*

video game *n* : videojuego *m*, juego *m* de video
video recorder → VCR
videotape¹ [ˈvɪdioˌteɪp] *vt* **-taped; -taping** : grabar en video, videograbar
videotape² *n* : videocinta *f*
vie [ˈvaɪ] *vi* **vied; vying** [ˈvaɪɪŋ] : competir, rivalizar
Vietnamese [viˌɛtnəˈmiːz, -ˈmiːs] *n* **1** : vietnamita *mf* **2** : vietnamita *m* (idioma) — **Vietnamese** *adj*
view¹ [ˈvjuː] *vt* **1** OBSERVE : mirar, ver, observar **2** CONSIDER : considerar, contemplar
view² *n* **1** SIGHT : vista *f* ⟨to come into view : aparecer⟩ **2** ATTITUDE, OPINION : opinión *f*, parecer *m*, actitud *f* ⟨in my view : en mi opinión⟩ **3** SCENE : vista *f*, panorama *f* **4** INTENTION : idea *f*, vista *f* ⟨with a view to : con vistas a, con la idea de⟩ **5 in view of** : dado que, en vista de (que)
viewer [ˈvjuːər] *n* : televidente *mf*; telespectador *m*, -dora *f* ⟨the show was watched by millions of viewers : el programa fue visto por millones de televidentes⟩
viewfinder [ˈvjuːˌfaɪndər] *n* : visor *m*
viewpoint [ˈvjuːˌpɔɪnt] *n* : punto *m* de vista
vigil [ˈvɪdʒəl] *n* **1** : vigilia *f*, vela *f* **2 to keep vigil** : velar
vigilance [ˈvɪdʒələnts] *n* : vigilancia *f*
vigilant [ˈvɪdʒələnt] *adj* : vigilante
vigilante [ˌvɪdʒəˈlænˌtiː] *n* : integrante *mf* de un comité de vigilancia (que actúa como policía)
vigilantly [ˈvɪdʒələntli] *adv* : con vigilancia
vigor [ˈvɪgər] *n* : vigor *m*, energía *f*, fuerza *f*
vigorous [ˈvɪgərəs] *adj* : vigoroso, enérgico — **vigorously** *adv*
Viking [ˈvaɪkɪŋ] *n* : vikingo *m*, -ga *f*
vile [ˈvaɪl] *adj* **viler; vilest 1** WICKED : vil, infame **2** REVOLTING : asqueroso, repugnante **3** TERRIBLE : horrible, atroz ⟨vile weather : tiempo horrible⟩ ⟨to be in a vile mood : estar de un humor de perros⟩
vileness [ˈvaɪlnəs] *n* : vileza *f*
vilify [ˈvɪləˌfaɪ] *vt* **-fied; -fying** : vilipendiar, denigrar, difamar
villa [ˈvɪlə] *n* : casa *f* de campo, quinta *f*
village [ˈvɪlɪdʒ] *n* : pueblo *m* (grande), aldea *f* (pequeña)
villager [ˈvɪlɪdʒ ər] *n* : vecino *m*, -na *f* (de un pueblo); aldeano *m*, -na *f* (de una aldea)
villain [ˈvɪlən] *n* : villano *m*, -na *f*; malo *m*, -la *f* (en ficción, películas, etc.)
villainess [ˈvɪlənɪs, -nəs] *n* : villana *f*
villainous [ˈvɪlənəs] *adj* : infame, malvado
villainy [ˈvɪləni] *n, pl* **-lainies** : vileza *f*, maldad *f*
vim [ˈvɪm] *n* : brío *m*, vigor *m*, energía *f*
vinaigrette [ˌvɪnɪˈɡrɛt] *n* : vinagreta *f*
vindicate [ˈvɪndəˌkeɪt] *vt* **-cated; -cating 1** EXONERATE : vindicar, disculpar **2** JUSTIFY : justificar
vindication [ˌvɪndəˈkeɪʃən] *n* : vindicación *f*, justificación *f*

vindictive [vɪn'dɪktɪv] *adj* : vengativo

vine ['vaɪn] *n* **1** GRAPEVINE : vid *f*, parra *f* **2** : planta *f* trepadora, enredadera *f*

vinegar ['vɪnɪɡər] *n* : vinagre *m*

vinegary ['vɪnɪɡəri] *adj* : avinagrado

vineyard ['vɪnjərd] *n* : viña *f*, viñedo *m*

vintage[1] ['vɪntɪdʒ] *adj* **1** : añejo (dícese de un vino) **2** CLASSIC : clásico, de época

vintage[2] *n* **1** : cosecha *f* ⟨the 1947 vintage : la cosecha de 1947⟩ **2** ERA : época *f*, era *f* ⟨slang of recent vintage : argot de la época reciente⟩

vinyl ['vaɪnəl] *n* : vinilo

viola [vi:'o:lə] *n* : viola *f*

violate ['vaɪə,leɪt] *vt* **-lated; -lating 1** BREAK : infringir, violar, quebrantar ⟨to violate the rules : violar las reglas⟩ **2** RAPE : violar **3** DESECRATE : profanar

violation [,vaɪə'leɪʃən] *n* **1** : violación *f*, infracción *f* (de una ley) **2** DESECRATION : profanación *f*

violator ['vaɪə,leɪtər] *n* : infractor *m*, -tora *f*

violence ['vaɪlənts, 'vaɪə-] *n* : violencia *f*

violent ['vaɪlənt, 'vaɪə-] *adj* : violento

violently ['vaɪləntli, 'vaɪə-] *adv* : violentamente, con violencia

violet ['vaɪlət, 'vaɪə-] *n* : violeta *f*

violin [,vaɪə'lɪn] *n* : violín *m*

violinist [,vaɪə'lɪnɪst] *n* : violinista *mf*

violoncello [,vaɪələn'tʃɛlo:, ,vi:-] → **cello**

VIP [,vi:,aɪ'pi:] *n*, *pl* **VIPs** [-'pi:z] : VIP *mf*, persona *f* de categoría

viper ['vaɪpər] *n* : víbora *f*

viral ['vaɪrəl] *adj* : viral, vírico ⟨viral pneumonia : pulmonía viral⟩

virgin[1] ['vərdʒən] *adj* **1** CHASTE : virginal ⟨the virgin birth : el alumbramiento virginal⟩ **2** : virgen, intacto ⟨a virgin forest : una selva virgen⟩ ⟨virgin wool : lana virgen⟩

virgin[2] *n* : virgen *mf*

virginal ['vərdʒənəl] *adj* : virginal

virginity [vər'dʒɪnəti] *n* : virginidad *f*

Virgo ['vər,ɡo:, 'vɪr-] *n* **1** : Virgo *m* (signo o constelación) **2** : Virgo *mf* (persona)

virile ['vɪrəl, -,aɪl] *adj* : viril, varonil

virility [və'rɪləti] *n* : virilidad *f*

virtual ['vərtʃuəl] *adj* : virtual ⟨a virtual dictator : un virtual dictador⟩ ⟨virtual reality : realidad virtual⟩

virtually ['vərtʃuəli, 'vərtʃəli] *adv* : en realidad, de hecho, casi

virtue ['vər,tʃu:] *n* **1** : virtud *f* **2 by virtue of** : en virtud de, debido a

virtuosity [,vərtʃu'asəti] *n*, *pl* **-ties** : virtuosismo *m*

virtuoso [,vərtʃu'o:so:, -zo:] *n*, *pl* **-sos** *or* **-si** [-,si:, -,zi:] : virtuoso *m*, -sa *f*

virtuous ['vərtʃuəs] *adj* : virtuoso, bueno — **virtuously** *adv*

virulence ['vɪrələnts, 'vɪrjə-] *n* : virulencia *f*

virulent ['vɪrələnt, 'vɪrjə-] *adj* : virulento

virus ['vaɪrəs] *n* : virus *m*

visa ['vi:zə, -sə] *n* : visa *f*

vis-à-vis [,vi:zə'vi:, -sə-] *prep* : con relación a, con respecto a

viscera ['vɪsərə] *npl* : vísceras *fpl*

visceral ['vɪsərəl] *adj* : visceral

viscosity [vɪs'kasəti] *n*, *pl* **-ties** : viscosidad *f*

viscous ['vɪskəs] *adj* : viscoso

vise ['vaɪs] *n* : torno *m* de banco, tornillo *m* de banco

visibility [,vɪzə'bɪləti] *n*, *pl* **-ties** : visibilidad *f*

visible ['vɪzəbəl] *adj* **1** : visible ⟨the visible stars : las estrellas visibles⟩ **2** OBVIOUS : evidente, patente

visibly ['vɪzəbli] *adv* : visiblemente

vision ['vɪʒən] *n* **1** EYESIGHT : vista *f*, visión *f* **2** APPARITION : visión *f*, aparición *f* **3** FORESIGHT : visión *f* (del futuro), previsión *f* **4** IMAGE : imagen *f* ⟨she had visions of a disaster : se imaginaba un desastre⟩

visionary[1] ['vɪʒə,nɛri] *adj* **1** FARSIGHTED : visionario, con visión de futuro **2** UTOPIAN : utópico, poco realista

visionary[2] *n*, *pl* **-ries** : visionario *m*, -ria *f*

visit[1] ['vɪzət] *vt* **1** : visitar, ir a ver **2** AFFLICT : azotar, afligir ⟨visited by troubles : afligido con problemas⟩ — *vi* : hacer (una) visita ⟨visiting hours : horas de visita⟩

visit[2] *n* : visita *f*

visitor ['vɪzətər] *n* : visitante *mf* (a una ciudad, etc.), visita *f* (a una casa)

visor ['vaɪzər] *n* : visera *f*

vista ['vɪstə] *n* : vista *f*

visual ['vɪʒuəl] *adj* : visual ⟨the visual arts : las artes visuales⟩ — **visually** *adv*

visualize ['vɪʒuə,laɪz] *vt* **-ized; -izing** : visualizar, imaginarse, hacerse una idea de — **visualization** [,vɪʒwələ'zeɪʃən] *n*

vital ['vaɪtəl] *adj* **1** : vital ⟨vital organs : órganos vitales⟩ **2** CRUCIAL : esencial, crucial, decisivo ⟨of vital importance : de suma importancia⟩ **3** LIVELY : enérgico, lleno de vida, vital

vitality [vaɪ'tæləti] *n*, *pl* **-ties** : vitalidad *f*, energía *f*

vitally ['vaɪtəli] *adv* : sumamente

vital statistics *npl* : estadísticas *fpl* demográficas

vitamin ['vaɪtəmən] *n* : vitamina *f* ⟨vitamin deficiency : carencia vitamínica⟩

vitriol ['vɪtriəl] *n* : vitriolo *m*

vitriolic [,vɪtri'alɪk] *adj* : mordaz, virulento

vivacious [və'veɪʃəs, vaɪ-] *adj* : vivaz, animado, lleno de vida

vivaciously [və'veɪʃəsli, vaɪ-] *adv* : con vivacidad, animadamente

vivacity [və'væsəti, vaɪ-] *n* : vivacidad *f*

vivid ['vɪvəd] *adj* **1** LIVELY : lleno de vitalidad **2** BRILLIANT : vivo, intenso ⟨vivid colors : colores vivos⟩ **3** INTENSE, SHARP : vívido, gráfico ⟨a vivid dream : un sueño vívido⟩

vividly ['vɪvədli] *adv* **1** BRIGHTLY : con colores vivos **2** SHARPLY : vívidamente

vividness ['vɪvədnəs] *n* **1** BRIGHTNESS : intensidad *f*, viveza *f* **2** SHARPNESS : lo gráfico, nitidez *f*

vivisection [,vɪvə'sɛkʃən, 'vɪvə,-] *n* : vivisección *f*

vixen ['vɪksən] *n* : zorra *f*, raposa *f*

V–neck ['viː,nɛk] *n* **1** : escote *m* en V, cuello *m* en V **2** : camisa *f* (etc.) con escote/cuello en V

vocabulary [voːˈkæbjə,lɛri] *n, pl* **-laries 1** : vocabulario *m* **2** LEXICON : léxico *m*

vocal ['voːkəl] *adj* **1** : vocal **2** LOUD, OUTSPOKEN : ruidoso, muy franco

vocal cords *npl* : cuerdas *fpl* vocales

vocalist ['voːkəlɪst] *n* : cantante *mf*, vocalista *mf*

vocalize ['voːkə,aɪz] *vt* **-ized; -izing** : vocalizar

vocation [voˈkeɪʃən] *n* : vocación *f* ⟨to have a vocation for : tener vocación de⟩

vocational [voˈkeɪʃənəl] *adj* : profesional ⟨vocational guidance : orientación profesional⟩

vociferous [voˈsɪfərəs] *adj* : ruidoso, vociferante

vodka ['vɑdkə] *n* : vodka *m*

vogue ['voːɡ] *n* : moda *f*, boga *f* ⟨to be in vogue : estar de moda, estar en boga⟩

voice[1] ['vɔɪs] *vt* **voiced; voicing** : expresar

voice[2] *n* **1** : voz *f* ⟨in a low voice : en voz baja⟩ ⟨a high/deep voice : una voz aguda/profunda⟩ ⟨to raise/lower one's voice : hablar más alto/bajo⟩ ⟨to lose one's voice : quedarse sin voz⟩ ⟨his voice is changing : le está cambiando la voz⟩ ⟨to have a good (singing) voice : tener una buena voz, cantar bien⟩ **2** WISH, OPINION : voz *f* ⟨the voice of the people : la voz del pueblo⟩ **3** SAY, INFLUENCE : voz *f* ⟨to have no voice : no tener voz, no tener ni voz ni voto⟩ **4** : voz *f* (en gramática) **5 to make one's voice heard** : hacerse oír

voice box → **larynx**

voiced ['vɔɪst] *adj* : sonoro

voice mail *n* : correo *m* de voz, buzón *m* de voz

void[1] ['vɔɪd] *vt* : anular, invalidar ⟨to void a contract : anular un contrato⟩

void[2] *adj* **1** EMPTY : vacío, desprovisto ⟨void of content : desprovisto de contenido⟩ **2** INVALID : inválido, nulo

void[3] *n* : vacío *m*

volatile ['vɑlətəl] *adj* : volátil, inestable

volatility [,vɑləˈtɪlətĭ] *n* : volatilidad *f*, inestabilidad *f*

volcanic [vɑlˈkænɪk] *adj* : volcánico

volcano [vɑlˈkeɪ,noː] *n, pl* **-noes** *or* **-nos** : volcán *m*

vole ['voːl] *n* : campañol *m*

volition [voˈlɪʃən] *n* : volición *f*, voluntad *f* ⟨of one's own volition : por voluntad propia⟩

volley ['vɑli] *n, pl* **-leys 1** : descarga *f* (de tiros) **2** : torrente *m*, lluvia *f* (de insultos, etc.) **3** : salva *f* (de aplausos) **4** : volea *f* (en deportes)

volleyball ['vɑli,bɔl] *n* : voleibol *m*; volibol *m Car, Hond, Mex*

volt ['voːlt] *n* : voltio *m*

voltage ['voːltɪD] *n* : voltaje *m*

voluble ['vɑljəbəl] *adj* : locuaz

volume ['vɑljəm, -,juːm] *n* **1** BOOK : volumen *m*, tomo *m* **2** SPACE : capacidad *f*, volumen *m* (en física) **3** AMOUNT : cantidad *f*, volumen *m* **4** LOUDNESS : volumen *m*

voluminous [vəˈluːmənəs] *adj* : voluminoso

voluntary ['vɑlən,tɛri] *adj* : voluntario — **voluntarily** [,vɑlənˈtɛrəli] *adv*

volunteer[1] [,vɑlənˈtɪr] *vt* : ofrecer, dar ⟨to volunteer one's assistance : ofrecer la ayuda⟩ — *vi* : ofrecerse, alistarse como voluntario

volunteer[2] *n* : voluntario *m*, -ria *f*

voluptuous [vəˈlʌptʃuəs] *adj* : voluptuoso

voluptuousness [vəˈlʌptʃuəsnəs] *n* : voluptuosidad *f*

vomit[1] ['vɑmət] *v* : vomitar

vomit[2] *n* : vómito *m*

voodoo ['vuː,duː] *n, pl* **voodoos** : vudú *m*

voracious [vɔˈreɪʃəs, və-] *adj* : voraz

voraciously [vɔˈreɪʃəsli, və-] *adv* : vorazmente, con voracidad

voracity [vɔˈræsəti, və-] *n* : voracidad *f*

vortex ['vɔr,tɛks] *n, pl* **vortices** ['vɔrtə,siːz] : vórtice *m*

vote[1] ['voːt] *v* **voted; voting** *vi* **1** : votar ⟨to vote Democratic/Republican : votar por los demócratas/republicanos⟩ **2 to vote against** : votar en contra de **3 to vote for** : votar, votar a favor de (una propuesta, etc.), votar por (un candidato) **4 to vote on** : someter a votación, votar sobre — *vt* **1** : votar **2 to vote down** : rechazar **3 to vote in** : elegir **4 to vote out** : no reelegir

vote[2] *n* **1** : voto *m* **2** SUFFRAGE : sufragio *m*, derecho *m* al voto

voter ['voːtər] *n* : votante *mf*

voting ['voːtɪŋ] *n* : votación *f*

vouch ['vautʃ] *vi* **to vouch for** : garantizar (algo), responder de (algo), responder por (alguien)

voucher ['vautʃər] *n* **1** RECEIPT : comprobante *m* **2** : vale *m* ⟨travel voucher : vale de viajar⟩

vow[1] ['vaʊ] *vt* : jurar, prometer, hacer voto de

vow[2] *n* : promesa *f*, voto *m* (en la religión) ⟨a vow of poverty : un voto de pobreza⟩

vowel ['vaʊəl] *n* : vocal *m*

voyage[1] ['vɔɪɪD] *vi* **-aged; -aging** : viajar

voyage[2] *n* : viaje *m*

voyager ['vɔɪɪD ər] *n* : viajero *m*, -ra *f*

voyeur [vwaˈjər, vɔɪˈər] *n* : mirón *m*, -rona *f*

vulgar ['vʌlɡər] *adj* **1** COMMON : ordinario, populachero, del vulgo **2** COARSE, CRUDE : grosero, de mal gusto, majadero *Mex* **3** INDECENT : indecente, colorado (dícese de un chiste, etc.)

vulgarity [,vʌlˈɡærəti] *n, pl* **-ties** : grosería *f*, vulgaridad *f*

vulgarly ['vʌlɡərli] *adv* : vulgarmente, groseramente

vulnerability [,vʌlnərəˈbɪləti] *n, pl* **-ties** : vulnerabilidad *f*

vulnerable ['vʌlnərəbəl] *adj* : vulnerable

vulture ['vʌltʃər] *n* : buitre *m*; zopilote *m CA, Mex*

vying → **vie**

W

w ['dʌbəlˌju:] *n, pl* **w's** *or* **ws** [-ˌju:z] : vigésima tercera letra del alfabeto inglés

wad¹ ['wɑd] *vt* **wadded; wadding** **1** : hacer un taco con, formar en una masa **2** STUFF : rellenar

wad² *n* : taco *m* (de papel), bola *f* (de algodón, etc.), fajo *m* (de billetes)

waddle¹ ['wɑdəl] *vi* **-dled; -dling** : andar como un pato

waddle² *n* : andar *m* de pato

wade ['weɪd] *v* **waded; wading** *vi* **1** : caminar por el agua **2 to wade through** : leer (algo) con dificultad — *vt or* **to wade across** : vadear

wading bird *n* : zancuda *f*, ave *f* zancuda

wafer ['weɪfər] *n* : barquillo *m*, galleta *f* de barquillo

waffle¹ ['wɑfəl] *vi* **waffled; waffling** VACILLATE : vacilar

waffle² *n* **1** : wafle *m* **2 waffle iron** : waflera *f*

waft ['wɑft, 'wæft] *vt* : llevar por el aire — *vi* : flotar

wag¹ ['wæɡ] *v* **wagged; wagging** *vt* : menear — *vi* : menearse, moverse

wag² *n* **1** : meneo *m* (de la cola) **2** JOKER, WIT : bromista *mf*

wage¹ ['weɪdʒ] *vt* **waged; waging** : hacer, librar ⟨to wage war : hacer la guerra⟩

wage² *n or* **wages** *npl* : sueldo *m*, salario *m* ⟨minimum wage : salario mínimo⟩

wage earner → **earner**

wager¹ ['weɪdʒ ər] *v* : apostar

wager² *n* : apuesta *f*

waggish ['wæɡɪʃ] *adj* : burlón, bromista (dícese de una persona), chistoso (dícese de un comentario)

waggle ['wæɡəl] *vt* **-gled; -gling** : menear, mover (de un lado a otro)

wagon ['wæɡən] *n* **1** : carro *m* (tirado por caballos) **2** CART : carrito *m* **3** → **station wagon**

waif ['weɪf] *n* : niño *m* abandonado, animal *m* sin hogar

wail¹ ['weɪl] *vi* : gemir, lamentarse

wail² *n* : gemido *m*, lamento *m*

wainscot ['weɪnskət, -ˌskɑt, -ˌskoːt] *or* **wainscoting** [-skɑɪŋ, -ˌskɑ-, -ˌskoː-] *n* : revestimiento *m* de paneles de madera

waist ['weɪst] *n* : cintura *f* (del cuerpo humano o de ropa), talle *m* (de ropa)

waistband ['weɪstˌbænd] *n* : cinturilla *f*

waistline ['weɪstˌlaɪn] → **waist**

wait¹ ['weɪt] *vi* **1** : esperar ⟨wait and see! : ¡espera y verás!⟩ ⟨I can't wait : me muero de ganas⟩ **2 to wait for** : esperar ⟨what are you waiting for? : ¿a qué esperas?⟩ **3 to wait on** : servir **4 to wait up (for someone)** : quedarse despierto esperando (a alguien) — *vt* **1** AWAIT : esperar ⟨wait your turn : espera a que te toque⟩ ⟨wait a minute : espere un momento⟩ **2** SERVE : servir, atender ⟨to wait tables : servir (a la mesa)⟩ **3 to wait out** : esperar hasta que pase

wait² *n* **1** : espera *f* **2 to lie in wait** : estar al acecho

waiter ['weɪtər] *n* : mesero *m*, camarero *m*, mozo *m* Arg, Chile, Col, Peru

waiting list *n* : lista *f* de espera

waiting room *n* : sala *f* de espera

waitress ['weɪtrəs] *n* : mesera *f*, camarera *f*, moza *f* Arg, Chile, Col, Peru

waive ['weɪv] *vt* **waived; waiving** : renunciar a ⟨to waive one's rights : renunciar a sus derechos⟩ ⟨to waive the rules : no aplicar las reglas⟩

waiver ['weɪvər] *n* : renuncia *f*

wake¹ ['weɪk] *v* **woke** ['woːk]; **woken** ['woːkən] *or* **waked; waking** *vi or* **to wake up** : despertar(se) ⟨he woke at noon : se despertó al mediodía⟩ ⟨wake up! : ¡despiértate!⟩ — *vt* : despertar

wake² *n* **1** VIGIL : velatorio *m*, velorio *m* (de un difunto) **2** TRAIL : estela *f* (de un barco, un huracán, etc.) **3** AFTERMATH : consecuencias *fpl* ⟨in the wake of : tras, como consecuencia de⟩

wakeful ['weɪkfəl] *adj* **1** SLEEPLESS : desvelado **2** VIGILANT : alerta, vigilante

wakefulness ['weɪkfəlnəs] *n* : vigilia *f*

waken ['weɪkən] → **awake**

walk¹ ['wɔk] *vi* **1** : caminar, andar, pasear ⟨you're walking too fast : estás caminando demasiado rápido⟩ ⟨to walk around the city : pasearse por la ciudad⟩ **2** : ir andando, ir a pie ⟨we had to walk home : tuvimos que ir a casa a pie⟩ **3** : recibir una base por bolas (dícese de un bateador) **4 to walk away** LEAVE : irse **5 to walk away** : salir ileso (de un accidente, etc.) **6 to walk away from** ABANDON : abandonar, retirarse de (negociaciones, etc.), rechazar (un acuerdo, etc.) **7 to walk away with** : ganar fácilmente (un premio, etc.) **8 to walk in on** INTERRUPT, SURPRISE : interrumpir, sorprender **9 to walk off** LEAVE : irse **10 to walk off with** : llevarse **11 to walk out** LEAVE : irse **12 to walk out** STRIKE : declararse en huelga **13 to walk out on** : abandonar — *vt* **1** : recorrer, caminar ⟨she walked two miles : caminó dos millas⟩ **2** ACCOMPANY : acompañar **3** : sacar a pasear (a un perro) **4** : darle una base por bolas (a un bateador) **5 to walk off** : caminar para aliviar (un calambre, etc.)

walk² *n* **1** : paseo *m*, caminata *f* ⟨to go for a walk : ir a caminar, dar un paseo⟩ **2** PATH : camino *m* **3** GAIT : andar *m* **4** : marcha *f* (en beisbol) **5 walk of life** : esfera *f*, condición *f*

walker ['wɔkər] *n* **1** : paseante *mf* **2** HIKER : excursionista *mf* **3** : andador *m* (aparato)

walking *n* : (el) caminar, (el) andar ⟨walking is good exercise : (el) caminar es buen ejercicio⟩

walking stick *n* : bastón *m*

walkout ['wɔkˌaʊt] *n* STRIKE : huelga *f*

walk out *vi* **1** STRIKE : declararse en huelga **2** LEAVE : salir, irse **3 to walk out on** : abandonar, dejar

walkway ['wɔk,weɪ] *n* **1** SIDEWALK : acera *f* **2** PATH : sendero *m* **3** PASSAGEWAY : pasadizo *m*

wall¹ ['wɔl] *vt* **1 to wall in** : cercar con una pared o un muro, tapiar, amurallar **2 to wall off** : separar con una pared o un muro **3 to wall up** : tapiar, condenar (una ventana, etc.)

wall² *n* **1** : pared *f* **2** : muro *m*, barda *f Mex* ⟨the walls of the city : las murallas de la ciudad⟩ **3** BARRIER : barrera *f* ⟨a wall of mountains : una barrera de montañas⟩ **4** : pared *f* (en anatomía) **5 to drive someone up the wall** *fam* : volver loco a alguien

walled ['wɔld] *adj* : amurallado

wallet ['wɑlət] *n* : billetera *f*, cartera *f*

wallflower ['wɔl,flauər] *n* **1** : alhelí *m* (flor) **2 to be a wallflower** : comer pavo

wallop¹ ['wɑləp] *vt* **1** TROUNCE : darle una paliza (a alguien) **2** SOCK : pegar fuerte

wallop² *n* : golpe *m* fuerte, golpazo *m*

wallow ['wɑ,loː] *vi* **1** : revolcarse ⟨to wallow in the mud : revolcarse en el lodo⟩ **2** DELIGHT : deleitarse ⟨to wallow in luxury : nadar en lujos⟩

wallpaper¹ ['wɔl,peɪpər] *vt* : empapelar

wallpaper² *n* : papel *m* pintado

wall–to–wall *adj* **1** FILLED : lleno ⟨it was wall-to-wall (with) people : estaba repleto de gente⟩ **2 wall–to–wall carpeting** : alfombra *f* (de pared a pared); moquette *f Arg, Uru*; moqueta *f Spain*

walnut ['wɔl,nʌt] *n* **1** : nuez *f* (fruta) **2** : nogal *m* (árbol y madera)

walrus ['wɔlrəs, 'wɑl-] *n, pl* **-rus** *or* **-ruses** : morsa *f*

waltz¹ ['wɔlts] *vi* **1** : bailar el vals **2** BREEZE : pasar con ligereza ⟨to waltz in : entrar tan campante⟩

waltz² *n* : vals *m*

wan ['wɑn] *adj* **wanner; wannest 1** PALLID : pálido **2** DIM : tenue ⟨wan light : luz tenue⟩ **3** LANGUID : lánguido ⟨a wan smile : una sonrisa lánguida⟩ — **wanly** *adv*

wand ['wɑnd] *n* : varita *f* (mágica)

wander ['wɑndər] *vi* **1** RAMBLE : deambular, vagar, vagabundear **2** STRAY : alejarse, desviarse, divagar ⟨she let her mind wander : dejó vagar la imaginación⟩ — *vt* : recorrer ⟨to wander the streets : vagar por las calles⟩

wanderer ['wɑndərər] *n* : vagabundo *m*, -da *f*; viajero *m*, -ra *f*

wanderlust ['wɑndər,lʌst] *n* : pasión *f* por viajar

wane¹ ['weɪn] *vi* **waned; waning 1** : menguar (dícese de la luna) **2** DECLINE : disminuir, decaer, menguar

wane² *n* **on the wane** : decayendo, en decadencia

wangle ['wæŋɡəl] *vt* **-gled; -gling** FINAGLE : arreglárselas para conseguir

wannabe ['wɑnə,biː] *n* : aspirante *mf* (a algo); imitador *m*, -dora *f* (de alguien)

want¹ ['wɑnt, 'wɔnt] *vt* **1** LACK : faltar **2** REQUIRE : requerir, necesitar **3** DESIRE : querer, desear

want² *n* **1** LACK : falta *f* **2** DESTITUTION : indigencia *f*, miseria *f* **3** DESIRE, NEED : deseo *m*, necesidad *f*

wanting ['wɑntɪŋ, 'wɔn-] *adj* **1** ABSENT : ausente **2** DEFICIENT : deficiente ⟨he's wanting in common sense : le falta sentido común⟩

wanton ['wɑntən, 'wɔn-] *adj* **1** LEWD, LUSTFUL : lascivo, lujurioso, licencioso **2** INHUMANE, MERCILESS : despiadado ⟨wanton cruelty : crueldad despiadada⟩

wapiti ['wɑpəˈti] *n, pl* **-ti** *or* **-tis** ELK : uapití *m*, wapití *m*

war¹ ['wɔr] *vi* **warred; warring** : combatir, batallar, hacer la guerra

war² *n* : guerra *f* ⟨to go to war : entrar en guerra⟩ ⟨to be at war : estar en guerra⟩

warble¹ ['wɔrbəl] *vi* **-bled; -bling** : gorjear, trinar

warble² *n* : trino *m*, gorjeo *m*

warbler ['wɔrblər] *n* : curruca *f*

ward¹ ['wɔrd] *vt* **to ward off** : desviar, protegerse contra

ward² *n* **1** : sala *f* (de un hospital, etc.) ⟨maternity ward : sala de maternidad⟩ **2** : distrito *m* electoral o administrativo (de una ciudad) **3** : pupilo *m*, -la *f* (de un tutor, etc.)

warden ['wɔrdən] *n* **1** KEEPER : guarda *mf*; guardián *m*, -diana *f* ⟨game warden : guardabosque⟩ **2** *or* **prison warden** : alcaide *m*

wardrobe ['wɔrd,roːb] *n* **1** CLOSET : armario *m* **2** CLOTHES : vestuario *m*, guardarropa *f*

ware ['wær] *n* **1** POTTERY : cerámica *f* **2 wares** *npl* GOODS : mercancía *f*, mercadería *f*

warehouse ['wær,haus] *n* : depósito *m*, almacén *m*, bodega *f Chile, Col, Mex*

warfare ['wɔr,fær] *n* **1** WAR : guerra *f* **2** STRUGGLE : lucha *f* ⟨the warfare against drugs : la lucha contra las drogas⟩

warhead ['wɔr,hɛd] *n* : ojiva *f*, cabeza *f* (de un misil)

warily ['wærəli] *adv* : cautelosamente, con cautela

wariness ['wærinəs] *n* : cautela *f*

warlike ['wɔr,laɪk] *adj* : belicoso, guerrero

warm¹ ['wɔrm] *vt* **1** HEAT : calentar, recalentar **2 to warm one's heart** : reconfortar a uno, alegrar el corazón **3 to warm up** : calentar (los músculos, un automóvil, etc.) — *vi* **1** : calentarse **2 to warm to** : tomarle simpatía (a alguien), entusiasmarse con (algo)

warm² *adj* **1** LUKEWARM : tibio, templado **2** : caliente, cálido, caluroso ⟨a warm wind : un viento cálido⟩ ⟨a warm day : un día caluroso, un día de calor⟩ ⟨warm hands : manos calientes⟩ **3** : caliente, que abriga ⟨warm clothes : ropa de abrigo⟩ ⟨I feel warm : tengo calor⟩ **4** CARING, CORDIAL : cariñoso, cordial **5** : cálido (dícese de colores) **6** FRESH : fresco, reciente ⟨a warm trail : un rastro reciente⟩ **7** (*used for riddles*) : caliente

warm–blooded ['wɔrm'blʌdəd] *adj* : de sangre caliente

warmhearted ['wɔrm'hɑrtəd] *adj* : cariñoso

warmly ['wɔrmli] *adv* 1 AFFECTIONATELY : calurosamente, afectuosamente 2 **to dress warmly** : abrigarse

warmonger ['wɔr,mɑŋɡər, -,mʌŋ-] *n* : belicista *mf*

warmth ['wɔrmpθ] *n* 1 : calor *m* 2 AFFECTION : cariño *m*, afecto *m* 3 ENTHUSIASM : ardor *m*, entusiasmo *m*

warm-up ['wɔrm,ʌp] *n* : calentamiento *m*

warn ['wɔrn] *vt* 1 CAUTION : advertir, alertar 2 INFORM : avisar, informar

warning ['wɔrnɪŋ] *n* 1 ADVICE : advertencia *f*, aviso *m* 2 ALERT : alerta *f*, alarma *f*

warp[1] ['wɔrp] *vt* 1 : alabear, combar 2 PERVERT : pervertir, deformar — *vi* : pandearse, alabearse, combarse

warp[2] *n* 1 : urdimbre *f* ⟨the warp and the weft : la urdimbre y la trama⟩ 2 : alabeo *m* (en la madera, etc.)

warrant[1] ['wɔrənt] *vt* 1 ASSURE : asegurar, garantizar 2 GUARANTEE : garantizar 3 JUSTIFY, MERIT : justificar, merecer

warrant[2] *n* 1 AUTHORIZATION : autorización *f*, permiso *m* ⟨an arrest warrant : una orden de detención⟩ 2 JUSTIFICATION : justificación *f*

warranty ['wɔrənti, ,wɔrən'ti:] *n*, *pl* **-ties** : garantía *f*

warren ['wɔrən] *n* : madriguera *f* (de conejos)

warrior ['wɔriər] *n* : guerrero *m*, -ra *f*

warship ['wɔr,ʃɪp] *n* : buque *m* de guerra

wart ['wɔrt] *n* : verruga *f*

wartime ['wɔr,taɪm] *n* : tiempo *m* de guerra

wary ['wæri] *adj* **warier; -est** : cauteloso, receloso ⟨to be wary of : desconfiar de⟩

was → be

wash[1] ['wɔʃ, 'wɑʃ] *vt* 1 CLEAN : lavar(se), limpiar, fregar ⟨to wash the dishes : lavar los platos⟩ ⟨to wash one's hands : lavarse las manos⟩ 2 DRENCH : mojar 3 LAP : bañar ⟨waves were washing the shore : las olas bañaban la orilla⟩ 4 CARRY, DRAG : arrastrar ⟨they were washed out to sea : fueron arrastrados por el mar⟩ 5 **to be/get washed out** : cancelarse por lluvia 6 **to wash away** : llevarse (un puente, etc.) 7 **to wash down** : lavar (paredes, etc.) 8 **to wash down** : tragarse (con agua, etc.) 9 **to wash off** : lavar 10 **to wash off** : quitar (la suciedad, etc.) 11 **to wash out** : lavar (un recipiente) 12 **to wash out** : destruir, inundar (una carretera, etc.) 13 **to wash out** : quitar (una mancha, etc.) — *vi* 1 : lavar(se) ⟨I'll wash, you dry : yo lavo y tú secas⟩ ⟨wash before dinner : lávate antes de cenar⟩ ⟨the dress washes well : el vestido se lava bien⟩ 2 **to wash over** : bañar ⟨relief washed over me : sentí un gran alivio⟩ 3 **to wash off/out** : quitarse 4 **to wash up** BATHE : lavarse 5 **to wash up/ashore** : ser arrojado por el mar

wash[2] *n* 1 : lavado *m* ⟨to give something a wash : lavar algo⟩ 2 LAUNDRY

: artículos *mpl* para lavar, ropa *f* sucia 3 : estela *f* (de un barco)

washable ['wɔʃəbəl, 'wɑ-] *adj* : lavable

washboard ['wɔʃ,bord, 'wɑʃ-] *n* : tabla *f* de lavar

washbowl ['wɔʃ,bo:l, 'wɑʃ-] *n* : lavabo *m*, lavamanos *m*

washcloth ['wɔʃ,klɔθ, 'wɑʃ-] *n* : toallita *f* (para lavarse)

washed-out ['wɔʃt'aut, 'wɑʃt-] *adj* 1 : desvaído (dícese de colores) 2 EXHAUSTED : agotado, desanimado

washed-up ['wɔʃt'ʌp, 'wɑʃt-] *adj* : acabado (dícese de una persona), fracasado (dícese de un negocio, etc.)

washer ['wɔʃər, 'wɑ-] *n* 1 → **washing machine** 2 : arandela *f* (de una llave, etc.)

washing ['wɔʃɪŋ, 'wɑ-] *n* WASH : ropa *f* para lavar

washing machine *n* : máquina *f* de lavar, lavadora *f*

washout ['wɔʃ,aut, 'wɑʃ-] *n* 1 : erosión *f* (de la tierra) 2 FAILURE : fracaso *m* ⟨she's a washout : es un desastre⟩

washroom ['wɔʃ,ru:m, 'wɑʃ-, -,rum] *n* : servicios *mpl* (públicos); baño *m*; sanitario *m* Col, Mex, Ven

wasn't ['wʌzənt] *contraction of* WAS NOT → be

wasp ['wɑsp] *n* : avispa *f*

WASP *or* **Wasp** ['wɑsp] *n* (*white Anglo-Saxon Protestant*) *sometimes disparaging* : persona *f* blanca, anglosajona, y protestante

waspish ['wɑspɪʃ] *adj* 1 IRRITABLE : irritable, irascible 2 CAUSTIC : cáustico, mordaz

waste[1] ['weɪst] *v* **wasted; wasting** *vt* 1 DEVASTATE : arrasar, arruinar, devastar 2 SQUANDER : desperdiciar, despilfarrar, malgastar ⟨to waste time : perder tiempo⟩ — *vi or* **to waste away** : consumirse, chuparse

waste[2] *adj* 1 BARREN : yermo, baldío 2 DISCARDED : de desecho 3 EXCESS : sobrante

waste[3] *n* 1 → **wasteland** 2 MISUSE : derroche *m*, desperdicio *m*, despilfarro *m* ⟨a waste of time : una pérdida de tiempo⟩ 3 RUBBISH : basura *f*, desechos *mpl*, desperdicios *mpl* 4 EXCREMENT : excremento *m*

wastebasket ['weɪst,bæskət] *or* **wastepaper basket** *n* : cesto *m* (de basura), papelera *f*, zafacón *m* Car

wasteful ['weɪstfəl] *adj* : despilfarrador, derrochador, pródigo

wastefulness ['weɪstfəlnəs] *n* : derroche *m*, despilfarro *m*

wasteland ['weɪst,lænd, -lənd] *n* : baldío *m*, yermo *m*, desierto *m*

wastepaper ['weɪst'peɪpər] *n* : papel *m* de desecho

wastepaper basket → **wastebasket**

watch[1] ['wɑtʃ] *vt* 1 OBSERVE : mirar, observar ⟨to watch television : mirar/ver la televisión⟩ ⟨watch this! : ¡mira!⟩ 2 MONITOR : vigilar 3 *or* **to watch over** : vigilar, cuidar (a niños, etc.) ⟨would you watch my things? : ¿me puedes cuidar/ vigilar las cosas?⟩ **4** : tener cuidado de, vigilar ⟨watch what you do : ten cuidado con lo que haces⟩ ⟨I have to watch my cholesterol : tengo que vigilar el colesterol⟩ — *vi* **1** OBSERVE : mirar, ver, observar **2 to watch for** AWAIT : esperar, quedar a la espera de **3 to watch out** : tener cuidado ⟨watch out! : ¡ten cuidado!, ¡ojo!⟩

watch² *n* **1** : guardia *f* ⟨to be on watch, to stand watch : estar de guardia⟩ **2** SURVEILLANCE : vigilancia *f* **3** LOOKOUT : guardia *mf*, centinela *f*, vigía *mf* **4** TIMEPIECE : reloj *m* **5 to keep watch on/over** : vigilar, cuidar

watchdog [ˈwɑtʃˌdɔɡ] *n* : perro *m* guardián

watcher [ˈwɑtʃər] *n* : observador *m*, -dora *f*

watchful [ˈwɑtʃfəl] *adj* : alerta, vigilante, atento

watchfulness [ˈwɑtʃfəlnəs] *n* : vigilancia *f*

watchmaker [ˈwɑtʃˌmeɪkər] *n* : relojero *m*, -ra *f*

watchmaking [ˈwɑtʃˌmeɪkɪŋ] *n* : relojería *f* (actividad)

watchman [ˈwɑtʃmən] *n, pl* **-men** [-mən, -ˌmɛn] : vigilante *m*, guarda *m*

watchtower [ˈwɑtʃˌtaʊər] *n* : atalaya *f*

watchword [ˈwɑtʃˌwərd] *n* **1** PASSWORD : contraseña *f* **2** SLOGAN : lema *m*, eslogan *m*

water¹ [ˈwɑtər, ˈwɑ-] *vt* **1** : regar (el jardín, etc.) **2 to water down** DILUTE : diluir, aguar — *vi* : lagrimear (dícese de los ojos), hacérsele agua la boca a uno ⟨my mouth is watering : se me hace agua la boca⟩

water² *n* **1** : agua *f* ⟨drinking water : agua potable⟩ ⟨running water : agua corriente⟩ **2 waters** *npl* : aguas *fpl* **3 not to hold water** : hacer agua por todos lados **4 to pass water** : orinar

water buffalo *n* : búfalo *m* de agua

watercolor [ˈwɑtərˌkʌlər, ˈwɑ-] *n* : acuarela *f*

watercourse [ˈwɑtərˌkors, ˈwɑ-] *n* : curso *m* de agua

watercress [ˈwɑtərˌkrɛs, ˈwɑ-] *n* : berro *m*

waterfall [ˈwɑtərˌfɔl, ˈwɑ-] *n* : cascada *f*, salto *m* de agua, catarata *f*

waterfowl [ˈwɑtərˌfaʊl, ˈwɑ-] *n* : ave *f* acuática

waterfront [ˈwɑtərˌfrʌnt, ˈwɑ-] *n* **1** : tierra *f* que bordea un río, un lago, o un mar **2** WHARF : muelle *m*

water heater *n* : calentador *m* de agua, bóiler *m Mex*

watering can *n* : regadera *f*

water lily *n* : nenúfar *m*

waterlogged [ˈwɑtərˌlɔɡd, ˈwɑtər-ˌlɑɡd] *adj* : lleno de agua, empapado, inundado (dícese del suelo)

watermark [ˈwɑtərˌmɑrk, ˈwɑ-] *n* **1** : marca *f* del nivel de agua **2** : filigrana *f* (en el papel)

watermelon [ˈwɑtərˌmɛlən, ˈwɑ-] *n* : sandía *f*

water moccasin → moccasin

waterpower [ˈwɑtərˌpaʊər, ˈwɑ-] *n* : energía *f* hidráulica

waterproof¹ [ˈwɑtərˌpruːf, ˈwɑ-] *vt* : hacer impermeable, impermeabilizar

waterproof² *adj* : impermeable, a prueba de agua

waterproofing *n* : impermeabilizante *nm* (sustancia química)

water repellent *n* : impermeabilizante *nm*

water–resistant *or* **water–repellent** *adj* : hidrófugo, impermeabilizado

watershed [ˈwɑtərˌʃɛd, ˈwɑ-] *n* **1** : línea *f* divisoria de aguas **2** BASIN : cuenca *f* (de un río)

waterskiing [ˈwɑtərˌskiːɪŋ, ˈwɑ-] *n* : esquí *m* acuático

waterspout [ˈwɑtərˌspaʊt, ˈwɑ-] *n* WHIRLWIND : tromba *f* marina

watertight [ˈwɑtərˌtaɪt, ˈwɑ-] *adj* **1** : hermético **2** IRREFUTABLE : irrebatible, irrefutable ⟨a watertight contract : un contrato sin lagunas⟩

waterwheel [ˈwɑtərˌʰwiːl, ˈwɑ-] *n* : noria *f*

waterway [ˈwɑtərˌweɪ, ˈwɑ-] *n* : vía *f* navegable

waterworks [ˈwɑtərˌwərks, ˈwɑ-] *npl* : central *f* de abastecimiento de agua

watery [ˈwɑtəri, ˈwɑ-] *adj* **1** : acuoso, como agua **2** : aguado, diluido ⟨watery soup : sopa aguada⟩ **3** : lloroso ⟨watery eyes : ojos llorosos⟩ **4** WASHED-OUT : desvaído (dícese de colores)

watt [ˈwɑt] *n* : vatio *m*

wattage [ˈwɑtɪd] *n* : vataje *m*

wave¹ [ˈweɪv] *v* **waved; waving** *vi* **1** : saludar con la mano, hacer señas con la mano ⟨she waved at him : lo saludó con la mano⟩ **2** FLUTTER, SHAKE : ondear, agitarse **3** UNDULATE : ondular — *vt* **1** SHAKE : agitar **2** BRANDISH : blandir **3** CURL : ondular, marcar (el pelo) **4** SIGNAL : hacerle señas a (con la mano) ⟨he waved farewell : se despidió con la mano⟩

wave² *n* **1** : ola *f* (de agua) **2** CURL : onda *f* (en el pelo) **3** : onda *f* (en física) **4** SURGE : oleada *f* ⟨a wave of enthusiasm : una oleada de entusiasmo⟩ **5** GESTURE : señal *f* con la mano, saludo *m* con la mano

wavelength [ˈweɪvˌlɛŋkθ] *n* : longitud *f* de onda

waver [ˈweɪvər] *vi* **1** VACILLATE : vacilar, fluctuar **2** FLICKER : parpadear, titilar, oscilar **3** FALTER : flaquear, tambalearse

wavy [ˈweɪvi] *adj* **wavier; -est** : ondulado

wax¹ [ˈwæks] *vi* **1** : crecer (dícese de la luna) **2** BECOME : volverse, ponerse ⟨to wax indignant : indignarse⟩ — *vt* : encerar

wax² *n* **1** BEESWAX : cera *f* de abejas **2** : cera *f* ⟨floor wax : cera para el piso⟩ **3** *or* **earwax** [ˈɪrˌwæks] : cerilla *f*, cerumen *m*

waxen [ˈwæksən] *adj* : de cera

waxy [ˈwæksi] *adj* **waxier; -est** : ceroso

way [ˈweɪ] *n* **1** PATH, ROAD : camino *m*, vía *f* ⟨they live across the way : viven enfrente⟩ **2** ROUTE : camino *m*, ruta *f* ⟨to go the wrong way : equivocarse de camino⟩ ⟨to lose one's way : perderse⟩ ⟨do you know the way? : ¿sabes el camino?⟩ ⟨can you tell me the way to . . . ? : ¿me puedes indicar cómo llegar a . . . ?⟩ ⟨I'm on my way : estoy de camino⟩ ⟨we should be on our way : tenemos que irnos⟩ ⟨on the way back : en el camino de regreso/vuelta⟩ ⟨the only way in/out : la única entrada/salida⟩ **3** : línea *f* de conducta, camino *m* ⟨he chose the easy way : optó por el camino fácil⟩ **4** MANNER, MEANS : manera *f*, modo *m*, forma *f* ⟨in the same way : del mismo modo, igualmente⟩ ⟨in no way : de ninguna manera⟩ ⟨to my way of thinking : a mi modo de ver⟩ ⟨the way she spends money, you would think she was rich! : gasta dinero como si fuera rica⟩ ⟨their way of life : su modo de vida⟩ **5** (*indicating a wish*) ⟨have it your way : como tú quieras⟩ ⟨to get one's own way : salirse uno con la suya⟩ **6** (*indicating progress*) ⟨we inched our way forward : avanzamos poco a poco⟩ ⟨to talk one's way out of something : librarse de algo (engatusándole a alguien)⟩ **7** (*indicating a condition or situation*) ⟨he's in a bad way : está muy mal de salud⟩ ⟨that's just the way things are : así son las cosas⟩ **8** (*indicating one of two alternatives*) ⟨either way : de cualquier manera⟩ ⟨you can't have it both ways : tienes que elegir⟩ **9** (*indicating a portion*) ⟨we split it three ways : lo dividimos en tres⟩ **10** RESPECT : aspecto *m*, sentido *m* ⟨in a way, it was a relief : en cierto modo fue un alivio⟩ ⟨in every way : en todo⟩ **11** CUSTOM : costumbre *f* ⟨to change/mend one's ways : dejar las malas costumbres, enmendarse⟩ ⟨to be set in one's ways : ser inflexible⟩ **12** PASSAGE : camino *m* ⟨to be/get in the way : estar/meterse en el camino⟩ ⟨get it out of the way! : ¡quítalo de en medio!⟩ ⟨to make way for, to clear the way for : abrirle paso a⟩ **13** DISTANCE : distancia *f* ⟨to come a long way : hacer grandes progresos⟩ ⟨he talked the whole way home : habló durante todo el camino a casa⟩ ⟨she ran all the way there : corrió hasta allí⟩ ⟨it stretches all the way along the beach : se extiende a lo largo de la playa⟩ ⟨we went all the way up : subimos hasta arriba⟩ ⟨we sat all the way at the back : nos sentamos al fondo⟩ ⟨you came all this way just to see me? : ¿viniste desde tan lejos sólo para verme?⟩ **14** DIRECTION : dirección *f* ⟨come this way : venga por aquí⟩ ⟨this way and that : de un lado a otro⟩ ⟨which way did he go? : ¿por dónde fue?⟩ **15 all the way** COMPLETELY : completamente **16 all the way** CONTINUOUSLY : en todo momento ⟨he was with us all the way : nos apoyó en todo momento⟩ ⟨all the way through the concert : durante todo el concierto⟩ **17 by the way** : a propósito, por cierto **18 by way of** VIA : vía, pasando por **19 by way of** *or* **in the way of** AS : a modo de, a manera de **20 every step of the way** : en todo momento **21 no way** : de ninguna manera, ni hablar **22 out of the way** REMOTE : remoto, recóndito **23 out of the way** FINISHED : acabado ⟨to get a task out of the way : quitar una tarea de en medio⟩ **24 the other way (around)** : al revés **25 there are no two ways about it** : no cabe la menor duda **26 to give way** COLLAPSE : romperse, hundirse, ceder **27 to give way to** : ceder a **28 to go out of one's way (to)** : tomarse muchas molestias (para), desvivirse (por) **29 to go someone's way** : salirle bien a alguien **30 to have a way of** : soler, tender a ⟨things have a way of working out : las cosas suelen arreglarse solas⟩ ⟨she has a way of exaggerating : tiende a exagerar las cosas⟩ **31 to have a way with** : saber como tratar a (los niños, los animales, etc.) ⟨to have a way with words : tener facilidad de palabra⟩ **32** → **under way 33 way to go!** *fam* : ¡bien hecho!

wayfarer [ˈweɪˌfærər] *n* : caminante *mf*

waylay [ˈweɪˌleɪ] *vt* **-laid** [-ˌleɪd]; **-laying** ACCOST : abordar

wayside [ˈweɪˌsaɪd] *n* : borde *m* del camino

wayward [ˈweɪwərd] *adj* **1** UNRULY : díscolo, rebelde **2** UNTOWARD : adverso

we [ˈwiː] *pron* : nosotros, nosotras

weak [ˈwiːk] *adj* **1** : débil ⟨weak arms/eyes : brazos/ojos débiles⟩ ⟨a weak leader/character : un líder/carácter débil⟩ ⟨a weak drug/signal/economy : una droga/señal/economía débil⟩ **2** GENTLE : flojo (dícese de un golpe), leve (dícese de un viento) **3** : flojo (dícese de un estudiante, etc.) **4** : flojo (dícese de una pieza, etc.) **5** : débil, flojo, endeble (dícese de un argumento, una excusa, etc.) ⟨a weak attempt : un intento tímido⟩ **6** DILUTED : aguado, diluido ⟨weak tea : té poco cargado⟩ **7** FAINT : tenue (dícese de los colores, las luces, los sonidos, etc.) **8** : poco pronunciado (dícese de la barbilla) **9** : regular (en gramática)

weaken [ˈwiːkən] *vt* : debilitar — *vi* : debilitarse, flaquear

weakling [ˈwiːklɪŋ] *n* : alfeñique *m fam*; debilucho *m*, -cha *f*

weakly[1] [ˈwiːkli] *adv* : débilmente

weakly[2] *adj* **weaklier; -est** : débil, enclenque

weakness [ˈwiːknəs] *n* **1** FEEBLENESS : debilidad *f* **2** FAULT, FLAW : flaqueza *f*, punto *m* débil

wealth [ˈwɛlθ] *n* **1** RICHES : riqueza *f* **2** PROFUSION : abundancia *f*, profusión *f*

wealthy [ˈwɛlθi] *adj* **wealthier; -est** : rico, acaudalado, adinerado

wean [ˈwiːn] *vt* **1** : destetar (a los niños o las crías) **2 to wean someone away from** : quitarle a alguien la costumbre de

weapon [ˈwɛpən] *n* : arma *f* ⟨biological/chemical weapon : arma biológica/

química⟩ ⟨weapon of mass destruction : arma de destrucción masiva⟩

weaponless ['wɛpənləs] *adj* : desarmado

weaponry ['wɛpənri] *n* : armamento *m*

wear[1] ['wær] *v* **wore** ['wor]; **worn** ['worn]; **wearing** *vt* **1** : llevar (ropa, un reloj, etc.), calzar (zapatos) ⟨to wear a smile : sonreír⟩ **2** *or* **to wear away** : gastar, desgastar, erosionar (rocas, etc.) ⟨the carpet was badly worn : la alfombra estaba muy gastada⟩ **3** : hacer (por el uso) ⟨he wore a hole in his pants : se le hizo un agujero en los pantalones⟩ **4 to wear down** DRAIN : agotar **5 to wear down** : convencer por cansancio **6 to wear on** IRRITATE : molestar, irritar **7 to wear one's heart on one's sleeve** : no ocultar uno sus sentimientos **8 to wear out** : gastar ⟨he wore out his shoes : gastó sus zapatos⟩ **9 to wear out** EXHAUST : agotar, fatigar ⟨to wear oneself out : agotarse⟩ **10 to wear through** : gastar (completamente) ⟨he wore through his shoes : se le hizo agujeros en los zapatos⟩ — *vi* **1** LAST : durar **2 to wear away** : desgastarse **3 to wear off** DIMINISH, VANISH : disminuir, desaparecer ⟨the drug wears off in a few hours : los efectos de la droga desaparecen después de unas horas⟩ **4 to wear on** CONTINUE, DRAG : continuar, alargarse **5 to wear out** : gastarse **6 to wear the pants** : llevar los pantalones **7 to wear thin** : gastarse (dícese de tela, etc.) **8 to wear thin** : agotarse (dícese de la paciencia, etc.), perder la gracia (dícese de un chiste)

wear[2] *n* **1** USE : uso *m* ⟨for everyday wear : para todos los días⟩ **2** CLOTHING : ropa *f* ⟨children's wear : ropa de niños⟩ **3** DETERIORATION : desgaste *m* ⟨to be the worse for wear : estar deteriorado⟩

wearable ['wærəbəl] *adj* : que puede ponerse (dícese de una prenda)

wear and tear *n* : desgaste *m*

weariness ['wɪrinəs] *n* : fatiga *f*, cansancio *m*

wearisome ['wɪrisəm] *adj* : aburrido, pesado, cansado

weary[1] ['wɪri] *v* **-ried; -rying** *vt* **1** TIRE : cansar, fatigar **2** BORE : hastiar, aburrir — *vi* : cansarse

weary[2] *adj* **wearier; -est 1** TIRED : cansado **2** FED UP : harto **3** BORED : aburrido

weasel ['wi:zəl] *n* : comadreja *f*

weather[1] ['wɛðər] *vt* **1** WEAR : erosionar, desgastar **2** ENDURE : aguantar, sobrellevar ⟨to weather the storm : capear el temporal⟩

weather[2] *n* **1** : tiempo *m* ⟨good/bad weather : buen/mal tiempo⟩ ⟨weather permitting : si hace buen tiempo⟩ ⟨weather forecast : pronóstico del tiempo, parte meteorológico⟩ **2 to be under the weather** : estar enfermo, no estar muy bien

weather–beaten ['wɛðər,bi:tən] *adj* : curtido

weatherman ['wɛðər,mæn] *n*, *pl* **-men** [-mən, -,mɛn] METEOROLOGIST : meteorólogo *m*, -ga *f*

weatherproof ['wɛðər,pru:f] *adj* : que resiste a la intemperie, impermeable

weather vane → **vane**

weave[1] ['wi:v] *v* **wove** ['wo:v] *or* **weaved; woven** ['wo:vən] *or* **weaved; weaving** *vt* **1** : tejer (tela) **2** INTERLACE : entretejer, entrelazar **3 to weave one's way through** : abrirse camino por — *vi* **1** : tejer **2** WIND : serpentear, zigzaguear

weave[2] *n* : tejido *m*, trama *f*

weaver ['wi:vər] *n* : tejedor *m*, -dora *f*

web[1] ['wɛb] *vt* **webbed; webbing** : cubrir o proveer con una red

web[2] *n* **1** COBWEB, SPIDERWEB : telaraña *f*, tela *f* de araña **2** ENTANGLEMENT, SNARE : red *f*, enredo *m* ⟨a web of intrigue : una red de intriga⟩ **3** : membrana *f* interdigital (de aves) **4** NETWORK : red *f* ⟨a web of highways : una red de carreteras⟩ **5 the Web** : la web

webbed ['wɛbd] *adj* : palmeado ⟨webbed feet : patas palmeadas⟩

webcam ['wɛb,kæm] *n* : webcam *f*

weblog → **blog**

webmaster *or* **Webmaster** ['wɛb,mæstər] *n* : webmaster *mf*

web page *or* **Web page** *n* : página *f* web

web site *or* **Web site** *n* : sitio *m* web

wed ['wɛd] *vt* **wedded; wedding 1** MARRY : casarse con **2** UNITE : ligar, unir

we'd ['wi:d] *contraction of* WE HAD, WE SHOULD *or* WE WOULD → **have, should, would**

wedding ['wɛdɪŋ] *n* : boda *f*, casamiento *m* ⟨wedding dress : traje de novia⟩ ⟨wedding ring : anillo de boda⟩

wedge[1] ['wɛdʒ] *vt* **wedged; wedging 1** : apretar (con una cuña) ⟨to wedge open : mantener abierto con una cuña⟩ **2** CRAM : meter, embutir

wedge[2] *n* **1** : cuña *f* **2** PIECE : porción *f*, trozo *m*

wedlock ['wɛd,lɑk] → **marriage**

Wednesday ['wɛnz,deɪ, -di] *n* : miércoles *m* ⟨today is Wednesday : hoy es miércoles⟩ ⟨(on) Wednesday : el miércoles⟩ ⟨(on) Wednesdays : los miércoles⟩ ⟨last Wednesday : el miércoles pasado⟩ ⟨next Wednesday : el miércoles que viene⟩ ⟨every other Wednesday : cada dos miércoles⟩ ⟨Wednesday afternoon/morning : miércoles por la tarde/mañana⟩

wee ['wi:] *adj* **1** : pequeño, minúsculo **2 the wee hours** → **hour**

weed[1] ['wi:d] *vt* **1** : desherbar **2 to weed out** : eliminar, quitar

weed[2] *n* : mala hierba *f*

weed killer *n* : herbicida *m*

weedy ['wi:di] *adj* **weedier; -est 1** : cubierto de malas hierbas **2** LANKY, SKINNY : flaco, larguirucho/pez

week ['wi:k] *n* : semana *f* ⟨last week : la semana pasada⟩ ⟨next week : la semana que viene⟩

weekday ['wi:k,deɪ] *n* : día *m* laborable

weekend ['wiːkˌɛnd] *n* : fin *m* de semana
weekly[1] ['wiːkli] *adv* : semanalmente
weekly[2] *adj* : semanal
weekly[3] *n, pl* **-lies** : semanario *m*
weep ['wiːp] *v* **wept** ['wɛpt]; **weeping** : llorar
weeping willow *n* : sauce *m* llorón
weepy ['wiːpi] *adj* **weepier; -est** : lloroso, triste
weevil ['wiːvəl] *n* : gorgojo *m*
weft ['wɛft] *n* : trama *f*
weigh ['weɪ] *vt* **1** : pesar **2** CONSIDER : considerar, sopesar **3 to weigh anchor** : levar anclas **4 to weigh down** : sobrecargar (con una carga), abrumar (con preocupaciones, etc.) **5 to weigh up** : hacerse una idea de — *vi* **1** : pesar ⟨it weighs 10 pounds : pesa 10 libras⟩ **2** COUNT : tener importancia, contar ⟨to weigh for/against : favorecer/perjudicar⟩ **3 to weigh in** : intervenir **4 to weigh on one's mind** : preocuparle a uno
weight[1] ['weɪt] *vt or* **to weight down 1** : poner peso en, sujetar con un peso **2** BURDEN : cargar, oprimir
weight[2] *n* **1** HEAVINESS : peso *m* ⟨to lose weight : bajar de peso, adelgazar⟩ **2** : peso *m* ⟨weights and measures : pesos y medidas⟩ **3** : pesa *f* ⟨to lift weights : levantar pesas⟩ **4** SINKER : plomo *m*, plomada *f* **5** BURDEN : peso *m*, carga *f* ⟨to take a weight off one's mind : quitarle un peso de encima a uno⟩ **6** IMPORTANCE : peso *m* **7** INFLUENCE : influencia *f*, autoridad *f* ⟨to throw one's weight around : hacer sentir su influencia⟩ **8 to pull one's weight** : poner uno de su parte
weightless ['weɪtləs] *adj* : ingrávido
weight lifting *n* : halterofilia *f*, levantamiento *m* de pesas
weighty ['weɪti] *adj* **weightier; -est 1** HEAVY : pesado **2** IMPORTANT : importante, de peso
weir ['wer, 'wɪr] *n* : dique *m*
weird ['wɪrd] *adj* **1** MYSTERIOUS : misterioso **2** STRANGE : extraño, raro — **weirdly** *adv*
weirdo ['wɪrˌdoː] *n, pl* **weirdos** : bicho *m* raro
welcome[1] ['wɛlkəm] *vt* **-comed; -coming** : darle la bienvenida a, recibir
welcome[2] *adj* : bienvenido ⟨to make someone welcome : acoger bien a alguien⟩ ⟨you're welcome! : ¡de nada!, ¡no hay de qué!⟩
welcome[3] *n* : bienvenida *f*, recibimiento *m*, acogida *f*
weld[1] ['wɛld] *v* : soldar
weld[2] *n* : soldadura *f*
welder ['wɛldər] *n* : soldador *m*, -dora *f*
welfare ['wɛlˌfær] *n* **1** WELL-BEING : bienestar *m* **2** : asistencia *f* social
well[1] ['wɛl] *vi or* **to well up** : brotar, manar
well[2] *adv* **better** ['bɛtər]; **best** ['bɛst] **1** RIGHTLY : bien, correctamente **2** SATISFACTORILY : bien ⟨to turn out well : resultar/salir bien⟩ ⟨well done! : ¡muy bien!⟩ **3** SKILLFULLY : bien ⟨she sings well : canta bien⟩ **4** (*indicating benevolence*) : bien ⟨to speak well of : hablar

bien de⟩ ⟨to wish someone well : desearle lo mejor a alguien⟩ ⟨he means well : tiene buenas intenciones⟩ **5** COMPLETELY : completamente ⟨well-hidden : completamente escondido⟩ **6** : bien ⟨I knew him well : lo conocía bien⟩ **7** CONSIDERABLY, FAR : muy, bastante ⟨well ahead : muy adelante⟩ ⟨well before the deadline : bastante antes de la fecha⟩ **8** CERTAINLY : bien ⟨you know very well that . . . : sabes muy bien que . . .⟩ ⟨he can well afford it : bien puede permitírselo⟩ **9** LIKELY : bien ⟨it could/may/might well be true : bien puede/podría/pudiera ser verdad⟩ **10** (*used for emphasis*) ⟨one might well ask if . . . : uno podría preguntarse si . . .⟩ ⟨I couldn't very well refuse! : ¿cómo iba a decir que no?⟩ **11 as well** ALSO : también **12 as well** (*indicating advisability*) ⟨we may/might as well get started : más vale que empecemos⟩ **13 as well** (*indicating equivalence*) ⟨I might as well have stayed home : bien podría haberme quedado en casa⟩ **14 → as well as 15 well and truly** : completamente
well[3] *adj* **1** SATISFACTORY : bien ⟨all is well : todo está bien⟩ **2** DESIRABLE : conveniente ⟨it would be well if you left : sería conveniente que te fueras⟩ **3** HEALTHY : bien, sano **4 it's just as well** : menos mal
well[4] *n* **1** : pozo *m* (de agua, petróleo, gas, etc.), aljibe *m* (de agua) **2** SOURCE : fuente *f* ⟨a well of information : una fuente de información⟩ **3 → stairwell**
well[5] *interj* **1** (*used to introduce a remark*) : bueno **2** (*used to express surprise*) : ¡vaya!
we'll ['wiːl, wɪl] *contraction of* WE SHALL *or* WE WILL **→ shall, will**
well—adjusted [ˌwɛləˈdʒʌstəd] *adj* : equilibrado (dícese de una persona)
well—balanced ['wɛlˈbælənst] *adj* : equilibrado
well—behaved ['wɛlbɪˈheɪvd] *adj* : (bien) educado, que se porta bien
well—being ['wɛlˈbiːɪŋ] *n* : bienestar *m*
well—bred ['wɛlˈbrɛd] *adj* : fino, (bien) educado
well—built ['wɛlˈbɪlt] *adj* : fornido
well—defined [ˌwɛldiˈfaɪnd] *adj* : bien definido
well—done ['wɛlˈdʌn] *adj* **1** : bien hecho ⟨well-done! : ¡bravo!⟩ **2** : bien cocido
well—dressed ['wɛlˈdrɛst] *adj* : bien vestido
well—founded ['wɛlˈfaʊndəd] *adj* : bien fundado
well—informed ['wɛlɪnˈfɔrmd] *adj* : bien informado
well—kept ['wɛlˈkɛpt] *adj* : bien cuidado
well—known ['wɛlˈnoːn] *adj* : famoso, bien conocido
well—made ['wɛlˈmeɪd] *adj* : sólido
well—mannered ['wɛlˈmænərd] *adj* : (bien) educado, de buenos modales
well—meaning ['wɛlˈmiːnɪŋ] *adj* : bienintencionado, que tiene buenas intenciones

well–nigh [ˈwɛlˈnaɪ] *adv* : casi ⟨well-nigh impossible : casi imposible⟩
well–off [ˈwɛlˈɔf] **1** → **well-to-do 2** FORTUNATE : afortunado
well–read [ˈwɛlˈrɛd] *adj* : culto
well–rounded [ˈwɛlˈraʊndəd] *adj* : completo, equilibrado
well–to–do [ˌwɛltəˈduː] *adj* : próspero, adinerado, rico
well–wisher [ˈwɛlˈwɪʃər] *n* ⟨a group of well-wishers gathered to say goodbye to him : un grupo de amigos/admiradores (etc.) se congregó para despedirlo⟩
well–worn [ˈwɛlˈworn] *adj* : muy gastado
Welsh [ˈwɛlʃ] *n* **1** : galés *m*, galesa *f* **2** : galés *m* (idioma) — **Welsh** *adj*
Welshman [ˈwɛlʃmən] *n, pl* **-men** [-mən, -ˌmɛn] : galés *m*
Welshwoman [ˈwɛlʃˌwʊmən] *n, pl* **-women** [-ˌwɪmən] : galesa *f*
welt [ˈwɛlt] *n* : verdugón *m*
welter [ˈwɛltər] *n* : fárrago *m*, revoltijo *m* ⟨a welter of data : un fárrago de datos⟩
wend [ˈwɛnd] *vi* **to wend one's way** : ponerse en camino, encaminar sus pasos
went → **go¹**
wept → **weep**
were → **be**
we're [ˈwɪr, ˈwər, ˈwiːər] *contraction of* WE ARE → **be**
weren't [ˈwərənt] *contraction of* WERE NOT → **be**
werewolf [ˈwɪrˌwʊlf, ˈwɛr-, ˈwər-, -ˌwʊlf] *n, pl* **-wolves** [-ˌwʊlvz, -ˌwʊlvz] : hombre *m* lobo
west¹ [ˈwɛst] *adv* : al oeste
west² *adj* : oeste, del oeste, occidental ⟨west winds : vientos del oeste⟩
west³ *n* **1** : oeste *m* **2 the West** : el Oeste, el Occidente
westbound [ˈwɛstˌbaʊnd] *adj* : que va hacia el oeste
westerly [ˈwɛstərli] *adv & adj* : del oeste
western¹ [ˈwɛstərn] *adj* **1** : Occidental, del Oeste **2** : occidental, oeste
western² *n* : western *m*
Westerner [ˈwɛstərnər] *n* : habitante *mf* del oeste
West Indian *n* : antillano *m*, -na *f* — **West Indian** *adj*
westward [ˈwɛstwərd] *adv & adj* : hacia el oeste
wet¹ [ˈwɛt] *vt* **wet** *or* **wetted; wetting** : mojar, humedecer
wet² *adj* **wetter; wettest 1** : mojado, húmedo ⟨wet clothes : ropa mojada⟩ ⟨wet paint : pintura fresca⟩ **2** RAINY : lluvioso
wet³ *n* **1** MOISTURE : humedad *f* **2** RAIN : lluvia *f*
wet blanket *n* : aguafiestas *mf*
wet nurse *n* : nodriza *f*
wet suit *n* : traje *m* de neopreno, traje *m* de buzo
we've [ˈwiːv] *contraction of* WE HAVE → **have**
whack¹ [ˈhwæk] *vt* : golpear (fuertemente), aporrear
whack² *n* **1** : golpe *m* fuerte, porrazo *m* **2** ATTEMPT : intento *m*, tentativa *f*

whale¹ [ˈhweɪl] *vi* **whaled; whaling** : cazar ballenas
whale² *n, pl* **whales** *or* **whale** : ballena *f*
whaleboat [ˈhweɪlˌboːt] *n* : ballenero *m*
whalebone [ˈhweɪlˌboːn] *n* : barba *f* de ballena
whaler [ˈhweɪlər] *n* **1** : ballenero *m*, -ra *f* **2** → **whaleboat**
wham [ˈhwæm] *interj* : zas!
wharf [ˈhworf] *n, pl* **wharves** [ˈhworvz] : muelle *m*, embarcadero *m*
what¹ [ˈhwat, ˈhwʌt] *adv* **1** HOW : cómo, qué, cuánto ⟨what does it matter? : ¿qué importa?⟩ **2 what with** : entre ⟨what with one thing and another : entre una cosa y otra⟩ **3 so what?** : ¿y qué?
what² *adj* **1** (*used in questions*) : qué ⟨what more do you want? : ¿qué más quieres?⟩ ⟨what color is it? : ¿de qué color es?⟩ **2** (*used in exclamations*) : qué ⟨what an idea! : ¡qué idea!⟩ **3** ANY, WHATEVER : cualquier ⟨give what help you can : da cualquier contribución que puedas⟩
what³ *pron* **1** (*used in direct questions*) : qué ⟨what happened? : ¿qué pasó?⟩ ⟨what does it cost? : ¿cuánto cuesta?⟩ ⟨what does this mean? : ¿que significa esto?⟩ ⟨what's it called? : ¿cómo se llama?⟩ ⟨what's the problem? : ¿cuál es el problema?⟩ ⟨what did you say? : ¿qué?, ¿cómo?⟩ ⟨what else did she say? : ¿qué más dijo?⟩ **2** : lo que, qué ⟨tell me what happened : dime qué pasó⟩ ⟨I don't know what to do : no sé qué hacer⟩ ⟨do what I tell you : haz lo que te digo⟩ ⟨guess what! : ¿sabes qué?⟩ **3 and/or what have you** : y no sé qué, y cosas por el estilo **4 what about** ⟨we're all going together — what about Kenny? : vamos todos juntos — ¿y Kenny?⟩ ⟨what about if . . . ? : ¿qué te parece si . . . ?⟩ **5 what for** WHY : por qué ⟨what did you do that for? : ¿por qué hiciste eso?⟩ **6 what if** : y si ⟨what if he knows? : ¿y si lo sabe?⟩ **7 what's more** : además **8 what's up?** *fam* : ¿qué pasa? **9 what's up?** (*used as a greeting*) *fam* : ¿qué hay?, ¿qué tal? **10 what's with . . . ?** *fam* : ¿a qué viene/vienen . . . ?
whatever¹ [hwatˈɛvər, ˌhwʌt-] *adj* **1** ANY : cualquier, cualquier . . . que ⟨whatever way you prefer : de cualquier manera que prefiera, como prefiera⟩ **2** (*in negative constructions*) ⟨there's no chance whatever : no hay ninguna posibilidad⟩ ⟨nothing whatever : nada en absoluto⟩
whatever² *pron* **1** ANYTHING : (todo) lo que ⟨I'll do whatever I want : haré lo que quiera⟩ **2** (*no matter what*) ⟨whatever it may be : sea lo que sea⟩ ⟨whatever happens : pase lo que pase⟩ **3** WHAT : qué ⟨whatever do you mean? : ¿qué quieres decir?⟩
whatnot [ˈhwatˌnat, ˈhwʌt-] *pron* : y qué sé yo ⟨diamonds, pearls, and whatnot : diamantes, perlas, y qué sé yo⟩
what's–his–name [ˈhwatsəzˌneɪm, ˈhwʌt-] *n* : fulano *m*
what's–her–name [ˈhwatsərˌneɪm, ˈhwʌt-] *n* : fulana *f*

whatsoever[1] [ˌʍɑtsoˈɛvər, ˌʍʌt-] *adj* → **whatever**[1]

whatsoever[2] *pron* → **whatever**[2]

wheat [ˈʍiːt] *n* : trigo *m*

wheaten [ˈʍiːtən] *adj* : de trigo

wheedle [ˈʍiːdəl] *vt* **-dled; -dling** CAJOLE : engatusar ⟨to wheedle something out of someone : sonsacarle algo a alguien⟩

wheel[1] [ˈʍiːl] *vt* : empujar (una bicicleta, etc.), mover (algo sobre ruedas) — *vi* **1** ROTATE : girar, rotar **2 to wheel around** TURN : darse la vuelta

wheel[2] *n* **1** : rueda *f* **2** *or* **steering wheel** : volante *m* (de automóviles, etc.), timón *m* (de barcos o aviones) **3 wheels** *npl* : maquinaria *f*, fuerza *f* impulsora ⟨the wheels of government : la maquinaria del gobierno⟩

wheelbarrow [ˈʍiːlˌbærˌoː] *n* : carretilla *f*

wheelchair [ˈʍiːlˌtʃær] *n* : silla *f* de ruedas

wheeze[1] [ˈʍiːz] *vi* **wheezed; wheezing** : resollar, respirar con dificultad

wheeze[2] *n* : resuello *m*

whelp[1] [ˈʍɛlp] *vi* : parir

whelp[2] *n* : cachorro *m*, -rra *f*

when[1] [ˈʍɛn] *adv* : cuándo ⟨when will you return? : ¿cuándo volverás?⟩ ⟨he asked me when I would be home : me preguntó cuándo estaría en casa⟩ ⟨say when : di basta/cuándo⟩

when[2] *conj* **1** (*referring to a particular time*) : cuando, en que ⟨when you are ready : cuando estés listo⟩ ⟨the days when I clean the house : los días en que limpio la casa⟩ **2** IF : cuando, si ⟨how can I go when I have no money? : ¿cómo voy a ir si no tengo dinero?⟩ **3** ALTHOUGH : cuando ⟨you said it was big when actually it's small : dijiste que era grande cuando en realidad es pequeño⟩

when[3] *pron* : cuándo ⟨since when are you the boss? : ¿desde cuándo eres el jefe?⟩

whence [ˈʍɛnts] *adv* : de donde

whenever[1] [ʍɛnˈɛvər] *adv* **1** : cuando sea ⟨tomorrow or whenever : mañana o cuando sea⟩ **2** (*in questions*) : cuándo

whenever[2] *conj* **1** : siempre que, cada vez que ⟨whenever I go, I'm disappointed : siempre que voy, quedo desilusionado⟩ **2** WHEN : cuando ⟨whenever you like : cuando quieras⟩

where[1] [ˈʍɛr] *adv* : dónde, adónde ⟨where is he? : ¿dónde está?⟩ ⟨where did they go? : ¿adónde fueron?⟩

where[2] *conj* : donde, adonde ⟨she knows where the house is : sabe donde está la casa⟩ ⟨she goes where she likes : va adonde quiera⟩

where[3] *pron* : donde ⟨Chicago is where I live : Chicago es donde vivo⟩

whereabouts[1] [ˈʍɛrəˌbauts] *adv* : dónde, por dónde ⟨whereabouts is the house? : ¿dónde está la casa?⟩

whereabouts[2] *ns & pl* : paradero *m*

whereas [ʍɛrˈæz] *conj* **1** : considerando que (usado en documentos legales) **2** : mientras que ⟨I like the white one whereas she prefers the black : me

gusta el blanco mientras que ella prefiere el negro⟩

whereby [ʍɛrˈbaɪ] *adv* : por lo cual

wherefore [ˈʍɛrˌfor] *adv* : por qué

wherein [ʍɛrˈɪn] *adv* : en el cual, en el que

whereof [ʍɛrˈʌv, -ɑv] *conj* : de lo cual

whereupon [ˈʍɛrəˌpɑn, -ˌpɔn] *conj* : con lo cual, después de lo cual

wherever[1] [ʍɛrˈɛvər] *adv* **1** WHERE : dónde, adónde **2** : en cualquier parte ⟨or wherever : o donde sea⟩

wherever[2] *conj* : dondequiera que, donde sea ⟨wherever you go : dondequiera que vayas⟩

wherewithal [ˈʍɛrwɪˌðɔl, -ˌθɔl] *n* : medios *mpl*, recursos *mpl*

whet [ˈʍɛt] *vt* **whetted; whetting 1** SHARPEN : afilar **2** STIMULATE : estimular ⟨to whet the appetite : estimular el apetito⟩

whether [ˈʍɛðər] *conj* **1** : si ⟨I don't know whether it is finished : no sé si está acabado⟩ ⟨we doubt whether he'll show up : dudamos que aparezca⟩ **2** (*used in comparisons*) ⟨whether I like it or not : tanto si quiero como si no⟩ ⟨whether he comes or he doesn't : venga o no⟩

whetstone [ˈʍɛtˌstoːn] *n* : piedra *f* de afilar

whey [ˈʍeɪ] *n* : suero *m* (de la leche)

which[1] [ˈʍɪtʃ] *adj* : qué, cuál ⟨which tie do you prefer? : ¿cuál corbata prefieres?⟩ ⟨which ones? : ¿cuáles?⟩ ⟨tell me which house is yours : dime qué casa es la tuya⟩

which[2] *pron* **1** : cuál ⟨which is the right answer? : ¿cuál es la respuesta correcta?⟩ **2** : que, el cual, la cual, los cuales, las cuales ⟨the cup which broke : la taza que se quebró⟩ ⟨the houses, which are made of brick . . . : las casas, las cuales son de ladrillo . . .⟩

whichever[1] [ʍɪtʃˈɛvər] *adj* : el (la) que, cualquiera que ⟨whichever book you like : cualquier libro que te guste⟩

whichever[2] *pron* : el que, la que, cualquiera que ⟨take whichever you want : toma el que quieras⟩ ⟨whichever I choose : cualquiera que elija⟩

whiff[1] [ˈʍɪf] *v* PUFF : soplar

whiff[2] *n* **1** PUFF : soplo *m*, ráfaga *f* **2** SNIFF : olor *m* **3** HINT : dejo *m*, pizca *f*

while[1] [ˈʍaɪl] *vt* **whiled; whiling** : pasar ⟨to while away the time : matar el tiempo⟩

while[2] *n* **1** TIME : rato *m*, tiempo *m* ⟨after a while : después de un rato⟩ ⟨in a while : dentro de poco⟩ **2 to be worth one's while** : valer la pena

while[3] *conj* **1** : mientras ⟨whistle while you work : silba mientras trabajas⟩ **2** WHEREAS : mientras que **3** ALTHOUGH : aunque ⟨while it's very good, it's not perfect : aunque es muy bueno, no es perfecto⟩

whim [ˈʍɪm] *n* : capricho *m*, antojo *m*

whimper[1] [ˈʍɪmpər] *vi* : lloriquear, gimotear

whimper[2] *n* : quejido *m*

whimsical ['hwɪmzɪkəl] *adj* **1** CAPRICIOUS : caprichoso, fantasioso **2** ERRATIC : errático — **whimsically** *adv*
whine[1] ['hwaɪn] *vi* **whined; whining** **1** : lloriquear, gimotear, gemir **2** COMPLAIN : quejarse
whine[2] *n* : quejido *m*, gemido *m*
whiner ['hwaɪnər] *n* : llorón *m*, -rona *f*
whiny ['hwaɪni] *adj* **whinier; -est** : ñoño
whinny[1] ['hwɪni] *vi* **-nied; -nying** : relinchar
whinny[2] *n, pl* **-nies** : relincho *m*
whip[1] ['hwɪp] *v* **whipped; whipping** *vt* **1** SNATCH : arrebatar ⟨she whipped the cloth from the table : arrebató el mantel de la mesa⟩ **2** LASH : azotar **3** MOVE, STIR : agitar (con fuerza) **4** FLING : lanzar, tirar (rápidamente) **5** *fam* DEFEAT : vencer, derrotar **6** INCITE : incitar, despertar, provocar ⟨to whip up enthusiasm : despertar el entusiasmo⟩ ⟨to whip up a controversy : provocar una polémica⟩ ⟨he whipped the crowd into a frenzy : enardeció a la multitud⟩ **7** BEAT : batir (huevos, crema, etc.) **8 to whip into shape** *fam* : poner en forma **9 to whip out** *fam* : sacar (rápidamente) **10 to whip up** *fam* PREPARE : improvisar, preparar (rápidamente) — *vi* **1** FLAP : agitarse **2** RACE : ir rápidamente ⟨I whipped through my chores : hice las tareas volando⟩ ⟨to whip past/by : pasar como una bala⟩
whip[2] *n* **1** : látigo *m*, azote *m*, fusta *f* (de jinete) **2** : miembro *m* de un cuerpo legislativo encargado de disciplina
whiplash ['hwɪp,læʃ] *n or* **whiplash injury** : traumatismo *m* cervical
whippet ['hwɪpət] *n* : galgo *m* pequeño, galgo *m* inglés
whir[1] ['hwər] *vi* **whirred; whirring** : zumbar
whir[2] *n* : zumbido *m*
whirl[1] ['hwərl] *vi* **1** SPIN : dar vueltas, girar ⟨my head is whirling : la cabeza me está dando vueltas⟩ **2 to whirl about** : arremolinarse, moverse rápidamente
whirl[2] *n* **1** SPIN : giro *m*, vuelta *f*, remolino *m* (dícese del polvo, etc.) **2** BUSTLE : bullicio *m*, torbellino *m* (de actividad, etc.) **3 to give it a whirl** : intentar hacer, probar
whirlpool ['hwərl,pu:l] *n* **1** : vorágine *f*, remolino *m* **2** *or* **whirlpool bath** : bañera *f* de hidromasaje
whirlwind[1] ['hwərl,wɪnd] *n* : remolino *m*, torbellino *m*, tromba *f*
whirlwind[2] *adj* : muy rápido
whisk[1] ['hwɪsk] *vt* **1** : llevar ⟨she whisked the children off to bed : llevó a los niños a la cama⟩ **2** : batir ⟨to whisk eggs : batir huevos⟩ **3 to whisk away** *or* **to whisk off** : sacudir
whisk[2] *n* **1** WHISKING : sacudida *f* (movimiento) **2** : batidor *m* (para batir huevos, etc.)
whisk broom *n* : escobilla *f*
whisker ['hwɪskər] *n* **1** : pelo *m* (de la barba o el bigote) **2 whiskers** *npl* : bigotes *mpl* (de animales)

whiskey *or* **whisky** ['hwɪski] *n, pl* **-keys** *or* **-kies** : whisky *m*
whisper[1] ['hwɪspər] *vi* : cuchichear, susurrar — *vt* : decir en voz baja, susurrar
whisper[2] *n* **1** WHISPERING : susurro *m*, cuchicheo *m* **2** RUMOR : rumor *m* **3** TRACE : dejo *m*, pizca *f*
whistle[1] ['hwɪsəl] *v* **-tled; -tling** *vi* : silbar, chiflar, pitar (dícese de un tren, etc.) — *vt* : silbar ⟨to whistle a tune : silbar una melodía⟩
whistle[2] *n* **1** WHISTLING : chiflido *m*, silbido *m* **2** : silbato *m*, pito *m* (instrumento)
whit ['hwɪt] *n* BIT : ápice *m*, pizca *f*
white[1] ['hwaɪt] *adj* **whiter; whitest** : blanco
white[2] *n* **1** : blanco *m* (color) **2** : clara *f* (de huevos) **3** : blanco *m* (del ojo) **4** *or* **white person** : blanco *m*, -ca *f*
white blood cell *n* : glóbulo *m* blanco
white chocolate *n* : chocolate *m* blanco
white–collar ['hwaɪt'kɑlər] *adj* **1** : de oficina **2 white–collar worker** : oficinista *mf*
whitefish ['hwaɪt,fɪʃ] *n* : pescado *m* blanco
white–hot *adj* : candente
white lie *n* : mentira *f* piadosa
whiten ['hwaɪtən] *vt* : blanquear — *vi* : ponerse blanco
whitener ['hwaɪtənər] *n* : blanqueador *m*
whiteness ['hwaɪtnəs] *n* : blancura *f*
white–tailed deer ['hwaɪt'teɪld] *n* : ciervo *f* de Virginia
whitewash[1] ['hwaɪt,wɔʃ] *vt* **1** : enjalbegar, blanquear ⟨to whitewash a fence : enjalbegar una valla⟩ **2** CONCEAL : encubrir (un escándalo, etc.)
whitewash[2] *n* **1** : jalbegue *m*, lechada *f* **2** COVER-UP : encubrimiento *m*
whither ['hwɪðər] *adv* : adónde
whittle ['hwɪtəl] *vt* **-tled; -tling** **1** : tallar (madera) **2 to whittle down** : reducir, recortar ⟨to whittle down expenses : reducir los gastos⟩
whiz[1] *or* **whizz** ['hwɪz] *vi* **whizzed; whizzing** **1** BUZZ : zumbar **2 to whiz by** : pasar muy rápido, pasar volando
whiz[2] *or* **whizz** *n, pl* **whizzes** **1** BUZZ : zumbido *m* **2 to be a whiz** : ser un prodigio, ser muy hábil
whiz kid *or* **whizz kid** *n* : prodigio *m*, genio *m*
who ['hu:] *pron* **1** (*used in direct and indirect questions*) : quién ⟨who is that? : ¿quién es ése?⟩ ⟨who did it? : ¿quién lo hizo?⟩ ⟨we know who they are : sabemos quiénes son⟩ **2** (*used in relative clauses*) : que, quien ⟨the lady who lives there : la señora que vive allí⟩ ⟨for those who wait : para los que esperan, para quienes esperan⟩
whodunit [hu:'dʌnɪt] *n* : novela *f* policíaca
whoever [hu:'evər] *pron* **1** : quienquiera que, quien ⟨whoever did it : quienquiera que lo hizo⟩ ⟨give it to whoever you want : dalo a quien quieras⟩ **2** (*used in questions*) : quién ⟨whoever could that be? : ¿quién podría ser?⟩

whole¹ [ˈhoːl] *adj* **1** UNHURT : ileso **2** INTACT : intacto, sano **3** ENTIRE : entero, íntegro ⟨the whole island : toda la isla⟩ ⟨whole milk : leche entera⟩ **4 a whole lot** : muchísimo

whole² *n* **1** : todo *m* **2 as a whole** : en conjunto **3 on the whole** : en general

wholehearted [ˈhoːlˈhɑrtəd] *adj* : sin reservas, incondicional — **wholeheartedly** *adv*

whole note *n* : semibreve *f*, redonda *f*

whole number *n* : entero *m*

wholesale¹ [ˈhoːlˌseɪl] *v* **-saled; -saling** *vt* : vender al por mayor — *vi* : venderse al por mayor

wholesale² *adv* : al por mayor

wholesale³ *adj* **1** : al por mayor ⟨wholesale grocer : tendero al por mayor⟩ **2** TOTAL : total, absoluto ⟨wholesale slaughter : matanza sistemática⟩

wholesale⁴ *n* : mayoreo *m*

wholesaler [ˈhoːlˌseɪlər] *n* : mayorista *mf*

wholesome [ˈhoːlsəm] *adj* **1** : sano ⟨wholesome advice : consejo sano⟩ **2** HEALTHY : sano, saludable

whole wheat *adj* : de trigo integral ⟨whole wheat bread : pan integral⟩

wholly [ˈhoːli] *adv* **1** COMPLETELY : completamente **2** SOLELY : exclusivamente, únicamente

whom [ˈhuːm] *pron* **1** (*used in direct questions*) : a quién ⟨whom did you choose? : ¿a quién elegiste?⟩ **2** (*used in indirect questions*) : de quién, con quién, en quién ⟨I don't know whom to consult : no sé con quién consultar⟩ **3** (*used in relative clauses*) : que, a quien ⟨the lawyer whom I recommended to you : el abogado que te recomendé⟩

whomever [huːmˈɛvər] *pron* WHOEVER : quienquiera, quien ⟨marry whomever you please : cásate con quien quieras⟩

whoop¹ [ˈʍuːp, ˈʍʊp] *vi* : gritar, chillar

whoop² *n* : grito *m*

whooping cough *n* : tos *f* ferina

whopper [ˈʍɑpər] *n* **1** : cosa *f* enorme **2** LIE : mentira *f* colosal

whopping [ˈʍɑpɪŋ] *adj* : enorme

whore [ˈhor] *n* : puta *f offensive*, ramera *f*

whorl [ˈʍorl, ˈʍərl] *n* : espiral *f*, línea *f* (de una huella digital)

whose¹ [ˈhuːz] *adj* **1** (*used in questions*) : de quién ⟨whose truck is that? : ¿de quién es ese camión?⟩ **2** (*used in relative clauses*) : cuyo ⟨the person whose work is finished : la persona cuyo trabajo está terminado⟩

whose² *pron* : de quién ⟨tell me whose it was : dime de quién era⟩

why¹ [ˈʍwaɪ] *adv* : por qué ⟨why did you do it? : ¿por qué lo hizo?⟩

why² *n, pl* **whys** REASON : porqué *m*, razón *f*

why³ *conj* : por qué ⟨I know why he left : yo sé por qué salió⟩ ⟨there's no reason why it should exist : no hay razón para que exista⟩

why⁴ *interj* (*used to express surprise*) : ¡vaya!, ¡mira!

Wicca [ˈwɪkə] *n* : wicca *f*

Wiccan [ˈwɪkən] *n* : wiccano *m*, -na *f* — **Wiccan** *adj*

wick [ˈwɪk] *n* : mecha *f*

wicked [ˈwɪkəd] *adj* **1** EVIL : malo, malvado **2** MISCHIEVOUS : travieso, pícaro ⟨a wicked grin : una sonrisa traviesa⟩ **3** TERRIBLE : terrible, horrible ⟨a wicked storm : una tormenta horrible⟩

wickedly [ˈwɪkədli] *adv* : con maldad

wickedness [ˈwɪkədnəs] *n* : maldad *f*

wicker¹ [ˈwɪkər] *adj* : de mimbre

wicker² *n* **1** : mimbre *m* **2** → **wickerwork**

wickerwork [ˈwɪkərˌwərk] *n* : artículos *mpl* de mimbre

wicket [ˈwɪkət] *n* **1** WINDOW : ventanilla *f* **2** *or* **wicket gate** : postigo *m* **3** : aro *m* (en croquet), palos *mpl* (en críquet)

wide¹ [ˈwaɪd] *adv* **wider; widest 1** WIDELY : por todas partes ⟨to travel far and wide : viajar por todas partes⟩ **2** COMPLETELY : completamente, totalmente ⟨wide open : abierto de par en par⟩ **3 wide apart** : muy separados

wide² *adj* **wider; widest 1** VAST : vasto, extensivo ⟨a wide area : una área extensiva⟩ **2** : ancho ⟨three meters wide : tres metros de ancho⟩ **3** BROAD : ancho, amplio **4** *or* **wide–open** : muy abierto **5 wide of the mark** : desviado, lejos del blanco

wide–awake [ˈwaɪdəˈweɪk] *adj* : (completamente) despierto

wide–eyed [ˈwaɪdˈaɪd] *adj* **1** : con los ojos muy abiertos **2** NAIVE : inocente, ingenuo

widely [ˈwaɪdli] *adv* : extensivamente, por todas partes

widen [ˈwaɪdən] *vt* : ampliar, ensanchar — *vi* : ampliarse, ensancharse

wide–ranging [ˈwaɪdˌreɪndɪŋ] *adj* EXTENSIVE, DIVERSE : amplio, diverso ⟨wide-ranging implications : implicaciones de gran alcance⟩ ⟨a wide-ranging discussion : una discusión que abarca muchos temas⟩

widescreen [ˈwaɪdˌskriːn] *adj* : de pantalla ancha

widespread [ˈwaɪdˈsprɛd] *adj* : extendido, extenso, difuso

widow¹ [ˈwɪˌdoː] *vt* : dejar viuda ⟨to be widowed : enviudar⟩

widow² *n* : viuda *f*

widower [ˈwɪdoʷər] *n* : viudo *m*

width [ˈwɪdθ] *n* : ancho *m*, anchura *f*

wield [ˈwiːld] *vt* **1** USE : usar, manejar ⟨to wield a broom : usar una escoba⟩ **2** EXERCISE : ejercer ⟨to wield influence : influir⟩

wiener [ˈwiːnər] → **frankfurter**

wife [ˈwaɪf] *n, pl* **wives** [ˈwaɪvz] : esposa *f*, mujer *f*

wifely [ˈwaɪfli] *adj* : de esposa, conyugal

wig [ˈwɪg] *n* : peluca *f*

wiggle¹ [ˈwɪɡəl] *v* **-gled; -gling** *vt* **1** : menear ⟨to wiggle one's hips : menear las caderas, menearse, contonearse⟩ **2** : mover (los dedos, etc.) — *vi* **1** : menearse, contonearse **2** SQUIRM, WRIGGLE : retorcerse

wiggle[2] *n* : meneo *m*, contoneo *m*

wiggly ['wɪɡəli] *adj* **wigglier; -est** **1** : que se menea **2** WAVY : ondulado

wigwag ['wɪɡ.wæɡ] *vi* **-wagged; -wagging** : comunicar por señales

wigwam ['wɪɡ.wɑm] *n* : wigwam *m*

wild[1] ['waɪld] *adv* **1** → **wildly** **2 to run wild** : descontrolarse

wild[2] *adj* **1** : salvaje, silvestre, cimarrón ⟨wild horses : caballos salvajes⟩ ⟨wild rice : arroz silvestre⟩ **2** DESOLATE : yermo, agreste **3** UNRULY : desenfrenado **4** CRAZY : loco, fantástico ⟨wild ideas : ideas locas⟩ **5** BARBAROUS : salvaje, bárbaro **6** ERRATIC : errático ⟨a wild throw : un tiro errático⟩ **7** FRENETIC : frenético **8** : extravagante ⟨to take/make a wild guess : adivinar, hacer una conjetura (al azar)⟩ **9 to be wild about** : estar loco por

wild[3] *n* → **wilderness**

wild boar *n* : jabalí *m*

wild card *n* **1** : factor *m* desconocido **2** : comodín *m* (carta) **3** *usu* **wildcard** : comodín *m* (símbolo)

wildcat ['waɪld.kæt] *n* **1** : gato *m* montés **2** BOBCAT : lince *m* rojo

wilderness ['wɪldərnəs] *n* : yermo *m*, desierto *m*

wildfire ['waɪld.faɪr] *n* **1** : fuego *m* descontrolado **2 to spread like wildfire** : propagarse como un reguero de pólvora

wildflower ['waɪld.flaʊər] *n* : flor *f* silvestre

wildfowl ['waɪld.faʊl] *n* : ave *f* de caza

wild goose chase *n fam* : misión *f* imposible o inútil ⟨it turned out to be a wild goose chase : resultó ser una pérdida de tiempo⟩

wildlife ['waɪld.laɪf] *n* : fauna *f*

wildly ['waɪldli] *adv* **1** FRANTICALLY : frenéticamente, como un loco **2** EXTREMELY : extremadamente ⟨wildly happy : loco de felicidad⟩

wile[1] ['waɪl] *vt* **wiled; wiling** LURE : atraer

wile[2] *n* : ardid *m*, artimaña *f*

will[1] ['wɪl] *v, past* **would** ['wʊd] *present s & pl* **will** *vt* WISH : querer ⟨do what you will : haz lo que quieras⟩ — *v aux* **1** (*expressing willingness*) ⟨no one would take the job : nadie aceptaría el trabajo⟩ ⟨I won't do it : no lo haré⟩ **2** (*expressing habitual action*) ⟨he will get angry over nothing : se pone furioso por cualquier cosa⟩ **3** (*forming the future tense*) ⟨tomorrow we will go shopping : mañana iremos de compras⟩ **4** (*expressing capacity*) ⟨the couch will hold three people : en el sofá cabrán tres personas⟩ **5** (*expressing determination*) ⟨I will go despite them : iré a pesar de ellos⟩ **6** (*expressing probability*) ⟨that will be the mailman : eso ha de ser el cartero⟩ **7** (*expressing inevitability*) ⟨accidents will happen : los accidentes ocurrirán⟩ **8** (*expressing a command*) ⟨you will do as I say : harás lo que digo⟩

will[2] *vt* **1** ORDAIN : disponer, decretar ⟨if God wills it : si Dios lo dispone, si Dios

quiere⟩ **2** : lograr a fuerza de voluntad ⟨they were willing him to succeed : estaban deseando que tuviera éxito⟩ **3** BEQUEATH : legar

will[3] *n* **1** DESIRE : deseo *m*, voluntad *f* **2** VOLITION : voluntad *f* ⟨free will : libre albedrío⟩ **3** WILLPOWER : voluntad *f*, fuerza *f* de voluntad ⟨a will of iron : una voluntad férrea⟩ **4** : testamento *m* ⟨to make a will : hacer testamento⟩

willful *or* **wilful** ['wɪlfəl] *adj* **1** OBSTINATE : obstinado, terco **2** INTENTIONAL : intencionado, deliberado — **willfully** *adv*

willing ['wɪlɪŋ] *adj* **1** INCLINED, READY : listo, dispuesto **2** OBLIGING : servicial, complaciente

willingly ['wɪlɪŋli] *adv* : con gusto

willingness ['wɪlɪŋnəs] *n* : buena voluntad *f*

willow ['wɪ.lo:] *n* : sauce *m*

willowy ['wɪlowi] *adj* : esbelto

willpower ['wɪl.paʊər] *n* : voluntad *f*, fuerza *f* de voluntad

willy-nilly [.wɪli'nɪli] *adv fam* : de cualquier manera

wilt ['wɪlt] *vi* **1** : marchitarse (dícese de las flores) **2** LANGUISH : debilitarse, languidecer

wily ['waɪli] *adj* **wilier; -est** : artero, astuto

wimp ['wɪmp] *n* **1** COWARD : gallina *f*, cobarde *mf* **2** WEAKLING : debilucho *m*, -cha *f*, alfeñique *m*

win[1] ['wɪn] *v* **won** ['wʌn]; **winning** *vi* : ganar — *vt* **1** : ganar, conseguir **2 to win over** : ganarse a **3 to win someone's confidence** : conquistar a alguien

win[2] *n* : triunfo *m*, victoria *f*

wince[1] ['wɪnts] *vi* **winced; wincing** : estremecerse, hacer una mueca de dolor

wince[2] *n* : mueca *f* de dolor

winch ['wɪntʃ] *n* : torno *m*

wind[1] ['wɪnd] *vt* : dejar sin aliento ⟨to be winded : quedarse sin aliento⟩

wind[2] ['waɪnd] *v* **wound** ['waʊnd]; **winding** *vi* **1** MEANDER : serpentear **2 to wind down** END : acabarse poco a poco **3 to wind down** UNWIND : relajarse **4 to wind up** END : terminar, acabar ⟨the meeting will be winding up soon : la reunión va a terminar pronto⟩ **5 to wind up** END UP : acabar, terminar ⟨to wind up doing something : acabar/terminar haciendo algo, acabar/terminar por hacer algo⟩ — *vt* **1** COIL, ROLL : envolver, enrollar **2** TURN : hacer girar ⟨to wind (up) a clock : darle cuerda a un reloj⟩ **3 to wind up** END : terminar, concluir

wind[3] ['wɪnd] *n* **1** : viento *m* ⟨against the wind : contra el viento⟩ **2** BREATH : aliento *m* **3** FLATULENCE : flatulencia *f*, ventosidad *f* **4 to get wind of** : enterarse de

wind[4] ['waɪnd] *n* **1** TURN : vuelta *f* **2** BEND : recodo *m*, curva *f*

windbreak ['wɪnd.breɪk] *n* : barrera *f* contra el viento, abrigadero *m*

windfall ['wɪnd.fɔl] *n* **1** : fruta *f* caída **2** : beneficio *m* imprevisto

wind instrument *n* : instrumento *m* de viento

windmill ['wɪnd,mɪl] *n* : molino *m* de viento

window ['wɪn,doː] *n* 1 : ventana *f* (de un edificio), ventanilla *f* (de un vehículo o avión), vitrina *f* (de una tienda) 2 → **windowpane** 3 : ventana *f* (en informática)

window box *n* : jardinera *f* de ventana

windowpane ['wɪn,doː,peɪn] *n* : vidrio *m*

window screen → **screen²**

window-shop ['wɪndo,ʃɑp] *vi* **-shopped; -shopping** : mirar las vitrinas

windowsill ['wɪn,doː,sɪl] *n* : alféizar *m* de la ventana

windpipe ['wɪnd,paɪp] *n* : tráquea *f*

windshield ['wɪnd,ʃiːld] *n* 1 : parabrisas *m* 2 **windshield wiper** : limpiaparabrisas *m*

windsurfing ['wɪnd,sərfɪŋ] *n* : windsurf *m*

windswept ['wɪnd,swɛpt] *adj* 1 : azotado por el viento 2 DISHEVELED : despeinado

windup ['waɪnd,ʌp] *n* : conclusión *f*

windy ['wɪndi] *adj* **windier; -est** 1 : ventoso ⟨it's windy : hace viento⟩ 2 VERBOSE : verboso, prolijo

wine¹ ['waɪn] *v* **wined; wining** *vi* : beber vino — *vt* **to wine and dine** : agasajar

wine² *n* : vino *m*

wineglass ['waɪn,glæs] *n* : copa *f* (de vino)

winery ['waɪnəri] *n, pl* **-eries** : bodega *f*

wineskin ['waɪn,skɪn] *n* : odre *m*, bota *f*

wine tasting *n* : degustación *f* de vinos

wing¹ ['wɪŋ] *vi* FLY : volar

wing² *n* 1 : ala *f* (de un ave o un avión) ⟨to take wing : levantar vuelo⟩ 2 : ala *f* (de un edificio) 3 FACTION : ala *f* ⟨the right wing of the party : el ala derecha del partido⟩ 4 **wings** *npl* : bastidores *mpl* (de un teatro) ⟨to be waiting in the wings : estar esperando su momento⟩ 5 **on the wing** : al vuelo, volando 6 **under one's wing** : bajo el cargo de uno ⟨to take someone under one's wing : encargarse de alguien⟩

winged ['wɪŋd, 'wɪŋəd] *adj* : alado

wink¹ ['wɪŋk] *vi* 1 : guiñar el ojo 2 BLINK : pestañear, parpadear 3 FLICKER : parpadear, titilar

wink² *n* 1 : guiño *m* (del ojo) 2 NAP : siesta *f* ⟨not to sleep a wink : no pegar el ojo⟩

winner ['wɪnər] *n* : ganador *m*, -dora *f*

winning ['wɪnɪŋ] *adj* 1 VICTORIOUS : ganador 2 CHARMING : encantador

winnings ['wɪnɪŋz] *npl* : ganancias *fpl*

winnow ['wɪ,noː] *vt* : aventar (el grano, etc.)

winsome ['wɪnsəm] *adj* CHARMING : encantador

winter¹ ['wɪntər] *adj* : invernal, de invierno

winter² *n* : invierno *m*

wintertime ['wɪntər,taɪm] *n* : invierno *m*

wintry ['wɪntri] *adj* **wintrier; -est** 1 WINTER : invernal, de invierno 2 COLD : frío ⟨she gave us a wintry greeting : nos saludó fríamente⟩

wipe¹ ['waɪp] *v* **wiped; wiping** *vt* 1 *or* **to wipe off** : limpiar, pasarle un trapo a ⟨to wipe one's feet : limpiarse los pies⟩ ⟨to wipe dry : secar⟩ 2 *or* **to wipe off** REMOVE : limpiar, quitar 3 *or* **to wipe clean** ERASE : borrar (un disco, etc.) 4 **to wipe away** REMOVE : limpiar (suciedad), secar (lágrimas), borrar (una memoria) 5 **to wipe down** : pasarle un trapo a 6 **to wipe out** ANNIHILATE : aniquilar, destruir 7 **to wipe up** : limpiar, secar (líquido, etc.) — *vi* **to wipe out** *fam* FALL : caerse (violentamente)

wipe² *n* : pasada *f* (con un trapo, etc.)

wire¹ ['waɪr] *vt* **wired; wiring** 1 : instalar el cableado en (una casa, etc.) 2 BIND : atar con alambre 3 TELEGRAPH : telegrafiar, mandarle un telegrama (a alguien)

wire² *n* 1 : alambre *m* ⟨barbed wire : alambre de púas⟩ 2 : cable *m* (eléctrico o telefónico) 3 TELEGRAM : telegrama *m*, cable *m*

wireless ['waɪrləs] *adj* : inalámbrico ⟨a wireless microphone : un micrófono inalámbrico⟩ ⟨wireless Internet access : acceso inalámbrico a Internet⟩

wiretap¹ ['waɪr,tæp] *vt* TAP : intervenir, pinchar *fam* (un teléfono)

wiretap² *n* TAP : micrófono *m* oculto (para la intervención telefónica)

wiretapping ['waɪr,tæpɪŋ] *n* : intervención *f* telefónica

wiring ['waɪrɪŋ] *n* : cableado *m*

wiry ['waɪri] *adj* **wirier; -est** 1 : hirsuto, tieso (dícese del pelo) 2 : esbelto y musculoso (dícese del cuerpo)

wisdom ['wɪzdəm] *n* 1 KNOWLEDGE : sabiduría *f* 2 JUDGMENT, SENSE : sensatez *f*

wisdom tooth *n* : muela *f* de juicio

wise¹ ['waɪz] *adj* **wiser; wisest** 1 LEARNED : sabio 2 SENSIBLE : sabio, sensato, prudente 3 KNOWLEDGEABLE : entendido, enterado ⟨they're wise to his tricks : conocen muy bien sus mañas⟩

wise² *n* : manera *f*, modo *m* ⟨in no wise : de ninguna manera⟩

wisecrack ['waɪz,kræk] *n* : broma *f*, chiste *m*

wisely ['waɪzli] *adv* : sabiamente, sensatamente

wish¹ ['wɪʃ] *vt* 1 : pedir (como deseo) ⟨I wish I were rich : ojalá fuera rica⟩ ⟨I wish I'd known : ojalá lo hubiera sabido⟩ ⟨I wish you'd be quiet! : ¿quieres callarte?⟩ 2 WANT : desear, querer ⟨I wish to be alone : quiero estar sólo⟩ 3 : desear ⟨they wished me well : me desearon lo mejor⟩ ⟨I wish you luck : te deseo suerte⟩ ⟨I wish you a Happy New Year! : ¡que tengas un feliz Año Nuevo!⟩ — *vi* 1 : pedir un deseo ⟨to wish upon a star : pedir un deseo a una estrella⟩ 2 : querer ⟨as you wish : como quiera⟩ 3 **to wish for** : pedir (como deseo)

wish² *n* 1 : deseo *m* ⟨to grant a wish : conceder un deseo⟩ 2 **wishes** *npl* : saludos *mpl*, recuerdos *mpl* ⟨to send best wishes : mandar muchos recuerdos⟩

wishbone ['wɪʃˌboːn] *n* : espoleta *f*

wishful ['wɪʃfəl] *adj* **1** HOPEFUL : deseoso, lleno de esperanza **2 wishful thinking** : ilusiones *fpl*

wishy–washy ['wɪʃiˌwɔʃi, -ˌwɑʃi] *adj* : insípido, soso

wisp ['wɪsp] *n* **1** BUNCH : manojo *m* (de paja) **2** STRAND : mechón *m* (de pelo) **3** : voluta *f* (de humo)

wispy ['wɪspi] *adj* **wispier; -est** : tenue, ralo (dícese del pelo)

wisteria [wɪs'tɪriə] *n* : glicinia *f*

wistful ['wɪstfəl] *adj* : anhelante, melancólico — **wistfully** *adv*

wistfulness ['wɪstfəlnəs] *n* : añoranza *f*, melancolía *f*

wit ['wɪt] *n* **1** INTELLIGENCE : inteligencia *f* **2** CLEVERNESS : ingenio *m*, gracia *f*, agudeza *f* **3** HUMOR : humorismo *m* **4** JOKER : chistoso *m*, -sa *f* **5 wits** *npl* : razón *f*, buen juicio *m* ⟨scared out of one's wits : muerto de miedo⟩ ⟨to be at one's wits' end : estar desesperado⟩

witch ['wɪtʃ] *n* **1** : bruja *f* **2** → **Wiccan**

witchcraft ['wɪtʃˌkræft] *n* **1** : brujería *f*, hechicería *f* **2** → **Wicca**

witch doctor *n* : hechicero *m*, -ra *f*

witchery ['wɪtʃəri] *n*, *pl* **-eries** WITCHCRAFT : brujería *f*, hechicería *f* **2** CHARM : encanto *m*

witch–hunt ['wɪtʃˌhʌnt] *n* : caza *f* de brujas

with ['wɪð, 'wɪθ] *prep* **1** : con ⟨I'm going with you : voy contigo⟩ ⟨coffee with milk : café con leche⟩ **2** AGAINST : con ⟨to argue with someone : discutir con alguien⟩ **3** (*used in descriptions*) : con, de ⟨the girl with red hair : la muchacha de pelo rojo⟩ **4** (*indicating manner, means, or cause*) : con ⟨to cut with a knife : cortar con un cuchillo⟩ ⟨fix it with tape : arréglalo con cinta⟩ ⟨with luck : con suerte⟩ ⟨trembling with fear : temblando de miedo⟩ **5** DESPITE : a pesar de, aún con ⟨even with all his work, the business failed : a pesar de todo su trabajo, el negocio fracasó⟩ **6** REGARDING : con respecto a, con ⟨the trouble with your plan : el problema con su plan⟩ **7** ACCORDING TO : según ⟨it varies with the season : varía según la estación⟩ **8** (*indicating support or understanding*) : con ⟨I'm with you all the way : estoy contigo hasta el final⟩

withdraw [wɪð'drɔ, wɪθ-] *v* **-drew** [-'druː]; **-drawn** [-'drɔn]; **-drawing** *vt* **1** REMOVE : retirar, apartar, sacar (dinero) **2** RETRACT : retractarse de — *vi* : retirarse, recluirse (de la sociedad)

withdrawal [wɪð'drɔəl, wɪθ-] *n* **1** : retirada *f*, retiro *m* (de fondos, etc.), retraimiento *m* (social) **2** RETRACTION : retractación *f* **3** *or* **withdrawal symptoms** : síndrome *m* de abstinencia

withdrawn [wɪð'drɔn, wɪθ-] *adj* : retraído, reservado, introvertido

wither ['wɪðər] *vt* : marchitar, agostar — *vi* **1** WILT : marchitarse **2** WEAKEN : decaer, debilitarse

withhold [wɪθ'hoːld, wɪð-] *vt* **-held** [-'hld];

-holding : retener (fondos), aplazar (una decisión), negar (permiso, etc.)

within¹ [wɪð'ɪn, wɪθ-] *adv* : dentro

within² *prep* **1** : dentro de ⟨within the limits : dentro de los límites⟩ ⟨within sight of : a la vista de⟩ **2** (*in expressions of distance*) : a menos de ⟨within 10 miles of the ocean : a menos de 10 millas del mar⟩ **3** (*in expressions of time*) : dentro de ⟨within an hour : dentro de una hora⟩ ⟨within a month of her birthday : a poco menos de un mes de su cumpleaños⟩

without¹ [wɪð'aʊt, wɪθ-] *adv* **1** OUTSIDE : fuera **2 to do without** : pasar sin algo

without² *prep* **1** OUTSIDE : fuera de **2** : sin ⟨without fear : sin temor⟩ ⟨he left without his briefcase : se fue sin su portafolios⟩

withstand [wɪθ'stænd, wɪð-] *vt* **-stood** [-'stʊd]; **-standing 1** BEAR : aguantar, soportar **2** RESIST : resistir, resistirse a

witless ['wɪtləs] *adj* : estúpido, tonto

witness¹ ['wɪtnəs] *vt* **1** SEE : presenciar, ver, ser testigo de **2** : atestiguar (una firma, etc.) — *vi* TESTIFY : atestiguar, testimoniar

witness² *n* **1** TESTIMONY : testimonio *m* ⟨to bear witness : atestiguar, testimoniar⟩ **2** : testigo *mf* ⟨witness for the prosecution : testigo de cargo⟩

witness stand *n* : estrado *m*

witticism ['wɪtəˌsɪzəm] *n* : agudeza *f*, ocurrencia *f*

witty ['wɪti] *adj* **wittier; -est** : ingenioso, ocurrente, gracioso

wives → **wife**

wizard ['wɪzərd] *n* **1** SORCERER : mago *m*, brujo *m*, hechicero *m* **2** : genio *m* ⟨a math wizard : un genio en matemáticas⟩

wizened ['wɪzənd, 'wiː-] *adj* : arrugado, marchito

wobble¹ ['wɑbəl] *vi* **-bled; -bling** : bambolearse, tambalearse, temblar (dícese de la voz)

wobble² *n* : tambaleo *m*, bamboleo *m*

wobbly ['wɑbəli] *adj* **wobblier; -est** : que se tambalea, inestable

woe ['woː] *n* **1** GRIEF, MISFORTUNE : desgracia *f*, infortunio *m*, aflicción *f* **2** **woes** *npl* TROUBLES : penas *fpl*, males *mpl*

woeful ['woːfəl] *adj* **1** SORROWFUL : afligido, apenado, triste **2** UNFORTUNATE : desgraciado, infortunado **3** DEPLORABLE : lamentable

woke¹, woken → **wake¹**

woke² ['woːk] *adj* : consciente de y sensible a los asuntos de justicia racial y social

wolf¹ ['wʊlf] *vt* *or* **to wolf down** : engullir

wolf² *n*, *pl* **wolves** ['wʊlvz] : lobo *m*, -ba *f*

wolfram ['wʊlfrəm] → **tungsten**

wolverine [ˌwʊlvəˈriːn] *n* : glotón *m* (animal)

woman ['wʊmən] *n*, *pl* **women** ['wɪmən] : mujer *f*

womanhood ['wʊmənˌhʊd] *n* **1** : condición *f* de mujer **2** WOMEN : mujeres *fpl*

womanizer [ˈwʊməˌnaɪzər] n : picaflor m
womanly [ˈwʊmənli] adj : femenino
womb [ˈwuːm] n : útero m, matriz f
won → **win**
wonder[1] [ˈwʌndər] vi **1** SPECULATE : preguntarse, pensar ⟨to wonder about : preguntarse por⟩ **2** MARVEL : asombrarse, maravillarse — vt : preguntarse ⟨I wonder if/whether they're coming : me pregunto si vendrán⟩
wonder[2] n **1** MARVEL : maravilla f, milagro m ⟨to work wonders : hacer maravillas⟩ **2** AMAZEMENT : asombro m
wonderful [ˈwʌndərfəl] adj : maravilloso, estupendo
wonderfully [ˈwʌndərfəli] adv : maravillosamente, de maravilla
wonderland [ˈwʌndərˌlænd, -lənd] n : país m de las maravillas
wonderment [ˈwʌndərmənt] n : asombro m
wondrous [ˈwʌndrəs] → **wonderful**
wont[1] [ˈwɔnt, ˈwoːnt, ˈwɑnt] adj : acostumbrado, habituado
wont[2] n : hábito m, costumbre f
won't [ˈwoːnt] contraction of WILL NOT → **will**[1]
woo [ˈwuː] vt **1** COURT : cortejar **2** : buscar el apoyo de (clientes, votantes, etc.)
wood[1] [ˈwʊd] adj : de madera
wood[2] n **1** or **woods** npl FOREST : bosque m **2** : madera f (materia) **3** FIREWOOD : leña f
woodchuck [ˈwʊdˌtʃʌk] n : marmota f de América
woodcut [ˈwʊdˌkʌt] n **1** : plancha f de madera (para imprimir imágenes) **2** : grabado m en madera
woodcutter [ˈwʊdˌkʌtər] n : leñador m, -dora f
wooded [ˈwʊdəd] adj : arbolado, boscoso
wooden [ˈwʊdən] adj **1** : de madera ⟨a wooden cross : una cruz de madera⟩ **2** STIFF : rígido, inexpresivo (dícese del estilo, de la cara, etc.)
woodland [ˈwʊdlənd, -ˌlænd] n : bosque m
woodpecker [ˈwʊdˌpɛkər] n : pájaro m carpintero
woodshed [ˈwʊdˌʃɛd] n : leñera f
woodsman [ˈwʊdzmən] n, pl **-men** [-mən, -ˌmɛn] → **woodcutter**
woodwind [ˈwʊdˌwɪnd] n : instrumento m de viento de madera
woodwork [ˈwʊdˌwərk] n : carpintería f
woodworking [ˈwʊdˌwərkɪŋ] n : carpintería f
woody [ˈwʊdi] adj **woodier; -est** **1** → **wooded** **2** : leñoso ⟨woody plants : plantas leñosas⟩ **3** : leñoso (dícese de la textura), a madera (dícese del aroma, etc.)
woof [ˈwʊf] → **weft**
wool [ˈwʊl] n : lana f
woolen[1] or **woollen** [ˈwʊlən] adj : de lana
woolen[2] or **woollen** n **1** : lana f (tela) **2** **woolens** npl : prendas fpl de lana
woolly [ˈwʊli] adj **woollier; -est** **1** : lanudo **2** CONFUSED : confuso, vago
woozy [ˈwuːzi] adj **woozier; -est** : mareado

word[1] [ˈwərd] vt : expresar, formular, redactar
word[2] n **1** : palabra f, vocablo m, voz f ⟨word for word : palabra por palabra⟩ ⟨words fail me : me quedo sin habla⟩ ⟨I can't understand a word she says : no entiendo ni una sola palabra de lo que dice⟩ **2** REMARK : palabra f ⟨by word of mouth : de palabra⟩ ⟨in a word : en una palabra⟩ ⟨in other words : en otras palabras⟩ ⟨in one's own words : en/con sus propias palabras⟩ ⟨in so many words : con esas palabras⟩ ⟨the last word : la última palabra⟩ ⟨to have a word with : hablar (dos palabras) con⟩ ⟨don't believe a word of it : no te creas ni una sola palabra⟩ ⟨don't say/breathe a word of this (to anyone) : de esto ni una palabra (a nadie)⟩ **3** COMMAND : orden f ⟨to give the word : dar la orden⟩ ⟨just say the word : no tienes más que decirlo⟩ **4** MESSAGE, NEWS : noticias fpl ⟨is there any word from her? : ¿hay noticias de ella?⟩ ⟨to send word : mandar un recado⟩ ⟨word has it that . . . : dicen que . . . , corre el rumor de que . . .⟩ **5** PROMISE : palabra f ⟨word of honor : palabra de honor⟩ ⟨to keep one's word : cumplir uno su palabra⟩ ⟨you have my word (on it) : te doy mi palabra⟩ ⟨take my word for it : te lo digo yo⟩ ⟨to take someone at his/her word : confiar en la palabra de alguien, fiarse de la palabra de alguien⟩ **6 words** npl QUARREL : palabra f, riña f ⟨to have words with : tener unas palabras con, reñir con⟩ **7 words** npl TEXT : letra f (de una canción, etc.) **8 from the word go** : desde el principio **9 to get a word in edgewise** : meter la cuchara **10 to have the last word** : tener/decir la última palabra **11 to put in a good word for someone** : recomendar a alguien **12 to put words into someone's mouth** : atribuirle a alguien algo que no dijo **13 to take the words out of someone's mouth** : quitarle las palabras de la boca a alguien **14 to waste words** : gastar saliva
wordiness [ˈwərdinəs] n : verbosidad f
wording [ˈwərdɪŋ] n : redacción f, lenguaje m (de un documento)
word processing n : procesamiento m de textos
word processor n : procesador m de textos
wordy [ˈwərdi] adj **wordier; -est** : verboso, prolijo
wore → **wear**[1]
work[1] [ˈwərk] v **worked** [ˈwərkt] or **wrought** [ˈrɔt]; **working** vi **1** LABOR : trabajar ⟨to work hard : trabajar mucho/duro⟩ ⟨to work full-time : trabajar a tiempo completo⟩ ⟨to work part-time : trabajar a/de medio tiempo⟩ ⟨to work overtime : trabajar horas extras⟩ **2** FUNCTION : funcionar, servir **3 to work around** : esquivar (un problema, etc.) **4 to work at** : esforzarse para mejorar ⟨she's working at controlling her temper : está tratando de apren-

der a controlar su mal genio⟩ ⟨you'll have to work harder at it : tendrás que esforzarte más⟩ **5 to work loose** : soltarse, desprenderse **6 to work on** : trabajar en (un proyecto, etc.) ⟨to work on a cure : trabajar para encontrar una cura⟩ ⟨she's working on (controlling) her temper : está tratando de aprender a controlar su mal genio⟩ **7 to work out** TURN OUT : resultar, salir **8 to work out** SUCCEED : dar resultado, salir bien **9 to work out** EXERCISE : hacer ejercicio **10 to work up to** (*indicating a gradual increase*) ⟨to work up to full speed : ir cobrando velocidad poco a poco⟩ — *vt* **1** : trabajar ⟨to work long hours : trabajar muchas horas⟩ ⟨to work weekends : trabajar los fines de semana⟩ ⟨to work nights : trabajar de noche⟩ ⟨to work the night shift : hacer el turno de noche⟩ ⟨she works two jobs : tiene dos empleos⟩ **2** : trabajar, labrar (la tierra, etc.) **3** : hacer trabajar (a alguien) **4** OPERATE : trabajar, operar **5** : hacer/conseguir (etc.) con esfuerzo ⟨gradually work in the flour : incorpore la harina poco a poco⟩ ⟨to work one's way up : lograr subir por sus propios esfuerzos⟩ **6** EFFECT : efectuar, llevar a cabo, obrar (milagros) **7** MANIPULATE, SHAPE : trabajar, formar ⟨work the dough : trabaje la masa⟩ ⟨a beautifully wrought vase : un florero bellamente elaborado⟩ **8** HANDLE : manejar (a alguien) ⟨he knows how to work a crowd/room : sabe conquistar al público⟩ **9 to work off** : pagar trabajando **10 to work out** DEVELOP, PLAN : idear, planear, desarrollar **11 to work out** RESOLVE : solucionar, resolver ⟨to work out the answer : calcular la solución⟩ **12 to work over** : darle una paliza a **13 to work up** : estimular, excitar ⟨don't work yourself up : no te agites⟩ **14 to work up** PRODUCE : generar ⟨to work up the courage to : armarse de valor para⟩ ⟨to work up a sweat : empezar a sudar⟩

work² *adj* : laboral

work³ *n* **1** : trabajo *m* ⟨work to do : trabajo que hacer⟩ ⟨the quality of his work : la calidad de su trabajo⟩ ⟨to bring work home : llevar trabajo a casa⟩ **2** EMPLOYMENT : trabajo *m*, empleo *m* ⟨out of work : desempleado⟩ ⟨line of work : profesión⟩ **3** : trabajo *m* (lugar) ⟨to go to work : ir a trabajar⟩ ⟨to leave work : salir del trabajo⟩ ⟨she's at work : está en el trabajo⟩ **4** EFFORT : trabajo *m* **5** DEED : obra *f*, labor *f* ⟨works of charity : obras de caridad⟩ **6** : obra *f* (de arte o literatura) **7** : obras *fpl* ⟨road work : obras viales⟩ **8** → **workmanship 9 works** *npl* FACTORY : fábrica *f* **10 works** *npl* MECHANISM : mecanismo *m* **11 the works** EVERYTHING : absolutamente todo *m* **12 at** ~ : WORKING : trabajando **13 at** ~ INVOLVED : en juego **14 in the works** : en trámite **15 it's all in a day's work** : es el pan nuestro de cada día **16 to have one's work cut**

out for one : tener mucho trabajo por delante **17 to make short work of** : hacer rápidamente

workable [ˈwərkəbəl] *adj* **1** : explotable (dícese de una mina, etc.) **2** FEASIBLE : factible, realizable

workaday [ˈwərkəˌdeɪ] *adj* : ordinario, banal

workaholic [ˌwərkəˈhɔlɪk] *n* : adicto *m*, -ta *f* al trabajo

workbench [ˈwərkˌbɛntʃ] *n* : mesa *f* de trabajo

workday [ˈwərkˌdeɪ] *n* **1** : jornada *f* laboral **2** WEEKDAY : día *m* hábil, día *m* laborable

worked up *adj* : agitado ⟨to get (all) worked up : agitarse⟩

worker [ˈwərkər] *n* : trabajador *m*, -dora *f*; obrero *m*, -ra *f*

workforce [ˈwərkˌfors] *n* **1** STAFF : mano *f* de obra **2** : fuerza *f* de trabajo, fuerza *f* laboral

working [ˈwərkɪŋ] *adj* **1** : que trabaja ⟨working mothers : madres que trabajan⟩ ⟨the working class : la clase obrera⟩ **2** : de trabajo ⟨working hours : horas de trabajo⟩ **3** FUNCTIONING : que funciona, operativo **4** SUFFICIENT : suficiente ⟨a working majority : una mayoría suficiente⟩ ⟨working knowledge : conocimientos básicos⟩

working–class [ˈwərkɪŋˈklæs] *adj* : obrero

workingman [ˈwərkɪŋˌmæn] *n, pl* **-men** [-mən, -ˌmɛn] : obrero *m*

workload [ˈwərkˌloːd] *n* : cantidad *f* de trabajo

workman [ˈwərkmən] *n, pl* **-men** [-mən, -ˌmɛn] **1** → **workingman 2** ARTISAN : artesano *m*

workmanlike [ˈwərkmənˌlaɪk] *adj* : bien hecho, competente

workmanship [ˈwərkmənˌʃɪp] *n* **1** WORK : ejecución *f*, trabajo *m* **2** CRAFTSMANSHIP : artesanía *f*, destreza *f*

workout [ˈwərkˌaʊt] *n* : ejercicios *mpl* físicos, entrenamiento *m*

workplace [ˈwərkˌples] *n* : lugar *m* de trabajo

workroom [ˈwərkˌruːm, -ˌrʊm] *n* : taller *m*

worksheet [ˈwərkˌʃiːt] *n* **1** : hoja *f* de ejercicios **2** : hoja *f* de cálculo (de impuestos, etc.)

workshop [ˈwərkˌʃɑp] *n* : taller *m* ⟨ceramics workshop : taller de cerámica⟩

workstation [ˈwərkˌsteɪʃən] *n* : estación *f* de trabajo (en informática)

world¹ [ˈwərld] *adj* : mundial, del mundo ⟨world championship : campeonato mundial⟩

world² *n* **1** : mundo *m* ⟨around the world : alrededor del mundo⟩ **2** : mundo *m* ⟨the industrialized world : el mundo industrializado⟩ **3** SOCIETY : mundo *m* ⟨the real world : la realidad⟩ **4** PEOPLE : mundo *m*, gente *f* ⟨to watch the world go by : ver pasar a la gente⟩ **5** REALM : mundo *m* ⟨the fashion world : el mundo de la moda⟩ **6** LIFE : mundo *m*, vida *f* ⟨his world fell apart : su mundo se derrumbó⟩ **7** PLANET : mundo *m*, planeta *f* **8 the world** EVERYTHING : todo *m* ⟨to mean the world to someone : ser todo para alguien⟩ **9 a world of** ⟨a world of difference : una diferencia enorme⟩ ⟨it'll do you a world of good : te hará la mar de bien⟩ **10 for all the world** *fam* EXACTLY : exactamente **11 (not) for the world** *fam* : por nada del mundo **12 in one's own world** *or* **in a world of one's own** *fam* : en su mundo **13 in the world** *fam* : del mundo ⟨the best in the world : el mejor del mundo⟩ ⟨what in the world . . .? : ¿qué diablos/demonios . . . ?⟩ **14 out of this world** *fam* : increíble, fantástico **15 the (whole) world over** *fam* : por/en/de todo el mundo **16 to have all the time in the world** : tener todo el tiempo del mundo **17 to come/ move up in the world** : prosperar, tener éxito **18 to think the world of someone** *fam* : tener a alguien en alta estima

world–famous *adj* : mundialmente famoso, de fama mundial

worldly [ˈwərldli] *adj* **worldlier; -est 1** : mundano ⟨worldly goods : bienes materiales⟩ **2** SOPHISTICATED : sofisticado, de mundo

worldwide[1] [ˈwərldˈwaid] *adv* : mundialmente, en todo el mundo

worldwide[2] *adj* : global, mundial

World Wide Web *n* : World Wide Web *f*, Red *f* (informática) mundial

worm[1] [ˈwərm] *vi* CRAWL : arrastrarse, deslizarse (como gusano) — *vt* **1** : desparasitar (un animal) **2 to worm one's way into** : introducirse en ⟨he wormed his way into her confidence : se ganó su confianza⟩ **3 to worm something out of someone** : sonsacarle algo a alguien

worm[2] *n* **1** : gusano *m*, lombriz *f* **2 worms** *npl* : lombrices *fpl* (parásitos)

worm–eaten [ˈwərmˌiːtən] *adj* : carcomido

wormy [ˈwərmi] *adj* **wormier; -est** : infestado de gusanos

worn *pp* → **wear**[1]

worn–out [ˈwornˈaut] *adj* **1** USED : gastado, desgastado **2** TIRED : agotado

worried [ˈwərid] *adj* : inquieto, preocupado

worrier [ˈwəriər] *n* : persona *f* que se preocupa mucho

worrisome [ˈwərisəm] *adj* **1** DISTURBING : preocupante, inquietante **2** : que se preocupa mucho (dícese de una persona)

worry[1] [ˈwəri] *v* **-ried; -rying** *vt* : preocupar, inquietar — *vi* : preocuparse, inquietarse, angustiarse

worry[2] *n, pl* **-ries** : preocupación *f*, inquietud *f*, angustia *f*

worrying [ˈwəriɪŋ] *adj* DISTURBING : preocupante, inquietante

worse[1] [ˈwərs] *adv* (*comparative of* BAD *or of* ILL) : peor

worse[2] *adj* (*comparative of* BAD *or of* ILL) : peor ⟨from bad to worse : de mal en peor⟩ ⟨to get worse : empeorar⟩ ⟨to feel worse : sentirse peor⟩

worse[3] *n* : estado *m* peor ⟨to take a turn for the worse : ponerse peor⟩ ⟨so much the worse : tanto peor⟩

worsen [ˈwərsən] *vt* : empeorar — *vi* : empeorar(se)

worship[1] [ˈwərʃəp] *v* **-shiped** *or* **-shipped; -shiping** *or* **-shipping** *vt* : adorar, venerar ⟨to worship God : adorar a Dios⟩ — *vi* : practicar una religión

worship[2] *n* : adoración *f*, culto *m*

worshiper *or* **worshipper** [ˈwərʃəpər] *n* : devoto *m*, -ta *f*; adorador *m*, -dora *f*

worst[1] [ˈwərst] *vt* DEFEAT : derrotar

worst[2] *adv* (*superlative of* ILL *or of* BAD *or* BADLY) : peor ⟨the worst dressed of all : el peor vestido de todos⟩

worst[3] *adj* (*superlative of* BAD *or of* ILL) : peor ⟨the worst movie : la peor película⟩

worst[4] *n* **the worst** : lo peor, el/la peor ⟨the worst is over : ya ha pasado lo peor⟩ ⟨if worst comes to worst : en el peor de los casos⟩

worst–case *adj* **a/the worst–case scenario** : el peor de los casos

worsted [ˈwʊstəd, ˈwərstəd] *n* : estambre *m*

worth[1] [ˈwərθ] *n* **1** : valor *m* (monetario) ⟨ten dollars' worth of gas : diez dólares de gasolina⟩ **2** MERIT : valor *m*, mérito *m*, valía *f* ⟨an employee of great worth : un empleado de gran valía⟩

worth[2] *prep* **to be worth** : valer ⟨her holdings are worth a fortune : sus propiedades valen una fortuna⟩ ⟨it's not worth it : no vale la pena⟩

worthiness [ˈwərðinəs] *n* : mérito *m*

worthless [ˈwərθləs] *adj* **1** : sin valor ⟨worthless trinkets : chucherías sin valor⟩ **2** USELESS : inútil

worthwhile [wərθˈhwail] *adj* : que vale la pena

worthy [ˈwərði] *adj* **worthier; -est 1** : digno ⟨worthy of promotion : digno de un ascenso⟩ **2** COMMENDABLE : meritorio, encomiable

would [ˈwʊd] (*past of* WILL) **1** (*expressing preference, desire, or willingness*) ⟨I would rather go alone than with her : preferiría ir sola que con ella⟩ ⟨I would like to help : me gustaría ayudar⟩ ⟨he would do anything for her : haría cualquier cosa por ella⟩ **2** (*expressing intent*) ⟨those who would ban certain books : aquellos que prohibirían ciertos libros⟩ **3** (*expressing habitual action*) ⟨he would often take his kids to the park : solía llevar a sus hijos al parque⟩ **4** (*expressing possibility or contingency*) ⟨I would go if I had the money : iría yo si tuviera el dinero⟩ ⟨I would if I could : lo haría si pudiera⟩ **5** (*offering or requesting advice*) ⟨if I were you, I would do it : yo en tu lugar lo haría⟩ ⟨what would you do? : ¿qué harías tú?⟩ **6** (*expressing probability*) ⟨she would have won if she hadn't tripped : habría ganado si no hubiera tropezado⟩ **7** (*expressing a request*) ⟨would you kindly help me with this? : ¿tendría la bondad de ayudarme con esto?⟩ ⟨would you mind waiting? : ¿le importaría esperar?⟩

would–be ['wʊd'bi:] *adj* : potencial ⟨a would-be celebrity : un aspirante a celebridad⟩

wouldn't ['wʊdənt] *contraction of* WOULD NOT → **would**

wound[1] ['wu:nd] *vt* : herir

wound[2] *n* : herida *f*

wound[3] ['waʊnd] → **wind**[2]

wove, woven → **weave**[1]

wow ['waʊ] *interj (expressing surprise or pleasure)* : ¡guau!, ¡híjole! *Mex*, ¡hala! *Spain*

wrangle[1] ['ræŋɡəl] *vi* -gled; -gling : discutir, reñir ⟨to wrangle over : discutir por⟩

wrangle[2] *n* : riña *f*, disputa *f*

wrap[1] ['ræp] *v* **wrapped; wrapping** *vt* 1 COVER : envolver, cubrir ⟨to wrap a package : envolver un paquete⟩ ⟨wrapped in mystery : envuelto en misterio⟩ 2 ENCIRCLE : rodear, ceñir ⟨to wrap one's arms around someone : estrechar a alguien⟩ 3 **to wrap up** FINISH : darle fin a (algo) — *vi* 1 COIL : envolverse, enroscarse 2 **to wrap up** DRESS : abrigarse ⟨wrap up warmly : abrígate bien⟩

wrap[2] *n* 1 WRAPPER : envoltura *f* 2 : prenda *f* que envuelve (como un chal, una bata, etc.)

wrapper ['ræpər] *n* : envoltura *f*, envoltorio *m*

wrapping ['ræpɪŋ] *n* : envoltura *f*, envoltorio *m*

wrath ['ræθ] *n* : ira *f*, cólera *f*

wrathful ['ræθfəl] *adj* : iracundo

wreak ['ri:k] *vt* : infligir, causar ⟨to wreak havoc : crear caos, causar estragos⟩

wreath ['ri:θ] *n, pl* **wreaths** ['ri:ðz, 'ri:θs] : corona *f* (de flores, etc.)

wreathe ['ri:ð] *vt* **wreathed; wreathing** 1 ADORN : coronar (de flores, etc.) 2 ENVELOP : envolver ⟨wreathed in mist : envuelto en niebla⟩

wreck[1] ['rɛk] *vt* : destruir, arruinar, estrellar (un automóvil), naufragar (un barco)

wreck[2] *n* 1 WRECKAGE : restos *mpl* (de un buque naufragado, un avión siniestrado, etc.) 2 RUIN : ruina *f*, desastre *m* ⟨this place is a wreck! : ¡este lugar está hecho un desastre!⟩ ⟨to be a nervous wreck : tener los nervios destrozados⟩

wreckage ['rɛkɪd] *n* : restos *mpl* (de un buque naufragado, un avión siniestrado, etc.), ruinas *fpl* (de un edificio)

wrecker ['rɛkər] *n* TOW TRUCK : grúa *f*

wren ['rɛn] *n* : chochín *m*

wrench[1] ['rɛntʃ] *vt* 1 PULL : arrancar (de un tirón) 2 SPRAIN, TWIST : torcerse (un tobillo, un músculo, etc.)

wrench[2] *n* 1 TUG : tirón *m*, jalón *m* 2 SPRAIN : torcedura *f* 3 *or* **monkey wrench** : llave *f* inglesa

wrest ['rɛst] *vt* : arrancar

wrestle[1] ['rɛsəl] *v* -tled; -tling *vi* 1 : luchar, practicar la lucha (en deportes) 2 STRUGGLE : luchar ⟨to wrestle with a dilemma : lidiar con un dilema⟩ — *vt* : luchar contra

wrestle[2] *n* STRUGGLE : lucha *f*

wrestler ['rɛsələr] *n* : luchador *m*, -dora *f*

wrestling ['rɛsəlɪŋ] *n* : lucha *f*

wretch ['rɛtʃ] *n* : infeliz *mf*; desgraciado *m*, -da *f*

wretched ['rɛtʃəd] *adj* 1 MISERABLE, UNHAPPY : desdichado, afligido ⟨I feel wretched : me siento muy mal⟩ 2 UNFORTUNATE : miserable, desgraciado, lastimoso ⟨wretched weather : tiempo espantoso⟩ 3 INFERIOR : inferior, malo

wretchedly ['rɛtʃədli] *adv* : miserablemente, lamentablemente

wriggle ['rɪɡəl] *vi* -gled; -gling : retorcerse, menearse

wring ['rɪŋ] *vt* **wrung** ['rʌŋ]; **wringing** 1 *or* **to wring out** : escurrir, exprimir (el lavado) 2 EXTRACT : arrancar, sacar (por la fuerza) 3 TWIST : torcer, retorcer 4 **to wring someone's heart** : partirle el corazón a alguien

wringer ['rɪŋər] *n* : escurridor *m*

wrinkle[1] ['rɪŋkəl] *v* -kled; -kling *vt* : arrugar — *vi* : arrugarse

wrinkle[2] *n* : arruga *f*

wrinkly ['rɪŋkəli] *adj* **wrinklier; -est** : arrugado

wrist ['rɪst] *n* 1 : muñeca *f* (en anatomía) 2 *or* **wristband** ['rɪst-,bænd] CUFF : puño *m*

wristwatch ['rɪst,wɑtʃ] *n* : reloj *m* de pulsera

writ ['rɪt] *n* : orden *f* (judicial)

write ['raɪt] *v* **wrote** ['ro:t]; **written** ['rɪtən]; **writing** *vi* 1 : escribir 2 **to write back** : contestar 3 **to write in** : escribir — *vt* 1 : escribir 2 **to write back** : contestar 3 **to write down** : apuntar, anotar 4 **to write in** INSERT : escribir, insertar 5 **to write into** : incluir (en un contrato, etc.) 6 **to write off** : declarar siniestro total (en contabilidad) 7 **to write off** DEDUCT : deducir, descontar (de los impuestos) 8 **to write off** : dar por perdido ⟨he wrote it off as a failure : lo consideró un fracaso⟩ 9 **to write out** : escribir 10 **to write out** : hacer (un cheque, una factura) 11 **to write someone out of** : eliminar a alguien de (un testamento, etc.) 12 **to write up** : redactar 13 **to write up** REPORT : ponerle una multa a (un conductor), darle una carta de amonestación a (un empleado)

write–off ['raɪt,ɔf] *n* 1 : cancelación *f* (de una deuda) 2 : siniestro *m* total, pérdida *f* total

writer ['raɪtər] *n* : escritor *m*, -tora *f*

writhe ['raɪð] *vi* **writhed; writhing** : retorcerse

writing ['raɪtɪŋ] *n* 1 : escritura *f* 2 HANDWRITING : letra *f* 3 **writings** *npl* WORKS : escritos *mpl*, obra *f*

writing paper *n* : papel *m* de carta

wrong[1] ['rɔŋ] *vt* **wronged; wronging** : ofender, ser injusto con

wrong[2] *adv* : mal, incorrectamente

wrong[3] *adj* **wronger** ['rɔŋər]; **wrongest** ['rɔŋəst] 1 EVIL, SINFUL : malo, injusto, inmoral ⟨it's wrong to lie : mentir está mal⟩ ⟨I've done nothing wrong : no he hecho nada malo⟩ **2** IMPROPER, UNSUITABLE : inadecuado, inapropiado, malo ⟨you're asking the wrong guy : no soy la persona indicada para responder⟩ **3** INCORRECT : malo, equivocado, incorrecto, erróneo ⟨a wrong answer : una mala respuesta, una respuesta equivocada⟩ ⟨I dialed the wrong number : me equivoqué de número (al marcar)⟩ ⟨the clock is wrong : el reloj anda mal⟩ **4 to be wrong** : equivocarse, estar equivocado ⟨I could be wrong : puede que esté equivocado⟩

wrong⁴ *n* **1** INJUSTICE : injusticia *f*, mal *m* **2** OFFENSE : ofensa *f*, agravio *m* (en derecho) **3 to be in the wrong** : haber hecho mal, estar equivocado

wrongdoer [ˈrɔŋˌduːər] *n* : malhechor *m*, -chora *f*

wrongdoing [ˈrɔŋˌduːɪŋ] *n* : fechoría *f*, maldad *f*

wrongful [ˈrɔŋfəl] *adj* **1** UNJUST : injusto **2** UNLAWFUL : ilegal

wrongly [ˈrɔŋli] *adv* **1** : injustamente **2** INCORRECTLY : erróneamente, incorrectamente

wrote → **write**

wrought [ˈrɔt] *adj* **1** SHAPED : formado, forjado ⟨wrought iron : hierro forjado⟩ **2** *or* **wrought up** : agitado, excitado

wrung → **wring**

wry [ˈraɪ] *adj* **wrier** [ˈraɪər]; **wriest** [ˈraɪəst] **1** TWISTED : torcido ⟨a wry neck : un cuello torcido⟩ **2** : irónico, sardónico (dícese del humor)

X

x¹ *n, pl* **x's** *or* **xs** [ˈɛksəz] **1** : vigésima cuarta letra del alfabeto inglés **2** : incógnita *f* (en matemáticas)

x² [ˈks] *vt* **x–ed** [ˈɛkst]; **x–ing** *or* **x'ing** [ˈɛksɪŋ] DELETE : tachar

xenon [ˈziːˌnɑn, ˈzɛ-] *n* : xenón *m*

xenophobe [ˈzɛnəˌfoːb, ˈziː-] *n* : xenófobo *m*, -ba *f*

xenophobia [ˌzɛnəˈfoːbiə, ˌziː-] *n* : xenofobia *f*

xenophobic [ˌzɛnəˈfoːbɪk, ˌziː-] *adj* : xenófobo

xerox [ˈzɪrˌɑks] *vt* : xerografiar

Xerox [ˈzɪrˌɑks] *trademark* se usa para una fotocopiadora

Xmas [ˈkrɪsməs] *n* : Navidad *f*

x–ray [ˈɛksˌreɪ] *vt* : radiografiar

X ray [ˈɛksˌreɪ] *n* **1** : rayo *m* X **2** : radiografía *f* (imagen)

xylophone [ˈzaɪləˌfoːn] *n* : xilófono *m*

Y

y [ˈwaɪ] *n, pl* **y's** *or* **ys** [ˈwaɪz] : vigésima quinta letra del alfabeto inglés

yacht¹ [ˈjɑt] *vi* : navegar (a vela), ir en yate ⟨to go yachting : irse a navegar⟩

yacht² *n* : yate *m*

yak [ˈjæk] *n* : yac *m*

yam [ˈjæm] *n* **1** : ñame *m* **2** SWEET POTATO : batata *f*, boniato *m*

yang [ˈjæŋ, ˈjɑŋ] *n* : yang *m* ⟨(the) yin and yang : el yin y el yang⟩

yank¹ [ˈjæŋk] *vt* : tirar de, jalar, darle un tirón a

yank² *n* : tirón *m*

Yankee [ˈjæŋki] *n* : yanqui *mf*

yap¹ [ˈjæp] *vi* **yapped; yapping 1** BARK, YELP : ladrar, gañir **2** CHATTER : cotorrear *fam*, parlotear *fam*

yap² *n* : ladrido *m*, gañido *m*

yard [ˈjɑrd] *n* **1** : yarda *f* (medida) **2** SPAR : verga *f* (de un barco) **3** COURTYARD : patio *m* **4** : jardín *m* (de una casa) **5** : depósito *m* (de mercancías, etc.)

yardage [ˈjɑrdɪʤ] *n* : medida *f* en yardas

yardarm [ˈjɑrdˌɑrm] *n* : penol *m*

yardstick [ˈjɑrdˌstɪk] *n* **1** : vara *f* **2** CRITERION : criterio *m*, norma *f*

yarn [ˈjɑrn] *n* **1** : hilado *m* **2** TALE : historia *f*, cuento *m* ⟨to spin a yarn : inventar una historia⟩

yawn¹ [ˈjɔn] *vi* **1** : bostezar **2** OPEN : abrirse

yawn² *n* : bostezo *m*

ye [ˈjiː] *pron* : vosotros, vosotras

yea¹ [ˈjeɪ] *adv* YES : sí

yea² *n* : voto *m* a favor

yeah [ˈjɛə, ˈjæə] *adv fam* YES : sí ⟨are you coming? yeah : ¿vienes? sí⟩ ⟨oh, yeah? : ¿ah, sí?⟩ ⟨it's true! yeah, right : ¡es verdad! sí, claro⟩

year [ˈjɪr] *n* **1** : año *m* ⟨last year : el año pasado⟩ ⟨he's ten years old : tiene diez años⟩ **2** : curso *m*, año *m* (escolar) **3 years** *npl* AGES : siglos *mpl*, años *mpl* ⟨I haven't seen them in years : hace siglos que no los veo⟩

yearbook [ˈjɪrˌbʊk] *n* : anuario *m*

year–end [ˈjɪrˈɛnd] *adj* : de fin de año

yearling [ˈjɪrlɪŋ, ˈjərlən] *n* : animal *m* menor de dos años

yearly¹ [ˈjɪrli] *adv* : cada año, anualmente

yearly² *adj* : anual

yearn [ˈjərn] *vi* : anhelar, ansiar

yearning [ˈjərnɪŋ] *n* : anhelo *m*

yeast [ˈjiːst] *n* : levadura *f*

yell¹ [ˈjɛl] *vi* : gritar, chillar — *vt* : gritar

yell² *n* : grito *m*, alarido *m* ⟨to let out a yell : dar un grito⟩

yellow¹ [ˈjɛlo] *vi* : ponerse amarillo, volverse amarillo

yellow² *adj* **1** : amarillo **2** COWARDLY : cobarde

yellow³ *n* : amarillo *m*

yellow fever *n* : fiebre *f* amarilla

yellowish [ˈjɛloɪʃ] *adj* : amarillento

yellow jacket *n* : avispa *f* (con rayas amarillas)

yelp¹ [ˈjɛlp] *vi* : dar un gañido (dícese de un animal), dar un grito (dícese de una persona)

yelp² *n* : gañido *m* (de un animal), grito *m* (de una persona)

yen [ˈjɛn] *n* **1** DESIRE : deseo *m*, ganas *fpl* **2** : yen *m* (moneda japonesa)

yeoman [ˈjoːmən] *n, pl* **-men** [-mən, -mɛn] : suboficial *mf* de marina

yes¹ [ˈjɛs] *adv* : sí ⟨to say yes : decir que sí⟩

yes² *n* : sí *m*

yesterday¹ [ˈjɛstərˌdeɪ, -di] *adv* : ayer

yesterday² *n* **1** : ayer *m* **2 the day before yesterday** : anteayer

yesteryear [ˈjɛstərˌjɪr] *n* of ~ : de antaño

yet¹ [ˈjɛt] *adv* **1** BESIDES, EVEN : aún ⟨yet more problems : más problemas aún⟩ ⟨yet again : otra vez⟩ **2** SO FAR : aún, todavía ⟨not yet : todavía no⟩ ⟨as yet : hasta ahora, todavía⟩ **3** : ya ⟨has he come yet? : ¿ya ha venido?⟩ **4** EVENTUALLY : todavía, algún día **5** NEVERTHELESS : sin embargo

yet² *conj* : pero

yew [ˈjuː] *n* : tejo *m*

Yiddish [ˈjɪdɪʃ] *n* : yiddish *m*, yidis *m* — **Yiddish** *adj*

yield¹ [ˈjiːld] *vt* **1** SURRENDER : ceder ⟨to yield the right of way : ceder el paso⟩ **2** PRODUCE : producir, dar, rendir (en finanzas) — *vi* **1** GIVE : ceder ⟨to yield under pressure : ceder por la presión⟩ **2** GIVE IN, SURRENDER : ceder, rendirse, entregarse

yield² *n* : rendimiento *m*, rédito *m* (en finanzas)

yin [ˈjɪn] *n* : yin *m* ⟨(the) yin and yang : el yin y el yang⟩

yodel¹ [ˈjoːdəl] *vi* **-deled** *or* **-delled; -deling** *or* **-delling** : cantar al estilo tirolés

yodel² *n* : canción *f* al estilo tirolés

yoga [ˈjoːgə] *n* : yoga *m*

yogurt [ˈjoːgərt] *n* : yogur *m*, yogurt *m*

yoke¹ [ˈjoːk] *vt* **yoked; yoking** : uncir (animales)

yoke² *n* **1** : yugo *m* (para uncir animales) ⟨the yoke of oppression : el yugo de la opresión⟩ **2** TEAM : yunta *f* (de bueyes)

yokel [ˈjoːkəl] *n* : palurdo *m*, -da *f*

yolk [ˈjoːk] *n* : yema *f* (de un huevo)

Yom Kippur [joːmˈkɪˈpʊr, jɑm-, -ˈkɪpər] *n* : el Día *m* del Perdón, Yom Kippur

yon [ˈjɑn] → **yonder**

yonder¹ [ˈjɑndər] *adv* : allá ⟨over yonder : allá lejos⟩

yonder² *adj* : aquel ⟨yonder hill : aquella colina⟩

yore [ˈjoːr] *n* **in days of yore** : antaño

you [ˈjuː] *pron* **1** (*used as subject — familiar*) : tú; vos *in some Latin American countries*; ustedes *pl*; vosotros, vosotras *pl Spain* **2** (*used as subject — formal*) : usted, ustedes *pl* **3** (*used as indirect object — familiar*) : te, les *pl* (se *before lo, la, los, las*), os *pl Spain* ⟨he told it to you : te lo contó⟩ ⟨I gave them to (all of, both of) you : se los di⟩ **4** (*used as indirect object — formal*) : lo *Spain sometimes* le, la; los *Spain sometimes* les, las *pl* **5** (*used after a preposition — familiar*) : ti; vos *in some Latin American countries*; ustedes *pl*; vosotros, vosotras *pl Spain* **6** (*used after a preposition — formal*) : usted, ustedes *pl* **7** (*used as an impersonal subject*) ⟨you never know : nunca se sabe⟩ ⟨you have to be aware : hay que ser consciente⟩ ⟨you mustn't do that : eso no se hace⟩ **8 with you** (*familiar*) : contigo; con ustedes *pl*; con vosotros, con vosotras *pl Spain* **9 with you** (*formal*) : con usted, con ustedes *pl*

you'd [ˈjuːd, ˈjud] *contraction of* YOU HAD *or* YOU WOULD → **have, would**

you'll [ˈjuːl, ˈjul] *contraction of* YOU SHALL *or* YOU WILL → **shall, will**

young¹ [ˈjʌŋ] *adj* **younger** [ˈjʌŋgər]; **youngest** [-gəst] **1** : joven, pequeño, menor ⟨young people : los jóvenes⟩ ⟨my younger brother : mi hermano menor⟩ ⟨she is the youngest : es la más pequeña⟩ **2** FRESH, NEW : tierno (dícese de las verduras), joven (dícese del vino) **3** YOUTHFUL : joven, juvenil

young² *npl* **1** : jóvenes *mfpl* (de los humanos), crías *fpl* (de los animales)

youngster [ˈjʌŋkstər] *n* **1** YOUTH : joven *mf* **2** CHILD : chico *m*, -ca *f*; niño *m*, -ña *f*

your [ˈjʊr, ˈjoːr, jər] *adj* **1** (*familiar singular*) : tu ⟨your cat : tu gato⟩ ⟨your books : tus libros⟩ ⟨wash your hands : lávate las manos⟩ **2** (*familiar plural*) : su, vuestro *Spain* ⟨your car : su coche, el coche de ustedes⟩ **3** (*formal*) : su ⟨your houses : sus casas⟩ **4** (*impersonal*) : el, la, los, las ⟨on your left : a la izquierda⟩

you're [ˈjʊr, ˈjoːr, ˈjər, ˈjuːər] *contraction of* YOU ARE → **be**

yours [ˈjʊrz, ˈjoːrz] *pron* **1** (*belonging to one person — familiar*) : (el) tuyo, (la) tuya, (los) tuyos, (las) tuyas ⟨those are mine; yours are there : ésas son mías; las tuyas están allí⟩ ⟨is this one yours? : ¿éste es tuyo?⟩ **2** (*belonging to more than one person — familiar*) : (el) suyo, (la) suya, (los) suyos, (las) suyas; (el) vuestro, (la) vuestra, (los) vuestros, (las) vuestras *Spain* ⟨our house and yours : nuestra casa y la suya⟩ **3** (*formal*) : (el) suyo, (la) suya, (los) suyos, (las) suyas

yourself [jərˈsɛlf] *pron, pl* **yourselves** [-ˈsɛlvz] **1** (*used reflexively — familiar*) : te, se *pl*, os *pl Spain* ⟨wash yourself : lávate⟩ ⟨you dressed yourselves : se vistieron, os vestisteis⟩ **2** (*used reflexively — formal*) : se ⟨did you hurt yourself? : ¿se hizo daño?⟩ ⟨you've gotten yourselves dirty : se ensuciaron⟩ 3 (*used for emphasis*) : tú mismo, tú misma; usted mismo, usted misma; ustedes mismos, ustedes mismas *pl*; vosotros mismos, vosotras mismas *pl Spain* ⟨you did it yourselves? : ¿lo hicieron ustedes mismos?, ¿lo hicieron por sí solos?⟩

youth ['ju:θ] *n, pl* **youths** ['ju:ðz, 'ju:θs] **1** : juventud *f* ⟨in her youth : en su juventud⟩ **2** BOY : joven *m* **3** : jóvenes *mfpl*, juventud *f* ⟨the youth of our city : los jóvenes de nuestra ciudad⟩

youthful ['ju:θfəl] *adj* **1** : de juventud **2** YOUNG : joven **3** JUVENILE : juvenil

youthfulness ['ju:θfəlnəs] *n* : juventud *f*

youth hostel → **hostel**

you've ['ju:v] *contraction of* YOU HAVE → **have**

yowl[1] ['jaʊl] *vi* : aullar

yowl[2] *n* : aullido *m*

yo–yo ['jo:,jo:] *n, pl* **-yos** : yoyo *m*, yoyó *m*

yucca ['jʌkə] *n* : yuca *f*

Yugoslavian [,ju:go'slaviən] *n* : yugoslavo *m*, -va *f* — **Yugoslavian** *adj*

yule ['ju:l] *n* CHRISTMAS : Navidad *f*

yuletide ['ju:l,taɪd] *n* : Navidades *fpl*

yup ['jʌp] *adv fam* → **yes**[1]

yuppie ['jʌpi] *n* : yuppy *mf*

Z

z ['zi:] *n, pl* **z's** *or* **zs** : vigésima sexta letra del alfabeto inglés

zany[1] ['zeɪni] *adj* **zanier; -est** : alocado, disparatado

zany[2] *n, pl* **-nies** : bufón *m*, -fona *f*

zap[1] ['zæp] *vt* **zapped; zapping** **1** ELIMINATE : eliminar **2** : enviar o transportar rápidamente — *vi* : ir rápidamente

zap[2] *n* **1** ZEST : sabor *m*, sazón *f* **2** BLAST : golpe *m* fuerte

zeal ['zi:l] *n* : fervor *m*, celo *m*, entusiasmo *m*

zealot ['zɛlət] *n* : fanático *m*, -ca *f*

zealous ['zɛləs] *adj* : celoso — **zealously** *adv*

zebra ['zi:brə] *n* : cebra *f*

zebu ['zi:,bu:, -,bju:] *n* : cebú *m*

zenith ['zi:nəθ] *n* **1** : cenit *m* (en astronomía) **2** PEAK : apogeo *m*, cenit *m* ⟨at the zenith of his career : en el apogeo de su carrera⟩

zeppelin ['zɛpləń, -pəlın] *n* : zepelín *m*

zero[1] ['zi:ro, 'zıro] *vi* **to zero in on** : apuntar hacia, centrarse en (un problema, etc.)

zero[2] *adj* : cero, nulo ⟨zero degrees : cero grados⟩ ⟨zero opportunities : oportunidades nulas⟩

zero[3] *n, pl* **-ros** : cero *m* ⟨below zero : bajo cero⟩

zest ['zɛst] *n* **1** GUSTO : entusiasmo *m*, brío *m* **2** FLAVOR : sabor *m*, sazón *f*

zestful ['zɛstfəl] *adj* : brioso

zesty ['zɛsti] *adj* **zestier; -est** **1** FLAVORFUL : sabroso, gustoso, picante **2** LIVELY : brioso

zigzag[1] ['zıg,zæg] *vi* **-zagged; -zagging** : zigzaguear

zigzag[2] *adv & adj* : en zigzag

zigzag[3] *n* : zigzag *m*

Zimbabwean [zɪm'babwiən, -bweɪ-] *n* : zimbabuense *mf* — **Zimbabwean** *adj*

zinc ['zıŋk] *n* : cinc *m*, zinc *m*

zing ['zıŋ] *n* **1** HISS, HUM : zumbido *m*, silbido *m* **2** ENERGY : brío *m*

zinnia ['zıniə, 'zi:-, -njə] *n* : zinnia *f*

Zionism ['zaɪə,nızəm] *n* : sionismo *m*

Zionist ['zaɪənıst] *n* : sionista *mf*

zip[1] ['zıp] *v* **zipped; zipping** *vt or* **to zip up** : cerrar el cierre de — *vi* **1** SPEED : pasarse volando ⟨the day zipped by : el día se pasó volando⟩ **2** HISS, HUM : silbar, zumbar

zip[2] *n* **1** ZING : zumbido *m*, silbido *m* **2** ENERGY : brío *m*

zip code *n* : código *m* postal

zipper ['zıpər] *n* : cierre *m*, cremallera *f*, zíper *m* CA, Mex

zippy ['zıpi] *adj* **zippier; -est** : brioso

zit ['zıt] *n* : grano *m*

zodiac ['zo:di,æk] *n* : zodíaco *m*

zombie ['zambi] *n* : zombi *mf*, zombie *mf*

zone[1] ['zo:n] *vt* **zoned; zoning** **1** : dividir en zonas **2** DESIGNATE : declarar ⟨to zone for business : declarar como zona comercial⟩

zone[2] *n* : zona *f*

zoo ['zu:] *n, pl* **zoos** : zoológico *m*, zoo *m*

zoological [,zo:ə'lɑdʒıkəl, ,zu:ə-] *adj* : zoológico

zoologist [zo'alədʒıst, zu:-] *n* : zoólogo *m*, -ga *f*

zoology [zo'alədʒi, zu:-] *n* : zoología *f*

zoom[1] ['zu:m] *vi* **1** : zumbar, ir volando ⟨to zoom past : pasar volando⟩ **2** CLIMB : elevarse ⟨the plane zoomed up : el avión se elevó⟩

zoom[2] *n* **1** : zumbido *m* ⟨the zoom of an engine : el zumbido de un motor⟩ **2** : subida *f* vertical (de un avión, etc.) **3** *or* **zoom lens** : zoom *m*

zucchini [zʊ'ki:ni] *n, pl* **-ni** *or* **-nis** : calabacín *m*, calabacita *f* Mex

Zulu ['zu:lu:] *n* **1** : zulú *mf* **2** : zulú *m* (idioma) — **Zulu** *adj*

zygote ['zaɪ,go:t] *n* : zigoto *m*, cigoto *m*

Common Spanish Abbreviations

SPANISH ABBREVIATION AND EXPANSION		ENGLISH EQUIVALENT	
abr.	abril	**Apr.**	April
a/c	a cargo de	**c/o**	care of
A.C., a.C.	antes de Cristo	**BC**	before Christ
A.D.	anno Domini	**AD**	anno Domini (in the year of our Lord)
a. de J.C.	antes de Jesucristo	**BC**	before Christ
admón.	administración	—	administration
a/f	a favor	—	in favor
ago.	agosto	**Aug.**	August
a.m.	ante meridiem (de la mañana)	**a.m., AM**	ante meridiem (before noon)
Apdo.	apartado (de correos)	—	P.O. box
aprox.	aproximadamente	**approx.**	approximately
Aptdo.	apartado (de correos)	—	P.O. box
Arq.	arquitecto	**arch.**	architect
A.T.	Antiguo Testamento	**O.T.**	Old Testament
atte.	atentamente	—	sincerely
atto., atta.	atento, atenta	—	kind, courteous
av., avda.	avenida	**Ave.**	Avenue
a/v.	a vista	—	on receipt
ayte.	ayudante	**asst.**	assistant
BID	Banco Interamericano de Desarrollo	**IDB**	Interamerican Development Bank
B⁰., B⁰	banco, barrio	—	Bank, District
blvar.	bulevar	**Blvd.**	Boulevard
BM	Banco Mundial	—	World Bank
br.	bulevar	**Blvd.**	Boulevard
c/, C/	calle	**St.**	Street
C	centígrado, Celsius	**C**	centigrade, Celsius
C.	compañía	**Co.**	Company
CA	corriente alterna	**AC**	alternating current
cap.	capítulo	**ch., chap.**	chapter
Cap.	capitán	**Capt.**	Captain
c/c	cuenta corriente	—	current account, checking account
c.c.	centímetros cúbicos	**cc, cu. cm**	cubic centimeters
CC	corriente continua	**DC**	direct current
CC	copia de carbón	**cc**	carbon copy
CCO	copia (de carbón) oculta	**bcc**	blind carbon copy
c/d	con descuento	—	with discount
Cd.	ciudad	—	city
CE	Comunidad Europea	**EC**	European Community
CEE	Comunidad Económica Europea	**EEC**	European Economic Community
cf.	compárese	**cf.**	compare
cg.	centígramo	**cg**	centigram

CGT	Confederación General de Trabajadores *or* del Trabajo	—	confederation of workers, union
CI	coeficiente intelectual *or* de inteligencia	IQ	intelligence quotient
Cía.	compañía	Co.	Company
cm.	centímetro	cm	centimeter
Cmte.	comandante	Cmdr.	Commander
Cnel.	coronel	Col.	Colonel
col.	columna	col.	column
Col. *Mex*	colonia	—	residential area
Com.	comandante	Cmdr.	Commander
comp.	compárese	comp.	compare
Cor.	coronel	Col.	Colonel
C.P.	código postal	—	zip code
CSF, c.s.f.	coste, seguro y flete	c.i.f.	cost, insurance, and freight
cta.	cuenta	ac., acct.	account
cte.	corriente	cur.	current
CTI	centro de tratamiento intensivo *Uru*	ICU	intensive care unit
c/u	cada uno, cada una	ea.	each
CV	caballo de vapor	hp	horsepower
D.	don	—	—
Da., D.ª	doña	—	—
dB	decibel, decibelio	dB	decibel
d.C.	después de Cristo	AD	anno Domini (in the year of our Lord)
dcha.	derecha	—	right
d. de J.C.	después de Jesucristo	AD	anno Domini (in the year of our Lord)
dep.	departamento	dept.	department
DF, D.F.	Distrito Federal	—	Federal District
dic.	diciembre	Dec.	December
dir.	director, directora	dir.	director
dir.	dirección	—	direction, address
DNI	*Arg, Spain* documento nacional de identidad	—	national identity card
Dña.	doña	—	—
dom., do.	domingo	Sun.	Sunday
dpto.	departamento	dept.	department
Dr.	doctor	Dr.	Doctor
Dra.	doctora	Dr.	Doctor
DSL	línea de abonado digital	DSL	digital subscriber line
dto.	descuento	—	discount
E, E.	Este, este	E	East, east
Ed.	editorial	—	publishing house
Ed., ed.	edición	Ed., ed.	edition
edif.	edificio	Bldg.	building
edo.	estado	st.	state
EEUU, EE.UU.	Estados Unidos	US, U.S.	United States
ej.	por ejemplo	ex.	for example
E.M.	esclerosis múltiple	MS	multiple sclerosis
ene.	enero	Jan.	January

et al.	et alii (y otros)	**et al.**	et alii (and others)
etc.	etcétera	**etc.**	et cetera
ext.	extensión	**ext.**	extension
F	Fahrenheit	**F**	Fahrenheit
f.a.b.	franco a bordo	**f.o.b.**	free on board
FAQ	pregunta(s) frecuente(s)	**FAQ**	frequently asked question(s)
FC	ferrocarril	**RR**	railroad
feb.	febrero	**Feb.**	February
FF AA, FF.AA.	Fuerzas Armadas	—	armed forces
FMI	Fondo Monetario Internacional	**IMF**	International Monetary Fund
g.	gramo	**g., gm, gr.**	gram
G	(talla) grande	**L**	large
GMT	tiempo medio de Greenwich, hora del meridiano de Greenwich	**GMT**	Greenwich Mean Time
G.P.	giro postal	**M.O.**	money order
gr.	gramo	**g., gm, gr.**	gram
Gral.	general	**Gen.**	General
h.	hora	**hr.**	hour
Hno(s).	hermano(s)	**Bro(s).**	Brother(s)
ib., ibid.	ibidem (en el mismo lugar)	**ibid.**	ibidem (in the same place)
I + D, I & D, I y D	investigación y desarrollo	**R & D**	research and development
i.e.	esto es, es decir	**i.e.**	that is
incl.	inclusive	**incl.**	inclusive, inclusively, including
Ing.	ingeniero, ingeniera	**eng.**	engineer
IPC	índice de precios al consumo	**CPI**	consumer price index
IVA	impuesto al valor agregado	**VAT**	value-added tax
izq.; izdo., izda.; izqdo., izqda.	izquierdo; izquierda	**l.**	Left
JJ.OO., JJ OO	Juegos Olímpicos	—	Olympics, Olympic Games
Jr.	Júnior	**Jr., Jun.**	Junior
juev.	jueves	**Thu., Thur., Thurs.**	Thursday
jul.	julio	**Jul.**	July
jun.	junio	**Jun.**	June
kg.	kilogramo	**kg**	kilogram
km.	kilómetro	**km**	kilometer
km/h	kilómetros por hora	**kph**	kilometers per hour
kv, kV	kilovatio	**kw, kW**	kilowatt
l.	litro	**l, lit.**	liter
lcdo., lcda.	licenciado, licenciada	—	—
ldo., lda.	licenciado, licenciada	—	—

LGBT	lesbianas, gays, bisexuales y transgénero	**LGBT**	lesbian, gay, bisexual, and transgender
LGBTQ	lesbianas, gays, bisexuales, transgénero y queer	**LGBTQ**	lesbian, gay, bisexual, transgender, and queer/questioning
Lic.	licenciado, licenciada	—	—
Ltda.	limitada	**Ltd.**	Limited
lun.	lunes	**Mon.**	Monday
m	masculino	**m**	masculine
m	metro	**m**	meter
m	minuto	**m**	minute
M	mediano, (talla) mediana	**M**	medium
mar.	marzo	**Mar.**	March
mart.	martes	**Tue., Tues.**	Tuesday
Méx.	mexicano, México	**Mex.**	Mexican, Mexico
mg.	miligramo	**mg**	milligram
miérc.	miércoles	**Wed.**	Wednesday
min	minuto	**min.**	minute
ml.	mililitro	**ml**	milliliter
mm.	milímetro	**mm**	millimeter
MN, M.N., m.n., m/n	moneda nacional	—	national currency
Mons.	monseñor	**Msgr.**	Monsignor
Mtra.	maestra	—	teacher
Mtro.	maestro	—	teacher
N, N.	Norte, norte	**N, no.**	North, north
NIP	número de identificación personal	**PIN**	personal identification number
n/	nuestro	—	our
N. de (la) R.	nota de (la) redacción	**Ed.**	editor's note
NE	nordeste	**NE**	northeast
NN.UU.	Naciones Unidas	**UN**	United Nations
n.°	número	**no.**	number
NO	noroeste	**NW**	northwest
nov.	noviembre	**Nov.**	November
N.T.	Nuevo Testamento	**N.T.**	New Testament
ntra., ntro.	nuestra, nuestro	—	our
NU	Naciones Unidas	**UN**	United Nations
núm.	número	**no.**	number
NY	Nueva York, New York	**NY**	New York
O, O.	Oeste, oeste	**W**	West, west
oct.	octubre	**Oct.**	October
OEA, O.E.A.	Organización de Estados Americanos	**OAS**	Organization of American States
OMS	Organización Mundial de la Salud	**WHO**	World Health Organization
ONG	organización no gubernamental	**NGO**	non-governmental organization
ONU	Organización de las Naciones Unidas	**UN**	United Nations
OTAN	Organización del Tratado del Atlántico Norte	**NATO**	North Atlantic Treaty Organization
p.	página	**p.**	page

P	(talla) pequeña	**S**	small
P, P.	padre	**Fr.**	Father
pág(s).	página(s)	**p(p)., pg(s).**	page(s)
Pat.	patente	**pat.**	patent
PBI	producto bruto interno	**GDP**	gross domestic product
PCL	pantalla de cristal líquido	**LCD**	liquid crystal display
P.D.	post data	**P.S.**	postscript
p. ej.	por ejemplo	**e.g.**	for example
PIB	producto interno bruto, producto interior bruto	**GDP**	gross domestic product
PIN	número de identificación personal	**PIN**	personal identification number
p.m.	post meridiem (de la tarde)	**p.m., PM**	post meridiem (afternoon)
PNB	Producto Nacional Bruto	**GNP**	gross national product
p°	paseo	**Ave.**	Avenue
p.p.	porte pagado	**ppd.**	postpaid
PP, p.p.	por poder, por poderes	**p.p.**	by proxy
PR	Puerto Rico	**PR**	Puerto Rico
prom.	promedio	**av., avg.**	average
pto.	punto	**pt.**	point
ptas., pts.	pesetas	**—**	—
PYME	Pequeña y Mediana Empresa	**—**	Small to Medium-Sized Business
Pza.	Plaza	**Sq.**	Square
q.e.p.d.	que en paz descanse	**R.I.P.**	(may he/she) rest in peace
R, R/	remite	**—**	sender
RAE	Real Academia Española	**—**	—
R & B	rhythm and blues, rhythm y blues	**R & B**	rhythm and blues
RCP	reanimación cardiopulmonar, resucitación cardiopulmonar	**CPR**	cardiopulmonary resuscitation
Rdo., Rda.	reverendo, reverenda	**Rev.**	Reverend
ref., ref.ª	referencia	**ref.**	reference
Rep.	República	**Rep.**	Republic
r.p.m.	revoluciones por minuto	**rpm**	revolutions per minute
Rte.	remite, remitente	**—**	sender
s.	siglo	**c., cent.**	century
s/	su, sus	**—**	his, her, your, their
S, S.	Sur, sur	**S, so.**	South, south
S.	san, santo	**St.**	Saint
Sr.	Sénior	**Sr.**	Senior
S.A.	Sociedad Anónima	**Inc.**	Incorporated (company)
sáb.	sábado	**Sat.**	Saturday
s/c	su cuenta	**—**	your account
SE	sudeste, sureste	**SE**	southeast

seg.	segundo, segundos	sec.	second, seconds
sep., sept.	septiembre	Sept.	September
s.e.u.o.	salvo error u omisión	—	errors and omissions excepted
Sgto.	sargento	Sgt.	Sergeant
S.L.	Sociedad Limitada	Ltd.	Limited (corporation)
S.M.	Su Majestad	HM	His Majesty, Her Majesty
SMS	servicio de mensajes cortos	SMS	Short Message Service
s/n	sin número	—	no (street) number
s.n.m.	sobre el nivel de mar	a.s.l.	above sea level
SO	sudoeste/suroeste	SW	southwest
S.R.C.	se ruega contestación	R.S.V.P.	please reply
ss.	siguientes	—	the following ones
SS, S.S.	Su Santidad	H.H.	His Holiness
Sta.	santa	St.	Saint
Sto.	santo	St.	Saint
t, t.	tonelada	t., tn.	ton
TAE	tasa anual efectiva	APR	annual percentage rate
tb.	también	—	also
tel., Tel.	teléfono	tel.	telephone
Tm.	tonelada métrica	MT	metric ton
Tn.	tonelada	t., tn.	ton
TOC	trastorno obsesivo-compulsivo	OCD	obsessive-compulsive disorder
trad.	traducido, traductor, traducción	tr., trans., transl.	translated, translator, translation
UCI	unidad de cuidados intensivos	ICU	intensive care unit
UE	Unión Europea	EU	European Union
Univ.	universidad	Univ., U.	University
Urb.	urbanización	—	residential area
UTI	unidad de terapia intensiva, unidad de tratamiento intensivo *Chile*	ICU	intensive care unit
v	versus	v., vs.	versus
v	verso	v., vs.	verse
v.	véase	viz.	see
Vda.	viuda	—	widow
v.g., v.gr.	verbigracia	e.g.	for example
vier., viern.	viernes	Fri.	Friday
V.M.	Vuestra Majestad	—	Your Majesty
VºBº, V.ºB.º	visto bueno	—	OK, approved
vol, vol.	volumen	vol.	volume
vra., vro.	vuestra, vuestro	—	your
www	world wide web, red mundial	www	World Wide Web

Abreviaturas comunes en inglés

ABREVIATURA INGLESA Y EXPANSIÓN		EQUIVALENTE ESPAÑOL	
AAA	American Automobile Association	—	—
AC	alternating current	**CA**	corriente alterna
AC	air-conditioning	—	aire acondicionado
ac., acct.	account	**cta.**	cuenta
AD	anno Domini (in the year of our Lord)	**A.D., d.C., d. de J.C.**	anno Domini, después de Cristo, después de Jesucristo
AK	Alaska	—	Alaska
aka	also known as	—	alias
AL, Ala.	Alabama	—	Alabama
Alas.	Alaska	—	Alaska
a.m., AM	ante meridiem (before noon)	**a.m.**	ante meridiem (de la mañana)
Am., Amer.	America, American	—	América, americano
amt.	amount	—	cantidad
anon.	anonymous	—	anónimo
ans.	answer	—	respuesta
Apr.	April	**abr.**	abril
approx.	approximately	**aprox.**	aproximadamente
APR	annual percentage rate	**TAE**	tasa anual efectiva
AR	Arkansas	—	Arkansas
arch.	architect	**Arq.**	arquitecto
Ariz.	Arizona	—	Arizona
Ark.	Arkansas	—	Arkansas
a.s.l.	above sea level	**s.n.m.**	sobre el nivel de mar
asst.	assistant	**ayte.**	ayudante
atty.	attorney	—	abogado, -da
Aug.	August	**ago.**	agosto
av.	average	**prom.**	promedio
Ave.	Avenue	**av., avda.**	avenida
avg.	average	**prom.**	promedio
AZ	Arizona	—	Arizona
BA	Bachelor of Arts	**Lic.**	Licenciado, -da en Filosofía y Letras
BA	Bachelor of Arts (degree)	—	Licenciatura en Filosofía y Letras
BC	before Christ	**a.C., A.C., a. de J.C.**	antes de Cristo, antes de Jesucristo
bcc	blind carbon copy	**CCO**	copia (de carbón) oculta
BCE	before the Christian Era, before the Common Era	—	antes de la era cristiana, antes de la era común
bet.	between	—	entre
Bldg.	Building	**edif.**	edificio
Blvd.	Boulevard	**blvar., br.**	bulevar
Br., Brit.	Britain, British	—	Gran Bretaña, británico
Bro(s).	Brother(s)	**Hno(s).**	hermano(s)
BS	Bachelor of Science	**Lic.**	Licenciado, -da en Ciencias
BS	Bachelor of Science (degree)	—	Licenciatura en Ciencias
c	carat	—	quilate

c	cent	—	centavo
c	centimeter	cm.	centímetro
c	century	s.	siglo
c	cup	—	taza
C	Celsius, centigrade	C	Celsius, centígrado
CA, Cal., Calif.	California	—	California
Can., Canad.	Canada, Canadian	—	Canadá, canadiense
cap.	capital	—	capital
cap.	capital	—	mayúscula
Capt.	Captain	Cap.	capitán
cc	cubic centimeters	c.c.	centímetros cúbicos
cc	carbon copy	CC	copia de carbón
cent.	century	s.	siglo
CEO	chief executive officer	—	presidente, -ta (de una corporación)
cf.	compare	cf.	compárese
CFO	chief financial officer	—	director financiero, directora financiera
cg	centigram	cg.	centígramo
ch., chap.	chapter	cap.	capítulo
CIA	Central Intelligence Agency	CIA	Agencia Central de Inteligencia
cm	centimeter	cm.	centímetro
Cmdr.	Commander	Com., Cmte.	comandante
Co.	Company	C., Cía.	compañía
co.	county	—	condado
CO	Colorado	—	Colorado
c/o	care of	a/c	a cargo de
COD	cash on delivery, collect on delivery	—	(pago) contra reembolso
col.	column	col.	columna
Col., Colo.	Colorado	—	Colorado
comp.	compare	comp.	compárese
Conn.	Connecticut	—	Connecticut
Corp.	Corporation	—	corporación
CPI	consumer price index	IPC	índice de precios al consumo
CPR	cardiopulmonary resuscitation	RCP	reanimación cardiopulmonar, resucitación cardiopulmonar
ct.	cent	—	centavo
CT	Connecticut	—	Connecticut
cu. cm	cubic centimeters	c.c.	centímetros cúbicos
D.A.	district attorney	—	fiscal (del distrito)
dB	decibel	dB	decibel, decibelio
DC	District of Columbia	—	—
DC	direct current	CC	corriente continua
DDS	Doctor of Dental Surgery	—	doctor de cirugía dental
DE	Delaware	—	Delaware
Dec.	December	dic.	diciembre
Del.	Delaware	—	Delaware
DHS	Department of Homeland Security	DHS	Departamento de Seguridad Nacional
dir.	director	dir.	director, directora
dir.	direction	dir.	dirección
DJ	disc jockey	—	disc jockey
dept.	department	dep., dpto.	departamento
DMD	Doctor of Dental Medicine	—	doctor de medicina dental

doz.	dozen	—	docena
Dr.	Doctor	**Dr., Dra.**	doctor, doctora
DSL	digital subscriber line	**DSL**	línea de abonado digital
DST	daylight saving time	—	—
DVM	Doctor of Veterinary Medicine	—	doctor de medicina veterinaria
E	East, east	**E, E.**	Este, este
ea.	each	**c/u**	cada uno, cada una
EC	European Community	**CE**	Comunidad Europea
EEC	European Economic Community	**CEE**	Comunidad Económica Europea
Ed., ed.	edition	**Ed., ed.**	edición
e.g.	for example	**v.g., v.gr., p.ej.**	verbigracia, por ejemplo
enc., encl.	enclosure	—	anexo
EMT	emergency medical technician	—	técnico, -ca en urgencias médicas
Eng.	England, English	—	Inglaterra, inglés
esp.	especially	—	especialmente
ER	emergency room	—	sala de urgencia(s), sala de emergencia(s)
EST	eastern standard time	—	—
etc.	et cetera	**etc.**	etcétera
ETA	estimated time of arrival	—	hora aproximada de llegada
et al.	et alii (and others)	**et al.**	et alii (y otros)
EU	European Union	**UE**	Unión Europea
ext.	extension	**ext.**	extensión
f	false	—	falso
f	female	**f**	femenino
F	Fahrenheit	**F**	Fahrenheit
FAQ	frequently asked question(s)	**FAQ**	pregunta(s) frecuente(s)
FBI	Federal Bureau of Investigation	**FBI**	Buró Federal de Investigaciones
Feb.	February	**feb.**	febrero
fem.	feminine	—	femenino
FEMA	Federal Emergency Agency	—	Agencia Federal para el Manejo de Emergencias
FL, Fla.	Florida	—	Florida
f.o.b.	free on board	**f.a.b.**	franco a bordo
Fr.	Father	**P, P.**	padre
Fri.	Friday	**vier., viern.**	viernes
ft.	feet, foot	—	pie(s)
FYI	for your information	—	para su información
g	gram	**g., gr.**	gramo
Ga., GA	Georgia	—	Georgia
gal.	gallon	—	galón
GDP	gross domestic product	**PBI, PIB**	producto bruto interno, producto interno bruto, producto interior bruto
Gen.	General	**Gral.**	general
GMT	Greenwich Mean Time	**GMT**	tiempo medio de Greenwich, hora del meridiano de Greenwich
GNP	gross national product	**PNB**	producto nacional bruto

gm	gram	**g., gr.**	gramo
Gov.	Governor	—	gobernador, -dora
govt.	government	—	gobierno
gr.	gram	**g., gr.**	gramo
H.H.	His Holiness	**SS, S.S.**	Su Santidad
HI	Hawaii	—	Hawai, Hawaii
hp	horsepower	**CV**	caballo de vapor
hr.	hour	**h.**	hora
HM	His Majesty, Her Majesty	**S.M.**	Su Majestad
HS	high school	—	colegio secundario
ht.	height	—	altura
Ia., IA	Iowa	—	Iowa
ibid.	ibidem (in the same place)	**ib., ibid.**	ibidem (en el mismo lugar)
ICE	Immigration and Customs Enforcement	**ICE**	Servicio de Inmigración y Control de Aduanas
ICU	intensive care unit	**UCI, UTI, CTI** *Uru*	unidad de cuidados intensivos, unidad de terapia intensiva, unidad de tratamiento intensivo *Chile*, centro de tratamiento intensivo *Uru*
ID	Idaho	—	Idaho
i.e.	that is	**i.e.**	esto es, es decir
IL, Ill.	Illinois	—	Illinois
IM	instant message	—	mensaje instantánea
IMF	International Monetary Fund	**FMI**	Fondo Monetario Internacional
in.	inch	—	pulgada
IN	Indiana	—	Indiana
Inc.	Incorporated (company)	**S.A.**	sociedad anónima
incl.	inclusive, inclusively, including	**incl.**	inclusive
Ind.	Indian, Indiana	—	Indiana
IQ	intelligence quotient	**CI**	coeficiente intelectual or de inteligencia
IRS	Internal Revenue Service	—	Servicio de Rentas Internas
ISP	Internet service provider	—	proveedor de servicios de Internet
Jan.	January	**ene.**	enero
Jul.	July	**jul.**	julio
Jun.	June	**jun.**	junio
Jr., Jun.	Junior	**Jr.**	Júnior
Kan., Kans.	Kansas	—	Kansas
kg	kilogram	**kg.**	kilogramo
km	kilometer	**km.**	kilómetro
kph	kilometers per hour	**km/h**	kilómetros por hora
KS	Kansas	—	Kansas
kw, kW	kilowatt	**kv, kV**	kilovatio
Ky., KY	Kentucky	—	Kentucky
l	liter	**l.**	litro
l.	left	**izq.**	izquierda
L	large	**G**	(talla) grande
La., LA	Louisiana	—	Louisiana, Louisiana
lb.	pound	—	libra
LCD	liquid crystal display	**PCL**	pantalla de cristal líquido

LGBT	lesbian, gay, bisexual, and transgender	**LGBT**	lesbianas, gays, bisexuales y transgénero
LGBTQ	lesbian, gay, bisexual, transgender, and queer/questioning	**LGBTQ**	lesbianas, gays, bisexuales, transgénero y queer
lit.	liter	**l.**	litro
LOL	laugh out loud, laughing out loud	—	reírse a carcajadas, riendo a carcajadas
Ltd.	Limited (corporation)	**S.L.**	Sociedad Limitada
m	male	**m**	masculino
m	meter	**m**	metro
m	mile	—	milla
M	medium	**M**	(talla) mediana
MA	Massachusetts	—	Massachusetts
Maj.	Major	—	mayor
Mar.	March	**mar.**	marzo
masc.	masculine	—	masculino
Mass.	Massachusetts	—	Massachusetts
Md., MD	Maryland	—	Maryland
M.D.	Doctor of Medicine	—	doctor de medicina
Me., ME	Maine	—	Maine
Mex.	Mexican, Mexico	**Méx.**	mexicano, México
mg	milligram	**mg.**	miligramo
mi.	mile	—	milla
MI, Mich.	Michigan	—	Michigan
min.	minute	**min**	minuto
Minn.	Minnesota	—	Minnesota
Miss.	Mississippi	—	Mississippi, Misisipí
ml	milliliter	**ml.**	mililitro
mm	millimeter	**mm.**	milímetro
MN	Minnesota	—	Minnesota
mo.	month	—	mes
M.O.	money order	**G.P.**	giro postal
Mo., MO	Missouri	—	Missouri
Mon.	Monday	**lun.**	lunes
Mont.	Montana	—	Montana
mpg	miles per gallon	—	millas por galón
mph	miles per hour	—	millas por hora
MS	Mississippi	—	Mississippi, Misisipí
MS	multiple sclerosis	**E.M.**	esclerosis múltiple
Msgr.	Monsignor	**Mons.**	monseñor
Mt.	Mount, Mountain	—	monte, montaña
MT	Montana	—	Montana
MT	Mountain Time	—	Hora de la(s) Montaña(s)
Mtn.	Mountain	—	montaña
N	North, north	**N, N.**	Norte, norte
NASA	National Aeronautics and Space Administration	—	—
NATO	North Atlantic Treaty Organization	**OTAN**	Organización del Tratado del Atlántico Norte
NC	North Carolina	—	Carolina del Norte, North Carolina
ND, N. Dak.	North Dakota	—	Dakota del Norte, North Dakota
NE	northeast	**NE**	nordeste
NE, Neb., Nebr.	Nebraska	—	Nebraska
Nev.	Nevada	—	Nevada

NGO	non-governmental organization	ONG	organización no gubernamental
NH	New Hampshire	—	Nueva Hampshire, Nuevo Hampshire, New Hampshire
NJ	New Jersey	—	Nueva Jersey, New Jersey
NM., N. Mex.	New Mexico	—	Nuevo México, New Mexico
no.	north	N, N.	norte
no.	number	n.°	número
Nov.	November	nov.	noviembre
NSA	National Security Agency	NSA	Agencia de Seguridad Nacional
N.T.	New Testament	N.T.	Nuevo Testamento
NV	Nevada	—	Nevada
NW	northwest	NO	noroeste
NY	New York	NY	Nueva York, New York
O	Ohio	—	Ohio
OAS	Organization of American States	OEA, O.E.A.	Organización de Estados Americanos
OCD	obsessive-compulsive disorder	TOC	trastorno obsesivo-compulsivo
Oct.	October	oct.	octubre
OH	Ohio	—	Ohio
OK, Okla.	Oklahoma	—	Oklahoma
OR, Ore., Oreg.	Oregon	—	Oregon
O.T.	Old Testament	A.T.	Antiguo Testamento
oz.	ounce, ounces	—	onza, onzas
p.	page	p., pág.	página
Pa., PA	Pennsylvania	—	Pennsylvania, Pensilvania
pat.	patent	pat.	patente
PD	police department	—	departamento de policía
PE	physical education	—	educación física
Penn., Penna.	Pennsylvania	—	Pennsylvania, Pensilvania
pg.	page	pág., p.	página
pgs.	pages	págs.	páginas
PhD	Doctor of Philosophy	—	doctor, -tora (en filosofía)
PIN	personal identification number	PIN, NIP	número de identificación personal
pkg.	package	—	paquete
p.m., PM	post meridiem (after noon)	p.m.	post meridiem (de la tarde)
P.O.	post office	—	oficina de correos, correo
pp.	pages	págs.	páginas
p.p.	by proxy	PP, p.p.	por poder, por poderes
ppd.	postpaid	p.p.	porte pagado
PR	Puerto Rico	PR	Puerto Rico
pres.	present	—	presente
Pres.	President	—	presidente, -ta
Prof.	Professor	—	profesor, -sora
P.S.	postscript	P.D.	postdata
P.S.	public school	—	escuela pública
pt.	pint	—	pinta

pt.	point	pto.	punto
PT	part-time, physical therapist, physical therapy	—	(de) medio tiempo, fisioterapeuta, fisioterapia
PTA	Parent-Teacher Association	—	—
PTO	Parent-Teacher Organization	—	—
q, qt.	quart	—	cuarto de galón
r.	right	dcha.	derecha
R & B	rhythm and blues	R & B	rhythm and blues, rhythm y blues
R & D	research and development	I + D, I & D, I y D	investigación y desarrollo
R & R	rest and recreation, rest and recuperation, rest and relaxation	—	descanso y recreo, descanso y recuperación, descanso y relajación
rd.	road	c/, C/	calle
RDA	recommended daily allowance	—	consumo diario recomendado
recd.	received	—	recibido
ref.	reference	ref., ref. a	referencia
Rep.	Republic	Rep.	República
Rev.	Reverend	Rdo., Rda.	reverendo, reverenda
RI	Rhode Island	—	Rhode Island
R.I.P.	(may he/she) rest in peace	q.e.p.d.	que en paz descanse
rpm	revolutions per minute	r.p.m.	revoluciones por minuto
RR	railroad	FC	ferrocarril
R.S.V.P.	please reply (répondez s'il vous plaît)	S.R.C.	se ruega contestación
rt.	right	dcha.	derecha
Rte.	Route	—	ruta
S	small	P	(talla) pequeña
S	South, south	S, S.	Sur, sur
S.A.	South America	—	Sudamérica, América del Sur
Sat.	Saturday	sáb.	sábado
SC	South Carolina	—	Carolina del Sur, South Carolina
SD, S. Dak.	South Dakota	—	Dakota del Sur, South Dakota
SE	southeast	SE	sudeste, sureste
sec.	second, seconds	seg.	segundo, segundos
Sept.	September	sep., sept.	septiembre
Sgt.	Sergeant	Sgto.	sargento
SMS	Short Message Service	SMS	servicio de mensajes cortos
so.	south	S, S.	sur
sq.	square	—	cuadrado
Sq.	Square	Pza.	Plaza
Sr.	Senior	Sr.	Sénior
Sr.	Sister (in religion)	—	sor
st.	state	—	estado
St.	Street	c/, C/	calle
St.	Saint	S.; Sto., Sta.	santo, santa

Sun.	Sunday	**dom., do.**	domingo
SW	southwest	**SO**	sudoeste, suroeste
t.	teaspoon	—	cucharadita
t.	ton	**t, t.**	tonelada
T, tb., tbsp.	tablespoon	—	cucharada (grande)
tel.	telephone	**tel., Tel.**	teléfono
Tenn.	Tennessee	—	Tennessee
Tex.	Texas	—	Texas
Thu., Thur., Thurs.	Thursday	**juev.**	jueves
TM	trademark	—	marca (de un producto)
tn.	ton	**t, t.**	tonelada
TN	Tennessee	—	Tennessee
tr., trans., transl.	translated, translator, translation	**trad.**	traducido, traductor, traducción
TSA	Transportation Security Administration	**TSA**	Administración de Seguridad en el Transporte
tsp.	teaspoon	—	cucharadita
Tue., Tues.	Tuesday	**mart.**	martes
TX	Texas	—	Texas
U.	University	**Univ.**	universidad
UN	United Nations	**NU, NN.UU.**	Naciones Unidas
Univ.	University	**Univ.**	universidad
US	United States	**EEUU, EE.UU.**	Estados Unidos
USA	United States of America	**EEUU, EE.UU.**	Estados Unidos de América
usu.	usually	—	usualmente
UT	Utah	—	Utah
v.	versus	**v**	versus
v.	verse	**v**	verso
Va., VA	Virginia	—	Virginia
VAT	value-added tax	**IVA**	impuesto al valor agregado
viz.	see	**v.**	véase
ver.	verse	**v**	verso
vol.	volume	**vol, vol.**	volumen
VP	vice president	—	vicepresidente, -ta
vs.	versus	**v**	versus
vs.	verse	**v**	verso
Vt., VT	Vermont	—	Vermont
W	West, west	**O, O.**	Oeste, oeste
WA, Wash.	Washington (state)	—	Washington
Wed.	Wednesday	**miérc.**	miércoles
WHO	World Health Organization	**OMS**	Organización Mundial de la Salud
WI, Wis., Wisc.	Wisconsin	—	Wisconsin
wt.	weight	—	peso
WV, W. Va.	West Virginia	—	Virginia del Oeste, West Virginia
www	World Wide Web	**www**	world wide web, red mundial
WY, Wyo.	Wyoming	—	Wyoming
yd.	yard	—	yarda
yr.	year	—	año

Spanish Numbers

Cardinal Numbers[1]

1	uno	28	veintiocho
2	dos	29	veintinueve
3	tres	30	treinta
4	cuatro	31	treinta y uno
5	cinco	40	cuarenta
6	seis	50	cincuenta
7	siete	60	sesenta
8	ocho	70	setenta
9	nueve	80	ochenta
10	diez	90	noventa
11	once	100	cien
12	doce	101	ciento uno
13	trece	200	doscientos
14	catorce	300	trescientos
15	quince	400	cuatrocientos
16	dieciséis	500	quinientos
17	diecisiete	600	seiscientos
18	dieciocho	700	setecientos
19	diecinueve	800	ochocientos
20	veinte	900	novecientos
21	veintiuno	1000	mil
22	veintidós	1001	mil uno
23	veintitrés	2000	dos mil
24	veinticuatro	100,000	cien mil
25	veinticinco	1,000,000	un millón
26	veintiséis	1,000,000,000	mil millones
27	veintisiete	1,000,000,000,000	un billón

[1]Most Spanish-speaking countries use either a decimal point (e.g., 38.25%) or a decimal comma (e.g., 38,25). In countries that use the decimal point, a different symbol (such as a comma, an apostrophe, or a space) is used as a thousands separator. Similarly, in countries where the decimal comma is preferred, a symbol other than a comma (such as a point, an apostrophe, or a space) is used to separate thousands.

Ordinal Numbers

1.º, 1.ª	primero, -ra[2]
2.º, 2.ª	segundo, -da
3.º, 3.ª	tercero, -ra[2]
4.º, 4.ª	cuarto, -ta
5.º, 5.ª	quinto, -ta
6.º, 6.ª	sexto, -ta
7.º, 7.ª	séptimo, -ma
8.º, 8.ª	octavo, -va
9.º, 9.ª	noveno, -na
10.º, 10.ª	décimo, -ma[3]
11.º, 11.ª	undécimo, -ma
12.º, 12.ª	duodécimo, -ma
13.º, 13.ª	decimotercero, -ra
14.º, 14.ª	decimocuarto, -ta
15.º, 15.ª	decimoquinto, -ta
16.º, 16.ª	decimosexto, -ta
17.º, 17.ª	decimoséptimo, -ma
18.º, 18.ª	decimoctavo, -va
19.º, 19.ª	decimonoveno, -na *or* decimonono, -na
20.º, 20.ª	vigésimo, -ma
21.º, 21.ª	vigésimoprimero, -ra[2]
30.º, 30.ª	trigésimo, -ma
40.º, 40.ª	cuadragésimo, -ma
50.º, 50.ª	quincuagésimo, -ma
60.º, 60.ª	sexagésimo, -ma
70.º, 70.ª	septuagésimo, -ma
80.º, 80.ª	octogésimo, -ma
90.º, 90.ª	nonagésimo, -ma
100.º, 100.ª	centésimo, -ma
1000.º, 1000.ª	milésimo, -ma
1,000,000.º, 1,000,000.ª	millonésimo, -ma
1,000,000,000.º, 1,000,000,000.ª	milmillonésimo, -ma

---

[2]The shortened forms of *primero* and *tercero* (which are *primer* and *tercer*, respectively) are abbreviated as *1.*er and *3.*er. Higher ordinals that end in these forms follow the same pattern (e.g., *vigésimoprimer → 21.*er).

[3]In informal Spanish speech and writing, higher ordinals are often replaced with their corresponding cardinal number: *el 35 aniversario de la compañía*, the company's 35th anniversary.

Números ingleses

Números cardinales

1	one	50	fifty
2	two	60	sixty
3	three	70	seventy
4	four	80	eighty
5	five	90	ninety
6	six	100	one hundred
7	seven	101	one hundred (and) one
8	eight	200	two hundred
9	nine	300	three hundred
10	ten	400	four hundred
11	eleven	500	five hundred
12	twelve	600	six hundred
13	thirteen	700	seven hundred
14	fourteen	800	eight hundred
15	fifteen	900	nine hundred
16	sixteen	1,000	one thousand
17	seventeen	1,001	one thousand (and) one
18	eighteen	2,000	two thousand
19	nineteen	10,000	ten thousand
20	twenty	100,000	one hundred thousand
21	twenty-one	1,000,000	one million
30	thirty	1,000,000,000	one billion
40	forty	1,000,000,000,000	one trillion

Números ordinales

1st	first	17th	seventeenth
2nd	second	18th	eighteenth
3rd	third	19th	nineteenth
4th	fourth	20th	twentieth
5th	fifth	21st	twenty-first
6th	sixth	30th	thirtieth
7th	seventh	40th	fortieth
8th	eighth	50th	fiftieth
9th	ninth	60th	sixtieth
10th	tenth	70th	seventieth
11th	eleventh	80th	eightieth
12th	twelfth	90th	ninetieth
13th	thirteenth	100th	hundredth
14th	fourteenth	1,000th	thousandth
15th	fifteenth	1,000,000th	millionth
16th	sixteenth	1,000,000,000th	billionth

Nations of the World
(Naciones del mundo)

Africa/África

Algeria	Argelia
Angola	Angola
Benin	Benin
Botswana	Botswana, Botsuana
Burkina Faso	Burkina Faso
Burundi	Burundi
Cameroon	Camerún
Cape Verde	Cabo Verde
Central African Republic	República Centroafricana
Chad	Chad
Comoros	Comores, Comoras
Congo, Democratic Republic of the	Congo, República Democrática del
Congo, Republic of the	Congo, República del
Côte d'Ivoire (Ivory Coast)	Costa de Marfil
Djibouti	Yibuti, Djibouti
Egypt	Egipto
Equatorial Guinea	Guinea Ecuatorial
Eritrea	Eritrea
Eswatini (Swaziland)	Esuatini (Suazilandia)
Ethiopia	Etiopía
Gabon	Gabón
Gambia	Gambia
Ghana	Ghana
Guinea	Guinea
Guinea-Bissau	Guinea-Bissau
Kenya	Kenya, Kenia
Lesotho	Lesotho, Lesoto
Liberia	Liberia
Libya	Libia
Madagascar	Madagascar
Malawi	Malawi, Malaui
Mali	Malí
Mauritania	Mauritania
Mauritius	Mauricio
Morocco	Marruecos
Mozambique	Mozambique
Namibia	Namibia
Niger	Níger
Nigeria	Nigeria
Rwanda	Ruanda
São Tomé and Principe	Santo Tomé y Príncipe
Senegal	Senegal
Seychelles	Seychelles
Sierra Leone	Sierra Leona
Somalia	Somalia

South Africa, Republic of	Sudáfrica, República de
South Sudan	Sudán del Sur
Sudan	Sudán
Tanzania	Tanzania, Tanzanía
Togo	Togo
Tunisia	Túnez
Uganda	Uganda
Zambia	Zambia
Zimbabwe	Zimbabwe, Zimbabue

Antarctica/Antártida

No independent countries

Asia/Asia

Afghanistan	Afganistán
Armenia	Armenia
Azerbaijan	Azerbaiyán, Azerbaiján
Bahrain	Bahrein
Bangladesh	Bangladesh
Bhutan	Bután, Bhután
Brunei	Brunei
Cambodia	Camboya
China	China
East Timor (Timor-Leste)	Timor Oriental
Georgia	Georgia
India	India
Indonesia	Indonesia
Iran	Irán
Iraq	Iraq, Irak
Israel	Israel
Japan	Japón
Jordan	Jordania
Kazakhstan	Kazajistán, Kazajstán
Korea, North	Corea del Norte
Korea, South	Corea del Sur
Kuwait	Kuwait
Kyrgyzstan	Kirguizistán, Kirguistán
Laos	Laos
Lebanon	Líbano
Malaysia	Malasia
Maldives	Maldivas
Mongolia	Mongolia
Myanmar (Burma)	Myanmar (Birmania)
Nepal	Nepal
Oman	Omán
Pakistan	Pakistán, Paquistán

Philippines	Filipinas
Qatar	Qatar
Saudi Arabia	Arabia Saudí, Arabia Saudita
Singapore	Singapur
Sri Lanka	Sri Lanka
Syria	Siria
Taiwan	Taiwán, Taiwan
Tajikistan	Tayikistán
Thailand	Tailandia
Turkey	Turquía
Turkmenistan	Turkmenistán
United Arab Emirates	Emiratos Árabes Unidos
Uzbekistan	Uzbekistán
Vietnam	Vietnam
Yemen	Yemen

Europe/Europa

Albania	Albania
Andorra	Andorra
Austria	Austria
Belarus	Belarús
Belgium	Bélgica
Bosnia and Herzegovina	Bosnia-Herzegovina
Bulgaria	Bulgaria
Croatia	Croacia
Cyprus	Chipre
Czech Republic	República Checa
Denmark	Dinamarca
Estonia	Estonia
Finland	Finlandia
France	Francia
Germany	Alemania
Greece	Grecia
Hungary	Hungría
Iceland	Islandia
Ireland	Irlanda
Italy	Italia
Kosovo	Kosovo
Latvia	Letonia
Liechtenstein	Liechtenstein
Lithuania	Lituania
Luxembourg	Luxemburgo
Macedonia	Macedonia
Malta	Malta
Moldova	Moldova
Monaco	Mónaco
Montenegro	Montenegro
Netherlands	Países Bajos

Norway	Noruega
Poland	Polonia
Portugal	Portugal
Romania	Rumanía, Rumania
Russia	Rusia
San Marino	San Marino
Serbia	Serbia
Slovakia	Eslovaquia
Slovenia	Eslovenia
Spain	España
Sweden	Suecia
Switzerland	Suiza
Ukraine	Ucrania
United Kingdom	Reino Unido
Vatican City	Ciudad del Vaticano

North America/Norteamérica

Antigua and Barbuda	Antigua y Barbuda
Bahamas	Bahamas
Barbados	Barbados
Belize	Belice
Canada	Canadá
Costa Rica	Costa Rica
Cuba	Cuba
Dominica	Dominica
Dominican Republic	República Dominicana
El Salvador	El Salvador
Grenada	Granada
Guatemala	Guatemala
Haiti	Haití
Honduras	Honduras
Jamaica	Jamaica
Mexico	México, Méjico
Nicaragua	Nicaragua
Panama	Panamá
Saint Kitts and Nevis	San Cristóbal y Nieves, Saint Kitts y Nevis
Saint Lucia	Santa Lucía
Saint Vincent and the Grenadines	San Vicente y las Granadinas
Trinidad and Tobago	Trinidad y Tobago
United States of America	Estados Unidos de América

Oceania/Oceanía

Australia	Australia
Fiji	Fiji, Fiyi
Kiribati	Kiribati

Marshall Islands	Islas Marshall
Micronesia, Federated States of	Estados Federados de Micronesia
Nauru	Nauru
New Zealand	Nueva Zelanda, Nueva Zelandia
Palau	Palaos
Papua New Guinea	Papúa Nueva Guinea, Papua Nueva Guinea
Samoa	Samoa
Solomon Islands	Islas Salomón
Tonga	Tonga
Tuvalu	Tuvalu
Vanuatu	Vanuatu

South America/Sudamérica

Argentina	Argentina
Bolivia	Bolivia
Brazil	Brasil
Chile	Chile
Colombia	Colombia
Ecuador	Ecuador
Guyana	Guyana
Paraguay	Paraguay
Peru	Perú
Suriname	Surinam
Uruguay	Uruguay
Venezuela	Venezuela

Metric System : Conversions
(Sistema métrico : conversiones)

Length

unit	number of meters	approximate U.S. equivalents	
millimeter	0.001	0.039	inch
centimeter	0.01	0.39	inch
meter	1	39.37	inches
kilometer	1,000	0.62	mile

Longitud

unidad	número de metros	equivalentes aproximados de los EEUU	
milímetro	0.001	0.039	pulgada
centímetro	0.01	0.39	pulgada
metro	1	39.37	pulgadas
kilómetro	1000	0.62	milla

Area

unit	number of square meters	approximate U.S. equivalents	
square centimeter	0.0001	0.155	square inch
square meter	1	10.764	square feet
hectare	10,000	2.47	acres
square kilometer	1,000,000	0.3861	square mile

Superficie

unidad	número de metros cuadrados	equivalentes aproximados de los EEUU	
centímetro cuadrado	0.0001	0.155	pulgada cuadrada
metro cuadrado	1	10.764	pies cuadrados
hectárea	10,000	2.47	acres
kilómetro cuadrado	1,000,000	0.3861	milla cuadrada

Volume

unit	number of cubic meters	approximate U.S. equivalents	
cubic centimeter	0.000001	0.061	cubic inch
cubic meter	1	1.307	cubic yards

Volumen

unidad	número de metros cúbicos	equivalentes aproximados de los EEUU	
centímetro cúbico	0.000001	0.061	pulgada cúbica
metro cúbico	1	1.307	yardas cúbicas

Capacity

unit	number of liters	approximate U.S. equivalents		
		CUBIC	DRY	LIQUID
liter	1	61.02 cubic inches	0.908 quart	1.057 quarts

Capacidad

unidad	número de litros	equivalentes aproximados de los EEUU		
		CÚBICO	SECO	LÍQUIDO
litro	1	61.02 pulgadas cúbicas	0.908 cuarto de galón	1.057 cuartos de galón

Mass and Weight

unit	number of grams	approximate U.S. equivalents	
milligram	0.001	0.015	grain
centigram	0.01	0.154	grain
gram	1	0.035	ounce
kilogram	1,000	2.2046	pounds
metric ton	1,000,000	1.102	short tons

Masa y peso

unidad	número de gramos	equivalentes aproximados de los EEUU	
miligramo	0.001	0.015	grano
centigramo	0.01	0.154	grano
gramo	1	0.035	onza
kilogramo	1000	2.2046	libras
tonelada métrica	1,000,000	1.102	toneladas cortas